2008

Writer's Market®

Robert Lee Brewer, Editor
Chuck Sambuchino, Assistant Editor

WRITER'S DIGEST BOOKS
CINCINNATI, OH

Complaint Procedure

If you feel you have not been treated fairly by a listing in *Writer's Market* or *Writer's Market Deluxe Edition*, we advise you to take the following steps:

- First try to contact the listing. Sometimes one phone call or a letter can quickly clear up the matter.
- Document all your correspondence with the listing. When you write to us with a complaint, provide the details of your submission, the date of your first contact with the listing and the nature of your subsequent correspondence.
- We will enter your letter into our files and attempt to contact the listing.
- The number and severity of complaints will be considered in our decision whether to delete the listing from the next edition.

Editorial Director, Writer's Digest Books: Jane Friedman
Managing Editor, Writer's Digest Market Books: Alice Pope

Writer's Market Web site: www.writersmarket.com
Writer's Digest Web site: www.writersdigest.com

2008 Writer's Market. Copyright © 2007 by Writer's Digest Books. Published by F + W Publications, 4700 East Galbraith Rd., Cincinnati, Ohio 45236. Printed and bound in the United States of America. All rights reserved. No part of this book may be reproduced in any form or by any electronic or mechanical means including information storage and retrieval systems without written permission from the publisher. Reviewers may quote brief passages to be printed in a magazine or newspaper.

Distributed in Canada by Fraser Direct
100 Armstrong Avenue
Georgetown, ON, Canada L7G 5S4
Tel: (905) 877-4411

Distributed in the U.K. and Europe by David & Charles
Brunel House, Newton Abbot, Devon, TQ12 4PU, England
Tel: (+44) 1626 323200, Fax: (+44) 1626 323319
E-mail: postmaster@davidandcharles.co.uk

Distributed in Australia by Capricorn Link
P.O. Box 704, Windsor, NSW 2756 Australia
Tel: (02) 4577-3555

Library of Congress Catalog Number 31-20772
ISSN: 0084-2729
ISBN-13: 978-1-58297-496-5
ISBN-13: 978-1-58297-497-2 (*Writer's Market Deluxe Edition*)
ISBN-10: 1-58297-496-9
ISBN-10: 1-58297-497-7 (*Writer's Market Deluxe Edition*)

Cover design and illustration by Josh Roflow
Interior design by Clare Finney
Production coordinated by Kristen Heller and Greg Nock
Illustrations ©Dominique Bruneton/PaintoAlto

Attention Booksellers: This is an annual directory of F + W Publications.
Return deadline for this edition is December 31, 2008.

Contents

TRADE JOURNALS

NEWSPAPERS

SCREENWRITING

PLAYWRITING

GREETING CARDS

CONTESTS & AWARDS

RESOURCES

INDEXES

From the Editor

Recently, I went through the history of *Writer's Market* from the early days in 1921 to today. There's always been a commitment to getting up-to-date, authoritative information, but I also noticed a pattern of providing a spectrum of possible ways for writers to sell their writing, whether by selling a short story to a magazine or a few lines to a greeting card company. As a writer, you *do* have a wide range of options to market yourself as a freelancer.

Knowing that sometimes you need to look to the past to improve the future, I made a decision to bring back some of those options to *Writer's Market*. This edition of *Writer's Market* includes screenwriting, playwriting, greeting card, and newspapers market listings. While these markets have always been online at WritersMarket.com, I felt they should be included in the book as well, especially for those writers who only use the book.*

This edition of *Writer's Market* is filled with those publishing opportunities, as well as some really great feature articles. The classics like "How Much Should I Charge?" on page 64, "Query Letter Clinic" on page 20, and "Minding the Details" on page 49 are included. There are some great new interviews with Seth Godin (page 40), Ben Olson (page 43), and Erik Larson (page 46). Plus, bestselling author Mary Roach has written an account of how she published her popular nonfiction book, *Stiff* (W.W. Norton), in "One Author's Path to Publication" on page 30.

From top to bottom, a lot of thought and hard work has gone into providing the best *Writer's Market* ever by looking at what's worked best in the past and pairing that up with the up-to-date information you need. As a writer myself, I would expect nothing less.

Until next we meet, keep writing and marketing what you write.

Robert Lee Brewer
Editor, *Writer's Market*
WritersMarket.com
writersmarket@fwpubs.com
www.myspace.com/writersmarket

P.S. *If you've only used the book in the past, check out our Web site at www.writersmarket.com, where we make daily updates to a searchable online database throughout the year.

How to Use *Writer's Market*

W*riter's Market* is here to help you decide where and how to submit your writing to appropriate markets. Each listing contains information about the editorial focus of the market, how it prefers material to be submitted, payment information, and other helpful tips.

WHAT'S INSIDE?

Since 1921, *Writer's Market* has been giving you the information you need to knowledgeably approach a market. We've continued to develop improvements to help you access that information more efficiently.

Navigational tools. We've designed the pages of *Writer's Market* with you, the user, in mind. Within the pages you will find **readable market listings** and **accessible charts and graphs**. One such chart can be found in the ever-popular **How Much Should I Charge?** on page 64. We've taken all of the updated information in this feature and put it into an easy-to-read and navigate chart, making it convenient for you to find the rates that accompany the freelance jobs you're seeking.

Tabs. You will also find user-friendly tabs for each section of *Writer's Market* so you can quickly find the section you need most. Once inside the Consumer Magazines, Trade Journals and Contests & Awards sections, you'll have subject headings at the top of the page to help guide and speed up your search.

Symbols. There are a variety of symbols that appear before each listing. A complete Key to Symbols appears on the back inside cover and on a removable bookmark. In Book Publishers, note the O‑ which quickly sums up a publisher's interests. In Consumer Magazines the O‑ zeroes in on what areas of that market are particularly open to freelancers—helping you break in. Other symbols let you know whether a listing is new to the book (N), a book publisher accepts only agented writers (A), comparative pay rates for a magazine (**$-$$$$**), and more.

Acquisition names, royalty rates and advances. In the Book Publishers section we identify acquisition editors with the boldface word **Acquisitions** to help you get your manuscript to the right person. Royalty rates and advances are also highlighted in boldface, as is other important information on the percentage of first-time writers and unagented writers the company publishes, the number of books published, and the number of manuscripts received each year.

Editors, pay rates, and percentage of material written by freelance writers. In the Consumer Magazines and Trade Journals sections, we identify to whom you should send your query or article with the boldface word **Contact**. The amount (percentage) of material accepted from freelance writers, and the pay rates for features, columns and departments, and fillers are also highlighted in boldface to help you quickly identify the information you need to know when considering whether to submit your work.

Query formats. We asked editors how they prefer to receive queries and have indicated in the listings whether they prefer them by mail, e-mail, fax or phone. Be sure to check an editor's individual preference before sending your query.

Articles. All of the articles, with the exception of a few standard pieces, are new to this edition. Newer, unpublished writers should be sure to read the articles in **The Basics** section, while more experienced writers should focus on those in the **Beyond the Basics** section. In addition, there is a section devoted to **Personal Views** featuring interviews with and articles by industry professionals and other career-oriented professionals, as well as best-selling authors.

Important Listing Information

Important

1. Listings are based on editorial questionnaires and interviews. They are not advertisements; publishers do not pay for their listings. The markets are not endorsed by *Writer's Market* editors. F+W Publications, Inc., Writer's Digest Books, and its employees go to great effort to ascertain the validity of information in this book. However, transactions between users of the information and individuals and/or companies are strictly between those parties.

2. All listings have been verified before publication of this book. If a listing has not changed from last year, then the editor said the market's needs have not changed and the previous listing continues to accurately reflect its policies.

3. *Writer's Market* reserves the right to exclude any listing.

4. When looking for a specific market, check the index. A market may not be listed for one of these reasons:
   - It doesn't solicit freelance material.
   - It doesn't pay for material.
   - It has gone out of business.
   - It has failed to verify or update its listing for this edition.
   - It hasn't answered *Writer's Market* inquiries satisfactorily. (To the best of our ability, and with our readers' help, we try to screen fraudulent listings.)

5. Individual markets that appeared in last year's edition but are not listed in this edition are included in the General Index, with a notation giving the reason for their exclusion.

2008 WRITER'S MARKET KEY TO SYMBOLS

 market new to this edition

 market accepts agented submissions only

 market does not accept unsolicited manuscripts

 Canadian market

market located outside of the U.S. and Canada

online opportunity

$ market pays 0-9¢/word or $0-$150/article

$$ market pays 10-49¢/word or $151-$750/article

$$$ market pays 50-99¢/word or $751-$1,500/article

$$$$ market pays $1/word or over $1,500/article

● comment from the editor of *Writer's Market*

tips to break into a specific market

ms, mss manuscript(s)

b&w black & white (photo)

SASE self-addressed, stamped envelope

SAE self-addressed envelope

IRC International Reply Coupon, for use in countries other than your own

(For words and expressions relating specifically to writing and publishing, see the Glossary in the back of this book.)

Find a handy pull-out bookmark, a quick reference to the icons used in this book, right inside the front cover.

IF WRITER'S MARKET IS NEW TO YOU . . .

A quick look at the **Contents** pages will familiarize you with the arrangement of *Writer's Market*. The three largest sections of the book are the market listings of Book Publishers; Consumer Magazines; and Trade Journals. You will also find other sections of market listings for Literary Agents; Newspapers; Screenwriting Markets; Playwriting Markets; Greeting Card Companies; and Contests & Awards.

Narrowing your search

After you've identified the market categories that interest you, you can begin researching specific markets within each section.

Book Publishers are categorized, in the **Book Publishers Subject Index**, according to types of books they are interested in. If, for example, you plan to write a book on a religious topic, simply turn to the Book Publishers Subject Index on page 1065 and look under the Religion subhead in Nonfiction for the names and page numbers of companies that publish such books.

Consumer Magazines and Trade Journals are categorized by subject within their respective sections to make it easier for you to identify markets for your work. If you want to publish an article dealing with retirement, you could look under the Retirement category of Consumer Magazines to find an appropriate market. You would want to keep in mind, however, that magazines in other categories might also be interested in your article. (For example, women's magazines publish such material.)

Interpreting the markets

Once you've identified companies or publications that cover the subjects in which you're interested, you can begin evaluating specific listings to pinpoint the markets most receptive to your work and most beneficial to you.

In evaluating an individual listing, first check the location of the company, the types of material it is interested in seeing, submission requirements, and rights and payment policies. Depending on your personal concerns, any of these items could be a deciding factor as you determine which markets you plan to approach. Many listings also include a reporting time, which lets you know how long it will typically take for the publisher to respond to your initial query or submission. (We suggest that you allow an additional two months for a response, just in case your submission is under further review or the publisher is backlogged.)

Check the Glossary on page 1061 for unfamiliar words. Specific symbols and abbreviations are explained in the Key to Symbols appearing on the inside cover, as well as on a removable bookmark. The most important abbreviation is SASE—self-addressed, stamped envelope. Always enclose a SASE when you send unsolicited queries, proposals or manuscripts.

A careful reading of the listings will reveal that many editors are very specific about their needs. Your chances of success increase if you follow directions to the letter. Often companies do not accept unsolicited manuscripts and return them unread. If a company does not accept unsolicited manuscripts, it is indicated in the listing with a (⊘) symbol. (Note: You may still be able to query a market that does not accept unsolicited manuscripts.)

Whenever possible, obtain writer's guidelines before submitting material. You can usually obtain guidelines by sending a SASE to the address in the listing. Magazines often post their guidelines on their Web sites, and many book publishers do so as well. Most of the listings indicate how writer's guidelines are made available. You should also familiarize yourself with the company's publications. Many of the listings contain instructions on how to obtain sample copies, catalogs or market lists. The more research you do upfront, the better your chances of acceptance, publication and payment.

Guide to listing features

Below is an example of the market listings you'll find in each section of *Writer's Market*. Note the callouts that identify various format features of the listing.

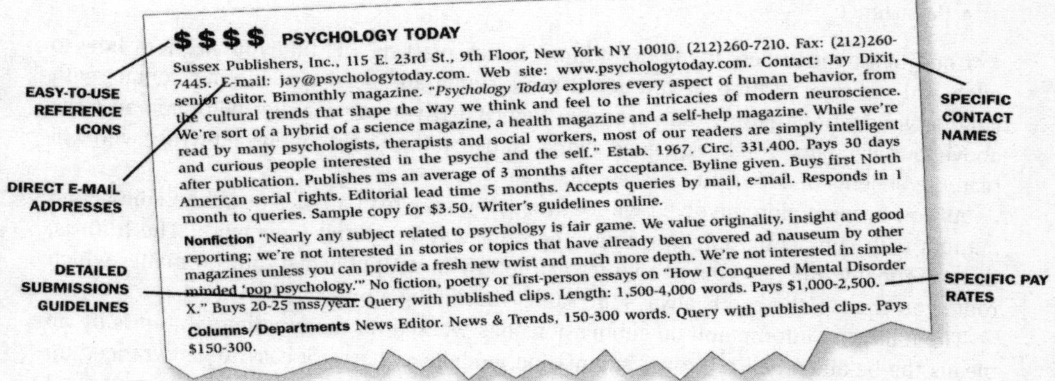

$ $ $ $ PSYCHOLOGY TODAY Sussex Publishers, Inc., 115 E. 23rd St., 9th Floor, New York NY 10010. (212)260-7210. Fax: (212)260-7445. E-mail: jay@psychologytoday.com. Web site: www.psychologytoday.com. Contact: Jay Dixit, senior editor. Bimonthly magazine. "*Psychology Today* explores every aspect of human behavior, from the cultural trends that shape the way we think and feel to the intricacies of modern neuroscience. We're sort of a hybrid of a science magazine, a health magazine and a self-help magazine. While we're read by many psychologists, therapists and social workers, most of our readers are simply intelligent and curious people interested in the psyche and the self." Estab. 1967. Circ. 331,400. Pays 30 days after publication. Publishes ms an average of 3 months after acceptance. Byline given. Buys first North American serial rights. Editorial lead time 5 months. Accepts queries by mail, e-mail. Responds in 1 month to queries. Sample copy for $3.50. Writer's guidelines online.

Nonfiction "Nearly any subject related to psychology is fair game. We value originality, insight and good reporting; we're not interested in stories or topics that have already been covered ad nauseum by other magazines unless you can provide a fresh new twist and much more depth. We're not interested in simple-minded 'pop psychology.'" No fiction, poetry or first-person essays on "How I Conquered Mental Disorder X." Buys 20-25 mss/year. Query with published clips. Length: 1,500-4,000 words. Pays $1,000-2,500.

Columns/Departments News Editor. News & Trends, 150-300 words. Query with published clips. Pays $150-300.

THE BASICS

Before Your First Sale

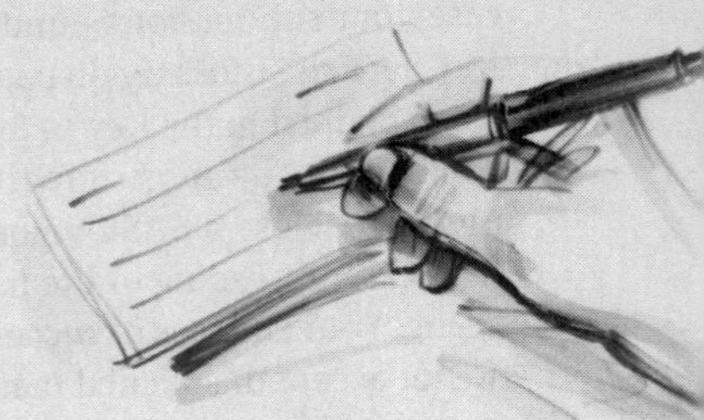

Everything in life has to start somewhere and that somewhere is always at the beginning. Stephen King, J.K. Rowling, John Grisham, Nora Roberts—they all had to start at the beginning. It would be great to say becoming a writer is as easy as waving a magic wand over your manuscript and ''Poof!'' you're published, but that's not how it happens. While there's no one true ''key'' to becoming successful, a long, well-paid writing career *can* happen when you combine four elements:

- Good writing
- Knowledge of writing markets
- Professionalism
- Persistence

Good writing is useless if you don't know which markets will buy your work or how to pitch and sell your writing. If you aren't professional and persistent in your contact with editors, your writing is just that—your writing. But if you are a writer who embraces the above four elements, you have a good chance at becoming a paid, published writer who will reap the benefits of a long and successful career.

As you become more involved with writing, you may read articles or talk to editors and authors with conflicting opinions about the right way to submit your work. The truth is, there are many different routes a writer can follow to get published, but no matter which route you choose, the end is always the same—becoming a published writer.

The following information on submissions has worked for many writers, but it is by no means the be-all-end-all of proper submission guidelines. It's very easy to get wrapped up in the specifics of submitting (Should I put my last name on every page of my manuscript?) and ignore the more important issues (Will this idea on ice fishing in Alaska be appropriate for a regional magazine in Seattle?). Don't allow yourself to become so blinded by submission procedures that you forget common sense. If you use your common sense and develop professional, courteous relations with editors, you will eventually find your own submission style.

DEVELOP YOUR IDEAS, THEN TARGET THE MARKETS

Writers often think of an interesting story, complete the manuscript, and then begin the search for a suitable publisher or magazine. While this approach is common for fiction, poetry and screenwriting, it reduces your chances of success in many nonfiction writing areas. Instead, try choosing categories that interest you and study those sections in *Writer's Market*. Select several listings you consider good prospects for your type of writing. Sometimes the individual listings will even help you generate ideas.

Next, make a list of the potential markets for each idea. Make the initial contact with markets using the method stated in the market listings. If you exhaust your list of possibilities, don't give up. Instead, reevaluate the idea or try another angle. Continue developing ideas and approaching markets. Identify and rank potential markets for an idea and continue the process.

As you submit to the various publications listed in *Writer's Market*, it's important to remember that every magazine is published with a particular audience and slant in mind. Probably the number one complaint we receive from editors is the submissions they receive are completely wrong for their magazines or book line. The first mark of professionalism is to know your market well. Gaining that knowledge starts with *Writer's Market*, but you should also do your own detective work. Search out back issues of the magazines you wish to write for, pick up recent issues at your local newsstand, or visit magazines' Web sites—anything that will help you figure out what subjects specific magazines publish. This research is also helpful in learning what topics have been covered ad nauseum—the topics you should stay away from or approach in a fresh way. Magazines' Web sites are invaluable as most post the current issue of the magazine, as well as back issues, and most offer writer's guidelines.

The same advice is true for submitting to book publishers. Research publisher Web sites for their submission guidelines, recently published titles and their backlist. You can use this information to target your book proposal in a way that fits with a publisher's other titles while not directly competing for sales.

Prepare for rejection and the sometimes lengthy wait. When a submission is returned, check your file folder of potential markets for that idea. Cross off the market that rejected the idea. If the editor has given you suggestions or reasons why the manuscript was not accepted, you might want to incorporate these suggestions when revising your manuscript. After revising your manuscript mail it to the next market on your list.

Take rejection with a grain of salt

Reminder

Rejection is a way of life in the publishing world. It's inevitable in a business that deals with such an overwhelming number of applicants for such a limited number of positions. Anyone who has published has lived through many rejections, and writers with thin skin are at a distinct disadvantage. A rejection letter is not a personal attack. It simply indicates your submission is not appropriate for that market. Writers who let rejection dissuade them from pursuing their dream or who react to an editor's "No" with indignation or fury do themselves a disservice. Writers who let rejection stop them do not get published. Resign yourself to facing rejection now. You will live through it, and you'll eventually overcome it.

QUERY AND COVER LETTERS

A query letter is a brief, one-page letter used as a tool to hook an editor and get him interested in your idea. When you send a query letter to a magazine, you are trying to get an editor to buy your idea or article. When you query a book publisher, you are attempting to get an editor interested enough in your idea to request your book proposal or your entire manuscript. (Note: Some book editors prefer to receive book proposals on first contact. Check individual listings for which method editors prefer.)

Here are some basic guidelines to help you create one that's polished and well-organized. For more tips see Query Letter Clinic on page 20.

- **Limit it to one page, single-spaced**, and address the editor by name (Mr. or Ms. and the surname). *Note*: Do not assume that a person is a Mr. or Ms. unless it is obvious from the name listed. For example, if you are contacting a D.J. Smith, do not assume that D.J. should be preceded by Mr. or Ms. Instead, address the letter to D.J. Smith.

- **Grab the editor's attention with a strong opening.** Some magazine queries, for example, begin with a paragraph meant to approximate the lead of the intended article.
- **Indicate how you intend to develop the article or book.** Give the editor some idea of the work's structure and content.
- **Let the editor know if you have photos** or illustrations available to accompany your magazine article.
- **Mention any expertise or training that qualifies you** to write the article or book. If you've been published before, mention it; if not, don't.
- **End with a direct request to write the article.** Or, if you're pitching a book, ask for the go-ahead to send in a full proposal or the entire manuscript. Give the editor an idea of the expected length and delivery date of your manuscript.

A common question that arises is: If I don't hear from an editor in the reported response time, how do I know when I can safely send the query to another market? Many writers find it helpful to indicate in their queries that if they don't receive a response from the editor (slightly after the listed reporting time), they will assume the editor is not interested. It's best to take this approach, particularly if your topic is timely.

A brief, single-spaced cover letter is helpful when sending a manuscript as it helps personalize the submission. However, if you have previously queried the editor, use the cover letter to politely and briefly remind the editor of that query—when it was sent, what it contained, etc. "Here is the piece on low-fat cooking that I queried you about on December 12. I look forward to hearing from you at your earliest convenience." Do not use the cover letter as a sales pitch.

If you are submitting to a market that accepts unsolicited manuscripts, a cover letter is useful because it personalizes your submission. You can, and should, include information about the manuscript, yourself, your publishing history, and your qualifications.

See Also

In addition to tips on writing queries, The Query Letter Clinic on page 20 offers eight example query letters, some that work and some that don't, as well as editors' comments on why the letters were either successful or failed to garner an assignment or contract.

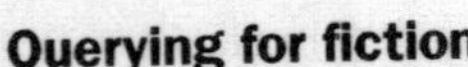

Querying for fiction

Fiction is sometimes queried, but more often editors prefer receiving material. Many fiction editors won't decide on a submission until they have seen the complete manuscript. When submitting a fiction book idea, most editors prefer to see at least a synopsis and sample

Query Letter Resources

For More Info

The following list of books provide you with more detailed information on writing query letters, cover letters, and book proposals. All titles are published by Writer's Digest Books.

- *Formatting & Submitting Your Manuscript, Edition 2*, by Cynthia Laufenberg and the Editors of Writer's Digest Books
- *How to Write Attention-Grabbing Query & Cover Letters*, by John Wood
- *How to Write a Book Proposal, 3rd Edition*, by Michael Larsen
- *Writer's Market Companion, 2nd Edition*, by Joe Feiertag and Mary Cupito

chapters (usually the first three). For fiction published in magazines, most editors want to see the complete short story manuscript. If an editor does request a query for fiction, it should include a description of the main theme and story line, including the conflict and resolution. Take a look at individual listings to see what editors prefer to receive.

NONFICTION BOOK PROPOSALS

Most nonfiction books are sold by a book proposal—a package of materials that details what your book is about, who its intended audience is, and how you intend to write the book. It includes some combination of a cover or query letter, an overview, an outline, author's information sheet, and sample chapters. Editors also want to see information about the audience for your book and about titles that compete with your proposed book.

Submitting a nonfiction book proposal

A proposal package should include the following items:

- **A cover or query letter.** This letter should be a short introduction to the material you include in the proposal.
- **An overview.** This is a brief summary of your book. It should detail your book's subject and give an idea of how that subject will be developed.
- **An outline.** The outline covers your book chapter by chapter and should include all major points covered in each chapter. Some outlines are done in traditional outline form, but most are written in paragraph form.
- **An author's information sheet.** This information should acquaint the editor with your writing background and convince him of your qualifications regarding the subject of your book.
- **Sample chapters.** Many editors like to see sample chapters, especially for a first book. Sample chapters show the editor how you write and develop ideas from your outline.
- **Marketing information.** Facts about how and to whom your book can be successfully marketed are now expected to accompany every book proposal. If you can provide information about the audience for your book and suggest ways the book publisher can reach those people, you will increase your chances of acceptance.
- **Competitive title analysis.** Check the *Subject Guide to Books in Print* for other titles on your topic. Write a one-or two-sentence synopsis of each. Point out how your book differs and improves upon existing topics.

For more information on nonfiction book proposals, read Michael Larsen's *How to Write a Book Proposal* (Writer's Digest Books).

A WORD ABOUT AGENTS

An agent represents a writer's work to publishers, negotiates contracts, follows up to see that contracts are fulfilled, and generally handles a writer's business affairs, leaving the writer free to write. Effective agents are valued for their contacts in the publishing industry, their knowledge about who to approach with certain ideas, their ability to guide an author's career, and their business sense.

While most book publishers listed in *Writer's Market* publish books by unagented writers, some of the larger houses are reluctant to consider submissions that have not reached them through a literary agent. Companies with such a policy are noted by an (A) icon at the beginning of the listing, as well as in the submission information within the listing.

Writer's Market includes a list of 85 literary agents who are all members of the Association of Authors' Representatives and who are also actively seeking new and established writers.

For a more comprehensive resource on finding and working with an agent, see *2008 Guide to Literary Agents*.

MANUSCRIPT FORMAT

You can increase your chances of publication by following a few standard guidelines regarding the physical format of your manuscript. It should be your goal to make your manuscript readable. Follow these suggestions as you would any other suggestions: Use what works for you and discard what doesn't.

In general, when submitting a manuscript, you should use white, $8\frac{1}{2} \times 11$, 20 lb. paper, and you should also choose a legible, professional looking font (i.e., Times New Roman)—no all-italic or artsy fonts. Your entire manuscript should be double-spaced with a $1\frac{1}{2}$-inch margin on all sides of the page. Once you are ready to print your manuscript, you should print either on a laser printer or an ink-jet printer.

ESTIMATING WORD COUNT

Many computers will provide you with a word count of your manuscript. Your editor will count again after editing the manuscript. Although your computer is counting characters, an editor or production editor is more concerned about the amount of space the text will occupy on a page. Several small headlines or subheads, for instance, will be counted the same by your computer as any other word of text. However, headlines and subheads usually employ a different font size than the body text, so an editor may count them differently to be sure enough space has been estimated for larger type.

For short manuscripts, it's often quickest to count each word on a representative page and multiply by the number of pages. You can get a very rough count by multiplying the number of pages in your manuscript by 250 (the average number of words on a double-spaced typewritten page).

PHOTOGRAPHS AND SLIDES

In some cases, the availability of photographs and slides can be the deciding factor as to whether an editor will accept your submission. This is especially true when querying a publication that relies heavily on photographs, illustrations or artwork to enhance the article (i.e., craft magazines, hobby magazines, etc.). In some instances, the publication may offer additional payment for photographs or illustrations.

Check the individual listings to find out which magazines review photographs and what their submission guidelines are. Most publications prefer you do not send photographs with your submission. However, if photographs or illustrations are available, you should indicate that in your query. As with manuscripts, never send the originals of your photographs or illustrations. Instead, send prints or duplicates of slides and transparencies. Also, more magazines and book publishers are using digital images.

SEND PHOTOCOPIES

If there is one hard-and-fast rule in publishing, it's this: *Never* send the original (or only) copy of your manuscript. Most editors cringe when they find out a writer has sent the only copy of their manuscript. You should always send photocopies of your manuscript.

Some writers choose to send a self-addressed, stamped postcard with a photocopied submission. In their cover letter they suggest if the editor is not interested in their manuscript, it may be tossed out and a reply sent on the postcard. This method is particularly helpful when sending your submissions to international markets.

Manuscript Formatting Sample

1 Type your real name (even if you use a pseudonym) and contact information

2 Double-space twice

3 Estimated word count and the rights you are offering

4 Type your title in capital letters, double-space and type "by," double-space again, and type your name (or pseudonym if you're using one)

5 Double-space twice, then indent first paragraph and start text of your manuscript

6 On subsequent pages, type your name, a dash, and the page number in the upper left or right corner

Your name
Your street address
City, State ZIP code
Day and evening phone numbers
E-mail address

50,000 words
World rights

TITLE
by
Your Name

You can increase your chances of publication by following a few standard guidelines regarding the physical format of your article or manuscript. It should be your goal to make your manuscript readable. Use these suggestions as you would any other suggestions: Use what works for you and discard what doesn't.

In general, when submitting a manuscript, you should use white, 8½x11, 20-lb. bond paper, and you should also choose a legible, professional-looking font (i.e., Times New Roman)—no all-italic or artsy fonts. Your entire manuscript should be double-spaced with a 1½-inch margin

Your Name - 2

on all sides of the page. Once you are ready to print your article or manuscript, you should print either on a laser printer or an ink-jet printer.

Remember, though, articles should either be written after you send a one-page query letter to an editor, and the editor then asks you to write the article. If, however, you are sending an article "on spec" to an editor, you should send both a query letter and the complete article.

Fiction is a little different from nonfiction articles, in that it is only sometimes queried, but more often not. Many fiction editors won't decide on a submission until they have seen the complete manuscript. When submitting a fiction book idea, most editors prefer to see at least a synopsis and sample chapters (usually the first three). For fiction that is published

The Basics

Mailing Manuscripts

- Fold manuscripts under five pages into thirds, and send in a #10 SASE.
- Mail manuscripts five pages or more unfolded in a 9×12 or 10×13 SASE.
- For return envelope, fold the envelope in half, address it to yourself, and add a stamp or, if going to Canada or another international destination, International Reply Coupons (available at most post office branches).
- Don't send by Certified Mail—this is a sign of an amateur.

MAILING SUBMISSIONS

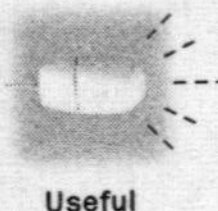

No matter what size manuscript you're mailing, always include a self-addressed, stamped envelope (SASE) with sufficient return postage. The Web site for the U.S. Postal Service (www.usps.com) and the Web site for the Canadian Post (www.canadapost.ca) both have postage calculators if you are unsure of how much postage you'll need to affix.

A book manuscript should be mailed in a sturdy, well-wrapped box. Enclose a self-addressed mailing label and paper clip your return postage to the label. However, be aware that some book publishers do not return unsolicited manuscripts, so make sure you know the practice of the publisher before sending any unsolicited material.

Types of mail service

There are many different mailing service options available to you whether you are sending a query letter or a complete manuscript. You can work with the U.S. Postal Service, United Parcel Service, Federal Express, or any number of private mailing companies. The following are the five most common types of mailing services offered by the U.S. Postal Service.

- **First Class** is a fairly expensive way to mail a manuscript, but many writers prefer it. First-Class mail generally receives better handling and is delivered more quickly than Standard mail.
- **Priority Mail** reaches its destination within two or three days.
- **Standard Mail** rates are available for packages, but be sure to pack your materials carefully because they will be handled roughly. To make sure your package will be returned to you if it is undeliverable, print "Return Postage Guaranteed" under your address.
- **Certified Mail** must be signed for when it reaches its destination.
- **Registered Mail** is a high-security method of mailing where the contents are insured. The package is signed in and out of every office it passes through, and a receipt is returned to the sender when the package reaches its destination.

THE BASICS

Freelance Newspaper Writing 101

by Feoshia Henderson

If you have a good story to tell, now more than ever, a newspaper can be the place to sell it.

Newspapers, like so many other businesses, have cut back on staff and other resources. But the boss still expects a steady stream of interesting stories to fill up those column inches. And to compete with the Internet and new media publications, many newspaper companies have started specialty magazines that depend on engaging feature articles.

This has created more opportunities for new and established freelance writers who are looking for welcoming, quality places to publish their work.

If you've never thought about writing for a newspaper, or just want some insight into what editors are looking for, read on. We've talked to newspaper editors around the country who work with freelance writers everyday to glean some key insight. Though editors and newspapers all have different needs, a few themes emerged when they were asked what makes a proposed article—and a writer—stand out.

You don't always have to be a pro

Pitching an article to a newspaper can be an intimidating prospect, especially if you're new to the market. But you might be surprised to find out that editors aren't always looking for highly experienced wordsmiths with extensive résumés. Of course, writers must have a grasp of basic journalistic writing style and grammar. Still, many editors say enthusiasm or proficiency in a particular subject is more prized in a freelance writer than a thick packet of published clips.

CityBeat, an alternative urban newsweekly in Cincinnati, Ohio, often looks for writers for their Arts and Entertainment section, especially for music and movie reviews. Travel, Home and Garden, and Lifestyle sections are common places where you'll frequently find freelance written articles. ''We tend to look for people who aren't trained writers. We'd rather have someone with expertise in a certain area and passion, and we can help with the writing part,'' says John Fox, editor and co-publisher of *CityBeat*.

That holds true for more traditional daily newspapers as well. John Bordsen, travel editor for *The Charlotte Observer* in North Carolina says: ''Some of the best writers I've used didn't have published clippings. When it comes to background, it's fair game.''

FEOSHIA HENDERSON is the northeastern Hamilton County suburban reporter for *The Cincinnati Enquirer*. Previous to joining the *Enquirer* staff, she worked for several daily and weekly newspapers in Kentucky. Henderson has been a professional freelance writer for six years and has written for *Louisville Magazine*, *Kentucky Monthly* and The Kentucky League of Cities' *City Magazine*, in addition to a monthly political column for *The Kentucky Gazette*.

Of course, experience does count for something, and it can give you an edge over other writers.

Jacqueline Palfy Klemond is senior editor for specialty publications for the South Dakota Argus Leader in Sioux Falls. She also directs the paper's Lifestyle feature staff. In addition to her newspaper duties, she oversees three magazines (topics include upscale living and pets) that the paper has published for the last three years. For her, experience is key.

"I look for someone who has been published before. Some people are very talented who haven't been published, but it's the first question I ask," says Klemond.

Sally Scherer, Lifestyles Editor for *The Lexington Herald Leader* in Kentucky says, "I would prefer to work with someone who has something already published so they can send clips."

So, get started!

Do your homework

Decision-makers say the most important step in taking an article from an idea to a published clip, is also the first step. Do some research before pitching a story to make sure it's a good fit for a particular paper. That will save your, and a potential editor's, time. It also will help you best decide what type of article the publication is likely to buy. Read through several issues of a newspaper you want to pitch, and examine the feature sections where those freelance articles usually land. Editors say they are less likely to rely on outside work for hard news stories, though there are some exceptions.

"They should study several previous issues by looking at our Web site to see what we do, and then bring me ideas they think I would be interested in," says Mary Corrado, Editor of *Inside*, a newsweekly that covers northside Chicago neighborhoods. *Inside* has writers' guidelines with specific instructions on its Web site, which a freelance writer should follow carefully.

When you read a paper, pay special attention to the tone of the writing. Is it irreverent? Formal? Edgy? Poetic? Does the newspaper print articles written in first-person or in a traditional news story style? Don't send in an essay or an opinion column if the newspaper doesn't usually print those types of feature articles. Make sure your particular writing style fits the publication to which you're offering ideas.

If you've done your homework it will show in your pitch. Technology makes freelance writing and research easier, more efficient and quicker to do from home, but it can have its drawbacks. Though tempting and easy to do because of e-mail and the Internet, don't send a speedy, generic query letter to dozens of different editors. Tailor your query letters to each newspaper to which you send it. Find the editor of the particular section you'd like to write for and address your letter specifically to that person. It will impress the editor, and give the query a better shot of someone actually taking the time to read it. Mention the publication by name and talk about other similar articles you've read.

"If I get a letter that is completely anonymous, one that says 'Dear Sir or Madam,' and they haven't bothered to look up my name, they are less likely to get the time of day," Scherer says. "Put some personality into it."

Tailoring your query may sound basic, but a lot of writers don't take the time to do it, editors say. If you do, you immediately stand apart from your competitors, who are many. That doesn't mean each query letter has to be radically different. Once you have a basic format, you can alter it to fit a particular newspaper.

"If you do your homework and send a query to the right person, there's a better chance of someone reading—it shows you're paying attention," *CityBeat* Editor Fox says. "It's pretty clear to me if somebody just goes through a list and they don't know what the paper is about."

Make it quick, but professional

Newspaper editors are like the rest of us: pressed for time. For many newspapers a query letter and clips sent by "snail mail" is a thing of the past, and unlike magazines that publish

THE BASICS

Publishing Poetry

A Reality Check

by Nancy Breen

As editor of *Poet's Market* (a directory, like *Writer's Market*, of magazines, journals, presses, contests and more, but geared to poets), I get a lot of questions about the whole process of writing and submitting poetry. Often similar questions are forwarded to me from *Writer's Market*. Regardless of the source, I try to treat all such queries with respect and genuine concern for passing along what I hope is valued information.

There are certain questions, though, that I dread to receive—because my answer invariably will lead to disillusionment and disappointment as I splash cold reality into the faces of unsuspecting (and uninformed) poets. Read further if you're curious what these questions are, and especially if you're an aspiring poet yourself.

Is there any money in poetry?

It really hurts to tell ambitious writers that their efforts will result in little monetary gain. However, that's the brutal truth about poetry: There's no money in it, at least not for the average hard-working (and even widely published) poet.

Most poetry appears in little magazines and literary journals. These markets are unlikely to pay cash for the poetry they print, offering instead a copy or two of the issue in which the poet's work appears (called a *contributor's copy*). Online literary magazines usually don't pay at all, although many poets see the worldwide exposure of Internet publication as a type of compensation. While there are a few larger literary magazines that do pay, they're quite prestigious and receive thousands of submissions per year while choosing a small percentage for publication. That means intense competition and high rates of rejection. The same is true of the few commercial magazines that publish poetry, such as *The New Yorker* and *The Atlantic Monthly*.

In truth, if you had a poem accepted by every paying magazine and journal, you probably still wouldn't make a decent income.

The situation in poetry book publishing is just as financially grim. Few of the "major" publishers put out many volumes of poetry; and those volumes usually are by our best known, established poets, talented up-and-comers, and major prizewinners. (A few celebrity poetry books may be in the mix; but, obviously, you have to become a celebrity *first* for publishers to take interest in your poetry.)

NANCY BREEN is the editor of *Poet's Market* (www.poetsmarket.com). Her poems have appeared in a number of journals, and she's published two chapbooks: *Rites and Observances* (Finishing Line Press) and *How Time Got Away* (Pudding House Publications).

Most poetry publishers are literary presses, often run through universities and colleges; or they're independent smaller presses. In either case, they don't have large sums of money to throw around for advances and royalties.

If you're disappointed, and even depressed by the low financial rewards of poetry publishing, ask yourself: When was the last time you bought a literary magazine or book of poetry? Few readers in America spend their dollars on poetry (and too often that includes the poets themselves).

Can you recommend a publisher for my 300-poem book manuscript?

First, reread the preceding section, especially the paragraphs about book publishers.

Next, if you haven't looked at the poetry shelves of your local bookstore lately, do a little market research. How many 300-poem books do you see? If you find one, is it by a single poet or is it an anthology? If the book is the work of one poet, review the biographical note for the poet's age, publishing history, academic background, awards won and hints about his or her standing in the literary community. If you don't have a similar biography as a poet, don't even think about trying to get such a massive collection of poems published.

Also, if you've never published any of your poems in literary magazines, don't start shopping for a book publisher just yet. The established route poets follow is to publish individual poems in magazines and journals (in print and online) before assembling a collection of any length. By publishing in magazines first, you establish some necessary credentials:

- You demonstrate you're familiar with the world of poetry publishing because you've been an active participant—publishers appreciate that.
- You prove that someone else has read and appreciated your work besides you, your friends and your family.
- You establish a track record of having worked successfully with editors.

There are occasional exceptions to the publish-in-magazines-first approach. The aforementioned celebrity poetry books are one example. And every few years there's a publishing phenomenon like Mattie Stepanek, the young boy with muscular dystrophy who sold millions of copies of his poetry books before his death at 14 in 2004. Such situations are unique unto themselves and represent exceptions, rather than the rule.

Keep in mind, too, that most poets progress from publishing in magazines to assembling a chapbook, rather than book manuscript. What is a chapbook? It's a soft cover publication of about 24-32 pages. Although bookstores don't stock chapbooks (even independent stores don't favor chapbooks because there's no spine showing the title—chapbooks are usually folded and saddle-stapled), chapbooks have become a very popular format. Production values range from simple to extravagant (depending on paper and cover stock), they can be produced and sold economically, and they're easy to offer for sale at readings. No, they don't make money for the poet *or* the press; but as I said earlier, money should never be a primary concern if you're serious about poetry.

Can you recommend an agent who can represent my poetry book?

As I said, there's little money in poetry. Agents work on commission, i.e., a percentage of what the poet is paid. Consequently, 15% of nothing doesn't make poetry attractive to agents.

As always, there may be exceptions. A highly successful poet may have an agent, especially if the poet does other writing that *does* benefit from representation. A beginning poet, though—especially a beginning poet with a manuscript of 300 previously unpublished poems—probably is not going to find an agent. In fact, any poet who comes across an agent who does express interest should be wary. Ask questions, do your homework, don't sign anything until you've thoroughly researched the agent. And *never* pay for representation.

How can I get my self-published book of poetry into bookstores?

Whether your book is truly self-published or printed by a vanity publisher or print-on-demand publisher (known as POD, wherein a publisher stores your book digitally and prints out copies as they're purchased), distribution is going to be a challenge. Bookstores usually work with professional distributors to stock their shelves, an avenue that may be closed to poets who self-publish. Similarly, vanity publishers can't get your books into bookstores without a distributor, no matter what they may claim. POD publishers may rely more on their own online bookstores and author Web sites than working with a distributor.

In most bookstores, a limited amount of shelf space is devoted to poetry. Sometimes independent bookstores (i.e., not owned by national chains) are more open to stocking small press and self-published books; this is especially true if the poet is a local author.

Poets shouldn't focus on bookstores as a sole source of sales. Other methods of selling include offering books through a personal Web site; scheduling readings at coffeehouses, bookstores or even your own church or community center (where you can offer your book for sale to the audience); and sending promotional postcards to potential customers with information about how to order by mail. To learn more, and to brainstorm additional ideas for selling and promotion, try your library for books on self-publishing; or enter "selling self-published books" or similar phrases into a search engine for a range of information and perspectives on the Web.

And about those anthologies...

No reality check for poets would be complete without a mention of those poetry operations that sponsor contests and Web sites, the ones that publish huge anthologies of "winning" poems. If you choose to participate, that's your decision, but be aware of these points:

- *Everyone* who submits a poem to such contests is "chosen" to appear in an anthology, so there's no quality standard.
- Having a poem published in such an anthology is *not* a legitimate publishing credit (that is, serious publishers don't take such publishing credits seriously).
- If your poem(s) appear in such an anthology, or on an associated public Web site, your work is considered "published" and cannot be submitted to any magazine or contest that does not accept previously published work.

Some poets appreciate the sense of community they find at such Web sites. They simply enjoy seeing their work in print and online, and they don't mind spending huge sums for copies of the anthologies (or for the plaques, coffee mugs and other merchandise that may be available). And that's their prerogative, as long as those poets aren't deceiving themselves about what such publication means. If they use their anthology appearances as selling points to prospective editors and publishers, though, they may find that they and their poetry are not going to be taken seriously.

What are your objectives?

Be realistic about what the world of poetry publishing has to offer and what you hope to achieve. If writing good poetry is more important to you than money, recognition and the other trappings of high stakes publication, then you're on the right path. If, on the other hand, you hope to achieve fame and fortune through your poetry, well—you need a reality check.

THE BASICS

Query Letter Clinic

Many great writers ask year after year, "Why is it so hard to get published?" In many cases, these writers have spent years—and possibly thousands of dollars on books and courses—developing their craft. They submit to the appropriate markets, yet rejection is always the end result. The culprit? A weak query letter.

The query letter is often the most important piece of the publishing puzzle. In many cases, it determines whether an editor or agent will even read your manuscript. A good query letter makes a good first impression; a bad query letter earns a swift rejection.

The elements of a query letter

A query letter should sell editors or agents on your idea or convince him to request your finished manuscript. The most effective query letters get into the specifics from the very first line. It's important to remember that the query is a call to action, not a listing of features and benefits.

In addition to selling your idea or manuscript, a query letter can include information on the availability of photographs or artwork. You can include a working title and projected word count. Depending on the piece, you might also mention whether a sidebar might be appropriate and the type of research you plan to conduct. If appropriate, include a tentative deadline and indicate whether the query is being simultaneously submitted.

Biographical information should be included as well, but don't overdo it unless your background actually helps sell the article or proves that you're the only person who could write your proposed piece.

Things to avoid in a query letter

The query letter is not a place to discuss pay rates. This step comes after an editor has agreed to take on your article or book. Besides making an unprofessional impression on an editor, it can also work to your disadvantage in negotiating your fee. If you ask for too much, an editor may not even contact you to see if a lower rate might work. If you ask for too little, you may start an editorial relationship where you are making far less than the normal rate.

You should also avoid rookie mistakes, such as mentioning that your work is copyrighted or including the copyright symbol on your work. While you want to make it clear that you've researched the market, avoid using flattery as a technique for selling your work. It often has the opposite effect of what you intend. In addition, don't hint that you can re-write the piece, as this only leads the editor to think there will be a lot of work involved in shaping up your writing.

Also, never admit several other editors or agents have rejected the query. Always treat your new audience as if they are the first place on your list of submission possibilities.

How to format your query letter

It's OK to break writing rules in a short story or article, but you should follow the rules when it comes to crafting an effective query. Here are guidelines for query writing.

- Use a normal font and typeface, such as Times New Roman and 10- or 12-point type.
- Include your name, address, phone number, e-mail address and Web site, if possible.
- Use a one-inch margin on paper queries.
- Address a specific editor or agent. (Note: The listings in *Writer's Market* provide a contact name for most submissions. It's wise to double-check contact names online or by calling.)
- Limit query letter to one single-spaced page.
- Include self-addressed, stamped envelope or postcard for response with post submissions.
- Use block paragraph format (no indentations).
- Thank the editor for considering your query.

When and how to follow up

Accidents do happen. Queries may not reach your intended reader. Staff changes or interoffice mail snafus may end up with your query letter thrown away. Or the editor may have set your query off to the side for further consideration and forgotten it. Whatever the case may be, there are some basic guidelines you should use for your follow-up communication.

Most importantly, wait until the reported response time, as indicated in *Writer's Market* or their submission guidelines, has elapsed before contacting an editor or agent. Then, you should send a short and polite e-mail describing the original query sent, the date it was sent, and asking if they received it or made a decision regarding its fate.

The importance of remaining polite and businesslike when following up cannot be stressed enough. Making a bad impression on an editor can often have a ripple effect—as that editor may share his or her bad experience with other editors at the magazine or publishing company.

How the clinic works

As mentioned earlier, the query letter is the most important weapon for getting an assignment or a request for your full manuscript. Published writers know how to craft a well-written, hard-hitting query. What follows are eight queries: four are strong; four are not. Detailed comments show what worked and what did not. As you'll see, there is no cut-and-dried ''good'' query format; every strong query works on its own merit.

Good Nonfiction Magazine Query

Jimmy Boaz, editor
American Organic Farmer's Digest
8336 Old Dirt Road
Macon, GA 00000

My name is only available on our magazine's Web site and on the masthead. So this writer has done her research.

Dear Mr. Boaz,

There are 87 varieties of organic crops grown in the United States, but there's only one farm producing 12 of these—Morganic Corporation.

Here's a story that hasn't been pitched before. I didn't know Morganic was so unique in the market. I'm interested to know more.

Located in the heart of Arkansas, this company spent the past decade providing great organic crops at a competitive price helping them grow into the ninth leading organic farming operation in the country. Along the way, they developed the most unique organic offering in North America.

As a seasoned writer with access to Richard Banks, the founder and president of Morganic, I propose writing a profile piece on Banks for your Organic Shakers department. After years of reading this riveting column, I believe the time has come to cover Morganic's rise in the organic farming industry.

The author has access to her interview subject, and she displays knowledge of the magazine by pointing out the correct section in which it would run.

The piece would run in the normal 800-1,200 word range with photographs available of Banks and Morganic's operation.

I've been published in *Arkansas Farmer's Deluxe*, *Organic Farming Today* and in several newspapers.

While I probably would've assigned this article based off the idea alone, her past credits do help solidify my decision.

Thank you for your consideration of this article. I hope to hear from you soon.

Sincerely,

Jackie Service
34 Good St.
Little Rock, AR 00000
jackie.service9867@email.com

Bad Nonfiction Magazine Query

This is sexist, and it doesn't address any contact specifically. It shows a complete lack of research on the part of the writer.

An over-the-top, bold claim by a writer who does not impress me with his publishing background.

Insults the magazine, and then reassures me he won't charge too much?

While I do assign material from time-to-time, I prefer writers pitch me on their own ideas after studying the magazine.

I'm sure people aren't going to be knocking down his door anytime soon.

Dear Gentlemen,

I'd like to write the next great article you'll ever publish. My writing credits include exposé pieces I've done for local and community newspapers and for my college English classes. I've been writing for years and years.

Your magazine may not be a big one like *Rolling Stone* or *Sports Illustrated*, but I'm willing to write an interview for you anyway. I know you need material, and I need money (but don't worry I won't charge too much).

Just give me some people to interview, and I'll do the best job you've ever read. It will be amazing, and I can re-write the piece for you if you don't agree. I'm willing to re-write 20 times if needed.

You better hurry up and assign me an article though, because I've sent out letters to lots of other magazines, and I'm sure to be filled up to capacity very soon.

Later gents,

Carl Bighead
76 Bad Query Lane
Big City, NY 00000

Good Fiction Magazine Query

Marcus West
88 Piano Drive
Lexington, KY 00000

August 8, 2007

Jeanette Curic, editor
Wonder Stories
45 Noodle Street
Portland, OR 00000

Dear Ms. Curic,

Please consider the following 1,200-word story, "Turning to the Melon," a quirky coming of age story with a little magical realism thrown in the mix.

After reading *Wonder Stories* for years, I think I've finally written something that would fit with your audience. My previous short story credits include *Stunned Fiction Quarterly* and *Faulty Mindbomb*.

Thank you in advance for considering "Turning to the Melon."

Sincerely,

Marcus West
(123) 456-7890
marcusw87452@email.com

Encl: Manuscript and SASE

Follows the format we established in our guidelines. Being able to follow directions is more important than many writers realize.

Story is in our word count, and the description sounds like the type of story we would consider publishing.

It's flattering to know he reads our magazine. While it won't guarantee publication, it does make me a little more hopeful that the story I'm reading will be a good fit. Also, good to know he's been published before.

I can figure it out, but it's nice to know what other materials were included in the envelope.

This letter is not flashy or gimmicky. It just gives me the basics and puts me in the right frame of mind to read the actual story.

Bad Fiction Magazine Query

We do not accept e-mail queries or submissions.

To: curic@wonderstories808.com
Subject: A Towering Epic Fantasy

This is a little too informal.

Hello there.

First off, what did he write? An epic novel or short story? Second, 25,000 words is way over our 1,500-word max.

I've written a great fantasy epic novel short story of about 25,000 words that may be included in your magazine if you so desire.

I'm lost for words.

More than 20 years, I've spent chained to my desk in a basement writing out the greatest story of our time. And it can be yours if you so desire to have it.

Money and movie rights? We pay moderate rates and definitely don't get involved in movies.

Just say the word, and I'll ship it over to you. We can talk money and movie rights after your acceptance. I have big plans for this story, and you can be part of that success.

Yours forever (if you so desire),

I'm sure the writer was just trying to be nice, but this is a little bizarre and kind of a scary stalker ending to the letter. I do not so desire any more contact with "Harry."

Harold
(or Harry for friends)

Good Nonfiction Book Query

Effective subject line. Lets me know exactly what to expect when I open the e-mail.

Good lead. Six kids and teaches high school. I already believe her.

Nice title that would fit well with others that we currently offer.

Her platform as a speaker definitely gets my attention.

25,000 e-mail subscribers? She must have a very good voice to gather that many readers.

To: corey@bigbookspublishing.com
Subject: Query: Become a Better Parent in 30 Days

Dear Mr. Corey,

As a parent of six and a high school teacher for more than a decade, I know first-hand that being a parent is difficult work. Even harder is being a good parent. My proposed title *Taking Care of Yourself and Your Kids: A 30-day Program to Become a Better Parent While Still Living Your Life* would show how to handle real-life situations and still be a good parent.

This book has been years in the making, as it follows the outline I've used successfully in my summer seminars I give on the topic to thousands of parents every year. It really works, because past participants contact me constantly to let me know what a difference my classes have made in their lives.

In addition to marketing and selling *Taking Care of Yourself and Your Kids* at my summer seminars, I would also be able to sell it through my Web site and promote it through my weekly e-newsletter with over 25,000 subscribers. Of course, it would also make a very nice trade title that I think would sell well in bookstores and possibly retail outlets, such as K-Mart, Wal-Mart and Target.

If you would like to look over my proposal, please just shoot an e-mail back.

Thank you for your consideration.

Sincerely,

Marilyn Parent
8647 Query St.
Norman, OK 00000
mparent8647@email.com
www.marilynsbetterparents.com

I was interested after the first paragraph, but every paragraph after made it impossible to not request her proposal.

Bad Nonfiction Book Query

The subject line is so vague, I almost deleted this e-mail as spam without even opening it.

This almost sounds like a sales pitch for a book. Maybe this is spam after all? The reason we don't publish such a book is easy—we don't do hobby titles.

I'm not going to open an attachment from an unknown sender via e-mail, especially of someone who's not the prettiest person. Also, copyrighting your work is the sign of an amateur.

1,000 possible buyers is a small market, and I'm not going to pay a writer to do research on a book proposal.

Not even a last name? Or contact information? At least, I won't feel guilty for not responding.

To: info@bigbookspublishing.com
Subject: a question for you

I really liked this book by Mega Book Publishers called *Build Better Trains in Your Own Backyard*. It was a great book that covered all the basics of model train building. My father and I would read from it together and assemble all the pieces, and it was magical like Christmas all through the year. Why wouldn't you want to publish such a book?

Well, here it is. I've already copyrighted the material for 1999 and can help you promote it if you want to send me on a worldwide book tour. As you can see from my attached digital photo, I'm not the prettiest person, but I am passionate.

There are at least 1,000 model train builders in the United States alone, and there might be even more than that. I haven't done enough research yet, because I don't know if this is an idea that appeals to you. If you give me maybe $500, I could do that research in a day and get back to you on it.

Anyway, this idea is a good one that brings back lots of memories for me.

Jacob

Good Fiction Book Query

Jeremy Mansfield, editor
Novels R Us Publishing
8787 Big Time Street
New York NY 00000

Dear Mr. Mansfield,

My 62,000-word novel, *Love in April*, is a psychologically complex thriller in the same mold as James Patterson, but with a touch of the supernatural a′ la Anne Rice.

Supernatural genre bending novels have been money in the bank lately with the emergence of the Anita Blake series and the Highlander series. *Love in April* comes from this same tradition, but like all bestselling fiction makes its own path.

Rebecca Frank is at the top of the modeling world, posing for magazines in exotic locales all over the world and living life to its fullest. Despite all her success, she feels something is missing in her life. Then she runs into Marcus Hunt, a wealthy bachelor with cold blue eyes and an ambiguous past.

Within 24 hours of meeting Marcus, Rebecca's understanding of the world turns upside down, and she finds herself fighting for her life and the love of a man who may not have the ability to return her the favor.

Filled with demons, serial killers, trolls, maniacal clowns and more, this novel will put Rebecca through a gauntlet of trouble and turmoil, leading up to a final climatic realization that may lead to her unraveling.

Love in April should fit in well with your other titles, such as *Bone Dead* and *Carry Me Home*, though it is a unique story. Your Web site mentioned supernatural suspense as a current interest, so I hope this is a good match.

My short fiction has appeared in many mystery magazines, including a prize-winning story in *The Mysterious Oregon Quarterly*. This novel is the first in a series that I'm working on (already half-way through the second).

As stated in your guidelines, I've included the first 30 pages. Thank you for considering *Love in April*.

Sincerely,

Merry Plentiful
54 Willow Road
East Lansing MI 00000
merry865423@email.com

Novel is correct length and has the suspense and supernatural elements we're seeking.

The quick summary sounds like something we would write on the back cover of our paperbacks. That's a good thing, because it identifies the triggers that draw a response out of our readers.

She mentions similar titles we've done and that she's done research on our Web site. She's not afraid to put in a little extra effort.

At the moment, I'm not terribly concerned that this book could become a series, but it is something good to file away in the back of my mind for future use.

Bad Fiction Book Query

Jeremy Mansfield
Novels R Us Publishing
8787 Big Time Street
New York NY 00000

Dear Editor,

My novel has an amazing twist ending that could make it a worldwide phenomenon overnight while you are sleeping. It has spectacular special effects that will probably lead to a multi-million dollar movie deal that will also spawn action figures, lunch boxes, and several other crazy subsidiary rights. I mean, we're talking big-time money here.

While I love to hear enthusiasm from a writer about his or her work, this kind of unchecked excitement is worrisome for an editor.

I'm not going to share the twist until I have a signed contract that authorizes me to a big bank account, because I don't want to have my idea stolen and used to promote whatever new initiative "The Man" has in mind for media nowadays. But let it be known that you will be rewarded handsomely for taking a chance on me.

I need to know the twist to make a decision on whether to accept the manuscript. Plus, I'm troubled by the paranoia and emphasis on making a lot of money.

Did you know that George Lucas once took a chance on an actor named Harrison Ford by casting him as Hans Solo in Star Wars? Look at how that's panned out. Ford went on to become a big actor in the Indiana Jones series, *The Fugitive*, *Blade Runner* and more. It's obvious that you taking a risk on me could play out in the same dramatic results.

I'm confused. Does he think he's Harrison Ford?

I realize you've got to make money, and guess what? I want to make money too. So we're on the same page, you and I. We both want to make money, and we'll stop at nothing to do so.

If you want me to start work on this amazing novel with an incredible twist ending, just send a one-page contract agreeing to pay me a lot of money if we hit it big. No other obligations will apply. If it's a bust, I won't sue you for millions.

So that's the twist: He hasn't even written it yet. I can't make a decision without a completed manuscript. There's no way I'm going to offer a contract for a novel that hasn't been written by someone with no experience or idea of how the publishing industry works.

Sincerely,

Kenzel Pain
92 Bad Writer Road
Austin TX 00000

PERSONAL VIEWS

Selling My First Book

How Stiff *Happened*

www.phyllischristopher.com

by Mary Roach

My journey toward the publication of my first book, *Stiff: The Curious Lives of Human Cadavers* (W.W. Norton), began in the fall of 2000. I'd been writing magazine articles and columns for 15 years. In all that time, I'd never been able to come up with an idea that seemed to merit a whole book and/or a topic that I could imagine sticking with for two years without losing interest. Here's what broke the spell. It's pretty pathetic. I worked in an office with a group of writers, and each January a few of us would go to lunch and make a list of predictions about our office mates for the coming year. The January prior, someone had predicted that by the end of the year I'd have a book deal. Round about October, I realized I had three months to write a book proposal and land a contract—or face the shame of not living up to the 1999 Mary prediction.

At the time I had this realization, I was writing a quirky, reported column for Salon.com. The column dealt, rather loosely, with medicine and the human body. I'd done three columns about cadaver research that got very high hit rates. Because my hit rates had been dropping over the past couple months, I'd been poking around for other cadaver material, hoping to jump-start my ratings. Before I had a chance to write any of them, the column got axed. So there I was, with four or five orphaned cadaver ideas and a pressing need to write a book proposal. Coincidentally, around that time I'd received an e-mail from an agent at William Morris, Jay Mandel, who was a fan of the column and wanted to know if I had any book ideas. I asked him if he thought that a book about the post-mortem careers of dead people might be a good idea. I expected him to say no. And really, I would have agreed with him. It was hard to imagine the scenario in which a person, browsing in a book store, stops and thinks, "Whoah, looky here. Book about cadaver research. This is what I'm going to read next." Strangely enough, Jay thought I should write the proposal.

I had no idea how to do this, of course. Jay sent me, by way of example, a proposal for a biography of Graham Parsons. This was not excessively helpful. Parsons is dead, but that's about it for similarities between the books. Nonetheless, the basics seemed pretty straightforward. Chapter outline is the meat of it. Throw in some grabby stuff up front to catch their attention, add some marketing-speak at the back end, make sure it sings. Mine wasn't long: maybe 15 pages double-spaced. I did not write a sample chapter, but rather included

---

MARY ROACH is the author of the *New York Times* bestsellers *Stiff: The Curious Lives of Human Cadavers* and *Spook: Science Tackles the Afterlife*, both published by WW Norton. Mary has written for *Outside, Wired, New Scientist, The New York Times Magazine*, and NPR's "All Things Considered." She is a frequent contributor at the *New York Times Book Review*, a former columnist for Salon.com and a contributing editor at the science magazine *Discover*.

the three cadaver-related Salon columns. I didn't do a lot of research for the proposal beyond the poking around I'd done for the Salon column. I figured that a proposal is essentially a sales tool, and that no one was going to hang on to it and check to see that the manuscript contained everything I'd proposed.

Enough editors liked the proposal that Jay urged me to come to New York (I live in California) and meet with some of them. So I did this. I bought a suit and borrowed a friend's winter coat that smelled faintly of mothballs. (I have not worn the suit since.) I spent two days in meetings with editors, maybe eight in all. There was one preemptive bid, a fairly generous one, on the last morning of meetings. Jay strongly advised turning it down. He wanted to take the book to auction. I remember saying—whining, really—"But isn't there a chance that no one else will bid? And that we will have turned away the only interested bidder?" Jay said, "Yes, there is. And we're going to take it." This is why we have agents. Agents got balls.

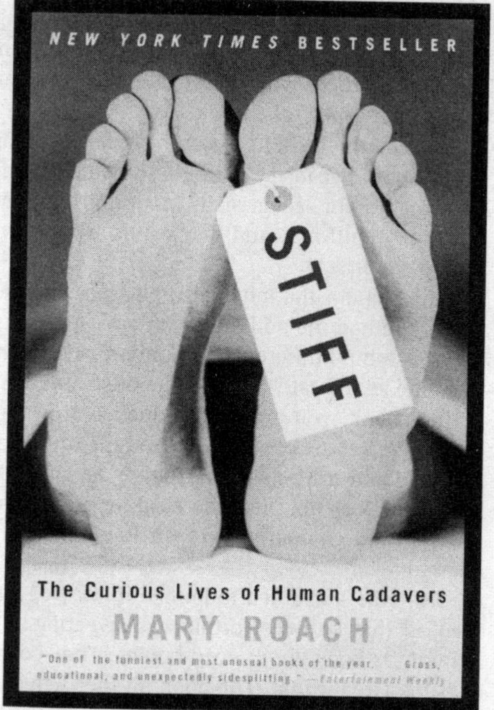

Stiff is Roach's bestselling first nonfiction title, covering what happens to body's after they're pronounced dead.

In the end, about a half dozen publishers bid on the book. A book about cadavers. By a woman who smells like mothballs. It was the most extraordinary thing that had ever happened to me. The bidding went on for two days, through, I think, three rounds. Jay called at the end of each round to update me: who had dropped out (all but three by the end of Round 1) and where the bids were at.

The highest bid was made by W.W. Norton (of *Norton Anthology of English Literature* fame). One of my office mates said, "Norton!? Aren't they a little highbrow for you?" And yes, they are. Which is partly why I was so thrilled to be going with them. A book about cadavers published by a more commercial publisher might have been dismissed as trashy. The fact that W.W. Norton was publishing this book, I think, made people in the industry take note. Jay told me that even if Norton had been the second-highest bidder—provided the difference between the top bids was relatively small—he would have advised signing with them. And I would have.

After the high of the deal, the panic set in. I had no idea how one goes about structuring a book. (I still don't.) My proposal had been half-baked and cavalier. I'd done almost no research. I spent about three months flailing and floundering, reporting on things I didn't end up using. At a certain point, though, it all began to gel and I had a sense of what this book was going to be and which chapters might go where. Even then, I remained skeptical that what I was producing was actually a book. It did not possess that Holy Grail of nonfiction, the "through line." There were no characters who hung around for more than a chapter, growing and changing and having epiphanies. I recall expressing my worries to a fellow nonfiction author. He said, "Yeah, but you know what? You're going to turn it in, and they're going to put a cover on it, and suddenly it will be a book. And no one will question it." And he was right. So far no one has figured it out. (Shhh.)

The hardest part of the book was persuading researchers to let me come to their labs and watch what they do. They had nothing to gain and a fair amount to lose, and I truly don't blame the people who turned me away. For me, this is always the hardest and most time-consuming aspect of a book.

I turned the book in a year from the date I signed the contract. I did not show it to anyone beforehand. Because what if I'd showed it to a friend or colleague, and they'd said, "I dunno, Mar, the humor seems really inappropriate"? My self-doubt is so solid that I would have cut the funny stuff out, and that would have been a mistake. I decided to see what my editor had to say first.

She was, for the most part, pleased. She didn't want the tone changed or the humor cut back. She had me add a chapter and edit one down by about half—both wise suggestions. We had a mild difference of opinion as to what the scope of the book should be, but in the end, she let me call it. This is the huge and wonderful difference between books and articles. With a book, you are the product; with an article, the magazine is the product. With an article, you must conform to the tone and goals of the magazine. With a book, you invent the tone and the goals. Your editor assumes that you are the best judge of how to treat the topic and does not push too hard for a major shift in your vision. It's heavenly. All told, the revisions, as compared to magazine revisions, were minor. It took about three weeks to get them done.

Stiff was scheduled to launch in May of 2003. There had been talk of a U.S. invasion of Iraq all that spring. Norton was sweating. This was not an ideal time to be launching a humorous book about dead bodies. They considered postponing publication, but decided it was too late for that. The book hit the shelves shortly after the "shock-and-awe" campaign. We lost some radio appearances ("Talk of the Nation" backed out), but in the end, the timing hardly mattered. The collective American attention span is so short that six weeks into the war, it had begun to fade from day-to-day conversation. There is actually more talk about Iraq now than there was then.

Norton did a superb job with the promotion of this book. In part it was the launch, which was a two-week tour with a lot of radio—the most valuable by far being NPR's "All Things Considered"—and a healthy hit of newspaper advertising. Plus good bookstore distribution to back it up. More importantly, when the book hit the *New York Times* extended bestseller list that August (talk about shock and awe) Norton was on top of it. They dived back in with more advertising, taking advantage of the buzz generated by the *Times* showing and always keeping on top of bookstore distribution.

Stiff continues to be a steady seller, with upwards of 400,000 copies in print. Ultimately, I think word-of-mouth is what made *Stiff* a hit, but word-of-mouth can't work its magic if the books aren't in the bookstores and the launch hasn't reached enough mouths. It's an elusive thing: that golden mix of marketing, buzz, subject matter, and writing that makes a book a hit. My second book, *Spook*, had a bigger launch but didn't sell as well. (More books were sold during the launch period, but it did not have the legs, as they say, that *Stiff* has had.)

A couple of more recent developments have helped *Stiff* keep selling. The book eventually made its way onto the book club circuit and onto a lot of high school reading lists. I couldn't have predicted either of these things. Indeed, I would have predicted, if asked, that neither would happen. But there you go. Books. They're a mystery.

PERSONAL VIEWS

Freelance Success Stories

compiled and judged by Robert Lee Brewer

In the past, *Writer's Market* has dedicated ample space to profiling successful and emerging writers in the typical third-person, article format. As we planned the 2008 edition, we thought, "Why not let successful writers present their own stories in their own voices?" This led to the first annual Freelance Success Stories contest (see the listing on page 985).

Our first contest was promoted exclusively online at WritersMarket.com and through other online channels, including newsletters, blogs, and message boards. There were 60 initial entrants and ultimately three winners: Jeff Yeager, Michelle Bermas, and John K. Borchardt. Another entrant, Kim Childress, provided a short sidebar for this edition of the book.

These stories are not presented as *the* one and only way to get published, or even as the three only ways (and a sidebar) to get published and find success. These stories are intended to serve as proof that regular people do find success in writing; to inspire new ideas for how you can use unique avenues and opportunities to find success; and to motivate you to create or add to your own success stories as a freelance writer.

After years of working on *Writer's Market* and WritersMarket.com, I felt sure our readers and subscribers would provide a wealth of success stories. Thank you for proving me right. I hope to read your success story for the 2009 edition of the book. In the meantime, please enjoy the winners of the 2008 contest.

THE STORY OF MY CHEAP SHOT

by Jeff Yeager

2005 was *my year,* despite the fact it was the year I officially dropped out.

That was the year I went from being a newbie freelance writer with fewer than 10 published clips in my file to being "one hot commodity," as my newly recruited literary agent put it, landing a healthy publishing contract with Random House's Broadway Books for my first book. It was the year Matt Lauer said on NBC's *Today Show* that I've "turned pinching pennies into an art form" and branded me the "Ultimate Cheapskate."

The morning I appeared on the *Today Show,* the local NBC producer from Columbus nonchalantly turned his back on me. But I could still hear most of the muffled cell phone call he'd just placed to the *Today Show* producer back in New York. The live broadcast from Bucyrus, Ohio's Bratwurst Festival—the culminating spot for the Show's inaugural weeklong

ROBERT LEE BREWER is the editor of *Writer's Market* and WritersMarket.com. He can be reached via e-mail at robert.brewer@fwpubs.com.

"Cheapskate Way" series—was scheduled to air in less than 10 minutes, and the local producer was visibly nervous.

"Well, yes, err, I guess we're ready. Ah, your, ah, on-air guy . . . I, I guess that's what he is . . . just arrived. Says his name is Jeff. Does that sound right?" Now I knew why he'd called.

"Yes, Jeff Yeager, that's right! Just checking. You know he arrived on a bicycle and all. Not what I'm normally used to, so I just wanted to make sure."

I couldn't fault the producer for questioning my credentials, because no one was more surprised than me to be standing there that sweaty August morning, ready to make my live television debut before six million viewers of America's most popular morning show. I asked if I could speak to the folks in New York, and the producer gladly passed me his cell phone, since, of course, I don't own one.

"Good morning," I said tentatively. "You know, I've never done this before. What exactly do you want me to say?" Pause.

"I don't really care, just so long as you're funny as hell," came the disembodied response from the Big Apple.

No pressure there.

I didn't even rank

If only I could take some credit for landing on the *Today Show* that morning. But the truth is, truly, funny as hell.

After 25 years of working in the nonprofit sector and living comfortably but frugally, I realized I could afford to quit my job to pursue whatever interests caught my fancy. I joined the ranks of what I call the "selfishly employed," those who have the financial freedom to pursue their passions as a livelihood, without inordinate worry over a paycheck.

I began to remember a time in life, in high school and college, when I expected that my future would be as a writer. Not the kind of business writing I'd been doing since I graduated and my nose met the grindstone, but the kind of story telling that was once my passion.

My rekindled interest in writing (along with other pastimes, like having an occasional beer with breakfast and sneaking into two matinees at the multiplex when I'd only paid for one) was pleasurable if not profitable. I only sold a few pieces, primarily financial tips and humorous stories about living the good life on less money.

One Sunday when Michelle Singletary, a nationally syndicated finance columnist with the *Washington Post*, announced her annual contest looking for the "Penny Pincher of the Year," I excerpted a few money saving suggestions from my writings and e-mailed them off. My wife Denise was certain that I'd win the $50 top prize, confident, based on our 21 years of marriage, that I am indeed America's cheapest man.

I'd at least had enough freelance writing experience to be a veteran of rejection, so I didn't get my hopes up, even though I'd submitted some of my best work to Singletary's contest. Later that summer, when the winners and dozens of "honorable mentions" were announced in the *Post*, I was not among them.

"See," I said to Denise with feigned good humor, "I don't even rank when it comes to being cheap."

But deep in my throat I was saying to myself, "See, I don't even rank when it comes to being a good enough writer to win a lousy $50 prize."

Unexpected success

It's often occurred to me that most good things in my life have happened when I'm only wearing underwear. Two weeks after learning of my defeat in the *Post*'s contest, I sat in my underwear one Wednesday morning opening a spam-ish sounding e-mail from nbctodayshow .com.

"You don't know me," the message began, "but first let me say that I think you should have won the 50 bucks." The message immediately had my undivided attention.

The *Today Show* producer went on to explain that they were starting a new weeklong "Cheapskate Way" series. Michelle Singletary was going to be a guest, and they'd asked Singletary if she knew of anyone who had a lighthearted take on the subject matter. Singletary passed along my (losing) contest entry to the *Today Show* folks.

What started out as a request to film me for a 10-second clip evolved into a segment just about me and my cheapskate ways, and then an offer to also do the live broadcast from Ohio. Apparently I was funny as hell, because I now appear fairly often on the show as a guest correspondent reporting on, well, all things cheap.

One hot commodity

Although I never aspired to be a television reporter—and still don't—I thought that my inadvertent TV exposure might kindle some interest in my writing. I contacted a few literary agents in New York (using my trusty *Writer's Market*, of course) and was excited to receive positive reactions from a number of them. I was most impressed with Stacey Glick, an accomplished agent with the firm Dystel & Goderich.

After signing on with D&G, Stacey painstakingly coached me through the six-month process of developing a proposal for my book, a book of financial wisdom and witticisms I'd been keeping a file of Post-It Note ideas on for most of my adult life. Now, though, it was time to make good on my mantra over all those years: "I could write a book."

I finished the proposal just in time for a much-anticipated overseas vacation my wife and I had been planning. Given my amateur standing as a writer, it seemed a safe bet to send out the proposal with the hope that in the months following our vacation I might find an interested publisher. As we took off on our flight to Athens, Greece, I felt a weight of mythical proportions lifted from my shoulders; my proposal was done and being circulated to 15 potential publishers by the omni-capable Stacey Glick.

"It's finally off my desk," I told Denise, "and the good news is it's way too early to start worrying about whether anyone will ever want to buy it. This is going to be the vacation of a lifetime."

The next day we landed in Athens, where we strolled hand-in-hand through the city's ancient marketplace. The sign for an internet café stood out among the centuries old shops of carpet merchants and spice vendors, and, with public Internet access still fairly uncommon in Greece, we decided to take the opportunity to check our e-mail.

Logging on, I emitted that same unenlightened "Huh?" I'd uttered that Wednesday morning when NBC first contacted me, but this time I was wearing more than just underwear. The e-mail from Stacey was titled "URGENT INTEREST!" and explained that, much to everyone's surprise, I'd gone from an "unheard of" to "one hot commodity" literally overnight. Of the 15 publishers who were sent my proposal, five eventually bid on the rights, with Broadway Books prevailing in a final "bidding war."

Fittingly, the Ultimate Cheapskate agreed to sell the rights to his book via telephone from a tourist class hotel in Sparta, Greece, home of the legendary Spartans, the measure of all cheapskates down through the ages.

Cheap shot

If you'd asked me that Sunday morning when I entered the contest in the *Washington Post*, "What's the best thing that can happen, Jeff?" I would have responded, with genuine enthusiasm, "I could win 50 bucks!"

Well, I didn't, which goes to show you why life is so great sometimes. Sometimes things just work out and you get a shot, even if it is a cheap shot.

ANYTHING FOR THE STORY

by Michelle Bermas

"You want to go up in a hot air balloon when you're seven months pregnant?" my obstetrician asked.

"I wouldn't ask if it weren't important," I said. "I'm a freelance writer."

Her lips curved into a grin as her eyes met mine, questioning, judging, wondering just what the hell kind of mother-to-be would consider such a thing?

I should have said, "I'm going on a tiger safari in the Serengetthi."

Spotting an opportunity

Writers understand that when a spark of an idea ignites inside of you, you must either act immediately or it will fizzle out. I had been published in local newspapers but wanted to crack into a bigger market.

It all began when I saw a poster for a Hot Air Balloon Festival, to be held locally at the (now defunct) South Weymouth Naval Air Station. This rare event in Massachusetts was a great writing opportunity. I queried both the *Boston Globe* newspaper and *Balloon Life* magazine and both editors said yes. Needless to say, I didn't mention my pregnancy.

My first interview was with a local historian about the naval base. He supplied me with its rich history complete with black and white photographs. Then, I interviewed Ted Hilliard, one of the balloonists. Hilliard fell in love with ballooning after buying his teenage daughter her first, used balloon. Though skeptical, I soon wore Ted down and he agreed to take me on a 10-minute ride the following week. I wanted the full experience of flying high above the trees so I could genuinely write about it, especially for *Balloon Life*.

Taking flight

The day of the flight, it was 62 degrees and the sun was shining; it was a good day to fly. I waddled over to the balloon around 6 a.m. Crews blew up the envelopes (the bag of the balloon) as John Mellencamp sang "Paper in Fire" on a distant radio. The sky was dappled with a few balloons hovering over their liftoff site.

"Come on, it's time," I heard someone shout. Within moments, our eagle balloon was pulling toward the sky, and I watched men jump effortlessly into the basket. It took mere seconds before they were untying the ropes.

"Hey," I shouted, "Wait for me." So much for a pee break. I would just have to hold it for 10 minutes, and ignore my bladder. The balloon was hovering two feet off the ground. How was I going to do this, I thought.

"There's no graceful way to get into a balloon," Ted shouted.

I had one chance to get in. "I'm ready, I'm ready," I shouted over the noise. I raised my leg and flung myself over the lip of the basket. Two men helped pull me inside. The basket swayed under my added weight like a clock pendulum. My feet were just under me when I felt the lift of the balloon. It's like when your belly jumps when you drive over a hill too fast. We rose steadily and I wondered if I had made a wise choice. The shadow of the balloon was outlined in the trees and I began to relax, it'd be over before I knew it.

"This is amazing," I said to no one in particular.

Soon we were a thousand feet above the town. People waved and cars honked. Cattle looked like plastic toys. A coyote ran into the woods. We drifted over matchbox size houses. I felt like ET in the front of little Elliot's basket, riding his bicycle home. I've never considered myself a thrill seeker, but I love adventure, experiencing something new and getting a great story. I've flown my father's Cessna, rode in a glider plane drifting on air pockets, scuba dived with sharks and high-roped in the Connecticut woods.

Finding a place to land

"The wind is picking up a little and I don't see a good place to land," Ted said. He talked on his cell phone with the chase crew below. Their job was to follow our balloon in their pickup truck and drive us back when we landed. Then he said, "If I spit, I'm not being disgusting, I'm checking the wind."

I enjoyed sailing over farms, houses and cranberry bogs. The baby kicked a few times and I felt happy.

Sirens sounded and we all looked down and saw a police car had pulled over our chase crew. Then we saw them pointing up at us.

"Ever been caught speeding in a hot air balloon before?" I asked. "Hey, let's toss down our drivers licenses." No one laughed.

Ted said, "The police were worried about us landing. We should have found a place 30 minutes ago."

I'd lost all track of time.

"We're three towns away from our liftoff spot," a man said.

"I'm gonna bring her down slowly. There's a farm up ahead in Bridgewater," he said.

"Bridgewater!" I shouted. It was at least 40 minutes driving time back to the naval base. Now I had to pee very badly.

"You'll need to duck so you don't get hit by tree branches," said Ted. The other men seemed indifferent. I hunched down like I was painting my toenails for prom night. Of course, crouching is impossible with such a big belly.

I heard one man say, "Owww" when a branch hit his head and knocked off his John Deere hat. Then everyone joined me now, squatting.

"When we land, Michelle, I want you to stay in the basket. The men will jump out and stabilize us. We'll hit the ground and then bump back up," Ted said.

I peered over the edge. We were sinking fast. My mom was right—what was I thinking? The cows were getting larger and the barn wasn't cute anymore. After 45 minutes of flight we were going to land in a hayfield. We bumped down, the men jumped out, and the basket swung wildly. Then we floated back up as they grabbed for the ropes to anchor us. After the men helped me out, I thought, *The baby is safe and I've got a great story.*

"Hello earth," I said. "Glad to see you again."

Success and lessons learned

When *The Boston Globe* published my article, I was very proud. Also, *Balloon Life* published my interview with Ted Hilliard, "A Real Life Bear—Grizzly or Teddy? You decide." They also published my sidebar, "Hot in New England, First Annual on a Naval Base," about the festival.

This assignment taught me so much; sometimes I have to rein in the "leap and the net will appear" mentality. The experience and clips outweighed the low pay, but it was a stupid thing to do, albeit exciting. Now as a mother, I'm horrified I took such a risk and thank God no one was hurt. I had my concerns but kept reasoning it was safe; this was my story that no one could duplicate; and it was *The Boston Globe.* (A side note: My son is now four years old and wild as a bobcat. I have no idea where he gets it.)

I've grown as a writer since that time. My latest magazine short was on underwater rugby and I didn't dip a toe in the water once.

STUMBLING INTO MY FIRST BOOK SALE

by John K. Borchardt

Walking down the trade show aisle I was surrounded by book publishers' booths stocked with books, books, books. My long-standing desire to write a book hit me again with full force. I had always been intimidated by the process of getting published and the poor odds of throwing a book proposal over the transom—frightened to the point that I did not make appointments to talk to book publishers' representatives when attending writer's conferences. But now, here I was at a national science conference, and my desire to write a book struck again with full force.

I summoned up the courage to walk up to one of the publisher's booths, that of the American Chemical Society's ACS Books, and asked if there was an editor I could talk to about a book I wanted to write. The saleslady called over acquisitions editor Cheryl Brown and my journey to becoming a published book author began.

Amidst the noise and bustle of people at the booth and in the trade show aisles, I described my book idea. That wasn't hard; I'd been mulling it over for the past two years. My idea was for a book customized for scientists and engineers on how to get a job and keep it once you had it. After discussing the book idea, Cheryl asked me about my qualifications. Basically I fit the profile of the typical reader I was targeting with my book—an industrial chemist concerned about job security in a world of corporate downsizing, mergers and outsourcing. I also described my experience writing more than 200 articles on job-hunting and achieving career success published in ACS magazines and other magazines targeting engineers, college students and career women.

Cheryl concluded our 15-minute conversation by promising to send me an ACS book proposal form. Despite my aching feet from traipsing what seemed like miles of trade show aisles, I was walking on cloud nine.

However, pessimism soon set in. I didn't see the editor take notes during our conversation. Maybe she just said she'd send me the book proposal forms to get rid of me. Maybe she'd forget. The relief I felt when the forms arrived by e-mail soon after the conference quickly dissipated when I read them. Not only did I need to do a considerable of research to complete the forms but I also had to write an entire chapter of the book.

I gritted my teeth and set to it. I did a very thorough job of completing the form, in particular describing the book's target readers, the magazines they read and the conferences they attended. Rather than pick an easy chapter to write, I picked a hard one—a chapter on job-hunting titled "Working With Your References." I wanted to demonstrate that I could make a dull topic interesting and readable. If I could, I hoped the editors reviewing my proposal would believe I could write a readable, interesting book.

The pay off

The strategy worked! After a couple of months I received my contract and began writing while still working fulltime. My editor, Barbara Pralley, sensed my nervousness and was very supportive assuring me that I would complete my manuscript before she would have her first baby. This didn't happen and she was back at work after the birth of her daughter while I was still writing. I was so proud when I submitted my manuscript, which was then sent out to six reviewers.

I received their comments and suggestions for changes about three months later. This led to the most difficult part of the project—making the many changes they requested or writing justifications for not making the changes. This done, I proudly submitted my manuscript only to learn that Oxford University Press—USA was taking over management of ACS Books. Each of more than 75 book projects in progress would receive detailed scrutiny before publication could occur. Most of the projects were cancelled, but mine survived although publication was delayed by about 10 months.

Finally, more than a year after I had submitted my revisions I came home from work to find a carton sitting in front of my door. I saw it was from Oxford University Press and eagerly ripped it open. There in all their glory were 10 author's copies of my book, *Career Management for Scientists and Engineers*. The book cover was even in my favorite color: blue.

The importance of follow through

However, the story doesn't end here. Even before my book was published I should have been reading about what authors could do to promote sales of their book. Instead I assumed that the publisher would do whatever was needed. Despite excellent reviews in trade magazines and on Amazon.com, sales were sluggish. The book was out for more than a year before I began learning how to do my part. I learned some effective techniques for promoting my book, particularly by distributing flyers at science and engineering conferences. I even sold a copy I was carrying to an insurance agent while on an airplane. From Silicon Valley, he wanted to better understand his many scientist and engineer customers.

Book sales picked up—probably not due to many sales to insurance agents—and the publisher told me that a second printing was planned. I suggested an updated, second edition instead. I sent a detailed description of the many changes I was planning, in particular describing many developments in job-hunting using the Internet. Taking the time and trouble to do a thorough job worked. There will be a second edition. And I owe it all to a moment of courage in a tradeshow aisle.

Delivering Articles Like Babies

My wackiest sale went to *Dolphin Log* magazine. They had published an article of mine in the past, and the editor had two pages to fill. She called to see if I could send them something. "I need someone who can write well and write fast," she explained.

I was flattered. Unfortunately, I was in the hospital experiencing complications from the birth of my second son at the time. I told her I couldn't do anything new, but I had an article I had been submitting on throwing an eco-friendly block party.

She bought it over the phone, and I faxed a copy from the hospital.

—*Kim Childress*

PERSONAL VIEWS

Seth Godin

'You Don't Need to Be Perfect—Just Remarkable'

by Anthony Tedesco

I don't know how to break this to you, but: There's a good chance Seth Godin, author of seven best-selling books including *Purple Cow* and *Free Prize Inside*, is already three big ideas ahead of your next big idea. Mine too. It's nothing to be ashamed of. Godin's famously bald head seems to double as his own personal crystal ball. He's proven himself prophetic over and over again, anticipating and changing the way the world thinks about marketing, work and even change itself. He's a successful author, columnist, blogger, entrepreneur and marketing consultant who's been so effective for businesses that Successful Meetings chose him as one of their 21 Speakers for the Next Century.

But what can writers learn from an author who helps businesses? Everything. Whether the purist literary scribe in you likes it or not, writing is business. To best sell books and articles, you've got to see not only your editors and publishers as clients, but your potential readers as consumers. And according to Godin, we've all got to start treating our consumers better, as individuals we earnestly care about it, instead of as money we're trying to coax.

It can't be about you and your success. For Godin, the money is clearly a fringe benefit that comes from forging ahead of the status quo, and for putting people and ideas first, even if it means getting the good word to them as fast as possible for free.

Fear not: The success will come. Godin practices what he preaches, and his results say the rest. *Permission Marketing: Turning Strangers into Friends and Friends into Customers* was an Amazon.com Top 100 bestseller for a year, a *New York Times* business book bestseller, and it spent four months on the *Business Week* bestseller list. *Unleashing the Ideavirus: How to Turn Your Ideas into Marketing Epidemics* is one of the most popular e-books ever written, touting more than 1 million downloads. It hit #4 on the Amazon Japan bestseller list, and #5 in the United States.

Godin's *The Big Red Fez: How to Make Any Web Site Better* was the #1 e-book worldwide on Amazon for almost a year before it was published in paperback in 2002. His latest book, *Small is the New Big* ("and 183 other riffs, rants, and remarkable business ideas") is already being celebrated by readers and critics alike.

What's his secret? Godin's not telling. Success needs just enough of your own fingerprint to make it work for whatever your own groundbreaking idea happens to be. But it's the idea that's the key—bird's eye right down to the benefits for every reader, consumer, person—

ANTHONY TEDESCO is cofounder of The Student Publishing Program (www.225pm.org), coauthor of Online Markets for Writers (www.MarketsForWriters.com) and publisher of free e-books for writers, including *Top Writers Share Their Best Writing Advice* and *Top 250 Free Resources for Writers* (available at www.MarketsForWriters.com/wm2008).

and below, Seth Godin has given us insights on how writers and authors can best get to, write, and spread their ideas, with the ultimate karmic result of success.

Could you share the advice that's helped you most with your own writing?

A) Write like you talk. If you don't talk well, learn to change that. It's easier than changing your writing. B) Write nonfiction for your readers, not for you. And C) Be brief.

Could you share the tips/tricks you've found most helpful for overcoming writer's block?

What's that?

No one ever gets speaking block, have you noticed that?

Do you need a book to build a platform, or a platform to write a book?

Platform first. It would be great if a book could help you build a platform, but that's a total crapshoot these days.

Do you have a process for developing a book idea and/or deciding which projects to take on, and how important do you think this process is to the success of a writer?

It depends on how prolific you are. I choose topics by three criteria: A) How important is it to me to get the word out? B) Can I live with it for a year of writing? And C) Can I live with being the ''author'' of that idea for the rest of my life?

Do you think there's one ''silver bullet'' that will ensure writers find success?

Yes, but I'm not going to tell you what it is.

(I think it starts with the definition of success. If your goal is to make a living, go do something else. If your goal is to spread ideas, then write early and often and make it free and put it online. Good ideas spread.)

Could you share the free resources you've found most helpful as a writer and author, and let us know why they've been so helpful?

Wikipedia is numbers 1, 2 and 3.

Learning how to search with Google is a great skill. And I love Google Answers, though they've cancelled it. Librarians like to help, especially if you ask nicely, and the Editorial Freelancers Association is a great free place to find a freelance copy editor.

What marketing plan would you recommend for an author who has time but not money to spend?

Build a blog and a squidoo lens [www.squidoo.com]. Contribute to bulletin boards and forum. Give help, don't ask. Build a permission database of people who want to hear from you. *Then* write.

What's the best book marketing plan when the budget is somewhere around ''sky's the limit''?

Same.

Malcolm Gladwell wrote the foreword to your book, *Unleashing the Ideavirus*. Is there any particular one of Malcolm's innovative concepts from *The Tipping Point* and/or *Blink* that's helped you develop some of your own breakthroughs?

I stole relentlessly from *The Tipping Point*. Everyone who is reading this should read both of his books. For one thing, he is an absolutely brilliant writer.

For *Small Is the New Big*, you've successfully repositioned and resold your blog entries and columns into another promising book. Could you give other bloggers and columnists advice on how they too might accomplish this feat?
Don't be in such a hurry to write for the moment. I try to write blog posts that'll last.

Whether or not a writer has book aspirations, what's the secret to writing a successful blog or column?
You must understand that people don't have to read you. They have other choices. They are not captive. Please treat us that way.

What's the biggest mistake writers make while trying to market their books?
They think that just because they worked hard, they deserve an audience.

Could you share advice on how best to self-publish and promote e-books? Are your e-books done primarily to promote your print books, and to eventually become print books?
I don't write to make money, and I especially don't write e-books to make money. I create them in Word, print to PDF, add some links and distribute them for free. They spread. When they spread, they help support my main goal, which is spreading ideas.

How can authors and freelance writers best incorporate the advantages of permission marketing?
Do people want to hear from you? Why? What's in it for them? If they truly do, then make it easy for them sign up (RSS, e-mail, etc.) and nurture that asset. That's it. You can get more for free by writing to free@permission.com.

In your book, *The Big Moo*, you stress the importance of being remarkable rather than being perfect. Could you explain that distinction as well as how writers and authors can best pursue remarkableness?
When I did a dozen books for Scholastic, they obsessed about serial commas. This is nuts. Nobody ever had a bestseller because their serial commas were correct. Yes, you need to be functionally literate. But no, you don't need to be perfect. Just remarkable. Noteworthy. Worth spreading.

Could you give examples of how authors could promote themselves using viral marketing, or other ideavirus marketing vehicles? Are there certain tools/ vehicles that have to be in place before the frenzy?
The frenzy is usually random and unpredictable. Instead, go for the groundswell. And the groundswell happens when you write something that needs to be read!

Ben Olson

'I'm Just a Guy Who Lives, and Writes About It'

by Sherry Ramsey

To get his creative-writing mind flowing, 25-year-old author Ben Olson (*Wanderlost*, 2006, Alphar) puts himself in some strange situations. He's gone on hitchhiking jaunts, road trips, and adventures that have gotten him attacked by lonely truckers, a water buffalo in Thailand, and menopausal women. But Olson thrives on this kind of challenge; in fact, he relishes it. "I like putting myself in a position that I'll have to get out of," says Olson. "It always produces the most interesting consequences, but I have to do it, you know? I have to purge myself, then I come back, and I'm fine."

Raised in Sandpoint, Idaho, Olson is regularly published in a small paper called the *Sandpoint Reader*. In January 2006, he found himself in a local bar at closing time, on open mic night. For hours he'd listened to poets, guitar players, singers and people who just liked the sound of their own voices, and he wondered why he hung around letting himself go stagnant.

"Sometimes I just need to shake things up. I thought, 'Why don't I take a train around the country so I can see, and observe, and write, and not be in control of where I'm going?' So that's what I did." The following day, Olson packed a bag, went to the train station and purchased a $385 rail pass from Amtrak. This allowed him to come and go on the train, anywhere, anytime for 30 days.

Alone, Olson jumped on the train with no destination in mind and traveled to Sacramento, Chicago, Washington, D.C., and New Orleans among others. Through the train window he watched the scenery change from trees and mountains, to flat prairies, to a crowded metropolis, and wrote about what he saw. At each stop along the way, passengers left and boarded, a constant flow of new characters for his journal. He watched them, wondered about them, and wrote about them. "I guess it's the anonymity that I love," says Olson. "Just being another face in the crowd, like an invisible camera lens, capturing the things we do when attention isn't upon us." He e-mailed his musings back to the *Sandpoint Reader*, and they were published each week in his absence. For an entire month the people of Sandpoint lived the adventure through Olson's eyes.

Wanting to visit friends along the way, he got off the train and hitchhiked. "I love the beauty of hitchhiking," says Olson. "You stick out your thumb, and never know what's coming your way." But he's found there are times when hitchhiking has its disadvantages,

---

SHERRY RAMSEY is a professional freelance writer, published regularly in *North Idaho Lifestyle Magazine, Idaho Magazine, The Spokane Spokesman Review, The River Journal*, and other regional publications. Ramsey is a member of the Society of Children's Book Writers & Illustrators, Idaho Press Club, President of Idaho Writer's League Sandpoint Chapter, and First Vice President of Idaho Writer's League Coeur d'Alene Chapter.

like the time two lonely truckers picked him up on the side of the road. "They were propositioning me. I had to shove one, and jump out of the rig at 1:30 in the morning; it was scary."

During his trip, he found old friends, partied like only someone in his 20s can, and moved on. His writing slump was gone, as he faced new and unreal situations. "There's something about the motion that gets my mind in gear," says Olson. "It never matters where I'm going, or what for, it's just the idea that I'm on the move. It helps my writing because it quiets down the restless urge I always get when bored and jaded in one place."

He found himself in New Orleans a few months after hurricane Katrina. "The tracks were washed out and refugees were everywhere; the buses, and trains were full," says Olson. "I actually had to sleep in the streets that night, behind a factory with broken glass all over the place. I was scared shitless the whole time. So the next morning I hitchhiked eight hundred miles to Jacksonville, Florida—it took two days."

Finding himself flat broke, ten miles from the nearest town, at 1:30 a.m. after bailing on the truckers, Olson decided it was time to go home. "I knew that was the climax. It was the weirdest it could get, and the best it could get. I had to go home and rest."

He made his way to the nearest train station and started home, with nothing but a can of peanut butter, and water to sustain him on his journey. Back in Idaho, Olson crashed in his cabin for six days catching up on much needed sleep. When he surfaced from his stupor, he decided to try to sell his train ramblings as a novel. He gathered the articles that were published in his absence, and sent them out with a query letter.

"I write fiction because I have to. I like the protection it allows," says Olson. "I bought a copy of *Writer's Market* and fired off dozens of queries, but of course, no one accepted them. I still have the stacks of rejection letters as most writers do."

But in April 2006, Olson received an e-mail from Tom Moore of Alphar Publishing. Moore liked the writing and wanted to run it by the literary board. Not long after, another e-mail came containing a book contract.

"I've been wanting to do this for so long it was almost anti-climactic. I was sitting there in a sleeping bag when the contract came." Moore asked Olson if he could have the book written by June 1, less than six weeks away, with a launch date for winter 2007.

"I wrote *Wanderlost* in 37 days," says Olson. "I had my notes and articles, but I had to put it all together into fiction, with characters and dialog. I stocked up on cigarettes, holed up in my cabin and just cranked it out. It almost drove me insane. I don't think this is the way writing a book is supposed to happen."

His book was launched July 7, 2006, over a year ahead of schedule. "Everyone is congratulating me, but I'm still broke. I'm not getting showered with money or national attention. I'm just the same as I was before."

So what kind of training does someone need to go on a trip in January, and have a book on the shelves by July? "I haven't had any formal training or writing courses; in fact, I'm not trained to do anything," says Olson. "Everything I've ever done—a writer, a photographer, a film producer, a golf pro—it was all something that I stumbled into. I'd just wedge my toes in the door and wriggle myself in, conning everyone into thinking I knew what I was doing when, really, I had no clue. I'm not a scholar—I'm just a guy who lives, and writes about it."

But he always knew he was meant to write. "I began reading at a very early age, and was fascinated by books—the smell of the aging paper, the way they feel in your back pocket, resisting the urge to skip ahead to the bottom of the page during a tense portion of writing. All I've ever wanted to do is write exactly what I want to write and get some idiot to pay me for it. I wanted to etch my name into immortality like the greats I pored through—Hemingway, Kerouac, Thompson, Steinbeck, Orwell, Huxley."

Olson doesn't have a set writing schedule. His mind and heart tell him when he has something to say. "I write on bar napkins. They litter my desk, full of gibberish, and quotes, and ideas. I use them because I can capture moments exactly as they are—the way people talk," says Olson. "Carrying a notebook doesn't have the same effect, because then you're prepared to write. It's like taking a photo of someone who sits there looking at the camera, putting on their fake camera smiles. That's not real, it's just their facade. Stealing a handful of napkins and a pen from the cocktail waitress when inspiration hits is more real, more organic; therefore, more important."

So what form of inspiration will Olson use to write his next book—spend a month on the streets with the homeless, infiltrate the mob, live with cannibals?

Olson laughs at the thought. "I wouldn't rule any of those out, but I've already started my next book. It's going to be about my hitchhiking travels." For Ben Olson, the cure for writer's block is change, excitement, and new territory. Having the guts to take off and try the unknown, plunged him into an adventure that sparked his first novel.

"I've been writing this book in my head for five years, I just couldn't find the catalyst to propel it. This trip was it, and I knew it."

PERSONAL VIEWS

Erik Larson

A Commitment to Fact-filled Storytelling

Photo by Mary Cairns

by Joanna Masterson

With a background writing for *The Wall Street Journal, Time, Harper's, The New Yorker* and *The Atlantic Monthly*, best-selling nonfiction author Erik Larson is no stranger to capturing the details that make a story truly stand out.

Perhaps even more intriguing is his ability to make nonfiction read like fiction, without fudging any of the facts. Nowhere is this commitment to both historical research and narrative prose more apparent than in Larson's trio of books: *Isaac's Storm, Devil in the White City* (both Crown) and, most recently, *Thunderstruck* (Three Rivers Press).

Isaac's Storm follows weatherman Isaac Cline as he deals with the hurricane that devastated Galveston, Texas, in 1900; *Devil in the White City* counters the story of Chicago World's Fair architect Daniel Burnham with that of murderer H.H. Holmes; and *Thunderstruck* connects British murderer Dr. H.H. Crippen with the invention of wireless communication in late 19th-century Europe.

Now a veteran of *The New York Times* bestseller list, Larson admits his entry into publishing wasn't quite so notable. His first book, *Naked Consumer*, explored the topic of companies spying on consumers, and his second book, *Lethal Passage*, served as a study of American gun culture. Neither garnered much of a national audience, but fortunately for millions of readers, Larson didn't give up.

How did you break into publishing?

The transition into books was kind of easy. I had an idea for a book, so I put together a 25-page proposal for *Naked Consumer*. I sent it to about 10 different agents at the same time. A couple of people rejected the idea. One agent liked the idea so she sent it out to publishers. Unfortunately, that first book went nowhere. Nobody bought it and nobody read it. One guy reviewed it and he hated it, but it gave me the bug and I had a mechanism in place for doing the next book.

At what point did you secure your agent, David Black?

I had two agents before David Black. I felt somewhat dissatisfied, so, once I felt clear of obligation in terms of royalty checks, I started looking for another agent. I called a lot of my newspaper friends to ask about their agents. A couple of them had David Black and felt he

---

JOANNA MASTERSON, previously the editor of *2007 Guide to Literary Agents* (Writer's Digest Books), now writes for a trade magazine in Arlington, Virginia.

was terrific. He was instrumental in helping me figure out how to write historical true stories. He really hammered me to think in terms of story and narrative, how to break a story down into its components and tell it with the suspense it had at the time.

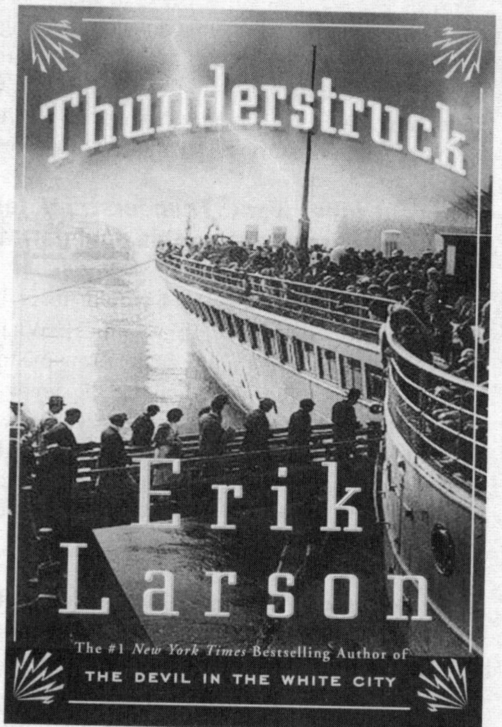

Thunderstruck is Larson's latest historical nonfiction book, which places scientific achievement side-by-side with a notorious murder.

How did your journalism background help prepare you for writing proposals and book-length manuscripts?

Journalism was invaluable to me. It gave me daily writing experience. There is no substitute for putting words together every day. I was a Sunday feature writer . . . so it gave me a nice test bed for writing longer stuff.

David Black insists on a really high level of preparation. My proposals typically run 80 pages and include a sample chapter, statement of intent and a chapter-by-chapter outline. A proposal takes about three to six months to do. The first proposal took forever and I was getting more and more frustrated. I was ready to dump [Black] . . . thank God I didn't. When you have something that thoroughly prepared, the publisher knows if they don't bite it's going out the next day for someone else.

How do you tackle and organize your research?

To me, the key is immersing myself. My MO, like with *Devil in the White City*, is to go to a place like the Chicago Historical Society and, rather than spending months there, photocopy what might be valuable. It's more cost effective to do this and process it in my office than to stay there and read through everything.

I have an arcane indexing process where anything worthwhile is indexed on a cover sheet so I know where things are in that document. I maintain for all my books a master chronology for all my research, so by the time I'm done I have this really detailed—usually around 70 pages—chronology. That's an outline. It's a very powerful instrument because it shows me where the juxtapositions are. From that I can kind of roughly shape what a chapter ought to include.

I also use a trick I learned from my former newspaper bureau chief: I take the rough draft and separate the dual narratives with scissors and move components around. It's a very powerful technique because you always find duplications. A natural structure almost invariable appears. Once I have everything glued back together, I go back to writing.

How do you make your writing appealing to fiction readers?

You can't just choose an event and then write a narrative nonfiction book about the subject. There has to be some inherently powerful narrative line—an arc. It's what any novel has to have, but nonfiction can't get by without it either.

The classic narrative is the Burnham story [from *Devil in the White City*]: His partner dies and he has to continue against an accumulating set of obstacles nobody could have foreseen. You need to find that kind of arc, and as you do your research you break the story down to its DNA—or chronology—so the story as you write it unfolds as it occurred, like you don't know how it ends. It's what novelists do all the time and it's doable in nonfiction. You just have to pick your story very carefully, and you have to go the distance.

Like your other work, *Thunderstruck* follows the lives of two very different men. What draws you to this dual narrative storytelling device and how do you keep it fresh?

It has never been deliberate. I would never have wanted to only write a book about the world's fair or the killer [H.H. Holmes]. What I found very striking was the juxtaposition between the two. The duality really drew me to the book. After *Devil in the White City* I went storming around the house saying I'll never do another dual narrative again. It makes a writer's life instantly harder because you're writing two different books, and then have to make those two books work together. I discarded idea after idea . . . because it's hard to find the right idea that provides that narrative arc . . . and then one day I was musing about wireless and stumbled onto a Web site about wireless that mentioned Crippen. I thought, here we go again.

Your books are very detail oriented in terms of setting. How do you authentically recreate a city and time period?

The key is detail and choosing details that will light the imagination. When I read about the past, I try to be very mindful of what surprised me and what delighted and fascinated me. I make note of that reaction in my notes. Two to three years later when you're sick of your material because it's lost any newness, it helps to have in your notes what you thought was moving or funny.

Normally I don't do online research—I find it dry and uninteresting and there's so much garbage. But with *Thunderstruck*, there were a couple Web sites I found very interesting. One gave maps and personal anecdotes about all the sections of London. It was as though I had a research assistant working on my behalf back in time.

What do you find to be the most challenging and rewarding parts of publicity?

The most challenging thing is doing a talk every night. Public speaking is hard because even though I do it and I think I'm good at it, it's stressful. I know what I want to say, but for the 10 minutes before the speech, it's very nerve racking.

It's very satisfying meeting people who love your book. I have three teenage daughters, so it's nice out on the road to be treated like an adult. It's hard being away from the family, though.

Are you already drumming up a new idea for your next book?

I never take a break, so right now I'm in the midst of looking [for a new topic]. I swear to God I'm not going to do another dual narrative. This is really the toughest part of my career. You feel so unproductive. But the best elixir for anxiety about your current book is work. When you're working, everything else falls into the background.

Do you have any advice for writers?

When you're writing, never binge. Stop while you're ahead. Some days I stop mid-sentence or mid-paragraph because it gives me a spot the next morning where I can instantly be productive. I sit there and am immediately writing. It's a great technique. Also, if you have a problem with a passage, read your material over just before you go to bed. By morning, more often than not it will be solved.

BEYOND THE BASICS

Minding the Details

Writers who've been successful in getting their work published know that publishing requires two different mind-sets. The first is the actual act of writing the manuscript. The second is the business of writing—the marketing and selling of the manuscript. This shift in perspective is necessary if you want to become a successful career writer. You must keep the business side of the industry in mind as you develop your writing.

Each of the following sections and accompanying sidebars discusses a writing business topic that affects anyone selling a manuscript. Our treatment of the business topics that follow is necessarily limited, so look for short blocks of information and resources throughout this section to help you further research the content.

CONTRACTS AND AGREEMENTS

If you've worked as a freelance writer, you know contracts and agreements vary from publisher to publisher. Some magazine editors work only by verbal agreement, as do many agents; others have elaborate documents you must sign in duplicate and return to the editor before you even begin the assignment. It is essential that you consider all of the elements involved in a contract, whether verbal or written, and know what you stand to gain and lose by agreeing to the contract. Maybe you want to repurpose the article and resell it to a market that is different from the first publication to which you sold it. If that's the case, then you need to know what rights to sell.

In contract negotiations, the writer is usually interested in licensing the work for a particular use, but limiting the publisher's ability to make other uses of the work in the future. It's in the publisher's best interest, however, to secure as many rights as possible, both now and

Contracts and Contract Negotiation

For More Info

- **The Authors Guild** (www.authorsguild.org), 31 E. 32nd St., 7th Floor, New York NY 10016. (212)563-5904. Fax: (212)564-5363. E-mail: staff@authorsguild.org.
- **National Writers Union** (www.nwu.org), 113 University Place, 6th Floor, New York NY 10003. (212)254-0279. Fax: (212)254-0673. E-mail: nwu@wu.org.

later on. Those are the basic positions of both parties. The contract negotiation involves compromising on questions relating to those basic points—and the amount of compensation to be given the writer for his work. If at any time you are unsure about any part of the contract, it is best to consult a lawyer who specializes in media law and contract negotiation.

A contract is rarely a take-it-or-leave-it proposition. If an editor tells you his company will allow no changes to the contract, you will then have to decide how important the assignment is to you. However, most editors are open to negotiations, so you need to learn how to compromise on points that don't matter to you, and stand your ground on those that do matter.

RIGHTS AND THE WRITER

A creative work can be used in many different ways. As the author of the work, you hold all rights to the work in question. When you agree to have your work published, you are granting a publisher the right to use your work in any number of ways. Whether that right is to publish the manuscript for the first time in a publication, or to publish it as many times and in many different ways as a publisher wishes, is up to you—it all depends on the agreed-upon terms. As a general rule, the more rights you license away, the less control you have over your work and the money you're paid. You should strive to keep as many rights to your work as you can.

Writers and editors sometimes define rights in a number of different ways. Below you will find a classification of terms as they relate to rights.

- **First Serial Rights**—Rights that the writer offers a newspaper or magazine to publish the manuscript for the first time in any periodical. All other rights remain with the writer. Sometimes the qualifier "North American" is added to these rights to specify a geographical limitation to the license.

  When content is excerpted from a book scheduled to be published, and it appears in a magazine or newspaper prior to book publication, this is also called first serial rights.
- **One-Time Rights**—Nonexclusive rights (rights that can be licensed to more than one market) purchased by a periodical to publish the work once (also known as simultaneous rights). That is, there is nothing to stop the author from selling the work to other publications at the same time.
- **Second Serial (Reprint) Rights**—Nonexclusive rights given to a newspaper or magazine to publish a manuscript after it has already appeared in another newspaper or magazine.
- **All Rights**—This is exactly what it sounds like. "All rights" means an author is selling every right he has to a work. If you license all rights to your work, you forfeit the right to ever use the work again. If you think you may want to use the article again, you should avoid submitting to such markets or refuse payment and withdraw your material.
- **Electronic Rights**—Rights that cover a broad range of electronic media, from online magazines and databases to CD-ROM magazine anthologies and interactive games. The contract should specify if—and which—electronic rights are included. The presumption is unspecified rights remain with the writer.
- **Subsidiary Rights**—Rights, other than book publication rights, that should be covered in a book contract. These may include various serial rights; movie, TV, audiotape, and other electronic rights; translation rights, etc. The book contract should specify who controls the rights (author or publisher) and what percentage of sales from the licensing of these rights goes to the author.
- **Dramatic, TV, and Motion Picture Rights**—Rights for use of material on the stage, on TV, or in the movies. Often a one-year option to buy such rights is offered (generally for 10 percent of the total price). The party interested in the rights then tries to sell the idea to other people—actors, directors, studios, or TV networks. Some properties are

optioned numerous times, but most fail to become full productions. In those cases, the writer can sell the rights again and again.

Sometimes editors don't take the time to specify the rights they are buying. If you sense that an editor is interested in getting stories, but doesn't seem to know what his and the writer's responsibilities are, be wary. In such a case, you'll want to explain what rights you're offering (preferably one-time or first serial rights only) and that you expect additional payment for subsequent use of your work.

The Copyright Law that went into effect January 1, 1978, states writers are primarily selling one-time rights to their work unless they—and the publisher—agree otherwise in writing. Book rights are covered fully by contract between the writer and the book publisher.

SELLING SUBSIDIARY RIGHTS

The primary right in book publishing is the right to publish the book itself. All other rights (movie rights, audio rights, book club rights, etc.) are considered secondary, or subsidiary, to the right to print publication. In contract negotiations, authors and their agents traditionally try to avoid granting the publisher subsidiary rights they feel comfortable marketing themselves. Publishers, on the other hand, want to obtain as many of the subsidiary rights as they can.

Larger agencies have experience selling subsidiary rights, and many authors represented by such agents prefer to retain those rights and let their agents do the selling. On the other

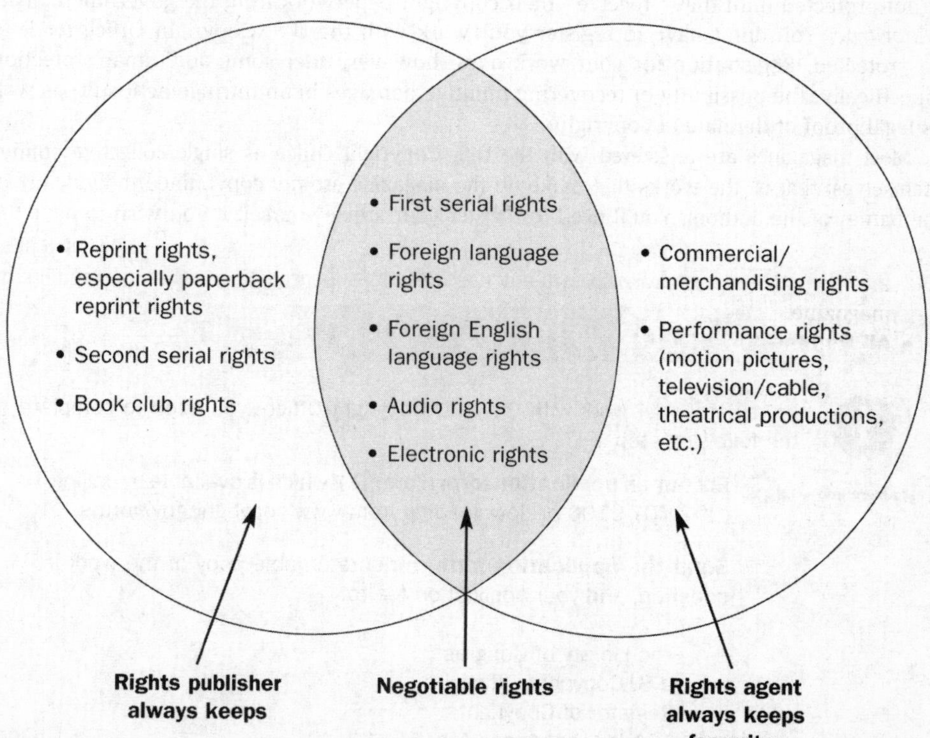

Some subsidiary rights are always granted to the publisher. Some should always be retained by the author. The remainder are negotiable, and require knowledgeable advice from a literary agent or attorney in deciding whether it is more advantageous to grant the rights to the publisher or to reserve them.

hand, book publishers have subsidiary rights departments whose sole job is to exploit the subsidiary rights the publisher was able to retain during the contract negotiation.

The marketing of electronic rights can be tricky. With the proliferation of electronic and multimedia formats, publishers, agents, and authors are going to great lengths to make sure contracts specify exactly which electronic rights are being conveyed (or retained). Compensation for these rights is a major source of conflict because many book publishers seek control of them, and many magazines routinely include electronic rights in the purchase of all rights, often with no additional payment.

COPYRIGHT

Copyright law exists to protect creators of original works. It is also designed to encourage the production of creative works by ensuring that artists and writers hold the rights by which they can profit from their hard work.

The moment you finish a piece of writing—or in fact, the second you begin to pen the manuscript—the law recognizes only you can decide how the work is used. Copyright protects your writing, recognizes you (its sole creator) as its owner, and grants you all the rights and benefits that accompany ownership. With very few exceptions, anything you write today will enjoy copyright protection for your lifetime, plus 70 years. Copyright protects "original works of authorship" that are fixed in a tangible form of expression. *Copyright law cannot protect titles, ideas, and facts.*

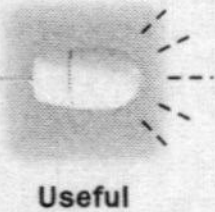

Useful Websites

Some writers are under the mistaken impression that a registered copyright with the U.S. Copyright Office (www.copyright.gov) is necessary to protect their work, and that their work is not protected until they "receive" their copyright paperwork from the government. *This is not true*. You don't have to register your work with the U.S. Copyright Office for it to be protected. Registration for your work does, however, offer some additional protection (specifically, the possibility of recovering punitive damages in an infringement suit) as well as legal proof of the date of copyright.

Most magazines are registered with the U.S. Copyright Office as single collective entities themselves; that is, the works that make up the magazine are *not* copyrighted individually in the names of the authors. You'll need to register your article yourself if you wish to have the

Beyond the Basics

Filing for Copyright

For More Info

To register your work with the U.S. Copyright Office, you need to complete the following steps.

1. **Fill out an application form** (Form TX), which is available by calling (202)707-9100 or downloading from www.copyright.gov/forms.
2. **Send the application form,** a nonreturnable copy of the work in question, and your application fee to:

   The Library of Congress
   U.S. Copyright Office
   Register of Copyrights
   101 Independence Ave. SE
   Washington DC 20559-6222

additional protection of copyright (your name, the year of first publication, and the copyright symbol ©) appended to any published version of your work. You may use the copyright symbol regardless of whether your work has been registered with the U.S. Copyright Office.

One thing you need to pay particular attention to is work-for-hire arrangements. If you sign a work-for-hire agreement, you are agreeing that your writing will be done as a work for hire, and you will not control the copyright of the completed work—the person or organization who hired you will be the copyright owner. These agreements and transfers of exclusive rights must appear in writing to be legal. In fact, it's a good idea to get every publishing agreement you negotiate in writing before the sale.

FINANCES AND TAXES

You will find that as your writing business expands, so will your need to keep track of writing-related expenses and incomes. Keeping a close eye on these details will prove very helpful when it comes time to report your income to the IRS. It will also help you pay as little tax as possible and keep you aware of the state of your freelance writing as a business. This means you need to set up a detailed tracking and organizing system to log all expenses and income. Without such a system, your writing as a business will eventually fold. If you dislike handling finance-related tasks, you can always hire a professional to oversee these duties for you. However, even if you do hire a professional, you still need to keep all original records.

The following tips will help you keep track of the finance-related tasks associated with your freelance business.

- Keep accurate records.
- Separate your writing income and expenses from your personal income and expenses.
- Maintain a separate bank account and credit card for business-related expenses.
- Record every transaction (expenses and earnings) related to your writing.
- Begin keeping records when you make your first writing-related purchase.
- Establish a working, detailed system of tracking expenses and income. Include the date; the source of income (or the vendor of your purchase); a description of what was sold or bought; how the payment was rendered (cash, check, credit card); and the amount of the transaction.
- Keep all check stubs and receipts (cash purchases and credit cards).
- Set up a record-keeping system, such as a file folder system, to store all receipts.

Tax Information

Important

While we cannot offer you tax advice or interpretations, we can suggest several sources for the most current information.

- Check the IRS Web site (www.irs.gov).
- Call your local IRS office.
- Obtain basic IRS publications by phone or by mail; most are available at libraries and some post offices.

BEYOND THE BASICS

Launching Your Freelance Business

by I.J. Schecter

Starting something from scratch takes guts, faith and a healthy dose of stubborn optimism. Some would argue that deciding to launch a freelance writing practice requires a touch of masochism, too. But let's look at this rationally. First, you aren't starting from scratch; you're starting with talent, knowledge, skill, connections, and, probably, the moral support of a good number of people. Second, starting a writing business is no more or less difficult than starting any other type of business, whether a bakery, real estate brokerage or piano-tuning service. Third, you're peddling an extremely valuable product. Most businesses figure out pretty fast that if they don't know how to communicate, they're going to have a hard time winning customers. And in today's world of short attention spans and stimulus overload, the ability to communicate succinctly and powerfully is more valuable than ever.

Pre-work

Before putting your name out there, there are a few things you need to take care of. At the top of the list is getting business cards and letterhead printed. When you do start to tell people about your practice, the last thing you want is to be stuck without a card to hand over. And after you do offer it, hopefully prompting a discussion about your potential client's needs, you'll want to send a follow-up letter immediately—but on your own stationery, not some generic one. From the moment you decide to freelance professionally, you must think of yourself as a brand. Most writers feel hesitant about marketing themselves in any specific way because they don't want to cut off other opportunities. But when you're starting out, establishing a firm brand perception—that is, a clear statement about what you do and why it's valuable—is more important than appearing able do it all. Demonstrate expertise in a few specific areas, and others will inevitably find their way into your lap.

Selling yourself

Almost all writers share an aversion to self-selling—but it's mostly a function of unfair conditioning. That is, they assume they hate marketing themselves before they even try because other writers have convinced them one can't be a good writer and a good salesman at the same time.

The truth is plenty of good writers are natural salesmen, too, but they feel the superficial selling part undermines the authentic writing part. Take a moment to think about it and

---

I.J. SCHECTER (www.ijschecter.com) is an award-winning writer, interviewer and essayist. His bestselling collection, *Slices: Observations from the Wrong Side of the Fairway* (John Wiley & Sons), is available in bookstores and online.

Where Is Your Stapler?

Many writers and other artists claim that their extreme lack of organization is simply an occupational hazard. Others practically boast about it, claiming it as a distinct imprint of creativity. Whether or not creative types are naturally disinclined toward self-organization, the sooner you decide to get organized and stay organized, the more successful you and your practice will become. Why? Two reasons, one physical, the other mental. Physically speaking, when your work environment is organized, you spend more time writing and less time trying to locate the calculator or paper clips or this file or that folder. Simple odds dictate that using your time more productively will lead to more work.

The mental aspect is just as important. We all know how aggravating it is having to scramble to find that copy of the current contract for that magazine when we've forgotten what the word count was, or trying desperately to remember where we put the CD with the backup copy of that article after the electrical storm has wiped out our operating system with the deadline looming. It stands to reason that the less energy you need to put into non-writing activities, the more energy you can direct toward your actual work, improving its overall quality and thereby making you a more desirable commodity. Sure, a little anxiety can be healthy for writing, but it should be anxiety borne of the drive to produce stellar work, not anxiety based on wondering where the stamps got to for the umpteenth time.

Organizing yourself is probably a lot easier than you imagine, and you might even be surprised at how good a little structure makes you feel. Start small: Buy a box of multicolored file folders, some labels, some CDs or a memory stick, and several upright magazine files. Label one of the magazine files **Contracts**, then place in it different file folders labeled with the subject area for a given contract. For me, these folders include, among others, Bridal, Fitness, Golf, Men's, Gardening, and, of course, Writing and Publishing. Label another of the magazine files **Current Assignments** and a third **Story Ideas**, and populate them as you did the first. Use consistent colors for specific topics—in other words, gardening always gets a yellow file folder whether it's in the **Story Ideas** or the **Contracts** file. This will make for easy cross-referencing. And that's just a start. Odds are this small bit of organization will spur you, and soon you'll be creating files for every aspect of your work—character sketches, source notes, dialogue snippets, conferences and retreats, news items. "Organization is everything," says freelancer Heather Cook, author of *Rookie Reiner: Surviving and Thriving in the Show Pen* (Trafalgar Square Books). "From maintaining accurate records for tax purposes to structuring a weekly plan to include marketing and administrative tasks, it allows me to stay focused and efficient—and that makes my overall work better."

you'll realize all businesspeople have to market themselves just like writers do. A restaurateur needs to do more than just open his doors to generate traffic. An investment broker must go beyond merely getting a license if he hopes to succeed. A psychologist wanting to build a practice ought to take a few steps in addition to simply hanging a shingle. And a writer needs to do more than just write. "This job is about sales as much as it is about writing," says Toronto-based freelancer Ian Harvey. "One of the simple rules guiding my practice is this: Hustle, hustle, hustle."

So how does a writer generate buzz? There are several ways: letters, flyers, brochures, newsletters, blogs, samples, cold calls, and so on. When I launched my practice, the first thing I did (after getting business cards and letterhead printed, of course) was to send out hundreds of introductory letters—to those I knew, to those I didn't know, to people, to businesses . . . to just about everyone whose address I could get. I discriminated little in this initial blitz, though naturally with each letter I dropped into the mailbox I became even more nervous that all the money, time and effort I was expending might lead nowhere.

Then I received a phone call. One of my letters had gone to a high school acquaintance working at a company that manufactured and distributed musical compilations on CD. She had received my letter just as her boss was looking for a writer to help write snappy liner notes. Years later, this company remains one of my biggest corporate clients.

Another of my letters went to an old colleague. He had become the head of an executive degree program at a local university and was preparing to design the program brochure, for which a writer was sorely needed. I won the assignment, which led to another three.

The lesson? You truly never know where work is going to come from. More important, you can't count on finding yourself in the right place at the right time; you have to create the possibility of being there.

Growing pains

There are two parts to selling yourself. First is developing the nerve to do it. Second is developing the right type of skin: rhino. "Rejections are part of the game," says Harvey, "but this is the only game in which rejection doesn't mean no. It means not now, or not for me, or not for me right now. It doesn't mean no forever." While it's fair to spend a little time—very little—getting annoyed or frustrated at rejection, it's best to take that annoyed or frustrated energy and pour it into something productive. Few businesses explode overnight; the ones that end up successful demand lots of grunt work up front, reach a minimum threshold after a few years, and then begin to grow in earnest.

It's imperative you commit to the up-front part. "Most businesses fail because the proprietors underestimate the amount of work required to get the business off the ground and overestimate the revenue in the first year or two," says Paul Lima, a professional writer for over 25 years and author of *The Six-Figure Freelancer*. Adds Vancouver-based freelancer Teresa Murphy, author of more than 1,000 magazine articles, "You need the ability to work 15 hours a day and love it, day in and day out. That means holidays, summer weekends and all-nighters when clients have rush projects. I've worked Boxing Day, New Year's Eve, Easter Sunday until midnight."

Of course, if you've decided to take the plunge in the first place, no doubt you've got this much passion and then some, because, like these professionals, you've realized that, despite the challenges of the writing life, nothing in the world makes you feel happier or more fulfilled.

Gaining, and sustaining, momentum

Investing the time and energy at the outset will lead to a point of critical mass—that first small group of people interested in your work, the first pebble in your pond. This could include a magazine editor, the president of a company or a friend needing some editing help. To help that first small ripple expand outward, you need to embed two vital behavioral principles.

1. Overdelivery. Whether you're writing an article for your local newspaper, a marketing brochure for a multinational conglomerate or an essay for your best friend's medical school application, do the very best job you can. Your writing is judged every time you put pen to paper or fingers to keys. Force yourself to knock the ball out of the park at every opportunity and you'll develop the kind of reputation that leads to positive word of mouth, constant repeat business and sparkling testimonials.

2. Professionalism. From editors to executives, just about everyone is stretched thin these days—and that's why being known as someone easy to work with can distinguish you from other writers who also deliver solid work. Acting like a professional means a number of things. Dressing a certain way. Acting a certain way. Hitting deadlines. Returning calls and e-mails promptly.

It also means not ever being petty, spiteful or antagonistic. Following the publication of my first short story collection, I lucked into a chance to set up a small table at a prominent outdoor literary festival. Beside me was the editor of an esteemed literary journal—along with her large dog, in a cage a few feet behind us. The dog began barking his head off just as people starting checking out the book tables, and he didn't stop for an hour, scaring off just about anyone who wandered anywhere near me and my book. The woman did nothing. I didn't just want to offer her a few choice words; I wanted to write her a scathing letter several pages long. Friends and family urged me to resist, and, though it was hard, I did. A few years later, when I sent this editor a story for consideration in her journal, she accepted it (though she had no recollection of me from the festival), creating a writing credit that remains one of my most important. The moral? In this business just like any other, people, and circumstances, will irk you—but in almost every case it behooves you to take the high road. Reacting emotionally can only harm you; staying cool can only benefit you.

The numbers game

Writing is dynamic and fluid; it can be endlessly revised, massaged, tweaked, twisted and reversed back over itself. For this reason, it's essential that you get every one of your assignments in writing (no pun intended; OK, slightly intended). Commercial assignments will usually come with a contract; corporate assignments almost never will. To address this, prepare two versions of your own standard agreement. For commercial gigs, this document should include a brief description of the assignment, word count, pay rate, and deadline, along with all the other legal bits you can find by looking up any typical freelance contract. For corporate assignments, it should include a more detailed description of the project (including each piece of work if there are multiple parts), the agreed timeline, the fee (either an overall flat rate or an hourly rate), and, crucially, a definition of completion. For example, in my standard corporate agreement, I have a clause indicating that, for the agreed-upon fee, I will deliver the described work by the noted deadline and then allow two rounds of requested revisions or suggestions from the client, after which I will start charging extra. This creates clear mutual expectations between the client and me and helps avoid awkward conversations

Tax Tip

Sure, self-employment doesn't come with medical and dental, but it does offer plenty of opportunities for tax write-offs. Among the expenses you can potentially deduct are car, phone, restaurant meals, postage, magazine purchases, and, if you work from home, a portion of your monthly mortgage (or rent) and utilities. Have a chat with your accountant about this and hold onto your receipts so calculations are easy come tax season. You'll be glad you did.

toward the end of the project when the senior partner tries to add an arbitrary comma for the third time.

For corporate work, you'll also have to develop the skill of estimating. It's one thing to name an hourly rate when a potential client first asks; it's another to try to come up with a total number of hours based on his incredibly vague description of the assignment. But come up with one you must—only to be met with, in some cases, a response gently questioning why the work ought to take so long. Here we have a quandary: By and large, people vastly underestimate how long good writing actually takes. I've found the best way to deal with this is to be truthful. I tell my clients up front that writing and communications work tends to take quite a bit longer than non-writers imagine, and that, in fact, most projects end up taking 20 percent more hours than I initially estimate because the client themselves didn't realize going in how much would be involved. As long as I deliver good work, this ceases to be an issue.

How much or how little should you charge for your work? It depends—based on your experience, where you live, and a host of other factors. (See page 64 for a range of rates for different types of writing projects.) Make sure, before you enter any negotiation, that you've decided upon the lowest figure you're willing to accept. Or, as freelancer Colette van Haaren puts it, "You need three things in this business: a good nose to sniff out stories, a thick skin for when rejection hits, and a backbone for when you have to negotiate."

Sure, I'm working—in my head

Only about half my time is spent actually working on assignments. The other half is spent crafting queries, doing research, maintaining correspondence, or, to be honest, just brainstorming. My favorite part of being a writer is that I can work anywhere, since so much of

Answering the Question

Friends familiar with your long-time desire to write may good-naturedly tease you about the risk of giving up your thankless but stable 9-to-5 grind to tackle something so daunting. Former colleagues may wonder aloud about your decision. Busybody aunts will gossip about how no one makes money writing and what a nice doctor or lawyer you would have made.

Change their perception by embracing and celebrating your decision rather than timidly defending it. When people ask, "So what are you doing now?" answer with pride and conviction. Don't say, "I thought I'd give freelancing a go and see how it works out" or "I'm going to try being a freelance writer, though I'm not really sure what that means." Have your "elevator speech"—a business term for the 30-second spiel that describes what you do—always at the ready. When people ask me what I do, I respond, "I'm a freelance writer and communications consultant." If they want to know more, I tell them my practice is divided evenly between commercial writing, like magazine features, and corporate writing, which entails everything from marketing brochures to ghostwriting business books. Suddenly they're intrigued. They see writing as a real, viable, honest-to-goodness business—not because I've dropped figures but because I've spoken about it in a clear, confident manner. Let's stop apologizing for being writers. I love being one, and I bet you do, too. Tell anyone who asks.

the work is done between my ears. Often someone will ask me a question, and, when I don't answer, my wife will murmur to him or her, "Oh, he's just working." And she's right.

I also believe, however, that the luxury of being able to do mental work represents an important responsibility. During spells when my plate isn't full with deadlines, I don't rest on my laurels. Instead, I record ideas, I query like crazy, I read other writers, I think about new marketing angles. In short, given the nature of my profession, I have no excuse for down time. "If you don't care about your business, no one else will," says freelancer Sharon Aschaiek. "Use slow times to indirectly generate more work—develop new pitches, follow up with previous editors and clients, explore new marketing avenues. Even use the time to take care of accounting and administrative issues. Just don't let yourself get complacent."

The bottom line

Is freelancing hard work? Sure—damned hard. But it's no harder than any other profession. Like every job, it requires a combination of skill, thoroughness and dependability. The difference is you don't have anyone defining the parameters of the job for you or providing incentives to succeed. The discipline and drive have to come solely from you. Or, in the words of full-time freelancer and book author Lisa Bendall, "All the talent in the world won't help if you aren't willing to put in the time at your desk and actually work. You've got to crack your own whip."

Now get cracking!

BEYOND THE BASICS

Reduce, Reuse, Recycle

Creating New Material From Old Ideas

by Joanna Masterson

When it comes to writing full-time for magazines, newspapers and Web sites, successful freelancers understand one thing: There's no shame in cashing in on old ideas. In fact, repurposing previously published articles is a great way to develop story pitches and maintain a steady flow of paychecks.

REPURPOSING YOUR MATERIAL

Submit reprints

The easiest way to extend the lifetime of an article is by selling it as a reprint. Doing so requires no extra work other than submitting the article to new publications. Some publications have a policy against reprints, but many accept them and will pay freelancers a reduced rate. Authors must ensure the initial publisher only purchased first rights to the article, and not all rights. Authors also are responsible for informing subsequent publications that the article was first printed elsewhere.

Change the scope

There are many ways to tap into markets that don't accept straight reprints without writing a brand-new article. The key is to make it look like a new story without investing a lot of time and energy. Often, the best first step is to rewrite the lead. Doing so not only puts a fresh face on the piece, but also provides an opportunity to point it in a new direction.

The story's scope can be narrowed dramatically by cutting out quotes and detailed examples, thus shortening the overall length. The information could be summed up even more to serve as a sidebar to another article.

If the article is short to begin with, add more detail by doing supplementary research or interviewing new sources. This can be a good approach if the piece was first published in a newspaper or on a Web site and the author is interested in breaking into magazines, which often demand more in-depth articles.

Jay Copp, a Chicagoland-based freelance writer and editor of *The Lion Magazine,* finds himself becoming a mini-expert when first getting into a story. "You don't know much about the topic, so you immerse yourself in it," he says. "When you do a second story, it's a lot easier and your comfort level increases. You already know the sources, which saves you time."

Copp remembers a specific assignment for *West Suburban Living Magazine* in which he

---

JOANNA MASTERSON was previously the editor of *2007 Guide to Literary Agents* (Writer's Digest Books). She now writes for a trade magazine in Arlington, Virginia.

interviewed a host of parents and sports psychologists on "how much is too much" when it comes to youth sports. "I accumulated a lot of material, but there's only so much you can use in one story. I ended up pitching it to *Chicago Parent*, too, but as 10 tips for parents with kids involved in youth sports. It was pretty easy to do another article without finding many new sources or repeating myself."

Change the tone

Altering the article's tone can give it new life as well. Try making a serious piece more accessible to readers by using conversational writing, or turn a first-person essay into a straightforward how-to article. Again, this can prove effective for writers wanting to target a variety of media. Writing for the Web is quite different than magazine and newspaper writing, but basic article ideas easily cross these boundaries.

Gather ideas

Old articles are useful even if the actual text can't be repurposed. To spur story ideas, authors periodically should look through their clips to see if any articles can be updated. This is particularly effective on stories related to trends. If something was hot a few years ago, do some digging to see if it's still going strong or if something new has replaced it. Or, if something new popped up a few months ago, keep an eye out for evidence of it becoming a larger trend and use the original article as background information.

Plan ahead

One way to ensure longevity from an article topic is to plan ahead. While writing the first piece, have an idea of what would or would not be included in a secondary article. Set aside information while it's fresh on the brain and start looking for publications that would be interested in an iteration of the original article.

Copp recalls a local article he did on being a frugal shopper, a topic he figured would make a great national story as well. "I waited a while and some of the Internet sites and sources disappeared, so the story was stale," he says. "If you are going to take a story and rework it, you've got to do it fairly quickly."

Another helpful hint is to interview the same source for two different articles. Authors should make their intentions known to the source and try to get enough quotes to fuel two different articles.

BORROWING FROM OTHERS

Be fair

Some of these same techniques can be applied to other writers' work, but with a few caveats. First, it is never acceptable to plagiarize someone's work. Stealing a basic story idea is quite different from stealing the idea, sources, headline and lead.

The point is to use published articles as a brainstorming tool. For example, look through national publications for ideas that can be given a local angle. If a national study was reported in *BusinessWeek* or *USA Today* and evidence of the study can be seen in local communities, use the study as background material and talk to local sources about its impact on nearby areas.

This concept can be reversed as well, from small scale to large scale. If something interesting is happening in the community and there's evidence of it happening in other communities, try pitching a trend article to state, regional or national publications.

Copp regularly cuts out and files clips from newspapers and magazines, paying close attention to personality profiles. Any person of distinction, he explains, has certain credentials—a church affiliation or an alma mater—and those credentials almost always match up with a publication.

Repurposing Books

It's not just magazine articles ideas that can be recycled—books can be repurposed, too. Just look at *Eats, Shoots & Leaves: Why, Commas Really Do Make a Difference!* (Putnam Juvenile 2006), co-authored by Lynn Truss and Bonnie Timmons. After Truss' similarly titled grammar book proved a home run in the adult market, Putnam approached her about doing a children's version.

"When the original *Eats, Shoots & Leaves* came out and got such great attention, we thought about ways to make punctuation fun in a visual way and approached Truss about the picture book," says Susan Kochan, senior editor at Putnam. "The adult book has some hilarious and visual examples of how punctuation can change the meaning of a sentence and it seemed natural to show kids how that could look."

Other examples of books repurposed for the children's market include: *Chew on This*, by Eric Schlosser and Charles Wilson (based on Schlosser's *Fast Food Nation*); *The Revenge of the Whale*, by Nathaniel Philbrick (based on *In the Heart of the Sea*); and *The Cod's Tale* and *The Story of Salt*, both by Mark Kurlansky and S.D. Schindler (based on Kurlansky's *Cod: A Biography of the Fish That Changed the World* and *Salt: A World History*).

Kochan sees the adaptation of books as a way to expand the audience for interesting content. "The picture book adaptations of Kurlansky's books have tons of information that is fascinating to kids and touches on parts of history, geology, geography and more that they are learning in school," she says. "Kurlansky saw a topic in a unique way that was popular with adults and—when boiled down into a different format—also popular with kids."

Repurposing nonfiction seems to work best when switching from an adult to a children's market. Fiction, Kochan notes, is more about voice and character, which tend to be geared toward a particular age group right from the start.

Successful published authors have the best odds of re-issuing a book in a new market, but unpublished authors can apply the concept of repurposing to their work as well. It's never wise to shape a book to fit a certain trendy market, but if there's an old manuscript sitting in the bottom of a drawer or a new one stuck at the halfway point, try giving it a different twist. A fresh perspective may illuminate the possibility of writing for a new audience or tackling a new genre. If nothing else, it will help get some creative juices flowing.

Unpublished nonfiction authors could use repurposing as a selling point in their proposals as well. Keep in mind that agents and editors only want to hear details on one book in a proposal; however, briefly mentioning the sales potential of a second, related book could be a creative way to show the topic's versatility. This only should be done if the repurposed book has real merit, as false promises and gimmicks do more harm than good in the publishing industry.

"What could you possibly write that's new about Fred Rogers?" Copp asks. Well, he found out Mr. Rogers was a Presbyterian and pitched an idea to a Presbyterian publication talking about the TV star from a more religious perspective. "When you want to pitch a celebrity article, you have to come up with a new angle," he says. "And a lot of times these people are glad to talk about it."

Be smart

Second, authors should never recycle an article idea that was originally printed in the same publication they want to pitch. Most publications have precious editorial space to fill and can't waste it covering the same topics over and over again.

However, it always pays off to review a publication's archives (look online or request back issues, if necessary). Doing so gives freelancers valuable insight into the publication's style and what types of articles it likes to print. When it comes time to pitch a story idea, mention how it relates to or fits with the rest of the publication's content. It will show the editor a commitment to reading the publication and formulating appropriate ideas.

Authors shouldn't limit inspiration to traditional print articles. Watch news and other TV programs, listen to the radio and pay attention to Web content and blogs. These resources not only are helpful brainstorming tools, but also can provide expert sources on a variety of topics.

BEYOND THE BASICS

How Much Should I Charge?

by Lynn Wasnak

If you're a beginning freelance writer, or don't know many other freelancers, you may wonder how anyone manages to earn enough to eat and pay the rent by writing or performing a mix of writing-related tasks. Yet, smart full-time freelance writers and editors annually gross $35,000 and up—sometimes up into the $150,000-200,000 range. These top-earning freelancers rarely have names known to the general public. (Celebrity writers earn fees far beyond the rates cited in this survey.) But, year after year, they sustain themselves and their families on a freelance income, while maintaining control of their hours and their lives.

Such freelancers take writing and editing seriously—it's their business.

Periodically, they sit down and think about the earning potential of their work, and how they can make freelancing more profitable and fun. They know their numbers: what it costs to run their business; what hourly rate they require; how long a job will take. Unless there's a real bonus (a special clip, or a chance to try something new) these writers turn down work that doesn't meet the mark and replace it with a better-paying project.

If you don't know your numbers, take a few minutes to figure them out. Begin by choosing your target annual income—whether it's $25,000 or $100,000. Add in fixed expenses: social security, taxes, and office supplies. Don't forget health insurance and something for your retirement. Once you've determined your annual gross target, divide it by 1,000 billable hours—about 21 hours per week—to determine your target hourly rate.

Remember—this rate is flexible. You can continue doing low-paying work you love as long as you make up for the loss with more lucrative jobs. But you must monitor your rate of earning if you want to reach your goal. If you slip, remind yourself you're in charge. As a freelancer, you can raise prices, chase better-paying jobs, work extra hours, or adjust your spending."

"Sounds great," you may say. "But how do I come up with 1,000 billable hours each year? I'm lucky to find a writing-related job every month or two, and these pay a pittance."

That's where business attitude comes in: network, track your time, join professional organizations, and study the markets. Learn how to query, then query like mad. Take chances by reaching for the next level. Learn to negotiate for a fee you can live on—your plumber does! Then get it in writing.

You'll be surprised how far you can go, and how much you can earn, if you believe in your skills and act on your belief. The rates that follow are a guide to steer you in the right direction.

LYNN WASNAK (www.lynnwasnak.com) has freelanced full time for nearly three decades as a writer, editor, and small publisher. Her international newsletter for childhood trauma survivors, ManyVoices (www.manyvoicespress.com), is now in its 17th year.

This report is based on input from sales finalized in 2005 and 2006 only. The data is generated from voluntary surveys completed by members of numerous professional writers' and editors' organizations and specialty groups. We thank these responding groups, listed below, and their members for generously sharing information. If you would like to contribute your input, e-mail lwasnak@fuse.net for a survey.

Organizations

For More Info

For more information on determining freelance pay rates, negotiating contracts, etc., you can visit the following organizations' Web sites. (*Editor's note: A special thank you to the members of the organizations listed below for their thoughtful responses to our survey.*)

- **American Literary Translators Association (ALTA):** www.literarytranslators.org
- **American Medical Writers Association (AMWA):** www.amwa.org
- **American Society of Journalists and Authors (ASJA):** www.asja.org
- **American Society of Media Photographers (ASMP):** www.asmp.org
- **American Society of Picture Professionals (ASPP):** www.aspp.com
- **American Translators Association (ATA):** www.atanet.org
- **Association of Independents in Radio (AIR):** www.airmedia..org
- **Association of Personal Historians (APH):** www.personalhistorians.org
- **The Cartoon Bank:** www.cartoonbank.com
- **Editorial Freelancers Association (EFA):** www.the-efa.org
- **Freelance Success (FLX):** www.freelancesuccess.com
- **International Association of Business Communicators (IABC):** www.iabc.com
- **Investigative Reporters & Editors (IRE):** www.ire.org
- **Media Communicators Association International (MCA-I):** www.mca-i.org
- **National Association of Science Writers (NASW):** www.nasw.org
- **National Cartoonists Society (NCS):** www.reuben.org/main.asp
- **National Writers Union (NWU):** www.nwu.org
- **Society of Professional Journalists (SPJ):** www.spj.org
- **Society for Technical Communication (STC):** www.stc.org
- **Washington Independent Writers (WIW):** www.washwriter.org
- **Women in Film (WIF):** www.wif.org
- **Writers Guild of America East (WGAE):** www.wgae.org
- **Writers Guild of America West (WGA):** www.wga.org

Advertising, Copywriting & Public Relations

	PER HOUR			PER PROJECT			OTHER		
	HIGH	LOW	AVG	HIGH	LOW	AVG	HIGH	LOW	AVG
Advertising copywriting	$150	$35	$92	$9,000	$150	$2,278	$3/word	25¢/word	$1.63/word
Advertorials	$180	$50	$97	n/a	n/a	n/a	$3/word $1,875/page	75¢/word $300/page	$1.92/word $550/page
Book jacket copywriting	$100	$40	$71	$700	$350	$500	$1/word	50¢/word	75¢/word
Campaign development or product launch	$150	$50	$89	$8,750	$1,500	$4,250	n/a	n/a	n/a
Catalog copywriting	$100	$25	$60	n/a	n/a	n/a	$350/item	$25/item	$84/item
Copyediting for advertising	$100	$20	$58	n/a	n/a	n/a	$1/word	25¢/word	65¢/word
Direct-mail copywriting	$150	$50	$87	$50,000	$600	$8,248	$4/word $1,200/page	$1/word $200/page	$1.50/word $400/page
E-mail ad copywriting	$100	$50	$80	$3,500	$200	$836	n/a	n/a	$2/word
Event promotions/publicity	$85	$50	$63	n/a	n/a	n/a	n/a	n/a	$500/day
Fundraising campaign brochure	$110	$69	$91	$3,500	$300	$1,525	n/a	n/a	$1/word
Political campaigns, public relations	$125	$45	$88	n/a	n/a	n/a	n/a	n/a	n/a
Press kits	$180	$30	$96	$5,000	$1,000	$2,334	$2/word	50¢/word	$1.30/word
Press/news release	$180	$35	$97	$1,500	$125	$479	$500/page	$150/page	$297/page
Public relations for businesses	$180	$50	$89	n/a	n/a	n/a	$500/day	$200/day	$367/day
Public relations for government	$90	$50	$64	n/a	n/a	n/a	n/a	n/a	n/a
Public relations for organizations or nonprofits	$80	$20	$53	n/a	n/a	n/a	n/a	n/a	n/a
Public relations for schools or libraries	$80	$50	$60	n/a	n/a	n/a	n/a	n/a	n/a
Speech writing/editing (general)[1]	$167	$43	$81	$10,000	$2,700	$5,480	n/a	n/a	n/a

1 Per project figures based on 30-minute speech.

	PER HOUR			PER PROJECT			OTHER		
	HIGH	LOW	AVG	HIGH	LOW	AVG	HIGH	LOW	AVG
Speech writing for government officials	$200	$30	$86	n/a	n/a	n/a	n/a	n/a	$4,500/ 20 min
Speech writing for political candidates	$150	$60	$92	n/a	n/a	n/a	n/a	n/a	$650/15 min
Audiovisuals & Electronic Communications									
Book summaries (narrative synopsis) for film producers[1]	n/a	n/a	n/a	n/a	n/a	n/a	$1,269/15 min $34/page	$2,114/30 min $15/page	$4,006/60 min $20/page
Business film scripts[2] (training and info)	$150	$85	$100	n/a	$600	n/a	$500/run min	$50/run min	$229/run min
Copyediting audiovisuals	$88	$22	$36	n/a	n/a	n/a	n/a	n/a	$50/page
Corporate product film	$150	$85	$129	n/a	n/a	n/a	$500/run min	$100/run min	$300/run min
Educational/training film scripts	$110	$75	$96	n/a	n/a	n/a	$500/run min	$100/run min	$300/run min
Movie novelization	$100	$35	$68	$15,000	$3,000	$6,750	n/a	n/a	n/a
Radio commercials/PSAs	$85	$30	$56	n/a	n/a	n/a	$850/run min	$120/run min	$504/run min
Radio editorials & essays (no production)	$70	$50	$60	n/a	n/a	n/a	$200/run min	$45/run min	$109/run min
Radio interviews (3 minute interview)	n/a	n/a	n/a	$1,500	$150	$400	n/a	n/a	n/a
Radio stories (over 2 minutes with sound production)	$1,500	$100	$400	n/a	n/a	n/a	n/a	n/a	n/a
Screenwriting (original screenplay)	n/a	n/a	n/a	$106,070	$56,500	$81,285	n/a	n/a	n/a
Script synopsis for agent or film producer	n/a	n/a	n/a	$75	$60	$65	n/a	n/a	n/a
Script synopsis for business	$70	$45	$58	$100	$60	$75	n/a	n/a	n/a

1 Other figures based on length of speech (min=minute).

2 Run min=run minute.

	PER HOUR			PER PROJECT			OTHER		
	HIGH	LOW	AVG	HIGH	LOW	AVG	HIGH	LOW	AVG
Scripts for nontheatrical films for education, business, industry	$125	$55	$80	$5,000	$3,000	$4,083	$500/run min	$100/run min	$300/run min
TV commercials/PSAs[1]	$85	$60	$73	n/a	n/a	n/a	$2,500/ 30 sec spot	$150/ 30 sec spot	$963/ 30 sec spot
TV news story/feature[2]	$100	$70	$90	n/a	n/a	n/a	n/a	n/a	n/a
TV scripts (nontheatrical)	$150	$35	$89	$20,000	$10,000	$15,000	$1,000/day	$550/day	$800/day
TV scripts (teleplay/MOW)[3]	n/a	n/a	n/a	n/a	n/a	n/a	$500/run min	$100/run min	$300/run min
Book Publishing									
Abstracting and abridging	$125	$35	$75	n/a	n/a	n/a	$2/word	$1/word	$1.50/word
Anthology editing	$80	$23	$52	$7,900	$4,000	$5,967	n/a	n/a	n/a
Book proposal consultation	$100	$40	$57	$1,500	$250	$792	n/a	n/a	n/a
Book proposal writing	$100	$40	$65	$10,000	$500	$4,512	n/a	n/a	n/a
Book query critique	$100	$50	$60	$300	$200	$250	n/a	n/a	n/a
Book query writing	n/a	n/a	n/a	$500	$120	$200	n/a	n/a	n/a
Children's book writing (advance against royalties)	n/a	n/a	n/a	n/a	n/a	n/a	$4,000	$1,500	$2,920
Children's book writing (work for hire)	$75	$50	$63	n/a	n/a	n/a	$5/word	$1/word	$3/word
Content editing (scholarly)	$125	$30	$51	$15,000	$525	$6,119	$20/page	$4/page	$6/page
Content editing (textbook)	$100	$23	$52	$4,500	$500	$1,859	$9/page	$3/page	$4/page
Content editing (trade)	$125	$19	$49	$20,000	$1,000	$7,988	$40/page	$3.75/page	$7.50/page
Copyediting	$75	$20	$34	$5,500	$2,000	$3,500	$6/page	$1/page	$4.10/page
Fiction book writing (own)	n/a	n/a	n/a	n/a	n/a	n/a	$40,000	$525	$14,203

1 30 sec spot=30-second spot

2 $1,201 Writers Guild of America minimum/story.

3 TV scripts 30 minutes or less average $6,535/story, $19,603 with teleplay; TV scripts 60 minutes or less average $11,504/story, $28,833 with teleplay.

	PER HOUR			PER PROJECT			OTHER		
	HIGH	LOW	AVG	HIGH	LOW	AVG	HIGH	LOW	AVG
Ghostwriting, as told to[1]	$100	$50	$73	$80,000	$5,500	$22,800	n/a	n/a	n/a
Ghostwriting, no credit	$115	$30	$70	$100,000	$5,000	$36,229	$3/word	50¢/word	$1.65/word
Indexing	$40	$22	$30	n/a	n/a	n/a	$5/page	$2/page	$3.69/page
Manuscript evaluation and critique	$100	$36	$72	$2,000	$150	$835	n/a	n/a	n/a
Nonfiction book writing (collaborative)	$100	$70	$85	$75,000	$1,300	$25,297	n/a	n/a	n/a
Nonfiction book writing (own) (advance against royalties)	n/a	n/a	n/a	n/a	n/a	n/a	$50,000	$4,000	$17,909
Novel synopsis (general)	$60	$30	$45	$400	$150	$275	$30/page	$10/page	$20/page
Proofreading	$75	$15	$30	n/a	n/a	n/a	$5/page	$2/page	$3.09/page
Research for writers or book publishers	$150	$15	$46	n/a	n/a	n/a	$600/day	$450/day	$525/day
Rewriting	$120	$25	$63	$50,000	$4,000	$14,500	n/a	n/a	n/a
Translation (fiction)[2]	n/a	n/a	n/a	$10,000	$7,000	$8,500	12¢	6¢	9¢
Translation (nonfiction)	n/a	n/a	n/a	n/a	n/a	n/a	15¢	8¢	10¢
Translation (poetry)	n/a	n/a	n/a	n/a	n/a	n/a	$15/page	$0/page	$7.50/page
Business									
Annual reports	$180	$45	$87	$15,000	$500	$6,147	$600/day	$400/day	$494/day
Associations and organizations (writing for)	$125	$20	$68	n/a	n/a	n/a	$400/day	$300/day	$350/day
Brochures, fliers, booklets for business	$150	$30	$86	$15,000	$300	$2,777	$2/word $800/page	25¢/word $50/page	$1.28/word $387/page
Business & sales letters	$150	$36	$81	$2,000	$150	$762	$2/word	$1/word	$1.42/page
Business & government research	$100	$35	$69	n/a	n/a	n/a	n/a	n/a	n/a

1 Per project figures do not include royalty arrangements, which vary from publisher to publisher.

2 Other figures in cents are per target word.

	PER HOUR			PER PROJECT			OTHER		
	HIGH	LOW	AVG	HIGH	LOW	AVG	HIGH	LOW	AVG
Business editing (general)	$150	$25	$72	n/a	n/a	n/a	n/a	n/a	n/a
Business plan	$150	$50	$88	$15,000	$1,000	$6,000	n/a	n/a	$1/word
Business-writing seminars	$200	$60	$103	$8,600	$550	$2,450	n/a	n/a	n/a
Catalogs for businesses	$90	$35	$65	$10,000	$2,000	$5,000	$1,500/page	$200/page	$684/page
Consultation on communications	$180	$70	$120	n/a	n/a	n/a	$1,200/day	$500/day	$740/day
Copyediting for businesses	$125	$25	$61	n/a	n/a	n/a	$4/page	$2/page	$3/page
Corporate histories	$180	$35	$87	$35,000	$1,000	$12,500	$2/word	$1/word	$1.50/word
Corporate periodicals, editing	$125	$40	$70	n/a	n/a	n/a	n/a	n/a	n/a
Corporate periodicals, writing	$135	$50	$93	$7,500	$1,000	$4,000	$3/word	$1/word	$1.75/word
Corporate profile	$180	$65	$102	n/a	n/a	n/a	$2/word	$1/word	$1.50/word
Ghostwriting for business (usually trade magazine articles for business columns)	$135	$25	$96	n/a	n/a	$750	$2/word n/a	50¢/word n/a	$1/word $500/day
Government writing	$75	$20	$50	n/a	n/a	n/a	$1/word	25¢/word	63¢/word
Grant proposal writing for nonprofits	$150	$43	$96	$3,000	$500	$1,767	n/a	n/a	n/a
Newsletters, desktop publishing/production	$135	$35	$76	n/a	n/a	n/a	$750/page	$150/page	$391/page
Newsletters, editing	$100	$30	$63	n/a	n/a	$3,600	$230/page	$150/page	$185/page
Newsletters, writing[1]	$125	$30	$82	$5,000	$800	$2,000	$5/word	$1/word	$2/word
Translation (commercial for government agencies, technical)	n/a	n/a	n/a	n/a	n/a	n/a	$1.40/ target line	$1/ target line	$1.20/ target line
Computer, Scientific & Technical									
Computer-related manual writing	$165	$60	$105	n/a	n/a	n/a	n/a	n/a	n/a

1 Per project figures based on four-page newsletters.

	PER HOUR			PER PROJECT			OTHER		
	HIGH	LOW	AVG	HIGH	LOW	AVG	HIGH	LOW	AVG
E-mail copywriting	$100	$35	$73	n/a	n/a	n/a	$2/word	30¢/word	$1.12/word
Medical and science editing	$125	$30	$66	n/a	n/a	n/a	$4/page	$3/page	$3.50/page
Medical and science proofreading	$125	$18	$51	n/a	n/a	n/a	n/a	n/a	n/a
Medical and science writing	$180	$30	$98	$5,000	$1,000	$2,875	$2/word	25¢/word	90¢/word
Online editing	$110	$30	$58	n/a	n/a	n/a	$4/page	$3/page	$3.50/page
Technical editing	$100	$33	$72	n/a	n/a	n/a	n/a	n/a	n/a
Technical writing	$125	$30	$84	n/a	n/a	n/a	n/a	n/a	n/a
Web page design	$150	$50	$90	$4,000	$500	$2,000	n/a	n/a	n/a
Web page editing	$100	$32	$62	n/a	n/a	n/a	n/a	n/a	n/a
Web page writing	$150	$30	$83	$7,000	$100	$1,251	$1.25/word	35¢/word	86¢/word
White Papers	$135	$45	$107	n/a	n/a	n/a	n/a	n/a	n/a
Editorial/Design Packages[1]									
Desktop publishing	$125	$20	$57	$2,500	$800	$1,650	$150/page	$35/page	$92/page
Greeting card ideas	n/a	n/a	n/a	n/a	n/a	n/a	$300/card	$50/card	$125/card
Photo brochures[2]	$75	$65	$70	$15,000	$400	$4,913	n/a	n/a	n/a
Photo research	$70	$20	$39	n/a	n/a	n/a	n/a	n/a	n/a
Photography (corporate-commercial)	n/a	n/a	n/a	n/a	n/a	n/a	$2,500/day	$1,000/day	$2,000/day
Picture editing	$100	$40	$70	n/a	n/a	n/a	$65/picture	$35/picture	$45/picture
Slides/Overhead	$100	$50	$55	$2,500	$500	$1,000	$90/slide	$50/slide	$63/slide
Educational & Literary Services									
Educational consulting and designing business/adult education courses	$100	$35	$68	n/a	n/a	n/a	$1,000/day	$600/day	$800/day

1 For more information about photography rates, see *2007 Photographer's Market*.

2 Per project figures based on 4 pages/8 photos

Beyond the Basics

	PER HOUR			PER PROJECT			OTHER		
	HIGH	LOW	AVG	HIGH	LOW	AVG	HIGH	LOW	AVG
Educational grant and proposal writing	$100	$35	$56	$15,000	$500	$8,084	n/a	n/a	n/a
Manuscript evaluation for theses/ dissertations	$100	$15	$38	$1,500	$200	$500	n/a	n/a	n/a
Poetry manuscript critique	$90	$30	$85	n/a	n/a	n/a	n/a	n/a	n/a
Presentations at national conventions (by well-known authors)	$500	$125	$294	n/a	n/a	n/a	$30,000/ event	$1,000/ event	$5,000/ event
Presentations at regional writers' conferences	n/a	n/a	n/a	n/a	n/a	n/a	$1,000/ event	$50/ event	$336/ event
Presentations to local groups, librarians or teachers	n/a	n/a	n/a	n/a	n/a	n/a	$400/event	$50/event	$228/event
Presentations to school classes (5-day visiting artists program)	n/a	n/a	n/a	n/a	n/a	n/a	$3,400	$2,500	$2,750
Readings by poets, fiction writers (highest fees for celebrity writers)	n/a	n/a	n/a	n/a	n/a	n/a	$3,000/event	$50/event	$200/event
Short story manuscript critique	$115	$35	$72	n/a	n/a	n/a	$175/story	$50/story	$115/story
Teaching college course/seminar (includes adult education)	$125	$35	$84	$5,000	$550	$2,502	$550/day	$150/day	$367/day
Writers' workshops	$220	$30	$75	n/a	n/a	n/a	$4,400/event	$250/event	$1,663/event
Writing for scholarly journals	$60	$40	$50	n/a	n/a	n/a	$450/article	$100/article	$252/article
Magazines & Trade Journals[1]									
Article manuscript critique	$100	$40	$64	n/a	n/a	n/a	n/a	n/a	n/a
Arts reviewing	n/a	n/a	n/a	$300	$100	$167	$1/word	10¢/word	78¢/word
Book reviews	n/a	n/a	n/a	$500	$50	$190	$1/word	15¢/word	48¢/word
City magazine, calendar of events column	n/a	n/a	n/a	n/a	n/a	n/a	$250/column n/a	$50/column n/a	$134/column 75¢/word
Consultation on magazine editorial	$150	$50	$90	n/a	n/a	n/a	n/a	n/a	$450/day

1 For specific pay rate information for feature articles, columns/departments, fillers, etc., see individual market listings.

	PER HOUR			PER PROJECT			OTHER		
	HIGH	LOW	AVG	HIGH	LOW	AVG	HIGH	LOW	AVG
Consumer magazine column	n/a	n/a	n/a	n/a	n/a	n/a	$1.50/word $2,500/column	37¢/word $75/column	84¢/word $717/column
Consumer magazine feature articles	n/a	n/a	n/a	$11,700	$100	$2,993	$3/word	14¢/word	$1.28/word
Content editing	$125	$20	$48	n/a	n/a	n/a	$6,500/issue	$2,000/issue	$4,250/issue
Copyediting magazines	$75	$25	$40	n/a	n/a	n/a	$10/page	$2.90/page	$6.30/page
Fact checking	$125	$20	$41	n/a	n/a	n/a	n/a	n/a	n/a
Ghostwriting articles (general)	$200	$50	$100	$3,500	$1,100	$2,088	$2/word	60¢/word	$1.08/word
Magazine research	$50	$20	$37	n/a	n/a	n/a	$500/item	$100/item	$225/item
Proofreading	$75	$20	$34	n/a	n/a	n/a	n/a	n/a	n/a
Reprint fees	n/a	n/a	n/a	$1,500	$25	$397	$1.50/word	10¢/word	59¢/word
Rewriting	$125	$20	$60	n/a	n/a	n/a	n/a	n/a	n/a
Trade journal column	$70	$35	$56	n/a	n/a	n/a	$1/word $600/column	27¢/word $250/column	78¢/word $342/column
Trade journal feature article	$100	$44	$75	$2,000	$150	$962	$3/word	17¢/word	95¢/word
Miscellaneous									
Cartoons (gag, plus illustration)	n/a	n/a	n/a	n/a	n/a	n/a	$575	$15	$100
Comedy writing for nightclub entertainers	n/a	n/a	n/a	n/a	n/a	n/a	$150/joke $500/group	$5/joke $100/group	$50/joke $250/group
Craft projects with instructions	n/a	n/a	n/a	$300	$50	$175	n/a	n/a	n/a
Encyclopedia articles	n/a	n/a	n/a	n/a	n/a	n/a	$2,000/article 35¢/word	$50/article 15¢/word	$300/article 25¢/word
Family histories	$80	$30	$65	$30,000	$7,000	$17,400	n/a	n/a	n/a
Gagwriting for cartoonists	n/a	n/a	n/a	n/a	n/a	n/a	n/a	n/a	$30/gag
Institutional history (church school)	n/a	n/a	$50	n/a	n/a	n/a	$125/page	$75/page	$100/page
Manuscript typing	n/a	n/a	$20	n/a	n/a	n/a	$3/page	$1/page	$1.27/page

	PER HOUR			PER PROJECT			OTHER		
	HIGH	LOW	AVG	HIGH	LOW	AVG	HIGH	LOW	AVG
Résumés	n/a	n/a	n/a	$500	$200	$300	n/a	n/a	n/a
Writing contest judging[1]	n/a	n/a	$50	$250	$0	$55	$20/entry	$10/entry	$15/entry
Newspapers									
Arts reviewing	n/a	n/a	n/a	$200	$15	$93	60¢/word	10¢/word	37¢/word
Book reviews	n/a	n/a	n/a	$200	$15	$98	60¢/word	25¢/word	40¢/word
Column, local	n/a	n/a	n/a	n/a	n/a	n/a	$250/column	$50/column	$103/column
Copyediting	$35	$25	$30	n/a	n/a	n/a	n/a	n/a	n/a
Editing/manuscript evaluation	n/a	n/a	$35	n/a	n/a	n/a	n/a	n/a	n/a
Feature	n/a	n/a	n/a	$1,000	$75	$338	$1.50/word	10¢/word	54¢/word
Obituary copy	n/a	n/a	n/a	n/a	n/a	n/a	$225/story	$35/story	$112/story
Proofreading	$25	$18	$20	n/a	n/a	n/a	n/a	n/a	n/a
Reprints	n/a	n/a	n/a	$300	$50	$163	n/a	n/a	n/a
Stringing	n/a	n/a	n/a	n/a	n/a	n/a	$2,400/story	$40/story	$378/story
Syndicated column, self-promoted (rate depends on circulation)	n/a	n/a	n/a	n/a	n/a	n/a	$35/insertion	$4/insertion	$8/insertion

1 Some pay in gift certificates or books. Judging of finalists may be duty included in workshop speaker's fee.

BEYOND THE BASICS

Editor FAQs

by Robert Lee Brewer

The publishing world is filled with so many nooks and crannies that even the most experienced writers have common questions about various topics, such as co-authoring, self-publishing, ghostwriting and more. I know, because writers tend to ask me the same questions whether I'm speaking at a bookstore or a writer's conference, or fielding questions through WritersMarket.com. Here are some of those most frequently asked questions with my most frequently given answers.

What's the trick to getting published?

There really *is* no trick to getting published. There's no tried-and-true gimmick that will build your career for you. Making it as a writer requires a lot of hard work, discipline and perseverance.

The first step is always to work on the craft of writing. You can improve your craft by participating in writer's groups, attending writer's conferences, taking online courses, or going to workshops at local universities. Instructional books on technique (many can be found online at www.WritersDigest.com) can provide exercises, spark ideas, and give advice on plotting, characterization and more.

Once your work is at a publishable level, you should sit down with a pad of paper and outline what your long-term goals are. Then, identify some short-term goals you think will get you there.

It's hard to get somewhere without knowing where you're going, so don't discount this step in the process of becoming a successful writer. Sure, you can change directions if you see a better destination along the way, but it's important that you always have a goal in mind. Your goals will help direct which skills you need to focus on the most and will play an important role in how your writing is crafted.

How does co-authoring work?

In a situation where you wish to co-author a book or article, I suggest defining the roles of each author upfront to avoid ambiguity, hurt feelings, or disputes during the writing process and later on during the submission process. Make sure each author agrees on the goals, responsibilities, rights, compensation and deadlines for the project. Communication throughout the process is key.

ROBERT LEE BREWER is the editor of *Writer'sMarket* and WritersMarket.com. He can be reached via e-mail at robert.brewer@fwpubs.com.

When contacting a publisher or agent, it's best to elect one main contact person to avoid confusion. This person should be good at communicating with the publisher or agent and the other co-author or authors.

What about ghostwriting?

Ghostwriting is the process where you take another person's ideas and write an article or book for them, either under their name or "as told to." Authoritative experts with no writing experience use this process, as well as celebrities with stories to tell.

Ghostwriting is not a glamorous job, since you usually don't get credit or recognition, but it does pay the bills for many hard-working and organized writers. As with co-authoring, be sure to get goals, rights, payment, responsibilities, deadlines and other details ironed out before starting any project.

Whether you are looking for a ghostwriter or you wish to become one, the following Web sites can help: www.freelancewriting.com; www.craigslist.org; www.writers-editors.com. On these Web sites, you can look for job openings or post one.

Should I hire an editor or book doctor?

Some writers hire professional editors to strengthen their manuscripts before submitting to publishers or agents. These editors can check for content, flow, do line-by-line edits, offer general critiques, and more (or less—on a case-by-case basis). However, it is often hard to evaluate how good an editor is until you've already invested a good deal of time and money into the process. A much more affordable and possibly more effective solution is to join a writing group in your area or attend a writing workshop that addresses your type of writing. Writer's conferences also offer critiques by professional writers, editors and agents. If these options are not available, then you could try hiring a graduate student from a local college.

You can hunt down possible editors online at the following Web sites: www.writerseditors.com; www.freelancewriting.com; www.absolutewrite.com. Also, check out classified ads in the back of the *Writer's Digest* magazine.

When do I need an agent?

First, you only need an agent if you are writing a book or a screenplay. Second, nonfiction writers need a completed book proposal together before hunting down an agent, and fiction writers need a completed manuscript. Third, agents are most helpful for selling to the larger book publishers, so if you're writing a book that will only appeal to academics or a very small audience, using an agent will not make as much sense.

A good agent will place your work with a publisher; negotiate the best package of subsidiary rights, advance money, and royalty terms possible; help you develop your career as a writer for the short-and long-term; and many also provide guidance in the development of writing projects and promotional opportunities.

For more information on agents, check out *2008 Guide to Literary Agents*, edited by Chuck Sambuchino (Writer's Digest Books). In addition to over 500 listings, this resource is filled with articles explaining how to find and work with an appropriate agent.

Is self-publishing a better option for writers?

Self-publishing is definitely tied up in the whole equation of determining your goals as a writer. Many writers envision publishing a book that will be sold in bookstores, and possibly as a bestseller. If that's your goal, then self-publishing should only be used as a last resort.

Unless you're writing for a very specialized audience or trying to publish a book of poetry, then I suggest trying to get an agent first. If that doesn't work out, try submitting directly to book publishers. If that doesn't work, maybe you need to revise your query letter or manuscript and try again. This is especially true if you keep hearing the same comments and suggestions from agents and editors.

If you've exhausted all these options and you still think you can reach an audience, then self-publishing could be an option for you. However, make sure you research all your self-publishing options to save time, money and headaches. Self-publishing is a very rough road for any writer and often turns into a full-time job with a very low rate of success.

How do I handle a pseudonym?

Many writers working under a pseudonym wonder if they have to deceive their publishers and live a double life. The best policy is to bring your pseudonym up at the beginning of your communication with an agent or editor. In your initial query or cover letter, use your real name, but explain in one sentence somewhere in that letter (and not in the first paragraph) that you write under a pen name. That way payment can be made to your real name, helping you avoid any possible taxation or banking snafus. Also, to avoid confusion, use your pseudonym on the actual manuscript.

Should I copyright my work before submitting?

For all practical and legal purposes, your work is protected by copyright once you put it on paper (or save it electronically). While registering your copyright will add an extra level of protection for your writing against possible manuscript thieves, it is not necessary and can often label you as an amateur. Most cases of plagiarism occur after a work has been published

Word Count Guidelines

Use the average word lengths below to help you decide what kind of manuscript you've written. As the formats for the delivery of content evolve, so do the rules (for example, the recent explosion of blogging). Always check the specific guidelines of a market listing before submitting. The word lengths below are not rigid guidelines—just the norms.

If you're writing fiction, then:

Up to 1,000 words = short-story, flash fiction or vignette
1,000-6,000 words = short story
6,000-15,000 words = long story or novelette
15,000-45,000 = novella
45,000-120,000 words = novel (though most commonly 50,000-80,000 words)

Anything more than 120,000 words will probably need to be broken up into a series of books or condensed.

If you're writing nonfiction, then:

less than 1,000 words = filler, sidebar or review
1,000-6,000 words = feature article
20,000-200,000 words = book length (though most commonly 50,000-100,000 words)

Nonfiction lengths can vary dramatically, depending on art and design elements (whether advertisements or sidebars) that run with the text.

and is under the protection of copyright. Do not write that your work is copyrighted or include a copyright symbol on your manuscript or in your query or cover letter; this will generally get your submission rejected before it is even read.

How do I know a publisher won't steal my work?

As in life, there are no guarantees in publishing. However, it is rare to hear an actual first-person account of an editor or agent stealing someone else's work before it is published. Most people who relay these tall tales of publishing will say "a friend of a friend" had her work stolen by an editor. While there may be a case or two where this has happened, you probably have better odds of winning the lottery than having your work stolen. Whether that's a good or bad thing is open to interpretation.

In addition, *Writer's Market* strives to list only reputable publishers and viable markets within its pages. From including screening questions in our questionnaires to scanning online writer groups and responding to writer complaints, we work to maintain the highest quality directory available to writers trying to get published and paid for their writing. (If you feel you have not been treated fairly by a listing in the book, please follow the Complaint Procedure found on the copyright page of this book—next to the Table of Contents.)

BEYOND THE BASICS

Publishers and Their Imprints

The publishing world is in constant transition. With all the buying, selling, reorganizing, consolidating, and dissolving, it's hard to keep publishers and their imprints straight. To help make sense of these changes, here's a breakdown of major publishers (and their divisions)—who owns whom and which imprints are under each company umbrella. Keep in mind that this information changes frequently. The Web site of each publisher is provided to help you keep an eye on this ever-evolving business.

HARLEQUIN ENTERPRISES

www.eharlequin.com

Harlequin

Harlequin American Romance
Harlequin Bianca
Harlequin Blaze
Harlequin Deseo
Harlequin Everlasting Love
Harlequin Ginger Blossom
Harlequin Historical
Harlequin Intrigue
Harlequin Jazmin
Harlequin Julia
Harlequin Medical Romance
Harlequin NEXT
Harlequin Presents
Harlequin Romance
Harlequin Superromance

HQN Books

LUNA

Mills & Boon

Mills & Boon Historical Romance
Mills & Boon Medical Romance
Mills & Boon Modern Xtra-Sensual

MIRA

Kimani Press

Kimani Press Arabesque Inspirational Romance
Kimani Press Arabesque Romance
Kimani Press Kimani Romance
Kimani TRU
Kimani Press New Spirit
Kimani Press Romance Sepia

Red Dress Ink

Silhouette

Silhouette Bombshell
Silhouette Desire
Silhouette Nocturne
Silhouette Romance
Silhouette Romantic Suspense
Silhouette Special Edition

SPICE

Steeple Hill

Steeple Hill Café
Steeple Hill Love Inspired

Steeple Hill Love Inspired Historical
Steeple Hill Love Inspired Suspense
Steeple Hill Women's Fiction

Worldwide Library
Rogue Angel
Worldwide Mystery

HARPERCOLLINS

www.harpercollins.com

HarperCollins Australia/New Zealand
Angus & Robertson
Collins
Fourth Estate
Harper Perennial
HarperCollins
HarperSports
Voyager

HarperCollins Canada
HarperCollinsPublishers
HarperPerennial Canada
HarperTrophyCanada
Phyllis Bruce Books

HarperCollins Children's Books Group
Amistad
Eos
Greenwillow Books
HarperCollins Children's Audio
HarperCollins Children's Books
HarperFestival
HarperEntertainment
HarperTeen
HarperTrophy
Joanna Cotler books
Julie Andrews Collection
Katherine Tegen Books
Laura Geringer Books
Rayo

HarperCollins General Books Group
Amistad
Avon
Avon A
Avon Red
Caedmon
Collins
Collins Design
Dark Alley
Ecco
Eos
Harper Paperbacks
Harper Perennial
Harper Perennial Modern Classics
HarperAudio
HarperCollins
HarperCollins e-Books
HarperEntertainment
HarperLuxe
HarperSanFrancisco
HarperTorch
Morrow Cookbooks
Rayo
William Morrow

HarperCollins UK
Collins
General Books
- HarperFiction
  - Voyager
- HarperNonfiction
  - HarperCollins Audio
  - HarperEntertainment
  - HarperSport
  - HarperThorsons Harper Element
  - Tolkien and Estates
- HarperCollins Children's Books

Press Books
- FourthEstate
- HarperPerennial
- HarperPress

Zondervan
Vida
Zonderkidz
Zondervan

Beyond the Basics

HOLTZBRINCK PUBLISHERS

www.holtzbrinck.com

Farrar, Straus & Giroux
Faber & Faber, Inc.
Farrar, Straus & Giroux Books for Young Readers
Hill & Wang (division)
North Point Press

Henry Holt and Co. LLC
Books for Young Readers
Metropolitan Books
Owl Books
Times Books

Pan MacMillan
Boxtree
MacMillan
MacMillan Children's Books
Campbell Books
Priddy Books
Pan
Picador
Sidgwick & Jackson

St. Martin's Press
Griffin Books
Let's Go
Minotaur
St. Martin's Paperbacks
St. Martin's Press
Thomas Dunne Books
Truman Talley Books

Tom Doherty Associates
Forge
Tor Books

PENGUIN GROUP (USA), INC.

www.penguingroup.com

Penguin Adult Division
Ace Books
Alpha Books
Avery
Berkley Books
Dutton
Gotham Books
HPBooks
Hudson Street Press
Jeremy P. Tarcher
Jove
New American Library
Penguin
Penguin Press
Perigree
Plume
Portfolio
Putnam
Riverhead Books
Sentinel
Viking

Young Readers Division
Dial Books for Young Readers
Dutton Children's Books
Firebird
Frederick Warne
Grosset & Dunlap
Philomel
Price Stern Sloan
Puffin Books
Putnam
Razorbill
Speak
Viking Children's Books

RANDOM HOUSE, INC.

www.randomhouse.com

Bantam Dell Publishing Group
Bantam Hardcover
Bantam Mass Market
Bantam Trade Paperback
Crimeline
Delacorte Press

Dell
Delta
Domain
DTP
Fanfare
Island
Spectra
The Dial Press

Crown Publishing Group
Clarkson Potter
Crown Business
Crown Publishers, Inc.
Harmony Books
Potter Style
Potter Craft
Shaye Arehart Books
Three Rivers Press

Doubleday Broadway Publishing Group
Broadway Books
Currency
Doubleday
Doubleday Image
Doubleday Religious Publishing
Harlem Moon
Main Street Books
Morgan Road Books
Spiegel & Grau
Nan A. Talese

Knopf Publishing Group
Alfred A. Knopf
Anchor Books
Everyman's Library
Pantheon Books
Schocken Books
Vintage Books

Random House Publishing Group
Ballantine Books
Del Rey
Del Rey/Lucas Books
Fawcett
Ivy
The Modern Library
One World
Random House Trade Group
Random House Trade Paperbacks
Reader's Circle
Striver's Row Books
Villard Books
Wellspring

Random House Audio Publishing Group
Listening Library
Random House Audio
Random House Audio Assets
Random House Audio Dimensions
Random House Price-less
Random House Audio Roads
Random House Audio Voices

Random House Children's Books
Golden Books
Kids@Random

Random House Direct, Inc.
Bon Apetit
Gourmet Books
Pillsbury

Random House Information Group
Fodor's Travel Publications
Living Language
Prima Games
The Princeton Review
Random House Español
Random House Puzzles & Games
Random House Reference Publishing

Random House International
Areté
McClelland & Stewart Ltd.
Plaza & Janés
Random House Australia
Random House of Canada Ltd.
Random House of Mondadori
Random House South Africa
Random House South America
Random House United Kingdom
Transworld UK
Verlagsgruppe Random House

Random House Large Print

Random House Value Publishing

Waterbrook Press
Fisherman Bible Study Guides
Shaw Books
Waterbrook Press

SIMON & SCHUSTER

www.simonsays.com

Simon & Schuster Adult Publishing
Atria Books
Free Press
Howard Books
Pocket Books
Scribner
Simon & Schuster
Strebor
The Touchstone & Fireside Group

Simon & Schuster Audio
Pimsleur
Simon & Schuster Audioworks
Simon & Schuster Sound Ideas

Simon & Schuster Children's Publishing
Aladdin Paperbacks
Atheneum Books for Young Readers
Libros Para Niños
Little Simon®
Little Simon Inspirations
Margaret K. McElderry Books
Simon & Schuster Books for Young Readers
Simon Pulse
Simon Spotlight®
Simon Spotlight Entertainment

Simon & Schuster International
Simon & Schuster Australia
Simon & Schuster Canada
Simon & Schuster UK

HACHETTE BOOK GROUP USA

www.twbookmark.com

Center Street

FaithWords

Hachette Book Group Digital Media
Hachette Audio

Little, Brown and Company
Back Bay Books
Bulfinch Press

Little, Brown Books for Young Readers
LB Kids
Megan Tingley Books

Grand Central Publishing
Business Plus
5-Spot
Forever
Orbit
Springboard Press
Twelve
Vision
Wellness Central
Yen Press

MARKETS

Literary Agents

The 85 literary agencies listed in this section are either actively seeking new clients (◻) or seeking both new and established writers (◪), and they all generate 98 to 100 percent of their income from commission on sales.

All 85 agencies are members of the Association of Authors' Representatives (AAR), which means they do not charge for reading, critiquing, or editing. Some agents in this section may charge clients for office expenses such as photocopying, foreign postage, long-distance phone calls, or express mail services. Make sure you have a clear understanding of what these expenses are before signing any agency agreement.

FOR MORE . . .

The *2008 Guide to Literary Agents* (Writer's Digest Books) offers more than 650 listings for both literary and script agents, as well as information on writers' conferences. It also offers a wealth of information on the author/agent relationship and other related topics.

SUBHEADS

Each listing is broken down into subheads to make locating specific information easier. In the first section, you'll find contact information for each agency. Further information is provided which indicates an agency's size, its willingness to work with a new or previously unpublished writer, and its general areas of interest.

Member Agents Agencies comprised of more than one agent list member agents and their individual specialties to help you determine the most appropriate person for your query letter.

Represents Here agencies specify what nonfiction and fiction subjects they consider.

O⁻ Look for the key icon to quickly learn an agent's areas of specialization or specific strengths.

How to Contact In this section agents specify the type of material they want to receive, how they want to receive it, and how long you should wait for their response.

Recent Sales To give a sense of the types of material they represent, agents provide specific titles they've sold.

Terms Provided here are details of an agent's commission, whether a contract is offered, and what additional office expenses you might have to pay if the agent agrees to represent you. Standard commissions range from 10-15 percent for domestic sales, and 15-20 percent for foreign or dramatic sales.

Writers' Conferences Here agents list the conferences they attend.

Tips Agents offer advice and additional instructions for writers looking for representation.

N DOMINICK ABEL LITERARY AGENCY, INC.

146 W. 82nd St., #1B, New York NY 10024. (212)877-0710. Fax: (212)595-3133. E-mail: agency@dalainc.com. Estab. 1975. Member of AAR. Represents 100 clients. Currently handles: adult nonfiction books; adult novels.

How to Contact Query with SASE.

Terms Agent receives 15% commission on domestic sales; 20% commission on foreign sales.

N ADAMS LITERARY

7845 Colony Road C4, #215, Charlotte NC 28226. (212)786-9140. Fax: (212)786-9170. E-mail: info@adamsliterary.com. Web site: www.adamsliterary.com. **Contact:** Tracey Adams. Estab. 2004. Member of AAR.

- Prior to becoming an agent, Ms. Adams worked in the marketing and editorial departments of Greenwillow Books and Margaret K. McElderry Books.

Member Agents Tracey Adams; Josh Adams.

Adams Literary is a full-service literary agency exclusively representing children's book authors and artists. "Although we remain absolutely dedicated to finding new talent, we must announce that, until further notice, we can no longer accept unsolicited manuscripts. We also cannot accept queries or submissions via e-mail."

How to Contact Please visit this agency's Web site for updates regarding submissions policy, as it is in flux. No e-mail or fax queries.

Recent Sales Two novels, by Cynthia Lord (Scholastic).

N ALIVE COMMUNICATIONS, INC.

7680 Goddard St., Suite 200, Colorado Springs CO 80920. (719)260-7080. Fax: (719)260-8223. Web site: www.alivecom.com. Estab. 1989. Member of AAR, Authors Guild. Represents 100+ clients. 5% of clients are new/unpublished writers. Currently handles: 50% nonfiction books; 35% novels; 5% novellas; 10% juvenile books.

Member Agents Rick Christian, president (blockbusters, bestsellers); Lee Hough (popular/commercial nonfiction and fiction, thoughtful spirituality, children's); Beth Jusino (thoughtful/inspirational nonfiction, women's fiction/nonfiction, Christian living).

Represents Nonfiction books, novels, short story collections, novellas. **Considers these nonfiction areas:** Biography/autobiography; business/economics; child guidance/parenting; how-to; memoirs; religious/inspirational; self-help/personal improvement; women's issues/studies. **Considers these fiction areas:** Action/adventure; contemporary issues; detective/police/crime; family saga; historical; humor/satire; literary; mainstream/contemporary; mystery/suspense; religious/inspirational; thriller.

This agency specializes in fiction, Christian living, how-to and commercial nonfiction. Actively seeking inspirational, literary and mainstream fiction, and work from authors with established track records and platforms. Does not want poetry, young adult paperbacks, scripts or dark themes.

How to Contact Query with SASE. Be advised that this agency works primarily with well-established, bestselling, and career authors. Returns materials only with SASE. Obtains most new clients through recommendations from others.

Recent Sales Sold 300+ titles in the last year. A spiritual memoir, by Eugene Peterson (Viking); A biography of Rwandan president Paul Kagame, by Stephen Kinzer; *Ever After*, by Karen Klingsbury (Zondervan).

Terms Agent receives 15% commission on domestic sales; 15% commission on foreign sales. Offers written contract; 2-month notice must be given to terminate contract.

Tips "Rewrite and polish until the words on the page shine. Endorsements and great connections may help, provided you can write with power and passion. Network with publishing professionals by making contacts, joining critique groups, and attending writers' conferences in order to make personal connections and to get feedback. Alive Communications, Inc., has established itself as a premiere literary agency. We serve an elite group of authors who are critically acclaimed and commercially successful in both Christian and general markets."

MIRIAM ALTSHULER LITERARY AGENCY

53 Old Post Road N., Red Hook NY 12571. (845)758-9408. **Contact:** Miriam Altshuler. Estab. 1994. Member of AAR. Represents 40 clients. Currently handles: 45% nonfiction books; 45% novels; 5% story collections; 5% juvenile books.

- Ms. Altshuler has been an agent since 1982.

Represents Nonfiction books, novels, short story collections, juvenile books. **Considers these nonfiction areas:** Biography/autobiography; ethnic/cultural interests; history; language/literature/criticism; memoirs; multicultural; music/dance; nature/environment; popular culture; psychology; sociology; theater/film; women's issues/studies. **Considers these fiction areas:** Literary; mainstream/contemporary; multicultural.

- Does not want self-help, mystery, how-to, romance, horror, spiritual, fantasy, poetry, screenplays, science fiction or techno-thriller.

How to Contact Query with SASE. Prefers to read materials exclusively. If no SASE is included, no response will be sent. No unsolicited mss. No e-mail or fax queries. Considers simultaneous queries. Responds in 3 weeks to mss. Returns materials only with SASE. Obtains most new clients through recommendations from others.

Terms Agent receives 15% commission on domestic sales; 20% commission on foreign sales. Charges clients for overseas mailing, photocopies, overnight mail when requested by author.

Writers' Conferences Bread Loaf Writers' Conference; Washington Independent Writers Conference; North Carolina Writers' Network Conference.

THE AMPERSAND AGENCY

Ryman's Cottages, Little Tew, Oxfordshire OX7 4JJ United Kingdom. (44)(16)868-3677. Fax: (44)(16)868-3449. E-mail: peter@theampersandagency.co.uk. Web site: www.theampersandagency.co.uk. **Contact:** Peter Buckman. Estab. 2003. Member of AAR. Represents 35 clients. 75% of clients are new/unpublished writers.

- Prior to opening his agency, Mr. Buckman was a writer and publisher in England and America.

Member Agents Peter Buckman (literary fiction and nonfiction); Peter Janson-Smith (crime, thrillers, biography); Anne-Marie Doulton (historical and women's fiction).

Represents Nonfiction books, novels, juvenile books, scholarly books. **Considers these nonfiction areas:** Animals; biography/autobiography; cooking/foods/nutrition; current affairs; education; ethnic/cultural interests; government/politics/law; health/medicine; history; humor/satire; language/literature/criticism; memoirs; military/war; music/dance; popular culture; psychology; theater/film; translation; true crime/investigative. **Considers these fiction areas:** Action/adventure; comic books/cartoon; confession; detective/police/crime; ethnic; family saga; fantasy; historical; juvenile; literary; mainstream/contemporary; mystery/suspense; romance; thriller; young adult; glitz.

- "Being a new agency, we specialize in new writers, although we also represent well-established names. We are small, experienced, and professional. We know what we like, respond quickly, and enjoy working with the writers we take on to present their work in the best possible way. We also offer a foreign rights service and have well-established contacts on both sides of the Atlantic in film, TV, broadcasting, and publishing." Actively seeking commercial and literary fiction and nonfiction. Does not want science fiction or works with only regional appeal.

How to Contact Submit outline, 1-2 sample chapters. Accepts queries via e-mail. Considers simultaneous queries. Responds in 1 week to queries; 1 month to mss. Returns materials only with SASE. Obtains most new clients through recommendations, writers' handbooks, word of mouth.

Recent Sales Sold 14 titles in the last year. *Q&A*, by Vikas Swarup (Scribner/Doubleday); *My Side of the Story*, by Will Davis (Bloomsbury); *Digging Up the Dead*, by Dr. Druin Burch (Chatoo & Windus); *Neptune's Daughter*, by Beryl Kingston (Transita). Other clients include Geoff Baker, Max Barron, Rob Buckman, Anna Crosbie, Andrew Cullen, Tom Darke, Francis Ellen, Justin Elliott, Cora Harrison, Georgette Heyer, Michael Hutchinson, Jim McKenna, Euan Macpherson, Bolaji Odofin, Rosie Orr, Philip Purser, Penny Rumble, Nick van Bloss, Mike Walters, Norman Welch, Kirby Wright.

Terms Agent receives 10-15% commission on domestic sales; 20% commission on foreign sales. Offers written contract. "By agreement with the author, we charge for extra photocopying in the case of multiple submissions and for any lawyers or other profesional fees required by a negotiation."

BETSY AMSTER LITERARY ENTERPRISES

P.O. Box 27788, Los Angeles CA 90027-0788. **Contact:** Betsy Amster. Estab. 1992. Member of AAR. Represents more than 65 clients. 35% of clients are new/unpublished writers. Currently handles: 65% nonfiction books; 35% novels.

- Prior to opening her agency, Ms. Amster was an editor at Pantheon and Vintage for 10 years, and served as editorial director for the Globe Pequot Press for 2 years.

Represents Nonfiction books, novels. **Considers these nonfiction areas:** Biography/autobiography; child guidance/parenting; ethnic/cultural interests; gardening; health/medicine; history; money/finance; psychology; sociology; women's issues/studies. **Considers these fiction areas:** Ethnic; literary; mystery/suspense (quirky); thriller (quirky); women's (high quality).

- Actively seeking strong narrative nonfiction, particularly by journalists; outstanding literary fiction (the next Richard Ford or Jhumpa Lahiri); witty, intelligent commerical women's fiction (the next Elinor Lipman or Jennifer Weiner); mysteries that open new worlds to us; and high-profile self-help and psychology, preferably research based. Does not want to receive poetry, children's books, romances, Western, science fiction or action/adventure.

How to Contact For fiction, send query, first 3 pages, SASE. For nonfiction, send query or proposal with SASE.

No e-mail or fax queries. Considers simultaneous queries. Responds in 1 month to queries; 2 months to mss. Obtains most new clients through recommendations from others, solicitations, conferences.

Recent Sales *The Blessing of a B Minus*, by Dr. Wendy Mogel (Scribner); *Winners and Lovers: Balancing Love and Power in All Your Relationships*, by Dr. Elaine N. Aron (Little, Brown); *Wild Indigo and Wild Inferno*, by Sandi Ault (Berkley Prime Crime); *Mona Lisa in Camelot: Jacqueline Kennedy and the True Story of the Painting's High-Stakes Journey to America*, by Margaret Leslie Davis (DaCapo); *The Girl I Left Behind: A Narrative History of the Sixties*, by Judith Nies (HarperCollins); *The Battle for Wine and Love (Or How I Saved the World from Parkerization)*, by Alice Feiring (Harcourt); *Mutts*, by Sharon Montrose (Stewart, Tabori & Chang); *A Vicky Hill Exclusive!*, by Hannah Dennison (Berkley Prime Crime); *100 Trees and How They Got Their Names*, by Diana Wells (Algonquin). Other clients include Dr. Linda Acredolo and Dr. Susan Goodwyn, Dwight Allen, Barbara DeMarco-Barrett, Robin Chotzinoff, Rob Cohen & David Wollock, Phil Doran, Ruth Andrew Ellenson, Maria Amparo Escandon, Paul Mandelbaum, Joy Nicholson, Christopher Noxon, Edward Schneider and R.J. Smith.

Terms Agent receives 15% commission on domestic sales; 20% commission on foreign sales. Offers written contract, binding for 1 year; 3-month notice must be given to terminate contract. Charges for photocopying, postage, long distance phone calls, messengers, galleys/books used in submissions to foreign and film agents and to magazines for first serial rights.

Writers' Conferences Squaw Valley Writers' Workshop; San Diego State University Writers' Conference; UCLA Extension Writers' Program; The Loft Literary Center.

BALKIN AGENCY, INC.

P.O. Box 222, Amherst MA 01004. (413)548-9835. Fax: (413)548-9836. E-mail: rick62838@crocker.com. **Contact:** Rick Balkin, president. Estab. 1972. Member of AAR. Represents 50 clients. 10% of clients are new/unpublished writers. Currently handles: 85% nonfiction books; 5% scholarly books; 5% textbooks; 5% reference books.

- Prior to opening his agency, Mr. Balkin served as executive editor with Bobbs-Merrill Company.

Represents Nonfiction books, scholarly books, textbooks. **Considers these nonfiction areas:** Animals; anthropology/archaeology; current affairs; health/medicine; history; how-to; language/literature/criticism; nature/environment; popular culture; science/technology; sociology; translation; biography.

This agency specializes in adult nonfiction. No fiction, poetry, screenplays or computer books.

How to Contact Query with SASE, submit proposal package, outline. Accepts e-mail queries. No fax queries. Responds in 1 week to queries; 2 weeks to mss. Returns materials only with SASE. Obtains most new clients through recommendations from others.

Recent Sales Sold 30 titles in the last year. *The Many Faces of God*, by (W.W. Norton Co.); *A Perfect Mess*, by Eric Abrahamson and David H. Freedman (Little Brown); *1491*, by Charles Mann (Knopf).

Terms Agent receives 15% commission on domestic sales; 20% commission on foreign sales. Offers written contract, binding for 1 year. This agency charges clients for photocopying and express or foreign mail.

Tips "I do not take on books described as bestsellers or potential bestsellers. Any nonfiction work that is either unique, paradigmatic, a contribution, truly witty, or a labor of love is grist for my mill."

N THE PAULA BALZER AGENCY

55 Eastern Parkway, #5H, Brooklyn NY 11238. (347)787-4131. E-mail: info@pbliterary.com. Web site: www.pbliterary.com. **Contact:** Paula Balzer. Member of AAR. Represents 35 clients. 50% of clients are new/unpublished writers. Currently handles: 50% nonfiction books; 50% novels.

- Prior to her current position, Ms. Balzer was with Carlisle & Company, as well as Sarah Lazin Books.

Represents Nonfiction books, novels. **Considers these nonfiction areas:** Biography/autobiography; child guidance/parenting; cooking/foods/nutrition; current affairs; education; gay/lesbian issues; government/politics/law; history; how-to; humor/satire; memoirs; popular culture; psychology; science/technology; self-help/personal improvement; women's issues/studies. **Considers these fiction areas:** Erotica; family saga; gay/lesbian; glitz; historical; horror; humor/satire; literary; mainstream/contemporary; mystery/suspense; thriller; women's.

Humor and popular culture.

How to Contact Query with SASE, submit proposal package, author bio, 50 sample pages. Accepts e-mail queries. No fax queries. Responds in 3 weeks to queries; 4-6 weeks to mss. Returns materials only with SASE. Obtains most new clients through recommendations from others.

Recent Sales *Separated*, by Sheldon Rusch (Berkley); *Pledged: The Secret Life of Sororities*, by Alexandra Robbins (Hyperion); *Quarterlife Crisis: The Unique Challenges of Life in Your Twenties*, by Alexandra Robbins (Penguin Putnam); *Dear Mrs. Lindbergh: A Novel*, by Kathleen Hughes (W.W. Norton & Company).

Terms Agent receives 15% commission on domestic sales; 20% commission on foreign sales. Offers written contract.

LORETTA BARRETT BOOKS, INC.

101 Fifth Ave., New York NY 10003. (212)242-3420. Fax: (212)807-9579. E-mail: query@lorettabarrettbooks.com. Web site: www.lorettabarrettbooks.com. **Contact:** Loretta A. Barrett, Nick Mullendore. Estab. 1990. Member of AAR. Currently handles: 50% nonfiction books; 50% novels.

- Prior to opening her agency, Ms. Barrett was vice president and executive editor at Doubleday and editor-in-chief of Anchor Books.

Represents Nonfiction books, novels. **Considers these nonfiction areas:** Biography/autobiography; child guidance/parenting; current affairs; ethnic/cultural interests; government/politics/law; health/medicine; history; memoirs; money/finance; multicultural; nature/environment; popular culture; psychology; religious/inspirational; science/technology; self-help/personal improvement; sociology; spirituality; sports; women's issues/studies; nutrition; creative nonfiction. **Considers these fiction areas:** Action/adventure; contemporary issues; detective/police/crime; ethnic; family saga; historical; literary; mainstream/contemporary; mystery/suspense; psychic/supernatural; thriller.

This agency specializes in general interest books. No children's, juvenile, science fiction, or fantasy.

How to Contact Query with SASE. Accepts e-mail queries. No fax queries. Considers simultaneous queries. Responds in 2-3 weeks to queries. Returns materials only with SASE.

Recent Sales *Spiritual Progress*, by Thomas D. Williams (Hachette); *The Hazards of Space Travel*, by Neil Comins (Ballantine); *Mother Angelica's Little Book of Life Lessons*, by Raymond Arroyo (Doubleday) and more.

Terms Agent receives 15% commission on domestic sales; 20% commission on foreign sales. Offers written contract. Charges clients for shipping and photocopying.

N FAYE BENDER LITERARY AGENCY

337 W. 76th St., #E1, New York NY 10023. E-mail: info@fbliterary.com. Web site: www.fbliterary.com. **Contact:** Faye Bender. Estab. 2004. Member of AAR.

Represents Nonfiction books, novels, juvenile books. **Considers these nonfiction areas:** Memoirs; popular culture; women's issues/studies; young adult; narrative; health; biography; popular science. **Considers these fiction areas:** Literary; young adult (middle-grade); women's; commercial.

"I choose books based on the narrative voice and strength of writing. I work with previously published and first-time authors." Does not want receive genre fiction (Western, romance, horror, fantasy, science fiction).

How to Contact Query with SASE and 10 sample pages via mail or e-mail. No fax queries.

Recent Sales *Science Experiments*, by Karen Romano Young (National Geographic Society); *The Last Beach Bungalow*, by Jennie Nash (Berkley).

Tips "Please keep your letters to the point, include all relevant information, and have a bit of patience."

MEREDITH BERNSTEIN LITERARY AGENCY

2095 Broadway, Suite 505, New York NY 10023. (212)799-1007. Fax: (212)799-1145. Estab. 1981. Member of AAR. Represents 85 clients. 20% of clients are new/unpublished writers. Currently handles: 50% nonfiction books; 50% fiction.

- Prior to opening her agency, Ms. Bernstein served at another agency for 5 years.

Represents Nonfiction books, novels. **Considers these nonfiction areas:** Any area of nonfiction in which the author has an established platform. **Considers these fiction areas:** Literary; mystery/suspense; romance; thriller; women's.

This agency does not specialize. It is very eclectic.

How to Contact Query with SASE. No e-mail or fax queries. Considers simultaneous queries. Obtains most new clients through recommendations from others, conferences, developing/packaging ideas.

Recent Sales Three untitled novels of suspense, by Nancy Pickard (Ballantine); *Why Women Lie*, by Susan Baresh; *Bride's Diplomacy Guide*, by Sharon Naylor (Adams); *Mortgage Brokering*, by Darrin Seppinni (McGraw, Hill).

Terms Agent receives 15% commission on domestic sales; 20% commission on foreign sales. Charges clients $75 disbursement fee/year.

Writers' Conferences Southwest Writers' Conference; Rocky Mountain Fiction Writers' Colorado Gold; Pacific Northwest Writers' Conference; Willamette Writers' Conference; Surrey International Writers' Conference; San Diego State University Writers' Conference.

BLEECKER STREET ASSOCIATES, INC.

532 LaGuardia Place, #617, New York NY 10012. (212)677-4492. Fax: (212)388-0001. **Contact:** Agnes Birnbaum. Estab. 1984. Member of AAR, RWA, MWA. Represents 60 clients. 20% of clients are new/unpublished writers. Currently handles: 75% nonfiction books; 25% novels.

- Prior to becoming an agent, Ms. Birnbaum was a senior editor at Simon & Schuster, Dutton/Signet, and other publishing houses.

Represents Nonfiction books, novels. **Considers these nonfiction areas:** Animals; biography/autobiography; business/economics; child guidance/parenting; computers/electronic; cooking/foods/nutrition; current affairs; ethnic/cultural interests; government/politics/law; health/medicine; history; how-to; memoirs; military/war; money/finance; nature/environment; New Age/metaphysics; popular culture; psychology; religious/inspirational; science/technology; self-help/personal improvement; sociology; sports; true crime/investigative; women's issues/studies. **Considers these fiction areas:** Ethnic; historical; literary; mystery/suspense; romance; thriller; women's.

O→ "We're very hands-on and accessible. We try to be truly creative in our submission approaches. We've had especially good luck with first-time authors." Does not want to receive science fiction, westerns, poetry, children's books, academic/scholarly/professional books, plays, scripts, or short stories.

How to Contact Query with SASE. No email, phone, or fax queries. Considers simultaneous queries. Responds in 2 weeks to queries; 1 month to mss. Returns materials only with SASE. Obtains most new clients through recommendations from others, solicitations, conferences, "plus, I will approach someone with a letter if his/her work impresses me."

Recent Sales Sold 20 titles in the last year. *Following Sarah*, by Daniel Brown (Morrow); *Biology of the Brain*, by Paul Swingle (Rutgers University Press); *Tripoli*, by David Smethurst (Ballantine); *Phantom Warrior*, by Bryant Johnson (Berkley).

Terms Agent receives 15% commission on domestic sales; 25% commission on foreign sales. Offers written contract; 1-month notice must be given to terminate contract. Charges for postage, long distance, fax, messengers, photocopies (not to exceed $200).

Tips "Keep query letters short and to the point; include only information pertaining to the book or background as a writer. Try to avoid superlatives in description. Work needs to stand on its own, so how much editing it may have received has no place in a query letter."

THE BLUMER LITERARY AGENCY, INC.

350 Seventh Ave., Suite 2003, New York NY 10001-5013. (212)947-3040. **Contact:** Olivia B. Blumer. Estab. 2002. Member of AAR. Represents 34 clients. 60% of clients are new/unpublished writers. Currently handles: 67% nonfiction books; 33% novels.

- Prior to becoming an agent, Ms. Blumer spent 25 years in publishing (subsidiary rights, publicity, editorial).

Represents Nonfiction books, novels. **Considers these nonfiction areas:** Agriculture/horticulture; animals; anthropology/archaeology; art/architecture/design; biography/autobiography; business/economics; cooking/foods/nutrition; ethnic/cultural interests; health/medicine; how-to; humor/satire; language/literature/criticism; memoirs; money/finance; nature/environment; photography; popular culture; psychology; religious/inspirational; self-help/personal improvement; true crime/investigative; women's issues/studies; New Age/metaphysics; crafts/hobbies; interior design/decorating. **Considers these fiction areas:** Detective/police/crime; ethnic; family saga; feminist; historical; humor/satire; literary; mainstream/contemporary; mystery/suspense; regional; thriller.

O→ Actively seeking quality fiction, practical nonfiction, and memoir with a larger purpose.

How to Contact Query with SASE. No e-mail or fax queries. Responds in 3 weeks to queries; 4-6 weeks to mss. Returns materials only with SASE. Obtains most new clients through recommendations from others, but significant exceptions have come from the slush pile.

Recent Sales *The Color of Law*, by Mark Gimenez; *Still Life with Chickens*, by Catherine Goldhammer; *Demolition Desserts*, by Elizabeth Falkner; *Fat* by Jennifer McLagan; *Carpool Diem*, by Nancy Star. Other clients include Joan Anderson, Marialisa Calta, Ellen Rolfes, Laura Karr, Liz McGregor, Lauri Ward, Susann Cokal, Dennis L. Smith, Sharon Pywell, Sarah Turnbull, Naomi Duguid, Jeffrey Alford.

Terms Agent receives 15% commission on domestic sales; 20% commission on foreign sales. Charges for photocopying, overseas shipping, FedEx/UPS.

N THE BLYTHE AGENCY

25 Washington St., Ste 614, Brooklyn NY 11201. (718)781-6489. Web site: www.blythe-agency.com. **Contact:** Rolph Blythe. Estab. 2006. Member of AAR.

- Prior to his current position, Mr. Blythe was an agent with Dunow, Carlson & Lerner Literary Agency.

Represents Nonfiction books, novels. **Considers these nonfiction areas:** Biography/autobiography; history; memoirs; narrative nonfiction. **Considers these fiction areas:** Detective/police/crime; literary; mystery/suspense; thriller.

O→ Actively seeking unique, voice-driven fiction, biography, history, science, lifestyle, and mystery and crime books. Does not want to receive screenplays, poetry, children's or Christian/inspirational.

How to Contact Query with SASE, submit synopsis, 1-2 (50-75 pp.) sample chapter(s), author bio. Writers can query through the Web site form. This agency only responds if interested. No e-mail or fax queries. Responds in 4-6 weeks to queries. Obtains most new clients through recommendations from others, solicitations.
Recent Sales *Four-Letter Words and Other Secrets of Crossword Puzzle Champions*, by Michelle Arnot (Perigee); *Madly*, by William Benton.
Terms Agent receives 15% commission on domestic sales; 20% commission on foreign sales.

BOOKENDS, LLC

Web site: www.bookends-inc.com; bookendslitagency.blogspot.com. **Contact:** Jessica Faust, Jacky Sach, Kim Lionetti. Estab. 1999. Member of AAR. Represents 50+ clients. 10% of clients are new/unpublished writers. Currently handles: 50% nonfiction books; 50% novels.
Member Agents Jessica Faust (Fiction: romance, erotica, chick lit, women's fiction, mysterious and suspense. Nonfiction: business, finance, career, parenting, psychology, women's issues, self-help, health, sex); Jacky Sach (mysteries, women's fiction, suspense, self-help, spirituality, alternative and mainstream health, business and career, addiction, chick-lit nonfiction).
Represents Nonfiction books, novels. **Considers these nonfiction areas:** Business/economics; child guidance/parenting; ethnic/cultural interests; gay/lesbian issues; health/medicine; how-to; money/finance; New Age/metaphysics; psychology; religious/inspirational; self-help/personal improvement; sex; spirituality; true crime/investigative; women's issues/studies. **Considers these fiction areas:** Detective/police/crime (cozies); mainstream/contemporary; mystery/suspense; romance; thriller; women's; chick lit.

- BookEnds does not want to receive children's books, screenplays, science fiction, poetry, or technical/military thrillers.

How to Contact Review Web site for guidelines.
Recent Sales *1,000 Wine Secrets*, by Carolyn Hammond (Sourcebooks); *Wolf Tales III*, by Kate Douglas (Kensington Aphrodisia); *Women at Ground Zero*, by Mary Carouba and Susan Hagen (Alpha Books).

BRANDT & HOCHMAN LITERARY AGENTS, INC.

1501 Broadway, Suite 2310, New York NY 10036. (212)840-5760. Fax: (212)840-5776. **Contact:** Gail Hochman. Estab. 1913. Member of AAR. Represents 200 clients.
Member Agents Carl Brandt; Gail Hochman; Marianne Merola; Charles Schlessiger; Bill Contardi.
Represents Nonfiction books, novels, short story collections, juvenile books, journalism. **Considers these nonfiction areas:** Biography/autobiography; current affairs; ethnic/cultural interests; government/politics/law; history; women's issues/studies. **Considers these fiction areas:** Contemporary issues; ethnic; historical; literary; mainstream/contemporary; mystery/suspense; romance; thriller; young adult.
How to Contact Query with SASE. No e-mail or fax queries. Considers simultaneous queries. Responds in 1 month to queries. Returns materials only with SASE. Obtains most new clients through recommendations from others.
Recent Sales *Season of Betrayal*, by Margaret Lowrie Robertson (Harcourt); *The Misremembered Man*, by Christina McKenna (Toby Press). Other clients include Scott Turow, Carlos Fuentes, Ursula Hegi, Michael Cunningham, Mary Pope Osborne, Julia Glass.
Terms Agent receives 15% commission on domestic sales; 20% commission on foreign sales. Charges clients for ms duplication or other special expenses agreed to in advance.
Tips "Write a letter which will give the agent a sense of you as a professional writer—your long-term interests as well as a short description of the work at hand."

BRICK HOUSE LITERARY AGENTS

80 Fifth Ave., Suite 1101, New York NY 10011. Web site: www.brickhouselit.com. **Contact:** Sally Wofford-Girand. Member of AAR.
Member Agents Sally Wofford-Girand; Judy Heiblum; Melissa Sarver, assistant.
Represents Nonfiction books, novels. **Considers these nonfiction areas:** Ethnic/cultural interests; history; memoirs; women's issues/studies; biography; science; natural history. **Considers these fiction areas:** Literary.
How to Contact Query via mail or e-mail.

CURTIS BROWN, LTD.

10 Astor Place, New York NY 10003-6935. (212)473-5400. Web site: www.curtisbrown.com. Alternate address: Peter Ginsberg, president at CBSF, 1750 Montgomery St., San Francisco CA 94111. (415)954-8566. Member of AAR; signatory of WGA.
Member Agents Laura Blake Peterson; Emilie Jacobson, senior vice president; Maureen Walters, senior vice president; Ginger Knowlton, vice president; Mitchell Waters; Elizabeth Harding; Holly Frederick; Timothy Knowlton, CEO; Ginger Clark; Katherine Fausset.

Represents Nonfiction books, novels, short story collections, juvenile books. **Considers these nonfiction areas:** Agriculture/horticulture; americana; animals; anthropology/archaeology; art/architecture/design; biography/autobiography; business/economics; child guidance/parenting; computers/electronic; cooking/foods/nutrition; crafts/hobbies; current affairs; education; ethnic/cultural interests; gardening; gay/lesbian issues; government/politics/law; health/medicine; history; how-to; humor/satire; interior design/decorating; juvenile nonfiction; language/literature/criticism; memoirs; military/war; money/finance; multicultural; music/dance; nature/environment; New Age/metaphysics; philosophy; photography; popular culture; psychology; recreation; regional; religious/inspirational; science/technology; self-help/personal improvement; sex; sociology; software; spirituality; sports; theater/film; translation; travel; true crime/investigative; women's issues/studies; young adult; creative nonfiction. **Considers these fiction areas:** Action/adventure; comic books/cartoon; confession; contemporary issues; detective/police/crime; erotica; ethnic; experimental; family saga; fantasy; feminist; gay/lesbian; glitz; gothic; hi-lo; historical; horror; humor/satire; juvenile; literary; mainstream/contemporary; military/war; multicultural; multimedia; mystery/suspense; New Age; occult; picture books; plays; poetry; psychic/supernatural; regional; religious/inspirational; romance; science fiction; short story collections; spiritual; sports; thriller; translation; westerns/frontier; young adult; women's.

How to Contact Query individual agent with SASE. Prefers to read materials exclusively. *No unsolicited mss.* No e-mail or fax queries. Responds in 3 weeks to queries; 5 weeks to mss. Obtains most new clients through recommendations from others, solicitations, conferences.

N MARIA CARVAINIS AGENCY, INC.

1350 Avenue of the Americas, Suite 2905, New York NY 10019. (212)245-6365. Fax: (212)245-7196. E-mail: mca@mariacarvainisagency.com. **Contact:** Maria Carvainis, Donna Bagdasarian. Estab. 1977. Member of AAR, Authors Guild, Women's Media Group, ABA, MWA, RWA; signatory of WGA. Represents 75 clients. 10% of clients are new/unpublished writers. Currently handles: 35% nonfiction books; 65% novels.

- Prior to opening her agency, Ms. Carvainis spent more than 10 years in the publishing industry as a senior editor with Macmillan Publishing, Basic Books, Avon Books, and Crown Publishers. Ms. Carvainis has served as a member of the AAR Board of Directors and AAR Treasurer, as well as serving as chair of the AAR Contracts Committee. She presently serves on the AAR Royalty Committee. Ms. Bagdasarian began her career as an academic at Boston University, then spent 5 years with Addison Wesley Longman as an acquisitions editor before joining the William Morris Agency in 1998. She has represented a breadth of projects, ranging from literary fiction to celebrity memoir.

Member Agents Maria Carvainis, president/literary agent; Donna Bagdasarian, literary agent; Moira Sullivan, literary associate/subsidiary rights manager; Christopher Jaskot, literary assistant.

Represents Nonfiction books, novels. **Considers these nonfiction areas:** Biography/autobiography; business/economics; history; memoirs; science/technology (pop science); women's issues/studies. **Considers these fiction areas:** Historical; literary; mainstream/contemporary; mystery/suspense; thriller; young adult; women's; middle grade.

O→ Does not want to receive science fiction or children's picture books.

How to Contact Query with SASE. Responds in up to 3 to mss. Obtains most new clients through recommendations from others, conferences, query letters.

Recent Sales *Simply Magic*, by Mary Balogh (Bantam Dell); *Save Your Own*, by Elizabeth Brink (Houghton Mifflin); *Ricochet*, by Sandra Brown (Simon & Schuster); *The Marriage Wager*, by Candace Camp (Mira); *Jeb: America's Next Bush*, by S.V. Date (Penguin Group/Tarcher Imprint); *A Widow's Curse*, by Phillip DePoy (St. Martin's Press); *A Falconer's Voice*, by Tim Gallagher (Houghton Mifflin); *Into the Dark*, by Cindy Gerard (St. Martin's Press); *Picture Perfect*, by D. Anne Love (Simon & Schuster Children's Publishing). Other clients include Sue Erikson Bloland, David Bottoms, Pam Conrad, John Faunce, Samantha James, Lucy Lehrer, Dushan Zaric and Jason Kosmas.

Terms Agent receives 15% commission on domestic sales; 20% commission on foreign sales. Offers written contract. Charges clients for foreign postage and bulk copying.

Writers' Conferences BookExpo America; Frankfurt Book Fair; London Book Fair; Mystery Writers of America; Thrillerfest; Romance Writers of America.

CASTIGLIA LITERARY AGENCY

1155 Camino Del Mar, Suite 510, Del Mar CA 92014. (858)755-8761. Fax: (858)755-7063. Estab. 1993. Member of AAR, PEN. Represents 50 clients. Currently handles: 55% nonfiction books; 45% novels.

Member Agents Julie Castiglia; Winifred Golden; Sally Van Haitsma.

Represents Nonfiction books, novels. **Considers these nonfiction areas:** Animals; anthropology/archaeology; biography/autobiography; business/economics; child guidance/parenting; cooking/foods/nutrition; current affairs; ethnic/cultural interests; health/medicine; history; language/literature/criticism; money/finance; nature/environment; psychology; religious/inspirational; science/technology; self-help/personal improvement; women's issues/studies. **Considers these fiction areas:** Ethnic; literary; mainstream/contemporary; mystery/suspense; women's.

O→ Does not want to receive horror, screenplays, poetry or academic nonfiction.

How to Contact Query with SASE. No fax queries. Returns materials only with SASE. Obtains most new clients through recommendations from others, solicitations, conferences.

Recent Sales Sold 26 titles in the last year. *Big Brown*, by Greg Neimann (Wiley); *From Baghdad With Love*, by Jay Kopelman with Melinda Roth (Lyons Press); *Illuminations*, by Mark Tompkins (Ten Speed/Celestial Arts); *Midnight Brunch*, by Marta Acosta (S&S); *Teardrops*, by Doug Keister (Gibbs Smith); *Orphan's Journey*, by Robert Buettner (Little, Brown/Orbit).

Terms Agent receives 15% commission on domestic sales; 25% commission on foreign sales. Offers written contract; 6-week notice must be given to terminate contract.

Writers' Conferences Santa Barbara Writers' Conference; Southern California Writers' Conference; Surrey International Writers' Conference; San Diego State University Writers' Conference; Willamette Writers' Conference.

Tips "Be professional with submissions. Attend workshops and conferences before you approach an agent."

JANE CHELIUS LITERARY AGENCY

548 Second St., Brooklyn NY 11215. (718)499-0236. Fax: (718)832-7335. E-mail: queries@janechelius.com. Web site: www.janechelius.com. Member of AAR.

Represents Nonfiction books, novels. **Considers these nonfiction areas:** Humor/satire; women's issues/studies; popular science; parenting; medicine; biography; natural history; narrative. **Considers these fiction areas:** Literary; mystery/suspense; women's; men's adventure.

O→ Does not want to receive children's books, stage plays, screenplays, or poetry.

How to Contact Query with synopsis, cover letter, SASE. Accepts e-mail queries. *No unsolicited chapters or mss.* Responds in 3-4 weeks to queries.

THE CHOATE AGENCY, LLC

1320 Bolton Road, Pelham NY 10803. E-mail: choateagency@optonline.net. **Contact:** Mickey Choate. Member of AAR.

Represents Nonfiction books, novels. **Considers these nonfiction areas:** History; memoirs (by journalists, military or political figures); biography; cookery/food; journalism; military science; narrative; politics; general science; wine/spirits. **Considers these fiction areas:** Historical; mystery/suspense; thriller; select literary fiction.

O→ Does not want to receive chick lit, cozies or romance.

How to Contact Query with brief synopsis and bio. This agency prefers e-queries, but accepts snail mail queries with SASE. Accepts e-mail queries. No fax queries.

Recent Sales *The King of Lies*, by John Hart (St. Martin's Minotaur); *Heart-Shaped Box*, by Joe Hill (William Morrow); *Simply Michael Mina*, by Michael Mina (Bulfinch/Little, Brown).

CINE/LIT REPRESENTATION

P.O. Box 802918, Santa Clarita CA 91380-2918. (661)513-0268. Fax: (661)513-0915. E-mail: cinelit@msn.com. **Contact:** Mary Alice Kier. Member of AAR.

Member Agents Mary Alice Kier; Anna Cottle.

Represents Nonfiction books, novels.

O→ Actively seeking mainstream, thrillers, mysteries, supernatural, horror, narrative nonfiction, environmental, adventure, biography, travel and pop culture. Does not want to receive Western's, sci-fi or romance.

How to Contact Query with SASE. Accepts e-mail queries. No fax queries.

Recent Sales *Solos and Souvenir of Cold Springs*, by Kitty Burns Florey; *Snow In July*, by Heather Barbieri; *The Sound of Her Name*, by Mary Morgan; *Bait and Switch*, by Larry Brooks; *The Last Giant of Beringia*, by Dan O'Neill.

THE CREATIVE CULTURE, INC.

72 Spring St., Suite 304, New York NY 10012. (212)680-3510. Fax: (212)680-3509. Web site: www.thecreativeculture.com. **Contact:** Debra Goldstein. Estab. 1998. Member of AAR.

- Prior to opening her agency, Ms. Goldstein and Ms. Gerwin were agents at the William Morris Agency; Ms. Naples was a senior editor at Simon & Schuster.

Member Agents Debra Goldstein (self-help, creativity, fitness, inspiration, lifestyle); Mary Ann Naples (health/nutrition, lifestyle, narrative nonfiction, practical nonfiction, literary fiction, animals/vegetarianism); Laura Nolan (literary fiction, parenting, self-help, psychology, women's studies, current affairs, science); Karen Gerwin; Emmanuelle Alspaugh (romance, general nonfiction, fiction).

Represents Nonfiction books, novels.

O→ Does not want to receive children's, poetry, screenplays or science fiction.

How to Contact Query with bio, book description, 5-7 sample pages (fiction only), SASE. Accepts e-mail queries. No fax queries. Responds in 2 months to queries.

Recent Sales *Dr. Neal Barnard's Program for Reversing Diabetes*, by Neil Barnard (Rodale); *The Power of Patience: How to Slow the Rush and Enjoy More Happiness, Success, and Peace of Mind Every Day*, by M.J. Ryan (Broadway Books); *The Secret Lives of Curious Virgins: My Life as a Reluctant Good Girl*, by Carlene Bauer (HarperCollins). Other clients include David Awbrey, Tom Hughes, Brenda McClain, Paula Chaffee Scardamalia.

LIZA DAWSON ASSOCIATES

350 Seventh Ave., Ste. 2003, New York NY 10001. (212)465-9071. Member of AAR, MWA, Women's Media Group. Represents 50+ clients. 15% of clients are new/unpublished writers. Currently handles: 60% nonfiction books; 40% novels.

- Prior to becoming an agent, Ms. Dawson was an editor for 20 years, spending 11 years at William Morrow as vice president and 2 years at Putnam as executive editor. Ms. Bladell was a senior editor at HarperCollins and Avon. Ms. Miller is an *Essence*-bestselling author and niche publisher. Ms. Olswanger is an author.

Member Agents Liza Dawson, LDawson@lizadawsonassociates.com; Anna Olswanger, anna@olswanger.com; Havis Dawson, HDawson@lizadawsonassociates.com.

Represents Nonfiction books, novels and gift books (Olswanger only). **Considers these nonfiction areas:** Biography/autobiography; health/medicine; history; memoirs; psychology; sociology; women's issues/studies; politics; business; parenting. **Considers these fiction areas:** Fantasy (Blasdell only); historical; literary; mystery/suspense; regional; science fiction (Blasdell only); thriller; African-American (Miller only).

O→ This agency specializes in readable literary fiction, thrillers, mainstream historicals, women's fiction, academics, historians, business, journalists and psychology. Does not want to receive Western, sports, computers or juvenile.

How to Contact Query with SASE. Responds in 3 week to queries; 6 weeks to mss. Obtains most new clients through recommendations from others, conferences.

Recent Sales Sold 40 titles in the last year. *Going for It*, by Karen E. Quinones Miller (Warner); *Mayada: Daughter of Iraq*, by Jean Sasson (Dutton); *It's So Much Work to Be Your Friend: Social Skill Problems at Home and at School*, by Richard Lavoie (Touchstone); *WORDCRAFT: How to Write Like a Professional*, by Jack Hart (Pantheon); *...And a Time to Die: How Hospitals Shape the End of Life Experience*, by Dr. Sharon Kaufman (Scribner); *Zeus: A Biography*, by Tom Stone (Bloomsbury).

Terms Agent receives 15% commission on domestic sales; 20% commission on foreign sales. Offers written contract. Charges clients for photocopying and overseas postage.

N DEFIORE & CO.

72 Spring St., Suite 304, New York NY 10012. (212)925-7744. Fax: (212)925-9803. E-mail: info@defioreandco.com. Web site: www.defioreandco.com. **Contact:** Brian DeFiore. Estab. 1999. Member of AAR. Represents 55 clients. 50% of clients are new/unpublished writers. Currently handles: 70% nonfiction books; 30% novels.

- Prior to becoming an agent, Mr. DeFiore was publisher of Villard Books (1997-1998), editor-in-chief of Hyperion (1992-1997), and editorial director of Delacorte Press (1988-1992).

Member Agents Brian DeFiore (popular nonfiction, business, pop culture, parenting, commercial fiction); Laurie Abkemeier (memoir, parenting, business, how-to/self-help, popular science); Kate Garrick (literary fiction, crime, pop culture, politics, history, psychology, narrative nonfiction).

Represents Nonfiction books, novels. **Considers these nonfiction areas:** Biography/autobiography; business/economics; child guidance/parenting; cooking/foods/nutrition; money/finance; multicultural; popular culture; psychology; religious/inspirational; self-help/personal improvement; sports. **Considers these fiction areas:** Ethnic; literary; mainstream/contemporary; mystery/suspense; thriller.

How to Contact Query with SASE. Considers simultaneous queries. Responds in 3 weeks to queries; 2 months to mss. Returns materials only with SASE. Obtains most new clients through recommendations from others.

Recent Sales Sold 35 titles in the last year. *Marley and Me*, by John Grogan; *Post Secret*, by Frank Warren; *Bitter Is the New Black*, by Jen Lancaster; *All for a Few Perfect Waves*, by David Rensin; *Seemed Like a Good Idea at the Time*, by David Goodwillie; *Lights Out*, by Jason Starr; *The Alpha Solution*, by Dr Ronald Glassman; *The $64 Tomato*, by Bill Alexander; *The Extraordinary Adventures of Alfred Kropp*, by Rick Yancey. Other clients include Loretta LaRoche, Joel Engel, Robin McMillan, Jessica Teich, Ronna Lichtenberg, Jimmy Lerner, Lou Manfredini, Norm Green, Lisa Kusel, Michael Walter, Stephen Graham Jones.

Terms Agent receives 15% commission on domestic sales; 20% commission on foreign sales. Offers written contract; 10-day notice must be given to terminate contract. Charges clients for photocopying and overnight delivery (deducted only after a sale is made).

Writers' Conferences Maui Writers Conference; Pacific Northwest Writers Conference; North Carolina Writers' Network Fall Conference.

SANDRA DIJKSTRA LITERARY AGENCY

1155 Camino del Mar, PMB 515, Del Mar CA 92014. (858)755-3115. Fax: (858)794-2822. E-mail: sdla@dijkstraagency.com. **Contact:** Taryn Fagerness. Estab. 1981. Member of AAR, Authors Guild, PEN West, Poets and Editors, MWA. Represents 100+ clients. 30% of clients are new/unpublished writers. Currently handles: 50% nonfiction books; 45% novels; 5% juvenile books.

Member Agents Sandra Dijkstra; Jill Marsal; Taryn Fagerness.

Represents Nonfiction books, novels. **Considers these nonfiction areas:** Americana; animals (pets); anthropology/archaeology; business/economics; child guidance/parenting; cooking/foods/nutrition; ethnic/cultural interests; gay/lesbian issues; government/politics/law; health/medicine; history; juvenile nonfiction; language/literature/criticism; military/war; money/finance; nature/environment; psychology; regional; religious/inspirational; science/technology; self-help/personal improvement; sociology; travel; women's issues/studies; Asian studies; art; accounting; biography; environmental studies; technology; transportation. **Considers these fiction areas:** Erotica; ethnic; literary; mainstream/contemporary; mystery/suspense; picture books; thriller.

This agency specializes in quality fiction including women's and multicultural fiction, mystery/thrillers, children's literature, narrative nonfiction, psychology, self-help, science, health, business, memoirs, biography, current affairs and history. Does not want to receive Western, sci-fi or poetry.

How to Contact Submit for fiction, send brief synopsis and 50 sample pages, SASE. No e-mail or fax queries. Responds in 4-6 weeks to queries. Obtains most new clients through recommendations from others, solicitations, conferences.

Recent Sales *Firewife*, by Tinling Choong; *Palace of Illusions*, by Chitra Divakaruni; *The Longevity Bible*, by Dr. Gary Small; *The American Resting Place*, by Marilyn Yalom.

Terms Agent receives 15% commission on domestic sales; 20% commission on foreign sales. Offers written contract. Charges clients for expenses "to cover domestic costs so that we can spend time selling books instead of accounting expenses. We also charge for the photocopying of the full manuscript or nonfiction proposal and for foreign postage."

Writers' Conferences "We have attended Squaw Valley Writers' Workshop, Santa Barbara Writers' Conference, Asilomar, Southern California Writers' Conference, and Rocky Mountain Fiction Writers' Colorado Gold, to name a few. We also speak regularly for writers groups such as PEN West and the Independent Writers Association."

Tips "Be professional and learn the standard procedures for submitting your work. Be a regular patron of bookstores, and study what kind of books are being published. Read. Check out your local library and bookstores—you'll find lots of books on writing and the publishing industry that will help you. At conferences, ask published writers about their agents. Don't believe the myth that an agent has to be in New York to be successful—we've already disproved it!"

DUNHAM LITERARY, INC.

156 Fifth Ave., Suite 625, New York NY 10010-7002. (212)929-0994. Web site: www.dunhamlit.com. **Contact:** Jennie Dunham. Estab. 2000. Member of AAR. Represents 50 clients. 15% of clients are new/unpublished writers. Currently handles: 25% nonfiction books; 25% novels; 50% juvenile books.

- Prior to opening her agency, Ms. Dunham worked as a literary agent for Russell & Volkening. The Rhoda Weyr Agency is now a division of Dunham Literary, Inc.

Represents Nonfiction books, novels, short story collections, juvenile books. **Considers these nonfiction areas:** Anthropology/archaeology; biography/autobiography; ethnic/cultural interests; government/politics/law; health/medicine; history; language/literature/criticism; nature/environment; popular culture; psychology; science/technology; women's issues/studies. **Considers these fiction areas:** Ethnic; juvenile; literary; mainstream/contemporary; picture books; young adult.

How to Contact Query with SASE. No e-mail or fax queries. Responds in 1 week to queries; 2 months to mss. Obtains most new clients through recommendations from others, solicitations.

Recent Sales *America the Beautiful*, by Robert Sabuda; *Dahlia*, by Barbara McClintock; *Living Dead Girl*, by Tod Goldberg; *In My Mother's House*, by Margaret McMulla; *Black Hawk Down*, by Mark Bowden; *Look Back All the Green Valley*, by Fred Chappell; *Under a Wing*, by Reeve Lindbergh; *I Am Madame X*, by Gioia Diliberto.

Terms Agent receives 15% commission on domestic sales; 20% commission on foreign sales.

DYSTEL & GODERICH LITERARY MANAGEMENT

1 Union Square W., Suite 904, New York NY 10003. (212)627-9100. Fax: (212)627-9313. E-mail: miriam@dystel.com. Web site: www.dystel.com. **Contact:** Miriam Goderich. Estab. 1994. Member of AAR. Represents 300

clients. 50% of clients are new/unpublished writers. Currently handles: 65% nonfiction books; 25% novels; 10% cookbooks.

• Dystel & Goderich Literary Management recently acquired the client list of Bedford Book Works.

Member Agents Stacey Glick; Jane Dystel; Miriam Goderich; Michael Bourret; Jim McCarthy; Lauren Abramo; Adina Kahn.

Represents Nonfiction books, novels, cookbooks. **Considers these nonfiction areas:** Animals; anthropology/archaeology; biography/autobiography; business/economics; child guidance/parenting; cooking/foods/nutrition; current affairs; education; ethnic/cultural interests; gay/lesbian issues; government/politics/law; health/medicine; history; humor/satire; military/war; money/finance; New Age/metaphysics; popular culture; psychology; religious/inspirational; science/technology; true crime/investigative; women's issues/studies. **Considers these fiction areas:** Action/adventure; detective/police/crime; ethnic; family saga; gay/lesbian; literary; mainstream/contemporary; mystery/suspense; thriller.

O━ This agency specializes in cookbooks and commercial and literary fiction and nonfiction.

How to Contact Query with SASE. Considers simultaneous queries. Responds in 1 month to queries; 6 weeks to mss. Obtains most new clients through recommendations from others, solicitations, conferences.

Terms Agent receives 15% commission on domestic sales; 19% commission on foreign sales. Offers written contract. Charges for photocopying. Galley charges and book charges from the publisher are passed on to the author.

Writers' Conferences Whidbey Island Writers' Conference; Backspace Writers' Conference; Iowa Summer Writing Festival; Pacific Northwest Writers' Association; Pike's Peak Writers' Conference; Santa Barbara Writers' Conference; Harriette Austin Writers' Conference; Sandhills Writers' Conference; Denver Publishing Institute; Love Is Murder.

Tips "Work on sending professional, well-written queries that are concise and addressed to the specific agent the author is contacting. No dear Sirs/Madam."

THE ELAINE P. ENGLISH LITERARY AGENCY

4701 41st St. NW, Suite D, Washington DC 20016. (202)362-5190. Fax: (202)362-5192. E-mail: elaine@elaineenglish.com. Web site: www.elaineenglish.com. **Contact:** Elaine English. Member of AAR. Represents 16 clients. 25% of clients are new/unpublished writers. Currently handles: 100% novels.

• Ms. English has been working in publishing for more than 20 years. She is also an attorney specializing in media and publishing law.

Represents Novels. **Considers these fiction areas:** Historical; multicultural; mystery/suspense; romance (single title, historical, contemporary, romantic, suspense, chick lit, erotic); thriller; general women's fiction. The agency is slowly but steadily acquiring in all mentioned areas.

O━ Actively seeking women's fiction, including single-title romances. Does not want to receive any science fiction, time travel, children's, or young adult.

How to Contact Prefers e-queries sent to queries@elaineenglish.com. If requested, submit synopsis, first 3 chapters, SASE. Accepts e-mail queries. No fax queries. Responds in 6-12 weeks to queries; 6 months to requested ms. Returns materials only with SASE. Obtains most new clients through recommendations from others, conferences, submissions.

Recent Sales *The Blue-Eyed Devil*, by Diane Whiteside (Kensington).

Terms Agent receives 15% commission on domestic sales; 20% commission on foreign sales. Offers written contract; 30-day notice must be given to terminate contract. Charges only for copying and postage; generally taken from proceeds.

Writers' Conferences RWA National Conference; SEAK Medical & Legal Fiction Writing Conference; Novelists, Inc; Malice Domestic; Washington Romance Writers Retreat, among others.

FELICIA ETH LITERARY REPRESENTATION

555 Bryant St., Suite 350, Palo Alto CA 94301-1700. (650)375-1276. Fax: (650)401-8892. E-mail: feliciaeth@aol.com. **Contact:** Felicia Eth. Estab. 1988. Member of AAR. Represents 25-35 clients. Currently handles: 85% nonfiction books; 15% adult novels.

Represents Nonfiction books, novels. **Considers these nonfiction areas:** Animals; anthropology/archaeology; biography/autobiography; business/economics; child guidance/parenting; current affairs; ethnic/cultural interests; gay/lesbian issues; government/politics/law; health/medicine; history; nature/environment; popular culture; psychology; science/technology; sociology; true crime/investigative; women's issues/studies. **Considers these fiction areas:** Ethnic; feminist; gay/lesbian; literary; mainstream/contemporary; thriller.

O━ This agency specializes in high-quality fiction (preferably mainstream/contemporary) and provocative, intelligent, and thoughtful nonfiction on a wide array of commercial subjects.

How to Contact Query with SASE, outline. Considers simultaneous queries. Responds in 3 weeks to queries; 4-6 weeks to mss.

Recent Sales Sold 7-10 titles in the last year. *Jane Austen in Boca*, by Paula Marantz Cohen (St. Martin's Press); *Why Gender Matters*, by Dr. Leonard Sax (Doubleday/Random House); *Anna Maria Violino*, by Barbara Quick (HarperCollins).
Terms Agent receives 15% commission on domestic sales; 20% commission on foreign sales; 20% commission on dramatic rights sales. Charges clients for photocopying and express mail service.
Writers' Conferences National Coalition of Independent Scholars Conference.
Tips "For nonfiction, established expertise is certainly a plus—as is magazine publication—though not a prerequisite. I am highly dedicated to those projects I represent, but highly selective in what I choose."

DIANA FINCH LITERARY AGENCY

116 W. 23rd St., Suite 500, New York NY 10011. (646)375-2081. E-mail: diana.finch@verizon.net. **Contact:** Diana Finch. Estab. 2003. Member of AAR. Represents 45 clients. 20% of clients are new/unpublished writers. Currently handles: 65% nonfiction books; 25% novels; 5% juvenile books; 5% multimedia.

- Prior to opening her agency, Ms. Finch worked at Ellen Levine Literary Agency for 18 years.

Represents Nonfiction books, novels, scholarly books. **Considers these nonfiction areas:** Biography/autobiography; business/economics; child guidance/parenting; computers/electronic; current affairs; ethnic/cultural interests; government/politics/law; health/medicine; history; how-to; humor/satire; juvenile nonfiction; memoirs; military/war; money/finance; music/dance; nature/environment; photography; popular culture; psychology; science/technology; self-help/personal improvement; sports; theater/film; translation; true crime/investigative; women's issues/studies. **Considers these fiction areas:** Action/adventure; detective/police/crime; ethnic; historical; literary; mainstream/contemporary; thriller; young adult.

O━ Actively seeking narrative nonfiction, popular science, and health topics. Does not want romance, mysteries, or children's picture books.

How to Contact Query with SASE or via e-mail (no attachments). No phone or fax queries. Considers simultaneous queries. Returns materials only with SASE. Obtains most new clients through recommendations from others.
Recent Sales *Armed Madhouse*, by Greg Palast (Penguin US/UK); *The Bush Agenda*, by Antonia Juhasz; *Journey of the Magi*, by Tudor Parfitt (Farrar, Straus & Giroux); *Radiant Days*, by Michael FitzGerald (Shoemaker & Hoard); *The Queen's Soprano*, by Carol Dines (Harcourt Young Adult); *Was the 2004 Election Stolen?*, by Steven Freeman and Joel Bleifuss (Seven Stories); *Lipstick Jihad*, by Azadeh Moaveni (Public Affairs); *Great Customer Connections*, by Rich Gallagher (Amacom). Other clients include Daniel Duane, Thomas Goltz, Hugh Pope, Owen Matthews, Dr. Robert Marion.
Terms Agent receives 15% commission on domestic sales; 20% commission on foreign sales. Offers written contract. "I charge for photocopying, overseas postage, galleys, and books purchased, and try to recap these costs from earnings received for a client, rather than charging outright."
Tips "Do as much research as you can on agents before you query. Have someone critique your query letter before you send it. It should be only 1 page and describe your book clearly—and why you are writing it—but also demonstrate creativity and a sense of your writing style."

N FLETCHER & PARRY

78 Fifth Ave., 3rd Floor, New York NY 10011. (212)614-0778. Fax: (212)614-0728. **Contact:** Christy Fletcher, Emma Parry. Estab. 2003. Member of AAR.
Represents Nonfiction books, novels. **Considers these nonfiction areas:** Current affairs; history; memoirs; sports; travel; African American; narrative; science; biography; business; health; lifestyle. **Considers these fiction areas:** Literary; young adult; commercial.

O━ Does not want genre fiction.

How to Contact Query with SASE. Responds in 4-6 weeks to queries.
Recent Sales *Let Them In: The Case for Open Borders*, by Jason Riley (Gotham); *The Vanishing Act of Esme Lennox*, by Maggie O'Farrell (Harcourt).

N FOLIO LITERARY MANAGEMENT, LLC

505 Eighth Ave., Suite 603, New York NY 10018. Web site: www.foliolit.com. Alternate address: 1627 K St. NW, Suite 1200, Washington DC 20006. Estab. 2006. Member of AAR. Represents 100+ clients.

- Prior to creating Folio Literary Management, Mr. Hoffman worked for several years at another agency; Mr. Kleinman was an agent at Graybill & English; Ms. Wheeler was an agent at Creative Media Agency; Ms. Fine was an agent at Vigliano Associates and Trident Media Group; Ms. Cartwright-Niumata was an editor at Simon & Schuster, HarperCollins, and Avalon Books; Ms. Becker worked as a copywriter, journalist and author.

Member Agents Scott Hoffman; Jeff Kleinman; Paige Wheeler; Celeste Fine; Erin Cartwright-Niumata, Laney K. Becker.
Represents Nonfiction books, novels, short story collections. **Considers these nonfiction areas:** Animals

(equestrian); business/economics; child guidance/parenting; history; how-to; humor/satire; memoirs; military/war; nature/environment; popular culture; psychology; religious/inspirational; science/technology; self-help/personal improvement; women's issues/studies; narrative nonfiction; art; espionage; biography; crime; politics; health/fitness; lifestyle; relationship; culture; cookbooks. **Considers these fiction areas:** Erotica; fantasy; literary; mystery/suspense; religious/inspirational; romance; science fiction; thriller (psychological); young adult; women's; Southern; legal; edgy crime.

How to Contact Query with SASE or via e-mail (no attachments). Read agent bios online for specific submission guidelines. Responds in 1 month to queries.

Recent Sales Sold more than 100 titles in the last year. *Finn*, by Jon Clinch (Random House); *A Killing Tide*, by P.J. Alderman (Dorchester); *The Inn on Half Moon Bay*, by Diane Tyrrel (Berkley); *The Biography of Kenny Chesney*, by Holly Gleason (Center Street); *Color of the Sea*, by John Hamamura (Thomas Dunne Books/St. Martin's Press); *The 30-Day Diabetes Miracle* (Perigee); *Meow Is for Murder*, by Linda O. Johnston (Berkley Prime Crime); *Wildlife's Scotland Yard*, by Laurel Neme (Joseph Henry Press); *Mockingbird*, by Charles J. Shields (Henry Holt); *Under the Mask*, by Heidi Ardizzone (Norton); *The Culture Code*, by Dr. Clotaire Rapaille (Doubleday).

JEANNE FREDERICKS LITERARY AGENCY, INC.

221 Benedict Hill Road, New Canaan CT 06840. (203)972-3011. Fax: (203)972-3011. E-mail: jeanne.fredericks@gmail.com. **Contact:** Jeanne Fredericks. Estab. 1997. Member of AAR, Authors Guild. Represents 90 clients. 10% of clients are new/unpublished writers. Currently handles: 100% nonfiction books.

- Prior to opening her agency, Ms. Fredericks was an agent and acting director with the Susan P. Urstadt, Inc. Agency.

Represents Nonfiction books. **Considers these nonfiction areas:** Animals; biography/autobiography; child guidance/parenting; cooking/foods/nutrition; gardening; health/medicine (alternative health); history; how-to; interior design/decorating; money/finance; nature/environment; photography; psychology; self-help/personal improvement; sports (not spectator sports); women's issues/studies.

O→ This agency specializes in quality adult nonfiction by authorities in their fields. Does not want to receive children's books or fiction.

How to Contact Query first with SASE, then send outline/proposal, 1-2 sample chapters, SASE. No fax queries. Accepts short e-mail queries (no attachments). Considers simultaneous queries. Responds in 3-5 weeks to queries; 2-4 months to mss. Returns materials only with SASE. Obtains most new clients through recommendations from others, solicitations, conferences.

Recent Sales *American Quilts*, by Robert Shaw (Sterling); *Lilias! Yoga Gets Better with Age*, by Lilias Folan (Rodale); *Homescaping*, by Anne Halpin (Rodale); *The Big Steal*, by Emyl Jenkins (Algonquin); *Creating Optimism in Your Child*, by Bob Murray, PhD, and Alice Fortinberry, MS (McGraw-Hill); *Waking the Warrior Goddess*, by Christine Horner, MD (Basic Health); *Healing the Heart with EECP*, by Debra Braverman, MD (Celestial Arts); *Melanoma, Rev. Ed.*, by Catherine Poole and Dupont Guerry, MD (Yale); *Bodywork*, by Thomas Claire (Basic Health); *Treasure Ship: The Legend and Legacy of S.S. Brother Jonathan*, by Dennis M. Powers (Citadel); *Integral Health*, by Elliott Dacher, MD (Basic Health); *Glut: The Deep History of Computer Science*, by Alex Wright (Joseph Henry Press); *Building Within Nature*, by Andy and Sally Wasowski (University of Minnesota Press); *No Limit: From the Cardroom to the Boardroom, Revised Edition*, by Donald Krause (Amacom); *Into Brown Bear Country*, by Will Troyer (University of Alaska Press).

Terms Agent receives 15% commission on domestic sales; 25% commission on foreign sales with co-agent; without co-agent receives 20% commission on foreign sales. Offers written contract, binding for 9 months; 2-month notice must be given to terminate contract. Charges client for photocopying of whole proposals and mss, overseas postage, priority mail, express mail services.

Writers' Conferences Connecticut Press Club Biennial Writer's Conference; ASJA Writers' Conference; BookExpo America; Garden Writers' Association Annual Symposium.

Tips "Be sure to research competition for your work and be able to justify why there's a need for your book. I enjoy building an author's career, particularly if he/she is professional, hardworking, and courteous. Aside from 17 years of agenting experience, I've had 10 years of editorial experience in adult trade book publishing that enables me to help an author polish a proposal so that it's more appealing to prospective editors. My MBA in marketing also distinguishes me from other agents."

N GELFMAN SCHNEIDER LITERARY AGENTS, INC.

250 W. 57th St., Suite 2515, New York NY 10107. (212)245-1993. Fax: (212)245-8678. E-mail: mail@gelfmanschneider.com. **Contact:** Jane Gelfman, Deborah Schneider. Estab. 1981. Member of AAR. Represents 300+ clients. 10% of clients are new/unpublished writers.

Represents Nonfiction books, novels. **Considers these nonfiction areas:** Biography; health; lifestyle; politics; science. **Considers these fiction areas:** Literary; mainstream/contemporary; mystery/suspense; women's.

O→ Does not want to receive romance, science fiction, westerns, or children's books.

How to Contact Query with SASE. Send queries via snail mail only. No e-mail or fax queries. Responds in 1 month to queries; 2 months to mss.

Terms Agent receives 15% commission on domestic sales; 20% commission on foreign sales; 15% commission on dramatic rights sales. Offers written contract. Charges clients for photocopying and messengers/couriers.

N BARRY GOLDBLATT LITERARY, LLC

320 Seventh Ave., #266, Brooklyn NY 11215. Fax: (718)360-5453. **Contact:** Barry Goldblatt. Member of AAR.

Represents Juvenile books. **Considers these fiction areas:** Picture books; young adult; middle grade.

How to Contact Query with SASE. No e-mail queries.

Recent Sales The Chasing Yesterday trilogy, by Robin Wasserman (Scholastic); *Rabbit and Squirrel*, by Kara LaReau (Harcourt); *Go Go Gorillas*, by Julia Durango (Simon & Schuster Children's).

N IRENE GOODMAN LITERARY AGENCY

80 Fifth Ave., Suite 1101, New York NY 10011. Web site: www.irenegoodman.com. **Contact:** Irene Goodman, Miriam Kriss. Member of AAR.

Represents Nonfiction books, novels. **Considers these nonfiction areas:** History; parenting, social issues, francophilia, anglophilia, Judaica, lifestyles, cooking, memoir. **Considers these fiction areas:** Historical; literary; mystery/suspense; romance; thriller; young adult; women's; chick lit; modern urban fantasies.

How to Contact Query with 1-3 chapters, synopsis, SASE. No e-mail or fax queries. Accepts e-mail queries. No fax queries. Responds in 1 month to mss.

N THE JOY HARRIS LITERARY AGENCY, INC.

156 Fifth Ave., Suite 617, New York NY 10010. (212)924-6269. Fax: (212)924-6609. **Contact:** Joy Harris. Member of AAR. Represents more than 100 clients. Currently handles: 50% nonfiction books; 50% novels.

Represents Nonfiction books, novels. **Considers these fiction areas:** Ethnic; experimental; family saga; feminist; gay/lesbian; glitz; hi-lo; historical; humor/satire; literary; mainstream/contemporary; multicultural; multimedia; mystery/suspense; regional; short story collections; spiritual; translation; young adult; women's.

O→ No screenplays.

How to Contact Query with sample chapter, outline/proposal, SASE. Accepts fax queries. No e-mail queries. Considers simultaneous queries. Responds in 2 months to queries. Returns materials only with SASE. Obtains most new clients through recommendations from clients and editors.

Recent Sales This agency prefers not to share information on specific sales.

Terms Agent receives 15% commission on domestic sales; 20% commission on foreign sales. Charges clients for some office expenses.

RICHARD HENSHAW GROUP

22 West 23rd St., Fifth Floor, New York NY 10010. (212)414-1172. Fax: (212)414-1182. E-mail: submissions@henshaw.com. Web site: www.rich.henshaw.com. **Contact:** Rich Henshaw. Estab. 1995. Member of AAR, SinC, MWA, HWA, SFWA, RWA. Represents 35 clients. 20% of clients are new/unpublished writers. Currently handles: 35% nonfiction books; 65% novels.

- Prior to opening his agency, Mr. Henshaw served as an agent with Richard Curtis Associates, Inc.

Represents Nonfiction books, novels. **Considers these nonfiction areas:** Animals; biography/autobiography; business/economics; child guidance/parenting; computers/electronic; cooking/foods/nutrition; current affairs; gay/lesbian issues; government/politics/law; health/medicine; how-to; humor/satire; military/war; money/finance; music/dance; nature/environment; New Age/metaphysics; popular culture; psychology; science/technology; self-help/personal improvement; sociology; sports; true crime/investigative; women's issues/studies. **Considers these fiction areas:** Action/adventure; detective/police/crime; ethnic; family saga; fantasy; glitz; historical; horror; humor/satire; literary; mainstream/contemporary; mystery/suspense; psychic/supernatural; romance; science fiction; sports; thriller.

O→ This agency specializes in thrillers, mysteries, science fiction, fantasy and horror.

How to Contact Query with SASE. Responds in 3 weeks to queries; 6 weeks to mss. Obtains most new clients through recommendations from others, solicitations, conferences.

Recent Sales *Blindfold Game*, by Dana Stabenow (St. Martin's Press); *A Deeper Sleep*, by Dana Stabenow (St. Martin's Press); *The Drowning Man*, by Margaret Coel (Berkley); *The History of the Ancient World*, by Susan Wise Bauer (Norton); *Stone Butterfly*, by James D. Doss (St. Martin's Press); *Box Like the Pros*, by Joe Frazier and William Dettloff (HarperCollins); *The Raven Prince*, by Elizabeth Hoyt (Warner). Other clients include Jessie Wise, Peter van Dijk, Jay Caselberg, Judith Laik.

Terms Agent receives 15% commission on domestic sales; 20% commission on foreign sales. No written contract. 100% of business is derived from commissions on ms sales. Charges clients for photocopying and book orders.

Tips "While we do not have any reason to believe that our submission guidelines will change in the near future, writers can find up-to-date submission policy information on our Web site. Always include a SASE with correct return postage."

HOPKINS LITERARY ASSOCIATES

2117 Buffalo Rd., Suite 327, Rochester NY 14624-1507. (585)352-6268. **Contact:** Pam Hopkins. Estab. 1996. Member of AAR, RWA. Represents 30 clients. 5% of clients are new/unpublished writers. Currently handles: 100% novels.

Represents Novels. **Considers these fiction areas:** Romance (historical, contemporary, category); women's.

- This agency specializes in women's fiction, particularly historical, contemporary, and category romance, as well as mainstream work.

How to Contact Submit outline, 3 sample chapters. No e-mail or fax queries. Considers simultaneous queries. Responds in 2 weeks to queries; 1 month to mss. Returns materials only with SASE. Obtains most new clients through recommendations from others, solicitations, conferences.

Recent Sales Sold 50 titles in the last year. *Lady of Sin*, by Madeline Hunter (Bantam); *Silent in the Grave*, by Deanna Raybourn (Mira); *Passion*, by Lisa Valdez (Berkley).

Terms Agent receives 15% commission on domestic sales; 20% commission on foreign sales. No written contract.

Writers' Conferences RWA National Conference.

IMPRINT AGENCY, INC.

240 West 35th St., Suite 500, New York NY 10001. Web site: www.imprintagency.com. **Contact:** Stephany Evans, president. Member of AAR.

- Prior to her current position, Ms. Evans began agenting in 1990 with Sandra Martin/Paraview; Ms. Reid formerly ran her own agency, JetReid.

Member Agents Stephany Evans, sevans@imprintagency.com (health and wellness, spirituality, psychology/self-help, mind/body, pregnancy and parenting, lifestyle, popular reference, narrative nonfiction, women's fiction, both literary and commercial—including chick lit, mystery and light suspense); Gary Heidt, gheidt@imprintagency.com (mystery, thriller, romance, literary fiction, multicultural, speculative, humorous, satirical); Mhays@imprintagency.com (sophisticated women's fiction—think urban chick lit, pop culture, lifestyle, animals, and absorbing nonfiction accounts); Janet Reid, jreid@imprintagency.com.

Represents Nonfiction books, novels. **Considers these nonfiction areas:** Government/politics/law; health/medicine; history; music/dance; psychology; self-help/personal improvement; spirituality; relationship, parapsychology, parenting, pregancy, narrative nonfiction, lifestyle. **Considers these fiction areas:** Literary; multicultural; mystery/suspense; thriller; young adult; women's (chick-lit); commercial.

- "Special areas of interest include alternative health and healing, spirituality, popular psychology, transpersonal psychology, parapsychology, pets, women's issues, history, popular science, parenting, multicultural issues, home decor and narrative nonfiction. We are not looking for historicals, Western's, fantasies, science fiction, plays, poetry or children's books."

How to Contact Query with SASE, proposal package, outline, outline/proposal, publishing history, author bio. No attachments on e-mails. If interested, the agency will contact you. Accepts e-mail queries. No fax queries.

Recent Sales Sold more than 25 titles in the last year. *Baby Proof*, by Emily Giffin (St. Martin's Press); *Crossing Into Medicine Country*, by David Carson (Arcade); *Rollergirl: Totally True Tales From the Track*, by Melissa Joulwan (Simon & Schuster); *The Pirate Primer*, by George Choundras (Writer's Digest Books). Agent receives 15% commission on domestic sales; 20% commission on foreign sales.

HARVEY KLINGER, INC.

300 W. 55th St., New York NY 10019. (212)581-7068. E-mail: queries@harveyklinger.com. Web site: www.harveyklinger.com. **Contact:** Harvey Klinger. Estab. 1977. Member of AAR. Represents 100 clients. 25% of clients are new/unpublished writers. Currently handles: 50% nonfiction books; 50% novels.

Member Agents David Dunton (popular culture, music-related books, literary fiction, crime novels, thrillers); Sara Crowe (children's and young adult authors, adult fiction and nonfiction, foreign rights sales); Andrea Somberg (literary fiction, commercial fiction, romance, sci-fi/fantasy, mysteries/thrillers, young adult, middle grade, quality narrative nonfiction, popular culture, how-to, self-help, humor, interior design, cookbooks, health/fitness); Nikki Van De Car (science fiction/fantasy, horror, romance, literary fiction, popular culture, how-to, memoir).

Represents Nonfiction books, novels. **Considers these nonfiction areas:** Biography/autobiography; cooking/foods/nutrition; health/medicine; psychology; science/technology; self-help/personal improvement; spirituality; sports; true crime/investigative; women's issues/studies. **Considers these fiction areas:** Action/adventure; detective/police/crime; family saga; glitz; literary; mainstream/contemporary; mystery/suspense; thriller.

O→ This agency specializes in big, mainstream, contemporary fiction and nonfiction.

How to Contact Query with SASE. No phone or fax queries. Accepts e-mail queries. No fax queries. Responds in 2 months to queries and mss. Obtains most new clients through recommendations from others.

Recent Sales *Breakable You*, By Brian Morton; *The Money In You!*, by Julie Stav; *The Mercy Seller*, by Brenda Vantrease; *A Country Music Christmas*, by Edie Hand and Buddy Killen; *Keep Climbing*, by Sean Swarner; *The Cubicle Survival Guide*, by James F. Thomspon; *Cookie Sensations*, by Meaghan Mountford; *Stranger*, by Justine Musk; *Laird Of The Mist*, by Paula Quinn. Other clients include Barbara Wood, Terry Kay, Barbara De Angelis, Jeremy Jackson.

Terms Agent receives 15% commission on domestic sales; 25% commission on foreign sales. Offers written contract. Charges for photocopying mss and overseas postage for mss.

N ◪ BARBARA S. KOUTS, LITERARY AGENT

P.O. Box 560, Bellport NY 11713. (631)286-1278. Fax: (631) 286-1538. **Contact:** Barbara Kouts. Estab. 1980. Member of AAR. Represents 50 clients. 10% of clients are new/unpublished writers.

Represents Juvenile books.

O→ This agency specializes in children's books.

How to Contact Query with SASE. Considers simultaneous queries. Responds in 1 week to queries; 2 months to mss. Obtains most new clients through recommendations from others, solicitations, conferences.

Terms Agent receives 10% commission on domestic sales; 20% commission on foreign sales. This agency charges clients for photocopying.

Tips "Write, do not call. Be professional in your writing."

N ◪ STUART KRICHEVSKY LITERARY AGENCY, INC.

381 Park Ave. S., Suite 914, New York NY 10016. (212)725-5288. Fax: (212)725-5275. E-mail: query@skagency.com. Member of AAR.

Member Agents Stuart Krichevsky; Shana Cohen (science fiction, fantasy); Kathryne Wick.

Represents Nonfiction books, novels.

How to Contact Submit query, synopsis, 1 sample page via e-mail (no attachments). Snail mail queries also acceptable. No fax queries. Obtains most new clients through recommendations from others, solicitations.

Recent Sales Untitled, by C.J. Chivers (Simon & Schuster); *American Islam*, by Paul M. Barrett (Farrar, Straus and Giroux); *The Nabokov's Nutcracker: Knowing and Loving the Parts of Speech*, by Ben Yagoda (Broadway Books).

◪ MICHAEL LARSEN/ELIZABETH POMADA, LITERARY AGENTS

1029 Jones St., San Francisco CA 94109-5023. (415)673-0939. E-mail: larsenpoma@aol.com. Web site: www.larsen-pomada.com. **Contact:** Mike Larsen, Elizabeth Pomada. Estab. 1972. Member of AAR, Authors Guild, ASJA, PEN, WNBA, California Writers Club, National Speakers Association. Represents 100 clients. 40-45% of clients are new/unpublished writers. Currently handles: 70% nonfiction books; 30% novels.

- Prior to opening their agency, Mr. Larsen and Ms. Pomada were promotion executives for major publishing houses. Mr. Larsen worked for Morrow, Bantam and Pyramid (now part of Berkley); Ms. Pomada worked at Holt, David McKay and The Dial Press. Mr. Larsen is the author of the third editions of *How to Write a Book Proposal* and *How to Get a Literary Agent*.

Member Agents Michael Larsen (nonfiction); Elizabeth Pomada (fiction, narrative nonfiction, nonfiction for women); Laurie McLean, laurie@agentsavant.com (fantasy, science, romance, middle-grade and YA fiction).

Represents Adult book-length fiction and nonfiction that will interest New York publishers or are irresistibly written or conceived. **Considers these nonfiction areas:** Anthropology/archaeology; art/architecture/design; biography/autobiography; business/economics; cooking/foods/nutrition; current affairs; ethnic/cultural interests; gay/lesbian issues; government/politics/law; health/medicine; history; how-to; humor/satire; memoirs; money/finance; music/dance; nature/environment; New Age/metaphysics; popular culture; psychology; religious/inspirational; science/technology; self-help/personal improvement; sociology; sports; theater/film; travel; true crime/investigative; women's issues/studies; futurism. **Considers these fiction areas:** Action/adventure; contemporary issues; detective/police/crime; ethnic; experimental; family saga; fantasy; feminist; gay/lesbian; glitz; historical; humor/satire; literary; mainstream/contemporary; mystery/suspense; religious/inspirational; romance (contemporary, gothic, historical); chick lit.

O→ "We have diverse tastes. We look for fresh voices and new ideas. We handle literary, commercial and genre fiction, and the full range of nonfiction books." Actively seeking commercial, genre and literary fiction. Does not want to receive children's books, plays, short stories, screenplays, pornography, poetry or stories of abuse.

How to Contact Query with SASE, submit first 10 pages of completed novel, 2-page synopsis, SASE. Make sure the query is 1 page. For nonfiction, send a promotion plan done according to the advice on the Web site. Accepts e-mail queries. No fax queries. Responds in 2 weeks to queries; 2 months to mss.

Recent Sales Sold at least 15 titles in the last year. *Banana Hear Summer*, by Merlinda Bobis (Bantam); *Guerilla Marketing: Secrets for Making Big Profits from Your Small Business, 4th edition*, by Jay Levinson (Houghton Mifflin); *The Tender Carnivore: How to Be a Thoughtful Meat-Eater*, by Catherine Friend (Marlowe).

Terms Agent receives 15% commission on domestic sales; 20% (30% for Asia) commission on foreign sales. May charge for printing, postage for multiple submissions, foreign mail, foreign phone calls, galleys, books, legal fees.

Writers' Conferences BookExpo America; Santa Barbara Writers' Conference; San Francisco Writers' Conference.

Tips "We love helping writers get the rewards and recognition they deserve. If you can write books that meet the needs of the marketplace and you can promote your books, now is the best time ever to be a writer. We must find new writers to make a living, so we are very eager to hear from new writers whose work will interest large houses, and nonfiction writers who can promote their books. For a list of recent sales, helpful info, and three ways to make yourself irresistible to any publisher, please visit our Web site."

NANCY LOVE LITERARY AGENCY

250 E. 65th St., New York NY 10021-6614. (212)980-3499. Fax: (212)308-6405. E-mail: nloveag@aol.com. **Contact:** Nancy Love. Estab. 1984. Member of AAR. Represents 60-80 clients. 25% of clients are new/unpublished writers. Currently handles: 90% nonfiction books; 10% novels.

- This agency is not taking on any new fiction writers at this time.

Represents Nonfiction books. **Considers these nonfiction areas:** Biography/autobiography; child guidance/parenting; cooking/foods/nutrition; current affairs; ethnic/cultural interests; government/politics/law; health/medicine; history; how-to; nature/environment; popular culture; psychology; religious/inspirational; science/technology; self-help/personal improvement; sociology; spirituality; travel (armchair only, no how-to); true crime/investigative; women's issues/studies.

O→ This agency specializes in adult nonfiction. Actively seeking narrative nonfiction.

How to Contact Query with SASE. No e-mail or fax queries. Considers simultaneous queries. Responds in 3 weeks to queries; 6 weeks to mss. Returns materials only with SASE. Obtains most new clients through recommendations from others, solicitations.

Recent Sales Sold 18 titles in the last year. *Say Good-bye to Knee Pain*, by Marian Betancourt and Joe Hofannin (Pocket); *Texas Hill Country Cookbook*, by Scott Cohen and Marian Betancourt (Globe Pequot); *The Monster in the Corner Office*, by Patricia King (Adams); *Shooting Star*, by Cynthia Riggs (St. Martin's); *Indian Pipes*, by Cynthia Riggs (St. Martin's Press); *Overthrow*, by Stephen Kinzer (Henry Holt); *Don't Panic*, by Stanton Peele (Crown); *Overcoming Obesity with Surgery*, by James Weber (M. Evans/Rowman & Littlefield); *How to Think Like a Terrorist*, by Mike German (Potomac Books).

Terms Agent receives 15% commission on domestic sales; 20% commission on foreign sales. Offers written contract. Charges clients for photocopying if it runs more than $20.

Tips "Nonfiction authors and/or collaborators must be an authority in their subject area and have a platform. Send an SASE if you want a response."

LOWENSTEIN-YOST ASSOCIATES

121 W. 27th St., Suite 601, New York NY 10001. (212)206-1630. Fax: (212)727-0280. Web site: www.lowensteinyost.com. **Contact:** Barbara Lowenstein or Nancy Yost. Estab. 1976. Member of AAR. Represents 150 clients. 20% of clients are new/unpublished writers. Currently handles: 60% nonfiction books; 40% novels.

Member Agents Barbara Lowenstein, president (nonfiction interests include narrative nonfiction, health, money, finance, travel, multicultural, popular culture and memoir; fiction interests include literary fiction and women's fiction); Nancy Yost, vice president (mainstream/contemporary fiction, mystery, suspense, contemporary/historical romance, thriller, women's fiction); Norman Kurz, business affairs; Zoe Fishman, foreign rights (young adult, literary fiction, narrative nonfiction); Rachel Vater (fantasy, young adult, women's fiction); Natanya Wheeler (narrative nonfiction, literary fiction, historical, women's fiction, birds).

Represents Nonfiction books, novels. **Considers these nonfiction areas:** Animals; anthropology/archaeology; biography/autobiography; business/economics; child guidance/parenting; current affairs; education; ethnic/cultural interests; government/politics/law; health/medicine; history; how-to; language/literature/criticism; memoirs; money/finance; multicultural; nature/environment; popular culture; psychology; self-help/personal improvement; sociology; travel; women's issues/studies; music; narrative nonfiction; science; film. **Considers these fiction areas:** Detective/police/crime; erotica; ethnic; feminist; historical; literary; mainstream/contemporary; mystery/suspense; romance (contemporary, historical, regency); thriller; women's; fantasy, young adult.

O→ This agency specializes in health, business, creative nonfiction, literary fiction and commercial fiction—especially suspense, crime and women's issues. "We are a full-service agency, handling domestic and foreign rights, film rights and audio rights to all of our books."

How to Contact Query with SASE. Prefers to read materials exclusively. For fiction, send outline and first chapter. *No unsolicited mss.* Responds in 4 weeks to queries. Returns materials only with SASE. Obtains most new clients through recommendations from others, solicitations, conferences.

Recent Sales *Body After Baby*, by Jackie Keller (Avery); *Creating Competitive Advantage*, by Jaynie Smith & Bill Flanagan (Doubleday); *To Keep a Husband*, by Lindsay Graves (Ballantine); *The Notorious Mrs. Winston*, by Mary Mackey (Berkley); *Gleason's Gym Total Body Boxing Workout for Women*, by Hector Roca & Bruce Silverglade (Fireside); *More Than A Champion: A Biography of Mohammed Ali*, by Ishmael Reed (Shaye Areheart); *Dreams of A Caspian Rain*, by Gina Nahai; *House of Dark Delights*, by Louisa Burton (Bantam); a new thriller by Perri O'Shaugnessy (Pocket); the debut thriller by N.P.R. writer Susan Arnout Smith (St. Martin's); *Sworn to Silence*, by Linda Castillo; *Thinner or Pretty on the Outside*, by Valerie Frankel; *In the Stars*, by Eileen Cook; *The Dark Lantern*, by Gerri Brightwell. Other clients include Stephanie Laurens, Dr. Ro, Penny McFall, Deborah Crombie, Liz Carlyle, Suzanne Enoch, Gaelen Foley, Tamar Myers, Sandi K. Shelton, Kathryn Smith, Cheyenne McCray, Barbara Keesling.

Terms Agent receives 15% commission on domestic sales; 20% commission on foreign sales. Offers written contract. Charges for large photocopy batches, messenger service, international postage.

Writers' Conferences Malice Domestic; Bouchercon; RWA National Conference.

Tips "Know the genre you are working in and read! Also, please see our Web site for details on which agent to query for your project."

N ◪ LYONS LITERARY, LLC

116 West 23rd St., Suite 500, New York NY 10011. (212)851-8428. Fax: (212)851-8405. E-mail: info@lyonsliterary.com. Web site: www.lyonsliterary.com. **Contact:** Jonathan Lyons. Estab. 2007. Member of AAR, The Author's Guild, American Bar Association, New York State Bar Associaton, New York State Intellectual Property Law Section. Represents 36 clients. 15% of clients are new/unpublished writers. Currently handles: 60% nonfiction books; 36% novels; 2% story collections; 2% poetry.

Represents Nonfiction books, novels, short story collections. **Considers these nonfiction areas:** Animals; biography/autobiography; business/economics; child guidance/parenting; cooking/foods/nutrition; crafts/hobbies; current affairs; ethnic/cultural interests; gay/lesbian issues; government/politics/law; health/medicine; history; how-to; humor/satire; memoirs; military/war; money/finance; multicultural; music/dance; nature/environment; popular culture; psychology; science/technology; self-help/personal improvement; sociology; sports; translation; travel; true crime/investigative; women's issues/studies. **Considers these fiction areas:** Action/adventure; comic books/cartoon; confession; detective/police/crime; ethnic; experimental; family saga; fantasy; feminist; gay/lesbian; glitz; historical; horror; humor/satire; literary; mainstream/contemporary; mystery/suspense; psychic/supernatural; regional; science fiction; sports; thriller; women's; chick lit.

O→ "With my legal expertise and experience selling domestic and foreign language book rights, paperback reprint rights, audio rights, film/TV rights and permissions, I am able to provide substantive and personal guidance to my clients in all areas relating to their projects. In addition, with the advent of new publishing technology, Lyons Literary, LLC is situated to address the changing nature of the industry while concurrently handling authors' more traditional needs."

How to Contact Query with SASE, submit outline, synopsis, author bio, SASE. No phone queries. Accepts e-mail queries. No fax queries. Considers simultaneous queries. Responds in 8 weeks to queries; 12 weeks to mss. Returns materials only with SASE. Obtains most new clients through recommendations from others.

Recent Sales Sold more than 30 titles in the last year. This agency prefers not to share information on specific sales.

Terms Agent receives 15% commission on domestic sales; 20% commission on foreign sales. Offers written contract.

Writers' Conferences Agents and Editors Conference.

Tips "Please submit electronic queries through our Web site submission form."

◪ CAROL MANN AGENCY

55 Fifth Ave., New York NY 10003. (212)206-5635. Fax: (212)675-4809. E-mail: will@carolmannagency.com. **Contact:** Will Sherlin. Estab. 1977. Member of AAR. Represents roughly 200 clients. 15% of clients are new/unpublished writers. Currently handles: 90% nonfiction books; 10% novels.

Member Agents Carol Mann; Will Sherlin; Laura Yorke.

Represents Nonfiction books, novels. **Considers these nonfiction areas:** Anthropology/archaeology; art/architecture/design; biography/autobiography; business/economics; child guidance/parenting; current affairs; ethnic/cultural interests; government/politics/law; health/medicine; history; money/finance; popular culture; psychology; self-help/personal improvement; sociology; sports; women's issues/studies; music. **Considers these fiction areas:** Literary; commercial.

O→ This agency specializes in current affairs, self-help, popular culture, psychology, parenting, and history. Does not want to receive genre fiction (romance, mystery, etc.).

How to Contact Query with outline/proposal, SASE. Responds in 3 weeks to queries.

Recent Sales Clients include novelists Paul Auster and Marita Golden; National Book Award Winner Tim Egan, Hannah Storm, and Willow Bay; Pulitzer Prize-winner Fox Butterfield; bestselling essayist Shelby Steele; sociologist Dr. William Julius Wilson; economist Thomas Sowell; bestselling diet doctors Mary Dan and Michael Eades; ACLU president Nadine Strossen; pundit Mona Charen; memoirist Lauren Winner; photography project editors Rick Smolan and David Cohen (*America 24/7*); Kevin Liles, executive vice president of Warner Music Group and former president of Def Jam Records; and Jermaine Dupri.

Terms Agent receives 15% commission on domestic sales; 20% commission on foreign sales. Offers written contract.

N MARTIN LITERARY MANAGEMENT

17328 Ventura Blvd., Suite 138, Encino (LA) CA 91316. (818)595-1130. Fax: (818)715-0418. E-mail: sharlene@martinliterarymanagement.com. Web site: www.MartinLiteraryManagement.com. **Contact:** Sharlene Martin. Estab. 2002. Member of AAR. 75% of clients are new/unpublished writers. Currently handles: 100% nonfiction books.

- Prior to becoming an agent, Ms. Martin worked in film/TV production and acquisitions.

Represents Nonfiction books. **Considers these nonfiction areas:** Biography/autobiography; business/economics; child guidance/parenting; current affairs; health/medicine; history; how-to; humor/satire; memoirs; popular culture; psychology; religious/inspirational; self-help/personal improvement; true crime/investigative; women's issues/studies.

O→ This agency has strong ties to film/TV. Actively seeking nonfiction that is highly commercial and that can be adapted to film.

How to Contact Query with SASE, submit outline, 2 sample chapters. Prefers e-mail queries. Will request supporting materials if interested. No phone queries. Do not send materials unless requested. Submission guidelines defined on Web site. Accepts e-mail queries. No fax queries. Considers simultaneous queries. Responds in 1 week to queries; 3-4 weeks to mss. Returns materials only with SASE. Obtains most new clients through recommendations from others.

Recent Sales *Prince of Darkness—Richard Perle: The Kingdom, The Power, and the End of Empire in America*, by Alan Weisman (Union Square Press/Sterling); *Truth At Last: The Real Story of James Earl Ray*, by John Larry Ray with Lyndon Barsten (Lyons Press).

Terms Agent receives 15% commission on domestic sales; 25% commission on foreign sales. Offers written contract, binding for 1 year; 1-month notice must be given to terminate contract. Charges author for postage and copying if material is not sent electronically. 99 percent of materials are sent electronically to minimize charges to author for postage and copying.

Tips "Have a strong platform for nonfiction. Please don't call. I welcome e-mail. I'm very responsive when I'm interested in a query and work hard to get my clients materials in the best possible shape before submissions. Do your homework prior to submission and only submit your best efforts. Please review our Web site carefully to make sure we're a good match for your work."

MARGRET MCBRIDE LITERARY AGENCY

7744 Fay Ave., Suite 201, La Jolla CA 92037. (858)454-1550. Fax: (858)454-2156. E-mail: staff@mcbridelit.com. Web site: www.mcbrideliterary.com. **Contact:** Michael Daley, submissions manager. Estab. 1980. Member of AAR, Authors Guild. Represents 55 clients.

- Prior to opening her agency, Ms. McBride worked at Random House, Ballantine Books, and Warner Books.

Represents Nonfiction books, novels. **Considers these nonfiction areas:** Biography/autobiography; business/economics; cooking/foods/nutrition; current affairs; ethnic/cultural interests; government/politics/law; health/medicine; history; how-to; money/finance; music/dance; popular culture; psychology; science/technology; self-help/personal improvement; sociology; women's issues/studies; style. **Considers these fiction areas:** Action/adventure; detective/police/crime; ethnic; historical; humor/satire; literary; mainstream/contemporary; mystery/suspense; thriller; westerns/frontier.

O→ This agency specializes in mainstream fiction and nonfiction. Does not want to receive screenplays, romance, poetry, or children's/young adult.

How to Contact Query with synopsis, bio, SASE. No e-mail or fax queries. Considers simultaneous queries. Responds in 4-6 weeks to queries; 6-8 weeks to mss. Returns materials only with SASE.

Recent Sales *Accelerants*, by Michael Boylan (Portfolio); *You Call the Shots*, by Cameron Johnson; *From Hope to Higher Ground*, by Gov. Mike Huckabee; *Extraordinary Weddings*, by Colin Cowie.

Terms Agent receives 15% commission on domestic sales; 25% commission on foreign sales. Charges for overnight delivery and photocopying.

N MENZA-BARRON AGENCY

1170 Broadway, Suite 807, New York NY 10001. (212)889-6850. **Contact:** Claudia Menza, Manie Barron. Estab. 1983. Member of AAR. Represents 100 clients. 50% of clients are new/unpublished writers.

Represents Nonfiction books, novels. **Considers these nonfiction areas:** Current affairs; education; ethnic/cultural interests (especially African-American); health/medicine; history; multicultural; music/dance; photography; psychology; theater/film.

This agency specializes editorial assistance and African-American fiction and nonfiction.

How to Contact Query with SASE. Responds in 2-4 weeks to queries; 2-4 months to mss. Returns materials only with SASE.

Recent Sales This agency prefers not to share information on specific sales.

Terms Agent receives 15% commission on domestic sales; 20% (if co-agent is used) commission on foreign sales; 20% commission on dramatic rights sales. Offers written contract.

NELSON LITERARY AGENCY

1020 15th St., Suite 26L, Denver CO 80202. (303)463-5301. E-mail: query@nelsonagency.com. Web site: www.nelsonagency.com. **Contact:** Kristin Nelson. Estab. 2002. Member of AAR.

- Prior to opening her own agency, Ms. Nelson worked as a literary scout and subrights agent for agent Jody Rein.

Represents Novels, select nonfiction. **Considers these nonfiction areas:** Memoirs; narrative nonfiction. **Considers these fiction areas:** Literary; romance (includes fantasy with romantic elements, science fiction, fantasy, young adult); women's; chick lit (includes mysteries); commercial/mainstream.

NLA specializes in representing commercial fiction and high caliber literary fiction. Actively seeking Latina writers who tackle contemporary issues in a modern voice (think *Dirty Girls Social Club*). Does not want short story collections, mysteries (except chick lit), thrillers, Christian, horror, or children's picture books.

How to Contact Query by e-mail only.

Recent Sales *Schemes of Love*, by Sherry Thomas (Bantam Dell); *The Camelot Code*, by Mari Mancusi (Dutton Children's); *Magic Lost, Trouble Found*, by Lisa Shearin (Ace); *Magellan's Witch*, by Carolyn Jewel (Hachette/Warner); *No Place Safe*, by Kim Reid (Kensington); *Plan B*, by Jennifer O'Connell (MTV/Pocket Books); *Code of Love*, by Cheryl Sawyer (NAL/Penguin Group); *Once Upon Stilettos*, by Shanna Swendson (Ballantine); *I'd Tell You I Love You But Then I'd Have to Kill You*, by Ally Carter (Hyperion Children's); *An Accidental Goddess*, by Linnea Sinclair (Bantam Spectra). Other clients include Paula Reed, Becky Motew, Jack McCallum, Jana Deleon.

L. PERKINS ASSOCIATES

5800 Arlington Ave., Riverdale NY 10471. (718)543-5344. Fax: (718)543-5354. E-mail: lperkinsagency@yahoo.com. **Contact:** Lori Perkins, Amy Stout (jrlperkinsagency@yahoo.com). Estab. 1990. Member of AAR. Represents 90 clients. 10% of clients are new/unpublished writers.

- Ms. Perkins has been an agent for 20 years. She is also the author of *The Insider's Guide to Getting an Agent* (Writer's Digest Books), as well as three other nonfiction books. She has also edited two anthologies.

Represents Nonfiction books, novels. **Considers these nonfiction areas:** Popular culture. **Considers these fiction areas:** Erotica; fantasy; horror; literary (dark); science fiction.

Most of Ms. Perkins' clients write both fiction and nonfiction. "This combination keeps my clients publishing for years. I am also a published author, so I know what it takes to write a good book." Actively seeking a Latino *Gone With the Wind* and *Waiting to Exhale*, and urban ethnic horror. Does not want to receive anything outside of the above categories (westerns, romance, etc.).

How to Contact Query with SASE. Considers simultaneous queries. Responds in 12 weeks to queries; 3-6 months to mss. Returns materials only with SASE. Obtains most new clients through recommendations from others, solicitations, conferences.

Recent Sales Sold 100 titles in the last year. *How to Make Love Like a Porn Star: A Cautionary Tale*, by Jenna Jameson (Reagan Books); *Everything But . . .?*, by Rachel Krammer Bussel (Bantam); *Dear Mom, I Always Wanted You to Know*, by Lisa Delman (Perigee Books); *The Illustrated Ray Bradbury*, by Jerry Weist (Avon); *The Poet in Exile*, by Ray Manzarek (Avalon); *Behind Sad Eyes: The Life of George Harrison*, by Marc Shapiro (St. Martin's Press).

Terms Agent receives 15% commission on domestic sales; 20% commission on foreign sales. No written contract. Charges clients for photocopying.

Writers' Conferences San Diego State University Writers' Conference; NECON; BookExpo America; World Fantasy Convention.

Tips "Research your field and contact professional writers' organizations to see who is looking for what. Finish your novel before querying agents. Read my book, *An Insider's Guide to Getting an Agent*, to get a sense of how agents operate. Read agent blogs—litsoup.blogspot.com and missnark.blogspot.com.

AARON M. PRIEST LITERARY AGENCY

708 Third Ave., 23rd Floor, New York NY 10017-4103. (212)818-0344. Fax: (212)573-9417. Estab. 1974. Member of AAR. Currently handles: 25% nonfiction books; 75% novels.

Member Agents Aaron Priest, querypriest@aaronpriest.com (thrillers and fiction); Lisa Erbach Vance, queryvance@aaronpriest.com (general fiction, mystery, thrillers, historical fiction, up market women's fiction, narrative nonfiction, memoir); Lucy Childs, querychilds@aaronpriest.com (literary and commercial fiction, memoir, historical fiction, upscale commercial women's fiction); Nicole Kenealy, querykenealy@aaronpriest.com (chick-lit/commercial women's fiction, literary fiction,young adult fiction and nonfiction).

Represents Commercial fiction, literary fiction, some nonfiction.

How to Contact Query with SASE, submit publishing history, author bio. Make sure your query is one page. Paste first chapter into body e-mail. Do not query more than one agent here. Accepts e-mail queries. No fax queries. Considers simultaneous queries. Responds in 3 weeks, only if interested.

Recent Sales *She is Me*, by Kathleen Schine; *Killer Smile*, by Lisa Scottoline.

Terms Agent receives 15% commission on domestic sales. This agency charges for photocopying and postage expenses.

PSALTIS LITERARY

Post Office: Park West Finance, P.O. Box 20736, New York NY 10025. E-mail: psaltisliterary@mpsaltis.com. Web site: www.mpsaltis.com. **Contact:** Michael Psaltis. Member of AAR. Represents 30-40 clients.

Represents Nonfiction books, novels. **Considers these nonfiction areas:** Biography/autobiography; business/economics; cooking/foods/nutrition; health/medicine; history; memoirs; popular culture; psychology; science/technology. **Considers these fiction areas:** Mainstream/contemporary.

How to Contact Submit outline/proposal. Responds in 2-4 weeks to queries; 6-8 weeks to mss.

Recent Sales *Hometown Appetites*, by Kelly Alexander and Cindy Harris (Gotham Books); *A Life in Twilight*, by Mark Wolverton (Joseph Henry Press); *Cooked*, by Jeff Henderson (William Morrow).

Terms Agent receives 15% commission on domestic sales; 20% commission on foreign sales. Offers written contract.

RAINES & RAINES

103 Kenyon Road, Medusa NY 12120. (518)239-8311. Fax: (518)239-6029. **Contact:** Theron Raines (member of AAR); Joan Raines; Keith Korman. Represents 100 clients.

Represents Nonfiction books, novels. **Considers these nonfiction areas:** All subjects. **Considers these fiction areas:** Action/adventure; detective/police/crime; fantasy; historical; mystery/suspense; picture books; science fiction; thriller; westerns/frontier.

How to Contact Query with SASE. Responds in 2 weeks to queries.

Terms Agent receives 15% commission on domestic sales; 20% commission on foreign sales. Charges for photocopying.

HELEN REES LITERARY AGENCY

376 North St., Boston MA 02113-2013. (617)227-9014. Fax: (617)227-8762. E-mail: reesagency@reesagency.com. **Contact:** Joan Mazmanian, Ann Collette, Helen Rees, Lorin Rees. Estab. 1983. Member of AAR, PEN. Represents more than 100 clients. 50% of clients are new/unpublished writers. Currently handles: 60% nonfiction books; 40% novels.

Member Agents Ann Collette (literary fiction, women's studies, health, biography, history); Helen Rees (business, money/finance/economics, government/politics/law, contemporary issues, literary fiction); Lorin Rees (business, money/finance, management, history, narrative nonfiction, science, literary fiction, memoir).

Represents Nonfiction books, novels. **Considers these nonfiction areas:** Biography/autobiography; business/economics; current affairs; government/politics/law; health/medicine; history; money/finance; women's issues/studies. **Considers these fiction areas:** Historical; literary; mainstream/contemporary; mystery/suspense; thriller.

How to Contact Query with SASE, outline, 2 sample chapters. No unsolicited e-mail submissions. No multiple submissions. No e-mail or fax queries. Responds in 3-4 weeks to queries. Obtains most new clients through recommendations from others, conferences, submissions.

Recent Sales Sold more than 35 titles in the last year. *Get Your Shipt Together*, by Capt. D. Michael Abrashoff;

Overpromise and Overdeliver, by Rick Berrara; *Opacity*, by Joel Kurtzman; *America the Broke*, by Gerald Swanson; *Murder at the B-School*, by Jeffrey Cruikshank; *Bone Factory*, by Steven Sidor; *Father Said*, by Hal Sirowitz; *Winning*, by Jack Welch; *The Case for Israel*, by Alan Dershowitz; *As the Future Catches You*, by Juan Enriquez; *Blood Makes the Grass Grow Green*, by Johnny Rico; *DVD Movie Guide*, by Mick Martin and Marsha Porter; *Words That Work*, by Frank Luntz; *Stirring It Up*, by Gary Hirshberg; *Hot Spots*, by Martin Fletcher; *Andy Grove: The Life and Times of an American*, by Richard Tedlow; *Girls Most Likely To*, by Poonam Sharma.
Terms Agent receives 15% commission on domestic sales; 20% commission on foreign sales.

REGAL LITERARY AGENCY

1140 Broadway, Penthouse, New York NY 10001. (212)684-7900. Fax: (212)684-7906. E-mail: Shannon@regal-literary.com. Web site: www.regal-literary.com. **Contact:** Shannon Firth, Marcus Hoffmann. Estab. 2002. Member of AAR. Represents 100 clients. 20% of clients are new/unpublished writers. Currently handles: 48% nonfiction books; 46% novels; 6% poetry.

- Prior to becoming agents, Mr. Regal was a musician; Mr. Steinberg was a filmmaker and screenwriter; Ms. Reid and Ms. Schott Pearson were magazine editors; Mr. Hoffman worked in the publishing industry in London.

Member Agents Joseph Regal (literary fiction, science, history, memoir); Peter Steinberg (literary and commercial fiction, history, humor, memoir, narrative nonfiction, young adult); Bess Reed (literary fiction, narrative nonfiction, self-help); Lauren Schott Pearson (literary fiction, commercial fiction, memoir, narrative nonfiction, thrillers, mysteries); Markus Hoffmann (foreign rights manager, literary fiction, mysteries, thrillers, international fiction, science, music). Michael Psaltis of Psaltis Literary also works with Regal Literary agents to form the Culinary Cooperative—a joint-venture agency dedicated to food writing, cookbooks, and all things related to cooking. Recent sales include *Cooked* (William Morrow); *Carmine's Family Style* (St. Martin's Press); *Fish On a First-Name Basis* (St. Martin's Press); *The Reverse Diet* (John Wiley & Sons); and *The Seasoning of a Chef* (Doubleday/Broadway).
Represents Nonfiction books, novels, short story collections, novellas. **Considers these nonfiction areas:** Anthropology/archaeology; art/architecture/design; biography/autobiography; business/economics; cooking/foods/nutrition; current affairs; ethnic/cultural interests; gay/lesbian issues; history; humor/satire; language/literature/criticism; memoirs; military/war; music/dance; nature/environment; photography; popular culture; psychology; religious/inspirational; science/technology; sports; translation; women's issues/studies. **Considers these fiction areas:** Comic books/cartoon; detective/police/crime; ethnic; historical; literary; mystery/suspense; thriller; contemporary.

O→ "We have discovered more than a dozen successful literary novelists in the last 5 years. We are small, but are extraordinarily responsive to our writers. We are more like managers than agents, with an eye toward every aspect of our writers' careers, including publicity and other media." Actively seeking literary fiction and narrative nonfiction. Does not want romance, science fiction, horror, or screenplays.

How to Contact Query with SASE, 5-15 sample pages. No phone calls. No e-mail or fax queries. Considers simultaneous queries. Responds in 2-3 weeks to queries; 4-12 to mss. Returns materials only with SASE. Obtains most new clients through recommendations from others, unsolicited submissions.
Recent Sales Sold 20 titles in the last year. *The Stolen Child*, by Keith Donohue (Nan Talese/Doubleday); *What Elmo Taught Me*, by Kevin Clash (HarperCollins); *The Affected Provincial's Companion*, by Lord Breaulove Swells Whimsy (Bloomsbury); *The Three Incestuous Sisters*, by Audrey Niffenegger (Abrams); *The Traveler*, by John Twelve Hawks (Doubleday). Other clients include James Reston Jr., Tony Earley, Dennie Hughes, Mark Lee, Jake Page, Cheryl Bernard, Daniel Wallace, John Marks, Keith Scribner, Cathy Day, Alicia Erian, Gregory David Roberts, Dallas Hudgens, Tim Winton, Ian Spiegelman, Brad Barkley, Heather Hepler, Gavin Edwards, Sara Voorhees, Alex Abella.
Terms Agent receives 15% commission on domestic sales; 20% commission on foreign sales. No written contract. Charges clients for typical/major office expenses, such as photocopying and foreign postage.

JODIE RHODES LITERARY AGENCY

8840 Villa La Jolla Drive, Suite 315, La Jolla CA 92037-1957. **Contact:** Jodie Rhodes, president. Estab. 1998. Member of AAR. Represents 50 clients. 60% of clients are new/unpublished writers. Currently handles: 60% nonfiction books; 35% novels; 5% middle grade/young adult books.

- Prior to opening her agency, Ms. Rhodes was a university-level creative writing teacher, workshop director, published novelist, and vice president/media director at the N.W. Ayer Advertising Agency.

Member Agents Jodie Rhodes; Clark McCutcheon (fiction); Bob McCarter (nonfiction).
Represents Nonfiction books, novels. **Considers these nonfiction areas:** Biography/autobiography; child guidance/parenting; ethnic/cultural interests; government/politics/law; health/medicine; history; memoirs; military/war; science/technology; women's issues/studies. **Considers these fiction areas:** Ethnic; family saga; historical; literary; mainstream/contemporary; mystery/suspense; thriller; young adult; women's.

O→ Actively seeking witty, sophisticated women's books about career ambitions and relationships; edgy/trendy YA and teen books; narrative nonfiction on groundbreaking scientific discoveries, politics, economics, military and important current affairs by prominent scientists and academic professors. Does not want to receive erotica, horror, fantasy, romance, science fiction, religious/inspirational, or children's books (does accept young adult/teen).

How to Contact Query with brief synopsis, first 30-50 pages, SASE. Do not call. Do not send complete ms unless requested. This agency does not return unrequested material weighing a pound or more that requires special postage. Include e-mail address with query. No e-mail or fax queries. Considers simultaneous queries. Responds in 3 weeks to queries. Returns materials only with SASE. Obtains most new clients through recommendations from others, agent sourcebooks.

Recent Sales Sold 40 titles in the last year. *A Matter of Gravity*, by John Moffat (Harpercollins); *A Girl Named Indie*, by Kavita Daswani (Simon and Schuster); *First Six Minutes of Life on Earth*, by Christina Reed (John Wiley & Sons); *Flak Jacket Rock*, by Dean Kohler (HarperCollins); *Roots and Wings*, by Many Ly (Random House); *The Art of Solving Crime*, by Max Houck (Praeger); *Murder at the Universe*, by Dan Craig (Midnight Ink); *Into Jerusalem*, by Craig Eisendrath (The Permanent Press); *Preventing Alzheimer's* by Marwan Sabbagh (John Wiley and Sons); *The Genie Machine*, by Robert Plotkin (Stanford University Press); *Take Charge of Your Diabetes*, by Sarfraz Zaidi (Da Capo Press).

Terms Agent receives 15% commission on domestic sales; 20% commission on foreign sales. Offers written contract; 1-month notice must be given to terminate contract. Charges clients for fax, photocopying, phone calls, postage. Charges are itemized and approved by writers upfront.

Tips "Think your book out before you write it. Do your research, know your subject matter intimately, and write vivid specifics, not bland generalities. Care deeply about your book. Don't imitate other writers. Find your own voice. We never take on a book we don't believe in, and we go the extra mile for our writers. We welcome talented, new writers."

N RIGHTS UNLIMITED, INC.

6 W. 37th St., Fourth Floor, New York NY 10018. E-mail: submissions@rightsunlimited.com. Web site: www.rightsunlimited.com. Estab. 1985. Member of AAR. Represents 100+ clients.

Member Agents Desmond Sansevere; Diane Dreher; Ben Salmon; Ryan Dreher.

Represents Nonfiction books, novels. **Considers these nonfiction areas:** Business/economics; current affairs; health/medicine; history; humor/satire; memoirs; popular culture; self-help/personal improvement; sociology; travel; women's issues/studies; celebrity biography; career development; alternative culture; diet/fitness; alternative medicine; inspiration; relationships; gender/sexuality; lifestyle; cookbooks; gift books. **Considers these fiction areas:** Fantasy; literary; multicultural; mystery/suspense; romance (contemporary); science fiction; thriller (international); women's (mainstream); chick lit; mommy lit; quirky/edgy fiction; crime.

O→ No textbooks or poetry.

How to Contact Query with SASE or via e-mail (no attachments). For nonfiction, send query letter, bio, outline, SASE. For fiction, send query letter, bio, synopsis, first 10 pages, SASE. Responds in 1 month to queries.

Recent Sales *Driving the Career Highway*, by Janice Reals-Ellig and William J. Morin (Nelson Business); *101 Things To Do Before You Get a Job*, by Lindsey Pollak (Harper Business); *Health by Water*, by Alexa Fleckenstein and Roanne Weisman (Contemporary).

Terms Agent receives 15% commission on domestic sales; 20% commission on foreign sales; 20% commission on dramatic rights sales.

N ANGELA RINALDI LITERARY AGENCY

P.O. Box 7877, Beverly Hills CA 90212-7877. (310)842-7665. Fax: (310)837-8143. E-mail: amr@rinaldiliterary.com. Web site: www.rinaldiliterary.com. **Contact:** Angela Rinaldi. Estab. 1994. Member of AAR. Represents 50 clients. Currently handles: 50% nonfiction books; 50% novels.

- Prior to opening her agency, Ms. Rinaldi was an editor at NAL/Signet, Pocket Books and Bantam, and the manager of book development for *The Los Angeles Times*.

Represents Nonfiction books, novels, TV and motion picture rights (for clients only). **Considers these nonfiction areas:** Biography/autobiography; business/economics; health/medicine; money/finance; self-help/personal improvement; true crime/investigative; women's issues/studies; books by journalists and academics. **Considers these fiction areas:** Literary; commercial; upmarket women's fiction; suspense.

O→ Actively seeking commercial and literary fiction. Does not want to receive scripts, poetry, category romances, children's books, Western's, science fiction/fantasy, technothrillers or cookbooks.

How to Contact For fiction, send first 3 chapters, brief synopsis, SASE. For nonfiction, query with SASE or send outline/proposal, SASE. Do not send certified or metered mail. Brief e-mail inquiries are OK (no attachments). Considers simultaneous queries. Please advise if it is a multiple submission. Responds in 6 weeks to queries. Returns materials only with SASE.

Recent Sales *My First Crush*, by Linda Kaplan (Lyons Press); *Rescue Me*, by Megan Clark (Kensington); *The Blood Orange Tree*, by Drusilla Campbell (Kensington); *Indivisible by Two: Great Tales of Twins, Triplets and Quads*, by Dr. Nancy Segal (Harvard University Press); *Zen Putting*, by Dr. Joseph Parent (Gotham Books); *Bone Lake*, by Drusilla Campbell (Madison Park Press).

Terms Agent receives 15% commission on domestic sales; 20% commission on foreign sales. Offers written contract. Charges clients for photocopying.

RLR ASSOCIATES, LTD.

Literary Department, 7 W. 51st St., New York NY 10019. (212)541-8641. Fax: (212)541-6052. E-mail: info@rlrassociates.net. Web site: www.rlrliterary.net. **Contact:** Jennifer Unter, Tara Mark, Scott Gould. Member of AAR. Represents 50 clients. 25% of clients are new/unpublished writers. Currently handles: 70% nonfiction books; 25% novels; 5% story collections.

Represents Nonfiction books, novels, short story collections, scholarly books. **Considers these nonfiction areas:** Animals; anthropology/archaeology; art/architecture/design; biography/autobiography; business/economics; child guidance/parenting; cooking/foods/nutrition; current affairs; education; ethnic/cultural interests; gay/lesbian issues; government/politics/law; health/medicine; history; humor/satire; interior design/decorating; language/literature/criticism; memoirs; money/finance; multicultural; music/dance; nature/environment; photography; popular culture; psychology; religious/inspirational; science/technology; self-help/personal improvement; sociology; sports; translation; travel; true crime/investigative; women's issues/studies. **Considers these fiction areas:** Action/adventure; comic books/cartoon; detective/police/crime; ethnic; experimental; family saga; feminist; gay/lesbian; historical; horror; humor/satire; literary; mainstream/contemporary; multicultural; mystery/suspense; sports; thriller.

> ''We provide a lot of editorial assistance to our clients and have connections.'' Actively seeking fiction, current affairs, history, art, popular culture, health and business. Does not want to receive science fiction, fantasy, screenplays or illustrated children's stories.

How to Contact Query with SASE. Considers simultaneous queries. Responds in 4-8 weeks to queries. Returns materials only with SASE. Obtains most new clients through recommendations from others.

Recent Sales Other clients include Shelby Foote, The Grief Recovery Institute, Don Wade, Don Zimmer, The Knot.com, David Plowden, PGA of America, Danny Peary, Goerge Kalinsky, Peter Hyman, Daniel Parker, Lee Miller, Elise Miller, Nina Planck, Karyn Bosnak.

Terms Agent receives 15% commission on domestic sales; 20% commission on foreign sales. Offers written contract.

Tips ''Please check out our Web site for more details on our agency.''

B.J. ROBBINS LITERARY AGENCY

5130 Bellaire Ave., North Hollywood CA 91607-2908. (818)760-6602. E-mail: robbinsliterary@aol.com. **Contact:** (Ms.) B.J. Robbins. Estab. 1992. Member of AAR. Represents 40 clients. 50% of clients are new/unpublished writers. Currently handles: 50% nonfiction books; 50% novels.

Represents Nonfiction books, novels. **Considers these nonfiction areas:** Biography/autobiography; current affairs; ethnic/cultural interests; health/medicine; how-to; humor/satire; memoirs; music/dance; popular culture; psychology; self-help/personal improvement; sociology; sports; theater/film; travel; true crime/investigative; women's issues/studies. **Considers these fiction areas:** Detective/police/crime; ethnic; literary; mainstream/contemporary; mystery/suspense; sports; thriller.

How to Contact Query with SASE, submit outline/proposal, 3 sample chapters, SASE. Accepts e-mail queries (no attachments). No fax queries. Considers simultaneous queries. Responds in 2-6 weeks to queries; 6-8 weeks to mss. Returns materials only with SASE. Obtains most new clients through conferences, referrals.

Recent Sales Sold 15 titles in the last year. *Getting Stoned with Savages*, by J. Maarten Troost (Broadway); *Hot Water*, by Kathryn Jordan (Berkley); *Between the Bridge and the River*, by Craig Ferguson (Chronicle); *I'm Proud of You*, by Tim Madigan (Gotham); *Man of the House*, by Chris Erskine (Rodale); *Bird of Another Heaven*, by James D. Houston (Knopf); *Tomorrow They Will Kiss*, by Eduardo Santiago (Little, Brown).

Terms Agent receives 15% commission on domestic sales; 20% commission on foreign sales. Offers written contract; 3-month notice must be given to terminate contract. 100% of business is derived from commissions on ms sales. This agency charges clients for postage and photocopying (only after sale of ms).

Writers' Conferences Squaw Valley Writers Workshop; San Diego State University Writers' Conference; Santa Barbara Writers' Conference.

THE ROSENBERG GROUP

23 Lincoln Ave., Marblehead MA 01945. (781)990-1341. Fax: (781)990-1344. Web site: www.rosenberggroup.com. **Contact:** Barbara Collins Rosenberg. Estab. 1998. Member of AAR, recognized agent of the RWA. Represents

25 clients. 15% of clients are new/unpublished writers. Currently handles: 30% nonfiction books; 30% novels; 10% scholarly books; 30% college textbooks.

• Prior to becoming an agent, Ms. Rosenberg was a senior editor for Harcourt.

Represents Nonfiction books, novels, textbooks (college textbooks only). **Considers these nonfiction areas:** Current affairs; popular culture; psychology; sports; women's issues/studies; women's health; food/wine/beverages. **Considers these fiction areas:** Romance; women's.

O→ Ms. Rosenberg is well-versed in the romance market (both category and single title). She is a frequent speaker at romance conferences. Actively seeking romance category or single title in contemporary chick lit, romantic suspense, and the historical subgenres. Does not want to receive inspirational or spiritual romances.

How to Contact Query with SASE. No e-mail or fax queries. Responds in 2 weeks to queries; 4-6 weeks to mss. Returns materials only with SASE. Obtains most new clients through recommendations from others, solicitations, conferences.

Recent Sales Sold 21 titles in the last year.

Terms Agent receives 15% commission on domestic sales; 15% commission on foreign sales. Offers written contract; 1-month notice must be given to terminate contract. Charges maximum of $350/year for postage and photocopying.

Writers' Conferences RWA National Conference; BookExpo America.

RITA ROSENKRANZ LITERARY AGENCY

440 West End Ave., Suite 15D, New York NY 10024-5358. (212)873-6333. **Contact:** Rita Rosenkranz. Estab. 1990. Member of AAR. Represents 30 clients. 30% of clients are new/unpublished writers. Currently handles: 99% nonfiction books; 1% novels.

• Prior to opening her agency, Ms. Rosenkranz worked as an editor in major New York publishing houses.

Represents Nonfiction books. **Considers these nonfiction areas:** Animals; anthropology/archaeology; art/architecture/design; biography/autobiography; business/economics; child guidance/parenting; computers/electronic; cooking/foods/nutrition; crafts/hobbies; current affairs; ethnic/cultural interests; gay/lesbian issues; government/politics/law; health/medicine; history; how-to; humor/satire; interior design/decorating; language/literature/criticism; military/war; money/finance; music/dance; nature/environment; New Age/metaphysics; photography; popular culture; psychology; religious/inspirational; science/technology; self-help/personal improvement; sports; theater/film; women's issues/studies.

O→ This agency focuses on adult nonfiction, stresses strong editorial development and refinement before submitting to publishers, and brainstorms ideas with authors. Actively seeking authors who are well paired with their subject, either for professional or personal reasons.

How to Contact Submit proposal package, outline, SASE. No e-mail or fax queries. Considers simultaneous queries. Responds in 2 weeks to queries. Obtains most new clients through solicitations, conferences, word of mouth.

Recent Sales Sold 35 titles in the last year. *Forbidden Fruit: True Love Stories from the Underground Railroad*, by Betty DeRamus (Atria Books); *Business Class: Etiquette Essentials for Success at Work*, by Jacqueline Whitmore (St. Martin's Press); *Olive Trees and Honey: A Treasury of Vegetarian Recipes from Jewish Communities Around the World*, by Gil Marks (Wiley); *20 Strengths Adoptive Parents Must Discover*, by Sherrie Eldridge (Bantom Dell); *Baseball Hall of Fame Museum*, by Bert Sugar (Running Press).

Terms Agent receives 15% commission on domestic sales; 20% commission on foreign sales. Offers written contract, binding for 3 years; 3-month written notice must be given to terminate contract. 100% of business is derived from commissions on ms sales. Charges clients for photocopying. Makes referrals to editing services.

Tips "Identify the current competition for your project to make sure the project is valid. A strong cover letter is very important."

THE PETER RUBIE LITERARY AGENCY

240 W. 35th St., Suite 500, New York NY 10001. (212)279-1776. Fax: (212)279-0927. E-mail: peterrubie@prlit.com. Web site: www.prlit.com. **Contact:** Peter Rubie (peterrubie@prlit.com); June Clark (pralit@aol.com); and Amy Tipton (assist@prlit.com). Estab. 2000. Member of AAR. Represents 130 clients. 20% of clients are new/unpublished writers.

• Prior to opening his agency, Mr. Rubie authored two novels and a number of nonfiction books. He was also the fiction editor at Walker and Co. Ms. Clark is the author of several books and plays, and previously worked in cable TV marketing and promotion. Ms. Tipton is also a writer and has worked as a literary assistant and office manager at several agencies.

Member Agents Peter Rubie (crime, science fiction, fantasy, literary fiction, thrillers, narrative/serious nonfiction, business, self-help, how-to, popular, food/wine, history, commercial science, music, education, parenting); June Clark (celebrity biographies, parenting, pets, women's issues, teen nonfiction, how-to, self-help, offbeat business, food/wine, commercial New Age, pop culture, entertainment, gay/lesbian); Amy Tipton (edgy/gritty fiction, urban, women's fiction, memoir and young adult).

Represents Nonfiction books, novels. **Considers these nonfiction areas:** Business/economics; current affairs; ethnic/cultural interests; gay/lesbian issues; how-to; popular culture; science/technology; self-help/personal improvement; TV; creative nonfiction (narrative); health/nutrition; cooking/food/wine; music; theater/film; prescriptive New Age; parenting/education; pets; commercial academic material. **Considers these fiction areas:** Fantasy; historical; literary; science fiction; thriller.

How to Contact For fiction, submit short synopsis, first 30-40 pages. For nonfiction, submit 1-page overview of the book, TOC, outline, 1-2 sample chapters. Accepts e-mail queries. No fax queries. Responds in 2 months to queries; 3 months to mss. Returns materials only with SASE. Obtains most new clients through recommendations from others.

Recent Sales Sold 50 titles in the last year. *Walking Money*, by James Born (Putnam); *Atherton*, by Patrick Carman (Little, Brown); *One Nation Under God*, by James P. Moore (Doubleday); *28 Days*, by Gabrielle Lichterman (Adams); *Shattered Dreams*, by Harlan Ullman (Carroll & Graf); *Chef on Fire*, by Joseph Carey (Taylor); *Laughing with Lucy*, by Madelyn Pugh Davis (Emis); *Read My Hips*, by Eve Marx (Adams); *Black Comedians*, Black Comedy, by Darryl Littleton.

Terms Agent receives 15% commission on domestic sales; 20% commission on foreign sales. Offers written contract. Charges clients for photocopying and some foreign mailings.

Tips "We look for writers who are experts, have a strong platform and reputation in their field, and have an outstanding prose style. Be professional and open-minded. Know your market and learn your craft. Go to our Web site for up-to-date information on clients and sales."

RUSSELL & VOLKENING

50 W. 29th St., #7E, New York NY 10001. (212)684-6050. Fax: (212)889-3026. Web site: www.randvinc.com. **Contact:** Timothy Seldes, Jesseca Salky. Estab. 1940. Member of AAR. Represents 140 clients. 20% of clients are new/unpublished writers. Currently handles: 45% nonfiction books; 50% novels; 3% story collections; 2% novellas.

Represents Nonfiction books, novels, short story collections. **Considers these nonfiction areas:** Anthropology/archaeology; art/architecture/design; biography/autobiography; business/economics; cooking/foods/nutrition; current affairs; education; ethnic/cultural interests; gay/lesbian issues; government/politics/law; health/medicine; history; language/literature/criticism; military/war; money/finance; music/dance; nature/environment; photography; popular culture; psychology; science/technology; sociology; sports; theater/film; true crime/investigative; women's issues/studies; creative nonfiction. **Considers these fiction areas:** Action/adventure; detective/police/crime; ethnic; literary; mainstream/contemporary; mystery/suspense; picture books; sports; thriller.

O→ This agency specializes in literary fiction and narrative nonfiction.

How to Contact Query with SASE, submit synopsis, several pages. No e-mail or fax queries. Responds in 4 weeks to queries.

Recent Sales *Digging to America*, by Anne Tyler (Knopf); *Get a Life*, by Nadine Gardiner; *The Franklin Affair*, by Jim Lehrer (Random House).

Terms Agent receives 15% commission on domestic sales; 20% commission on foreign sales. Charges clients for standard office expenses relating to the submission of materials.

Tips "If the query is cogent, well written, well presented, and is the type of book we'd represent, we'll ask to see the manuscript. From there, it depends purely on the quality of the work."

N THE SAGALYN AGENCY

4922 Fairmont Ave., Suite 200, Bethesda MD 20814. (301)718-6440. Fax: (301)718-6444. E-mail: query@sagalyn.com. Web site: www.sagalyn.com. Estab. 1980. Member of AAR. Currently handles: 85% nonfiction books; 5% novels; 10% scholarly books.

- Prior to becoming an agent, Ms. Sagalyn worked for ICM and had her own agency in Washington, D.C.

Member Agents Raphael Sagalyn.

Represents Nonfiction books. **Considers these nonfiction areas:** Biography/autobiography; business/economics; history; memoirs; popular culture; religious/inspirational; science/technology; journalism.

O→ Does not want to receive stage plays, screenplays, poetry, science fiction, fantasy, romance, children's books or young adult books.

How to Contact Please send e-mail queries only (no attachments). Include 1 of these words in the subject line: query, submission, inquiry. Accepts e-mail queries. No fax queries.

Recent Sales *Intrinsic Motivation: The New Logic of Rewards*, by Daniel Pink (Riverhead); *Sexpertise*, by Robin Sawyer (Simon Spotlight Entertainment); see Web site for more sales information.

Tips "We receive 1,000-1,200 queries a year, which in turn lead to 2 or 3 new clients. Query via e-mail only."

VICTORIA SANDERS & ASSOCIATES

241 Avenue of the Americas, Suite 11 H, New York NY 10014. (212)633-8811. Fax: (212)633-0525. E-mail: queriesvsa@hotmail.com. Web site: www.victoriasanders.com. **Contact:** Victoria Sanders, Diane Dickensheid. Estab. 1993. Member of AAR; signatory of WGA. Represents 135 clients. 25% of clients are new/unpublished writers. Currently handles: 50% nonfiction books; 50% novels.

Represents Nonfiction books, novels. **Considers these nonfiction areas:** Biography/autobiography; current affairs; ethnic/cultural interests; gay/lesbian issues; government/politics/law; history; humor/satire; language/literature/criticism; music/dance; popular culture; psychology; theater/film; translation; women's issues/studies. **Considers these fiction areas:** Action/adventure; contemporary issues; ethnic; family saga; feminist; gay/lesbian; literary; thriller.

How to Contact Query by e-mail only.

Recent Sales Sold 20+ titles in the last year. *Faithless, Triptych & Skin Privilege*, by Karin Slaughter (Delacorte); *Jewels: 50 Phenomenal Black Women Over 50*, by Connie Briscoe and Michael Cunningham (Bulfinch); *B Mother*, by Maureen O'Brien (Harcourt); *Vagablonde*, by Kim Green (Warner); *Next Elements*, by Jeff Chang (Basic Civitas); *The Ties That Bind*, by Dr. Bertice Berry.

Terms Agent receives 15% commission on domestic sales; 20% commission on foreign sales. Offers written contract. Charges for photocopying, messenger, express mail. If in excess of $100, client approval is required.

Tips "Limit query to letter (no calls) and give it your best shot. A good query is going to get a good response."

THE SEYMOUR AGENCY

475 Miner St., Canton NY 13617. (315)386-1831. E-mail: marysue@slic.com. Web site: www.theseymouragency.com. **Contact:** Mary Sue Seymour. Estab. 1992. Member of AAR, RWA, Authors Guild; signatory of WGA. Represents 50 clients. 5% of clients are new/unpublished writers. Currently handles: 50% nonfiction books; 50% fiction.

- Ms. Seymour is a retired New York State certified teacher.

Represents Nonfiction books, novels. **Considers these nonfiction areas:** Business/economics; health/medicine; how-to; self-help/personal improvement; Christian books; cookbooks; any well-written nonfiction that includes a proposal in standard format and 1 sample chapter. **Considers these fiction areas:** Religious/inspirational (Christian books); romance (any type).

How to Contact Query with SASE, synopsis, first 50 pages for romance. Accepts e-mail queries. No fax queries. Considers simultaneous queries. Responds in 1 month to queries; 3 months to mss. Returns materials only with SASE.

Recent Sales Two romance books, by Tracy Willouer; two romance books, by Kimberly Kaye Terry; Maryanne Raphael's authorized biograohy of Mother Teresa; *Interference*, by Shelley Wernlein; *The Doctor's Daughter*, by Donna MacQuigg.

Terms Agent receives 12-15% commission on domestic sales.

Writers' Conferences BookExpo America; Start Your Engines; Romantic Times Convention; ICE Escape Writers Conference; Spring Into Romance; Silicon Valley RWA Conference; Put Your Heart in a Book; RWA National.

DENISE SHANNON LITERARY AGENCY, INC.

20 W. 22nd St., Suite 1603, New York NY 10010. (212)414-2911. Fax: (212)414-2930. E-mail: info@deniseshannonagency.com. Web site: www.deniseshannonagency.com. **Contact:** Denise Shannon. Estab. 2002. Member of AAR.

- Prior to opening her agency, Ms. Shannon worked for 16 years with Georges Borchardt and International Creative Management.

Represents Nonfiction books, novels. **Considers these nonfiction areas:** Biography/autobiography; business/economics; health/medicine; narrative nonfiction; politics; journalism; social history. **Considers these fiction areas:** Literary.

"We are a boutique agency with a distinguished list of fiction and nonfiction authors."

How to Contact Query with SASE. Submit query with description of project, bio, SASE. Accepts e-mail queries (submissions@deniseshannonagency.com).

Recent Sales *The God of Animals*, by Aryn Kyle (Scribner); *Organic, Inc.: The Marketing of Innocence*, by Samuel Fromartz (Harcourt); *Absurdistan*, by Gary Shteyngart (Random House); *The Visible World*, by Mark Slouka (Houghton Mifflin).

Tips Query to the e-mail address submissions@deniseshannonagency.com.

WENDY SHERMAN ASSOCIATES, INC.

450 Seventh Ave., Suite 2307, New York NY 10123. (212)279-9027. Fax: (212)279-8863. Web site: www.wsherman.com. **Contact:** Wendy Sherman. Estab. 1999. Member of AAR. Represents 50 clients. 30% of clients are new/unpublished writers. Currently handles: 50% nonfiction books; 50% novels.

- Prior to opening the agency, Ms. Sherman worked for The Aaron Priest agency and served as vice president, executive director, associate publisher, subsidiary rights director, and sales and marketing director in the publishing industry.

Member Agents Wendy Sherman; Michelle Brower.

Represents Nonfiction books, novels. **Considers these nonfiction areas:** Psychology; narrative; practical. **Considers these fiction areas:** Literary; women's (suspense).

O-ᴛ "We specialize in developing new writers, as well as working with more established writers. My experience as a publisher has proven to be a great asset to my clients."

How to Contact Query with SASE or send outline/proposal, 1 sample chapter. No e-mail queries. Considers simultaneous queries. Responds in 1 month to queries. Returns materials only with SASE. Obtains most new clients through recommendations from others.

Recent Sales *America's Boy: A Memoir*, by Wade Rouse; *Marked Man*, by William Lashner; *The Vanishing Point*, by Mary Sharratt; *Spooning: The Cooking Club Divas Turn Up The Heat*, by Darri Stephens and Megan DeSales; *The Kindergarten Wars: The Battle To Get Into America's Best Private Schools*, by Alan Eisenstock; *The Judas Field: A Novel Of The Civil War*, by Howard Bahr. Other clients include Fiction clients include: William Lashner, Nani Power, DW Buffa, Howard Bahr, Suzanne Chazin, Sarah Stonich, Ad Hudler, Mary Sharratt, Libby Street, Heather Estay, Darri Stephens, Megan Desales. Nonfiction clients include: Rabbi Mark Borovitz, Alan Eisenstock, Esther Perel, Clifton Leaf, Maggie Estep, Greg Baer, Martin Friedman, Lundy Bancroft, Alvin Ailey Dance, Lise Friedman, Liz Landers, Vicky Mainzer.

Terms Agent receives 15% commission on domestic sales; 20% commission on foreign sales. Offers written contract.

Tips "The bottom line is: Do your homework. Be as well prepared as possible. Read the books that will help you present yourself and your work with polish. You want your submission to stand out."

SPENCERHILL ASSOCIATES

P.O. Box 374, Chatham NY 12037. (518)392-9293. Fax: (518)392-9554. E-mail: ksolem@klsbooks.com; jennifer@klsbooks.com. **Contact:** Karen Solem or Jennifer Schober. Estab. 2001. Member of AAR. Represents 40 clients. 5% of clients are new/unpublished writers. Currently handles: 5% nonfiction books; 90% novels; 5% novellas.

- Prior to becoming an agent, Ms. Solem was editor-in-chief at HarperCollins and an associate publisher.

Member Agents Karen Solem; Jennifer Schober (new agent actively seeking clients).

Represents Nonfiction books, novels. **Considers these nonfiction areas:** Animals; religious/inspirational. **Considers these fiction areas:** Detective/police/crime; historical; mainstream/contemporary; religious/inspirational; romance; thriller.

O-ᴛ "We handle mostly commercial women's fiction, historical novels, romance (historical, contemporary, paranormal), thrillers, and mysteries. We also represent Christian fiction and nonfiction." No poetry, science fiction, juvenile, or scripts.

How to Contact Query with SASE, proposal package, outline. Responds in 1 month to queries. Returns materials only with SASE.

Recent Sales Sold 225 titles in the last year.

Terms Agent receives 15% commission on domestic sales; 20% commission on foreign sales. Offers written contract; 3-month notice must be given to terminate contract.

STEELE-PERKINS LITERARY AGENCY

26 Island Ln., Canandaigua NY 14424. (585)396-9290. Fax: (585)396-3579. E-mail: pattiesp@aol.com. **Contact:** Pattie Steele-Perkins. Member of AAR, RWA. Currently handles: 100% novels.

Represents Novels. **Considers these fiction areas:** Romance and women's, including multicultural and inspirational.

How to Contact Submit outline, 3 sample chapters, SASE. Considers simultaneous queries. Responds in 6 weeks to queries. Returns materials only with SASE. Obtains most new clients through recommendations from others, queries/solicitations.

Recent Sales This agency prefers not to share information on specific sales.

Terms Agent receives 15% commission on domestic sales. Offers written contract, binding for 1 year; 1-month notice must be given to terminate contract.

Writers' Conferences RWA National Conference; BookExpo America; CBA Convention; Romance Slam Jam.

Tips "Be patient. E-mail rather than call. Make sure what you are sending is the best it can be."

PAM STRICKLER AUTHOR MANAGEMENT

1 Water St., New Paltz NY 12561. (845)255-0061. Web site: www.pamstrickler.com. **Contact:** Pamela Dean Strickler. Member of AAR.

- Prior to opening her agency, Ms. Strickler was senior editor at Ballantine Books..

O⇁ Specializes in romance and women's fiction. Does not want to receive nonfiction or children's books.

How to Contact Query via e-mail with 1-page letter including brief plot description and first 10 pages of ms (no attachments). *No unsolicited mss.*

Recent Sales *Lady Dearing's Masquerade*, by Elena Greene (New American Library); *Her Body of Work*, by Marie Donovan (Harlequin/Blaze); *Deceived*, by Nicola Cornick (Harlequin/HQN).

N ◪ EMMA SWEENEY AGENCY, LLC

245 East 80th St., New York NY 10021. E-mail: queries@emmasweeneyagency.com; info@emmasweeneyagency.com. Web site: www.emmasweeneyagency.com. **Contact:** Eva Talmadge. Estab. 2006. Member of AAR, Women's Media Group. Represents 50 clients. 5% of clients are new/unpublished writers. Currently handles: 30% nonfiction books; 70% novels.

- Prior to becoming an agent, Ms. Sweeney was a subsidiary rights assistant at William Morrow. Since 1990, she has been a literary agent, and was most recently an agent with Harold Ober Associates.

Member Agents Emma Sweeney, president; Eva Talmadge, rights manager; Lauren Carnali, editorial assistant (lauren@emmasweeneyagency.com).

Represents Nonfiction books, novels. **Considers these nonfiction areas:** Agriculture/horticulture; animals; biography/autobiography; cooking/foods/nutrition; memoirs. **Considers these fiction areas:** Literary; mystery/suspense; thriller; women's.

O⇁ ''Please note that we specialize in quality fiction and nonfiction. Our primary areas of interest include literary and women's fiction, mysteries and thrillers, science, history, biography, memoir, religious studies and the natural sciences.'' Does not want to receive romance, Western's or screenplays.

How to Contact See Web site for submission and contact information. No snail mail queries. Accepts e-mail queries. No fax queries.

Recent Sales *Water for Elephants*, by Sara Gruen (Algonquin); *The Joy of Living*, by Yongey Mingyur Rinpoche (Harmony Books); *The River Wife*, by Jonis Agee (Random House).

Terms Agent receives 15% commission on domestic sales; 10% commission on foreign sales.

Writers' Conferences Nebraska Writers' Conference; Words and Music Festival in New Orleans.

N ◪ TESSLER LITERARY AGENCY, LLC

27 W. 20th St., Suite 1003, New York NY 10011. (212)242-0466. Fax: (212)242-2366. Web site: www.tessleragency.com. **Contact:** Michelle Tessler. Member of AAR.

- Prior to forming her own agency, Ms. Tessler worked at Carlisle & Co. (now a part of Inkwell Management). She has also worked at the William Morris Agency and the Elaine Markson Literary Agency..

O⇁ The Tessler Agency is a full-service boutique agency that represents writers of high-quality nonfiction and literary and commercial fiction.

How to Contact Submit query through Web site only.

N ◪ 2M COMMUNICATIONS, LTD.

121 W. 27 St., #601, New York NY 10001. (212)741-1509. Fax: (212)691-4460. E-mail: morel@bookhaven.com. Web site: www.2mcommunications.com. **Contact:** Madeleine Morel. Estab. 1982. Member of AAR. Represents 100 clients. 20% of clients are new/unpublished writers. Currently handles: 100% nonfiction books.

- Prior to becoming an agent, Ms. Morel worked at a publishing company.

Represents Nonfiction books. **Considers these nonfiction areas:** Biography/autobiography; child guidance/parenting; ethnic/cultural interests; health/medicine; history; self-help/personal improvement; women's issues/studies; music; cookbooks.

O⇁ This agency specializes in exclusively and non-exclusively representing professional ghost writers and collaborators. This agency's writers have penned multiple bestsellers. They work closely with other leading literary agents and editors whose high-profile authors require confidential associations.

How to Contact Query with SASE, submit outline, 3 sample chapters. Considers simultaneous queries. Responds in 1 week to queries; 1 month to mss. Obtains most new clients through recommendations from others, solicitations.

Recent Sales Sold 25 titles in the last year. *How Do You Compare?*, by Andy Williams (Penguin Putnam); *Hormone Wisdom*, by Theresa Dale (John Wiley); *Irish Dessert Cookbook*, by Margaret Johnson (Chronicle).

Terms Agent receives 15% commission on domestic sales; 20% commission on foreign sales. Offers written contract, binding for 2 years. Charges clients for postage, photocopying, long-distance calls, faxes.

N ◪ VERITAS LITERARY AGENCY

510 Sand Hill Circle, Menlo Park CA 94025. E-mail: agent@veritasliterary.com. Web site: www.veritasliterary.com. **Contact:** Katherine Boyle. Member of AAR.

Represents Nonfiction books, novels. **Considers these nonfiction areas:** Current affairs; government/politics/law; memoirs; popular culture; women's issues/studies; narrative nonfiction, art and music biography, natural history, health and wellness, psychology, serious religion (no New Age) and popular science. **Considers these fiction areas:** Contemporary and literary fiction only.

O→ Does not want to receive romance, sci-fi, poetry or children's books.

How to Contact Query with SASE. This agency prefers a short query letter with no attachments. Accepts e-mail queries. No fax queries. *Sickened* by Julie Gregory; *Hedwig and Berti,* by Frieda Arkin; *American Sideshow,* by Marc Hartzman.

WALES LITERARY AGENCY, INC.

P.O. Box 9428, Seattle WA 98109-0428. (206)284-7114. E-mail: waleslit@waleslit.com. Web site: www.waleslit.com. **Contact:** Elizabeth Wales, Josie di Bernardo. Estab. 1988. Member of AAR, Book Publishers' Northwest, Pacific Northwest Booksellers Association, PEN. Represents 65 clients. 10% of clients are new/unpublished writers. Currently handles: 60% nonfiction books; 40% novels.

- Prior to becoming an agent, Ms. Wales worked at Oxford University Press and Viking Penguin.

Member Agents Elizabeth Wales; Neal Swain.

O→ This agency specializes in narrative nonfiction and quality mainstream and literary fiction. Does not handle screenplays, children's literature, genre fiction, or most category nonfiction.

How to Contact Query with cover letter, writing sample (about 30 pages), SASE. No phone or fax queries. Prefers regular mail queries, but accepts 1-page e-mail queries with no attachments. Considers simultaneous queries. Responds in 3 weeks to queries; 6 weeks to mss. Returns materials only with SASE.

Recent Sales *Fashion Statements*, edited by Michelle Tea (Seal Press/Avalon); *The Mom and Pop Store: Minding the American Dream*, by Robert Specter (Walker Books); *The Million Dollar Chicken: How I Won the Grand Prize at the Pillsbury Bake-Off*, by Ellie Mathews (Berkley/Penguin).

Terms Agent receives 15% commission on domestic sales; 20% commission on foreign sales.

Writers' Conferences Pacific Northwest Writers Conference; Willamette Writers Conference.

Tips "We are especially interested in work that espouses a progressive cultural or political view, projects a new voice, or simply shares an important, compelling story. We also encourage writers living in the Pacific Northwest, West Coast, Alaska, and Pacific Rim countries, and writers from historically underrepresented groups, such as gay and lesbian writers and writers of color, to submit work (but does not discourage writers outside these areas). Most importantly, whether in fiction or nonfiction, the agency is looking for talented storytellers."

TED WEINSTEIN LITERARY MANAGEMENT

307 Seventh Ave., Suite 2407, Dept. GLA, New York NY 10001. Web site: www.twliterary.com. **Contact:** Ted Weinstein. Estab. 2001. Member of AAR. Represents 50 clients. 50% of clients are new/unpublished writers. Currently handles: 100% nonfiction books.

Represents Nonfiction books by a wide range of journalists, academics, and other experts. **Considers these nonfiction areas:** Biography/autobiography; business/economics; current affairs; government/politics/law; health/medicine; history; popular culture; science/technology; self-help/personal improvement; travel; lifestyle, narrative journalism, popular science.

How to Contact Please visit Web site for detailed guidelines before submitting. Accepts e-mail queries. No fax queries. Responds in 3 weeks to queries.

Terms Agent receives 15% commission on domestic sales; 20% commission on foreign sales; 20% commission on dramatic rights sales. Offers written contract, binding for 1 year. Charges clients for photocopying and express shipping.

Tips "Send e-queries only. See the Web site for guidelines."

WRITERS HOUSE

21 W. 26th St., New York NY 10010. (212)685-2400. Fax: (212)685-1781. Web site: www.writershouse.com. Estab. 1974. Member of AAR. Represents 440 clients. 50% of clients are new/unpublished writers. Currently handles: 25% nonfiction books; 40% novels; 35% juvenile books.

Member Agents Albert Zuckerman (major novels, thrillers, women's fiction, important nonfiction); Amy Berkower (major juvenile authors, women's fiction, art/decorating, psychology); Merrilee Heifetz (quality children's fiction, science fiction/fantasy, popular culture, literary fiction); Susan Cohen (juvenile/young adult fiction and nonfiction, Judaism, women's issues); Susan Ginsburg (serious and popular fiction, true crime, narrative nonfiction, personality books, cookbooks); Michele Rubin (serious nonfiction); Robin Rue (commercial fiction and nonfiction, young adult fiction); Jodi Reamer (juvenile/young adult fiction and nonfiction, adult commercial fiction, popular culture); Simon Lipskar (literary and commercial fiction, narrative nonfiction); Steven Malk (juvenile/young adult fiction and nonfiction); Dan Lazar (commercial and literary fiction, pop culture, narrative nonfiction, women's interest, memoirs, Judaica and humor); Rebecca Sherman (juvenile, young adult); Ken Wright (juvenile, young adult).

Represents Nonfiction books, novels, juvenile books. **Considers these nonfiction areas:** Animals; art/architecture/design; biography/autobiography; business/economics; child guidance/parenting; cooking/foods/nutrition; health/medicine; history; humor/satire; interior design/decorating; juvenile nonfiction; military/war; money/finance; music/dance; nature/environment; psychology; science/technology; self-help/personal improvement; theater/film; true crime/investigative; women's issues/studies. **Considers these fiction areas:** Action/adventure; contemporary issues; detective/police/crime; erotica; ethnic; family saga; fantasy; feminist; gay/lesbian; gothic; hi-lo; historical; horror; humor/satire; juvenile; literary; mainstream/contemporary; military/war; multicultural; mystery/suspense; New Age; occult; picture books; psychic/supernatural; regional; romance; science fiction; short story collections; spiritual; sports; thriller; translation; westerns/frontier; young adult; women's; cartoon.

O→ This agency specializes in all types of popular fiction and nonfiction. Does not want to receive scholarly, professional, poetry, plays, or screenplays.

How to Contact Query with SASE. No e-mail or fax queries. Responds in 1 month to queries. Obtains most new clients through recommendations from authors and editors.

Recent Sales Sold 200-300 titles in the last year. *Moneyball*, by Michael Lewis (Norton); *Cut and Run*, by Ridley Pearson (Hyperion); *Report from Ground Zero*, by Dennis Smith (Viking); *Northern Lights*, by Nora Roberts (Penguin/Putnam); Captain Underpants series, by Dav Pilkey (Scholastic); Junie B. Jones series, by Barbara Park (Random House). Other clients include Francine Pascal, Ken Follett, Stephen Hawking, Linda Howard, F. Paul Wilson, Neil Gaiman, Laurel Hamilton, V.C. Andrews, Lisa Jackson, Michael Gruber, Chris Paolini, Barbara Delinsky, Ann Martin, Bradley Trevor Greive, Erica Jong, Kyle Mills, Andrew Guess, Tim Willocks.

Terms Agent receives 15% commission on domestic sales; 20% commission on foreign sales. Offers written contract, binding for 1 year. Agency charges fees for copying mss/proposals and overseas airmail of books.

Tips "Do not send manuscripts. Write a compelling letter. If you do, we'll ask to see your work."

SUSAN ZECKENDORF ASSOC., INC.

171 W. 57th St., New York NY 10019. (212)245-2928. **Contact:** Susan Zeckendorf. Estab. 1979. Member of AAR. Represents 15 clients. 25% of clients are new/unpublished writers. Currently handles: 50% nonfiction books; 50% novels.

- Prior to opening her agency, Ms. Zeckendorf was a counseling psychologist.

Represents Nonfiction books, novels. **Considers these nonfiction areas:** Biography/autobiography; child guidance/parenting; health/medicine; history; music/dance; psychology; science/technology; sociology; women's issues/studies. **Considers these fiction areas:** Detective/police/crime; ethnic; historical; literary; mainstream/contemporary; mystery/suspense; thriller.

O→ Actively seeking mysteries, literary fiction, mainstream fiction, thrillers, social history, parenting, classical music, and biography. Does not want to receive science fiction, romance, or children's books.

How to Contact Query with SASE. No e-mail or fax queries. Considers simultaneous queries. Responds in 10 days to queries; 3 weeks to mss. Returns materials only with SASE.

Recent Sales *How to Write a Damn Good Mystery*, by James N. Frey (St. Martin's Press); *The Handscrabble Chronicles* (Berkley); *Haunted Heart: A Biography of Susannah McCorkle*, by Linda Dahl (University of Michigan Press); *Garden of Aloes*, by Gayle Jandrey (Permanent Press).

Terms Agent receives 15% commission on domestic sales; 20% commission on foreign sales. Charges for photocopying and messenger services.

Writers' Conferences Frontiers in Writing Conference; Oklahoma Festival of Books.

Tips "We are a small agency giving lots of individual attention. We respond quickly to submissions."

MARKETS

Book Publishers

The markets in this year's Book Publishers section offer opportunities in nearly every area of publishing. Large, commercial houses are here as are their smaller counterparts.

The **Book Publishers Subject Index** on page 1065 is the best place to start your search. You'll find it in the back of the book, before the General Index. Subject areas for both fiction and nonfiction are broken out for all of the book publisher listings, including Canadian publishers and small presses.

When you have compiled a list of publishers interested in books in your subject area, read the detailed listings. Pare down your list by cross-referencing two or three subject areas and eliminating the listings only marginally suited to your book. When you have a good list, send for those publishers' catalogs and manuscript guidelines, or check publishers' Web sites, which often contain catalog listings, manuscript preparation guidelines, current contact names, and other information helpful to prospective authors. You want to use this information to make sure your book idea is in line with a publisher's list but is not a duplicate of something already published.

You should also visit bookstores and libraries to see if the publisher's books are well represented. When you find a couple of books the house has published that are similar to yours, write or call the company to find out who edited those books. This extra bit of research could be the key to getting your proposal to precisely the right editor.

Publishers prefer different methods of submission on first contact. Most like to see a one-page query with SASE, especially for nonfiction. Others will accept a brief proposal package that might include an outline and/or a sample chapter. Some publishers will accept submissions from agents only. Each listing in the Book Publishers section includes specific submission methods, if provided by the publisher. Make sure you read each listing carefully to find out exactly what the publisher wants to receive.

When you write your one-page query, give an overview of your book, mention the intended audience, the competition for your book (check local bookstore shelves), and what sets your book apart from the competition. You should also include any previous publishing experience or special training relevant to the subject of your book. For more on queries, read "Query Letter Clinic" on page 20.

Personalize your query by addressing the editor individually and mentioning what you know about the company from its catalog or books. Never send a form letter as a query. Envelopes addressed to "Editor" or "Editorial Department" end up in the dreaded slush pile. Under the heading **Acquisitions**, we list the names of editors who acquire new books for each company, along with the editors' specific areas of expertise. Try your best to send your query to the appropriate editor. Editors move around all the time, so it's in your best interest to look online or call the publishing house to make sure the editor you are addressing your query to is still employed by that publisher.

Author-subsidy publishers' not included

Writer's Market is a reference tool to help you sell your writing, and we encourage you to work with publishers that pay a royalty. Subsidy publishing involves paying money to a publishing house to publish a book. The source of the money could be a government, foundation or university grant, or it could be the author of the book. If one of the publishers listed in this book offers you an author-subsidy arrangement (sometimes called "cooperative publishing," "co-publishing," or "joint venture"); or asks you to pay for part or all of the cost of any aspect of publishing (editing services, manuscript critiques, printing, advertising, etc.); or asks you to guarantee the purchase of any number of the books yourself, we would like you to inform us of that company's practices immediately.

INFORMATION AT-A-GLANCE

There are a number of icons at the beginning of each listing to quickly convey certain information. In the Book Publisher sections, these icons identify new listings (N), Canadian markets ( ), publishers that accept agented submissions only (A), and publishers who do not accept unsolicited manuscripts ( ). Different sections of *Writer's Market* include other symbols; check the back inside cover for an explanation of all the symbols used throughout the book.

How much money? What are my odds?

We've also highlighted important information in boldface, the "quick facts" you won't find in any other market guide but should know before you submit your work. These items include: how many manuscripts a publisher buys per year; how many manuscripts from first-time authors; how many manuscripts from unagented writers; the royalty rate a publisher pays; and how large an advance is offered. Standard royalty rates for paperbacks generally range from 7½ to 12½ percent, and from 10 to 15 percent for hardcovers . Royalty rates for children's books are often lower, generally ranging from 5 to 10 percent; 10 percent for picture books (split between the author and the illustrator).

Publishers, their imprints, and how they are related

In this era of big publishing—and big mergers—the world of publishing has grown even more intertwined. A "family tree" on page 79 lists the imprints and divisions of the largest conglomerate publishers.

Keep in mind that most of the major publishers listed in this family tree do not accept unagented submissions or unsolicited manuscripts. You will find many of these publishers and their imprints listed within the Book Publishers section, and many contain only basic contact information. If you are interested in pursuing any of these publishers, we advise you to see each publisher's Web site for more information.

For a list of publishers according to their subjects of interest, see the Nonfiction and Fiction sections of the Book Publishers Subject Index. Information on book publishers listed in the previous edition of *Writer's Market*, but not included in this edition, can be found in the General Index.

A.D. BANKER & CO., LLC

5000 College Blvd., #120, Overland Park KS 66211-1629. (800)866-2468. Fax: (913)451-1214. E-mail: curriculum@mail.adbanker.com. Web site: www.adbanker.com. **Acquisitions:** Janet Hensley, product development manager; Michelle Jain, course developer. Estab. 1978. Publishes trade paperback and electronic originals and reprints. **Publishes 95 titles/year. Receives 20 queries and 5 mss/year. 90% of books from first-time authors; 90% from unagented writers. Pays 10% royalty on retail price.** Publishes book 6 months after acceptance of ms. Accepts simultaneous submissions. Responds in 1 month to queries; 1 month to proposals; 1 month to mss. Book catalog and ms guidelines free.

Nonfiction Technical, textbook. Subjects include accounting, insurance, investment, retirement, securities. "We need comprehensive texts on any insurance topic, including annuities, life insurance, estate and financial planning, excess and surplus lines, living trusts, long term care, managed care, Medicare supplements, qualified plans, retirement planning, Social Security, risk management, professional liability, and personal and commercial lines." Submit proposal package including outline, 1 sample chapter(s), author bio, or submit complete ms. Reviews artwork/photos as part of ms package. Send photocopies or e-copies.

Recent Title(s) *California Property and Casualty Study Manual, 2005 Ed.*, by Ken Scheneman; *North Carolina Life and Health Study Manual, 2005 Ed.*, by Ken Scheneman and Michelle Jain.

Tips "Our target audience consists of licensed professionals and trainees in occupations that have entrance exams, licensing or continuing education requirements, including the accounting, insurance, law, and investment securities industries. All of our demand is for texts that can be approved for credit. Manuscripts must have at least 100 pages and 75 multiple choice questions to receive credit. Our editors will help writers improve promising completed submissions."

⊘ ABDO PUBLISHING CO.

8000 W. 78th St., Suite 310, Edina MN 55439. (800)800-1312. Fax: (952)831-1632. E-mail: info@abdopub.com. Web site: www.abdopub.com. **Acquisitions:** Paul Abdo, editor-in-chief. Estab. 1985. Publishes hardcover originals. **Publishes 300 titles/year.**

Imprints ABDO & Daughters; Buddy Books; Checkerboard Library; SandCastle.

- *No unsolicited mss.*
- O→ ABDO publishes nonfiction children's books (pre-kindergarten to 8th grade) for school and public libraries—mainly history, sports, biography, geography, science, and social studies.

Nonfiction Biography, children's/juvenile, how-to. Subjects include animals, history, science, sports, geography, social studies. Submit résumé to pabdo@abdopub.com.

Recent Title(s) *Lewis and Clark*, by John Hamilton (children's nonfiction); *Tiger Woods*, by Paul Joseph (children's biography).

ABI PROFESSIONAL PUBLICATIONS

P.O. Box 17446, Clearwater FL 33762. (727)556-0950. Fax: (727)556-2560. Web site: www.abipropub.com. **Acquisitions:** Art Brown, publisher/editor-in-chief (prosthetics, rehabilitation, dental/medical research). Publishes hardcover and trade paperback originals. **Publishes 10 titles/year. Receives 20-30 queries and 5-10 mss/year. 25% of books from first-time authors; 100% from unagented writers. Pays royalty on revenues generated. Offers small advance.** Publishes book 1+ years after acceptance of ms. Accepts simultaneous submissions. Responds in 6 months to queries.

- No registered, certified, return-receipt submissions accepted.

Nonfiction Reference, technical, textbook. Subjects include health/medicine. Submit proposal package including outline, representative sample chapter(s), author bio, or submit complete ms. Reviews artwork/photos as part of ms package. Send photocopies.

Recent Title(s) *Managing Spinal Cord Injury*, by Suzanne L. Groah.

Tips Audience is allied health professionals, dentists, researchers, patients undergoing physical rehabilitation. "We will not review electronic submissions."

ABINGDON PRESS

Imprint of The United Methodist Publishing House, 201 Eighth Ave. S., Nashville TN 37203. (615)749-6000. Fax: (615)749-6512. Web site: www.abingdonpress.com. President/Publisher: Neil M. Alexander. Senior Vice President/Publishing: Harriett Jane Olson. **Acquisitions:** Robert Ratcliff, senior editor (professional clergy and academic); Judy Newman St. John (children's); Ron Kidd, senior editor (general interest). Estab. 1789. Publishes hardcover and paperback originals; church supplies. **Publishes 120 titles/year. Receives 3,000 queries and 250 mss/year. Small% of books from first-time authors; 85% from unagented writers. Pays 7½% royalty on retail price.** Publishes book 2 years after acceptance of ms. Does not accept simultaneous submissions. Responds in 2 months to queries. Book catalog free; ms guidelines online.

Imprints Dimensions for Living; Cokesbury; Abingdon Press.

O-π Abingdon Press, America's oldest theological publisher, provides an ecumenical publishing program dedicated to serving the Christian community—clergy, scholars, church leaders, musicians, and general readers—with quality resources in the areas of Bible study, the practice of ministry, theology, devotion, spirituality, inspiration, prayer, music and worship, reference, Christian education, and church supplies.

Nonfiction Children's/juvenile, gift book, reference, textbook, religious-lay, and professional, scholarly. Subjects include education, religion, theology. Query with outline and samples only.

Recent Title(s) *A History of Preaching*, by Edwards; *Global Bible Commentary*, edited by Patte; *Sanctuary*, by Stevens.

HARRY N. ABRAMS, INC.

Subsidiary of La Martiniere Groupe, 115 W. 18th St., New York NY 10011. (212)206-7715. Fax: (212)645-8437. E-mail: submissions@abramsbooks.com. Web site: www.abramsbooks.com. **Acquisitions:** Managing Editor. Estab. 1949. Publishes hardcover and "a few" paperback originals. **Publishes 250 titles/year.** Does not accept simultaneous submissions. Responds in 6 months (if interested) to queries.

O-π "We publish *only* high-quality illustrated art books, i.e., art, art history, museum exhibition catalogs, written by specialists and scholars in the field."

Nonfiction Illustrated book. Subjects include art/architecture, nature/environment, recreation (outdoor). Requires illustrated material for art and art history, museums. Submit queries, proposals, and mss via mail with SASE. No e-mail submissions. Reviews artwork/photos as part of ms package.

Recent Title(s) *1001 Reasons to Love Horses*, by Sheri Seggerman and Mary Tiegreen; *About NYC*, by Joanne Dugan; *Mother Teresa: A Life of Dedication*, by Raghu Rai.

Tips "We are one of the few publishers who publish almost exclusively illustrated books. We consider ourselves the leading publishers of art books and high-quality artwork in the U.S. Once the author has signed a contract to write a book for our firm the author must finish the manuscript to agreed-upon high standards within the schedule agreed upon in the contract."

ABSEY & CO.

23011 Northcrest Dr., Spring TX 77389. (281)257-2340. Fax: (281)251-4676. E-mail: abseyandco@aol.com. Web site: www.absey.com. **Acquisitions:** Edward Wilson, editor-in-chief. New York Offices: 45 W. 21st St., Suite 5A, New York NY 10010. Publishes hardcover, trade paperback, and mass market paperback originals. **Publishes 6-10 titles/year. 50% of books from first-time authors; 50% from unagented writers. Royalty and advance vary.** Publishes book 1 year after acceptance of ms. Does not accept simultaneous submissions. Responds in 3 months to queries; 9 months to mss. Ms guidelines online.

O-π "Our goal is to publish original, creative works of literary merit." Currently emphasizing educational, young adult literature. De-emphasizing self-help.

Nonfiction Subjects include education, language/literature (language arts), general nonfiction. "We will not open anything without a return address. All submissions sent without return or insufficient postage are discarded." Query with SASE.

Fiction Juvenile, mainstream/contemporary, short story collections. "Since we are a small, new press, we are looking for book-length manuscripts with a firm intended audience." Query with SASE.

Poetry Publishes the Writers and Young Writers Series. Interested in thematic poetry collections of literary merit. Query.

Recent Title(s) *Saving the Scrolls*, by Mary Kerry; *Where I'm From*, by George Ella Lyon (poetry); *Regular Lu*, by Robin Nelson.

Tips "We work closely and attentively with authors and their work." Does not download mss or accept e-mail submissions.

ACADEMY CHICAGO PUBLISHERS

363 W. Erie St., Suite 7E., Chicago IL 60610-3125. (312)751-7300. Fax: (312)751-7306. E-mail: info@academychicago.com. Web site: www.academychicago.com. **Acquisitions:** Anita Miller, editorial director/senior editor. Estab. 1975. Publishes hardcover and some paperback originals and trade paperback reprints. **Publishes 10 titles/year. Pays 7-10% royalty on wholesale price.** Publishes book 18 months after acceptance of ms. Book catalog and ms guidelines online.

O-π "We publish quality fiction and nonfiction. Our audience is literate and discriminating. No novelized biography, history, or science fiction."

Nonfiction Biography. Subjects include history, travel. No religion or self-help. Submit proposal package including outline, author bio, 3 sample chapters.

Fiction Historical, mainstream/contemporary, military/war, mystery. "We look for quality work, but we do not publish experimental, avant garde novels." Submit proposal package including synopsis, 3 sample chapters.

Tips "At the moment, we are looking for good nonfiction; we certainly want excellent original fiction, but we are swamped. No fax queries, no disks. No electronic submissions. We are always interested in reprinting good out-of-print books."

ACE SCIENCE FICTION AND FANTASY

Imprint of The Berkley Publishing Group, Penguin Group (USA), Inc., 375 Hudson St., New York NY 10014. (212)366-2000. Web site: www.penguin.com. **Acquisitions:** Anne Sowards, editor; Jessica Webb, editorial assistant. Estab. 1953. Publishes hardcover, paperback, and trade paperback originals and reprints. **Publishes 75 titles/year. Pays royalty. Offers advance.** Publishes book 1-2 years after acceptance of ms. Does not accept simultaneous submissions. Responds in 2 months to queries; 6 months to mss. Ms guidelines for #10 SASE.

O→ Ace publishes science fiction and fantasy exclusively.

Fiction Fantasy, science fiction. No other genre accepted. No short stories. Query first with SASE.

Recent Title(s) *Od Magic*, by Patricia A. McKillip; *Accelerando*, by Charles Stross.

N ACTA PUBLICATIONS

5559 W. Howard St., Skokie IL 60077. (847)676-2282. Fax: (847)676-2287. E-mail: acta@actapublications.com. Web site: www.actapublications.com. **Acquisitions:** Andrew Yankech. Estab. 1958. Publishes trade paperback originals. **Publishes 12 titles/year. Receives 100 queries and 25 mss/year. 50% of books from first-time authors; 90% from unagented writers. Pays 10-12% royalty on wholesale price.** Publishes book 1 year after acceptance of ms. Does not accept simultaneous submissions. Responds in 1 month to proposals. Book catalog and ms guidelines available online or with #10 SASE.

O→ ACTA publishes nonacademic, practical books aimed at the mainline religious market.

Nonfiction Self-help. Subjects include religion, spirituality. Submit outline, 1 sample chapter. Reviews artwork/photos as part of ms package. Send photocopies.

Recent Title(s) *Three Saints*, by Joan Williams (history/women's spirituality); *Running Into the Arms of God*, by Patrick Hannon (inspirational/spirituality); *Now What Did I Do?*, by Lynn Cassella-Kapusinski (self-help/family).

Tips "Don't send a submission unless you have examinedour catalog or several of our books."

ADAMS MEDIA

Division of F+W Publications, Inc., 57 Littlefield St., Avon MA 02322. (508)427-7100. Fax: (800)872-5628. E-mail: submissions@adamsmedia.com. Web site: www.adamsmedia.com. **Acquisitions:** Gary M. Krebs, executive publishing director; Paula Munier, director of product development; Jill Alexander, senior editor; Jennifer Kushnier, editor. Estab. 1980. Publishes hardcover originals, trade paperback originals and reprints. **Publishes 230 titles/year. Receives 5,000 queries and 1,500 mss/year. 40% of books from first-time authors; 40% from unagented writers. Pays standard royalty or makes outright purchase. Offers variable advance.** Publishes book 12-18 months after acceptance of ms. Accepts simultaneous submissions. Responds in 3 months to queries. Ms guidelines online.

O→ Adams Media publishes commercial nonfiction, including self-help, inspiration, women's issues, pop psychology, relationships, business, careers, parenting, New Age, gift books, cookbooks, how-to, reference. Does not return unsolicited materials. Does not accept electronic submissions.

Recent Title(s) *The List*; *The DNA of Leadership*; *Dieting Sucks.*

ADAMS-BLAKE PUBLISHING

8041 Sierra St., #102, Fair Oaks CA 95628. (916)962-9296. Web site: www.adams-blake.com. Vice President: Paul Raymond. **Acquisitions:** Monica Blane, senior editor. Estab. 1992. Publishes trade paperback originals and reprints. **Publishes 10-15 titles/year. Receives 150 queries and 90 mss/year. 90% of books from first-time authors; 90% from unagented writers. Pays 10% royalty on wholesale price.** Publishes book 6 months after acceptance of ms. Accepts simultaneous submissions. Responds in 3 months to mss. Ms guidelines online.

O→ Adams-Blake Publishing is looking for business, technology, and finance titles, as well as data that can be bound/packaged and sold to specific industry groups at high margins. "We publish technical and training material we can sell to the corporate market. We are especially looking for 'high ticket' items that sell to the corporate market for prices between $100-300." Currently emphasizing technical, computers, technology. De-emphasizing business, management.

Nonfiction How-to, technical. Subjects include business/economics, computers/electronic, health/medicine, money/finance, software. Query with sample chapters or complete ms. Reviews artwork/photos as part of ms package. Send photocopies.

Recent Title(s) *Computer Money*, by Alan N. Canton; *Success From Home! The Word Processing Business*, by Diana Ennen.

Tips "We will take a chance on material the big houses reject. Since we sell the majority of our material directly, we can publish material for a very select market. This year we seek niche market material that we can Docutech and sell direct to the corporate sector. Author should include a marketing plan. Sell us on the project!''

AERONAUTICAL PUBLISHERS

1 Oakglade Circle, Hummelstown PA 17036-9525. (717)566-0468. Fax: (717)566-6423. E-mail: possibilitypress@aol.com. Web site: www.aeronauticalpublishers.com. **Acquisitions:** Mike Markowski, publisher; Marjie Markowski, editor-in-chief. Estab. 1981. Publishes trade paperback originals. **Pays variable royalty.** Responds in 2 months to queries. Ms guidelines online.

Imprints American Aeronautical Archives, Aviation Publishers.

O‒ ''Our mission is to help people learn more about aviation and model aviation through the written word.''

Nonfiction How-to, technical, general. Subjects include history (aviation), hobbies, recreation, radio control, free flight, indoor models, micro radio control, homebuilt aircraft, ultralights, and hang gliders. Prefers submission by mail. Include SASE.

Recent Title(s) *Flying Models*, by Don Ross; *Those Magnificent Fast Flying Machines*, by C.B. Hayward.

Tips ''Our focus is on books of short to medium length that will serve the emerging needs of the hobby. We also want to help youth get started, while enhancing everyone's enjoyment of the hobby. We are looking for authors that are passionate about the hobby, and will champion the messages of their books.''

ALASKA NORTHWEST BOOKS

Graphic Arts Center Publishing, P.O. Box 10306, Portland OR 97296-0306. (503)226-2402. Fax: (503)223-1410. Web site: www.gacpc.com. **Acquisitions:** Tim Frew, executive editor. Estab. 1959. Publishes hardcover and trade paperback originals and reprints. **Publishes 12 titles/year. 10% of books from first-time authors; 90% from unagented writers. Pays 10-14% royalty on net revenues. Buys mss outright (rarely). Offers advance.** Publishes book an average of 2 years after acceptance of ms. Accepts simultaneous submissions. Responds in 6 months to queries. Book catalog for 9×12 SAE with 6 first-class stamps; ms guidelines online.

Nonfiction Children's/juvenile, cookbook. Subjects include nature/environment, recreation, sports, travel, Native American culture, adventure, the arts. ''All written for a general readership, not for experts in the subject.'' Submit outline, sample chapter(s).

Recent Title(s) *The Winterlake Lodge Cookbook: Culinary Adventures in the Wilderness*; *Portrait of the Alaska Railroad*; *Big-Enough Anna: The Little Sled Dog Who Braved the Arctic* (children's book).

Tips ''Book proposals that are professionally written and polished with a clear understanding of the market, receive our most careful consideration. We are looking for originality. We publish a wide range of books for a wide audience. Some of our books are clearly for travelers, others for those interested in outdoor recreation or various regional subjects. If I were a writer trying to market a book today, I would research the competition (existing books) for what I have in mind, and clearly (and concisely) express why my idea is different and better. I would describe the book buyers (and readers)—where they are, how many of them are there, how they can be reached (organizations, publications), why they would want or need my book.''

ALEXANDER BOOKS

Imprint of Creativity, Inc., 65 Macedonia Rd., Alexander NC 28701. (828)252-9515. Fax: (828)255-8719. E-mail: pat@abooks.com. Web site: www.abooks.com. **Acquisitions:** Editor. Publishes hardcover originals, and trade paperback originals and reprints. **Pays royalty on net receipts.** Book catalog and ms guidelines online.

Imprints Farthest Star (science fiction from established professionals only); Mountain Church (Christian books from a mainly Protestant viewpoint); Blue/Gray Books (American Civil War); Elephant Books (cookbooks, books about elephants); Worldcomm (genealogical reference, how-to of all types); Land of the Sky (books about Asheville, North Carolina and the surrounding Southern Mountains).

- No e-mail or phone submissions.

O‒ Alexander Books publishes mostly nonfiction national titles, both new and reprints.

Nonfiction Biography, how-to, reference, self-help. Subjects include computers/electronic, government/politics, history, regional, religion, travel, collectibles. ''We are interested in large, niche markets.'' Query, or submit 3 sample chapters and proposal package, including marketing plans with SASE. Reviews artwork/photos as part of ms package. Send photocopies.

Fiction ''Unless you are a big name, do not submit.'' Query with SASE, or submit synopsis, 3 sample chapters.

Recent Title(s) *Sanders Price Guide to Autographs, 5th Ed.*, by Sanders and Roberts; *Birthright*, by Mike Resnick.

Tips ''Send well-proofed manuscripts in final form. We will not read first rough drafts. Know your market.''

ALGONQUIN BOOKS OF CHAPEL HILL

Workman Publishing, P.O. Box 2225, Chapel Hill NC 27515-2225. (919)967-0108. Web site: www.algonquin.com. **Acquisitions:** Editorial Department. Publishes hardcover originals. **Publishes 24 titles/year.** query by mail before submitting work. No phone, e-mail or fax queries or submissions. Visit our Web site for full submission policy to queries. Ms guidelines online.

O→ Algonquin Books publishes quality literary fiction and literary nonfiction.

ALGORA PUBLISHING

222 Riverside Dr., 16th Floor, New York NY 10025-6809. (212)678-0232. Fax: (212)666-3682. E-mail: editors@algora.com. Web site: www.algora.com. **Acquisitions:** Martin DeMers, editor (sociology/philosophy/economics); Claudiu A. Secara, publisher (philosophy/international affairs). Publishes hardcover and trade paperback originals and reprints. **Publishes 25 titles/year. Receives 1,500 queries and 800 mss/year. 20% of books from first-time authors; 85% from unagented writers. Pays 7-12% royalty on net receipts. Offers $0-1,000 advance.** Publishes book 10-18 months after acceptance of ms. Accepts simultaneous submissions. Responds in 1-2 months to queries; 1-2 months to proposals; 2-3 months to mss. Book catalog and ms guidelines online.

O→ Algora Publishing is an academic-type press, focusing on works by North and South American, European, Asian, and African authors for the educated general reader.

Nonfiction General nonfiction for the educated reader. Subjects include anthropology/archeology, creative nonfiction, education, government/politics, history, language/literature, military/war, money/finance, music/dance, nature/environment, philosophy, psychology, religion, science, sociology, translation, women's issues/studies, economics. Query by e-mail (preferred) or submit proposal package including outline, 3 sample chapters or complete ms.

Recent Title(s) *Washington Diplomacy*, by John Shaw (international politics); *The Case for the Living Wage*, by Jerold Waltman (political economy); *Electoral Laws and Their Political Consequences*, by Bernard Grofman and Arend Lijphart (political science).

Tips "We welcome first-time writers; we help craft an author's raw manuscript into a literary work."

ALLWORTH PRESS

10 E. 23rd St., Suite 510, New York NY 10010-4402. Fax: (212)777-8261. E-mail: pub@allworth.com. Web site: www.allworth.com. Publisher: Tad Crawford. **Acquisitions:** Nicole Potter-Talling, senior editor. Estab. 1989. Publishes hardcover and trade paperback originals. **Publishes 36-40 titles/year. Offers advance.** Does not accept simultaneous submissions. Responds in 1 month to queries; 2 months to proposals. Book catalog and ms guidelines free.

O→ Allworth Press publishes business and self-help information for artists, designers, photographers, authors and film and performing artists, as well as books about business, money and the law for the general public. The press also publishes the best of classic and contemporary writing in art and graphic design. Currently emphasizing photography, graphic & industrial design, performing arts, fine arts and crafts, et al.

Nonfiction How-to, reference. Subjects include art/architecture, business/economics, film/cinema/stage, music/dance, photography, film, television, graphic design, performing arts, writing, as well as business and legal guides for the public. Query.

Recent Title(s) *Business & Legal Forms for Fine Artists, 3rd Ed.*, by Tad Crawford; *Letters From Backstage*, by Michael Kostroff; *Profitable Photography in the Digital Age*, by Dan Heller.

Tips "We are trying to give ordinary people advice to better themselves in practical ways—as well as helping creative people in the fine and commercial arts."

ALTHOS PUBLISHING

404 Wake Chapel Rd., Fuquay-Varina NC 27526-1936. (919)557-2260. Fax: (919)557-2261. E-mail: info@althos.com. Web site: www.althos.com. Publisher: Lawrence Harte. **Acquisitions:** Karen Bunn. Publishes hardcover and trade paperback originals. **Publishes 50 titles/year. Receives 200 queries/year. Pays 10% royalty on sales.** Publishes book 1-3 months after acceptance of ms. Responds in 3 months to proposals; 6 months to mss. Book catalog online; ms guidelines free.

O→ Althos publishes books that solve problems, reduce cost, or save time.

Nonfiction Textbook. Subjects include telecommunications. Query with SASE. Reviews artwork/photos as part of ms package. Send photocopies.

AMACOM BOOKS

American Management Association, 1601 Broadway, New York NY 10019-7406. (212)586-8100. Fax: (212)903-8168. Web site: www.amanet.org; www.amacombooks.org. President and Publisher: Hank Kennedy. **Acquisitions:** Adrienne Hickey, editor-in-chief (management, human resources, leadership, organizational development, strategic planning); Ellen Kadin, executive editor (marketing, customer service, careers, manufacturing, communication skills); Jacquie Flynn, executive editor (training, science, technology, self-help, finance); Christina Parisi, senior acquisitions editor (real estate, project management, sales, supply chain management). Estab. 1923. Publishes hardcover and trade paperback originals, professional books.

O→ AMACOM is the publishing arm of the American Management Association, the world's largest training organization for managers and their organizations. AMACOM books are intended to enhance readers' personal and professional growth, and to help readers meet the challenges of the future by conveying emerging trends and cutting-edge thinking.

Nonfiction Self-help. Subjects include business/economics, science, current affairs. Publishes books for consumer and professional markets, including general business, management, strategic planning, human resources, manufacturing, project management, training, finance, sales, marketing, customer service, career, technology applications, history, real estate, parenting, communications and biography. Submit proposals including brief book description and rationale, TOC, author bio, intended audience, competing books and sample chapters. Proposals returned with SASE only.

Recent Title(s) *The 7 Hidden Reasons Employees Leave*, by Leigh Brannam; *The Power of Charm*, by Brian Tracy; *The Nature of Leadership*, by B. Joseph White.

AMBER BOOKS PUBLISHING

Imprint of Amber Communications Group, Inc., 1334 E. Chandler Blvd., Suite 5-D67, Phoenix AZ 85048. (480)460-1660. E-mail: amberbk@aol.com. Web site: www.amberbooks.com. **Acquisitions:** Tony Rose, publisher. Estab. 1998. Publishes trade paperback and mass market paperback originals. Book catalog free or online.

Imprints Busta Books (celebrity bio); Amber/Wiley (personal finance, beauty); Colossus Books (personalities, history-making topics); Ambrosia Books (nonfiction, fiction, novels, docu-dramas).

O→ "Amber Books is the nation's largest African-American publisher of self-help and Career Guide books."

Nonfiction Biography (celebrity), children's/juvenile, how-to, self-help, Career Guides. Subjects include fashion/beauty, multicultural, personal finance, relationship advice. Submit proposal or outline with author biography. Please do not e-mail or mail mss unless requested by publisher. Reviews artwork/photos as part of ms package. Send photocopies.

Fiction Historic docudramas. Wants African-American topics and interest. Submit proposal or outline with author biography. Please do not e-mail or mail mss unless requested by publisher. Reviews artwork/photos as part if ms package. Send photocopies.

Recent Title(s) *101 Real Money Questions*, by Jesse B. Brown; *The African-American Women's Guide to Successful Make-Up and Skin Care*, by Alfred Fornay (revised); *The Jennifer Lopez Story*, by Stacy-Deanne.

Tips "The goal of Amber Books is to expand our catalog comprised of self-help books, and celebrity bio books; and expand our fiction department in print and on software, which pertain to, about, and for the African-American population."

AMERICA WEST PUBLISHERS

P.O. Box 2208, Carson City NV 89702-2208. (775)885-0700. Fax: (877)726-2632. E-mail: global@nohoax.com. Web site: www.nohoax.com. **Acquisitions:** George Green, president. Estab. 1985. Publishes hardcover and trade paperback originals and reprints. **Publishes 20 titles/year. 90% of books from first-time authors; 90% from unagented writers. Pays 10% royalty on wholesale price. Offers $300 average advance.** Publishes book 6 months after acceptance of ms. Accepts simultaneous submissions. Responds in 1 month to queries. Book catalog and ms guidelines free.

Imprints Bridger House Publishers, Inc.

O→ America West seeks the "other side of the picture," political cover-ups, and new health alternatives.

Nonfiction Subjects include business/economics, government/politics, health/medicine (holistic self-help), New Age, UFO-metaphysical. Submit outline, sample chapter(s). Reviews artwork/photos as part of ms package.

Recent Title(s) *Day of Deception*, by William Thomas.

Tips "We currently have materials in all bookstores that have areas of UFOs; also political and economic nonfiction."

AMERICAN ATHEIST PRESS

P.O. Box 5733, Parsippany NJ 07054-6733. (908)276-7300. Fax: (908)276-7402. E-mail: editor@atheists.org. Web site: www.atheists.org. **Acquisitions:** Frank Zindler, editor. Estab. 1963. Publishes trade paperback originals and reprints. Publishes monthly journal, *American Atheist*, for which articles of interest to Atheists are needed. **Publishes 12 titles/year. 40-50% of books from first-time authors; 100% from unagented writers. Pays 5-10% royalty on retail price.** Publishes book within 2 years after acceptance of ms. Accepts simultaneous submissions. Responds in 4 months to queries. Book catalog for $6^1/_2 \times 9^1/_2$ SAE; ms guidelines for 9×12 SAE.

Imprints Gustav Broukal Press.

"We are interested in books that will help atheists gain a deeper understanding of atheism, improve their ability to critique religious propaganda, and assist them in fighting to maintain the 'wall of separation between state and church.' " Currently emphasizing the politics of religion, science and religion. De-emphasizing Biblical criticism (but still doing some).

Nonfiction Biography, general nonfiction, reference, general. Subjects include government/politics, history (of religion and Atheism, of the effects of religion historically), philosophy (from an Atheist perspective, particularly criticism of religion), religion, Atheism (particularly the lifestyle of Atheism; the history of Atheism; applications of Atheism). "We would like to see more submissions dealing with the histories of specific religious sects, such as the L.D.S., the Worldwide Church of God, etc." Submit outline, sample chapter(s). Reviews artwork/photos as part of ms package.

Fiction Humor (satire of religion or of current religious leaders), anything of particular interest to Atheists. "We rarely publish any fiction. But we have occasionally released a humorous book. No mainstream. For our press to consider fiction, it would have to tie in with the general focus of our press, which is the promotion of Atheism and free thought." Submit outline, sample chapter(s).

Recent Title(s) *Living in the Light: Freeing Your Child from the Dark Ages*, by Anne Stone (rearing Atheist children); *The Jesus the Jews Never Knew (Against the Historicity of Jesus)*, by Frank R. Zindler; *Illustrated Stories From the Bible (That They Won't Tell You in Sunday School)*, by Paul Farrell.

Tips "We will need more how-to types of material—how to argue with creationists, how to fight for state/church separation, etc. We have an urgent need for literature for young Atheists."

AMERICAN BAR ASSOCIATION PUBLISHING

321 N. Clark St., Chicago IL 60610. (312)988-5000. Fax: (312)988-6030. Web site: www.ababooks.org. **Acquisitions:** Kathleen A. Welton, director book publishing. Estab. 1878. Publishes hardcover and trade paperback originals. **Publishes 100 titles/year. Receives 50 queries/year. 20% of books from first-time authors; 95% from unagented writers. Pays 5-15% royalty on net receipts.** Publishes book 6 months after acceptance of ms. Accepts simultaneous submissions. Responds in 1 month to queries; 1 month to proposals; 3 months to mss. Book catalog and ms guidelines online.

"We are interested in books that help lawyers practice law more effectively, whether it's help in handling clients, structuring a real estate deal, or taking an antitrust case to court."

Nonfiction All areas of legal practice. How-to (in the legal market), reference, technical. Subjects include business/economics, computers/electronic, money/finance, software, legal practice. "Our market is not, generally, the public. Books need to be targeted to lawyers who are seeking solutions to their practice problems. We rarely publish scholarly treatises." Query with SASE.

Recent Title(s) *McElhaney's Trial Notebook*; *How to Start a Law Practice*; *Advocacy Words*.

Tips "ABA books are written for busy, practicing lawyers. The most successful books have a practical, reader-friendly voice. If you can build in features like checklists, exhibits, sample contracts, flow charts, and tables of cases, please do so." The Association also publishes over 50 major national periodicals in a variety of legal areas. Contact Kathleen Welton, director of book publishing, at the above address for guidelines.

AMERICAN CHEMICAL SOCIETY

Publications/Books Division, 1155 16th St. NW, Washington DC 20036. (202)452-2120. Fax: (202)452-8913. E-mail: b_hauserman@acs.org. Web site: pubs.acs.org/books/. **Acquisitions:** Bob Hauserman, acquisitions editor. Estab. 1876. Publishes hardcover originals. **Publishes 35 titles/year. Pays royalty.** Accepts simultaneous submissions. Responds in 2 months to proposals. Book catalog free; ms guidelines online.

American Chemical Society publishes symposium-based books for chemistry.

Nonfiction Technical, semi-technical. Subjects include science. "Emphasis is on meeting-based books."

Recent Title(s) *Infrared Analysis of Peptides and Proteins*, edited by Singh.

AMERICAN CORRECTIONAL ASSOCIATION

206 N. Washington St., Suite 200, Alexandria VA 22314. (703)224-0194. Fax: (703)224-0179. E-mail: aliceh@aca.org. Web site: www.aca.org. **Acquisitions:** Alice Heiserman, manager of publications and research. Estab. 1870. Publishes trade paperback originals. **Publishes 18 titles/year. 90% of books from first-time authors; 100% from unagented writers. Pays 10% royalty on net receipts.** Publishes book 1 year after acceptance of ms. Responds in 4 months to queries. Book catalog free; ms guidelines online.

American Correctional Association provides practical information on jails, prisons, boot camps, probation, parole, community corrections, juvenile facilities and rehabilitation programs, substance abuse programs, and other areas of corrections.

Nonfiction "We are looking for practical, how-to texts or training materials written for the corrections profession. We are especially interested in books on management, development of first-line supervisors, and security-threat group/management in prisons." How-to, reference, technical, textbook, correspondence courses. Subjects include corrections and criminal justice. No autobiographies or true-life accounts by current or former inmates or correctional officers, theses, or dissertations. No fiction or poetry. Query with SASE. Reviews artwork/photos as part of ms package.

Recent Title(s) *TRY: Treatment Readiness for Youth at Risk*; *Changing Criminal Thinking*; *Becoming a Model Warden*.

Tips Authors are professionals in the field and corrections. "Our audience is made up of corrections professionals and criminal justice students. No books by inmates or former inmates." This publisher advises out-of-town freelance editors, indexers, and proofreaders to refrain from requesting work from them.

AMERICAN COUNSELING ASSOCIATION

5999 Stevenson Ave., Alexandria VA 22304. (703)823-9800. Fax: (703)823-4786. E-mail: cbaker@counseling.org. Web site: www.counseling.org. **Acquisitions:** Carolyn C. Baker, director of publications. Estab. 1952. Publishes paperback originals. Accepts simultaneous submissions. Responds in 1 month to queries. Ms guidelines free.

O→ The American Counseling Association is dedicated to promoting public confidence and trust in the counseling profession. "We publish scholarly texts for graduate level students and mental health professionals. We do not publish books for the general public."

Nonfiction Reference, scholarly, textbook (for professional counselors). Subjects include education, gay/lesbian, health/medicine, multicultural, psychology, religion, sociology, spirituality, women's issues/studies. ACA does not publish self-help books or autobiographies. Query with SASE, or submit proposal package including outline, 2 sample chapters, vitae.

Recent Title(s) *Multicultural Issues in Counseling, 3rd Ed.*, edited by Courtland C. Lee; *ACA Ethical Standards Casebook, 6th Ed.*, by Barbara Herlihy and Gerald Corey.

Tips "Target your market. Your books will not be appropriate for everyone across all disciplines."

AMERICAN FEDERATION OF ASTROLOGERS

6535 S. Rural Rd., Tempe AZ 85283. (480)838-1751. Fax: (480)838-8293. E-mail: afa@msn.com. Web site: www.astrologers.com. Estab. 1938. Publishes trade paperback originals and reprints. **Publishes 10-15 titles/year. Receives 10 queries and 20 mss/year. 50% of books from first-time authors; 100% from unagented writers. Pays 10% royalty.** Publishes book 10 months after acceptance of ms. Accepts simultaneous submissions. Responds in 6 months to mss. Book catalog and ms guidelines free.

O→ American Federation of Astrologers publishes astrology books, calendars, charts, and related aids.

Nonfiction Subjects include astrology. Submit complete ms.

Recent Title(s) *The Vertex*, by Donna Henson; *Financial Astrology*, by David Williams; *Forensic Astrology*, by Dave Cambell.

AMERICAN QUILTER'S SOCIETY

Schroeder Publishing, P.O. Box 3290, Paducah KY 42002-3290. (270)898-7903. Fax: (270)898-1173. E-mail: editor@aqsquilt.com. Web site: www.americanquilter.com. **Acquisitions:** Nicole Chambers, executive book editor (primarily how-to and patterns, but other quilting books sometimes published). Estab. 1984. Publishes hardcover and trade paperback originals. **Publishes 20 titles/year. Receives 300 queries/year. 60% of books from first-time authors; 100% from unagented writers. Pays 5% royalty on retail price.** Publishes book 11 months after acceptance of ms. Accepts simultaneous submissions. Responds in same day to queries; 2 months to proposals. Book catalog and ms guidelines free or online.

O→ American Quilter's Society publishes how-to and pattern books for quilters (beginners through intermediate skill level).

Nonfiction Coffee table book, how-to, reference, technical (about quilting). Subjects include creative nonfiction, hobbies (about quilting). Query with SASE, or submit proposal package including outline, 1 sample chapter, photos or sketches of all patterns. Reviews artwork/photos as part of ms package. Photocopies; slides, drawings and e-mailed JPG files are also acceptable for a proposal.

Recent Title(s) *Birds N Roses*, by Margaret Docherty; *Clever Banners, Panels & Postcards*, by Mary Mayne.

AMERICAN SOCIETY FOR TRAINING AND DEVELOPMENT

1640 King St., Alexandria VA 22313. (800)628-2783. Fax: (703)683-9591. E-mail: mmorrow@astd.org. Web site: www.astd.org. **Acquisitions:** Mark Morrow, manager, acquisitions and author relations. Estab. 1944. Publishes trade paperback originals. **Publishes 16-20 titles/year. Receives 50 queries and 25-50 mss/year. 25% of books from first-time authors; 99% from unagented writers. Pays 10% royalty on net receipts.** Publishes book up to 1 year after acceptance of ms. Accepts simultaneous submissions. Responds in 1 month to queries; 1 month to proposals; 1 month to mss. Book catalog and ms guidelines free.

Nonfiction Trade books for training and performance improvement professionals. Subjects include training and development, leadership, management, professional development. Submit proposal package including outline, 1 sample chapter. Reviews artwork/photos as part of ms package.

Recent Title(s) *Lies About Learning*, by Larry Israelite; *10 Steps to Successful Stategic Planning*, by Susan Barksolale and Teri Lund; *Crash and Learn*, by Jim Smith, Jr.

Tips Audience includes workplace learning professionals including frontline trainers, training managers and executives; performance professionals, including performance consultants; organizational development and human resource development professionals. "Send a good proposal targeted to our audience providing how-to advice that readers can apply now!"

AMERICAN WATER WORKS ASSOCIATION

6666 W. Quincy Ave., Denver CO 80235. (303)734-3419. Fax: (303)794-7310. E-mail: cmurcray@awwa.org. Web site: www.awwa.org/communications/books. **Acquisitions:** Colin Murcray, senior acquisitions editor. Estab. 1881. Publishes hardcover and trade paperback originals. Does not accept simultaneous submissions. Responds in 4 months to queries. Book catalog and ms guidelines free.

O→ AWWA strives to advance and promote the safety and knowledge of drinking water and related issues to all audiences—from kindergarten through post-doctorate.

Nonfiction Subjects include nature/environment, science, software, drinking water- and wastewater-related topics, operations, treatment, sustainability. Query with SASE, or submit outline, author bio, 3 sample chapters. Reviews artwork/photos as part of ms package. Send photocopies.

Recent Title(s) *The Evolving Water Utility*, by Gary Westerhoff, et. al.

Tips "See Web site to download submission instructions."

AMG PUBLISHERS

6815 Shallowford Rd., Chattanooga TN 37421-1755. (423)894-6060. Fax: (423)894-9511. E-mail: danp@amginternational.org. Web site: www.amgpublishers.com. **Acquisitions:** Dan Penwell, manager of product development and acquisitions. Publishes hardcover and trade paperback originals, electronic originals, and audio Bible and book originals. **Publishes 25-35 titles/year; imprint publishes 20 titles/year. Receives 2,000 queries and 500 mss/year. 25% of books from first-time authors; 40% from unagented writers. Pays 10-14% royalty on wholesale price.** Publishes book 12-15 months after acceptance of ms. Accepts simultaneous submissions. Responds in 1 week to queries; 6 months to proposals; 6 months to mss. Book catalog and ms guidelines online.

Imprints Living Ink.

Nonfiction Reference, Bible study workbook, Bibles, commentaries. Looking for books that facilitate interaction with Bible, encourage and facilitate spiritual growth. Subjects include Christian living, women's, men's, and family issues, single and divorce issues, devotionals, inspirationals, prayer, contemporary issues, Biblical reference, applied theology and apologetics and bible studies." Prefer queries by e-mail. "We are looking for youth/young teen fantasy fiction that contains spiritual truths."

Recent Title(s) *Eye of the Oracle*, by Bryan Davis; *The Faith of America's First Ladies*, by Jane Cook; *Battlefields and Blessings*, by Terry Tuley.

Tips "AMG is open to well-written, niche books that meet immediate needs in the lives of adults and young adults."

AMHERST MEDIA, INC.

175 Rano St., Suite 200, Buffalo NY 14207. (716)874-4450. Fax: (716)874-4508. E-mail: amherstmed@aol.com. Web site: www.AmherstMedia.com. **Acquisitions:** Craig Alesse, publisher. Estab. 1974. Publishes trade paperback originals and reprints. **Publishes 30 titles/year. 60% of books from first-time authors; 90% from unagented writers. Pays 6-8% royalty on retail price. Offers advance.** Publishes book 1 year after acceptance of ms. Accepts simultaneous submissions. Responds in 2 months to queries. Book catalog and ms guidelines free.

O→ Amherst Media publishes how-to photography books.

Nonfiction How-to. Subjects include photography. "Looking for well-written and illustrated photo books." Query with outline, 2 sample chapters, and SASE. Reviews artwork/photos as part of ms package.

Recent Title(s) *Portrait Photographer's Handbook*, by Bill Hurter.

Tips "Our audience is made up of beginning to advanced photographers. If I were a writer trying to market a book today, I would fill the need of a specific audience and self-edit in a tight manner."

[A] ANDREWS MCMEEL UNIVERSAL

4520 Main St., Kansas City MO 64111-7701. (816)932-6700. **Acquisitions:** Christine Schillig, vice president/editorial director. Estab. 1973. Publishes hardcover and paperback originals. **Publishes 200 titles/year. Pays royalty on retail price, or net receipts. Offers advance.**

O-ᴿ Andrews McMeel publishes general trade books, humor books, miniature gift books, calendars, and stationery products.

Nonfiction How-to, humor, inspirational. Subjects include contemporary culture, general trade, relationships. Also produces gift books. *Agented submissions only.*

Recent Title(s) *The Complete Calvin and Hobbes*, by Bill Watterson.

ANKER PUBLISHING CO., INC.

P.O. Box 249, Bolton MA 01740-0249. (978)779-6190. Fax: (978)779-6366. E-mail: info@ankerpub.com. Web site: www.ankerpub.com. **Acquisitions:** James D. Anker, president and publisher. Publishes hardcover and paperback professional books. **Publishes 10 titles/year. Pays royalty. Offers advance.** Publishes book 4 months after acceptance of ms. Accepts simultaneous submissions.

O-ᴿ Publishes professional development books for higher education faculty and administrators.

Nonfiction Professional development. Subjects include education. Query with SASE, or submit proposal package including outline, 3 sample chapters.

APA BOOKS

American Psychological Association, 750 First St., NE, Washington DC 20002-4242. (800)374-2721 or (202)336-5792. E-mail: books@apa.org. Web site: www.apa.org/books. Publishes hardcover and trade paperback originals. Book catalog and ms guidelines online.

Imprints Magination Press (children's books).

Nonfiction Reference, scholarly, textbook, professional. Subjects include education, gay/lesbian, multicultural, psychology, science, social sciences, sociology, women's issues/studies. Submit cv and prospectus with TOC, intended audience, selling points, and outside competition.

Recent Title(s) *The Dependent Patient: A Practitioner's Guide*, by Robert F. Bornstein, PhD; *A Place to Call Home: After-School Programs for Urban Youth*, by Barton J. Hirsch, PhD; *Law & Mental Health Professionals: Ohio*, by Leon VandeCreek, PhD and Marshall Kapp, JD.

Tips "Our press features scholarly books on empirically supported topics for professionals and students in all areas of psychology."

APPALACHIAN MOUNTAIN CLUB BOOKS

5 Joy St., Boston MA 02108. (617)523-0655. Fax: (617)523-0722. E-mail: amcpublications@outdoors.org. Web site: www.outdoors.org. **Acquisitions:** Editor-in-Chief. Estab. 1897. Publishes hardcover and trade paperback originals. Accepts simultaneous submissions. Ms guidelines online.

O-ᴿ Appalachian Mountain Club publishes hiking guides, paddling guides, nature, conservation, and mountain-subject guides for America's Northeast. "We connect recreation to conservation and education."

Nonfiction Subjects include nature/environment, recreation, regional (Northeast outdoor recreation), literary nonfiction, guidebooks. Query with proposal and SASE. Reviews artwork/photos as part of ms package. Send photocopies or transparencies.

Recent Title(s) *Women on High*; *Northeastern Wilds*; *Massachusetts Trail Guide.*

Tips "Our audience is outdoor recreationists, conservation-minded hikers and canoeists, family outdoor lovers, armchair enthusiasts. Visit our Web site for proposal submission guidelines and more information."

A-R EDITIONS, INC.

8551 Research Way, Suite 180, Middleton WI 53562. (608)836-9000. Fax: (608)831-8200. Web site: www.areditions.com. **Acquisitions:** Paul L. Ranzini, managing editor (Recent Researches Series); James L. Zychowicz, managing editor (Computer Music and Digital Audio Series). Estab. 1962. **Publishes 30 titles/year. Receives 40 queries and 30 mss/year. 75% of books from first-time authors; 100% from unagented writers. Pays royalty or honoraria.** Does not accept simultaneous submissions. Responds in 1 month to queries; 3 months to proposals; 6 months to mss. Book catalog and ms guidelines online.

O-ᴿ A-R Editions publishes modern critical editions of music based on current musicological research. Each edition is devoted to works by a single composer or to a single genre of composition. The contents are chosen for their potential interest to scholars and performers, then prepared for publication according to the standards that govern the making of all reliable, historical editions.

Nonfiction Subjects include computers/electronic, music/dance, software, historical music editions. Computer Music and Digital Audio Series titles deal with issues tied to digital and electronic media, and include both textbooks and handbooks in this area. Query with SASE, or submit outline.

Recent Title(s) *New Digital Musical Instruments*, by Eduardo Mirando and Marcelo Wanderley; *Charles Ives: 129 Songs*, edited by H. Wiley Hitchcock.

ARABESQUE

BET Books, 850 Third Ave., 16th Floor, New York NY 10022. (212)407-1500. Web site: www.bet.com/books. **Acquisitions:** Karen Thomas, editorial director. Publishes mass market paperback originals. Accepts simultaneous submissions. Responds in 3 months to mss. Book catalog for #10 SASE; ms guidelines online.

Arabesque publishes contemporary romances about African-American couples.

Fiction Multicultural (romance), romance. "Arabesque books must be 85,000-100,000 words in length, and are contemporary genre romances only." Submit proposal package including synopsis, 3 sample chapters.

Recent Title(s) *His 1-800 Wife*, by Shirley Hailstock.

Tips "Please do not phone to see if your manuscript was received or returned, or to find out what we thought of it. A self-addressed, stamped postcard can be enclosed with your submission if you want confirmation of its arrival. Specify whether you would like your manuscript returned or recycled if it is not right for us."

ARCADE PUBLISHING

116 John St., Suite 2810, New York NY 10038. (212)475-2633. Fax: (212)353-8148. Web site: www.arcadepub.com. **Acquisitions:** Richard Seaver, president/editor-in-chief; Jeannette Seaver, publisher/executive editor; Cal Barksdale, senior editor; Casey Ebro, editor; James Jayo, assistant editor; Tessa Aye, editorial assistant. Estab. 1988. Publishes hardcover originals, trade paperback reprints. **Publishes 35 titles/year. 5% of books from first-time authors. Pays royalty on retail price. 10 author's copies. Offers advance.** Publishes book within 18 months after acceptance of ms. Responds in 2 months to queries. Book catalog and ms guidelines for #10 SASE.

Arcade prides itself on publishing top-notch literary nonfiction and fiction, with a significant proportion of foreign writers.

Nonfiction Biography, general nonfiction, general nonfiction. Subjects include history, memoirs, nature/environment, travel, popular science, current events. *Agented submissions only.* Reviews artwork/photos as part of ms package. Send photocopies.

Fiction Literary, mainstream/contemporary, short story collections. No romance, historical, science fiction. *Agented submissions only.*

Recent Title(s) *It Might Have Been What He Said*, by Eden Collinsworth; *Witness to Nuremberg*, by Richard Sonnenfeldt; *The Zebra Murders*, by Prentice Earl Sanders and Bennett Cohen.

ARCHEBOOKS PUBLISHING

ArcheBooks Publishing Inc., 9101 W. Sahara Ave., Suite 105-112, Las Vegas NV 89117. (800)358-8101. Fax: (702)987-0256. E-mail: info@archebooks.com. Submissions E-mail: publisher@archebooks.com. Web site: www.archebooks.com. **Acquisitions:** Robert E. Gelinas, publisher. Estab. 2003. Publishes hardcover originals, electronic originals and hardcover reprints. **Publishes 30-40 titles/year; imprint publishes 30-40 titles/year. Receives 100+ queries and 50+ mss/year. 90% of books from first-time authors. Pays royalty on retail price. Minimum of $2,500, subject to negotiation and keeping prior history and corporate policy in mind.** Publishes book 6-9 months after acceptance of ms. Does not accept simultaneous submissions. All submissions must be online only. Responds in 1 month to queries; 1 month to proposals; 1 month to mss. Book catalog and ms guidelines online.

Nonfiction Subjects include history, true crime. *Agented submissions only.* Reviews artwork/photos as part of ms package. Digital e-mail attachments.

Fiction Adventure, fantasy, historical, horror, humor, literary, mainstream/contemporary, military/war, mystery, romance, science fiction, suspense, western, young adult. "Writers should be prepared to participate in very aggressive and orchestrated marketing and promotion campaigns, using all the promotional tools and training that we provide, at no charge. We're expanding in all areas." *Agented submissions only.*

Recent Title(s) *The Don Juan Con*, by Sara Williams; *The Mustard Seed*, by Robert E. Gelinas; *The Planters*, by Bill Rogers.

Tips "Learn to write a good book proposal. An article on this topic can be found for free on our Web site in the Author's Corner section of Writer's Resources."

ARKANSAS RESEARCH, INC.

P.O. Box 303, Conway AR 72033. (501)470-1120. E-mail: desmond@arkansasresearch.com. **Acquisitions:** Desmond Walls Allen, owner. Estab. 1985. Publishes trade paperback originals and reprints. **Publishes 30 titles/year. 10% of books from first-time authors; 100% from unagented writers. Pays 5-10% royalty on retail price.** Publishes book 6 months after acceptance of ms. Does not accept simultaneous submissions. Responds in 1 month to queries. Book catalog for $1; ms guidelines free.

"Our company opens a world of information to researchers interested in the history of Arkansas."

Nonfiction All Arkansas-related subjects. How-to (genealogy), reference. Subjects include Americana, ethnic, history, hobbies (genealogy), military/war, regional. "We don't print autobiographies or genealogies about 1 family." Query with SASE. Reviews artwork/photos as part of ms package. Send photocopies.

Recent Title(s) *Life & Times From The Clay County Courier Newspaper Published at Corning, Arkansas, 1893-1900.*

ARROW PUBLICATIONS, LLC

9112 Paytley Bridge Lane, Potomac MD 20854-4432. Fax: (301)299-9423. E-mail: arrow_info@arrowpub.com. Submissions E-mail: roman.comic1@sympatico.ca. Web site: www.arrowpub.com; www.myromancestory.com. **Acquisitions:** Tom King, managing editor (romance/adventure/mystery); Maryan Gibson, acquisition editor (romance/adventure/mystery). Estab. 1987. Publishes romance fiction in a graphic novel format. **Publishes 50 titles/year. Receives 150 queries and 100 mss/year. 80% of books from first-time authors; 100% from unagented writers. Makes outright purchase of $600-1,000.** Publishes book 4-6 months after acceptance of ms. Does not accept simultaneous submissions. Responds in 1 month to queries; 1 month to mss. Ms guidelines online.

Fiction Adventure, fantasy, humor, mystery, romance, suspense. "We are looking for outlines of stories heavy on romance with elements of adventure/intrigue/mystery. We will consider other romance genres as long as the romance element is strong. Humorous love stories are always appreciated. We need true-to-life romances between consenting adults, with believable conflicts and well-defined characterizations. We publish illustrated romance stories, so we are looking for good dialogue writers. Each story is formatted into a script of 70-75 panels, comprising narrative, dialogue, and art direction." Query with SASE, or submit proposal package including synopsis.

Recent Title(s) *The Hunted*, by Jennifer Savage (romance/adventure); *Tales of Your New Life*, by Nic Anders and Taylor Ashley Subrosa (romance/fantasy); *Coming Home*, by April Harbringer (romance/mystery).

Tips "Our audience is primarily women 18 and older. View sample stories and review guidelines online. Send query with outline first. We do not publish full-length novels."

ARTE PUBLICO PRESS

University of Houston, 452 Cullen Performance Hall, Houston TX 77204-2004. Fax: (713)743-3080. Web site: www.artepublicopress.com. **Acquisitions:** Nicolas Kanellos, editor. Estab. 1979. Publishes hardcover originals, trade paperback originals and reprints. **Publishes 36 titles/year. Receives 1,000 queries and 2,000 mss/year. 50% of books from first-time authors; 80% from unagented writers. Pays 10% royalty on wholesale price. Provides 20 author's copies; 40% discount on subsequent copies. Offers $1,000-3,000 advance.** Publishes book 2 years after acceptance of ms. Accepts simultaneous submissions. Responds in 1 month to queries; 1 month to proposals; 4 months to mss. Book catalog free; ms guidelines online.

Imprints Piñata Books.

- "We are a showcase for Hispanic literary creativity, arts and culture. Our endeavor is to provide a national forum for U.S.-Hispanic literature."

Nonfiction Children's/juvenile, reference. Subjects include ethnic, language/literature, regional, translation, women's issues/studies. Hispanic civil rights issues for new series: The Hispanic Civil Rights Series. Query with SASE, or submit outline, 2 sample chapters.

Fiction Ethnic, literary, mainstream/contemporary, written by U.S.-Hispanic authors. Query with SASE, or submit outline/proposal, synopsis, 2 sample chapters, or submit complete ms.

Poetry Submit 10 sample poems.

Recent Title(s) *Shadows and Supposes*, by Gloria Vando (poetry); *Home Killings*, by Marcos McPeek Villatoro (mystery); *Message to Aztlár*, by Rodolfo "Corky" Gonzales (Hispanic Civil Rights Series book).

ASA, AVIATION SUPPLIES & ACADEMICS

7005 132nd Pl. SE, Newcastle WA 98059. (425)235-1500. E-mail: feedback@asa2fly.com. Web site: www.asa2fly.com. Does not accept simultaneous submissions. Book catalog free.

- ASA is an industry leader in the development and sales of aviation supplies, publications, and software for pilots, flight instructors, flight engineers and aviation technicians. All ASA products are developed by a team of researchers, authors and editors.

Nonfiction All subjects must be related to aviation education and training. How-to, technical. Subjects include education. "We are primarily an aviation publisher. Educational books in this area are our specialty; other aviation books will be considered." Query with outline. Send photocopies.

Recent Title(s) *The Savvy Flight Instructor: Secrets of the Successful CFI*, by Greg Brown.

Tips "Two of our specialty series include ASA's *Focus Series*, and ASA *Aviator's Library*. Books in our *Focus Series* concentrate on single-subject areas of aviation knowledge, curriculum and practice. The *Aviator's Library* is comprised of titles of known and/or classic aviation authors or established instructor/authors in the industry, and other aviation specialty titles."

ASCE PRESS

1801 Alexander Bell Dr., Reston VA 20191-4400. (703)295-6275. Fax: (703)295-6278. E-mail: ascepress@asce.org. Web site: www.pubs.asce.org. Estab. 1989. **Pays royalty on net receipts.** Accepts simultaneous submissions. Request ASCE Press book proposal submission guidelines; ms guidelines online.

O→ ASCE Press publishes technical volumes that are useful to both practicing civil engineers and civil engineering students. "We publish books by individual authors and editors to advance the civil engineering profession." Currently emphasizing construction, geotechnical, structural engineering, water/environmental, management and engineering history. De-emphasizing highly specialized areas with narrow scope.

Nonfiction "We are looking for topics that are useful and instructive to the engineering practitioner." Subjects include civil engineering. Query with proposal, sample chapters, CV, TOC, and target audience.

Recent Title(s) *Engineering With the Spreadsheet*, by Craig T. Christy; *Designed for Dry Feet*, by Robert J. Hoeksema; *Preparing for Design-Build Projects*, by Douglas D. Gransberg.

Tips "As a traditional publisher of scientific and technical materials, ASCE Press applies rigorous standards to the expertise, scholarship, readability and attractiveness of its books."

ASSOCIATION FOR SUPERVISION AND CURRICULUM DEVELOPMENT

1703 N. Beauregard St., Alexandria VA 22311. (703)575-5693. Fax: (703)575-5400. E-mail: swillis@ascd.org. Web site: www.ascd.org. **Acquisitions:** Scott Willis, acquisitions director. Estab. 1943. Publishes trade paperback originals. **Publishes 24-30 titles/year. Receives 100 queries and 100 mss/year. 50% of books from first-time authors; 95% from unagented writers. Pays negotiable royalty on actual monies received.** Publishes book 1 year after acceptance of ms. Accepts simultaneous submissions. Responds in 3 months to proposals. Book catalog and ms guidelines free or online.

O→ ASCD publishes high-quality professional books for educators.

Nonfiction Subjects include education (for professional educators). Submit outline, 2 sample chapters. Reviews artwork/photos as part of ms package. Send photocopies.

Recent Title(s) *Leadership for the Learning: How to Help Students Succeed*, by Carl Glickman; *The Multiple Intelligences of Reading and Writing*, by Thomas Armstrong; *Educating Oppositional and Defiant Children*, by Philip S. Hall, Nancy D. Hall.

A ⊘ ATHENEUM BOOKS FOR YOUNG READERS

Imprint of Simon & Schuster, 1230 Avenue of the Americas, New York NY 10020. (212)698-2715. Fax: (212)698-2796. Web site: www.simonsayskids.com. Estab. 1960. Publishes hardcover originals. Accepts simultaneous submissions. Ms guidelines for #10 SASE.

O→ Atheneum Books for Young Readers publishes books aimed at children, pre-school through high school.

Nonfiction Biography, children's/juvenile, humor, self-help. Subjects include Americana, animals, art/architecture, business/economics, government/politics, health/medicine, history, music/dance, nature/environment, photography, psychology, recreation, religion, science, sociology, sports, travel. "Do remember, most publishers plan their lists as much as two years in advance. So if a topic is 'hot' right now, it may be 'old hat' by the time we could bring it out. It's better to steer clear of fads. Some writers assume juvenile books are for 'practice' until you get good enough to write adult books. Not so. Books for young readers demand just as much professionalism in writing as adult books. So save those 'practice' manuscripts for class, or polish them before sending them. *Query only for all submissions. We don't accept unsolicited mss. It is recommended that you find an agent to represent your work.*"

Fiction All in juvenile versions. Adventure, ethnic, experimental, fantasy, gothic, historical, horror, humor, mainstream/contemporary, mystery, science fiction, sports, suspense, western, Animal. "We have few specific needs except for books that are fresh, interesting and well written. Fad topics are dangerous, as are works you haven't polished to the best of your ability. We also don't need safety pamphlets, ABC books, coloring books and board books. In writing picture book texts, avoid the coy and 'cutesy,' such as stories about characters with alliterative names." *Query only. No unsolicited mss.* No "paperback romance type" fiction.

Recent Title(s) *Billy and the Rebel*, by Deborah Hopkinson, illustrated by Brian Floca; *Imagine a Day*, by Sarah L. Thomson, illustrated by Rob Gonsalves; *Seeds*, written and illustrated by Ken Robbins.

ATRIAD PRESS, LLC

13820 Methuen Green, Dallas TX 75240. (972)671-0002. E-mail: editor@atriadpress.com. Web site: www.atriadpress.com; www.hauntedencounters.com. President: Ginnie Bivona. **Acquisitions:** Mitchel Whitington, senior editor. Estab. 2002. Publishes trade paperback originals. Accepts simultaneous submissions. Book catalog and ms guidelines online.

O→ "We are currently accepting submissions for three different series: The Haunted Encounters Series (submissions@atriadpress.com); Encuentros Encantados (hector@atriadpress.com); Ghostly Tales from America's Jails (jails@atriadpress.com)."

Nonfiction Ghost stories, haunted experiences. Does not want UFO or angels. Submit proposal package including outline, author bio, 3 sample chapters, via mail or e-mail.
Recent Title(s) *Haunted Encounters: Real-Life Stories of Supernatural Experiences* (anthology).
Tips "The market for ghost stories is huge! It seems to be very broad—and ranges from young to old. Currently, our books are for adults, but we would consider the teen market. Please check your manuscript carefully for errors in spelling and structure."

AUDIO RENAISSANCE

Division of Holtzbrinck Publishers, 175 Fifth Ave., New York NY 10010. (646)307-5000. Fax: (917)534-0980. Web site: www.audiorenaissance.com. Estab. 1988.

- "Audio Renaissance publishes audio editions of the best fiction and nonfiction among the Holtzbrinck trade publishers. It has a strong tradition in the self-help, personal growth, and business categories."

Recent Title(s) *The World Is Flat*, by Thomas L. Friedman; *Housekeeping*, by Marilynne Robinson; *Running With Scissors*, by Augusten Burroughs.

AUGSBURG BOOKS

Imprint of Augsburg Fortress Publishers, P.O. Box 1209, Minneapolis MN 55440-1209. (612)330-3300. E-mail: booksub@augsburgfortress.org; lutheranvoices@augsburgfortress.org. Web site: www.augsburgbooks.com. Publishes trade and mass market paperback originals and reprints, hardcover picture books. **Pays royalty.** Book catalog for 9×12 SAE with 3 first-class stamps; ms guidelines online.

- Augsburg Books is the publishing house of the Evangelical Lutheran Church in America. Augsburg Books are meant to nurture faith in daily life, enhancing the lives of Christians in their homes, churches, and schools.

Nonfiction Subjects include religion, spirituality (adult), grief/healing/wholeness, parenting, interactive books for children and families, seasonal and picture books. Query with SASE, or submit proposal package.
Recent Title(s) *The Passion of the Lord: African American Reflections*, edited by Matthew V. Johnson, Sr. and James A. Noel; *Two Worlds Are Ours: An Introduction to Christian Mysticism*, by John Macquarrie.

AVALON BOOKS

Thomas Bouregy & Co., Inc., 160 Madison Ave., 5th Floor, New York NY 10016. (212)598-0222. Fax: (212)979-1862. E-mail: editorial@avalonbooks.com. Web site: www.avalonbooks.com. **Acquisitions:** Erin Cartwright-Niumata, editorial director; Susan McCarty, associate editor. Estab. 1950. Publishes hardcover originals. **Publishes 60 titles/year. Pays 15% royalty. Offers $1,000+ advance.** Publishes book 10-12 months after acceptance of ms. Responds in 1 month to queries. Ms guidelines online.
Fiction "We publish wholesome contemporary romances, mysteries, historical romances and westerns. Our books are read by adults as well as teenagers, and the characters are all adults. All mysteries are contemporary. We publish contemporary romances (4 every 2 months), historical romances (2 every 2 months), mysteries (2 every 2 months) and westerns (2 every 2 months). Submit first 3 sample chapters, a 2-3 page synopsis and SASE. The manuscripts should be 40,000-70,000 words. Manuscripts that are too long will not be considered. The books shall be wholesome fiction, without graphic sex, violence or strong language. We are actively looking for romantic comedy, chick lit." Query with SASE.
Recent Title(s) *Promises*, by Carolyn Brown (historical romance); *Christmas in Carol*, by Sheila Roberts (contemporary romantic comedy); *Realm of Darkness*, by Cynthia Danielewski (mystery).

AVALON TRAVEL PUBLISHING

Avalon Publishing Group, 1400 65th St., Suite 250, Emeryville CA 94608. (510)595-3664. Fax: (510)595-4228. E-mail: acquisitions@avalonpub.com. Web site: www.travelmatters.com. Estab. 1973. Publishes trade paperback originals. **Publishes 100 titles/year. Receives 5,000 queries/year. 25% of books from first-time authors; 95% from unagented writers. Pays royalty on net receipts. Offers up to $17,000 advance.** Publishes book an average of 9 months after acceptance of ms. Accepts simultaneous submissions. Responds in 4 months to queries; 4 months to proposals. Ms guidelines online.

- "Avalon travel guides feature a combination of practicality and spirit, offering a traveler-to-traveler perspective perfect for planning an afternoon hike, around-the-world journey, or anything in between. ATP publishes 7 major series. Each one has a different emphasis and a different geographic coverage. We're currently expanding our coverage, with a focus on European and Asian destinations. Our main areas of interest are North America, Central America, South America, the Caribbean, and the Pacific. At any given moment, we are seeking to acquire only a handful of specific titles in each of our major series. Check online guidelines for current needs. Follow guidelines closely."

Nonfiction Subjects include regional, travel.

Recent Title(s) *Moon Handbooks Florida Gulf Coast*, by Laura Reiley; *Moon Handbooks Panama*, by William Friar; *Living Abroad in Costa Rica*, by Erin Van Rheenen.
Tips "Please note that ATP is only looking for books that fit into current series and is not interested in the following genres: fiction, children's books, and travelogues/travel diaries."

AVANT-GUIDE

Empire Press Media, 444 Madison Ave., 35th Floor, New York NY 10022. E-mail: editor@avantguide.com. Web site: www.avantguide.com. **Acquisitions:** Dan Levine, editor-in-chief (travel). Estab. 1997. Publishes trade paperback and electronic originals. **Publishes 20 titles/year. Receives 200 queries and 10 mss/year. 20% of books from first-time authors; 100% from unagented writers. Makes outright purchase of $10,000-30,000.** Publishes book 10 months after acceptance of ms. Accepts simultaneous submissions. Responds in 1 month to queries; 1 month to proposals; 1 month to mss. Book catalog free; ms guidelines online.
Nonfiction Subjects include travel (guide books). "Avant-Guide books live at the intersection of travel and style. They co-opt the best aspects of the guidebook genre—namely, being thorough and trustworthy. Then they add dynamic prose, innovative design and a brutally honest cosmopolitan perspective. Each new title in this boutique travel guidebook series is comprehensive in scope and includes authoritative reports on essential sights, hip new restaurants, nightclubs, hotels, and shops—all while making a fashion statement all its own. Avant-Guide is the first and only travel guidebook series for globally aware travelistas." Query by e-mail.
Tips "Avant-Guide readers are style-conscious, well-dressed, well-traveled city dwelling 25-49 year old men and women. They are sophisticated, brand-savvy, well-heeled, 21st century consumers searching for understated, cutting edge experiences. While they like to travel stylishly, our readers are busy people who don't have time to wade through exhaustive lists. When they travel they want to know only about the best hotels, restaurants, shops and nightlife. Our core audience resides in affluent city areas and gentrified multi-ethnic areas. They are predominantly single or unmarried-couples, highly qualified executives and creative professionals."

[A] AVON BOOKS

HarperCollins, 10 E. 53rd St., New York NY 10022. Web site: www.avonbooks.com. **Acquisitions:** Editorial Submissions. Estab. 1941. Publishes hardcover trade and mass market paperback originals and reprints. **Royalty negotiable. Offers advance.** Accepts simultaneous submissions. Ms guidelines for #10 SASE.
Fiction Romance (contemporary, historical). *Agented submissions only.*
Recent Title(s) *Night Train to Lisbon*, by Emily Grayson; *Dirty South*, by Ace Atkins; *Sandstorm*, by James Rollins.

[N] BACKCOUNTRY GUIDES

Imprint of The Countryman Press, P. O. Box 748, Woodstock VT 05091-0748. (802)457-4826. Fax: (802)457-1678. E-mail: countrymanpress@wwnorton.com. Web site: www.countrymanpress.com. **Acquisitions:** Kermit Hummel, editorial director. Estab. 1973. Publishes trade paperback originals. **Publishes 50 titles/year.** Accepts simultaneous submissions. Responds in 3 months to proposals. Book catalog free; ms guidelines online.
Nonfiction Subjects include nature/environment, recreation (bicycling, hiking, canoeing, kayaking, fly fishing, walking, guidebooks, and series), sports, travel, food, gardening, country living, New England history. Query with SASE, or submit proposal package including outline, 2-3 sample chapters, market analysis. Reviews artwork/photos as part of ms package. Send transparencies.
Recent Title(s) *The King Arthur Flour Cookie Companion*; *Grand Canyon Wild*, by John Annerino; *50 Hikes in Arizona*, by Martin Tessmer.
Tips "Look at our existing series of guidebooks to see how your proposal fits in."

⊘ BAKER ACADEMIC

Division of Baker Publishing Group, P.O. Box 6287, Grand Rapids MI 49516-6287. (616)676-9185. Fax: (616)676-2315. Web site: www.bakeracademic.com. Editorial Director: Jim Kinney. Estab. 1939. Publishes hardcover and trade paperback originals. **Publishes 50 titles/year. 10% of books from first-time authors; 85% from unagented writers. Offers advance.** Publishes book 1 year after acceptance of ms. Book catalog for $9^1/_2 \times 12^1/_2$ SAE with 3 first-class stamps; ms guidelines for #10 SASE.

- "Baker Academic publishes religious academic and professional books for students and church leaders. Most of our authors and readers are Christians with academic interests, and our books are purchased from all standard retailers." Does not accept unsolicited queries.

Nonfiction Illustrated book, multimedia, reference, scholarly, textbook, dictionary, encyclopedia, reprint, professional book, CD-ROM. Subjects include anthropology/archeology, education, psychology, religion, women's issues/studies, Biblical studies, Christian doctrine, books for pastors and church leaders, contemporary issues.
Recent Title(s) *Apostle Paul*, by Udo Schnelle; *Dictionary for Theological Interpretation of the Bible*, edited by Kevin Vanhoorer, et al; *The American Evangelical Story*, by Douglas Sweeney.

BAKER BOOKS

Imprint of Baker Publishing Group, P.O. Box 6287, Grand Rapids MI 49516-6287. (616)676-9185. Fax: (616)676-9573. Web site: www.bakerbooks.com. Estab. 1939. Publishes hardcover and trade paperback originals, and trade paperback reprints. Does not accept unsolicited proposals. Book catalog for $9^{1}/_{2} \times 12^{1}/_{2}$ SAE with 3 first-class stamps; ms guidelines for #10 SASE.

"Baker Books publishes popular religious nonfiction reference books and professional books for church leaders. Most of our authors and readers are evangelical Christians, and our books are purchased from Christian bookstores, mail-order retailers, and school bookstores." Does not accept unsolicited queries.

Nonfiction Biography, multimedia, reference, self-help, textbook, CD-ROM. Subjects include child guidance/parenting, psychology, religion, women's issues/studies, Christian doctrine, books for pastors and church leaders, seniors' concerns, singleness, contemporary issues.

Recent Title(s) *Praying Backwards*, by Bryan Chapell; *The Scandal of the Evangelical Conscience*, by Ronald J. Sider; *The Invisible War*, by Chip Ingram.

BAKER PUBLISHING GROUP

P.O. Box 6287, Grand Rapids MI 49516-6287. (616)676-9185. Fax: (616)676-2315. Web site: www.bakerpublishinggroup.com.

Imprints Baker Academic; Baker Books; Bethany House; Brazos Press; Chosen; Fleming H. Revell.

- *Does not accept unsolicited queries.*

BALLANTINE PUBLISHING GROUP

Imprint of Random House, Inc., 1745 Broadway, 18th Floor, New York NY 10019. (212)782-9000. Web site: www.randomhouse.com. Estab. 1952. Publishes hardcover, trade paperback, mass market paperback originals. Ms guidelines online.

Imprints Ballantine Books, Ballantine Reader's Circle, Del Rey, Del Rey/Lucas Books, Fawcett, Ivy, One World, Wellspring.

Ballantine Books publishes a wide variety of nonfiction and fiction.

Nonfiction Biography, general nonfiction, gift book, how-to, humor, self-help. Subjects include animals, child guidance/parenting, community, cooking/foods/nutrition, creative nonfiction, education, gay/lesbian, health/medicine, history, language/literature, memoirs, military/war, recreation, religion, sex, spirituality, travel, true crime, women's issues/studies. *Agented submissions only.* Reviews artwork/photos as part of ms package. Send photocopies.

Fiction Confession, ethnic, fantasy, feminist, gay/lesbian, historical, humor, literary, mainstream/contemporary (women's), military/war, multicultural, mystery, romance, short story collections, spiritual, suspense, general fiction. *Agented submissions only.*

BANTAM BOOKS FOR YOUNG READERS

Imprint of Random House Children's Books/Random House, Inc., 1745 Broadway, New York NY 10019. (212)782-9000. Web site: www.randomhouse.com/kids.

- Not seeking mss at this time.

BANTAM DELL PUBLISHING GROUP

Random House, Inc., 1745 Broadway, New York NY 10019. (212)782-9000. Web site: www.bantamdell.com. Estab. 1945. Publishes hardcover, trade paperback and mass market paperback originals; mass market paperback reprints. Accepts simultaneous submissions.

Imprints Bantam Hardcover; Bantam Mass Market; Bantam Trade Paperback; Crimeline; Delacorte Press; Dell; Delta; The Dial Press; Domain; DTP; Fanfare; Island; Spectra.

Bantam Dell is a division of Random House, publishing both fiction and nonfiction. *No unsolicited mss*; send one-page queries.

Nonfiction Biography, how-to, humor, self-help. Subjects include Americana, child guidance/parenting, cooking/foods/nutrition, government/politics, health/medicine, history, military/war, New Age, philosophy, psychology, religion, science, sociology, spirituality, sports, true crime, women's issues/studies, fitness, mysticism/astrology.

Fiction Adventure, fantasy, historical, horror, literary, military/war, mystery, science fiction, suspense, women's fiction, general commercial fiction.

Recent Title(s) *The Glass Lake*, by Maeve Binchy; *Diabesity*, by Francine R. Kaufman, MD; *Charming Billy*, by Alice McDermott.

BANTAM DOUBLEDAY DELL BOOKS FOR YOUNG READERS

Random House Children's Publishing, Random House, Inc., 1745 Broadway, New York NY 10019. (212)782-9000. Fax: (212)782-8234. Web site: www.randomhouse.com/kids. Vice President/Publisher: Beverly Horowitz. **Acquisitions:** Michelle Poploff, editorial director. Publishes hardcover, trade paperback and mass market paperback series originals, trade paperback reprints. **Publishes 300 titles/year. Receives thousands queries/year. 10% of books from first-time authors; small% from unagented writers. Pays royalty. Offers varied advance.** Publishes book 2 years after acceptance of ms. Does not accept simultaneous submissions. Responds in 2 months to queries. Book catalog for 9×12 SASE.

Imprints Delacorte Press Books for Young Readers; Doubleday Books for Young Readers; Dell Laurel Leaf (YA); Dell Yearling (middle grade).

O-ᴿ "Bantam Doubleday Dell Books for Young Readers publishes award-winning books by distinguished authors and the most promising new writers." The best way to break in to this market is through its 2 contests, the Delacrote/Yearling Contest and the Delacorte Press Contest for a First Young Adult Novel.

Nonfiction Children's/juvenile. "Bantam Doubleday Dell Books for Young Readers publishes a very limited number of nonfiction titles." *No unsolicited mss.*

Fiction Adventure, fantasy, historical, humor, juvenile, mainstream/contemporary, mystery, picture books, suspense, chapter books, middle-grade. *No unsolicited mss.* Accepts unsolicited queries only.

Recent Title(s) *Sisterhood of the Traveling Pants*, by Ann Brashares; *Cuba 15*, by Nancy Osa.

BARBOUR PUBLISHING, INC.

P.O. Box 719, Uhrichsville OH 44683. (740)922-6045. Fax: (740)922-5948. Web site: www.barbourpublishing.com. **Acquisitions:** Paul Muckley, editorial director (nonfiction); Rebecca Germany, senior editor (women's fiction). Estab. 1981. Publishes hardcover, trade paperback and mass market paperback originals and reprints. **Publishes 200 titles/year. Receives 500 queries and 1000 mss/year. 40% of books from first-time authors; 90% from unagented writers. Pays 0-12% royalty on net price or makes outright purchase of $500-5,000. Offers $500-5,000 advance.** Publishes book 2 years after acceptance of ms. Accepts simultaneous submissions. Responds in 1 month to queries. Book catalog online or for 9×12 SAE with 2 first-class stamps; ms guidelines for #10 SASE or online.

Imprints Heartsong Presents (contact Rebecca Germany, managing editor).

O-ᴿ Barbour Books publishes inspirational/devotional material that is nondenominational and evangelical in nature; Heartsong Presents publishes Christian romance. "We're a Christian evangelical publisher."

Nonfiction Reference, devotional. Subjects include child guidance/parenting, cooking/foods/nutrition, money/finance, religion (evangelical Christian), women's issues/studies, inspirational/Christian living. "We look for book ideas with mass appeal—nothing in narrowly-defined niches. If you can appeal to a wide audience with an important message, creatively presented, we'd be interested to see your proposal." Submit outline, 3 sample chapters, SASE. Reviews artwork/photos as part of ms package. Send photocopies.

Fiction Romance (historical and contemporary), suspense, women's issues. "Heartsong romance is 'sweet'—no sex, no bad language. Other genres may be 'grittier'—real-life stories. All must have Christian faith as an underlying basis. Common writer's mistakes are a sketchy proposal, an unbelieveable story, and a story that doesn't fit our guidelines for inspirational romances." Submit synopsis, 3 sample chapters, SASE.

Recent Title(s) *Daily Wisdom for Working Women*, by Michelle Medlock Adams and Gena Maselli (devotional); *Dead as a Scone*, by Ron and Janet Benrey (fiction); *Mommy's Locked in the Bathroom*, by Cynthia Sumner (women's issues).

Tips "Audience is evangelical/Christian conservative, nondenominational, young and old. We're looking for great concepts, not necessarily a big name author or agent. We want to publish books that will sell millions, not just 'flash in the pan' releases. Send us your ideas!"

BAREFOOT BOOKS

2067 Massachusettes Ave., Cambridge MA 02140. Web site: www.barefootbooks.com. **Acquisitions:** Submissions Editor. Publishes hardcover and trade paperback originals. **Publishes 30 titles/year. Receives 2,000 queries and 3,000 mss/year. 35% of books from first-time authors; 60% from unagented writers. Pays 2½-5% royalty on retail price, or makes outright purchase of $5.99-19.99. Offers advance.** Publishes book 2 years after acceptance of ms. Accepts simultaneous submissions. Responds in 4 months to queries; 4 months to proposals; 4 months to mss. Book catalog for 9×12 SAE stamped with $1.80 postage; ms guidelines online.

O-ᴿ "We are a small, independent publishing company that publishes high-quality picture books for children of all ages and specializes in the work of artists and writers from many cultures. We focus on themes that support independence of spirit, encourage openness to others, and foster a life-long love of learning. Prefers full manuscript."

Fiction Juvenile. Barefoot Books only publishes children's picture books and anthologies of folktales. "We do not publish novels. We encourage authors to send their full manuscript. Always include SASE."

Recent Title(s) *We All Went on Safari: A Counting Journey Through Tanzania*, by Laurie Krebs (early learning picture book); *The Fairie's Gift*, by Tanya Robyn Batt (picture book); *The Lady of Ten Thousand Names: Goddess Stories From Many Cultures*, by Burleigh Mutén (illustrated anthology).

Tips "Our audience is made up of children and parents, teachers and students, of many different ages and cultures. Since we are a small publisher, and we definitely publish for a 'niche' market, it is helpful to look at our books and our Web site before submitting, to see if your book would fit into the type of book we publish."

BARRICADE BOOKS, INC.

185 Bridge Plaza N., Suite 308A, Fort Lee NJ 07024-5900. (201)944-7600. Fax: (201)944-6363. **Acquisitions:** Carole Stuart, publisher. Estab. 1991. Publishes hardcover and trade paperback originals, trade paperback reprints. **Publishes 30 titles/year. Receives 200 queries and 100 mss/year. 80% of books from first-time authors; 50% from unagented writers. Pays 10-12% royalty on retail price for hardcover. Offers advance.** Publishes book 18 months after acceptance of ms. Responds in 1 month to queries.

O━ Barricade Books publishes nonfiction, "mostly of the controversial type, and books we can promote with authors who can talk about their topics on radio and television and to the press."

Nonfiction Biography, reference. Subjects include business/economics, ethnic, gay/lesbian, government/politics, health/medicine, history, nature/environment, psychology, sociology, true crime, women's issues/studies. Query with SASE, or submit outline, 1-2 sample chapters. Material will not be returned or responded to without SASE. Reviews artwork/photos as part of ms package. Send photocopies.

Recent Title(s) *Sharks in the Desert*, by John Smith; *Palm Springs Confidential*, by Howard Johns.

Tips "Do your homework. Visit bookshops to find publishers who are doing the kinds of books you want to write. Always submit to a person—not just 'Editor.' Always enclose a SASE or you may not get a response."

BARRON'S EDUCATIONAL SERIES, INC.

250 Wireless Blvd., Hauppauge NY 11788. (800)645-3476. Fax: (631)434-3723. E-mail: waynebarr@barronseduc.com. Web site: barronseduc.com. **Acquisitions:** Wayne Barr, acquisitions editor. Estab. 1941. Publishes hardcover, paperback and mass market originals and software. **Publishes 400 titles/year. Receives 2,000 queries/year. 25% of books from first-time authors; 75% from unagented writers. Pays 12-14% royalty on net receipts. Offers $3-4,000 advance.** Publishes book 18 months after acceptance of ms. Accepts simultaneous submissions. Responds in 3 months to queries; 8 months to mss. Book catalog free; ms guidelines online.

O━ Barron's tends to publish series of books, both for adults and children. "We are always on the lookout for creative nonfiction ideas for children and adults."

Nonfiction Student test prep guides. Subjects include business/economics, child guidance/parenting, education, health/medicine, hobbies, language/literature, New Age, sports, translation, adult education, foreign language, review books, guidance, pets. Query with SASE, or submit outline, 2-3 sample chapters. Reviews artwork/photos as part of ms package.

Recent Title(s) *Hex Appeal*, by Lucy Summers; *Teachable Moments*, by Edie Weinthal.

Tips "Audience is mostly educated self-learners and hobbyists. The writer has the best chance of selling us a book that will fit into one of our series. Children's books have less chance for acceptance because of the glut of submissions. SASE must be included for the return of all materials. Please be patient for replies."

BASIC BOOKS

Perseus Books, 387 Park Ave. S., 12th Floor, New York NY 10016. (212)340-8100. Web site: www.basicbooks.com. **Acquisitions:** Editor. Estab. 1952. Publishes hardcover and trade paperback originals and reprints. Accepts simultaneous submissions. Responds in at least 3 months to queries. Book catalog and ms guidelines free.

O━ "We want serious nonfiction by leading scholars, intellectuals, and journalists. No poetry, romance, children's books, conventional thrillers, or conventional horror."

Nonfiction Subjects include history, psychology, sociology, politics, current affairs. Submit proposal package including outline, sample chapter(s), TOC, cv, SASE. No e-mail or disk submissions.

Recent Title(s) *The Mystery of Capital*, by Hernando de Soto (economics); *The Hidden Hitler*, by Lothar Machton (history/biography); *The Truth Will Set You Free*, by Alice Miller (psychology).

BASIC HEALTH PUBLICATIONS, INC.

28812 Top of the World Dr., Laguna Beach CA 92651. (949)715-7327. Fax: (949)715-7328. Web site: www.basichealthpub.com. **Acquisitions:** Norman Goldfind, publisher. Estab. 2001. Publishes trade paperback and mass market paperback originals and reprints. Accepts simultaneous submissions. Book catalog online; ms guidelines for #10 SASE.

Nonfiction Booklets, trade paperback, mass market paperback, hardcover. Subjects include health/medicine. "We are very highly focused on health, alternative medicine, nutrition, and fitness. Must be well researched and documented with appropriate references. Writing should be aimed at lay audience but also be able to cross over to professional market." Submit proposal package including outline, 2-3 sample chapters, introduction.

Recent Title(s) *The Sinatra Solution: Metabolic Cardiology*, by Stephen Sinatra, MD; *Umbilical Cord Stem Cell Therapy: The Gift of Life From Healthy Newborns*, by David Steenblock, MSDD, and Anthony F. Payne, PhD.

Tips "Our audience is over 30, well educated, middle to upper income. We prefer writers with professional credentials (M.D.s, Ph.D.s, N.D.s, etc.), or writers with backgrounds in health and medicine."

BATTELLE PRESS

505 King Ave., Columbus OH 43201. (614)424-6393. Fax: (614)424-3819. E-mail: press@battelle.org. Web site: www.battelle.org/bookstore. **Acquisitions:** Joe Sheldrick. Estab. 1980. Publishes hardcover and paperback originals and markets primarily by direct mail. **Publishes 15 titles/year. Pays 10% royalty on wholesale price.** Publishes book 6 months after acceptance of ms. Accepts simultaneous submissions. Responds in 1 month to queries. Book catalog free; ms guidelines online.

- Battelle Press strives to be a primary source of books and software on science and technology management.

Nonfiction Subjects include science. "We are looking for management, leadership, project management and communication books specifically targeted to engineers and scientists." Query with SASE. Returns submissions with SASE only by writer's request. Reviews artwork/photos as part of ms package. Send photocopies.
Recent Title(s) *Communications Guide*; *Technically Speaking*.
Tips Audience consists of engineers, researchers, scientists and corporate researchers and developers.

BAYLOR UNIVERSITY PRESS

P.O. Box 97363, Waco TX 76798. (254)710-3164. Fax: (254)710-3440. Web site: www.baylorpress.com. **Acquisitions:** Carey C. Newman, editor. Publishes hardcover and trade paperback originals. **Publishes 30 titles/year. Pays 10% royalty on wholesale price.** Publishes book 1 year after acceptance of ms. Accepts simultaneous submissions. Responds in 2 months to proposals. Ms guidelines online.

- "We publish contemporary and historical scholarly works on religion and public life." Currently emphasizing religious studies.

Nonfiction Subjects include politics/society, rhetoric/religion, sociology/religion, Judaism/Christianity, religion/higher education, Christianity/literature. Submit outline, 1-3 sample chapters.
Recent Title(s) *Building Jewish in the Roman East*, by Peter Richardson; *Encyclopedia of Evangelicalism*, by Randall Balmer; *Not Quite American? The Shaping of Muslim Identity in the United States*, by Yvonne Yazbeck Haddad.

BAYWOOD PUBLISHING CO., INC.

26 Austin Ave., P.O. Box 337, Amityville NY 11701. (631)691-1270. Fax: (631)691-1770. E-mail: baywood@baywood.com. Web site: www.baywood.com. **Acquisitions:** Stuart Cohen, managing editor. Estab. 1964. **Publishes 25 titles/year. Pays 7-15% royalty on retail price. Offers advance.** Publishes book within 1 year after acceptance of ms. Does not accept simultaneous submissions. Book catalog and ms guidelines free or online.

- Baywood Publishing publishes original and innovative books in the humanities and social sciences, including areas such as health sciences, gerontology, death and bereavement, psychology, technical communications and archeology.

Nonfiction Scholarly, technical, scholarly. Subjects include anthropology/archeology, computers/electronic, education, health/medicine, nature/environment, psychology, sociology, women's issues/studies, gerontology, imagery, labor relations, death/dying, drugs. Submit proposal package.
Recent Title(s) *Common Threads: Nine Widows' Journeys Through Love, Loss and Healing*, by Diane S. Kaimann; *Invitation to the Life Course: Toward New Understandings of Later Life*, edited by Richard A. Settersten, Jr; *Exploding Steamboats, Senate Debates and Technical Reports: The Convergence of Technology, Politics and Rhetoric in the Steamboat Bill of 1838*, by R. John Brockmann.

BEACON HILL PRESS OF KANSAS CITY

Nazarene Publishing House, P.O. Box 419527, Kansas City MO 64141. (816)931-1900. Fax: (816)753-4071. **Acquisitions:** Judi Perry, consumer editor. Publishes hardcover and paperback originals. **Publishes 30 titles/year. Pays royalty.** Publishes book 1 year after acceptance of ms. Responds in 3 months to queries.

- "Beacon Hill Press is a Christ-centered publisher that provides authentically Christian resources faithful to God's word and relevant to life."

Nonfiction Accent on holy living; encouragement in daily Christian life. Subjects include applied Christianity, spiritual formation, leadership resources, contemporary issues, and Christian care. No fiction, autobiography, poetry, short stories, or children's picture books. Query with SASE, or submit proposal package. Average ms length: 30,000-60,000.
Recent Title(s) *When God Takes Too Long*, by Joe Bentz.

BEACON PRESS

25 Beacon St., Boston MA 02108-2892. (617)742-2110. Fax: (617)723-3097. E-mail: cvyce@beacon.org. Web site: www.beacon.org. Director: Helene Atwan. **Acquisitions:** Gayatri Patnaik, senior editor (African-American,

Asian-American, Latino, Native American, Jewish, and gay and lesbian studies, anthropology); Joanne Wyckoff, executive editor (child and family issues, environmental concerns); Amy Caldwell, senior editor (poetry, gender studies, gay/lesbian studies, and Cuban studies); Christopher Vyce, assistant editor; Brian Halley, assistant editor. Estab. 1854. Publishes hardcover originals and paperback reprints. **Publishes 60 titles/year. 10% of books from first-time authors. Pays royalty. Offers advance.** Accepts simultaneous submissions. Responds in 3 months to queries.

Imprints Bluestreak Series (innovative literary writing by women of color).

O→ Beacon Press publishes general interest books that promote the following values: the inherent worth and dignity of every person; justice, equity, and compassion in human relations; acceptance of one another; a free and responsible search for truth and meaning; the goal of world community with peace, liberty, and justice for all; respect for the interdependent web of all existence. Currently emphasizing innovative nonfiction writing by people of all colors. De-emphasizing poetry, children's stories, art books, self-help.

Nonfiction Scholarly. Subjects include anthropology/archeology, child guidance/parenting, education, ethnic, gay/lesbian, nature/environment, philosophy, religion, women's issues/studies, world affairs. General nonfiction including works of original scholarship, religion, women's studies, philosophy, current affairs, anthropology, environmental concerns, African-American, Asian-American, Native American, Latino, and Jewish studies, gay and lesbian studies, education, legal studies, child and family issues, Irish studies. *Strongly prefers agented submissions.* Query with SASE, or submit outline, sample chapter(s), résumé, CV. *Strongly prefers referred submissions, on exclusive.*

Recent Title(s) *Radical Equation*, by Robert Moses and Charles Cobb; *All Souls*, by Michael Patrick McDonald; *Speak to Me*, by Marcie Hershman.

Tips "We probably accept only 1 or 2 manuscripts from an unpublished pool of 4,000 submissions/year. No fiction, children's book, or poetry submissions invited. An academic affiliation is helpful."

BEARMANOR MEDIA

P.O. Box 71426, Albany GA 31708. (229)436-4265. E-mail: books@benohmart.com. Web site: www.bearmanormedia.com. Estab. 2001. Publishes trade paperback originals and reprints. **Publishes 25 titles/year.** Accepts simultaneous submissions. Book catalog for #10 SASE; ms guidelines by e-mail.

Nonfiction Autobiography, biography, general nonfiction. Subjects include old-time radio, voice actors, old movies, classic television. Query with SASE, or submit proposal package including outline, list of credits on the subject.

Recent Title(s) *Son of Harpo Speaks*, by Bill Marx.

Tips "My readers love the past. Radio, old movies, old television. My own tastes include voice actors and scripts, especially of radio and television no longer available. I prefer books on subjects that haven't previously been covered as full books. Doesn't matter to me if you're a first-time author or have a track record. Just know your subject!"

⊘ BEDFORD/ST. MARTIN'S

Division of Holtzbrinck Publishers, Boston Office: 75 Arlington St., Boston MA 02116. (617)399-4000. Fax: (617)426-8582. Web site: www.bedfordstmartins.com. New York Office: 33 Irving Place, New York NY 10003. (212)375-7000. Fax: (212)614-1885. Estab. 1981. **Publishes 200 titles/year.** Book catalog online.

O→ College publisher specializing in English (composition, development, literature, and linguistics); history; communications; business and technical writing; and music.

BEHRMAN HOUSE, INC.

11 Edison Place, Springfield NJ 07081. (973)379-7200. Fax: (973)379-7280. Web site: www.behrmanhouse.com. **Acquisitions:** Editorial Committee. Estab. 1921. Accepts simultaneous submissions. Responds in 3 months to queries. Book catalog free; ms guidelines online.

O→ "Behrman House publishes quality books and supplementary materials of Jewish content—history, Bible, philosophy, holidays, ethics, Israel, Hebrew—for the classroom and the reading public."

Nonfiction Children's/juvenile (ages 1-18), reference, textbook. Subjects include ethnic, philosophy, religion. "We want Jewish textbooks for the el-hi market." Query with SASE, or submit résumé, 2 sample chapters, TOC, target audience. No electronic submissions.

Recent Title(s) *Great Israel Scavenger Hunt*, by Scott Blumenthal (Israel); *Rediscovering the Jewish Holidays*, by Nina Beth Cardin and Gila Gevirtz (Jewish Holidays).

FREDERIC C. BEIL, PUBLISHER, INC.

609 Whitaker St., Savannah GA 31401. (912)233-2446. Fax: (912)233-6456. E-mail: beilbook@beil.com. Web site: www.beil.com. **Acquisitions:** Mary Ann Bowman, editor. Estab. 1982. Publishes hardcover originals and

reprints. **Publishes 13 titles/year. Receives 3,500 queries and 13 mss/year. 80% of books from first-time authors; 100% from unagented writers. Pays 7½% royalty on retail price.** Publishes book 20 months after acceptance of ms. Accepts simultaneous submissions. Responds in 1 week to queries. Book catalog free.
Imprints The Sandstone Press; Hypermedia, Inc.

O→ Frederic C. Beil publishes in the fields of history, literature, and biography.

Nonfiction Biography, children's/juvenile, general nonfiction, illustrated book, reference, general trade. Subjects include art/architecture, history, language/literature, book arts. Query with SASE. Reviews artwork/photos as part of ms package. Send photocopies.
Fiction Historical, literary, regional, short story collections, biography. Query with SASE.
Recent Title(s) *Joseph Jefferson: Dean of the American Theatre*, by Arthur Bloom; *Goya, Are You With Me Now?*, by H.E. Francis.
Tips "Our objectives are (1) to offer to the reading public carefully selected texts of lasting value; (2) to adhere to high standards in the choice of materials and in bookmaking craftsmanship; (3) to produce books that exemplify good taste in format and design; and (4) to maintain the lowest cost consistent with quality."

N BELLWETHER-CROSS PUBLISHING

Imprint of Star Publishing Co., Inc., 940 Emmett Ave., #3, Belmont CA 94002. (650)591-3505. Fax: (650)591-3898. Web site: www.starpublishing.com.
Nonfiction Reference, textbook. Submit cover letter and complete ms with SASE. Reviews artwork/photos as part of ms package. Send photocopies.
Recent Title(s) *Transitional Science*, by H. Sue Way and Gaines B. Jackson; *Daring to Be Different: A Manager's Ascent to Leadership*, by James A. Hatherley.

BENTLEY PUBLISHERS

1734 Massachusetts Ave., Cambridge MA 02138-1804. (617)423-4595. Fax: (617)876-9235. Web site: www.bentleypublishers.com. Estab. 1950. Publishes hardcover and trade paperback originals and reprints. Does not accept simultaneous submissions. Book catalog and ms guidelines for 9×12 SAE with 4 first-class stamps. Proposal guidelines online.

O→ Bentley Publishers publishes books for automotive enthusiasts. "We are interested in books that showcase good research, strong illustrations, and valuable technical information."

Nonfiction Automotive subjects only. How-to, technical, theory of operation. Subjects include sports (motor sports). Query with SASE, or submit sample chapter(s), author bio, synopsis, target market. Reviews artwork/photos as part of ms package.
Recent Title(s) *Alex Zanardi: My Sweetest Victory*, by Alex Zanardi and Gianluca Gasparini; *Porsche Boxster Service Manual: 1997-2004*, by Bentley Publishers; *Mercedes-Benz Technical Companion*, by Staff of *The Star* with Mercedes-Benz Club of America.
Tips "Our audience is composed of serious, intelligent automobile, sports car, and racing enthusiasts, automotive technicians and high-performance tuners."

A ⊘ THE BERKLEY PUBLISHING GROUP

Penguin Putnam, Inc., 345 Hudson St., New York NY 10014. (212)366-2000. Web site: www.penguinputnam.com. Estab. 1955. Publishes paperback and mass market originals and reprints. **Publishes more than 500 titles/year.** Does not accept simultaneous submissions.
Imprints Ace; Berkley; Jove.

- *Currently not accepting unsolicited submissions.*

O→ The Berkley Publishing Group publishes a variety of general nonfiction and fiction including the traditional categories of romance, mystery and science fiction.

Nonfiction Biography, general nonfiction, how-to, reference, self-help. Subjects include business/economics, child guidance/parenting, creative nonfiction, gay/lesbian, health/medicine, history, New Age, psychology, true crime, women's issues/studies, job-seeking communication, positive thinking, general commercial publishing. No memoirs or personal stories. *Prefers agented submissions.*
Fiction Adventure, historical, literary, mystery, romance, spiritual, suspense, western, young adult. No occult fiction. *Prefers agented submissions.*
Recent Title(s) *Visions in Death*, by Norah Roberts; *Dark Secret*, by Christine Feehan.

BERRETT-KOEHLER PUBLISHERS, INC.

235 Montgomery St., #650, San Francisco CA 94104. (415)288-0260. Fax: (415)362-2512. E-mail: bkpub@bkpub.com. Web site: www.bkconnection.com. **Acquisitions:** Jeevan Sivasubramaniam. Publishes hardcover originals, trade paperback originals, mass market paperback originals, hardcover reprints, trade paperback reprints. **Publishes 40 titles/year. Receives 1,300 queries and 800 mss/year. 20-30% of books from first-time authors;**

70% from unagented writers. Pays 10-20% royalty. Publishes book 10 months after acceptance of ms. Accepts simultaneous submissions. Responds in 1 month to queries; 1 month to proposals; 1 month to mss. Book catalog and ms guidelines online.
Nonfiction General nonfiction, gift book, how-to, humor, scholarly, self-help, textbook. Subjects include business/economics, community, government/politics, New Age, spirituality, world affairs. Submit proposal package including outline, author bio, 1-2 sample chapters. Hard-copy proposals only. Do not e-mail, fax, or phone please. Reviews artwork/photos as part of ms package. Send photocopies or originals with SASE.
Recent Title(s) *Alternatives to Globalization*, by Jerry Mander & IFG (current affairs); *Leadership and the New Science*, by Margaret Wheatley (business); *Confessions of an Economic Hit Man*, by John Perkins (*New York Times* bestseller).
Tips "Our audience is business leaders, OD consultants, academics, economists, political leaders, and people with a popular platform. Use common sense, do your research, know what kind of books we publish, address the query properly, try not to have coffee-mug stains on your cover letter."

N BET BOOKS

850 3rd Ave., New York NY 10022. Web site: www.bet.com/books. **Acquisitions:** Glenda Howard, senior editor (Sepia and New Spirit); Karen Thomas, editorial director (Arabesque). Estab. 1998. Responds in 2-4 months to queries.
Imprints Arabesque (romance with predominantly African-American characters); Sepia (contemporary novels—thrillers, mystery, adventure, urban life); New Spirit (inspirational novels and motivational nonfiction in which characters overcome challenges through faith).
Tips "Please do not phone to see if your manuscript was received or returned, or to find out what we thought of it. A self-addressed, stamped postcard can be enclosed with your submission if you want confirmation of its arrival. Specify whether you would like your manuscript returned or recycled if it is not right for us."

BETHANY HOUSE PUBLISHERS

11400 Hampshire Ave. S., Minneapolis MN 55438. (952)829-2500. Fax: (952)996-1304. Web site: www.bethanyhouse.com. Estab. 1956. Publishes hardcover and trade paperback originals, mass market paperback reprints. **Publishes 90-100 titles/year. 2% of books from first-time authors; 50% from unagented writers. Pays royalty on net price. Offers advance.** Publishes book 1 year after acceptance of ms. Accepts simultaneous submissions. Responds in 3 months to queries. Book catalog for 9×12 SAE with 5 first-class stamps; ms guidelines online.

- *All unsolicited mss returned unopened.*
- Bethany House Publishers specializes in books that communicate Biblical truth and assist people in both spiritual and practical areas of life. "While we do not accept unsolicited queries or proposals via telephone or e-mail, we will consider 1-page queries sent by fax and directed to Adult Nonfiction, Adult Fiction, or Young Adult/Children."

Nonfiction Children's/juvenile, gift book, how-to, reference, self-help, spiritual growth. Subjects include child guidance/parenting, Biblical disciplines, personal and corporate renewal, emerging generations, devotional, marriage and family, applied theology, inspirational.
Fiction Historical, young adult, contemporary.
Recent Title(s) *Under God*, by Toby Mae and Michael Tait (nonfiction); *Candle in the Darkness*, by Lynn Austin (fiction); *God Called a Girl*, by Shannon Kubiak Primicerio (YA nonfiction).
Tips "Bethany House Publishers' publishing program relates Biblical truth to all areas of life—whether in the framework of a well-told story, of a challenging book for spiritual growth, or of a Bible reference work. We are seeking high quality fiction and nonfiction that will inspire and challenge our audience."

A BEYOND WORDS PUBLISHING, INC.

20827 NW Cornell Rd., Suite 500, Hillsboro OR 97124-9808. (503)531-8700. Fax: (503)531-8773. Web site: www.beyondword.com. **Acquisitions:** Cynthia Black, editor-in-chief. Estab. 1984. Publishes hardcover and trade paperback originals and paperback reprints. **Publishes 10-15 titles/year.** Accepts simultaneous submissions.

- No electronic submissions or queries. Does not accept unagented manuscripts.

Nonfiction Wants body, mind and spirit, focusing on holistic living, spiritual parenting, spiritual lifestyles, native wisdom and spiritual needs.
Tips "*Beyond Words* markets to cultural, creative people, mostly women ages 30-60. Study our list before you submit and check out our Web site to make sure your book is a good fit for our list."

BIG IDEA, INC.

P.O. Box 1299, Batavia IL 60510. E-mail: cindy.kenney@bigidea.com. Web site: www.bigidea.com. **Acquisitions:** Cindy Kenney, senior managing editor (curriculum, children's books). Estab. 1992. Publishes hardcover originals. **Publishes 20 titles/year. Receives 1,500 queries and 1,000 mss/year. 5% of books from first-time authors; 50% from unagented writers. Pays no royalties.** Publishes book 20 months after acceptance of ms. Accepts simultaneous submissions. Responds in 3-6 months to queries; 3-6 months to proposals; 3-6 months to mss.

Nonfiction Children's/juvenile, coffee table book, gift book, humor, illustrated book, reference, textbook, novelty. Subjects include child guidance/parenting, creative nonfiction, education, religion. Nonfiction is geared toward the gift market or family/parenting tools. Material must be highly innovative and creative. Query with SASE.

Fiction Humor, juvenile, picture books, religious, young adult. Submit complete ms for children's books and curriculum lessons. Otherwise, query with SASE.

Recent Title(s) *A VeggieTales Bible Dictionary*, by Cindy Kenney and Karen Brothers (resource); *Lord of the Beans*, by Phil Vischer (picture book); *Mess Detectives*, by Doug Peterson (storybook).

Tips "Audience includes parents and children ages 3 through teen. All submissions must conform to the Big Idea style and be highly innovative, witty, and fun."

⊘ BLACKBIRCH PRESS, INC.

Thomson Gale, 15822 Bernardo Center Dr., Suite C, San Diego CA 92127. Web site: www.galegroup.com/blackbirch/. **Acquisitions:** Publisher. Estab. 1992. Publishes hardcover and trade paperback originals. Accepts simultaneous submissions. Replies only if interested to queries. Ms guidelines free.

O━ Blackbirch Press publishes educational nonfiction books for elementary and middle school students.

Nonfiction Biography, children's/juvenile, illustrated book, reference. Subjects include animals, anthropology/archeology, art/architecture, education, health/medicine, history, nature/environment, science, sports, travel, women's issues/studies. Publishes in series—6-8 books at a time. "No proposals for adult readers, please." *No unsolicited mss or proposals. No phone calls.* Query with SASE. Cover letters and résumés are useful for identifying new authors. Reviews artwork/photos as part of ms package. Send photocopies.

Recent Title(s) *A Whale on Her Own: The True Story of Wilma the Whale*, by Brian Skerry; *Flies*, by Elaine Pascoe.

Tips "We cannot return submissions or send guidelines/replies without an enclosed SASE."

⊘ BLEAK HOUSE BOOKS

953 E. Johnson St., Madison WI 53703. (608)259-8370. Web site: www.bleakhousebooks.com. **Acquisitions:** Julie Kuczynski, mystery editor; Alison Embley, literary editor. Estab. 1995. **Publishes 6-10 titles/year. Receives 250+ queries and 50 mss/year. 50% of books from first-time authors; 90% from unagented writers. Pays 7½-15% royalty on wholesale price. Offers $500-4,000 advance.** Publishes book 12-18 months after acceptance of ms. Accepts simultaneous submissions. Responds in 1-2 months to queries; 2-3 months to mss. Book catalog online.

Fiction Literary, mystery. "We are looking for gritty mystery/crime/suspense. Characters should be psychologically complex, flawed, and human. We are rarely interested in cozies and are never interested in animals or inanimate objects that solve mysteries. We want books that are part of a planned series, and we want authors that understand the business of publishing. We are also looking for dark and quirky literary fiction. Tell us a story that hasn't been told before. The most important thing is the quality of writing. Just because your best friends and family loved the book doesn't mean it's going to go over big with everybody else." Query with SASE. *All unsolicited mss returned unopened.*

Recent Title(s) *Blood of the Lamb*, by Michael Lister; *A Prayer for Dawn*, by Nathan Singer; *The Nail Knot*, by John Galligan.

Tips "Our audience is made up of 2 groups. The first is mystery readers—a group dedicated to quality books that have a satisfaying conclusion to the age old questions of 'Whoodunit?' The second group reads books to get a different perspective on the human condition, to live through characters they haven't seen or heard from before. These readers aren't afraid of a book that is quirky or disturbed. Do not call us about submission guidelines, your query letter, or anything else that can be answered in this book or others like it. Make sure your book is finished before contacting us. Our job is to clean up small stuff, not help rewrite a book. We are very loyal to our authors and work closely with our authors. We expect an author to be ready to work hard. It's a two way street."

BLOOMBERG PRESS

Imprint of Bloomberg L.P., 731 Lexington Ave., New York NY 10022. Web site: www.bloomberg.com/books. Estab. 1995. Publishes hardcover and trade paperback originals. **Publishes 18-22 titles/year. Receives 200 queries and 20 mss/year. 45% from unagented writers. Pays negotiable, competitive royalty. Offers negotiable advance.** Publishes book 9 months after acceptance of ms. Accepts simultaneous submissions. With SASE, responds in 1 month to queries. Book catalog for 10×13 SAE with 5 first-class stamps.

Imprints Bloomberg Professional Library.

O→ Bloomberg Press publishes professional books for practitioners in the financial markets. "We publish commercially successful, very high-quality books that stand out clearly from the competition by their brevity, ease of use, sophistication, and abundance of practical tips and strategies; books readers need, will use, and appreciate."

Nonfiction How-to, reference, technical. Subjects include business/economics, money/finance, professional books on finance, investment and financial services, and books for financial advisors. "We are looking for authorities and for experienced service journalists. Do not send us unfocused books containing general information already covered by books in the marketplace. We do not publish business, management, leadership, or career books." Submit outline, sample chapter(s), SAE with sufficient postage, or submit complete ms.

Tips "*Bloomberg Professional Library*: Audience is upscale, financial professionals—traders, dealers, brokers, planners and advisors, financial managers, money managers, company executives, sophisticated investors. Authors are experienced financial journalists and/or financial professionals nationally prominent in their specialty for some time who have proven an ability to write a successful book. Research Bloomberg and look at our books in a library or bookstore, and peruse our Web site."

BLOOMSBURY CHILDREN'S BOOKS

Imprint of Bloomsbury USA, 175 Fifth Ave., Suite 315, New York NY 10010. (646)307-5858. Fax: (212)982-2837. E-mail: bloomsburykids@bloomsburyusa.com. Web site: www.bloomsburyusa.com. **Publishes 60 titles/year. 25% of books from first-time authors. Pays royalty. Offers advance.** Accepts simultaneous submissions. Responds in 6 months to queries; 6 months to mss. Book catalog and ms guidelines online.

- No phone calls or e-mails.

Fiction Adventure, fantasy, historical, humor, juvenile, multicultural, mystery, picture books, poetry, science fiction, sports, suspense, young adult, animal, anthology, concept, contemporary, folktales, problem novels. "We publish picture books, chapter books, middle grade, and YA novels, and some nonfiction." Query with SASE, or submit synopsis, first 3 chapters with SASE.

Recent Title(s) *Where Is Coco Going?*, by Sloane Tanen (picture books); *Once Upon a Curse*, by E.D. Baker (middle grade); *Enna Burning*, by Shannon Hale (young adult fantasy).

Tips "Do not send originals or only copy. Be sure your work is appropriate for us. Familiarize yourself with our list by going to bookstores or libraries."

BNA BOOKS

Imprint of The Bureau of National Affairs, Inc., 1231 25th St. NW, Washington DC 20037. (202)452-4343. Fax: (202)452-4997. E-mail: books@bna.com. Web site: www.bnabooks.com. **Acquisitions:** Jim Fattibene, acquisitions manager. Estab. 1929. Publishes hardcover and softcover originals. Accepts simultaneous submissions. Book catalog and ms guidelines online.

O→ BNA Books publishes professional reference books written by lawyers, for lawyers.

Nonfiction Legal reference. Subjects include labor and employment law, intellectual property law, health law, legal practice, labor relations, arbitration and ADR, occupational safety and health law, employee benefits law. No fiction, biographies, bibliographies, cookbooks, religion books, humor, or trade books. Submit detailed TOC or outline, cv, intended market, estimated word length.

Recent Title(s) *Computer and Intellectual Property Crime: Federal & State Law, 2004 Cumulative Supplement*; *Patent Litigation Strategies Handbooks, 2004 Cumulative Supplement*; *Pharmaceutical Patent Law*.

Tips "Our audience is made up of practicing lawyers and law librarians. We look for authoritative and comprehensive treatises that can be supplemented or revised every year or 2 on legal subjects of interest to those audiences."

BOA EDITIONS, LTD.

260 East Ave., Rochester NY 14604. (585)546-3410. Fax: (585)546-3913. E-mail: info@boaeditions.org. Web site: www.boaeditions.org. Estab. 1976. Publishes hardcover and trade paperback originals. **Publishes 11-13 titles/year. Receives 1,000 queries and 700 mss/year. 15% of books from first-time authors; 90% from unagented writers. Negotiates royalties. Offers variable advance.** Publishes book 18 months after acceptance of ms. Accepts simultaneous submissions. Responds in 1 week to queries; 5 months to mss. Ms guidelines online.

O→ BOA Editions publishes distinguished collections of poetry, fiction and poetry in translation. "Our goal is to publish the finest American contemporary poetry, fiction and poetry in translation."

Poetry BOA offers a first book poetry prize of $1,500 and book publication for the winner. For guidelines, see the home page of our Web site.

Recent Title(s) *Owner of the House*, by Louis Simpson; *Book of My Nights*, by Li-Young Lee.

Tips "Readers who, like Whitman, expect of the poet to 'indicate more than the beauty and dignity which always attach to dumb real objects . . . They expect him to indicate the path between reality and their souls,' are the audience of BOA's books."

BONUS BOOKS, INC.

9255 Sunset Blvd., #711, Los Angeles CA 90069. E-mail: submissions@bonusbooks.com. Web site: www.bonusbooks.com. **Acquisitions:** Editor. Estab. 1985. Publishes hardcover and trade paperback originals and reprints. Accepts simultaneous submissions. Responds in 6-8 weeks to queries. Book catalog for 9X11 SAE; ms guidelines for #10 SASE.

O→ Bonus Books publishes quality nonfiction in a variety of categories, including entertainment/pop culture, games/gambling, sports/sports biography, regional (Chicago), broadcasting, fundraising.

Nonfiction Biography, self-help. Subjects include business/economics, cooking/foods/nutrition, education, health/medicine, hobbies, money/finance, regional, sports (gambling), women's issues/studies, pop culture, automotive/self-help, current affairs, broadcasting, business/self-help, Chicago people and places, collectibles, education/self-help, fundraising, handicapping winners, home and health, entertainment. Query with SASE, or submit outline, author bio, 2-3 sample chapters, TOC, SASE. All submissions and queries must include SASE. Reviews artwork/photos as part of ms package.

Recent Title(s) *America's Right Turn*, by David Franke and Richard A. Viguerie; *The On Position*, by Katie Moran; *In the Midst of Wolves*, by Keith Remer.

BOWTIE PRESS

BowTie, Inc., P.O. Box 6050, Mission Viejo CA 92690. E-mail: bowtiepress@fancypubs.com. Web site: www.bowtiepress.com. **Acquisitions:** Karla Austin, business operations manager (adult nonfiction); Art Stickney, acquisitions editor (adult nonfiction). Estab. 1995. Publishes hardcover and trade paperback originals. **Publishes 30 titles/year. Receives 250 queries and 50 mss/year. 20% of books from first-time authors; 90% from unagented writers. Payment varies from author to author.** Publishes book 1 year after acceptance of ms. Accepts simultaneous submissions. Responds in 1 month to queries; 2 months to proposals; 3 months to mss. Book catalog and ms guidelines online.

Imprints Kennel Club Books (Andrew DePrisco); Doral Publishing (Art Stickney).

Nonfiction Coffee table book, general nonfiction, gift book, how-to, illustrated book, reference. Subjects include agriculture/horticulture, animals, gardening, nature/environment, science, marine subjects, crafts, education. Submit proposal package including outline, sample chapter(s). Reviews artwork/photos as part of ms package. Send photocopies.

BOYDS MILLS PRESS

Highlights for Children, 815 Church St., Honesdale PA 18431-1895. (570)253-1164. Web site: www.boydsmillspress.com. Publisher: Kent L. Brown. **Acquisitions:** Larry Rosler, editorial director. Estab. 1990. Publishes hardcover originals and trade paperback reprints. **Publishes 50 titles/year. Receives 10,000 queries and 7,500 mss/year. 40% of books from first-time authors; 60% from unagented writers. Pays royalty on retail price. Offers variable advance.** Accepts simultaneous submissions. Responds in 1 month to mss. Book catalog online.

Imprints Wordsong (poetry); Calkins Creek Books (American history).

O→ Boyds Mills Press, the book-publishing arm of *Highlights for Children*, publishes a wide range of children's books of literary merit, from preschool to young adult. Currently emphasizing picture books and novels (but no fantasy, romance, or horror). Time between acceptance and publication depends on acceptance of ms.

Nonfiction Children's/juvenile. Subjects include agriculture/horticulture, animals, ethnic, history, nature/environment, sports, travel. "Nonfiction should be accurate, tailored to young audience. Prefer simple, narrative style, but in compelling, evocative language. Too many authors overwrite for the young audience and get bogged down in minutiae. Boyds Mills Press is not interested in manuscripts depicting violence, explicit sexuality, racism of any kind, or which promote hatred. We also are not the right market for self-help books." Query with SASE, or submit proposal package including outline. Reviews artwork/photos as part of ms package.

Fiction Adventure, ethnic, historical, humor, juvenile, mystery, picture books, young adult (adventure, animal, contemporary, ethnic, historical, humor, mystery, sports). "We look for imaginative stories or concepts with simple, lively language that employs a variety of literary devices, including rhythm, repitition, and when composed properly, rhyme. The stories may entertain or challenge, but the content must be age appropriate for children. For middle and young adult fiction we look for stories told in strong, considered prose driven by well-imagined characters." No fantasy, romance, horror. Query with SASE. Submit outline/synopsis and 3 sample chapters for novel or complete ms for picture book.

Poetry "Poetry should be appropriate for young audiences, clever, fun language, with easily understood meaning. Too much poetry is either too simple and static in meaning, or too obscure." Collections should have a unifying theme.

Recent Title(s) *Rat*, by Jan Cheripko (novel); *The Alligator in the Closet*, by David Harrison (poetry); *The President Is Shot* (nonfiction).

Tips "Our audience is pre-school to young adult. Concentrate first on your writing. Polish it. Then—and only then—select a market. We need primarily picture books with fresh ideas and characters—avoid worn themes of 'coming-of-age,' 'new sibling,' and self-help ideas. We are always interested in multicultural settings. Please—no anthropomorphic characters."

⊘ BRANDEN PUBLISHING CO., INC.

P.O. Box 812094, Wellesley MA 02482. (781)235-3634. Fax: (781)790-1056. Web site: www.brandenbooks.com. **Acquisitions:** Adolph Caso, editor. Estab. 1909. Publishes hardcover and trade paperback originals, reprints, and software. **Publishes 15 titles/year. 80% of books from first-time authors; 90% from unagented writers. Pays 5-10% royalty on net receipts. 10 author's copies. Offers $1,000 maximum advance.** Publishes book 10 months after acceptance of ms. Responds in 1 month to queries.

Imprints International Pocket Library and Popular Technology; Four Seas and Brashear; Branden Books.

O→ Branden publishes books by or about women, children, military, Italian-American, or African-American themes.

Nonfiction Biography, children's/juvenile, general nonfiction, illustrated book, reference, technical, textbook. Subjects include Americana, art/architecture, computers/electronic, contemporary culture, education, ethnic, government/politics, health/medicine, history, military/war, music/dance, photography, sociology, software, classics. Especially looking for "about 10 manuscripts on national and international subjects, including biographies of well-known individuals. Currently specializing in Americana, Italian-American, African-American." No religion or philosophy. *No unsolicited mss.* Paragraph query only with author's vita and SASE. No telephone, e-mail, or fax inquiries. Reviews artwork/photos as part of ms package.

Fiction Ethnic (histories, integration), historical, literary, military/war, religious (historical-reconstructive), short story collections. Looking for "contemporary, fast pace, modern society." No science, mystery, experimental, horor, or pornography. *No unsolicited mss.* Query with SASE. Paragraph query only with author's vita and SASE. No telephone, e-mail, or fax inquiries.

Recent Title(s) *Gilber Van Zandt*, by Marilyn Sequin; *The Wisdom of Angels*, by Martha Cummings; *Kaso Verb Conjugation System*, by Adolph Caso (English, Spanish, Italian).

BRENNER MICROCOMPUTING, INC.

Imprint of Brenner Information Group, P.O. Box 721000, San Diego CA 92172. (858)538-0093. Fax: (858)538-0380. E-mail: brenner@brennerbooks.com. Web site: www.brennerbooks.com. **Acquisitions:** Jenny Hanson, acquisitions manager (pricing & ranges). Estab. 1982. Publishes trade paperback and electronic originals. **Publishes 15 titles/year. Receives 1 ms and 10 queries/year. 5% of books from first-time authors; 95% from unagented writers. Pays 5-15% royalty on wholesale price, or retail price, or net receipts. Offers $0-1,000 advance.** Publishes book 1 year after acceptance of ms. Accepts simultaneous submissions. Responds in 1 month to queries; 1 month to proposals; 1 month to mss. Book catalog free; ms guidelines for #10 SASE.

Nonfiction How-to, reference, self-help, technical. Subjects include time statistics and pricing for small businesses.

BREVET PRESS, INC.

P.O. Box 82, 124 S. Main, Worthington SD 57077-0082. **Acquisitions:** Donald P. Mackintosh, publisher (business); Peter E. Reid, managing editor (technical); A. Melton, editor (Americana); B. Mackintosh, editor (history). Estab. 1972. Publishes hardcover and paperback originals and reprints. **Publishes 15 titles/year. 50% of books from first-time authors; 100% from unagented writers. Pays 5% royalty. Offers $1,000 average advance.** Publishes book 1 year after acceptance of ms. Accepts simultaneous submissions. Responds in 2 months to queries. Book catalog free.

O→ Brevet Books seeks nonfiction with "market potential and literary excellence."

Nonfiction Technical. Subjects include Americana, business/economics, history. Query with SASE. Reviews artwork/photos as part of ms package. Send photocopies.

Tips "Keep sexism out of the manuscripts."

BRISTOL PUBLISHING ENTERPRISES

2714 McCone Ave., Hayward CA 94545. (800)346-4889. Fax: (800)346-7064. E-mail: orders@bristolpublishing.com. Web site: bristolcookbooks.com. Estab. 1988. Publishes trade paperback originals. Accepts simultaneous submissions. Book catalog online.

Imprints Nitty Gritty cookbooks; The Best 50 Recipe Series; Pet Care Series.

Nonfiction Cookbook, craft books, pet care books. Subjects include cooking/foods/nutrition. Send a proposal, or query with possible outline, brief note about author's background, sample of writing, or chapter from ms.

Recent Title(s) *The Best 50 Chocolate Recipes*, by Christie Katona; *No Salt, No Sugar, No Fat*, by Jacqueline Williams and Goldie Silverman (revised edition); *Wraps and Roll-Ups*, by Dona Z. Meilach (revised edition).
Tips Readers of cookbooks are novice cooks. ''Our books educate without intimidating. We require our authors to have some form of background in the food industry.''

BROADMAN & HOLMAN PUBLISHERS

Lifeway Christian Resources, 127 Ninth Ave. N., Nashville TN 37234. (615)251-2644. Fax: (615)251-3752. Web site: www.broadmanholman.com. Publisher: David Shepherd. **Acquisitions:** Leonard G. Goss, acquisitions editor. Estab. 1934. Publishes hardcover and paperback originals. **Publishes 90-100 titles/year. Pays negotiable royalty.** Accepts simultaneous submissions. Responds in 9-12 months to queries; 9-12 months to mss. Ms guidelines online.

O→ Broadman & Holman Publishers publishes books that provide biblical solutions that spiritually transform individuals and cultures. Currently emphasizing inspirational/gift books, general Christian living and books on Christianity and society.

Nonfiction Gift book, reference, textbook, devotional journals, juvenile. Subjects include religion, spirituality. Christian living, devotionals, prayer, women, youth, spiritual growth, Christian history, parenting, home school, biblical studies, science and faith, current events, marriage and family concerns, church life, pastoral helps, preaching, evangelism. ''Materials in these areas must be suited for an evangelical Christian readership.'' No poetry, biography, or sermons. Query with SASE.
Fiction Adventure, mystery, religious (general religious, inspirational, religious fantasy, religious mystery/suspense, religious thriller, religious romance), western. ''We publish fiction in all the main genres. We want not only a very good story, but also one that sets forth Christian values. Nothing that lacks a positive Christian emphasis (but do not preach, however); nothing that fails to sustain reader interest.'' Query with SASE.
Recent Title(s) *A Greater Freedom*, by Oliver North; *The Beloved Disciple*, by Beth Moore; *Against All Odds*, by Chuck Norris.

BROADWAY BOOKS

Imprint of Doubleday Broadway Publishing Group, Random House, Inc., 1745 Broadway, New York NY 10019. (212)782-9000. Web site: www.broadwaybooks.com. Estab. 1995. Publishes hardcover and trade paperback books.

O→ Broadway publishes general interest nonfiction and fiction for adults.

Nonfiction Biography, cookbook, general nonfiction, illustrated book, reference, General interest adult books. Subjects include business/economics, child guidance/parenting, contemporary culture, cooking/foods/nutrition, gay/lesbian, government/politics, health/medicine, history, memoirs, money/finance, multicultural, New Age, psychology, sex, spirituality, sports, travel (narrative), women's issues/studies, current affairs, motivational/inspirational, popular culture, consumer reference. *Agented submissions only.*
Fiction Publishes a limited list of commercial fiction, mainly chick lit. *Agented submissions only.*
Recent Title(s) *A Short History of Nearly Everything*, by Bill Bryson; *The Automatic Millionaire*, by David Bach; *Babyville*, by Jane Green.

BUCKNELL UNIVERSITY PRESS

Taylor Hall, Bucknell University, Lewisburg PA 17837. (570)577-1552. E-mail: clingham@bucknell.edu. Web site: www.departments.bucknell.edu/univ_press. **Acquisitions:** Greg Clingham, director. Estab. 1969. Publishes hardcover originals. **Publishes 35-40 titles/year.** Does not accept simultaneous submissions. Book catalog free; ms guidelines online.

O→ ''In all fields, our criteria are scholarly excellence, critical originality, and interdisciplinary and theoretical expertise and sensitivity.''

Nonfiction Scholarly. Subjects include art/architecture, history, language/literature, philosophy, psychology, religion, sociology, English and American literary criticism, literary theory and cultural studies, historiography, art history, modern languages, classics, anthropology, ethnology, cultural and political geography, Hispanic and Latin American studies. Series: Bucknell Studies in Eighteenth-Century Literature and Culture, Bucknell Series in Latin American Literature and Theory, Eighteenth-Century Scotland. Submit proposal package including cv, SASE.
Recent Title(s) *The Selected Essays of Donald Greene*, edited by John Lawrence Abbott; *Brazilian Science Fiction: Cultural Myths and Nationhood in the Land of the Future*, by M. Elizabeth Ginway; *Borges and Translation: The Irreverence of Periphery*, by Sergio Waisman.

BUILDERBOOKS.COM™

National Association of Home Builders, 1201 15th St. NW, Washington DC 20005-2800. (800)368-5242. Fax: (202)266-8559. E-mail: publishing@nahb.com. Web site: www.builderbooks.com. Managing Director: Larry

Fox, ext. 8201. Senior Editor: Doris M. Thennyson, ext. 8368. Managing Editor: Aaron White, ext. 8476 (safety; multifamily; seniors housing; business and construction management for remodelers, builders, developers and others; land development; customer relations; computerization; construction how-to; economics; legal issues; marketing and selling for builders, remodelers, developers, suppliers, manufacturers and their sales and marketing directors). Publishes "books and electronic products for builders, remodelers, developers, sales and marketing professionals, manufacturers, suppliers, and consumers in the residential construction industry. Writers must be experts." **Publishes 20 titles/year. 33% of books from first-time authors; 99% from unagented writers. Pays royalty.** Publishes book 6-12 months after acceptance of ms. Does not accept simultaneous submissions. Responds in 1-2 months to queries. Book catalog free or on Web site; ms guidelines by e-mail.

Nonfiction "We prefer a detailed outline on a strong residential construction industry topic. Our readers like step-by-step how-to books and electronic products, no history or philosophy of the industry." How-to, reference, technical. Subjects include safety, multifamily, seniors housing, remodeling, land development, business and construction management, customer service, computerization, financial management, and sales and marketing. Query first. E-mail queries accepted. Include electronic and hard copy artwork/photos as part of ms package. Send photocopies.

Recent Title(s) *Building Community: Live, Gather, Play*, by Tom Kopf; *Customer Service for Home Builders*, by Carol Smith; *Jobsite Phrasebook, English/Spanish*, by Kent Shepard.

Tips Audience is primarily home builders, remodelers, developers, sales and marketing professionals, manufactuers, suppliers, and consumers in the residential construction industry. Ask for a sample outline.

⊘ BULFINCH PRESS

Time Life Bldg., 1271 Avenue of the Americas, New York NY 10020. (212)522-8700. Web site: www.bulfinchpress.com. Publishes hardcover and trade paperback originals. Accepts simultaneous submissions.

- *No unsolicited mss.* It is suggested that you enlist the help of an agent.

O-ᵣ Bulfinch Press publishes large format art books. "We are the home of Ansel Adams and Irving Penn."

Nonfiction Coffee table book, cookbook, gift book, illustrated book. Subjects include art/architecture, cooking/foods/nutrition, gardening, photography, interior design, lifestyle. Query with SASE.

Recent Title(s) *Brunscwig & Fils Up Close: From Grand Rooms to Your Rooms*, by Murray Douglas and Chippy Irvine; *The Party Planner*, by David Tutera; *Gardens to Go: Creating & Designing a Container Garden*, by Sydney Eddison.

BURFORD BOOKS

32 Morris Ave., Springfield NJ 07081. (973)258-0960. Fax: (973)258-0113. **Acquisitions:** Peter Burford, publisher. Estab. 1997. Publishes hardcover originals, trade paperback originals and reprints. **Publishes 12 titles/year. Receives 300 queries and 200 mss/year. 30% of books from first-time authors; 60% from unagented writers. Pays royalty on wholesale price.** Publishes book 18 months after acceptance of ms. Accepts simultaneous submissions. Responds in 1 month to queries; 1 month to proposals; 2 months to mss. Book catalog and ms guidelines free.

O-ᵣ Burford Books publishes books on all aspects of the outdoors, from backpacking to sports, practical and literary.

Nonfiction How-to, illustrated book. Subjects include animals, cooking/foods/nutrition, hobbies, military/war, nature/environment, recreation, sports, travel. Query with SASE, or submit outline. Reviews artwork/photos as part of ms package. Send photocopies.

Recent Title(s) *Saltwater Fishing*, by Jim Freda; *One Hundred Stretches*, by Jim Brown.

BUTTE PUBLICATIONS, INC.

P.O. Box 1328, Hillsboro OR 97123-1328. (503)648-9791. Fax: (503)693-9526. E-mail: service@buttepublications.com. Web site: www.buttepublications.com. Estab. 1992. **Publishes several titles/year.** Accepts simultaneous submissions. Responds in 6 or more months to mss. Book catalog and ms guidelines for #10 SASE or online; ms guidelines online.

O-ᵣ Butte Publications, Inc., publishes classroom books related to deafness and language.

Nonfiction Children's/juvenile, textbook. Subjects include education (all related to field of deafness and education). Submit proposal package, including author bio, synopsis, market survey, 2-3 sample chapters, SASE and ms (if completed). Reviews artwork/photos as part of ms package. Send photocopies.

Fiction Submit complete ms.

Recent Title(s) *Cajun's Song*, by Darlene Toole; *Diccionario Visual Plus*, by Virginia McKinney; *Slangman Guides*, by Davie Burke.

Tips "Audience is students, teachers, parents, and professionals in the arena dealing with deafness and hearing loss. We are not seeking autobiographies or novels."

CANDLEWICK PRESS

2067 Massachusetts Ave., Cambridge MA 02140. (617)661-3330. Fax: (617)661-0565. Web site: www.candlewick.com. President/Publisher: Karen Lotz. **Acquisitions:** Deb Wayshak, senior editor (fiction); Joan Powers, editor-at-large (picture books); Liz Bicknell, editorial director/associate publisher (poetry, picture books, fiction); Mary Lee Donovan, executive editor (picture books, nonfiction/fiction); Sarah Ketchersid, editor (board, toddler). Estab. 1991. Publishes hardcover and trade paperback originals and reprints. **Publishes 200 titles/year. 5% of books from first-time authors.**

Candlewick Press publishes high-quality, illustrated children's books for ages infant through young adult. "We are a truly child-centered publisher."

Nonfiction Children's/juvenile. "Good writing is essential; specific topics are less important than strong, clear writing." *No unsolicited mss.*

Fiction Juvenile, picture books, young adult. *No unsolicited mss.*

Recent Title(s) *Dragonology*, by Dr. Ernest Drake; *Feed*, by M.T. Anderson (National Book Award finalist); *Encyclopedia Prehistorica: Dinosaurs*, by Robert Sabuda and Matthew Reinhart.

Tips "*We no longer accept unsolicited mss.* See our Web site for further information about us."

C&T PUBLISHING

1651 Challenge Dr., Concord CA 94520-5206. (925)677-0377. Fax: (925)677-0373. E-mail: ctinfo@ctpub.com. Web site: www.ctpub.com. Estab. 1983. Publishes hardcover and trade paperback originals. **Publishes 70 titles/year.** Accepts simultaneous submissions. Responds in 3 months to queries. Book catalog free; proposal guidelines online.

"C&T publishes well-written, beautifully designed books on quilting and fiber crafts, embroidery, dollmaking, knitting and paper crafts."

Nonfiction How-to (quilting), illustrated book. Subjects include hobbies, quilting books, occasional quilt picture books, quilt-related crafts, wearable art, needlework, fiber and surface embellishments, other books relating to fabric crafting and paper crafting. Extensive proposal guidelines are available on the company's Web site.

Recent Title(s) *Puzzle Quilts*, by Paula Nadelstern; *Fast Knits Fat Needles*, by Sally Harding.

Tips "In our industry, we find that how-to books have the longest selling life. Quiltmakers, sewing enthusiasts, needle artists, fiber artists and paper crafters are our audience. We like to see new concepts or techniques. Include some great samples, and you'll get our attention quickly. Dynamic design is hard to resist, and if that's your forte, show us what you've done."

CANON PRESS

P.O. Box 8729, Moscow ID 83843. (208)892-8074. Fax: (208)892-8143. E-mail: submissions@canonpress.org. Web site: www.canonpress.org. **Acquisitions:** J. C. Evans. Estab. 1988. Publishes hardcover and trade paperback originals. **Publishes 10 titles/year. Receives 500 queries and 250 mss/year. 10% of books from first-time authors; 100% from unagented writers. Pays 5-10% royalty on wholesale price, or retail price.** Publishes book 18 months after acceptance of ms. Accepts simultaneous submissions. Book catalog and ms guidelines online.

- *No unsolicited mss.*

Nonfiction Subjects include creative nonfiction, education, humanities, language/literature, religion. "As we are generally dissatisfied with contemporary, evangelical Christian nonfiction, we recommend visiting our Web site and perusing our recent titles before submitting."

Fiction Adventure, historical, humor, juvenile, literary, poetry, poetry in translation, religious, short story collections.

Poetry "As we are generally dissatisfied with contemporary, evangelical Christian poetry (or lack thereof), we recommend perusing our Web site and new titles before submitting."

Recent Title(s) *My Life for Yours* (family living); *Trinity & Reality* (apologetics); *Miniature & Morals* (literary criticism).

Tips "We seek to encourage Christians with God-honoring, Biblical books. Writers should possess a Trinitarian understanding of the good, true, and beautiful, and their submissions should reflect their understanding."

CAPITAL BOOKS

22841 Quicksilver Dr., Dulles VA 20166. (703)661-1571. Fax: (703)661-1547. E-mail: jennifer@booksintl.com. Web site: www.capital-books.com. **Acquisitions:** Kathleen Hughes, publisher (reference, how-to, lifestyle, regional travel, business, women's studies). Estab. 1998. Publishes hardcover and trade paperback originals, and trade paperback reprints. **Publishes 30 titles/year. Receives 300 queries and 400 mss/year. 30% of books from first-time authors; 90% from unagented writers. Pays 1-10% royalty on net receipts. Offers up to $5,000 advance.** Publishes book 9-12 months after acceptance of ms. Accepts simultaneous submissions.

Responds in 6 months to queries; 6 months to proposals; 6 months to mss. Book catalog free; ms guidelines online.

Nonfiction General nonfiction, how-to, reference, self-help. Subjects include animals, business/economics, child guidance/parenting, contemporary culture, cooking/foods/nutrition, gardening, health/medicine, money/finance, multicultural, nature/environment, psychology, regional, social sciences, travel, women's issues/studies. "We are looking for lifestyle and business books by experts with their own marketing and sales outlets." No religious titles, fiction, or children's books. Submit proposal package including outline, 3 sample chapters, query letter. Reviews artwork/photos as part of ms package. Send photocopies.

Recent Title(s) *Mental Agility*, by Rob Jolles; *More Alive With Color*, by Leatrice Eiseman.

Tips "Our audience is comprised of enthusiastic readers who look to books for answers and information. Do not send fiction, children's books, or religious titles. Please tell us how you, the author, can help market and sell the book."

⊘ CAPSTONE PRESS

151 Good Counsel Dr., P.O. Box 669, Mankato MN 56002. (507)345-8100. Fax: (507)625-4662. Web site: www.capstonepress.com. Publishes hardcover originals. Book catalog online.

Imprints Edge Books; Blazers Books; Snap Books, Pebble Books; Graphic Library; A+ Books; Pebble Plus; Yellow Umbrella Books; First Facts; Fact Finders; Spanish/Bilingual.

O→ Capstone Press publishes nonfiction children's books for schools and libraries.

Nonfiction Children's/juvenile. Subjects include Americana, animals, child guidance/parenting, cooking/foods/nutrition, health/medicine, history, military/war, multicultural, nature/environment, recreation, science, sports. "We do not accept proposals or manuscripts. Authors interested in writing for Capstone Press should send cover letter stating subject interest/specialty, résumé, up to 3 samples of writing (unpublished samples preferred)."

Tips Audience is made up of elementary, middle school, and high school students who are just learning how to read, who are experiencing reading difficulties, or who are learning English. Capstone Press does not publish unsolicited mss submitted by authors, nor entertains proposals. Instead, Capstone hires freelance authors to write on nonfiction topics selected by the company. Do not send book proposals. Do not send fiction.

CARDOZA PUBLISHING

857 Broadway, 3rd Floor, New York NY 10003. E-mail: submissions@cardozapub.com. Web site: www.cardozapub.com. **Acquisitions:** Acquisitions Editor (gaming, gambling, card and casino games, and board games). Estab. 1981. Publishes trade paperback originals and reprints. **Publishes 35-40 titles/year. Receives 20-30 queries and 20-30 mss/year. 50% of books from first-time authors; 90% from unagented writers. Pays 5-6% royalty on retail price. Offers $1,000-10,000 advance.** Publishes book 7 months after acceptance of ms. Accepts simultaneous submissions. Responds in 1-2 months to queries; 1-2 months to proposals; 2-3 months to mss. Book catalog online; ms guidelines by e-mail.

Nonfiction How-to. Subjects include hobbies, gaming, gambling, backgammon chess, card games. "Cardoza Publishing publishes exclusively gaming and gambling titles. In the past, we have specialized in poker and chess titles. While we always need more of those, we are currently seeking more books on various noncasino card games, such as bridge, hearts, spades, gin rummy, or canasta." Query with SASE, or submit complete ms. Reviews artwork/photos as part of ms package. Send photocopies.

Recent Title(s) *Super System*, by Doyle Brunson (poker); *Championship Hold 'Em*, by Tom McEvoy and T.J. Cloutier (poker); *Ken Warren Teaches Texas Hold 'Em*, by Ken Warren (poker).

Tips Audience is professional and recreational gamblers, chess players, card players. "We prefer not to deal with agents whenever possible. We publish only titles in a very specific niche market; please do not send us material that will not be relevant to our business."

THE CAREER PRESS, INC.

P.O. Box 687, 3 Tice Rd., Franklin Lakes NJ 07417. (201)848-0310 or (800)227-3371. E-mail: mlewis@careerpress.com. Web site: www.careerpress.com; www.newpagebooks.com. **Acquisitions:** Michael Lewis, acquisitions editor. Estab. 1985. Publishes hardcover and paperback originals. Does not accept simultaneous submissions. Ms guidelines online.

Imprints New Page Books.

O→ Career Press publishes books for adult readers seeking practical information to improve themselves in careers, college, finance, parenting, retirement, spirituality and other related topics, as well as management philosophy titles for a small business and management audience. New Page Books publishes in the areas of New Age, self-help, health, parenting, general nonfiction and weddings/entertaining. Currently de-emphasizing Judaica.

Nonfiction How-to, reference, self-help. Subjects include business/economics, money/finance, recreation, nutrition. "Look through our catalog; become familiar with our publications. We like to select authors who are specialists on their topic." Submit outline, author bio, 1-2 sample chapters, marketing plan, SASE. Or, send complete ms (preferred).

Recent Title(s) *The Wisdom of Ginsu®*, by Barry Beecher and Edward Valenti; *Supernetworking for Sales Pros*, by Michael Salmon; *How to Win Any Argument*, by Robert Mayer.

CAROLRHODA BOOKS, INC.

Imprint of Lerner Publishing Group, 241 First Ave. N., Minneapolis MN 55401-1607. (612)332-3344. *No phone calls.* Fax: (612)332-7615. Web site: www.lernerbooks.com. **Acquisitions:** Zelda Wagner, fiction submissions editor; Jennifer Zimian, nonfiction submissions editor. Estab. 1959. Publishes hardcover originals. Accepts simultaneous submissions. Book catalog for 9×12 SAE with $3.85 postage; ms guidelines online.

- Accepts submissions from November 1-30 only. Submissions received at other times of the year will be returned to sender.

O→ Carolrhoda Books is a children's publisher focused on producing high-quality, socially conscious nonfiction and fiction books with unique and well-developed ideas and angles for young readers that help them learn about and explore the world around them.

Nonfiction Carolrhoda Books seeks creative children's nonfiction. Biography. Subjects include ethnic, nature/environment, science. "We are always interested in adding to our biography series. Books on the natural and hard sciences are also of interest." Query with SASE. Prefers to receive complete ms, outline, résumé. Reviews artwork/photos as part of ms package. Send photocopies.

Fiction Historical, juvenile, multicultural, picture books, young reader, middle grade and young adult fiction. "We continue to add fiction for middle grades and 8-10 picture books per year. Not looking for folktales or anthropomorphic animal stories." Carolrhoda does not publish alphabet books, puzzle books, song books, textbooks, workbooks, religious subject matter, or plays. Query with SASE. Prefers to receive complete ms, outline, and a few sample chapters.

Recent Title(s) *Blackberry Stew*, by Isabell Monk, illustrated by Janice Lee Porter; *A Style All Her Own*, by Laurie Friedman, illustrated by Sharon Watts; *Tooth Fairy's First Night*, by Anne Bowen, illustrated by Jon Berkeley.

[A] CARROLL & GRAF PUBLISHERS, INC.

Avalon Publishing Group, 245 W. 17th St., 11th Floor, New York NY 10011-5300. (212)981-9919. Fax: (646)375-2571. Web site: www.avalonpub.com. Publisher: Will Balliett. Estab. 1982. Publishes hardcover and trade paperback originals. Responds in a timely fashion to queries.

O→ Carroll and Graf Publishers offers quality fiction and nonfiction for a general readership.

Nonfiction Publish general trade books. Subjects include contemporary culture, history, memoirs, military/war, psychology, sports, true crime, current affairs, adventure/exploration. *Agented submissions only.*

Fiction Literary, mainstream/contemporary, mystery, suspense, thriller. No romance. *Agented submissions only.* Query with SASE.

Recent Title(s) *The Politics of Truth*, by Joseph Wilson; *Hiding the Elephant*, by Jim Steinmeyer.

CARSON-DELLOSA PUBLISHING CO., INC.

P.O. Box 35665, Greensboro NC 27425-5665. (336)632-0084. Fax: (336)856-9414. Web site: www.carsondellosa.com. **Acquisitions:** Jennifer Bonnett, book acquistions. **Publishes 80-90 titles/year. 15-20% of books from first-time authors; 95% from unagented writers. Makes outright purchase.** Accepts simultaneous submissions. Responds in 3 months to proposals. Book catalog online; ms guidelines free.

Nonfiction We publish supplementary educational materials, such as teacher resource books, workbooks, and activity books. Subjects include education (including Christian education). No textbooks or trade children's books, please. Submit proposal package including sample chapters or pages, SASE. Reviews artwork/photos as part of ms package. Send photocopies.

Tips "Our audience consists of pre-K through grade 8 educators, parents, and students. Ask for our submission guidelines and a catalog before you send us your materials. We do not publish fiction or nonfiction storybooks."

CARSTENS PUBLICATIONS, INC.

Hobby Book Division, P.O. Box 700, Newton NJ 07860-0700. (973)383-3355. Fax: (973)383-4064. E-mail: hal@carstens-publications.com. Web site: www.carstens-publications.com. **Acquisitions:** Harold H. Carstens, publisher. Estab. 1933. Publishes paperback originals. **Publishes 8 titles/year. 100% from unagented writers. Pays 10% royalty on retail price. Offers advance.** Publishes book 1 year after acceptance of ms. Responds in 2 months to queries. Book catalog for #10 SASE.

O→ Carstens specializes in books about railroads, model railroads, and airplanes for hobbyists.

Nonfiction Subjects include model railroading, toy trains, model aviation, railroads, and model hobbies. "Au-

thors must know their field intimately because our readers are active modelers. Writers cannot write about somebody else's hobby with authority. If they do, we can't use them. Our railroad books presently are primarily photographic essays on specific railroads." Query with SASE. Reviews artwork/photos as part of ms package.
Recent Title(s) *Pennsylvania Railroad Lines East*, by Steve Stewart and Dave Augsburger; *Track Design*, by Bill Schopp.
Tips "We need lots of good photos. Material must be in model, hobby, railroad, and transportation field only."

CARTWHEEL BOOKS

Imprint of Scholastic Trade Division, 557 Broadway, New York NY 10012. (212)343-6100. Web site: www.scholastic.com. Vice President/Editorial Director: Ken Geist. Estab. 1991. Publishes novelty books, easy readers, board books, hardcover and trade paperback originals. Accepts simultaneous submissions. Book catalog for 9×12 SASE; ms guidelines free.

- Cartwheel Books publishes innovative books for children, up to age 8. "We are looking for 'novelties' that are books first, play objects second. Even without its gimmick, a Cartwheel Book should stand alone as a valid piece of children's literature."

Nonfiction Children's/juvenile. Subjects include animals, history, music/dance, nature/environment, recreation, science, sports. "Cartwheel Books publishes for the very young, therefore nonfiction should be written in a manner that is accessible to preschoolers through 2nd grade. Often writers choose topics that are too narrow or 'special' and do not appeal to the mass market. Also, the text and vocabulary are frequently too difficult for our young audience." Accepts mss from agents, previously published authors only. Reviews artwork/photos as part of ms package. Please do not send original artwork.
Fiction Humor, juvenile, mystery, picture books. "Again, the subject should have mass market appeal for very young children. Humor can be helpful, but not necessary. Mistakes writers make are a reading level that is too difficult, a topic of no interest or too narrow, or manuscripts that are too long." Accepts mss from agents, previously published authors only.
Tips Audience is young children, ages 0-8. "Know what types of books the publisher does. Some manuscripts that don't work for one house may be perfect for another. Check out bookstores or catalogs to see where your writing would 'fit' best."

CATHOLIC UNIVERSITY OF AMERICA PRESS

620 Michigan Ave. NE, Washington DC 20064. (202)319-5052. Fax: (202)319-4985. E-mail: cua-press@cua.edu. Web site: cuapress.cua.edu. **Acquisitions:** Dr. Gregory F. Lanave, acquisitions editor (philosophy, theology); Dr. David J. McGonagle, director (all other fields). Estab. 1939. **Publishes 30-35 titles/year. 50% of books from first-time authors; 100% from unagented writers. Pays variable royalty on net receipts.** Publishes book 18 months after acceptance of ms. Responds in 5 days to queries. Book catalog on request; ms guidelines online.

- The Catholic University of America Press publishes in the fields of history (ecclesiastical and secular), literature and languages, philosophy, political theory, social studies, and theology. "We have interdisciplinary emphasis on patristics, medieval studies, and Irish studies. Our principal interest is in works of original scholarship intended for scholars and other professionals, and for academic libraries, but we will also consider manuscripts whose chief contribution is to offer a synthesis of knowledge of the subject which may be of interest to a wider audience or suitable for use as supplementary reading material in courses."

Nonfiction Scholarly. Subjects include government/politics, history, language/literature, philosophy, religion, Church-state relations. No unrevised doctoral dissertations. Length: 40,000-120,000 words. Query with outline, sample chapter, cv, and list of previous publications.
Recent Title(s) *Mediapolitik: How the Mass Media Have Transformed World Politics*, by Lee Edwards.
Tips "Scholarly monographs and works suitable for adoption as supplementary reading material in courses have the best chance."

CATO INSTITUTE

1000 Massachusetts Ave. NW, Washington DC 20001. (202)842-0200. Web site: www.cato.org. **Acquisitions:** Gene Healy, senior editor. Estab. 1977. Publishes hardcover originals, trade paperback originals and reprints. **Publishes 12 titles/year. 25% of books from first-time authors; 90% from unagented writers. Makes outright purchase of $1,000-10,000. Offers advance.** Publishes book 9 months after acceptance of ms. Accepts simultaneous submissions. Responds in 3 months to queries. Book catalog online.

- Cato Institute publishes books on public policy issues from a free-market or libertarian perspective.

Nonfiction Scholarly. Subjects include business/economics, education, government/politics, health/medicine, money/finance, sociology, public policy, foreign policy, monetary policy. Query with SASE.
Recent Title(s) *Toward Liberty*, edited by David Boaz; *Voucher Wars*, by Clint Bolick.

CAXTON PRESS

312 Main St., Caldwell ID 83605-3299. (208)459-7421. Fax: (208)459-7450. Web site: caxtonpress.com. Publisher: Scott Gipson. **Acquisitions:** Wayne Cornell, editor (Western Americana, regional nonfiction). Estab. 1907. Publishes hardcover and trade paperback originals. **Publishes 6-10 titles/year. 50% of books from first-time authors; 60% from unagented writers. Pays royalty. Offers advance.** Publishes book 18 months after acceptance of ms. Accepts simultaneous submissions. Responds in 3 months to queries. Book catalog for 9×12 SAE; ms guidelines online.

- "Western Americana nonfiction remains our focus. We define Western Americana as almost any topic that deals with the people or culture of the west, past and present." Currently emphasizing regional issues—primarily Pacific Northwest. De-emphasizing "coffee table" or photograph-intensive books.

Nonfiction Biography, children's/juvenile, cookbook, scholarly. Subjects include Americana, history, regional. "We need good Western Americana, especially the Northwest, emphasis on serious, narrative nonfiction." Query. Reviews artwork/photos as part of ms package.

Recent Title(s) *Necktie Parties*, by Diane Goeres-Gardner; *Our Ladies of the Tenderloin*, by Linda Wommack; *Hobbled Stirrups*, by Jane Burnett Smith.

Tips "Books to us never can or will be primarily articles of merchandise to be produced as cheaply as possible and to be sold like slabs of bacon or packages of cereal over the counter. If there is anything that is really worthwhile in this mad jumble we call the 21st century, it should be books."

CELESTIAL ARTS

Ten Speed Press, P.O. Box 7123-S, Berkeley CA 94707. (510)559-1600. Fax: (510)524-1629. Web site: www.tenspeed.com. Estab. 1966. Publishes trade paperback originals and reprints. Accepts simultaneous submissions. Responds in 6-8 weeks to queries. Book catalog and ms guidelines online.

- Celestial Arts publishes nonfiction for a forward-thinking, open-minded audience interested in psychology, self-help, spirituality, health and parenting.

Nonfiction Cookbook, how-to, reference, self-help. Subjects include child guidance/parenting, cooking/foods/nutrition, education, health/medicine, New Age, psychology, women's issues/studies. "We specialize in parenting, alternative health, how-to and spirituality. And please, no poetry!" Submit proposal package including outline, author bio, 1-2 sample chapters, SASE. Reviews artwork/photos as part of ms package. Send photocopies.

Recent Title(s) *Addiction to Love*, by Susan Peabody; *Your Right to Know*, by Andrew Kimbrell; *Girls Speak Out*, by Andrea Johnston.

Tips Audience is fairly well-informed, interested in psychology and sociology-related topics, open-minded, innovative, forward-thinking. "The most completely thought-out (developed) proposals earn the most consideration."

CENTERSTREAM PUBLICATIONS

P.O. Box 17878, Anaheim Hills CA 92817. (714)779-9390. Fax: (714)779-9390. E-mail: centerstrm@aol.com. Web site: www.centerstream-usa.com. **Acquisitions:** Ron Middlebrook, Cindy Middlebrook, owners. Estab. 1980. Publishes music hardcover and mass market paperback originals, trade paperback and mass market paperback reprints. **Publishes 12 titles/year. Receives 15 queries and 15 mss/year. 80% of books from first-time authors; 100% from unagented writers. Pays 10-15% royalty on wholesale price. Offers $300-3,000 advance.** Publishes book 8 months after acceptance of ms. Accepts simultaneous submissions. Responds in 3 months to queries. Book catalog and ms guidelines for #10 SASE.

- Centerstream publishes music history and instructional books, all instruments plus DVDs.

Nonfiction Subjects include music history and music instruction. Query with SASE.

Recent Title(s) *Guitar Chord Shapes of Charlie Christian.*

CHALICE PRESS

1221 Locust St., Suite 670, St. Louis MO 63103. (314)231-8500 or (615)452-3311. Fax: (314)231-8524 or (615)452-7781. E-mail: submissions@cbp21.com. Web site: www.chalicepress.com. **Acquisitions:** Dr. Trent C. Butler, editorial director. Publishes hardcover and trade paperback originals. **Publishes 35 titles/year. Receives 300 queries and 250 mss/year. 10% of books from first-time authors; 100% from unagented writers. Pays 14% royalty on net receipts.** Publishes book 1 year after acceptance of ms. Accepts simultaneous submissions. Responds in 1 month to queries; 2 months to proposals; 3 months to mss. Book catalog and ms guidelines online.

Nonfiction Textbook. Subjects include religion, Christian spirituality. Submit proposal package including outline, 1-2 sample chapters.

Recent Title(s) *Solving the Da Vinci Code Mystery*, by Brandon Gilvin; *Chalice Introduction to the New Testament*, edited by Dennis E. Smith; *Martin Luther King on Creative Living*, by Michael G. Long.

Tips "We publish for professors, church ministers, and lay Christian readers."

CHARISMA HOUSE

Strang Communications, 600 Rinehart Rd., Lake Mary FL 32746. (407)333-0600. Fax: (407)333-7100. E-mail: charismahouse@strang.com. Web site: www.charismahouse.com. **Acquisitions:** Acquisitions Assistant. Publishes hardcover and trade paperback originals. **Publishes 40-50 titles/year. Receives 600 mss/year. 2% of books from first-time authors; 95% from unagented writers. Pays 4-18% royalty on retail price. Offers $1,500-5,000 advance.** Publishes book 18 months after acceptance of ms. Accepts simultaneous submissions. Responds in 3 months to proposals. Ms guidelines online.

Imprints Creation House (customized publications of Christian fiction and nonfiction); Siloam (emphasizing health and fitness from the Christian perspective—topics include fitness, diet and nutrition, conventional and alternative medicine, and emotional and relationship health).

O‑ Charisma House publishes nonfiction books about Christian living, the work of the Holy Spirit, prayer, scripture, adventures in evangelism and missions, and popular theology. "We now accept fiction submissions for speculative and historical fiction that focuses on the supernatural interventions of God."

Recent Title(s) *The Thorn in the Flesh*, by R.T. Kendall (nonfiction); *My Spiritual Inheritance*, by Juanita Bynum (nonfiction).

Tips "Request book proposal guidelines or go to our Web site before sending submissions."

CHARLES RIVER MEDIA

25 Thomson Place, Boston MA 02210. (617)757-7900. Fax: (617)757-7969. E-mail: info@charlesriver.com. Web site: www.charlesriver.com. **Acquisitions:** David Pallai, president (networking, Internet related); Jenifer Niles, publisher (computer graphics, animation, game programming). Publishes hardcover and trade paperback originals. **Publishes 60 titles/year. Receives 1,000 queries and 250 mss/year. 20% of books from first-time authors; 90% from unagented writers. Pays 5-20% royalty on wholesale price. Offers $3,000-20,000 advance.** Publishes book 4 months after acceptance of ms. Accepts simultaneous submissions. Responds in 2 weeks to queries. Book catalog for #10 SASE; ms guidelines online.

O‑ "Our publishing program concentrates on 6 major areas: Internet, networking, game development, programming, engineering, and graphics. The majority of our titles are considered intermediate, not high-level research monographs, and not for lowest-level general users."

Nonfiction Multimedia (Win/Mac format), reference, technical. Subjects include computers/electronic. Query with SASE, or submit proposal package including outline, résumé, 2 sample chapters. Reviews artwork/photos as part of ms package. Send photocopies or GIF, TIFF, or PDF files.

Recent Title(s) *Game Programming Gems*; *Professional Web Design 2/E*.

Tips "We are very receptive to detailed proposals by first-time or nonagented authors. Consult our Web site for proposal outlines. Manuscripts must be completed within 6 months of contract signing."

CHARLESBRIDGE PUBLISHING, SCHOOL DIVISION

85 Main St., Watertown MA 02472. (800)225-3214. Fax: (800)926-5775. E-mail: schooleditorial@charlesbridge.com. Web site: www.charlesbridge.com/school. **Acquisitions:** Elena Dworkin Wright, vice president school division. Estab. 1980. Publishes educational curricula and hardcover and paperback nonfiction and fiction children's picture books. **Publishes 20 titles/year. 10-20% of books from first-time authors; 80% from unagented writers. Royalty and advance vary.** Publishes book 2 years after acceptance of ms. Ms guidelines online.

O‑ "We're looking for compelling story lines, humor and strong educational content."

Nonfiction Children's/juvenile, textbook. Subjects include education, multicultural, nature/environment, science, math, astronomy, physical science, problem solving. Submit complete ms.

Fiction Multicultural, nature, science, social studies, bedtime, etc. Non-rhyming stories. Submit complete ms.

Recent Title(s) *Really Rabbits*, by Virginia Kroll; *Sir Cumference and the Sword in the Cone*, by Cindy Neuschwander; *Zachary Zormer, Shape Transformer*, by Joanne Anderson Reisberg.

CHARLESBRIDGE PUBLISHING, TRADE DIVISION

85 Main St., Watertown MA 02472. (617)926-0329. Fax: (617)926-5720. Web site: www.charlesbridge.com. **Acquisitions:** Submissions Editors. Estab. 1980. Publishes hardcover and trade paperback nonfiction and fiction, children's books for the trade and library markets. **Publishes 30 titles/year. 10-20% of books from first-time authors; 80% from unagented writers. Pays royalty. Offers advance.** Publishes book 2-4 years after acceptance of ms. Ms guidelines online.

Imprints Charlesbridge.

O‑ "We're always interested in innovative approaches to a difficult genre, the nonfiction picture book."

Nonfiction Children's/juvenile. Subjects include animals, creative nonfiction, history, multicultural, nature/

environment, science, social science. Strong interest in nature, environment, social studies, and other topics for trade and library markets. *Exclusive submissions only.*

Fiction "Strong stories with enduring themes." *Exclusive submissions only.*

Recent Title(s) *A Mother's Journey*, by Sandra Markle; *Ace Lacewing*, by David Biedrzycki; *Aggre and Ben*, by Lori Ries.

CHELSEA GREEN PUBLISHING CO.

P.O. Box 428, 85 N. Main St., White River Junction VT 05001-0428. (802)295-6300. Fax: (802)295-6444. Web site: www.chelseagreen.com. **Acquisitions:** John Barstow, editor-in-chief. Estab. 1984. Publishes hardcover and trade paperback originals and reprints. **Publishes 12-15 titles/year. Receives 300-400 queries and 200-300 mss/year. 30% of books from first-time authors; 80% from unagented writers. Pays royalty on publisher's net. Offers $2,500-10,000 advance.** Publishes book 18 months after acceptance of ms. Responds in 2 weeks to queries; 1 month to proposals; 1 month to mss. Book catalog free or online; ms guidelines online.

O→ Chelsea Green publishes and distributes books relating to issues of sustainability with a special concentration on books about nature, the environment, independent living and enterprise, organic gardening, renewable energy, alternative or natural building techniques, and the politics of sustainability. The books reflect positive options in a world of environmental turmoil. Emphasizing food/agriculture/gardening, innovative shelter and natural building, renewable energy, sustainable business, and enterprise. De-emphasizing nature/natural history.

Nonfiction Cookbook, how-to, reference, technical. Subjects include agriculture/horticulture, art/architecture, cooking/foods/nutrition, gardening, health/medicine, money/finance, nature/environment, forestry, current affairs/politics. Query with SASE, or submit proposal package including outline, 1-2 sample chapters. Reviews artwork/photos as part of ms package.

Recent Title(s) *The Slow Food Guide to New York City*, by Slow Food USA; *The Straw Bale House*, by Steen, Steen, Bainbridge; *Gaia's Garden*, by Toby Hemenway.

Tips "Our readers are passionately enthusiastic about ecological solutions for contemporary challenges in construction, energy harvesting, agriculture, and forestry. Our books are also carefully and handsomely produced to give pleasure to bibliophiles of a practical bent. It would be very helpful for prospective authors to have a look at several of our current books, as well as our catalog and Web site. For certain types of book, we are the perfect publisher, but we are exceedingly focused on particular areas."

CHELSEA HOUSE PUBLISHERS

Haights Cross Communications, 132 W. 31st St., 17th Floor, New York NY 10001. (800)848-BOOK. Fax: (800)780-7300. E-mail: editorial@factsonfile.com. Web site: www.chelseahouse.com. **Acquisitions:** Editorial Assistant. Publishes hardcover originals and reprints. Accepts simultaneous submissions. Book catalog online; ms guidelines for #10 SASE.

O→ "We publish curriculum-based nonfiction books for middle school and high school students."

Nonfiction Biography (must be common format, fitting under a series umbrealla), children's/juvenile. Subjects include Americana, animals, anthropology/archeology, ethnic, gay/lesbian, government/politics, health/medicine, history, hobbies, language/literature, military/war, multicultural, music/dance, nature/environment, recreation, regional, religion, science, sociology, sports, travel, women's issues/studies. "We are interested in expanding our topics to include more on the physical, life and environmental sciences." Query with SASE, or submit proposal package including outline, 2-3 sample chapter(s), résumé. Reviews artwork/photos as part of ms package. Send photocopies.

Recent Title(s) *Futuristics: Looking Ahead, Vol. 1* (Tackling Tomorrow Today series); *Hepatitis* (Deadly Disease & Epidemics series); *South Africa: A State of Apartheid* (Arbitrary Borders series).

Tips "Know our product. Do not waste your time or ours by sending something that does not fit our market. Be professional. Send clean, clear submissions that show you read the preferred submission format. Always include SASE."

CHICAGO REVIEW PRESS

814 N. Franklin, Chicago IL 60610-3109. (312)337-0747. Fax: (312)337-5110. E-mail: csherry@chicagoreviewpress.com. Submissions E-mail: ytaylor@chicagoreviewpress.com. Web site: www.chicagoreviewpress.com. **Acquisitions:** Cynthia Sherry, associate publisher (general nonfiction, children's); Yuval Taylor, senior editor (African-American and performing arts); Jerome Pohlen, senior editor (educational resources). Estab. 1973. Publishes hardcover and trade paperback originals, and trade paperback reprints. **Publishes 40-50 titles/year. Receives 400 queries and 800 mss/year. 50% of books from first-time authors; 50% from unagented writers. Pays 7-12½% royalty. Offers $3,000-10,000 average advance.** Publishes book 18 months after acceptance of ms. Accepts simultaneous submissions. Responds in 3 months to queries. Book catalog for $3.50; ms guidelines for #10 SASE or online at Web site.

Imprints Lawrence Hill Books; A Cappella Books (contact Yuval Taylor); Zephyr Press (contact Jerome Pohlen).

O→ Chicago Review Press publishes intelligent nonfiction on timely subjects for educated readers with special interests.

Nonfiction Children's/juvenile (activity books only), how-to. Subjects include art/architecture, child guidance/parenting, creative nonfiction, education, gardening (regional), health/medicine, history, hobbies, memoirs, multicultural, nature/environment, recreation, regional, music. Query with outline, TOC, and 1-2 sample chapters. Reviews artwork/photos as part of ms package.

Recent Title(s) *In Plain Sight: The Startling Truth Behind the Elizabeth Smart Investigation*, by Tom Smart and Lee Benson.

Tips "Along with a table of contents and 1-2 sample chapters, also send a cover letter and a list of credentials with your proposal. Also, provide the following information in your cover letter: audience, market, and competition—who is the book written for and what sets it apart from what's already out there."

CHILD WELFARE LEAGUE OF AMERICA

P.O. Box 932831, Atlanta GA 31193. Web site: www.cwla.org/pubs. **Acquisitions:** Acquisitions Editor. Publishes hardcover and trade paperback originals. Book catalog and ms guidelines online.

Imprints CWLA Press (child welfare professional publications); Child & Family Press (children's books and parenting books for the general public).

O→ CWLA is a privately supported, nonprofit, membership-based organization committed to preserving, protecting, and promoting the well-being of all children and their families.

Nonfiction Children's/juvenile. Subjects include child guidance/parenting, sociology. Submit complete ms and proposal with outline, TOC, sample chapter, intended audience, and SASE.

Recent Title(s) *Can You Hear Me Smiling*, by Aariane R. Jackson; *A Look in the Mirror: Freeing Yourself from the Body Image Blues*, by Valerie Rainon McManus; *A Pocket Full of Kisses*, by Audrey Penn.

Tips "We are looking for positive, kid-friendly books for ages 3-9. We are looking for books that have a positive message—a feel-good book."

N CHILDREN'S PRESS/FRANKLIN WATTS

Imprint of Scholastic, Inc., 90 Old Sherman Turnpike, Danbury CT 06816. Web site: publishing.grolier.com. Estab. 1946. Publishes nonfiction hardcover originals. Book catalog for #10 SASE.

O→ Children's Press publishes 90% nonfiction for the school and library market, and 10% early reader fiction and nonfiction. "Our books support textbooks and closely relate to the elementary and middle-school curriculum." Franklin Watts publishes nonfiction for middle and high school curriculum.

Nonfiction Biography, children's/juvenile, reference. Subjects include animals, anthropology/archeology, art/architecture, ethnic, health/medicine, history, hobbies, multicultural, music/dance, nature/environment, science, sports, general children's nonfiction. "We publish nonfiction books that supplement the school curriculum." No fiction, poetry, folktales, cookbooks or novelty books. Query with SASE.

Recent Title(s) *Arctic Tundra*, by Salvatore Tocci; *My Birthday Cake*, by Olivia George, illustrated by Martha Avilés; *You Have Healthy Bones!*, by Susan DerKazarian.

Tips Most of this publisher's books are developed inhouse; less than 5% come from unsolicited submissions. However, they publish several series for which they always need new books. Study catalogs to discover possible needs.

CHIPPEWA PUBLISHING LLC

678 Dutchman Dr. #3, Chippewa Falls WI 54729. E-mail: submissions@chippewapublishing.com. Web site: www.chippewapublishing.com. **Acquisitions:** Kimberly Burton, executive managing editor. Estab. 2004. Publishes trade paperback and electronic originals and MP3 audiobooks. Focus is on electronic copies. **Publishes 45 titles/year; imprint publishes 12 titles/year. 45% of books from first-time authors; 90% from unagented writers. Pays 40% royalty on net for electronic copies and 15% net on paperback. Anthology payments negotiated depending on story size.** Does not accept simultaneous submissions. Book catalog and writer's guidelines online.

Fiction Adventure, erotica, ethnic, experimental, fantasy, gay/lesbian, gothic, historical, horror, humor, juvenile, mainstream/contemporary, military/war, mystery, occult, romance (dark), science fiction, short story collections, suspense, young adult. "We specialize in dark romance, horror, science fiction, fantasy, and erotica, but we accept other titles too." Submit complete ms.

Recent Title(s) *The Hunted*, by Marianne Lacroix; *He Came From Venus*, by Ella Scopilo; *Masterpiece*, by Nancy S. Ward.

Tips "Our audience loves to be shocked by what they read. Our romance books take it beyond a simple kiss; our horror takes it beyond just blood and guts. We enjoy an exciting story. Edit your work before sending it to us and do not use passive voice. We will return manuscripts with excessive passive voice and general mistakes.

If it is a good story, we'll let you know and ask you to try again. Please be professional. We are very busy and so are you. We do not accept hard copy submissions. Please e-mail your submission following the writer's guidelines on the Web site."

CHIVALRY BOOKSHELF

3305 Mayfair Ln., Highland Village TX 75077. (978)418-4774. Fax: (978)418-4774. E-mail: chronique_editor@yahoo.com. Submissions E-mail: csr@chivalrybookshelf.com. Web site: www.chivalrybookshelf.com. **Acquisitions:** Brian R. Price, publisher (history, art, philosophy, political science, military, martial arts, fencing); Gregory Mele, martial arts editor (martial arts, fencing, history). Estab. 1996. Publishes hardcover and trade paperback originals and reprints. **Publishes 12 titles/year. Receives 75 queries and 25 mss/year. 50% of books from first-time authors; 90% from unagented writers. Pays 5-12% royalty.** Publishes book 6 months after acceptance of ms. Does not accept simultaneous submissions. Responds in 1 month to queries; 1 month to proposals; 2 months to mss. Book catalog free; ms guidelines online.

Nonfiction Biography, booklets, children's/juvenile, coffee table book, general nonfiction, gift book, how-to, humor, illustrated book, scholarly, technical. Subjects include art/architecture, creative nonfiction, education, government/politics, history, military/war, recreation, sports (martial arts/fencing especially), translation. "Chivalry Bookshelf began focusing on new works and important reprints relating to arms and armour, medieval knighthood, and related topics. Since then, we have become the largest publisher of books relating to 'Western' or 'historical' martial arts, including translations, interpretations, and fascimile reproductions done in partnership with major museums such as the J. Paul Getty Museum and the British Royal Armouries. During 2006, we are expanding our history and military line dramatically and will be seeking manuscripts, especially translations and biographies, relating to classical, medieval, Renaissance, or pre-21st century history. During 2007 we plan to launch a new imprint dealing with modern politics and military issues. Manuscripts that deal with military memoirs, arms and armour, martial arts, and medieval history will receive particular consideration." Query with SASE, or submit proposal package including outline, 1 sample chapter, sample illustrations, or submit complete ms. Reviews artwork/photos as part of ms package.

Recent Title(s) *The Medieval Art of Swordsmanship*, translated and interpreted by Dr. Jeffrey L. Forgeng, co-published with the British Royal Armouries (art history); *Deeds of Arms*, by Dr. Stephen Muhlberger (scholarly/popular translation); *Arte of Defence*, by William E. Wilson (historical fencing).

Tips "The bulk of our books are intended for serious amateur scholars and students of history and martial arts. The authors we select tend to have a strong voice, are well read in their chosen field, and submit relatively clean manuscripts."

CHRISTIAN ED. PUBLISHERS

P.O. Box 26639, San Diego CA 92196. (858)578-4700. Fax: (858)578-2431. Web site: www.christianedwarehouse.com. **Acquisitions:** Janet Ackelson, assistant editor. **Publishes 80 titles/year. Makes outright purchase of 3¢/word.** Responds in 3 months on assigned material to mss. Book catalog for 9×12 SAE with 4 first-class stamps; ms guidelines for #10 SASE.

> O━ Christian Ed. Publishers is an independent, nondenominational, evangelical company founded over 50 years ago to produce Christ-centered curriculum materials based on the Word of God for thousands of churches of different denominations throughout the world. "Our mission is to introduce children, teens, and adults to a personal faith in Jesus Christ, and to help them grow in their faith and service to the Lord. We publish materials that teach moral and spiritual values while training individuals for a lifetime of Christian service." Currently emphasizing Bible curriculum for preschool-preteen ages.

Nonfiction Children's/juvenile. Subjects include education (Christian), religion. "All subjects are on assignment." Query with SASE.

Fiction "All writing is done on assignment." Query with SASE.

Recent Title(s) *All-Stars for Jesus: Bible Curriculum for Preteens.*

Tips "Read our guidelines carefully before sending us a manuscript. All writing is done on assignment only and must be age appropriate (preschool-6th grade)."

CHRONICLE BOOKS

85 Second St., 6th Floor, San Francisco CA 94105. (415)537-4200. Fax: (415)537-4460. E-mail: frontdesk@chroniclebooks.com. Web site: www.chroniclebooks.com. **Acquisitions:** Jay Schaefer (fiction); Bill LeBlond (cookbooks); Alan Rapp (art and design); Sarah Malarkey (licensing and popular culture); Jodi Davis (sex, fitness and pop culture); Steve Mockus (popular culture); Debra Lande (gift books); Victoria Rock (children's). Estab. 1966. Publishes hardcover and trade paperback originals. **Publishes 175 titles/year.** Publishes book 18 months after acceptance of ms. Accepts simultaneous submissions. Responds in 3 months to queries. Book catalog for 11X14 SAE with 5 first-class stamps; ms guidelines online.

Imprints Chronicle Books for Children; GiftWorks (ancillary products, such as stationery, gift books).

"Inspired by the enduring magic and importance of books, our objective is to create and distribute exceptional publishing that is instantly recognizable for its spirit, creativity and value. This objective informs our business relationships and endeavors, be they with customers, authors, suppliers or colleagues."

Nonfiction Coffee table book, cookbook, gift book. Subjects include art/architecture, cooking/foods/nutrition, gardening, nature/environment, photography, recreation, regional, design, pop culture, interior design. Query or submit outline/synopsis with artwork and sample chapters.

Fiction Submit complete ms.

Recent Title(s) *The Beatles Anthology*, by The Beatles; *Worst-Case Scenario Survival Handbook*, by David Borgenicht and Joshua Piven.

CHRONICLE BOOKS FOR CHILDREN

680 Second St., San Francisco CA 94107. (415)537-4400. Fax: (415)537-4415. Web site: www.chroniclekids.com. **Acquisitions:** Victoria Rock, associate publisher. Publishes hardcover and trade paperback originals. **Publishes 50-60 titles/year. Receives 30,000 queries/year. 6% of books from first-time authors; 25% from unagented writers. Pays 8% royalty. Offers variable advance.** Publishes book 18-24 months after acceptance of ms. Accepts simultaneous submissions. Responds in 2-4 weeks to queries; 6 months to mss. Book catalog for 9×12 SAE with 3 first-class stamps; ms guidelines online.

Chronicle Books for Children publishes an eclectic mixture of traditional and innovative children's books. "Our aim is to publish books that inspire young readers to learn and grow creatively while helping them discover the joy of reading. We're looking for quirky, bold artwork and subject matter." Currently emphasizing picture books. De-emphasizing young adult.

Nonfiction Biography, children's/juvenile (for ages 8-12), illustrated book, picture books (for ages up to 8 years). Subjects include animals, art/architecture, multicultural, nature/environment, science. Query with synopsis and SASE. Reviews artwork/photos as part of ms package.

Fiction Mainstream/contemporary, multicultural, young adult, picture books; middle grade fiction; young adult projects. "We do not accept proposals by fax, via e-mail, or on disk. When submitting artwork, either as a part of a project or as samples for review, do not send original art. Please be sure to include an SASE large enough to hold your materials. Projects submitted without an appropriate SASE will be recycled." Query with SASE. Send complete ms with SASE for picture books.

Recent Title(s) *The Man Who Went to the Far Side of the Moon*; *Just a Minute*; *Ruby's Wish*.

Tips "We are interested in projects that have a unique bent to them—be it in subject matter, writing style, or illustrative technique. As a small list, we are looking for books that will lend our list a distinctive flavor. Primarily we are interested in fiction and nonfiction picture books for children ages up to eight years, and nonfiction books for children ages up to twelve years. We publish board, pop-up, and other novelty formats as well as picture books. We are also interested in early chapter books, middle grade fiction, and young adult projects."

CLARION BOOKS

Houghton Mifflin Co., 215 Park Ave. S., New York NY 10003. Web site: www.houghtonmifflinbooks.com. **Acquisitions:** Dinah Stevenson, vice president and publisher; Jennifer B. Greene, senior editor (contemporary fiction, picture books for all ages, nonfiction); Jennifer Wingertzahn, editor (fiction, picture books); Lynne Polvino, associate editor (fiction, nonfiction, picture books). Estab. 1965. Publishes hardcover originals for children. *No multiple submissions.* **Publishes 50 titles/year. Pays 5-10% royalty on retail price. Offers minimum of $4,000 advance.** Publishes book 2 years after acceptance of ms. Responds in 2 months to queries. Ms guidelines for #10 SASE or online.

Clarion Books publishes picture books, nonfiction, and fiction for infants through grade 12. Avoid telling your stories in verse unless you are a professional poet.

Nonfiction Biography, children's/juvenile, photo essay. Subjects include Americana, history, language/literature, nature/environment, photography, holiday. No unsolicited mss. Query with SASE, or submit proposal package including sample chapter(s), SASE. Reviews artwork/photos as part of ms package. Send photocopies.

Fiction Adventure, historical, humor, suspense, strong character studies, contemporary. Clarion is highly selective in the areas of historical fiction, fantasy, and science fiction. A novel must be superlatively written in order to find a place on the list. Mss that arrive without an SASE of adequate size will *not* be responded to or returned. Accepts fiction translations. Submit complete ms. No queries, please. Send to only *one* Clarion editor.

Recent Title(s) *Lizzie Bright and the Buckminster Boy*, by Gary D. Schmidt (fiction); *One Green Apple*, by Eve Bunting (picture book); *Good Brother, Bad Brother*, by James Cross Giblin (nonfiction).

Tips Looks for "freshness, enthusiasm—in short, life."

CLARKSON POTTER

The Crown Publishing Group, Random House, Inc., 1745 Broadway, 13th Floor, New York NY 10019. (212)782-9000. Web site: www.clarksonpotter.com. Estab. 1959. Publishes hardcover and trade paperback originals. Accepts agented submissions only. Does not accept simultaneous submissions.

- Clarkson Potter specializes in publishing cooking books, decorating and other around-the-house how-to subjects.

Nonfiction Biography, how-to, humor, self-help, crafts, cooking and foods, decorating, design gardening. Subjects include art/architecture, child guidance/parenting, cooking/foods/nutrition, language/literature, memoirs, nature/environment, photography, psychology, translation. *Agented submissions only.* Query or submit outline and sample chapter with tearsheets from magazines and artwork copies (e.g.—color photocopies or duplicate transparencies).

Recent Title(s) *Ranch House Style*, by Katherine Samon; *Half-Scratch Magic*, by Linda West Eckhardt and Katherine West Defoyd; *Wildflowers*, by David Stark and Avi Adler.

CLEIS PRESS

P.O. Box 14697, San Francisco CA 94114. (415)575-4700. Fax: (415)575-4705. Web site: www.cleispress.com. **Acquisitions:** Frederique Delacoste. Estab. 1980. Publishes trade paperback originals and reprints. **Publishes 20 titles/year. 10% of books from first-time authors; 90% from unagented writers. Pays variable royalty on retail price.** Publishes book 2 years after acceptance of ms. Responds in 1 month to queries.

- Cleis Press specializes in feminist and gay/lesbian fiction and nonfiction.

Nonfiction Subjects include gay/lesbian, women's issues/studies, sexual politics, erotica, human rights, African-American studies. "We are interested in books on topics of sexuality, human rights and women's and gay and lesbian literature. Please consult our Web site first to be certain that your book fits our list." Query or submit outline and sample chapters.

Fiction Feminist, gay/lesbian, literary. "We are looking for high quality fiction by women and men." No romances. Submit complete ms. *Writer's Market* recommends sending a query with SASE first.

Recent Title(s) *Deconstructing Tyrone* (nonfiction); *Jia* (fiction); *Whole Lesbian Sex Book* (nonfiction).

Tips "Be familiar with publishers' catalogs; be absolutely aware of your audience; research potential markets; present fresh new ways of looking at your topic; avoid 'PR' language and include publishing history in query letter."

COFFEE HOUSE PRESS

27 N. Fourth St., Suite 400, Minneapolis MN 55401. (612)338-0125. Fax: (612)338-4004. Web site: www.coffeehousepress.org. Publisher: Allan Kornblum. **Acquisitions:** Chris Fischbach, senior editor. Estab. 1984. Publishes hardcover and trade paperback originals. **Publishes 12 titles/year.** Responds in 4-6 weeks to queries; up to 6 months to mss. Book catalog and ms guidelines online.

Fiction Seeks literary novels, short story collections and poetry. No genre fiction or antholgies. Query first with outline, samples (20-30 pages) and SASE.

Poetry Full-length collections.

Recent Title(s) *The Impossibly*, by Laird Hunt; *The California Poem*, by Eleni Sikelianos; *Circle K Cycles*, by Karen Tei Yamashita.

Tips "Look for our books at stores and libraries to get a feel for what we like to publish. No phone calls, e-mails, or faxes."

COLLECTORS PRESS, INC.

P.O. Box 230986, Portland OR 97281-0986. (503)684-3030. Fax: (503)684-3777. Web site: www.collectorspress.com. **Acquisitions:** Lindsay Burt, acquisitions editor. Estab. 1992. Publishes hardcover and trade paperback originals. **Publishes 20 titles/year. Receives 500 queries and 200 mss/year. 75% of books from first-time authors; 75% from unagented writers. Pays royalty.** Publishes book 1 year after acceptance of ms. Responds in 1 month to queries. Book catalog and ms guidelines free.

- Collectors Press, Inc., publishes award-winning popular-culture coffee table and gift books that are graphically driven and appeal to a broad audience. We also have a strong cookbook publishing program focused on Americana cooking.

Nonfiction Cookbook, illustrated book, reference. Subjects include art/architecture, cooking/foods/nutrition, photography, nostalgic pop culture, science-fiction art, fantasy art, graphic design, comic art, magazine art, historical art, poster art, genre-specific art. Submit proposal package, including market research, outline, 2 sample chapters, and SASE. Reviews artwork/photos as part of ms package. Send transparencies or very clear photos.

Recent Title(s) *The Good Home Cookbook*; *70s Fashion Fiascos.*

Tips "Please carefully review our submissions guidelines posted on our Web site before submitting your manuscript."

COLLEGE PRESS PUBLISHING CO.

P.O. Box 1132/223, 223 W. 3rd St., Joplin MO 64801. (800)289-3300. Fax: (417)623-8250. E-mail: jmcclarnon@collegepress.com. Web site: www.collegepress.com. **Acquisitions:** Acquisitions Editor. Estab. 1959. Publishes hardcover and trade paperback originals and reprints. Accepts simultaneous submissions. Responds in 3 months to proposals; 2 months to mss. Book catalog for 9×12 SAE with 5 first-class stamps; ms guidelines online.

Imprints HeartSpring Publishing (nonacademic Christian, inspirational, devotional and Christian fiction).

- "College Press is an evangelical Christian publishing house primarily associated with the Christian churches/Church of Christ."

Nonfiction Seeks Bible studies, topical studies, apologetic studies, historical biographies of Christians, and Sunday/Bible school curriculum. No poetry, games/puzzles, or any book without a Christian message. Query with SASE, or submit proposal package including outline, author bio, synopsis, TOC, target audience.

Recent Title(s) *Encounters With Christ*, by Mark E. Moore.

Tips "Our core market is Christian Churches/Churches of Christ and conservative evangelical Christians. Have your material critically reviewed prior to sending it. Make sure that it is non-Calvinistic and that it leans more amillennial (if it is apocalyptic writing)."

COMMON COURAGE PRESS

One Red Barn Rd. Box 702, Monroe ME 04951. (207)525-0900. Fax: (207)525-3068. Web site: www.commoncouragepress.com. Publisher: Greg Bates. Estab. 1991. Publishes hardcover and trade paperback originals and trade paperback reprints. Accepts simultaneous submissions. Book catalog and ms guidelines online.

- "Nonfiction leftist, activist, political, history, feminist, media issues are our niche. *We are not taking unsolicited mss at this time.*"

Nonfiction Reference, textbook. Subjects include anthropology/archeology, creative nonfiction, ethnic, gay/lesbian, government/politics, health/medicine, history, military/war, multicultural, nature/environment, science. Query with SASE or submit proposal package, including outline. Reviews artwork/photos as part of ms package.

Recent Title(s) *New Military Humanism*, by Noam Chomsky (leftist political); *Rogue State*, by William Blum (leftist political).

Tips Audience consists of left-wing activists, college audiences.

CONCORDIA PUBLISHING HOUSE

3558 S. Jefferson Ave., St. Louis MO 63118-3968. (314)268-1187. Fax: (314)268-1329. Web site: www.cph.org. **Acquisitions:** Peggy Kuethe, senior editor (children's product, adult devotional, teaching resources); Dawn Weinstock, managing production editor (adult nonfiction on Christian spirituality and culture, academic works of interest in Lutheran markets). Estab. 1869. Publishes hardcover and trade paperback originals. **Publishes 50 titles/year.** Ms guidelines online.

- Concordia publishes Protestant, inspirational, theological, family, and juvenile material. All mss must conform to the doctrinal tenets of The Lutheran Church—Missouri Synod. No longer publishes fiction.

Nonfiction Children's/juvenile, adult. Subjects include child guidance/parenting (in Christian context), religion, inspirational.

Recent Title(s) *Is God Listening? Making God Part of Your Life*, by Andrew E. Steinmann (Christian living); *Mommy Promises*, by Julie Stiegemer (children's picture).

Tips "Call for information about what we are currently accepting."

CONSORTIUM PUBLISHING

640 Weaver Hill Rd., West Greenwich RI 02817-2261. (401)397-9838. Fax: (401)392-1926. John M. Carlevale, chief of publications. Estab. 1990. Publishes trade paperback originals and reprints. **Publishes 12 titles/year. Receives 150 queries and 50 mss/year. 50% of books from first-time authors; 95% from unagented writers. Pays 10-15% royalty.** Publishes book 3 months after acceptance of ms. Responds in 2 months to queries. Book catalog and ms guidelines for #10 SASE.

- Consortium publishes books for all levels of the education market.

Nonfiction Autobiography, how-to, humor, illustrated book, reference, self-help, technical, textbook. Subjects include business/economics, child guidance/parenting, education, government/politics, health/medicine, history, music/dance, nature/environment, psychology, science, sociology, women's issues/studies. Query, or submit proposal package, including TOC, outline, 1 sample chapter, and SASE. Reviews artwork/photos as part of ms package. Send photocopies.

Recent Title(s) *Teaching the Child Under Six, 4th Ed.*, by James L. Hymes, Jr. (education).

Tips Audience is college and high school students and instructors, elementary school teachers and other trainers.

CONTINUUM INTERNATIONAL PUBLISHING GROUP, LTD.

80 Maiden Lane, Suite 704, New York NY 10038. (212)953-5858. Fax: (212)953-5944. E-mail: info@continuumbooks.com. Web site: www.continuumbooks.com. **Acquisitions:** Frank Oveis, VP/senior editor (religious, current affairs); Evander Lomke, VP/senior editor (literary criticism, performing arts, social thought, women's studies); David Barker, editorial director (film, music, pop culture); Gabriella Page-Fort, publishing services supervisor. Publishes hardcover originals and paperback textbooks. Does not accept simultaneous submissions. Book catalog and ms guidelines free.

O→ Continuum publishes textbooks, monographs, and reference works in religious studies, the humanities, arts, and social sciences for students, teachers, and professionals worldwide.

Nonfiction Reference, technical, textbook. Subjects include anthropology/archeology, business/economics, education, film/cinema/stage (performance), government/politics, history, language/literature, music/dance (popular), philosophy, religion, sociology, linguistics. Submit outline.

Recent Title(s) *Jazz Writings*, by Philip Larkin; *Heavenly Touch*, by Abraham Joshua Heschel; *When the War Came Home*, by Stacy Bannerman.

⊘ COPPER CANYON PRESS

P.O. Box 271, Port Townsend WA 98368. (360)385-4925. Fax: (360)385-4985. E-mail: poetry@coppercanyonpress.org. Web site: www.coppercanyonpress.org. **Acquisitions:** Michael Wiegers, editor. Estab. 1972. Publishes trade paperback originals and occasional cloth-bound editions. **Publishes 18 titles/year. Receives 2,000 queries and 1,500 mss/year. 10% of books from first-time authors; 95% from unagented writers. Pays royalty.** Publishes book 2 years after acceptance of ms. Responds in 4 months to queries. Book catalog free; ms guidelines online.

O→ Copper Canyon Press is dedicated to publishing poetry in a wide range of styles and from a full range of the world's cultures.

Poetry "First, second, and third book manuscripts are considered only for our Hayden Carruth Award, presented annually." Send SASE for entry form in September of each year. *No unsolicited mss.*

Recent Title(s) *Steal Away*, by C.D. Wright; *Nightworks*, by Marvin Bell; *The Complete Poems of Kenneth Rexroth*.

CORNELL UNIVERSITY PRESS

Sage House, 512 E. State St., Ithaca NY 14850. (607)277-2338. Fax: (607)277-2374. Web site: www.cornellpress.cornell.edu. Estab. 1869. Publishes hardcover and paperback originals. **Publishes 150 titles/year. Pays royalty. Offers $0-5,000 advance.** Publishes book 1 year after acceptance of ms. Accepts simultaneous submissions. Book catalog and ms guidelines online.

Imprints Comstock (contact Heidi Steinmetz Lovette); ILR Press (contact Frances Benson).

O→ Cornell Press is an academic publisher of nonfiction with particular strengths in anthropology, Asian studies, biological sciences, classics, history, labor and business, literary criticism, politics and international relations, women's studies, Slavic studies, philosophy and security studies. Currently emphasizing sound scholarship that appeals beyond the academic community.

Nonfiction Biography, reference, scholarly, textbook. Subjects include agriculture/horticulture, anthropology/archeology, art/architecture, business/economics, education, ethnic, gay/lesbian, government/politics, history, language/literature, military/war, music/dance, philosophy, regional, sociology, translation, women's issues/studies, classics, life sciences. Submit résumé, cover letter, and prospectus.

Recent Title(s) *The Audubon Society Guide to Attracting Birds*, by Stephen Kress; *Darfur: The Ambiguous Genocide, revised edition*, by Gerard Prunier; *Nursing Against the Odds*, by Suzanne Gordon.

CORWIN PRESS, INC.

2455 Teller Rd., Thousand Oaks CA 91320. (800)818-7243. Fax: (805)499-2692. E-mail: robb.clouse@corwinpress.com. Web site: www.corwinpress.com. **Acquisitions:** Robb Clouse, editorial director; Lizzie Brenkus, acquisitions editor (administration); Cathy Hernandez, acquisitions editor (content, curriculum); Kylee Liegl, acquisitions editor (content, curriculum and exceptional education); Rachel Livsey, senior acquisitions editor (staff development, diversity and research methods); Kathleen McLane, consulting acquisitions editor (exceptional education); Stacy Wagner, associate acquisitions editor (early childhood education and school counseling); Jean Ward, consulting senior acquisitions editor (teaching); Faye Zucker, executive editor (teaching). Estab. 1990. Publishes hardcover and paperback originals. **Publishes 240 titles/year.** Publishes book 7 months after acceptance of ms. Responds in 1-2 months to queries. Ms guidelines online.

O→ Corwin Press, Inc., publishes leading-edge, user-friendly publications for education professionals.

Nonfiction Professional-level publications for administrators, teachers, school specialists, policymakers, researchers and others involved with preK-12 education. Subjects include education. Seeking fresh insights, conclusions, and recommendations for action. Prefers theory or research-based books that provide real-world examples and practical, hands-on strategies to help busy educators be successful. No textbooks that simply summarize existing knowledge or mass-market books. Query with SASE.

THE COUNTRYMAN PRESS

P.O. Box 748, Woodstock VT 05091-0748. (802)457-4826. Fax: (802)457-1678. E-mail: countrymanpress@wwnorton.com. Web site: www.countrymanpress.com. Editorial Director: Kermit Hummel. Estab. 1973. Publishes hardcover originals, trade paperback originals and reprints. **Publishes 35 titles/year. Receives 1,000 queries/year. 30% of books from first-time authors; 70% from unagented writers. Pays 5-15% royalty on retail price. Offers $1,000-5,000 advance.** Publishes book 18 months after acceptance of ms. Accepts simultaneous submissions. Responds in 2 months to proposals. Book catalog free; ms guidelines online.

Imprints Backcountry Guides, Berkshire House.

O‑ Countryman Press publishes books that encourage physical fitness and appreciation for and understanding of the natural world, self-sufficiency, and adventure.

Nonfiction ''We publish several series of regional recreation guidebooks—hiking, bicycling, walking, fly-fishing, canoeing, kayaking—and are looking to expand them. We're also looking for books of national interest on travel, gardening, rural living, nature, and fly-fishing.'' General nonfiction, how-to, guidebooks; general nonfiction. Subjects include cooking/foods/nutrition, gardening, history, nature/environment, recreation, regional, travel, country living. Submit proposal package including outline, author bio, 3 sample chapters, market information, SASE. Reviews artwork/photos as part of ms package. Send photocopies.

Recent Title(s) *The King Arthur Flour Cookie Companion*; *The Green Mountain Spinnery Knitting Book*; *Dog Friendly Washington DC and the Mid-Atlantic States*.

COVENANT COMMUNICATIONS, INC.

Box 416, American Fork UT 84003-0416. (801)756-1041. Web site: www.covenant-lds.com. **Publishes 60+ titles/year. 35% of books from first-time authors; 100% from unagented writers. Pays 6½-15% royalty on retail price.** Publishes book 6-12 months after acceptance of ms. Responds in 4 months to mss. Ms guidelines online.

O‑ Currently emphasizing inspirational, devotional, historical, biography. Our fiction is also expanding, and we are looking for new approaches to LDS literature and storytelling.

Nonfiction Biography, children's/juvenile, coffee table book, gift book, humor, illustrated book, multimedia (CD-ROM), reference, scholarly. Subjects include child guidance/parenting, creative nonfiction, history, memoirs, religion (LDS or Mormon), spirituality. Submit complete ms with synopsis and 1-page cover letter.

Fiction ''We publish exclusively to the 'Mormon' (The Church of Jesus Christ of Latter-Day Saints) market. All work must appeal to that audience.'' Adventure, historical, humor, juvenile, literary, mainstream/contemporary, mystery, picture books, regional, religious, romance, spiritual, suspense, young adult. Submit complete ms with synopsis and 1-page cover letter.

Recent Title(s) *Between Husband and Wife*, by Brinley and Lamb (marriage/self-help); *Timeless Waltz*, by Anita Stansfield (fiction); *The Book of Mormon* (on DVD).

Tips ''Our audience is exclusively LDS (Latter-Day Saints, 'Mormon').''

COWLEY PUBLICATIONS

4 Brattle St., Cambridge MA 02138. (800)225-1534. Fax: (617)441-0120. E-mail: cowley@cowley.org. Web site: www.cowley.org. Estab. 1979. Publishes trade paperback originals. **Publishes 16-20 titles/year. Receives 500 queries and 300 mss/year. 50% of books from first-time authors; 90% from unagented writers. Pays 10-15% royalty on wholesale price. Offers $0-5,000 advance.** Publishes book 12-18 months after acceptance of ms. Accepts simultaneous submissions. Responds in 2 months to queries; 3 months to proposals; 4 months to mss. Book catalog and ms guidelines online.

Nonfiction General nonfiction. Subjects include religion, spirituality. ''We publish books and resources for those seeking spiritual and theological formation. We are committed to developing a new generation of writers and teachers who will encourage people to think and pray in new ways about spirituality, reconciliation, and the future. We are interested in the many ways that faith and spirituality intersect with the world, in arts, social concerns, ethics, and so on.'' Query with SASE, or submit proposal package including outline, 1 sample chapter, other materials as specified online.

Poetry ''We consider poetry by invitation only.''

Recent Title(s) *The Comforting Whirlwind*, by Bill McKibben; *The Soul of the Night*, by Chet Raymo; *Ridiculous Packaging*, by Karen Favreau.

Tips ''We envision an audience of committed Christians and spiritual seekers of various denominations and faiths. Familiarize yourself with our catalog and our outlook on spiritual and theological formation. Prepare proposals/manuscripts that are of professional caliber and demonstrate an understanding of and commitment to your book's reader.''

CQ PRESS

Division of Congressional Quarterly, Inc., 1255 22nd St. NW, Suite 400, Washington DC 20037. (202)729-1800. E-mail: ckiino@cqpress.com. Web site: www.cqpress.com. **Acquisitions:** Doug Goldenberg-Hart, Shana Wagger (library/reference); Clarisse Kiino (college), Barbara Rogers (staff directories). Estab. 1945. Publishes hardcover and online paperback titles. Accepts simultaneous submissions. Book catalog free.

Imprints College, Library/Reference, Staff Directories; CQ Electronic Library/CQ Researcher.

O➛ CQ Press seeks "to educate the public by publishing authoritative works on American and international politics, policy, and people."

Nonfiction "We are interested in American government, public administration, comparative government, and international relations." Reference, textbook (all levels of college political science texts), information directories (on federal and state governments, national elections, international/state politics and governmental issues). Subjects include government/politics, history. Submit proposal package including outline.

Tips "Our books present important information on American government and politics, and related issues, with careful attention to accuracy, thoroughness, and readability."

CRAFTSMAN BOOK CO.

6058 Corte Del Cedro, Carlsbad CA 92009-9974. (760)438-7828 or (800)829-8123. Fax: (760)438-0398. Web site: www.craftsman-book.com. **Acquisitions:** Laurence D. Jacobs, editorial manager. Estab. 1957. Publishes paperback originals. **Publishes 12 titles/year. 85% of books from first-time authors; 98% from unagented writers. Pays 7½-12½% royalty on wholesale price or retail price.** Publishes book 2 years after acceptance of ms. Accepts simultaneous submissions. Responds in 2 months to queries. Book catalog and ms guidelines free.

O➛ Publishes how-to manuals for professional builders. Currently emphasizing construction software.

Nonfiction All titles are related to construction for professional builders. How-to, technical. Subjects include building, construction. Query with SASE. Reviews artwork/photos as part of ms package.

Recent Title(s) *Steel-Frame House Construction*, by Tim Waite.

Tips "The book should be loaded with step-by-step instructions, illustrations, charts, reference data, forms, samples, cost estimates, rules of thumb, and examples that solve actual problems in the builder's office and in the field. The book must cover the subject completely, become the owner's primary reference on the subject, have a high utility-to-cost ratio, and help the owner make a better living in his chosen field."

CREATIVE HOMEOWNER

24 Park Way, Upper Saddle River NJ 07458. (201)934-7100. Fax: (201)934-8971. E-mail: info@creativehomeowner.com. Web site: www.creativehomeowner.com. Estab. 1978. Publishes trade paperback originals. Book catalog free.

O➛ Creative Homeowner is the one source for the largest selection of quality home-related how-to books, idea books, booklets, and project plans.

Nonfiction How-to, illustrated book. Subjects include gardening, crafts/hobbies, home remodeling/building, home repairs, home decorating/design, ideas, inspiration. Query, or submit proposal package, including competitive books (short analysis), outline, and SASE. Reviews artwork/photos as part of ms package.

Recent Title(s) *The Painted Home*, by Kerry Skinner; *So Simple Window Style*, by Gail Abbott and Cate Burren; *The Smart Approach to Baby Rooms*, by Joanne Still.

⊘ CRICKET BOOKS

Imprint of Carus Publishing, 140 S. Dearborn St., Suite 1450, Chicago IL 60603. (603)924-7209. Fax: (603)924-7380. Web site: www.cricketbooks.net. **Acquisitions:** Submissions Editor. Estab. 1999. Publishes hardcover originals. **Publishes 10 titles/year. Receives 1,500 queries and 5,000 mss/year. Open to first-time authors. Pays up to 10% royalty on retail price. Offers $1,500 and up advance.** Publishes book 18 months after acceptance of ms. Accepts simultaneous submissions. Responds in 4 months to queries; 4 months to proposals; 6 months to mss. Ms guidelines online.

- *Currently not accepting queries or ms.* Check Web site for submissions details and updates.

O➛ Cricket Books publishes picture books, chapter books, and middle-grade novels.

Nonfiction Children's/juvenile. Send proposal, including sample chapters, TOC, and description of competition.

Fiction Juvenile (adventure, easy-to-read, fantasy/science fiction, historical, horror, mystery/suspense, problem novels, sports, western), early chapter books and middle-grade fiction. Submit complete ms.

Recent Title(s) *Dream-of-Jade*, by Lloyd Alexander; *Hercules*, by Geraldine McCaughrean; *Double-Dare to Be Scared*, by Robert San Souci.

Tips "Take a look at the recent titles to see what sort of materials we're interested in, especially for nonfiction. Please note that we aren't doing the sort of strictly educational nonfiction that other publishers specialize in."

THE CROSSROAD PUBLISHING COMPANY

16 Penn Plaza, Suite 1550, New York NY 10001. Fax: (212)868-2171. E-mail: editor@crossroadpublishing.com. Web site: www.cpcbooks.com. **Acquisitions:** Nancy Neal. Estab. 1980. Publishes hardcover and trade paperback originals and reprints. **Publishes 45 titles/year; imprint publishes 10 titles/year. Receives 1,000 queries and 200 mss/year. 10% of books from first-time authors; 75% from unagented writers. Pays 6-14% royalty on wholesale price.** Publishes book 14 months after acceptance of ms. Accepts simultaneous submissions. Responds in 6 weeks to queries; 6 weeks to proposals; 6 weeks to mss. Book catalog free; ms guidelines online.

Imprints Crossroad (trade); Herder (classroom/academic).

Nonfiction Autobiography, biography, general nonfiction, gift book, reference, scholarly, self-help, textbook. Subjects include creative nonfiction, ethnic, philosophy, religion, spirituality, women's issues/studies. "We want hopeful, well-written books on religion and spirituality." Query with SASE.

Recent Title(s) *Secularity and the Gospel*, by Ronald Rolheiser.

Tips "Refer to our Web site and catalog for a sense of the range and kinds of books we offer. Follow our application guidelines as posted on our Web site."

Ⓐ CROWN BUSINESS

Random House, Inc., 1745 Broadway, New York NY 10019. (212)572-2275. Fax: (212)572-6192. E-mail: crownbiz@randomhouse.com. Web site: www.randomhouse.com/crown. Estab. 1995. Publishes hardcover and trade paperback originals. Accepts simultaneous submissions. Book catalog online.

- *Agented submissions only.*

Nonfiction Subjects include business/economics, money/finance, management, technology. Query with proposal package including outline, 1-2 sample chapters, market analysis and SASE.

Recent Title(s) *Life 2.0*, by Rich Karlgaard; *Confronting Reality*, by Larry Bossidy and Ram Charan; *You're In Charge—Now What?*, by Thomas J. Neff and James M. Citrin.

Ⓐ ⊘ CROWN PUBLISHING GROUP

Imprint of Random House, Inc., 1745 Broadway, New York NY 10019. (212)782-9000. Web site: www.randomhouse.com/crown. Estab. 1933. Publishes popular fiction and nonfiction hardcover originals.

Imprints Bell Tower; Clarkson Potter; Crown Business; Crown Forum; Harmony Books; Shaye Arehart Books; Three Rivers Press.

- *Agented submissions only.* See Web site for more details.

Recent Title(s) *Confidence*, by Rosabeth Moss Kanter; *The Future for Investors*, by Jeremy Siegel.

CSLI PUBLICATIONS

Ventura Hall, Stanford University, Stanford CA 94305-4115. (650)723-1839. Fax: (650)725-2166. E-mail: pubs@csli.stanford.edu. Web site: cslipublications.stanford.edu. Publishes hardcover and scholarly paperback originals. Does not accept simultaneous submissions. Book catalog free; ms guidelines online.

- *No unsolicited mss.*
- O┳ "CSLI Publications, part of the Center for the Study of Language and Information, specializes in books in the study of language, information, logic, and computation."

Nonfiction Reference, technical, textbook, scholarly. Subjects include anthropology/archeology, computers/electronic, language/literature (linguistics), science, logic, cognitive science. Query with SASE or by email.

Recent Title(s) *Handbook of French Semantics*, edited by Francis Corblin and Henriëtte de Swart; *Geometry & Meaning*, by Dominic Widdows.

CUMBERLAND HOUSE PUBLISHING

431 Harding Industrial Dr., Nashville TN 37211. (615)832-1171. Fax: (615)832-0633. E-mail: information@cumberlandhouse.com. Web site: www.cumberlandhouse.com. Estab. 1996. Publishes hardcover, trade paperback and mass market originals and reprints. Accepts simultaneous submissions. Responds in 4-6 months to mss. Book catalog for 8×10 SAE with 4 first-class stamps; ms guidelines online.

Imprints Cumberland House Hearthside; Highland Books; WND Books.

- Accepts mss by US mail only. No electronic or telephone queries will be accepted.
- O┳ Cumberland House publishes "market specific books. We evaluate in terms of how sure we are that we can publish the book successfully and then the quality or uniqueness of a project." No longer seeking to acquire fiction titles.

Nonfiction Cookbook, gift book, how-to, humor, reference. Subjects include Americana, cooking/foods/nutrition, government/politics, history, military/war, recreation, regional, sports, travel, current affairs, popular culture, civil war. Query with SASE, or submit proposal package including outline, 1 sample chapter, synopsis, résumé, SASE. Reviews artwork/photos as part of ms package. Send photocopies only; not original copies.

Recent Title(s) *Earl Hamner*, by James E. Person, Jr; *Atomic Iran*, by Jerome Corsi; *Love Signs*, by Gregory E. Lang.
Tips Audience is "adventuresome people who like a fresh approach to things. Writers should tell what their idea is, why it's unique and why somebody would want to buy it—but don't pester us."

CURRENCY

1745 Broadway, New York NY 10019. (212)782-9000. Web site: www.randomhouse.com/doubleday/currency. Estab. 1989.

Currency publishes "business books for people who want to make a difference, not just a living."
Nonfiction Subjects include marketing, investment. *Agented submissions only.*
Recent Title(s) *It's Not What You Say . . . It's What You Do*; *Shift: Inside Nissan's Historic Revival*; *The Fred Factor*.

DA CAPO PRESS

Perseus Books Group, 11 Cambridge Center, Cambridge MA 02142. Web site: www.dacapopress.com. Estab. 1975. Publishes hardcover originals and trade paperback originals and reprints. **Publishes 115 titles/year; imprint publishes 115 titles/year. Receives 500 queries and 300 mss/year. 25% of books from first-time authors; 1% from unagented writers. Pays 7-15% royalty. Offers $1,000-225,000 advance.** Publishes book 1 year after acceptance of ms. Accepts simultaneous submissions. Responds in 2-3 months to queries; 2-3 months to proposals; 2-3 months to mss. Book catalog and ms guidelines online.
Nonfiction Autobiography, biography, general nonfiction, gift book. Subjects include art/architecture, contemporary culture, creative nonfiction, government/politics, history, language/literature, memoirs, military/war, social sciences, sports, translation, travel, world affairs. Does not accept electronic submissions or take phone calls regarding submissions. Query with SASE, or submit proposal package including outline, 3 sample chapters, cv. Reviews artwork/photos as part of ms package. Send photocopies.
Recent Title(s) *The Longest Winter*, by Adam Kershaw; *Da Capo Best Music Writing 2005*, edited by JT Leroy; *Friday Night Lights*, by H.G. Bissinger.

DARBY CREEK PUBLISHING

7858 Industrial Pkwy., Plain City OH 43064. Web site: www.darbycreekpublishing.com. Estab. 2002. Publishes hardcover, trade paperback, and mass market paperback originals and reprints. **Publishes 10-12 titles/year. Receives 500 queries and 750 mss/year. 25% of books from first-time authors; 75% from unagented writers. Pays royalty on retail price.** Publishes book 12-18 months after acceptance of ms. Accepts simultaneous submissions. Responds in 1 month to queries; 2 months to proposals; 2 months to mss. Book catalog and ms guidelines online.
Nonfiction Children's/juvenile, general nonfiction, illustrated book, hi-lo. Subjects include animals, anthropology/archeology, creative nonfiction, history, hobbies, nature/environment, science, social sciences, sports. "We are not a school library publisher. We do not do nonfiction series." Query with SASE, or submit complete ms. Reviews artwork/photos as part of ms package. Send photocopies.
Fiction Adventure, hi-lo, historical, humor, juvenile, mainstream/contemporary, multicultural, mystery, short story collections, sports, suspense, young adult. "We only want the highest-quality fiction for middle grade, hi-lo and young adults. We are not focused on picture books." Submit proposal package including synopsis, 2 sample chapters, or submit complete ms.
Recent Title(s) *Albino Animals*, by Kelly Milner Halls (photo/science); *Miracle: The True Story of the Wreck of the Sea Venture*, by Gail Karwoski (history); *Dog Days*, by David Lubar (realistic fiction).
Tips "We are looking for the 'Aha!' nonfiction title—the one no one else has done yet. All submissions should be comparable to or better than well-reviewed titles."

JONATHAN DAVID PUBLISHERS, INC.

68-22 Eliot Ave., Middle Village NY 11379-1194. (718)456-8611. Fax: (718)894-2818. E-mail: info@jdbooks.com. Web site: www.jdbooks.com. **Acquisitions:** Alfred J. Kolatch, editor-in-chief. Estab. 1948. Publishes hardcover and trade paperback originals and reprints. **Publishes 20-25 titles/year. 50% of books from first-time authors; 90% from unagented writers. Pays royalty, or makes outright purchase.** Publishes book 18 months after acceptance of ms. Responds in 1 month to queries; 1 month to proposals; 2 months to mss. Book catalog and ms guidelines online.

Jonathan David publishes "popular Judaica." Currently emphasizing projects geared toward children.
Nonfiction Biography, children's/juvenile, coffee table book, cookbook, gift book, how-to, humor, illustrated book, reference, self-help. Subjects include cooking/foods/nutrition, creative nonfiction, ethnic, multicultural, religion, sports. Query with SASE, or submit proposal package including outline, résumé, 3 sample chapters. Reviews artwork/photos as part of ms package. Send photocopies.
Recent Title(s) *Great Jews in Entertainment*, by Darryl Lyman.

DAW BOOKS, INC.

Distributed by Penguin Group (USA), 375 Hudson St., 3rd Floor, New York NY 10014-3658. (212)366-2096. Fax: (212)366-2090. E-mail: daw@us.penguingroup.com. Web site: www.dawbooks.com. Publishers: Elizabeth R. Wollheim and Sheila E. Gilbert. **Acquisitions:** Peter Stampfel, submissions editor. Estab. 1971. Publishes hardcover and paperback originals and reprints. **Publishes 60-80 titles/year. Pays in royalties with an advance negotiable on a book-by-book basis.** Responds in 3 months to mss. Ms guidelines online.

- Simultaneous submissions "returned unread at once, unless prior arrangements are made by agent."

O→ DAW Books publishes science fiction and fantasy.

Fiction Fantasy, science fiction. "We are interested in science fiction and fantasy novels. We need science fiction more than fantasy right now, but we're still looking for both. We like character-driven books with appealing characters. We accept both agented and unagented manuscripts. Long books are absolutely not a problem. We are not seeking collections of short stories or ideas for anthologies. We do not want any nonfiction manuscripts." Submit entire ms, cover letter, SASE. Simultaneous submissions "returned unread at once unless prior arrangements are made by agent."

Recent Title(s) *The Wizard of London*, by Mercedes Lacky (fantasy); *Shadowmarch*, by Tad Williams (fantasy); *Pretender*, by C.J. Cherryh (science fiction).

[N] DEAD END STREET, LLC

813 Third St., Hoquiam WA 98550. Web site: deadendstreet.com. Estab. 1997. Publishes all genres and seeks "cutting edge authors who represent the world's dead end streets." Accepts simultaneous submissions. Responds in 1 month to queries. Book catalog and ms guidelines online.

O→ "Accepts fiction, nonfiction, and screenplay submissions. Submit 500-word synopsis through the online form. If interested, we will request the full manuscript within 30 days. If you are not contacted within 30 days, it's because we cannot pursue your project. At this time, we're particularly interested in screenplays for features and shorts."

IVAN R. DEE, PUBLISHER

Imprint of The Rowman & Littlefield Publishing Group, 1332 N. Halsted St., Chicago IL 60622-2694. (312)787-6262. Fax: (312)787-6269. E-mail: elephant@ivanrdee.com. Submissions E-mail: editorial@ivanrdee.com. Web site: www.ivanrdee.com. **Acquisitions:** Ivan R. Dee, president; Hilary Meyer, managing editor. Estab. 1988. Publishes hardcover originals and trade paperback originals and reprints. **Publishes 50 titles/year. 10% of books from first-time authors; 70% from unagented writers. Pays royalty. Offers advance.** Publishes book 8 months after acceptance of ms. Accepts simultaneous submissions. Responds in 1 month to queries; 1 month to proposals; 1 month to mss. Book catalog free.

Imprints Elephant Paperbacks; New Amsterdam Books; J.S. Sanders Books.

O→ Ivan R. Dee publishes serious nonfiction for general-informed readers.

Nonfiction Biography. Subjects include art/architecture, government/politics, history, language/literature, world affairs, contemporary culture, baseball. "We publish history, biography, literature and letters, theater and drama, politics and current affairs, and literary baseball." Submit outline, sample chapter(s). Reviews artwork/photos as part of ms package.

Recent Title(s) *Terrible Fate*, by Benjamin Lieberman; *Moral Imagination*, by Gertrude Himmelfarb; *Essential Chaplin*, by Richard Schickel.

Tips "We publish for an intelligent lay audience and college course adoptions."

[A] DEL REY BOOKS

Imprint of Random House Publishing Group, 1745 Broadway, 18th Floor, New York NY 10019. (212)782-9000. E-mail: delrey@randomhouse.com. Web site: www.randomhouse.com. Estab. 1977. Publishes hardcover, trade paperback, and mass market originals and mass market paperback reprints. **Pays royalty on retail price. Offers competitive advance.** Does not accept simultaneous submissions.

O→ Del Rey publishes top level fantasy, alternate history, and science fiction.

Fiction Fantasy (should have the practice of magic as an essential element of the plot), science fiction (well-plotted novels with good characterizations, exotic locales and detailed alien creatures), alternate history. *Agented submissions only.*

Recent Title(s) *The Salmon of Doubt*, by Douglas Adams; *Weapons of Choice*, by John Birmingham; *The Zenith Angle*, by Bruce Sterling.

Tips "Del Rey is a reader's house. Pay particular attention to plotting, strong characters, and dramatic, satisfactory conclusions. It must be/feel believable. That's what the readers like. In terms of mass market, we basically created the field of fantasy bestsellers. Not that it didn't exist before, but we put the mass into mass market."

DELACORTE BOOKS FOR YOUNG READERS

Imprint of Random House Children's Books/Random House, Inc., 1745 Broadway, New York NY 10019. (212)782-9000. Web site: www.randomhouse.com.

- Although not currently seeking unsolicited mss, mss are being sought for 2 contests: Delacorte Dell Yearling Contest for a First Middle-Grade Novel and Delacorte Press Contest for a First Young Adult Novel. Submission guidelines can be found online.

DELL DRAGONFLY BOOKS FOR YOUNG READERS

Imprint of Random House Children's Books/Random House, Inc., 1745 Broadway, New York NY 10019. (212)782-9000. Web site: www.randomhouse.com.

- Quality reprint paperback imprint for paperback books. *Does not accept mss.*

DELL LAUREL LEAF BOOKS FOR YOUNG READERS

Imprint of Random House Children's Books/Random House, Inc., 1745 Broadway, New York NY 10019. (212)782-9000. Web site: www.randomhouse.com.

- Quality reprint paperback imprint for young adult paperback books. *Does not accept mss.*

DELL YEARLING BOOKS FOR YOUNG READERS

Imprint of Random House Children's Books/Random House, Inc., 1745 Broadway, New York NY 10019. (212)782-9000. Web site: www.randomhouse.com.

- Quality reprint paperback imprint for middle grade paperback books. *Does not accept unsolicited mss.*

DEVORSS & CO.

DeVorss Publications, P.O. Box 1389, Camarillo CA 93011-1389. E-mail: editorial@devorss.com. Web site: www.devorss.com. Publishes hardcover and trade paperback originals and reprints. **Receives 700 queries and 300 mss/year. 95% of books from first-time authors; 100% from unagented writers. 10% maximum royalty on retail price.** Publishes book 6 months after acceptance of ms. Accepts simultaneous submissions. Responds in 1 month to mss. Book catalog for #10 SASE; ms guidelines for #10 SASE.

Nonfiction Children's/juvenile, gift book, self-help, body, mind, and spirit. Subjects include creative nonfiction, philosophy, psychology, spirituality, Body, Mind, and Spirit. Query with SASE. Reviews artwork/photos as part of ms package. Send photocopies.

Recent Title(s) *Little Green Apples*, by O.C. Smith and James Shaw.

Tips "Our audience is people using their mind to improve health, finances, relationships, life changes, etc. Ask for guidelines first. Don't submit outlines, proposals, or manuscripts. Don't call. Please send submissions and inquiries by mail only."

DIAL BOOKS FOR YOUNG READERS

Imprint of Penguin Group USA, 345 Hudson St., 14th Floor, New York NY 10014. (212)366-2000. Web site: www.penguinputnam.com. President/Publisher: Nancy Paulsen. Associate Publisher/Editorial Director: Lauri Hornik. **Acquisitions:** Submissions Editor. Estab. 1961. Publishes hardcover originals. **Publishes 50 titles/year. Receives 5,000 queries/year. 20% of books from first-time authors. Pays royalty. Offers varies advance.** Does not accept simultaneous submissions. Responds in 4 months to queries. Book catalog for 9 X12 SAE with 4 first-class stamps.

- Dial Books for Young Readers publishes quality picture books for ages 18 months-8 years; lively, believable novels for middle readers and young adults; and occasional nonfiction for middle readers and young adults.

Nonfiction Children's/juvenile, illustrated book. Accepts unsolicited queries.

Fiction Adventure, fantasy, juvenile, picture books, young adult. Especially looking for "lively and well-written novels for middle grade and young adult children involving a convincing plot and believable characters. The subject matter or theme should not already be overworked in previously published books. The approach must not be demeaning to any minority group, nor should the roles of female characters (or others) be stereotyped, though we don't think books should be didactic, or in any way message-y. No topics inappropriate for the juvenile, young adult, and middle grade audiences. No plays." Query with SASE. Accepts unsolicited queries and up to 10 pages for longer works and unsolicited mss for picture books.

Recent Title(s) *A Cool Moonlight*, by Angela Johnson; *A Year Down Yonder*, by Richard Peck; *A Penguin Pup for Pinkerton*, by Steven Kellogg.

Tips "Our readers are anywhere from preschool age to teenage. Picture books must have strong plots, lots of action, unusual premises, or universal themes treated with freshness and originality. Humor works well in these books. A very well-thought-out and intelligently presented book has the best chance of being taken on. Genre isn't as much of a factor as presentation."

DK PUBLISHING, INC.

(formerly Dorling Kindersley), Pearson Plc, 375 Hudson St., New York NY 10014. (212)213-4800. Web site: www.dk.com. **Pays royalty or flat fee.**

- Publishes picture books for middle-grade and older readers. Also, illustrated reference books for adults and children.

Fiction *Agented submissions only.*

DNA PRESS & NARTEA PUBLISHING

(formerly ACEN Press), DNA Press, P.O. Box 572, Eagleville PA 19408. Fax: (501)694-5495. E-mail: info@dnapress.com. Web site: www.dnapress.com. **Acquisitions:** Xela Schenk, operations manager. Estab. 1998. Publishes hardcover and trade paperback originals. **Publishes 10 titles/year; imprint publishes 5 titles/year. Receives 500 queries and 400 mss/year. 90% of books from first-time authors; 100% from unagented writers. Pays 10-15% royalty.** Publishes book 8 months after acceptance of ms. Accepts simultaneous submissions. Responds in 6 weeks to mss. Book catalog and ms guidelines free.

- Book publisher for young adults, children, and adults.

Nonfiction Children's/juvenile (explaining science), how-to. Subjects include education, health/medicine, science, sports, travel. "We publish books for children which teach scientific concepts as part of the general context; or how-to for adults which carry scientific knowledge and contribute to learning." Submit complete ms. Reviews artwork/photos as part of ms package. Send photocopies.

Fiction Juvenile, science fiction, young adult. "All books should be oriented to explaining science even if they do not fall 100% under the category of science fiction." Submit complete ms.

Recent Title(s) *Virgil's End*; *Feebie Brainiac and the Lysis Virus*; *The Prometheus Project.*

Tips "Quick response, great relationships, high commission/royalty."

TOM DOHERTY ASSOCIATES LLC

Subsidiary of Holtzbrinck Publishers, 175 Fifth Ave., 14th Floor, New York NY 10010. Fax: (212)388-0191. E-mail: inquiries@tor.com. Web site: www.tor-forge.com. **Acquisitions:** Patrick Nielsen Hayden (science fiction and fantasy); Melissa Singer (mainstream fiction). Estab. 1980. Publishes hardcover trade, paperback, and mass market originals. Does not accept simultaneous submissions. Book catalog and ms guidelines online.

Imprints Forge Books; Orb Books; Tor.

Nonfiction Biography.

Fiction Fantasy, horror, mystery, romance (paranormal), science fiction, suspense, western, techno thrillers, American historicals, true crime. Submit synopsis, first 3 chapters, cover letter stating genre and previous book sales or publications (if relevant).

Recent Title(s) *Gardens of the Moon*, by Steven Erikson (fantasy); *Ringworld's Children*, by Larry Nevin (science fiction).

DOLLAR$MART BOOKS

4320-C Ridgecrest, #150, Rio Rancho NM 87124. (505)681-2880. **Acquisitions:** Cheryl Gorder, publisher (financial education and business); Robin, editor (spirituality and New Age). Estab. 1985. Publishes trade paperback and electronic originals. **Publishes 12 titles/year. Receives 500 queries and 500 mss/year. 90% of books from first-time authors; 90% from unagented writers. Pays 10-15% royalty on retail price, or makes outright purchase of $500-3,000.** Publishes book 3 months after acceptance of ms. Accepts simultaneous submissions. Responds in 1 month to queries; 1 month to mss. Book catalog free; ms guidelines for #10 SASE.

Nonfiction How-to, reference, self-help. Subjects include business/economics, education, money/finance, New Age, spirituality, real estate. Submit complete ms. Reviews artwork/photos as part of ms package. Send photocopies.

Fiction "The only fiction we publish is 'spiritual warrior' type." Submit complete ms.

Recent Title(s) *Dollar$mart Resource Guide for Kids*; *Dollar$mart Kid's Education at Home*; *Leave Fear at the Door.*

Tips "We would prefer to see complete manuscripts, and we will return manuscripts if they are accompanied by an envelope with sufficient postage."

DORCHESTER PUBLISHING CO., INC.

200 Madison Ave., Suite 2000, New York NY 10016. (212)725-8811. Fax: (212)532-1054. Web site: www.dorchesterpub.com. **Offers advance.** Does not accept simultaneous submissions. Ms guidelines online.

Imprints Love Spell (romance); Leisure Books (romance, westerns, horror, thrillers); Making It (chick lit).

- No submissions via e-mail or fax.

DOUBLEDAY BOOKS FOR YOUNG READERS

Imprint of Random House Children's Books/Random House, Inc., 1745 Broadway, New York NY 10019. (212)782-9000. Web site: www.randomhouse.com/kids.

- Trade picture book list, from preschool to age 8. Not accepting any unsolicited book mss at this time.

DOUBLEDAY BROADWAY PUBLISHING GROUP

Imprint of Random House, Inc., 1745 Broadway, New York NY 10019. (212)782-9000. Fax: (212)782-9700. Web site: www.randomhouse.com. Estab. 1897. Publishes hardcover originals. **Receives thousands of queries and thousands of mss/year. Pays royalty on retail price. Offers advance.** Does not accept simultaneous submissions.

Imprints Broadway Books; Currency; Doubleday; Doubleday Image; Doubleday Religious Publishing; Main Street Books; Nan A. Talese.

- *Does not accept any unagented submissions.* No exceptions.

O‑ Doubleday publishes high-quality fiction and nonfiction.

Nonfiction Biography. Subjects include Americana, anthropology/archeology, business/economics, computers/electronic, education, ethnic, government/politics, health/medicine, history, language/literature, money/finance, nature/environment, philosophy, religion, science, sociology, software, sports, translation, women's issues/studies. *Agented submissions only.*

Fiction Adventure, confession, ethnic, experimental, feminist, gay/lesbian, historical, humor, literary, mainstream/contemporary, religious, short story collections. *Agented submissions only.*

DOUBLEDAY RELIGIOUS PUBLISHING

Imprint of Doubleday Broadway Publishing Group, Division of Random House, Inc., 1745 Broadway, New York NY 10019. (212)782-9000. Web site: www.randomhouse.com. Estab. 1897. Publishes hardcover and trade paperback originals and reprints. Accepts simultaneous submissions. Book catalog for SAE with 3 first-class stamps.

Imprints Image Books; Anchor Bible Commentary; Anchor Bible Reference; Galilee; New Jerusalem Bible; Three Leaves Press.

Nonfiction Historical, philosophical, religious. *Agented submissions only.*

Fiction Religious. *Agented submissions only.*

DOUBLEDAY/IMAGE

Doubleday Broadway Publishing Group, Random House, Inc., 1745 Broadway, New York NY 10019. (212)782-9000. Fax: (212)302-7985. Web site: www.randomhouse.com. **Acquisitions:** Trace Murphy, executive editor. Estab. 1956. Publishes hardcover, trade and mass market paperback originals and reprints. **Publishes 12 titles/year. Receives 500 queries and 300 mss/year. 10% of books from first-time authors. Pays royalty on retail price. Offers varied advance.** Publishes book 18 months after acceptance of ms. Accepts simultaneous submissions. Responds in 3 months to proposals.

O‑ Image Books has grown from a classic Catholic list to include a variety of current and future classics, maintaining a high standard of quality as the finest in religious paperbacks. Also publishes Doubleday paperbacks/hardcovers for general religion, spirituality, including works based in Buddhism, Islam, Judaism.

Nonfiction Biography, how-to, reference. Subjects include philosophy, religion, women's issues/studies. Query with SASE. Will review photocopies of artwork/photos.

Recent Title(s) *Papal Sin*, by Garry Wills; *Soul Survivor*, by Philip Yancey; *The Lamb's Supper*, by Scott Hahn.

LISA DREW BOOKS

Imprint of Scribner, Simon & Schuster Adult Publishing Group, 1230 Avenue of the Americas, New York NY 10020. (212)698-7000. Web site: www.simonsays.com. **Acquisitions:** Lisa Drew, publisher. Publishes hardcover originals. **Publishes 10-14 titles/year. Receives 600 queries/year. 10% of books from first-time authors. Pays royalty on retail price. Offers variable advance.** Publishes book 1 year after acceptance of ms.

- Accepts simultaneous agented submissions. Responds in 1 month.

O‑ "We publish narrative nonfiction. We do not want how-to books, fiction or self-help."

Nonfiction Subjects include government/politics, history, women's issues/studies. *No unsolicited material. Agented submissions only.*

🅐 THOMAS DUNNE BOOKS

Imprint of St. Martin's Press, 175 Fifth Ave., New York NY 10010. (212)674-5151. Web site: www.stmartins.com. Publishes hardcover and trade paperback originals, and reprints. Accepts simultaneous submissions. Book catalog and ms guidelines free.

O→ Thomas Dunne publishes a wide range of fiction and nonfiction. Accepts submissions from agents only.

Nonfiction Biography. Subjects include government/politics, history, sports, political commentary. "Author's attention to detail is important. We get a lot of manuscripts that are poorly proofread and just can't be considered." Agents submit query, or an outline and 100 sample pages. Reviews artwork/photos as part of ms package. Send photocopies.

Fiction Mainstream/contemporary, mystery, suspense, thrillers, women's. Agents submit query, or submit synopsis and 100 sample pages.

Recent Title(s) *Snobs*, by Julian Fellowes; *Can't Stop Won't Stop*, by Jeff Chang; *Travels With My Donkey*, by Tim Moore.

🅐 ⊘ DUTTON ADULT TRADE

Imprint of Penguin Group (USA), Inc., 375 Hudson St., New York NY 10014. (212)366-2000. Web site: www.penguinputnam.com. Estab. 1852. Publishers hardcover originals. **Pays royalty. Offers negotiable advance.** Accepts simultaneous submissions. Book catalog for #10 SASE.

O→ Dutton publishes hardcover, original, mainstream, and contemporary fiction and nonfiction in the areas of memoir, self-help, politics, psychology, and science for a general readership.

Nonfiction General nonfiction, humor, reference, self-help, Memoir. *Agented submissions only. No unsolicited mss.*

Fiction Adventure, historical, literary, mainstream/contemporary, mystery, short story collections, suspense. *Agented submissions only. No unsolicited mss.*

Tips "Write the complete manuscript and submit it to an agent or agents. They will know exactly which editor will be interested in a project."

DUTTON CHILDREN'S BOOKS

Imprint of Penguin Group (USA), Inc., 345 Hudson St., New York NY 10014. (212)414-3700. Fax: (212)414-3397. Web site: www.penguin.com. **Acquisitions:** Stephanie Owens Lurie, president and publisher (picture books and fiction); Maureen Sullivan, executive editor (books for all ages with distinctive narrative style); Lucia Monfried, senior editor (picture books, easy-to-read books, fiction). Estab. 1852. Publishes hardcover originals as well as novelty formats. **Publishes 100 titles/year. 15% of books from first-time authors. Pays royalty on retail price. Offers advance.**

O→ Dutton Children's Books publishes high-quality fiction and nonfiction for readers ranging from preschoolers to young adults on a variety of subjects. Currently emphasizing middle-grade and young adult novels that offer a fresh perspective. De-emphasizing photographic nonfiction and picture books that teach a lesson.

Nonfiction Children's/juvenile, for preschoolers to young adults. Subjects include animals, history (US), nature/environment, science. Query with SASE.

Fiction Dutton Children's Books has a diverse, general interest list that includes picture books; easy-to-read books; and fiction for all ages, from "first chapter" books to young adult readers. Query with SASE.

Recent Title(s) *The Best Pet of All*, by David LaRochelle (picture book); *The Schwa Was Here*, by Neal Shusterman (novel); *Looking for Alaska*, by John Green (young adult novel).

EAKIN PRESS

P.O. Drawer 90159, Austin TX 78709-0159. (512)288-1771. Fax: (512)288-1813. Web site: www.eakinpress.com. **Acquisitions:** Virginia Messer, publisher. Estab. 1978. Publishes hardcover and paperback originals and reprints. Accepts simultaneous submissions. Responds in up to 1 year to queries. Book catalog for $1.25; ms guidelines online.

- No electronic submissions.

O→ Eakin specializes in Texana and Western Americana for adults and juveniles. Currently emphasizing women's studies.

Nonfiction Biography, cookbook (regional). Subjects include Americana (Western), business/economics, cooking/foods/nutrition, ethnic, history, military/war, regional, sports, African American studies, Civil War, Texas history. Juvenile nonfiction: includes biographies of historic personalities, prefer with Texas or regional interest, or nature studies; and easy-read illustrated books for grades 1-3. Submit sample chapter(s), author bio, synopsis, publishing credits, SASE.

Fiction Historical, juvenile. Juvenile fiction for grades K-12, preferably relating to Texas and the Southwest or

contemporary. No adult fiction. Query or submit outline/synopsis, author bio, publishing credits, and sample chapters. For children's books or books under 100 pgs, send complete ms.
Recent Title(s) *Sam Houston Slept Here*, by Bill O'Neal; *Grape Man of Texas*, by Sherrie S. McLeRoy and Roy E. Renfro, Jr., PhD; *Playbills and Popcorn*, by Michael A. Jenkins.

EASTERN WASHINGTON UNIVERSITY PRESS

705 W. 1st Ave., Spokane WA 99201. (509)623-4285. Fax: (509)623-4283. E-mail: ewupress@ewu.edu. Web site: ewupress.ewu.edu. **Acquisitions:** Chris Howell, senior editor (poetry, fiction); Ivar Nelson, director (nonfiction); Pamela Holway, managing editor. Estab. 1994. Publishes hardcover and trade paperback originals and reprints. **Publishes 14 titles/year. Receives 150 queries/year. 25% of books from first-time authors. Pays 10% royalty.** Publishes book 2-4 years after acceptance of ms. Accepts simultaneous submissions. Responds in 1-2 months to queries; 3 months to proposals; 6-9 months to mss. Book catalog and ms guidelines free.
Nonfiction Subjects include anthropology/archeology, history, language/literature, nature/environment, philosophy, regional, translation.
Fiction Accepts novels and entries for the short fiction contest. Query before sending complete ms.
Poetry Accepts any poetry.
Tips "Submit complete ms in hard copy—no digital ms submissions. May query by e-mail."

ECLIPSE PRESS

The Blood-Horse, Inc., 3101 Beaumont Centre Circle, Lexington KY 40513. Web site: www.eclipsepress.com. **Acquisitions:** Jacqueline Duke, editor (equine). Estab. 1916. Publishes hardcover and trade paperback originals. **Publishes 12-15 titles/year. Receives 100 queries and 50 mss/year. 20% of books from first-time authors; 40% from unagented writers. Pays 10-15% royalty on net receipts, or makes outright purchase. Offers $3,000-12,000 advance.** Publishes book 18 months after acceptance of ms. Accepts simultaneous submissions. Responds in 2-3 months to queries; 2-3 months to proposals; 2-3 months to mss. Book catalog free.
Nonfiction Subjects include sports (equine, equestrian). "We only accept nonfiction works on equine and equestrian topics." Query with SASE, or submit outline, sample chapter(s). Reviews artwork/photos as part of ms package.
Tips "Our audience is sports, horse, and racing enthusiasts."

EDUCATOR'S INTERNATIONAL PRESS, INC.

18 Colleen Rd., Troy NY 12180. (518)271-9886. Fax: (518)266-9422. E-mail: bill@edint.com. Web site: www.edint.com. **Acquisitions:** William Clockel, publisher. Estab. 1996. Publishes hardcover and trade paperback originals and reprints. Accepts simultaneous submissions. Book catalog and ms guidelines free.

O→ Educator's International publishes books in all aspects of education, broadly conceived, from prekindergarten to postgraduate. "We specialize in texts, professional books, videos and other materials for students, faculty, practitioners and researchers. We also publish a full list of books in the areas of women's studies, and social and behavioral sciences."

Nonfiction Textbook, supplemental texts; conference proceedings. Subjects include education, gay/lesbian, language/literature, philosophy, psychology, software, women's issues/studies. Submit TOC, outline, 2-3 chapters, résumé with SASE. Reviews artwork/photos as part of ms package.
Recent Title(s) *Journal of Curriculum and Pedagogy*; *Democratic Responses in an Era of Standardization* (Relationship and the Arts in Teacher Education).
Tips Audience is professors, students, researchers, individuals, libraries.

EDUCATORS PUBLISHING SERVICE

P.O. Box 9031, Cambridge MA 02139-9031. (617)547-6706. Fax: (617)547-3805. Web site: www.epsbooks.com. **Acquisitions:** Charles H. Heinle, vice president, Publishing Group. Estab. 1952. **Publishes 26 titles/year. Receives 200 queries and 200 mss/year. 50% of books from first-time authors; 90% from unagented writers. Pays 5-10% royalty on retail price.** Publishes book 8 months (minimum) after acceptance of ms. Accepts simultaneous submissions. Responds in 1 month to queries; 3 months to proposals; 3 months to mss. Book catalog and ms guidelines online.

O→ EPS accepts queries from educators writing for a school market, authoring materials (primarily K-8) in the reading and language areas. "We are interested in materials following pedagogical restraints (such as decodable texts and leveled readers) that we can incorporate into ongoing or future projects, or that form a complete program in themselves."

Nonfiction Workbooks (language arts) and some professional books. Subjects include education (reading comprehension, phonics vocabulary development and writing), supplementary texts and workbooks (reading and language arts). Query with SASE.

Recent Title(s) *Words Are Wonderful, Book 3*, by Dorothy Grant Hennings; *Ten Essential Vocabulary Strategies*, by Lee Mountain; *Write About Me*, by Elsie Wilmerding.
Tips Student (K-8) audiences.

EDUPRESS, INC.

W5527 State Road 106, P.O. Box 800, Fort Atkinson WI 53538-0800. (920)563-9571. E-mail: edupress@highsmith.com. Web site: www.edupressinc.com. Estab. 1979. Publishes trade paperback originals. Book catalog and ms guidelines free.

- Edupress, Inc., publishes supplemental resources for classroom curriculum. Currently emphasizing more science, math, language arts emphasis than in the past.

Nonfiction Subjects include education (resources for pre-school through middle school).
Tips Audience is classroom teachers and homeschool parents.

EERDMANS BOOKS FOR YOUNG READERS

William B. Eerdmans Publishing Co., 255 Jefferson Ave. SE, Grand Rapids MI 49503. (616)459-4591. Fax: (616)776-7638. Web site: www.eerdmans.com/youngreaders. **Acquisitions:** Judy Zylstra, editor. Publishes picture books and middle reader and young adult fiction and nonfiction. **Publishes 12-15 titles/year. Receives 4,000 queries/year. Pays 5-7½% royalty on retail price.** Publishes book Publishes middle reader and YA books in 1 year; publishes picture books in 2-3 years after acceptance of ms. Accepts simultaneous submissions. Responds in 6 weeks to queries. Book catalog for #10 SASE; ms guidelines online.

- No queries or submissions via e-mail or fax. Eerdmans is no longer accepting, considering, or returning unsolicited mss that are not clearly indicated on the outside envelope to be exclusive submissions.
- "We publish books for children and young adults that deal with spiritual themes—but never in a preachy or heavy-handed way. Some of our books are clearly religious, while others (especially our novels) look at spiritual issues in very subtle ways. We look for books that are honest, wise and hopeful." Currently emphasizing general picture books (also picture book biographies), novels (middle reader and YA). De-emphasizing retellings of Bible stories. "We also have been expanding to publish books for library, school and general trade markets."

Nonfiction Children's/juvenile, picture books, middle reader, young adult nonfiction. "Do not send illustrations unless you are a professional illustrator." Submit complete mss for picture books and novels or biographies under 200 pages with SASE. For longer books, send query letter and 3 or 4 sample chapters with SASE. Reviews artwork/photos as part of ms package. Send color photocopies rather than original art.
Fiction Juvenile, picture books, young adult, middle reader. "Do not send illustrations unless you are a professional illustrator." Submit complete mss for picture books and novels or biographies under 200 pages with SASE. For longer books, send query letter and 3 or 4 sample chapters with SASE.
Recent Title(s) *Mississippi Morning*, by Ruth Vanderzee, illustrated by Floyd Cooper; *Something to Tell Grandcows*, by Eileen Spinelli, illustrated by Bill Slarin; *Going for the Record*, by Julie A. Swanson.

ELEPHANT BOOKS

65 Macedonia Rd., Alexander NC 28701. (828)252-9515. Fax: (828)255-8719. E-mail: pat@abooks.com. Web site: abooks.com. **Acquisitions:** Editor. Publishes trade paperback originals and reprints. Book catalog and ms guidelines online.

- No e-mail or phone submissions.

Nonfiction Cookbook, books about elephants. Subjects include cooking/foods/nutrition, history, military/war (Civil War). Query, or submit outline with 3 sample chapters and proposal package, including potential marketing plans with SASE. Reviews artwork/photos as part of ms package. Send photocopies.

ELSEVIER, INC.

Reed-Elsevier (USA) Inc., 30 Corporate Dr., Suite 400, Burlington MA 01803. (800)470-1199. Fax: (781)904-2640. Web site: www.bh.com. **Acquisitions:** Jim DeWolf, vice president of professional publishing (engineering, electronics, computing, media and visual, security); Joanne Tracy, publisher (Focal Press); Theron Shreve, publisher (Digital Press); Susan Pioli, publishing director (medical); Mark Listewnik, senior acquisitions editor (security). Estab. 1975. Publishes hardcover and trade paperback originals. **Publishes 350 titles/year; imprint publishes 40-50 titles/year. 25% of books from first-time authors; 95% from unagented writers. Pays 10-12% royalty on wholesale price. Offers modest advance.** Publishes book 9 months after acceptance of ms. Responds in 1 month to proposals. Book catalog free; ms guidelines online.
Imprints Butterworth-Heinemann/Academic Press (engineering, business); Morgan Kauffman/Digital Press (computing); Focal Press (media and visual technology); Newnes (electronics); Butterworth Heinemann Security; Acadmic Press (life sciences, physical science).

O→ Elsevier publishes technical professional and academic books in technology, medicine and business; no fiction.

Nonfiction How-to (in our selected areas), reference, technical, textbook. Subjects include business/economics, computers/electronic, health/medicine, photography, science, security/criminal justice, audio-video broadcast, communication technology. Query with SASE, or submit outline, 1-2 sample chapters, information on competing books and how yours is different/better. Reviews artwork/photos as part of ms package. Send photocopies.

Tips Elsevier has been serving professionals and students for over 5 decades. "We remain committed to publishing materials that forge ahead of rapidly changing technology and reinforce the highest professional standards. Our goal is to give you the competitive advantage in this rapidly changing digital age."

EMPIRE PUBLISHING SERVICE

P.O. Box 1344, Studio City CA 91614-0344. **Acquisitions:** Joseph Witt. Estab. 1960. Publishes hardcover reprints and trade paperback originals and reprints. **Publishes 40 titles/year; imprint publishes 15 titles/year. Receives 500 queries and 85 mss/year. 50% of books from first-time authors; 95% from unagented writers. Pays 6-10% royalty on retail price. Offers variable advance.** Publishes book up to 2 years after acceptance of ms. Does not accept simultaneous submissions. Responds in 1 month to queries; 2 months to proposals; up to 1 year to mss. Book catalog for #10 SASE; ms guidelines for $1 or #10 SASE.

Imprints Gaslight Publications; Gaslight Books; Empire Publications; Empire Books; Empire Music.

O→ "Submit only Sherlock Holmes, performing arts and health."

Nonfiction How-to, humor, reference, technical, textbook. Subjects include health/medicine, humor, music/dance, Sherlock Holmes. Query with SASE. Reviews artwork/photos as part of ms package. Send photocopies.

Fiction Historical (pre-18th century), mystery (Sherlock Holmes). Query with SASE.

Recent Title(s) *Sherlock Holmes and the Adventure of the Clothesline*, by Carolyn Wells; *Elementary My Dear Watson*, by William Alan Landes; *The Magic of Food*, by James Cohen.

ENCOUNTER BOOKS

900 Broadway, Suite 400, New York NY 10003-1239. (212)871-6310. Fax: (212)871-6311. E-mail: read@encounterbooks.com. Web site: www.encounterbooks.com. **Acquisitions:** Roger Kimball. Hardcover originals and trade paperback reprints. Accepts simultaneous submissions. Book catalog free or online; ms guidelines online.

- *Accepts agented material only. No unsolicited mss/queries.* Reading period is March 1-November 1.

O→ Encounter Books publishes serious nonfiction—books that can alter our society, challenge our morality, stimulate our imaginations—in the areas of history, politics, religion, biography, education, public policy, current affairs, and social sciences.

Nonfiction Biography, reference. Subjects include child guidance/parenting, education, ethnic, government/politics, health/medicine, history, language/literature, memoirs, military/war, multicultural, philosophy, psychology, religion, science, sociology, women's issues/studies, gender studies. Submit proposal package, including outline and 1 sample chapter, SASE. Do not send via e-mail.

Recent Title(s) *Black Rednecks and White Liberals*, by Thomas Sowell; *The Prince of the City*, by Fred Siegel.

ENSLOW PUBLISHERS, INC.

40 Industrial Rd., Box 398, Berkeley Heights NJ 07922. (973)771-9400. Web site: www.enslow.com. **Acquisitions:** Brian D. Enslow, editor. Estab. 1977. Publishes hardcover originals. 10% require freelance illustration. **Publishes 250 titles/year. Pays royalty on net price with advance or flat fee. Offers advance.** Publishes book 1 year after acceptance of ms. Responds in 1 month to queries. Ms guidelines for #10 SASE.

O→ Enslow publishes hardcover nonfiction series books for young adults and school-age children.

Nonfiction Biography, children's/juvenile, reference. Subjects include health/medicine, history, recreation (Sports), science, sociology. Interested in new ideas for series of books for young people. No fiction, fictionalized history, or dialogue.

Recent Title(s) *TV News: Can It Be Trusted?*, by Ray Spangenburg and Kit Moser; *Resisters and Rescuers—Standing Up Against the Holocaust*, by Linda Jacobs Attman.

Tips "We love to receive résumés from experienced writers with good research skills who can think like young people."

ENTREPRENEUR PRESS

2445 McCabe Way, Irvine CA 92614. (949)261-2325. Fax: (949)261-7729. Web site: www.entrepreneurpress.com. **Acquisitions:** Karen Thomas, assistant acquisition editor. Publishes quality hardcover and trade paperbacks. **Publishes 50+ titles/year. Receives 1,200 queries and 600 mss/year. 40% of books from first-time authors; 60% from unagented writers. Pays competitive net royalty.** Accepts simultaneous submissions. Ms guidelines online.

Nonfiction Subjects include business/economics, start-up, marketing, finance, personal finance, accounting, motivation, leadership, and management. Query with SASE, or submit proposal package including outline, author bio, 2 sample chapters, preface or executive summary, competition. Reviews artwork/photos as part of ms package. Send transparencies.

Recent Title(s) *Million Dollar Habits*, by Brian Tracy; *Guerilla Marketing in 30 Days Workbook*, by Jay Conrad Levinson and Al Lautenslager.

Tips "We publish books in real estate, careers, Ebay series and online business."

EVAN-MOOR EDUCATIONAL PUBLISHERS

18 Lower Ragsdale Dr., Monterey CA 93940-5746. (800)976-1915. Fax: (800)777-4332. E-mail: editorial@evan-moor.com. Web site: www.evan-moor.com. **Acquisitions:** Acquisitions Editor. Estab. 1979. Publishes teaching materials. **Publishes 40-60 titles/year.** Accepts simultaneous submissions. Responds in 3 months to queries. Book catalog and ms guidelines free or on Web site.

- "Our books are teaching ideas, lesson plans, and blackline reproducibles for grades pre-K through 6th in all curriculum areas except music and bilingual." Currently emphasizing writing/language arts, practice materials for home use. De-emphasizing thematic materials. "We do not publish children's literary fiction or literary nonfiction."

Nonfiction Subjects include education, teaching materials, grades pre-K through 6th. No children's fiction or nonfiction literature. Submit proposal package, including outline and 3 sample chapters, résumé, SASE.

Recent Title(s) *Basic Phonics Skills*; *Read and Understand Poetry*; *U.S. Facts & Fun*.

Tips "Writers should know how classroom/educational materials differ from trade publications. They should request catalogs and submission guidelines before sending queries or manuscripts. Visiting our Web site will give writers a clear picture of the type of materials we publish."

EXCELSIOR CEE PUBLISHING

P.O. Box 5861, Norman OK 73070. (405)329-3909. Fax: (405)329-6886. **Acquisitions:** J.C. Marshall. Estab. 1989. Publishes hardcover and trade paperback originals. **Publishes 15 titles/year. Receives 400 queries/year. Pays royalty, or makes outright purchase (both negotiable); will consider co-op publishing some titles.** Publishes book 1 year after acceptance of ms. Accepts simultaneous submissions. Responds in 1 month to queries. Book catalog for #10 SASE.

- "All of our books speak to the reader through words of feeling—whether they are how-to, educational, humor, or memoir, the reader comes away with feeling, truth, and inspiration." Currently emphasizing how-to, family history, memoirs, inspiration. De-emphasizing childrens.

Nonfiction Biography, gift book, how-to, humor, self-help, inspiration. Subjects include Americana, education, history, language/literature, memoirs, women's issues/studies, general nonfiction, writing. Query with SASE.

Recent Title(s) *Goodbye Kite*, by Lois Redpath; *About Face . . . Forward March*, by Robert Seikel; *Oklahoma Jim*, by James Shears.

Tips "We have a general audience, bookstore browsers interested in nonfiction reading. We publish titles that have a mass appeal and can be enjoyed by a large reading public."

FACTS ON FILE, INC.

132 W. 31st St., 17th Floor, New York NY 10001. (212)967-8800. Fax: (212)967-9196. E-mail: llikoff@factsonfile.com. Web site: www.factsonfile.com. **Acquisitions:** Laurie Likoff, editorial director (science, fashion, natural history); Frank Darmstadt (science & technology, nature, reference); Nicole Bowen, senior editor (American history, women's studies, young adult reference); James Chambers, trade editor (health, pop culture, true crime, sports); Jeff Soloway, acquisitions editor (language/literature). Estab. 1941. Publishes hardcover originals and reprints. **Publishes 135-150 titles/year. 25% from unagented writers. Pays 10% royalty on retail price. Offers $5,000-10,000 advance.** Accepts simultaneous submissions. Responds in 2 months to queries. Book catalog free; ms guidelines online.

Imprints Checkmark Books.

- Facts on File produces high-quality reference materials on a broad range of subjects for the school library market and the general nonfiction trade.

Nonfiction "We publish serious, informational books for a targeted audience. All our books must have strong library interest, but we also distribute books effectively to the trade. Our library books fit the junior and senior high school curriculum." Reference. Subjects include contemporary culture, education, health/medicine, history, language/literature, multicultural, recreation, religion, sports, careers, entertainment, natural history, popular culture. No computer books, technical books, cookbooks, biographies (except YA), pop psychology, humor, fiction or poetry. Query or submit outline and sample chapter with SASE. No submissions returned without SASE.

Tips "Our audience is school and public libraries for our more reference-oriented books and libraries, schools and bookstores for our less reference-oriented informational titles."

FAIRLEIGH DICKINSON UNIVERSITY PRESS

285 Madison Ave., Madison NJ 07940. (973)443-8564. Fax: (973)443-8364. E-mail: fdupress@fdu.edu. Web site: www.fdu.edu/fdupress. **Acquisitions:** Harry Keyishian, director. Estab. 1967. Publishes hardcover originals and occasional paperbacks. **Publishes 30-40 titles/year. 33% of books from first-time authors; 95% from unagented writers.** Publishes book approximately 1 year after acceptance of ms. Responds in 2 weeks to queries.

- "Contract is arranged through Associated University Presses of Cranbury, New Jersey. We are a selection committee only." Nonauthor subsidy publishes 2% of books.
- O━ Fairleigh Dickinson publishes scholarly books for the academic market, in the humanities and social sciences.

Nonfiction Biography, reference, scholarly, scholarly books. Subjects include art/architecture, business/economics, ethnic, film/cinema/stage, gay/lesbian, government/politics, history, music/dance, philosophy, psychology, sociology, women's issues/studies, Civil War, film, Jewish studies, literary criticism, scholarly editions. Looking for scholarly books in all fields; no nonscholarly books. Query with outline, detailed abstract, and sample chapters (if possible). Reviews artwork/photos as part of ms package. Send only copies of illustrations during the evaluation process.

Recent Title(s) *The Carlyle Encyclopedia*, edited by Mark Cummings; *Sleuthing Ethnicity: The Detective in Multiethnic Crime Fiction*, edited by D. Fischer-Hornung and Monika Mueller; *Whig's Progress: Tom Wharton Between Revolutions*, by J. Kent Clark.

Tips "Research must be up to date. Poor reviews result when bibliographies and notes don't reflect current research. We follow *Chicago Manual of Style* (15th edition) in scholarly citations. We welcome collections of unpublished conference papers or essay collections, if they relate to a strong central theme and have scholarly merit. For further details, consult our online catalogue."

FAITH KIDZ BOOKS

Cook Communications Ministries, 4050 Lee Vance View, Colorado Springs CO 80918. (800)708-5550. Web site: www.cookministries.com. **Acquisitions:** Mary McNeil, senior acquisitions editor. Publishes hardcover and paperback originals. Accepts simultaneous submissions. Responds in 6 months to queries.

- Not currently accepting unsolicited book proposals.
- O━ Faith Kidz Books publishes inspirational works for children, ages 0-12, with a strong underlying Christian theme or clearly stated Biblical value, designed to foster spiritual growth in children and positive interaction between parent and child. Currently emphasizing Bible storybooks, Christian living books, life issue books, early readers, and picture books.

Nonfiction Biography, children's/juvenile. Subjects include religion (Bible stories, devotionals), picture books on nonfiction subjects.

Fiction Historical, juvenile, picture books, religious, toddler books. "Picture books, devotionals, Bible storybooks, for an age range of 1-12. We're particularly interested in materials for beginning readers." No teen fiction. Previously published or agented authors preferred.

Recent Title(s) *God Is There*, by Dan Foote; *Baby Bible 123*.

N FALLS MEDIA

565 Park Ave., Suite 11e, New York NY 10021. Fax: (952)487-5309. Web site: www.wouldyourather.com. **Acquisitions:** Justin Heimberg, president (humor, gift, nonfiction); David Gomberg, president (children's, illustrated, young adult). Estab. 2004. Publishes hardcover, trade and mass market paperback originals. **Publishes 10-20 titles/year. Receives 200 queries and 50 mss/year. 50% of books from first-time authors; 50% from unagented writers. Pays 7-20% royalty on retail price.** Publishes book 6 months after acceptance of ms. Accepts simultaneous submissions. Book catalog online.

Nonfiction Children's/juvenile, coffee table book, general nonfiction, gift book, how-to, humor, illustrated book, multimedia, reference, self-help, socially interactive books, games. Subjects include creative nonfiction, education, hobbies, regional, sex, sports, travel, women's issues/studies, college market. "We specialize in hip, young audiences. We like books that are socially interactive or offer an experience beyond just reading." Submit proposal package including outline, 2 sample chapter(s), any visuals or illustrations. Reviews artwork/photos as part of ms package. Send photocopies or scanned artwork or design.

Fiction Adventure, comic books, erotica, fantasy, humor, juvenile, multimedia, picture books, science fiction, young adult. "Our emphasis is on high concept for hip, young audiences." Submit proposal package including synopsis.

Recent Title(s) *The Hip Grandma's Handbook*, by Linda Oatman-High (humor/reference).

Tips "Our audience is Gen X, Gen Y, college, young adult, professionals, pop culture fans."

FANTAGRAPHICS BOOKS

7563 Lake City Way NE, Seattle WA 98115. (206)524-1967. Fax: (206)524-2104. E-mail: fbicomix@fantagraphics.com. Web site: www.fantagraphics.com. Co-owners: Gary Groth, Kim Thompson. **Acquisitions:** Submissions Editor. Estab. 1976. Publishes original trade paperbacks. Responds in 2-3 months to queries. Book catalog and ms guidelines online.

O-- Publishes comics for thinking readers. Does not want mainstream genres of superhero, vigilante, horror, fantasy, or science fiction.

Fiction Comic books. ''Fantagraphics is an independent company with a modus operandi different from larger, factory-like corporate comics publishers. If your talents are limited to a specific area of expertise (i.e. inking, writing, etc.), then you will need to develop your own team before submitting a project to us. We want to see an idea that is fully fleshed-out in your mind, at least, if not on paper. Submit a minimum of 5 fully-inked pages of art, a synopsis, SASE, and a brief note stating approximately how many issues you have in mind.''

Recent Title(s) *In My Darkest Hour*, by Wilfred Santiago; *When We Were Very Maakies*, by Tony Millionaire.

Tips ''Take note of the originality and diversity of the themes and approaches to drawing in such Fantagraphics titles as *Love & Rockets* (stories of life in Latin America and Chicano L.A.), *Palestine* (journalistic autobiography in the Middle East), *Eightball* (surrealism mixed with kitsch culture in stories alternately humorous and painfully personal), and *Naughty Bits* (feminist humor and short stories which both attack and commiserate). Try to develop your own, equally individual voice; originality, aesthetic maturity, and graphic storytelling skill are the signs by which Fantagraphics judges whether or not your submission is ripe for publication.''

FARRAR, STRAUS & GIROUX BOOKS FOR YOUNG READERS

Farrar Straus Giroux, Inc., 19 Union Square W., New York NY 10003. (212)741-6900. Fax: (212)633-2427. Web site: www.fsgkidsbooks.com. **Acquisitions:** Margaret Ferguson, editorial director. Estab. 1946. Publishes hardcover originals and trade paperback reprints. **Publishes 75 titles/year. Receives 6,000 queries and mss/year. 5% of books from first-time authors; 50% from unagented writers. Pays royalty. Pays 2-6% royalty on retail price for paperbacks, 3-10% for hardcovers. Offers $3,000-25,000 advance.** Publishes book 18 months after acceptance of ms. Accepts simultaneous submissions. Responds in 2 months to queries; 4 months to mss. Book catalog for 9×12 SAE with $1.95 postage; ms guidelines online.

Imprints Frances Foster Books; Melanie Kroupa Books.

O-- ''We publish original and well-written material for all ages.''

Fiction Juvenile, picture books, young adult, nonfiction. ''Do not query picture books; just send manuscript. Do not fax or e-mail queries or manuscripts.'' Query with SASE.

Recent Title(s) *Jack Adrift*, by Jack Gantos (ages 10 up); *The Canning Season*, by Polly Horvath (National Book Award); *Tree of Life*, by Peter Sis (all ages).

Tips Audience is full age range, preschool to young adult. Specializes in literary fiction.

FATCAT PRESS

P.O. Box 130281, Ann Arbor MI 48113. E-mail: editorial@fatcatpress.com. Submissions E-mail: inbox@fatcatpress.com. Web site: www.fatcatpress.com. **Acquisitions:** Ellen Bauerle, publisher/acquiring editor (technology, mysteries, Buddhist studies, travel, science fiction). Estab. 2003. Publishes electronic originals and occasional reprints. **Publishes 20 titles/year. Receives 360 queries and 120 mss/year. 60% of books from first-time authors; 95% from unagented writers. Pays 50% royalty on net receipts.** Publishes book 3 months after acceptance of ms. Does not accept simultaneous submissions. Responds in 1 month to queries; 1 month to proposals; 1 month to mss. Book catalog and ms guidelines online.

Nonfiction General nonfiction. Subjects include travel, eastern religion and spirituality, technology and society. ''Prospective authors must follow submission information on our Web site. We only publish in specific areas, as noted there.'' Query with SASE, or submit proposal package including outline, 2 sample chapters, current e-mail address.

Fiction Fantasy, mystery, science fiction. ''We want top-flight writing, unusual points of view, unusual characters.'' Query via e-mail, or submit complete ms.

Tips ''Our readers are educated, well read, and technologically competent. Many travel extensively.''

[A] [⊘] FAWCETT

The Ballantine Publishing Group, A Division of Random House, Inc., 1745 Broadway, New York NY 10019. E-mail: bfi@randomhouse.com. Web site: www.randomhouse.com. Estab. 1955. Publishes paperback originals and reprints.

O-- Major publisher of mystery mass market and trade paperbacks.

Fiction Mystery. *Agented submissions only. All unsolicited mss returned unopened.*

FREDERICK FELL PUBLISHERS, INC.

2131 Hollywood Blvd., Suite 305, Hollywood FL 33020. (954)925-5242. Fax: (954)925-5244. E-mail: info@fellpub.com. Web site: www.fellpub.com. **Acquisitions:** Barbara Newman, senior editor. Publishes hardcover and trade paperback originals. **Publishes 40 titles/year. Receives 4,000 queries and 1,000 mss/year. 95% of books from first-time authors; 95% from unagented writers. Pays negotiable royalty on retail price. Offers up to $10,000 advance.** Publishes book 1 year after acceptance of ms. Accepts simultaneous submissions. Responds in 1 month to queries; 3 months to proposals. Ms guidelines online.

- "Fell has just launched 25 titles in the *Know-It-All* series. We will be publishing over 125 titles in all genres. Prove to us that your title is the best in this new exciting nonfiction format."

Nonfiction "We are reviewing in all categories. Advise us of the top three competitive titles for your work and the reasons why the public would benefit by having your book published." How-to, reference, self-help. Subjects include business/economics, child guidance/parenting, education, ethnic, film/cinema/stage, health/medicine, hobbies, money/finance, spirituality. Submit proposal package, including outline, 3 sample chapters, author bio, publicity ideas, market analysis. Reviews artwork/photos as part of ms package. Send photocopies.

Recent Title(s) *Secrets of Mind Power*, by Harry Lorayne; *Greatest Salesman in the World*, by Og Mandino (illustrated edition).

Tips "We are most interested in well-written, timely nonfiction with strong sales potential. We will not consider topics that appeal to a small, select audience. Learn markets and be prepared to help with sales and promotion. Show us how your book is unique or better than the competition."

THE FEMINIST PRESS AT THE CITY UNIVERSITY OF NEW YORK

365 Fifth Ave., Suite 5406, New York NY 10016. (212)817-7920. Fax: (212)817-1593. E-mail: fhowe@gc.cuny.edu. Web site: www.feministpress.org. **Acquisitions:** Florence Howe. Estab. 1970. Publishes hardcover and trade paperback originals and reprints. Publishes no original fiction; exceptions are anthologies and international works. Accepts simultaneous submissions. Book catalog and ms guidelines online.

- Our primary mission is to publish works of fiction by women which preserve and extend women's literary traditions. We emphasize work by multicultural/international women writers.

Nonfiction Subjects include ethnic, gay/lesbian, government/politics, health/medicine, history, language/literature, memoirs, multicultural, music/dance, sociology, translation, women's issues/studies. "We look for nonfiction work which challenges gender-role stereotypes and documents women's historical and cultural contributions. Note that we generally publish for the college classroom as well as the trade." Send e-mail queries only, limited to 200 words with "Submission" as the subject line. "We regret that submissions are no longer accepted through the mail and unsolicited packages will be discarded."

Fiction Ethnic, feminist, gay/lesbian, literary, short story collections, women's. "The Feminist Press publishes only fiction reprints by classic American women authors and imports and translations of distinguished international women writers. Rarely publishes original fiction." Needs fiction by "U.S. women of color writers from 1920-1970 who have fallen out of print." Query by e-mail only; limit 200 words with "Submission" as the subject line.

Recent Title(s) *The Stories of Fannie Hurst*, by Fannie Hurst; edited by Susan Koppelman; *Developing Power*, by Arvonne S. Fraser and Irene Tinker; *Bunny Lake Is Missing*, by Evelyn Piper.

Tips We cannot accept telephone inquiries regarding proposed submissions.

FERGUSON PUBLISHING CO.

Imprint of Facts on File, 132 W. 31st St., 17th Floor, New York NY 10001. (800)322-8755. E-mail: editorial@factsonfile.com. Web site: www.fergpubco.com. **Acquisitions:** Editorial Director. Estab. 1940. Publishes hardcover and trade paperback originals. **Publishes 50 titles/year. Pays by project.** Responds in 6 months to queries. Ms guidelines online.

- "We are primarily a career education publisher that publishes for schools and libraries. We need writers who have expertise in a particular career or career field (for possible full-length books on a specific career or field)."

Nonfiction "We publish work specifically for the elementary/junior high/high school/college library reference market. Works are generally encyclopedic in nature. Our current focus is career encyclopedias. We consider manuscripts that cross over into the trade market." Reference. Subjects include careers. "No mass market, poetry, scholarly, or juvenile books, please." Query or submit an outline and 1 sample chapter.

Recent Title(s) *Ferguson Career Biographies: Colin Powell, Bill Gates, etc.* (20 total books in series); *Careers in Focus: Geriatric Care, Design, etc.*

Tips "We like writers who know the market—former or current librarians or teachers or guidance counselors."

FIRE ENGINEERING BOOKS & VIDEOS

Imprint of PennWell Corp., 1421 S. Sheridan Rd., Tulsa OK 74112. (918)831-9420. Fax: (918)831-9555. E-mail: bookproposals@pennwell.com. Web site: www.pennwellbooks.com. **Acquisitions:** Jerry Naylis, supervising editor. Publishes hardcover and softcover originals. Does not accept simultaneous submissions. Responds in 1 month to proposals. Book catalog free.

O— Fire Engineering publishes textbooks relevant to firefighting and training. Currently emphasizing strategy and tactics, reserve training, preparedness for terrorist threats, natural disasters, first response to fires and emergencies.

Nonfiction Reference, technical, textbook. Subjects include firefighter training, public safety. Submit proposal via e-mail.

Recent Title(s) *Fire Officer's Handbook of Tactics, Third Ed.*, by John Norman; *Emergency Rescue Shoring Techniques*, by John O'Connell.

Tips "No human-interest stories; technical training only."

FOCAL PRESS

Imprint of Elsevier (USA), Inc., 30 Corporate Dr., Suite 400, Burlington MA 01803. Fax: (781)221-1615. Web site: www.focalpress.com. **Acquisitions:** Joanne Tracy, publishing director; for further editorial contacts, visit the contacts page on the company's Web site. Estab. US, 1981; UK, 1938. Publishes hardcover and paperback originals and reprints. **Publishes 80-120 UK-US titles/year; entire firm publishes over 1,000 titles/year. 25% of books from first-time authors; 90% from unagented writers. Pays 10-12% royalty on net receipts. Offers modest advance.** Publishes book 6 months after acceptance of ms. Accepts simultaneous submissions. Responds in 2 months to queries. Book catalog for #10 SASE; ms guidelines online.

O— Focal Press provides excellent books for students, advanced amateurs, and working professionals involved in all areas of media technology. Topics of interest include photography (digital and traditional techniques), film/video, audio, broadcasting, and cinematography, through to journalism, radio, television, video, and writing. Currently emphasizing graphics, gaming, animation, and multimedia.

Nonfiction How-to, reference, scholarly, technical, textbook, media arts. Subjects include film/cinema/stage, photography, film, cinematography, broadcasting, theater and performing arts, audio, sound and media technology. "We do not publish collections of photographs or books composed primarily of photographs." Query preferred, or submit outline and sample chapters. Reviews artwork/photos as part of ms package.

Recent Title(s) *Adobe Photoshop CS2 for Photographers*, by Martin Evening (nonfiction).

[A] FODOR'S TRAVEL PUBLICATIONS, INC.

Imprint of Random House, Inc., 1745 Broadway, New York NY 10019. Web site: www.fodors.com. **Acquisitions:** Editorial Director. Estab. 1936. Publishes trade paperback originals. **Most titles are collective works, with contributions as works for hire. Most contributions are updates of previously published volumes.** Accepts simultaneous submissions. Responds in 2 months to queries. Book catalog free.

O— Fodor's publishes travel books on many regions and countries.

Nonfiction How-to (travel), illustrated book (travel), travel guide. Subjects include travel. "We are interested in unique approaches to favorite destinations. Writers seldom review our catalog or our list and often query about books on topics that we're already covering. Beyond that, it's important to review competition and to say what the proposed book will add. Do not send originals without first querying as to our interest in the project. We're not interested in travel literature or in proposals for general travel guidebooks." *Agented submissions only.* Submit proposal and résumé via mail.

Recent Title(s) *Fodor's Cape Code 2005*; *Fodor's German for Travelers, 3rd Ed.* (phrase book); *Solo Traveler: Tales & Tips for Great Trips*, by Lea Lane.

Tips "In preparing your query or proposal, remember that it's the only argument Fodor's will hear about why your book will be a good one, and why you think it will sell; and it's also best evidence of your ability to create the book you propose. Craft your proposal well and carefully so that it puts your best foot forward."

[N] [A] FOGHORN PUBLISHERS

The Scribes Ink, Inc., P.O. Box 8286, Manchester CT 06040-0286. (860)216-5622. Fax: (860)290-8291. E-mail: foghornpublisher@aol.com. **Acquisitions:** Dr. Aaron D. Lewis, publisher. Publishes hardcover and trade paperback originals. **Publishes 10-20 titles/year. Receives 200 queries and 1,000 mss/year. 60% of books from first-time authors. Pays 9-15% royalty on wholesale price.** Publishes book 3 months after acceptance of ms. Accepts simultaneous submissions. Responds in 1 month to queries; 1 month to proposals; 1 month to mss. Ms guidelines free.

Nonfiction Audiocassettes, self-help. Subjects include history, money/finance, religion, spirituality, health/wellness, natural healing. *Agented submissions only.*

Fiction Religious, spiritual. *Agented submissions only.*

Recent Title(s) *The Laws of Thinking*, by E. Bernaro Jordan (spritual/self-help); *What in Hell Is Holding You Back*, by Edward Stephens (Christian living).

FORDHAM UNIVERSITY PRESS

University Box L, Bronx NY 10458. (718)817-4795. Fax: (718)817-4785. Web site: www.fordhampress.com. **Acquisitions:** Helen Tartar, editorial director. Publishes hardcover and trade paperback originals and reprints. Book catalog and ms guidelines free.

> "We are a publisher in humanities, accepting scholarly monographs, collections, occasional reprints and general interest titles for consideration. No fiction."

Nonfiction Biography, textbook, scholarly. Subjects include anthropology/archeology, art/architecture, education, film/cinema/stage, government/politics, history, language/literature, military/war (World War II), philosophy, regional (New York), religion, science, sociology, translation, business, Jewish studies, media, music. Submit query letter, CV, SASE.

Recent Title(s) *The Search for Major Plagge*, by Michael Good; *Red Tail Captured, Red Tail Free*, by Alexander Jefferson, with Lewis Carlson.

Tips "We have an academic and general audience."

FORT ROSS INC. RUSSIAN-AMERICAN PUBLISHING PROJECTS

26 Arthur Place, Yonkers NY 10701. (914)375-6448. Fax: (914)375-6439. E-mail: fort.ross@verizon.net. Submissions E-mail: vkartsev2000@yahoo.com. Web site: www.fortrossinc.com. **Acquisitions:** Dr. Vladimir P. Kartsev, executive director. Estab. 1992. Publishes paperback originals. **Publishes 10 titles/year. Receives 100 queries and 100 mss/year. Pays 4-7% royalty on wholesale price or makes outright purchase of $500-1,500. Offers $500-$1,000; negotiable advance.** Publishes book 1 year after acceptance of ms. Accepts simultaneous submissions. Responds in 1 month to queries; 1 month to proposals; 3 months to mss.

> "Generally, we publish Russia-related books in English or Russian. Sometimes we publish various fiction and nonfiction books in collaboration with the East European publishers in translation. We are looking mainly for well-established authors."

Nonfiction Biography, illustrated book (for adults and children), reference.

Fiction Adventure, fantasy (space fantasy, sword and sorcery), horror, mainstream/contemporary, mystery (amateur sleuth, police procedural, private eye/hardboiled), romance (contemporary, futuristic/time travel), science fiction (hard science/technological, soft/sociological), suspense. Query with SASE.

Recent Title(s) *Cosack Galloped Far Away*, by Nikolas Feodoroff; *Verses*, by Filip Novikov; *Bay of Cross*, by Yury Egorov (in Russian).

FORTRESS PRESS

P.O. Box 1209, Minneapolis MN 55440-1209. (612)330-3300. E-mail: booksub@augsburgfortress.org. Web site: www.fortresspress.com. Publishes hardcover and trade paperback originals. **Pays royalty on retail price.** Accepts simultaneous submissions. Book catalog free (call 1-800-328-4648); ms guidelines online.

> Fortress Press publishes academic books in Biblical studies, theology, Christian ethics, church history, and professional books in pastoral care and counseling.

Nonfiction Subjects include religion, women's issues/studies, church history, African-American studies. Query with annotated TOC, brief cv, sample pages, SASE. Please study guidelines before submitting.

Recent Title(s) *God & Power: Counter-Apocalyptic Journeys*, by Catherine Keller; *New Testament Theology: Communion and Community*, by Philip F. Esler; *Radical Wisdom: A Feminist Mystical Theology*, by Beverly J. Lanzetta.

FORUM PUBLISHING CO.

383 E. Main St., Centerport NY 11721. (631)754-5000. Fax: (631)754-0630. Web site: www.forum123.com. **Acquisitions:** Martin Stevens. Estab. 1981. Publishes trade paperback originals. **Publishes 12 titles/year. Receives 200 queries and 25 mss/year. 75% of books from first-time authors; 75% from unagented writers. Makes outright purchase of $250-750.** Publishes book 4 months after acceptance of ms. Accepts simultaneous submissions. Responds in 1 month to mss. Book catalog free.

> "Forum publishes only business titles."

Nonfiction Subjects include business/economics, money/finance. Submit outline. Reviews artwork/photos as part of ms package. Send photocopies.

Recent Title(s) *Selling Information By Mail*, by Glen Gilcrest; *Secrets of Successful Advertising*.

WALTER FOSTER PUBLISHING, INC.

23062 La Cadena Dr., Laguna Hills CA 92653. (800)426-0099. Fax: (949)380-7575. E-mail: info@walterfoster.com. Web site: www.walterfoster.com. Publishes trade paperback originals. Accepts simultaneous submissions. Book catalog free.

> Walter Foster publishes instructional how-to/craft instruction as well as licensed products.

Nonfiction How-to. Subjects include arts and crafts. Submit proposal package, including query letter, color photos/examples of artwork. Reviews artwork/photos as part of ms package. Submit color photocopies or color photos. Samples cannot be returned.

Recent Title(s) *Glass Painting; Ceramic Painting; Paper Crafts* (art instruction).

FOX CHAPEL PUBLISHING

1970 Broad St., East Petersburg PA 17520. (717)560-4703. Fax: (717)560-4702. E-mail: editors@foxchapelpublishing.com. Web site: www.foxchapelpublishing.com. **Acquisitions:** Alan Giagnocavo, publisher; Peg Couch, acquisitions editor; Gretchen Bacon, editor. Publishes hardcover and trade paperback originals and trade paperback reprints. **Publishes 25-40 titles/year. 50% of books from first-time authors; 100% from unagented writers. Pays royalty or makes outright purchase. Offers variable advance.** Publishes book 6-18 months after acceptance of ms. Accepts simultaneous submissions. Responds in 2 months to queries.

O→ Fox Chapel publishes woodworking and woodcarving titles for professionals and hobbyists.

Nonfiction Subjects include woodworking, wood carving, scroll saw and woodturning. Write for query submission guidelines. Reviews artwork/photos as part of ms package. Send photocopies.

Recent Title(s) *Woodworker's Pocket Reference; Little Book of Whittling; Great Book of Fairy Patterns.*

Tips "We're looking for knowledgeable artists, woodworkers first, writers second to write for us. Our market is for avid woodworking hobbyists and professionals."

[A] FREE PRESS

Simon & Schuster, 1230 Avenue of the Americas, New York NY 10020. (212)698-7000. Fax: (212)632-4989. Web site: www.simonsays.com. Publisher: Martha Levin. **Acquisitions:** Bruce Nichols, vice president/senior editor (history/serious nonfiction); Leslie Meredith, vice president/senior editor (psychology/sprituality/self-help); Fred Hills (business/serious nonfiction); Amy Scheibe, senior editor (literary fiction); Elizabeth Stein, senior editor (history, current events, biography, memoir); Dominick Anfuso, vice president/editorial director (self-help/serious nonfiction). Estab. 1947. **Publishes 85 titles/year. 15% of books from first-time authors; 10% from unagented writers. Pays variable royalty. Offers advance.** Publishes book 1 year after acceptance of ms. Responds in 2 months to queries.

O→ The Free Press publishes nonfiction.

Nonfiction *Does not accept unagented submissions.* Query with 1-3 sample chapters, outline before submitting mss.

Recent Title(s) *Against All Enemies*, by Richard Clarke; *The 8th Habit*, by Stephen R. Covey.

FREE SPIRIT PUBLISHING, INC.

217 Fifth Ave. N., Suite 200, Minneapolis MN 55401-1299. (612)338-2068. Fax: (612)337-5050. E-mail: acquisitions@freespirit.com. Web site: www.freespirit.com. Publisher: Judy Galbraith. **Acquisitions:** Acquisitions Editor. Estab. 1983. Publishes trade paperback originals and reprints. **Publishes 18-24 titles/year. 25% of books from first-time authors; 50% from unagented writers. Offers advance.** Book catalog and ms guidelines online.

Imprints Self-Help for Kids®; Learning to Get Along® Series; Self-Help for Teens®; Laugh & Learn™ Series; How Rude!™ Handbooks for Teens; Adding Assets Series for Kids.

O→ "We believe passionately in empowering kids to learn to think for themselves and make their own good choices."

Nonfiction Children's/juvenile (young adult), self-help (parenting). Subjects include child guidance/parenting, education (pre-K-12, study and social skills, special needs, differentiation but not textbooks or basic skills books like reading, counting, etc.), health/medicine (mental/emotional health for/about children), psychology (for/about children), sociology (for/about children). "Many of our authors are educators, mental health professionals, and youth workers involved in helping kids and teens." No fiction or picture storybooks, poetry, single biographies or autobiographies, books with mythical or animal characters, or books with religious or New Age content. Query with cover letter stating qualifications, intent, and intended audience and how your book stands out from the field, along with outline, 2 sample chapters, résumé, SASE. Do not send original copies of work.

Recent Title(s) *100 Things Guys Need to Know; Too Stressed to Think?; 26 Big Things Small Hands Do.*

Tips "Our books are issue-oriented, jargon-free, and solution-focused. Our audience is children, teens, teachers, parents and youth counselors. We are especially concerned with kids' social and emotional well-being and look for books with ready-to-use strategies for coping with today's issues at home or in school—written in everyday language. We are not looking for academic or religious materials, or books that analyze problem's with the nation's school systems. Instead, we want books that offer practical, positive advice so kids can help themselves and parents and teachers can help kids succeed."

FUTURE HORIZONS

721 W. Abram St., Arlington TX 76013. (817)277-0727. Fax: (817)277-2270. E-mail: kelly@futurehorizons-autism.com. Web site: www.futurehorizons-autism.com. **Acquisitions:** Kelly Gilpin. Publishes hardcover origi-

nals, trade paperback originals and reprints. **Publishes 10 titles/year. Receives 250 queries and 125 mss/year. 75% of books from first-time authors; 95% from unagented writers. Pays 10% royalty, or makes outright purchase.** Publishes book 2 months after acceptance of ms. Accepts simultaneous submissions. Responds in 1 month to queries; 2 months to proposals. Book catalog free; ms guidelines online.

Nonfiction Children's/juvenile (pertaining to autism), cookbook (for autistic individuals), humor (about autism), self-help (detailing with autism/Asperger's syndrome). Subjects include education (about autism/Asperger's syndrome), autism. Submit proposal package including outline. Reviews artwork/photos as part of ms package. Send photocopies.

Recent Title(s) *Unwritten Rules of Social Relationships*, by Dr. Temple Grandin and Sean Barron; *Ten Things Every Child With Autism Wishes You Knew*, by Ellen Notbohm.

Tips Audience is parents, teachers, professionals dealing with individuals with autism or Asperger's syndrome. "Books that sell well, have practical and useful information on how to help individuals and/or care givers of individuals with autism. Personal stories, even success stories, are usually not helpful to others in a practical way."

GENESIS PRESS, INC.

P.O. Box 101, Columbus MS 39701. (888)463-4461. Fax: (662)329-9399. E-mail: books@genesis-press.com. Web site: www.genesis-press.com. Estab. 1993. Publishes hardcover and trade paperback originals and reprints. Responds in 2 months to queries; 4 months to mss. Ms guidelines online.

Imprints Indigo (romance); Black Coral (fiction); Indigo Love Spectrum (interracial romance); Indigo After Dark (erotica); Obsidian (thriller/myster); Indigo Glitz (love stories for young adults); Indigo Vibe (for stylish audience under 35 years old); Mount Blue (Christian); Inca Books (teens); Sage (self-help/inspirational).

O→ Genesis Press is the largest privately owned African-American publisher in the country, focusing on African American, Hispanic, Asian, and interracial fiction.

Nonfiction Autobiography, biography, self-help. Submit outline, 3 sample chapters, SASE.

Fiction Adventure, erotica, ethnic, multicultural, mystery, romance, science fiction, women's. Submit synopsis, 3 sample chapters, SASE.

Recent Title(s) *Falling*, by Natalie Dunbar; *Hearts Awakening*, by Veronica Parker.

Tips "Be professional. Always include a cover letter and SASE. Follow the submission guidelines posted on our Web site or send SASE for a copy."

GGC, INC./PUBLISHING

5107 13th St. NW, Washington DC 20011. (202)541-9700. Fax: (202)541-9750. E-mail: info@ggcinc.com. Web site: www.gogardner.com. **Acquisitions:** Garth Gardner, publisher (computer graphics, animation cartoons); Bonney Ford, editor (GGC, art, animation). Publishes trade paperback reprints. **Publishes 10 titles/year; imprint publishes 2 titles/year. Receives 50 queries and 25 mss/year. 80% of books from first-time authors; 70% from unagented writers. Pays 10-15% royalty on wholesale price or makes outright purchase.** Publishes book 3 months after acceptance of ms. Accepts simultaneous submissions. Responds in 1 month to queries. Book catalog and ms guidelines online.

O→ GGC publishes books on the subjects of computer graphics, animation, new media, multimedia, art, cartoons, drawing.

Nonfiction How-to, multimedia, reference, self-help, technical, textbook. Subjects include art/architecture, education, history, computer graphics. Submit proposal package including 2 sample chapter(s), résumé, cover letter. Reviews artwork/photos as part of ms package. Send photocopies.

Recent Title(s) *Gardner's Guide to Creating 2D Animation in a Small Studio*, by Bill Davis; *Career Diary of a Composer*, by Patrick Smith; *Gardner's Guide to Drawing for Animation*, by David Brain.

THE GLOBE PEQUOT PRESS, INC.

P.O. Box 480, Guilford CT 06437. (203)458-4500. Fax: (203)458-4604. Web site: www.globepequot.com. President/Publisher: Linda Kennedy. **Acquisitions:** Shelley Wolf, submissions editor. Estab. 1947. Publishes paperback originals, hardcover originals and reprints. **Publishes 600 titles/year. 30% of books from first-time authors; 70% from unagented writers. Average print order for a first book is 4,000-7,500. Makes an outright purchase, or pays 10% royalty on net price. Offers advance.** Publishes book 1 year after acceptance of ms. Accepts simultaneous submissions. Responds in 3 months to queries. Ms guidelines online.

O→ Globe Pequot is the largest publisher of regional travel books, local interest titles and outdoor recreation guidebooks in the United States and offers the broadest selection of titles of any vendor in these markets.

Nonfiction Regional travel guidebooks, outdoor recreation guides, natural history field guides, topics of local interest and state pride, popular western and women's history. Subjects include cooking/foods/nutrition (regional), history (popular, regional), nature/environment, recreation (outdoor), regional travel. No doctoral theses, fiction, genealogies, travel memoirs, poetry, or textbooks. Submit brief synopsis of work, TOC, or outline, sample chapter, résumé/vita, definition of target audience, and an analysis of competing titles. Reviews artwork/photos as part of ms package. Do not send originals.

Recent Title(s) *Insiders' Guide to Columbus, Ohio*; *Larry Bloom's Connecticut Notebook*; *A FalconGuide to Saguaro National Park*.

DAVID R. GODINE, PUBLISHER, INC.

9 Hamilton Place, Boston MA 02108. (617)451-9600. Fax: (617)350-0250. E-mail: info@godine.com. Web site: www.godine.com. Estab. 1970. Publishes hardcover and trade paperback originals and reprints. **Publishes 35 titles/year. Pays royalty on retail price.** Publishes book 3 years after acceptance of ms. Book catalog for 5×8 SAE with 3 first-class stamps.

- "Our particular strengths are books about the history and design of the written word, literary essays, and the best of world fiction in translation. We also have an unusually strong list of children's books, all of them printed in their entirety with no cuts, deletions, or side-stepping to keep the political watch-dogs happy."

Nonfiction Biography, children's/juvenile, coffee table book, cookbook, illustrated book. Subjects include Americana, art/architecture, gardening, nature/environment, photography, literary criticism, book arts, typography. *No unsolicited mss.* Query with SASE.

Fiction Historical, literary. *No unsolicited mss.* Query with SASE.

Tips "Please visit our Web site for more information about our books and detailed submission policy. No phone calls, please."

THE GRADUATE GROUP

P.O. Box 370351, West Hartford CT 06137-0351. (860)233-2330. Fax: (860)233-2330. E-mail: graduategroup@hotmail.com. Web site: www.graduategroup.com. **Acquisitions:** Mara Whitman, partner; Amy Gibson, partner; Robert Whitman, vice president. Estab. 1964. Publishes trade paperback originals. **Publishes 50 titles/year. Receives 100 queries and 70 mss/year. 60% of books from first-time authors; 85% from unagented writers. Pays 20% royalty on retail price.** Publishes book 3 months after acceptance of ms. Accepts simultaneous submissions. Responds in 1 month to queries. Book catalog free; ms guidelines online.

- "The Graduate Group helps college and graduate students better prepare themselves for rewarding careers and helps people advance in the workplace." Currently emphasizing test preparation, career advancement, and materials for prisoners, law enforcement, books on unique careers.

Nonfiction Reference. Subjects include business/economics, education, government/politics, health/medicine, money/finance, law enforcement. Submit complete ms and SASE with sufficient postage.

Recent Title(s) *Real Life 101: Winning Secrets You Won't Find in Class*, by Debra Yergen; *Getting In: Applicant's Guide to Graduate School Admissions*, by David Burrell.

Tips Audience is career planning offices; colleges, graduate schools, and public libraries. "We are open to all submissions, especially those involving career planning, internships, and other nonfiction titles. Looking for books on law enforcement, books for prisoners, and reference books on subjects/fields students would be interested in. We want books on helping students and others to interview, pass tests, gain opportunity, understand the world of work, network, build experience, prepare for advancement, prepare to enter business, improve personality, and build relationships."

GRAYWOLF PRESS

2402 University Ave., Suite 203, St. Paul MN 55114. Web site: www.graywolfpress.org. Editor/Publisher: Fiona McCrae. Executive Editor: Anne Czarniecki. Poetry Editor: Jeffrey Shotts. **Acquisitions:** Katie Dublinski, editorial manager (nonfiction, fiction). Estab. 1974. Publishes trade cloth and paperback originals. **Publishes 23 titles/year. Receives 3,000 queries/year. 20% of books from first-time authors; 50% from unagented writers. Pays royalty on retail price. Offers $1,000-25,000 advance.** Publishes book 18 months after acceptance of ms. Responds in 3 months to queries. Book catalog free; ms guidelines online.

- Graywolf Press is an independent, nonprofit publisher dedicated to the creation and promotion of thoughtful and imaginative contemporary literature essential to a vital and diverse culture.

Nonfiction Subjects include contemporary culture, language/literature, culture. Query with SASE.

Fiction Short story collections, literary novels. "Familiarize yourself with our list first." No genre books (romance, western, science fiction, suspense). Query with SASE. "Please do not fax or e-mail queries or submissions."

Poetry "We are interested in linguistically challenging work." Query with SASE.

Recent Title(s) *The Long Meadow*, by Vijay Seshaudri; *Wounded*, by Percival Everett; *Dictionary Days*, by Ilan Stavans.

GREAT QUOTATIONS PUBLISHING

8102 Lemont Rd., #300, Woodridge IL 60517. (630)390-3580. **Acquisitions:** Tami Suits, acquisitions editor (humor, relationships, Christian); Jan Stob, acquisitions editor (children's). Estab. 1991. **Publishes 30 titles/year. Receives 1,500 queries and 1,200 mss/year. 50% of books from first-time authors; 80% from unagented writers. Pays 3-8% royalty on net receipts.** Publishes book 6 months after acceptance of ms. Accepts simultaneous submissions. Responds in 6 months with SASE to queries. Book catalog for $2; ms guidelines for #10 SASE.

- Great Quotations seeks original material for the following general categories: humor, inspiration, motivation, success, romance, tributes to mom/dad/grandma/grandpa, etc. Currently emphasizing humor, relationships. De-emphasizing poetry, self-help. "We publish new books twice a year, in July and in January."

Nonfiction Humor, illustrated book, self-help. Subjects include business/economics, child guidance/parenting, nature/environment, religion, sports, women's issues/studies. "We look for subjects with identifiable markets, appealing to the general public. We publish humorous books or others requiring multicolor illustration on the inside. We don't publish highly controversial subject matter." Submit outline, 2 sample chapter(s). Reviews artwork/photos as part of ms package. Send photocopies or transparencies.

Recent Title(s) *Stress or Sanity*; *If My Teacher Sleeps at School*.

Tips "Our books are physically small and generally a very quick read. They are available at gift shops and book shops throughout the country. We are aware that most of our books are bought on impulse and given as gifts. We need strong, clever, descriptive titles; beautiful cover art; and brief, positive, upbeat text. Be prepared to submit final manuscript on computer disk, according to our specifications. (It is not necessary to try to format the typesetting of your manuscript to look like a finished book.)"

⊘ GREENHAVEN PRESS, INC.

15822 Bernardo Center Dr., Suite C, San Diego CA 92127. E-mail: chandra.howard@thomson.com. Web site: www.gale.com/greenhaven. **Acquisitions:** Chandra Howard, senior aquisitions editor. Estab. 1970. Publishes approximately 220 anthologies/year; all anthologies are works for hire. **Makes outright purchase of $1,500-3,000.**

- Greenhaven Press publishes hardcover educational, (nontrade) nonfiction anthologies on contemporary issues, scientific discoveries, and history for high school and college readers. These anthologies serve as supplementary educational material for high school and college libraries and classrooms. Currently emphasizing social-issue anthologies.

Nonfiction "We produce tightly formatted anthologies on contemporary issues and history for high school and college-level readers. We are looking for freelance book editors to research and compile these anthologies; we are not interested in submissions of single-author manuscripts. Each series has specific requirements. Potential book editors should familiarize themselves with our catalog and anthologies." Send query letter and résumé. *No unsolicited ms.*

Recent Title(s) *Opposing Viewpoints: Israel*; *At Issue: Does the World Hate the U.S.?*; *The Bill of Rights: Freedom of Speech*.

⊘ GREENWILLOW BOOKS

HarperCollins Publishers, 1350 Avenue of the Americas, New York NY 10019. (212)261-6500. Web site: www.harperchildrens.com/hch. Estab. 1974. Publishes hardcover originals and reprints.

- Greenwillow Books publishes quality picture books and fiction for young readers of all ages, and nonfiction primarily for children under seven years of age.

Fiction Juvenile. Fantasy, humor, literary, mystery, picture books.

Recent Title(s) *The Train of States*, by Peter Sis; *If Not for the Cat*, by Jack Prelutsky, illustrated by Ted Rand; *Happy Haunting, Amelia Bedelia*, by Herman Parish, illustrated by Lynn Sweat.

Tips "Currently not accepting unsolicited mail, mss or queries."

⊘ GREENWOOD PRESS

Greenwood Publishing Group, 88 Post Rd. W., Box 5007, Westport CT 06881. (203)226-3571. Fax: (203)222-1502. E-mail: editorial@greenwood.com. Web site: www.greenwood.com. **Acquisitions:** Gary Kuris, editorial director; Emily Birch, managing editor. Publishes hardcover originals. **Publishes 200 titles/year. Receives 1,000 queries/year. 25% of books from first-time authors. Pays variable royalty on net price. Offers rare advance.** Publishes book 1 year after acceptance of ms. Accepts simultaneous submissions. Responds in 6 months to queries. Book catalog and ms guidelines online.

- Greenwood Press publishes reference materials for high school, public and academic libraries in the humanities and the social and hard sciences.

Nonfiction Reference, scholarly. Subjects include humanities, social sciences, humanities and the social and hard sciences. Query with proposal package, including scope, organization, length of project, whether complete ms is available or when it will be, cv or résumé and SASE. *No unsolicited mss.*

Recent Title(s) *All Things Shakespeare*, by Kirstin Olsen.

GREENWOOD PUBLISHING GROUP

Reed-Elsevier (USA) Inc., 88 Post Rd. W., Box 5007, Westport CT 06881-5007. (203)226-3571. Fax: (203)222-6009. E-mail: editorial@greenwood.com. Web site: www.greenwood.com. **Acquisitions:** See Web site for list of contact editors by subject area. **Pays variable royalty on net price.** Accepts simultaneous submissions. Book catalog and ms guidelines online.

Imprints Praeger (general nonfiction in the social sciences, business, and humanities for public library patrons); Greenwood Press (reference titles for middle, high school, public, and academic libraries); Praeger Security International (nonfiction dealing with security studies broadly defined).

O→ The Greenwood Publishing Group consists of 3 distinguished imprints with one unifying purpose: to provide the best possible reference and general interest resources in the humanities and the social and hard sciences.

Nonfiction Reference, scholarly, general interest. Subjects include business/economics, child guidance/parenting, education, government/politics, history, humanities, language/literature, music/dance, psychology, religion, social sciences, sociology, sports, women's issues/studies. Query with proposal package, including scope, organization, length of project, whether a complete ms is available or when it will be, CV or résumé and SASE.

Recent Title(s) *Relationship Sabotage*, by William J. Matta; *Global Business Etiquette*, by Jeannette S. Martin and Lillian H. Chaney; *The Sound of Stevie Wonder*, by James E. Perone.

Tips ''No interest in fiction, drama, poetry—looking for reference materials and materials for educated general readers. Many of our authors are college professors who have distinguished credentialsa and who have published research widely in their fields.'' Greenwood Publishing maintains an excellent Web site, providing complete catalog, ms guidelines and editorial contacts.

Ⓐ ⊘ GROSSET & DUNLAP PUBLISHERS

Penguin Putnam Inc., 345 Hudson St., New York NY 10014. Web site: www.penguingroup.com. President/Publisher: Debra Dorfman. Estab. 1898. Publishes hardcover (few) and mass market paperback originals. **Publishes 100-125 titles/year. Pays royalty. Offers advance.** Does not accept simultaneous submissions.

- *Not currently accepting submissions.*

O→ Grosset & Dunlap publishes children's books that show children that reading is fun, with books that speak to their interests, and that are affordable so that children can build a home library of their own. Focus on licensed properties, series and readers.

Nonfiction Children's/juvenile. Subjects include nature/environment, science. *Agented submissions only.*

Fiction Juvenile. *Agented submissions only.*

Recent Title(s) *Winner Takes All!*, by Maria Gallagher; *A Light From Within: Zenda*, by Ken Petti, John Amodeo, and Cassandra Westwood.

Tips ''Nonfiction that is particularly topical or of wide interest in the mass market; new concepts for novelty format for preschoolers; and very well-written easy readers on topics that appeal to primary graders have the best chance of selling to our firm.''

GROUP PUBLISHING, INC.

1515 Cascade Ave., Loveland CO 80538. (970)669-3836. Fax: (970)679-4370. E-mail: kloesche@grouppublishing.com. Web site: www.group.com. **Acquisitions:** Kerri Loesche, editorial assistant/copyright coordinator. Estab. 1974. Publishes trade paperback originals. **Publishes 40 titles/year. Receives 500 queries and 500 mss/year. 40% of books from first-time authors; 95% from unagented writers. Pays up to 10% royalty on wholesale price or makes outright purchase or work for hire. Offers up to $1,000 advance.** Publishes book 18 months after acceptance of ms. Accepts simultaneous submissions. Responds in 1 month to queries; 6 months to proposals; 6 months to mss. Book catalog for 9×12 SAE with 2 first-class stamps; ms guidelines online.

O→ ''Our mission is to equip churches to help children, youth, and adults grow in their relationship with Jesus.''

Nonfiction How-to, multimedia, textbook (pastor/Sunday school teacher/youth leader). Subjects include education, religion. ''We're an interdenominational publisher of resource materials for people who work with adults, youth or children in a Christian church setting. We also publish materials for use directly by youth or children (such as devotional books, workbooks or Bibles stories). Everything we do is based on concepts of active and interactive learning as described in *Why Nobody Learns Much of Anything at Church: And How to Fix It*, by Thom and Joani Schultz. We need new, practical, hands-on, innovative, out-of-the-box ideas—things that no one's doing . . . yet.'' Query with SASE, or submit proposal package including outline, 3 sample chapters, cover letter, introduction to book, and sample activities if appropriate.

Recent Title(s) *An Unstoppable Force*, by Erwin McManus; *The 1 Thing*™, by Thom and Joani Schultz (effective teaching and learning).

Tips "Our audience consists of pastors, Christian education directors, youth leaders, and Sunday school teachers."

GRYPHON HOUSE, INC.

P.O. Box 207, Beltsville MD 20704. (301)595-9500. Fax: (301)595-0051. Web site: www.gryphonhouse.com. **Acquisitions:** Kathy Charner, editor-in-chief. Estab. 1971. Publishes trade paperback originals. **Publishes 12-15 titles/year. Pays royalty on wholesale price.** Does not accept simultaneous submissions. Responds in 3-6 months to queries. Ms guidelines online.

O→ Gryphon House publishes books that teachers and parents of young children (birth-age 8) consider essential to their daily lives.

Nonfiction Children's/juvenile, how-to. Subjects include child guidance/parenting, education (early childhood). Currently emphasizing reading; de-emphasizing after-school activities. Submit outline, 2-3 sample chapters, SASE.

Recent Title(s) *Reading Games*, by Jackie Silberg; *Primary Art*, by Mary Ann Kohl; *Preschool Math*, by Robert Williams, Debra Cunningham and Joy Lubawy.

GRYPHON PUBLICATIONS

P.O. Box 209, Brooklyn NY 11228. **Acquisitions:** Gary Lovisi, owner/publisher. Publishes trade paperback originals and reprints. **Publishes 10 titles/year. Receives 500 queries and 1,000 mss/year. 20% of books from first-time authors; 90% from unagented writers. Makes outright purchase by contract, price varies. Offers no advance.** Publishes book 1-2 years after acceptance of ms. Responds in 1 month to queries to queries. Book catalog and ms guidelines for #10 SASE.

Imprints Paperback Parade Magazine; Hardboiled Magazine; Gryphon Books; Gryphon Doubles.

O→ "I publish very genre-oriented work (science fiction, crime, pulps) and nonfiction on these topics, authors and artists. It's best to query with an idea first."

Nonfiction Reference, scholarly, bibliography. Subjects include hobbies, language/literature, book collecting. "We need well-written, well-researched articles, but query first on topic and length. Writers should not submit material that is not fully developed/researched." Query with SASE. Reviews artwork/photos as part of ms package. Send photocopies; slides, transparencies may be necessary later.

Fiction Crime, hard-boiled fiction. "We want cutting-edge fiction, under 3,000 words with impact." For short stories, query or submit complete ms. For novels, send 1-page query letter with SASE.

Recent Title(s) *Barsom: Edgar Rice Burroughs & the Martian Myth*, by Richard A. Lysoff; *Sherlock Holmes & the Terror Out of Time*, by Ralph Vaughan; *A Trunk Full of Murder*, by Julius Fast.

Tips "We are very particular about novels and book-length work. A first-timer has a better chance with a short story or article. On anything over 4,000 words do not send manuscript, send only query letter with SASE."

HALF HALT PRESS, INC.

P.O. Box 67, Boonsboro MD 21713. (301)733-7119. Fax: (301)733-7408. E-mail: mail@halfhaltpress.com. Web site: www.halfhaltpress.com. **Acquisitions:** Elizabeth Carnes, publisher. Estab. 1986. Publishes 90% hardcover and trade paperback originals and 10% reprints. **Publishes 15 titles/year. 25% of books from first-time authors; 50% from unagented writers. Pays 10-12½% royalty on retail price.** Publishes book 1 year after acceptance of ms. Does not accept simultaneous submissions. Responds in 1 month to queries. Book catalog for 6×9 SAE 2 first-class stamps.

O→ "We publish high-quality nonfiction on equestrian topics, books that help riders and trainers do something better."

Nonfiction How-to. Subjects include animals (horses), sports. "We need serious instructional works by authorities in the field on horse-related topics, broadly defined." Query with SASE. Reviews artwork/photos as part of ms package.

Recent Title(s) *Dressage in Harmony*, by Walter Zettl.

Tips "Writers have the best chance selling us well-written, unique works that teach serious horse people how to do something better. If I were a writer trying to market a book today, I would offer a straightforward presentation, letting the work speak for itself, without hype or hard sell. Allow the publisher to contact the writer, without frequent calling to check status. They haven't forgotten the writer but may have many different proposals at hand; frequent calls to 'touch base,' multiplied by the number of submissions, become an annoyance. As the publisher/author relationship becomes close and is based on working well together, early impressions may be important, even to the point of being a consideration in acceptance for publication."

HANSER GARDNER PUBLICATIONS

6915 Valley Ave., Cincinnati OH 45244. (513)527-8894. Fax: (513)527-8801. Web site: www.hansergardner.com. **Acquisitions:** Woody Chapman (metalworking—wchapman@gardnerweb.com); Christine Strohm (plastics—cstrohm@gardnerweb.com). Estab. 1993. Publishes hardcover and paperback originals, and digital educational and training programs. **Publishes 10-15 titles/year. Receives 100 queries and 10-20 mss/year. 50% of books from first-time authors; 100% from unagented writers. Pays 10-15% royalty on net receipts.** Publishes book 10 months after acceptance of ms. Accepts simultaneous submissions. Responds in 2 weeks to queries; 1 month to proposals; 1 month to mss. Book catalog free; ms guidelines online.

O→ Hanser Gardner publishes books and electronic media for the manufacturing (both metalworking and plastics) industries. Publications range from basic training materials to advanced reference books.

Nonfiction "We publish how-to texts, references, and technical books, and computer-based learning materials for the manufacturing industries. Titles include award-winning management books, encyclopedic references, and leading references." Submit outline, sample chapter(s), résumé, preface, and comparison to competing or similar titles.

Recent Title(s) *Modern Machine Shop's Handbook for the Metalworking Industries*, by W. Chapman; *Polymer Extrusion, 4th Ed.*, by Chris Rauwendaal.

Tips "E-mail submissions speed up response time."

⊘ HARCOURT, INC., CHILDREN'S BOOKS DIVISION

525 B St., Suite 1900, San Diego CA 92101. (619)231-6616. Fax: (619)699-6777. Web site: www.harcourtbooks.com/childrensbooks. Estab. 1919. Publishes hardcover originals and trade paperback reprints.

Imprints Harcourt Children's Books; Red Wagon Books; Harcourt Young Classics; Green Light Readers; Voyager Books/Libros Viajeros; Harcourt Paperbacks; Odyssey Classics; Magic Carpet Books.

O→ Harcourt, Inc., owns some of the world's most prestigious publishing imprints—imprints which distinguish quality products for the juvenile, educational, scientific, technical, medical, professional and trade markets worldwide.

Nonfiction *No unsolicited mss or queries.* No phone calls.

Fiction Young adult. *No unsolicited mss or queries.* No phone calls.

Recent Title(s) *Tails*, by Matthew Van Fleet; *The Leaf Man*, by Lois Ehlert; *Each Little Bird That Sings*, Deborah Wiles.

Ⓐ ⊘ HARCOURT, INC., TRADE DIVISION

525 B St., Suite 1900, San Diego CA 92101. (619)699-6560. Fax: (619)699-5555. Web site: www.harcourtbooks.com. **Acquisitions:** Rebecca Saletan, editor-in-chief; David Hough, managing editor; Drenka Willen, senior editor (poetry, fiction in translation, history); Andrea Schulz (nonfiction, American fiction, history, science); Ann Patty (American fiction); Tim Bent (nonfiction). Also: 15 E. 26th St., New York NY 10010. Publishes hardcover and trade paperback originals and trade paperback reprints. **Publishes 120 titles/year. 5% of books from first-time authors; 5% from unagented writers. Pays 6-15% royalty on retail price. Offers $2,000 minimum advance.** Accepts simultaneous submissions. Book catalog for 9×12 SAE; ms guidelines online.

Imprints Harvest Books (contact Andre Bernard).

O→ Harcourt, Inc., owns some of the world's most prestigious publishing imprints—imprints which distinguish quality products for the juvenile, educational, scientific, technical, medical, professional, and trade markets worldwide. Currently emphasizing science and math.

Nonfiction Biography, children's/juvenile, coffee table book, general nonfiction, gift book, illustrated book, multimedia, reference, technical. Subjects include anthropology/archeology, art/architecture, child guidance/parenting, creative nonfiction, education, ethnic, gay/lesbian, government/politics, health/medicine, history, language/literature, memoirs, military/war, multicultural, philosophy, psychology, religion, science, sociology, spirituality, sports, translation, travel, women's issues/studies. Published all categories except business/finance (university texts), cookbooks, self-help, sex. *No unsolicited mss. Agented submissions only.*

Fiction Historical, mystery, picture books. *Agented submissions only.*

Recent Title(s) *Life of Pi*, by Yann Martel (fiction); *The Time Traveler's Wife*, by Audrey Niffenegger (fiction); *Odd Girl Out*, by Rachel Simmons (nonfiction).

Ⓐ HARPERBUSINESS

Imprint of HarperCollins General Books Group, 10 E. 53rd St., New York NY 10022. (212)207-7000. Web site: www.harpercollins.com. Estab. 1991. Publishes hardcover, trade paperback originals and reprints. **Pays royalty on retail price. Offers advance.** Accepts simultaneous submissions.

O→ HarperBusiness publishes "the inside story on ideas that will shape business practices with cutting-edge information and visionary concepts."

Nonfiction Biography (economics). Subjects include business/economics, Marketing subjects. "We don't publish how-to, textbooks or things for academic market; no reference (tax or mortgage guides), our reference department does that. Proposals need to be top notch. We tend not to publish people who have no business standing. Must have business credentials.'' *Agented submissions only.*

Recent Title(s) *The Flight of the Creative Class*, by Richard Florida; *Fortune Favors the Bold*, by Lester C. Thurow; *Reinventing the Wheel*, by Steve Kemper.

HARPERCOLLINS

10 E. 53rd St., New York NY 10022. (212)207-7000. Web site: www.harpercollins.com. Publishes hardcover and paperback originals and paperback reprints. **Pays royalty. Offers negotiable advance.**

Imprints HarperCollins Australia/New Zealand: Angus & Robertson, Fourth Estate, HarperBusiness, HarperCollins, HarperPerenniel, HarperReligious, HarperSports, Voyager; **HarperCollins Canada**: HarperFlamingoCanada, PerennialCanada; **HarperCollins Children's Books Group:** Amistad, Julie Andrews Collection, Avon, Joanna Cotler Books, Eos, Laura Geringer Books, Greenwillow Books, HarperAudio, HarperCollins Children's Books, HarperFestival, HarperTempest, HarperTrophy, Rayo, Katherine Tegen Books; **HarperCollins General Books Group:** Access, Amistad, Avon, Caedmon, Ecco, Eos, Fourth Estate, HarperAudio, HarperBusiness, HarperCollins, HarperEntertainment, HarperLargePrint, HarperResource, HarperSanFrancisco, HarperTorch, Harper Design International, Perennial, PerfectBound, Quill, Rayo, ReganBooks, William Morrow, William Morrow Cookbooks; **HarperCollins UK:** Collins Bartholomew, Collins, HarperCollins Crime & Thrillers, Collins Freedom to Teach, HarperCollins Children,s Books, Thorsons/Element, Voyager Books; **Zondervan:**: Inspirio, Vida, Zonderkidz, Zondervan.

''HarperCollins, one of the largest English language publishers in the world, is a broad-based publisher with strengths in academic, business and professional, children's, educational, general interest, and religious and spiritual books, as well as multimedia titles.''

Nonfiction *Agented submissions only.*

Fiction Adventure, fantasy, gothic, historical, literary, mystery, science fiction, suspense, western. ''We look for a strong story line and exceptional literary talent.'' *Agented submissions only. All unsolicited mss returned unopened.*

Recent Title(s) *Don't Know Much About Mummies*, by Kenneth C. Davis; *Looking for Jaguar*, by Susan Katz; *Runny Babbit*, by Shel Silverstein.

Tips ''We do not accept any unsolicited material.''

HARPERCOLLINS CHILDREN'S BOOKS GROUP

Imprint of HarperCollins Children's Books Group, 1350 Avenue of the Americas, New York NY 10019. (212)261-6500. Web site: www.harperchildrens.com. Publishes hardcover and paperback originals.

Imprints Amistad; Julie Andrews Collection; Avon; Joanna Cotler Books; Eos; Laura Geringer Books; Greenwillow Books; HarperAudio; HarperCollins Children's Books; HarperFestival; HarperTempest; HarperTrophy; Rayo; Katherine Tegen Books.

No unsolicited mss and/or unagented mss or queries. ''The volume of these submissions is so large that we cannot give them the attention they deserve. Such submissions will not be reviewed or returned.''

Nonfiction Picture books, middle grade, young adult, board books, novelty books, TV/Movie tie-ins. *No unsolicited mss or queries. Agented submissions only.*

Fiction Picture books, young adult, chapter books, middle grade, early readers. *Agented submissions only. No unsolicited mss or queries.*

Recent Title(s) *A Dance of Sisters*, by Tracey Porter; *Down the Rabbit Hole*, by Peter Abrahams; *California Holiday*, by Kate Cann.

HARPERCOLLINS GENERAL BOOKS GROUP

Division of HarperCollins Publishers, 10 E. 53 St., New York NY 10022. (212)207-7000. Fax: (212)207-7633. Web site: www.harpercollins.com.

Imprints Access; Amistad; Avon; Caedmon; Dark Alley; Ecco; Eos; Fourth Estate; HarperAudio; HarperBusiness; HarperCollins; HarperEntertainment; HarperLargePrint; HarperResource; HarperSanFranciso; HarperTorch; Harper Design International; Perennial; PerfectBound; Quill; Rayo; ReganBooks; William Morrow; William Morrow Cookbooks.

- See Web site for further details.

HARPERENTERTAINMENT

HarperCollins Publishers, 10 E. 53rd St., New York NY 10022. (212)207-7000. Web site: www.harpercollins.c om. Estab. 1997.

''HarperEntertainment is dedicated to publishing sports, movie and TV tie-ins, celebrity bios and books reflecting trends in popular culture.''

Nonfiction Biography, children's/juvenile, humor, Movie and TV tie-ins. Subjects include film/cinema/stage, humor. "The bulk of our work is done by experienced writers for hire, but we are open to original ideas." Query with SASE.

Fiction Humor, juvenile, Movie and TV tie-ins. Query with SASE.

Recent Title(s) *Chore Whore*, by Heather H. Howard; *Dizzy*, by Donald L. Maggin; *Thoroughbred #71: Calamity Jinx*, by Joanna Campbell.

Tips "We are demanding about the quality of proposals; in addition to strong writing skills and thorough knowledge of the subject matter, we require a detailed analysis of the competition."

HARVARD BUSINESS SCHOOL PRESS

Imprint of Harvard Business School Publishing Corp., 60 Harvard Way, Boston MA 02163. (617)783-7400. Fax: (617)783-7489. E-mail: bookpublisher@hbsp.harvard.edu. Web site: www.hbsp.harvard.edu. Director: David Goehring. **Acquisitions:** Hollis Heimbouch, editorial director; Kirsten Sandberg, executive editor; Melinda Adams Merino, executive editor; Jeff Kehoe, senior editor; Jacque Murphy, senior editor; Astrid Sandoval, associate editor. Estab. 1984. Publishes hardcover originals and several paperback series. **Publishes 40-50 titles/year. Pays escalating royalty on retail price. Advances vary depending on author and market for the book.** Accepts simultaneous submissions. Responds in 1 month to proposals; 1 month to mss. Book catalog and ms guidelines online.

- The Harvard Business School Press publishes books for senior and general managers and business scholars. HBS Press is the source of the most influential ideas and conversations that shape business worldwide.

Nonfiction Trade and professional. Subjects include business, general management, strategy, leadership, marketing, innovation, human resources. Submit proposal package including outline, sample chapter(s).

Recent Title(s) *Blue Ocean Strategy*, by Chan Keni and Renee Manborgue; *Resonant Leadership*, by Richard Boyatzis and Annie McKee; *The Ultimate Question*, by Fred Reichheld.

Tips "We do not publish books on real estate, personal finance or business parables."

THE HARVARD COMMON PRESS

535 Albany St., Boston MA 02118-2500. (617)423-5803. Fax: (617)695-9794. Web site: www.harvardcommonpress.com. Publisher/President: Bruce P. Shaw. **Acquisitions:** Valerie Cimino, executive editor. Estab. 1976. Publishes hardcover and trade paperback originals and reprints. **Publishes 16 titles/year. 20% of books from first-time authors; 40% from unagented writers. Pays royalty. Offers average $2,500-10,000 advance.** Publishes book 1 year after acceptance of ms. Accepts simultaneous submissions. Responds in 2 months to queries. Book catalog for 9×12 SAE with 3 first-class stamps; ms guidelines for #10 SASE or online.

Imprints Gambit Books.

- "We want strong, practical books that help people gain control over a particular area of their lives." Currently emphasizing cooking, child care/parenting, health. De-emphasizing general instructional books, travel.

Nonfiction Subjects include child guidance/parenting, cooking/foods/nutrition, health/medicine. "A large percentage of our list is made up of books about cooking, child care, and parenting; in these areas we are looking for authors who are knowledgeable, if not experts, and who can offer a different approach to the subject. We are open to good nonfiction proposals that show evidence of strong organization and writing, and clearly demonstrate a need in the marketplace. First-time authors are welcome." Submit outline. Reviews artwork/photos as part of ms package.

Recent Title(s) *Icebox Desserts*, by Lauren Chattman; *Pie*, by Ken Haedrich; *Not Your Mother's Slow Cooker Cookbook*, by Beth Hensperger and Julie Kaufmann.

Tips "We are demanding about the quality of proposals; in addition to strong writing skills and thorough knowledge of the subject matter, we require a detailed analysis of the competition."

HARVEST HOUSE PUBLISHERS

990 Owen Loop N., Eugene OR 97402. (541)343-0123. Fax: (541)302-0731. Web site: www.harvesthousepublishers.com. Estab. 1974. Publishes hardcover, trade paperback, and mass market paperback originals and reprints. **Publishes 160 titles/year. Receives 1,500 queries and 1,000 mss/year. 1% of books from first-time authors. Pays royalty.** Book catalog free.

Nonfiction Reference, self-help. Subjects include anthropology/archeology, business/economics, child guidance/parenting, health/medicine, money/finance, religion, women's issues/studies, Bible studies. *No unsolicited mss.*

Fiction *No unsolicited mss, proposals, or artwork. Agented submissions only.*

Recent Title(s) *Power That Changes Everything*, by Stormie Omartian; *Why Is the Sky Blue*, by Susan Meissner; *Living With Passion and Purpose*, by Elizabeth George.

Tips "For first time/nonpublished authors we suggest building their literary résumé by submitting to magazines, or perhaps accruing book contributions."

HASTINGS HOUSE/DAYTRIPS PUBLISHERS

LINI LLC, P.O. Box 908, Winter Park FL 32790-0908. (407)339-3600. Fax: (407)339-5900. E-mail: hastings_daytrips@earthlink.net. Web site: www.hastingshousebooks.com. Publisher: Peter Leers. **Acquisitions:** Earl Steinbicker, senior travel editor (edits Daytrips Series). Publishes trade paperback originals and reprints. **Publishes 20 titles/year. Receives 600 queries and 900 mss/year. 10% of books from first-time authors; 40% from unagented writers. Pays 8-10% royalty on net receipts.** Publishes book 6-10 months after acceptance of ms. Responds in 2 months to queries.

O→ "We are primarily focused on expanding our Daytrips Travel Series (facts/guide) nationally and internationally." Currently de-emphasizing all other subjects.

Nonfiction Subjects include travel. Submit outline. Query.

Recent Title(s) *Daytrips Eastern Australia*, by James Postell; *Daytrips Italy*, by Earl Steinbicker (5th edition); *Daytrips Scotland & Wales*, by Judith Frances Duddle.

[A] HAY HOUSE, INC.

P.O. Box 5100, Carlsbad CA 92018-5100. (760)431-7695. Fax: (760)431-6948. E-mail: jvermooten@hayhouse.com. Web site: www.hayhouse.com. Editorial Director: Jill Kramer. **Acquisitions:** Jessica Vermooten. Estab. 1985. Publishes hardcover and trade paperback originals. **Publishes 50 titles/year. Pays standard royalty.** Publishes book 14-16 months after acceptance of ms. Accepts simultaneous submissions. Responds in 2 months to mss. No e-mail submissions; ms guidelines online.

Imprints Hay House Lifestyles; New Beginnings Press; Smiley Books.

O→ "We publish books, audios, and videos that help heal the planet."

Nonfiction Biography, self-help. Subjects include cooking/foods/nutrition, education, health/medicine, money/finance, nature/environment, New Age, philosophy, psychology, sociology, women's issues/studies, mind/body/spirit. "Hay House is interested in a variety of subjects as long as they have a positive self-help slant to them. No poetry, children's books, or negative concepts that are not conducive to helping/healing ourselves or our planet." *Agented submissions only.*

Recent Title(s) *Inspiration*, by Dr. Wayne W. Dyer; *Yes, You Can Be a Successful Income Investor!*, by Ben Stein and Phil Demuth; *Secrets & Mysteries of the World*, by Sylvia Browne.

Tips "Our audience is concerned with our planet, the healing properties of love, and general self-help principles. If I were a writer trying to market a book today, I would research the market thoroughly to make sure there weren't already too many books on the subject I was interested in writing about. Then I would make sure I had a unique slant on my idea. Simultaneous submissions from agents must include SASEs. No e-mail submissions."

HAZELDEN PUBLISHING AND EDUCATIONAL SERVICES

P.O. Box 176, Center City MN 55012. (651)257-4010. Web site: www.hazelden.org. Editorial Director: Rebecca Post. Estab. 1954. Publishes trade paperback originals and educational materials (videos, workbooks, pamphlets, etc.) for treatment centers, schools, hospitals, and correctional institutions. **Publishes 100 titles/year. Receives 2,500 queries and 2,000 mss/year. 30% of books from first-time authors; 50% from unagented writers. Pays 8% royalty on retail price. Offers variable advance.** Publishes book 1 year after acceptance of ms. Accepts simultaneous submissions. Responds in 6 months to queries. Book catalog and ms guidelines online.

O→ Hazelden is a trade, educational and professional publisher specializing is psychology, self-help, and spiritual books that help enhance the quality of people's lives. Products include gift books, curriculum, workbooks, audio and video, computer-based products, and wellness products. "We specialize in books on addiction/recovery, spirituality/personal growth, and prevention topics related to chemical and mental health."

Nonfiction How-to, multimedia, self-help. Subjects include child guidance/parenting, memoirs, psychology, sex (sexual addiction), spirituality, addiction/recovery, eating disorders, codependency/family issues. Query with SASE.

Recent Title(s) *Clean*, by Chris Beckman; *The Lois Wilson Story*, by William E. Borchert; *Moth*, by Dirk Johnson.

Tips Audience includes "consumers and professionals interested in the range of topics related to chemical and emotional health, including spirituality, self-help, and addiction recovery."

HEALTH COMMUNICATIONS, INC.

3201 SW 15th St., Deerfield Beach FL 33442. (954)360-0909. Fax: (954)360-0034. Web site: www.hcibooks.com. **Acquisitions:** Bret Witter, editorial director; Allison Janse, executive editor; Amy Hughes, religion editor; Elisabeth Rinaldi, editor. Estab. 1976. Publishes hardcover and trade paperback nonfiction only. **Publishes 50 titles/year.** Responds in 3 months to queries; 3 months to proposals. Ms guidelines online.

"We are the Life Issues Publisher. Health Communications, Inc., strives to help people grow and improve their lives, from physical and emotional health to finances and interpersonal relationships."

Nonfiction Self-help. Subjects include child guidance/parenting, health/medicine, psychology, women's issues/studies.

Recent Title(s) *The Reallionaire*, by Farrah Gray; *What the Bleep Do We Know*, by William Arntz, Betsy Chasse and Mark Vincente; *The Germ Freak's Guide to Outwitting Colds and Flu*, by Allison Janse.

WILLIAM S. HEIN & CO., INC.

1285 Main St., Buffalo NY 14209-1987. (716)882-2600. Fax: (716)883-8100. E-mail: mail@wshein.com. Web site: www.wshein.com. **Acquisitions:** Sheila Jarrett, publications manager. Estab. 1961. **Publishes 50 titles/year. Receives 80 queries and 40 mss/year. 20% of books from first-time authors; 100% from unagented writers. Pays 10-20% royalty on net price.** Publishes book 9 months after acceptance of ms. Accepts simultaneous submissions. Responds in 2 months to queries. Book catalog online; ms guidelines for #10 SASE.

William S. Hein & Co. publishes reference books for law librarians, legal researchers, and those interested in legal writing. Currently emphasizing legal research, legal writing, and legal education.

Nonfiction Law, reference, scholarly. Subjects include education, government/politics, women's issues/studies, world affairs, legislative histories.

Recent Title(s) *1000 Days to the Bar*, by Dennis J. Tonsing; *Librarian's Copyright Companion*, by James S. Heller.

HEINEMANN

Reed Elsevier (USA) Inc., 361 Hanover St., Portsmouth NH 03801-3912. (603)431-7894. Fax: (603)431-7840. E-mail: proposals@heinemann.com. Web site: www.heinemann.com. Estab. 1977. Publishes hardcover and trade paperback originals. **Publishes 80-100 titles/year. 50% of books from first-time authors; 75% from unagented writers. Pays royalty on wholesale price. Offers variable advance.** Does not accept simultaneous submissions. Responds in 6-8 weeks to proposals. Book catalog free; ms guidelines online.

Imprints Boynton/Cook Publishers.

Heinemann specializes in professional resources for educators and theater professionals. "Our goal is to offer a wide selecton of books that satisfy the needs and interests of educators from kindergarten to college." Currently emphasizing literacy education, social studies, mathematics, science, K-12 education through technology, drama and drama education.

Nonfiction "Our goal is to provide books that represent leading ideas within our niche markets. We publish very strictly within our categories. We do not publish classroom textbooks." Query with SASE, or submit proposal package including outline, 1-2 sample chapters, TOC.

Recent Title(s) *Word Matters*, by Irene Fountas and Gay-Su Pinnell.

Tips "Keep your queries (and manuscripts!) short, study the market, be realistic and prepared to promote your book."

N HELLGATE PRESS

P.O. Box 3727, Central Point OR 97502. (541)855-5566. E-mail: harley@hellgatepress.com. Web site: www.hellgatepress.com. **Acquisitions:** Harley B. Patrick, editor. Estab. 1996. **Publishes 15-20 titles/year. Pays royalty.** Publishes book 6-8 months after acceptance of ms. Responds in 2 months to queries.

Hellgate Press specializes in military history, other military topics, and travel adventure.

Nonfiction Subjects include history, memoirs, military/war, travel adventure. Query/proposal only with SASE or by e-mail. *Do not send mss.* Reviews artwork/photos as part of ms package. Send photocopies.

Recent Title(s) *XVIII Airborne Corps in Desert Storm*, by Charles Lane Toomey; *Charlie Battery*, by Andrew Lubin; *My Life in Capitals*, by Bobbie Bergesen.

HENDRICKSON PUBLISHERS, INC.

140 Summit St., P.O. Box 3473, Peabody MA 01961-3473. Fax: (978)531-8146. E-mail: editorial@hendrickson.com. Web site: www.hendrickson.com. **Acquisitions:** Shirley Decker-Lucke, editorial director. Estab. 1983. Publishes trade reprints and scholarly material in the areas of New Testament; Hebrew Bible; religion and culture; patristics; Judaism; and practical, historical, and Biblical theology. **Publishes 35 titles/year. Receives 800 queries/year. 10% of books from first-time authors; 90% from unagented writers.** Publishes book an average of 1 year after acceptance of ms. Does not accept simultaneous submissions. Responds in 3-4 months to queries. Book catalog and ms guidelines for #10 SASE.

Hendrickson is an academic publisher of books that "give insight into Bible understanding (academically) and encourage spiritual growth (popular trade)." Currently emphasizing Biblical helps and reference, ministerial helps, Biblical studies and de-emphasizing fiction and biography.

Nonfiction Reference. Subjects include religion. "We will consider any quality manuscript specifically related to Biblical studies and related fields." Submit outline, sample chapter(s), and CV.

Recent Title(s) *Getting the Gospels*, by Steven L. Bridge.

JOSEPH HENRY PRESS

National Academy Press, 500 5th St., NW, Lockbox 285, Washington DC 20001. (202)334-3336. Fax: (202)334-2793. E-mail: jrobbins@nas.edu. Web site: www.jhpress.org. **Acquisitions:** Jeffrey Robbins, senior editor. Publishes hardcover and trade paperback originals. **Publishes 15-20 titles/year. Receives 200 queries and 60 mss/year. 30% of books from first-time authors; 50% from unagented writers. Pays standard trade book list-price royalties. Offers occasional, varying royalty advance.** Publishes book 1 year after acceptance of ms. Accepts simultaneous submissions. Responds in 1 month to queries.

- Submit to: Jeffrey Robbins, senior editor, The Joseph Henry Press, 4701 Willard Ave. #1731, Chevy Chase MD 02148. (301)654-5188. Fax: (301)654-8931.

  O→ "The Joseph Henry Press seeks manuscripts in general science and technology that will appeal to young scientists and established professionals or to interested lay readers within the overall categories of science, technology and health. We'll be looking at everything from astrophysics to the environment to nutrition."

Nonfiction Technical. Subjects include health/medicine, nature/environment, psychology, technology, nutrition, physical sciences. Submit proposal package including author bio, TOC, prospectus (via mail or e-mail), SASE.

Recent Title(s) *Prime Obsession: Berhard Riemann and the Greatest Unsolved Problem in Mathematics*, by John Derbyshire; *Einstein Defiant: Genius Versus Genius in the Quantum Revolution*, by Edmund Blair Bolles; *Mendel in the Kitchen: A Scientist's View of Genetically Modified Foods*, by Nina V. Fedoroff and Nancy Marie Brown.

[N] HERITAGE BOOKS, INC.

65 E. Main St., Westminster MD 21157. (410)876-0371. E-mail: submissions@heritagebooks.com. **Acquisitions:** Editorial Director. Estab. 1978. Publishes hardcover and paperback originals and reprints. **Publishes 200 titles/year. 25% of books from first-time authors; 100% from unagented writers. Pays 10% royalty on list price.** Accepts simultaneous submissions. Responds in 3 months to queries. Book catalog and ms guidelines free.

O→ "Our goal is to celebrate life by exploring all aspects of American life: settlement, development, wars, and other significant events, including family histories, memoirs, etc." Currently emphasizing early American life, early wars and conflicts, ethnic studies.

Nonfiction Biography, how-to (genealogical, historical), reference, scholarly. Subjects include Americana, ethnic (origins and research guides), history, memoirs, military/war, regional (history). Query with SASE. Submit outline via e-mail. Reviews artwork/photos as part of ms package.

Tips "The quality of the book is of prime importance; next is its relevance to our fields of interest."

HEYDAY BOOKS

Box 9145, Berkeley CA 94709-9145. Fax: (510)549-1889. E-mail: heyday@heydaybooks.com. Web site: www.heydaybooks.com. **Acquisitions:** Jeannine Gendar, editorial director. Estab. 1974. Publishes hardcover originals, trade paperback originals and reprints. **Publishes 12-15 titles/year. Receives 200 submissions/year. 50% of books from first-time authors; 90% from unagented writers. Pays 8% royalty on net price.** Publishes book 10 months after acceptance of ms. Does not accept simultaneous submissions. Responds in 2 months to queries; 2 months to mss. Book catalog for 7×9 SAE with 3 first-class stamps.

O→ Heyday Books publishes nonfiction books and literary anthologies with a strong California focus. "We publish books about Native Americans, natural history, history, literature, and recreation, with a strong California focus."

Nonfiction Books about California only. Subjects include Americana, ethnic, history, nature/environment, recreation, regional, travel. Query with outline and synopsis. Reviews artwork/photos as part of ms package.

Recent Title(s) *Dark God of Eros: A William Everson Reader*, edited by Albert Gelpi; *The High Sierra of California*, by Gary Snyder and Tom Killion; *Under the Fifth Sun: Latino Literature from California*, edited by Rick Heidre.

⊘ HIDDENSPRING

997 Macarthur Blvd., Mahwah NJ 07430. (201)825-7300. Fax: (201)825-8345. Web site: www.hiddenspringbooks.com. **Acquisitions:** Paul McMahon, managing editor (nonfiction/spirituality). Publishes hardcover and trade paperback originals and reprints. **Publishes 10-12 titles/year. 5% of books from first-time authors; 10% from unagented writers. Royalty varies. Offers variable advance.**

- *Currently not accepting unsolicited submissions.*

  O→ "Books should always have a spiritual angle—nonfiction with a spiritual twist."

Nonfiction Biography, self-help. Subjects include Americana, art/architecture, creative nonfiction, ethnic, history, multicultural, psychology, religion.

Recent Title(s) *Frances of Assisi*, by Adrian House; *Traveling With the Saints*, by Lucinda Vardey; *Becoming Who You Are*, by James Martin, SJ.

HILL AND WANG

Farrar Straus & Giroux, Inc., 19 Union Square W., New York NY 10003. (212)741-6900. Fax: (212)633-9385. Web site: www.fsgbooks.com. **Acquisitions:** Thomas LeBien, publisher; Elisabeth Sifton, editor; June Kim, assistant editor. Estab. 1956. Publishes hardcover and trade paperbacks. **Publishes 12 titles/year. Receives 1,500 queries/year. 50% of books from first-time authors; 50% from unagented writers. Pays 10% royalty on retail price to 5,000 copies sold, 12½% to 10,000 copies, 15% thereafter on hardcover; 7½% on retail price for paperback.** Publishes book 1 year after acceptance of ms. Accepts simultaneous submissions. Book catalog free.

- Hill and Wang publishes serious nonfiction books, primarily in history, science, mathematics and the social sciences. "We are not considering new fiction, drama, or poetry."

Nonfiction Subjects include government/politics, history (American). Submit outline, sample chapter(s). SASE and a letter explaining rationale for book.

HILL STREET PRESS

191 E. Broad St., Suite 209, Athens GA 30601-2848. (706)613-7200. Fax: (706)613-7204. E-mail: editorial@hillstreetpress.com. Web site: www.hillstreetpress.com. **Acquisitions:** Judy Long, editor-in-chief. Estab. 1998. Publishes hardcover originals, trade paperback originals and reprints. **Publishes 20 titles/year. Receives 300 queries/year. 5% of books from first-time authors; 2% from unagented writers. Pays 9-12½% royalty on wholesale price.** Publishes book 1 year after acceptance of ms. Accepts simultaneous submissions. Responds in 1 month to queries; 3 months to proposals; 6 months to mss. Book catalog and ms guidelines online.

- "HSP is a Southern regional press. While we are not a scholarly or academic press, our nonfiction titles must meet the standards of research for an exacting general audience."

Nonfiction Biography, coffee table book, cookbook, gift book, humor, illustrated book. Subjects include Americana, cooking/foods/nutrition, creative nonfiction, gardening, gay/lesbian, history, memoirs, nature/environment, recreation, regional (Southern), sports, travel. Submit proposal package including outline, résumé, 3 sample chapters.

Fiction Must have a strong connection with the American South. Gay/lesbian, historical, humor, literary, mainstream/contemporary, military/war, regional (southern US), religious, sports, African-American. "Reasonable length projects (50,000-85,000 words) stand a far better chance of review. Do not submit proposals for works in excess of 125,000 words in length." No short stories. "No cornball moonlight-and-magnolia stuff." Query with SASE, or submit proposal package including résumé, synopsis, 3 sample chapters, press clips. "Let us know at the point of submission if you are represented by an agent."

Recent Title(s) *Strange Birds in the Tree of Heaven*, by Karen Salyer McElmurray (literary fiction); *The Worst Day of My Life, So Far*, by M.A. Harper (literary fiction); *How I Learned to Snap* (memoir).

Tips "Audience is discerning with an interest in the fiction, history, current issues, and food of the American South"

HIPPOCRENE BOOKS, INC.

171 Madison Ave., New York NY 10016. (212)685-4371. Fax: (212)779-9338. E-mail: hippocrene.books@verizon.net. Web site: www.hippocrenebooks.com. President/Publisher: George Blagowidow. **Acquisitions:** Rebecca Cole, editor (food and wine); Robert Martin, editor (foreign language, dictionaries, language guides); Sophie Fels, editor (history, nonfiction). Estab. 1971. Publishes hardcover and trade paperback originals. **Publishes 60-80 titles/year. 10% of books from first-time authors; 95% from unagented writers. Pays 6-10% royalty on retail price. Offers $1,500 advance.** Publishes book 16 months after acceptance of ms. Accepts simultaneous submissions. Responds in 2 months to queries. Book catalog for 9×12 SAE with 5 first-class stamps; ms guidelines for #10 SASE.

- "We focus on ethnic-interest and language-related titles, particularly on less frequently published languages and often overlooked cultures." Currently emphasizing concise foreign language dictionaries.

Nonfiction Biography, cookbook, reference. Subjects include cooking/foods/nutrition, ethnic, history, language/literature, military/war, multicultural, travel. No contemporary fiction or memoir. Submit proposal package including outline, 2 sample chapters, TOC.

Recent Title(s) *Yoruba Practical Dictionary*; *A History of the Islamic World*; *Secrets of Colombian Cooking.*

Tips "Our recent successes in publishing general books considered midlist by larger publishers are making us more of a general trade publisher. We continue to do well with reference books like dictionaries and other language related titles. We ask for proposal, sample chapter, and table of contents. If we are interested, we will reply with a request for more material."

N HISTORY PUBLISHING COMPANY, INC.

P.O. Box 700, Palisades NY 10964. Fax: (845)359-8282. E-mail: historypublish@aol.com. Web site: www.historypublishing.com. **Acquisitions:** Don Bracken, editorial director (history); Tom Cameron, senior editor (contemporary affairs). Estab. 2001. Publishes hardcover and trade paperback originals and reprints; also, electronic reprints. **Publishes 20 titles/year; imprint publishes 10 titles/year. Pays 10-15% royalty on wholesale price. Offers $0-2,000 advance.** Publishes book 1 year after acceptance of ms. Accepts simultaneous submissions. Responds in 1 month to queries; 1 month to proposals; 2 months to mss. Ms guidelines by e-mail.

Imprints Today's Books (contact Don Bracken).

Nonfiction Autobiography, biography, general nonfiction, how-to. Subjects include Americana, business/economics, contemporary culture, creative nonfiction, government/politics, history, military/war, social sciences, sociology, world affairs. Query with SASE, or submit proposal package including outline, 3 sample chapter(s), or submit complete ms. Reviews artwork/photos as part of ms package. Send photocopies.

Recent Title(s) *Career of Gold*; *The Words of War*; *Men in Blue and Gold*.

Tips "We focus on an audience interested in the events that shaped the world we live in and the events of today that continue to shape that world. Focus on interesting and serious events that will appeal to the contemporary reader. That reader likes easy-to-read history that flows from one page to the next. If you have a good story, we will help you develop it and guide you to a finish."

HOLIDAY HOUSE, INC.

425 Madison Ave., New York NY 10017. (212)688-0085. Fax: (212)421-6134. Editor-in-Chief: Regina Griffin. Estab. 1935. Publishes hardcover originals and paperback reprints. **Publishes 60 titles/year. 2-5% of books from first-time authors; 50% from unagented writers. Pays royalty on list price, range varies. Offers Flexible, depending on whether the book is illustrated. advance.** Publishes book 1-2 years after acceptance of ms. Does not accept simultaneous submissions. Ms guidelines for #10 SASE.

- Holiday House publishes children's and young adult books for the school and library markets. "We have a commitment to publishing first-time authors and illustrators. We specialize in quality hardcovers from picture books to young adult, both fiction and nonfiction, primarily for the school and library market." Currently emphasizing literary middle-grade novels.

Nonfiction Subjects include Americana, history, science, Judaica. Query with SASE. Reviews artwork/photos as part of ms package. Send photocopies—no originals.

Fiction Adventure, historical, humor, literary, mainstream/contemporary, Judaica and holiday, animal stories for young readers. Children's books only. Query with SASE. "No phone calls, please."

Tips "We need novels with strong stories and writing."

HENRY HOLT & CO. BOOKS FOR YOUNG READERS

Imprint of Henry Holt & Co., LLC, 175 Fifth Ave., New York NY 10010. (646)307-5057. Web site: www.henryholt.com. Vice President, Publisher and Editorial Director: Laura Godwin. Executive Editor: Christy Ottaviano. Editor-at-Large: Nina Ignatowicz. Editor: Reka Simonsen. Editor: Kate Farrell. **Acquisitions:** Submissions Editor. Estab. 1866 (Holt). Publishes hardcover originals of picture books, chapter books, middle grade and young adult novels. **Publishes 70-80 titles/year. 10% of books from first-time authors; 50% from unagented writers. Pays royalty on retail price. Offers $3,000 and up advance.** Publishes book 18-36 months after acceptance of ms. Book catalog for 8½×11 SAE with $1.75 postage; ms guidelines online.

- Please do not send SASE. No response unless interested in publication.
- "Henry Holt Books for Young Readers publishes highly original and cutting-edge fiction and nonfiction for all ages, from the very young to the young adult."

Nonfiction Children's/juvenile, illustrated book. Submit complete ms.

Fiction Adventure, fantasy, historical, mainstream/contemporary, multicultural, picture books, young adult. Juvenile: adventure, animal, contemporary, fantasy, history, multicultural. Picture books: animal, concept, history, mulitcultural, sports. Young adult: contemporary, fantasy, history, multicultural, nature/environment, problem novels, sports. Submit complete ms.

Recent Title(s) *Hondo and Fabian*, by Peter McCarty; *Keeper of the Night*, by Kimberly Willis Holt.

Ø HENRY HOLT & CO. LLC

Holtzbrinck Publishers, 115 W. 18th St., New York NY 10011. (646)307-5095. Fax: (212)633-0748. Web site: www.henryholt.com. Estab. 1866. Does not accept simultaneous submissions.

Imprints Books for Young Readers; John Macrae Books; Metropolitan Books; Owl Books; Times Books.

- *Does not accept unsolicited queries or mss.*
- Holt is a general-interest publisher of quality fiction and nonfiction.

Recent Title(s) *The Many Lives of Marilyn Monroe*, by Sarah Churchwell; *Science Friction: Where the Known Meets the Unknown*, by Michael Shermer; *American Mafia: A History of Its Rise to Power*, by Thomas Reppetto.

HONOR BOOKS

Cook Communications Ministries, 4050 Lee Vance View, Colorado Springs CO 80918. (719)536-0100. E-mail: info@honorbooks.com. Web site: www.honorbooks.com. Publishes hardcover and trade paperback originals. **Pays royalty on wholesale price, makes outright purchase or assigns work for hire. Offers negotiable advance.**

- *Currently closed to book proposals.*
- "We are a Christian publishing house with a mission to inspire and encourage people to draw near to God and to enjoy His love and grace. We are no longer accepting unsolicited mss from writers." Currently emphasizing humor, personal and spiritual growth, children's books, devotions, personal stories.

Nonfiction Subjects include religion, motivation, devotionals. Subjects are geared toward the "felt needs" of people. No autobiographies or teaching books.

Recent Title(s) *Welcome Home*, by Liz Cowen Furman; *Breakfast for the Soul*, by Judy Couchman.

Tips "Our books are for busy, achievement-oriented people who are looking for a balance between reaching their goals and knowing that God loves them unconditionally. Our books encourage spiritual growth, joyful living and intimacy with God. Write about what you are for and not what you are against. We look for scripts that are biblically based and which inspire readers."

HOUGHTON MIFFLIN BOOKS FOR CHILDREN

Imprint of Houghton Mifflin Trade & Reference Division, 222 Berkeley St., Boston MA 02116. (617)351-5959. Fax: (617)351-1111. E-mail: children's_books@hmco.com. Web site: www.houghtonmifflinbooks.com. **Acquisitions:** Erica Zappy, associate editor; Kate O'Sullivan, editor; Anne Rider, executive editor; Margaret Raymo, editorial director. Publishes hardcover originals and trade paperback originals and reprints. **Publishes 100 titles/year. Receives 5,000 queries and 14,000 mss/year. 10% of books from first-time authors; 60% from unagented writers. Pays 5-10% royalty on retail price. Offers variable advance.** Publishes book 18-24 months after acceptance of ms. Accepts simultaneous submissions. Responds in 4-6 months to queries. Book catalog for 9×12 SASE with 3 first-class stamps; ms guidelines online.

Imprints Sandpiper Paperback Books; Graphia.

- Does not respond to or return mss unless interested.
- "Houghton Mifflin gives shape to ideas that educate, inform, and above all, delight."

Nonfiction Biography, children's/juvenile, humor, illustrated book. Subjects include animals, anthropology/archeology, art/architecture, ethnic, history, language/literature, music/dance, nature/environment, science, sports. Interested in innovative books and subjects about which the author is passionate. Query with SASE, or submit sample chapter(s), synopsis. Reviews artwork/photos as part of ms package. Send photocopies.

Fiction Adventure, ethnic, historical, humor, juvenile (early readers), literary, mystery, picture books, suspense, young adult, board books. Submit complete ms.

Recent Title(s) *The Red Book*, by Barbara Lehman; *Actual Size*, by Steve Jenkins; *Dairy Queen*, by Catherine Gilbert Murdock.

Tips "Faxed or e-mailed manuscripts and proposals are not considered. Complete submission guidelines available on Web site."

HOUGHTON MIFFLIN CO.

222 Berkeley St., Boston MA 02116. (617)351-5000. Web site: www.hmco.com. **Acquisitions:** Submissions Editor. Estab. 1832. Publishes hardcover originals and trade paperback originals and reprints. Accepts simultaneous submissions. Book catalog online.

Imprints American Heritage Dictionaries; Clarion Books; Great Source Education Group; Houghton Mifflin; Houghton Mifflin Books for Children; Houghton Mifflin Paperbacks; Mariner Books; McDougal Littell; Peterson Field Guides; Riverside Publishing; Sunburst Technology; Taylor's Gardening Guides; Edusoft; Promissor; Walter Lorraine Books; Kingfisher.

- "Houghton Mifflin gives shape to ideas that educate, inform and delight. In a new era of publishing, our legacy of quality thrives as we combine imagination with technology, bringing you new ways to know."

Nonfiction Audiocassettes, autobiography, biography, children's/juvenile, cookbook, general nonfiction, gift book, how-to, illustrated book, reference, self-help. Subjects include agriculture/horticulture, animals, anthropology/archeology, cooking/foods/nutrition, ethnic, gardening, gay/lesbian, health/medicine, history, memoirs, military/war, social sciences. "We are not a mass market publisher. Our main focus is serious nonfiction. We do practical self-help but not pop psychology self-help." *Agented submissions only.*

Fiction Literary. "We are not a mass market publisher. Study the current list." *Agented submissions only.*

Recent Title(s) *The Namesake*, by Jhumpa Lahiri; *The Plot Against America*, by Philip Roth.

Tips "Our audience is high end literary."

HOUSE OF COLLECTIBLES

Imprint of Random House, Inc., 1745 Broadway, 15th Floor, New York NY 10019. E-mail: houseofcollectibles@randomhouse.com. Web site: www.houseofcollectibles.com. Publishes trade and mass market paperback originals. **Royalty on retail price varies. Offers varied advance.** Does not accept simultaneous submissions. Book catalog free.

Imprints Official Price Guide series.

O→ "One of the premier publishing companies devoted to books on a wide range of antiques and collectibles, House of Collectibles publishes books for the seasoned expert and the beginning collector alike."

Nonfiction How-to (related to collecting antiques and coins), reference. Subjects include art/architecture (fine art), sports, comic books, American patriotic memorabilia, clocks, character toys, coins, stamps, costume jewelry, knives, books, military, glassware, records, arts and crafts, Native American collectibles, pottery, fleamarkets. Accepts unsolicited proposals.

Recent Title(s) *The Official Price Guide to Records*, by Jerry Osborne; *The One-Minute Coin Expert*, by John Travers.

Tips "We have been publishing price guides and other books on antiques and collectibles for over 35 years and plan to meet the needs of collectors, dealers, and appraisers well into the 21st century."

HUDSON HILLS PRESS, INC.

74-2 Union St., Box 205, Manchester VT 05254. (802)362-6450. Fax: (802)362-6459. E-mail: sbutterfield@hudsonhills.com. Web site: www.hudsonhills.com. **Acquisitions:** Sarah Butterfield, assistant to publisher. Estab. 1978. Publishes hardcover and paperback originals. **Publishes 15+ titles/year. 15% of books from first-time authors; 90% from unagented writers. Pays 4-6% royalty on retail price. Offers $3,500 average advance.** Publishes book 1 year after acceptance of ms. Accepts simultaneous submissions. Responds in 2 months to queries. Book catalog for 6×9 SAE with 2 first-class stamps.

O→ Hudson Hills Press publishes books about art and photography, including monographs.

Nonfiction Subjects include art/architecture, photography. Query first, then submit outline and sample chapters. Reviews artwork/photos as part of ms package.

Recent Title(s) *Systems of Color*, by Ida Kohlmeyer.

HUNTER HOUSE

P.O. Box 2914, Alameda CA 94501. (510)865-5282. Fax: (510)865-4295. E-mail: acquisitions@hunterhouse.com. Web site: www.hunterhouse.com. **Acquisitions:** Jeanne Brondino, acquisitions editor; Kiran S. Rana, publisher. Estab. 1978. Publishes trade paperback originals and reprints. **Publishes 24 titles/year. Receives 200-300 queries and 100 mss/year. 50% of books from first-time authors; 80% from unagented writers. Pays 12% royalty on net receipts, defined as selling price. Offers $500-3,000 advance.** Publishes book 1-2 years after acceptance of ms. Accepts simultaneous submissions. Responds in 2 months to queries; 3 months to proposals. Book catalog for 8½×11 SAE with 3 first-class stamps; ms guidelines online.

O→ Hunter House publishes health books (especially women's health), self-help health, sexuality and couple relationships, violence prevention and intervention. De-emphasizing reference, self-help psychology.

Nonfiction Subjects include health/medicine, self-help, women's health, fitness, relationships, sexuality, personal growth, and violence prevention. "Health books (especially women's health) should focus on self-help health or current issues that are inadequately covered and be written for the general population. Family books: Our current focus is sexuality and couple relationships, and alternative lifestyles to high stress. Community topics include violence prevention/violence intervention. We also publish specialized curricula for counselors and educators in the areas of violence prevention and trauma in children." Query with proposal package, including synopsis, TOC, and chapter outline, sample chapter, target audience information, competition, and what distinguishes the book. Reviews artwork/photos as part of ms package. Send photocopies, proposals generally not returned, requested mss returned with SASE. Reviews artwork/photos as part of ms package.

Recent Title(s) *The Cortisol Connection*, by Shawn Talbott; *Tantric Sex for Women*, by Christa Schulte; *How to Spot a Dangerous Man*, by Sandra Brown.

Tips Audience is concerned people who are looking to educate themselves and their community about real-life issues that affect them. "Please send as much information as possible about who your audience is, how your book addresses their needs, and how you reach that audience in your ongoing work."

HUNTER PUBLISHING, INC.

P.O. Box 746, Walpole MA 02081. Fax: (772)546-8040. E-mail: hunterp@bellsouth.net. Web site: www.hunterpublishing.com. President: Michael Hunter. **Acquisitions:** Kim Andre, editor; Lissa Dailey. Estab. 1985. **Publishes 100 titles/year. 10% of books from first-time authors; 75% from unagented writers. Pays royalty. Offers negotiable advance.** Publishes book 5 months after acceptance of ms. Accepts simultaneous submis-

sions. Responds in 3 weeks to queries; 1 month to mss. Book catalog for #10 SAE with 4 first-class stamps.
Imprints Adventure Guides; Romantic Weekends Guides; Alive Guides.

O→ Hunter Publishing publishes practical guides for travelers going to the Caribbean, US, Europe, South America, and the far reaches of the globe.

Nonfiction Reference. Subjects include regional, travel (travel guides). ''We need travel guides to areas covered by few competitors: Caribbean Islands, South and Central America, Europe, Asia from an active 'adventure' perspective.'' No personal travel stories or books not directed to travelers. Query, or submit outline/synopsis and sample chapters. Reviews artwork/photos as part of ms package.
Recent Title(s) *Adventure Guide to Canada's Atlantic Provinces*, by Barbara Radcliffe-Rogers.
Tips ''Guides should be destination-specific, rather than theme-based alone. Thus, 'Travel with Kids' is too broad; 'Italy with Kids' is OK. Make sure the guide doesn't duplicate what other guide publishers do.''

IBEX PUBLISHERS

P.O. Box 30087, Bethesda MD 20824. (301)718-8188. Fax: (301)907-8707. E-mail: info@ibexpub.com. Web site: www.ibexpub.com. Publishes hardcover and trade paperback originals and reprints. **Publishes 10-12 titles/year. Payment varies.** Accepts simultaneous submissions. Book catalog free.
Imprints Iranbooks Press.

O→ IBEX publishes books about Iran and the Middle East.

Nonfiction Biography, cookbook, reference, textbook. Subjects include cooking/foods/nutrition, language/literature. Query with SASE, or submit propsal package, including outline and 2 sample chapters.
Poetry Translations of Persian poets will be considered.

ICONOGRAFIX, INC.

1830A Hanley Rd., P.O. Box 446, Hudson WI 54016. (715)381-9755. Fax: (715)381-9756. E-mail: dcfrautschi@iconografixinc.com. Web site: www.enthusiastbooks.com. **Acquisitions:** Dylan Frautschi, acquisitions manager (transportation). Estab. 1992. Publishes trade paperback originals. **Publishes 24 titles/year. Receives 100 queries and 20 mss/year. 50% of books from first-time authors; 100% from unagented writers. Pays 8-12% royalty on wholesale price. Offers $1,000-3,000 advance.** Publishes book 1 year after acceptance of ms. Accepts simultaneous submissions. Responds in 1 month to queries; 3 months to proposals; 3 months to mss. Book catalog and ms guidelines free.

O→ Iconografix publishes special, historical-interest photographic books for transportation equipment enthusiasts. Currently emphasizing emergency vehicles, buses, trucks, railroads, automobiles, auto racing, construction equipment, snowmobiles.

Nonfiction Interested in photo archives. Coffee table book, illustrated book (photographic), photo albums. Subjects include Americana (photos from archives of historic places, objects, people), history, hobbies, military/war, transportation (older photos of specific vehicles). Query with SASE, or submit proposal package, including outline. Reviews artwork/photos as part of ms package. Send photocopies.
Recent Title(s) *Trolley Buses Around the World*, by William A. Luke; *Vintage Snowmobilia*, by Jon D. Bertolinol.

ILR PRESS

Cornell University Press, Sage House, 512 E. State St., Ithaca NY 14850. (607)277-2338. Fax: (607)277-2374. **Acquisitions:** Frances Benson, editorial director (fgb2@cornell.edu). Estab. 1945. Publishes hardcover and trade paperback originals and reprints. **Publishes 10-15 titles/year. Pays royalty.** Does not accept simultaneous submissions. Responds in 2 months to queries. Book catalog free.

O→ ''We are interested in manuscripts with innovative perspectives on current workplace issues that concern both academics and the general public.''

Nonfiction Subjects include business/economics, government/politics, history, sociology. All titles relate to labor relations and/or workplace issues including relevant work in the fields of history, sociology, political science, economics, human resources, and organizational behavior. Developing a new series on the work of health care. Query with SASE, or submit outline, sample chapter(s), cv.
Recent Title(s) *Code Green: Money-driven Hospitals and the Dismantling of Nursing*, by Dana Beth Weinberg; *The Working Class Majority: America's Best Kept Secret*, by Michael Zweig; *State of Working America*, by Lawrence Mishel, et. al.
Tips ''Manuscripts must be well documented to pass our editorial evaluation, which includes review by academics in related fields.''

INCENTIVE PUBLICATIONS, INC.

2400 Crestmoor Rd., Suite 211, Nashville TN 37215. (615)385-2934. Fax: (615)385-2967. E-mail: comments@incentivepublications.com. Web site: www.incentivepublications.com. **Acquisitions:** Patience Camplair, editor. Estab. 1970. Publishes paperback originals. **Publishes 25-30 titles/year. 25% of books from first-time authors;**

100% from unagented writers. Pays royalty, or makes outright purchase. Publishes book an average of 1 year after acceptance of ms. Responds in 1 month to queries. Ms guidelines online.

O- Incentive publishes developmentally appropriate teacher/parent resource materials and educational workbooks for children in grades K-12. Currently emphasizing primary material. Also interested in character education, English as a second language programs, early learning, current technology, related materials.

Nonfiction Subjects include education. Teacher resource books in pre-K through 12th grade. Query with synopsis and detailed outline.

Recent Title(s) *The Ready to Learn Book Series*, by Imogene Forte (Grades pre K-K); *Drumming to the Beat of a Different Marcher*, by Debbie Silver; *As Reading Programs Come and Go, This Is What You Need to Know*, by Judith Cochran.

INDIANA HISTORICAL SOCIETY PRESS

450 W. Ohio St., Indianapolis IN 46202-3269. (317)233-6073. Fax: (317)233-0857. **Acquisitions:** Submissions Editor. Estab. 1830. Publishes hardcover and paperback originals. **Publishes 10 titles/year.** Responds in 1 month to queries.

Nonfiction Biography. Subjects include agriculture/horticulture, art/architecture, business/economics, ethnic, government/politics, history, military/war, sports, children's books. All topics must relate to Indiana. "We seek book-length manuscripts that are solidly researched and engagingly written on topics related to Indiana: biography, history, literature, music, politics, transportation, sports, agriculture, architecture, and children's books." Query with SASE.

Recent Title(s) *Gus Grissom: The Lost Astronaut*, by Ray E. Boomhower; *Skirting the Issue: Stories of Indiana's Historical Women Artists*, by Judith Vale Newton and Carol Ann Weiss; *Affectionately Yours: The Civil War Home-Front Letters of the Ovid Butler Family*, edited by Barbara Butler Davis.

INFORMATION TODAY, INC.

143 Old Marlton Pike, Medford NJ 08055. (609)654-6266. Fax: (609)654-4309. E-mail: jbryans@infotoday.com. Web site: www.infotoday.com. **Acquisitions:** John B. Bryans, editor-in-chief/publisher. Publishes hardcover and trade paperback originals. **Publishes 15-20 titles/year. Receives 200 queries and 30 mss/year. 30% of books from first-time authors; 90% from unagented writers. Pays 10-15% royalty on wholesale price. Offers $500-2,500 advance.** Publishes book 9 months after acceptance of ms. Accepts simultaneous submissions. Responds in 1 month to queries; 2 months to proposals; 3 months to mss. Book catalog free or on Web site; proposal guidelines free or via e-mail as attachment.

Imprints ITI (academic, scholarly, library science); CyberAge Books (high-end consumer and business technology books—emphasis on Internet/WWW topics including online research).

O- "We look for highly-focused coverage of cutting-edge technology topics, written by established experts and targeted to a tech-savvy readership. Virtually all our titles focus on how information is accessed, used, shared, and transformed into knowledge that can benefit people, business, and society." Currently emphasizing Internet/online technologies, including their social significance; biography, how-to, technical, reference, scholarly. De-emphasizing fiction.

Nonfiction Biography, how-to, multimedia, reference, self-help, technical, scholarly. Subjects include business/economics, computers/electronic, education, science, Internet and cyberculture, library and information science. Query with SASE. Reviews artwork/photos as part of ms package. Send photocopies.

Recent Title(s) *The Visible Employee*, by Jeffrey M. Stanton and Kathryn R. Stam; *Teach Beyond Your Reach*, by Robin Neidorf; *The Traveler's Wife*, by Randolph Hock.

Tips "Our readers include scholars, academics, indexers, librarians, information professionals (ITI imprint), as well as high-end consumer and business users of Internet/WWW/online technologies, and people interested in the marriage of technology with issues of social significance (i.e., cyberculture)."

⊘ INNER OCEAN PUBLISHING, INC.

P.O. Box 1239, Makawao HI 96768. (808)573-8000. Fax: (808)573-0700. E-mail: info@innerocean.com. Web site: www.innerocean.com. **Acquisitions:** Karen Bouris, publisher; John Elder, executive publisher. Estab. 1999. Publishes hardcover originals and trade paperback originals and reprints. **Publishes 20+ titles/year. Pays 10-15% roaylty on net sales. Offers modest advance.** Accepts simultaneous submissions. Responds in 2-3 months to queries. Book catalog free; ms guidelines online.

Nonfiction General trade. Subjects include spirituality, women's issues/studies, personal growth, sexuality, environmental, and political call to action. Query with SASE. *Do not send ms.*

Recent Title(s) *If Women Ruled the World*; *Awake in the Wild*; *Deeksha.*

Tips Audience is a wide range of readers interested in improving their lives through self-awareness, personal empowerment, and community involvement.

INNER TRADITIONS

Bear & Co., P.O. Box 388, Rochester VT 05767. (802)767-3174. Fax: (802)767-3726. E-mail: submissions@gotoit.com. Web site: www.innertraditions.com. Managing Editor: Jeanie Levitan. **Acquisitions:** Jon Graham, editor. Estab. 1975. Publishes hardcover and trade paperback originals and reprints. **Publishes 60 titles/year. Receives 5,000 queries/year. 10% of books from first-time authors; 20% from unagented writers. Pays 8-10% royalty on net receipts. Offers $1,000 average advance.** Publishes book 1 year after acceptance of ms. Responds in 3 months to queries; 6 months to mss. Book catalog free; ms guidelines online.

Imprints Destiny Audio Editions; Destiny Books; Destiny Recordings; Healing Arts Press; Inner Traditions; Inner Traditions En Español; Inner Traditions India; Park Street Press; Bear & Company; Bear Cub; Bindu Books.

O━ Inner Traditions publishes works representing the spiritual, cultural and mythic traditions of the world and works on alternative medicine and holistic health that combine contemporary thought with the knowledge of the world's great healing traditions. Currently emphasizing secret society research, alternative Christianity, indigenous spirituality, ancient history.

Nonfiction ''We are interested in the relationship of the spiritual and transformative aspects of world cultures.'' Subjects include animals, art/architecture, child guidance/parenting, contemporary culture, ethnic, fashion/beauty, health/medicine (alternative medicine), history (ancient history and mythology), music/dance, nature/environment, New Age, philosophy (esoteric), psychology, religion (world religions), sex, spirituality, women's issues/studies, indigenous cultures, ethnobotany business. No fiction. Query or submit outline and sample chapters with SASE. Does not return mss without SASE. Reviews artwork/photos as part of ms package.

Recent Title(s) *Science and the Akashic Field*, by Ervin Laszlo; *The Knights Templar in the New World*, by William F. Mann; *The Secret Teachings of Plants*, by Stephen Harrod Buhner.

Tips ''We are not interested in autobiographical stories of self-transformation. We do accept electronic submissions (via e-mail). We are not currently looking at fiction.''

INTERLINK PUBLISHING GROUP, INC.

46 Crosby St., Northampton MA 01060. (413)582-7054. Fax: (413)582-7057. E-mail: info@interlinkbooks.com. Web site: www.interlinkbooks.com. **Acquisitions:** Michel Moushabeck, publisher. Estab. 1987. Publishes hardcover and trade paperback originals. **Publishes 50 titles/year. 30% of books from first-time authors; 50% from unagented writers. Pays 6-8% royalty on retail price. Offers small advance.** Publishes book 18 months after acceptance of ms. Accepts simultaneous submissions. Responds in 3-6 months to queries. Book catalog free; ms guidelines online.

Imprints Crocodile Books, USA; Interlink Books; Olive Branch Press.

O━ Interlink publishes a general trade list of adult fiction and nonfiction with an emphasis on books that have a wide appeal while also meeting high intellectual and literary standards.

Nonfiction Subjects include world travel, world history and politics, ethnic cooking, world music. Submit outline and sample chapters.

Fiction Ethnic, international. ''Adult—We are looking for translated works relating to the Middle East, Africa or Latin America.'' No science fiction, romance, plays, erotica, fantasy, horror. Query with SASE, or submit outline, sample chapter(s).

Recent Title(s) *House of the Winds*, by Mia Yun.

Tips ''Any submissions that fit well in our publishing program will receive careful attention. A visit to our Web site, your local bookstore, or library to look at some of our books before you send in your submission is recommended.''

INTERNATIONAL CITY/COUNTY MANAGEMENT ASSOCIATION

777 N. Capitol St., NE, Suite 500, Washington DC 20002. (202)962-4262. Fax: (202)962-3500. Web site: www.icma.org. **Acquisitions:** Christine Ulrich, editorial director. Estab. 1914. Publishes hardcover and paperback originals. **Publishes 10-15 titles/year. Receives 50 queries and 20 mss/year. 20% of books from first-time authors; 100% from unagented writers. Makes negotiable outright purchase. Offers occasional advance.** Publishes book 18 months after acceptance of ms. Responds in 2 months to queries. Book catalog and ms guidelines online.

O━ ''Our mission is to create excellence in local government by developing and fostering professional local government management worldwide.''

Nonfiction Reference, textbook, training manuals. Subjects include government/politics. Query with outline and 1 sample chapter. Reviews artwork/photos as part of ms package. Send photocopies.

Recent Title(s) *Capital Budgeting and Finance: A Guide for Local Governments*; *The Effective Local Government Manager*.

Tips ''Our mission is to enhance the quality of local government and to support and assist professional local administrators in the United States and other countries.''

INTERNATIONAL FOUNDATION OF EMPLOYEE BENEFIT PLANS

P.O. Box 69, Brookfield WI 53008-0069. (262)786-6700. Fax: (262)786-8780. E-mail: books@ifebp.org. Web site: www.ifebp.org. **Acquisitions:** Dee Birschel, senior director of publications. Estab. 1954. Publishes trade paperback originals. **Publishes 10 titles/year. 15% of books from first-time authors; 80% from unagented writers. Pays 5-15% royalty on wholesale and retail price.** Publishes book 1 year after acceptance of ms. Responds in 3 months to queries. Book catalog free; ms guidelines for #10 SASE.

- IFEBP publishes general and technical monographs on all aspects of employee benefits—pension plans, health insurance, etc.

Nonfiction Subjects limited to health care, pensions, retirement planning and employee benefits and compensation. Reference, technical, textbook. Subjects include consumer information. Query with outline.

Recent Title(s) *Managing Pharmacy Benefits*, by Randy Vogenberg and Joanne Sica; *Effective Benefit Communication*, by Ann Black.

Tips "Be aware of interests of employers and the marketplace in benefits topics, for example, how AIDS affects employers, healthcare cost containment."

INTERNATIONAL MEDICAL PUBLISHING

1313 Dolley Madison Blvd., Suite 302, McLean VA 22101. (703)356-2037. Fax: (703)734-8987. E-mail: contact@medicalpublishing.com. Web site: www.medicalpublishing.com. **Acquisitions:** Thomas Masterson, MD, editor. Estab. 1991. Publishes mass market paperback originals. **Publishes 30 titles/year. Receives 100 queries and 20 mss/year. 5% of books from first-time authors; 100% from unagented writers. Pays royalty on gross receipts.** Publishes book 8 months after acceptance of ms. Responds in 2 months to queries.

- IMP publishes books to make life easier for doctors in training. "We're branching out to also make life easier for people with chronic medical problems."

Nonfiction Reference, textbook. Subjects include health/medicine. "We distribute only through medical and scientific bookstores. Think about practical material for doctors-in-training. We are interested in handbooks. Online projects are of interest." Query with outline.

Recent Title(s) *Healthy People 2010*, by the US Department of Health and Human Services; *Day-by-Day Diabetes*, by Resa Levetan.

INTERNATIONAL PRESS

P.O. Box 43502, Somerville MA 02143. (617)623-3855. Fax: (617)623-3101. E-mail: orders@intlpress.com. Submissions E-mail: info@intlpress.com. Web site: www.intlpress.com. **Acquisitions:** Lisa Lin, general manager (research math and physics). Estab. 1992. Publishes hardcover originals and reprints. **Publishes 12 titles/year. Receives 200 queries and 500 mss/year. 10% of books from first-time authors; 100% from unagented writers. Pays 3-10% royalty.** Publishes book 6 months after acceptance of ms. Does not accept simultaneous submissions. Responds in 5 months to queries; 5 months to proposals; 1 year to mss. Book catalog free; ms guidelines online.

Nonfiction Reference, scholarly. Subjects include science. "All our books will be in research mathematics. Authors need to provide ready to print latex files." Submit complete ms. Reviews artwork/photos as part of ms package. EPS files.

Recent Title(s) *Collected Works on Ricci Flow*; *Current Developments in Mathematics*; *Surveys in Differential Geometry*.

Tips "Audience is PhD mathematicians, researchers and students."

INTERNATIONAL SOCIETY FOR TECHNOLOGY IN EDUCATION (ISTE)

175 W. Broadway, Suite 300, Eugene OR 97401. (541)434-8928. E-mail: books@iste.org. Web site: www.iste.org. **Acquisitions:** Scott Harter, acquisitions and development editor. Publishes trade paperback originals. **Publishes 10 titles/year. Receives 100 queries and 40 mss/year. 75% of books from first-time authors; 95% from unagented writers. Pays 10% royalty on retail price.** Publishes book 6-9 months after acceptance of ms. Accepts simultaneous submissions. Responds in 2 weeks to queries; 1 month to proposals; 1 month to mss. Book catalog and ms guidelines online.

- Currently emphasizing books on educational technology standards, curriculum integration, professional development, and assessment. De-emphasizing software how-to books.

Nonfiction Reference, technical, curriculum. Subjects include educational technology, curriculum design, educational administration. Submit proposal package including outline, sample chapter(s), TOC, vita. Reviews artwork/photos as part of ms package. Send photocopies.

Recent Title(s) *1-to-1 Learning*, by Pamela Livingtson; *Nets.S Resources for Student Assessment*, by Peggy Kelly and John Haber; *Digital-Age Literary for Teachers*, by Susan Brooks-Young.

Tips "Our audience is K-12 teachers, teacher educators, technology coordinators, and school and district administrators."

INTERNATIONAL WEALTH SUCCESS

P.O. Box 186, Merrick NY 11570-0186. (516)766-5850. Fax: (516)766-5919. **Acquisitions:** Tyler G. Hicks, editor. Estab. 1967. **Publishes 10 titles/year. 100% of books from first-time authors; 100% from unagented writers. Pays 10% royalty on wholesale or retail price. Offers usual advance of $1,000, but this varies depending on author's reputation and nature of book. Buys all rights.** Publishes book 4 months after acceptance of ms. Responds in 1 month to queries. Book catalog and ms guidelines for 9×12 SAE with 3 first-class stamps.

O⊸ "Our mission is to publish books, newsletters, and self-study courses aimed at helping beginners and experienced business people start, and succeed in, their own small business in the fields of real estate, import-export, mail order, licensing, venture capital, financial brokerage, etc. The large number of layoffs and downsizings have made our publications of greater importance to people seeking financial independence in their own business, free of layoff threats and snarling bosses."

Nonfiction How-to, self-help. Subjects include business/economics, financing, business success, venture capital, etc. "Techniques, methods, sources for building wealth. Highly personal, how-to-do-it with plenty of case histories. Books are aimed at wealth builders and are highly sympathetic to their problems. These publications present a wide range of business opportunities while providing practical, hands-on, step-by-step instructions aimed at helping readers achieve their personal goals in as short a time as possible while adhering to ethical and professional business standards." Length: 60,000-70,000 words. Query. Reviews artwork/photos as part of ms package.

Recent Title(s) *How to Buy and Flip Real Estate for a Profit*, by Rod L. Griffin.

Tips "With the mass layoffs in large and medium-size companies there is an increasing interest in owning your own business. So we focus on more how-to, hands-on material on owning—and becoming successful in—one's own business of any kind. Our market is the BWB—Beginning Wealth Builder. This person has so little money that financial planning is something they never think of. Instead, they want to know what kind of a business they can get into to make some money without a large investment. Write for this market and you have millions of potential readers. Remember—there are a lot more people without money than with money."

⊘ INTERVARSITY PRESS

P.O. Box 1400, Downers Grove IL 60515. (630)734-4000. Fax: (630)734-4200. E-mail: submissions@ivpress.com. Web site: www.ivpress.com. **Acquisitions:** David Zimmerman, associate editor (general); Andy Le Peau, editorial director; Jim Hoover, associate editorial director (academic, reference); Cindy Bunch, senior editor (Bible study, Christian living); Joel Scandrett (academic, reference); Gary Deddo, associate editor (academic); Dan Reid, senior editor (reference, academic); Al Hsu, associate editor (general). Estab. 1947. Publishes hardcover originals, trade paperback and mass market paperback originals. **Publishes 90-100 titles/year. Receives 1,500 queries and 1,000 mss/year. 15% of books from first-time authors; 85% from unagented writers. Pays negotiable flat fee or royalty on retail price. Offers negotiable advance.** Publishes book 18 months after acceptance of ms. Accepts simultaneous submissions. Responds in 3 months to proposals. Book catalog for 9×12 SAE and 5 first-class stamps; ms guidelines online.

Imprints IVP Academic (contact Gary Deddo for academic or Dan Reid for reference); IVP Connect (contact Cindy Bunch); IVP Books (contact Al Hsu).

O⊸ InterVarsity Press publishes a full line of books from an evangelical Christian perspective targeted to an open-minded audience. "We serve those in the university, the church, and the world, by publishing books from an evangelical Christian perspective."

Nonfiction Subjects include religion. Query with SASE. *No unsolicited mss.*

Recent Title(s) *Spiritual Disciplines Handbook*, by Adele Ahlberg Calhoun; *Fabricating Jesus*, by Craig A. Evans.

INTERWEAVE PRESS

201 E. 4th St., Loveland CO 80537. (970)669-7672. Fax: (970)667-8317. Web site: www.interweave.com. **Acquisitions:** Tricia Waddell, book editorial director. Estab. 1975. Publishes hardcover and trade paperback originals. **Publishes 25-30 titles/year. 60% of books from first-time authors; 85% from unagented writers. Pays 10% royalty on net receipts.** Publishes book 1-2 years after acceptance of ms. Accepts simultaneous submissions. Responds in 2 months to queries. Book catalog online; ms guidelines free.

O⊸ Interweave Press publishes instructive titles relating to the fiber arts and beadwork topics.

Nonfiction Subjects limited to fiber arts—spinning, knitting, crochet, dyeing and weaving—and beadwork topics. How-to, technical. Submit outline, sample chapter(s). Reviews artwork/photos as part of ms package.

Recent Title(s) *One Skein: 30 Quick Projects to Knit and Crochet*, by Leigh Radford.

Tips "We are looking for very clear, informally written, technically correct manuscripts, generally of a how-to nature, in our specific fiber and beadwork fields only. Our audience includes a variety of creative self-starters who appreciate inspiration and clear instruction. They are often well educated and skillful in many areas."

THE INVISIBLE COLLEGE PRESS

P.O. Box 209, Woodbridge VA 22194-0209. (703)590-4005. E-mail: submissions@invispress.com. Web site: www.invispress.com. **Acquisitions:** Dr. Phillip Reynolds, editor (nonfiction); Paul Mossinger, submissions editor (fiction). Publishes trade paperback originals and reprints. **Publishes 12 titles/year. Receives 120 queries and 30 mss/year. 75% of books from first-time authors; 75% from unagented writers. Pays 10-25% royalty on wholesale price. Offers $100 advance.** Publishes book 4 months after acceptance of ms. Accepts simultaneous submissions. Responds in 1 month to queries; 1 month to proposals; 3 months to mss. Book catalog and ms guidelines online.

Nonfiction Reference. Subjects include creative nonfiction, government/politics, religion, spirituality, conspiracy. "We only publish nonfiction related to conspiracies, UFOs, government cover-ups, and the paranormal." Query with SASE, or submit proposal package including outline, 1 sample chapter.

Fiction Experimental, fantasy, gothic, horror, literary, mainstream/contemporary, occult, religious, science fiction, spiritual, suspense, conspiracy. "We only publish fiction related to conspiracies, UFOs, government cover-ups, and the paranormal." Query with SASE, or submit proposal package including synopsis, 1 sample chapter.

Recent Title(s) *UFO Politics at the White House*, by Larry Bryant (nonfiction); *City of Pillars*, by Dominic Peloso (fiction); *The Third Day*, by Mark Graham (fiction).

Tips "Our audience tends to be fans of conspiracies and UFO mythology. They go to UFO conventions, they research who shot JFK, they believe that they are being followed by Men in Black, they wear aluminum-foil hats to stop the CIA from beaming them thought-control rays. We are only interested in work dealing with established conspiracy/UFO mythology. Rosicrucians, Illuminatti, Men in Black, Area 51, Atlantis, etc. If your book doesn't sound like an episode of the *X-Files*, we probably won't consider it."

JAIN PUBLISHING CO.

P.O. Box 3523, Fremont CA 94539. (510)659-8272. Fax: (510)659-0501. E-mail: mail@jainpub.com. Web site: www.jainpub.com. **Acquisitions:** M. Jain, editor-in-chief. Estab. 1989. Publishes hardcover and paperback originals and reprints. **Publishes 12-15 titles/year. Receives 300 queries/year. 100% from unagented writers. Pays 5-15% royalty on net sales.** Publishes book 1-2 years after acceptance of ms. Responds in 3 months to mss. Book catalog and ms guidelines online.

- Jain Publishing Co. publishes college textbooks and supplements, as well as professional and scholarly references, ebooks and ecourses.

Nonfiction Reference, textbook. Subjects include humanities, social sciences, Asian studies, medical, business, scientific/technical. Submit proposal package including publishing history. Reviews artwork/photos as part of ms package. Send photocopies.

Recent Title(s) *A Student Guide to College Composition*, by William Murdiek.

JEWISH LIGHTS PUBLISHING

LongHill Partners, Inc., P.O. Box 237, Sunset Farm Offices, Rt. 4, Woodstock VT 05091. (802)457-4000. Fax: (802)457-4004. Web site: www.jewishlights.com. Editor: Stuart Matlins. **Acquisitions:** Acquisitions Editor. Estab. 1990. Publishes hardcover and trade paperback originals, trade paperback reprints. **Publishes 30 titles/year. 30% of books from first-time authors; 99% from unagented writers. Pays royalty on net sales, 10% on first printing, then increases.** Publishes book 1 year after acceptance of ms. Accepts simultaneous submissions. Responds in 3 months to queries. Book catalog and ms guidelines online.

- "People of all faiths and backgrounds yearn for books that attract, engage, educate and spiritually inspire. Our principal goal is to stimulate thought and help all people learn about who the Jewish people are, where they come from, and what the future can be made to hold."

Nonfiction Children's/juvenile, illustrated book, reference, self-help. Subjects include business/economics (with spiritual slant, finding spiritual meaning in one's work), health/medicine (healing/recovery, wellness, aging, life cycle), history, nature/environment, philosophy, religion (theology), spirituality (and inspiration), women's issues/studies. "We do *not* publish haggadot, biography, poetry, or cookbooks." Submit proposal package, including cover letter, TOC, 2 sample chapters and SASE (postage must cover weight of ms). Reviews artwork/photos as part of ms package. Send photocopies.

Tips "We publish books for all faiths and backgrounds that also reflect the Jewish wisdom tradition."

JIST PUBLISHING, INC.

8902 Otis Ave., Indianapolis IN 46216-1033. (317)613-4200. Fax: (317)613-4304. E-mail: info@jist.com. Web site: www.jist.com. **Acquisitions:** Susan Pines, associate publisher (career reference and career assessment mss); Lori Cates Hand, acquisitions and development editor (trade mss); Randy Haubner, acquisitions editor (workbook mss and all KIDSRIGHTS/JIST Life mss). Estab. 1981. Publishes practical, self-directed tools and training materials that are used in employment and training education, and business settings. Whether reference books, trade books, assessment tools, workbooks, or videos, JIST products foster self-directed job-search attitudes and behaviors. Trade and institutional hardcover and paperback originals and reprints. **Publishes 50 titles/year. Receives 150 submissions/year. 25% of books from first-time authors. Pays 5-10% royalty on wholesale price or makes outright purchase (negotiable).** Publishes book 1-2 years after acceptance of ms. Accepts simultaneous submissions. Responds in 5-6 months to queries. Book catalog and ms guidelines online.

Imprints JIST Works (job search, career development, and occupational information titles); Park Avenue (education, business, self-help, and life skills titles); Your Domain Publishing (public domain and government agency data and information titles); JIST Life (adults); KIDSRIGHTS (children).

O→ "Our purpose is to provide quality job search, career development, occupational, character education, and life skills information, products, and services that help people manage and improve their lives and careers—and the lives of others."

Nonfiction Specializes in job search, career development, occupational information, character education, and domestic abuse topics. "We want text/workbook formats that would be useful in a school or other institutional setting. We also publish trade titles for all reading levels. Will consider books for professional staff and educators, appropriate software and videos." Query with SASE. Reviews artwork/photos as part of ms package.

Recent Title(s) *The Very Quick Job Search, Third Ed.*, by Michael Farr; *Young Person's Occupational Outlook Handbook, Fourth Ed.*, by the editors of JIST; *Gallery of Best Résumés, Third Ed.*, by David Noble.

Tips "Our primary audience is institutions and staff who work with people of all reading and academic skill levels, making career and life decisions, and people who are looking for jobs."

THE JOHNS HOPKINS UNIVERSITY PRESS

2715 N. Charles St., Baltimore MD 21218. (410)516-6900. Fax: (410)516-6968. E-mail: tcl@press.jhu.edu. Web site: www.press.jhu.edu. **Acquisitions:** Trevor Lipscombe, editor-in-chief (physics, astronomy, mathematics; tcl@press.jhu.edu); Jacqueline C. Wehmueller, executive editor (consumer health, history of medicine, education; jwehmueller@press.jhu.edu); Henry Y.K. Tom, executive editor (social sciences; htom@press.jhu.edu); Wendy Harris, senior acquisitions editor (clinical medicine, public health, health policy; wharris@press.jhu.edu); Robert J. Brugger, senior acquisitions editor (American history, history of science and technology, regional books; rbrugger@press.jhu.edu); Vincent J. Burke, acquisitions editor (biology; vjb@press.jhu.edu); Michael B. Lonegro, acquisitions editor (humanities, classics, and ancient studies; mlonegro@press.jhu.edu). Estab. 1878. Publishes hardcover originals and reprints, and trade paperback reprints. **Publishes 140 titles/year. Pays royalty.** Publishes book 1 year after acceptance of ms.

Nonfiction Biography, general nonfiction, reference, scholarly, textbook. Subjects include government/politics, health/medicine, history, humanities, regional, religion, science, social sciences. Submit proposal package including outline, 1 sample chapter, curriculum vita. Reviews artwork/photos as part of ms package. Send photocopies.

Recent Title(s) *In Albert's Shadow*, by Milan Popovic (collection of letters); *An Alliance at Risk*, by Laurent Cohen-Tanugi, translated by George A. Holoch, Jr. (international relations); *Living With Rheumatoid Arthritis*, by Tammi L. Shlotzhauer, MD, and James L. McGuire, MD (health).

JOSSEY-BASS/PFEIFFER

John Wiley & Sons, Inc., 989 Market St., San Francisco CA 94103. (415)433-1740. Fax: (415)433-0499. Web site: www.josseybass.com; www.pfeiffer.com. **Acquisitions:** Paul Foster, publisher (public health and health administration, education K-12, higher and adult education, trade psychology, conflict resolustion, parenting, relationships, Judaica religion and spirituality); Cedric Crocker, publisher (business, nonprofit and public management, training and human resources developement). **Publishes 250 titles/year. Pays variable royalties. Offers occasional advance.** Publishes book 1 year after acceptance of ms. Accepts simultaneous submissions. Responds in 2-3 months to queries. Ms guidelines online.

Nonfiction Subjects include business/economics, education, health/medicine, money/finance, psychology, religion. Jossey-Bass publishes first-time and unagented authors. Publishes books on topics of interest to a wide range of readers: business & management, conflict resolution, mediation and negotiation, K-12 education, higher and adult education, healthcare management, psychology/behavioral healthcare, nonprofit & public management, religion, human resources & training. Also publishes 25 periodicals.

Recent Title(s) *No More Misbehavin'*, by Michele Borba; *Hidden Wholeness*, by Parker Palmer; *Teaching With Fire*, by Sam Intrator.

JUDAICA PRESS

123 Ditmas Ave., Brooklyn NY 11218. (718)972-6200. Fax: (718)972-6204. E-mail: info@judaicapress.com. Web site: www.judaicapress.com. **Acquisitions:** Nachum Shapiro, managing editor. Estab. 1963. Publishes hardcover and trade paperback originals and reprints. **Publishes 12 titles/year.** Responds in 3 months to queries. Book catalog in print and online.

O-ᵣ "We cater to the Orthodox Jewish market."

Nonfiction "Looking for Orthodox Judaica in all genres." Children's/juvenile, cookbook, textbook, outreach books. Subjects include religion (Bible commentary), prayer, holidays, life cycle. Submit ms with SASE.

Fiction Novels.

Recent Title(s) *Scattered Pieces*, by Allison Cohen; *The Practical Guide to Kashrus*, by Rabbi Shaul Wagschal; *How Mitzvah Giraffe Got His Long, Long Neck*, by David Sokoloff.

JUDSON PRESS

P.O. Box 851, Valley Forge PA 19482-0851. (610)768-2118. Fax: (610)768-2441. E-mail: acquisitions@judsonpress.com. Web site: www.judsonpress.com. Publisher: Laura Alden. **Acquisitions:** Randy Frame. Estab. 1824. Publishes hardcover and paperback originals. **Publishes 12-15 titles/year. Receives 750 queries/year. Pays royalty or makes outright purchase.** Publishes book 10 months after acceptance of ms. Accepts simultaneous submissions. Responds in 3 months to queries. Book catalog for 9×12 SAE with 4 first-class stamps; ms guidelines for #10 SASE.

O-ᵣ "Our audience is mostly church members and leaders who seek to have a more fulfilling personal spiritual life and want to serve Christ in their churches and other relationships. We have a large African-American readership." Currently emphasizing worship resources/small group resources. De-emphasizing biography, poetry.

Nonfiction Adult religious nonfiction of 30,000-80,000 words. Subjects include multicultural, religion. Query with SASE, or submit outline, sample chapter(s).

Recent Title(s) *The Gospel According to Dr. Seuss*, by James W. Kemp; *The Real Deal*, by Billie Montgomery Cook; *40 Days to a Life of G.O.L.D.*, by Ed Gray.

Tips "Writers have the best chance selling us practical books assisting clergy or laypersons in their ministry and personal lives. Our audience consists of Protestant church leaders and members. Be sensitive to our workload and adapt to the market's needs. Books on multicultural issues are very welcome. Also seeking books that heighten awareness and sensitivity to issues related to the poor and to social justice."

KALMBACH PUBLISHING CO.

21027 Crossroads Circle, P.O. Box 1612, Waukesha WI 53187-1612. (262)796-8776. Fax: (262)798-6468. E-mail: books@kalmbach.com. Web site: corporate.kalmbach.com. **Acquisitions:** Mark Thompson, editor-in-chief (hobbies); Pat Lantier, executive editor (jewelry and crafts). Estab. 1934. Publishes paperback originals and reprints. **Publishes 40-50 titles/year. 50% of books from first-time authors; 99% from unagented writers. Pays 7% royalty on net receipts. Offers $2,500 advance.** Publishes book 18 months after acceptance of ms. Responds in 2 months to queries.

Nonfiction Kalmbach publishes reference materials and how-to publications for hobbyists, jewelry-makers, and crafters. Concentration in the railfan, model railroading, plastic modeling, and toy train collecting/operating hobbies. Focus on beading, wirework, and one-of-a-kind artisan creations for jewelry-making and crafts and in the railfan, model railroading, plastic modeling and toy train collecting/operating hobbies. Query with 2-3 page detailed outline, sample chapter with photos, drawings, and how-to text. Reviews artwork/photos as part of ms package.

Recent Title(s) *The Model Railroader's Guide to Coal Railroading*, by Tony Koester; *Polymer Pizzazz: 27 Great Polymer Clay Jewelry Projects*.

Tips "Our how-to books are highly visual in their presentation. Any author who wants to publish with us must be able to furnish good photographs and rough drawings before we'll consider his or her book."

[A] ⊘ KENSINGTON PUBLISHING CORP.

850 Third Ave., 16th Floor, New York NY 10022. (212)407-1500. Fax: (212)935-0699. Web site: www.kensingtonbooks.com. **Acquisitions:** Michaela Hamilton, editor-in-chief (thrillers, mysteries, mainstream fiction, true crime, current events); Kate Duffy, editorial director, romance and women's fiction (historical romance, Regency romance, Brava erotic romance, women's contemporary fiction); John Scognamiglio, editorial director, fiction (historical romance, Regency romance, women's contemporary fiction, gay and lesbian fiction and nonfiction, mysteries, suspense, mainstream fiction); Karen Thomas, editorial director, Dafina Books (African-American fiction and nonfiction); Audrey LaFehr, editorial director (women's fiction, thrillers); Gene Brissie, editor-in-chief, Citadel Press (narrative nonfiction, business, pop culture, how-to, biography, cooking, history and military history); Bob Shuman, senior editor, Citadel Press (politics, military, wicca, business, Judaica, sports); Jeremie Ruby-Strauss, senior editor (nonfiction, pop culture, pop reference, true crime); Gary Goldstein, senior editor (westerns, true crime, military, sports, how-to, narrative nonfiction); Richard Ember, editor, Citadel Press (biography, film, sports, New Age, spirituality); Miles Lott, assistant editor (mainstream fiction, thrillers, horror, women's fiction, general nonfiction, popular culture, entertainment); Hilary Sares, consulting editor (historical romance, Regency romance, women's fiction). Estab. 1975. Publishes hardcover and trade paperback originals,

mass market paperback originals and reprints. **Publishes over 500 titles/year. Receives 5,000 queries and 2,000 mss/year. 10% of books from first-time authors. Pays 6-15% royalty on retail price, or makes outright purchase. Offers $2,000 and up advance.** Publishes book 9-12 months after acceptance of ms. Accepts simultaneous submissions. Responds in 1 month to queries; 1 month to proposals; 4 months to mss. Book catalog online.

Imprints Kensington Books; Brava Books; Citadel Press; Dafina Books; Pinnacle Books; Zebra Books.

- Kensington recently purchased the assets of Carol Publishing Group.

O━ Kensington focuses on profitable niches and uses aggressive marketing techniques to support its books.

Nonfiction Biography, cookbook, gift book, how-to, humor, illustrated book, reference, self-help. Subjects include Americana, animals, business/economics, child guidance/parenting, contemporary culture, cooking/foods/nutrition, gay/lesbian, health/medicine (alternative), history, hobbies, memoirs, military/war, money/finance, multicultural, nature/environment, philosophy, psychology, recreation, regional, sex, sports, travel, true crime, women's issues/studies, pop culture, true crime, current events. *Agented submissions only. No unsolicited mss.* Reviews artwork/photos as part of ms package. Send photocopies.

Fiction Ethnic, gay/lesbian, historical, horror, mainstream/contemporary, multicultural, mystery, occult, romance (contemporary, historical, regency), suspense, western (epic), thrillers, women's. No science fiction/fantasy, experimental fiction, business texts or children's titles. *Agented submissions only. No unsolicited mss.*

Recent Title(s) *Sullivan's Law*, by Nancy Taylor Rosenberg (fiction); *Sex, Lies, and Politics*, by Larry Flynt (nonfiction).

Tips Agented submissions only, except for submissions to romance lines. For those lines, query with SASE or submit proposal package including 3 sample chapters, synopsis.

KENT STATE UNIVERSITY PRESS

P.O. Box 5190, Kent OH 44242-0001. (330)672-7913. Fax: (330)672-3104. Web site: www.kentstateuniversitypress.com. **Acquisitions:** Joanna H. Craig, editor-in-chief. Estab. 1965. Publishes hardcover and paperback originals and some reprints. **Publishes 30-35 titles/year. Nonauthor subsidy publishes 20% of books. Standard minimum book contract on net sales.** Responds in 4 months to queries. Book catalog free.

O━ Kent State publishes primarily scholarly works and titles of regional interest. Currently emphasizing US history, US literary criticism.

Nonfiction Biography, general nonfiction, scholarly. Subjects include anthropology/archeology, art/architecture, history, language/literature, regional, true crime, literary criticism, material culture, textile/fashion studies, US foreign relations. Especially interested in scholarly works in history (US and world) and US literary studies of high quality, any titles of regional interest for Ohio, scholarly biographies and general nonfiction. Send a letter of inquiry before submitting mss. Decisions based on in-house readings and 2 by outside scholars in the field of study. Enclose return postage.

KNOPF PUBLISHING GROUP

Imprint of Random House, Inc., 1745 Broadway, New York NY 10019. Web site: www.aaknopf.com. **Acquisitions:** Senior Editor. Estab. 1915. Publishes hardcover and paperback originals. **Royalty and advance vary.** Accepts simultaneous submissions. Responds in 2-6 months to queries. Book catalog for $7\frac{1}{2} \times 10\frac{1}{2}$ SAE with 5 first-class stamps; ms guidelines online.

Imprints Alfred A. Knopf; Everyman's Library; Pantheon Books; Schocken Books; Vintage Anchor Publishing (Vintage Books, Anchor Books).

- "We usually only accept work through an agent, but you may still send a query to our slush pile."

O━ Knopf is a general publisher of quality nonfiction and fiction.

Nonfiction General nonfiction, scholarly, book-length nonfiction, including books of scholarly merit. Subjects include general scholarly nonfiction. "A good nonfiction writer should be able to follow the latest scholarship in any field of human knowledge, and fill in the abstractions of scholarship for the benefit of the general reader by means of good, concrete, sensory reporting." Preferred length: 50,000-150,000 words. Submit query, 25-50 page sample, SASE. Reviews artwork/photos as part of ms package.

Fiction Publishes book-length fiction of literary merit by known or unknown writers. Length: 40,000-150,000 words. Submit query, 25-50 page sample, SASE.

Recent Title(s) *Soldiers and Slaves*, by Roger Cohen; *The Power of the Dog*, by Don Winslow; *Falling Water Rising*, by Franklin Toker.

KRAUSE PUBLICATIONS

Imprint of F+W Publications, Inc., 700 E. State St., Iola WI 54990. (715)445-2214. Fax: (715)445-4087. Web site: www.krause.com. **Acquisitions:** Acquisitions Editor. Publishes hardcover and trade paperback originals. **Publishes 170 titles/year. Receives 400 queries and 40 mss/year. 10% of books from first-time authors; 90% from unagented writers. Pays 9-12% royalty on net or makes outright purchase of $2,000-10,000.**

Offers $1,500-4,000 advance. Publishes book 18 months after acceptance of ms. Does not accept simultaneous submissions. Responds in 3 months to proposals; 2 months to mss. Book catalog for free or on Web site; ms guidelines free.

O→ "We are the world's largest hobby and collectibles publisher."

Nonfiction How-to, illustrated book, reference, technical, price guides. Subjects include hobbies (antiques, collectibles, toys), sports (outdoors, hunting, fishing), coins, firearms, knives, records, sewing, quilting, ceramics. Submit proposal package, including outline, 1-3 sample chapters, and letter explaining your project's unique contributions. Reviews artwork/photos as part of ms package. Send sample photos.

Recent Title(s) *Easy-to-Sew Playful Toys*, by Debra Quartermain (how-to); *The ABC's of Reloading*, by Bill Chevalier (how-to/reference).

Tips Audience consists of serious hobbyists. "Your work should provide a unique contribution to the special interest."

KREGEL PUBLICATIONS

Kregel, Inc., P.O. Box 2607, Grand Rapids MI 49501. (616)451-4775. Fax: (616)451-9330. Web site: www.kregelpublications.com. **Acquisitions:** Dennis R. Hillman, publisher. Estab. 1949. Publishes hardcover and trade paperback originals and reprints. **Publishes 90 titles/year. Receives 1,000 queries and 300 mss/year. 20% of books from first-time authors; 70% from unagented writers. Pays 8-16% royalty on wholesale price. Offers negotiable advance.** Publishes book 16 months after acceptance of ms. Ms guidelines online.

Imprints Editorial Portavoz (Spanish-language works); Kregel Academic & Professional; Kregel Kidzone.

O→ "Our mission as an evangelical Christian publisher is to provide—with integrity and excellence—trusted, Biblically-based resources that challenge and encourage individuals in their Christian lives. Works in theology and Biblical studies should reflect the historic, orthodox Protestant tradition."

Nonfiction "We serve evangelical Christian readers and those in career Christian service."

Fiction Religious (children's, general, inspirational, mystery/suspense, relationships), young adult. Fiction should be geared toward the evangelical Christian market. Wants "books with fast-paced, contemporary storylines presenting a strong Christian message in an engaging, entertaining style."

Recent Title(s) *Clopper, The Christmas Donkey*, by Emily King; *The Case for the Resurrection of Jesus*, by Gary Habermas and Michael Licona; *Firestorm*, by Jeanette Windle (mystery).

Tips "Our audience consists of conservative, evangelical Christians, including pastors and ministry students."

KRIEGER PUBLISHING CO.

P.O. Box 9542, Melbourne FL 32902-9542. (321)724-9542. Fax: (321)951-3671. E-mail: info@krieger-publishing.com. Web site: www.krieger-publishing.com. **Acquisitions:** Sharan B. Merriam and Ronald M. Cervero, series editor (adult education); David E. Kyvig, series director (local history); James B. Gardner, series editor (public history). Also publishes in the fields of history and space sciences. Estab. 1969. Publishes hardcover and paperback originals and reprints. **Publishes 30 titles/year. 30% of books from first-time authors; 100% from unagented writers. Pays royalty on net price.** Publishes book 9-18 months after acceptance of ms. Responds in 3 months to queries. Book catalog free.

Imprints Anvil Series; Orbit Series; Public History; Professional Practices in Adult Education and Lifelong Learning Series.

O→ "We are a short-run niche publisher providing accurate and well-documented scientific and technical titles for text and reference use, college level and higher."

Nonfiction Reference, technical, textbook, scholarly. Subjects include agriculture/horticulture, animals, education (adult), history, nature/environment, science (space), herpetology, chemistry, physics, engineering, veterinary medicine, natural history, math. Query with SASE. Reviews artwork/photos as part of ms package.

Recent Title(s) *The Contemporary Constitution*, by Joseph A. Melusky; *Snakes of the Americas*, by Bob L. Tipton.

WENDY LAMB BOOKS

Imprint of Random House Children's Books/Random House, Inc., 1745 Broadway, New York NY 10019. (212)782-9000. Web site: www.randomhouse.com. Estab. 2001. Publishes hardcover originals. **Pays royalty.** Accepts simultaneous submissions. Ms guidelines for #10 SASE.

- Literary fiction and nonfiction for readers 8-15. Query with SASE.

Nonfiction Children's/juvenile.

Fiction Juvenile (ages 2-18).

Poetry Submit 4 sample poems.

Tips "A query letter should briefly describe the book you want to write, the intended age group, and your publishing credentials, if any. If you like, you may send no more than 5 pages of the manuscript of shorter works (picture books) and a maximum of 10 pages of longer works (novels). Please do not send more than the specified amount. Also, do not send cassette tapes, videos, or other materials along with your query or excerpt. Manuscript pages will not be returned. Do not send original art."

LARK BOOKS

67 Broadway, Asheville NC 28801. (828)253-0467. Fax: (828)253-7952. Web site: www.larkbooks.com. President/Publisher: Carol Taylor. **Acquisitions:** Nicole McConville, submissions coordinator. Estab. 1976. Publishes hardcover and trade paperback originals and reprints. **Publishes 60 titles/year. Receives 300 queries and 100 mss/year. 80% of books from first-time authors; 90% from unagented writers. Offers up to $4,000 advance.** Publishes book 1 year after acceptance of ms. Accepts simultaneous submissions. Responds in 3 months to queries. Ms guidelines online.

- Lark Books publishes high quality, highly illustrated books, primarily in the crafts/leisure markets celebrating the creative spirit. We work closely with bookclubs. Our books are either how-to, 'gallery' or combination books."

Nonfiction Children's/juvenile, coffee table book, how-to, illustrated book. Subjects include hobbies, nature/environment, photography, crafts, books for enthusiasts. Query first. If asked, submit outline and 1 sample chapter, sample projects, TOC, visuals. Reviews artwork/photos as part of ms package. Send transparencies.

Recent Title(s) *Exquisite Little Knits, Design!*.

Tips "We publish both first-time and seasoned authors. In either case, we need to know that you have substantial expertise on the topic of the proposed book—that we can trust you to know what you're talking about. If you're great at your craft but not so great as a writer, you might want to work with us as a coauthor or as a creative consultant."

LAWYERS & JUDGES PUBLISHING CO.

P.O. Box 30040, Tucson AZ 85751-0040. (520)323-1500. Fax: (520)323-0055. E-mail: sales@lawyersandjudges.com. Web site: www.lawyersandjudges.com. **Acquisitions:** Steve Weintraub, president. Estab. 1963. Publishes professional hardcover and trade paperback originals. **Publishes 20 titles/year. Receives 200 queries and 60 mss/year. 15% of books from first-time authors; 100% from unagented writers. Pays 7-10% royalty on net receipts.** Publishes book 5 months after acceptance of ms. Accepts simultaneous submissions. Responds in 1 month to queries. Book catalog and ms guidelines free.

- Lawyers & Judges is a highly specific publishing company, reaching the legal, accident reconstruction, insurance, and medical fields.

Nonfiction Reference. Subjects include law, insurance, forensics, accident reconstruction. Submit proposal package including outline, sample chapter(s).

Recent Title(s) *Human Factors in Traffic Safety*; *Forensic Science Today*; *Terrorism Law, 3rd Ed.*

LEE & LOW BOOKS

95 Madison Ave., New York NY 10016. (212)779-4400. Fax: (212)532-6035. Web site: www.leeandlow.com. **Acquisitions:** Louise May, editor-in-chief. Estab. 1991. Publishes hardcover originals—picture books, middle-grade works only. **Publishes 12-16 titles/year. Pays royalty. Offers advance.** Accepts simultaneous submissions. Responds in 4 months to queries; 4 months to mss. Book catalog and ms guidelines online.

- "Our goals are to meet a growing need for books that address children of color, and to present literature that all children can identify with. We only consider multicultural children's books." Currently emphasizing material for 5-12 year olds. Sponsors a yearly New Voices Award for first-time picture book authors of color. Contest rules online at Web site or for SASE.

Nonfiction Children's/juvenile, illustrated book. Subjects include ethnic, multicultural.

Fiction Ethnic, juvenile, multicultural, illustrated. "We do not consider folktales, fairy tales, or animal stories." Send complete ms with cover letter or through an agent.

Recent Title(s) *John Lewis in the Lead*, by Jim Haskins and Kathleen Benson; *George Crum and the Saratoga Chip*, by Gaylia Taylor.

Tips "Of special interest are stories set in contemporary America. We are interested in fiction as well as nonfiction."

LEGACY PRESS

Imprint of Rainbow Publishers, P.O. Box 70130, Richmond VA 23255. (800)323-7337. **Acquisitions:** Christy Scannell, editor,. Estab. 1997. **Publishes 20 titles/year. Receives 250 queries and 100 mss/year. 50% of books from first-time authors. Pays royalty based on wholesale price. Offers negotiable advance.** Publishes book 1-3 years after acceptance of ms. Accepts simultaneous submissions. Book catalog for 9×12 SAE with 2 first-class stamps; ms guidelines for #10 SASE.

- "Legacy Press strives to publish Bible-based materials that inspire Christian spiritual growth and development in children." Currently emphasizing nonfiction for kids, particularly pre-teens and more specifically girls, although we are publishing boys and girls 2-12. No picture books, fiction without additional activities, poetry or plays.

Nonfiction Subjects include creative nonfiction, education, hobbies, religion. Submit outline, 3-5 sample chapters, market analysis, SASE.

Recent Title(s) *God and Me!* (series for girls); *Gotta Have God* (series for boys); *The Christian Girl's Guide To . . .* (series for girls).

Tips "We are looking for Christian versions of general market nonfiction for kids, as well as original ideas."

LEGEND BOOKS

69 Lansing St., Auburn NY 13021. (315)258-8012. **Acquisitions:** Joseph P. Berry, editor. Publishes paperback monographs, scholarly books, and college textbooks. **Publishes 15 titles/year. Receives 100 queries and 60 mss/year. 50% of books from first-time authors; 100% from unagented writers. Pays 20% royalty on net sales.** Publishes book 9 months after acceptance of ms. Accepts simultaneous submissions. Responds in 2 months to queries; 2 months to proposals; 2 months to mss.

O→ Legend Books publishes a variety of books used in the college classroom, including workbooks. However, it does not publish any books on mathematics or hard sciences.

Nonfiction Biography, scholarly, textbook, community/public affairs, speech/mass communication. Subjects include business/economics, child guidance/parenting, community, education, government/politics, health/medicine, history, humanities, philosophy, psychology, recreation, social sciences, sociology, sports, journalism, public relations, television. Query with SASE, or submit complete ms (include SASE if ms is to be returned). Reviews artwork/photos as part of ms package. Send photocopies.

Recent Title(s) *The Conversion of the King of Bissau*, by Timothy Coates, PhD (world history); *Values, Society & Evolution*, by H. James Birx, PhD (anthropology and sociology).

Tips "We seek college professors who actually teach courses for which their books are designed."

LEHIGH UNIVERSITY PRESS

B040 Christmas-Saucon Hall, 14 E. Packer Ave., Lehigh University, Bethlehem PA 18015. (610)758-3933. Fax: (610)758-6331. E-mail: inlup@lehigh.edu. Web site: www.lehigh.edu/library/lup. **Acquisitions:** Scott Paul Gordon, director. Estab. 1985. Publishes hardcover originals. **Publishes 10 titles/year. Receives 90-100 queries and 50-60 mss/year. 70% of books from first-time authors; 100% from unagented writers. Pays royalty.** Publishes book 18 months after acceptance of ms. Accepts simultaneous submissions. Responds in 3 months to queries. Book catalog and ms guidelines free.

O→ "Currently emphasizing works on 18th-century studies, history of technology, and literary criticism. Accepts all subjects of academic merit."

Nonfiction Lehigh University Press is a conduit for nonfiction works of scholarly interest to the academic community. Biography, reference, scholarly. Subjects include Americana, art/architecture, history, language/literature, science. Submit proposal package including 1 sample chapter and current CV.

Recent Title(s) *Francis Johnson*, by Charles K. Jones; *Reading and Riding*, by Eileen S. DeMarco; *Negotiator*, by Philip J. Bigger.

LEISURE BOOKS

Imprint of Dorchester Publishing Co., 200 Madison Ave., Suite 2000, New York NY 10016. (212)725-8811. Fax: (212)532-1054. Web site: www.dorchesterpub.com. **Acquisitions:** Leah Hultenschmidt, editor; Alicia Condon, editorial director; Don D'Auria, executive editor (westerns, thrillers, horror); Christopher Keeslar, senior editor. Estab. 1970. Publishes mass market paperback originals and reprints. Publishes romances, westerns, horror, chick lit and thrillers only. **Publishes 240 titles/year. 20% of books from first-time authors; 20% from unagented writers. Pays royalty on retail price. Offers negotiable advance.** Publishes book 18 months after acceptance of ms. Does not accept simultaneous submissions. Responds in 6 months to queries. Book catalog for free by calling (800)481-9191; ms guidelines online.

Imprints Love Spell (romance); Leisure (romance, western, thriller, horror); Making It (chick lit).

O→ Leisure Books/Love Spell is seeking historical, contemporary, time travel, paranormal romances and romantic suspense.

Fiction Horror, romance, suspense, western, chick lit. "All historical romance should be set pre-1900. Westerns should take place West of the Mississippi River before 1900. No sweet romance, science fiction or cozy mysteries." Query with SASE, or submit synopsis, first 3 chapters. "All manuscripts must be typed, double-spaced on one side, and left unbound."

Recent Title(s) *A Knight's Honor*, by Connie Mason (romance); *The Lake*, by Richard Laymon (horror); *Calendar Girl*, by Naomi Neale (chick lit).

LERNER PUBLISHING CO.

241 First Ave. N., Minneapolis MN 55401. (612)332-3344. Fax: (612)332-7615. Web site: www.lernerbooks.com. **Acquisitions:** Jennifer Zimian, nonfiction submissions editor; Zelda Wagner, fiction submissions editor. Estab. 1959. Publishes hardcover originals, trade paperback originals and reprints. Accepts simultaneous submissions. Book catalog for 9×12 SAE with $4.05 postage; ms guidelines online.

Imprints Millbrook Press; Twenty-First-Century Books; Carolrhoda Books; First Avenue Editions (paperback reprints for hard/soft deals only); Lerner Publications; LernerClassroom; Kar-Ben Publishing.

- Only accepts subsmissions in November. Anything sent in another month will be returned unopened.
- "Our goal is to publish children's books that educate, stimulate and stretch the imagination, foster global awareness, encourage critical thinking and inform, inspire and entertain."

Nonfiction Biography, children's/juvenile. Subjects include art/architecture, ethnic, history, nature/environment, science, sports. Query with SASE, or submit outline, 1-2 sample chapters.

Fiction Young adult (problem novels, sports, adventure, mystery). Looking for "well-written middle grade and young adult. *No adult fiction or single short stories*." Query with SASE, or submit outline, synopsis, 2 sample chapters.

Recent Title(s) *Secrets of a Civil War Submarine*, by Sally M. Walker; *Heart to Heart With Mallory*, by Laurie Friedman.

Tips "No alphabet, puzzle, song or text books, religious subject matter or plays. Submissions are accepted in the months of November only. Work received in any other month will be returned unopened. SASE required for authors who wish to have their material returned or business-sized SASE for response only. Submissions without an SASE will receive no reply. Please allow 5-7 months for a response. No phone calls."

⊘ ARTHUR A. LEVINE BOOKS

Imprint of Scholastic Inc., 557 Broadway, New York NY 10012. (212)343-4436. Web site: www.arthuralevinebooks.com. **Acquisitions:** Arthur Levine, editorial director. **Publishes 10-14 titles/year. Pays variable royalty on retail price. Offers variable advance.** Book catalog for 9×12 SASE.

Fiction Juvenile, picture books, young adult, middle grade novels. Query with SASE. *All unsolicited mss returned unopened*. "We are willing to work with first-time authors, with or without an agent. However, we only accept query letters."

Recent Title(s) *The Guild of Geniuses*, by Dan Santat; *Millicent Min, Girl Genius*, by Lisa Yee; *The Story of a Seagull and the Cat Who Taught Her How to Fly*, by Luis Sepulveda.

LIBRARIES UNLIMITED, INC.

88 Post Rd. W., Westport CT 06881. (800)225-5800. Fax: (203)222-1502. Web site: www.lu.com. **Acquisitions:** Barbara Ittner, acquisitions editor (public library titles); Sharon Coatney (school library titles); Sue Easun (academic library titles). Estab. 1964. Publishes hardcover and paperback originals. **Publishes 100 titles/year. Receives 400 queries and 100 mss/year. 50% of books from first-time authors; 100% from unagented writers.** Publishes book 9 months after acceptance of ms. Accepts simultaneous submissions. Responds in 1 month to queries; 2 months to proposals; 2 months to mss. Book catalog and ms guidelines online.

- Libraries Unlimited publishes resources for libraries, librarians, and educators. "We are currently emphasizing readers' advisory guides, academic reference works, readers' theatre, literary and technology resources."

Nonfiction Biography (collections), reference, textbook. Subjects include agriculture/horticulture, anthropology/archeology, art/architecture, business/economics, education, ethnic, health/medicine, history, language/literature, music/dance, philosophy, psychology, religion, science, sociology, women's issues/studies, technology. "We are interested in library applications and tools for all subject areas." Submit proposal package including outline, résumé, 1 sample chapter. Reviews artwork/photos as part of ms package. Send photocopies.

Recent Title(s) *Information Literacy: Essential Skills for the Information Age*, by Michael B. Eisenberg, Carrie A. Lowe, and Kathleen L. Spitzer; *Picture This! Using Picture Books for Character Education in the Classroom*, by Claire Gatrell Stephens.

Tips "We welcome any ideas that combine professional expertise, writing ability, and innovative thinking. Audience is librarians (school, public, academic, and special) and teachers (K-12)."

LIGUORI PUBLICATIONS

One Liguori Dr., Liguori MO 63057. (636)464-2500. Fax: (636)464-8449. Web site: www.liguori.org. Publisher: Harry Grile. **Acquisitions:** Daniel Michaels, acquisitions editor. Estab. 1947. Publishes paperback originals and reprints under the Ligouri and Libros Ligouri imprints. **Publishes 20-25 titles/year. Pays royalty, or makes outright purchase. Offers varied advance.** Publishes book 2 years after acceptance of ms. Does not accept simultaneous submissions. Responds in 2 months to queries; 2 months to proposals; 3 months to mss. Ms guidelines online.

Imprints Libros Liguori; Liguori Books; Liguori/Triumph; Liguori Lifespan.

O→ Liguori Publications, faithful to the charism of St. Alphonsus, is an apostolate within the mission of the Denver Province. Its mission, a collaborative effort of Redemptorists and laity, is to spread the gospel of Jesus Christ primarily through the print and electronic media. It shares in the Redemptorist priority of giving special attention to the poor and the most abandoned. Currently emphasizing practical spirituality, prayers and devotions, "how-to" spirituality.

Nonfiction Mss with Catholic sensibility. Self-help. Subjects include religion, spirituality. Mostly adult audience; limited children/juvenile. Query with SASE, or submit outline, 1 sample chapter.

LILLENAS PUBLISHING CO.

Imprint of Lillenas Drama Resources, P.O. Box 419527, Kansas City MO 64109. (816)931-1900. Fax: (816)412-8390. E-mail: drama@lillenas.com. Web site: www.lillenasdrama.com. **Acquisitions:** Kim Messer, product manager (Christian drama). Publishes mass market paperback and electronic originals. **Publishes 50+ titles/year; imprint publishes 12+ titles/year. Pays royalty on wholesale price, or makes outright purchase.**

Nonfiction Plays, collections of scripts. Subjects include religion, life issues. Query with SASE, or submit complete ms.

Ⓐ ⊘ LITTLE, BROWN AND CO. ADULT TRADE BOOKS

1271 Avenue of the Americas, New York NY 10020. (212)522-8700. Fax: (212)522-2067. Web site: www.twbookmark.com. Estab. 1837. Publishes hardcover originals and paperback originals and reprints.

- *Does not accept unsolicited mss.*

Recent Title(s) *The Way Out*, by Craig Childs; *The True and Outstanding Adventures of the Hunt Sisters*, by Elisabeth Robinson; *Searching for the Sound*, by Phil Lesh.

Ⓐ ⊘ LITTLE, BROWN AND CO., INC.

1271 Avenue of the Americas, New York NY 10017. Web site: www.twbookgroup.com. **Acquisitions:** Editorial Department, Trade Division. Estab. 1837. Publishes adult and juvenile hardcover and paperback originals, and reprints. **Pays royalty. Offers varying advance.** Does not accept simultaneous submissions. Ms guidelines online.

Imprints Little, Brown and Co. Adult Trade; Bulfinch Press; Back Bay; Little, Brown Books for Young Readers.

- *No unsolicited submissions. Agented submissions only.*

O→ "The general editorial philosophy for all divisions continues to be broad and flexible, with high quality and the promise of commercial success as always the first considerations."

Nonfiction Autobiography, biography, cookbook. Subjects include contemporary culture, cooking/foods/nutrition, history, memoirs, nature/environment, science, sports.

Fiction Experimental, literary, mainstream/contemporary, mystery, short story collections, suspense, thrillers/espionage, translations.

Ⓐ ⊘ LITTLE SIMON

Imprint of Simon & Schuster Children's Publishing Division, Simon & Schuster, 1230 Avenue of the Americas, New York NY 10020. (212)698-1295. Fax: (212)698-2794. Web site: www.simonsayskids.com. Publishes novelty and branded books only. **Offers advance and royalties.**

- *Currently not accepting unsolicited mss.*

O→ "Our goal is to provide fresh material in an innovative format for preschool to age 8. Our books are often, if not exclusively, format driven."

Nonfiction "We publish very few nonfiction titles." Children's/juvenile. No picture books. Query with SASE.

Fiction "Novelty books include many things that do not fit in the traditional hardcover or paperback format, such as pop-up, board book, scratch and sniff, glow in the dark, lift the flap, etc." Children's/juvenile. No picture books. Large part of the list is holiday-themed.

Recent Title(s) *Mother's Day Ribbons*, by Michelle Knudsen, illustrated by John Wallace; *Dear Zoo*, by Rod Campbell; *My Blankie*, by Patricia Ryan Lampl, illustrated by Valeria Petrone.

LLEWELLYN PUBLICATIONS

Imprint of Llewellyn Worldwide, Ltd., 2143 Wooddale Dr., Woodbury MN 55125. (800)THE-MOON. Fax: (651)291-1908. E-mail: billk@llewellyn.com. Web site: www.llewellyn.com. **Acquisitions:** Acquisitions Editor. Estab. 1901. Publishes trade and mass market paperback originals. **Publishes 100 titles/year. 30% of books from first-time authors; 90% from unagented writers. Pays 10% royalty on wholesale price, or retail price.** Accepts simultaneous submissions. Responds in 3 months to queries. Book catalog for 9×12 SAE with 4 first-class stamps.

Llewellyn publishes New Age fiction and nonfiction exploring "new worlds of mind and spirit." Currently emphasizing astrology, alternative health and healing, tarot. De-emphasizing fiction, channeling.

Nonfiction How-to, self-help. Subjects include cooking/foods/nutrition, health/medicine, nature/environment, New Age, psychology, women's issues/studies. Submit outline, sample chapter(s). Reviews artwork/photos as part of ms package.

Fiction "Authentic and educational, yet entertaining." Occult, spiritual (metaphysical).

Recent Title(s) *Authentic Spirituality*, by Richard N. Potter; *You Are Psychic*, by Debra Katz.

LOFT PRESS, INC.

P.O. Box 150, Fort Valley VA 22652. (540)933-6210. Web site: www.loftpress.com. **Acquisitions:** Ann A. Hunter, editor-in-chief. Publishes hardcover and trade paperback originals and reprints. **Publishes 12-20 titles/year; imprint publishes 6-8 titles/year. Receives 200 queries and 150 mss/year. 50% of books from first-time authors; 100% from unagented writers. Pays royalty on net receipts.** Publishes book 6 months after acceptance of ms. Ms guidelines online.

Imprints Punch Press, Eschat Press, Far Muse Press (for all contact Stephen R. Hunter, publisher).

Nonfiction Biography, coffee table book, how-to, technical, textbook. Subjects include Americana, art/architecture, business/economics, computers/electronic, government/politics, history, language/literature, memoirs, philosophy, regional, religion, science. Submit proposal package including outline, 1 sample chapter(s). Reviews artwork/photos as part of ms package. Send photocopies.

Fiction Literary, plays, poetry, poetry in translation, regional, short story collections. Submit proposal package including 1 sample chapter(s), synopsis.

Poetry Submit 5 sample poems.

Recent Title(s) *Who Is God*, by Mohan Rao; *Telly the White-Liver Woman*, by Isaac Chin; *Zula Remembers*, by Zula Dietrich.

LOUISIANA STATE UNIVERSITY PRESS

P.O. Box 25053, Baton Rouge LA 70894-5053. (225)578-6434. Fax: (225)578-6461. Web site: www.lsu.edu/lsupress. Director: MaryKatherine Callaway. Estab. 1935. Publishes hardcover and paperback originals, and reprints. Publishes 12 poetry titles per year and 1 work of original fiction as part of the Yellow Shoe Fiction series. **Publishes 80-90 titles/year. 33% of books from first-time authors; 95% from unagented writers. Pays royalty.** Publishes book 1 year after acceptance of ms. Does not accept simultaneous submissions. Responds in 1 month to queries. Book catalog and ms guidelines free.

Nonfiction Biography. Subjects include art/architecture, ethnic, government/politics, history, language/literature, music/dance, photography, regional, women's issues/studies, geography and environmental studies. Query with SASE, or submit outline, sample chapter(s).

Recent Title(s) *Habitat*, by Brendan Galvin (poetry); *If the Sky Falls*, by Nicholas Montemarano (fiction); *Toxic Drift* (history/environmental studies).

Tips "Our audience includes scholars, intelligent laymen, general audience."

LOVE INSPIRED

Imprint of Steeple Hill, 233 Broadway, Suite 1001, New York NY 10279. (212)553-4200. Fax: (212)227-8969. Web site: www.steeplehill.com. **Acquisitions:** Joan Marlow Golan, executive editor (inspirational fiction); Krista Stroever, associate senior editor (inspirational fiction); Melissa Endlich, editor (inspirational fiction); Diane Dietz, assistant editor (inspirational fiction). Estab. 1997. Publishes mass market paperback originals. **Publishes 78-90 titles/year. Pays royalty on retail price. Offers advance.** Does not accept simultaneous submissions. Responds in 3 months to queries; 3 months to proposals; 3 months to mss. Ms guidelines online.

Fiction Religious, romance. "The Love Inspired line is a series of contemporary, inspirational romances that feature Christian characters facing the many challenges of life and love in today's world. We only publish inspirational romance between 60,000 and 65,000 words." Query with SASE.

Recent Title(s) *Blessed Vows*, by Jillian Hart; *Sugar Plums for Dry Creek*, by Janet Tronstad.

Tips "Please read our guidelines."

LOVE INSPIRED SUSPENSE

Imprint of Steeple Hill, 233 Broadway, Suite 1001, New York NY 10279. (212)553-4200. Fax: (212)227-8969. Web site: www.steeplehill.com. **Acquisitions:** Joan Marlow Golan, executive editor (inspirational fiction); Krista Stroever, associate senior editor (inspirational fiction); Melissa Endlich, editor (inspirational fiction); Diane Dietz, assistant editor (inspirational fiction). Estab. 1997. Publishes mass market paperback originals. **Publishes 78-90 titles/year. Pays royalty on retail price. Offers advance.** Does not accept simultaneous submissions. Responds in 3 months to queries; 3 months to proposals; 3 months to mss. Ms guidelines online.

Fiction Religious, romance, suspense. "This new brand is a series of edge-of-the-seat, comtemporary romantic suspense tales or intrigue and romance featuring Christian characters facing challenges to their faith and to their lives. We only publish novels between 60,000 and 65,000 words." Query with SASE.

Recent Title(s) *Die Before Nightfall*, by Shirlee McCoy; *Under Cover of Darkness*, by Elizabeth White.

Tips "Please read our guidelines."

LOVE SPELL

Imprint of Dorchester Publishing Co., Inc., 200 Madison Ave., Suite 2000, New York NY 10016. (212)725-8811. Fax: (212)532-1054. Web site: www.dorchesterpub.com. **Acquisitions:** Leah Hultenschmidt, editor; Christopher Keeslar, senior editor; Alicia Condon, editorial director. Publishes mass market paperback originals. **Publishes 48 titles/year. Receives 1,500-2,000 queries and 150-500 mss/year. 30% of books from first-time authors; 25-30% from unagented writers. Pays royalty on retail price. Offers variable advance.** Publishes book 1 year after acceptance of ms. Does not accept simultaneous submissions. Responds in 8 months to mss. Book catalog for free or by calling (800)481-9191; ms guidelines online.

- Love Spell publishes the many sub-genres of romance: time-travel, paranormal, futuristic and romantic suspense. "Despite the exotic settings, we are still interested in character-driven plots."

Fiction Romance (futuristic, time travel, paranormal, romantic suspense), whimsical contemporaries. "Books industry-wide are getting shorter; we're interested in 90,000 words." Query with SASE, or submit synopsis. No material will be returned without SASE. No queries by fax or e-mail. "All manuscripts must be typed, double-spaced on one side, and left unbound."

Recent Title(s) *The Deadliest Denial*, by Colleen Thompson; *Shadow Touch*, by Marjorie M. Liu.

LOYOLA PRESS

3441 N. Ashland Ave., Chicago IL 60657-1397. (773)281-1818. Fax: (773)281-0152. E-mail: editorial@loyolapress.com. Web site: www.loyolapress.org. **Acquisitions:** Joseph Durepos, acquisitions editor. Publishes hardcover and trade paperback. **Publishes 20-30 titles/year. Receives 500 queries/year. Pays standard royalties. Offers reasonable advance.** Accepts simultaneous submissions. Book catalog and ms guidelines online.

Imprints Loyola Classics (new editions of classic Catholic literature).

Nonfiction Subjects include religion, spirituality, inspirational, prayer, Catholic life, parish and adult faith formation resources with a special focus on Ignatian spirituality and Jesuit history. Query with SASE.

Recent Title(s) *My Life With the Saints*, by James Martin, S.J; *Heroic Leadership*, by Chris Lowney; *The Shoemaker's Gospel*, by Daniel Brent.

Tips "We're looking for motivated authors who have a passion for the Catholic tradition, to prayer and spirituality, and to helping readers respond to the existence of God in their lives."

[N] LRP PUBLICATIONS, INC.

P.O. Box 980, Horsham PA 19044. (215)784-0860. Fax: (215)784-9639. E-mail: custserve@lrp.com. Web site: www.lrp.com. **Acquisitions:** See Web site for contacts by product group. Estab. 1977. Publishes hardcover and trade paperback originals. **Pays royalty.** Does not accept simultaneous submissions. Book catalog and ms guidelines free.

Nonfiction Reference. Subjects include business/economics, education. Submit proposal package including outline.

THE LYONS PRESS

Imprint of The Globe Pequot Press, Inc., Box 480, 246 Goose Lane, Guilford CT 06437. (203)458-4500. Fax: (203)458-4668. Web site: www.lyonspress.com. **Acquisitions:** Jay Cassell, editorial director (fishing, hunting, survival, military, history); Tom McCarthy, senior editor (sports & fitness, history, outdoor adventure, current events); George Donahue, senior editor (military history, martial arts, narrative nonfiction, sports, current affairs); Ann Treistman, senior editor (narrative nonfiction, adventure, sports, animals, cooking); Jay McCullough, editor (narrative nonfiction, adventure, military, espionage, international current events, history); Holly Rubino, associate editor (narrative nonfiction, home); Lilly Golden, editor-at-large (nature, narrative nonfiction); Lisa Purcell, editor-at-large (history, adventure, narrative nonfiction); Steve Price, editor-at-large (equestrian). Estab. 1984 (Lyons & Burford), 1997 (The Lyons Press). Publishes hardcover and trade paperback originals and reprints. **Publishes 300 titles/year. 50% of books from first-time authors; 30% from unagented writers. Pays 5-10% royalty on wholesale price. Offers $2,000-7,000 advance.** Publishes book 1 year after acceptance of ms. Accepts simultaneous submissions. Responds in 2 months to queries; 2 months to proposals; 3 months to mss. Book catalog and ms guidelines online.

- The Lyons Press has teamed up to develop books with The Explorers Club, Orvis, L.L. Bean, *Field & Stream*, Outward Bound, Buckmasters, and *Golf Magazine*.
- The Lyons Press publishes practical and literary books, chiefly centered on outdoor subjects—natural history, all sports, gardening, horses, fishing, hunting, survival, self-reliant living.

Nonfiction Biography, how-to, reference. Subjects include agriculture/horticulture, Americana, animals, cooking/foods/nutrition, history, military/war, nature/environment, recreation, sports, adventure, fitness. "Visit our Web site and note the featured categories." Query with SASE, or submit proposal package including outline, 3 sample chapters. marketing description. Reviews artwork/photos as part of ms package. Send photocopies or nonoriginal prints.
Recent Title(s) *Believe*, by Buck Brannaman (horses); *The Orvis Ultimate Book of Fly Fishing*, by Tom Rosenbauer (fishing); *Lost in Tibet*, by Richard Starks and Miriam Murcutt (adventure/military history).

⊘ MACADAM/CAGE PUBLISHING, INC.

155 Sansome St., Suite 550, San Francisco CA 94104. (415)986-7502. Fax: (415)986-7414. Web site: www.macadamcage.com. Publisher: David Poindexter. **Acquisitions:** Manuscript Submissions. Estab. 1999. Publishes hardcover and trade paperback originals. **Publishes 25-30 titles/year. Receives 5,000 queries and 1,500 mss/year. 75% of books from first-time authors; 50% from unagented writers. Pays negotiable royalties. Offers negotiable advance.** Publishes book up to 1 year after acceptance of ms. Accepts simultaneous submissions.

- *No unsolicited mss accepted at this time.*

O→ MacAdam/Cage publishes quality works of literary fiction that are carefully crafted and tell a bold story. De-emphasizing romance, poetry, Christian or New Age mss.

Nonfiction Biography. Subjects include history, memoirs, science, social sciences. "Narrative nonfiction that reads like fiction." No self-help or New Age. No unsolicited mss accepted at this time.
Fiction Historical, literary, mainstream/contemporary. No electronic or faxed submissions. No romance, science fiction, Christian, New Age. No unsolicited submissions accepted at this time.
Recent Title(s) *How to be Lost*, by Amanda Eyre Ward (fiction); *The Time Traveler's Wife*, by Audrey Niffenegger (fiction); *Pinkerton's Sister*, by Peter Rushforth (fiction).
Tips "We like to keep in close contact with writers. We publish for readers of quality fiction and nonfiction."

Ⓐ ⊘ MARINER BOOKS

Houghton Mifflin Trade Division, 222 Berkeley St., Boston MA 02116. (617)351-5000. Fax: (617)351-1202. Web site: www.hmco.com. Estab. 1997. Publishes trade paperback originals and reprints. **Pays royalty on retail price, or makes outright purchase. Offers variable advance.** Book catalog free.

O→ Houghton Mifflin books give shape to ideas that educate, inform and delight. Mariner has an eclectic list that notably embraces fiction.

Nonfiction Biography. Subjects include education, government/politics, history, nature/environment, philosophy, science, sociology, political thought. *Agented submissions only.*
Fiction Literary, mainstream/contemporary. *Agented submissions only.*
Recent Title(s) *The End of Oil*, by Paul Roberts (politics/environment); *The Namesake*, by Jhumpa Lahiri (literary fiction); *Bury the Chains*, by Adam Hochschild (history).

⊘ MARLOWE & CO.

Imprint of Avalon Publishing Group, 245 W. 17th St., 11th Floor, New York NY 10011. (212)981-9919. Fax: (212)375-2571. Web site: www.avalonpub.com. Publisher: Matthew Lore. Estab. 1994.

O→ Marlowe & Co. publishes widely in the areas of health and fitness, food and cooking, psychology and personal growth, religion and spirituality, current affairs, pregnancy and parenting, and folklore and mythology.

Nonfiction Self-help. Subjects include health and fitness, food and cooking, psychology and personal growth, religion and spirituality, current affairs, pregnancy and parenting, and folklore and mythology. *No unsolicited mss.*
Recent Title(s) *Anti-Aging Plan*, by Roy L. Walford, MD and Lisa Walford; *Away With Wrinkles*, by Nick Lowe; *Bike for Life*, by Roy M. Wallack and Bill Katovsky.

MARVEL COMICS

10 E. 40th St., New York NY 10016. Web site: www.marvel.com. Publishes hardcover originals and reprints, trade paperback reprints, mass market comic book originals, electronic reprints. **Pays on a per page work for hire basis or creator-owned which is then contracted. Pays negotiable advance.** Does not accept simultaneous submissions. Responds in 3-5 weeks to queries. Ms guidelines online.
Fiction Adventure, comic books, fantasy, horror, humor, science fiction, young adult. "Our shared universe needs new heroes and villains; books for younger readers and teens needed." Submit inquiry letter, idea submission form (download from Web site), SASE.
Tips Marvel currently appeals to 12-30 year-old males. "We'd like to expand that both up and down the age range. We're looking for strong voices and people who have read things beyond the last 40 years of comics publishing. Life experience helps a lot."

MC PRESS

125 N. Woodland Trail, Double Oak TX 75077. Fax: (682)831-0701. E-mail: mlee@mcpressonline.com. Web site: www.mcpressonline.com. **Acquisitions:** Merrikay Lee, president (computer). Estab. 2001. Publishes trade paperback originals. **Publishes 40 titles/year; imprint publishes 20 titles/year. Receives 100 queries and 50 mss/year. 5% of books from first-time authors; 5% from unagented writers. Pays 10-16% royalty on wholesale price.** Publishes book 5 months after acceptance of ms. Accepts simultaneous submissions. Responds in 1 month to queries; 1 month to proposals; 1 month to mss. Book catalog and ms guidelines free.

Imprints MC Press, IBM Press.

Nonfiction Technical. Subjects include computers/electronic. "We specialize in computer titles targeted at IBM technologies." Submit proposal package including outline, 2 sample chapter(s), abstract. Reviews artwork/photos as part of ms package. Send photocopies.

Recent Title(s) *Understanding the IBM Web Facing Tool*, by Claus Weiss and Emily Bruner (computer); *Eclipse Step-by-Step*, by Jae Pluta (computer).

MCBOOKS PRESS

ID Booth Building, 520 N. Meadow St., Ithaca NY 14850. (607)272-2114. Fax: (607)273-6068. E-mail: jackie@mcbooks.com. Web site: www.mcbooks.com. Publisher: Alexander G. Skutt. **Acquisitions:** Jackie Swift, editorial director. Estab. 1979. Publishes trade paperback and hardcover originals and reprints. **Publishes 20 titles/year. Pays 5-10% royalty on retail price. Offers $1,000-5,000 advance.** Accepts simultaneous submissions. Responds in 3 months to queries; 3 months to proposals. online.

- "We can only consider the highest quality projects in our narrow interest areas."
- Currently emphasizing vegetarian, sports memoirs and unique events, upstate regional New York.

Nonfiction Subjects include vegetarian titles (no recipe books) and lesser known sports. "While we still publish historical fiction, our list is full for the immediate future. Authors' ability to promote a plus." *No unsolicited mss.* Query with SASE.

Fiction Historical, nautical, naval and military historical. Query with SASE.

Recent Title(s) *Tenacious*, by Julian Stockwin; *Inside the Ropes*, by Arthur Mercante; *Better Than Peanut Butter & Jelly, 2nd Ed.*, by Marty Mattare and Wendy Muldawer.

MARGARET K. MCELDERRY BOOKS

Imprint of Simon & Schuster Children's Publishing Division, Simon & Schuster, 1230 Sixth Ave., New York NY 10020. (212)698-2761. Fax: (212)698-2797. Web site: www.simonsayskids.com. **Acquisitions:** Emma D. Dryden, vice president/editorial director; Karen Wojtyla, senior editor; Sarah Sevier, associate editor. Estab. 1971. Publishes quality material for preschoolers to 18-year-olds. Publishes hardcover originals. **Publishes 30 titles/year. Receives 4,000 queries/year. 15% of books from first-time authors; 50% from unagented writers. Average print order is 5,000-10,000 for a first middle grade or young adult book; 7,500-20,000 for a first picture book. Pays royalty on hardcover retail price: 10% fiction; picture book, 5% author and 5% illustrator. Offers $5,000-8,000 advance for new authors.** Publishes book up to 3 years after acceptance of ms. Ms guidelines for #10 SASE.

- "We are more interested in superior writing and illustration than in a particular 'type' of book." Currently emphasizing young picture books and funny middle grade fiction.

Nonfiction Biography, children's/juvenile. Subjects include history, adventure. "Read. The field is competitive. See what's been done and what's out there before submitting. Looks for originality of ideas, clarity and felicity of expression, well-organized plot and strong characterization (fiction) or clear exposition (nonfiction); quality. Accept query letters with SASE only." *No unsolicited mss.*

Fiction Adventure, fantasy, historical, mainstream/contemporary, mystery, picture books, young adult (or middle grade), All categories (fiction and nonfiction) for juvenile and young adult. "We will consider any category. Results depend on the quality of the imagination, the artwork, and the writing." *No unsolicited mss.* Send query letter with SASE only for picture books; query letter with first 3 chapters, SASE for middle grade and young adult novels.

Poetry *No unsolicited mss.* Query, or submit 3 sample poems.

Recent Title(s) *Bear Stays Up for Christmas*, by Karma Wilson, illustrated by Jane Chapman (picture book); *Indigo's Star*, by Hilary McKay (middle-grade fiction); *The Legend of Buddy Bush*, by Shelia P. Moses (teen fiction).

Tips "Read! The children's book field is competitive. See what's been done and what's out there before submitting. We look for high quality: an originality of ideas, clarity and felicity of expression, a well-organized plot, and strong character-driven stories."

MCFARLAND & CO., INC., PUBLISHERS

Box 611, Jefferson NC 28640. (336)246-4460. Fax: (336)246-5018. E-mail: info@mcfarlandpub.com. Web site: www.mcfarlandpub.com. **Acquisitions:** Steve Wilson, executive editor (automotive, general); Virginia Tobiassen, editorial development chief (general, medieval history, bilingual works); Gary Mitchem, acquisitions editor (general, baseball). Estab. 1979. Publishes hardcover and "quality" paperback originals; a "nontrade" publisher. **Publishes 290 titles/year. 70% of books from first-time authors; 95% from unagented writers. Pays 10-12½% royalty on net receipts.** Publishes book 10 months after acceptance of ms. Responds in 1 month to queries. Ms guidelines online.

- McFarland publishes serious nonfiction in a variety of fields, including general reference, performing arts, sports (particularly baseball); women's studies, librarianship, literature, Civil War, history and international studies. Currently emphasizing medieval history, automotive history, Spanish-English bilingual works. De-emphasizing memoirs.

Nonfiction Reference (and scholarly), scholarly, professional monographs. Subjects include art/architecture, business/economics, contemporary culture, ethnic, film/cinema/stage, health/medicine, history, music/dance, recreation, sociology, sports (very strong), women's issues/studies (very strong), world affairs, African-American studies (very strong), chess, Civil War, drama/theater, cinema/radio/TV (very strong), librarianship (very strong), pop culture, world affairs (very strong). Reference books are particularly wanted—fresh material (i.e., not in head-to-head competition with an established title). "We prefer manuscripts of 250 or more double-spaced pages or at least 75,000 words." No fiction, New Age, exposés, poetry, children's books, devotional/inspirational works, Bible studies, or personal essays. Query with SASE, or submit outline, sample chapter(s). Reviews artwork/photos as part of ms package.

Recent Title(s) *Broadway Musicals, 1943-2004*, by John Stewart; *The Jordan Automobile*, by James H. Lackey; *The Christmas Encyclopedia, 2nd Ed.*, by William D. Crump.

Tips "We want well-organized knowledge of an area in which there is not information coverage at present, plus reliability so we don't feel we have to check absolutely everything. Our market is worldwide and libraries are an important part." McFarland also publishes the *Journal of Information Ethics* and *North Korean Review*.

MCGRAW-HILL TRADE

Imprint of The McGraw-Hill Companies, 2 Penn Plaza, New York NY 10121-2298. Web site: www.books.mcgraw-hill.com. Publisher: Philip Ruppel. Editor-in-Chief: Jeffrey Krames. **Acquisitions:** Jonathan Eaton, editorial director (International Marine/Ragged Mountain Press); Barbara Gilson, editorial director (Schaum's Outlines). Accepts simultaneous submissions. Ms guidelines online.

- Publisher not responsible for returning mss or proposals.
- McGraw Hill Trade is a publishing leader in business/investing, management, careers, self-help, consumer health, language reference, test preparation, sports/recreation, and general interest titles.

Nonfiction How-to, reference, self-help, technical. Subjects include business/economics, child guidance/parenting, education (study guides), health/medicine, money/finance, sports (fitness), management, consumer reference, English and foreign language reference. "Current, up-to-date, original ideas are needed. Good self-promotion is key." Submit proposal package including outline, concept of book, competition and market info, cv.

Recent Title(s) *World Out of Balance*, by Paul A. Laudicina; *You Play to Win the Game*, by Herman Edwards and Shelly Smith; *SAT Vocabulary Express*, by Jacqueline Byrne and Michael Ashley.

MCGRAW-HILL/OSBORNE MEDIA

The McGraw-Hill Companies, 2100 Powell St., 10th Floor, Emeryville CA 94608. (800)227-0900. Web site: www.osborne.com. Estab. 1979. Publishes computer trade paperback originals. Book catalog and ms guidelines online.

- Publishes self-paced computer training materials.

Nonfiction Reference, technical. Subjects include computers/electronic, software (and hardware). Submit proposal package including outline, sample chapter(s), résumé, competition analysis, SASE. Reviews artwork/photos as part of ms package.

Tips "A leader in self-paced training and skills development tools on information technology and computers."

N ME & MI PUBLISHING

English-Spanish Foundation, 128 South County Farm, Wheaton IL 60187. Fax: (630)588-9804. E-mail: m3@memima.com. Web site: www.memima.com. **Acquisitions:** Mark Wesley, acquisition editor (pre-K-1). Estab. 2001. Publishes hardcover originals. **Publishes 10 titles/year. Receives 30 queries and 30 mss/year. 30% of books from first-time authors; 70% from unagented writers. Pays 5% royalty on wholesale price, or makes outright purchase of $1,000-3,000.** Publishes book 1 year after acceptance of ms. Accepts simultaneous submissions. Responds in 1 month to queries; 3 months to proposals; 4 months to mss. Book catalog online; ms guidelines by e-mail.

Nonfiction Children's/juvenile. Subjects include ethnic, language/literature, multicultural. Submit complete ms. Reviews artwork/photos as part of ms package. Send photocopies.

Tips "Our audience is pre-K to 2nd grade. Our books are bilingual (Spanish and English)."

MEADOWBROOK PRESS

5451 Smetana Dr., Minnetonka MN 55343. (952)930-1100. Fax: (952)930-1940. Web site: www.meadowbrookpress.com. **Acquisitions:** Submissions Editor. Estab. 1975. Publishes trade paperback originals and reprints. **Publishes 12 titles/year. Receives 1,500 queries/year. 10% of books from first-time authors. Pays 7½% royalty. Offers small advance.** Publishes book 18 months-2 years after acceptance of ms. Accepts simultaneous submissions. Responds only if interested to queries. Book catalog for #10 SASE; ms guidelines online.

- Meadowbrook is a family-oriented press which specializes in parenting and pregnancy books, children's poetry books.

Nonfiction How-to, reference. Subjects include child guidance/parenting, cooking/foods/nutrition, pregnancy, childbirth, party planning, children's activities, relationships. "We prefer a query first; then we will request an outline and/or sample material." Send for guidelines. No children's fiction, academic, or biography. Query or submit outline with sample chapters.

Poetry Children's poetry books.

Recent Title(s) *Tinkle, Tinkle, Little Tot*, by Bruce Lansky, Robert Pottle and friends (childcare); *The Official Lamaze Guide*, by Judith Lothion and Charlotte DeVries (pregnancy).

Tips "Always send for guidelines before submitting material. Always submit nonreturnable copies; we do not respond to queries or submissions unless interested."

MENASHA RIDGE PRESS

P.O. Box 43673, Birmingham AL 35243. (205)322-0439. E-mail: rhelms@menasharidge.com. Web site: www.menasharidge.com. **Acquisitions:** Molly Merkle, associate publisher (travel, reference); Russell Helms, senior acquisitions editor. Publishes hardcover and trade paperback originals. **Publishes 20 titles/year. 30% of books from first-time authors; 85% from unagented writers. Pays varying royalty. Offers varying advance.** Publishes book 1 year after acceptance of ms. Accepts simultaneous submissions. Responds in 2 months to queries. Book catalog for 9×12 SAE with 4 first-class stamps.

- Menasha Ridge Press publishes "distinctive books in the areas of outdoor sports, travel, and diving. Our authors are among the best in their fields."

Nonfiction How-to, humor, travel guides. Subjects include recreation (outdoor), sports (adventure), travel, outdoors. "Most concepts are generated in-house, but a few come from outside submissions." Submit proposal package including résumé, synopsis. Reviews artwork/photos as part of ms package.

Recent Title(s) *Sex in the Outdoors*, by Buck Tilton.

Tips Audience is 25-60, 14-18 years' education, white collar and professional, $30,000 median income, 75% male, 55% east of the Mississippi River.

MENC

The National Association for Music Education, 1806 Robert Fulton Dr., Reston VA 20191-4348. Fax: (703)860-9443. E-mail: ashleyo@menc.org. Web site: www.menc.org. **Acquisitions:** Frances Ponick, director of publications; Ashley Opp, assistant acquisitions editor. Estab. 1907. Publishes hardcover and trade paperback originals. **Publishes 15 titles/year. Receives 75 queries and 50 mss/year. 40% of books from first-time authors; 100% from unagented writers. Pays royalty on retail price.** Publishes book 1-2 years after acceptance of ms. Does not accept simultaneous submissions. Responds in 2 months to queries; 4 months to proposals. Book catalog and ms guidelines online.

Nonfiction General nonfiction, how-to, reference, scholarly, textbook. Subjects include child guidance/parenting, education, multicultural, music/dance, music education. Mss evaluated by professional music educators. Submit proposal package including outline, 1-3 sample chapter(s), author bio, CV, marketing strategy.

Tips "Look online for book proposal guidelines. No telephone calls. We are committed to music education books that will serve as the very best resources for music educators, students and their parents."

MERIWETHER PUBLISHING, LTD.

885 Elkton Dr., Colorado Springs CO 80907-3557. (719)594-4422. Fax: (719)594-9916. E-mail: merpeds@aol.com. Web site: www.meriwetherpublishing.com; www.contemporarydrama.com. **Acquisitions:** Arthur Zapel, Theodore Zapel, Rhonda Wray, editors. Estab. 1969. Publishes paperback originals and reprints. **50% of books from first-time authors; 90% from unagented writers. Pays 10% royalty, or makes outright purchase.** Publishes book 6-12 months after acceptance of ms. Accepts simultaneous submissions. Responds in 3 weeks to queries; 2 months to mss. Book catalog and ms guidelines for $2 postage.

- Meriwether publishes theater/arts books, games and videos; speech resources; plays, skits, and musicals; and drama resources for gifted students. "We specialize in books on the theatre arts and religious plays for Christmas, Easter, and youth activities. We also publish musicals for high school performers and churches." Currently emphasizing how-to books for theatrical arts and church youth activities.

Nonfiction "We publish unusual textbooks or trade books related to the communication of performing arts and how-to books on staging, costuming, lighting, etc." How-to, reference, textbook. Subjects include performing arts, theater/drama. "We prefer mainstream religion theatre titles." Query, or submit outline/synopsis and sample chapters.

Fiction Plays and musical comedies for middle grades through college only. Mainstream/contemporary, plays (and musicals), religious (children's plays and religious Christmas and Easter plays), suspense, all in playscript format, comedy. Query with SASE.

Recent Title(s) *100 Great Monologs*, by Rebecca Young; *Group Improvisation*, by Peter Gwinn; *112 Acting Games*, by Gavin Levy.

Tips "Our educational books are sold to teachers and students at college, high school, and middle school levels. Our religious books are sold to youth activity directors, pastors, and choir directors. Our trade books are directed at the public with a tie to the performing arts. Another group of buyers is the professional theater, radio, and TV category. We focus more on books of plays and short scenes and textbooks on directing, staging, make-up, lighting, etc."

MERRIAM PRESS

218 Beech St., Bennington VT 05201-2611. (802)447-0313. E-mail: ray@merriam-press.com. Web site: www.merriam-press.com. Publishes hardcover and softcover originals and reprints. **Publishes 12+ titles/year. 70-90% of books from first-time authors; 95% from unagented writers. Pays 10% royalty on actual selling price.** Publishes book 1 year or less after acceptance of ms. Does not accept simultaneous submissions. Responds quickly (e-mail preferred) to queries. Book catalog for $1 or visit Web site to view all available titles and access writer's guidelines and info.

O→ Merriam Press publishes only military history - particularly World War II history.

Nonfiction Biography, illustrated book, reference, technical. Subjects include military/war (World War II). Query with SASE or by e-mail first. Reviews artwork/photos as part of ms package. Send photocopies or on floppy disk/CD.

Recent Title(s) *Playing for Time*, by Lodwock Alford; *A Doctor's Vietnam Journal*, by Carl E. Bartecchi; *Letters From the Front*, by Robert Lowery.

Tips "Our books are geared for military historians, collectors, model kit builders, wargamers, veterans, general enthusiasts. We do not publish any fiction or poetry, only WWII military history."

METAL POWDER INDUSTRIES FEDERATION

105 College Rd. E., Princeton NJ 08540. (609)452-7700. Fax: (609)987-8523. E-mail: info@mpif.org. Web site: www.mpif.org. **Acquisitions:** Jim Adams, director of technical services; Peggy Lebedz, assistant publications manager. Estab. 1946. Publishes hardcover originals. **Publishes 10 titles/year. Pays 3-12½% royalty on wholesale or retail price. Offers $3,000-5,000 advance.** Responds in 1 month to queries.

O→ Metal Powder Industries publishes monographs, textbooks, handbooks, design guides, conference proceedings, standards, and general titles in the field of powder metallurgy or particulate materials.

Nonfiction Work must relate to powder metallurgy or particulate materials. Technical, textbook.

Recent Title(s) *Advances in Powder Metallurgy and Particulate Materials* (conference proceeding).

MICHIGAN STATE UNIVERSITY PRESS

1405 S. Harrison Rd., Manly Miles Bldg., Suite 25, East Lansing MI 48823-5202. (517)355-9543. Fax: (517)432-2611. E-mail: msupress@msu.edu. Web site: www.msupress.msu.edu. **Acquisitions:** Martha Bates, acquisitions editor. Estab. 1947. Publishes hardcover and softcover originals. **Pays variable royalty.** Does not accept simultaneous submissions. Book catalog and ms guidelines for 9×12 SASE or online.

- Distributes books for: University of Calgary Press, Penumbra Press, National Museum of Science (UK), African Books Collective, University of Alberta Press, University of Manitoba Press.

O→ Michigan State University publishes scholarly books that further scholarship in their particular field. In addition, they publish nonfiction that addresses, in a more contemporary way, social concerns, such as diversity, civil rights, and the environment. They also publish literary fiction and poetry.

Nonfiction Scholarly. Subjects include Americana (American studies), business/economics, creative nonfiction, ethnic (Afro-American studies), government/politics, history (contemporary civil rights), language/literature, regional (Great Lakes regional, Canadian studies), women's issues/studies. Submit proposal/outline and sample chapter. Reviews artwork/photos as part of ms package.

Recent Title(s) *5 Years of the 4th Genre*, edited by Martha A. Bates; *Jewish Life in the Industrial Promised Land, 1855-2005*, by Nora Faires and Nancy Hanflik; *My Father on a Bicycle*, by Patricia Clark.

N MICROSOFT PRESS

E-mail: 4bkideas@microsoft.com. Web site: www.microsoft.com/learning/books. **Acquisitions:** Editor. Book proposal guidelines available online.

O→ "We place a great deal of emphasis on your proposal. A proposal provides us with a basis for evaluating the idea of the book and how fully your book fulfills its purpose."

Nonfiction How-to, multimedia, technical. Subjects include software. "A book proposal should consist of the following information: a table of contents, a résumé with author biography, a writing sample, and a questionnaire."

MILKWEED EDITIONS

1011 Washington Ave. S., Suite 300, Minneapolis MN 55415. (612)332-3192. Fax: (612)215-2550. Web site: www.milkweed.org. **Acquisitions:** Daniel Slager, editor-in-chief; The Editors, first readers (fiction, nonfiction, children's fiction, poetry). Estab. 1980. Publishes hardcover originals and paperback originals and reprints. **Publishes 20 titles/year. 30% of books from first-time authors; 70% from unagented writers. Pays 6% royalty on retail price. Offers varied advance.** Publishes book 1-2 years after acceptance of ms. Accepts simultaneous submissions. Responds in 6 months to queries; 6 months to mss. Book catalog for $1.50 postage; ms guidelines online.

Imprints Milkweeds for Young Readers.

- Reads poetry in January and June only, but accepts submissions year round.

O→ Milkweed Editions publishes literary fiction for adults and middle grade readers, nonfiction, and poetry. "Our vision is focused on giving voice to writers whose work is of the highest literary quality and whose ideas engender personal reflection and cultural action."

Nonfiction Literary. Subjects include nature/environment, human community. Submit complete ms with SASE.

Fiction Literary. Novels for adults and for readers 8-13. High literary quality. For adult readers: literary fiction, nonfiction, poetry, essays. For children (ages 8-13): literary novels. Translations welcome for both audiences. No romance, mysteries, science fiction. Send for guidelines first, then submit complete ms.

Recent Title(s) *Ordinary Wolves*, by Seth Kantner (fiction); *Postcards from Ed*, by Edward Abbey (nonfiction); *Willow Room, Green Door*, by Deborah Keenan (poetry).

Tips "We are looking for excellent writing with the intent of making a humane impact on society. Send for guidelines. Acquaint yourself with our books in terms of style and quality before submitting. Many factors influence our selection process, so don't get discouraged. Nonfiction is focused on literary writing about the natural world, including living well in urban environments."

MINNESOTA HISTORICAL SOCIETY PRESS

Minnesota Historical Society, 345 Kellogg Blvd. W., St. Paul MN 55102-1906. (651)296-2264. Fax: (651)297-1345. Web site: www.mnhs.org/mhspress. **Acquisitions:** Gregory M. Britton, director; Ann Regan, editor-in-chief. Estab. 1849. Publishes hardcover and trade paperback originals, trade paperback reprints. **Publishes 25 titles/year; imprint publishes 1-4 titles/year. Receives 200 queries and 75 mss/year. 50% of books from first-time authors; 85% from unagented writers. Royalties are negotiated. Offers advance.** Publishes book 14 months after acceptance of ms. Accepts simultaneous submissions. Responds in 1 month to queries. Book catalog free.

Imprints Borealis Books.

O→ Minnesota Historical Society Press publishes both scholarly and general interest books that contribute to the understanding of the Midwest.

Nonfiction Regional works only. Biography, coffee table book, cookbook, illustrated book, reference, scholarly. Subjects include anthropology/archeology, art/architecture, cooking/foods/nutrition, ethnic, history, memoirs, photography, regional, women's issues/studies. Query with SASE, or submit proposal package including outline, 1 sample chapter. Reviews artwork/photos as part of ms package. Send photocopies.

Recent Title(s) *Hot Dish Heaven: Classic Casseroles from Midwestern Kitchens*, by Ann L. Burckhardt; *A/A Guide to the Twin Cities*, by Larry Millett; *Crossing Hoffa: A Teamster's Story*, by Steven J. Harper.

Tips A regional connection is required.

⊘ MITCHELL LANE PUBLISHERS, INC.

P.O. Box 196, Hockessin DE 19707. (302)234-9426. Fax: (302)234-4742. **Acquisitions:** Barbara Mitchell, publisher. Estab. 1993. Publishes hardcover and library bound originals. **Publishes 85 titles/year. Receives 100 queries and 5 mss/year. 0% of books from first-time authors; 90% from unagented writers. Makes outright purchase on work-for-hire basis.** Publishes book 1 year after acceptance of ms. Does not accept simultaneous submissions. Responds only if interested to queries. Book catalog free.

O→ "Mitchell Lane publishes quality nonfiction for children and young adults."

Nonfiction Biography, children's/juvenile. Subjects include ethnic, multicultural. Query with SASE. *All unsolicited mss discarded.*

Recent Title(s) *Tiki Barber* (A Robbie Reader); *Extreme Cycling With Dale Holmes* (Extreme Sports); *Hurricane Katrina, 2005* (Natural Disasters).

Tips "We hire writers on a 'work-for-hire' basis to complete book projects we assign. Send résumé and writing samples that do not need to be returned."

MODERN LANGUAGE ASSOCIATION OF AMERICA

26 Broadway, 3rd Floor, New York NY 10004-1789. (646)576-5000. Fax: (646)458-0030. Director of MLA Book Publications: David G. Nicholls. **Acquisitions:** Joseph Gibaldi, director of book acquisitions and development; Sonia Kane, acquisitions editor; Joshua Shanholtzer, assistant acquisitions editor. Estab. 1883. Publishes hardcover and paperback originals. **Publishes 15 titles/year. 100% from unagented writers. Pays 4-8% royalty on net receipts.** Publishes book 1 year after acceptance of ms. Does not accept simultaneous submissions. Responds in 2 months to mss. Book catalog free.

- The MLA publishes on current issues in literary and linguistic research and teaching of language and literature at postsecondary level.

Nonfiction Reference, scholarly, professional. Subjects include education, language/literature, translation (with companion volume in foreign language, for classroom use). No critical monographs. Query with SASE, or submit outline.

Recent Title(s) *A Research Guide for Undergraduates*, by Nancy L. Baker and Nancy Huling; *Electronic Textual Editing*, edited by Lou Burnard, Katherine O'Brien O'Keeffe, and John Unsworth.

MOODY PUBLISHERS

Moody Bible Institute, 820 N. LaSalle Blvd., Chicago IL 60610. (312)329-8047. Fax: (312)329-2019. Web site: www.moodypublishers.org. Vice President/Executive Editor: Greg Thornton. **Acquisitions:** Acquisitions Coordinator. Estab. 1894. Publishes hardcover, trade, and mass market paperback originals. **Publishes 60 titles/year; imprint publishes 5-10 titles/year. Receives 1,500 queries and 2,000 mss/year. 1% of books from first-time authors; 80% from unagented writers. Royalty varies. Offers $1,000-10,000 advance.** Publishes book 9-12 months after acceptance of ms. Does not accept simultaneous submissions. Responds in 2-3 months to queries. Book catalog for 9×12 SAE with 4 first-class stamps; ms guidelines for SASE and on Web site.

Imprints Northfield Publishing; Lift Every Voice (African American-interest).

- "The mission of Moody Publishers is to educate and edify the Christian and to evangelize the non-Christian by ethically publishing conservative, evangelical Christian literature and other media for all ages around the world; and to help provide resources for Moody Bible Institute in its training of future Christian leaders."

Nonfiction Children's/juvenile, gift book, general Christian living. Subjects include child guidance/parenting, money/finance, religion, spirituality, women's issues/studies. "We are no longer reviewing queries or unsolicited manuscripts unless they come to us through an agent. Unsolicited proposals will be returned only if proper postage is included. We are not able to acknowledge the receipt of your unsolicited proposal." *Agented submissions only.*

Fiction Fantasy, historical, mystery, religious (children's religious, inspirational, religious mystery/suspense), science fiction, young adult (adventure, fantasy/science fiction, historical, mystery/suspense, series). Query with 1 chapter and SASE.

Recent Title(s) *The Rats of Hamelin*, by Adam and Keith McCune; *Admission*, by Travis Thrasher; *Dawn of a Thousand Nights*, by Tricia Goyer.

Tips "In our fiction list, we're looking for Christian storytellers rather than teachers trying to present a message. Your motivation should be to delight the reader. Using your skills to create beautiful works is glorifying to God."

MORGAN REYNOLDS PUBLISHING

620 S. Elm St., Suite 223, Greensboro NC 27406. (336)275-1311. Fax: (336)275-1152. E-mail: editorial@morganreynolds.com. Web site: www.morganreynolds.com. Founder/Publisher: John Riley. **Acquisitions:** Casey Cornelius, editor-in-chief. Estab. 1994. Publishes hardcover originals. **Publishes 35 titles/year. Receives 250-300 queries and 100-150 mss/year. 50% of books from first-time authors; 100% from unagented writers. Pays advance and 10% royalty.** Publishes book 12-18 months after acceptance of ms. Accepts simultaneous submissions. Responds in 3 months to queries. Book catalog and ms guidelines online.

- Morgan Reynolds publishes nonfiction books for young-adult readers. "We prefer lively, well-written biographies of interesting, contemporary and historical figures for our biography series. Books for our Great Events Series should be insightful and exciting looks at critical periods." Currently emphasizing great scientists and scientific subjects, world history, and world writers. De-emphasizing sports figures.

Nonfiction "We do not always publish the obvious subjects. Don't shy away from less-popular subjects." Biography. Subjects include Americana (young-adult oriented), business/economics, government/politics, history, language/literature, military/war, money/finance, women's issues/studies. No picture books or fiction. Query with SASE.

Recent Title(s) *Best of Times*, by Peggy Cervantes; *Nikola Tesla and the Taming of Electricity*, by Lisa J. Aldrich; *Dark Dreams*, by Nancy Whitelaw.

Tips "Read our writer's guidelines, look at our books, and visit our Web site."

MORNINGSIDE HOUSE, INC.

Morningside Bookshop, 260 Oak St., Dayton OH 45410. (937)461-6736. Fax: (937)461-4260. E-mail: msbooks@erinet.com. Web site: www.morningsidebooks.com. **Acquisitions:** Robert J. Younger, publisher. Publishes hardcover and trade paperback originals. **Publishes 10 titles/year; imprint publishes 5 titles/year. Receives 30 queries and 10 mss/year. 20% of books from first-time authors; 80% from unagented writers. Pays 10% royalty on retail price. Offers $1,000-2,000 advance.** Publishes book 15 months after acceptance of ms. Accepts simultaneous submissions. Book catalog for $5 or on Web site.

Imprints Morningside Press;, Press of Morningside Bookshop.

- Morningside publishes books for readers interested in the history of the American Civil War.

Nonfiction Subjects include history, military/war. Query with SASE, or submit complete ms. Reviews artwork/photos as part of ms package. Send photocopies.

Recent Title(s) *The Mississippi Brigade of Brig. Gen. Joseph R. Davis*, by T.P. Williams; *The 16th Michigan Infantry*, by Kim Crawford.

Tips "We are only interested in previously unpublished material."

N MOTORCYCLING

P.O. Box 560989, Rockledge FL 32955. (321)690-2224. Fax: (321)690-0853. Web site: www.bfpbooks.com. **Acquisitions:** Acquisitions Editor. Publishes trade paperback originals and limited hardback. **Publishes 15-25 titles/year. Receives 100 queries and 50 mss/year. 50% of books from first-time authors; 99% from unagented writers. Pays 7-11% royalty on retail price.** Publishes book 3 months after acceptance of ms. Responds in 1 month to queries. Ms guidelines online.

- Motorcycling (BFP, Inc.) publishes books on motorcycling and motorcycling history.

Nonfiction General interest relating to touring, guide books, how-to subjects, and motorcycling history. "We are interested in any title related to these fields. Query with a list of ideas. Include phone number. Our title plans rarely extend past 6 months, although we know the type and quantity of books we will publish over the next 2 years. We prefer good knowledge with simple-to-understand writing style containing a well-rounded vocabulary." Query with SASE. Reviews artwork/photos as part of ms package. Send photocopies or JPEG files on CD.

Tips "All of our staff and editors are riders. As such, we publish what we would want to read relating to the subject. Our audience in general are active riders at the beginner and intermediate level of repair knowledge and riding skills, and history buffs wanting to learn more about the history of motorcycles in this country. Many are people new to motorcycles, attempting to learn all they can before starting out on that first long ride or even buying their first bike. Keep it easy and simple to follow. Use motorcycle jargon sparingly. Do not use complicated technical jargon, terms, or formulas without a detailed explanation of the same. Use experienced riders and mechanics as a resource for knowledge. Please read our guidelines before submitting your manuscript."

MOUNTAIN PRESS PUBLISHING CO.

P.O. Box 2399, Missoula MT 59806-2399. (406)728-1900 or (800)234-5308. Fax: (406)728-1635. E-mail: info@mtnpress.com. Web site: www.mountain-press.com. **Acquisitions:** Gwen McKenna, editor (history); Jennifer Carey, editor (Roadside Geology, Field Guides, and Tumblweed Series, natural history, science). Estab. 1948. Publishes hardcover and trade paperback originals. **Publishes 15 titles/year. 50% of books from first-time authors; 90% from unagented writers. Pays 7-12% royalty on wholesale price.** Publishes book 2 years after acceptance of ms. Responds in 3 months to queries. Book catalog online.

- Expanding children's/juvenile nonfiction titles.
- "We are expanding our Roadside Geology, Geology Underfoot, and Roadside History series (done on a state-by-state basis). We are interested in well-written regional field guides—plants and flowers—and readable history and natural history."

Nonfiction How-to. Subjects include animals, history (Western), nature/environment, regional, science (Earth science). "No personal histories or journals." Query with SASE, or submit outline, sample chapter(s). Reviews artwork/photos as part of ms package.

Recent Title(s) *Plants of the Lewis and Clark Expedition*, by H. Wayne Phillips; *Loons: Diving Birds of the North*, by Donna Love; *Encyclopedia of Indian Wars*, by Gregory F. Michno.

Tips "Find out what kind of books a publisher is interested in and tailor your writing to them; research markets and target your audience. Research other books on the same subjects. Make yours different. Don't present your manuscript to a publisher—sell it. Give the information needed to make a decision on a title. Please learn what we publish before sending your proposal. We are a 'niche' publisher."

N THE MOUNTAINEERS BOOKS

1001 SW Klickitat Way, Suite 201, Seattle WA 98134-1162. (206)223-6303. Fax: (206)223-6306. E-mail: mbooks@mountaineersbooks.org. Web site: www.mountaineersbooks.org. **Acquisitions:** Cassandra Conyers, acquisitions editor. Estab. 1961. Publishes 95% hardcover and trade paperback originals and 5% reprints. **Publishes 40 titles/year. Receives 150-250 submissions/year. 25% of books from first-time authors; 98% from unagented writers. Pays royalty on net receipts. Offers advance.** Publishes book 1 year after acceptance of ms. Does not accept simultaneous submissions. Responds in 3 months to queries. Book catalog for 9×12 SAE with $1.33 postage first-class stamps; ms guidelines online.

- See the Contests and Awards section for information on the Barbara Savage/'Miles From Nowhere' Memorial Award for outstanding adventure narratives offered by Mountaineers Books.

O→ Mountaineers Books specializes in expert, authoritative books dealing with mountaineering, hiking, backpacking, skiing, snowshoeing, etc. These can be either how-to-do-it or where-to-do-it (guidebooks). Currently emphasizing regional conservation and natural history.

Nonfiction How-to (outdoor), guidebooks for national and international adventure travel. Subjects include nature/environment, recreation, regional, sports (non-competitive self-propelled), translation, travel, natural history, conservation. Accepts nonfiction translations. Looks for "expert knowledge, good organization." Also interested in nonfiction adventure narratives. Does *not* want to see "anything dealing with hunting, fishing or motorized travel." Submit outline, 2 sample chapter(s), author bio.

Recent Title(s) *Best Hikes with Dogs: Western Washington*, by Nelson; *Backpacker: More Everyday Wisdom*, by Berger; *Detectives on Everest*, by Hemmleb and Simonson.

Tips "The type of book the writer has the best chance of selling to our firm is an authoritative guidebook (*in our field*) to a specific area not otherwise covered; or a how-to that is better than existing competition (again, *in our field*)."

MOYER BELL, LTD.

549 Old North Rd., Kingston RI 02881-1220. (401)783-5480. Fax: (401)284-0959. E-mail: contact@moyerbellbooks.com. Web site: www.moyerbellbooks.com. Publisher: Britt Bell. Estab. 1984. Book catalog online.

O→ Moyer Bell publishes literature, reference, and art books.

A THE MYSTERIOUS PRESS

Imprint of Warner Books, 1271 Avenue of the Americas, New York NY 10020. (212)522-7200. Fax: (212)522-7990. Web site: www.mysteriouspress.com. **Acquisitions:** Kristen Weber, editor. Estab. 1976. Publishes hardcover, trade paperback and mass market editions. **Publishes 20 titles/year. Pays standard, but negotiable, royalty on retail price. Offers negotiable advance.** Publishes book an average of 1 year after acceptance of ms. Ms guidelines online.

O→ The Mysterious Press publishes well-written crime/mystery/suspense fiction.

Fiction Mystery, suspense, Crime/detective novels. No short stories. *Agented submissions only.*

Recent Title(s) *Sacred Cows*, by Karen E. Olson; *Sudden Death*, by David Rosenfelt.

NAVAL INSTITUTE PRESS

US Naval Institute, 291 Wood Ave., Annapolis MD 21402-5034. (410)268-6110. Fax: (410)295-1084. E-mail: esecunda@usni.org. Web site: www.usni.org. Press Director: Mark Gatlin. **Acquisitions:** Paul Wilderson, executive editor; Tom Cutler, senior acquisitions editor; Eric Mills, acquisitions editor. Estab. 1873. **Publishes 80-90 titles/year. 50% of books from first-time authors; 90% from unagented writers.** Ms guidelines online.

O→ The Naval Institute Press publishes trade and scholarly nonfiction and some fiction. "We are interested in national and international security, naval, military, military jointness, intelligence, and special warfare, both current and historical."

Nonfiction Submit proposal package with outline, author bio, TOC, description/synopsis, sample chapter(s), page/word count, number of illustrations, ms completion date, intended market; or submit complete ms. Send SASE with sufficient postage for return of ms.

Fiction Submit complete ms. Send SASE with sufficient postage for return of ms.

NAVPRESS PUBLISHING GROUP

P.O. Box 35001, Colorado Springs CO 80935. Fax: (719)260-7223. E-mail: bookeditorial@navpress.com. Web site: www.navpress.com. Estab. 1975. Publishes hardcover, trade paperback and mass market paperback originals and reprints. **Publishes 50 titles/year. Pays royalty.** Book catalog free.

Imprints Piñion Press.

Nonfiction Reference, self-help, inspirational, Christian living, Bible studies. Subjects include business/economics, child guidance/parenting, religion, sociology, spirituality, marriage. Submit outline, author bio, 2-3 sample chapters, competition summary, audience profile, SASE.
Fiction Submit outline, author bio, 2-5 sample chapters, reader profile, word count.
Recent Title(s) *Ask Me Anything: Provocative Answers for College Students*, by J. Budziszewski; *5 Minute Theologian: Maximum Truth in Minimum Time*, by Rick Cornish.

NEAL-SCHUMAN PUBLISHERS, INC.

100 William St., Suite 2004, New York NY 10038-4512. (212)925-8650. Fax: (212)219-8916. E-mail: janice@neal-schuman.com. Web site: www.neal-schuman.com. **Acquisitions:** Paul Seeman, assistant director of publishing. Estab. 1976. Publishes trade paperback originals. **Publishes 30 titles/year. 75% of books from first-time authors; 90% from unagented writers. Pays 10% royalty on net receipts. Offers infrequent advance.** Publishes book 4 months after acceptance of ms. Does not accept simultaneous submissions. Responds in 1 month to proposals. Book catalog and ms guidelines free.

- "Neal-Schuman publishes books about library management, information literary titles, the Internet and information technology." Especially soliciting proposals for undergraduate information studies, knowledge management textbooks.

Nonfiction Reference, technical, textbook, professional, storytime guides, youth services. Subjects include computers/electronic, education, software, Internet guides, library and information science. "We are looking for many books about the Internet." Submit proposal package including outline, sample chapter(s), résumé, preface.
Recent Title(s) *The Virtual Reference Handbook*, by Diane K. Kovacs; *Information Literary Collaborations That Work*, by Trudie E. Jacobson and Thomas P. Mackey; *The Compleye Copyright Liability Handbook*, by Tomas A. Lipinski.

THOMAS NELSON, INC.

Box 141000, Nashville TN 37214-1000. (615)889-9000. Web site: www.thomasnelson.com. **Acquisitions:** Acquisitions Editor. Publishes hardcover and paperback orginals. **Publishes 100-150 titles/year. Rates negotiated for each project. Offers advance.** Publishes book 1-2 years after acceptance of ms. Accepts simultaneous submissions.
Imprints Nelson Books; W Publishing; Rutledge Hill Press; J. Countryman; Cool Springs Press; Reference & Electronic Publishing; Editorial Caribe; Nelson Curriculum; Tommy Nelson; Nelson Current; WestBow Press.

- *Does not accept unsolicited mss.* No phone queries.
- Thomas Nelson publishes Christian lifestyle nonfiction and fiction, and general nonfiction.

Nonfiction Cookbook, reference, self-help. Subjects include business/economics (business development), cooking/foods/nutrition, gardening, health/medicine (and fitness), religion, spirituality, adult inspirational, motivational, devotional, Christian living, prayer and evangelism, Bible study, personal development, political, biography/autobiography.
Fiction Publishes authors of commercial fiction who write for adults from a Christian perspective.
Recent Title(s) *Live Like You Were Dying*, with Tim McGraw; *Epic*, by John Eldredge; *When the Enemy Strikes*, by Charles Stanley.

TOMMY NELSON

Imprint of Thomas Nelson, Inc., P.O. Box 141000, Nashville TN 37214-1000. (615)889-9000. Fax: (615)902-2219. Web site: www.tommynelson.com. Publishes hardcover and trade paperback originals. **Publishes 50-75 titles/year.** Does not accept simultaneous submissions. Ms guidelines online.

- *Does not accept unsolicited mss.*
- Tommy Nelson publishes children's Christian nonfiction and fiction for boys and girls up to age 14. "We honor God and serve people through books, videos, software and Bibles for children that improve the lives of our customers."

Nonfiction Children's/juvenile. Subjects include religion (Christian evangelical).
Fiction Adventure, juvenile, mystery, picture books, religious. "No stereotypical characters."
Recent Title(s) *Hermie the Common Caterpillar*, by Max Lucado; *Bible for Me Series*, by Andy Holmes; *Shaoey and Dot*, by Mary Beth and Steven Curtis Chapman.
Tips "Know the Christian Booksellers Association market. Check out the Christian bookstores to see what sells and what is needed."

NEW HARBINGER PUBLICATIONS

5674 Shattuck Ave., Oakland CA 94609. (510)652-0215. Fax: (510)652-5472. E-mail: proposals@newharbinger.com. Web site: www.newharbinger.com. **Acquisitions:** Catharine Sutker, acquisitions manager. Estab. 1973.

Publishes 48 titles/year. Receives 1,000 queries and 300 mss/year. 60% of books from first-time authors; 75% from unagented writers. Pays 10% royalty on net receipts. Publishes book 1 year after acceptance of ms. Accepts simultaneous submissions. Responds in 2 weeks to queries; 1 month to proposals; 2 months to mss. Book catalog free; ms guidelines online.

O→ "We look for psychology and health self-help books that teach readers how to master essential life skills. Mental health professionals who want simple, clear explanations or important psychological techniques and health issues also read our books. Thus, our books must be simple ane easy to understand but also complete and authoritative. Most of our authors are therapists or other helping professionals."

Nonfiction Self-help (psychology/health). Subjects include health/medicine, psychology, women's issues/studies, psycho spirituality, anger management, anxiety, coping, mindfulness skills. "Authors need to be qualified psychotherapists or health practitioners to publish with us." Submit proposal package including outline, 2 sample chapters, competing titles, and a compelling, supported reason why the book is unique.

Recent Title(s) *The Gift of ADHD*, by Lara Honos-Webb, PhD; *Get Out of Your Mind and Into Your Life*, by Steven C. Hayes, PhD; *Five Good Minutes*, by Jeffrey Brantley, MD, and Wendy Millstine.

Tips Audience includes psychotherapists and lay readers wanting step-by-step strategies to solve specific problems. "Our definition of a self-help psychology or health book is one that teaches essential life skills. The primary goal is to train the reader so that, after reading the book, he or she can deal more effectively with health and/or psychological challenges."

NEW HOPE PUBLISHERS

Woman's Missionary Union, P.O. Box 12065, Birmingham AL 35202-2065. (205)991-4950. Fax: (205)991-4015. E-mail: new_hope@wmu.org. Web site: www.newhopepublishers.com. **Acquisitions:** Acquisitions Editor. **Publishes 20-28 titles/year. Receives several hundred queries/year. 25% of books from first-time authors; small% from unagented writers. Pays royalty on net receipts.** Publishes book 2 years after acceptance of ms. Book catalog for 9×12 SAE with 3 first-class stamps.

O→ "Our vision is the encouragement of Christian believers to a radical commitment to God's mission." This market does not accepy unsoliticied mss.

Nonfiction "We publish books dealing with all facets of Christian life for women and families, including health, discipleship, missions, ministry, Bible studies, spiritual development, parenting, and marriage. We currently do not accept adult fiction or children's picture books. We are particularly interested in niche categories and books on lifestyle development and change." Children's/juvenile (religion). Subjects include child guidance/parenting (from Christian perspective), education (Christian church), health/medicine (Christian), multicultural, religion (spiritual development, Bible study, life situations from Christian perspective, ministry), women's issues/studies (Christian), church leadership, evangelism. Prefers a query and prospectus.

Recent Title(s) *Trolls and Truth*, by Jimmy Dorrell; *Street Signs*, by Ray Bakke and Jon Sharpe; *Church Nanny*, by Gigi Schweikert.

NEW HORIZON PRESS

P.O. Box 669, Far Hills NJ 07931. (908)604-6311. Fax: (908)604-6330. E-mail: nhp@newhorizonpressbooks.com. Web site: www.newhorizonpressbooks.com. **Acquisitions:** Dr. Joan S. Dunphy, publisher (nonfiction, social issues, true crime). Estab. 1983. Publishes hardcover and trade paperback originals. **Publishes 12 titles/year. 90% of books from first-time authors; 50% from unagented writers. Pays standard royalty on net receipts. Offers advance.** Publishes book within 2 years after acceptance of ms. Accepts simultaneous submissions. Book catalog free; ms guidelines online.

Imprints Small Horizons.

O→ New Horizon publishes adult nonfiction featuring true stories of uncommon heroes, true crime, social issues, and self help.

Nonfiction Biography, children's/juvenile, how-to, self-help. Subjects include child guidance/parenting, creative nonfiction, government/politics, health/medicine, nature/environment, psychology, women's issues/studies, true crime. Submit proposal package including outline, résumé, author bio, 3 sample chapters, photo, marketing information.

Recent Title(s) *Missing: The Oregon City Girls*, by Linda O'Neal, Philip Tennyson and Rick Watson; *Faces of Evil*, by Lois Gibson and Deanie Francis Mills; *Clueless*, by Bobbie Reid.

Tips "We are a small publisher, thus it is important that the author/publisher have a good working relationship. The author must be willing to promote his book."

NEW SEEDS BOOKS

Imprint of Shambhala Publications, 300 Massachusetts Ave., Boston MA 02115. Fax: (617)236-1563. E-mail: editor@newseeds-books.com. Web site: www.newseeds-books.com. **Acquisitions:** David O'Neal, senior editor. Estab. 2005. Publishes hardcover and trade paperback originals, as well as hardcover and trade paperback reprints. **Publishes 90-100 (Shambhala); 10 (New Seeds Books) titles/year. Pays 7.5-15% royalty on retail price.** Publishes book 1 year after acceptance of ms. Accepts simultaneous submissions. Responds in 3 months to queries; 3 months to proposals; 3 months to mss. Ms guidelines by e-mail.

Nonfiction Autobiography, biography, general nonfiction, gift book. Subjects include religion, spirituality, contemplative Christianity. New Seeds publishes works exemplifying the wisdom of Christianity, with a special emphasis on the traditions of contemplation and prayer. Query with SASE, or submit proposal package including outline, author bio, 2 sample chapters, or submit complete ms. Reviews artwork/photos as part of ms package. Send photocopies.

Recent Title(s) *Where God Happens: Discovering Christ in One Another*, by Rowan Williams; *The Unknown Sayings of Jesus*, by Marvin Meyer; *Love Burning in the Soul*, by James Harpur.

N NEW SPIRIT

Imprint of BET Books, 850 Third Ave., 16th Floor, New York NY 10022. Web site: www.bet.com/books. **Acquisitions:** Glenda Howard, senior editor. Responds in 4 months to proposals.

Nonfiction "Our nonfiction books objective is to encourage and motivate readers by offering messages advocating personal growth, empowerment, and strong personal relationships." Submit proposal package including outline, 3 sample chapters.

Fiction "We are looking to acquire fiction novels that are well crafted, and will feature strong characters who overcome challenges and obstacles through the power of prayer and faith. The New Spirit fiction titles will appeal to a broad audience because they will address contemporary issues such as love, betrayal, tragedy, and triumph over adversity, while keeping a spiritual message throughout." Submit proposal package including synopsis, 3 sample chapters.

Tips "Please do not phone to see if your manuscript was received or returned, or to find out what we thought of it. A self-addressed, stamped postcard can be enclosed with your submission if you want confirmation of its arrival. Specify whether you would like your manuscript returned or recycled if it is not right for us."

NEW WIN PUBLISHING

Division of Academic Learning Co., LLC, 9682 Telstar Ave., Suite 110, El Monte CA 91731. (626)448-4422. E-mail: info@academiclearningcompany.com. Web site: www.newwinpublishing.com. **Acquisitions:** Arthur Chou, acquisitions editor. Publishes hardcover and trade paperback originals and reprints. **Publishes 20 titles/year; imprint publishes 6-8 titles/year. Pays 10% royalty on retail price.** Publishes book 6 months after acceptance of ms. Accepts simultaneous submissions. Responds in 1 month to queries; 1 month to proposals; 1 month to mss. Book catalog online; ms guidelines by e-mail.

Imprints Winchester Press; WBusiness Books; Z Health Books.

Nonfiction Children's/juvenile, coffee table book, cookbook, how-to, self-help. Subjects include business/economics, child guidance/parenting, cooking/foods/nutrition, health/medicine, hobbies. Submit proposal package including outline, 2 sample chapter(s), cover letter, or submit complete ms. Reviews artwork/photos as part of ms package. Send photocopies.

Recent Title(s) *Great Salespeople Aren't Born, They're Hired*, by Joe Miller (business/self-help); *Eat Smart*, by Dale Figtree (nutrition/juvenile).

NEW WORLD LIBRARY

14 Pamaron Way, Novato CA 94949. (415)884-2100. Fax: (415)884-2199. Web site: www.newworldlibrary.com. Publisher: Marc Allen. **Acquisitions:** Submissions Editor. Estab. 1979. Publishes hardcover and trade paperback originals and reprints. **Publishes 35-40 titles/year.** Accepts simultaneous submissions. Responds in 3 months to queries. Book catalog free; ms guidelines online.

Imprints Nataraj; H.J. Kramer; Amber-Allen Publishing.

- Does not accept e-mail submissions. No longer accepting unsolicited children's mss.
- "NWL is dedicated to publishing books and audio projects that inspire and challenge us to improve the quality of our lives and our world."

Nonfiction Gift book, self-help. Subjects include alternative lifestyles (health), business/economics (prosperity), ethnic (African/American, Native American), health/medicine (natural), money/finance, nature/environment, psychology, religion, spirituality, women's issues/studies, personal growth, parenting. Submit outline, author bio, 2-3 sample chapters, SASE. Reviews artwork/photos as part of ms package. Send photocopies.

Recent Title(s) *Coaching the Artist Within*, by Eric Maisel; *Forever Ours*, by Janis Amatuzio.

NEWMARKET PRESS

18 E. 48th St., New York NY 10017. (212)832-3575. Fax: (212)832-3629. E-mail: mailbox@newmarketpress.com. Web site: www.newmarketpress.com. President/Publisher: Esther Margolis. **Acquisitions:** Editorial De-

partment. Publishes hardcover and trade paperback originals and reprints. **Publishes 15-20 titles/year. Pays royalty. Offers varied advance.** Accepts simultaneous submissions. Ms guidelines for #10 SASE or online.

O→ Currently emphasizing movie tie-in/companion books, health, psychology, parenting. De-emphasizing fiction.

Nonfiction Biography, coffee table book, general nonfiction, reference, self-help. Subjects include child guidance/parenting, cooking/foods/nutrition, health/medicine, history, psychology, business/personal finance, film/performing arts. Submit proposal package including complete ms, or 1-3 sample chapters, TOC, marketing info, author credentials, SASE.

Recent Title(s) *Condi*, by Antonia Felix; *Hotel Rwanda: Bringing the True Story of an African Hero to Film*, edited by Terry George; *In Good Company*, by Paul Weitz.

NO STARCH PRESS, INC.

555 De Haro St., Suite 250, San Francisco CA 94107. (415)863-9900. Fax: (415)863-9950. E-mail: info@nostarch.com. Web site: www.nostarch.com. **Acquisitions:** William Pollock, publisher. Estab. 1994. Publishes trade paperback originals. **Publishes 20-25 titles/year. Receives 100 queries and 5 mss/year. 80% of books from first-time authors; 90% from unagented writers. Pays 10-15% royalty on wholesale price. Offers advance.** Publishes book 4 months after acceptance of ms. Accepts simultaneous submissions. Book catalog free.

Imprints Linux Journal Press.

O→ No Starch Press, Inc., is an independent publishing company committed to producing easy-to-read and information-packed computer books. Currently emphasizing open source, Web development, computer security issues, programming tools, and robotics. "More stuff, less fluff."

Nonfiction How-to, reference, technical. Subjects include computers/electronic, hobbies, software (Open Source). Submit outline, author bio, 1 sample chapter, market rationale. Reviews artwork/photos as part of ms package. Send photocopies.

Recent Title(s) *Hacking: The Art of Exploitation*, by Jon Erickson; *Art of Assembly Language*, by Randall Hyde; *Hacking the XBox*, by Andrew "bunnie" Huang.

Tips "No fluff—content, content, content or just plain fun. Understand how your book fits into the market. Tell us why someone, anyone, will buy your book. Be enthusiastic."

NOLO

950 Parker St., Berkeley CA 94710. (510)549-1976. Fax: (510)859-0025. E-mail: acquisitions@nolo.com. Web site: www.nolo.com. **Acquisitions:** Editorial Department. Estab. 1971. Publishes trade paperback originals. **Publishes 75 new editions and 15 new titles/year. 20% of books from first-time authors. Pays 10-12% royalty on net receipts. Offers advance.** Accepts simultaneous submissions. Responds in 3 weeks to queries; 5 weeks to proposals. Ms guidelines online.

O→ "We publish practical, do-it-yourself books, software and various electronic products on financial and legal issues that affect individuals, small business, and nonprofit organizations. We specialize in helping people handle their own legal tasks; i.e., write a will, file a small claims lawsuit, start a small business or nonprofit, or apply for a patent."

Nonfiction General nonfiction, how-to, reference, self-help, child guidance/parenting. Subjects include business/economics, money/finance, legal guides in various topics including employment, small business, intellectual property, parenting and education, finance and investment, landlord/tenant, real estate, and estate planning. Query with SASE, or submit outline, 1 sample chapter.

Recent Title(s) *Credit Repair*, by Robin Leonard; *The Small Business Start-Up Kit*, by Pevi Pakroo; *Effective Fundraising for Nonprofits*, by Ilona Bray.

NORTH POINT PRESS

Imprint of Farrar Straus & Giroux, Inc., 19 Union Square W., New York NY 10003. (212)741-6900. E-mail: fsg.editorial@fsgbooks.com. Web site: www.fsgbooks.com. Estab. 1980. Publishes hardcover and paperback originals. **Pays standard royalty. Offers varied advance.** Accepts simultaneous submissions. Ms guidelines for #10 SASE.

O→ "We are a broad-based literary trade publisher—high quality writing only."

Nonfiction Subjects include history, nature/environment, religion (no New Age), travel, cultural criticism, music, cooking/food. "Be familiar with our list. No genres." Query with SASE, or submit outline, 1-2 sample chapters.

Recent Title(s) *Chocolate: A Bittersweet Saga of Dark and Light*, by Mort Rosenblum; *In Fond Remembrance of Me*, by Howard Norman.

NORTHERN ILLINOIS UNIVERSITY PRESS

2280 Bethany Rd., DeKalb IL 60115-2854. (815)753-1826. Fax: (815)753-1845. Web site: www.niupress.niu.edu. Director/Editor-in-Chief: Mary L. Lincoln. **Acquisitions:** Melody Herr, acquisitions editor (history, politics).

Estab. 1965. **Publishes 20-22 titles/year. Pays 10-15% royalty on wholesale price. Offers advance.** Does not accept simultaneous submissions. Book catalog free.

O⊸ NIU Press publishes scholarly work and books of general interest to the informed public. "We publish mainly history, politics, anthropology, and other social sciences. We are interested also in studies on the Chicago area and Midwest, and in literature in translation." Currently emphasizing history, the social sciences, and cultural studies.

Nonfiction "Publishes mainly history, political science, social sciences, philosophy, literary and cultural studies, and regional studies." Subjects include anthropology/archeology, government/politics, history, language/literature, philosophy, regional, social sciences, translation, cultural studies. No collections of previously published essays or unsolicited poetry. Query with SASE, or submit outline, 1-3 sample chapters.

Recent Title(s) *Illinois: A History of the Land and Its People.*

NORTHWORD BOOKS FOR YOUNG READERS

Imprint of T&N Children's Publishing, 11571 K-Tel Dr., Minnetonka MN 55343. (952)933-7537. Fax: (952)933-3630. Web site: www.tnkidsbooks.com. **Acquisitions:** Kristen McCurry (children's books). Estab. 1984. Publishes children's nonfiction trade hardcovers and paperback originals. **Publishes 16-20 titles/year. 25% of books from first-time authors; 50% from unagented writers. Pays 5% royalty on list price. Offers $2,000 and up advance.** Publishes book 1-2 years after acceptance of ms. Accepts simultaneous submissions. Responds in 3 months to queries. Ms guidelines for #10 SASE.

O⊸ NorthWord Books for Young Readers exclusively publishes nonfiction nature, wildlife, natural history, and outdoor titles for children.

Nonfiction Formats include board books, picture books and series. Submit complete ms.

Recent Title(s) *Zebras*, by Jill Anderson (ages 3-6); *What Do Roots Do?*, by Kathleen V. Kudlinski (ages 5-8); *Let's Rock*, by Linda Kranz (ages 6-12).

W.W. NORTON CO., INC.

500 Fifth Ave., New York NY 10110. Fax: (212)869-0856. E-mail: manuscripts@wwnorton.com. Web site: www.wwnorton.com. **Acquisitions:** Starling Lawrence, editor-in-chief; Robert Weil, executive editor; Edwin Barber; Jill Bialosky (literary fiction, biography, memoirs); Amy Cherry (history, biography, women's issues, African-American, health); Carol Houck-Smith (literary fiction, creative nonfictions, memoir/biography); Angela von der Lippe (trade nonfiction, behavioral sciences, earth sciences, astronomy, neuro-science, education); Jim Mairs (history, biography, illustrated books); Alane Mason (serious nonfiction cultural and intellectual history, illustrated books, literary fiction and memoir); W. Drake McFeely, president (nonfiction, particularly science and social science); Maria Guarnaschelli (cookbooks, food & travel writing, literary fiction, memoir, serious nonfiction—esepcially language, psychology, physics, history, math, nature). Estab. 1923. Publishes hardcover and paperback originals and reprints. **Publishes 300 titles/year. Pays royalty. Offers advance.** Does not accept simultaneous submissions. Responds in 2 months to queries. Ms guidelines online.

Imprints Backcountry Publication; Countryman Press; W.W. Norton.

O⊸ General trade publisher of fiction, poetry and nonfiction, educational and professional books. "W. W. Norton Co. strives to carry out the imperative of its founder to 'publish books not for a single season, but for the years' in the areas of fiction, nonfiction and poetry."

Nonfiction Autobiography, biography, reference, self-help. Subjects include agriculture/horticulture, art/architecture, business/economics, child guidance/parenting, community, computers/electronic, cooking/foods/nutrition, government/politics, health/medicine, history, hobbies, language/literature, memoirs, music/dance, nature/environment, photography, psychology, religion, science, sports, travel, antiques and collectibles, current affairs, family, games, law, mystery, nautical subjects, poetry, political science, sailing, transportation. College Department: Subjects include biological sciences, economics, psychology, political science and computer science. Professional Books specializes in psychotherapy. "We are not interested in considering books from the following categories: juvenile or young adult, religious, occult or paranormal, and arts and crafts." Query with SASE, or submit 2-3 sample chapters, 1 of which should be the first chapter. Please give a brief description of your submission, your writing credentials, and any experience, professional or otherwise, which is relevant to your submission. No phone calls. Address envelope and letter to The Editors.

Fiction Literary, poetry, poetry in translation, religious. High-qulity literary fiction. "We are not interested in considering books from the following categories: juvenile or young adult, religious, occult or paranormal, genre fiction (formula romances, sci-fi or westerns)." Accepts e-mail submissions. No phone calls.

Recent Title(s) *Guns, Germs and Steel*, by Jared Diamond; *Island*, by Alistir MacLeod.

NURSESBOOKS.ORG

American Nurses Association, 8515 Georgia Ave., Suite 400, Silver Spring MD 20901-3492. (301)628-5212. Fax: (301)628-5003. E-mail: eric.wurzbacher@ana.org. Web site: www.nursesbooks.org. **Acquisitions:** Rosanne

Roe, publisher; Eric Wurzbacher, editor/project manager. Publishes professional paperback originals and reprints. **Publishes 10 titles/year. Receives 50 queries and 8-10 mss/year. 75% of books from first-time authors; 100% from unagented writers. Pays 12% royalty on net receipts.** Publishes book 4 months after acceptance of ms. Does not accept simultaneous submissions. Responds in 3 months to proposals; 3 months to mss. Book catalog online; ms guidelines free.

O→ Nursebooks.org publishes books designed to help professional nurses in their work and careers. Through the publishing program, Nursebooks.org provides nurses in all practice settings with publications that address cutting-edge issues and form a basis for debate and exploration of this century's most critical health care trends.

Nonfiction Reference, technical, textbook, handbooks; resource guides. Subjects include advanced practice, computers, continuing education, ethics, health care policy, nursing administration, psychiatric and mental health, quality, nursing history, workplace issues, key clinical topics, such as geriatrics, pain management, public health, spirituality and home health. Submit outline, 1 sample chapter, CV, list of 3 reviewers and paragraph on audience and how to reach them. Reviews artwork/photos as part of ms package. Send photocopies.

Recent Title(s) *Florence Nightingale Today: Healing, Leadership, and Global Action*; *Genetics Nursing Portfolios: A New Model for Credentialing*; *Faith Community Nursing Handbook*.

OAK KNOLL PRESS

310 Delaware St., New Castle DE 19720. (302)328-7232. Fax: (302)328-7274. E-mail: oakknoll@oakknoll.com. Web site: www.oakknoll.com. **Acquisitions:** John Von Hoelle, director of publishing. Estab. 1976. Publishes hardcover and trade paperback originals and reprints. **Publishes 40 titles/year. Receives 250 queries and 100 mss/year. 50% of books from first-time authors; 100% from unagented writers.** Publishes book 12 months after acceptance of ms. Accepts simultaneous submissions. Ms guidelines online.

O→ Oak Knoll specializes in books about books and manuals on the book arts—preserving the art and lore of the printed word.

Nonfiction How-to. Subjects include book arts, printing, papermaking, bookbinding, book collecting, etc. Reviews artwork/photos as part of ms package. Send photocopies.

Recent Title(s) *ABC for Book Collectors, 8th Ed.*, by John Carter and Nicolas Barker; *Early Type Specimens*, by John Lane; *The Great Libraries*, by Konstantinos Staikos.

OHIO STATE UNIVERSITY PRESS

1070 Carmack Rd., Columbus OH 43210-1002. (614)292-6930. Fax: (614)292-2065. E-mail: ohiostatepress@osu.edu. Web site: www.ohiostatepress.org. **Acquisitions:** Malcolm Litchfield, director; Sandy Crooms, acquisitions editor. Estab. 1957. **Publishes 30 titles/year. Pays royalty. Offers advance.** Responds in 3 months to queries. Ms guidelines online.

O→ The Ohio State University Press publishes scholarly nonfiction, and offers short fiction and short poetry prizes. Currently emphasizing history, literary studies, political science, women's health, classics, Victoria studies.

Nonfiction General nonfiction, scholarly. Subjects include business/economics, education, government/politics, history (American), language/literature, multicultural, regional, sociology, women's issues/studies, criminology, literary criticism, women's health. Query with SASE.

Recent Title(s) *Saving Lives*, by Albert Goldbarth (poetry); *Ohio: History of People*, by Andrew Cayton (nonfiction).

[A] ONE WORLD BOOKS

Ballantine Publishing Group, Inc., 1745 Broadway, 18th Floor, New York NY 10019. (212)782-9000. Fax: (212)572-4949. Web site: www.randomhouse.com. Estab. 1991. Publishes hardcover, trade and mass market paperback originals and trade paperback reprints. Accepts simultaneous submissions.

O→ "All One World Books must be specifically written for either an African-American, Asian, Native American, or Hispanic audience. No exceptions."

Nonfiction Biography, cookbook, how-to, humor, self-help. Subjects include Americana, cooking/foods/nutrition, creative nonfiction, ethnic, government/politics, history, memoirs, multicultural, philosophy, psychology, recreation, travel, women's issues/studies, African-American studies. *Agented submissions only.*

Fiction Adventure, comic books, confession, erotica, ethnic, historical, humor, literary, mainstream/contemporary, multicultural, mystery, regional, romance, suspense, strong need for commercial women's fiction. No poetry. *Agented submissions only.*

Recent Title(s) *A One Woman Man*, by Travis Hunter; *Space Between the Stars*, by Deborah Santana; *Black Titan*, by Carol Jenkins and Elizabeth Gardner Hines.

Tips All books must be written in English.

N ORANGE FRAZER PRESS, INC.

P.O. Box 214, Wilmington OH 45177. (937)382-3196. Fax: (937)383-3159. Web site: www.orangefrazer.com. **Acquisitions:** Marcy Hawley, editor. Publishes hardcover and trade paperback originals and reprints. **Publishes 25 titles/year. Receives 50 queries and 40 mss/year. 50% of books from first-time authors; 99% from unagented writers. Pays 10-12% royalty on wholesale price. Offers advance.** Publishes book 18 months after acceptance of ms. Accepts simultaneous submissions. Responds in 2 months to queries; 1 month to proposals; 1 month to mss. Book catalog free.

- Orange Frazer Press accepts Ohio-related nonfiction only; corporate histories; town celebrations; anniversary books.

Nonfiction Accepts Ohio nonfiction only. Biography, coffee table book, cookbook, gift book, humor, illustrated book, reference, textbook. Subjects include art/architecture, cooking/foods/nutrition, education, history, memoirs, nature/environment, photography, recreation, regional (Ohio), sports, travel, women's issues/studies. Submit proposal package including outline, 1 sample chapter(s), SASE. Reviews artwork/photos as part of ms package. Send photocopies or transparencies.

Recent Title(s) *CHAD: I Can't Be Stopped*; *The Art of Table Dancing*.

Tips "We do many high-end company and corporate histories."

ORCHARD BOOKS

Imprint of Scholastic Trade Division, 557 Broadway, New York NY 10012. (212)343-6100. Web site: www.scholastic.com. Estab. 1987. Publishes hardcover and trade paperback originals.

- Orchard specializes in children's picture books. Currently emphasizing picture books and middle grade novels (ages 8-12). De-emphasizing young adult.

Nonfiction Children's/juvenile, illustrated book. Subjects include animals, history, nature/environment. "*No unsolicited mss.* Be as specific and enlightening as possible about your book." Query with SASE. Reviews artwork/photos as part of ms package. Send photocopies.

Fiction Picture books, young adult, middle reader; novelty. *No unsolicited mss.* Query with SASE.

Recent Title(s) *Katie's Sunday Afternoon*, by James Mayhew; *The Wheels on the Race Car*, by Alexander Zane, illustrated by James Warhola; *What's Going On In There?*, by Geoffrey Grahn.

Tips "Go to a bookstore and read several Orchard Books to get an idea of what we publish. Write what you feel and query us if you think it's 'right.' It's worth finding the right publishing match."

OREGON STATE UNIVERSITY PRESS

500 Kerr, Corvallis OR 97331-2122. (541)737-3873. Fax: (541)737-3170. Web site: oregonstate.edu/dept/press. **Acquisitions:** Mary Elizabeth Braun, acquiring editor. Estab. 1962. Publishes hardcover and paperback originals. **Publishes 12-15 titles/year. 75% of books from first-time authors. Pays royalty on net receipts.** Publishes book 1 year after acceptance of ms. Does not accept simultaneous submissions. Responds in 3 months to queries. Book catalog for 6×9 SAE with 2 first-class stamps; ms guidelines online.

Nonfiction Publishes scholarly books in history, biography, geography, literature, natural resource management, with strong emphasis on Pacific or Northwestern topics. Reference, scholarly. Subjects include regional, science. Submit outline, sample chapter(s).

Recent Title(s) *Gathering Moss: A Natural & Cultural History of Mosses*, by Robin Wall Kimmerer; *Oregon's Promise: An Interpretive History*, by David Peterson del Mar; *Living with Earthquakes in the Pacific Northwest*, by Robert S. Yeats.

N O'REILLY MEDIA

1005 Gravenstein Highway N., Sebastopol CA 95472. (707)827-7000. Fax: (707)829-0104. E-mail: proposals@oreilly.com. Web site: www.oreilly.com. **Acquisitions:** Acquisitions Editor. Ms guidelines online.

- "We're always looking for new authors and new book ideas. Our ideal author has real technical competence and a passion for explaining things clearly."

Nonfiction How-to, technical. Subjects include computers/electronic. "At the same time as you might say that our books are written 'by and for smart people,' they also have a down to earth quality. We like straight talk that goes right to the heart of what people need to know." Submit proposal package including outline, publishing history, author bio.

Tips "It helps if you know that we tend to publish 'high end' books rather than books for dummies, and generally don't want yet another book on a topic that's already well covered."

OUR SUNDAY VISITOR PUBLISHING

200 Noll Plaza, Huntington IN 46750-4303. (260)356-8400. Fax: (260)359-9117. E-mail: booksed@osv.com. Web site: www.osv.com. President/Publisher: Greg Erlandson. Editorial Director: Beth McNamara. Editorial Development Manager: Jacquelyn Lindsey. **Acquisitions:** Michael Dubruiel, Kelley Renz, acquisitions editors.

Estab. 1912. Publishes paperback and hardbound originals. **Publishes 30-40 titles/year. 10% of books from first-time authors; 90% from unagented writers. Pays variable royalty on net receipts. Offers $1,500 average advance.** Publishes book 1-2 years after acceptance of ms. Does not accept simultaneous submissions. Responds in 3 months to queries. Book catalog for 9×12 SAE; ms guidelines for #10 SASE or online.

- "We are a Catholic publishing company seeking to educate and deepen our readers in their faith." Currently emphasizing reference, apologetics, and catechetics. De-emphasizing inspirational.

Nonfiction Catholic viewpoints on family, prayer, and devotional books, and Catholic heritage books. Reference. Prefers to see well-developed proposals as first submission with annotated outline and definition of intended market. Reviews artwork/photos as part of ms package.

Recent Title(s) *De-Coding DaVinci*, by Amy Welborn.

Tips "Solid devotional books that are not first person, or lives of the saints and catechetical books have the best chance of selling to our firm. Make it solidly Catholic, unique, without pious platitudes."

THE OVERLOOK PRESS

141 Wooster St., New York NY 10012. (212)673-2210. Fax: (212)673-2296. Web site: www.overlookpress.com. Publisher: Peter Mayer. Estab. 1971. Publishes hardcover and trade paperback originals and hardcover reprints. **Publishes 100 titles/year.** Does not accept simultaneous submissions. Book catalog free.

- Overlook Press publishes fiction, children's books, and nonfiction.

Nonfiction Biography. Subjects include art/architecture, film/cinema/stage, history, regional (New York State), current events, design, health/fitness, how-to, lifestyle, martial arts. No pornography. *Agented submissions only.*

Fiction Literary, some commercial, foreign literature in translation. *Agented submissions only.*

Recent Title(s) *Dragon's Eye*, by Andy Oakes; *The Brontes*, by Juliet Barker; *Triomf*, translated from the Afrikaans by Leon de Kock.

THE OVERMOUNTAIN PRESS

P.O. Box 1261, Johnson City TN 37605. (423)926-2691. Fax: (423)232-1252. E-mail: submissions@overmtn.com. Web site: www.overmountainpress.com. Publisher: Beth Wright; Managing Editor: Daniel Lewis. Estab. 1970. Publishes hardcover and trade paperback originals and reprints. Accepts simultaneous submissions. Responds in 1-4 months to mss. Book catalog free; ms guidelines online.

Imprints Silver Dagger Mysteries.

- The Overmountain Press publishes primarily Appalachian history. Audience is people interested in history of Tennessee, Virginia, North Carolina, Kentucky, and all aspects of this region—Revolutionary War, Civil War, county histories, historical biographies, etc.

Nonfiction Regional works only. Coffee table book, cookbook. Subjects include Americana, cooking/foods/nutrition, ethnic, history, military/war, nature/environment, photography, regional, women's issues/studies, Native American, ghostlore, guidebooks, folklore. Submit proposal package including outline, 3 sample chapters, marketing suggestions. Reviews artwork/photos as part of ms package. Send photocopies.

Fiction Picture books (must have regional flavor). Submit complete ms.

Tips "Please, no phone calls."

RICHARD C. OWEN PUBLISHERS, INC.

P.O. Box 585, Katonah NY 10536. (914)232-3903. Web site: www.rcowen.com. **Acquisitions:** Janice Boland, director, children's books; Amy Finney, project editor (professional development, teacher-oriented books). Estab. 1982. Publishes paperback originals. **Pays 5% royalty on wholesale price. Books for Young Learners Anthologies: flat fee for all rights.** Publishes book 2-5 years after acceptance of ms. Accepts simultaneous submissions. Responds in 1 month to proposals; 5 months to mss. Ms guidelines online.

- "Due to high volume and long production time, we are currently limiting to nonfiction submissions only."

Nonfiction Children's/juvenile. Subjects include animals, art/architecture, fashion/beauty, gardening, history, music/dance, nature/environment, recreation, science, sports, women's issues/studies, contemporary culture. "Our books are for kindergarten, first- and second-grade children to read on their own. The stories are very brief—under 1,000 words—yet well structured and crafted with memorable characters, language, and plots." Send for ms guidelines, then submit complete ms with SASE via mail only or visit Web site.

Poetry "Poems that excite children are fun, humorous, fresh, and interesting. If rhyming, must be without force or contrivance. Poems should tell a story or evoke a mood or atmostphere and have rhythmic language." No jingles. Submit complete ms.

Tips "We don't respond to queries or e-mails. Please do not fax or e-mail us. Because our books are so brief it is better to send entire manuscript. We publish story books with inherent educational value for young readers—books they can read with enjoyment and success. We believe students become enthusiastic, independent, lifelong learners when supported and guided by skillful teachers using good books. The professional development work we do and the books we publish support these beliefs."

OWL BOOKS

Henry Holt & Co., Inc., 115 W. 18th St., New York NY 10011. (212)886-9200. Fax: (212)633-0748. Web site: www.henryholt.com. Estab. 1996. Publishes paperback originals and reprints. Accepts simultaneous submissions. Ms guidelines online.

"We are looking for original, great ideas that have commercial appeal, but that you can respect."

Nonfiction Biography, self-help. Subjects include health/medicine, history (American, military), regional, science, women's issues/studies, current affairs, parenting, business/finance. *Agented submissions only.*

Recent Title(s) *The G Spot*, by Alice Kahn Ladas, Beverly Whipple, and John D. Perry; *The Gluten-Free Gourmet Cooks Comfort Foods*, by Bette Hagman; *I'm OK, You're My Parents*, by Dale Atkins, PhD.

P & R PUBLISHING CO.

P.O. Box 817, Phillipsburg NJ 08865. Fax: (908)454-0859. Web site: www.prpbooks.com. Estab. 1930. Publishes hardcover originals and trade paperback originals and reprints. **Publishes 40 titles/year. Receives 300 queries and 100 mss/year. 5% of books from first-time authors; 95% from unagented writers. Pays 10-14% royalty on wholesale price.** Accepts simultaneous submissions. Responds in 1 month to queries; 2 months to proposals; 4 months to mss. Book catalog free; ms guidelines online.

Nonfiction Biography, booklets, children's/juvenile, gift book, scholarly. Subjects include history, religion, spirituality, translation. Query with SASE.

Recent Title(s) *Justification and the New Perspectives on Paul*, by Guy Waters (Biblical studies); *The Afternoon of Life*, by Elyse Fitzpatrick (women); *Rebel's Keep*, by Douglas Bond (children's historical fiction).

Tips "Our audience is evangelical Christians, other Christians, and seekers. All of our publications are consistent with Biblical teaching, as summarized in the Westminster Standards."

PACIFIC PRESS PUBLISHING ASSOCIATION

Trade Book Division, P.O. Box 5353, Nampa ID 83653-5353. (208)465-2500. Fax: (208)465-2531. E-mail: booksubmissions@pacificpress.com. Web site: www.pacificpress.com. **Acquisitions:** Tim Lale, acquisitions editor (children's stories, biography, Christian living, spiritual growth); David Jarnes, book editor (theology, doctrine, inspiration). Estab. 1874. Publishes hardcover and trade paperback originals and reprints. **Publishes 35 titles/year. 35% of books from first-time authors; 100% from unagented writers. Pays 8-16% royalty on wholesale price.** Publishes book up to 2 years after acceptance of ms. Does not accept simultaneous submissions. Responds in 3 months to queries. Ms guidelines online.

"We publish books that fit Seventh-day Adventist beliefs only. All titles are Christian and religious. For guidance, see www.adventist.org/beliefs/index.html. Our books fit into the categories of this retail site: www.adventistbookcenter.com."

Nonfiction Biography, booklets, children's/juvenile, cookbook (vegetarian), how-to, humor. Subjects include child guidance/parenting, cooking/foods/nutrition (vegetarian only), health/medicine, history, nature/environment, philosophy, religion, spirituality, women's issues/studies, family living, Christian lifestyle, Bible study, Christian doctrine, eschatology. Query with SASE or e-mail, or submit 3 sample chapters, cover letter with overview of book. Electronic submissions accepted. Reviews artwork/photos as part of ms package.

Fiction Religious. "Pacific Press rarely publishes fiction, but we're interested in developing a line of Seventh-day Adventist fiction in the future. Only proposals accepted; no full manuscripts."

Recent Title(s) *Who's Afraid of the Judgment?*, by Roy Gane (doctrine); *Rainbow Over Hell*, by Sharon Fujimoto-Johnson (historical biography); *Plagues in the Palace*, by Bradley Booth (children's).

Tips "Our primary audience is members of the Seventh-day Adventist denomination. Almost all are written by Seventh-day Adventists. Books that do well for us relate the Biblical message to practical human concerns and focus more on the experiential rather than theoretical aspects of Christianity. We are assigning more titles, using less unsolicited material—although we still publish manuscripts from freelance submissions and proposals."

PALADIN PRESS

7077 Winchester Circle, Boulder CO 80301. (303)443-7250. Fax: (303)442-8741. E-mail: editorial@paladin-press.com. Web site: www.paladin-press.com. President/Publisher: Peder C. Lund. **Acquisitions:** Jon Ford, editorial director. Estab. 1970. Publishes hardcover originals and paperback originals and reprints. **Publishes 50 titles/year. 50% of books from first-time authors; 95% from unagented writers. Pays 10-15% royalty on net receipts. Offers advance.** Publishes book 1 year after acceptance of ms. Accepts simultaneous submissions. Responds in 2 months to proposals. Book catalog free.

Imprints Sycamore Island Books; Flying Machines Press; Outer Limits Press; Romance Book Classics.

- Paladin Press publishes the "action library" of nonfiction in military science, police science, weapons, combat, personal freedom, self-defense, survival.

Nonfiction "Paladin Press primarily publishes original manuscripts on military science, weaponry, self-defense, personal privacy, financial freedom, espionage, police science, action careers, guerrilla warfare, and fieldcraft." How-to, reference. Subjects include government/politics, military/war. "If applicable, send sample photographs and line drawings with complete outline and sample chapters." Query with SASE.

Recent Title(s) *Surviving Workplace Violence: What to Do Before a Violent Incident; What to Do When the Violence Explodes*, by Loren W. Christensen.

Tips "We need lucid, instructive material aimed at our market and accompanied by sharp, relevant illustrations and photos. As we are primarily a publisher of 'how-to' books, a manuscript that has step-by-step instructions, written in a clear and concise manner (but not strictly outline form) is desirable. No fiction, first-person accounts, children's, religious, or joke books. We are also interested in serious, professional videos and video ideas (contact Michael Rigg)."

PALGRAVE MACMILLAN

St. Martin's Press, 175 Fifth Ave., New York NY 10010. (212)982-3900. Fax: (212)777-6359. Web site: www.palgrave-usa.com. **Acquisitions:** Airié Stuart (history, business, economics, current events, psychology, biography); Anthony Wahl (political science, current events, Asian studies, international relations); Farideh Koohi-Kamali (literature, anthropology, cultural studies, performing arts, Islamic World & Middle East); Amanda Johnson (education, religion, women's studies/history); Ella Pearce (African studies, Latin American studies); Alessandra Bastagli (American history, American studies, world history); Heather Van Dusen (political science, political economy, political theory). Publishes hardcover and trade paperback originals. Accepts simultaneous submissions. Book catalog and ms guidelines online.

- Palgrave wishes to "expand on our already successful academic, trade, and reference programs so that we will remain at the forefront of publishing in the global information economy of the 21st century. We publish high-quality academic works and a distinguished range of reference titles, and we expect to see many of our works available in electronic form. We do not accept fiction or poetry."

Nonfiction Biography, reference, scholarly. Subjects include business/economics, creative nonfiction, education, ethnic, gay/lesbian, government/politics, history, language/literature, military/war, money/finance, multicultural, music/dance, philosophy, regional, religion, sociology, spirituality, translation, women's issues/studies, humanities, social studies, film/cinema/stage, contemporary culture, general nonfiction, world affairs. "We are looking for good solid scholarship." Query with proposal package including outline, 3-4 sample chapters, prospectus, cv and SASE. Reviews artwork/photos as part of ms package.

Recent Title(s) *Future Jihad*, by Walid Phares; *Billions*, by Tom Doctoroff; *AIDS in Asia*, by Susan Houter.

PANTHEON BOOKS

Imprint of Knopf Publishing Group, Division of Random House, Inc., 1745 Broadway 21-2, New York NY 10019. (212)782-9000. Fax: (212)572-6030. Web site: www.pantheonbooks.com. **Acquisitions:** Adult Editorial Department. Estab. 1942. Publishes hardcover and trade paperback originals and trade paperback reprints. **Pays royalty. Offers advance.** Does not accept simultaneous submissions.

- "We only accept mss submitted by an agent. You may still send a 20-50 page sample and a SASE to our slushpile. Allow 2-6 months for a response."
- Pantheon Books publishes both Western and non-Western authors of literary fiction and important nonfiction.

Nonfiction Autobiography, biography, general nonfiction, literary; international. Subjects include government/politics, history, memoirs, science, travel.

Fiction Quality fiction, including graphic novels and fairytales/folklore.

Recent Title(s) *In the Company of Cheerful Ladies*, by Alexander McCall Smith; *The Way Home*, by Ernestine Bradley; *Reef Madness*, by David Dobbs.

PARACLETE PRESS

P.O. Box 1568, Orleans MA 02653. (508)255-4685. Fax: (508)255-5705. Web site: www.paracletepress.com. **Acquisitions:** Editorial Review Committee. Estab. 1981. Publishes hardcover and trade paperback originals. **Publishes 20 titles/year. Receives 250 mss/year.** Publishes book up to 2 years after acceptance of ms. Does not accept simultaneous submissions. Responds in 2 months to queries; 2 months to mss. Book catalog for $8\frac{1}{2} \times 11$ SASE; ms guidelines for #10 SASE.

- Publisher of devotionals, new editions of classics, books on prayer, Christian living, spirituality, fiction, compact discs, and videos.

Nonfiction Subjects include religion. Query with SASE, or submit 2-3 sample chapters, TOC, chapter summaries.

Recent Title(s) *The Jesus Creed*, by Scot McKnight; *Engaging the World With Merton*, by M. Basil Pennington, O.C.S.O; *The Illuminated Heart*, by Frederica Mathewes-Green.

PARAGON HOUSE PUBLISHERS

1925 Oakcrest Ave., Suite 7, St. Paul MN 55113-2619. (651)644-3087. Fax: (651)644-0997. E-mail: paragon@paragonhouse.com. Web site: www.paragonhouse.com. **Acquisitions:** Rosemary Yokoi, acquisitions editor. Estab. 1962. Publishes hardcover and trade paperback originals and trade paperback reprints. **Publishes 12-15 titles/year; imprint publishes 2-5 titles/year. Receives 1,500 queries and 150 mss/year. 7% of books from first-time authors; 90% from unagented writers. Offers $500-1,500 advance.** Publishes book 1 year after acceptance of ms. Accepts simultaneous submissions. Ms guidelines online.

Imprints *Series*: Paragon Issues in Philosophy, Genocide and Holocaust Studies; Omega Books.

- ''We publish general-interest titles and textbooks that provide the readers greater understanding of society and the world.'' Currently emphasizing religion, philosophy, economics, and society.''

Nonfiction Biography, reference, textbook. Subjects include child guidance/parenting, government/politics, memoirs, multicultural, nature/environment, philosophy, religion, sex, sociology, women's issues/studies, world affairs. Submit proposal package including outline, 2 sample chapters, market breakdown, SASE.

Recent Title(s) *Inman's War*, by Jeffrey Copeland; *Catholic Spirituality in Focus*, by George E. Saint-Laurent; *World Religions in a Postmodern World*, by Henry Ruf.

PARKWAY PUBLISHERS, INC.

Box 3678, Boone NC 28607. (828)265-3993. Fax: (828)265-3993. E-mail: parkwaypub@hotmail.com. Web site: www.parkwaypublishers.com. **Acquisitions:** Rao Aluri, president. Publishes hardcover and trade paperback originals. **Publishes 10-12 titles/year. Receives 15-20 queries and 20 mss/year. 75% of books from first-time authors; 100% from unagented writers.** Publishes book 8 months after acceptance of ms. Does not accept simultaneous submissions.

- Parkway publishes books on the local history and culture of western North Carolina. ''We are located on Blue Ridge Parkway and our primary industry is tourism. We are interested in nonfiction books which present the history and culture of western North Carolina to the tourist market.'' Will consider fiction if it highlights the region.

Nonfiction Technical. Subjects include history, biography, tourism, and natural history. Query with SASE, or submit complete ms.

Recent Title(s) *Shuffletown USA and Orville Hicks: Mountain Stories, Mountain Roots.*

PAULINE BOOKS AND MEDIA

Daughters of St. Paul, 50 St. Paul's Ave., Boston MA 02130. (617)522-8911. Fax: (617)541-9805. E-mail: editorial@pauline.org. Web site: www.pauline.org. **Acquisitions:** Sr. Donna William Giaimo, FSP; Sr. Madonna Therese, acquisitions editor. Estab. 1948. Publishes trade paperback originals and reprints. Does not accept simultaneous submissions. Responds in 2-3 months to queries. Book catalog for 9×12 SAE with 4 first-class stamps; ms guidelines online.

- Submissions are evaluated on adherence to Gospel values, harmony with the Catholic tradition, relevance of topic, and quality of writing.

Nonfiction Subjects include spirituality, scripture, catechetics, family life, teacher resources, lives of the saints, mariology, prayer, peer pressure, substance abuse, self-esteem,. No biography/autobiography, poetry, or strictly nonreligious works considered. Submit 2-3 sample chapters, query, synopsis, SASE.

Fiction Bible stories, prayerbooks, coloring/activity books. Children only. No strictly nonreligious works considered. Submit synopsis, 2-3 sample chapters, query, SASE.

Recent Title(s) *Lent: An Uncommon Love Story*, by Antoinette Bosco; *Experiencing Bereavement*, by Helen Alexander; *Saint Jude*, by Michael Aquilina III.

PEACHTREE CHILDREN'S BOOKS

Peachtree Publishers, Ltd., 1700 Chattahoochee Ave., Atlanta GA 30318-2112. (404)876-8761. Fax: (404)875-2578. E-mail: hello@peachtree-online.com. Web site: www.peachtree-online.com. **Acquisitions:** Helen Harriss, submissions editor. Publishes hardcover and trade paperback originals. **Publishes 30 titles/year. 25% of books from first-time authors; 25% from unagented writers. Pays royalty on retail price; Advance varies.** Publishes book 1 year or more after acceptance of ms. Accepts simultaneous submissions. Responds in 6 months to queries; 6 months to mss. Book catalog for 6 first-class stamps; ms guidelines online.

Imprints Freestone; Peachtree Jr.

- ''We publish a broad range of subjects and perspectives, with emphasis on innovative plots and strong writing.''

Nonfiction Children's/juvenile. Subjects include animals, child guidance/parenting, creative nonfiction, education, ethnic, gardening, health/medicine, history, language/literature, multicultural, music/dance, nature/environment, recreation, regional, science, social sciences, sports, travel. No e-mail or fax queries of mss. Submit complete ms with SASE, or summary and 3 sample chapters with SASE.

Fiction Juvenile, picture books, young adult. Looking for very well-written middle grade and young adult novels. No collections of poetry or short stories; no romance or science fiction. Submit complete ms with SASE.

Recent Title(s) *Dad, Jackie and Me*, by Myron Uhlberg (children's picture book); *Yellow Star*, by Carmen Agra Deedy (children's picture book); *Dog Sense*, by Sneed Collard (middle reader).

PEACHTREE PUBLISHERS

1700 Chattahoochee Ave., Atlanta GA 30318-2112. (404)876-8761. Fax: (404)875-2578. E-mail: hello@peachtree-online.com. Web site: www.peachtree-online.com. **Acquisitions:** Helen Harriss, submissions editor. Estab. 1978. Publishes hardcover and trade paperback originals. **Publishes 30 titles/year. 25% of books from first-time authors; 75% from unagented writers. Pays royalty. Royalty varies. Offers advance.** Publishes book 1 year or more after acceptance of ms. Accepts simultaneous submissions. Responds in 6 months to queries; 6 months to mss. Book catalog for 9×12 SAE with 6 first-class stamps; ms guidelines online.

Imprints Peachtree Children's Books (Peachtree Jr., FreeStone).

- Peachtree Publishers specializes in children's books, middle reader and books, young adult, regional guidebooks, parenting and self-help.

Nonfiction Children's/juvenile, general nonfiction, self-help, regional guides. Subjects include health/medicine, recreation. No technical or reference. No e-mail or fax submissions or queries. Submit outline, 3 sample chapters, or submit complete ms. Include SASE for response.

Fiction Juvenile, young adult. "Absolutely no adult fiction! We are seeking young adult and juvenile works, including mystery and historical fiction, of high literary merit." No adult fiction, fantasy, science fiction, or romance. No collections of poetry or short stories. Query with SASE. Query, submit outline/synopsis, and 3 sample chapters, or submit complete ms with SASE. Inquires/submissions by US Mail only. E-mail and fax will not be answered.

Recent Title(s) *Around Atlanta With Children*, by Denise Black and Janet Schwartz; *Yellow Star*, by Carmen Agra Deedy; *Surviving Jamestown: The Adventures of Young Sam Collier*, by Gail Langer Karwoski.

PENGUIN GROUP (USA), Inc.

375 Hudson St., New York NY 10014. (212)366-2000. Web site: www.penguin.com. General interest publisher of both fiction and nonfiction.

Imprints Penguin Adult Division: Ace Books, Alpha Books, Avery, Berkley Books, Dutton, Gotham Books, HPBooks, Hudson Street Press, Jove, New American Library, Penguin, The Penguin Press, Perigee, Plume, Portfolio, G.P. Putnam's Sons, Riverhead, Sentinel, Jeremy P. Tarcher, Viking; **Penguin Children's Division:** Dial Books for Young Readers, Dutton Children's Books, Firebird, Grosset & Dunlap, Philomel, Price Stern Sloan, Puffin Books, G.P. Putnam's Sons, Speak, Viking Children's Books, Frederick Warne.

- *No unsolicited mss.* Submit work through a literary agent. Exceptions are DAW Books and G.P. Putnam's Sons Books for Young Readers, which are accepting submissions. See individual listings for more information.

Recent Title(s) *Predator*, by Patricia Cornwell; *Red Lily*, by Nora Roberts; *On Beauty*, by Zadie Smith.

PERENNIAL

HarperCollins Publishers, 10 E. 53rd St., New York NY 10022. (212)207-7000. Web site: www.harpercollins.com. **Acquisitions:** Acquisitions Editor. Estab. 1963. Publishes trade paperback originals and reprints. Book catalog free.

- "Perennial publishes a broad range of adult literary fiction and nonfiction paperbacks that create a record of our culture."

Nonfiction Subjects include Americana, animals, business/economics, child guidance/parenting, cooking/foods/nutrition, education, ethnic, gay/lesbian, history, language/literature, military/war, money/finance, music/dance, nature/environment (and environment), philosophy, psychology (self-help psychotherapy), recreation, regional, religion (spirituality), science, sociology, sports, translation, travel, women's issues/studies, mental health, health, classic literature. "Our focus is ever-changing, adjusting to the marketplace. Mistakes writers often make are not giving their background and credentials - why they are qualified to write the book. A proposal should explain why the author wants to write this book; why it will sell; and why it is better or different from others of its kind." *Agented submissions only.*

Fiction Ethnic, feminist, literary. *Agented submissions only.*

Poetry Don't send poetry unless you have been published in several established literary magazines already. *Agented submissions only.*

Recent Title(s) *Bradbury Stories*, by Ray Bradbury; *Ugly Americans*, by Ben Mezrich; *Goodnight Steve McQueen*, by Louise Wener.

Tips "See our Web site for a list of titles or write to us for a free catalog."

PERIGEE BOOKS

Imprint of Penguin Group (USA), Inc., 375 Hudson St., New York NY 10014. (212)366-2000. Publisher: John Duff. **Acquisitions:** Marian Lizzi, senior editor (health, reference, childcare, cookbooks); Meg Leder, editor (personal growth, crafts, lifestyle, women's issues); Christel Winkler, associate editor (career reference, lifestyle). Editors also acquire for Putnam for hard/soft joint ventures in all areas of prescriptive nonfiction. Publishes hardcover and trade paperback originals and reprints. **Publishes 55-60 titles/year. Receives hundreds queries/year. 30% of books from first-time authors; 10% from unagented writers. Pays 6-7½% royalty. Offers $5,000-150,000 advance.** Publishes book within 18 months after acceptance of ms. Accepts simultaneous submissions. Responds in 2 months to queries. Book catalog free; ms guidelines given on contract.

- Publishes in all areas of self-help and how-to. Currently emphasizing popular psychology, women's issues in health, fitness, and careers and lifestyles.

Nonfiction How-to, reference (popular), self-help, prescriptive books. Subjects include child guidance/parenting, cooking/foods/nutrition, health/medicine, hobbies, money/finance (personal finance), psychology, sex, sports, women's issues/studies, career, fashion/beauty. Prefers agented mss, but accepts unsolicited queries. Query with SASE, or submit outline.

PETER PAUPER PRESS, INC.

202 Mamaroneck Ave., White Plains NY 10601-5376. E-mail: bpaulding@peterpauper.com. **Acquisitions:** Barbara Paulding, editorial director. Estab. 1928. Publishes hardcover originals. **Publishes 40-50 titles/year. Receives 100 queries and 150 mss/year. 5% from unagented writers. Makes outright purchase only. Offers advance.** Publishes book 1 year after acceptance of ms. Does not accept simultaneous submissions. Responds in 2 months to queries. Ms guidelines for #10 SASE or may request via e-mail.

- PPP publishes small and medium format, illustrated gift books for occasions and in celebration of specific relationships such as mom, sister, friend, teacher, grandmother, granddaughter. PPP has expanded into the following areas: books for teens and tweens, activity books for children, books on popular topics of nonfiction for adults and licensed books by best-selling authors.

Nonfiction Gift book. Subjects include specific relationships or special occasions (graduation, Mother's Day, Christmas, etc.). "We do not publish fiction or poetry. We publish brief, original quotes, aphorisms, and wise sayings. Please do not send us other people's quotes." Query with SASE.

Recent Title(s) *The Little Pink Book of Frozen Drinks*; *Spit Happens!*; *Brianiac's Sudoku*.

Tips "Our readers are primarily female, age 10 and over, who are likely to buy a 'gift' book or gift book set in a stationery, gift, book, or boutique store or national book chain. Writers should become familiar with our previously published work. We publish only small- and medium-format, illustrated, hardcover gift books and sets of between 1,000-4,000 words. We have much less interest in work aimed at men."

PETERSON'S

2000 Lenox Dr., Princeton Pike Corporate Center, 3rd Floor, Lawrenceville NJ 08648. (609)896-1800. Web site: www.petersons.com. Estab. 1966. Publishes trade and reference books. **Pays royalty. Offers advance.** Does not accept simultaneous submissions. Book catalog free.

- "Peterson's publishes guides to graduate and professional programs, colleges and universities, financial aid, distance learning, private schools, summer programs, international study, executive education, job hunting and career opportunities, educational and career test prep, as well as online products and services offering educational and career guidance and information for adult learners and workplace solutions for education professionals."

Nonfiction Authored titles; education directories; career directories. Subjects include business/economics, education, careers. Looks for "appropriateness of contents to our markets, author's credentials, and writing style suitable for audience."

Recent Title(s) *Best College Admissions Essays, 3rd Ed.*; *Study Abroad 2005, 12th Ed.*; *Summer Opportunities for Kids & Teenagers 2005, 22nd Ed.*

Tips Many of Peterson's reference works are updated annually. Peterson's markets strongly to libraries and institutions, as well as to the corporate sector.

PFLAUM PUBLISHING GROUP

N90 W16890 Roosevelt Dr., Menomonee Falls WI 53051-7933. (262)502-4222. Fax: (262)502-4224. E-mail: kcannizzo@pflaum.com. **Acquisitions:** Karen A. Cannizzo, editorial director. Other Address: 2621 Dryden Rd.,

Suite 300, Dayton OH 45439. Fax: (937)293-1310. **Publishes 20 titles/year. Payment may be outright purchase, royalty, or down payment plus royalty.** Book catalog and ms guidelines free.

O→ "Pflaum Publishing Group, a division of Peter Li, Inc., serves the specialized market of religious education, primarily Roman Catholic. We provide high quality, theologically sound, practical, and affordable resources that assist religious educators of and ministers to children from preschool through senior high school."

Nonfiction Religious education programs and catechetical resources. Query with SASE.

Recent Title(s) *Absolutely Advent*; *Totally Lent*.

PHAIDON PRESS

180 Varick St., Suite 1420, New York NY 10014. (212)652-5400. Fax: (212)652-5410. Web site: www.phaidon.com. **Acquisitions:** Editorial Submissions. Publishes hardcover and trade paperback originals and reprints. **Publishes 100 titles/year. Receives 500 mss/year. 40% of books from first-time authors; 90% from unagented writers. Pays royalty on wholesale price, if appropriate. Offers advance, if appropriate.** Publishes book 1 year after acceptance of ms. Accepts simultaneous submissions. Responds in 3 months to proposals. Book catalog free; ms guidelines online.

Imprints Phaidon.

Nonfiction Subjects include art/architecture, photography, design. Submit proposal package and outline, or submit complete ms. Reviews artwork/photos as part of ms package. Send photocopies.

PHI DELTA KAPPA INTERNATIONAL

P.O. Box 789, Bloomington IN 47402. (812)339-1156. Fax: (812)339-0018. E-mail: information@pdkintl.org. Web site: www.pdkintl.org. **Acquisitions:** Donovan R. Walling, director of publications. Estab. 1906. Publishes hardcover and trade paperback originals. **Publishes 24-30 titles/year. Receives 100 queries and 50-60 mss/year. 50% of books from first-time authors; 100% from unagented writers. Pays honorarium of $500-5,000.** Publishes book 9 months after acceptance of ms. Does not accept simultaneous submissions. Responds in 3 months to proposals. Book catalog and ms guidelines free.

O→ "We publish books for educators—K-12 and higher education. Our professional books are often used in college courses but are never specifically designed as textbooks."

Nonfiction How-to, reference, scholarly, essay collections. Subjects include child guidance/parenting, education, legal issues. Query with SASE, or submit outline, 1 sample chapter. Reviews artwork/photos as part of ms package.

Recent Title(s) *The Nation's Report Card*, edited by Lyle V. Jones and Ingram Olkin; *Evaluating Principals*, by James E. Green.

PIA/GATFPRESS

Graphic Arts Technical Foundation, 200 Deer Run Rd., Sewickley PA 15143-2600. (412)741-6860. Fax: (412)741-2311. E-mail: tdestree@piagatf.org. Submissions E-mail: awoodall@piagatf.org. Web site: www.gain.net. **Acquisitions:** Tom Destree, editor in chief; Amy Woodall, managing editor (graphic arts, communication, book publishing, printing). Estab. 1924. Publishes trade paperback originals and hardcover reference texts. **Publishes 20 titles/year. 50% of books from first-time authors; 100% from unagented writers. Pays 5-15% royalty on wholesale price.** Publishes book 18 months after acceptance of ms. Responds in 1 month to queries. Book catalog for 9×12 SAE with 2 first-class stamps; ms guidelines for #10 SASE.

O→ "PIA/GATF's mission is to serve the graphic communications community as the major resource for technical information and services through research and education." Currently emphasizing career guides for graphic communications and turnkey training curriculums."

Nonfiction How-to, reference, technical, textbook. Subjects include printing/graphic communications, electronic publishing. "We primarily want textbook/reference books about printing and related technologies. However, we are expanding our reach into electronic communications." Query with SASE, or submit outline, sample chapters, and SASE. Reviews artwork/photos as part of ms package.

Recent Title(s) *Color and Its Reproduction, 3rd Ed.*, by Gary G. Field; *To Be a Profitable Printer*, by Michael Moffit.

Tips "We are publishing titles that are updated more frequently, such as *On-Demand Publishing*. Our scope now includes reference titles geared toward general audiences interested in computers, imaging, and Internet, as well as print publishing."

PICADOR USA

Subsidiary of Holtzbrinck Publishers Holdings LLC, 175 Fifth Ave., New York NY 10010. (212)674-5151. Fax: (212)253-9627. Web site: www.picadorusa.com. Estab. 1994. Publishes hardcover and trade paperback originals and reprints.

• *No unsolicited mss or queries. Agented submissions only.*

O¬ Picador publishes high-quality literary fiction and nonfiction.

Recent Title(s) *Housekeeping*, by Marilynne Robinson; *Life on the Outside*, by Jennifer Gonnerman; *Dry*, by Augusten Burroughs.

PICTON PRESS

Picton Corp., P.O. Box 1347, Rockland ME 04841-1347. (207)596-7766. Fax: (207)596-7767. E-mail: sales@pictonpress.com. Web site: www.pictonpress.com. Publishes hardcover and mass market paperback originals and reprints, and CDs. **Publishes 30 titles/year. Receives 30 queries and 15 mss/year. 50% of books from first-time authors; 100% from unagented writers. Pays 0-10% royalty on wholesale price, or makes outright purchase.** Publishes book 6 months after acceptance of ms. Does not accept simultaneous submissions. Responds in 2 months to queries; 2 months to proposals; 3 months to mss. Book catalog free.

Imprints Cricketfield Press; New England History Press; Penobscot Press; Picton Press.

O¬ "Picton Press is one of America's oldest, largest, and most respected publishers of genealogical and historical books specializing in research tools for the 17th, 18th, and 19th centuries."

Nonfiction Reference, textbook. Subjects include Americana, history, hobbies, genealogy, vital records. Query with SASE, or submit outline.

Recent Title(s) *Norden: A Guide to Scandinavian Genealogical Research in a Digital World*, by Art Jura.

THE PILGRIM PRESS

700 Prospect Ave. E., Cleveland OH 44115-1100. (216)736-3755. Fax: (216)736-2207. E-mail: tstaveteig@thepilgrimpress.com. Web site: www.thepilgrimpress.com. **Acquisitions:** Timothy G. Staveteig, publisher. Publishes hardcover and trade paperback originals. **Publishes 55 titles/year. 60% of books from first-time authors; 80% from unagented writers. Pays standard royalties. Offers advance.** Publishes book an average of 18 months after acceptance of ms. Does not accept simultaneous submissions. Responds in 3 months to queries. Book catalog and ms guidelines online.

Nonfiction Scholarly. Subjects include business/economics, gay/lesbian, government/politics, nature/environment, religion, ethics, social issues with a strong commitment to justice—addressing such topics as public policy, sexuality and gender, human rights and minority liberation—primarily in a Christian context, but not exclusively.

Tips "We are concentrating more on academic and trade submissions. Writers should send books about contemporary social issues. Our audience is liberal, open-minded, socially aware, feminist, church members and clergy, teachers, and seminary professors."

PLAYERS PRESS, INC.

P.O. Box 1132, Studio City CA 91614-0132. (818)789-4980. **Acquisitions:** Robert W. Gordon, vice president, editorial. Estab. 1965. Publishes hardcover originals and trade paperback originals and reprints. **Publishes 35-70 titles/year. 15% of books from first-time authors; 80% from unagented writers. Pays royalty on wholesale price. Offers advance.** Publishes book 3 months-2 years after acceptance of ms. Does not accept simultaneous submissions. Book catalog for 9×12 SAE with 6 first-class stamps; ms guidelines for #10 SASE.

O¬ Players Press publishes support books for the entertainment industries: theater, film, television, dance and technical. Currently emphasizing plays for all ages, theatre crafts, monologues and short scenes for ages 5-9, 11-15, and musicals.

Nonfiction Children's/juvenile, theatrical drama/entertainment industry. Subjects include film/cinema/stage, performing arts, costume, theater crafts, film crafts, dance. Needs quality plays and musicals, adult or juvenile. Query with SASE. Reviews music as part of ms package.

Fiction Plays: Subject matter includes adventure, confession, ethnic, experimental, fantasy, historical, horror, humor, mainstream, mystery, religious romance, science fiction, suspense, western. Submit complete ms for theatrical plays only. Plays must be previously produced. "No novels or story books are accepted."

Recent Title(s) *Women's Wear of the 1930's*, by Hopper/Countryman; *Rhyme Tyme*, by William-Alan Landes; *Borrowed Plumage*, by David Crawford.

Tips "Plays, entertainment industry texts, theater, film and TV books have the only chances of selling to our firm."

PLEASANT COMPANY PUBLICATIONS

8400 Fairway Place, Middleton WI 53562. Fax: (608)828-4768. Web site: www.americangirl.com. **Acquisitions:** Submissions Editor. Estab. 1986. Publishes hardcover and trade paperback originals. **Publishes 50-60 titles/year. Receives 500 queries and 800 mss/year. 90% from unagented writers. Offers varying advance.** Publishes book 3-12 months after acceptance of ms. Accepts simultaneous submissions. Responds in 3 months to queries; 4 months to mss. Book catalog for #10 SASE; ms guidelines for for SASE or on the Web site.

O→ Pleasant Company publishes fiction and nonfiction for girls 7-12. Not accepting fictional mss at this time. "We recommend checking our updated writer's guidelines online for possible changed."

Nonfiction Children's/juvenile (for girls 7-12), how-to. Subjects include contemporary lifestyle, activities. Query with SASE.

Recent Title(s) *Very Funny, Elizabeth!*, by Valerie Tripp; *Marisol*, by Gary Soto.

PLUME

Division of Penguin Group (USA), Inc., 375 Hudson St., New York NY 10014. (212)366-2000. Web site: www.penguinputnam.com. Estab. 1970. Publishes paperback originals and reprints. **Pays in royalties and author's copies. Offers advance.** Accepts simultaneous submissions. Book catalog for SASE.

Nonfiction Serious and historical nonfiction, including pop culture, current events, politics. *Agented submissions only.*

Fiction "All kinds of commercial and litearary fiction, including mainstream, historical, New Age, western, erotica, gay. Full-length novels and collections." *Agented submissions only.*

Recent Title(s) *Leonard Maltin's Classic Movie Guide*, by Leonard Maltin; *Summer in the City*, by Robyn Sisman; *Swimming Naked*, by Stacy Sims.

POCKET BOOKS

Simon & Schuster, 1230 Avenue of the Americas, New York NY 10020. (212)698-7000. Web site: www.simonsays.com. Estab. 1939. Publishes paperback originals and reprints, mass market and trade paperbacks. Does not accept simultaneous submissions. Book catalog free; ms guidelines online.

O→ Pocket Books publishes commercial fiction and genre fiction (WWE, Downtown Press, Star Trek).

Nonfiction Reference. Subjects include cooking/foods/nutrition. *Agented submissions only.*

Fiction Mystery, romance, suspense (psychological suspense, thriller), western, *Star Trek* novels. *Agented submissions only.*

Recent Title(s) *My Wicked Highlander*, by Jen Holling; *The Givenchy Code*, by Julie Kenner; *Awaken Me Darkly*, by Gena Showalter.

POISONED PEN PRESS

6962 E. 1st Ave., #103, Scottsdale AZ 85251. (480)945-3375. Fax: (480)949-1707. E-mail: editor@poisonedpenpress.com. Submissions E-mail: editor@poisonedpenpress.com. Web site: www.poisonedpress.com. Estab. 1996. Publishes hardcover originals, and hardcover and trade paperback reprints. **Publishes 36 titles/year. Receives 1,000 queries and 300 mss/year. 35% of books from first-time authors; 65% from unagented writers. Pays 9-15% royalty on retail price.** Publishes book 6-8 months after acceptance of ms. Does not accept simultaneous submissions. Responds in 2-3 months to queries; 2-3 months to proposals; 6 months to mss. Book catalog and ms guidelines online.

O→ "Our publishing goal is to offer well-written mystery novels of crime and/or detection where the puzzle and its resolution are the main forces that move the story forward."

Fiction Mystery. Mss should generally be longer than 65,000 words and shorter than 100,000 words. Does not want novels "centered on serial killers, spousal or child abuse, drugs, or extremist groups, although we do not entirely rule such works out." Query with SASE, or submit synopsis, first 30 pages. "We must receive both the synopsis and manuscript pages electronically as separate attachments to an e-mail message or as a disk or CD which we will not return."

Tips Audience is adult readers of mystery fiction.

POTOMAC BOOKS, INC.

22841 Quicksilver Dr., Dulles VA 20166. (703)661-1548. Fax: (703)661-1547. Web site: www.potomacbooksinc.com. **Acquisitions:** Don McKeon, vice president/publisher; Don Jacobs, acquisitions editor (general inquiries). Estab. 1984. Publishes hardcover and trade paperback originals and reprints. **Publishes 60 titles/year. Receives 900 queries/year. 20% of books from first-time authors; 70% from unagented writers. Pays royalty on wholesale price. Offers five figure maximum advance.** Publishes book 1 year after acceptance of ms. Accepts simultaneous submissions. Responds in 2 months to queries. Book catalog free; send 9×12 SAE with 4 first-class stamps for ms guidelines.

Imprints Potomac Sports.

O→ Potomac Books specializes in national and international affairs, history (especially military and diplomatic), intelligence, biography, reference, and sports. "We are particularly interested in authors who can communicate a sophisticated understanding of their topic to general readers, as well as specialists."

Nonfiction Subjects include government/politics, history, military/war, sports, world affairs, national and international affairs, intelligence studies. When submitting nonfiction, be sure to include sufficient biographical information (e.g., track records of previous publications), and "make clear in the query letter how your work might differ from other such works already published and with which yours might compete.'' Query letter should provide a summary of the project, a description of the author's credentials and an analysis of the work's competition. SASE must be included to receive a response. No e-mail submissions, please.

Recent Title(s) *Shattered Sword*, by Jonathan Parshall and Anthony Tully; *Wrigley Field*, by Stuart Shea.

Tips ''Our audience consists of general nonfiction readers, as well as students, scholars, policymakers and the military.''

PRACTICE MANAGEMENT INFORMATION CORP. (PMIC)

4727 Wilshire Blvd., #300, Los Angeles CA 90010. (323)954-0224. Fax: (323)954-0253. E-mail: arthur.gordon@pmicmail.com. Web site: www.medicalbookstore.com. **Acquisitions:** Arthur Gordon, managing editor. Estab. 1986. Publishes hardcover originals. **Publishes 21 titles/year. Receives 100 queries and 50 mss/year. 10% of books from first-time authors; 90% from unagented writers. Pays 12½% royalty on net receipts. Offers $1,000-5,000 advance.** Publishes book 18 months after acceptance of ms. Does not accept simultaneous submissions. Responds in 6 months to queries.

Imprints PMIC; Health Information Press (HIP).

O— PMIC helps healthcare workers understand the business of medicine by publishing books for doctors, medical office and hospital staff, medical managers, insurance coding/billing personnel. HIP seeks to simplify health care for consumers.

Nonfiction Reference, technical, textbook, medical practice management, clinical. Subjects include business/economics, health/medicine, science. Submit proposal package including outline, résumé, 3-5 sample chapters, letter stating who is the intended audience and the need/market for such a book.

Recent Title(s) *ICD-9-CM Coding Made Easy*, by James Davis; *Medicare Rules & Regulations*, by Maxine Lewis; *Medical Practice Forms*, by Keith Borglum.

PRB PRODUCTIONS

963 Peralta Ave., Albany CA 94706-2144. (510)526-0722. Fax: (510)527-4763. E-mail: prbprdns@aol.com. Web site: www.prbpro.com; www.prbmusic.com. **Acquisitions:** Peter R. Ballinger and Leslie Gold, publishers (early and contemporary music for instruments and voices). **Publishes 10-15 titles/year. Pays 10% royalty on retail price.** Accepts simultaneous submissions. Responds in 1 month to queries; 3 months to mss. Book catalog free on request or on Web site.

Nonfiction Textbook, sheet music. Subjects include music/dance. Query with SASE, or submit complete ms.

Recent Title(s) *Two String Quartets*, by Nathaniel Stookey (contemporary); *Complete Madrigals of John Wilbye*; *G.P. Telemann, Jesu, meine Freude, Cantata for SATB Soloists/Chorus, Chamber Orchestra*, edited by Ann Kersting-Meulman.

Tips Audience is music schools, universities, libraries, professional music educators, and amateur/professional musicians.

PRESTWICK HOUSE, INC.

P.O. Box 658, Clayton DE 19938. Web site: www.prestwickhouse.com. Estab. 1980.

Nonfiction Reference, textbook, teaching supplements. Subjects include grammar, writing, test taking. Submit proposal package including outline, résumé, 1 sample chapter, TOC.

Tips ''We market our books primarily for middle and high school English teachers. Submissions should address a direct need of grades 7-12 language arts teachers. Current and former English teachers are encouraged to submit materials developed and used by them successfully in the classroom.''

⊘ PRICE STERN SLOAN, INC.

Penguin Group (USA), 345 Hudson, New York NY 10014. (212)414-3590. Fax: (212)414-3396. Web site: www.penguinputnam.com. Estab. 1963. **Publishes 75 titles/year. Makes outright purchase. Offers advance.** Does not accept simultaneous submissions. Book catalog for 9×12 SAE with 5 first-class stamps; ms guidelines for #10 SASE.

Imprints Mad Libs; Mad Libs Jr; Mr. Men & Little Miss; Serendipity; Wee Sing.

O— Price Stern Sloan publishes quirky mass market novelty series for children as well as licensed tie-in books.

Nonfiction Children's/juvenile, humor. ''Most of our titles are unique in concept as well as execution.'' Do not send *original* artwork or ms. *No unsolicited mss.*

Fiction ''Quirky, funny picture books, novelty books and quirky full color series.''

Recent Title(s) *123 Look at Me!*, by Roberta Intrater.

Tips ''Price Stern Sloan has a unique, humorous, off-the-wall feel.''

PROFESSIONAL PUBLICATIONS, INC.

1250 Fifth Ave., Belmont CA 94002-3863. (650)593-9119. Fax: (650)592-4519. E-mail: acquisitions@ppi2pass.com. Web site: www.ppi2pass.com. Estab. 1975. Publishes hardcover, electronic and paperback originals, video and audio cassettes, CD-ROMs and DVDs. **Publishes 10 titles/year.** Publishes book 4-18 months after acceptance of ms. Accepts simultaneous submissions. Responds in 1 month to queries. Book catalog and ms guidelines free.

> O→ PPI publishes professional career, reference, and licensing preparation materials. Professional Publications wants only professionals practicing in the field to submit material. Currently emphasizing engineering, interior design, architecture, landscape architecture and LEED exam review.

Nonfiction Multimedia, reference, technical, textbook. Subjects include science, architecture, landscape architecture, engineering mathematics, engineering, land surveying, interior design, greenbuilding, sustainable development, and other professional licensure and development subjects. Especially needs "review and reference books for all professional licensing examinations." Please submit ms and proposal outlining market potential, etc. Proposal template available upon request. Reviews artwork/photos as part of ms package.

Recent Title(s) *Six-Minute Solutions for the Civil PE Exam*, various authors; *LEED NC Sample Exam*; *Work With Anyone Anywhere*.

Tips "We specialize in books for working professionals and those who want to enter the profession: engineers, architects, land surveyors, interior designers, etc. The more technically complex the manuscript, the happier we are. We love equations, tables of data, complex illustrations, mathematics, etc. Demonstrating your understanding of the market, competition, and marketing ideas will help sell us on your proposal."

PROMETHEUS BOOKS

59 John Glenn Dr., Amherst NY 14228-2197. (800)421-0351. Fax: (716)564-2711. E-mail: slmitchell@prometheusbooks.com. Web site: www.prometheusbooks.com. **Acquisitions:** Steven L. Mitchell, editor-in-chief. Estab. 1969. Publishes hardcover originals, trade paperback originals and reprints. Accepts simultaneous submissions. Responds in 1 month to queries; 2 months to proposals; 3 months to mss. Book catalog free or online; ms guidelines for #10 SASE.

Imprints Humanity Books (scholarly and professional monographs in philosophy, social science, sociology, archaeology, black stuides, womens studies, Marxist studies, etc.).

> O→ "Prometheus Books is a leading independent publisher in philosophy, popular science, and critical thinking. We publish authoritative and thoughtful books by distinguished authors in many categories. We are a niche, or specialized, publisher that features critiques of the paranormal and pseudoscience, critiques of religious extremism and right wing fundamentalism and creationism; Biblical and Koranic criticism: human sexuality, etc. Currently emphasizing popular science, health, psychology, social science."

Nonfiction Biography, children's/juvenile, reference, self-help, general, historical, popular. Subjects include education, government/politics, health/medicine, history, language/literature, New Age (critiquing of), philosophy, psychology, religion (not religious, but critiquing), contemporary issues, current events, Islamic studies, law, popular science, critiques of the paranormal and UFO sightings, sexuality. "Ask for a catalog, go to the library or our Web site, look at our books and others like them to get an idea of what our focus is." Submit proposal package including outline, synopsis, potential market, tentative ms length, résumé, and a well-developed query letter with SASE. Reviews artwork/photos as part of ms package. Send photocopies.

Recent Title(s) *Affirmations*, by Paul Kurtz; *Should Parents Be Licensed?*, edited by Peg Tittle; *Of Molecules and Men*, by Francis Crick.

Tips "Audience is highly literate with multiple degrees; an audience that is intellectually mature and knows what it wants. They are aware, and we try to provide them with new information on topics of interest to them in mainstream and related areas."

PRUFROCK PRESS, INC.

5926 Balcones Dr., Ste. 220, Austin TX 78731. (512)300-2220. Fax: (513)300-2221. E-mail: info@prufrock.com. Web site: www.prufrock.com. Publisher: Joel McIntosh. **Acquisitions:** Larry Elwood, Jennifer Robins. Publishes trade paperback originals and reprints. Does not accept simultaneous submissions. Book catalog and ms guidelines free.

> O→ "Prufrock Press publishes exciting, innovative and current resources supporting the education of gifted and talented learners."

Nonfiction How-to, textbook, scholarly. Subjects include child guidance/parenting, education. "We publish for the education market. Our readers are typically teachers or parents of gifted and talented children. Our product line is built around professional development books for teachers and activity books for gifted children. Our products support innovative ways of making learning more fun and exciting for gifted and talented children." Submit book prospectus (download form on Web site).

Recent Title(s) *Hands-on Ecology*, by Colleen Kessler; *Logic on Meadow Brooklane*, by Bonnie Risby; *Philosophy for Teens*, by Sharon M. Kaye and Paul Thomson.
Tips "We are looking for practical, classroom-ready materials that encourage children to creatively learn and think."

PUFFIN BOOKS

Imprint of Penguin Group (USA), Inc., 345 Hudson St., New York NY 10014. (212)366-2000. Web site: www.penguinputnam.com. Publishes trade paperback originals and reprints. **Publishes 225 titles/year. Royalty varies. Offers varies advance.** Does not accept simultaneous submissions. Book catalog for 9×12 SAE with 7 first-class stamps.

- Puffin Books publishes high-end trade paperbacks and paperback reprints for preschool children, beginning and middle readers, and young adults.

Nonfiction Biography, children's/juvenile, illustrated book, Young children's concept books (counting, shapes, colors). Subjects include education (for teaching concepts and colors, not academic), history, women's issues/studies. *No unsolicited mss.*
Fiction Picture books, young adult, middle grade, easy-to-read grades 1-3. "We publish mostly paperback reprints. We do very few original titles. We do not publish original picture books." *No unsolicited mss.*
Recent Title(s) *America the Beautiful*, by Katherine Bates, illustrated by Wendell Minor; *Travel Team*, by Mike Lupica.
Tips "Our audience ranges from little children 'first books' to young adult (ages 14-16). An original idea has the best luck."

PURDUE UNIVERSITY PRESS

South Campus Courts, Bldg. E, 509 Harrison St., West Lafayette IN 47907-2025. (765)494-2038. E-mail: pupress@purdue.edu. Web site: www.thepress.purdue.edu. Director: Thomas Bacher. **Acquisitions:** Margaret Hunt, managing editor. Estab. 1960. Publishes hardcover and trade paperback originals and trade paperback reprints. **Publishes 20-25 titles/year.** Does not accept simultaneous submissions. Book catalog and ms guidelines for 9×12 SASE.
Imprints PuP Books (juvenile reprint series that brings back to publication out-of-print stories illuminating other times in American history)

- "We look for books that look at the world as a whole and offer new thoughts and insights into the standard debate." Currently emphasizing technology, human-animal issues, business. De-emphasizing literary studies.

Nonfiction "We publish work of quality scholarship and titles with regional (Midwest) flair. Especially interested in innovative contributions to the social sciences and humanities that break new barriers and provide unique views on current topics. Expanding into veterinary medicine, technology, and business topics." Biography, scholarly. Subjects include agriculture/horticulture, Americana, business/economics, government/politics, health/medicine, history, language/literature, philosophy, regional, science, social sciences, sociology. "Always looking for new authors who show creativity and thoroughness of research." Print and electronic projects accepted. Query before submitting.
Recent Title(s) *Flies in the Face of Fashion, Mites Make Right, and Other Bugdacious Tales*, by Tom Turpin; *Murder He Wrote*, by Donald Bain; *The Golden Bridge*, by Patty Dobbs Gross.

G.P. PUTNAM'S SONS BOOKS FOR YOUNG READERS

Penguin Young Readers Group, Penguin Group USA, 345 Hudson St., 14th Floor, New York NY 10014. (212)414-3610. Web site: www.penguin.com. Publishes hardcover originals. **Pays standard royalty. Offers negotiable advance.** Accepts simultaneous submissions. Ms guidelines for SASE.
Nonfiction Submit 1-2 sample chapters, query letter, synopsis, TOC, SASE.
Fiction Children's picture books (ages 0-8); middle-grade fiction and illustrated chapter books (ages 7-10); older middle-grade fiction (ages 10-14); some young adult (14-18). Particularly interested in middle-grade fiction with strong voice, literary quality, high interest for audience, poignancy, humor, unusual settings or plots. Historical fiction OK. No series or activity books, no board books. Submit proposal package including 1-3 sample chapters, synopsis, query letter, SASE. Send complete ms for picture books. No response without SASE.

G.P. PUTNAM'S SONS HARDCOVER

Imprint of Penguin Group (USA), Inc., 375 Hudson, New York NY 10014. (212)366-2000. Fax: (212)366-2664. Web site: www.penguinputnam.com. Publishes hardcover originals. **Pays variable royalties on retail price. Offers varies advance.** Accepts simultaneous submissions. Request book catalog through mail order department.
Nonfiction Biography, cookbook, self-help. Subjects include animals, business/economics, child guidance/

parenting, contemporary culture, cooking/foods/nutrition, health/medicine, military/war, nature/environment, religion, science, sports, travel, women's issues/studies, celebrity-related topics. *Agented submissions only. No unsolicited mss.*

Fiction Adventure, literary, mainstream/contemporary, mystery, suspense, women's. *Agented submissions only. No unsolicited mss.*

Recent Title(s) *A Voice for the Dead*, by James Starrs and Katherine Ramsland; *Prince of Fire*, by Daniel Silva.

QUE

Pearson Education, 800 E. 96th St., Indianapolis IN 46240. (317)581-3500. E-mail: proposals@quepublishing.com. Web site: www.quepublishing.com. Publisher: Paul Boger. Estab. 1981. Publishes hardcover, trade paperback and mass market paperback originals and reprints. **Publishes 100 titles/year. 80% from unagented writers. Pays variable royalty on wholesale price or makes work-for-hire arrangements. Offers varying advance.** Accepts simultaneous submissions. Book catalog and ms guidelines online.

Nonfiction Subjects include computers/electronic. Submit proposal package including résumé, TOC, writing sample, competing titles.

Recent Title(s) *MySQL, 3rd Ed.*, by Paul Dubois; *Absolute Beginner's Guide to Project Management*, by Greg Horine; *Teach Yourself to Create Web Pages*, by Preston Gralla and Matt Brown.

QUILL DRIVER BOOKS/WORD DANCER PRESS

1254 Commerce Ave., Sanger CA 93657. (559)876-2170. Fax: (559)876-2180. Web site: www.quilldriverbooks.com. **Acquisitions:** Stephen Blake Mettee, publisher. Publishes hardcover and trade paperback originals and reprints. **Publishes 10-12 (Quill Driver Books: 6-8/year, Word Dancer Press: 4/year) titles/year. 50% of books from first-time authors; 95% from unagented writers. Pays 4-10% royalty on retail price. Offers $500-5,000 advance.** Publishes book 9 months after acceptance of ms. Accepts simultaneous submissions. Responds in 1 month to queries; 1 month to proposals; 3 months to mss. Book catalog and ms guidelines for #10 SASE.

> "We publish a modest number of books per year, each of which, we hope, makes a worthwhile contribution to the human community, and we have a little fun along the way. We are strongly emphasizing our book series: The Best Half of Life series—on subjects which will serve to enhance the lifestyles, life skills, and pleasures of living for those over 50."

Nonfiction Biography, general nonfiction, how-to, reference, general. Subjects include regional (California), writing, aging. Query with SASE, or submit proposal package. Reviews artwork/photos as part of ms package. Send photocopies.

Recent Title(s) *Live Longer, Live Better*, by Peter H. Gott, MD; *The California Wine Country Diet*, by Haven Logan, PhD; *Dr. Ruth's Sex After 50*, by Dr. Ruth K. Westheimer.

QUITE SPECIFIC MEDIA GROUP, LTD.

7373 Pyramid Place, Hollywood CA 90046. (323)851-5797. Fax: (323)851-5798. E-mail: info@quitespecificmedia.com. Web site: www.quitespecificmedia.com. **Acquisitions:** Ralph Pine, editor-in-chief. Estab. 1967. Publishes hardcover originals, trade paperback originals and reprints. **Publishes 12 titles/year. Receives 300 queries and 100 mss/year. 75% of books from first-time authors; 85% from unagented writers. Pays royalty on wholesale price. Offers varies advance.** Publishes book 18 months after acceptance of ms. Accepts simultaneous submissions. Responds to queries. Book catalog online; ms guidelines free.

Imprints Costume & Fashion Press; Drama Publishers; By Design Press; Entertainment Pro; Jade Rabbit.

> Quite Specific Media Group is an umbrella company of 5 imprints specializing in costume and fashion, theater and design.

Nonfiction For and about performing arts theory and practice: acting, directing; voice, speech, movement; makeup, masks, wits; costumes, sets, lighting, sound; design and execution; technical theater, stagecraft, equipment; stage management; producing; arts management, all varieties; business and legal aspects; film, radio, television, cable, video; theory, criticism, reference; theater and performance history; costume and fashion. How-to, multimedia, reference, textbook, guides; manuals; directories. Subjects include fashion/beauty, film/cinema/stage, history, translation. Accepts nonfiction and technical works in translations also. Query by e-mail please. Reviews artwork/photos as part of ms package.

RAGGED MOUNTAIN PRESS

The McGraw Hill Companies, P.O. Box 220, Camden ME 04843-0220. (207)236-4837. Fax: (207)236-6314. Web site: www.raggedmountainpress.com. Editorial Director: Jonathan Eaton. **Acquisitions:** Bob Holtzman, acquisitions/ms submissions. Estab. 1993. Publishes hardcover and trade paperback originals and reprints. Accepts simultaneous submissions. Ms guidelines online.

Imprints International Marine (books about boats and the sea).

O→ Ragged Mountain Press publishes books that take you off the beaten path.

Nonfiction "Ragged Mountain publishes nonconsumptive outdoor and environmental issues books of literary merit or unique appeal." How-to (outdoor-related), humor, guidebooks, essays. Subjects include cooking/ foods/nutrition, nature/environment, recreation, sports, team sports, adventure, camping, fly fishing, snowshoeing, backpacking, canoeing, outdoor cookery, skiing, snowboarding, survival skills, wilderness know-how, birdwatching, natural history, climbing, kayaking. "Be familiar with the existing literature. Find a subject that hasn't been done or has been done poorly, then explore it in detail and from all angles." Submit outline, rationale, cv, suggested reviewers, competition and market information. Reviews artwork/photos as part of ms package. Send photocopies.

Recent Title(s) *Stitch-and-Glue Boatbuilding*, by Chris Kulczycki; *In the Wake of the Jomon*, by Jon Turk; *The Complete RV Handbook*, by Jayne Freeman.

N RAILROADING

Imprint of Far Horizons Media Company, P.O. Box 560989, Rockledge FL 32956. (321)690-2224. Fax: (321)690-0853. Web site: www.bfpbooks.com. Publishes trade paperback originals and limited hardback. **Publishes 15-25 titles/year. Receives 100 queries and 50 mss/year. 50% of books from first-time authors; 99% from unagented writers. Pays 7-11% royalty on retail price.** Publishes book 3-4 months after acceptance of ms. Responds in 1 month to queries. Ms guidelines online.

- Railroading (BFP, Inc.) publishes books on model railroading and railroad history.

Nonfiction General nonfiction (relating to model railroading and railroad history), how-to, reference. "We are interested in any title related to these fields. Query with a list of ideas. Include phone number. This is a fast-changing market. Our title plans rarely extend past 6 months, although we know the type and quantity of books we will publish over the next 2 years. We prefer good knowledge with simple-to-understand writing style containing a well-rounded vocabulary." Query with SASE. Reviews artwork/photos as part of ms package. Send photocopies or JPEG files on CD.

Recent Title(s) *Track Plans for Beginners in N-Scale*; *Track Plans for Beginners in HO-Scale*; *Track Plans for Beginners in O-Scale*.

Tips "All of our staff and editors are model railroaders. As such, we publish what we would want to read relating to the subject. Our audience in general are active model railroaders at the beginner and intermediate level, and history buffs wanting to learn more about the history of railroads in this country. Many are people new to the hobby, attempting to learn all they can before starting their first layout. Keep it easy and simple to follow. Use railroad terms and jargon sparingly. Do not use complicated technical jargon, terms, or formulas without detailed explanation of the same. Use experienced craftsmen as a resource for knowledge. Please read our guidelines before submitting your manuscript."

N A ⊘ RANDOM HOUSE AUDIO PUBLISHING GROUP

Subsidiary of Random House, Inc., 1745 Broadway, New York NY 10019. (212)782-9720. Fax: (212)782-9600. Web site: www.randomhouse.com.

Imprints Listening Library; Random House Audible; Random House Audio; Random House Audio Assets; Random House Audio Dimensions; Random House Audio Roads; Random House Audio Voices; Random House Price-less.

O→ Audio publishing for adults and children, offering titles in both abridged and unabridged formats on cassettes, compact discs, and by digital delivery.

Recent Title(s) *Confronting Reality*, by Larry Bossidy and Ram Charan; *To the Last Man*, by Jeff Shaara; *Dragon Rider*, by Cornelia Funke.

A ⊘ RANDOM HOUSE CHILDREN'S BOOKS

Imprint of Random House, Inc., 1745 Broadway, New York NY 10019. (212)782-9000. Web site: www.randomhouse.com. Estab. 1925.

Imprints BooksReportsNow.com, GoldenBooks.com, Junie B. Jones, Kids@Random, Seusville, Teachers@Random, Teens@Random; **Knopf/Delacorte/ Dell Young Readers Group:** Bantam, Crown, David Fickling Books, Delacorte Press, Dell Dragonfly, Dell Laurel-Leaf, Dell Yearling, Doubleday, Alfred A. Knopf, Wendy Lamb Books; **Random House Young Readers Group:** Akiko, Arthur, Barbie, Beginner Books, The Berenstain Bears, Bob the Builder, Disney, Dragon Tales, First Time Books, Golden Books, Landmark Books, Little Golden Books, Lucas Books, Mercer Mayer, Nickelodeon, Nick, Jr., pat the bunny, Picturebacks, Precious Moments, Richard Scarry, Sesame Street Books, Step Into Reading, Stepping Stones, Star Wars, Thomas the Tank Engine and Friends.

- Only accepts unsolicited mss through Delacorte Dell Yearling Contest for a First Middle Grade Novel and Delacorte Press Contest for a First Young Adult Novel. Otherwise, submit through a literary agent.

Recent Title(s) *Toad Heaven*, by Morris Gleitzman; *The Haunting*, by Joan Lowery Nixon; *Melanie in Manhattan*, by Carol Weston.

RANDOM HOUSE DIRECT, INC.

Affiliate of Random House, Inc., 1745 Broadway, New York NY 10019. Web site: www.randomhouse.com.

Imprints Bon Apetit; Gourmet Books; Pillsbury.

RANDOM HOUSE, INC.

Division of Bertelsmann Book Group, 1745 Broadway, New York NY 10019. (212)782-9000. Web site: www.randomhouse.com. Estab. 1925. **Pays royalty. Offers advance.**

Imprints Ballantine Publishing Group: Ballantine Books, Ballantine Reader,s Circle, Del Rey, Del Rey/Lucas Books, Fawcett, Ivy, One World, Wellspring; **Bantam Dell Publishing Group:** Bantam Hardcover, Bantam Mass Market, Bantam Trade Paperback, Crimeline, Delacorte Press, Dell, Delta, The Dial Press, Domain, DTP, Fanfare, Island, Spectra; **Crown Publishing Group:** Bell Tower, Clarkson Potter, Crown Business, Crown Forum, Crown Publishers, Inc., Harmony Books, Shaye Arehart Books, Three Rivers Press; **Doubleday Broadway Publishing Group:** Broadway Books, Currency, Doubleday, Doubleday Image, Doubleday Religious Publishing, Main Street Books, Nan A. Talese; **Knopf Publishing Group:** Alfred A. Knopf, Everyman,s Library, Pantheon Books, Schocken Books, Vintage Anchor Publishing (Vintage Books, Anchor Books); **Random House Audio Publishing Group:** Listening Library, Random House Audible, Random House Audio, Random House Audio Assets, Random House Audio Dimensions, Random House Audio Roads, Random House Audio Voices, Random House Price-less; **Random House Children,s Books:** BooksReportsNow.com, GoldenBooks.com, Junie B. Jones, Kids@Random, Seusville, Teachers@Random, Teens@Random, Knopf/Delacorte/Dell Young Readers Group (Alfred A. Knopf, Bantam, Crown, David Fickling Books, Delacorte Press, Dell Dragonfly, Dell Laurel-Leaf, Dell Yearling Books, Doubleday, Wendy Lamb Books), Random House Young Readers Group (Akiko, Arthur, Barbie, Beginner Books, The Berenstain Bears, Bob the Builder, Disney, Dragon Tales, First Time Books, Golden Books, Landmark Books, Little Golden Books, Lucas Books, Mercer Mayer, Nickelodeon, Nick, Jr., pat the bunny, Picturebacks, Precious Moments, Richard Scarry, Sesame Street Books, Step Into Reading, Stepping Stones, Star Wars, Thomas the Tank Engine and Friends), **Random House Direct, Inc.:** Bon Appetit, Gourmet Books, Pillsbury; **Random House Information Group:** Fodor,s Travel Publications, House of Collectibles, Living Language, Prima Games, The Princeton Review, Random House Espanol, Random House Puzzles & Games, Random House Reference; **Random House International:** Arete, McClelland & Stewart Ltd., Plaza & Janes, Random House Australia, Random House of Canada Ltd., Random House Mondadori, Random House South Africa, Random House South America, Random House United Kingdom, Transworld UK, Verlagsgruppe Random House; **Random House Value Publishing:** Children,s Classics, Crescent, Derrydale, Gramercy, Testament, Wings; **Waterbrook Press:** Fisherman Bible Study Guides, Shaw Books, Waterbrook Press.

- *Agented submissions only. No unsolicited mss.*

"Random House has long been committed to publishing the best literature by writers both in the United States and abroad."

RANDOM HOUSE INFORMATION GROUP

Division of Random House, Inc., 1745 Broadway, New York NY 10019. (212)782-9000. Web site: www.randomhouse.com.

Imprints Fodor's Travel Publications; Living Language; House of Collectibles; Prima Games; The Princeton Review; Random House Español; Random House Puzzles & Games; Random House Reference Publishing.

RANDOM HOUSE INTERNATIONAL

Division of Random House, Inc., 1745 Broadway, New York NY 10019. (212)572-6106. Fax: (212)572-6045. Web site: www.randomhouse.com.

Imprints Arete; McClelland & Stewart Ltd; Plaza & Janes; Random House Australia; Random House of Canada Ltd; Random House Mondadori; Random House South Africa; Random House South America; Random House United Kingdom; Transworld UK; Verlagsgruppe Random House.

Recent Title(s) *Saturday*, by Ian McEwan (Random House Australia); *The Family Tree*, by Carole Cadwalladr (Transworld UK); *The Bird Factory*, by David Layton (McClelland & Stewart).

RANDOM HOUSE LARGE PRINT

Division of Random House, Inc., 1745 Broadway, New York NY 10019. (212)782-9720. Fax: (212)782-9600. Web site: www.randomhouse.com. Estab. 1990. **Publishes 60 titles/year.**

Acquires and publishes general interest fiction and nonfiction in large print editions.

RANDOM HOUSE PUBLISHING GROUP

Division of Random House, Inc., 1745 Broadway, New York NY 10019. (212)782-9000. Web site: www.randomhouse.com. Estab. 1925. Publishes hardcover and paperback trade books. **Publishes 120 titles/year.**

Imprints Ballantine Books; Del Rey; Modern Library; One World; Presidio Press; Random House; Random House Trade Paperbacks; Villard.

- See Web site for details.

0→ "Random House is the world's largest English-language general trade book publisher. It includes an array of prestigious imprints that publish some of the foremost writers of our time—in hardcover, trade paperback, mass market paperback, electronic, multimedia and other formats."

Nonfiction *Agented submissions only.*

Fiction *Agented submissions only.*

RANDOM HOUSE VALUE PUBLISHING

Affiliate of Random House, Inc., 1745 Broadway, New York NY 10019. (212)940-7422. Fax: (212)572-2114. Web site: www.randomhouse.com. Estab. 1933. Publishes hardcover and illustrated/nonillustrated nonfiction, adult fiction, and gifts.

Imprints Children's Classics; Crescent; Derrydale; Gramercy; Testament; Wings.

Recent Title(s) *The Celebrate-Your-Life Quote Book*, by Allen Klein; *The Complete Mom's Little Instruction Book*, by Annie Pigeon; *Paris Boulangerie-Patisserie*, by Linda Dannenberg.

RANDOM HOUSE/GOLDEN BOOKS FOR YOUNG READERS GROUP

Imprint of Random House Children's Books/Random House, Inc., 1745 Broadway, New York NY 10019. (212)782-9000. Web site: www.randomhouse.com/kids. Vice President/Publisher: Kate Klimo. Vice President/ Associate Publisher (Random House): Mallory Loehr. Estab. 1935. Publishes hardcover, trade paperback, and mass market paperback originals and reprints. **Publishes 375 titles/year. Receives 1,000 queries/year. Pays 1-6% royalty, or makes outright purchase. Offers variable advance.** Accepts simultaneous submissions. Book catalog free.

Imprints Beginner Books; Disney; First Time Books; Landmark Books; Picturebacks; Sesame Workshop; Step into Reading; Stepping Stones; Little Golden Books.

- Color & activity; board & novelty; fiction and nonfiction for beginning readers; hardcover and paperback fiction for kids ages 7-YA.

0→ "Our aim is to create books that nurture the hearts and minds of children, providing and promoting quality books and a rich variety of media that entertain and educate readers from birth to 16 years."

Nonfiction Children's/juvenile. Subjects include animals, history, nature/environment, science, sports, popular culture. *No unsolicited mss. Agented submissions only.*

Fiction Horror, juvenile, mystery, picture books, young adult. "Familiarize yourself with our list. We look for original, unique stories. Do something that hasn't been done." *Agented submissions only. No unsolicited mss.*

Recent Title(s) *The Best Place to Read*, by Debbie Bertram & Susan Bloom; *Top-Secret, Personal Beeswax: A Journal by Junie B. (and Me)*, by Barbara Park; *The Pup Speaks Up*, by Anna Jane Hays.

RED DRESS INK

Harlequin Enterprises, Ltd., 233 Broadway, New York NY 10279. Web site: www.eharlequin.com; www.reddressink.com. **Acquisitions:** Margaret O'Neill Marbury, senior editor; Farrin Jacobs, associate editor. Also: P.O. Box 5190, Buffalo NY 14240-5190. Publishes hardcover and trade paperback originals. Accepts simultaneous submissions. Book catalog and ms guidelines online.

Fiction Adventure, confession, humor, literary, mainstream/contemporary, multicultural, regional, romance, short story collections, contemporary women's fiction. Red Dress Ink publishes "stories that reflect the lifestyles of today's urban, single women. They show life as it is, with a strong touch of humor, hipness and energy." Word length: 80,000-110,000 words. Point of view: no restriction but must have a strong female protagonist. Tone: vibrant. Query with SASE.

Recent Title(s) *Sleeping Over*, by Stacey Ballis; *Lisa Maria Takes Off*, by Susan Hubbard; *Love Like That*, by Amanda Hill.

Tips Audience is women 18-55. "These books are *Ally McBeal* meets *Sex and the City, Bridget Jones's Diary* meets *The Girls' Guide to Hunting and Fishing*. The style of writing is light, highly accessible, clever, funny and full of witty observations. The dialogue is sharp and true-to-life. These are characters you can immediately identify with in a story you just can't put down!"

RED WHEEL/WEISER AND CONARI PRESS

368 Congress St., Boston MA 02210. (617)542-1324. Fax: (617)482-9676. Web site: www.redwheelweiser.com. **Acquisitions:** Pat Bryce, acquisitions editor. Estab. 1956. Publishes hardcover and trade paperback originals and reprints. **Publishes 60-75 titles/year; imprint publishes 20-25 titles/year. Receives 2,000 queries and 2,000 mss/year. 20% of books from first-time authors; 50% from unagented writers. Pays royalty.** Publishes

book 1 year after acceptance of ms. Accepts simultaneous submissions. Responds in 3 months to queries; 3-6 months to proposals; 3-6 months to mss. Book catalog free; ms guidelines online.

Imprints Red Wheel; Conari Press; Weiser.

Nonfiction Gift book, self-help, inspirational, esoteric subjects including magic, Wicca, astrology, tarot. Subjects include New Age, spirituality, women's issues/studies, parenting. Query with SASE, or submit proposal package including outline, 2 sample chapters, TOC. Reviews artwork/photos as part of ms package. Send photocopies.

Recent Title(s) *The Blackberry Tea Club*, by Barbara Herrick; *What Is Goth?*, by Voltaire; *Shining Through*, by Hugh Prather.

REFERENCE SERVICE PRESS

5000 Windplay Dr., Suite 4, El Dorado Hills CA 95762. (916)939-9620. Fax: (916)939-9626. E-mail: info@rspfunding.com. Web site: www.rspfunding.com. **Acquisitions:** Stuart Hauser, acquisitions editor. Estab. 1977. Publishes hardcover originals. **Publishes 10-20 titles/year. 100% from unagented writers. Pays 10% royalty. Offers advance.** Publishes book 6 months after acceptance of ms. Accepts simultaneous submissions. Responds in 2 months to queries. Book catalog for #10 SASE.

- "Reference Service Press focuses on the development and publication of financial aid resources in any format (print, electronic, e-book, etc.). We are interested in financial aid publications aimed at specific groups (e.g., minorities, women, veterans, the disabled, undergraduates majoring in specific subject areas, specific types of financial aid, etc.)."

Nonfiction Specializes in financial aid opportunities for students in or having these characteristics: women, minorities, veterans, the disabled, etc. Subjects include agriculture/horticulture, art/architecture, business/economics, education, ethnic, health/medicine, history, religion, science, sociology, women's issues/studies, disabled. Submit outline, sample chapter(s).

Recent Title(s) *Financial Aids for Women, 2005-2007*.

Tips "Our audience consists of librarians, counselors, researchers, students, re-entry women, scholars, and other fundseekers."

REGNERY PUBLISHING, INC.

Subsidiary of Eagle Publishing, One Massachusetts Ave., NW, Washington DC 20001. (202)216-0600. Web site: www.regnery.com. Publisher: Marji Ross. **Acquisitions:** Harry Crocker, executive editor. Estab. 1947. Publishes hardcover and paperback originals and reprints. **Publishes 30 titles/year. Pays 8-15% royalty on retail price. Offers $0-50,000+ advance.** Publishes book 1 year after acceptance of ms. Responds in 3 months to queries; 3 months to proposals; 3 months to mss.

Imprints Gateway Editions; Capital Press.

- Regnery publishes current affairs books from a conservative point of view.

Nonfiction Biography, current affairs. Subjects include business/economics, government/politics, history, money/finance, national security. *Agented submissions only. No unsolicited mss.*

Recent Title(s) *Men in Black*; *Winning the Future*; *The Final Days*.

Tips "We seek high-impact, headline-making, best-seller treatments of pressing current issues by established experts in the field."

FLEMING H. REVELL PUBLISHING

Division of Baker Book House, P.O. Box 6287, Grand Rapids MI 49516. (800)877-2665. Fax: (800)398-3111. Web site: www.bakerbooks.com. Estab. 1870. Publishes hardcover, trade paperback and mass market paperback originals. Book catalog and ms guidelines online.

- *No longer accepts unsolicited mss.*
- Revell publishes to the heart (rather than to the head). For 125 years, Revell has been publishing evangelical books for the personal enrichment and spiritual growth of general Christian readers.

Nonfiction How-to, self-help. Subjects include child guidance/parenting, religion, Christian living, marriage.

Fiction Historical, religious, suspense, contemporary.

Recent Title(s) *Suddenly Unemployed*, by Helen Kooiman Hosier; *The Bride's Handbook*, by Amy J. Tol; *Just Give Me a Little Peace and Quiet*, by Lorilee Craker.

RFF PRESS

Resources for the Future, 1616 P St., NW, Washington DC 20036. (202)328-5086. Fax: (202)328-5002. E-mail: rffpress@rff.org. Web site: www.rffpress.org. **Acquisitions:** Don Reisman, publisher. Publishes hardcover, trade paperback and electronic originals. **Publishes 20 titles/year. Pays royalty on wholesale price.** Publishes book 6 months after acceptance of ms. Accepts simultaneous submissions. Responds in 1 month to queries; 1 month to proposals; 2 months to mss. Book catalog online; ms guidelines free.

Nonfiction "We focus on social science approaches to environmental and natural resource issues." Reference,

technical, textbook, trade. Subjects include agriculture/horticulture, business/economics, government/politics, history, nature/environment, science, urban planning/land-use policy. "We do not publish works that are purely opinion driven. Inquire via e-mail or letter; no phone calls." Submit proposal package including outline. Reviews artwork/photos as part of ms package. Send photocopies.
Recent Title(s) *Northern Landscapes*, by Daniel Nelson; *Zoned Out*; *Determining the Economic Value of Water*, by Robert A. Young.
Tips Audience is scholars, policy makers, activists, businesses, government, the general public. Distributed by Johns Hopkins University Press.

RIO NUEVO PUBLISHERS

Imprint of Treasure Chest Books, P.O. Box 5250, Tucson AZ 85703. Fax: (520)624-5888. E-mail: info@rionuevo.com. Submissions E-mail: theresak@rionuevo.com. Web site: www.rionuevo.com. **Acquisitions:** Theresa Kennedy, acquiring editor (adult nonfiction titles about the Southwest). Estab. 1975. Publishes hardcover and trade paperback originals and reprints. **Publishes 12-20 titles/year. Receives 20 queries and 10 mss/year. 30% of books from first-time authors; 100% from unagented writers. Pays 7-10% royalty on net receipts, or makes outright purchase. Offers $1,000-4,000 advance.** Publishes book 1 year after acceptance of ms. Accepts simultaneous submissions. Responds in 6 months to queries; 6 months to proposals; 6 months to mss. Book catalog online; ms guidelines by e-mail.
Nonfiction Cookbook, general nonfiction, gift book, illustrated book. Subjects include animals, cooking/foods/nutrition, gardening, history, nature/environment, regional, religion, spirituality, travel. "We cover the Southwest but prefer titles that are not too narrow in their focus. We want our books to be of broad enough interest that people from other places will also want to read them." Query with SASE, or submit proposal package including outline, 2 sample chapters. Reviews artwork/photos as part of ms package. Send photocopies.
Recent Title(s) *Yard Full of Sun: The Story of a Gardener's Obsession That Got a Little Out of Hand*; *The Prickley Pear Cookbook*; *Clouds for Dessert: Sweet Treats From the Wild West.*
Tips "We have a general audience of intelligent people interested in the Southwest—nature, history, culture. Many of our books are sold in gift shops throughout the region; we are also distributed nationally by W.W. Norton."

RIVER CITY PUBLISHING

River City Publishing, LLC, 1719 Mulberry St., Montgomery AL 36106. (334)265-6753. Fax: (334)265-8880. E-mail: jgilbert@rivercitypublishing.com. Web site: www.rivercitypublishing.com. **Acquisitions:** Jim Gilbert, editor. Estab. 1989. Publishes hardcover and trade paperback originals and reprints. **Publishes 8 titles/year. Receives 1,250 queries and 200 mss/year. 20% of books from first-time authors; 75% from unagented writers. Pays 10% royalty on net revenue. Offers $500-5,000 advance.** Publishes book 1 year after acceptance of ms. Accepts simultaneous submissions. Responds in 3 months to queries; 4 months to proposals; 1 year to mss. Ms guidelines free.
Imprints Starrhill Press; Elliott & Clark; River City Kids.
Nonfiction Autobiography, biography. Subjects include art/architecture, creative nonfiction, government/politics, history, memoirs, regional, sports, travel. Submit proposal package including outline, 2 sample chapters, author's bio/résumé. Reviews artwork/photos as part of ms package. Send photocopies.
Fiction Ethnic, historical, literary, multicultural, poetry, regional (southern), short story collections. Submit proposal package including résumé, synopsis, author bio, 3 sample chapters.
Recent Title(s) *Murder Creek*, by Joe Formichella (true crime); *The Bear Bryant Funeral Train: Resurrected Edition*, by Brad Vice (short fiction).

ROC BOOKS

Imprint of New American Library, A Division of Penguin Putnam, Inc., 375 Hudson St., New York NY 10014. (212)366-2000. Web site: www.penguinputnam.com. Publishes mass market, trade, and hardcover originals. **Pays royalty. Offers negotiable advance.** Accepts simultaneous submissions.

"We're looking for books that are a good read, that people will want to pick up time and time again."
Fiction Fantasy, horror, science fiction. "Roc tries to strike a balance between fantasy and science fiction. We strongly discourage unsolicited submissions."
Recent Title(s) *Dreams Made Flesh*, by Anne Bishop; *The Protector's War*, by S.M. Stirling.

ROUTLEDGE

part of Taylor and Francis LLC, 270 Madison Ave., New York NY 10016. (212)216-7800. Web site: routledge.com. **Acquisitions:** Mary MacInnes, vice president/publisher. Estab. 1836. **Publishes 2,000 titles/year. 10% of books from first-time authors; 95% from unagented writers. Pays royalty. Offers advance.** Publishes book 1 year after acceptance of ms. Accepts simultaneous submissions. Ms guidelines online.

Imprints Theatre Arts Books.

O-r The Routledge list includes humanities, social sciences, reference, monographs, reference works, hardback and paperback upper-level texts, scholarly research, student supplementary books. Does not respond to unsolicited proposals.

Nonfiction Reference, textbook. Subjects include education, ethnic, gay/lesbian, government/politics, history, music/dance, psychology, literary criticism, social sciences, geography, cultural studies, urban studies and planning.

ROWMAN & LITTLEFIELD PUBLISHING GROUP

4501 Forbes Blvd., Suite 200, Lanham MD 20706. (301)459-3366. Fax: (301)429-5748. Web site: www.rowmanlittlefield.com. Editorial Director: Jeremy Langford. **Acquisitions:** See Web site for a detailed list of editors and addresses by subject area. Estab. 1949. Publishes hardcover and trade paperback originals and reprints. **Offers advance.** Does not accept simultaneous submissions. Ms guidelines online.

Imprints Lexington Books; Rowman & Littlefield Publishers; Madison Books; Scarecrow Press; Cooper Square.

Recent Title(s) *Crime, Punishment, and Policing in China*, by Børge Bakken; *The Making of Arab News*, by Noha Mellor; *African Americans in the U.S. Economy*, edited by Cecilia A. Conrad, John Whitehead, Patrick Mason, and James Stewart.

RUTGERS UNIVERSITY PRESS

100 Joyce Kilmer Ave., Piscataway NJ 08854-8099. (732)445-7762. Fax: (732)445-7039. Web site: rutgerspress.rutgers.edu. **Acquisitions:** Leslie Mitchner, editor-in-chief/associate director (humanities); Adi Hovav, editor (social sciences); Doreen Valentine, editor (science, health & medicine); Kendra Boileau, editor (history, American studies, Asian-American studies). Estab. 1936. Publishes hardcover and trade paperback originals, and reprints. **Publishes 90 titles/year. Receives 1,500 queries and 300 mss/year. 30% of books from first-time authors; 70% from unagented writers. Pays 7½-15% royalty. Offers $1,000-10,000 advance.** Publishes book 1 year after acceptance of ms. Responds in 1 month to proposals. Book catalog online or with SASE; ms guidelines online.

O-r "Our Press aims to reach audiences beyond the academic community with accessible scholarly and regional books."

Nonfiction Reference. Subjects include art/architecture (art history), ethnic, film/cinema/stage, gay/lesbian, government/politics, health/medicine, history, multicultural, nature/environment, regional, religion, sociology, women's issues/studies, African-American studies, Asian-American studies, history of science and technology, literature, literary criticism, human evolution, ecology, media studies. Books for use in undergraduate courses. Submit outline, 2-3 sample chapters. Reviews artwork/photos as part of ms package. Send photocopies.

Recent Title(s) *Snapshots of Bloomsbury*, by Maggie Humm; *Pump and Dump*, by Robert Tillman and Michael L. Indergaard; *Being Jewish in the New Germany*, by Jeffrey M. Peck.

Tips Both academic and general audiences. "Many of our books have potential for undergraduate course use. We are more trade-oriented than most university presses. We are looking for intelligent, well-written, and accessible books. Avoid overly narrow topics."

RUTLEDGE HILL PRESS

Imprint of Thomas Nelson, P.O. Box 141000, Nashville TN 37214-1000. (615)902-2333. Fax: (615)902-2340. Web site: www.rutledgehillpress.com. **Acquisitions:** Lawrence Stone, publisher. Estab. 1982. Publishes hardcover and trade paperback originals and reprints. **Publishes 40-50 titles/year. Receives 1,000 submissions/year. 40% of books from first-time authors; 80% from unagented writers. Pays royalty. Offers advance.** Publishes book 10 months after acceptance of ms. Responds in 2 months to queries. Book catalog for 9×12 SASE; ms guidelines for #10 SASE.

O-r "We are a publisher of market-specific books, focusing on particular genres or regions."

Nonfiction "We have recently made a strategic decision to focus our publishing in 4 areas: cookbooks, how-to books, health and nutrition, and gift and inspirational (not religious) books. The book should have a unique marketing hook. Books built on new ideas and targeted to a specific U.S. region are welcome. Please, no fiction, children's, academic, poetry or religious works, and we won't even look at *Life's Little Instruction Book* spinoffs or copycats." Submit cover letter that includes brief marketing strategy and author bio, outline, and sample chapters. Reviews artwork/photos as part of ms package.

Recent Title(s) *A Gentleman Entertains*, by John Bridges and Bryan Curtis; *101 Secrets a Good Dad Knows*, by Walter Browder and Sue Ellen Browder; *I Hope You Dance*, by Tia Sillers and Mark Sanders.

SAE INTERNATIONAL

Society of Automotive Engineers, 400 Commonwealth Dr., Warrendale PA 15096. (724)776-4841. E-mail: writeabook@sae.org. Web site: www.sae.org. **Acquisitions:** Jeff Worsinger, product developer; Martha Swiss, product developer; Kris Hattman, product developer; Erin Moore, associate product developer; Matt Miller, product manager; Theresa Wertz, product manager; Emily Kroll, associate product developer. Estab. 1905. Publishes hardcover and trade paperback originals, Web and CD-ROM based electronic product. **Publishes 30-40 titles/ year. Receives 250 queries and 75 mss/year. 30-40% of books from first-time authors; 100% from unagented writers. Pays royalty. Offers possible advance.** Publishes book 9-10 months after acceptance of ms. Accepts simultaneous submissions. Responds in 2 months to queries. Book catalog free; ms guidelines online.

O⇁ "Automotive means anything self-propelled. We are a professional society serving this area, which includes aircraft, spacecraft, marine, rail, automobiles, trucks, and off-highway vehicles." Currently emphasizing engineering.

Nonfiction Biography, multimedia (CD-ROM, Web-based), reference, technical, textbook. Query with SASE. Reviews artwork/photos as part of ms package. Send photocopies.

Recent Title(s) *Hands-On Race Car Engineer*; *Ferrari Formula 1*.

Tips "Audience is automotive engineers, technicians, car buffs, aerospace engineers, technicians, and historians."

SAFARI PRESS, INC.

15621 Chemical Lane, Bldg. B, Huntington Beach CA 92649-1506. (714)894-9080. Fax: (714)894-4949. E-mail: info@safaripress.com. Web site: www.safaripress.com. **Acquisitions:** Jacqueline Neufeld, editor. Estab. 1985. Publishes hardcover originals and reprints, and trade paperback reprints. **Publishes 25-30 titles/year. 70% of books from first-time authors; 80% from unagented writers. Pays 8-15% royalty on wholesale price.** Does not accept simultaneous submissions. Book catalog for $1; ms guidelines online.

- The editor notes that she receives many mss outside the areas of big-game hunting, wingshooting, and sporting firearms, and these are always rejected.

O⇁ Safari Press publishes books only on big-game hunting, sporting, firearms, and wingshooting; this includes African, North American, European, Asian, and South American hunting and wingshooting. Does not want books on 'outdoors' topics (hiking, camping, canoeing, etc.).

Nonfiction Biography (of hunters), how-to (hunting and wingshooting stories), hunting adventure stories. Subjects include hunting, firearms, wingshooting, "We discourage autobiographies, unless the life of the hunter or firearms maker has been exceptional. We routinely reject manuscripts along the lines of 'Me and my buddies went hunting for . . . and a good time was had by all!" No outdoors topics (hiking, camping, canoeing, fishing, etc.). Query with SASE, or submit outline.

Recent Title(s) *Royal Quest: The Hunting Saga of H.I.H. Prince Abdorreza of Iran*; *The Best of Holland & Holland: England's Premier Gunmaker*; *Safari Guide 2007-2008*.

SAINT MARY'S PRESS

702 Terrace Heights, Winona MN 55987-1318. (800)533-8095. Fax: (800)344-9225. E-mail: submissions@smp.org. Web site: www.smp.org. Ms guidelines online or by e-mail.

Nonfiction Subjects include religion (prayers), spirituality. Titles for Catholic youth and their parents, teachers, and youth ministers. Query with SASE, or submit proposal package including outline, 1 sample chapter, SASE. Brief author biography.

Recent Title(s) *The Catholic Faith Handbook for Youth*; *The Total Faith Initiative*; *Take Ten: Daily Bible Reflections for Teens*.

Tips "Request product catalog and/or do research online of Saint Mary Press book lists before submitting proposal."

⊘ SANTA MONICA PRESS LLC

P.O. Box 1076, Santa Monica CA 90406. Web site: www.santamonicapress.com. **Acquisitions:** Acquistions Editor. Estab. 1991. Publishes trade paperback originals. **Publishes 15 titles/year. 25% of books from first-time authors; 75% from unagented writers. Pays 4-10% royalty on wholesale price. Offers $500-2,500 advance.** Publishes book 6-18 months after acceptance of ms. Accepts simultaneous submissions. Responds in 1-2 months to proposals. Book catalog for 9×12 SASE with $1.06 postage; ms guidelines online.

O⇁ "At Santa Monica Press, we're not afraid to cast a wide editorial net. Our vision extends from lively and modern how-to books to offbeat looks at popular culture, from film history to literature."

Nonfiction Biography, gift book, how-to, humor, illustrated book, reference. Subjects include Americana, creative nonfiction, film/cinema/stage, health/medicine, language/literature, memoirs, music/dance, spirituality, sports, travel, contemporary culture, film/cinema/stage, general nonfiction. *All unsolicited mss returned unopened.* Submit proposal package, including outline, 2-3 sample chapters, biography, marketing and publicity plans, analysis of competitive titles, SASE with appropriate postage. Reviews artwork/photos as part of ms package. Send photocopies.

Recent Title(s) *The Bad Driver's Handbook*, by Zack Arnstein and Larry Arnstein; *The Ruby Slippers, Madonna's Bra, and Einstein's Brain*, by Chris Epting; *L.A. Noir*, by Alan Silver and James Ursini.
Tips "Visit our Web site before submitting to get a clear idea of the types of books we publish. Carefully analyze your book's competition and tell us what makes your book different—and what makes it better. Also let us know what promotional and marketing opportunities you, as the author, bring to the project."

SARABANDE BOOKS, INC.

2234 Dundee Rd., Suite 200, Louisville KY 40205. (502)458-4028. Fax: (502)458-4065. E-mail: info@sarabandebooks.org. Web site: www.sarabandebooks.org. **Acquisitions:** Sarah Gorham, editor-in-chief. Estab. 1994. Publishes hardcover and trade paperback originals. **Publishes 10 titles/year. Receives 500 queries and 3,000 mss/year. 35% of books from first-time authors; 75% from unagented writers. Pays royalty. 10% on actual income received. Also pays in author's copies. Offers $500-1,000 advance.** Publishes book 18 months after acceptance of ms. Accepts simultaneous submissions. Book catalog free; contest guidelines for #10 SASE or on Web site.

O→ "Sarabande Books was founded to publish poetry, short fiction, and creative nonfiction. We look for works of lasting literary value. We are actively seeking creative nonfiction." Accepts submissions through contests only.

Fiction Literary, short story collections, novellas, short novels (300 pages maximum, 150 pages minimum).
Poetry "Poetry of superior artistic quality; otherwise no restraints or specifications."
Recent Title(s) *Portrait of My Mother Who Posed Nude in Wartime*, by Marjorie Sandor; *October*, by Louise Glck.
Tips Sarabande publishes for a general literary audience. "Know your market. Read—and buy—books of literature." Sponsors contests for poetry and fiction.

SAS PUBLISHING

SAS Campus Dr., Cary NC 27513-2414. (919)531-0585. Fax: (919)677-4444. E-mail: saspress@sas.com. Web site: support.sas.com/saspress. **Acquisitions:** Julie M. Platt, editor-in-chief. Estab. 1976. Publishes hardcover and trade paperback originals. **Publishes 40 titles/year. 50% of books from first-time authors; 100% from unagented writers. Payment negotiable. Offers negotiable advance.** Does not accept simultaneous submissions. Responds in 2 weeks to queries. Book catalog and ms guidelines via Web site or with SASE; ms guidelines online.

O→ SAS publishes books for SAS and JMP software users, "both new and experienced."

Nonfiction Technical, textbook. Subjects include software, statistics. "SAS Publishing jointly Wiley and SAS Business Series titles. Through SAS, we also publish books by SAS users on a variety of topics relating to SAS software. SAS titles enhance users' abilities to use SAS effectively. We're interested in publishing manuscripts that describe or illustrate using any of SAS products, including JMP software. Books must be aimed at SAS or JMP users, either new or experienced. Tutorials are particularly attractive, as are descriptions of user-written applications for solving real-life business, industry or academic problems. Books on programming techniques using SAS are also desirable. Manuscripts must reflect current or upcoming software releases, and the author's writing should indicate an understanding of SAS and the technical aspects covered in the manuscript." Query with SASE, or submit outline, sample chapter(s). Reviews artwork/photos as part of ms package.
Recent Title(s) *The Little SAS Book: A Primer, Third Ed.*, by Lora D. Delwiche and Susan J. Slaughter; *SAS for Mixed Models, 2nd Ed.*, by Ramon Littell, George Milliken, Walter Stroup, Russell Wolfinger and Oliver Schenberger.
Tips "If I were a writer trying to market a book today, I would concentrate on developing a manuscript that teaches or illustrates a specific concept or application that SAS users will find beneficial in their own environments or can adapt to their own needs."

SASQUATCH BOOKS

119 S. Main, Suite 400, Seattle WA 98104. (206)467-4300. Fax: (206)467-4301. E-mail: custserve@sasquatchbooks.com. Web site: www.sasquatchbooks.com. President: Chad Haight. **Acquisitions:** Gary Luke, editorial director; Terence Maikels, acquisitions editor; Heidi Lenze, acquisitions editor. Estab. 1986. Publishes regional hardcover and trade paperback originals. **Publishes 30 titles/year. 20% of books from first-time authors; 75% from unagented writers. Pays royalty on cover price. Offers wide range advance.** Publishes book 6 months after acceptance of ms. Does not accept simultaneous submissions. Responds in 3 months to queries. Book catalog for 9×12 SAE with 2 first-class stamps; ms guidelines online.

O→ Sasquatch Books publishes books for a West Coast regional audience—Alaska to California. Currently emphasizing outdoor recreation, cookbooks, and history.

Nonfiction "We are seeking quality nonfiction works about the Pacific Northwest and West Coast regions (including Alaska to California). The literature of place includes how-to and where-to as well as history and narrative nonfiction.'' Reference. Subjects include animals, art/architecture, business/economics, cooking/foods/nutrition, gardening, history, nature/environment, recreation, regional, sports, travel, women's issues/studies, outdoors. Query first, then submit outline and sample chapters with SASE.

Recent Title(s) *Out of Left Field*, by Art Thiel; *Book Lust*, by Nancy Pearl; *The Traveling Curmudgeon*, by Jon Winokur.

Tips ''We sell books through a range of channels in addition to the book trade. Our primary audience consists of active, literate residents of the West Coast.''

SCARECROW PRESS, INC.

Imprint of Rowman & Littlefield Publishing Group, 4501 Forbes Blvd., Suite 200, Lanham MD 20706. (301)459-3366. Fax: (301)429-5748. Web site: www.scarecrowpress.com. Vice President/Publisher: Edward Kurdyla. **Acquisitions:** Martin Dillon, acquisitions editor (information studies, interdisciplinary studies, general reference); Bruce Phillips, acquisitions editor (music); Stephen Ryan (film and theater); Kim Tabor (young adult literature). Estab. 1955. Publishes hardcover originals. **Publishes 165 titles/year. 70% of books from first-time authors; 99% from unagented writers. Pays 8% royalty on net of first 1,000 copies; 10% of net price thereafter.** Publishes book 18 months after acceptance of ms. Does not accept simultaneous submissions. Responds in 2 months to queries. Catalog and ms guidelines online.

- Scarecrow Press publishes several series: Historical Dictionaries (includes countries, religions, international organizations, and area studies); Studies and Documentaries on the History of Popular Entertainment (forthcoming); Society, Culture and Libraries. ''Emphasis is on any title likely to appeal to libraries.'' Currently emphasizing jazz, Africana, and educational issues of contemporary interest.

Nonfiction Reference (criminology, guides, military history, bibliographies), scholarly. Subjects include film/cinema/stage, language/literature, religion, sports, annotated bibliographies, handbooks and biographical dictionaries in the areas of women's studies and ethnic studies, parapsychology, fine arts and handicrafts, genealogy, sports history, music, movies, stage, library and information science. Query with SASE.

SCHIFFER PUBLISHING, LTD.

4880 Lower Valley Rd., Atglen PA 19310. (610)593-1777. Fax: (610)593-2002. E-mail: info@schifferbooks.com. Web site: www.schifferbooks.com. **Acquisitions:** Tina Skinner. Estab. 1975. **Publishes 10-20 titles/year. Pays royalty on wholesale price.** Responds in 2 weeks to queries. Book catalog free; ms guidelines online.

Nonfiction Art-quality illustrated regional histories. Looking for informed, entertaining writing and lots of subject areas to provide points of entry into the text for non-history buffs who buy a beautiful book because they are from, or love, an area. Full color possible in the case of historic postcards. Fax or e-mail outline, photos, and book proposal.

Recent Title(s) *Antique Enameled Jewelry*, by Dale Nicholls with Robin Allison; *Mannequins*, by Steven M. Richman; *The Long Campaign*, by John W. Lambert.

Tips ''We want to publish books for towns or cities with relevant population or active tourism to support book sales. A list of potential town vendors is a helpful start toward selling us on your book idea.''

SCHOCKEN BOOKS

Imprint of Random House, Inc., a Division of Bertlesmann AG, 1745 Broadway, New York NY 10019. (212)572-2838. Fax: (212)572-6030. Web site: www.schocken.com. Estab. 1945. Publishes hardcover and trade paperback originals and reprints. **Publishes 9-12 titles/year. Small% of books from first-time authors; small% from unagented writers. Offers varied advance.** Accepts simultaneous submissions.

- ''Schocken publishes quality Judaica in all areas—fiction, history, biography, current affairs, spirituality and religious practices, popular culture, and cultural studies.''

Recent Title(s) *One People Two Worlds*, by Ammiel Hirsch and Yosef Reinman; *The Rebbe's Army*, by Sue Fishkoff; *Reading the Women of the Bible*, by Tikva Frymer-Kensky.

SCHOLASTIC LIBRARY PUBLISHING

A division of Scholastic, Inc., 90 Old Sherman Turnpike, Danbury CT 06816. (203)797-3500. Fax: (203)797-3197. Web site: www.scholastic.com/librarypublishing. Estab. 1895. Publishes hardcover and trade paperback originals. Does not accept simultaneous submissions.

Imprints Grolier;, Children's Press; Franklin Watts; Grolier Online.

- *This publisher accepts agented submissions only.*
- ''Scholastic Library is a leading publisher of reference, educational, and children's books. We provide parents, teachers, and librarians with the tools they need to enlighten children to the pleasure of learning and prepare them for the road ahead.''

🅰 SCHOLASTIC PRESS

Imprint of Scholastic, Inc., 557 Broadway, New York NY 10012. (212)343-6100. Fax: (212)343-4713. Web site: www.scholastic.com. **Acquisitions:** Elizabeth Szabla, editorial director; Kara LaReau, executive editor; Lauren Thompson, senior editor; Leslie Budnick and Jennifer Rees, editors. Publishes hardcover originals. **Publishes 30 titles/year. Receives 2,500 queries/year. 5% of books from first-time authors. Pays royalty on retail price. Offers variable advance.** Publishes book 18-24 months after acceptance of ms. Does not accept simultaneous submissions. Responds in 3 months to queries; 6-8 months to mss.

O-ᵣ Scholastic Press publishes "fresh, literary picture book fiction and nonfiction; fresh, literary nonseries or nongenre-oriented middle grade and young adult fiction." Currently emphasizing "subtly handled treatments of key relationships in children's lives; unusual approaches to commonly dry subjects, such as biography, math, history, or science." De-emphasizing fairy tales (or retellings), board books, genre, or series fiction (mystery, fantasy, etc.).

Nonfiction Children's/juvenile, general interest. *Agented submissions and previously published authors only.*

Fiction Juvenile, picture books, novels. Wants "fresh, exciting picture books and novels—inspiring, new talent." *Agented submissions and previously published authors only.*

SCHROEDER PUBLISHING CO., INC.

P.O. Box 3009, Paducah KY 42002-3009. (270)898-6211. Fax: (270)898-8890. E-mail: editor@collectorbooks.com. Web site: www.collectorbooks.com. Estab. 1973. Publishes hardcover and trade paperback orginals. **Publishes 95 titles/year; imprint publishes 65 (Collector Books); 30 (American Quilter's Society) titles/year. Receives 150 queries and 100 mss/year. 60% of books from first-time authors; 100% from unagented writers. Pays 5% royalty on retail price.** Publishes book 6 months after acceptance of ms. Accepts simultaneous submissions. Responds in 1 month to queries; 1 month to proposals; 1 month to mss. Book catalog and ms guidelines online.

Imprints Collector Books, American Quilter's Society.

Nonfiction Coffee table book, general nonfiction, gift book, how-to, illustrated book, reference, self-help, textbook. Subjects include hobbies, antiques and collectibles. Submit proposal package including outline, 2 sample chapter(s). Reviews artwork/photos as part of ms package. Send transparencies or prints.

Recent Title(s) *Schroeder's Antiques Price Guide*, by Sharon Huxford (reference); *Vintage Golf Club Collectibles*, by Ronald John (reference); *Collector's Encyclopedia of Depression Glass*, by Gene Florence (reference).

Tips Audience consists of collectors, garage sale and flea market shoppers, antique dealers, E-bay shoppers, and quilters.

🅰 SCRIBNER

Imprint of Simon & Schuster Adult Publishing Group, 1230 Avenue of the Americas, New York NY 10020. (212)698-7000. Web site: www.simonsays.com. **Acquisitions:** Nan Graham (literary fiction, nonfiction); Sarah McGrath (fiction, nonfiction); Susanne Kirk (fiction); Lisa Drew (nonfiction); Alexis Gargagliano (fiction, nonfiction); Brant Rumble (fiction, nonfiction); Colin Harrison (fiction, nonfiction). Publishes hardcover originals. **Publishes 70-75 titles/year. Receives thousands queries/year. 20% of books from first-time authors; 0% from unagented writers. Pays 7½-15% royalty. Offers variable advance.** Publishes book 9 months after acceptance of ms. Accepts simultaneous submissions. Responds in 3 months to queries.

Imprints Lisa Drew Books; Scribner Classics (reprints only); Scribner Poetry (by invitation only).

Nonfiction Biography. Subjects include education, ethnic, gay/lesbian, health/medicine, history, language/literature, nature/environment, philosophy, psychology, religion, science, criticism. *Agented submissions only.*

Fiction Literary, mystery, suspense. *Agented submissions only.*

Recent Title(s) *That Old Ace in the Hole*, by Annie Proulx; *Cosmopolis*, by Don DeLillo; *Random Family*, by Adrian Nicole LeBlanc.

SELF-COUNSEL PRESS

1704 N. State St., Bellingham WA 92225. (360)676-4530. Web site: www.self-counsel.com. **Acquisitions:** Richard Day, managing editor. Estab. 1971. Publishes trade paperback originals. **Publishes 30 titles/year. Receives 1,500 queries/year. 30% of books from first-time authors; 90% from unagented writers. Pays 10% royalty on net receipts. Offers rare advance.** Publishes book 8 months after acceptance of ms. Accepts simultaneous submissions. Responds in 2 months to queries. Book catalog via Web site or upon request; ms guidelines online.

O-ᵣ Self-Counsel Press publishes a range of quality self-help books written in practical, nontechnical style by recognized experts in the fields of business, financial, or legal guidance for people who want to help themselves.

Nonfiction How-to, reference, self-help. Subjects include business/economics, computers/electronic, money/finance, legal issues for lay people. Submit proposal package including outline, résumé, 2 sample chapters.

Recent Title(s) *Write Your Legal Will in 3 Easy Steps*, by Craig Waters; *Start & Run an Event Planning Business*, by Cindy Lemaise and M. Foster Walker; *Family Medical History Kit*, by Self-Counsel Press.

SEPIA

Imprint of BET Books, 850 Third Ave., 16th Floor, New York NY 10022. Web site: www.bet.com/books. **Acquisitions:** Glenda Howard, senior editor. Responds in 4 months to proposals.

Fiction Historical, mainstream/contemporary. ''Manuscripts submitted in consideration for Sepia should be 90,000-100,000 words in length. We will review both contemporary and historical novels that display strong characters with intriguing plots.'' Submit proposal package including synopsis, 3 sample chapters.

Tips ''Please do not phone to see if your manuscript was received or returned, or to find out what we thought of it. A self-addressed, stamped postcard can be enclosed with your submission if you want confirmation of its arrival. Specify whether you would like your manuscript returned or recycled if it is not right for us.''

SEVEN STORIES PRESS

140 Watts St., New York NY 10013. (212)226-8760. Fax: (212)226-1411. E-mail: info@sevenstories.com. Web site: www.sevenstories.com. **Acquisitions:** Daniel Simon; Anna Lui. Estab. 1995. Publishes hardcover and trade paperback originals. **Publishes 40-50 titles/year. 15% of books from first-time authors; 50% from unagented writers. Pays 7-15% royalty on retail price. Offers advance.** Publishes book 1-3 years after acceptance of ms. Accepts simultaneous submissions. Book catalog and ms guidelines free.

- Seven Stories Press publishes literary fiction and political nonfiction for social justice. Currently emphasizing politics, social justice, biographies, foreign writings.

Nonfiction Biography. Subjects include general nonfiction. Responds only if interested. Query with SASE. *All unsolicited mss returned unopened.*

Fiction Literary. Query with SASE. *All unsolicited mss returned unopened.*

Recent Title(s) *A Man Without a Country*, by Kurt Vonnegut; *Fledgling*, by Octavia E. Butler; *Abolition Democracy*, by Angela Y. Davis.

SHEED & WARD BOOK PUBLISHING

Imprint of Rowman & Littlefield Publishing Group, 4501 Forbes Blvd., Suite 200, Lanham MD 20706. (301)459-3366. Fax: (301)429-5747. Web site: www.sheedandward.com. Editors: John Loudon and Ross Miller. **Acquisitions:** Sarah Johnson. Publishes hardcover and paperback originals. Does not accept simultaneous submissions. Book catalog free or on Web site; ms guidelines online.

- ''We are looking for books that help our readers, most of whom are college educated, gain access to the riches of the Catholic/Christian tradition. We publish in the areas of history, biography, spirituality, prayer, ethics, ministry, justice, liturgy.''

Nonfiction Biography. Subjects include religion, spirituality, family life, theology, ethics. Submit proposal package including outline, 2 sample chapters, strong cover letter indicating why the project is unique and compelling. Reviews artwork/photos as part of ms package. Send photocopies.

Recent Title(s) *Becoming Fully Human*, by Joan Chittister, OSB; *Exploring Catholic Literature*, by Mary R. Reichardt.

Tips ''We prefer that writers get our author guidelines either from our Web site or via mail before submitting proposals.''

SIERRA CLUB BOOKS

85 Second St., San Francisco CA 94105. (415)977-5500. Fax: (415)977-5792. E-mail: books.publishing@sierraclub.org. Web site: www.sierraclub.org/books. **Acquisitions:** Danny Moses, editor-in-chief. Estab. 1962. Publishes hardcover and paperback originals and reprints. **Publishes approximately 15 titles/year. 50% from unagented writers. Pays royalty. Offers $5,000-15,000 average advance.** Publishes book 1 year after acceptance of ms. Accepts simultaneous submissions. Responds in 1 month to queries; 2 months to proposals; 3 months to mss. Book catalog and ms guidelines online.

Imprints Sierra Club Books for Children.

- *Currently not accepting unsolicited mss* or proposals for children's books.
- The Sierra Club was founded to help people to explore, enjoy, and preserve the nation's forests, waters, wildlife, and wilderness. The books program publishes quality trade books about the outdoors and the protection of the natural world.

Nonfiction General nonfiction. Subjects include nature/environment. A broad range of environmental subjects: outdoor adventure, women in the outdoors; literature, including travel and works on the spiritual aspects of the natural world; natural history and current environmental issues. Does not want ''proposals for large, color-photographic books without substantial text; how-to books on building things outdoors; books on motorized travel; or any but the most professional studies of animals.'' No fiction or poetry. Query with SASE. Reviews artwork/photos as part of ms package. Send photocopies.

Recent Title(s) *Paper or Plastic*, by Daniel Imhoff; *Legacy*, by Nancy Kittle and John Hart; *The Quest for Environmental Justice*, edited by Robert D. Bullard.

⊘ SILHOUETTE BOOKS

233 Broadway, New York NY 10279. (212)553-4200. Fax: (212)227-8960. Web site: www.eharlequin.com. Director, Global Series Editorial: Randall Toye. Executive Editor, Silhouette Books: Mary-Theresa Hussey. **Acquisitions:** Gail Chasan, senior editor (Silhouette Special Edition); Melissa Jeglinski, senior editor (Silhouette Desire); Patience Smith, associate senior editor (Silhouettee Intimate Moments); Natashya Wilson, associate senior editor (Silhouette Bombshell). Estab. 1979. Publishes mass market paperback originals. **Publishes over 350 titles/year. Pays royalty. Offers advance.** Publishes book 1-3 years after acceptance of ms. Does not accept simultaneous submissions. Ms guidelines online.

Imprints Silhouette Desire (contemporary adult romances, 50,000-55,000 words); Silhouette Intimate Moments (contemporary adult romantic suspense, 60,000-65,000 words); Silhouette Bombshell (contemporary adult suspense/adventure fiction, 70,000-75,000 words); Silhouette Special Edition (contemporary adult romances, 60,000-65,000 words).

- O→ Silhouette publishes contemporary adult romances.

Fiction Romance (contemporary romance for adults). ''We are interested in seeing submissions for all our lines. No manuscripts other than the types outlined. Manuscript should follow our general format, yet have an individuality and life of its own that will make them stand out in the readers' minds.'' *No unsolicited mss*. Send query letter, 2 page synopsis, and SASE to head of line.

Recent Title(s) *Marrying Molly*, by Christine Rimmer; *AKA Goddess*, by Evelyn Vaughn.

Tips ''The romance market is constantly changing, so when you read for research, read the latest books and those that have been recommended to you by people knowledgeable in the genre. We are actively seeking new authors for all our lines, contemporary and historical.''

SILMAN-JAMES PRESS

3624 Shannon Rd., Los Angeles CA 90027. (323)661-9922. Fax: (323)661-9933. E-mail: silmanjamespress@earth link.net. Web site: www.silmanjamespress.com. Publishes trade paperback originals and reprints. **Pays variable royalty on retail price.** Book catalog free.

Imprints Siles Press (publishes chess books and other nonfiction subjects).

Nonfiction Pertaining to film, theatre, music, peforming arts. Biography, how-to, reference, technical, textbook. Submit proposal package including outline, 1+ sample chapter(s). Will accept phone queries. Reviews artwork/photos as part of ms package. Send photocopies.

Recent Title(s) *John Carpenter: The Prince of Darkness*, by Gilles Boulenger; *Screenplay: Writing the Picture*, by Robin U. Russin and William Missouri Downs; *Total Directing*, by Tom Kingdon.

Tips ''Our audience ranges from people with a general interest in film (fans, etc.) to students of film and performing arts to industry professionals. We will accept 'query' phone calls.''

⊘ SILVER DAGGER MYSTERIES

The Overmountain Press, 325 Walnut St., Johnson City TN 37605. E-mail: contactsd@silverdaggermysteries.c om. Web site: www.silverdaggermysteries.com. Estab. 1999. Publishes hardcover and trade paperback originals and reprints. Accepts simultaneous submissions. Book catalog and ms guidelines online.

- *Currently closed to submissions.*
- O→ Silver Dagger publishes mysteries that take place in the American South. Emphasizing cozies, police procedurals, hard-boiled detectives.

Fiction Mystery (amateur sleuth, cozy, police procedural, private eye/hardboiled), young adult (mystery). ''We look for average-length books of 60-80,000 words.'' No horror or science fiction. *All unsolicited mss returned unopened.*

Recent Title(s) *Death by Dissertation*, by Dean James; *Execute the Office*, by Daniel Bailey; *Criminal Appetite*, presented by Jeffrey Marks.

SILVER LAKE PUBLISHING

111 E. Wishkah St., Aberdeen WA 98520. (360)532-5758. Fax: (360)532-5728. E-mail: publisher@silverlakepub. com. Web site: www.silverlakepub.com. Estab. 1998. Publishes hardcover and trade paperback originals and reprints. **Pays royalty.** Accepts simultaneous submissions. Responds in 6-8 weeks to proposals. Book catalog and ms guidelines free.

Nonfiction How-to, reference. Subjects include business/economics, money/finance. No fiction or poetry. Submit outline, résumé, 2 sample chapters, cover letter, synopsis. Submit via mail only.

Recent Title(s) *The Fresh Politics Reader*, by Taylor W. Buley; *88% of Americans Are Abnormal*, by Dave Oatley; *Shroud of Silence*, by Frank Feldinger.

SIMON & SCHUSTER BOOKS FOR YOUNG READERS

Imprint of Simon & Schuster Children's Publishing, 1230 Avenue of the Americas, New York NY 10020. (212)698-7000. Fax: (212)698-2796. Web site: www.simonsayskids.com. **Acquisitions:** Elizabeth Law, vice president/associate publisher; Kevin Lewis, executive editor; Paula Wiseman, editorial director. Publishes hardcover originals. **Publishes 75 titles/year. Pays variable royalty on retail price.** Publishes book 2-4 years after acceptance of ms. Accepts simultaneous submissions. Responds in 2 months to queries; 2 months to mss. Ms guidelines for #10 SASE.

Imprints Paula Wiseman Books.

- *No unsolicited mss.* Queries are accepted via mail.
- "We publish high-quality fiction and nonfiction for a variety of age groups and a variety of markets. Above all, we strive to publish books that we are passionate about."

Nonfiction Children's/juvenile. Subjects include history, nature/environment, biography. Query with SASE only. *All unsolicited mss returned unopened.*

Fiction Fantasy, historical, humor, juvenile, mystery, picture books, science fiction, young adult (adventure, historical, mystery, contemporary fiction). Query with SASE only. *All unsolicited mss returned unopened.*

Recent Title(s) *Duck for President*, by Doreen Cronin; *Spiderwick*, by Holly Black, illustrated by Tony Di Terlizzi; *Shrimp*, by Rachel Cohn.

SIMON & SCHUSTER CHILDREN'S PUBLISHING

Division of Simon & Schuster, Inc., 1230 Avenue of the Americas, New York NY 10020. (212)698-7000. Web site: www.simonsays.com. Publishes hardcover and paperback fiction, nonfiction, trade, library, mass market titles, and novelty books for preschool through young adult readers. **Publishes 650 titles/year.**

Imprints Aladdin Paperbacks; Atheneum Books for Young Readers (Richard Jackson Books, Anne Schwartz Books); Libros Para Ninos; Little Simon; Margaret K. McElderry Books; Simon & Schuster Books for Young Readers (Paula Wiseman Books); Simon Pulse; Simon Spotlight; Simon Spotlight Entertainment.

SIMON & SCHUSTER, INC.

1230 Avenue of the Americas, New York NY 10020. (212)698-7000. Web site: www.simonsays.com. **Pays royalty. Offers advance.** Ms guidelines online.

Imprints Simon & Schuster Adult Publishing Group: Atria Books (Washington Square Press), The Free Press (Simon & Schuster Source, Wall Street Journal Books), Kaplan, Pocket Books (Downtown Press, MTV Books, Paraview Pocket, Pocket Star, Star Trek, VH-1 Books, World Wrestling Entertainment), Scribner (Lisa Drew Books, Scribner Classics, Scribner Paperback Fiction), Simon & Schuster (Simon & Schuster Classic Editions), Simon & Schuster Trade Paperbacks (Fireside, Libros en Espanol, Touchstone) **Simon & Schuster Australia:** Audio, Fireside, Kangaroo Press, Martin Books, Pocket Books, Scribner, Simon & Schuster, Touchstone; **Simon & Schuster Children's Publishing:** Aladdin Paperbacks; Atheneum Books for Young Readers (Richard Jackson Books, Anne Schwartz Books), Libros Para Ninos, Little Simon, Margaret K. McElderry Books, Simon & Schuster Books for Young Readers (Paula Weisman Books), Simon Pulse, Simon Spotlight and Simon Spotlight Entertainment; **Simon & Schuster Audio** (Encore, Nightingale-Conant, Pimsleur Language Programs, Simon & Schuster Audioworks, Simon & Schuster Sound Ideas); **Simon & Schuster Online**; **Simon & Schuster UK:** Fireside, The Free Press, Martin Books, Pocket Books, Scribner, Simon & Schuster, Simon & Schuster Audio, Touchstone, Town House.

- See Web site for more details.

SKINNER HOUSE BOOKS

The Unitarian Universalist Association, 25 Beacon St., Boston MA 02108. (617)742-2100 ext. 601. Fax: (617)742-7025. Web site: www.uua.org/skinner. **Acquisitions:** Mary Benard, project editor. Estab. 1975. Publishes trade paperback originals and reprints. **Publishes 10-20 titles/year. 50% of books from first-time authors; 100% from unagented writers. Pays 5-10% royalty on net receipts.** Publishes book 1 year after acceptance of ms. Does not accept simultaneous submissions. Responds in 3 months to queries. Book catalog for 6×9 SAE with 3 first-class stamps; ms guidelines online.

- "We publish titles in Unitarian Universalist faith, liberal religion, history, biography, worship, and issues of social justice. We also publish inspirational titles of poetic prose and meditations. Writers should know that Unitarian Universalism is a liberal religious denomination committed to progressive ideals." Currently emphasizing social justice concerns.

Nonfiction Biography, self-help. Subjects include gay/lesbian, memoirs, religion, women's issues/studies, inspirational, church leadership. Query with SASE. Reviews artwork/photos as part of ms package. Send photocopies.

Recent Title(s) *In Nature's Honor*, by Patricia Montley; *Simply Pray*, by Erik Wikstrom; *Faith Without Certainty*, by Paul Rasor.
Tips "From outside our denomination, we are interested in manuscripts that will be of help or interest to liberal churches, Sunday School classes, parents, ministers, and volunteers. Inspirational/spiritual and children's titles must reflect liberal Unitarian Universalist values. Fiction for youth is being considered."

GIBBS SMITH, PUBLISHER

P.O. Box 667, Layton UT 84041. (801)544-9800. Fax: (801)546-8853. E-mail: info@gibbs-smith.com. Web site: www.gibbs-smith.com. **Acquisitions:** Suzanne Taylor, editorial director, humor. Estab. 1969. Publishes hardcover and trade paperback originals. **Publishes 80 titles/year. Receives 3,000-4,000 queries/year. 50% of books from first-time authors; 75% from unagented writers. Pays 8-14% royalty on gross receipts. Offers advance based on first year saleability projections.** Publishes book 1-2 years after acceptance of ms. Accepts simultaneous submissions. Responds in 1 month to queries; 10 weeks to proposals; 10 weeks to mss. Book catalog for 9×12 SAE and $2.13 in postage; ms guidelines online.

O→ "We publish books that enrich and inspire humankind." Currently emphasizing interior decorating and design, home reference. De-emphasizing novels and short stories.

Nonfiction Humor, illustrated book, textbook, children's. Subjects include art/architecture, nature/environment, regional, interior design, cooking, business, western, outdoor/sports/recreation. Query with SASE, or submit outline, several completed chapters, author's cv. Reviews artwork/photos as part of ms package. Send sample illustrations, if applicable.
Fiction Only short works oriented to gift market. No novels or short stories. Submit synopsis with sample illustration, if applicable. Send query letter or short gift book ms directly to the editorial director.
Recent Title(s) *Secrets of French Design*, by Betty Lou Phillips (nonfiction); *101 More Things to Do with a Slow Cooker*, by Stephanie Ashcraft and Janet Eyring (cookbook).

SOCRATES MEDIA, LLC

227 W. Monroe, Suite 500, Chicago IL 60606. (312)762-5600. Fax: (312)762-5601. Web site: www.socrates.com. **Acquisitions:** Paul Barrett, VP/general manager. Publishes trade paperback and electronic originals. Accepts simultaneous submissions. Book catalog free.

O→ Publishes self-help business forms, legal forms, software, books, kits, and certificates.

Nonfiction How-to. Subjects include business/economics, money/finance, real estate, law. Submit complete ms.
Tips "Our audience is interested in business, legal, and financial matters."

SOHO PRESS, INC.

853 Broadway, New York NY 10003. (212)260-1900. Fax: (212)260-1902. E-mail: soho@sohopress.com. Web site: www.sohopress.com. **Acquisitions:** Laura Hruska, editor-in-chief; Katie Herman, editor. Estab. 1986. Publishes hardcover and trade paperback originals. Accepts simultaneous submissions. Ms guidelines online.

O→ Soho Press publishes primarily fiction, as well as some narrative literary nonfiction. No electronic submissions.

Nonfiction Autobiography, biography, narrative. Subjects include contemporary culture, history, memoirs, military/war, travel (armchair). No self-help, how-to, or cookbooks. Submit outline, sample chapter(s), publishing history, SASE.
Fiction Adventure, ethnic, feminist, historical, literary, mainstream/contemporary, mystery (primarily police procedural series with foreign/exotic settings), suspense. Submit outline, publishing history, synopsis, 3 sample chapters, SASE.
Recent Title(s) *Billy Boyle*, by James R. Benn; *The Texicans*, by Nina Vida; *Chinatown Beat*, by Henry Chang.
Tips "Soho Press publishes discerning authors for discriminating readers, finding the strongest possible writers and publishing them."

SOUNDPRINTS

Division of Trudy Corp., 353 Main Ave., Norwalk CT 06851. Web site: www.soundprints.com. Publishes hardcover and trade paperback originals. **Publishes 30 titles/year; imprint publishes 10 titles/year. Receives 500 queries and 500 mss/year. 10% of books from first-time authors; 100% from unagented writers. Makes outright purchase of $500-1,000.** Book catalog for #10 SASE.

O→ "Whether your children are fascinated by life in the blue ocean or the green grass of their own backyards, Soundprints storybooks, read-along audiobooks, and adorable stuffed toys offer something to delight every child."

Nonfiction Children's/juvenile. Subjects include animals, nature/environment. Query with SASE.
Fiction Query with SASE.

Recent Title(s) *Pepper: A Snowy Search; Pteranodon Soars; Red Bat at Sleepy Hollow Lane.*
Tips "Before submitting, you should have a knowledge of what we publish."

⊘ SOURCEBOOKS, INC.

P.O. Box 4410, Naperville IL 60567. (630)961-3900. Fax: (630)961-2168. Web site: www.sourcebooks.com. Publisher: Dominique Raccah. **Acquisitions:** Todd Stocke, VP/editorial director (nonfiction trade); Deborah Werksman (Sourcebooks Hysteria, Sourcebooks Casablanca); Michael Bowen (Sphinx Publishing). Estab. 1987. Publishes hardcover and trade paperback originals. **Publishes 150 titles/year. 30% of books from first-time authors; 25% from unagented writers. Pays royalty on wholesale price. Offers advance.** Publishes book 1 year after acceptance of ms. Accepts simultaneous submissions. Responds in 3 months to queries. Book catalog and ms guidelines online.

Imprints Sourcebooks Casablanca (love/relationships); Sourcebooks Hysteria (women's humor/gift book); Sourcebooks Landmark; Sourcebooks MediaFusion (multimedia); Sphinx Publishing (self-help legal).

- Sourcebooks publishes many forms of nonfiction titles, generally in the how-to and reference areas, including books on parenting, self-help/psychology, business, and health. Focus is on practical, useful information and skills. It also continues to publish in the reference, New Age, history, current affairs, and travel categories. Currently emphasizing gift, women's interest, history, reference.

Nonfiction "We seek unique books on traditional subjects and authors who are smart and aggressive." Biography, gift book, how-to, illustrated book, multimedia, reference, self-help, technical, textbook. Subjects include art/architecture, business/economics, child guidance/parenting, history, military/war, money/finance, psychology, science, sports, women's issues/studies, contemporary culture. Books for small business owners, entrepreneurs, and students. "A key to submitting books to us is to explain how your book helps the reader, why it is different from the books already out there (please do your homework), and the author's credentials for writing this book. Books likely to succeed with us are self-help, parenting and childcare, psychology, women's issues, how-to, history, reference, biography, humor, gift books, or books with strong artwork." Query with SASE, 2-3 sample chapters (not the first). *No complete mss.* Reviews artwork/photos as part of ms package.

Recent Title(s) *Let Every Nation Know*, by Robert Dallek and Terry Golway; *The Last Nine Innings*, by Charles Euchner.

Tips "Our market is a decidedly trade-oriented bookstore audience. We also have very strong penetration into the gift-store market. Books which cross over between these 2 very different markets do extremely well with us. Our list is a solid mix of unique and general audience titles and series-oriented projects. In other words, we are looking for products that break new ground either in their own areas or within the framework of our series of imprints. We love to develop books in new areas or develop strong titles in areas that are already well developed."

SOUTHERN ILLINOIS UNIVERSITY PRESS

P.O. Box 3697, Carbondale IL 62902-3697. (618)453-6626. Fax: (618)453-1221. Web site: www.siu.edu/~siupress. **Acquisitions:** Karl Kageff, editor-in-chief (film, regional and US history, rhetoric); Kristine Priddy, editor (theater, composition); Sylvia Rodrigue, executive editor (Civil War, Reconstruction); Bridget Brown, assistant editor (poetry, popular culture). Estab. 1956. Publishes hardcover and trade paperback originals and reprints. **Publishes 50-60 titles/year. Receives 700 queries and 300 mss/year. 40% of books from first-time authors; 99% from unagented writers. Pays 5-10% royalty on wholesale price. Rarely offers advance.** Publishes book 1-1½ years after acceptance of ms. Does not accept simultaneous submissions. Responds in 2 months to queries. Book catalog and ms guidelines free.

Imprints Shawnee Books; Shawnee Classics (regional reprint); Crab Orchard Series in Poetry; Theater in the Americas; Studies in Rhetorics and Feminisms; Studies in Writing and Rhetoric.

- "Scholarly press specializes in film and theater studies, rhetoric and composition studies, American history, Civil War, regional and nonfiction trade, poetry. No fiction." Currently emphasizing film, theater and American history, especially Civil War.

Recent Title(s) *The Lincoln Family Album*, by Mark E. Neely Jr. and Harold Holzer; *Shattered Sense of Innocence: The 1955 Murders of Three Chicago Children*, by Richard C. Lindberg and Gloria Jean Sykes; *Federico Fellini as Auteur: Seven Aspects of His Films*, by John C. Stubbs.

A ⊘ SPECTRA BOOKS

Subsidiary of Random House, Inc., 1745 Broadway, New York NY 10019. (212)782-8632. Fax: (212)782-9174. Web site: www.bantamdell.com. Estab. 1985. Publishes hardcover originals, paperback originals, and trade paperbacks. **Pays royalty. Offers negotiable advance.** Accepts simultaneous submissions.

- Accepts agented submissions only.

Fiction Fantasy, literary, science fiction. Needs include novels that attempt to broaden the traditional range of science fiction and fantasy. Strong emphasis on characterization. Especially well-written, traditional science

fiction and fantasy will be considered. No fiction without at least some element of speculation or the fantastic.
Recent Title(s) *The Mysteries*, by Lisa Tuttle; *Pashazade*, by Jon Courtenay Grimwood; *A Secret Atlas*, by Michael A. Stackpole.

THE SPEECH BIN, INC.

1965 25th Ave., Vero Beach FL 32960-3062. (561)770-0007. **Acquisitions:** Jan J. Binney, senior editor. Estab. 1984. Publishes trade paperback originals. **Publishes 10-20 titles/year. Receives 500 mss/year. 50% of books from first-time authors; 90% from unagented writers. Pays negotiable royalty on wholesale price. Offers advance.** Publishes book 1 year after acceptance of ms. Does not accept simultaneous submissions. Responds in 3 months to queries. Book catalog for 9×12 SASE.

- Publishes professional materials for specialists in rehabilitation, particularly speech-language pathologists and audiologists, special educators, occupational and physical therapists, and parents and caregivers of children and adults with developmental and post-trauma disabilities."

Nonfiction Booklets, children's/juvenile (preschool-teen), how-to, illustrated book, reference, textbook, games for children and adults. Subjects include education, health/medicine, communication disorders, education for handicapped persons. Query with SASE, or submit outline, sample chapter(s). Reviews artwork/photos as part of ms package. Send photocopies.
Fiction "Booklets or books for children and adults about handicapped persons, especially with communication disorders." Query with SASE, or submit outline, sample chapter(s), synopsis.
Recent Title(s) *I Can Say S*; *I Can Say R*.
Tips "Books and materials must be clearly presented and well written. We have added books and materials for use by other allied health professionals. We are also looking for more materials for use in treating adults and very young children with communication disorders. Please do not fax or e-mail manuscripts to us or call and tell us about your manuscript." The Speech Bin is increasing their number of books published per year and is especially interested in reviewing treatment materials for adults and adolescents.

SPENCE PUBLISHING CO.

111 Cole St., Dallas TX 75207. (214)939-1700. Fax: (214)939-1800. E-mail: muncy@spencepublishing.com. Web site: www.spencepublishing.com. **Acquisitions:** Mitchell Muncy, editor-in-chief. Estab. 1995. Publishes hardcover and trade paperback originals.

- *No longer accepting unsolicited proposals.*

SPI BOOKS

99 Spring St., 3rd Floor, New York NY 10012. (212)431-5011. Fax: (212)431-8646. E-mail: publicity@spibooks.com. Web site: www.spibooks.com. **Acquisitions:** Ian Shapolsky, acquisitions editor (pop culture, how-to, exposé, entertainment, Judaica, business, conspiracy, children's); Jill Olofsson, acquisitions editor (how-to, self-help, health). Estab. 1991. Publishes hardcover and trade paperback originals and reprints. **Publishes 20-30 titles/year. 5% of books from first-time authors; 50% from unagented writers. Pays 6-15% royalty on retail price. Offers $1,000-10,000 advance.** Publishes book 3-6 months after acceptance of ms. Accepts simultaneous submissions. Responds in 2 months to queries; 2 months to proposals; 2 months to mss. Book catalog online; ms guidelines free.
Nonfiction Autobiography, biography, children's/juvenile, coffee table book, cookbook, general nonfiction, gift book, how-to, humor, illustrated book, reference, scholarly, self-help, textbook. Subjects include Americana, animals, business/economics, child guidance/parenting, community, contemporary culture, cooking/foods/nutrition, creative nonfiction, education, ethnic, government/politics, health/medicine, history, hobbies, humanities, language/literature, memoirs, military/war, money/finance, multicultural, music/dance, nature/environment, New Age, philosophy, psychology, regional, religion, sex, social sciences, sociology, spirituality, sports, translation, travel, women's issues/studies, world affairs, exposé, conspiracy. "Aside from a quality editorial product, we request a marketing plan, suggested by the author, to supplement our own ideas for successfully marketing/promoting their book." Query with SASE, or submit proposal package including outline, sample chapter(s). Reviews artwork/photos as part of ms package. Send photocopies.
Recent Title(s) *Don't Be a Slave to What You Crave*, by Dr. Daisy Merey (health); *Princess Diana: The Hidden Evidence*, by King & Beveridge (conspiracy); *Steve Martin: The Magic Years*, by Morris Walker (biography).
Tips "Advise us how to reach the market for the legions of interested buyers of your book. Be specific if you can help us target marketing opportunities and promotional possibilities, particularly those that are not obvious. Also, let us know if there are any friends/contacts/connections you can draw upon to assist us in getting the message out about the significance of your book."

ST. ANTHONY MESSENGER PRESS

28 W. Liberty St., Cincinnati OH 45202-6498. (513)241-5615. Fax: (513)241-0399. E-mail: books@americancatholic.org. Web site: www.americancatholic.org. Publisher: The Rev. Jeremy Harrington, O.F.M. **Acquisitions:**

Lisa Biedenbach, editorial director. Estab. 1970. Publishes trade paperback originals. **Publishes 20-25 titles/year; imprint publishes 12-15 titles/year. Receives 300 queries and 50 mss/year. 5% of books from first-time authors; 99% from unagented writers. Pays 10-12% royalty on net receipts. Offers $1,000 average advance.** Publishes book 18 months after acceptance of ms. Responds in 2 months to queries; 2 months to proposals; 2 months to mss. Book catalog for 9×12 SAE with 4 first-class stamps; ms guidelines online.

Imprints Servant Books.

O→ "St. Anthony Messenger Press/Franciscan Communications seeks to communicate the word that is Jesus Christ in the styles of Saints Francis and Anthony. Through print and electronic media marketed in North America and worldwide, we endeavor to evangelize, inspire, and inform those who search for God and seek a richer Catholic, Christian, human life. Our efforts help support the life, ministry, and charities of the Franciscan Friars of St. John the Baptist Province, who sponsor our work." Currently emphasizing prayer/spirituality.

Nonfiction Family-based religious education programs. Subjects include church history and practices, Catholic identity and teaching, prayer and spirituality resources, Scripture study. Query with SASE, or submit outline, Attn: Lisa Biedenbach. Reviews artwork/photos as part of ms package.

Recent Title(s) *Life With Mother Teresa*, by Sebastian Vazhakala, MC; *Franciscan Prayer*, by Ilia Delio, OSF; *Spirituality of Sport*, by Susan Saint Sing.

Tips "Our readers are ordinary 'folks in the pews' and those who minister to and educate these folks. Writers need to know the audience and the kind of books we publish. Manuscripts should reflect best and current Catholic theology and doctrine." St. Anthony Messenger Press especially seeks books which will sell in bulk quantities to parishes, teachers, pastoral ministers, etc. They expect to sell at least 5,000 to 7,000 copies of a book.

ST. AUGUSTINE'S PRESS

P.O. Box 2285, South Bend IN 46680-2285. (219)-291-3500. Fax: (219)291-3700. E-mail: bruce@staugustine.net. Web site: www.staugustine.net. **Acquisitions:** Bruce Fingerhut, president (philosophy). Publishes hardcover originals and trade paperback originals and reprints. **Publishes 30 titles/year. Receives 200 queries and 100 mss/year. 5% of books from first-time authors; 95% from unagented writers. Pays 6-20% royalty. Offers $500-5,000 advance.** Publishes book 8 months after acceptance of ms. Accepts simultaneous submissions. Responds in 2-6 months to queries; 3-8 months to proposals; 4-8 months to mss. Book catalog free.

Imprints Carthage Reprints.

O→ "Our market is scholarly in the humanities. We publish in philosophy, religion, cultural history, and history of ideas only."

Nonfiction Biography, textbook. Subjects include history (of ideas), philosophy, religion. Query with SASE. Reviews artwork/photos as part of ms package. Send photocopies.

Recent Title(s) *Introduction to the Summa Theologiae of Thomas Aquinas*, by John of St. Thomas (medieval philosophy); *The American Catholic Voter: 200 Years of Political Impact*, by George J. Marlin (cultural history); *A Theater of Envy: William Shakespeare*, by René Girard (philosophy of literature).

Tips Scholarly and student audience.

ST. MARTIN'S PRESS, LLC

Holtzbrinck Publishers, 175 Fifth Ave., New York NY 10010. (212)674-5151. Fax: (212)420-9314. Web site: www.stmartins.com. Estab. 1952. Publishes hardcover, trade paperback and mass market originals. **Publishes 1,500 titles/year. Pays royalty. Offers advance.** Ms guidelines online.

Imprints Minotaur; Thomas Dunne Books; Griffin; Palgrave MacMillan (division); Priddy Books; St. Martin's Press Paperback & Reference Group; St. Martin's Press Trade Division; Truman Talley Books.

O→ General interest publisher of both fiction and nonfiction.

Nonfiction Biography, cookbook, reference, scholarly, self-help, textbook. Subjects include business/economics, cooking/foods/nutrition, sports, general nonfiction, contemporary culture, true crime. *Agented submissions only. No unsolicited mss.*

Fiction Fantasy, historical, horror, literary, mainstream/contemporary, mystery, science fiction, suspense, western (contemporary), general fiction; thriller. *Agented submissions only. No unsolicited mss.*

ST PAULS/ALBA HOUSE

Society of St. Paul, 2187 Victory Blvd., Staten Island NY 10314-6603. (718)761-0047. Fax: (718)761-0057. E-mail: edmund_lane@juno.com. Web site: www.stpauls.us. **Acquisitions:** Edmund C. Lane, SSP, acquisitions editor. Estab. 1957. Publishes trade paperback and mass market paperback originals and reprints. **Publishes 22 titles/year. Receives 250 queries and 150 mss/year. 10% of books from first-time authors; 100% from unagented writers. Pays 5-10% royalty.** Publishes book 10 months after acceptance of ms. Does not accept simultaneous submissions. Responds in 1 month to queries; 1 month to proposals; 2 months to mss. Book catalog and ms guidelines free.

Nonfiction Reference, scholarly, textbook, religious biographies. Subjects include philosophy, religion, spirituality. "Alba House is the North American publishing division of St. Paul, an International Roman Catholic Missionary Religious Congregation dedicated to spreading the Gospel message via the media of communications." Does not want fiction, children's books, poetry, personal testimonies, or autobiographies. Submit complete ms. Reviews artwork/photos as part of ms package. Send photocopies.

Recent Title(s) *Those Mysterious Priests*, by Fulton J. Sheen (spirituality); *Captured Fire*, by S. Joseph Krempa (homiletics).

Tips "Our audience is educated Roman Catholic readers interested in matters related to the Church, spirituality, Biblical and theological topics, moral concerns, lives of the saints, etc."

STACKPOLE BOOKS

5067 Ritter Rd., Mechanicsburg PA 17055. Fax: (717)796-0412. E-mail: jschnell@stackpolebooks.com. Web site: www.stackpolebooks.com. **Acquisitions:** Judith Schnell, editorial director (fly fishing, sports); Chris Evans, editor (history); Mark Allison, editor (nature); Ed Skender, editor (military guides); Kyle Weaver, editor (Pennsylvania/regional). Estab. 1935. Publishes hardcover and paperback originals and reprints. **Publishes 100 titles/year. Offers industry standard advance.** Publishes book 1 year after acceptance of ms. Does not accept simultaneous submissions. Responds in 1 month to queries.

O→ "Stackpole maintains a growing and vital publishing program by featuring authors who are experts in their fields."

Nonfiction Subjects include history, military/war, nature/environment, recreation, sports, wildlife, outdoor skills, fly fishing, paddling, climbing. Query with SASE. Does not return unsolicited mss. Reviews artwork/photos as part of ms package.

Recent Title(s) *Mayflies*; *Careers With Animals*; *In the Company of Moose*.

Tips "Stackpole seeks well-written, authoritative manuscripts for specialized and general trade markets. Proposals should include chapter outline, sample chapter, illustrations, and author's credentials."

STANDARD PUBLISHING

Standex International Corp., 8121 Hamilton Ave., Cincinnati OH 45231. (513)931-4050. Web site: www.standardpub.com. Editorial Directors: Mark Taylor, adult ministry resources; Ruth Frederick, children and youth ministry resources; Diane Stortz, family resources. Estab. 1866. Publishes hardcover and paperback originals and reprints. **Pays royalty.** Publishes book 18 months after acceptance of ms. Does not accept simultaneous submissions. Responds in 3 months to queries. Ms guidelines online.

O→ Standard specializes in religious books for children through adults and religious education.

Nonfiction Children's/juvenile, illustrated book, reference. Subjects include education, picture books, Christian education (teacher training, working with volunteers), quiz, puzzle, crafts (to be used in Christian education), Christian living. Query with SASE.

Recent Title(s) *Second Guessing God*, by Brian Jones; *Devotions by Dead People*, by Lynn Lusby Pratt; *My Little Good Night Storybook*, by Susan Lingo.

STANFORD UNIVERSITY PRESS

1450 Page Mill Rd., Palo Alto CA 94304-1124. (650)723-9434. Fax: (650)725-3457. E-mail: info@www.sup.org. Web site: www.sup.org. **Acquisitions:** Muriel Bell (Asian studies, US foreign policy, Asian-American studies); Amanda M. Moran (law, political science, public policy); Martha Cooley (economics, finance, business); Kate Wahl (sociology, anthropology, education, Middle Eastern studies). Estab. 1925. **Pays variable royalty (sometimes none). Offers occasional advance.** Does not accept simultaneous submissions. Ms guidelines online.

O→ Stanford University Press publishes scholarly books in the humanities and social sciences, along with professional books in business, economics and management science; also high-level textbooks and some books for a more general audience.

Nonfiction Scholarly, textbook, professional books. Subjects include anthropology/archeology, business/economics, ethnic (studies), gay/lesbian, government/politics, history, humanities, language/literature, nature/environment, philosophy, psychology, religion, science, social sciences, sociology, political science, law, education, history and culture of China, Japan and Latin America, European history, linguistics, geology, medieval and classical studies. Query with prospectus and an outline. Reviews artwork/photos as part of ms package.

Recent Title(s) *Culture and Public Action*; *The Sovereignty Revolution*; *Maps, Myths, and Men*.

Tips "The writer's best chance is a work of original scholarship with an argument of some importance."

STEEPLE HILL WOMEN'S FICTION

Imprint of Steeple Hill, 233 Broadway, Suite 1001, New York NY 10279. (212)553-4200. Fax: (212)227-8969. Web site: www.steeplehill.com. **Acquisitions:** Joan Marlow Golan, executive editor (inspirational fiction);

Krista Stroever, associate senior editor (inspirational fiction); Melissa Endlich, editor (inspirational fiction); Diane Dietz, assistant editor (inspirational fiction). Estab. 1997. Publishes hardcover, trade paperback, and mass market paperback originals. **Publishes 78-90 titles/year. Pays royalty on retail price. Offers advance.** Does not accept simultaneous submissions. Responds in 3 months to queries; 3 months to proposals; 3 months to mss. Ms guidelines online.

Imprints Steeple Hill Café; Steeple Hill Women's Fiction.

Fiction Literary, mystery, religious, romance, chick lit. "This program is dedicated to publishing inspirational Christian women's fiction that depicts the struggles characters encounter as they learn important lessons about trust and the power of faith. See listing for subgenres. The Steeple Hill Café line is a new subbrand within the Steeple Hill Women's Fiction Program, and it is dedicated to publishing inspirational fiction for the hip, modern women of faith. These distinctively smart and spirited books will depict the unique and varied situations women encounter as they learn important lessons about life, love, and the power of faith." Query with SASE.

Recent Title(s) *Hideaway*, by Hannah Alexander; *The Whitney Chronicles*, by Judy Baer.

Tips "Please read our guidelines."

STENHOUSE PUBLISHERS

480 Congress St., Portland ME 04101-3400. Web site: www.stenhouse.com. **Acquisitions:** William Varner, senior editor. Estab. 1993. Publishes paperback originals. **Publishes 15 titles/year. Receives 300 queries/year. 30% of books from first-time authors; 99% from unagented writers. Pays royalty on wholesale price. Offers very modest advance.** Accepts simultaneous submissions. Responds in 2 weeks to queries; 1 month to mss. Book catalog free or online; ms guidelines online.

O→ Stenhouse publishes exclusively professional books for teachers, K-12.

Nonfiction Subjects include education (specializing in literacy). "All our books are a combination of theory and practice." No children's books or student texts. Query with SASE, or submit outline. Reviews artwork/photos as part of ms package. Send photocopies.

Recent Title(s) *Reconsidering Read-Aloud*, by Mary Lee Hahn; *Writing for Real*, by Ross M. Burkhardt; *Knowing How*, by Mary C. McMackin and Barbara Seigel.

STERLING PUBLISHING

387 Park Ave. S., New York NY 10016. (212)532-7160. Fax: (212)213-2495. Web site: www.sterlingpub.com. **Acquisitions:** Category Editor (i.e., Craft Editor or Children's Editor). Estab. 1949. Publishes hardcover and paperback originals and reprints. **Pays royalty. Offers advance.** Does not accept simultaneous submissions. Ms guidelines online.

Imprints Sterling/Chapelle; Lark; Sterling/Tamos; Sterling/Prolific Impressions.

O→ Sterling publishes highly illustrated, accessible, hands-on, practical books for adults and children.

Nonfiction Publishes nonfiction only. Children's/juvenile, how-to, humor, reference, adult. Subjects include alternative lifestyles, animals, art/architecture, ethnic, gardening, health/medicine, hobbies, New Age, recreation, science, sports, fiber arts, games and puzzles, children's humor, children's science, nature and activities, pets, wine, home decorating, dolls and puppets, ghosts, UFOs, woodworking, crafts, medieval, Celtic subjects, alternative health and healing, new consciousness. Submit outline, publishing history, 1 sample chapter, SASE. Reviews artwork/photos as part of ms package. Send photocopies.

Recent Title(s) *AARP Crash Course in Estate Planning*, by Michael Palermo and Ric Edelman.

STIPES PUBLISHING LLC

P.O. Box 526, Champaign IL 61824-9933. (217)356-8391. Fax: (217)356-5753. E-mail: stipes@soltec.net. Web site: www.stipes.com. **Acquisitions:** Benjamin H. Watts, (engineering, science, business); Robert Watts (agriculture, music, and physical education). Estab. 1925. Publishes hardcover and paperback originals. **Publishes 15-30 titles/year. 50% of books from first-time authors; 95% from unagented writers. Pays 15% maximum royalty on retail price.** Publishes book 4 months after acceptance of ms. Does not accept simultaneous submissions. Responds in 2 months to queries. Ms guidelines online.

O→ Stipes Publishing is "oriented towards the education market and educational books with some emphasis in the trade market."

Nonfiction Technical (some areas), textbook (on business/economics, music, chemistry, CADD, agriculture/horticulture, environmental education, recreation, physical education). Subjects include agriculture/horticulture, business/economics, music/dance, nature/environment, recreation, science. "All of our books in the trade area are books that also have a college text market. No books unrelated to educational fields taught at the college level." Submit outline, 1 sample chapter.

Recent Title(s) *The AutoCAD 2004 Workbook*, by Philip Age and Ronald Sutliff.

STOEGER PUBLISHING CO.

17603 Indian Head Hwy., Suite 200, Accokeek MD 20607. (301)283-6300. Fax: (301)283-4783. Web site: www.stoegerindustries.com. **Acquisitions:** Jay Langston, publisher. Estab. 1925. Publishes hardback and trade paperback originals. **Publishes 12-15 titles/year. Royalty varies, depending on ms. Offers advance.** Accepts simultaneous submissions. Responds in 2 months to queries. Book catalog online.

O→ Stoeger publishes books on hunting, shooting sports, fishing, cooking, nature, and wildlife.

Nonfiction Specializes in reference and how-to books that pertain to hunting, fishing, and appeal to gun enthusiasts. How-to, reference. Subjects include cooking/foods/nutrition, sports. Submit outline, sample chapter(s).

Fiction Specializes in outdoor-related fiction.

Recent Title(s) *Escape in Iraq: The Thomas Hamill Story*; *Gun Trader's Guide, 26th Ed.*; *Hunting Whitetails East & West*.

STOREY PUBLISHING, LLC

210 MASS MoCA Way, North Adams MA 01247. (413)346-2100. Fax: (413)346-2196. Web site: www.storey.com. **Acquisitions:** Deborah Balmuth, editorial director (building, cooking, mind/body/spirit); Deborah Burns (horses, farming, animals, nature); Gwen Steege (gardening, crafts). Estab. 1983. Publishes hardcover and trade paperback originals and reprints. **Publishes 40 titles/year. Receives 600 queries and 150 mss/year. 25% of books from first-time authors; 80% from unagented writers. Pays royalty, or makes outright purchase. Offers advance.** Publishes book within 2 years after acceptance of ms. Accepts simultaneous submissions. Responds in 1 month to queries; 3 months to proposals; 3 months to mss. Book catalog free; ms guidelines online.

O→ "We publish practical information that encourages personal independence in harmony with the environment."

Nonfiction Subjects include animals, gardening, nature/environment, home, mind/body/spirit, birds, beer and wine, crafts, building, cooking. Reviews artwork/photos as part of ms package.

Recent Title(s) *Mom's Best One-Dish Suppers*, by Andrea Chesman; *Cleaning Plain & Simple*, by Donna Smallin; *Incredible Vegetables From Self-Watering Containers*, by Edward C. Smith.

STYLUS PUBLISHING, LLC

22883 Quicksilver Dr., Sterling VA 20166. Web site: styluspub.com. **Acquisitions:** John von Knorring, publisher. Estab. 1996. Publishes hardcover and trade paperback originals. **Publishes 10-15 titles/year. Receives 50 queries and 6 mss/year. 50% of books from first-time authors; 100% from unagented writers. Pays 5-10% royalty on wholesale price. Offers advance.** Publishes book 6 months after acceptance of ms. Does not accept simultaneous submissions. Responds in 1 month to queries. Book catalog free; ms guidelines online.

O→ "We publish in higher education (diversity, professional development, distance education, teaching, administration)."

Nonfiction Scholarly. Subjects include education. Query or submit outline, 1 sample chapter with SASE. Reviews artwork/photos as part of ms package. Send photocopies.

Recent Title(s) *What Makes Racial Diversity Work in Higher Education*; *Taking Ownership of Accreditation*; *The Art of Changing the Brain*.

SUN BOOKS/SUN PUBLISHING

P.O. Box 5588, Santa Fe NM 87502-5588. (505)471-5177. E-mail: info@sunbooks.com. Web site: www.sunbooks.com. **Acquisitions:** Skip Whitson, director. Publishes trade paperback originals and reprints. **Publishes 10-15 titles/year. 5% of books from first-time authors; 90% from unagented writers. Pays 5% royalty on retail price, or makes outright purchase.** Publishes book 16 months after acceptance of ms. Responds in 2 months to queries; 2 months to proposals; 6 months to mss. Book catalog online.

Nonfiction Biography, cookbook, how-to, humor, illustrated book, reference, self-help, technical. Subjects include Americana, anthropology/archeology, business/economics, cooking/foods/nutrition, creative nonfiction, education, government/politics, health/medicine, history, language/literature, memoirs, money/finance, multicultural, nature/environment, philosophy, psychology, regional, religion, sociology, travel, women's issues/studies, metaphysics, motivational, inspirational, Oriental studies. Query with SASE, preferably via e-mail. Reviews artwork/photos as part of ms package. Send photocopies.

Recent Title(s) *Eight Pillars of Prosperity*, by James Allen; *Ambition and Success*, by Orson Swett Marden; *Cheerfulness as a Life Power*, by Orson Swett Marden.

SYRACUSE UNIVERSITY PRESS

621 Skytop Road, Suite 110, Syracuse NY 13244-5290. (315)443-5534. Fax: (315)443-5545. Web site: syracuseuniversitypress.syr.edu. **Acquisitions:** Peter B. Webber, director. Estab. 1943. **Publishes 50 titles/year. 25% of books from first-time authors; 75% from unagented writers. Pays royalty on net receipts.** Publishes book

an average of 15 months after acceptance of ms. Does not accept simultaneous submissions. Book catalog for 9×12 SAE with 3 first-class stamps; ms guidelines online.

Currently emphasizing television, Jewish studies, Middle East topics. De-emphasizing peace studies.

Nonfiction Subjects include regional. ''Special opportunity in our nonfiction program for freelance writers of books on New York state, sports history, Jewish studies, the Middle East, religious studies, television, and popular culture. Provide precise descriptions of subjects, along with background description of project. The author must make a case for the importance of his or her subject.'' Submit query with SASE or online, or submit outline and 2 sample chapters. Reviews artwork/photos as part of ms package.

Recent Title(s) *A Time Between Ashes and Roses*, by Adonis, translated from Arabic by Shawkat M. Toorawa; *In the Path of Hizbullah*, by A. Nizar Hamzeh; *Encyclopedia NYS*.

Tips ''We're seeking well-written and well-researched books that will make a significant contribution to the subject areas listed above and will be well-received in the marketplace.''

NAN A. TALESE

Imprint of Doubleday, 1745 Broadway, New York NY 10019. (212)782-8918. Fax: (212)782-8448. Web site: www.nanatalese.com. **Acquisitions:** Nan A. Talese, publisher and editorial director; Lorna Owen, editor; Luke Epplin, associate editor. Publishes hardcover originals. **Publishes 15 titles/year. Receives 400 queries and 400 mss/year. Pays variable royalty on retail price. Offers varying advance.** *Agented submissions only.*

Nan A. Talese publishes nonfiction with a powerful guiding narrative and relevance to larger cultural interests, and literary fiction of the highest quality.

Nonfiction Biography. Subjects include contemporary culture, history, philosophy, sociology.

Fiction Literary. Well-written narratives with a compelling story line, good characterization and use of language. ''We like stories with an edge.''

Recent Title(s) *Saturday*, by Ian McEwan; *Albion: The Origins of the English Imagination*, by Peter Ackroyd; *Oryx and Crake*, by Margaret Atwood.

Tips ''Audience is highly literate people interested in story, information and insight. We want well-written material submitted by agents only. See our Web site.''

JEREMY P. TARCHER, INC.

Imprint of Penguin Group (USA), Inc., 375 Hudson St., New York NY 10014. (212)366-2000. Web site: www.penguinputnam.com. Publisher: Joel Fotinos. **Acquisitions:** Mitch Horowitz, executive editor; Sara Carder, senior editor. Estab. 1972. Publishes hardcover and trade paperback originals and reprints. **Publishes 40-50 titles/year. Receives 1,000 queries and 1,000 mss/year. 20% of books from first-time authors; 20% from unagented writers. Pays royalty. Offers advance.** Accepts simultaneous submissions.

Tarcher's vision is to publish ideas and works about human consciousness that are large enough to include all aspects of human experience.

Nonfiction Self-help, spirituality, social issues. Subjects include gay/lesbian, health/medicine, nature/environment, philosophy, psychology, religion, women's issues/studies, Eastern and Western religions, metaphysics, politics. Query with SASE.

Recent Title(s) *The Faith of George W. Bush*, by Stephen Mansfield; *The European Dream*, by Jeremy Rifkin; *The Secret Teachings of All Ages*, by Manly P. Hall.

Tips ''Our audience seeks personal growth through books. Understand the imprint's focus and categories.''

TAYLOR TRADE PUBLISHING

5360 Manhattan Circle, #101, Boulder CO 80303. (303)543-7835. E-mail: tradeeditorial@rowman.com. Web site: www.rlpgtrade.com. **Acquisitions:** Dulcie Wilcox, acquisitions editor. Publishes hardcover originals, trade paperback originals and reprints. **Publishes 70 titles/year. 15% of books from first-time authors; 65% from unagented writers. Pays 10-15% royalty on net receipts.** Publishes book 1 year after acceptance of ms. Responds in 2 months to queries.

Nonfiction Self-help, field guides. Subjects include child guidance/parenting, cooking/foods/nutrition, gardening, health/medicine, history (Texas/Western, general), nature/environment, sports, contemporary affairs, music, film, theater, art, nature writing, exploration, women's studies, African-American studies, literary studies. All proposals may be sent via e-mail. Query with SASE, or submit outline, sample chapter(s).

TEACHER CURRICULUM LLC

P.O. Box 1161, Spokane Valley WA 99211-1615. Fax: (509)533-1915. E-mail: dennisr@goteachit.com. Submissions E-mail: swd509@earthlink.net. Web site: www.goteachit.com. Estab. 2004. Publishes electronic originals. **Publishes 1,000 titles/year. Receives 500 queries and 500 mss/year. 90% of books from first-time authors; 100% from unagented writers. Pays 10-20% royalty on retail price.** Publishes book 3 months after acceptance of ms. Accepts simultaneous submissions. Responds in 1 month to queries; 1 month to mss. Book catalog online.

Nonfiction Booklets, children's/juvenile, reference, textbook, traditional or non-traditional curriculum. Subjects include animals, education, history, social sciences, world affairs, curriculum. "We generally write using established templates or formats. We accept ideas for development into our formats." Submit proposal package including outline, and clearly state object of curriculum. Reviews artwork/photos as part of ms package. Send photocopies.

Fiction Adventure, comic books, confession, erotica, ethnic, experimental, fantasy, feminist, gay/lesbian, gothic, hi-lo, historical, horror, humor, juvenile, literary, mainstream/contemporary, military/war, multicultural, multimedia, mystery, occult, picture books, plays, poetry, poetry in translation, regional, religious, romance, science fiction, short story collections, spiritual, sports, suspense, western, young adult. "We publish curriculum in any of the above areas. We publish original fiction, but it must be developed into a usable curriculum for use in a classroom." Submit synopsis, curriculum outline.

Poetry "We publish original poetry with a usable curriculum for use in primary and secondary classrooms." Submit any sample poems.

Recent Title(s) *Hamlet Educational Games Package*, by Annella Rice; *The Crucible Complete Teaching Unit*, by Ron Price.

Tips "Go to our Web site and order a product in the specific area of interest."

N TEACHERS COLLEGE PRESS

1234 Amsterdam Ave., New York NY 10027. (212)678-3929. Fax: (212)678-4149. Web site: www.teacherscollegepress.com. Director: Carole P. Saltz. **Acquisitions:** Brian Ellerbeck, executive acquisitions editor. Estab. 1904. Publishes hardcover and paperback originals and reprints. **Publishes 60 titles/year. Pays industry standard royalty. Offers advance.** Publishes book 1 year after acceptance of ms. Does not accept simultaneous submissions. Responds in 2 months to queries. Book catalog free; ms guidelines online.

O→ Teachers College Press publishes a wide range of educational titles for all levels of students: early childhood to higher education. "Publishing books that respond to, examine, and confront issues pertaining to education, teacher training, and school reform."

Nonfiction Subjects include computers/electronic, education, film/cinema/stage, government/politics, history, philosophy, sociology, women's issues/studies. "This university press concentrates on books in the field of education in the broadest sense, from early childhood to higher education: good classroom practices, teacher training, special education, innovative trends and issues, administration and supervision, film, continuing and adult education, all areas of the curriculum, computers, guidance and counseling, and the politics, economics, philosophy, sociology, and history of education. We have recently added women's studies to our list. The Press also issues classroom materials for students at all levels, with a strong emphasis on reading and writing and social studies." Submit outline, sample chapter(s).

Recent Title(s) *Cultural Miseducation: In Search of a Democratic Solution*, by Jane Roland Martin.

TEACHING & LEARNING CO.

1204 Buchanan St., P.O. Box 10, Carthage IL 62321-0010. (217)357-2591. Fax: (217)357-6789. E-mail: customerservice@teachinglearning.com. Web site: www.teachinglearning.com. **Acquisitions:** Jill Day, vice president of production. Estab. 1994. **Publishes 60 titles/year. Receives 25 queries and 200 mss/year. 25% of books from first-time authors; 98% from unagented writers. Pays royalty.** Accepts simultaneous submissions. Responds in 3 months to queries; 9 months to proposals; 9 months to mss. Book catalog and ms guidelines free.

O→ Teaching & Learning Co. publishes teacher resources (supplementary activity/idea books) for grades pre K-8. Currently emphasizing "more math for all grade levels, more primary science material."

Nonfiction Children's/juvenile. Subjects include art/architecture, education, language/literature, science, teacher resources in language arts, reading, math, science, social studies, arts and crafts, responsibility education. No picture books or storybooks. Submit table of contents, introduction, 3 sample chapters with SASE. Reviews artwork/photos as part of ms package. Send photocopies.

Recent Title(s) *Group Project Student Role Sheets*, by Christine Boardman Moen (nonfiction); *Poetry Writing Handbook*, by Greta Barclay Lipson, Ed.D. (poetry); *Four Square Writing Methods (3 books)*, by Evan and Judith Gould.

Tips "Our books are for teachers and parents of pre K-8th grade children."

TEMPLE UNIVERSITY PRESS

1601 N. Broad St., USB 305, Philadelphia PA 19122-6099. (215)204-8787. Fax: (215)204-4719. E-mail: tempress@temple.edu. Web site: www.temple.edu/tempress/. **Acquisitions:** Alex Holzman, director; Janet Francendese, editor-in-chief; Micah Kleit, executive editor. Estab. 1969. **Publishes 60 titles/year. Offers advance.**

Publishes book 10 months after acceptance of ms. Does not accept simultaneous submissions. Responds in 2 months to queries. Book catalog free; ms guidelines online.

- "Temple University Press has been publishing useful books on Asian-Americans, law, gender issues, film, women's studies and other interesting areas for nearly 30 years."

Nonfiction Subjects include ethnic, government/politics, health/medicine, history, photography, regional (Philadelphia), sociology, labor studies, urban studies, Latin American/Latino, Asian American, African American studies, public policy, women's studies. "No memoirs, fiction or poetry." Query with SASE. Reviews artwork/photos as part of ms package.

Recent Title(s) *From Black Power to Hip Hop*, by Patricia Hill Collins; *Animal Passions and Beastly Virtues*, by Mar Bekoff.

TEN SPEED PRESS

P.O. Box 7123, Berkeley CA 94707. (510)559-1600. Fax: (510)524-1052. E-mail: info@tenspeed.com. Web site: www.tenspeed.com. **Acquisitions:** Phil Wood, president; Lorena Jones, Ten Speed Press publisher; Aaron Wehmer, Ten Speed Press editorial director; Jo Ann Deck, Celestial Arts/Crossing Press publisher. Estab. 1971. Publishes trade paperback originals and reprints. **Publishes 120 titles/year; imprint publishes 70 titles/year. 40% of books from first-time authors; 40% from unagented writers. Pays 15-20% royalty on net receipts. Offers $2,500 average advance.** Publishes book 1 year after acceptance of ms. Accepts simultaneous submissions. Responds in 3 months to queries. Book catalog for 9×12 SAE with 6 first-class stamps; ms guidelines online.

Imprints Celestial Arts; Crossing Press; Tricycle Press.

- Ten Speed Press publishes authoritative books for an audience interested in innovative ideas. Currently emphasizing cookbooks, career, business, alternative education, and offbeat general nonfiction gift books.

Nonfiction Subjects include business/economics, child guidance/parenting, cooking/foods/nutrition, gardening, health/medicine, money/finance, nature/environment, New Age (mind/body/spirit), recreation, science. "No fiction." Query with SASE, or submit proposal package including sample chapter(s).

Recent Title(s) *How to Be Happy, Dammit*, by Karen Salmansohn; *The Bread Baker's Apprentice*, by Peter Reinhart.

Tips "We like books from people who really know their subject, rather than people who think they've spotted a trend to capitalize on. We like books that will sell for a long time, rather than nine-day wonders. Our audience consists of a well-educated, slightly weird group of people who like food, the outdoors, and take a light, but serious, approach to business and careers. Study the backlist of each publisher you're submitting to and tailor your proposal to what you perceive as their needs. Nothing gets a publisher's attention like someone who knows what he or she is talking about, and nothing falls flat like someone who obviously has no idea who he or she is submitting to."

TEXAS A&M UNIVERSITY PRESS

College Station TX 77843-4354. (979)845-1436. Fax: (979)847-8752. E-mail: fdl@tampress.tamu.edu. Web site: www.tamu.edu/upress. **Acquisitions:** Mary Lenn Dixon, editor-in-chief (presidential studies, anthropology, borderlands, western history); Shannon Davies, senior editor (natural history, agriculture). Estab. 1974. **Publishes 60 titles/year. Pays royalty.** Publishes book 1 year after acceptance of ms. Does not accept simultaneous submissions. Responds in 1 month to queries. Book catalog free; ms guidelines online.

- Texas A&M University Press publishes a wide range of nonfiction, scholarly trade, and crossover books of regional and national interest, "reflecting the interests of the university, the broader scholarly community, and the people of our state and region."

Nonfiction Subjects include agriculture/horticulture, anthropology/archeology, art/architecture, business/economics, government/politics, history (American and Western), language/literature (Texas and western), military/war, nature/environment, regional (Texas and the Southwest), Mexican-US borderlands studies, nautical archaeology, ethnic studies, presidential studies, business history. Query with SASE.

Recent Title(s) *The White House World*, edited by Martha Joynt Kuma and Terry Sullivan.

Tips Proposal requirements are posted on the Web site.

TEXAS STATE HISTORICAL ASSOCIATION

2.306 Richardson Hall, University Station, Austin TX 78712. (512)471-1525. Fax: (512)471-1551. Web site: www.tsha.utexas.edu. **Acquisitions:** J. Kent Calder, director of publications. Estab. 1897. Publishes hardcover and trade paperback originals and reprints. **Publishes 8 titles/year. Receives 50 queries and 50 mss/year. 10% of books from first-time authors; 95% from unagented writers. Pays 10% royalty on net cash proceeds.** Publishes book 1 year after acceptance of ms. Does not accept simultaneous submissions. Responds in 2-3 months to mss. Book catalog and ms guidelines free.

O‑‑ "We are interested in scholarly historical articles and books on any aspect of Texas history and culture."
Nonfiction Biography, coffee table book, illustrated book, reference, scholarly. Subjects include history. Query with SASE. Reviews artwork/photos as part of ms package. Send photocopies.
Recent Title(s) *Sea of Mud: The Retreat of the Mexican Army after San Jacinto*, by Gregg J. Dimmick; *Civil War and Revolution on the Rio Grande Frontier: A Narrative and Photographic History*, by Jerry Thompson and Lawrence T. Jones III.

THUNDER'S MOUTH PRESS

Imprint of Avalon Publishing Group, 245 W. 17th St., New York NY 10011. (646)375-2570. Fax: (646)375-2571. Web site: www.thundersmouth.com. **Acquisitions:** Acquisitions Editor. Estab. 1982. Publishes hardcover and trade paperback originals and reprints, almost exclusively nonfiction. **Publishes 70-80 titles/year. Receives 4,000 queries/year. 15% from unagented writers. Pays 7-10% royalty on retail price. Offers $2,500 average advance.** Publishes book 8 months after acceptance of ms. Does not accept simultaneous submissions. Responds in 2 months to queries.
Nonfiction Biography. Subjects include government/politics, popular culture. *No unsolicited mss.*
Recent Title(s) *Chance*, by Amir Aczel.

TILBURY HOUSE, PUBLISHERS

Imprint of Harpswell Press, Inc., 2 Mechanic St., Gardiner ME 04345. (207)582-1899. Fax: (207)582-8227. E-mail: tilbury@tilburyhouse.com. Web site: www.tilburyhouse.com. Publisher: Jennifer Bunting (New England, maritime, children's). **Acquisitions:** Audrey Maynard, children's book editor. Estab. 1990. Publishes hardcover originals, trade paperback originals. **Publishes 10 titles/year. Pays royalty.** Book catalog free; ms guidelines online.
Nonfiction Regional adult biography/history/maritime/nature, and children's picture books that deal with issues, such as bullying, multiculturalism, etc. Submit complete ms. Reviews artwork/photos as part of ms package. Send photocopies.
Recent Title(s) *Playing War*, by Kathy Beckwith; *Thanks to the Animals*, by Allen Sockabasin.

MEGAN TINGLEY BOOKS

Imprint of Little, Brown & Co., 1271 Avenue of the Americas, New York NY 10020. (212)522-8700. Fax: (212)522-7997. Web site: www.lb-kids.com. **Acquisitions:** Megan Tingley, editor-in-chief; Nancy Consescu, assistant editor. Publishes hardcover and trade paperback originals and reprints. **Publishes 80-100 titles/year; imprint publishes 10-20 titles/year. Receives 500-1,000 queries and 500-1,000 mss/year. 2% of books from first-time authors; 5% from unagented writers. Pays 0-15% royalty on retail price, or makes outright purchase.** Publishes book 1-2 years after acceptance of ms. Accepts simultaneous submissions. Responds in 1 month to queries; 6-8 weeks to proposals; 6-8 weeks to mss.

O‑‑ Megan Tingley Books is an imprint of the children's book department of Little, Brown and Company. Currently looking for all formats with special interest in humor, music, multicultural, supernatural, narrative nonfiction, poetry, and unusual art styles. No fairy tales.

Nonfiction Children's/juvenile. Subjects include animals, art/architecture, cooking/foods/nutrition, creative nonfiction, ethnic, gay/lesbian, history, language/literature, memoirs, multicultural, music/dance, photography. *Agented submissions and queries only.* Ideally, books should be about a subject that hasn't been dealt with for children before. Reviews artwork/photos as part of ms package. Send photocopies. No original pieces.
Fiction Picture books, middle grade, young adult. Adventure, fantasy, gay/lesbian, historical, humor, multicultural, suspense, political, chick lit. *Agented submissions only.* No genre novels (romance, mystery, science fiction, etc.).
Recent Title(s) *Luna*, by Julie Ann Peters; *Harlem Stomp!*, by Laban Carrick Hill; *You Read to Me, I'll Read to You*, by Mary Ann Hoberman; illustrated by Michael Emberley.
Tips "Do your research. Know our submission policy. Do not fax or call."

TORAH AURA PRODUCTIONS

4423 Fruitland Ave., Los Angeles CA 90058. (800)238-6724. Fax: (323)585-0327. E-mail: misrad@torahaura.com. Web site: www.torahaura.com. **Acquisitions:** Jane Golub. Estab. 1982. Publishes hardcover and trade paperback originals. **Publishes 25 titles/year; imprint publishes 10 titles/year. Receives 5 queries and 10 mss/year. 2% of books from first-time authors; 100% from unagented writers. Pays 10% royalty on wholesale price.** Publishes book 2-3 years after acceptance of ms. Accepts simultaneous submissions. Responds in 6 months to mss. Book catalog free.

O‑‑ Torah Aura only publishes educational materials for Jewish classrooms.

Nonfiction Children's/juvenile, textbook. Subjects include language/literature (Hebrew), religion (Jewish). No picture books. Query with SASE. Reviews artwork/photos as part of ms package. Send photocopies.

Fiction Juvenile, religious, young adult. All fiction must have Jewish interest. No picture books. Query with SASE. Reviews artwork/photos as part of ms package. Send photocopies.
Recent Title(s) *I Have Some Questions About God*, by Rabbis Bradley Shavit Artson, Ed Feinstein, Elyse Frishman, Joshua Hammerman, Jeffrey K. Salkin, and Sybil Sheridan; *Let's Talk About God*, by Dorothy K. Kripke.

TOWER PUBLISHING

588 Saco Rd., Standish ME 04084. (207)642-5400. Fax: (207)642-5463. E-mail: info@towerpub.com. Web site: www.towerpub.com. **Acquisitions:** Michael Lyons, president. Estab. 1772. Publishes hardcover originals and reprints, trade paperback originals. **Publishes 22 titles/year. Receives 60 queries and 30 mss/year. 10% of books from first-time authors; 90% from unagented writers. Pays royalty on net receipts.** Publishes book 6 months after acceptance of ms. Accepts simultaneous submissions. Responds in 1 month to queries; 2 months to proposals; 2 months to mss. Book catalog and ms guidelines online.

O→ Tower Publishing specializes in business and professional directories and legal books.

Nonfiction Reference. Subjects include business/economics. Looking for legal books of a national stature. Query with SASE, or submit outline.

TRAFALGAR SQUARE BOOKS

P.O. Box 257, N. Pomfret VT 05053-0257. (802)457-1911. Fax: (802)457-1913. E-mail: tsquare@sover.net. Web site: www.horseandriderbooks.com. Publisher: Caroline Robbins. **Acquisitions:** Martha Cook, managing editor. Estab. 1985. Publishes hardcover and trade paperback originals and reprints. **Publishes 10 titles/year. Pays royalty. Offers advance.** Responds in 2 months to queries.

O→ "We publish high quality instructional books for horsemen and horsewomen, always with the horse's welfare in mind."

Nonfiction "We publish books for intermediate to advanced riders and horsemen." Subjects include animals (horses). Query with SASE, or submit proposal package including outline, publishing history, 1-2 sample chapters, TOC, and audience for book's subject.
Recent Title(s) *Bombproof Your Horse*, by Rick Pelicano; *Clinton Anderson's Down Under Horsemanship*, by Clinton Anderson; *The Ultimate Horse Behavior and Training Book*, by Linda Tellington-Jones.

TRANSNATIONAL PUBLISHERS, INC.

410 Saw Mill River Rd., Ardsley NY 10502. (914)693-5100. Fax: (914)693-4430. E-mail: info@transnationalpubs.com. Web site: www.transnationalpubs.com. Publisher: Heike Fenton. Estab. 1980. **Publishes 45-50 titles/year. Receives 40-50 queries and 30 mss/year. 60% of books from first-time authors; 95% from unagented writers. Pays royalty.** Publishes book 6-9 months after acceptance of ms. Accepts simultaneous submissions. Responds in 1 month to queries. Book catalog and ms guidelines free.

O→ "We provide specialized international law publications for the teaching of law and law-related subjects in law school classroom, clinic, and continuing legal education settings." Currently emphasizing any area of international law that is considered a current issue/event.

Nonfiction Reference, technical, textbook. Subjects include business/economics, government/politics, women's issues/studies, international law. Query with SASE, or submit proposal package including sample chapter(s), TOC, and introduction.
Recent Title(s) *The Jurisprudence on the Rights of the Child*, edited by Cynthia Price Cohen; *The Legislative History of the International Criminal Court*, by M. Cherif Bassiouni; *Humanitarian Intervention*, by Fernando Tesón.

TRICYCLE PRESS

P.O. Box 7123, Berkeley CA 94707. (510)559-1600. Web site: www.tenspeed.com. **Acquisitions:** Nicole Geiger, publisher; Abigail Samoun, project editor. Estab. 1993. Publishes hardcover and trade paperback originals. **Publishes 18-20 titles/year. 20% of books from first-time authors; 60% from unagented writers. Pays 15-20% royalty on net receipts. Offers $0-9,000 advance.** Publishes book 1-2 years after acceptance of ms. Accepts simultaneous submissions. Responds in 4-6 months to mss. Book catalog for 9×12 SASE with 3 first-class stamps or visit the Web site; ms guidelines online.

O→ "Tricycle Press looks for something outside the mainstream; books that encourage children to look at the world from a possibly alternative angle. We have been trying to publish educational books with strong trade appeal and high quality middle grade fiction."

Nonfiction Biography, children's/juvenile, gift book, humor, illustrated book, picture books. Subjects include animals, art/architecture, creative nonfiction, film/cinema/stage, gardening, health/medicine, multicultural, music/dance, nature/environment, photography, science, travel, health, geography, math. Submit 2-3 chapters, or 20 pages and TOC. Reviews artwork/photos as part of ms package. Send photocopies.
Fiction Preteen. "One-off middle grade novels—quality fiction, 'tween fiction." Board books and picture books:

Submit complete ms. Middle grade books and other longer projects: Send complete outline and 2-3 sample chapters (ages 9-14).

Recent Title(s) *Yesterday I Had the Blues*, by Jeron Frame, illustrated by Gregory Christie; *The Young Adventurer's Guide to Everest: From Avalanche to Zopkio*, by Jonathan Chester; *The Bossqueen, Little Big Bark, and the Sentinel Pup*, by Sarah Jordan.

TRIUMPH BOOKS

542 Dearborn St., Suite 750, Chicago IL 60605. (312)939-3330. Fax: (312)663-3557. Web site: www.triumphbooks.com. Editorial Director: Thomas Bast. **Acquisitions:** Mike Emmerich. Estab. 1989. Publishes hardcover originals and trade paperback originals and reprints. Accepts simultaneous submissions. Book catalog free.

Nonfiction Biography, coffee table book, gift book, humor, illustrated book. Subjects include recreation, sports, health, sports business/motivation. Query with SASE. Reviews artwork/photos as part of ms package. Send photocopies.

Recent Title(s) *It's Only Me: The Ted Williams We Hardly Knew*, by John Underwood; *For the Love of NASCAR*, by Michael Fresina; *Bobby Jones and the Quest for the Grand Slam*, by Catherine Lewis.

TRUMAN STATE UNIVERSITY PRESS

100 E. Normal St., Kirksville MO 63501-4221. (660)785-7336. Fax: (660)785-4480. E-mail: tsup@truman.edu. Web site: tsup.truman.edu. **Acquisitions:** Barbara Smith-Mandell (American studies, poetry); Michael Wolfe (early modern studies). **Publishes 10 titles/year. Pays 7% royalty on net receipts.** Ms guidelines online.

Nonfiction Early modern, American studies, poetry.

Recent Title(s) *A Rebel on the Road*; *Voices of the Heart.*

TWISTED SHIFT

3300 Fresno Place, Schertz TX 78154.Submissions E-mail: submissions@twistedshift.com. Web site: www.twistedshift.com. Owner/Chief Editor: Dorothy Ellis. Estab. 2005. Publishes electronic originals and reprints. **Publishes 24-36 titles/year. Pays 32-37% royalty on retail price.** Does not accept simultaneous submissions. Responds in 1-2 weeks to queries; 2-4 weeks to proposals; 2-5 months to mss. online; ms guidelines online.

> O‑ Twisted Shift is an e-publisher dedicated to everything regarding human transformation. "We are currently seeking creative, well-written fiction featuring human transformation. This means stories about werewolves, vampires, giants, shrinking - absolutely any storyline which contains an integral scene where a human being physically changes into something else. Stories can be 1,000-130,000 words."

Fiction Adventure, erotica, ethnic, experimental, fantasy, feminist, gay/lesbian, gothic, hi-lo, historical, horror, humor, literary, multicultural, mystery, occult, regional, romance, science fiction, short story collections, suspense, western, paranormal. For stories over 10,000 words: Query by e-mail with complete synopsis and the first 3 chapters. For stories under 10,000 words: Submit the complete ms.

Tips "Review our Web site to understand what we sell. Please read and follow our online guidelines. We get several submissions in every batch that completely ignore them, and we're never impressed."

TWO DOT

Imprint of The Globe Pequot Press., 825 Great Northern Blvd., Suites 327 & 328, Helena MT 59601. (406)442-6597. Fax: (406)457-5461. Web site: www.globepequot.com. **Acquisitions:** Erin Turner, executive editor. Publishes hardcover and trade paperback originals. **Publishes 20 titles/year. 30% of books from first-time authors; 80% from unagented writers. Pays royalty on net price.** Accepts simultaneous submissions. Responds in 3 months to queries. Book catalog and ms guidelines online.

> O‑ "Two Dot looks for lively writing for a popular audience, well-researched, on regional themes." Currently emphasizing popular history, western history, regional history, biography collections, western Americana. De-emphasizing scholarly writings, memoirs, fiction, poetry.

Nonfiction Subjects include Americana (western), history, regional. Three state-by-state series of interest: More than Petticoats (notable women); It Happened In . . . (state histories); and Outlaw Tales (by state). Submit outline, 1-2 sample chapter(s), SASE. Reviews artwork/photos as part of ms package. Send photocopies.

Recent Title(s) *Hearts West*, by Chris Enss; *The Lady Rode Bucking Horses*, by Dee Marvine; *More Than Petticoats*, by Greta Anderson.

TYNDALE HOUSE PUBLISHERS, INC.

351 Executive Dr., Carol Stream IL 60188. (800)323-9400. Fax: (800)684-0247. Web site: www.tyndale.com. **Acquisitions:** Manuscript Review Committee. Estab. 1962. Publishes hardcover and trade paperback originals and mass paperback reprints. **Pays negotiable royalty. Offers negotiable advance.** Accepts simultaneous submissions. Ms guidelines for 9 × 12 SAE and $2.40 for postage or visit Web site.

Tyndale House publishes "practical, user-friendly Christian books for the home and family."

Nonfiction Children's/juvenile, self-help (Christian growth). Subjects include child guidance/parenting, religion, devotional/inspirational, theology/Bible doctrine, contemporary/critical issues. Prefers agented submissions. *No unsolicited mss.*

Fiction Romance, Christian (children's, general, inspirational, mystery/suspense, thriller, romance). Christian truths must be woven into the story organically. No short story collections. Youth books: character building stories with Christian perspective. Especially interested in ages 10-14. "We primarily publish Christian historical romances, with occasional contemporary, suspense, or standalones." *Agented submissions only. No unsolicited mss.*

Recent Title(s) *Danzig Passage*, by Bodie & Brock Thoene; *Croutons for Breakfast*, by Lissa Halls Johnson and Kathy Wierenga; *Stolen Secrets*, by Jerry B. Jenkins and Chris Fabry.

UNITY HOUSE

Unity, 1901 NW Blue Pkwy., Unity Village MO 64065-0001. (816)524-3550, ext. 3190. Fax: (816)347-5536. Web site: www.unityonline.org. Estab. 1903. Publishes hardcover and trade paperback originals and reprints. **Publishes 5 titles/year. 30% of books from first-time authors; 95% from unagented writers. Pays 10-15% royalty on net receipts. Offers advance.** Publishes book 13 months after acceptance of ms. Does not accept simultaneous submissions. Responds in 2-6 months to mss. Ms guidelines online.

"Unity House publishes metaphysical Christian books based on Unity principles, as well as inspirational books on metaphysics and practical spirituality. All manuscripts must reflect a spiritual foundation and express the Unity philosophy, practical Christianity, universal principles, and/or metaphysics."

Nonfiction "Writers should be familiar with principles of metaphysical Christianity but not feel bound by them. We are interested in works in the related fields of holistic health, spiritual psychology, and the philosophy of other world religions." Reference (spiritual/metaphysical), self-help, inspirational. Subjects include health/medicine (holistic), philosophy (perennial/New Thought), psychology (transpersonal), religion (spiritual/metaphysical Bible interpretation/modern Biblical studies). Full mss requested along with author background.

Fiction Spiritual, visionary fiction, inspirtational, metaphysical. Query with SASE.

Recent Title(s) *Looking in for Number One*, by Alan Cohen; *That's Just How My Spirit Travels*, by Rosemary Fillmore Rhea.

UNIVERSITY OF ALABAMA PRESS

Box 870380, Tuscaloosa AL 35487. (205)348-5180. Fax: (205)348-9201. Web site: www.uapress.ua.edu. **Acquisitions:** Daniel J.J. Ross, director (American history, Southern history and culture, American military history, American religious history, Latin American history, Jewish studies); Daniel Waterman, acquisitions editor for humanities (American literature and criticism, rhetoric and communication, literary journalism, African-American studies, women's studies, public administration, theater, natural history and environmental studies, regional studies, including regional trade titles); Judith Knight, senior acquisitions editor (American archaeology, Caribbean archaeology, historical archaeology, ethnohistory, anthropology). Estab. 1945. Publishes nonfiction hardcover and paperbound originals, and fiction paperback reprints. **Publishes 55-60 titles/year. 70% of books from first-time authors; 95% from unagented writers. Offers advance.** Responds in 2 weeks to queries. Book catalog free.

Nonfiction Biography, scholarly. Subjects include anthropology/archeology, community, government/politics, history, language/literature, religion, translation. Considers upon merit almost any subject of scholarly interest, but specializes in communications, military history, public administration, literary criticism and biography, history, Jewish studies, and American archeology. Accepts nonfiction translations. Query with SASE. Reviews artwork/photos as part of ms package.

Fiction Reprints of works by contemporary, Southern writers. Query with SASE.

Tips Please direct inquiry to appropriate acquisitions editor. University of Alabama Press responds to an author within 2 weeks upon receiving the ms. If they think it is unsuitable for Alabama's program, they tell the author at once. If the ms warrants it, they begin the peer-review process, which may take 2-4 months to complete. During that process, they keep the author fully informed.

UNIVERSITY OF ALASKA PRESS

P.O. Box 756240, Fairbanks AK 99775-6240. (907)474-5831 or (888)252-6657. Fax: (907)474-5502. E-mail: fypress@uaf.edu. Web site: www.uaf.edu/uapress. Estab. 1967. Publishes hardcover originals, trade paperback originals and reprints. **Publishes 10 titles/year. Pays 7½% royalty on net receipts.** Publishes book within 2 years after acceptance of ms. Responds in 2 months to queries. Book catalog free; ms guidelines online.

Imprints Classic Reprints; Oral Biographies; Rasmuson Library Historical Translation Series.

"The mission of the University of Alaska Press is to encourage, publish, and disseminate works of scholarship that will enhance the store of knowledge about Alaska and the North Pacific Rim, with a special emphasis on the circumpolar regions."

Nonfiction Biography, reference, scholarly nonfiction relating to Alaska-circumpolar regions. Subjects include Americana (Alaskana), animals, anthropology/archeology, art/architecture, education, ethnic, government/politics, health/medicine, history, language/literature, military/war, nature/environment, regional, science, translation, women's issues/studies. Northern or circumpolar only. Query with SASE and proposal. Reviews artwork/photos as part of ms package.

Recent Title(s) *Gold Rush Grub*, by Ann Chandonnet; *Geology of Southeast Alaska*, by Harold Stowell; *Into Brown Bear Country*, by Will Troyer.

Tips "Writers have the best chance with scholarly nonfiction relating to Alaska, the circumpolar regions and North Pacific Rim. Our audience is made up of scholars, historians, students, libraries, universities, individuals, and the general Alaskan public."

THE UNIVERSITY OF ARKANSAS PRESS

201 Ozark Ave., Fayetteville AR 72701-1201. (479)575-3246. Fax: (479)575-6044. E-mail: uapress@uark.edu. Web site: www.uapress.com. **Acquisitions:** Lawrence J. Malley, director and editor-in-chief. Estab. 1980. Publishes hardcover and trade paperback originals and reprints. **Publishes 30 titles/year. 30% of books from first-time authors; 95% from unagented writers. Pays royalty on net receipts.** Publishes book 1 year after acceptance of ms. Responds in 3 months to proposals. Book catalog and ms guidelines on Web site or on request.

O━ The University of Arkansas Press publishes series on Ozark studies, the Civil War in the West, poetry and poetics, and sport and society.

Nonfiction Subjects include government/politics, history (Southern), humanities, nature/environment, regional, Arkansas, African-American studies, Middle Eastern studies, poetry/poetics. Accepted mss must be submitted on disk. Query with SASE, or submit outline, sample chapter(s), résumé.

Recent Title(s) *Reading With Oprah*, by Kathleen Rooney; *Looking Back to See*, by Maxine Brown; *Chattahoochee*, by Patrick Phillips.

UNIVERSITY OF CALIFORNIA PRESS

2120 Berkeley Way, Berkeley CA 94720-1012. (510)642-4247. Fax: (510)643-7127. E-mail: askucp@ucpress.edu. Web site: www.ucpress.edu. **Acquisitions:** Lynne Withey (public health); Reed Malcolm (religion, politics, Asian studies); Niels Hooper (history); Deborah Kirshman (museum copublications); Sheila Levine (food, regional); Jenny Wapner (natural history, organismal biology); Naomi Schneider (sociology, politics, anthropology, Latin American studies); Blake Edgar (biology, archaeology, viticulture & enology); Stephanie Fay (art); Stan Holwitz (anthropology, public health, Jewish studies); Laura Cerruti (literature, poetry, classics); Mary Francis (music, film); Chuck Crumly (evolution, environment, ecology, biology). Estab. 1893. Publishes hardcover and paperback originals and reprints. **Offers advance.** Response time varies, depending on the subject. Enclose return postage to queries. Ms guidelines online.

O━ University of California Press publishes mostly nonfiction written by scholars.

Nonfiction Scholarly. Subjects include history, nature/environment, translation, art, literature, natural sciences, some high-level popularizations. No length preference. Submit sample chapter(s), letter of introduction, cv, TOC.

Fiction Publishes fiction only in translation.

Recent Title(s) *William Dean Howells: A Writer's Life*, by Susan Goodman and Carl Dawson; *A History of Wine in America: From Prohibition to the Present*, by Thomas Pinney; *Biology of Gila Monsters and Beaded Lizards*, by Daniel Beck.

UNIVERSITY OF GEORGIA PRESS

330 Research Dr., Athens GA 30602-4901. (706)369-6130. Fax: (706)369-6131. E-mail: books@ugapress.uga.edu. Web site: www.ugapress.org. Estab. 1938. Publishes hardcover originals, trade paperback originals, and reprints. **Publishes 85 titles/year. Offers rare, varying advance.** Publishes book 1 year after acceptance of ms. Does not accept simultaneous submissions. Responds in 2 months to queries. Book catalog and ms guidelines for #10 SASE or online.

Nonfiction Biography. Subjects include government/politics, history (American), nature/environment, regional, environmental studies, literary nonfiction. Query with SASE, or submit author bio, 1 sample chapter. Reviews artwork/photos as part of ms package. Send if essential to book.

Fiction Short story collections published in Flannery O'Connor Award Competition. Query #10 SASE for guidelines and submission periods. Charges $20 submission fee. "No phone calls accepted."

Recent Title(s) *Equiano, the African: Biography of a Self-Made Man*, by Vincent Carretta; *The Civil Rights Movement in American Memory*, edited by Renee Romano and Leigh Raiford; *Sabbath Creole*, by Juddun Mitcham.

UNIVERSITY OF ILLINOIS PRESS

1325 S. Oak St., Champaign IL 61820-6903. (217)333-0950. Fax: (217)244-8082. E-mail: sears@uillinois.edu. Web site: www.press.uillinois.edu. **Acquisitions:** Willis Regier, director (literature, classics, classical music, sports history); Joan Catapano, associate director and editor-in-chief (women's studies, film, African-American studies); Laurie Matheson (American history, labor history, American music, American studies). Estab. 1918. Publishes hardcover and trade paperback originals and reprints. **Publishes 150 titles/year. 35% of books from first-time authors; 95% from unagented writers. Pays 0-10% royalty on net receipts. Offers $1,000-1,500 (rarely) advance.** Publishes book 1 year after acceptance of ms. Responds in 1 month to queries. Book catalog for 9×12 SAE with 2 first-class stamps; ms guidelines online.

- University of Illinois Press publishes "scholarly books and serious nonfiction" with a wide range of study interests. Currently emphasizing American history, especially immigration, labor, African-American, and military; American religion, music, women's studies, and film.

Nonfiction Biography, reference, scholarly, scholarly. Subjects include Americana, animals, cooking/foods/nutrition, government/politics, history (especially American history), language/literature, military/war, music/dance (especially American music), philosophy, regional, sociology, sports, translation, film/cinema/stage. Always looking for "solid, scholarly books in American history, especially social history; books on American popular music, and books in the broad area of American studies." Query with SASE, or submit outline.

Recent Title(s) *Philosophical Writings*, by Simone de Beauvoir (philosophy); *March of the Machines: The Breakthrough in Artificial Intelligence*, by Kevin Warwick (nonfiction); *Myths American Lives By*, by Richard T. Hughes (nonfiction).

Tips "As a university press, we are required to submit all manuscripts to rigorous scholarly review. Manuscripts need to be clearly original, well written, and based on solid and thorough research. We cannot encourage memoirs or autobiographies."

UNIVERSITY OF MISSOURI PRESS

2910 LeMone Blvd., Columbia MO 65201. (573)882-7641. Fax: (573)884-4498. Web site: www.umsystem.edu/upress. **Acquisitions:** (Mr.) Clair Willcox and Gary Kass, acquisitions editors; Beverly Jarrett, editor-in-chief (history, literature, political philosophy, intellectual history, women's studies, African-American studies). Estab. 1958. Publishes hardcover and paperback originals and paperback reprints. **Publishes 65 titles/year. 40-50% of books from first-time authors; 90% from unagented writers. Pays up to 10% royalty on net receipts.** Publishes book within 1 year after acceptance of ms. Responds immediately to queries; 3 months to mss. Book catalog free; ms guidelines online.

- University of Missouri Press publishes primarily scholarly nonfiction in the humanities and social sciences. Currently emphasizing American history, political philosophy, literary criticism, African-American studies, women's studies.

Nonfiction Scholarly. Subjects include history (American), regional (studies of Missouri and the Midwest), social sciences, women's issues/studies, political philosophy, African-American studies. Consult *Chicago Manual of Style.* No mathematics or hard sciences. Query with SASE, or submit outline, sample chapter(s).

Recent Title(s) *Where the Southern Cross the Yellow Dog*, by Louis D. Rubin; *I Hid It Under the Sheets*, Gerald Eskenazi.

UNIVERSITY OF NEBRASKA PRESS

1111 Lincoln Mall, Lincoln NE 68588-0630. (800)755-1105. Fax: (402)472-6214. E-mail: pressmail@unl.edu. Web site: nebraskapress.unl.edu. Director: Gary Dunham. Managing Editor: Beth Ina. Sports Editor: Rob Taylor. History Editor: Heather Lundine. . **Acquisitions:** Ladette Randolph, associate director for development. Publishes hardcover and trade paperback originals and trade paperback reprints. Book catalog free; ms guidelines online.

Imprints Bison Books (paperback reprints of classic books).

- "We primarily publish nonfiction books and scholarly journals, along with a few titles per season in contemporary and regional prose and poetry. On occasion, we reprint previously published fiction of established reputation, and we have several programs to publish literary works in translation."

Nonfiction Biography, cookbook, reference, textbook. Subjects include agriculture/horticulture, animals, anthropology/archeology, creative nonfiction, history, memoirs, military/war, multicultural, nature/environment, religion, sports, translation, women's issues/studies, Native American studies, American Lives series, experimental fiction by American-Indian writers. Submit book proposal with overview, audience, format, detailed chapter outline, sample chapters, sample bibliography, timetable, CV.

Fiction Series and translation only. Occasionaly reprints fiction of established reputation.

Poetry Contemporary, regional.

Recent Title(s) *Mad Seasons*, by Karra Porter; *The Broidered Garment*, by Hilda Martinsen Neihardt; *New Perspectives on Native North America*, by Sergei A. Kan and Pauline Turner Strong.

UNIVERSITY OF NEVADA PRESS

MS 166, Reno NV 89557. (775)784-6573. Fax: (775)784-6200. Web site: www.unpress.nevada.edu. **Acquisitions:** Joanne O'Hare, director. Estab. 1961. Publishes hardcover and paperback originals and reprints. **Publishes 25 titles/year.** Does not accept simultaneous submissions. Ms guidelines online.

Nonfiction Subjects include anthropology/archeology, ethnic (studies), history (regional and natural), nature/environment, regional (history and geography), western literature, current affairs, gambling and gaming, Basque studies. No juvenile books. Submit proposal. No online submissions. Reviews artwork/photos as part of ms package. Send photocopies.

Fiction Submit proposal package including outline, synopsis, 2-4 sample chapters.

UNIVERSITY OF NEW MEXICO PRESS

1312 Baschart Rd. SE, Albuquerque NM 87106. (505)277-2346 or (800)249-7737. E-mail: unmpress@unm.edu. Web site: www.unmpress.com. **Acquisitions:** Maya Allen-Gallegos, managing editor; David Holtby, editor-in-chief; Elizabeth Hadas, editor. Also: Editorial Dept., University of New Mexico Press, MSC11 6290, Albuquerque NM 87131-0001. Estab. 1929. Publishes hardcover originals and trade paperback originals and reprints. **Pays variable royalty. Offers advance.** Does not accept simultaneous submissions. Book catalog free; ms guidelines online.

> O→ "The Press is well known as a publisher in the fields of anthropology, archeology, Latin American studies, photography, architecture and the history and culture of the American West, fiction, some poetry, Chicano/a studies and works by and about American Indians. We focus on American West, Southwest and Latin American regions."

Nonfiction Biography, children's/juvenile, illustrated book, multimedia, scholarly. Subjects include Americana, anthropology/archeology, art/architecture, creative nonfiction, ethnic, gardening, gay/lesbian, government/politics, history, language/literature, memoirs, military/war, multicultural, music/dance, nature/environment, photography, regional, religion, science, translation, travel, women's issues/studies, contemporary culture, cinema/stage, true crime, general nonfiction. "No how-to, humor, juvenile, self-help, software, technical or textbooks." Query with SASE. Reviews artwork/photos as part of ms package. Send photocopies.

Recent Title(s) *Jemez Spring*, by Rudolfo Anaya; *The Cherokee Nation*, by Robert J. Conley; *Blood of Our Earth*, by Dan C. Jones.

THE UNIVERSITY OF NORTH CAROLINA PRESS

116 S. Boundary St., Chapel Hill NC 27514. (919)966-3561. Fax: (919)966-3829. E-mail: uncpress@unc.edu. Web site: www.uncpress.unc.edu. **Acquisitions:** David Perry, editor-in-chief (regional trade, Civil War); Charles Grench, senior editor (American history, European history, law and legal studies, business and economic history, classics, political or social science); Elaine Maisner, senior editor (Latin American studies, religious studies, anthropology, regional trade, folklore); Sian Hunter, senior editor (literary studies, gender studies, American studies, African American studies, social medicine, Appalachian studies, media studies); Mark Simpson-Vos, associate editor (electronic publishing and special projects, American-Indian studies). Publishes hardcover originals, trade paperback originals and reprints. **Publishes 90 titles/year. Receives 500 queries and 200 mss/year. 50% of books from first-time authors; 90% from unagented writers. Pays variable royalty on wholesale price. Offers variable advance.** Publishes book 1 year after acceptance of ms. Responds in 3-4 weeks to queries; 3-4 weeks to proposals; 2 weeks to mss. Book catalog free or on Web site; ms guidelines online.

> O→ "UNC Press publishes nonfiction books for academic and general audiences. We have a special interest in trade and scholarly titles about our region. We do not, however, publish original fiction, drama, or poetry, memoirs of living persons, or festshriften."

Nonfiction Biography, cookbook, multimedia (CD-ROM). Subjects include Americana, anthropology/archeology, art/architecture, cooking/foods/nutrition, gardening, government/politics, health/medicine, history, language/literature, military/war, multicultural, music/dance, nature/environment, philosophy, photography, regional, religion, translation, women's issues/studies, African-American studies, American studies, cultural studies, Latin-American studies, American-Indian studies, media studies, gender studies, social medicine, Appalachian studies. Submit proposal package including outline, CV, cover letter, abstract, and TOC. Reviews artwork/photos as part of ms package. Send photocopies.

UNIVERSITY OF NORTH TEXAS PRESS

P.O. Box 311336, Denton TX 76203-1336. Fax: (940)565-4590. E-mail: rchrisman@unt.edu; kdevinney@unt.edu. Web site: www.unt.edu/untpress. Director: Ronald Chrisman. **Acquisitions:** Karen DeVinney, managing editor. Estab. 1987. Publishes hardcover and trade paperback originals and reprints. **Publishes 14-16 titles/year. Receives 500 queries/year. 95% from unagented writers. Pays 7-10% royalty on net receipts.** Publishes book 1-2 years after acceptance of ms. Does not accept simultaneous submissions. Responds in 1 month to queries. Book catalog for 8½×11 SASE; ms guidelines online.

O→ "We are dedicated to producing the highest quality scholarly, academic, and general interest books. We are committed to serving all peoples by publishing stories of their cultures and experiences that have been overlooked. Currently emphasizing military history, Texas history and Texas literature, Mexican-American studies."

Nonfiction Subjects include agriculture/horticulture, Americana, ethnic, government/politics, history, language/literature, military/war, nature/environment, regional, women's issues/studies. Query with SASE. Reviews artwork/photos as part of ms package. Send photocopies.

Fiction "The only fiction we publish is the winner of the Katherine Anne Porter Prize in Short Fiction, an annual, national competition with a $1,000 prize, and publication of the winning manuscript each Fall."

Poetry "The only poetry we publish is the winner of the Vassar Miller Prize in Poetry, an annual, national competition with a $1,000 prize and publication of the winning manuscript each Spring." Query.

Recent Title(s) *California Voices:The Oral Memoirs of Josi Maria Amador.*

Tips "We publish series called War and the Southwest; Texas Folklore Society Publications; the Western Life Series; practical guide series; Al-Filo: Mexican-American studies; North Texas crime and criminal justice; Katherine Anne Porter Prize in Short Fiction."

UNIVERSITY OF OKLAHOMA PRESS

2800 Venture Dr., Norman OK 73069. E-mail: ceranklin@ou.edu. Web site: www.oupress.com. **Acquisitions:** Charles E. Rankin, editor-in-chief. Estab. 1928. Publishes hardcover and paperback originals and reprints. **Publishes 90 titles/year. Pays standard royalty.** Does not accept simultaneous submissions. Responds promptly to queries. Book catalog for 9×12 SAE with 6 first-class stamps.

Imprints Plains Reprints.

O→ University of Oklahoma Press publishes books for both scholarly and nonspecialist readers.

Nonfiction Subjects include political science (Congressional, area and security studies), history (regional, military, natural), language/literature (American Indian, US West), American Indian studies, classical studies. Query with SASE, or submit outline, résumé, 1-2 sample chapters. Use *Chicago Manual of Style* for ms guidelines. Reviews artwork/photos as part of ms package.

Recent Title(s) *The Uncivil War: Irregular Warfare in the Upper South, 1861-1865,* by Robert R. Mackey (history); *Ojibwa Warrior,* by Dennis Banks and Richard Erdoes (American Indian studies); *Oklahoma Breeding Bird Atlas,* by Dan L. Reinking (natural history).

⊘ UNIVERSITY OF PENNSYLVANIA PRESS

3905 Spruce St., Philadelphia PA 19104. (215)898-6261. Fax: (215)898-0404. Web site: www.upenn.edu/pennpress. Director: Eric Halpern. **Acquisitions:** Jerome Singerman, humanities editor; Peter Agree, editor-in-chief; Jo Joslyn, art and architecture editor; Robert Lockhart, history editor; Bill Finan, development editor. Estab. 1890. Publishes hardcover and paperback originals, and reprints. **Publishes 100+ titles/year. 20-30% of books from first-time authors; 95% from unagented writers. Royalty determined on book-by-book basis. Offers advance.** Publishes book 10 months after delivery of ms after acceptance of ms. Does not accept simultaneous submissions. Responds in 3 months to queries. Book catalog and ms guidelines online.

Nonfiction "Serious books that serve the scholar and the professional, student and general reader." Scholarly. Subjects include Americana, art/architecture, history (American, art), sociology, anthropology, literary criticism, cultural studies, ancient studies, medieval studies, urban studies, human rights. Follow the *Chicago Manual of Style. No unsolicited mss.* Query with SASE, or submit outline, résumé. Reviews artwork/photos as part of ms package. Send photocopies.

UNIVERSITY OF SCRANTON PRESS

University of Scranton, Smufit Hall, 445 Madison Ave., Scranton PA 18510. Web site: www.scrantonpress.com. **Acquisitions:** Richard W. Rousseau, director. Estab. 1981. Publishes paperback originals. Does not accept simultaneous submissions. Book catalog and ms guidelines free.

Imprints Ridge Row Press.

O→ The University of Scranton Press, a member of the Association of Jesuit University Presses, publishes primarily scholarly monographs in theology, philosophy, and the culture and history of Northeast Pennsylvania.

Nonfiction Looking for clear editorial focus: theology/religious studies; philosophy/philosophy of religion; scholarly treatments; the culture of Northeast Pennsylvania. Scholarly monographs. Subjects include art/architecture, language/literature, philosophy, regional, religion, sociology. Query with SASE, or submit outline, 2 sample chapters.

Poetry Only poetry related to Northeast Pennsylvania.

Recent Title(s) *Not My Kid 2*, by Mary Muscari, PhD; *Jesuit Generals*, by Thomas E. Zeyen, SJ; *Becoming a Bar Mitzvah*, by Arnine Cumsky Weiss.

THE UNIVERSITY OF TENNESSEE PRESS

600 Henley St., UT Conference Center, Suite 110, Knoxville TN 37902. (865)974-3321. Fax: (865)974-3724. E-mail: custserv@utpress.org. Web site: www.utpress.org. **Acquisitions:** Scot Danforth, acquisitions editor (scholarly books); Jennifer Siler, director (regional trades, fiction). Estab. 1940. **Publishes 35 titles/year. 35% of books from first-time authors; 99% from unagented writers. Pays negotiable royalty on net receipts.** Does not accept simultaneous submissions. Book catalog for 12X16 SAE with 2 first-class stamps; ms guidelines online.

O→ "Our mission is to stimulate scientific and scholarly research in all fields; to channel such studies, either in scholarly or popular form, to a larger number of people; and to extend the regional leadership of the University of Tennessee by stimulating research projects within the South and by nonuniversity authors."

Nonfiction Scholarly, American studies only. Subjects include Americana, anthropology/archeology (historical), art/architecture (vernacular), history, language/literature, regional, religion (history sociology, anthropology, biography only), women's issues/studies, African-American studies, Appalachian studies, folklore/folklife, material culture. Prefers "scholarly treatment and a readable style. Authors usually have PhDs." Submissions in other fields, and submissions of poetry, textbooks, plays and translations are not invited. Submit outline, author bio, 2 sample chapters. Reviews artwork/photos as part of ms package.
Fiction Query with SASE, or submit synopsis, author bio.
Recent Title(s) *Dictionary of Smoky Mountain English*, by Michael B. Montgomery and Joseph S. Hall.
Tips "Our market is in several groups: scholars; educated readers with special interests in given scholarly subjects; and the general educated public interested in Tennessee, Appalachia, and the South. Not all our books appeal to all these groups, of course, but any given book must appeal to at least one of them."

UNIVERSITY OF TEXAS PRESS

P.O. Box 7819, Austin TX 78713-7819. (512)471-7233. Fax: (512)232-7178. E-mail: utpress@uts.cc.utexas.edu. Web site: www.utexaspress.com. **Acquisitions:** Theresa May, assistant director/editor-in-chief (social sciences, Latin American studies); James Burr, sponsoring editor (humanities, classics); William Bishel, sponsoring editor (natural sciences, Texas history); Allison Faust, sponsoring editor (Texana, geography, art, music). Estab. 1952. **Publishes 90 titles/year. 50% of books from first-time authors; 99% from unagented writers. Pays royalty on net receipts. Offers occasional advance.** Publishes book 18-24 months after acceptance of ms. Does not accept simultaneous submissions. Responds in 3 months to queries. Book catalog free; ms guidelines online.

O→ "In addition to publishing the results of advanced research for scholars worldwide, UT Press has a special obligation to the people of its state to publish authoritative books on Texas. We do not publish fiction or poetry, except as invited by a series editor, and some Latin American and Middle Eastern literature in translation."

Nonfiction Biography, scholarly. Subjects include anthropology/archeology, art/architecture, ethnic, film/cinema/stage, history, language/literature, nature/environment, regional, science, translation, women's issues/studies, natural history, American, Latin American, Native American, Latino, and Middle Eastern studies; classics and the ancient world, film, contemporary regional architecture, geography, ornithology, biology. Also uses specialty titles related to Texas and the Southwest, national trade titles and regional trade titles. Query with SASE, or submit outline, 2 sample chapters. Reviews artwork/photos as part of ms package.
Fiction No poetry. Query with SASE, or submit outline, 2 sample chapters.
Recent Title(s) *The Memory of Bones*, by Houston; *Who Guards the Guardians and How*, by Bruneau; *Women Embracing Islam*, edited by van Nieuwkerk.
Tips "It's difficult to make a manuscript over 400 double-spaced pages into a feasible book. Authors should take special care to edit out extraneous material. We look for sharply focused, in-depth treatments of important topics."

UNIVERSITY PRESS OF KANSAS

2502 Westbrooke Circle, Lawrence KS 66045-4444. (785)864-4154. Fax: (785)864-4586. E-mail: upress@ku.edu. Web site: www.kansaspress.ku.edu. **Acquisitions:** Michael J. Briggs, editor-in-chief (military history, political science, law); Kalyani Fernando, acquisitions editor (western history, American studies, environmental studies, women's studies); Fred M. Woodward, director, (political science, presidency, regional). Estab. 1946. Publishes hardcover originals, trade paperback originals and reprints. **Publishes 55 titles/year. Receives 600 queries/year. 20% of books from first-time authors; 98% from unagented writers. Pays 5-15% royalty on net receipts. Offers selective advance.** Publishes book 10 months after acceptance of ms. Does not accept simultaneous submissions. Responds in 1 month to proposals. Book catalog and ms guidelines free.

- The University Press of Kansas publishes scholarly books that advance knowledge and regional books that contribute to the understanding of Kansas, the Great Plains, and the Midwest.

Nonfiction Biography, scholarly. Subjects include Americana, anthropology/archeology, government/politics, history, military/war, nature/environment, regional, sociology, women's issues/studies. "We are looking for books on topics of wide interest based on solid scholarship and written for both specialists and informed general readers. Do not send unsolicited, complete manuscripts." Submit outline, sample chapter(s), cover letter, cv, prospectus. Reviews artwork/photos as part of ms package. Send photocopies.

Recent Title(s) *Hillary Rodham Clinton*, by Gil Troy; *In the Name of National Security*, by Louis Fisher; *Red Storm Over the Balkans*, by David M. Glantz.

UNIVERSITY PRESS OF MISSISSIPPI

3825 Ridgewood Rd., Jackson MS 39211-6492. (601)432-6205. Fax: (601)432-6217. E-mail: press@ihl.state.ms.us. Web site: www.upress.state.ms.us. **Acquisitions:** Craig Gill, editor-in-chief (regional studies, art, folklore, fiction, memoirs); Seetha Srinivasan, director (African-American studies, popular culture, literature). Estab. 1970. Publishes hardcover and paperback originals and reprints. **Publishes 60 titles/year. 20% of books from first-time authors; 90% from unagented writers. Competitive royalties and terms. Offers advance.** Publishes book 1 year after acceptance of ms. Does not accept simultaneous submissions. Responds in 3 months to queries.

- "University Press of Mississippi publishes scholarly and trade titles, as well as special series, including: American Made Music; Conversations with Comic Artists; Conversations with Filmmakers; Faulkner and Yoknapatawpha; Literary Conversations; Studies in Popular Culture; Hollywood Legends; Understanding Health and Sickness."

Nonfiction Biography, scholarly. Subjects include Americana, art/architecture, ethnic (minority studies), government/politics, health/medicine, history, language/literature, music/dance, photography, regional (Southern), folklife, literary criticism, popular culture with scholarly emphasis, literary studies. "We prefer a proposal that describes the significance of the work and a chapter outline." Submit outline, sample chapter(s), cv.

Fiction Commissioned trade editions by prominent writers.

Recent Title(s) *Katherine Anne Porter*, by Darlene Harbour Unrue; *Salvation Run*, by Mary Gardner.

UNIVERSITY PRESS OF NEW ENGLAND

1 Court St., Suite 250, Lebanon NH 03766. (603)448-1533. Fax: (603)448-7006. E-mail: university.press@dartmouth.edu. Web site: www.upne.com. Director: Richard Abel. **Acquisitions:** Phyllis Deutsch, editor-in-chief; Ellen Wicklum, editor; John Landrigan, editor. Estab. 1970. Publishes hardcover and paperback originals. **Publishes 90 titles/year. Pays standard royalty. Offers occasional advance.** Responds in 2 months to queries. Book catalog and ms guidelines for 9×12 SASE and 5 first-class stamps; ms guidelines online.

Imprints Brandeis University Press; Dartmouth College Press; University of New Hampshire Press; Northeastern University Press; Tufts University Press; University of Vermont Press; University Press of New England; Hardscrabble Books (fiction of New England).

Nonfiction Subjects include Americana, art/architecture, nature/environment, regional (New England), decorative arts and material culture, African-American studies, music, American studies, Jewish studies, criminal justice. Submit outline, 1-2 sample chapters. No electronic submissions.

Fiction Literary. Only New England novels, literary fiction, and reprints (New England and African American). Query with SASE, or submit sample chapter(s).

Recent Title(s) *Harvard's Civil War*, by Richard F. Miller; *American Playgrounds*, by Susan G. Solomon; *Running the Bulls*, by Cathie Pelletier.

UPSTART BOOKS

Highsmith Press, P.O. Box 800, Fort Atkinson WI 53538-0800. (920)563-9571. Fax: (920)563-4801. E-mail: mmulder@highsmith.com. Web site: www.highsmith.com. **Acquisitions:** Matt Mulder, director of publications. Estab. 1990. Publishes hardcover and paperback originals. **Publishes 20 titles/year. Receives 500-600 queries and 400-500 mss/year. 30% of books from first-time authors; 100% from unagented writers. Pays 10-12% royalty on net receipts. Offers $250-1,000 advance.** Publishes book 6 months after acceptance of ms. Accepts simultaneous submissions. Responds in 1 month to queries; 2 months to proposals. Book catalog and ms guidelines online.

Imprints Alleyside Press, Upstart Books (creative supplemental reading, library and critical thinking skills materials designed to expand the learning environment).

- Upstart Books publishes educational resources to meet the practical needs of librarians, educators, readers, library users, media specialists, schools and related institutions, and to help them fulfill their valuable functions.

Nonfiction Children's/juvenile, reference. Subjects include education, language/literature, multicultural. "We are primarily interested in manuscripts that stimulate or strengthen reading, library and information-seeking skills and foster critical thinking." Query with outline and 1-2 sample chapters. Reviews artwork/photos as part of ms package. Send transparencies.

Fiction "Our current emphasis is on storytelling collections for preschool-grade 6. We prefer stories that can be easily used by teachers and children's librarians, multicultural topics, and manuscripts that feature fold and cut, flannelboard, tangram, or similar simple patterns that can be reproduced. No longer accepting children's picture book mss.

Recent Title(s) *Finger Tales*, by Joan Hilyer Phelps; *Characters with Character*, by Diane Findlay.

THE URBAN LAND INSTITUTE

1025 Thomas Jefferson St. NW, Washington DC 20007-5201. (202)624-7000. Fax: (202)624-7140. Web site: www.uli.org. **Acquisitions:** Rachelle Levitt, executive vice president/publisher. Estab. 1936. Publishes hardcover and trade paperback originals. **Publishes 15-20 titles/year. 2% of books from first-time authors; 100% from unagented writers. Pays 10% royalty on gross sales. Offers $1,500-2,000 advance.** Publishes book 6 months after acceptance of ms. Does not accept simultaneous submissions. Book catalog and ms guidelines via Web site or 9×12 SAE.

O→ The Urban Land Institute publishes technical books on real estate development and land planning.

Nonfiction Technical. Subjects include money/finance, design and development. "The majority of manuscripts are created in-house by research staff. We acquire 2 or 3 outside authors to fill schedule and subject areas where our list has gaps. We are not interested in real estate sales, brokerages, appraisal, making money in real estate, opinion, personal point of view, or manuscripts negative toward growth and development." Query with SASE. Reviews artwork/photos as part of ms package.

Recent Title(s) *Trammel Crow; Housing for Niche Markets.*

URJ PRESS

633 Third Ave., New York NY 10017-6778. (212)650-4120. Fax: (212)650-4119. E-mail: press@urj.org. Web site: www.urjpress.com. **Acquisitions:** Rabbi Hara Person, editor (subjects related to Judaism). Publishes hardcover and trade paperback originals. **Publishes 22 titles/year. Receives 500 queries and 400 mss/year. 70% of books from first-time authors; 90% from unagented writers. Pays 3-5% royalty on retail price, or makes outright purchase of $500-2,000. Offers $500-2,000 advance.** Publishes book 9 months after acceptance of ms. Does not accept simultaneous submissions. Responds in 2 months to queries; 6 months to proposals; 6 months to mss. Book catalog and ms guidelines free or on Web site.

O→ URJ Press publishes books related to Judaism.

Nonfiction Biography, children's/juvenile, coffee table book, cookbook, gift book, how-to, illustrated book, multimedia (CD), reference, textbook. Subjects include art/architecture (synagogue), child guidance/parenting (Jewish), cooking/foods/nutrition (Jewish), education (Jewish), ethnic (Judaism), government/politics, history (Jewish), language/literature (Hebrew), military/war (as relates to Judaism), music/dance, nature/environment, philosophy (Jewish), religion (Judaism only), sex (as it relates to Judaism), spirituality (Jewish). Submit proposal package including outline, author bio, 1-2 sample chapters.

Fiction Jewish, liberal content. Picture book length only. Juvenile, children's picture books. Submit complete ms with author bio.

Recent Title(s) *Talmud for Everyday Living: Employer-Employee Relations*, by Hillel Gamoran (nonfiction); *The Gift of Wisdom*, by Steven E. Steinbock (textbook for grades 5-7); *Solomon and the Trees*, by Matt Biers-Ariel (picture book).

Tips "Look at some of our books. Have an understanding of the Reform Judaism community. In addition to bookstores, we sell to Jewish congregations and Hebrew day schools."

UTAH STATE UNIVERSITY PRESS

7800 Old Main Hill, Logan UT 84322-7800. (435)797-1362. Fax: (435)797-0313. Web site: www.usu.edu/usupress. **Acquisitions:** Michael Spooner, director (composition, poetry); John Alley, editor (history, folklore, fiction). Estab. 1972. Publishes hardcover and trade paperback originals and reprints. **Publishes 18 titles/year. 8% of books from first-time authors. Pays royalty on net receipts.** Publishes book 18 months after acceptance of ms. Does not accept simultaneous submissions. Responds in 1 month to queries. Book catalog free; ms guidelines online.

O→ Utah State University Press publishes scholarly works in the academic areas noted below. Currently interested in book-length scholarly mss dealing with folklore studies, composition studies, Native American studies, and history.

Nonfiction Biography, reference, scholarly, textbook. Subjects include history (of the West), regional, folklore, the West, Native-American studies, studies in composition and rhetoric. Query with SASE. Reviews artwork/photos as part of ms package. Send photocopies.

Recent Title(s) *Alaska's Daughter: An Eskimo Memoir of the Early Twentieth Century*, by Elizabeth Bernhardt Pinson; *Building the Goodly Fellowship of Faith: A History of the Episcopal Church in Utah, 1867-1996*, by Frederick Quinn; *Once Upon a Virus: AIDS Legends and Vernacular Risk Perception*, by Diane E. Goldstein.
Tips Utah State University Press also sponsors the annual May Swenson Poetry Award.

VANDERBILT UNIVERSITY PRESS

VU Station B 351813, Nashville TN 37235. (615)322-3585. Fax: (615)343-8823. E-mail: vupress@vanderbilt.edu. Web site: www.vanderbilt.edu/vupress. **Acquisitions:** Michael Ames, director. Publishes hardcover originals and trade paperback originals and reprints. **Publishes 20-25 titles/year. Receives 500 queries/year. 25% of books from first-time authors; 90% from unagented writers. Pays 8% royalty on net receipts. Offers rare advance.** Publishes book 10 months after acceptance of ms. Accepts simultaneous submissions. Responds in 2 weeks to proposals. Book catalog free; ms guidelines online.

- Also distributes for and co-publishes with Country Music Foundation.
- "Vanderbilt University Press publishes books on healthcare, social sciences, education, and regional studies, for both academic and general audiences that are intellectually significant, socially relevant, and of practical importance."

Nonfiction Biography, scholarly, textbook. Subjects include Americana, anthropology/archeology, education, ethnic, government/politics, health/medicine, history, language/literature, multicultural, music/dance, nature/environment, philosophy, women's issues/studies. Submit prospectus, sample chapter, cv. Reviews artwork/photos as part of ms package. Send photocopies.
Recent Title(s) *Lost Delta Found*, edited by Robert Gordon and Bruce Nemerov.
Tips "Our audience consists of scholars and educated, general readers."

VENTURE PUBLISHING, INC.

1999 Cato Ave., State College PA 16801. (814)234-4561. Fax: (814)234-1651. E-mail: vpublish@venturepublish.com. Web site: www.venturepublish.com. Estab. 1978. Publishes hardcover and paperback originals and reprints. **Pays royalty on wholesale price. Offers advance.** Does not accept simultaneous submissions. Book catalog and ms guidelines for SASE or online.

- Venture Publishing produces quality educational publications, also workbooks for professionals, educators, and students in the fields of recreation, parks, leisure studies, therapeutic recreation and long term care.

Nonfiction Scholarly (college academic), textbook, professional. Subjects include nature/environment (outdoor recreation management and leadership texts), recreation, sociology (leisure studies), long-term care nursing homes, therapeutic recreation. "Textbooks and books for recreation activity leaders high priority." Submit 1 sample chapter, book proposal, competing titles.
Recent Title(s) *Bordeom Busters: Themed Special Events to Dazzle and Delight Your Group*, by Annette C. Moore; *Constraints to Leisure*, edited by Edgar L. Jackson; *Introduction to Therapeutic Receration: U.S. & Canadian Perspectives*, by Kenneth E. Mobily and Lisa J. Ostiguy.

VERSO

180 Varick St., 10th Floor, New York NY 10014-4606. (212)807-9680. Fax: (212)807-9152. E-mail: versony@versobooks.com. Web site: www.versobooks.com. **Acquisitions:** Editorial Department. Estab. 1970. Publishes hardcover and trade paperback originals. **Pays royalty. Offers advance.** Accepts simultaneous submissions. Book catalog free; ms guidelines online.

- "Our books cover economics, politics, cinema studies, and history (among other topics), but all come from a critical, Leftist viewpoint, on the border between trade and academic."

Nonfiction Illustrated book. Subjects include business/economics, government/politics, history, philosophy, sociology, women's issues/studies. Submit proposal package.
Recent Title(s) *Planet of Slums*, by Mike Davis; *George and Martha*, by Karen Finley; *High Water Everywhere*, by Alexander Cockburn and Jeffry St. Clair.

⊘ VIKING CHILDREN'S BOOKS

Imprint of Penguin Group (USA), Inc., 345 Hudson St., New York NY 10014-3657. (212)414-3600. Fax: (212)414-3399. Web site: www.us.penguingroup.com. **Acquisitions:** Catherine Frank, senior editor; Tracy Gates, executive editor; Joy Peskin, senior editor; Anne Gunton, associate editor; Janet Pascal, editor; Kendra Levin, editorial assistant. Publishes hardcover originals. **Publishes 70 titles/year. Pays 2-10% royalty on retail price or flat fee. Offers negotiable advance.** Publishes book 1-2 years after acceptance of ms. Responds in 6 months to queries; 6 months to mss. *Does not accept unsolicited submissions.*

- Viking Children's Books publishes high-quality trade books for children including fiction, nonfiction and picture books for pre-schoolers through young adults.

Nonfiction Children's/juvenile. Query with SASE, or submit outline, 3 sample chapters, SASE.
Fiction Juvenile, picture books, young adult. For picture books, submit complete ms and SASE. For novels, submit outline with 3 sample chapters and SASE.
Recent Title(s) *Just Listen*, by Sarah Dessen; *Llama Llama Red Pajama*, by Anna Dewdney.

VILLARD BOOKS

Imprint of Random House Publishing Group, 1745 Broadway, New York NY 10019. (212)572-2600. Web site: www.atrandom.com. Estab. 1983. Publishes hardcover and trade paperback originals. **Pays negotiable royalty. Offers negotiable advance.** Accepts simultaneous submissions.

"Villard Books is the publisher of savvy and sometimes quirky, best-selling hardcovers and trade paperbacks."

Nonfiction General nonfiction. Subjects include commercial nonfiction. *Agented submissions only.*
Fiction Commercial fiction. *Agented submissions only.*
Recent Title(s) *Serpent Girl*, by Matthew Carnahan; *Mr. Lucky*, by James Swain; *Swing*, by Rupert Holmes.

VINTAGE BOOKS & ANCHOR BOOKS

Division of Random House, Inc., 1745 Broadway Ave., New York NY 10019. Web site: www.vintagebooks.com; www.anchorbooks.com. Publishes trade paperback originals and reprints. Accepts simultaneous submissions.
Nonfiction Subjects include history, science, sociology, women's issues/studies.
Fiction Literary, mainstream/contemporary, short story collections. *Agented submissions only.*
Recent Title(s) *The Dew Breaker*, by Edwidge Danticat; *A Distant Shore*, by Caryl Phillips; *Operating Instructions*, by Anne Lammott.

VINTAGE ROMANCE PUBLISHING

107 Clearview Circle, Goose Creek SC 29445. E-mail: editor@vrpublishing.com. Submissions E-mail: submissions@vrpublishing.com. Web site: www.vrpublishing.com. **Acquisitions:** Dawn Carrington, editor (historical romance and nonfiction). Estab. 2004. Publishes hardcover, trade paperback and mass market originals and trade paperback reprints. **Publishes 24 titles/year; imprint publishes 5 titles/year. Receives 250 queries and 25 mss/year. 75% of books from first-time authors; 98% from unagented writers. Pays 6% royalty on retail price.** Publishes book 8 months after acceptance of ms. Does not accept simultaneous submissions. Responds in 1 month to queries; 3 months to proposals; 4-5 months to mss. Book catalog and ms guidelines online.
Imprints Vintage Heat; Kid's Corner.
Nonfiction Children's/juvenile, reference. Subjects include Americana, history, memoirs. "All nonfiction should relate to some aspect of history and historical romance, i.e., the history of the Regency period, the history of old romance or true love stories from earlier times." Query with SASE, or submit proposal package including outline, 2 sample chapter(s). Reviews artwork/photos as part of ms package. Send photocopies.
Fiction Historical, humor, juvenile, mystery, picture books, religious, romance, western. "All fiction submissions should have a minimum of 30% romance." Query with SASE.
Recent Title(s) *Old School Romance*, by Conrad V. Sucatre (history of romance books); *A Pair of Wings*, by Lorna K. Grant (WWII romance); *Traces of Love*, by various poets (love poem anthology).
Tips "Audience comprised of avid readers of historical romances, history books, romance readers, parents, poets, lovers of poetry. Please review our detailed submission guidelines prior to submitting. Please be prepared to submit a detailed marketing plan and be prepared to actually promote and market your work upon acceptance."

VITAL HEALTH PUBLISHING

P.O. Box 152, Ridgefield CT 06877. (203)894-1882. Fax: (203)894-8408. E-mail: info@vitalhealthbooks.com. Web site: www.vitalhealthbooks.com. **Acquisitions:** David Richard, publishing director (health, nutrition, ecology, creativity). Estab. 1997. Publishes trade paperback originals and reprints. **Publishes 10 titles/year; imprint publishes 5-6 titles/year. Receives 150 queries and 25 mss/year. 25% of books from first-time authors; 90% from unagented writers. Pays 15-20% royalty on wholesale price for top authors; pays in copies 30-40% of the time. Offers $1,000-5,000 advance.** Publishes book 6-8 months after acceptance of ms. Does not accept simultaneous submissions. Responds in 2 months to queries; 1-3 months to proposals; 2-4 months to mss. Book catalog online.
Imprints Vital Health Publishing; Enhancement Books.

Nonfiction books for a health-conscious, well-educated, creative audience.

Nonfiction Audiocassettes, children's/juvenile, cookbook, self-help. Subjects include health/medicine, music/dance, New Age, philosophy, spirituality. "All titles must be related to health. Because we have a holistic philosophy, this includes nutrition, ecology, creativity, and spirituality. Submit proposal package including outline, 1 sample chapter, cover letter describing the project. Reviews artwork/photos as part of ms package. Send photocopies or color prints.

Recent Title(s) *Cultivate Health from Within: Dr. Shahani's Guide to Probiotics*, by Khem Shahani, Ph.D. (nonfiction); *Our Children's Health*, by Bonnie Minsky, L.C.N. (nonfiction); *The Color Pathway to the Soul: The Diamond Color Meditation*, by John Diamond, M.D.

Tips "View our Web site to compare our titles to your manuscript."

VIVISPHERE PUBLISHING

675 Dutchess Turnpike, Poughkeepsie NY 12603. (845)463-1100, ext. 314. Fax: (845)463-0018. Web site: www.vivisphere.com. **Acquisitions:** Lisa Mays. Estab. 1995. Publishes paperback originals and paperback reprints. **Pays royalty.** Publishes book 3-12 months after acceptance of ms. Accepts simultaneous submissions. Responds in 3 months to queries. Book catalog free; ms guidelines free or online.

O→ Cookbooks should have a particular slant or appeal to a certain niche. Also publish out-of-print books.

Nonfiction Cookbook, self-help. Subjects include history, military/war, New Age, game of bridge. Query with SASE.

Fiction Feminist, gay/lesbian, historical, horror, literary, mainstream/contemporary, military/war, science fiction, western. Query with SASE.

WADSWORTH PUBLISHING CO.

10 Davis Dr., Belmont CA 94002. (650)595-2350. Fax: (650)637-7544. Web site: www.thomson.com. **Acquisitions:** Sean Wakely, president; Steve Wainwright, editor (philosophy/religion); Holly Allen, publisher (communications, radio/TV/film/theater); David Tatum, editor (political science); Clark Baxter, publisher (history/music); Annie Mitchell, editor (communications and speech); Lin Marshall, editor (sociology/anthropology [upper level]); Lisa Gebo, senior editor (psychology and helping professions); Dan Alpert, editor (education/special education); Vicki Knight, publisher (psychology); Peter Marshall, publisher (health/nutrition); Michele Sordi, editor (psychology); Marianne Tafliner, senior editor (psychology). Estab. 1956. Publishes hardcover and paperback originals and software. **Publishes 300 titles/year. 35% of books from first-time authors; 99% from unagented writers. Pays 5-15% royalty on net receipts.** Publishes book 1 year after acceptance of ms. Accepts simultaneous submissions. Book catalog and ms guidelines via Web site or with SASE.

O→ Wadsworth publishes college-level textbooks in social sciences, humanities, education, and college success.

Nonfiction Multimedia, textbook, multimedia products: higher education only. Subjects include anthropology/archeology, education, health/medicine, language/literature, music/dance, nature/environment, philosophy, psychology, religion (studies), science, sociology, software, nutrition, counseling, criminal justice, speech and mass communications, broadcasting, TV and film productions, college success. Query with SASE, or submit outline, sample chapter(s), synopsis.

J. WESTON WALCH, PUBLISHER

P.O. Box 658, Portland ME 04104-0658. (207)772-3105. Fax: (207)774-7167. Web site: www.walch.com. **Acquisitions:** Susan Blair, editor-in-chief. Estab. 1927. **Publishes 100 titles/year. Receives 300 submissions/year. 10% of books from first-time authors; 95% from unagented writers. Pays 5-8% royalty on flat rate.** Publishes book 6 months after acceptance of ms. Accepts simultaneous submissions. Responds in 2 months to queries. Book catalog for 9×12 SAE with 5 first-class stamps; ms guidelines for #10 SASE.

O→ "We focus on English/language arts, math, social studies and science teaching resources for middle school through adult assessment titles."

Nonfiction Formats include teacher resources, reproducibles. Subjects include education (mathematics, middle school, social studies, remedial and special education), government/politics, history, language/literature, science, social sciences, technology. Most titles are assigned by us, though we occasionally accept an author's unsolicited submission. We have a great need for author/artist teams and for authors who can write at third- to seventh-grade levels. Looks for sense of organization, writing ability, knowledge of subject, skill of communicating with intended audience. We do *not* want textbooks or anthologies. All authors should have educational writing experience. *Query first.* Query with SASE. Reviews artwork/photos as part of ms package.

WALKER AND CO.

Walker Publishing Co., 104 Fifth Ave., 7th Floor, New York NY 10011. (212)727-8300. Fax: (212)727-0984. Web site: www.walkeryoungreaders.com. **Acquisitions:** Submissions to Adult Nonfiction Editor limited to agents, published authors, and writers wtih professional credentials in their field of expertise. Children's books to "Submissions Editor-Juvenile." Estab. 1959. Publishes hardcover trade originals. Does not accept simultaneous submissions. Book catalog for 9×12 SAE with 3 first-class stamps.

O→ Walker publishes general nonfiction on a variety of subjects, as well as children's books.

Nonfiction Autobiography, biography, Adult. Subjects include business/economics, health/medicine, history (science and technology), nature/environment, science, sports. *Adult: agented submissions only*; Juvenile: send synopsis.

Fiction Juvenile, mystery (adult), picture books. Query with SASE. Send complete ms for picture books.

Recent Title(s) *Blood Red Horse*, by K.M. Grant; *The Driving Book*, by Karen Gravelle; *Shelf Life*, by Robert Corbet.

WATERBROOK PRESS

Subsidiary of Random House, 12265 Oracle Blvd., Suite 200, Colorado Springs CO 80921. (719)590-4999. Fax: (719)590-8977. Web site: www.waterbrookpress.com. Estab. 1996. Publishes hardcover and trade paperback originals. **Publishes 70 titles/year. Receives 2,000 queries/year. 15% of books from first-time authors. Pays royalty.** Publishes book 11 months after acceptance of ms. Accepts simultaneous submissions. Responds in 2-3 months to queries; 2-3 months to proposals; 2-3 months to mss. Book catalog online.

Nonfiction General nonfiction, self-help, juvenile. Subjects include child guidance/parenting, health/medicine, money/finance, religion, spirituality. "We publish books on unique topics with a Christian perspective." *Agented submissions only.*

Fiction Adventure, historical, literary, mainstream/contemporary, mystery, religious (inspirational, religious mystery/suspense, religious thriller, religious romance), romance (contemporary, historical), science fiction, spiritual, suspense. *Agented submissions only.*

Recent Title(s) *Every Young Woman's Battle*, by Shannon Ethridge; *Homestead*, by Jane Kirkpatrick; *Dinner With a Perfect Stranger*, by David Gregory.

WATSON-GUPTILL PUBLICATIONS

Imprint of Billboard Publications, Inc., 770 Broadway, New York NY 10003. (646)654-5000. Fax: (646)654-5486. Web site: www.watsonguptill.com. **Acquisitions:** Candace Raney, executive editor (fine art, art technique, pop culture, graphic design); Bob Nirkind, executive editor (Billboard-music, popular culture); Joy Acquilino, senior editor (crafts); Victoria Craven, senior editor (Amphoto-photography, lifestyle, architecture); Julie Mazur (children's books). Publishes hardcover and trade paperback originals and reprints. **Receives 150 queries and 50 mss/year. 50% of books from first-time authors; 75% from unagented writers. Pays royalty on wholesale price.** Publishes book 9 months after acceptance of ms. Responds in 2 months to queries; 3 months to proposals. Book catalog free; ms guidelines online.

Imprints Watson-Guptill; Amphoto; Whitney Library of Design; Billboard Books; Back Stage Books.

O→ Watson-Guptill is an arts book publisher.

Nonfiction How-to (instructionals). Subjects include art/architecture, music/dance, photography, lifestyle, pop culture, theater. "Writers should be aware of the kinds of books (arts, crafts, graphic designs, instructional) Watson-Guptill publishes before submitting. Although we are growing and will consider new ideas and approaches, we will not consider a book if it is clearly outside of our publishing program." Query with SASE, or submit proposal package including outline, 1-2 sample chapters. Reviews artwork/photos as part of ms package. Send photocopies or transparencies.

Recent Title(s) *Manga Mania Shoujo*, by Christopher Hart; *Scared! How to Draw Horror Comic Characters*, by Steve Miller and Bryan Baugh; *Days of Hope and Dreams: An Intimate Portrait of Bruce Springsteen*, by Frank Stefanko.

Tips "We are an art book publisher."

WESLEYAN UNIVERSITY PRESS

215 Long Lane, Middletown CT 06459. (860)685-7711. Fax: (860)685-7712. E-mail: stamminen@wesleyan.edu. Web site: www.wesleyan.edu/wespress. Director: Suzanna Tamminen. **Acquisitions:** Eric Levy. Estab. 1959. Publishes hardcover originals and paperbacks. Accepts simultaneous submissions. Book catalog free; Ms guidelines online or with #10 SASE.

O→ Wesleyan University Press is a scholarly press with a focus on poetry, music, dance and cultural studies.

Nonfiction Biography, scholarly, textbook. Subjects include music/dance, film/TV & media studies, science fiction studies, dance and poetry. Submit proposal package including outline, sample chapter(s), cover letter, CV, TOC, anticipated length of ms and date of completion. Reviews artwork/photos as part of ms package. Send photocopies.

Poetry "We do not accept unsolicited manuscripts."

Recent Title(s) *Sex and the Slayer*, by Lorna Jarrett; *Door in the Mountain*, by Jean Valentine; *The Begum's Millions*, by Jules Verne.

WESTCLIFFE PUBLISHERS

P.O. Box 1261, Englewood CO 80150. (303)935-0900. Fax: (303)935-0903. E-mail: editor@westcliffepublishers.com. Web site: www.westcliffepublishers.com. Linda Doyle, associate publisher. **Acquisitions:** Jenna Samelson, managing editor. Estab. 1981. Publishes hardcover originals, trade paperback originals, and reprints. **Publishes 18 titles/year. Receives 100 queries and 60 mss/year. 50% of books from first-time authors; 100% from unagented writers. Pays royalty on retail price. Offers advance.** Publishes book 18 months after acceptance of ms. Accepts simultaneous submissions. Responds in 1 month to queries. Book catalog free; ms guidelines online.

"Westcliffe Publishers produces the highest quality in regional photography and essays for our outdoor guidebooks, coffee table-style books, and calendars. As an eco-publisher our mission is to foster environmental awareness by showing the beauty of the natural world." Strong concentration on color guide books, outdoor sports, history.

Nonfiction Coffee table book, gift book, illustrated book, reference. Subjects include Americana, animals, gardening, history, nature/environment, photography, regional, sports (outdoor), travel. "Writers need to do their market research to justify a need in the marketplace." Submit proposal package including outline. Westcliffe will contact you for photos, writing samples.

Recent Title(s) *Colorado: 1870-2000*, by John Fielder; *Haunted Texas Vacations*, by Lisa Farwell.

Tips Audience are nature and outdoors enthusiasts and photographers. "Just call us!"

WESTMINSTER JOHN KNOX PRESS

Division of Presbyterian Publishing Corp., 100 Witherspoon St., Louisville KY 40202-1396. Fax: (502)569-5113. Web site: www.wjkbooks.com. **Acquisitions:** Lori Dowell. Publishes hardcover and paperback originals and reprints. **Publishes 100 titles/year. Receives 2,500 queries and 750 mss/year. 10% of books from first-time authors. Pays royalty on retail price.** Does not accept simultaneous submissions. Proposal guidelines online.

"All WJK books have a religious/spiritual angle, but are written for various markets—scholarly, professional, and the general reader." Westminster John Knox is affiliated with the Presbyterian Church USA. No phone queries.

Nonfiction Subjects include religion, spirituality. Submit proposal package according to the WJK book proposal guidelines found online.

WHITAKER HOUSE PUBLISHERS

1030 Hunt Valley Circle, New Kensington PA 15068. E-mail: publisher@whitakerhouse.com. Web site: www.whitakerhouse.com. **Acquisitions:** Tom Cox, managing editor. Estab. 1970. **Publishes 35 titles/year. Receives 250 queries and 100 mss/year. 60% from unagented writers. Pays 6-25% royalty on wholesale price.** Publishes book 7 months after acceptance of ms. Does not accept simultaneous submissions. Responds in 3 months to queries; 3 months to proposals; 3 months to mss. Book catalog online.

Nonfiction Accepts submissions on any topic as long as they have a Christian perspective. Audiocassettes, autobiography, biography, children's/juvenile, coffee table book, general nonfiction, gift book, how-to, humor, multimedia, reference, scholarly, self-help. **All unsolicited mss returned unopened.**

Fiction All fiction must have a Christian perspective. Adventure, ethnic, fantasy, historical, humor, juvenile, literary, mainstream/contemporary, multicultural, multimedia, mystery, religious, romance, science fiction, spiritual, sports, suspense, young adult. **All unsolicited mss returned unopened.**

Recent Title(s) *The Most Important Person on Earth*, by Dr. Myles Munroe; *It's Your Time*, by Bishop Eddie Long; *Divine Revelation of Spiritual Warfare*, by Mary K. Baxter.

Tips "Audience includes those seeking uplifting and inspirational fiction and nonfiction."

WHITEHORSE PRESS

107 E. Conway Rd., Center Conway NH 03813-4012. (603)356-6556. Fax: (603)356-6590. **Acquisitions:** Dan Kennedy, publisher. Estab. 1988. Publishes trade paperback originals. **Publishes 10-20 titles/year. Pays 10% royalty on wholesale price.** Does not accept simultaneous submissions. Responds in 1 month to queries.

Nonfiction "We are actively seeking nonfiction books to aid motorcyclists in topics such as motorcycle safety, restoration, repair, and touring. We are especially interested in technical subjects related to motorcycling." How-to, reference. Subjects include travel. Query with SASE.

Recent Title(s) *Essential Guide to Motorcycle Maintenence*, by Mark Zimmerman (trade paperback).

Tips "We like to discuss project ideas at an early stage and work with authors to develop those ideas to fit our market."

ALBERT WHITMAN AND CO.

6340 Oakton St., Morton Grove IL 60053-2723. (847)581-0033. Web site: www.albertwhitman.com. **Acquisitions:** Kathleen Tucker, editor-in-chief. Estab. 1919. Publishes hardcover originals and paperback reprints.

Publishes 30 titles/year. 20% of books from first-time authors; 70% from unagented writers. Pays 10% royalty for novels; 5% for picture books. Offers advance. Publishes book an average of 18 months after acceptance of ms. Accepts simultaneous submissions. Responds in 6 weeks to queries; 3-4 months to mss. Book catalog for 8×10 SAE with 3 first-class stamps; ms guidelines for #10 SASE.

O→ Albert Whitman publishes good books for children on a variety of topics: holidays (i.e., Halloween), special needs (such as diabetes), and problems like divorce. The majority of our titles are picture books with less than 1,500 words." De-emphasizing bedtime stories.

Nonfiction All books are for ages 2-12. Children's/juvenile, illustrated book. Subjects include animals, anthropology/archeology, art/architecture, computers/electronic, cooking/foods/nutrition, ethnic, gardening, health/medicine, history, hobbies, language/literature, music/dance, nature/environment, photography, recreation, religion, science, sports, travel, social studies, math. Submit complete ms if ms is picture book length; otherwise query with SASE.

Fiction All books are for ages 2-12. Adventure, ethnic, fantasy, historical, humor, mystery, holiday, concept books (to help children deal with problems), family. Currently emphasizing picture books; de-emphasizine folf tales and bedtime stories. No young adult and adult books. Submit complete ms for picture books; for longer works submit query with outline and sample chapters.

Recent Title(s) *Pumpkin Jack*, by Will Hubbell.

Tips "We sell mostly to libraries, but our bookstore sales are growing. We recommend you study our catalog, or visit our Web site before submitting your work."

WHITSTON PUBLISHING CO., INC.

P.O. Box 38263, Albany NY 12203. (518)869-9110. Fax: (518)452-2154. Web site: www.whitston.com. **Acquisitions:** Michael Laddin, publisher. Estab. 1969. Publishes hardcover and trade paperback originals. **Publishes 15-25 titles/year. Receives 500 queries/year. 20% of books from first-time authors; 100% from unagented writers. Pays royalities after sale of 500 copies.** Publishes book 1-2 years after acceptance of ms. Does not accept simultaneous submissions. Responds in 6 months to queries.

O→ Whitston focuses on literature, politics, history, business, and the sciences.

Nonfiction "We publish nonfiction books in the humanities. We also publish reference bibliographies and indexes." Subjects include art/architecture, business/economics, government/politics, health/medicine, history, language/literature, social sciences. Query with SASE. Reviews artwork/photos as part of ms package.

Recent Title(s) *Mark Twain Among the Scholars; Autobiographies by Americans of Color; Into the Dragon's Teeth: Warriors' Tales of the Battle of the Bulge.*

MARKUS WIENER PUBLISHERS, INC.

231 Nassau St., Princeton NJ 08542. (609)921-1141. **Acquisitions:** Shelley Frisch, editor-in-chief. Estab. 1981. Publishes hardcover and trade paperback originals and reprints. **Publishes 15 titles/year; imprint publishes 5 titles/year. Receives 50-150 queries and 50 mss/year. Pays 8-10% royalty on net receipts.** Publishes book 1 year after acceptance of ms. Does not accept simultaneous submissions. Responds in 2 months to queries; 2 months to proposals. Book catalog free.

Imprints Princeton Series on the Middle East; Topics in World History.

O→ Markus Wiener publishes textbooks on history subjects and regional world history.

Nonfiction Textbook. Subjects include history, world affairs, Caribbean studies, Middle East, Africa.

Recent Title(s) *History of Puerto Rico*, by Fernando Pico; *The New Face of Lebanon*, by William Morris.

MICHAEL WIESE PRODUCTIONS

11288 Ventura Blvd., Suite 621, Studio City CA 91604. (818)379-8799 or (206)283-2948. Fax: (818)986-3408. E-mail: kenlee@mwp.com. Web site: www.mwp.com. **Acquisitions:** Ken Lee, vice president. Estab. 1981. Publishes trade paperback originals. Accepts simultaneous submissions. Book catalog online.

O→ Michael Wiese publishes how-to books for professional film or video makers, film schools and bookstores.

Nonfiction How-to. Subjects include professional film and videomaking. Call before submitting.

Recent Title(s) *Filmmaking for Teens*, by Troy Lanier and Clay Nichols; *The Hollywood Standard*, by Christopher Riley; *The Working Director*, by Charles Wilkinson.

Tips Audience is professional filmmakers, writers, producers, directors, actors and university film students.

WILDCAT CANYON PRESS

Council Oak Books, 2105 E. 15th St., Suite B, Tulsa OK 74105. (918)743-2665. Fax: (918)743-4288. Web site: www.counciloakbooks.com. **Acquisitions:** Acquisitions Editor. Accepts simultaneous submissions. Responds in 6 months to queries. Book catalog and ms guidelines online.

O→ Wildcat Canyon Press publishes quality books on relationships, women's issues, home and family, and personal growth.

Nonfiction Gift book, self-help, lifestyle. Query with SASE, or submit proposal package including outline, sample chapter(s), author bio, SASE. Reviews artwork/photos as part of ms package. Send photocopies.

Recent Title(s) *Brenda's Bible*, by Brenda Kinsel; *Growing Season: A Healing Journey Into the Heart of Nature*, by Arlene Bernstein.

Tips "We are looking for fun and practical book projects that work well in both the traditional bookstore and gift markets."

WILDERNESS PRESS

1200 Fifth St., Berkeley CA 94710. (510)558-1666. Fax: (510)558-1696. E-mail: editor@wildernesspress.com. Web site: www.wildernesspress.com. **Acquisitions:** Managing Editor. Estab. 1967. Publishes paperback originals. **Publishes 12 titles/year.** Publishes book 8-12 months after acceptance of ms. Responds in 2 months to queries. Book catalog and ms guidelines online.

O→ "Wilderness Press has a long tradition of publishing the highest quality, most accurate hiking and other outdoor activity guidebooks."

Nonfiction How-to (outdoors). Subjects include nature/environment, recreation, trail guides for hikers and backpackers. "We publish books about the outdoors and some general travel guides. Many are trail guides for hikers and backpackers, but we also publish climbing, kayaking, and other outdoor activity guides, how-to books about the outdoors and urban walking books. The manuscript must be accurate. The author must research an area in person. If writing a trail guide, you must walk all the trails in the area your book is about. Outlook must be strongly conservationist. Style must be appropriate for a highly literate audience." Download proposal guidelines from Web site.

Recent Title(s) *Best of California's Missions, Mansions and Museums*; *Stairway Walks in San Francisco*; *Walking Brooklyn*.

JOHN WILEY & SONS, INC.

111 River St., Hoboken NJ 07030. (201)748-6000. Fax: (201)748-6088. Web site: www.wiley.com. **Acquisitions:** Editorial Department. Estab. 1807. Publishes hardcover originals, trade paperback originals and reprints. **Pays competitive rates. Offers advance.** Accepts simultaneous submissions. Book catalog and ms guidelines online.

Imprints Jossey-Bass (business/management, leadership, human resource development, education, health, psychology, religion, and public and nonprofit sectors).

O→ The General Interest group publishes nonfiction books for the consumer market.

Nonfiction Biography, children's/juvenile, reference, narrative nonfiction. Subjects include history, memoirs, psychology, science (popular), African American interest, health/self-improvement, technical, medical. Submit proposal package, or submit complete ms. See Web site for more details.

Recent Title(s) *Bordeaux and Its Wines, 17th Ed.*, by Charles Cocks; *Penthouse Living*, by Jonathan Bell; *Prevention of Type 2 Diabetes*, edited by Manfred Ganz.

WILLIAM ANDREW, INC.

13 Eaton Ave., Norwich NY 13815. (607)337-5000. Fax: (607)337-5090. E-mail: mtreloar@williamandrew.com. Web site: www.williamandrew.com. **Acquisitions:** Millicent Treloar, senior editor. Estab. 1989. Publishes hardcover originals. Accepts simultaneous submissions. Book catalog online.

O→ "We are looking for authors who want to write a book or compile data that can be employed by readers in day-to-day activities."

Nonfiction Reference, scholarly, technical, databooks, handbooks, literature reviews, patent reviews, data compilations, comprehensive fundamentals overviews, consultant-style training and evaluative works. Subject areas include agricultural/food technology, coatings/paints formulations, cosmetics/toiletries, diffusion/thin films, health/safety, industrial chemicals, MEMS/nanotechnology, materials engineers, packaging, plastics, processing/manufacturing, surface engineering. Submit outline with book propsal, SASE. Reviews artwork/photos as part of ms package. Send photocopies.

Recent Title(s) *Nanostructured Materials*, by Koch; *Handbook of Molded Part Shrinkage and Warpage*, by Fischer; *Fluoroplastics, Volumes 1 and 2*, by Ebnesajjad.

WILLIAM MORROW

HarperCollins, 10 E. 53rd St., New York NY 10022. (212)207-7000. Fax: (212)207-7145. Web site: www.harperco llins.com. **Acquisitions:** Acquisitions Editor. Estab. 1926. **Pays standard royalty on retail price. Offers varying advance.** Book catalog free.

O→ William Morrow publishes a wide range of titles that receive much recognition and prestige. A most selective house.

Nonfiction Biography, cookbook, general nonfiction, how-to. Subjects include art/architecture, cooking/foods/nutrition, history. Length 50,000-100,000 words. *No unsolicited mss or proposals. Agented submissions only.*
Fiction Publishes adult ficiton. Morrow accepts only the highest quality submissions in adult fiction. *No unsolicited mss or proposals. Agented submissions only.*
Recent Title(s) *Serpent on the Crown*, by Elizabeth Peters; *The Baker's Apprentice*, by Judith R. Hendricks; *Freakonomics*, by Steven D. Levitt and Stephen J. Dubner.

WILLOW CREEK PRESS

P.O. Box 147, 9931 Highway 70 W., Minocqua WI 54548. (715)358-7010. Fax: (715)358-2807. E-mail: andread@willowcreekpress.com. Web site: www.willowcreekpress.com. **Acquisitions:** Andrea Donner, managing editor. Estab. 1986. Publishes hardcover and trade paperback originals and reprints. **Publishes 25 titles/year. Receives 400 queries and 150 mss/year. 15% of books from first-time authors; 50% from unagented writers. Pays 6-15% royalty on wholesale price. Offers $2,000-5,000 advance.** Publishes book within 18 months after acceptance of ms. Accepts simultaneous submissions. Responds in 2 months to queries. Ms guidelines online.

O→ "We specialize in nature, outdoor, and sporting topics, including gardening, wildlife, and animal books. Pets, cookbooks, and a few humor books and essays round out our titles." Currently emphasizing pets (mainly dogs and cats), wildlife, outdoor sports (hunting, fishing). De-emphasizing essays, fiction.

Nonfiction Coffee table book, cookbook, how-to, humor, illustrated book, reference. Subjects include animals, cooking/foods/nutrition, gardening, nature/environment, recreation, sports, travel, wildlife, pets. Submit outline, 1 sample chapter, SASE. Reviews artwork/photos as part of ms package.
Recent Title(s) *Why Babies Do That*; *Horse Tails & Trails*; *The Little Book of Lap Dogs*.

WILSHIRE BOOK CO.

9731 Variel Ave., Chatsworth CA 91311-4315. (818)700-1522. Fax: (818)700-1527. E-mail: mpowers@mpowers.com. Web site: www.mpowers.com. Publisher: Melvin Powers. **Acquisitions:** Rights Department. Estab. 1947. Publishes trade paperback originals and reprints. **Publishes 25 titles/year. Receives 1,200 queries/year. 70% of books from first-time authors; 90% from unagented writers. Pays standard royalty. Offers advance.** Publishes book 6-9 months after acceptance of ms. Accepts simultaneous submissions. Responds in 2 months.
Nonfiction How-to, humor, self-help, motivational/inspiration, recovery. Subjects include psychology, personal success, entrepreneurship, Internet marketing, mail order, horsmanship. Minimum 30,000 words. Submit 3 sample chapters, or submit complete ms. Include outline, author bio, analysis of book's competition and SASE. No e-mail or fax submissions. Reviews artwork/photos as part of ms package. Send photocopies.
Fiction Adult allegories that teach principles of psychological growth or offer guidance in living. Minimum 30,000 words. No standard fiction. Submit 3 sample chapters, or submit complete ms. Include outline, author bio, analysis of book's competition and SASE. No e-mail or fax queries.
Recent Title(s) *The Dragon Slayer with a Heavy Heart*, by Marcia Powers; *The Secret of Overcoming Verbal Abuse*, by Albert Ellis, PhD, and Marcia Grad Powers; *The Princess Who Believed in Fairy Tales*, by Marcia Grad.
Tips "We are vitally interested in all new material we receive. Just as you are hopeful when submitting your manuscript for publication, we are hopeful as we read each one submitted, searching for those we believe could be successful in the marketplace. Writing and publishing must be a team effort. We need you to write what we can sell. We suggest you read the successful books similar to the one you want to write. Analyze them to discover what elements make them winners. Duplicate those elements in your own style, using a creative new approach and fresh material, and you will have written a book we can catapult onto the bestseller list. You are welcome to telephone or e-mail us for immediate feedback on any book concept you may have. To learn more about us and what we publish—and for complete manuscript guidelines—visit our Web site."

WISDOM PUBLICATIONS

199 Elm St., Somerville MA 02144. (617)776-7416, ext. 28. Fax: (617)776-7841. E-mail: editorial@wisdompubs.org. Web site: www.wisdompubs.org. Publisher: Timothy McNeill. **Acquisitions:** David Kittlestrom, senior editor. Estab. 1976. Publishes hardcover originals and trade paperback originals and reprints. **Publishes 20-25 titles/year. Receives 300 queries/year. 50% of books from first-time authors; 95% from unagented writers. Pays 4-8% royalty on wholesale price. Offers advance.** Publishes book within 2 years after acceptance of ms. Does not accept simultaneous submissions. Book catalog and ms guidelines online.

O→ Wisdom Publications is dedicated to making available authentic Buddhist works for the benefit of all. "We publish translations, commentaries, and teachings of past and contemporary Buddhist masters and original works by leading Buddhist scholars." Currently emphasizing popular applied Buddhism, scholarly titles.

Nonfiction Reference, self-help, textbook (Buddhist). Subjects include philosophy (Buddhist or comparative

Buddhist/Western), psychology, religion, Buddhism, Tibet. Query with SASE. Reviews artwork/photos as part of ms package. Send photocopies.

Poetry Buddhist. Query.

Recent Title(s) *Essence of the Heart Sutra*, by The Dalai Lama.

Tips "We are basically a publisher of Buddhist books—all schools and traditions of Buddhism. Please see our catalog or our Web site before you send anything to us to get a sense of what we publish."

WIZARDS OF THE COAST

Subsidiary of Hasbro, Inc., P.O. Box 707, Renton WA 98057-0707. (425)226-6500. Web site: www.wizards.com. **Acquisitions:** Peter Archer, director. Publishes hardcover and trade paperback originals and trade paperback reprints. Wizard of the Coast publishes games as well, including Dungeons & Dragons® role-playing game. **Pays based on royalty, flat fee, or work-for hire assignment.** Accepts simultaneous submissions. Responds in 4 months to queries. Ms guidelines online.

Imprints Dragonlance; Forgotten Realms; Magic: The Gathering; Eberron.

- Wizards of the Coast publishes only science fiction and fantasy shared-world titles. Currently emphasizing solid fantasy writers. De-emphasizing gothic fiction.

Fiction Fantasy, short story collections. "We currently publish work-for-hire novels set in our trademarked worlds. We also accept submissions for speculative fiction, such as fantasy, science fiction, horror, alternate history and magical realism. No violent or gory fantasy or science fiction." Query with author credentials, synopsis, 10-page writing sample, and SASE.

Recent Title(s) *The City of Splendors*, by Ed Greenwood; *Promise of the Witch-King*, by R.A. Salvatore; *Empire of Blood*, by Richard A. Knaak.

Tips "Our audience is largely comprised of highly imaginative 12-30 year-old males."

WOODLAND PUBLISHING, INC.

448 E. 800 North, Orem UT 84097. (801)434-8113. Fax: (801)334-1913. Web site: www.woodlandpublishing.com. Estab. 1974. Publishes perfect bound and trade paperback originals. **Offers advance.** Accepts simultaneous submissions. Book catalog and ms guidelines for #10 SASE or via e-mail.

- "Our readers are interested in herbs and other natural health topics. Most of our books are sold through health food stores."

Nonfiction Subjects include health/medicine (alternative). Query with SASE and author credentials.

Recent Title(s) *Soy Smart Health, 2nd Ed.*, by Rita Elkins, MH; *100 and Healthy*, by W. Shaffer Fox.

Tips "Our readers are interested in herbs and other natural health topics. Most of our books are sold through health food stores."

WORDWARE PUBLISHING, INC.

2320 Los Rios Blvd., Suite 200, Plano TX 75074. (972)423-0090. Fax: (972)881-9147. E-mail: tmcevoy@wordware.com. Web site: www.wordware.com. President: Russell A. Stultz. **Acquisitions:** Wes Beckwith, acquisitions editor. Estab. 1983. Publishes trade paperback and mass market paperback originals. **Publishes 20-25 titles/year. Receives 75-100 queries and 30-50 mss/year. 40% of books from first-time authors; 95% from unagented writers. Royalties/advances negotiated per project.** Publishes book 6 months after acceptance of ms. Accepts simultaneous submissions. Responds in 2 weeks to queries. Book catalog free; ms guidelines online.

- Wordware publishes computer/electronics books covering a broad range of technologies for professional programmers and developers with special emphasis in game development, animation, and modeling.

Nonfiction Reference, technical, textbook. Subjects include computers/electronic. "Wordware publishes advanced titles for developers and professional programmers." Submit proposal package including 2 sample chapters, TOC, target audience summation, competing books.

Recent Title(s) *3DS Max Lighting; Modeling a Character in 3DS Max, 2nd Ed.; LightWave 3D 8 Character Animation; Essential LightWave 3D 8; OpenGL Game Development.*

WORKMAN PUBLISHING CO.

225 Varick St., New York NY 10014. (212)254-5900. Fax: (212)254-8098. Web site: www.workman.com. Editor-in-Chief: Susan Bolotin. **Acquisitions:** Suzanne Rafer, executive editor (cookbook, child care, parenting, teen interest); Ruth Sullivan, Margot Herrera, Richard Rosen, senior editors. Raquel Jaramillo, senior editor (juvenile). Estab. 1967. Publishes hardcover and trade paperback originals. **Publishes 40 titles/year. Receives thousands of queries/year. Open to first-time authors. Pays variable royalty on retail price. Offers variable advance.** Publishes book approximately 1 year after acceptance of ms. Accepts simultaneous submissions. Responds in 5 months to queries. Ms guidelines online.

Imprints Algonquin, Artisan, Greenwich Workshop Press, Storey, Timber.

"We are a trade paperback house specializing in a wide range of popular nonfiction. We publish no adult fiction and very little children's fiction. We also publish a full range of full-color wall and Page-A-Day calendars."

Nonfiction Cookbook, gift book, how-to, humor. Subjects include business/economics, child guidance/parenting, cooking/foods/nutrition, gardening, health/medicine, sports, travel. Query with SASE first for guidelines. Reviews artwork/photos as part of ms package.

Recent Title(s) *Your Personal Penguin*, by Sandra Boynton; *Is It Hot in Here? Or Is It Me?*, by Pat Wingert and Barbara Kantrowitz; *Girl's Guide to Absolutely Everything*, by Melissa Kirsch.

Tips "No phone calls, please. We do not accept submissions via fax or e-mail."

N WORLD AUDIENCE

25 Sickles St., #6E, New York NY 10040. (347)523-9727. Fax: (347)523-9727. E-mail: strozier@worldaudience.org. Submissions E-mail: submissions@worldaudience.org. Web site: www.worldaudience.org. **Acquisitions:** M. Stefan Strozier, chief editor (plays, poetry, novel); Hareendran Kalliukeel, editor (short stories and novels). Estab. 2004. **Publishes 100 titles/year; imprint publishes 60 titles/year. Receives 8,000 queries and 4,000 mss/year. 80% of books from first-time authors; 95% from unagented writers. Pays 15-50% royalty.** Publishes book 3 months after acceptance of ms. Accepts simultaneous submissions. Responds in 1 month to queries. online at www.worldaudience.org, or available for #10 SASE; available at www.worldaudience.org, or by sending an e-mail to info@worldaudience.org.

Imprints Mock Frog Design Press (Australia); Skive Magazine and books.

Nonfiction How-to, humor. Subjects include Americana, art/architecture, language/literature, military/war, sex, spirituality, translation, travel, world affairs. "Nonfiction should be niche and unusual." Submit proposal package including outline, 3 sample chapter(s). Reviews artwork/photos as part of ms package.jpg files.Experimental, horror, humor, literary, military/war, plays, poetry, poetry in translation, short story collections, spiritual. "We seek excellent writing ability first and foremost." Submit proposal package including 3 sample chapter(s), synopsis.

Poetry "We seek formal poetry." Submit 5 sample poems.

Recent Title(s) *The Great Book of Theatre Quotes*, by Louis Phillips (quotations); *The Biting Age*, by Ernest Pempsey (satire); *Still in Soil*, by Kyle Torke (poetry).

Tips "A world audience reached through the Internet *and* traditional distribution." Prepare packages neatly.

WRITER'S DIGEST BOOKS

Imprint of F+W Publications, Inc., 4700 E. Galbraith Rd., Cincinnati OH 45236. (513)531-2690, ext. 1408. E-mail: jane.friedman@fwpubs.com. Web site: www.wdeditors.com. **Acquisitions:** Jane Friedman, editorial director. Estab. 1920. Publishes hardcover originals and trade paperbacks. **Publishes 25-30 titles/year. Receives 300 queries and 50 mss/year. 30% from unagented writers. Pays 10-20% royalty on net receipts. Offers average $5,000 and up advance.** Publishes book 18 months after acceptance of ms. Accepts simultaneous submissions. Responds in 3 months to queries. Book catalog for 9×12 SAE with 6 first-class stamps.

- Writer's Digest Books accepts query letters and complete proposals via mail or e-mail at jane.friedman@fwpubs.com.

Writer's Digest Books is the premiere source for books about writing, publishing instructional and reference books for writers. Typical mss are 80,000 words. E-mail queries strongly preferred; no phone calls please.

Nonfiction How-to, reference, instructional books for writers. "Our instruction books stress results and how specifically to achieve them. Should be well-researched, yet lively and readable. We do not want to see books telling readers how to crack specific nonfiction markets: *Writing for the Computer Market* or *Writing for Trade Publications*, for instance. We are most in need of fiction-technique books written by published authors. Be prepared to explain how the proposed book differs from existing books on the subject." No fiction or poetry. Query with SASE, or submit outline, sample chapter(s), SASE. E-mail queries preferred.

Recent Title(s) *Your First Novel*, by Ann Rittenberg and Laura Whitcomb; *3 A.M. Epiphany*, by Brian Kitely; *The Pirate Primer*, by George Choundras.

Tips "Most queries we receive are either too broad (how to write fiction) or too niche (how to write erotic horror), and don't reflect a knowledge of our large backlist of 150 titles. We rarely publish new books on journalism, freelancing, magazine article writing or marketing/promotion. We are actively seeking: light or humorous reads about the writing life, superbly written; interactive and visual writing instruction books, similar to *Pocket Muse*, by Monica Wood; and general reference works that appeal to an audience beyond writers, such as specialized word finders, eccentric dictionaries, or pocket guides."

WRITINGCAREER.COM

P.O. Box 14061, Surfside Beach SC 29575. Web site: www.writingcareer.com. **Acquisitions:** Brian Konradt, publisher (how-to). Estab. 2003. Publishes electronic originals and reprints. **Publishes 12 titles/year. 100%**

from unagented writers. Pays 50% royalty on retail price. Publishes book 1 month after acceptance of ms. Accepts simultaneous submissions. Responds in 1 month to queries. Book catalog and ms guidelines online.
Nonfiction Subjects include writing, freelancing, screenwriting, editing, marketing, copywriting, style guides, etc. "We are a niche market with specific needs. We only publish nonfiction how-to books on the creative and business aspects of writing." Query at www.writingcareer.com/epublishing.shtml.
Recent Title(s) *Writing Industry Reports*, by Jennie S. Bev; *Freelance Writing for Vet Hospitals*, by Stanley Burkhardt.
Tips WritingCareer.com targets writers—freelancers, staff writers, hobbyists—who want to master their writing, marketing, and business skills. "Browse our book titles at WritingCareer.com to better understand what we publish and sell."

YALE UNIVERSITY PRESS

302 Temple St., New Haven CT 06511. (203)432-0960. Fax: (203)432-0948. Web site: www.yale.edu/yup. **Acquisitions:** Jonathan Brent, editorial director (literature, literary studies, theater); Jean E. Thomson Black (science, medicine); Lauren Shapiro (reference books); Keith Condon (education, behavioral/social sciences); Michelle Komie (art, architecture); Patricia Fidler, publisher (art, architecture); Mary Jane Peluso, publisher (languages, ESL); John Kulka (literature, literary studies, philosophy, political science); Michael O'Malley (business, economics, law); Christopher Rogers (history). Also: P.O. Box 209040, New Haven CT 06520-9040. Estab. 1908. Publishes hardcover and trade paperback originals. Accepts simultaneous submissions. Book catalog and ms guidelines online.

Yale University Press publishes scholarly and general interest books.

Nonfiction Biography, illustrated book, reference, scholarly, textbook. Subjects include Americana, anthropology/archeology, art/architecture, business/economics, education, health/medicine, history, language/literature, military/war, music/dance, philosophy, psychology, religion, science, sociology, women's issues/studies. "Our nonfiction has to be at a very high level. Most of our books are written by professors or journalists, with a high level of expertise. Submit proposals only. We'll ask if we want to see more. *No unsolicited mss.* We won't return them." Submit sample chapters, cover letter, prospectus, cv, table of contents, SASE. Reviews artwork/photos as part of ms package. Send photocopies.
Poetry Publishes 1 book each year. Submit to Yale Series of Younger Poets Competition. Open to poets under 40 who have not had a book previously published. Submit ms of 48-64 pages by November 15. Rules and guidelines available online or with SASE. Submit complete ms.
Recent Title(s) *Methodism: Empire of the Spirit*, by David Hempton; *A Drawing Manual*, by Thomas Eakins; *The Eighties: America in the Age of Reagan*, by John Ehrman.
Tips "Audience is scholars, students and general readers."

ZEBRA BOOKS

Kensington, 850 Third Ave., 16th Floor, New York NY 10022. (212)407-1500. Web site: www.kensingtonbooks.com. Publishes hardcover originals, trade paperback and mass market paperback originals and reprints. Accepts simultaneous submissions. Book catalog online.

Zebra Books is dedicated to women's fiction, which includes, but is not limited to romance.

Fiction Mostly historical romance. Some contemporary romance, westerns, horror, and humor. *Agented submissions only.*
Recent Title(s) *Calder Promise*, by Janet Dailey; *Come Up and See Me Sometime*, by Lucy Monroe; *A Perfect Wedding*, by Anne Robins.

MARKETS

Canadian Book Publishers

Canadian book publishers share the same mission as their U.S. counterparts—publishing timely books on subjects of concern and interest to a targetable audience. Most of the publishers listed in this section, however, differ from U.S. publishers in that their needs tend toward subjects specific to Canada or intended for a Canadian audience. Some are interested in submissions from Canadian writers only. There are many regional publishers that concentrate on region-specific subjects.

U.S. writers hoping to do business with Canadian publishers should follow specific paths of research to find out as much about their intended markets as possible. The listings will inform you about what kinds of books the Canadian companies publish and tell you whether they are open to receiving submissions from writers in the U.S. To further target your markets and see specific examples of the books these houses are publishing, send for catalogs from publishers, or check their Web sites.

Once you have determined which publishers will accept your work, it is important to understand the differences that exist between U.S. mail and Canadian mail. U.S. postage stamps are useless on mailings originating outside of the U.S. When enclosing a SASE for return of your query or manuscript from a Canadian publisher, you must include International Reply Coupons (IRCs) or Canadian postage stamps.

For a list of publishers according to their subjects of interest, see the Nonfiction and Fiction sections of the Book Publishers' Subject Index. Information on book publishers listed in the previous edition of *Writer's Market*, but not included in this edition, can be found in the General Index.

ANNICK PRESS, LTD.

15 Patricia Ave., Toronto ON M2M 1H9 Canada. (416)221-4802. Fax: (416)221-8400. E-mail: annickpress@annickpress.com. Web site: www.annickpress.com. **Acquisitions:** Rick Wilks, director; Colleen MacMillan, associate publisher. Publishes picture books, juvenile and YA fiction and nonfiction; specializes in trade books. **Publishes 25 titles/year. Receives 5,000 queries and 3,000 mss/year. 20% of books from first-time authors; 80-85% from unagented writers.** Publishes book 2 years after acceptance of ms. Book catalog and ms guidelines online.

- *Does not accept unsolicited mss.*
- Annick Press maintains "a commitment to high quality books that entertain and challenge. Our publications share fantasy and stimulate imagination, while encouraging children to trust their judgment and abilities."

Recent Title(s) *Mimus*, by Lilli Thal; *Evil Masters*, by Laura Scandiffio.

ARSENAL PULP PRESS

Suite 200, 341 Water St., Vancouver BC V6B 1B8 Canada. (604)687-4233. Fax: (604)687-4283. E-mail: info@arsenalpulp.com. Web site: www.arsenalpulp.com. **Acquisitions:** Brian Lam, publisher. Estab. 1980. Publishes trade paperback originals, and trade paperback reprints. Rarely publishes non-Canadian authors. **Publishes 20 titles/year. Receives 500 queries and 300 mss/year. 40% of books from first-time authors; 100% from unagented writers.** Publishes book 1 year after acceptance of ms. Accepts simultaneous submissions. Responds in 2 months to queries; 4 months to proposals; 4 months to mss. Book catalog for 9×12 SAE with IRCs or online; ms guidelines online.

Nonfiction Cookbook, illustrated book, literary, cultural studies. Subjects include art/architecture, cooking/foods/nutrition, creative nonfiction, ethnic (Canadian, aboriginal issues), gay/lesbian, history (cultural), language/literature, multicultural, regional (British Columbia), sex, sociology, travel, women's issues/studies, film. Submit proposal package including outline, 2-3 sample chapters. Reviews artwork/photos as part of ms package.

Fiction Ethnic (general), feminist, gay/lesbian, literary, multicultural, short story collections. No children's books or genre fiction, i.e., westerns, romance, horror, mystery, etc. Submit proposal package including outline, synopsis, 2-3 sample chapters.

Recent Title(s) *The Greenpeace to Amchitka*, by Robert Hunter (nonfiction); *La Dolce Vegan*, by Sarah Kramer (nonfiction cookbook); *Song of the Loon*, by Richard Amory (fiction).

BOREALIS PRESS, LTD.

8 Mohawk Crescent, Napean ON K2H 7G6 Canada. (613)829-0150. Fax: (613)829-7783. E-mail: drt@borealispress.com. Web site: www.borealispress.com. **Acquisitions:** Frank M. Tierney. Estab. 1972. Publishes hardcover and paperback originals and reprints. **Publishes 20 titles/year. 80% of books from first-time authors; 95% from unagented writers. Pays 10% royalty on net receipts; plus 3 free author's copies.** Publishes book 18 months after acceptance of ms. Does not accept simultaneous submissions. Responds in 2 months to queries; 4 months to mss. Book catalog and ms guidelines online.

Imprints Tecumseh Press.

- "Our mission is to publish work which will be of lasting interest in the Canadian book market." Currently emphasizing Canadian fiction, nonfiction, drama, poetry. De-emphasizing children's books.

Nonfiction Biography, children's/juvenile, reference. Subjects include government/politics, history, language/literature, regional. "Only material Canadian in content." Looks for "style in tone and language, reader interest, and maturity of outlook." Query with SASE, or submit outline, 2 sample chapters. *No unsolicited mss.* Reviews artwork/photos as part of ms package.

Fiction Adventure, ethnic, historical, juvenile, literary, mainstream/contemporary, romance, short story collections, young adult. "Only material Canadian in content and dealing with significant aspects of the human situation." Query with SASE, or submit synopsis, 1-2 sample chapters. *No unsolicited mss.*

Recent Title(s) *Canada's Governors General At Play*, by James Noonan; *James McGill of Montreal*, by John Cooper; *Musk Oxen of Gango*, by Mary Burpee.

THE BOSTON MILLS PRESS

132 Main St., Erin ON N0B 1T0 Canada. (519)833-2407. Fax: (519)833-2195. E-mail: books@bostonmillspress.com. Web site: www.bostonmillspress.com. President: John Denison. **Acquisitions:** Noel Hudson, managing editor. Estab. 1974. Publishes hardcover and trade paperback originals. **Publishes 20 titles/year. 40% of books from first-time authors; 95% from unagented writers. Pays 8% royalty on retail price. Offers advance.** Publishes book 6 months-2 years after acceptance of ms. Accepts simultaneous submissions. Responds in 2 months to queries. Book catalog free.

O-→ Boston Mills Press publishes specific market titles of Canadian and American interest including history, transportation, and regional guidebooks. "We like very focused books aimed at the North American market."

Nonfiction Coffee table book, gift book, illustrated book. Subjects include Americana, art/architecture, cooking/foods/nutrition, creative nonfiction, gardening, history, military/war, nature/environment, photography, recreation, regional, sports, travel, Canadiana. "We're interested in anything to do with Canadian or American history—especially transportation." No autobiographies. Query with SASE. Reviews artwork/photos as part of ms package. Send photocopies.

BROADVIEW PRESS, INC.

P.O. Box 1243, Peterborough ON K9J 7H5 Canada. (705)743-8990. Fax: (705)743-8353. E-mail: customerservice@broadviewpress.com. Web site: www.broadviewpress.com. **Acquisitions:** See Editorial Guidelines online. Estab. 1985. **Publishes over 60 titles/year. Receives 500 queries and 200 mss/year. 10% of books from first-time authors; 99% from unagented writers. Pays royalty.** Publishes book 1 year after acceptance of ms. Accepts simultaneous submissions. Responds in 1 month to queries; 2 months to proposals; 4 months to mss. Book catalog free; ms guidelines online.

O-→ "We publish in a broad variety of subject areas in the arts and social sciences. We are open to a broad range of political and philosophical viewpoints, from liberal and conservative to libertarian and Marxist, and including a wide range of feminist viewpoints."

Nonfiction Biography, reference, textbook. Subjects include anthropology/archeology, gay/lesbian, history, language/literature, philosophy, religion, sociology, women's issues/studies, politics. "All titles must have some potential for university or college-level course use. Crossover titles are acceptable." Query with SASE, or submit proposal package. Reviews artwork/photos as part of ms package. Send photocopies.

Recent Title(s) *Philosophical Conversations*, by Robert M. Martin.

Tips "Our titles often appeal to a broad readership; we have many books that are as much of interest to the general reader as they are to academics and students."

CARSWELL THOMSON

One Corporate Plaza 2075 Kennedy Rd., Scarborough ON M1T 3V4 Canada. (416)298-5024. Fax: (416)298-5094. E-mail: robert.freeman@thomson.com. Web site: www.carswell.com. **Acquisitions:** Robert Freeman, vice president, legal, accounting and finance, and corporate groups. Publishes hardcover originals. **Publishes 150-200 titles/year. 30-50% of books from first-time authors. Pays 5-15% royalty on wholesale price.** Publishes book 6 months after acceptance of ms. Accepts simultaneous submissions. Responds in 3 months to queries. Book catalog and ms guidelines free.

O-→ Carswell Thomson is Canada's national resource of information and legal interpretations for law, accounting, tax and business professionals.

Nonfiction Reference (legal, tax). "Canadian information of a regulatory nature is our mandate." Submit proposal package including outline, résumé.

Tips Audience is Canada and persons interested in Canadian information; professionals in law, tax, accounting fields; business people interested in regulatory material.

COACH HOUSE BOOKS

401 Huron St. on bpNichol Lane, Toronto ON M5S 2G5 Canada. (416)979-2217. Fax: (416)977-1158. Web site: www.chbooks.com. **Acquisitions:** Alana Wilcox, editor. Publishes trade paperback originals by Canadian authors. **Publishes 16 titles/year. 80% of books from first-time authors; 100% from unagented writers. Pays 10% royalty on retail price.** Publishes book 1 year after acceptance of ms. Does not accept simultaneous submissions. Responds in 6 months to queries. Ms guidelines online.

- *All unsolicited mss returned unopened.*

Nonfiction Books about Toronto. Query with SASE.

Fiction Experimental, literary, plays. "Consult Web site for submissions policy."

Poetry Consult Web site for guidelines. Query.

Recent Title(s) *Portable Altamount*, by Brian Joseph Davis (poetry); *Your Secrets Sleep With Me*, by Darren O'Donnell (fiction); *Goodness*, by Michael Redhill (drama).

Tips "We are not a general publisher, and publish only Canadian poetry, fiction, artist books and drama. We are interested primarily in innovative or experimental writing."

COTEAU BOOKS

Thunder Creek Publishing Co-operative Ltd., 2517 Victoria Ave., Regina SK S4P 0T2 Canada. (306)777-0170. Fax: (306)522-5152. E-mail: coteau@coteaubooks.com. Web site: www.coteaubooks.com. **Acquisitions:** Geoffrey Ursell, publisher. Estab. 1975. Publishes trade paperback originals and reprints. **Publishes 16 titles/year.**

Receives 200 queries and 200 mss/year. 25% of books from first-time authors; 90% from unagented writers. Pays 10% royalty on retail price. Publishes book 1 year after acceptance of ms. Does not accept simultaneous submissions. Responds in 3 months to queries; 3 months to mss. Book catalog free; ms guidelines online.

"Our mission is to publish the finest in Canadian fiction, nonfiction, poetry, drama, and children's literature, with an emphasis on Saskatchewan and prairie writers." De-emphasizing science fiction, picture books.

Nonfiction Coffee table book, reference. Subjects include creative nonfiction, ethnic, history, language/literature, memoirs, regional, sports, travel. Canadian authors only. Submit author bio, 3-4 sample chapters, SASE.

Fiction Ethnic, fantasy, feminist, gay/lesbian, historical, humor, juvenile, literary, mainstream/contemporary, multicultural, multimedia, mystery, plays, poetry, regional, short story collections, spiritual, sports, young adult, novels, short fiction, middle years. *Canadian authors only*. No science fiction. No children's picture books. Submit author bio, 3-4 sample chapters, SASE.

Poetry Submit 20-25 sample poems, or submit complete ms.

Recent Title(s) *The Kalifax Trilogy*, juvenile fiction series for ages 9 and up; *Penelope's Way*, by Blanche Howard (novel); *A Song for Nettie Johnson*, by Gloria Swaii (novel).

Tips "Look at past publications to get an idea of our editorial program. We do not publish romance, horror, or picture books but are interested in juvenile and teen fiction from Canadian authors. Submissions, even queries, must be made in hard copy only. We do not accept simultaneous/multiple submissions."

DUNDURN PRESS, LTD.

3 Church St., Suite 500, Toronto ON M5E 1M2 Canada. (416)214-5544. Fax: (416)214-5556. E-mail: info@dundurn.com. Web site: www.dundurn.com. **Acquisitions:** Barry Jowett (fiction); Tony Hawke (nonfiction). Estab. 1972. Publishes hardcover and trade paperback originals and reprints. **Receives 600 queries/year. 25% of books from first-time authors; 50% from unagented writers. Pays 10% royalty on net receipts.** Publishes book an average of 1 year after acceptance of ms. Accepts simultaneous submissions. Responds in 3 months to queries. Ms guidelines online.

Dundurn publishes books by Canadian authors.

Nonfiction Subjects include art/architecture, history (Canadian and military), music/dance (drama), regional, art history, theater, serious and popular nonfiction. Submit cover letter, synopsis, cv, sample chapters, SASE/IRC, or submit complete ms.

Fiction Literary, mystery, young adult. "No romance, science fiction, or experimental." Submit sample chapters, synopsis, author bio, SASE/IRCs, or submit complete ms.

Recent Title(s) *Now You Know Almost Everything*, by Doug Lennox; *Viking Terror*, by Tom Henighan; *The Women of Beaver Hall*, by Evelyn Walters.

ECRITS DES FORGES

C.P. 335, 1497 Laviolette, Trois-Rivieres QC G9A 5G4 Canada. (819)379-9813. Fax: (819)376-0774. Web site: www.ecritsdesforges.com. **Acquisitions:** Gaston Bellemare, president. Estab. 1971. Publishes hardcover originals. **Publishes 40 titles/year. Receives 30 queries and 1,000 mss/year. 10% of books from first-time authors; 90% from unagented writers. Pays 10-30% royalty. Offers 50% advance.** Publishes book 9 months after acceptance of ms. Accepts simultaneous submissions. Responds in 9 months to queries. Book catalog free.

Ecrits des Forges publishes only poetry written in French.

Poetry Submit 20 sample poems.

Recent Title(s) *Feux D'Octobre*, by Francesc Parcerisas; *Dés L'Origine*, by Bernard Pozier; *Un Homme*, by Jean Boë.

ECW PRESS

2120 Queen St. E., Suite 200, Toronto ON M4E 1E2 Canada. (416)694-3348. Fax: (416)698-9906. E-mail: info@ecwpress.com. Web site: www.ecwpress.com. **Acquisitions:** Jack David, president (nonfiction); Michael Holmes, literary editor (fiction, poetry); Jennifer Hale, associate editor (pop culture, entertainment). Estab. 1979. Publishes hardcover and trade paperback originals. **Publishes 40 titles/year; imprint publishes 6 titles/year. Receives 500 queries and 300 mss/year. 30% of books from first-time authors. Pays 8-12% royalty on net receipts. Offers $300-5,000 advance.** Publishes book 18 months after acceptance of ms. Accepts simultaneous submissions. Book catalog free; ms guidelines online.

ECW publishes nonfiction about people or subjects that have a substantial fan base. Currently emphasizing books about music, gambling, TV and movie stars.

Nonfiction Biography (popular), general nonfiction, humor. Subjects include business/economics, creative nonfiction, gay/lesbian, government/politics, health/medicine, history, memoirs, money/finance, regional, sex, sports, women's issues/studies, contemporary culture, Wicca, gambling, TV and movie stars. Submit proposal package including outline, 4-5 sample chapters, IRC, SASE. Reviews artwork/photos as part of ms package. Send photocopies.

Fiction "We publish literary fiction and poetry from Canadian authors exclusively. Literary, mystery, poetry, short story collections, suspense. Visit company Web site to view submission guidelines.

Poetry "We publish Canadian poetry exclusively." Query, or submit 4-5 sample poems.

Recent Title(s) *Too Close to the Falls*, by Catherine Gildiner; *Ghost Rider*, by Neil Peart; *Ashland*, by Gil Anderson (poetry).

Tips "Visit our Web site and read a selection of our books."

EDGE SCIENCE FICTION AND FANTASY PUBLISHING

Box 1714, Calgary AB T2P 2L7 Canada. (403)254-0160. Fax: (403)254-0456. Web site: www.edgewebsite.com. Estab. 1996. Publishes hardcover and trade paperback originals. **Publishes 6-8 titles/year. Receives 400 mss/year. 70% of books from first-time authors; 75% from unagented writers. Pays 10% royalty on wholesale price. Offers negotiable advance.** Publishes book 18 months after acceptance of ms. Does not accept simultaneous submissions. Responds in 1 month to queries; 1 month to proposals; 4-5 months to mss. Ms guidelines online.

"We want to encourage, produce, and promote thought-provoking and well-written science fiction and fantasy literature."

Fiction Fantasy (space fantasy, sword and sorcery), science fiction (hard science/technological, soft/sociological). "We are looking for all types of fantasy and science fiction, except juvenile/young adult, horror, erotica, religious fiction, short stories, dark/gruesome fantasy, or poetry." Submit outline, 3 sample chapter(s), synopsis. Check Web site or send SAE & IRCS for guidelines.

Recent Title(s) *The Black Chalice*, by Marie Jakober; *Eclipse*, by K.A. Bedford; *Stealing Magic*, by Tanya Huff.

Tips "Send us your best, polished, completed manuscript. Use proper manuscript format. Take the time before you submit to get a critique from someone who can offer you useful advice. When in doubt, visit our Web site for helpful resources, FAQs, and other tips."

FERNWOOD PUBLISHING, LTD.

32 Ocenavista Lane, Site 2A, Box 5, Black Pointe NS B0J 1B0 Canada. (902)857-1388. E-mail: info@fernwoodbooks.ca. Web site: www.fernwoodbooks.ca. **Acquisitions:** Errol Sharpe, publisher (social science); Wayne Antony, editor (social science). Publishes trade paperback originals. **Publishes 15-20 titles/year. Receives 80 queries and 30 mss/year. 40% of books from first-time authors; 100% from unagented writers. Pays 7-10% royalty on wholesale price. Offers advance.** Publishes book 1 year after acceptance of ms. Accepts simultaneous submissions. Responds in 6 weeks to proposals. Ms guidelines online.

"Fernwood's objective is to publish critical works which challenge existing scholarship."

Nonfiction Reference, textbook, scholarly. Subjects include agriculture/horticulture, anthropology/archeology, business/economics, education, ethnic, gay/lesbian, government/politics, health/medicine, history, language/literature, multicultural, nature/environment, philosophy, regional, sex, sociology, sports, translation, women's issues/studies, contemporary culture, world affairs. "Our main focus is in the social sciences and humanities, emphasizing labor studies, women's studies, gender studies, critical theory and research, political economy, cultural studies, and social work—for use in college and university courses." Submit proposal package including outline, sample chapter(s). Reviews artwork/photos as part of ms package. Send photocopies.

Recent Title(s) *Challenges and Perils: Social Democracy in Neoliberal Times*, edited by William K. Carroll and R.S. Ratner; *Empire With Imperialism: The Global Dynamics of Neoliberal Capitalism*, by James Petras, Henry Veltmeyer, Luciano Vasapollo and Mauro Casadio; *Cultivating Utopia: Organic Farmers in a Conventional Landscape*, by Kregg Hetherington.

GOOSE LANE EDITIONS

469 King St., Fredericton, New Brunswick E3B 1E5 Canada. (506)450-4251. Fax: (506)459-4991. Web site: www.gooselane.com. **Acquisitions:** Laurel Boone, editorial director. Estab. 1954. Publishes hardcover and paperback originals and occasional reprints. **Publishes 16-20 titles/year. 20% of books from first-time authors; 60% from unagented writers. Pays 8-10% royalty on retail price. Offers $500-3,000, negotiable advance.** Does not accept simultaneous submissions. Responds in 6 months to queries.

Goose Lane publishes literary fiction and nonfiction from well-read and highly skilled Canadian authors.

Nonfiction Biography, illustrated book. Subjects include art/architecture, history, language/literature, nature/environment, regional, women's issues/studies. Query with SASE.

Fiction Literary (novels), short story collections, contemporary. "Our needs in fiction never change: Substantial, character-centered literary fiction." No children's, YA, mainstream, mass market, genre, mystery, thriller, confessional or science fiction. Query with SAE with Canadian stamps or IRCs. No US stamps.

Recent Title(s) *The Nettle Spinner*, by Kathryn Kuitenbrouwer; *Ideas*, edited by Bernie Lucht.

Canadian Publishers

Tips "Writers should send us outlines and samples of books that show a very well-read author with highly developed literary skills. Our books are almost all by Canadians living in Canada; we seldom consider submissions from outside Canada. If I were a writer trying to market a book today, I would contact the targeted publisher with a query letter and synopsis, and request manuscript guidelines. Purchase a recent book from the publisher in a relevant area, if possible. Always send an SASE with IRCs or suffient return postage in Canadian stamps for reply to your query and for any material you'd like returned should it not suit our needs."

GUERNICA EDITIONS

Box 117, Station P, Toronto ON M5S 2S6 Canada. (416)658-9888. Fax: (416)657-8885. E-mail: guernicaeditions@cs.com. Web site: www.guernicaeditions.com. **Acquisitions:** Antonio D'Alfonso, editor/publisher (poetry, nonfiction, novels); Ken Scambray, editor (US reprints). Estab. 1978. Publishes trade paperback originals, reprints, and software. **Publishes 25 titles/year. Receives 750 mss/year. 20% of books from first-time authors; 99% from unagented writers. Pays 8-10% royalty on retail price, or makes outright purchase of $200-5,000. Offers $200-2,000 advance.** Publishes book 15 months after acceptance of ms. Does not accept simultaneous submissions. Responds in 1 month to queries; 6 months to proposals; 1 year to mss. Book catalog online.

Guernica Editions is an independent press dedicated to the bridging of cultures. "We do original and translations of fine works. We are seeking essays on authors and translations with less emphasis on poetry."

Nonfiction Biography. Subjects include art/architecture, creative nonfiction, ethnic, film/cinema/stage, gay/lesbian, government/politics, history, language/literature, memoirs, multicultural, music/dance, philosophy, psychology, regional, religion, sex, translation, women's issues/studies. Query with SASE. *All unsolicited mss returned unopened.* Reviews artwork/photos as part of ms package. Send photocopies.

Fiction Erotica, feminist, gay/lesbian, literary, multicultural, plays, poetry, poetry in translation. "We wish to open up into the fiction world and focus less on poetry. We specialize in European, especially Italian, translations." Query with SASE. *All unsolicited mss returned unopened.*

Poetry Feminist, gay/lesbian, literary, multicultural, poetry in translation. "We wish to have writers in translation. Any writer who has translated Italian poetry is welcomed. Full books only. No single poems by different authors, unless modern, and used as an anthology. First books will have no place in the next couple of years." Query.

Recent Title(s) *Surface Roots*, by Kenneth Scambray; *Naked in the Sanctuary*, by Julie Roorda; *Prague Memories*, by Tecia Werbowski.

HARLEQUIN ENTERPRISES, LTD.

225 Duncan Mill Rd., Don Mills ON M3B 3K9 Canada. (416)445-5860. Web site: www.eharlequin.com. US address: 233 Broadway, Suite 1001, New York NY 10279. (212)553-4200. UK address: Eton House, 18-24 Paradise Rd., Richmond Surrey TW9 1SR United Kingdom. Estab. 1949. Publishes mass market paperback, trade paperback, and hardcover originals and reprints. **Publishes 1,500 titles/year. Pays royalty. Offers advance.** Publishes book 1-2 years after acceptance of ms. Responds in 6 weeks to queries; 3 months to mss. Ms guidelines online.

Imprints Harlequin Books; Silhouette; MIRA; Luna; HQN Books; Mills & Boon; Steeple Hill Books; Red Dress Ink; Steeple Hill Café.

- Web sites: www.eharlequin.com; www.mirabooks.com; www.reddressink.com; www.steeplehill.com; www.luna-books.com.

Fiction Considers all types of serious romance and strong, mainstream, women's fiction. For series, query with SASE. MIRA accepts *agented submissions only*.

Tips "The quickest route to success is to check www.eharlequin.com, the other Web sites listed above, or write or call for submission guidelines. We acquire first novelists. Before submitting, read as many current titles in the imprint or line of your choice as you can. It's very important to know the genre, what readers are looking for, and the series or imprint most appropriate for your submission."

HARPERCOLLINS CANADA, LTD.

2 Bloor St. E., 20th Floor, Toronto ON M4W 1A8 Canada. (416)975-9334. Fax: (416)975-5223. Web site: www.harpercollins.ca. Estab. 1989.

Imprints HarperCollinsPublishers; HarperPerennialCanada (trade paperbacks); HarperTrophyCanada (children's); Phyllis Bruce Books.

- HarperCollins Canada is not accepting unsolicited material at this time.

Recent Title(s) *Hope Diamond*, by Richard Kurin; *Madame Zee*, by Pearl Luke; *Real Life Entertaining*, by Jennifer Rubell.

Canadian Publishers

HERITAGE HOUSE PUBLISHING CO., LTD.

#6 356 Simcoe St., Victoria BC V8V 1L1 Canada. Phone/Fax: (250)360-0829. E-mail: publisher@heritagehouse.ca. Web site: www.heritagehouse.ca. **Acquisitions:** Rodger Touchie, publisher/president. Publishes trade paperback originals. **Publishes 10-12 titles/year. Receives 200 queries and 60 mss/year. 50% of books from first-time authors; 100% from unagented writers. Pays 9% royalty. Offers advance.** Publishes book 1 year after acceptance of ms. Does not accept simultaneous submissions. Responds in 2 months to queries. Book catalog for #10 SASE; ms guidelines online.

> Heritage House is primarily a regional publisher of Western Canadiana and the Pacific Northwest. "We aim to publish and distribute good books that entertain and educate our readership regarding both historic and contemporary Western Canada and the Pacific Northwest."

Nonfiction Biography, how-to, illustrated book. Subjects include animals, anthropology/archeology, cooking/foods/nutrition, history, nature/environment, recreation, regional, sports. Writers should include a sample of their writing, an overview sample of photos or illustrations to support the text, and a brief letter describing who they are writing for. Query with SASE, or submit outline, 2-3 sample chapters. Reviews artwork/photos as part of ms package. Send photocopies.

Fiction Children's books. Very limited—only author/illustrator collaboration.

Recent Title(s) *Simply the Best: Insights and Strategies From Great Hockey Coaches*, by Mike Johnson and Ryan Walters; *Fortress of the Grizzlies: The Khutzeymateen Grizzly Bear Sanctuary*, by Dan Wakeman and Wendy Shymanski; *Mountie Makers: Putting the Canadian in RCMP*, by Bob Teather.

Tips "Our books appeal to residents and visitors to the northwest quadrant of the continent. Present your material only after you have done your best."

HOUSE OF ANANSI PRESS

110 Spadina Ave., Suite 801, Toronto ON M5V 2K4 Canada. Fax: (416)363-1017. Web site: www.anansi.ca. **Acquisitions:** Lynn Henry, publisher. Estab. 1967. Publishes hardcover and trade paperback originals and paperback reprints. **Publishes 10-15 titles/year. Receives 750 queries/year. 5% of books from first-time authors; 50% from unagented writers. Pays 8-15% royalty on retail price. Offers $500-2,000 advance.** Publishes book 18 months after acceptance of ms. Accepts simultaneous submissions. Responds in 2 months to queries; 3 months to proposals; 4 months to mss. Book catalog free; ms guidelines online.

> "Our mission is to publish the best new literary writers in Canada and to continue to grow and adapt along with the Canadian literary community while maintaining Anansi's rich history."

Nonfiction Biography. Subjects include anthropology/archeology, gay/lesbian, government/politics, history, language/literature, philosophy, science, sociology, women's issues/studies. "Our nonfiction list is literary, but not overly academic. Some writers submit academic work better suited for university presses or pop-psychology books, which we do not publish." Query with SASE, or submit outline, 2 sample chapters. Reviews artwork/photos as part of ms package. Send photocopies.

Fiction Ethnic (general), experimental, feminist, gay/lesbian, literary, short story collections. "We publish literary fiction by Canadian authors. Authors must have been published in established literary magazines and/or journals. We only want to consider sample chapters." Query with SASE, or submit outline, synopsis, 2 sample chapters.

Poetry "We only publish book-length works by Canadian authors. Poets must have a substantial résumé of published poems in literary magazines or journals. We only want samples from a manuscript." Submit 10-15 sample poems.

Recent Title(s) *Alligator*, by Lisa Moore; *Moving Targets*, by Margaret Atwood; *A Short History of Progress*, by Ronald Wright.

Tips "Submit often to magazines and journals. Read and buy other writers' work. Know and be a part of your writing community."

INSOMNIAC PRESS

192 Spadina Ave., Suite 403, Toronto ON M5T 2C2 Canada. (416)504-6270. Fax: (416)504-9313. E-mail: mike@insomniacpress.com. Web site: www.insomniacpress.com. **Acquisitions:** Mike O'Connor, publisher. Estab. 1992. Publishes trade paperback originals and reprints, mass market paperback originals, and electronic originals and reprints. **Publishes 20 titles/year. Receives 250 queries and 1,000 mss/year. 50% of books from first-time authors; 80% from unagented writers. Pays 10-15% royalty on retail price. Offers $500-1,000 advance.** Publishes book 6 months after acceptance of ms. Accepts simultaneous submissions. Responds in 1 week to queries; 2 months to proposals; 2 months to mss. Ms guidelines online.

Nonfiction Gift book, humor, self-help. Subjects include business/economics, creative nonfiction, gay/lesbian, government/politics, health/medicine, language/literature, money/finance, multicultural, religion, true crime. Very interested in areas such as true crime and well-written and well-researched nonfiction on topics of wide interest. Query via e-mail, submit proposal package including outline, 2 sample chapters, or submit complete ms. Reviews artwork/photos as part of ms package. Send photocopies.

Fiction Comic books, ethnic, experimental, gay/lesbian, humor, literary, mainstream/contemporary, multicultural, mystery, poetry, suspense. We publish a mix of commercial (mysteries) and literary fiction. Query via e-mail, submit proposal package including synopsis or submit complete ms.

Poetry "Our poetry publishing is limited to 2-4 books per year and we are often booked up a year or two in advance." Submit complete ms.

Recent Title(s) *Belong*, by Jennifer Morton; *Certifiable*, by David McGimpsey; *Creating Love*, by Samantha Stevens.

Tips "We envision a mixed readership that appreciates up-and-coming literary fiction and poetry as well as solidly researched and provocative nonfiction. Peruse our Web site and familiarize yourself with what we've published in the past."

INSTITUTE OF PSYCHOLOGICAL RESEARCH, INC.

34 Fleury St. W., Montréal QC H3L 1S9 Canada. (514)382-3000. Fax: (514)382-3007. **Acquisitions:** Robert Chevrier, advisor. Estab. 1958. Publishes hardcover and trade paperback originals and reprints. **Publishes 12 titles/year. 10% of books from first-time authors; 100% from unagented writers. Pays 10-12% royalty.** Publishes book 6 months after acceptance of ms. Responds in 2 months to queries.

Institute of Psychological Research publishes psychological tests and science textbooks for a varied professional audience.

Nonfiction Textbook. Subjects include philosophy, psychology, science, translation. "We are looking for psychological tests in French or English." Query with SASE, or submit complete ms.

Recent Title(s) *Épreuve individuelle d'habileté mentale*, by Jean-Marc Chevrier (intelligence test).

Tips "Psychologists, guidance counselors, professionals, schools, school boards, hospitals, teachers, government agencies and industries comprise our audience."

KEY PORTER BOOKS

6 Adelaide St. E, 10th Floor, Toronto ON M5C 1H6 Canada. (416)862-7777. Fax: (416)862-2304. E-mail: info@keyporter.com. Web site: www.keyporter.com. **Acquisitions:** Jordan Fenn, publisher. Estab. 1979. Publishes hardcover and trade paperback originals and reprints. **Publishes 100 titles/year. Receives 1,000 queries and 500 mss/year. Pays royalty.** Accepts simultaneous submissions. Responds in 4 months to queries; 6 months to proposals; 6 months to mss.

Imprints Key Porter Kids; L&OD.

Key Porter specializes in autobiography, biography, children's, cookbook, gift book, how-to, humor, illustrated book, self-help, young adult. Subjects include art, architecture, business, economics, parenting, food, creative nonfiction, gardening, general nonfiction, politics, health, history, humanities, memoirs, military, personal finance, nature, environment, photography, psychology, science, social sciences, sociology, sports, translation, travel, women's issues, world affairs, and literary fiction. Query with SASE. Reviews artwork/photos as part of ms package. Send photocopies.

KUNATI INC.

2600 Skymark Ave., Building 12, Suite 103, Mississauga ON L4W 5B2 Canada. Fax: (905)625-8987. E-mail: info@kunati.com. Submissions E-mail: query@kunati.com. Web site: www.kunati.com. **Acquisitions:** James McKinnon, editor-in-chief (all commercial categories, edgy fiction, literary fiction, memoir, humor); Derek Armstrong, publisher (thrillers, mystery, suspense, non-slasher horror, historical epic, fantasy epic, science fiction, true crime). Alternate Address: 6901 Bryan Dairy Rd., Suite 150, Largo FL 33777. Estab. 2005. Publishes hardcover originals and trade paperbacks. **Publishes 26 titles/year. Receives 1,200 queries and 450 mss/year. 80% of books from first-time authors; 75% from unagented writers. Pays 10-15% royalty.** Publishes book 8 months after acceptance of ms. Accepts simultaneous submissions. Responds in 1 month to queries; 2-3 months to proposals; 2 months to mss. You can get a catalog and ms guidelines online, for #10 SASE, or via e-mail.

"Unless you have an absolutely stunning voice, your best opportunity to make us sit up and pay attention is to submit only the most quirky, different, funky, controversial, hiarious, and bizarre material—anything but academic or mainstream. On the other hand, do not bother submitting extremism, quackery, or memoirs without truth. There's a fine line between fun and silly; either entertain to the extreme or present new ideas."

Nonfiction How-to, humor, self-help. Subjects include creative nonfiction, gardening, health/medicine, memoirs, money/finance, multicultural, nature/environment, New Age, philosophy, psychology, religion, science, sex, social sciences, sociology, spirituality, sports, women's issues/studies, world affairs. Query with outline, 3 sample chapters, SASE via mail or e-mail. Reviews artwork/photos as part of ms package. Send photocopies.

Fiction Adventure, confession, erotica, ethnic, experimental, fantasy, gay/lesbian, gothic, historical, horror, humor, juvenile, literary, mainstream/contemporary, multicultural, mystery, occult, science fiction, sports, suspense, young adult. "We don't pay attention to category or genre. If it's edgy, we're interested." Query with short synopsis (that discloses the story's outcome), 3 sample chapters, SASE via mail or e-mail.

Recent Title(s) *Toonamint of Champions*, by Todd Sentell; *Rabid*, by T.K. Kenyon; *Whale Song*, by Cheryl Kaye Tardiff.

Tips "Our books cover all audiences. Our only requirement is literary quality of writing; therefore, our focus is on the thoughtful and hopeless hip, or the educated and ceaselessly cynical. Your query letter and synopsis should be your best writing ever."

LEXISNEXIS CANADA, INC.

123 Commerce Valley Dr. E., Suite 700, Markham ON L3T 7W8 Canada. (905)479-2665. Fax: (905)479-2826. E-mail: info@lexisnexis.ca. Web site: www.lexisnexis.ca. **Acquisitions:** Product Development Director. **Publishes 100 titles/year. 50% of books from first-time authors; 100% from unagented writers. Pays 5-15% royalty on wholesale price.** Publishes book 4 months after acceptance of ms. Accepts simultaneous submissions. Responds in 1 month to queries. Book catalog free; ms guidelines online.

- LexisNexis Canada, Inc., publishes professional reference material for the legal, business, and accounting markets under the Butterworths imprint and operates the Quicklaw and LexisNexis online services.

Nonfiction Multimedia (CD-ROM, Quicklaw, and LexisNexis online services), reference (legal and law for business), legal and accounting newspapers.

Recent Title(s) *The Canada-U.S. Tax Treaty Text and Commentary*, by Vern Krishna; *The Public Purchasing Law Handbook*, by Robert C. Worthington; *Corporate Law in Quebec*, by Stephan Rousseau.

Tips Audience is legal community, business, medical, accounting professions.

N LIFETIME BOOKS

Subsidiary of Barclay Road Inc., 5005 Jean Talon, #200, Montreal QC H3S 1G2 Canada. (514)807-5245. Fax: (206)350-5392. E-mail: pub@barclayroad.com. Web site: www.barclayroad.com. **Acquisitions:** Barb Leonard, editor (general). Estab. 1998. Publishes hardcover, trade paperback and electronic originals and reprints. **Publishes 5 titles/year. Pays 3-15% royalty on retail price.** Publishes book 18 months after acceptance of ms. Accepts simultaneous submissions. Responds in 6 months to queries; 8 months to proposals; 8 months to mss. Book catalog online; ms guidelines by e-mail.

Nonfiction Autobiography, biography, booklets, children's/juvenile, cookbook, general nonfiction, how-to, humor, self-help. Subjects include Americana, animals, art/architecture, business/economics, computers/electronic, cooking/foods/nutrition, gardening, health/medicine, history, hobbies, memoirs, military/war, money/finance, New Age, philosophy, photography, science, software, spirituality, sports, translation, women's issues/studies, world affairs, magic. Submit complete ms. Reviews artwork/photos as part of ms package. Send photocopies.

Fiction Adventure, historical, juvenile, military/war, short story collections, sports, western, young adult. Submit complete ms.

Recent Title(s) *Vitamins for the Spirit*, by Robert J. Danzig; *Magic Secrets of David Blaine*, by Herbert Becker.

LONE PINE PUBLISHING

10145 81st Ave., Edmonton AB T6E 1W9 Canada. (403)433-9333. Fax: (403)433-9646. Web site: www.lonepinepublishing.com. **Acquisitions:** Nancy Foulds, editorial director. Estab. 1980. Publishes trade paperback originals and reprints. **Publishes 30-40 titles/year. 75% of books from first-time authors; 95% from unagented writers. Pays royalty.** Does not accept simultaneous submissions. Responds in 3 months to queries. Book catalog free.

Imprints Lone Pine; Home World; Pine Candle; Pine Cone; Ghost House Books.

- Lone Pine publishes natural history and outdoor recreation—including gardening—titles and some popular history and ghost story collections by region. "'The World Outside Your Door' is our motto—helping people appreciate nature and their own special place." Currently emphasizing ghost stories by region and gardening by region.

Nonfiction Subjects include animals, gardening, nature/environment, recreation, regional. The list is set for the next year and a half, but we are interested in seeing new material. Query with SASE, or submit outline, sample chapter(s). Reviews artwork/photos as part of ms package.

Recent Title(s) *Birds of New York State*, by Bob Budliger and Gregory Kennedy; *Best Garden Plants for Montana*, by Dr. Bob Gough, Cheryl Moore-Gough and Laura Peters; *Ghost Stories of North Carolina*, by Edrick Thay.

Tips "Writers have their best chance with recreational or nature guidebooks. Most of our books are strongly regional in nature."

MCCLELLAND & STEWART, LTD.

The Canadian Publishers, 75 Sherbourne St., Toronto ON M5A 2P9 Canada. (416)598-1114. Fax: (416)598-7764. E-mail: editorial@mcclelland.com. Web site: www.mcclelland.com. Publishes hardcover, trade paperback, and mass market paperback originals and reprints. **Publishes 80 titles/year. Receives 1,500 queries/year. 10% of books from first-time authors; 30% from unagented writers. Pays 10-15% royalty on retail price (hardcover rates). Offers advance.** Publishes book 1 year after acceptance of ms. Responds in 3 months to proposals.

Imprints McClelland & Stewart; New Canadian Library; Douglas Gibson Books; Emblem Editions (Ellen Seligman, editor).

Nonfiction "We publish books primarily by Canadian authors." Subjects include art/architecture, business/economics, gay/lesbian, government/politics, health/medicine, history, language/literature, military/war, music/dance, nature/environment, philosophy, photography, psychology, recreation, religion, science, sociology, sports, translation, travel, women's issues/studies, Canadiana. Submit outline. *All unsolicited mss returned unopened.*

Fiction Literary novels (some short story collections, including novels with a historical setting) and some crime writing. "We publish work by established authors, as well as the work of new and developing authors." Query. *All unsolicited mss returned unopened.*

Poetry "Only Canadian poets should apply. We publish only 4 titles each year." Query. *No unsolicted mss.*

Recent Title(s) *Runaway*, by Alice Munro; *Norman Bray in the Performance of His Life*, by Trevor Cole; *The Mysteries*, by Robert McGill.

MIRA BOOKS

Imprint of Harlequin, 225 Duncan Mill Rd., Don Mills ON M3B 3K9 Canada. Web site: www.mirabooks.com. Publishes hardcover, trade paperback, and mass market originals. **Pays royalty. Offers advance.**

Fiction Relationship novels; political, psychological and legal thrillers; family sagas; commercial literary fiction. *Agented submissions only.*

Recent Title(s) *Killing Kelly*, by Heather Graham; *Me & Emma*, by Elizabeth Flock; *Criminal Intent*, by Laurie Breton.

MUSSIO VENTURES PUBLISHING LTD.

5811 Beresford St., Burnaby BC V5J1K1 Canada. (604)438-3474. Fax: (604)438-3470. Web site: www.backroadmapbooks.com. Estab. 1993. **Publishes 5 titles/year. Receives 5 queries and 2 mss/year. 25% of books from first-time authors; 0% from unagented writers. Makes outright purchase of $2,000-4,800. Offers $1,000 advance.** Publishes book 12 months after acceptance of ms. Accepts simultaneous submissions. Responds in 1 month to queries; 1 month to proposals; 1 month to mss. Book catalog free.

Nonfiction Map and Guide books. Subjects include nature/environment, maps and guides. Submit proposal package including outline/proposal, 1 sample chapter. Reviews artwork/photos as part of ms package. Send photocopies or Digital files.

Recent Title(s) *Nova Scotia Backroad Mapbook*, by Linda Akosmitis; *Northern BC Backroad Mapbook*, by Trent Ernst.

Tips "Audience includes outdoor recreation enthusiasts and travellers. Provide a proposal including an outline and samples."

NAPOLEON PUBLISHING/RENDEZVOUS PRESS

178 Willowdale Ave., Suite 201, Toronto ON M2N 4Y8 Canada. (416)730-9052. Fax: (416)730-8096. Web site: www.rendezvouspress.com. **Acquisitions:** A. Thompson, editor. Estab. 1990. Publishes hardcover and trade paperback originals and reprints. **Publishes 12 titles/year; imprint publishes 6 titles/year. Receives 200 queries and 100 mss/year. 50% of books from first-time authors; 80% from unagented writers.** Publishes book 18 months after acceptance of ms. Accepts simultaneous submissions. Responds in 1 month to queries; 3 months to proposals; 6 months to mss. Book catalog and ms guidelines online.

- Napoleon is not accepting children's novels, biographies or picture book mss at this time. Rendezvous is not accepting mysteries. Check Web site for updates.

O→ Rendezvous publishes adult fiction. Napoleon publishes children's books.

Nonfiction Query with SASE, or submit outline, 1 sample chapter(s).

Recent Title(s) *Death in the Age of Steam*, by Mel Bradshaw; *The Dead Don't Get Out Much*, by M.J. Maffini; *The Fragrant Garden*, by Day's Lee.

Tips "Canadian resident authors only."

NATURAL HERITAGE/NATURAL HISTORY, INC.

P.O. Box 95, Station O, Toronto ON M4A 2M8 Canada. (416)694-7907. Fax: (416)690-0819. E-mail: info@naturalheritagebooks.com. Submissions E-mail: submissions@naturalheritagebooks.com. Web site: www.naturalheri-

tagebooks.com. **Acquisitions:** Barry Penhale, publisher. Publishes trade paperback originals. **Publishes 10-12 titles/year. 50% of books from first-time authors; 85% from unagented writers. Pays 8-10% royalty on retail price.** Publishes book 2-3 years after acceptance of ms. Accepts simultaneous submissions. Responds in 4 months to queries; 6 months to proposals; 6 months to mss. Book catalog free; ms guidelines online.
Imprints Natural Heritage Books.

O→ Currently emphasizing heritage, history, nature.

Nonfiction Subjects include ethnic, history, nature/environment, recreation, regional. Submit outline.
Fiction Children's (age 8-12), biography/memoir. Query with SASE.
Recent Title(s) *Canoeing a Continent: On the Trail of Alexander Mackenzie*, by Max Finkelstein (nonfiction); *Algonquin Wildlife: Lessons in Survival*, by Norm Quinn (nonfiction); *The Underground Railroad: Next Stop, Toronto!*, by Adrienne Shadd, Afua Cooper, and Karolyn Smardz Frost (young adult nonfiction).
Tips "We are a Canadian publisher in the natural heritage and history fields. We publish only Canadian authors or books with significant Canadian content."

NEW SOCIETY PUBLISHERS

P.O. Box 189, Gabriola Island BC V0R 1X0 Canada. (250)247-9737. Fax: (250)247-7471. E-mail: info@newsociety.com. Web site: www.newsociety.com. **Acquisitions:** Chris Plant, editor. Publishes trade paperback originals and reprints and electronic originals. **Publishes 25 titles/year. Receives 300 queries and 200 mss/year. 50% of books from first-time authors; 80% from unagented writers. Pays 10-12% royalty on wholesale price. Offers $0-5,000 advance.** Publishes book 9 months after acceptance of ms. Accepts simultaneous submissions. Responds in 1 month to queries; 2 months to proposals. Book catalog free or online; ms guidelines online.
Nonfiction Biography, how-to, illustrated book, self-help. Subjects include business/economics, child guidance/parenting, creative nonfiction, education, government/politics, memoirs, nature/environment, philosophy, regional, sustainability, open building. Query with SASE, or submit proposal package including outline, 2 sample chapters. Reviews artwork/photos as part of ms package. Send photocopies.
Recent Title(s) *The Party's Over: Oil, War & the Fate of Industrial Societies*, by Richard Heinberg (current affairs).
Tips Audience is activists, academics, progressive business people, managers. "Don't get an agent!"

NEWEST PUBLISHERS LTD.

201, 8540-109 St., Edmonton AB T6G 1E6 Canada. (780)432-9427. Fax: (780)433-3179. E-mail: info@newestpress.com. Web site: www.newestpress.com. **Acquisitions:** Amber Rider, general manager. Estab. 1977. Publishes trade paperback originals. **Publishes 13-16 titles/year. 40% of books from first-time authors; 85% from unagented writers. Pays 10% royalty.** Publishes book 2-3 years after acceptance of ms. Accepts simultaneous submissions. Responds in 6-8 months to queries. Book catalog for 9×12 SASE; ms guidelines online.

O→ NeWest publishes Western Canadian fiction, nonfiction, poetry, and drama.

Nonfiction Literary/essays (Western Canadian authors, Western Canadian and Northern themes). Subjects include ethnic, government/politics, history (Western Canada), nature/environment (northern), Canadiana. Query.
Fiction Literary. "Our press is interested in Western Canadian writing." Submit complete ms.
Recent Title(s) *Big Rig 2*, by Don McTavish (nonfiction); *The Far Away Home*, by Marci Densiule (short fiction); *Always Someone to Kill the Doves*, by Fred Flahiff (nonfiction).

NOVALIS

Bayard Presse Canada, 10 Lower Spadina Ave., Suite 400, Toronto ON M5V 2Z2 Canada. (416)363-3303. Fax: (416)363-9409. E-mail: cservice@novalis.ca. Web site: www.novalis.ca. **Acquisitions:** Kevin Burns, commissioning editor; Michael O'Hearn, publisher; Anne Louise Mahoney, managing editor. Editorial offices: Novalis, St. Paul University, 223 Main St., Ottawa ON, K1S 1C4, Canada. Phone: (613)782-3039. Fax: (613)751-4020. E-mail: kburns@ustpaul.ca. Publishes hardcover and trade paperback originals and trade paperback reprints. **Publishes 40 titles/year. 20% of books from first-time authors. Pays 10-15% royalty on wholesale price. Offers $300-2,000 advance.** Publishes book 12-18 months after acceptance of ms. Responds in 2 months to queries; 1 month to proposals; 3 months to mss. Book catalog for free or online; ms guidelines free.

O→ "Novalis publishes books about faith, religion, and spirituality in their broadest sense. Based in the Catholic tradition, our interest is strongly ecumenical. Regardless of their denominational perspective, our books speak to the heart, mind, and spirit of people seeking to deepen their faith and understanding."

Nonfiction Biography, children's/juvenile, gift book, humor, illustrated book, reference, self-help. Subjects include child guidance/parenting, education (Christian or Catholic), memoirs, multicultural, nature/environment, philosophy, religion, spirituality. Query with SASE.

Recent Title(s) *Restless Churches*, by Reginald W. Bibby; *Drawn to the Mystery of Jesus Through the Gospel of John*, by Jean Vanier; *At the Edge of Our Longing*, by James Conlon.

ORCA BOOK PUBLISHERS

P.O. Box 5626, Stn. B, Victoria BC V8R 6S4 Canada. Fax: (877)408-1551. E-mail: orca@orcabook.com. Web site: www.orcabook.com. **Acquisitions:** Maggie DeVries, editor (picture books, young readers); Andrew Wooldridge, editor (juvenile fiction, teen fiction); Bob Tyrrell, publisher (YA, teen). Estab. 1984. Publishes hardcover and trade paperback originals, and mass market paperback originals and reprints. **Publishes 30 titles/year. Receives 2,500 queries and 1,000 mss/year. 20% of books from first-time authors; 75% from unagented writers. Pays 10% royalty.** Publishes book 12-18 months after acceptance of ms. Does not accept simultaneous submissions. Responds in 1 month to queries; 1 month to proposals; 1-2 months to mss. Book catalog for $8\frac{1}{2} \times 11$ SASE; ms guidelines online.

- Only publishes Canadian authors.

Nonfiction Subjects include multicultural, picture books. Query with SASE.

Fiction Hi-lo, juvenile (5-9 years), literary, mainstream/contemporary, young adult (10-18 years). "Ask for guidelines, find out what we publish." Looking for childrens fiction. No romance, science fiction. Query with SASE, or submit proposal package including outline, synopsis, 2-5 sample chapters, SASE.

Recent Title(s) *Before Wings*, by Beth Goobie (teen fiction); *No Two Snowflakes*, by Sheree Fitch (picture book).

Tips "Our audience is for students in grades K-12. Know our books, and know the market."

PEMMICAN PUBLICATIONS, INC.

150 Henry Ave., Winnipeg MB R3B 0J7 Canada. (204)589-6346. Fax: (204)589-2063. Web site: www.pemmican.mb.ca. **Acquisitions:** Rihiannen Margarita, managing editor (First Nations, Metis, and Inuit culture and heritage. Estab. 1980. Publishes trade paperback originals and reprints, and electronic reprints. **Publishes 7-10 titles/year. Receives 120 queries and 120 mss/year. 50% of books from first-time authors; 100% from unagented writers. Pays 10% royalty on retail price.** Publishes book 1-2 years after acceptance of ms. Accepts simultaneous submissions. Responds in 1 month to queries; 1 month to proposals; 1 year to mss. Book catalog and ms guidelines free.

Nonfiction Autobiography, biography, children's/juvenile, coffee table book, general nonfiction, illustrated book, reference, scholarly. Subjects include alternative lifestyles, creative nonfiction, education, ethnic, government/politics, history, language/literature, military/war, nature/environment, spirituality. "All of our books are culture and heritage related (Aboriginal), Metis, First Nations, or Inuit. Submit proposal package including outline and 3 sample chapters, or submit complete ms. Reviews artwork/photos as part of ms package. Send photocopies.

Fiction Adventure, ethnic, fantasy, historical, juvenile, literary, military/war, multicultural, mystery, picture books, short story collections, spiritual, sports, suspense, western, young adult. "All manuscripts must be culture and heritage related." Submit proposal package including 3 sample chapters, or submit complete ms.

Poetry "Must be a Metis, First Nations, or Inuit author." Submit 10 sample poems, or submit complete ms.

Recent Title(s) *My Children Are My Reward*, by Alex Harpelle (biography); *The Tobanz*, by Edgar Desjarlais (young adult sports); *The Dream Catcher Pool*, by Jane Chartrand (children's fiction).

Tips Audience is anyone who has an interest in Metis, First Nations, and Inuit culture. No agent is necessary.

PLAYWRIGHTS CANADA PRESS

215 Spadina Ave., Suite 230, Toronto ON M5T 2C7 Canada. (416)703-0013. Fax: (416)408-3402. Web site: www.playwrightscanada.com. **Acquisitions:** Annie Gibson. Estab. 1984. Publishes paperback originals and reprints of plays. **50% of books from first-time authors; 50% from unagented writers. Pays 10% royalty on retail price.** Publishes book 6 months-1 year after acceptance of ms. Responds in 2-3 months to queries. Ms guidelines online.

- Playwrights Canada Press only publishes drama by Canadian citizens or landed immigrants that has been professionally produced. Submit complete ms.

Recent Title(s) *An Anglophone Is Coming to Dinner*, by George Rideout; *Bella Donna*, by David Copelin; *Cold Meat Party*, by Brad Fraser.

PRODUCTIVE PUBLICATIONS

P.O. Box 7200 Station A, Toronto ON M5W 1X8 Canada. (416)483-0634. Fax: (416)322-7434. **Acquisitions:** Iain Williamson, owner. Estab. 1985. Publishes trade paperback originals. **Publishes 24 titles/year. Receives 160 queries and 40 mss/year. 80% of books from first-time authors; 100% from unagented writers. Pays 10% royalty on wholesale price.** Publishes book 6 months after acceptance of ms. Accepts simultaneous submissions. Responds in 1 month to queries; 1 month to proposals; 3 months to mss. Book catalog free.

O→ "Productive Publications publishes books to help readers succeed and to help them meet the challenges of the new information age and global marketplace." Interested in books on business, computer software, the Internet for business purposes, investment, stock market and mutual funds, etc. Currently emphasizing computers, software, small business, business management, entrepreneurship. De-emphasizing jobs, how to get employment.

Nonfiction How-to, reference, self-help, technical. Subjects include business/economics (small business and management), computers/electronic, money/finance, software (business). "We are interested in small business/entrepreneurship/self-help (business)—100-300 pages." Submit outline. Reviews artwork/photos as part of ms package. Send photocopies.

Recent Title(s) *How to Deliver Excellent Customer Service: A Step-by-Step Guide for Every Business*, by Julie Olley; *Market Your Professional Service*, by Jerome Shure.

Tips "We are looking for books written by knowledgeable, experienced experts who can express their ideas clearly and simply."

RAINCOAST BOOK DISTRIBUTION, LTD.

9050 Shaughnessy St., Vancouver BC V6P 6E5 Canada. (604)323-7128. Fax: (604)323-2600. E-mail: info@raincoast.com. Web site: raincoast.com. Publisher: Michelle Benjamin. Publishes hardcover and trade paperback originals and reprints. **Publishes 60 titles/year. Receives 3,000 queries/year. 10% of books from first-time authors; 40% from unagented writers. Pays 8-12% royalty on retail price. Offers $1,000-6,000 advance.** Publishes book within 2 years after acceptance of ms. Book catalog for #10 SASE.

Imprints Raincoast Books; Polestar Books (fiction, poetry, literary nonfiction).

Nonfiction Children's/juvenile, coffee table book, gift book. Subjects include animals, art/architecture, ethnic, history, nature/environment, photography, recreation, regional, sports, travel. *No unsolicited mss.* Query with SASE.

Fiction Literary, short story collections, young adult. *No unsolicited mss.*

Recent Title(s) *Redress*, by Roy Miki; *Black*, by George Elliott Clarke; *A War Against Truth*, by Paul William Roberts.

ROCKY MOUNTAIN BOOKS

406-13th Ave. NE, Calgary AB T2E 1C2 Canada. (403)249-9490. Fax: (403)249-2968. E-mail: rmb@heritagehouse.ca. Web site: www.rmbooks.com. **Acquisitions:** Fraser Seely, publisher. Publishes trade paperback originals. **Publishes 15 titles/year. Receives 30 queries/year. 75% of books from first-time authors; 100% from unagented writers. Pays 12-17% royalty on net receipts. Rarely offers advance.** Publishes book 1 year after acceptance of ms. Accepts simultaneous submissions. Responds in 2 months to queries. Book catalog and ms guidelines free.

O→ Rocky Mountain Books publishes books on outdoor recreation, mountains, and mountaineering in Western Canada.

Nonfiction Biography, how-to. Subjects include nature/environment, recreation, regional, travel. "Our main area of publishing is outdoor recreation guides to Western and Northern Canada." Query with SASE.

Recent Title(s) *Caves of the Canadian Rockies and Columbia Mountains*, by Jon Rollins; *Exploring Prince George*, by Mike Nash.

RONSDALE PRESS

3350 W. 21st Ave., Vancouver BC V6S 1G7 Canada. (604)738-4688. Fax: (604)731-4548. Web site: www.ronsdalepress.com. **Acquisitions:** Ronald B. Hatch, director (fiction, poetry, social commentary); Veronica Hatch, managing director (children's literature). Estab. 1988. Publishes trade paperback originals. **Publishes 10 titles/year. Receives 300 queries and 800 mss/year. 60% of books from first-time authors; 95% from unagented writers. Pays 10% royalty on retail price.** Publishes book 6 months after acceptance of ms. Accepts simultaneous submissions. Responds in 2 weeks to queries; 1 month to proposals; 3 months to mss. Book catalog for #10 SASE; ms guidelines online.

O→ Canadian authors only. Ronsdale publishes fiction, poetry, regional history, biography and autobiography, books of ideas about Canada, as well as young adult historical fiction.

Nonfiction Biography, children's/juvenile. Subjects include history (Canadian), language/literature, nature/environment, regional.

Fiction Literary, short story collections, novels. *Canadian authors only.* Query with at least the first 80 pages. Short story collections must have some previous magazine publication.

Poetry "Poets should have published some poems in magazines/journals and should be well-read in contemporary masters." Submit complete ms.

Recent Title(s) *Red Goodwin*, by John Wilson (YA historical fiction); *When Eagles Call*, by Susan Dobbie (novel).

Tips "Ronsdale Press is a literary publishing house, based in Vancouver, and dedicated to publishing books from across Canada, books that give Canadians new insights into themselves and their country. We aim to publish the best Canadian writers."

SCHOLASTIC CANADA, LTD.

604 King St. W., Toronto ON M5V 1E1 Canada. (416)915-3500. Fax: (416)849-7912. Web site: www.scholastic.ca. Publishes hardcover and trade paperback originals. **Publishes 40 titles/year; imprint publishes 4 titles/year. 3% of books from first-time authors; 50% from unagented writers. Pays 5-10% royalty on retail price. Offers $1,000-5,000 (Canadian) advance.** Publishes book 1 year after acceptance of ms. Does not accept simultaneous submissions. Responds in 3 months to queries; 6 months to proposals. Book catalog for $8\frac{1}{2} \times 11$ SAE with 2 first-class stamps (IRC or Canadian stamps only).

Imprints North Winds Press; Les Editions Scholastic.

- Scholastic publishes books by Canadians and/or about Canada. Currently emphasizing Canadian interest, middle-grade fiction.

Nonfiction Biography, children's/juvenile. Subjects include history, hobbies, nature/environment, recreation, science, sports. *Agented submissions only. No unsolicited mss.*

Fiction Juvenile (middle grade), young adult. *No unsolicited mss. Agented submissions only.* Canadian authors only.

Recent Title(s) *Dear Canada: No Safe Harbour*, by Julie Lawson; *Terry Fox: A Story of Hope*, by Maxine Trottier; *Moon and Star*, by Robin Muller.

J. GORDON SHILLINGFORD PUBLISHING INC.

P.O. Box 86, RPO Corydon Ave., Winnipeg MB R3M 3S3 Canada. Phone/Fax: (204)779-6967. E-mail: jgshill@allstream.net. Web site: www.jgshillingford.com. **Acquisitions:** Catherine Hunter, poetry editor; Glenda MacFarlone, drama editor. Estab. 1993. Publishes trade paperback originals. **Publishes 14 titles/year. Receives 100 queries and 50 mss/year. 15% of books from first-time authors; 60% from unagented writers. Pays 10% royalty on retail price.** Accepts simultaneous submissions. Responds in 3-6 months to queries. Book catalog and ms guidelines online.

Imprints Scirozzo Drama (theater); The Muses Company (poetry); Watson & Dwyer Publishing (Canadian social history); J. Gordon Shillingford (politics, religion, true crime, biography).

Nonfiction Biography, general nonfiction, humor. Subjects include government/politics, religion, true crime, social history. Query with CV, 20-page sample, SASE.

Fiction Plays (professionally produced), poetry (by published poets). Query with CV, 20-page sample, SASE.

Recent Title(s) *Molly's Veil*, by Sharon Bajer; *Unfamiliar Weather*, by Chris Hutchinson; *Eating the Wedding Gifts: Lean Years After Marriage Break-Up*, by Barbara Murphy.

THOMPSON EDUCATIONAL PUBLISHING, INC.

6 Ripley Ave., Suite 200, Toronto ON M6S 3N9 Canada. (416)766-2763. Fax: (416)766-0398. E-mail: publisher@thompsonbooks.com. Web site: www.thompsonbooks.com. **Acquisitions:** Keith Thompson, president. **Publishes 10 titles/year. Receives 15 queries and 10 mss/year. 80% of books from first-time authors; 100% from unagented writers. Pays 10% royalty on net receipts.** Publishes book 1 year after acceptance of ms. Does not accept simultaneous submissions. Responds in 1 month to queries. Book catalog free; ms guidelines online.

- Thompson Educational specializes in high-quality educational texts in the social sciences and humanities.

Nonfiction Textbook. Subjects include business/economics, education, ethnic, government/politics, multicultural, sociology, sports, women's issues/studies. Submit outline, résumé, 1 sample chapter.

Recent Title(s) *Social Work: A Critical Turn*, edited by Steven Hick, Jan Foot and Richard Pozzuto.

TURNSTONE PRESS

607-100 Arthur St., Winnipeg MB R3B 1H3 Canada. (204)947-1555. Fax: (204)942-1555. E-mail: info@ravenstonebooks.com. Web site: www.ravenstonebooks.com. **Acquisitions:** Todd Besant, managing editor; Sharon Caseburg, acquisitions editor. Estab. 1976. Publishes trade paperback originals, mass market for literary mystery imprint. **Publishes 10-12 titles/year. Receives 800 mss/year. 25% of books from first-time authors; 75% from unagented writers. Pays 10% royalty on retail price and 10 author's copies. Offers advance.** Publishes book 18 months-2 years after acceptance of ms. Does not accept simultaneous submissions. Responds in 4 months to queries. Book catalog for #10 SASE; ms guidelines online.

Imprints Ravenstone (literary mystery fiction).

- Turnstone Press is a literary press that publishes Canadian writers with an emphasis on writers from, and writing on, the Canadian West. Currently emphasizing novels, nonfiction travel, adventure travel, poetry. Does not consider formula or mainstream work.

Nonfiction Subjects include travel, adventure travel, cultural/social issues, Canadian literary criticism. Query with SASE, literary cv, and 50-page sample.
Fiction Literary, regional (Western Canada), short story collections, contemporary, novels. *Canadian authors only*. Query with SASE, literary cv, and 50-page sample.
Poetry Submit complete ms.
Recent Title(s) *Kornukopia*, by David Annandale (action/thriller); *Leaving Wyoming*, by Brent Robillard (novel); *Loving Gertrude Stein*, by Deborah Schnitzer (poetry).
Tips "Writers are encouraged to view our list and check if submissions are appropriate. Although we publish new authors, we prefer first-time authors to have publishing credits in literary magazines. We would like to see more adventure travel, as well as eclectic novels. We would like to see 'nonformula' writing for the Ravenstone imprint, especially literary thrillers, urban mystery, and noir."

THE UNIVERSITY OF ALBERTA PRESS

Ring House 2, Edmonton AB T6G 2E1 Canada. (780)492-3662. Fax: (780)492-0719. E-mail: michael.luski@ualberta.ca. Web site: www.uap.ualberta.ca. **Acquisitions:** Michael Luski. Estab. 1969. Publishes orginals and reprints. **Publishes 18-25 titles/year. Royalties are negotiated.** Publishes book within 2 years (usually) after acceptance of ms. Does not accept simultaneous submissions. Responds in 3 months to queries. Ms guidelines online.

- "We do not accept unsolicited novels, short story collections, or poetry. Please see our Web site for details."

Nonfiction Biography, scholarly, textbook. Subjects include business/economics, health/medicine, history, language/literature, nature/environment, regional, natural history, social policy. Submit cover letter, word count, CV, 1 sample chapter, TOC.
Recent Title(s) *Mapper of Mountains*, by I.S. Maclaren with Eric Higgs and Gabrielle Zezulka-Mailloux; *Leaving Shadows*, by Lisa Grekul; *Woman Behind the Painter*, edited by Juliet McMaster.

UNIVERSITY OF CALGARY PRESS

2500 University Dr. NW, Calgary AB T2N 1N4 Canada. (403)220-7578. Fax: (403)282-0085. Web site: www.uofcpress.com. **Acquisitions:** Walter Hildebrandt, director. Publishes hardcover and trade paperback originals and reprints. **Publishes up to 30 titles/year.** Publishes book 20 months after acceptance of ms. Does not accept simultaneous submissions. Responds in 1 month to queries; 2 months to proposals; 2 months to mss. Book catalog free; ms guidelines online.
Nonfiction Scholarly. Subjects include art/architecture, philosophy, travel, women's issues/studies, world affairs. Canadian studies, post-modern studies, native studies, history, international relations, artic studies, Africa, Latin American and Caribbean studies, and heritage of the Canadian and American heartland. The UC Press has recently launched the "Beyond Boundaries" series that takes an in-depth look at critical issues in the areas of Canadian defense and strategic studies.
Recent Title(s) *Trade Negotiations in Agriculture*, edited by William Kerr and James Gaistord.

UNIVERSITY OF OTTAWA PRESS

542 King Edward, Ottawa ON K1N 6N5 Canada. (613)562-5246. Fax: (613)562-5247. E-mail: press@uottawa.ca. Web site: www.uopress.uottawa.ca. **Acquisitions:** Eric Nelson, assistant editor. Estab. 1936. **Publishes 25 titles/year. 20% of books from first-time authors; 95% from unagented writers. Pays 5-10% royalty on net receipts.** Publishes book 6-12 months after acceptance of ms. Does not accept simultaneous submissions. Responds in 1 month to queries; 6 months to mss. Book catalog and ms guidelines free.

- The University of Ottawa Press publishes books for scholarly and serious nonfiction audiences. They were the first bilingual university in Canada. Currently emphasizing French in North America, language rights, translation, Canadian studies, criminology, international development, governance. De-emphasizing medieval studies.

Nonfiction Reference, scholarly, textbook. Subjects include education, government/politics, history, philosophy, religion, sociology, translation, women's studies, Canadian literature. Submit outline, sample chapter(s), CV.
Recent Title(s) *Ashore and Afloat: The British Navy and the Halifax Naval Yard Before 1820*, by Julian Gwyn; *Canada's Religions*, by Robert Choquette; *The Diary of Abraham Ulrikab*, edited by Hartmut Lutz.
Tips "No unrevised theses! Envision audience of academic specialists and readers of serious nonfiction."

VÉHICULE PRESS

Box 125, Place du Parc Station, Montreal QC H2X 4A3 Canada. (514)844-6073. Fax: (514)844-7543. Web site: www.vehiculepress.com. **Acquisitions:** Simon Dardick, president/publisher. Estab. 1973. Publishes trade paperback originals by Canadian authors only. **Publishes 15 titles/year. 20% of books from first-time authors;**

95% from unagented writers. Pays 10-15% royalty on retail price. Offers $200-500 advance. Publishes book 1 year after acceptance of ms. Responds in 4 months to queries. Book catalog for 9×12 SAE with IRCs.

Imprints Signal Editions (poetry); Dossier Quebec (history, memoirs); Esplanade Editions (fiction).

- Canadian authors only.

O→ "Montreal's Véhicule Press has published the best of Canadian and Quebec literature—fiction, poetry, essays, translations, and social history."

Nonfiction Autobiography, biography. Subjects include government/politics, history, language/literature, memoirs, regional, sociology. Especially looking for Canadian social history. Query with SASE. Reviews artwork/photos as part of ms package.

Fiction Contact Andrew Steinmetz. Feminist, literary, regional, short story collections. No romance or formula writing. Query with SASE.

Poetry Contact Carmine Starnino with SASE.

Recent Title(s) *Mirabel*, by Pierre Nepreu, translated by Judith Cowan; *Seventeen Tomatoes*, by Jasprect Singh; *The Man Who Killed Houdini*, by Don Bell.

N WEIGL EDUCATIONAL PUBLISHERS, LIMITED

6325 10th St. SE, Calgary AB T2H 2Z9 Canada. (403)233-7747. Fax: (403)233-7769. E-mail: info@weigl.com. Web site: www.weigl.com. **Acquisitions:** Linda Weigl, president/publisher. Publishes hardcover originals and reprints, school library softcover. **Publishes 104 titles/year. 100% from unagented writers. Makes outright purchase.** Responds ASAP to queries. Book catalog free.

O→ Textbook publisher catering to juvenile and young adult audience (K-12).

Nonfiction Children's/juvenile, textbook, library series. Subjects include animals, education, government/politics, history, nature/environment, science. Query with SASE.

Recent Title(s) *Indigenous Peoples*; *Natural Wonders*; *Science Matters*.

WHITECAP BOOKS, LTD.

351 Lynn Ave., North Vancouver BC V7J 2C4 Canada. (604)980-9852. Fax: (604)980-8197. Web site: www.whitecap.ca. Publishes hardcover and trade paperback originals. **Publishes 20 titles/year. Receives 500 queries and 1,000 mss/year. 20% of books from first-time authors; 90% from unagented writers. Pays royalty. Offers negotiated advance.** Publishes book 18 months after acceptance of ms. Accepts simultaneous submissions. Responds in 3 months to proposals.

O→ Whitecap Books publishes a wide range of nonfiction with a Canadian and international focus. Currently emphasizing children's nonfiction, natural history. De-emphasizing children's illustrated fiction.

Nonfiction Children's/juvenile, coffee table book, cookbook. Subjects include animals, cooking/foods/nutrition, gardening, history, nature/environment, recreation, regional, travel. "We require an annotated outline. Writers should take the time to research our list and read the submission guidelines on our Web site. This is especially important for children's writers." Submit outline, 1 sample chapter, SASE. Reviews artwork/photos as part of ms package. Send photocopies.

Recent Title(s) *The Canadian Housewife*, by Rosemary Neering (nonfiction); *Chef at Home*, by Michael Smith (nonfiction); *Eleven Lazy Llamas*, by Diana Bonder (children's illustrated fiction).

Tips "We want well-written, well-researched material that presents a fresh approach to a particular topic."

WORLDWIDE MYSTERY

Division of Harlequin Books, 225 Duncan Mill Rd., Don Mills ON M3B 3K9 Canada. (416)445-5860. Estab. 1979. Publishes paperback reprints.

O→ Publishes reprints only. Do not send original material.

Fiction Mystery (amateur sleuth, cozies, police procedural, private eye).

Recent Title(s) *Crazy Eights*, by Elizabeth Gunn; *Thicker Than Water*, by Rett MacPherson; *Too Late for Angels*, by Mignon F. Ballard.

Canadian Publishers

MARKETS

Small Presses

Small press is a relative term. Compared to the dozen or so conglomerates, the rest of the book publishing world may seem to be comprised of small presses. A number of the publishers listed in the Book Publishers section consider themselves small presses and cultivate the image. For our classification, small presses are those that publish, on average, less than 10 books per year.

The publishing opportunities are slightly more limited with the companies listed here than with those in the Book Publishers section. Not only are they publishing fewer books, but small presses are usually not able to market their books as effectively as larger publishers, and their print runs and royalty arrangements are usually smaller.

However, realistic small press publishers don't try to compete with Penguin Group (USA), Inc., or Random House. Most small press publishers get into book publishing for the love of it, not solely for the profit. Of course, every publisher, small or large, wants successful books, but small press publishers often measure success in different ways.

Many writers actually prefer to work with small presses. Since small publishing houses are usually based on the publisher's commitment to the subject matter, and since they work with far fewer authors than the conglomerates, small press authors and their books usually receive more personal attention than the larger publishers can afford to give them. Promotional dollars at the big houses tend to be siphoned toward a few books each season that they have decided are likely to succeed, leaving hundreds of ''midlist'' books underpromoted. Since small presses only commit to a very small number of books every year, they are vitally interested in the promotion and distribution of each book.

Just because they publish fewer titles than large publishing houses does not mean small press editors have the time to look at complete manuscripts. In fact, the editors with smaller staffs often have even less time for submissions. The procedure for contacting a small press with your book idea is exactly the same as it is for a larger publisher. Send a one-page query with SASE first. If the press is interested in your proposal, be ready to send an outline or synopsis, and/or a sample chapter or two.

For more information on small presses, see *Novel & Short Story Writer's Market* and *Poet's Market* (Writer's Digest Books).

For a list of publishers according to their subjects of interest, see the Nonfiction and Fiction sections of the Book Publishers Subject Index. Information on book publishers listed in the previous edition of *Writer's Market*, but not included in this edition, can be found in the General Index.

A.T. PUBLISHING

23 Lily Lake Rd., Highland NY 12528. (845)691-2021. **Acquisitions:** Anthony Prizzia, publisher (education); John Prizzia, publisher. Estab. 2001. Publishes trade paperback originals. **Publishes 1-3 titles/year. Receives 5-10 queries and 5-10 mss/year. 100% of books from first-time authors; 100% from unagented writers. Pays 15-25% royalty on retail price, or makes outright purchase of $500-2,500. Offers $500-1,000 advance.** Accepts simultaneous submissions. Responds in 1 month to queries; 2 months to proposals; 4 months to mss.

Nonfiction How-to. Subjects include cooking/foods/nutrition, education, recreation, science, sports. Query with SASE, or submit complete ms. Reviews artwork/photos as part of ms package. Send photocopies.

Recent Title(s) *The Portion Principle*, by Kaitlin Lonie; *The Waiter and Waitress's Guide to a Bigger Income*, by Anthony Thomas (how-to); *Why Is the Teacher's Butt So Big?*, by Debra Craig.

Tips Audience is people interested in a variety of topics, general. ''Submit typed manuscript for consideration, including a SASE for return of manuscript.''

ADDICUS BOOKS, INC.

P.O. Box 45327, Omaha NE 68145. (402)330-7493. Web site: www.addicusbooks.com. **Acquisitions:** Acquisitions Editor. Estab. 1994. **Publishes 10 nonfiction titles/year. 90% of books from first-time authors; 95% from unagented writers. Pays royalty as a percentage of net. Offers advance.** Publishes book 9 months after acceptance of ms. Accepts simultaneous submissions. Responds in 1 month to proposals. Ms guidelines online.

O⊸ Addicus Books, Inc. seeks mss with strong national or regional appeal.

Nonfiction Subjects include Americana, business/economics, health/medicine, psychology, regional, true crime, true crime. ''We are expanding our line of consumer health titles.'' Query with SASE. Do not send entire ms unless requested. When querying electronically, send only 1-page e-mail, giving an overview of your book and its market. Please do not send attachments unless invited to do so. Additional submission guidelines online.

Recent Title(s) *Overcoming Metabolic Syndrome*, by Scott Isaacs, MD; *Understanding Your Living Will*, by Fred Mirarchi.

Tips ''We are looking for quick-reference books on health topics. Do some market research to make sure the market is not already flooded with similar books. We're also looking for good true-crime manuscripts, with an interesting story, with twists and turns, behind the crime.''

ALEF DESIGN GROUP

4423 Fruitland Ave., Los Angeles CA 90058. (800)238-6724. Fax: (323)585-0327. Web site: www.alefdesign.com. **Acquisitions:** Jane Golub. Estab. 1990. Publishes hardcover and trade paperback originals. **Publishes 2-5 titles/year. Receives 30 queries and 30 mss/year. 80% of books from first-time authors; 100% from unagented writers. Pays 10% royalty.** Publishes book 3 years after acceptance of ms. Does not accept simultaneous submissions. Responds in 6 months to mss. Ms guidelines for 9×12 SAE with 10 first-class stamps.

O⊸ The Alef Design Group publishes books of *Judaic interest only*.

Nonfiction Children's/juvenile, textbook. Subjects include language/literature (Hebrew), religion (Jewish). Query with SASE. Reviews artwork/photos as part of ms package. Send photocopies.

Fiction Juvenile, religious, young adult. ''We publish books of Judaic interest only.'' Query with SASE.

Recent Title(s) *Talmud with Training Wheels* (nonfiction); *Let's Talk About God*, by Dorothy K. Kripke (juvenile nonfiction).

ALPINE PUBLICATIONS

38262 Linman Road, Crawford CO 81415. (970)921-5005. Fax: (970)921-5081. E-mail: alpinepubl@aol.com. Web site: alpinepub.com. **Acquisitions:** Ms. B.J. McKinney, publisher. Estab. 1975. Publishes hardcover and trade paperback originals and reprints. **Publishes 6-10 titles/year. 40% of books from first-time authors; 95% from unagented writers. Pays 8-15% royalty on wholesale price. Offers advance.** Publishes book 18 months after acceptance of ms. Accepts simultaneous submissions. Responds in 1-3 weeks to queries; 1 month to proposals; 1 month to mss. Book catalog free; ms guidelines online.

Imprints Blue Ribbon Books.

Nonfiction How-to, illustrated book, reference. Subjects include animals. ''Alpine specializes in books that promote the enjoyment of and responsibility for companion animals with emphasis on dogs and horses.'' Reviews artwork/photos as part of ms package. Send photocopies.

Recent Title(s) *New Secrets of Successful Show Dog Handling*, by Peter Green and Mario Migliorini (dog); *Training for Trail Horse Classes*, by Laurie Truskauskas (horse); *The Japanese Chin*, by Elisabeth Legl (dogs).

Tips ''Our audience is pet owners, breeders, exhibitors, veterinarians, animal trainers, animal care specialists, and judges. Look up some of our titles before you submit. See what is unique about our books. Write your proposal to suit our guidelines.''

AMBASSADOR BOOKS, INC.

91 Prescott St., Worcester MA 01605. (508)756-2893. Fax: (508)757-7055. Web site: www.ambassadorbooks.com. **Acquisitions:** Mr. Chris Driscoll, acquisitions editor. Publishes hardcover and trade paperback originals. **Publishes 9 titles/year. Receives 2,000 queries and 100 mss/year. 50% of books from first-time authors; 90% from unagented writers. Pays 8-10% royalty on retail price.** Publishes book 1 year after acceptance of ms. Accepts simultaneous submissions. Responds in 3-4 months to queries. Book catalog free or online.

O- "We are a Christian publishing company looking for books of intellectual and/or spiritual excellence."

Nonfiction Books with a spiritual theme. Biography, children's/juvenile, illustrated book, self-help. Subjects include creative nonfiction, regional, religion, spirituality, sports, Catholic and Christian books. Query with SASE, or submit complete ms. Reviews artwork/photos as part of ms package. Send photocopies.

Fiction Books with a spiritual/religious theme. Juvenile, literary, picture books, religious, spiritual, sports, young adult, women's. Query with SASE, or submit complete ms.

Recent Title(s) *A Child's Bedtime Companion*, by Sandy Henry, illustrated by Vera Pavlova; *Praying for a Miracle*, by Gilda D'Agostrio.

AMERICAN CATHOLIC PRESS

16565 S. State St., South Holland IL 60473. (312)331-5845. Fax: (708)331-5484. E-mail: acp@acpress.org. Web site: www.acpress.org. **Acquisitions:** Rev. Michael Gilligan, PhD, editorial director. Estab. 1967. Publishes hardcover originals and hardcover and paperback reprints. **Publishes 4 titles/year. Makes outright purchase of $25-100.** Does not accept simultaneous submissions. Ms guidelines online.

Nonfiction Subjects include education, music/dance, religion, spirituality. "We publish books on the Roman Catholic liturgy—for the most part, books on religious music and educational books and pamphlets. We also publish religious songs for church use, including Psalms, as well as choral and instrumental arrangements. We are interested in new music, meant for use in church services. Books, or even pamphlets, on the Roman Catholic Mass are especially welcome. We have no interest in secular topics and are not interested in religious poetry of any kind."

Tips "Most of our sales are by direct mail, although we do work through retail outlets."

N THE AMWELL PRESS

P.O. Box 5385, Clinton NJ 08809-0385. (908)638-9033. Fax: (908)638-4728. Corporate Secretary: Genevieve Symonds. **Acquisitions:** James Rikhoff, president. Estab. 1976. Publishes hardcover originals. **Publishes 4 titles/year.** Publishes book 18 months after acceptance of ms. Responds in 2 months to queries.

O- The Amwell Press publishes hunting and fishing nonfiction, but not how-to books on these subjects.

Nonfiction Subjects include hunting and fishing stories/literature (not how-to). Mostly limited editions. No fiction. Query with SASE.

Recent Title(s) *Handy to Home*, by Tom Hennessey; *Beyond Hill Country*, by Rikhoff and Sullivan; *A Quail Hunter's Odyssey*, by Dr. Joseph Greenfield.

ANACUS PRESS

Imprint of Finney Co., 8075 215th St. W, Lakeville MN 55044. (952)469-6699. Fax: (952)469-1968. E-mail: feedback@finney-hobar.com. Web site: www.anacus.com. **Acquisitions:** Alan Krysan, president (bicycling guides, travel). Publishes trade paperback originals. **Publishes variable number of titles/year. Pays 10% royalty on wholesale price. Offers $500 advance.** Book catalog online.

Nonfiction Subjects include recreation, regional, travel (travel guides, travelogue). Query with SASE.

Recent Title(s) *Bed, Breakfast & Bike Florida*, by Dale V. Lally, Jr. (travel guide).

Tips Audience is cyclists and armchair adventurers.

ANCHORAGE PRESS PLAYS, INC.

P.O. Box 2901, Louisville KY 40201. Phone/Fax: (502)583-2288. E-mail: applays@bellsouth.net. Web site: www.applays.com. **Acquisitions:** Marilee Miller, publisher. Estab. 1935. Publishes hardcover and trade paperback originals. **Publishes up to 10 titles/year. 50% of books from first-time authors; 80% from unagented writers. Pays 10-15% royalty. Playwrights also receive 50-75% royalties.** Publishes book 1-2 years after acceptance of ms. Accepts simultaneous submissions. Responds in 1 year to mss. Book catalog and ms guidelines online.

O- "We are an international agency for plays for young people. First in the field since 1935. We are primarily a publisher of theatrical plays with limited textbooks."

Nonfiction Textbook, plays. Subjects include education, theater, child drama, plays. "We are looking for texts for teachers of drama/theater." Query. Reviews artwork/photos as part of ms package.

Recent Title(s) *Curtain Time is Magic Time*, by Michael H. Hibbard; *The Rose of Treason*, by James DeVita; *The Pied Piper of Hamelin*, by Tim Wright.

Small Presses

ANHINGA PRESS

P.O. Box 10595, Tallahassee FL 32302. (850)422-1408. Fax: (850)442-6323. E-mail: info@anhinga.org. Web site: www.anhinga.org. **Acquisitions:** Rick Campbell or Joann Gardner, editors. Publishes hardcover and trade paperback originals. **Publishes 5 titles/year. Pays 10% royalty on retail price. Offers Anhinga Prize of $2,000.** Accepts simultaneous submissions. Responds in 3 months to queries; 3 months to proposals; 3 months to mss. Book catalog for #10 SASE or online; ms guidelines online.

O— Publishes only full-length collections of poetry (60-80 pages). No individual poems or chapbooks.

Poetry Query with SASE and 10-page sample (not full ms) by mail. No e-mail queries.

Recent Title(s) *Blood Almanac*, by sandy Langhorn; *Morning of the Red Admirals*, by Robert Dana; *Dubious Angels*, by Keith Ratzlaff.

ARCHIMEDES PRESS, INC.

6 Berkley Rd., Glenville NY 12302. (518)265-3269. Fax: (518)384-1313. E-mail: archimedespress@verizon.net. Web site: www.archimedespress.com. President: Kim Gorham. **Acquisitions:** Richard DiMaggio, chief editor. Estab. 2002. Publishes broad-based hardcover, trade paperback, and mass market paperback originals. **Publishes 3-6 titles/year. Pays 5-15% royalty.** Publishes book 6 months after acceptance of ms. Does not accept simultaneous submissions. Responds in 2 months to queries.

O— Looking for quality nonfiction, business, self-improvement. Also desire funny, up-beat titles.

Nonfiction General nonfiction, how-to, illustrated book, multimedia, self-help. Subjects include alternative lifestyles, business/economics, child guidance/parenting, community, cooking/foods/nutrition, creative nonfiction, education, government/politics, history, humanities, language/literature, money/finance, photography, sex, social sciences, travel. "E-mail submissions acceptable. Please snail mail complete manuscripts. If a consumer wants it, so do we." Query with SASE, or submit sample chapter(s), marketing plan, SASE, or submit complete ms. Reviews artwork/photos as part of ms package. Send photocopies.

Recent Title(s) *Real Estate Professionals Liability Review*; *Financial Empowerment Infomercials*.

Tips "Our audience is the consumer, plain and simple. That means everyone. We are a small press and try hard to avoid the limitations of the industry. While agented submissions are preferred, they are not necessary with professional submissions. We want fresh, creative ideas and will accept unsolicited manuscripts. These, however, will not be returned without a SASE. E-mails are OK. No phone calls, please."

ARDEN PRESS, INC.

P.O. Box 418, Denver CO 80201-0418. (303)697-6766. Fax: (303)697-3443. **Acquisitions:** Susan Conley, publisher. Estab. 1980. Publishes hardcover and trade paperback originals and reprints. **Publishes 4-6 titles/year. 20% of books from first-time authors; 80% from unagented writers. Pays 8-15% royalty on wholesale price. Offers $2,000 average advance.** Publishes book 6 months after acceptance of ms. Accepts simultaneous submissions. Responds in 2 months to queries. Ms guidelines free.

O— Arden Press publishes nonfiction on women's history and women's issues. "We sell to general and women's bookstores as well as public and academic libraries. Many of our titles are adopted as texts for use in college courses."

Nonfiction Subjects include women's issues/studies. No personal memoirs or autobiographies. Query with outline/synopsis and sample chapters.

Recent Title(s) *Whatever Happened to the Year of the Woman?*, by Amy Handlin.

Tips "Writers have the best chance selling us nonfiction on women's subjects. If I were a writer trying to market a book today, I would learn as much as I could about publishers' profiles *then* contact those who publish similar works."

ART DIRECTION BOOK CO., INC.

456 Glenbrook Rd., Glenbrook CT 06096-1800. (203)353-1441. Fax: (203)353-1371. **Acquisitions:** Don Barron, editorial director. Estab. 1959. Publishes hardcover and paperback originals. **Publishes 2 titles/year. Pays 10% royalty on retail price. Offers average $1,000 advance.** Publishes book 1 year after acceptance of ms. Does not accept simultaneous submissions. Responds in 3 months to queries. Book catalog for 6×9 SAE.

Imprints Infosource Publications.

O— Art Direction Book Co. is interested in books for the professional advertising art field—books for art directors, designers, etc; also entry-level books for commercial and advertising art students in such fields as typography, photography, paste-up, illustration, clip-art, design, layout, and graphic arts.

Nonfiction Textbook, commercial art, ad art how-to. Subjects include art/architecture. Query with outline and 1 sample chapter. Reviews artwork/photos as part of ms package.

Recent Title(s) *The Write Book.*

ASIAN HUMANITIES PRESS

Jain Publishing Co., P.O. Box 3523, Fremont CA 94539. (510)659-8272. Fax: (510)659-0501. E-mail: mail@jainpub.com. Web site: www.jainpub.com. **Acquisitions:** M. Jain, editor-in-chief. Estab. 1989. Publishes hardcover and trade paperback originals and reprints. **Publishes 6 titles/year. 100% from unagented writers. Pays 5-15% royalty on net receipts.** Publishes book 1-2 years after acceptance of ms. Does not return proposal material. Responds in 3 months to mss. Book catalog and ms guidelines online.

O→ Asian Humanities Press publishes in the areas of humanities and social sciences pertaining to Asia, commonly categorized as "Asian Studies." Currently emphasizing undergraduate-level textbooks.

Nonfiction Reference, textbook, general trade books. Subjects include language/literature, philosophy, psychology, religion, spirituality, Asian classics, social sciences, art/culture. Submit proposal package including vita, list of prior publications. Reviews artwork/photos as part of ms package. Send photocopies.

Recent Title(s) *Adhidharmasamuccaya*, by Walpola Rahula.

AVANYU PUBLISHING, INC.

P.O. Box 27134, Albuquerque NM 87125. (505)341-1280. Fax: (505)341-1281. Web site: www.avanyu-publishing.com. **Acquisitions:** J. Brent Ricks, president. Estab. 1984. Publishes hardcover and trade paperback originals and reprints. **Publishes 4 titles/year. 30% of books from first-time authors; 90% from unagented writers. Pays 8% maximum royalty on wholesale price. Offers advance.** Publishes book 1 year after acceptance of ms. Does not accept simultaneous submissions. Responds in 2 months to queries. Book catalog for #10 SASE.

O→ Avanyu publishes highly-illustrated, history-oriented books on American Indians and adventures in the Southwest.

Nonfiction Biography, children's/juvenile, coffee table book, illustrated book, reference, scholarly. Subjects include Americana (Southwest), anthropology/archeology, art/architecture, ethnic, history, multicultural, photography, regional, sociology, spirituality. Query with SASE. Reviews artwork/photos as part of ms package.

Recent Title(s) *Kachinas Spirit Beings of the Hopi*; *Mesa Verde Ancient Architecture*; *Hopi Snake Ceremonies*.

Tips "Our audience consists of libraries, art collectors, and history students. We publish subjects dealing with modern and historic American Indian matters of all kinds."

BANCROFT PRESS

P.O. Box 65360, Baltimore MD 21209-9945. (410)358-0658. Fax: (410)764-1967. E-mail: bruceb@bancroftpress.com. Web site: www.bancroftpress.com. **Acquisitions:** Bruce Bortz, editor and publisher (health, investments, politics, history, humor, literary novels, mystery/thrillers, young adult). Publishes hardcover and trade paperback originals. **Publishes 6 titles/year. Pays 6-8% royalty. Pays various royalties on retail price. Offers $750 advance.** Publishes book up to 3 years after acceptance of ms. Accepts simultaneous submissions. Responds in 6-12 months to queries; 6-12 months to proposals; 6-12 months to mss. Ms guidelines online.

O→ Bancroft Press is a general trade publisher. "We are currently moving into soley publishing young adult fiction and nonfiction as well as adult fiction for young adults (single titles and series). Please, nothing that would be too graphic for anyone under 17 years old."

Nonfiction "Our No. 1 priority is publishing books appropriate for young adults, ages 10-18. All quality books on any subject that fit that category will be considered." Biography, how-to, humor, self-help. Subjects include business/economics, government/politics, health/medicine, money/finance, regional, sports, women's issues/studies, popular culture, essays. "We advise writers to visit the Web site." Submit proposal package including outline, 2 sample chapters, competition/market survey.

Fiction "Our No. 1 priority is publishing books appropriate for young adults, ages 10-18. All quality books on any subject that fit that category will be considered." Ethnic (general), feminist, gay/lesbian, historical, humor, literary, mainstream/contemporary, military/war, mystery (amateur sleuth, cozy, police procedural, private eye/hardboiled), regional, science fiction (hard science/technological, soft/sociological), young adult (historical, problem novels, series), thrillers. Query by e-mail or by mail with SASE, outline, 2 sample chapters. Or, submit complete ms.

Recent Title(s) *Like We Care*, by Tom Matthews; *Finding the Forger*, by Libby Sternberg; *Gradebusters*, by Stephen Schmidtz, PhD.

BARNEGAT LIGHT PRESS

Pine Barrens Press, P.O. Box 607, 3959 Rt. 563, Chatsworth NJ 08019-0607. (609)894-4415. Fax: (609)894-2350. **Acquisitions:** R. Marilyn Schmidt, publisher. Publishes trade paperback originals. **Publishes 4 titles/year. Receives 50 queries and 30 mss/year. No first-time authors; 100% from unagented writers. Makes outright purchase.** Publishes book 6 months after acceptance of ms. Responds in 1 month to queries. Book catalog free or online.

Imprints Pine Barrens Press.

O→ "We are a regional publisher emphasizing the mid-Atlantic region. Areas concerned are mid-Atlantic gardening, cooking, and travel."

Nonfiction Cookbook, how-to, illustrated book. Subjects include agriculture/horticulture, cooking/foods/nutrition, gardening, regional, travel. Query with SASE. Reviews artwork/photos as part of ms package. Send photocopies.

Recent Title(s) *Towns Lost But Not Forgotten*, by R. Marilyn Schmidt; *Seashorer Gardening With Native Plants*, by R. Marilyn Schmidt.

BARNWOOD PRESS

4604 47th Ave. S, Seattle WA 98118. E-mail: barnwoodpress@earthlink.net. Web site: www.barnwoodpress.org. **Acquisitions:** Tom Koontz, editor. Estab. 1975. Publishes original trade paperbacks. **Publishes 2 titles/year. Pays 10% of run.** Responds in 1 month to queries.

Poetry Query first with a few sample poems and cover letter with brief bio and publication credits.

N BEAR STAR PRESS

185 Hollow Oak Dr., Cohasset CA 95973. (530)891-0360. Web site: www.bearstarpress.com. **Acquisitions:** Beth Spencer, publisher/editor. Estab. 1996. Publishes trade paperback originals. **Publishes 1-3 titles/year. Pays $1,000, and 25 copies to winner of annual Dorothy Brunsman contest.** Publishes book 9 months after acceptance of ms. Accepts simultaneous submissions. Responds in 2 weeks to queries. Ms guidelines online.

O→ "Bear Star is committed to publishing the best poetry it can attract. Each year it sponsors a contest open to poets from Western and Pacific states. From time to time we add to our list other poets from our target area whose work we admire."

Poetry Wants well-crafted poems. No restrictions as to form, subject matter, style, or purpose. "Poets should enter our annual book competition. Other books are occasionally solicited by publisher, sometimes from among contestants who didn't win." Query, or submit complete ms.

Recent Title(s) *Keel Bone*, by Mata Khosla; *The Soup of Something Missing*, by Rick Bursky; *Death of a Mexican and Other Poems*, by Manuel Paul Lopez.

Tips "Send your best work, consider its arrangement. A 'wow' poem early keeps me reading."

BEEMAN JORGENSEN, INC.

7510 Allisonville Rd., Indianapolis IN 46250. (317)841-7677. Fax: (317)849-2001. **Acquisitions:** Brett Johnson, president (automotive/auto racing). Publishes hardcover and trade paperback originals and hardcover reprints. **Publishes 4 titles/year. Receives 10 queries/year. 50% of books from first-time authors; 100% from unagented writers. Pays 15-30% royalty on wholesale price. Offers up to $1,000 advance.** Publishes book 8 months after acceptance of ms. Responds in 1 month to queries; 2 months to proposals. Book catalog free.

Nonfiction Publishes books on automobiles and auto racing. Coffee table book, illustrated book, reference. Subjects include sports (auto racing). Query with SASE, or submit proposal package including outline, 1 sample chapter.

Recent Title(s) *Drag Racing Basics*, by Cindy Crawford (illustrated book); *Road America*, by Tom Schultz (illustrated book); *Porshe 356, Guide to D-I-Y Restoration*, by Jim Kellogg (illustrated book).

Tips Audience is automotive enthusiasts, specific marque owners/enthusiasts, auto racing fans, and participants.

BICK PUBLISHING HOUSE

307 Neck Rd., Madison CT 06443. (203)245-0073. Fax: (203)245-5990. E-mail: bickpubhse@aol.com. Web site: www.bickpubhouse.com. **Acquisitions:** Dale Carlson, president (psychology); Hannah Carlson (special needs, disabilities); Irene Ruth (wildlife). Estab. 1994. Publishes trade paperback originals. **Publishes 4 titles/year. Receives 100 queries and 100 mss/year. 55% of books from first-time authors; 55% from unagented writers. Pays 10% royalty on net receipts. Offers $500-1,000 advance.** Publishes book 1 year after acceptance of ms. Responds in 1 month to queries; 2 months to proposals; 3 months to mss. Book catalog free; ms guidelines for #10 SASE.

O→ Bick Publishing House publishes step-by-step, easy-to-read professional information for the general adult public about physical, psychological, and emotional disabilities or special needs. Currently emphasizing science, psychology for teens.

Nonfiction Subjects include health/medicine (disability/special needs), psychology, young adult or teen science, psychology, wildlife rehabilitation. Query with SASE, or submit proposal package including outline, résumé, 3 sample chapters.

Recent Title(s) *The Courage to Lead Support Groups: Mental Illnesses and Addictions*, by Hannah Carlson; *In and Out of Your Mind Teen Science*, by Dale Carlson; *Who Said What, Philosophy Quotes for Teens: What Are You Doing With Your Life?*, by J. Krishnamurti.

BKMK PRESS

University of Missouri-Kansas City, 5101 Rockhill Rd., Kansas City MO 64110-2499. (816)235-2558. Fax: (816)235-2611. E-mail: bkmk@umkc.edu. Web site: www.umkc.edu/bkmk. **Acquisitions:** Ben Furnish, managing editor. Estab. 1971. Publishes trade paperback originals. Accepts simultaneous submissions. Responds in 4-6 months to queries. Ms guidelines online.

O→ BkMk Press publishes fine literature. Reading period January-June.

Nonfiction Creative nonfiction essays. Query with SASE.

Fiction Literary, short story collections. Query with SASE.

Poetry Submit 10 sample poems.

Recent Title(s) *I'll Never Leave You*, by H.E. Francis; *Circe, After Hours*, by Marilyn Kallet; *A Bed of Nails*, by Ron Tanner.

Tips "We skew toward readers of literature, particularly contemporary writing. Because of our limited number of titles published per year, we discourage apprentice writers or 'scattershot' submissions."

BLACK DOME PRESS CORP.

1011 Route 296, Hensonville NY 12439. (518)734-6357. Fax: (518)734-5802. E-mail: blackdomep@aol.com. Web site: www.blackdomepress.com. Estab. 1990. Publishes cloth and trade paperback originals and reprints. Accepts simultaneous submissions. Book catalog online.

Nonfiction Subjects include history, nature/environment, photography, regional (New York state), Native Americans, grand hotels, geneology, colonial life, quilting, architecture, railroads. New York state regional material only. Submit proposal package including outline, author bio.

Recent Title(s) *Kaaterskill Clove: Where Nature Met Art*, by Raymond Beecher; *The Catskill Park: Inside the Blue Line*, by Norman J. Van Valkenburgh and Christopher W. Olney.

Tips "Our audience is comprised of New York state residents, tourists, and visitors."

BLACK HERON PRESS

P.O. Box 95676, Seattle WA 98145. Web site: www.blackheronpress.com. **Acquisitions:** Jerry Gold, publisher. Estab. 1984. Publishes hardcover and trade paperback originals. **Publishes 4-6 titles/year.** Accepts simultaneous submissions.

O→ "Black Heron Press publishes primarily literary fiction."

Fiction Literary. "We don't want to see fiction written for the mass market. If it sells to the mass market, fine, but we don't see ourselves as a commercial press." Submit first 30-40 pages of the book, SASE. No e-mail queries.

Recent Title(s) *Temping*, by Kirby Olson; *New Light*, by Annette Gilson; *A Grey Moon Over China*, by Thomas A. Day.

Tips "Readers should look at some of our books before submitting—they are easily available. Most submissions we see are done competently but have been sent to the wrong place. We do not publish self-help books or romances."

BLUE POPPY PRESS

Imprint of Blue Poppy Enterprises, Inc., 5441 Western Ave., #2, Boulder CO 80301-2733. (303)447-8372. Fax: (303)245-8362. E-mail: info@bluepoppy.com. Web site: www.bluepoppy.com. **Acquisitions:** Bob Flaws, editor-in-chief. Estab. 1981. Publishes hardcover and trade paperback originals. **Publishes 3-4 titles/year. Receives 50 queries and 5-10 mss/year. 30-40% of books from first-time authors; 100% from unagented writers. Pays 8-12% royalty.** Publishes book 1 year after acceptance of ms. Does not accept simultaneous submissions. Responds in 1 month to queries. Book catalog free; ms guidelines online.

O→ Blue Poppy Press is dedicated to expanding and improving the English language literature on acupuncture and Asian medicine for both professional practitioners and lay readers.

Nonfiction Self-help, technical, textbook (related to acupuncture and Oriental medicine). Subjects include ethnic, health/medicine. "We only publish books on acupuncture and Oriental medicine by authors who can read Chinese and have a minimum of 5 years clinical experience. We also require all our authors to use Wiseman's *Glossary of Chinese Medical Terminology* as their standard for technical terms." Query with SASE, or submit outline, 1 sample chapter.

Recent Title(s) *The Successful Chinese Herbalist*, by Bob Flaws and Honora Lee Wolfe; *Understanding the Difficult Patient*, by Nancy Bilello.

Tips Audience is "practicing acupuncturists, interested in alternatives in healthcare, preventive medicine, Chinese philosophy, and medicine."

BLUE RAVEN PRESS

219 SE Main St., Suite 506, Minneapolis MN 55414. (612)331-8039. Fax: (612)331-8115. E-mail: barbarajgislason @blueravenpress.com. Web site: www.blueravenpress.com. **Acquisitions:** Barbara J. Gislason, Esq., publisher

(nonfiction and fiction). Estab. 2002. Publishes hardcover, trade paperback, and mass market paperback originals. **Publishes 2-3 titles/year. 10% of books from first-time authors; 90% from unagented writers. Typically pays 5% royalty on retail price. Offers $3,000-5,000 advance.** Publishes book 18 months after acceptance of ms. Does not accept simultaneous submissions. Responds in 6 months to queries; 9 months to proposals; 2 months to mss. Ms guidelines online.

O-- "We are particularly looking for groundbreaking nonfiction and fiction on the subject of animals that is powerfully written. Blue Raven Press books must express ideas and tell stories powerful enough to change people's views about animals without overt sentimentality. All of our writers communicate effectively and compellingly about animals."

Nonfiction "Our nonfiction authors may be formally trained in animal subjects and/or may write from life experience." Query with SASE, or submit proposal package including outline, 3 sample chapters, analysis of competition, marketing ideas, and author platform/background. If you are a published author whose prior book has sold at least 5,000 copies, submit complete ms. Reviews artwork/photos as part of ms package. Send 1 photocopy.

Fiction "Our fiction authors enable readers to suspend disbelief through compelling characterizations, skillfully revealing what lies beneath the surface, and competent world-building." Query with SASE, or submit proposal package including synopsis, 3 sample chapters, author background and marketing ideas. If you are a published author who's sold at least 5,000 copies of a prior book, submit complete ms.

Tips "Our audience comprises people who take responsibility for the world around them, as well as people who are fascinated by, or who strongly bond with, animals."

N BLUEBRIDGE

Imprint of United Tribes Media, Inc., 240 W. 35th St., Suite 500, New York NY 10001. (212)244-4166. Fax: (212)279-0927. E-mail: janguerth@aol.com. Web site: www.bluebridgebooks.com. **Acquisitions:** Jan-Erik Guerth, publisher (general nonfiction). Estab. 2004. Publishes hardcover and trade paperback originals. **Publishes 6-8 titles/year. Receives 1,000 queries and 200 mss/year. 5% of books from first-time authors; 20% from unagented writers. Pays variable royalty on wholesale price. Offers variable advance.** Publishes book 1-2 years after acceptance of ms. Accepts simultaneous submissions. Responds in 1 month to queries; 1 month to proposals; 2 months to mss. Book catalog for #10 SASE.

Nonfiction General nonfiction. Subjects include Americana, anthropology/archeology, art/architecture, business/economics, child guidance/parenting, contemporary culture, creative nonfiction, ethnic, gardening, gay/lesbian, government/politics, health/medicine, history, humanities, language/literature, multicultural, music/dance, nature/environment, philosophy, psychology, religion, science, social sciences, sociology, spirituality, travel, women's issues/studies, world affairs. BlueBridge is an independent publisher of international nonfiction based in New York City. The BlueBridge mission: Thoughtful Books for Mind and Spirit. Query with SASE or preferably by e-mail.

Recent Title(s) *Horse*, by J. Edward Chamberlin; *The Door of No Return*, by William St. Clair.

Tips "We target a broad general audience."

A BOOK PEDDLERS

2828 Hedberg Drive, Minnetonka MN 55305. (952)544-1154. Fax: (952)544-1153. E-mail: vlansky@bookpeddlers.com. Web site: www.bookpeddlers.com. **Acquisitions:** Vicki Lansky, publisher/editor. Publishes hardcover and trade paperback originals. **Publishes several titles/year. Receives 50 queries and 10 mss/year. 0% of books from first-time authors; 0% from unagented writers. Pays 10% royalty on wholesale price. Offers advance.** Publishes book 1 year after acceptance of ms. Accepts simultaneous submissions. Responds in 1 week to queries. Book catalog for #10 SASE; ms guidelines online.

Nonfiction Children's/juvenile, gift book, how-to, self-help. "We accept no fiction and practically nothing that is sent to us. A writer must be very on target for our consideration." Query with SASE.

Recent Title(s) *Coming Clean*, by Schar War (dirty little secrets from a professional housecleaner).

Tips "See submission guidelines on Web site."

BREAKAWAY BOOKS

P.O. Box 24, Halcottsville NY 12438. (212)898-0408. E-mail: information@breakawaybooks.com. Web site: www.breakawaybooks.com. **Acquisitions:** Garth Battista, publisher. Estab. 1994. Publishes hardcover and trade paperback originals. **Publishes 8-10 titles/year. Receives 400 queries and 100 mss/year. 35% of books from first-time authors; 75% from unagented writers. Offers advance.** Publishes book 9 months after acceptance of ms. Accepts simultaneous submissions. Responds in 1 month to queries; 1 month to proposals; 2 months to mss. Book catalog and ms guidelines free and online.

O-- "Breakaway Books is a sports literature specialty publisher—only fiction and narrative nonfiction. No how-tos."

Small Presses

Nonfiction Subjects include sports (narrative only, not how-to). Query with SASE or by e-mail.
Fiction Short story collections (sports stories). Query with SASE, or submit complete ms.
Recent Title(s) *God on the Starting Line*, by Marc Bloom; *The Art of Bicycling*, edited by Justin Belmont; *American Miler*, by Dr. Paul Kiell.
Tips Audience is intelligent, passionately committed to athletes. "We're starting a new children's book line—only children's books dealing with running, cycling, swimming, triathlon, plus boating (canoes, kayaks and sailboats)."

BREWERS PUBLICATIONS

Imprint of Brewers Association, 736 Pearl St., Boulder CO 80302. (303)447-0816. Fax: (303)447-2825. E-mail: ray@brewersassociation.org. Web site: beertown.org. **Acquisitions:** Ray Daniels, publisher. Estab. 1986. Publishes hardcover and trade paperback originals. **Publishes 2 titles/year. 50% of books from first-time authors; 100% from unagented writers. Pays royalty on net receipts. Offers small advance.** Publishes book 9 months after acceptance of ms. Accepts simultaneous submissions. Responds in 3 months to relevant queries. Only those submissions relevant to our needs will receive a response to queries. Ms guidelines online.

O→ Brewers Publications is the largest publisher of books on beer-related subjects.

Nonfiction "We only publish nonfiction books of interest to amateur and professional brewers. Our authors have many years of brewing experience and in-depth practical knowledge of their subject. We are not interested in fiction, drinking games or beer/bar reviews. If your book is not about how to make beer, then do not waste your time or ours by sending it. Those determined to fit our needs will subscribe to and read *Zymurgy* and *The New Brewer*." Query first with proposal and sample chapter.
Recent Title(s) *Radical Brewing*, by Randy Mosher; *Brew Like a Monk*, by Stan Hieronymus; *Wild Brews*, by Jeff Sparrow.

N BRIGHT MOUNTAIN BOOKS, INC.

206 Riva Ridge Dr., Fairview NC 28730. (828)628-1768. Fax: (828)628-1755. E-mail: booksbmb@charter.net. **Acquisitions:** Cynthia F. Bright, editor. Publishes trade paperback originals and reprints. **Publishes 3 titles/year. Pays royalty.** Responds in 1 month to queries; 3 months to mss.
Imprints Historical Images.
Nonfiction Biography. Subjects include history, regional. "Our current emphasis is on regional titles set in the Southern Appalachians and Carolinas, which can include nonfiction by local writers." Query with SASE.
Recent Title(s) *The Carolina Mountains*, by Margaret W. Marley; *Roadside Revenants*, by Michael Renegar.

N BRIGHTON PUBLICATIONS, INC.

P.O. Box 120706, St. Paul MN 55112-0706. (800)536-2665. Fax: (651)636-2220. E-mail: sharon@partybooks.com. Web site: www.partybooks.com. **Acquisitions:** Sharon E. Dlugosch, editor. Estab. 1977. Publishes trade paperback originals. **Receives 100 queries and 100 mss/year. 50% of books from first-time authors; 100% from unagented writers. Pays 10% royalty on wholesale price.** Accepts simultaneous submissions. Responds in 3 months to queries. Book catalog and ms guidelines for #10 SASE.

O→ Brighton Publications publishes books on celebration or seasonal how-to parties and anything that will help to give a better party such as activities, games, favors, and themes. Currently emphasizing games for meetings, annual parties, picnics, etc., celebration themes, and party/special event planning.

Nonfiction How-to. Subjects include games, tabletop, party themes. "We're interested in topics telling how to live any part of life well." Query with SASE, or submit outline, 2 sample chapter(s).
Recent Title(s) *Installation Ceremonies for Every Group: 26 Memorable Ways to Install New Officers*, by Pat Hines; *Meeting Room Games: Getting Things Done in Committees*, by Nan Booth.

BULL PUBLISHING CO.

P.O. Box 1377, Boulder CO 80306. (800)676-2855. Fax: (303)545-6354. E-mail: jim.bullpubco@comcast.net. Web site: www.bullpub.com. **Acquisitions:** James Bull, publisher (self-care, nutrition, women's health, weight control); Lansing Hays, publisher (self-help, psychology). Estab. 1974. Publishes hardcover and trade paperback originals. **Publishes 6-8 titles/year. Pays 10-16% royalty on wholesale price (net to publisher).** Publishes book 6 months after acceptance of ms. Book catalog free.

O→ Bull Publishing publishes health and nutrition books for the public with an emphasis on self-care, nutrition, women's health, weight control and psychology.

Nonfiction How-to, self-help. Subjects include cooking/foods/nutrition, education, health/medicine, women's issues/studies. Subjects include self-care, nutrition, fitness, child health and nutrition, health education, mental health. "We look for books that fit our area of strength: responsible books on health that fill a substantial public need, and that we can market primarily through professionals." Submit outline, sample chapter(s). Reviews artwork/photos as part of ms package.
Recent Title(s) *Child of Mine, 3rd Ed.*, by Ellyn Satter; *Hormonal Balance*, by Scott Isaacs.

Small Presses

CAMINO BOOKS, INC.

P.O. Box 59026, Philadelphia PA 19102. (215)413-1917. Fax: (215)413-3255. Web site: www.caminobooks.com. **Acquisitions:** E. Jutkowitz, publisher. Estab. 1987. Publishes hardcover and trade paperback originals. **Publishes 8 titles/year. 20% of books from first-time authors. Pays 6-12% royalty on net receipts. Offers $2,000 average advance.** Publishes book 1 year after acceptance of ms. Responds in 2 weeks to queries. Ms guidelines online.

O→ Camino Books, Inc., publishes nonfiction of regional interest to the Mid-Atlantic states.

Nonfiction Biography, children's/juvenile, cookbook, how-to. Subjects include agriculture/horticulture, Americana, art/architecture, child guidance/parenting, cooking/foods/nutrition, ethnic, gardening, government/politics, history, regional, travel. Query with SASE, or submit outline, sample chapter(s).

Tips "The books must be of interest to readers in the Middle Atlantic states, or they should have a clearly defined niche, such as cookbooks."

CAROUSEL PRESS

P.O. Box 6038, Berkeley CA 94706-0038. (510)527-5849. Web site: www.carousel-press.com. **Acquisitions:** Carole T. Meyers, editor/publisher. Estab. 1976. Publishes trade paperback originals and reprints. **Publishes 1-2 titles/year. Pays 10-15% royalty on wholesale price. Offers $1,000 advance.** Responds in 1 month to queries.

Nonfiction Subjects include travel, travel-related. Query with SASE.

Recent Title(s) *Dream Sleeps: Castle & Palace Hotels of Europe*, by Pamela L. Barrus.

CHURCH GROWTH INSTITUTE

P.O. Box 7, Elkton MD 21922-0007. (434)525-0022. Fax: (434)525-0608. E-mail: cgimail@churchgrowth.org. Web site: www.churchgrowth.org. **Acquisitions:** Cindy Spear, administrator/resource development director. Estab. 1978. Publishes electronic books (pdf), 3-ring-bound manuals, mixed media resource packets. **Publishes 3 titles/year. Pays 6% royalty on retail price.** Publishes book 1 year after acceptance of ms. Accepts simultaneous submissions. Responds in 3 months to queries. Book catalog for 9×12 SAE with 4 first-class stamps; ms guidelines given after query and outline is received.

O→ "Our mission is to provide practical resources to help pastors, churches, and individuals reach their potential for Christ; to promote spiritual and numerical growth in churches, thereby leading Christians to maturity and lost people to Christ; and to equip pastors so they can equip their church members to do the work of the ministry."

Nonfiction "Material should originate from a conservative Christian view and cover topics that will help churches grow, through leadership training, self-evaluation, and new or unique ministries, or enhancing existing ministries. Self-discovery inventories regarding spiritual growth, relationship improvement, etc., are hot items." How-to. Subjects include education, religion (church-growth related), ministry, how-to manuals, spiritual growth, relationship-building, evangelism. "Accepted manuscripts will be adapted to our resource packet, manual, or inventory format. All material must be practical and easy for the average Christian to understand." Query, or submit outline and brief explanation of what the packet will accomplish in the local church and whether it is leadership or lay oriented. Queries accepted by mail or e-mail. No phone queries. Reviews artwork/photos as part of ms package. Send photos or images on CD (in TIFF, EPS, or PDF format).

Recent Title(s) *Ministry Descriptions*; *Ask Me to Pray for You*; *Marriage Communication Assessment*.

Tips "We are not accepting textbooks. Concentrate on how-to manuals and ministry evaluation and diagnostic tools and spiritual or relationship-oriented 'inventories' for individual Christians."

CLARITY PRESS, INC.

3277 Roswell Rd. NE, #469, Atlanta GA 30305. (877)613-1495. Fax: (404)231-3899 and (877)613-7868. E-mail: claritypress@usa.net. Web site: www.claritypress.com. **Acquisitions:** Diana G. Collier, editorial director (contemporary social justice issues). Estab. 1984. Publishes hardcover and trade paperback originals. **Publishes 4 titles/year.** Accepts simultaneous submissions. Submit by e-mail, no SASE. Responds in 1 month to queries.

Nonfiction Publishes books on contemporary issues in US, Middle East and Africa. Subjects include ethnic, world affairs, human rights/socio-economic and minority issues. No fiction. Query with synopsis, TOC, résumé, publishing history.

Recent Title(s) *The Power of Israel in the United States*, by James Petras; *Biowarfare and Terrorism*, by Francis A. Boyle.

Tips "Check our titles on the Web site."

CLOVER PARK PRESS

P.O. Box 5067, Santa Monica CA 90409-5067. (310)452-7657. E-mail: cloverparkpr@earthlink.net. Web site: www.cloverparkpress.com. **Acquisitions:** Martha Grant, acquisitions editor. Estab. 1991. Publishes hardcover and trade paperback originals. **Publishes 6-10 titles/year. Receives 800 queries and 500 mss/year. 80% from unagented writers. Pays royalty, or makes outright purchase. Offers modest advance.** Publishes book less than 1 year after acceptance of ms. Accepts simultaneous submissions. Responds in 2 months to queries; 2 months to proposals; 4 months to mss. Book catalog online; ms guidelines for #10 SASE.

Nonfiction Biography, general nonfiction. Subjects include creative nonfiction, memoirs, multicultural, nature/environment, regional, science, travel, women's issues/studies, world affairs. ''We are accepting queries in the above subjects in order to expand our list.'' Query with SASE, or submit proposal package including outline, author bio, 30-50 pages (including the first chapter), SASE.

Recent Title(s) *Last Moon Dancing: A Memoir of Love and Real Life in Africa*, by Monique Maria Schmidt.

Tips ''Our audience is women, high school, and college students, readers with curiosity about the world. Initial contact by e-mail or query letter. We welcome good writing. Have patience, we will respond.''

CONSUMER PRESS

13326 SW 28 St., Suite 102, Ft. Lauderdale FL 33330. (954)370-9153. E-mail: info@consumerpress.com. **Acquisitions:** Joseph Pappas, editorial director. Estab. 1989. Publishes trade paperback originals. **Publishes 2-5 titles/year. Pays royalty on wholesale price or on retail price, as per agreement.** Does not accept simultaneous submissions. Book catalog free.

Imprints Women's Publications.

Nonfiction How-to, self-help. Subjects include child guidance/parenting, health/medicine, money/finance, women's issues/studies, homeowner guides, building/remodeling, food/nutrition. Query with SASE.

Recent Title(s) *The Ritalin Free Child*, by Diana Hunter; *Before You Hire a Contractor, 2nd Ed.*, by Steve Gonzalez, CRC; *Food Smart: Understanding Nutrition in the 21st Century*, by Diana Hunter.

CORNELL MARITIME PRESS, INC.

P.O. Box 456, Centreville MD 21617-0456. (410)758-1075. Fax: (410)758-6849. Web site: www.cmptp.com. **Acquisitions:** Marci McGuinness Andrews, managing editor. Estab. 1938. Publishes hardcover originals and quality paperbacks. **Publishes 7-9 titles/year. 80% of books from first-time authors; 99% from unagented writers.** Publishes book 1 year after acceptance of ms. Responds in 2 months to queries.

Imprints Tidewater (regional history, outdoor sports, and wildlife of the Chesapeake Bay and the Delmarva Peninsula).

> O⊸ Cornell Maritime Press publishes books for the merchant marine and a few recreational boating books for professional mariners and yachtsmen. Cornell also publishes a line of leathercraft books.

Nonfiction How-to (on maritime subjects), technical, manuals. Subjects include marine subjects (highly technical). Look online for current acquisition needs and submission guidelines.

Recent Title(s) *Off the Hook*, by Lenny Rudow; *Nautical Rules of the Road*, by Farnsworth, Young and Browne.

COTTONWOOD PRESS, INC.

109-B Cameron Dr., Fort Collins CO 80525. (800)864-4297. Fax: (970)204-0761. E-mail: cottonwood@cottonwoodpress.com. Web site: www.cottonwoodpress.com. **Acquisitions:** Cheryl Thurston, editor. Estab. 1986. Publishes trade paperback originals. **Publishes 2-8 titles/year. Receives 50 queries and 40 mss/year. 50% of books from first-time authors; 100% from unagented writers. Pays 10-12% royalty on net receipts.** Publishes book 1 year after acceptance of ms. Accepts simultaneous submissions. Responds in 1 month to queries; 1 month to proposals; 3 months to mss. Book catalog for 10×12 SAE with 2 first-class stamps; ms guidelines online.

> O⊸ Cottonwood Press publishes creative and practical materials for English and language arts teachers, grades 5-12. ''We believe English should be everyone's favorite subject.''

Nonfiction Textbook. Subjects include education, language/literature. ''We are always looking for truly original, creative materials for teachers.'' Query with SASE, or submit outline, 1-3 sample chapters.

Recent Title(s) *Phunny Stuph—Proofreading Exercises With a Sense of Humor*, by M.S. Samston; *Twisting Arms—Teaching Students to Write to Persuade*, by Dawn DiPrince; *Rock & Rap in Middle School*, by Sheree Sevilla and Suzanne Stansbury.

Tips ''We publish only supplemental textbooks for English/language arts teachers, grades 5-12, with an emphasis upon middle school and junior high materials. Don't assume we publish educational materials for all subject areas. We do not. Never submit anything to us before looking at our catalog. We have a very narrow focus and a distinctive style. Writers who don't understand that are wasting their time. On the plus side, we are eager to work with new authors who show a sense of humor and a familiarity with young adolescents.''

N CREATRIX BOOKS, LLC

Creatrix! LLC, P.O. Box 366, Cottage Grove WI 53527. Web site: www.creatrixbooks.com. Estab. 2004. Publishes hardcover and trade paperback originals and reprints. **Publishes 3-6 titles/year; imprint publishes 1-3 titles/**

year. **Pays 6-8% royalty on retail price.** Publishes book 1-2 years after acceptance of ms. Does not accept simultaneous submissions. Book catalog and ms guidelines online.

Imprints Creatrix Resource Library, LLC; Creatrix Vision Spun Fiction, LLC.

Nonfiction General nonfiction, how-to, multimedia, reference, scholarly, self-help, technical. Subjects include alternative lifestyles, anthropology/archeology, contemporary culture, ethnic, gay/lesbian, health/medicine, history, multicultural, nature/environment, New Age, philosophy, psychology, religion, sociology, spirituality, women's issues/studies, pagan/Wiccan. "All subjects must be written from a feminist spiritual perspective. We are looking for well-researched material written in a style accessible to the layperson. Footnotes, references and bibliographies are encouraged." Submit proposal package including outline, 3 sample chapter(s), author bio.

Fiction Adventure, ethnic, fantasy, feminist, gay/lesbian, historical, humor, literary, multicultural, occult, religious, spiritual. "We are a feminist spiritual press. We are looking for literary-style, woman-centered stories, especially those that present alternatives to the patriarchal paradigm. We want substantial plots of visionary fiction with a feminist spiritual tone." Submit proposal package including 3 sample chapter(s), synopsis.

Recent Title(s) *Wild Girls: The Path of the Young Goddess*, by Patricia Monaghan (instructional manual); *She Who Walks the Labyrinth*, by K. Sojourner.

Tips "Our main readers are educated women between the ages of 27-70 years who are spiritual seekers. Our secondary market is the daughters of these women and college-age women. We are Wiccan but open to any spiritual path that empowers women. Strong, complicated female characters matter in our fiction."

CROSSQUARTER PUBLISHING GROUP

P.O. Box 86, Crookston MN 56716. (218)281-8065. E-mail: info@crossquarter.com. Web site: www.crossquarter.com. **Acquisitions:** Anthony Ravenscroft. Publishes trade paperback originals and reprints. **Publishes 5-10 titles/year. Receives 1,200 queries/year. 90% of books from first-time authors. Pays 8-10% royalty on wholesale or retail price.** Publishes book 1-2 years after acceptance of ms. Accepts simultaneous submissions. Responds in 3 months to queries. Book catalog for $1.75; ms guidelines online.

- Query letters are required. *No unsolicited mss.*
- "We emphasize personal sovereignty, self responsibility and growth with pagan or pagan-friendly emphasis for young adults and adults."

Nonfiction Biography, how-to, self-help. Subjects include health/medicine, nature/environment, New Age, philosophy, psychology, religion (pagan only), spirituality, autobiography. Query with SASE. Reviews artwork/photos as part of ms package. Send photocopies.

Fiction Science fiction, visionary fiction. Query with SASE.

Recent Title(s) *Polyamory*, by Anthony Ravenscroft; *Extinction*, by John Lee Schneider.

Tips "Audience is earth-conscious people looking to grow into balance of body, mind, heart and spirit."

CYCLE PUBLISHING

Van der Plas Publications, 1282 Seventh Ave., San Francisco CA 94122. (415)665-8214. Fax: (415)753-8572. E-mail: rvdp@vanderplas.net. Web site: www.cyclepublishing.com. **Acquisitions:** Rob van der Plas, publisher/editor. Estab. 1997. Publishes hardcover and trade paperback originals. **Publishes 4 titles/year.** Accepts simultaneous submissions. Book catalog and ms guidelines for #10 SASE.

Nonfiction How-to, technical. Subjects include recreation, sports, manufactured homes. Submit complete ms. Reviews artwork/photos as part of ms package.

Recent Title(s) *Mountain Bike Maintenance*; *Buying a Manufactured Home*.

Tips "Writers have a good chance selling us books with better and more illustrations and a systematic treatment of the subject. First check what is on the market and ask yourself whether you are writing something that is not yet available and wanted."

JOHN DANIEL AND CO.

Daniel & Daniel, Publishers, Inc., P.O. Box 2790, McKinleyville CA 95519. (707)839-3495. Fax: (707)839-3242. E-mail: dandd@danielpublishing.com. Web site: www.danielpublishing.com. **Acquisitions:** John Daniel, publisher. Estab. 1980. Publishes hardcover originals and trade paperback originals. Publishes poetry, fiction and nonfiction. **Publishes 4 or fewer titles/year. Pays 10% royalty on wholesale price. Offers $0-500 advance.** Publishes book 1 year after acceptance of ms. Accepts simultaneous submissions. Responds in 1 month to queries; 1 month to proposals; 2 months to mss. Book catalog and ms guidelines online.

Nonfiction Biography, essay. Subjects include creative nonfiction, memoirs. "We seldom publish books over 70,000 words. Other than that, we're looking for books that are important and well-written." Query with SASE, or submit proposal package including outline, 50 pages.

Fiction Literary, short story collections. Publishes poetry, fiction and nonfiction; specializes in belles lettres, literary memoir. Query with SASE, or submit proposal package including synopsis, 50 pages.

Poetry "We publish very little poetry, I'm sorry to say." Query, or submit complete ms.

Recent Title(s) *Out of the Kitchen: Adventures of a Food Writer*, by Jeannette Ferrary (memoir); *Yellow Swing*, by Rosalind Brackenbury (poetry).
Tips "Audience includes literate, intelligent general readers. We are very small and very cautious, and we publish fewer books each year, so any submission to us is a long shot. But we welcome your submissions, by mail or e-mail only, please. We don't want submissions by phone, fax or disk."

DANTE UNIVERSITY OF AMERICA PRESS, INC.

P.O. Box 812158, Wellesley MA 02482. Fax: (781)790-1056. E-mail: danteu@danteuniversity.org. Web site: www.danteuniversity.org/dpress.html. **Acquisitions:** Adolph Caso, president. Estab. 1975. Publishes hardcover and trade paperback originals and reprints. **Publishes 5 titles/year. 50% of books from first-time authors; 50% from unagented writers. Pays royalty. Offers negotiable advance.** Publishes book 10 months after acceptance of ms. Responds in 2 months to queries.

> O⇁ "The Dante University Press exists to bring quality, educational books pertaining to our Italian heritage as well as the historical and political studies of America. Profits from the sale of these publications benefit the Foundation, bringing Dante University closer to a reality."

Nonfiction Biography, reference, scholarly, reprints. Subjects include history (Italian-American), humanities, translation (from Italian and Latin), general scholarly nonfiction, Renaissance thought and letter, Italian language and linguistics, Italian-American culture, bilingual education. Query with SASE. Reviews artwork/photos as part of ms package.
Fiction Translations from Italian and Latin. Query with SASE.
Poetry "There is a chance that we would use Renaissance poetry translations."
Recent Title(s) *The Prince*, by Machiavelli (social sciences); *The Kaso Dictionary—English-Italian* (reference).

MAY DAVENPORT, PUBLISHERS

26313 Purissima Rd., Los Altos Hills CA 94022. (650)947-1275. Fax: (650)947-1373. E-mail: mdbooks@earthlink.net. Web site: www.maydavenportpublishers.com. **Acquisitions:** May Davenport, editor/publisher. Estab. 1976. Publishes hardcover and paperback originals. **Publishes 4 titles/year. 95% of books from first-time authors; 100% from unagented writers. Pays 15% royalty on retail price. Offers no advance.** Publishes book 1 year after acceptance of ms. Responds in 1 month to queries. Book catalog and ms guidelines for #10 SASE.
Imprints md Books (nonfiction and fiction).

> O⇁ May Davenport publishes "literature for teenagers (before they graduate from high schools) as supplementary literary material in English courses nationwide." Looking particularly for authors able to write for the "teen Internet" generation who don't like to read in-depth. Currently emphasizing more upper-level subjects for teens.

Nonfiction Subjects include Americana, language/literature, humorous memoirs for chldren/young adults. "For children ages 6-8: stories to read with pictures to color in 500 words. For preteens and young adults: Exhibit your writing skills and entertain them with your literary tools." Query with SASE.
Fiction Humor, literary. "We want to focus on novels junior and senior high school teachers can share with their reluctant readers in their classrooms." Query with SASE.
Recent Title(s) *Matthew Livingston & the Prison of Souls*, by Marco Conell; *Surviving Sarah*, by Dinah Leigh (nonfiction).
Tips "Just write your fictional novel humorously. If you can't write that way, create youthful characters so teachers, as well as 15-18-year-old high school readers, will laugh at your descriptive passages and contemporary dialogue. Avoid 1-sentence paragraphs. The audience we want to reach is past Nancy Drew and Hardy Boy readers."

DAWN PUBLICATIONS

12402 Bitney Springs Rd., Nevada City CA 95959. (530)274-7775. Fax: (530)274-7778. Web site: www.dawnpub.com. **Acquisitions:** Glenn Hovemann, editor. Estab. 1979. Publishes hardcover and trade paperback originals. **Publishes 6 titles/year. Receives 550 queries and 2,500 mss/year. 15% of books from first-time authors; 90% from unagented writers. Pays royalty on net receipts. Offers advance.** Publishes book 1 to 2 years after acceptance of ms. Accepts simultaneous submissions. Responds in 2 months to queries. Book catalog and ms guidelines online.

> O⇁ Dawn Publications is dedicated to inspiring in children a sense of appreciation for all life on earth. Dawn looks for nature awareness and appreciation titles that promote a relationship with the natural world and specific habitats, usually through inspiring treatment and nonfiction.

Nonfiction Children's/juvenile. Subjects include animals, nature/environment. Query with SASE.
Recent Title(s) *The Web at Dragonfly Pond*, by Brian "Fox" Ellis; *City Beats*, by S. Kelly Rammell; *If You Were My Baby*, by Fran Hodgkins.
Tips Publishes mostly "creative nonfiction" with lightness and inspiration.

DBS PRODUCTIONS

P.O. Box 1894, Charlottesville VA 22903. (800)745-1581. Fax: (434)293-5502. E-mail: robert@dbs-sar.com. Web site: www.dbs-sar.com. **Acquisitions:** Bob Adams, publisher. Estab. 1989. Publishes hardcover and trade paperback originals. **Publishes 6 titles/year. Receives 5 queries/year. 5% of books from first-time authors; 100% from unagented writers. Pays 5-20% royalty on retail price.** Publishes book 1 year after acceptance of ms. Does not accept simultaneous submissions. Responds in 2 months to queries. Book catalog on request or on Web site; ms guidelines for #10 SASE.

O→ dbS Productions produces search and rescue and outdoor first-aid related materials and courses. It offers a selection of publications, videotapes, management kits and tools, and instructional modules.

Nonfiction Technical, textbook. Subjects include health/medicine. Submit proposal package including outline, 2 sample chapters. Reviews artwork/photos as part of ms package. Send photocopies.

Recent Title(s) *Field Operations Guide for Search and Rescue, 2nd Ed.*, by R. Koester.

N DEMONTREVILLE PRESS, INC.

P.O. Box 835, Lake Elmo MN 55042-0835. E-mail: publisher@demontrevillepress.com. Web site: www.demontrevillepress.com. **Acquisitions:** Kevin Clemens, publisher (automotive fiction and nonfiction). Estab. 2006. Publishes trade paperback originals and reprints. **Publishes 4 titles/year. Receives 150 queries and 100 mss/year. 90% of books from first-time authors; 90% from unagented writers. Pays 10% royalty on wholesale price.** Publishes book 18 months after acceptance of ms. Accepts simultaneous submissions. Responds in 2 months to queries; 3 months to proposals; 6 months to mss. Book catalog and ms guidelines online.

Nonfiction Biography, technical. Subjects include creative nonfiction, history, automotive. ''We want collections of essays dealing with automotive and motorcycle adventure.'' Submit proposal package including outline, 3 sample chapter(s), author bio. Reviews artwork/photos as part of ms package. Do not send photos until requested.

Fiction Adventure, mystery, sports, young adult, automotive, motorcycle. ''We want short story or novel length automotive or motorcycle historicals and/or adventures.'' Submit proposal package including 3 sample chapter(s), synopsis, author bio.

Tips ''Automotive and motorcyle enthusiasts, adventurers, and history buffs make up our audience. You should be an enthusiast if you wish to write for Demontreville Press.''

⊘ THE DENALI PRESS

P.O. Box 021535, Juneau AK 99802-1535. (907)586-6014. Fax: (907)463-6780. E-mail: denalipress@alaska.com. Web site: www.denalipress.com. **Acquisitions:** Alan Schorr, editorial director; Sally Silvas-Ottumwa, editorial associate. Estab. 1986. Publishes trade paperback originals. **Publishes 5 titles/year. 50% of books from first-time authors; 80% from unagented writers. Pays 10% royalty on wholesale price, or makes outright purchase. Offers advance.** Publishes book 1 year after acceptance of ms. Accepts simultaneous submissions. Responds in 1 month to queries.

O→ The Denali Press looks for reference works suitable for the educational, professional, and library market. "Though we publish books on a variety of topics, our focus is most broadly centered on multiculturalism, public policy, Alaskana, and general reference works."

Nonfiction Reference. Subjects include Americana, anthropology/archeology, ethnic, government/politics, history, multicultural, recreation, regional. ''We need reference books—ethnic, refugee, and minority concerns.'' Query with SASE, or submit outline, sample chapter(s). *All unsolicited mss returned unopened.*

Recent Title(s) *Winning Political Campaigns: A Comprehensive Guide to Electoral Success*, by William S. Bike.

DIALOGUE PUBLISHING INC.

16990 Cherry Crossing Dr., Colorado Springs CO 80291-3406. (719)495-3755. Fax: (719)527-0843. E-mail: info@dialoguepublishing.com. Web site: www.dialoguepublishing.com. **Acquisitions:** Sue Hamilton, president (mainstream and women's fiction, mystery, nonfiction). Estab. 2004. Publishes harcover originals and trade paperback originals. **Publishes 2 titles/year. Receives 500 queries and 12 mss/year. 90% of books from first-time authors; 100% from unagented writers. Pays 10-15% royalty.** Publishes book 6-8 months after acceptance of ms. Accepts simultaneous submissions. Responds in 3 months to queries; 3 months to proposals; 2 months to mss. Book catalog and ms guidelines online.

Nonfiction General nonfiction. Subjects include health/medicine. Query with SASE, or submit proposal package including outline, author bio, 3 sample chapters, any marketing ideas.

Fiction Literary, mainstream/contemporary, mystery, suspense, women's. Query with SASE, or submit proposal package including synopsis, author bio, 3 sample chapters, any marketing ideas.

Tips ''I am looking for strong female heroines from unpublished writers who have participated in writers' workshops and conferences to hone their craft.''

DIAMOND EYES PUBLISHING

P.O. Box 7276, Woodland Park CO 80863. (888)769-9931. E-mail: info@depublishing.com. Submissions E-mail: submit@depublishing.com. Web site: www.depublishing.com. **Acquisitions:** Jessica Adriel, senior editor (fiction). Estab. 1999. Publishes trade paperback originals. **Publishes 6 titles/year. Receives 1,000 queries and 50 mss/year. 80% of books from first-time authors; 100% from unagented writers. Pays 8-10% royalty on net receipts.** Publishes book 1 year after acceptance of ms. Accepts simultaneous submissions. Responds in 2 months to queries; 4 months to mss. Book catalog and ms guidelines online.

Nonfiction General nonfiction, self-help. Subjects include money/finance, religion, true crime, motivational books, workbooks, church dramas, plays. "Diamond Eyes is looking for 'How-to Manuals' that can be marketed to churches. We are especially interested in leadership ideas for teens, and ideas for how to grow/develop a drama department. We are looking for short plays to comprise for churches or youth organizations. Biblical finance or controversial biblical topics welcome. Authors should note that we have a charismatic viewpoint on most issues." Query via e-mail.

Fiction Mainstream/contemporary, plays, young adult. "Trident Books is seeking fresh ideas for mainstream fiction, or any story that teaches a moral or lesson. Books are marketed toward a secular audience but teach a moral or ethical virtue. We are also interested in books that possess supernatural perspectives or characters. Lauren's Box is a women's fiction imprint of Diamond Eyes and is looking for authors who write about everyday characters who embrace grief, trauma, divorce, or any other issue except medical that women face today. We are looking for romance novels as well. Submit your ideas on all subjects if you are looking for a publisher who is interested in the purpose of your book and not just publishing another title." Query via e-mail.

Poetry "We only publish the winners of our contest. The winners will be published in a gift book along with inspirational photos. The fee to enter the contest is $7/poem. There is no deadline. Our goal is to enhance the meaning and purpose of poetry by sharing the beauty of the writer through their own expression. We welcome poems on various topics. Entrants can view the topics on our Web site."

Recent Title(s) *Writing His Way*, by Jessica Adriel (Christian writing manual); *Drawing Marissa.*

Tips "We are a Christian publisher looking for fiction that has a message and provides the reader with more than just entertainment. Read a few articles on query letters, and know how the industry works. Understand that writing talent is secondary to how an author conducts him/herself. Your query is your first impression. Do not rush; be more than prepared when you send out your query and pray."

DOWN THE SHORE PUBLISHING

Box 100, West Creek NJ 08092. Fax: (609)597-0422. E-mail: info@down-the-shore.com. Web site: www.down-the-shore.com. Publishes hardcover and trade paperback originals and reprints. **Publishes 6-10 titles/year. Pays royalty on wholesale or retail price, or makes outright purchase.** Accepts simultaneous submissions. Responds in 3 months to queries. Book catalog for 8×10 SAE with 2 first-class stamps or on Web site; ms guidelines online.

O→ "Bear in mind that our market is regional—New Jersey, the Jersey Shore, the mid-Atlantic, and seashore and coastal subjects."

Nonfiction Children's/juvenile, coffee table book, gift book, illustrated book. Subjects include Americana, art/architecture, history, nature/environment, regional. Query with SASE, or submit proposal package including 1-2 sample chapters, synopsis. Reviews artwork/photos as part of ms package. Send photocopies.

Fiction Regional. Query with SASE, or submit proposal package including synopsis, 1-2 sample chapters.

Poetry "We do not publish poetry, unless it is to be included as part of an anthology."

Recent Title(s) *Four Seasons at the Shore*; *The Oyster Singer*, by Larry Savadove.

Tips "Carefully consider whether your proposal is a good fit for our established market."

DUQUESNE UNIVERSITY PRESS

600 Forbes Ave., Pittsburgh PA 15282. (412)396-6610. Fax: (412)396-5984. Web site: www.dupress.duq.edu. **Acquisitions:** Susan Wadsworth-Booth, director. Estab. 1927. Publishes hardcover and trade paperback originals. **Publishes 8-12 titles/year. Receives 500 queries and 75 mss/year. 30% of books from first-time authors; 95% from unagented writers. Pays royalty on net price. Offers (some) advance.** Publishes book 1 year after acceptance of ms. Responds in 1 month to proposals; 3 months to mss. Book catalog and ms guidelines for #10 SASE; ms guidelines online.

O→ Duquesne publishes scholarly monographs in the fields of literary studies (medieval & Renaissance), continental philosophy, ethics, religious studies and existential psychology.

Nonfiction Scholarly (academic). Subjects include language/literature, philosophy (continental), psychology (existential), religion. "We look for quality of scholarship." For scholarly books, query or submit outline, 1 sample chapter, and SASE.

Recent Title(s) *What Is the West?*, by Philippe Nemo; *Freud's Traumatic Memory*, by Mary Marcel; *The Philosopher's Gaze*, by David Levin.

EAGLE'S VIEW PUBLISHING

6756 North Fork Rd., Liberty UT 84310. (801)745-0905. Fax: (801)393-4647. E-mail: eglcrafts@aol.com. Web site: www.eaglesviewpub.com. **Acquisitions:** Denise Knight, editor-in-chief. Estab. 1982. Publishes trade paperback originals. **Publishes 2-4 titles/year. Receives 40 queries and 20 mss/year. 90% of books from first-time authors; 100% from unagented writers. Pays 8-10% royalty on net selling price.** Publishes book 1 year or more after acceptance of ms. Accepts simultaneous submissions. Responds in 1 year to proposals. Book catalog and ms guidelines for $4.

- Eagle's View primarily publishes how-to craft books with a subject related to historical or contemporary Native American/Mountain Man/frontier crafts/bead crafts. Currently emphasizing bead-related craft books. De-emphasizing history except for historical Indian crafts.

Nonfiction How-to, Indian, mountain man, and American frontier (history and craft). Subjects include anthropology/archeology (Native American crafts), ethnic (Native American), history (American frontier historical patterns and books), hobbies (crafts, especially beadwork). "We are expanding from our Indian craft base to more general, but related, crafts. We prefer to do photography in-house." Submit outline, 1-2 sample chapters. Reviews artwork/photos as part of ms package. Send photocopies or sample illustrations.

Recent Title(s) *Treasury of Beaded Jewelry*, by Mary Ellen Harte; *Beads and Beadwork of the American Indian*, by William C. Orchard; *Hemp Masters: Getting Knotty*, by Max Lunger.

Tips "We will not be publishing any new beaded earrings books for the forseeable future. We are interested in other craft projects using seed beads, especially books that feature a variety of items, not just different designs for 1 item."

EARTH-LOVE PUBLISHING HOUSE LTD.

3440 Youngfield St., Suite 353, Wheat Ridge CO 80033. (303)233-9660. Fax: (303)233-9354. **Acquisitions:** Laodeciae Augustine, director. Publishes trade paperback originals. **Publishes 1-2 titles/year. Pays 6-10% royalty on wholesale price.** Does not accept simultaneous submissions. Responds in 1 month to queries; 1 month to proposals; 3 months to mss.

Nonfiction Reference. Subjects include minerals. Query with SASE.

Recent Title(s) *Love Is in the Earth—Kaleidoscope Pictorial Supplement Z*, by Melody (mineral reference); *Loves Is in the Earth—Crystal Tarot for the Millennium*, by Melody; *Love Is in the Earth—Reality Checque*, by Melody.

EASTLAND PRESS

P.O. Box 99749, Seattle WA 98139. (206)217-0204. Fax: (206)217-0205. E-mail: info@eastlandpress.com. Web site: www.eastlandpress.com. **Acquisitions:** John O'Connor, managing editor. Estab. 1981. Publishes hardcover and trade paperback originals. **Publishes 3-4 titles/year. Receives 25 queries/year. 30% of books from first-time authors; 90% from unagented writers. Pays 12-15% royalty on receipts.** Publishes book 2 years after acceptance of ms. Accepts simultaneous submissions. Responds in 1 month to queries. Book catalog free.

- Eastland Press is interested in textbooks for practitioners of alternative medical therapies primarily Chinese and physical therapies, and related bodywork.

Nonfiction Reference, textbook, alternative medicine (Chinese and physical therapies, and related bodywork). Subjects include health/medicine. "We prefer that a manuscript be completed or close to completion before we will consider publication. Proposals are rarely considered, unless submitted by a published author or teaching institution." Submit outline and 2-3 sample chapters. Reviews artwork/photos as part of ms package. Send photocopies.

Recent Title(s) *Anatomy of Breathing*, by Blandine Calais-Germain; *The Fasciae: Anatomy, Dysfunction & Treatment*, by Serge Paoletti; *Chinese Herbal Medicine*, by Dan Bensky.

ELYSIAN EDITIONS

Imprint of Princeton Book Co., Publishers, 614 Route 130, Hightstown NJ 08520. (609)426-0602. Fax: (609)426-1344. E-mail: elysian@aosi.com. Web site: www.dancehorizons.com/elysian.html. **Acquisitions:** Charles Woodford (fitness, yoga, travel, memoir, true adventure). Publishes hardcover and trade paperback originals and reprints. **Publishes 1-3 titles/year. Receives 100 queries and 30 mss/year. 25% of books from first-time authors; 50% from unagented writers. Pays royalty on retail price. Offers negotiable advance.** Publishes book 9-12 months after acceptance of ms. Accepts simultaneous submissions. Responds in 3 weeks to queries; 3 weeks to proposals; 1 month to mss. Book catalog free or on Web site; ms guidelines free.

Nonfiction Biography. Subjects include memoirs, travel, true adventure, fitness, yoga. Submit proposal package including outline, 3 sample chapters. Reviews artwork/photos as part of ms package. Send photocopies.

Recent Title(s) *Paris Discovered: Explorations in the City of Light*; *Inner Focus, Outer Strength: Imagery and Exercise for Health, Strength, and Beauty.*

ERIE CANAL PRODUCTIONS

4 Farmdale St., Clinton NY 13323. E-mail: eriecanal@juno.com. Web site: www.eriecanalproductions.com. **Acquisitions:** Scott Fiesthumel, president. Estab. 2001. Publishes trade paperback originals. **Publishes 1-2 titles/year. 50% of books from first-time authors; 100% from unagented writers. Pays negotiable royalty on net profits.** Responds in 1 month to queries. Book catalog free.

Nonfiction Biography, general nonfiction. Subjects include Americana, history, sports. Query with SASE. *All unsolicited mss returned unopened.*

Recent Title(s) *The Legend of Wild Bill Setley*, by Tony Kissel; *S. Fiesthumel* (biography); *Diamond Dynasty*, by Billy Mills.

Tips "We publish nonfiction books that look at historical places, events, and people along the traditional route of the Erie Canal through New York State."

ETC PUBLICATIONS

700 E. Vereda Sur, Palm Springs CA 92262-4816. (760)325-5352. Fax: (760)325-8841. **Acquisitions:** Dr. Richard W. Hostrop, publisher (education and social sciences); Lee Ona S. Hostrop, editorial director (history and works suitable below the college level). Estab. 1972. Publishes hardcover and paperback originals. **Publishes 6-12 titles/year. 75% of books from first-time authors; 90% from unagented writers. Offers 5-15% royalty, based on wholesale and retail price.** Publishes book 9 months after acceptance of ms.

ETC publishes works that "further learning as opposed to entertainment."

Nonfiction Textbook, educational management, gifted education, futuristics. Subjects include education, translation (in above areas). Submit complete ms with SASE. Reviews artwork/photos as part of ms package.

Recent Title(s) *The Artilect War*; *The Cosmists vs. The Terrans.*

Tips "Special consideration is given to those authors who are capable and willing to submit their completed work in camera-ready, typeset form. We are particularly interested in works suitable for both the Christian school market and homeschoolers; e.g., state history texts below the high school level with a Christian-oriented slant."

EXCALIBUR PUBLICATIONS

P.O. Box 89667, Tucson AZ 85752-9667. (520)575-9057. E-mail: excalibureditor@earthlink.net. **Acquisitions:** Alan M. Petrillo, editor. Publishes trade paperback originals. **Publishes 4-6 titles/year. Pays royalty or makes outright purchase.** Responds in 1 month to queries; 1 month to mss.

Excalibur publishes historical and military works from all time periods.

Nonfiction Subjects include history (military), military/war (strategy and tactics, as well as the history of battles, firearms, arms, and armour), historical personalities. "We are seeking well-researched and documented works. Unpublished writers are welcome." Query with synopsis, first chapter, SASE. Include notes on photos, illustrations, and maps.

Recent Title(s) *Famous Faces of World War II*, by Robert Van Osdol; *Present Sabers: A History of the U.S. Horse Cavalry*, by Allan Heninger; *Japanese Rifles of World War II*, by Duncan O. McCollum.

Tips "Know your subject matter, and present it in a clear and precise manner. Please give us a brief description of your background or experience as it relates to your submission, as well as any marketing insight you might have on your subject."

EXECUTIVE EXCELLENCE PUBLISHING

1806 North 1120 West, Provo UT 84604. (801)375-4060. Fax: (801)377-5960. E-mail: editorial@eep.com. Web site: www.eep.com. **Acquisitions:** Ken Shelton, editor in chief. Estab. 1984. Publishes hardcover and trade paperback originals and trade paperback reprints. **Publishes 4 titles/year. Receives 300 queries and 150 mss/year. 35% of books from first-time authors; 95% from unagented writers. Pays 15% on cash received and 50% of subsidary right proceeds.** Publishes book 6-9 months after acceptance of ms. Accepts simultaneous submissions. Responds in 1 month to queries; 1 month to proposals; 1 month to mss. Book catalog free or on Web site.

Executive Excellence publishes business and self-help titles. "We help you—the busy person, executive or entrepreneur—to find a wiser, better way to live your life and lead your organization." Currently emphasizing business innovations for general management and leadership (from the personal perspective). De-emphasizing technical or scholarly textbooks on operational processes and financial management or workbooks.

Nonfiction Self-help. Subjects include business/economics, leadership/management, entrepreneurship, career, motivational. Submit proposal package, including outline, 1-2 sample chapters and author bio, company information.

Recent Title(s) *Why Lead?*, by Phil Harkins/Phil Swift; *Monopolize Your Marketplace*, by Richard Harshaw.

Tips "Executive Excellence Publishing is an established publishing house with a strong niche in the marketplace.

Our magazines, *Leadership Excellence, Sales and Service Excellence* and *Personal Excellence*, are distributed monthly in countries across the world. Our authors are on the cutting edge in their fields of leadership, self-help and business and organizational development. We are always looking for strong new talent with something to say, and a burning desire to say it. We expect authors to invest in their work. We do not offer all-expense paid ego trips."

N FAIRVIEW PRESS

2450 Riverside Ave., Minneapolis MN 55454. (612)672-4774. Fax: (612)672-4980. E-mail: press@fairview.org. Web site: www.fairviewpress.org. **Acquisitions:** Steve Deger, acquisitions and marketing. Estab. 1988. Publishes hardcover and trade paperback originals and reprints. **Publishes 8-12 titles/year. Receives 3,000 queries and 1,500 mss/year. 40% of books from first-time authors; 65% from unagented writers. Advance and royalties negotiable.** Publishes book 1 year after acceptance of ms. Accepts simultaneous submissions. Responds in 6 months to proposals. Book catalog free; ms guidelines online.

- Fairview Press publishes books and related materials that educate individuals and families about their physical, emotional, and spiritual health and motivate them to make positive changes in themselves and their communities.

Nonfiction Submit proposal package including outline, author bio, 2 sample chapters, marketing ideas, SASE. Reviews artwork/photos as part of ms package. Send photocopies.

Tips Audience is general reader.

N FATHER'S PRESS

2424 SE 6th St., Lee's Summit MO 64063. E-mail: mikesmitley2@yahoo.com. Submissions E-mail: fatherspress@yahoo.com. Web site: www.fatherspress.com. **Acquisitions:** Mike Smitley, owner (fiction, nonfiction). Estab. 2006. Publishes hardcover, trade paperback, and mass market paperback originals and reprints. **Publishes 6-10 titles/year. Pays 10-15% royalty on wholesale price.** Publishes book 6 months after acceptance of ms. Does not accept simultaneous submissions. Responds in 1 month to queries; 1 month to proposals; 3 months to mss. Ms guidelines online.

Nonfiction Autobiography, biography, children's/juvenile, coffee table book, cookbook, general nonfiction, gift book, humor, illustrated book. Subjects include Americana, animals, cooking/foods/nutrition, creative nonfiction, history, hobbies, memoirs, military/war, nature/environment, recreation, regional, religion, sports, travel, women's issues/studies, world affairs. Query with SASE. **All unsolicited mss returned unopened.** Reviews artwork/photos as part of ms package. Send photocopies.

Fiction Adventure, historical, humor, juvenile, literary, mainstream/contemporary, military/war, mystery, regional, religious, suspense, western, young adult. Query with SASE. **All unsolicited mss returned unopened.**

Recent Title(s) *The Christian and the Struggle With Truth*, by Charles Scheele (Christian); *Dead Files*, by Mike Smitley (mystery/suspense).

FIELDSTONE ALLIANCE, INC.

60 Plato Blvd. E., Suite 150, St. Paul MN 55107. (651)556-4500. E-mail: vhyman@fieldstonealliance.org. Web site: www.fieldstonealliance.org. **Acquisitions:** Vincent Hyman, director. Publishes professional trade paperback originals. **Publishes 6 titles/year. Receives 30 queries and 15 mss/year. 75% of books from first-time authors; 100% from unagented writers. Pays 10% royalty on net receipts. Offers advance.** Publishes book 18 months after acceptance of ms. Accepts simultaneous submissions. Responds in 6 weeks to queries; 6 weeks to proposals; 3 months to mss. Book catalog and ms guidelines online.

- Fieldstone Alliance emphasizes community development, nonprofit organization management, and books for foundations and grant makers. Actively seeking authors and editorial outside vendors of color.

Nonfiction Subjects include nonprofit management, funder's guides, board guides, organizational development, community building. "We are seeking manuscripts that report 'best practice' methods using handbook or workbook formats for nonprofit and community development managers." Submit 3 sample chapters, complete topical outline, and full proposal based on online guidelines. Phone query OK before submitting proposal with detailed chapter outline, SASE, statement of the goals of the book, statement of unique selling points, identification of audience, author qualification, competing publications, marketing potential.

Recent Title(s) *The Accidental Techie*; *A Funder's Guide to Evaluation*; *Benchmarking for Nonprofits.*

Tips "Writers must be practitioners with a passion for their work in nonprofit management or community building and experience presenting their techniques at conferences. Writers receive preference if they can demonstrate the capacity to help sell their books via trainings, a large established e-mail or client list, or other direct connections with customers, who are largely nonprofit leaders, managers and consultants. We seek practical, not academic books. Our books identify professional challenges faced by our audiences and offer practical, step-by-step solutions. Never send us a manuscript without first checking our online guidelines. Queries showing evidence that the author has not reviewed our guidelines will be ignored."

FILTER PRESS, LLC

P.O. Box 95, Palmer Lake CO 80133-0095. (719)481-2420. Fax: (719)481-2420. E-mail: info@filterpressbooks.com. Web site: www.filterpressbooks.com. **Acquisitions:** Doris Baker, president. Estab. 1957. Publishes trade paperback originals and reprints. **Publishes 4-6 titles/year. Pays 10-12% royalty on wholesale price.** Publishes book 1 year after acceptance of ms.

O— Filter Press specializes in nonfiction of the West.

Nonfiction Subjects include Americana, anthropology/archeology, ethnic, history, regional, crafts and crafts people of the Southwest. Query with outline and SASE. Reviews artwork/photos as part of ms package.

Recent Title(s) *Touching Tomorrow*, by Debra Faulkner; *Enos Mills*, by John Stansfield.

FINNEY COMPANY, INC.

8075 215th St. W, Lakeville MN 55044. (952)469-6699. Fax: (952)469-1968. E-mail: feedback@finney-hobar.com. Web site: www.finney-hobar.com. **Acquisitions:** Alan E. Krysan, president. Publishes trade paperback originals. **Publishes 2 titles/year. Pays 10% royalty on wholesale price. Offers advance.** Publishes book 1 year after acceptance of ms. Responds in 8-10 weeks to queries.

Nonfiction Reference, textbook. Subjects include business/economics, education, career exploration/development. Finney publishes career development educational materials. Query with SASE. Reviews artwork/photos as part of ms package.

Recent Title(s) *Planning My Career*, by Capozziello; *On the Job*, edited by Laurie Diethelm, et. al.

FOOTPRINT PRESS, INC.

303 Pine Glen Ct., Englewood FL 34223. Phone/Fax: (941)474-8316. E-mail: info@footprintpress.com. Web site: www.footprintpress.com. **Acquisitions:** Sue Freeman, publisher (New York state recreation). Publishes trade paperback originals. **Publishes 1 titles/year. Pays 10% royalty on wholesale price.** Accepts simultaneous submissions. Responds in 1 month to queries; 1 month to proposals; 2 months to mss. Book catalog and ms guidelines for #10 SASE or online.

O— Footprint Press publishes books pertaining to outdoor recreation in New York state.

Nonfiction How-to. Subjects include recreation, regional, sports. Query with SASE.

Recent Title(s) *Cobblestone Quest*, by Rich and Sue Freeman.

FORWARD MOVEMENT

300 W. 4th St., Cincinnati OH 45202-2666. (513)721-6659. Fax: (513)721-0729. Web site: www.forwardmovement.org. Estab. 1934. Book catalog and ms guidelines free.

O— "Forward Movement was established 'to help reinvigorate the life of the church.' Many titles focus on the life of prayer, where our relationship with God is centered, death, marriage, baptism, recovery, joy, the Episcopal Church and more." Currently emphasizing prayer/spirituality.

Nonfiction "We are an agency of the Episcopal Church." Biography, children's/juvenile, reference, self-help (about religion and prayer). Subjects include religion. Query with SASE or submit complete ms.Juvenile.

Recent Title(s):; *De-Cluttering as a Spiritual Activity*, by Donna Schaper; *A Letter Never Sent*, by Alanson B. Houghton.

Tips Audience is primarily Episcopalians and other Christians.

FRONT ROW EXPERIENCE

540 Discovery Bay Blvd., Discovery Bay CA 94514-9454. (925)634-5710. Fax: (925)634-5710. E-mail: service@frontrowexperience.com. Web site: www.frontrowexperience.com. **Acquisitions:** Frank Alexander, editor. Estab. 1974. Publishes trade paperback originals and reprints. **Publishes 1-2 titles/year. Pays 10% royalty on net receipts.** Accepts simultaneous submissions. Responds in 1 month to queries.

Imprints Kokono.

O— Front Row publishes books on movement education and coordination activities for pre-K to 6th grade.

Nonfiction Subjects include movement education, perceptual-motor development, sensory motor development, hand-eye coordination activities. Query.

Recent Title(s) *Perceptual-Motor Lesson Plans, Level 2.*

Tips "Be on target—find out what we want, and only submit queries."

⊘ GAY SUNSHINE PRESS and LEYLAND PUBLICATIONS

P.O. Box 410690, San Francisco CA 94141-0690. Web site: www.leylandpublications.com. **Acquisitions:** Winston Leyland, editor. Estab. 1970. Publishes hardcover originals, trade paperback originals and reprints. **Pub-**

lishes 2-3 titles/year. Pays royalty, or makes outright purchase.** Responds in 6 weeks to queries; 2 months to mss. Book catalog for $1.

O→ Gay history, sex, politics, and culture are the focus of the quality books published by Gay Sunshine Press. Leyland Publications publishes books on popular aspects of gay sexuality and culture.

Nonfiction "We're interested in innovative literary nonfiction which deals with gay lifestyles." How-to. No long personal accounts, academic or overly formal titles. Query with SASE. *All unsolicited mss returned unopened.*

Fiction Interested in innovative well-written novels on gay themes; also short story collections. Erotica, experimental, historical, literary, mystery, science fiction, All gay male material only. "We have a high literary standard for fiction. We desire fiction on gay themes of high literary quality and prefer writers who have already had work published in books or literary magazines. We also publish erotica¢short stories and novels." Query with SASE. *All unsolicited mss returned unopened.*

Recent Title(s) *Out of the Closet Into Our Hearts: Celebration of Our Gay/Lesbian Family Members.*

GEM GUIDES BOOK CO.

315 Cloverleaf Dr., Suite F, Baldwin Park CA 91706-6510. (626)855-1611. Fax: (626)855-1610. E-mail: gembooks@aol.com. Web site: www.gemguidesbooks.com. **Acquisitions:** Kathy Mayerski, editor. Estab. 1965. **Publishes 6-8 titles/year. 60% of books from first-time authors; 100% from unagented writers. Pays 6-10% royalty on retail price.** Publishes book 1 year after acceptance of ms. Accepts simultaneous submissions. Responds in 5 months to queries.

Imprints Gembooks.

O→ "Gem Guides prefers nonfiction books for the hobbyist in rocks and minerals; lapidary and jewelry-making; travel and recreation guide books for the West and Southwest; and other regional local interest." Currently emphasizing how-to, field guides, West/Southwest regional interest. De-emphasizing stories, history, poetry.

Nonfiction Subjects include history (Western), hobbies (rockhounding, prospecting, lapidary, jewelry craft), nature/environment, recreation, regional (Western US), science (earth), travel. Query with outline/synopsis and sample chapters with SASE. Reviews artwork/photos as part of ms package.

Recent Title(s) *Fee Mining and Mineral Adventures in the Eastern U.S.*, by James Martin Monaco and Jeannette Hathaway Monaco; *Geology Trails of Northern California*, by Robin C. Johnson and Dot Loftsrom; *Baby's Day Out in Southern California: Fun Places to Go Wwith Babies and Toddlers*, by JoBea Holt.

Tips "We have a general audience of people interested in recreational activities. Publishers plan and have specific book lines in which they specialize. Learn about the publisher and submit materials compatible with that publisher's product line."

⊘ GIFTED EDUCATION PRESS

10201 Yuma Court, Manassas VA 20109. (703)369-5017. E-mail: mfisher345@comcast.net. Web site: www.giftedpress.com. **Acquisitions:** Maurice Fisher, publisher. Estab. 1981. Publishes trade paperback originals. **Publishes 5 titles/year. Receives 20 queries and 10 mss/year. 90% of books from first-time authors; 100% from unagented writers. Pays 10% royalty on retail price.** Publishes book 4 months after acceptance of ms. Accepts simultaneous submissions. Responds in 1 month to queries; 1 month to proposals; 1 month to mss. Book catalog and ms guidelines online.

O→ Searching for rigorous texts on teaching science, math and humanities to gifted students.

Nonfiction Textbook, subject matter guides in different fields of education. Subjects include child guidance/parenting, computers/electronic, education, history, humanities, philosophy, science, teaching, math, biology, Shakespeare, chemisty, physics, creativity. Query with SASE. *All unsolicited mss returned unopened.* Reviews artwork/photos as part of ms package.

Recent Title(s) *Snibbles*, by Judy Michelett; *Laboratory Physics Experiments for the Gifted*, by Raja Almukahhal; *Why Don't Birds Get Lost?*, by Franklin H. Bronson.

Tips Audience includes teachers, parents, gifted program supervisors, professors. "Be knowledgeable about your subject. Write clearly and don't use educational jargon."

⊘ GOLLEHON PRESS, INC.

6157 28th St. SE, Grand Rapids MI 49546. (616)949-3515. Fax: (616)949-8674. E-mail: john@gollehonbooks.com. Web site: www.gollehonbooks.com. Editor: John Gollehon. **Acquisitions:** Lori Adams, editor. Publishes hardcover, trade paperback, and mass market paperback originals. **Publishes 6-8 titles/year. Receives 100 queries and 30 mss/year. 85% of books from first-time authors; 90% from unagented writers. Pays 7% royalty on retail price. Offers $500-1,000 advance.** Publishes book usually 6 months after acceptance of ms. Accepts simultaneous submissions. Responds in 1 month (if interested) to proposals; 2 months to mss. Book catalog and ms guidelines online.

O→ Currently emphasizing theology (life of Christ), political, current events, pets (dogs only, rescue/heroic), self-help, and gardening. *No unsolicited mss*; brief proposals only with first 5 pages of Chapter 1. "Writer must have strong credentials to author work."

Nonfiction See information listed above for current needs. Submit brief proposal package only with bio and first 5 pages of Chapter 1. "We do not return materials unless we specifically request the full manuscript." Reviews artwork/photos as part of ms package. Writer must be sure he/she owns all rights to photos, artwork, illustrations, etc., submitted for consideration (all submissions must be free of any third-party claims). Never send original photos or art.

Tips "Mail brief book proposal, bio, and a few sample pages only. We will request a full manuscript if interested. We cannot respond to all queries. Full manuscript will be returned if we requested it, and if writer provides SASE. We do not return proposals. Simultaneous submissions are encouraged."

GRAND CANYON ASSOCIATION

P.O. Box 399, 4 Tonto St., Grand Canyon AZ 86023. (928)638-7021. Fax: (928)638-2484. E-mail: tberger@grandcanyon.org. Web site: www.grandcanyon.org. **Acquisitions:** Todd R. Berger, managing editor (Grand Canyon-related geology, natural history, outdoor activities, human history, photography, ecology, etc., posters, postcards and other nonbook products). Estab. 1932. Publishes hardcover originals and reprints, and trade paperback originals and reprints. **Publishes 6 titles/year. Receives 100 queries/year. 70% of books from first-time authors; 99% from unagented writers. Pays royalty on wholesale price, or makes outright purchase.** Publishes book 1 month-1 year after acceptance of ms. Accepts simultaneous submissions. Responds in 2 months to queries; 2 months to proposals; 2 months to mss. Book catalog online; ms guidelines by e-mail.

Nonfiction Autobiography, biography, booklets, children's/juvenile, coffee table book, general nonfiction, gift book, how-to, illustrated book, scholarly. Subjects include animals, anthropology/archeology, art/architecture, creative nonfiction, history, nature/environment, photography, recreation, regional, science, sports, travel, geology. Grand Canyon Association (GCA) is a nonprofit organization established in 1932 to support education, research, and other programs for the benefit of Grand Canyon National Park and its visitors. GCA operates bookstores throughout the park, publishes books and other materials related to the Grand Canyon region, supports wildlife surveys and other research, funds acquisitions for the park's research library, and produces a wide variety of free publications and exhibits for park visitors. Since 1932, GCA has provided Grand Canyon National Park with over $23 million in financial support. Query with SASE, or submit proposal package including outline, 3-4 sample chapters, list of publication credits, and samples of previous work, or submit complete ms. Reviews artwork/photos as part of ms package. Send transparencies, color or b&w prints, or digital samples of images.

Recent Title(s) *Carving Grand Canyon*, by Wayne Ranney (geology); *Earth Notes*, by Peter Friederici (nature/environment); *Life in Stone*, by Christa Sadler (fossils).

Tips "All books, articles, and other products must be about the Grand Canyon. We also publish some things, to a much lesser extent, on the surrounding region, particularly geology-related titles with a connection to the Grand Canyon."

GREAT POTENTIAL PRESS

P.O. Box 5057, Scottsdale AZ 85261. (602)954-4200. Fax: (602)954-0185. E-mail: info@giftedbooks.com. Web site: www.giftedbooks.com. **Acquisitions:** Janet Gore, editor (gifted curriculum in schools); James Webb, president (parenting and social and emotional needs). Estab. 1986. Publishes trade paperback originals. **Publishes 4-5 titles/year. Receives 10 queries and 10-15 mss/year. 25% of books from first-time authors; 100% from unagented writers. Pays 10% royalty on retail price.** Publishes book 6-12 months after acceptance of ms. Accepts simultaneous submissions. Responds in 2 months to queries; 3 months to proposals; 4 months to mss. Book catalog free or on Web site; ms guidelines online.

O→ Great Potential Press publishes books on the social/emotional/interpersonal/creative needs of gifted and talented children and adults for parents and teachers of gifted and talented youngsters. Currently emphasizing books regarding gifted and talented children, their parents and teachers. De-emphasizing research-based books.

Nonfiction Biography, children's/juvenile, humor, reference, self-help, textbook, assessment scales, advocacy, parenting tips. Subjects include child guidance/parenting, education, multicultural, psychology, translation, travel, women's issues/studies, gifted/talented children and adults. No research-based books, dissertations. Submit proposal package, including preface or introduction, TOC, outline, 3 sample chapters and an explanation of how work differs from similar published books.

Recent Title(s) *Misdiagnosis and Dual Diagnoses of Gifted Children and Adults*, by James T. Webb, PhD; *Being Smart about Gifted Children*, by Dona J. Matthews, PhD and Joanne F. Foster, EdD; *Grandparents' Guide to Gifted Children*, by James T. Webb, PhD.

Tips "Manuscripts should be clear, cogent, and well-written and should pertain to gifted, talented, and creative persons and/or issues."

GREENE BARK PRESS

P.O. Box 1108, Bridgeport CT 06601. (203)372-4861. Fax: (203)371-5856. Web site: www.greenebarkpress.com. **Acquisitions:** Thomas J. Greene, publisher; Tara Maroney, associate publisher. Estab. 1991. Publishes hardcover originals. **Publishes 1-5 titles/year. Receives 100 queries and 6,000 mss/year. 60% of books from first-time authors; 100% from unagented writers. Pays 10-15% royalty on wholesale price.** Publishes book 1 year after acceptance of ms. Accepts simultaneous submissions. Responds in 2 months to queries; 6 months to mss. Book catalog for $2; ms guidelines for SASE.

- Greene Bark Press only publishes books for children and young adults, mainly picture and read-to books. "All of our titles appeal to the imagination and encourage children to read and explore the world through books. We only publish children's fiction—all subjects—but in reading picture book format appealing to ages 3-9 or all ages."

Fiction Juvenile. Submit complete ms. No queries or ms by e-mail.
Recent Title(s) *The Magical Trunk*, by Gigi Tegge; *Hey! There's a Goblin Under My Throne!*, by Rhett Ransom Pennell; *Edith Ellen Eddy*, by Julee-Ann Granger.
Tips Audience is "children who read to themselves and others. Mothers, fathers, grandparents, godparents who read to their respective children, grandchildren. Include SASE, be prepared to wait, do not inquire by telephone."

HACHAI PUBLISHING

762 Park Place, Brooklyn NY 11216. (718)633-0100. Web site: www.hachai.com. **Acquisitions:** Devorah Leah Rosenfeld, editor. Estab. 1988. Publishes hardcover originals. **Publishes 4 titles/year. Makes outright purchase of $600 and up.** Accepts simultaneous submissions. Responds in 2 months to mss. Book catalog free; ms guidelines online.

- "Hachai is dedicated to producing high quality Jewish children's literature, ages 2-10. Story should promote universal values such as sharing, kindness, etc."

Nonfiction Children's/juvenile. Subjects include ethnic, religion. Submit complete ms, SASE. Reviews artwork/photos as part of ms package. Send photocopies.
Recent Title(s) *Shadowplay*, by Leah Shollar; *What Do I Say?*, by Malky Goldberg; *Fayga Finds the Way*, by Batsheva Brandeis.
Tips "We are looking for books that convey the traditional Jewish experience in modern times or long ago; traditional Jewish observance such as Sabbath and holidays and mitzvos such as mezuzah, blessings etc; positive character traits (middos) such as honesty, charity, respect, sharing, etc. We are also interested in historical fiction for young readers (7-10) written with a traditional Jewish perspective and highlighting the relevance of Torah in making important choices. Please, no animal stories, romance, violence, preachy sermonizing."

HATALA GEROPRODUCTS

P.O. Box 42, Greentop MO 63546. E-mail: editor@geroproducts.com. Web site: www.geroproducts.com. **Acquisitions:** Mark Hatala, Ph.D., president (psychology, romance, relationships). Estab. 2002. Publishes hardcover and trade paperback originals. **Publishes 3-4 titles/year. Receives 120 queries and 50 mss/year. 30% of books from first-time authors; 80% from unagented writers. Pays 5-7½% royalty on retail price. Offers $250-500 advance.** Publishes book 18 months after acceptance of ms. Accepts simultaneous submissions. Responds in 1 month to queries; 2 months to proposals; 2 months to mss. Ms guidelines online.
Nonfiction How-to, humor, self-help, senior relationships, style, estate planning, gardening, pets and romance. Subjects include health/medicine, psychology, sex, travel, senior, advice. "Books should be of interest to older (60+) adults. Romance, relationships, advice, travel, how-to books are most appropriate. All books are larger print; so manuscripts should be around 50,000 words." Query with SASE, or submit proposal package including outline, 3 sample chapters, SASE.
Fiction Erotica, romance. Query with SASE, or submit proposal package including synopsis, 3 sample chapters, SASE.
Recent Title(s) *Seniors in Love*, by Robert Wolley (senior relationships); *ABC's of Aging*, by Dr. Ruth Jacobs (self-help); *Romance is in the Air*, by Ginger Binkley (romance).
Tips "Audience is men and women (but particularly women) over age 60. Books need to be pertinent to the lives of older Americans."

HAWK PUBLISHING GROUP

7107 S. Yale Ave., #345, Tulsa OK 74136. (918)492-3677. Fax: (918)492-2120. Web site: www.hawkpub.com. Estab. 1999. Publishes hardcover and trade paperback originals. **Publishes 6-8 titles/year. 25% of books from**

first-time authors; 50% from unagented writers. Pays royalty. Publishes book 1-2 years after acceptance of ms. Accepts simultaneous submissions. Ms guidelines online.

"Please visit our Web site and read the submission guidelines before sending anything to us. The best way to learn what might interest us is to visit the Web site, read the information there, look at the books, and perhaps even read a few of them."

Nonfiction Looking for subjects of broad appeal and interest.

Fiction Looking for good books of all kinds. Not interested in juvenile, poetry, or short story collections. Does not want childrens or young adult books. Submissions will not be returned, so send only copies. No SASE. No submissions by e-mail or by "certified mail or any other service that requires a signature." Replies "only if interested. If you have not heard from us within 3 months after the receipt of your submission, you may safely assume that we were not able to find a place for it in our list."

HEALTH PRESS NA INC.

P.O. Box 37470, Albuquerque NM 87176. (505)888-1394. Fax: (505)888-1521. E-mail: goodbooks@healthpress.com. Web site: www.healthpress.com. **Acquisitions:** K. Frazer, editor. Estab. 1988. Publishes hardcover and trade paperback originals. **Publishes 8 titles/year. 90% of books from first-time authors; 90% from unagented writers. Pays standard royalty on wholesale price.** Publishes book 1 year after acceptance of ms. Accepts simultaneous submissions. Responds in 3 months to proposals. Book catalog free; ms guidelines online.

Health Press publishes books by healthcare professionals on cutting-edge patient education topics.

Nonfiction How-to, reference, self-help, textbook. Subjects include education, health/medicine. Submit proposal package including outline, résumé, 3 complete sample chapters. Reviews artwork/photos as part of ms package. Send photocopies.

Recent Title(s) *Keeping a Secret: A Story About Juvenile Rheumatoid Arthritis*; *Peanut Butter Jam: A Story About Peanut Allergy*; *Health and Nutrition Secrets*.

HEALTH PROFESSIONS PRESS

P.O. Box 10624, Baltimore MD 21285-0624. (410)337-9585. Fax: (410)337-8539. E-mail: acquis@healthpropress.com. Web site: www.healthpropress.com. **Acquisitions:** Mary Magnus, director of publications (aging, long-term care, health administration). Publishes hardcover and trade paperback originals. **Publishes 6-8 titles/year. Receives 70 queries and 12 mss/year. 50% of books from first-time authors; 100% from unagented writers. Pays 8-18% royalty on wholesale price.** Publishes book 10 months after acceptance of ms. Accepts simultaneous submissions. Responds in 1 month to queries; 3 months to proposals; 4 months to mss. Book catalog free or online; ms guidelines online.

"We are a specialty publisher. Our primary audiences are professionals, students, and educated consumers interested in topics related to aging and eldercare."

Nonfiction How-to, reference, self-help, textbook. Subjects include health/medicine, psychology. Query with SASE, or submit proposal package including outline, résumé, 1-2 sample chapters, cover letter.

Recent Title(s) *Caring for People With Challenging Behaviors*; *Movement With Meaning*; *Promoting Family Involvement in Long-Term Care Settings*.

HENDRICK-LONG PUBLISHING CO., INC.

10635 Tower oaks D., Houston TX 77070. (832)912-7323. Fax: (832)912-7353. E-mail: hendrick-long@worldnet.att.net. Web site: hendricklongpublishing.com. **Acquisitions:** Vilma Long. Estab. 1969. Publishes hardcover and trade paperback originals and hardcover reprints. **Publishes 4 titles/year. 90% from unagented writers. Pays royalty. Pays royalty on selling price. Offers advance.** Publishes book 18 months after acceptance of ms. Does not accept simultaneous submissions. Responds in 3 months to queries. Book catalog for 8½×11 or 9×12 SASE with 4 first-class stamps; ms guidelines online.

Hendrick-Long publishes historical fiction and nonfiction about Texas and the Southwest for children and young adults.

Nonfiction Biography, children's/juvenile. Subjects include history, regional. Query, or submit outline and 2 sample chapters. Reviews artwork/photos as part of ms package. Send photocopies.

Fiction Juvenile, young adult. Query with SASE, or submit outline, synopsis, 2 sample chapters.

Recent Title(s) *Native Americans of Texas* (paperback, teacher's guide and workbook editions).

HENSLEY PUBLISHING

6116 E. 32nd St., Tulsa OK 74135-5494. (918)664-8520. E-mail: editorial@hensleypublishing.com. Web site: www.hensleypublishing.com. **Acquisitions:** Acquisitions Department. Publishes trade paperback originals. **Publishes 5 titles/year. Receives 200 queries/year. 50% of books from first-time authors; 50% from unagented writers.** Publishes book 18 months after acceptance of ms. Responds in 2 months to queries. Ms guidelines online.

0→ Hensley Publishing publishes Bible studies that offer the reader a wide range of topics. Currently emphasizing 192-page (8½×11) workbook studies.

Nonfiction Subjects include child guidance/parenting, money/finance, religion, women's issues/studies, marriage/family. "We publish only Bible studies. We do not want to see anything non-Christian." No New Age, poetry, plays, sermon collections. Query with synopsis and sample chapters.

Recent Title(s) *So You're a Christian! Now What?*, by Catherine Painter; *Walking With God*, by Mindy Ferguson.

Tips "Submit something that crosses denominational lines directed toward the large Christian market, not small specialized groups. We serve an interdenominational market—all Christian persuasions. Our goal is to get readers back into studying the Bible instead of studying about the Bible."

HIGH PLAINS PRESS

P.O. Box 123, 539 Cassa Rd., Glendo WY 82213. (307)735-4370. Fax: (307)735-4590. E-mail: editor@highplainspress.com. Web site: www.highplainspress.com. **Acquisitions:** Nancy Curtis, publisher. Estab. 1986. Publishes hardcover and trade paperback originals. **Publishes 4 titles/year. Receives 300 queries and 200 mss/year. 80% of books from first-time authors; 95% from unagented writers. Pays 10% royalty on wholesale price. Offers $200-800 advance.** Publishes book 2 years after acceptance of ms. Accepts simultaneous submissions. Responds in 1 month to queries; 3 months to proposals; 3 months to mss. Book catalog for 9×12 SASE; ms guidelines online.

0→ "What we sell best is history of the Old West, particularly things relating to Wyoming. We also publish 1 book of poetry a year in our Poetry of the American West series."

Nonfiction "We focus on books of the American West, mainly history. We like books on the history and culture of Wyoming and the West." Biography. Subjects include Americana, art/architecture, history, nature/environment, regional. Submit outline, 3 sample chapters. Reviews artwork/photos as part of ms package. Send photocopies.

Poetry "We only seek poetry closely tied to the Rockies. Do not submit single poems." Query, or submit complete ms.

Recent Title(s) *The Last Eleven Days of Earl Durand*, by Jerred Metz; *Beasts in the Snow: Poetry of the American West*, by Jane Wohl.

N LAWRENCE HILL BOOKS

Chicago Review Press, 814 N. Franklin St., 2nd Floor, Chicago IL 60610. (312)337-0747. Fax: (312)337-5110. **Acquisitions:** Yuval Taylor, senior editor. Publishes hardcover originals and trade paperback originals and reprints. **Publishes 3-10 titles/year. Receives 20 queries and 10 mss/year. 40% of books from first-time authors; 50% from unagented writers. Pays 7½-12½% royalty on retail price. Offers $3,000-10,000 advance.** Publishes book 1 year after acceptance of ms. Accepts simultaneous submissions. Responds in 1 month to queries; 2 months to proposals; 2 months to mss. Book catalog free.

Nonfiction Biography, reference, general nonfiction. Subjects include ethnic, government/politics, history, multicultural. Submit proposal package including outline, 2 sample chapters.

Recent Title(s) *The Thunder of Angels*, by Donnie Williams with Wayne Greenhaw.

N HIS WORK CHRISTIAN PUBLISHING

P.O. Box 5732, Ketchikan AK 99901. Fax: (614)388-0664. E-mail: hiswork@hisworkpub.com. Submissions E-mail: editor@hisworkpub.com. Web site: www.hisworkpub.com. **Acquisitions:** Angela J. Perez, acquisitions editor. Estab. 2005. Publishes trade paperback and electronic originals and reprints; also, hardcover originals. **Publishes 3-5 titles/year. Receives 24 queries and 16 mss/year. 100% of books from first-time authors; 100% from unagented writers. Pays 10-20% royalty on wholesale price.** Publishes book 1 year after acceptance of ms. Accepts simultaneous submissions. Responds in 1-3 months to queries; 1 month to proposals; 1-2 months to mss. Book catalog and ms guidelines online.

Nonfiction Autobiography, biography, children's/juvenile, cookbook, general nonfiction, how-to, illustrated book, self-help. Subjects include child guidance/parenting, cooking/foods/nutrition, creative nonfiction, gardening, health/medicine, history, hobbies, language/literature, memoirs, money/finance, music/dance, photography, recreation, religion, sports. "We only accept Christian material or material that does not go against Christian standards. This is a very strict policy that we enforce. Please keep this in mind before deciding to submit your work to us." Submit proposal package including outline, 3 sample chapter(s), or submit complete ms. Reviews artwork/photos as part of ms package. Send photocopies.

Fiction Humor, juvenile, mystery, picture books, poetry, religious, short story collections, sports, suspense, young adult. Submit proposal package including 3 sample chapter(s), synopsis, or submit complete ms.

Poetry "We only plan to publish 1-2 titles per year in poetry. Send us only your best work." Submit 15 sample poems.

Small Presses

Recent Title(s) *Things I Wonder*, by Jennifer Smith (children's picture book); *Teach Me to Tie*, by Angela J. Perez (children's picture book); *A Half-Husband's Journey*, by Josh D. Wilson (poetry).
Tips "Audience is children and adults who are looking for the entertainment and relaxation you can only get from jumping into a good book. Submit only your best work to us. Submit only in the genres we are interested in publishing. Do not submit work that is not suitable for a Christian audience."

HOBAR PUBLICATIONS

A division of Finney Co., 8075 215th St. W, Lakeville MN 55044. (952)469-6699. Fax: (952)469-1968. E-mail: feedback@finney-hobar.com. Web site: www.finney-hobar.com. **Acquisitions:** Alan E. Krysan, president. Publishes trade paperback originals. **Publishes 4-6 titles/year. Receives 30 queries and 10 mss/year. 35% of books from first-time authors; 100% from unagented writers. Pays 10% royalty on wholesale price. Offers advance.** Publishes book 6-12 months after acceptance of ms. Accepts simultaneous submissions. Responds in 8-10 weeks to queries.

O-π Hobar publishes career and technical educational materials.

Nonfiction How-to, illustrated book, reference, technical, textbook, handbooks, field guides. Subjects include agriculture/horticulture, animals, business/economics, education, gardening, nature/environment, science, building trades. Query with SASE. Reviews artwork/photos as part of ms package.
Recent Title(s) *E.M. Young*, by Dr. Hiram Drache; *National Safety Tractor and Machinery*; *Operation Program Student Manual*, by Penn State, The Ohio State University and the National Safety Council.

HOHM PRESS

P.O. Box 31, Prescott AZ 86302. (800)381-2700. Fax: (928)717-1779. Web site: www.hohmpress.com. **Acquisitions:** Regina Sara Ryan, managing editor. Estab. 1975. Publishes hardcover and trade paperback originals. **Publishes 6-8 titles/year. 50% of books from first-time authors. Pays 10% royalty on net sales.** Publishes book 18 months after acceptance of ms. Accepts simultaneous submissions. Responds in 3 months to queries.

O-π Hohm Press publishes a range of titles in the areas of transpersonal psychology and spirituality, herbistry, alternative health methods, and nutrition. Currently emphasizing health alternatives. Not interested in personal health survival stories.

Nonfiction Subjects include health/medicine (natural/alternative health), philosophy, religion (Hindu, Buddhist, Sufi, or translations of classic texts in major religious traditions), yoga. "We look for writers who have an established record in their field of expertise. The best buy of recent years came from 2 women who fully substantiated how they could market their book. We believed they could do it. We were right." No children's books please. Query with SASE. No e-mail inquiries, please.
Poetry "We are not accepting poetry at this time except for translations of recognized religious/spiritual classics."

HOWELLS HOUSE

P.O. Box 9546, Washington DC 20016-9546. (202)333-2182. **Acquisitions:** W.D. Howells, publisher. Estab. 1988. Publishes hardcover and trade paperback originals and reprints. **Publishes 4 titles/year; imprint publishes 2-3 titles/year. Receives 2,000 queries and 300 mss/year. 50% of books from first-time authors; 60% from unagented writers. Pays 15% net royalty or makes outright purchase. May offer advance.** Publishes book 8 months after acceptance of ms. Does not accept simultaneous submissions. Responds in 2 months to proposals.
Imprints The Compass Press; Whalesback Books.

O-π "Our interests are institutions and institutional change."

Nonfiction Biography, illustrated book, textbook. Subjects include Americana, anthropology/archeology, art/architecture, business/economics, education, government/politics, history, photography, science, sociology, translation, women's issues/studies. Query.
Fiction Historical, literary, mainstream/contemporary. Query.

IDYLL ARBOR, INC.

39129 264th Ave. SE, Enumclaw WA 98022. (360)825-7797. Fax: (360)825-5670. E-mail: editors@idyllarbor.com. Web site: www.idyllarbor.com. **Acquisitions:** Tom Blaschko. Publishes hardcover and trade paperback originals, and trade paperback reprints. **Publishes 6 titles/year. 50% of books from first-time authors; 100% from unagented writers. Pays 8-15% royalty on wholesale price or retail price.** Publishes book 1 year after acceptance of ms. Accepts simultaneous submissions. Responds in 1 month to queries; 2 months to proposals; 6 months to mss. Book catalog and ms guidelines free.
Imprints Issues Press; Pine Winds Press.

O-π Idyll Arbor publishes practical information on the current state and art of healthcare practice. Currently emphasizing therapies (recreational, aquatic, occupational, music, horticultural), activity directors in long-term care facilities, and social service professionals.

Nonfiction Reference, technical, textbook. Subjects include health/medicine (for therapists, social service providers and activity directors), psychology, recreation (as therapy), horticulture (used in long-term care activities or health care therapy). "Idyll Arbor is currently developing a line of books under the imprint Issues Press, which treats emotional issues in a clear-headed manner. The latest books are *Female Sex Offenders: What Therapists, Law Enforcement and Child Protective Services Need to Know* and *Situational Mediation: Sensible Conflict Resolution*. Another series of *Personal Health* books explains a condition or a closely related set of medical or psychological conditions. The target audience is the person or the family of the person with the condition. We want to publish a book that explains a condition at the level of detail expected of the average primary care physician so that our readers can address the situation intelligently with specialists. We look for manuscripts from authors with recent clinical experience. Good grounding in theory is required, but practical experience is more important." Query preferred with outline and 1 sample chapter. Reviews artwork/photos as part of ms package. Send photocopies.
Recent Title(s) *The Safe Approach: Controlling Risk for Workers in the Helping Professions*, by Charles Ennis and Janet Douglas; *Aquatic Therapy: Techniques and Interventions*, by Luis G. Vargas.
Tips "The books must be useful for the health practitioner who meets face to face with patients or the books must be useful for teaching undergraduate and graduate level classes. We are especially looking for therapists with a solid clinical background to write on their area of expertise."

ILLUMINATION ARTS

P.O. Box 1865, Bellevue WA 98009. (425)644-7185. Fax: (425)644-9274. E-mail: liteinfo@illumin.com. Web site: www.illumin.com. **Acquisitions:** Ruth Thompson, editorial director (ms submissions). Publishes hardcover originals. **Publishes 1-4 titles/year. Pays royalty on wholesale price. Offers advance for artists.** Book catalog and ms guidelines online.

O→ Illumination Arts publishes inspirational/spiritual (not religious) children's picture books.

Nonfiction Children's/juvenile. "Our books are all high quality and exquisitely illustrated. Stories need to be exciting and inspirational for children." Submit complete ms with SASE. Reviews artwork/photos as part of ms package. Send photocopies.
Fiction Picture books (children's). Prefer under 1,000 words; 1,500 words max. No electronic submissions.
Recent Title(s) *Am I a Color Too?*, by Heidi Cole and Nancy Vogl; *Mrs. Murphy's Marvelous Mansion*, by Emma Perry Roberts.
Tips "A smart writer researches publishing companies thoroughly before submitting and then follows submission guidelines closely."

IMAGES SI, INC.

Imprint of Images Publishing, 109 Woods of Arden Rd., Staten Island NY 10312. (718)966-3694. Fax: (718)966-3695. Web site: www.imagesco.com/publishing/index.html. **Acquisitions:** Acquisitions Editor. Estab. 1990. Publishes 2 audio books/year. 10% of stories from first-time authors. 75% of stories from unagented writers. Publishes stories 6 months-2 years after acceptence. **Pays flat fee for short stories.** Accepts simultaneous submissions. Responds in 2-6 months to queries; 2-6 months to mss. Publisher's catalog and writer's guidelines online.

O→ "We are currently looking for hard science fiction short stories only for our line of audio books."

Fiction Needs hard science fiction for audiocassetes and CDs. Query with SASE.
Recent Title(s) *Kirlian Photography*, by John Iovine; *Centauri III*, by George L. Griggs.

IMPACT PUBLISHERS, INC.

P.O. Box 6016, Atascadero CA 93423-6016. (805)466-5917. Fax: (805)466-5919. E-mail: info@impactpublishers.com. Web site: www.impactpublishers.com. **Acquisitions:** Freeman Porter, acquisitions editor. Estab. 1970. Publishes trade paperback originals. **Publishes 6-10 titles/year. Receives 250 queries and 250 mss/year. 20% of books from first-time authors; 60% from unagented writers. Pays 10% royalty on net receipts. Offers advance.** Publishes book 12-18 months after acceptance of ms. Accepts simultaneous submissions. Responds in 5 months to proposals. Book catalog free; ms guidelines online.
Imprints Little Imp Books; Rebuilding Books; Practical Therapist series.

O→ "Our purpose is to make the best human services expertise available to the widest possible audience: children, teens, parents, couples, individuals seeking self-help and personal growth, and human service professionals." Currently emphasizing books on divorce recovery for The Rebuilding Books Series. De-emphasizing children's books.

Nonfiction "All our books are written by qualified human service professionals and are in the fields of mental health, personal growth, relationships, aging, families, children, and professional psychology." Children's/juvenile, self-help. Subjects include child guidance/parenting, health/medicine, psychology (professional), caregiving/eldercare. "We do not publish general fiction for children, poetry, or New Age/spiritual works."

Small Presses

Submit proposal package, including short résumé or vita, book description, audience description, outline, 1-3 sample chapters, and SASE.

Recent Title(s) *Moved by the Spirit*, by Jeffrey Kottler and John Carlson; *Your Child's Divorce*, by Marsha Temlock.

Tips "Don't call to see if we have received your submission. Include a self-addressed, stamped postcard if you want to know if your manuscript arrived safely. We prefer a nonacademic, readable style. We publish only popular and professional psychology and self-help materials written in 'everyday language' by professionals with advanced degrees and significant experience in the human services. Our theme is 'psychology you can use, from professionals you can trust.' "

INFO NET PUBLISHING

21142 Canada Rd., Unit 1-C, Lake Forest CA 92630. (949)458-9292. Fax: (949)462-9595. E-mail: herb@infonetpublishing.com. Web site: www.infonetpublishing.com. **Acquisitions:** Herb Wetenkamp, president. Estab. 1987. Publishes hardcover and trade paperback originals. **Publishes 6 titles/year. Receives 50 queries and 20 mss/year. 80% of books from first-time authors; 85% from unagented writers. Pays 7-10% royalty on wholesale price, or makes outright purchase of $1,000-5,000. Offers $1,000-2,000 advance in some cases.** Publishes book 10 months after acceptance of ms. Accepts simultaneous submissions. Responds in 2 months to queries. Book catalog for 10×12 SAE with 2 first-class stamps; ms guidelines for #10 SASE.

- Info Net publishes for easily identified niche markets; specific markets with some sort of special interest, hobby, avocation, profession, sport, or lifestyle. New emphasis on collectibles and a series of books on retailing with CD-Roms.

Nonfiction Biography, children's/juvenile, gift book, how-to, reference, self-help, technical. Subjects include Americana (and collectibles), business/economics (retailing), history, hobbies, military/war, nature/environment (and environment), recreation, regional, sports, travel, women's issues/studies, aviation/aircraft archaeology. "We are looking for specific niche market books, not general titles, other than self-help. Do not repeat same formula as other books. In other words, offer something new." Submit outline, 3 sample chapters, proposal package, including demographics, marketing plans/data with SASE. Reviews artwork/photos as part of ms package. Send photocopies.

Recent Title(s) *Aircraft Wrecks in the Mountains and Deserts of California, 3rd Ed.*

Tips "Please check to be sure similar titles are not already published covering the exact same subject matter. Research the book you are proposing."

INSTITUTE OF POLICE TECHNOLOGY AND MANAGEMENT

University of North Florida, 12000 Alumni Dr., Jacksonville FL 32224-2678. (904)620-4786. Fax: (904)620-2453. E-mail: rhodge@unf.edu. Web site: www.iptm.org. **Acquisitions:** Richard C. Hodge, editor. Estab. 1980. Usually publishes trade paperback originals. **Publishes 8 titles/year. Receives 30 queries and 12 mss/year. 50% of books from first-time authors; 100% from unagented writers. Pays 25% royalty on actual sale price, or makes outright purchase of $300-2,000.** Publishes book 6 months after acceptance of ms. Does not accept simultaneous submissions. Responds in 3 weeks to queries.

- "Our publications are principally for law enforcement. Will consider works in nearly every area of law enforcement."

Nonfiction Illustrated book, reference, technical, textbook. Subjects include traffic crash investigation and reconstruction, management and supervision, criminal investigations, security. "Our authors are mostly active or retired law enforcement officers with excellent, up-to-date knowledge of their particular areas. However, some authors are highly regarded professionals in other specialized fields that in some way intersect with law enforcement." Reviews artwork/photos as part of ms package.

Tips "Manuscripts should not be submitted before the author has contacted IPTM's editor by e-mail or telephone. It is best to make this contact before completing a lengthy work such as a manual."

INTERCULTURAL PRESS, INC.

100 City Hall Plaza, Suite 501, Boston MA 02180. E-mail: submissions@interculturalpress.com. Web site: www.interculturalpress.com. **Acquisitions:** Judy Carl-Hendrick, managing editor. Estab. 1980. Publishes hardcover and paperback originals. **Publishes 8-12 titles/year. 50% of books from first-time authors; 95% from unagented writers. Pays royalty. Offers small advance occasionally.** Publishes book within 18 months after acceptance of ms. Accepts simultaneous submissions. Responds in 1 month to queries. Book catalog free; ms guidelines online.

- Intercultural Press publishes materials related to intercultural relations, including the practical concerns of living and working in foreign countries, the impact of cultural differences on personal and professional relationships, and the challenges of interacting with people from unfamiliar cultures, whether at home or abroad. Currently emphasizing international business.

Nonfiction "We want books with an international or domestic intercultural or multicultural focus, including those on business operations (how to be effective in intercultural business activities), education (textbooks for teaching intercultural subjects, for instance), and training (for Americans abroad or foreign nationals coming to the United States)." Reference, textbooks, theory. Subjects include world affairs, business, education, diversity and multicultural, relocation and cultural adaptation, culture learning, training materials, country-specific guides. "Our books are published for educators in the intercultural field, business people engaged in international business, managers concerned with cultural diversity in the workplace, and anyone who works in an occupation where cross-cultural communication and adaptation are important skills. No manuscripts that don't have an intercultural focus." Accepts nonfiction translations. Submit proposals, outline, résumé, cv, and potential market information.
Recent Title(s) *The Cultural Imperative: Global Trends in the 21st Century*, by Richard D. Lewis; *Exploring Culture: Excercises, Stories and Synthetic Cultures*, by Gert Jan Hofstede, Paul B. Pedersen and Geert Hofstede.

N INTERNATIONAL PUBLISHERS CO., INC.

239 W. 23 St., New York NY 10011. (212)366-9816. Fax: (212)366-9820. E-mail: service@intpubnyc.com. Web site: www.intpubnyc.com. **Acquisitions:** Betty Smith, president. Estab. 1924. Publishes hardcover originals, trade paperback originals and reprints. **Publishes 5-6 titles/year. Receives 50-100 mss/year. 10% of books from first-time authors. Pays 5-7½% royalty on paperbacks; 10% royalty on cloth.** Publishes book 6 months after acceptance of ms. Accepts simultaneous submissions. Responds in 1 month to queries; 6 months to mss. Book catalog and ms guidelines for SAE with 60– postage.

O→ International Publishers Co., Inc., emphasizes books based on Marxist science.

Nonfiction Subjects include art/architecture, government/politics, history, philosophy, economics, social sciences, Marxist-Leninist classics. "Books on labor, black studies, and women's studies based on Marxist science have high priority." Query, or submit outline, sample chapters, and SASE. Reviews artwork/photos as part of ms package.
Recent Title(s) *Choice: A Doctor's Experience with the Abortion Dilemma*, by Don Sloan, M.D; *People vs. Profits: Selections from the Writings of Victor Perlo*.
Tips No fiction or poetry.

IRON GATE PUBLISHING

P.O. Box 999, Niwot CO 80544-0999. (303)530-2551. Fax: (303)530-5273. E-mail: editor@irongate.com. Web site: www.irongate.com; www.reunionsolutions.com. **Acquisitions:** Dina C. Carson, publisher (how-to, genealogy). Publishes hardcover and trade paperback originals. **Publishes 6-10 titles/year; imprint publishes 2-6 titles/year. Receives 100 queries and 20 mss/year. 30% of books from first-time authors; 10% from unagented writers. Pays royalty on a case-by-case basis.** Publishes book 1 year after acceptance of ms. Accepts simultaneous submissions. Responds in 2 months to proposals. Book catalog and writer's guidelines free or online.
Imprints Reunion Solutions Press; KinderMed Press.

O→ "Our readers are people who are looking for solid, how-to advice on planning reunions or self-publishing a genealogy."

Nonfiction Subjects include hobbies, genealogy, reunions, party planning. Query with SASE, or submit proposal package, including outline, 2 sample chapters, and marketing summary. Reviews artwork/photos as part of ms package. Send photocopies.
Recent Title(s) *The Genealogy and Local History Researcher's Self-Publishing Guide*; *Reunion Solutions: Everything You Need to Know to Plan a Family, Class, Military, Association or Corporate Reunion*.
Tips "Please look at the other books we publish and tell us in your query letter why your book would fit into our line of books."

ITALICA PRESS

595 Main St., Suite 605, New York NY 10044-0047. (212)935-4230. Fax: (212)838-7812. E-mail: inquiries@italicapress.com. Web site: www.italicapress.com. **Acquisitions:** Ronald G. Musto and Eileen Gardiner, publishers. Estab. 1985. Publishes trade paperback originals. **Publishes 6 titles/year. Receives 600 queries and 60 mss/year. 5% of books from first-time authors; 100% from unagented writers. Pays 7-15% royalty on wholesale price. author's copies.** Publishes book 1 year after acceptance of ms. Accepts simultaneous submissions. Responds in 1 month to queries; 4 months to mss. Book catalog and ms guidelines online.

O→ Italica Press publishes English translations of modern Italian fiction and medieval and Renaissance nonfiction.

Nonfiction Subjects include translation. "We publish English translations of medieval and Renaissance source materials and English translations of modern Italian fiction." Query with SASE. Reviews artwork/photos as part of ms package. Send photocopies.

Fiction Translations of 20th century Italian fiction. Query with SASE.
Poetry Poetry titles are always translations and generally dual language.
Tips "We are interested in considering a wide variety of medieval and Renaissance topics (not historical fiction), and for modern works we are only interested in translations from Italian fiction by well-known Italian authors."

ALICE JAMES BOOKS

238 Main St., Farmington ME 04938. (207)778-7071. Fax: (207)778-7071. E-mail: ajb@umf.maine.edu. Web site: www.alicejamesbooks.org. **Acquisitions:** April Ossmann, executive director. Publishes trade paperback originals. **Publishes 6 titles/year. Receives 1,000 mss/year. 50% of books from first-time authors; 99% from unagented writers. Pays through competition awards.** Publishes book 1 year after acceptance of ms. Accepts simultaneous submissions. Responds in 1 month to queries; 4 months to mss. Book catalog for free or on Web site; ms guidelines for #10 SASE or on Web site.

O→ Alice James Books is a nonprofit poetry press.

Poetry Query.
Recent Title(s) *Here, Bullet*, by Brian Turner; *Gloryland*, by Anne Marie Macari; *Goest*, by Cole Swensen.
Tips "Send SASE for contest guidelines or check Web site. Do not send work without consulting current guidelines."

N JAMESON BOOKS, INC.

722 Columbus St., P.O. Box 738, Ottawa IL 61350. (815)434-7905. Fax: (815)434-7907. **Acquisitions:** Jameson G. Campaigne, publisher/editor. Estab. 1986. Publishes hardcover originals. **Publishes 6 titles/year. Receives 500 queries and 300 mss/year. 33% of books from first-time authors; 33% from unagented writers. Pays 6-15% royalty on retail price. Offers $1,000-25,000 advance.** Publishes book 1 year after acceptance of ms. Accepts simultaneous submissions. Responds in 6 months to queries.

O→ Jameson Books publishes conservative politics and economics, Chicago area history, and biographies.

Nonfiction Biography. Subjects include business/economics, government/politics, history, regional (Chicago area). Query with SASE, or submit 1 sample chapter. Submissions not returned without SASE.
Fiction Very well-researched western (frontier pre-1850). Interested in pre-cowboy "mountain men" in American west, before 1820 in east frontier fiction. No cowboys, no science fiction, mystery, poetry, et al. Query with SASE, or submit outline, synopsis, 1 sample chapter.
Recent Title(s) *Politics as a Noble Calling*, by F. Clifton White (memoirs); *Capitalism*, by George Reisman; *The Citizen's Guide to Fighting Government*, by Steve Symms and Larry Grupp.

N JILLETT PUBLICATIONS

70 Woodland Hills, South Berwick ME 03908. E-mail: bud@jillett.com. Web site: publications.jillett.com. **Acquisitions:** Bud Jillett, editor-in-chief. Estab. 2004. Publishes hardcover and trade paperback originals. **Publishes 2 titles/year; imprint publishes 2 titles/year. Receives 10 queries and 5 mss/year. 50% of books from first-time authors; 100% from unagented writers. Pays 10-15% royalty on gross. Will consider outright purchase.** Publishes book 6-18 months after acceptance of ms. Accepts simultaneous submissions. Responds in 1 month to queries; 1 month to proposals; 1 month to mss. Book catalog and ms guidelines online.

Nonfiction General nonfiction, how-to, humor, illustrated book, self-help. Subjects include art/architecture, creative nonfiction, hobbies, New Age, spirituality. "Jillett Publications is currently expanding its line of spiritual titles. We're also looking for interesting, funny, and fringe ideas. See our Web site for current title descriptions. Are you really good at reading body language? Any tips for lip reading? Do you have an original and funny cartoon series? Know any tricks for living in the nooks and crannies of society? Do you have a brilliant idea for opting out of the proverbial rat race? These are the types of topics we're interested in." Query by e-mail or with SASE to postal address; submit proposal with outline, sample chapters, and any marketing information or ideas; or submit completed ms. Reviews artwork/photos as part of ms package. Send photocopies or PDF drawings, JPEGs.
Recent Title(s) *Beetles & Bones*, by Rob Graves.
Tips "Our audience is at least slightly bored with life's trodden paths. They are self-reliant individuals with a sense of humor. If they grew up in the 60's, they probably owned a lava lamp. If they are from the 70's, they were mildly amused by the disco era and would be completely aghast these days by anybody with a disco ball. If their formitive years were in the 80's, they'd love to own an original Apple computer with a case signed by Steve Wozniak. If they grew up in the 90's, they are not as impressed by video games as they are by the Martian Rover landings. Please read and be interested in the subject area you write about. Tell us why your idea is original and why people will buy your book if we publish it. Passion about your project will go a long way."

KAEDEN BOOKS

P.O. Box 16190, Rocky River OH 44116. (800)890-7323. Fax: (440)617-1403. E-mail: info@kaeden.com. Web site: www.kaeden.com. Estab. 1986. Publishes paperback originals. **Publishes 8-16 titles/year. Pays flat fee**

or royalty by individual arrangement with author depending on book. Ms guidelines online.

O-ₜ Children's book publisher for education K-3 market: reading stories, fiction/nonfiction, chapter books, science, math, and social studies materials, also poetry.

Nonfiction Grades K-3 only. Needs all subjects, especially biography, science, nature, and history. Send complete ms and SASE. Only responds "if interested."

Fiction Grades K-3 only. Adventure, ethnic, fantasy, historical, humor, mystery, science fiction (soft/sociological), short story collections, sports, suspense (amateur sleuth). Send a disposable copy of ms and SASE. Responds only "if interested."

Tips "Our line is expanding with two particular areas of interest. First is nonfiction early readers for K-2 (up to 9,000 words). Second is early chapter books for grades 1 and 2 (up to 1,000-1,500). Material must be suitable for use in the public school classroom, be multicultural, and be high interest with appropriate word usage and a positive tone for the respective grade."

B. KLEIN PUBLICATIONS

P.O. Box 6578, Delray Beach FL 33482. (561)496-3316. Fax: (561)496-5546. **Acquisitions:** Bernard Klein, editor-in-chief. Estab. 1946. Publishes hardcover and paperback originals. **Publishes 5 titles/year. Pays 10% royalty on wholesale price.** Accepts simultaneous submissions. Responds in 2 months to queries. Book catalog for #10 SASE.

O-ₜ B. Klein Publications specializes in directories, annuals, who's who books, bibliography, business opportunity, reference books. Markets books by direct mail and mail order.

Nonfiction How-to, reference, self-help, directories; bibliographies. Subjects include business/economics, hobbies. Query with SASE, or submit outline, sample chapter(s).

Recent Title(s) *Guide to American Directories*, by Bernard Klein; *Mail Order Business Directory*.

N KOMENAR PUBLISHING

1756 Lacassie Ave., Suite 202, Walnut Creek CA 94596-7002. (510)444-2261. Fax: (510)834-2141. Web site: www.komenarpublishing.com. **Acquisitions:** Charlotte Cook, president (fiction: mainstream, literary, mystery, historical, science fiction). Estab. 2005. Publishes hardcover originals. **Publishes 2-4 titles/year. Receives 100 queries and 40 mss/year. 100% of books from first-time authors; 100% from unagented writers. Pays royalty. Pays 20% royalties after the first 7,500 books have sold.** Publishes book 1 year after acceptance of ms. Accepts simultaneous submissions. Responds in 1-3 months to queries; 1-3 months to mss. Book catalog and ms guidelines online.

Fiction Adventure, ethnic, experimental, fantasy, historical, humor, literary, mainstream/contemporary, multicultural, mystery, science fiction, suspense. KOMENAR Publishing believes a novel should be a compelling read. Readers are entitled to stories with strong forward momentum, engaging and dynamic characters, and evocative settings. The story must begin in the first chapter. Submit proposal package including author bio, cover letter, first 10 pages of ms. See Web site for additional details.

Recent Title(s) *Over the Edge*, by Marc Paul Kaplan (literary crime thriller); *My Half of the Sky*, by Jana McBurney-Lin (literary mainstream).

Tips "Our audience is comprised of habitual readers. Any experimental craft choices should be applied to the story, not to font, margins or punctuation. Chapters of our books are online. Read a couple. Charlotte Cook is likely to call promising authors. It's a good idea to have some familiarity with our books."

LAKE CLAREMONT PRESS

P.O. Box 25291, Chicago IL 60625. (773)728-1600. Fax: (773)728-1613. E-mail: sharon@lakeclaremont.com. Web site: www.lakeclaremont.com. **Acquisitions:** Sharon Woodhouse, publisher. Publishes trade paperback originals. **Publishes 5-7 titles/year. Receives 300 queries and 50 mss/year. 50% of books from first-time authors; 100% from unagented writers. Pays 10-15% royalty on wholesale price. Offers $500-1,000 advance.** Publishes book 4-12 months after acceptance of ms. Accepts simultaneous submissions. Responds in 1 month to queries; 2 months to proposals; 2-6 months to mss. Book catalog online.

O-ₜ "We specialize in books on the Chicago area and its history, and may consider regional titles for the Midwest. We also like nonfiction books on ghosts and cemeteries."

Nonfiction Subjects include Americana, ethnic, history, nature/environment (regional), regional, travel, women's issues/studies, film/cinema/stage (regional), urban studies. Query with SASE, or submit proposal package, including outline and 2 sample chapters, or submit complete ms (e-mail queries and proposals preferred).

Recent Title(s) *Today's Chicago Blues*, by Karen Hanson; *The Politics of Place*, by Joseph Schwieterman and Dana Caspall.

Tips "Please include a market analysis in proposals (who would buy this book and where) and an analysis of similar books available for different regions. Please know what else is out there."

LANGMARC PUBLISHING

P.O. Box 90488, Austin TX 78709-0488. (512)394-0989. Fax: (512)394-0829. E-mail: langmarc@booksails.com. Web site: www.langmarc.com. **Acquisitions:** Lois Qualben, president (inspirational). Publishes trade paperback originals. **Publishes 3-5 titles/year; imprint publishes 1 titles/year. Receives 150 queries and 80 mss/year. 60% of books from first-time authors; 80% from unagented writers. Pays 10-14% royalty on wholesale price.** Publishes book 18 months after acceptance of ms. Accepts simultaneous submissions. Responds in 3 months to queries. Book catalog free; ms guidelines online.

Imprints North Sea Press; Harbor Lights Series.

Nonfiction Self-help, inspirational. Subjects include child guidance/parenting, education. Query with SASE. Reviews artwork/photos as part of ms package. Send photocopies.

Recent Title(s) *Penny's From Heaven*; *Tragic Redemption*; *Don't Call Me Shy*.

LARSON PUBLICATIONS/PBPF

4936 Rt. 414, Burdett NY 14818-9729. (607)546-9342. Fax: (607)546-9344. E-mail: larson@lightlink.com. Web site: www.larsonpublications.org. **Acquisitions:** Paul Cash, director. Estab. 1982. Publishes hardcover and trade paperback originals. **Publishes 4-5 titles/year. 5% of books from first-time authors. Pays variable royalty. Seldom offers advance.** Publishes book 1-2 years after acceptance of ms. Accepts simultaneous submissions. Responds in 4-6 months to queries. Visit Web site for book catalog.

Nonfiction Subjects include philosophy, psychology, religion, spirituality. Query with SASE and outline.

Recent Title(s) *Astronoesis*, by Anthony Damiani.

Tips "We look for original studies of comparative spiritual philosophy or personal fruits of independent (transsectarian viewpoint) spiritual research/practice."

LIFE CYCLE BOOKS

P.O. Box 1008, Niagara Falls NY 14304. (416)690-5860. Fax: (416)690-8532. Web site: www.lifecyclebooks.com. **Acquisitions:** Paul Broughton, general manager. Estab. 1973. Publishes trade paperback originals and reprints, and mass market reprints. **Publishes 6 titles/year. Receives 100+ queries/year. 50% of books from first-time authors; 100% from unagented writers. Pays 8-10% royalty on wholesale price. Offers $250-1,000 advance.** Publishes book 1 year after acceptance of ms. Does not accept simultaneous submissions. Responds in 1 month to queries; 1 month to proposals; 1 month to mss. Book catalog online.

Nonfiction Booklets, children's/juvenile, reference, scholarly. Subjects include health/medicine, religion, social sciences, women's issues/studies. "We specialize in human life issues." Query with SASE, or submit complete ms. Reviews artwork/photos as part of ms package.

Recent Title(s) *Don't Panic: How to Tell Your Parents You're Pregnant*, by Elaine Depaw; *Men and Abortion: A Path to Healing*, by Catherine T. Coyle, PhD.

LIGHTHOUSE POINT PRESS

100 First Ave., Suite 525, Pittsburgh PA 15222-1517. (412)323-9320. Fax: (412)323-9334. E-mail: info@yearick-millea.com. **Acquisitions:** Ralph W. Yearick, publisher (business/career/general nonfiction). Publishes hardcover and trade paperback originals and trade paperback reprints. **Publishes 1-2 titles/year. Pays 5-10% royalty on retail price.** Does not accept simultaneous submissions. Responds in 6 months to queries.

O━ Lighthouse Point Press specializes in business/career nonfiction titles.

Nonfiction Reference. Subjects include business/economics. "We are open to all types of submissions related to general nonfiction, but most interested in business/career manuscripts." Submit proposal package including outline, 1-2 sample chapters, or submit complete ms.

Recent Title(s) *A Passion for Winning: Fifty Years of Promoting Legendary People and Products*, by Aaron D. Cushman (business/public relations); *On Track to Quality*, by Dr. James K. Todd (business).

Tips "When submitting a manuscript or proposal, please tell us what you see as the target market/audience for the book. Also, be very specific about what you are willing to do to promote the book."

⊘ LINTEL

24 Blake Lane, Middletown NY 10940. (845)342-5224. **Acquisitions:** Joan Dornhoefer, editorial assistant. Estab. 1978. Publishes hardcover originals and reprints and trade paperback originals. **Pays royalty. Authors get 100 copies originally, plus royalties after expenses cleared. Offers advance.** Publishes book 6-8 months after acceptance of ms. Accepts simultaneous submissions. Responds in 2 months to queries; 3 months to mss.

- No unsolicited mss.

Nonfiction "So far all our nonfiction titles have been textbooks." Query with SASE.

Fiction Experimental, feminist, gay/lesbian, regional (short fiction). Query with SASE. Accepts photocopied submissions.

Poetry Submit 5 sample poems.

Recent Title(s) *Writing a Television Play, Second Edition*, Michelle Cousin (textbook); *June*, Mary Sanders Smith (fiction); *Love's Mainland*, by Walter James Miller.

LOST HORSE PRESS

105 Lost Horse Lane, Sandpoint ID 83864. (208)255-4410. Fax: (208)255-1560. E-mail: losthorsepress@mindspring.com. Web site: www.losthorsepress.org. **Acquisitions:** Christine Holbert, editor. Estab. 1998. Publishes hardcover and paperback originals. **Publishes 4 titles/year.** Publishes book 1-2 years after acceptance of ms.

- *Does not accept unsolicited mss.*

Fiction Literary, poetry, regional (Pacific Northwest), short story collections.

Recent Title(s) *Composing Voices*, by Robert Pack (poetry); *Thistle*, by Melissa Kwasny; *A Change of Maps*, by Carolyne Wright.

THE MAGNI GROUP, INC.

7106 Wellington Point Rd., McKinney TX 75070. (972)540-2050. Fax: (972)540-1057. E-mail: info@magnico.com. Web site: www.magnico.com. **Acquisitions:** Evan Reynolds, president. Publishes hardcover originals and trade paperback reprints. **Publishes 5-10 titles/year. Receives 20 queries and 10-20 mss/year. 50% of books from first-time authors; 80% from unagented writers. Pays royalty on wholesale price, or makes outright purchase. Offers advance.** Publishes book 6 months after acceptance of ms. Does not accept simultaneous submissions. Responds in 2 months to queries. Book catalog and ms guidelines online.

Imprints Magni Publishing.

Nonfiction Cookbook, how-to, self-help. Subjects include child guidance/parenting, cooking/foods/nutrition, health/medicine, money/finance, sex. Submit complete ms. Reviews artwork/photos as part of ms package. Send photocopies.

Recent Title(s) *Natural Remedies From Around the World*; *Natural Cures for Your Dog & Cat.*

MAGNUS PRESS

P.O. Box 2666, Carlsbad CA 92018. (760)806-3743. Fax: (760)806-3689. E-mail: magnuspres@aol.com. Web site: www.magnuspress.com. **Acquisitions:** Warren Angel, editorial director. Estab. 1997. Publishes trade paperback originals and reprints. **Publishes 1-3 titles/year; imprint publishes 1-3 titles/year. Receives 200 queries and 220 mss/year. 44% of books from first-time authors; 89% from unagented writers. Pays 6-15% royalty on retail price.** Publishes book 1 year after acceptance of ms. Accepts simultaneous submissions. Responds in 1 month to queries; 1 month to proposals; 1 month to mss. Book catalog and ms guidelines for #10 SASE.

Imprints Canticle Books.

Nonfiction Christian books, popularly written Bible studies, inspirational, devotional. Subjects include religion (from a Christian perspective.). "Writers must be well-grounded in Biblical knowledge and must be able to communicate effectively with the lay person." Submit proposal package including outline, sample chapter(s), author bio.

Recent Title(s) *Sports Stories and the Bible*, by Stan Nix (inspirational).

Tips Magnus Press's audience is mainly Christian lay persons, but also includes anyone interested in spirituality and/or Biblical studies and the church. "Study our listings and catalog; learn to write effectively for an average reader; read any one of our published books."

MARINE TECHNIQUES PUBLISHING

126 Western Ave., Suite 266, Augusta ME 04330-7252. (207)622-7984. Fax: (207)621-0821. E-mail: promariner@midmaine.com. Web site: www.marinetechpublishing.com. **Acquisitions:** James L. Pelletier, president/owner (commercial marine or maritime international); Christopher S. Pelletier, vice president operations (national and international maritime related properties); Jenelle M. Pelletier, editor-in-chief (national and international maritime related properties). **Publishes 3-5 titles/year. Receives 5-20 queries and 1-4 mss/year. 15% of books from first-time authors. Pays 25-55% royalty on wholesale or retail price.** Publishes book 6-12 months after acceptance of ms. Accepts simultaneous submissions. Responds in 2 months to queries; 4 months to proposals; 6 months to mss. Book catalog free.

Publishes only books related to the commercial marine industry.

Nonfiction Reference, self-help, technical, maritime company directories. Subjects include the commerical maritime industry only. Submit proposal package, including ms, with all photos (photocopies OK).

Fiction Must be commercial maritime/marine related. Submit complete ms.

Poetry Must be related to maritime/marine subject matter. Submit complete ms.

Tips Audience consists of commercial marine/maritime firms, persons employed in all aspects of the marine/maritime commercial and recreational fields, persons interested in seeking employment in the commercial marine industry; firms seeking to sell their products and services to vessel owners, operators, and managers;

shipyards, vessel repair yards, recreational and yacht boat building and national and international parts in the commercial marine industry worldwide, etc.

MARLOR PRESS, INC.

4304 Brigadoon Dr., St. Paul MN 55126. (651)484-4600. E-mail: marlin.marlor@minn.net. **Acquisitions:** Marlin Bree, publisher. Estab. 1981. Publishes trade paperback originals. **Publishes 6 titles/year. Receives 100 queries and 25 mss/year. Pays 8-10% royalty on wholesale price.** Publishes book 1 year after acceptance of ms. Does not accept simultaneous submissions. Responds in 3-6 weeks to queries.

O→ Currently emphasizing general interest nonfiction children's books and nonfiction boating books.

Nonfiction Subjects include travel, boating. "Primarily how-to stuff." *No unsolicited mss.* No anecdotal reminiscences or biographical materials. No fiction or poetry. Query first; submit outline with sample chapters only when requested. Do not send full ms. Reviews artwork/photos as part of ms package.

Recent Title(s) *London for the Independent Traveler*, by Ruth Humleker; *Kid's Magic Secrets*, by Loris Bree; *Notable New York*, by Stephen W. Plumb.

MAUPIN HOUSE PUBLISHING, INC.

2416 NW 71 Place, Gainesville FL 32653. (800)524-0634. Fax: (352)373-5546. E-mail: info@maupinhouse.com. Web site: www.maupinhouse.com. **Acquisitions:** Julia Graddy, publisher. Publishes trade paperback originals and reprints. **Publishes 7 titles/year. Pays 10% royalty on retail price.** Responds in 1-2 weeks to queries.

O→ Maupin House publishes professional resource books for language arts teachers K-12.

Nonfiction How-to. Subjects include education, language/literature, writing workshop, reading instruction. "We are looking for practical, in-classroom resource materials, especially in the field of language arts and writing workshop. Classroom teachers are our top choice as authors." Query with SASE or via e-mail.

Recent Title(s) *Models for Teaching Writing Craft Target Skills; Discovering Voice.*

MCDONALD & WOODWARD PUBLISHING CO.

431-B E. College St., Granville OH 43023-1310. (740)321-1140. Fax: (740)321-1141. Web site: www.mwpubco.com. **Acquisitions:** Jerry N. McDonald, managing partner/publisher. Estab. 1986. Publishes hardcover and trade paperback originals. **Publishes 8 titles/year. Receives 100 queries and 20 mss/year. 50% of books from first-time authors; 100% from unagented writers. Pays 10% royalty on net receipts.** Publishes book 1 year after acceptance of ms. Accepts simultaneous submissions. Responds in 2 weeks to queries. Book catalog online.

O→ "McDonald & Woodward publishes books in natural and cultural history." Currently emphasizing travel, natural and cultural history, and natural resource conservation.

Nonfiction Biography, coffee table book, illustrated book. Subjects include Americana, anthropology/archeology, ethnic, history, nature/environment, science, travel. Query with SASE, or submit outline, sample chapter(s). Reviews artwork/photos as part of ms package. Send photocopies.

Recent Title(s) *The Carousel Keepers: An Oral History of American Carousels*, by Carrie Papa; *Pitcher Plants of America*, by Stewart McPherson; *The Teeth of the Lion: The Story of the Beloved and Despised Dandelion*, by Anita Sanchez.

Tips "We are especially interested in additional titles in our Guides to the American Landscape Series. Should consult titles in print for guidance. We want well-organized, clearly written, substantive material."

MEDICAL GROUP MANAGEMENT ASSOCIATION

104 Inverness Terrace E., Englewood CO 80112. (303)799-1111. Fax: (303)397-1823. E-mail: maust@mgma.com. Submissions E-mail: experts@mgma.com. Web site: www.mgma.com. **Acquisitions:** Marilee Aust, senior manager (finance, risk management, information management, governance, and organizational dynamics); Craig Wibert, information services manager (human resources, business and clinical operations, professional ethics/responsibility). Estab. 1926. Publishes hardcover, trade paperback, and electronic originals, and trade paperback reprints. **Publishes 6 titles/year; imprint publishes 3 titles/year. Receives 20 queries and 6 mss/year. 30% of books from first-time authors; 100% from unagented writers. Pays 8-17% royalty on net sales (twice a year). Offers $2,000-5,000. advance.** Publishes book 6 months after acceptance of ms. Accepts simultaneous submissions. Responds in 1 month to queries; 2 months to proposals; 2 months to mss. Book catalog online; writer's guidelines online or via e-mail.

Nonfiction Audiocassettes, how-to, multimedia, reference, scholarly, technical, textbook. Subjects include business/economics, education, health/medicine. Submit proposal package including outline, 5 sample chapters, or submit complete ms. Reviews artwork/photos as part of ms package. Send photocopies.

Recent Title(s) *Electronic Health Records*, by Margret Amatakul and Steve Lazarus.

Tips "Audience includes medical practice administrators, executives, physician leaders, office managers, and health administration faculty. Our books are geared at the business side of medicine. We also accept opinion papers, monographs, and white papers on topics of this nature."

MESSIANIC JEWISH PUBLISHERS

6120 Day Long Lane, Clarksville MD 21029. (410)531-6644. E-mail: website@messianicjewish.net. Web site: www.messianicjewish.net. **Acquisitions:** Janet Chaier, managing editor. Publishes hardcover and trade paperback originals and reprints. **Publishes 6-12 titles/year. Pays 7-15% royalty on wholesale price.** Ms guidelines by e-mail.

Nonfiction Jewish themes only. Gift book, reference. Subjects include religion (Messianic Judaism, Jewish roots of the Christian faith). Text must demonstrate keen awareness of Jewish culture and thought, and Biblical literacy. Query with SASE. Unsolicited mss are not returned.

Fiction "We publish very little fiction. Jewish or Biblical themes are a must." Religious. Text must demonstrate keen awareness of Jewish culture and thought. Query with SASE. Unsolicited mss are not returned.

Recent Title(s) *Blessing the King of the Universe: Transforming Your Life Through the Practice of Biblical Praise*, by Irene Lipson (religious reference/devotional); *The Distortion: 2,000 Years of Misrepresenting the Relationship Between Jesus the Messiah and the Jewish People*, by Dr. John Fischer and Dr. Patrice Fischer (nonfiction); *Celebrations of the Bible: A Messianic Children's Curriculum*.

Tips "Our audience is Christians, Messianic Jews, and Jewish people of all backgrounds. Be familiar with titles we have already published and the kind of books we consider."

MEYERBOOKS, PUBLISHER

P.O. Box 427, Glenwood IL 60425-0427. (708)757-4950. **Acquisitions:** David Meyer, publisher. Estab. 1976. Publishes hardcover and trade paperback originals and reprints. **Publishes 2 titles/year. Pays 10-15% royalty on wholesale or retail price.** Responds in 3 months to queries.

Imprints David Meyer Magic Books; Waltham Street Press.

- "We are currently publishing books on stage magic history. We only consider subjects which have never been presented in book form before. We are not currently considering books on health, herbs, cookery, or general Americana."

Nonfiction Reference. Subjects include history of stage magic. Query with SASE.

Recent Title(s) *Inclined Toward Magic: Encounters With Books, Collectors and Conjurors' Lives*, by David Meyer; *Houdini and the Indescribable Phenomenon*, by Robert Lund.

MID-LIST PRESS

4324 12th Ave S., Minneapolis MN 55407-3218. (612)822-3733. Fax: (612)823-8387. Web site: www.midlist.org. Publisher: Lane Stiles. Estab. 1989. Publishes hardcover and trade paperback originals. **Publishes 6 titles/year. Pays 40-50% royalty on net receipts.** Publishes book 12-18 months after acceptance of ms. Accepts simultaneous submissions. Ms guidelines online.

- Mid-List Press publishes books of high literary merit and fresh artistic vision by new and emerging writers.

Fiction General fiction. No children's, juvenile, romance, young adult. See guidelines.

Recent Title(s) *The Woman Who Never Cooked*, by Mary L. Tabor (short fiction); *A Doorless Knocking Into Night*, by Lexi Rudnitsky (poetry); *Rose City: A Memoir of Work*, by Jean Harper (creative nonfiction).

Tips Mid-List Press is an independent press. Mid-List Press publishes fiction, poetry, and creative nonfiction.

MILKWEEDS FOR YOUNG READERS

Milkweed Editions, 1011 Washington Ave. S., Suite 300, Minneapolis MN 55415. (612)332-3192. Fax: (612)215-2550. Web site: www.milkweed.org. **Acquisitions:** The editors. Estab. 1984. Publishes hardcover and trade paperback originals. **Publishes 3-4 titles/year. 25% of books from first-time authors; 50% from unagented writers. Pays 6% royalty on retail price. Offers variable advance.** Publishes book 1 year after acceptance of ms. Accepts simultaneous submissions. Responds in 6 months to queries. Book catalog for $1.50; ms guidelines for #10 SASE or on the Web site.

- "We are looking first of all for high quality literary writing. We publish books with the intention of making a humane impact on society."

Fiction Adventure, fantasy, historical, humor, mainstream/contemporary, animal, environmental. Query with SASE.

Recent Title(s) *Perfect*, by Natasha Friend; *Trudy*, by Jessica Lee Anderson.

N MOMENTUM BOOKS, LLC

117 W. Third St., Royal Oak MI 48067. (800)758-1870. Fax: (248)691-4531. E-mail: info@momentumbooks.com. Web site: www.momentumbooks.com. **Acquisitions:** Franklin Foxx, editor. Estab. 1987. **Publishes 6 titles/year. Receives 100 queries and 30 mss/year. 95% of books from first-time authors; 100% from unagented writers. Pays 10-15% royalty.** Does not accept simultaneous submissions. Ms guidelines online.

O→ Momentum Books publishes regional books and general interest nonfiction.

Nonfiction Subjects include cooking/foods/nutrition, history, sports, travel, automotive, current events. Submit proposal package including outline, 3 sample chapters, marketing outline.

Recent Title(s) *From Soupy to Nuts*, by Tim Kiska; *Bob-Lo*, by Annessa Carlisle; *Death's Door*, by Steve Lehto.

MOUNT IDA PRESS

152 Washington Ave., Albany NY 12210. (518)426-5935. Fax: (518)426-4116. **Acquisitions:** Diana S. Waite, publisher. Publishes trade paperback original illustrated books. Does not accept simultaneous submissions.

O→ Mount Ida Press specializes in high-quality publications on regional history, architecture, and building technology.

Recent Title(s) *Fort Orange Club, 1880-2005.*

[N] MOUNT OLIVE COLLEGE PRESS

Mount Olive College, 634 Henderson St., Mount Olive NC 28365. (919)658-2502. **Acquisitions:** Dr. Pepper Worthington, director (nonfiction, fiction, poetry, children's stories). Estab. 1990. Publishes trade paperback originals. **Publishes 3 titles/year. Receives 2,500 queries/year. 75% of books from first-time authors.** Does not accept simultaneous submissions.

Nonfiction Biography, children's/juvenile, general nonfiction, scholarly, self-help. Subjects include creative nonfiction, history, humanities, language/literature, memoirs, philosophy, psychology, religion, sociology, travel, women's issues/studies. Submit sample chapter(s), 3 sample chapters. Reviews artwork/photos as part of ms package. Send photocopies.

Fiction Literary, poetry, religious, short story collections, spiritual. Submit 3 sample chapters.

Poetry Submit 10 sample poems.

[N] MYSTIC RIDGE BOOKS

Subsidiary of Mystic Ridge Productions, Inc., P.O. Box 66930, Albuquerque NM 87193-6930. (505)899-2121. Web site: www.mysticridgebooks.com. **Acquisitions:** Richard Brown, president (books of quality, unique to their subject, of a marketable nature). Estab. 1999. Publishes hardcover, trade paperback, and mass market paperback originals, and trade paperback and mass market paperback reprints. **Publishes 6+ titles/year. Receives 500+ queries and 200+ mss/year. 50% of books from first-time authors; 90% from unagented writers. Pays 10% royalty on wholesale price.** Publishes book 9 months after acceptance of ms. Accepts simultaneous submissions. Responds in 3 months to queries; 3 months to proposals; 3 months to mss. Book catalog online.

O→ Please - no inquiries by phone, and no queries by certified mail or e-mail.

Nonfiction Audiocassettes, autobiography, biography, children's/juvenile, cookbook, how-to, humor, self-help, general nonfiction. Subjects include Americana, animals, anthropology/archeology, business/economics, child guidance/parenting, contemporary culture, cooking/foods/nutrition, creative nonfiction, government/politics, health/medicine, history, hobbies, language/literature, memoirs, money/finance, philosophy, psychology, recreation, science, sex, social sciences, spirituality, translation, women's issues/studies. "The writer should have a unique angle on a subject (it would be a plus if they are an expert in their field). The topic should not be too narrow a market; in other words, the target readership should be fairly large. The writer must also be a good self-promoter, willing to be proactive in getting publicity." Query with SASE. Reviews artwork/photos as part of ms package. Send photocopies.

Fiction Young adult. This publisher is only looking for juvenile fiction at this time. Query with SASE.

Recent Title(s) *Baring It All*, edited by Layla Shilkret (nonfiction—women's erotica); *Cutting Edge Blackjack*, by Richard Harvey (nonfiction—games/gaming); *The Fuzzy Escape Artists*, by Michael Isaacs (children's picture book).

Tips "An agent is not necessary. Quality is key. It is helpful if the author has a dynamic, charismatic personality, who is intent on developing a high, public profile."

NATUREGRAPH PUBLISHERS, INC.

P.O. Box 1047, Happy Camp CA 96039. (530)493-5353. Fax: (530)493-5240. E-mail: nature@sisqtel.net. Web site: www.naturegraph.com. Keven Brown, editor. **Acquisitions:** Barbara Brown, editor-in-chief. Estab. 1946. Publishes trade paperback originals. **Publishes 3 titles/year. Pays 8-10% royalty on wholesale price.** Accepts simultaneous submissions. Responds in 1 month to queries; 2 months to mss. Book catalog free.

O→ "Naturegraph publishes books to help people learn about the natural world and Native American culture. Not so technically written to scare away beginners." Emphasizing natural history and Native American history (but not political).

Nonfiction Primarily publishes nonfiction for the layman in natural history (biology, geology, ecology, astronomy); American Indian (historical and contemporary); outdoor living (backpacking, wild edibles, etc.). How-

Small Presses

to. Subjects include ethnic, nature/environment, science (natural history: biology, geology, ecology, astronomy), crafts. "Our primary niches are nature and Native American subjects with adult level, nontechnical language, and scientific accuracy. First, send for our free catalog. Study what kind of books we have already published." Query with SASE, or submit outline, 2 sample chapters.

Recent Title(s) *Enjoying the Native American-Style Flute; The Winds Erase Your Footprints.*

Tips "Please—always send a stamped reply envelope. Publishers get hundreds of manuscripts yearly; not just yours."

THE NAUTICAL & AVIATION PUBLISHING CO.

2055 Middleburg Lane, Mt. Pleasant SC 29464. (843)856-0561. Fax: (843)856-3164. **Acquisitions:** Melissa A. Pluta, acquisitions editor. Estab. 1979. Publishes hardcover originals and reprints. **Publishes 5-10 titles/year. Receives 200 queries/year. Pays 10-12% royalty on net receipts. Offers rare advance.** Accepts simultaneous submissions. Responds in 3 weeks to queries. Book catalog free.

O→ The Nautical & Aviation Publishing Co. publishes naval and military history, fiction, and reference.

Nonfiction Reference. Subjects include military/war (American), naval history. Query with SASE, or submit 3 sample chapters, synopsis. Reviews artwork/photos as part of ms package.

Fiction Historical, military/war (Revolutionary War, War of 1812, Civil War, WW I and II, Persian Gulf, and Marine Corps history). Looks for "novels with a strong military history orientation." Submit complete ms with cover letter and brief synopsis.

Recent Title(s) *The Civil War in the Carolinas*, by Dan L. Morrill; *Christopher and the Quasi War With France*, by William P. Mack; *A Guide to Airborne Weapons*, by David Crosby.

Tips "We are primarily a nonfiction publisher, but we will review historical fiction of military interest with strong literary merit."

NEW ENGLAND CARTOGRAPHICS, INC.

P.O. Box 9369, North Amherst MA 01059. (413)549-4124. Fax: (413)549-3621. E-mail: geolopes@crocker.com. Web site: www.necartographics.com. **Acquisitions:** Chris Ryan, editor; Valerie Vaughan. Publishes trade paperback originals and reprints. **Publishes 3 titles/year. Pays 5-10% royalty on retail price.** Accepts simultaneous submissions. Responds in 2 weeks to queries.

Nonfiction Subjects include nature/environment, recreation, regional, sports. "We are interested in specific 'where to' in the area of outdoor recreation guidebooks of the northeast US" Topics of interest are hiking/backpacking, skiing, canoeing, rail-trails, etc. Query with SASE, or submit sample chapter(s). Reviews artwork/photos as part of ms package. Send photocopies.

Recent Title(s) *Waterfalls of Massachussetts*, by Joseph Bushee, Jr; *Hiking the SuAsCo Watershed*, by Jill Phelps-Kern; *Birding Western Massachussetts*, by Robert Tougias.

NEW VICTORIA PUBLISHERS

P.O. Box 27, Norwich VT 05055-0027. (802)649-5297. Fax: (802)649-5297. E-mail: newvic@aol.com. Web site: www.newvictoria.com. **Acquisitions:** Claudia McKay, editor. Estab. 1976. Publishes trade paperback originals. **Publishes 1-2 titles/year. 50% of books from first-time authors; large% from unagented writers. Pays 10% royalty.** Publishes book 1 year after acceptance of ms. Does not accept simultaneous submissions. Book catalog free; ms guidelines for SASE.

O→ "New Victoria is a nonprofit literary and cultural organization producing the finest in lesbian fiction and nonfiction." Emphasizing mystery. De-emphasizing coming-of-age stories.

Nonfiction Biography. Subjects include gay/lesbian, history (feminist), women's issues/studies. "We are interested in feminist history or biography and interviews with or topics relating to lesbians." No poetry. Submit outline, sample chapter(s).

Fiction Adventure, erotica, fantasy, feminist, historical, humor, mystery (amateur sleuth), romance, science fiction, western. "Looking for strong feminist characters, also strong plot and action. We will consider most anything if it is well written and appeals to a lesbian/feminist audience. Hard copy only—no disks." Submit outline, sample chapter(s), synopsis.

Recent Title(s) *Theoretically Dead*, by Tinker Marks (mystery); *Circles of Power*, by Barbara Summerhawk.

Tips "Try to appeal to a specific audience and not write for the general market. We're still looking for well-written, hopefully humorous, lesbian fiction and well-researched biography or nonfiction."

⊘ NEW VOICES PUBLISHING

Division of KidsTerrain, Inc., P.O. Box 560, Wilmington MA 01887. (978)658-2131. Fax: (978)988-8833. E-mail: rschiano@kidsterrain.com. Web site: www.kidsterrain.com. **Acquisitions:** Rita Schiano, executive editor (children's books). Estab. 2000. Publishes hardcover and trade paperback originals. **Publishes 5 titles/year. 95% of books from first-time authors; 95% from unagented writers. Pays 10-15% royalty on wholesale**

price. Publishes book 1 year after acceptance of ms. Does not accept simultaneous submissions. Responds in 1 month to queries; 3 months to proposals; 3 months to mss. Book catalog and ms guidelines online.

O→ The audience for this company is children ages 4-9, and is not accepting unsolicited mss at this time.

Nonfiction Children's/juvenile, illustrated book. Subjects include child guidance/parenting.
Fiction Juvenile. Query with SASE.
Recent Title(s) *Reaching Home*, by Ron Breazeale.
Tips "Know, specifically, what your story/book is about."

NEWSAGE PRESS

P.O. Box 607, Troutdale OR 97060-0607. (503)695-2211. Fax: (503)695-5406. E-mail: info@newsagepress.com. Web site: www.newsagepress.com. **Acquisitions:** Maureen R. Michelson, publisher; Sherry Wachter, marketing and communications. Estab. 1985. Publishes trade paperback originals. Ms guidelines online.

O→ "We focus on nonfiction books. No 'how to' books or cynical, despairing books." Currently emphasizing books that explore the animal/human bond and death and grieving, and are written intelligently. Photo-essay books in large format are no longer published by Newsage Press. No novels or other forms of fiction.

Nonfiction Subjects include animals, multicultural, nature/environment, women's issues/studies, death/dying. Submit 2 sample chapters, proposal (no more than 10 pgs), SASE.
Recent Title(s) *Looking Like the Enemy: My Story of Imprisonment in a Japanese-American Internment Camp*, by Mary Matsuda Gruenewald; *Whales: Touching the Mystery*, by Doug Thompson.

NEXT DECADE, INC.

39 Old Farmstead Rd., Chester NJ 07930. (908)879-6625. Fax: (908)879-2920. E-mail: barbara@nextdecade.com. Web site: www.nextdecade.com. **Acquisitions:** Barbara Kimmel, president (reference); Carol Rose, editor. Publishes trade paperback originals. **Publishes 2-4 titles/year. Pays 8-15% royalty on wholesale price.** Responds in 1 month to queries. Book catalog and ms guidelines online.

Nonfiction Reference. Subjects include health/medicine (women's), money/finance, multicultural, senior/retirement issues, real estate.
Recent Title(s) *Retire in Style*, by Warren Bland, PhD; *The Hysterectomy Hoax*, by Stanley West, MD.
Tips "We publish books that simplify complex subjects. We are a small, award-winning press that successfully publishes a handful of books each year."

NODIN PRESS

530 N. Third St., Suite 120, Minneapolis MN 55401. (612)333-6300. Fax: (612)333-6303. E-mail: nstill4402@aol.com. **Acquisitions:** Norton Stillman, publisher. Publishes hardcover and trade paperback originals. **Publishes 5 titles/year. Receives 20 queries and 20 mss/year. 75% of books from first-time authors; 100% from unagented writers. Pays 7½% royalty.** Publishes book 6 months after acceptance of ms. Accepts simultaneous submissions. Responds in 6 months to queries. Book catalog and ms guidelines free.

O→ Nodin Press publishes Minnesota regional titles: nonfiction, memoir, sports, poetry.

Nonfiction Biography, regional guide book. Subjects include history (ethnic), regional, sports, travel. Query with SASE.
Poetry Regional (Minnesota poets). Submit 10 sample poems.
Recent Title(s) *The Great Dan Patch and the Remarkable Mr. Savage*, by Tim Brady; *Tending the Earth, Mending the Spirit*, by Connie Guldman and Richard Mahler; *Kodiak Kings*, by Jason Wood.

NOMAD PRESS

2456 Christian St., White River Junction VT 05001. (802)649-1995. Fax: (802)649-2667. E-mail: info@nomadpress.net. Web site: www.nomadpress.net. Publisher: Alex Kahan. **Acquisitions:** Acquisitions Editor. Publishes trade paperback originals. **Publishes 8+ titles/year. 10% of books from first-time authors; 90% from unagented writers. Pays royalty on retail price, or makes outright purchase. Offers negotiable advance.** Publishes book 1 year after acceptance of ms. Does not accept simultaneous submissions. Responds in 1-2 months to mss. Book catalog and ms guidelines online.

Nonfiction Parenting, how-to, teaching/education, children's activity/science titles. Subjects include child guidance/parenting, sports, teacher training/education, writing/journalism.
Recent Title(s) *Make a Real Living as a Freelance Writer*, by Jenna Glatzer (journalism/career); *Playing the Game: Inside Athletic Recruiting in the Ivy League*, by Chris Lincoln (sports); *How to Handle School Snafus: A Go Parents! Guide*, by Carmella Van Vleet (parenting).

NORTH CAROLINA OFFICE OF ARCHIVES AND HISTORY

Historical Publications Section, 4622 Mail Service Center, Raleigh NC 27699-4622. (919)733-7442. Fax: (919)733-1439. E-mail: donna.kelly@ncmail.net. Web site: www.ncpublications.com. **Acquisitions:** Donna E. Kelly, administrator (North Carolina and southern history). Publishes hardcover and trade paperback originals. **Publishes 4 titles/year. Receives 20 queries and 25 mss/year. 5% of books from first-time authors; 100% from unagented writers. Makes one-time payment upon delivery of completed ms.** Publishes book 2 years after acceptance of ms. Accepts simultaneous submissions. Responds in 1 week to queries; 1 week to proposals; 2 months to mss. Ms guidelines for $3.

O→ "We publish *only* titles that relate to North Carolina. The North Carolina Office of Archives and History also publishes the *North Carolina Historical Review*, a scholarly journal of history."

Nonfiction Hardcover and trade paperback books relating to North Carolina. Subjects include history (related to North Carolina), military/war (related to North Carolina), regional (North Carolina and Southern history). Query with SASE. Reviews artwork/photos as part of ms package. Send photocopies.

Recent Title(s) *African Americans in North Carolina*, edited by Alan D. Watson; *A Johnny-Reb Band From Salem*, by Harry H. Hall; *The Old North State Fact Book*, edited by C. Daniel Crews and Lisa D. Bayley.

Tips Audience is public school and college teachers and students, librarians, historians, genealogists, North Carolina citizens, tourists.

⊘ NORTHLAND PUBLISHING, INC.

P.O. Box 1389, Flagstaff AZ 86002-1389. (928)774-5251. Fax: (928)774-0592. Web site: www.northlandbooks.com. **Acquisitions:** Claudine Randazzo, managing editor; Theresa Howell, managing children's editor (picture books, especially with Southwest appeal). Estab. 1958. Publishes hardcover and trade paperback originals. **Publishes 8-10 titles/year; imprint publishes 8-10 titles/year. 20% of books from first-time authors; 20% from unagented writers. Pays royalty. Offers advance.** Publishes book 1-2 years after acceptance of ms. Accepts simultaneous submissions. Responds in 3 months to queries. Call for book catalog; ms guidelines online.

Imprints Rising Moon (books for children); Luna Rising (bilingual Spanish/English books for children).

O→ "Northland Publishing acquires nonfiction books intended for general trade audiences on the American West and Southwest, including Native American arts, crafts, and culture; Mexican culture; regional cookery; Western lifestyle; and interior design and architecture. Northland is not accepting poetry or fiction at this time."

Nonfiction Query with SASE, or submit outline, 2-3 sample chapters. No fax or e-mail submissions.

Fiction Picture books. Submit complete ms.

Recent Title(s) *Indian Yell*, by Michael Blake; *Family Home of the New West*, by Eliza Cross Castaneda.

Tips "Our audience is composed of general-interest readers."

NOVA PRESS

11659 Mayfield Ave., Suite 1, Los Angeles CA 90049. (310)207-4078. Fax: (310)571-0908. E-mail: novapress@aol.com. Web site: www.novapress.net. **Acquisitions:** Jeff Kolby, president. Estab. 1993. Publishes trade paperback originals. **Publishes 4 titles/year. Pays 10-22½% royalty on net receipts.** Publishes book 6 months after acceptance of ms. Book catalog free.

O→ Nova Press publishes only test prep books for college entrance exams (SAT, GRE, GMAT, LSAT, etc.), and closely related reference books, such as college guides and vocabulary books.

Nonfiction How-to, self-help, technical, test prep books for college entrance exams. Subjects include education, software.

Recent Title(s) *The MCAT Chemistry Book*, by Ajikumar Aryangat.

⊘ OBERLIN COLLEGE PRESS

50 N. Professor St., Oberlin College, Oberlin OH 44074. (440)775-8408. Fax: (440)775-8124. E-mail: oc.press@oberlin.edu. Web site: www.oberlin.edu/ocpress. Managing Editor: Linda Slocum. **Acquisitions:** David Young, David Walker, editors. Publishes hardcover and trade paperback originals. **Publishes 2-3 titles/year. Pays 7½-10% royalty.** Does not accept simultaneous submissions. Responds promptly to queries.

Imprints *FIELD: Contemporary Poetry & Poetics*, a magazine published twice annually, FIELD Translation Series, FIELD Poetry Series, FIELD Editions.

Poetry *FIELD Magazine*—submit up to 5 poems with SASE for response; FIELD Translation Series—query with SASE and sample poems; FIELD Poetry Series—*no unsolicited mss*. Enter mss in FIELD Poetry Prize held annually in May. Send SASE for guidelines after February 1.

Recent Title(s) *Red Studio*, by Mary Cornish.

PACESETTER PUBLICATIONS

P.O. Box 101330, Denver CO 80250-1330. (303)722-7200. Fax: (303)733-2626. E-mail: jsabah@aol.com. Web site: www.joesabah.com. **Acquisitions:** Joe Sabah, editor (how-to). Publishes trade paperback originals and reprints. **Publishes 3 titles/year. Pays 10-15% royalty. Offers $500-2,000 advance.** Does not accept simultaneous submissions. Responds in 1 month to queries.

Nonfiction How-to, self-help. Subjects include money/finance. Query with SASE, or submit proposal package including outline, 2 sample chapters.

Recent Title(s) *How to Get the Job You Really Want and Get Employers to Call You.*

N PALARI PUBLISHING

P.O. Box 9288, Richmond VA 23227-0288. (866)570-6724. Fax: (866)570-6724. E-mail: dave@palaribooks.com. Web site: www.palaribooks.com. **Acquisitions:** David Smitherman, fiction publisher. Estab. 1998. Publishes hardcover and trade paperback originals. **Pays royalty.** Publishes book 1 year after acceptance of ms. Does not accept simultaneous submissions. Responds in 1 month to queries; 2-3 months to mss. Ms guidelines online.

- Member of Publishers Marketing Association.

O‑‑ Small publisher specializing in quirky fiction and nonfiction. Distributes titles through Baker & Taylor, Ingram, Amazon, mail order and Web site. Promotes titles through book signings, direct mail and the Internet. Published 2 debut authors in the last year.

Fiction Adventure, ethnic, gay/lesbian, historical, literary, mainstream/contemporary, multicultural. "Tell why your idea is unique or interesting. Make sure we are interested in your genre before submitting." Query with SASE, or submit author bio, estimated word count, list of publishing credits. Accepts queries via e-mail, fax. Often comments on rejected mss.

Recent Title(s) *Poor Man's Philanthropist: The Thomas Cannon Story* (inspirational); *The 7 Most Powerful Selling Secrets* (business); *The Guessing Game* (mystery).

Tips "Send a good bio. I'm interested in a writer's experience and unique outlook on life."

PARADISE RESEARCH PUBLICATIONS, INC.

P.O. Box 837, Kihei HI 96753-0837. (808)874-4876. Fax: (808)874-4876. E-mail: dickb@dickb.com. Web site: www.dickb.com/index.shtml. Publishes trade paperback originals. **Publishes 3 titles/year. Receives 5 queries and 1 mss/year. 20% of books from first-time authors; 100% from unagented writers. Pays 10% royalty.** Publishes book 3 months after acceptance of ms. Accepts simultaneous submissions. Responds in 1 month to queries. Book catalog online.

O‑‑ Paradise Research Publications wants only books on Alcoholics Anonymous and its spiritual roots.

Nonfiction Self-help. Subjects include health/medicine, psychology, religion, spirituality. Query with SASE.

PARALLAX PRESS

P.O. Box 7355, Berkeley CA 94707. (510)525-0101, ext. 113. Fax: (510)525-7129. E-mail: rachel@parallax.org. Web site: www.parallax.org. **Acquisitions:** Rachel Neumann, senior editor. Estab. 1985. Publishes hardcover and trade paperback originals. **Publishes 5-8 titles/year.** Does not accept simultaneous submissions. Responds in 6-8 weeks to queries. Book catalog for 1 SAE with 3 first-class stamps; Ms guidelines for #10 SASE or online.

O‑‑ "We focus primarily on engaged Buddhism."

Nonfiction Children's/juvenile, coffee table book, self-help. Subjects include multicultural, religion (Buddhism), spirituality. Query with SASE, or submit 1 sample chapter, 1-page proposal. Reviews artwork/photos as part of ms package. Send photocopies.

Recent Title(s) *Journeying East*, by Victoria Jean Dimidjian; *Touching the Earth*, by Thich Nhat Hanh; *Wild Grace*, by Eric Alan.

PEACE HILL PRESS

Affiliate of W.W. Norton, 18021 The Glebe Ln., Charles City VA 23030. E-mail: info@peacehillpress.com. Web site: www.peacehillpress.com. **Acquisitions:** Peter Buffington, acquisitions editor. Estab. 2001. Publishes hardcover and trade paperback originals. **Publishes 4-8 titles/year. Pays 6-10% royalty on retail price. Offers $500-1,000 advance.** Publishes book 18 months after acceptance of ms. Accepts simultaneous submissions.

Nonfiction Children's/juvenile. Subjects include education, history, language/literature. Submit proposal package including outline, 1 sample chapter(s). Reviews artwork/photos as part of ms package. Send photocopies.

Fiction Historical, juvenile, picture books, young adult.

Recent Title(s) *The Story of the World, Vol. 2, revised ed.*, by Susan Wise Bauer.

PENMARIN BOOKS, INC.

1044 Magnolia Way, Roseville CA 95661. (916)771-5869. Fax: (916)771-5879. E-mail: ginny@penmarin.com. Web site: www.penmarin.com. **Acquisitions:** Virginia Ray, editorial director. Estab. 1987. Publishes hardcover and trade paperback originals. **Publishes 4 titles/year. Receives 200 queries and 100 mss/year. 40% of books from first-time authors; 60% from unagented writers. Pays 7-15% royalty on retail price. Offers $3,000-**

10,000 advance. Publishes book 1 year after acceptance of ms. Accepts simultaneous submissions. Responds in 1 week to queries; 1 month to proposals. Book catalog and ms guidelines online.

Nonfiction Autobiography (celebrity), biography (celebrity), general nonfiction, self-help. Subjects include child guidance/parenting, contemporary culture, health/medicine, history, psychology, world affairs, investigative journalism. Submit proposal package including outline, 1-3 sample chapters, and all material listed in proposal/submission guidelines on Web site. Query by e-mail first. Reviews artwork/photos as part of ms package. Send photocopies.

Recent Title(s) *Marilyn, Joe and Me*, by June DiMaggio.

PICCADILLY BOOKS, LTD.

P.O. Box 25203, Colorado Springs CO 80936-5203. (719)550-9887. Web site: www.piccadillybooks.com. **Acquisitions:** Submissions Department. Estab. 1985. Publishes hardcover originals and trade paperback originals and reprints. **Publishes 5-8 titles/year. 70% of books from first-time authors; 95% from unagented writers. Pays 6-10% royalty on retail price.** Publishes book 1 year after acceptance of ms. Accepts simultaneous submissions. Responds only if interested, unless accompanied by a SASE to queries.

O→ Picadilly publishes nonfiction, diet, nutrition, and health-related books with a focus on alternative and natural medicine.

Nonfiction How-to, reference, self-help. Subjects include cooking/foods/nutrition, health/medicine, performing arts, writing, small business. "Do your research. Let us know why there is a need for your book, how it differs from other books on the market, and how you will promote the book." No phone calls. Submit outline and sample chapters.

Recent Title(s) *Heart Frauds*, by Charles T. McGee, MD.

Tips "We publish nonfiction, general interest, self-help books currently emphasizing alternative health."

PINEY CREEK PRESS

P.O. Box 227, Roaring Spring PA 16673. Phone/Fax: (814)276-3935. E-mail: pineycrk@pennswoods.net. **Acquisitions:** Patty A. Wilson, executive editor (US regional ghost stories, folklore collections and historical short stories); Scott Crownover, associate editor (regional ghost stories, folklore, history—particularly mid-Atlantic). Estab. 1999. Publishes mass market paperback originals and reprints. **Publishes 1-3 titles/year. Receives 250 queries and 100 mss/year. 90% of books from first-time authors; 100% from unagented writers. Offers $500-1,500 advance.** Publishes book 4-7 months after acceptance of ms. Accepts simultaneous submissions. Responds in 1-3 months to queries; 1-5 months to proposals; 1-6 months to mss. Book catalog for #10 SASE; ms guidelines for #10 SASE.

Imprints "Currently we have our main line of ghost story collections under the main imprint of Piney Creek Press; however, we are hoping to open two new imprints this year—one for folklore collections and one for historical collections with regional themes. Be creative with these. One book slated for publication right now is *Pennsylvania Ghost Guide*, Vol. 3."

O→ "The audience for our books is people who have specific interests, such as ghost stories or folklore, and people who have a general interest in history."

Nonfiction "We focus on regional collections of ghost stories, folklore and historical collections of stories. We are currently hoping to increase the regional collections of ghost stories, and add a line of regional folklore collections and historical collections. We will be particularly interested in any collection with an unusual theme such as ghost stories from a state along with recipes from haunted sites or historical stories all from a region that have a theme such as lost treasures or military goofs." Submit proposal package including outline, 3 sample chapters, photos or illustrations if there are any. Reviews artwork/photos as part of ms package. Send photocopies.

Recent Title(s) *The Pennsylvania Ghost Guide, Vol. 1 & 2*, by Patty A. Wilson.

Tips "Know the market that you are sending to and then listen to the editor. Editors are not the enemy—they have a job to do and will help you with good advice."

PLANNERS PRESS

Imprint of the American Planning Association, 122 S. Michigan Ave., Chicago IL 60603. Fax: (312)431-9985. E-mail: slewis@planning.org. Web site: www.planning.org. **Acquisitions:** Sylvia Lewis, director of publications. Estab. 1978. Publishes hardcover and trade paperback originals. **Publishes 4-6 titles/year. Receives 20 queries and 6-8 mss/year. 50% of books from first-time authors; 100% from unagented writers. Pays 10-12% royalty on retail price. Offers advance.** Publishes book 1 year after acceptance of ms. Does not accept simultaneous submissions. Responds in 1 month to queries; 2 months to proposals; 2 months to mss. Book catalog and ms guidelines free.

O→ "Our books have a narrow audience of city planners and often focus on the tools of city planning."

Nonfiction Technical (public policy and city planning). Subjects include government/politics. Submit 2 sample chapters and TOC. Reviews artwork/photos as part of ms package. Send photocopies.

Recent Title(s) *Smart Growth in a Changing World; True Urbanism: Living in and Near the Center; The High Cost of Free Parking.*

PLANNING/COMMUNICATIONS

7215 Oak Ave., River Forest IL 60305-1935. (708)366-5200. Fax: (708)366-5280. E-mail: dl@planningcommunications.com. Web site: jobfindersonline.com; dreamitdoit.net. **Acquisitions:** Daniel Lauber, president. Estab. 1979. Publishes hardcover, trade, and mass market paperback originals, trade paperback reprints. **Publishes 3-6 titles/year. Receives 30 queries and 20 mss/year. 50% of books from first-time authors; 100% from unagented writers. Pays 10-16% royalty on net receipts.** Publishes book 1 year after acceptance of ms. Accepts simultaneous submissions. Responds in 3 months to queries. Book catalog for $2 or free on Web site; ms guidelines online.

O-x Planning/Communications publishes books on careers, improving your life, dream fulfillment, ending discrimination, sociology, urban planning, and politics.

Nonfiction Self-help. Subjects include business/economics (careers), education, government/politics, money/finance, sociology, ending discrimination, careers, résumés, cover letters, interviewing. Submit outline, 3 sample chapters, SASE. Reviews artwork/photos as part of ms package. Send photocopies.

Recent Title(s) *Dream It Do It: Inspiring Stories of Dreams Come True*, by Sharon Cook and Graciela Sholander; *How to Get a Job in Europe*, by Cheryl Matherly and Robert Sanborn; *International Job Finder*, by Daniel Lauber and Kraig Rice.

Tips "Our editorial mission is to publish books that can make a difference in people's lives—books of substance, not glitz."

N Ø PLATYPUS MEDIA, LLC

627 A St. NE, Washington DC 20002. (202)546-1674. Fax: (202)546-2356. E-mail: info@platypusmedia.com. Web site: www.platypusmedia.com. **Acquisitions:** Tracey Kilby, editorial assistant (children's—early childhood and science, birth, lactation). Estab. 2000. Publishes hardcover and trade paperback originals. **Publishes 3-4 titles/year. Receives 100 queries and 250 mss/year. 5% of books from first-time authors; 100% from unagented writers. Pays royalty on wholesale price, or makes outright purchase.** Publishes book 9 months after acceptance of ms. Accepts simultaneous submissions. Responds in 2-4 months to queries; 2-4 months to proposals; 2-4 months to mss. Book catalog free; ms guidelines online.

O-x "All content should focus on family closeness and child development."

Nonfiction Booklets, children's/juvenile. Subjects include child guidance/parenting, education, health/medicine, women's issues/studies, breastfeeding, childbirth, children's science books. Query with SASE. *All unsolicited mss returned unopened.* Reviews artwork/photos as part of ms package. Send photocopies.

Fiction Juvenile. Query with SASE. *All unsolicited mss returned unopened.*

Recent Title(s) *One Minute Mysteries*, by Eric Yoder and Natalie Yoder; *Look What I See! Where Can I Be? Visiting China*, by Dia L. Michels; *I Was Born to Be a Brother*, by Zaydek G. Michels-Gualtieri.

Tips "Audience includes parents, children, teachers, and parenting professionals. We publish just a handful of books each year and most are generated in-house."

PLEXUS PUBLISHING, INC.

143 Old Marlton Pike, Medford NJ 08055-8750. (609)654-6500. Fax: (609)654-4309. E-mail: jbryans@plexuspublishing.com. Web site: www.plexuspublishing.com. **Acquisitions:** John B. Bryans, editor-in-chief/publisher. Estab. 1977. Publishes hardcover and paperback originals. **Publishes 4-5 titles/year. 70% of books from first-time authors; 90% from unagented writers. Pays 10-15% royalty on net receipts. Offers $500-1,000 advance.** Accepts simultaneous submissions. Responds in 3 months to proposals. Book catalog and book proposal guidelines for 10×13 SAE with 4 first-class stamps.

O-x Plexus publishes regional-interest (southern New Jersey and the greater Philadelphia area) fiction and nonfiction including mysteries, field guides, nature, travel and history. Also a limited number of titles in health/medicine, biology, ecology, botany, astronomy.

Nonfiction Query with SASE.

Fiction Mysteries and literary novels with a strong regional (southern New Jersey) angle. Query with SASE.

Recent Title(s) *The Philadelphian*, by Richard Powell; *Boardwalk Empire*, by Nelson Johnson.

POSSIBILITY PRESS

One Oakglade Circle, Hummelstown PA 17036-9525. (717)566-0468. Fax: (717)566-6423. E-mail: info@possibilitypress.com. Web site: www.possibilitypress.com. **Acquisitions:** Mike Markowski, publisher; Marjie Markowski, editor-in-chief. Estab. 1981. Publishes trade paperback originals. **Publishes 4-6 titles/year. 90% of books from first-time authors; 95% from unagented writers. Royalties vary.** Responds in 1 month to queries. Ms guidelines online.

Imprints Aeronautical Publishers; Possibility Press.

O→ "Our mission is to help the people of the world grow and become the best they can be, through the written and spoken word."

Nonfiction How-to, self-help, inspirational. Subjects include psychology (pop psychology), business, success/ motivation, inspiration, entrepreneurship, sales marketing, network, MLM and home-based business topics, and human interest success stories. Prefers submissions to be mailed. Include SASE.

Fiction Parables that teach lessons about life and success.

Recent Title(s) *Ask!*, by Bill McGrane; *Dynamic Synergy!*, by Emerson Klees; *No Excuse!*, by Jay Rifenbary.

Tips "Our focus is on creating and publishing short- to medium-length bestsellers written by authors who speak and consult. We're looking for kind and compassionate authors who are passionate about making a difference in the world, and will champion their mission to do so, especially by public speaking."

N PULSE GUIDES

ASDavis Media Group, P.O. Box 590780, San Francisco CA 94159-0780. E-mail: christina@pulseguides.com. Web site: www.pulseguides.com. **Acquisitions:** Christina Henry, acquisitions editor. Estab. 1998. Publishes trade paperback originals. **Publishes 8 titles/year; imprint publishes 6 (fun single city destination); 2 (historic) titles/year. Makes outright purchase of $15,000-20,000. Offers $5,000 advance.** Does not accept simultaneous submissions. Responds in 2 months to queries; 2 months to proposals; 2 months to mss. Book catalog free.

Imprints Fun Seeker's Guides; Greenline Historical Travel Guides; Pulse Guides.

Nonfiction Subjects include history, travel. Submit proposal package including outline. Reviews artwork/photos as part of ms package.

Recent Title(s) *The 25 Best World War II Sites: European Theater*, by Chuck Thompson (travel); *The Fun Seeker's Athens*, by Coral Davenport and Jane Foster (travel); *The Fun Seeker's Miami*, by Gretchen Schmidt (travel).

Tips Audience is adult travelers.

QUEST BOOKS

Imprint of Theosophical Publishing House, 306 W. Geneva Rd., Wheaton IL 60187. (630)665-0130. Fax: (630)665-8791. E-mail: permissions@questbooks.net. Web site: www.questbooks.net. **Acquisitions:** Karen Schweizer. Publishes hardcover originals and trade paperback originals and reprints. **Publishes 8-10 titles/ year. Receives 600 queries/year. 50% of books from first-time authors; 90% from unagented writers. Pays royalty. Offers varying advance.** Publishes book 20 months after acceptance of ms. Accepts simultaneous submissions. Responds in 2 months to queries. Book catalog free; ms guidelines online.

O→ "Quest Books is the imprint of the Theosophical Publishing House, the publishing arm of the Theosophical Society in America. Since 1965, Quest books has sold millions of books by leading cultural thinkers on such increasingly popular subjects as transpersonal psychology, comparative religion, deep ecology, spiritual growth, the development of creativity, and alternative health practices."

Nonfiction Subjects include anthropology/archeology, art/architecture, health/medicine, music/dance, nature/ environment, philosophy (holistic), psychology (transpersonal), religion (Eastern and Western), science, spirituality (Native American, etc.), travel, women's issues/studies, biography, self-help, theosophy, comparative religion, men's and women's spirituality, holistic implications in science, health and healing, yoga, meditation, astrology. "Our speciality is high-quality spiritual nonfiction with a self-help aspect. Great writing is a must. We seldom publish 'personal spiritual awakening' stories. No submissions accepted that do not fit the needs outlined above." Accepts nonfiction translations. No fiction, poetry, children's books, or any literature based on channeling or personal psychic impressions. Query with SASE, or submit proposal package including sample chapter(s), author bio, TOC. Prefers online submissions; no attachments please. Reviews artwork/photos as part of ms package. Send photocopies.

Recent Title(s) *The Yoga of Time Travel*; *In Search of P.D. Ouspensley*; *The Zen of Listening*.

Tips "Our audience includes cultural creatives, seekers in all religions, students of religion, general public, professors, and health professionals. Read a few recent Quest titles. Know our books and our company goals. Explain how your book or proposal relates to other Quest titles. Quest gives preference to writers with established reputations/successful publications."

QUICK PUBLISHING, LLC

1610 Long Leaf Circle, St. Louis MO 63146. (314)432-3435. Fax: (314)993-4485. E-mail: quickpublishing@sbcglobal.net. **Acquisitions:** Angie Quick. Publishes trade paperback and hardback originals. **Publishes 2-5 titles/ year. Pays 8-10% royalty on net receipts.** Ms guidelines online.

Nonfiction Scientific, outdoor guides, regional books, and self-help, including child guidance/parenting, education, senior/aging.

Recent Title(s) *Kicking Depression's Ugly Butt*, by Dr. Robert Westermeyer; *Molecular Biology Made Simple and Fun, Third Ed.*, by David P. Clark and Lonnie D. Russell.

N QUINTESSENTIAL BOOKS

P.O. Box 8755, Kansas City MO 64114. Web site: www.quintessentialbooks.com. **Acquisitions:** Laura C. Lucas, acquisitions editor (business); Susan Simon, acquisitions editor (fiction and general nonfiction). Estab. 1991. Publishes hardcover, trade paperback, and mass market paperback originals and reprints. **Publishes 5-10 titles/year. Receives 150 queries and 25 mss/year. 25% of books from first-time authors; 25% from unagented writers. Pays 5-10% royalty on net revenues.** Publishes book 18 months after acceptance of ms. Accepts simultaneous submissions. Responds in 3-4 months to queries; 2 months to proposals; 2 months to mss. Ms guidelines online.

Nonfiction Biography, general nonfiction, how-to, humor, scholarly, self-help. Subjects include Americana, business/economics, child guidance/parenting, community, contemporary culture, creative nonfiction, education, government/politics, health/medicine, history, humanities, language/literature, memoirs, military/war, money/finance, nature/environment, philosophy, psychology, religion, science, social sciences, spirituality, world affairs. "Nonfiction writers must address significant topics in a fresh way, must speak boldly on controversial issues, and must be clear and accurate. Manuscripts on medicine, mental health, and nutrition will only be accepted from credentialed health professionals. We will not consider books on the occult or eschatology." Query with SASE. Reviews artwork/photos as part of ms package. electronic files.

Fiction Adventure, historical, humor, literary, mainstream/contemporary, military/war, mystery, religious, short story collections, spiritual, suspense, western. "Fiction writers must exhibit an understanding of human hearts and relationships, must create a complex and credible world for the reader, and must have multi-faceted characters and aesthetic depth." Does not want romance or children's books. Query with SASE.

Recent Title(s) *Fatal Illusions*, by James R. Lucas (business).

Tips "Our audience is intelligent, discerning and widely read. They value the truth, practicality and literary merit."

N RED EYE PRESS, INC.

P.O. Box 65751, Los Angeles CA 90065. **Acquisitions:** James Goodwin, president. Publishes trade paperback originals. **Publishes 2 titles/year. Pays 8-12% royalty on retail price. Offers $1-2,000 advance.**

O━ No unsolicited submissions.

Nonfiction How-to, reference. Subjects include gardening.

Recent Title(s) *Great Labor Quotations—Sourcebook and Reader*, Peter Bollen.

Tips "We publish how-to and reference works that are the standard for their genre, authoritative, and able to remain in print for many years."

N RED ROCK PRESS

459 Columbus Ave., Suite 114, New York NY 10024. Fax: (212)362-6216. E-mail: info@redrockpress.com. Web site: www.redrockpress.com. **Acquisitions:** Ilene Barth. Estab. 1998. Publishes hardcover and trade paperback originals. **Publishes 6-8 titles/year. Pays royalty on wholesale price. The amount of the advance offered depends on the project.** Does not accept simultaneous submissions. Responds in 3-4 months to queries. Book catalog for #10 SASE.

Nonfiction Coffee table book, gift book, humor, illustrated book. Subjects include creative nonfiction. "All our books are pegged to gift-giving holidays."

Recent Title(s) *I Love You Because . . .*; *The Christmas Flower Boo.*

REFERENCE PRESS INTERNATIONAL

P.O. Box 4126, Greenwich CT 06831. (203)622-6860. **Acquisitions:** Cheryl Lacoff, senior editor. Publishes hardcover and trade paperback originals. **Publishes 6 titles/year. Receives 50 queries and 20 mss/year. 75% of books from first-time authors; 90% from unagented writers. Pays royalty, or makes outright purchase. Offers determined by project advance.** Publishes book 6 months after acceptance of ms. Accepts simultaneous submissions. Responds in 3 months to queries.

O━ Reference Press specializes in gift books, instructional, reference, and how-to titles.

Nonfiction Gift book, how-to, illustrated book, multimedia (audio, video, CD-ROM), reference, technical, instructional. Subjects include anything related to the fine arts or crafts field. "Follow the guidelines as stated concerning subjects and types of books we're looking for." Query with SASE, or submit outline, 1-3 sample chapters. Reviews artwork/photos as part of ms package. photocopies, not originals.

Recent Title(s) *Who's Who in the Peace Corps* (alumni directory).

RISING MOON

Imprint of Northland Publishing, Inc., P.O. Box 1389, Flagstaff AZ 86002-1389. (928)774-5251. Fax: (928)774-0592. E-mail: editorial@northlandpub.com. Web site: www.risingmoonbooks.com. **Acquisitions:** Theresa Howell, kids editor. Estab. 1988. Publishes hardcover and trade paperback originals. **Publishes 8-12 titles/year. 20% of books from first-time authors; 20% from unagented writers. Pays royalty. Sometimes pays flat fee. Offers advance.** Publishes book 1-2 years after acceptance of ms. Accepts simultaneous submissions. Responds in 3 months to queries. Call for book catalog; ms guidelines online.

O→ Rising Moon's objective is to provide children with entertaining and informative books that follow the heart and tickle the funny bone. Rising Moon is no longer publishing middle-grade children's fiction.

Fiction Picture books (with Southwest or Latino themes). "We are looking for exceptional stories with wide appeal to add to our line of Southwest-themed books." Submit complete ms with SASE of adequate size and postage. No e-mail submissions.

Recent Title(s) *Do Princesses Wear Hiking Boots?*, by Carmela Lavigna Coyle, illustrated by Mike Gordon.

Tips "Our audience is composed of regional Southwest-interest readers."

N RIVER'S BEND PRESS

P.O. Box 606, Stillwater MN 55082. E-mail: editor@riversbendpress.com. Web site: www.riversbendpress.com. **Acquisitions:** William Schmaltz. Estab. 2001. Publishes hardcover, trade paperback, and mass market paperback originals. **Publishes 4 titles/year. Receives 250 queries and 200 mss/year. 90% of books from first-time authors; 100% from unagented writers. Pays 15-20% royalty on net receipts. Offers $500 advance.** Publishes book 9-12 months after acceptance of ms. Accepts simultaneous submissions. Responds in 3-6 weeks to queries; 3-6 months to mss. Book catalog and ms guidelines online.

Nonfiction Autobiography, biography, general nonfiction, humor, illustrated book, reference, scholarly. Subjects include Americana, anthropology/archeology, art/architecture, creative nonfiction, ethnic, history, hobbies, humanities, language/literature, memoirs, military/war, translation, objectivism. No children's stories, religious stories, or self-help/abuse/recovery stories. Query with SASE, or submit first 3 chapters. Reviews artwork/photos as part of ms package. Send photocopies.

Fiction Adventure, comic books, historical, humor, literary, mainstream/contemporary, military/war, mystery, short story collections, suspense, western, young adult, gen-X. No children's stories, religious stories or epic battles between heaven and hell.

Recent Title(s) *When White is Black*, by John A. Martin Jr. (memoir); *Black Tuesday's Child*, by Donald Mace Williams (fiction).

Tips "We are willing to consider anything that's well written, except heaven/hell stories and demons."

ROSE PUBLISHING

4733 Torrance Blvd., #259, Torrance CA 90503. (310)353-2100. Fax: (310)353-2116. E-mail: lynnette@rose-publishing.com. Web site: www.rose-publishing.com. **Acquisitions:** Carol R. Witte, editor. **Publishes 25-30 titles/year. 5% of books from first-time authors; 100% from unagented writers. Makes outright purchase.** Publishes book 18 months after acceptance of ms. Accepts simultaneous submissions. Responds in 3 months to proposals; 2 months to mss. Book catalog for $1.29 in postage.

O→ "We publish Bible reference materials in wall chart, pamphlet, and Powerpoint form, easy-to-understand and appealing to children, teens or adults on Bible study, prayer, basic beliefs, sharing the gospel, creation, apologetics, marriage, family and teens."

Nonfiction Reference, pamphlets, group study books. Subjects include religion, science, sex, spirituality, Bible studies, Christian history, counseling aids, cults/occult, curriculum, Christian discipleship, stewardship, evangelism/witnessing, Christian living, marriage, prayer, creation, singles issues. No fiction or poetry. Submit proposal package including outline, photocopies of chart contents or poster artwork. Reviews artwork/photos as part of ms package. Send photocopies.

Recent Title(s) *Bible & Christian History Time Lines*; *Questions & Answers on Mormonism*; *Jehovah's Witnesses*.

Tips Audience includes both church (Bible study leaders, Sunday school teachers [all ages], pastors, youth leaders), and home (parents, home schoolers, children, youth, high school, and college). Open to topics that supplement Sunday School curriculum or Bible study, junior high materials, Bible study, reasons to believe, books of the Bible.

SAFER SOCIETY PRESS

P.O. Box 340, Brandon VT 05733. (802)247-3132. Fax: (802)247-4233. Web site: www.safersociety.org. **Acquisitions:** Gaen Murphree, editorial director. Estab. 1985. Publishes trade paperback originals. **Publishes 3-4 titles/year. Receives 15-20 queries and 15-20 mss/year. 90% of books from first-time authors; 100% from unagented writers. Pays 10% royalty on retail price.** Publishes book 1 year after acceptance of ms. Accepts simultaneous submissions. Book catalog free; ms guidelines online.

O→ "Our mission is the prevention and treatment of sexual abuse."
Nonfiction Self-help (sex abuse prevention and treatment). Subjects include psychology (sexual abuse). "We are a small, nonprofit, niche press. We want well-researched books dealing with any aspect of sexual abuse: treatment, prevention, understanding; works on subject in Spanish." Memoirs generally not accepted. Query with SASE, submit proposal package, or complete ms. Reviews artwork/photos as part of ms package. Send photocopies.
Recent Title(s) *Footprints*, by Krishan G. Hansen, MSW, and Timothy J. Kahn, MSW; *Choices*, by Charlene Steen, PhD, JD.
Tips Audience is persons working in mental health/persons needing self-help books. Pays small fees or low royalties.

SALINA BOOKSHELF

1254 W. University Ave., Suite 130, Flagstaff AZ 86001. (928)527-0070. Fax: (928)526-0386. E-mail: jessier@salinabookshelf.com. Web site: www.salinabookshelf.com. **Acquisitions:** Jessie Ruffenach, editor. Publishes trade paperback originals and reprints. **Publishes 4-5 titles/year. 50% of books from first-time authors; 100% from unagented writers. Pays varying royalty. Offers advance.** Publishes book 1 year after acceptance of ms. Accepts simultaneous submissions. Responds in 3 months to queries.
Nonfiction Children's/juvenile, textbook (Navajo language). Subjects include education, ethnic, science. "We publish childrens' bilingual readers. Nonfiction should be appropriate to science and social studies curriculum grades 3-8." Query with SASE. Reviews artwork/photos as part of ms package. Send photocopies.
Fiction Juvenile. "Submissions should be in English or Navajo. All our books relate to the Navajo language and culture." Query with SASE.
Poetry "We accept poetry in English/Southwest language for children." Submit 3 sample poems.
Recent Title(s) *Dine Bizaad: Speak, Read, Write Navajo*, by Irvy W. Goossen.

SALVO PRESS

P.O. Box 7396, Beaverton OR 97007. E-mail: info@salvopress.com. Web site: www.salvopress.com. **Acquisitions:** Scott Schmidt, publisher. Estab. 1998. Publishes hardcover and paperback originals and e-books in most formats. **Publishes 3 titles/year. Receives 500 queries/year. 50% of books from first-time authors; 80% from unagented writers. Pays 10% royalty.** Publishes book 9 months after acceptance of ms. Does not accept simultaneous submissions. Responds in 1 month to queries; 2 months to mss. Book catalog and ms guidelines online.
Fiction Adventure, literary, mystery (amateur sleuth, police procedural, private/hard boiled), science fiction (hard science/technological), suspense, espionage, thriller. "Our needs change. Check our Web site." Query with SASE.
Recent Title(s) *Global Shot*, by Trevor Scott; *The Devil's Racket*, by Tom Wallace.

[N] SANDLAPPER PUBLISHING CO., INC.

P.O. Box 730, Orangeburg SC 29116-0730. (803)531-1658. Fax: (803)534-5223. E-mail: agallman1@bellsouth.net. Web site: www.sandlapperpublishing.com. **Acquisitions:** Amanda Gallman, managing editor. Estab. 1982. Publishes hardcover and trade paperback originals and reprints. **Publishes 6 titles/year. 80% of books from first-time authors; 95% from unagented writers. Pays 15% maximum royalty on net receipts.** Publishes book 20 months after acceptance of ms. Does not accept simultaneous submissions. Responds in 3 months to queries. Book catalog and ms guidelines for 9×12 SAE with 4 first-class stamps.
O→ "We are an independent, regional book publisher specializing in educational nonfiction relating to South Carolina." Emphasizing history and travel.
Nonfiction Biography, children's/juvenile (ages 9-14), cookbook, humor, illustrated book, reference, textbook. Subjects include cooking/foods/nutrition, history, humor, regional, culture and cuisine of the Southeast especially South Carolina. "We are looking for manuscripts that reveal under-appreciated or undiscovered facets of the rich heritage of our region. If a manuscript doesn't deal with South Carolina or the Southeast, the work is probably not appropriate for us. We don't do self-help books, children's books about divorce, kidnapping, etc., and absolutely no religious manuscripts." No phone calls. Query with SASE, or submit outline, sample chapter(s). Reviews artwork/photos as part of ms package.
Recent Title(s) *Lowcountry Scenes*, by Jon Wongrey.
Tips "Our readers are South Carolinians, visitors to the region's tourist spots, and friends and family that live out-of-state. We are striving to be a leading regional publisher for South Carolina. We will be looking for more history, travel and biography."

SCHREIBER PUBLISHING, INC.

P.O. Box 4193, Rockville MD 20849. (301)424-7737. Fax: (301)424-2336. E-mail: spbooks@aol.com. Web site: www.schreiberpublishing.com. President: Morry Schreiber. **Acquisitions:** Linguistics Editor; Judaica Editor.

Publishes hardcover and trade paperback originals and reprints. **Publishes 8 titles/year. Receives 40 queries and 12 mss/year. 80% of books from first-time authors; 95% from unagented writers. Pays negotiable royalty on retail price.** Publishes book 6 months after acceptance of ms. Accepts simultaneous submissions. Responds in 1 month to queries; 1 month to proposals; 1 month to mss. Book catalog free or on Web site; ms guidelines free.

O┳ Schreiber publishes reference books and dictionaries for better language and translation work, as well as Judaica books emphasizing Jewish culture and religion. Currently emphasizing multicultural dictionaries and parochial books.

Nonfiction Biography, children's/juvenile, coffee table book, gift book, humor, multimedia (CD-ROM), reference, textbook. Subjects include history, language/literature, memoirs, money/finance, multicultural, religion, science, translation. Query with SASE, or submit proposal package including outline, 1 sample chapter, and TOC. Reviews artwork/photos as part of ms package. Send photocopies.

Recent Title(s) *Ask the Bible*, by Morry Soffer; *Spanish Business Dictionary*.

SCRIBLERUS PRESS

548 E. 82nd St., #1B, New York NY 10028. E-mail: editor@scriblerus.net. Web site: www.scriblerus.net. **Acquisitions:** Sean Miller, editor. Estab. 2005. Publishes hardcover, trade paperback, and electronic originals. **Publishes 1-5 titles/year. Receives 100 queries/year. Pays 15-25% royalty on wholesale price.** Publishes book 6 months after acceptance of ms. Accepts simultaneous submissions. Responds in 1 month to queries; 2 months to mss. Ms guidelines online.

- Accepts queries via e-mail only. Snail mail will be refused.

Fiction Experimental, literary. Submit proposal package including synopsis, author bio, 3 sample chapters.

Recent Title(s) *The Empire Menaced*, by Dearth Nadir/Xiao En.

SEAWORTHY PUBLICATIONS, INC.

626 W. Pierre Lane, Port Washington WI 53074. (262)268-9250. Fax: (262)268-9208. E-mail: publisher@seaworthy.com. Web site: www.seaworthy.com. **Acquisitions:** Joseph F. Janson, publisher. Publishes trade paperback originals, hardcover originals, and reprints. **Publishes 8 titles/year. Receives 150 queries and 40 mss/year. 60% of books from first-time authors; 100% from unagented writers. Pays 15% royalty on wholesale price. Offers $1,000 advance.** Publishes book 6 months after acceptance of ms. Does not accept simultaneous submissions. Responds in 1 month to queries. Book catalog on Web site or for #10 SASE; ms guidelines online.

O┳ Seaworthy Publications is a nautical book publisher that primarily publishes books of interest to recreational boaters and bluewater cruisers, including cruising guides, how-to books about boating. Currently emphasizing how-to.

Nonfiction Illustrated book, reference, technical. Subjects include hobbies (sailing, boating), regional (boating guide books). Regional guide books, first-person adventure, reference, technical—all dealing with boating. Query with SASE, or submit 3 sample chapters, TOC. Prefers electronic query via e-mail. Reviews artwork/photos as part of ms package. Send photocopies or color prints.

Recent Title(s) *The Solitude of the Open Sea*, by Gregory Newell Smith.

Tips "Our audience consists of sailors, boaters, and those interested in the sea, sailing, or long-distance cruising."

[N] SILVER MOON PRESS

381 Park Avenue South, Suite 1121, New York NY 10016. (212)242-6499. Fax: (212)242-6799. **Acquisitions:** Hope Killcoyne, managing editor. Publishes hardcover originals. **Publishes 1-2 prep workbooks and 1-2 historical fiction titles/year. Receives 600 queries and 400 mss/year. 60% of books from first-time authors; 70% from unagented writers. Pays 7-10% royalty. Offers 500-1,000 advance.** Publishes book 18 months after acceptance of ms. Accepts simultaneous submissions. Responds in 6-12 months to queries; 6-12 months to proposals; 6-12 months to mss. Book catalog for 9×12 SASE; ms guidelines for #10 SASE.

O┳ Publishes educational material for grades 3-8.

Nonfiction Biography, test-prep material. Subjects include education, history, language/literature, multicultural. Query with SASE, or submit proposal package including outline, first pages of manuscript.

Fiction Historical, multicultural, biographical. Query with SASE, or submit proposal package including synopsis.

Recent Title(s) *Ambush in the Wilderness*, by Kris Hemphill (historical fiction); *Brothers of the Falls*, by Joanna Emery (historical fiction); *Leo Politi: Artist of the Angels*, by Ann Stalcup (biography).

SOCIETY OF MANUFACTURING ENGINEERS

One SME Dr., P.O. Box 930, Dearborn MI 48121. (313)425-3280. Fax: (313)425-3417. E-mail: sbollinger@sme.org. Web site: www.sme.org. **Acquisitions:** Manager. Publishes hardcover and trade paperback originals. **Publishes 6 titles/year. Receives 20 queries and 10 mss/year. 90% of books from first-time authors; 100%**

from unagented writers. Pays 10% or more royalty on wholesale or retail price. Publishes book 8 months after acceptance of ms. Responds in 1 month to queries; 1 month to proposals; 1 month to mss. Book catalog and ms guidelines online.

Nonfiction "Seeking manuscripts that would assist manufacturing practitioners in increasing their productivity, quality, and/or efficiency." Technical, textbook. Subjects include engineering, industry. Reviews artwork/photos as part of ms package. Send photocopies.

Recent Title(s) *Hitchhiker's Guide to Lean*; *Quick Die Change*.

Tips Audience is "manufacturing practitioners and management, individuals wishing to advance their careers in the industry or to enhance productivity, quality, and efficiency within a manufacturing operation."

ST. BEDE'S PUBLICATIONS

St. Scholastica Priory, P.O. Box 545, Petersham MA 01366-0545. (978)724-3213. Fax: (978)724-3216. President: Sister Mary Clare Vincent. **Acquisitions:** Acquisitions Editor. Estab. 1977. Publishes hardcover originals, trade paperback originals and reprints. **Publishes 3-4 titles/year. 30-40% of books from first-time authors; 98% from unagented writers. Pays 5-10% royalty on wholesale price, or retail price.** Publishes book 2 years after acceptance of ms. Accepts simultaneous submissions. Responds in 2 months to queries. Book catalog and ms guidelines for 9×12 SAE with 2 first-class stamps.

- St. Bede's Publications is owned and operated by the Roman Catholic nuns of St. Scholastica Priory. The publications are seen as an apostolic outreach. Their mission is to make available to everyone quality books on spiritual subjects such as prayer, scripture, theology, and the lives of holy people.

Nonfiction Textbook (theology). Subjects include history, philosophy, religion, sex, spirituality, translation, prayer, hagiography, theology, church history, related lives of saints. No submissions unrelated to religion, theology, spirituality, etc., and no poetry, fiction, or children's books. Does not return submissions without adequate postage. Query, or submit outline and sample chapters with SASE.

Recent Title(s) *Reading the Gospels with Gregory the Great*, translated by Santha Bhattacharji; *Why Catholic?*, by Father John Pasquini.

Tips "There seems to be a growing interest in monasticism among lay people, and we will be publishing more books in this area. For our theology/philosophy titles our audience is scholars, colleges and universities, seminaries, etc. For our other titles (i.e. prayer, spirituality, lives of saints, etc.) the audience is above-average readers interested in furthering their knowledge in these areas."

N STEMMER HOUSE PUBLISHERS

4 White Brook Rd., Gilsum NH 03448. (800)345-6665. Fax: (603)357-2073. E-mail: pbs@pathwaybook.com. Estab. 1975. **Imprint publishes 2 titles/year. Offers advance.** Publishes book 1-2 years after acceptance of ms. Accepts simultaneous submissions. Book catalog for 5½×8½ SAE with 2 first-class stamps; ms guidelines for #10 SASE.

Imprints The International Design Library®; The NatureEncyclopedia Series.

Nonfiction Biography, children's/juvenile, illustrated book. Subjects include animals, multicultural, nature/environment, arts. Query with SASE.

STRATA PUBLISHING, INC.

P.O. Box 1303, State College PA 16804. (814)234-8545. Web site: www.stratapub.com. **Acquisitions:** Kathleen Domenig, publisher (speech communication, journalism, mass communication, political science). Publishes college textbooks. **Publishes 1-3 titles/year. Pays royalty on wholesale price.** Publishes book about 1 year after acceptance of ms. Responds in 1 month to queries; 3 months to proposals; 3 months to mss. Book catalog and ms guidelines online.

Nonfiction Textbook. Subjects include speech, journalism, mass communication. Query with SASE, or submit proposal package including outline, 2 sample chapters.

Recent Title(s) *Readings in Rhetorical Criticism, 2nd Ed.*, by Carl R. Burgchardt; *Freedom of Speech in the United States, 5th Ed.*, by Thomas L. Tedford and Dale A. Herbeck; *Argumentation*, by James A. Herrick.

Tips "Please visit our Web site for a description of our publishing needs and manuscript submission guidelines."

SUCCESS PUBLISHING

3419 Dunham Rd., Warsaw NY 14569-9735. **Acquisitions:** Allan H. Smith, president (home-based business); Ginger Smith (business); Dana Herbison (home/craft); Robin Garretson (fiction). Estab. 1982. Publishes mass market paperback originals. **Publishes 6 titles/year. Receives 10 mss/year. 90% of books from first-time authors; 100% from unagented writers. Pays 7-12% royalty. Offers $500-1,000 advance.** Publishes book 10 months after acceptance of ms. Accepts simultaneous submissions. Responds in 2 months to queries. Book catalog and ms guidelines for #10 SAE with 2 first-class stamps.

O→ Success publishes guides that focus on the needs of the home entrepreneur to succeed as a viable business. Currently emphasizing starting a new business. De-emphasizing self-help/motivation books. Success Publishing notes that it is looking for ghostwriters.

Nonfiction Children's/juvenile, how-to, self-help. Subjects include business/economics, child guidance/parenting, hobbies, money/finance, craft/home-based business. "We are looking for books on how-to subjects such as home business and sewing." Query with SASE.

Recent Title(s) *How to Find a Date/Mate*, by Dana Herbison.

Tips "Our audience is made up of housewives, hobbyists, and owners of home-based businesses."

SWEDENBORG FOUNDATION PUBLISHERS

320 North Church St., West Chester PA 19380. (610)430-3222. Fax: (610)430-7982. E-mail: editor@swedenborg.com. Web site: www.swedenborg.com. **Acquisitions:** Mary Lou Bertucci, senior editor. Estab. 1849. Publishes trade paperback originals and reprints. **Publishes 5 titles/year.** Does not accept simultaneous submissions. Responds in 1 month to queries; 3 months to proposals; 3 months to mss. Book catalog free; ms guidelines online.

Imprints Chrysalis Books; Swedenborg Foundation Press.

O→ "The Swedenborg Foundation publishes books by and about Emanuel Swedenborg (1688-1772), his ideas, how his ideas have influenced others, and related topics. A Chrysalis book is a spiritually focused book presented with a nonsectarian perspective that appeals to open-minded, well-educated seekers of all traditions. Appropriate topics include—but are not limited to—science, mysticism, spiritual growth and development, wisdom traditions, healing and spirituality, as well as subjects that explore Swedenborgian concepts, such as: near-death experience, angels, Biblical interpretation, mysteries of good and evil, etc. Although Chrysalis Books explore topics of general spirituality, a work must actively engage the thought of Emanuel Swedenborg and show an understanding of his philosophy in order to be accepted for publication."

Nonfiction Self-help, spiritual growth and development. Subjects include philosophy, psychology, religion, science. Query with SASE, or submit proposal package including outline, sample chapter(s), synopsis. "I personally prefer e-mail." Reviews artwork/photos as part of ms package. Send photocopies.

Recent Title(s) *Healing as a Sacred Path: A Story of Personal, Medical, and Spiritual Transformation*, by L. Robert Keck; *Emanuel Swedenborg: Visionary Savant in the Age of Reason*, by Ernst Benz; *Kant on Swedenborg*, edited and translated by Gregory Johnson.

THE SYSTEMSWARE CORPORATION

973 Russell Ave., Suite D, Gaithersburg MD 20879. (301)948-4890. Fax: (301)926-4243. **Acquisitions:** Pat White, editor. Estab. 1987. Does not accept simultaneous submissions.

Nonfiction Technical, textbook. Subjects include computers/electronic, software. "We specialize in innovative books and periodicals on Knowledge Engineering or Applied Artificial Intelligence and Knowledge Based Systems. We also develop intelligent procurement-related software packages for large procurement systems." Query with SASE.

TCU PRESS

P.O. Box 298300, TCU, Fort Worth TX 76129. (817)257-7822. Fax: (817)257-5075. **Acquisitions:** Judy Alter, director; James Ward Lee, acquisitions editor; Susan Petty, editor. Estab. 1966. Publishes hardcover originals, some reprints. **Publishes 9-12 titles/year. 10% of books from first-time authors; 75% from unagented writers. Pays 10% royalty on net receipts.** Publishes book 16 months after acceptance of ms. Does not accept simultaneous submissions. Responds in 3 months to queries.

O→ TCU publishes "scholarly works and regional titles of significance focusing on the history and literature of the American West."

Nonfiction Biography, coffee table book, scholarly. Subjects include Americana, art/architecture, contemporary culture, ethnic, history, language/literature, multicultural, regional, women's issues/studies, American studies, criticism. Query with SASE. Reviews artwork/photos as part of ms package.

Fiction Historical, young adult, contemporary. No mysteries or science fiction.

Recent Title(s) *Adventures With a Texas Humanist*, by James Ward Lee; *Jim Courtright of Fort Worth: His Life and Legend*, by Robert K. Dearment; *Texas Literary Outlaws*, by Steven L. Davis.

Tips "Regional and/or Texana nonfiction has best chance of breaking into our firm. Our list focuses on the history of literature of the American West, although recently we have branched out into literary criticism, women's studies, and Mexican-American studies."

N TECHNICAL ANALYSIS OF STOCKS & COMMODITIES

Technical Analysis, Inc., 4757 California Ave. SW, Seattle WA 98116-4499. (206)938-0570. E-mail: editor@traders.com. Web site: www.traders.com. **Acquisitions:** Jayanthi Gopalakrishnan, editor. Estab. 1982. Publishes

trade paperback originals and reprints. **Makes outright purchase.** Responds in 6 months to queries.
Nonfiction Publishes business and economics books and software about using charts and computers to trade stocks, options, mutual funds or commodity futures. "Know the industry and the markets using technical analysis." Query with SASE.
Recent Title(s) *Charting the Stock Market*, by Hutson, Weis, Schroeder (technical analysis).
Tips "Only traders and technical analysts really understand the industry. First consideration for publication will be given to material, regardless of topic, that presents the subject in terms that are easily understandable by the novice trader. One of our prime considerations is to instruct, and we must do so in a manner that the lay person can comprehend. This by no means bars material of a complex nature, but the author must first establish the groundwork."

TIA CHUCHA PRESS

℅ Tia Chucha's Centro Cultural, 12737 Glenoaks Blvd., #22, Sylmar CA 91342. **Acquisitions:** Luis Rodriguez, director. Publishes trade paperback originals. **Publishes 2-4 titles/year. Receives 25-30 queries and 150 mss/year. Pays 10% royalty on wholesale price.** Publishes book 1 year after acceptance of ms. Does not accept simultaneous submissions. Responds in 9 months to mss. Ms guidelines free.
Poetry "No restrictions as to style or content. We do cross-cultural and performance-oriented poetry. It has to work on the page, however." Submit complete ms.
Recent Title(s) *My Sweet Unconditional*, by Ariel Robello; *Frozen Accident*, by Alfred Arteaga.
Tips Audience is "those interested in strong, multicultural, urban poetry—the best of bar-cafe poetry. Send letter of inquiry with 2-3 samples of your best work."

TIDEWATER PUBLISHERS

Cornell Maritime Press, Inc., P.O. Box 456, Centreville MD 21617-0456. (410)758-1075. Fax: (410)758-6849. Web site: www.cmptp.com. **Acquisitions:** Michelle M. Slavin, managing editor. Estab. 1938. Publishes hardcover and paperback originals. **Publishes 7-9 titles/year. 41% of books from first-time authors; 99% from unagented writers. Pays 7½-15% royalty on retail price.** Publishes book 1 year after acceptance of ms. Does not accept simultaneous submissions. Responds in 2 months to queries.

- Tidewater Publishers issues adult nonfiction and photography works related to the Chesapeake Bay area, Delmarva, or Maryland in general.

Nonfiction Regional subjects only. Cookbook, how-to, illustrated book, reference. Subjects include art/architecture, history, regional, sports, boating, outdoor recreation.
Recent Title(s) *Fishing the Chesapeake*, by Lenny Rudow; *Bodine's Chesapeake Bay Country*, by Jennifer Bodine.
Tips "Our acquisition needs change frequently. Be sure to check our Web site under 'Submission Guidelines' for current requirements."

TOP PUBLICATIONS, LTD.

3100 Independence Parkway, Suite 311-349, Plano TX 75075. (972)490-9686. Fax: (972)233-0713. E-mail: info@toppub.com. Submissions E-mail: submissions@toppub.com. Web site: www.toppub.com. **Acquisitions:** Bill Manchee, editor. Estab. 1999. Publishes harcover originals. **Publishes 4 titles/year. Receives 200 queries and 20 mss/year. 90% of books from first-time authors; 95% from unagented writers. Pays 15-20% royalty on wholesale price. Offers $500-2,500 advance.** Publishes book 8 months after acceptance of ms. Accepts simultaneous submissions. Responds in 6 months to queries; 6 months to mss. Book catalog free; ms guidelines online.
Fiction Adventure, historical, horror, juvenile, mainstream/contemporary, military/war, mystery, poetry, regional, romance, science fiction, short story collections, suspense, young adult. "It is imperative that our authors realize they will be required to promote their book extensively for it to be a success. Unless they are willing to make this commitment, they shouldn't submit to TOP."
Recent Title(s) *Cactus Island*, by William Manchee; *Keeper of the Island*, by H.J. Ralles; *LAndmarked for Murder*, by LA Chapter of Sisters in Crime.
Tips "Because of the intense competition in this industry, we recommend that our authors write books that appeal to a large mainstream audience to make marketing easier and increase the chances of success. Be patient and don't get your hopes up. We only publish a few titles a year so the odds at getting published at TOP are slim. If we reject your work, don't give it a second thought. It probably doesn't have any reflection on your work. We have to pass on a lot of good material each year simply by the limitations of our time and budget."

THE TRINITY FOUNDATION

PO Box 68, Unicoi TN 37692. (423)743-0199. Fax: (423)743-2005. E-mail: jrob1517@aol.com. Web site: www.trinityfoundation.org. **Acquisitions:** John Robbins. Publishes hardcover and paperback originals and reprints.

Publishes 5 titles/year. Publishes book 9 months after acceptance of ms. Responds in 1 month to queries; 1 month to proposals; 3 months to mss. Book catalog online.

Nonfiction "Only books that conform to the philosophy and theology of the Westminster Confession of Faith." Textbooks subjects include business/economics, education, government/politics, history, philosophy, religion, science. Query with SASE.

TURTLE BOOKS

866 United Nations Plaza, Suite #525, New York NY 10017. (212)644-2020. Fax: (212)223-4387. Web site: www.turtlebooks.com. **Acquisitions:** John Whitman, publisher (children's picture books). Publishes hardcover and trade paperback originals. **Publishes 6-8 titles/year. Receives 3,000 mss/year. 25% of books from first-time authors; 50% from unagented writers. Pays royalty on retail price. Offers advance.** Publishes book 12 months after acceptance of ms. Accepts simultaneous submissions.

O→ Turtle Books publishes only children's picture books (ie, no chapter books, YA or adult).

Nonfiction Children's/juvenile, illustrated book. Subjects include animals, education, history, language/literature, multicultural, nature/environment, regional, any subject suitable for a children's picture book. Submit complete ms. Reviews artwork/photos as part of ms package. Send photocopies, no original art.

Fiction Adventure, ethnic, fantasy, historical, multicultural, regional, sports, western. Subjects suitable for children's picture books. "We are looking for good stories which can be illustrated as children's picture books." Submit complete ms. Please do not send queries.

Poetry Must be suitable for an illustrated children's book format. Submit complete ms.

Recent Title(s) *Finding Daddy: A Story of the Great Depression*, by Jo Harper; *The Crab Man*, by Patricia Van West; *Alphabet Fiesta*, by Anne Miranda (children's picture books).

Tips "Our preference is for stories rather than concept books. We will consider only children's picture book manuscripts."

⊘ UMI (URBAN MINISTRIES, INC.)

1551 Regency Court, Calumet City IL 60409. Fax: (708)868-6759. Estab. 1970. Publishes trade paperback originals and reprints. **Publishes 2-3 titles/year.** Does not accept simultaneous submissions.

- *"We no longer accept unsolicited manuscripts."*

Nonfiction Illustrated book, reference, scholarly. Subjects include education (religious/Christian), religion (Christian), spirituality (Christian), Christian living, Christian doctrine, theology. "The books we publish are generally those we have a specific need for (i.e., Vacation Bible School curriculum topics); to complement an existing resource or product line; or those with a potential to develop into a curriculum." Query with SASE, or submit proposal package including outline, 2-3 sample chapters, letter why UMI should publish the book and why the book will sell.

Recent Title(s) *Family Ties: Restoring Unity in the African American Family*; *Strategies for Educating African American Children*; *Strategies for Educating African American Adults*.

Tips "Our audience is comprised of Christians, mostly African Americans."

THE UNIVERSITY OF AKRON PRESS

374B Bierce Library, Akron OH 44325-1703. (330)972-5342. Fax: (330)972-8364. E-mail: uapress@uakron.edu. Web site: www.uakron.edu/uapress. **Acquisitions:** Elton Glaser, director. Estab. 1988. Publishes hardcover and trade paperback originals. **Publishes 8-12 titles/year. Receives 400-500 queries and 100 mss/year. 40% of books from first-time authors; 100% from unagented writers. Pays 5-10% royalty. Offers (possible) advance.** Publishes book 10-12 months after acceptance of ms. Responds in 2 months to queries; 2 months to proposals; 3 months to mss. Book catalog free; ms guidelines online.

O→ "The University of Akron Press strives to be the University's ambassador for scholarship and creative writing at the national and international levels." Currently emphasizing technology and the environment, Ohio history and culture, poetry, history of law, political science, and international, political, and economic history. De-emphasizing fiction.

Nonfiction Scholarly. Subjects include history, regional, science, environment, technology, law, political science. "We publish mostly in our 4 nonfiction series: Technology and the Environment; Ohio History and Culture; Law, Politics and Society, and International, Political, and Economic History." Query with SASE. Reviews artwork/photos as part of ms package. Send photocopies.

Poetry Follow the guidelines and submit mss only for the contest: www.uakron.edu/uapress/poetry.html.

Recent Title(s) *The Destruction of Young Lawyers*, by Douglas Litowitz; *The Elections of 2000*, edited by Mary K. Kirtz, Mark J. Kasoff, Rick Farmer and John C. Green.

Tips "We have mostly an audience of general educated readers, with a more specialized audience of public historians, sociologists and political scientists for the scholarly series."

VANDERWYK & BURNHAM

P.O. Box 2789, Acton MA 01720. (978)263-7595. Fax: (978)263-0696. Web site: www.vandb.com. **Acquisitions:** Meredith Rutter, publisher. Publishes hardcover and trade paperback originals. **Publishes 3-6 titles/year. Pays royalty on net receipts. Offers $500-2,000 advance.** Accepts simultaneous submissions. Responds in 3 months to queries. Ms guidelines online.

Nonfiction Subjects include psychology, narrative nonfiction, contemporary issues, aging. "We publish books that make a difference in people's lives, including motivational books about admirable people and programs, and self-help books for people 40 and over." Query by e-mail with no attachments or submit proposal package, including résumé, publishing history, synopsis, competing books.

Recent Title(s) *Hidden in Plain Sight: Getting to the Bottom of Puzzling Emotions*; *You're Only Young Twice*; *10 Do-overs to Reawaken Your Spirit.*

WASHINGTON STATE UNIVERSITY PRESS

P.O. Box 645910, Pullman WA 99164-5910. (800)354-7360. Fax: (509)335-8568. E-mail: wsupress@wsu.edu. Web site: www.wsupress.wsu.edu. **Acquisitions:** Glen Lindeman, editor. Estab. 1928. Publishes hardcover originals, trade paperback originals and reprints. **Publishes 8-10 titles/year. 40% of books from first-time authors. Most books from unagented writers. Pays 5% royalty graduated according to sales.** Publishes book 18 months after acceptance of ms. Responds in 2 months to queries. Ms guidelines online.

- WSU Press publishes books on the history, pre-history, culture, and politics of the West, particularly the Pacific Northwest.

Nonfiction Biography. Subjects include cooking/foods/nutrition (history), government/politics, history, nature/environment, regional, essays. "We seek manuscripts that focus on the Pacific Northwest as a region. No poetry, novels, literary criticism, how-to books. We welcome innovative and thought-provoking titles in a wide diversity of genres, from essays and memoirs to history, archaeology, and political science." Submit outline, sample chapter(s). Reviews artwork/photos as part of ms package.

Recent Title(s) *Lewis and Clark Lexicon of Discovery*; *Color: Latino Voices in the Pacific Northwest*; *Washington State Government and Politics.*

Tips "We have developed our marketing in the direction of regional and local history and have attempted to use this as the base upon which to expand our publishing program. In regional history, the secret is to write a good narrative—a good story—that is substantiated factually. It should be told in an imaginative, clever way. Have visuals (photos, maps, etc.) available to help the reader envision what has happened. Tell the regional history story in a way that ties it to larger, national, and even international events. Weave it into the large pattern of history."

WESTERN PSYCHOLOGICAL SERVICES

12031 Wilshire Blvd., Los Angeles CA 90025. (310)478-2061. Fax: (310)478-7838. E-mail: bthomas@wpspublish.com. Web site: www.wpspublish.com; www.creativetherapystore.com. **Acquisitions:** Brian Thomas, marketing manager. Estab. 1948. Publishes trade paperback originals. **Publishes 6 titles/year. Receives 60 queries and 30 mss/year. 75% of books from first-time authors; 80% from unagented writers. Pays 5-10% royalty on wholesale price.** Publishes book 1 year after acceptance of ms. Accepts simultaneous submissions. Responds in 2 months to queries. Book catalog free; ms guidelines online.

- Western Psychological Services publishes practical books and games used by therapists, counselors, social workers, and others in the helping professionals working with children and adults.

Nonfiction Testing, addictions, special education, autism, speech-language-hearing, marriage and family therapy, neuropsychology, school psychology, occupational therapy, sensory integration. Subjects include child guidance/parenting, education, psychology, mulicultural issues. Submit complete ms. Reviews artwork/photos as part of ms package. Send photocopies.

Fiction Children's books dealing with feelings, anger, social skills, autism, family problems, etc. Submit complete ms.

Recent Title(s) *Sensory Integration and the Child*, by A. Jean Ayres, PhD; *To Be Me*, by Rebecca Etlinger.

WESTERNLORE PRESS

P.O. Box 35305, Tucson AZ 85740. (520)297-5491. Fax: (520)297-1722. **Acquisitions:** Lynn R. Bailey, editor. Estab. 1941. **Publishes 6-12 titles/year. Pays standard royalty on retail price.** Does not accept simultaneous submissions. Responds in 2 months to queries.

- Westernlore publishes Western Americana of a scholarly and semischolarly nature.

Nonfiction Biography, scholarly. Subjects include Americana, anthropology/archeology, history, regional, historic sights, restoration, ethnohistory pertaining to the American West. Re-publication of rare and out-of-print books. Length: 25,000-100,000 words. Query with SASE.

Recent Title(s) *Too Tough to Die*, by Bailey; *Men & Women of American Mining*, by Bailey & Chaput (2 volumes); *Cochise County Stalwarts, Vol. I & II*, by Bailey & Chaput.

WESTWINDS PRESS

Imprint of Graphic Arts Center Publishing Company, P.O. Box 10306, Portland OR 97296-0306. (503)226-2402. Fax: (503)223-1410. Web site: www.gacpc.com. **Acquisitions:** Tim Frew, executive editor. Estab. 1999. Publishes hardcover and trade paperback originals and reprints. **Publishes 5-7 titles/year. 10% of books from first-time authors; 90% from unagented writers. Pays 10-14% royalty on net receipts, or makes outright purchase. Offers advance.** Publishes book an average of 2 years after acceptance of ms. Accepts simultaneous submissions. Responds in 6 months to queries. Book catalog for 9×12 SAE with 6 first-class stamps; ms guidelines online.

Nonfiction Children's/juvenile, cookbook. Subjects include history, memoirs, regional (Western regional states—nature, travel, cookbooks, Native American culture, adventure, outdoor recreation, sports, the arts, and children's books), guidebooks.

Recent Title(s) *Salmon* (Northwest Homegrown cookbook series); *The Exploding Whale* (memoir); *Portland Confidential* (true crime).

Tips "Book proposals that are professionally written and polished with a clear understanding of the market receive our most careful consideration. We are looking for originality. We publish a wide range of books for a wide audience. Some of our books are clearly for travelers, others for those interested in outdoor recreation or various regional subjects. If I were a writer trying to market a book today, I would research the competition (existing books) for what I have in mind, and clearly (and concisely) express why my idea is different and better. I would describe the book buyers (and readers)—where they are, how many of them are there, how they can be reached (organizations, publications), why they would want or need my book."

WHITFORD PRESS

Imprint of Schiffer Publishing, Ltd., 4880 Lower Valley Rd., Atglen PA 19310. (610)593-1777. **Acquisitions:** Mary Whitford. Estab. 1975. **Publishes 2-6 titles/year. Pays royalty on wholesale price.** Responds in 2 weeks to queries. Book catalog free.

Nonfiction Regional ghost story compilations with historic and contemporary accounts of paranormal activity. Entertaining writing, originality, and an exciting assortment of tales make these books sell.

Tips "We want to publish books for towns or cities with relevant population or active tourism to support book sales. A list of potential town vendors is a helpful start toward selling us on your book idea."

N WHITTLER'S BENCH PRESS

Dram Tree Books, P.O. Box 7183, Wilmington NC 28406. E-mail: dramtreebooks@ec.rr.com. Web site: www.dramtreebooks.com. **Acquisitions:** Fiction Editor. Estab. 2005. Publishes trade paperback originals and reprints. **Publishes 2-6 titles/year. 90% of books from first-time authors; 100% from unagented writers. Pays 10-15% royalty on retail price. Offers $250-500 advance.** Publishes book 1 year after acceptance of ms. Does not accept simultaneous submissions. Responds in 2 months to queries; 2 months to proposals; 4 months to mss. Ms guidelines by e-mail.

Fiction Adventure, historical, humor, military/war, mystery, regional, suspense. "Our main focus is on historical fiction, mysteries and humorous novels—and all of it must have some link to North Carolina. When submitting humorous novels you must make us laugh. Think in terms of books by authors like Michael Malone, T.R. Pearson, Clyde Edgerton, Terry Pratchett, etc." Query with SASE, or submit proposal package including 3 sample chapter(s), synopsis.

Tips "Our readers are looking for compelling stories that will transport them away from the pressures of the 'real' world for however long they spend with our stories. The North Carolina tie-in is an important part of what will be a Whittler's Bench Press title. Remember they'll be paying good money to be entertained, so give them a story that satisfies. If historical fiction, make sure you get the history right. Finally, always remember: It must have a North Carolina angle of some kind."

WINDWARD PUBLISHING

Imprint of Finney Company, 8075 215th St. W., Lakeville MN 55044. (952)469-6699. Fax: (952)469-1968. E-mail: feedback@finney-hobar.com. Web site: www.finney-hobar.com. **Acquisitions:** Alan E. Krysan, president. Estab. 1973. Publishes trade paperback originals. **Publishes 6-10 titles/year. Receives 120 queries and 50 mss/year. 50% of books from first-time authors; 100% from unagented writers. Pays 10% royalty on wholesale price. Offers advance.** Publishes book 6-12 months after acceptance of ms. Accepts simultaneous submissions. Responds in 8-10 weeks to queries.

O→ Windward publishes illustrated natural history and recreation books.

Nonfiction Illustrated book, handbooks, field guides. Subjects include agriculture/horticulture, animals, garden-

Small Presses

ing, nature/environment, recreation, science, sports, natural history. Query with SASE. Reviews artwork/photos as part of ms package.

Recent Title(s) *Nighlight*, by Jeannine Anderson; *Space Station Science*, by Marianne Dyson; *Wild Beach*, by Marion Coste.

WISH PUBLISHING

P.O. Box 10337, Terre Haute IN 47801. (812)299-5700. Fax: (928)447-1836. E-mail: holly@wishpublishing.com. Web site: www.wishpublishing.com. **Acquisitions:** Holly Kondras, president. Publishes hardcover and trade paperback originals. **Publishes 5-10 titles/year. Pays 10-18% royalty on wholesale price.** Accepts simultaneous submissions. Responds in 2 months to queries; 2 months to proposals; 2 months to mss. Book catalog and ms guidelines free or online.

Nonfiction Biography, children's/juvenile, reference. Subjects include health/medicine, sports, women's issues/studies. Query with SASE, or submit proposal package including outline, author bio, 2 sample chapters. Reviews artwork/photos as part of ms package. Send photocopies.

Recent Title(s) *Hard Fought Victories: Women Coaches Making a Difference* (sports); *Total Fitness for Women* (fitness); *Girls' Basketball: Building a Winning Team* (sports).

Tips Audience is women and girls who play sports, and their coaches, parents, and supporters.

WOLF DEN BOOKS

5783 S.W. 40th St., Miami FL 33155. E-mail: info@wolfdenbooks.com. Web site: www.wolfdenbooks.com. **Acquisitions:** Gail Shivel (literary criticism); S.L. Harrison (journalism, history, political science). Estab. 2000. Publishes hardcover, trade paperback and electronic originals and reprints. **Publishes 3 titles/year. Receives 6 queries and 3 mss/year. 100% from unagented writers. Pays 5-7½% royalty on retail price.** Publishes book 1 year after acceptance of ms. Accepts simultaneous submissions. Book catalog online; ms guidelines by e-mail.

- Do not send postage; mss are not returned.

Nonfiction General nonfiction, reference, scholarly, textbook. Subjects include history, language/literature, political science, literary biography. "Thoughtful, idea-rich, factual, common sense prose is sought in the areas of literary criticism, political science, history and journalism." Submit complete ms. Reviews artwork/photos as part of ms package. Send photocopies.

Recent Title(s) *The Columbiad*, by Joel Barlow; *Selected Pseudonymous Writings*, compiled by S.L. Harrison.

N WORD WARRIORS PRESS

3808 Blaisdell Ave. S., #309, Minneapolis MN 55409. Web site: www.wordwarriorspress.com. **Acquisitions:** Gail Cerridwen, managing editor (creative nonfiction). Estab. 2003. Publishes trade paperback originals. **Publishes 1-2 titles/year. Receives 100 queries and 170 mss/year. 100% of books from first-time authors; 100% from unagented writers. Pays 6-8% royalty on retail price.** Publishes book 9 months after acceptance of ms. Accepts simultaneous submissions. Responds in 2 months to queries; 2 months to proposals; 4 months to mss. Ms guidelines online.

Nonfiction Autobiography, journals. Subjects include alternative lifestyles, contemporary culture, creative nonfiction, ethnic, gay/lesbian, memoirs, multicultural, sex, women's issues/studies. "We publish only authors in their 20s or late teens, especially those people and stories not well represented in mainstream publishing. We welcome raw, honest, edgy, and uncensored writing styles." Submit proposal package including outline, 2 sample chapter(s), or submit complete ms. Reviews artwork/photos as part of ms package. Send photocopies.

Fiction Ethnic, experimental, feminist, gay/lesbian, gothic, literary, mainstream/contemporary, multicultural, short story collections, young adult. "Right now, we're publishing creative nonfiction (mostly written in the style of fiction). But we're also interested in edgy, experimental fiction for future publications." Submit proposal package including 2 sample chapter(s), synopsis, or submit complete ms.

Recent Title(s) *Stranger in My Skin*, by Alysa Phillips (memoir); *Outlet or a Heaven Full of Televisions*, by Scott Sundvall (memoir); *Yesterday's Warrior*, by Heather Harrison (memoir).

Tips "Our target audience is younger and alternative people. We're especially interested right now in seeing personal experiences for any upcoming prison anthology. We'd also like to see more submissions from POC and LGBT authors."

WORLD LEISURE

P.O. Box 160, Hampstead NH 03841. (617)569-1966. E-mail: leocha@worldleisure.com. Web site: www.worldleisure.com. **Acquisitions:** Charles Leocha, president. Estab. 1977. Publishes trade paperback originals. **Publishes 3-5 titles/year. Pays royalty, or makes outright purchase.** Accepts simultaneous submissions. Responds in 2 months to queries. Book catalog and ms guidelines online.

O→ World Leisure specializes in travel books, activity guidebooks, and self-help titles.

Nonfiction Self-help. Subjects include recreation, sports (skiing/snowboarding), travel. "We will be publishing annual updates to *Ski Snowboard Europe* and *Ski Snowboard America & Canada*. Writers planning any winter resort stories should contact us for possible add-on assignments at areas not covered by our staff." Submit outline, intro sample chapter(s), annotated TOC, SASE.

Recent Title(s) *Ski Snowboard America*, by Charles Leocha; *Ski Snowboard Europe*, by Charles Leocha.

N YMAA PUBLICATION CENTER

4354 Washington St., Roslindale MA 02131. (617)323-7215. Fax: (617)323-7417. E-mail: ymaa@aol.com. **Acquisitions:** David Ripianzi, director. Estab. 1982. Publishes trade paperback originals and reprints. **Publishes 6 titles/year. Receives 50 queries and 20 mss/year. 25% of books from first-time authors; 100% from unagented writers. Pays 10% royalty on net receipts.** Publishes book 18 months after acceptance of ms. Accepts simultaneous submissions. Responds in 3 months to proposals. Book catalog online; ms guidelines free.

O→ "YMAA publishes books on Chinese Chi Kung (Qigong), Taijiquan, (Tai Chi) and Asian martial arts. We are expanding our focus to include books on healing, wellness, meditation and subjects related to Asian culture and Asian medicine." De-emphasizing fitness books.

Nonfiction "We are most interested in Asian martial arts, Chinese medicine, and Chinese Qigong. We publish Eastern thought, health, meditation, massage, and East/West synthesis." How-to, multimedia, self-help. Subjects include ethnic, health/medicine (Chinese), history, philosophy, spirituality, sports, Asian martial arts, Chinese Qigong. "We no longer publish or solicit books for children. We also produce instructional DVDs and videos to accompany our books on traditional Chinese martial arts, meditation, massage, and Chi Kung." Submit proposal package including outline, author bio, 1 sample chapter, SASE. Reviews artwork/photos as part of ms package. Send photocopies and 1-2 originals to determine quality of photo/line art. "We are excited to announce a new category: **martial arts fiction**. We are seeking mss that bring the venerated tradition of true Asian martial arts to readers. Your novel length ms should be a thrilling story that conveys insights into true martial techniques and philosophies."

Recent Title(s) *The Way of the Sanchin Kata*, by Kris Wilder; *Sunrise Tai Chi*, by Ramel Rones; *The Cutting Season*, by Arthur Rosenfeld.

Tips "If you are submitting health-related material, please refer to an Asian tradition. Learn about author publicity options as your participation is mandatory."

MARKETS

Consumer Magazines

Selling your writing to consumer magazines is as much an exercise of your marketing skills as it is of your writing abilities. Editors of consumer magazines are looking not only for good writing, but for good writing which communicates pertinent information to a specific audience—their readers.

Approaching the consumer magazine market

Marketing skills will help you successfully discern a magazine's editorial slant, and write queries and articles that prove your knowledge of the magazine's readership. You can gather clues about a magazine's readership—and establish your credibility with the magazine's editor—in a number of ways:

- **Read** the magazine's listing in *Writer's Market*.
- **Study** a magazine's writer's guidelines.
- **Check** a magazine's Web site.
- **Read** several current issues of the target magazine.
- **Talk** to an editor by phone.

Writers who can correctly and consistently discern a publication's audience and deliver stories that speak to that target readership will win out every time over writers who submit haphazardly.

What editors want

In nonfiction, editors continue to look for short feature articles covering specialized topics. Editors want crisp writing and expertise. If you are not an expert in the area about which you are writing, make yourself one through research. Always query before sending your manuscript. Don't e-mail or fax a query to an editor unless the listing mentions it is acceptable to do so.

Fiction editors prefer to receive complete manuscripts. Writers must keep in mind that marketing fiction is competitive, and editors receive far more material than they can publish. For this reason, they often do not respond to submissions unless they are interested in using the story. More comprehensive information on fiction markets can be found in *Novel & Short Story Writer's Market* (Writer's Digest Books).

Payment

Most magazines listed here have indicated pay rates; some give very specific payment-per-word rates, while others state a range. **(Note: All of the magazines listed in the Consumer**

Magazines section are paying markets. However, some of the magazines are not identified by payment icons ($-$$$$) because the magazines preferred not to disclose specific payment information.) Any agreement you come to with a magazine, whether verbal or written, should specify the payment you are to receive and when you are to receive it. Some magazines pay writers only after the piece in question has been published (on publication). Others pay as soon as they have accepted a piece and are sure they are going to use it (on acceptance). In *Writer's Market*, those magazines that pay on acceptance have been highlighted with the phrase **pays on acceptance** set in bold type.

So what is a good pay rate? There are no standards; the principle of supply and demand operates at full throttle in the business of writing and publishing. As long as there are more writers than opportunities for publication, wages for freelancers will never skyrocket. Rates vary widely from one market to the next. Smaller circulation magazines and some departments of the larger magazines will pay a lower rate.

Editors know the listings in *Writer's Market* are read and used by writers with a wide range of experience, from those unpublished writers just starting out, to those with a successful, profitable freelance career. As a result, many magazines publicly report pay rates in the lower end of their actual pay ranges. Experienced writers will be able to successfully negotiate higher pay rates for their material. Newer writers should be encouraged that as their reputation grows (along with their clip file), they will be able to command higher rates. The article "How Much Should I Charge?" on page 64, gives you an idea of pay ranges for different freelance jobs, including those directly associated with magazines.

INFORMATION AT-A-GLANCE

In the Consumer Magazines section, icons identify comparative payment rates (**$-$$$$**); new listings (N); and magazines that do not accept unsolicited manuscripts (⊘). Different sections of *Writer's Market* include other symbols; check the inside back cover for an explanation of all the symbols used throughout the book.

Important information is highlighted in boldface—the "quick facts" you won't find in any other market book, but should know before you submit your work. The word **Contact** identifies the appropriate person to query at each magazine. We also highlight what percentage of the magazine is freelance written; how many manuscripts a magazine buys per year of nonfiction, fiction, poetry, and fillers; and respective pay rates in each category.

Information on publications listed in the previous edition of *Writer's Market*, but not included in this edition, can be found in the General Index.

ANIMAL

$ $ AKC GAZETTE

American Kennel Club, 260 Madison Ave., New York NY 10016. Web site: www.akc.org/pubs/index.cfm. **85% freelance written.** Monthly magazine. "Geared to interests of fanciers of purebred dogs as opposed to commercial interests or pet owners. We require solid expertise from our contributors—we are *not* a pet magazine." Estab. 1889. Circ. 60,000. Pays on publication. Publishes ms an average of 6 months after acceptance. Byline given. Offers 10% kill fee. Buys first North American serial, electronic, international rights. Submit seasonal material 6 months in advance. Accepts queries by mail. Responds in 2 months to queries. Writer's guidelines for #10 SASE.

Nonfiction General interest, how-to, humor, interview/profile, photo feature, travel, dog art, training and canine performance sports. No poetry, tributes to individual dogs, or fiction. **Buys 30-40 mss/year.** Length: 1,000-3,000 words. **Pays $300-500.** Pays expenses of writers on assignment.

Photos Photo contest guidelines for #10 SASE. State availability with submission. Reviews color transparencies, prints. Buys one-time rights. Pays $50-200/photo. Captions, identification of subjects, model releases required.

Fiction Annual short fiction contest only. Guidelines for #10 SASE.

Tips "Contributors should be involved in the dog fancy or be an expert in the area they write about (veterinary, showing, field trialing, obedience training, dogs in legislation, dog art or history or literature). All submissions are welcome but author must be a credible expert or be able to interview and quote the experts. Veterinary articles must be written by or with veterinarians. Humorous features or personal experiences relative to purebred dogs should have broader applications. For features, know the subject thoroughly and be conversant with jargon peculiar to the sport of dogs."

$ $ THE AMERICAN QUARTER HORSE JOURNAL

P.O. Box 32470, Amarillo TX 79120. (806)376-4811. Fax: (806)349-6400. E-mail: aqhajrnl@aqha.org. Web site: www.aqha.com. Editor-in-Chief: Jim Jennings. **Contact:** Jim Bret Campbell, editor. **30% freelance written.** Prefers to work with published/established writers. Monthly official publication of the American Quarter Horse Association. Estab. 1948. Circ. 70,000. **Pays on acceptance.** Publishes ms an average of 3 months after acceptance. Byline given. Buys first North American serial rights. Submit seasonal material 6 months in advance. Accepts queries by mail, e-mail, fax. Responds in 2 weeks to queries.

- Break in by "writing about topics tightly concentrated on the Quarter Horse industry while maintaining strong journalistic skills."

Nonfiction Book excerpts, essays, how-to (fitting, grooming, showing, or anything that relates to owning, showing, or breeding), interview/profile (feature-type stories—must be about established horses or people who have made a contribution to the business), new product, opinion, personal experience, photo feature, technical (equine updates, new surgery procedures, etc.), travel, informational (educational clinics, current news). **Buys 40 mss/year.** Length: 800-2,000 words. **Pays $150-600.**

Photos Reviews $2^1/_4 \times 2^1/_4$, 4×5, or 35mm transparencies, 4×5 glossy prints.

- The online magazine carries original content not found in the print edition. Contact: Jim Bret Campbell.

Tips "Writers must have a knowledge of the horse business."

$ $ APPALOOSA JOURNAL

Appaloosa Horse Club, 2720 West Pullman Rd., Moscow ID 83843-0903. (208)882-5578. Fax: (208)882-8150. E-mail: journal@appaloosa.com. Web site: www.appaloosajournal.com. **Contact:** Diane Rice, editor. **40% freelance written.** Monthly magazine covering Appaloosa horses. Estab. 1946. Circ. 25,000. Pays on publication. Publishes ms an average of 3 months after acceptance. Byline given. Buys first North American serial, electronic rights. Responds in 1 month to queries; 2 months to mss. Sample copy for free. Writer's guidelines online.

- *Appaloosa Journal* no longer accepts material for columns.

Nonfiction Historical/nostalgic, interview/profile, photo feature. **Buys 15-20 mss/year.** Query with or without published clips or send complete ms. Length: 800-1,800 words. **Pays $200-400.**

Photos Send photos with submission. Payment varies. Captions, identification of subjects required.

- The online magazine carries original content not found in the print edition. Contact: Jennie Archer, online editor.

Tips "Articles by writers with horse knowledge, news sense, and photography skills are in great demand. If it's a strong article about an Appaloosa, the writer has a pretty good chance of publication. A good understanding of the breed and the industry, breeders, and owners is helpful. Make sure there's some substance and a unique twist."

$ $ AQUARIUM FISH INTERNATIONAL

Fishkeeping—the Art and the Science, (formerly *Aquarium Fish Magazine*), Bowtie, Inc., P.O. Box 6050, Mission Viejo CA 92690. Fax: (949)855-3045. E-mail: aquariumfish@bowtieinc.com. Web site: www.aquariumfish.com.

Editor: Russ Case. Managing Editor: Patricia Knight. **Contact:** Brian Wheeler, assistant editor. **90% freelance written.** Monthly magazine covering fish and other aquatic pets. "Our focus is on beginning and intermediate fish keeping; we also run one advanced saltwater article per issue. Most of our articles concentrate on general fish and aquarium care, but we will also consider other types of articles that may be helpful to those in the fishkeeping hobby. Freshwater and saltwater tanks, and ponds are covered." Estab. 1988. Pays on publication. Byline given. Buys first North American serial, electronic rights. Accepts queries by mail, e-mail, fax. Responds in 1 month to queries; 6 months to mss. Writer's guidelines for #10 SASE.

Nonfiction General interest (species profiles, natural history with home care info), interview/profile (of well-known people in fish keeping), new product (press releases only for Product Showcase section), photo feature, caring for fish in aquariums. Special issues: "We do have 1 annual; freelancers should query." No fiction, anthropomorphism, articles on sport fishing, or animals that cannot be kept as pets (i.e., whales, dolphins, manatees, etc.). **Buys 60 mss/year.** Query with or without published clips or send complete ms. Length: 1,500-2,000 words. **Pays 20¢/word.**

Photos Send for digital image requirements. State availability with submission. Reviews 35mm transparencies, 4×5 prints. Buys first North American serial rights. Offers $15-200/photo. Identification of subjects required.

Fillers Facts, gags to be illustrated by cartoonist, newsbreaks. **Buys variable number/year.** Length: 50-200 words.

Tips "Take a look at our guidelines before submitting. Writers are not required to provide photos for submitted articles, but we do encourage it, if possible. It helps if writers are involved in fish keeping themselves. Our writers tend to be experienced fish keepers, detailed researchers, and some scientists."

ARABIAN STUDS & STALLIONS ANNUAL

Vink Publishing, P.O. Box 8369, Woolloongabba QLD 4102 Australia. (61)(7)3334-8000. Fax: (61)(7)3391-5118. E-mail: sharon@vinkpub.com. Web site: www.arabianhorse.com.au. **Contact:** Sharon Meyers, editor. Annual magazine covering Arabian horses.

- Query before submitting.

THE AUSTRALIAN ARABIAN HORSE NEWS

Vink Publishing, P.O. Box 8369, Woolloongabba QLD 4102 Australia. (61)(7)3334-8000. Fax: (61)(7)3391-5118. E-mail: sharon@vinkpub.com. Web site: www.arabianhorse.com.au. **Contact:** Sharon Meyers, editor. Quarterly magazine covering Australian Arabian horses.

- Query before submitting.

$ BIRDING WORLD

Sea Lawn, Coast Road, Cley next the Sea, Holt Norfolk NR25 7RZ United Kingdom. (44)(126)374-0913. E-mail: steve@birdingworld.co.uk. Web site: www.birdingworld.co.uk. **Contact:** Steve Gantlett. Monthly magazine publishing notes about birds and birdwatching. The emphasis is on rarer British and Western Palearctic birds with topical interest. Estab. 1988. Accepts queries by mail, e-mail. Sample copy for £4.50. Writer's guidelines by e-mail.

Articles and notes on the following subjects are welcome: identification, descriptions of recent rarities, birding accounts, and letters on any subjects of interest to birders.

Nonfiction Pays £2-4/100 words for unsolicited articles.

Photos Reviews digital images, drawings, maps, graphs, paintings. Pays £10-30/color photos; £5-25/b&w photos.

$ $ CAT FANCY

For the Love of Cats, Fancy Publications, a division of BowTie Inc., P.O. Box 6050, Mission Viejo CA 92690. (949)855-8822. E-mail: query@catfancy.com. Web site: www.catfancy.com. **Contact:** Susan Logan, editor. **90% freelance written.** Monthly magazine covering all aspects of responsible cat ownership. Estab. 1965. Pays on publication. Buys first North American serial rights. Editorial lead time 6 months. Responds in 3 months to queries. Writer's guidelines online.

- *Cat Fancy* does not accept unsolicited mss and only accepts queries from January-May. Queries sent after May will be returned or discarded.

Nonfiction Engaging presentation of expert, up-to-date information. Must be cat oriented. Writing should not be gender specific. How-to, humor, photo feature, travel, behavior, health, lifestyle, cat culture, entertainment. **Buys 70 mss/year.** Query with published clips. Length: 300-1,000 words. **Pays $50-450.**

Photos Seeking photos of happy, healthy, well-groomed cats and kittens in indoor settings. Buys one-time rights. Negotiates payment individually. Captions, identification of subjects, model releases required.

Tips "No fiction or poetry. Please read recent issues to become acquainted with our style and content. Show us in your query how you can contribute something new and unique. No phone queries."

$ $ THE CHRONICLE OF THE HORSE

P.O. Box 46, Middleburg VA 20118-0046. (540)687-6341. Fax: (540)687-3937. E-mail: staff@chronofhorse.com. Web site: www.chronofhorse.com. Editor: Tricia Booker. Managing Editor: Beth Rasin. **Contact:** Molly Sorge, assistant editor. **80% freelance written.** Weekly magazine covering horses. "We cover English riding sports, including horse showing, grand prix jumping competitions, steeplechase racing, foxhunting, dressage, endurance riding, handicapped riding, and combined training. We are the official publication for the national governing bodies of many of the above sports. We feature news, how-to articles on equitation and horse care and interviews with leaders in the various fields." Estab. 1937. Circ. 18,000. Pays for features on acceptance; news and other items on publication. Publishes ms an average of 4 months after acceptance. Byline given. Buys first North American serial rights, makes work-for-hire assignments. Submit seasonal material 3 months in advance. Accepts queries by mail, e-mail. Responds in 5-6 weeks to queries. Sample copy for $2 and 9×12 SAE. Writer's guidelines online.

O━ Break in by "clearing a small news assignment in your area ahead of time."

Nonfiction General interest, historical/nostalgic (history of breeds, use of horses in other countries and times, art, etc.), how-to (trailer, train, design a course, save money, etc.), humor (centered on living with horses or horse people), interview/profile (of nationally known horsemen or the very unusual), technical (horse care, articles on feeding, injuries, care of foals, shoeing, etc.). Special issues: Steeplechase Racing (January); American Horse in Sport and Grand Prix Jumping (February); Horse Show (March); Intercollegiate (April); Kentucky 4-Star Preview (April); Junior and Pony (April); Dressage (June); Horse Care (July); Combined Training (August); Hunt Roster (September); Amateur (November); Stallion (December). No poetry, Q&A interviews, clinic reports, Western riding articles, personal experience or wild horses. **Buys 300 mss/year.** Query with or without published clips or send complete ms. Length: 6-7 pages. **Pays $150-250.**

Photos State availability with submission. Reviews prints or color slides; accepts color for b&w reproduction. Buys one-time rights. Pays $25-30. Identification of subjects required.

Columns/Departments Dressage, Combined Training, Horse Show, Horse Care, Racing over Fences, Young Entry (about young riders, geared for youth), Horses and Humanities, Hunting, Vaulting, Handicapped Riding, Trail Riding, 1,000-1,225 words; News of major competitions ("clear assignment with us first"), 1,500 words. Query with or without published clips or send complete ms. **Pays $25-200.**

Tips "Get our guidelines. Our readers are sophisticated, competitive horsemen. Articles need to go beyond common knowledge. Freelancers often attempt too broad or too basic a subject. We welcome well-written news stories on major events, but clear the assignment with us."

$ COONHOUND BLOODLINES

The Complete Magazine for the Houndsman and Coon Hunter, United Kennel Club, Inc., 100 E. Kilgore Rd., Kalamazoo MI 49002-5584. (269)343-9020. Fax: (269)343-7037. E-mail: vrand@ukcdogs.com. Web site: www.ukcdogs.com. **Contact:** Vicki Rand, editor. **40% freelance written.** Monthly magazine covering all aspects of the 6 Coonhound dog breeds. "Writers must retain the 'slang' particular to dog people and to our readers—many of whom are from the South." Estab. 1925. Circ. 16,000. Pays on publication. Publishes ms an average of 6 months after acceptance. Byline given. Buys first North American serial rights, makes work-for-hire assignments. Editorial lead time 6 months. Submit seasonal material 6 months in advance. Accepts queries by mail, e-mail, fax, phone. Accepts simultaneous submissions. Responds in 6 weeks to queries. Sample copy for $4.50.

Nonfiction General interest, historical/nostalgic, humor, interview/profile, new product, personal experience, photo feature, breed-specific. Special issues: Six of our 12 issues are each devoted to a specific breed of Coonhound. Treeing Walker (February); English (July); Black & Tan (April); Bluetick (May); Redbone (June); Plott Hound (August), 1,000-3,000 words and photos. **Buys 12-36 mss/year.** Query. Length: 1,000-5,000 words. **Pays variable amount.** Sometimes pays expenses of writers on assignment.

Photos State availability with submission. Reviews contact sheets. Buys one-time rights. Negotiates payment individually. Captions, identification of subjects required.

Fiction Must be about the Coonhound breeds or hunting with hounds. Adventure, historical, humorous, mystery. **Buys 3-6 mss/year.** Query. Length: 1,000-3,000 words. **Pay varies.**

Tips "Hunting with hounds is a two-century old American tradition and an important part of the American heritage, especially east of the Mississippi. It covers a lifestyle as well as a wonderful segment of the American population, many of whom still live by honest, friendly values."

$ $ DOG FANCY

P.O. Box 6050, Mission Viejo CA 92690-6050. Fax: (949)855-3045. E-mail: barkback@dogfancy.com. Web site: www.dogfancy.com. **95% freelance written.** Monthly magazine for men and women of all ages interested in all phases of dog ownership. Estab. 1970. Circ. 250,000. Pays on publication. Publishes ms an average of 6 months after acceptance. Byline given. Offers kill fee. Buys first North American serial, nonexclusive electronic and other rights. Submit seasonal material 6 months in advance. Accepts queries by mail. Responds in 2 months to queries. Sample copy for $5.50. Writer's guidelines online.

Nonfiction General interest, how-to, humor, inspirational, interview/profile, photo feature, travel. "No stories written from a dog's point of view." **Buys 100 mss/year.** Query. Length: 800-1,200 words. **Pays $200-500.**

Photos State availability with submission. Reviews transparencies, slides. Offers no additional payment for photos accepted with ms.

Columns/Departments Health and Medicine; Training and Behavior, 500 words. **Buys 24 mss/year.** Query by mail only. **Pays $200-250.**

Tips "We're looking for the unique experience that enhances the dog/owner relationship. Medical articles are assigned to veterinarians. Note that we write for a lay audience (nontechnical), but we do assume a certain level of intelligence. Read the magazine before making a pitch. Make sure your query is clear, concise, and relevant."

N $ DOGS IN CANADA

Apex Publishing, Ltd., 89 Skyway Ave., Suite 200, Etobicoke ON M9W 6R4 Canada. (416)798-9778. Fax: (416)798-9671. E-mail: editor@dogsincanada.com. Web site: www.dogsincanada.com. Managing Editor: Beth Marley. **Contact:** Kelly Caldwell, editor-in-chief. **90% freelance written.** Monthly magazine covering dogs. "*Dogs in Canada* is considered a reliable and authoritative source of information about dogs. The mix of content must satisfy a diverse readership, including knowledgeable dog owners and fanciers as well as those who simply love dogs." Estab. 1889. Circ. 41,769. **Pays on acceptance.** Publishes ms an average of 3 months after acceptance. Byline given. Offers 50% kill fee. Buys first North American serial, first, electronic rights. Editorial lead time 4 months. Submit seasonal material 6 months in advance. Accepts queries by mail, e-mail, fax. Accepts previously published material. Responds in 6 weeks to queries; 2 months to mss. Writer's guidelines for #10 SASE or via e-mail.

Nonfiction Book excerpts, historical/nostalgic, humor, interview/profile. Does not want articles written from the dog's point of view. **Buys less than 10 mss/year.** Query with or without published clips or send complete ms. Length: 500-1,800 words. **Pays $100.** Sometimes pays expenses of writers on assignment.

Photos Bill Whitehead, art director. State availability of or send photos with submission. Reviews contact sheets, negatives, transparencies, 5×7 prints, GIF/JPEG files. Rights negotiated individually. Negotiates payment individually. Identification of subjects, model releases required.

Poetry Buys less than 10 poems/year. Submit maximum 2 poems.

Fillers Anecdotes, short humor. **Buys less than 10/year.** Length: 150-500 words.

Tips "If high quality photos are available to complement the piece, that helps us considerably. Also, we have covered virtually all of the basics of dog health, nutrition, behavior, etc. Queries with new ideas or a fresh approach will catch our attention."

N $ DOGS IN CANADA ANNUAL

Apex Publishing, Ltd., 89 Skyway Ave., Suite 200, Etobicoke ON M9W 6R4 Canada. (416)798-9778. Fax: (416)798-9671. E-mail: editor@dogsincanada.com. Web site: www.dogsincanada.com. Managing Editor: Beth Marley. **Contact:** Kelly Caldwell, editor-in-chief. **25% freelance written.** Annual magazine covering dogs. Also a small cats section. "*Dogs in Canada Annual* is a reliable source of information about dogs. Our mix of content must satisfy a diverse readership, including knowledgeable dog owners, breed enthusiasts, and average pet owners who simply love their dogs." Estab. 1975. Circ. 107,919. **Pays on acceptance.** Publishes ms an average of 6 months after acceptance. Byline given. Offers 50% kill fee. Buys first North American serial, first, electronic rights. Editorial lead time 5 months. Submit seasonal material 6 months in advance. Accepts queries by mail, e-mail, fax. Responds in 6 weeks to queries; 2 months to mss. Writer's guidelines for #10 SASE or by e-mail.

Nonfiction Interview/profile, photo feature, travel. Does not want anything written from the dog's perspective. **Buys less than 10 mss/year.** Query with or without published clips or send complete ms. Length: 500-1,500 words. **Pays $100.** Sometimes pays expenses of writers on assignment.

Photos Bill Whitehead, art director. State availability of or send photos with submission. Reviews contact sheets, negatives, transparencies, 5×7 prints, GIF/JPEG files. Rights negotiated individually. Negotiates payment individually. Identification of subjects, model releases required.

Columns/Departments Query with or without published clips. **Pays $100.**

Fillers Anecdotes, facts, short humor. **Buys less than 10/year.** Length: 150-500 words. **Pays $100.**

Tips "An interesting idea or fresh approach is preferred, as past Annuals have covered most of the basics regarding pet health, behavior, etc. Query with published samples."

N $ $ EQUESTRIAN MAGAZINE

The Official Magazine of Equestrian Sport Since 1937, United States Equestrian Federation (USEF), 4047 Iron Works Parkway, Lexington KY 40511. (859)258-2472. Fax: (859)231-6662. E-mail: bsosby@usef.org. Web site:

www.usef.org. **Contact:** Brian Sosby, editor. **10-30% freelance written.** Magazine published 10 times/year covering the equestrian sport. Estab. 1937. Circ. 77,000. Pays on publication. Byline given. Offers 50% kill fee. Buys first North American serial, first rights. Editorial lead time 1-5 months. Accepts queries by mail, e-mail, fax, phone. Sample copy and writer's guidelines free.

Nonfiction Interview/profile, technical, all equestrian-related. **Buys 20-30 mss/year.** Query with published clips. Length: 500-3,500 words. **Pays $200-500.**

Photos State availability with submission. Reviews contact sheets. Buys one-time rights. Offers $50-200/photo. Captions, identification of subjects, model releases required.

Columns/Departments Horses of the Past (famous equines); Horse People (famous horsemen/women), both 500-1,000 words. **Buys 20-30 mss/year.** Query with published clips. **Pays $100.**

Tips "Write via e-mail in first instance with samples, résumé, then mail original clips."

$ EQUINE JOURNAL

103 Roxbury St., Keene NH 03431-8801. (603)357-4271. Fax: (603)357-7851. E-mail: editorial@equinejournal.com. Web site: www.equinejournal.com. **Contact:** Kathleen Labonville, managing editor. **90% freelance written.** Monthly tabloid covering horses—all breeds, all disciplines. "To educate, entertain, and enable amateurs and professionals alike to stay on top of new developments in the field. Covers horse-related activities from all corners of New England, New York, New Jersey, Pennsylvania, and the Midwest." Estab. 1988. Circ. 26,000. Pays on publication. Byline given. Buys first North American serial, electronic rights. Editorial lead time 4 months. Accepts queries by mail, e-mail, fax, phone. Responds in 2 months to queries. Writer's guidelines online.

Nonfiction General interest, how-to, interview/profile. **Buys 100 mss/year.** Query with published clips or send complete ms. Length: 1,500-2,200 words.

Photos Send photos with submission. Reviews prints. Pays $10.

Columns/Departments Horse Health (health-related topics), 1,200-1,500 words. **Buys 12 mss/year.** Query.

N EQUUS

656 Quince Orchard Rd., Suite 600, Gaithersburg MD 20878-1409. (301)977-3900. Fax: (301)990-9015. E-mail: equuslts@aol.com. Web site: www.equisearch.com. Editor: Laurie Prinz. Monthly magazine covering equine behavior. Provides the latest information from the world's top veternarians, equine researchers, riders, and trainers. Circ. 149,482. Accepts queries by mail. Writer's guidelines online.

Nonfiction Features on healthcare, behavior, training techniques, veterinary breakthroughs, exercise physiology, etc. Send complete ms. Length: 1,600-3,000 words. **Payment depends on quality, length, and complexity of the story.**

Columns/Departments The Medical Front (research/technology/treatments), 200-400 words; Hands On (everyday horse care), 100-400 words; Roundup (industry news stories), 100-400 words; True Tales (experiences/relationships with horses), 700-2,000 words; Case Report (equine illness/injury), 1,000-2,500 words. Send complete ms. **Payment depends on quality, length, and complexity of the story.**

$ $ FIELD TRIAL MAGAZINE

Androscoggin Publishing, Inc., P.O. Box 98, Milan NH 03588. (603)449-6767. Fax: (603)449-2462. E-mail: birddog@wildblue.net. Web site: www.fielddog.com/ftm. **Contact:** Craig Doherty, editor. **75% freelance written.** Quarterly magazine covering field trials for pointing dogs. "Our readers are knowledgeable sports men and women who want interesting and informative articles about their sport." Estab. 1997. Circ. 6,000. Pays on publication. Publishes ms an average of 6 months after acceptance. Byline given. Buys first North American serial rights. Editorial lead time 3 months. Submit seasonal material 6 months in advance. Accepts queries by mail, e-mail, fax. Accepts simultaneous submissions. Responds in 2 weeks to queries; 2 months to mss. Sample copy for free. Writer's guidelines online.

Nonfiction Book excerpts, essays, general interest, historical/nostalgic, how-to, interview/profile, opinion, personal experience. No hunting articles. **Buys 12-16 mss/year.** Query. Length: 1,000-3,000 words. **Pays $100-300.**

Photos Send photos with submission. Buys one-time rights. Offers no additional payment for photos accepted with ms. Captions, identification of subjects required.

Fiction Fiction that deals with bird dogs and field trials. **Buys 4 mss/year.** Send complete ms. Length: 1,000-2,500 words. **Pays $100-250.**

Tips "Make sure you have correct and accurate information—we'll work with a writer who has good solid info even if the writing needs work."

$ $ THE GAITED HORSE

The One Magazine for All Gaited Horses, P.O. Box 488, Chattaroy WA 99003. E-mail: tgheditor@thegaitedhorse.com. Web site: www.thegaitedhorse.com. **Contact:** Rhonda Hart Poe, editor. Quarterly magazine. "Subject matter must relate in some way to gaited horses.'' Estab. 1998. Circ. 15,000. Pays on publication. Publishes ms an average of 2 months after acceptance. Byline given. Buys first North American serial rights, makes work-for-hire assignments. Editorial lead time 4 months. Submit seasonal material 4 months in advance. Accepts queries by mail, e-mail. Accepts simultaneous submissions. Responds in 6 weeks to queries; 1 month to mss. Sample copy for $3. Writer's guidelines online.

Nonfiction Wants anything related to gaited horses, lifestyles, art, etc. Book excerpts, essays, exposé, general interest (gaited horses), historical/nostalgic, how-to, humor, interview/profile, new product, personal experience, photo feature, travel. **Buys 25 mss/year.** Query or send complete ms. Length: 1,000-2,500 words. **Pays $50-300.**

Photos State availability of or send photos with submission. Reviews prints (3×5 or larger). Buys one-time rights. Negotiates payment individually. Captions, identification of subjects, model releases required.

Columns/Departments Legal Paces (equine owners rights & responsibilities); Horse Cents (financial advice for horse owners); Health Check (vet advice); Smoother Trails (trail riding), all 500-1,000 words. **Buys 24 mss/year.** Query. **Pays $100.**

Fillers Anecdotes, short humor, NewsBits. **Buys 20/year.** Length: 5-300 words. **Pays $10-50.**

Tips ''We are actively seeking to develop writers from within the various gaited breeds and equine disciplines. If you have a unique perspective on these horses, we would love to hear from you. Submit a query that targets any aspect of gaited horses and you'll have my attention.''

$ THE GREYHOUND REVIEW

P.O. Box 543, Abilene KS 67410-0543. (785)263-4660. Fax: (785)263-4689. E-mail: nga@ngagreyhounds.com. Web site: www.ngagreyhounds.com. Editor: Gary Guccione. **Contact:** Tim Horan, managing editor. **20% freelance written.** Monthly magazine covering greyhound breeding, training, and racing. Estab. 1911. Circ. 3,500. **Pays on acceptance.** Byline given. Buys first rights. Submit seasonal material 2 months in advance. Responds in 2 weeks to queries; 1 month to mss. Sample copy for $3. Writer's guidelines free.

Nonfiction ''Articles must be targeted at the greyhound industry: from hard news, to special events at racetracks, to the latest medical discoveries.'' How-to, interview/profile, personal experience. Do not submit gambling systems. **Buys 24 mss/year.** Query. Length: 1,000-10,000 words. **Pays $85-150.**

Reprints Send photocopy. Pays 100% of amount paid for original article.

Photos State availability with submission. Reviews digital images. Buys one-time rights. Pays $10-50 photo. Identification of subjects required.

$ HORSE CONNECTION

Horse Connection, LLC, 380 Perry St., Suite 210, Castle Rock CO 80104. (303)663-1300. Fax: (303)663-1331. Web site: www.horseconnection.com. **Contact:** Geoff Young, publisher. **90% freelance written.** Magazine published 12 times/year covering horse owners and riders. ''Our readers are horse owners and riders. They specialize in English riding. We primarily focus on show jumping and hunters, dressage, and three-day events, with additional coverage of driving, polo, and endurance.'' Estab. 1995. Circ. 25,000. Pays on publication. Publishes ms an average of 1 month after acceptance. Byline given. Buys first, second serial (reprint) rights. Editorial lead time 3 months. Submit seasonal material 3 months in advance. Accepts queries by e-mail. Responds in 1 month to queries. Sample copy for $3.50 or online. Writer's guidelines for #10 SASE or online.

Nonfiction Humor, interview/profile, personal experience, event reports. No general interest stories about horses. Nothing negative. No western, racing, or breed specific articles. No ''my first pony'' stories. **Buys 30-50 mss/year.** Query with published clips. Length: 500-1,000 words. **Pays $25 for assigned articles; $75 for unsolicited articles.** Sometimes pays expenses of writers on assignment.

Reprints Accepts previously published submissions.

Photos State availability with submission. Buys one-time rights. Negotiates payment individually.

Tips ''Please read the magazine. We are currently focused on the western states and we like stories about English riders from these states.''

$ $ HORSE ILLUSTRATED

The Magazine for Responsible Horse Owners, BowTie, Inc., P.O. Box 6050, Mission Viejo CA 92690-6050. (949)855-8822. Fax: (949)855-3045. Web site: www.horseillustrated.com. **Contact:** Moira Harris, editor. **90% freelance written.** Prefers to work with published/established writers but will work with new/unpublished writers. Monthly magazine covering all aspects of horse ownership. ''Our readers are adults, mostly women, between the ages of 18 and 40; stories should be geared to that age group and reflect responsible horse care.'' Estab. 1976. Circ. 216,930. Pays on publication. Publishes ms an average of 8 months after acceptance. Byline given. Buys one-time rights, requires first North American rights among equine publications. Submit seasonal material 6 months in advance. Accepts queries by mail. Responds in 3 months to queries. Writer's guidelines for #10 SASE.

Nonfiction "We are looking for authoritative, in-depth features on trends and issues in the horse industry. Such articles must be queried first with a detailed outline of the article and clips. We rarely have a need for fiction." General interest, historical/nostalgic, how-to (horse care, training, veterinary care), inspirational, photo feature. No "little girl" horse stories, "cowboy and Indian" stories or anything not *directly* relating to horses. **Buys 20 mss/year.** Query or send complete ms. Length: 1,000-2,000 words. **Pays $200-400.**
Photos Send photos with submission. Reviews 35mm and medium format transparencies, 4×6 prints.
Tips "Freelancers can break in at this publication with feature articles on Western and English training methods; veterinary and general care how-to articles; and horse sports articles. We rarely use personal experience articles. Submit photos with training and how-to articles whenever possible. We have a very good record of developing new freelancers into regular contributors/columnists. We are always looking for fresh talent, but certainly enjoy working with established writers who 'know the ropes' as well. We are accepting less unsolicited freelance work—much is now assigned and contracted."

$ $ $ THE HORSE

Your Guide To Equine Health Care, P.O. Box 919003, Lexington KY 40591-9003. (859)276-6771. Fax: (859)276-4450. E-mail: kherbert@thehorse.com. Web site: www.thehorse.com. Managing Editor: Christy West. **Contact:** Kimberly S. Herbert, editor. **85% freelance written.** Monthly magazine covering equine health and care. *The Horse* is an educational/news magazine geared toward the hands-on horse owner. Estab. 1983. Circ. 55,000. **Pays on acceptance.** Publishes ms an average of 6 months after acceptance. Byline given. Buys first world and electronic rights Accepts queries by mail, e-mail. Responds in 3 months to queries. Sample copy for $3.95 or online. Writer's guidelines online.

O→ Break in with short horse health news items.

Nonfiction How-to, technical, topical interviews. "No first-person experiences not from professionals; this is a technical magazine to inform horse owners." **Buys 90 mss/year.** Query with published clips. Length: 250-4,000 words. **Pays $60-850 for assigned articles.**
Photos Send photos with submission. Reviews transparencies. Offers $35-350. Captions, identification of subjects required.
Columns/Departments News Front (news on horse health), 100-500 words; Equinomics (economics of horse ownership); Step by Step (feet and leg care); Nutrition; Reproduction; Back to Basics, all 1,500-2,200 words. **Buys 50 mss/year.** Query with published clips. **Pays $50-450.**

The Web site carries original content not found in the print edition—mostly news items.

Tips "We publish reliable horse health care and management information from top industry professionals and researchers around the world. Manuscript must be submitted electronically or on disk."

N HORSE-CANADA

225 Industrial Parkway S., Box 670, Aurora ON L4G 4J9 Canada. (905)727-0107. Fax: (905)841-1530. E-mail: lbenson@primus.ca. Web site: www.horse-canada.com. Publisher: Jennifer Anstey. **Contact:** Lee Benson, managing editor. **80% freelance written.** National magazine for horse lovers of all ages. Readers are committed horse owners with many different breeds involved in a variety of disciplines—from beginner riders to industry professionals. *Horsepower* is for horse-crazy kids and is inserted into *Horse Canada* to entertain and educate future equestrians. Circ. 20,000. Buys all rights. Editorial lead time 2 months. Accepts queries by e-mail. Writer's guidelines online.
Nonfiction Health and management topics, training tips, rural living, and hot industry issues. Query. Length: 750-1,500 words. **Payment varies.**
Photos State availability of or send photos with submission.
Columns/Departments The Tail End (humor). **Payment varies.**

$ I LOVE CATS

I Love Cats Publishing, 16 Meadow Hill Lane, Armonk NY 10504. (908)222-0990. Fax: (908)222-8228. E-mail: ilovecatseditor@sbcglobal.net. Web site: www.iluvcats.com. **Contact:** Lisa Allmendinger, editor. **100% freelance written.** Bimonthly magazine. "*I Love Cats* is a general interest cat magazine for the entire family. It caters to cat lovers of all ages. The stories in the magazine include fiction, nonfiction, how-to, humorous, and columns for the cat lover." Estab. 1989. Circ. 25,000. Pays on publication. Publishes ms an average of 2 years after acceptance. Byline given. Must sign copyright consent form. Buys all rights. Editorial lead time 6 months. Submit seasonal material 9 months in advance. Accepts queries by mail, e-mail. Responds in 3 months to queries. Sample copy for $5. Writer's guidelines online.
Nonfiction Essays, general interest, how-to, humor, inspirational, interview/profile, new product, opinion, personal experience, photo feature. No poetry. **Buys 50 mss/year.** Send complete ms. Length: 500-1,000 words. **Pays $50-100, or contributor copies or other premiums if requested.** Sometimes pays expenses of writers on assignment.

Photos Please send copies; art will no longer be returned. Send photos with submission. Buys all rights. Offers no additional payment for photos accepted with ms. Identification of subjects required.
Fiction Adventure, fantasy, historical, humorous, mainstream, mystery, novel excerpts, slice-of-life vignettes, suspense. "This is a family magazine. No graphic violence, pornography, or other inappropriate material. *I Love Cats* is strictly 'G-rated.' " **Buys 50 mss/year.** Send complete ms. Length: 500-1,000 words. **Pays $25-100.**
Fillers Anecdotes, facts, short humor. **Buys 25/year. Pays $25.**
Tips "Please keep stories short and concise. Send complete manuscript with photos, if possible. I buy lots of first-time authors. Nonfiction pieces with color photos are always in short supply. With the exception of the standing columns, the rest of the magazine is open to freelancers. Be witty, humorous, or offer a different approach to writing."

$ MINIATURE DONKEY TALK

Miniature Donkey Talk, Inc., 1338 Hughes Shop Rd., Westminster MD 21158-2911. (410)875-0118. Fax: (410)857-9145. E-mail: minidonk@qis.net. Web site: www.miniaturedonkey.net. **Contact:** Bonnie Gross, editor. **65% freelance written.** Quarterly magazine covering donkeys, with articles on healthcare, promotion, and management of donkeys for owners, breeders, or donkey lovers. Estab. 1987. Circ. 4,925. **Pays on acceptance.** Publishes ms an average of 4 months after acceptance. Byline given. Buys first, second serial (reprint) rights. Editorial lead time 2 months. Submit seasonal material 3 months in advance. Accepts queries by mail, e-mail, fax. Accepts previously published material. Responds in 2 weeks to queries; 1 month to mss. Sample copy for $5. Writer's guidelines free.
Nonfiction "We accept breeder profiles—either of yourself or another breeder. We cover nonshow events such as fairs, donkey gatherings, holiday events, etc. We want relevant, informative equine health pieces. We much prefer they deal specifically with donkeys, but will consider articles geared toward horses. If at all possible, substitute the word 'horse' for 'donkey.' We reserve the right to edit, change, delete, or add to health articles. Please be careful with the accuracy of advice or training material, as well as farm management articles and fictional stories on donkeys." Book excerpts, humor, interview/profile, personal experience. **Buys 6 mss/year.** Query with published clips. Length: 700-5,000 words. **Pays $25-150.**
Photos State availability with submission. Reviews 3×5 prints. Buys one-time rights. Offers no additional payment for photos accepted with ms. Identification of subjects required.
Columns/Departments Humor, 2,000 words; Healthcare, 2,000-5,000 words; Management, 2,000 words. **Buys 50 mss/year.** Query. **Pays $25-100.**
Tips "Simply send your manuscript. If on topic and appropriate, good possibility it will be published. No fiction or poetry."

$ $ MUSHING

Stellar Communications, Inc., P.O. Box 246, Fairbanks AK 99709. (917)929-6118. E-mail: editor@mushing.com. Web site: www.mushing.com. Publisher: Todd Hoener. **Contact:** Amanda Byrd, managing editor. Bimonthly magazine covering all aspects of the growing sports of dogsledding, skijoring, carting, dog packing, and weight pulling. "*Mushing* promotes responsible dog care through feature articles and updates on working animal health care, safety, nutrition, and training." Estab. 1987. Circ. 6,000. Pays within 3 months of publication. Publishes ms an average of 4 months after acceptance. Byline given. Buys first, second serial (reprint) rights. Submit seasonal material 4 months in advance. Accepts queries by mail, e-mail, fax, phone. Responds in 8 months to queries. Sample copy for $5 ($6 US to Canada). Writer's guidelines online.
Nonfiction "We consider articles on canine health and nutrition, sled dog behavior and training, musher profiles and interviews, equipment how-to's, trail tips, expedition and race accounts, innovations, sled dog history, current issues, personal experiences, and humor." Historical/nostalgic, how-to. Special issues: Iditarod and Long-Distance Racing (January/February); Ski or Sprint Racing (March/April); Health and Nutrition (May/June); Musher and Dog Profiles, Summer Activities (July/August); Equipment, Fall Training (September/October); Races and Places (November/December). Query with or without published clips. Considers complete ms with SASE. Length: 1,000-2,500 words. **Pays $50-250.** Sometimes pays expenses of writers on assignment.
Photos "We look for good b&w and quality color for covers and specials." Send photos with submission. Reviews contact sheets, negatives, transparencies, prints. Buys one-time and second reprint rights. Pays $20-165/photo. Captions, identification of subjects, model releases required.
Columns/Departments Query with or without published clips or send complete ms.
Fillers Anecdotes, facts, newsbreaks, short humor, cartoons, puzzles. Length: 100-250 words. **Pays $20-35.**
Tips "Read our magazine. Know something about dog-driven, dog-powered sports."

$ $ PAINT HORSE JOURNAL

American Paint Horse Association, P.O. Box 961023, Fort Worth TX 76161-0023. (817)834-2742. Fax: (817)222-8466. E-mail: bhill@apha.com. Web site: www.painthorsejournal.com. **Contact:** Breanne Hill, editor. **10%**

freelance written. Works with a small number of new/unpublished writers each year. Monthly magazine for people who raise, breed and show Paint Horses. Estab. 1966. Circ. 30,000. **Pays on acceptance.** Byline given. Offers negotiable kill fee. Buys first North American serial rights. Submit seasonal material 3 months in advance. Accepts queries by mail, e-mail, fax. Sample copy for $4.50. Writer's guidelines online.

Nonfiction General interest (personality pieces on well-known owners of Paints), historical/nostalgic (Paint Horses in the past—particular horses and the breed in general), how-to (train and show horses), photo feature (Paint Horses). **Buys 4-5 mss/year.** Query. Length: 1,000-2,000 words. **Pays $100-650.**

Photos Photos must illustrate article and must include registered Paint Horses. Send photos with submission. Reviews 35mm or larger transparencies, 3×5 or larger color glossy prints, digital images on CD or DVD. Offers no additional payment for photos accepted with accompanying ms. Captions required.

Tips "Well-written first person articles are welcomed. Submit items that show a definite understanding of the horse business. Be sure you understand precisely what a Paint Horse is as defined by the American Paint Horse Association. Use proper equine terminology. Photos with copy are almost always essential."

$ $ REPTILES

The World's Leading Reptile Magazine, BowTie, Inc., P.O. Box 6050, Mission Viejo CA 92690. E-mail: reptiles@bowtieinc.com. Web site: www.reptilesmagazine.com. Editor: Russ Case. Managing Editor: Clay Jackson. **Contact:** Kara Sutton-Jones, associate editor. **20% freelance written.** Monthly magazine covering reptiles and amphibians. "*Reptiles* covers a wide range of topics relating to reptiles and amphibians, including breeding, captive care, field herping, etc." Estab. 1992. Pays on publication. Publishes ms an average of 6-8 months after acceptance. Byline given. Offers 20% kill fee. Buys first North American serial, electronic rights. Accepts queries by mail, e-mail. Responds in 2 weeks to queries; 1-2 months to mss. Sample copy and writer's guidelines online.General interest, historical/nostalgic, how-to, interview/profile, personal experience, photo feature, travel. **Buys 10 mss/year.** Query. Length: 1,000-2,000 words. **Pays $250-600.**

Tips "Keep in mind that *Reptiles* has a very knowledgeable readership when it comes to herps. While we accept freelance articles, the bulk of what we publish comes from 'herp people.' Do your research, interview experts, etc., for the best results."

$ ROCKY MOUNTAIN RIDER MAGAZINE

Regional All-Breed Horse Monthly, P.O. Box 1011, Hamilton MT 59840. (406)363-4085. Fax: (406)363-1056. Web site: www.rockymountainrider.com. **Contact:** Natalie Riehl, editor. **90% freelance written.** Monthly magazine for horse owners and enthusiasts. Estab. 1993. Circ. 15,000. Pays on publication. Publishes ms an average of 6 months after acceptance. Byline given. Buys one-time rights. Submit seasonal material 6 months in advance. Accepts simultaneous submissions. Responds in 1 month to queries; 2 months to mss. Sample copy for free. Writer's guidelines for #10 SASE.

Nonfiction Book excerpts, essays, general interest, historical/nostalgic, humor, interview/profile, new product, personal experience, photo feature, equine medical. **Buys 100 mss/year.** Send complete ms. Length: 500-2,000 words. **Pays $15-90.**

Photos Send photos with submission. Reviews 3×5 prints, e-mail digital photos. Buys one-time rights. Pays $5/photo. Captions, identification of subjects required.

Poetry Light verse, traditional. **Buys 25 poems/year.** Submit maximum 10 poems. Length: 6-36 lines. **Pays $10.**

Fillers Anecdotes, facts, gags to be illustrated by cartoonist, short humor. Length: 200-750 words. **Pays $15.**

Tips "*RMR* is looking for positive, human interest stories that appeal to an audience of horsepeople. We accept profiles of unusual people or animals, history, humor, anecdotes, cowboy poetry, coverage of regional events, and new products. We aren't looking for many 'how-to' or training articles, and are not currently looking at any fiction."

N $ $ TROPICAL FISH HOBBYIST MAGAZINE

TFH Publications, Inc., One TFH Plaza, Neptune City NJ 07753. (732)988-8400. Fax: (732)988-9635. E-mail: editor@tfh.com. Web site: www.tfhmagazine.com. Editor: David Boruchowitz. **Contact:** Albert Connelly, managing editor. **90% freelance written.** Monthly magazine covering tropical fish. Estab. 1952. Circ. 35,000. **Pays on acceptance.** Byline given. Buys all rights. Editorial lead time 3 months. Submit seasonal material 6 months in advance. Accepts queries by e-mail. Responds immediately on electronic queries to queries. Writer's guidelines online.

Nonfiction "We cover any aspect of aquarium science, aquaculture, and the tropical fish hobby. Our readership is diverse—from neophytes to mini reef specialists. We require well-researched, well-written, and factually accurate copy, preferably with photos." **Buys 100-150 mss/year. Pays $100-250.**

Photos State availability with submission. Reviews prints, slides, high-resolution digital images. Buys multiple nonexclusive rights. Negotiates payment individually. Identification of subjects, model releases required.

Tips "With few exceptions, all communication and submission must be electronic. We want factual, interesting, and relevant articles about the aquarium hobby written by people who are obviously knowledgeable. We publish an enormous variety of article types. Review several past issues to get an idea of the scope."

$ $ USDF CONNECTION

United States Dressage Federation, 4051 Iron Works Parkway, Lexington KY 40511. E-mail: connection@usdf.org. Web site: www.usdf.org. **Contact:** Jennifer Bryant, editor. **40% freelance written.** Monthly magazine covering dressage (an equestrian sport). "All material must relate to the sport of dressage in the US." Estab. 2000. Circ. 35,000. **Pays on acceptance.** Publishes ms an average of 3 months after acceptance. Byline given. Offers 50% kill fee. Buys first North American serial, second serial (reprint) rights. Editorial lead time 3 months. Submit seasonal material 6 months in advance. Accepts queries by mail, e-mail. Accepts previously published material. Responds in 1 month to queries; 1-2 months to mss. Sample copy for $5. Writer's guidelines online.
Nonfiction Book excerpts, essays, how-to, interview/profile, opinion, personal experience. Does not want general interest equine material or stories that lack a US dressage angle. **Buys 40 mss/year.** Query. Length: 650-3,000 words. **Pays $100-500 for assigned articles; $100-300 for unsolicited articles.** Sometimes pays expenses of writers on assignment.
Photos State availability with submission. Reviews prints, GIF/JPEG files. Buys one-time rights. Negotiates payment individually. Captions, identification of subjects required.
Columns/Departments Amateur Hour (profiles of adult amateur USDF members), 1,200-1,500 words; Under 21 (profiles of young USDF members), 1,200-1,500 words; Veterinary Connection (dressage-related horse health), 1,500-2,500 words; Mind-Body-Spirit Connection (rider health/fitness, sport psychology), 1,500-2,500 words. **Buys 24 mss/year.** Query with published clips. **Pays $150-400.**
Tips "Know the organization and the sport. Most successful contributors are active in the horse industry and bring valuable perspectives and insights to their stories and images."

$ $ ZOO VIEW

Greater Los Angeles Zoo Association, 5333 Zoo Dr., Los Angeles CA 90027. E-mail: bposada@lazoo.org. Web site: www.lazoo.org. Managing Editor: Sandy Masuo. **Contact:** Brenda Posada, director of publications. **20% freelance written.** Quarterly magazine covering animals, wildlife and conservation. "The zoo's mission is 'nurturing wildlife and enriching the human experience.' Our readers are knowledgeable and passionate about animals and respectful of nature and the environment. Our primary focus is on the plants and animals at the Los Angeles Zoo." Estab. 1965. Circ. 70,000. **Pays on acceptance.** Publishes ms an average of 2 months after acceptance. Byline given. Offers 25% kill fee. Buys first, electronic rights. Editorial lead time 2 months. Accepts queries by mail. Responds in 8-10 weeks to queries. Sample copy for 9×12 SAE with 3 first class stamps or $2. Writer's guidelines free.
Nonfiction General interest, interview/profile. Does not want "my trip to the zoo" or articles that anthropomorphize animals (give them human characteristics). **Buys 4-10 mss/year.** Query with published clips. Length: 750-2,500 words. **Pays $75-300.**
Photos State availability with submission. Buys one-time rights. Offers no additional payment for photos accepted with ms. Identification of subjects required.
Tips "Demonstrate in your query or samples a lively, engaging writing style and a knowledge of your proposed subject."

ART & ARCHITECTURE

$ $ AMERICAN ARTIST

VNU Business Media, 770 Broadway, New York NY 10003-9595. (646)654-5506. E-mail: mail@myamericanartist.com. Web site: www.myamericanartist.com. **Contact:** M. Stephen Doherty, editor-in-chief. Monthly magazine covering art. Written to provide information on outstanding representational artists living in the US. Estab. 1937. Circ. 116,526. Editorial lead time 18 weeks. Accepts queries by mail. Responds in 6-8 weeks to queries. Sample copy for $3.95. Writer's guidelines by e-mail.
Nonfiction Essays, exposé, interview/profile, personal experience, technical. Query with published clips and résumé. Length: 1,500-2,000 words. **Pays $500.**

$ $ AMERICAN INDIAN ART MAGAZINE

American Indian Art, Inc., 7314 E. Osborn Dr., Scottsdale AZ 85251. (480)994-5445. Fax: (480)945-9533. E-mail: info@aiamagazine.com. Web site: www.aiamagazine.com. **97% freelance written.** Works with many new/unpublished writers/year. Quarterly magazine covering Native American art, historic and contemporary, including new research on any aspect of Native American art north of the US-Mexico border. Estab. 1975. Circ.

22,000. Pays on publication. Publishes ms an average of 6 months after acceptance. Byline given. Buys first, one-time rights. Responds in 6 weeks to queries; 3 months to mss. Writer's guidelines for #10 SASE or online.
Nonfiction New research on any aspect of Native American art. No previously published work or personal interviews with artists. **Buys 12-18 mss/year.** Query. Length: 6,000-7,000 words. **Pays $150-300.**
Photos An article usually requires 8-15 photographs. Buys one-time rights. Fee schedules and reimbursable expenses are decided upon by the magazine and the author.
Tips "The magazine is devoted to all aspects of Native American art. Some of our readers are knowledgeable about the field and some know very little. We seek articles that offer something to both groups. Articles reflecting original research are preferred to those summarizing previously published information."

$ $ $ AMERICANSTYLE MAGAZINE

The Rosen Group, 3000 Chestnut Ave., Suite 304, Baltimore MD 21211. (410)889-3093. Fax: (410)243-7089. E-mail: hoped@rosengrp.com. Web site: www.americanstyle.com. **Contact:** Hope Daniels, editor-in-chief. **80% freelance written.** Bimonthly magazine covering arts, crafts, travel, and interior design. "*AmericanStyle* is a full-color lifestyle publication for people who love art. Our mandate is to nurture collectors with information that will increase their passion for contemporary art and craft and the artists who create it. *AmericanStyle*'s primary audience is contemporary craft collectors and enthusiasts. Readers are college-educated, age 35+, high-income earners with the financial means to collect art and craft, and to travel to national art and craft events in pursuit of their passions." Estab. 1994. Circ. 60,000. Pays on publication. Publishes ms an average of 9 months after acceptance. Buys first North American serial rights. Editorial lead time 9 months. Submit seasonal material at least 1 year in advance. Accepts queries by mail, e-mail, fax. Sample copy for $3. Writer's guidelines online.

O→ *AmericanStyle* is especially interested in freelance ideas about arts travel, profiles of contemporary craft collectors, and established studio craft artists.

Nonfiction Specialized arts/crafts interests. Length: 600-1,200 words. **Pays $500-800.** Sometimes pays expenses of writers on assignment.
Photos Send photos with submission. Reviews oversized transparencies, 35mm slides, low resolution e-images. Negotiates payment individually. Captions required.
Columns/Departments Portfolio (profiles of emerging and established artists); Arts Walk; Origins; One on One, all 600-900 words. Query with published clips. **Pays $500-700.**
Tips "This is not a hobby-crafter magazine. Country crafts or home crafting is not our market. We focus on contemporary American craft art, such as ceramics, wood, fiber, glass, metal."

N ARCHITECTURAL DIGEST

The International Magazine of Interior Design, Conde Nast Publications, Inc., 6300 Wilshire Blvd., Suite 1100, Los Angeles CA 90048. (323)965-3700. Fax: (323)937-1458. Web site: www.architecturaldigest.com. **Contact:** Submissions Editor. Monthly magazine covering architecture. A global magazine that offers a look at the homes of the rich and famous. Other topics include travel, shopping, automobiles, and technology. Estab. 1920. Circ. 821,992. Accepts queries by mail. Sample copy for $5 on newstands.
Nonfiction Send 3 samples of your work with a brief cover letter. Include a paragraph on who else you've written for and a paragraph on any story ideas you have for *Architectural Digest*. Query with published clips.

$ $ $ ART & ANTIQUES

TransWorld Publishing, Inc., 2100 Powers Ferry Rd., Suite 300, Atlanta GA 30339. (770)955-5656. Fax: (770)952-0669. E-mail: pverbanas@billian.com. Editor: Barbara S. Tapp. **Contact:** Patti Verbanas, executive editor. **90% freelance written.** Monthly magazine covering fine art and antique collectibles and the people who collect them and/or create them. "*Art & Antiques* is the authoritative source for elegant, sophisticated coverage of the treasures collectors love, the places to discover them, and the unique ways collectors use them to enrich their environments." Circ. 125,800. **Pays on acceptance.** Byline given. Offers 25% kill fee or $250. Buys all rights. Editorial lead time 8 months. Submit seasonal material 8 months in advance. Accepts queries by mail, e-mail. Responds in 6 weeks to queries; 2 months to mss. Sample copy and writer's guidelines free.
Nonfiction "We publish 1 'interior design with art and antiques' focus feature a month." Essays. Special issues: Living with art & antiques (April); English art & antiques (May); paintings (June); modernism (September); decorative arts (December); contemporary art (February). **Buys 200 mss/year.** Query with or without published clips. Length: 150-1,200 words. **Pays $150-1,200 for assigned articles.** Pays $50 toward expenses of writers on assignment.
Photos Scouting shots. Send photos with submission. Reviews contact sheets, transparencies, prints. Captions, identification of subjects required.
Columns/Departments Art & Antiques News (trend coverage and timely news of issues and personalities), 100-350 words; Preview/Review (thoughts and criticisms on a variety of worldwide art exhibitions throughout

the year), 600-800 words; Market Value (experts highlight popular to undiscovered areas of collecting), 600-800 words; Emerging Artist (an artist on the cusp of discovery), 600-800 words; Discoveries (collections in lesser-known museums and homes open to the public), 800-900 words; Today's Masters (peek into the studio of an artist who is currently hot or is a revered veteran allowing the reader to watch the artist in action), 800-900 words; Then & Now (the best reproductions being created today and the craftspeople behind the work), 800-900 words; World View (major art and antiques news worldwide; visuals preferred but not necessary), 600-800 words; Traveling Collector (hottest art and antiques destinations, dictated by those on editorial calendar; visuals preferred but not necessary), 800-900 words; Essay (first-person piece tackling a topic in a nonacademic way; visuals preferred but not necessary); A&A Insider (a how-to column on collecting topics); Art and Design (highlights 1 genre of decorative arts and shows revolutionary and innovative designs of that genre over the decades). **Buys 200 mss/year.** Query by mail only with or without published clips. **Pays $150-900.**

Fillers Facts, newsbreaks. **Buys 22/year.** Length: 150-300 words. **Pays $150-300.**

The online magazine carries original content not found in the print edition, though there is no payment at this time.

Tips "Send scouting shots with your queries. We are a visual magazine and no idea will be considered without visuals. We are good about responding to writers in a timely fashion—excessive phone calls are not appreciated, but do check in if you haven't heard from us in 2 months. We like colorful, lively and creative writing."

$ $ ART PAPERS

Atlanta Art Papers, Inc., P.O. Box 5748, Atlanta GA 31107-0748. (404)588-1837. Fax: (404)588-1836. E-mail: editor@artpapers.org. Web site: www.artpapers.org. **Contact:** Sylvie Fortin, editor-in-chief. **95% freelance written.** Bimonthly magazine covering contemporary art and artists. "*Art Papers*, about regional and national contemporary art and artists, features a variety of perspectives on current art concerns. Each issue presents topical articles, interviews, reviews from across the US, and an extensive and informative artists' classified listings section. Our writers and the artists they cover represent the scope and diversity of the country's art scene." Estab. 1977. Circ. 12,000. Pays on publication. Publishes ms an average of 3 months after acceptance. Byline given. Not copyrighted. Buys all rights. Editorial lead time 2 months. Submit seasonal material 2 months in advance.

Nonfiction Feature articles and reviews. **Buys 240 mss/year. Pays $60-325; unsolicited articles are on spec.**

Photos Send photos with submission. Reviews color slides, b&w prints. Offers no additional payment for photos accepted with ms. Identification of subjects required.

Columns/Departments Buys 8-10 mss/year. Query. **Pays $100-175.**

$ ART TIMES

Commentary and Resource for the Fine and Performing Arts, P.O. Box 730, Mount Marion NY 12456-0730. (845)246-6944. Fax: (845)246-6944. E-mail: info@arttimesjournal.com. Web site: www.arttimesjournal.com. **Contact:** Raymond J. Steiner, editor. **10% freelance written.** Monthly tabloid covering the arts (visual, theater, dance, music, literary, etc.). "*Art Times* covers the art fields and is distributed in locations most frequented by those enjoying the arts. Our copies are distributed throughout the Northeast as well as in most of the galleries of Soho, 57th Street and Madison Avenue in the metropolitan area; locations include theaters, galleries, museums, cultural centers and the like. Our readers are mostly over 40, affluent, art-conscious and sophisticated. Subscribers are located across US and abroad (Italy, France, Germany, Greece, Russia, etc.)." Estab. 1984. Circ. 27,000. Pays on publication. Publishes ms an average of 3 years after acceptance. Byline given. Buys first North American serial, first rights. Submit seasonal material 8 months in advance. Accepts simultaneous submissions. Responds in 6 months to queries; 6 months to mss. Sample copy for 9×12 SAE and 6 first-class stamps. Writer's guidelines for #10 SASE or online.

Fiction Raymond J. Steiner, fiction editor. "We're looking for short fiction that aspires to be literary." Adventure, ethnic, fantasy, historical, humorous, mainstream, science fiction, contemporary. "We seek quality literary pieces. Nothing violent, sexist, erotic, juvenile, racist, romantic, political, off-beat, or related to sports or juvenile fiction." **Buys 8-10 mss/year.** Send complete ms. Length: 1,500 words maximum. **Pays $25 maximum (honorarium) and 1 year's free subscription.**

Poetry "We prefer well-crafted 'literary' poems. No excessively sentimental poetry." Raymond J. Steiner, poetry editor. Avant-garde, free verse, haiku, light verse, traditional, poet's niche. **Buys 30-35 poems/year.** Submit maximum 6 poems. Length: 20 lines maximum. **Offers contributor copies and 1 year's free subscription.**

Tips "Be advised that we are presently on an approximate 3-year lead for short stories, 2-year lead for poetry. We are now receiving 300-400 poems and 40-50 short stories per month. We only publish 2-3 poems and 1 story each issue. Be familiar with *Art Times* and its special audience. *Art Times* has literary leanings with articles written by a staff of scholars knowledgeable in their respective fields. Although an 'arts' publication, we observe no restrictions (other than noted) in accepting fiction/poetry other than a concern for quality writing—subjects can cover anything and not specifically arts."

$ $ ARTLINK

Australia's Leading Contemporary Art Quarterly, Artlink Australia, 363 Esplande, Henley Beach SA 5022 Australia. (61)(8)8356-8511. Fax: (61)(8)8235-1280. E-mail: info@artlink.com.au. Web site: www.artlink.com.au. **Contact:** Stephanie Britton, executive editor. Quarterly magazine covering contemporary art in Australia. Estab. 1981. Writer's guidelines online.

Nonfiction General interest. Write or e-mail the editor with your CV and 2-3 examples of previously published writing. **Pays $250/1,000 words.**

Tips "Because *Artlink* is a themed magazine which tries to make art relevant across society, we often need to find contributors who have expert knowledge of subjects outside of the art area who can put the work of artists in a broader context."

ARTNEWS

ABC, 48 W. 38th St., New York NY 10018. (212)398-1690. Fax: (212)819-0394. E-mail: info@artnews.com. Web site: www.artnews.com. Monthly magazine. "*ARTnews* reports on art, personalities, issues, trends and events that shape the international art world. Investigative features focus on art ranging from old masters to contemporary, including painting, sculpture, prints, and photography. Regular columns offer exhibition and book reviews, travel destinations, investment and appreciation advice, design insights, and updates on major art world figures." Estab. 1902. Circ. 84,012. Accepts queries by mail, e-mail, fax, phone.

$ $ $ $ AZURE DESIGN, ARCHITECTURE AND ART

460 Richmond St. W., Suite 601, Toronto ON M5V 1Y1 Canada. (416)203-9674. Fax: (416)203-9842. E-mail: azure@azureonline.com. Web site: www.azuremagazine.com. **Contact:** Nelda Rodger, editor. **75% freelance written.** Magazine covering design and architecture. Estab. 1985. Circ. 20,000. Pays on publication. Publishes ms an average of 1 month after acceptance. Offers variable kill fee. Buys first rights. Editorial lead time up to 45 days. Responds in 6 weeks to queries.

Nonfiction Buys 25-30 mss/year. Length: 350-2,000 words. **Pays $1/word (Canadian).**

Columns/Departments Trailer (essay/photo on something from the built environment); and Forms & Functions (coming exhibitions, happenings in world of design), both 300-350 words. **Buys 30 mss/year.** Query. **Pays $1/word (Canadian).**

Tips "Try to understand what the magazine is about. Writers must be well versed in the field of architecture and design. It's very unusual to get something from someone I haven't worked quite closely with and gotten a sense of who the writer is. The best way to introduce yourself is by sending clips or writing samples and describing what your background is in the field."

$ BOMB MAGAZINE

New Arts Publications, 80 Hanson Place, Suite 703, Brooklyn NY 11217. (718)636-9100. Fax: (718)636-9200. E-mail: info@bombsite.com. Web site: www.bombsite.com. Editor: Betsy Sussler. Managing Editor: Brian McMullen. Quarterly magazine providing interviews between artists, writers, musicians, directors and actors. Written, edited and produced by industry professionals and funded by those interested in the arts. Publishes "work which is unconventional and contains an edge, whether it be in style or subject matter." Estab. 1981. Circ. 36,000. Pays on publication. Publishes ms an average of 3-6 months after acceptance. Buys first, one-time rights. Editorial lead time 3-4 months. Accepts queries by mail. Responds in 3-5 months to mss. Sample copy for $7, plus $1.59 postage and handling. Writer's guidelines by e-mail.

Fiction Send completed ms with SASE. Experimental, novel excerpts, contemporary. No genre: romance, science fiction, horror, western. Length: less than 25 pages. **Pays $100, and contributor's copies.**

Poetry Send completed ms with SASE. Submit maximum 4-6 poems. Length: No more than 25 pages in length.

Tips "Mss should be typed, double-spaced, proofread and should be final drafts. Purchase a sample issue before submitting work."

N $ $ C

international contemporary art, C The Visual Arts Foundation, P.O. Box 5, Station B, Toronto ON M5T 2T2 Canada. (416)539-9495. Fax: (416)539-9903. E-mail: editor@cmagazine.com. Web site: www.cmagazine.com. **Contact:** Rosemary Heather, editor. **80% freelance written.** Quarterly magazine covering international contemporary art. "*C* provides a vital and vibrant forum for the presentation of contemporary art and the discussion of issues surrounding art in our culture, including feature articles, reviews and reports, as well as original artists' projects." Estab. 1983. Circ. 7,000. Pays on publication. Publishes ms an average of 4 months after acceptance. Byline given. Offers kill fee. Editorial lead time 3 months. Accepts queries by mail, e-mail, fax. Accepts simultaneous submissions. Responds in 6 weeks to queries; 4 months to mss. Sample copy for $10 (US). Writer's guidelines for #10 SASE.

Nonfiction Essays, general interest, opinion, personal experience. **Buys 50 mss/year.** Length: 1,000-3,000 words. **Pays $150-500 (Canadian), $105-350 (US).**
Photos State availability of or send photos with submission. Reviews 35mm transparencies or 8×10 prints. Buys one-time rights; shared copyright on reprints. Offers no additional payment for photos accepted with ms. Captions required.
Columns/Departments Reviews (review of art exhibitions), 500 words. **Buys 30 mss/year.** Query. **Pays $125 (Canadian).**

$ $ DIRECT ART MAGAZINE

Slow Art Productions, P.O. Box 503, Phoenicia NY 12464. E-mail: directartmag@aol.com. Web site: www.slowart.com. **75% freelance written.** Semiannual fine art magazine covering alternative, anti-establishment, left-leaning fine art. Estab. 1998. Circ. 10,000. **Pays on acceptance.** Byline sometimes given. Buys one-time, electronic rights. Editorial lead time 2 months. Submit seasonal material 3 months in advance. Accepts queries by mail, e-mail. Accepts simultaneous submissions. Responds in 2 weeks to queries; 1 month to mss. Sample copy for 9×12 SAE and 10 first-class stamps. Writer's guidelines for #10 SASE.
Nonfiction Essays, exposé, historical/nostalgic, how-to, humor, inspirational, interview/profile, opinion, personal experience, photo feature, technical. **Buys 4-6 mss/year.** Query with published clips. Length: 1,000-3,000 words. **Pays $100-500.**
Reprints Accepts previously published submissions.
Photos State availability of or send photos with submission. Reviews 35mm slide transparencies, digital files on CD (TIF format). Buys one-time rights. Negotiates payment individually.
Columns/Departments Query with published clips. **Pays $100-500.**

EASTERN ART REPORT

Eastern Art Publishing, P.O. Box 13666, London England SW14 8WF United Kingdom. (44)(208)392-1122. Fax: (44)(208)392-1422. E-mail: ear@eapgroup.com. Web site: www.eapgroup.com. Editor/Publisher: Sajid Rizvi. **Contact:** Managing Editor. *EAR* has a worldwide readership—from scholars to connoisseurs—with varying knowledge of or interest in the historical, philosophical, practical, or theoretical aspects of Eastern art. Estab. 1989. Accepts queries by mail, e-mail, fax. Writer's guidelines online
Nonfiction International Diary (art-related news, previews, reviews); Art market reports written from an individual perspective; books previews and reviews. Query.
Photos Reviews illustrations, electronic images of at least 300 dpi.

$ ESPACE

Sculpture, Centre de Diffusion 3D, 4888 St. Denis, Montreal QC H2J 2L6 Canada. (514)844-9858. Fax: (514)844-3661. E-mail: espace@espace-sculpture.com. Web site: www.espace-sculpture.com. **Contact:** S. Fisette, editor. **95% freelance written.** Quarterly magazine covering sculpture events. "Canada's only sculpture publication, *Espace* represents a critical tool for the understanding of contemporary sculpture. Published 4 times a year, in English and French, *Espace* features interviews, in-depth articles, and special issues related to various aspects of three dimensionality. Foreign contributors guarantee an international perspective and diffusion." Estab. 1987. Circ. 1,400. Pays on publication. Publishes ms an average of 3 months after acceptance. Byline given. Buys all rights. Editorial lead time 5 months. Submit seasonal material 3 months in advance. Accepts queries by mail. Accepts simultaneous submissions. Sample copy for free.
Nonfiction Essays, exposé. **Buys 60 mss/year.** Query. Length: 1,000-1,400 words. **Pays $60/page.**
Reprints Accepts previously published submissions.
Photos Send photos with submission. Reviews transparencies, prints. Offers no additional payment for photos accepted with ms.

LA ARCHITECT

The Magazine of Design in Southern California, Balcony Media, Inc., 512 E. Wilson, Suite 213, Glendale CA 91206. (818)956-5313. Fax: (818)956-5904. E-mail: jennifer@balconypress.com. Web site: www.laarch.com. **Contact:** Jennifer Caterino, editor. **80% freelance written.** Bimonthly magazine covering architecture, interiors, landscape, and other design disciplines. "*L.A. Architect* is interested in architecture, interiors, product, graphics, and landscape design as well as news about the arts. We encourage designers to keep us informed on projects, techniques, and products that are innovative, new, or nationally newsworthy. We are especially interested in new and renovated projects that illustrate a high degree of design integrity and unique answers to typical problems in the urban cultural and physical environment." Estab. 1999. Circ. 20,000. Pays on publication. Publishes ms an average of 3 months after acceptance. Byline given. Makes work-for-hire assignments. Editorial lead time 4 months. Submit seasonal material 4 months in advance. Accepts queries by mail, e-mail, fax. Responds in 1 month to queries; 1 month to mss. Sample copy for $5.95. Writer's guidelines online.

Nonfiction Book excerpts, essays, historical/nostalgic, interview/profile, new product. **Buys 20 mss/year.** Length: 500-2,000 words. **Payment negotiable.**

Photos State availability with submission. Buys one-time rights. Offers no additional payment for photos accepted with ms. Captions, identification of subjects, model releases required.

Tips "Our magazine focuses on contemporary and cutting-edge work either happening in Southern California or designed by a Southern California designer. We like to find little-known talent that has not been widely published. We are not like *Architectural Digest* in flavor so avoid highly decorative subjects. Each project, product, or event should be accompanied by a story proposal or brief description and select images. Do not send original art without our written request; we make every effort to return materials we are unable to use, but this is sometimes difficult and we must make advance arrangements for original art."

$ $ THE MAGAZINE ANTIQUES

Brant Publications, 575 Broadway, New York NY 10012. (212)941-2800. Fax: (212)941-2819. **Contact:** Allison Ledes, editor. **75% freelance written.** Monthly magazine. "Articles should present new information in a scholarly format (with footnotes) on the fine and decorative arts, architecture, historic preservation, and landscape architecture." Estab. 1922. Circ. 61,754. Pays on publication. Publishes ms an average of 6 months after acceptance. Byline given. Buys all rights. Editorial lead time 6 months. Submit seasonal material 6 months in advance. Responds in 3 weeks to queries; 6 months to mss. Sample copy for $10.50 for back issue; $5 for current issue.

Nonfiction Historical/nostalgic, scholarly. **Buys 50 mss/year.** Length: 2,850-3,500 words. **Pays $250-500.** Sometimes pays expenses of writers on assignment.

Photos State availability with submission. Reviews contact sheets, negatives, transparencies, prints. Buys one-time rights. Captions, identification of subjects required.

$ $ $ $ METROPOLIS

The Magazine of Architecture and Design, Bellerophon Publications, 61 W. 23rd St., 4th Floor, New York NY 10010. (212)627-9977. Fax: (212)627-9988. E-mail: edit@metropolismag.com. Web site: www.metropolismag.com. Executive Editor: Martin Pedersen. **80% freelance written.** Monthly magazine (combined issue July/August) for consumers interested in architecture and design. Estab. 1981. Circ. 45,000. Pays 60-90 days after acceptance. Publishes ms an average of 3 months after acceptance. Byline given. Makes work-for-hire assignments. Submit seasonal material 3 months in advance. Accepts queries by mail, e-mail, fax. Responds in 8 months to queries. Sample copy for $7. Writer's guidelines online.

Nonfiction Martin Pedersen, executive editor. Essays (design, architecture, urban planning issues and ideas), interview/profile (of multi-disciplinary designers/architects). No profiles on individual architectural practices, information from public relations firms, or fine arts. **Buys 30 mss/year.** Length: 1,500-4,000 words. **Pays $1,500-4,000.**

Photos Reviews contact sheets, 35mm or 4×5 transparencies, 8×10 b&w prints. Buys one-time rights. Payment offered for certain photos. Captions required.

Columns/Departments The Metropolis Observed (architecture, design, and city planning news features), 100-1,200 words, **pays $100-1,200**; Perspective (opinion or personal observation of architecture and design), 1,200 words, **pays $1,200**; Enterprise (the business/development of architecture and design), 1,500 words, **pays $1,500**; In Review (architecture and book review essays), 1,500 words, **pays $1,500**. Direct queries to Belinda Lanks, managing editor. **Buys 40 mss/year.** Query with published clips.

The online magazine carries original content not found in the print edition. Contact: Randi Greenberg (randi@metropolismag.com).

Tips "*Metropolis* strives to tell the story of design to a lay person with an interest in the built environment, while keeping the professional designer engaged. The magazine examines the various design disciplines (architecture, interior design, product design, graphic design, planning, and preservation) and their social/cultural context. We're looking for the new, the obscure, or the wonderful. Also, be patient and don't expect an immediate answer after submission of query."

$ $ MIX

Independent Art and Culture Magazine, Parallelogramme Artist-Run Culture and Publishing, Inc., 401 Richmond St., Suite 446, Toronto ON M5V 3A8 Canada. (416)506-1012. Fax: (416)506-0141. E-mail: info@mixmagazine.com. Web site: www.mixmagazine.com. **95% freelance written.** Quarterly magazine covering Artist-Run gallery activities. "*Mix* represents and investigates contemporary artistic practices and issues, especially in the progressive Canadian artist-run scene." Estab. 1975. Circ. 3,500. Pays on publication. Publishes ms an average of 6 months after acceptance. Byline given. Offers 40% kill fee. Buys first North American serial rights. Editorial lead time 6 months. Submit seasonal material 4 months in advance. Accepts queries by mail, e-mail, fax. Responds in 2 months to queries; 3 months to mss. Sample copy for $6.95, 8½×10¼ SAE and 6 first-class stamps. Writer's guidelines online.

Nonfiction Essays, interview/profile. **Buys 12-20 mss/year.** Query with published clips. Length: 750-3,500 words. **Pays $100-450.**
Reprints Send photocopy of article and information about when and where the article previously appeared.
Photos State availability with submission. Buys one-time rights. Captions, identification of subjects required.
Columns/Departments Features, 1,000-3,000 words; Art Reviews, 500 words. Query with published clips. **Pays $100-450.**
Tips "Read the magazine and other contemporary art magazines. Understand the idea 'artist-run.' We're not interested in 'artsy-phartsy' editorial, but rather pieces that are critical, dynamic, and would be of interest to nonartists too."

$ $ MODERNISM MAGAZINE

199 George St., Lambertville NJ 08530. (609)397-4104. Fax: (609)397-4409. E-mail: andrea@modernismmagazine.com. Web site: www.modernismmagazine.com. Publisher: David Rago. **Contact:** Andrea Truppin, editor-in-chief. **70% freelance written.** Quarterly magazine covering 20th century art and design. "We are interested in objects and the people who created them. Our coverage begins in the 1920s with Art Deco and related movements, and ends with 1980s Post-Modernism, leaving contemporary design to other magazines. Our emphasis is on the decorative arts—furniture, pottery, glass, textiles, metalwork, and so on—but we're moving toward more coverage of interiors." Estab. 1998. Circ. 20,000. Pays on publication. Publishes ms an average of 4 months after acceptance. Byline given. Offers 25% kill fee. Buys all rights. Editorial lead time 6 months. Submit seasonal material 6 months in advance. Accepts queries by mail, e-mail, fax. Accepts previously published material. Accepts simultaneous submissions. Responds in 1 month to queries. Sample copy for $6.95. Writer's guidelines free.
Nonfiction Book excerpts, essays, historical/nostalgic, interview/profile, new product, photo feature. "No first-person." **Buys 20 mss/year.** Query with published clips. Length: 2,000-2,500 words. **Pays $400 for assigned articles.**
Reprints Accepts previously published submissions.
Photos State availability of or send photos with submission. Reviews contact sheets, transparencies, prints. Buys one-time rights. Negotiates payment individually. Captions, identification of subjects required.
Tips "Articles should be well researched, carefully reported, and directed at a popular audience with a special interest in the Modernist movement. Please don't assume readers have prior familiarity with your subject; be sure to tell us the who, what, why, when, and how of whatever you're discussing."

N SOUTHWEST ART

5444 Westheimer Rd., Suite 1440, Houston TX 77056. (713)296-7900. Fax: (713)850-1314. E-mail: southwestart@southwestart.com. Web site: www.southwestart.com. **Contact:** Kristin Bucher, editor. **60% freelance written.** Monthly magazine directed to art collectors interested in artists, market trends, and art history of the American West. Estab. 1971. Circ. 60,000. **Pays on acceptance.** Publishes ms an average of 1 year after acceptance. Byline given. Submit seasonal material 8 months in advance. Accepts queries by mail, fax. Responds in 6 months to mss.
Nonfiction Book excerpts, interview/profile. No fiction or poetry. **Buys 70 mss/year.** Query with published clips. Length: 1,400-1,600 words.
Photos Photographs, color print-outs, and videotapes will not be considered. Reviews 35mm, $2^1/_4 \times 2^1/_4$, 4×5 transparencies. Negotiates rights. Captions, identification of subjects required.
Tips "Research the Southwest art market, send slides or transparencies with queries, and send writing samples demonstrating knowledge of the art world."

$ $ WATERCOLOR

VNU Business Media, 770 Broadway, New York NY 10003. (646)654-5506. E-mail: mail@myamericanartist.com. Web site: www.myamericanartist.com. **Contact:** M. Stephen Doherty, editor-in-chief. Quarterly magazine devoted to watermedia artists. Circ. 80,000. Editorial lead time 4 months.
Nonfiction Essays, exposé, interview/profile, personal experience, technical. Query with published clips. Length: 1,500-2,000 words. **Pays $500.**

$ $ WILDLIFE ART

The Art Journal of the Natural World, Pothole Publications, Inc., Box 219, 611 Main St., Ramona CA 92065. Fax: (760)788-9454. E-mail: rmscott-blair@wildlifeartmag.com. Web site: www.wildlifeartmag.com. Editor: Rose Marie Scott-Blair. **60% freelance written.** Bimonthly magazine. "*Wildlife Art* is the world's foremost magazine of the natural world, featuring wildlife, landscape, and western art. Features living artists as well as wildlife art masters, illustrators, and conservation organizations. Special emphasis on landscape and plein-air paintings. Audience is collectors, galleries, museums, show promoters worldwide." Estab. 1982. Circ. 30,000.

Pays on publication. Publishes ms an average of 6 months after acceptance. Byline given. Offers negotiable kill fee. Buys second serial (reprint) rights. Accepts queries by mail, e-mail. Responds in 6 months to queries. Sample copy for 9×12 SAE and 10 first-class stamps. Writer's guidelines online.

Nonfiction General interest, historical/nostalgic, interview/profile. **Buys 40 mss/year.** Query with published clips, include artwork samples. Length: 800-1,500 words. **Pays $150-500.**

Tips "Best way to break in is to offer concrete story ideas, new talent, a new unique twist of artistic excellence."

ASSOCIATIONS

$ $ $ $ AMERICAN EDUCATOR

American Federation of Teachers, 555 New Jersey Ave., Washington DC 20001. (202)879-4420. Fax: (202)879-4534. E-mail: amered@aft.org. Web site: www.aft.org/american_educator/index.html. **Contact:** Ruth Wattenberg, editor. **50% freelance written.** Quarterly magazine covering education, condition of children, and labor issues. "*American Educator*, the quaterly magazine of the American Federation of Teachers, reaches over 800,000 public school teachers, higher education faculty, and education researchers and policymakers. The magazine concentrates on significant ideas and practices in education, civics, and the condition of children in America and around the world." Estab. 1977. Circ. 850,000. Pays on publication. Publishes ms an average of 2-6 months after acceptance. Byline given. Offers 50% kill fee. Buys one-time, electronic rights. Editorial lead time 1 year. Submit seasonal material 6 months in advance. Accepts queries by mail, e-mail, fax. Accepts previously published material. Accepts simultaneous submissions. Responds in 2 months to queries; 6 months to mss. Sample copy and writer's guidelines online.

Nonfiction Book excerpts, essays, historical/nostalgic, interview/profile, discussions of educational research. No pieces that are not supportive of the public schools. **Buys 8 mss/year.** Query with published clips. Length: 1,000-7,000 words. **Pays $750-3,000 for assigned articles; $300-1,000 for unsolicited articles.** Pays expenses of writers on assignment.

Photos State availability with submission. Reviews contact sheets, negatives, transparencies, 8×10 prints, GIF/JPEG files. Buys one-time rights. Negotiates payment individually. Captions, identification of subjects, model releases required.

N $ $ DAC NEWS

Official Publication of the Detroit Athletic Club, Detroit Athletic Club, 241 Madison Ave., Detroit MI 48226. (313)442-1034. Fax: (313)442-1047. E-mail: kenv@thedac.com. **Contact:** Kenneth Voyles, editor/publisher. **20% freelance written.** Magazine published 10 times/year. "*DAC News* is the magazine for Detroit Athletic Club members. It covers club news and events, plus general interest features." Estab. 1916. Circ. 5,000. Pays on publication. Publishes ms an average of 3 months after acceptance. Byline given. Buys one-time rights, makes work-for-hire assignments. Editorial lead time 3 months. Submit seasonal material 3 months in advance. Accepts queries by mail, phone. Responds in 1 month to queries. Sample copy for free.

Nonfiction General interest, historical/nostalgic, photo feature. "No politics or social issues—this is an entertainment magazine. We do not acccept unsolicited manuscripts or queries for travel articles." **Buys 2-3 mss/year.** Length: 1,000-2,000 words. **Pays $100-500.** Sometimes pays expenses of writers on assignment.

Photos Illustrations only. State availability with submission. Reviews transparencies, 4×6 prints. Buys one-time rights. Negotiates payment individually. Captions, identification of subjects, model releases required.

Tips "Review our editorial calendar. It tends to repeat from year to year, so a freelancer with a fresh approach to one of these topics will get our attention quickly. It helps if articles have some connection with the DAC, but this is not absolutely necessary. We also welcome articles on Detroit history, Michigan history, or automotive history."

$ $ $ DCM

Data Center Management: Bringing Insight and Ideas to the Data Center Community, AFCOM, 742 E. Chapman Ave., Orange CA 92866. Fax: (714)997-9743. E-mail: cstichter@afcom.com. Web site: www.afcom.com. Executive Editor: Jill Eckhaus. **Contact:** Chelsey Stichter, managing editor. **50% freelance written.** Bimonthly magazine covering data center management. "*DCM* is the slick, 4-color, bimonthly publication for members of AFCOM, the leading association for data center management." Estab. 1988. Circ. 4,000 worldwide. Pays on acceptance for assigned articles and on publication for unsolicited articles. Publishes ms an average of 3 months after acceptance. Byline given. Offers 0-10% kill fee. Buys all rights. Editorial lead time 6-12 months. Submit seasonal material 6 months in advance. Responds in 1-3 weeks to queries; 1-3 months to mss. Writer's guidelines online.

- Prefers queries by e-mail.

Nonfiction How-to, technical, management as it relates to and includes examples of data centers and data center managers. Special issues: "The January/February issue is the annual 'Emerging Technologies' issue. Articles for this issue are visionary and product neutral.'' No product reviews or general tech articles. **Buys 15+ mss/year.** Query with published clips. Length: 2,000 word maximum. **Pays 50¢/word and up, based on writer's expertise.**

Photos ''We rarely consider freelance photos.'' State availability with submission. Reviews TIFF/PDF/GIF/JPEG files. Buys one-time rights. Offers no additional payment for photos accepted with ms. Identification of subjects, model releases required.

Tips ''See 'Top 10 Reasons for Rejection' and editorial guidelines online.''

$ $ THE ELKS MAGAZINE

425 W. Diversey Parkway, Chicago IL 60614-6196. (773)755-4740. E-mail: elksmag@elks.org. Web site: www.elks.org/elksmag. Editor: Cheryl T. Stachura. **Contact:** Anna L. Idol, managing editor. **25% freelance written.** Magazine published 10 times/year with basic mission of being the ''voice of the Elks.'' All material concerning the news of the Elks is written in-house. Estab. 1922. Circ. 1,037,000. **Pays on acceptance.** Buys first North American serial rights. Responds in 1 month with a yes/no on ms purchase. Responds in 2 weeks to queries. Sample copy for 9×12 SAE with 5 first-class stamps or online. Writer's guidelines online.

- Accepts queries by mail, but purchase decision is based on final mss only.

Nonfiction ''We're really interested in seeing manuscripts on business, technology, sports, health, Americana, science, history, or just intriguing topics.'' No fiction, religion, controversial issues, first-person, fillers, or verse. **Buys 20-30 mss/year.** Send complete ms. Length: 1,500-2,500 words. **Pays 25¢/word.**

Photos If possible, please advise where photographs may be found. Photographs taken and submitted by the writer are paid for separately at $25 each. Send transparencies, slides. Pays $475 for one-time cover rights.

Tips ''Please try us first. We'll get back to you soon.''

N $ $ HUMANITIES

National Endowment for the Humanities, 1100 Pennsylvania Ave. NW, Washington DC 20506. (202)606-8435. Fax: (202)606-8451. E-mail: alifson@neh.gov. Web site: www.neh.gov. Editor: Mary Lou Beatty (mbeatty@neh.gov). **Contact:** Anna Gillis, writer-editor. **50% freelance written.** Bimonthly magazine covering news in the humanities focused on projects that receive financial support from the agency. Estab. 1980. Circ. 6,000. Pays on publication. Publishes ms an average of 2 months after acceptance. Byline given. Not copyrighted. Buys all rights, makes work-for-hire assignments. Editorial lead time 3 months. Submit seasonal material 4 months in advance. Accepts queries by mail, e-mail, fax, phone. Accepts previously published material. Sample copy online.

Nonfiction Book excerpts, historical/nostalgic, interview/profile, photo feature. **Buys 25 mss/year.** Query with published clips. Length: 400-2,500 words. **Pays $300-400.** Sometimes pays expenses of writers on assignment.

Photos Contact mbiernik@neh.gov. Buys one-time rights. Offers no additional payment for photos accepted with ms; negotiates payment individually. Identification of subjects, model releases required.

Columns/Departments In Focus (directors of state humanities councils), 700 words; Breakout (special activities of state humanities councils), 750 words. **Buys 12 mss/year.** Query with published clips. **Pays $300.**

$ $ ⊘ KIWANIS

3636 Woodview Trace, Indianapolis IN 46268. (317)875-8755. Fax: (317)879-0204. E-mail: magazine@kiwanis.org. Web site: www.kiwanis.org. **10% freelance written.** Magazine published 6 times/year for business and professional persons and their families. Estab. 1917. Circ. 240,000. **Pays on acceptance.** Publishes ms an average of 6 months after acceptance. Byline given. Offers 40% kill fee. Buys first rights. Accepts queries by mail, e-mail, fax. Responds in 1 month to queries. Sample copy and writer's guidelines for 9×12 SAE with 5 first class stamps. Writer's guidelines online.

- No unsolicited mss.

Nonfiction Articles about social and civic betterment, small-business concerns, children, science, education, religion, family, health, recreation, etc. Emphasis on objectivity, intelligent analysis, and thorough research of contemporary issues. Positive tone preferred. Concise, lively writing, absence of clichés, and impartial presentation of controversy required. Articles must include information and quotations from international sources. ''We have a continuing need for articles that concern helping youth, particularly prenatal through age 5: day care, developmentally appropriate education, early intervention for at-risk children, parent education, safety and health. No fiction, personal essays, profiles, travel pieces, fillers, or verse of any kind. A light or humorous approach is welcomed where the subject is appropriate and all other requirements are observed.'' **Buys 20 mss/year.** Length: 500-1,200 words. **Pays $300-600.** Sometimes pays expenses of writers on assignment.

Photos ''We accept photos submitted with manuscripts. Our rate for a manuscript with good photos is higher than for one without.'' Buys one-time rights. Identification of subjects, model releases required.

Tips ''We will work with any writer who presents a strong feature article idea applicable to our magazine's audience and who will prove he or she knows the craft of writing. First, obtain writer's guidelines and a sample copy. Study for general style and content. When querying, present detailed outline of proposed manuscript's focus and editorial intent. Indicate expert sources to be used, as well as possible Kiwanis sources for quotations and anecdotes. Present a well-researched, smoothly written manuscript that contains a 'human quality' with the use of anecdotes, practical examples, quotations, etc.''

$ $ LEGACY MAGAZINE

National Association for Interpretation, P.O. Box 2246, Fort Collins CO 80522. (970)484-8283. Fax: (970)484-8179. Web site: www.interpnet.com/interpnet/miscpages/publication.htm. **80% freelance written.** Bimonthly magazine covering heritage interpretation (national parks, museums, nature centers, aquaria, etc.). ''The National Association for Interpretation's premier publication, *Legacy Magazine* offers a thought-provoking look at the field of heritage interpretation through articles about individuals who interpret natural and cultural history, biographies of important figures in or related to the field, discussions of interpretive sites, and trends in interpretation. The magazine, published 6 times a year, appeals to those interested in learning about natural or cultural heritage and interpretive sites around the world.'' Estab. 1989. Circ. 5,000. Pays on publication. Publishes ms an average of 4 months after acceptance. Byline given. Offers 80% kill fee. Buys first North American serial rights. Editorial lead time 6 months. Submit seasonal material 4 months in advance. Accepts queries by mail, e-mail, fax, phone. Accepts simultaneous submissions. Responds in 1 month to queries; 4 months to mss. Sample copy online. Writer's guidelines by e-mail.

Nonfiction Essays, historical/nostalgic, opinion, personal experience, photo feature, travel, heritage interpretation. **Buys 12-20 mss/year.** Query. Length: 500-2,500 words. **Pays $75-350.** Sometimes pays expenses of writers on assignment.

Photos State availability with submission. Reviews contact sheets, 4×6 prints, GIF/JPEG files. Buys one-time rights. Offers $75-100/photo. Captions required.

Columns/Departments Visitor's View (review of personal experience at a heritage interpretation site), 500 words. **Buys 6 mss/year.** Query. **Pays $75-150.**

Tips ''Please review the article descriptions in our writer's guidelines before submitting a query.''

$ $ THE LION

300 W. 22nd St., Oak Brook IL 60523-8815. (630)571-5466. Fax: (630)571-8890. E-mail: rkleinfe@lionsclubs.org. Web site: www.lionsclubs.org. **Contact:** Robert Kleinfelder, senior editor. **35% freelance written.** Works with a small number of new/unpublished writers each year. Monthly magazine covering service club organization for Lions Club members and their families. Estab. 1918. Circ. 490,000. **Pays on acceptance.** Publishes ms an average of 5 months after acceptance. Byline given. Buys all rights. Accepts queries by mail, e-mail, fax, phone. Responds in 1 month to queries. Sample copy and writer's guidelines free.

Nonfiction Welcomes humor, if sophisticated but clean; no sensationalism. Prefers anecdotes in articles. Photo feature (must be of a Lions Club service project), informational (issues of interest to civic-minded individuals). No travel, biography, or personal experiences. **Buys 40 mss/year.** Length: 500-1,500 words. **Pays $100-750.** Sometimes pays expenses of writers on assignment.

Photos Purchased with accompanying ms. ''Photos should be at least 5×7 glossies; color prints or slides are preferred. We also accept digital photos by e-mail. Be sure photos are clear and as candid as possible.'' Total purchase price for ms includes payment for photos accepted with ms. Captions required.

Tips ''Send detailed description of proposed article. Query first and request writer's guidelines and sample copy. Incomplete details on how the Lions involved actually carried out a project and poor quality photos are the most frequent mistakes made by writers in completing an article assignment for us. No gags, fillers, quizzes, or poems are accepted. We are geared increasingly to an international audience. Writers who travel internationally could query for possible assignments, although only locally related expenses could be paid.''

$ $ $ THE MEETING PROFESSIONAL

Meeting Professionals International, 3030 LBJ Freeway, Suite 1700, Dallas TX 75234. Fax: (972)702-3096. E-mail: publications@mpiweb.org. Web site: www.themeetingprofessional.org. Associate Publisher: Colin Rorrie Jr. Editor-in-Chief: Tom Domine. **Contact:** Kirsten Rockwood, publications coordinator. **60% freelance written.** Monthly magazine covering the global meeting idustry. ''*The Meeting Professional* delivers strategic editorial content on meeting industry trends, opportunities and items of importance in the hope of fostering professional development and career enhancement. The magazine is mailed monthly to 20,000 MPI members and 10,000 qualified nonmember subscribers and meeting industry planners. It is also distributed at major industry shows, such as IT&ME and EIBTM, at MPI conferences, and upon individual request.'' Circ. 30,000. **Pays on acceptance.** Publishes ms an average of 2-3 months after acceptance. Byline given. Offers a negotiable kill fee. Buys all rights. Editorial lead time 2 months. Submit seasonal material 3 months in advance. Accepts queries by e-mail. Sample copy for free. Writer's guidelines by e-mail.

Nonfiction General interest, how-to, interview/profile, travel, industry-related. No duplications from other industry publications. **Buys 60 mss/year.** Query with published clips. Length: 1,000-2,500 words. **Pays 50-75¢/word for assigned articles.**

Tips "Understand and have experience within the industry. Writers who are familiar with our magazine and our competitors are better able to get our attention, send better queries, and get assignments."

$ $ PENN LINES

Pennsylvania Rural Electric Association, 212 Locust St., Harrisburg PA 17108. E-mail: peter_fitzgerald@prea.com. Web site: www.prea.com/pennlines/plonline.htm. **Contact:** Peter Fitzgerald, senior editor. Monthly magazine covering rural life in Pennsylvania. News magazine of Pennsylvania electric cooperatives. Features should be balanced, and they should have a rural focus. Electric cooperative sources (such as consumers) should be used. Estab. 1966. Circ. 140,000. Pays on publication. Publishes ms an average of 3 months after acceptance. Byline given. Buys first rights. Editorial lead time 4 months. Submit seasonal material 4 months in advance. Accepts queries by mail, e-mail. Sample copy and writer's guidelines online.

Nonfiction General interest, historical/nostalgic, how-to, interview/profile, travel (rural PA only). **Buys 6 mss/year.** Query or send complete ms. Length: 500-2,000 words. **Pays $300-650.**

Photos Reviews transparencies, prints, GIF/JPEG files. Buys one-time rights and right to publish online. Negotiates payment individually. Captions required.

Tips "Find topics of statewide interest to rural residents. Detailed information on *Penn Lines'* readers, gleaned from a reader survey, is available online."

$ $ PERSPECTIVES IN HEALTH

Pan American Health Organization, 525 23rd St. NW, Washington DC 20037-2895. (202)974-3122. Fax: (202)974-3143. E-mail: eberwind@paho.org. Web site: www.paho.org. **Contact:** Donna Eberwine, editor. **80% freelance written.** Magazine published 3 times/year covering international public health with a focus on the Americas. "*Perspectives in Health*, the popular magazine of the Pan American Health Organization (PAHO), was created in 1996 to serve as a forum on current issues in the area of international public health and human development. PAHO works with the international community, government institutions, nongovernmental organizations, universities, community groups, and others to strengthen national and local public health systems and to improve the health and well-being of the peoples of the Americas." Estab. 1996. Circ. 10,000. **Pays on acceptance.** Publishes ms an average of 6 months after acceptance. Byline given. Buys first North American serial rights and electronic rights to post articles on the PAHO Web site. Editorial lead time 2 months. Accepts queries by mail, e-mail, fax, phone. Responds in 2 months to faxed/mailed queries; 1 week to e-mail queries. Sample copy and writer's guidelines free.

- Each issue of *Perspectives in Health* is published in English and Spanish.

Nonfiction Subject matter: Culturally insightful and scientifically sound articles related to international public health and human development issues and programs affecting North America, Latin America, and the Caribbean. The story angle should have wide relevancy—i.e., capturing national and particularly international concerns, even if the setting is local—and should be high in human interest content: "international public health with a human face." General topics may include (but are not limited to) AIDS and other sexually transmitted diseases, maternal and child health, the environment, food and nutrition, cardiovascular diseases, cancer, mental health, oral health, violence, veterinary health, disaster preparedness, health education and promotion, substance abuse, water and sanitation, and issues related to the health and well-being of women, adolescents, workers, the elderly, and minority groups in the countries of the Americas. Historical pieces on the region's public health "trail blazers" and innovators are also welcome. General interest, historical/nostalgic, interview/profile, opinion, personal experience, photo feature. No highly technical, highly bureaucratic articles. **Buys 12 mss/year.** Query with or without published clips or send complete ms. Length: 1,500-3,000 words. **Pays $250.** Sometimes pays expenses of writers on assignment.

Photos State availability with submission. Reviews contact sheets, negatives, transparencies, prints. Buys one-time rights. Negotiates payment individually. Captions, identification of subjects, model releases required.

Columns/Departments Last Word, 750 words. **Buys 2 mss/year.** Query with or without published clips or send complete ms. **Pays $100.**

Tips "*Perspectives* puts the human face on international public health issues and programs. All facts must be documented. Quote people involved with the programs described. Get on-site information—not simply an Internet-researched story."

$ $ RECREATION NEWS

Official Publication of the RecGov.org, 730 Heston Lane, Bel Air MD 21014. (410)638-6901. Fax: (410)638-6902. Web site: www.recreationnews.com. **85% freelance written.** Monthly guide to leisure-time activities for federal and private industry workers covering outdoor recreation, travel, fitness and indoor pasttimes. Estab. 1979. Circ. 110,000. Pays on publication. Publishes ms an average of 8 months after acceptance. Byline given. Buys first, second serial (reprint) rights. Submit seasonal material 10 months in advance. Accepts queries by mail, e-mail, fax, phone. Accepts previously published material. Accepts simultaneous submissions. Responds in 2 months to queries. Sample copy and writer's guidelines for 9×12 SAE with $1.05 in postage.

Nonfiction Historical/nostalgic (Washington-related), personal experience (with recreation, life in Washington), travel (mid-Atlantic travel only), sports; hobbies. Special issues: skiing (December). **Buys 45 mss/year.** Query with published clips. Length: 800-2,000 words. **Pays $50-300.**

Reprints Send tearsheet or typed ms with rights for sale noted and information about when and where the material previously appeared. Pays $50.

Photos Call for details.

Tips "Our writers generally have a few years of professional writing experience and their work runs to the lively and conversational. We like more manuscripts in a wide range of recreational topics, including the off-beat. The areas of our publication most open to freelancers are general articles on travel and sports, both participational and spectator, also historic in the DC area. In general, stories on sites visited need to include info on nearby places of interest and places to stop for lunch, to shop, etc."

N THE ROTARIAN

Rotary International, One Rotary Center, 1560 Sherman Ave., Evanston IL 60201-3698. (847)866-3000. Fax: (847)866-9732. E-mail: rotarian@rotaryintl.org. Web site: www.rotary.org. **Contact:** Janice Chambers, travel (chamberj@rotaryintl.org); Cary Silver, health (silverc@rotary.org); Tiffany Woods, management/finance (woodst@rotaryintl.org). **40% freelance written.** Monthly magazine for Rotarian business and professional men and women and their families, schools, libraries, hospitals, etc. Articles should appeal to an international audience and in some way help Rotarians help other people. The organization's rationale is one of hope, encouragement, and belief in the power of individuals talking and working together. Estab. 1911. Circ. 510,000. **Pays on acceptance.** Byline sometimes given. Kill fee negotiable. Buys one-time, all rights. Editorial lead time 4-8 months. Accepts queries by mail, e-mail. Accepts previously published material. Sample copy for $1 (e-mail edbrookc@rotaryintl.org). Writer's guidelines online.

- "Break in with a short item (200-600 words) in the Fields Reports section, which focuses on Rotarians participating in innovative, successful programs/projects. Field Reports can also include short profiles of Rotrians, scholarship/grant recipients, and exchange students.

Nonfiction General interest, humor, inspirational, photo feature, technical (science), travel (lifestyle), sports, business/finance, environmental, health/medicine, social issues. No fiction, religious, or political articles. Query with published clips. Length: 1,500-2,500 words. **Pays negotiable rate.**

Reprints Send tearsheet, photocopy or typed ms with rights for sale noted and information about when and where the material previously appeared. Negotiates payment.

Photos State availability with submission. Reviews contact sheets, transparencies. Buys one-time rights.

Columns/Departments Health; Management; Finance; Travel, all 550-900 words. Query.

Tips "The chief aim of *The Rotarian* is to report Rotary International news. Most of this information comes through Rotary channels and is staff written or edited. The best field for freelance articles is in the general interest category. We prefer queries with a Rotary angle. These stories run the gamut from humor pieces and how-to stories to articles about such significant concerns as business management, technology, world health, and the environment."

N SCOTTISH HOME & COUNTRY MAGAZINE

Scottish Women's Rural Institutes, 42 Heriot Row, Edinburgh Scotland EH3 6ES United Kingdom. (44)(131)225-1724. Fax: (44)(131)225-8129. E-mail: magazine@swri.demon.co.uk. Web site: www.swri.org.uk/magazine.html. **Contact:** Liz Ferguson. Monthly publication that keeps readers in touch with SWRI news and rural events throughout Scotland. Editorial lead time 1 month. Sample copy for £1.35. Writer's guidelines by e-mail

- SWRI members are not normally paid for submissions.
- Articles accompanied by photographs or illustrations have an advantage. Pictures of any relevant events/activities are always of interest.

Nonfiction Crafts, personal histories, social history, health, travel, cookery, general women's interests. Does not want articles on religion or party politics. Send complete ms. Length: 500-1,000 words.

$ $ $ SCOUTING

Boy Scouts of America, 1325 W. Walnut Hill Lane, P.O. Box 152079, Irving TX 75015-2079. Web site: www.scoutingmagazine.org. **80% freelance written.** Magazine published 6 times/year covering Scouting activities for adult leaders of the Boy Scouts, Cub Scouts, and Venturing. Estab. 1913. Circ. 1,000,000. Pays on acceptance for major features and some shorter features. Publishes ms an average of 18 months after acceptance. Byline given. Buys first North American serial rights. Editorial lead time 1 year. Submit seasonal material 1 year in advance. Accepts queries by mail. Accepts previously published material. Accepts simultaneous submissions.

Responds in 1 month to queries; 2 months to mss. Sample copy for $2.50 and 9×12 SAE with 4 first-class stamps or online. Writer's guidelines online.

O→ Break in with "a profile of an outstanding Scout leader who has useful advice for new volunteer leaders (especially good if the situation involves urban Scouting or Scouts with disabilities or other extraordinary roles)."

Nonfiction Program activities, leadership techniques and styles, profiles, inspirational, occasional general interest for adults (humor, historical, nature, social issues, trends). Inspirational, interview/profile. **Buys 20-30 mss/year.** Query with published clips and SASE. Length: 600-1,200 words. **Pays $750-1,000 for major articles, $300-500 for shorter features.** Pays expenses of writers on assignment.

Reprints Send photocopy of article and information about when and where the article previously appeared. "First-person accounts of meaningful Scouting experiences (previously published in local newspapers, etc.) are a popular subject."

Photos State availability with submission. Reviews transparencies, prints. Buys one-time rights. Identification of subjects required.

Columns/Departments Way It Was (Scouting history), 600-750 words; Family Talk (family—raising kids, etc.), 600-750 words. **Buys 8-12 mss/year.** Query. **Pays $300-500.**

Fillers "Limited to personal accounts of humorous or inspirational Scouting experiences." Anecdotes, short humor. **Buys 15-25/year.** Length: 50-150 words. **Pays $25 on publication.**

Tips "*Scouting* magazine articles are mainly about successful program activities conducted by or for Cub Scout packs, Boy Scout troops, and Venturing crews. We also include features on winning leadership techniques and styles, profiles of outstanding individual leaders, and inspirational accounts (usually first person) of *Scouting*'s impact on an individual, either as a youth or while serving as a volunteer adult leader. Because most volunteer Scout leaders are also parents of children of Scout age, *Scouting* is also considered a family magazine. We publish material we feel will help parents in strengthening their families (because they often deal with communicating and interacting with young people, many of these features are useful to a reader in both roles as parent and Scout leader)."

$ $ SOUTH AMERICAN EXPLORER

South American Explorers, 126 Indian Creek Rd., Ithaca NY 14850. (607)277-0488. Fax: (607)277-6122. E-mail: don@saexplorers.org. Web site: www.saexplorers.org. **Contact:** Don Montague, editor-in-chief. **80% freelance written.** Quarterly travel/scientific/educational journal covering exploration, conservation, anthropology, ethnography, field sports, natural history, history, archeology, linguistics, and just about anything relating to South America. "The *South American Explorer* goes primarily (but not exclusively) to members of the South American Explorers. Readers are interested in all the above subjects as well as endangered peoples, wildlife protection, volunteer opportunities, etc." Estab. 1977. Circ. 10,000. Pays on publication. Publishes ms an average of 2-3 months after acceptance. Byline given. Buys first rights. Editorial lead time 3 months. Accepts queries by mail, e-mail, fax, phone. Accepts previously published material. Accepts simultaneous submissions. Responds in 1 month to queries.

Nonfiction All content must relate to South America in some way. Book excerpts, essays, exposé, general interest, historical/nostalgic, how-to, humor, inspirational, interview/profile, new product, opinion, personal experience, photo feature, religious, technical, travel. No "My South American Vacation," "The Extraterrestrial Origins of Machu Picchu," "Encounters with the Amazon Yeti," "My Journal of Traveling Through South America." **Buys 20 mss/year.** Query with or without published clips or send complete ms. Length: 1,000-4,500 words. **Pays $50-400 for assigned articles; $50-300 for unsolicited articles.**

Photos Send photos with submission. Reviews contact sheets, negatives, transparencies, prints, GIF/JPEG files. Buys one-time rights. Negotiates payment individually. Captions required.

Columns/Departments Assignment Desk; South American Explorers; Book Reviews; Movie Reviews; News Shorts; Tips and Notes; Cyber Page. **Buys 6 mss/year.** Send complete ms. **Pays $50-250.**

Fillers Length: 500-1,500 words.

N $ $ THE TOASTMASTER

Toastmasters International, P.O. Box 9052, Mission Viejo CA 92690. (949)858-8255. E-mail: sfrey@toastmasters.org. Web site: www.toastmasters.org. **Contact:** Suzanne Frey. **50% freelance written.** Monthly magazine on public speaking, leadership, and club concerns. "This magazine is sent to members of Toastmasters International, a nonprofit educational association of men and women throughout the world who are interested in developing their communication and leadership skills. Members range from novice to professional speakers and from a wide variety of ethnic and cultural backgrounds, as Toastmasters is an international organization." Estab. 1933. Circ. 210,000. **Pays on acceptance.** Publishes ms an average of 1 year after acceptance. Byline given. Buys first, second serial (reprint), all rights. Submit seasonal material 3-4 months in advance. Accepts previously published material. Accepts simultaneous submissions. Responds in 6-8 weeks to queries. Sample copy for 9×12 SASE with 4 first-class stamps. Writer's guidelines online.

Nonfiction "Toastmasters members are requested to view their submissions as contributions to the organization. Sometimes asks for book excerpts and reprints without payment, but original contribution from individuals outside Toastmasters will be paid for at stated rates." How-to, humor, interview/profile (well-known speakers and leaders), communications, leadership, language use. **Buys 50 mss/year.** Query with published clips by mail or e-mail (preferred). Length: 700-2,000 words. **Pays $250-350.** Sometimes pays expenses of writers on assignment.

Reprints Send ms with rights for sale noted and information about when and where the material previously appeared. Pays 50-70% of amount paid for an original article.

Tips "We are looking primarily for how-to articles on subjects from the broad fields of communications and leadership which can be directly applied by our readers in their self-improvement and club programming efforts. Concrete examples are useful. Avoid sexist or nationalist language. Articles with obvious political or religious slants will not be accepted."

N $ TRAIL & TIMBERLINE

The Colorado Mountain Club, 710 10th St., Suite 200, Golden CO 80401. (303)996-2745. Fax: (303)279-9690. E-mail: beckwt@cmc.org. Web site: www.cmc.org. **Contact:** Tom Beckwith, editor/publications manager. **80% freelance written.** Official quarterly publication for the Colorado Mountain Club. "Articles in *Trail & Timberline* conform to the mission statement of the Colorado Mountain Club to unite the energy, interest, and knowledge of lovers of the Colorado mountains, to collect and disseminate information, to stimulate public interest, and to encourage preservation of the mountains of Colorado and the Rocky Mountain region." Estab. 1918. Circ. 10,500. Pays on publication. Publishes ms an average of 2 months after acceptance. Byline given. Buys all rights. Editorial lead time 6 months. Submit seasonal material 6 months in advance. Accepts queries by mail, e-mail. Accepts previously published material. Responds in 1 week to queries; 1 month to mss. Sample copy for $5. Writer's guidelines online.

Nonfiction Essays, humor, opinion (Switchbacks), personal experience, photo feature, travel (Trip Reports). **Buys 10-15 mss/year.** Send complete ms. Length: 500-2,000 words. **Pays $50.**

Photos Send photos with submission. Reviews contact sheets, 35mm transparencies, 3×5 or larger prints, GIF/JPEG files. Buys one-time rights. Offers no additional payment for photos accepted with ms. Captions, identification of subjects, model releases required.

Poetry Jared Smith, poetry editor. Avant-garde, free verse, traditional. **Buys 6-12 poems/year.**

Tips "Writers should be familiar with the purposes and ethos of the Colorado Mountain Club before querying. Writer's guidelines are available and should be consulted—particularly for poetry submissions. All submissions must conform to the mission statement of the Colorado Mountain Club."

$ $ U MAG

A Magazine for Young USAA Members, USAA, 9800 Fredericksburg Rd., San Antonio TX 78288. Fax: (210)498-0030. E-mail: shari.biediger@usaa.com. **Contact:** Shari Biediger, senior editor. **75% freelance written.** Quarterly magazine covering money, safety, history, human interest, military related. Estab. 1995. Circ. 439,000. **Pays on acceptance.** Publishes ms an average of 6 months after acceptance. Buys all rights. Editorial lead time 6 months. Submit seasonal material 9 months in advance. Accepts queries by mail, e-mail, fax. Accepts simultaneous submissions. Sample copy and writer's guidelines free.

Nonfiction General interest, historical/nostalgic, how-to, humor, interview/profile, personal experience. Nothing religious. **Buys 4-6 mss/year.** Query with published clips. Length: 250-500 words.

Fiction Adventure, historical, humorous. Buys 1 ms/year.

Fillers Anecdotes, facts, gags to be illustrated by cartoonist, short humor. **Buys 2/year.**

Tips "Write for a tween audience (ages 8-12). Shouldn't sound like textbook material."

$ $ U-TURN

For Teen USAA Members, USAA, 9800 Fredericksburg Rd., San Antonio TX 78288. Fax: (210)498-0030. E-mail: shari.biediger@usaa.com. **Contact:** Shari Biediger, senior editor. **85% freelance written.** Quarterly magazine covering driving, college prep, lifestyle, and money. Estab. 1998. Circ. 545,000. **Pays on acceptance.** Publishes ms an average of 6 months after acceptance. Offers 30% kill fee. Buys all rights. Editorial lead time 6 months. Submit seasonal material 9 months in advance. Accepts queries by mail, e-mail, fax. Responds in 6 weeks to queries; 6 months to mss. Sample copy and writer's guidelines free.

Nonfiction How-to, humor, interview/profile. **Buys 6 mss/year.** Query with published clips. Length: 250-500 words. Sometimes pays expenses of writers on assignment.

Tips "Read other magazines targeted at this age group (13-17)."

$ $ $UPDATE

New York Academy of Sciences, 2 E. 63rd St., New York NY 10021. Web site: www.nyas.org. **40% freelance written.** Magazine published 7 times/year covering science, health issues. Scientific newsletter for members of the New York Academy of Sciences. Estab. 2001. Circ. 25,000. Pays on publication. Publishes ms an average of 1 month after acceptance. Byline sometimes given. Not copyrighted. Buys first, electronic rights, makes work-for-hire assignments. Editorial lead time 2 months. Submit seasonal material 2 months in advance. Accepts queries by mail. Sample copy online.

Nonfiction All articles "must be science or medical related in every case." Book excerpts, essays, general interest, historical/nostalgic, interview/profile, technical. No science fiction, any pieces exceeding 1,000 words, or subjects that aren't current. **Buys 6-7 mss/year.** Query. Length: 300-1,000 words. **Pays $200-1,200.** Sometimes pays expenses of writers on assignment.

Photos State availability with submission. Reviews GIF/JPEG files. Buys one-time rights. Negotiates payment individually. Captions, identification of subjects, model releases required.

Tips "Submit detailed summary or outline of the proposed article's content. Subject matter must be current and topical, as well as scientific, technical, or medical in nature. We prefer interviews with noted scientific and medical researchers whose work is cutting edge and credible. Articles should be relatively brief and contain some 'news' element, i.e., important recent development or unusual, attention-getting element. All sources must be identified and credible."

$ $VFW MAGAZINE

Veterans of Foreign Wars of the United States, 406 W. 34th St., Kansas City MO 64111. (816)756-3390. Fax: (816)968-1169. E-mail: kpetrovic@vfw.org. Web site: www.vfw.org. **Contact:** Rich Kolb, editor-in-chief. **40% freelance written.** Monthly magazine on veterans' affairs, military history, patriotism, defense, and current events. "*VFW Magazine* goes to its members worldwide, all having served honorably in the armed forces overseas from World War II through the war on terrorism." Circ. 1,800,000. **Pays on acceptance.** Byline given. Offers 50% kill fee. Buys first rights. Submit seasonal material 6 months in advance. Accepts queries by mail, e-mail, fax. Responds in 2 months to queries. Sample copy for 9×12 SAE with 5 first-class stamps.

- Break in with "fresh and innovative angles on veterans' rights; stories on little-known exploits in US military history. Will be particularly in the market for Vietnam War battle accounts during 2005. Upbeat articles about severely disabled veterans who have overcome their disabilities; feel-good patriotism pieces; current events as they relate to defense policy; and health and retirement pieces are always welcome."

Nonfiction Veterans' and defense affairs, recognition of veterans and military service, current foreign policy, American armed forces abroad, and international events affecting US national security are in demand. **Buys 25-30 mss/year.** Query with 1-page outline, résumé, and published clips. Length: 1,000 words. **Pays up to $500 maximum unless otherwise negotiated.**

Photos Send photos with submission. Reviews contact sheets, negatives, color (2¼×2¼) preferred transparencies, 5×7 or 8×10 b&w prints. Buys first North American rights. Captions, identification of subjects required.

Tips "Absolute accuracy and quotes from relevant individuals are a must. Bibliographies useful if subject required extensive research and/or is open to dispute. Counsult *The Associated Press Stylebook* for correct grammar and punctuation. Please enclose a 3-sentence biography describing your military service and your military experience in the field in which you are writing. No phone queries."

N VINTAGE SNOWMOBILE MAGAZINE

Vintage Snowmobile Club of America, P.O. Box 130, Grey Eagle MN 56336. E-mail: mike@vsca.com. Web site: www.vsca.com. **Contact:** Mike Meagher. **75% freelance written.** Quarterly magazine covering vintage snowmobiles and collectors. *Vintage Snowmobile Magazine* deals with vintage snowmobiles and is sent to members of the Vintage Snowmobile Club of America. Estab. 1987. Circ. 2,400. **Pays on acceptance.** Publishes ms an average of 3 months after acceptance. Byline sometimes given. Buys first North American serial rights. Editorial lead time 2 months. Submit seasonal material 3 months in advance. Accepts queries by mail, e-mail, fax, phone.

Nonfiction General interest, historical/nostalgic, humor, photo feature, coverage of shows. Query with published clips. Length: 200-2,000 words.

Photos Send photos with submission. Reviews 3×5 prints, GIF/JPEG files. Buys all rights. Negotiates payment individually.

Columns/Departments Featured Sleds Stories, 500 words. Query with published clips.

N WALK MAGAZINE

The Ramblers' Association, 2nd Floor, Camelford House, 87-90 Albert Embankment, London England SE1 7TW United Kingdom. (44)(207)339-8500. Fax: (44)(207)339-8501. E-mail: chriso@ramblers.org.uk. Web site:

www.ramblers.org.uk. **Contact:** Chris Ord, editor. Quarterly magazine that encourages people to participate in walking, educates people about the countryside, and promotes wider access to—and protection of—the countryside. The magazine is distributed to Ramblers' Association members, organizations, and individuals who want to stay informed on the group's policies. Circ. 140,000. Pays on publication. Editorial lead time 6 weeks. Accepts queries by mail. Sample copy online or for a SASE (A4 and 73 pence). Writer's guidelines by e-mail

- Book reviews, news stories, and articles on policy issues are normally written in-house.

Nonfiction Feature articles should promote an interest in walking, but should not just profile a location. Articles should describe why a particular walk is special to the writer. It helps if the walk can be accessed by public transportation. Query with synopsis/outline, published clips, SASE. Length: 500-800 words. **Payment is negotiable.**

Photos Send photos with submission. Reviews 300 dpi digital images, 35mm or medium format color slides. Payment is negotiated. Captions required.

ASTROLOGY, METAPHYSICAL & NEW AGE

$ $ $ $ BODY & SOUL

Martha Stewart Living Omnimedia, 42 Pleasant St., Watertown MA 02472. (617)926-0200. Editor-in-Chief: Alanna Fincke. Managing Editor: Donna Coco. **Contact:** Editorial Department. **60% freelance written.** Magazine published 8 times/year emphasizing "personal fulfillment and healthier lifestyles. The audience we reach is primarily female, college-educated, 25-55 years of age, concerned about personal growth, health, earth-friendly living and balance in personal life." Estab. 1974. Circ. 400,000. Publishes ms an average of 6 months after acceptance. Byline given. Offers 25% kill fee. Buys first North American serial, electronic rights. Editorial lead time 6-8 months. Submit seasonal material 1 year in advance. Accepts queries by mail. Accepts simultaneous submissions. Responds in 2 months to queries. Sample copy for $5 and 9×12 SAE.

O→ No phone calls. The process of decision making takes time and involves more than one editor. An answer cannot be given over the phone. Do not send completed, full-length mss. These will be returned or rejected, unread. Send short queries, résumés and clips only.

Nonfiction How-to, inner growth, spiritual, health news, environmental issues, fitness, natural beauty. **Buys 50 mss/year.** Query with published clips. Length: 100-2,500 words. **Pays 75¢-$1.25/word.** Pays expenses of writers on assignment.

Columns/Departments Health, beauty, fitness, home, healthy eating, personal growth, and spirituality, 600-1,300 words. **Buys 50 mss/year.** Query with published clips. **Pays 75¢-$1.25/word.**

Tips "Read the magazine and get a sense of the type of writing run in column. In particular, we are looking for new or interesting approaches to subjects such as mind-body fitness, earth-friendly products, Eastern and herbal medicine, self-help, community, healthy eating, etc. No e-mail or phone queries, please. Begin with a query, résumé and published clips—we will contact you for the manuscript. A query is 1-2 paragraphs—if you need more space than that to present the idea, then you don't have a clear grip on it."

$ $ FATE MAGAZINE

P.O. Box 460, Lakeville MN 55044. Fax: (952)891-6091. E-mail: fate@fatemag.com. Web site: www.fatemag.com. **Contact:** Editor. **70% freelance written.** Estab. 1948. Circ. 20,000. Pays after publication. Byline given. Buys all rights. Responds in 3 months to queries.

Nonfiction Personal psychic and mystical experiences, 350-500 words. **Pays $25.** Articles on parapsychology, Fortean phenomena, cryptozoology, spiritual healing, flying saucers, new frontiers of science, and mystical aspects of ancient civilizations, 500-3,000 words. Must include complete authenticating details. Prefers interesting accounts of single events rather than roundups. "We very frequently accept manuscripts from new writers; the majority are people's first-person accounts of their own psychic/mystical/spiritual experiences. We do need to have all details, where, when, why, who and what, included for complete documentation. We ask for a notarized statement attesting to truth of the article." Query. **Pays 10¢/word.**

Photos Buys slides, prints, or digital photos/illustrations with ms. Pays $10.

Fillers Fillers are especially welcomed and must be be fully authenticated also, and on similar topics. Length: 50-300 words.

Tips "We would like more stories about current paranormal or unusual events."

$ MAGICAL BLEND MAGAZINE

A Primer for the 21st Century, 55 Independence Circle, #202, Chico CA 95973. (530)893-9037. Fax: (530)893-9076. E-mail: editor@magicalblend.com. Web site: www.magicalblend.com. **50% freelance written.** Bimonthly magazine covering social and mystical transformation. "*Magical Blend* endorses no one pathway to spiritual growth, but attempts to explore many alternative possibilities to help transform the planet." Estab.

1980. Circ. 100,000. Pays on publication. Publishes ms an average of 2 months after acceptance. Byline given. Responds in 2-6 months to mss. Sample copy for free. Writer's guidelines for #10 SASE.

O→ Break in by "writing a great article that gives our readers something they can use in their daily lives or obtain 'name' interviews."

Nonfiction "Articles must reflect our standards; see our magazine." Book excerpts, essays, general interest, inspirational, interview/profile, religious, travel. No poetry or fiction. **Buys 24 mss/year.** Send complete ms. Length: 1,000-2,000 words. **Pays $35-100.**

Photos State availability with submission. Reviews transparencies. Buys all rights. Negotiates payment individually. Identification of subjects, model releases required.

Fillers Newsbreaks. **Buys 12-20/year.** Length: 300-450 words. **Pays variable rate.**

$ NEW YORK SPIRIT MAGAZINE

107 Sterling Place, Brooklyn NY 11217. (718)638-3733. Fax: (718)230-3459. E-mail: office@nyspirit.com. Web site: www.nyspirit.com. Bimonthly tabloid covering spirituality and personal growth and transformation. "We are a magazine that caters to the holistic health community in New York City." Circ. 50,000. **Pays on acceptance.** Publishes ms an average of 3 months after acceptance. Byline given. Buys first rights. Editorial lead time 1 month. Accepts previously published material. Accepts simultaneous submissions. Responds in 1 month to queries. Sample copy for 8×10 SAE and 10 first-class stamps. Writer's guidelines online.

Nonfiction Essays, how-to, humor, inspirational, interview/profile, photo feature. **Buys 30 mss/year.** Query with or without published clips. Length: 1,000-3,500 words. **Pays $150 maximum.**

Photos State availability with submission. Model releases required.

Columns/Departments Fitness (new ideas in staying fit), 1,500 words. **Pays $150.**

Fiction Humorous, mainstream, inspirational. **Buys 5 mss/year.** Query with published clips. Length: 1,000-3,500 words. **Pays $150.**

Tips "Be vivid and descriptive. We are very interested in hearing from new writers."

N $ NEWWITCH

BBI, Inc., P.O. Box 641, Point Arena CA 95468. (707)882-2052. Fax: (707)882-2793. E-mail: meditor@newwitch.com. Web site: www.newwitch.com. Editor: Anne Niven, editor-in-chief. **Contact:** Kenaz Filan, managing editor. Quarterly magazine covering paganism, wicca and earth religions. "*newWitch* is dedicated to witches, wiccans, neo-pagans, and various other earth-based, pre-Christian, shamanic, and magical practitioners. We hope to reach not only those already involved in what we cover, but the curious and completely new as well." Estab. 2002. Circ. 15,000. Pays on publication. Byline given. Offers 100% kill fee. Buys first world wide periodical and nonexclusive electronic rights. Editorial lead time 3-4 months. Submit seasonal material 6 months in advance. Accepts queries by mail, e-mail, fax, phone. Accepts previously published material. Responds in 1-2 weeks to queries; 1 month to mss. Sample copy for $6. Writer's guidelines online.

Nonfiction "Particularly interested in how-to spellcrafting and material for solitary pagans and wiccans." Book excerpts, essays, historical/nostalgic, how-to, humor, inspirational, interview/profile, new product, opinion, personal experience, photo feature, religious, travel. Query with or without published clips or send complete ms. Length: 1,000-4,000 words. **Pays 2¢/word minimum.** Sometimes pays expenses of writers on assignment.

Photos State availability with submission. Reviews GIF/JPEG files. Buys first world wide periodical and nonexclusive electronic rights. Negotiates payment individually; offers no additional payment for photos accepted with ms. Identification of subjects, model releases required.

Fiction Adventure, erotica, ethnic, fantasy, historical, horror, humorous, mainstream, mystery, novel excerpts, religious, romance, suspense. Does not want "faction" (fictionalized retellings of real events). Avoid gratuitous sex, violence, sentimentality and pagan moralizing. "Don't beat our readers with the Rede or the Threefold Law." **Buys 3-4 mss/year.** Send complete ms. Length: 1,000-5,000 words. **Pays 2¢/word minimum.**

Poetry Avant-garde, free verse, haiku, light verse, traditional. Submit maximum 3-5 poems. **Pays $15.**

Tips "Read the magazine, do your research, write the piece, send it in. That's really the only way to get started as a writer: everything else is window dressing."

$ PANGAIA

Earthwise Spirituality, Blessed Bee, Inc., P.O. Box 641, Point Arena CA 95468. Fax: (707)882-2793. E-mail: info@pangaia.com. Web site: www.pangaia.com. Editor: Anne Newkirk Niven. Managing Editor: Elizabeth Barrette. **50% freelance written.** Quarterly magazine of Earth spirituality covering Earth-based religions. "We publish articles pertinent to an Earth-loving readership. Mysticism, science, humor, tools all are described." Estab. 1994. Circ. 10,000. Pays on publication. Publishes ms an average of 6 months after acceptance. Byline given. Offers $10 kill fee. Buys first North American serial, electronic rights. Editorial lead time 6 months. Submit seasonal material 6 months in advance. Accepts queries by mail, e-mail. Responds in 2-8 weeks to queries. Sample copy for $5. Writer's guidelines online.

Nonfiction Book excerpts, essays, how-to, humor, inspirational, interview/profile, photo feature, religious, Reviews. Special issues: Contact editor for upcoming themes. No material on unrelated topics. **Buys 30 mss/year.** Query. Length: 500-5,000 words. **Pays 3-5¢/word.** Sometimes pays with contributor copies or other premiums rather than a cash payment if negotiated/requested by writer. Sometimes pays expenses of writers on assignment. 1¢/word.

Photos State availability with submission. Reviews 5×7 prints, GIF/JPEG files. Buys one-time rights. Negotiates payment individually. Model releases required.

Fiction Ethnic, fantasy, religious, science fiction, Pagan/Gaian. No grim or abstract stories. **Buys 5 mss/year.** Send complete ms. Length: 500-5,000 words. **Pays 3-5¢/word.**

Poetry Will consider most forms. Free verse, traditional. "Avoid clichés like the burning times. Do not send forms with rhyme/meter unless those features are executed perfectly." **Buys 12 poems/year.** Submit maximum 5 poems. Length: 3-100 lines. **$11.**

Tips "Share a spiritual insight that can enlighten others. Back up your facts with citations where relevant, and make those facts sound like the neatest thing since self-lighting charcoal. Explain how to solve a problem; offer a new way to make the world a better place. We would also like to see serious scholarship on nature religion topics, material of interest to intermediate or advanced practicioners, which is both accurate and engaging."

$ SHAMAN'S DRUM

A Journal of Experiential Shamanism, Cross-Cultural Shamanism Network, P.O. Box 270, Williams OR 97544. (541)846-1313. Fax: (541)846-1204. **Contact:** Timothy White, editor. **75% freelance written.** Quarterly educational magazine of cross-cultural shamanism. "*Shaman's Drum* seeks contributions directed toward a general but well-informed audience. Our intent is to expand, challenge, and refine our readers' and our understanding of shamanism in practice. Topics include indigenous medicineway practices, contemporary shamanic healing practices, ecstatic spiritual practices, and contemporary shamanic psychotherapies. Our overall focus is cross-cultural, but our editorial approach is culture-specific—we prefer that authors focus on specific ethnic traditions or personal practices about which they have significant firsthand experience. We are looking for examples of not only how shamanism has transformed individual lives but also practical ways it can help ensure survival of life on the planet. We want material that captures the heart and feeling of shamanism and that can inspire people to direct action and participation, and to explore shamanism in greater depth." Estab. 1985. Circ. 10,000. Publishes ms an average of 6 months after acceptance. Byline given. Buys first North American serial, first rights. Editorial lead time 1 year. Accepts previously published material. Responds in 3 months to queries. Sample copy for $7. Writer's guidelines for #10 SASE.

Nonfiction Book excerpts, essays, interview/profile (please query), opinion, personal experience, photo feature. No fiction, poetry, or fillers. **Buys 16 mss/year.** Send complete ms. Length: 5,000-8,000 words. **Pays 5¢/word, "depending on how much we have to edit."**

Reprints Send ms with rights for sale noted and information about when and where the material previously appeared. Pays 50% of amount paid for an original article.

Photos Send photos with submission. Reviews contact sheets, transparencies, All size prints. Buys one-time rights. Offers $40-50/photo. Identification of subjects required.

Columns/Departments Judy Wells, Earth Circles. Timothy White, Reviews. Earth Circles (news format, concerned with issues, events, organizations related to shamanism, indigenous peoples, and caretaking Earth); Reviews (in-depth reviews of books about shamanism or closely related subjects such as indigenous lifestyles, ethnobotany, transpersonal healing, and ecstatic spirituality), 500-1,500 words. **Buys 8 mss/year.** Query. **Pays 5¢/word.**

Tips "All articles must have a clear relationship to shamanism, but may be on topics which have not traditionally been defined as shamanic. We prefer original material that is based on, or illustrated with, first-hand knowledge and personal experience. Articles should be well documented with descriptive examples and pertinent background information. Photographs and illustrations of high quality are always welcome and can help sell articles."

$ WHOLE LIFE TIMES

6464 W. Sunset Blvd., Suite 1080, Los Angeles CA 90028. (323)464-1285. Fax: (323)464-8838. E-mail: editor@wholelifetimes.com. Web site: www.wholelifetimes.com. **Contact:** Eliza Thomas, editor-in-chief. Monthly tabloid for cultural creatives. Estab. 1979. Circ. 58,000. Pays within 1-2 months after publication. Byline given. Buys first North American serial rights. Accepts queries by mail, e-mail. Sample copy for $3. Writer's guidelines for #10 SASE.

Nonfiction Social justice, food health, alternative healing, eco-travel, political issues, spiritual, conscious business, leading-edge information, relevant celebrity profiles. Special issues: Healing Arts, Food and Nutrition, Spirituality, New Beginnings, Relationships, Longevity, Arts/Cultures Travel, Vitamins and Supplements, Women's Issues, Sexuality, Science and Metaphysics, Environment/Simple Living. **Buys 60 mss/year.** Query with published clips or send complete ms. **Payment varies.**

Reprints Send ms with rights for sale noted and information about when and where the material previously appeared. Pays 50% of amount paid for an original article.

Columns/Departments Healing; Parenting; Finance; Food; Personal Growth; Relationships; Humor; Travel; Politics; Sexuality; Spirituality; and Psychology. Length: 750-1,200 words.

Tips ''Queries should be professionally written and show an awareness of current topics of interest in our subject area. We welcome investigative reporting and are happy to see queries that address topics in a political context. We are especially looking for articles on health and nutrition. No monthly columns sought.''

AUTOMOTIVE & MOTORCYCLE

$ AMERICAN MOTORCYCLIST

American Motorcyclist Association, 13515 Yarmouth Dr., Pickerington OH 43147. (614)856-1900. Fax: (614)856-1920. E-mail: gparsons@ama-cycle.org. Web site: www.ama-cycle.org. **Contact:** Grant Parsons, managing editor. **10% freelance written.** Monthly magazine for ''enthusiastic motorcyclists investing considerable time and money in the sport. We emphasize the motorcyclist, not the vehicle.'' Estab. 1947. Circ. 260,000. Pays on publication. Byline given. Buys first North American serial rights. Editorial lead time 3 months. Submit seasonal material 4 months in advance. Accepts queries by mail, e-mail. Responds in 5 weeks to queries; 6 weeks to mss. Sample copy for $1.25. Writer's guidelines free.

Nonfiction Interview/profile (with interesting personalities in the world of motorcycling), personal experience, travel. **Buys 8 mss/year.** Query with or without published clips or send complete ms. Length: 1,000-2,500 words. **Pays minimum $8/published column inch.**

Photos Send photos with submission. Reviews transparencies, prints. Buys one-time rights. Pays $50/photo minimum. Captions, identification of subjects required.

Tips ''Our major category of freelance stories concerns motorcycling trips to interesting North American destinations. Prefers stories of a timeless nature.''

$ $ AUTO RESTORER

BowTie, Inc., 3 Burroughs, Irvine CA 92618. (949)855-8822. Fax: (949)855-3045. E-mail: tkade@fancypubs.com. Web site: www.autorestorermagazine.com. **Contact:** Ted Kade, editor. **85% freelance written.** Monthly magazine covering auto restoration. ''Our readers own old cars and they work on them. We help our readers by providing as much practical, how-to information as we can about restoration and old cars.'' Estab. 1989. Pays on publication. Publishes ms an average of 3 months after acceptance. Buys first North American serial, one-time rights. Submit seasonal material 4 months in advance. Accepts queries by mail, e-mail, fax. Responds in 2 months to queries. Sample copy for $7. Writer's guidelines free.

Nonfiction How-to (auto restoration), new product, photo feature, technical, product evaluation. **Buys 60 mss/year.** Query with or without published clips. Length: 200-2,500 words. **Pays $150/published page, including photos and illustrations.**

Photos Technical drawings that illustrate articles in black ink are welcome. Send photos with submission. Reviews contact sheets, transparencies, 5×7 prints. Offers no additional payment for photos accepted with ms.

Tips ''Query first. Interview the owner of a restored car. Present advice to others on how to do a similar restoration. Seek advice from experts. Go light on history and nonspecific details. Make it something that the magazine regularly uses. Do automotive how-tos.''

⊘ AUTOMOBILE MAGAZINE

Primedia Broad Reach Magazines, 120 E. Liberty St., 2nd Floor, Ann Arbor MI 48104. (734)994-3500. Web site: www.automobilemag.com. Editor: Gavin Conway. Monthly magazine covering automobiles. Edited for the automotive enthusiast interested in the novelty as well as the tradition of all things automotive. Circ. 644,000. Editorial lead time 6 weeks.

- Query before submitting.

N $ $ AUTOMOBILE QUARTERLY

The Connoisseur's Magazine of Motoring Today, Yesterday, and Tomorrow, Automobile Heritage Publishing & Communications LLC, 800 E. 8th St., New Albany IN 47150. Fax: (812)948-2816. Web site: www.autoquarterly.com. **85% freelance written.** Quarterly magazine covering ''automotive history, with excellent photography.'' Estab. 1962. Circ. 8,000. **Pays on acceptance.** Publishes ms an average of 1 year after acceptance. Byline given. Buys first international serial rights. Editorial lead time 9 months. Responds in 1 month to queries; 2 months to mss. Sample copy for $19.95.

Nonfiction Historical/nostalgic, photo feature, technical, biographies. **Buys 25 mss/year.** Query. Length: 2,500-5,000 words. **Pays approximately 35¢/word or more.** Sometimes pays expenses of writers on assignment.

Photos State availability with submission. Reviews 4×5; 35mm; 120 transparencies; historical prints. Buys perpetual rights of published photography per work-for-hire freelance agreement.

Tips "Please query, with clips, via snail mail. No phone calls, please. Study *Automobile Quarterly*'s unique treatment of automotive history first."

$ $ $ $ AUTOWEEK

Crain Communications, Inc., 1155 Gratiot Ave., Detroit MI 48207. (313)446-6000. Fax: (313)446-1027. Web site: www.autoweek.com. Editor: Dutch Mandel. Managing Editor: Roger Hart. **Contact:** Bob Gritzinger, news editor. 3% freelance written, all by regular contributors. Weekly magazine. "*AutoWeek* is the country's only weekly magazine for the auto enthusiast." Estab. 1958. Circ. 350,000. Pays on publication. Publishes ms an average of 1 month after acceptance. Byline given. Buys all rights. Accepts queries by mail, fax.

Nonfiction Historical/nostalgic, interview/profile. **Buys 5 mss/year.** Query. Length: 100-400 words. **Pays $1/word.**

$ $ BACKROADS

Motorcycles, Travel & Adventure, Backroads, Inc., P.O. Box 317, Branchville NJ 07826. (973)948-4176. Fax: (973)948-0823. E-mail: editor@backroadsusa.com. Web site: www.backroadsusa.com. Managing Editor: Shira Kamil. **Contact:** Brian Rathjen, editor/publisher. **80% freelance written.** Monthly tabloid covering motorcycle touring. "*Backroads* is a motorcycle tour magazine geared toward getting motorcyclists on the road and traveling. We provide interesting destinations, unique roadside attractions and eateries, plus Rip & Ride Route Sheets. We cater to all brands. If you really ride, you need *Backroads*." Estab. 1995. Circ. 40,000. Pays on publication. Byline given. Buys one-time rights. Editorial lead time 1 month. Submit seasonal material 3 months in advance. Accepts queries by mail, e-mail, fax. Sample copy for $4. Writer's guidelines online.

Nonfiction Shira Kamil, editor/publisher. Essays (motorcycle/touring), new product, opinion, personal experience, travel. "No long diatribes on 'How I got into motorcycles.' " Query. Length: 500-2,500 words. **Pays 10¢/word minimum for assigned articles; 5¢/word minimum for unsolicited articles.** Pays writers contributor copies or other premiums for short pieces.

Photos Send photos with submission. Offers no additional payment for photos accepted with ms.

Columns/Departments We're Outta Here (weekend destinations), 500-750 words; Great All-American Diner Run (good eateries with great location), 300-800 words; Thoughts from the Road (personal opinion/insights), 250-500 words; Mysterious America (unique and obscure sights), 300-800 words; Big City Getaway (day trips), 500-750 words. **Buys 20-24 mss/year.** Query. **Pays $75/article.**

Fillers Facts, newsbreaks. Length: 100-250 words.

Tips "We prefer destination-oriented articles in a light, layman's format, with photos (digital images on CD). Stay away from any name-dropping and first-person references."

$ $ $ ✪ CANADIAN BIKER MAGAZINE

735 Market St., Victoria BC V8T 2E2 Canada. (250)384-0333. Fax: (250)384-1832. E-mail: edit@canadianbiker.com. Web site: canadianbiker.com. **Contact:** John Campbell, editor. **65% freelance written.** Magazine covering motorcycling. "A family-oriented motorcycle magazine whose purpose is to unite Canadian motorcyclists from coast to coast through the dissemination of information in a non-biased, open forum. The magazine reports on new product, events, touring, racing, vintage and custom motorcycling as well as new industry information." Estab. 1980. Circ. 20,000. Publishes ms an average of 1 year after acceptance. Byline given. Buys first rights. Editorial lead time 3 months. Accepts queries by mail, e-mail, fax, phone. Responds in 6 weeks to queries; 6 months to mss. Sample copy for $5 or online. Writer's guidelines free.

Nonfiction All nonfiction must include photos and/or illustrations. General interest, historical/nostalgic, how-to, interview/profile (Canadian personalities preferred), new product, technical, travel. **Buys 12 mss/year.** Query with or without published clips or send complete ms. Length: 500-1,500 words. **Pays $100-200 for assigned articles; $80-150 for unsolicited articles.**

Photos State availability of or send photos with submission. Reviews 4×4 transparencies, 3×5 prints. Buys one-time rights. Negotiates payment individually. Captions, identification of subjects, model releases required.

Tips "We're looking for more racing features, rider profiles, custom sport bikes, quality touring stories, 'extreme' riding articles. Contact editor first before writing anything. Have original ideas, an ability to write from an authoritative point of view, and an ability to supply quality photos to accompany text. Writers should be involved in the motorcycle industry and be intimately familiar with some aspect of the industry which would be of interest to readers. Observations of the industry should be current, timely, and informative."

$$$$ CAR AND DRIVER

Hachette Filipacchi Magazines, Inc., 2002 Hogback Rd., Ann Arbor MI 48105-9795. (734)971-3600. Fax: (734)971-9188. E-mail: editors@caranddriver.com. Web site: www.caranddriver.com. Monthly magazine for auto enthusiasts; college-educated, professional, median 24-35 years of age. Estab. 1956. Circ. 1,300,000. **Pays on acceptance.** Byline given. Offers 25% kill fee. Buys first North American serial rights. Accepts queries by mail, e-mail, fax. Responds in 2 months to queries.

Nonfiction Seek stories about people and trends, including racing. Two recent freelance purchases include news-feature on cities across America banning "cruising" and feature on how car companies create "new car smells." All road tests are staff-written. "Unsolicited manuscripts are not accepted. Query letters must be addressed to the Managing Editor. Rates are generous, but few manuscripts are purchased from outside." **Buys 1 mss/year. Pays max $3,000/feature; $750-1,500/short piece.** Pays expenses of writers on assignment.

Photos Color slides and b&w photos sometimes purchased with accompanying ms.

Tips "It is best to start off with an interesting query and to stay away from nuts-and-bolts ideas because that will be handled in-house or by an acknowledged expert. Our goal is to be absolutely without flaw in our presentation of automotive facts, but we strive to be every bit as entertaining as we are informative. We do not print this sort of story: 'My Dad's Wacky, Lovable Beetle.' "

N CAR CRAFT

Primedia Enthusiast Group, 6420 Wilshire Blvd., Los Angeles CA 90048-5502. (323)782-2000. Fax: (323)782-2223. E-mail: carcraft@primedia.com. Web site: www.carcraft.com. Editor-in-Chief: David Freiburger. **Contact:** Douglas R. Glad, editor. Monthly magazine. Created to appeal to drag racing and high performance auto owners. Circ. 383,334. Editorial lead time 3 months.

N $$$ CELEBRITY CAR MAGAZINE

duPont Publishing, Inc., 3051 Tech Dr., St. Petersburg FL 33716. (727)573-9339. Fax: (727)489-0279. E-mail: dkenny@dupontregistry.com. Web site: www.dupontregistry.com. **Contact:** David Kenny, editor-in-chief. **90% freelance written.** Quarterly magazine covering celebrities and cars. "*Celebrity Car* is about automotive style and access to a world of exciting cars, offering insight into the celebrities and their automobiles. *Celebrity Car* profiles the automobile collections of musicians, athletes, movie and television stars and industry personalities—all with a passion for cars—in full-color photographs with their vehicles." Estab. 2003. Circ. 120,000. **Pays on acceptance.** Publishes ms an average of 2 months after acceptance. Byline given. Offers $100 kill fee. Makes work-for-hire assignments. Editorial lead time 2 months. Accepts queries by e-mail. Sample copy for free. Writer's guidelines free

Nonfiction Interview/profile, automotive luxury. Query. Length: 750-1,000 words. **Pays $750.** Sometimes pays expenses of writers on assignment.

$$ CLASSIC TRUCKS

Primedia/McMullen Argus Publishing, 774 S. Placentia Ave., Placentia CA 92870. E-mail: rob.fortier@primedia.com. Web site: www.classictrucks.com. **Contact:** Rob Fortier, editor. Monthly magazine covering classic trucks from the 1930s to 1973. Estab. 1994. Circ. 60,000. Pays on publication. Byline given. Buys first North American serial rights. Editorial lead time 4 months. Submit seasonal material 4 months in advance. Writer's guidelines free.

Nonfiction How-to, interview/profile, new product, technical, travel. Query. Length: 1,500-5,000 words. **Pays $75-200/page; $100/page maximum for unsolicited articles.**

Photos Send photos with submission. Reviews transparencies, 5×7 prints. Buys one-time rights. Negotiates payment individually. Captions, identification of subjects, model releases required.

Columns/Departments Buys 24 mss/year. Query.

$$$ FOUR WHEELER MAGAZINE

6420 Wilshire Blvd., Los Angeles CA 90048. E-mail: fourwheelereditor@primedia.com. Web site: www.fourwheeler.com. **Contact:** Douglas McColloch, editorial director. **20% freelance written.** Works with a small number of new/unpublished writers each year. Monthly magazine covering four-wheel-drive vehicles, back-country driving, competition, and travel adventure. Estab. 1963. Circ. 355,466. Pays on publication. Publishes ms an average of 4 months after acceptance. Buys all rights. Submit seasonal material 4 months in advance. Accepts queries by mail. Sample copy not available.

Nonfiction 4WD competition and travel/adventure articles, technical, how-tos, and vehicle features about unique four-wheel drives. "We like the adventure stories that bring four wheeling to life in word and photo: mud-running deserted logging roads, exploring remote, isolated trails or hunting/fishing where the 4×4 is a necessity for success." Query with photos. Length: 1,200-2,000 words; average 4-5 pages when published. **Pays $200-300/feature vehicles; $350-600/travel and adventure; $100-800/technical articles.**

Photos Requires professional quality color slides and b&w prints for every article. Prefers Kodachrome 64 or Fujichrome 50 in 35mm or 2¼ formats. "Action shots a must for all vehicle features and travel articles." Captions required.
Tips "Show us you know how to use a camera as well as the written word. The easiest way for a new writer/photographer to break into our magazine is to read several issues of the magazine, then query with a short vehicle feature that will show his or her potential as a creative writer/photographer."

$ $ ⊘ FRICTION ZONE

Motorcycle Travel and Information, 60166 Hop Patch Spring Rd., Mountain Center CA 92561. (909)659-9500. E-mail: editor@friction-zone.com. Web site: www.friction-zone.com. **60% freelance written.** Monthly magazine covering motorcycles. Estab. 1999. Circ. 26,000. Pays on publication. Publishes ms an average of 1 month after acceptance. Byline given. Buys first North American serial rights. Editorial lead time 6 weeks. Submit seasonal material 2 months in advance. Sample copy for $4.50 or on Web site.
Nonfiction General interest, historical/nostalgic, how-to, humor, inspirational, interview/profile, new product, opinion, photo feature, technical, travel, medical (relating to motorcyclists), book reviews (relating to motorcyclists). Does not accept first-person writing. **Buys 1 mss/year.** Query. Length: 1,000-3,000 words. **Pays 20¢/word.** Sometimes pays expenses of writers on assignment.
Photos Send photos with submission. Reviews negatives, slides. Buys one-time rights. Offers $15/published photo. Captions, identification of subjects, model releases required.
Columns/Departments Health Zone (health issues relating to motorcyclists); Motorcycle Engines 101 (basic motorcycle mechanics); Road Trip (California destination review including hotel, road, restaurant), all 2,000 words. **Buys 60 mss/year.** Query. **Pays 20¢/word.**
Fiction "We want stories concerning motorcycling or motorcyclists. No 'first-person' fiction." Query. Length: 1,000-2,000 words. **Pays 20¢/word.**
Fillers Anecdotes, facts, gags to be illustrated by cartoonist, newsbreaks, short humor. Length: 2,000-3,000 words. **Pays 20¢/word.**
Tips "Query via e-mail with sample writing. Visit our Web site for more detailed guidelines."

⊘ HOT ROD MAGAZINE

Primedia Enthusiast Group, 6420 Wilshire Bvld., Los Angeles CA 90048-5515. (323)782-2000. Fax: (323)782-2223. E-mail: hotrod@primedia.com. Web site: www.hotrod.com. Editor: David Freiburger. Monthly magazine covering hot rods. Focuses on 50s and 60s cars outfitted with current drive trains and the nostalgia associated with them. Circ. 700,000. Editorial lead time 3 months.

- Query before submitting.

$ $ IN THE WIND

Paisano Publications, LLC, P.O. Box 3000, Agoura Hills CA 91376-3000. (818)889-8740. Fax: (818)889-1252. E-mail: photos@easyriders.net. Web site: www.easyriders.com. Editor: Kim Peterson. **50% freelance written.** Quarterly magazine. "Geared toward the custom (primarily Harley-Davidson) motorcycle rider and enthusiast, *In the Wind* is driven by candid pictorial-action photos of bikes being ridden, and events." Estab. 1978. Circ. 90,000. Pays on publication. Publishes ms an average of 9 months after acceptance. Byline given. Buys all rights. Editorial lead time 6 months. Accepts queries by mail, e-mail. Responds in 2 weeks to queries; 2 months to mss. Sample copy not available.
Nonfiction Photo feature, event coverage. No long-winded tech articles. **Buys 6 mss/year.** Length: 750-1,000 words. **Pays $250-600.** Sometimes pays expenses of writers on assignment.
Photos Send SASE for return. Send photos with submission. Reviews transparencies, digital images, b&w, color prints. Buys all rights. Identification of subjects, model releases, on obviously posed and partially nude photos, required.
Tips "Know the subject. Looking for submissions from people who ride their own bikes."

⊘ LATINOS ON WHEELS

On Wheels, Inc., 585 E. Larned St., Suite 100, Detroit MI 48226-4369. (313)963-2209. Fax: (313)963-7778. E-mail: editor@onwheelsinc.com. Web site: www.onwheelsinc.com/lowmagazine. Editor: Valerie Menard. Quarterly magazine. Supplement to leading Latino newspapers in the US. Provides Latino car buyers and car enthusiasts with the most relevant automotive trends. Circ. 500,000.

- Query before submitting.

⊘ LOWRIDER MAGAZINE

Primedia Enthusiast Group, 2400 E. Katella Ave., 11th Floor, Anaheim CA 92806. E-mail: ralph.fuentes@primedia.com. Web site: www.lowridermagazine.com. Editor: Ralph Fuentes. Monthly magazine covering the national and international lowriding scene with high impact, full-color vehicle and event features. Circ. 212,500. Editorial lead time 3 months.

- Query before submitting.

MOTOR TREND

Primedia, 6420 Wilshire Blvd., 7th Floor, Los Angeles CA 90048. Web site: www.motortrend.com. **5-10% freelance written.** Only works with published/established writers. Monthly magazine for automotive enthusiasts and general interest consumers. Estab. 1949. Circ. 1,250,000. Publishes ms an average of 3 months after acceptance. Buys all rights. Accepts queries by mail. Responds in 1 month to queries. Sample copy not available.

Nonfiction "Automotive and related subjects that have national appeal. Emphasis on domestic and imported cars, road tests, driving impressions, auto classics, auto, travel, racing, and high-performance features for the enthusiast. Packed with facts. Freelancers should confine queries to photo-illustrated exotic drives and other feature material; road tests and related activity are handled in house. A fact-filled query is suggested for all freelancers."

Photos Buys photos of prototype cars and assorted automotive matter.

NEW ZEALAND 4WD

Adrenalin Publishing Ltd., P.O. Box 65-092, Mairangi Bay Auckland New Zealand. (64)(9)478-4771. Fax: (64)(9)478-4779. E-mail: editor@nz4wd.co.nz. Web site: www.nz4wd.co.nz. **Contact:** John Oxley, editor. Magazine published 11 times/year covering topics of interest to 4WD vehicle buyers and drivers, including vehicle selection, accessories/upgrading, 4WD clubs/sports, lifestyle activities associated with 4WD, adventure and track stories, and technical articles. Estab. 1996.

- Query before submitting.

OUTLAW BIKER

Art & Ink Enterprises, Inc., 820 Hamilton St., #C-6, Charlotte NC 28206. (704)333-3331. Fax: (704)333-3433. E-mail: inked@skinartmag.com. Web site: www.outlawbiker.com. **50% freelance written.** Magazine published 4 times/year covering bikers and their lifestyle. "All writers must be insiders of biker lifestyle. Features include coverage of biker events, profiles, and humor." Estab. 1983. Circ. 150,000. Pays on publication. Publishes ms an average of 3 months after acceptance. Byline given. Buys first rights. Editorial lead time 3 months. Submit seasonal material 5 months in advance. Accepts queries by mail, e-mail, fax. Accepts previously published material. Accepts simultaneous submissions. Responds in 2 weeks to queries; 2 months to mss. Sample copy for $5.98. Writer's guidelines for #10 SASE.

Nonfiction Historical/nostalgic, humor, new product, personal experience, photo feature, travel. Special issues: Daytona Special, Sturgis Special (annual bike runs). "No first time experiences—our readers already know." **Buys 10-12 mss/year.** Send complete ms. Length: 100-1,000 words.

Photos Send photos with submission. Reviews transparencies, prints. Buys one-time rights. Offers $0-10/photo. Captions, identification of subjects, model releases required.

Columns/Departments Buys 10-12 mss/year. Send complete ms.

Fiction Adventure, erotica, fantasy, historical, humorous, romance, science fiction, slice-of-life vignettes, suspense. No racism. **Buys 10-12 mss/year.** Send complete ms. Length: 500-2,500 words.

Poetry Avant-garde, free verse, haiku, light verse, traditional. **Buys 10-12 poems/year.** Submit maximum 12 poems. Length: 2-1,000 lines.

Fillers Anecdotes, facts, gags to be illustrated by cartoonist, newsbreaks, short humor. **Buys 10-12/year.** Length: 500-2,000 words.

Tips "Writers must be insiders of the biker lifestyle. Manuscripts with accompanying photographs as art are given higher priority."

PETERSEN'S CUSTOM CLASSIC TRUCKS

Primedia Enthusiast Group, 774 S. Placentia Ave., Placentia CA 92870. E-mail: brian.smith@primedia.com. Web site: www.customclassictrucks.com. **Contact:** D. Brian Smith, editor. Bimonthly magazine. Contains a compilation of technical articles, historical reviews, coverage of top vintage truck events and features dedicated to the fast growing segment of the truck market that includes vintage pickups and sedan deliveries. Circ. 104,376.

POPULAR HOT RODDING

Primedia Enthusiast Group, 774 S. Placentia Ave., Placentia CA 92870. E-mail: johnny.hunkins@primedia.com. Web site: www.popularhotrodding.com. Editor: John Hunkins. Monthly magazine for the automotive enthusiast; highlights features that emphasize performance, bolt-on accessories, replacement parts, safety, and the sport of drag racing. Circ. 182,000.

- Query before submitting.

$ $ RIDER MAGAZINE

Ehlert Publishing Group, 2575 Vista Del Mar Dr., Ventura CA 93001. E-mail: editor@ridermagazine.com. Web site: www.ridermagazine.com. **Contact:** Mark Tuttle, editor. **60% freelance written.** Monthly magazine covering motorcycling. "*Rider* serves the all-brand motorcycle lifestyle/enthusiast with a slant toward travel and touring." Estab. 1974. Circ. 127,000. Pays on publication. Publishes ms an average of 6-12 months after acceptance. Byline given. Offers 25% kill fee. Buys first North American serial, electronic rights. Editorial lead time 3 months. Submit seasonal material 6 months in advance. Accepts queries by mail. Responds in 2 months to queries. Sample copy for $2.95. Writer's guidelines by e-mail.

- "The articles we do buy often share the following characteristics: 1) The writer queried us in advance by regular mail (not by telephone or e-mail) to see if we needed or wanted the story; 2) The story was well written and of proper length; 3) The story had sharp, uncluttered photos taken with the proper film—*Rider* does not buy stories without photos."

Nonfiction General interest, historical/nostalgic, how-to, humor, interview/profile, personal experience, travel. Does not want to see "fiction or articles on 'How I Began Motorcycling.' " **Buys 40-50 mss/year.** Query. Length: 750-1,800 words. **Pays $150-750.**

Photos Send photos with submission. Reviews contact sheets, transparencies, high quality prints, high resolution (4MP+) digital images. Buys one-time and electronic rights. Offers no additional payment for photos accepted with ms. Captions required.

Columns/Departments Favorite Rides (short trip), 850-1,100 words. **Buys 12 mss/year.** Query. **Pays $150-750.**

Tips "We rarely accept manuscripts without photos (slides or b&w prints). Query first. Follow guidelines available on request. We are most open to favorite rides, feature stories (must include excellent photography) and material for 'Rides, Rallies and Clubs.' Include a map, information on routes, local attractions, restaurants, and scenery in favorite ride submissions."

$ $ ROAD KING

Parthenon Publishing, 28 White Bridge Rd., Suite 209, Nashville TN 37205. Fax: (615)627-2197. Web site: www.roadking.com. **Contact:** Nancy Henderson, managing editor. **25% freelance written.** Bimonthly magazine covering the trucking industry. Pays 3 weeks from acceptance. Publishes ms an average of 3 months after acceptance. Byline given. Offers 30% kill fee. Buys first North American serial, all electronic rights. Editorial lead time 3-4 months. Submit seasonal material 4 months in advance. Accepts queries by mail, fax. Accepts simultaneous submissions. Responds in 3-4 weeks to queries. Sample copy for #10 SASE. Writer's guidelines free.

Nonfiction Book excerpts, general interest, how-to, new product, health. **Buys 12 mss/year.** Query with published clips. Length: 100-1,000 words. **Pays $50-500.** Pays expenses of writers on assignment.

Photos Michael Nott, art director. Send photos with submission. Negotiates payment individually.

$ $ ROADBIKE

TAM Communications, 1010 Summer St., Stamford CT 06905. (203)425-8777. Fax: (203)425-8775. E-mail: ericp@roadbikemag.com. **Contact:** Eric Putter, editor. **40% freelance written.** Monthly magazine covering motorcycling tours, project and custom bikes, products, news, and tech. Estab. 1993. Circ. 50,000. Pays on publication. Publishes ms an average of 6 months after acceptance. Byline given. Editorial lead time 4 months. Submit seasonal material 6 months in advance. Accepts queries by mail, e-mail, fax. Writer's guidelines free.

Nonfiction How-to (motorcycle tech, travel, camping), interview/profile (motorcycle related), new product, photo feature (motorcycle events or gathering places with maximum of 1,000 words text), travel. No fiction. **Buys 100 mss/year.** Query with or without published clips or send complete ms. Length: 1,000-2,500 words. **Pays $15-400.**

Photos Send photos with submission (high resolution digital images only). Buys one-time rights. Offers no additional payment for photos accepted with ms. Captions required.

Fillers Facts.

⊘ SPORT COMPACT CAR

Primedia Enthusiast Group, 2400 E. Katella Ave., 11th Floor, Anaheim CA 92806. (714)939-2584. Web site: www.sportcompactcarweb.com. Editor: Edward Loh. Monthly magazine for owners and potential buyers of new compacts who seek inside information regarding performance, personalization, and cosmetic enhancement of the vehicles. Circ. 117,000. Editorial lead time 4 months.

- Query before submitting.

SPORT RIDER

Primedia Enthusiast Group, 6420 Wilshire Blvd., Los Angeles CA 90048. (323)782-2584. Fax: (323)782-2372. E-mail: srmail@primedia.com. Web site: www.sportrider.com. Bimonthly magazine for enthusiast of sport/street motercycles and emphasizes performance, both in the motorcycle and the rider. Circ. 108,365.

- Query before submitting.

SPORT TRUCK

Primedia Enthusiast Group, 774 S. Placentia Ave., Suite 700, Placentia CA 92806. E-mail: mike.finnegan@primedia.com. Web site: www.sporttruck.com. Editor: Mike Finnegan. Monthly magazine. Covers the entire range of light duty trucks and sport utility vehicles with an emphasis on performance and personalization. Circ. 200,357.

SUPER CHEVY

Primedia Enthusiast Group, 774 S. Placentia Ave., Placentia CA 92870. (714)939-2540. E-mail: terry.cole@primedia.com. Web site: www.superchevy-web.com. Editor: Terry Cole. Monthly magazine covering various forms of motorsports where Cheverolet cars and engines are in competition. Circ. 198,995.

- Query before submitting.

TRUCK TREND

The SUV & Pickup Authority, Primedia, 260 Madison Ave., 8th Floor, New York NY 10016. (212)726-4300. Web site: www.trucktrend.com. **Contact:** Mark Williams, editor. **60% freelance written.** Bimonthly magazine covering light trucks, SUVs, minivans, vans, and travel. "*Truck Trend* readers want to know about what's new in the world of sport-utilities, pickups, and vans. What to buy, how to fix up, and where to go." Estab. 1998. Circ. 125,000. Pays on publication. Publishes ms an average of 3 months after acceptance. Byline given. Buys all rights. Editorial lead time 5 months. Submit seasonal material 6 months in advance. Accepts queries by mail. Sample copy for #10 SASE. Writer's guidelines not available.

Nonfiction How-to, travel. **Buys 12 mss/year.** Query. Length: 500-1,800 words.

Photos Send photos with submission. Reviews transparencies. Buys all rights. Offers no additional payment for photos accepted with ms. Captions, identification of subjects, model releases required.

The online magazine carries original content not found in the print edition.

Tips "Know the subject/audience. Start by using a previous story as a template. Call the editor for advice after flushing out the story. Understand the editor is looking for freelancers to make life easier."

$ TRUCKIN'

Primedia Enthusiast Group, 2400 E. Katella Ave., Suite 700, Anaheim CA 92806. Fax: (714)978-6390. Web site: www.truckinweb.com. Editor: Steve Warner. Monthly magazine. Written for pickup drivers and enthusiasts. Circ. 186,606. Editorial lead time 3 months.

AVIATION

$ $ $ $ AIR & SPACE MAGAZINE

Smithsonian Institution, P.O. Box 37012, MRC 951, Washington DC 20013-7012. (202)275-1230. Fax: (202)275-1886. E-mail: editors@si.edu. Web site: www.airspacemag.com. **Contact:** Paul Hoversten (features); Patricia Trenner, senior editor (departments). **80% freelance written.** Bimonthly magazine covering aviation and aerospace for a nontechnical audience. "The emphasis is on the human rather than the technological, on the ideas behind the events. Features are slanted to a technically curious, but not necessarily technically knowledgeable, audience. We are looking for unique angles to aviation/aerospace stories, history, events, personalities, current and future technologies, that emphasize the human-interest aspect." Estab. 1985. Circ. 225,000. **Pays on acceptance.** Byline given. Offers kill fee. Buys first North American serial rights. Accepts queries by mail, e-mail, fax. Responds in 3 months to queries. Sample copy for $7. Writer's guidelines online.

"We're looking for 'reader service' articles—a collection of helpful hints and interviews with experts that would help our readers enjoy their interest in aviation. An example: An article telling readers how they could learn more about the space shuttle, where to visit, how to invite an astronaut to speak to their schools, what books are most informative, etc. A good place to break in is our 'Soundings' department."

Nonfiction The editors are actively seeking stories covering space and general or business aviation. Book excerpts, essays, general interest (on aviation/aerospace), historical/nostalgic, humor, photo feature, technical. **Buys 50 mss/year.** Query with published clips. Length: 1,500-3,000 words. **Pays $1,500-3,000.** Pays expenses of writers on assignment.
Photos Refuses unsolicited material. State availability with submission. Reviews 35 mm transparencies, digital files.
Columns/Departments Above and Beyond (first person), 1,500-2,000 words; Flights and Fancy (whimsy), approximately 800 words. Soundings (brief items, timely but not breaking news), 500-700 words. **Buys 25 mss/year.** Query with published clips. **Pays $150-300.**
Tips "We continue to be interested in stories about space exploration. Also, writing should be clear, accurate, and engaging. It should be free of technical and insider jargon, and generous with explanation and background. The first step every aspiring contributor should take is to study recent issues of the magazine."

N 🌐 AUSTRALIAN FLYING

Yaffa Publishing, 17-21 Bellevue St., Surry Hills NSW 2010 Australia. (61)(2)9281-2333. Fax: (61)(2)9281-2750. E-mail: shelleyross@yaffa.com.au. Web site: www.yaffa.com.au. Bimonthly magazine offering hands-on tips to better flying as well as the latest technologies, accessories and techniques, and all the relevant news that affects the day to day operation of the industry.
Nonfiction General interest, how-to, interview/profile, new product, technical. Query.

N $ AUTOPILOT MAGAZINE

The AutoPilot Franchise Systems, 1954 Airport Rd., Suite 250, Atlanta GA 30341. (770)422-1505. Fax: (770)255-1016. E-mail: scaddell@autopilotmagazine.com. Web site: www.autopilotmagazine.com. Editor: Brenda Tran. **Contact:** Sallie Caddell and Elizabeth Partridge, managing editors. **70% freelance written.** Bimonthly magazine covering aviation. "*AutoPilot Magazine* is a lifestyle magazine for the aviation enthusiast. We currently have four editions circulating, including Alabama, Georgia, Florida and the Mid-Atlantic region. This magazine differs from other aviation publications, because its focus is specifically on the pilot." Estab. 2000. Circ. 90,000 for all four editions. **Pays on acceptance.** Byline given. Buys second serial (reprint) rights. Editorial lead time 2-3 weeks. Accepts queries by mail, e-mail, fax, phone. Sample copy for free. Writer's guidelines free
Nonfiction Book excerpts, essays, historical/nostalgic, personal experience, photo feature, travel. Query. Length: 500-900 words. **Pays $100.**
Columns/Departments Airport Spotlight (general aviation airports), 500-800 words; Pilot Profiles, 500-800 words; Notable Aviation Organizations, 900 words; Aviation Museums, 900 words; Aviation Memorials, 600 words. **Pays $100.**
Fillers Anecdotes.
Tips "Please e-mail with a current résumé and 2 writing samples."

$ $ AVIATION HISTORY

Weider History Group, 741 Miller Dr., SE, Suite D-2, Leesburg VA 20175-8920. (703)771-9400. Fax: (703)779-8345. Web site: www.thehistorynet.com. **95% freelance written.** Bimonthly magazine covering military and civilian aviation from first flight to the jet age. It aims to make aeronautical history not only factually accurate and complete, but also enjoyable to a varied subscriber and newsstand audience. Estab. 1990. Circ. 60,000. Pays on publication. Publishes ms an average of 2 years after acceptance. Byline given. Buys all rights. Editorial lead time 6 months. Submit seasonal material 1 year in advance. Accepts queries by mail, e-mail, fax. Accepts simultaneous submissions. Responds in 3 months to queries; 6 months to mss. Sample copy for $5. Writer's guidelines for #10 SASE or online.
Nonfiction Historical/nostalgic, interview/profile, personal experience. **Buys 24 mss/year.** Query. Length: Feature articles should be 3,500-4,000 words, each with a 500-word sidebar, author's biography, and book suggestions for further reading. **Pays $300.**
Photos State availability of art and photos with submissions, cite sources. "We'll order." Reviews contact sheets, negatives, transparencies. Buys one-time rights. Identification of subjects required.
Columns/Departments People and Planes; Enduring Heritage; Aerial Oddities; Art of Flight, all 2,000 words. **Pays $150**. Book reviews, 300-750 words, **pays minimum $40.**
Tips "Choose stories with strong art possibilities. Include a hard copy as well as an IBM- or Macintosh-compatible floppy disk. Write an entertaining, informative, and unusual story that grabs the reader's attention and holds it. All stories must be true. We do not publish fiction or poetry."

N $ BALLOON LIFE

9 Madeline Ave., Westport CT 06880. (203)629-1241. E-mail: bill_armstrong@balloonlife.com. Web site: www.balloonlife.com. **Contact:** Bill Armstrong. **75% freelance written.** Monthly magazine covering sport of hot air

ballooning. "Readers participate as pilots, crew, and official observers at events and spectators." Estab. 1986. Circ. 7,000. Pays on publication. Publishes ms an average of 3-4 months after acceptance. Byline given. Offers 50-100% kill fee. Buys first North American serial rights. Submit seasonal material 4 months in advance. Accepts queries by mail, e-mail. Accepts simultaneous submissions. Responds in 2 weeks to queries. Sample copy for 9×12 SAE with $2 postage. Writer's guidelines online.

Nonfiction Book excerpts, general interest, how-to (flying hot air balloons, equipment techniques), interview/profile, new product, technical, events/rallies, safety seminars, balloon clubs/organizations, letters to the editor. **Buys 150 mss/year.** Query with or without published clips or send complete ms. Length: 1,000-1,500 words. **Pays $50-200.**

Photos Send photos with submission. Reviews transparencies, prints, high-resolution digital images. Buys nonexclusive, all rights. Offers $15/inside photos, $50/cover. Captions, identification of subjects required.

Columns/Departments Crew Quarters (devoted to some aspect of crewing), 900 words; Preflight (a news and information column), 300-500 words; **pays $50**. Logbook (balloon events that have taken place in last 3-4 months), 300-500 words; **pays $20**. **Buys 60 mss/year.** Send complete ms.

Tips "This magazine slants toward the technical side of ballooning. We are interested in articles that help to educate and provide safety information. Also stories with manufacturers, important individuals, and/or historic events and technological advances important to ballooning. The magazine attempts to present how-to articles on flying, business opportunities, weather, equipment, etc. Both our feature stories and Logbook sections are where most manuscripts are purchased."

$ $ CESSNA OWNER MAGAZINE

Jones Publishing, Inc., N7450 Aanstad Rd., P.O. Box 5000, Iola WI 54945. (715)445-5000. Fax: (715)445-4053. E-mail: carie@cessnaowner.org. Web site: www.cessnaowner.org. **Contact:** Stacy Ganzer, editor. **50% freelance written.** Monthly magazine covering Cessna single and twin-engine aircraft. "*Cessna Owner Magazine* is the official publication of the Cessna Owner Organization (C.O.O.). Therefore, our readers are Cessna aircraft owners, renters, pilots, and enthusiasts. Articles should deal with buying/selling, flying, maintaining, or modifying Cessnas. The purpose of our magazine is to promote safe, fun, and affordable flying." Estab. 1975. Circ. 6,000. Pays on publication. Publishes ms an average of 3 months after acceptance. Byline given. Buys first, one-time, second serial (reprint) rights, makes work-for-hire assignments. Editorial lead time 1 month. Submit seasonal material 3 months in advance. Accepts queries by mail, e-mail, fax, phone. Accepts previously published material. Responds in 2 weeks to queries; 1 month to mss. Sample copy and writer's guidelines free or on Web site.

Nonfiction "We are always looking for articles about Cessna aircraft modifications. We also need articles on Cessna twin-engine aircraft. April, July, and October are always big issues for us because we attend various airshows during these months and distribute free magazines. Feature articles on unusual, highly modified, or vintage Cessnas are especially welcome during these months. Good photos are also a must." Historical/nostalgic (of specific Cessna models), how-to (aircraft repairs and maintenance), new product, personal experience, photo feature, technical (aircraft engines and airframes). Special issues: Engines (maintenance, upgrades); Avionics (purchasing, new products). **Buys 48 mss/year.** Query. Length: 1,500-2,000 words. **Pays 12¢/word.**

Reprints Send mss via e-mail with rights for sale noted and information about when and where the material previously appeared.

Photos Send photos with submission. Reviews 3×5 and larger prints. Captions, identification of subjects required.

FLYING MAGAZINE

Hachette Filipacchi Media U.S., Inc., 1633 Broadway, 45th Floor, New York NY 10019. (212)767-6000. Fax: (212)767-4932. E-mail: flyedit@hfmus.com. Web site: www.flyingmag.com. Monthly magazine covering aviation. Edited for active pilots through coverage of new product development and application in the general aviation market. Estab. 1927. Circ. 277,875. Editorial lead time 3 months. Accepts queries by mail, e-mail, fax. Sample copy for $4.99.

- *Flying* is almost entirely staff written; use of freelance material is limited.

Nonfiction "We are looking for the most unusual and best-written material that suits *Flying*. Most subjects in aviation have already been done so fresher ideas and approaches to stories are particularly valued. We buy 'I Learned About Flying From That' articles, as well as an occasional feature with and without photographs supplied." Send complete ms.

$ $ ⊘ GENERAL AVIATION NEWS

Flyer Media, Inc., P.O. Box 39099, Lakewood WA 98439-0099. (888)333-5937. Fax: (253)471-9911. E-mail: janice@generalaviationnews.com. Web site: www.generalaviationnews.com. **Contact:** Janice Wood, editor. **30% freelance written.** Prefers to work with published/established writers who are pilots. Biweekly tabloid covering general, regional, national, and international aviation stories of interest to pilots, aircraft owners, and aviation enthusiasts. Estab. 1949. Circ. 35,000. Pays 1 month after publication. Publishes ms an average of 3 months after acceptance. Byline given. Buys first North American serial, second serial (reprint) rights. Submit seasonal material 6 months in advance. Accepts queries by mail, e-mail, fax, phone. Responds in 2 months to queries. Sample copy for $3.50. Writer's guidelines online.

- Always query first. Unsolicited mss will not be considered.
- O→ Break in by having "an aviation background, including a pilot's license, being up to date on current events, and being able to write. A 1,000-word story with good photos is the best way to see your name in print."

Nonfiction "News is covered by our staff. What we're looking for from freelancers is personality features, including stories of people who use their aircraft in an unusual way, builder and pilot reports, and historical features." **Buys 100 mss/year.** Query with published clips. Length: 500-2,000 words. **Pays $75-500.** Sometimes pays expenses of writers on assignment.

Photos Shoot clear, up-close photos, preferably color prints or slides. Send photos with submission. Payment negotiable. Captions, identification of subjects required.

Tips "The longer the story, the less likely it is to be accepted. If you are covering controversy, send us both sides of the story. Most of our features and news stories are assigned in response to a query."

$ $ PIPERS MAGAZINE

Jones Publishing, Inc., N7450 Aanstad Rd., P.O. Box 5000, Iola WI 54945. (715)445-5000. Fax: (715)445-4053. E-mail: carie@piperowner.org. Web site: www.piperowner.org. **Contact:** Stacy Ganzer, editor. **50% freelance written.** Monthly magazine covering Piper single and twin engine aircraft. "*Pipers Magazine* is the official publication of the Piper Owner Society (P.O.S). Therefore, our readers are Piper aircraft owners, renters, pilots, mechanics, and enthusiasts. Articles should deal with buying/selling, flying, maintaining, or modifying Pipers. The purpose of our magazine is to promote safe, fun and affordable flying." Estab. 1988. Circ. 5,000. Pays on publication. Publishes ms an average of 3 months after acceptance. Buys first, one-time, second serial (reprint) rights, makes work-for-hire assignments. Editorial lead time 1 month. Submit seasonal material 3 months in advance. Accepts queries by mail, e-mail, fax, phone. Accepts previously published material. Responds in 2 weeks to queries; 1 month to mss. Sample copy for free. Writer's guidelines free.

Nonfiction "We are always looking for articles about Piper aircraft modifications. We also are in need of articles on Piper twin engine aircraft, and late-model Pipers. April, July, and October are always big issues for us, because we attend airshows during these months and distribute free magazines." Feature articles on unusual, highly-modified, vintage, late-model, or ski/float equipped Pipers are especially welcome. Good photos are a must. Historical/nostalgic (of specific models of Pipers), how-to (aircraft repairs and maintenance), new product, personal experience, photo feature, technical (aircraft engines and airframes). **Buys 48 mss/year.** Query. Length: 1,500-2,000 words. **Pays 12¢/word.**

Reprints Send mss by e-mail with rights for sale noted and information about when and where the material previously appeared.

Photos Send photos with submission. Reviews transparencies, 3×5 and larger prints. Offers no additional payment for photos accepted. Captions, identification of subjects required.

$ $ PLANE AND PILOT

Werner Publishing Corp., 12121 Wilshire Blvd., 12th Floor, Los Angeles CA 90025. (310)820-1500. Fax: (310)826-5008. E-mail: editors@planeandpilotmag.com. Web site: www.planeandpilotmag.com. **80% freelance written.** Monthly magazine covering general aviation. "We think a spirited, conversational writing style is most entertaining for our readers. We are read by private and corporate pilots, instructors, students, mechanics and technicians—everyone involved or interested in general aviation." Estab. 1964. Circ. 150,000. Pays on publication. Publishes ms an average of 4 months after acceptance. Byline given. Offers kill fee. Buys all rights. Submit seasonal material 4 months in advance. Accepts previously published material. Responds in 4 months to queries. Sample copy for $5.50. Writer's guidelines online.

Nonfiction How-to, new product, personal experience, technical, travel, pilot efficiency, pilot reports on aircraft. **Buys 75 mss/year.** Query. Length: 1,200 words. **Pays $200-500.** Pays expenses of writers on assignment.

Reprints Send tearsheet, photocopy or typed ms with rights for sale noted and information about when and where the material previously appeared. Pays 50% of amount paid for original article.

Photos Submit suggested heads, decks and captions for all photos with each story. Submit b&w photos, 8×10 prints with glossy finish. Submit color photos in the form of 2¼×2¼, 4×5 or 35mm transparencies in plastic sleeves. Buys all rights. Offers $50-300/photo.

Columns/Departments Readback (any newsworthy items on aircraft and/or people in aviation), 1,200 words;

Jobs & Schools (a feature or an interesting school or program in aviation), 900-1,000 words. **Buys 30 mss/year.** Send complete ms. **Pays $200-500.**
Tips "Pilot proficiency articles are our bread and butter. Manuscripts should be kept under 1,800 words—1,200 words is ideal."

SKY

Pace Communications, Inc., 1301 Carolina St., Greensboro NC 27401. (336)378-6065. Fax: (336)383-5699. Web site: www.delta-sky.com. Monthly magazine. Circ. 500,000. Editorial lead time 6 months. Sample copy for $7.50.
Tips "With all correspondence, please include your address and a daytime telephone number."

N $ $ SOUTHERN AVIATOR

Flyer Media, 11120 Gravelly Lake Dr., SW #7, Lakewood WA 98499. (800)426-8538. Fax: (253)471-9911. E-mail: janice@generalaviationnews.com. Web site: www.southern-aviator.com. **Contact:** Janice Wood, editor. **20% freelance written.** Monthly magazine covering southern aviation. Circ. 25,000. Byline given. Buys first North American serial rights. Editorial lead time 3-5 months. Accepts queries by e-mail. Accepts simultaneous submissions. Writer's guidelines free
Nonfiction General interest, how-to, interview/profile, technical, travel. Query. Length: 700-1,000 words. **Pays $75-250.**
Photos Send photos with submission. Reviews JPEG/EPS/TIFF files (300 dpi).

BUSINESS & FINANCE

NATIONAL

$ $ $ $ BUSINESS 2.0 MAGAZINE

Time, Inc., One California St., 29th Floor, San Francisco CA 94111. E-mail: freelancers@business2.com. Web site: www.business2.com. **Contact:** Josh Quittner, editor. Monthly magazine covering business administration. Estab. 1998. Circ. 600,000. Pays on publication. Publishes ms an average of 3 months after acceptance. Byline given. Offers 20% kill fee. Buys all rights. Editorial lead time 2 months. Submit seasonal material 4 months in advance. Accepts queries by e-mail. Accepts simultaneous submissions.

- Break in with fresh ideas on business transformation—from the way companies are conceived and financed to how they develop markets and retain customers.

Nonfiction Buys 40-50 mss/year. Query with published clips. Length: 150-3,000 words. **Pays $1/word.** Pays expenses of writers on assignment.

N $ $ $ $ CORPORATE BOARD MEMBER

Board Member Inc., 475 Park Ave. S., 19th Floor, New York NY 10016. E-mail: cleinster@boardmember.com. Web site: www.boardmember.com. **Contact:** Colin Leinster, editor. **100% freelance written.** Bimonthly magazine covering corporate governance. "Our readers are the directors and top executives of publicly-held US corporations. We look for detailed and preferably narrative stories about how individual boards have dealt with the challenges that face them on a daily basis: reforms, shareholder suits, CEO pay, firing and hiring CEOs, setting up new boards, firing useless directors. We're happy to light fires under the feet of boards that are asleep at the switch. We also do service-type pieces, written in the second person, advising directors about new wrinkles in disclosure laws, for example." Estab. 1999. Circ. 60,000. **Pays on acceptance.** Publishes ms an average of 3 months after acceptance. Byline given. Offers 25% kill fee. Buys all rights. Editorial lead time 4-5 months. Submit seasonal material 4-5 months in advance. Accepts queries by e-mail. Responds in 1 week to queries; 1 week to mss. Sample copy online. Writer's guidelines by e-mail.
Nonfiction Special issues: Best Law Firms in America (July/August); What Directors Think (November/December). Does not want views from 35,000 feet, pontification, opinion, humor, anything devoid of reporting. **Buys 100 mss/year.** Query. Length: 650-2,500 words. **Pays $1,200-5,000.** Pays expenses of writers on assignment.
Tips "Don't suggest stories you can't deliver."

$ $ DOLLARS AND SENSE: THE MAGAZINE OF ECONOMIC JUSTICE

Economic Affairs Bureau, 29 Winter St., Boston MA 02108. (617)447-2177. Fax: (617)477-2179. E-mail: dollars@dollarsandsense.org. Web site: www.dollarsandsense.org. **Contact:** Amy Gluckman or Chris Sturr, co-editors. **10% freelance written.** Bimonthly magazine covering economic, environmental, and social justice. "We explain the workings of the US and international economics, and provide left perspectives on current economic affairs. Our audience is a mix of activists, organizers, academics, unionists, and other socially concerned people.'' Estab. 1974. Circ. 8,000. Pays on publication. Publishes ms an average of 4 months after acceptance. Byline given. Editorial lead time 3 months. Submit seasonal material 2 months in advance. Accepts queries by mail, e-mail, fax, phone. Sample copy for $5 or on Web site. Writer's guidelines online.

Nonfiction Exposé, political economics. **Buys 6 mss/year.** Query with published clips. Length: 700-2,500 words. **Pays $0-200.** Sometimes pays expenses of writers on assignment.

Photos State availability with submission. Buys one-time rights. Negotiates payment individually. Captions, identification of subjects required.

Tips ''Be familiar with our magazine and the types of communities interested in reading us. *Dollars and Sense* is a progressive economics magazine that explains in a popular way both the workings of the economy and struggles to change it. Articles may be on the environment, the World Bank, community organizing, urban conflict, inflation, unemployment, union reform, welfare, changes in government regulation—a broad range of topics that have an economic theme. Find samples of our latest issue on our homepage.''

$ $ ENTREPRENEUR MAGAZINE

Entrepreneur Media, 2445 McCabe Way, Suite 400, Irvine CA 92614. E-mail: kaxelton@entrepreneur.com. Web site: www.entrepreneur.com. **Contact:** Karen Axelton, executive editor. **60% freelance written.** *Entrepreneur* readers already run their own businesses. They have been in business for several years and are seeking innovative methods and strategies to improve their business operations. They are also interested in new business ideas and opportunities, as well as current issues that affect their companies. Circ. 600,000. **Pays on acceptance.** Publishes ms an average of 5 months after acceptance. Byline given. Buys first worldwide rights. Submit seasonal material 6 months in advance. Accepts queries by mail, e-mail. Responds in 3 months to queries. Sample copy for $7.20. Writer's guidelines online.

Nonfiction How-to (information on running a business, dealing with the psychological aspects of running a business, profiles of unique entrprenuers), current news/trends (and their effect on small business). **Buys 10-20 mss/year.** Query with published clips. Length: 1,800 words. **Payment varies.**

Photos ''Ask for photos or transparencies when interviewing entrepreneurs; send them with the article.'' Buys one-time rights.

Columns/Departments Snapshots (profiles of interesting entrepreneurs who exemplify innovation in their marketing/sales technique, financing method or management style, or who have developed an innovative product/service or technology); Money Smarts (financial management); Marketing Smarts; Web Smarts (Internet news); Tech Smarts; Management Smarts; Viewpoint (first-person essay on entrepreneurship), all 300 words. **Pays $1/word.**

Tips ''Read several issues of the magazine! Study the feature articles versus the columns. Probably 75 percent of our freelance rejections are for article ideas covered in one of our regular columns. Go beyond the typical, flat 'business magazine query'—how to write a press release, how to negotiate with vendors, etc.—and instead investigate a current trend and develop a story on how that trend affects small business. In your query, mention companies you'd like to use to illustrate examples and sources who will provide expertise on the topic.''

⊘ FORBES

Forbes, Inc., 60 5th Ave., New York NY 10011. Web site: www.forbes.com. Biweekly magazine. Edited for top business management professionals and for those aspiring to positions of corporate leadership. Circ. 1,000,000. Editorial lead time 2 months

- Query before submitting.

⊘ FORTUNE

Time, Inc., 1271 Avenue of the Americas, New York NY 10020. (212)522-1212. Fax: (212)522-0810. E-mail: fortunemail_letters@fortunemail.com. Web site: www.fortune.com. Managing Editor: Eric Pooley. Biweekly magazine. Edited primarily for high-demographic business people. Specializes in big stories about companies, business personalities, technology, managing, Wall Street, media, marketing, personal finance, politics and policy. Circ. 1,066,000. Editorial lead time 6 weeks. Sample copy not available

- Does not accept freelance submissions.

$ $ $ $ HISPANIC BUSINESS

Hispanic Business, Inc., 425 Pine Ave., Santa Barbara CA 93117. (805)964-4554. Fax: (805)964-6139. Web site: www.hispanicbusiness.com. **Contact:** Editorial. **40-50% freelance written.** Monthly magazine covering Hispanic business. ''For more than 2 decades, *Hispanic Business* magazine has documented the growing affluence and power of the Hispanic community. Our magazine reaches the most educated, affluent Hispanic business and community leaders. Stories should have relevance for the Hispanic business community.'' Estab. 1979. Circ. 220,000 (rate base); 990,000 (readership base). Pays on publication. Publishes ms an average of 1 month after acceptance. Byline given. Offers 50% kill fee. Buys all rights. Editorial lead time 1-3 months. Submit seasonal material 2 months in advance. Accepts queries by mail. Accepts simultaneous submissions. Responds in 3 weeks to queries; 1 month to mss. Sample copy for free

Nonfiction Interview/profile, travel. **Buys 120 mss/year.** Query résumé and published clips. Length: 650-2,000 words. **Pays $50-1,500.** Sometimes pays expenses of writers on assignment

Photos State availability with submission. Reviews GIF/JPEG files. Buys all rights. Negotiates payment individually. Captions required

Columns/Departments Tech Pulse (technology); Money Matters (financial), both 800 words. **Buys 40 mss/year.** Query with résumé and published clips. **Pays $50-450.**

Tips "E-mail or snail mail queries with résumé and published clips are the most effective."

⊘ MONEY

Time, Inc., 1271 Avenue of the Americas, 17th Floor, New York NY 10020. (212)522-1212. Fax: (212)522-0189. E-mail: managing_editor@moneymail.com. Web site: money.cnn.com. Monthly magazine covering finance. *Money* magazine offers sophisticated coverage in all aspects of personal finance for individuals, business executives, and personal investors. Estab. 1972. Circ. 1,967,420

- *Money* magazine does not accept unsolicited manuscripts and almost never uses freelance writers.

$ $ $ MYBUSINESS MAGAZINE

Hammock Publishing, 3322 W. End Ave., Suite 700, Nashville TN 37203. Web site: www.mybusinessmag.com. **75% freelance written.** Bimonthly magazine for small businesses. "We are a guide to small business success, however that is defined in the new small business economy. We explore the methods and minds behind the trends and celebrate the men and women leading the creation of the new small business economy." Estab. 1999. Circ. 600,000. **Pays on acceptance.** Publishes ms an average of 4 months after acceptance. Byline given. Offers 30% kill fee. Buys first North American serial, electronic rights. Editorial lead time 4 months. Submit seasonal material 5 months in advance. Accepts queries by mail. Accepts simultaneous submissions. Responds in 3 weeks to queries. Sample copy free. Writer's guidelines online.

Nonfiction Book excerpts, how-to (small business topics), new product. **Buys 8 mss/year.** Query with published clips. Length: 200-1,800 words. **Pays $75-1,000.** Pays expenses of writers on assignment.

Tips *MyBusiness* is sent bimonthly to the 600,000 members of the National Federation of Independent Business. "We're here to help small business owners by giving them a range of how-to pieces that evaluate, analyze, and lead to solutions."

$ $ THE NETWORK JOURNAL

Black Professional and Small Business News, The Network Journal Communication, 39 Broadway, Suite 2120, New York NY 10006. (212)962-3791. Fax: (212)962-3537. E-mail: editors@tnj.com. Web site: www.tnj.com. **25% freelance written.** Monthly magazine covering business and career articles. *The Network Journal* caters to black professionals and small-business owners, providing quality coverage on business, financial, technology and career news germane to the black community. Estab. 1993. Circ. 25,000. Pays on publication. Byline given. Buys all rights. Editorial lead time 2 months. Submit seasonal material 3 months in advance. Accepts queries by mail, e-mail, fax, phone. Accepts previously published material. Accepts simultaneous submissions. Sample copy for $1 or online. Writer's guidelines for SASE or online.

Nonfiction How-to, interview/profile. Send complete ms. Length: 1,200-1,500 words. **Pays $150-200.** Sometimes pays expenses of writers on assignment.

Photos Send photos with submission. Buys one-time rights. Offers $25/photo. Identification of subjects required.

Columns/Departments Book reviews, 700-800 words; career management and small business development, 800 words. **Pays $100.**

Tips "We are looking for vigorous writing and reporting for our cover stories and feature articles. Pieces should have gripping leads, quotes that actually say something and that come from several sources. Unless it is a column, please do not submit a 1-source story. Always remember that your article must contain a nutgraph—that's usually the third paragraph telling the reader what the story is about and why you are telling it now. Editorializing should be kept to a minimum. If you're writing a column, make sure your opinions are well-supported."

PERDIDO

Leadership with a Conscience, High Tide Press, 3650 W. 183rd St., Homewood IL 60430-2603. (708)206-2054. Fax: (708)206-2044. E-mail: editor1@hightidepress.com. Web site: www.perdidomagazine.com. **Contact:** Mary Rundell-Holmes, editor. **60% freelance written.** Quarterly magazine covering leadership and management. "We are concerned with what's happening in organizations that are mission-oriented—as opposed to merely profit-oriented. *Perdido* is focused on helping conscientious leaders put innovative ideas into practice. We seek pragmatic articles on management techniques as well as essays on social issues relating to the workplace (not politics or religion). The readership of *Perdido* is comprised mainly of CEOs, executive directors, vice presidents, and program directors of nonprofit and for-profit organizations. We try to make the content of *Perdido* accessible to all decision-makers, whether in the nonprofit or for-profit world, government, or academia. *Perdido* actively pursues diverse opinions and authors from many different fields." Estab. 1994. Circ. 3,000. Pays on publication. Publishes ms an average of 3 months after acceptance. Byline given. Buys first North American serial, second serial (reprint) rights. Submit seasonal material 6 months in advance. Accepts queries by mail, e-mail, fax, phone. Accepts previously published material. Accepts simultaneous submissions. Responds in 2 months to queries. Call or e-mail for sample copy and writer's guidelines.

Nonfiction Book excerpts, humor, interview/profile, informative articles. **Buys 6-10 mss/year.** Query with published clips. Length: 1,000-3,000 words.

Photos State availability with submission. Reviews 5×7 prints. Buys one-time rights. Negotiates payment individually. Captions, identification of subjects, model releases required.

Columns/Departments Book Review (new books on management/leadership), 800 words.

Tips "Potential writers for *Perdido* should rely on the magazine's motto—Leadership with a Conscience—as a starting point. We're looking for thoughtful reflections on management that help people succeed. While instructive articles are good, we avoid step-by-step recipes. Data and real life examples are very important."

$ $ $ $ PROFIT

Your Guide to Business Success, 1 Mt. Pleasant Rd., 11th Floor, Toronto ON M4Y 2Y5 Canada. (416)764-1402. Fax: (416)764-1404. Web site: www.profitguide.com. **80% freelance written.** Magazine published 6 times/year covering small and medium businesses. "We specialize in specific, useful information that helps our readers manage their businesses better. We want Canadian stories only." Estab. 1982. Circ. 110,000. **Pays on acceptance.** Publishes ms an average of 2 months after acceptance. Byline given. Offers variable kill fee. Buys first North American serial, electronic rights. Submit seasonal material 6 months in advance. Accepts queries by mail, fax, phone. Responds in 1 month to queries; 6 weeks to mss. Sample copy for 9×12 SAE with 84¢ postage. Writer's guidelines free.

Nonfiction How-to (business management tips), strategies and Canadian business profiles. **Buys 50 mss/year.** Query with published clips. Length: 800-2,000 words. **Pays $500-2,000.** Pays expenses of writers on assignment.

Columns/Departments Finance (info on raising capital in Canada), 700 words; Marketing (marketing strategies for independent business), 700 words. **Buys 80 mss/year.** Query with published clips. **Pays $150-600.**

Tips "We're wide open to freelancers with good ideas and some knowledge of business. Read the magazine and understand it before submitting your ideas—which should have a Canadian focus."

SMARTMONEY MAGAZINE

1755 Broadway, 2nd Floor, New York NY 10019. E-mail: editors@smartmoney.com. Web site: www.smartmoney.com.

- Query before submitting.

$ $ TECHNICAL ANALYSIS OF STOCKS & COMMODITIES

The Traders' Magazine, Technical Analysis, Inc., 4757 California Ave. SW, Seattle WA 98116-4499. (206)938-0570. Fax: (206)938-1307. E-mail: editor@traders.com. Web site: www.traders.com. Publisher: Jack K. Hutson. **Contact:** Jayanthi Gopalakrishnan, editor. **85% freelance written.** Magazine covers methods of investing and trading stocks, bonds and commodities (futures), options, mutual funds, and precious metals using technical analysis. Estab. 1982. Circ. 65,000. Pays on publication. Publishes ms an average of 6 months after acceptance. Byline given. Buys all rights. Responds in 2 months to queries. Sample copy for $8. Writer's guidelines online

- Eager to work with new/unpublished writers.

Nonfiction How-to (trade), humor (cartoons), technical (trading and software aids to trading), reviews, utilities, real world trading (actual case studies of trades and their results). "No newsletter-type, buy-sell recommendations. The article subject must relate to technical analysis, charting or a numerical technique used to trade securities or futures. Almost universally requires graphics with every article." **Buys 150 mss/year.** Query with published clips or send complete ms. Length: 1,000-4,000 words. **Pays $100-500.**

Reprints Send tearsheet with rights for sale noted and information about when and where the material previously appeared

Photos Christine M. Morrison, art director. State availability with submission. Buys one time and reprint rights. Pays $60-350 for b&w or color negatives with prints or positive slides. Captions, identification of subjects, model releases required

Columns/Departments Length: 800-1,600 words. **Buys 100 mss/year.** Query. **Pays $50-300.**

Fillers Karen Wasserman, fillers editor. Must relate to trading stocks, bonds, options, mutual funds, commodities, or precious metals. Cartoons on investment humor. **Buys 20/year.** Length: 500 words. **Pays $20-50.**

Tips "Describe how to use technical analysis, charting, or computer work in day-to-day trading of stocks, bonds, commodities, options, mutual funds, or precious metals. A blow-by-blow account of how a trade was made, including the trader's thought processes, is the very best-received story by our subscribers. One of our primary considerations is to instruct in a manner that the layperson can comprehend. We are not hypercritical of writing style."

REGIONAL

$ $ ALASKA BUSINESS MONTHLY

Alaska Business Publishing, 501 W. Northern Lights Blvd., Suite 100, Anchorage AK 99503-2577. (907)276-4373. Fax: (907)279-2900. E-mail: editor@akbizmag.com. Web site: www.akbizmag.com. **Contact:** Debbie Cutler, editor. **80% freelance written.** Magazine covering Alaska-oriented business and industry. "Our audience is Alaska businessmen and women who rely on us for timely features and up-to-date information about doing business in Alaska." Estab. 1985. Circ. 11,500. Pays on publication. Publishes ms an average of 4 months after acceptance. Byline given. Offers $50 kill fee. Buys all rights. Editorial lead time 5 months. Submit seasonal material 5 months in advance. Accepts queries by mail, e-mail, fax. Accepts previously published material. Responds in 1 month to queries. Sample copy for 9×12 SAE and 4 first-class stamps. Writer's guidelines free.

Nonfiction General interest, how-to, interview/profile, new product (Alaska), opinion. No fiction, poetry, or anything not pertinent to Alaska. **Buys approximately 130 mss/year.** Send complete ms. Length: 500-2,000 words. **Pays $150-300.** Sometimes pays expenses of writers on assignment.

Photos State availability with submission.

Columns/Departments Required Reading (business book reviews); Right Moves; Alaska this Month; Monthly Calendars (all Alaska related), all 500-1,200 words. **Buys 12 mss/year.** Send complete ms. **Pays $50-75.**

Tips "Send a well-written manuscript on a subject of importance to Alaska businesses. We seek informative, entertaining articles on everything from entrepreneurs to heavy industry. We cover all Alaska industry to include mining, tourism, timber, transportation, oil and gas, fisheries, finance, insurance, real estate, communications, medical services, technology, and construction. We also cover Native and environmental issues, and occasionally feature Seattle and other communities in the Pacific Northwest."

N $ $ $ $ ALBERTA VENTURE

Venture Publishing Inc., 10259 - 105 St., Edmonton AB T5J 1E3 Canada. (780)990-0839. E-mail: feedback@albertaventure.com. Web site: www.albertaventure.com. Managing Editor: Tracy Hyatt. **Contact:** Michael McCullough, editor. **70% freelance written.** Monthly magazine covering business in Alberta. "Our readers are mostly business owners and managers in Alberta who read the magazine to keep up with trends and run their businesses better." Estab. 1997. Circ. 35,000. Pays on publication. Publishes ms an average of 2 months after acceptance. Byline given. Offers 30% kill fee. Buys first North American serial, electronic rights. Editorial lead time 3 months. Submit seasonal material 3 months in advance. Accepts queries by e-mail. Responds in 2 weeks to queries. Sample copy online. Writer's guidelines by e-mail.

Nonfiction How-to, business narrative related to Alberta. Does not want company or product profiles. **Buys 75 mss/year.** Query. Length: 1,000-3,000 words. **Pays $300-2,000 (Canadian).** Pays expenses of writers on assignment.

Photos Contact Alfredo Zelcer, art director. State availability with submission. Reviews GIF/JPEG files. Buys one-time rights. Negotiates payment individually. Identification of subjects required.

$ $ ATLANTIC BUSINESS MAGAZINE

Communications Ten, Ltd., P.O. Box 2356, Station C, St. John's NL A1C 6E7 Canada. (709)726-9300. Fax: (709)726-3013. E-mail: dchafe@atlanticbusinessmagazine.com. Web site: www.atlanticbusinessmagazine.com. **Contact:** Dawn Chafe, editor. **80% freelance written.** Bimonthly magazine covering business in Atlantic Canada. "We discuss positive business developments, emphasizing that the 4 Atlantic provinces are a great place to do business." Estab. 1989. Circ. 30,000. Pays within 30 days of publication. Publishes ms an average of 2 months after acceptance. Byline given. Buys one-time rights. Editorial lead time 6 months. Accepts queries by mail, e-mail, fax. Sample copy and writer's guidelines free.

Nonfiction Exposé, general interest, interview/profile, new product. "We don't want religious, technical, or scholarly material. We are not an academic magazine. We are interested only in stories concerning business topics specific to the 4 Canadian provinces of Nova Scotia, New Brunswick, Prince Edward Island, and Newfoundland and Labrador." **Buys 36 mss/year.** Query with published clips. Length: 1,200-2,500 words. **Pays $300-750.** Sometimes pays expenses of writers on assignment.

Photos Send photos with submission. Reviews contact sheets, transparencies, prints. Buys one-time rights. Negotiates payment individually. Captions, identification of subjects required.

Columns/Departments Query with published clips.

Tips "Writers should submit their areas of interest as well as samples of their work and, if possible, suggested story ideas."

BCBUSINESS

Canada Wide Magazines & Communications, Ltd., 4180 Lougheed Hwy., 4th Floor, Burnaby BC V5C 6A7 Canada. (604)299-7311. Fax: (604)299-9188. E-mail: bcb@canadawide.com; ttjaden@canadawide.com. Web site: www.bcbusinessmagazine.com. Associate Editor: David Jordan. **Contact:** Tracy Tjaden, managing editor. **80% freelance written.** Monthly magazine covering significant issues and trends shaping the province's business environment. Stories are lively, topical and extensively researched. Circ. 30,000. Pays 2 weeks prior to being published. Publishes ms an average of 2 months after acceptance. Byline given. Offers kill fee. Buys first rights. Editorial lead time 4 months. Submit seasonal material 4 months in advance. Accepts queries by e-mail. Accepts simultaneous submissions. Responds in 6 weeks to queries. Writer's guidelines free.

Nonfiction Query with published clips. Length: 1,500-2,000 words. Sometimes pays expenses of writers on assignment.

Photos State availability with submission.

$ BLUE RIDGE BUSINESS JOURNAL

Landmark, Inc., 347 W. Campbell Ave., Roanoke VA 24016. (540)777-6462. Fax: (540)777-6471. E-mail: dan@bizjournal.com. Web site: www.roanokebiz.com. **Contact:** Dan Smith, editor. **75% freelance written.** Monthly. "We take a regional slant on national business trends, products, methods, etc. Interested in localized features and news stories highlighting business activity." Estab. 1989. Circ. 15,000. **Pays on acceptance.** Publishes ms an average of 1 month after acceptance. Byline given. Buys all rights. Editorial lead time 10 days. Accepts queries by mail, e-mail, fax. Accepts previously published material. Responds immediately to queries. Call the editor for sample copies and/or writer's guidelines. Writers must live in our region.

Nonfiction Regional business. Special issues: Health Care and Hospitals; Telecommunications; Building and Construction; Investments; Personal Finance and Retirement Planning; Guide to Architectural; Engineering and Construction Services; and Manufacturing and Industry. No columns or stories that are not pre-approved. **Buys 120-150 mss/year.** Query. Length: 500-2,000 words.

Photos State availability with submission. Buys all rights. Offers $10/photo. Captions, identification of subjects required.

Tips "Talk to the editor. Offer knowledgeable ideas (if accepted they will be assigned to that writer). We need fast turnaround, accurate reporting, neat dress, non-smokers. More interested in writing samples than educational background."

BUSINESS LONDON

P.O. Box 7400, London ON N5Y 4X3 Canada. (519)472-7601. Fax: (519)473-7859. E-mail: editorial@businesslondon.ca. Web site: www.businesslondon.ca. **Contact:** Gord Delamont, editor. **70% freelance written.** Monthly magazine covering London business. "Our audience is primarily small and medium businesses and entrepreneurs. Focus is on success stories and how to better operate your business." Estab. 1987. Circ. 14,000. Pays on publication. Publishes ms an average of 3 months after acceptance. Byline given. Offers 50% kill fee. Buys first rights. Editorial lead time 3 months. Accepts queries by e-mail. Responds in 3 months to mss. Sample copy for #10 SASE. Writer's guidelines free.

Nonfiction How-to (business topics), humor, interview/profile, new product (local only), personal experience (must have a London connection). **Buys 30 mss/year.** Query with published clips. Length: 250-1,500 words.

Photos Send photos with submission. Reviews contact sheets, transparencies. Buys one-time rights. Negotiates payment individually. Identification of subjects required.

Tips "Phone with a great idea. The most valuable things a writer owns are ideas. We'll take a chance on an unknown if the idea is good enough."

BUSINESS NH MAGAZINE

670 N. Commercial St., Suite 110, Manchester NH 03101. (603)626-6354. Fax: (603)626-6359. E-mail: edit@businessnhmagazine.com. Web site: www.businessnhmagazine.com. Publisher: Sean Mahoney. Managing Editor: Matthew J. Mowry. Associate Editor: Mark Laliberte. **25% freelance written.** Monthly magazine covering business, politics, and people of New Hampshire. "Our audience consists of the owners and top managers of New Hampshire businesses." Estab. 1983. Circ. 15,000. Pays on publication. Publishes ms an average of 2 months after acceptance. Byline given. Accepts queries by e-mail, fax.

Nonfiction How-to, interview/profile. "No unsolicited manuscripts; interested in New Hampshire writers only." **Buys 24 mss/year.** Query with published clips and résumé. Length: 750-2,500 words. **Payment varies.**

Photos Both b&w and color photos are used. Buys one-time rights. Payment varies.
Tips "I always want clips and résumés with queries. Freelance stories are almost always assigned. Stories must be local to New Hampshire."

N $ $ CINCY BUSINESS MAGAZINE

People, Passions, Pursuits, Great Lakes Publishing Co., Cincinnati Club Building, 30 Garfield Place, Suite 440, Cincinnati OH 45202. (513)479-0713. Fax: (513)421-2542. E-mail: news@cincybusinessmag.com. Web site: www.cincybusinessmag.com. Editor: Felix Winternitz. **Contact:** Greg Loomis, managing editor. **80% freelance written.** Bimonthly magazine covering Cincinnati business, through colorful profiles of CEOs. "*Cincy Business* is written for an audience of Cincinnati business decision makers and CEOs. We don't cover business news per se, but rather, strive to give a sense of the business community through people profiles. We are as interested in what CEOs do in their offtime as at work. We publish stories on business leaders and their hobbies, collections, charitable pursuits, etc." Estab. 2004. Circ. 15,300. Pays on publication. Publishes ms an average of 3 months after acceptance. Byline given. Offers 100% kill fee. Buys all rights. Editorial lead time 3 months. Submit seasonal material 4 months in advance. Accepts queries by mail, e-mail, fax, phone. Accepts previously published material. Responds in 2 weeks to queries; 1 month to mss. Sample copy online.
Nonfiction General interest, interview/profile. Does not want stock advice. **Buys 80 mss/year.** Query with or without published clips or send complete ms. Length: 500-1,000 words. **Pays $150-500.**
Tips "Getting access to a CEO is always the challenge. If you can bring us a CEO who is willing to be profiled, that's a great way to break into the publication."

N $ $ CORPORATE CONNECTICUT MAGAZINE

The Corporate World at Eye Level, Corporate World LLC, P.O. Box 290726, Wethersfield CT 06129. Web site: www.corpct.com. Managing Editor: Russ Jones. **Contact:** Chris Brunson, editor. **50% freelance written.** Quarterly magazine covering regional reporting, global coverage of corporate/business leaders, entreprenuers. "*Corporate Connecticut* is devoted to people who make business happen in the private sector and who create innovative change across public arenas. Centered in the Northeast between New York and Boston, Connecticut is positioned in a coastal corridor with a dense affluent population who are highly mobile, accomplished and educated." Estab. 2001. Pays on publication. Publishes ms an average of 2-3 months after acceptance. Byline given. Offers 25% kill fee. Buys first North American serial, electronic, all, negotiable rights. Editorial lead time 3-6 months. Submit seasonal material 10-12 months in advance. Accepts queries by mail, e-mail. Responds in 2 weeks to queries. Sample copy for #10 SASE.
Nonfiction "Interested in pieces on hedge funds, venture capital, high-end travel." Query with published clips. **Pays 35¢/word minimum with varying fees for excellence.**
Photos State availability with submission.
Tips "Review our online content to get a general feel for the publication. Aim high with content, do research, pitch a unique angle with a global perspective on business and people."

$ CRAIN'S DETROIT BUSINESS

Crain Communications, Inc., 1155 Gratiot, Detroit MI 48207-2997. (313)446-1654. Fax: (313)446-1687. E-mail: sselby@crain.com. Web site: www.crainsdetroit.com. Publisher: Mary Kramer. Executive Editor: Cindy Goodaker. **Contact:** Michelle Martinez, special sections editor. **10% freelance written.** Weekly tabloid covering business in the Detroit metropolitan area—specifically Wayne, Oakland, Macomb, Washtenaw, and Livingston counties. Estab. 1985. Circ. 150,000. Pays on publication. Publishes ms an average of 1 month after acceptance. Byline given. Buys all rights. Accepts queries by mail, e-mail. Sample copy for $1.50. Writer's guidelines online.

- *Crain's Detroit Business* uses only area writers and local topics.

Nonfiction New product, technical, business. **Buys 20 mss/year.** Query with published clips. Length: 30-40 words/column inch. **Pays $10-15/column inch.** Pays expenses of writers on assignment.
Photos State availability with submission.
Tips "Contact special sections editor in writing with background and, if possible, specific story ideas relating to our type of coverage and coverage area."

$ IN BUSINESS WINDSOR

Cornerstone Publications, Inc., 1775 Sprucewood Ave., Unit 1, LaSalle ON N9J 1X7 Canada. (519)250-2880. Fax: (519)250-2881. E-mail: gbaxter@inbusinesswindsor.com. Web site: www.inbusinesswindsor.com. **Contact:** Gary Baxter, general manager/publisher. **70% freelance written.** Monthly magazine covering business. "We focus on issues/ideas which are of interest to businesses in and around Windsor and Essex County (Ontario). Most stories deal with business and finance; occasionally we will cover health and sports issues that affect our readers." Estab. 1988. Circ. 10,000. **Pays on acceptance.** Byline given. Buys first rights. Editorial lead time 3 months. Submit seasonal material 3 months in advance. Accepts queries by mail, e-mail, fax. Responds in 2 weeks to queries; 1 month to mss. Sample copy for $3.50.

Nonfiction General interest, how-to, interview/profile. **Buys 25 mss/year.** Query with published clips. Length: 800-1,500 words. **Pays $70-150.** Sometimes pays expenses of writers on assignment.

N $ $ INGRAM'S

Show-Me Publishing, Inc., P.O. Box 411356, Suite 1014, Kansas City MO 64141-1356. (816)842-9994. Fax: (816)474-1111. E-mail: editorial@ingramsonline.com. Web site: www.ingramsonline.com. Editor-in-Chief/ Publisher: Joe Sweeney. **Contact:** Jack Cashill, executive editor. **50% freelance written.** Monthly magazine covering Kansas City business/executive lifestyle for upscale, affluent business executives and professionals. Looking for sophisticated writing with style and humor when appropriate. Estab. 1974. Circ. 96,000. Pays 1 month after publication. Publishes ms an average of 2 months after acceptance. Byline given. Buys first, electronic rights. Editorial lead time 2 months. Submit seasonal material 3 months in advance. Accepts queries by mail, fax. Responds in 6 weeks to queries. Sample copy for $3.

- Only accepts local writers; guest columnist are not paid articles.

Nonfiction "All articles must have a Kansas City angle. We don't accept unsolicited manuscripts except for opinion column." General interest, how-to (business and personal finance related), interview/profile (Kansas City execs, politicians, celebrities), opinion, technical. **Buys 30 mss/year.** Query with published clips. Length: 500-3,000 words. **Pays $175-350.** Sometimes pays expenses of writers on assignment.

Columns/Departments Say So (opinion), 1,500 words. **Buys 12 mss/year. Pays $100 max.**

All articles published are also published on the Web site, and writers must agree to those terms.

Tips "Writers must understand the publication and the audience—knowing what appeals to a business executive, entrepreneur, or professional in Kansas City. Do not call."

$ $ THE LANE REPORT

Lane Communications Group, 210 E. Main St., 14th Floor, Lexington KY 40507. (859)244-3500. Fax: (859)244-3555. E-mail: editorial@lanereport.com. Web site: www.kybiz.com. Associate Editor: Karen Baird. **Contact:** Andy Olsen, managing editor. **70% freelance written.** Monthly magazine covering statewide business. Estab. 1986. Circ. 15,000. Pays on publication. Byline given. Buys one-time rights. Editorial lead time 6 weeks. Submit seasonal material 3 months in advance. Accepts queries by mail, e-mail, fax. Accepts previously published material. Accepts simultaneous submissions. Responds in 1 month to queries. Sample copy and writer's guidelines free.

Nonfiction Essays, interview/profile, new product, photo feature. No fiction. **Buys 30-40 mss/year.** Query with published clips. Length: 500-2,000 words. **Pays $150-375.** Sometimes pays expenses of writers on assignment.

Photos State availability with submission. Reviews contact sheets, negatives, transparencies, prints, digital images. Buys one-time rights. Negotiates payment individually. Identification of subjects required.

Columns/Departments Technology and Business in Kentucky; Advertising; Exploring Kentucky; Perspective; Spotlight on the Arts, all less than 1,000 words.

Tips "As Kentucky's only statewide business and economics publication, we look for stories that incorporate perspectives from the Commonwealth's various regions and prominent industries—tying it into the national picture when appropriate. We also look for insightful profiles and interviews of Kentucky's entrepreneurs and business leaders."

N $ MERCER BUSINESS MAGAZINE

White Eagle Publishing Company, 2550 Kuser Rd., Trenton State NJ 08691. (609)586-2056. Fax: (609)586-8052. E-mail: maggih@mercerbusiness.com. Web site: www.mercerchamber.org. **Contact:** Maggi S. Hill, managing editor. **100% freelance written.** Monthly magazine covering national and local business-related, theme-based topics. "*Mercer Business* is a Chamber of Commerce publication, so the slant is pro-business primarily. Also covers nonprofits, education and other related issues." Estab. 1924. Circ. 8,500. Pays on publication. Publishes ms an average of 1 month after acceptance. Byline given. Makes work-for-hire assignments. Editorial lead time 6 weeks. Submit seasonal material 6 weeks in advance. Accepts queries by e-mail. Accepts simultaneous submissions. Responds in 1 week to queries. Sample copy for #10 SASE. Writer's guidelines by e-mail.

Nonfiction Humor. Query with published clips. Length: 1,000-1,800 words. **Pays $150 for assigned articles.** Sometimes pays expenses of writers on assignment.

Photos State availability of or send photos with submission. Offers no additional payment for photos accepted with ms. Captions, identification of subjects, model releases required.

Fillers Gags to be illustrated by cartoonist. **Buys 24/year.** Length: 300-500 words.

Tips "Query with cover letter preferred after perusal of editorial calendar."

$$$$ OREGON BUSINESS

MEDIAmerica, Inc., 610 SW Broadway, Suite 200, Portalnd OR 97205. (503)223-0304. Fax: (503)221-6544. E-mail: queries@oregonbusiness.com. Web site: www.oregonbusiness.com. **Contact:** Robin Doussard, editor. **15-25% freelance written.** Monthly magazine covering business in Oregon. "Our subscribers inlcude owners of small and medium-sized businesses, government agencies, professional staffs of banks, insurance companies, ad agencies, attorneys and other service providers. We accept *only* stories about Oregon businesses, issues and trends." Estab. 1981. Circ. 50,000. Pays on publication. Byline given. Buys first North American serial, electronic rights. Editorial lead time 2 months. Accepts queries by mail, e-mail. Sample copy for $4. Writer's guidelines online.

Nonfiction Features should focus on "major trends shaping the state; noteworthy businesses, practices, and leaders; stories with sweeping implications across industry sectors." Query with résumé and 2-3 published clips. Length: 1,200-3,000 words.

Columns/Departments First Person (opinion piece on an issue related to business), 750 words; Around the State (recent news and trends, and how they might shape the future), 100-600 words; Business Tools (practical, how-to suggestions for business managers and owners), 400-600 words; In Character (profile of interesting or "quirky" member of the business community), 850 words. Query with résumé and 2-3 published clips

Tips "An *Oregon Business* story must meet at least 2 of the following criteria: **Size and location**: The topic must be relevant to Northwest businesses. Featured companies (including franchises) must be based in Oregon or Southwest Washington. **Service**: Our sections (1,200 words) are reserved largely for service pieces focusing on finance, marketing, management or other general business topics. These stories are meant to be instructional, emphasizing problem-solving by example. **Trends**: These are sometimes covered in a section piece, or perhaps a feature story. We aim to be the state's leading business publication so we want to be the first to spot trends that affect Oregon companies. **Exclusivity or strategy**: of an event, whether it's a corporate merger, a dramatic turnaround, a marketing triumph or a PR disaster."

N $$ PACIFIC COAST BUSINESS TIMES

14 E. Carrillo St., Suite A, Santa Barbara CA 93101. (805)560-6950. Fax: (805)560-8399. E-mail: newsroom@pacbiztimes.com. Web site: www.pacbiztimes.com. Editor: Henry Dubroff. **Contact:** Rose Medlock, managing editor. **10% freelance written.** Weekly tabloid covering financial news specific to Santa Barbara, Ventura, San Luis Obispo counties in California. Estab. 2000. Circ. 5,000. Byline given. Buys all rights. Editorial lead time 1 month. Accepts queries by e-mail, phone. Sample copy for free. Writer's guidelines free.

Nonfiction Interview/profile, opinion, personal finance. Does not want first person, promo or fluff pieces. **Buys 20 mss/year.** Query. Length: 500-800 words. **Pays $75-175.** Pays expenses of writers on assignment.

Columns/Departments Harvey Mackay (management), 600 words. Query. **Pays $10-50.**

N $$ PRAIRIE BUSINESS

Grand Forks (ND) Herald, Forum Communications Company, 205 4th Ave. N., Fargo ND 58102. (701)232-8893. Fax: (701)280-9092. E-mail: rick@prairiebizmag.com. Web site: www.prairiebizmag.com. **Contact:** Rick Killion, editor. **30% freelance written.** Monthly magazine covering business on the Northern Plains (North Dakota, South Dakota, Minnesota). "We attempt to be a resource for business owners/managers, policymakers, educators, and nonprofit administrators, acting as a catalyst for growth in the region by reaching out to an audience of decisionmakers within the region and also venture capitalists, site selectors, and angel visitors from outside the region." Estab. 2000. Circ. 20,000. Pays within 2 weeks of mailing date. Publishes ms an average of 1-2 months after acceptance. Byline given. Buys all rights. Editorial lead time 2 months. Submit seasonal material 2 months in advance. Accepts queries by e-mail. Accepts previously published material. Accepts simultaneous submissions. Responds in 2 weeks to queries. Sample copy for free. Writer's guidelines free.

Nonfiction Interview/profile, technical. Does not want articles that are blatant self-promotion for any interest without providing value for readers. **Buys 36 mss/year.** Query. Length: 800-1,500 words. **Pays 10-15¢/word.**

Photos Send photos with submission. Reviews GIF/JPEG files (hi-res). Buys one-time rights. Offers $20-250/photo. Captions, identification of subjects required.

N PROVIDENCE BUSINESS NEWS

220 W. Exchange St., Suite 210, Providence RI 02903. (401)273-2201, ext. 215. Fax: (401)274-0670. E-mail: murphy@pbn.com. Web site: www.pbn.com. **Contact:** Mark S. Murphy, editor. Business magazine covering news of importance to the Providence area.

- Query before submitting.

$ ROCHESTER BUSINESS JOURNAL

Rochester Business Journal, Inc., 45 E. Ave., Suite 500, Rochester NY 14604. (585)546-8303. Fax: (585)546-3398. Web site: www.rbjdaily.com. **10% freelance written.** Weekly tabloid covering local business. "The

Rochester Business Journal is geared toward corporate executives and owners of small businesses, bringing them leading-edge business coverage and analysis first in the market.'' Estab. 1984. Circ. 10,000. Pays on publication. Publishes ms an average of 1 month after acceptance. Byline given. Buys first, second serial (reprint), electronic rights. Editorial lead time 6 weeks. Accepts queries by mail, fax. Responds in 1 week to queries. Sample copy for free or by e-mail. Writer's guidelines online.

Nonfiction How-to (business topics), news features, trend stories with local examples. Do not query about any topics that do not include several local examples—local companies, organizations, universities, etc. **Buys 110 mss/year.** Query with published clips. Length: 1,000-2,000 words. **Pays $150.**

Tips ''The *Rochester Business Journal* prefers queries from local published writers who can demonstrate the ability to write for a sophisticated audience of business readers. Story ideas should be about business trends illustrated with numerous examples of local companies participating in the change or movement.''

N $ SOMERSET BUSINESS MAGAZINE

White Eagle Printing Company, 2550 Kuser Rd., Trenton State NJ 08691. (609)586-2056. Fax: (609)586-8052. E-mail: maggih@sombusmag.com. Web site: www.scbp.org. **Contact:** Maggi S. Hill, managing editor. **100% freelance written.** Monthly magazine covering national and local business-related, theme-based topics. ''*Somerset Business Magazine* is a Chamber of Commerce publication, so the slant is pro-business primarily. Also covers nonprofits, education and other related issues.'' Estab. 1924. Circ. 6,500. Pays on publication. Publishes ms an average of 1 month after acceptance. Makes work-for-hire assignments. Editorial lead time 6 weeks. Submit seasonal material 6 weeks in advance. Accepts queries by e-mail. Accepts simultaneous submissions. Responds in 1 week to queries. Sample copy for #10 SASE. Writer's guidelines by e-mail.

Nonfiction Humor. Query with published clips. Length: 1,000-1,800 words. **Pays $150 for assigned articles.** Sometimes pays expenses of writers on assignment.

Photos State availability of or send photos with submission. Offers no additional payment for photos accepted with ms. Captions, identification of subjects, model releases required.

Tips ''Query with cover letter preferred after perusal of editorial calendar.''

$ $ VERMONT BUSINESS MAGAZINE

2 Church St., Burlington VT 05401-4445. (802)863-8038. Fax: (802)863-8069. E-mail: mcq@vermontbiz.com. Web site: www.vermontbiz.com. **Contact:** Timothy McQuiston, editor. **80% freelance written.** Monthly tabloid covering business in Vermont. Circ. 8,000. Pays on publication. Publishes ms an average of 1 month after acceptance. Byline given. Buys one-time rights. Responds in 2 months to queries. Sample copy for 11×14 SAE and 7 first-class stamps.

Nonfiction Business trends and issues. **Buys 200 mss/year.** Query with published clips. Length: 800-1,800 words. **Pays $100-200.**

Reprints Send tearsheet and information about when and where the material previously appeared.

Photos Send photos with submission. Reviews contact sheets. Offers $10-35/photo. Identification of subjects required.

Tips ''Read daily papers and look for business angles for a follow-up article. We look for issue and trend articles rather than company or businessman profiles. Note: Magazine accepts Vermont-specific material only. The articles must be about Vermont.''

CAREER, COLLEGE & ALUMNI

$ $ AMERICAN CAREERS

Career Communications, Inc., 6701 W. 64th St., Overland Park KS 66202. (800)669-7795. Fax: (913)362-7788. Web site: www.carcom.com. **Contact:** Mary Pitchford, editor. **50% freelance written.** Student publication covering careers, career statistics, skills needed to get jobs. ''*American Careers* provides career, salary, and education information to middle school and high school students. Self-tests help them relate their interests and abilities to future careers. Articles on résumés, interviews, etc., help them develop employability skills.'' Estab. 1989. Circ. 500,000. Pays 1 month after acceptance. Byline given. Buys all rights, makes work-for-hire assignments. Accepts queries by mail. Accepts simultaneous submissions. Sample copy for $3. Writer's guidelines for #10 SASE.

- Break in by ''sending us query letters with samples and résumés. We want to 'meet' the writer before making an assignment.''

Nonfiction Career and education features related to career paths, including arts and communication, business, law, government, finance, construction, technology, health services, human services, manufacturing, engineering, and natural resources and agriculture. ''No preachy advice to teens or articles that talk down to students.'' **Buys 20 mss/year.** Query by mail only with published clips. Length: 300-1,000 words. **Pays $100-450.**

Photos State availability with submission. Buys all rights. Negotiates payment individually. Captions, identification of subjects, model releases required.

Tips "Letters of introduction or query letters with samples and résumés are ways we get to know writers. Samples should include how-to articles and career-related articles. Articles written for teenagers also would make good samples. Short feature articles on careers, career-related how-to articles, and self-assessment tools (10-20 point quizzes with scoring information) are primarily what we publish."

N $ $ THE BLACK COLLEGIAN

The Career & Self Development Magazine for African-American Students, IMDiversity, Inc., 140 Carondelet St., New Orleans LA 70130. Web site: www.black-collegian.com. **25% freelance written.** Semiannual magazine for African-American college students and recent graduates with an interest in career and job information, African-American cultural awareness, personalities, history, trends, and current events. Estab. 1970. Circ. 122,000. Pays 1 month after publication. Byline given. Buys one-time rights. Submit seasonal material 2 months in advance. Accepts queries by mail. Responds in 6 months to queries. Sample copy for $5 (includes postage) and 9×12 SAE. Writer's guidelines for #10 SASE.

Nonfiction Material on careers, sports, black history, news analysis. Articles on problems and opportunities confronting African-American college students and recent graduates. Book excerpts, exposé, general interest, historical/nostalgic, how-to (develop employability), inspirational, interview/profile, opinion, personal experience. Query. Length: 900-1,900 words. **Pays $100-500 for assigned articles.**

Photos State availability of or send photos with submission. Reviews 8×10 prints. Captions, identification of subjects, model releases required.

Tips Articles are published under primarily 5 broad categories: job hunting information, overviews of career opportunities and industry reports, self-development information, analyses and investigations of conditions and problems that affect African-Americans, and celebrations of African-American success.

N BROWN ALUMNI MAGAZINE

Brown University, 71 George St., Providence RI 02912. (401)863-2873. Fax: (401)863-9599. E-mail: alumni_magazine@brown.edu. Web site: www.brownalumnimagazine.com. Editor: Norman Boucher (norman_boucher@brown.edu). **Contact:** Elizabeth Smith, office manager (elizabeth_g_smith@brown.edu). Bimonthly magazine covering the world of Brown University and its alumni. "We are an editorially independent, general interest magazine covering the on-campus world of Brown University and the off-campus world of its alumni." Estab. 1900. Circ. 80,000. **Pays on acceptance.** Publishes ms an average of 3 months after acceptance. Byline given. Buys North American serial and Web rights. Editorial lead time 3 months. Submit seasonal material 4 months in advance. Accepts queries by mail, e-mail, fax. Responds in several weeks to queries. Sample copy for free. Writer's guidelines online.

Nonfiction Book excerpts, essays, exposé, general interest, historical/nostalgic, humor, interview/profile, opinion, personal experience, photo feature, travel, profiles. No articles unconnected to Brown or its alumni. **Buys 50 mss/year.** Query with published clips. Length: 150-4,000 words.

Photos State availability with submission. Reviews contact sheets, transparencies, prints. Buys one-time rights. Negotiates payment individually. Captions, identification of subjects required.

Columns/Departments P.O.V. (essays by Brown alumni), 750 words. Send complete ms.

Tips "Be imaginative and be specific. A Brown connection is required for all stories in the magazine, but a Brown connection alone does not guarantee our interest. Ask yourself: Why should readers care about your proposed story? Also, we look for depth and objective reporting, not boosterism."

$ $ CIRCLE K MAGAZINE

3636 Woodview Trace, Indianapolis IN 46268-3196. (317)875-8755. Fax: (317)879-0204. E-mail: ckimagazine@kiwanis.org. Web site: www.circlek.org. **Contact:** Kasey Jackson, executive editor. **60% freelance written.** Magazine published 6 times/year. "Our readership consists almost entirely of above-average college students interested in voluntary community service and leadership development. They are politically and socially aware and have a wide range of interests." Circ. 12,000. **Pays on acceptance.** Byline given. Buys first North American serial rights. Accepts queries by mail, e-mail, fax. Responds in 2 weeks to queries. Sample copy for large SAE with 3 first-class stamps or on Web site. Writer's guidelines online.

- Break in by offering "fresh ideas for stories dealing with college students who are not only concerned with themselves. Our readers are concerned with making their communities better."

Nonfiction Articles published in *Circle K* are of 2 types—serious and light nonfiction. "We are interested in general interest articles on topics concerning college students and their lifestyles, as well as articles dealing with careers, community concerns, and leadership development. No first-person confessions, family histories, or travel pieces." Query. Length: 1,500-2,000 words. **Pays $150-400.**

Photos Purchased with accompanying ms; total price includes both photos and ms. Captions required.

Tips "Query should indicate author's familiarity with the field and sources. Subject treatment must be objective and in-depth, and articles should include illustrative examples and quotes from persons involved in the subject or qualified to speak on it. We are open to working with new writers who present a good article idea and demonstrate that they've done their homework concerning the article subject itself, as well as concerning our magazine's style. We're interested in college-oriented trends, for example: entrepreneur schooling, high-tech classrooms, music, leisure, and health issues."

$ $ CONCORDIA UNIVERSITY MAGAZINE

Concordia University, 1455 de Maisonneuve Blvd. W., FB520, Montreal QC H3G 1M8 Canada. (514)848-2424, ext. 3826. Fax: (514)848-4510. E-mail: howard.bokser@concordia.ca. Web site: www.magazine.concordia.ca. **Contact:** Howard Bokser, editor. **60% freelance written.** Quarterly magazine covering matters relating to Concordia University and its alumni. "We only cover topics related to research and teaching at Concordia, and student or administrator news, and we profile university alumni." Estab. 1977. Circ. 85,000. **Pays on acceptance.** Publishes ms an average of 1 month after acceptance. Byline given. Offers 50% kill fee. Not copyrighted. Buys first rights. Editorial lead time 2 months. Submit seasonal material 2 months in advance. Accepts queries by mail, e-mail. Accepts previously published material. Accepts simultaneous submissions. Responds in 1 month to queries; 1 month to mss. Sample copy online. Writer's guidelines free.

Nonfiction Book excerpts, general interest, historical/nostalgic, humor, interview/profile, opinion, personal experience, photo feature. **Buys 10 mss/year.** Query with published clips. Length: 1,500-2,000 words. **Pays $350-450.** Sometimes pays expenses of writers on assignment.

Photos State availability with submission. Reviews contact sheets, 2x2 transparencies, 4×6 prints, GIF/JPEG files. Buys one-time rights. Negotiates payment individually. Identification of subjects required.

Columns/Departments End Piece (opinion or essay), 650 words. **Buys 4 mss/year.** Query with published clips. **Pays $275.**

$ $ EQUAL OPPORTUNITY

The Nation's Only Multi-Ethnic Recruitment Magazine for African-American, Hispanic, Native-American & Asian-American College Grads, Equal Opportunity Publications, Inc., 445 Broad Hollow Rd., Suite 425, Melville NY 11747. (631)421-9421. Fax: (631)421-0359. E-mail: jschneider@eop.com. Web site: www.eop.com. **Contact:** James Schneider, editor. **70% freelance written.** Prefers to work with published/established writers. Triannual magazine covering career guidance for minorities. "Our audience is 90% college juniors and seniors; 10% working graduates. An understanding of educational and career problems of minorities is essential." Estab. 1967. Circ. 11,000. Pays on publication. Publishes ms an average of 6 months after acceptance. Byline given. Buys first rights. Editorial lead time 6 months. Submit seasonal material 6 months in advance. Accepts queries by mail, e-mail, fax, phone. Accepts previously published material. Responds in 2 weeks to queries; 1 month to mss. Sample copy and writer's guidelines for 9×12 SAE with 5 first-class stamps.

- Distributed through college guidance and placement offices.

Nonfiction General interest (specific minority concerns), how-to (job hunting skills, personal finance, better living, coping with discrimination), interview/profile (minority role models), opinion (problems of minorities), personal experience (professional and student study experiences), technical (on career fields offering opportunities for minorites), coverage of minority interests. **Buys 10 mss/year.** Query with or without published clips or send complete ms. Length: 1,000-2,000 words. **Pays 10¢/word.** Sometimes pays expenses of writers on assignment.

Reprints Send information about when and where the material previously appeared. Pays 10¢/word.

Photos Reviews 35mm color slides and b&w. Buys all rights. Captions, identification of subjects required.

Tips "Articles must be geared toward questions and answers faced by minority and women students. We would like to see role-model profiles of professions."

$ $ $ $ HARVARD MAGAZINE

Harvard Magazine, Inc., 7 Ware St., Cambridge MA 02138. (617)495-5746. Fax: (617)495-0324. Web site: www.harvardmagazine.com. **Contact:** John S. Rosenberg, editor. **35-50% freelance written.** Bimonthly magazine for Harvard University faculty, alumni, and students. Estab. 1898. Circ. 245,000. Pays on publication. Publishes ms an average of 4 months after acceptance. Byline given. Buys one-time print and Web site rights. Editorial lead time 1 year. Accepts queries by mail, fax. Responds in 1 month to queries; 1 month to mss. Sample copy online. Writer's guidelines not available.

Nonfiction Book excerpts, essays, interview/profile, journalism on Harvard-related intellectual subjects. **Buys 20-30 mss/year.** Query with published clips. Length: 800-10,000 words. **Pays $250-2,000.** Pays expenses of writers on assignment.

$ $ $ $ NOTRE DAME MAGAZINE

University of Notre Dame, 538 Grace Hall, Notre Dame IN 46556-5612. (574)631-5335. Fax: (574)631-6767. E-mail: ndmag@nd.edu. Web site: www.nd.edu/~ndmag. Managing Editor: Carol Schaal. **Contact:** Kerry Temple, editor. **75% freelance written.** Quarterly magazine covering news of Notre Dame and education and issues affecting contemporary society. "We are a university magazine with a scope as broad as that found at a university, but we place our discussion in a moral, ethical, and spiritual context reflecting our Catholic heritage." Estab. 1972. Circ. 150,000. **Pays on acceptance.** Publishes ms an average of 1 year after acceptance. Byline given. Buys first, electronic rights. Accepts queries by mail, e-mail, fax. Responds in 2 months to queries. Sample copy online. Writer's guidelines online.

Nonfiction Opinion, personal experience, religious. **Buys 35 mss/year.** Query with published clips. Length: 600-3,000 words. **Pays $250-3,000.** Sometimes pays expenses of writers on assignment.

Photos State availability with submission. Buys one-time and electronic rights. Identification of subjects, model releases required.

Columns/Departments Perspectives (essays, deal with a wide array of issues—some topical, some personal, some serious, some light). Query with or without published clips or send complete ms.

The online version carries original content not found in the print edition and includes writer's guidelines. Contact: Carol Schaal.

Tips "The editors are always looking for new writers and fresh ideas. However, the caliber of the magazine and frequency of its publication dictate that the writing meet very high standards. The editors value articles strong in storytelling quality, journalistic technique, and substance. They do not encourage promotional or nostalgia pieces, stories on sports, or essays that are sentimentally religious."

$ $ OREGON QUARTERLY

The Northwest Perspective from the University of Oregon, 130 Chapman Hall, 5228 University of Oregon, Eugene OR 97403-5228. (541)346-5048. Fax: (541)346-5571. E-mail: gmaynard@uoregon.edu. Web site: www.uoregon.edu/~oq. Managing Editor: Ross West. **Contact:** Guy Maynard, editor. **50% freelance written.** Quarterly magazine covering people and ideas at the University of Oregon and the Northwest. Estab. 1919. Circ. 100,000. **Pays on acceptance.** Publishes ms an average of 3 months after acceptance. Byline given. Offers 20% kill fee. Buys first North American serial rights. Accepts queries by mail, e-mail. Accepts previously published material. Responds in 2 months to queries. Sample copy for 9×12 SAE with 4 first-class stamps or on Web site. Writer's guidelines online.

Break in to the magazine with a profile (400 or 800 words) of a University of Oregon alumnus. Best to query first.

Nonfiction Northwest issues and culture from the perspective of UO alumni and faculty. **Buys 30 mss/year.** Query with published clips. Length: 500-3,000 words. **Pays 20¢/word.** Sometimes pays expenses of writers on assignment.

Reprints Send photocopy and information about when and where the material previously appeared. Pays 50% of amount paid for an original article.

Photos State availability with submission. Reviews 8×10 prints. Buys one-time rights. Offers $10-25/photo. Identification of subjects required.

Fiction Publishes novel excerpts.

Tips "Query with strong, colorful lead; clips."

N THE PENN STATER

Penn State Alumni Association, Hintz Family Alumni Center, University Park PA 16802. (814)865-2709. Fax: (814)863-5690. E-mail: pennstater@psu.edu. Web site: www.alumni.psu.edu. **Contact:** Tina Hay, editor. **60% freelance written.** Bimonthly magazine covering Penn State and Penn Staters. Estab. 1910. Circ. 130,000. **Pays on acceptance.** Publishes ms an average of 4 months after acceptance. Byline given. Offers 50% kill fee. Buys first North American serial, second serial (reprint) rights. Editorial lead time 3 months. Submit seasonal material 8 months in advance. Accepts queries by mail, e-mail, fax. Accepts previously published material. Accepts simultaneous submissions. Responds in 3 months to queries. Sample copy and writer's guidelines free.

Nonfiction Stories must have Penn State connection. Book excerpts (by or about Penn Staters), general interest, historical/nostalgic, interview/profile, personal experience, photo feature, book reviews, science/research. No unsolicited mss. **Buys 20 mss/year.** Query with published clips. Length: 200-3,000 words. **Pays competitive rates.** Pays expenses of writers on assignment.

Reprints Send photocopy and information about when and where the material previously appeared. Payment varies.

Photos Send photos with submission. Captions required.

Tips "We are especially interested in attracting writers who are savvy in creative nonfiction/literary journalism. Most stories must have a Penn State tie-in. No phone calls, please."

$ $ THE PURDUE ALUMNUS

Purdue Alumni Association, Dick and Sandy Dauch Alumni Center, 403 W. Wood St., West Lafayette IN 47907-2007. (765)494-5175. Fax: (765)494-9179. E-mail: alumnus@purdue.edu. Web site: www.purdue.edu/PAA. **Contact:** Sharon Martin, editor. **50% freelance written.** Prefers to work with published/established writers; works with small number of new/unpublished writers each year. Bimonthly magazine covering subjects of interest to Purdue University alumni. Estab. 1912. Circ. 65,000. Pays on publication. Publishes ms an average of 2 months after acceptance. Byline given. Buys first rights, makes work-for-hire assignments. Submit seasonal material 6 months in advance. Accepts queries by mail. Accepts previously published material. Accepts simultaneous submissions. Responds in 3 months to queries. Sample copy for 9×12 SAE with 2 first-class stamps. Writer's guidelines online.

Nonfiction Focus is on alumni, campus news, issues, and opinions of interest to 65,000 members of the Alumni Association. Feature style, primarily university-oriented. Issues relevant to education. General interest, historical/nostalgic, humor, interview/profile, personal experience. **Buys 12-20 mss/year.** Length: 1,500-2,500 words. **Pays $250-500 for assigned articles.** Pays expenses of writers on assignment.

Photos State availability with submission. Reviews 5×7 prints, b&w contact sheets.

Tips "We have more than 350,000 living, breathing Purdue alumni. If you can find a good story about one of them, we're interested. We use local freelancers to do campus pieces."

$ $ QUEEN'S ALUMNI REVIEW

Queen's University, 99 University Ave., Kingston ON K7L 3N6 Canada. Fax: (613)533-6828. E-mail: cuthberk@post.queensu.ca. Web site: alumnireview.queensu.ca. **Contact:** Ken Cuthbertson, editor. **25% freelance written.** Quarterly magazine. Estab. 1927. Circ. 103,000. Pays on publication. Publishes ms an average of 3 months after acceptance. Byline given. Buys electronic, first world serial rights. Editorial lead time 3 months. Submit seasonal material 9 months in advance. Accepts queries by mail, e-mail. Responds in 2 weeks to queries; 2 weeks to mss. Sample copy and writer's guidelines online.

Nonfiction "We publish feature articles, columns, and articles about alumni, faculty, and staff who are doing unusual or worthwile things." Does not want religious or political rants, travel articles, how-to, or general interest pieces that do not refer to or make some reference to our core audience." **Buys 10 mss/year.** Query with or without published clips or send complete ms. Length: 200-2,500 words. **Pays 50¢/word (Canadian) for assigned articles.** Sometimes pays expenses of writers on assignment.

Photos Send photos with submission. Reviews transparencies, prints, GIF/JPEG files. Offers $25 minimum or negotiates payment individually. Identification of subjects required.

Columns/Departments "Potential freelancers should study our magazine before submitting a query for a column." **Buys 10 mss/year.** Query with published clips or send complete ms. **Pays 50¢/word (Canadian).**

Tips "We buy freelance material, but our budget is limited, and so we choose carefully. All articles should have a Queen's angle—one that shows how Queen's alumni, faculty, staff, or friends of the university are involved and engaged in the world. We also look for topical articles that start Queen's specific and go from there to look at issues of a wide topical interest. The writing should be professional, snappy, informative, and engaging. We always have far more editorial material in hand than we can ever publish. Study our magazine before you submit a query. Our circulation is primarily in Canada, but we also have readers in the US, UK, Hong Kong, Australia, and elsewhere. Our readers are young and old, male and female, well educated, well traveled, and sophisticated. We look for material that will appeal to a broad constituency."

$ $ RIPON COLLEGE MAGAZINE

P.O. Box 248, Ripon WI 54971-0248. (920)748-8322. Fax: (920)748-9262. E-mail: dammr@ripon.edu. Web site: www.ripon.edu. **Contact:** Ric Damm, editor. **15% freelance written.** Quarterly magazine that "contains information relating to Ripon College and is mailed to alumni and friends of the college." Estab. 1851. Circ. 14,000. Pays on publication. Publishes ms an average of 3 months after acceptance. Byline given. Makes work-for-hire assignments. Accepts queries by mail, e-mail, fax, phone. Responds in 2 weeks to queries.

Nonfiction Historical/nostalgic, interview/profile. **Buys 4 mss/year.** Query with or without published clips or send complete ms. Length: 250-1,000 words. **Pays $25-350.**

Photos State availability with submission. Reviews contact sheets. Buys one-time rights. Offers additional payment for photos accepted with ms. Captions, model releases required.

Tips "Story ideas must have a direct connection to Ripon College."

RUTGERS MAGAZINE

Rutgers University, 96 Davidson Rd., Piscataway NJ 08854-8062. (732)445-3710. Fax: (732)445-5925. E-mail: rutgersmagazine@ur.rutgers.edu. **Contact:** Renee Olson, editor. **30% freelance written.** Published 3 times/year. University magazine of general interest, but articles must have a Rutgers University or alumni tie-in. Circ. 70,000. **Pays on acceptance.** Publishes ms an average of 4 months after acceptance. Byline given. Offers kill fee. Buys first North American serial rights. Submit seasonal material 8 months in advance. Accepts queries by mail, e-mail, fax.

Nonfiction Essays, general interest, historical/nostalgic, interview/profile, photo feature, science/research; art/humanities. No fillers/shorts, how-to articles, or articles without a Rutgers connection. **Buys 10-15 mss/year.** Query with published clips. Length: 1,000-4,000 words. **Payment varies.**

Photos State availability with submission. Buys one-time rights. Payment varies. Identification of subjects required.

Columns/Departments Sports; Alumni Profiles (related to Rutgers), all 1,200-1,800 words. **Buys 4-6 mss/year.** Query with published clips. **Pays competitively.**

Tips "Send an intriguing query backed by solid clips. We'll evaluate clips and topic for most appropriate use."

TRANSFORMATIONS

A Journal of People and Change, Worcester Polytechnic Institute, 100 Institute Rd., Worcester MA 01609-2280. Web site: www.wpi.edu/+transformations. **Contact:** Charna Westervelt, editor. **60% freelance written.** Quarterly alumni magazine covering science and engineering/education/business personalities and related technologies and issues for 30,000 alumni, primarily engineers, scientists, entrepreneurs, managers, media. Estab. 1897. Circ. 38,000. Pays on publication. Publishes ms an average of 6 months after acceptance. Byline given. Buys one-time rights. Accepts queries by mail, e-mail. Accepts previously published material. Accepts simultaneous submissions. Responds in 1 month to queries. Sample copy online.

Nonfiction Interview/profile (alumni in engineering, science, etc.), photo feature, features on people and programs at WPI. Query with published clips. Length: 300-2,000 words. **Pays negotiable rate.** Sometimes pays expenses of writers on assignment.

Photos State availability with submission. Reviews contact sheets. Pays negotiable rate. Captions required.

Tips "Submit outline of story, story idea, or published work. Features are most open to freelancers with excellent narrative skills, and an ability to understand and convey complex technologies in an engaging way. Keep in mind that this is an alumni magazine, so most articles focus on the college and its graduates."

CHILD CARE & PARENTAL GUIDANCE

$ $ $ AMERICAN BABY MAGAZINE

For expectant and new parents, Meredith Corp., 375 Lexington Ave., 9th Floor, New York NY 10017. Web site: www.americanbaby.com. **70% freelance written.** Monthly magazine covering health, medical and childcare concerns for expectant and new parents, particularly those having their first child or those whose child is between the ages of birth and 2 years old. Mothers are the primary readers, but fathers' issues are equally important. Estab. 1938. Circ. 2,000,000. **Pays on acceptance.** Publishes ms an average of 6 months after acceptance. Byline given. Offers 25% kill fee. Buys first North American serial rights. Editorial lead time 5 months. Submit seasonal material 6 months in advance. Accepts queries by mail. Accepts previously published material. Responds in 3 months to queries; 3 months to mss. Sample copy for 9×12 SAE with 6 first-class stamps. Writer's guidelines for #10 SASE.

- Prefers to work with published/established writers; works with a small number of new/unpublished writers each year.

Nonfiction Full-length articles should offer helpful expert information on some aspect of pregnancy or child care; should cover a common problem of child-raising, along with solutions; or should give expert advice on a psychological or practical subject. Articles about products, such as toys and nursery furniture, are not accepted, as these are covered by staff members. Book excerpts, essays, general interest, how-to (some aspect of pregnancy or child care), humor, new product, personal experience, fitness, beauty, health. "No 'hearts and flowers' or fantasy pieces." **Buys 60 mss/year.** Query with or without published clips or send complete ms. Length: 1,000-2,000 words. **Pays $750-1,200 for assigned articles; $600-800 for unsolicited articles.** Pays expenses of writers on assignment.

Reprints Send photocopy and information about when and where the material previously appeared. Pays 50%.

Photos State availability with submission. Reviews transparencies, Prints. Buys one-time rights. Identification of subjects, model releases required.

Columns/Departments Personal essays (700-1,000 words) and shorter items for Crib Notes (news and features) and Health Briefs (50-150 words) are also accepted. **Pays $200-1,000.**

Tips "Get to know our style by thoroughly reading a recent issue of the magazine. Don't send something we recently published. Our readers want to feel connected to other parents, both to share experiences and to learn from one another. They want reassurance that the problems they are facing are solvable and not uncommon. They want to keep up with the latest issues affecting their new family, particularly health and medical news, but they don't have a lot of spare time to read. We forgo the theoretical approach to offer quick-to-read, hands-on information that can be put to use immediately. A simple, straightforward, clear approach is mandatory.''

$ATLANTA PARENT/ATLANTA BABY

2346 Perimeter Park Dr., Suite 100, Atlanta GA 30341. (770)454-7599. Fax: (770)454-7699. Web site: www.atlantaparent.com. Publisher: Liz White. **50% freelance written.** Pays on publication. Publishes ms an average of 3 months after acceptance. Byline given. Buys one-time rights. Submit seasonal material 6 months in advance. Accepts queries by mail, e-mail. Accepts previously published material. Responds in 4 months to queries. Sample copy for $3.

Nonfiction General interest, how-to, humor, interview/profile, travel. Special issues: Private School (January); Camp (February); Birthday Parties (March and September); Maternity and Mothering (May and October); Childcare (July); Back-to-School (August); Teens (September); Holidays (November/December). No religious or philosophical discussions. **Buys 60 mss/year.** Query with or without published clips or send complete ms. Length: 800-1,500 words. **Pays $5-50.** Sometimes pays expenses of writers on assignment.

Reprints Send tearsheet or photocopy with rights for sale noted and information about when and where the material previously appeared. **Pays $30-50.**

Photos State availability of or send photos with submission. Reviews 3×5 photos. Buys one-time rights. Offers $10/photo.

Tips ''Articles should be geared to problems or situations of families and parents. Should include down-to-earth tips and be clearly written. No philosophical discussions. We're also looking for well-written humor.''

N $$$$BABY STEPS

iVillage, 500 7th Ave., 14th Floor, New York NY 10018. Web site: www.ivillage.com. Editor: Sally Tusa. **Contact:** Stacey Felsen, articles editor. **90% freelance written.** Semiannual magazine covering baby's first year of life. ''*Baby Steps* helps parents care for and raise their new baby—from the very first diaper change through the milestone first birthday celebration. Its writers, healthcare professionals who treat young children every day, serve as an expert resource for parents on the essentials of infant care, growth and development.'' Estab. 2001. Circ. 2,700,000. **Pays on acceptance.** Publishes ms an average of 6 months after acceptance. Byline given. Buys all rights. Editorial lead time 8 months. Submit seasonal material 8 months in advance. Accepts queries by mail. Accepts simultaneous submissions. Sample copy for free.

Nonfiction Book excerpts, how-to, new product, personal experience, health. **Buys 20 mss/year.** Query with published clips. Length: 1,500-2,500 words. **Pays 50¢-$1.25/word.** Sometimes pays expenses of writers on assignment.

N $$$$BABY TALK

Time, Inc., 530 Fifth Ave., 4th Floor, New York NY 10036. (212)522-4327. Fax: (212)522-8699. E-mail: letters@babytalk.com. Web site: www.babytalk.com. **Contact:** Editor. Magazine published 10 times/year. *Baby Talk* is written primarily for women who are considering pregnancy or who are expecting a child, and parents of children from birth through 18 months, with the emphasis on pregnancy through first 6 months of life. Estab. 1935. Circ. 2,000,000. Byline given. Accepts queries by mail. Responds in 2 months to queries.

Nonfiction Features cover pregnancy, the basics of baby care, infant/toddler health, growth and development, juvenile equipment and toys, work and day care, marriage and sex—approached from a how-to, service perspective. The message—Here's what you need to know and why—is delivered with smart, crisp style. The tone is confident and reassuring (and, when appropriate, humorous and playful), with the backing of experts. In essence, *Baby Talk* is a training manual of parents facing the day-to-day dilemmas of new parenthood. No phone calls. Query with SASE. Length: 1,000-2,000 words. **Pays $500-2,000 depending on length, degree of difficulty, and the writer's experience.**

Columns/Departments 100-1,250 words. Query with SASE. **Pays $100-1,000.**

Tips ''Please familiarize yourself with the magazine before submitting a query. Take the time to focus your story idea; scattershot queries are a waste of everyone's time. WE do not accept poetry.''

N $$BIRMINGHAM PARENT

Evans Publishing LLC, 115-C Hilltop Business Dr., Pelham AL 35124. (205)739-0090. Fax: (205)739-0073. E-mail: editor@birminghamparent.com. Web site: www.birminghamparent.com. **Contact:** Carol Muse Evans, publisher/editor. **75% freelance written.** Monthly magazine covering family issues, parenting, education, babies to teens, health care, anything involving parents raising children. ''We are a free, local parenting publication in central Alabama. All of our stories carry some type of local slant. Parenting magazines abound: we are the source for the local market.'' Estab. 2004. Circ. 40,000. Pays within 30 days of publication. Publishes ms an average of 3-4 months after acceptance. Byline given. Offers 20% kill fee. Buys first North American serial, second serial (reprint), electronic rights. Editorial lead time 3-4 months. Submit seasonal material 4 months in advance. Accepts queries by e-mail. Accepts previously published material. Accepts simultaneous submissions. Responds in 2-3 weeks to queries; 2-3 months to mss. Sample copy for $3. Writer's guidelines online.

Nonfiction Book excerpts, general interest, how-to, interview/profile, parenting. Does not want first person pieces. "Our pieces educate and inform: we don't take stories without sources." **Buys 24 mss/year.** Query with or without published clips or send complete ms. Length: 350-2,500 words. **Pays $50-350 for assigned articles; $35-200 for unsolicited articles.**

Photos State availability with submission. Reviews GIF/JPEG files. Buys one-time rights. Negotiates payment individually; offers no additional payment for photos accepted with ms. Captions, identification of subjects, model releases required.

Columns/Departments Parenting Solo (single parenting), 650 words; Baby & Me (dealing with newborns or pregnancy), 650 words; Teens (raising teenagers), 650-1,500 words. **Buys 36 mss/year.** Query with published clips or send complete ms. **Pays $35-200.**

Tips "We have a local slant. Figure out a way you can present your story so that you can add local slant to it, or suggest to us how to do so. Please no first person opinion pieces—no '10 great gifts for teachers,' for example, without sources. We expect some sources for our informative stories."

$ CHESAPEAKE FAMILY

Jefferson Communications, 929 West St., Suite 307, Annapolis MD 21401. (410)263-1641. Fax: (410)280-0255. E-mail: editor@chesapeakefamily.com. Web site: www.chesapeakefamily.com. **Contact:** Susan Jenkins, editor. **80% freelance written.** Monthly magazine covering parenting. "*Chesapeake Family* is a free, regional parenting publication serving readers in the Anne Arundel, Calvert, Prince George's, and Queen Anne's counties of Maryland. Our goal is to identify tips, resources, and products that will make our readers' lives easier. We answer the questions they don't have time to ask, doing the research for them so they have the information they need to make better decisions for their families' health, education, and well-being. Articles must have local angle and resources." Estab. 1990. Circ. 40,000. Publishes ms an average of 2 months after acceptance. Byline given. Buys first, one-time, second serial (reprint), electronic rights, makes work-for-hire assignments. Editorial lead time 3-6 months. Submit seasonal material 4 months in advance. Accepts queries by mail, e-mail, fax. Accepts previously published material. Accepts simultaneous submissions. Writer's guidelines online.

Nonfiction How-to (parenting topics: sign your kids up for sports, find out if your child needs braces, etc.), interview/profile (local personalities), travel (family-fun destinations). No general, personal essays (however, personal anecdotes leading into a story with general applicability is fine). **Buys 25 mss/year.** Send complete ms. Length: 800-1,200 words. **Pays $75-125; $35-50 for unsolicited articles.**

Photos State availability with submission. Reviews prints, GIF/JPEG files. Offers no additional payment for photos accepted with ms, unless original, assigned photo is selected for the cover. Model releases required.

Columns/Departments Buys 25 mss/year. Pays $35-50.

Tips "A writer's best chance is to know the issues specific to our local readers. Know how to research the issues well, answer the questions our readers need to know, and give them information they can act on—and present it in a friendly, conversational tone."

$ $ CHICAGO PARENT

Wednesday Journal, Inc., 141 S. Oak Park Ave., Oak Park IL 60302-2972. (708)386-5555. Fax: (708)524-8360. E-mail: sschultz@chicagoparent.com. Web site: www.chicagoparent.com. **Contact:** Susy Schultz, editor. **60% freelance written.** Monthly tabloid. "*Chicago Parent* has a distinctly local approach. We offer information, inspiration, perspective and empathy to Chicago-area parents. Our lively editorial mix has a 'we're all in this together' spirit, and articles are thoroughly researched and well written." Estab. 1988. Circ. 125,000 in 3 zones covering the 6-county Chicago metropolitan area. Pays on publication. Publishes ms an average of 2 months after acceptance. Byline given. Offers 10-50% kill fee. Buys first, electronic rights. Editorial lead time 4 months. Submit seasonal material 4 months in advance. Accepts queries by mail. Responds in 6 weeks to queries. Sample copy for $3.95 and 11×17 SAE with $1.65 postage. Writer's guidelines for #10 SASE.

- Break in by "writing 'short stuff' items (front-of-the-book short items on local people, places and things of interest to families)." Local writers only.

Nonfiction Essays, exposé, how-to (parent-related), humor, interview/profile, travel, local interest; investigative features. Special issues: include Chicago Baby and Healthy Child. "No pot-boiler parenting pieces, simultaneous submissions, previously published pieces or non-local writers (from outside the 6-county Chicago metropolitan area)." **Buys 40-50 mss/year.** Query with published clips. Length: 200-2,500 words. **Pays $25-300 for assigned articles; $25-100 for unsolicited articles.** Pays expenses of writers on assignment.

Photos State availability with submission. Reviews contact sheets, negatives, prints. Buys one-time rights. Offers $0-40/photo; negotiates payment individually. Captions, identification of subjects required.

Columns/Departments Healthy Child (kids' health issues), 850 words; Getaway (travel pieces), up to 1,200 words; other columns not open to freelancers. **Buys 30 mss/year.** Query with published clips or send complete ms. **Pays $100.**

Tips "We don't like pot-boiler parenting topics and don't accept many personal essays unless they are truly compelling."

$$$$ CHILD

Meredith Corporation, 375 Lexington Ave., New York NY 10014. (212)499-2000. Web site: www.child.com. Editor-in-Chief: Miriam Arond. Managing Editor: Dawn Roode. **Contact:** Submissions. **75% freelance written.** Magazine published 10 times/year covering parenting. Estab. 1986. Circ. 865,000. **Pays on acceptance.** Byline given. Offers 25% kill fee. Buys first, all rights. Editorial lead time 6 months. Submit seasonal material 7 months in advance. Accepts queries by mail. Responds in 2 months to queries. Sample copy for $3.50. Writer's guidelines for #10 SASE.

Nonfiction Book excerpts, essays, interview/profile, personal experience, travel, health, timely trend stories on topics that affect today's parents. No poetry or fiction. **Buys 40-50 feature, 20-30 short mss/year.** Query with published clips. Length: 650-2,500 words. **Pays $1/word and up for assigned articles.** Sometimes pays expenses of writers on assignment.

Columns/Departments What I Wish Every Parent Knew (personal essay); How They Do It (highlighting the experience of real parents in unique situations, explaining how they keep their lives in balance). **Buys 10 mss/year.** Query with published clips. **Pays $1/word and up.**

Tips "Stories should include opinions from experts as well as anecdotes from parents to illustrate the points being made. Lifestyle is key. Send a well-written query that meets our editorial needs. *Child* receives too many inappropriate submissions. Please study the magazine carefully before submitting."

N $$ COLUMBUS PARENT MAGAZINE

Consumer News Service, 5300 Crosswind Dr., Columbus OH 43216. Fax: (614)461-7527. E-mail: columbusparent@thisweeknews.com. Web site: www.columbusparent.com. **Contact:** Donna Willis, editor. **50% freelance written.** Monthly magazine covering parenting. "A hip, reliable resource for Central Ohio parents who are raising children from birth to 18." Estab. 1988. Circ. 60,000. Pays on publication. Publishes ms an average of 2 months after acceptance. Byline given. Offers 10% kill fee. Buys all rights. Editorial lead time 3 months. Submit seasonal material 5 months in advance. Accepts queries by mail, e-mail, fax. Sample copy and writer's guidelines online

Nonfiction General interest, how-to, interview/profile, new product. Does not want personal essays. **Buys 80 mss/year.** Send complete ms. Length: 500-900 words. **Pays 10¢/word.**

Photos State availability with submission. Buys one-time rights. Offers no additional payment for photos accepted with ms. Identification of subjects required

Tips "Your best bet for breaking in is to be an Ohio resident."

$ CONNECTICUT'S COUNTY KIDS

Journal Register Co., 1175 Post Rd. E., Westport CT 06880-5224. (203)226-8877, ext. 125. Fax: (203)221-7540. E-mail: countykids@ctcentral.com. Web site: www.countykids.com. **Contact:** Linda Greco, editor. **80-90% freelance written.** Monthly tabloid covering parenting. "We publish positive articles (nonfiction) that help parents of today raise children." Estab. 1987. Circ. 30,000. Pays on publication. Publishes ms an average of 2 months after acceptance. Byline given. Buys first North American serial, first, one-time, second serial (reprint) rights. Editorial lead time 6 weeks. Submit seasonal material 2-3 months in advance. Accepts queries by e-mail. Accepts previously published material. Writer's guidelines by e-mail.

Nonfiction Essays, general interest, humor, inspirational, new product, opinion, personal experience. Special issues: Birthday; Maternity; Birthing Services. No fiction. **Buys 24-35 mss/year.** Send complete ms. Length: 600-1,500 words. **Pays $40-100 for assigned articles; $25-40 for unsolicited articles.**

Columns/Departments Mom's View (humorous experiences), 800-1,000 words; Pediatric Health (medical situations), 800 words; Active Family (events shared as a family), 800 words. **Buys 15-20 mss/year.** Send complete ms. **Pays $25-40.**

Tips "We like to use Connecticut writers when we can, but we do use writers from all over the US. We like all kinds of writing styles."

$$ EXPECTING

Family Communications, 65 The East Mall, Toronto ON M8Z 5W3 Canada. (416)537-2604. Fax: (416)538-1794. E-mail: susanp@parentscanada.com. **Contact:** Susan Pennell-Sebekos, editor. **100% freelance written.** Semiannual digest-sized magazine. Writers must be Canadian health professionals. Articles address all topics relevant to expectant parents. Estab. 1995. Circ. 100,000. **Pays on acceptance.** Publishes ms an average of 6 months after acceptance. Byline given. Buys all rights. Editorial lead time 6 months. Accepts queries by mail, e-mail. Responds in 2 months to queries.

Nonfiction Medical. **Buys 6 mss/year.** Query with published clips. Length: 1,000-2,000 words. **Pays $300 (more for some articles).** Sometimes pays expenses of writers on assignment.

Photos State availability with submission. Buys all rights. Negotiates payment individually. Identification of subjects required.

$$$$ FAMILYFUN

Disney Publishing, Inc., 47 Pleasant St., Northampton MA 01060. (413)585-0444. Fax: (413)586-5724. E-mail: letters.familyfun@disney.com. Web site: www.familyfun.com. **Contact:** Features Editor. Magazine covering activities for families with kids ages 3-12. "*FamilyFun* is about all the great things families can do together. Our writers are either parents or authorities in a covered field." Estab. 1991. Circ. 1,850,000. **Pays on acceptance.** Byline sometimes given. Offers 25% kill fee. Makes work-for-hire assignments. Editorial lead time 6 months. Submit seasonal material 6 months in advance. Accepts simultaneous submissions. Responds in 3 months to queries. Sample copy for $5. Writer's guidelines online.

Nonfiction Book excerpts, essays, general interest, how-to (crafts, cooking, educational activities), humor, interview/profile, personal experience, photo feature, travel. **Buys dozens of mss/year.** Query with published clips. Length: 850-3,000 words. **Pays $1.25/word.** Pays expenses of writers on assignment.

Photos State availability with submission. Reviews contact sheets, negatives, transparencies. Buys all rights. Offers $75-500/photo. Identification of subjects, model releases required.

Columns/Departments Family Almanac, Nicole Blasenak, associate editor (simple, quick, practical, inexpensive ideas and projects—outings, crafts, games, nature activities, learning projects, and cooking with children), 200-400 words; query or send ms; **pays per word or $200 for ideas.** Family Traveler, Adrienne Stolarz, assistant editor (brief, newsy items about family travel, what's new, what's great, and especially, what's a good deal), 100-125 words; send ms; **pays per word or $50 for ideas.** My Great Idea, Mary Giles, senior editor (explains fun and inventive ideas that have worked for writer's own family), 1,000 words; query or send ms; **pays $1,250 on acceptance.** Also publishes best letters from writers and readers following column, send to My Great Idea: From Our Readers Editor, 100-150 words, **pays $75 on publication. Buys 60-80 letters/year; 10-12 mss/year.**

Tips "Many of our writers break into *FF* by writing for Family Almanac or Family Traveler (front-of-the-book departments)."

$ GRAND RAPIDS FAMILY

Gemini Publications, 549 Ottawa Ave., NW, Suite 201, Grand Rapids MI 49503. (616)459-4545. Fax: (616)459-4800. E-mail: cvalade@geminipub.com. Web site: www.grfamily.com. **Contact:** Carole Valade, editor. Monthly magazine covering local parenting issues. "*Grand Rapids Family* seeks to inform, instruct, amuse, and entertain its readers and their families." Circ. 30,000. Pays on publication. Byline given. Offers $25 kill fee. Buys first North American serial, simultaneous, all rights, makes work-for-hire assignments. Editorial lead time 3 months. Submit seasonal material 4 months in advance. Accepts simultaneous submissions. Responds in 2 months to queries; 6 months to mss. Writer's guidelines for #10 SASE.

Nonfiction "The publication recognizes that parenting is a process that begins before conception/adoption and continues for a lifetime. The issues are diverse and ever changing. *Grand Rapids Family* seeks to identify these issues and give them a local perspective, using local sources and resources." Query. **Pays $25-50.**

Photos State availability with submission. Reviews contact sheets. Buys one-time or all rights. Offers $25/photo. Captions, identification of subjects, model releases required.

Columns/Departments Pays $25.

$ GWINNETT PARENTS MAGAZINE

3651 Peachtree Pkwy., Suite 325, Suwanee GA 30024. (678)935-5116. Fax: (678)935-5115. E-mail: editor@gwinnettparents.com. Web site: www.gwinnettparents.com. **Contact:** Terrie Porter, editor. "Our mission is to provide the most comprehensive source of parenting information and local resources for families living in and around Gwinnett County, Georgia." Pays on publication. Publishes ms an average of 1-4 weeks after acceptance. Buys nonexclusive online archival rights rights. Editorial lead time 2 months. Accepts queries by e-mail. Responds in 3-4 weeks to queries. Sample copy by e-mail (paulp@gwinnettparents.com).

- Articles that are well written, concise, timely, and professionally presented have the best chance of being published. Topics with a local flair are preferable to those citing sources and incidents, or quoting individuals, from areas outside Gwinnett County.

Nonfiction Send queries with a brief bio via e-mail with "Editorial Submission" in the subject line. Length: 500-1,500 words. **Pays $50 for department articles; $75 for features.**

Photos Accepts color or b&w high resolution images. No images from the Internet. Identification of subjects, photo credit required.

$HOME EDUCATION MAGAZINE

P.O. Box 1083, Tonasket WA 98855. (509)486-1351. Web site: www.homeedmag.com. **Contact:** Helen Hegener, managing editor. **80% freelance written.** Bimonthly magazine covering home-based education. "We feature articles which address the concerns of parents who want to take a direct involvement in the education of their children—concerns such as socialization, how to find curriculums and materials, testing and evaluation, how to tell when your child is ready to begin reading, what to do when homeschooling is difficult, teaching advanced subjects, etc." Estab. 1983. Circ. 32,000. Pays on publication. Publishes ms an average of 4 months after acceptance. Byline given. Buys first North American serial, first, one-time, electronic rights. Submit seasonal material 6 months in advance. Accepts queries by mail. Responds in 2 months to queries. Sample copy for $6.50. Writer's guidelines for #10 SASE or via e-mail.

O→ Break in by "reading our magazine, understanding how we communicate with our readers, having an understanding of homeschooling, and being able to communicate that understanding clearly."

Nonfiction Essays, how-to (related to homeschooling), humor, interview/profile, personal experience, photo feature, technical. **Buys 40-50 mss/year.** Query with or without published clips or send complete ms. Length: 750-2,500 words. **Pays $50-100.** Sometimes pays expenses of writers on assignment.

Photos Send photos with submission. Reviews enlargements, 35mm prints, CD-ROMs. Buys one-time rights. Pays $100/cover; $12/inside photos. Identification of subjects required.

Tips "We would like to see how-to articles (that don't preach, just present options); articles on testing, accountability, working with the public schools, socialization, learning disabilities, resources, support groups, legislation, and humor. We need answers to the questions that homeschoolers ask. Please, no teachers telling parents how to teach. Personal experience with homeschooling is the preferred approach."

$HOMESCHOOLING TODAY

P.O. Box 436, Katy TX 77450. (281)579-0033. E-mail: management@homeschooltoday.com. Web site: www.homeschooltoday.com. **75% freelance written.** Bimonthly magazine covering homeschooling. "We are a practical magazine for homeschoolers with a broadly Christian perspective." Estab. 1992. Circ. 25,000. Pays on publication. Publishes ms an average of 1 year after acceptance. Byline given. Offers 25% kill fee. Buys first rights. Editorial lead time 6 months. Submit seasonal material 1 year in advance. Accepts simultaneous submissions. Responds in 2 months to mss. Sample copy and writer's guidelines free.

Nonfiction Book excerpts, how-to, inspirational, interview/profile, new product. No fiction or poetry. **Buys 30 mss/year.** Send complete ms. Length: 500-2,500 words. **Pays 8¢/word.**

Photos State availability with submission. Buys one-time rights. Offers no additional payment for photos accepted with ms. Captions, identification of subjects required.

N $KIDS LIFE MAGAZINE

Kids Life Publishing of Tuscaloosa, LLC, 1426 22nd Ave., Tuscaloosa AL 35401. Fax: (205)345-1632. E-mail: kidslife@comcast.net. Web site: www.kidslifemagazine.com. Editor: Brian Turner. **Contact:** Mary Jane Turner, publisher. **50% freelance written.** Bimonthly magazine covering family and child. "*Kids Life Magazine* is a one-stop place for families containing everything the Tuscaloosa area offers our children." Estab. 1996. Circ. 30,000. Pays on publication. Byline given. Not copyrighted. Buys simultaneous rights. Editorial lead time 2 months. Submit seasonal material 4 months in advance. Accepts queries by e-mail. Accepts previously published material. Accepts simultaneous submissions. Sample copy for free. Writer's guidelines online.

Nonfiction "We want anything child and family related." Personal experience. **Buys 12 mss/year. Pays up to $25.**

Photos Send photos with submission. Reviews GIF/JPEG files. Offers no additional payment for photos accepted with ms.

Columns/Departments Reel Life with Jane (movie reviews), 1,000 words; Single Parenting, 750 words; Spiritual, 725 words. **Buys 3 mss/year. Pays $0-20.**

Fillers Facts, gags to be illustrated by cartoonist, short humor. Length: 500 words.

Tips "E-mail submissions. We welcome anyone wanting to be published."

N $$$$LAMAZE PARENTS

iVillage, 500 7th Ave., 14th Floor, New York NY 10018. Web site: www.ivillage.com. Editor: Sally Tusa. **Contact:** Stacey Felsen, articles editor. **90% freelance written.** Semiannual magazine covering 3rd trimester of pregnancy and childbirth. "*Lamaze Parents*, an official magazine of Lamaze International, is the only magazine that supports an expectant woman's choice to give birth naturally. Its expert advice and evidence-based information empower her to feel confident in her body's ability to experience childbirth the Lamaze way." Estab. 1990. Circ. 2,400,000. **Pays on acceptance.** Publishes ms an average of 6 months after acceptance. Byline given. Buys all rights. Editorial lead time 8 months. Submit seasonal material 8 months in advance. Accepts queries by mail. Accepts simultaneous submissions. Sample copy for free.

Nonfiction Book excerpts, essays, how-to, inspirational, new product, opinion, personal experience, health. **Buys 20 mss/year.** Query with published clips. Length: 1,500-2,500 words. **Pays 50¢-$1.25/word.** Sometimes pays expenses of writers on assignment.

N $ $ $ $ LAMAZE PREGNANCY

iVillage, 500 7th Ave., 14th Floor, New York NY 10018. Web site: www.ivillage.com. Editor: Sally Tusa. **Contact:** Stacey Felsen, articles editor. **90% freelance written.** Semiannual magazine covering 1st and 2nd trimesters of pregnancy. "*Lamaze Pregnancy*, an official magazine of Lamaze International, introduces expectant women to the Lamaze philosophy of childbirth during the earliest weeks of their pregnancy. Nurses, childbirth educators and other experts in the field show women how to strengthen their body and build their confidence during the first and second trimesters so they have the healthiest pregnancy possible in preparation for a natural labor and birth." Estab. 2006. Circ. 1,000,000. **Pays on acceptance.** Publishes ms an average of 6 months after acceptance. Byline given. Buys all rights. Editorial lead time 8 months. Submit seasonal material 8 months in advance. Accepts queries by mail. Accepts simultaneous submissions. Sample copy for free.

Nonfiction Book excerpts, essays, how-to, inspirational, new product, opinion, personal experience, health. **Buys 20 mss/year.** Query with published clips. Length: 1,500-2,500 words. **Pays 50¢-$1.25/word.** Sometimes pays expenses of writers on assignment.

$ $ METRO PARENT MAGAZINE

Metro Parent Publishing Group, 24567 Northwestern Hwy., Suite 150, Southfield MI 48075. (248)352-0990. Fax: (248)352-5066. E-mail: sdemaggio@metroparent.com. Web site: www.metroparent.com. **Contact:** Susan DeMaggio, editor. **75% freelance written.** Monthly magazine covering parenting, women's health, education. "We are a local magazine on parenting topics and issues of interest to Detroit-area parents. Related issues: *Ann Arbor Parent; African/American Parent; Metro Baby Magazine.*" Circ. 85,000. Pays on publication. Publishes ms an average of 3 months after acceptance. Byline given. Buys first rights. Editorial lead time 3 months. Submit seasonal material 3 months in advance. Accepts queries by mail, e-mail. Accepts previously published material. Accepts simultaneous submissions. Responds in 2 weeks to queries; 3 months to mss. Sample copy for $2.50.

Nonfiction Essays, humor, inspirational, personal experience. **Buys 100 mss/year.** Send complete ms. Length: 1,500-2,500 words. **Pays $50-300 for assigned articles.**

Photos State availability with submission. Buys one-time rights. Offers $100-200/photo or negotiates payment individually. Captions required.

Columns/Departments Women's Health (latest issues of 20-40 year olds), 750-900 words; Solo Parenting (advice for single parents); Family Finance (making sense of money and legal issues); Tweens 'N Teens (handling teen issues), 750-800 words. **Buys 50 mss/year.** Send complete ms. **Pays $75-150.**

$ METROFAMILY MAGAZINE

Inprint Publishing, 306 S. Bryant C-152, Edmond OK 73034. (405)340-1404. E-mail: editor@metrofamilymagazine.com. Web site: www.metrofamilymagazine.com. Publisher: Sarah Taylor. **Contact:** Denise Springer, editor. **60% freelance written.** Monthly tabloid covering parenting. "*MetroFamily Magazine* provides local parenting and family fun information for our Central Oklahoma readers. Send us (by e-mail only) informative, helpful how-tos parents can use and relate to. Keep it light and bring on the humor." Circ. 30,000. Pays on publication. Publishes ms an average of 2-3 months after acceptance. Byline given. Offers 100% kill fee. Buys first North American serial, second serial (reprint), simultaneous, electronic rights. Editorial lead time 2-3 months. Submit seasonal material 3 months in advance. Accepts queries by e-mail. Accepts previously published material. Accepts simultaneous submissions. Responds in 3 weeks to queries; 1 month to mss. Sample copy for 10×13 SAE and 3 first-class stamps. Writer's guidelines for #10 SASE.

Nonfiction How-to (parenting issues, education), humor, travel. No poetry, fiction (except for humor column), or anything that doesn't support good, solid family values. Send complete ms. Length: 300-600 words. **Pays $25-50, plus 1 contributor copy.**

Photos State availability with submission. Reviews GIF/JPEG files. Buys one-time rights. Negotiates payment individually. Captions, identification of subjects, model releases required.

Columns/Departments You've Just Gotta Laugh, humor (600 words). **Buys 12 mss/year.** Send complete ms. **Pays $25-35.**

Fillers Facts, short humor. **Buys 12/year.** Length: 300-600 words. **Pays $25-35.**

$ METROKIDS MAGAZINE

The Resource for Delaware Valley Families, Kidstuff Publications, Inc., 4623 S. Broad St., Philadelphia PA 19122. (215)291-5560. Fax: (215)291-5563. E-mail: editor@metrokids.com. Web site: www.metrokids.com. **Contact:** Tom Livingston, executive editor. **25% freelance written.** Monthly tabloid providing information for parents and kids in Philadelphia and surrounding counties, South Jersey, and Delaware. Estab. 1990. Circ.

130,000. Pays on publication. Byline given. Buys one-time rights. Submit seasonal material 4 months in advance. Accepts queries by e-mail. Accepts previously published material. Writer's guidelines by e-mail.

- Responds only if interested.

Nonfiction General interest, how-to, new product, travel, parenting, health. Special issues: Educator's Edition—field trips, school enrichment, teacher, professional development (March & September); Camps (December & June); Special Kids—children with special needs (August); Vacations and Theme Parks (May & June); What's Happening—guide to events and activities (January); Kids 'N Care—guide to childcare (July). **Buys 40 mss/year.** Query with published clips. Length: 800-1,500 words. **Pays $50.** Sometimes pays expenses of writers on assignment.

Reprints E-mail summary or complete article and information about when and where the material previously appeared. Pays $35, or $50 if localized after discussion.

Columns/Departments Techno Family (CD-ROM and Web site reviews); Body Wise (health); Style File (fashion and trends); Woman First (motherhood); Practical Parenting (financial parenting advice); Kids 'N Care (toddlers and daycare); Special Kids (disabilities), all 800-1,000 words. **Buys 25 mss/year.** Query. **Pays $1-50.**

Tips "We prefer e-mail queries or submissions. Because they're so numerous, we don't reply unless interested. We are interested in feature articles (on specified topics) or material for our regular departments (with a regional/seasonal base). Articles should cite expert sources and the most up-to-date theories and facts. We are looking for a journalistic style of writing. We are also interested in finding local writers for assignments."

N $ $ $ $ PARENTING MAGAZINE

Time, Inc., 530 Fifth Ave., 4th Floor, New York NY 10036. (212)522-1212. Fax: (212)522-8699. Web site: www.parenting.com. Editor-in-Chief: Janet Chan. Executive Editor: Lisa Bain. Assistant Editor: Amy Roberts. **Contact:** Articles Editor. Magazine published 10 times/year for mothers of children from birth to 12, and covering both the emotional and practical aspects of parenting. Estab. 1987. Circ. 2,100,000. **Pays on acceptance.** Byline given. Offers 25% kill fee. Buys a variety of rights, including electronic rights. Writer's guidelines for #10 SASE.

Nonfiction Book excerpts, personal experience, child development/behavior/health; investigative reports. **Buys 20-30 mss/year.** Query with or without published clips. Length: 1,000-2,500 words. **Pays $1,000-3,000.** Pays expenses of writers on assignment.

Columns/Departments Query to the specific departmental editor. **Buys 50-60 mss/year.** Query. **Pays $50-400.**

Tips "The best guide for writers is the magazine itself. Please familiarize yourself with it before submitting a query."

N PARENTS

Meredith Corp., 375 Lexington Ave., New York NY 10017. (212)499-2000. Fax: (212)499-2077. Web site: www.parents.com. Articles Editor: Mary Hickey. Monthly magazine. Estab. 1926. Circ. 1,700,000. **Pays on acceptance.** Offers 25% kill fee. Submit seasonal material 6-8 months in advance. Accepts queries by mail, e-mail. Responds in 6 weeks to queries. Writer's guidelines online.

Nonfiction "Before you query us, please take a close look at our magazine at the library or newsstand. This will give you a good idea of the different kinds of stories we publish, as well as their tempo and tone. In addition, please take the time to look at the masthead to make sure you are directing your query to the correct department." Query with published clips.

Columns/Departments As They Grow (issues on different stages of development), 1,000 words.

Tips "We're a national publication, so we're mainly interested in stories that will appeal to a wide variety of parents. We're always looking for compelling human-interest stories, so you may want to check your local newspaper for ideas. Keep in mind that we can't pursue stories that have appeared in competing national publications."

N $ $ PARENT:WISE AUSTIN

Pleticha Publishing Inc., 5501-A Balcones Dr., Suite 102, Austin TX 78731. (512)459-8698. Fax: (512)532-6885. Web site: www.parentwiseaustin.com. **Contact:** Kim Pleticha, editor. **25% freelance written.** Monthly magazine covering parenting news, features and issues; mothering issues; maternal feminism; feminism as it pertains to motherhood and work/life balance; serious/thoughtful essays about the parenting experience; humor articles pertaining to the parenting experience. "*Parent:Wise Austin* targets educated, thoughtful readers who want solid information about the parenting experience. We seek to create a warm, nurturing community by providing excellent, well researched articles, thoughtful essays, humor articles, and other articles appealing to parents. Our readers demand in-depth, well written articles; we do not accept, nor will we print, 're-worked' articles on boiler plate topics." Estab. 2004. Circ. 32,000. Pays on publication. Publishes ms an average of 2 months after acceptance. Byline given. Buys first North American serial, electronic rights. Editorial lead time 6 months. Submit seasonal material 6 months in advance. Accepts queries by e-mail. Accepts simultaneous submissions. Responds in 1 week to queries; 1 month to mss. Sample copy for 8×10 SAE and 3 first-class stamps. Writer's guidelines online

Nonfiction Essays, humor, opinion, personal experience, travel, hard news, features on parenting issues. Special issues: Mother's Day issue (May); Father's Day issue (June). Does not want "boiler plate" articles or generic articles that have been "customized" for our market. **Buys 12-20 mss/year.** Query with published clips. Length: 500-5,000 words. **Pays $50-200.** Sometimes pays expenses of writers on assignment

Photos Contact Nisa Sharma, art director. State availability with submission. Reviews JPEG files. Buys one-time and electronic rights. Offers no additional payment for photos accepted with ms. Captions, identification of subjects, model releases required

Columns/Departments My Life as a Parent (humor), 500-700 words; Essay (first-person narrative), 500-1,000 words. **Buys 24-50 mss/year.** Send complete ms. **Pays $50.**

Poetry Avant-garde, free verse, haiku, light verse, traditional. Does not want poetry that does not pertain to parenting or the parenting experience. **Buys 3-5 poems/year.** Submit maximum 3 poems. Length: 25 lines

Tips "We are much more likely to accept an Essay or a My Life as a Parent (humor) article than a cover article. Cover articles generally are assigned months in advance to seasoned journalists who know our market; humor and essay articles are accepted without a query and generally publish within a couple of months of acceptance. For cover articles, we prefer detailed queries (e.g., the theme of the article; who you plan to interview; what you hope to 'discover' or how you plan to educate readers) and clips of previous work. Please e-mail queries, clips and questions to the editor. No phone calls."

$ PEDIATRICS FOR PARENTS

Pediatrics for Parents, Inc., 120 Western Ave., Gloucester MA 01930. (215)253-4543. Fax: (973)302-4543. E-mail: richsagall@pedsforparents.com. **Contact:** Richard J. Sagall, editor. **50% freelance written.** Monthly newsletter covering children's health. "*Pediatrics For Parents* emphasizes an informed, common-sense approach to childhood health care. We stress preventative action, accident prevention, when to call the doctor and when and how to handle a situation at home. We are also looking for articles that describe general, medical and pediatric problems, advances, new treatments, etc. All articles must be medically accurate and useful to parents with children—prenatal to adolescence." Estab. 1981. Circ. 20,000. Pays on publication. Publishes ms an average of 4 months after acceptance. Byline given. Buys first North American serial, electronic rights. Accepts queries by mail, e-mail, fax. Accepts previously published material. Accepts simultaneous submissions. Responds in 1 month to queries. Sample copy and writer's guidelines online.

Nonfiction Medical. No first person or experience. **Buys 25 mss/year.** Query with or without published clips or send complete ms. Length: 1,000-1,500 words. **Pays $10-25.**

Reprints Accepts previously published submissions.

N $ PIKES PEAK PARENT

The Gazette/Freedom Communications, 30 S. Prospect St., Colorado Springs CO 80903. Fax: (719)476-1625. E-mail: parent@gazette.com. Web site: www.pikespeakparent.com. **Contact:** Lisa Carpenter, editor. **10% freelance written.** Monthly tabloid covering parenting, family and grandparenting. "We prefer stories with local angle and local stories. We do not accept unsolicited manuscripts." Estab. 1994. Circ. 35,000. Pays on publication. Byline given. Buys first North American serial, electronic rights. Editorial lead time 3 months. Submit seasonal material 4 months in advance. Accepts queries by e-mail. Accepts previously published material. Accepts simultaneous submissions. Responds in 1 month to queries. Sample copy online.

Nonfiction Essays, general interest, how-to, medical related to parenting. **Buys 10 mss/year.** Query with published clips. Length: 800-1,000 words. **Pays $20-120.**

Tips "Local, local, local—with a fresh slant."

$ $ $ PLUM MAGAZINE

Groundbreak Publishing, 276 Fifth Ave., Suite 302, New York NY 10001. (212)725-9201. Fax: (212)725-9203. E-mail: editor@plummagazine.com. Web site: www.plummagazine.com. **Contact:** Editor. **90% freelance written.** Annual magazine covering health and lifestyle for pregnant women over age 35. Published in conjunction with the American College of Obstetricians and Gynecologists, *Plum* is a patient education tool meant to be an adjunct to obstetrics care. It presents information on preconception, prenatal medical care, nutrition, fitness, beauty, fashion, decorating, and travel. It also covers newborn health with articles on baby wellness, nursery necessities, postpartum care, and more. Estab. 2004. Circ. 450,000. Pays on publication. Publishes ms an average of 3-6 months after acceptance. Byline sometimes given. Offers 20% kill fee. Buys all rights. Editorial lead time 6 months. Submit seasonal material 8 months in advance. Accepts queries by e-mail. Responds in 6 weeks to queries. Sample copy for $7.95. Writer's guidelines by e-mail.

Nonfiction Essays, how-to, interview/profile. Query with published clips. Length: 300-3,500 words. **Pays 75¢-$1/word.**

N $ SACRAMENTO PARENT

Reaching Greater Sacramento & the Sierra Foothills, Family Publishing Inc., 457 Grass Valley Hwy., Suite 5, Auburn CA 95603. (530)888-0573. Fax: (530)888-1536. E-mail: amy@sacramentoparent.com. Web site: www.sacramentoparent.com. Managing Editor: Shelly Bokman. **Contact:** Amy Crelly, editor. **50% freelance written.** Monthly magazine covering parenting in the Sacramento region. "We look for articles that promote a developmentally appropriate, healthy and peaceful environment for children." Estab. 1992. Circ. 50,000. Pays on publication. Publishes ms an average of 2 months after acceptance. Byline given. Offers 10% kill fee. Buys first North American serial, electronic rights. Editorial lead time 3 months. Submit seasonal material 4 months in advance. Accepts queries by e-mail. Sample copy for free. Writer's guidelines by e-mail.

Nonfiction All articles should be related to parenting. Book excerpts, general interest, how-to, humor, interview/profile, opinion, personal experience. **Buys 36 mss/year.** Query. Length: 300-1,000 words. **Pays $30-100.**

Columns/Departments Let's Go! (Sacramento regional family-friendly day trips/excursions/activities), 600 words. **Pays $25-45.**

$ SAN DIEGO FAMILY MAGAZINE

San Diego County's Leading Resource for Parents & Educators Who Care!, P.O. Box 23960, San Diego CA 92193-3960. (619)685-6970. Fax: (619)685-6978. Web site: www.sandiegofamily.com. **Contact:** Tara Trewary, editor. **75% freelance written.** Monthly magazine for parenting and family issues. "*SDFM* strives to provide informative, educational articles emphasizing positive parenting for our typical readership of educated mothers, ages 25-45, with an upper-level income. Most articles are factual and practical, a few are humor and personal experience. Editorial emphasis is uplifting and positive." Estab. 1982. Circ. 120,000. Pays on publication. Byline given. Buys first, one-time, second serial (reprint) rights. Editorial lead time 2 months. Submit seasonal material 3 months in advance. Accepts previously published material. Responds in 1 month to queries. Sample copy for $4.50 with 9×12 SAE. Writer's guidelines online.

- No e-mail or fax queries accepted.

Nonfiction How-to, interview/profile (influential or noted persons or experts included in parenting or the welfare of children), parenting, new baby help, enhancing education, family activities, articles of specific interest to San Diego. "No rambling, personal experience pieces." **Buys 75 mss/year.** Send complete ms. Length: 800-1,200 words. **Pays $1.25/column inch.**

Reprints Send ms with rights for sale noted and information about when and where the material previously appeared. Will respond only if SASE is included.

Photos State availability with submission. Identification of subjects required.

Fillers Facts, newsbreaks (specific to family market). **Buys 10/year.** Length: 50-200 words. **Pays $1.25/column inch minimum.**

N $ SCHOLASTIC PARENT AND CHILD

Scholastic, Inc., 557 Broadway, New York NY 10012. (212)343-6100. Fax: (212)343-4801. E-mail: parentandchild@scholastic.com. Web site: parentandchildonline.com. Editor-in-Chief: Pam Abrams. Bimonthly magazine. Published to keep active parents up-to-date on children's learning and development while in pre-school or child-care enviroment. Circ. 1,224,098. Editorial lead time 10 weeks. Sample copy not available.

N TIDEWATER PARENT

Portfolio Publishing, 258 Granby St., Norfolk VA 23510. (757)222-3900. Fax: (757)222-3919. E-mail: jenny.odonnell@portfolioweekly.com. Web site: www.tidewaterparent.com. Publisher: Mary-Louise Scott. **Contact:** Jenny O'Donnell, editor. **85% freelance written.** Monthly tabloid targeting families in the Hampton Roads area. "All our readers are parents of children ages 0-11. Our readers demand stories that will help them tackle the challenges and demands they face daily as parents." Estab. 1980. Pays on publication. Byline given. Buys first North American serial rights. Editorial lead time 2 months. Submit seasonal material 3 months in advance. Accepts queries by mail, e-mail, fax. Accepts previously published material. Accepts simultaneous submissions. Responds in 1 month to queries; 4 months to mss. Sample copy for free. Writer's guidelines free.

Nonfiction Essays, general interest, historical/nostalgic, how-to, humor, interview/profile, personal experience, religious, travel. No poetry or fiction. **Buys 60 mss/year.** Query with or without published clips or send complete ms. Length: 500-3,000 words.

Photos State availability of or send photos with submission. Buys one-time rights. Negotiates payment individually. Captions required.

Columns/Departments Music and Video Software (reviews), both 600-800 words; also Where to Go, What to Do, Calendar Spotlight and Voices. **Buys 36 mss/year.** Send complete ms.

Tips "Articles for *Tidewater Parent* should be informative and relative to parenting. An informal, familiar tone is preferable to a more formal style. Avoid difficult vocabulary and complicated sentence structure. A conversational tone works best. Gain your reader's interest by using real-life situations, people or examples to support what you're saying."

$ $ $ $ TODAY'S PARENT

Today's Parent Group, One Mt. Pleasant Rd., 8th Floor, Toronto ON M4Y 2Y5 Canada. (416)764-2883. Fax: (416)764-2801. E-mail: sarah.moore@tpg.rogers.com. Web site: www.todaysparent.com. **Contact:** Sarah Moore, managing editor. Monthly magazine for parents with children up to the age of 12. Circ. 175,000. Editorial lead time 5 months.

Nonfiction Runs features with a balance between the practical and the philosophical, the light-hearted and the investigative. All articles should be grounded in the reality of Canadian family life. Length: 1,800-2,500 words. **Pays $1,500-2,200.**

Columns/Departments Profile (Canadian who has accomplished something remarkable for the benefit of children), 250 words; **pays $250.** Your Turn (parents share their experiences), 800 words; **pays $200.** Beyond Motherhood (deals with topics not directly related to parenting), 700 words; **pays $800.** Education (tackles straightforward topics and controversial or complex topics), 1,200 words; **pays $1,200-1,500.** Health Behavior (child development and discipline), 1,200 words; **pays $1,200-1,500.** Slice of Life (explores lighter side of parenting), 750 words; **pays $650.**

Tips "Because we promote ourselves as a Canadian magazine, we use only Canadian writers."

$ $ $ $ TODAY'S PARENT PREGNANCY & BIRTH

One Mt. Pleasant Rd., 8th Floor, Toronto ON M4Y 2Y5 Canada. (416)764-2883. Fax: (416)764-2801. Web site: www.todaysparent.com. **Contact:** Editor. **100% freelance written.** Magazine published 3 times/year. "*P&B* helps, supports and encourages expectant and new parents with news and features related to pregnancy, birth, human sexuality and parenting." Estab. 1973. Circ. 200,000. **Pays on acceptance.** Publishes ms an average of 8 months after acceptance. Buys first North American serial rights. Editorial lead time 6 months. Responds in 6 weeks to queries. Writer's guidelines for SASE.

Nonfiction Features about pregnancy, labor and delivery, post partum issues. **Buys 12 mss/year.** Query with published clips. Length: 1,000-2,500 words. **Pays up to $1/word.** Sometimes pays expenses of writers on assignment.

Photos State availability with submission. Rights negotiated individually. Pay negotiated individually.

Tips "Our writers are professional freelance writers with specific knowledge in the childbirth field. *P&B* is written for a Canadian audience using Canadian research and sources."

N $ $ TOLEDO AREA PARENT NEWS

Adams Street Publishing, 1120 Adams St., Toledo OH 43624-1509. (419)244-9859. Fax: (419)244-9871. E-mail: editor@toldeoparent.com. Web site: www.toledoparent.com. **Contact:** Collette Jacobs, publisher. Monthly tabloid for Northwest Ohio/Southeast Michigan parents. Estab. 1992. Circ. 40,000. Pays on publication. Publishes ms an average of 1 month after acceptance. Byline given. Editorial lead time 3 months. Accepts queries by mail, e-mail, fax. Responds in 1 month to queries. Sample copy for $1.50.

Break in with "local interest articles—Ohio/Michigan regional topics and examples preferred."

Nonfiction "We use only local writers by assignment. We accept queries and opinion pieces only. Send cover letter to be considered for assignments." General interest, interview/profile, opinion. **Buys 10 mss/year.** Length: 1,000-2,500 words. **Pays $75-125.**

Photos State availability with submission. Buys all rights. Negotiates payment individually. Identification of subjects required.

Tips "We love humorous stories that deal with common parenting issues or features on cutting-edge issues."

TREASURE VALLEY FAMILY MAGAZINE

Family Magazine & Media, Inc., 13191 W. Scotfield St., Boise ID 83713-0899. (208)938-2119. Fax: (208)938-2117. E-mail: magazine@tresurevalleyfamily.com. Web site: www.treasurevalleyfamily.com. **Contact:** Liz Buckingham, editor. **90% freelance written.** Monthly magazine covering parenting, education, child development. "Geared to parents with children 12 years and younger. Focus on education, interest, activities for children. Positive parenting and healthy families." Estab. 1993. Circ. 20,000. Pays on publication. Publishes ms an average of 3 months after acceptance. Byline given. Offers 50% kill fee. Buys first North American serial rights. Editorial lead time 3 months. Submit seasonal material 3 months in advance. Accepts queries by mail, e-mail. Accepts simultaneous submissions. Responds in 2 months to queries. Sample copy for $2. Writer's guidelines online.

Nonfiction Special issues: Family Health and Wellness (January); Early Childhood Education (February); Secondary and Higher Education (March); Summer Camps (April); Youth Sports Guide (May); Family Recreation and Fairs & Festivals (June/July); Back-to-School and extra-curricular Activities (August/September); Teens and College Planning (October); Birthday Party Fun (November); Youth in the Arts and Holiday Traditions (December). Query with published clips. Length: 1,000-1,300 words.

Photos State availability with submission. Buys one-time rights. Negotiates payment individually. Captions required.

Columns/Departments Crafts, travel, finance, parenting. Length: 700-1,000 words. Query with published clips.

$ $ TWINS

The Magazine for Parents of Multiples, The Business Word, Inc., 11211 E. Arapahoe Rd., Suite 101, Centennial CO 80112-3851. (303)967-0111. Fax: (303)290-9025. E-mail: twins.editor@businessword.com. Web site: www.twinsmagazine.com. **Contact:** Susan Alt, editor-in-chief. **80% freelance written.** Bimonthly magazine covering parenting multiples. "*TWINS* is an international publication that provides informational and educational articles regarding the parenting of twins, triplets, and more. All articles must be multiple specific and have an upbeat, hopeful, and/or positive ending." Estab. 1984. Circ. 55,000. Pays on publication. Byline given. Buys first North American serial rights. Editorial lead time 6 months. Submit seasonal material 8 months in advance. Accepts queries by mail, e-mail, fax. Response time varies to queries. Sample copy for $5 or on Web site. Writer's guidelines online.

Nonfiction Interested in seeing twin-specific discipline articles. Personal experience (first-person parenting experience), professional experience as it relates to multiples. Nothing on cloning, pregnancy reduction, or fertility issues. **Buys 12 mss/year.** Query with or without published clips or send complete ms. Length: 650-1,300 words. **Pays $25-250 for assigned articles; $25-100 for unsolicited articles.**

Photos State availability with submission. Offers no additional payment for photos accepted with ms. Identification of subjects required.

Columns/Departments Special Miracles (miraculous stories about multiples with a happy ending), 800-850 words. **Buys 8-10 mss/year.** Query with or without published clips or send complete ms. **Pays $40-75.**

Tips "All department articles must have a happy ending, as well as teach a lesson helpful to parents of multiples."

$ WESTERN NEW YORK FAMILY

Western New York Family, Inc., 3147 Delaware Ave., Suite B, Buffalo NY 14217. (716)836-3486. Fax: (716)836-3680. E-mail: michele@wnyfamilymagazine.com. Web site: www.wnyfamilymagazine.com. **Contact:** Michele Miller, editor/publisher. **90% freelance written.** Monthly magazine covering parenting in Western New York State. "Readership is largely composed of families with children ages newborn to 14 years. Although most subscriptions are in the name of the mother, 91% of fathers also read the publication. Strong emphasis is placed on how and where to find family-oriented events, as well as goods and services for children, in the Buffalo/Niagara Falls area." Estab. 1984. Circ. 22,500. Pays on publication. Publishes ms an average of 3 months after acceptance. Byline given. Buys one-time, second serial (reprint), simultaneous rights. Editorial lead time 2 months. Submit seasonal material 3 months in advance. Accepts previously published material. Accepts simultaneous submissions. Responds only if interested to queries. Sample copy for $2.50 and 9×12 SAE with $1.06 postage. Writer's guidelines online.

- Break in with either a "cutting edge" topic that is new and different in its relevance to current parenting challenges and trends or a "timeless" topic which is "evergreen" and can be kept on file to fill last minute holes.

Nonfiction How-to (craft projects for kids, holiday, costume, etc.), humor (as related to parenting), personal experience (parenting related), travel (family destinations). Special issues: Birthday Celebrations (January); Cabin Fever (February); Seeking Spring/Eldercare Guide (March); Having a Baby/Home Buying, Building & Beautifying; (April); Mother's Day (May); Father's Day (June); Summer Fun (July and August); Back to School (September); Halloween Happenings (October); Family Issues (November); and Holiday Happenings/Exploring Education (December). **Buys 125 mss/year.** Send complete ms by mail or e-mail. Unsolicited e-mail attachments are not accepted; paste text of article into body of e-mail. Length: 750-3,000 words. **Pays $50-150 for assigned articles; $35-50 for unsolicited articles.** Sometimes pays expenses of writers on assignment.

Reprints Accepts previously published submissions.

Photos State availability with submission. Reviews 3×5 prints, JPEG files via e-mail. Buys one-time rights. Offers no additional payment for photos accepted with ms. Captions, identification of subjects, model releases required.

Tips "We are interested in well-researched, nonfiction articles on surviving the newborn, preschool, school age, and adolescent years. Our readers want practical information on places to go and things to do in the Buffalo area and nearby Canada. They enjoy humorous articles about the trials and tribulations of parenthood as well as 'how-to' articles (i.e., choosing a musical instrument for your child, keeping your sanity while shopping with preschoolers, ideas for holidays and birthdays, etc.). Articles on making a working parent's life easier are of great interest as are articles written by fathers. We also need more material on preteen and young teen (13-

15) issues. More material on multicultural families and their related experiences, traditions, etc., would be of interest in 2005. Our annual 'Eldercare Guide: Caring for Our Aging Parents' has become very popular, and more material is needed on that subject."

WHAT'S UP KIDS? FAMILY MAGAZINE

496 Metler Rd., Ridgeville ON L0S 1M0 Canada. E-mail: susan@whatsupkids.com. Web site: www.whatsupkids.com. **Contact:** Paul Baswick, editor. **95% freelance written.** Bimonthly magazine covering topics of interest to young families. "Editorial is aimed at parents of kids birth-age 14. Kids Fun Section offers a section just for kids. We're committed to providing top-notch content." Estab. 1995. Circ. 200,000. Pays 30 days after publication. Publishes ms an average of 4-6 months after acceptance. Byline given. Buys first North American serial rights. Editorial lead time 6 months. Submit seasonal material 6 months in advance. Accepts queries by e-mail. Responds in 2 weeks if interested, by e-mail to queries. Writer's guidelines online.

Nonfiction Service articles for families. No religious (one sided), personal experience, ADHD, bullying or anything that's "all the talk." **Buys 50 mss/year.** Query with published clips. Length: 300-900 words. **Pays variable amount for assigned articles.** Sometimes pays expenses of writers on assignment.

Columns/Departments Understanding Families; Learning Curves; Family Finances; Baby Steps, all 400-600 words. **Buys variable number of mss/year.** Query with published clips. **Payment varies.**

Tips "We only accept submissions from Canadian writers. Writers should send cover letter, clips, and query. Please do not call, and include e-mail address on all queries."

WORKING MOTHER MAGAZINE

60 E. 42nd St., Suite 2700, New York NY 10165. Web site: www.workingmother.com. Editor-in-Chief: Suzanne Riss. **Contact:** Editorial Department. **90% freelance written.** Prefers to work with published/established writers; works with a small number of new/unpublished writers each year. Monthly magazine for women who balance a career, home, and family. Circ. 925,000. Publishes ms an average of 4 months after acceptance. Byline given. Offers kill fee. Buys all rights. Submit seasonal material 6 months in advance. Accepts queries by mail. Sample copy for $5; available by calling (800)925-0788. Writer's guidelines online.

Nonfiction Humor, service, child development, material pertinent to the working mother's predicament. **Buys 9-10 mss/year.** Query with published clips. Length: 700-1,500 words.

Tips "We are looking for pieces that help the reader. In other words, we don't simply report on a trend without discussing how it specifically affects our readers' lives and how they can handle the effects. Where can they look for help if necessary?"

COMIC BOOKS

$ THE COMICS JOURNAL

Fantagraphics Books, 7563 Lake City Way NE, Seattle WA 98115. (206)524-1967. Fax: (206)524-2104. E-mail: dean@tcj.com. Web site: www.tcj.com. **Contact:** Michael Dean, managing editor; Dirk Deppey, Web site contact. Monthly magazine covering the comics medium from an arts-first perspective. *The Comics Journal* is one of the nation's most respected single-arts magazines, providing its readers with an eclectic mix of industry news, professional interviews, and reviews of current work. Due to its reputation as the American magazine with an interest in comics as an art form, the *Journal* has subscribers worldwide, and in this country serves as an important window into the world of comics for several general arts and news magazines. Byline given. Buys exclusive rights to articles that run in print or online versions for 6 months after initial publication. Rights then revert back to the writer. Accepts queries by mail, e-mail. Writer's guidelines online.

Nonfiction "We're not the magazine for the discussion of comic 'universes,' character re-boots, and Spider-Man's new costume—beyond, perhaps, the business or cultural implications of such events." Essays, general interest, how-to, humor, interview/profile, opinion. Send complete ms. Length: 2,000-3,000 words. **Pays 4¢/word, and 1 contributor's copy.**

Columns/Departments On Theory, Art and Craft (2,000-3,000 words); Firing Line (1,000-5,000 words); Bullets (400 words or less). Send complete ms. **Pays 4¢/word, and 1 contributor's copy.**

Tips "Like most magazines, the best writers guideline is to look at the material within the magazine and give something that approximates that material in terms of approach and sophistication. Anything else is a waste of time."

CONSUMER SERVICE & BUSINESS OPPORTUNITY

CONSUMER REPORTS

Consumers Union of U.S., Inc., 101 Truman Ave., Yonkers NY 10703-1057. (914)378-2000. Fax: (914)378-2904. Web site: www.consumerreports.org. **Contact:** Robert Tiernan, managing editor. **5% freelance written.**

Monthly magazine. "*Consumer Reports* is the leading product-testing and consumer-service magazine in the US. We buy very little freelance material, mostly from proven writers we have used before for finance and health stories." Estab. 1936. Circ. 14,000,000. **Pays on acceptance.** Publishes ms an average of 2 months after acceptance. Offers negotiable kill fee. Buys all rights. Editorial lead time 4 months. Submit seasonal material 6 months in advance. Accepts queries by mail.

Nonfiction Technical, personal finance, personal health. **Buys 12 mss/year.** Query. Length: 1,000 words. **Pays variable rate.**

N $ $ $ $ CONSUMERS DIGEST

Consumers Digest Communications LLC, 520 Lake-Cook Rd., Suite 500, Deerfield IL 60015. (847)607-3000. Fax: (847)607-3009. E-mail: rdzierwa@consumersdigest.com. Web site: www.consumersdigest.com. **Contact:** Rich Dzierwn, editor. **95% freelance written.** Bimonthly magazine covering consumer matters, new products/services. "*Consumers Digest* is designed to provide opinions and recommendations in regard to consumer issues." Estab. 1959. **Pays on acceptance.** Publishes ms an average of 2 months after acceptance. Byline given. Offers 50% kill fee. Buys all rights, makes work-for-hire assignments. Editorial lead time 3-4 months. Submit seasonal material 8 months in advance. Accepts queries by mail, e-mail.

Nonfiction Exposé, general interest, new product. **Buys 70 mss/year.** Query. Length: 1,300-3,500 words. **Pays 75¢-$1/word.** Sometimes pays expenses of writers on assignment.

$ $ HOME BUSINESS MAGAZINE

United Marketing & Research Co., Inc., P.O. Box 807, Lakeville MN 55044. E-mail: editor@homebusinessmag.com. Web site: www.homebusinessmag.com. **Contact:** Stacy Henderson, online editor. **75% freelance written.** "*Home Business Magazine* covers every angle of the home-based business market including: cutting edge editorial by well-known authorities on sales and marketing, business operations, the home office, franchising, business opportunities, network marketing, mail order and other subjects to help readers choose, manage and prosper in a home-based business; display advertising, classified ads and a directory of home-based businesses; technology, the Internet, computers and the future of home-based business; home-office editorial including management advice, office set-up, and product descriptions; business opportunities, franchising and work-from-home success stories." Estab. 1993. Circ. 105,000. Publishes ms an average of 6 months after acceptance. Makes work-for-hire assignments. Editorial lead time 6 months. Submit seasonal material 6 months in advance. Accepts queries by e-mail. Accepts previously published material. Accepts simultaneous submissions. Sample copy for 9×12 SAE and 8 first-class stamps. Writer's guidelines for #10 SASE.

Nonfiction Book excerpts, general interest, how-to (home business), inspirational, interview/profile, new product, personal experience, photo feature, technical, mail order, franchise, business management, internet, finance network marketing. No non-home business related topics. **Buys 40 mss/year.** Send complete ms. Length: 200-1,000 words. **Pays 20¢/published word for work-for-hire assignments; 50-word byline for unsolicited articles.**

Photos Offers no additional payment for photos accepted with ms. Identification of subjects required.

Columns/Departments Marketing & Sales; Money Corner; Home Office; Management; Technology; Working Smarter; Franchising; Network Marketing, all 650 words. Send complete ms.

Tips "Send complete information by e-mail. We encourage writers to submit Feature Articles (2-3 pages) and Departmental Articles (1 page). Please submit polished, well-written, organized material. It helps to provide subheadings within the article. Boxes, lists, and bullets are encouraged because they make your article easier to read, use, and reference by the reader. A primary problem in the past is that articles do not stick to the subject of the title. Please pay attention to the focus of your article and to your title. Please don't call to get the status of your submission. We will call if we're interested in publishing the submission."

KIPLINGER'S PERSONAL FINANCE

1729 H St. NW, Washington DC 20006. (202)887-6400. Fax: (202)331-1206. Web site: www.kiplinger.com. Editor: Fred W. Frailey. **Contact:** Dayl Sanders, office manager. **10% freelance written.** Prefers to work with published/established writers. Monthly magazine for general, adult audience intersted in personal finance and consumer information. "*Kiplinger's* is a highly trustworthy source of information on saving and investing, taxes, credit, home ownership, paying for college, retirement planning, automobile buying, and many other personal finance topics." Estab. 1947. Circ. 800,000. **Pays on acceptance.** Publishes ms an average of 2 months after acceptance. Buys all rights. Responds in 1 month to queries.

Nonfiction "Most material is staff-written, but we accept some freelance. Thorough documentation is required for fact-checking." Query with published clips. Pays expenses of writers on assignment.

Tips "We are looking for a heavy emphasis on personal finance topics. Currently most work is provided by in-house writers."

CONTEMPORARY CULTURE

$ $ A&U

America's AIDS Magazine, Art & Understanding, Inc., 25 Monroe St., Suite 205, Albany NY 12210-2729. (888)245-4333. Fax: (888)790-1790. E-mail: chaelneedle@mac.com. Web site: www.aumag.org. **Contact:** Chael Needle, managing editor. **50% freelance written.** Monthly magazine covering cultural, political, and medical responses to AIDS/HIV. Estab. 1991. Circ. 205,000. Pays 3 months after publication. Publishes ms an average of 3 months after acceptance. Byline given. Offers 20% kill fee. Buys first North American serial rights. Editorial lead time 6 months. Accepts queries by mail, fax, phone. Accepts simultaneous submissions. Responds in 1 month to queries; 2 months to mss. Sample copy for $5. Writer's guidelines online.

Nonfiction Book excerpts, essays, general interest, how-to, humor, interview/profile, new product, opinion, personal experience, photo feature, travel, reviews (film, theater, art exhibits, video, music, other media), medical news. **Buys 12 mss/year.** Query with published clips. Length: 800-1,200 words. **Pays $150-300 for assigned articles.** Sometimes pays expenses of writers on assignment.

Photos State availability with submission. Reviews contact sheets, up to 4×5 transparencies, 5×7 to 8×10 prints. Buys one-time rights. Captions, identification of subjects, model releases required.

Columns/Departments The Culture of AIDS (reviews of books, music, film), 300 words; Viewpoint (personal opinion), 750 words. **Buys 6 mss/year.** Send complete ms. **Pays $50-150.**

Fiction Unpublished work only; accepts prose, poetry, and drama. Send complete ms. Length: less than 1,500 words. **Pays $100.**

Poetry Any length/style (shorter works preferred). **Pays $25.**

Tips "We're looking for more articles on youth and HIV/AIDS; more international coverage; more small-town America coverage."

$ $ $ ADBUSTERS

Journal of the Mental Environment, The Media Foundation, 1243 W. 7th Ave., Vancouver BC V6H 1B7 Canada. (604)736-9401. Fax: (604)737-6021. Web site: www.adbusters.org. Managing Editor: Tim Querengesser. **Contact:** Kalle Lasn, editor. **50% freelance written.** Bimonthly magazine. "We are an activist journal of the mental environment." Estab. 1989. Circ. 90,000. Pays 1 month after publication. Byline given. Buys first rights. Accepts queries by mail, e-mail, fax. Accepts simultaneous submissions. Writer's guidelines online.

Nonfiction Essays, exposé, interview/profile, opinion. **Buys variable mss/year.** Query. Length: 250-3,000 words. **Pays $100/page for unsolicited articles; 50¢/word for solicited articles.**

Fiction Inquire about themes.

Poetry Inquire about themes.

$ $ THE AMERICAN SCHOLAR

Phi Beta Kappa, 1606 New Hampshire Ave. NW, Washington DC 20009. (202)265-3808. Fax: (202)265-0083. E-mail: scholar@pbk.org. Editor: Robert Wilson. **Contact:** Jean Stipicevic, managing editor. **100% freelance written.** Quarterly journal. "Our intent is to have articles written by scholars and experts but written in nontechnical language for an intelligent audience. Material covers a wide range in the arts, sciences, current affairs, history, and literature." Estab. 1932. Circ. 30,000. Pays on publication. Publishes ms an average of 1 year after acceptance. Byline given. Offers 50% kill fee. Buys first rights. Editorial lead time 6 months. Submit seasonal material 6 months in advance. Accepts queries by mail, e-mail, fax. Responds in 2 weeks to queries; 2 months to mss. Sample copy for $9. Writer's guidelines for #10 SASE or via e-mail.

Nonfiction Essays, historical/nostalgic, humor. **Buys 40 mss/year.** Query. Length: 3,000-5,000 words. **Pays $500 maximum.**

Poetry "We're not considering any unsolicited poetry." Contact Sandra Costich, poetry editor.

$ BOSTON REVIEW

35 Medford St., Suite 302, Somerville MA 02135. (617)591-0505. Fax: (617)591-0440. E-mail: review@bostonreview.net. Web site: www.bostonreview.net. Editors: Deb Chasman and Josh Cohen. **Contact:** Joshua J. Friedman, managing editor. **90% freelance written.** Bimonthly magazine of cultural and political analysis, reviews, fiction, and poetry. "The editors are committed to a society and culture that foster human diversity and a democracy in which we seek common grounds of principle amidst our many differences. In the hope of advancing these ideals, the *Review* acts as a forum that seeks to enrich the language of public debate." Estab. 1975. Circ. 20,000. Publishes ms an average of 4 months after acceptance. Byline given. Buys first North American serial, first rights. Accepts simultaneous submissions. Responds in 4 months to queries. Sample copy for $5 or online. Writer's guidelines online.

Nonfiction Critical essays and reviews. "We do not accept unsolicited book reviews. If you would like to be considered for review assignments, please send your résumé along with several published clips." **Buys 50 mss/year.** Query with published clips.

Fiction Conact Junot Diaz, fiction editor. "I'm looking for stories that are emotionally and intellectually substantive and also interesting on the level of language. Things that are shocking, dark, lewd, comic, or even insane are fine so long as the fiction is *controlled* and purposeful in a masterly way. Subtlety, delicacy, and lyricism are attractive too." Ethnic, experimental, contemporary, prose poem. "No romance, erotica, genre fiction." **Buys 5 mss/year.** Send complete ms. Length: 1,200-5,000 words. **Pays $25-300, and 5 contributor's copies.**

Poetry Reads poetry between September 15 and May 15 each year. Contact Benjamin Paloff and Timothy Donnelly, poetry editors.

N $ $ BROKEN PENCIL

The Magazine of Zine Culture and the Independent Arts, P.O. Box 203, Station P, Toronto ON M5S 2S7 Canada. E-mail: editor@brokenpencil.com. Web site: www.brokenpencil.com. Managing Editor: Audrey Gagnon. **Contact:** Lindsay Gibb, editor. **80% freelance written.** Quarterly magazine covering arts and culture. "*Broken Pencil* is one of the few magazines in the world devoted exclusively to underground culture and the independent arts. We are a great resource and a lively read! *Broken Pencil* reviews the best zines, books, Web sites, videos and artworks from the underground and reprints the best articles from the alternative press. From the hilarious to the perverse, *Broken Pencil* challenges conformity and demands attention." Estab. 1995. Circ. 5,000. Pays on publication. Publishes ms an average of 2-3 months after acceptance. Byline given. Buys first rights. Accepts queries by mail, e-mail. Writer's guidelines online.

Nonfiction Essays, general interest, historical/nostalgic, humor, interview/profile, opinion, personal experience, photo feature, travel, reviews. Does not want anything about mainstream art and culture. **Buys 8 mss/year.** Query with published clips. Length: 400-2,500 words. **Pays $100-400.** Sometimes pays expenses of writers on assignment.

Photos Send photos with submission. Reviews prints, GIF/JPEG files. Buys one-time rights. Negotiates payment individually. Identification of subjects required.

Columns/Departments Contact Erin Kobayashi, books editor; James King, ezines editor; Terence Dick, music editor; Lindsay Gibb, film editor. Books (book reviews and feature articles); Ezines (ezine reviews and feature articles); Music (music reviews and feature articles); Film (film reviews and feature articles), all 200-300 words for reviews and 1,000 words for features. **Buys 8 mss/year.** Query with published clips. **Pays $100-400.**

Fiction Contact Hal Niedzviecki, fiction editor. "We're particularly interested in work from emerging writers." Adventure, condensed novels, confessions, erotica, ethnic, experimental, fantasy, historical, horror, humorous, mystery, novel excerpts, romance, science fiction, slice-of-life vignettes. **Buys 8 mss/year.** Send complete ms. Length: 500-3,000 words.

Tips "Write in to receive a list of upcoming themes and then pitch us stories based around those themes. If you keep your ear to the ground in the alternative and underground arts communities, you will be able to find content appropriate for *Broken Pencil*."

$ CANADIAN DIMENSION

Dimension Publications, Inc., 91 Albert St., Room 2-B, Winnipeg MB R3B 1G5 Canada. (204)957-1519. Fax: (204)943-4617. E-mail: info@canadiandimension.com. Web site: www.canadiandimension.com. **80% freelance written.** Bimonthly magazine covering socialist perspective. "We bring a socialist perspective to bear on events across Canada and around the world. Our contributors provide in-depth coverage on popular movements, peace, labour, women, aboriginal justice, environment, third world and eastern Europe." Estab. 1963. Circ. 3,000. Pays on publication. Publishes ms an average of 6 months after acceptance. Accepts previously published material. Accepts simultaneous submissions. Responds in 6 weeks to queries. Sample copy for $2. Writer's guidelines online.

Nonfiction Interview/profile, opinion, reviews; political commentary and analysis; journalistic style. **Buys 8 mss/year.** Length: 500-2,000 words. **Pays $25-100.**

Reprints Send ms with rights for sale noted and information about when and where the material previously appeared.

N $ $ COFFEEHOUSE DIGEST

Repton Media LLC, P.O. Box 1091, Sugarloaf CA 92386-1091. (877)600-1276. Fax: (775)255-1908. E-mail: info@coffeehousedigest.com. Web site: www.coffeehousedigest.com. **Contact:** Lorren Repton, managing editor. **100% freelance written.** Bimonthly magazine covering the coffeehouse lifestyle. "We reach an eclectic group of individuals, so our editorial schedule is varied and most certainly not themed. We want cutting edge articles to interest everyone who may walk into a coffee house, but no article longer than it takes to savor a talle latte." Estab. 2006. Circ. 100,000. Pays on publication. Byline given. Offers 50% kill fee. Buys first North American serial, electronic rights, makes work-for-hire assignments. Editorial lead time 3 months. Submit seasonal material 1 year in advance. Accepts queries by e-mail. Accepts simultaneous submissions. Responds in 1 month to queries; 3 months to mss. Sample copy for 6×9 SAE and 3 first-class stamps.

Nonfiction Exposé, general interest, historical/nostalgic, how-to, humor, interview/profile, new product, opinion, technical, travel. Does not want humdrum pieces you can find in any magazine. **Buys 36 mss/year.** Query. Length: 1,000 words. **Pays 10¢/word.**

Photos State availability of or send photos with submission. Reviews GIF/JPEG files. Buys one-time rights. Offers no additional payment for photos accepted with ms. Captions, identification of subjects, model releases required.

Columns/Departments Percolations (caffeine-induced revelations); The Grind (working world related, whether employee or employer); Blogophile (blogger's insight, best of online communities); Java Junket (not necessarily coffee-related travel); Wired UP (technology); Bon Appetit (anything food or drink related); Spilling the Beans (self-help), all 450 words. Cafe Culture (profiles of coffee houses around the world and happenings); Steaming Reviews (books, music, movies), both 250 words. Barista's Brews (profiles of baristas, tips and how-to's); Extremes (anything to the extreme, example sports); Overdrive (for motorheads, anything with a motor or transportation related); Frothed (opinion), all 450 words. **Buys 120 mss/year.** Query. **Pays 10¢/word.**

Tips "Be sure to read our editorial schedule online and understand the concept of our magazine. We don't just feature stories about coffee, and we are not a trade publication. Come up with some unique storylines for our departments. Accompanying photos or graphics a big plus to get published."

$ $ $ COMMENTARY

American Jewish Committee, 165 E. 56th St., New York NY 10022. (212)891-1400. Fax: (212)891-6700. Web site: www.commentarymagazine.com. Editor: Neal Kozodoy. Managing Editor: Gary Rosen. Monthly magazine. Estab. 1945. Pays on publication. Publishes ms an average of 2 months after acceptance. Byline given. Buys all rights. Accepts queries by mail.

Nonfiction Essays, opinion. **Buys 4 mss/year.** Query. Length: 2,000-8,000 words. **Pays $400-1,200.**

Tips "Unsolicited manuscripts must be accompanied by a self-addressed, stamped envelope."

N $ $ COMMON GROUND

Common Ground Publishing, 204-4381 Fraser St., Vancouver BC V5V 4G4 Canada. (604)733-2215. Fax: (604)733-4415. E-mail: editor@commonground.ca. Web site: www.commonground.ca. Senior Editor: Joseph Roberts. **90% freelance written.** Monthly tabloid covering health, environment, spirit, creativity, and wellness. "We serve the cultural creative community." Estab. 1982. Circ. 65,900. Pays on publication. Publishes ms an average of 1 month after acceptance. Byline given. Buys one-time, second serial (reprint) rights. Editorial lead time 2 months. Submit seasonal material 3 months in advance. Accepts queries by e-mail. Accepts simultaneous submissions. Responds in 6 weeks to queries; 3 months to mss. Sample copy for $5. Writer's guidelines online.

Nonfiction Topics include health, personal growth, creativity, spirituality, ecology, or short inspiring stories on environment themes. Book excerpts, how-to, inspirational, interview/profile, opinion, personal experience, travel, call to action. **Buys 12 mss/year.** Send complete ms. Length: 500-2,500 words. **Pays 10¢/word (Canadian).**

Reprints Accepts previously published submissions.

Photos State availability with submission. Buys one-time rights. Captions, photo credits required.

$ $ $ FIRST THINGS

Institute on Religion & Public Life, 156 Fifth Ave., Suite 400, New York NY 10010. (212)627-1985. Fax: (212)627-2184. E-mail: ft@firstthings.com. Web site: www.firstthings.com. **Contact:** Joseph Bottum, editor. **70% freelance written.** "Intellectual journal published 10 times/year containing social and ethical commentary in broad sense, religious and ethical perspectives on society, culture, law, medicine, church and state, morality and mores." Estab. 1990. Circ. 32,000. Pays on publication. Publishes ms an average of 4 months after acceptance. Byline given. Buys all rights. Editorial lead time 2 months. Submit seasonal material 5 months in advance. Responds in 3 weeks to mss. Sample copy and writer's guidelines for #10 SASE.

Nonfiction Essays, opinion. **Buys 60 mss/year.** Send complete ms. Length: 1,500-6,000 words. **Pays $400-1,000.** Sometimes pays expenses of writers on assignment.

Poetry Joseph Bettum, poetry editor. Traditional. **Buys 25-30 poems/year.** Length: 4-40 lines. **Pays $50.**

Tips "We prefer complete manuscripts (hard copy, double-spaced) to queries, but will reply if unsure."

N $ $ $ FLAUNT MAGAZINE

1422 N. Highland Ave., Los Angeles CA 90028. (323)836-1000. E-mail: info@flauntmagazine.com. Web site: www.flaunt.com. Managing Editor: Lucy Kim. **Contact:** Dale Brasel and Hugh MacDonald, editors. **40% freelance written.** Monthly magazine covering culture, arts, entertainment, music, fashion and film. "*Flaunt* features the bold work of emerging photographers, writers, artists and musicians. The quality of the content is mirrored in the sophisticated, interactive format of the magazine, using advanced printing techniques, fold-out articles, beautiful papers and inserts to create a visually stimulating, surprisingly readable, and intelligent book that pushes the magazine into the realm of art-object. *Flaunt* magazine has for the last 8 years made it a point to break new ground, earning itself a reputation as an engine of the avant-garde and an outlet for the culture of the cutting edge. *Flaunt* takes pride in reinventing itself each month, while consistently representing a hybrid of all that is interesting in entertaiment, fashion, music, design, film, art and literature.'' Estab. 1998. Circ. 100,000. Publishes ms an average of 3 months after acceptance. Byline given. Buys one-time rights. Editorial lead time 3 months. Submit seasonal material 3 months in advance. Accepts queries by mail, e-mail. Accepts simultaneous submissions. Responds in 2 weeks to queries; 1 month to mss. Writer's guidelines by e-mail.

Nonfiction Book excerpts, essays, exposé, general interest, historical/nostalgic, humor, interview/profile, new product, opinion, personal experience, photo feature, travel. Special issues: September and March (fashion issues); February (men's issue); May (music issue). **Buys 20 mss/year.** Query with published clips. Length: 500-5,000 words. **Pays $0-1,000.** Sometimes pays expenses of writers on assignment.

Photos Contact Lee Corbin, art director. State availability with submission. Reviews contact sheets, transparencies, prints, GIF/JPEG files. Buys one-time rights. Identification of subjects, model releases required.

Fiction Contact Andrew Pogany, senior editor. **Buys 4 mss/year.** Length: 500-5,000 words. **Pays $0-500.**

$ $ FRANCE TODAY

The Journal of French Travel & Culture, 944 Market St., Suite 200, San Francisco CA 94102. (415)981-9088. Fax: (415)981-9177. E-mail: asenges@francetoday.com. Web site: www.francetoday.com. **Contact:** Anne Sengès, managing editor. **70% freelance written.** Tabloid published 10 times/year covering contemporary France. ''*France Today* is a feature publication on contemporary France including sociocultural analysis, business, trends, current events, food, wine, and travel.'' Estab. 1989. Circ. 12,000. Pays on publication. Byline given. Buys first North American serial, second serial (reprint) rights. Submit seasonal material 4 months in advance. Accepts queries by mail, e-mail, fax. Accepts previously published material. Responds in 3 months to queries. Sample copy for 10×13 SAE with 5 first-class stamps.

Nonfiction Essays, exposé, general interest, humor, interview/profile, personal experience, travel, historical. Special issues: Paris, France on the Move, France On a Budget, Summer Travel, France Adventure. ''No travel pieces about well-known tourist attractions.'' Query with published clips, or articles sent on spec. Length: 500-1,500 words. **Pays 10¢/word.**

Reprints Send ms with rights for sale noted and information about when and where the material previously appeared. Payment varies.

Photos Buys one-time rights. Offers $25/photo. Identification of subjects required.

N $ $ HEADS MAGAZINE

Worldwide Heads, P.O. Box 1319, Hudson QC J0P 1H0 Canada. E-mail: editor@headsmagazine.com. Web site: www.headsmagazine.com. **Contact:** Editor. **100% freelance written.** Magazine published every 6 weeks covering the marijuana lifestyle. ''*Heads Magazine* is a counter-culture publication concerning the lifestyle surrounding marijuana use and propogation.'' Estab. 2000. Circ. 75,000. Pays 3 months after publication. Publishes ms an average of 3 months after acceptance. Byline given. Buys all rights. Editorial lead time 3 months. Submit seasonal material 4 months in advance. Accepts queries by mail, e-mail, fax. Accepts simultaneous submissions. Sample copy for $5 (US) or online at Web site. Writer's guidelines for $5 (US) or by e-mail.

- The editor will contact the writer only if query/ms is usable.

Nonfiction Book excerpts, exposé, general interest, how-to (grow info), humor, interview/profile, new product, opinion, personal experience, photo feature, travel. **Buys 150 mss/year.** Query with published clips or send complete ms. Length: 600-1,500 words. **Pays $50-200.**

Photos Send photos with submission. Reviews contact sheets, prints, GIF/JPEG files. Buys all rights. Negotiates payment individually. Captions, model releases required.

Columns/Departments Marijuana Notes & News (news items about marijuana), 80-150 words; Heads Destination (travel stories), 1,000-2,000 words; Heads Musician (feature story about a musician—pot oriented), 1,000-2,000 words; Ahead of Their Times (groundbreaking member of the counter-culture), 600-1,000 words. **Buys 64 mss/year.** Send complete ms. **Pays $50-200.**

Fillers Facts, newsbreaks. Length: 50-150 words. **Pays $5-15.**

N $ $ KARMA MAGAZINE

2880 Zanker Rd., Suite 203, San Jose CA 95134. E-mail: editorial@karmamagazine.com. Web site: www.karmamagazine.com. **Contact:** Eric Eslao, editor. **75% freelance written.** Quarterly magazine covering nightlife culture. ''*Karma* is the premier nightlife resource for those who choose to live it up, while remaining on the periphery of cultural insights. It highlights the lifestyles and interests of dedicated nightlife-revelers through comprehensive reviews of clubs, bars, and restaurants around the world. It also includes thought-provoking celebrity profiles and intelligent editorals of art, culture and news accented by quality, stylized photography. *Karma* engages readers with full access to nightlife culture from around the globe, providing a sure grasp on what makes urbanites tick.'' Estab. 2003. Circ. 50,000. Pays on publication. Publishes ms an average of 3 months after acceptance. Byline given. Buys first North American serial, first, one-time, electronic, all rights. Editorial lead time 3 months. Submit seasonal material 3 months in advance. Accepts queries by e-mail. Accepts simultaneous submissions. Responds in 1 month to queries. Sample copy online.

Nonfiction Essays, general interest, how-to, interview/profile, new product, opinion, photo feature, technical, travel. No self-congratulatory or self-obsessed personal experiences about the nightclub scene; no story ideas without original angles. Query with published clips. Length: 100-2,500 words. **Pays 25¢/word.** Sometimes pays expenses of writers on assignment.

Photos State availability with submission. Reviews contact sheets, prints, GIF/JPEG/PDF files. Buys one-time rights or all rights. Negotiates payment individually. Captions, identification of subjects required.

Columns/Departments Features (celebrity interviews and profiles/news in the club industry), 1,500-2,500 words; Zen (nightlife and pop culture trends—art/music/film/product reviews), 50-500 words; Locus (hot-spot reviews of clubs/bars/restaurants), 500-1,000 words. Each issue, *Karma* also features an off-the-beaten path international destination.

$$$$ MOTHER JONES

Foundation for National Progress, 222 Sutter St., 6th Floor, San Francisco CA 94108. (415)321-1700. Fax: (415)321-1701. Web site: www.motherjones.com. **Contact:** Alastair Paulin, senior editor. **80% freelance written.** Bimonthly magazine covering politics, investigative reporting, social issues, and pop culture. ''*Mother Jones* is a 'progressive' magazine—but the core of its editorial well is reporting (i.e., fact-based). No slant required. MotherJones.com is an online sister publication.'' Estab. 1976. Circ. 235,000. Pays on publication. Publishes ms an average of 4 months after acceptance. Byline given. Offers 33% kill fee. Buys first North American serial, first, one-time, electronic rights. Editorial lead time 4 months. Submit seasonal material 6 months in advance. Responds in 2 months to queries. Sample copy for $6 and 9×12 SAE. Writer's guidelines online.

Nonfiction Exposé, interview/profile, photo feature, current issues, policy, investigative reporting. **Buys 70-100 mss/year.** Query with published clips. Length: 2,000-5,000 words. **Pays $1/word.** Sometimes pays expenses of writers on assignment.

Columns/Departments Outfront (short, newsy and/or outrageous and/or humorous items), 200-800 words; Profiles of ''Hellraisers,'' 500 words. **Pays $1/word.**

Tips ''We're looking for hard-hitting, investigative reports exposing government cover-ups, corporate malfeasance, scientific myopia, institutional fraud or hypocrisy; thoughtful, provocative articles which challenge the conventional wisdom (on the right or the left) concerning issues of national importance; and timely, people-oriented stories on issues such as the environment, labor, the media, healthcare, consumer protection, and cultural trends. Send a great, short query and establish your credibility as a reporter. Explain what you plan to cover and how you will proceed with the reporting. The query should convey your approach, tone and style, and should answer the following: What are your specific qualifications to write on this topic? What 'ins' do you have with your sources? Can you provide full documentation so that your story can be fact-checked?''

N $$$ THE NEW CANADIAN MAGAZINE

Canadian Culture, Business and Politics, The NewCanadian Publishing Inc., 151 Jean-Leman, Suite 2001, Candiac Quebec J5R 4V5 Canada. (450)444-0341. Fax: (514)221-2427. E-mail: editorial@newcanadian.com. Web site: www.newcanadian.com. **Contact:** Amy Luft, editorial manager. **80% freelance written.** Quarterly magazine covering Canadian culture, business, and politics. This magazine is a modern and thought-provoking take on social issues of concern to an intelligent and affluent Canadian reader. Estab. 2002. Circ. 30,000. Pays on publication. Publishes ms an average of 3 months after acceptance. Byline given. Buys all rights, with the exception of personal stories rights. Editorial lead time 4-5 months. Submit seasonal material 5 months in advance. Accepts queries by e-mail. Accepts simultaneous submissions. Responds in 2-3 weeks to queries. Sample copy online. Writer's guidelines not available; editor will answer any questions via e-mail if requested.

Nonfiction Essays, general interest, historical/nostalgic, interview/profile, personal experience, travel. **Buys 50-60 mss/year.** Query with published clips. Length: 800-2,500 words. **Pays $240-1,250.** Sometimes pays expenses of writers on assignment.

Photos State availability with submission. Reviews prints, GIF/JPEG files. Buys all rights. Mainly offers no additional payment for photos accepted with ms; occasionally will negotiate payment individually. Captions, identification of subjects, model releases required.

Columns/Departments Routes (historical and cultural overview of various Canadian cultural communities), 1,800-2,000 words; Features (thought-provoking modern social issue), 1,800-2,500 words; Business, 1,800-

2,000 words; Lifestyle, 1,200-1,800 words; Destination (travel stories in Canada and worldwide), 1,500-2,000 words. **Buys 50-60 mss/year.** Query with published clips. **Pays $240-1,250.**

Tips "Articles should discuss timeless social issues with a modern hook. Let us know why you're the best person to write it, and what insight you have into this issue. Also, submissions are all well-received for our Routes section."

N $ $ $ NEW ENGLAND WATERSHED

A New England Journal of Thought, Culture and Art, New England Watershed Publications Inc., P.O. Box 36, Hatfield MA 01038. (413)247-3201. E-mail: publisher@newenglandwatershed.com. Web site: www.newenglandwatershed.com. Editor: Russell Powell. **Contact:** Jeanne Braham, poetry editor. **67% freelance written.** Quarterly magazine covering New England culture, art and ideas. "We are interested in ideas, art, culture and history pertaining to the New England experience, especially throughout the Connecticut River corridor from Canada to Long Island Sound." Estab. 2005. Circ. 3,000. Pays on publication. Publishes ms an average of 3 months after acceptance. Byline given. Offers 20% kill fee. Buys first North American serial rights. Editorial lead time 3 months. Submit seasonal material 6 months in advance. Accepts queries by mail, e-mail. Accepts previously published material. Accepts simultaneous submissions. Responds in 4-6 weeks to queries; 1-3 months to mss. Sample copy for $7.95 and 8 First-Class stamps. Writer's guidelines online

Nonfiction New Englanders can write about any topic relating to their passion or expertise. People from outside the region need to write about events, ideas and people that inform the contemporary New England experience. "We place a premium on ideas." Book excerpts, essays, historical/nostalgic, humor, interview/profile, opinion, personal experience, photo feature. **Buys 15-20 mss/year.** Query. Length: 500-3,500 words. **Pays $200-1,000 for assigned articles; $200-800 for unsolicited articles.** Sometimes pays expenses of writers on assignment

Photos Contact Russell Powell, editor. State availability with submission. Reviews contact sheets, prints, GIF/JPEG files. Buys one-time rights. Offers no additional payment for photos accepted with ms. Identification of subjects required

Poetry Contact Jeanne Braham, poetry editor. **Buys 15-20 poems/year.** Submit maximum 5 poems. **Pays $25-75.**

Tips "We are interested in new ideas, well-expressed. Don't tell us something we already know, and if you can easily imagine your piece in another magazine, it is probably not for us. We want to fully articulate what it means to live and work in New England, and confront the challenges of our age in meaningful ways."

$ NEW HAVEN ADVOCATE

News & Arts Weekly, New Mass Media, Inc., 900 Chapel St., Suite 1100, New Haven CT 06510. (203)789-0010. Fax: (203)787-1418. E-mail: pbass@newhavenadvocate.com. Web site: www.newhavenadvocate.com. **Contact:** Tom Gogola, managing editor. **10% freelance written.** Weekly tabloid. "Alternative, investigative, cultural reporting with a strong voice. We like to shake things up." Estab. 1975. Circ. 55,000. Pays on publication. Byline given. Buys one-time rights. Buys on speculation. Editorial lead time 1 month. Submit seasonal material 2 months in advance. Accepts simultaneous submissions. Responds in 1 month to queries. Sample copy not available.

Nonfiction Book excerpts, essays, exposé, general interest, humor, interview/profile. **Buys 15-20 mss/year.** Query with published clips. Length: 750-2,000 words. **Pays $50-150.** Sometimes pays expenses of writers on assignment.

Photos State availability with submission. Buys one-time rights. Captions, identification of subjects, model releases required.

Tips "Strong local focus; strong literary voice, controversial, easy-reading, contemporary, etc."

N THE OLDIE MAGAZINE

Oldie Publications Ltd, 65 Newman St., London England W1T 3EG United Kingdom. (44)(207)436-8801. E-mail: editorial@theoldie.co.uk. Web site: www.theoldie.co.uk. Editor: Richard Ingrams. Assistant Editor: Meg Mendez. **Contact:** Jeremy Lewis, features editor. Accepts queries by mail. Responds in 2-3 weeks to mss. Sample copy by e-mail. Writer's guidelines online.

Nonfiction Send complete ms. Length: 600-1,000 words.

Photos Send photocopies of photographs, cartoons, and illustrations.

Columns/Departments Modern Life (puzzling aspects of today's world); Anorak (owning up to an obsession); The Old Un's Diary (oldun@theoldie.co.uk).

Fiction Buys up to 3 short stories/year. Send complete ms.

$ POETRY CANADA MAGAZINE

2431 Cyprus Ave., Brighton ON L7P 1G5 Canada. Web site: www.poetrycanada.com. **90% freelance written.** Quarterly magazine promoting culture and diversity through art, photography, poetry, and articles. Despite its

Canadian root, writers from around the world can submit poetry, book reviews, and articles that will help to advance and inspire the reader to learn more about their craft, society, and environment. Estab. 2003. Circ. 500. Pays on publication. Publishes ms an average of 3-12 months after acceptance. Byline given. Buys one-time, electronic rights. Editorial lead time 3-12 months. Submit seasonal material 6 months in advance. Accepts queries by e-mail. Responds in 3 days to queries. Sample copy and writer's guidelines online.

Nonfiction General interest, historical/nostalgic, how-to, humor, inspirational, photo feature, art feature. **Buys 60-100 mss/year.** Length: 25-800 words. **Pays $5-100 and a contributor copy.**

Columns/Departments Book Reviews; Top Ways To; Dead Poets Society; Poets Practice; Interviews. **Buys 12-15 mss/year. Pays $5-100.**

Poetry All types and styles; no line limit.

$ $ SHEPHERD EXPRESS

Alternative Publications, Inc., 413 N. Second St., Suite 150, Milwaukee WI 53203. (414)276-2222. Fax: (414)276-3312. E-mail: editor@shepherd-express.com. Web site: www.shepherd-express.com. **50% freelance written.** Weekly tabloid covering "news and arts with a progressive news edge and a hip entertainment perspective." Estab. 1982. Circ. 58,000. Pays on publication. Publishes ms an average of 2 weeks after acceptance. Submit seasonal material 1 month in advance. Accepts simultaneous submissions. Sample copy for $3.

Nonfiction Book excerpts, essays, exposé, opinion. **Buys 200 mss/year.** Query with published clips or send complete ms. Length: 900-2,500 words. **Pays $35-300 for assigned articles; $10-200 for unsolicited articles.** Sometimes pays expenses of writers on assignment.

Photos State availability with submission. Reviews prints. Buys one-time rights. Negotiates payment individually. Captions, identification of subjects, model releases required.

Columns/Departments Opinions (social trends, politics, from progressive slant), 800-1,200 words; Books Reviewed (new books only: Social trends, environment, politics), 600-1,200 words. **Buys 10 mss/year.** Send complete ms.

Tips "Include solid analysis with point of view in tight but lively writing. Nothing cute. Do not tell us that something is important, tell us why."

$ $ $ THE SUN

The Sun Publishing Co., 107 N. Roberson St., Chapel Hill NC 27516. (919)942-5282. Fax: (919)932-3101. Web site: www.thesunmagazine.org. **Contact:** Sy Safransky, editor. **90% freelance written.** Monthly magazine. "We are open to all kinds of writing, though we favor work of a personal nature." Estab. 1974. Circ. 70,000. Pays on publication. Publishes ms an average of 6-12 months after acceptance. Byline given. Buys first, one-time rights. Accepts previously published material. Responds in 3-6 months to queries; 3-6 months to mss. Sample copy for $5. Writer's guidelines online.

Nonfiction Book excerpts, essays, general interest, opinion, personal experience, spiritual, interview. **Buys 50 mss/year.** Send complete ms. Length: 7,000 words maximum. **Pays $300-1,500.** Complimentary subscription is given in addition to payment (applies to payment for *all* works, not just nonfiction).

Reprints Send photocopy and information about when and where the material previously appeared. Pays 50% of amount paid for original article or story.

Photos Send photos with submission. Reviews b&w prints. Buys one-time rights. Offers $100-400/photo. Model releases required.

Fiction "We avoid stereotypical genre pieces like science fiction, romance, western, and horror. Read an issue before submitting." Literary. **Buys 20 mss/year.** Send complete ms. Length: 7,000 words maximum. **Pays $300-1,000.**

Poetry Free verse, prose poems, short and long poems. **Buys 24 poems/year.** Submit maximum 6 poems. **Pays $50-250.**

UTNE READER

1624 Harmon Place, Suite 330, Minneapolis MN 55403. (612)338-5040. Fax: (612)338-6043. E-mail: editor@utne.com. Web site: www.utne.com. Accepts queries by mail, e-mail. Writer's guidelines online.

Reprints Send tearsheet or photocopy with rights for sale noted and information about when and where the material previously appeared.

Tips "State the theme(s) clearly, let the narrative flow, and build the story around strong characters and a vivid sense of place. Give us rounded episodes, logically arranged. We do not publish fiction or poetry."

⊘ VANITY FAIR

Conde Nast Publications, Inc., 4 Times Square, Floor 22, New York NY 10036. (212)286-8180. Fax: (212)286-6707. E-mail: vfmail@vf.com. Web site: www.condenet.com. Editors: Graydon Carter and David Friend. Managing Editor: Chris Garrett. Monthly magazine. "*Vanity Fair* is edited for readers with an interest in contemporary society." Circ. 1,131,144. Sample copy not available.

- Does not buy freelance material or use freelance writers.

$ YES!

A Journal of Positive Futures, Positive Futures Network, P.O. Box 10818, Bainbridge Island WA 98110. (206)842-0216. Fax: (206)842-5208. E-mail: editors@yesmagazine.org. Web site: www.futurenet.org. Executive Editor: Sarah Ruth van Gelder. Quarterly magazine covering sustainability and community. "Interested in stories on building a positive future: sustainability, overcoming divisiveness, community organizing, social movement, etc." Estab. 1996. Circ. 55,000. Pays on publication. Byline given. Editorial lead time 4 months. Accepts queries by mail. Accepts previously published material. Accepts simultaneous submissions. Responds in 1 month to queries; 3 months to mss. Sample copy and writer's guidelines online.

Nonfiction "Please check Web site for a detailed call for submission before each issue." Book excerpts, essays, humor, interview/profile, personal experience, photo feature, technical, environmental. Query with published clips. Length: 1,500-2,500 words. **Pays up to $100/page for original, researched material.** Pays writers with 1-year subsciption and 2 contributor copies.

Reprints Send photocopy or typed ms with rights for sale noted and information about when and where the material previously appeared.

Photos State availability with submission. Reviews contact sheets, negatives, transparencies, prints. Buys one-time rights. Identification of subjects required.

Tips "Read and become familiar with the publication's purpose, tone and quality. We are about facilitating the creation of a better world. We are looking for writers who want to participate in that process. *Yes!* is less interested in bemoaning the state of our problems than in highlighting promising solutions. We are highly unlikely to accept submissions that simply state the author's opinion on what needs to be fixed and why. Our readers know *why* we need to move towards sustainability; they are interested in *how* to do so."

DISABILITIES

$ $ ABILITIES

Canada's Lifestyle Magazine for People with Disabilities, Canadian Abilities Foundation, 401-340 College St., Toronto ON M5T 3A9 Canada. (416)923-1885. Fax: (416)923-9829. E-mail: able@abilities.ca. Web site: www.abilities.ca. Editor: Raymond Cohen. **Contact:** Jaclyn Law, managing editor. **50% freelance written.** Quarterly magazine covering disability issues. "*Abilities* provides information, inspiration, and opportunity to its readers with articles and resources covering health, travel, sports, products, technology, profiles, employment, recreation, and more." Estab. 1987. Circ. 45,000. Pays on publication. Publishes ms an average of 3 months after acceptance. Byline given. Offers 50% kill fee. Buys first rights. Editorial lead time 3 months. Submit seasonal material 4 months in advance. Accepts queries by mail, e-mail, fax. Responds in 3 months to queries. Sample copy for free. Writer's guidelines for #10 SASE, online, or by e-mail.

Nonfiction Book excerpts, general interest, how-to, humor, inspirational, interview/profile, new product, opinion, personal experience, photo feature, travel. Does not want "articles that 'preach to the converted'—contain info that people with disabilities likely already know, such as what it's like to have a disability." **Buys 30-40 mss/year.** Query or send complete ms. Length: 500-2,500 words. **Pays $50-400 (Canadian) for assigned articles; $50-300 (Canadian) for unsolicited articles.**

Reprints Sometimes accepts previously published submissions (if stated as such).

Photos State availability with submission.

Columns/Departments The Lighter Side (humor), 700 words; Profile, 1,200 words.

Tips "Do not contact by phone—send something in writing. Send a great idea that we haven't done before, and make a case for why you'd be able to do a good job with it. Must be Canadian-focused. Be sure to include a relevant writing sample."

$ $ $ $ ARTHRITIS TODAY

Arthritis Foundation, 1330 W. Peachtree St. NW, Suite 100, Atlanta GA 30309. (404)872-7100. Fax: (404)872-9559. E-mail: contactus@arthritis.org. Web site: www.arthritis.org. Editor: Marcy O'Koon Moss. Managing Editor: Lissa Poirot. Medical Editor: Donna Siegfried. **50% freelance written.** Bimonthly magazine covering living with arthritis and the latest in research/treatment. "*Arthritis Today* is a consumer health magazine and is written for the more than 70 million Americans who have arthritis and for the millions of others whose lives are touched by an arthritis-related disease. The editorial content is designed to help the person with arthritis live a more productive, independent, and pain-free life. The articles are upbeat and provide practical advice, information, and inspiration." Estab. 1987. Circ. 650,000. **Pays on acceptance.** Byline given. Offers kill fee.

Buys first North American serial, second serial (reprint), electronic rights. Editorial lead time 6 months. Submit seasonal material 6 months in advance. Accepts queries by mail, e-mail, fax. Accepts simultaneous submissions. Responds in 2 months to queries. Sample copy for 9×11 SAE with 4 first-class stamps. Writer's guidelines online.

Nonfiction General interest, how-to (tips on any aspect of living with arthritis), inspirational, new product (arthritis related), opinion, personal experience, photo feature, technical, travel (tips, news), service, nutrition, general health, lifestyle. **Buys 12 unsolicited mss/year.** Query with published clips. Length: 150-2,500 words. **Pays $100-2,500.** Pays expenses of writers on assignment.

Photos Send photos with submission. Reviews prints. Buys one-time rights. Negotiates payment individually. Identification of subjects required.

Columns/Departments Nutrition, 100-600 words; Fitness, 100-600 words; Balance (emotional coping), 100-600 words; MedWatch, 100-800 words; Solutions, 100-600 words; Life Makeover, 400-600 words.

Fillers Facts, gags to be illustrated by cartoonist, short humor. **Buys 2/year.** Length: 40-100 words. **Pays $80-150.**

Tips "Our readers are already well informed. We need ideas and writers that give in-depth, fresh, interesting information that truly adds to their understanding of their condition and their quality of life. Quality writers are more important than good ideas. The staff generates many of our ideas but needs experienced, talented writers who are good reporters to execute them. Please provide published clips. In addition to articles specifically about living with arthritis, we look for articles to appeal to an older audience on subjects such as hobbies, general health, lifestyle, etc."

$ $ CAREERS & THE DISABLED

Equal Opportunity Publications, 445 Broad Hollow Rd., Suite 425, Melville NY 11747. (631)421-9421. Fax: (631)421-0359. E-mail: jschneider@eop.com. Web site: www.eop.com. **Contact:** James Schneider, editor. **60% freelance written.** Magazine published 6 times/year offering "role-model profiles and career guidance articles geared toward disabled college students and professionals, and promotes personal and professional growth." Estab. 1967. Circ. 10,000. Pays on publication. Publishes ms an average of 6 months after acceptance. Byline given. Buys first North American serial rights. Editorial lead time 6 months. Submit seasonal material 6 months in advance. Accepts queries by mail, e-mail, fax, phone. Accepts previously published material. Accepts simultaneous submissions. Responds in 3 weeks to queries. Sample copy for 9×12 SAE with 5 first-class stamps.

Nonfiction Essays, general interest, how-to, interview/profile, new product, opinion, personal experience. **Buys 30 mss/year.** Query. Length: 1,000-2,500 words. **Pays 10¢/word.** Sometimes pays expenses of writers on assignment.

Reprints Accepts previously published submissions and information about when and where the material previously appeared.

Photos Reviews transparencies, prints. Buys one-time rights. Captions, identification of subjects, model releases required.

Tips "Be as targeted as possible. Role-model profiles and specific career guidance strategies that offer advice to disabled college students are most needed."

$ $ DIABETES HEALTH

6 School St., Suite 160, Fairfax CA 94930. (415)258-2828. Fax: (415)258-2822. Web site: www.diabetesinterview.com. Editor-in-Chief: Scott King. **40% freelance written.** Monthly tabloid covering diabetes care. "*Diabetes Interview* covers the latest in diabetes care, medications, and patient advocacy. Personal accounts are welcome as well as medical-oriented articles by MDs, RNs, and CDEs (certified diabetes educators)." Estab. 1991. Circ. 40,000. Pays on publication. Publishes ms an average of 2 months after acceptance. Byline given. Buys all rights. Editorial lead time 2 months. Submit seasonal material 2 months in advance. Accepts queries by mail, e-mail, fax, phone. Sample copy online. Writer's guidelines free.

Nonfiction Essays, how-to, humor, inspirational, interview/profile, new product, opinion, personal experience. **Buys 25 mss/year.** Send complete ms. Length: 500-1,500 words. **Pays 20¢/word.**

Reprints Accepts previously published submissions.

Photos State availability of or send photos with submission. Negotiates payment individually.

Tips "Be actively involved in the diabetes community or have diabetes. However, writers need not have diabetes to write an article, but it must be diabetes-related."

$ $ DIABETES SELF-MANAGEMENT

R.A. Rapaport Publishing, Inc., 150 W. 22nd St., Suite 800, New York NY 10011-2421. (212)989-0200. Fax: (212)989-4786. E-mail: editor@diabetes-self-mgmt.com. Web site: www.diabetesselfmanagement.com. **Contact:** Ingrid Strauch, managing editor. **20% freelance written.** Bimonthly magazine. "We publish how-to health care articles for motivated, intelligent readers who have diabetes and who are actively involved in their own health care management. All articles must have immediate application to their daily living." Estab. 1983. Circ. 480,000. Pays on publication. Byline given. Offers 20% kill fee. Buys all rights. Submit seasonal material 6 months in advance. Accepts queries by mail, e-mail, fax. Responds in 6 weeks to queries. Sample copy for $4 and 9×12 SAE with 6 first-class stamps or online. Writer's guidelines for #10 SASE.

O━ Break in by having extensive knowledge of diabetes. "We are extremely generous regarding permission to republish."

Nonfiction How-to (exercise, nutrition, diabetes self-care, product surveys), technical (reviews of products available, foods sold by brand name, pharmacology), travel (considerations and prep for people with diabetes). No personal experiences, personality profiles, exposés, or research breakthroughs. **Buys 10-12 mss/year.** Query with published clips. Length: 2,000-2,500 words. **Pays $400-700 for assigned articles; $200-700 for unsolicited articles.**

Tips "The rule of thumb for any article we publish is that it must be clear, concise, useful, and instructive, and it must have immediate application to the lives of our readers. If your query is accepted, expect heavy editorial supervision."

$DIALOGUE

Blindskills, Inc., P.O. Box 5181, Salem OR 97304-0181. (800)860-4224; (503)581-4224. Fax: (503)581-0178. E-mail: info@blindskills.com. Web site: www.blindskills.com. **Contact:** Carol M. McCarl, publisher. **60% freelance written.** Bimonthly journal covering visually impaired people. Estab. 1962. Circ. 1,100. Pays on publication. Publishes ms an average of 6 months after acceptance. Byline given. Buys first rights. Editorial lead time 3 months. Accepts queries by e-mail. One free sample on request. Available in large print, Braille, 4-track audio cassette, and e-mail. $42 annually, all formats, all subscribers. Writer's guidelines online.

O━ Break in by "using accurate punctuation, grammar, and structure, and writing about pertinent subject matter."

Nonfiction Mostly features material written by visually impaired writers. Essays, general interest, historical/nostalgic, how-to (life skills methods used by visually impaired people), humor, interview/profile, personal experience, sports, recreation, hobbies. No controversial, explicit sex, religious, or political topics. **Buys 80 mss/year.** Send complete ms. Length: 200-1,000. **Pays $15-35 for assigned articles; $15-25 for unsolicited articles.**

Columns/Departments All material should be relative to blind and visually impaired readers. Living with Low Vision, 1,000 words; Hear's How (dealing with sight loss), 1,000 words. Technology Answer Book, 800 words. **Buys 80 mss/year.** Send complete ms. **Pays $10-25.**

$KALEIDOSCOPE

Exploring the Experience of Disability Through Literature and the Fine Arts, Kaleidoscope Press, 701 S. Main St., Akron OH 44311-1019. (330)762-9755. Fax: (330)762-0912. E-mail: mshiplett@udsakron.org. Web site: www.udsakron.org. **Contact:** Gail Willmott, editor-in-chief. **75% freelance written.** Eager to work with new/unpublished writers. Semiannual magazine. Subscribers include individuals, agencies, and organizations that assist people with disabilities and many university and public libraries. Appreciates work by established writers as well. Especially interested in work by writers with a disability, but features writers both with and without disabilities. "Writers without a disability must limit themselves to our focus, while those with a disability may explore any topic (although we prefer original perspectives about experiences with disability)." Estab. 1979. Circ. 1,000. Pays on publication. Byline given. Buys first rights. Rights return to author upon publication. Accepts queries by mail, fax. Accepts previously published material. Accepts simultaneous submissions. Responds in 3 weeks to queries; 6 months to mss. Sample copy for $6 prepaid. Writer's guidelines online.

O━ Submit photocopies with SASE for return of work. Please type submissions (double spaced, pages numbered and name on each page). Include SASE with sufficient postage for return of work. All submissions should be accompanied by an autobiographical sketch. May include art or photos that enhance works, prefer b&w with high contrast.

Nonfiction Articles related to disability. Book excerpts, essays, humor, interview/profile, personal experience, book reviews, articles related to disability. **Buys 8-15 mss/year.** Length: 5,000 words maximum. **Pays $25-125, plus 2 copies.**

Reprints Send ms with rights for sale noted and information about when and where the material previously appeared. Reprints permitted with credit given to original publication.

Photos Send photos with submission.

Fiction Fiction Editor. Short stories, novel excerpts. Traditional and experimental styles. Works should explore experiences with disability. Use people-first language. "We look for well-developed plots, engaging characters, and realistic dialogue. We lean toward fiction that emphasizes character and emotions rather than action-oriented narratives. No fiction that is stereotypical, patronizing, sentimental, erotic, or maudlin. No romance, religious or dogmatic fiction; no children's literature." Length: 5,000 words maximum. **Pays $10-125, and 2 contributor's copies; additional copies $6.**

Poetry "Do not get caught up in rhyme scheme. High quality with strong imagery and evocative language." Reviews any style. **Buys 12-20 poems/year.** Submit maximum 5 poems.

Tips "Articles and personal experiences should be creative rather than journalistic and with some lepth. Writers should use more than just the simple facts and chronology of an experience with disability. Inqui about future themes of upcoming issues. Sample copy very helpful. Works should not use stereotyping, pa onizing, or offending language about disability. We seek fresh imagery and thought-provoking language."

N $ $ PN

Paralyzed Veterans of America, 2111 E. Highland Ave., Suite 180, Phoenix AZ 85016. Fax: (602)224 07. E-mail: info@pnnews.com. Web site: www.pn-magazine.com. Editor: Cliff Crase. **Contact:** Mary Van eire, editorial coordinator. Monthly magazine covering news and information for wheelchair users. "Writin ust pertain to people with disabilities—specifically mobility impairments." Estab. 1946. Circ. 40,000. Pays on li-cation. Publishes ms an average of 2-4 months after acceptance. Byline given. Buys one-time rights. Edi al lead time 3 months. Submit seasonal material 3 months in advance. Accepts queries by mail, e-mail, fax. Sa copy for free. Writer's guidelines free.

Nonfiction How-to, interview/profile, new product, opinion. **Buys 10-12 mss/year.** Query with or witho published clips or send complete ms. Length: 1,200-2,500 words. **Pays $25-250.**

$ $ SPECIALIVING

P.O. Box 1000, Bloomington IL 61702. (309)820-9277. E-mail: gareeb@aol.com. Web site: www.specialiving.com. **Contact:** Betty Garee, managing editor. **90% freelance written.** Quarterly magazine covering the physically disabled/mobility impaired. Estab. 2001. Circ. 12,000. Pays on publication. Byline given. Buys one-time rights. Editorial lead time 3 months. Submit seasonal material 6 months in advance. Accepts queries by mail, e-mail, fax, phone. Accepts simultaneous submissions. Responds in 3 weeks to queries. Sample copy for $3.

Nonfiction How-to, humor, inspirational, interview/profile, new product, personal experience, technical, travel. **Buys 40 mss/year.** Query. Length: 800 words. **Pays 10¢/word.** Pays in contributor copies, only if requested.

Photos State availability with submission. Reviews GIF/JPEG files. Buys one-time rights. Offers $10/photo; $50/cover photo. Captions, identification of subjects required.

Columns/Departments Shopping Guide; Items. **Buys 10 mss/year.** Query. **Pays $50.**

N $ $ SPORTS N SPOKES

Paralyzed Veterans of America, 2111 E. Highland Ave., Suite 180, Phoenix AZ 85016. Fax: (602)224-0507. E-mail: info@pnnews.com. Web site: www.sportsnspokes.com. Editor: Cliff Crase. **Contact:** Brenda Martin, editorial coordinator. Bimonthly magazine covering wheelchair sports and recreation. "Writing must pertain to wheelchair sports and recreation." Estab. 1974. Circ. 25,000. Pays on publication. Publishes ms an average of 2-3 months after acceptance. Byline given. Buys first rights. Editorial lead time 2-3 months. Submit seasonal material 2-3 months in advance. Accepts queries by mail, e-mail, fax. Sample copy for free. Writer's guidelines free.

Nonfiction General interest, interview/profile, new product. **Buys 5-6 mss/year.** Query with or without published clips or send complete ms. Length: 1,200-2,500 words. **Pays $20-250.**

ENTERTAINMENT

$ CINEASTE

America's Leading Magazine on the Art and Politics of the Cinema, Cineaste Publishers, Inc., 304 Hudson St., 6th Floor, New York NY 10013-1015. (212)366-5720. Fax: (212)366-5724. E-mail: cineaste@cineaste.com. **Contact:** Gary Crowdus, editor-in-chief. **30% freelance written.** Quarterly magazine covering motion pictures with an emphasis on social and political perspective on cinema. Estab. 1967. Circ. 11,000. Pays on publication. Publishes ms an average of 4 months after acceptance. Byline given. Offers 50% kill fee. Buys first North American serial rights. Editorial lead time 3 months. Submit seasonal material 4 months in advance. Accepts queries by mail, e-mail, fax. Responds in 1 month to queries. Sample copy for $5. Writer's guidelines for #10 SASE.

O⊸ Break in by "being familiar with our unique editorial orientation—we are not just another film magazine."

Nonfiction Book excerpts, essays, exposé, historical/nostalgic, humor, interview/profile, opinion. **Buys 20-30 mss/year.** Query with published clips. Length: 2,000-5,000 words. **Pays $30-100.**

Photos State availability with submission. Reviews transparencies, 8×10 prints. Buys one-time rights. Offers no additional payment for photos accepted with ms. Identification of subjects required.
Columns/Departments Homevideo (topics of general interest or a related group of films); A Second Look (new interpretation of a film classic or a reevaluation of an unjustly neglected release of more recent vintage); Lost and Found (film that may or may not be released or otherwise seen in the US but which is important enough to be brought to the attention of our readers), all 1,000-1,500 words. Query with published clips. **Pays $50 minimum.**
Tips "We dislike academic jargon, obtuse Marxist terminology, film buff trivia, trendy 'buzz' phrases, and show biz references. We do not want our writers to speak of how they have 'read' or 'decoded' a film, but to view, analyze, and interpret. The author's processes and quirks should be secondary to the interests of the reader. Warning the reader of problems with specific films is more important to us than artificially 'puffing' a film because its producers or politics are agreeable. One article format we encourage is an omnibus review of several current films, preferably those not reviewed in a previous issue. Such an article would focus on films that perhaps share a certain political perspective, subject matter, or generic concerns (i.e., films on suburban life, or urban violence, or revisionist Westerns). Like individual film reviews, these articles should incorporate a very brief synopsis of plots for those who haven't seen the films. The main focus, however, should be on the social issues manifested in each film, and how it may reflect something about the current political/social/esthetic climate."

N $ $ COLUMBIA CITY PAPER

Columbia's Only Locally Owned Alt Weekly, Columbia City Paper, LLC, 701 Gervais St., Suite 150-218, Columbia SC 29201. (803)256-6670. Fax: (803)461-4640. E-mail: submissions@columbiacitypaper.com. Web site: www.columbiacitypaper.com. Paul Blake, publisher; Corey Hutchins, news editor; Sean Rayford, music editor. **Contact:** Todd Morehead, managing editor. **20% freelance written.** Biweekly newspaper. This publication is an alternative newsweekly. Circ. 20,000+. Pays on publication. Byline given. Buys one-time, second serial (reprint), simultaneous, electronic rights. Editorial lead time 2 weeks. Accepts queries by mail, e-mail. Accepts previously published material. Accepts simultaneous submissions. Responds in 1 month to queries. Writer's guidelines online.
Nonfiction Exposé, general interest, humor, interview/profile (politicians, regional weirdos), regional sports with a quirky twist. Query. Length: 300-4,000 words. **Pays varied price.**
Photos Sean Rayford. State availability with submission. Reviews JPG, TIF. Buys one-time rights. Identification of subjects required.
Columns/Departments Tight Ends (quirky regional sports, 700 words); Talkback! (op/ed, 100-700 words); Letters to the Reader (humurous rant in four sentences addressed to the general populace and sometimes inanimate objects, 50 words maximum). Query.
Fillers Writer should query with ideas. Newsbreaks, short humor. Length: 200-700 words.
Tips "Columbia City Paper offers a progressive voice to fly in the face of conservatism. Definitely read a few back issues to familiarize yourself with the tone of the paper. We recommend breaking in with offbeat news briefs or in-depth exposé pieces. Above all, send your best work and pull no punches. Imagine if Lenny Bruce and Bob Woodward moved to the South to start an alternative newsweekly."

$ DANCE INTERNATIONAL

Scotiabanti Dance Centre, 677 Davie St., Vancouver BC V6B 2G6 Canada. (604)681-1525. Fax: (604)681-7732. E-mail: danceint@direct.ca. Web site: www.danceinternational.org. **Contact:** Maureen Riches, editor. **100% freelance written.** Quarterly magazine covering dance arts. "Articles and reviews on current activities in world dance, with occasional historical essays; reviews of dance films, video, and books." Estab. 1973. Circ. 4,500. Pays on publication. Publishes ms an average of 3 months after acceptance. Byline given. Offers 50% kill fee. Buys one-time rights. Editorial lead time 3 months. Submit seasonal material 6 weeks in advance. Accepts queries by mail, e-mail, fax, phone. Responds in 2 weeks to queries; 1 month to mss. Sample copy for $7. Writer's guidelines for #10 SASE.
Nonfiction Book excerpts, essays, historical/nostalgic, interview/profile, personal experience, photo feature. **Buys 100 mss/year.** Query. Length: 1,200-2,200 words. **Pays $40-150.**
Photos Send photos with submission. Reviews prints. Offers no additional payment for photos accepted with ms. Identification of subjects required.
Columns/Departments Dance Bookshelf (recent books reviewed), 700-800 words; Regional Reports (events in each region), 1,200 words. **Buys 100 mss/year.** Query. **Pays $80.**
Tips "Send résumé and samples of recent writings."

$ DANCE SPIRIT

Lifestyle Media, Inc., 110 William St., 23rd Floor, New York NY 10038. (646)459-4800. Fax: (646)459-4900. E-mail: sjarrett@lifestylemedia.com. Web site: www.dancespirit.com. **Contact:** Sara Jarrett, editor-in-chief. **50%**

freelance written. Monthly magazine covering all dance disciplines. "*Dance Spirit* is a special interest teen magazine for girls and guys who study and perform either through a studio or a school dance performance group." Estab. 1997. Circ. 100,000. Pays on publication. Publishes ms an average of 4 months after acceptance. Byline given. Offers 25% kill fee. Buys all rights. Editorial lead time 3 months. Submit seasonal material 8 months in advance. Accepts queries by e-mail. Responds in 3 months to queries; 4 months to mss. Sample copy for $4.95.

Nonfiction Personal experience, photo feature, dance-related articles only. **Buys 100 mss/year.** Query with published clips. Length: 500-1,200 words. **Pays $150.** Sometimes pays expenses of writers on assignment.

Photos Reviews transparencies. Buys all rights. Negotiates payment individually. Captions, identification of subjects, model releases required.

Columns/Departments Ballet; Jazz; Tap; Swing; Hip Hop; Lyrical; Dance Team; Health; Beauty; Los Angeles and New York City Focuses; Choreography; Celebrities; Nutrition.

The online magazine carries original content not found in the print edition. Contact: Sara Jarrett.

Tips "Reading the magazine can't be stressed enough. We look for writers with a dance background and experienced dancers/choreographers to contribute; succinct writing style, hip outlook."

$ $ DIRECTED BY

The Cinema Quarterly, Visionary Media, P.O. Box 1722, Glendora CA 91740-1722. Fax: (309)276-0309. E-mail: visionarycinema@yahoo.com. Web site: www.directed-by.com. **Contact:** Carsten Dau, editor. **10% freelance written.** Quarterly magazine covering the craft of directing a motion picture. "Our articles are for readers particularly knowledgeable about the art and history of movies from the director's point of view. Our purpose is to communicate our enthusiasm and interest in the craft of cinema." Estab. 1998. Circ. 42,000. Pays on publication. Publishes ms an average of 3 months after acceptance. Byline given. Offers 25% kill fee. Buys all rights. Editorial lead time 3 months. Submit seasonal material 3 months in advance. Accepts queries by mail, e-mail. Accepts simultaneous submissions. Responds in 6 weeks to queries. Sample copy for $5. Writer's guidelines free or by e-mail.

Nonfiction Interview/profile, photo feature, on-set reports. No gossip, celebrity-oriented material, or movie reviews. **Buys 5 mss/year.** Query. Length: 500-7,500 words. **Pays $50-750.** Sometimes pays expenses of writers on assignment.

Photos State availability with submission. Reviews contact sheets. Buys all rights. Offers no additional payment for photos accepted with ms. Captions, identification of subjects required.

Columns/Departments Trends (overview/analysis of specific moviemaking movements/genres/subjects), 1,500-2,000 words; Focus (innovative take on the vision of a contemporary director), 1,500-2,000 words; Appreciation (overview of deceased/foreign director), 1,000-1,500 words; Final Cut (spotlight interview with contemporary director), 3,000 words; Perspectives (interviews/articles about film craftspeople who work with a featured director), 1,500-2,000 words. **Buys 5 mss/year.** Query. **Pays $50-750.**

Tips "We have been inundated with 'shelf-life' article queries and cannot publish even a small fraction of them. As such, we have restricted our interest in freelancers to writers who have direct access to a notable director of a current film which has not been significantly covered in previous issues of magazines; said director must be willing to grant an exclusive peronal interview to *DIRECTED BY*. This is a tough task for a writer, but if you are a serious freelancer and have access to important filmmakers, we are interested in you."

DISNEY MAGAZINE

Disney Publishing Worldwide, 244 Main St., Northampton MA 01060-3886. (413)585-0444. Fax: (413)587-9335. E-mail: letters.familyfun@disney.com. Web site: www.disneymagazine.com. Quarterly magazine. Circ. 480,000.

- Does not buy freelance material or use freelance writers.

EAST END LIGHTS

The Quarterly Magazine for Elton John Fans, 4040 Creditview Rd., Mississauga ON L5C 3Y8 Canada. (416)760-3426. Fax: (905)566-7369. E-mail: eastendlights@sympatico.ca. Web site: www.eastendlights.com. **90% freelance written.** Quarterly magazine covering Elton John. "In one way or another, a story must relate to Elton John, his activities or associates (past and present). We appeal to discriminating Elton fans. No gushing fanzine material. No current concert reviews." Estab. 1990. Circ. 1,700. Pays 3 weeks after publication. Publishes ms an average of 3 months after acceptance. Byline given. Buys first, second serial (reprint) rights. Submit seasonal material 6 months in advance. Accepts queries by mail, e-mail, fax. Accepts previously published material. Responds in 2 months to queries. Sample copy for $5.

Nonfiction Book excerpts, essays, exposé, general interest, historical/nostalgic, humor, interview/profile. **Buys 20 mss/year.** Query with or without published clips or send complete ms. Length: 400-1,000 words.

Reprints Send tearsheet or photocopy with rights for sale noted and information about when and where the material previously appeared.

Photos State availability with submission. Reviews negatives, 5×7 prints, high-resolution digital files. Buys one-time and all rights.

Columns/Departments Clippings (nonwire references to Elton John in other publications), maximum 200 words. **Buys 12 mss/year.** Send complete ms.

Tips "Approach us with a well-thought-out story idea. We prefer interviews with Elton-related personalities—past or present. Try to land an interview we haven't done. We are particularly interested in music/memorabilia collecting of Elton material."

N ⊘ ENTERTAINMENT WEEKLY

Time, Inc., 1675 Broadway, 30th Floor, New York NY 10019. (212)522-5600. Fax: (212)522-0074. Web site: www.ew.com. Editor: Norman Pearlstine. Weekly magazine. Written for readers who want the latest reviews, previews and updates of the entertainment world. Circ. 1,600,000. Editorial lead time 4 weeks. Sample copy not available.

- Does not buy freelance material or use freelance writers.

$ $ FANGORIA

Horror in Entertainment, Starlog Communications, Inc., 1372 Broadway, 2nd Floor, New York NY 10018. (212)634-0318. Fax: (212)889-7933. Web site: www.fangoria.com. **Contact:** Anthony Timpone, editor. **95% freelance written.** Works with a small number of new/unpublished writers each year. Magazine published 10 times/year covering horror films, TV projects, comics, videos, and literature, and those who create them. "We provide an assignment sheet (deadlines, info) to writers, thus authorizing queried stories that we're buying." Estab. 1979. Pays on publication. Publishes ms an average of 3 months after acceptance. Byline given. Buys all rights. Submit seasonal material 4 months in advance. Accepts queries by mail. Responds in 6 weeks to queries. Sample copy for $9 and 10×13 SAE with 4 first-class stamps. Writer's guidelines for #10 SASE.

O→ Break in by "reading the magazine regularly and exhibiting a professional view of the genre."

Nonfiction Book excerpts, interview/profile of movie directors, makeup FX artists, screenwriters, producers, actors, noted horror/thriller novelists and others—with genre credits; special FX and special makeup FX how-it-was-dones (on filmmaking only). Occasional "think" pieces, opinion pieces, reviews, or sub-theme overviews by industry professionals. Avoids most articles on science-fiction films. **Buys 120 mss/year.** Query with published clips. Length: 1,000-3,500 words. **Pays $100-250.** Sometimes pays expenses of writers on assignment.

Photos State availability with submission. Reviews transparencies, prints (b&w, color) electronically. Captions, identification of subjects required.

Columns/Departments Monster Invasion (exclusive, early information about new film productions; also mini-interviews with filmmakers and novelists). Query with published clips. **Pays $45-75.**

▣ The online magazine carries original content not found in the print edition.

Tips "Other than recommending that you study one or several copies of *Fangoria*, we can only describe it as a horror film magazine consisting primarily of interviews with technicians and filmmakers in the field. Be sure to stress the interview subjects' words—not your own opinions as much. We're very interested in small, independent filmmakers working outside of Hollywood. These people are usually more accessible to writers, and more cooperative. *Fangoria* is also sort of a de facto bible for youngsters interested in movie makeup careers and for young filmmakers. We are devoted only to reel horrors—the fakery of films, the imagery of the horror fiction of a Stephen King or a Clive Barker—we do not want nor would we ever publish articles on real-life horrors, murders, etc. A writer must enjoy horror films and horror fiction to work for us. If the photos in *Fangoria* disgust you, if the sight of (stage) blood repels you, if you feel 'superior' to horror (and its fans), you aren't a writer for us and we certainly aren't the market for you. We love giving new writers their first chance to break into print in a national magazine. We are currently looking for Arizona- and Las Vegas-based correspondents, as well as writers stationed in Spain (especially Barcelona), southern US cities, and Eastern Europe."

FILM COMMENT

Film Society of Lincoln Center, 70 Lincoln Center Plaza, New York NY 10023. (212)875-5610. E-mail: editor@filmlinc.com; chang@filmlinc.com. Web site: www.filmlinc.com. **Contact:** Chris Chang, senior editor. **100% freelance written.** Bimonthly magazine covering film criticism and film history. Estab. 1962. Circ. 30,000. Pays on publication. Byline given. Editorial lead time 6 weeks. Accepts queries by mail, e-mail, fax, phone. Accepts simultaneous submissions.

Nonfiction Essays, historical/nostalgic, interview/profile, opinion. **Buys 100 mss/year.** Send complete ms. We respond to queries, but rarely assign a writer we don't know. Length: 800-8,000 words.

Photos State availability with submission. Buys one-time rights. No additional payment for photos accepted with ms.

Tips "We are more or less impervious to 'hooks,' don't worry a whole lot about 'who's hot who's not,' or tying in with next fall's surefire big hit. (We think people should write about films they've seen, not films that haven't even been finished.) We appreciate good writing (writing, not journalism) on subjects in which the writer has some personal investment and about which he or she has something noteworthy to say. Demonstrate ability and inclination to write *FC*-worthy articles. We read and consider everything we get, and we do print unknowns and first-timers. Probably the writer with a shorter submission (1,000-2,000 words) has a better chance than with an epic article that would fill half the issue."

N $ $ FLICK MAGAZINE

Your Movie Souvenir, Decipher, Inc., 253 Granby St., Norfolk VA 23510. (757)623-3600. Fax: (757)623-8368. E-mail: julie.matthews@decipher.com. Web site: www.flickmagazine.com. Managing Editor: Julie Matthews. **Contact:** Peter Lobred, vice president, publishing. **30-40% freelance written.** Mini-magazine distributed in movie theaters that comes out in conjunction with selected movies covering one specific movie per issue. "*Flick*'s mission is to match the passion and personality of fans, taking readers inside Hollywood and increasing their connection to the film they are about to view." Estab. 2005. Circ. 2.5 million. **Pays on acceptance.** Publishes ms an average of 4 months after acceptance. Makes work-for-hire assignments. Editorial lead time 4-5 months. Accepts queries by mail, e-mail.

Nonfiction Essays, humor, interview/profile, opinion, personal experience. Query. Length: 500-1,000 words. **Pays $200-500.** Sometimes pays expenses of writers on assignment.

Photos Art Director (jeff.hellerman@decipher.com).

Columns/Departments Pays $200-500. Gags to be illustrated by cartoonist, short humor. **Buys 5-10/year. Pays $200-500.**

Tips "Writing for *Flick* is about research, story angles, subject knowledge, and access to movie cast and crew."

N ⊘ GLOBE

American Media, Inc., 1000 American Media Way, Boca Raton FL 33464. (561)997-7733. Fax: (561)989-1004. E-mail: newstips@globefl.com. Web site: www.globemagazine.com. Weekly tabloid. "*Globe* is edited for an audience interested in a wide range of human-interest stories, with particular emphasis on celebrities." Circ. 631,705.

- Does not buy freelance material or use freelance writers.

N $ IN TOUCH WEEKLY

Bauer Magazine Limited Partnership, 270 Sylvan Ave., Englewood Cliffs NJ 07632. (201)569-6699. E-mail: contactintouch@intouchweekly.com. Web site: www.intouchweekly.com. Editor: Richard Spencer. Managing Editor: Kathryn Walsh. **10% freelance written.** Weekly magazine covering celebrity news and entertainment. Estab. 2002. Circ. 1,300,000. Pays on publication. Buys all rights. Editorial lead time 1 week. Accepts queries by mail, e-mail, phone.

Nonfiction Interview/profile, gossip. **Buys 1,300 mss/year.** Query. Length: 100-1,000 words. **Pays $50.**

INTERVIEW

Brant Publications, Inc., 575 Broadway, 5th Floor, New York NY 10012. (212)941-2900. Fax: (212)941-2934. E-mail: brantinter@aol.com. Web site: www.interviewmagazine.com. Editor: Ingrid Sischy. Monthly magazine. Explores the inside world of music, film, fashion, art, TV, photography, sports, contemporary life and politics through celebrity interviews. Circ. 200,000. Editorial lead time 2 months. Sample copy not available.

$ $ MOVIEMAKER MAGAZINE

MovieMaker Publishing Co., 121 Fulton St., Fifth Floor, New York NY 10038. (212)766-4100. Fax: (212)766-4102. E-mail: jwood@moviemaker.com. Web site: www.moviemaker.com. **Contact:** Jennifer Wood, editor. **95% freelance written.** Bimonthly magazine covering film, independent cinema, and Hollywood. "*MovieMaker*'s editorial is a progressive mix of in-depth interviews and criticism, combined with practical techniques and advice on financing, distribution, and production strategies. Behind-the-scenes discussions with Hollywood's top moviemakers, as well as independents from around the globe, are routinely found in *MovieMaker*'s pages." Estab. 1993. Circ. 55,000. Pays within 1 month of publication. Publishes ms an average of 2 months after acceptance. Byline given. Offers variable kill fee. Buys all rights. Editorial lead time 3 months. Submit seasonal material 4 months in advance. Accepts queries by mail, e-mail, fax. Accepts simultaneous submissions. Responds in 2 months to queries; 2 months to mss. Sample copy online. Writer's guidelines by e-mail.

Nonfiction Jennifer Wood, managing editor. Exposé, general interest, historical/nostalgic, how-to, interview/profile, new product, technical. **Buys 10 mss/year.** Query with published clips. Length: 800-3,000 words. **Pays $75-500 for assigned articles.**

Photos State availability with submission. Rights purchased negotiable. Payment varies for photos accepted with ms. Identification of subjects required.
Columns/Departments Jennifer Wood, managing editor. Documentary; Home Cinema (home video/DVD reviews); How They Did It (first-person filmmaking experiences); Festival Beat (film festival reviews); World Cinema (current state of cinema from a particular country). Query with published clips. **Pays $75-300.**
Tips "The best way to begin working with *MovieMaker* is to send a list of 'pitches' along with your résumé and clips. As we receive a number of résumés each week, we want to get an early sense of not just your style of writing, but the kinds of subjects that interest you most as they relate to film. E-mail is the preferred method of correspondence, and please allow 2 months before following up on a query or résumé. Queries should be submitted in writing, rather than phone calls."

N $ $ $ OK! MAGAZINE

Northern & Shell North America Limited, 475 Fifth Ave., 2nd Floor, New York NY 10017. Fax: (212)672-0801. E-mail: editor@ok-magazine.com. Web site: www.ok-magazine.com. Editor: Sarah Ivens. Managing Editor: Martin Smith. **Contact:** Katie Caperton, editorial manager; Rob Chilton, features director. **10% freelance written.** Weekly magazine covering entertainment news. "We are a celebrity friendly magazine. We strive not to show celebrities in a negative light. We consider ourselves a cross between *People* and *In Style*." Estab. 2005. Circ. 1,000,000. Pays after publication. Publishes ms an average of 1 month after acceptance. Byline sometimes given. Buys first North American serial, first, one-time rights. Editorial lead time 2 weeks. Accepts queries by mail, e-mail, fax.
Nonfiction Interview/profile, photo feature. **Buys 50 mss/year.** Query with published clips. Length: 500-2,000 words. **Pays $100-1,000.**
Photos Contact Maria Collazo, photography director.

⊘ PREMIERE MAGAZINE

Hachette Filipacchi Magazines, 1633 Broadway, 41st Floor, New York NY 10019. (212)767-5400. Fax: (212)767-5450. Web site: www.premiere.com. Magazine published 10 times/year.

- Does not buy freelance material or use freelance writers.

$ $ RUE MORGUE

Horror in Culture & Entertainment, Marrs Media, Inc., 700 Queen St. E., Toronto ON M4M 1G9 Canada. E-mail: info@rue-morgue.com. Web site: www.rue-morgue.com. Editor: Rod Gudino. Associate Editor: Mary Beth Hollyer. **Contact:** Jen Vuckovic, managing editor. **50% freelance written.** Bimonthly magazine covering horror entertainment. "A knowledge of horror entertainment (films, books, games, toys, etc.)." Estab. 1997. Pays on publication. Publishes ms an average of 4 months after acceptance. Byline given. Buys all rights. Editorial lead time 2 months. Submit seasonal material 4 months in advance. Accepts queries by e-mail. Responds in 6 weeks to queries; 2 months to mss. Writer's guidelines by e-mail.
Nonfiction Essays, exposé, historical/nostalgic, interview/profile, new product, travel. No fiction. Reviews done by staff writers. **Buys 10 mss/year.** Query with published clips or send complete ms. Length: 500-2,000 words. **Pays $75-300.**
Columns/Departments Classic Cut (historical essays on classic horror films, books, games, comic books, music), 500-700 words. **Buys 1-2 mss/year.** Query with published clips. **Pays $60.**
Tips "The editors are most responsive to special interest articles and analytical essays on cultural/historical topics relating to the horror genre—published examples: Leon Theremin, Soren Kierkegaard, Horror in Fine Art, Murderbilia."

⊘ SOAP OPERA DIGEST

Primedia Broad Reach Magazines, 216 Madison Ave., 10th Floor, New York NY 10016. Web site: www.soapdigest.com. Weekly magazine for the daytime and primetime soap opera viewer. Circ. 1,040,142.

- Does not buy freelance material or use freelance writers.

$ $ $ $ SOUND & VISION

Hachette Filipacchi Media U.S., Inc., 1633 Broadway, New York NY 10019. (212)767-6000. Fax: (212)767-5615. E-mail: soundandvision@hfmus.com. Web site: www.soundandvisionmag.com. Editor-in-Chief: Mike Mettler. Entertainment Editor: Ken Richardson. **Contact:** Michael Gaughn, features editor. **40% freelance written.** Published 10 times/year. Provides readers with authoritative information on the home entertainment technologies and products that will impact their lives. Estab. 1958. Circ. 400,000. **Pays on acceptance.** Publishes ms an average of 4 months after acceptance. Byline given. Buys first North American serial, electronic rights. Accepts queries by mail, e-mail, fax. Sample copy for 9×12 SAE and 11 first-class stamps.
Nonfiction Home theater, audio, video and multimedia equipment plus movie, music, and video game reviews,

how-to-buy and how-to-use A/V gear, interview/profile. **Buys 25 mss/year.** Query with published clips. Length: 1,500-3,000 words. **Pays $1,000-1,500.**

Tips "Send proposals or outlines, rather than complete articles, along with published clips to establish writing ability. Publisher assumes no responsibility for return or safety of unsolicited art, photos, or manuscripts."

STAR MAGAZINE

American Media, Inc., 1000 American Media Way, Boca Raton FL 33464. E-mail: letters@starmagazine.com. Web site: www.starmagazine.com.

- Query before submitting.

$ $ TAKE ONE

Film & Television in Canada, Canadian Independent Film & Television Publishing Association, 252-128 Danforth Ave., Toronto ON M4K 1N1 Canada. (416)944-1096. Fax: (416)465-4356. E-mail: editor@takeonemagazine.ca. Web site: www.takeonemagazine.ca. **Contact:** Wyndham Wise, editor-in-chief. **100% freelance written.** Quarterly magazine covering Canadian film and television. "*Take One* is a special interest magazine that focuses exclusively on Canadian cinema, filmmakers, and Canadian television." Estab. 1992. Circ. 5,000/issue. Pays on publication. Publishes ms an average of 2 months after acceptance. Byline given. Offers 50% kill fee. Buys one-time, electronic rights. Editorial lead time 3 months. Submit seasonal material 3 months in advance. Accepts queries by mail, e-mail, fax, phone. Sample copy online.

Nonfiction Essays, historical/nostalgic, interview/profile, opinion. Query. Length: 2,000-4,000 words. **Pays 12¢/word.** Sometimes pays expenses of writers on assignment.

$ TELE REVISTA

Su Mejor Amiga, Teve Latino Publishing, Inc., P.O. Box 142179, Coral Gables FL 33114-5170. (305)445-1755. Fax: (305)445-3907. E-mail: info@telerevista.com. Web site: www.telerevista.com. **Contact:** Ana Pereiro, editor. **100% freelance written.** Monthly magazine covering Hispanic entertainment (US and Puerto Rico). "We feature interviews, gossip, breaking stories, behind-the-scenes happenings, etc." Estab. 1986. Pays on publication. Publishes ms an average of 3 months after acceptance. Byline sometimes given. Buys all rights. Editorial lead time 2 months. Submit seasonal material 3 months in advance. Accepts queries by mail, e-mail, fax. Sample copy for free.

Nonfiction Exposé, interview/profile, opinion, photo feature. **Buys 200 mss/year.** Query. **Pays $25-75.**

Photos State availability of or send photos with submission. Buys all rights. Negotiates payment individually. Captions required.

Columns/Departments Buys 60 mss/year. Query. **Pays $25-75.**

Fillers Anecdotes, facts, gags to be illustrated by cartoonist, newsbreaks, short humor.

TV GUIDE

Gemstar-TV Guide Ineternational, Inc., 1211 Avenue of the Americas, 4th Floor, New York NY 10036. (212)852-7500. Fax: (212)852-7470. Web site: www.tvguide.com. Weekly magazine. Focuses on all aspects of network, cable, and pay television programming and how it affects and reflects audiences. Circ. 9,097,762.

- Does not buy freelance material or use freelance writers.

VARIETY

Reed Business Information, 5700 Wilshire Blvd., Suite 120, Los Angeles CA 90036. (323)965-4476. Fax: (323)857-0494. E-mail: news@reedbusiness.com. Web site: www.variety.com. Editor-in-Chief: Peter Bart. Deputy Editor: Elizabeth Guider. Weekly magazine. Circ. 34,000.

- Does not buy freelance material or use freelance writers.

XXL MAGAZINE

Harris Publications, 1115 Broadway, 8th Floor, New York NY 10010. (212)807-7100. Fax: (212)620-7787. E-mail: xxl@harris-pub.com. Web site: www.xxlmag.com. Publisher: Dennis S. Page. Editor-in-Chief: Elliott Wilson. **Contact:** Juleyka Lantigua, managing editor; Vanessa Satten, deputy editor; Dave Bry, features editor; Bonsu Thompson, music editor; Leah Rose, associate music editor; Jermaine Hall, contributing editor. **50% freelance written.** Monthly magazine. "*XXL* is hip-hop on a higher level, an upscale urban lifestyle magazine." Estab. 1997. Circ. 350,000. Pays on publication. Byline given. Buys all rights. Editorial lead time 2 months. Submit seasonal material 3 months in advance. Accepts queries by mail.

Nonfiction Interview/profile, music, entertainment, luxury materialism. Query with published clips. Length: 200-5,000 words.

Photos State availability with submission. Reviews contact sheets, transparencies, prints. Captions, model releases required.

Tips Please send clips, query, and cover letter by mail.

ETHNIC & MINORITY

N $ $ $ $ AARP SEGUNDA JUVENTUD

AARP, 601 E St. NW, Washington DC 20049. (202)434-6749. E-mail: segundajuventud@aarp.org. Web site: www.aarpsegundajuventud.org. **75% freelance written.** Bimonthly magazine geared toward 50+ Hispanics. "With fresh and relevant editorial content and a mission of inclusiveness and empowerment, *AARP Segunda Juventud* serves more than 800,000 Hispanic AARP members and their families in all 50 states, the District of Columbia, Puerto Rico, and the US Virgin Islands." Estab. 2002. Circ. 800,000. **Pays on acceptance.** Publishes ms an average of 4 months after acceptance. Byline given. Offers 33.33% kill fee. Buys exclusive first worldwide rights. Editorial lead time 2-12 months. Submit seasonal material 4-12 months in advance. Accepts queries by mail, e-mail. Accepts simultaneous submissions. Responds in 4 months to queries; 4 months to mss. Sample copy online.

Nonfiction "Must have a Hispanic angle targeting the 50+ audience." General interest, interview/profile, new product, travel, reviews (book, film, music). **Buys 36 mss/year.** Query with published clips. Length: 200-1,500 words. **Pays $1-2/word.** Sometimes pays expenses of writers on assignment.

Photos Send photos with submission. Reviews contact sheets, negatives, transparencies, prints, GIF/JPEG files. Negotiates payment individually. Captions, identification of subjects, model releases required.

Columns/Departments Health; Finance; Travel; Celebrity profile; Encore (Hispanic 50+ individuals re-inventing themselves). **Buys 24 mss/year.** Query with published clips. **Pays $1-2/word.**

Fillers Facts. **Buys 6/year.** Length: 200-250 words. **Pays $1-2/word.**

Tips "Look closely at the last 6 issues to get familiar with the magazine topics. Don't submit queries for topics already covered. Write lively but succinct queries that demonstrate you have done your research into our magazine and our demographic, the 50+ Hispanic."

N $ AIM MAGAZINE

Aim Publishing Co., P.O. Box 390, Milton WA 98354. (253)815-9030. E-mail: submissions@aimmagazine.org. Web site: aimmagazine.org. **Contact:** Ruth Apilado, editor. **75% freelance written.** Works with a small number of new/unpublished writers each year. Quarterly magazine on social betterment that promotes racial harmony and peace for high school, college, and general audience. Publishes material "to purge racism from the human bloodstream through the written word." Estab. 1975. Circ. 10,000. Pays on publication. Publishes ms an average of 3 months after acceptance. Byline given. Offers 60% kill fee. Buys first, one-time rights. Submit seasonal material 6 months in advance. Accepts queries by mail, e-mail. Accepts simultaneous submissions. Responds in 2 months to queries; 1 month to mss. Sample copy and writer's guidelines for $4 and 9×12 SAE with $1.70 postage or online.

Nonfiction Exposé (education), general interest (social significance), historical/nostalgic (Black or Indian), how-to (create a more equitable society), interview/profile (one who is making social contributions to community), book reviews, reviews of plays. No religious material. **Buys 16 mss/year.** Send complete ms. Length: 500-800 words. **Pays $25-35.**

Photos Reviews b&w prints. Captions, identification of subjects required.

Fiction Contact Ruth Apilado, associate editor. "Fiction that teaches the brotherhood of man." Ethnic, historical, mainstream, suspense. Open. No religious mss. **Buys 20 mss/year.** Send complete ms. Length: 1,000-1,500 words. **Pays $25-35.**

Poetry Avant-garde, free verse, light verse. No "preachy" poetry. **Buys 20 poems/year.** Submit maximum 5 poems. Length: 15-30 lines. **Pays $3-5.**

Fillers Anecdotes, newsbreaks, short humor. **Buys 30/year.** Length: 50-100 words. **Pays $5.**

Tips "Interview anyone of any age who unselfishly is making an unusual contribution to the lives of less fortunate individuals. Include photo and background of person. We look at the nations of the world as part of one family. Short stories and historical pieces about Blacks and Indians are the areas most open to freelancers. Subject matter of submission is of paramount concern for us rather than writing style. Articles and stories showing the similarity in the lives of people with different racial backgrounds are desired."

$ $ AMBASSADOR MAGAZINE

National Italian American Foundation, 1860 19th St. NW, Washington DC 20009. (202)387-0600. Fax: (202)387-0800. E-mail: monica@niaf.org. Web site: www.niaf.org. **Contact:** Monica Soladay. **50% freelance written.** Quarterly magazine for Italian-Americans covering Italian-American history and culture. "We publish nonfiction articles on little-known events in Italian-American history and articles on Italian-American culture, traditions, and personalities living and dead." Estab. 1989. Circ. 25,000. Pays on approval of final draft. Byline given. Offers $50 kill fee. Buys second serial (reprint) rights. Editorial lead time 3 months. Accepts queries by mail, e-mail, fax. Accepts previously published material. Accepts simultaneous submissions. Responds in 2 months to queries. Sample copy and writer's guidelines free.

Nonfiction Historical/nostalgic, interview/profile, photo feature. **Buys 12 mss/year.** Send complete ms. Length: 800-1,500 words. **Pays $250 for photos and article.**
Photos Send photos with submission. Reviews contact sheets, prints. Buys one-time rights. Offers no additional payment for photos accepted with ms. Captions, identification of subjects required.
Tips "Good photos, clear prose, and a good storytelling ability are all prerequisites."

$ $ $ B'NAI B'RITH MAGAZINE

(formerly *The B'nai B'rith IJM*), B'nai B'rith International, 2020 K St. NW, Washington DC 20006. (202)857-2708. Fax: (202)857-2781. E-mail: ijm@bnaibrith.org. Web site: bnaibrith.org. **Contact:** Elana Harris, managing editor. **90% freelance written.** Quarterly magazine "specializing in social, political, historical, religious, cultural, 'lifestyle,' and service articles relating chiefly to the Jewish communities of North America and Israel. Write for the American Jewish audience, i.e., write about topics from a Jewish perspective, highlighting creativity and innovation in Jewish life." Estab. 1886. Circ. 110,000. Pays on publication. Publishes ms an average of 6 months after acceptance. Byline given. Offers 25% kill fee. Buys first rights. Editorial lead time 3 months. Submit seasonal material 5 months in advance. Accepts queries by mail, e-mail, fax. Accepts simultaneous submissions. Responds in 1 month to queries; 6 weeks to mss. Sample copy for $2. Writer's guidelines for #10 SASE or by e-mail.
Nonfiction General interest pieces of relevance to the Jewish community of US and abroad. Interview/profile, photo feature, religious, travel. "No Holocaust memoirs, first-person essays/memoirs, fiction, or poetry." **Buys 14-20 mss/year.** Query with published clips. Length: 1,000-2,500 words. **Pays $300-800 for assigned articles; $300-700 for unsolicited articles.** Sometimes pays expenses of writers on assignment.
Photos "Rarely assigned." Buys one-time rights.
Columns/Departments Up Front (book, CD reviews, small/short items with Jewish interest), 150-200 words. **Buys 3 mss/year.** Query. **Pays $50.**
Tips "Know what's going on in the Jewish world. Look at other Jewish publications also. Writers should submit clips with their queries. Read our guidelines carefully and present a good idea expressed well. Proofread your query letter."

$ CELTIC HERITAGE

Clansman Publishing, Ltd., 1657 Barrington St., Suite 122, Halifax NS B3J 2A1 Canada. (902)425-4944. Fax: (902)835-0080. E-mail: editorial@celticheritage.ns.ca. Web site: www.celticheritage.ns.ca. **Contact:** Alexa Thompson, managing editor. **95% freelance written.** Bimonthly magazine covering culture of North Americans of Celtic descent. "The magazine chronicles the stories of Celtish people who have settled in North America, with a focus on the stories of those who are not mentioned in history books. We also feature Gaelic language articles, history of Celtic people, traditions, music, and folklore. We profile Celtic musicians and include reviews of Celtic books, music, and videos." Estab. 1987. Circ. 5,000 (per issue). Pays 2 months after publication. Publishes ms an average of 2 months after acceptance. Byline given. Buys all rights. Editorial lead time 2 months. Submit seasonal material 3 months in advance. Accepts queries by mail, e-mail, fax, phone. Accepts previously published material. Responds in 1 week to queries; 1 month to mss. Sample copy for free. Writer's guidelines online.
Nonfiction Essays, general interest, historical/nostalgic, interview/profile, opinion, personal experience, travel, Gaelic language, Celtic music reviews, profiles of Celtic musicians, Celtic history, traditions, and folklore. No fiction, poetry, historical stories already well publicized. **Buys 100 mss/year.** Query or send complete ms. Length: 800-2,500 words. **Pays $50-75 (Canadian). All writers receive a complimentary subscription.** "We have, on rare occasion, run an advertisement for a writer in lieu of payment."
Photos State availability with submission. Reviews 35mm transparencies, 5×7 prints, JPEG files (200 dpi). "We do not pay for photographs." Captions, identification of subjects, model releases required.
Columns/Departments Query. **Pays $50-75 (Canadian).**
Fillers Anecdotes, facts. **Buys 2-3/year.** Length: 300-500 words. **Pays $30-50 (canadian).**
Tips "The easiest way to get my attention is to submit a query by e-mail. We are so short staffed that we do not have much time to start a correspondence by regular post."

N $ $ EAST WEST MAGAZINE

East West, Life + Style, EW Woman, LLC, P.O. Box 13624, Scottsdale AZ 85267. Fax: (480)502-4363. E-mail: editor@eastwestmagazine.com. Web site: www.eastwestmagazine.com. Editor: Anita Malik. **Contact:** Ellen Horowitz, managing editor. **80% freelance written.** Bimonthly magazine covering Asian American/East West lifestyle. "*East West Magazine* appeals to professional, educated women and men between the ages of 20-50, individuals who are Asian American and those who have some interest in or connection to Eastern influences in our Western society, whether it be via travel, food choices, alternative health remedies, spiritual practices or fashion." Estab. 2004. Circ. 15,000. Pays on publication. Publishes ms an average of 2 months after acceptance. Byline given. Offers 50% kill fee. Buys first North American serial, electronic rights, makes work-for-hire assignments. Editorial lead time 4 months. Submit seasonal material 3 months in advance. Accepts queries by e-mail, fax. Accepts simultaneous submissions. Responds in 2 weeks to queries; 1 month to mss. Sample copy by e-mail. Writer's guidelines free.

Nonfiction Contact Anita Malik, editor-in-chief. Interview/profile, opinion, photo feature, technical, travel, health. Query with published clips. Length: 300-1,200 words. **Pays 10-20¢/word.**

Columns/Departments Contact Ellen Horowitz, managing editor. Money (financial tips, advice, how-to), 800 words; Releases (movie/music reviews), 300 words. **Buys 10 mss/year.** Query with published clips. **Pays 10-20¢/word.**

Tips "*East West* is currently aiming to bring in lively and engaging articles in the areas of health, food, money and relationships. We are seeking writers with creative and interesting ideas who offer a fresh new perspective."

N $ FILIPINAS

A Magazine for All Filipinos, Filipinas Publishing, Inc., 1486 Huntington Ave., Suite 300, South San Francisco CA 94080. (650)872-8650. Fax: (650)872-8651. E-mail: editorial@filipinasmag.com. Web site: www.filipinasmag.com. **Contact:** Mona Lisa Yuchengco, editor/publisher. Monthly magazine focused on Filipino-American affairs. "*Filipinas* answers the lack of mainstream media coverage of Filipinos in America. It targets both Filipino immigrants and American-born Filipinos, gives in-depth coverage of political, social, and cultural events in the Philippines and in the Filipino-American community. Features role models, history, travel, food and leisure, issues, and controversies." Estab. 1992. Circ. 40,000. Pays on publication. Publishes ms an average of 5 months after acceptance. Byline given. Offers $10 kill fee. Buys first, all rights. Editorial lead time 2 months. Submit seasonal material 4 months in advance. Accepts queries by mail, e-mail, fax. Responds in 3 weeks to queries; 5 months to mss. Writer's guidelines for 9½×4 SASE or on Web site.

- *Unsolicited mss will not be paid.*
- O→ Break in with "a good idea outlined well in the query letter. Also, tenacity is key. If one idea is shot down, come up with another."

Nonfiction Interested in seeing "more issue-oriented pieces, unusual topics regarding Filipino-Americans, and stories from the Midwest and other parts of the country other than the coasts." Exposé, general interest, historical/nostalgic, inspirational, interview/profile, opinion, personal experience, travel. No academic papers. **Buys 80-100 mss/year.** Query with published clips. Length: 800-1,500 words. **Pays $50-75.**

Photos State availability with submission. Reviews 2¼×2¼ and 4×5 transparencies. Offers $15-25/photo. Captions, identification of subjects required.

Columns/Departments Cultural Currents (Filipino traditions and beliefs), 1,000 words; New Voices (first-person essays by Filipino Americans ages 10-25), 800 words; First Person (open to all Filipinos), 800 words. Query with published clips. **Pays $50-75.**

$ $ GERMAN LIFE

Zeitgeist Publishing, Inc., 1068 National Hwy., LaVale MD 21502. (301)729-6190. Fax: (301)729-1720. E-mail: mslider@germanlife.com. Web site: www.germanlife.com. **Contact:** Mark Slider, editor. **50% freelance written.** Bimonthly magazine covering German-speaking Europe. "*German Life* is for all interested in the diversity of German-speaking culture—past and present—and in the various ways that the US (and North America in general) has been shaped by its German immigrants. The magazine is dedicated to solid reporting on cultural, historical, social, and political events." Estab. 1994. Circ. 40,000. Pays on publication. Byline given. Buys first North American serial rights. Editorial lead time 4 months. Submit seasonal material 6 months in advance. Accepts queries by mail, e-mail. Responds in 2 months to queries; 3 months to mss. Sample copy for $4.95 and SAE with 4 first-class stamps. Writer's guidelines online.

Nonfiction General interest, historical/nostalgic, interview/profile, photo feature, travel. Special issues: Oktoberfest-related (October); Seasonal Relative to Germany, Switzerland, or Austria (December); Travel to German-speaking Europe (April). **Buys 50 mss/year.** Query with published clips. Length: 800-1,500 words. **Pays $200-500 for assigned articles; $200-350 for unsolicited articles.**

Photos State availability with submission. Reviews color transparencies, 5×7 color or b&w prints. Buys one-time rights. Offers no additional payment for photos accepted with ms. Identification of subjects required.

Columns/Departments German-Americana (regards specific German-American communities, organizations, and/or events past or present), 1,200 words; Profile (portrays prominent Germans, Americans, or German-Americans), 1,000 words; At Home (cuisine, etc. relating to German-speaking Europe), 800 words; Library (reviews of books, videos, CDs, etc.), 300 words. **Buys 30 mss/year.** Query with published clips. **Pays $50-150.**

Fillers Facts, newsbreaks. Length: 100-300 words. **Pays $50-150.**

Tips "The best queries include several informative proposals. Writers should avoid overemphasizing autobiographical experiences/stories."

$ HERITAGE FLORIDA JEWISH NEWS

207 O'Brien Rd., Suite 101, Fern Park FL 32730. (407)834-8787. E-mail: heritagefl@aol.com. Web site: www.heritagefl.com. **Contact:** Lyn Payne, associate editor. **20% freelance written.** Weekly tabloid on Jewish subjects of local, national and international scope, except for special issues. "Covers news of local, national and international scope of interest to Jewish readers and not likely to be found in other publications." Estab. 1976. Circ. 3,500. Pays on publication. Byline given. Buys first North American serial, first, one-time, second serial (reprint), simultaneous rights. Submit seasonal material 3 months in advance. Accepts queries by e-mail. Accepts previously published material. Responds in 1 month to queries. Sample copy for $1 and 9×12 SASE.

Nonfiction "Especially needs articles for these annual issues: Rosh Hashanah, Financial, Chanukah, Celebration (wedding and bar mitzvah), Passover, Health and Fitness, House and Home, Back to School, Travel and Savvy Seniors. No fiction, poems, first-person experiences." General interest, interview/profile, opinion, photo feature, religious, travel. **Buys 50 mss/year.** Send query only. Length: 500-1,000 words. **Pays 75¢/column inch.**

Reprints Send ms with rights for sale noted.

Photos State availability with submission. Reviews 8×10 prints. Buys one-time rights. Offers $5/photo. Captions, identification of subjects required.

$ HORIZONS

The Jewish Family Journal, Targum Press, 22700 W. Eleven Mile Rd., Southfield MI 48034. Fax: (888)298-9992. E-mail: horizons@netvision.net.il. Web site: www.targum.com. Managing Editor: Moshe Dombey. **Contact:** Miriam Zakon, chief editor. **100% freelance written.** Quarterly magazine covering the Orthodox Jewish family. "We include fiction and nonfiction, memoirs, essays, historical, and informational articles—all of interest to the Orthodox Jew." Estab. 1994. Circ. 5,000. Pays 4-6 weeks after publication. Publishes ms an average of 6 months after acceptance. Byline given. Buys one-time rights. Editorial lead time 6 months. Submit seasonal material 8 months in advance. Accepts queries by mail, e-mail, fax. Accepts simultaneous submissions. Responds in 1 week to queries; 2 months to mss. Writer's guidelines available.

Nonfiction Essays, historical/nostalgic, humor, inspirational, interview/profile, opinion, personal experience, photo feature, travel. **Buys 150 mss/year.** Send complete ms. Length: 350-3,000 words. **Pays $5-150.**

Photos State availability with submission. Buys one-time rights. Offers no additional payment for photos accepted with ms.

Fiction Historical, humorous, mainstream, slice-of-life vignettes. Nothing not suitable to Orthodox Jewish values. **Buys 10-15 mss/year.** Send complete ms. Length: 300-3,000 words. **Pays $20-100.**

Poetry Free verse, haiku, light verse, traditional. **Buys 30-35 poems/year.** Submit maximum 4 poems. Length: 3-28 lines. **Pays $5-10.**

Fillers Anecdotes, short humor. **Buys 20/year.** Length: 50-120 words. **Pays $5.**

Tips "*Horizons* publishes for the Orthodox Jewish market and therefore only accepts articles that are of interest to this market. We do not accept submissions dealing with political issues or Jewish legal issues. The tone is light and friendly and we therefore do not accept submissions that are of a scholarly nature. Our writers must be very familiar with our market. Anything that is not suitable for our readership doesn't stand a chance, no matter how high its literary merit."

$ INTERNATIONAL EXAMINER

622 S. Washington, Seattle WA 98104. (206)624-3925. Fax: (206)624-3046. E-mail: editor@iexaminer.org. Web site: www.iexaminer.org. **Contact:** Nhien Nguyen, managing editor. **75% freelance written.** Biweekly journal of Asian-American news, politics, and arts. "We write about Asian-American issues and things of interest to Asian-Americans. We do not want stuff about Asian things (stories on your trip to China, Japanese Tea Ceremony, etc. will be rejected). Yes, we are in English." Estab. 1974. Circ. 12,000. Pays on publication. Publishes ms an average of 1 month after acceptance. Buys one-time rights. Editorial lead time 1 month. Submit seasonal material 2 months in advance. Accepts simultaneous submissions. Writer's guidelines for #10 SASE.

Nonfiction Essays, exposé, general interest, historical/nostalgic, humor, interview/profile, opinion, personal experience, photo feature. **Buys 100 mss/year.** Query by mail, fax, or e-mail with published clips. Length: 750-5,000 words depending on subject. **Pays $25-100.** Sometimes pays expenses of writers on assignment.

Reprints Accepts previously published submissions (as long as not published in same area). Send typed ms with rights for sale noted and information about when and where the material previously appeared. Payment negotiable.

Photos State availability with submission. Reviews contact sheets. Buys one-time rights. Negotiates payment individually. Captions, identification of subjects required.

Fiction Asian-American authored fiction by or about Asian-Americans. Novel excerpts. **Buys 1-2 mss/year.** Query.

Tips "Write decent, suitable material on a subject of interest to the Asian-American community. All submissions are reviewed; all good ones are contacted. It helps to call and run an idea by the editor before or after sending submissions."

$ $ ITALIAN AMERICA

Official Publication of the Order Sons of Italy in America, 219 E St. NE, Washington DC 20002. (202)547-2900. Fax: (202)546-8168. E-mail: ddesanctis@osia.org. Web site: www.osia.org. **Contact:** Dr. Dona De Sanctis, editor/deputy executive director. **20% freelance written.** Quarterly magazine. "*Italian America* provides timely information about OSIA, while reporting on individuals, institutions, issues, and events of current or historical significance in the Italian-American community." Estab. 1996. Circ. 65,000. Pays on publication. Publishes ms an average of 3 months after acceptance. Byline given. Offers 50% kill fee. Buys worldwide nonexclusive rights. Editorial lead time 3 months. Accepts queries by mail, e-mail, fax. Accepts simultaneous submissions. Sample copy for free. Writer's guidelines online.

Nonfiction Historical/nostalgic (little known historical facts that must relate to Italian Americans), interview/profile, opinion, current events. **Buys 8 mss/year.** Query with published clips. Length: 750-1,000 words. **Pays $50-250.**

Tips "We pay particular attention to the quality of graphics that accompany the stories. We are interested in little known facts about historical/cultural Italian America."

$ $ JEWISH ACTION

Union of Orthodox Jewish Congregations of America, 11 Broadway, New York NY 10004. (212)613-8146. Fax: (212)613-0646. E-mail: ja@ou.org. Web site: www.ou.org/publications/ja/. Editor: Nechama Carmel. **Contact:** Dassi Zeidel, assistant editor. **80% freelance written.** Quarterly magazine covering a vibrant approach to Jewish issues, Orthodox lifestyle, and values. Circ. 40,000. Pays 2 months after publication. Byline given. Not copyrighted. Submit seasonal material 4 months in advance. Responds in 3 months to queries. Sample copy online. Writer's guidelines for #10 SASE or by e-mail.

- Prefers queries by e-mail. Mail and fax OK.

O━ Break in with a query for "Just Between Us" column.

Nonfiction Current Jewish issues, history, biography, art, inspirational, humor, music, book reviews. "We are not looking for Holocaust accounts. We welcome essays about responses to personal or societal challenges." **Buys 30-40 mss/year.** Query with published clips. Length: 1,000-3,000 words. **Pays $100-400 for assigned articles; $75-150 for unsolicited articles.**

Photos Send photos with submission. Identification of subjects required.

Columns/Departments Just Between Us (personal opinion on current Jewish life and issues), 1,000 words. **Buys 4 mss/year.**

Fiction Must have relevance to Orthodox reader. Length: 1,000-2,000 words.

Poetry Buys limited number of poems/year. Pays $25-75.

Tips "Remember that your reader is well educated and has a strong commitment to Orthodox Judaism. Articles on the holidays, Israel, and other common topics should offer a fresh insight. Because the magazine is a quarterly, we do not generally publish articles which concern specific timely events."

N $ JULUKA

P.O. Box 4675, Palo Verdes Peninsula CA 90274. (866)458-5852. Fax: (310)707-2255. E-mail: info@julukanews.com. Web site: www.julukanews.com. Publisher: Ruan Wannenburg. **Contact:** Charlene Avis, managing editor. Published in the US for those interested in South Africa. Helps South Africans adapt to life in a new country and provides a forum for networking and exchanging ideas, opinions, and resources. Editorial lead time 1 month. Accepts queries by e-mail.

Nonfiction Humor, interview/profile, opinion, personal experience, travel, news, book reviews. **Pays 5¢/word.** Sometimes pays expenses of writers on assignment.

Photos Send photos with submission.

Columns/Departments Travel, 520 words; Art & Culture (artist profiles/gallery events), 200-400 words; Culture Shock (personal stories about life in North American/stories about emigrating), 500 words; Sports 200-400 words; Human Interest (personal experiences), 300-1,000 words; Guest Editorial, 150-350 words; Reader Profiles, 400-800 words; Money Matters (financial news), 150-300 words; News You Can Use (law/insurance/financial planning), 250-350 words.

$ KHABAR

The Community Magazine, Khabar, Inc., 3790 Holcomb Bridge Rd., Suite 101, Norcross GA 30092. (770)451-7666. Fax: (770)234-6115. E-mail: parthiv@khabar.com. Web site: www.khabar.com. **Contact:** Parthiv N. Parekh, editor. **50% freelance written.** Monthly magazine covering the Asian and Indian community in Georgia. "Content relating to Indian-American and/or immigrant experience." Estab. 1992. Circ. 26,000. Pays on publication. Publishes ms an average of 2 months after acceptance. Offers 25% kill fee. Buys one-time, second serial (reprint), simultaneous, electronic rights. Editorial lead time 2 months. Submit seasonal material 2 months in advance. Accepts queries by e-mail. Accepts previously published material. Accepts simultaneous submissions. Sample copy for free. Writer's guidelines by e-mail.

Nonfiction Essays, interview/profile, opinion, personal experience, travel. **Buys 5 mss/year.** Query with or without published clips or send complete ms. Length: 750-4,000 words. **Pays $50-125 for assigned articles; $50-100 for unsolicited articles.**

Reprints Accepts previously published submissions.

Photos State availability of or send photos with submission. Negotiates payment individually. Captions, identification of subjects required.

Columns/Departments Book Review, 1,200 words; Music Review, 800 words; Spotlight (profiles), 1,200-3,000 words. **Buys 5 mss/year.** Query with or without published clips or send complete ms. **Pays $50-100.**

Fiction Ethnic. **Buys 5 mss/year.** Query with or without published clips or send complete ms. **Pays $50-100.**

Tips "Ask for our 'editorial guidelines' document by e-mail or otherwise by writing to us."

$ $ $ $ LATINA MAGAZINE

Latina Media Ventures, 1500 Broadway, 7th Floor, New York NY 10036. (212)642-0200. E-mail: editor@latina.com. Web site: www.latina.com. Managing Editor: Lisa Loverro. **40-50% freelance written.** Monthly magazine covering Latina lifestyle. "*Latina Magazine* is the leading bilingual lifestyle publication for Hispanic women in the US today. Covering the best of Latino fashion, beauty, culture, and food, the magazine also features celebrity profiles and interviews." Estab. 1996. Circ. 250,000. Pays on publication. Publishes ms an average of 2-3 months after acceptance. Byline given. Offers 25% kill fee. Buys first, second serial (reprint), electronic rights. Editorial lead time 3 months. Submit seasonal material 4-5 months in advance. Accepts queries by e-mail. Responds in 1 month to queries; 1-2 months to mss. Sample copy online.

- Editors are in charge of their individual sections and pitches should be made directly to them. Do not make pitches directly to the editor-in-chief or the editorial director as they will only be routed to the relevant section editor.

Nonfiction Essays, how-to, humor, inspirational, interview/profile, new product, personal experience. Special issues: The 10 Latinas Who Changed the World (December). "We do not feature an extensive amount of celebrity content or entertainment content, and freelancers should be sensitive to this. The magazine does not contain book or album reviews, and we do not write stories covering an artist's new project. We do not attend press junkets and do not cover press conferences. Please note that we are a lifestyle magazine, not an entertainment magazine." **Buys 15-20 mss/year.** Query with published clips. Length: 300-2,200 words. **Pays $1/word.** Pays expenses of writers on assignment.

Photos State availability with submission. Reviews contact sheets, transparencies, GIF/JPEG files. Buys one-time rights. Negotiates payment individually. Identification of subjects required.

Tips "*Latina*'s features cover a wide gamut of topics, including fashion, beauty, wellness, and personal essays. The magazine runs a wide variety of features on news and service topics (from the issues affecting Latina adolescents to stories dealing with anger). If you are going to make a pitch, please keep the following things in mind. All pitches should include statistics or some background reporting that demonstrates why a developing trend is important. Also, give examples of women who can provide a personal perspective. Profiles and essays need to have a strong personal journey angle. We will not cover someone just because they are Hispanic. When pitching stories about a particular person, please let us know the following: timeliness (Is this someone who is somehow tied to breaking news events? Has their story been heard?); the 'wow' factor (Why is this person remarkable? What elements make this story a standout? What sets your subject apart from other women?); target our audience (please note that the magazine targets acculturated, English-dominant Latina women between the ages of 18-39)."

$ $ $ MOMENT

The Magazine of Jewish Culture, Politics and Religion, 4115 Wisconsin Ave. NW, Suite 102, Washington DC 20016. (202)364-3300. Fax: (202)364-2636. E-mail: editor@momentmag.com. Web site: www.momentmag.com. **90% freelance written.** Bimonthly magazine. "*Moment* is an independent Jewish bimonthly general interest magazine that specializes in cultural, political, historical, religious, and lifestyle articles relating chiefly to the North American Jewish community and Israel." Estab. 1975. Circ. 65,000. Pays on publication. Publishes ms an average of 6 months after acceptance. Byline given. Buys first North American serial rights. Editorial lead time 3 months. Submit seasonal material 6 months in advance. Accepts queries by mail, e-mail, fax. Accepts simultaneous submissions. Responds in 1 month to queries; 3 months to mss. Sample copy for $4.50 and SAE. Writer's guidelines online.

Nonfiction "We look for meaty, colorful, thought-provoking features and essays on Jewish trends and Israel. We occasionally publish book excerpts, memoirs, and profiles." **Buys 25-30 mss/year.** Query with published clips. Length: 2,500-7,000 words. **Pays $200-1,200 for assigned articles; $40-500 for unsolicited articles.**

Photos State availability with submission. Buys one-time rights. Negotiates payment individually. Identification of subjects required.

Columns/Departments 5765 (snappy pieces about quirky events in Jewish communities, news and ideas to improve Jewish living), 250 words maximum; Olam (first-person pieces, humor, and colorful reportage), 600-1,500 words; Book reviews (fiction and nonfiction) are accepted but generally assigned, 400-800 words. **Buys 30 mss/year.** Query with published clips. **Pays $50-250.**

Tips "Stories for *Moment* are usually assigned, but unsolicited manuscripts are often selected for publication. Successful features offer readers an in-depth journalistic treatment of an issue, phenomenon, institution, or individual. The more the writer can follow the principle of 'show, don't tell,' the better. The majority of the submissions we receive are about The Holocaust and Israel. A writer has a better chance of having an idea accepted if it is not on these subjects."

N $ $ NA'AMAT WOMAN

Magazine of NA'AMAT USA, The Women's Labor Zionist Organization of America, 350 Fifth Ave., Suite 4700, New York NY 10118. (212)563-5222. Fax: (212)563-5710. **Contact:** Judith A. Sokoloff, editor. **80% freelance written.** Magazine published 4 times/year covering Jewish themes and issues, Israel, women's issues, and social and political issues. "Magazine covering a wide variety of subjects of interest to the Jewish community—including political and social issues, arts, profiles, and many articles about Israel and women's issues. Fiction must have a Jewish theme. Readers are the American Jewish community." Estab. 1926. Circ. 20,000. Pays on publication. Byline given. Buys first North American serial, first, one-time, second serial (reprint) rights, makes work-for-hire assignments. Accepts queries by mail, fax. Responds in 3 months to queries; 3 months to mss. Sample copy for 9×11½ SAE and $1.20 postage. Writer's guidelines for #10 SASE.

Nonfiction "All articles must be of particular interest to the Jewish community." Exposé, general interest (Jewish), historical/nostalgic, interview/profile, opinion, personal experience, photo feature, travel, art, music, social, and political issues, Israel. **Buys 20 mss/year.** Query with or without published clips or send complete ms. **Pays 10-15¢/word.**

Photos State availability with submission. Buys one-time rights. Pays $25-55 for 4×5 or 5×7 prints. Captions, identification of subjects required.

Columns/Departments Buys 20 mss/year. Query with published clips or send complete ms. **Pays 10¢/word.**

Fiction "Intelligent fiction with Jewish slant. No maudlin nostalgia or trite humor." Ethnic, historical, humorous, novel excerpts, women-oriented. **Buys 3 mss/year.** Query with published clips or send complete ms. Length: 2,000-3,000 words. **Pays 10¢/word and 2 contributor's copies.**

$ $ NATIVE PEOPLES MAGAZINE

5333 N. 7th St., Suite C-224, Phoenix AZ 85014. (602)265-4855. Fax: (602)265-3113. E-mail: dgibson@nativepeoples.com. Web site: www.nativepeoples.com. **Contact:** Daniel Gibson, editor. Bimonthly magazine covering Native Americans. "High-quality reproduction with full color throughout. The primary purpose of this magazine is to offer a sensitive portrayal of the arts and lifeways of Native peoples of the Americas." Estab. 1987. Circ. 50,000. Pays on publication. Byline given. Buys one-time, nonexclusive web and reprint rights rights. Accepts queries by mail, e-mail, fax. Responds in 2 months to queries. Writer's guidelines online.

Nonfiction All features by freelancers. Of the departments, Pathways (travel section), History and Viewpoint (opinion) most open to freelancers. Interview/profile (of interesting and leading Natives from all walks of life, with an emphasis on arts), personal experience. **Buys 35 mss/year.** Length: 1,000-2,500 words. **Pays 25¢/word.**

Photos State availability with submission. Reviews transparencies, prefers high res digital images and 35mm slides. Inquire for details. Buys one-time rights and nonexclusive Web and reprint rights. Offers $45-150/page rates, $250/cover photos. Identification of subjects required.

Tips "We are focused upon authenticity and a positive portrayal of present-day Native American life and cultural practices. Our stories portray role models of Native people, young and old, with a sense of pride in their heritage and culture. Therefore, it is important that the Native American point of view be incorporated in each story."

$ $ RUSSIAN LIFE

RIS Publications, P.O. Box 567, Montpelier VT 05601. (802)223-4955. Fax: (802)223-6105. Web site: www.russialife.net. **Contact:** Paul Richardson, publisher. **75% freelance written.** Bimonthly magazine covering Russian culture, history, travel, and business. "Our readers are informed Russophiles with an avid interest in all things Russian. But we do not publish personal travel journals or the like." Estab. 1956. Circ. 15,000. Pays on publication. Publishes ms an average of 3-6 months after acceptance. Byline given. Buys first rights. Editorial lead time 2 months. Submit seasonal material 3 months in advance. Accepts queries by mail. Accepts previously published material. Responds in 1 month to queries. Sample copy for 9×12 SAE and 6 first-class stamps. Writer's guidelines online.

Break in with a "good travel essay piece covering remote regions of Russia."

Nonfiction General interest, photo feature, travel. No personal stories, i.e., "How I came to love Russia." **Buys 15-20 mss/year.** Query. Length: 1,000-6,000 words. **Pays $100-300.**

Reprints Accepts previously published submissions rarely.

Photos Send photos with submission. Reviews contact sheets. Buys one-time rights. Negotiates payment individually. Captions required.

The online magazine carries original content not found in the print editions.

Tips "A straightforward query letter with writing sample or manuscript (not returnable) enclosed."

$ $ SCANDINAVIAN REVIEW

The American-Scandinavian Foundation, 58 Park Ave., New York NY 10016. (212)879-9779. E-mail: editor@amscan.org. Web site: www.amscan.org. **75% freelance written.** Triannual magazine for contemporary Scandinavia. Audience: Members, embassies, consulates, libraries. Slant: Popular coverage of contemporary affairs in Scandinavia. Estab. 1913. Circ. 4,000. Pays on publication. Publishes ms an average of 2 months after acceptance. Byline given. Buys first North American serial, second serial (reprint) rights. Editorial lead time 3 months. Submit seasonal material 3 months in advance. Accepts previously published material. Responds in 6 weeks to queries. Sample copy online. Writer's guidelines free.

Nonfiction General interest, interview/profile, photo feature, travel (must have Scandinavia as topic focus). Special issues: Scandinavian travel. No pornography. **Buys 30 mss/year.** Query with published clips. Length: 1,500-2,000 words. **Pays $300 maximum.**

Photos Reviews 3×5 transparencies, prints. Buys one-time rights. Pays $25-50/photo; negotiates payment individually. Captions required.

N $ TODAY'S LATINO MAGAZINE

217 N. Broad St., Middletown DE 19709. (302)376-1129. Fax: (302)376-1129. E-mail: info@todayslatino.com. Web site: www.todayslatino.com. Managing Editor: Hector Correa. **Contact:** Milton Delgado, editor. **80% freelance written.** Quarterly magazine covering issues and stories affecting latinos. "We seek to inform, educate, and entertain the upwardly mobile Latino and English speaking people interested in our rich culture and language." Estab. 2003. Circ. 7,000. Pays on publication. Publishes ms an average of 2 months after acceptance. Byline given. Buys one-time rights. Editorial lead time 1 month. Submit seasonal material 2 months in advance. Accepts queries by mail, e-mail, phone. Accepts previously published material. Sample copy for free. Writer's guidelines free.

Nonfiction Length: 500-1,500 words. **Pays $75-125.** Sometimes pays expenses of writers on assignment.

Photos Send photos with submission. Reviews TIFF/JPEG files. Buys one-time rights. Pays $25-100. Captions, identification of subjects, model releases required.

Columns/Departments Politics; Celebrities; Travel, all 1,000 words. **Buys 10 mss/year.** Query with or without published clips. **Pays $75-125.**

Fiction Ethnic. Does not want vulgar, street urban. Buys 1 ms/year. Send complete ms.

Poetry Avant-garde, free verse, traditional. Does not want vulgar writing. **Buys 4 poems/year.** Submit maximum 4 poems. Length: 5-20 lines.

Fillers Anecdotes, facts, newsbreaks, short humor. **Buys 4/year.** Length: 500-750 words. **Pays $75-100.**

Tips "I really appreciate a professional writer who can write in English and Spanish, and whose style would be attractive for the professional Latino."

UPSCALE MAGAZINE

Bronner Brothers, 600 Bronner Brothers Way SW, Atlanta GA 30310. (404)758-7467. E-mail: info@upscalemag.com. Web site: www.upscalemagazine.com. Monthly magazine covering topics for "upscale African-American/black interests. *Upscale* offers to take the reader to the 'next level' of life's experience. Written for the black reader and consumer, *Upscale* provides information in the realms of business, news, lifestyle, fashion and beauty, and arts and entertainment." Estab. 1989. Circ. 250,000. Pays on publication. Publishes ms an average of 4 months after acceptance. Byline given. Offers 25% kill fee. Buys first North American serial rights. Editorial lead time 3-4 months. Accepts queries by mail. Accepts simultaneous submissions. Responds in 1 month to queries. Sample copy and writer's guidelines online.

Photos State availability with submission. Negotiates payment individually. Captions, identification of subjects, model releases required.

Columns/Departments News & Business (factual, current); Lifestyle (travel, home, wellness, etc.); Beauty & Fashion (tips, trends, upscale fashion, hair); and Arts & Entertainment (artwork, black celebrities, entertainment). **Buys 6-10 mss/year.** Query with published clips. **Payment different for each department.**

Tips "Make queries informative and exciting. Include entertaining clips. Be familiar with issues affecting black readers. Be able to write about them with ease and intelligence."

$ WINDSPEAKER

Aboriginal Multi-Media Society of Alberta, 13245-146 St., Edmonton AB T5L 4S8 Canada. (800)661-5469. Fax: (780)455-7639. E-mail: edwind@ammsa.com. Web site: www.ammsa.com. **Contact:** Debora Steel, editor-in-chief. **25% freelance written.** Monthly tabloid covering native issues. "Focus on events and issues that affect and interest native peoples, national or local." Estab. 1983. Circ. 27,000. Pays on publication. Publishes ms an average of 1 month after acceptance. Byline given. Offers kill fee. Buys first rights. Editorial lead time 1 month. Submit seasonal material 2 months in advance. Accepts queries by mail, e-mail, phone. Accepts simultaneous submissions. Sample copy for free. Writer's guidelines online.

Nonfiction Opinion, photo feature, travel, news interview/profile, reviews: books, music, movies. Special issues: Powwow (June); Travel supplement (May). **Buys 200 mss/year.** Query with published clips and SASE or by phone. Length: 500-800 words. **Pays $3-3.60/published inch.** Sometimes pays expenses of writers on assignment.

Photos Send photos with submission. Buys one-time rights. Offers $25-100/photo. Will pay for film and processing. Identification of subjects required.

Tips "Knowledge of Aboriginal culture and political issues is a great asset."

FOOD & DRINK

BON APPETIT

America's Food and Entertaining Magazine, Conde Nast Publications, Inc., 4 Times Square, 15th Floor, New York NY 10036. (212)286-2106. Fax: (212)286-2363. Web site: www.bonappetit.com. Editor-in-Chief: Barbara Fairchild. **Contact:** Victoria von Biel, executive editor. **50% freelance written.** Monthly magazine covering fine food, restaurants, and home entertaining. "*Bon Appetit* readers are upscale food enthusiasts and sophisticated travelers. They eat out often and entertain 4-6 times a month." Estab. 1956. Circ. 1,300,000. **Pays on acceptance.** Byline given. Buys all rights. Submit seasonal material 1 year in advance. Accepts queries by mail. Responds in 6 weeks to queries. Writer's guidelines for #10 SASE.

Nonfiction Travel (food-related), food feature, personal essays. "No cartoons, quizzes, poetry, historic food features, or obscure food subjects." **Buys 50 mss/year.** Query with résumé and published clips. No phone calls or e-mails. Length: 150-2,000 words. **Pays $100 and up.** Pays expenses of writers on assignment.

Photos Never send photos.

Tips "Writers must have a good knowledge of *Bon Appetit* and the related topics of food, travel, and entertaining (as shown in accompanying clips). A light, lively style is a plus."

COOK'S ILLUSTRATED

Boston Common Press, 17 Station St., Brookline MA 02445-7995. (617)232-1000. Fax: (617)232-1572. E-mail: cooks@bcpress.com. Web site: cooksillustrated.com. Bimonthly magazine. Circ. 500,000.

- Does not buy freelance material or use freelance writers.

FOOD & WINE

American Express Publishing Corp., 1120 Avenue of the Americas, 9th Floor, New York NY 10036. (212)382-5600. Fax: (212)764-2177. Web site: www.foodandwine.com. **Contact:** Dana Cowin, editor-in-chief. Monthly magazine for the reader who enjoys the finer things in life. Editorial focuses on upscale dining, covering resturants, entertaining at home, and travel destinations. Circ. 964,000. Editorial lead time 6 months.

- Does not buy freelance material or use freelance writers.

$ $ $ $ GOURMET

The Magazine of Good Living, Conde Nast Publications, Inc., 4 Times Square, New York NY 10036. (212)286-2860. Fax: (212)286-2672. Web site: www.gourmet.com. Editor-in-Chief: Ruth Reichl. Monthly magazine for sophisticated readers who have a passion for food and travel. Byline given. Offers 25% kill fee. Accepts queries by mail. Responds in 2 months to queries. Sample copy for free.

Nonfiction Looking for articles on reminiscence, single foods, and ethnic cuisines. **Buys 25-30 mss/year.** Query with published clips. Length: 200-3,000 words. Pays expenses of writers on assignment.

$ $ HOME COOKING

House of White Birches, 306 E. Parr Rd., Berne IN 46711. (260)589-4000 ext. 337. Fax: (260)589-8093. E-mail: editor@homecookingmagazine.com. Web site: www.homecookingmagazine.com. Associate Editor: Barb Sprunger. **Contact:** Alice Robinson and Judy Shaw, editors. **35% freelance written.** Bimonthly magazine. Circ. 58,000. Pays within 45 days of acceptance. Publishes ms an average of 4 months after acceptance. Byline given. Buys all rights. Editorial lead time 6 months. Submit seasonal material 6 months in advance. Accepts queries

by mail, e-mail. Responds in 1 month to queries. Sample copy for 6×9 SAE and 5 first-class stamps.
Nonfiction How-to, humor, personal experience, recipes, all in food/cooking area. No health/fitness or travel articles. **Buys 36 mss/year.** Query or send complete ms. Length: 200-350 words, plus 6-10 recipes. **Pays $75-200 for assigned articles; $25-200 for unsolicited articles.**
Columns/Departments Pinch of Sage (hints for the home cook), 200-500 words; Kitchen Know-How, 250-1,000 words. **Buys 12 mss/year.** Query or send complete ms.
Tips "You must request our writer's guidelines and editorial calendar for issue themes. We will gladly e-mail or mail them to you. Please follow our guidelines and schedule for all submissions."

N $ $ KASHRUS MAGAZINE

The Bimonthly for the Kosher Consumer and the Trade, The Kashrus Institute, P.O. Box 204, Parkville Station, Brooklyn NY 11204. (718)336-8544. **Contact:** Rabbi Yosef Wikler, editor. **25% freelance written.** Prefers to work with published/established writers, but will work with new/unpublished writers. Bimonthly magazine covering the kosher food industry and food production as well as Jewish life in all parts of the world. Estab. 1980. Circ. 10,000. Pays on publication. Publishes ms an average of 2 months after acceptance. Byline given. Offers 50% kill fee. Buys first, second serial (reprint) rights. Submit seasonal material 2 months in advance. Accepts queries by mail, phone. Accepts previously published material. Accepts simultaneous submissions. Responds in 1 week to queries; 2 weeks to mss. Sample copy for $2.
Nonfiction General interest, interview/profile, new product, personal experience, photo feature, religious, technical, travel. Special issues: International Kosher Travel (October); Passover Shopping Guide (March); Domestic Kosher Travel Guide (June). **Buys 8-12 mss/year.** Query with published clips. Length: 1,000-1,500 words. **Pays $100-250 for assigned articles; up to $100 for unsolicited articles.** Sometimes pays expenses of writers on assignment.
Reprints Send tearsheet or photocopy and information about when and where the material previously appeared. Pays 25-50% of amount paid for an original article.
Photos No guidelines; send samples or call. State availability with submission. Buys one-time rights. Offers no additional payment for photos accepted with ms.
Columns/Departments Book Review (cookbooks, food technology, kosher food), 250-500 words; People In the News (interviews with kosher personalities), 1,000-1,500 words; Regional Kosher Supervision (report on kosher supervision in a city or community), 1,000-1,500 words; Food Technology (new technology or current technology with accompanying pictures), 1,000-1,500 words; Travel (international, national—must include Kosher information and Jewish communities), 1,000-1,500 words; Regional Kosher Cooking, 1,000-1,500 words. **Buys 8-12 mss/year.** Query with published clips. **Pays $50-250.**
Tips "*Kashrus Magazine* will do more writing on general food technology, production, and merchandising as well as human interest travelogs and regional writing in 2007 than we have done in the past. Areas most open to freelancers are interviews, food technology, cooking and food preparation, dining, regional reporting, and travel, but we also feature healthy eating and lifestyles, redecorating, catering, and hospitals and health care. We welcome stories on the availability and quality of kosher foods and services in communities across the US and throughout the world. Some of our best stories have been by non-Jewish writers about kosher observance in their region. We also enjoy humorous articles. Just send a query with clips and we'll try to find a storyline that's right for you, or better yet, call us to discuss a storyline."

KRAFT FOOD & FAMILY

Redwood Custom Communications, 37 Front St. E., Toronto ON M5E 1B3 Canada. (416)360-7339. Fax: (416)360-8846. Web site: www.kraftkitchens.com. Published 5 times/year "*Kraft Food & Family* is published by Kraft Foods and is directed to Kraft consumers in the United States. The magazine provides simple, realistic food ideas and solutions for time-challenged mothers and working women."

- Does not buy freelance material or use freelance writers.

SAVEUR

World Publications, Inc., 304 Park Ave. S., 8th Floor, New York NY 10010. (212)219-7400. Web site: www.saveur.com. Magazine published 8 times/year covering exotic foods. Written for sophisticated, upscale lovers of food, wine, travel, and adventure. Estab. 1994. Circ. 390,589. Accepts queries by mail. Sample copy for $5 at newsstands. Writer's guidelines by e-mail.
Nonfiction Query with published clips.
Columns/Departments Query with published clips.
Tips "Queries and stories should be detailed and specific, and personal ties to the subject matter are important—let us know why you should be the one to write the story. Familiarize yourself with our departments, and the magazine style as a whole, and pitch your stories accordingly. Also, we rarely assign restaurant-based pieces, and the selections 'Classis' and 'Source' are almost always staff-written."

TASTE OF HOME

Reader's Digest Association, Inc., 5400 S. 60th St., Greendale WI 53129. (414)423-0100. Fax: (414)423-8463. E-mail: editors@tasteofhome.com. Web site: www.tasteofhome.com. Editor: Ann Kaiser. Bimonthly magazine. "*Taste of Home* is dedicated to home cooks, from beginners to the very experienced. Editorial includes recipes and serving suggestions, interviews and ideas from the publication's readers and field editors based around the country, and reviews of new cooking tools and gadgets." Circ. 3.5 million.

- Does not buy freelance material or use freelance writers.

N TEA A MAGAZINE

Olde English Tea Company, Inc., 3 Devotion Rd., P.O. Box 348, Scotland CT 06264. (860)456-1145. Fax: (860)456-1023. E-mail: teamag@teamag.com. Web site: www.teamag.com. Editor: Pearl Dexter. **Contact:** Jobina Miller, assistant to the editor. **75% freelance written.** Quarterly magazine covering anything tea related. "*Tea A Magazine* is an exciting magazine all about tea, both as a drink and for its cultural significance in art, music, literature, history and society." Estab. 1994. Circ. 9,500. Pays on publication. Publishes ms an average of 1 year after acceptance. Byline given. Buys all rights. Editorial lead time 9 months. Submit seasonal material 6 months in advance. Responds in 6 months to mss. Writer's guidelines by e-mail.

Nonfiction Book excerpts, essays, general interest, historical/nostalgic, how-to, humor, interview/profile, personal experience, photo feature, travel. Send complete ms. **Pays negotiable amount.** Sometimes pays expenses of writers on assignment.

Photos Send photos with submission. Reviews prints, GIF/JPEG files (300 dpi). Buys all rights. Negotiates payment individually. Captions, identification of subjects required.

Columns/Departments Readers' Stories (personal experience involving tea); Book Reviews (review on tea books). Send complete ms. **Pays negotiable amount.**

Fiction Does not want anything that is not tea related. Send complete ms. **Pays negotiable amount.**

Poetry Avant-garde, free verse, haiku, light verse, traditional. Does not want anything that is not tea related.

Tips "Please submit full manuscripts with photos and make sure it is tea related."

N $ $ $ $ WINE ENTHUSIAST MAGAZINE

Wine Enthusiast Companies, 103 Fairview Park Dr., Elmsford NY 10523. E-mail: tmoriarty@wineenthusiast.net. Web site: www.wineenthusiast.com/mag. Editor: Adam Strum. **Contact:** Tim Moriarty, managing editor. **40% freelance written.** Monthly magazine covering the lifestyle of wine. "Our readers are upscale and educated, but not necessarily super-sophisticated about wine itself. Our informal, irreverent approach appeals to savvy enophiles and newbies alike." Estab. 1988. Circ. 80,000. **Pays on acceptance.** Byline given. Offers 25% kill fee. Buys first North American serial rights. Editorial lead time 4 months. Submit seasonal material 5 months in advance. Accepts queries by e-mail. Responds in 2 weeks to queries; 2 months to mss.

Nonfiction Essays, humor, interview/profile, new product, personal experience. **Buys 5 mss/year. Pays $750-2,500 for assigned articles; $750-2,000 for unsolicited articles.**

Photos Send photos with submission. Reviews GIF/JPEG files. Offers $135-400/photo.

$ $ WINE PRESS NORTHWEST

P.O. Box 2608, Tri-Cities WA 99302. (509)582-1564. Fax: (509)585-7221. E-mail: edegerman@winepressnw.com. Web site: www.winepressnw.com. **Contact:** Eric Degerman, managing editor. **50% freelance written.** Quarterly magazine covering Pacific Northwest wine (Washington, Oregon, British Columbia, Idaho). "We focus narrowly on Pacific Northwest wine. If we write about travel, it's where to go to drink NW wine. If we write about food, it's what goes with NW wine. No beer, no spirits." Estab. 1998. Circ. 12,000. Pays on publication. Publishes ms an average of 3 months after acceptance. Byline given. Offers 20% kill fee. Buys first North American serial, electronic rights. Editorial lead time 3 months. Submit seasonal material 3 months in advance. Accepts queries by mail, e-mail, fax. Accepts simultaneous submissions. Responds in 1 month to queries. Sample copy free or online. Writer's guidelines free.

Nonfiction General interest, historical/nostalgic, interview/profile, new product, photo feature, travel. No "beer, spirits, non-NW (California wine, etc.)" **Buys 30 mss/year.** Query with published clips. Length: 1,500-2,500 words. **Pays $300.** Sometimes pays expenses of writers on assignment.

Photos State availability with submission. Reviews contact sheets. Buys one-time rights. Negotiates payment individually. Identification of subjects required.

Tips "Writers must be familiar with *Wine Press Northwest* and should have a passion for the region, its wines, and cuisine."

$ $ $ WINE SPECTATOR

M. Shanken Communications, Inc., 387 Park Ave. S., 8th Floor, New York NY 10016. (212)684-4224. Fax: (212)684-5424. E-mail: winespec@mshanken.com. Web site: www.winespectator.com. **Contact:** Thomas Matthews, executive editor. **20% freelance written.** Prefers to work with published/established writers. Monthly news magazine. Estab. 1976. Circ. 350,000. Pays within 30 days of publication. Publishes ms an average of 2 months after acceptance. Byline given. Buys all rights, makes work-for-hire assignments. Submit seasonal material 4 months in advance. Accepts queries by mail, fax. Responds in 3 months to queries. Writer's guidelines for #10 SASE.

Nonfiction General interest (news about wine or wine events), interview/profile (of wine, vintners, wineries), opinion, photo feature, travel, dining and other lifestyle pieces. No "winery promotional pieces or articles by writers who lack sufficient knowledge to write below just surface data." Query. Length: 100-2,000 words. **Pays $100-1,000.**

Photos Send photos with submission. Buys all rights. Pays $75 minimum for color transparencies. Captions, identification of subjects, model releases required.

The online magazine carries original content not found in the print edition. Contact: Dana Nigro, news editor.

Tips "A solid knowledge of wine is a must. Query letters essential, detailing the story idea. New, refreshing ideas which have not been covered before stand a good chance of acceptance. *Wine Spectator* is a consumer-oriented news magazine, but we are interested in some trade stories; brevity is essential."

GAMES & PUZZLES

$ THE BRIDGE BULLETIN

American Contract Bridge League, 2990 Airways Blvd., Memphis TN 38116-3847. (901)332-5586, ext. 1291. Fax: (901)398-7754. E-mail: editor@acbl.org. Web site: www.acbl.org. Editor: Brent Manley. Managing Editor: Paul Linxwiler. **Contact:** Editor. **20% freelance written.** Monthly magazine covering duplicate (tournament) bridge. Estab. 1938. Circ. 155,000. Pays on publication. Publishes ms an average of 3 months after acceptance. Byline given. Buys first, second serial (reprint) rights. Editorial lead time 2 months. Accepts queries by mail, e-mail. Accepts previously published material. Accepts simultaneous submissions.

Break in with a "humorous piece about bridge."

Nonfiction Book excerpts, essays, how-to (play better bridge), humor, interview/profile, new product, personal experience, photo feature, technical, travel. **Buys 6 mss/year.** Query. Length: 500-2,000 words. **Pays $100/page.**

Photos Color required. State availability with submission. Buys all rights. Negotiates payment individually. Identification of subjects required.

Tips "Articles must relate to contract bridge in some way. Cartoons on bridge welcome."

$ $ CHESS LIFE

United States Chess Federation, P.O. Box 3967, Crossville TN 38557-3967. (931)787-1234. Fax: (931)787-1200. E-mail: dlucas@uschess.org. Web site: www.uschess.org. **Contact:** Daniel Lucas, editor. **15% freelance written.** Works with a small number of new/unpublished writers/year. Monthly magazine. "*Chess Life* is the official publication of the United States Chess Federation, covering news of most major chess events, both here and abroad, with special emphasis on the triumphs and exploits of American players." Estab. 1939. Circ. 85,000. Publishes ms an average of 6 months after acceptance. Byline given. Buys first rights. Submit seasonal material 6 months in advance. Accepts queries by mail, e-mail, fax, phone. Accepts simultaneous submissions. Responds in 3 months to mss. Sample copy and writer's guidelines for 9×11 SAE with 5 first-class stamps.

Nonfiction All must have some relation to chess. General interest, historical/nostalgic, humor, interview/profile (of a famous chess player or organizer), photo feature (chess centered), technical. No "stories about personal experiences with chess." **Buys 30-40 mss/year.** Query with samples if new to publication. Length: 3,000 words maximum. **Pays $100/page (800-1,000 words).** Sometimes pays expenses of writers on assignment.

Reprints Send tearsheet, photocopy or typed ms with rights for sale noted and information about when and where the material previously appeared.

Photos Reviews b&w contact sheets and prints, and color prints and slides. Buys all or negotiable rights. Pays $25-100 inside; covers negotiable. Captions, identification of subjects, model releases required.

Fillers Submit with samples and clips. Buys first or negotiable rights to cartoons and puzzles. **Pays $25 upon acceptance.**

Tips "Articles must be written from an informed point of view—not from view of the curious amateur. Most of our writers are specialized in that they have sound credentials as chess players. Freelancers in major population areas (except New York and Los Angeles, which we already have covered) who are interested in short personality profiles and perhaps news reporting have the best opportunities. We're looking for more personality pieces on chess players around the country; not just the stars, but local masters, talented youths, and dedicated volunteers. Freelancers interested in such pieces might let us know of their interest and their range. Could be we know of an interesting story in their territory that needs covering. Examples of published articles include a locally produced chess television program, a meeting of chess set collectors from around the world, chess in our prisons, and chess in the works of several famous writers."

ELECTRONIC GAMING MONTHLY

Ziff-Davis Media, Inc., 101 2nd St., 8th Floor, San Francisco CA 94105. (415)547-8000. Fax: (415)547-8777. Web site: www.egmmag.com. Monthly magazine. Focuses on electronic games for console video game units. Circ. 600,000. Sample copy not available.

GAMEPRO

IDG Entertainment, 555 12th St., Oakland CA 94607. (510)768-2700. Fax: (510)768-2701. Web site: www.gamepro.com. Monthly magazine. "*GamePro* is the industry leader among independent multiplatform video gaming magazines." Circ. 517,000. Byline given.

- Contact specific editor. Mostly staff written.

Nonfiction New product. Query.

$ $ $ INQUEST GAMER

151 Wells Ave., Congers NY 10920-2036. (845)268-2000. Fax: (845)268-0053. E-mail: inquisition@wizarduniverse.com. Web site: www.wizarduniverse.com. **Contact:** Kyle Ackerman, editor. Monthly magazine covering all gaming, particularly video and computer gaming, collectible and miniature gaming, and role-playing and board games. Pays on publication. Publishes ms an average of 2 months after acceptance. Byline given. Buys one-time, all rights. Accepts queries by mail, e-mail, fax, phone. Responds in 6 weeks to mss. Sample copy for $5. Writer's guidelines for #10 SASE.

O→ Break in with short news pieces.

Nonfiction Interview/profile (Q&As with big-name personalities or properties in gaming). No advertorials or stories on older, non-current games. **Buys 60 mss/year.** Query with published clips. Length: 2,000-4,000 words. **Pays $350-1,000.**

Columns/Departments Technical columns on how to play currently popular games. **Buys 100 mss/year.** Query with published clips. **Pays $50-250.**

Tips "*InQuest* is always looking for good freelance news and feature writers who are interested in card, roleplaying, or electronic games. A love of fantasy or science fiction books, movies, or art is desirable. Experience is preferred; sense of humor a plus; a flair for writing mandatory. Above all you must be able to find interesting new angles to a story, work hard, and meet deadlines."

N ✚ WOMAN POKER PLAYER MAGAZINE

915 Chester St., New Westminster BC V3L 4N4 Canada. (609)628-2358. Fax: (516)977-9409. E-mail: editorial@womanpokerplayer.com. Web site: www.womanpokerplayer.com. Editor: Barbara Enright. **Contact:** Manjann Morrison, managing editor. **80% freelance written.** Bimonthly magazine covering poker. "*Woman Poker Player* is for the woman who enjoys poker. We are a lifestyle publication that also covers fashion and wellness." Estab. 2005. Circ. 35,000. Pays on publication. Publishes ms an average of 2 months after acceptance. Byline sometimes given. Buys all rights. Editorial lead time 1 month. Submit seasonal material 1 month in advance. Accepts queries by e-mail. Accepts simultaneous submissions. Sample copy for free.

Nonfiction Book excerpts, humor, interview/profile, poker. Query. Length: 1,100-2,000 words. **Pays variable amount.**

Photos State availability with submission. Reviews contact sheets, GIF/JPEG files. Buys one-time rights. Negotiates payment individually. Captions, model releases required.

Fiction Condensed novels, poker. Query. Length: 1,000-2,000 words.

Fillers Facts, gags to be illustrated by cartoonist. **Buys 6/year.**

Tips "Send pitch via e-mail stating writing experience."

GAY & LESBIAN INTEREST

$ $ THE ADVOCATE

Liberation Publications, Inc., 6922 Hollywood Blvd., Suite 1000, Los Angeles CA 90028-6148. (323)871-1225. Fax: (323)467-6805. E-mail: newsroom@advocate.com. Web site: www.advocate.com. **Contact:** Bruce Steele, editor-in-chief. Biweekly magazine covering national news events with a gay and lesbian perspective on the issues. Estab. 1967. Circ. 120,000. Pays on publication. Byline given. Buys first North American serial rights. Responds in 1 month to queries. Sample copy for $3.95. Writer's guidelines by e-mail.

Nonfiction "Here are elements we look for in all articles: *Angling*: An angle is the one editorial tool we have to attract a reader's attention. An *Advocate* editor won't make an assignment unless he or she has worked out a very specific angle with you. Once you've worked out the angle with an editor, don't deviate from it without letting the editor know. Some of the elements we look for in angles are: a news hook; an open question or controversy; a 'why' or 'how' element or novel twist; national appeal; and tight focus. *Content*: Lesbian and gay news stories in all areas of life: arts, sciences, financial, medical, cyberspace, etc. *Tone*: Tone is the element that makes an emotional connection. Some characteristics we look for: toughness; edginess; fairness and even-handedness; multiple perspectives.'' Exposé, interview/profile, news reporting and investigating. Special issues: gays on campus, coming out interviews with celebrities, HIV and health. Query. Length: 1,200 words. **Pays $550.**

Columns/Departments Arts & Media (news and profiles of well-known gay or lesbians in entertainment) is most open to freelancers, 750 words. Query. **Pays $100-500.**

Tips ''*The Advocate* is a unique newsmagazine. While we report on gay and lesbian issues and are published by one of the country's oldest and most established gay-owned companies, we also play by the rules of mainstream-not-gay-community-journalism.''

N $BENT MAGAZINE

Top Down Productions LLC, 233 Kaymar Dr., Amherst NY 14228-3008. E-mail: query@bent-magazine.com. Web site: www.bent-magazine.com. Co-Editor: Angie Carruthers. **Contact:** Christine Syphrit, co-editor. **100% freelance written.** Bimonthly magazine covering homoerotic romantic literature. ''*BENT Magazine* seeks to provide quality romantic fiction and articles of interest to fans of yaoi and slash. All fiction works must focus on a homosexual male main character and/or male/male romance.'' Estab. 2006. Circ. 40. Pays on publication. Publishes ms an average of 1 month after acceptance. Byline given. Buys first North American serial, first, one-time, second serial (reprint), electronic rights. Editorial lead time 2 months. Submit seasonal material 2 months in advance. Accepts queries by e-mail. Accepts previously published material. Accepts simultaneous submissions. Responds in 1 week to queries; 2-4 months to mss. Sample copy and writer's guidelines online.

Nonfiction Book excerpts, essays, general interest, historical/nostalgic, new product, opinion, reviews. Does not want personal experience testimonials. **Buys 36 mss/year.** Query with or without published clips or send complete ms. Length: 1,000-5,000 words. **Pays $5.**

Columns/Departments Manga Reviews; Book/Movie/Anime Reviews, 1,000 words. **Buys 24 mss/year.** Query with or without published clips or send complete ms. **Pays $5.**

Fiction Adventure, erotica, fantasy, historical, horror, humorous, mainstream, mystery, novel excerpts, romance, science fiction, serialized novels, slice-of-life vignettes, suspense, western. Does not want stories that contain heterosexual sex. ''We are not interested in just-the-sex stories with no development of plot or characters.'' **Buys 48 mss/year.** Query with or without published clips or send complete ms. Length: 1,000-50,000 words. **Pays $5-30.**

Tips ''Stories in the sample issue provide a good generalization of what we are looking for. If unsure whether a submission meets the needs of the magazine, please query first with a brief summary/description of the intended work.''

$ $CURVE MAGAZINE

Outspoken Enterprises, Inc., 1550 Bryant St., Suite 510, San Francisco CA 94103. Fax: (415)863-1609. E-mail: editor@curvemag.com. Web site: www.curvemag.com. Editor-in-Chief: Frances Stevens. **Contact:** Diane Anderson-Minshall, executive editor. **60% freelance written.** Magazine published 10 times/year covering lesbian entertainment, culture, and general interest categories. ''We want dynamic and provocative articles that deal with issues, ideas, or cultural moments that are of interest or relevance to gay women.'' Estab. 1990. Circ. 80,000. Pays on publication. Byline given. Offers 25% kill fee. Buys first North American serial rights. Editorial lead time 6 months. Submit seasonal material 6 months in advance. Accepts queries by mail, e-mail, fax. Sample copy for $3.95 with $2 postage. Writer's guidelines online.

Nonfiction General interest, photo feature, travel, celebrity interview/profile. Special issues: Sex (February); Travel (March); Fashion + Design (April); Weddings (May); Pride (June); Music (August); School (September); Travel (October); Money/Careers (November); Gift Guide (December). No fiction or poetry. **Buys 100 mss/year.** Query. Length: 200-2,000 words. **Pays 15¢/word.**

Photos Send hi-res photos with submission. Buys one-time rights. Offers $25-100/photo; negotiates payment individually. Captions, identification of subjects, model releases required.

Tips ''Feature articles generally fit into 1 of the following categories: Celebrity profiles (lesbian, bisexual, or straight women who are icons for the lesbian community or actively involved in coalition-building with the lesbian community); community segment profiles—i.e., lesbian firefighters, drag kings, sports teams (multiple interviews with a variety of women in different parts of the country representing a diversity of backgrounds); noncelebrity profiles (activities of unknown or low-profile lesbian and bisexual activists/political leaders, athletes, filmmakers, dancers, writers, musicians, etc.); controversial issues (spark a dialogue about issues that divide us as a community, and the ways in which lesbians of different backgrounds fail to understand and support one another). We are not interested in inflammatory articles that incite or enrage readers without offering a channel for action, but we do look for challenging, thought-provoking work. The easiest way to get published in *Curve* is with a front-of-the-book piece for our Curvatures section, topical/fun/newsy pop culture articles that are 100-350 words.''

$ECHO MAGAZINE

ACE Publishing, Inc., P.O. Box 16630, Phoenix AZ 85011-6630. (602)266-0550. Fax: (602)266-0773. E-mail: editor@echomag.com. Web site: www.echomag.com. **Contact:** Buddy Early, managing editor. **30-40% freelance written.** Biweekly magazine covering gay and lesbian issues. ''*Echo Magazine* is a newsmagazine for gay, lesbian, bisexual, and transgendered persons in the Phoenix metro area and throughout the state of Arizona. Editorial content needs to be pro-gay, that is, supportive of GLBT equality in all areas of American life.'' Estab. 1989. Circ. 15,000-18,000. Pays on publication. Publishes ms an average of less than 1 month after acceptance. Byline given. Buys all rights. Editorial lead time 1-2 months. Submit seasonal material 1-2 months in advance. Accepts queries by e-mail. Responds in 2 weeks to queries; 1 month to mss. Sample copy online. Writer's guidelines by e-mail.

Nonfiction Book excerpts, essays, historical/nostalgic, humor, interview/profile, opinion, personal experience, photo feature, travel. Special issues: Pride Festival (April); Arts issue (August); Holiday Gift/Decor (December). No ''articles on topics unrelated to our GLBT readers, or anything that is not pro-gay.'' **Buys 10-20 mss/year.** Query. Length: 500-2,000 words. **Pays $30-40.**

Photos State availability with submission. Reviews contact sheets, GIF/JPEG files. Buys all rights. Negotiates payment individually. Captions, identification of subjects, model releases required.

Columns/Departments Guest Commentary (opinion on GLBT issues), 500-1,000 words; Arts/Entertainment (profiles of GLBT or relevant celebrities, or arts issues), 800-1,500 words. **Buys 5-10 mss/year.** Query. **Pays $30-40.**

Tips ''Know Phoenix (or other areas of Arizona) and its GLBT community. Please don't send nongay-related or nonpro-gay material. Research your topics thoroughly and write professionally. Our print content and online contenty are very similar.''

$THE GAY & LESBIAN REVIEW

Gay & Lesbian Review, Inc., P.O. Box 180300, Boston MA 02118. (617)421-0082. E-mail: editor@glreview.com. Web site: www.glreview.com. **100% freelance written.** Bimonthly magazine covers gay and lesbian history, culture, and politics. ''In-depth essays on GLBT history, biography, the arts, political issues, written in clear, lively prose targeted to the 'literate nonspecialist.' '' Estab. 1994. Circ. 12,000. Pays on publication. Byline given. Buys first rights. Editorial lead time 2 months. Accepts queries by mail, e-mail, phone. Accepts simultaneous submissions. Sample copy for free. Writer's guidelines free.

Nonfiction Essays, historical/nostalgic, humor, interview/profile, opinion, book reviews. Does not want fiction, memoirs, personal reflections. Query. Length: 1,500-5,000 words. **Pays $100.** ''Writer can waive payment for five gift subscriptions.''

Poetry Avant-garde, free verse, traditional.

Tips ''We prefer that a proposal be e-mailed before a completed draft is sent.''

$$$$GENRE

Genre Publishing, 213 W. 35th St., Suite 402, New York NY 10001. (212)594-8181. Fax: (212)594-8263. E-mail: genre@genremagazine.com. Web site: www.genremagazine.com. Editor: Bill Henning. **60% freelance written.** Monthly magazine. ''*Genre*, America's best-selling gay men's lifestyle magazine, covers entertainment, fashion, travel, and relationships in a hip, upbeat, upscale voice.'' Estab. 1991. Circ. 50,000. Pays on publication. Publishes ms an average of 3 months after acceptance. Byline given. Offers 25% kill fee. Buys first North American serial, electronic rights. Editorial lead time 10 weeks. Submit seasonal material 10 weeks in advance. Accepts queries by mail, e-mail, fax. May only respond if interested to queries. Sample copy for $6.95 ($5 plus $1.95 postage).

Nonfiction Essays, exposé, general interest, historical/nostalgic, how-to, humor, inspirational, interview/profile, new product, opinion, personal experience, photo feature, religious, travel, relationships, fashion. Not interested in articles on 2 males negotiating a sexual situation or coming out stories. **Buys variable number mss/year.** Query with published clips. Length: 500-1,500 words. **Pays $150-1,600.**

Photos State availability with submission. Reviews contact sheets, 3×5 or 5×7 prints. Buys one-time rights. Negotiates payment individually. Model releases required.

Columns/Departments Body (how to better the body); Mind (how to better the mind); Spirit (how to better the spirit), all 700 words; Reviews (books, movies, music, travel, etc.), 500 words. **Buys variable number of mss/year.** Query with published clips or send complete ms. **Pays $200 maximum.**

Fiction Adventure, experimental, horror, humorous, mainstream, mystery, novel excerpts, religious, romance, science fiction, slice-of-life vignettes, suspense. **Buys 10 mss/year.** Send complete ms. Length: 2,000-4,000 words.

Tips "Like you, we take our journalistic responsibilities and ethics very seriously, and we subscribe to the highest standards of the profession. We expect our writers to represent original work that is not libelous and does not infringe upon the copyright or violate the right of privacy of any other person, firm or corporation."

$ $ GIRLFRIENDS MAGAZINE

Lesbian Culture, Politics, and Entertainment, 3415 César Chávez, Suite 101, San Francisco CA 94110. (415)648-9464. Fax: (415)648-4705. E-mail: staff@girlfriendsmag.com. Web site: www.girlfriendsmag.com. **Contact:** Editor. Monthly lesbian magazine. "*Girlfriends* provides its readers with intelligent, entertaining and visually pleasing coverage of culture, politics, and entertainment—all from an informed and critical lesbian perspective." Estab. 1994. Circ. 75,000. Pays on publication. Publishes ms an average of 6 months after acceptance. Byline given. Offers 50% kill fee. Buys first rights and use for advertising/promoting *Girlfriends*. Editorial lead time 3 months. Submit seasonal material 6 months in advance. Accepts queries by mail, e-mail. Accepts simultaneous submissions. Responds in 3 weeks to queries; 2 months to mss. Sample copy for $4.95 plus $1.50 postage or online. Writer's guidelines online.

- *Girlfriends* is not accepting fiction, poetry or fillers.

O‑‑ Break in by sending a letter detailing interests and story ideas, plus résumé and published samples.

Nonfiction Book excerpts, essays, exposé, historical/nostalgic, humor, interview/profile, new product, opinion, personal experience, photo feature, religious, technical, travel, investigative features. Special issues: Sex, music, bridal, sports and Hollywood issues, breast cancer issue. Special features: Best lesbian restaurants in the US; best places to live. **Buys 20-25 mss/year.** Query with published clips. Length: 1,000-3,500 words. **Pays 15¢/word.**

Reprints Send photocopy or typed ms with rights for sale noted and information about when and where the material previously appeared. Negotiable payment.

Photos Send photos with submission. Reviews contact sheets, 4×5 or 2¼×2¼ transparencies, prints. Buys one-time rights. Offers $30-50/photo. Captions, identification of subjects, model releases required.

Columns/Departments Book reviews, 900 words; Music reviews, 600 words; Travel, 600 words; Opinion pieces, 1,000 words; Humor, 600 words. Query with published clips. **Pays 15¢/word.**

Tips "Be unafraid of controversy—articles should focus on problems and debates raised in lesbian culture, politics, and sexuality. Avoid being 'politically correct.' We don't just want to know what's happening in the lesbian world, we want to know how what's happening in the world affects lesbians."

$ $ THE GUIDE

To Gay Travel, Entertainment, Politics, and Sex, Fidelity Publishing, P.O. Box 990593, Boston MA 02115. (617)266-8557. Fax: (617)266-1125. E-mail: letters@guidemag.com. Web site: www.guidemag.com. **25% freelance written.** Monthly magazine on the gay and lesbian community. Estab. 1981. Circ. 30,000. **Pays on acceptance.** Publishes ms an average of 2 months after acceptance. Offers negotiable kill fee. Buys first rights. Submit seasonal material 2 months in advance. Accepts queries by mail, e-mail. Accepts previously published material. Accepts simultaneous submissions. Responds in 3 months to queries. Sample copy for 9×12 SAE and 8 first-class stamps. Writer's guidelines for #10 SASE.

Nonfiction Book excerpts (if yet unpublished), essays, exposé, general interest, historical/nostalgic, humor, interview/profile, opinion, personal experience, photo feature, religious. **Buys 24 mss/year.** Query with or without published clips or send complete ms. Length: 500-5,000 words. **Pays $85-240.**

Reprints Occasionally buys previously published submissions. Pays 100% of amount paid for an original article.

Photos Send photos with submission. Reviews contact sheets. Buys one-time rights. Pays $15/image used. Captions, identification of subjects, model releases required.

Tips "Brevity, humor, and militancy appreciated. Writing on sex, political analysis, and humor are particularly appreciated. We purchase very few freelance travel pieces; those that we do buy are usually on less commercial destinations."

$ HX MAGAZINE

Two Queens, Inc., 230 W. 17th St., 8th Floor, New York NY 10011. (212)352-3535. E-mail: info@hx.com. Web site: www.hx.com. **25% freelance written.** Weekly magazine covering gay New York City nightlife and entertainment. Estab. 1991. Circ. 39,000. Pays on publication. Publishes ms an average of 1 month after acceptance. Byline given. Buys first North American serial, second serial (reprint), electronic rights. Editorial lead time 2 months. Submit seasonal material 2 months in advance.

Nonfiction General interest, arts and entertainment, celebrity profiles, reviews. **Buys 50 mss/year.** Query with published clips. Length: 500-2,000 words. **Pays $50-150; $25-100 for unsolicited articles.**

Reprints Send tearsheet or photocopy with rights for sale noted and information about when and where the material previously appeared. Pays 50% of amount paid for an original article.
Photos State availability with submission. Reviews contact sheets, negatives, 8×10 prints. Buys one-time, reprint and electronic reprint rights. Captions, identification of subjects, model releases required.
Columns/Departments Buys 200 mss/year. Query with published clips. **Pays $25-125.**

$ $ INSTINCT MAGAZINE

Instinct Publishing, 11440 Ventura Blvd., Suite 200, Studio City CA 91604. (818)286-0071. Fax: (818)286-0077. E-mail: editor@instinctmag.com. Web site: www.instinctmag.com. Editor: Mike Wood. **60% freelance written.** Gay men's monthly lifestyle and entertainment magazine. "*Instinct* is a blend of *Cosmo* and *Maxim* for gay men. We're smart, sexy, irreverent, and we always have a sense of humor—a unique style that has made us the #1 gay men's magazine in the US." Estab. 1997. Circ. 100,000. Pays on publication. Byline given. Offers 20% kill fee. Buys all rights. Editorial lead time 2 months. Accepts queries by mail, e-mail. Accepts simultaneous submissions. Sample copy and writer's guidelines online.
Nonfiction "Be inventive and specific—an article on 'dating' isn't saying much unless there is a really great hook." Exposé, general interest, humor, interview/profile (celebrity and non-celebrity), travel, basically anything of interest to gay men will be considered. Does not want first-person accounts or articles. Query with published clips or send complete ms. Length: 850-3,000 words. **Pays $150-300.** Sometimes pays expenses of writers on assignment.
Photos Buys all rights. Negotiates payment individually. Captions, identification of subjects, model releases required.
Columns/Departments Health (gay, off-kilter), 800 words; Fitness (irreverent), 500 words; Movies, Books (edgy, sardonic), 800 words; Music, Video Games (indie, underground), 800 words. **Pays $150-250.**
Tips "While *Instinct* publishes a wide variety of features and columns having to do with gay men's issues, we maintain our signature irreverent, edgy tone throughout. When pitching stories (e-mail is preferred), be as specific as possible, and try to think beyond the normal scope of 'gay relationship' features. An article on 'Dating Tips,' for example, will not be considered, while an article on 'Tips on Dating Two Guys At Once' is more our slant. We rarely accept finished articles. We keep a special eye out for pitches on investigational/exposé-type stories geared toward our audience."

$ $ METROSOURCE

MetroSource Publishing, Inc., 180 Varick St., 5th Floor, New York NY 10014. (212)691-5127. Fax: (212)741-2978. Web site: www.metrosource.com. **70% freelance written.** Magazine published 6 times/year. "*MetroSource* is an upscale, glossy, 4-color lifestyle magazine targeted to an urban, professional gay and lesbian readership." Estab. 1990. Circ. 120,000. Pays on publication. Publishes ms an average of 2 months after acceptance. Byline given. Editorial lead time 3 months. Submit seasonal material 4 months in advance. Accepts queries by mail, e-mail, fax, phone. Accepts simultaneous submissions. Sample copy for $5.
Nonfiction Exposé, interview/profile, opinion, photo feature, travel. **Buys 20 mss/year.** Query with published clips. Length: 1,000-2,500 words. **Pays $100-600.**
Photos State availability with submission. Negotiates payment individually. Captions, model releases required.
Columns/Departments Book, film, television, and stage reviews; health columns; and personal diary and opinion pieces. Word lengths vary. Query with published clips. **Pays $200.**

OUT

245 W. 17th St., Suite 1200, New York NY 10011. (212)242-8100. Fax: (212)242-8364. E-mail: editor@out.com. Web site: www.out.com. Editor-in-Chief: Aaron Hicklin. **Contact:** Department Editor. **70% freelance written.** Monthly national magazine covering gay and lesbian general-interest topics. "Our subjects range from current affairs to culture, from fitness to finance." Estab. 1992. Circ. 120,000. Pays on publication. Publishes ms an average of 3 months after acceptance. Byline given. Offers 25% kill fee. Buys first North American serial rights. second serial (reprint) rights for anthologies (additional fee paid) and 30-day reprint rights (additional fee paid if applicable) Editorial lead time 3 months. Submit seasonal material 5 months in advance. Accepts queries by mail. Accepts simultaneous submissions. Responds in 6 weeks to queries; 2 months to mss.
Nonfiction Book excerpts, essays, exposé, general interest, historical/nostalgic, humor, interview/profile, new product, opinion, personal experience, photo feature, fashion/lifestyle. **Buys 200 mss/year.** Query with published clips and SASE. Length: 50-1,500 words. **Pays variable rate.** Sometimes pays expenses of writers on assignment.
Photos State availability with submission. Reviews contact sheets, transparencies, prints. Buys one-time rights. Negotiates payment individually. Captions, identification of subjects, model releases required.
Tips "*Out*'s contributors include editors and writers from the country's top consumer titles: skilled reporters, columnists, and writers with distinctive voices and specific expertise in the fields they cover. But while published

clips and relevant experience are a must, the magazine also seeks out fresh, young voices. The best guide to the kind of stories we publish is to review our recent issues. Is there a place for the story you have in mind? Be aware of our long lead time. No phone queries, please."

N $ OUTLOOKS

Outlooks Publication Inc., #1B, 1230A 17th Ave. SW, Calgary Alberta T2T 0B8 Canada. (403)228-1157. Fax: (403)228-7735. E-mail: main@outlooks.ca. Web site: www.outlooks.ca. **Contact:** Roy Heale, editor. **100% freelance written.** Monthly national lifestyle publication for Canada's gay and lesbian community. Estab. 1997. Circ. 37,500. Pays on publication. Publishes ms an average of 2 months after acceptance. Byline given. Offers 50% kill fee. Buys first rights. Editorial lead time 2 months. Submit seasonal material 3 months in advance. Accepts queries by e-mail. Accepts simultaneous submissions. Responds in 2 weeks to queries. Sample copy online. Writer's guidelines free.

Nonfiction Essays, general interest, humor, interview/profile, photo feature, travel. Query with published clips. Length: 1,000-1,200 words. **Pays $100-120.** Sometimes pays expenses of writers on assignment.

Photos State availability with submission. Reviews contact sheets. Buys one-time rights. Negotiates payment individually. Captions required.

Columns/Departments Book, movie, and music reviews (600-700 words). **Buys 120 mss/year.** Query with published clips.

Fiction Adventure, erotica, humorous. **Buys 10 mss/year.** Query with published clips. Length: 1,200-1,600 words. **Pays $120-160.**

OUTSMART

Up & Out Communications, 3406 Audubon Place, Houston TX 77006. (713)520-7237. Fax: (713)522-3275. Web site: www.outsmartmagazine.com. **50% freelance written.** Monthly magazine concerned with gay, lesbian, bisexual, and transgender issues. "*OutSmart* offers vibrant and thoughtful coverage of the stories that appeal most to an educated gay audience." Estab. 1994. Circ. 60,000. Pays on publication. Byline given. Buys one-time, simultaneous rights. Permission to publish on Web site. Editorial lead time 3 months. Submit seasonal material 4 months in advance. Accepts queries by mail, e-mail, fax. Responds in 6 weeks to queries; 2 months to mss. Sample copy and writer's guidelines online.

Nonfiction Historical/nostalgic, interview/profile, opinion, personal experience, photo feature, travel, health/wellness; local/national news. **Buys 24 mss/year.** Send complete ms. Length: 450-2,000 words. **Negotiates payment individually.**

Reprints Send photocopy.

Photos State availability with submission. Reviews 4×6 prints. Buys one-time rights. Negotiates payment individually. Identification of subjects required.

The online magazine carries original content not found in the print edition and includes writer's guidelines.

Tips "*OutSmart* is a mainstream publication that covers culture, politics, personalities, and entertainment as well as local and national news and events. We work to address the diversity of the lesbian, gay, bisexual, and transgender community, fostering understanding among all our readers."

$ $ SCENE

Lund Entertainment, Inc., P.O. Box 20099, Worcester MA 01602. (508)753-3177. Fax: (508)753-1067. E-mail: elfman@scenemag.net. Web site: www.scenemag.net. **Contact:** Lois Elfman, editor-in-chief. **50% freelance written.** Bimonthly magazine geared toward a readership of gay men 25 and older. It is a combination of celebrity news, other light news, serious news, and in-depth features. Estab. 2005. Circ. 33,000. Pays 1 month after publication. Publishes ms an average of 2-3 months after acceptance. Byline given. Buys all rights. Editorial lead time 2-3 months. Submit seasonal material 3 months in advance. Accepts queries by e-mail. Accepts simultaneous submissions. Responds in 2 weeks to queries. Sample copy for #10 SASE.

Nonfiction General interest, interview/profile. No lists, opinion pieces, personal experience pieces, product reviews, or sex stories. Query with published clips. Length: 150-2,000 words. Sometimes pays expenses of writers on assignment.

Photos State availability with submission. Buys one-time rights. Pays $15/published photo. Identification of subjects required.

Tips "Don't suggest articles about straight entertainers who are popular with gay audiences. Try to be innovative. Bring the editor a great story from your area that a national audience might not instantly know. Do not compare *Scene* to any other gay magazine."

N $ SWERVE

Manitoba's GLBT Magazine, Swerve Media Inc., 200-63 Albert St., Winnipeg MB R3B 1G4 Canada. (204)942-4599. Fax: (204)947-0554. E-mail: swervemedia@mts.net. Web site: www.swervemedia.org. Managing Editor:

April Friesen. **Contact:** Charles Melvin, editor. **95% freelance written.** Monthly magazine covering any topic of interest to GLBT readers. "*Swerve* is a free publication that provides information, analysis, and amusement through words and imagery produced for the gay, lesbian, bisexual, transgender, two-spirit, and queer community and its allies." Estab. 1994. Circ. 10,000. Pays on publication. Publishes ms an average of 1 month after acceptance. Byline given. Buys one-time rights. Editorial lead time 1 month. Accepts queries by mail, e-mail, fax, phone. Accepts previously published material. Accepts simultaneous submissions. Responds in 2 weeks to queries. Sample copy and writer's guidelines online.

Nonfiction Essays, exposé, general interest, historical/nostalgic, how-to, humor, inspirational, interview/profile, opinion, personal experience, photo feature, religious, technical, travel. Query. Length: 600-1,200 words. **Pays $24-48.**

Photos State availability with submission. Buys one-time rights. Offers $10/photo. Identification of subjects required.

Columns/Departments Staying Alive (health-related issues); News Inside Out (historical background of GLBT news stories); Urban Explorer (profiles of any gay-friendly cities), all 600 words. **Buys 6-10 mss/year.** Query. **Pays $24-48.**

$ $ XTRA

Toronto's Lesbian & Gay Biweekly, Pink Triangle Press, 491 Church St., Suite 200, Toronto ON M4Y 2C6 Canada. (416)925-6665. Fax: (416)925-6503. E-mail: info@xtra.ca. Web site: www.xtra.ca. Editor-in-Chief: David Walberg. **Contact:** Paul Gallant, managing editor. **80% freelance written.** Biweekly tabloid covering gay, lesbian, bisexual and transgender issues, news, arts and events of interest in Toronto. "*Xtra* is dedicated to lesbian and gay sexual liberation. We publish material that advocates this end, according to the mission statement of the not-for-profit organization Pink Triange Press, which operates the paper." Estab. 1984. Circ. 45,000. Pays on publication. Byline given. Buys first North American serial, electronic rights. Editorial lead time 1 month. Accepts queries by e-mail. Accepts previously published material. Accepts simultaneous submissions. Responds in 2 weeks to queries. Sample copy online. Writer's guidelines by e-mail.

Nonfiction Book excerpts, essays, interview/profile, opinion, personal experience, travel. US-based stories or profiles of straight people who do not have a direct connection to the LGBT community. Query with published clips. Length: 200-1,600 words. Sometimes pays expenses of writers on assignment.

Photos Send photos with submission. Buys Internet rights. Offers $60 minimum. Captions, identification of subjects, model releases required.

Columns/Departments *Xtra* rarely publishes unsolicited columns. **Buys 6 mss/year.** Query with published clips.

GENERAL INTEREST

$ $ THE AMERICAN LEGION MAGAZINE

P.O. Box 1055, Indianapolis IN 46206-1055. (317)630-1200. Fax: (317)630-1280. E-mail: magazine@legion.org. Web site: www.legion.org. Editorial Administrator: Brandy Ballenger. **Contact:** John Raughter, editor. **70% freelance written.** Prefers to work with published/established writers, but works with a small number of new/unpublished writers each year. Monthly magazine. "Working through 15,000 community-level posts, the honorably discharged wartime veterans of The American Legion dedicate themselves to God, country and traditional American values. They believe in a strong defense; adequate and compassionate care for veterans and their families; community service; and the wholesome development of our nation's youth. We publish articles that reflect these values. We inform our readers and their families of significant trends and issues affecting our nation, the world and the way we live. Our major features focus on the American flag, national security, foreign affairs, business trends, social issues, health, education, ethics and the arts. We also publish selected general feature articles, articles of special interest to veterans, and question-and-answer interviews with prominent national and world figures." Estab. 1919. Circ. 2,550,000. **Pays on acceptance.** Publishes ms an average of 6 months after acceptance. Byline given. Buys first North American serial rights. Accepts queries by mail, e-mail, fax. Responds in 2 months to queries. Sample copy for $3.50 and 9×12 SAE with 6 first-class stamps. Writer's guidelines for #10 SASE.

Nonfiction Well-reported articles or expert commentaries cover issues/trends in world/national affairs, contemporary problems, general interest, sharply-focused feature subjects. Monthly Q&A with national figures/experts. General interest, interview/profile. No regional topics or promotion of partisan political agendas. No personal experiences or war stories. **Buys 50-60 mss/year.** Query with SASE should explain the subject or issue, article's angle and organization, writer's qualifications, and experts to be interviewed. Length: 300-2,000 words. **Pays 40¢/word and up.**

Photos On assignment.

Tips "Queries by new writers should include clips/background/expertise; no longer than 1½ pages. Submit suitable material showing you have read several issues. *The American Legion Magazine* considers itself '*the* magazine for a strong America.' Reflect this theme (which includes economy, educational system, moral fiber, social issues, infrastructure, technology and national defense/security). We are a general interest, national magazine, not a strictly military magazine. We are widely read by members of the Washington establishment and other policy makers."

AMERICAN PROFILE

Publishing Group of America, 341 Cool Springs Blvd., Suite 400, Franklin TN 37067. (615)468-6000. Fax: (615)468-6100. E-mail: editorial@americanprofile.com. Web site: www.americanprofile.com. **90% freelance written.** Weekly magazine with national and regional editorial celebrating the people, places, and experiences of hometowns across America. The 4-color magazine is distributed through small to medium-size community newspapers. Estab. 2000. Circ. 7,000,000. **Pays on acceptance.** Byline given. Buys first, electronic, 6-month exclusive rights rights. Editorial lead time 6 months. Submit seasonal material 1 year in advance. Accepts queries by mail. Responds in 1 month to queries; 1 month to mss. Writer's guidelines online.

O→ "In addition to a query, first-time writers should include 2-3 published clips."

Nonfiction General interest, how-to, interview/profile. No fiction, nostalgia, poetry, essays. **Buys 250 mss/year.** Query with published clips. Length: 400-1,200 words. Pays expenses of writers on assignment.

Photos State availability with submission. Reviews transparencies. Buys one-time rights, nonexclusive after 6 months. Negotiates payment individually. Captions, identification of subjects, model releases required.

Columns/Departments Health; Family; Finances; Home; Gardening.

Tips "Please visit the Web site to see our content and writing style."

$ $ $ $ THE ATLANTIC MONTHLY

600 New Hampshire Ave. NW, Washington DC 20037. (202)266-7000. Fax: (202)266-7075. E-mail: letters@theatlantic.com. Web site: www.theatlantic.com. **Contact:** C. Michael Curtis, senior editor (fiction); Don Peck, senior editor (nonfictiion); David Barber (poetry). Monthly magazine of arts and public affairs. General magazine for an educated readership with broad cultural interests. Estab. 1857. Circ. 400,000. **Pays on acceptance.** Byline given. Buys first North American serial rights. Accepts queries by mail. Responds in 2 months to mss. Writer's guidelines online.

Nonfiction Reportage preferred. Book excerpts, essays, general interest, humor, personal experience, religious, travel. Query with or without published clips or send complete ms. All unsolicited mss must be accompanied by SASE. Length: 1,000-6,000 words. **Payment varies.** Sometimes pays expenses of writers on assignment.

Fiction "Seeks fiction that is clear, tightly written with strong sense of 'story' and well-defined characters. No longer publishes fiction in the regular magazine. Instead, it will appear in a special newsstand-only fiction issue." Literary and contemporary fiction. Send complete ms. Length: 2,000-6,000 words.

Poetry Contact Peter Davison, poetry editor. **Buys 40-60 poems/year.**

Tips Writers should be aware that this is not a market for beginner's work (nonfiction and fiction), nor is it truly for intermediate work. Study this magazine before sending only your best, most professional work. When making first contact, "cover letters are sometimes helpful, particularly if they cite prior publications or involvement in writing programs. Common mistakes: melodrama, inconclusiveness, lack of development, unpersuasive characters and/or dialogue."

$ ⊘ BIBLIOPHILOS

A Journal of History, Literature, and the Liberal Arts, The Bibliophile Publishing Co., Inc., 200 Security Building, Fairmont WV 26554. (304)366-8107. **Contact:** Dr. Gerald J. Bobango, editor. **65-70% freelance written.** Quarterly literary magazine concentrating on 19th century American and European history and literature. "We see ourself as a forum for new and unpublished writers, historians, philosophers, literary critics and reviewers, and those who love animals. Audience is academic-oriented, college graduate, who believes in traditional Aristotelian-Thomistic thought and education, and has a fair streak of the Luddite in him/her. Our ideal reader owns no television, has never sent nor received e-mail, and avoids shopping malls at any cost. He loves books." Estab. 1981. Circ. 400. Pays on publication. Publishes ms an average of 1 year after acceptance. Byline given. Buys first North American serial rights. Editorial lead time 6 months. Submit seasonal material 6 months in advance. Accepts queries by mail. Responds in 2 weeks to queries; 1 month to mss. Sample copy for $5.25. Writer's guidelines for 9½×4 SAE with 2 first-class stamps.

- Query first only, unaccompanied by any ms.

O→ Break in with "either prose or poetry which is illustrative of man triumphing over and doing without technology, pure Ludditism, if need be. Send material critical of the socialist welfare state, constantly expanding federal government (or government at all levels), or exposing the inequities of affirmative action, political correctness, and the mass media packaging of political candidates. We want to see a pre-1960 worldview."

Nonfiction Book excerpts, essays, general interest, historical/nostalgic, humor, interview/profile, opinion, personal experience, photo feature, travel, book review-essay, literary criticism. Special issues: Upcoming theme issues include an annual all book-review issue, containing 10-15 reviews and review-essays, or poetry about books and reading. Does not want to see "anything that Oprah would recommend, or that Erma Bombeck or Ann Landers would think humorous or interesting. No 'I found Jesus and it changed my life' material." **Buys 25-30 mss/year.** Query by mail only first, not with any ms included. Length: 1,500-3,000 words. **Pays $5-35.**

Photos State availability with submission. Reviews b&w 4×6 prints. Buys one-time rights. Negotiates payment individually. Identification of subjects required.

Columns/Departments Features (fiction and nonfiction, short stories), 1,500-3,000 words; Poetry (batches of 5, preferably thematically related), 3-150 lines; Reviews (book reviews or review essays on new books or individual authors, current and past), 1,000-1,500 words; Opinion (man triumphing over technology and technocrats, the facade of modern education, computer fetishism), 1,000-1,500 words. **Buys 20 mss/year.** Query by mail only. **Pays $25-40.**

Fiction Contact Gerald J. Bobango, editor. Adventure, ethnic, historical, horror, humorous, mainstream, mystery, novel excerpts, romance, slice-of-life vignettes, suspense, western, utopian, Orwellian. "No 'I remember Mama, who was a saint and I miss her terribly'; no gay or lesbian topics; no drug culture material; nothing harping on political correctness; nothing to do with healthy living, HMOs, medical programs, or the welfare state, unless it is against statism in these areas." **Buys 25-30 mss/year.** Length: 1,500-3,000 words. **Pays $25-40.**

Poetry "Formal and rhymed verse gets read first." Free verse, light verse, traditional, political satire, doggerel.

Tips "Query first. Do not send material unsolicited. We shall not respond if you do."

$ CAPPER'S

Ogden Publications, Inc., 1503 SW 42nd St., Topeka KS 66609-1265. (785)274-4300. Web site: www.cappers.com. **25% freelance written.** Works with a small number of new/unpublished writers each year. Monthly tabloid emphasizing home and family for readers who live mainly in the rural Midwest. "*Capper's* is upbeat, focusing on the homey feelings people like to share, as well as hopes and dreams." Estab. 1879. Circ. 200,000. Pays for poetry and fiction on acceptance; articles on publication. Publishes ms an average of 2-12 months after acceptance. Byline given. Buys first rights. Submit seasonal material 4 months in advance. Accepts queries by mail. Responds in 2-3 months to queries; 6 months to mss. Sample copy and writer's guidelines online.

Nonfiction General interest, historical/nostalgic (local museums, etc.), inspirational, travel, nostalgic, human interest, family-oriented. **Buys 75 mss/year.** Send complete ms. Length: 900 words maximum. **Pays $2.50/printed inch. Pays additional $5 if used on Web site.**

Reprints Accepts occasionally from noncompeting venues. Send typed ms with rights for sale noted and information about when and where the material previously appeared.

Photos Send photos with submission. Buys one-time rights. Pays $5-15 for b&w glossy prints; $20-40 for color prints (inside); $40 for cover. Captions required.

Columns/Departments Send complete ms. **Pays approximately $2/printed inch. Payment for recipes is $5. Hints used earn $2 gift certificate.**

Fiction "We buy very few fiction pieces—longer than short stories, shorter than novels." Adventure, historical, humorous, mainstream, mystery, romance, serialized novels, western. No explicit sex, violence, profanity, or alcohol use. **Buys 4-5 mss/year.** Length: 7,500-50,000 words. **Pays $100-400.**

Poetry "The poems that appear in *Capper's* are not too difficult to read. They're easy to grasp. We're looking for everyday events and down-to-earth themes." Free verse, light verse, traditional, nature, inspiration. **Buys 150 poems/year.** Submit maximum 5-6 poems. Length: 4-16 lines. **Pays $10-15.**

Tips "Study a few issues of our publication. Most rejections are for material that is too long, unsuitable or out of character for our magazine (too sexy, too much profanity, wrong kind of topic, etc.). On occasion, we must cut material to fit column space. No electronic submissions."

$ $ $ $ DIVERSION

300 W. 57th St., New York NY 10019. (212)969-7500. Fax: (212)969-7563. E-mail: shartford@hearst.com. Web site: www.diversion.com. **Contact:** Shari Hartford. Monthly magazine covering travel and lifestyle, edited for physicians. "*Diversion* offers an eclectic mix of interests beyond medicine. Regular features include stories on domestic and foreign travel destinations, food and wine, cars, gardening, photography, books, electronic gear, and the arts. Although *Diversion* doesn't cover health subjects, it does feature profiles of doctors who excel at nonmedical pursuits or who engage in medical volunteer work." Estab. 1973. Circ. 190,000. Pays 3 months after acceptance. Byline given. Offers 25% kill fee. Editorial lead time 6 months. Responds in 1 month to queries. Sample copy for $4.50. Guidelines available.

O→ Break in by "querying with a brief proposal describing the focus of the story. It should be on a topic in which you have demonstrated expertise."

Nonfiction "We get so many travel and food queries that we're hard pressed to even read them all. Far better to query us on culture, the arts, sports, technology, etc." Query with proposal, published clips, and author's credentials. Length: 1,800-2,000 words. **Pays 50¢-$1/word.**

Columns/Departments Travel, food & wine, photography, gardening, cars, technology. Length: 1,200 words.

Ø EBONY

Johnson Publishing Co., Inc., 820 S. Michigan Ave., Chicago IL 60605. Web site: www.ebonyjet.com. Monthly magazine covering topics ranging from education and history to entertainment, art, government, health, travel, sports and social events. African-American oriented consumer interest magazine. Circ. 1,728,986. Editorial lead time 3 months.

- Query before submitting.

N $ $ FASHION FORUM

The Substance of Style, Business Journals, Inc., 185 Madison Ave., 5th Floor, New York NY 10016. (212)710-7442. E-mail: roberthp@busjour.com. Web site: www.busjour.com. Editor: Karen Alberg Grossman. **Contact:** Robert Haynes-Peterson, managing editor. **70% freelance written.** Semiannual magazine covering luxury fashion (mens 80%, womens 20%), luxury lifestyle. "*Forum* directly targets a very upscale reader interested in profiles and service pieces on upscale designers, new fashion trends and traditional suiting. Lifestyle articles—including wine and spirits, travel, cars, boating, sports, collecting, etc.—are upscale top of the line (ie, don't write how expensive taxis are)." Circ. 150,000. Pays on publication. Publishes ms an average of 3-4 months after acceptance. Byline given. Offers 50% kill fee. Buys all rights. Editorial lead time 6 months. Submit seasonal material 6 months in advance. Accepts queries by mail, e-mail. Responds in 2-3 weeks to queries. Writer's guidelines by e-mail

Nonfiction General interest, interview/profile, travel, luxury lifestyle trends, fashion service pieces. Does not want personal essays. "We run a few but commission them. No fiction or single product articles. In other words, an article should be on whats new in Italian wines, not about one superspecial brand." **Buys 20-25 mss/year.** Query. Length: 600-1,500 words. **Pays $300-500.**

Photos State availability with submission. Reviews GIF/JPEG files. Buys one-time rights. Offers no additional payment for photos accepted with ms

Columns/Departments Travel, 1,000-1,500 words; Wine + Spirits, 600-1,200 words; Gourmet, 600-1,200 words; Wheels, 600 words. **Buys 10-15 mss/year.** Query. **Pays $300-500.**

Tips "Be prepared to write like you know the upscale lifestyle. Even if you only own one jacket, or stay in hostels, remember our readers, for the most part, don't even know about hostels! Experience in a specific category, or direct access to designers for profiles is a huge in!"

$ $ $ $ HARPER'S MAGAZINE

666 Broadway, 11th Floor, New York NY 10012. (212)420-5720. Fax: (212)228-5889. Web site: www.harpers.org. Editor: Roger Hodge. **90% freelance written.** Monthly magazine for well-educated, socially concerned, widely read men and women who value ideas and good writing. "*Harper's Magazine* encourages national discussion on current and significant issues in a format that offers arresting facts and intelligent opinions. By means of its several shorter journalistic forms—Harper's Index, Readings, Forum, and Annotation—as well as with its acclaimed essays, fiction, and reporting, *Harper's* continues the tradition begun with its first issue in 1850: to inform readers across the whole spectrum of political, literary, cultural, and scientific affairs." Estab. 1850. Circ. 230,000. **Pays on acceptance.** Publishes ms an average of 3 months after acceptance. Offers negotiable kill fee. Rights purchased vary with author and material. Accepts previously published material. Responds in 6 weeks to queries. Sample copy for $5.95.

Nonfiction "For writers working with agents or who will query first only, our requirements are: public affairs, literary, international and local reporting, and humor." Publishes 1 major report/issue. Length: 4,000-6,000 words. Publishes 1 major essay/issue. Length: 4,000-6,000 words. "These should be construed as topical essays on all manner of subjects (politics, the arts, crime, business, etc.) to which the author can bring the force of passionate and informed statement." Humor. No interviews; no profiles. **Buys 2 mss/year.** Query. Length: 4,000-6,000 words.

Reprints Accepted for Readings section. Send typed ms with rights for sale noted and information about when and where the article previously appeared.

Photos Occasionally purchased with ms; others by assignment. Stacey Clarkson, art director. State availability with submission. Pays $50-500.

Fiction Will consider unsolicited fiction. Humorous. **Buys 12 mss/year.** Query. Length: 3,000-5,000 words. **Generally pays 50¢-$1/word.**

Tips "Some readers expect their magazines to clothe them with opinions in the way that Bloomingdale's dresses them for the opera. The readers of *Harper's Magazine* belong to a different crowd. They strike me as the kind of people who would rather think in their own voices and come to their own conclusions."

N $ $ INDUSTRY MAGAZINE

Industry Publications, LLC, 1768 Park Center Dr., Suite 280, Orlando FL 32835. Fax: (407)290-0120. E-mail: knye@industrymagazine.com. Web site: www.industrymagazine.com. Editor: Matt Scanlon. Managing Editor: Ashely Burns. **Contact:** Kim Nye, associate editor. **80% freelance written.** Bimonthly magazine covering fashion, entertainment, people, culture. "*Industry* combines all the power and swoop of a national, luxury lifestyle, general interest title with the inimitable flair of its regional franchises. Specifically directed at well-educated, affluent, sophisticated residents of its franchise cities, *Industry* offers what typical regional books cannot; content that is at once national and local in scope." Estab. 2002. Circ. 250,000. Pays on publication. Publishes ms an average of 1 month after acceptance. Byline given. Offers 33% kill fee. Buys first rights. Editorial lead time 3 months. Submit seasonal material 5 months in advance. Accepts queries by e-mail, fax. Responds in 1 month to queries. Sample copy by e-mail.

- *Industry Magazine* has editions in Orlando; Tampa Bay; Sarasota; Palm Beach; El Paso; Kansas City; Los Angeles; Staten Island; Phoenix.

Nonfiction General interest, humor, interview/profile, new product, travel, fashion. Does not want stale, PR-type product descriptions. Writers should be witty, but sophisticated and opinionated. **Buys 500 mss/year.** Query with published clips. Length: 450-2,000 words. **Pays $275-600.** Sometimes pays expenses of writers on assignment.

Photos Contact Kristen Papa, photo editor. Send photos with submission. Reviews GIF/JPEG files (300 dpi or higher). Buys one-time rights. Offers no additional payment for photos accepted with ms. Identification of subjects required.

Columns/Departments Night Owl (local nightlife for specific regions), 450-600 words; iSpot (places local elite/highrollers are seen), 800 words; Art Scene (local art scene in specific regions), 450-600 words; Restaurant Review (local restaurants in specific regions). **Buys 300 mss/year.** Query. **Pays $275-300.**

Tips "Pitch ideas based on what you see in the magazine. Do not forget to send clips with your pitch, even if it is not a magazine article. I need to know how well you can write."

$ $ $ $ NATIONAL GEOGRAPHIC MAGAZINE

1145 17th St. NW, Washington DC 20036. (202)857-7000. Fax: (202)492-5767. Web site: www.nationalgeographic.com. Editor-in-Chief: Chris Johns. **Contact:** Oliver Payne, senior editor. **60% freelance written.** Prefers to work with published/established writers. Monthly magazine for members of the National Geographic Society. "Timely articles written in a compelling, 'eyewitness' style. Arresting photographs that speak to us of the beauty, mystery, and harsh realities of life on earth. Maps of unprecedented detail and accuracy. These are the hallmarks of *National Geographic* magazine. Since 1888, the *Geographic* has been educating readers about the world." Estab. 1888. Circ. 6,800,000.

- Before querying, study recent issues and check a *Geographic Index* at a library since the magazine seldom returns to regions or subjects covered within the past 10 years.

Nonfiction *National Geographic* publishes general interest, illustrated articles on science, natural history, exploration, cultures and geographical regions. Of the freelance writers assigned, a few are experts in their fields; the remainder are established professionals. Fewer than 1% of unsolicited queries result in assignments. Query (500 words with clips of published articles) by mail to Senior Assitant Editor Oliver Payne. Do not send mss. Length: 2,000-8,000 words. Pays expenses of writers on assignment.

Photos Query in care of the Photographic Division.

- The online magazine carries original content not included in the print edition. Contact: Valerie May, online editor.

Tips "State the theme(s) clearly, let the narrative flow, and build the story around strong characters and a vivid sense of place. Give us rounded episodes, logically arranged."

$ $ $ THE NEW YORK TIMES MAGAZINE

229 W. 43rd St., New York NY 10036. (212)556-1234. Fax: (212)556-3830. E-mail: magazine@nytimes.com. Web site: www.nytimes.com/pages/magazine. *The New York Times Magazine* appears in *The New York Times* on Sunday. The *Arts and Leisure* section appears during the week. The *Op Ed* page appears daily.

- Because of the volume of submissions for the Lives column, the magazine cannot return or respond to unsolicited manuscripts.

Nonfiction *Arts & Leisure*: Wants "to encourage imaginativeness in terms of form and approach—stressing ideas, issues, trends, investigations, symbolic reporting and stories delving deeply into the creative achievements and processes of artists and entertainers—and seeks to break away from old-fashioned gushy, fan magazine stuff."

Length: 1,500-2,000 words. **Pays $100-350**, depending on length. Address unsolicited articles with SASE to the Arts & Leisure Articles Editor. *Op Ed* page: "The Op Ed page is always looking for new material and publishes many people who have never been published before. We want material of universal relevance which people can talk about in a personal way. When writing for the Op Ed page, there is no formula, but the writing itself should have some polish. Don't make the mistake of pontificating on the news. We're not looking for more political columnists." Length: 750 words. **Pays $150.**

NEW YORK TIMES UPFRONT

Scholastic, Inc., 557 Broadway, New York NY 10012-3999. Web site: www.upfrontmagazine.com. Biweekly magazine collaboration between *The New York Times* and Scholastic, Inc. designed as a news magazine specifically for teenagers. Circ. 200,000. Editorial lead time 1-2 months.

- Query before submitting.

THE NEW YORKER

4 Times Square, New York NY 10036. (212) 286-5900. Web site: www.newyorker.com. A quality weekly magazine of distinct news stories, articles, essays, and poems for a literate audience. Estab. 1925. Circ. 1,000,000. **Pays on acceptance.** Accepts queries by mail, e-mail. Responds in 3 months to mss. Writer's guidelines online.

- *The New Yorker* receives approximately 4,000 submissions per month.
- Paste submissions into the body of the e-mail: fiction@newyorker.com (fiction); talkofthetown@newyorker.com (Talk of the Town); shouts@newyorker.com (Shouts & Murmurs); poetry@newyorker.com (poetry); newsbreaks@newyorker.com (newsbreaks).

Fiction Publishes 1 ms/issue. Send complete ms. **Payment varies.**

Poetry Send poetry to "Poetry Department." Submit maximum 6 poems.

Tips "Be lively, original, not overly literary. Write what you want to write, not what you think the editor would like."

$ $ $ NEWSWEEK

251 W. 57th St., 17th Floor, New York NY 10019. E-mail: letters@newsweek.com. Web site: www.newsweek.com. *Newsweek* is edited to report the week's developments on the newsfront of the world and the nation through news, commentary and analysis. Circ. 3,180,000. Buys non-exclusive world-wide rights.

Columns/Departments myturn@newsweek.com. Accepts unsolicited mss for My Turn, a column of personal opinion. The 850- 900-word essays for the column must be original, not published elsewhere, and contain verifiable facts. Only responds if interested. **Pays $1,000 on publication.**

N $ $ NYCPLUS

Community Media, LLC, 487 Greenwich St., #6A, New York NY 10013. (212)229-1890. Fax: (212)229-2790. E-mail: jennie@squigglefish.com. Web site: www.nycplus.com. **Contact:** Jennie Green or Jerry Tallmer, editors. **100% freelance written.** Monthly magazine. "We are looking for well-written stories of substance that relate in some way to our 50+ theme. All genres." Estab. 2005. Circ. 50,000. Pays on publication. Publishes ms an average of 3-6 months after acceptance. Byline given. Buys first rights. Editorial lead time 2-3 months. Submit seasonal material 4-5 months in advance. Accepts queries by e-mail. Accepts simultaneous submissions. Responds in 2 months to queries; 2 months to mss. Sample copy online. Writer's guidelines by e-mail.

Nonfiction Essays, general interest, historical/nostalgic, humor, inspirational, interview/profile, opinion, personal experience. **Buys 110 mss/year.** Query. Length: 900-4,000 words. **Pays $100-300.**

Columns/Departments Memory (personal experience/nostalgia), 800-1,100 words; Mind/Body (50+), 1,000-1,200 words; Food (old and new), 1,000-1,200 words; Work (2nd career/nonretirement), 1,200-1,600 words.

Fiction Humorous, mainstream, slice-of-life vignettes.

Tips "Go to our Web site and read as much content as you can."

$ $ $ THE OLD FARMER'S ALMANAC

Yankee Publishing, Inc., P.O. Box 520, 1121Main St., Dublin NH 03444. (603)563-8111. Fax: (603)563-8252. Web site: www.almanac.com. **Contact:** Janice Stillman, editor. **95% freelance written.** Annual magazine covering weather, gardening, history, oddities, lore. "*The Old Farmer's Almanac* is the oldest continuously published periodical in North America. Since 1792, it has provided useful information for people in all walks of life: tide tables for those who live near the ocean; sunrise tables and planting charts for those who live on the farm or simply enjoy gardening; recipes for those who like to cook; and forecasts for those who don't like the question of weather left up in the air. The words of the *Almanac*'s founder, Robert B. Thomas, guide us still: 'Our main endeavor is to be useful, but with a pleasant degree of humour.' " Estab. 1792. Circ. 3,750,000. **Pays on acceptance.** Publishes ms an average of 9 months after acceptance. Byline given. Offers 25% kill fee. Buys first

North American serial, electronic, all rights. Editorial lead time 6 months. Submit seasonal material 1 year in advance. Accepts queries by mail. Responds in 3 weeks to queries; 2 months to mss. Sample copy for $5 at bookstores or online. Writer's guidelines online.

Nonfiction General interest, historical/nostalgic, how-to (garden, cook, save money), humor, weather, natural remedies, obscure facts, history, popular culture. No personal weather recollections/accounts, personal/family histories. Query with published clips. Length: 800-2,500 words. **Pays 65¢/word.** Sometimes pays expenses of writers on assignment.

Fillers Anecdotes, short humor. **Buys 1-2/year.** Length: 100-200 words. **Pays $25.**

The online magazine carries original content not found in the print edition.

Tips "*The Old Farmer's Almanac* is a reference book. Our readers appreciate obscure facts and stories. Read it. Think differently. Read writer's guidelines online."

$ $ $ OPEN SPACES

Open Spaces Publications, Inc., PMB 134, 6327-C SW Capitol Hwy., Portland OR 97239-1937. (503)227-5764. Fax: (503)227-3401. E-mail: info@open-spaces.com. Web site: www.open-spaces.com. President: Penny Harrison. Managing Editor: James Bradley. **Contact:** Elizabeth Arthur, editor. **95% freelance written.** Quarterly general interest magazine. "*Open Spaces* is a forum for informed writing and intelligent thought. Articles are written by experts in various fields. Audience is varied (CEOs and rock climbers, politicos and university presidents, etc.) but is highly educated and loves to read good writing." Estab. 1997. Pays on publication. Publishes ms an average of 6 months after acceptance. Byline given. Offers 20% kill fee. Rights purchased vary with author and material. Editorial lead time 9 months. Accepts queries by mail, fax. Accepts simultaneous submissions. Sample copy for $10. Writer's guidelines online.

Nonfiction Essays, general interest, historical/nostalgic, how-to (if clever), humor, interview/profile, personal experience, travel. **Buys 35 mss/year.** Send complete ms. Length: 1,500-2,500 words; major articles up to 6,000 words. **Pays variable amount.**

Photos State availability with submission. Buys one-time rights. Captions, identification of subjects required.

Columns/Departments Contact David Williams, departments editor. Books (substantial topics such as the Booker Prize, The Newbery, etc.); Travel (must reveal insight); Sports (past subjects include rowing, and swing dancing); Unintended Consequences, 1,500-2,500 words. **Buys 20-25 mss/year.** Send complete ms. **Payment varies.**

Fiction Contact Ellen Teicher, fiction editor. "Quality is far more important than type. Read the magazine. Excellence is the issue—not subject matter." **Buys 8 mss/year.** Length: 2,000-6,000 words. **Payment varies.**

Poetry "Again, quality is far more important than type." Contact Susan Juve-Hu Bucharest, poetry editor. Submit maximum 3 poems with SASE.

Fillers Anecdotes, short humor, cartoons; interesting or amusing Northwest facts; expressions, etc.

Tips "*Open Spaces* reviews all manuscripts submitted in hopes of finding writing of the highest quality. We present a Northwest perspective as well as a national and international one. Best advice is read the magazine."

$ $ $ $ PARADE

Parade Publications, Inc., 711 Third Ave., New York NY 10017. (212)450-7000. Fax: (212)450-7284. Web site: www.parade.com. Executive Editor: Janice Kaplan. Editor: Lee Kravitz. **Contact:** Sharon Male, articles editor. **95% freelance written.** Weekly magazine for a general interest audience. Estab. 1941. Circ. 81,000,000. **Pays on acceptance.** Publishes ms an average of 5 months after acceptance. Kill fee varies in amount. Buys worldwide exclusive rights for 7 days, plus nonexclusive electronic and other rights in perpetuity. Editorial lead time 1 month. Accepts queries by mail, e-mail, fax. Accepts simultaneous submissions. Sample copy and writer's guidelines online.

Nonfiction Publishes general interest (on health, trends, social issues or anything of interest to a broad general audience), interview/profile (of news figures, celebrities and people of national significance), and "provocative topical pieces of news value." Spot news events are not accepted, as *Parade* has a 2-month lead time. No fiction, fashion, travel, poetry, cartoons, nostalgia, regular columns, personal essays, quizzes, or fillers. Unsolicited queries concerning celebrities, politicians or sports figures are rarely assigned. **Buys 150 mss/year.** Query with published clips. Length: 1,200-1,500 words. **Pays very competitive amount.** Pays expenses of writers on assignment.

Tips "If the writer has a specific expertise in the proposed topic, it increases the chances of breaking in. Send a well-researched, well-written 1-page proposal and enclose a SASE. Do not submit completed manuscripts."

PEOPLE

Time, Inc., 1271 Avenue of the Americas, New York NY 10020. (212)522-1212. Fax: (212)522-1359. E-mail: editor@people.com. Web site: www.people.com. Editor-in-Chief: Noman Pearlstine. Managing Editor: Larry

Hackett. Weekly magazine. Designed as a forum for personality journalism through the use of short articles on contemporary news events and people. Circ. 3,617,127. Editorial lead time 3 months. Sample copy not available.

- Does not buy freelance materials or use freelance writers.

$ THE POLISHING STONE

Refining the Life You Live Into the Life You Love, 3616 Colby Ave., #707, Everett WA 98201. E-mail: submissions @polishingstone.com. Web site: www.polishingstone.com. **Contact:** Lee Revere. **50% freelance written.** Magazine published 5 times/year "*The Polishing Stone* takes an optimistic and realistic look at the environment and quality of life: whole foods, alternative health, earth-friendly and handcrafted products, mindful parenting, relationships, and social and environmental issues. We focus on healthy lifestyles that are close to the earth, sustainable, and in balance. The issues we cover are serious, but we seek a tone of ease because our personal beliefs lean toward hopefulness about possibilities and opportunities for healing. Facts are encouraged as an accurate assessment of a situation, but should not overshadow the offering of solutions and inspiration. In a world where reporting has become synonymous with shock tactics, speaking from the heart is an effective alternative." Estab. 2004. Pays on publication. Publishes ms an average of 4 months after acceptance. Byline given. Buys first North American serial rights. Editorial lead time 4 months. Submit seasonal material 4 months in advance. Accepts queries by mail. Accepts simultaneous submissions. Responds in 1 month to queries; 2 months to mss. Sample copy and writer's guidelines online.

- "Our readers range from those relatively new to taking charge of their own health and that of our planet, to that tighter core of people who are dedicated environmentalists. Regardless, they want an accurate recap of the situation and straightforward solutions—dished out with as light a hand as possible."

Nonfiction Book excerpts, essays, general interest, how-to (accepted for the following columns: Whole Foods, From the Ground Up, Everything Herbal, With our Hands and Treading Lightly), humor, inspirational, interview/profile, new product, personal experience. Special issues: The Polishing Stone is published in February, April, July, September and December. Articles often relate to the season in which they appear. "We do not accept travel, religious or technical articles, or any article that focuses on problems without offering solutions. We do not publish reprints." **Buys 75 mss/year.** Query with published clips. Length: 200-1,600 words.

Columns/Departments Whole Foods (preparation of primarily vegetarian foods); From the Ground Up (earth-friendly gardening); Everything Herbal (information about the healing power of herbs); A Balance of Health (practical alternatives for returning to balanced health); Treading Lightly (sustainable products, processes and services); With our Hands (artisans share design for simple hand-made products); Life out Loud (an honest look at how children shape us); Looking Within (spiritual and psychological insights); In Community (the people responsible for healing/changing communities); This Spinning Earth (information and inspiration to heal the earth); In Print & On Screen (reviews of books and movies that explain and encourage). **Buys 75 mss/year.** Query with published clips or send complete ms. **Pays $25-100.**

Poetry Free verse, haiku, light verse. **Buys 5-10 poems/year.** Submit maximum 4 poems. Length: 5-25 lines.

Fillers Anecdotes, facts, short humor. **Buys 10-20/year.** Length: 50-175 words. **Pays $10.**

Tips If previously published, send query letter and clips. Otherwise, send a completed ms of no more than 1,600 words. Send both queries and completed mss by mail only. "We want to give new writers a chance, especially those who are willing to do the work. For queries, this means providing a clear description of your topic, angle, sources, lead, and reason why the article is a good fit for *The Polishing Stone*. Completed manuscripts should be carefully edited and fact-checked prior to submission. As always, read our magazine as a guide to our content and writing style. Draw on your own experiences and expertise and share from the heart."

PORTLAND MAGAZINE

Maine's City Magazine, 722 Congress St., Portland ME 04102. (207)775-4339. Fax: (207)775-2334. E-mail: staff@portlandmonthly.com. Web site: www.portlandmagazine.com. **Contact:** Colin Sargent, editor & publisher. "Monthly city lifestyle magazine—fiction, style, business, real estate, controversy, fashion, cuisine, interviews and art relating to the Maine area." Estab. 1985. Circ. 100,000. Pays on publication. Buys first North American serial rights.

Fiction Colin Sargent, editor. Send complete ms. Length: 700 words or less.

$ $ READER'S DIGEST

The Reader's Digest Association, Inc., Box 100, Pleasantville NY 10572-0100. Web site: www.rd.com. Monthly magazine.

Columns/Departments Life in These United States; All in a Day's Work; Humor in Uniform, **pays $300**. Laughter, the Best Medicine; Quotable Quotes, **pays $100**. Address your submission to the appropriate humor category.

Tips "Full-length, original articles are usually assigned to regular contributors to the magazine. We do not accept or return unpublished manuscripts. We do, however, accept 1-page queries that clearly detail the article idea—with special emphasis on the arc of the story, your interview access to the main characters, your access to special documents, etc. We look for dramatic narratives, articles about everyday heroes, crime dramas, adventure stories. Do include a separate page of your writing credits. We are not interested in poetry, fiction, or opinion pieces. Please submit article proposals on the Web site."

$$$$ READER'S DIGEST (CANADA)

1125 Stanley St., Montreal QC H3B 5H5 Canada. (514)940-0751. Fax: (514)940-7332. E-mail: originals@rd.com; editor@rd.com. Web site: www.readersdigest.ca. **30-50% freelance written.** Monthly magazine of general interest articles and subjects. Estab. 1948. Circ. 1,000,000. **Pays on acceptance for original works.** Pays on publication for "pickups." Byline given. Offers $500 (Canadian) kill fee. Buys one-time rights (for reprints), all rights (for original articles). Submit seasonal material 5 months in advance. Accepts queries by mail, e-mail. Accepts previously published material. Writer's guidelines online.

- Only responds to queries if interested. Prefers Canadian subjects.

Nonfiction "We're looking for true stories that depend on emotion and reveal the power of our relationships to help us overcome adversity; also for true first-person accounts of an event that changed a life for the better or led to new insight. No fiction, poetry or articles too specialized, technical or esoteric—read *Reader's Digest* to see what kind of articles we want." General interest, how-to (general interest), humor (jokes), inspirational, personal experience, travel (adventure), crime, health. Query with published clips. Length: 2,000-2,500 words. **Pays $1.50-2.50/word (CDN) depending on story type.** Pays expenses of writers on assignment.

Reprints Query. Payment is negotiable.

Photos State availability with submission.

The online magazine carries original content not found in the print edition.

Tips "*Reader's Digest* usually finds its freelance writers through other well-known publications in which they have previously been published. There are guidelines available and writers should read *Reader's Digest* to see what kind of stories we look for and how they are written. We do not accept unsolicited manuscripts."

$ REUNIONS MAGAZINE

P.O. Box 11727, Milwaukee WI 53211-0727. (414)263-4567. Fax: (414)263-6331. E-mail: reunions@execpc.com. Web site: www.reunionsmag.com. **Contact:** Edith Wagner, editor. **75% freelance written.** Bimonthly magazine covering reunions—all aspects and types. "*Reunions Magazine* is primarily for people actively planning family, class, military, and other reunions. We want easy, practical ideas about organizing, planning, researching/searching, attending, or promoting reunions." Estab. 1990. Circ. 20,000. Pays on publication. Publishes ms an average of 1 year after acceptance. Byline given. Buys one-time rights. Editorial lead time 6 months. Submit seasonal material 1 year in advance. Accepts queries by mail, e-mail, fax. Accepts previously published material. Responds in about 1 year to queries. Sample copy and writer's guidelines for #10 SASE or online.

Nonfiction "We can't get enough about reunion activities, particularly family reunions with multigenerational activities. We would also like more reunion food-related material." Needs reviewers for books, videos, software (include your requirements). Special features: Ethnic/African-American family reunions; food, kids stuff, theme parks, small venues (bed & breakfasts, dormitories, condos); golf, travel and gaming features; themes, cruises, ranch reunions and reunions in various US locations. Historical/nostalgic, how-to, humor, interview/profile, new product, personal experience, photo feature, travel. **Buys 50 mss/year.** Query with published clips. Length: 500-2,500 (prefers work on the short side). **Pays $25-50.** Often rewards with generous copies.

Reprints Send tearsheet, photocopy or typed ms with rights for sale noted and information about when and where the material previously appeared. Usually pays $10.

Photos Always looking for vertical cover photos screaming: "Reunion!" Prefers print or e-mail pictures. State availability with submission. Reviews contact sheets, negatives, 35mm transparencies, prints, TIFF/JPEG files (300 dpi or higher) as e-mail attachments. Offers no additional payment for photos accepted with ms. Captions, identification of subjects, model releases required.

Fillers Must be reunion-related. Anecdotes, facts, short humor. **Buys 20-40/year.** Length: 50-250 words. **Pays $5.**

The online magazine carries original content and includes writer's guidelines and articles. Contact: Edith Wagner, online editor.

Tips "All copy must be reunion-related with strong, real reunion examples and experiences. Write a lively account of an interesting or unusual reunion, either upcoming or soon after while it's hot. Tell readers why the reunion is special, what went into planning it, and how attendees reacted. Our 'Masterplan' section, about family reunion planning, is a great place for a freelancer to start by telling her/his own reunion story. Send us how-tos or tips about any of the many aspects of reunion organizing or activities. Open your minds to different types of reunions—they're all around!"

$ $ $ $ ROBB REPORT

The Magazine for the Luxury Lifestyle, Curtco Media Labs, 1 Acton Place, Acton MA 01720. (978)264-7500. Fax: (978)264-7505. E-mail: miken@robbreport.com. Web site: www.robbreport.com. **Contact:** Mike Nolan, editor. **60% freelance written.** Monthly magazine. "We are a lifestyle magazine geared toward active, affluent readers. Addresses upscale autos, luxury travel, boating, technology, lifestyles, watches, fashion, sports, investments, collectibles." Estab. 1976. Circ. 111,000. Pays on publication. Byline given. Offers 25% kill fee. Buys first North American serial, all rights. Submit seasonal material 5 months in advance. Accepts queries by mail, fax. Responds in 2 months to queries; 1 month to mss. Sample copy for $10.95, plus shipping and handling. Writer's guidelines for #10 SASE.

Nonfiction New product (autos, boats, aircraft, watches, consumer electronics), travel (international and domestic), dining. Special issues: Home (October); Recreation (March). **Buys 60 mss/year.** Query with published clips. Length: 500-2,000 words. **Pays $1/word.** Sometimes pays expenses of writers on assignment.

Photos State availability with submission. Buys one-time rights. Payment depends on article.

Tips "Show zest in your writing, immaculate research, and strong thematic structure, and you can handle most any assignment. We want to put the reader there, whether the article is about test driving a car, fishing for marlin, or touring a luxury home. The best articles will be those that tell compelling stories. Anecdotes should be used liberally, especially for leads, and the fun should show in your writing."

$ $ THE SATURDAY EVENING POST

The Saturday Evening Post Society, 1100 Waterway Blvd., Indianapolis IN 46202. (317)634-1100. Fax: (317)637-0126. Web site: www.satevepost.org. Medical/Fitness Editor: Cory SerVaas, MD. **30% freelance written.** Bimonthly general interest, family-oriented magazine focusing on physical fitness, preventive medicine. "Ask almost any American if he or she has heard of *The Saturday Evening Post*, and you will find that many have fond recollections of the magazine from their childhood days. Many readers recall sitting with their families on Saturdays awaiting delivery of their *Post* subscription in the mail. *The Saturday Evening Post* has forged a tradition of 'forefront journalism.' *The Saturday Evening Post* continues to stand at the journalistic forefront with its coverage of health, nutrition, and preventive medicine." Estab. 1728. Circ. 350,000. Pays on publication. Publishes ms an average of 3 months after acceptance. Byline given. Buys all rights. Submit seasonal material 4 months in advance. Accepts queries by mail, fax. Accepts simultaneous submissions. Responds in 3 weeks to queries; 6 weeks to mss.

Nonfiction Book excerpts, how-to (gardening, home improvement), humor, interview/profile, medical, health, fitness. "No political articles or articles containing sexual innuendo or hypersophistication." **Buys 25 mss/year.** Query with or without published clips or send complete ms. Length: 2,500-3,000 words. **Pays $25-400.** Sometimes pays expenses of writers on assignment.

Photos State availability with submission. Reviews negatives, transparencies. Buys one-time or all rights. Offers $50 minimum, negotiable maximum per photo. Identification of subjects, model releases required.

Columns/Departments Travel (destinations); Post Scripts (well-known humorists); Post People (activities of celebrities). Length 750-1,500. **Buys 16 mss/year.** Query with published clips or send complete ms. **Pays $150 minimum, negotiable maximum.**

Fiction Fiction Editor.

Poetry Light verse.

Fillers Post Scripts Editor. Anecdotes, short humor. **Buys 200/year.** Length: 300 words. **Pays $15.**

Tips "Areas most open to freelancers are Health, Fitness, Research Breakthroughs, Nutrition, Post Scripts, and Travel. For travel we like text-photo packages, pragmatic tips, side bars, and safe rather than exotic destinations. Query by mail, not phone. Send clips."

$ $ $ $ SMITHSONIAN MAGAZINE

MRC 951, P.O. Box 37012, Washington DC 20013-7012. (202)275-2000. Web site: www.smithsonianmag.com. **90% freelance written.** Monthly magazine for associate members of the Smithsonian Institution; 85% with college education. "*Smithsonian Magazine's* mission is to inspire fascination with all the world has to offer by featuring unexpected and entertaining editorial that explores different lifestyles, cultures and peoples, the arts, the wonders of nature and technology, and much more. The highly educated, innovative readers of *Smithsonian* share a unique desire to celebrate life, seeking out the timely as well as timeless, the artistic as well as the academic, and the thought-provoking as well as the humorous." Circ. 2,300,000. **Pays on acceptance.** Publishes ms an average of 6 months after acceptance. Offers 33% kill fee. Buys first North American serial rights. Editorial lead time 2 months. Submit seasonal material 3 months in advance. Responds in 3 weeks to queries. Sample copy for $5. Writer's guidelines online.

- "We consider focused subjects that fall within the general range of Smithsonian Institution interests, such as: cultural history, physical science, art and natural history. We are always looking for offbeat subjects and profiles. We do not consider fiction, poetry, political and news events, or previously published articles. We publish only 12 issues a year, so it is difficult to place an article in *Smithsonian*, but please be assured that all proposals are considered.''

Nonfiction ''Our mandate from the Smithsonian Institution says we are to be interested in the same things which now interest or should interest the institution: Cultural and fine arts, history, natural sciences, hard sciences, etc.'' **Buys 120-130 feature (up to 5,000 words) and 12 short (500-650 words) mss/year.** Use online submission form. **Pays various rates per feature, $1,500 per short piece.** Pays expenses of writers on assignment.

Photos Purchased with or without ms and on assignment. ''Illustrations are not the responsibility of authors, but if you do have photographs or illustration materials, please include a selection of them with your submission. In general, 35mm color transparencies or black-and-white prints are perfectly acceptable. Photographs published in the magazine are usually obtained through assignment, stock agencies, or specialized sources. No photo library is maintained and photographs should be submitted only to accompany a specific article proposal.'' Send photos with submission. Pays $400/full color page. Captions required.

Columns/Departments Last Page humor, 550-700 words. Use online submission form. **Pays $1,000-1,500.**

Tips ''Send proposals through online submission form only. No e-mail or mail queries, please.''

$ SOFA INK QUARTERLY

Sofa Ink, 1825 SE 7th Ave., Portland OR 97214. E-mail: acquisitions@sofaink.com. Web site: www.sofaink.com. Editor: Linda M. Meyer. **Contact:** David Cowsert, publisher. **95% freelance written.** Quarterly magazine. ''The magazine is distributed primarily to waiting rooms and lobbies of medical facilities. All of our stories and poetry have positive endings. We like to publish a variety of genres with a focus on good storytelling and word-mastery that does not include swearing, profaning deity, gore, excessive violence or gratuitous sex.'' Estab. 2005. Circ. 650. **Pays on acceptance.** Publishes ms an average of 3 months after acceptance. Byline given. Buys first North American serial rights. Submit seasonal material 4 months in advance. Accepts queries by mail, e-mail. Accepts simultaneous submissions. Responds in 1-3 months to queries; 1-3 months to mss. Sample copy for $6. Writer's guidelines online.

Nonfiction Essays, general interest, historical/nostalgic, humor, inspirational, interview/profile, personal experience. Send complete ms. Length: 7,500 words. **Pays $5, plus 3 contributor copies.**

Photos Buys one-time rights. Offers no additional payment for photos accepted with ms. Identification of subjects, model releases required.

Fiction Adventure, ethnic, experimental, fantasy, historical, humorous, mainstream, mystery, romance, science fiction, slice-of-life vignettes, suspense, western. Does not want erotic, religious. **Buys 24-30 mss/year.** Send complete ms. Length: 7,500 words. **Pays $5.**

Poetry Avant-garde, free verse, haiku, light verse, traditional. **Buys 9-15 poems/year.** Submit maximum 5 poems.

Tips ''Follow the content guidelines. Electronic submissions should be in a Word attachment rather than in the body of the message.''

N $ SOMA

SOMA Magazine, Inc., 888 O'Farrell St., Suite 103, San Francisco CA 94109. E-mail: info@somamagazine.com. Web site: www.somamagazine.com. Editor: Patrick Knowles. **Contact:** Mila Zuo, managing editor. **5% freelance written.** Monthly magazine covering the arts, music, film, fashion, design, architecture, nightlife, etc. ''*SOMA* explores the contemporary landscape through insightful writing.'' Estab. 1986. Circ. 115,000. Pays on publication. Publishes ms an average of 1-3 months after acceptance. Byline given. Offers $30 kill fee. Buys first North American serial rights. Editorial lead time 3 months. Submit seasonal material 3 months in advance. Accepts queries by e-mail. Accepts simultaneous submissions. Responds in 3 months to queries. Sample copy for $3.50. Writer's guidelines free.

⊘ TIME

Time Inc. Magazine, Time & Life Bldg., 1271 Avenue of the Americas, New York NY 10020. (212)522-1212. Fax: (212)522-0323. E-mail: letters@time.com. Web site: www.time.com. **Contact:** Jim Kelly, managing editor. Weekly magazine. ''*Time* covers the full range of information that is important to people today—breaking news, national and world affairs, business news, societal and lifestyle issues, culture and entertainment news and reviews.'' Estab. 1923. Circ. 4,150,000. Sample copy not available.

- *Time* does not accept unsolicited material for publication. The magazine is entirely staff written and produced.

N $ $ $ $ TOWN & COUNTRY

The Hearst Corp., 1700 Broadway, New York NY 10019. (212)903-5000. Fax: (212)262-7107. Web site: www.townandcountrymag.com. Editor-in-Chief: Pamela Fiori. **40% freelance written.** Monthly lifestyle magazine.

"*Town & Country* is a lifestyle magazine for the affluent market. Features focus on fashion, beauty, travel, interior design, and the arts, as well as individuals' accomplishments and contributions to society." Estab. 1846. Circ. 488,000. **Pays on acceptance.** Byline given. Offers 25% kill fee. Buys first North American serial, electronic rights. Accepts queries by mail. Responds in 2 months to queries.

Nonfiction "We're looking for engaging service articles for a high income, well-educated audience, in numerous categories: travel, personalities, interior design, fashion, beauty, jewelry, health, city news, the arts, philanthropy." General interest, interview/profile, travel. Rarely publishes work not commissioned by the magazine. Does not publish poetry, short stories, or fiction. **Buys 25 mss/year.** Query by mail only with relevant clips before submitting. Length: Column items, 100-300 words; feature stories, 800-2,000 words. **Pays $2/word.**

Tips "We have served the affluent market for over 150 years, and our writers need to be expert in the needs and interests of that market. Most of our freelance writers start by doing short pieces for our front-of-book columns, then progress from there."

HEALTH & FITNESS

$ $ AMERICAN FITNESS

15250 Ventura Blvd., Suite 200, Sherman Oaks CA 91403. (818)905-0040. Fax: (818)990-5468. Web site: www.afaa.com. Publisher: Roscoe Fawcett. **Contact:** Dr. Meg Jordan, editor. **75% freelance written.** Bimonthly magazine covering exercise and fitness, health, and nutrition. "We need timely, in-depth, informative articles on health, fitness, aerobic exercise, sports nutrition, age-specific fitness, and outdoor activity." Absolutely no first-person accounts. Need well-reserched articles for professional readers. Circ. 42,000. Pays 30 days after publication. Publishes ms an average of 6 months after acceptance. Byline given. Submit seasonal material 4 months in advance. Accepts queries by mail, fax. Accepts previously published material. Accepts simultaneous submissions. Responds in 2 months to queries. Sample copy for $4.50 and SAE with 6 first-class stamps.

Nonfiction Needs include health and fitness, including women's issues (pregnancy, family, pre- and post-natal, menopause, and eating disorders); new research findings on exercise techniques and equipment; aerobic exercise; sports nutrition; sports medicine; innovations and trends in aerobic sports; tips on teaching exercise and humorous accounts of fitness motivation; physiology; youth and senior fitness. Historical/nostalgic (history of various athletic events), inspirational, interview/profile (fitness figures), new product (plus equipment review), personal experience (successful fitness story), photo feature (on exercise, fitness, new sport), travel (activity adventures). No articles on unsound nutritional practices, popular trends, or unsafe exercise gimmicks. **Buys 18-25 mss/year.** Query with published clips or send complete ms. Length: 800-1,200 words. **Pays $200 for features, $80 for news.** Sometimes pays expenses of writers on assignment.

Photos Sports, action, fitness, aquatic aerobics competitions, and exercise class. "We are especially interested in photos of high-adrenalin sports like rock climbing and mountain biking." Reviews transparencies, prints. Usually buys all rights; other rights purchased depend on use of photo. Pays $35 for transparencies. Captions, identification of subjects, model releases required.

Columns/Departments Research (latest exercise and fitness findings); Alternative paths (nonmainstream approaches to health, wellness, and fitness); Strength (latest breakthroughs in weight training); Clubscene (profiles and highlights of fitness club industry); Adventure (treks, trails, and global challenges); Food (low-fat/nonfat, high-flavor dishes); Homescene (home-workout alternatives); Clip 'n' Post (concise exercise research to post in health clubs, offices or on refrigerators). Length: 800-1,000 words. Query with published clips or send complete ms. **Pays $100-200.**

Tips "Make sure to quote scientific literature or good research studies and several experts with good credentials to validate exercise trend, technique, or issue. Cover a unique aerobics or fitness angle, provide accurate and interesting findings, and write in a lively, intelligent manner. Please, no first-person accouts of 'how I lost weight or discovered running.' *AF* is a good place for first-time authors or regularly published authors who want to sell spin-offs or reprints."

N $ $ AMERICAN HEALTH & FITNESS

CANUSA Publishing, 5775 McLaughlin Rd., Mississauga ON L5R 3P9 Canada. Fax: (905)507-2372. E-mail: editorial@ahfmag.com. Web site: www.ahfmag.com. Bimonthly magazine. "*American Health & Fitness* is designed to help male fitness enthusiasts (18-39) stay fit, strong, virile, and healthy through sensible diet and exercise." Estab. 2000. Circ. 310,000. **Pays on acceptance.** Publishes ms an average of 6 months after acceptance. Byline given. Buys all rights. Editorial lead time 4 months. Submit seasonal material 6 months in advance. Accepts queries by mail, e-mail, fax. Responds in 4 months to queries; 4 months to mss. Sample copy for $5.

Nonfiction How-to, humor, inspirational, interview/profile, new product, personal experience, photo feature, bodybuilding and weight training, health & fitness tips, diet, medical advice, workouts, nutrition. **Buys 80-100 mss/year.** Query or send complete ms. Length: 800-1,500 words. **Pays 25-45¢/word.**

Photos Send photos with submission. Reviews 35mm transparencies, 8×10 prints. Buys all rights. Offers $35 and up/photo. Captions, identification of subjects required.
Columns/Departments Personal Training; Strength & Conditioning; Fitness; Longevity; Natural Health; Sex. **Buys 40 mss/year.** Query or send complete ms.
Fillers Anecdotes, facts, gags to be illustrated by cartoonist, newsbreaks (fitness, nutrition, health), short humor. **Buys 50-100/year.** Length: 100-200 words.

$ $ ASCENT MAGAZINE

Yoga for an Inspired Life, Timeless Books, 837 Rue Gilford, Montreal QC H2J 1P1 Canada. (514)499-3999. Fax: (514)499-3904. E-mail: info@ascentmagazine.com. Web site: www.ascentmagazine.com. Editor: Sarah E. Truman. **Contact:** Anurag Dhir, managing editor. **75% freelance written.** Quarterly magazine covering engaged spirituality, with a focus on yoga philosophy and practice. "*Ascent* publishes unique and personal perspectives on yoga and spirituality. Our goal is to explore what it means to be truly human, to think deeply, and live a meaningful life in today's world." Estab. 1999. Circ. 6,000. Pays on publication. Publishes ms an average of 3 months after acceptance. Byline given. Offers 20% kill fee. Buys first North American serial, with exclusive rights for 6 months after publication rights. Editorial lead time 4 months. Submit seasonal material 6 months in advance. Accepts queries by e-mail. Responds in 1 month to queries; 1 month to mss. Sample copy for $5. Writer's guidelines online.
Nonfiction Essays, interview/profile, personal experience, photo feature, spiritual. Special issues: Liberation (Fall); Health & Healing (Winter); Family (Spring). No academic articles or promotional articles for specific yoga school or retreats. **Buys 30 mss/year.** Query with published clips. Length: 800-3,500 words. **Pays 20¢/word (Canadian).** Sometimes pays expenses of writers on assignment.
Photos Contact Joe Ollmann, designer. Reviews GIF/JPEG files. Buys one-time rights. Negotiates payment individually.
Columns/Departments Reviews (books and CDs), 500 words. **Buys 10 mss/year.** Query based on online guidelines. **Pays $50-150 (Canadian).**
Tips "*Ascent* publishes mainly personal, reflective nonfiction. Make sure to tell us how you will bring a personal, intimate tone to your article. Send a detailed query with writing samples. Give us a good idea of your potential as a writer."

N $ $ BETTER HEALTH

Hospital of Saint Raphael, 1450 Chapel St., New Haven CT 06511. (203)789-3972. Fax: (203)789-4053. E-mail: cboynton@srhs.org. Web site: www.srhs.org. **Contact:** Cynthia Wolfe Boynton, editor/publishing director. **90% freelance written.** Prefers to work with published/established writers; will consider new/unpublished writers. Bimonthly magazine devoted to health, wellness, medicine, fitness, and nutrition. Estab. 1979. Circ. 500,000. **Pays on acceptance.** Byline given. Offers 20% kill fee. Buys first North American serial rights. Accepts queries by mail. Responds in 1 month to queries. Sample copy for $2.50. Writer's guidelines online.
Nonfiction Wellness/prevention issues are of primary interest. New medical techniques or nonmainstream practices are not considered. Does not want fillers, poems, quizzes, seasonal, heavy humor, inspirational, personal experience, or any material advocating birth control, abortion, or any other issues at odds with Catholic church doctrine. **Buys 30 mss/year.** Query with published clips. Length: 1,500-3,000 words. **Pays $250-700.** Sometimes pays expenses of writers on assignment.

$ $ $ BETTER NUTRITION

Active Interest Media, 300 Contintental Blvd., Suite 650, El Segundo CA 90245-5067. (310)356-4100. Fax: (310)356-4110. E-mail: editorial@betternutrition.com. Web site: www.betternutrition.com. Editor-in-Chief: Nicole Brechka. **57% freelance written.** Monthly magazine covering nutritional news and approaches to optimal health. "The new *Better Nutrition* helps people (men, women, families, old and young) integrate nutritious food, the latest and most effective dietary supplements, and exercise/personal care into healthy lifestyles." Estab. 1938. Circ. 460,000. Pays on publication. Publishes ms an average of 2 months after acceptance. Byline given. Buys varies according to article rights. Editorial lead time 3 months. Accepts queries by mail, e-mail. Sample copy for free.
Nonfiction Each issue has multiple features, clinical research crystallized into accessible articles on nutrition, health, alternative medicine, disease prevention. **Buys 120-180 mss/year.** Query. Length: 400-1,200 words. **Pays $400-1,000.**
Photos State availability with submission. Reviews 4×5 transparencies, 3×5 prints. Buys one time rights or non-exclusive reprint rights. Negotiates payment individually. Captions, identification of subjects, model releases required.
Tips "Be on top of what's newsbreaking in nutrition and supplementation. Interview experts. Fact-check, fact-check, fact-check. Send in a résumé (including Social Security/IRS number), a couple of clips, and a list of article possibilities."

$ $ CLIMBING

Primedia Enthusiast Group, 0326 Highway 133, Suite 190, Carbondale CO 81623. (970)963-9449. Fax: (970)963-9442. Web site: www.climbing.com. Editor-in-Chief: Jonathan Thesenga. Magazine published 9 times/year covering climbing and mountaineering. Provides features on rock climbing and mountaineering worldwide. Estab. 1970. Circ. 51,000. Pays on publication. Editorial lead time 6 weeks. Accepts queries by e-mail. Sample copy for $4.99. Writer's guidelines online.

Nonfiction SASE returns. Interview/profile (interesting climbers), personal experience (climbing adventures), surveys of different areas. Query. Length: 1,500-3,500 words. **Pays 35¢/word.**

Photos State availability with submission. Reviews negatives, 35mm transparencies, prints, digital submissions on CD. Pays $25-800.

Columns/Departments Query. **Payment varies.**

$ $ DELICIOUS LIVING!

Feel Good/Live Well, New Hope Natural Media, 1401 Pearl St., Suite 200, Boulder CO 80302. (303)939-8440. Fax: (303)939-9886. E-mail: delicious@newhope.com. Web site: www.healthwell.com. **85% freelance written.** Monthly magazine covering natural products, nutrition, alternative medicines, herbal medicines. "*Delicious Living!* magazine empowers natural foods store shoppers to make health-conscious choices in their lives. Our goal is to improve consumers' perception of the value of natural methods in achieving health. To do this, we educate consumers on nutrition, disease prevention, botanical medicines and natural personal care products." Estab. 1985. Circ. 420,000. **Pays on acceptance.** Publishes ms an average of 6 months after acceptance. Byline given. Offers 20% kill fee. Editorial lead time 6 months. Submit seasonal material 8 months in advance. Accepts simultaneous submissions. Responds in 3 months to queries. Sample copy and writer's guidelines free.

Nonfiction Book excerpts, how-to, interview/profile, personal experience (regarding natural or alternative health), health nutrition, herbal medicines, alternative medicine, environmental. **Buys 150 mss/year.** Query with published clips. Length: 500-2,000 words. **Pays $100-700 for assigned articles; $50-300 for unsolicited articles.**

Photos State availability with submission. Reviews 3×5 prints. Buys one-time rights. Offers no additional payment for photos accepted with ms. Identification of subjects required.

Columns/Departments Herbs (scientific evidence supporting herbal medicines), 1,500 words; Nutrition (new research on diet for good health), 1,200 words; Dietary Supplements (new research on vitamins/minerals, etc.), 1,200 words. Query with published clips. **Pays $100-500.**

Tips "Highlight any previous health/nutrition/medical writing experience. Demonstrate a knowledge of natural medicine, nutrition, or natural products. Health practitioners who demonstrate writing ability are ideal freelancers."

⊘ FIT PREGNANCY

Weider Publications, Inc., 21100 Erwin St., Woodland Hills CA 91367-3712. Web site: www.fitpregnancy.com. Bimonthly magazine. Circ. 505,000.

- Does not buy freelance material.

$ $ $ $ FITNESS MAGAZINE

Meredith Corp., 375 Lexington Ave., New York NY 10017-5514. Web site: www.fitnessmagazine.com. Editor-in-Chief: Denise Brodey. Monthly magazine for women in their 20s and 30s who are interested in fitness and living a healthy life. Circ. 1.5 million. **Pays on acceptance.** Byline given. Offers 20% kill fee. Buys first North American serial rights. Responds in 2 months to queries.

- Do not call.

Nonfiction "We need timely, well-written nonfiction articles on exercise and fitness, beauty, health, diet/nutrition, and psychology. We always include boxes and sidebars in our stories." **Buys 60-80 mss/year.** Query. Length: 1,500-2,500 words. **Pays $1,500-2,500.** Pays expenses of writers on assignment.

Reprints Send photocopy. Negotiates fee.

Columns/Departments Buys 30 mss/year. Query. **Pays $800-1,500.**

Tips "Our pieces must get inside the mind of the reader and address her needs, hopes, fears and desires. *Fitness* acknowledges that getting and staying fit is difficult in an era when we are all time-pressured."

$ $ HEALING LIFESTYLES & SPAS

P.O. Box 271207, Louisville CO 80027. (202)441-9557. Fax: (303)926-4099. E-mail: editorial@healinglifestyles.com. Web site: www.healinglifestyles.com. Editor: Melissa B. Williams. **90% freelance written.** "*Healing Lifestyles & Spas* is a bimonthly magazine committed to healing, health, and living a well-rounded, more natural life. In each issue we cover retreats, spas, organic living, natural food, herbs, beauty, yoga, alternative medicine, bodywork, spirituality, and features on living a healthy lifestyle." Estab. 1996. Circ. 45,000. Pays on publication.

Publishes ms an average of 2-10 months after acceptance. Editorial lead time 6 months. Submit seasonal material 6-9 months in advance. Accepts queries by mail, e-mail. Responds in 6 weeks to queries.

Nonfiction "We will consider all in-depth features relating to spas, retreats, lifestyle issues, mind/body well being, yoga, enlightening profiles, and women's health issues." Travel (domestic and international). No fiction or poetry. Query. Length: 1,000-2,000 words. **Pays $150-500, depending on length, research, experience, and availability and quality of images.**

Photos "If you will be providing your own photography, you must use slide film or provide a Mac-formatted CD with image resolution of at least 300 dpi." Send photos with submission. Captions required.

Columns/Departments All Things New & Natural (short pieces outlining new health trends, alternative medicine updates, and other interesting tidbits of information), 50-200 words; Urban Retreats (focuses on a single city and explores its spas and organic living features), 1,200-1,600 words; Health (features on relevant topics ranging from nutrition to health news and updates), 900-1,200 words; Food (nutrition or spa-focused food articles and recipes), 1,000-1,200 words; Ritual (highlights a specific at-home ritual), 500 words; Seasonal Spa (focuses on a seasonal ingredient on the spa menu), 500-700 words; Spa Origins (focuses on particular modalities and healing beliefs from around the world, 1,000-1,200 words; Yoga, 400-800 words; Retreat (highlights a spa or yoga retreat), 500 words; Spa a la carte (explores a new treatment or modality on the spa menu), 600-1,000 words; Insight (focuses on profiles, theme-related articles, and new therapies, healing practices, and newsworthy items), 1,000-2,000 words. Query.

$ $ $ $ HEALTH

Time, Inc., Southern Progress Corp., 2100 Lakeshore Dr., Birmingham AL 35209. (205)445-6000. Fax: (205)445-5123. E-mail: health@timeinc.com. Web site: www.health.com. Vice President/Editor: Doug Crichton. Magazine published 10 times/year covering health, fitness, and nutrition. "Our readers are predominantly college-educated women in their 30s, 40s, and 50s. Edited to focus not on illness, but on wellness news, events, ideas, and people." Estab. 1987. Circ. 1,360,000. **Pays on acceptance.** Byline given. Offers 33% kill fee. Buys first publication and online rights. Accepts queries by mail, fax. Accepts simultaneous submissions. Responds in 2 months to queries to mss. Sample copy for $5 to Back Issues. Writer's guidelines for #10 SASE or via e-mail.

Nonfiction No unsolicited mss. **Buys 25 mss/year.** Query with published clips and SASE. Length: 1,200 words. **Pays $1.50-2/word.** Pays expenses of writers on assignment.

Columns/Departments Body, Mind, Fitness, Beauty, Food.

Tips "We look for well-articulated ideas with a narrow focus and broad appeal. A query that starts with an unusual local event and hooks it legitimately to some national trend or concern is bound to get our attention. Use quotes, examples and statistics to show why the topic is important and why the approach is workable. We need to see clear evidence of credible research findings pointing to meaningful options for our readers. Stories should offer practical advice and give clear explanations."

$ $ HEPATITIS

Management and Treatment—A Practical Guide for Patients, Families, and Friends, Quality Publishing, Inc., 523 N. Sam Houston Tollway E., Suite 300, Houston TX 77060. (281)272-2744. Fax: (281)847-5440. E-mail: gdrushel@hepatitismag.com. Web site: www.hepatitismag.com. **Contact:** Managing Editor. **70-80% freelance written.** Quarterly magazine covering Hepatitis health news. Estab. 1999. Circ. 25,000. Pays on publication. Publishes ms an average of 2 months after acceptance. Byline given. Buys first North American serial, electronic rights. Editorial lead time 6 months. Submit seasonal material 4 months in advance. Accepts queries by mail, e-mail. Accepts simultaneous submissions. Responds in 6 weeks to queries. Sample copy and writer's guidelines free.

Nonfiction Inspirational, interview/profile, new product, personal experience. "We do not want any one-source or no-source articles." **Buys 42-48 mss/year.** Query with or without published clips. Length: 1,500-2,500 words. Sometimes pays expenses of writers on assignment.

Photos Send photos with submission. Reviews transparencies, prints, GIF/JPEG files. Rights negotiated, usually purchases one-time rights. Offers no additional payment for photos accepted with ms. Identification of subjects required.

Columns/Departments General news or advice on Hepatitis written by a doctor or healthcare professional, 1,500-2,000 words. **Buys 12-18 mss/year.** Query. **Pays $375-500.**

Tips "Be specific in your query. Show me that you know the topic you want to write about, and show me that you can write a solid, well-rounded story."

$ $ $ LET'S LIVE MAGAZINE

Basic Media Group, Inc., 11050 Santa Monica Blvd., 3rd Floor, Los Angeles CA 90025-3594. (310)445-7500. Fax: (310)445-7583. E-mail: info@letslivemag.com. Web site: www.letsliveonline.com. Editor-in-Chief: Beth Salmon. **Contact:** Ayn Nix, senior editor. **95% freelance written.** Monthly magazine emphasizing health and preventive medicine. "We're especially looking for stories that profile a hot, new supplement with growing research to validate its benefits to health and wellness." Estab. 1933. Circ. 1,700,000. Pays within 1 month. Publishes ms an average of 4 months after acceptance. Byline given. Buys all rights. Submit seasonal material 6 months in advance. Accepts queries by mail, e-mail, fax. Responds in 2 months to queries; 3 months to mss. Sample copy for $5 and 10×13 SAE with 6 first-class stamps or on Web site. Writer's guidelines for #10 SASE.

O→ The editors are looking for more cutting-edge, well-researched natural health information that is substantiated by experts and well-respected scientific research literature. Works with a small number of new/unpublished writers each year; expertise in health field helpful.

Nonfiction Mss must be well-researched, reliably documented and written in a clear, readable style. General interest (effects of vitamins, minerals, herbs and nutrients in improvement of health or afflictions), historical/nostalgic (documentation of experiments or treatments establishing value of nutrients as boon to health), how-to (enhance natural beauty, exercise/bodybuilding, acquire strength and vitality, improve health of adults and/or children and prepare tasty, health meals), interview/profile (benefits of research in establishing prevention as key to good health, background and/or medical history of preventive medicine, MDs or PhDs, in advancement of nutrition), opinion (views of orthomolecular doctors or their patients on balue of health foods toward maintaining good health). "No pre-written articles or mainstream medicine pieces such as articles on drugs or surgery." **Buys 2-4 mss/year.** Query with published clips and SASE. Length: 800-1,400 words. **Pays $700-1,200 for features.**

Photos Send photos with submission. Reviews transparencies, prints. Pays $50 for 8×10 color prints, 35mm transparencies. Captions, model releases required.

Columns/Departments Natural Medicine Chest. Query with published clips and SASE. **Payment varies.**

Tips "We want writers with experience in researching nonsurgical medical subjects and interviewing experts with the ability to simplify technical and clinical information for the layman. A captivating lead and structural flow are essential. The most frequent mistakes made by writers are in writing articles that are too technical, in poor style, written for the wrong audience (publication not thoroughly studied), or have unreliable documentation or overzealous faith in the topic reflected by flimsy research and inappropriate tone."

$ $ $ $ MAMM MAGAZINE

Courage, Respect & Survival, MAMM, LLC, 54 W. 22nd St., 4th Floor, New York NY 10010. (646)365-1355. Fax: (646)365-1369. E-mail: editorial@mamm.com. Web site: www.mamm.com. **80% freelance written.** Magazine published 10 times/year covering cancer prevention, treatment, and survival for women. "*MAMM* gives its readers the essential tools and emotional support they need before, during and after diagnosis of breast, ovarian and other gynecologic cancers. We offer a mix of survivor profiles, conventional and alternative treatment information, investigative features, essays, and cutting-edge news." Estab. 1997. Circ. 100,000. Pays within 30 days of publication. Publishes ms an average of 3 months after acceptance. Byline given. Offers 50% kill fee. Buys exclusive rights up to 3 months after publishing. Submit seasonal material 3-4 months in advance. Accepts simultaneous submissions. Sample copy and writer's guidelines free.

Nonfiction Book excerpts, essays, exposé, how-to, humor, inspirational, interview/profile, opinion, personal experience, photo feature, historic/nostalgic. **Buys 90 mss/year.** Query with published clips. Length: 200-3,000 words. **Pays $100-3,000.** Negotiates coverage of expenses of writers on assignment.

Photos Send photos with submission. Reviews contact sheets, negatives. Buys first rights. Negotiates payment individually. Identification of subjects required.

Columns/Departments Opinion (cultural/political); International Dispatch (experience); Q and A (interview format), all 600 words. **Buys 30 mss/year.** Query with published clips. **Pays $400-800.**

$ $ $ $ MEN'S HEALTH

Rodale, 33 E. Minor St., Emmaus PA 18098. (610)967-5171. Fax: (610)967-7725. E-mail: mhletters@rodale.com. Web site: www.menshealth.com. Editor-in-Chief: David Zinczenko. Executive Editor: Peter Moore. **Contact:** Bill Stieg, senior editor. **50% freelance written.** Magazine published 10 times/year covering men's health and fitness. "*Men's Health* is a lifestyle magazine showing men the practical and positive actions that make their lives better, with articles covering fitness, nutrition, relationships, travel, careers, grooming, and health issues." Estab. 1986. Circ. 1,600,000. **Pays on acceptance.** Offers 25% kill fee. Buys all rights. Accepts queries by mail, fax. Responds in 3 weeks to queries. Writer's guidelines for #10 SASE.

O→ Freelancers have the best chance with the front-of-the-book piece, Malegrams.

Nonfiction "Authoritative information on all aspects of men's physical and emotional health. We rely on writers to seek out the right experts and to either tell a story from a first-person vantage or get good anecdotes." **Buys 30 features/year; 360 short mss/year.** Query with published clips. Length: 1,200-4,000 words for features, 100-300 words for short pieces. **Pays $1,000-5,000 for features; $100-500 for short pieces.**

Columns/Departments Length: 750-1,500 words. **Buys 80 mss/year. Pays $750-2,000.**

The online magazine carries original content not included in the print edition. Contact: Rob Gerth, online editor.

Tips "We have a wide definition of health. We believe that being successful in every area of your life is being healthy. The magazine focuses on all aspects of health, from stress issues and nutrition, to exercise and sex. It is 50% staff written, 50% from freelancers. The best way to break in is not by covering a particular subject, but by covering it within the magazine's style. There is a very particular tone and voice to the magazine. A writer has to be a good humor writer as well as a good service writer. Prefers mail queries. No phone calls, please."

$ $ $ MUSCLE & FITNESS

Weider Health & Fitness, 21100 Erwin St., Woodland Hills, CA 91367. (818)884-6800. Fax: (818)595-0463. Web site: www.muscle-fitness.com. Editor-in-Chief: Jeff O'Connell. Executive Editor: Maureen Meyers Farrar. **50% freelance written.** Monthly magazine covering bodybuilding and fitness for healthy, active men and women. It contains a wide range of features and monthly departments devoted to all areas of bodybuilding, health, fitness, sport, injury prevention and treatment, and nutrition. Editorial fulfills 2 functions: information and entertainment. Special attention is devoted to how-to advice and accuracy. Estab. 1950. Circ. 500,000. Pays on publication. Publishes ms an average of 2 months after acceptance. Editorial lead time 5 months. Submit seasonal material 6 months in advance. Accepts queries by mail. Accepts previously published material. Responds in 1 month to queries.

Nonfiction "All features and departments are written on assignment." Book excerpts, how-to (training), humor, interview/profile, photo feature. **Buys 120 mss/year.** Does not accept unsolicited mss. Length: 800-1,800 words. **Pays $400-1,000 for assigned articles.** Pays expenses of writers on assignment.

Reprints Send photocopy with rights for sale noted and information about when and where the material previously appeared. Payment varies.

Photos State availability with submission.

Tips "Know bodybuilders and bodybuilding. Read our magazine regularly (or at least several issues), come up with new information or a new angle on our subject matter (bodybuilding training, psychology, nutrition, diets, fitness, sports, etc.), then pitch us in terms of providing useful, unique, how-to information for our readers. Send a 1-page query letter (as described in *Writer's Market*) to sell us on your idea and on you as the best writer for that article. Send a sample of your published work."

$ $ $ OXYGEN!

Serious Fitness for Serious Women, Canusa Products/St. Ives, Inc., 5775 McLaughlin Rd., Mississauga ON L5R 3P7 Canada. (905)507-3545. Fax: (905)507-2372. E-mail: editorial@oxygenmag.com. Web site: www.oxygenmag.com. **Contact:** Kerrie Lee Brown, editor-in-chief. **70% freelance written.** Monthly magazine covering women's health and fitness. "*Oxygen* encourages various exercise, good nutrition to shape and condition the body." Estab. 1997. Circ. 340,000. **Pays on acceptance.** Publishes ms an average of 4 months after acceptance. Byline given. Offers 25% kill fee. Buys all rights. Editorial lead time 3 months. Submit seasonal material 6 months in advance. Accepts queries by mail, fax. Responds in 5 weeks to queries; 2 months to mss. Sample copy for $5.

Break in with "a really strong query proving that it is well researched."

Nonfiction Exposé, how-to (training and nutrition), humor, inspirational, interview/profile, new product, personal experience, photo feature. No "poorly researched articles that do not genuinely help the readers towards physical fitness, health and physique." **Buys 100 mss/year.** Send complete ms. Length: 1,400-1,800 words. **Pays $250-1,000.** Sometimes pays expenses of writers on assignment.

Photos State availability of or send photos with submission. Reviews contact sheets, 35mm transparencies, prints. Buys all rights. Offers $35-500. Identification of subjects required.

Columns/Departments Nutrition (low-fat recipes), 1,700 words; Weight Training (routines and techniques), 1,800 words; Aerobics (how-tos), 1,700 words. **Buys 50 mss/year.** Send complete ms. **Pays $150-500.**

Tips "Every editor of every magazine is looking, waiting, hoping and praying for the magic article. The beauty of the writing has to spring from the page; the edge imparted has to excite the reader because of its unbelievable information."

N $ $ $ $ PHYSICAL

Franklin Publications, 11050 Santa Monica Blvd., Los Angeles CA 90025. (310)445-7505. Fax: (310)445-7587. Web site: www.physicalmag.com. **90% freelance written.** Monthly magazine covering physical fitness, sports nutrition, and body building. Directed at a very active, mostly male reader with emphasis on the physical lifestyle—good nutrition, regular exercise, and dietary supplementation of sports nutrition. Estab. 1998. Circ. 600,000. **Pays on acceptance.** Publishes ms an average of 4-5 months after acceptance. Byline given. Buys first North American serial, electronic rights. Editorial lead time 6 months. Submit seasonal material 6 months in advance. Accepts queries by mail, e-mail, fax. Accepts simultaneous submissions. Responds in 1 month to queries; 4 months to mss. Sample copy for free. Writer's guidelines by e-mail.

Nonfiction General interest, how-to (exercise, build muscle, lose weight, etc.), inspirational, personal experience, technical, sports training, nutrition, workouts. No "soft girlie topics, gear or boy toys, automobiles, or electronics." **Buys 100-120 mss/year.** Query with or without published clips. Length: 800-1,800 words. **Pays $500-1,500 for assigned articles; $0-1,000 for unsolicited articles.** Sometimes pays expenses of writers on assignment.

Photos Buys one-time rights. Negotiates payment individually. Captions, identification of subjects, model releases required.

Tips "Keep our reader in mind—buyer of sports nutrition and health food, vitamins, and herbal products at General Nutrition Centers. Articles should promote the physical lifestyle of nutrition and exercise."

$$$$ POZ

CDM Publishing, LLC, 500 Fifth Ave., Suite 320, New York NY 10110. (212)242-2163. Fax: (212)675-8505. E-mail: poz-editor@poz.com. Web site: www.poz.com. Managing Editor: Jennifer Morton. **Contact:** Angelo Ragaza, editor. **75% freelance written.** Monthly national magazine for people impacted by HIV and AIDS. "*POZ* is a trusted source of conventional and alternative treatment information, investigative features, survivor profiles, essays and cutting-edge news for people living with AIDS and their caregivers. *POZ* is a lifestyle magazine with both health and cultural content." Estab. 1994. Circ. 100,000. Pays 30 days after publication. Publishes ms an average of 3 months after acceptance. Byline given. Offers 25% kill fee. Buys first rights. Editorial lead time 4 months. Submit seasonal material 4 months in advance. Accepts simultaneous submissions. Sample copy and writer's guidelines free.

Nonfiction Book excerpts, essays, exposé, historical/nostalgic, how-to, humor, inspirational, interview/profile, opinion, personal experience, photo feature. **Buys 180 mss/year.** Query with published clips. "We take unsolicited mss on speculation only." Length: 200-3,000 words. **Pays $1/word.** Sometimes pays expenses of writers on assignment.

Photos Send photos with submission. Reviews contact sheets, negatives. Buys first rights. Negotiates payment individually. Identification of subjects required.

⊘ PREVENTION

Rodale, Inc., 33 E. Minor St., Emmaus PA 18098-0099. E-mail: prevention@rodale.com. Web site: www.prevention.com. Editor-in-Chief: Liz Vaccariello. Deputy Executive Editor: Lisa Davis. Monthly magazine covering health and fitness. Written to motivate, inspire and enable male and female readers ages 35 and over to take charge of their health, to become healthier and happier, and to improve the lives of family and friends. Estab. 1950. Circ. 3,150,000.

- *Prevention* does not accept, nor do they acknowledge, unsolicited submissions.

N ⊘ PREVENTION'S GUIDE TO WEIGHT LOSS

Rodale, Inc., 33 E. Minor St., Emmaus PA 18098-0001. (610)967-5171. Fax: (610)967-7726. E-mail: preventionspecials@rodale.com. Web site: www.prevention.com. Executive Editor: Cindi Caciolo. Biannual magazine. Edited to help readers make the positive lifestyle changes necessary to shed weight permanently and in the most healthful manner possible. Circ. 425,000. Sample copy not available.

- Does not buy freelance material or use freelance writers.

PREVENTION'S GUIDE: WALKING FIT

Rodale, Inc., 33 E. Minor St., Emmaus PA 18098-0001. (610)967-5171. Fax: (610)967-7654. E-mail: preventionspecials@rodale.com. Web site: www.prevention.com. Executive Editor: Cindi Caciolo. Biannual magazine. Serves as a guide for those looking to experience the many benefits of fitness walking. Circ. 650,000. Sample copy not available.

PREVENTION'S GUIDE: FIT AND FIRM AT 35 PLUS

Rodale, Inc., 33 E. Minor St., Emmaus PA 18098-7726. (610)967-5171. Fax: (610)967-7654. E-mail: preventionspecials@rodale.com. Web site: www.prevention.com. Executive Editor: Cindi Caciolo. Semiannual magazine. Targeted to the 35+ women who want to look and feel their best. Circ. 650,000. Sample copy not available.

$$$$ SHAPE MAGAZINE

Weider Publications, Inc., 21100 Erwin St., Woodland Hills CA 91367. (818)595-0593. Fax: (818)704-7620. Web site: www.shapemag.com. Executive Editor: Trisha Calvo. Deputy Editor: A.J. Hanley. **Contact:** Leslie Ryan, Fitness/Gear; Kim Acosta, Health; Gabrielle Gayogoy, Time Out/SYL Quiz/Lifestyle/Psychology; Monica Gullon, Food/Nutrition/Books; Lindsay Morris, Travel/Internet/Fitness Bonus; Liz Koppelman, beauty; Violet

Moon Gaynor, Fashion. **70% freelance written.** Prefers to work with published/established writers. Monthly magazine covering health, fitness, nutrition, and beauty for women ages 18-34. "*Shape* reaches women who are committed to healthful, active lifestyles. Our readers are participating in a variety of fitness-related activities, in the gym, at home and outdoors, and they are also proactive about their health and are nutrition conscious." Estab. 1981. Circ. 1,600,000. **Pays on acceptance.** Offers 33% kill fee. Buys second serial (reprint), all rights. Submit seasonal material 8 months in advance. Accepts queries by mail. Responds in 2 months to queries. Sample copy for 9×12 SAE and 4 first-class stamps. Writer's guidelines online.

Nonfiction "We use some health and fitness articles written by professionals in their specific fields." Book excerpts, exposé (health, fitness, nutrition related), how-to (get fit), health/fitness, recipes. "We rarely publish celebrity question and answer stories, celebrity profiles, or menopausal/hormone replacement therapy stories." **Buys 27 features/year; 36-54 short mss/year.** Query with published clips. Length: 2,500 words/features; 1,000 words/shorter pieces. **Pays $1.50/word (on average).**

Tips "Review a recent issue of the magazine. Not responsible for unsolicited material. We reserve the right to edit any article."

N $ $ $ SPIRITUALITY & HEALTH MAGAZINE

The Soul Body Connection, Spirituality & Health Publishing, Inc., 74 Trinity Place, New York NY 10006. E-mail: editor@spiritualityhealth.com. Web site: www.spiritualityhealth.com. Editor: Robert Owens Scott. **Contact:** Betsy Robinson, managing editor. Bimonthly magazine covering research-based spirituality and health. "We look for formally credentialed writers in their fields. We are nondenominational and nonproselytizing. We are not New Age. We appreciate well-written work that offers spiritual seekers from all different traditions help in their unique journeys." Estab. 1998. Circ. 70,000. **Pays on acceptance.** Byline given. Offers 50% kill fee. Buys first North American serial, electronic rights. Editorial lead time 4 months. Submit seasonal material 6 months in advance. Accepts queries by e-mail. Accepts simultaneous submissions. Responds in 3-4 months to queries; 2-4 months to mss. Sample copy and writer's guidelines online.

- "The most open department is Updates & Observations. Read it to see what we use. (All back issues are on teh Web site.) News must be current with a four-month lead time."

Nonfiction Book excerpts, how-to, opinion (With credentials for topic in guest column), news shorts. Special issues: "We don't have an editorial calendar, but we're in the general market for what we call 'short inspirational collages.' For example, we are about to publish a compilation of peace quotes from famous people. We have also done reader-collections of wisdom tips. These are pieces that are curated more than written." Does not want proselytizing, New Age cures with no scientific basis, "how I recovered from a disease" personal essays, psychics, advice columns, profiles of individual healers or practitioners, pieces promoting "one way" or "guru," reviews, poetry or columns. Query with or without published clips or send complete ms. Length: 300 words for news shorts, otherwise 700 -1,500 words. Sometimes pays expenses of writers on assignment.

Columns/Departments Guest/credentialed opinion pieces (550-800 words) and What Goes On There Really (500-70 words). Read samples of both on the Web site. **Buys 6 mss/year.** Send complete ms.

Tips "Start by pitching really interesting, well-researched news shorts for Updates & Observations. Before you pitch, do a search of our Web site to see if we've already covered it. We are horribly slow answering since we meet only once every couple months to discuss new queries. But when a new cutting-edge research-based news piece comes in, the editors tend to move faster."

N $ $ ⊘ VIBRANT LIFE

A Magazine for Healthful Living, Review and Herald Publishing Association, 55 W. Oak Ridge Dr., Hagerstown MD 21740-7390. (301)393-4019. Fax: (301)393-4055. E-mail: vibrantlife@rhpa.org. Web site: www.vibrantlife.com. **Contact:** Charles Mills, editor. **80% freelance written.** Enjoys working with published/established writers; works with a small number of new/unpublished writers each year. Bimonthly magazine covering health articles (especially from a prevention angle and with a Christian slant). "The average length of time between acceptance of a freelance-written manuscript and publication of the material depends upon the topics: some immediately used; others up to 2 years." Estab. 1885. Circ. 30,000. **Pays on acceptance.** Byline given. Offers 50% kill fee. Buys first serial, first world serial, or sometimes second serial (reprint) rights. Submit seasonal material 9 months in advance. Accepts queries by mail, e-mail, fax. Accepts previously published material. Responds in 1 month to queries. Sample copy for $1. Writer's guidelines online.

- Currently closed to submissions.

Nonfiction "We seek practical articles promoting better health and a more fulfilled life. We especially like features on breakthroughs in medicine, and most aspects of health. We need articles on how to integrate a person's spiritual life with their health. We'd like more in the areas of exercise, nutrition, water, avoiding addictions of all types, and rest—all done from a wellness perspective." Interview/profile (with personalities on health). **Buys 50-60 feature articles/year and 6-12 short mss/year.** Send complete ms. Length: 500-1,500 words for features, 25-250 words for short pieces. **Pays $75-300 for features, $50-75 for short pieces.**

Reprints Send tearsheet and information about when and where the material previously appeared. Pays 50% of amount paid for an original article.
Photos Not interested in b&w photos. Send photos with submission. Reviews 35mm transparencies.
Columns/Departments Pays $75-175.
Tips "*Vibrant Life* is published for baby boomers, particularly young professionals, age 40-55. Articles must be written in an interesting, easy-to-read style. Information must be reliable; no faddism. We are more conservative than other magazines in our field. Request a sample copy, and study the magazine and writer's guidelines."

$ $ $ $ VIM & VIGOR

America's Family Health Magazine, 1010 E. Missouri Ave., Phoenix AZ 85014-2601. (602)395-5850. Fax: (602)395-5853. E-mail: stephaniec@mcmurry.com. **Contact:** Stephanie Conner, senior editor. **90% freelance written.** Quarterly magazine covering health and healthcare. Estab. 1985. Circ. 800,000. **Pays on acceptance.** Publishes ms an average of 6 months after acceptance. Byline given. Buys all rights. Sample copy for 9×12 SAE with 8 first-class stamps. Writer's guidelines for #10 SASE.
Nonfiction "Absolutely no complete manuscripts will be accepted/returned. All articles are assigned. Send published samples for assignment consideration. Any queries regarding story ideas will be placed on the following year's conference agenda and will be addressed on a topic-by-topic basis." Health, disease, medical breakthroughs, exercise/fitness trends, wellness, healthcare. Send published clips and résumé by mail or e-mail. Length: 500-1,200 words. **Pays 90¢-$1/word.** Pays expenses of writers on assignment.
Tips "Writers must have consumer healthcare experience."

WEIGHT WATCHERS MAGAZINE

W/W Publishing Group, 747 3rd Ave., 24th Floor, New York NY 10017. (212)207-8800. Fax: (212)588-1733. E-mail: wwmeditor@wwpublishinggroup.com. Web site: www.weightwatchers.com. Editorial Director: Nancy Gagliardi. Executive Editor: Geri Anne Fennessey. Associate Editor: Jennifer Fields. Editor: Barbara Brody. **70% freelance written.** Bimonthly magazine mostly for women interested in weight loss, including healthy lifestyle/behavior information/advice, news on health, nutrition, fitness, beauty, fashion, psychology and food/recipes. Estab. 1968. Circ. 1,200,000. **Pays on acceptance.** Offers 25% kill fee. Buys first North American serial rights. Editorial lead time 3-12 months. Accepts queries by mail.
Nonfiction Covers diet, nutrition, motivation/psychology, food, spas, and products for both the kitchen and an active lifestyle. Articles have an authoritative, yet friendly tone. How-to and service information crucial for all stories. Query with published clips. Length: 700-1,500 words.
Columns/Departments Accepts editorial in health, fitness, diet, inspiration, nutrition.
Tips "Well-developed, tightly written queries always a plus, as are trend pieces. We're always on the lookout for a fresh angle on an old topic. Sources must be reputable; we prefer subjects to be medical professionals with university affiliations who are published in their field of expertise. Lead times require stories to be seasonal, long-range, and forward-looking. We're looking for fresh, innovative stories that yield worthwhile information for women interested in losing weight—the latest exercise alternatives, a suggestion of how they can reduce stress, nutritional information that may not be common knowledge, reassurance about their lifestyle or health concerns, etc. Familiarity with the Weight Watchers philosophy/program is a plus."

N $ $ WHJ/HRHJ

Williamsburg Health Journal/Hampton Roads Health Journal, Rian Enterprises, LLC, 4808 Courthouse St., Williamsburg VA 23188. Fax: (757)645-4473. E-mail: info@williamsburghealth.com. Web site: www.williamsburghealth.com. **Contact:** Page E. Bishop, editor. **30% freelance written.** Monthly tabloid covering health and insurance. "*WHJ* provides family-friendly health advice and how-to. No controversial subject matter. Objective, empowering, honest, entertaining." Estab. 2005. Circ. 40,000. Pays on publication. Publishes ms an average of 1-2 months after acceptance. Byline given. Not copyrighted. Buys first rights. Editorial lead time 4 months. Submit seasonal material 6 months in advance. Accepts queries by mail, e-mail, fax. Accepts previously published material. Accepts simultaneous submissions. Responds in 2 weeks to queries; 1 month to mss. Sample copy and writer's guidelines online
Nonfiction Book excerpts, essays, exposéé, general interest, historical/nostalgic, how-to, humor, inspirational, interview/profile, new product, opinion, personal experience, photo feature, technical, travel. Does not want promotion of products, religious material, anything over 2,000 words. **Buys 100 mss/year.** Query with published clips. Length: 400-1,000 words. **Pays 15¢/word.** Sometimes pays expenses of writers on assignment
Photos Contact Brian M. Freer, publisher. State availability with submission. Reviews GIF/JPEG files. Buys one-time rights. Negotiates payment individually. Captions, identification of subjects required
Tips "Submit samples of your best health and science writing. Generate new slants on well-established health topics. Be objective. Entertain. Surprise us!"

$$$$ YOGA JOURNAL

475 Sasome St., Suite 850, San Francisco CA 94111. (510)841-9200. Web site: www.yogajournal.com. **Contact:** Matthew Solan, senior editor; Todd Jones, senior editor; Phil Catalfo, senior editor; Nora Isaacs, managing editor; Vasela Simic, copy editor. **75% freelance written.** Bimonthly magazine covering the practice and philosophy of yoga. Estab. 1975. Circ. 130,000. Pays within 90 days of acceptance. Publishes ms an average of 10 months after acceptance. Byline given. Offers kill fee on assigned articles. Buys first North American serial rights. Submit seasonal material 4 months in advance. Accepts queries by mail. Accepts previously published material. Responds in 3 months to queries. Sample copy for $4.99. Writer's guidelines online.

Nonfiction "Yoga is a main concern, but we also highlight other conscious living/New Age personalities and endeavors (nothing too 'woo-woo'). In particular we welcome articles on the following themes: 1) Leaders, spokepersons, and visionaries in the yoga community; 2) The practice of hatha yoga; 3) Applications of yoga to everyday life; 4) Hatha yoga anatomy and kinesiology, and therapeutic yoga; 5) Nutrition and diet, cooking, and natural skin and body care." Book excerpts, how-to (yoga, exercise, etc.), inspirational, interview/profile, opinion, photo feature, travel (yoga-related). Does not want unsolicited poetry or cartoons. "Please avoid New Age jargon and in-house buzz words as much as possible." **Buys 50-60 mss/year.** Query with SASE. Length: 3,000-5,000 words. **Pays $800-2,000.**

Reprints Send tearsheet or photocopy with rights for sale noted and information about when and where the material previously appeared.

Columns/Departments Health (self-care; well-being); Body-Mind (hatha Yoga, other body-mind modalities, meditation, yoga philosophy, Western mysticism); Community (service, profiles, organizations, events), all 1,500-2,000 words. **Pays $400-800.** Living (books, video, arts, music), 800 words. **Pays $200-250.** World of Yoga, Spectrum (brief yoga and healthy living news/events/fillers), 150-600 words. **Pays $50-150.**

Tips "Please read our writer's guidelines before submission. Do not e-mail or fax unsolicited manuscripts."

HISTORY

AMERICAN HERITAGE

90 Fifth Ave., New York NY 10011. (212)367-3100. E-mail: mail@americanheritage.com. Web site: www.americanheritage.com. **Contact:** Richard Snow, editor. **70% freelance written.** Magazine published 6 times/year. "*American Heritage* writes from a historical point of view on politics, business, art, current and international affairs, and our changing lifestyles. The articles are written with the intent to enrich the reader's appreciation of the sometimes nostalgic, sometimes funny, always stirring panorama of the American experience." Circ. 350,000. **Pays on acceptance.** Publishes ms an average of 6-12 months after acceptance. Byline given. Buys first North American serial, all rights. Submit seasonal material 1 year in advance. Responds in 2 months to queries. Writer's guidelines for #10 SASE.

O→ Before submitting material, "check our index to see whether we have already treated the subject."

Nonfiction Wants "historical articles by scholars or journalists intended for intelligent lay readers rather than for professional historians." Emphasis is on authenticity, accuracy, and verve. "Interesting documents, photographs, and drawings are always welcome. Style should stress readability and accuracy." **Buys 10-15 unsolicited mss/year.** Query. Length: 1,500-6,000 words. **Payment varies.** Sometimes pays expenses of writers on assignment.

Tips "We have over the years published quite a few 'firsts' from young writers whose historical knowledge, research methods, and writing skills met our standards. The scope and ambition of a new writer tell us a lot about his or her future usefulness to us. A major article gives us a better idea of the writer's value. Everything depends on the quality of the material. We don't really care whether the author is 20 and unknown, or 80 and famous, or vice versa. No phone calls, please."

⊘ AMERICAN HISTORY

Weider History Group, 741 Miller Dr., Suite D-2, Leesburg VA 20175-8994. (703)771-9400. Fax: (703)779-8345. Web site: www.historynet.com. **60% freelance written.** Bimonthly magazine of cultural, social, military, and political history published for a general audience. Estab. 1966. Circ. 95,000. **Pays on acceptance.** Byline given. Buys first rights. Responds in 10 weeks to queries. Sample copy and guidelines for $5 (includes 3rd class postage) or $4 and 9×12 SAE with 4 first-class stamps. Writer's guidelines for #10 SASE.

Nonfiction Features events in the lives of noteworthy historical figures and accounts of important events in American history. Also includes pictorial features on artists, photographers, and graphic subjects. "Material is presented on a popular rather than a scholarly level." **Buys 20 mss/year.** Query by mail only with published clips and SASE. Length: 2,000-4,000 words depending on type of article.

Photos Welcomes suggestions for illustrations.

Tips "Key prerequisites for publication are thorough research and accurate presentation, precise English usage, and sound organization, a lively style, and a high level of human interest. *Unsolicited manuscripts not considered.* Inappropriate materials include: fiction, book reviews, travelogues, personal/family narratives not of national significance, articles about collectibles/antiques, living artists, local/individual historic buildings/landmarks, and articles of a current editorial nature. Currently seeking articles on significant Civil War subjects. No phone, fax, or e-mail queries, please.''

AMERICAN LEGACY

Forbes, Inc., 28 W. 23rd St., 10th Floor, New York NY 10010-5254. (212)367-3100. Fax: (212)367-3151. E-mail: apeterson@forbes.com. Web site: www.americanlegacymagazine.net. Editor: Audrey Peterson. Quarterly magazine spotlighting the historical and cultural achievements of African American men and women throughout history. Editorial lead time 6 months.

- Query before submitting.

$ $ AMERICA'S CIVIL WAR

Weider History Group, 741 Miller Dr., Suite D-2, Leesburg VA 20175-8994. (703)771-9400. Fax: (703)779-8345. Web site: www.historynet.com. **95% freelance written.** Bimonthly magazine covering ''popular history and straight historical narrative for both the general reader and the Civil War buff covering strategy, tactics, personalities, arms and equipment.'' Estab. 1988. Circ. 78,000. Pays on publication. Byline given. Buys all rights. Accepts queries by mail, e-mail, fax. Sample copy for $5. Writer's guidelines for #10 SASE.

Nonfiction Historical/nostalgic, book notices, preservation news. **Buys 24 mss/year.** Query. Length: 3,500-4,000 words and a 500-word sidebar. **Pays $300 and up.**

Photos Send photos with submission or cite sources. Captions, identification of subjects required.

Columns/Departments Personality (profiles of Civil War personalities); Men & Material (about weapons used); Commands (about units); Eyewitness to War (historical letters and diary excerpts). Length: 2,000 words. **Buys 24 mss/year.** Query. **Pays $150 and up.**

Tips ''All stories must be true. We do not publish fiction or poetry. Write an entertaining, well-researched, informative and unusual story that grabs the reader's attention and holds it. Include suggested readings in a standard format at the end of your piece. Manuscript must be typed, double-spaced on one side of standard white 8½×11, 16 to 30 pound paper—no onion skin paper or dot matrix printouts. All submissions are on speculation. Prefer subjects to be on disk (IBM- or Macintosh-compatible floppy disk) as well as a hard copy. Choose stories with strong art possibilities.''

$ THE ARTILLERYMAN

Historical Publications, Inc., 234 Monarch Hill Rd., Tunbridge VT 05077. (802)889-3500. Fax: (802)889-5627. E-mail: mail@civilwarnews.com. **Contact:** Kathryn Jorgensen, editor. **60% freelance written.** Quarterly magazine covering antique artillery, fortifications, and crew-served weapons 1750-1900 for competition shooters, collectors, and living history reenactors using artillery. ''Emphasis on Revolutionary War and Civil War but includes everyone interested in pre-1900 artillery and fortifications, preservation, construction of replicas, etc.'' Estab. 1979. Circ. 2,000. Pays on publication. Publishes ms an average of 6 months after acceptance. Byline given. Not copyrighted. Buys one-time rights. Accepts queries by mail, e-mail, fax. Accepts previously published material. Accepts simultaneous submissions. Responds in 3 weeks to queries. Sample copy and writer's guidelines for 9×12 SAE with 4 first-class stamps.

- Break in with a historical or travel piece featuring artillery—the types and history of guns and their use.

Nonfiction Interested in ''artillery only, for sophisticated readers. Not interested in other weapons, battles in general.'' Historical/nostalgic, how-to (reproduce ordnance equipment/sights/implements/tools/accessories, etc.), interview/profile, new product, opinion (must be accompanied by detailed background of writer and include references), personal experience, photo feature, technical (must have footnotes), travel (where to find interesting antique cannon). **Buys 24-30 mss/year.** Send complete ms. Length: 300 words minimum. **Pays $20-60.** Sometimes pays expenses of writers on assignment.

Reprints Send tearsheet or photocopy and information about when and where the material previously appeared. Pays 100% of amount paid for an original article.

Photos Send photos with submission. Pays $5 for 5×7 and larger b&w prints. Captions, identification of subjects required.

Tips ''We regularly use freelance contributions for Places-to-Visit, Cannon Safety, The Workshop, and Unit Profiles departments. Also need pieces on unusual cannon or cannon with a known and unique history. To judge whether writing style and/or expertise will suit our needs, writers should ask themselves if they could knowledgeably talk artillery with an expert. Subject matter is of more concern than writer's background.''

BRITISH HERITAGE

Weider History Group, 741 Miller Dr., Suite D-2, Leesburg VA 20175-8994. (703)771-9400. Fax: (703)779-8345. E-mail: dana.huntley@weiderhistorygroup.com. Web site: www.thehistorynet.com. Editor: Dana Huntley. Bimonthly magazine covering British heritage. Presents comprehensive information and background of British culture for admirers and those interested in learning about life (past and present) in England, Scotland, and Wales. Circ. 77,485. **Pays on acceptance.** Buys all rights. Editorial lead time 6 months. Accepts queries by e-mail. Sample copy not available.

Nonfiction British history, culture, travel. **Buys 50 mss/year.** Query by e-mail. Length: 2,000-2,500 words.

Columns/Departments Timeline; Hands Across the Sea; Streetlights of London, all 1,000-1,200 words.

Tips "The first rule still stands: Know thy market."

$ $ $ CIVIL WAR TIMES

Weider History Group, 741 Miller Dr. SE, Suite D-2, Leesburg VA 20175. (703)779-8371. Fax: (703)779-8345. Web site: www.historynet.com. **90% freelance written.** Works with a small number of new/unpublished writers each year. Magazine published 6 times/year. "*Civil War Times* is the full-spectrum magazine of the Civil War. Specifically, we look for nonpartisan coverage of battles, prominent military and civilian figures, the home front, politics, military technology, common soldier life, prisoners and escapes, period art and photography, the naval war, blockade-running, specific regiments, and much more." Estab. 1962. Circ. 108,000. Pays on acceptance and on publication. Publishes ms an average of 18 months after acceptance. Buys unlimited usage rights. Submit seasonal material 1 year in advance. Responds in 3-6 months to queries. Sample copy for $6. Writer's guidelines for #10 SASE.

Nonfiction Interview/profile, photo feature, Civil War historical material. "Don't send us a comprehensive article on a well-known major battle. Instead, focus on some part or aspect of such a battle, or some group of soldiers in the battle. Similar advice applies to major historical figures like Lincoln and Lee. Positively no fiction or poetry." **Buys 20 freelance mss/year.** Query with clips and SASE. **Pays $75-800.**

Tips "We're very open to new submissions. Send query after examining writer's guidelines and several recent issues. Include photocopies of photos that could feasibly accompany the article. Confederate soldiers' diaries and letters are especially welcome."

$ GOOD OLD DAYS

America's Premier Nostalgia Magazine, House of White Birches, 306 E. Parr Rd., Berne IN 46711. Fax: (260)589-8093. E-mail: editor@goodolddaysonline.com. Web site: www.goodolddaysonline.com. **Contact:** Ken Tate, editor. **75% freelance written.** Monthly magazine of first person nostalgia, 1935-1960. "We look for strong narratives showing life as it was in the first half of the 20th century. Our readership is comprised of nostalgia buffs, history enthusiasts, and the people who actually lived and grew up in this era." Pays on contract. Publishes ms an average of 8 months after acceptance. Byline given. Prefers all rights, but will negotiate for First North American serial and one-time rights. Submit seasonal material 10 months in advance. Responds in 2 months to queries. Sample copy for $2. Writer's guidelines online.

- Queries accepted, but are not necessary.

Nonfiction Regular features: Good Old Days on Wheels (auto, plane, horse-drawn, tram, bicycle, trolley, etc.); Good Old Days In the Kitchen (favorite foods, appliances, ways of cooking, recipes); Home Remedies (herbs and poultices, hometown doctors, harrowing kitchen table operations). Historical/nostalgic, humor, personal experience, photo feature, favorite food/recipes, year-round seasonal material, biography, memorable events, fads, fashion, sports, music, literature, entertainment. No fiction accepted. **Buys 350 mss/year.** Query or send complete ms. Length: 500-1,500 words. **Pays $20-100, depending on quality and photos.**

Photos "Send original or professionally copied photographs. Do not submit laser-copied prints." Send photos with submission. Identification of subjects required.

Tips "Most of our writers are not professionals. We prefer the author's individual voice, warmth, humor, and honesty over technical ability."

N $ $ HISTORY MAGAZINE

Moorshead Magazines, 500-505 Consumers Rd., Toronto ON M2J 4V8 Canada. E-mail: magazine@history-magazine.com. Web site: www.history-magazine.com. Editor: Halvor Moorshead. **Contact:** Victoria King, deputy editor. **90% freelance written.** Bimonthly magazine covering social history. "A general interest history magazine, focusing on social history up to the outbreak of World War II." Estab. 1999. Pays on publication. Publishes ms an average of 6 months after acceptance. Byline given. Buys electronic, world serial rights rights. Editorial lead time 6 months. Submit seasonal material 6 months in advance. Accepts queries by mail, e-mail. Responds in 1 month to queries; 1 month to mss. Sample copy and writer's guidelines online.

Nonfiction Book excerpts, historical/nostalgic. Does not want first-person narratives or revisionist history. **Buys 50 mss/year.** Query. Length: 400-2,500 words. **Pays $50-250.**

Photos State availability with submission. Reviews GIF/JPEG files. Buys one-time rights. Negotiates payment individually. Captions required.

Tips "A love of history helps a lot and a willingness to work with us to present interesting articles on the past to our readers."

N $ $ KANSAS JOURNAL OF MILITARY HISTORY

P.O. Box 828, Topeka KS 66601. (785)357-0510. Fax: (785)357-0579. E-mail: karen@ksjournal.com. Web site: www.ksjournal.com. Managing Editor: Deb Goodrich. **Contact:** Tom Goodrich, editor. **20% freelance written.** Quarterly magazine that celebrates and explores the military history of Kansas and its territories and the Kansans who have served here and abroad, and promotes tourism by showcasing historic sites and landmarks. Estab. 2004. Circ. 4,000. Pays on publication. Publishes ms an average of 6 months after acceptance. Byline given. Buys first North American serial rights. Editorial lead time 6 months. Submit seasonal material 1 year in advance. Accepts queries by mail, e-mail. Accepts previously published material. Accepts simultaneous submissions. Responds in 2 weeks to queries; 2 months to mss. Sample copy and writer's guidelines online.

Nonfiction Book excerpts, essays, historical/nostalgic, humor, interview/profile, opinion, personal experience, photo feature. Special issues: Lights, Camera, Kansas: movie stills, posters, etc. relating to film in Kansas. Does not want to receive fiction or poetry. **Buys 10 mss/year.** Query with published clips. Length: 500-1,500 words. **Pays $50-200.**

Photos Send photos with submission. Reviews contact sheets, GIF/JPEG files. Buys one-time rights. Offers no additional payment for photos accepted with ms. Captions, identification of subjects, model releases required.

Columns/Departments Hand to Hand (opinion, pro/con, historic figures), 800-1,000 words. **Buys 5 mss/year. Pays $50-200.**

Fillers Anecdotes, facts, gags to be illustrated by cartoonist, short humor. **Buys 20/year.** Length: 200-300 words. **Pays $25-50.**

Tips "We are interested in history that is fun, compelling, and interesting—not academic. The audience is made up of military members, veterans, tourists, and history buffs (novice and knowledgeable)."

$ LEBEN

A Journal of Reformed Life, City Seminary Press, 2150 River Plaza Dr., #150, Sacramento CA 95833. E-mail: editor@leben.us. Web site: www.leben.us. **Contact:** Wayne Johnson, editor. **40% freelance written.** Quarterly magazine presenting the people and events of Christian history from a Reformation perspective. "We are not a theological journal, per se, but rather a popular history magazine." Estab. 2004. Circ. 5,000. **Pays on acceptance.** Publishes ms an average of 6 months after acceptance. Byline given. Offers 25% kill fee. Buys first North American serial, second serial (reprint), electronic rights. Editorial lead time 6 months. Submit seasonal material 6 months in advance. Accepts queries by e-mail. Accepts previously published material. Accepts simultaneous submissions. Responds in 3 weeks to queries; 2 months to mss. Sample copy for $1.50 (order online or request via e-mail). Writer's guidelines by e-mail.

Nonfiction Historical/nostalgic, reformed biography. Does not want articles that argue theological issues. There is a place for that, but not in a popular history/biography magazine aimed at general readership. Query. Length: 500-2,500 words. **Pays up to $100.**

Tips "Visit our Web site and read our publication. We are a niche magazine, but one a person knowledgeable about the Reformation should be able to write for."

MHQ

The Quarterly Journal of Military History, Weider History Group, 741 Miller Dr., Suite D-2, Leesburg VA 20175-8994. (703)771-9400. Fax: (703)779-8345. Web site: www.historynet.com. Editor: Rod Paschall. **Contact:** Nicholas W. Wood, associate editor. **100% freelance written.** Quarterly journal covering military history. "*MHQ* offers readers in-depth articles on the history of warfare from ancient times into the 21st century. Authoritative features and departments cover military strategies, philosophies, campaigns, battles, personalities, weaponry, espionage and perspectives, all written in a lively and readable style. Articles are accompanied by classic works of art, photographs and maps. Readers include serious students of military tactics, strategy, leaders and campaigns, as well as general world history enthusiasts. Many readers are currently in the military or retired officers." Estab. 1988. Circ. 22,000. Pays on publication. Byline given. Buys all rights. Editorial lead time 1 year. Submit seasonal material 1 year in advance. Accepts queries by mail, e-mail, fax. Accepts simultaneous submissions. Sample copy for $23 (hardcover), $13 (softcover); some articles on Web site. Writer's guidelines for #10 SASE or via e-mail.

Nonfiction Historical/nostalgic, personal experience, photo feature. No fiction or stories pertaining to collectibles or reenactments. **Buys 50 mss/year.** Query preferred; also accepts complete ms. Length: 1,500-6,000 words.

Photos Send photos/art with submission. Reviews transparencies, prints. Buys all rights. Negotiates payment individually. Identification of subjects required.

Columns/Departments Artists on War (description of artwork of a military nature); Experience of War (first-person accounts of military incidents); Strategic View (discussion of military theory, strategy); Arms & Men (description of military hardware or unit), all up to 2,500 words. **Buys 20 mss/year.** Send complete ms.

Tips "All stories must be true—we publish no fiction. Although we are always looking for variety, some subjects—World War II, the American Civil War, and military biography, for instance—are the focus of so many proposals that we are forced to judge them by relatively rigid criteria. We are always glad to consider articles on these subjects. However, less common ones—medieval, Asian, or South American military history, for example—are more likely to attract our attention. The likelihood that articles can be effectively illustrated often determines the ultimate fate of manuscripts. Many otherwise excellent articles have been rejected due to a lack of suitable art or photographs. Regular departments—columns on strategy, tactics, and weaponry—average 1,500 words. While the information we publish is scholarly and substantive, we prefer writing that is light, anecdotal, and above all, engaging, rather than didactic."

MILITARY HISTORY

Weider History Group, 741 Miller Dr., Suite D-2, Leesburg VA 20175-8994. (703)771-9400. Fax: (703)779-8345. Web site: www.historynet.com. **Contact:** Michael Robbins, editor. **95% freelance written.** Magazine published 10 times/year covering all military history of the world. "We strive to give the general reader accurate, highly readable, often narrative popular history, richly accompanied by period art." Circ. 112,000. Pays 30 days after publication. Byline given. Buys all rights. Submit seasonal material 1 year in advance. Accepts queries by mail, e-mail, fax. Sample copy for $5. Writer's guidelines for #10 SASE.

Nonfiction "The best way to break into our magazine is to write an entertaining, informative, and unusual story that grabs the reader's attention and holds it." Historical/nostalgic, interview/profile (military figures of commanding interest), personal experience (only occasionally). **Buys 30 mss/year.** Query with published clips. "Submit a short, self-explanatory query summarizing the story proposed, its highlights, and/or significance. State also your own expertise, access to sources, or proposed means of developing the pertinent information." Length: 4,000 words with a 500-word sidebar.

Columns/Departments Intrigue; Weaponry; Perspectives; Personality; Reviews (books, video, CD-ROMs, software—all relating to military history). Length: 2,000 words. **Buys 24 mss/year.** Query with published clips.

Tips "We would like journalistically 'pure' submissions that adhere to basics, such as full name at first reference, same with rank, and definition of prior or related events, issues cited as context or obscure military 'hardware.' Read the magazine, discover our style, and avoid subjects already covered. Pick stories with strong art possibilities (real art and photos), send photocopies, tell us where to order the art. Avoid historical overview; focus upon an event with appropriate and accurate context. Provide bibliography. Tell the story in popular but elegant style. Submissions must be in digital format."

$ $ PERSIMMON HILL

National Cowboy & Western Heritage Museum, 1700 NE 63rd St., Oklahoma City OK 73111. (405)478-6404. Fax: (405)478-4714. E-mail: editor@nationalcowboymuseum.org. Web site: www.nationalcowboymuseum.o rg. **Contact:** M.J. Van Deventer, editor. **70% freelance written.** Prefers to work with published/established writers; works with a small number of new/unpublished writers each year. Quarterly magazine for an audience interested in Western art, Western history, ranching, and rodeo, including historians, artists, ranchers, art galleries, schools, and libraries. Estab. 1970. Circ. 15,000. Pays on publication. Publishes ms an average of 18 months after acceptance. Byline given. Buys first rights. Responds in 3 months to queries. Sample copy for $10.50, including postage. Writer's guidelines for #10 SASE or on Web site.

O‐ "We need more material on rodeo, both contemporary and historical. And we need more profiles on contemporary working ranches in the West."

Nonfiction Historical and contemporary articles on famous Western figures connected with pioneering the American West, Western art, rodeo, cowboys, etc. (or biographies of such people), stories of Western flora and animal life and environmental subjects. "We want thoroughly researched and historically authentic material written in a popular style. May have a humorous approach to subject. No broad, sweeping, superficial pieces; i.e., the California Gold Rush or rehashed pieces on Billy the Kid, etc." **Buys 50-75 mss/year.** Query by mail only with clips. Length: 1,500 words. **Pays $150-300.**

Photos Purchased with ms or on assignment. Reviews color transparencies, glossy b&w prints. Pays according to quality and importance for b&w and color photos. Captions required.

Tips "Send us a story that captures the spirit of adventure and indvidualism that typifies the Old West or reveals a facet of the Western lifestyle in comtemporary society. Excellent illustrations for articles are essential! We lean towards scholarly, historical, well-researched articles. We're less focused on Western celebrities than some of the other contemporary Western magazines."

PRESERVATION MAGAZINE

National Trust for Historic Preservation, 1785 Massachusetts Ave. NW, Washington DC 20036. (202)588-6388. Fax: (202)588-6266. E-mail: preservation@nthp.org. Web site: www.preservationonline.org. **Contact:** Arnold Berke, executive editor. **75% freelance written.** Prefers to work with published/established writers. Bimonthly magazine covering preservation of historic buildings and neighborhoods in the US. "We cover subjects related in some way to place. Most entries are features, department, or opinion pieces." Circ. 250,000. Pays on publication. Publishes ms an average of 2 months after acceptance. Byline given. Offers variable kill fee. Buys one-time rights. Accepts queries by mail, e-mail, fax. Responds in 2 months to queries.

Nonfiction Book excerpts, essays, historical/nostalgic, humor, interview/profile, opinion, photo feature, travel, features, news. **Buys 30 mss/year.** Query with published clips. Length: 500-3,500 words. Sometimes pays expenses of writers on assignment.

The online magazine carries original content not found in the print edition. Contact: Margaret Foster.

Tips "Do not send or propose histories of buildings, descriptive accounts of cities or towns, or long-winded treatises. Best bet for breaking in is via Preservation Online, Reporter (news features, 500-1,000 words), House Rules (brief profile or article, 500-800 words)."

N $ $ $ TIMELINE

Ohio Historical Society, 1982 Velma Ave., Columbus OH 43211-2497. (614)297-2360. Fax: (614)297-2367. E-mail: timeline@ohiohistory.org. **Contact:** David A. Simmons, editor. **90% freelance written.** Works with a small number of new/unpublished writers each year. Quarterly magazine covering history, prehistory, and the natural sciences, directed toward readers in the Midwest. Estab. 1984. Circ. 7,000. **Pays on acceptance.** Publishes ms an average of 1 year after acceptance. Byline given. Offers $75 minimum kill fee. Buys first North American serial, all rights. Submit seasonal material 6 months in advance. Accepts queries by mail, e-mail, fax. Responds in 3 weeks to queries; 6 weeks to mss. Sample copy for $12 and 9×12 SAE. Writer's guidelines for #10 SASE.

Nonfiction Topics include the traditional fields of political, economic, military, and social history; biography; the history of science and technology; archaeology and anthropology; architecture; the fine and decorative arts; and the natural sciences including botany, geology, zoology, ecology, and paleontology. Book excerpts, essays, historical/nostalgic, interview/profile (of individuals), photo feature. **Buys 22 mss/year.** Query. Length: 1,500-6,000 words. Also vignettes of 500-1,000 words. **Pays $100-800.**

Photos Submissions should include ideas for illustration. Send photos with submission. Reviews contact sheets, transparencies, 8×10 prints. Buys one-time rights. Captions, identification of subjects, model releases required.

Tips "We want crisply written, authoritative narratives for the intelligent lay reader. An Ohio slant may strengthen a submission, but it is not indispensable. Contributors must know enough about their subject to explain it clearly and in an interesting fashion. We use high-quality illustration with all features. If appropriate illustration is unavailable, we can't use the feature. The writer who sends illustration ideas with a manuscript has an advantage, but an often-published illustration won't attract us."

N $ $ TRACES OF INDIANA AND MIDWESTERN HISTORY

Indiana Historical Society, 450 W. Ohio St., Indianapolis IN 46202-3269. (317)232-1877. Fax: (317)233-0857. E-mail: rboomhower@indianahistory.org. Web site: www.indianahistory.org. **Contact:** Ray E. Boomhower, managing editor. **80% freelance written.** Quarterly magazine on Indiana history. "Conceived as a vehicle to bring to the public good narrative and analytical history about Indiana in its broader contexts of region and nation, *Traces* explores the lives of artists, writers, performers, soldiers, politicians, entrepreneurs, homemakers, reformers, and naturalists. It has traced the impact of Hoosiers on the nation and the world. In this vein, the editors seek nonfiction articles that are solidly researched, attractively written, and amenable to illustration, and they encourage scholars, journalists, and freelance writers to contribute to the magazine." Estab. 1989. Circ. 10,000. Publishes ms an average of 6 months after acceptance. Byline given. Buys one-time rights. Submit seasonal material 1 year in advance. Responds in 3 months to mss. Writer's guidelines online.

Nonfiction Book excerpts, historical essays, historical photographic features on topics of biography, literature, folklore, music, visual arts, politics, economics, industry, transportation, and sports. **Buys 20 mss/year.** Send complete ms. Length: 2,000-4,000 words. **Pays $100-500.**

Photos Send photos with submission. Reviews contact sheets, transparencies, photocopies, prints. Buys one-time rights. Pays "reasonable photographic expenses." Captions, identification of subjects, permissions required.

Tips "Freelancers should be aware of prerequisites for writing history for a broad audience. Should have some awareness of this magazine and other magazines of this type published by Midwestern historical societies. Preference is given to subjects with an Indiana connection and authors who are familiar with *Traces*. Quality of potential illustration is also important."

N TRAINS

Kalmbach Publishing Co., P.O. Box 1612, Waukesha WI 53187-1612. (262)796-8776. Fax: (262)796-1142. E-mail: editor@trainsmag.com. Web site: www.trainsmag.com. Editor: Jim Wrinn. Monthly magazine. that appeals to consumers interested in learning about the function and history of the railroad industry. Circ. 100,000. Editorial lead time 2 months.

- Query before submitting.

$ $ $ TRUE WEST

True West Publishing, Inc., P.O. Box 8008, Cave Creek AZ 85327. (888)687-1881. Fax: (480)575-1903. E-mail: editor@twmag.com. Web site: twmag.com. Executive Editor: Bob Boze Bell. **Contact:** Meghan Saar, managing editor. **70% freelance written.** Works with a small number of new/unpublished writers each year. Magazine published 10 times/year covering Western American history from prehistory 1800 to 1930. ''We want reliable research on significant historical topics written in lively prose for an informed general audience. More recent topics may be used if they have a historical angle or retain the Old West flavor of trail dust and saddle leather.'' Estab. 1953. Pays on publication. Byline given. Buys first North American serial rights. Editorial lead time 3 months. Accepts queries by mail, e-mail. Sample copy for $3. Writer's guidelines online.

- No unsolicited mss.

O→ ''We are looking for historically accurate stories on the Old West that make you wonder 'What happens next?'"

Nonfiction No fiction, poetry, or unsupported, undocumented tales. **Buys 30 mss/year.** Query. Length: 1,000-3,000 words. **Pays $50-800.**

Photos State availability with submission. Reviews contact sheets, negatives, 4×5 transparencies, 4×5 prints. Buys one-time rights. Offers $20/photo. Captions, identification of subjects, model releases required.

Columns/Departments Book Reviews, 50-60 words (no unsolicited reviews). **Pays $25.**

Fillers Anecdotes, facts, gags to be illustrated by cartoonist, newsbreaks, short humor. **Buys 30/year.** Length: 50-600 words.

Tips ''Read our magazines and follow our guidelines. A freelancer is most likely to break in with us by submitting thoroughly researched, lively prose on relatively obscure topics or by being assigned to write for 1 of our departments. First-person accounts rarely fill our needs. Historical accuracy and strict adherence to the facts are essential. We much prefer material based on primary sources (archives, court records, documents) and should not be based mainly on secondary sources (published books, magazines, and journals). Art is also a huge selling point for us.''

VIETNAM

Weider History Group, 741 Miller Dr., Suite D-2, Leesburg VA 20175-8994. (703)771-9400. Fax: (703)779-8345. Web site: www.historynet.com. **90% freelance written.** Bimonthly magazine providing in-depth and authoritative accounts of the many complexities that made the war in Vietnam unique, including the people, battles, strategies, perspectives, analysis, and weaponry. Estab. 1988. Circ. 46,000. Pays on publication. Byline given. Buys all rights. Accepts queries by mail, fax. Sample copy for $5. Writer's guidelines for #10 SASE.

Nonfiction Historical/nostalgic (military), interview/profile, personal experience. ''Absolutely no fiction or poetry; we want straight history, as much personal narrative as possible, but not the gung-ho, shoot-'em-up variety, either.'' **Buys 24 mss/year.** Query. Length: 4,000 words maximum; sidebars 500 words.

Photos Send photos with submission or state availability and cite sources. Identification of subjects required.

Columns/Departments Arsenal (about weapons used, all sides); Personality (profiles of the players, all sides); Fighting Forces (various units or types of units: air, sea, rescue); Perspectives. Length: 2,000 words. Query.

Tips ''Choose stories with strong art possibilities. Send hard copy plus an IBM- or Macintosh-compatible floppy disk. All stories must be true. We do not publish fiction or poetry. All stories should be carefully researched third-person articles or firsthand accounts that give the reader a sense of experiencing historical events.''

$ $ WILD WEST

Weider History Group, 741 Miller Dr., SE, Suite D-2, Leesburg VA 20175-8920. (703)771-9400. Fax: (703)779-8345. Web site: www.historynet.com. **95% freelance written.** Bimonthly magazine covering the history of the American frontier, from its eastern beginnings to its western terminus. ''*Wild West* covers the popular (narrative) history of the American West—events, trends, personalities, anything of general interest.'' Estab. 1988. Circ. 83,500. Pays on publication. Publishes ms an average of 2 years after acceptance. Byline given. Not copyrighted. Buys all rights. Editorial lead time 10 months. Submit seasonal material 1 year in advance. Accepts queries by mail, e-mail. Accepts simultaneous submissions. Responds in 3 months to queries; 6 months to mss. Sample copy for $6. Writer's guidelines for #10 SASE or online.

Nonfiction Historical/nostalgic (Old West). No excerpts, travel, etc. Articles can be ''adapted from'' book. No fiction or poetry—nothing current. **Buys 36 mss/year.** Query. Length: 3,500 words with a 500-word sidebar. **Pays $300.**

Photos State availability with submission. Reviews negatives, transparencies. Buys one-time rights. Offers no additional payment for photos accepted with ms. Captions, identification of subjects required.

Columns/Departments Gunfighters & Lawmen, 2,000 words; Westerners, 2,000 words; Warriors & Chiefs, 2,000 words; Western Lore, 2,000 words; Guns of the West, 1,500 words; Artists West, 1,500 words; Books Reviews, 250 words. **Buys 36 mss/year.** Query. **Pays $150 for departments; book reviews paid by the word, minimum $40.**

Tips "Always query the editor with your story idea. Successful queries include a description of sources of information and suggestions for color and b&w photography or artwork. The best way to break into our magazine is to write an entertaining, informative, and unusual story that grabs the reader's attention and holds it. We favor carefully researched, third-person articles that give the reader a sense of experiencing historical events. Include a hard copy as well as an IBM- or Macintosh-compatible floppy disk."

$ $ WORLD WAR II

Weider History Group, 741 Miller Dr., Suite D-2, Leesburg VA 20175-8994. (703)771-9400. Fax: (703)779-8345. Web site: www.historynet.com. **95% freelance written.** Prefers to work with published/established writers. Bimonthly magazine covering military operations in World War II—events, personalities, strategy, national policy, etc. Estab. 1986. Circ. 146,000. Pays on publication. Byline given. Buys all rights. Accepts queries by mail, e-mail, fax. Sample copy for $5. Writer's guidelines for #10 SASE.

Nonfiction World War II military history. Submit anniversary-related material 1 year in advance. No fiction. **Buys 24 mss/year.** Query. Length: 4,000 words with a 500-word sidebar. **Pays $300 and up.**

Photos For photos and other art, send photocopies and cite sources. "We'll order." State availability with submission. Captions, identification of subjects required.

Columns/Departments Undercover (espionage, resistance, sabotage, intelligence gathering, behind the lines, etc.); Personality (WWII personalities of interest); Armament (weapons, their use and development); Commands (unit histories); One Man's War (personal profiles), all 2,000 words. Book reviews, 300-750 words. **Buys 30 (plus book reviews) mss/year.** Query. **Pays $150 and up.**

Tips "List your sources and suggest further readings in standard format at the end of your piece—as a bibliography for our files in case of factual challenge or dispute. All submissions are on speculation. Include a hard copy as well as an IBM- or Macintosh-compatible floppy disk. All stories must be true. We do not publish fiction or poetry. Stories should be carefully researched."

HOBBY & CRAFT

N $ $ ANTIQUE & COLLECTIBLES SHOWCASE

Trajan Publishing Corporation, P.O. Box 28103, Lakeport PO, 600 Ontario St., St. Catherines ON L2N 7P8 Canada. E-mail: acseditor@rogers.com. Web site: www.antiqueandcollectiblesshowcase.ca. **Contact:** Judy Penz Sheluk, editor. **75% freelance written.** Bimonthly magazine covering antiques and contemporary collectibles. "Preference is given to Canadian writers, but US writers will be considered if they have a unique angle on a story of interest to Canadian readers." Estab. 2003. Circ. 5,500. Pays on publication. Publishes ms an average of 2-3 months after acceptance. Byline given. Buys first North American serial, electronic rights, makes work-for-hire assignments. Editorial lead time 1-3 months. Submit seasonal material 6 months in advance. Accepts queries by mail, e-mail. Responds in 1 month to queries. Sample copy for $5 (Canadian). Writer's guidelines online.

Nonfiction General interest, how-to, interview/profile, opinion. Does not want poetry, book reports or self-promotion. **Buys 30 mss/year.** Query. Length: 500-1,500 words. **Pays $50-225.**

Photos Send photos with submission. Reviews GIF/JPEG files. Offers no additional payment for photos accepted with ms.

Columns/Departments Antiquing in the 21st Century (modern perspective from knowledgeable sources), 750 words; Decorating With Antiques (how to use Great Aunt Gerdie's bookcase), 750 words. **Buys 25 mss/year.** Query. **Pays $50-150.**

Tips "Antiques are old, but your ideas and your writing shouldn't be. We want to entertain the reader. Form pitches based on the guidelines. Show e-mail subject as Freelance Query."

$ $ ANTIQUE TRADER

Krause Publications, a Division of F+W Publications, Inc., 700 E. State St., Iola WI 54990-0001. (715)445-2214. Fax: (715)445-4087. E-mail: antiquetrader@fwpubs.com. Web site: www.antiquetrader.com. **Contact:** Patricia DuChene, associate editor. **60% freelance written.** Weekly tabloid covering antiques. "We publish quote-heavy stories of timely interest in the antiques field. We cover antiques shows, auctions, and news events." Estab. 1957. Circ. 30,000. Pays on publication. Publishes ms an average of 1-3 months after acceptance. Byline given. Offers 50% kill fee. Buys exclusive rights. Editorial lead time 2 months. Accepts queries by mail, e-mail, fax. Responds in 1 week to queries; 2 months to mss. Sample copy for cover price, plus postage. Writer's guidelines online.

Nonfiction Book excerpts, general interest, interview/profile, personal experience, show and auction coverage. Does not want the same, dry textbook, historical stories on antiques that appear elsewhere. "I want personality and timeliness." **Buys 1,000+ mss/year.** Query with or without published clips or send complete ms. Length: 750-1,200 words. **Pays $50-200, plus contributor copy.**

Photos State availability with submission. Reviews transparencies, prints, GIF/JPEG files. Buys one-time rights. Offers no additional payment for photos accepted with ms. Identification of subjects required.

Columns/Departments Dealer Profile (interviews with interesting antiques dealers), 750-1,200 words; Collector Profile (interviews with interesting collectors), 750-1,000 words. **Buys 30-60 mss/year.** Query with or without published clips or send complete ms.

N $ $ ANTIQUES & COLLECTING MAGAZINE

Lightner Publishing, 1006 S. Michigan Ave., Chicago IL 60605. Fax: (312)939-0053. E-mail: editor@acmagazine.com. Web site: www.acmagazine.com. **Contact:** Therese Nolan, editor. **75% freelance written.** Monthly magazine covering antiques and collectibles. Estab. 1931. Circ. 16,000. Pays on publication. Publishes ms an average of 6 months after acceptance. Byline given. Buys first North American serial rights. Editorial lead time 2 months. Submit seasonal material 3 months in advance. Accepts queries by mail, e-mail, fax. Accepts simultaneous submissions. Sample copy for free. Writer's guidelines online

Nonfiction General interest, historical/nostalgic, interview/profile, personal experience. **Buys 48-60 mss/year.** Query with or without published clips or send complete ms. Length: 800-1,600 words. **Pays $50-250.**

Photos State availability of or send photos with submission. Reviews contact sheets, transparencies, prints, GIF/JPEG files. Buys one-time rights. Offers no additional payment for photos accepted with ms. Captions, identification of subjects required

Fiction Historical, humorous, slice-of-life vignettes. **Buys 1-5 mss/year.** Query with or without published clips or send complete ms. **Pays $50-250.**

Fillers Anecdotes, facts, short humor.

$ AUTOGRAPH COLLECTOR

Odyssey Publications, 510-A South Corona Mall, Corona CA 92879. (951)734-9636. Fax: (951)371-7139. E-mail: editorev@telus.net. Web site: www.autographcollector.com. **Contact:** Ev Phillips, editor. **80% freelance written.** Monthly magazine covering the autograph collecting hobby. "The focus of *Autograph Collector* is on documents, photographs, or any collectible item that has been signed by a famous person, whether a current celebrity or historical figure. Articles stress how and where to locate celebrities and autograph material, authenticity of signatures and what they are worth." Byline given. Offers negotiable kill fee. Buys all rights. Editorial lead time 2 months. Submit seasonal material 3 months in advance. Accepts queries by mail, e-mail, fax, phone. Responds in 2 weeks to queries. Sample copy and writer's guidelines free.

Nonfiction "Articles must address subjects that appeal to autograph collectors and should answer 6 basic questions: Who is this celebrity/famous person? How do I go about collecting this person's autograph? Where can I find it? How scarce or available is it? How can I tell if it's real? What is it worth?" Historical/nostalgic, how-to, interview/profile, personal experience. **Buys 25-35 mss/year.** Query. Length: 1,600-2,000 words. **Pays 5¢/word.** Sometimes pays expenses of writers on assignment.

Photos State availability with submission. Reviews transparencies, prints. Buys one-time rights. Offers $3/photo. Captions, identification of subjects required.

Columns/Departments Buys 90-100 mss/year. Query. **Pays $50 or as determined on a per case basis.**

Fillers Anecdotes, facts. **Buys 20-25/year.** Length: 200-300 words. **Pays $15.**

Tips "Ideally writers should be autograph collectors themselves and know their topics thoroughly. Articles must be well-researched and clearly written. Writers should remember that *Autograph Collector* is a celebrity-driven magazine and name recognition of the subject is important."

$ $ BEAD & BUTTON

Kalmbach Publishing, P.O. Box 1612, Waukesha WI 53187. E-mail: web@beadandbutton.com. Web site: www.beadandbutton.com. **50% freelance written.** "*Bead & Button* is a bimonthly magazine devoted to techniques, projects, designs and materials relating to beads, buttons, and accessories. Our readership includes both professional and amateur bead and button makers, hobbyists, and enthusiasts who find satisfaction in making beautiful things." Estab. 1994. Circ. 80,000. **Pays on acceptance.** Publishes ms an average of 4 months after acceptance. Byline given. Offers $75 kill fee. Buys all rights. Accepts queries by mail, e-mail, fax. Writer's guidelines online.

Nonfiction Historical/nostalgic (on beaded jewelry history), how-to (make beaded jewelry and accessories), humor, inspirational, interview/profile. **Buys 24-30 mss/year.** Send complete ms. Length: 750-3,000 words. **Pays $75-300.**

Photos Send photos with submission. Offers no additional payment for photos accepted with ms. Identification of subjects required.

Columns/Departments Chic & Easy (fashionable jewelry how-to); Beginner (easy-to-make jewelry how-to); Simply Earrings (fashionable earring how-to); Fun Fashion (trendy jewelry how-to), all 1,000 words. **Buys 12 mss/year.** Send complete ms. **Pays $75-150.**

Tips "*Bead & Button* magazine primarily publishes how-to articles by the artists who have designed the piece. We publish 2 profiles and 1 historical piece per issue. These would be the only applicable articles for non-artisan writers. Also our humorous and inspirational endpiece might apply."

$ $ BLADE MAGAZINE

The World's #1 Knife Publication, Krause Publications, a Division of F+W Publications, Inc., 700 E. State St., Iola WI 54990-0001. (715)445-2214. Fax: (715)445-4087. E-mail: bladeeditor@fwpubs.com. Web site: www.blademag.com. Editor: Steve Shackleford. **Contact:** Missy Beyer, ad sales. **5% freelance written.** Monthly magazine covering working and using collectible, popular knives. "*Blade* prefers in-depth articles focusing on groups of knives, whether military, collectible, high-tech, pocket knives or hunting knives, and how they perform." Estab. 1973. Circ. 39,000. Pays on publication. Publishes ms an average of 9 months after acceptance. Byline given. Buys all rights. Editorial lead time 9 months. Submit seasonal material 9 months in advance. Accepts queries by mail, e-mail, fax. Responds in 3 months to queries; 6 months to mss. Sample copy for $4.99. Writer's guidelines for 8×11 SAE with 3 first-class stamps.

Nonfiction General interest, historical/nostalgic, how-to, interview/profile, new product, photo feature, technical. Query with or without published clips or send complete ms. Length: 700-1,400 words. **Pays $200-300.**

Photos Send photos with submission. Reviews transparencies, prints, digital images (300 dpi at 1200x1200 pixels). Buys all rights. Offers no additional payment for photos accepted with ms. Captions, identification of subjects required.

Fillers Anecdotes, facts, newsbreaks. **Buys 1-2/year.** Length: 50-200 words. **Pays $25-50.**

Tips "We are always willing to read submissions from anyone who has read a few copies and studied the market. The ideal article for us is a piece bringing out the romance, legend, and love of man's oldest tool—the knife. We like articles that place knives in peoples' hands—in life saving situations, adventure modes, etc. (Nothing gory or with the knife as the villain.) People and knives are good copy. We are getting more well-written articles from writers who are reading the publication beforehand. That makes for a harder sell for the quickie writer not willing to do his homework. Go to knife shows and talk to the makers and collectors. Visit knifemakers' shops and knife factories. Read anything and everything you can find on knives and knifemaking."

$ BREW YOUR OWN

The How-to Homebrew Beer Magazine, Battenkill Communications, 5053 Main St., Suite A, Manchester Center VT 05255. (802)362-3981. Fax: (802)362-2377. E-mail: edit@byo.com. Web site: www.byo.com. **Contact:** Chris Colby, editor. **85% freelance written.** Monthly magazine covering home brewing. "Our mission is to provide practical information in an entertaining format. We try to capture the spirit and challenge of brewing while helping our readers brew the best beer they can." Estab. 1995. Circ. 40,000. **Pays on acceptance.** Publishes ms an average of 4 months after acceptance. Byline given. Offers 25% kill fee. Buys all rights. Editorial lead time 3 months. Submit seasonal material 3 months in advance. Accepts queries by mail, e-mail, fax. Responds in 2 months to queries. Writer's guidelines online.

- Break in by "sending a detailed query in 1 of 2 key areas: how to brew a specific, interesting style of beer (with step-by-step recipes), or how to build your own specific piece of brewing equipment."

Nonfiction Informational pieces on equipment, ingredients, and brewing methods. Historical/nostalgic, how-to (home brewing), humor (related to home brewing), interview/profile (of professional brewers who can offer useful tips to home hobbyists), personal experience, trends. **Buys 75 mss/year.** Query with published clips or description of brewing expertise. Length: 800-3,000 words. **Pays $50-150, depending on length, complexity of article, and experience of writer.** Sometimes pays expenses of writers on assignment.

Photos State availability with submission. Reviews contact sheets, transparencies, 5×7 prints, slides, and electronic images. Buys all rights. Negotiates payment individually. Captions required.

Columns/Departments News (humorous, unusual news about homebrewing), 50-250 words; Last Call (humorous stories about homebrewing), 700 words. **Buys 12 mss/year.** Query with or without published clips. **Pays $50.**

Tips "*Brew Your Own* is for anyone who is interested in brewing beer, from beginners to advanced all-grain brewers. We seek articles that are straightforward and factual, not full of esoteric theories or complex calculations. Our readers tend to be intelligent, upscale, and literate."

N $ $ CANADIAN WOODWORKING

Develop Your Skills-Tool Your Shop-Build Your Dreams, Sawdust Media, Inc., 51 Maple Ave. N., RR #3, Burford ON N0E 1A0 Canada. (519)449-2444. Fax: (519)449-2445. E-mail: letters@canadianwoodworking.com. Web site: www.canadianwoodworking.com. **Contact:** Carl Duguay, editor (carl@canadianwoodworking.com). **20% freelance written.** Bimonthly magazine covering woodworking. Estab. 1999. Pays on publication. Byline given. Offers 50% kill fee. Buys all rights. Accepts queries by e-mail. Sample copy online. Writer's guidelines by e-mail.

Nonfiction How-to, humor, inspirational, new product, personal experience, photo feature, technical. Does not want profile on a woodworker. Query. Length: 500-4,000 words. **Pays $100-600 for assigned articles; $50-400 for unsolicited articles.**

Photos State availability with submission. Buys all rights. Negotiates payment individually.

$ $ CERAMICS MONTHLY

735 Ceramic Place, Suite 100, Westerville OH 43081. (614)895-4213. Fax: (614)891-8960. E-mail: editorial@ceramicsmonthly.org. Web site: www.ceramicsmonthly.org. **Contact:** René Fairchild, assistant editor. **70% freelance written.** Monthly magazine (except July and August) covering the ceramic art and craft field. "Each issue includes articles on potters and ceramics artists from throughout the world, exhibitions, and production processes, as well as critical commentary, book and video reviews, clay and glaze recipes, kiln designs and firing techniques, advice from experts in the field, and ads for available materials and equipment. While principally covering contemporary work, the magazine also looks back at influential artists and events from the past." Estab. 1953. Circ. 39,000. Pays on publication. Byline given. Editorial lead time 3 months. Submit seasonal material 6 months in advance. Accepts queries by mail, e-mail, fax, phone. Responds in 2 months to mss. Writer's guidelines online.

Nonfiction Essays, how-to, interview/profile, opinion, personal experience, technical. **Buys 100 mss/year.** Send complete ms. Length: 500-3,000 words. **Pays 10¢/word.**

Photos Send photos with submission. Reviews original slides or 2¼ or 4×5 transparencies. Offers $25 for photos. Captions required.

Columns/Departments Upfront (workshop/exhibition review), 500-1,000 words. **Buys 20 mss/year.** Send complete ms.

$ $ CLASSIC TOY TRAINS

Kalmbach Publishing Co., 21027 Crossroads Circle, Waukesha WI 53187. (262)796-8776. Fax: (262)796-1142. E-mail: editor@classictoytrains.com. Web site: www.classictoytrains.com. **Contact:** Neil Besougloff, editor. **80% freelance written.** Magazine published 9 times/year covering collectible toy trains (O, S, Standard) like Lionel and American Flyer, etc. "For the collector and operator of toy trains, *CTT* offers full-color photos of layouts and collections of toy trains, restoration tips, operating information, new product reviews and information, and insights into the history of toy trains." Estab. 1987. Circ. 60,000. **Pays on acceptance.** Publishes ms an average of 1 year after acceptance. Byline given. Buys all rights. Editorial lead time 3 months. Submit seasonal material 6 months in advance. Accepts queries by mail, e-mail. Responds in 3 weeks to queries; 1 month to mss. Sample copy for $5.95, plus postage. Writer's guidelines online.

Nonfiction General interest, historical/nostalgic, how-to (restore toy trains; design a layout; build accessories; fix broken toy trains), interview/profile, personal experience, photo feature, technical. **Buys 90 mss/year.** Query. Length: 500-5,000 words. **Pays $75-500.** Sometimes pays expenses of writers on assignment.

Photos Send photos with submission. Reviews 4×5 transparencies, 5×7 prints or 35mm slides preferred. Also accepts hi-res digital photos. Buys all rights. Offers no additional payment for photos accepted with ms or $15-75/photo. Captions required.

Tips "It's important to have a thorough understanding of the toy train hobby; most of our freelancers are hobbyists themselves. One-half to two-thirds of *CTT*'s editorial space is devoted to photographs; superior photography is critical."

$ COLLECTORS NEWS

P.O. Box 306, Grundy Center IA 50638. (319)824-6981. Fax: (319)824-3414. E-mail: lkruger@thepioneergroup.com. Web site: collectors-news.com. **Contact:** Linda Kruger, managing editor. **20% freelance written.** Works with a small number of new/unpublished writers each year. Monthly magazine-size publication on offset, glossy cover, covering antiques, collectibles, and nostalgic memorabilia. Estab. 1959. Circ. 9,000. Pays on publication. Publishes ms an average of 1 year after acceptance. Byline given. Buys first rights, makes work-for-hire assignments. Submit seasonal material 3 months in advance. Accepts queries by mail, e-mail, fax, phone. Responds in 2 weeks to queries; 6 weeks to mss. Sample copy for $4 and 9×12 SAE. Writer's guidelines free.

O→ Break in with articles on collecting online; history and values of collectibles and antiques; collectors with unique and/or extensive collections; using collectibles in the home decor; and any 20th century and timely subjects.

Nonfiction General interest (collectibles, antique to modern), historical/nostalgic (relating to collections or collectors), how-to (display your collection, care for, restore, appraise, locate, add to, etc.), interview/profile (covering individual collectors and their hobbies, unique or extensive; celebrity collectors, and limited edition artists), technical (in-depth analysis of a particular antique, collectible, or collecting field), travel (''hot'' antiquing places in the US). Special issues: 12-month listing of antique and collectible shows, flea markets, and conventions (January includes events January-December; June includes events June-May); Care & Display of Collectibles (September); holidays (October-December). **Buys 36 mss/year.** Query with sample of writing. Length: 800-1,000 words. **Pays $1.10/column inch.**

Photos ''Articles must be accompanied by photographs for illustration.'' A selection of 2-8 images is suggested. ''Articles are eligible for full-color front page consideration when accompanied by high resolution electronic images. Only 1 article is highlighted on the cover/month. Any article providing a color photo selected for front page use receives an additional $25.'' Reviews color or b&w digital images. Buys first rights. Payment for photos included in payment for ms. Captions required.

Tips ''Present a professionally written article with quality illustrations—well-researched and documented information.''

COUNTRY ALMANAC

Harris Publications, Inc., 1115 Broadway, New York NY 10010. (212)807-7100. Fax: (212)463-9958. E-mail: countryletters@yahoo.com. Web site: www.countryalmanacmag.com. Editor: Jodi Zucker. Quarterly magazine. Home service magazine containing articles ranging from country living, crafts, home-spun decorating, food, and outdoor hobbies. Circ. 300,000. Editorial lead time 4-5 months.

$ CQ AMATEUR RADIO

The Radio Amateur's Journal, CQ Communications, Inc., 25 Newbridge Rd., Hicksville NY 11801. (516)681-2922. Fax: (516)681-2926. E-mail: cq@cq-amateur-radio.com. Web site: www.cq-amateur-radio.com. Managing Editor: Gail Schieber. **Contact:** Richard Moseson, editor. **40% freelance written.** Monthly magazine covering amateur (ham) radio. ''*CQ* is published for active ham radio operators and is read by radio amateurs in over 100 countries. All articles must deal with amateur radio. Our focus is on operating and on practical projects. A thorough knowledge of amateur radio is required.'' Estab. 1945. Circ. 60,000. Pays on publication. Publishes ms an average of 6 months after acceptance. Byline given. Buys first North American serial rights. Editorial lead time 4 months. Submit seasonal material 4 months in advance. Accepts queries by mail, e-mail, fax. Responds in 3 weeks to queries; 3 months to mss. Sample copy for free. Writer's guidelines online.

Nonfiction Historical/nostalgic, how-to, interview/profile, personal experience, technical, all related to amateur radio. **Buys 50-60 mss/year.** Query. Length: 2,000-4,000 words. **Pays $40/published page.**

Photos State availability with submission. Reviews contact sheets, 4×6 prints, TIFF or JPEG files with 300 dpi resolution. Buys one-time rights. Offers no additional payment for photos accepted with ms. Captions, identification of subjects, model releases required.

Tips ''You must know and understand ham radio and ham radio operators. Most of our writers (95%) are licensed hams. Because our readers span a wide area of interests within amateur radio, don't assume they are already familiar with your topic. Explain. At the same time, don't write down to the readers. They are intelligent, well-educated people who will understand what you're saying when written and explained in plain English.''

N $ $ CREATING KEEPSAKES

Scrapbook Magazine, Primedia Enthusiast Group, 14850 Pony Express Rd., Bluffdale UT 84065. (801)984-2070. E-mail: marianne.madsen@primedia.com. Web site: www.creatingkeepsakes.com. **Contact:** Marianne Madsen. Monthly magazine covering scrapbooks. Written for scrapbook lovers and those with a box of photos high in the closet. Circ. 100,000. Editorial lead time 6 weeks. Accepts queries by mail, e-mail. Sample copy not available. Writer's guidelines online.

Nonfiction Accepts articles on a variety of scrapbook and keepsake topics. Query with 2 visuals to illustrate your suggested topic. Length: 800-1,200 words.

Tips ''Should we opt to pursue the article you've proposed, we will ask you to supply the complete article on disk in WordPerfect, Word or ASCII format. Please supply a paper copy as well. The article should be lively and easy to read, contain solid content, and be broken up with subheads or sidebars as appropriate. We will provide additional guidelines to follow upon acceptance of your query.''

N CREATIVE KNITTING

(formerly Knitting Digest), House of White Birches, 306 E. Parr Rd., Berne IN 46711. (260)589-4000. Fax: (260)589-8093. E-mail: editor@creativeknittingmagazine.com. Web site: www.creativeknittingmagazine.com. **Contact:** Bobbie Matela, editor. Bimonthly magazine covering knitting designs and patterns. "We print only occasional articles, but are always open to knitting designs and proposals." Estab. 1993. Circ. 50,000. Pays within 6 months. Publishes ms an average of 11 months after acceptance. Byline given. Buys all rights. Accepts queries by mail, e-mail. Responds in 2 months to queries; 6 months to mss. Writer's guidelines for #10 SASE.

Nonfiction How-to (knitting skills), technical (knitting field). **Buys 4-6 mss/year.** Send complete ms. Length: 500 words maximum. **Pays variable amount. Also pays in contributor copies.**

Tips "Clear concise writing. Humor is appreciated in this field, as much as technical tips. The magazine is a digest, so space is limited. All submissions must be typed and double-spaced."

$ $ DOLLHOUSE MINIATURES

Madavor Media, 420 Boylston St., 5th Floor, Boston MA 02116. (800)437-5828. Web site: www.dhminiatures.com. Editor: Terrence Lynch. **80% freelance written.** Monthly magazine covering dollhouse scale miniatures. "*Dollhouse Miniatures* is America's best-selling miniatures magazine and the definitive resource for artisans, collectors, and hobbyists. It promotes and supports the large national and international community of miniaturists through club columns, short reports, and by featuring reader projects and ideas." Estab. 1971. Circ. 25,000. **Pays on acceptance.** Byline given. Buys all rights. Editorial lead time 6 months. Submit seasonal material 6 months in advance. Accepts queries by mail. Responds in 1 month to queries; 2 months to mss. Sample copy for $4.95. Writer's guidelines online.

Nonfiction How-to (miniature projects of various scales in variety of media), interview/profile (artisans, collectors), photo feature (dollhouses, collections, museums). No articles on miniature shops or essays. **Buys 50-60 mss/year.** Query with or without published clips or send complete ms. Length: 500-1,500 words. **Pays $50-350 for assigned articles; $0-200 for unsolicited articles.**

Photos Send photos with submission. Reviews 35mm slides and larger, 3×5 prints. Buys all rights. Photos are paid for with ms. Seldom buys individual photos. Captions, identification of subjects required.

Tips "Familiarity with the miniatures hobby is very helpful. Accuracy to scale is extremely important to our readers. A complete package (manuscripts/photos) has a better chance of publication."

$ $ DOLLS

Jones Publishing, Inc., 217 Passaic Ave., Hasbrouck Heights NJ 07684. (715)445-5000. Fax: (715)445-4053. E-mail: nrdollsmagazine@earthlink.net. Web site: www.jonespublishing.com. Assistant Editor: Trina Laube. **Contact:** Nayda Rondon, editor. **75% freelance written.** Magazine published 10 times/year covering dolls, doll artists, and related topics of interest to doll collectors and enthusiasts. "*Dolls* enhances the joy of collecting by introducing readers to the best new dolls from around the world, along with the artists and designers who create them. It keeps readers up-to-date on shows, sales and special events in the doll world. With beautiful color photography, *Dolls* offers an array of easy-to-read, informative articles that help our collectors select the best buys." Estab. 1982. Circ. 100,000. Pays on publication. Byline given. Buys first North American serial rights. Accepts queries by mail, e-mail. Responds in 1 month to queries.

Nonfiction Historical/nostalgic, how-to, interview/profile, new product, photo feature. **Buys 55 mss/year.** Query with published clips or send complete ms. Length: 750-1,200 words. **Pays $75-300.**

Photos Send photos with submission. Reviews transparencies. Buys one-time rights. Offers no additional payment for photos accepted with ms. Captions, identification of subjects, model releases required.

Tips "Know the subject matter and artists. Having quality artwork and access to doll artists for interviews are big pluses. We need original ideas of interest to doll lovers."

$ $ FIBERARTS

Contemporary Textile Art and Craft, Interweave Press, 201 E. Fourth St., Loveland CO 80537. (970)613-4679. Fax: (970)669-6117. E-mail: lizg@fiberarts.com. Web site: www.fiberarts.com. **Contact:** Liz Good, assistant editor. **85% freelance written.** Magazine published 5 times/year covering textiles as art and craft (contemporary trends in fiber sculpture, weaving, quilting, surface design, stitchery, papermaking, basketry, felting, wearable art, knitting, fashion, crochet, mixed textile techniques, ethnic dying, eccentric tidbits, etc.) for textile artists, craftspeople, collectors, teachers, museum and gallery staffs, and enthusiasts. Estab. 1975. Circ. 27,000. Pays on publication. Publishes ms an average of 4 months after acceptance. Byline given. Buys first rights. Accepts queries by mail. Sample copy for $6.99. Writer's guidelines online.

Nonfiction "Please be very specific about your proposal. Also, an important consideration in accepting an article is the kind of photos that you can provide as illustration. We like to see photos in advance." Essays, interview/profile (artist), opinion, personal experience, photo feature, technical, education, trends, exhibition reviews, textile news, book reviews, ethnic. Query with brief synopsis, SASE, and visuals. No phone queries. Length: 250-2,000 words. **Pays $70-550.**

Photos Color slides, large-format transparencies, or 300 dpi (5-inch-high) TIFF images must accompany every query. The more photos to choose from, the better. Please include caption information. The names and addresses of those mentioned in the article or to whom the visuals are to be returned are necessary.

Columns/Departments Commentary (thoughtful opinion on a topic of interest to our readers), 400 words; News and Notes; Profiles; The Creative Process; Travel and Traditions; Collecting; Reviews (exhibits and shows; summarize quality, significance, focus and atmosphere, then evaluate selected pieces for aesthetic quality, content and technique—because we have an international readership, brief biographical notes or quotes might be pertinent for locally or regionally known artists). (Do not cite works for which visuals are unavailable; you are not eligible to review a show in which you have participated as an artist, organizer, curator or juror.)

Tips "Our writers are usually familiar with textile techniques and textile-art history, but expertise in historical textiles, art, or design can also qualify a new writer. The writer should also be familiar with *Fiberarts* magazine. The professional is essential to the editorial depth of *Fiberarts* and must find timely information in the pages of the magazine, but our editorial philosophy is that the magazine must provide the non-professional textile enthusiast with the inspiration, support, useful information, and direction to keep him or her excited, interested, and committed. Although we address serious issues relating to the fiber arts as well as light, we're looking for an accessible rather than overly scholarly tone."

$ FIBRE FOCUS

Magazine of the Ontario Handweavers and Spinners, 3212 S. Service Rd. W., Oakville ON L6L 6T1 Canada. Web site: www.ohs.on.ca. **Contact:** Pat Hood, editor. **90% freelance written.** Quarterly magazine covering handweaving, spinning, basketry, beading, and other fibre arts. "Our readers are weavers and spinners who also do dyeing, knitting, basketry, feltmaking, papermaking, sheep raising, and craft supply. All articles deal with some aspect of these crafts." Estab. 1957. Circ. 1,000. Pays within 30 days after publication. Byline given. Buys one-time rights. Editorial lead time 6 months. Submit seasonal material 6 months in advance. Accepts previously published material. Responds in 1 month to queries. Sample copy for $8 Canadian. Writer's guidelines online.

Nonfiction How-to, interview/profile, new product, opinion, personal experience, technical, travel, book reviews. **Buys 40-60 mss/year.** Length: Varies. **Pays $30 Canadian/published page.**

Photos Send photos with submission. Buys one-time rights. Offers additional payment for photos accepted with ms. Captions, identification of subjects required.

Tips "Visit the OHS Web site for current information."

$ $ FINE BOOKS & COLLECTIONS

OP Media, LLC, P.O. Box 106, Eureka CA 95502. E-mail: scott@finebooksmagazine.com. Web site: www.finebooksmagazine.com. **Contact:** P. Scott Brown, managing editor. **90% freelance written.** Bimonthly magazine covering used and antiquarian bookselling and book collecting. "We cover all aspects of selling and collecting out-of-print books. We emphasize good writing, interesting people, and unexpected view points." Estab. 2002. Circ. 5,000. Pays on publication. Publishes ms an average of 4 months after acceptance. Byline given. Offers negotiable kill fee. Buys first North American serial, second serial (reprint), electronic rights, makes work-for-hire assignments. Editorial lead time 4 months. Submit seasonal material 4 months in advance. Accepts queries by mail, e-mail. Accepts previously published material. Accepts simultaneous submissions. Responds in 1 month to queries; 2 months to mss. Sample copy for $6.50. Writer's guidelines online.

Nonfiction Book excerpts, essays, exposé, general interest, historical/nostalgic, how-to, humor, opinion, personal experience, photo feature, travel. Does not want tales of the "gold in my attic" vein; stories emphasizing books as an investment. **Buys 40 mss/year.** Query with published clips. Length: 1,000-5,000 words. **Pays $100-400.** Sometimes pays expenses of writers on assignment.

Photos State availability with submission. Reviews GIF/JPEG files. Buys one-time, plus nonexclusive electronic rights. Negotiates payment individually. Captions, identification of subjects required.

Columns/Departments Digest (news about collectors, booksellers, and bookselling), 350 words; Book Reviews (reviews of books about books, writers, publishers, collecting), 400-800 words.

Tips "Tell compelling stories about people and the passion for book collecting. We aim to make academic writing on books accessible to a broad audience and to enliven the writing of aficionados with solid editing and story development."

$ $ FINE TOOL JOURNAL

Antique & Collectible Tools, Inc., 27 Fickett Rd., Pownal ME 04069. (207)688-4962. Fax: (207)688-4831. E-mail: ceb@finetoolj.com. Web site: www.finetoolj.com. **Contact:** Clarence Blanchard, president. **90% freelance written.** Quarterly magazine specializing in older or antique hand tools from all traditional trades. Readers are primarily interested in woodworking tools, but some subscribers have interests in such areas as leatherworking, wrenches, kitchen, and machinist tools. Readers range from beginners just getting into the hobby to advanced collectors and organizations. Estab. 1970. Circ. 2,500. Pays on publication. Publishes ms an average of 6 months after acceptance. Byline given. Offers $50 kill fee. Buys first, second serial (reprint) rights. Editorial lead time 9 months. Submit seasonal material 6 months in advance. Accepts queries by mail. Accepts previously published material. Responds in 2 months to queries; 3 months to mss. Sample copy for $5. Writer's guidelines for #10 SASE.

Nonfiction "We're looking for articles about tools from all trades. Interests include collecting, preservation, history, values and price trends, traditional methods and uses, interviews with collectors/users/makers, etc. Most articles published will deal with vintage, pre-1950, hand tools. Also seeking articles on how to use specific tools or how a specific trade was carried out. However, how-to articles must be detailed and not just of general interest. We do on occasion run articles on modern toolmakers who produce traditional hand tools." General interest, historical/nostalgic, how-to (make, use, fix and tune tools), interview/profile, personal experience, photo feature, technical. **Buys 24 mss/year.** Send complete ms. Length: 400-2,000 words. **Pays $50-200.** Pays expenses of writers on assignment.

Photos Send photos with submission. Reviews 4×5 prints. Buys all rights. Negotiates payment individually. Identification of subjects, model releases required.

Columns/Departments Stanley Tools (new finds and odd types), 300-400 words; Tips of the Trade (how to use tools), 100-200 words. **Buys 12 mss/year.** Send complete ms. **Pays $30-60.**

Tips "The easiest way to get published in the *Journal* is to have personal experience or know someone who can supply the detailed information. We are seeking articles that go deeper than general interest and that knowledge requires experience and/or research. Short of personal experience, find a subject that fits our needs and that interests you. Spend some time learning the ins and outs of the subject and with hard work and a little luck you will earn the right to write about it."

$ $ FINE WOODWORKING

The Taunton Press, P.O. Box 5506, Newtown CT 06470-5506. (800)926-8776. Fax: (203)270-6753. E-mail: achristiana@taunton.com. Web site: www.taunton.com. Publisher: Anatole Burkin. Editor: Asa Christiana. **Contact:** Betsy Engel. Bimonthly magazine on woodworking in the small shop. "All writers are also skilled woodworkers. It's more important that a contributor be a woodworker than a writer. Our editors (also woodworkers) will provide assistance and travel to shops to shoot all photography needed." Estab. 1975. Circ. 270,000. **Pays on acceptance.** Byline given. Offers variable kill fee. Buys first rights and rights to republish in other forms and media, as well as use in promo pieces. Submit seasonal material 6 months in advance. Accepts simultaneous submissions. Responds in 1 month to queries. Writer's guidelines free and online.

> O‑ "We're looking for good articles on almost all aspects of woodworking from the basics of tool use, stock preparation and joinery, to specialized techniques and finishing. We're especially keen on articles about shop-built tools, jigs and fixtures, or any stage of design, construction, finishing and installation of cabinetry and furniture. Whether the subject involves fundamental methods or advanced techniques, we look for high-quality workmanship, thoughtful designs, and safe and proper procedures."

Nonfiction How-to (woodworking). **Buys 120 mss/year.** Send article outline, any helpful drawings or photos, and proposal letter. **Pays $150/magazine page for assigned articles.** Sometimes pays expenses of writers on assignment.

Columns/Departments Fundamentals (basic how-to and concepts for beginning woodworkers); Master Class (advanced techniques); Finish Line (finishing techniques); Question & Answer (woodworking Q&A); Methods of Work (shop tips); Tools & Materials (short reviews of new tools). **Buys 400 mss/year. Pays $10-150/ published page.**

Tips "Look for authors guidelines and follow them. Stories about woodworking reported by non-woodworkers are *not* used. Our magazine is essentially reader-written by woodworkers."

$ FINESCALE MODELER

Kalmbach Publishing Co., P.O. Box 1612, Waukesha WI 53187. Web site: www.finescale.com. **Contact:** Matt Usher, editor. **80% freelance written.** Eager to work with new/unpublished writers. Magazine published 10 times/year "devoted to how-to-do-it modeling information for scale model builders who build non-operating aircraft, tanks, boats, automobiles, figures, dioramas, and science fiction and fantasy models." Circ. 60,000. **Pays on acceptance.** Publishes ms an average of 14 months after acceptance. Byline given. Buys all rights. Responds in 6 weeks to queries; 3 months to mss. Sample copy for 9×12 SAE and 3 first-class stamps.

> O‑ *Finescale Modeler* is especially looking for how-to articles for auto and aircraft modelers.

Nonfiction How-to (build scale models), technical (research information for building models). Query or send complete ms. Length: 750-3,000 words. **Pays $60/published page minimum.**

Photos Send photos with submission. Reviews transparencies, color prints. Buys one-time rights. Pays $7.50

minimum for transparencies and $5 minimum for color prints. Captions, identification of subjects required.
Columns/Departments *FSM* Showcase (photos plus description of model); *FSM* Tips and Techniques (model building hints and tips). **Buys 25-50 mss/year.** Send complete ms. **Pays $25-50.**
Tips "A freelancer can best break in first through hints and tips, then through feature articles. Most people who write for *FSM* are modelers first, writers second. This is a specialty magazine for a special, quite expert audience. Essentially, 99% of our writers will come from that audience."

$ $ THE HOME SHOP MACHINIST

2779 Aero Park Dr., Traverse City MI 49686. (616)946-3712. Fax: (616)946-3289. E-mail: nknopf@villagepress.com. Web site: www.homeshopmachinist.net. **Contact:** Neil Knopf, editor. **95% freelance written.** Bimonthly magazine covering machining and metalworking for the hobbyist. Circ. 34,000. Pays on publication. Publishes ms an average of 2 years after acceptance. Byline given. Buys first North American serial rights. Responds in 2 months to queries. Sample copy for free. Writer's guidelines for 9×12 SASE.
Nonfiction How-to (projects designed to upgrade present shop equipment or hobby model projects that require machining), technical (should pertain to metalworking, machining, drafting, layout, welding or foundry work for the hobbyist). No fiction or "people" features. **Buys 40 mss/year.** Query with or without published clips or send complete ms. Length: open—"whatever it takes to do a thorough job." **Pays $40/published page, plus $9/published photo.**
Photos Send photos with submission. Pays $9-40 for 5×7 b&w prints; $70/page for camera-ready art; $40 for b&w cover photo. Captions, identification of subjects required.
Columns/Departments Book Reviews; New Product Reviews; Micro-Machining; Foundry. Length: 600-1,500 words. **Buys 25-30 mss/year.** Query. **Pays $40-70.**
Fillers Machining tips/shortcuts. **Buys 12-15/year.** Length: 100-300 words. **Pays $30-48.**
Tips "The writer should be experienced in the area of metalworking and machining; should be extremely thorough in explanations of methods, processes—always with an eye to safety; and should provide good quality b&w photos and/or clear dimensioned drawings to aid in description. Visuals are of increasing importance to our readers. Carefully planned photos, drawings and charts will carry a submission to our magazine much farther along the path to publication."

$ $ KITPLANES

For Designers, Builders, and Pilots of Experimental Aircraft, A Primedia Publication, 239 New Rd., Suite B-201, Parsippany NJ 07054. (973)227-7660. Fax: (973)227-7630. E-mail: editorial@kitplanes.com. Web site: www.kitplanes.com. **Contact:** Brian Clark, editor. **80% freelance written.** Eager to work with new/unpublished writers. Monthly magazine covering self-construction of private aircraft for pilots and builders. Estab. 1984. Circ. 72,000. Pays on publication. Publishes ms an average of 3 months after acceptance. Byline given. Buys complete rights, except book rights. Submit seasonal material 6 months in advance. Accepts queries by mail, e-mail. Responds in 2 weeks to queries; 6 weeks to mss. Sample copy for $6. Writer's guidelines online.
Nonfiction "We are looking for articles on specific construction techniques, the use of tools—both hand and power—in aircraft building, the relative merits of various materials, conversions of engines from automobiles for aviation use, and installation of instruments and electronics." General interest, how-to, interview/profile, new product, personal experience, photo feature, technical. No general-interest aviation articles, or "My First Solo" type of articles. **Buys 80 mss/year.** Query. Length: 500-3,000 words. **Pays $70-600 including story photos for assigned articles.**
Photos State availability of or send photos with submission. Buys one-time rights. Pays $300 for cover photos. Captions, identification of subjects required.
Tips "*Kitplanes* contains very specific information—a writer must be extremely knowledgeable in the field. Major features are entrusted only to known writers. I cannot emphasize enough that articles must be directed at the individual aircraft builder. We need more 'how-to' photo features in all areas of homebuilt aircraft."

N $ $ KNIVES ILLUSTRATED

The Premier Cutlery Magazine, 265 S. Anita Dr., Suite 120, Orange CA 92868. (714)939-9991. Fax: (714)939-9909. E-mail: editorial@knivesillustrated.com. Web site: www.knivesillustrated.com. **Contact:** J. Bruce Voyles, editor. **40-50% freelance written.** Bimonthly magazine covering high-quality factory and custom knives. "We publish articles on different types of factory and custom knives, how-to make knives, technical articles, shop tours, articles on knife makers and artists. Must have knowledge about knives and the people who use and make them. We feature the full range of custom and high tech production knives, from miniatures to swords, leaving nothing untouched. We're also known for our outstanding how-to articles and technical features on equipment, materials and knife making supplies. We do not feature knife maker profiles as such, although we do spotlight some makers by featuring a variety of their knives and insight into their background and philosophy." Estab. 1987. Circ. 35,000. Pays on publication. Byline given. Editorial lead time 3 months. Accepts queries

by mail, e-mail, fax. Responds in 2 weeks to queries. Sample copy available. Writer's guidelines for #10 SASE.
Nonfiction General interest, historical/nostalgic, how-to, interview/profile, new product, photo feature, technical. **Buys 35-40 mss/year.** Query. Length: 400-2,000 words. **Pays $100-500.**
Photos Send photos with submission. Reviews 35mm, 2¼ × 2¼, 4×5 transparencies, 5×7 prints, electronic images in TIFF, GIF or JPEG Mac format. Negotiates payment individually. Captions, identification of subjects, model releases required.
Tips "Most of our contributors are involved with knives, either as collectors, makers, engravers, etc. To write about this subject requires knowledge. Writers can do OK if they study some recent issues. If you are interested in submitting work to *Knives Illustrated* magazine, it is suggested you analyze at least 2 or 3 different editions to get a feel for the magazine. It is also recommended that you call or mail in your query to determine if we are interested in the topic you have in mind. While verbal or written approval may be given, all articles are still received on a speculation basis. We cannot approve any article until we have it in hand, whereupon we will make a final decision as to its suitability for our use. Bear in mind we do not suggest you go to the trouble to write an article if there is doubt we can use it promptly."

LAPIDARY JOURNAL

300 Chesterfield Parkway, Suite 100, Malvern PA 19355. (610)232-5700. Fax: (610)232-5756. E-mail: ljeditorial@interweave.com. Web site: www.lapidaryjournal.com. **70% freelance written.** Monthly magazine covering gem, bead and jewelry arts. "Our audience is hobbyists who usually have some knowledge of and proficiency in the subject before they start reading. Our style is conversational and informative. There are how-to projects and profiles of artists and materials." Estab. 1947. Circ. 53,000. **Pays on acceptance.** Publishes ms an average of 4 months after acceptance. Byline given. Buys one-time and worldwide rights. Editorial lead time 3 months. Accepts queries by mail, e-mail. Sample copy online.
Nonfiction Looks for conversational and lively narratives with quotes and anecdotes; Q&As; interviews. How-to (jewelry/craft), interview/profile, new product, personal experience, technical, travel. Special issues: Bead Annual, Jewelry Design issue, Jewelry Arts Awards, Bead Arts Awards, Gemmy's, Annual Buyers' Directory. **Buys 100 mss/year.** Query. Length: 1,500-2,500 words preferred; 1,000-3,500 words acceptable; longer works occasionally published serially.
Reprints Send photocopy.
Tips "Some knowledge of jewelry, gemstones and/or minerals is a definite asset. Step-by-Step is a section within *Lapidary Journal* that offers illustrated, step-by-step instruction in gem cutting, jewelry making, and beading. Please request a copy of the Step-by-Step guidelines for greater detail."

$ $ THE LEATHER CRAFTERS & SADDLERS JOURNAL

331 Annette Court, Rhinelander WI 54501-2902. (715)362-5393. Fax: (715)362-5391. E-mail: tworjournal@newnorth.net. Co-Publisher: Dorothea Reis. **Contact:** William R. Reis, editor/co-publisher. **100% freelance written.** Bimonthly magazine. "A leather-working publication with how-to, step-by-step instructional articles using full-size patterns for leathercraft, leather art, custom saddle, boot and harness making, etc. A complete resource for leather, tools, machinery, and allied materials, plus leather industry news." Estab. 1990. Circ. 8,000. Pays on publication. Publishes ms an average of 4 months after acceptance. Byline given. Buys first North American serial, second serial (reprint) rights. Submit seasonal material 6 months in advance. Accepts queries by mail, e-mail, fax, phone. Accepts previously published material. Accepts simultaneous submissions. Responds in 1 month to mss. Sample copy for $6. Writer's guidelines for #10 SASE.

O→ Break in with a how-to, step-by-step leather item article from beginner through masters and saddlemaking.

Nonfiction "I want only articles that include hands-on, step-by-step, how-to information." How-to (crafts and arts, and any other projects using leather). **Buys 75 mss/year.** Send complete ms. Length: 500-2,500 words. **Pays $20-250 for assigned articles; $20-150 for unsolicited articles.**
Reprints Send tearsheet or photocopy. Pays 50% of amount paid for an original article.
Photos Send good contrast color print photos and full-size patterns and/or full-size photo-carve patterns with submission. Lack of these reduces payment amount. Captions required.
Columns/Departments Beginners; Intermediate; Artists; Western Design; Saddlemakers; International Design; and Letters (the open exchange of information between all peoples). Length: 500-2,500 words on all. **Buys 75 mss/year.** Send complete ms. **Pays $5-20.**
Tips "We want to work with people who understand and know leathercraft and are interested in passing on their knowledge to others. We would prefer to interview people who have achieved a high level in leathercraft skill."

$ LINN'S STAMP NEWS

Amos Press, P.O. Box 29, Sidney OH 45365. (937)498-0801. Fax: (937)498-0886. Web site: www.linns.com. **50% freelance written.** Weekly tabloid on the stamp collecting hobby. All articles must be about philatelic

Consumer Magazines

collectibles. Our goal at *Linn's* is to create a weekly publication that is indispensable to stamp collectors. Estab. 1928. Circ. 39,000. Pays within 1 month of publication. Publishes ms an average of 3 months after acceptance. Byline given. Buys first print and electronic rights. Submit seasonal material 2 months in advance. Responds in 6 weeks to queries. Sample copy for free. Writer's guidelines online.

Nonfiction General interest, historical/nostalgic, how-to, interview/profile, technical, club and show news, current issues, auction realization and recent discoveries. ''No articles merely giving information on background of stamp subject. Must have philatelic information included.'' **Buys 50 mss/year.** Send complete ms. Length: 500 words maximum. **Pays $50.** Sometimes pays expenses of writers on assignment.

Photos Good illustrations a must. Provide captions on a separate sheet of paper. Send scans with submission. Reviews digital color at twice actual size (300 dpi). Buys all rights. Offers no additional payment for photos accepted with ms. Captions required.

Tips ''Check and double check all facts. Footnotes and bibliographies are not appropriate to newspaper style. Work citation into the text. Even though your subject might be specialized, write understandably. Explain terms. *Linn's* features are aimed at a broad audience of relatively novice collectors. Keep this audience in mind. Provide information in such a way to make stamp collecting more interesting to more people.''

$ LOST TREASURE, INC.

P.O. Box 451589, Grove OK 74345. (918)786-2182. Fax: (918)786-2192. E-mail: managingeditor@losttreasure.com. Web site: www.losttreasure.com. **Contact:** Jann Clark, managing editor. **75% freelance written.** Monthly and annual magazines covering lost treasure. Estab. 1966. Circ. 55,000. Pays on publication. Byline given. Buys all rights. Accepts queries by mail, e-mail, fax. Responds in 1 month to queries; 2 months to mss. Sample copy for #10 SASE. Writer's guidelines for 10×13 SAE with $1.47 postage or online.

Nonfiction *Lost Treasure* is composed of lost treasure stories, legends, how-to articles, treasure hunting club news, who's who in treasure hunting, tips. Length: 500-1,200 words. *Treasure Cache*, an annual, contains stories about documented treasure caches with a sidebar from the author telling the reader how to search for the cache highlighted in the story. **Buys 225 mss/year.** Query on *Treasure Cache* only. Length: 1,000-2,000 words. **Pays 4¢/word.**

Photos Color or b&w prints, hand-drawn or copied maps, art with source credit with mss will help sell your story.We are always looking for cover photos with or without accompanying ms. Pays $100/published cover photo. Must be vertical 35mm color slides or negatives. Pays $5/published photo. Captions required.

Tips ''We are only interested in treasures that can be found with metal detectors. Queries welcome but not required. If you write about famous treasures and lost mines, be sure we haven't used your selected topic recently—the story must have a new slant or new information. Source documentation required. How-tos should cover some aspect of treasure hunting and how-to steps should be clearly defined. If you have a *Treasure Cache* story we will, if necessary, help the author with the sidebar telling how to search for the cache in the story. *Lost Treasure* articles should coordinate with theme issues when possible.''

MCCALL'S QUILTING

Primedia Enthusiast Group, 741 Corporate Circle, Suite A, Golden CO 80401. (303)278-1010. Fax: (303)277-0370. Web site: www.mccallsquilting.com. Publisher: Tina Battock. **Contact:** Beth Hayes, editor. Bimonthly magazine covering quiltmaking. Attracts quilters of all skill levels with a variety of complete, how-to quilting projects, including bed size quilts, wall hangings, wearables, and small projects. Estab. 1993. Circ. 162,000. Buys limited exclusive copyright license. Editorial lead time 6-9 months. Submit seasonal material 6-9 months in advance. Accepts queries by mail. Sample copy for $5.95. Writer's guidelines by e-mail.

Tips ''For any design or article, include a detailed description of the project to help us make an informed decision.''

$ MODEL RAILROADER

P.O. Box 1612, Waukesha WI 53187. Fax: (262)796-1142. E-mail: mrmag@mrmag.com. Web site: www.trains.com. **Contact:** Terry Thompson, editor/publisher. Monthly magazine for hobbyists interested in scale model railroading. ''We publish articles on all aspects of model-railroading and on prototype (real) railroading as a subject for modeling.'' Byline given. Buys exclusive rights. Accepts queries by mail, e-mail, fax. Responds in 2 months to queries.

O━ ''Study publication before submitting material.'' First-hand knowledge of subject almost always necessary for acceptable slant.

Nonfiction Wants construction articles on specific model railroad projects (structures, cars, locomotives, scenery, benchwork, etc.). Also photo stories showing model railroads. Query. **Pays base rate of $90/page.**

Photos Buys photos with detailed descriptive captions only. Pays $15 and up, depending on size and use.

Tips ''Before you prepare and submit any article, you should write us a short letter of inquiry describing what you want to do. We can then tell you if it fits our needs and save you from working on something we don't want.''

$ MONITORING TIMES

Grove Enterprises, Inc., 7540 Hwy. 64 W., Brasstown NC 28902-0098. (828)837-9200. Fax: (828)837-2216. E-mail: editor@monitoringtimes.com. Web site: www.monitoringtimes.com. Publisher: Robert Grove. **Contact:** Rachel Baughn, editor. **15% freelance written.** Monthly magazine for radio hobbyists. Estab. 1982. Circ. 15,000. Pays on publication. Publishes ms an average of 4 months after acceptance. Byline given. Buys first North American serial, second serial (reprint) rights. Submit seasonal material 4 months in advance. Accepts queries by mail, e-mail. Accepts previously published material. Responds in 1 month to queries. Sample copy for 9×12 SAE and 9 first-class stamps. Writer's guidelines online.

Break in with a shortwave station profile or topic, or scanning topics of broad interest.

Nonfiction General interest, how-to, humor, interview/profile, personal experience, photo feature, technical. **Buys 50 mss/year.** Query. Length: 1,500-3,000 words. **Pays average of $50/published page.**

Reprints Send photocopy and information about when and where the material previously appeared. Pays 50% of amount paid for an original article.

Photos Send photos with submission. Buys one-time rights. Captions required.

Tips "Need articles on radio communications systems and shortwave broadcasters. We are accepting more technical projects."

N $ NATIONAL COMMUNICATIONS MAGAZINE

Norm Schrein, Inc., P.O. Box 291918, Kettering OH 45429. (937)299-7226. Fax: (937)299-1323. E-mail: norm@bearcat1.com. Web site: www.nat-com.org. Managing Editor: Peggy Lockhart. **Contact:** Norm Schrein, editor. **100% freelance written.** Bimonthly magazine covering radio as a hobby. Estab. 1990. Circ. 5,000. Pays on publication. Publishes ms an average of 2 months after acceptance. Byline given. Buys all rights. Editorial lead time 2 months. Submit seasonal material 2 months in advance. Accepts queries by phone. Accepts previously published material. Accepts simultaneous submissions. Sample copy for $4.

Nonfiction How-to, interview/profile, new product, personal experience, photo feature, technical. Does not want articles off topic of the publication's audience (radio hobbyists). **Buys 2-3 mss/year.** Query. Length: 300 words. **Pays $75+.**

Photos Send photos with submission. Reviews GIF/JPEG files. Buys all rights. Offers no additional payment for photos accepted with ms. Captions, identification of subjects required.

⊘ OLD CARS PRICE GUIDE

Krause Publications, a Division of F+W Publications, Inc., 700 E. State St., Iola WI 54990-0001. (715)445-2214. Fax: (715)445-4087. E-mail: oldcarspg@fwpubs.com. Web site: www.oldcarspriceguide.net. Editor: Ron Kowalke. Bimonthly magazine covering collector vehicle values. Estab. 1978. Circ. 60,000. Sample copy for free.

- This publication is testing a new format and is not accepting freelance submissions at this time.

PACK-O-FUN

Projects For Kids & Families, Clapper Communications, 2400 Devon Ave., Des Plaines IL 60018-4618. (847)635-5800. Web site: www.pack-o-fun.com. Bimonthly magazine covering crafts and activities for kids and those working with kids. Estab. 1951. Circ. 102,000. Pays 45 days after signed contract. Byline given. Buys all rights. Editorial lead time 6 months. Submit seasonal material 6 months in advance. Accepts queries by mail, e-mail, fax. Accepts previously published material. Accepts simultaneous submissions. Responds in 2 months to queries. Sample copy for $9.95 or online.

Nonfiction "We request fun, constructive, inexpensive crafts and activities. Projects must be original, and complete instructions are required upon acceptance." **Payment negotiable.**

Reprints Send tearsheet and information about when and where the material previously appeared.

Photos Photos of project may be submitted in place of project at query stage.

Tips "*Pack-O-Fun* is looking for original how-to projects for kids and those working with kids. Write simple instructions for crafts to be done by children ages 5-13 years. We're looking for recyclable ideas for throwaways. We accept fiction if accompanied by a craft or in skit form (appropriate for classrooms, scouts, or Bible school groups). It would be helpful to check out our magazine before submitting."

$ $ PAPERCRAFTS MAGAZINE

Primedia Magazines, 14850 Pony Express Rd., Bluffdale UT 84065. (801)984-2070. Fax: (801)984-2080. E-mail: editor@papercraftsmag.com. Web site: www.papercraftsmag.com. Magazine published 10 times/year designed to help readers make creative and rewarding handmade crafts. The main focus is fresh, craft-related projects our reader can make and display in her home or give as gifts. Estab. 1978. Circ. 300,000. **Pays on acceptance.** Byline given. Buys all rights. Editorial lead time 6 months. Accepts queries by mail, e-mail. Responds in 1 month to queries. Writer's guidelines for #10 SASE.

Nonfiction How-to. **Buys 300 mss/year.** Query with photo or sketch of how-to project. Do not send the actual project until request. **Pays $100-500 for assigned articles.**

Tips "We are looking for projects that are fresh, innovative, and in sync with today's trends. We accept projects made with a variety of techniques and media. Projects can fall in several categories, ranging from home decor to gifts, garden accessories to jewelry, and other seasonal craft projects. Submitted projects must be original, never-before-published, copyright-free work that use readily available materials."

$ PIECEWORK MAGAZINE

Interweave Press, Inc., 201 E. 4th St., Loveland CO 80537-5655. (970)669-7672. Fax: (970)667-8317. E-mail: piecework@interweave.com. Web site: www.interweave.com. **90% freelance written.** Bimonthly magazine covering needlework history. "*PieceWork* celebrates the rich tradition of needlework and the history of the people behind it. Stories and projects on embroidery, cross-stitch, knitting, crocheting, and quilting, along with other textile arts, are featured in each issue." Estab. 1993. Circ. 60,000. Pays on publication. Byline given. Offers 30% kill fee. Buys first North American serial rights. Editorial lead time 6 months. Submit seasonal material 6 months in advance. Accepts queries by mail, e-mail, fax, phone. Responds in 6 months to queries. Sample copy and writer's guidelines free.

Nonfiction Book excerpts, historical/nostalgic, how-to, interview/profile, new product. No contemporary needlework articles. **Buys 25-30 mss/year.** Send complete ms. Length: 1,000-5,000 words. **Pays $100/printed page.**

Photos State availability of or send photos with submission. Reviews transparencies, prints. Buys one-time rights. Captions, identification of subjects, model releases required.

Tips "Submit a well-researched article on a historical aspect of needlework complete with information on visuals and suggestion for accompanying project."

$ POPULAR COMMUNICATIONS

CQ Communications, Inc., 25 Newbridge Rd., Hicksville NY 11801. (516)681-2922. Fax: (516)681-2926. E-mail: popularcom@aol.com. Web site: www.popular-communications.com. **Contact:** Harold Ort, editor. **25% freelance written.** Monthly magazine covering the radio communications hobby. Estab. 1982. Circ. 40,000. Pays on publication. Publishes ms an average of 6 months after acceptance. Byline given. Buys first North American serial rights. Editorial lead time 3 months. Submit seasonal material 6 months in advance. Accepts queries by mail, e-mail. Responds in 1 month to queries; 2 months to mss. Sample copy for free. Writer's guidelines for #10 SASE.

Nonfiction General interest, how-to (antenna construction), humor, new product, photo feature, technical. **Buys 6-10 mss/year.** Query. Length: 1,800-3,000 words. **Pays $35/printed page.**

Photos State availability with submission. Negotiates payment individually. Captions, identification of subjects, model releases required.

Tips "Either be a radio enthusiast or know one who can help you before sending us an article."

$$$$ POPULAR MECHANICS

Hearst Corp., 300 W. 57th St., New York NY 10019. (212)649-2000. E-mail: popularmechanics@hearst.com. Web site: www.popularmechanics.com. **Contact:** Don Chaikin (auto); Glenn Derene (technology, electronics, computers); Roy Berendsohn (home); Jennifer Bogo (science). **Up to 50% freelance written.** Monthly magazine on technology, science, automotive, home, outdoors. "We are a men's service magazine that addresses the diverse interests of today's male, providing him with information to improve the way he lives. We cover stories from do-it-yourself projects to technological advances in aerospace, military, automotive and so on." Estab. 1902. Circ. 1,200,000. Publishes ms an average of 6 months after acceptance. Offers 25% kill fee. Submit seasonal material 6 months in advance.

- **Pays $1/word and up.**

$$ POPULAR WOODWORKING

F+W Publications, Inc., 4700 E. Galbraith Rd., Cincinnati OH 45236. (513)531-2690, ext. 1348. E-mail: megan.fitzpatrick@fwpubs.com. Web site: www.popularwoodworking.com. Publisher: Steve Shanesy. Editor: Christopher Schwarz. **Contact:** Megan Fitzpatrick, managing editor. **45% freelance written.** Magazine published 7 times/year. "*Popular Woodworking* invites woodworkers of all levels into a community of professionals who share their hard-won shop experience through in-depth projects and technique articles, which help the readers hone their existing skills and develop new ones. Related stories increase the readers' understanding and enjoyment of their craft. Any project submitted must be aesthetically pleasing, of sound construction, and offer a challenge to readers. On the average, we use 4 freelance features per issue. Our primary needs are 'how-to' articles on woodworking. Our secondary need is for articles that will inspire discussion concerning woodworking. Tone of articles should be conversational and informal, as if the writer is speaking directly to the reader.

Our readers are the woodworking hobbyist and small woodshop owner. Writers should have an extensive knowledge of woodworking, or be able to communicate information gained from woodworkers." Estab. 1981. Circ. 200,000. **Pays on acceptance.** Publishes ms an average of 10 months after acceptance. Byline given. Buys first world rights rights. Submit seasonal material 6 months in advance. Accepts queries by mail, e-mail, fax, phone. Accepts previously published material. Responds in 2 months to queries. Sample copy for $4.50 and 9×12 SAE with 6 first-class stamps or online. Writer's guidelines online.

O→ "The project must be well-designed, well-constructed, well-built and well-finished. Technique pieces must have practical application."

Nonfiction How-to (on woodworking projects, with plans), humor (woodworking anecdotes), technical (woodworking techniques). No tool reviews. **Buys 40 mss/year.** Query with or without published clips or send complete ms. **Pay starts at $150/published page.**

Reprints Send photocopy with rights for sale noted and information about when and where the material previously appeared. Pays 25% of amount paid for an original article.

Photos Photographic quality affects acceptance. Need sharp close-up color photos of step-by-step construction process. Send photos with submission. Reviews digital images. Captions, identification of subjects required.

Columns/Departments Tricks of the Trade (helpful techniques), Out of the Woodwork (thoughts on woodworking as a profession or hobby, can be humorous or serious), 500-1,500 words. **Buys 20 mss/year.** Query.

Tips "Write an 'Out of the Woodwork' column for us and then follow up with photos of your projects. Submissions should include materials list, complete diagrams (blueprints not necessary), and discussion of the step-by-step process. We have become more selective on accepting only practical, attractive projects with quality construction. We are also looking for more original topics for our other articles."

N $QST

American Radio Relay League, 225 Main St., Newington CT 06111. (860)594-0200. Fax: (860)594-0259. E-mail: qst@arrl.org. Web site: www.arrl.org. Editor: Steve Ford. **Contact:** Joel Kleinman, managing editor. **90% freelance written.** Monthly magazine covering amateur radio. "*QST* is an ARRL membership journal covering subjects of interest to amateur ('ham') radio operators." Estab. 1915. Circ. 150,000. Pays on publication. Publishes ms an average of 6 months after acceptance. Byline given. Buys all rights. Editorial lead time 6 months. Submit seasonal material 6 months in advance. Accepts queries by mail, e-mail, fax, phone. Responds in 1 week to queries; 1 month to mss. Sample copy not available. Writer's guidelines online.

Nonfiction General interest, how-to, technical. Query. Length: 900-3,000 words. **Pays $65-125.** Sometimes pays expenses of writers on assignment.

Photos Send photos with submission. Reviews GIF/JPEG files. Buys all rights. Offers no additional payment for photos accepted with ms. Captions, identification of subjects required.

Tips "Submissions must relate to amateur 'ham' radio."

N QUILT MAKER

Primedia Enthusiast Group, 741 Corporate Circle, Suite A, Golden CO 80401. (303)278-1010. Fax: (303)277-0370. E-mail: quiltmaker@primedia.com. Web site: www.quiltmaker.com. Editor: Brenda Bauermeister Groelz. Bimonthly magazine for quilters that provides original and appealing designs, patters, and instructions for the successful completion of a quilt and/or quilting projects. Circ. 145,000. Editorial lead time 6 months. Accepts queries by mail. Writer's guidelines online.

O→ Original quilt designs may be submitted to the magazine through its design contest. Winners get $150 and publication credit in the magazine.

Nonfiction

Photos High-resolution digital photos of complete quilts may be submitted for the Sew to Speak column (sewtospeak@quiltmaker.com).

$ $THE QUILTER

All American Crafts, Inc., 7 Waterloo Rd., Stanhope NJ 07874. (973)347-6900. E-mail: editors@thequiltermag.com. Web site: www.thequiltermag.com. **Contact:** Laurette Koserowski, editor. **45% freelance written.** Bimonthly magazine on quilting. Estab. 1988. Pays on publication. Publishes ms an average of 6 months after acceptance. Byline given. Submit seasonal material 6 months in advance. Accepts queries by mail, phone. Responds in 2 months to queries. Sample copy for 9×12 SAE and 4 first-class stamps. Writer's guidelines online.

Nonfiction Quilts and quilt patterns with instructions, quilt-related projects, interview/profile, photo feature—all quilt related. Query with published clips. Length: 350-1,000 words. **Pays 10-12¢/word.**

Photos Send photos with submission. Reviews transparencies, prints. Buys one-time or all rights. Offers $10-15/photo. Captions, identification of subjects required.

Columns/Departments Feature Teacher (qualified quilt teachers with teaching involved—with slides); Profile (award-winning and interesting quilters). Length: 1,000 words maximum. **Pays 10¢/word, $15/photo.**

QUILTER'S NEWSLETTER MAGAZINE

Primedia Enthusiast Group, 741 Corporate Circle, Suite A, Golden CO 80401. (303)278-1010. Fax: (303)277-0370. Web site: www.quiltersnewsletter.com. Publisher: Tina Battock. **Contact:** Jan Magee, senior editor. Magazine published 10 times/year covering quilt making. Written for quilt enthusiasts. Estab. 1969. Circ. 185,000. Pays on publication. Accepts queries by mail. Sample copy and writer's guidelines online.

Nonfiction SASE Returns. Historical/nostalgic, how-to (design techniques, presentation of a single technique or concept with step-by-step approach), interview/profile, new product, reviews (quilt books and videos). Send complete ms.

Photos Color only, no b&w. Reviews 2×2, 4×5 or larger transparencies, 35mm slides, digital hi-res photos (300 dpi or higher). Negotiates payment individually. Captions required.

Tips "Our decision will be based on the freshness of the material, the interest of the material to our readers, whether we have recently published similar material or already have something similar in our inventory, how well it fits into the balance of the material we have on hand, how much rewriting or editing we think it will require, and the quality of the slides, photos or illustrations you include."

N $ $ QUILTER'S WORLD

185 Sweet Rd., Lincoln ME 04457. (260)794-3290. E-mail: editor@quilters-world.com. Web site: www.quilters-world.com. **Contact:** Sandra L. Hatch, editor. **100% freelance written.** Works with a small number of new/unpublished writers each year. Bimonthly magazine covering quilting. "*Quilter's World* is a general quilting publication. We accept articles about special quilters, techniques, coverage of unusual quilts at quilt shows, special interest quilts, human interest articles and patterns. We include 12-15 patterns in every issue. Reader is 30-70 years old, midwestern." Circ. 130,000. Pays 45 days after acceptance. Byline given. Buys all rights. Submit seasonal material 10 months in advance. Accepts queries by mail, e-mail. Responds in 3 months to queries. Writer's guidelines online.

Nonfiction How-to, interview/profile (quilters), new product (quilt products), photo feature, technical. Query or send complete ms. **Pays $50-550.**

Photos State availability with submission. Reviews Color slides. Captions required.

Tips "Read several recent issues for style and content."

$ QUILTWORKS TODAY

Chitra Publications, 2 Public Ave., Montrose PA 18801. (570)278-1984. Fax: (570)278-2223. E-mail: chitraed@epix.net. Web site: www.quilttownusa.com. **Contact:** Connie Ellsworth, production manager. **40% freelance written.** Bimonthly magazine covering quilting, traditional and contemporary. "We seek articles with 1 or 2 magazine pages of text, and quilts that illustrate the content. (Each page of text is approximately 750 words, 6,500 characters, or 3 double-spaced typewritten pages.) Please submit double-spaced manuscripts with wide margins. Submit your article in both hard copy and on a MacIntosh formatted disk, or if using a PC, save as MS-DOS text." Estab. 2002. Circ. 70,000. Pays on publication. Publishes ms an average of 6 months after acceptance. Byline given. Buys second serial (reprint) rights. Submit seasonal material 8 months in advance. Accepts queries by mail, e-mail, fax. Responds in 1 month to queries; 2 months to mss. Writer's guidelines online.

Nonfiction How-to (for various quilting techniques), interview/profile, new product, personal experience, photo feature, instructional, quilting education. **Buys 12-18 mss/year.** Query or send complete ms. **Pays $75/full page of published text.**

Reprints Send photocopy and information about when and where the material previously appeared.

Photos Send photos with submission. Reviews 35mm slides and larger transparenices (color). Offers $20/photo. Captions, identification of subjects required.

Tips "Our publication appeals to new and experienced traditional quilters."

N $ $ RAILMODEL JOURNAL

Golden Bell Press, Inc., 2403 Champa St., Denver CO 80205. (303)296-1600. Fax: (303)295-2159. Web site: www.railmodeljournal.com. **Contact:** Robert Schleicher, editor. **80% freelance written.** Monthly magazine for advanced model railroaders. "We use step-by-step how-to articles with photos of realistic and authentic models." Estab. 1989. Circ. 15,000. Pays on publication. Byline given. Buys first, second serial (reprint) rights. Editorial lead time 6 months. Submit seasonal material 6 months in advance. Responds in 4 months to queries; 8 months to mss. Sample copy for $5.50. Writer's guidelines free.

Nonfiction Historical/nostalgic, how-to, photo feature, technical. No beginner articles or anything that could even be mistaken for a toy train. **Buys 70-100 mss/year.** Query. Length: 200-5,000 words. **Pays $60-800.** Sometimes pays expenses of writers on assignment.

Photos Send photos with submission. Reviews contact sheets, 35mm transparencies, 5×7 prints. Buys one-time and reprint rights. Captions, identification of subjects, model releases required.

Tips "Writers must understand dedicated model railroaders who recreate 100% of their model cars, locomotives, buildings, and scenes from specific real-life prototypes. Close-up photos are a must."

$ RENAISSANCE MAGAZINE

One Controls Dr., Shelton CT 06484. (800)232-2224. Fax: (800)775-2729. E-mail: editor@renaissancemagazine.com. Web site: www.renaissancemagazine.com. **Contact:** Managing editor. **90% freelance written.** Bimonthly magazine covering the history of the Middle Ages and the Renaissance. "Our readers include historians, reenactors, roleplayers, medievalists, and Renaissance Faire enthusiasts." Estab. 1996. Circ. 33,000. Pays on publication. Publishes ms an average of 1 year after acceptance. Byline given. Buys first North American serial rights. Editorial lead time 6 months. Submit seasonal material 4 months in advance. Accepts queries by mail, e-mail, fax, phone. Accepts previously published material. Responds in 3 weeks to queries; 2 months to mss. Sample copy for $9. Writer's guidelines online.

- The editor reports an interest in seeing costuming "how-to" articles; and Renaissance Festival "insider" articles.

O‑ Break in by submitting short (500-1,000 word) articles as fillers or querying on upcoming theme issues.

Nonfiction Essays, exposé, historical/nostalgic, how-to, interview/profile, new product, opinion, photo feature, religious, travel. **Buys 25 mss/year.** Query or send ms. Length: 1,000-5,000 words. **Pays 8¢/word.**

Photos State availability with submission. Reviews contact sheets, negatives, transparencies, prints. Buys all rights. Pays $7.50/photo. Captions, identification of subjects, model releases required.

Tips "Send in all articles in the standard manuscript format with photos/slides or illustrations for suggested use. Writers *must* be open to critique, and all historical articles should also include a recommended reading list. A SASE must be included to receive a response to any submission."

$ $ ROCK & GEM

The Earth's Treasures, Minerals and Jewelry, Miller Magazines, Inc., 290 Maple Court, Suite 232, Ventura CA 93003-7783. (805)644-3824, ext. 29. Fax: (805)644-3875. E-mail: editor@rockngem.com. Web site: www.rockngem.com. **Contact:** Lynn Varon, managing editor. **99% freelance written.** Monthly magazine covering rockhounding field trips, how-to lapidiary projects, minerals, fossils, gold prospecting, mining, etc. "This is not a scientific journal. Its articles appeal to amateurs, beginners, and experts, but its tone is conversational and casual, not stuffy. It's for hobbyists." Estab. 1971. Circ. 55,000. Pays on publication. Byline given. Buys first worldwide serial and electronic reprint rights. Editorial lead time 4 months. Submit seasonal material 6 months in advance. Accepts queries by mail. Writer's guidelines online.

- Contributor agreement required.

Nonfiction General interest, how-to, personal experience, photo feature, travel. Does not want to see "The 25th Anniversary of the Pet Rock," or anything so scientific that it could be a thesis. **Buys 156-200 mss/year.** Send complete ms. Length: 2,000-4,000 words. **Pays $100-250.**

Photos Accepts prints, slides or digital art on disk or CD only (provide thumbnails). Send photos with submission. Offers no additional payment for photos accepted with ms. Captions required.

Tips "We're looking for more how-to articles and field trips with maps. Read writers guidelines very carefully and follow all instructions in them. Then be patient. Your manuscript may be published within a month or even a year from date of submission."

$ SCALE AUTO

Kalmbach Publishing Co., 21027 Crossroads Circle, P.O. Box 1612, Waukesha WI 53187-1612. (262)796-8776. Fax: (262)796-1383. E-mail: jhaught@kalmbach.com. Web site: www.scaleautomag.com. **Contact:** Jim Haught, editor. **70% freelance written.** Bimonthly magazine covering model car building. "We are looking for model builders, collectors, and enthusiasts who feel their models and/or modeling techniques and experiences would be of interest and benefit to our readership." Estab. 1979. Circ. 35,000. Pays on publication. Publishes ms an average of 1 year after acceptance. Byline given. Buys all rights. Editorial lead time 4 months. Submit seasonal material 4 months in advance. Accepts queries by mail, e-mail, fax, phone. Responds in 3 months to queries; 3 months to mss. Sample copy and writer's guidelines online.

Nonfiction Book excerpts, historical/nostalgic, how-to (build models, do different techniques), interview/profile, personal experience, photo feature, technical. Query or send complete ms. Length: 750-3,000 words. **Pays $60/published page.**

Photos When writing how-to articles be sure to take photos during the project. Send photos with submission.

Reviews negatives, 35mm color transparencies, color glossy. Buys all rights. Negotiates payment individually. Captions, identification of subjects, model releases required.

Columns/Departments Buys 50 mss/year. Query. **Pays $60/page.**

Tips "First and foremost, our readers like how-to material: how-to paint, how-to scratchbuild, how-to chop a roof, etc. Basically, our readers want to know how to make their own models better. Therefore, any help or advice you can offer is what modelers want to read. Also, the more photos you send, taken from a variety of views, the better choice we have in putting together an outstanding article layout. Send us more photos than you would ever possibly imagine we could use. This permits us to pick and choose the best of the bunch."

$ $ SEW NEWS

Creating for You and Your Home, Primedia Enthusiast Group, 741 Corporate Circle, Suite A, Golden CO 80401. (303)278-1010. Fax: (303)277-0370. E-mail: sewnews@sewnews.com. Web site: www.sewnews.com. **Contact:** Marla Stefanelli, editor. **70% freelance written.** Works with a small number of new/unpublished writers each year. Monthly magazine covering fashion, gift, and home-dec sewing. "Our magazine is for the beginning home sewer to the professional dressmaker. It expresses the fun, creativity, and excitement of sewing." Estab. 1980. Circ. 185,000. **Pays on acceptance.** Publishes ms an average of 6 months after acceptance. Byline given. Buys all rights. Submit seasonal material 6 months in advance. Accepts queries by mail, e-mail, fax. Responds in 2 months to mss. Sample copy for $5.99. Writer's guidelines for #10 SAE with 2 first-class stamps or online.

- All stories submitted to *Sew News* must be on disk or by e-mail.

Nonfiction How-to (sewing techniques), interview/profile (interesting personalities in home-sewing field). **Buys 200-240 mss/year.** Query with published clips if available. Length: 500-2,000 words. **Pays $25-500 for assigned articles.**

Photos Prefers digital images, color photos, or slides. Send photos with submission. Buys all rights. Payment included in ms price. Identification of subjects required.

The online magazine carries some original content not found in the print edition and includes writer's guidelines. *Sew News* has a free online newsletter.

Tips "Query first with writing sample and outline of proposed story. Areas most open to freelancers are how-to and sewing techniques; give explicit, step-by-step instructions, plus rough art. We're using more home decorating and soft craft content."

$ SHUTTLE SPINDLE & DYEPOT

Handweavers Guild of America, Inc., 1255 Buford Hwy., Suite 211, Suwanee GA 30024. (678)730-0010. Fax: (678)730-0836. E-mail: hga@weavespindye.org. Web site: www.weavespindye.org. Assistant Editor: Trish Fowler. Advertising Manager: Dorothy Holt. **Contact:** Sandra Bowles, editor-in-chief. **60% freelance written.** Quarterly magazine. "Quarterly membership publication of the Handweavers Guild of America, Inc., *Shuttle Spindle & Dyepot* magazine seeks to encourage excellence in contemporary fiber arts and to support the preservation of techniques and traditions in fiber arts. It also provides inspiration for fiber artists of all levels and develops public awareness and appreciation of the fiber arts. *Shuttle Spindle & Dyepot* appeals to a highly educated, creative, and very knowledgeable audience of fiber artists and craftsmen, weavers, spinners, dyers, and basket makers." Estab. 1969. Circ. 30,000. Pays on publication. Publishes ms an average of 6 months after acceptance. Byline given. Buys first North American serial, second serial (reprint), electronic rights. Editorial lead time 8 months. Submit seasonal material 8 months in advance. Accepts queries by mail, e-mail, fax, phone. Sample copy for $7.50 plus shipping. Writer's guidelines online.

Articles featuring up-and-coming artists, new techniques, cutting-edge ideas and designs, fascinating children's activities, and comprehensive fiber collections are a few examples of "best bet" topics.

Nonfiction Inspirational, interview/profile, new product, personal experience, photo feature, technical, travel. "No self-promotional and no articles from those without knowledge of area/art/artists." **Buys 40 mss/year.** Query with published clips. Length: 1,000-2,000 words. **Pays $75-150.**

Photos State availability with submission. Offers no additional payment for photos accepted with ms. Captions, identification of subjects, model releases required.

Columns/Departments Books and Videos, News and Information, Calendar and Conference, Travel and Workshop (all fiber/art related).

Tips "Become knowledgeable about the fiber arts and artists. The writer should provide an article of importance to the weaving, spinning, dyeing and basket making community. Query by telephone (once familiar with publication) by appointment helps editor and writer.

$ $ SPORTS COLLECTORS DIGEST

Voice for the Hobby, Krause Publications, a Division of F + W Publications, Inc., 700 E. State St., Iola WI 54990. (715)445-2214. Fax: (715)445-4087. E-mail: scd@fwpubs.com. Web site: www.sportscollectorsdigest.com.; www.krause.com. **Contact:** T.S. O'Connell, editor. **10% freelance written.** Weekly tabloid covering sports collectibles. Estab. 1973. Circ. 30,000. Pays on publication. Publishes ms an average of 2 months after acceptance. Byline given. Makes work-for-hire assignments. Editorial lead time 2 months. Submit seasonal material 1 month in advance. Accepts queries by e-mail. Sample copy for free.

Nonfiction General interest (new card issues, research older sets), historical/nostalgic (old stadiums, old collectibles, etc.), how-to (buy cards, sell cards and other collectibles, display collectibles, ways to get autographs, jerseys and other memorabilia), interview/profile (well-known collectors, ball players—but must focus on collectibles), new product (new card sets), personal experience (what I collect and why-type stories). No non-collecting sports stories. "We are not competing with *The Sporting News*, *Sports Illustrated*, or your daily paper. Sports collectibles only." **Buys 50-75 mss/year.** Query. Length: 300-3,000 words. **Pays $100-200.**

Reprints Send tearsheet. Pays 100% of amount paid for an original article.

Photos Unusual collectibles. Send photos with submission. Buys all rights. Pays $25-150 for b&w prints. Identification of subjects required.

Columns/Departments Length: 500-1,500 words. **Buys 100-150 mss/year.** Query. **Pays $90-150.**

Tips "Sports collectibles submissions only, e-mailed or mailed to T.S. O'Connell (oconnellt@krause.com)."

$ SUNSHINE ARTIST

America's Premier Show & Festival Publication, Palm House Publishing Inc., 4075 L.B. McLeod Rd., Suite E, Orlando FL 32811. (800)597-2573. Fax: (407)228-9862. E-mail: editor@sunshineartist.com. Web site: www.sunshineartist.com. Monthly magazine covering art shows in the US. "We are the premiere marketing/reference magazine for artists and crafts professionals who earn their living through art shows nationwide. We list more than 2,000 shows monthly, critique many of them, and publish articles on marketing, selling and other issues of concern to professional show circuit artists." Estab. 1972. Circ. 12,000. Pays on publication. Publishes ms an average of 3 months after acceptance. Byline given. Buys first North American serial rights. Responds in 2 months to queries. Sample copy for $5.

Nonfiction "We publish articles of interest to artists and crafts professionals who travel the art show circuit. Current topics include marketing, computers, and RV living." No how-to. **Buys 5-10 freelance mss/year.** Query with or without published clips or send complete ms. Length: 1,000-2,000 words. **Pays $50-150.**

Reprints Send photocopy and information about when and where the material previously appeared.

Photos Send photos with submission. Offers no additional payment for photos accepted with ms. Captions, identification of subjects, model releases required.

$ $ TATTOO REVUE

Art & Ink Enterprises, Inc., 5 Marine View Plaza, Suite 207, Hoboken NJ 07030. (201)653-2700. Fax: (201)653-7892. E-mail: laurenblake@skinartmag.com. Web site: www.skinart.com. Editor: Lauren Blake. **Contact:** Managing Editor. **25% freelance written.** Interview and profile magazine published 4 times/year covering tattoo artists, their art and lifestyle. "All writers must have knowledge of tattoos. Features include interviews with tattoo artists and collectors." Estab. 1990. Circ. 100,000. Pays on publication. Publishes ms an average of 3 months after acceptance. Byline given. Buys one-time rights. Editorial lead time 3 months. Submit seasonal material 5 months in advance. Accepts queries by mail, e-mail, fax. Responds in 2 weeks to queries. Sample copy for $5.98. Writer's guidelines for #10 SASE.

Nonfiction Book excerpts, historical/nostalgic, humor, interview/profile, photo feature. Special issues: Publishes special convention issues—dates and locations provided upon request. "No first-time experiences—our readers already know." **Buys 10-30 mss/year.** Query with published clips or send complete ms. Length: 500-2,500 words. **Pays $25-200.**

Photos Send photos with submission. Reviews transparencies, prints. Buys one-time rights. Offers $0-10/photo. Captions, identification of subjects, model releases required.

Columns/Departments **Buys 10-30 mss/year.** Query with or without published clips or send complete ms. **Pays $25-50.**

Fillers Anecdotes, facts, gags to be illustrated by cartoonist, newsbreaks, short humor. **Buys 10-20/year.** Length: 50-2,000 words.

The online magazine carries original content not found in the print edition. Contact: Lauren Blake.

Tips "All writers must have knowledge of tattoos! Either giving or receiving."

$ $ TEDDY BEAR REVIEW

Jones Publishing, Inc., N7450 Aanstad Rd., P.O. Box 5000, Iola WI 54945. (715)445-5000. E-mail: editor@teddybearreview.com. Web site: www.teddybearreview.com. **65% freelance written.** Works with a small number of new/unpublished writers each year. Bimonthly magazine on teddy bears for collectors, enthusiasts and bearmakers. Estab. 1985. Payment upon publication on the last day of the month the issue is mailed. Byline given. Contact editor for copy of freelance contributor agreement. Submit seasonal material 6 months in advance. Sample copy and writer's guidelines for $2 and 9×12 SAE.

Nonfiction Historical/nostalgic, how-to, interview/profile. No articles from the bear's point of view. **Buys 30-40 mss/year.** Query with published clips. Length: 900-1,500 words. **Pays $100-350.**
Photos Send photos with submission. Reviews transparencies, prints. Buys one-time rights. Offers no additional payment for photos accepted with ms. Captions required.
Tips "We are interested in good, professional writers around the country with a strong knowledge of teddy bears. Historical profile of bear companies, profiles of contemporary artists, and knowledgeable reports on museum collections are of interest."

$ $ THREADS

Taunton Press, 63 S. Main St., P.O. Box 5506, Newtown CT 06470. (203)426-8171. Fax: (203)426-3434. E-mail: th@taunton.com. Web site: www.threadsmagazine.com. Bimonthly magazine covering sewing, garment construction, home decor and embellishments (quilting and embroidery). "We're seeking proposals from hands-on authors who first and foremost have a skill. Being an experienced writer is of secondary consideration." Estab. 1985. Circ. 129,000. Byline given. Offers $150 kill fee. Buys one-time, second serial (reprint) rights. Editorial lead time 4 months. Responds in 1-2 months to queries. Writer's guidelines for free or online.
Nonfiction "We prefer first-person experience." **Pays $150/page.**
Columns/Departments Product reviews; Book reviews; Tips; Closures (stories of a humorous nature). Query. **Pays $150/page.**
Tips "Send us a proposal (outline) with photos of your own work (garments, samples, etc.)."

$ $ TOY CARS & MODELS

Krause Publications, a Division of F + W Publications, Inc., 700 E. State St., Iola WI 54990-0001. Fax: (715)445-4087. E-mail: contacttoycars@fwpubs.com. Web site: www.toycarsmag.com. **Contact:** Merry Dudley, editor. **90% freelance written.** Monthly magazine covering die-cast metal, plastic, resin, and white-metal model cars. "*Toy Cars & Models* provides comprehensive coverage of the model car hobby without bias toward scale, subject, manufacturer or material. Each month, *TC&M* offers columns and news stories featuring models made of die-cast, white metal, plastic, resin and more while getting readers in touch with the manufacturers, distributors and retailers who sell these model cars." Estab. 1998. Circ. 20,000. Pays on publication. Publishes ms an average of 1 year after acceptance. Byline given. Offers kill fee. Editorial lead time 3 months. Submit seasonal material 3 months in advance. Accepts queries by mail, e-mail, fax. Accepts simultaneous submissions. Responds in 1 month to queries; 2 months to mss. Writer's guidelines free.
Nonfiction Essays, general interest, historical/nostalgic, how-to (build models, assemble collections, protect/display collection), interview/profile, new product, photo feature, technical. Query. Length: 300-1,500 words. **Pays $50-200 for assigned articles; $50-100 for unsolicited articles.**
Photos Send photos with submission. Reviews transparencies, 3×5 prints, GIF/JPEG files (300 resolution, 4 inches wide). Buys negotiable rights. No additional payment for photos accepted with ms. Captions, identification of subjects, model releases required.
The online magazine carries original content not found in the print version. Contact: Merry Dudley, online editor.
Tips "Our magazine is for serious hobbyists looking for info about kit building, model quality, new products, and collectible value."

$ $ TOY FARMER

Toy Farmer Publications, 7496 106 Ave. SE, LaMoure ND 58458-9404. (701)883-5206. Fax: (701)883-5209. E-mail: info@toyfarmer.com. Web site: www.toyfarmer.com. President/Publisher: Cathy Scheibe. **Contact:** Cheryl Hegvik, editorial assistant. **70% freelance written.** Monthly magazine covering farm toys. Estab. 1978. Circ. 27,000. Pays on publication. Byline given. Buys first North American serial rights. Editorial lead time 3 months. Submit seasonal material 3 months in advance. Accepts queries by mail, e-mail, fax, phone. Accepts previously published material. Responds in 1 month to queries; 2 months to mss. Sample copy for $4. Writer's guidelines available upon request.

- Youth involvement is strongly encouraged.

Nonfiction General interest, historical/nostalgic, interview/profile, new product, personal experience, technical, book introductions. **Buys 100 mss/year.** Query with published clips. Length: 800-1,500 words. **Pays 10¢/word.** Sometimes pays expenses of writers on assignment.
Photos Must be 35mm originals or very high resolution digital images. State availability with submission. Buys one-time rights. Offers no additional payment for photos accepted with ms.

$ $ TOY SHOP

Krause Publications, a Division of F + W Publications, Inc., 700 E. State St., Iola WI 54990-0001. (715)445-4612. Fax: (715)445-4087. E-mail: toyshop@fwpubs.com. Web site: www.toyshopmag.com. **Contact:** Tom Bartsch,

editor. **20% freelance written.** Biweekly tabloid covering toys. "Our publication features writing that's easy to understand and lively." Estab. 1988. Circ. 15,000. Pays on publication. Publishes ms an average of 3 months after acceptance. Byline given. Offers kill fee. Editorial lead time 2 months. Submit seasonal material 2 months in advance. Accepts queries by mail, e-mail, phone. Accepts previously published material. Accepts simultaneous submissions. Responds in 1 week to queries; 1 month to mss. Sample copy for free. Writer's guidelines free.
Nonfiction General interest, historical/nostalgic, humor, interview/profile, personal experience. **Buys 60 mss/year.** Query. Length: 600-800 words. **Pays $125-175.** Sometimes pays expenses of writers on assignment.
Reprints Send photocopy and information about when and where the material previously appeared.
Photos Send photos with submission. Reviews 5×7 prints, GIF/JPEG files. Offers no additional payment for photos accepted with ms. Captions, identification of subjects required.
Columns/Departments Buys 20 mss/year. Query. **Pays $125-175.**
Tips "Submit well-worded queries. Know our magazine and style before submitting."

$ $TOY TRUCKER & CONTRACTOR

Toy Farmer Publications, 7496 106th Ave. SE, LaMoure ND 58458-9404. (701)883-5206. Fax: (701)883-5209. E-mail: info@toyfarmer.com. Web site: www.toytrucker.com. President/Publisher: Cathy Scheibe. **Contact:** Cheryl Hegvik, editorial assistant. **40% freelance written.** Monthly magazine covering collectible toys. "We are a magazine on hobby and collectible toy trucks and construction pieces." Estab. 1990. Circ. 6,500. Pays on publication. Byline given. Buys first North American serial rights. Editorial lead time 3 months. Submit seasonal material 3 months in advance. Accepts queries by mail, e-mail, fax, phone. Accepts previously published material. Responds in 1 month to queries; 2 months to mss. Sample copy for $4. Writer's guidelines available on request.
Nonfiction Historical/nostalgic, interview/profile, new product, personal experience, technical. **Buys 35 mss/year.** Query. Length: 800-1,400 words. **Pays 10¢/word.** Sometimes pays expenses of writers on assignment.
Photos Must be 35mm originals or very high resolution digital images. Send photos with submission. Offers no additional payment for photos accepted with ms. Captions, identification of subjects, model releases required.
Tips "Send sample work that would apply to our magazine. Also, we need more articles on collectors, builders, model kit enthusiasts and small company information. We have regular columns, so a feature should not repeat what our columns do."

TUFF STUFF

Krause Publications, a Division of F+W Publications, Inc., 700 E. State St., Iola WI 54990-0001. (715)445-2214. Fax: (715)445-4087. E-mail: tuffstuff@fwpubs.com. Web site: www.tuffstuff.com. Editor: Scott Kelnhofer. **Contact:** Scott Fragale, managing editor (scott.fragale@fwpubs.com). Monthly magazine covering sports collectibles. "Collectibles expertise is necessary." Estab. 1984. Circ. 140,000. Pays on publication. Publishes ms an average of 2 months after acceptance. Byline given. Offers negotiable kill fee. Makes work-for-hire assignments. Editorial lead time 3 months. Submit seasonal material 3 months in advance. Accepts queries by e-mail. Sample copy for free. Writer's guidelines not available.
Photos State availability with submission. Reviews GIF/JPEG files. Buys one-time rights. Negotiates payment individually.
Tips "No general interest sports submissions. Collectibles writers only."

⊘ VOGUE KNITTING

Soho Publishing Co., Inc., 233 Spring St., 8th Floor, New York NY 10013. (212)937-2555. Fax: (646)336-3960. E-mail: miriam@sohopublishingco.com. Web site: www.vogueknitting.com. Quarterly magazine created for participants in and enthusiasts of high fashion knitting. Circ. 175,000.

- Query before submitting.

$WESTERN & EASTERN TREASURES

People's Publishing Co., Inc., P.O. Box 219, San Anselmo CA 94979. E-mail: treasurenet@prodigy.net. Web site: www.treasurenet.com. **Contact:** Rosemary Anderson, managing editor. **100% freelance written.** Monthly magazine covering hobby/sport of metal detecting/treasure hunting. "*Western & Eastern Treasures* provides concise, yet comprehensive coverage of every aspect of the sport/hobby of metal detecting and treasure hunting with a strong emphasis on current, accurate information; innovative, field-proven advice and instruction; and entertaining, effective presentation." Estab. 1966. Circ. 50,000. Pays on publication. Publishes ms an average of 3 months after acceptance. Byline given. Buys all rights. Editorial lead time 4 months. Submit seasonal material 3-4 months in advance. Responds in 3 months to mss. Sample copy for 9×12 SAE and 5 first-class stamps. Writer's guidelines for #10 SASE.
Nonfiction How-to (tips and finds for metal detectorists), interview/profile (only people in metal detecting), personal experience (positive metal detector experiences), technical (only metal detecting hobby-related), help-

ing in local community with metal detecting skills (i.e., helping local police locate evidence at crime scenes—all volunteer basis). Special issues: Silver & Gold Annual (editorial deadline February each year)—looking for articles 1,500 words maximum, plus photos on the subject of locating silver and/or gold using a metal detector. No fiction, poetry, or puzzles. **Buys 150+ mss/year.** Send complete ms. Length: 600-1,500 words. **Pays 2¢/word for assigned articles.** Sometimes pays in contributor copies as trade for advertising space.
Photos Steve Anderson, vice president. Send photos with submission. Reviews 35mm transparencies, prints, digital scans (minimum 300 dpi). Buys all rights. Offers $5 minimum/photo. Captions, identification of subjects required.

N $ $ WOOD MAGAZINE

Meredith Corporation, 1716 Locust St., Des Moines IA 50309. E-mail: jim.harrold@meredith.com. Web site: www.woodmagazine.com. Editor: Bill Krier. Managing Editor: Marlen Kemmet. **Contact:** Jim Harrold, executive editor. **3% freelance written.** Magazine published 7 times/year covering woodworking. "*Wood* manuscripts are friendly, informative, authoritative in the subject of woodworking, and full of helpful service-related content." Estab. 1984. Circ. 550,000. Pays on publication. Byline given. Buys all rights. Editorial lead time 2 months. Submit seasonal material 1 year in advance. Accepts queries by e-mail. Responds in 3 weeks to queries; 3 weeks to mss.
Nonfiction "Looking for woodworking pieces." Does not want nonwoodworking. **Buys 3-4 mss/year.** Query. Length: 500-2,000 words. **Pays $300/page.** Pays expenses of writers on assignment.
Photos Reviews GIF/JPEG files. Buys all rights. Negotiates payment individually. Model releases required.

$ $ WOODSHOP NEWS

Soundings Publications, Inc., 10 Bokum Rd., Essex CT 06426-1185. (860)767-8227. Fax: (860)767-0645. E-mail: editorial@woodshopnews.com. Web site: www.woodshopnews.com. **Contact:** Tod Riggio, editor. **20% freelance written.** Monthly tabloid "covering woodworking for professionals. Solid business news and features about woodworking companies. Feature stories about interesting professional woodworkers. Some how-to articles." Estab. 1986. Circ. 60,000. Pays on publication. Publishes ms an average of 3 months after acceptance. Byline given. Buys first North American serial rights. Submit seasonal material 4 months in advance. Accepts queries by mail, e-mail, fax. Responds in 1 month to queries. Sample copy online. Writer's guidelines free.

- *Woodshop News* needs writers in major cities in all regions except the Northeast. Also looking for more editorial opinion pieces.

Nonfiction How-to (query first), interview/profile, new product, opinion, personal experience, photo feature. Key word is "newsworthy." No general interest profiles of "folksy" woodworkers. **Buys 15-25 mss/year.** Query with published clips or send complete ms. Length: 100-1,200 words. **Pays $50-500 for assigned articles; $40-250 for unsolicited articles.** Pays expenses of writers on assignment.
Photos Send photos with submission. Reviews contact sheets, prints. Buys one-time rights. Captions, identification of subjects required.
Columns/Departments Pro Shop (business advice, marketing, employee relations, taxes, etc., for the professional written by an established professional in the field); Finishing (how-to and techniques, materials, spraybooths, staining; written by experienced finishers), both 1,200-1,500 words. **Buys 18 mss/year.** Query. **Pays $200-300.**
Tips "The best way to start is a profile of a professional woodworker in your area. Find a unique angle about the person or business and stress this as the theme of your article. Avoid a broad, general-interest theme that would be more appropriate to a daily newspaper. Our readers are professional woodworkers who want more depth and more specifics than would a general readership. If you are profiling a business, we need standard business information such as gross annual earnings/sales, customer base, product line and prices, marketing strategy, etc. Color 35mm or high-res digital photos are a must."

$ $ WOODWORK

A Magazine For All Woodworkers, Ross Periodicals, 42 Digital Dr., #5, Novato CA 94949. (415)382-0580. Fax: (415)382-0587. E-mail: woodwork@rossperiodicals.com. Web site: www.woodwork-mag.com. Publisher: Tom Toldrian. **Contact:** John Lavine, editor. **90% freelance written.** Bimonthly magazine covering woodworking. "We are aiming at a broad audience of woodworkers, from the enthusiast to professional. Articles range from intermediate to complex. We cover such subjects as carving, turning, furniture, tools old and new, design, techniques, projects, and more. We also feature profiles of woodworkers, with the emphasis being always on communicating woodworking methods, practices, theories, and techniques. Suggestions for articles are always welcome." Estab. 1986. Circ. 50,000. Pays on publication. Byline given. Buys first North American serial, second serial (reprint) rights. Accepts queries by mail, e-mail, fax. Sample copy for $5 and 9×12 SAE with 6 first-class stamps. Writer's guidelines for #10 SASE.
Nonfiction How-to (simple or complex, making attractive furniture), interview/profile (of established wood-

workers that make attractive furniture), photo feature (of interest to woodworkers), technical (tools, techniques). "Do not send a how-to unless you are a woodworker." Query. Length: 1,500-2,000 words. **Pays $150/published page.**

Photos Send photos with submission. Reviews 35mm slides. Buys one-time rights. Pays higher page rate for photos accepted with ms. Captions, identification of subjects required.

Columns/Departments Tips and Techniques column, **pays $35-75.** Interview/profiles of established woodworkers (bring out woodworker's philosophy about the craft, opinions about what is happening currently). Good photos of attractive furniture a must. Section on how-to desirable. Query with published clips.

Tips "Our main requirement is that each article must directly concern woodworking. If you are not a woodworker, the interview/profile is your best chance. Good writing is essential, as are good photos. The interview must be entertaining, but informative and pertinent to woodworkers' interests. Include sidebar written by the profile subject."

HOME & GARDEN

$ THE ALMANAC FOR FARMERS & CITY FOLK

Greentree Publishing, Inc., 840 S. Rancho Dr., Suite 4-319, Las Vegas NV 89106. (702)387-6777. Fax: (702)385-1370. Web site: www.thealmanac.com. **30-40% freelance written.** Annual almanac of "down-home, folksy material pertaining to farming, gardening, homemaking, animals, etc." Deadline: March 31. Estab. 1983. Circ. 300,000. Pays on publication. Publishes ms an average of 6 months after acceptance. Byline given. Buys first North American serial rights. Sample copy for $4.99.

O→ Break in with short, humorous solutions to everyday problems; gardening; or how-to pieces.

Nonfiction Essays, general interest, historical/nostalgic, how-to (any home or garden project), humor. No fiction or controversial topics. "Please, no first-person pieces!" **Buys 30-40 mss/year.** No queries please. Editorial decisions made from ms only. Send complete ms by mail. Length: 350-1,400 words. **Pays $45/page.**

Poetry Buys 1-6 poems/year. Pays $45 for full pages or $15 for short poems.

Fillers Uses 60/year. Anecdotes, facts, short humor, gardening hints. Length: 125 words maximum. **Pays $15 for short fillers or page rate for longer fillers.**

Tips "Typed submissions essential as we scan manuscript. Short, succinct material is preferred. Material should appeal to a wide range of people and should be on the 'folksy' side, preferably with a thread of humor woven in. No first-person pieces (using 'I' or 'my')."

$ $ THE AMERICAN GARDENER

A Publication of the American Horticultural Society, 7931 E. Boulevard Dr., Alexandria VA 22308-1300. (703)768-5700. Fax: (703)768-7533. E-mail: editor@ahs.org. Web site: www.ahs.org. Managing Editor: Mary Yee. **Contact:** David J. Ellis, editor. **60% freelance written.** Bimonthly magazine covering gardening and horticulture. "*The American Gardener* is the official publication of the American Horticultural Society (AHS), a national, nonprofit, membership organization for gardeners, founded in 1922. The AHS mission is 'to open the eyes of all Americans to the vital connection between people and plants, and to inspire all Americans to become responsible caretakers of the earth, to celebrate America's diversity through the art and science of horticulture, and to lead this effort by sharing the society's unique national resources with all Americans." All articles in *The American Gardener* are also published on members-only Web site. Estab. 1922. Circ. 36,000. Pays on publication. Publishes ms an average of 6 months after acceptance. Byline given. Offers 25% kill fee. Buys first North American serial rights. Editorial lead time 4 months. Submit seasonal material at least 1 year in advance. Accepts queries by mail. Responds in 3 months to queries. Sample copy for $5. Writer's guidelines by e-mail and online.

Nonfiction "Feature-length articles include in-depth profiles of individual plant groups; profiles of prominent American horticulturists and gardeners (living and dead); profiles of unusual public or private gardens; descriptions of historical developments in American gardening; descriptions of innovative landscape design projects (especially relating to use of regionally native plants or naturalistic gardening); and descriptions of important plant breeding and research programs tailored to a lay audience. We run a few how-to articles; these should address relatively complex or unusual topics that most other gardening magazines won't tackle—photography must be provided." **Buys 30 mss/year.** Query with published clips. Length: 1,500-2,500 words. **Pays $300-550, depending on complexity and author's experience.**

Reprints Rarely purchases second rights. Send photocopy of article with information about when and where the material previously appeared. Payment varies.

Photos E-mail or check Web site for guidelines before submitting. Must be accompanied by postage-paid return mailer. Buys one-time print rights, plus limited rights to run article on members-only Web site. Offers $75-300/photo. Identification of subjects required.

Columns/Departments Conservationist's Notebook (addresses issues in plant conservation that are relevant or of interest to gardeners); Natural Connections (explains a natural phenomenon—plant and pollinator relationships, plant and fungus relationships, parasites—that may be observed in nature or in the garden), 750-1,200 words. **Buys 10 mss/year.** Query with published clips. **Pays $100-250.**

Tips "The majority of our readers are advanced, passionate amateur gardeners; about 20 percent are horticultural professionals. Most prefer not to use synthetic chemical pesticides. Our articles are intended to bring this knowledgeable group new information, ranging from the latest scientific findings that affect plants, to in-depth profiles of specific plant groups, and the history of gardening and gardens in America."

$ $ ATLANTA HOMES AND LIFESTYLES

Weisner Publishing, LLC, 1100 Johnson Ferry Rd., Suite 595, Atlanta GA 30342. (404)252-6670. Fax: (404)252-6673. Web site: www.atlantahomesmag.com. **Contact:** Oma Blaise, editor-in-chief. **65% freelance written.** Magazine published 8 times/year. "*Atlanta Homes and Lifestyles* is designed for the action-oriented, well-educated reader who enjoys his/her shelter, its design and construction, its environment, and living and entertaining in it." Estab. 1983. Circ. 33,091. Pays on publication. Publishes ms an average of 6 months after acceptance. Byline given. Buys all rights. Accepts queries by mail, fax. Responds in 3 months to queries. Sample copy for $3.95. Writer's guidelines online.

Nonfiction Interview/profile, new product, photo feature, well-designed homes, gardens, local art, remodeling, food, preservation, entertaining. "We do not want articles outside respective market area, not written for magazine format, or that are excessively controversial, investigative or that cannot be appropriately illustrated with attractive photography." **Buys 35 mss/year.** Query with published clips. Length: 500-1,200 words. **Pays $100-500.** Sometimes pays expenses of writer on assignment.

Photos Most photography is assigned. State availability with submission. Reviews transparencies. Buys one-time rights. Pays $40-50/photo. Captions, identification of subjects, model releases required.

Columns/Departments Short Takes (newsy items on home and garden topics); Quick Fix (simple remodeling ideas); Cheap Chic (stylish decorating that is easy on the wallet); Digging In (outdoor solutions from Atlanta's gardeners); Big Fix (more extensive remodeling projects); Real Estate News. Length: 350-500 words. Query with published clips. **Pays $50-200.**

Tips "Query with specific new story ideas rather than previously published material."

$ $ AUSTIN HOME & LIVING

Publications & Communications, Inc., 11675 Jollyville Rd., Suite 150, Austin TX 78759. (512)381-0576. Fax: (512)331-3950. E-mail: bronas@pcinews.com. Web site: www.austinhomeandliving.com. Editor: Taylor Bowles. **Contact:** Brona Stockton, associate publisher. **75% freelance written.** Bimonthly magazine. "*Austin Home & Living* showcases the homes found in Austin and provides tips on food, gardening, and decorating." Estab. 1994. Circ. 20,000. Pays on publication. Publishes ms an average of 4 months after acceptance. Byline given. Offers 100% kill fee. Buys all rights. Editorial lead time 4 months. Submit seasonal material 6 months in advance. Accepts queries by mail, e-mail, fax. Responds in 1 month to queries; 2 months to mss. Sample copy for free. Writer's guidelines online.

Nonfiction How-to, interview/profile, new product, travel. **Buys 18 mss/year.** Query with published clips. Length: 500-2,000 words. **Pays $200 for assigned articles.** Pays expenses of writers on assignment.

Photos State availability of or send photos with submission. Reviews negatives, transparencies, prints. Buys all rights. Offers no additional payment for photos accepted with ms. Captions required.

🌐 AUSTRALIAN HOME BEAUTIFUL

Pacific Magazines, Private Bag 9700, North Sydney NSW 2059 Australia. (61)(2)9464-3218. Fax: (61)(2)9464-3263. E-mail: homebeautiful@pacificmags.com.au. Web site: www.homebeautiful.com.au. Monthly magazine filled with loads of practical information, shopping details and aspirational images.

Nonfiction General interest, how-to, new product, photo feature. Query.

$ BACKHOME

Your Hands-On Guide to Sustainable Living, Wordsworth Communications, Inc., P.O. Box 70, Hendersonville NC 28793. (828)696-3838. Fax: (828)696-0700. E-mail: backhome@ioa.com. Web site: www.backhomemagazine.com. **Contact:** Lorna K. Loveless, editor. **80% freelance written.** Bimonthly magazine. *BackHome* encourages readers to take more control over their lives by doing more for themselves: productive organic gardening; building and repairing their homes; utilizing alternative energy systems; raising crops and livestock; building furniture; toys and games and other projects; creative cooking. *BackHome* promotes respect for family activities, community programs, and the environment. Estab. 1990. Circ. 26,000. Pays on publication. Publishes ms an average of 1 year after acceptance. Byline given. Offers $25 kill fee at publisher's discretion. Buys first North American serial rights. Editorial lead time 3 months. Submit seasonal material 6 months in advance. Accepts queries by mail, e-mail, fax, phone. Accepts previously published material. Responds in 6 weeks to queries; 2 months to mss. Sample copy $5 or online. Writer's guidelines online.

- The editor reports an interest in seeing "more alternative energy experiences, *good* small houses, workshop projects (for handy persons, not experts), and community action others can copy."

O— Break in by writing about personal experience (especially in overcoming challenges) in fields in which *BackHome* focuses.

Nonfiction How-to (gardening, construction, energy, homebusiness), interview/profile, personal experience, technical, self-sufficiency. No essays or old-timey reminiscences. **Buys 80 mss/year.** Query. Length: 750-5,000 words. **Pays $35 (approximately)/printed page.**

Reprints Send photocopy and information about when and where the material previously appeared. Pays $35/printed page.

Photos Send photos with submission. Reviews color prints, 35mm slides, JPEG photo attachments of 300 dpi. Buys one-time rights. Offers additional payment for photos published. Identification of subjects required.

Tips "Very specific in relating personal experiences in the areas of gardening, energy, and homebuilding how-to. Third-person approaches to others' experiences are also acceptable but somewhat less desirable. Clear color photo prints, especially those in which people are prominent, help immensely when deciding upon what is accepted."

BATHROOM YEARBOOK

Universal Magazines, Ltd., Unit 5, 6-8 Byfield St., North Ryde NSW 2113 Australia. (61)(2)9887-0367. Fax: (61)9805-0714. E-mail: mgardener@universalmagazines.com.au. Web site: www.completehome.com.au. Editor: Melanie Gardener. Annual magazine covering all the latest bathroom products and designs.

Nonfiction General interest, new product, photo feature. Query.

$$$$ BETTER HOMES AND GARDENS

1716 Locust St., Des Moines IA 50309-3023. (515)284-3044. Fax: (515)284-3763. Web site: www.bhg.com. Editor-in-Chief: Gayle Butler. Editor (Building): Laura O' Neil. Editor (Food & Nutrition): Nancy Hopkins. Editor (Garden/Outdoor Living): Doug Jimerson. Editor (Health): Christian Millman. Editor (Education & Parenting): Stephen George. Editor (Automotive): Lamont Olson. Editor (Home Design): Oma Ford. Editor (Features and Family Matters): Stephen George. **10-15% freelance written.** Magazine "providing home service information for people who have a serious interest in their homes." "We read all freelance articles, but much prefer to see a letter of query rather than a finished manuscript." Estab. 1922. Circ. 7,605,000. **Pays on acceptance.** Buys all rights.

Nonfiction Travel, education, gardening, health, cars, home, entertainment. "We do not deal with political subjects or with areas not connected with the home, community, and family." No poetry or fiction. **Pay rates vary.**

Tips "Most stories published by this magazine go through a lengthy process of development involving both editor and writer. Some editors will consider only query letters, not unsolicited manuscripts. Direct queries to the department that best suits your storyline."

$$ BIRDS & BLOOMS

Reiman Publications, 5925 Country Lane, Greendale WI 53129. (414)423-0100. E-mail: editors@birdsandblooms.com. Web site: www.birdsandblooms.com. **15% freelance written.** Bimonthly magazine focusing on the "beauty in your own backyard. *Birds & Blooms* is a sharing magazine that lets backyard enthusiasts chat with each other by exchanging personal experiences. This makes *Birds & Blooms* more like a conversation than a magazine, as readers share tips and tricks on producing beautiful blooms and attracting feathered friends to their backyards." Estab. 1995. Circ. 1,900,000. Pays on publication. Publishes ms an average of 7 months after acceptance. Byline given. Buys all rights. Editorial lead time 2 months. Submit seasonal material 4 months in advance. Accepts queries by mail, e-mail. Accepts simultaneous submissions. Responds in 2 months to queries; 2 months to mss. Sample copy for $2, 9×12 SAE and $1.95 postage. Writer's guidelines for #10 SASE.

Nonfiction Essays, how-to, humor, inspirational, personal experience, photo feature, natural crafting and plan items for building backyard accents. No bird rescue or captive bird pieces. **Buys 12-20 mss/year.** Send complete ms. Length: 250-1,000 words. **Pays $100-400.**

Photos Trudi Bellin, photo coordinator. Send photos with submission. Reviews transparencies, prints. Buys one-time rights. Identification of subjects required.

Columns/Departments Backyard Banter (odds, ends and unique things); Bird Tales (backyard bird stories); Local Lookouts (community backyard happenings), all 200 words. **Buys 12-20 mss/year.** Send complete ms. **Pays $50-75.**

Fillers Anecdotes, facts, gags to be illustrated by cartoonist. **Buys 25/year.** Length: 10-250 words. **Pays $10-75.**

Tips "Focus on conversational writing—like you're chatting with a neighbor over your fence. Manuscripts full of tips and ideas that people can use in backyards across the country have the best chance of being used. Photos that illustrate these points also increase chances of being used."

CANADIAN GARDENING MAGAZINE

Transcontinental Media G.P., 25 Sheppard Ave. W., Suite 100, Toronto ON M2N 6S7 Canada. E-mail: satterthwaite@canadiangardening.com. Web site: www.canadiangardening.com. Acting Managing Editor: Helen Catellier. **Contact:** Aldona Satterthwaite, editor-in-chief. Mostly freelance written. Magazine published 8 times/year covering Canadian gardening. "*Canadian Gardening* is a national magazine aimed at the avid home gardener. Our readers are city gardeners with tiny lots, country gardeners with rolling acreage, indoor gardeners, rooftop gardeners, and enthusiastic beginners and experienced veterans. Estab. 1990. Circ. 152,000. **Pays on acceptance.** Byline given. Offers 25-50% kill fee. Buys electronic rights. Editorial lead time 4 months. Submit seasonal material 4 months in advance. Accepts queries by mail, e-mail, fax. Accepts simultaneous submissions. Responds in 4 months to queries. Writer's guidelines online.

Nonfiction How-to (planting and gardening projects), humor, personal experience, technical, plant and garden profiles, practical advice. **Buys 100 mss/year.** Query. Length: 200-1,500 words. **Pays variable amount.** Sometimes pays expenses of writers on assignment.

Photos Send image samples with submission. Reviews color photocopies and PDFs. Negotiates payment individually.

$ $ CANADIAN HOMES & COTTAGES

The In-Home Show, Ltd., 2650 Meadowvale Blvd., Unit 4, Mississauga ON L5N 6M5 Canada. (905)567-1440. Fax: (905)567-1442. E-mail: jnaisby@homesandcottages.com. Web site: www.homesandcottages.com. Managing Editor: Steven Chester. **Contact:** Janice Naisby, editor-in-chief. **75% freelance written.** Magazine published 6 times/year covering building and renovating; "technically comprehensive articles." Estab. 1987. Circ. 79,000. Pays on publication. Publishes ms an average of 2 months after acceptance. Byline given. Offers 10% kill fee. Buys first North American serial rights. Editorial lead time 3 months. Submit seasonal material 3 months in advance. Accepts queries by mail. Sample copy for SAE. Writer's guidelines for #10 SASE.

Nonfiction Looking for how-to projects and simple home improvement ideas. Humor (building and renovation related), new product, technical. **Buys 32 mss/year.** Query. Length: 1,000-2,000 words. **Pays $300-750.** Sometimes pays expenses of writers on assignment.

Photos Send photos with submission. Reviews transparencies, prints. Buys one-time rights. Negotiates payment individually. Captions, identification of subjects required.

Tips "Read our magazine before sending in a query. Remember that you are writing to a Canadian audience."

N CANADIAN LIVING

Transcontinental Publications, 25 Sheppard Ave. W., Suite 100, Toronto ON M2N 6S7 Canada. (416)733-7600. Web site: www.canadianliving.com. **Contact:** Submissions Editor. Monthly magazine covering Canadian lifestyles. Written as a family lifestyle magazine with emphasis on practical information for women at home and in business. Circ. 542,815. Editorial lead time 3 months. Accepts queries by mail, e-mail. Sample copy not available. Writer's guidelines by e-mail.

Nonfiction General interest, how-to, interview/profile. Travel articles or features dealing with career or workplace issues. Query. Length: 750-2,500 words.

N $ $ THE CANADIAN ORGANIC GROWER

129 Beech Hill Rd., Weldon NB E4H 4N5 Canada. E-mail: janet@cog.ca. Web site: www.cog.ca. **Contact:** Janet Wallace, editor. **100% freelance written.** Quarterly magazine covering organic gardening and farming. "We publish articles that are of interest to organic gardeners, farmers and consumers in Canada. We're always looking for practical how-to articles, as well as farmer profiles. At times, we include news about the organic community, recipes and stories about successful marketing strategies." Estab. 1975. Circ. 4,000. Pays on publication. Publishes ms an average of 2-3 months after acceptance. Byline given. Buys first North American serial rights. Editorial lead time 6 months. Submit seasonal material 6 months in advance. Accepts queries by mail, e-mail. Accepts previously published material. Responds in 3 weeks to queries; 1 month to mss. Sample copy and writer's guidelines online.

Nonfiction Essays, general interest, how-to (garden, farm, market, process organic food), interview/profile, new product, opinion, technical. Does not want rants. **Buys 25 mss/year.** Query. Length: 500-2,500 words. **Pays $50-250 for assigned articles; $50-200 for unsolicited articles.**

Photos State availability with submission. Reviews prints, GIF/JPEG files. Buys one-time rights. Negotiates payment individually. Captions, identification of subjects required.

Columns/Departments Organic Certification; Organic Livestock, both 750 words. Query. **Pays $50-100.**

N $ CAROLINA HOMES & INTERIORS

MediaServices, Inc., P.O. Box 22617, Charleston SC 29413. (843)881-1481. Fax: (843)849-6717. E-mail: editorial@carolinahomes.net. Web site: www.carolinahomes.net. **Contact:** Andrew Mosier, managing editor. **80% freelance written.** Quarterly magazine covering coastal Carolina homes and lifestyles. "We feature the finest in coastal living. Highlighting builders, designers, communities, vendors and the many recreational alternatives in the Carolinas, coastal Georgia and Florida, *CH&I* is the region's premiere home and lifestyle guide." Estab. 1983. Circ. 65,000. Pays 30 days after publication. Publishes ms an average of 2 months after acceptance. Byline given. Offers 50% kill fee. Buys one-time rights. Editorial lead time 2 months. Submit seasonal material 4 months in advance. Accepts queries by mail, e-mail. Accepts previously published material. Accepts simultaneous submissions. Responds in 2 weeks to queries; 1-2 months to mss. Sample copy for free. Writer's guidelines by e-mail.

Nonfiction Exposé, general interest, historical/nostalgic, how-to, inspirational, interview/profile, new product, personal experience, technical, travel. **Buys 50 mss/year.** Query with published clips. Length: 300-2,000 words. **Pays $30.** Sometimes pays expenses of writers on assignment.

Columns/Departments Inner Beauty, 300 words; Outer Beauty, 300 words; Coastal Custom Builders, 600 words; Hot Retirement Towns, 400 words; Things to Do, 500 words; Four!, 500 words; Day Trips, 750 words; Smiling Faces, 600 words; Important People, 600 words; Top, maximum 300 words; Night Out, 750 words. **Buys 50 mss/year.** Query with published clips. **Pays $30.**

Tips "Be creative. Story ideas should reflect the beauty of the region. All writers are welcome, but local writers are preferred. New writers are encouraged to query."

$ $ $ $ COASTAL LIVING

Southern Progress Corp., 2100 Lakeshore Dr., Birmingham AL 35209. (205)445-6007. Fax: (205)445-8655. E-mail: mamie_walling@timeinc.com. Web site: www.coastalliving.com. **Contact:** Mamie Walling. Bimonthly magazine for those who live or vacation along our nation's coasts. The magazine emphasizes home design and travel, but also covers a wide variety of other lifestyle topics and coastal concerns. Estab. 1997. Circ. 660,000. **Pays on acceptance.** Offers 25% kill fee. Responds in 2 months to queries. Sample copy and writer's guidelines online.

Nonfiction The magazine is roughly divided into 5 areas, with regular features, columns and departments for each area. **Currents** offers short, newsy features of 25-200 words written mostly by staff members on new products, seaside events, beach fashions, etc. **Travel** includes outdoor activities, nature experiences, and lodging and dining stories. **Homes** places the accent on casual living, with warm, welcoming houses and rooms designed for living. **Food & Entertainment** is divided into *In the Coastal Kitchen* (recipes and tips) and *Seafood Primer* (basics of buying and preparing seafood). The **Lifestyle** section is a catch all of subjects to help readers live better and more comfortably: *The Good Life* (profiles of people who have moved to the coast), *Coastal Character* (profile of someone connected to a coastal environment), *Collectibles* (treasured items/accessories with a marine connection), *So You Want to Live In . . .* (profiles of coastal communities), etc. Query with clips and SASE. **Pays $1/word.**

Photos State availability with submission.

Tips "Query us with ideas that are very specifically targeted to the columns that are currently in the magazine."

$ $ COLORADO HOMES & LIFESTYLES

Wiesner Publishing, LLC, 7009 S. Potomac St., Centennial CO 80112-4029. (303)397-7600. Fax: (303)397-7619. E-mail: mdakotah@coloradohomesmag.com. Web site: www.coloradohomesmag.com. **75% freelance written.** Upscale shelter magazine published 9 times/year containing beautiful homes, landscapes, architecture, calendar, antiques, etc. All of Colorado is included. Geared toward home-related and lifestyle areas, personality profiles, etc. Estab. 1981. Circ. 36,000. **Pays on acceptance.** Publishes ms an average of 3 months after acceptance. Byline given. Offers 15% kill fee. Buys first North American serial rights. Editorial lead time 3 months. Submit seasonal material 1 year in advance. Accepts queries by mail, e-mail. Accepts simultaneous submissions. Responds in 2 months to queries. Sample copy for #10 SASE.

Nonfiction Fine homes and furnishings, regional interior design trends, shopping information, interesting personalities and lifestyles—all with a Colorado slant. No personal essays, religious, humor, technical. **Buys 50-75 mss/year.** Query with published clips. Length: 900-1,500 words. **Pays $200-400.** Sometimes pays expenses of writers on assignment.

Photos Send photos with submission. Reviews transparencies, b&w glossy prints, CDs, digital images, slides. Identification of subjects, title and caption suggestions appreciated. photographic credits required.

Tips "Send query, lead paragraph, clips. Send ideas for story or stories. Include some photos, if applicable. The more interesting and unique the subject, the better. A frequent mistake made by writers is failure to provide material with a style and slant appropriate for the magazine, due to poor understanding of the focus of the magazine."

$ $ CONCRETE HOMES

Publications and Communications, Inc. (PCI), 11675 Jollyville Rd., Suite 150, Austin TX 78759. Fax: (512)331-3950. E-mail: homes@pcinews.com. Web site: concretehomesmagazine.com. Editor: Taylor Bowles. **Contact:** Brona Stockton, associate publisher. **85% freelance written.** Bimonthly magazine covering homes built with concrete. "*Concrete Homes* is a publication designed to be informative to consumers, builders, contractors, architects, etc., who are interested in concrete homes. The magazine profiles concrete home projects (they must be complete) and offers how-to and industry news articles." Estab. 1999. Circ. 25,000. Pays on publication. Publishes ms an average of 2 months after acceptance. Byline given. Offers 100% kill fee. Buys all rights. Editorial lead time 2 months. Submit seasonal material 3-4 months in advance. Accepts queries by mail, e-mail. Accepts simultaneous submissions. Responds in 1 month to queries; 1 month to mss. Sample copy and writer's guidelines online.

Nonfiction How-to, interview/profile, new product, technical. **Buys 30-40 mss/year.** Query or query with published clips. Length: 800-2,000 words. **Pays $200-250.** Sometimes pays expenses of writers on assignment.

Photos State availability with submission. Reviews 8×10 transparencies, prints, GIF/JPEG files. Buys all rights. Offers no additional payment for photos accepted with ms. Captions required.

Tips "Demonstrate awareness of concrete homes and some knowledge of the construction/building industry."

$ $ $ $ COTTAGE LIFE

Quarto Communications, 54 St. Patrick St., Toronto ON M5T 1V1 Canada. (416)599-2000. Fax: (416)599-4070. E-mail: editorial@cottagelife.com. Web site: www.cottagelife.com. Editor: Penny Caldwell. **Contact:** Liann Bobechko, assistant editor. **80% freelance written.** Bimonthly magazine. "*Cottage Life* is written and designed for the people who own and spend time at waterfront cottages throughout Canada and bordering US states, with a strong focus on Ontario. The magazine has a strong service slant, combining useful 'how-to' journalism with coverage of the people, trends, and issues in cottage country. Regular columns are devoted to boating, fishing, watersports, projects, real estate, cooking, design and decor, nature, personal cottage experience, and environmental, political, and financial issues of concern to cottagers." Estab. 1988. Circ. 70,000. **Pays on acceptance.** Publishes ms an average of 2 months after acceptance. Byline given. Offers 50-100% kill fee. Buys first North American serial rights. Sample copy not available. Writer's guidelines online.

Nonfiction Book excerpts, exposé, historical/nostalgic, how-to, humor, interview/profile, personal experience, photo feature, technical. **Buys 90 mss/year.** Query with published clips and SAE with Canadian postage or IRCs. Length: 150-3,500 words. **Pays $100-3,000.** Pays expenses of writers on assignment.

Columns/Departments On the Waterfront (front department featuring short news, humor, human interest, and service items), 400 words maximum. **Pays $50-400.** Cooking, Real Estate, Fishing, Nature, Watersports, Decor, Personal Experience, and Issues, all 150-1,200 words. **Pays $100-1,200.** Query with published clips and SAE with Canadian postage or IRCs, or by e-mail.

Tips "If you have not previously written for the magazine, the 'On the Waterfront' section is an excellent place to break in."

N $ $ COTTAGE STYLE

Harris Publications, 1115 Broadway, New York NY 10010. Managing Editor: Ellen Wolynec. **Contact:** Ashley Womble (ashley@harris-pub.com). **60% freelance written.** Quarterly magazine covering cottages, cabins and bungalows. Estab. 2001. Pays on publication. Publishes ms an average of 6-12 months after acceptance. Byline given. Offers 50% kill fee. Buys first rights. Editorial lead time 6-12 months. Submit seasonal material 12 months in advance. Accepts queries by mail, e-mail. Responds in 4-6 weeks to queries; 2-4 months to mss.

Nonfiction General interest, how-to, interview/profile, craft, decorating, gardening. Does not want articles that do not lend themselves to photographic illustration. *Cottage Style* is a photo-driven magazine. **Buys 70-100 mss/year.** Query. **Pays $100-500.** Sometimes pays expenses of writers on assignment.

Photos State availability with submission. Reviews transparencies, GIF/JPEG files (300 dpi at 4×5 or bigger). Buys one-time rights. Offers $75-150/photo. Captions, identification of subjects, model releases required.

Tips "All articles must have information (or sources) that are useful (and current) that readers can use to copy the look or lifestyle discussed."

COUNTRY DECORATING IDEAS

Harris Publications, Inc., 1115 Broadway, New York NY 10010. (212)807-7100. E-mail: countryletters@yahoo.com. Web site: www.countrydecoratingideas.com. Quarterly magazine featuring do-it-yourself ideas and affordable advice on country decorating for the home. Circ. 360,183. Editorial lead time 2 months.

- Query before submitting.

$ $ $ $ COUNTRY HOME

Meredith Corp., 1716 Locust St., Des Moines IA 50309-3023. (515)284-3000. Fax: (515)284-2552. E-mail: countryh@meredith.com; carol.sheehan@meredith.com. Web site: www.countryhome.com. Editor-in-Chief: Carol

Sheehan. **Contact:** Assignments Editor. Magazine published 10 times/year for people interested in the country way of life. "*Country Home* magazine is a lifestyle publication created for readers who share passions for American history, style, craftsmanship, tradition, and cuisine. These people, with a desire to find a simpler, more meaningful lifestyle, live their lives and design their living spaces in ways that reflect those passions." Estab. 1979. Circ. 1,250,000. Pays on completion of assignment. Publishes ms an average of 5 months after acceptance. Byline given. Submit seasonal material 6 months in advance. Accepts queries by mail. Responds in 6 weeks to queries. Sample copy for $4.95. Writer's guidelines not available. Editorial calendar online.

"We are not responsible for unsolicited manuscripts, and we do not encourage telephone queries."

Nonfiction Architecture and Design, Families at Home, Travel, Food and Entertaining, Art and Antiques, Gardens and Outdoor Living, Personal Reflections. Query by mail only with writing samples and SASE. Length: 750-1,500 words. **Pays $500-1,500.**

Columns/Departments Length: 500-750 words. Include SASE. Query with published clips. **Pays $300-500.**

The online magazine carries original content not found in the print edition. Contact: Susan Weaver, online editor.

COUNTRY LIVING

The Hearst Corp., 224 W. 57th St., New York NY 10019. (212)649-3500. Monthly magazine covering home design and interior decorating with an emphasis on country style. "A lifestyle magazine for readers who appreciate the warmth and traditions associated with American home and family life. Each monthly issue embraces American country decorating and includes features on furniture, antiques, gardening, home building, real estate, cooking, entertaining and travel." Estab. 1978. Circ. 1,600,000.

Nonfiction Subjects covered include decorating, collecting, cooking, entertaining, gardening/landscaping, home building/remodeling/restoring, travel, and leisure activities. **Buys 20-30 mss/year.** Send complete ms and SASE. **Payment varies.**

Columns/Departments Query first.

Tips "Know the magazine, know the market, and know how to write a good story that will interest *our* readers."

COUNTRY SAMPLER

707 Kautz Rd., St. Charles IL 60174. (630)377-8000. Fax: (630)377-8194. Web site: www.sampler.com. Bimonthly magazine. "*Country Sampler* is a country decorating, antiques, and collectibles magazine and a country product catalog." Estab. 1984. Circ. 300,000. Accepts queries by mail, fax.

Nonfiction "Furniture, accessories, and decorative accents created by artisans throughout the country are displayed and offered for purchase directly from the maker. Fully decorated room settings and home tours show the readers how to use the items in their homes to achieve the warmth and charm of the country look."

Tips "Send photos and story idea for a country-style house tour. Story should be regarding decorating tips and techniques."

N $ $ $ $ D HOME AND GARDEN MAGAZINE

D Magazine Partners, 4311 Oak Lawn Ave., Dallas TX 75219. (214)939-3636. Fax: (214)748-4153. E-mail: rogerb@dmagazine.com. Web site: www.dhomeandgarden.com. Editor: Christine Allison. **Contact:** Roger Brooks, managing editor. **50% freelance written.** Magazine published 7 times/year covering Dallas home and garden. Estab. 1999. Circ. 25,000. **Pays on acceptance.** Publishes ms an average of 2-3 months after acceptance. Byline given. Offers 25% kill fee. Buys all rights. Editorial lead time 2-3 months. Submit seasonal material 2-3 months in advance. Accepts queries by mail, e-mail, fax, phone. Sample copy online. Writer's guidelines free.

Nonfiction Special issues: Green issue (January/February). Does not want anything not specific to Dallas. **Buys 3-5 mss/year.** Query. Length: 800-2,000 words. **Pays $400-1,500.** Sometimes pays expenses of writers on assignment.

Photos Contact Andrea Tomek, art director. State availability with submission. Reviews contact sheets, GIF/JPEG files. Buys one-time rights. Negotiates payment individually. Identification of subjects required.

N $ $ DREAM HOUSE MAGAZINE

Western Canada's Premier fine home and lifestyle publication, Dream House Publications, Ltd., 106-873 Beatty St., Vancouver BC V6B 2M6 Canada. (604)681-3463. Fax: (604)681-3494. E-mail: tracey@dreamhousemag.com. Web site: www.dreamhousemag.com. **Contact:** Tracey Ellis, editor. **50% freelance written.** Magazine published 8 times/year covering fine homes, luxury lifestyle. "*Dream House Magazine* serves its readers the best of the best in fine homes and luxury lifestyles." Estab. 2001. Circ. 28,000. Pays within 30 days of publication. Publishes ms an average of 1 month after acceptance. Byline given. Offers 50% kill fee. Buys first North American serial rights. Editorial lead time 3 months. Submit seasonal material 1 month in advance. Accepts queries by mail, e-mail. Writer's guidelines free.

Nonfiction General interest, historical/nostalgic, humor, interview/profile, new product, photo feature, travel.

Does not want memoirs. Query with published clips. Length: 500-800 words. **Pays 25-35¢/word.**
Photos Send photos with submission. Reviews TIFF files only (300 dpi at 8×10). Buys one-time rights. Offers no additional payment for photos accepted with ms.
Columns/Departments Finance; Real Estate; Insurance, all 500-800 words. Query with published clips.
Tips "Read magazine. Study our audience. Be well connected in the luxury marketplace."

$ $ EARLY AMERICAN LIFE

Firelands Media Group LLC, P.O. Box 221228, Shaker Heights OH 44122-0996. E-mail: queries@firelandsmedia.com. Web site: www.ealonline.com. **Contact:** Jeanmarie Andrews, executive editor. **60% freelance written.** Bimonthly magazine for "people who are interested in capturing the warmth and beauty of the 1600-1840 period and using it in their homes and lives today. They are interested in antiques, traditional crafts, architecture, restoration, and collecting." Estab. 1970. Circ. 90,000. **Pays on acceptance.** Publishes ms an average of 1 year after acceptance. Byline given. Buys worldwide rights. Accepts queries by mail, e-mail. Responds in 3 months to queries. Sample copy and writer's guidelines for 9×12 SAE with $2.50 postage.

- Break in "by offering highly descriptive, entertaining, yet informational articles on social culture, decorative arts, antiques, or well-restored and appropriately furnished homes that reflect middle-class American life prior to 1850."

Nonfiction "Social history (the story of the people, not epic heroes and battles), travel to historic sites, antiques and reproductions, restoration, architecture, and decorating. We try to entertain as we inform. We're always on the lookout for good pieces on any of our subjects. Would like to see more on how real people did something great to their homes." **Buys 40 mss/year.** Query with or without published clips or send complete ms. Length: 750-3,000 words. **Pays $350-700, additionally for photos.**
Tips "Our readers are eager for ideas on how to bring early America into their lives. Conceive a new approach to satisfy their related interests in arts, crafts, travel to historic sites, and especially in houses decorated in the Early American style. Write to entertain and inform at the same time. We are visually oriented, so writers are asked to supply images or suggest sources for illustrations."

$ $ $ FINE GARDENING

Taunton Press, 63 S. Main St., P.O. Box 5506, Newtown CT 06470-5506. (203)426-8171. Fax: (203)426-3434. E-mail: fg@taunton.com. Web site: www.finegardening.com. **Contact:** Todd Meier, editor-in-chief. Bimonthly magazine. "High-value magazine on landscape and ornamental gardening. Articles written by avid gardeners—first person, hands-on gardening experiences." Estab. 1988. Circ. 200,000. **Pays on acceptance.** Publishes ms an average of 6 months after acceptance. Byline given. Buys all rights. Editorial lead time 1 year. Submit seasonal material 1 year in advance. Accepts queries by mail, e-mail, fax. Sample copy not available. Writer's guidelines free.
Nonfiction How-to, personal experience, photo feature, book reviews. **Buys 60 mss/year.** Query. Length: 1,000-3,000 words. **Pays $300-1,200.**
Photos Send photos with submission. Reviews digital images. Buys serial rights.
Columns/Departments Book, video and software reviews (on gardening); Last Word (essays/serious, humorous, fact or fiction). Length: 250-500 words. **Buys 30 mss/year.** Query. **Pays $50- 200.**
Tips "It's most important to have solid first-hand experience as a gardener. Tell us what you've done with your own landscape and plants."

$ $ FINE HOMEBUILDING

The Taunton Press, 63 S. Main St., P.O. Box 5506, Newtown CT 06470-5506. (203)426-8171. Fax: (203)426-3434. E-mail: fh@taunton.com. Web site: www.taunton.com. Bimonthly magazine for builders, architects, contractors, owner/builders and others who are seriously involved in building new houses or reviving old ones. Estab. 1981. Circ. 300,000. Pays half on acceptance, half on publication. Publishes ms an average of 1 year after acceptance. Byline given. Offers on acceptance payment as kill fee. Buys first rights. Reprint rights Responds in 1 month to queries. Sample copy not available. Writer's guidelines for SASE and on Web site.
Nonfiction "We're interested in almost all aspects of home building, from laying out foundations to capping cupolas." Query with outline, description, photographs, sketches and SASE. **Pays $150/published page.**
Photos "Take lots of work-in-progress photos. Color print film, ASA 400, from either Kodak or Fuji works best. If you prefer to use slide film, use ASA 100. Keep track of the negatives; we will need them for publication. If you're not sure what to use or how to go about it, feel free to call for advice."
Columns/Departments Tools & Materials, Reviews, Questions & Answers, Tips & Techniques, Cross Section, What's the Difference?, Finishing Touches, Great Moments, Breaktime, Drawing Board (design column). Query with outline, description, photographs, sketches and SASE. **Payment varies.**
Tips "Our chief contributors are home builders, architects and other professionals. We're more interested in your point of view and technical expertise than your prose style. Adopt an easy, conversational style and define

any obscure terms for non-specialists. We try to visit all our contributors and rarely publish building projects we haven't seen, or authors we haven't met."

$ GARDEN COMPASS

Streamopolis, 1450 Front St., San Diego CA 92101. (619)239-2202. Fax: (619)239-4621. E-mail: editor@gardencompass.com. Web site: www.gardencompass.com. **Contact:** Sharon Asakawa, editor. **70% freelance written.** Bimonthly magazine covering gardening. *Garden Compass* is "entertaining and offers sound practical advice for West Coast gardeners." Estab. 1992. Circ. 112,000. Pays on publication. Publishes ms an average of 10 weeks after acceptance. Byline given. Offers $50 kill fee. Not copyrighted. Buys first North American serial rights. Editorial lead time 6 months. Submit seasonal material 6 months in advance. Accepts queries by mail, e-mail. Accepts simultaneous submissions. Responds in 1 month to queries. Sample copy for free.

Photos State availability of or send photos with submission. Reviews contact sheets, transparencies, GIF/JPEG files. Buys one-time rights. Negotiates payment individually. Identification of subjects required.

Columns/Departments Pest Patrol (plant posts/diseases), 400-800 words; e-Gardening (garden info on the Web), 400-800 words; Book Review (gardening books), 400-600 words; Fruit Trees, 800-1,200 words. Query with published clips. **Payment varies.**

Fillers Anecdotes, facts, newsbreaks. Length: 30-150 words. **Pays $25.**

⊘ THE HERB COMPANION

Ogden Publications, Inc., 1503 SW 42nd St., Topeka KS 66609. (785)274-4300. Fax: (785)274-4305. E-mail: editor@herbcompanion.com. Web site: www.herbcompanion.com. **Contact:** K.C. Compton, editor. **80% freelance written.** Bimonthly magazine about herbs: culture, history, culinary, crafts and some medicinal use for both experienced and novice herb enthusiasts. Pays on publication. Byline given. Buys all rights. Editorial lead time 4 months. Accepts queries by mail, e-mail, fax. Responds in 2 months to queries. Sample copy for $6. Writer's guidelines online.

- *Do not send unsolicited mss.*

Nonfiction Practical horticultural, original recipes, historical, herbal crafts, helpful hints, and book reviews. How-to, interview/profile. Submit by mail only detailed query or ms. Length: 4 pages or 1,000 words. **Pays according to length, story type, and experience.**

Photos Returns photos and artwork. Send photos with submission. Reviews transparencies.

Tips "New approaches to familiar topics are especially welcome. Technical accuracy is essential. Please use scientific as well as popular names for plants and cover the subject in depth while avoiding overly academic presentation. Information should be made accessible to the reader, and we find this is best accomplished by writing from direct personal experience where possible and always in an informal style."

$ HOME DIGEST

Your Guide to Home and Life Improvement, Home Digest International, Inc., 115 George St., Unit 604, Oakville ON L6J 0A2 Canada. (905)844-3361. Fax: (905)849-4618. E-mail: homedigesteditor@sympatico.ca. Web site: www.homedigest.ca. **Contact:** William Roebuck, editor. **10% freelance written.** Quarterly magazine covering home and life management for families in the greater Toronto region. "*Home Digest* has a strong service slant, combining useful how-to journalism with coverage of the trends and issues of home ownership and family life. In essence, our focus is on the concerns of families living in their own homes." Estab. 1995. Circ. 670,000. Pays on publication. Publishes ms an average of 3 months after acceptance. Byline given. Buys first North American serial rights and the rights to archive articles on the magazine's Web site. Editorial lead time 3 months. Submit seasonal material 5 months in advance. Accepts queries by mail, e-mail. Accepts previously published material. Accepts simultaneous submissions. Responds in 1 month to queries. Sample copy for 9×6 SAE and 2 Canadian first-class stamps. Writer's guidelines online.

Nonfiction General interest, how-to (home renovation tips, decorating tips), humor (living in Toronto). No opinion, fashion, or beauty. **Buys 4 mss/year.** Query. Length: 350-700 words. **Pays $35-100 (Canadian).**

Photos Send photos with submission. Reviews prints, JPEGs. Buys one-time rights. Pays $10-20/photo. Captions, identification of subjects, model releases required.

Columns/Departments Household Hints (tested tips that work); Home Renovation Tips; all 300-350 words. **Buys 4-6 mss/year.** Query. **Pays $40-50 (Canadian).**

Tips "Base your ideas on practical experiences. We're looking for 'uncommon' advice that works."

N ⊘ HOME MAGAZINE

Hachette Filipacchi Media U.S., Inc., 1633 Broadway, New York NY 10019. E-mail: homemag@hfnm.com. Web site: www.homemag.com. Monthly magazine written for the American home owner and home enthusiast. Circ. 1,020,938.

- Query before submitting.

$ $ $ $ HORTICULTURE

Gardening at Its Best, F+W Publications, Inc., 98 N. Washington St., Boston MA 02114. (617)742-5600. Fax: (617)367-6364. E-mail: sara.begg@hortmag.com. Web site: www.hortmag.com. **Contact:** Sara Begg, senior editor. Bimonthly magazine. "*Horticulture*, the country's oldest gardening magazine, is designed for active amateur gardeners. Our goal is to offer a blend of text, photographs and illustrations that will both instruct and inspire readers." Circ. 240,000. Byline given. Offers kill fee. Buys first North American serial, one-time rights. Submit seasonal material 10 months in advance. Accepts queries by mail, e-mail, fax. Responds in 3 months to queries. Sample copy not available. Writer's guidelines for SASE or by e-mail.

Nonfiction "We look for an encouraging personal experience, anecdote and opinion. At the same time, a thorough article should to some degree place its subject in the broader context of horticulture." **Buys 15 mss/year.** Query with published clips, subject background material and SASE. Length: 1,000-2,000 words. **Pays $600-1,500.** Pays expenses of writers on assignment if previously arranged with editor.

Columns/Departments Query with published clips, subject background material and SASE. Include disk where possible. **Pays $50-750.**

Tips "We believe every article must offer ideas or illustrate principles that our readers might apply on their own gardens. No matter what the subject, we want our readers to become better, more creative gardeners."

$ $ $ $ HOUSE BEAUTIFUL

The Hearst Corp., 1700 Broadway, New York NY 10019. (212)903-5084. Web site: www.housebeautiful.com. Editor: Mark Mayfield. Monthly magazine. Targeted toward affluent, educated readers ages 30-40. Covers home design and decoration, gardening and entertaining, interior design, architecture and travel. Circ. 865,352. Editorial lead time 3 months. Sample copy not available.

KITCHEN YEARBOOK

Universal Magazines, Ltd., Unit 5, 6-8 Byfield St., North Ryde NSW 2113 Australia. (61)(2)9887-0367. Fax: (61)(2)9887-0350. E-mail: mgardener@universalmagazines.com.au. Web site: www.completehome.com.au. Editor: Melanie Gardener. Annual magazine covering the year's most innovative and inspiring kitchen designs

Nonfiction General interest, how-to, inspirational, new product, photo feature. Query.

KITCHENS & BATHROOMS QUARTERLY

Universal Magazines, Ltd., Unit 5, 6-8 Byfield St., North Ryde NSW 2113 Australia. (61)(2)9887-0367. Fax: (61)(2)9887-0350. E-mail: mgardener@universalmagazines.com.au. Web site: www.completehome.com.au. Editor: Melanie Gardener. Quarterly magazine for planning, designing, building or renovating your kitchen or bathroom.

Nonfiction General interest, how-to, new product, photo feature. Query.

$ $ $ LAKESTYLE

Celebrating Life on the Water, Bayside Publications, Inc., P.O. Box 170, Excelsior MN 55331. (952)470-1380. Fax: (952)470-1389. E-mail: editor@lakestyle.com. Web site: www.lakestyle.com. **50% freelance written.** Quarterly magazine. "*Lakestyle* is committed to celebrating the lifestyle chosen by lake home and cabin owners." Estab. 2000. Circ. 40,000. Pays on publication. Publishes ms an average of 3 months after acceptance. Byline given. Offers 10% kill fee. Buys all rights. Editorial lead time 2 months. Submit seasonal material 3 months in advance. Accepts queries by mail, e-mail, fax, phone. Accepts previously published material. Responds in 3 weeks to queries; 1 month to mss. Sample copy for $5. Writer's guidelines online.

Nonfiction Essays, historical/nostalgic, how-to, humor, inspirational, interview/profile, new product, photo feature. No direct promotion of product. **Buys 15 mss/year.** Query with or without published clips or send complete ms. Length: 500-2,500 words. **Pays 25-50¢/word for assigned articles; 10-25¢/word for unsolicited articles.** Sometimes pays expenses of writers on assignment.

Photos State availability of or send photos with submission. Rights purchased vary. Offers no additional payment for photos accepted with ms. Captions, identification of subjects, model releases required.

Columns/Departments Lakestyle Entertaining (entertaining ideas); Lakestyle Gardening (gardening ideas); On the Water (boating/playing on the lake); Hidden Treasures (little known events); At the Cabin (cabin owner's information); all approximately 1,000 words. **Buys 10 mss/year.** Query with or without published clips or send complete ms. **Pays 10-25¢/word.**

Tips "*Lakestyle* is interested in enhancing the lifestyle chosen by our readers, a thorough knowledge of cabin/lake home issues helps writers fulfill this goal."

N LOG HOME LIVING

Home Buyer Publications, Inc., 4125 Lafayette Center Dr., Suite 100, Chantilly VA 20151. (703)222-9411. Fax: (703)222-3209. E-mail: editor@loghomeliving.com. Web site: www.loghomeliving.com. **Contact:** Editor. **90% freelance written.** Monthly magazine for enthusiasts who are dreaming of, planning for, or actively building a log home. Estab. 1989. Circ. 132,000. **Pays on acceptance.** Publishes ms an average of 6 months after acceptance. Byline given. Offers $100 kill fee. Buys first North American serial, second serial (reprint) rights.

Editorial lead time 6 months. Submit seasonal material 6 months in advance. Accepts queries by mail, e-mail. Accepts previously published material. Responds in 6 weeks to queries. Sample copy for $4. Writer's guidelines online.

Nonfiction How-to (build or maintain log home), interview/profile (log home owners), personal experience, photo feature (log homes), technical (design/decor topics), travel. **Buys 60 mss/year.** Query with SASE. Length: 1,000-2,000 words. **Payment depends on length, nature of the work and writer's expertise.** Pays expenses of writers on assignment.

Reprints Send tearsheet, photocopy or typed ms and information about when and where the material previously appeared.

Photos State availability with submission. Reviews contact sheets, 4×5 transparencies, 4×6 prints. Buys one-time rights. Negotiates payment individually.

Tips "*Log Home Living* is devoted almost exclusively to modern manufactured and handcrafted kit log homes. Our interest in historical or nostalgic stories of very old log cabins, reconstructed log homes, or one-of-a-kind owner-built homes is secondary and should be queried first."

MIDWEST HOME AND GARDEN

U.S. Trust Bldg., 730 S. Second Ave., Suite 600, Minneapolis MN 55402. Fax: (612)371-5801. E-mail: kmeewes@mnmo.com. Web site: www.midwesthomemag.com. **Contact:** Kori Meewes. **50% freelance written.** "*Midwest Home and Garden* is an upscale shelter magazine showcasing innovative architecture, interesting interior design, and beautiful gardens of the Midwest." Estab. 1997. Circ. 80,000. **Pays on acceptance.** Byline given. Accepts queries by mail, e-mail, fax. Writer's guidelines online.

Nonfiction Profiles of regional designers, architects, craftspeople related to home and garden. Photo-driven articles on home decor and design, and gardens. Book excerpts, essays, how-to (garden and design), interview/profile (brief), new product, photo feature. Query with résumé, published clips, and SASE. Length: 300-1,000 words. **Payment negotiable.**

Columns/Departments Back Home (essay on home/garden topics), 800 words; Design Directions (people and trends in home and garden), 300 words.

Tips "We are always looking for great new interior design, architecture, and gardens—in Minnesota and in the Midwest."

N $ $ MILWAUKEE HOME & FINE LIVING

Trails Media Group, Inc., 6525 W. Bluemound Rd., Milwaukee WI 53213. (414)771-9945. Fax: (414)771-9975. E-mail: mheditor@wistrails.com. Web site: www.milwaukee-home.com. Assistant Editor: Lori Nadolski. **Contact:** Manya Kaczkowski, editor. **80% freelance written.** Bimonthly magazine covering homes, gardens, art, furnishings, food, fashion. Estab. 2004. Circ. 17,500. Pays on publication. Publishes ms an average of 6 months after acceptance. Byline given. Offers 25% kill fee. Buys first North American serial, electronic rights. Editorial lead time 6 months. Submit seasonal material 1 year in advance. Accepts queries by mail, e-mail. Responds in 6 weeks to queries. Sample copy for 10×13 SAE and 2 first-class stamps. Writer's guidelines online.

Nonfiction General interest, historical/nostalgic, interview/profile, new product, photo feature. **Buys 80 mss/year.** Query with published clips. Length: 100-1,200 words. **Pays $25-360.** Sometimes pays expenses of writers on assignment.

Columns/Departments Insights (home furnishings, trends, tips, products); Fine Living (travel, fashion, dining, local events), both 200 words. **Pays $25-360.**

Tips "Please submit queries on local topics relating to specific homes and gardens, and products that can be obtained in the Milwaukee, Wisconsin, 7-county area. Read the magazine for style and content."

$ $ MOUNTAIN LIVING

Network Communications, 1777 S. Harrison St., Suite 1200, Denver CO 80210. (303)248-2062. Fax: (303)248-2064. E-mail: irawlings@mountainliving.com. Web site: www.mountainliving.com. **Contact:** Irene Rawlings, editor-in-chief. **50% freelance written.** Magazine published 8 times/year covering "shelter and lifestyle issues for people who live in, visit, or hope to live in the mountains." Estab. 1994. Circ. 48,000. **Pays on acceptance.** Publishes ms an average of 4 months after acceptance. Byline given. Buys one-time magazine rights, plus right to run piece online. Editorial lead time 6 months. Submit seasonal material 8-12 months in advance. Accepts queries by mail, e-mail, phone. Responds in 6 weeks to queries; 2 months to mss. Sample copy for $5 or on Web site.

Nonfiction Photo feature, travel, home features. **Buys 30 mss/year.** Query with published clips. Length: 500-1,000 words. **Pays $250-500.** Sometimes pays expenses of writers on assignment.

Photos Provide photos (slides, transparencies, or on disk, saved as TIFF and at least 300 dpi). State availability with submission. Buys one-time rights plus rights to run photo on Web site. Negotiates payment individually.

Columns/Departments ML Recommends; Short Travel Tips; New Product Information; Art; Insider's Guide;

Entertaining. Length: 300-800 words. **Buys 35 mss/year.** Query with published clips. **Pays $50-500.**

Tips "A deep understanding of and respect for the mountain environment is essential. Think out of the box. We love to be surprised. Write a brilliant, short query, and always send clips. Before you query, read the magazine to get a sense of who we are and what we like."

N $$$$ ORGANIC GARDENING

Rodale, 33 E. Minor St., Emmaus PA 18098. (610)967-8363. Fax: (610)967-7722. E-mail: og@rodale.com. Web site: www.organicgardening.com. **75% freelance written.** Bimonthly magazine. "*Organic Gardening* is for gardeners who enjoy gardening as an integral part of a healthy lifestyle. Editorial shows readers how to grow flowers, edibles, and herbs, as well as information on ecological landscaping. Also covers organic topics including soil building and pest control." Estab. 1942. Circ. 300,000. Pays between acceptance and publication. Byline given. Buys all rights. Accepts queries by mail, fax. Responds in 3 months to queries. Sample copy not available.

Nonfiction Query with published clips and outline. **Pays up to $1/word for experienced writers.**

The online magazine carries original content not found in the print edition.

Tips "If you have devised a specific technique that's worked in your garden, have insight into the needs and uses of a particular plant or small group of plants, or have designed whole gardens that integrate well with their environment, and, if you have the capacity to clearly describe what you've learned to other gardeners in a simple but engaging manner, please send us your article ideas. Read a recent issue of the magazine thoroughly before you submit your ideas. If you have an idea that you believe fits with our content, send us a 1-page description of it that will grab our attention in the same manner you intend to entice readers into your article. Be sure to briefly explain why your idea is uniquely suited to our magazine. (We will not publish an article that has already appeared elsewhere. Also, please tell us if you are simultaneously submitting your idea to another magazine.) Tell us about the visual content of your idea—that is, what photographs or illustrations would you suggest be included with your article to get the ideas and information across to readers? If you have photographs, let us know. If you have never been published before, consider whether your idea fits into our Gardener to Gardener department. The shorter, narrowly focused articles in the department and its conversational tone make for a more accessible avenue into the magazine for inexperienced writers."

N RENOVATE & EXTEND

(formerly *Extend*), Universal Magazines, Ltd., Unit 5, 6-8 Byfield St., North Ryde NSW 2113 Australia. (61)(2)9887-0367. Fax: (61)(2)9805-0714. E-mail: sgolight@bigpond.net.au. Web site: www.completehome.com.au. Editor: Suni Golightly. Quarterly magazine featuring a mix of home extension and renovation projects that add style, value and space to homes.

Nonfiction General interest, how-to, inspirational, new product, photo feature. Query.

$$ SAN DIEGO HOME/GARDEN LIFESTYLES

McKinnon Enterprises, Box 719001, San Diego CA 92171-9001. (858)571-1818. Fax: (858)571-6379. E-mail: carlson@sdhg.net; ditler@sdhg.net. **Contact:** Wayne Carlson, editor; Eva Ditler, managing editor. **50% freelance written.** Monthly magazine covering homes, gardens, food, intriguing people, real estate, art, culture, and local travel for residents of San Diego city and county. Estab. 1979. Circ. 50,000. Pays on publication. Publishes ms an average of 3 months after acceptance. Byline given. Buys first North American serial rights. Submit seasonal material 3 months in advance. Accepts queries by mail, e-mail, fax, phone. Responds in 3 months to queries. Sample copy for $4.

Nonfiction Residential architecture and interior design (San Diego-area homes only), remodeling (must be well-designed—little do-it-yourself), residential landscape design, furniture, other features oriented toward upscale readers interested in living the cultured good life in San Diego. Articles must have a local angle. Query with published clips. Length: 700-2,000 words. **Pays $50-350 for assigned articles.**

Tips "No out-of-town, out-of-state subject material. Most freelance work is accepted from local writers. Gear stories to the unique quality of San Diego. We try to offer only information unique to San Diego—people, places, shops, resources, etc."

$$ SEATTLE HOMES & LIFESTYLES

Network Communications, Inc., 1221 E. Pike St., Suite 305, Seattle WA 98122-3930. (206)322-6699. Fax: (206)322-2799. E-mail: gisellesmith@seattlehomesmag.com. Web site: www.seattlehomesmag.com. **Contact:** Giselle Smith, editor-in-chief. **60% freelance written.** Magazine published 10 times/year covering home design and lifestyles. "*Seattle Homes and Lifestyles* showcases the finest homes and gardens in the Northwest, and the personalities and lifestyles that make this region special. We try to help our readers take full advantage of the resources the region has to offer with in-depth coverage of events, entertaining, shopping, food, and wine. And we write about it with a warm, personal approach that underscores our local perspective." Estab. 1996. Circ. 30,000. **Pays on acceptance.** Publishes ms an average of 2 months after acceptance. Byline given. Offers

25% kill fee. Buys first, electronic rights. Editorial lead time 3 months. Submit seasonal material 4 months in advance. Accepts previously published material. Accepts simultaneous submissions. Responds in 4 months to queries.

Nonfiction General interest, how-to (decorating, cooking), interview/profile, photo feature. "No essays, travel stories, sports coverage." **Buys 95 mss/year.** Query with published clips via mail. Length: 300-1,500 words. **Pays $150-400.**

Photos State availability with submission. Reviews contact sheets, transparencies, prints. Buys one-time rights. Negotiates payment individually. Captions, identification of subjects, model releases required.

Tips "We're always looking for experienced journalists with clips that demonstrate a knack for writing engaging, informative features. We're also looking for writers knowledgeable about architecture and decorating who can communicate a home's flavor and spirit through the written word. Since all stories are assigned by the editor, please do not submit manuscripts. Send a résumé and 3 published samples of your work. Story pitches are not encouraged. Please mail all submissions—do not e-mail or fax. Please don't call—we'll call you if we have an assignment. Writers from the Seattle area only."

N $ $ $ SMART HOMEOWNER

Navigator Publishing, P.O. Box 569, Portland ME 04112. (207)772-2466. Fax: (207)772-2879. E-mail: editors@smarthomeownermag.com. Web site: www.smarthomeownermag.com. **Contact:** Bob Freeman, editor. **75% freelance written.** Bimonthly magazine covering smart residential building practices, greenbuilding, energy efficiency, healthy home building and home automation. "We tell our readers how to build better homes. Primarily, we focus on 3 areas of residential home building: greenbuilding (eco-friendly building), energy efficiency, and healthy home building. We focus on products and systems homeowners can use to build better homes. We are not a DIY magazine, but rather strive to educate our readers about the options available to them if they are building or remodeling a home. Among the subjects we cover: Energy Star appliances, reclaimed flooring, nontoxic building materials, energy-efficient windows and doors, mold-resistant building materials, efficient heating and cooling systems, and anything else for residential building that is innovative, durable and nontoxic, and that results in a more efficient, healthy, comfortable home." Pays half before publication; half on publication. Publishes ms an average of 2-4 months after acceptance. Byline given. Offers $150 kill fee. Buys first North American serial, all rights, makes work-for-hire assignments. Editorial lead time 4 months. Submit seasonal material 4 months in advance. Accepts queries by mail, e-mail, fax. Accepts simultaneous submissions. Responds in 2 weeks to queries; 1 month to mss. Sample copy online. Writer's guidelines free.

Nonfiction General interest, interview/profile, new product, technical. Special issues: Green Issue (May/June); Home Energy Issue (September/October), both annual issues. Does not want DIY articles or anything that's too far out of the mainstream. "We are a mainstream greenbuilding magazine." **Buys 45 mss/year.** Query with or without published clips. Length: 800-2,400 words. **Pays $400-1,200.** Sometimes pays expenses of writers on assignment.

Photos State availability with submission. Reviews contact sheets, GIF/JPEG files. Buys one-time rights. Negotiates payment individually.

Columns/Departments Greenbuilding (residential green/eco-friendly residential building); Home Tech (home automation, energy efficient controls), 1,000-1,400 words. **Buys 18-25 mss/year.** Query. **Pays $500-700.**

Tips "We're particularly interested in what we call 'whole-house' articles, which focus on a single home and the resident homeowners."

SOUTHERN ACCENTS

Southern Progress Corp., 2100 Lakeshore Dr., Birmingham AL 35209. (205)445-6000. Fax: (205)445-6990. Web site: www.southernaccents.com. **Contact:** Dawn Cannon, managing editor. "*Southern Accents* celebrates the finest of the South." Estab. 1977. Circ. 370,000. Accepts queries by mail. Responds in 2 months to queries.

Nonfiction "Each issue features the finest homes and gardens along with a balance of features that reflect the affluent lifestyles of its readers, including architecture, antiques, entertaining, collecting, and travel." Query by mail with SASE, bio, clips, and photos.

Tips "Query us only with specific ideas targeted to our current columns."

⊘ MARTHA STEWART LIVING

Time Publishing, Inc., 11 W. 42nd St., 25th Floor, New York NY 10036. E-mail: mstewart@marthastewart.com. Web site: www.marthastewart.com. **Contact:** Editorial. Monthly magazine offering readers a unique combination of inspiration and how-to information focusing on our 8 core areas: Home, Cooking & Entertaining, Gardening, Crafts, Holidays, Keeping, Weddings, and Baby.

- Query before submitting.

$ $ $ STYLE AT HOME

Transcontinental Media, G.P., 25 Sheppard Ave. W., Suite 100, Toronto ON M2N 6S7 Canada. (416)733-7600. Fax: (416)218-3632. E-mail: letters@styleathome.com. Associate Editor: Laurie Grassi. **Contact:** Gail Johnston

Habs, editor-in-chief. **85% freelance written.** Magazine published 12 times/year. "The number one magazine choice of Canadian women aged 25 to 54 who have a serious interest in decorating. Provides an authoritative, stylish collection of inspiring and accessible Canadian interiors, decor projects; reports on style design trends." Estab. 1997. Circ. 230,000. **Pays on acceptance.** Byline given. Offers 50% kill fee. Buys first, electronic rights. Editorial lead time 4 months. Submit seasonal material 6 months in advance. Accepts queries by e-mail. Responds in 1 month to queries; 2 weeks to mss. Writer's guidelines by e-mail.

O━ Break in by "familiarizing yourself with the type of interiors we show. Be very up to date with the design and home decor market in Canada. Provide a lead to a fabulous home or garden."

Nonfiction Interview/profile, new product. "No how-to; these are planned in-house." **Buys 80 mss/year.** Query with published clips; include scouting shots with interior story queries. Length: 300-700 words. **Pays $300-1,000.** Sometimes pays expenses of writers on assignment.

Columns/Departments Humor (fun home decor/renovating experiences), 500 words. Query with published clips. **Pays $250-500.**

$ $ $ SU CASA

At Home in the Southwest, Hacienda Press, 4100 Wolcott Ave. NE, Suite B, Albuquerque NM 87109. (505)344-1783. Fax: (505)345-3295. E-mail: cpoling@sucasamagazine.com. Web site: www.sucasamagazine.com. **Contact:** Charles Poling, editor. **80% freelance written.** Magazine published 5 times/year covering southwestern homes, building, design, architecture for the reader comtemplating building, remodeling, or decorating a Santa Fe style home. Su Casa is tightly focused on Southwestern home building, architecture and design. "In particular, we feature New Mexico homes. We also cover alternative construction, far-out homes and contemporary design." Estab. 1995. Circ. 40,000. **Pays on acceptance.** Publishes ms an average of 6 months after acceptance. Byline given. Offers 50% kill fee. Buys one-time, second serial (reprint) rights. Editorial lead time 6-9 months. Submit seasonal material 9 months in advance. Accepts queries by mail, e-mail, fax, phone. Responds in 1 week to queries; 1 month to mss. Sample copy for free. Writer's guidelines free.

- All the departments are assigned long term. "We encourage writers to pitch feature story ideas. We don't cover trends or concepts, but rather homes that express them."

Nonfiction Book excerpts, essays, interview/profile, personal experience, photo feature. Special issues: The summer issue covers kitchen and bath topics. Does not want how-to articles, product reviews or features, no trends in southwest homes. **Buys 30 mss/year.** Query with published clips. Length: 1,000-2,500 words. **Pays $250-1,000.** Sometimes pays expenses of writers on assignment.

Photos State availability of or send photos with submission. Reviews GIF/JPEG files. Buys one-time rights. Offers $25-150/photo. Captions, identification of subjects, model releases, property releases required.

$ $ TEXAS GARDENER

The Magazine for Texas Gardeners, by Texas Gardeners, Suntex Communications, Inc., P.O. Box 9005, Waco TX 76714-9005. (254)848-9393. Fax: (254)848-9779. E-mail: info@texasgardener.com. Web site: www.texasgardener.com. **Contact:** Chris Corby, editor. **80% freelance written.** Works with a small number of new/unpublished writers each year. Bimonthly magazine covering vegetable and fruit production, ornamentals, and home landscape information for home gardeners in Texas. Estab. 1981. Circ. 20,000. Pays on publication. Publishes ms an average of 4 months after acceptance. Byline given. Buys first North American serial, all rights. Submit seasonal material 6 months in advance. Accepts queries by mail, e-mail, fax. Responds in 2 months to queries. Sample copy for $2.95 and SAE with 5 first-class stamps. Writer's guidelines for #10 SASE.

Nonfiction "We use articles that relate to Texas gardeners. We also like personality profiles on hobby gardeners and professional horticulturists who are doing somehting unique." How-to, humor, interview/profile, photo feature. **Buys 50-60 mss/year.** Query with published clips. Length: 800-2,400 words. **Pays $50-200.**

Photos "We prefer superb color and b&w photos; 90% of photos used are color." Send photos with submission. Reviews contact sheets, $2\frac{1}{4} \times 2\frac{1}{4}$ or 35mm color transparencies, 8×10 b&w prints. Pays negotiable rates. Identification of subjects, model releases required.

Columns/Departments Between Neighbors. **Pays $25.**

Tips "First, be a Texan. Then come up with a good idea of interest to home gardeners in this state. Be specific. Stick to feature topics like 'How Alley Gardening Became a Texas Tradition.' Leave topics like 'How to Control Fire Blight' to the experts. High quality photos could make the difference. We would like to add several writers to our group of regular contributors and would make assignments on a regular basis. Fillers are easy to come up with in-house. We want good writers who can produce accurate and interesting copy. Frequent mistakes made by writers in completing an article assignment for us are that articles are not slanted toward Texas gardening, show inaccurate or too little gardening information, or lack good writing style."

N $ $ $ $ THIS OLD HOUSE MAGAZINE

Time4Media/Time Inc., 1185 Avenue of the Americas, 27th Floor, New York NY 10036. Web site: www.thisoldhouse.com. Editor: Scott Omelianuk (scott_omelianunk@timeinc.com). Managing Editors: Laura Goldstein,

Kathryn Keller. **Contact:** Michael Stolper, assistant to the editor. **40% freelance written.** Magazine published 10 times/year covering home design, renovation, and maintenance. "*This Old House* is the ultimate resource for readers whose homes are their passions. The magazine's mission is threefold: to inform with lively service journalism and reporting on innovative new products and materials, to inspire with beautiful examples of fine craftsmanship and elegant architectural design, and to instruct with clear step-by-step projects that will enhance a home or help a homeowner maintain one. The voice of the magazine is not that of a rarefied design maven or a linear Mr. Fix It, but rather that of an eyes-wide-open, in-the-trenches homeowner who's eager for advice, tools, and techniques that'll help him realize his dream of a home." Estab. 1995. Circ. 960,000. **Pays on acceptance.** Publishes ms an average of 3-6 months after acceptance. Byline given. Buys all rights. Editorial lead time 3-12 months. Submit seasonal material 1 year in advance. Accepts queries by mail, e-mail.

Nonfiction Essays, how-to, new product, technical, must be house-related. **Buys 70 mss/year.** Query with published clips. Length: 250-2,500 words. **Pays $1/word.** Sometimes pays expenses of writers on assignment.

Columns/Departments Around the House (news, new products), 250 words. **Pays $1/word.**

N TIMBER HOME LIVING

(formerly Timber Frame Homes), 4125 Lafayette Center Dr., Suite 100, Chantilly VA 20151. (703)222-9411. E-mail: editor@timberhomeliving.com. Web site: www.timberhomeliving.com. **Contact:** Mike McCarthy, editor. **75% freelance written.** Quarterly magazine for people who own or are planning to build contemporary timber frame homes. It is devoted exclusively to timber frame homes that have a freestanding frame and wooden joinery. Our interest in historical, reconstructed timber frames and one-of-a-kind owner-built homes is secondary and should be queried first. Estab. 1991. Circ. 92,500. **Pays on acceptance.** Publishes ms an average of 3 months after acceptance. Byline given. Offers $100 kill fee. Buys first North American serial, second serial (reprint) rights. Accepts queries by mail, e-mail. Sample copy for $4. Writer's guidelines online.

Nonfiction General interest, how-to (construction advice), interview/profile (timber home owners), new product, photo feature, technical (design/decor). No historical articles. **Buys 15 mss/year.** Query with SASE. Length: 1,200-1,400 words. **Payment depends on the story's length, the nature of the work, and the expertise of the writer.** Sometimes pays expenses of writers on assignment.

Photos State availability with submission. Reviews contact sheets, transparencies, prints. Buys one-time rights. Negotiates payment individually.

TRADITIONAL HOME

Meredith Corp., 1716 Locust St., Des Moines 50309-3023. (515)284-3762. Fax: (515)284-2083. E-mail: traditionalhome@meredith.com. Web site: www.traditionalhome.com. Senior Decorating Editor: Candace Manroe. Senior Architecture Editor: Amy Elbert. Entertaining and Travel Editor: Carroll Stoner. Senior Features and Antiques Editor: Doris Athineos. Garden Editor: Ethne Clarke. Magazine published 8 times/year. Features articles on building and decorating homes in the traditional style. Estab. 1978. Circ. 950,000. Editorial lead time 6 months. Sample copy not available.

$ $ UNIQUE HOMES

Network Communications, Inc., 327 Wall St., Princeton NJ 08540. (609)688-1110. Fax: (609)688-0201. E-mail: lkim@uniquehomes.com. Web site: www.uniquehomes.com. Editor: Kathleen Carlin-Russell. **Contact:** Lauren Baier Kim, managing editor. **30% freelance written.** Bimonthly magazine covering luxury real estate for consumers and the high-end real estate industry. "Our focus is the luxury real estate market, i.e., the business of buying and selling luxury homes, as well as regional real estate market trends." Pays on publication. Publishes ms an average of 3 months after acceptance. Byline given. Buys all rights. Editorial lead time 4 months. Submit seasonal material 4 months in advance. Accepts queries by mail, e-mail, fax. Responds in 1 month to queries; 4 months to mss. Sample copy online. Writer's guidelines not available.

Nonfiction Looking for high-end luxury real estate profiles on cities and geographical regions. Luxury real estate, interior design, landscaping, home features. Special issues: Golf Course Living; Resort Living; Ski Real Estate; Farms, Ranches and Country Estates; Waterfront Homes; International Homes. **Buys 36 mss/year.** Query with published clips and résumé. Length: 500-1,500 words. **Pays $150-500.**

Photos State availability with submission. Reviews transparencies, prints. Buys all rights. Offers no additional payment for photos accepted with ms. Captions required.

Tips "For profiles on specific geographical areas, seeking writers with an in-depth personal knowledge of the luxury real estate trends in those locations. Writers with in-depth knowledge of the high-end residential market (both domestic and abroad) are especially needed."

⊘ VERANDA

The Hearst Corp., 455 E. Paces Ferry Rd. NE, Suite 216, Atlanta GA 30305-3319. (404)261-3603. Fax: (404)364-9772. Web site: www.veranda.com. Bimonthly magazine. Written as an interior design magazine featuring creative design across the country and around the world. Circ. 380,890. Editorial lead time 5 months.

- Does not buy freelance materials or use freelance writers.

N $ $ VICTORIAN HOMES

Y-Visionary Publishing, LP, 265 S. Anita Dr., Suite 120, Orange CA 92868-3310. E-mail: editorial@victorianhomes.com. Web site: www.victorianhomesmag.com. **90% freelance written.** Bimonthly magazine covering Victorian home restoration and decoration. "*Victorian Homes* is read by Victorian home owners, restorers, house museum management, and others interested in the Victorian revival. Feature articles cover home architecture, interior design, furnishings, and the home's history. Photography is very important to the feature." Estab. 1981. Circ. 100,000. **Pays on acceptance.** Publishes ms an average of 1 year after acceptance. Byline given. Offers $50 kill fee. Buys first North American serial, one-time rights. Editorial lead time 4 months. Submit seasonal material 1 year in advance. Accepts queries by mail, e-mail, fax. Accepts simultaneous submissions. Responds in 6 weeks to queries; 2 months to mss. Sample copy and writer's guidelines for SAE.

O→ Break in with "access to good photography and reasonable knowledge of the Victorian era."

Nonfiction "Article must deal with structures—no historical articles on Victorian people or lifestyles." How-to (create period style curtains, wall treatments, bathrooms, kitchens, etc.), photo feature. **Buys 30-35 mss/year.** Query. Length: 800-1,800 words. **Pays $300-500.** Sometimes pays expenses of writers on assignment.

Photos State availability with submission. Reviews 2¼×2¼ transparencies. Buys one-time rights. Negotiates payment individually. Captions required.

$ $ WATER GARDENING

The Magazine for Pondkeepers, The Water Gardeners, Inc., P.O. Box 607, St. John IN 46373. (219)374-9419. Fax: (219)374-9052. E-mail: wgmag@watergardening.com. Web site: www.watergardening.com. **50% freelance written.** Bimonthly magazine. *Water Gardening* is for hobby water gardeners. "We prefer articles from a first-person perspective." Estab. 1996. Circ. 25,000. Pays on publication. Publishes ms an average of 6 months after acceptance. Byline given. Offers 50% kill fee. Buys first North American serial rights. Editorial lead time 6 months. Submit seasonal material 6-12 months in advance. Accepts queries by mail, e-mail, fax. Responds in 1 month to queries; 3 months to mss. Sample copy for $3. Writer's guidelines for #10 SASE.

Nonfiction How-to (construct, maintain, improve ponds, water features), interview/profile, new product, personal experience, photo feature. **Buys 18-20 mss/year.** Query. Length: 600-1,500 words.

Photos State availability with submission. Reviews contact sheets, 3×5 transparencies, 3×5 prints. Buys one-time rights. Negotiates payment individually. Captions, identification of subjects, model releases required.

HUMOR

$ FUNNY TIMES

A Monthly Humor Review, Funny Times, Inc., P.O. Box 18530, Cleveland Heights OH 44118. (216)371-8600. Fax: (216)371-8696. E-mail: ft@funnytimes.com. Web site: www.funnytimes.com. **Contact:** Raymond Lesser, Susan Wolpert, editors. **50% freelance written.** Monthly tabloid for humor. "*Funny Times* is a monthly review of America's funniest cartoonists and writers. We are the *Reader's Digest* of modern American humor with a progressive/peace-oriented/environmental/politically activist slant." Estab. 1985. Circ. 74,000. Pays on publication. Publishes ms an average of 3 months after acceptance. Byline given. Buys one-time, second serial (reprint) rights. Editorial lead time 2 months. Accepts previously published material. Accepts simultaneous submissions. Responds in 3 months to mss. Sample copy for $3 or 9×12 SAE with 3 first-class stamps (83¢ postage). Writer's guidelines online.

Nonfiction "We only publish humor or interviews with funny people (comedians, comic actors, cartoonists, etc.). Everything we publish is very funny. If your piece isn't extremely funny then don't bother to send it. Don't send us anything that's not outrageously funny. Don't send anything that other people haven't already read and told you they laughed so hard they peed their pants." Essays (funny), humor, interview/profile, opinion (humorous), personal experience (absolutely funny). **Buys 60 mss/year.** Send complete ms. Length: 500-700 words. **Pays $60 minimum.**

Reprints Accepts previously published submissions.

Columns/Departments Query with published clips.

Fiction Ray Lesser and Susan Wolpert, editors. "Anything funny." **Buys 6 mss/year.** Query with published clips. Length: 500-700 words. **Pays $50-150.**

Fillers Short humor. **Buys 6/year. Pays $20.**

Tips "Send us a small packet (1-3 items) of only your very funniest stuff. If this makes us laugh we'll be glad to ask for more. We particularly welcome previously published material that has been well-received elsewhere."

$ $ MAD MAGAZINE

1700 Broadway, New York NY 10019. (212)506-4850. E-mail: submissions@madmagazine.com. Web site: www.madmag.com. **Contact:** *MAD* Submissions Editor. **100% freelance written.** Monthly magazine "always on the lookout for new ways to spoof and to poke fun at hot trends." Estab. 1952. **Pays on acceptance.** Publishes ms an average of 6 months after acceptance. Byline given. Buys all rights. Submit seasonal material 6 months in advance. Responds in 10 weeks to queries. Sample copy and writer's guidelines online.

Nonfiction "Submit a premise with 3 or 4 examples of how you intend to carry it through, describing the action and visual content. Rough sketches desired but not necessary. One-page gags: 2- to 8-panel cartoon continuities as minimum very funny, maximum hilarious!" Satire, parody. "We're not interested in formats we're already doing or have done to death like 'what they say and what they really mean.' Don't send previously published submissions, riddles, advice columns, TV or movie satires, book manuscripts, top 10 lists, articles about Alfred E. Neuman, poetry, essays, short stories or other text pieces." **Buys 400 mss/year. Pays minimum of $500/page.**

Tips "Have fun! Remember to think visually! Surprise us! Freelancers can best break in with satirical nontopical material. Include SASE with each submission. Originality is prized. We like outrageous, silly and/or satirical humor."

INFLIGHT

$ $ $ HEMISPHERES

Pace Communications for United Airlines, Pace Communications, 1301 Carolina St., Greensboro NC 27401. (336)383-5690. E-mail: hemiedit@aol.com. Web site: www.hemispheresmagazine.com. **95% freelance written.** Monthly magazine for the educated, sophisticated business and recreational frequent traveler on an airline that spans the globe. "*Hemispheres* is an inflight magazine that interprets 'inflight' to be a mode of delivery rather than an editorial genre. As such, Hemispheres' task is to engage, intrigue and entertain its primary readers—an international, culturally diverse group of affluent, educated professionals and executives who frequently travel for business and pleasure on United Airlines. The magazine offers a global perspective and a focus on topics that cross borders as often as the people reading the magazine. That places our emphasis on ideas, concepts, and culture rather than products. We present that perspective in a fresh, artful and sophisticated graphic enviroment." Estab. 1992. Circ. 500,000. **Pays on acceptance.** Publishes ms an average of 4-6 months after acceptance. Byline given. Offers 20% kill fee. Buys first worldwide rights. Editorial lead time 8 months. Submit seasonal material 8 months in advance. Accepts queries by mail. Responds in 2 months to queries; 4 months to mss. Sample copy for $7.50. Writer's guidelines for #10 SASE.

Nonfiction "Keeping 'global' in mind, we look for topics that reflect a modern appreciation of the world's cultures and environment. No 'What I did (or am going to do) on a trip.' " General interest, humor, personal experience. Query with published clips. Length: 500-3,000 words. **Pays 50¢/word and up.**

Photos Reviews photos "only when we request them." State availability with submission. Buys one-time rights. Negotiates payment individually. Captions, identification of subjects, model releases required.

Columns/Departments Making a Difference (Q&A format interview with world leaders, movers, and shakers. A 500-600 word introduction anchors the interview. "We want to profile an international mix of men and women representing a variety of topics or issues, but all must truly be making a difference. No puffy celebrity profiles."); 15 Fascinating Facts (a snappy selection of 1- or 2-sentence obscure, intriguing, or travel-service-oriented items that the reader never knew about a city, state, country, or destination.); Executive Secrets (things that top executives know); Case Study (Business strategies of international companies or organizations. No lionizations of CEOs. Strategies should be the emphasis. "We want international candidates."); Weekend Breakway (Takes us just outside a major city after a week of business for several activities for a physically active, action-packed weekend. This isn't a sedentary "getaway" at a "property."); Roving Gourmet (Insider's guide to interesting eating in major city, resort area, or region. The slant can be anything from ethnic to expensive; not just "best." The 4 featured eateries span a spectrum from "hole in the wall," to "expense account lunch," and on to "big deal dining."); Collecting (occasional 800-word story on collections and collecting that can emphasize travel); Eye on Sports (global look at anything of interest in sports); Vintage Traveler (options for mature, experienced travelers); Savvy Shopper (Insider's tour of best places in the world to shop. Savvy Shopper steps beyond all those stories that just mention the great shopping at a particular destination. A shop-by-shop, gallery-by-gallery tour of the best places in the world.); Science and Technology (Substantive, insightful stories on how technology is changing our lives and the business world. Not just another column on audio components or software. No gift guides!); Aviation Journal (For those fascinated with aviation. Topics range widely.); Terminal Bliss (a great airports guide series); Grape And Grain (wine and spirits with emphasis on education, not one-upmanship); Show Business (films, music, and entertainment); Musings (humor or just curious musings); Quick Quiz (tests to amuse and educate); Travel Trends (brief, practical, invaluable, global, trend-oriented); Book Beat (Tackles topics like the Wodehouse Society, the birth of a book, the competition between local bookshops and national chains. Please, no review proposals.); What the World's Reading (residents explore how current bestsellers tell us what their country is thinking). Length: 1,400 words. Query with published clips. **Pays 50¢/word and up.**

Fiction Adventure, ethnic, historical, humorous, mainstream, mystery, explorations of those issues common to all people but within the context of a particular culture. **Buys 14 mss/year.** Send complete ms. Length: 1,000-4,000 words. **Pays 50¢/word and up.**

Tips "We increasingly require writers of 'destination' pieces or departments to 'live whereof they write.' Increasingly want to hear from US, UK, or other English-speaking/writing journalists (business & travel) who reside outside the US in Europe, South America, Central America, and the Pacific Rim—all areas that United flies. We're not looking for writers who aim at the inflight market. *Hemispheres* broke the fluffy mold of that tired domestic genre. Our monthly readers are a global mix on the cutting edge of the global economy and culture. They don't need to have the world filtered by US writers. We want a Hong Kong restaurant writer to speak for that city's eateries, so we need English-speaking writers around the globe. That's the 'insider' story our readers respect. We use resident writers for departments such as Roving Gourmet, Savvy Shopper, On Location, 3 Perfect Days, and Weekend Breakaway, but authoritative writers can roam in features. Sure we cover the US, but with a global view: No 'in this country' phraseology. 'Too American' is a frequent complaint for queries. We use UK English spellings in articles that speak from that tradition and we specify costs in local currency first before US dollars. Basically, all of above serves the realization that today, 'global' begins with respect for 'local.' That approach permits a wealth of ways to present culture, travel, and business for a wide readership. We anchor that with a reader-service mission that grounds everything in 'how to do it.' "

$ $ HORIZON AIR MAGAZINE

Paradigm Communications Group, 2701 First Ave., Suite 250, Seattle WA 98121. Fax: (206)448-6939. **Contact:** Michele Andrus Dill, editor. **90% freelance written.** Monthly inflight magazine covering travel, business, and leisure in the Pacific Northwest. "*Horizon Air Magazine* serves a sophisticated audience of business and leisure travelers. Stories must have a Northwest slant." Estab. 1990. Circ. 440,000/month. Pays on publication. Publishes ms an average of 1 year after acceptance. Byline given. Offers 33% kill fee. Buys first North American serial, electronic rights. Editorial lead time 6 months. Submit seasonal material 5 months in advance. Accepts queries by mail, fax. Sample copy for 10×12 SASE. Writer's guidelines for #10 SASE.

- Responds only if interested, so include e-mail and phone number but no need to include SASE for queries.

Nonfiction Essays (personal), general interest, historical/nostalgic, how-to, humor, interview/profile, personal experience, photo feature, travel, business. Special issues: Meeting planners' guide, golf, gift guide. No material unrelated to the Pacific Northwest. **Buys approximately 36 mss/year.** Query with published clips or send complete ms. Length: 1,500-3,000 words. **Pays $300-700.** Sometimes pays expenses of writers on assignment.

Photos State availability with submission. Reviews transparencies, prints. Buys one-time rights. Negotiates payment individually. Captions, identification of subjects, model releases required.

Columns/Departments Region (Northwest news/profiles), 200-400 words; Air Time (personal essays), 700 words. **Buys 15 mss/year.** Query with published clips. **Pays $100 (Region), $250 (Air Time).**

$ $ SKYLIGHTS

The Inflight Magazine of Spirit Airlines, Worth International Media Group, Inc., 5979 NW 151 St., Suite 120, Miami Lakes FL 33014. (305)828-0123. Fax: (305)828-0799. Web site: www.worthit.com. Executive Editor: Gretchen Schmidt; Managing Editor: Millie Acebal Rousseau. **Contact:** Skylights Editorial Department. Bimonthly magazine. Like Spirit Airlines, *Skylights* will be known for its practical and friendly sensibility. This publication is a clean, stylish, user-friendly product. This is not an old-school airline, and *Skylights* is not an old-school inflight. Circ. 5.5 million. Pays on publication. Byline sometimes given. Buys first North American serial rights. Editorial lead time 3-6 months. Submit seasonal material 4 months in advance. Accepts queries by mail. Responds in 4-6 weeks to queries. Writer's guidelines via e-mail at millie@worthit.com.

O→ "We're not going to bore readers with ponderous dissertations on weighty or esoteric topics, ho-hum something-for-everyone destination pieces, the stuffy de rigueur which-mutual-funds-to-watch business article. Instead, we're going to give readers the quick and practical lowdown on where they're going, what's going on once they get there, where they can sleep, eat, play, buy, relax. We'll present who and what they're talking about—names, faces, music, movies, books, gadgets, fashion—in chatty culture-current language. Our voice reflects a youthful sassy edge that—while never speaking down to our readers—amuses and delights our wide-ranging readership. Our readers are both leisure and business travelers."

Nonfiction General interest, humor, interview/profile, new product, travel. No first-person accounts or weighty topics. Stories should be practical and useful, but not something-for-everyone-type articles. **Buys 18 mss/year.** Query with published clips. Length: 350-1,200 words. **Pays 25-40¢/word.**

Photos State availability with submission. Reviews GIF/JPEG files. Buys one-time rights. Negotiaties payment individually. Captions, identification of subjects, model releases required.

Columns/Departments Events calendar (based on Spirit destinations), 1,200 words; Gizmos (latest and greatest gadgets), 250-word descriptions; Biz (bizz buzz), 650-800 words; Fast Reads (quick finds, books, movies, music, food, wine); Skybuys (hot buys and smart shopping options), 150-word descriptions; Beauty and Health Story (specific aspects of staying well), 800 words. **Buys 36 mss/year.** Query with published clips. **25-40¢/word.**

Fillers Crossword puzzles, think and do ideas for kids (entertainment for children, such as new DVDs). Length: 250-400 words. **Pays 25-40¢/word.**

$ $ $ $ SOUTHWEST AIRLINES SPIRIT

4333 Amon Carter Blvd., Fort Worth TX 76155. (817)967-1803. Fax: (817)931-3015. E-mail: editors@spiritmag.com. Web site: www.spiritmag.com. **Contact:** Ross McCammon, editor. Monthly magazine for passengers on Southwest Airlines. Estab. 1992. Circ. 380,000. **Pays on acceptance.** Byline given. Buys first North American serial, electronic rights. Responds in 1 month to queries.

Nonfiction "Seeking lively, accessible, entertaining, relevant, and trendy travel, business, lifestyle, sports, celebrity, food, tech-product stories on newsworthy/noteworthy topics in destinations served by Southwest Airlines; well-researched and reported; multiple source only. Experienced magazine professionals only." **Buys about 40 mss/year.** Query by mail only with published clips. Length: 1,500 words (features). **Pays $1/word.** Pays expenses of writers on assignment.

Columns/Departments Length: 800-900 words. **Buys about 21 mss/year.** Query by mail only with published clips.

Fillers Buys 12/year. Length: 250 words. **Pays variable amount.**

Tips "*Southwest Airlines Spirit* magazine reaches more than 2.8 million readers every month aboard Southwest Airlines. Our median reader is a college-educated, 32- to 40-year-old traveler with a household income around $90,000. Writers must have proven magazine capabilities, a sense of fun, excellent reporting skills, a smart, hip style, and the ability to provide take-away value to the reader in sidebars, charts, and/or lists."

$ $ SPIRIT OF ALOHA

The Inflight Magazine of Aloha Airlines, Honolulu Publishing Co., Ltd., 707 Richards St., Suite 525, Honolulu HI 96813. (808)524-7400. Fax: (808)531-2306. E-mail: tchapman@honpub.com. Web site: www.spiritofaloha.com. **Contact:** Tom Chapman, editor. **80% freelance written.** Bimonthly magazine covering Hawaii. Estab. 1978. Circ. 100,000. **Pays on acceptance.** Publishes ms an average of 2 months after acceptance. Byline given. Buys first rights. Editorial lead time 2 months. Submit seasonal material 4 months in advance. Accepts queries by mail, e-mail. Responds in up to 1 month to queries. Writer's guidelines by e-mail.

Nonfiction Should be related to Hawaii. **Buys 40 mss/year.** Query with published clips. Length: 1,500-2,500 words. **Pays $600 and up.**

Photos State availability with submission. Reviews transparencies. Buys one-time rights. Negotiates payment individually. Captions, identification of subjects, model releases required.

$ $ $ $ US AIRWAYS MAGAZINE

Pace Communications, 1301 Carolina St., Greensboro NC 27401. E-mail: edit@usairwaysmag.com. Web site: www.usairwaysmag.com. Editor: Lance Elko. **Contact:** Submissions Editor. Monthly magazine for travelers on US Airways. "We focus on travel, lifestyle and pop culture." Estab. 2006. Circ. 441,000. **Pays on acceptance.** Publishes ms an average of 4 months after acceptance. Byline given. Buys exclusive worldwide rights for all media for 120 days rights. Editorial lead time 3 months. Accepts queries by mail, e-mail. Responds in 6 weeks to queries; 1 month to mss. Sample copy for $7.50 or online. Writer's guidelines online.

Nonfiction Features are highly visual, focusing on some ususual or unique angle of travel, food, business, or other topic approved by a US Airways editor. General interest, personal experience, travel, food, lifestyle, sports. **Buys 200-350 mss/year.** Query with published clips. Length: 100-1,500 words. **Pays $100-1,500.** Sometimes pays expenses of writers on assignment.

Photos State availability with submission. Reviews contact sheets, negatives, transparencies. Buys one-time rights. Negotiates payment individually. Identification of subjects, model releases required.

Columns/Departments Several columns are authored by a single writer under long-term contract with US Airways Magazine. Departments open to freelance pitches include: All Over the Map; Alter Ego; Straight Talk; Hands On; Shelf Life; In Gear; Get Personal; and Get Away. All of these departments may be viewed on the magazine's Web site.

Tips "We look for smart, pithy writing that addresses travel, lifestyle and pop culture. Study the magazine for content, style and tone. Queries for story ideas should be to the point and presented clearly. Any written correspondence should include a SASE."

$ $ $ WASHINGTON FLYER MAGAZINE

1707 L St., NW, Suite 800, Washington DC 20036. (202)331-9393. Fax: (202)331-2043. E-mail: lauren@themagazinegroup.com. Web site: www.fly2dc.com. **Contact:** Lauren Paige Kennedy, editor-in-chief. **60% freelance written.** Bimonthly magazine for business and pleasure travelers at Washington National and Washington Dulles International airports INSI. "Primarily affluent, well-educated audience that flies frequently in and out of Washington, DC." Estab. 1989. Circ. 182,000. **Pays on acceptance.** Byline given. Offers 25% kill fee. Buys first North American serial rights. Submit seasonal material 4 months in advance. Accepts queries by mail, e-mail, fax. Responds in 10 weeks to queries. Sample copy for 9×12 SAE with $2 postage. Writer's guidelines online.

> O→ "First understand the magazine—from the nuances of its content to its tone. Best departments to get your foot in the door are 'Washington Insider' and 'Mini Escapes.' The former deals with new business, the arts, sports, etc. in Washington. The latter: getaways that are within 4 hours of Washington by car. Regarding travel, we're less apt to run stories on sedentary pursuits (i.e., inns, B&Bs, spas). Our readers want to get out and discover an area, whether it's DC or Barcelona. Action-oriented activities work best. Also, the best way to pitch is via e-mail. Our mail is sorted by interns, and sometimes I never get queries. E-mail is so immediate, and I can give a more personal response."

Nonfiction One international destination feature per issue, determined 6 months in advance. One feature per issue on aspect of life in Washington. General interest, interview/profile, travel, business. No personal experiences, poetry, opinion or inspirational. **Buys 20-30 mss/year.** Query with published clips. Length: 800-1,200 words. **Pays $500-900.**

Photos State availability with submission. Reviews negatives, almost always color transparencies. Buys one-time rights. Considers additional payment for top-quality photos accepted with ms. Identification of subjects required.

Columns/Departments Washington Insider; Travel; Hospitality; Airports and Airlines; Restaurants; Shopping, all 800-1,200 words. Query. **Pays $500-900.**

Tips "Know the Washington market and issues relating to frequent business/pleasure travelers as we move toward a global economy. With a bimonthly publication schedule it's important that stories remain viable as possible during the magazine's 2-month 'shelf life.' No telephone calls, please and understand that most assignments are made several months in advance. Queries are best sent via e-mail."

WILD BLUE YONDER

1099 18th St., Suite 500, Denver CO 80202. (303)296-0339. Fax: (303)296-3410. E-mail: editorial@gowildblueyonder.com. Web site: www.gowildblueyonder.com. **60% freelance written.** Prefers queries via e-mail. "Don't waste the editor's time. Know the route and the publication before you query." Pays 10 days after publication. Offers $25 kill fee. Sample copy for $5. Writer's guidelines online.

Fiction Send complete ms.

JUVENILE

$ $ AMERICAN GIRL

8400 Fairway Place, Middleton WI 53562. Web site: www.americangirl.com. **Contact:** Magazine Department Assistant. **5% freelance written.** Bimonthly 4-color magazine covering hobbies, crafts and profiles of interest to girls ages 8-12. "We want thoughtfully developed children's literature with good characters and plots." Estab. 1992. Circ. 700,000. **Pays on acceptance.** Byline given for larger features, not departments. Offers 50% kill fee. Buys first North American serial, all rights. Editorial lead time 6 months. Submit seasonal material 6 months in advance. Accepts queries by mail. Accepts previously published material. Accepts simultaneous submissions. Responds in 3 months to queries. Sample copy for $4.50 (check made out to *American Girl*) and 9×12 SAE with $1.98 postage. Writer's guidelines online.

> O→ Best opportunity for freelancers is the Girls Express section. "We're looking for short profiles of girls who are into sports, the arts, interesting hobbies, cultural activities, and other areas. A key: The girl must be the 'star' and the story must be from her point of view. Be sure to include the age of the girls you're pitching to us. If you have any photo leads, please send those, too. We also welcome how-to stories—how to send away for free things, hot ideas for a cool day, how to write the President and get a response. In addition, we're looking for easy crafts that can be explained in a few simple steps. Stories in Girls Express have to be told in no more than 175 words. We prefer to receive ideas in query form rather than finished manuscripts."

Nonfiction Pays $300 minimum for feature articles. Pays expenses of writers on assignment.

Photos "We prefer to shoot." State availability with submission. Buys all rights.

Columns/Departments Girls Express (short profiles of girls with unusual and interesting hobbies that other girls want to read about), 175 words; Brain Waves (puzzles, games, etc.—especially looking for seasonal). Query.

Fiction Adventure, humorous, slice-of-life vignettes. No romance, science fiction, fantasy. **Buys 6 mss/year.** Query with published clips. Length: 2,300 words maximum. **Pays $500 minimum.**

N $ AQUILA MAGAZINE

New Leaf Publishing Ltd, Studio 2, Willowfield Studios, 67a Willowfield Rd., Eastbourne, East Sussex England BN22 8AP United Kingdom. (44)(132)343-1313. Fax: (44)(132)373-1136. E-mail: info@aquila.co.uk. Web site: www.aquila.co.uk. **Contact:** Janet Thomson. Magazine for children 8-12 years old. Circ. 40,000. Sample copy for £5.

"We aim to provide quality ideals and to encourage children to develop caring and thoughtful attitudes toward others and their environment."

Nonfiction Contact the editor to discuss ideas. Features are only likely to be of interest if they are highly original in presentation and content and use specialist/inside knowledge. Query. Length: 600-800 words. **Pays £50-75.**

Fiction Submit either 1 short story or a 2-4 instalments of a story. Each instalment must be satisfying to read in its own right, but also include an ending that tempts the reader to return for the next part. Length: 1,000-1,500 words. **Pays £90/short story; £80/episode for a serial.**

$ BABYBUG

Carus Publishing Co., 140 S. Dearborn, Suite 1450, Chicago IL 60603. (312)701-1720. Web site: www.cricketmag.com. Editor-in-Chief: Marianne Carus. Editorial Director/Editor: Alice Letvin. Art Director: Suzanne Beck. **50% freelance written.** Board-book magazine published monthly except for combined May/June and July/August issues. "*Babybug* is 'the listening and looking magazine for infants and toddlers,' intended to be read aloud by a loving adult to foster a love of books and reading in young children ages 6 months-3 years." Estab. 1994. Circ. 45,000. Pays on publication. Byline given. Accepts simultaneous submissions. Responds in 3 months to mss. Writer's guidelines online.

Nonfiction Basic words and concepts. **Buys 10-20 mss/year.** Submit complete ms, SASE. Length: 10 words maximum. **Pays $25 minimum.**

Photos "Artists should submit review samples (tearsheets/photocopies) of artwork to be kept in our illustrator files." Author-illustrators may submit a complete ms with art samples. The ms will be evaluated for quality of concept and text before the art is considered. Buys all rights; the physical artwork remains the property of the illustrator and may be used for self promotion. Pays $500/spread; $250/page.

Fiction Stories must be simple and concrete. **Buys 10-20 mss/year.** Length: 2-8 short sentences. **$25 minimum.**

Poetry Rhythmic, rhyming. Length: 8 lines maximum. **$25 minimum.**

Tips "Imagine having to read your story or poem—out loud—50 times or more! That's what parents will have to do. Babies and toddlers demand, 'Read it again!' Your material must hold up under repetition. And humor is much appreciated by all."

$$$$ BOYS' LIFE

Boy Scouts of America, P.O. Box 152079, Irving TX 75015-2079. (972)580-2366. Fax: (972)580-2079. Web site: www.boyslife.org. **Contact:** Michael Goldman, senior editor. **75% freelance written.** Prefers to work with published/established writers; works with small number of new/unpublished writers each year. Monthly magazine covering activities of interest to all boys ages 6-18. Most readers are Boy Scouts or Cub Scouts. "*Boys' Life* covers Boy Scout activities and general interest subjects for ages 6-18, Boy Scouts, Cub Scouts and others of that age group." Estab. 1911. Circ. 1,300,000. **Pays on acceptance.** Publishes ms an average of 1 year after acceptance. Buys one-time rights. Accepts queries by mail. Responds in 2 months to queries. Sample copy for $3.60 and 9×12 SAE. Writer's guidelines for #10 SASE or online.

Nonfiction Subject matter is broad, everything from professional sports to American history to how to pack a canoe. Look at a current list of the BSA's more than 100 merit badge pamphlets for an idea of the wide range of subjects possible. Uses strong photo features with about 500 words of text. Separate payment or assignment for photos. How-to, photo feature, hobby and craft ideas. **Buys 60 mss/year.** Query with SASE. No phone queries. Length: Major articles run 500-1,500 words; preferred length is about 1,000 words, including sidebars and boxes. **Pays $400-1,500.** Pays expenses of writers on assignment.

Columns/Departments "Science, nature, earth, health, sports, space and aviation, cars, computers, entertainment, pets, history, and music are some of the columns for which we use 300-750 words of text. This is a good place to show us what you can do." **Buys 75-80 mss/year.** Query. **Pays $250-300.**

Fiction Adventure, humorous, mystery, science fiction, western, sports. **Buys 12-15 mss/year.** Send complete ms. Length: 1,000-1,500 words. **Pays $750 minimum.**

Tips "We strongly recommend reading at least 12 issues of the magazine before you submit queries. We are a good market for any writer willing to do the necessary homework."

$ BREAD FOR GOD'S CHILDREN

Bread Ministries, Inc., P.O. Box 1017, Arcadia FL 34265. (863)494-6214. Fax: (863)993-0154. E-mail: bread@sunline.net. Editor: Judith M. Gibbs. **Contact:** Donna Wade, editorial secretary. **10% freelance written.** Published 6-8 times/year. "An interdenominational Christian teaching publication published 6-8 times/year written to aid children and youth in leading a Christian life." Estab. 1972. Circ. 10,000. Pays on publication. Publishes ms an average of 6 months after acceptance. Byline given. Buys first rights. Accepts queries by mail. Accepts simultaneous submissions. Responds in 6 months to mss. Three sample copies for 9×12 SAE and 5 first-class stamps. Writer's guidelines for #10 SASE.

- Break in with a good story about a 6-10 year old gaining insight into a spiritual principle—without an adult preaching the message to him.

Reprints Send tearsheet and information about when and where the material previously appeared.

Columns/Departments Let's Chat (children's Christian values), 500-700 words; Teen Page (youth Christian values), 600-800 words; Idea Page (games, crafts, Bible drills). **Buys 5-8 mss/year.** Send complete ms. **Pays $30.**

Fiction "We are looking for writers who have a solid knowledge of Biblical principles and are concerned for the youth of today living by those principles. Our stories must be well written, with the story itself getting the message across—no preaching, moralizing, or tag endings." No fantasy, science fiction, or nonChristian themes. **Buys 15-20 mss/year.** Send complete ms. Length: 600-800 words (young children), 900-1,500 words (older children). **Pays $40-50.**

Tips "We're looking for more submissions on healing miracles and reconciliation/restoration. Follow usual guidelines for careful writing, editing, and proofreading. We get many manuscripts with misspellings, poor grammar, careless typing. Know your subject—writer should know the Lord to write about the Christian life. Study the publication and our guidelines."

$ CADET QUEST MAGAZINE

P.O. Box 7259, Grand Rapids MI 49510-7259. (616)241-5616. Fax: (616)241-5558. E-mail: submissions@calvinistcadets.org. Web site: www.calvinistcadets.org. **Contact:** G. Richard Broene, editor. **40% freelance written.** Works with a small number of new/unpublished writers each year. Magazine published 7 times/year. "*Cadet Quest Magazine* shows boys 9-14 how God is at work in their lives and in the world around them." Estab. 1958. Circ. 9,000. **Pays on acceptance.** Publishes ms an average of 4-11 months after acceptance. Byline given. Buys first North American serial, one-time, second serial (reprint), simultaneous rights. Rights purchased vary with author and material. Accepts previously published material. Accepts simultaneous submissions. Responds in 2 months to submissions to queries. Sample copy for 9×12 SASE. Writer's guidelines for #10 SASE.

- Accepts submissions by mail, or by e-mail (must include ms in text of e-mail). Will not open attachments.

Nonfiction Articles about young boys' interests: sports (articles about athletes and developing Christian character through sports; photos appreciated), outdoor activities (camping skills, nature study, survival exercises; practical 'how to do it' approach works best. 'God in nature' themes appreciated), science, crafts, and problems. Emphasis is on a Christian perspective. How-to, humor, inspirational, interview/profile, personal experience, informational. Special issues: Write for new themes list in February. **Buys 20-25 mss/year.** Send complete ms. Length: 500-1,500 words. **Pays 2-5¢/word.**

Reprints Send ms with rights for sale noted. Payment varies.

Photos Pays $20-30 for photos purchased with ms.

Columns/Departments Project Page (uses simple projects boys 9-14 can do on their own made with easily accessible materials; must provide clear, accurate instructions).

Fiction "Considerable fiction is used. Fast-moving stories that appeal to a boy's sense of adventure or sense of humor are welcome." Adventure, religious, spiritual, sports, comics. "Avoid preachiness. Avoid simplistic answers to complicated problems. Avoid long dialogue and little action." No fantasy, science fiction, fashion, horror or erotica. Send complete ms. Length: 900-1,500 words. **Pays 4-6¢/word, and 1 contributor's copy.**

Fillers Any type of puzzles.

Tips "Best time to submit stories/articles is early in calendar year (February-April). Also remember readers are boys ages 9-14. Stories must reflect or add to the theme of the issue and be from a Christian perspective."

$ $ CALLIOPE

Exploring World History, Cobblestone Publishing Co., 30 Grove St., Suite C, Peterborough NH 03458-1454. (603)924-7209. Fax: (603)924-7380. Web site: www.cobblestonepub.com. **Contact:** Rosalie F. Baker, editor. **50% freelance written.** Magazine published 9 times/year covering world history (East and West) through 1800 AD for 8- 14-year-old kids. Articles must relate to the issue's theme. Lively, original approaches to the subject are the primary concerns of the editors in choosing material. Estab. 1990. Circ. 12,000. Pays on publication. Byline given. Buys all rights. Accepts queries by mail. If interested, responds 5 months before publication date to mss. Sample copy for $5.95, $2 shipping and handling, and 10×13 SASE. Writer's guidelines online.

O-ᵣ "Break in with a well-written query on a topic that relates directly to an upcoming issue's theme, a writing sample that is well-researched and concise, and a bibliography that includes new research."

Nonfiction Plays, biographies, in-depth nonfiction. Essays, general interest, historical/nostalgic, how-to (crafts/woodworking), humor, interview/profile, personal experience, photo feature, technical, travel, recipes. No religious, pornographic, biased, or sophisticated submissions. **Buys 30-40 mss/year.** Query with writing sample, 1-page outline, bibliography, SASE. Length: 700-800/feature articles; 300-600 words/supplemental nonfiction. **Pays 20-25¢/word.**

Photos If you have photographs pertaining to any upcoming theme, please contact the editor by mail or fax, or send them with your query. You may also send images on speculation. Reviews b&w prints, color slides. Buys one-time rights. Pays $15-100/b&w; $25-100/color; cover fees are negotiated.

Fiction Adventure, historical, biographical, retold legends. **Buys 10 mss/year.** Length: 800 words maximum. **Pays 20-25¢/word.**

Poetry Serious and light verse considered. Must have clear, objective imagery. Length: 100 lines maximum. **Pays on an individual basis.**

Fillers Crossword and other word puzzles (no word finds), mazes, and picture puzzles that use the vocabulary of the issue's theme or otherwise relate to the theme. **Pays on an individual basis.**

Tips "Authors are urged to use primary resources and up-to-date scholarly resources in their bibliography. In all correspondence, please include your complete address and a telephone number where you can be reached."

$ CHARACTERS

Kids Short Story Outlet, Davis Publications, P.O. Box 708, Newport NH 03773-0708. (603)863-5896. Fax: (603)863-8198. E-mail: hotdog@nhvt.net. **Contact:** Cindy Davis, editor. **100% freelance written.** Quarterly magazine for kids. "We accept submissions by all, but when space is limited, give preference to ones written by kids." Estab. 2003. Pays on publication. Publishes ms an average of 6 months after acceptance. Byline given. Not copyrighted. Buys one-time, second serial (reprint) rights. Editorial lead time 4 months. Submit seasonal material 6 months in advance. Accepts previously published material. Accepts simultaneous submissions. Responds in 2 weeks to queries; 1 month to mss. Sample copy for $5. Writer's guidelines by e-mail or snail mail.

Fiction All genres accepted. **Buys 40 mss/year.** Send complete ms. Length: 1,500 words maximum. **Pays $5, plus contributor copy.**

$ $ ⊘ CHILDREN'S PLAYMATE MAGAZINE

Children's Better Health Institute, 1100 Waterway Blvd., Indianapolis IN 46202. (317)634-1100. Fax: (317)684-8094. Web site: www.childrensplaymatemag.org. **40% freelance written.** Eager to work with new/unpublished writers. Magazine published 8 times/year for children ages 6-8. "We are looking for articles, poems, and activities with a health, fitness, or nutrition theme. We try to present our material in a positive light, and we try to incorporate humor and a light approach wherever possible without minimizing the seriousness of what we are saying." Estab. 1929. Circ. 114,907. Pays on publication. Byline given. Buys all rights. Submit seasonal material 8 months in advance. Responds in 3 months to queries. Sample copy for $1.75. Writer's guidelines for SASE or online.

- Closed to submissions until further notice.

O-ᵣ Include word count. Material will not be returned unless accompanied by a SASE.

Nonfiction "We are especially interested in material concerning sports and fitness, including profiles of famous amateur and professional athleters; 'average' atheletes (especially children) who have overcome obstacles to excel in their areas; and new or unusual sports, particularly those in which children can participate. Nonfiction articles dealing with health subjects should be fresh and creative. Avoid encyclopedic or 'preachy' approach. We try to present our health material in a positive manner, incorporate humor and a light approach wherever possible without minimizing the seriousness of the message." Interview/profile (famous amateurs and professional athletes), photo feature, recipes (ingredients should be healthful). **Buys 25 mss/year.** Send complete ms. Length: 300-700 words. **Pays up to 17¢/word.**

Photos State availability with submission. Buys one-time rights. $15 minimum. Captions, model releases required.

Fiction Terry Harshman, editor. Not buying much fiction right now except for rebus stories of 100-300 words and occasional poems. Vocabulary suitable for ages 6-8. Include word count. No adult or adolescent fiction. Send complete ms. Length: 300-700 words. **Pays minimum of 17¢/word and 10 contributor's copies.**

Fillers Recipes, puzzles, dot-to-dots, color-ins, hidden pictures, mazes. Prefers camara-ready activities. Activity guidelines for #10 SASE. **Buys 25/year. Pays variable amount.**

Tips "We would especially like to see more holiday stories, articles, and activities. Please send seasonal material at least 8 months in advance."

$ $ COBBLESTONE

Discover American History, Cobblestone Publishing, 30 Grove St., Suite C, Peterborough NH 03458. Fax: (603)924-7380. Web site: www.cobblestonepub.com. **Contact:** Meg Chorlian, editor. Magazine published monthly from September-May covering American history for children ages 8-14. Prefers to work with published/established writers. "Each issue presents a particular theme, making it exciting as well as informative. Half of all subscriptions are for schools." All material must relate to monthly theme. Estab. 1979. Circ. 27,000. Pays on publication. Byline given. Offers 50% kill fee. Buys all rights. Accepts queries by mail. Sample copy for $5.95, $2 shipping and handling, 10×13 SASE. Writer's guidelines online.

Nonfiction Historical/nostalgic, how-to (crafts/woodworking), interview/profile, personal experience, plays, biography, recipes, activities. No material that editorializes rather than reports. **Buys 80 mss/year.** Query with writing sample, 1-page outline, bibliography, SASE. Length: 700-800 words/feature articles; 300-600 words/supplemental nonfiction; 700 words maximum/activities. **Pays 20-25¢/word.**

Photos Reviews contact sheets, transparencies, prints. Buys one-time rights. $15-100/b&w; $25-100/color; cover fees are negotiated. Captions, identification of subjects required.

Fiction Adventure, historical, biographical, retold legends. **Buys 5 mss/year.** Length: 800 words maximum. **Pays 20-25¢/word.**

Poetry Serious and light verse considered. Must have clear, objective imagery. Free verse, light verse, traditional. **Buys 3 poems/year.** Length: 50 lines maximum.

Fillers Crossword and other word puzzles (no word finds), mazes, and picture puzzles that useg the vocabulary of the issue's theme or otherwise relate to the theme. **Pays on an individual basis.**

Tips "Review theme lists and past issues to see what we're looking for."

$ $ CRICKET

Carus Publishing Co., 140 S. Dearborn St., Chicago IL 60603. (312)701-1720, ext. 10. Web site: www.cricketmag.com. Editor-in-Chief: Marianne Carus. Editorial Director: Alice Letvin. Contributing Editor: Deborah Vetter. Editor: Lonnie Plecha. Senior Art Director: Karen Kohn. **Contact:** Submissions Editor. Monthly magazine for children ages 9-14. *Cricket* is looking for more fiction and nonfiction for the older end of its 9-14 age range, as well as contemporary stories set in other countries. It also seeks humorous stories and mysteries (not detective spoofs), fantasy and original fairy tales, stand-alone excerpts from unpublished novels, and well-written/researched science articles. Estab. 1973. Circ. 73,000. Pays on publication. Byline given. Accepts queries by mail. Accepts previously published material. Responds in 4-6 months to mss. Writer's guidelines online.

Nonfiction Adventure, biography, architecture, geography, history, natural history, foreign culture, travel, science, archaeology, sports, technology. A bibliography is required for all nonfiction articles. Submit complete ms, SASE. Length: 200-1,500 words. **Pays 25¢/word maximum.** with rights for sale noted and information about when and where the material previously appeared.

Photos Commissions all art separately from the text. Tearsheets/photocopies of both color and b&w work are considered. Accepts artwork done in pencil, pen and ink, watercolor, acrylic, oil, pastels, scratchboard, and woodcut. Does not want work that is overly caricatured or cartoony. "It is especially helpful to see pieces showing young people, animals, action scenes, and several scenes from a narrative showing a character in different situations and emotional states."

Fiction Fantasy, historical, humorous, mystery, science fiction, realistic, contemporary, folk tales, fairy tales, legends, myths. No didactic, sex, religious, or horror stories. **Buys 75-100 mss/year.** Length: 200-2,000 words. **Pays 25¢/word maximum, and 6 contributor's copies; $2.50 charge for extras.**

Poetry Serious, humorous, nonsense rhymes. **Buys 20-30 poems/year.** Length: 50 lines maximum. **Pays $3/line maximum.**

Fillers Crossword puzzles, logic puzzles, math puzzles, crafts, recipes, science experiments, games and activities from other countries, plays, music, art.

N $ ⊘ DISCOVERIES

Word Action Publishing Co., 2923 Troost Ave., Kansas City MO 64109. (816)931-1900, ext. 8220. Fax: (816)412-8306. E-mail: kdadams@wordaction.com. Editor: Virginia Folsom. **Contact:** Kimberly Adams, assistant editor. **80% freelance written.** Weekly Sunday school take-home paper. "Our audience is third and fourth graders. We require that the stories relate to the Sunday school lesson for that week." Circ. 18,000. **Pays on acceptance.** Publishes ms an average of 1-2 year after acceptance. Byline given. Buys multi-use rights. Accepts queries by mail, e-mail, fax. Accepts previously published material. Accepts simultaneous submissions. Responds in 6 weeks to queries. Sample copy for SASE. Writer's guidelines for SASE.

- Closed to submissions until after the fall of 2007.

O→ "Query before sending submissions. Make sure content is Biblically correct and relevant where necessary."

Fiction Submit contemporary, true-to-life portrayals of 8-10 year olds, written for a third- to fourth-grade reading level. Religious themes. Must relate to our theme list. No fantasy, science fiction, abnormally mature or precocious children, personification of animals. Nothing preachy. No unrealistic dialogue. **Buys 50 mss/year.** Send complete ms. **Pays $25.**

Fillers Spot cartoons, puzzles (related to the theme), trivia (any miscellaneous area of interest to 8-10 year olds). Length: 50-100 words. **Pays $15 for trivia, puzzles, and cartoons.**

Tips "Follow our theme list and read the Bible verses that relate to the theme."

$ $ FACES

People, Places and Cultures, Cobblestone Publishing, 30 Grove St., Suite C, Peterborough NH 03458. (603)924-7209. Fax: (603)924-7380. E-mail: facesmag@yahoo.com. Web site: www.cobblestonepub.com. **Contact:** Elizabeth Crooker Carpentiere, editor. **90-100% freelance written.** Publishes monthly throughout the schoolyear, *Faces* covers world culture for ages 9-14. "It stands apart from other children's magazines by offering a solid look at one subject and stressing strong editorial content, color photographs throughout, and original illustrations. *Faces* offers an equal balance of feature articles and activities, as well as folktales and legends." Estab. 1984. Circ. 15,000. Pays on publication. Byline given. Offers 50% kill fee. Buys all rights. Accepts queries by mail, e-mail. Accepts simultaneous submissions. Sample copy for $5.95, $2 shipping and handling, 10×13 SASE. Writer's guidelines for SASE or on Web site.

O-┐ All material must relate to the theme of a specific upcoming issue in order to be considered.

Nonfiction Interviews, personal accounts, in-depth nonfiction highlighting an aspect of the featured culture. Historical/nostalgic, humor, interview/profile, personal experience, photo feature, travel, recipes, activities, crafts. **Buys 45-50 mss/year.** Query with writing sample, 1-page outline, bibliography, SASE. Length: 800 words/feature articles; 300-600/supplemental nonfiction; up to 700 words/activities. **Pays 20-25¢/word.**

Photos Contact the editor by mail or fax, or send photos with your query. You may also send images on speculation. . Reviews contact sheets, transparencies, prints. Buys one-time rights. Pays $15-100/b&w; $25-100/color; cover fees are negotiated. Captions, identification of subjects, model releases required.

Fiction Ethnic, historical, retold legends/folktales, original plays. Length: 800 words maximum. **Pays 20-25¢/word.**

Poetry Serious and light verse considered. Must have clear, objective imagery. Length: 100 lines maximum. **Pays on an individual basis.**

Fillers Crossword and other word puzzles (no word finds), mazes, and picture puzzles that use the vocabulary of the issue's theme or otherwise relate to the theme. **Pays on an individual basis.**

$ $ THE FRIEND

50 E. North Temple, Salt Lake City UT 84150-3226. Fax: (801)240-2270. **Contact:** Vivian Paulsen, managing editor. **50% freelance written.** Eager to work with new/unpublished writers as well as established writers. Monthly publication of The Church of Jesus Christ of Latter-Day Saints for children ages 3-11. Circ. 275,000. **Pays on acceptance.** Buys all rights. Submit seasonal material 1 year in advance. Responds in 2 months to mss. Sample copy and writer's guidelines for $1.50 and 9×12 SAE with 4 first-class stamps.

Nonfiction "*The Friend* is interested in only stories based on true experiences." Special issues: Christmas, Easter. Submit complete ms with SASE. No queries, please. Length: 1,000 words maximum. **Pays $100-250.**

Poetry Serious, humorous, holiday. Any form with child appeal. **Pays $25 minimum.**

Tips "Do you remember how it feels to be a child? Can you write stories that appeal to children ages 3-11 in today's world? We're interested in stories with an international flavor and those that focus on present-day problems. Send material of high literary quality slanted to our editorial requirements. Let the child solve the problem—not some helpful, all-wise adult. No overt moralizing. Nonfiction should be creatively presented—not an array of facts strung together. Beware of being cutesy."

$ FUN FOR KIDZ

Bluffton News Printing & Publishing, 101 N. Main St., Bluffton OH 45817. Web site: www.funforkidzmagazines.com. Editor: Marilyn Edwards. **Contact:** Bethany Sneed, associate editor. **60% freelance written.** Bimonthly magazine. "We feature children involved in wholesome activities." Pays on publication. Publishes ms an average of up to 4 years after acceptance. Byline given. Buys first, one-time, second serial (reprint), electronic rights. Accepts queries by mail. Accepts simultaneous submissions. Responds in 4-6 weeks to queries; 2 months to mss. Sample copy for $6. Writer's guidelines for #10 SASE or online.

Nonfiction "Follow our theme list for article needs. We are always looking for creative activities to go with our themes." **Buys about 18 mss/year.** Send complete ms. ; **Pays 5¢/word.**

Photos Send photos with submission. Buys one-time rights. Offers $5 maximum/photo. **Buys about 10 mss/year.** Send complete ms. Length: Maxiumum 600 words. **Pays 5¢/word.**

Poetry "Poetry must follow our pre-set themes." Free verse, haiku, light verse, traditional. **Buys about 12 poems/year.**

Tips "Read our guidelines to learn about the kind of material we look for. Always include a SASE when sending in manuscripts for consideration."

$ GUIDE

True Stories Pointing to Jesus, Review and Herald Publishing Association, 55 W. Oak Ridge Dr., Hagerstown MD 21740. (301)393-4037. Fax: (301)393-4055. E-mail: guide@rhpa.org. Web site: www.guidemagazine.org. **Contact:** Randy Fishell, editor, or Rachel Whitaker, associate editor. **90% freelance written.** Weekly magazine featuring all-true stories showing God's involvement in 10- to 14-year-olds' lives. Estab. 1953. Circ. 32,000. **Pays on acceptance.** Publishes ms an average of 8 months after acceptance. Byline given. Buys first North American serial, second serial (reprint) rights. Editorial lead time 8 months. Submit seasonal material 8 months in advance. Accepts queries by mail, e-mail, fax. Responds in 1 month to queries. Sample copy for 6×9 SAE and 2 first-class stamps. Writer's guidelines online.

- Prefers electronic ms submissions.

O→ Break in with "a true story that shows in a clear way that God is involved in a 10- to 14-year-old's life."

Nonfiction Religious. "No fiction. Nonfiction should set forth a clearly evident spiritual application." **Buys 300 mss/year.** Send complete ms. Length: 500-1,200 words. **Pays $25-125.**

Reprints Send photocopy. Pays 50% of usual rates.

Fillers Anecdotes, games, puzzles, religious. **Buys 75/year. Pays $25-40.**

Tips "The majority of 'misses' are due to the lack of a clearly evident (not 'preachy') spiritual application."

$ HIGH ADVENTURE

General Council of the Assemblies of God/Royal Rangers, 1445 N. Boonville Ave., Springfield MO 65802-1894. (417)862-2781, ext. 4181. Fax: (417)831-8230. E-mail: royalrangers@ag.org. Web site: www.royalrangers.ag.org. **Contact:** John Hicks, editor. **60-70% freelance written.** Quarterly magazine. Estab. 1971. Circ. 87,000. Pays on publication. Publishes ms an average of 6-12 months after acceptance. Buys one-time, electronic rights. Buys first or all rights. Editorial lead time 3 months. Submit seasonal material 3 months in advance. Accepts queries by mail, e-mail, fax. Accepts previously published material. Accepts simultaneous submissions. Responds in 4-6 weeks to queries; 3-6 months to mss. Sample copy and writer's guidelines for 9×12 SAE and 2 first-class stamps. Writer's guidelines for SASE, by e-mail or fax. Editorial calendar for #10 SASE.

Nonfiction General interest, historical/nostalgic, humor, inspirational, personal experience, religious. No objectionable language, innuendo, immoral, or non-Christian materials. **Buys 10-12 mss/year.** Send complete ms. Length: 200-1,000 words. **Pays 6¢/word for assigned articles.**

Fiction Adventure, historical, humorous, religious, camping. No objectionable language, innuendo, immoral, or non-Christian materials. **Buys 30 mss/year.** Send complete ms. Length: 200-1,000 words. **Pays 6¢/word, plus 3 contributor's copies.**

Fillers Anecdotes, facts, short humor. **Buys 25-30/year.** Length: 25-100 words. **Pays 6¢/word.**

Tips "Consider the (middle/upper elementary) average age of readership when making a submission."

$ HIGHLIGHTS FOR CHILDREN

803 Church St., Honesdale PA 18431-1824. (570)253-1080. Fax: (570)251-7847. Web site: www.highlights.com. Editor: Christine French Clark. **Contact:** Manuscript Submissions. **80% freelance written.** Monthly magazine for children ages 2-12. "This book of wholesome fun is dedicated to helping children grow in basic skills and knowledge, in creativeness, in ability to think and reason, in sensitivity to others, in high ideals, and worthy ways of living—for children are the world's most important people. We publish stories for beginning and advanced readers. Up to 500 words for beginners (ages 3-7), up to 800 words for advanced (ages 8-12)." Estab. 1946. Circ. 2,000,000. **Pays on acceptance.** Buys all rights. Accepts queries by mail. Responds in 2 months to queries. Sample copy for free. Writer's guidelines for SASE or on Web site.

Nonfiction "We need articles on science, technology, and nature written by persons with strong backgrounds in those fields. Contributions always welcomed from new writers, especially engineers, scientists, historians, teachers, etc., who can make useful, interesting facts accessible to children. Also writers who have lived abroad and can interpret the ways of life, especially of children, in other countries in ways that will foster world brotherhood. Sports material, arts features, biographies, and articles of general interest to children. Direct, original approach, simple style, interesting content, not rewritten from encyclopedias. State background and qualifications for writing factual articles submitted. Include references or sources of information. Articles geared toward our younger readers (3-7) especially welcome, up to 500 words. Also buys original party plans for children ages 4-12, clearly described in 300-600 words, including drawings or samples of items to be illustrated. Also, novel but tested ideas in crafts, with clear directions. Include samples. Projects must require only free or inexpensive, easy-to-obtain materials. Especially desirable if easy enough for early primary grades. Also, fingerplays with lots of action, easy for very young children to grasp and to dramatize. Avoid wordiness. We need creative-thinking puzzles that can be illustrated, optical illusions, brain teasers, games of physical agility, and other 'fun' activities." Query. Length: 800 words maximum. **Pays $50 for party plans; $25 for craft ideas; $25 for fingerplays; $150 and up for articles.**

Photos Reviews color 35mm slides, photos, or electronic files.

Fiction Unusual, meaningful stories appealing to both girls and boys, ages 2-12. "Vivid, full of action. Engaging plot, strong characterization, lively language." Prefers stories in which a child protagonist solves a dilemma through his or her own resources. Seeks stories that the child ages 8-12 will eagerly read, and the child ages 2-7 will like to hear when read aloud (500-800 words). "Stories require interesting plots and a number of illustration possiblities. Also need rebuses (picture stories 125 words or under), stories with urban settings, stories for beginning readers (100-500 words), sports and humorous stories and mysteries. We also would like to see more material of 1-page length (300-400 words), both fiction and factual. War, crime, and violence are taboo." Adventure, fantasy, historical, humorous, animal, contemporary, folktales, multi-cultural, problem-solving, sports. "No war, crime or violence." Send complete ms. **Pays $150 minimum.**

The online magazine carries original content not found in the print edition.

Tips "We are pleased that many authors of children's literature report that their first published work was in the pages of *Highlights*. It is not our policy to consider fiction on the strength of the reputation of the author. We judge each submission on its own merits. With factual material, however, we do prefer that writers be authorities in their field or people with first-hand experience. In this manner we can avoid the encyclopedic article that merely restates information readily available elsewhere. We don't make assignments. Query with simple letter to establish whether the nonfiction subject is likely to be of interest. A beginning writer should first become familiar with the type of material that *Highlights* publishes. Include special qualifications, if any, of author. Write for the child, not the editor. Write in a voice that children understand and relate to. Speak to today's kids, avoiding didactic, overt messages. Even though our general principles haven't changed over the years, we are contemporary in our approach to issues. Avoid worn themes."

$ $ HUMPTY DUMPTY'S MAGAZINE

Children's Better Health Institute, P.O. Box 567, Indianapolis IN 46206-0567. (317)636-8881. Fax: (317)684-8094. E-mail: plybarger@cbhi.org. Web site: www.humptydumptymag.org. **Contact:** Phyllis Lybarger, editor. **25% freelance written.** Magazine published 8 times/year covering health, nutrition, hygiene, fitness, and safety for children ages 4-6. "Our publication is designed to entertain and to educate young readers in healthy lifestyle habits. Fiction, poetry, pencil activities should have an element of good nutrition or fitness." Estab. 1948. Circ. 350,000. Pays on publication. Publishes ms an average of 8 months after acceptance. Byline given. Buys all rights. Editorial lead time 8 months. Submit seasonal material 10 months in advance. Accepts simultaneous submissions. Sample copy for $2.95. Writer's guidelines for SASE or on Web site.

- All work is on speculation only; queries are not accepted nor are stories assigned.

Nonfiction "Material must have a health theme—nutrition, safety, exercise, hygiene. We're looking for articles that encourage readers to develop better health habits without preaching. Very simple factual articles that creatively teach readers about their bodies. We use several puzzles and activities in each issue—dot-to-dot, hidden pictures, and other activities that promote following instructions, developing finger dexterity, and working with numbers and letters." Include word count. **Buys 3-4 mss/year.** Send complete ms. Length: 300 words maximum. **Pays 22¢/word.**

Photos Send photos with submission. Buys all rights. Offers no additonal payment for photos accepted with ms.

Columns/Departments Mix & Fix (no-cook recipes), 100 words. All ingredients must be nutritious—low fat, no sugar, etc.—and tasty. **Buys 8 mss/year.** Send complete ms. **Payment varies.**

Fiction Phyllis Lybarger, editor. "We use some stories in rhyme and a few easy-to-read stories for the beginning reader. All stories should work well as read-alouds. Currently we need health/sports/fitness stories. We try to present our health material in a positive light, incorporating humor and a light approach wherever possible. Avoid stereotyping. Characters in contemporary stories should be realistic and reflect good, wholesome values." Include word count. Juvenile health-related material. "No inanimate talking objects, animal stories, or science fiction." **Buys 4-6 mss/year.** Send complete ms. Length: 350 words maximum. **Pays 22¢/word for stories, plus 10 contributor's copies.**

Tips "We would like to see more holiday stories, articles, and activities. Please send seasonal material at least eight months in advance."

$ $ JACK AND JILL

Children's Better Health Institute, P.O. Box 567, Indianapolis IN 46206-0567. (317)636-8881. Fax: (317)684-8094. E-mail: cbhiseif@tcon.net. Web site: www.jackandjillmag.org. **Contact:** Daniel Lee, editor. **50% freelance written.** Bimonthly Magazine published 8 times/year for children ages 7-10. "Material will not be returned unless accompanied by SASE with sufficient postage." No queries. May hold material being seriously considered for up to 1 year. Estab. 1938. Circ. 200,000. Pays on publication. Publishes ms an average of 8 months after acceptance. Byline given. Buys all rights. Submit seasonal material 8 months in advance. Responds in 10 weeks to mss. Sample copy for $2.95. Writer's guidelines online.

- Closed to submissions until further notice.

O→ Break in with nonfiction about ordinary kids with a news hook—something that ties in with current events, matters the kids are seeing on television and in mainstream news—i.e., space exploration, scientific advances, sports, etc.

Nonfiction "Because we want to encourage youngsters to read for pleasure and for information, we are interested in material that will challenge a young child's intelligence and be enjoyable reading. Our emphasis is on good health, and we are in particular need of articles, stories, and activities with health, safety, exercise, and nutrition themes. We try to present our health material in a positive light—incorporating humor and a light approach wherever possible without minimizing the seriousness of what we are saying. Straight factual articles are OK if they are short and interestingly written. We would rather see, however, more creative alternatives to the straight factual article. Items with a news hook will get extra attention. We'd like to see articles about interesting kids involved in out-of-the-ordinary activities. We're also interested in articles about people with unusual hobbies for our Hobby Shop department." **Buys 10-15 mss/year.** Send complete ms. Length: 500-800 words. **Pays 17¢/word minimum.**

Photos When appropriate, photos should accompany ms. Reviews sharp, contrasting b&w glossy prints. Sometimes uses color slides, transparencies, or good color prints. Buys one-time rights. Pays $15/photo.

Fiction May include, but is not limited to, realistic stories, fantasy, adventure—set in past, present, or future. "All stories need a well-developed plot, action, and incident. Humor is highly desirable. Stories that deal with a health theme need not have health as the primary subject." Adventure, historical, humorous, mystery, science fiction, sports. Wants health-related stories with a subtle lesson. **Buys 20-25 mss/year.** Send complete ms. Length: 500-800 words. **Pays 15¢/word minimum.**

Fillers Puzzles (including various kinds of word and crossword puzzles), poems, games, science projects, and creative craft projects. "We get a lot of these. To be selected, an item needs a little extra spark and originality. Instructions for activities should be clearly and simply written and accompanied by models or diagram sketches. We also have a need for recipes. Ingredients should be healthful; avoid sugar, salt, chocolate, red meat, and fats as much as possible. In all material, avoid references to eating sugary foods, such as candy, cakes, cookies, and soft drinks."

Tips "We are constantly looking for new writers who can tell good stories with interesting slants—stories that are not full of out-dated and time-worn expressions. We like to see stories about kids who are smart and capable, but not sarcastic or smug. Problem-solving skills, personal responsibility, and integrity are good topics for us. Obtain current issues of the magazine and study them to determine our present needs and editorial style."

$ $ $ JUNIOR SCHOLASTIC

Scholastic, Inc., 557 Broadway, New York NY 10012-3902. (212)343-6100. Fax: (212)343-6945. E-mail: junior@scholastic.com. Web site: www.juniorscholastic.com. Magazine published 18 times/year. Edited for students ages 11-14. Circ. 535,000. Editorial lead time 6 weeks.

$ $ LADYBUG

The Magazine for Young Children, Carus Publishing Co., 140 S. Dearborn, Suite 1450, Chicago IL 60603. (312)701-1720. Web site: www.cricketmag.com. Editor-in-Chief: Marianne Carus. Editorial Director/Editor: Alice Letvin. Managing Art Director: Suzanne Beck. Monthly magazine for children ages 2-6. "We look for quality literature and nonfiction." Estab. 1990. Circ. 125,000. Pays on publication. Byline given. Accepts previously published material. Responds in 6 months to mss. Writer's guidelines online.

O→ *Ladybug* needs imaginative activities based on concepts and interesting, appropriate nonfiction. See sample issues.

Nonfiction Concepts, vocabulary, simple explanations of things in a young child's world. **Buys 35 mss/year.** Send complete ms, SASE. Length: 400-700 words. **Pays 25¢/word ($25 minimum).**

Photos "Artists should submit tearsheets/photocopies of artwork to be kept in our illustrator files." Buys all rights; physical art remains the property of the illustrator and may be used for artist's self promotion. $500/spread; $250/page.

Fiction Read-aloud stories, picture stories, original retellings of folk and fairy tales, multicultural stories. **Buys 30 mss/year.** Length: 800 words maximum. **Pays 25¢/word ($25 minimum).**

Poetry Light verse, traditional, humorous, rhythmic, rhyming, serious, active. **Buys 40 poems/year.** Submit maximum 5 poems. Length: 20 lines maximum. **Pays $3/line ($25 minimum).**

Fillers Learning activities, games, crafts, songs, finger games. See back issues for types, formats, and length.

Tips "Reread manuscript before sending in. Keep within specified word limits. Study back issues before submitting to learn about the types of material we're looking for. Writing style is paramount. We look for rich, evocative language and a sense of joy or wonder. Remember that you're writing for preschoolers—be age-appropriate, but not condescending or preachy. A story must hold enjoyment for both parent and child through repeated read-aloud sessions. Remember that people come in all colors, sizes, physical conditions, and have special needs. Be inclusive!"

$ NATURE FRIEND

Carlisle Press, 2673 TR 421, Sugarcreek OH 44681. (330)852-1900. Fax: (330)852-3285. **Contact:** Marvin Wengerd, editor. **80% freelance written.** Monthly magazine covering nature. "*Nature Friend* includes stories, puzzles, science experiments, nature experiments—all submissions need to honor God as creator." Estab. 1983. Circ. 13,000. Pays on publication. Byline given. Buys first, one-time rights. Editorial lead time 4 months. Submit seasonal material 3 months in advance. Accepts simultaneous submissions. Responds in 6 months to mss. Sample copy and writer's guidelines for $4 postage paid.

O→ Break in with a "conversational story about a nature subject that imparts knowledge and instills Christian values."

Nonfiction How-to (nature, science experiments), photo feature, articles about interesting/unusual animals. No poetry, evolution, animals depicted in captivity. **Buys 50 mss/year.** Send complete ms. Length: 250-900 words. **Pays 5¢/word.**

Photos Send photos with submission. Reviews prints. Buys one-time rights. Offers $20-75/photo. Captions, identification of subjects required.

Columns/Departments Learning By Doing, 500-900 words. **Buys 12 mss/year.** Send complete ms.

Fillers Facts, puzzles, short essays on something current in nature. **Buys 35/year.** Length: 150-250 words. **Pays 5¢/word.**

Tips "We want to bring joy and knowledge to children by opening the world of God's creation to them. We endeavor to create a sense of awe about nature's creator and a respect for His creation. I'd like to see more submissions on hands-on things to do with a nature theme (not collecting rocks or leaves—real stuff). Also looking for good stories that are accompanied by good photography."

$ $ NEW MOON

The Magazine for Girls & Their Dreams, New Moon Publishing, Inc., 2 W. First St., #101, Duluth MN 55802. (218)728-5507. Fax: (218)728-0314. E-mail: girl@newmoon.org. Web site: www.newmoon.org. **Contact:** Editorial Department. **25% freelance written.** Bimonthly magazine covering girls ages 8-14, edited by girls aged 8-14. "In general, all material should be pro-girl and feature girls and women as the primary focus. *New Moon* is for every girl who wants her voice heard and her dreams taken seriously. *New Moon* celebrates girls, explores the passage from girl to woman, and builds healthy resistance to gender inequities. The *New Moon* girl is true to herself and *New Moon* helps her as she pursues her unique path in life, moving confidently into the world." Estab. 1992. Circ. 30,000. Pays on publication. Publishes ms an average of 6 months after acceptance. Byline given. Buys all rights. Editorial lead time 6 months. Submit seasonal material 8 months in advance. Accepts queries by mail, e-mail, fax. Accepts simultaneous submissions. Responds in 2 months to mss. Sample copy for $7 or online. Writer's guidelines for SASE or online.

O→ Adult writers can break in with "Herstory articles about less well-known women from all over the world, especially if it relates to one of our themes. Same with Women's Work articles. Girls can break in with essays and articles (nonfiction) that relate to a theme."

Nonfiction Essays, general interest, humor, inspirational, interview/profile, opinion, personal experience (written by girls), photo feature, religious, travel, multicultural/girls from other countries. No fashion, beauty, or dating. **Buys 20 mss/year.** Query with or without published clips or send complete ms. Length: 600 words. **Pays 6-12¢/word.**

Photos State availability with submission. Buys one-time rights. Negotiates payment individually. Captions, identification of subjects required.

Columns/Departments Women's Work (profile of a woman and her job relating the the theme), 600 words; Herstory (historical woman relating to theme), 600 words. **Buys 10 mss/year.** Query. **Pays 6-12¢/word.**

Fiction Prefers girl-written material. All girl-centered. Adventure, fantasy, historical, humorous, slice-of-life vignettes. **Buys 6 mss/year.** Send complete ms. Length: 1,200-1,400 words. **Pays 6-12¢/word.**

Poetry No poetry by adults.

Tips "We'd like to see more girl-written feature articles that relate to a theme. These can be about anything the girl has done personally, or she can write about something she's studied. Please read *New Moon* before submitting to get a sense of our style. Writers and artists who comprehend our goals have the best chance of publication. We love creative articles—both nonfiction and fiction—that are not condescending to our readers. Keep articles to suggested word lengths; avoid stereotypes. Refer to our guidelines and upcoming themes."

$ $ POCKETS

The Upper Room, 1908 Grand Ave., P.O. Box 340004, Nashville TN 37203-0004. (615)340-7333. Fax: (615)340-7267. E-mail: pockets@upperroom.org. Web site: www.pockets.org. Editor: Lynn W. Gilliam. **Contact:** Laurette Wolfe, editorial assistant. **60% freelance written.** Monthly (except February) magazine covering children's and families' spiritual formation. "We are a Christian, inter-denominational publication for children 6-11 years of age. Each issue reflects a specific theme." Estab. 1981. Circ. 96,000. **Pays on acceptance.** Publishes ms an average of 1 year-18 months after acceptance. Byline given. Buys first North American serial rights. Submit seasonal material 1 year in advance. Accepts previously published material. Responds in 6 weeks to mss. Each issue reflects a specific theme. Sample copy, writers' guidelines and themes available with a 9×12 SASE with 4 First-Class stamps attached to envelope.

• *Pockets* publishes fiction and poetry, as well as short-short stories (no more than 600 words) for children 5-7. Eager to work with new/unpublished writers.

Nonfiction Seek biographical sketches, famous or unknown, whose lives reflect their Christian commitment and are of particular interest to children. Write in a way that appeals to children. We welcome retold scripture stories that remain true to the Bible and are related to the theme. **Buys 10 mss/year.** Length: 400-1,000 words. **Pays 14¢/word.**

Reprints Accepts one-time previously published submissions. Send typed ms with rights for sale noted and information about when and where the material previously appeared.

Photos Close-up photos of children actively involved in activites are preferred. Send photos with submission. Reviews contact sheets, transparencies, prints, digital images (300 dpi). Buys one-time rights. Pays $25/photo.

Columns/Departments Poetry and Prayer (related to themes), maximum 24 lines; Pocketsful of Love (family communications activities), 300 words; Peacemakers at Work (profiles of children working for peace, justice, and ecological concerns), 300-800 words. **Pays 14¢/word**. Activities/Games (related to themes). **Pays $25 and up**. Kids Cook (simple recipes children can make alone or with minimal help from an adult). **Pays $25. Buys 20 mss/year.**

Fiction "Submissions do not need to be overtly religious. They should reflect daily living, lifestyle, and problem-solving based on living as faithful disciples. They should help children experience the Christian life that is not always a neatly wrapped moral package but is open to the continuing revelation of God's will for their lives." Adventure, ethnic, historical, religious, slice-of-life vignettes. No violence, science fiction, romance, fantasy, or talking animal stories. **Buys 25-30 mss/year.** Send complete ms. Length: 600-1,400 words. **Pays 14¢/word, plus 2-5 contributor's copies.**

Poetry **Buys 14 poems/year.** Length: 4-24 lines. **Pays $2/line, $25 minimum.**

▣ The online magazine carries original content not found in the print edition and includes writers' guidelines, themes, and annual fiction-writing contest guidelines. Contact: Cary Graham, editorial assistant.

Tips "Theme stories, role models, and retold scripture stories are most open to freelancers. Poetry is also open. It is very helpful if writers read our writers' guidelines and themes on our Web site."

SCHOLASTIC DYNAMATH

Scholastic, Inc., 557 Broadway, New York NY 10012-3902. (212)343-6100. Fax: (212)343-6945. E-mail: dynamath@scholastic.com. Web site: www.scholastic.com. Magazine published 8 times/year featuring nonfiction and fiction-based exercises. Intended to show 3rd through 6th graders that math can be fun and relevent to their lives. Circ. 200,000.

SCHOLASTIC MATH MAGAZINE

Scholastic, Inc., 557 Broadway, New York NY 10012-3902. (212)343-6100. Fax: (212)343-4459. E-mail: mathmag@scholastic.com. Web site: www.scholastic.com. Monthly magazine aimed at increasing sixth through ninth graders' interest in mathmatics. Circ. 200,000.

SCHOLASTIC NEWS

Scholastic, Inc., 557 Broadway, New York NY 10012-3902. (212)343-6100. Fax: (212)343-4459. Web site: www.scholasticnews.com. Published weekly during the school year Edited for teachers and instructors of children through the 6th grade. Covers current events, vocabulary, reading comprehension, geography, and more. Circ. 3,500,000.

SCIENCE WORLD

Scholastic, Inc., 557 Broadway, New York NY 10012-3902. (212)343-6100. Fax: (212)343-6945. E-mail: scienceworld@scholastic.com. Web site: www.scholastic.com. Editor: Patty Janes. Biweekly magazine. Science publication for students grades 7-10. Circ. 404,597. Editorial lead time 3 weeks.

$ SHINE BRIGHTLY

GEMS Girls' Clubs, P.O. Box 7259, Grand Rapids MI 49510. (616)241-5616. Fax: (616)241-5558. E-mail: christina@gemsgc.org. Web site: www.gemsgc.org. Editor: Jan Boone. **Contact:** Christina Malone, managing editor. **80% freelance written.** Works with new and published/established writers. Monthly magazine. "Our purpose is to lead girls into a living relationship with Jesus Christ and to help them see how God is at work in their lives and the world around them. Puzzles, crafts, stories, and articles for girls ages 9-14." Estab. 1971. Circ. 16,000. Pays on publication. Publishes ms an average of 1 year after acceptance. Byline given. Buys first North American serial, second serial (reprint), simultaneous rights. Submit seasonal material 1 year in advance. Accepts previously published material. Accepts simultaneous submissions. Responds in 2 months to queries. Sample copy for 9×12 SAE with 3 first class stamps and $1. Writer's guidelines online.

Nonfiction "We do not want easy solutions or quick character changes from good to bad. No pietistic characters. No 'new girl at school starting over after parents' divorce' stories. Constant mention of God is not necessary if the moral tone of the story is positive. We do not want stories that always have a happy ending." Needs include: biographies and autobiographies of "heroes of the faith," informational (write for issue themes), multicultural materials. Humor, inspirational, interview/profile, personal experience (avoid the testimony approach), photo feature (query first), religious, travel, adventure, mystery. **Buys 35 unsolicited mss/year.** Send complete ms. Length: 100-900 words. **Pays 3¢/word, plus 2 copies.**

Reprints Send ms with rights for sale noted and information about when and where the material previously appeared.

Photos Purchased with or without ms. Appreciate multicultural subjects. Reviews 5×7 or 8×10 clear color glossy prints. Pays $25-50 on publication.

Columns/Departments How-to (crafts); puzzles and jokes; quizzes. Length: 200-400 words. Send complete ms. **Pay varies.**

Fiction Adventure, ethnic, historical, humorous, mystery, religious, romance, slice-of-life vignettes, suspense. **Buys 20 mss/year.** Send complete ms. Length: 400-900 words. **Pays up to $35.**

Poetry Free verse, haiku, light verse, traditional. **Pays $5-15.**

Tips "Prefers not to see anything on the adult level, secular material, or violence. Writers frequently oversimplify the articles and often write with a Pollyanna attitude. An author should be able to see his/her writing style as exciting and appealing to girls ages 9-14. The style can be fun, but also teach a truth. Subjects should be current and important to *SHINE brightly* readers. Use our theme update as a guide. We would like to receive material with a multicultural slant."

$ SPARKLE

GEMS Girls' Clubs, P.O. Box 7259, Grand Rapids MI 49510. (616)241-5616. Fax: (616)241-5558. E-mail: sarahv@gemsgc.org. Web site: www.gemsgc.org. Editor: Jan Boone. **Contact:** Sarah Vanderaa, managing editor. **80% freelance written.** Magazine published 3 times/year that helps girls in first through third grades grow in a stronger relationship with Jesus Christ. "We try to help them see God through the use of crafts, puzzles, games, stories, articles, poems, and Bible lessons." Estab. 2002. Circ. 3,000. Pays on publication. Byline given. Offers $20 kill fee. Buys first North American serial, first, one-time, second serial (reprint), simultaneous rights. Editorial lead time 3 months. Submit seasonal material 1 year in advance. Accepts queries by mail. Accepts previously published material. Accepts simultaneous submissions. Responds in 3 weeks to queries; 3 months to mss. Sample copy for 9X13 SAE and 3 first-class stamps. Writer's guidelines for #10 SASE or online.

Nonfiction How-to (crafts/recipes), humor, inspirational, personal experience, photo feature, religious, travel. Constant mention of God is not necessary if the moral tone of the story is positive. **Buys 9 mss/year.** Send complete ms. Length: 100-400 words. **Pays $20/article.**

Photos Send photos with submission. Reviews at least 5×7 clear color glossy prints, GIF/JPEG files on CD. Buys one-time rights. Offers $25-50/photo. Identification of subjects required.

Columns/Departments Crafts; puzzles and jokes; quizzes, all 200-400 words. Send complete ms. **Payment varies.**

Fiction Adventure, ethnic, fantasy, humorous, mystery, religious, slice-of-life vignettes. **Buys 6 mss/year.** Send complete ms. Length: 100-400 words. **Pays $20/story.**

Poetry Free verse, haiku, light verse, traditional. "We do not wish to see anything that is too difficult for a first grader to read. We wish it to remain light. The style can be fun, but also teach a truth. No violence or secular material." **Buys 2 poems/year.** Submit maximum 4 poems.

Fillers Facts, short humor. **Buys 2/year.** Length: 50-150 words. **Pays $10-15.**

Tips "Writers frequently should oversimplify the articles and often write with a "Pollyanna" attitude. Authors should see their writing style as exciting and appealing to girls ages 6-9. Subjects should be current and important to *Sparkle* readers. Use our theme as a guide. We would like to receive material with a multicultural slant."

$ $ SPIDER

The Magazine for Children, Cricket Magazine Group, 70 East Lake St., Suite 300, Chicago IL 60601. (312)701-1720. Fax: (312)701-1728. Web site: www.cricketmag.com. Editor-in-Chief: Marianne Carus. Editorial Director: Alice Letvin. Managing Art Director: Suzanne Beck. **Contact:** Submissions Editor. **85% freelance written.** Monthly reading and activity magazine for children ages 6 to 9. "*Spider* introduces children to the highest quality stories, poems, illustrations, articles, and activities. It was created to foster in beginning readers a love of reading and discovery that will last a lifetime. We're looking for writers who respect children's intelligence." Estab. 1994. Circ. 70,000. Pays on publication. Byline given. Accepts previously published material. Accepts simultaneous submissions. Responds in 6 months to mss. Writer's guidelines online.

Nonfiction Nature, animals, science, foreign culture, history, fine arts and music, humanities topics. Submit complete ms, bibliography, SASE. Length: 300-800 words. **Pays up to 25¢/word.**

Reprints Send photocopy with rights for sale noted and information about when and where the material previously appeared.

Photos For art samples, it is especially helpful to see pieces showing children, animals, action scenes, and several scenes from a narrative showing a character in different situations. Send photocopies/tearsheets. Also considers photo essays (prefers color, but b&w is also accepted). Reviews contact sheets, transparencies, 8_10 prints. Captions, identification of subjects, model releases required.

Fiction Stories should be easy to read. Fantasy, humorous, science fiction, folk tales, fairy tales, fables, myths. Length: 300-1,000 words. **Pays up to 25¢/word.**

Poetry Free verse, traditional, serious, humorous, nonsense rhymes. Submit maximum 5 poems. Length: 20 lines maximum. **Pays $3/line maximum.**

Fillers Recipes, crafts, puzzles, games, brainteasers, math and word activities. Length: 1-4 pages. **Pays Other.**

Tips "We'd like to see more of the following: engaging nonfiction, fillers, and 'takeout page' activities; folktales, fairy tales, science fiction, and humorous stories. Most importantly, do not write down to children."

$ STONE SOUP

The Magazine by Young Writers and Artists, Children's Art Foundation, P.O. Box 83, Santa Cruz CA 95063-0083. (831)426-5557. Fax: (831)426-1161. E-mail: editor@stonesoup.com. Web site: www.stonesoup.com. **Contact:** Ms. Gerry Mandel, editor. **100% freelance written.** Bimonthly magazine of writing and art by children, including fiction, poetry, book reviews, and art by children through age 13. Audience is children, teachers, parents, writers, artists. "We have a preference for writing and art based on real-life experiences; no formula stories or poems." Estab. 1973. Circ. 20,000. Pays on publication. Publishes ms an average of 4 months after acceptance. Buys all rights. Submit seasonal material 6 months in advance. Sample copy for $5 or online. Writer's guidelines online.

- Don't send queries, just submissions. No e-mail submissions. "Please do not enclose a SASE. We only respond to work we want to publish. If you do not hear from us within 6 weeks, it means we could not use your work."

Nonfiction Historical/nostalgic, personal experience, book reviews. **Buys 12 mss/year. Pays $40.**

Fiction Adventure, ethnic, experimental, fantasy, historical, humorous, mystery, science fiction, slice-of-life vignettes, suspense. "We do not like assignments or formula stories of any kind." **Buys 60 mss/year.** Send complete ms. Length: 150-2,500 words. **Pays $40 for stories. Authors also receive 2 copies, a certificate, and discounts on additional copies and on subscriptions.**

Poetry Avant-garde, free verse. **Buys 12 poems/year. Pays $40/poem.**

- The online magazine carries original content not found in the print edition and includes writer's guidelines. Contact: Ms. Gerry Mandel, online editor.

Tips "All writing we publish is by people ages 13 and under. We do not publish any writing by adults. We can't emphasize enough how important it is to read a couple of issues of the magazine. We have a strong preference for writing on subjects that mean a lot to the author. If you feel strongly about something that happened to you or something you observed, use that feeling as the basis for your story or poem. Stories should have good descriptions, realistic dialogue, and a point to make. In a poem, each word must be chosen carefully. Your poem should present a view of your subject, and a way of using words that are special and all your own."

$ $ U.S. KIDS

A Weekly Reader Magazine, Children's Better Health Institute, P.O. Box 567, Indianapolis IN 46206-0567. (317)636-8881. Fax: (317)684-8094. Web site: www.cbhi.org/magazines/uskids/index.shtml. **Contact:** Daniel Lee, editor. **50% freelance written.** Magazine published 8 times/year featuring "kids doing extraordinary things, especially activities related to health, sports, the arts, interesting hobbies, the environment, computers, etc." Estab. 1987. Circ. 230,000. Pays on publication. Publishes ms an average of 4 months after acceptance. Byline given. Buys all rights. Editorial lead time 6 months. Submit seasonal material 6 months in advance. Responds in 4 months to mss. Sample copy for $2.95 or online. Writer's guidelines for #10 SASE.

• *U.S. Kids* is being retargeted to a younger audience. Closed to submissions until further notice.
Nonfiction Especially interested in articles with a health/fitness angle. General interest, how-to, interview/profile, science, kids using computers, multicultural. **Buys 16-24 mss/year.** Send complete ms. Length: 400 words maximum. **Pays up to 25¢/word.**
Photos State availability with submission. Reviews contact sheets, negatives, transparencies, color photocopies, or prints. Buys one-time rights. Negotiates payment individually. Captions, identification of subjects, model releases required.
Columns/Departments Real Kids (kids doing interesting things); Fit Kids (sports, healthy activities); Computer Zone. Length: 300-400 words. Send complete ms. **Pays up to 25¢/word.**
Fiction Buys very little fictional material. **Buys 1-2 mss/year.** Send complete ms. Length: 400 words. **Pays up to 25¢/word.**
Poetry Light verse, traditional, kid's humorous, health/fitness angle. **Buys 6-8 poems/year.** Submit maximum 6 poems. Length: 8-24 lines. **Pays $25-50.**
Fillers Facts, newsbreaks, short humor, puzzles, games, activities. Length: 200-500 words. **Pays 25¢/word.**
Tips "We are retargeting the magazine for first-, second-, and third-graders, and looking for fun and informative articles on activities and hobbies of interest to younger kids. Special emphasis on fitness, sports, and health. Availability of good photos a plus."

LITERARY & "LITTLE"

$ AFRICAN AMERICAN REVIEW

Saint Louis University, Humanities 317, 3800 Lindell Blvd., St. Louis MO 63108. (314)977-3703. Fax: (314)977-1514. E-mail: keenanam@slu.edu. Web site: aar.slu.edu. Editor: Jocelyn Moody. **Contact:** Aileen Keenan, managing editor. **65% freelance written.** Quarterly magazine covering African-American literature and culture. "Essays on African-American literature, theater, film, art and culture generally; interviews; poetry and fiction by African-American authors; book reviews." Estab. 1967. Circ. 2,067. Pays on publication. Publishes ms an average of 1 year after acceptance. Byline given. Buys first North American serial rights. Editorial lead time 1 year. Responds in 1 month to queries; 6 months to mss. Sample copy for $12. Writer's guidelines online.
Nonfiction Essays, interview/profile. **Buys 30 mss/year.** Query. Length: 3,500-6,000 words. **Pays $50-90.** Pays in contributors copies, offprints and honorarium.
Photos State availability with submission. Pays $100 for covers. Captions required.
Fiction Jocelyn Moody, editor. Ethnic, experimental, mainstream. "No children's/juvenile/young adult/teen." **Buys 5 mss/year.** Length: 2,500-5,000 words. **Pays $25-50, 1contributor's copy and 10 offprints.**

$ AGNI

Creative Writing Program, Boston University, 236 Bay State Rd., Boston MA 02215. (617)353-7135. Fax: (617)353-7134. E-mail: agni@bu.edu. Web site: www.agnimagazine.org. **Contact:** Sven Birkerts, editor. Biannual magazine. "Eclectic literary magazine publishing first-rate poems, essays, translations, and stories." Estab. 1972. Circ. 4,000. Pays on publication. Publishes ms an average of 6 months after acceptance. Byline given. Buys first North American serial rights. Rights to reprint in *AGNI* anthology (with author's consent). Editorial lead time 1 year. Accepts queries by mail. Accepts simultaneous submissions. Responds in 2 weeks to queries; 4 months to mss. Sample copy for $10 or online. Writer's guidelines online.
• Reading period September 1-May 31 only.
Fiction Stories, prose poems. "No science fiction or romance." **Buys 6-12 mss/year. Pays $10/page up to $150, 2 contributor's copies, 1-year subscription, and 4 gift copies.**
Poetry Buys more than 60 poems/year. Submit maximum 5 poems. **Pays $20-150.**
The online magazine carries original content not found in the print edition. Contact: Sven Birkerts, editor.
Tips "We're looking for extraordinary translations from little-translated languages. It is important to look at a copy of *AGNI* before submitting, to see if your work might be compatible. Please write for guidelines or a sample."

$ $ ALASKA QUARTERLY REVIEW

ESB 208, University of Alaska-Anchorage, 3211 Providence Dr., Anchorage AK 99508. (907)786-6916. E-mail: aqr@uaa.alaska.edu. Web site: www.uaa.alaska.edu/aqr. **Contact:** Ronald Spatz, executive editor. **95% freelance written.** Semiannual magazine publishing fiction, poetry, literary nonfiction, and short plays in traditional and experimental styles. *AQR* "publishes fiction, poetry, literary nonfiction and short plays in traditional and experimental styles." Estab. 1982. Circ. 3,500. Honorariums on publication when funding permits. Publishes ms an average of 6 months after acceptance. Byline given. Buys first North American serial rights. Upon request, rights will be transferred back to author after publication. Accepts queries by mail. Responds in 1 month to queries; 6 months to mss. Sample copy for $6. Writer's guidelines online.

- *Alaska Quarterly* reports they are always looking for freelance material and new writers.

Nonfiction Literary nonfiction: essays and memoirs. **Buys 0-5 mss/year.** Query. Length: 1,000-20,000 words. **Pays $50-200 subject to funding.** Pays in contributor's copies and subscription when funding is limited.

Fiction Ronald Spatz, fiction editor. Experimental and traditional literary forms. No romance, children's, or inspirational/religious. Publishes novel excerpts. **Buys 20-26 mss/year**. Also publishes drama: experimental and traditional one-act plays. **Buys 0-2 mss/year.** Experimental, contemporary, prose poem. "If the works in *Alaska Quarterly Review* have certain characteristics, they are these: freshness, honesty, and a compelling subject. What makes a piece stand out from the multitude of other submissions? The voice of the piece must be strong—idiosyncratic enough to create a unique persona. We look for the demonstration of craft, making the situation palpable and putting it in a form where it becomes emotionally and intellectually complex. One could look through our pages over time and see that many of the pieces published in the *Alaska Quarterly Review* concern everyday life. We're not asking our writers to go outside themselves and their experiences to the absolute exotic to catch our interest. We look for the experiential and revelatory qualities of the work. We will, without hesitation, champion a piece that may be less polished or stylistically sophisticated, if it engages me, surprises me, and resonates for me. The joy in reading such a work is in discovering something true. Moreover, in keeping with our mission to publish new writers, we are looking for voices our readers do not know, voices that may not always be reflected in the dominant culture and that, in all instances, have something important to convey." Length: not exceeding 100 pages. **Pays $50-200 subject to funding; pays in contributor's copies and subscriptions when funding is limited.**

Poetry Avant-garde, free verse, traditional. No light verse. **Buys 10-30 poems/year.** Submit maximum 10 poems. **Pays $10-50 subject to availability of funds; pays in contributor's copies and subscriptions when funding is limited.**

Tips "All sections are open to freelancers. We rely almost exclusively on unsolicited manuscripts. *AQR* is a nonprofit literary magazine and does not always have funds to pay authors."

$ AMERICAN BOOK REVIEW

The Writer's Review, Inc., Campus Box 4241, Illinois State University, Normal IL 61790-4241. (309)438-2127. Fax: (309)438-3523. E-mail: americanbookreview@llstu.edu. Web site: www.litline.org/abr. Editor/Publisher: Charles B. Harris. **Contact:** Joe Amato, managing editor. Bimonthly magazine covering book reviews. "We specialize in reviewing books published by independent presses." Estab. 1977. Circ. 15,000. Pays on publication. Publishes ms an average of 2-4 months after acceptance. Byline given. Offers $50 kill fee. Buys one-time rights. Editorial lead time 1 month. Accepts queries by mail, e-mail, fax, phone. Responds in 2 weeks to queries; 1-2 months to mss. Sample copy for $4. Writer's guidelines online.

Nonfiction Book reviews. Does not want fiction, poetry, or interviews. Query with published clips. Length: 750-1,250 words. **Pays $50.**

Tips "Most of our reviews are assigned, but we occasionally accept unsolicited reviews. Send query and samples of published reviews."

$ ANCIENT PATHS

Christian Literary Magazine, P.O. Box 7505, Fairfax Station VA 22039. E-mail: ssburris@msn.com. Web site: www.editorskylar.com. **Contact:** Skylar Hamilton Burris, editor. **99% freelance written.** Biennial magazine with subtle Christian and universal religious themes. "*Ancient Paths* publishes quality fiction, creative nonfiction and poetry for a literate Christian audience. Religious themes are usually subtle, and the magazine has non-Christian readers as well as some content by non-Christian authors. However, writers should be comfortable appearing in a Christian magazine." Estab. 1998. Circ. 200. Pays on publication. Publishes ms an average of 6 months after acceptance. Byline given. Not copyrighted. Buys one-time rights. Accepts previously published material. Accepts simultaneous submissions. Responds in 4-5 weeks to mss. Sample copy for $5; make checks payable to Skylar Burris. Writer's guidelines online.

- *Ancient Paths* is published in January of odd-numbered years. The submission period is March 1, 2007-June 1, 2008.

Fiction Fantasy, historical, humorous, mainstream, mystery, novel excerpts, religious, science fiction, slice-of-life vignettes, western, literary. No retelling of Bible stories. Literary fiction favored over genre fiction. **Buys 4-10 mss/year.** Send complete ms. Length: 250-2,500 words. **Pays $6, 1 copy, and discount on additional copies.**

Poetry Free verse, traditional. No avant-garde, prose poetry, forced rhyme or poor meter. **Buys 25-60 poems/year.** Submit maximum 5 poems. Length: 4-60 lines. **Pays $2/poem, 1 copy, and discount on additional copies.**

Tips "Make the reader think as well as feel. Do not simply state a moral message; no preaching, nothing didactic. You should have something meaningful to say, but be subtle. Show, don't tell."

$ANTIETAM REVIEW

Washington County Arts Council, 14 W. Washington St., Hagerstown MD 21740. (301)791-3132. Fax: (240)420-1754. E-mail: antietamreview@washingtoncountyarts.com (queries only). Web site: www.washingtoncountyarts.com. **Contact:** Mary Jo Vincent, managing editor. **90% freelance written.** Annual magazine covering fiction, poetry, and b&w photography. Estab. 1982. Circ. 1,000. Buys first North American serial rights. Sample copy for $6.30 (back issue); $8.40 (current issue).

Photos Seeks b&w photos. All subject matter is considered. Contact via mail or e-mail for photo guidelines.

Fiction Condensed novels, ethnic, experimental, novel excerpts, short stories of a literary quality. No religious, romance, erotica, confession, or horror. Length: Maximum 5,000 words. **Pays $50-100 and 2 contributor's copies.**

Poetry Avant-garde, free verse, traditional. No haiku, religious or rhyme. Submit maximum 3 poems. Length: 30 lines maximum. **Pays $25/poem and 2 contributor copies.**

Tips "We seek high-quality, well-crafted work with significant character development and shift. We look for work that is interesting, involves the reader, and teaches us a new way to view the world. A manuscript stands out because of its energy and flow. Most of our submissions reflect the times (news/current events) more than industry trends. Works should have a compelling voice, originality, and magic. Contributors are encouraged to review past issues."

$ THE ANTIGONISH REVIEW

St. Francis Xavier University, P.O. Box 5000, Antigonish NS B2G 2W5 Canada. (902)867-3962. Fax: (902)867-5563. E-mail: tar@stfx.ca. Web site: www.antigonishreview.com. Co-Editors: Gerald Trites and Jeanette Lynes. **Contact:** Bonnie McIsaac, office manager. **100% freelance written.** Quarterly magazine. Literary magazine for educated and creative readers. Estab. 1970. Circ. 850. Pays on publication. Publishes ms an average of 8 months after acceptance. Byline given. Offers variable kill fee. Rights retained by author. Editorial lead time 4 months. Submit seasonal material 4 months in advance. Accepts queries by mail, fax. Responds in 1 month to queries; 6 months to mss. Sample copy for $7 or online. Writer's guidelines for #10 SASE or online.

Nonfiction Essays, interview/profile, book reviews/articles. No academic pieces. **Buys 15-20 mss/year.** Query. Length: 1,500-5,000 words. **Pays $50-150.**

Fiction Literary. Contemporary, prose poem. No erotica. **Buys 35-40 mss/year.** Send complete ms. Length: 500-5,000 words. **Pays $50 for stories.**

Poetry Buys 100-125 poems/year. Submit maximum 5 poems. **Pays in copies.**

Tips "Send for guidelines and/or sample copy. Send ms with cover letter and SASE with submission."

$ANTIOCH REVIEW

P.O. Box 148, Yellow Springs OH 45387-0148. Web site: www.review.antioch.edu. **Contact:** Robert S. Fogarty, editor. Quarterly magazine for general, literary, and academic audience. "Literary and cultural review of contemporary issues, and literature for general readership." Estab. 1941. Circ. 5,100. Pays on publication. Publishes ms an average of 10 months after acceptance. Byline given. Buys first, one-time rights. Responds in 3-6 months to mss. Sample copy for $7. Writer's guidelines online.

Nonfiction "Contemporary articles in the humanities and social sciences, politics, economics, literature, and all areas of broad intellectual concern. Somewhat scholarly, but never pedantic in style, eschewing all professional jargon. Lively, distinctive prose insisted upon. We *do not* read simultaneous submissions." Length: 2,000-8,000 words. **Pays $15/printed page.**

Fiction Fiction editor. "Quality fiction only, distinctive in style with fresh insights into the human condition." Experimental, contemporary. No science fiction, fantasy, or confessions. Length: generally under 8,000. **Pays $15/printed page.**

Poetry "No light or inspirational verse." **Pays $15/printed page.**

$ ARC

Canada's National Poetry Magazine, Arc Poetry Society, P.O. Box 81060, Ottawa ON K1P 1B1 Canada. E-mail: arc@arcpoetry.ca. Web site: www.arcpoetry.ca. **Contact:** Anita Lahey, editor. Semiannual magazine featuring poetry, poetry-related articles, and criticism. "Our focus is poetry, and Canadian poetry in general, although we do publish writers from elsewhere. We are looking for the best poetry from new and established writers. We often have special issues. Send a SASE for upcoming special issues and contests." Estab. 1978. Circ. 1,500. Pays on publication. Publishes ms an average of 6 months after acceptance. Byline given. Buys one-time rights. Responds in 4 months to queries. Writer's guidelines for #10 SASE.

Nonfiction Essays, interview/profile, book reviews. Query first. Length: 500-4,000 words. **Pays $40/printed page (Canadian), and 2 copies.**

Photos Query first. Buys one-time rights. Pays $300 for 10 photos.

Poetry Avant-garde, free verse. E-mail submissions not accepted. **Buys 60 poems/year.** Submit maximum 5 poems. **Pays $40/printed page (Canadian).**

Tips "Please include brief biographical note with submission."

$ ARTS & LETTERS

Journal of Contemporary Culture, Georgia College & State University, Campus Box 89, Milledgeville GA 31061. E-mail: al@gcsu.edu. Web site: al.gcsu.edu. **Contact:** Martin Lammon, editor. Semiannual magazine covering poetry, fiction, creative nonfiction, and commentary on contemporary culture. "The journal features the mentors interview series and the world poetry translation series. Also, it is the only journal nationwide to feature authors and artists that represent such an eclectic range of creative work." Estab. 1999. Circ. 1,500. Pays on publication. Publishes ms an average of 6-12 months after acceptance. Rights revert to author after publication. Responds in 2 months to mss. Sample copy for $5, plus $1 for postage. Writer's guidelines online.

Nonfiction Karen Salyer McElmurray, creative nonfiction editor. Looking for creative nonfiction.

Fiction Allen Gee, fiction editor. No genre fiction. **Buys 6 mss/year.** Length: 3,000-7,500 words. **Pays $50 minimum or $10/published page.**

Poetry Alice Friman, poetry editor.

Tips "An obvious, but not gimmicky, attention to fresh usage of language. A solid grasp of the craft of story writing. Fully realized work."

$ $ ⊘ BACKWARDS CITY REVIEW

Backwards City Publications, P.O. Box 41317, Greensboro NC 27404-1317. E-mail: editors@backwardscity.net. Web site: www.backwardscity.net. Founders/Editors: Jaimee Hills, Patrick Egan, Don Ezra Cruz, Tom Christopher, Gerry Canavan. **Contact:** Genre Editor. **100% freelance written.** Semiannual magazine covering literature. "*The Backwards City Review* was founded by 5 graduates of the Greensboro Writing Program with 1 goal in mind: to create a journal that caters to the world above, beyond, around, near, within-sight-of and slightly out of tune with conventional literary outlets. Cities are built upon need. In the physical world, they collect around resources: a spring, a bay, fertile soil. Imaginary cities collect around ideas: a style of art, a search for information, a game, a movie, a band, a book, a political ideal. It is these new cities that nourish us and make it possible for us to live. In our Backwards City, there is no mayor, and we eat all our meals at 1 long table." Estab. 2004. Circ. 500. Pays on publication. Publishes ms an average of 6 months after acceptance. Byline given. Buys first North American serial, electronic, anthology rights. Editorial lead time 6 months. Accepts queries by mail, e-mail. Accepts simultaneous submissions. Responds in 3-6 months to queries; 3-6 months to mss. Sample copy for $7. Writer's guidelines online.

- *Backwards City Review* is temporarily closed to submissions.

Nonfiction Essays. No religious/inspiration. **Buys 2-4 mss/year.** Send complete ms. Length: 10,000 words maximum. **Pays $0-400 (when available). Pays in contributor copies for noncontest entries.**

Photos State availability with submission. Reviews contact sheets, prints, slides. Buys one-time rights. Negotiates payment individually.

Fiction Experimental, mainstream. No religious/inspirational. Interested in well-written stories that may be a little off the beaten path. Publishes short shorts/flash fiction. **Buys 8-20 mss/year.** Send complete ms. Length: Length: 10,000 words maximum. **Pays $0-400 (when available). Pays in contributor copies for noncontest entries.**

Poetry Avant-garde, free verse, haiku, traditional, literary. No concrete or visual poetry. **Buys 40-80 poems/year.** Submit maximum 10 pages poems. **Pays in contributor copies.**

Tips "Check our Web site and read our guidelines. Read a sample issue before submitting. Send us your best work."

BELLINGHAM REVIEW

Mail Stop 9053, Western Washington University, Bellingham WA 98225. (360)650-4863. E-mail: bhreview@cc.wwu.edu. Web site: www.wwu.edu/~bhreview. Editor: Brenda Miller. **Contact:** Poetry, Fiction, or Creative Nonfiction Editor. **100% freelance written.** Semiannual nonprofit magazine. *Bellingham Review* seeks literature of palpable quality; stories, essays, and poems that nudge the limits of form or execute traditional forms exquisitely. Estab. 1977. Circ. 1,600. Pays on publication when funding allows. Publishes ms an average of 6 months after acceptance. Byline given. Buys first North American serial rights. Editorial lead time 6 months. Accepts simultaneous submissions. Responds in 3 months to mss. Sample copy for $7. Writer's guidelines online.

Nonfiction Nonfiction Editor. Essays, personal experience. Does not want anything nonliterary. **Buys 4-6 mss/**

year. Send complete ms. Length: 9,000 words maximum. **Pays as funds allow, plus contributor copies.**
Fiction Fiction Editor. Literary short fiction. Experimental, humorous. Does not want anything nonliterary. **Buys 4-6 mss/year.** Send complete ms. Length: 9,000 words maximum. **Pays as funds allow.**
Poetry Poetry Editor. Avant-garde, free verse, traditional. Will not use light verse. **Buys 10-30 poems/year.** Submit maximum 3 poems. **Pays as funds allow.**
Tips "Open submission period is from October 1-February 1. Manuscripts arriving between February 2 and September 30 will be returned unread." The *Bellingham Review* holds 3 annual contests: the 49th Parallel Poetry Award, the Annie Dillard Award in Nonfiction, and the Tobias Wolff Award in Fiction. Submissions December 1-March 15. See the individual listings for these contests under Contests & Awards for full details.

$ BLACK WARRIOR REVIEW

P.O. Box 862936, Tuscaloosa AL 35486-0027. (205)348-4518. Web site: www.webdelsol.com/bwr. **90% freelance written.** Semiannual magazine of fiction, poetry, essays, art, comics and reviews. "We publish contemporary fiction, poetry, reviews, essays, and art for a literary audience. We publish the freshest work we can find." Estab. 1974. Circ. 2,000. Pays on publication. Publishes ms an average of 6 months after acceptance. Byline given. Buys first rights. Accepts simultaneous submissions. Responds in 4 months to mss. Sample copy for $10. Writer's guidelines online.
Nonfiction Shoode Hargis, nonfiction editor. Interview/profile, literary/personal essays. **Buys 5 mss/year.** No queries; send complete ms. **Pays up to $100, copies, and a 1-year subscription.**
Fiction Luke Southworth, fiction editor. Publishes novel excerpts if under contract to be published. One story/chapter per envelope, please. Contemporary, short and short-short fiction. Want "work that is conscious of form and well-crafted. We are open to good experimental writing and short-short fiction. No genre fiction please." **Buys 10 mss/year. Pays up to $150, copies, and a 1-year subscription.**
Poetry Dave Welch, poetry editor. **Buys 35 poems/year.** Submit maximum 7 poems. **Pays up to $75, copies, and a 1-year subscription.**
Tips "Read *BWR* before submitting. Send us only your best work. Address all submissions to the appropriate genre editor."

N ⊘ BOOKLIST

American Library Association, 50 E. Huron St., Chicago IL 60611. (312)280-5715. Fax: (312)337-6787. E-mail: booklist@ala.org. Web site: www.ala.org/booklist. **Contact:** Bill Ott, editor. **30% freelance written.** Biweekly magazine covering library selection, book publishing. Estab. 1905. Circ. 26,000. Pays on publication. Publishes ms an average of 6 weeks after acceptance. Byline given. Buys all rights. Editorial lead time 3 months. Submit seasonal material 6 months in advance. Accepts queries by mail, fax. Sample copy for free. Writer's guidelines online.

- *Booklist* does not accept unsolicited mss.

Nonfiction No unsolicited mss. Reviews must be assigned by editors. Query with published clips. Length: 140-200 words. **Payment varies for assigned articles.**
Columns/Departments Writers & Readers (established writers talk about writing for the library audience), 1,000 words. **Buys 4 mss/year.** Query with published clips. **Payment varies.**
Tips "Already-published reviewers are the best prospects. Must demonstrate an understanding of the subject matter and of the public and/or school library markets. Unsolicited reviews or articles are not welcome."

$ $ BOULEVARD

Opojaz, Inc., 6614 Clayton Rd., PMB 325, Richmond Heights MO 63117. (314)862-2643. Fax: (314)862-2982. **Contact:** Richard Burgin, editor. **100% freelance written.** Triannual magazine covering fiction, poetry, and essays. "*Boulevard* is a diverse literary magazine presenting original creative work by well-known authors, as well as by writers of exciting promise." Estab. 1985. Circ. 11,000. Pays on publication. Publishes ms an average of 9 months after acceptance. Byline given. Offers no kill fee. Buys first North American serial rights. Accepts queries by mail, phone. Accepts simultaneous submissions. Responds in 2 weeks to queries; 3 months to mss. Sample copy for $8. Writer's guidelines online.

O‐ Break in with "a touching, intelligent, and original story, poem or essay."

Nonfiction Book excerpts, essays, interview/profile, opinion, photo feature. "No pornography, science fiction, children's stories, or westerns." **Buys 10 mss/year.** Send complete ms. Length: 10,000 words maximum. **Pays $20/page, minimum $150.**
Fiction Confessions, experimental, mainstream, novel excerpts. "We do not want erotica, science fiction, romance, western, or children's stories." **Buys 20 mss/year.** Send complete ms. Length: 8,000 words maximum. **$20/page; minimum $150.**
Poetry Avant-garde, free verse, haiku, traditional. "Do not send us light verse." **Buys 80 poems/year.** Submit maximum 5 poems. Length: 200 lines. **$25-250 (sometimes higher).**

Tips "Read the magazine first. The work *Boulevard* publishes is generally recognized as among the finest in the country. We continue to seek more good literary or cultural essays. Send only your best work."

N BRAIN, CHILD

The Magazine for Thinking Mothers, March Press, P.O. Box 714, Lexington VA 24450. E-mail: editor@brainchildmag.com. Web site: www.brainchildmag.com. Co-Editors: Jennifer Niesslein and Stephanie Wilkinson. **90% freelance written.** Quarterly magazine covering the experience of motherhood. "*Brain, Child* reflects modern motherhood—the way it really is. We like to think of *Brain, Child* as a community, for and by mothers who like to think about what raising kids does for (and to) the mind and soul. *Brain, Child* isn't your typical parenting magazine. We couldn't cupcake-decorate our way out of a paper bag. We are more 'literary' than 'how-to,' more *New Yorker* than *Parents*. We shy away from expert advice on childrearing in favor of first-hand reflections by great writers (Jane Smiley, Barbara Ehrenreich, Anne Tyler) on life as a mother. Each quarterly issue is full of essays, features, humor, reviews, fiction, art, cartoons, and our readers' own stories. Our philosophy is pretty simple: Motherhood is worthy of literature. And there are a lot of ways to mother, all of them interesting. We're proud to be publishing articles and essays that are smart, down to earth, sometimes funny, and sometimes poignant." Estab. 2000. Circ. 36,000. Pays on publication. Publishes ms an average of 6 months after acceptance. Byline given. Buys first North American serial, electronic, and *Brain, Child* anthology rights. Editorial lead time 3 months. Submit seasonal material 6 months in advance. Accepts queries by mail, e-mail. Accepts simultaneous submissions. Responds in 1 month to queries; 1-3 months to mss. Sample copy and writer's guidelines online.

Nonfiction Essays (including debate), humor, in-depth features. No how-to articles, advice, or tips. **Buys 40-50 mss/year.** Query with published clips for features and debate essays; send complete ms for essays. Length: 800-5,000 words. **Payment varies.** Sometimes pays expenses of writers on assignment.

Photos State availability with submission. Reviews contact sheets, prints, GIF/JPEG files. Model releases required.

Fiction "We publish fiction that has a strong motherhood theme." Mainstream, literary. No genre fiction. **Buys 4 mss/year.** Send complete ms. Length: 800-5,000 words. **Payment varies.**

$ BRAVE HEARTS

Ogden Publications, 1503 SW 42nd St., Topeka KS 66609-1265. Web site: www.braveheartsmagazine.com. **100% freelance written.** Quarterly magazine covering inspirational topics. "*Brave Hearts* is written by and for ordinary people who have an inspirational message to share on an issue's topic." Estab. 2001. Circ. 1,000. Pays on publication. Publishes ms an average of 6 months after acceptance. Byline given. Buys all rights. Editorial lead time 3 months. Submit seasonal material 6 months in advance. Responds in 1 month to queries. Sample copy for $4.95. Writer's guidelines online.

Nonfiction Essays (short), general interest, humor, inspirational, personal experience, photo feature. Does not want overly religious, opinion, negative situations (sex/drugs/violence). Send complete ms. Length: 300-900 words. **Pays $5-12.**

Photos Send photos with submission. Reviews prints. Buys all rights. Pays maximum $5/photo. Captions, identification of subjects required.

Poetry Free verse, light verse, traditional. Does not want negative situations (sex/drugs/violence). **Buys 30+ poems/year.** Submit maximum 5 poems. **Pays $10.**

Tips "Be succinct and on topic. Indicate in your cover letter which topic/issue that submission is on. Be inspirational, yet not overtly religious. Topics for upcoming issues are printed on the inside cover of each issue."

$ $ BRICK

A Literary Journal, Brick, Box 537, Station Q, Toronto ON M4T 2M5 Canada. Web site: www.brickmag.com. Publisher: Michael Redhill. **90% freelance written.** Semiannual magazine covering literature and the arts. "We publish literary nonfiction of a very high quality on a range of arts and culture subjects." Estab. 1978. Circ. 4,000. Pays on publication. Publishes ms an average of 3 months after acceptance. Byline given. Buys first world, first serial, one-time English language rights. Editorial lead time 5 months. Responds in 6 months to mss. Sample copy for $12, plus $3 shipping. Writer's guidelines online.

Nonfiction Essays, historical/nostalgic, interview/profile, opinion, travel. No fiction, poetry, personal real-life experience, or book reviews. **Buys 30-40 mss/year.** Send complete ms. Length: 250-2,500 words. **Pays $75-500 (Canadian).**

Photos State availability with submission. Reviews transparencies, prints, TIFF/JPEG files. Buys one-time rights. Offers $25-50/photo.

Tips "*Brick* is interested in polished work by writers who are widely read and in touch with contemporary culture. The magazine is serious, but not fusty. We like to feel the writer's personality in the piece, too."

N $ BUTTON

New England's Tiniest Magazine of Poetry, Fiction and Gracious Living, P.O. Box 77, Westminster MA 01473. E-mail: sally@moonsigns.net. Web site: www.moonsigns.net. **Contact:** Sally Cragin, editor. **10% freelance written.** Annual literary magazine. "*Button* is New England's tiniest magazine of poetry, fiction, and gracious living, published once a year. As 'gracious living' is on the cover, we like wit, brevity, cleverly-conceived essay/recipe, poetry that isn't sentimental or song lyrics. I started *Button* so that a century from now, when people read it in landfils or, preferably, libraries, they'll say, 'Gee, what a great time to have lived. I wish I lived back then.' " Estab. 1993. Circ. 1,500. Pays on publication. Publishes ms an average of 3-9 months after acceptance. Byline given. Buys first North American serial rights. Editorial lead time 6 months. Responds in 1 month to queries; 2 months to mss. Sample copy for $2.50. Writer's guidelines online.

Nonfiction Personal experience, cooking stories. Does not want "the tired, the trite, the sexist, the multiply-folded, the single-spaced, the sentimental, the self-pitying, the swaggering, the infantile (i.e., coruscated whimsy and self-conscious quaint), poems about Why You Can't Be together and stories about How Complicated Am I. Before you send us anything, sit down and read a poem by Stanley Kunitz or a story by Evelyn Waugh, Louisa May Alcott, or anyone who's visited the poles, and if you still think you've written a damn fine thing, have at it. A word-count on the top of the page is fine—a copyright or 'all rights reserved' reminder makes you look like a beginner." **Buys 1-2 mss/year.** Length: 300-2,000 words. **Pays $10 and up, depending on length of piece.**

Fiction W.M. Davies, fiction editor. Seeking quality fiction. "No genre fiction, science fiction, techno-thriller." Wants more of "anything Herman Melville, Henry James, or Betty MacDonald would like to read." **Buys 1-2 mss/year.** Send complete ms. Length: 300-2,000 words. **Pays $25.**

Poetry Seeking quality poetry. Free verse, traditional. **Buys 2-4 poems/year.** Submit maximum 3 poems. **Pays $10-25.**

Tips "*Button* writers have been widely published elsewhere, in virtually all the major national magazines. They include, Ralph Lombreglia, Lawrence Millman, They Might Be Giants, Combustible Edison, Sven Birkerts, Stephen McCauley, Amanda Powell, Wayne Wilson, David Barber, Romayne Dawnay, Brendan Galvin, and Diana DerHovanessian. It's $2 for a sample, which seems reasonable. Follow the guidelines, make sure you read your work aloud, and don't inflate or deflate your publications and experience. We've published plenty of new folks, but on the merits of the work."

$ $ THE CAPILANO REVIEW

2055 Purcell Way, North Vancouver BC V7J 3H5 Canada. E-mail: tcr@capcollege.bc.ca. Web site: www.thecapilanoreview.ca. **100% freelance written.** "Triannual visual and literary arts magazine that publishes only what the editors consider to be the very best fiction, poetry, drama, or visual art being produced. *TCR* editors are interested in fresh, original work that stimulates and challenges readers. Over the years, the magazine has developed a reputation for pushing beyond the boundaries of traditional art and writing. We are interested in work that is new in concept and in execution." Estab. 1972. Circ. 900. Pays on publication. Publishes ms an average of within 1 year after acceptance. Byline given. Buys first North American serial rights. Accepts queries by mail. Responds in 4 months to mss. Sample copy for $10 (outside of Canada, USD). Writer's guidelines for #10 SASE with IRC or Canadian stamps or online.

Fiction Send complete ms with SASE and Canadian postage or IRCs. Experimental, novel excerpts, literary. "No traditional, conventional fiction. Want to see more innovative, genre-blurring work." **Buys 10-15 mss/year.** Length: 8,000 words. **Pays $50-200.**

Poetry Submit maximum 6-8 poems (with SASE and Canadian postage or IRCs). Avant-garde, free verse. **Buys 40 poems/year. Pays $50-200.**

$ THE CHATTAHOOCHEE REVIEW

Georgia Perimeter College, 2101 Womack Rd., Dunwoody GA 30338-4497. (770)274-5147. Web site: www.chattahoochee-review.org. **Contact:** Marc Fitten, editor. Quarterly magazine. "We publish a number of Southern writers, but *Chattahoochee Review* is not by design a regional magazine. All themes, forms, and styles are considered as long as they impact the whole person: heart, mind, intuition, and imagination." Estab. 1980. Circ. 1,350. Pays on publication. Publishes ms an average of 3 months after acceptance. Byline given. Buys first rights. Accepts queries by mail. Responds in 2 weeks to queries; 4 months to mss. Sample copy for $6. Writer's guidelines online.

Nonfiction "We look for distinctive, honest personal essays and creative nonfiction of any kind, including the currently popular memoiristic narrative. We publish interviews with writers of all kinds: literary, academic, journalistic, and popular. We also review selected current offerings in fiction, poetry, and nonfiction, including works on photography and the visual arts. We do not often, if ever, publish technical, critical, theoretical, or scholarly work about literature, although we are interested in essays written for general readers about writers, their careers, and their work." Essays (interviews with authors, reviews). **Buys 10 mss/year.** Send complete ms. Length: 5,000 words maximum.

Photos State availability with submission. Buys one-time rights. Negotiates payment individually. Identification of subjects required.

Fiction Accepts all subject matter except juvenile, science fiction, and romance. **Buys 12 mss/year.** Send complete ms. Length: 6,000 words maximum. **Pays $20/page, $250 max and 2 contributor's copies.**

Poetry Avant-garde, free verse, haiku, light verse, traditional. **Buys 60 poems/year.** Submit maximum 5 poems. **Pays $50/poem.**

Tips "Become familiar with our journal and the type of work we regularly publish."

CHELSEA

Chelsea Associates, P.O. Box 773 Cooper Station, New York NY 10276-0773. Web site: www.chelseamag.org. **Contact:** Alfredo de Palchi, editor. **70% freelance written.** Semiannual magazine. "We stress style, variety, originality. No special biases or requirements. Flexible attitudes, eclectic material. We take an active interest, as always, in cross-cultural exchanges, superior translations, and are leaning toward cosmopolitan, interdisciplinary techniques, but maintain no strictures against traditional modes." Estab. 1958. Circ. 2,200. Pays on publication. Publishes ms an average of 6 months after acceptance. Byline given. Buys first North American serial rights. Accepts queries by mail. Responds in 3-5 months to mss. Sample copy for $6. Writer's guidelines and contest guidelines available for #10 SASE.

- *Chelsea* also sponsors fiction and poetry contests. Poetry Deadline: December 15; Fiction Deadline: June 15. Send SASE for guidelines.

Nonfiction Essays, book reviews (query first with sample). **Buys 6 mss/year.** Send complete ms with SASE. Length: 6,000 words.

Fiction Mainstream, novel excerpts, literary. **Buys 12 mss/year.** Send complete ms. Length: 5,000-6,000 words.

Poetry Avant-garde, free verse, traditional. **Buys 60-75 poems/year.**

Tips "We only accept written correspondence. We are looking for more super translations, first-rate fiction, and work by writers of color. No need to query; submit complete manuscript. We suggest writers look at a recent issue of *Chelsea*."

$ $ CHICKEN SOUP FOR THE SOUL

101 Stories to Open the Heart and Rekindle the Spirit, Chicken Soup for the Soul Enterprises, Inc., P.O, Box 30880, Santa Barbara CA 93130. (805)563-2935. Fax: (805)563-2945. E-mail: blomonaco@chickensoup.com. Web site: www.chickensoup.com. **95% freelance written.** Paperback with 8-12 publications/year featuring inspirational, heartwarming, uplifting short stories. Estab. 1993. Circ. Over 40 titles; 60 million books in print. Pays on publication. Publishes ms an average of 8 months after acceptance. Byline given. Buys one-time rights. Accepts queries by mail, e-mail, fax. Accepts previously published material. Accepts simultaneous submissions. Responds upon consideration to queries. Sample copy not available. Writer's guidelines online.

Nonfiction Humor, inspirational, personal experience, religious. Special issues: Traveling sisterhood, Mother-Daughter stories, Christian teen, Christmas stories, stories by and/or about men on love, kindness, parenting, family, Nascar racing, athletes, teachers, fishing, adoption, volunteers. No sermon, essay, eulogy, term paper, journal entry, political, or controversial issues. **Buys 1,000 mss/year.** Send complete ms. Length: 300-1,200 words. **Pays $200.**

Poetry Traditional. No controversial poetry. **Buys 50 poems/year.** Submit maximum 5 poems. **Pays $50.**

Fillers Anecdotes, facts, gags to be illustrated by cartoonist, short humor. **Buys 50/year. Pays $200.**

Tips "We prefer submissions to be sent via our Web site. Print submissions should be on $8^{1}/_{2} \times 11$ paper in 12 point Times New Roman font. Type author's contact information on the first page of story. Stories are to be nonfiction. No anonymous or author unknown submissions are accepted. We do not return submissions."

$ THE CINCINNATI REVIEW

P.O. Box 210069, Cincinnati OH 45221-0069. (513)556-3954. E-mail: editors@cincinnatireview.com. Web site: www.cincinnatireview.com. Managing Editor: Nicola Mason. **Contact:** Don Bogen, poetry editor; Brock Clarke, fiction editor. **100% freelance written.** Semiannual magazine. "A journal devoted to publishing the best new literary fiction and poetry as well as book reviews, essays, and interviews." Estab. 2003. Pays on publication. Publishes ms an average of 6 months after acceptance. Byline given. Buys first North American serial, electronic rights. Accepts queries by mail. Responds in 2 weeks to queries; 6 weeks to mss. Sample copy for $7 (back issue) or $9 (current issue), subscription for $15. Writer's guidelines online.

- Reads submissions September 1-May 31.

Nonfiction Book excerpts, essays, interview/profile, new book fiction and poetry reviews. Query. Length: 1,000-5,000 words. **Pays $25/page.**

Columns/Departments Book Reviews; Literary Fiction; Poetry, 1,500 words. **Buys 20 mss/year.** Query. **Pays $25/page.**

Fiction Brock Clarke, fiction editor. Literary. Does not want genre fiction. **Buys 13 mss/year.** Query. Length: 125-10,000 words. **Pays $25/page.**

Poetry Don Bogen, poetry editor. Avant-garde, free verse, traditional. **Buys 120 poems/year.** Submit maximum 10 poems. **Pays $30/page.**

N $ $ CITY SLAB

Urban Tales of the Grotesque, City Slab Publications, 1705 Summit Ave., #314, Seattle WA 98122. (206)226-7430. E-mail: submission@cityslab.com. Web site: www.cityslab.com. **Contact:** Dave Lindschmidt, editor. **90% freelance written.** Quarterly magazine covering horror and horror/crime mix. "*City Slab* magazine is hard-edged, adult fiction." Estab. 2002. Pays on publication. Publishes ms an average of 3 months after acceptance. Byline given. Buys first North American serial rights. Accepts queries by mail, e-mail. Responds in 3 weeks to queries; 2 months to mss. Sample copy for $6. Writer's guidelines online.

Nonfiction Essays, interview/profile, photo feature. **Buys 4 mss/year.** Send complete ms. Length: 2,000-3,000 words. **Pays $50-100, plus contributor copies.**

Photos State availability of or send photos with submission. Reviews JPEG files. Buys one-time rights. Offers no additional payment for photos accepted with ms. Model releases required.

Fiction "*City Slab* wants to publish well thought out, literary-quality horror." Erotica, experimental, horror. Does not want to see children/youth in sexually oriented stories. **Buys 24 mss/year.** Send complete ms. Length: 5,000 words maximum. **Pays 1-10¢/word.**

Tips "Read not only the horror greats—Barker, King, Campbell, Lovecraft, etc.—but also the classics—Dickens, Hemingway, Oates, Steinbeck—to see how a great tale is woven. Recently published fiction by Gerard Hoaurner, Christa Faust, and P.D. Cacek."

$ COLORADO REVIEW

Center for Literary Publishing, Department of English, Colorado State University, Fort Collins CO 80523. (970)491-5449. E-mail: creview@colostate.edu. Web site: coloradoreview.colostate.edu. **Contact:** Stephanie G'Schwind, editor. Literary magazine published 3 times/year. Estab. 1956. Circ. 1,100. Pays on publication. Publishes ms an average of 1 year after acceptance. Byline given. Buys first North American serial rights. Rights revert to author upon publication. Editorial lead time 1 year. Responds in 2 months to mss. Sample copy for $10. Writer's guidelines online.

- Mss are read from September 1 to April 30. Mss recieved between May 1 and August 30 will be returned unread. Send no more than 1 story at a time.

Nonfiction Personal essays, creative nonfiction. **Buys 6-9 mss/year.** Send complete ms. **Pays $5/page.**

Fiction Short fiction. No genre fiction. Ethnic, experimental, mainstream, contemporary. **Buys 15-20 mss/year.** Send complete ms. Length: under 30 ms pages. **Pays $5/page.**

Poetry Considers poetry of any style. Send no more than 5 poems at one time. Don Revell or Jorie Graham, poetry editors. **Buys 60-100 poems/year. Pays $5/page.**

$ $ CONFRONTATION

A Literary Journal, Long Island University, Brookville NY 11548. (516)299-2720. Fax: (516)299-2735. E-mail: mtucker@liu.edu. Assistant to Editor: Jonna Semeik. **Contact:** Martin Tucker, editor-in-chief. **75% freelance written.** Semiannual magazine. "We are eclectic in our taste. Excellence of style is our dominant concern." Estab. 1968. Circ. 2,000. Pays on publication. Publishes ms an average of 1 year after acceptance. Byline given. Offers kill fee. Buys first North American serial, first, one-time, all rights. Accepts queries by mail, e-mail, phone. Accepts simultaneous submissions. Responds in 3 weeks to queries; 2 months to mss. Sample copy for $3. Writer's guidelines not available.

- *Confrontation* does not read mss during June, July, or August.

Nonfiction Essays, personal experience. **Buys 15 mss/year.** Send complete ms. Length: 1,500-5,000 words. **Pays $100-300 for assigned articles; $15-300 for unsolicited articles.**

Photos State availability with submission. Buys one-time rights. Offers no additional payment for photos accepted with ms.

Fiction "We judge on quality, so genre is open." Experimental, mainstream, novel excerpts, slice-of-life vignettes, contemporary, prose poem. "No 'proselytizing' literature or genre fiction." **Buys 60-75 mss/year.** Send complete ms. Length: 6,000 words. **Pays $25-250.**

Poetry Avant-garde, free verse, haiku, light verse, traditional. **Buys 60-75 poems/year.** Submit maximum 6 poems. Length: Open. **Pays $10-100.**

Tips "Most open to fiction and poetry. Study our magazine."

$ THE CONNECTICUT POETRY REVIEW

The Connecticut Poetry Review Press, P.O. Box 392, Stonington CT 06378. Managing Editor: Harley More. **Contact:** J. Claire White. **60% freelance written.** Annual magazine covering poetry/literature. Estab. 1981. Circ. 500. **Pays on acceptance.** Byline sometimes given. Buys first rights. Editorial lead time 4 months. Submit seasonal material 4 months in advance. Accepts queries by mail. Responds in 1 month to queries; 3 months to mss. Sample copy for $5 and #10 SASE. Writer's guidelines for #10 SASE.

Nonfiction Book excerpts, essays. **Buys 18 mss/year.**

Fiction Experimental.

Poetry Avant-garde, free verse, haiku, traditional. No light verse. **Buys 20-30 poems/year.** Submit maximum 4 poems. Length: 3-25 lines. **Pays $5-10.**

N $ CONTEMPORARY VERSE 2

The Canadian Journal of Poetry and Critical Writing, Contemporary Verse 2, Inc., 207-100 Arthur St., Winnipeg MB R3B 1H3 Canada. (204)949-1365. Fax: (204)942-5754. E-mail: cv2@mb.sympatico.ca. Web site: www.contemporaryverse2.ca. **Contact:** Clarise Foster, managing editor. **75% freelance written.** Quarterly magazine covering poetry and critical writing about poetry. "*CV2* publishes poetry of demonstrable quality as well as critical writing in the form of interviews, essays, articles, and reviews. With the critical writing we tend to create a discussion of poetry which will interest a broad range of readers, including those who might be skeptical about the value of poetry." Estab. 1975. Circ. 600. Pays on publication. Byline given. Offers 50% kill fee. Not copyrighted. Buys first North American serial, second serial (reprint) rights. Editorial lead time 3-6 months. Submit seasonal material 3-6 months in advance. Accepts queries by mail, e-mail, phone. Responds in 2-3 weeks to queries; 3-8 months to mss. Sample copy for $8. Writer's guidelines online.

Nonfiction Essays, interview/profile, book reviews. No content that is not about poetry. **Buys 10-30 mss/year.** Query. Length: 800-3,000 words. **Pays $40-130 for assigned articles.** Pays in contributor copies only if requested by the author.

Poetry Avant-garde, free verse. No rhyming verse, traditionally inspirational. **Buys 110-120 poems/year.** Submit maximum 6 poems. **Pays $20/poem.**

N $ CRAB ORCHARD REVIEW

A Journal of Creative Works, Southern Illinois University at Carbondale, English Department, Faner Hall, Carbondale IL 62901-4503. (618)453-6833. Fax: (618)453-8224. Web site: www.siu.edu/~crborchd. "We are a general interest literary journal published twice/year. We strive to be a journal that writers admire and readers enjoy. We publish fiction, poetry, creative nonfiction, fiction translations, interviews and reviews." Estab. 1995. Circ. 2,200. Publishes ms an average of 9-12 months after acceptance. Buys first North American serial rights. Accepts simultaneous submissions. Responds in 3 weeks to queries; 9 months to mss. Sample copy for $8. Writer's guidelines for #10 SASE.

Fiction Jon Tribble, managing editor. Ethnic, excerpted novel. No science fiction, romance, western, horror, gothic or children's. Wants more nove excerpts that also stand alone as pieces. Length: 1,000-6,500 words. **Pays $100 minimum; $20/page maximum, 2 contributor's copies and a year subscription.**

Tips "We publish two issues per volume—one has a theme (we read from May to November for the theme issue), the other doesn't (we read from January through April for the nonthematic issue). Consult our Web site for information about our upcoming themes."

$ CREATIVE NONFICTION

Creative Nonfiction Foundation, 5501 Walnut St., Suite 202, Pittsburgh PA 15232. (412)688-0304. Fax: (412)688-0262. E-mail: information@creativenonfiction.org. Web site: www.creativenonfiction.org. **Contact:** Lee Gutkind, editor. **100% freelance written.** Magazine published 3 times/year covering nonfiction—personal essay, memoir, literary journalism. "*Creative Nonfiction* is the first journal to focus exclusively upon the genre of creative nonfiction. It publishes personal essay, memoir, and literary journalism on a broad range of subjects. Interviews with prominent writers and commentary about the genre also appear on its pages." Estab. 1993. Circ. 4,000. Pays on publication. Publishes ms an average of 1 year after acceptance. Byline given. Buys all rights. Editorial lead time 6 months. Accepts simultaneous submissions. Responds in 6 months to mss. Sample copy for $10. Writer's guidelines online.

Nonfiction Essays, interview/profile, personal experience, narrative journalism. No poetry, fiction. **Buys 30 mss/year.** Send complete ms. Length: 5,000 words maximum. **Pays $10/page—more if grant money available for assigned articles.**

Tips "Points to remember when submitting to *Creative Nonfiction:* strong reportage; well-written prose, attentive to language, rich with detail and distinctive voice; an informational quality or 'teaching element'; a compelling, focused, sustained narrative that's well-structured and conveys meaning. Manuscripts will not be accepted via fax or e-mail."

$ DESCANT

Descant Arts & Letters Foundation, P.O. Box 314, Station P, Toronto ON M5S 2S8 Canada. (416)593-2557. Fax: (416)593-9362. E-mail: info@descant.ca. Web site: descant.ca. Editor: Karen Mulhallen. **Contact:** Mark Lalibente, managing editor. Quarterly journal. Estab. 1970. Circ. 1,200. Pays on publication. Publishes ms an average of 16 months after acceptance. Editorial lead time 1 year. Accepts queries by mail, e-mail, phone. Sample copy for $8.50 plus postage. Writer's guidelines online.

- Pays $100 honorarium, plus 1-year's subscription for accepted submissions of any kind.

Nonfiction Book excerpts, essays, interview/profile, personal experience, historical.
Photos State availability with submission. Reviews contact sheets, prints. Buys one-time rights. Offers no additional payment for photos accepted with ms.
Fiction Karen Mulhallen, editor. Short stories or book excerpts. Maximum length 6,000 words; 3,000 words or less preferred. Ethnic, experimental, historical, humorous. No gothic, religious, beat. Send complete ms. **Pays $100 (Canadian); additional copies $8.**
Poetry Free verse, light verse, traditional. Submit maximum 6 poems.
Tips "Familiarize yourself with our magazine before submitting."

$ DOWNSTATE STORY

1825 Maple Ridge, Peoria IL 61614. (309)688-1409. E-mail: ehopkins@prairienet.org. Web site: www.wiu.edu/users/mfgeh/dss. **Contact:** Elaine Hopkins, editor. Annual magazine covering short fiction with some connection with Illinois or the Midwest. Estab. 1992. Circ. 500. **Pays on acceptance.** Publishes ms an average of 1 year after acceptance. Buys first rights. Accepts simultaneous submissions. Responds "ASAP" to mss. Sample copy for $8. Writer's guidelines online.
Fiction Adventure, ethnic, experimental, historical, horror, humorous, mainstream, mystery, romance, science fiction, suspense, western. No porn. **Buys 10 mss/year.** Length: 300-2,000 words. **Pays $50.**
Tips Wants more political fiction. Publishes short shorts and literary essays.

$ DREAMS & VISIONS

Spiritual Fiction, Skysong Press, 35 Peter St. S., Orillia ON L3V 5A8 Canada. (705)329-1770. Fax: (705)329-1770. E-mail: skysong@bconnex.net. Web site: www.bconnex.net/~skysong. **Contact:** Steve Stanton, editor. **100% freelance written.** Semiannual magazine. "Innovative literary fiction for adult Christian readers." Estab. 1988. Circ. 300. Pays on publication. Publishes ms an average of 4 months after acceptance. Byline given. Buys first North American serial, one-time, second serial (reprint) rights. Editorial lead time 6 months. Accepts queries by mail, e-mail. Accepts simultaneous submissions. Responds in 3 weeks to queries; 3 months to mss. Sample copy for $4.95. Writer's guidelines online.
Fiction Experimental, fantasy, humorous, mainstream, mystery, novel excerpts, religious, science fiction, slice-of-life vignettes. "We do not publish stories that glorify violence or perversity. All stories should portray a Christian world view or expand upon Biblical themes or ethics in an entertaining or enlightening manner." **Buys 12 mss/year.** Send complete ms. Length: 2,000-6,000 words. **Pays 1¢/word.**

$ ELLIPSIS MAGAZINE

Westminster College of Salt Lake City, 1840 S. 1300 E., Salt Lake City UT 84105. (801)832-2321. E-mail: ellipsis@westminstercollege.edu. Web site: www.westminstercollege.edu/ellipsis. **Contact:** *Ellipsis* Editor. Annual magazine. *Ellipsis Magazine* needs good literary poetry, fiction, essays, plays and visual art. Estab. 1967. Circ. 2,500. Pays on publication. Publishes ms an average of 3 months after acceptance. Byline given. Not copyrighted. Buys first North American serial rights. Accepts queries by mail. Accepts simultaneous submissions. Responds in 6 months to mss. Sample copy for $7.50. Writer's guidelines online.

- Reads submissions August 1 to November 1.

Nonfiction Essays. Send ms with SASE and brief bio.
Fiction Needs good literary fiction and plays. Send complete ms. Length: 6,000 words. **Pays $50 per story and 1 contributor's copy; additional copies $3.50.**
Poetry All accepted poems are eligible for the *Ellipsis* Award which includes a $100 prize. Past judges have included Jorie Graham, Sandra Cisneros, and Stanley Plumly. Submit maximum 3-5 poems. Include SASE and brief bio.

$ EPOCH

Cornell University, 251 Goldwin Smith Hall, Cornell University, Ithaca NY 14853. (607)255-3385. Fax: (607)255-6661. Editor: Michael Koch. **Contact:** Joseph Martin, senior editor. **100% freelance written.** Magazine published 3 times/year. "Well-written literary fiction, poetry, personal essays. Newcomers always welcome. Open to mainstream and avant-garde writing." Estab. 1947. Circ. 1,000. Pays on publication. Publishes ms an average of 6 months after acceptance. Byline given. Offers 100% kill fee. Buys first North American serial rights. Editorial lead time 6 months. Submit seasonal material 8 months in advance. Accepts queries by mail. Responds in 2 weeks to queries; 6 weeks to mss. Sample copy for $5. Writer's guidelines for #10 SASE.

Nonfiction Send complete ms. Essays, interview. No inspirational. **Buys 6-8 mss/year.** Send complete ms. Length: Open. **Pays $5-10/printed page.**

Photos Send photos with submission. Reviews contact sheets, transparencies, any size prints. Buys one-time rights. Negotiates payment individually.

Fiction Ethnic, experimental, mainstream, novel excerpts, literary short stories. "No genre fiction. Would like to see more Southern fiction (Southern US)." **Buys 25-30 mss/year.** Send complete ms. Length: Open. **Pays $5 and up/printed page.**

Poetry Nancy Vieira Couto. Avant-garde, free verse, haiku, light verse, traditional, all types. **Buys 30-75 poems/year.** Submit maximum 7 poems.

Tips "Tell your story, speak your poem, straight from the heart. We are attracted to language and to good writing, but we are most interested in what the good writing leads us to, or where."

$ $ EVENT

Douglas College, P.O. Box 2503, New Westminster BC V3L 5B2 Canada. (604)527-5293. Fax: (604)527-5095. Web site: event.douglas.bc.ca. **Contact:** Ian Cockfield, assistant editor. **100% freelance written.** Magazine published 3 times/year containing fiction, poetry, creative nonfiction, notes on writing, and reviews. "We are eclectic and always open to content that invites involvement. Generally, we like strong narrative." Estab. 1971. Circ. 1,250. Pays on publication. Publishes ms an average of 8 months after acceptance. Byline given. Buys first North American serial rights. Accepts queries by mail, fax. Accepts simultaneous submissions. Responds in 1 month to queries; 6 months to mss. Sample copy for $5. Writer's guidelines online.

- *Event* does not read mss in July, August, December, and January. No e-mail submissions. All submissions must include SASE (Canadian postage or IRCs only).

Fiction "We look for readability, style, and writing that invites involvement." Submit maximum 2 stories. Humorous, contemporary. "No technically poor or unoriginal pieces." **Buys 12-15 mss/year.** Send complete ms. Length: 5,000 words maximum. **Pays $22/page up to $500.**

Poetry "We tend to appreciate the narrative and sometimes the confessional modes." Free verse, prose. No light verse. **Buys 30-40 poems/year.** Submit maximum 10 poems. **Pays $25-500.**

Tips "Write well and read some past issues of *Event*."

N $ FICTION

% Department of English, City College, 138th St. & Covenant Ave., New York NY 10031. (212)650-6319. E-mail: fiction@fictioninc.com. Web site: www.fictioninc.com. **Contact:** Mark J. Mirsky, editor. Semiannual magazine. "As the name implies, we publish only fiction; we are looking for the best new writing available, leaning toward the unconventional. *Fiction* has traditionally attempted to make accessible the unaccessible, to bring the experimental to a broader audience." Estab. 1972. Circ. 4,000. Publishes ms an average of 1 year after acceptance. Buys first rights. Accepts simultaneous submissions. Responds in 3 months to mss. Sample copy for $5. Writer's guidelines online.

- Reading period for unsolicited mss is September 15-April 15.

Fiction Experimental, humorous, contemporary, literary. translations. No romance, science fiction, etc. **Buys 24-40 mss/year.** Length: 5,000 words. **Pays $114.**

Tips "The guiding principle of *Fiction* has always been to go to terra incognita in the writing of the imagination and to ask that modern fiction set itself serious questions, if often in absurd and comedic voices, interrogating the nature of the real and the fantastic. It represents no particular school of fiction, except the innovative. Its pages have often been a harbor for writers at odds with each other. As a result of its willingness to publish the difficult, experimental, and unusual, while not excluding the well known, *Fiction* has a unique reputation in the US and abroad as a journal of future directions."

$ FIELD: CONTEMPORARY POETRY & POETICS

Oberlin College Press, 50 N. Professor St., Oberlin OH 44074-1091. (440)775-8408. Fax: (440)775-8124. E-mail: oc.press@oberlin.edu. Web site: www.oberlin.edu/ocpress. **Contact:** Linda Slocum, managing editor. **60% freelance written.** Biannual magazine of poetry, poetry in translation, and essays on contemporary poetry by poets. No electronic submissions. Estab. 1969. Circ. 1,500. Pays on publication. Byline given. Buys first rights. Editorial lead time 4 months. Accepts queries by mail, e-mail, fax, phone. Responds in 6 weeks to mss. Sample copy for $7. Writer's guidelines online.

Poetry **Buys 100 poems/year.** Submit maximum 5 with SASE poems. **Pays $15/page.**

Tips "Submit 3-5 of your best poems with a cover letter and SASE. No simultaneous submissions. Keep trying! Submissions are read year-round."

$ THE FIRST LINE

Blue Cubicle Press, LLC, P.O. Box 250382, Plano TX 75025-0382. E-mail: info@thefirstline.com. Web site: www.thefirstline.com. Co-editors: David LaBounty and Jeff Adams. **Contact:** Robin LaBounty, ms coordinator. **95% freelance written.** Quarterly magazine. *The First Line* is a magazine that explores the different directions writers can take when they start from the same place. All stories must be written with the first line provided by the magazine. Estab. 1999. Circ. 800. Pays on publication. Publishes ms an average of 1 month after acceptance. Byline given. Buys first North American serial, electronic rights. Editorial lead time 2 months. Accepts queries by mail, e-mail. Responds in 1 week to queries; 2 months to mss. Sample copy for $3.50. Writer's guidelines online.

Nonfiction Essays. **Buys 4-8 mss/year.** Query. Length: 600-1,000 words. **Pays $10.**

Fiction Adventure, ethnic, experimental, fantasy, historical, horror, humorous, mainstream, mystery, romance, science fiction, suspense, western. No stories that do not start with the issue's first sentence. **Buys 40-60 mss/year.** Send complete ms. Length: 300-3,000 words. **Pays $20.**

$ FIVE POINTS

A Journal of Literature and Art, Georgia State University, P.O. Box 3999, Atlanta GA 30302-3999. Fax: (404)651-3167. E-mail: info@langate.gsu.edu. Web site: www.webdelsol.com/Five_Points. Triannual *Five Points* is "committed to publishing work that compels the imagination through the use of fresh and convincing language." Estab. 1996. Circ. 2,000. Publishes ms an average of 6 months after acceptance. Buys first North American serial rights. Sample copy for $7. Editorial calendar online.

Fiction Megan Sexton, executive editor. **Pays $15/page minimum; $250 maximum, free subscription to magazine and 2 contributor's copies; additional copies $4.**

$ THE GEORGIA REVIEW

The University of Georgia, 012 Gilbert Hall, University of Georgia, Athens GA 30602-9009. (706)542-3481. Fax: (706)542-0047. E-mail: garev@uga.edu. Web site: www.uga.edu/garev. Managing Editor: Mindy Wilson. **Contact:** Stephen Covey, acting editor. **99% freelance written.** Quarterly journal. "Our readers are educated, inquisitive people who read a lot of work in the areas we feature, so they expect only the best in our pages. All work submitted should show evidence that the writer is at least as well-educated and well-read as our readers. Essays should be authoritative but accessible to a range of readers." Estab. 1947. Circ. 5,000. Pays on publication. Publishes ms an average of 6 months after acceptance. Byline given. Buys first North American serial rights. Accepts queries by mail. Responds in 2 weeks to queries; 3-4 months to mss. Sample copy for $8. Writer's guidelines online.

- No simultaneous or electronic submissions.

Nonfiction Essays. "For the most part we are not interested in scholarly articles that are narrow in focus and/or overly burdened with footnotes. The ideal essay for *The Georgia Review* is a provocative, thesis-oriented work that can engage both the intelligent general reader and the specialist." **Buys 12-20 mss/year.** Send complete ms. **Pays $40/published page.**

Photos Send photos with submission. Reviews 5×7 prints or larger. Buys one-time rights. Offers no additional payment for photos accepted with ms.

Fiction T.R. Hummer, editor. "We seek original, excellent writing not bound by type. Ordinarily we do not publish novel excerpts or works translated into English, and we strongly discourage authors from submitting these." **Buys 12-20 mss/year.** Send complete ms. Length: Open. **Pays $40/published page.**

Poetry "We seek original, excellent poetry." **Buys 60-75 poems/year.** Submit maximum 5 poems. **Pays $3/line.**

Tips "Unsolicited manuscripts will not be considered from May 1-August 15 (annually); all such submissions received during that period will be returned unread."

$ THE GETTYSBURG REVIEW

Gettysburg College, Gettysburg PA 17325. (717)337-6770. Fax: (717)337-6775. Web site: www.gettysburgreview.com. **Contact:** Peter Stitt, editor. Quarterly magazine. "Our concern is quality. Manuscripts submitted here should be extremely well written." Reading period September-May. Estab. 1988. Circ. 3,000. Pays on publication. Publishes ms an average of 6 months after acceptance. Byline given. Buys first North American serial rights. Editorial lead time 1 year. Submit seasonal material 9 months in advance. Accepts queries by mail, fax. Accepts simultaneous submissions. Responds in 1 month to queries; 3-6 months to mss. Sample copy for $7. Writer's guidelines online.

Nonfiction Essays. **Buys 20 mss/year.** Send complete ms. Length: 3,000-7,000 words. **Pays $30/page.**

Fiction Mark Drew, assisant editor. High quality, literary. Experimental, historical, humorous, mainstream, novel excerpts, serialized novels, contemporary. "We require that fiction be intelligent and esthetically written." **Buys 20 mss/year.** Send complete ms. Length: 2,000-7,000 words. **Pays $30/page.**

Poetry Buys 50 poems/year. Submit maximum 5 poems. **Pays $2.50/line.**

$ $ GLIMMER TRAIN STORIES

Glimmer Train Press, Inc., 1211 NW Glisan St., Suite 207, Portland OR 97209. (503)221-0836. Fax: (503)221-0837. E-mail: eds@glimmertrain.com. Web site: www.glimmertrain.org. **Contact:** Linda Swanson-Davies, co-editor. **90% freelance written.** Quarterly magazine of literary short fiction. "We are interested in well-written, emotionally-moving short stories, particularly by new and lightly published writers." Estab. 1991. Circ. 16,000. **Pays on acceptance.** Publishes ms an average of 18 months after acceptance. Byline given. Buys first rights. Responds in 3 months to mss. Sample copy for $11 on Web site. Writer's guidelines online.

Fiction "Open to stories of all themes, all subjects." **Buys 40 mss/year.** Length: up to 12,000. **Pays $700.**

Tips Use *Glimmer Train*'s online submission system on their Web site. See *Glimmer Train*'s contest listings in Contest and Awards section.

$ $ GRAIN LITERARY MAGAZINE

Saskatchewan Writers Guild, P.O. Box 67, Saskatoon SK S7K 3K1 Canada. (306)244-2828. Fax: (306)244-0255. E-mail: grainmag@sasktel.net. Web site: www.grainmagazine.ca. Buisiness Administrator: Bobbi Clackson-Walker. **Contact:** Kent Bruyneel, editor. **100% freelance written.** Quarterly magazine covering poetry, fiction, creative nonfiction, drama. "*Grain* publishes writing of the highest quality, both traditional and innovative in nature. The *Grain* editors' aim: To publish work that challenges readers; to encourage promising new writers; and to produce a well-designed, visually interesting magazine." Estab. 1973. Circ. 1,600. Pays on publication. Byline given. Buys first, canadian serial rights. Editorial lead time 6 months. Accepts queries by mail. Responds in 1 month to queries; 4 months to mss. Sample copy for $13 or online. Writer's guidelines for #10 SASE or online.

Nonfiction Interested in creative nonfiction.

Photos Submit 12-20 slides and b&w prints, short statement (200 words), and brief résumé. Reviews transparencies, prints. Pays $100 for front cover art, $30/photo.

Fiction David Carpenter, fiction editor. Literary fiction of all types. Experimental, mainstream, contemporary, prose poem. "No romance, confession, science fiction, vignettes, mystery." **Buys 40 mss/year.** Length: "No more than 30 pages." **Pays $40-175.**

Poetry "High quality, imaginative, well-crafted poetry. Submit maximum 8 poems and SASE with postage or IRC's. Avant-garde, free verse, haiku, traditional. No sentimental, end-line rhyme, mundane." **Buys 78 poems/year. Pays $40-175.**

Tips "Sweat the small stuff. Pay attention to detail, credibility. Make sure you have researched your piece and that the literal and metaphorical support one another."

N $ $ GUD MAGAZINE

Greatest Uncommon Denominator Magazine, Greatest Uncommon Denominator Publishing, P.O. Box 1537, Laconia NH 03247. E-mail: editor@gudmagazine.com. Web site: www.gudmagazine.com. Editors: Mike Coombes, Sal Coraccio, Kaolin Fire, Sue Miller. **Contact:** Editor. **99% freelance written.** Semiannual magazine covering literary content and art. "*GUD Magazine* transcends and encompasses the audiences of both genre and literary fiction by featuring fiction, art, poetry, essays and reports, and short drama." Estab. 2006. **Pays on acceptance.** Publishes ms an average of 6 months after acceptance. Byline given. Buys print and world wide electronic rights from the date of first publication until agreement is terminated in writing, by snail mail, by either party. Editorial lead time 6 months. Submit seasonal material 6 months in advance. Accepts queries by e-mail. Accepts previously published material. Accepts simultaneous submissions. Responds in 6 months to mss. Writer's guidelines online.

Nonfiction Book excerpts, essays, historical/nostalgic, humor, interview/profile, personal experience, photo feature, travel, interesting event. **Buys 2-4 mss/year.** Send complete ms. Length: 1-15,000 words. **Pays $450.**

Photos Send photos with submission. Reviews GIF/JPEG files. Buys all rights. Offers $12 for first rights; $5 for reprints. Model releases required.

Fiction Adventure, condensed novels, confessions, erotica, ethnic, experimental, fantasy, horror, humorous, novel excerpts, science fiction, serialized novels, suspense. **Buys 40 mss/year.** Send complete ms. Length: 1-15,000 words. **Pays $450.**

Poetry Avant-garde, free verse, haiku, light verse, traditional. Does not want "anything that rhymes 'love' with 'above.'" **Buys 12 poems/year.**

Fillers Comics. **Buys 10/year. Pays $5-12.**

Tips "We publish work in any genre, plus artwork, factual articles, and interviews. We'll publish something as short as 20 words or as long as 15,000, as long as it grabs us. Be warned: We read a lot. We've seen it all before. We are not easy to impress. Is your work original? Does it have something to say? Read it again. If you genuinely believe it to be so, send it. We do accept simultaneous sumbissions, as well as multiple submissions."

$ HAYDEN'S FERRY REVIEW

Arizona State University, Box 871502, Arizona State University, Tempe AZ 85287-1502. (480)965-1243. Fax: (480)965-2191. E-mail: hfr@asu.edu. Web site: www.asu.edu/clas/pipercwcenter/publications/haydensferryreview. **Contact:** Fiction, Poetry, or Art Editor. **85% freelance written.** Semiannual magazine. "*Hayden's Ferry Review* publishes the best quality fiction, poetry, and creative nonfiction from new, emerging, and established writers." Estab. 1986. Circ. 1,300. Pays on publication. Publishes ms an average of 6 months after acceptance. Byline given. Buys first North American serial rights. Editorial lead time 3 months. Accepts queries by mail. Accepts simultaneous submissions. Responds in 2 weeks to queries; 3 months to mss. Sample copy for $7.50. Writer's guidelines online.

- No electronic submissions.

Nonfiction Essays, interview/profile, personal experience. **Buys 2 mss/year.** Send complete ms. Length: Open. **Pays $25-100.**

Photos Send photos with submission. Reviews slides. Buys one-time rights. Offers $25/photo.

Fiction Editors change every 1-2 years. Ethnic, experimental, humorous, slice-of-life vignettes, contemporary, prose poem. **Buys 10 mss/year.** Send complete ms. Length: Open. **Pays $25-100.**

Poetry Avant-garde, free verse, haiku, light verse, traditional. **Buys 60 poems/year.** Submit maximum 6 poems. Length: Open. **Pays $25-100.**

$ THE HOLLINS CRITIC

P.O. Box 9538, Hollins University, Roanoke VA 24020-1538. E-mail: acockrell@hollins.edu. Web site: www.hollins.edu/academics/critic. Editor: R.H.W. Dillard. Managing Editor: Amanda Cockrell. **Contact:** Cathryn Hankla, poetry editor. **100% freelance written.** Magazine published 5 times/year. Estab. 1964. Circ. 400. Pays on publication. Publishes ms an average of 1 year after acceptance. Byline given. Buys first North American serial rights. Accepts queries by mail. Accepts simultaneous submissions. Responds in 2 months to mss. Sample copy for $2. Writer's guidelines for #10 SASE.

- No e-mail submissions. Send complete ms.

Poetry "We read poetry only from September 1-December 15." Avant-garde, free verse, traditional. **Buys 16-20 poems/year.** Submit maximum 5 poems. **Pays $25.**

Tips "We accept unsolicited poetry submissions; all other content is by prearrangement."

$ THE HUDSON REVIEW

A magazine of literature and the arts, The Hudson Review, Inc., 684 Park Ave., New York NY 10021. (212)650-0020. Fax: (212)774-1911. E-mail: info@hudsonreview.com. Web site: www.hudsonreview.com. Managing Editor: Ronald Koury. **Contact:** Paula Deitz, editor. **100% freelance written.** Quarterly magazine publishing fiction, poetry, essays, book reviews; criticism of literature, art, theatre, dance, film and music; and articles on contemporary cultural developments. Estab. 1948. Circ. 5,000. Pays on publication. Publishes ms an average of 6 months after acceptance. Byline given. Only assigned reviews are copyrighted. Editorial lead time 3 months. Accepts queries by mail. Responds in 2 months to queries; 3 months to mss. Sample copy for $9. Writer's guidelines for #10 SASE.

Nonfiction Paula Deitz. Essays, general interest, historical/nostalgic, opinion, personal experience, travel. **Buys 4-6 mss/year.** Send complete ms between January 1 and March 31 only. Length: 3,500 words maximum. **Pays 2½¢/word.**

Fiction Ronald Koury. Read between September 1 and November 30 only. **Buys 4 mss/year. Pays 2½¢/word.**

Poetry Read poems only between April 1 and June 30. Anne McPeak, associate editor. **Buys 12-20 poems/year.** Submit maximum 7 poems. **Pays 50¢/line.**

Tips "We do not specialize in publishing any particular 'type' of writing; our sole criterion for accepting unsolicited work is literary quality. The best way for you to get an idea of the range of work we publish is to read a current issue. We do not consider simultaneous submissions. Unsolicted manuscripts submitted outside of specified reading times will be returned unread. Do not send submissions via e-mail."

N $ HUNGER MOUNTAIN

The Vermont College Journal of Arts & Letters, Vermont College/Union Institute & University, 36 College St., Montpelier VT 05602. Fax: (802)828-8649. E-mail: hungermtn@tui.edu. Web site: www.hungermtn.org. **Contact:** Caroline Mercurio, managing editor. **30% freelance written.** Semiannual perfect-bound journal covering high quality fiction, poetry, creative nonfiction, interviews, photography, and artwork reproductions. Accepts high quality work from unknown, emerging, or successful writers and artists. No genre fiction, drama, children's writing, or academic articles, please. Estab. 2002. Pays on publication. Publishes ms an average of 1 year after acceptance. Byline given. Buys first North American serial rights. Submit seasonal material 6 months in advance. Accepts queries by mail. Responds in 1 month to queries; 3 months to mss. Sample copy for $10. Writer's guidelines for free, online, or by e-mail.

Nonfiction Creative nonfiction only. All book reviews and interviews will be solicited. Book excerpts, essays, opinion, personal experience, photo feature, religious, travel. Special issues: "We will publish special issues, hopefully yearly, but we do not know yet the themes of these issues." No informative or instructive articles, please. Query with published clips. **Pays $5/page (minimum $30).** Sometimes pays expenses of writers on assignment.
Photos Send photos with submission. Reviews contact sheets, transparencies, prints, GIF/JPEG files. Slides preferred. Buys one-time rights. Negotiates payment individually. Query with published clips. **Pays $25-100.**
Poetry Avant-garde, free verse, haiku, traditional, nature, narrative, experimental, etc. No light verse, humor/quirky/catchy verse, greeting card verse. **Buys 10 poems/year.**
Tips "We want high quality work! Submit in duplicate. Manuscripts must be typed, prose double-spaced. Poets submit at least 3 poems. No multiple genre submissions. We need more b&w photography and short shorts. Fresh viewpoints and human interest are very important, as is originality. We are committed to publishing an outstanding journal of arts & letters. Do not send entire novels, manuscripts, or short story collections. Do not send previously published work."

$ THE ICONOCLAST

1675 Amazon Rd., Mohegan Lake NY 10547-1804. **Contact:** Phil Wagner, editor. **90% freelance written.** Bimonthly literary magazine. "Aimed for a literate general audience with interests in fine (but accessible) fiction and poetry." Estab. 1992. Circ. 700. Pays on publication. Publishes ms an average of 9-12 months after acceptance. Byline given. Buys first North American serial rights. Editorial lead time 1-2 months. Accepts queries by mail. Responds in 2 weeks to queries; 1 month to mss. Sample copy for $5. Writer's guidelines for #10 SASE.
Nonfiction Essays, humor, reviews, literary/cultural matters. Does not want "anything that would be found in the magazines on the racks of supermarkets or convenience stores." **Buys 6-10 mss/year.** Query. Length: 250-2,500 words. **Pays 1¢/word.**
Photos Line drawings preferred. State availability with submission. Reviews 4×6, b&w prints. Buys one-time rights. Negotiates payment individually.
Columns/Departments Book reviews (fiction/poetry), 250-500 words. **Buys 6 mss/year.** Query. **Pays 1¢/word.**
Fiction Buys more fiction and poetry than anything else. Adventure, ethnic, experimental, fantasy, humorous, mainstream, novel excerpts, science fiction, literary. No character studies, slice-of-life, pieces strong on attitude/weak on plot. **Buys 25 mss/year.** Send complete ms. Length: 250-3,000 words. **Pays 1¢/word.**
Poetry Avant-garde, free verse, haiku, light verse, traditional. No religious, greeting card, beginner rhyming. **Buys 75 poems/year.** Submit maximum 4 poems. Length: 2-50 lines. **Pays $2-5.**
Tips "Professional conduct and sincerity help. Know it's the best you can do on a work before sending it out. Skill is the luck of the prepared. Everything counts. We love what we do, and are serious about it—and expect you to share that attitude. Remember: You're writing for paying subscribers. Ask Yourself: Would I pay money to read what I'm sending? We don't reply to submissions without a SASE, nor do we e-mail replies."

$ $ IMAGE

3307 Third Ave. W., Seattle WA 98119. (206)281-2988. E-mail: image@imagejournal.org. Web site: www.imagejournal.org. Editor: Gregory Wolfe. Managing Editor: Mary Kenagy. **50% freelance written.** Quarterly magazine covering the intersection between art and faith. *Image* is a unique forum for the best writing and artwork that is informed by—or grapples with—religious faith. "We have never been interested in art that merely regurgitates dogma or falls back on easy answers or didacticism. Instead, our focus has been on writing and visual artwork that embody a spiritual struggle, that seek to strike a balance between tradition and a profound openness to the world. Each issue explores this relationship through outstanding fiction, poetry, painting, sculpture, architecture, film, music, interviews, and dance. *Image* also features 4-color reproductions of visual art." Estab. 1989. Circ. 4,500. Pays on publication. Publishes ms an average of 8 months after acceptance. Byline given. Buys first North American serial rights. Accepts queries by mail, e-mail, phone. Responds in 1 month to queries; 2 months to mss. Sample copy for $16 or online. Writer's guidelines for #10 SASE or online.

O→ "We seek well-crafted essays, stories and poetry that use language in new and surprising ways and engage with timeless themes, like grace, redemption, and incarnation."

Nonfiction Essays. No sentimental, preachy, moralistic, or obvious essays. **Buys 10 mss/year.** Send complete ms. Length: 4,000-6,000 words. **Pays $10/page; $200 maximum for all prose articles.**
Fiction No sentimental, preachy, moralistic, obvious stories, or genre stories (unless they manage to transcend their genre). **Buys 8 mss/year.** Send complete ms. Length: 4,000-6,000 words. **Pays $10/page; $200 maximum.**
Poetry Buys 24 poems/year. Submit maximum 5 poems. **Pays $2/line; $150 maximum.**
Tips "Read the publication."

$ INDIANA REVIEW

Indiana University, Ballantine Hall 465, 1020 E. Kirkwood, Bloomington IN 47405-7103. (812)855-3439. E-mail: inreview@indiana.edu. Web site: www.indiana.edu/~inreview. **Contact:** Tracy Truels, editor. **100% freelance written.** Biannual magazine. "*Indiana Review*, a nonprofit organization run by IU graduate students, is a journal of previously unpublished poetry and fiction. Literary interviews and essays are also considered. We publish innovative fiction and poetry. We're interested in energy, originality, and careful attention to craft. While we publish many well-known writers, we also welcome new and emerging poets and fiction writers." Estab. 1976. Circ. 5,000. Pays on publication. Publishes ms an average of 3-6 months after acceptance. Byline given. Buys first North American serial rights. Accepts queries by mail, e-mail. Accepts simultaneous submissions. Responds in 2 or more weeks to queries; 4 or more months to mss. Sample copy for $9. Writer's guidelines online.

O‒ Break in with 500-1,000 word book reviews of fiction, poetry, nonfiction, and literary criticism published within the last 2 years.

Nonfiction Essays, interview/profile, creative nonfiction, reviews. No "coming of age/slice of life pieces." **Buys 5-7 mss/year.** Send complete ms. Length: 9,000 words maximum. **Pays $5/page ($10 minimum), plus 2 contributor's copies.**

Fiction Megan Savage, fiction editor. "We look for daring stories which integrate theme, language, character, and form. We like polished writing, humor, and fiction which has consequence beyond the world of its narrator." Ethnic, experimental, mainstream, novel excerpts, literary, short fictions, translations. No genre fiction. **Buys 14-18 mss/year.** Send complete ms. Length: 250-10,000 words. **Pays $5/page ($10 minimum), plus 2 contributor's copies.**

Poetry "We look for poems that are skillfull and bold, exhibiting an inventiveness of language with attention to voice and sonics." Experimental, free verse, prose poem, traditional form, lyrical, narrative. Cate Whetzel, poetry editor. **Buys 80 poems/year.** Submit maximum 6 poems. Length: 5 lines minimum. **Pays $5/page ($10 minimum), plus 2 contributor's copies.**

Tips "We're always looking for nonfiction essays that go beyond merely autobiographical revelation and utilize sophisticated organization and slightly radical narrative strategies. We want essays that are both lyrical and analytical where confession does not mean nostalgia. Read us before you submit. Often reading is slower in summer and holiday months. Only submit work to journals you would proudly subscribe to, then subscribe to a few. Take care to read the latest 2 issues and specifically mention work you identify with and why. Submit work that 'stacks up' with the work we've published." Offers annual poetry, fiction, short-short/prose-poem prizes. See Web site for details.

$ $ INKWELL

Manhattanville College, 2900 Purchase St., Purchase NY 10577. (914)323-7239. Fax: (914)323-3122. E-mail: inkwell@mville.edu. Web site: www.inkwelljournal.org. Editor: Alex Lindquist. **Contact:** Fiction editor; Poetry editor. **100% freelance written.** Semiannual magazine covering poetry, fiction, essays, artwork, and photography. Estab. 1995. Pays on publication. Publishes ms an average of 4 months after acceptance. Byline given. Buys first North American serial rights. Editorial lead time 4 months. Accepts simultaneous submissions. Responds in 1 month to queries; 4-6 months to mss. Sample copy for $6. Writer's guidelines free.

Nonfiction Book excerpts, essays, literary essays, memoirs. Does not want children's literature, erotica, pulp adventure, or science fiction. **Buys 3-4 mss/year.** Query with or without published clips or send complete ms. Length: 5,000 words maximum. **Pays $100-350.**

Photos Send photos/artwork with submission. Reviews 5×7 prints, GIF/JPEG files on diskette/cd. Buys one-time rights. Negotiates payment individually.

Fiction Mainstream, novel excerpts, literary. Does not want children's literature, erotica, pulp adventure, or science fiction. **Buys 20 mss/year.** Send complete ms. Length: 5,000 words maximum. **Pays $75-150.**

Poetry Avant-garde, free verse, traditional. Does not want doggerel, funny poetry, etc. **Buys 40 poems/year.** Submit maximum 5 poems. **Pays $5-10/page.**

Tips "We cannot accept electronic submissions or previously published work."

$ THE IOWA REVIEW

308 EPB, The University of Iowa, Iowa City IA 52242. Web site: iowareview.org. **Contact:** David Hamilton, editor. Triannual magazine "Stories, essays, and poems for a general readership interested in contemporary literature." Estab. 1970. Circ. 2,500. Pays on publication. Publishes ms an average of 8-12 months after acceptance. Buys first North American serial, nonexclusive anthology, classroom, and online serial rights. Responds in 3 months to mss. Sample copy for $8 and online. Writer's guidelines online.

- This magazine uses the help of colleagues and graduate assistants. Its reading period for unsolicited work is September 1-December 1. "From January through April, we read entries to our annual Iowa Awards competition. Check our Web site for further information."

Fiction "We are open to a range of styles and voices and always hope to be surprised by work we then feel we need." **Pays $25 for the first page and $15 for each additional page, plus 2 contributor's copies and a year-long subscription; additional copies 30% off cover price.**

Tips "We publish essays, reviews, novel excerpts, stories, and poems, and would like for our essays not always to be works of academic criticism. We have no set guidelines as to content or length, but strongly recommend that writers read a sample issue before submitting." **Buys 65-80 unsolicited ms/year.** Submit complete ms with SASE. **Pays $25 for the first page and $15 for each subsequent page of poetry or prose.**

$ IRREANTUM

A Review of Mormon Literature and Film, The Association for Mormon Letters, P.O. Box 1315, Salt Lake City UT 84110-1315. (801)355-3756. E-mail: editor@irreantum.org. Web site: www.irreantum.org. **Contact:** Scott Hatch or Valerie Holladay. Literary journal published 2 times/year. "While focused on Mormonism, *Irreantum* is a cultural, humanities-oriented magazine, not a religious magazine. Our guiding principle is that Mormonism is grounded in a sufficiently unusual, cohesive, and extended historical and cultural experience that it has become like a nation, an ethnic culture. We can speak of Mormon literature at least as surely as we can of a Jewish or Southern literature. *Irreantum* publishes stories, one-act dramas, stand-alone novel and drama excerpts, and poetry by, for, or about Mormons (as well as author interviews, essays, and reviews). The journal's audience includes readers of any or no religious faith who are interested in literary exploration of the Mormon culture, mindset, and worldview through Mormon themes and characters either directly or by implication. *Irreantum* is currently the only magazine devoted to Mormon literature." Estab. 1999. Circ. 500. Pays on publication. Publishes ms an average of 3-12 months after acceptance. Buys one-time, electronic rights. Accepts queries by e-mail. Accepts previously published material. Accepts simultaneous submissions. Responds in 2 weeks to queries; 2 months to mss. Sample copy for $6. Writer's guidelines by e-mail.

- Also publishes short shorts, literary essays, literary criticism, and poetry.

Fiction Adventure, ethnic, experimental, fantasy, historical, horror, humorous, mainstream, mystery, religious, romance, science fiction, suspense. **Buys 12 mss/year.** Length: 1,000-5,000 words. **Pays $0-100.**

Tips "*Irreantum* is not interested in didactic or polemnical fiction that primarily attempts to prove or disprove Mormon doctrine, history, or corporate policy. We encourage beginning writers to focus on human elements first, with Mormon elements introduced only as natural and organic to the story. Readers can tell if you are honestly trying to explore human experience or if you are writing with a propagandistic agenda either for or against Mormonism. For conservative, orthodox Mormon writers, beware of sentimentalism, simplistic resolutions, and foregone conclusions."

N $ ISLAND

P.O. Box 210, Sandy Bay Tasmania 7006 Australia. (61)(3)6226-2325. Fax: (61)(3)6226-2172. E-mail: island@tassie.net.au. Web site: www.islandmag.com. **Contact:** Gina Mercer, editor. Quarterly magazine. "*Island* seeks quality fiction, poetry, essays, and articles. A literary magazine with an environmental heart." Circ. 1,500. Buys one-time rights. Accepts queries by mail, e-mail. Sample copy for $8.95 (Australian). Writer's guidelines online.

Nonfiction Articles and reviews. **Pays $100 (Australian)/1,000 words.**

Fiction Length: 4,000 words. **Pays $100 (Australian).**

Poetry Pays $60.

$ THE JOURNAL

The Ohio State University, 164 W. 17th Ave., Columbus OH 43210. (614)292-4076. Fax: (614)292-7816. E-mail: thejournal@osu.edu. Web site: english.osu.edu/research/journals/thejournal/. **Contact:** Fiction Editor, Poetry Editor, Nonfiction Editor, Poetry Review Editor. **100% freelance written.** Semiannual magazine. "We're open to all forms; we tend to favor work that gives evidence of a mature and sophisticated sense of the language." Estab. 1972. Circ. 1,500. Pays on publication. Publishes ms an average of 1 year after acceptance. Byline given. Buys first North American serial rights. Accepts queries by mail. Accepts simultaneous submissions. Responds in 2 weeks to queries; 2 months to mss. Sample copy for $7 or online. Writer's guidelines online.

Nonfiction Essays, interview/profile. **Buys 2 mss/year.** Query. Length: 2,000-4,000 words. **Pays $20 maximum.**

Columns/Departments Reviews of contemporary poetry, 1,500 words maximum. **Buys 2 mss/year.** Query. **Pays $20.**

Fiction Novel excerpts, literary short stories. No romance, science fiction or religious/devotional. Length: Open. **Pays $20.**

Poetry Avant-garde, free verse, traditional. **Buys 100 poems/year.** Submit maximum 5 poems. **Pays $20.**

N $ KANSAS CITY VOICES

Whispering Prairie Press, P.O. Box 8342, Kansas City KS 66208-0342. E-mail: kcvoices@yahoo.com. Web site: kansascityvoices.tripod.com. Editor: Larry M. Schilb. **Contact:** Submissions Editor. **100% freelance written.** Annual magazine. "*Kansas City Voices* magazine publishes an eclectic mix of fiction, poetry, personal essays, articles and images of artwork. Though we like works that relate to Kansas City and the surrounding area, quality is our primary concern." Estab. 2003. Circ. 1,000. Pays on publication. Publishes ms an average of 6 months after acceptance. Byline given. Buys first North American serial rights. Accepts queries by mail. Accepts simultaneous submissions. Sample copy for $11.45. Writer's guidelines online.

Nonfiction Book excerpts, essays, general interest, historical/nostalgic, how-to, humor, inspirational, interview/profile, personal experience, photo feature, religious, travel. **Buys 10-15 mss/year.** Send complete ms. Length: 800-2,500 words. **Pays $20-100.**

Photos Send photos with submission. Offers no additional payment for photos accepted with ms.

Fiction Adventure, confessions, ethnic, experimental, fantasy, historical, horror, humorous, mainstream, mystery, novel excerpts, religious, romance, science fiction, slice-of-life vignettes, suspense, western. Send complete ms. Length: 2,500 words. **Pays $20-100.**

Poetry Avant-garde, free verse, light verse, traditional. Does not want haiku. Submit maximum 3 poems. Length: 35 lines maximum. **Pays $20-100.**

Tips "Familiarize yourself with the magazine, check the Web site and read the guidelines. We have a blind submissions policy, because we want quality work, whether or not it is by writers with long résumés. For fiction, we look for strong stories with active voices. Show, don't tell. Sending us your best work in a proofed, professionally formatted manuscript makes a great first impression."

$ THE KENYON REVIEW

Walton House, 104 College Dr., Gambier OH 43022. (740)427-5208. Fax: (740)427-5417. E-mail: kenyonreview@kenyon.edu. Web site: www.kenyonreview.org. **Contact:** David H. Lynn, editor. **100% freelance written.** Quarterly magazine covering contemporary literature and criticism. An international journal of literature, culture, and the arts dedicated to an inclusive representation of the best in new writing (fiction, poetry, essays, interviews, criticism) from established and emerging writers. Estab. 1939. Circ. 6,000. Pays on publication. Publishes ms an average of 1 year after acceptance. Byline given. Buys first rights. Editorial lead time 1 year. Submit seasonal material 1 year in advance. Responds in 3-4 months to queries; 4 months to mss. Sample copy $12, includes postage and handling. Please call or e-mail to order. Writer's guidelines online. Length: 3-15 typeset pages preferred. **Pays $30-40/page.**

Tips "We no longer accept mailed submissions. Work will only be read if it is submitted through our online program on our Web site. Reading period is September 1-January 31."

$ THE KIT-CAT REVIEW

244 Halstead Ave., Harrison NY 10528. (914)835-4833. E-mail: kitcatreview@gmail.com. **Contact:** Claudia Fletcher, editor. **100% freelance written.** Quarterly magazine. *The Kit-Cat Review* is named after the 18th Century Kit-Cat Club, whose members included Addison, Steele, Congreve, Vanbrugh, and Garth. Its purpose is to promote/discover excellence and originality. Estab. 1998. Circ. 500. Pays on publication. Publishes ms an average of 6-12 months after acceptance. Byline given. Buys first rights. Accepts queries by mail, phone. Accepts simultaneous submissions. Responds in 1 week to queries; 2 months to mss. Sample copy for $7 (payable to Claudia Fletcher). Writer's guidelines for SASE.

Nonfiction "Shorter pieces stand a better chance of publication." Book excerpts, essays, general interest, historical/nostalgic, humor, interview/profile, personal experience, travel. **Buys 6 mss/year.** Send complete ms with brief bio and SASE. Length: 5,000 words maximum. **Pays $25-100.**

Fiction Ethnic, experimental, novel excerpts, slice-of-life vignettes. No stories with "O. Henry-type formula endings. Shorter pieces stand a better chance of publication." No science fiction, fantasy, romance, horror, or new age. **Buys 20 mss/year.** Send complete ms. Length: 5,000 words maximum. **Pays $25-100 and 2 contributor's copies; additional copies $5.**

Poetry Free verse, traditional. No excessively obscure poetry. **Buys 100 poems/year. Pays $20-100.**

Tips "Obtaining a sample copy is strongly suggested. Include a short bio, SASE, and word count for fiction and nonfiction submissions."

N $ $ MAISONNEUVE

Maisonneuve Magazine Association, 400 de Maisonneuve Blvd. W., Suite 655, Montreal QC H3A 1L4 Canada. (514)482-5089. Fax: (514)482-6734. E-mail: submissions@maisonneuve.org. Web site: www.maisonneuve.org. Editor: Derek Webster. Managing Editor: Phillip Todd. **Contact:** Editorial Assistant. **90% freelance written.** Quarterly magazine covering eclectic curiousity. "What does *Maisonneuve* publish? The sky's the limit—hell, what's in a sky? Poems about nothing? Love 'em. Got a cousin who writes long diatribes against houseflies? How about a really good vignette on the way people walk? Photocopies of your childhood collection of gum-wrappers. Audiofiles of people talking at the Jackson Pollock retrospective. Sonnets to your beloved—they better be good. This is a young magazine, and we're still discovering our limits. You are invited to join in." Estab. 2002. Circ. under 10,000. Pays on publication. Publishes ms an average of 4-6 months after acceptance.

Byline given. Offers 25% kill fee. Buys first North American serial, electronic rights. Editorial lead time 4 months. Submit seasonal material 8 months in advance. Accepts simultaneous submissions. Responds in 2 weeks to queries; 2 months to mss. Sample copy and writer's guidelines online.

Nonfiction Essays, general interest, historical/nostalgic, humor, interview/profile, personal experience, photo feature. **Buys 20 mss/year.** Query with published clips. Length: 50-5,000 words. **Pays 10¢/word.** Sometimes pays expenses of writers on assignment.

Photos Contact Jenn McIntyre, art director. State availability with submission. Reviews GIF/JPEG files. Buys one-time rights. Negotiates payment individually. Captions, identification of subjects, model releases required.

Columns/Departments Open House (witty & whimsical), 800-1,200 words; Profiles + Interviews (character insights), 2,000 words; Studio (spotlight on visual artists/trends), 500 words; Manifesto (passionate calls for change), 800 words. **Buys 40-50 mss/year.** Query with published clips. **Pays 10¢/word.**

Fiction Adventure, confessions, ethnic, experimental, humorous, science fiction, slice-of-life vignettes. **Buys 4 mss/year.** Send complete ms. Length: 1,000-4,000 words. **Pays 10¢/word.**

Poetry Avant-garde, free verse, haiku, light verse, traditional. **Buys 16-32 poems/year.** Submit maximum unlimited poems. **Payment varies.**

Fillers Anecdotes, facts, short humor. **Buys 15/year.** Length: 50-150 words. **Pays payment varies.**

Tips ''*Maisonneuve* has been described as a new *New Yorker* for a younger generation, or as *Harper's* meets *Vice*, or as *Vanity Fair* without the vanity—but *Maisonneuve* is its own creature. *Maisonneuve*'s purpose is to keep its readers informed, alert, and entertained, and to dissolve artistic borders between regions, countries, languages and genres. It does this by providing a diverse range of commentary across the arts, sciences, daily and social life. The magazine has a balanced perspective, and 'brings the news' in a wide variety of ways. At its core, *Maisonneuve* asks questions about our lives and provides answers free of cant and cool.''

$ THE MALAHAT REVIEW

The University of Victoria, P.O. Box 1700, STN CSC, Victoria BC V8W 2Y2 Canada. (250)721-8524. E-mail: malahat@uvic.ca (for queries only). Web site: www.malahatreview.ca. **Contact:** John Barton, editor. **100% freelance written.** Eager to work with new/unpublished writers. Quarterly magazine covering poetry, fiction, and reviews. ''We try to achieve a balance of views and styles in each issue. We strive for a mix of the best writing by both established and new writers.'' Estab. 1967. Circ. 1,000. **Pays on acceptance.** Publishes ms an average of 6 months after acceptance. Byline given. Offers 100% kill fee. Buys second serial (reprint), first world rights. Accepts queries by mail. Responds in 2 weeks to queries; 3 months to mss. Sample copy for $12 (US). Writer's guidelines online.

Nonfiction ''Query first about review articles, critical essays, interviews, and visual art, which we generally solicit.'' Include SASE with Canadian postage or IRCs. **Pays $35/magazine page.**

Fiction ''General ficton and poetry.'' **Buys 20 mss/year.** Send complete ms. Length: 20 pages maximum. **Pays $30/magazine page.**

Poetry Avant-garde, free verse, traditional. **Buys 100 poems/year.** Length: 5-10 pages. **Pays $35/magazine page.**

Tips ''Please do not send more than 1 manuscript (the one you consider your best) at a time. See *The Malahat Review's* long poem and novella contests in Contest & Awards section.''

$ $ MANOA

A Pacific Journal of International Writing, English Dept., University of Hawaii, Honolulu HI 96822. (808)956-3070. Fax: (808)956-3083. E-mail: fstewart@hawaii.edu. Web site: manoajournal.hawaii.edu. **Contact:** Frank Stewart, editor. Semiannual magazine. ''High quality literary fiction, poetry, essays, personal narrative. Most of each issue is devoted to new work from Pacific and Asian nations. Our audience is primarily in the US, although expanding in Pacific countries. US writing need not be confined to Pacific settings or subjects.'' Estab. 1989. Circ. 2,500. Pays on publication. Byline given. Buys first North American serial, non-exclusive, one-time print rights. Editorial lead time 9 months. Accepts simultaneous submissions. Responds in 3 weeks to queries 1 month to poetry mss; 6 months to fiction to mss. Sample copy for $10 (US). Writer's guidelines online.

Nonfiction Book excerpts, essays, interview/profile, creative nonfiction or personal narrative related to literature or nature. No Pacific exotica. **Buys 1-2 mss/year.** Send complete ms. Length: 1,000-5,000 words. **Pays $25/ printed page.**

Fiction ''We're potentially open to anything of literary quality, though usually not genre fiction as such.'' Mainstream, contemporary, excerpted novel. No Pacific exotica. **Buys 1-2 in the US (excluding translation) mss/year.** Send complete ms. Length: 1,000-7,500 words. **Pays $100-500 normally ($25/printed page).**

Poetry No light verse. **Buys 10-20 poems/year.** Submit maximum 5-6 poems. **Pays $25/poem.**

Tips ''Although we are a Pacific journal, we are a general interest US literary journal, not limited to Pacific settings or subjects.''

$ THE MASSACHUSETTS REVIEW

South College, University of Massachusetts, Amherst MA 01003-9934. (413)545-2689. Fax: (413)577-0740. E-mail: massrev@external.umass.edu. Web site: www.massreview.org. **Contact:** Corwin Ericson, managing editor; Thomas Dumm, Ellen Watson, David Lenson, editors. Quarterly magazine. Estab. 1959. Circ. 1,200. Pays on publication. Publishes ms an average of 18 months after acceptance. Buys first North American serial rights. Accepts queries by mail. Accepts simultaneous submissions. Responds in 3 months to mss. Sample copy for $8. Writer's guidelines online.

- Does not respond to mss without SASE.

Nonfiction Articles on all subjects. No reviews of single books. Send complete ms or query with SASE. Length: 6,500 words maximum. **Pays $50.**

Fiction Short stories. Wants more prose less than 30 pages. **Buys 10 mss/year.** Send complete ms. Length: 25-30 pages maximum. **Pays $50.**

Poetry Submit maximum 6 poems. **Pays 35¢/line to $10 maximum.**

Tips "No manuscripts are considered June-October. No fax or e-mail submissions. No simultaneous submissions."

$ MICHIGAN QUARTERLY REVIEW

3574 Rackham Bldg., 915 E. Washington, University of Michigan, Ann Arbor MI 48109-1070. (734)764-9265. E-mail: mqr@umich.edu. Web site: www.umich.edu/~mqr. **Contact:** Laurence Goldstein, editor. **75% freelance written.** Quarterly magazine. "An interdisciplinary journal which publishes mainly essays and reviews, with some high-quality fiction and poetry, for an intellectual, widely read audience." Estab. 1962. Circ. 1,500. Pays on publication. Publishes ms an average of 1 year after acceptance. Byline given. Buys first serial rights. Accepts queries by mail. Responds in 2 months to queries; 2 months to mss. Sample copy for $4. Writer's guidelines online.

- The Laurence Goldstein Award is a $1,000 annual award to the best poem published in the *Michigan Quarterly Review* during the previous year. The Lawrence Foundation Award is a $1,000 annual award to the best short story published in the *Michigan Quarterly Review* during the previous year.

Nonfiction "*MQR* is open to general articles directed at an intellectual audience. Essays ought to have a personal voice and engage a significant subject. Scholarship must be present as a foundation, but we are not interested in specialized essays directed only at professionals in the field. We prefer ruminative essays, written in a fresh style and which reach interesting conclusions. We also like memoirs and interviews with significant historical or cultural resonance." **Buys 35 mss/year.** Query. Length: 2,000-5,000 words. **Pays $10/published page.**

Fiction Fiction Editor. No restrictions on subject matter or language. "We are very selective. We like stories which are unusual in tone and structure, and innovative in language. No genre fiction written for a market. Would like to see more fiction about social, political, cultural matters, not just centered on a love relationship or dysfunctional family." **Buys 10 mss/year.** Send complete ms. Length: 1,500-7,000 words. **Pays $10/published page.**

Poetry Buys 8 poems/issue **Pays $10/published page.**

Tips "Read the journal and assess the range of contents and the level of writing. We have no guidelines to offer or set expectations; every manuscript is judged on its unique qualities. On essays—query with a very thorough description of the argument and a copy of the first page. Watch for announcements of special issues which are usually expanded issues and draw upon a lot of freelance writing. Be aware that this is a university quarterly that publishes a limited amount of fiction and poetry that it is directed at an educated audience, one that has done a great deal of reading in all types of literature."

$ MID-AMERICAN REVIEW

Department of English, Box W, Bowling Green State University, Bowling Green OH 43403. (419)372-2725. Web site: www.bgsu.edu/midamericanreview. **Contact:** Michael Czyzniejewski, editor-in-chief. Willing to work with new/unpublished writers. Biannual magazine of "the highest quality fiction, poetry, and translations of contemporary poetry and fiction." Also publishes critical articles and book reviews of contemporary literature. "We try to put the best possible work in front of the biggest possible audience. We publish serious fiction and poetry, as well as critical studies in contemporary literature, translations and book reviews." Estab. 1981. Pays on publication when funding is available. Publishes ms an average of 6 months after acceptance. Byline given. Buys first North American serial, one-time rights. Accepts queries by mail, phone. Responds in 5 months to mss. Sample copy for $7 (current issue); $5 (back issue); $10 (rare back issues). Writer's guidelines online.

O→ "Grab our attention with something original—even experimental—but most of all, well-written."

Nonfiction Essays (articles focusing on contemporary authors and topics of current literary interest), short book reviews (500-1,000 words). **Pays $10/page up to $50, pending funding.**

Fiction Michael Czyzniejewski, fiction editor. Character-oriented, literary, experimental, short short. Experimental, Memoir, prose poem, traditional. "No genre fiction. Would like to see more short shorts." **Buys 12 mss/year.** Length: 6,000 words. **Pays $10/page up to $50, pending funding.**

Poetry Karen Craigo, poetry editor. Strong imagery and sense of visio. **Buys 60 poems/year. Pays $10/page up to $50, pending funding.**

Tips "We are seeking translations of contemporary authors from all languages into English; submissions must include the original and proof of permission to translate. We would also like to see more creative nonfiction."

N $ MILLER'S POND

H&H Press, 980 Locey Creek Rd., Middlebury Center PA 16935. (570)376-3361. Web site: www.millerspondpoetry.com. **Contact:** C.J. Houghtaling, publisher. **100% freelance written.** Annual magazine featuring poetry with poetry book/chapbook reviews and interviews of poets. E-mail submissions must be on the form from the Web site. Estab. 1998. Circ. 200. Pays on publication. Publishes ms an average of 1 year after acceptance. Byline given. Buys one-time rights. Editorial lead time 1 year. Accepts queries by mail. Accepts simultaneous submissions. Responds in 10 months to queries; 10 months to mss. Sample copy for $7, plus $3 postage. Writer's guidelines online.

Nonfiction Interview/profile (2,000 words), poetry chapbook reviews (500 words). **Buys 1-2 mss/year.** Query or send complete ms. **Pays $5.**

Poetry Free verse. No religious, horror, vulgar, rhymed, preachy, lofty, trite, overly sentimental. **Buys 30-35 poems/year.** Submit maximum 3-5 poems. Length: 40 lines maximum. **Pays $2.**

The online magazine carries original content not found in the print edition and includes writer's guidelines. No payment for material appearing online. Contact: Julie Damerell, online editor.

Tips "View our Web site to see what we like. Study the contemporary masters: Billy Collins, Maxine Kumin, Colette Inez, Vivian Shipley. Always enclose SASE."

$ $ $ THE MISSOURI REVIEW

357 McReynolds Hall, University of Missouri, Columbia MO 65211. (573)882-4474. Fax: (573)884-4671. E-mail: tmr@missourireview.com. Web site: www.missourireview.com. Associate Editor: Evelyn Somers. Poetry Editor: Jason Koo. Managing Editor: Richard Sowienski. **Contact:** Speer Morgan, editor. **90% freelance written.** Quarterly magazine. "We publish contemporary fiction, poetry, interviews, personal essays, cartoons, special features—such as History as Literature series and Found Text series—for the literary and the general reader interested in a wide range of subjects." Estab. 1978. Circ. 6,500. Offers signed contract. Byline given. Editorial lead time 6 months. Accepts queries by mail. Responds in 2 weeks to queries; 10 weeks to mss. Sample copy for $8.95 or online. Writer's guidelines online.

Nonfiction Evelyn Somers, associate editor. Book excerpts, essays. No literary criticism. **Buys 10 mss/year.** Send complete ms. **Pays $1,000.**

Fiction Ethnic, humorous, mainstream, novel excerpts, literary. No genre or flash fiction. **Buys 25 mss/year.** Send complete ms. Length: no preference. **Pays $30/printed page.**

Poetry Publishes 3-5 poetry features of 6-12 pages per issue. "Please familiarize yourself with the magazine before submitting poetry." Jason Koo, poetry editor. **Buys 50 poems/year. Pays $30/printed page.**

The online magazine carries original content not found in the print edition and includes writer's guidelines. Contact: Richard Sowienski, managing editor.

Tips "Send your best work."

$ MODERN HAIKU

An Independent Journal of Haiku and Haiku Studies, P.O. Box 68, Lincoln IL 62656. Web site: www.modernhaiku.org. **Contact:** Lee Gurga, editor. **85% freelance written.** Magazine published 3 times/year. "*Modern Haiku* publishes high quality material only. Haiku and related genres, articles on haiku, haiku book reviews, and translations compose its contents. It has an international circulation and is widely subscribed to by university, school, and public libraries. Estab. 1969. Circ. 625. Pays on acceptance for poetry; on publication for prose. Publishes ms an average of 3 months after acceptance. Byline given. Buys first North American serial rights. Editorial lead time 4 months. Accepts queries by mail. Responds in 1 week to queries; 2 weeks to mss. Sample copy for $8 in North America, $12 elsewhere. Writer's guidelines online.

Nonfiction Essays (anything related to haiku). **Buys 40 mss/year.** Send complete ms. **Pays $5/page.**

Columns/Departments Haiku & Senryu; Haibun; Articles (on haiku and related genres); book reviews (books of haiku or related genres), 4 pages maximum. **Buys 15 mss/year.** Send complete ms. **Pays $5/page.**

Poetry Haiku, senryu. Does not want "general poetry, sentimental, and pretty-pretty haiku or overtly pornographic." **Buys 500 poems/year.** Submit maximum 24 poems. **Pays $1.**

Tips "Study the history of haiku, read books about haiku, learn the aesthetics of haiku and methods of composition. Write about your sense perceptions of the suchness of entities; avoid ego-centered interpretations."

$ NEW ENGLAND REVIEW

Middlebury College, Middlebury VT 05753. (802)443-5075. E-mail: nereview@middlebury.edu. Web site: go.middlebury.edu/nereview. **Contact:** On envelope: Poetry, Fiction, or Nonfiction Editor; on letter: Stephen Donadio, editor. Quarterly magazine. Serious literary only. Reads September 1-May 31 (postmarked dates). Estab. 1978. Circ. 2,000. Pays on publication. Publishes ms an average of 6 months after acceptance. Byline given. Buys first North American serial, first, second serial (reprint) rights. Accepts simultaneous submissions. Responds in 2 weeks to queries; 3 months to mss. Sample copy for $8. Writer's guidelines online.

- No e-mail submissions.

Nonfiction Serious literary only. Rarely accepts previously published submissions (out of print or previously published abroad only.) **Buys 20-25 mss/year.** Send complete ms. Length: 7,500 words maximum, though exceptions may be made. **Pays $10/page ($20 minimum), and 2 copies.**

Fiction Send 1 story at a time, unless it is very short. Serious literary only, novel excerpts. **Buys 25 mss/year.** Send complete ms. Length: Prose length: 10,000 words maximum, double spaced. Novellas: 30,000 words maximum. **Pays $10/page ($20 minimum), and 2 copies.**

Poetry Buys 75-90 poems/year. Submit maximum 6 poems. **Pays $10/page ($20 minimum), and 2 copies.**

Tips "We consider short fiction, including shorts, short-shorts, novellas, and self-contained extracts from novels in both traditional and experimental forms. In nonfiction, we consider a variety of general and literary, but not narrowly scholarly essays; we also publish long and short poems; book reviews; screenplays; graphics; translations; critical reassessments; statements by artists working in various media; interviews; testimonies; and letters from abroad. We are committed to exploration of all forms of contemporary cultural expression in the US and abroad. With few exceptions, we print only work not published previously elsewhere."

$ NEW LETTERS

University of Missouri-Kansas City, University House, 5101 Rockhill Rd., Kansas City MO 64110-2499. (816)235-1168. Fax: (816)235-2611. E-mail: newletters@umkc.edu. Web site: www.newletters.org. Editor: Robert Stewart. **100% freelance written.** Quarterly magazine. "*New Letters* is intended for the general literary reader. We publish literary fiction, nonfiction, essays, poetry. We also publish art." Estab. 1934. Circ. 5,000. Pays on publication. Publishes ms an average of 6 months after acceptance. Byline given. Buys first North American serial rights. Editorial lead time 6 months. Submit seasonal material 6 months in advance. Accepts queries by mail. Responds in 1 month to queries; 3 months to mss. Sample copy for $10 or sample articles on Web site. Writer's guidelines online.

- Submissions are not read between May 1 and October 1.

Nonfiction Essays. No self-help, how-to, or nonliterary work. **Buys 8-10 mss/year.** Send complete ms. Length: 5,000 words maximum. **Pays $40-100.**

Photos Send photos with submission. Reviews contact sheets, 2x4 transparencies, prints. Buys one-time rights. Pays $10-40/photo.

Fiction Robert Stewart, editor. Ethnic, experimental, humorous, mainstream, contemporary. No genre fiction. **Buys 15-20 mss/year.** Send complete ms. Length: 5,000 words maximum. **Pays $30-75.**

Poetry Avant-garde, free verse, haiku, traditional. No light verse. **Buys 40-50 poems/year.** Submit maximum 6 poems. Length: Open. **Pays $10-25.**

Tips "We aren't interested in essays that are footnoted, or essays usually described as scholarly or critical. Our preference is for creative nonfiction or personal essays. We prefer shorter stories and essays to longer ones (an average length is 3,500-4,000 words). We have no rigid preferences as to subject, style, or genre, although commercial efforts tend to put us off. Even so, our only fixed requirement is on good writing."

$ $ THE NEW QUARTERLY

Canadian Writers & Writing, St. Jerome's University, 290 University Ave. N., Waterloo ON N2L 3G3 Canada. (519)884-8111, ext. 8290. E-mail: editor@newquarterly.net. Web site: www.newquarterly.net. Editor: Kim Jernigan. **95% freelance written.** Quarterly book covering Canadian fiction and poetry. "Emphasis on emerging writers and genres, but we publish more traditional work as well if the language and narrative structure are fresh." Estab. 1981. Circ. 1,000. Pays on publication. Publishes ms an average of 4 months after acceptance. Byline given. Buys first Canadian rights. Editorial lead time 6 months. Accepts queries by mail. Accepts simultaneous submissions. Responds in 2 weeks to queries; 4 months to mss. Sample copy for $16.50 (cover price, plus mailing). Writer's guidelines for #10 SASE or online.

- Open to Canadian writers only.

Fiction Kim Jernigan, Rae Crossman, Mark Spielmacher, Rosalynn Tyo, fiction editors. *Canadian work only.* "We are not interested in genre fiction. We are looking for innovative, beautifully crafted, deeply felt literary fiction." **Buys 20-25 mss/year.** Send complete ms. Length: 20 pages maximum. **Pays $200/story.**

Poetry *Canadian work only.* Lesley Elliott, Randi Patterson, John Vardon, Erin Noteboom, poetry editors. Avant-garde, free verse, traditional. **Buys 40 poems/year.** Submit maximum 5 poems. Length: 4½ inches typeset. **Pays $30/poem.**

Tips "Reading us is the best way to get our measure. We don't have preconceived ideas about what we're looking for other than that it must be Canadian work (Canadian writers, not necessarily Canadian content). We want something that's fresh, something that will repay a second reading, something in which the language soars and the feeling is complexly rendered."

$ THE NEW WRITER

P.O. Box 60, Cranbrook Kent TN17 2ZR United Kingdom. (44)(158)021-2626. Fax: (44)(158)021-2041. E-mail: editor@thenewwriter.com. Web site: www.thenewwriter.com. Publishes 6 issues per annum. Contemporary writing magazine which publishes "the best in fact, fiction and poetry." Estab. 1996. Circ. 1,500. Pays on publication. Publishes ms an average of 1 year after acceptance. Buys one-time rights. Accepts queries by e-mail, fax. Accepts simultaneous submissions. Responds in 2 months to queries; 4 months to mss. Sample copy for SASE and A4 SAE with IRCs only. Writer's guidelines for SASE.

Nonfiction Content should relate to writing. Query. Length: 1,000-2,000 words. **Pays £20-40.**

Fiction *No unsolicited mss.* Accepts fiction from subscribers only. "We will consider most categories apart from stories written for children. No horror, erotic, or cosy fiction." Query with published clips. Length: 2,000-5,000 words. **Pays £10 per story by credit voucher; additional copies for £1.50.**

Poetry Buys 50 poems/year. Submit maximum 3 poems. Length: 40 lines maximum. **Pays £3/poem.**

$ THE NORTH AMERICAN REVIEW

University of Northern Iowa, 1222 W. 27th St., Cedar Falls IA 50614-0516. (319)273-6455. Fax: (319)273-4326. E-mail: nar@uni.edu. Web site: www.webdelsol.com/northamreview/nar/. **Contact:** Grant Tracey, editor. **90% freelance written.** Bimonthly magazine. "The *NAR* is the oldest literary magazine in America and one of the most respected; though we have no prejudices about the subject matter of material sent to us, our first concern is quality." Estab. 1815. Circ. under 5,000. Pays on publication. Publishes ms an average of 1 year after acceptance. Byline given. Buys first North American serial, first rights. Accepts queries by mail. Responds in 4 months to mss. Sample copy for $5. Writer's guidelines online.

- This is the oldest literary magazine in the country and one of the most prestigious. Also one of the most entertaining—and a tough market for the young writer.

- Break in with the "highest quality poetry, fiction, and nonfiction on any topic, but particularly interested in the environment, gender, race, ethnicity, and class."

Nonfiction Ron Sandvik, nonfiction editor. No restrictions; highest quality only. Length: Open. **Pays $5/350 words; $20 minimum, $100 maximum.**

Fiction Grant Tracey, fiction editor. No restrictions; highest quality only. "No flat narrative stories where the inferiority of the character is the paramount concern." Wants to see more "well-crafted literary stories that emphasize family concerns." Length: Open. **Pays $5/350 words; $20 minimum, $100 maximum.**

Poetry No restrictions; highest quality only. Length: Open. **Pays $1/line; $20 minimum, $100 maximum.**

Tips "We like stories that start quickly and have a strong narrative arc. Poems that are passionate about subject, language, and image are welcome, whether they are traditional or experimental, whether in formal or free verse (closed or open form). Nonfiction should combine art and fact with the finest writing. We do not accept simultaneous submissions; these will be returned unread. We read poetry, fiction, and nonfiction year-round."

N $ NORTH CAROLINA LITERARY REVIEW

A Magazine of North Carolina Literature, Culture, and History, English Dept., East Carolina University, Greenville NC 27858-4353. (252)328-1537. Fax: (252)328-4889. E-mail: bauerm@mail.ecu.edu. Web site: www.ecu.edu/nclr. **Contact:** Margaret Bauer, editor. Annual magazine published in fall covering North Carolina writers, literature, culture, history. "Articles should have a North Carolina slant. First consideration is always for quality of work. Although we treat academic and scholarly subjects, we do not wish to see jargon-laden prose; our readers, we hope, are found as often in bookstores and libraries as in academia. We seek to combine the best elements of magazine for serious readers with best of scholarly journal." Estab. 1992. Circ. 750. Pays on publication. Publishes ms an average of 1 year after acceptance. Byline given. Buys first North American serial rights. Rights returned to writer on request. Editorial lead time 6 months. Accepts queries by mail, e-mail. Responds in 1 month to queries; 6 months to mss. Sample copy for $10-25. Writer's guidelines online.

- Break in with an article related to the special feature topic. Check the Web site for upcoming topics and deadlines.

Nonfiction North Carolina-related material only. Book excerpts, essays, exposé, general interest, historical/nostalgic, humor, interview/profile, opinion, personal experience, photo feature, travel, reviews, short narratives, surveys of archives. "No jargon-laden academic articles." **Buys 25-35 mss/year.** Query with published clips. Length: 500-5,000 words. **Pays $50-100 honorarium, extra copies, back issues or subscription (negotiable).**

Photos State availability with submission. Reviews 5×7 or 8×10 prints; snapshot size or photocopy OK. Buys one-time rights. Pays $25-250. Captions and identification of subjects required; releases (when appropriate) required.

Columns/Departments NC Writers (interviews, biographical/bibliographic essays); Reviews (essay reviews of North Carolina-related fiction, creative nonfiction, or poetry). Query with published clips. **Pays $50-100 honorarium, extra copies, back issues or subscription (negotiable).**

Fiction Must be either by a North Carolina-connected writer or set in North Carolina. **Buys 3-4 mss/year.** Query. Length: 5,000 words maximum. **$50-100 honorarium, extra copies, back issues or subscription (negotiable).**

Poetry *North Carolina poets only.* **Buys 8-10 poems/year.** Length: 30-150 lines. **$50-100 honorarium, extra copies, back issues or subscription (negotiable).**

Fillers Buys 2-5/year. Length: 50-500 words. **Pays $50-100 honorarium, extra copies, back issues or subscription (negotiable).**

Tips "By far the easiest way to break in is with special issue sections. We are especially interested in reports on conferences, readings, meetings that involve North Carolina writers, and personal essays or short narratives with a strong sense of place. See back issues for other departments. Interviews are probably the other easiest place to break in; no discussions of poetics/theory, etc., except in reader-friendly (accessible) language; interviews should be personal, more like conversations, that explore connections between a writer's life and his/her work."

$ NOTRE DAME REVIEW

University of Notre Dame, 840 Flanner Hall, Notre Dame IN 46556. (574)631-6952. Fax: (574)631-4795. E-mail: english.ndreview.1@nd.edu. Web site: www.nd.edu/~ndr/review.htm. Executive Editor: Kathleen J. Canavan. Poetry Editor: John Matthias. **Contact:** William O'Rourke, fiction editor. Semiannual magazine. "The *Notre Dame Review* is an indepenent, noncommercial magazine of contemporary American and international fiction, poetry, criticism, and art. We are especially interested in work that takes on big issues by making the invisible seen, that gives voice to the voiceless. In addition to showcasing celebrated authors like Seamus Heaney and Czelaw Milosz, the *Notre Dame Review* introduces readers to authors they may have never encountered before, but who are doing innovative and important work. In conjunction with the *Notre Dame Review*, the online companion to the printed magazine, the *Notre Dame Re-view* engages readers as a community centered in literary rather than commercial concerns, a community we reach out to through critique and commentary as well as aesthetic experience." Estab. 1995. Circ. 2,000. Pays on publication. Publishes ms an average of 6 months after acceptance. Buys first North American serial rights. Accepts simultaneous submissions. Responds in 4 or more months to mss. Sample copy for $6. Writer's guidelines online. **Buys 100 (90 poems, 10 stories) mss/year.** Length: 3,000 words. **Pays $5-25.**

Tips "We're looking for high quality work that takes on big issues in a literary way. Please read our back issues before submitting."

$ ONE-STORY

One-Story, LLC, P.O. Box 1326, New York NY 10156. Web site: www.one-story.com. **Contact:** Maribeth Batcha, publisher; Hannah Tinti, editor. **100% freelance written.** Literary magazine covering 1 short story. "*One-Story* is a literary magazine that contains, simply, 1 story. It is a subscription-only magazine. Every 3 weeks subscribers are sent *One-Story* in the mail. *One-Story* is artfully designed, lightweight, easy to carry, and ready to entertain on buses, in bed, in subways, in cars, in the park, in the bath, in the waiting rooms of doctor's offices, on the couch, or in line at the supermarket. Subscribers also have access to a Web site, where they can learn more about *One-Story* authors, and hear about *One-Story* readings and events. There is always time to read *One-Story*." Estab. 2002. Circ. 3,500. Pays on publication. Publishes ms an average of 3-6 months after acceptance. Byline given. Buys first North American serial rights. Buys the rights to publish excerpts on Web site and in promotional materials. Editorial lead time 3-4 months. Accepts simultaneous submissions. Responds in 2-6 months to mss. Sample copy for $5. Writer's guidelines online.

- Accepts submissions via Web site only.

Fiction Literary short stories. *One-Story* only accepts short stories. Do not send excerpts. Do not send more than 1 story at a time. **Buys 18 mss/year.** Send complete ms. Length: 3,000-8,000 words. **Pays $100.**

Tips "*One-Story* is looking for stories that are strong enough to stand alone. Therefore they must be very good. We want the best you can give. We want our socks knocked off."

N OTHER VOICES

University of Illinois at Chicago, 601 S. Morgan St., Chicago IL 60607. (312)413-2209. E-mail: othervoices@listserv.uic.edu. Web site: www.othervoicesmagazine.org. **Contact:** Gina Frangello and JoAnne Ruvoli, editors.

Semiannual magazine "publishing original, fresh, diverse stories and novel excerpts" for literate adults. Estab. 1985. Circ. 1,500. Buys one-time rights. Accepts simultaneous submissions. Responds in 10-12 weeks to mss. Sample copy for $7 (includes postage). Writer's guidelines for #10 SASE.

Fiction Humorous, contemporary, excerpted novel and one act-plays. Fiction only. "No taboos, except ineptitude and murkiness. No science fiction, romance, horror, chick lit or futuristic." Length: 5,000 words. **Pays in contributor's copies and modest cash gratuity.**

$ $ $ THE PARIS REVIEW

62 White Street, New York NY 10013. (212)861-0016. Fax: (212)861-4504. E-mail: queries@theparisreview.org. Web site: www.theparisreview.com. Editor: Philip Gourevitch. **Contact:** Fiction Editor, Poetry Editor. Quarterly magazine. "Fiction and poetry of superlative quality, whatever the genre, style or mode. Our contributors include prominent, as well as less well-known and previously unpublished writers. Writers at Work interview series includes important contemporary writers discussing their own work and the craft of writing." Pays on publication. Buys all, first english-language rights. Accepts queries by mail. Accepts simultaneous submissions. Responds in 4 months to mss. Sample copy for $15 (includes postage). Writer's guidelines online.

- Address submissions to proper department. Do not make submissions via e-mail.

Fiction Study the publication. Annual Aga Khan Fiction Contest award of $1,000. Send complete ms. Length: no limit. **Pays $500-1,000.**

Poetry Richard Howard, poetry editor.

$ $ PARNASSUS

Poetry in Review Foundation, 205 W. 89th St., #8-F, New York NY 10024. (212)362-3492. Fax: (212)875-0148. E-mail: parnew@aol.com. Web site: www.parnassuspoetry.com. Co-Editor: Ben Downing. **Contact:** Herbert Leibowitz, editor. Semiannual magazine covering poetry and criticism. Estab. 1972. Circ. 1,500. Pays on publication. Publishes ms an average of 5 months after acceptance. Byline given. Buys one-time rights. Accepts queries by mail. Responds in 2 months to mss. Sample copy for $15. Writer's guidelines not available.

Nonfiction Essays. **Buys 30 mss/year.** Query with published clips. Length: 1,500-7,500 words. **Pays $500.**

Poetry Accepts most types of poetry. Avant-garde, free verse, traditional. **Buys 3-4 unsolicited poems/year.**

Tips "Be certain you have read the magazine and are aware of the editor's taste. Blind submissions are a waste of everybody's time. We'd like to see more poems that display intellectual acumen and curiosity about history, science, music, etc., and fewer trivial lyrical poems about the self, or critical prose that's academic and dull. Prose should sing."

$ PLEIADES

Pleiades Press, Department of English & Philosophy, Central Missouri State University, Martin 336, Warrensburg MO 64093. (660)543-4425. Fax: (660)543-8544. E-mail: pleiades@cmsu1.cmsu.edu. Web site: www.cmsu.edu/englphil/pleiades. **Contact:** Kevin Prufer, editor. **100% freelance written.** Semiannual journal ($5^1/_2 \times 8^1/_2$ perfect bound). "We publish contemporary fiction, poetry, interviews, literary essays, special-interest personal essays, reviews for a general and literary audience." Estab. 1991. Circ. 3,000. Pays on publication. Publishes ms an average of 9 months after acceptance. Byline given. Buys first North American serial, second serial (reprint) rights. Occasionally requests rights for TV, radio reading, Web site. Editorial lead time 9 months. Accepts queries by mail. Accepts simultaneous submissions. Responds in 2 months to queries; 2 months to mss. Sample copy for $5 (back issue); $6 (current issue). Writer's guidelines for #10 SASE.

- Also sponsors the Lena-Miles Wever Todd Poetry Series competition, a contest for the best book ms by an American poet. The winner receives $1,000, publication by Pleiades Press, and distribution by Louisiana State University Press. Deadline September 30. Send SASE for guidelines.

Nonfiction Book excerpts, essays, interview/profile, reviews. "Nothing pedantic, slick, or shallow." **Buys 4-6 mss/year.** Send complete ms. Length: 2,000-4,000 words. **Pays $10.**

Fiction Susan Steinberg, fiction editor. Ethnic, experimental, humorous, mainstream, novel excerpts, magic realism. No science fiction, fantasy, confession, erotica. **Buys 16-20 mss/year.** Send complete ms. Length: 2,000-6,000 words. **Pays $10.**

Poetry Avant-garde, free verse, haiku, light verse, traditional. "Nothing didactic, pretentious, or overly sentimental." **Buys 40-50 poems/year.** Submit maximum 6 poems. **Pays $3/poem, and contributor copies.**

Tips "Show care for your material and your readers—submit quality work in a professional format. Include cover letter with brief bio and list of publications. Include SASE."

$ $ PLOUGHSHARES

Emerson College, Department M, 120 Boylston St., Boston MA 02116. Web site: www.pshares.org. **Contact:** Don Lee, editor. Triquarterly magazine for "readers of serious contemporary literature. Our mission is to present dynamic, contrasting views on what is valid and important in contemporary literature, and to discover and advance significant literary talent. Each issue is guest-edited by a different writer. We no longer structure issues around preconceived themes." Estab. 1971. Circ. 6,000. Pays on publication. Publishes ms an average of 6 months after acceptance. Offers 50% kill fee for assigned ms not published. kill fee. Buys first North American serial rights. Accepts simultaneous submissions. Responds in 5 months to mss. Sample copy for $9 (back issue). Writer's guidelines online.

- A competitive and highly prestigious market. Rotating and guest editors make cracking the line-up even tougher, since it's difficult to know what is appropriate to send. The reading period is August 1-March 31.

Nonfiction Essays (personal and literary; accepted only occasionally). Length: 6,000 words maximum. **Pays $25/printed page, $50-250.**

Fiction Mainstream. "No genre (science fiction, detective, gothic, adventure, etc.), popular formula, or commercial fiction whose purpose is to entertain rather than to illuminate." **Buys 25-35 mss/year.** Length: 300-6,000 words. **Pays $25/printed page, $50-250.**

Poetry Avant-garde, free verse, traditional, blank verse. Length: Open. **Pays $25/printed page, $50-250.**

Tips "We no longer structure issues around preconceived themes. If you believe your work is in keeping with our general standards of literary quality and value, submit at any time during our reading period."

$ POETRY

The Poetry Foundation, 444 N. Michigan Ave., Suite 1850, Chicago IL 60611-4034. (312)787-7070. Fax: (312)787-6650. E-mail: editors@poetrymagazine.org. Web site: www.poetrymagazine.org. Editor: Christian Wiman. Managing Editor: Helen Klaviter. Assistant Editor: Fred Sasaki. Reader: Christina Pugh. **Contact:** Editors. **100% freelance written.** Monthly magazine. Estab. 1912. Circ. 24,000. Pays on publication. Publishes ms an average of 9 months after acceptance. Byline given. Buys first serial rights. Accepts queries by mail. Responds in 1 month to queries; 1 month to mss. Sample copy for $5.50 or online at Web site. Writer's guidelines online.

Nonfiction Reviews (most are solicited). **Buys 14 mss/year.** Query. Length: 1,000-2,000 words. **Pays $150/page.**

Poetry All styles and subject matter. **Buys 180-250 poems/year.** Submit maximum 4 poems. Length: Open. **Pays $6-10/line ($150 minimum payment).**

N POETRY IRELAND REVIEW

Poetry Ireland, 2 Proud's Lane, Off St. Stephen's Green, Dublin 2 Ireland. 01-4789974. Fax: 01-4780205. E-mail: publications@poetryireland.ie. Web site: www.poetryireland.ie. Editor: Peter Sirr. Assistant Editor: Paul Lenehan. Quarterly literary magazine in book form. Estab. 1978. Circ. 2,000. Pays on publication. Not copyrighted. Accepts queries by mail, e-mail, fax, phone. Responds in 1 week to queries; 6 months to mss.

Poetry Avant-garde, free verse, haiku, traditional, contemporary. **Buys 150 poems/year.** Submit maximum 6 poems.

$ PRISM INTERNATIONAL

Department of Creative Writing, Buch E462 Main Mall, University of British Columbia, Vancouver BC V6T 1Z1 Canada. (604)822-2514. Fax: (604)822-3616. E-mail: prism@interchange.ubc.ca. Web site: prism.arts.ubc.ca. Executive Editors: Carla Elm Clement and Regan Taylor. **Contact:** Bren Simmers and Ben Hart, editors. **100% freelance written.** Works with new/unpublished writers. "A quarterly international journal of contemporary writing—fiction, poetry, drama, creative nonfiction and translation. Readership: public and university libraries, individual subscriptions, bookstores—a world-wide audience concerned with the contemporary in literature." Estab. 1959. Circ. 1,100. Pays on publication. Publishes ms an average of 4 months after acceptance. Buys first North American serial rights. Selected authors are paid an additional $10/page for digital rights. Accepts queries by mail, fax, phone. Responds in 4 months to queries; 3-6 months to mss. Sample copy for $10, more info online. Writer's guidelines online.

- Break in by "sending unusual or experimental work (we get mostly traditional submissions) and playing with forms (i.e., nonfiction, prose poetry, etc.)."

Nonfiction "Creative nonfiction that reads like fiction. Nonfiction pieces should be creative, exploratory, or experimental in tone rather than rhetorical, academic, or journalistic." No reviews, tracts, or scholarly essays. **Pays $20/printed page, and 1-year subscription.**

Fiction For Drama: one-acts preferred. Also interested in seeing dramatic monologues. Experimental, novel excerpts, traditional. New writing that is contemporary and literary. Short stories and self-contained novel excerpts. Works of translation are eagerly sought and should be accompanied by a copy of the original. Would like to see more translations. "No gothic, confession, religious, romance, pornography, or science fiction." **Buys 12-16 mss/year.** Send complete ms. Length: 25 pages maximum. **Pays $20/printed page, and 1-year subscription.**

Poetry **Buys 10 poems/issue.** Avant-garde, traditional. Submit maximum 6 poems. **Pays $40/printed page, and 1-year subscription.**

Tips "We are looking for new and exciting fiction. Excellence is still our No. 1 criterion. As well as poetry, imaginative nonfiction and fiction, we are especially open to translations of all kinds, very short fiction pieces and drama which work well on the page. Translations must come with a copy of the original language work. We pay an additional $10/printed page to selected authors whose work we place on our online version of *Prism*."

N $ QUARTERLY WEST

University of Utah, 255 S. Central Campus Dr., Room 3500, Salt Lake City UT 84112. E-mail: quarterlywest@yahoo.com. Web site: www.utah.edu/quarterlywest. **Contact:** Mike White and Paul Ketzle, co-editors. Semiannual magazine. "We publish fiction, poetry, and nonfiction in long and short formats, and will consider experimental as well as traditional works." Estab. 1976. Circ. 1,900. Pays on publication. Publishes ms an average of 6 months after acceptance. Buys first North American serial, all rights. Accepts queries by mail. Accepts simultaneous submissions. Responds in 6 months to mss. Sample copy for $7.50 or online. Writer's guidelines online.

Nonfiction Essays, interview/profile, personal experience, travel, book reviews. **Buys 6-8 mss/year.** Send complete ms. Length: 10,000 words maximum. **Pays $20-100.**

Fiction No preferred lengths; interested in longer, fuller short stories and short shorts. Ethnic, experimental, humorous, mainstream, novel excerpts, slice-of-life vignettes, short shorts, translations. No detective, science fiction or romance. **Buys 6-10 mss/year.** Send complete ms. **Pays $15-100, and 2 contributor's copies.**

Poetry Avant-garde, free verse, traditional. **Buys 40-50 poems/year.** Submit maximum 5 poems. **Pays $15-100.**

Tips "We publish a special section of short shorts every issue, and we also sponsor a biennial novella contest. We are open to experimental work—potential contributors should read the magazine! Don't send more than 1 story/submission. Biennial novella competition guidelines available upon request with SASE. We prefer work with interesting language and detail—plot or narrative are less important. We don't do Western themes or religious work."

$ $ QUEEN'S QUARTERLY

A Canadian Review, Queen's University, Kingston ON K7L 3N6 Canada. (613)533-2667. Fax: (613)533-6822. E-mail: qquarter@post.queensu.ca. Web site: info.queensu.ca/quarterly. **Contact:** Joan Harcourt, literary editor. **95% freelance written.** Quarterly magazine covering a wide variety of subjects, including science, humanities, arts and letters, politics, and history for the educated reader. "A general interest intellectual review, featuring articles, book reviews, poetry, and fiction." Estab. 1893. Circ. 3,000. Pays on publication. Publishes ms an average of 6-12 months after acceptance. Byline given. Buys first North American serial rights. Responds in 2-3 months to queries. Sample copy and writer's guidelines online.

Submissions can be sent as e-mail attachment or on hard copy with a SASE (Canadian postage).

Fiction Boris Castel, editor. Historical, mainstream, novel excerpts, short stories, women's. Length: 2,500-3,000 words. **Pays $100-300, 2 contributor's copies and 1-year subscription; additional copies $5.**

Poetry **Buys 25 poems/year.** Submit maximum 6 poems.

RARITAN

A Quarterly Review, 31 Mine St., New Brunswick NJ 08903. (732)932-7887. Fax: (732)932-7855. Editor: Jackson Lears. **Contact:** Stephanie Volmer, managing editor. Quarterly magazine covering literature, history, fiction, and general culture. Estab. 1981. Circ. 3,500. Pays on publication. Publishes ms an average of 1 year after acceptance. Byline given. Buys first North American serial rights. Editorial lead time 5 months. Accepts queries by mail.

- *Raritan* no longer accepts previously published or simultaneous submissions.

Nonfiction Book excerpts, essays. **Buys 50 mss/year.** Send complete ms. Length: 15-30 pages.

N $ RIVER STYX

Big River Association, 3547 Olive St., Suite 107, St. Louis MO 63103. (314)289-4090. Fax: (314)533-3345. Web site: www.riverstyx.org. Senior Editors: Quincy Troupe and Michael Castro. **Contact:** Richard Newman, editor. Triannual magazine. "*River Styx* publishes the highest quality fiction, poetry, interviews, essays, and visual art. We are an internationally distributed multicultural literary magazine." Mss read May-November. Estab. 1975. Pays on publication. Publishes ms an average of 1 year after acceptance. Byline given. Buys first North American serial, one-time rights. Accepts queries by mail. Accepts simultaneous submissions. Responds in 4 months to mss. Sample copy for $7. Writer's guidelines online.

Nonfiction Essays, interview/profile. **Buys 2-5 mss/year.** Send complete ms. **Pays 2 contributor copies, plus 1 year subscription; pays $8/page if funds are available.**

Photos Send photos with submission. Reviews 5×7 or 8×10 b&w and color prints and slides. Buys one-time rights. Pays 2 contributor copies, plus 1-year subscription; $8/page if funds are available.
Fiction Ethnic, experimental, mainstream, novel excerpts, short stories, literary. "No genre fiction, less thinly veiled autobiography." **Buys 6-9 mss/year.** Send complete ms. Length: no more than 23-30 manuscript pages. **Pays 2 contributor copies, plus 1-year subscription; $8/page if funds are available.**
Poetry Avant-garde, free verse, formal. No religious. **Buys 40-50 poems/year.** Submit maximum 3-5 poems. **Pays 2 contributor copies, plus a 1-year subscription; $8/page if funds are available.**

$ ROOM OF ONE'S OWN

A Canadian Quarterly of Women's Literature and Criticism, West Coast Feminist Literary Magazine Society, P.O. Box 46160, Station D, Vancouver BC V6J 5G5 Canada. Web site: www.roommagazine.com. **Contact:** Growing Room Collective. **100% freelance written.** Quarterly journal of feminist literature. "*Room of One's Own* is Canada's oldest feminist literary journal. Since 1975, *Room* has been a forum in which women can share their unique perspectives on the world, each other, and themselves." Estab. 1975. Circ. 1,000. Pays on publication. Publishes ms an average of 1 year after acceptance. Byline given. Buys first North American serial rights. Editorial lead time 9 months. Responds in 6 months to mss. Sample copy for $10 or online. Writer's guidelines online.
Nonfiction Reviews. **Buys 1-2 mss/year.** Send complete ms. Length: 500-1,500 words. **Pays $50 (Canadian), and a 1-year subscription.**
Fiction Feminist literature—short stories, creative nonfiction, essays by, for, and about women. "No humor, science fiction, romance." **Buys 40 mss/year.** Length: 2,000-5,000 words. **Pays $35 (Canadian), and a 1-year subscription.**
Poetry Avant-garde, free verse. "Nothing light, undeveloped." **Buys 40 poems/year.** Submit maximum 6 poems. Length: 3-80 lines. **Pays $50 (Canadian), and a 1-year subscription.**

N $ $ THE SAINT ANN'S REVIEW

A Journal of Contemporary Arts and Letters, Saint Ann's School, 129 Pierrepont St., Brooklyn NY 11201. (718)522-1660. Fax: (718)522-2599. E-mail: sareview@saintanns.k12.ny.us. Web site: www.saintannsreview.com. **Contact:** Beth Bosworth, editor. **100% freelance written.** Semiannual literary magazine. "We seek fully realized work, distinguished by power and craft." Estab. 2000. Circ. 2,000. Pays on publication. Publishes ms an average of 4 months after acceptance. Byline given. Buys first North American serial rights. Submit seasonal material 4 months in advance. Accepts queries by mail. Responds in 1 month to queries; 4 months to mss. Sample copy for $8. Writer's guidelines online.
Nonfiction Book excerpts (occasionally), essays, humor, interview/profile, personal experience, photo feature. **Buys 10 mss/year.** Query with or without published clips or send complete ms. Length: 7,500 words maximum. **Pays $40/published page, $250/maximum.**
Photos Send photos with submission. Reviews transparencies, prints, GIF/JPEG files, b&w art. Buys one-time rights. Offers $50/photo page or art page, $250 maximum.
Columns/Departments Book reviews, 1,500 words. **Buys 10 mss/year.** Send complete ms by mail only. **Pays $40/published page, $250 maximum.**
Fiction Ethnic, experimental, fantasy, historical, humorous, mainstream, slice-of-life vignettes, translations. **Buys 15 mss/year.** Length: 7,500 words maximum. **Pays $40/published page, $250 maximum.**
Poetry Avant-garde, free verse, haiku, light verse, traditional, translations. **Buys 30 poems/year.** Submit maximum 5 poems. **Pays $50/page, $250 maximum.**

N $ THE SAVAGE KICK LITERARY MAGAZINE

Murder Slim Press, 32c Lichfield Rd., Gt. Yarmouth Norfolk NR31 0EQ United Kingdom. E-mail: moonshine@murderslim.com. Web site: www.murderslim.com/savagekick.html. Managing Editors: Anna Caffrey, Pigmeat, Murder Slim. **Contact:** Moonshine. **100% freelance written.** Quarterly magazine. "*Savage Kick* primarily deals with viewpoints outside the mainstream . . . honest emotions told in a raw, simplistic way. It is recommended that you are very familiar with the *SK* style before submitting. We have only accepted 4 new writers in 12 months of the magazine. Ensure you have a distinctive voice and story to tell." Estab. 2005. Circ. 500+. **Pays on acceptance.** Publishes ms an average of up to 2 months after acceptance. Byline given. Buys all electronic rights for 3 months. Accepts queries by mail, e-mail. Accepts simultaneous submissions. Responds in 7-10 days to queries. Writer's guidelines free.
Nonfiction "We only accept articles in relation to the authors featured on our reading list." Interview/profile, personal experience. **Buys 10-20 mss/year.** Send complete ms. Length: 500-3,000 words. **Pays $25-35.**
Columns/Departments Buys up to 4 mss/year. Query. **Pays $25-35.**
Fiction Mystery, slice-of-life vignettes, crime. Real-life stories are preferred, unless the work is distinctively extreme within the crime genre. No mainstream fiction, Oprah-style fiction, Internet/chat language, teen issues,

excessive Shakespearean language, surrealism, overworked irony, or genre fiction (horror, fantasy, science fiction, western, erotica, etc.). **Buys 10-25 mss/year.** Send complete ms. Length: 500-6,000 words. **Pays $35.**

$ THE SEATTLE REVIEW

Box 354330, University of Washington, Seattle WA 98195. (206)543-2302. E-mail: seaview@u.washington.edu. Web site: depts.washington.edu/engl/seaview1.html. Semiannual magazine. "Includes general fiction, poetry, craft essays on writing, and one interview per issue with a Northwest writer." Estab. 1978. Circ. 1,000. Pays on publication. Buys first North American serial rights. Responds in 8 months to mss. Sample copy for $6. Writer's guidelines online.

- Editors accept submissions only from October 1 through May 31.

Fiction Colleen J. McElroy, editor. Wants more creative nonfiction. "We also publish a series called Writers and their Craft, which deals with aspects of writing fiction (also poetry)—point of view, characterization, etc, rather than literary criticism, each issue." Ethnic, experimental, fantasy, historical, horror, humorous, mainstream, mystery, novel excerpts, suspense, western, contemporary, feminist, gay, lesbian, literary, psychic/supernatural/occult, regional, translations. "Nothing in "bad taste (porn, racist, etc.). No genre fiction or science fiction." **Buys 4-10 mss/year.** Send complete ms. Length: 500-10,000 words. **Pays $0-100.**

Poetry Colleen J. McElroy, editor. Pros.

Tips "Beginners do well in our magazine if they send clean, well-written manuscripts. We've published a lot of 'first stories' from all over the country and take pleasure in discovery."

THE SEWANEE REVIEW

University of the South, 735 University Ave., Sewanee TN 37383-1000. (931)598-1246. E-mail: lcouch@sewanee.edu. Web site: www.sewanee.edu/sewanee_review. Managing Editor: Leigh Anne Couch. **Contact:** George Core. Quarterly magazine. "A literary quarterly, publishing original fiction, poetry, essays on literary and related subjects, and book reviews for well-educated readers who appreciate good American and English literature." Estab. 1892. Circ. 2,000. Pays on publication. Buys first North American serial, second serial (reprint) rights. Responds in 4-6 weeks to mss. Sample copy for $8.50 ($9.50 outside US). Writer's guidelines online.

- Does not read mss June 1-August 31.

Fiction Send query letter for essays and reviews. Send complete ms for fiction. Literary, contemporary. No erotica, science fiction, fantasy or excessively violent or profane material. **Buys 10-15 mss/year.** Length: 3,500-7,500 words.

Poetry Send complete ms. Submit maximum 6 poems. Length: 40 lines.

$ SHENANDOAH

The Washington and Lee University Review, Washington and Lee University, Mattingly House, 2 Lee Ave., Lexington VA 24450-2116. (540)458-8765. Fax: (540)458-8461. E-mail: shenandoah@wlu.edu. Web site: shenandoah.wlu.edu. **Contact:** Lynn Leech, managing editor. Triannual magazine. Estab. 1950. Circ. 2,000. Pays on publication. Publishes ms an average of 10 months after acceptance. Byline given. Buys first North American serial, one-time rights. Responds in 3 months to mss. Sample copy for $10. Writer's guidelines online.

Nonfiction Book excerpts, essays. **Buys 6 mss/year.** Send complete ms. **Pays $25/page ($250 max).**

Fiction Mainstream, novel excerpts. No sloppy, hasty, slight fiction. **Buys 15 mss/year.** Send complete ms. **Pays $25/page ($250 max).**

Poetry No inspirational, confessional poetry. **Buys 70 poems/year.** Submit maximum 6 poems. Length: Open. **Pays $2.50/line ($200 max).**

$ SOLEADO

Revista de Literatura y Cultura, Dept. of International Language and Culture Studies, IPFW, CM 267, 2101 E. Coliseum Blvd., Fort Wayne IN 46805. (260)481-6630. Fax: (260)481-6985. E-mail: summersj@ipfw.edu. Web site: users.ipfw.edu/summersj/Soleado-Web site/soleportada.htm. **Contact:** Jason Summers, editor. **100% freelance written.** Annual magazine covering Spanish-language literary, cultural, and creative writing. "Our readers are interested in literature and culture, from creative writing to personal essays and beyond. Spanish is of an ever-growing importance in the US and the world, and our readers and writers are people using that language. *Soleado* is a literary magazine, so academic treatises are not on the list of texts we would be excited to see. The focus of the magazine is on Spanish-language writing, although the national origin of the writer does not matter. The subject matter doesn't have to be Hispanic, either. The one exception to the Spanish-language requirement is that certain texts deal with the difficulties of being bilingual and/or bicultural are welcome to be written in 'Spanglish' when that usage is essential to the text." Estab. 2004. Pays on publication. Publishes ms an average of 8 months after acceptance. Byline given. Buys first North American serial, first, one-time, second serial (reprint), simultaneous, electronic, anthology rights. Editorial lead time 6 months. Submit seasonal material 1 year in advance. Accepts queries by mail, e-mail. Accepts previously published material. Responds in 1 week to queries; 3 months to mss. Sample copy and writer's guidelines online.

Nonfiction Book excerpts, essays, humor, interview/profile, opinion, personal experience, travel, translations, memoir, creative nonfiction. No how-to, general travel, inspirational, religious or anything written in English. All nonfiction must have a literary or cultural slant. **Buys up to 3 mss/year.** Query with or without published clips. **Pays maximum $50.**

Fiction "We are looking for good literary writing in Spanish, from Magical Realism a la García Márquez, to McOndo-esque writing similar to that of Edmundo Paz-Soldán and Alberto Fuguet, to Spanish pulp realism like that of Arturo Pérez-Reverte. Testimonials, experimental works like those of Diamela Eltit, and women's voices like Marcela Serrano and Zoé Valdés are also encouraged. We are not against any particular genre writing, but such stories do have to maintain their hold on the literary, as well as the genre, which is often a difficult task." Adventure, ethnic, experimental, fantasy, historical, humorous, mainstream, mystery, novel excerpts, science fiction, slice-of-life vignettes, suspense, translations, magical realism. **Buys 2-6 mss/year.** Query with or without published clips or send complete ms. Length: up to 8,000 words. **Pays $50.**

Poetry Avant-garde, free verse, light verse, traditional, translation. "Avoid poetry that takes us to places we have already seen. The best kind of poetry takes readers somewhere unexpected or via an unexpected path, departing from the familiar just when they thought they had things figured out." **Buys 10-15 poems/year.** Submit maximum 4 poems. Length: 400 words.

Fillers Short humor. **Buys up to 4/year.** Length: 1,000 words. **Pays $10.**

Tips "Whether you are or are not a native speaker of Spanish, have someone read over your manuscript for obvious grammatical errors, flow, and continuity of ideas. We are interested in literary translations into Spanish, as well as original writing. Query before sending submission as an e-mail attachment. We publish annually, and the reading period runs from September 1 to March 31 of the following year. Anything that comes between April and August won't get a reply until the new reading period begins."

$ THE SOUTHERN REVIEW

Louisiana State University, Old President's House, Baton Rouge LA 70803-5001. (225)578-5108. Fax: (225)578-5098. E-mail: southernreview@lsu.edu. Web site: www.lsu.edu/thesouthernreview. **Contact:** Donna Perreault, associate editor. **100% freelance written.** Works with a moderate number of new/unpublished writers each year. Quarterly magazine "with emphasis on contemporary literature in the US and abroad." Reading period: September-May. Estab. 1935. Circ. 2,900. Pays on publication. Publishes ms an average of 6 months after acceptance. Byline given. Buys first North American serial rights. Accepts queries by mail. Responds in 2 months to mss. Sample copy for $8. Writer's guidelines online.

Nonfiction Essays with careful attention to craftsmanship, technique, and seriousness of subject matter. "Willing to publish experimental writing if it has a valid artistic purpose. Avoid extremism and sensationalism. Essays should exhibit thoughtful and sometimes severe awareness of the necessity of literary standards in our time." Emphasis on contemporary literature. No footnotes. **Buys 25 mss/year.** Length: 4,000-10,000 words. **Pays $30/page.**

Fiction Short stories of lasting literary merit, with emphasis on style and technique; novel excerpts. "We emphasize style and substantial content. No mystery, fantasy or religious mss." Length: 4,000-8,000 words. **Pays $30/page.**

Poetry Length: 1-4 pages. **Pays $30/page.**

N $ STAND MAGAZINE

School of English, University of Leeds, Leeds LS2 9JT United Kingdom. (44)(113)343-4794. Fax: (44)(113)233-2791. E-mail: engstand@leeds.ac.uk. Web site: www.standmagazine.org. Editorial Assitant: Jeffrey Orr. Quarterly literary magazine. Pays £20 for the first poem or 1,000 words of prose and £5 for each additional piece published in the same issue of the magazine. Estab. 1952. Pays on publication. Accepts queries by mail. Accepts previously published material. Writer's guidelines online.

- US submissions can be made through the Virginia office (see separate listing).

N $ STORYTELLER

Canada's Short Story Magazine, Tyo Communications, 3687 Twin Falls Place, Ottawa ON K1V 1W6 Canada. E-mail: info@storytellermagazine.com. Web site: www.storytellermagazine.com. Managing Editor: Terry Tyo. **Contact:** Melanie Fogel, editor. **99% freelance written.** Quarterly magazine covering fiction. Estab. 1994. Circ. 1,000. Pays on publication. Publishes ms an average of 2-3 months after acceptance. Byline given. Buys first North American serial, second serial (reprint) rights. Accepts previously published material. Responds in 2-3 months to mss. Sample copy and writer's guidelines online.

Fiction Adventure, confessions, ethnic, experimental, fantasy, historical, horror, humorous, mainstream, mystery, romance, science fiction, serialized novels, slice-of-life vignettes, suspense, western. Does not want religious, erotica, hardcore genre, Americana, stories where nothing happens. **Buys 30-40 mss/year.** Send complete ms. Length: 2,000-6,000 words. **Pays 1/4-1/2¢/word.**

Tips "Write the kind of blurb for your story that you'd see on the dust jacket of a novel. If you can't make that blurb sound appealing, we probably don't want to see the story."

N $ $ THE STRAND MAGAZINE

P.O. Box 1418, Birmingham MI 48012-1418. (248)788-5948. Fax: (248)874-1046. E-mail: strandmag@strandmag.com. Web site: strandmag@strandmag.com. **Contact:** Andrew Gulli, editor. Quarterly magazine covering mysteries, short stories, essays, book reviews. "After an absence of nearly half a century, the magazine known to millions for bringing Sir Arthur Conan Doyle's ingenious detective, Sherlock Holmes, to the world has once again appeared on the literary scene. First launched in 1891, *The Strand*,included in its pages the works of some of the greatest writers of the 20th century: Agatha Christie, Dorothy Sayers, Margery Allingham, W. Somerset Maugham, Graham Greene, P.G. Wodehouse, H.G. Wells, Aldous Huxley and many others. In 1950, economic difficulties in England caused a drop in circulation which forced the magazine to cease publication." Estab. 1998. Circ. 50,000. **Pays on acceptance.** Publishes ms an average of 4 months after acceptance. Byline given. Buys first North American serial rights. Accepts queries by e-mail. Responds in 1 month to queries. Sample copy not available. Writer's guidelines for #10 SASE.

Fiction A.F. Gulli, editor. Horror, humorous, mystery, suspense, tales of the unexpected, tales of terror and the supernatural "written in the classic tradition of this century's great authors. "We are not interested in submissions with any sexual content." Length: 2,000-6,000 words. **Pays $50-175.**

Tips "No gratuitous violence, sexual content, or explicit language, please."

N $ $ $ SUBTROPICS

University of Florida, P.O. Box 112075, Gainesville FL 32611-2075. Web site: www.english.ufl.edu/subtropics. **Contact:** David Leavitt, fiction/nonfiction editor; Sidney Wade, poetry editor; Mark Mitchell, nonfiction editor. **100% freelance written.** Magazine published 3 times/year through the University of Florida's English department. *Subtropics* seeks to publish the best literary fiction, essays, and poetry being written today, both by established and emerging authors. "We will consider works of fiction of any length, from short shorts to novellas and self-contained novel excerpts. We give the same latitude to essays. We appreciate work in translation and, from time to time, republish important and compelling stories, essays, and poems that have lapsed out of print." Estab. 2005. **Pays on acceptance.** Publishes ms an average of 6 months after acceptance. Byline given. Buys first North American serial, one-time rights. Accepts queries by mail. Accepts simultaneous submissions. Responds in 1 month to queries; 2 months to mss. Writer's guidelines online.

Nonfiction Essays, literary nonfiction. No book reviews. **Buys 15 mss/year.** Send complete ms. **Pays $1,000.**

Fiction Literary fiction only, including short-shorts. No genre fiction. **Buys 20 mss/year.** Send complete ms. **Pays $500 for short-shorts; $1,000 for full stories.**

Poetry Buys 50 poems/year. Submit maximum 5 poems.

Tips "We publish longer works of fiction, including novellas and excerpts from forthcoming novels. Each issue will include a short-short story of about 250 words on the back cover. We are also interested in publishing works in translation for the magazine's English-speaking audience."

$ TAMPA REVIEW

University of Tampa Press, 401 W. Kennedy Blvd., Tampa FL 33606. (813)253-6266. Fax: (813)258-7593. Web site: tampareview.ut.edu. **Contact:** Richard B. Mathews, editor. Semiannual magazine published in hardback format. An international literary journal publishing art and literature from Florida and Tampa Bay as well as new work and translations from throughout the world. Estab. 1988. Circ. 500. Pays on publication. Publishes ms an average of 10 months after acceptance. Byline given. Buys first North American serial rights. Editorial lead time 18 months. Accepts queries by mail. Responds in 5 months to mss. Sample copy for $7. Writer's guidelines online.

Nonfiction Elizabeth Winston, nonfiction editor. General interest, interview/profile, personal experience, creative nonfiction. No "how-to" articles, fads, journalistic reprise, etc. **Buys 6 mss/year.** Send complete ms. Length: 250-7,500 words. **Pays $10/printed page.**

Photos State availability with submission. Reviews contact sheets, negatives, transparencies, prints, digital files. Buys one-time rights. Offers $10/photo. Captions, identification of subjects required.

Fiction Lisa Birnbaum and Kathleen Ochshorn, fiction editors. Ethnic, experimental, fantasy, historical, mainstream, literary. "We are far more interested in quality than in genre. Nothing sentimental as opposed to genuinely moving, nor self-conscious style at the expense of human truth." **Buys 6 mss/year.** Send complete ms. Length: 200-5,000 words. **Pays $10/printed page.**

Poetry Don Morrill and Martha Serpas, poetry editors. Avant-garde, free verse, haiku, light verse, traditional, visual/experimental. No greeting card verse, hackneyed, sing-song, rhyme-for-the-sake-of-rhyme. **Buys 45 poems/year.** Submit maximum 10 poems. Length: 2-225 lines.

Tips "Send a clear cover letter stating previous experience or background. Our editorial staff considers submissions between September and December for publication in the following year."

N $⊘ THEMA

Box 8747, Metairie LA 70011-8747. E-mail: thema@cox.net. Web site: members.cox.net/thema. **Contact:** Virginia Howard, editor. **100% freelance written.** Triannual magazine covering a different theme for each issue. Upcoming themes for SASE. "*Thema* is designed to stimulate creative thinking by challenging writers with unusual themes, such as 'bookstore cowboy' and 'umbrellas in the snow.' Appeals to writers, teachers of creative writing, and general reading audience." Estab. 1988. Circ. 350. **Pays on acceptance.** Publishes ms an average of within 6 months after acceptance. Byline given. Buys one-time rights. Accepts queries by mail. Accepts previously published material. Accepts simultaneous submissions. Responds in 1 week to queries; 5 months to mss. Sample copy for $8. Writer's guidelines for #10 SASE.

Reprints Send ms with rights for sale noted and information about when and where the material previously appeared. Pays the same amount paid for original.

Fiction Adventure, ethnic, experimental, fantasy, historical, humorous, mainstream, mystery, novel excerpts, religious, science fiction, slice-of-life vignettes, suspense, western, contemporary, sports, prose poem. "No erotica." **Buys 30 mss/year.** Length: fewer than 6,000 words preferred. **Pays $10-25.**

Poetry Avant-garde, free verse, haiku, light verse, traditional. "No erotica." **Buys 27 poems/year.** Submit maximum 3 poems. Length: 4-50 lines. **Pays $10.**

Tips "Be familiar with the themes. Don't submit unless you have an upcoming theme in mind. Specify the target theme on the first page of your manuscript or in a cover letter. Put your name on first page of manuscript only. (All submissions are judged in blind review after the deadline for a specified issue.) Most open to fiction and poetry. Don't be hasty when you consider a theme—mull it over and let it ferment in your mind. We appreciate interpretations that are carefully constructed, clever, subtle, and well thought out."

$ $ THE THREEPENNY REVIEW

P.O. Box 9131, Berkeley CA 94709. (510)849-4545. Web site: www.threepennyreview.com. **Contact:** Wendy Lesser, editor. **100% freelance written.** Works with small number of new/unpublished writers each year. Quarterly tabloid. "We are a general interest, national literary magazine with coverage of politics, the visual arts, and the performing arts as well." Estab. 1980. Circ. 9,000. **Pays on acceptance.** Publishes ms an average of 1 year after acceptance. Byline given. Buys first North American serial rights. Responds in 1 month to queries; 2 months to mss. Sample copy for $12 or online. Writer's guidelines online.

- Does not read mss from September to December.

Nonfiction Essays, exposé, historical/nostalgic, personal experience, book, film, theater, dance, music, and art reviews. **Buys 40 mss/year.** Query with or without published clips or send complete ms. Length: 1,500-4,000 words. **Pays $400.**

Fiction No fragmentary, sentimental fiction. **Buys 10 mss/year.** Send complete ms. Length: 800-4,000 words. **Pays $200 per poem or Table Talk piece.**

Poetry Free verse, traditional. No poems "without capital letters or poems without a discernible subject." **Buys 30 poems/year.** Submit maximum 5 poems. **Pays $200.**

Tips "Nonfiction (political articles, memoirs, reviews) is most open to freelancers."

$ $ $ TIN HOUSE

McCormack Communications, Box 10500, Portland OR 97210. (503)274-4393. Fax: (503)222-1154. Web site: www.tinhouse.com. Editor-in-Chief: Win McCormack. Managing Editor: Holly Macarthur. Editor: Rob Spillman. Senior Editor: Lee Montgomery. Poetry Editor: Brenda Shaunessy. **90% freelance written.** "We are a general interest literary quarterly. Our watchword is quality. Our audience includes people interested in literature in all its aspects, from the mundane to the exalted." Estab. 1998. Circ. 11,000. Pays on publication. Publishes ms an average of 6 months after acceptance. Byline given. Buys first North American serial, anthology rights. Editorial lead time 6 months. Submit seasonal material 6 months in advance. Accepts queries by mail. Accepts simultaneous submissions. Responds in 6 weeks to queries; 3 months to mss. Sample copy for $15. Writer's guidelines online.

Nonfiction Book excerpts, essays, interview/profile, personal experience. Send complete ms. Length: 5,000 words maximum. **Pays $50-800 for assigned articles; $50-500 for unsolicited articles.** Sometimes pays expenses of writers on assignment.

Columns/Departments Lost and Found (mini-reviews of forgotten or underappreciated books), up to 500 words; Readable Feasts (fiction or nonfiction literature with recipes), 2,000-3,000 words; Pilgrimage (journey to a personally significant place, especially literary), 2,000-3,000 words. **Buys 15-20 mss/year.** Send complete ms. **Pays $50-500.**

Fiction Rob Spillman, fiction editor. Experimental, mainstream, novel excerpts, literary. **Buys 15-20 mss/year.** Send complete ms. Length: 5,000 words maximum. **Pays $200-800.**

Poetry Brenda Shaunessy, poetry editor. Avant-garde, free verse, traditional. No prose masquerading as poetry. **Buys 40 poems/year.** Submit maximum 5 poems. **Pays $50-150.**

Tips "Remember to send a SASE with your submission."

$ $ VERBATIM

The Language Quarterly, Word, Inc., P.O. Box 597302, Chicago IL 60659. (773)478-2339. E-mail: editor@verbatimmag.com. Web site: www.verbatimmag.com. **Contact:** Erin McKean, editor. **75-80% freelance written.** Quarterly magazine covering language and linguistics. "*Verbatim* is the only magazine of language and linguistics for the lay person." Estab. 1974. Circ. 1,600. Pays on publication. Publishes ms an average of 6-9 months after acceptance. Byline given. Buys all rights. Editorial lead time 3 months. Submit seasonal material 6 months in advance. Accepts queries by mail, e-mail. Responds in 3 weeks to queries; 2 months to mss. Sample copy for 9×12 SAE and 6 first-class stamps. Writer's guidelines online.

Nonfiction Essays, humor, personal experience. Does not want puns or overly cranky prescriptivism. **Buys 24-28 mss/year.** Query. **Pays $25-400 for assigned articles; $25-300 for unsolicited articles.**

Poetry "We only publish poems explicitly about language. Poems written in language not enough." **Buys 4-6 poems/year.** Submit maximum 3 poems. Length: 3-75 lines. **Pays $25-50.**

Tips "Humorously write about an interesting language, language topic, or jargon. Also, when querying, include 3-4 lines of biographical information about yourself."

N $ $ VESTAL REVIEW

A flash fiction magazine, 2609 Dartmouth Dr., Vestal NY 13850. E-mail: submissions@vestalreview.net. Web site: www.vestalreview.net. **Contact:** Mark Budman, publisher/editor; Sue O'Neill, co-editor. Quarterly magazine specializing in flash fiction. "We accept only e-mail submissions." Circ. 1,500. Pays on publication. Publishes ms an average of 2-3 months after acceptance. Buys first North American serial, electronic rights. Accepts queries by e-mail. Accepts simultaneous submissions. Responds in 1 week to queries; 2 months to mss. Sample copy for $5. Writer's guidelines online.

Fiction Ethnic, horror, mainstream, speculative fiction. Does not read new submissions in March, June, September, and December. All submissions received during these months will be returned unopened. Length: 50-500 words. **Pays 3-10¢/word and 1 contributor's copy; additional copies $5.**

Tips "We like literary fiction, with a plot, that doesn't waste words. Don't send jokes masked as stories."

N $ THE VILLAGE RAMBLER MAGAZINE

The Flying Typewriter, P.O. Box 5070, Chapel Hill NC 27514-5001. (919)545-9789. Fax: (919)545-0921. E-mail: editor@villagerambler.com. Web site: www.villagerambler.com. **Contact:** Elizabeth Oliver, editor. **85% freelance written.** Bimonthly magazine. "*The Village Rambler Magazine* is distributed in North Carolina and features area and national talent. We are interested in fiction, poetry, and nonfiction." Estab. 2003. Circ. 3,000. Pays on publication. Publishes ms an average of 6-12 months after acceptance. Byline given. Buys first rights, makes work-for-hire assignments. Accepts queries by mail. Accepts previously published material. Responds in 1 month to queries; 4 months to mss. Sample copy for $8. Writer's guidelines for #10 SASE.

Nonfiction Book excerpts, essays, general interest, historical/nostalgic, humor, interview/profile, personal experience, photo feature. **Buys 24 mss/year.** Send complete ms. Length: 10,000 words maximum. **Pays $50, plus 1 contributor copy.**

Photos State availability with submission. Reviews 4×6 prints, GIF/JPEG files. Buys one-time rights. Negotiates payment individually. Captions, identification of subjects, model releases required.

Fiction Ethnic, experimental, historical, humorous, mainstream, novel excerpts, serialized novels, short shorts. No genre fiction (science fiction, horror, romance, or children's). **Buys 6-12 mss/year.** Send complete ms. Length: 10,000 words maximum. **Pays $50, plus 1 contributor copy.**

Poetry "We are open to all types of poetry." **Buys 12-18 poems/year.** Submit maximum 5 poems.

Tips "Send us your strongest work. We are interested in writing that knows its objective and achieves it with talent and technique."

$ VISIONS-INTERNATIONAL

Black Buzzard Press, 3503 Ferguson Lane, Austin TX 78754. (512)674-3977. **Contact:** B.R. Strahan, editor. **95% freelance written.** Magazine published 2 times/year featuring poetry, essays and reviews. Estab. 1979. Circ. 750. Pays on publication. Publishes ms an average of 6 months after acceptance. Byline given. Buys first North

American serial rights. Editorial lead time 2 months. Accepts queries by mail. Responds in 3 weeks to queries; 2 months to mss. Sample copy for $4.95. Writer's guidelines for #10 SASE.

Nonfiction Essays (by assignment after query reviews). Query. Length: 1 page maximum. **Pays $10 and complimentary copies.** Pays with contributor copies when grant money is unavailable.

Poetry Avant-garde, free verse, traditional, translations into English. No sentimental, religious, scurrilous, sexist, racist, amaturish, or over 3 pages. **Buys 110 poems/year.** Submit 3-6 poems Length: 2-120 lines.

Tips "Know your craft. We are not a magazine for amateurs. We also are interested in translation from modern poets writing in any language into English. No e-mail submissions please."

$ $ WEBER STUDIES

Voices and Viewpoints of the Contemporary West, Weber State University, 1214 University Circle, Ogden UT 84404-1214. (801)626-6616 or (801)626-6473. E-mail: weberstudies@weber.edu. Web site: weberstudies.weber.edu. Editor: Brad L. Roghaar. **Contact:** Kay Anderson, editorial assistant. **70% freelance written.** Magazine and online text archive published 3 times/year covering preservation of and access to wilderness, environmental cooperation, insight derived from living in the West, cultural diversity, changing federal involvement in the region, women and the West, implications of population growth, the contributions of individuals (scholars, artists and community leaders), a sense of place. "We seek works that provide insight into the environment and culture (both broadly defined) of the contemporary western US. We look for good writing that reveals human nature, as well as natural environment." Estab. 1981. Circ. 800-1,000. Pays on publication. Publishes ms an average of 6-12 months after acceptance. Byline given. Buys one-time, electronic rights. (copyrights revert to authors after publication) Editorial lead time 6 months. Submit seasonal material 6 months in advance. Accepts queries by mail, e-mail, phone. Accepts simultaneous submissions. Responds in 1 month to queries; 6-9 months to mss. Sample copy for $8. Writer's guidelines for #10 SASE, on Web site or by e-mail.

Nonfiction Essays, historical/nostalgic, interview/profile, opinion, personal experience, photo feature. **Buys 20-25 mss/year.** Send complete ms. Length: 5,000 words. **Pays $150-300, plus 1 contributor copy and 1-year subscription.**

Photos State availability with submission. Reviews 4×6 prints, 4×6 GIF/JPEG files at 300 dpi. Buys one-time rights. Negotiates pay individually. Captions, identification of subjects, model releases required.

Columns/Departments Send complete ms. **Pays $100-200.**

Fiction Adventure, ethnic, historical, humorous, mainstream, novel excerpts, religious, slice-of-life vignettes, western. Send complete ms. Length: 5,000 words. **Pays $150-300.**

Poetry Buys 15-20 sets of poems/year. Submit maximum 6 poems. **Pays $100-150.**

N $ WEST BRANCH

Bucknell Hall, Bucknell University, Lewisburg PA 17837-2029. (570)577-1853. Fax: (570)577-1885. E-mail: westbranch@bucknell.edu. Web site: www.bucknell.edu/westbranch. Managing Editor: Andrew Ciotola. **Contact:** Paula Closson Buck, editor. Semiannual literary magazine. "*West Branch* is an aesthetic conversation between the traditional and the innovative in poetry, fiction and nonfiction. It brings writers, new and established, to the rooms where they will be heard, and where they will, no doubt, rearrange the furniture." Pays on publication. Byline given. Buys first North American serial rights. Accepts queries by mail. Sample copy for $3. Writer's guidelines online.

Nonfiction Essays, general interest, literary. **Buys 4-5 mss/year.** Send complete ms. **Pays $20-100 ($10/page).**

Fiction Novel excerpts, short stories. No genre fiction. **Buys 10-12 mss/year.** Send complete ms. **Pays $20-100 ($10/page).**

Poetry Free verse, formal, experimental. **Buys 30-40 poems/year.** Submit maximum 6 poems. **Pays $20-100 ($10/page).**

Tips "Please send only 1 submission at a time and do not send another work until you have heard about the first. Send no more than 6 poems or 30 pages of prose at once. We accept simultaneous submissions if they are clearly marked as such, and if we are notified immediately upon acceptance elsewhere. Manuscripts must be accompanied by the customary return materials; we cannot respond by e-mail or postcard, except to foreign submissions. All manuscripts should be typed, with the author's name on each page; prose must be double-spaced. We recommend that you acquaint yourself with the magazine before submitting."

N $ WEST COAST LINE

A Journal of Contemporary Writing & Criticism, West Coast Review Publishing Society, 2027 E. Annex, 8888 University Dr., Simon Fraser University, Burnaby BC V5A 1S6 Canada. (604)291-4287. Fax: (604)291-4622. E-mail: wcl@sfu.ca. Web site: www.sfu.ca/west-coast-line. **Contact:** Roger Farr, managing editor. Triannual magazine of contemporary literature and criticism. Estab. 1990. Circ. 500. Pays on publication. Buys one-time rights. Editorial lead time 4 months. Accepts queries by mail, e-mail. Responds in up to 6 months to queries; up to 6 months to mss. Sample copy for $10. Writer's guidelines for SASE (US must include IRC).

Nonfiction Essays (literary/scholarly/critical), experimental prose. "No journalistic articles or articles dealing with nonliterary material." **Buys 8-10 mss/year.** Send complete ms. Length: 1,000-5,000 words. **Pays $8/page, 2 contributor's copies and a 1-year subscription.**

Fiction Experimental, novel excerpts. **Buys 3-6 mss/year.** Send complete ms. Length: 1,000-7,000 words. **Pays $8/page.**

Poetry Avant-garde. "No light verse, traditional." **Buys 10-15 poems/year.** Submit maximum maximum 5-6 poems.

Tips "Submissions must be either scholarly or formally innovative. Contributors should be familiar with current literary trends in Canada and the US. Scholars should be aware of current schools of theory. All submissions should be accompanied by a brief cover letter; essays should be formatted according to the MLA guide. The publication is not divided into departments. We accept innovative poetry, fiction, experimental prose, and scholarly essays."

$ WESTERN HUMANITIES REVIEW

University of Utah, English Department, 255 S. Central Campus Dr., Room 3500, Salt Lake City UT 84112-0494. (801)581-6070. Fax: (801)585-5167. E-mail: whr@mail.hum.utah.edu. Web site: www.hum.utah.edu/whr. **Contact:** David McGlynn, managing editor. Semiannual magazine for educated readers. Estab. 1947. Circ. 1,000. Pays on publication. Publishes ms an average of 1 year after acceptance. Buys all rights. Accepts simultaneous submissions. Sample copy for $10. Writer's guidelines online.

- Reads mss September 1-May 1. Mss sent outside these dates will be returned unread.

Nonfiction Barry Weller, editor-in-chief. Authoritative, readable articles on literature, art, philosophy, current events, history, religion, and anything in the humanities. Interdisciplinary articles encouraged. Departments on films and books. **Buys 4-5 unsolicited mss/year.** Send complete ms. **Pays $5/published page.**

Fiction Karen Brennan and Robin Hemley, fiction editors. Experimental. Does not want genre (romance, sci-fi, etc.). **Buys 8-12 mss/year.** Send complete ms. Length: 5,000 words. **Pays $5/published page (when funds available).**

Poetry Richard Howard, poetry editor.

Tips "Because of changes in our editorial staff, we urge familiarity with recent issues of the magazine. Inappropriate material will be returned without comment. We do not publish writer's guidelines because we think that the magazine itself conveys an accurate picture of our requirements. Please, no e-mail submissions."

N $ WINDSOR REVIEW

A Journal of the Arts, Dept. of English, University of Windsor, Windsor ON N9B 3P4 Canada. (519)253-3000. Fax: (519)971-3676. E-mail: uwrevu@uwindsor.ca. Web site: www.windsorreview.com. **Contact:** Laurie Gibson, editorial assistant. Semiannual magazine. "We try to offer a balance of fiction and poetry distinguished by excellence." Estab. 1965. Circ. 250. Pays on publication. Publishes ms an average of 6 months after acceptance. Buys one-time rights. Accepts queries by e-mail. Responds in 1 month to queries; 6 weeks to mss. Sample copy for $7 (US). Writer's guidelines online.

Fiction Alistair MacLeod, fiction editor. Literary. No genre fiction (science fiction, romance), "but would consider if writing is good enough." Send complete ms. Length: 1,000-5,000 words. **Pays $30, 1 contributor's copy and a free subscription.**

Poetry Submit maximum 6 poems.

Tips "Good writing, strong characters, and experimental fiction is appreciated."

$ $ THE YALE REVIEW

Yale University, P.O. Box 208243, New Haven CT 06520-8243. (203)432-0499. Fax: (203)432-0510. Web site: www.yale.edu. Associate Editor: Susan Bianconi. **Contact:** J.D. McClatchy, editor. **20% freelance written.** Quarterly magazine. Estab. 1911. Circ. 7,000. Pays prior to publication. Publishes ms an average of 6 months after acceptance. Buys one-time rights. Responds in 2 months to queries; 2 months to mss. Sample copy for $9, plus postage. Writer's guidelines online.

Nonfiction Authoritative discussions of politics, literature and the arts. No previously published submissions. Send complete ms with cover letter and SASE. Length: 3,000-5,000 words. **Pays $400-500.**

Fiction Buys quality fiction. Length: 3,000-5,000 words. **Pays $400-500.**

Poetry Pays $100-250.

$ ZAHIR

Unforgettable Tales, Zahir Publishing, 315 South Coast Hwy. 101, Suite U8, Encinitas CA 92024. E-mail: stempchin@zahirtales.com. Web site: www.zahirtales.com. **Contact:** Sheryl Tempchin, editor. **100% freelance written.** Triannual magazine covering speculative fiction. "We publish literary speculative fiction." Estab. 2003. Pays on publication. Publishes ms an average of 2-12 months after acceptance. Byline given. Buys first, second serial (reprint) rights. Accepts queries by e-mail. Accepts previously published material. Responds in 1-2 weeks to queries; 1-3 months to mss. Sample copy for $6.50 (US), $7.50 (Canada), $9.50 (international). Writer's guidelines for #10 SASE, by e-mail, or online.

Fiction Fantasy, science fiction, surrealism, magical realism. No children's stories or stories that deal with excessive violence or anything pornographic. **Buys 18-25 mss/year.** Send complete ms. Length: 6,000 words maximum. **Pays $10 and 2 contributor's copies.**

Tips "We look for great storytelling and fresh ideas. Let your imagination run wild and capture it in concise, evocative prose."

$$$ZOETROPE: ALL STORY

AZX Publications, The Sentinel Bldg., 916 Kearny St., San Francisco CA 94133. (415)788-7500. E-mail: info@all-story.com. Web site: www.all-story.com. **Contact:** Francis Ford Coppola, publisher; Michael Ray, editor. Quarterly magazine specializing in the best of contemporary short fiction. "*Zoetrope: All Story* presents a new generation of classic stories." Estab. 1997. Circ. 20,000. Publishes ms an average of 5 months after acceptance. Byline given. Buys first serial rights rights. Accepts queries by mail. Accepts simultaneous submissions. Responds in 8 months (if SASE included) to mss. Sample copy for $6.95. Writer's guidelines online.

- Does not accept submissions June 1-August 31.

Fiction Literary short stories, one-act plays. **Buys 25-35 mss/year.** Send complete ms. **Pays $1,000.**

Current and select back issues can be found online. "The Web site features current news, events, contests, workshops, writer's guidelines, and more. In addition, the site links to Francis Ford Coppola's Virtual Studio, which is host to an online workshop for short story writers."

$ZYZZYVA

The Last Word: West Coast Writers & Artists, P.O. Box 590069, San Francisco CA 94159-0069. (415)752-4393. Fax: (415)752-4391. E-mail: editor@zyzzyva.org. Web site: www.zyzzyva.org. **Contact:** Howard Junker, editor. **100% freelance written.** Works with a small number of new/unpublished writers each year. Magazine published in March, August, and November. "We feature work by writers currently living on the West Coast or in Alaska and Hawaii only. We are essentially a literary magazine, but of wide-ranging interests and a strong commitment to nonfiction." Estab. 1985. Circ. 3,500. **Pays on acceptance.** Publishes ms an average of 3 months after acceptance. Byline given. Buys first North American serial and one-time anthology rights. Accepts queries by mail, e-mail. Responds in 1 week to queries; 1 month to mss. Sample copy for $7 or online. Writer's guidelines online.

Nonfiction Book excerpts, general interest, historical/nostalgic, humor, personal experience. **Buys 50 mss/year.** Query by mail or e-mail. Length: Open. **Pays $50.**

Photos Reviews copies or slides only—scans at 300 dpi, 5½" wide.

Fiction Ethnic, experimental, humorous, mainstream. **Buys 20 mss/year.** Send complete ms. Length: 100-7,500 words. **Pays $50.**

Poetry Buys 20 poems/year. Submit maximum 5 poems. Length: 3-200 lines. **Pays $50.**

Tips "West Coast writers means those currently living in California, Alaska, Washington, Oregon, or Hawaii."

MEN'S

N $$$$CIGAR AFICIONADO

M. Shanken Communications, Inc., 387 Park Ave. S., 8th Floor, New York NY 10016. (212)684-4224. Fax: (212)684-5424. E-mail: gmott@mshanken.com. Web site: www.cigaraficionado.com. Assistant Managing Editor: Mike Marsh. **Contact:** Gordon Mott, editor. **75% freelance written.** Bimonthly magazine for affluent men. Estab. 1992. Circ. 275,000. **Pays on acceptance.** Publishes ms an average of 3-6 months after acceptance. Byline given. Offers 25% kill fee. Buys all rights. Editorial lead time 6 months. Submit seasonal material 6 months in advance. Accepts queries by e-mail. Responds in 1 month to queries; 2 months to mss. Sample copy for free.

Nonfiction General interest. Query. Length: 1,500-4,000 words. **Pays variable amount.** Pays expenses of writers on assignment.

Photos Contact Mary Galligun, photo editor.

N Ø DETAILS

Fairchild Publications, Inc., 7 W. 34th St., 4th Floor, New York NY 10001. (212)630-4000. Fax: (212)630-3815. E-mail: detailsletters@fairchildpub.com. Web site: www.details.com. Editor: Daniel Peres. Monthly lifestyle magazine for today's adult males. Circ. 425,000.

- Does not buy freelance material or use freelance writers.

$$$$ESQUIRE

Hearst Corp., 1790 Broadway, New York NY 10019. (212)649-4020. E-mail: esquire@hearst.com. Web site: www.esquire.com. Editor-in-Chief: David Granger. Monthly magazine covering the ever-changing trends in

American culture. Geared toward smart, well-off men. General readership is college educated and sophisticated, between ages 30 and 45. Written mostly by contributing editors on contract. Rarely accepts unsolicited mss. Estab. 1933. Circ. 720,000. Publishes ms an average of 2-6 months after acceptance. Retains first worldwide periodical publication rights for 90 days from cover date. Editorial lead time at least 2 months. Accepts simultaneous submissions. Writer's guidelines for SASE.

Nonfiction Focus is the ever-changing trends in American culture. Topics include current events and politics, social criticism, sports, celebrity profiles, the media, art and music, men's fashion. Queries must be sent by letter. **Buys 4 features and 12 shorter mss/year.** Length: Columns average 1,500 words; features average 5,000 words; short front of book pieces average 200-400 words. **Payment varies.**

Photos Uses mostly commissioned photography. Payment depends on size and number of photos.

Fiction "Literary excellence is our only criterion." Novel excerpts, short stories, memoirs, plays. No "pornography, science fiction or 'true romance' stories." Send complete ms.

Tips "A writer has the best chance of breaking in at *Esquire* by querying with a specific idea that requires special contacts and expertise. Ideas must be timely and national in scope."

⊘ FHM

For Him Magazine, Emap Metro, LLC, 110 5th Ave., 3rd Floor, New York NY 10011. (212)201-6700. Fax: (212)201-6980. E-mail: fhmedit@emapmetrousa.com. Web site: www.fhmus.com. Monthly magazine. Circ. 1,000,000.

- Does not buy freelance material or use freelance writers.

$ GC MAGAZINE

Handel Publishing, P.O. Box 331775, Fort Worth TX 76163. (817)640-1306. Fax: (817)633-9045. E-mail: rosa.gc@sbcglobal.net. Managing Editor: Rosa Flores. **80% freelance written.** Monthly magazine. "*GC Magazine* is a general entertainment magazine for men. We include entertainment celebrity interviews (movies, music, books) along with general interest articles for adult males." Estab. 1994. Circ. 53,000. Pays on publication. Publishes ms an average of 3 months after acceptance. Buys one-time rights. Editorial lead time 3 months. Submit seasonal material 6 months in advance. Accepts queries by mail, e-mail, fax. Accepts previously published material. Accepts simultaneous submissions. Responds in 3 months to queries. Sample copy for $1.50. Writer's guidelines for #10 SASE.

Nonfiction Book excerpts, essays, exposé, general interest, historical/nostalgic, how-to, humor, interview/profile, technical, travel, dating tips. **Buys 100 mss/year.** Query. Length: 1,000-2,000 words. **Pays 2¢/word.** Sometimes pays expenses of writers on assignment.

Reprints Accepts previously published submissions.

Photos State availability with submission. Reviews 3×5 prints, GIF/JPEG files. Buys one-time rights. Offers no additional payment for photos accepted with ms. Model releases required.

Columns/Departments Actress feature (film actress interviews), 2,500 words; Author feature (book author interviews), 1,500 words; Music feature (singer or band interviews), 1,500 words. **Buys 50 mss/year.** Query. **Pays 2¢/word.**

Tips "Submit material typed and free of errors. Writers should think of magazines like *Maxim* and *Details* when determining article ideas for our magazine. Our primary readership is adult males and we are seeking original and unique articles."

GQ

Conde Nast Publications, Inc., 4 Times Square, New York NY 10036. (212)286-2860. Fax: (212)286-7786. Web site: www.gq.com. Editorial Assistant: Sarah Wilson. Managing Editor: Martin Beiser. Senior Correspondent: Alan Richman. Senior Editor: Jason Gary. Senior Editor: John Gillies. Associate Editor: Brian Raftery. Monthly magazine covering subjects ranging from finance, food, entertainment, technology, celebrity profiles, sports and fashion. *Gentleman's Quarterly* is devoted to men's personal style and taste, from what he wears to the way he lives his life. Estab. 1957.

Nonfiction Interview/profile (celebrity).

$$$ INDY MEN'S MAGAZINE

The Guy's Guide to the Good Life, Table Moose Media, 8500 Keystone Crossing, Suite 100, Indianapolis IN 46240. (317)255-3850. Fax: (317)254-5944. E-mail: tim@indymensmagazine.com. Web site: www.indymensmagazine.com. **Contact:** Lou Harry, editor-in-chief. **50% freelance written.** Monthly magazine. Estab. 2002. Circ. 50,000. Pays on publication. Byline given. Offers 10% kill fee. Buys first North American serial rights. Editorial lead time 3 months. Submit seasonal material 1 year in advance. Accepts queries by mail. Accepts simultaneous submissions. Responds in 3 weeks to queries; 2 months to mss. Sample copy for $5. Writer's guidelines by e-mail.

Nonfiction Essays, travel. No generic pieces that could run anywhere. No advocacy pieces. **Buys 50 mss/year.** Query. Length: 100-2,000 words. **Pays $75-500 for assigned articles; $50-400 for unsolicited articles.** Sometimes pays expenses of writers on assignment.

Photos State availability with submission. Reviews contact sheets, transparencies, prints, GIF/JPEG files. Buys one-time rights. Negotiates payment individually. Identification of subjects required.

Columns/Departments Balls (opinionated sports pieces), 1,400 words; Dad Files (introspective parenting essays), 1,400 words; Men At Work (Indianapolis men and their jobs), 100-600 words; Trippin' (experiential travel), 1,500 words. **Buys 30 mss/year.** Query with published clips. **Pays $75-400.**

Fiction "The piece needs to hold our attention from the first paragraph." Adventure, fantasy, historical, horror, humorous, mainstream, mystery, science fiction, suspense. **Buys 12 mss/year.** Send complete ms. Length: 1,000-4,000 words. **Pays $50-250.**

Tips "We don't believe in wasting our reader's time, whether it's in a 50-word item or a 6,000-word Q&A. Our readers are smart, and they appreciate our sense of humor. Write to entertain and engage."

$ $ $ $ KING

Harris Publications, Inc., 1115 Broadway, 8th Floor, New York NY 10010. (212)467-9675. Fax: (212)807-0216. E-mail: siobhan@harris-pub.com. Web site: www.king-mag.com. Editor: Jermaine Hall. **Contact:** Siobhan O'Connor, deputy editor. **75% freelance written.** Men's lifestyle magazine published 10 times/year. "*King* is a general interest men's magazine with a strong editorial voice. Topics include lifestyle, entertainment, news, women, cars, music, fashion, investigative reporting." Estab. 2001. Circ. 270,000. Pays on publication. Byline given. Offers 25% kill fee. Buys all rights. Editorial lead time 2-3 months. Submit seasonal material 4 months in advance. Accepts queries by e-mail. Responds in 1 month to queries. Writer's guidelines free.

Nonfiction Essays, exposé, general interest. Does not want completed articles. Pitches only. Query with published clips. Length: 2,000-5,000 words. **Pays $1-2.50/word.** Sometimes pays expenses of writers on assignment.

MAXIM

Dennis Publishing, 1040 Avenue of the Americas, 16th Floor, New York NY 10018-3703. (212)302-2626. Fax: (212)302-2635. E-mail: editors@maximmag.com. Web site: www.maximonline.com. Editor: Keith Blanchard. Monthly magazine covering relationships, sex, women, careers and sports. Written for young, professional men interested in fun and informative articles. Circ. 2,500,000. Editorial lead time 5 months. Sample copy for $3.99 at newstands.

MEN'S JOURNAL

Wenner Media, Inc., 1290 Avenue of the Americas, 2nd Floor, New York NY 10104-0295. (212)484-1616. Fax: (212)484-3434. E-mail: letters@mensjournal.com. Web site: www.mensjournal.com. Features Editor: Bill Gifford. Monthly magazine covering general lifestyle for men, ages 25-49. "*Men's Journal* is for active men with an interest in participatory sports, travel, fitness, and adventure. It provides practical, informative articles on how to spend quality leisure time." Estab. 1992. Circ. 650,000. Accepts queries by mail, fax.

Nonfiction Features and profiles 2,000-7,000 words; shorter features of 400-1,200 words; equipment and fitness stories, 400-1,800 words. Book excerpts, essays, exposé, general interest, historical/nostalgic, how-to, humor, new product, personal experience, photo feature, travel. Query with SASE. **Payment varies.**

$ $ $ $ SMOKE MAGAZINE

Life's Burning Desires, Lockwood Publications, 26 Broadway, Floor 9M, New York NY 10004. (212)391-2060. Fax: (212)827-0945. E-mail: editor@smokemag.com. Web site: www.smokemag.com. Editor: Ted Hoyt. **50% freelance written.** Quarterly magazine covering cigars and men's lifestyle issues. "A large majority of *Smoke's* readers are affluent men, ages 28-50; active, educated and adventurous." Estab. 1995. Circ. 175,000. Pays 2 months after publication. Publishes ms an average of 3 months after acceptance. Byline given. Offers 25% kill fee. Buys first rights. Editorial lead time 2 months. Submit seasonal material 6 months in advance. Accepts queries by mail, e-mail. Accepts simultaneous submissions. Responds in 6 weeks to queries; 3 months to mss. Sample copy for $4.99.

O━ Break in with "good nonfiction that interests guys—beer, cuisine, true-crime, sports, cigars. Be original."

Nonfiction Essays, exposé, general interest, historical/nostalgic, how-to, humor, interview/profile, opinion, personal experience, photo feature, technical, travel, true crime. **Buys 8 mss/year.** Query with published clips. Length: 1,500-3,000 words. **Pays $500-1,200.** Sometimes pays expenses of writers on assignment.

Photos State availability with submission. Reviews $2\frac{1}{4} \times 2\frac{1}{4}$ transparencies. Negotiates payment individually. Identification of subjects required.

Columns/Departments Smoke Undercover (investigative journalism, personal experience); Smoke Screen (TV/

film/entertainment issues); Smoke City (cigar-related travel), all 1,500 words. **Buys 8 mss/year.** Query with published clips. **Pays $500-1,000.**

Tips "Send a short, clear query with clips. Go with your field of expertise: cigars, sports, music, true crime, etc."

STUFF

Dennis Publishing, 1040 Avenue of the Americas, 12th Floor, New York NY 10018. (212)372-3801. Fax: (212)354-4364. E-mail: editors@stuffmagazine.com. Web site: www.stuffmagazine.com. Editor-in-Chief: Jimmy Jellinek. Monthly magazine. Targeted towards American men who want sex, sports, gadgets, entertainment and humor. Circ. 1,200,000. Editorial lead time 3 months. Sample copy not available.

$ $ UMM (URBAN MALE MAGAZINE)

Canada's Only Lifestyle and Fashion Magazine for Men, UMM Publishing Inc., 70 George St., Suite 200, Ottawa ON K1N 5V9 Canada. (613)723-6216. Fax: (613)723-1702. E-mail: editor@umm.ca. Web site: www.umm.ca. **100% freelance written.** Bimonthly magazine covering men's interests. "Our audience is young men, aged 18-24. We focus on Canadian activities, interests, and lifestyle issues. Our magazine is fresh and energetic and we look for original ideas carried out with a spark of intelligence and/or humour (and you'd better spell humour with a 'u')." Estab. 1998. Circ. 90,000. Pays 1 month after publication. Publishes ms an average of 3 months after acceptance. Byline given. Buys first North American serial rights. Editorial lead time 3 months. Submit seasonal material 4 months in advance. Accepts queries by e-mail. Accepts simultaneous submissions. Responds in 6 weeks to queries; 6 weeks to mss.

Nonfiction Book excerpts, exposé, general interest, historical/nostalgic, how-to, humor, interview/profile, new product, personal experience, travel, adventure, cultural, sports, music. **Buys 80 mss/year.** Query with published clips. Length: 1,200-3,500 words. **Pays $100-400.** Sometimes pays expenses of writers on assignment.

Photos State availability with submission. Reviews contact sheets, prints. Buys one-time rights. Negotiates payment individually.

Fillers Anecdotes, facts, short humor. **Buys 35/year.** Length: 100-500 words. **Pays $50-150.**

Tips "Be familiar with our magazine before querying. We deal with all subjects of interest to young men, especially those with Canadian themes. We are very open-minded. Original ideas and catchy writing are key."

MILITARY

$ $ AIR FORCE TIMES

Army Times Publishing Co., 6883 Commercial Dr., Springfield VA 22159. (703)750-8646. Fax: (703)750-8601. E-mail: lbacon@airforcetimes.com. Web site: www.airforcetimes.com. **Contact:** Lance Bacon, managing editor. Weeklies edited separately for Army, Navy, Marine Corps, and Air Force military personnel and their families. They contain career information such as pay raises, promotions, news of legislation affecting the military, housing, base activities and features of interest to military people. Estab. 1940. **Pays on acceptance.** Byline given. Offers kill fee. Buys first rights. Accepts queries by mail, e-mail, phone. Accepts simultaneous submissions. Responds in 1 month to queries. Sample copy for #10 SASE. Writer's guidelines for #10 SASE.

Nonfiction Features of interest to career military personnel and their families. No advice pieces. **Buys 150-175 mss/year.** Query. Length: 750-2,000 words. **Pays $100-500.**

Columns/Departments Length: 500-900. **Buys 75 mss/year. Pays $75-125.**

The online magazines carry original content not found in the print editions. Web sites: www.armytimes.com; www.navytimes.com; www.airforcetimes.com; www.marinecorpstimes.com. Contact: Kent Miller, online editor.

Tips Looking for "stories on active duty, reserve and retired military personnel; stories on military matters and localized military issues; stories on successful civilian careers after military service."

N $ $ AIRFORCE

Air Force Productions, P.O Box 2460, Stn "D", Ottawa ON K1P 5W6 Canada. (613)232-2303. Fax: (613)232-2156. E-mail: vjohnson@airforce.ca. Web site: www.airforce.ca. **Contact:** Vic Johnson, editor. **5% freelance written.** Quarterly magazine covering Canada's air force heritage. Stories center on Canadian military aviation—past, present and future. Estab. 1977. Circ. 16,500. Pays on publication. Publishes ms an average of 6 months after acceptance. Byline given. Not copyrighted. Buys all rights. Editorial lead time 3 months. Submit seasonal material 3 months in advance. Accepts queries by mail, e-mail, fax, phone. Accepts previously published material. Accepts simultaneous submissions. Responds in 2 weeks to queries; 1 month to mss. Sample copy for free. Writer's guidelines by e-mail.

Nonfiction Historical/nostalgic, interview/profile, personal experience, photo feature. **Buys 2 mss/year.** Query

with published clips. Length: 1,500-3,500 words. Sometimes pays expenses of writers on assignment.
Photos Send photos with submission. Reviews prints, GIF/JPEG files. Buys one-time rights. Captions, identification of subjects required.
Fillers Anecdotes, facts. Length: About 800 words. **Pays negotiable.**
Tips "Writers should have a good background in Canadian military history."

$ $ ARMY MAGAZINE

2425 Wilson Blvd., Arlington VA 22201-3385. (703)841-4300. Fax: (703)841-3505. E-mail: armymag@ausa.org. Web site: www.ausa.org. **Contact:** Mary Blake French, editor-in-chief. **70% freelance written.** Prefers to work with published/established writers. Monthly magazine emphasizing military interests. Estab. 1904. Circ. 90,000. Pays on publication. Publishes ms an average of 5 months after acceptance. Byline given. Buys all rights. Submit seasonal material 3 months in advance. Accepts queries by mail. Sample copy for 9×12 SAE with $1 postage or online. Writer's guidelines for 9×12 SAE with $1 postage or online.

- *Army Magazine* looks for shorter articles.

Nonfiction "We would like to see more pieces about little-known episodes involving interesting military personalities. We especially want material lending itself to heavy, contributor-supplied photographic treatment. The first thing a contributor should recognize is that our readership is very savvy militarily. 'Gee-whiz' personal reminiscences get short shrift, unless they hold their own in a company in which long military service, heroism and unusual experiences are commonplace. At the same time, *Army* readers like a well-written story with a fresh slant, whether it is about an experience in a foxhole or the fortunes of a corps in battle." Historical/nostalgic (military and original), humor (military feature-length articles and anecdotes), interview/profile, photo feature. No rehashed history. No unsolicited book reviews. **Buys 40 mss/year.** Submit complete ms (hard copy and disk). Length: 1,000-1,500 words. **Pays 12-18¢/word.**
Photos Send photos with submission. Reviews prints, slides, high resolution digital photos. Buys all rights. Pays $50-100 for 8×10 b&w glossy prints; $50-350 for 8×10 color glossy prints and 35mm and high resolution digital photos. Captions required.

$ $ ARMY TIMES

Army Times Publishing Co., 6883 Commercial Dr., Springfield VA 22159. (703)750-9000. Fax: (703)750-8622. E-mail: aneill@armytimes.com. Web site: www.armytimes.com. **Contact:** Alex Neill, managing editor. Weekly for Army military personnel and their families containing career information such as pay raises, promotions, news of legislation affecting the military, housing, base activities and features of interest to military people. Estab. 1940. Circ. 230,000. **Pays on acceptance.** Byline given. Offers kill fee. Makes work-for-hire assignments. Accepts queries by mail, e-mail. Accepts simultaneous submissions. Responds in 1 month to queries. Sample copy and writer's guidelines for #10 SASE.

O→ Break in by "proposing specific feature stories that only you can write—things we wouldn't be able to get from 'generic' syndicated or wire material. The story must contain an element of mystery and/or surprise, and be entertaining as well as informative. Above all, your story must have a direct connection to military people's needs and interests."

Nonfiction Features of interest to career military personnel and their families: food, relationships, parenting, education, retirement, shelter, health, and fitness, sports, personal appearance, community, recreation, personal finance, entertainment. No advice please. **Buys 150-175 mss/year.** Query. Length: 750-2,000 words. **Pays $100-500.**
Columns/Departments Length: 500-900 words. **Buys 75 mss/year. Pays $75-125.**
Tips Looking for "stories on active duty, reserve and retired military personnel; stories on military matters and localized military issues; stories on successful civilian careers after military service."

N $ COMBAT HANDGUNS

Harris Outdoor Group, 1115 Broadway, New York NY 10010. (212)807-7100. Fax: (212)807-1479. E-mail: combat@harris-custsvc.com. Web site: www.combathandguns.com. Magazine published 8 times/year covering combat handguns. Written for handgun owners and collectors. Circ. 126,498. Editorial lead time 2 months. Accepts queries by mail, e-mail. Sample copy not available.
Nonfiction Query.
Photos Send photos with submission. Reviews GIF/JPEG files. Captions required.

$ $ MARINE CORPS TIMES

Army Times Publishing Co., 6883 Commercial Dr., Springfield VA 22159. (703)750-9000. Fax: (703)750-8767. E-mail: rcolenso@marinecorpstimes.com. Web site: www.marinecorpstimes.com. **Contact:** Rob Colenso, managing editor, *Marine Corps Times*. Weeklies edited separately for Army, Navy, Marine Corps, and Air Force military personnel and their families. They contain career information such as pay raises, promotions, news of legislation affecting the military, housing, base activities and features of interest to military people. Estab. 1940. Circ. 230,000 (combined). Pays on publication. Byline given. Offers kill fee. Buys first rights. Accepts queries by mail, e-mail, phone. Accepts simultaneous submissions. Responds in 1 month to queries. Sample copy for #10 SASE. Writer's guidelines for #10 SASE.

Nonfiction Features of interest to career military personnel and their families, including stories on current military operations and exercises. No advice pieces. **Buys 150-175 mss/year.** Query. Length: 750-2,000 words. **Pays $100-500.**

Columns/Departments Length: 500-900 words. **Buys 75 mss/year. Pays $75-125.**

The online magazines carry original content not found in the print editions. Web sites: www.armytimes.com; www.navytimes.com; www.airforcetimes.com. Contact: Kent Miller, online editor.

Tips Looking for "stories on active duty, reserve and retired military personnel; stories on military matters and localized military issues; stories on successful civilian careers after military service."

$ $ $ MILITARY OFFICER

201 N. Washington St., Alexandria VA 22314-2539. (800)234-6622. Fax: (703)838-8179. E-mail: editor@moaa.org. Web site: www.moaa.org. Editor: Col. Warren S. Lacy, USA-Ret. **Contact:** Managing Editor. **60% freelance written.** Prefers to work with published/established writers. Monthly magazine for officers of the 7 uniformed services and their families. Estab. 1945. Circ. 389,000. **Pays on acceptance.** Publishes ms an average of 1 year after acceptance. Byline given. Buys first North American serial rights. Accepts queries by e-mail. Responds in 3 months to queries. Sample copy and writer's guidelines online.

Nonfiction Current military/political affairs, finance, health and wellness, recent military history, travel, military family life-style. Emphasis now on current military and defense issues. "We rarely accept unsolicited manuscripts." **Buys 48 mss/year.** Query with résumé, sample clips. Length: 800-2,500 words. **Pays 80¢/word.**

Photos Query with list of stock photo subjects. Original slides and transparencies must be suitable for color separation. Reviews transparencies. Pays $20 for each 8×10 b&w photo (normal halftone) used. Pays $75-250 for inside color; $300 for cover.

$ $ NAVAL HISTORY

U.S. Naval Institute, 291 Wood Rd., Annapolis MD 21402-5034. (410)295-1079. Fax: (410)295-1049. E-mail: rlatture@usni.org. Web site: www.navalinstitute.org. Associate Editor: Jim Caiella. **Contact:** Richard G. Latture, editor-in-chief. **90% freelance written.** Bimonthly magazine covering naval and maritime history, worldwide. "We are committed, as a publication of the 130-year-old U.S. Naval Institute, to presenting the best and most accurate short works in international naval and maritime history. We do find a place for academicians, but they should be advised that a good story generally wins against a dull topic, no matter how well researched." Estab. 1988. Circ. 40,000. Pays on publication. Publishes ms an average of 2 years after acceptance. Byline given. Buys all rights. Editorial lead time 6 months. Submit seasonal material 6 months in advance. Accepts queries by mail, e-mail, fax, phone. Responds in 1 month to queries; 2 months to mss. Sample copy for $4.99 and SASE, or on Web site. Writer's guidelines online.

Nonfiction Book excerpts, essays, historical/nostalgic, humor, inspirational, interview/profile, personal experience, photo feature, technical. **Buys 50 mss/year.** Query. Length: 1,000-3,000 words. **Pays $300-500 for assigned articles; $75-400 for unsolicited articles.**

Photos State availability with submission. Reviews contact sheets, transparencies, 4×6 or larger prints, and digital submissions or CD-ROM. Buys one-time rights. Offers $10 minimum. Captions, identification of subjects, model releases required.

Fillers Anecdotes, newsbreaks (naval-related), short humor. **Buys 40-50/year.** Length: 50-1,000 words. **Pays $10-50.**

Tips "A good way to break in is to write a good, concise, exciting story supported by primary sources and substantial illustrations. Naval history-related news items (ship decommissionings, underwater archaeology, etc.) are also welcome. Because our story bank is substantial, competition is severe. Tying a topic to an anniversary many times is an advantage. We still are in need of Korean and Vietnam War-era material."

$ PARAMETERS

U.S. Army War College Quarterly, U.S. Army War College, 122 Forbes Ave., Carlisle PA 17013-5238. (717)245-4943. E-mail: parameters@carlisle.army.mil. Web site: www.carlisle.army.mil/usawc/parameters. **Contact:** Col. Robert H. Taylor, USA Ret., editor. **100% freelance written.** Prefers to work with published/established writers or experts in the field. Readership consists of senior leaders of US defense establishment, both uniformed and civilian, plus members of the media, government, industry and academia. Subjects include national and international security affairs, military strategy, military leadership and management, art and science of warfare, and military history with contemporary relevance. Estab. 1971. Circ. 13,500. Pays on publication. Publishes ms an average of 6 months after acceptance. Byline given. Accepts queries by mail, e-mail, phone. Responds in 6 weeks to queries. Sample copy free or online. Writer's guidelines online.

Nonfiction Prefers articles that deal with current security issues, employ critical analysis, and provide solutions or recommendations. Liveliness and verve, consistent with scholarly integrity, appreciated. Theses, studies, and academic course papers should be adapted to article form prior to submission. Documentation in complete endnotes. Send complete ms. Length: 4,500 words average. **Pays $200-300 average.**

Tips "Make it short; keep it interesting; get criticism and revise accordingly. Write on a contemporary topic. Tackle a subject only if you are an authority. No fax submissions." Encourage e-mail submissions.

$ $ PROCEEDINGS

U.S. Naval Institute, 291 Wood Rd., Annapolis MD 21402-5034. (410)268-6110. Fax: (410)295-7940. E-mail: articlesubmissions@navalinstitute.org. Web site: www.usni.org. Editor: Fred H. Rainbow. **Contact:** Gordon Keiser, senior editor. **80% freelance written.** Monthly magazine covering Navy, Marine Corps, Coast Guard issues. Estab. 1873. Circ. 100,000. **Pays on acceptance.** Publishes ms an average of 9 months after acceptance. Byline given. Buys all rights. Editorial lead time 3 months. Responds in 2 months to queries. Sample copy for $3.95. Writer's guidelines online.

Nonfiction Essays, historical/nostalgic, interview/profile, photo feature, technical. **Buys 100-125 mss/year.** Query with or without published clips or send complete ms. Length: 3,000 words. **Pays $60-150/printed page for unsolicited articles.**

Photos State availability of or send photos with submission. Reviews transparencies, prints. Buys one-time rights. Offers $25/photo maximum.

Columns/Departments Comment & Discussion (letters to editor), 750 words; Commentary (opinion), 900 words; Nobody Asked Me, But . . . (opinion), less than 1,000 words. **Buys 150-200 mss/year.** Query or send complete ms. **Pays $34-150.**

Fillers Anecdotes. **Buys 20/year.** Length: 100 words. **Pays $25.**

$ $ $ $ SOLDIER OF FORTUNE

The Journal of Professional Adventurers, 5735 Arapahoe Ave., Suite A-5, Boulder CO 80303-1340. (303)449-3750. E-mail: editorsof@aol.com. Web site: www.sofmag.com. **50% freelance written.** Monthly magazine covering military, paramilitary, police, combat subjects, and action/adventure. "We are an action-oriented magazine; we cover combat hot spots around the world. We also provide timely features on state-of-the-art weapons and equipment; elite military and police units; and historical military operations. Readership is primarily active-duty military, veterans, and law enforcement." Estab. 1975. Circ. 60,000. Byline given. Offers 25% kill fee. Buys first rights. Responds in 3 weeks to queries; 1 month to mss. Sample copy for $5. Writer's guidelines for #10 SASE.

Nonfiction Exposé, general interest, historical/nostalgic, how-to (on weapons and their skilled use), humor, interview/profile, new product, personal experience, photo feature (No. 1 on our list), technical, travel, combat reports, military unit reports, and solid Vietnam and Operation Iraqi Freedom articles. "No 'How I won the war' pieces; no op-ed pieces unless they are fully and factually backgrounded; no knife articles (staff assignments only). All submitted articles should have good art; art will sell us on an article." **Buys 75 mss/year.** Query with or without published clips or send complete ms. Send mss to articles editor; queries to managing editor. Length: 2,000-3,000 words. **Pays $150-250/page.**

Reprints Send disk copy, photocopy of article and information about when and where the material previously appeared. Pays 25% of amount paid for an original article.

Photos Send photos with submission. Reviews contact sheets, transparencies. Buys one-time rights. Pays $500 for cover photo. Captions, identification of subjects required.

Fillers Bulletin Board editor. Newsbreaks (military/paramilitary related has to be documented). Length: 100-250 words. **Pays $50.**

Tips "Submit a professionally prepared, complete package. All artwork with cutlines, double-spaced typed manuscript with 5.25 or 3.5 IBM-compatible disk, if available, cover letter including synopsis of article, supporting documentation where applicable, etc. Manuscript must be factual; writers have to do their homework and get all their facts straight. One error means rejection. Vietnam features, if carefully researched and art heavy, will always get a careful look. Combat reports, again, with good art, are No. 1 in our book and stand the best chance of being accepted. Military unit reports from around the world are well received, as are law-enforcement articles (units, police in action). If you write for us, be complete and factual; pros read *Soldier of Fortune*, and are very quick to let us know if we (and the author) err."

MUSIC

$ AMERICAN SONGWRITER MAGAZINE

1303 16th Ave. S., Nashville TN 37212. (615)321-6096. Fax: (615)321-6097. E-mail: info@americansongwriter.com. Web site: www.americansongwriter.com. **Contact:** Douglas Waterman, editor. **90% freelance written.**

Bimonthly magazine about songwriters and the craft of songwriting for many types of music, including pop, country, rock, metal, jazz, gospel, and r&b. Estab. 1984. Circ. 5,000. Pays on publication. Publishes ms an average of 2 months after acceptance. Offers 25% kill fee. Buys first North American serial rights. Accepts previously published material. Responds in 2 months to queries. Sample copy for $4. Writer's guidelines for #10 SASE or by e-mail.

Nonfiction General interest, interview/profile, new product, technical, home demo studios, movie and TV scores, performance rights organizations. **Buys 20 mss/year.** Query with published clips. Length: 300-1,200 words. **Pays $25-60.**

Reprints Send tearsheet or photocopy and information about when and where the material previously appeared. Pays same amount as paid for an original article.

Photos Send photos with submission. Reviews 3×5 prints. Buys one-time rights. Offers no additional payment for photos accepeted with ms. Identification of subjects required.

Tips "*American Songwriter* strives to present articles which can be read a year or 2 after they were written and still be pertinent to the songwriter reading them."

N BILLBOARD

VNU Business Media, 770 Broadway, 6th Floor, New York NY 10003-9593. (646)654-5220. Fax: (646)-654-4681. E-mail: info@billboard.com. Web site: www.billboard.com. Executive Editor: Ken Schlager. Features Editor: Marc Schiffman. Music Editor: Melinda Newman. Weekly magazine. Provides news, reviews, and statistics for all genres of music, including radio play, music video, related internet activity, and retail updates. Circ. 34,020. Editorial lead time 2 months.

BLACK BEAT

Dorchester Media, LLC, 333 7th Ave., 11th Floor, New York NY 10001. (212)780-3500. Fax: (212)979-4825. Web site: www.blackbeat.com. Editor-in-Chief: Danica Daniel. Bimonthly magazine covering the nouveau hip-hop culture and all the gloss that lifestyle promotes. Circ. 80,000.

BLENDER

The Ultimate Music Magazine, Dennis Publishing, 1040 Avenue of The Americas, New York NY 10018. (212)302-2626. Fax: (212)302-2635. E-mail: info@blender.com. Web site: www.blender.com. Editor-in-Chief: Craig Marks. Managing Editor: Adam Bell. Bimonthly magazine covering music for ages 18-34. "Discusses cutting-edge trends across several musical genres." Circ. 410,000. Byline given. Editorial lead time 2 months. Accepts queries by e-mail. Sample copy for $2.99.

Nonfiction Book excerpts, interview/profile (bands, musical artists), new product, reviews—CD, concert, film.

Photos Photography Editor: Tanya Martin.

$ $ BLUEGRASS UNLIMITED

Bluegrass Unlimited, Inc., P.O. Box 771, Warrenton VA 20188-0771. (540)349-8181 or (800)BLU-GRAS. Fax: (540)341-0011. E-mail: editor@bluegrassmusic.com. Web site: www.bluegrassmusic.com. Editor: Peter V. Kuykendall. **Contact:** Sharon McGraw, managing editor. **10% freelance written.** Prefers to work with published/established writers. Monthly magazine covering bluegrass, acoustic, and old-time country music. Estab. 1966. Circ. 27,000. Pays on publication. Publishes ms an average of 4 months after acceptance. Byline given. Offers negotiated kill fee. Buys first North American serial, one-time, second serial (reprint), all rights. Submit seasonal material 4 months in advance. Accepts queries by mail, e-mail, fax. Responds in 2 weeks to queries; 2 months to mss. Sample copy for free. Writer's guidelines for #10 SASE.

Nonfiction General interest, historical/nostalgic, how-to, interview/profile, personal experience, photo feature, travel. No "fan"-style articles. **Buys 30-40 mss/year.** Query with or without published clips. Length: Open. **Pays 10-13¢/word.**

Reprints Send photocopy with rights for sale noted and information about when and where the material previously appeared. Payment is negotiable.

Photos State availability of or send photos with submission. Reviews 35mm transparencies and 3×5, 5×7 and 8×10 b&w and color prints. Buys all rights. Pays $50-175 for transparencies; $25-60 for b&w prints; $50-250 for color prints. Identification of subjects required.

Fiction Ethnic, humorous. **Buys 3-5 mss/year.** Query. Length: Negotiable. **Pays 10-13¢/word.**

Tips "We would prefer that articles be informational, based on personal experience or an interview with lots of quotes from subject, profile, humor, etc."

$ $ CHAMBER MUSIC

Chamber Music America, 305 Seventh Ave., 5th Floor, New York NY 10001-6008. (212)242-2022. Fax: (212)242-7955. Web site: www.chamber-music.org. **Contact:** Editor. Bimonthly magazine covering chamber music. Estab. 1977. Circ. 13,000. Pays on publication. Publishes ms an average of 5 months after acceptance. Byline given. Offers kill fee. Buys first rights. Editorial lead time 4 months. Accepts queries by mail, phone.

Nonfiction Book excerpts, essays, humor, opinion, personal experience, issue-oriented stories of relevance to the chamber music fields written by top music journalists and critics, or music practitioners. No artist profiles, no stories about opera or symphonic work. **Buys 35 mss/year.** Query with published clips. Length: 2,500-3,500 words. **Pays $500 minimum.** Sometimes pays expenses of writers on assignment.

Photos State availability with submission. Offers no payment for photos accepted with ms.

$ CHART MAGAZINE

Canada's Music Magazine, Chart Communications, Inc., 41 Britain St., Suite 200, Toronto ON M5A 1R7 Canada. (416)363-3101. Fax: (416)363-3109. E-mail: chart@chartattack.com. Web site: www.chartattack.com. Editor: Nada Laskovski. **Contact:** Aaron Brophy, managing editor. **90% freelance written.** Monthly magazine. *Chart Magazine* has a "cutting edge attitude toward music and pop culture to fit with youth readership." Estab. 1990. Circ. 40,000 (paid). Pays on publication. Publishes ms an average of 3-6 months after acceptance. Byline given. Buys first North American serial, electronic rights. Editorial lead time 2 months. Submit seasonal material 3 months in advance. Accepts queries by mail, e-mail, fax, phone. Responds in 4-6 weeks to queries; 2-3 months to mss. Sample copy for $6 US (via mail order). Writer's guidelines free.

Nonfiction All articles must relate to popular music and/or pop culture. Book excerpts, essays, exposé, humor, interview/profile, personal experience, photo feature. Nothing that isn't related to popular music and pop culture (i.e., film, books, video games, fashion, etc., that would appeal to a hip youth demographic). Query with published clips and send complete ms. Length: varies. **Payment varies.**

Photos Steven Balaban, art director. Send photos with submission. Buys all rights. Negotiates payment individually.

N CHURCH MUSIC QUARTERLY

The Royal School of Church Music, 10 Elm Rd., Ewell Surrey KT17 2EU United Kingdom. (44)(208)393-5207. Fax: (44)(172)242-4849. E-mail: cmq@rscm.com. Web site: www.rscm.com. **Contact:** Esther Jones, editor. Quarterly publication that offers advice, information, and inspiration to church music enthusiasts around the world. Each issue offers a variety of articles and interviews by distinguished musicians, theologians, and scholars. Circ. 16,000. Accepts queries by e-mail. Writer's guidelines by e-mail.

- Does not pay for unsolcited articles. Pays £60/page upon publication for commissioned articles.

Nonfiction All articles must relate to church music and most have an educational element and fall into one of these categories: church music history, composer profiles, theology of music/liturgy, practical advice for church musicians/clergy, arts/education news, reports on developments in church music around the world. Submit ms, bio. Length: 1,400 words.

Photos Reviews prints, 300 dpi digital images.

$$$ GUITAR ONE

The Magazine You Can Play, 149 5th St., 9th Floor, New York NY 10010. (212)768-2966. Fax: (212)944-9279. E-mail: editors@guitaronemag.com. Web site: www.guitaronemag.com. **75% freelance written.** Monthly magazine covering guitar news, artists, music, gear. Estab. 1996. Circ. 140,000. Pays on publication. Publishes ms an average of 1 month after acceptance. Byline given. Offers 50% kill fee. Buys one-time rights. Editorial lead time 3 months. Accepts queries by mail, e-mail, fax. Accepts simultaneous submissions. Sample copy online.

Nonfiction Interview/profile (with guitarists). **Buys 15 mss/year.** Query with published clips. Length: 2,000-5,000 words. **Pays $300-1,200 for assigned articles; $150-800 for unsolicited articles.** Sometimes pays expenses of writers on assignment.

Photos State availability with submission. Reviews negatives, transparencies, prints. Buys one-time rights. Negotiates payment individually.

Tips "Find an interesting feature with a nice angle that pertains to guitar enthusiasts. Submit a well-written draft or samples of work."

$$ GUITAR PLAYER MAGAZINE

United Entertainment Media, Inc., 2800 Campus Dr., San Mateo CA 94403. (650)513-4300. Fax: (650)513-4616. E-mail: mmolenda@musicplayer.com. Web site: www.guitarplayer.com. **Contact:** Michael Molenda, editor-in-chief. **50% freelance written.** Monthly magazine for persons "interested in guitars, guitarists, manufacturers, guitar builders, equipment, careers, etc." Circ. 150,000. **Pays on acceptance.** Publishes ms an average of 3 months after acceptance. Byline given. Buys first serial and all reprint rights. Accepts queries by e-mail. Responds in 6 weeks to queries. Writer's guidelines for #10 SASE.

Nonfiction Publishes "wide variety of articles pertaining to guitars and guitarists: interviews, guitar craftsmen profiles, how-to features—anything amateur and professional guitarists would find fascinating and/or helpful.

In interviews with 'name' performers, be as technical as possible regarding strings, guitars, techniques, etc. We're not a pop culture magazine, but a magazine for musicians. The essential question: What can the reader take away from a story to become a better player?" **Buys 30-40 mss/year.** Query. Length: Open. **Pays $250-450.** Sometimes pays expenses of writers on assignment.

Photos Reviews 35 mm color transparencies, b&w glossy prints. Buys one-time rights. Payment varies.

N $ MUSIC FOR THE LOVE OF IT

67 Parkside Dr., Berkeley CA 94705. (510)654-9134. Fax: (510)654-4656. E-mail: tedrust@musicfortheloveofit.com. Web site: www.musicfortheloveofit.com. **Contact:** Ted Rust, editor. **20% freelance written.** Bimonthly newsletter covering amateur musicianship. "A lively, intelligent source of ideas and enthusiasm for a musically literate audience of adult amateur musicians." Estab. 1988. Circ. 600. Pays on publication. Publishes ms an average of 2 months after acceptance. Byline given. Buys one-time rights. Editorial lead time 1 month. Submit seasonal material 1 month in advance. Accepts queries by mail, e-mail, fax, phone. Responds in 1 week to queries; 1 month to mss. Sample copy for $6. Writer's guidelines online.

Break in with "a good article, written from a musician's point of view, with at least 1 photo."

Nonfiction Essays, historical/nostalgic, how-to, personal experience, photo feature. No concert reviews, star interviews, CD reviews. **Buys 6 mss/year.** Query. Length: 500-1,500 words. **Pays $50, or gift subscriptions.**

Photos State availability with submission. Reviews 4×6 prints or larger. Buys one-time rights. Offers no additional payment for photos accepted with ms. Identification of subjects required.

Tips "We're looking for more good how-to articles on musical styles. Love making music. Know something about it."

RELIX MAGAZINE

Music for the Mind, 104 W. 29th St., 11th Floor, New York NY 10001. (646)230-0100. Web site: www.relix.com. **Contact:** Aeve Baldwin, editor-in-chief. **30% freelance written.** Magazine published 8 times/year focusing on new and independent bands, classic rock, lifestyles, and music alternatives such as roots, improvisational music, psychedelia, and jambands. Estab. 1974. Circ. 100,000. Pays on publication. Publishes ms an average of 4 months after acceptance. Byline given. Buys one-time rights. Accepts queries by mail, e-mail. Responds in 3 months to queries. Sample copy for $5. Writer's guidelines online.

Nonfiction Feature topics include jambands, reggae, Grateful Dead, bluegrass, jazz, rock, experimental, electronic, and world music; also deals with environmental, cultural, and lifestyle issues. Historical/nostalgic, humor, interview/profile, photo feature, technical, live reviews, new artists, hippy lifestyles, food, mixed media, books. Query by e-mail with published clips if available or send complete ms. Length: 300-1,500 words. **Pays variable rates.**

Columns/Departments Query with published clips or send complete ms. **Pays variable rates.**

Tips "The best part of working with freelance writers is discovering new music we might never have stumbled across."

⊘ REVOLVER

Future US, Inc., 149 Fifth Ave., 9th Floor, New York NY 10010. Web site: www.revolvermag.com. Quarterly magazine covering artists from indie pop, classic rock, acid jazz, hip-hop, punk and more. Targets young men ages 18-34. Circ. 150,000.

- Query before submitting.

RIGHT ON!

Dorchester Media LLC, 333 7th Ave., 11th Floor, New York NY 10001. (212)780-3500, ext. 3516. Fax: (212)979-4825. Web site: www.rightonmag.com. Editor-in-Chief: Danica Daniel. Bimonthly magazine covering the hip-hop culture, entertainment, fashion, beauty, etc. "A truly sweet but street publication." Circ. 100,000.

⊘ ROLLING STONE

Wenner Media, 1290 Avenue of the Americas, New York NY 10104. (212)484-1616. Fax: (212)484-1664. E-mail: letters@rollingstone.com. Web site: www.rollingstone.com. Editor: Jann S. Wenner. Associate Editor: Evan Serpick. Biweekly magazine geared towards young adults interested in news of popular music, entertainment and the arts, current news events, politics and American culture. Circ. 1,254,200. Editorial lead time 1 month.

- Query before submitting.

SPIN

205 Lexington Ave., 3rd Floor, New York NY 10016. (212)231-7400. Fax: (212)231-7312. E-mail: feedback@spin.com. Web site: www.spin.com. Monthly magazine covering music and popular culture. "*Spin* covers progres-

sive rock as well as investigative reporting on issues from politics to pop culture. Editorial includes reviews, essays, profiles and interviews on a wide range of music from rock to jazz. It also covers sports, movies, politics, humor, fashion and issues—from AIDS research to the environment. The editorial focuses on the progressive new music scene and young adult culture more from an 'alternative' perspective as opposed to mainstream pop music. The magazine discovers new bands as well as angles for the familiar stars.'' Estab. 1985. Circ. 540,000.

Nonfiction Features are not assigned to writers who have not established a prior relationship with *Spin*. Cultural, political or social issues. New writers: submit complete ms with SASE. Established writers: query specific editor with published clips.

Columns/Departments Most open to freelancers: Exposure (short articles on popular culture, TV, movies, books), 200-500 words; Reviews (record reviews), 100 words; Noise (music and new artists). Query before submitting.

Tips ''The best way to break into the magazine is the Exposure and Reviews sections. We primarily work with seasoned, professional writers who have extensive national magazine experience and very rarely make assignments based on unsolicited queries.''

N $ $ $ SYMPHONY

American Symphony Orchestra League, 33 W. 60th St., Fifth Floor, New York NY 10023. (212)262-5161. Fax: (212)262-5198. E-mail: editor@symphony.org. Web site: www.symphony.org. **Contact:** Chester Lane, senior editor (clane@symphony.org); Rebecca Winzenried, editor-in-chief (rebeccaw@symphony.org). **50% freelance written.** Bimonthly magazine for the orchestra industry and classical music enthusiasts covering classical music, orchestra industry, musicians. Writers should be knowledgeable about classical music and have critical or journalistic/repertorial approach. Circ. 18,000. **Pays on acceptance.** Publishes ms an average of 2 months after acceptance. Byline given. Buys first, one-time rights. Editorial lead time 6 months. Submit seasonal material 8 months in advance. Accepts queries by mail, e-mail. Accepts simultaneous submissions. Writer's guidelines online.

Nonfiction Book excerpts, essays, inspirational, interview/profile, opinion, personal experience (rare), photo feature (rare), issue features, trend pieces (by assignment only; pitches welcome). Does not want to see reviews, interviews. **Buys 30 mss/year.** Query with published clips. Length: 1,500-3,500 words. **Pays $500-900.** Sometimes pays expenses of writers on assignment.

Photos Rarely commissions photos or illustrations. State availability of or send photos with submission. Reviews contact sheets, negatives, prints, electronic photos (preferred). Buys one-time rights. Offers no additional payment for photos accepted with ms. Captions, identification of subjects required.

Columns/Departments Repertoire (orchestral music—essays); Comment (personal views and opinions); Currents (electronic media developments); In Print (books); On Record (CD, DVD, video), all 1,000-2,500 words. **Buys 12 mss/year.** Query with published clips.

Tips ''We need writing samples before assigning pieces. We prefer to craft the angle with the writer, rather than adapt an existing piece. Pitches and queries should demonstrate a clear relevance to the American orchestra industry and should be timely.''

N $ $ $ $ VIBE

215 Lexington Ave., 6th Floor, New York NY 10016. (212)448-7300. Fax: (212)448-7400. Web site: www.vibe.com. Editor: Danyel Smith. Monthly magazine covering urban music and culture. ''*Vibe* chronicles and celebrates urban music and the youth culture that inspires and consumes it.'' Estab. 1993. Circ. 850,000. Pays on publication. Buys first North American serial rights. Editorial lead time 4 months. Responds in 2 months to queries. Sample copy available on newsstands. Writer's guidelines for #10 SASE.

Nonfiction Cultural, political or social issues. Query with published clips, résumé and SASE. Length: 800-3,000 words. **Pays $1/word.**

Columns/Departments Start (introductory news-based section), 350-740 words; Revolutions (music reviews), 100-800 words; Play (lifestyle). Query with published clips, résumé and SASE. **Pays $1/word.**

Tips ''A writer's best chance to be published in *Vibe* is through the Start or Revolutions sections. Keep in mind that *Vibe* is a national magazine, so ideas should have a national scope. People in Cali should care as much about the story as people in NYC. Also, *Vibe* has a 4-month lead time. What we work on today will appear in the magazine 4 or more months later. Stories must be timely with respect to this fact.''

MYSTERY

N $ GREAT MYSTERY AND SUSPENSE MAGAZINE

P.O. Box 8008, St. Joseph MO 64508-8008. E-mail: editor@greatmysteryandsuspense.com. Web site: www.greatmysteryandsuspense.com. **Contact:** Vicki Lipira, editor/co-publisher. **100% freelance written.** Quarterly magazine covering mystery and suspense. "Our mission is to help mystery/suspense writers publish and promote their work in a quality publication and to quelch the mystery lover's thirst for the sinister. What makes us different from some of the very few other mystery magazines is the word wholesome. We are looking for well-written, wholesome short stories by new and established writers who can weave suspense or mystery in an entertaining way." Estab. 2006. **Pays on acceptance.** Publishes ms an average of 3-6 months after acceptance. Byline given. Offers 50% kill fee. Buys first, second serial (reprint), electronic rights. Editorial lead time 6 months. Submit seasonal material 6 months in advance. Accepts queries by mail, e-mail. Accepts previously published material. Responds in 2-4 weeks to queries; 2-4 weeks to mss. Sample copy for 9×12 SASE. Writer's guidelines online.

Nonfiction Interview/profile. Query with published clips. **Pays $25.**

Fiction Mystery, suspense. **Buys 40-50 mss/year.** Send complete ms. Length: 750-2,500 words. **Pays $25-50.**

Poetry Free verse, traditional. **Buys 5-10 poems/year.** Submit maximum 2 poems. **Pays $5.**

Tips "We're open to anyone who can write a good mystery."

$ HARDBOILED

Gryphon Publications, P.O. Box 209, Brooklyn NY 11228. Web site: www.gryphonbooks.com. **Contact:** Gary Lovisi, editor. **100% freelance written.** Semiannual book covering crime/mystery fiction and nonfiction. "Hard-hitting crime fiction and private-eye stories—the newest and most cutting-edge work and classic reprints." Estab. 1988. Circ. 1,000. Pays on publication. Publishes ms an average of 18 months after acceptance. Byline given. Offers 100% kill fee. Buys first North American serial, one-time rights. Editorial lead time 1 year. Submit seasonal material 9 months in advance. Accepts queries by mail, fax. Accepts previously published material. Accepts simultaneous submissions. Responds in 2 weeks to queries; 1 month to mss. Sample copy for $10. Writer's guidelines for #10 SASE.

Nonfiction Book excerpts, essays, exposé. **Buys 4-6 mss/year.** Query. Length: 500-3,000 words. **Pays 1 copy.**

Reprints Query first.

Photos State availability with submission.

Columns/Departments Buys 2-4 mss/year. Query.

Fiction Mystery, hardboiled crime, and private-eye stories, all on the cutting edge. No "pastches, violence for the sake of violence." **Buys 40 mss/year.** Query with or without published clips or send complete ms. Length: 500-3,000 words. **Pays $5-50.**

Tips "Your best bet for breaking in is short hard crime fiction filled with authenticity and brevity. Try a subscription to *Hardboiled* to get the perfect idea of what we are after."

ALFRED HITCHCOCK'S MYSTERY MAGAZINE

Dell Magazines, 475 Park Ave. S., 11th Floor, New York NY 10016. (212)686-7188. Web site: www.themysteryplace.com. Editor: Linda Landrigan. **100% freelance written.** Monthly magazine featuring new mystery short stories. Estab. 1956. Circ. 100,000 readers. Pays on publication. Byline given. Buys first, foreign rights. Submit seasonal material 7 months in advance. Responds in 4 months to mss. Sample copy for $5. Writer's guidelines for SASE or on Web site.

Fiction Linda Landrigan, editor. Original and well-written mystery and crime fiction. "Because this is a mystery magazine, the stories we buy must fall into that genre in some sense or another. We are interested in nearly every kind of mystery: stories of detection of the classic kind, police procedurals, private eye tales, suspense, courtroom dramas, stories of espionage, and so on. We ask only that the story be about crime (or the threat or fear of one). We sometimes accept ghost stories or supernatural tales, but those also should involve a crime." No sensationalism. Send complete ms. Length: Up to 12,000 words. **Payment varies.**

Tips "No simultaneous submissions, please. Submissions sent to *Alfred Hitchcock's Mystery Magazine* are not considered for or read by *Ellery Queen's Mystery Magazine*, and vice versa."

$ ELLERY QUEEN'S MYSTERY MAGAZINE

Dell Magazines Fiction Group, 475 Park Ave. S., 11th Floor, New York NY 10016. (212)686-7188. Fax: (212)686-7414. E-mail: elleryqueen@dellmagazines.com. Web site: www.themysteryplace.com. **Contact:** Janet Hutchings, editor. **100% freelance written.** Magazine published 10 times/year featuring mystery fiction. "*Ellery Queen's Mystery Magazine* welcomes submissions from both new and established writers. We publish every kind of mystery short story: the psychological suspense tale, the deductive puzzle, the private eye case—the gamut of crime and detection from the realistic (including the policeman's lot and stories of police procedure) to the more imaginative (including 'locked rooms' and 'impossible crimes'). *EQMM* has been in continuous publication since 1941. From the beginning, 3 general criteria have been employed in evaluating submissions: We look for strong writing, an original and exciting plot, and professional craftsmanship. We encourage writers whose work meets these general criteria to read an issue of *EQMM* before making a submission." Estab. 1941. Circ. 180,780 readers. **Pays on acceptance.** Publishes ms an average of 6-12 months after acceptance. Byline given. Buys first North American serial rights. Accepts simultaneous submissions. Responds in 3 months to mss. Sample copy for $5. Writer's guidelines for SASE or online.

Fiction "We always need detective stories. Special consideration given to anything timely and original." Mystery. No explicit sex or violence, no gore or horror. Seldom publishes parodies or pastiches. **Buys up to 120 mss/year.** Send complete ms. Length: Most stories 2,500-8,000 words. Accepts longer and shorter submissions—including minute mysteries of 250 words, and novellas of up to 20,000 words from established authors. **Pays 5-8¢/word; occasionally higher for established authors.**

Poetry Short mystery verses, limericks. Length: 1 page, double spaced maximum.

Tips "We have a Department of First Stories to encourage writers whose fiction has never before been in print. We publish an average of 10 first stories every year."

NATURE, CONSERVATION & ECOLOGY

$ ALTERNATIVES JOURNAL

Canadian Environmental Ideas and Action, Alternatives, Inc., Faculty of Environmental Studies, University of Waterloo, Waterloo ON N2L 3G1 Canada. (519)888-4442. Fax: (519)746-0292. E-mail: editor@alternativesjournal.ca. Web site: www.alternativesjournal.ca. **Contact:** Tara Flynn, executive editor. **90% freelance written.** Quarterly magazine covering environmental issues with Canadian relevance. Estab. 1971. Circ. 4,800. Pays on publication. Publishes ms an average of 5 months after acceptance. Byline given. Offers 50% kill fee. Buys first rights. Editorial lead time 7 months. Submit seasonal material 5 months in advance. Accepts queries by mail, e-mail, fax. Accepts simultaneous submissions. Sample copy free for Canadian writers only. Writer's guidelines online.

Nonfiction Book excerpts, essays, exposé, humor, interview/profile, opinion. **Buys 50 mss/year.** Query with published clips. Length: 800-3,000 words. **Pays $50-150 (Canadian).** All contributors receive a free subscription in addition to payment. Sometimes pays expenses of writers on assignment.

Photos State availability with submission. Buys one-time rights. Offers $35-75/photo. Identification of subjects required.

$ $ $ AMERICAN FORESTS

American Forests, P.O. Box 2000, Washington DC 20013. E-mail: mrobbins@amfor.org. Web site: www.americanforests.org. **Contact:** Michelle Robbins, editor. **75% freelance written.** Quarterly magazine "of trees and forests published by a nonprofit citizens' organization that strives to help people plant and care for trees for ecosystem restoration and healthier communities." Estab. 1895. Circ. 25,000. **Pays on acceptance.** Publishes ms an average of 8 months after acceptance. Byline given. Buys one-time rights. Submit seasonal material 5 months in advance. Accepts queries by mail, e-mail. Accepts previously published material. Responds in 2 months to queries. Sample copy for $2. Writer's guidelines online.

- Break in with "stories that resonate with city dwellers who love trees, or small, forestland owners (private). This magazine is looking for more urban and suburban-oriented pieces.

Nonfiction All articles should emphasize trees, forests, forestry and related issues. General interest, historical/nostalgic, how-to, humor, inspirational. **Buys 8-12 mss/year.** Query. Length: 1,200-2,000 words. **Pays $250-1,000.**

Reprints Send tearsheet or typed ms with rights for sale noted and information about when and where the material previously appeared. Pays 50% of amount paid for original article.

Photos Originals only. Send photos with submission. Reviews 35mm or larger transparencies, glossy color prints. Buys one-time rights. Offers no additional payment for photos accompanying ms. Captions required.

Tips "We're looking for more good urban forestry stories, and stories that show cooperation among disparate elements to protect/restore an ecosystem. Query should have honesty and information on photo support. We *do not* accept fiction or poetry at this time."

N $ $ APPALACHIAN TRAILWAY NEWS

Appalachian Trail Conservancy, P.O. Box 807, Harpers Ferry WV 25425-0807. (304)535-6331. Fax: (304)535-2667. E-mail: editor@appalachiantrail.org. Web site: www.appalachiantrail.org. **40% freelance written.** Bimonthly magazine. Estab. 1925. Circ. 32,000. Pays on publication. Byline given. Buys first North American serial, second serial (reprint), web reprint rights. Responds in 2 months to queries. Sample copy and writer's guidelines online.

- Articles must relate to Appalachian Trail.

Nonfiction Publishes but does not pay for hiking "reflections." Essays, general interest, historical/nostalgic, how-to, humor, inspirational, interview/profile, photo feature, technical, travel. **Buys 5-10 mss/year.** Query with or without published clips, or send complete ms. Prefers e-mail queries. Length: 250-3,000 words. **Pays $25-300.** Pays expenses of writers on assignment.

Reprints Send photocopy with rights for sale noted and information about when and where the material previously appeared.

Photos State availability with submission. Reviews contact sheets, 5×7 prints, slides, digital images. Offers $25-125/photo; $250/cover. Identification of subjects required.

Tips "Contributors should display a knowledge of or interest in the Appalachian Trail. Those who live in the vicinity of the Trail may opt for an assigned story and should present credentials and subject of interest to the editor."

N $ $ $ THE ATLANTIC SALMON JOURNAL

The Atlantic Salmon Federation, P.O. Box 5200, St. Andrews NB E5B 3S8 Canada. Fax: (506)529-4985. E-mail: martinsilverstone@sympatico.ca. Web site: www.asf.ca. **Contact:** Martin Silverstone, editor. **50-68% freelance written.** Quarterly magazine covering conservation efforts for the Atlantic salmon, catering to the dedicated angler and conservationist. Circ. 11,000. Pays on publication. Publishes ms an average of 6 months after acceptance. Byline given. Buys first North American serial rights. Buys one-time rights to photos. Submit seasonal material 3 months in advance. Accepts simultaneous submissions. Responds in 2 months to queries. Sample copy for 9×12 SAE with $1 (Canadian), or IRC. Writer's guidelines free.

Nonfiction "We are seeking articles that are pertinent to the focus and purpose of our magazine, which is to inform and entertain our membership on all aspects of the Atlantic salmon and its environment, and conservation." Exposé, historical/nostalgic, how-to, humor, interview/profile, new product, opinion, personal experience, photo feature, technical, travel, conservation; science; research and management. **Buys 15-20 mss/year.** Query with published clips. Length: Length: 2,000 words. **Pays $400-800 for articles with photos.** Sometimes pays expenses of writers on assignment.

Photos State availability with submission. Pays $50 minimum; $350-500 for covers; $300 for 2-page spread; $175 for full page photo; $100 for ½-page photo. Captions, identification of subjects required.

Columns/Departments Fit To Be Tied (Conservation issues and salmon research; the design, construction and success of specific flies); interesting characters in the sport and opinion pieces by knowledgeable writers, 900 words; Casting Around (short, informative, entertaining reports, book reviews and quotes from the world of Atlantic salmon angling and conservation). Query. **Pays $50-300.**

Tips "Articles must reflect informed and up-to-date knowledge of Atlantic salmon. Writers need not be authorities, but research must be impeccable. Clear, concise writing is essential, and submissions must be typed."

$ $ THE BEAR DELUXE MAGAZINE

Orlo, P.O. Box 10342, Portland OR 97296. (503)242-1047. E-mail: bear@orlo.org. Web site: www.orlo.org. **Contact:** Tom Webb, editor. **80% freelance written.** Quarterly magazine. "*The Bear Deluxe Magazine* is a national independent environmental magazine publishing significant works of reporting, creative nonfiction, literature, visual art and design. Based in the Pacific Northwest, *The Bear Deluxe* reaches across cultural and political divides to engage readers on vital issues effecting the environment." Estab. 1993. Circ. 19,000. Pays on publication. Publishes ms an average of 6 months after acceptance. Byline given. Offers 25% kill fee. Buys first, one-time rights. Editorial lead time 6 months. Submit seasonal material 9 months in advance. Accepts queries by mail, e-mail. Accepts previously published material. Accepts simultaneous submissions. Responds in 3-6 months to mail queries. Only responds to e-mail queries if interested to queries. Sample copy for $3. Writer's guidelines for #10 SASE or on Web site.

Nonfiction Book excerpts, essays, exposé, general interest, interview/profile, new product, opinion, personal experience, photo feature, travel, artist profiles. Special issues: Publishes 1 theme/2 years. **Buys 40 mss/year.** Query with published clips. Length: 250-4,500 words. **Pays $25-400, depending on piece.** Sometimes pays expenses of writers on assignment.

Photos State availability with submission. Reviews contact sheets, transparencies, 8×10 prints. Buys one-time rights. Offers $30/photo. Identification of subjects, model releases required.

Columns/Departments Reviews (almost anything), 300 words; Front of the Book (mix of short news bits, found writing, quirky tidbits), 300-500 words; Portrait of an Artist (artist profiles), 1,200 words; Back of the Book (creative opinion pieces), 650 words. **Buys 16 mss/year.** Query with published clips. **Pays $25-400, depending on piece.**

Fiction "Stories must have some environmental context, but we view that in a broad sense." Adventure, condensed novels, historical, horror, humorous, mystery, novel excerpts, western. "No detective, children's or horror." **Buys 8 mss/year.** Query with or without published clips or send complete ms. Length: 750-4,500 words. **Pays free subscription to the magazine, contributor's copies and $25-400, depending on piece; additional copies for postage.**

Poetry Avant-garde, free verse, haiku, light verse, traditional. **Buys 16-20 poems/year.** Submit maximum 5 poems. Length: 50 lines maximum. **Pays $20, subscription, and copies.**

Fillers Facts, newsbreaks, short humor. **Buys 10/year.** Length: 100-750 words. **Pays $25, subscription, and copies.**

Tips "Offer to be a stringer for future ideas. Get a copy of the magazine and guidelines, and query us with specific nonfiction ideas and clips. We're looking for original, magazine-style stories, not fluff or PR. Fiction, essay, and poetry writers should know we have an open and blind review policy and should keep sending their best work even if rejected once. Be as specific as possible in queries."

$ BIRD WATCHER'S DIGEST

Pardson Corp., P.O. Box 110, Marietta OH 45750. (740)373-5285. Fax: (740)373-8443. E-mail: editor@birdwatchersdigest.com. Web site: www.birdwatchersdigest.com. **60% freelance written.** Works with a small number of new/unpublished writers each year. Bimonthly magazine covering natural history—birds and bird watching. "*BWD* is a nontechnical magazine interpreting ornithological material for amateur observers, including the knowledgeable birder, the serious novice and the backyard bird watcher; we strive to provide good reading and good ornithology." Estab. 1978. Circ. 90,000. Pays on publication. Publishes ms an average of 2 years after acceptance. Byline given. Buys one-time, second serial (reprint) rights. Submit seasonal material 6 months in advance. Accepts previously published material. Responds in 2 months to queries. Sample copy for $3.99 or online. Writer's guidelines online.

Nonfiction "We are especially interested in fresh, lively accounts of closely observed bird behavior and displays and of bird-watching experiences and expeditions. We often need material on backyard subjects such as bird feeding, housing, gardenening on less common species or on unusual or previously unreported behavior of common species." Book excerpts, how-to (relating to birds, feeding and attracting, etc.), humor, personal experience, travel (limited, we get many). No articles on pet or caged birds; none on raising a baby bird. **Buys 45-60 mss/year.** Send complete ms. Length: 600-3,500 words. **Pays from $100.**

Photos Send photos with submission. Reviews transparencies, prints. Buys one-time rights. Pays $75 minimum for transparencies.

Tips "We are aimed at an audience ranging from the backyard bird watcher to the very knowledgeable birder; we include in each issue material that will appeal at various levels. We always strive for a good geographical spread, with material from every section of the country. We leave very technical matters to others, but we want facts and accuracy, depth and quality, directed at the veteran bird watcher and at the enthusiastic novice. We stress the joys and pleasures of bird watching, its environmental contribution, and its value for the individual and society."

$ $ BIRDER'S WORLD

Enjoying Birds at Home and Beyond, Kalmbach Publishing Co., P.O. Box 1612, Waukesha WI 53187-1612. Fax: (262)798-6468. E-mail: mail@birdersworld.com. Web site: www.birdersworld.com. Editor: Charles J. Hagner. Associate Editor: Matt Mendenhall. Photo Editor: Ernie Mastroianni. **Contact:** Jessica Eskelsen, editorial associate. Bimonthly magazine for birdwatchers who actively look for wild birds in the field. "*Birder's World* concentrates on where to find, how to attract, and how to identify wild birds, and on how to understand what they do." Estab. 1987. Circ. 50,000. **Pays on acceptance.** Byline given. Buys one-time rights. Accepts queries by mail. Writer's guidelines online.

Nonfiction Essays, how-to (attracting birds), interview/profile, personal experience, photo feature (bird photography), travel (birding hotspots in North America and beyond), product reviews/comparisons, bird biology, endangered or threatened birds. No poetry, fiction, or puzzles. **Buys 60 mss/year.** Query with published clips. Length: 500-2,400 words. **Pays $200-450.**

Photos See photo guidelines online. State availability with submission. Buys one-time rights. Identification of subjects required.

$ $ $ CALIFORNIA WILD

Natural Science for Thinking Animals, California Academy of Sciences, 875 Howard St., San Francisco CA 94103. (415)321-8188. Fax: (415)321-8625. E-mail: kkhowell@calacademy.org. Web site: www.calacademy.org/calwild. **Contact:** Keith Howell, editor. **75% freelance written.** Quarterly magazine covering natural sciences and the environment. "Our readers' interests range widely from ecology to geology, from endangered species to anthropology, from field identification of plants and birds to armchair understanding of complex scientific issues." Estab. 1948. Circ. 32,000. Pays prior to publication. Publishes ms an average of 3 months after acceptance. Byline given. Offers 50% kill fee; maximum $200. Buys first North American serial, one-time rights. Editorial lead time 3 months. Submit seasonal material 6 months in advance. Accepts queries by mail, fax. Responds in 6 weeks to queries; 6 months to mss. Sample copy for 9×12 SASE or on Web site. Writer's guidelines online.

Nonfiction Personal experience, photo feature, biological, and earth sciences. Special issues: Mostly California pieces, but also from Pacific Ocean countries. No travel pieces. **Buys 20 mss/year.** Query with published clips. Length: 1,000-3,000 words. **Pays $250-1,000 for assigned articles; $200-800 for unsolicited articles.** Sometimes pays expenses of writers on assignment.
Photos State availability with submission. Reviews transparencies. Buys one-time rights. Offers $75-150/photo. Identification of subjects, model releases required.
Columns/Departments A Closer Look (unusual places); Wild Lives (description of unusual plant or animal); In Pursuit of Science (innovative student, teacher, young scientist), all 1,000-1,500 words; Skywatcher (research in astronomy), 2,000-3,000 words. **Buys 12 mss/year.** Query with published clips. **Pays $200-400.**
Tips "We are looking for unusual and/or timely stories about California environment or biodiversity."

$ $ $ CANADIAN WILDLIFE

350 Michael Cowpland Dr., Kanata ON K2M 2W1 Canada. (613)599-9594. Fax: (613)271-9591. E-mail: wild@cwf-fcf.org. Senior Editor: Andrea Fajrajsl. **Contact:** Asha Jhamandas, assistant editor. **90% freelance written.** Magazine published 5 times/year covering wildlife conservation. Includes topics pertaining to wildlife, endangered species, conservation, and natural history. When possible, it is beneficial if articles have a Canadian slant or the topic has global appeal. Estab. 1995. Circ. 15,000. **Pays on acceptance.** Publishes ms an average of 3 months after acceptance. Byline given. Offers 15% kill fee. Buys first North American serial rights. Editorial lead time 3 months. Submit seasonal material 4 months in advance. Accepts queries by mail, e-mail, fax. Responds in 6 weeks to queries; 2 months to mss. Sample copy for $5 (Canadian). Writer's guidelines free.
Nonfiction Book excerpts, interview/profile, photo feature, science/nature. No standard travel stories. **Buys 20 mss/year.** Query with published clips. Length: 800-2,500 words. **Pays $500-1,200 for assigned articles; $300-1,000 for unsolicited articles.**
Photos Send photos with submission. Reviews transparencies. Buys one-time rights. Negotiates payment individually. Captions, identification of subjects, model releases required.
Columns/Departments Vistas (science news), 200-500 words; Book Reviews, 100-150 words. **Buys 15 mss/year.** Query with published clips. **Pays $50-250.**
Tips "*Canadian Wildlife* is a benefit of membership in the Canadian Wildlife Federation. Nearly 15,000 people currently receive the magazine. The majority of these men and women are already well versed in topics concerning the environment and natural science; writers, however, should not make assumptions about the extent of a reader's knowledge of topics."

$ $ $ CONSCIOUS CHOICE

The Journal of Ecology & Natural Living, Conscious Enlightenment, LLC, 920 N. Franklin St., Suite 202, Chicago IL 60610-3179. Fax: (312)751-3973. E-mail: editor@consciouschoice.com. Web site: www.consciouschoice.com. **Contact:** Marla Donato, editor. **95% freelance written.** Monthly tabloid covering the environment, renewable energy, yoga, natural health and medicine, and personal growth and spirituality. Estab. 1988. Circ. 55,000. Pays on publication. Publishes ms an average of 6 months after acceptance. Byline given. Offers 50% kill fee. Buys first North American serial, electronic rights. Editorial lead time 6 months. Submit seasonal material 6 months in advance. Accepts queries by mail. Accepts simultaneous submissions. Responds in 6 weeks to queries; 1 month to mss. Sample copy online. Writer's guidelines free or by e-mail.
Nonfiction General interest (to cultural creatives), interview/profile (emphasis on narrative, story telling), environment. **Buys 24 mss/year.** Query with 2-3 published clips. Length: 1,800 words. **Pays $150-1,000.** Sometimes pays expenses of writers on assignment.

$ $ E THE ENVIRONMENTAL MAGAZINE

Earth Action Network, P.O. Box 5098, Westport CT 06881-5098. (203)854-5559. Fax: (203)866-0602. E-mail: info@emagazine.com. Web site: www.emagazine.com. **Contact:** Jim Motavalli, editor. **60% freelance written.** Bimonthly magazine. "*E Magazine* was formed for the purpose of acting as a clearinghouse of information, news, and commentary on environmental issues." Estab. 1990. Circ. 50,000. Pays on publication. Byline given. Buys first North American serial rights. Editorial lead time 3 months. Submit seasonal material 6 months in advance. Accepts queries by mail, e-mail, fax. Accepts simultaneous submissions. Sample copy for $5 or online. Writer's guidelines online.

- The editor reports an interest in seeing more investigative reporting.

Nonfiction On spec or free contributions welcome. Exposé (environmental), how-to, new product, book review, feature (in-depth articles on key natural environmental issues). **Buys 100 mss/year.** Query with published clips. Length: 100-4,000 words. **Pays 30¢/word.**
Photos State availability with submission. Reviews printed samples, e.g., magazine tearsheets, postcards, etc., to be kept on file. Buys one-time rights. Negotiates payment individually. Identification of subjects required.
Columns/Departments In Brief/Currents (environmental news stories/trends), 400-1,000 words; Conversations

(Q&As with environmental "movers and shakers"), 2,000 words; Tools for Green Living; Your Health; Eco-Travel; Eco-Home; Eating Right; Green Business; Consumer News (each 700-1,200 words). Query with published clips.

Contact: Jim Motavalli, online editor.

Tips "Contact us to obtain writer's guidelines and back issues of our magazine. Tailor your query according to the department/section you feel it would be best suited for. Articles must be lively, well researched, balanced, and relevant to a mainstream, national readership." On spec or free contributions welcome.

$ $ HIGH COUNTRY NEWS

High Country Foundation, P.O. Box 1090, Paonia CO 81428. (970)527-4898. E-mail: greg@hcn.org. Web site: www.hcn.org. **Contact:** Greg Hanscom, editor. **80% freelance written.** Weekly tabloid covering Rocky Mountain West, the Great Basin, and Pacific Northwest environment, rural communities, and natural resource issues in 10 western states for environmentalists, politicians, companies, college classes, government agencies, grass roots activists, public land managers, etc. Estab. 1970. Circ. 23,000. Pays on publication. Publishes ms an average of 2 months after acceptance. Byline given. Buys one-time rights. Accepts queries by mail. Responds in 1 month to queries. Sample copy for SAE or online. Writer's guidelines online.

Nonfiction Exposé (government, corporate), interview/profile, personal experience, photo feature (centerspread), reporting (local issues with regional importance). **Buys 100 mss/year.** Query. Length: up to 3,000 words. **Pays 20¢/word minimum.** Sometimes pays expenses of writers on assignment.

Reprints Send tearsheet and information about when and where the material previously appeared. Pays 15¢/word.

Photos Send photos with submission. Reviews b&w prints. Captions, identification of subjects required.

Columns/Departments Roundups (topical stories), 800 words; opinion pieces, 1,000 words.

Tips "We use a lot of freelance material, though very little from outside the Rockies. Familiarity with the newspaper is a must. Start by writing a query letter. We define 'resources' broadly to include people, culture, and aesthetic values, not just coal, oil, and timber."

$ $ $ MINNESOTA CONSERVATION VOLUNTEER

Minnesota Department of Natural Resources, 500 Lafeyette Rd., St. Paul MN 55155-4046. Web site: www.dnr.state.mn.us/magazine. **50% freelance written.** Bimonthly magazine covering Minnesota natural resources, wildlife, natural history, outdoor recreation, and land use. "*Minnesota Conservation Volunteer* is a donor-supported magazine advocating conservation and wise use of Minnesota's natural resources. Material must reflect an appreciation of nature and an ethic of care for the environment. We rely on a variety of sources in our reporting. More than 140,000 Minnesota households, businesses, schools, and other groups subscribe to this conservation magazine." Estab. 1940. Circ. 140,000. **Pays on acceptance.** Publishes ms an average of 2 months after acceptance. Byline given. Offers 30% kill fee. Buys first North American serial, rights to post to Web site, and archive rights. Editorial lead time 9 months. Submit seasonal material 9 months in advance. Accepts queries by mail, e-mail. Accepts previously published material. Responds in 1 month to queries; 2 months to mss. Sample copy free or on Web site. Writer's guidelines online.

Nonfiction Book excerpts, essays, exposé, general interest, historical/nostalgic, humor, interview/profile, opinion, personal experience, photo feature, travel, "Young Naturalist" for children. Does not publish poetry or uncritical advocacy. **Buys 10 mss/year.** Query with published clips. Length: up to 1,500 words. **Pays 50¢/word for full-length feature articles.** Pays expenses of writers on assignment.

Photos State availability with submission. Reviews 35mm or large format transparencies. Buys one-time rights, will negotiate for Web use separately. Offers $100/photo.

Columns/Departments Close Encounters (unusual, exciting, or humorous personal wildlife experience in Minnesota), up to 1,500 words; Sense of Place (first- or third-person essay developing character of a Minnesota place), up to 1,500 words; Viewpoint (well-researched and well-reasoned opinion piece), up to 1,500 words; Minnesota Profile (concise description of emblematic state species or geographic feature), 400 words. **Buys 10 mss/year.** Query with published clips. **Pays 50¢/word.**

Tips "In submitting queries, look beyond topics to *stories:* What is someone doing and why? How does the story end? In submitting a query addressing a particular issue, think of the human impacts and the sources you might consult. Summarize your idea, the story line, and sources in 2 or 3 short paragraphs. While topics must have relevance to Minnesota and give a Minnesota character to the magazine, feel free to round out your research with out-of-state sources."

$ $ $ NATIONAL PARKS

1300 19th St. NW, Suite 300, Washington DC 20036. (202)223-6722. Fax: (202)659-0650. E-mail: npmag@npca.org. Web site: www.npca.org/magazine/. Editor-in-chief: Linda Rancourt. **Contact:** Scott Kirkwood, senior editor. **60% freelance written.** Prefers to work with published/established writers. Quarterly magazine for a largely unscientific but highly educated audience interested in preservation of National Park System units, natural areas, and protection of wildlife habitat. Estab. 1919. Circ. 300,000. **Pays on acceptance.** Publishes ms an average of 2 months after acceptance. Offers 33% kill fee. Responds in 5 months to queries. Sample copy for $3 and 9×12 SASE or online. Writer's guidelines online.

Nonfiction All material must relate to US national parks. Exposé (on threats, wildlife problems in national parks), descriptive articles about new or proposed national parks and wilderness parks; natural history pieces describing park geology, wildlife or plants; new trends in park use; legislative issues. No poetry, philosophical essays, or first-person narratives. No unsolicited mss. Length: 1,500 words. **Pays $1,300 for 1,500-word features and travel articles.**

Photos No color prints or negatives. Send for guidelines. Not responsible for unsolicited photos. Send photos with submission. Reviews color slides. Pays $150-350 inside; $525 for covers. Captions required.

Tips "Articles should have an original slant or news hook and cover a limited subject, rather than attempt to treat a broad subject superficially. Specific examples, descriptive details, and quotes are always preferable to generalized information. The writer must be able to document factual claims, and statements should be clearly substantiated with evidence within the article. *National Parks* does not publish fiction, poetry, personal essays, or 'My trip to . . .' stories."

$ $ $ $ NATIONAL WILDLIFE

National Wildlife Federation, 11100 Wildlife Center Dr., Reston VA 20190. (703)438-6510. Fax: (703)438-6544. E-mail: pubs@nwf.org. Web site: www.nwf.org/nationalwildlife. **Contact:** Mark Wexler, editor. **75% freelance written.** Assigns almost all material based on staff ideas. Assigns few unsolicited queries. Bimonthly magazine. "Our purpose is to promote wise use of the nation's natural resources and to conserve and protect wildlife and its habitat. We reach a broad audience that is largely interested in wildlife conservation and nature photography." Estab. 1963. Circ. 650,000. **Pays on acceptance.** Publishes ms an average of 1 year after acceptance. Offers 25% kill fee. Buys all rights. Submit seasonal material 8 months in advance. Accepts queries by mail, e-mail, fax. Responds in 6 weeks to queries. Writer's guidelines for #10 SASE.

Nonfiction General interest (2,500 word features on wildlife, new discoveries, behavior, or the environment), how-to (particularly interested in gardening and green consumer pieces), interview/profile (people who have gone beyond the call of duty to protect wildlife and its habitat, or to prevent environmental contamination and people who have been involved in the environment or conservation in interesting ways), personal experience (outdoor adventure), photo feature (wildlife), short 700-word features on an unusual individual or new scientific discovery relating to nature. "Avoid too much scientific detail. We prefer anecdotal, natural history material." **Buys 50 mss/year.** Query with or without published clips. Length: 750-2,500 words. **Pays $800-3,000.** Sometimes pays expenses of writers on assignment.

Photos John Nuhn, photo editor. Send photos with submission. Reviews Kodachrome or Fujichrome transparencies. Buys one-time rights.

Tips "Writers can break in with us more readily by proposing subjects (initially) that will take only 1 or 2 pages in the magazine (short features)."

N $ $ $ $ NATURAL HISTORY

Natural History, Inc., 36 W. 25th St., 5th Floor, New York NY 10010. E-mail: nhmag@naturalhistorymag.com. Web site: www.naturalhistorymag.com. **15% freelance written.** Magazine published 10 times/year for well-educated audience: professional people, scientists, and scholars. Circ. 225,000. **Pays on acceptance.** Publishes ms an average of 3 months after acceptance. Byline given. Buys first North American serial rights. Becomes an agent for second serial (reprint) rights Submit seasonal material 6 months in advance.

Nonfiction "We are seeking new research on mammals, birds, invertebrates, reptiles, ocean life, anthropology, astronomy, preferably written by principal investigators in these fields. Our slant is toward unraveling problems in behavior, ecology, and evolution." **Buys 60 mss/year.** Query by mail or send complete ms. Length: 1,500-3,000 words. **Pays $500-2,500.**

Photos Rarely uses 8×10 b&w glossy prints; pays $125/page maximum. Much color is used; pays $300 for inside, and up to $600 for cover. Buys one-time rights.

Columns/Departments Journal (reporting from the field); Findings (summary of new or ongoing research); Naturalist At Large; The Living Museum (relates to the American Museum of Natural History); Discovery (natural or cultural history of a specific place).

Tips "We expect high standards of writing and research. We do not lobby for causes, environmental, or other. The writer should have a deep knowledge of his subject, then submit original ideas either in query or by manuscript."

$ $ $ NATURE CANADA

1 Nicholas St., Suite 606, Ottawa ON K1N 7B7 Canada. Fax: (613)562-3371. E-mail: magazine@naturecanada.ca. Web site: www.naturecanada.ca. **Contact:** Pamela Feeny, editor. Quarterly magazine covering conservation,

natural history and environmental/naturalist community. "Editorial content reflects the goals and priorities of Nature Canada as a conservation organization with a focus on our program areas: federally protected areas (national parks, national wildlife areas, etc.), endangered species, and bird conservation through Canada's important bird areas. Nature Canada is written for an audience interested in nature conservation. Nature Canada celebrates, preserves, and protects Canadian nature. We promote the awareness and understanding of the connection between humans and nature and how natural systems support life on Earth. We strive to instill a sense of ownership and belief that these natural systems should be protected." Estab. 1971. Circ. 27,000. Pays on publication. Publishes ms an average of 3 months after acceptance. Byline given. Offers $100 kill fee. Buys all Nature Canada rights (including electronic). Author retains resale rights elsewhere. Editorial lead time 4 months. Submit seasonal material 6 months in advance. Responds in 4 months to mss. Sample copy for $5. Writer's guidelines online.

Nonfiction Subjects include: Canadian conservation issues; nature education; reconnecting with nature; enviro-friendly lifestyles, products and consumer reports; federal protected areas; endangered species; birds; sustainable development; company and individual profiles; urban nature; how-to; natural history. **Buys 12 mss/year.** Query with published clips. Length: 650-2,000 words. **Pays up to 50¢/word (Canadian).**

Photos State availability with submission. Buys one-time rights. Offers $50-200/photo (Canadian). Identification of subjects required.

Tips "Our readers are well-educated and knowledgeable about nature and the environment so contributors should have a good understanding of the subject. We also deal exclusively with Canadian issues and species, except for those relating directly to our international program. E-mail queries preferred. Do not send unsolicited manuscripts. We receive many BC-related queries but need more for the rest of Canada, particularly SK, MB, QC and the Maritimes. Articles must focus on the positive and be supported by science when applicable. We are looking for strong, well-researched writing that is lively, entertaining, enlightening, provocative and, when appropriate, amusing."

N $ NEW YORK STATE CONSERVATIONIST

New York State Department of Environmental Conservation, 625 Broadway, Albany NY 12233-4502. (518)402-8047. Web site: www.theconservationist.org. Editor: David Nelson. **Contact:** Alex Hyatt, managing editor. **30% freelance written.** Bimonthly magazine covering outdoor education, environmental quality, hunting, fishing, wildlife profiles. Circ. 100,000. Pays on publication. Publishes ms an average of 2 months-5 years after acceptance. Byline given. Buys first North American serial rights. Editorial lead time 6 months. Submit seasonal material 6-12 months in advance. Accepts queries by mail. Accepts previously published material. Responds in 2-4 weeks to queries; 2 months to mss. Sample copy and writer's guidelines online.

Nonfiction Historical/nostalgic, personal experience, photo feature. **Buys 10 mss/year.** Query. **Pays $50-100.**

Photos Send photos with submission. Reviews transparencies. Buys one-time rights. Offers $15-100/photo. Captions, identification of subjects, model releases required.

Columns/Departments The Backpage (outdoor experiences, feel-good anectdotes), 700 words. **Buys 3 mss/year.** Query with published clips. **Pays $50.**

Tips "The more organized a writer is, the more likely we are to use the piece. Captions, photos, and solid writing don't hurt, either. People doing things in the outdoors. Well-researched wildlife profiles."

$ $ NORTHERN WOODLANDS MAGAZINE

Center for Woodlands Education, Inc., 1776 Center Rd., P.O. Box 471, Corinth VT 05039-0471. (802)439-6292. Fax: (802)439-6296. E-mail: anne@northernwoodlands.org. Web site: www.northernwoodlands.org. **Contact:** Anne Margolis. **40-60% freelance written.** Quarterly magazine covering natural history, conservation, and forest management in the Northeast. "*Northern Woodlands* strives to inspire landowners' sense of stewardship by increasing their awareness of the natural history and the principles of conservation and forestry that are directly related to their land. We also hope to increase the public's awareness of the social, economic, and environmental benefits of a working forest." Estab. 1994. Circ. 12,000. Pays 1 month prior to publication. Publishes ms an average of 6 months after acceptance. Byline given. Buys one-time rights. Editorial lead time 6 months. Submit seasonal material 6 months in advance. Accepts queries by mail, e-mail. Accepts previously published material. Accepts simultaneous submissions. Responds in 1 month to queries; 1-2 months to mss. Sample copy and writer's guidelines online.

Nonfiction Stephen Long, editor. Book excerpts, essays, how-to (related to woodland management), interview/profile (related to the Northeastern U.S.). No product reviews, first-person travelogues, cute animal stories, opinion, or advocacy pieces. **Buys 15-20 mss/year.** Query with published clips. Length: 500-3,000 words. **Pays 10¢/word.** Sometimes pays expenses of writers on assignment.

Photos State availability with submission. Reviews transparencies, prints, high res digital photos. Buys one-time rights. Offers $35-75/photo. Identification of subjects required.

Columns/Departments Stephen Long, editor. A Place in Mind (essays on places of personal significance), 600-

800 words. **Pays $150**. Knots and Bolts (seasonal natural history items or forest-related news items), 300-600 words. **Pays 10¢/word**. Wood Lit (book reviews), 600 words. **Pays $50**. Field Work (profiles of people who work in the woods, the wood-product industry, or conservation field), 1,500 words. **Pays 10¢/word**. **Buys 30 mss/year.** Query with published clips.

Poetry Jim Schley, poetry editor. Free verse, light verse, traditional. **Buys 4 poems/year.** Submit maximum 5 poems. **Pays $25.**

Tips "We will work with subject-matter experts to make their work suitable for our audience."

N $ $ OCEAN MAGAZINE

to Celebrate and Protect, P.O. Box 84, Rodanthe NC 27968-0084. (252)256-2296. E-mail: diane@oceanmag.org. Web site: www.oceanmag.org. **Contact:** Diane Buccheri, editor. **100% freelance written.** Quarterly magazine covering the ocean, its ecosystem, its creatures, recreation, pollution, energy sources, the love of it. "*OCEAN Magazine* serves to celebrate and protect the greatest, most comprehensive resource for life on earth, our world's ocean. *OCEAN* publishes articles, stories, poems, essays, and photography about the ocean—observations, experiences, scientific and environmental discussions—written with fact and feeling, illustrated with images from nature." Estab. 2003. Circ. 10,000. Pays on publication. Publishes ms an average of 2-4 months after acceptance. Byline given. Buys one-time rights. Editorial lead time 3 months. Submit seasonal material 3 months in advance. Accepts queries by mail, e-mail, phone. Accepts previously published material. Accepts simultaneous submissions. Responds in 2 weeks to queries; 1 month to mss. Sample copy and writer's guidelines online.

Nonfiction Book excerpts, essays, general interest, historical/nostalgic, inspirational, interview/profile, opinion, personal experience, photo feature, technical, travel, spiritual. Does not want poor writing. **Buys 24-36 mss/year.** Query. Length: 75-5,000 words. **Pays $75-500.**

Photos State availability with submission. Reviews 3×5, 4×6, 5×7 prints, JPEG files. Buys one-time rights. Negotiates payment individually. Identification of subjects, model releases required.

Fiction Adventure, fantasy, historical, novel excerpts, romance, slice-of-life vignettes. **Buys 1-2 mss/year.** Query. Length: 100-2,000 words. **Pays $75-400.**

Poetry Avant-garde, free verse, haiku, light verse, traditional. **Buys 12 poems/year.** Submit maximum 6 poems. **Pays $75-200.**

Fillers Anecdotes, facts. **Buys 4-12/year.** Length: 20-100 words. **Pays $25-50.**

Tips "Submit with a genuine love and concern for the ocean and its creatures."

$ $ $ $ ORION

The Orion Society, 187 Main St., Great Barrington MA 01230. E-mail: orion@orionsociety.org. Web site: www.oriononline.org. Editor: Jennifer Sahn. **Contact:** Submissions, *Orion* magazine. **90% freelance written.** Bimonthly magazine covering nature and culture. "*Orion* is a magazine about the issues of our time: how we live, what we value, what sustains us. *Orion* explores an emerging alternative worldview through essays, literary journalism, short stories, interviews, and reviews, as well as photo essays and portfolios of art." Estab. 1982. Circ. 22,000. Pays on publication. Publishes ms an average of 3-12 months after acceptance. Byline given. Buys first North American serial rights. Editorial lead time 3-9 months. Submit seasonal material 9 months in advance. Accepts queries by mail, e-mail. Accepts simultaneous submissions. Responds in 1-2 months to queries; 4-6 months to mss. Sample copy and writer's guidelines online.

Nonfiction Essays, exposé, historical/nostalgic, humor, personal experience, photo feature, reported feature. No "What I learned during my walk in the woods"; personal hiking/adventure/travel anecdotes; unsolicited poetry; writing that deals with the natural world in only superficial ways. **Buys 40-50 mss/year.** Send complete ms. Length: 2,000-4,500 words. **Pays $300-2,000.** Pays expenses of writers on assignment.

Photos State availability with submission. Reviews contact sheets, prints. Buys one-time rights. Negotiates payment individually.

Columns/Departments Point of View (opinion essay by a noted authority), 625 words; Sacred & Mundane (funny, ironic or awe-inspiring ways nature exists within or is created by contemporary culture), 200-600 words; Health & the Environment (emphasizes and explores relationship between human health and a healthy natural world, or forces that threaten both simultaneously), 1,300 words; Reviews (new books, films and recordings related to *Orion's* mission), 250-600 words; Coda (an endpaper), 650 words. **Buys 85 mss/year.** Send complete ms. **Pays $25-300.**

Fiction Ethnic, historical, humorous, mainstream, slice-of-life vignettes. No manuscripts that don't carry an environmental message or involve the landscape/nature as a major character. Buys up to 1 ms/year. Send complete ms. Length: 1,200-4,000 words. **Pays 10-20¢/word.**

Tips "We are most impressed by and most likely to work with writers whose submissions show they know our magazine. If you are proposing a story, your query must: 1. Be detailed in its approach and reflect the care you will give the story itself; 2. Define where in the magazine you believe the story would be appropriate; 3. Include three tear sheets of previously published work. If you are submitting a manuscript, it must be double-spaced, typed or printed in black ink. Please be sure your name and a page number appear on each page of your submission, and that we have your phone number and SASE."

N $ $ $ OUTDOOR AMERICA

Izaak Walton League of America, 707 Conservation Ln., Gaithersburg MD 20878-2983. (301)548-0150. Fax: (301)548-9409. E-mail: oa@iwla.org. Web site: www.iwla.org. **Contact:** Jason McGarvey, editor. Quarterly magazine covering national conservation efforts/issues related to and involving members of the Izaak Walton League. "A 4-color publication, *Outdoor America* is received by League members, as well as representatives of Congress and the media. Our audience, located predominantly in the midwestern and mid-Atlantic states, enjoys traditional recreational pursuits, such as fishing, hiking, hunting, and boating. All have a keen interest in protecting the future of our natural resources and outdoor recreation heritage." Estab. 1922. Circ. 40,000. **Pays on acceptance.** Publishes ms an average of 2 months after acceptance. Offers 1/3 original rate kill fee. Buys first North American serial rights. Accepts queries by mail, e-mail. Responds in 2 months to queries. Sample copy for $2.50. Writer's guidelines online.

Nonfiction Conservation and natural resources issue stories with a direct connection to the work and members of the Izaak Walton League. Features should be 2,000-3,000 words. Essays on outdoor ethics and conservation (1,500-2,000 words). No fiction, poetry, or unsubstantiated opinion pieces. Query or send ms for short columns/news pieces (500 words or less). Features are planned 6-12 months in advance. **Pays $1,000-1,500 for features.**

Photos Send tearsheets or nonreturnable samples. Pays $100-500.

N $ OUTDOORS SPECTACULAR

The Thrilling Variety Magazine of Fact and Fiction, P.O. Box 52022 NPO, 313 St. Anne's Rd., Winnipeg MB R2M 5P9 Canada. (204)955-0599. E-mail: editor@outdoorsspectacular.ca. Web site: www.outdoorsspectacular.ca. **Contact:** Brian G. Hanslip, editor/publisher. **75% freelance written.** Quarterly magazine covering outdoor tourism industry. Estab. 2005. Circ. 2,000. Pays on publication. Publishes ms an average of 3-9 months after acceptance. Byline given. Offers 50% or $25-50 kill fee. Buys first North American serial, first, one-time, second serial (reprint), electronic rights. Editorial lead time 3 months. Submit seasonal material 3 months in advance. Accepts queries by mail, e-mail. Accepts previously published material. Accepts simultaneous submissions. Responds in 1 month to queries; 1 month to mss. Sample copy for $3.95. Writer's guidelines online.

Nonfiction General interest, how-to (hunting, fishing, camping, traveling, etc.), humor, inspirational, interview/profile, new product, personal experience, photo feature, technical, travel, environmental, ecological, science, nature, wildlife. Does not want political, religious, tree-hugger propaganda, etc. **Buys 4-8 mss/year.** Send complete ms. Length: 500-2,000 words. **Pays $50-100.**

Photos Send photos with submission. Reviews 5×4 prints, GIF/JPEG files. Buys one-time rights. Offers no additional payment for photos accepted with ms.

Fiction "All fiction must have something to do with outdoors!" Adventure, experimental, horror, humorous, mystery, romance, science fiction, slice-of-life vignettes, suspense, cross genre, inspirational, psychological thrillers. Does not want erotica, splatterpunk, special interest, political, ethnic, confessions, religious. **Buys 4-8 mss/year.** Send complete ms. Length: 1,000-3,000 words. **Pays $50-100.**

Poetry Avant-garde, free verse, haiku, light verse, traditional. Does not want erotica, splatterpunk, special interest, political, ethnic, confessionals, religious, or tree-hugger propaganda. "We publish one poet per issue exclusively." See guidelines. **Buys 20 poems/year.** Submit maximum 5 poems. Length: 10-50 lines.

Fillers Facts, newsbreaks, short humor. **Buys 8-16/year.** Length: 250-500 words.

Tips "For nonfiction, follow the three E's of journalism: engage, entertain, educate. For fiction, delight, enchant, scare or thrill us. I like stories with a twist and/or surprise ending."

N $ $ $ $ SIERRA

85 Second St., 2nd Floor, San Francisco CA 94105. Web site: www.sierraclub.org. **Contact:** Managing Editor. Works with a small number of new/unpublished writers each year. Bimonthly magazine emphasizing conservation and environmental politics for people who are well educated, activist, outdoor-oriented, and politically well informed with a dedication to conservation. Estab. 1893. Circ. 695,000. **Pays on acceptance.** Publishes ms an average of 4 months after acceptance. Byline given. Offers negotiable kill fee. Buys first North American serial rights. Accepts queries by mail, fax. Accepts previously published material. Responds in 2 months to queries. Sample copy for $3 and SASE, or online. Writer's guidelines online.

- The editor reports an interest in seeing pieces on environmental "heroes," thoughtful features on new developments in solving environmental problems, and outdoor adventure stories with a strong environmental element.

Nonfiction Exposé (well-documented articles on environmental issues of national importance such as energy, wilderness, forests, etc.), general interest (well-researched nontechnical pieces on areas of particular environmental concern), interview/profile, photo feature (photo essays on threatened or scenic areas), journalistic treatments of semitechnical topic (energy sources, wildlife management, land use, waste management, etc.). No "My trip to . . ." or "Why we must save wildlife/nature" articles; no poetry or general superficial essays on environmentalism; no reporting on purely local environmental issues. **Buys 30-36 mss/year.** Query with published clips. Length: 1,000-3,000 words. **Pays $800-3,000.**

Reprints Send photocopy with rights for sale noted and information about when and where the material previously appeared. Payment negotiable.

Photos Send photos with submission. Buys one-time rights. Pays maximum $300 for transparencies; more for cover photos.

Columns/Departments Food for Thought (food's connection to environment); Good Going (adventure journey); Hearth & Home (advice for environmentally sound living); Body Politics (health and the environment); Profiles (biographical look at environmentalists); Hidden Life (exposure of hidden environmental problems in everyday objects); Lay of the Land (national/international concerns), 500-700 words; Mixed Media (essays on environment in the media; book reviews), 200-300 words. **Pays $50-500.**

The online magazine carries original content not found in the print edition and includes writer's guidelines.

Tips "Queries should include an outline of how the topic would be covered and a mention of the political appropriateness and timeliness of the article. Statements of the writer's qualifications should be included."

N $SOCKET SHOCKER MAGAZINE

SAMPLE Press, P.O. Box 471159, Fort Worth TX 76147. E-mail: info@socketshocker.com. Web site: www.socketshocker.com. **Contact:** Jennifer Farley, editor (submissions@socketshocker.com). **70% freelance written.** Quarterly magazine covering environment/ecology themes, organic living, and vegetarianism. "*Socket Shocker Magazine* is a progressive publication which considers writing in every genre, but the major underlying theme marbled throughout everything we print is steadfast (not radical) environmentalism, vegetarianism, animal and human (particularly women's) rights, organic living and natural health." Estab. 2006. Circ. 1,500. Pays on publication. Publishes ms an average of 3-6 months after acceptance. Byline given. Buys first North American serial, first, one-time, electronic rights. Editorial lead time 4 months. Submit seasonal material 4 months in advance. Accepts queries by mail, e-mail. Responds in 6 weeks to queries. Writer's guidelines online.

Nonfiction Essays, exposé, general interest, how-to (organic gardening, organic/vegetarian cooking, recycling, composting, etc.), humor, inspirational, interview/profile, opinion, personal experience, shorts, brief news items or full length articles related to the world of liberal activism, environmentalism, vegetarianism, political cartoons. Does not want hate-related or sexist articles and essays, erotica, or gratuitous violence. **Buys 40 mss/year.** Send complete ms. Length: 500-3,500 words. **Pays ½¢/word.** Sometimes pays expenses of writers on assignment.

Photos Send photos with submission. Reviews prints, JPEG files. Buys first time rights. Offers 50¢/photo. Captions, identification of subjects, model releases required.

Columns/Departments The Green House Effect (natural house-cleaning methods), 500-1,500 words; Fourth Estate (environmentalism vs. government issues), 1,500-2,000 words; Art Party (profiles new talent in art and writing), 1,000-2,500 words; Veg Out (low-fat, organic vegetarian/vegan recipes with photos and anecdotes), 1,000-2,500 words. **Buys 15-25 mss/year.** Send complete ms. **Pays ½¢/word.**

Fiction Humorous, mainstream. Does not want erotica. **Buys 4-8 mss/year.** Send complete ms. Length: 1,000-2,500 words. **Pays ½¢/word.**

Poetry Avant-garde, free verse, light verse, traditional. Does not want love or angst-ridden poetry. **Buys 10-12 poems/year.** Submit maximum 3 poems. Length: 4-35 lines. **Pays ½¢/word.**

Fillers Anecdotes, facts, newsbreaks, short humor. **Buys 30-40/year.** Length: 50-500 words. **Pays ½¢/word.**

Tips "A freelancer can best approach and break into *Socket Shocker Magazine* by being sincere and earnest in their writing. The magazine's ethical stance is very clear, but we do not want radical or extremist slants in articles. Everything should be clear and factual, relevant to environmentalist, vegetarian and artistic readers, and present both sides of any story."

N $ $WHISPER IN THE WOODS

Nature Journal, Turning Leaf Productions, LLC, P.O. Box 1014, Traverse City MI 49685-1014. (231)943-0153. E-mail: editor@whisperinthewoods.com. Web site: www.whisperinthewoods.com. Editor: Kimberli Bindschatel. Managing Editor: Denise Baker. **100% freelance written.** Quarterly literary art journal covering nature, art and photography. "We focus on the appreciation of the beauty of nature." Estab. 2002. Circ. 10,000. Pays on publication. Publishes ms an average of 9 months after acceptance. Byline sometimes given. Offers 20% kill fee. Buys first North American serial rights. Editorial lead time 1 year. Submit seasonal material 1 year in advance. Accepts queries by mail. Accepts previously published material. Accepts simultaneous submissions. Sample copy for $8. Writer's guidelines online.

Nonfiction Essays, inspirational, personal experience, photo feature, travel. Query with published clips. Length: 600-1,500 words. **Pays $20-300.**

Photos State availability with submission. Reviews contact sheets, GIF/JPEG files. Buys one-time rights. Captions required.

Poetry Denise Baker, managing editor. Avant-garde, free verse, haiku, light verse, traditional. **Buys 4 poems/year.** Submit maximum 5 poems. **Pays $25-40.**

Tips "Carefully follow submission guidelines."

$ $ $ $ WILDLIFE CONSERVATION

2300 Southern Blvd., Bronx NY 10460. E-mail: nsimmons@wcs.org. Web site: www.wcs.org. **Contact:** Nancy Simmons, senior editor. Bimonthly magazine for environmentally aware readers. Offers 25% kill fee. Buys first North American serial rights. Accepts simultaneous submissions. Responds in 1 month to queries. Sample copy for $4.95 (plus $1 postage). Writer's guidelines available for SASE or via e-mail.

Nonfiction "We want well-reported articles on conservation issues, conservation successes, and straight natural history based on author's research." **Buys 30 mss/year.** Query with published clips. Length: 300-2,000 words. **Pays $1/word for features and department articles, and $150 for short pieces.**

PERSONAL COMPUTERS

BASELINE

Ziff Davis Media, Inc., 28 E. 28th St., New York NY 10016. (212)503-5435. Fax: (212)503-5454. E-mail: baseline @ziffdavis.com. Web site: www.baselinemag.com. Editor-in-Chief: Tom Steinert-Threlkeld. Managing Editor: Anna Maria Virzi. **Contact:** Elizabeth Bennett, associate editor. Monthly magazine covering "pricing, planning, and managing the implementation of next generation IT solutions. *Baseline* is edited for senior IT and coroporate management business leaders." Circ. 125,000. Editorial lead time 3 months.

- Managing Editor Maria Virzi says, "Most of the reporting and writing is done by staff writers and editors."

$ EZ TECH: WINDOWS XP

Future Network USA, 150 N. Hill Dr., Suite 40, Brisbane CA 94005. (415)468-4684. Fax: (415)468-4686. E-mail: editor@eztechguides.com. Web site: futurenetworkusa.com/publications/eztechguides.html. **Contact:** Robert Strohmeyer, editor. **80% freelance written.** Bimonthly magazine covering Microsoft Windows XP and related software and hardware. "*EZ Tech: Windows XP* is America's leading Windows XP resource, packed with in-depth tutorials, advice, and news about Microsoft's Windows XP operating system and its related hardware and software." Estab. 2003. **Pays on acceptance.** Publishes ms an average of 2 months after acceptance. Byline given. Offers 10% kill fee. Buys all rights. Editorial lead time 3 months. Submit seasonal material 3 months in advance. Accepts queries by e-mail. Responds in 2-3 weeks to queries. Sample copy online. Writer's guidelines by e-mail.

- "Our international team of seasoned technology writers brings authority, humor, and expertise to readers whose technology experience levels range from beginner to itermediate. We are the smart person's alternative to technical manuals, and we satisfy our readers' desires for both information and enteratinment through lively, crisp copy that redefines what a technology magazine can be."

Nonfiction How-to, new product, technical. **Buys 60 mss/year.** Query with published clips. Length: 500-8,000 words. **Pays 25-50¢/word.** Sometimes pays expenses of writers on assignment.

Tips "We're looking for writers who are absolute experts with Windows XP and can bring the world of technology to life with fun, exciting, and entertaining copy. Our magazine is the smart person's alternative to the technical manual, and we need writers who can speak to an audience of intelligent readers who are too busy for jargon. If you're a world-class Windows XP geek with a flair for the written word and an astoundingly nuanced sense of humor, we welcome your pitches. Your query should demonstrate both your technical expertise and your writing voice, and should be accompanied by clips from a major technology publication. Hint: We are a technology magazine, and you will be judged on your use of technology in communicating with us. Clips should be sent as PDF attachments of URLs. Please do not send queries via snail mail. First-time writers and hobbyists need not apply."

INFOWORLD

Lead with Knowledge, InfoWorld Media Group, 501 2nd St., Suite 500, San Francisco CA 94107. Web site: www.infoworld.com. Editor-in-Chief: Steve Fox. Weekly magazine. "*InfoWorld* provides in-depth technical analysis on key products, solutions, and technologies for sound buying decisions and business gain." Circ. 220,000. Editorial lead time 2 months. Accepts queries by e-mail.

- Contact specific editor.

Nonfiction Reviews, features, and news.

$ $ $ LAPTOP

Bedford Communications, 1410 Broadway, 21st Floor, New York NY 10018. (212)807-8220. Fax: (212)807-1098. E-mail: ccummings@bedfordmags.com. Web site: www.laptopmag.com. Editor-in-Chief: Mark Spoonauer. **Contact:** Corrine Cummings, assistant editor. **60% freelance written.** Monthly magazine covering mobile computing, such as laptop computers, PDAs, software, and peripherals; industry trends. "Publication is geared toward the mobile technology laptop computer buyer, with an emphasis on the small office." Estab. 1991. Pays on publication. Publishes ms an average of 3 months after acceptance. Byline given. Offers 20% kill fee. Buys all rights. Editorial lead time 4 months. Accepts queries by e-mail. Responds in 4 months to queries. Sample copy online. Writer's guidelines not available.

Nonfiction How-to (e.g., how to install a CD-ROM drive), technical, hands-on reviews, features. **Buys 80-100 mss/year.** Length: 300-3,500 words. **Pays $150-1,250.** Sometimes pays expenses of writers on assignment.

Tips "Send résumé with feature-length clips (technology-related, if possible) to editorial offices. Unsolicited manuscripts are not accepted or returned."

$ $ $ $ MACADDICT

Imagine Media, 150 North Hill Dr., Suite 40, Brisbane CA 94005. (415)468-4684. Fax: (415)468-4686. E-mail: editor@macaddict.com. Web site: www.macaddict.com. **Contact:** Rik Myslewski, editor-in-chief. **35% freelance written.** Monthly magazine covering Macintosh computers. "*MacAddict* is a magazine for Macintosh computer enthusiasts of all levels. Writers must know, love and own Macintosh computers." Estab. 1996. Circ. 160,000. Pays on publication. Publishes ms an average of 3 months after acceptance. Byline given. Buys all rights. Editorial lead time 3 months. Submit seasonal material 2 months in advance. Accepts queries by mail, e-mail. Responds in 1 month to queries.

Nonfiction How-to, new product, technical. No humor, case studies, personal experience, essays. **Buys 30 mss/year.** Query with or without published clips. Length: 250-7,500 words. **Pays $50-2,500.**

Columns/Departments Reviews (always assigned), 300-750 words; How-to's (detailed, step-by-step), 500-2,500 words; features, 1,000-3,500 words. **Buys 20 mss/year.** Query with or without published clips. **Pays $50-2,500.**

The online magazine carries original content not found in the print edition. Contact: Niko Coucouvanis, online editor.

Tips "Send us an idea for a short one to two page how-to and/or send us a letter outlining your publishing experience and areas of Mac expertise so we can assign a review to you (reviews editor is Roman Loyola). Your submission should have great practical hands-on benefit to a reader, be fun to read in the author's natural voice, and include lots of screenshot graphics. We require electronic submissions. Impress our reviews editor with well-written reviews of Mac products and then move up to bigger articles from there."

$ $ $ $ MACLIFE

Imagine Media, 150 North Hill Drive, Suite 40, Brisbane CA 94005. (415)468-4684. Fax: (415)468-4686. E-mail: editor@macaddict.com. Web site: www.maclife.com. **Contact:** Rik Myslewski, editor-in-chief. **35% freelance written.** Monthly magazine covering Macintosh computers. "*MacLife* is a magazine for Macintosh computer enthusiasts of all levels. Writers must know, love and own Macintosh computers." Estab. 1996. Circ. 160,000. Pays on publication. Publishes ms an average of 3 months after acceptance. Byline given. Buys all rights. Editorial lead time 3 months. Submit seasonal material 2 months in advance. Accepts queries by mail, e-mail. Responds in 1 month to queries.

- This publication was formerly titled "MacAddict."

Nonfiction How-to, new product, technical. No humor, case studies, personal experience, essays. **Buys 30 mss/year.** Query with or without published clips. Length: 250-7,500 words. **Pays $50-2,500.**

Columns/Departments Reviews (always assigned), 300-750 words; How-to's (detailed, step-by-step), 500-2,500 words; features, 1,000-3,500 words. **Buys 20 mss/year.** Query with or without published clips. **Pays $50-2,500.**

The online magazine carries original content not found in the print edition. Contact: Niko Coucouvanis, online editor.

Tips "Send us an idea for a short one to two page how-to and/or send us a letter outlining your publishing experience and areas of Mac expertise so we can assign a review to you (reviews editor is Roman Loyola). Your submission should have great practical hands-on benefit to a reader, be fun to read in the author's natural voice, and include lots of screenshot graphics. We require electronic submissions. Impress our reviews editor with well-written reviews of Mac products and then move up to bigger articles from there."

ONLINE MAGAZINE

Information Today, Inc., P.O. Box 78225, Indianapolis IN 46278. (317)870-1994. Fax: (317)870-1996. E-mail: marydee@infotoday.com. Web site: www.infotoday.com/online. **Contact:** Marydee Ojala, editor. Bimonthly magazine for librarians and other professionals who routinely use online services for information delivery, research, and knowledge management. "*Online* provides evaluation and informed opinion about selecting, using, and managing electronic information products, as well as industry and professional information about online database systems." Estab. 1977. Circ. 9,000. Byline given. Editorial lead time 3-4 months. Sample copy and writer's guidelines online.

- Unaccepted mss will not be returned.

Nonfiction Query. **Pays variable amount.**

Tips Read online guidelines.

PC GAMER

Future Network USA, 150 N. Hill Dr., Suite 40, Brisbane CA 94005. (415)468-4684. Fax: (415)468-4686. E-mail: editor@pcgamer.com. Web site: www.pcgamer.com. Monthly magazine. Accepts queries by e-mail.

Nonfiction General interest, new product. Query.

Tips "Audience is serious Windows-based gamers."

⊘ PC MAGAZINE

Ziff-Davis Media, Inc., 28 E. 28th St., New York NY 10016. (212)503-3500. Fax: (212)503-5799. E-mail: pcmag@ziffdavis.com. Web site: www.pcmag.com. Editor-in-Chief: Jim Louderback. Managing Editor: Paul Ross. Magazine published 22 times/year. Circ. 1,228,658. Editorial lead time 4 months.

- Query before submitting.

⊘ PC WORLD

PC World Communications, Inc., 501 2nd St., Suite 600, San Francisco CA 94107. (415)243-0500. Fax: (415)442-1891. E-mail: letters@pcworld.com. Web site: www.pcworld.com. Editor-in-Chief: Harry McCracken. Managing Editor: Kimberly Brinson. Senior Associate Editor: Narasu Rebbapragada or Eric Butterfield. Senior Editor: Anush Yegyazarian. **Contact:** Article Proposals. Monthly magazine covering personal computers. "*PC World* was created to give PC-proficient managers advice on which technology products to buy, tips on how to use those products most efficiently, news about the latest technological developments, and alerts regarding current problems with products and manufacturers." Circ. 1,100,000. Editorial lead time 3 months. Accepts queries by mail. Sample copy not available. Writer's guidelines by e-mail.

- "We have very few opportunities for writers who are not already contributing to the magazine."
- O━ "One way we discover new talent is by assigning short tips and how-to pieces."

Nonfiction How-to, reviews, news items, features. Query. **Payment varies.**

Tips "Once you're familiar with *PC World*, you can write us a query letter. Your letter should answer the following questions as specifically and consisely as possible. What is the problem, technique, or product you want to discuss? Why will *PC World* readers be interested in it? Which section of the magazine do you think it best fits? What is the specific audience for the piece (e.g., database or LAN users, desktop publishers, and so on)?"

$ $ $ SMART COMPUTING

Sandhills Publishing, 131 W. Grand Dr., Lincoln NE 68521. (800)544-1264. Fax: (402)479-2104. E-mail: editor@smartcomputing.com. Web site: www.smartcomputing.com. Editor: Rod Scher. **Contact:** Ron Kobler, editor-in-chief. **45% freelance written.** Monthly magazine. "We focus on plain-English computing articles with an emphasis on tutorials that improve productivity without the purchase of new hardware." Estab. 1990. Circ. 200,000. **Pays on acceptance.** Publishes ms an average of 2 months after acceptance. Byline given. Offers 25% kill fee. Buys all rights. Editorial lead time 4 months. Submit seasonal material 4 months in advance. Accepts queries by mail, e-mail. Accepts simultaneous submissions. Responds in 1 month to queries. Sample copy for $7.99. Writer's guidelines for #10 SASE.

- O━ Break in with "any article containing little-known tips for improving software and hardware performance and Web use. We're also seeking clear reporting on key trends changing personal technology."

Nonfiction How-to, new product, technical. No humor, opinion, personal experience. **Buys 250 mss/year.** Query with published clips. Length: 800-3,200 words. **Pays $240-960.** Pays expenses of writers on assignment up to $75.

Photos Send photos with submission. Buys all rights. Offers no additional payment for photos accepeted with ms. Captions required.

Tips "Focus on practical, how-to computing articles. Our readers are intensely productivity-driven. Carefully review recent issues. We receive many ideas for stories printed in the last 6 months."

WIRED MAGAZINE

Condé Nast Publications, 520 Third St., 3rd Floor, San Francisco CA 94107-1815. (415)276-5000. Fax: (415)276-5150. E-mail: submit@wiredmag.com. Web site: www.wired.com/wired. Publisher: Dean Shutte. Editor-in-chief: Chris Anderson. Managing Editor: Rebecca Smith Hurd. Editor: Blaise Zerega. **Contact:** Chris Baker, editorial assistant. **95% freelance written.** Monthly magazine covering technology and digital culture. "We cover the digital revolution and related advances in computers, communications and lifestyles." Estab. 1993. Circ. 500,000. Pays on publication. Publishes ms an average of 3 months after acceptance. Byline given. Offers 25% kill fee. Buys all rights for items less than 1,000 words, first North American serial rights for pieces over 1,000 words. Editorial lead time 3 months. Responds in 3 weeks to queries. Sample copy for $4.95. Writer's guidelines by e-mail.

Nonfiction Essays, interview/profile, opinion. "No poetry or trade articles." **Buys 85 features, 130 short pieces, 200 reviews, 36 essays, and 50 other mss/year.** Query. Pays expenses of writers on assignment.

Tips "Send query letter with clips to Chris Baker. Read the magazine. We get too many inappropriate queries. We need quality writers who understand our audience, and who understand how to query."

PHOTOGRAPHY

N 🌐 AUSTRALIAN PHOTOGRAPHY

Australia's Best-Selling Photo Magazine, Yaffa Publishing, 17-21 Bellevue St., Surry Hills NSW 2010 Australia. (61)(2)9281-2333. Fax: (61)(2)9281-2750. E-mail: yaffa@yaffa.com.au. Web site: www.yaffa.com.au. Monthly magazine covering both traditional and digital photography. Estab. 1950.

Nonfiction General interest, how-to, interview/profile, new product, technical. Query.

$ NATURE PHOTOGRAPHER

Nature Photographer Publishing Co., Inc., P.O. Box 220, Lubec ME 04652. (207)733-4201. Fax: (207)733-4202. E-mail: nature_photographer@yahoo.com. Web site: www.naturephotographermag.com. **Contact:** Helen Longest-Saccone, editor-in-chief/photo editor. Quarterly magazine written by field contributors and editors; write to above address to become a "Field Contributor." *Nature Photographer* emphasizes nature photography that uses low-impact and local less-known locations, techniques and ethics. Articles include how-to, travel to worldwide wilderness locations, and how nature photography can be used to benefit the environment and environmental education of the public. Estab. 1990. Circ. 35,000. Pays on publication. Buys one-time rights. Submit seasonal material 8 months in advance. Accepts queries by e-mail. Accepts simultaneous submissions. Responds in 2 months to queries. Sample copy for 9×12 SAE and 6 first-class stamps. Writer's guidelines by e-mail.

Nonfiction How-to (exposure, creative techniques, techniques to make photography easier, low-impact techniques, macro photography, wildlife, scenics, flowers), photo feature, technical, travel. No articles about photographing in zoos or on game farms. **Buys 56-72 mss/year.** Length: 750-2,500 words. **Pays $75-150.**

Photos Send photos upon request. Do not send with submission. Reviews 35mm and digital images on CD (both scanned and digitally captured images) transparencies. Buys one-time rights. Offers no additional payment for photos accepted with ms. Identification of subjects required.

Tips "Must have good, solid research and knowledge of subject. Be sure to obtain guidelines before submitting query. If you have not requested guidelines within the last year, request an updated version because *Nature Photographer* is now written by editors and field contributors, and guidelines will outline how you can become a field contributor."

$ $ PC PHOTO

Werner Publishing Corp., 12121 Wilshire Blvd., 12th Floor, Los Angeles CA 90025. (310)820-1500. Fax: (310)826-5008. E-mail: pceditors@wernerpublishing.com. Web site: www.pcphotomag.com. Managing Editor: Chris Robinson. **Contact:** Rob Sheppard, editor. **60% freelance written.** Bimonthly magazine covering digital photography. "Our magazine is designed to help photographers better use digital technologies to improve their photography." Estab. 1997. Circ. 175,000. Pays on publication. Publishes ms an average of 4 months after acceptance. Byline given. Buys one-time rights. Editorial lead time 6 months. Submit seasonal material 6 months in advance. Accepts queries by mail. Responds in 1 month to queries. Sample copy for #10 SASE or online. Writer's guidelines online.

Nonfiction How-to, personal experience, photo feature. **Buys 30 mss/year.** Query. Length: 1,200 words. **Pays $500 for assigned articles; approximately $400 for unsolicited articles.**

Photos Do not send original transparencies or negatives. Send photos with submission. Buys one-time rights. Offers $100-200/photo.

Tips "Since *PCPHOTO* is a photography magazine, we must see photos before any decision can be made on an article, so phone queries are not appropriate. Ultimately, whether we can use a particular piece or not will depend greatly on the photographs and how they fit in with material already in our files. We take a fresh look at the modern photographic world by encouraging photography and the use of new technologies. Editorial is intended to demystify the use of modern equipment by emphasizing practical use of the camera and the computer, highlighting the technique rather than the technical."

$ $ PHOTO TECHNIQUES

Preston Publications, Inc., 6600 W. Touhy Ave., Niles IL 60714. (847)647-2900. Fax: (847)647-1155. E-mail: slewis@prestonpub.com. Web site: www.phototechmag.com. **50% freelance written.** Prefers to work with experienced photographer-writers; happy to work with excellent photographers whose writing skills are lacking. Bimonthly publication covering photochemistry, lighting, optics, processing, and printing, Zone System, digital imaging/scanning/printing, special effects, sensitometry, etc. Aimed at serious amateurs. Article conclusions should be able to be duplicated by readers. Estab. 1979. Circ. 30,000. Pays within 3 weeks of publication. Publishes ms an average of 8 months after acceptance. Byline given. Buys one-time rights. Sample copy for $5. Writer's guidelines by e-mail.

Nonfiction How-to, photo feature, technical (product review), special interest articles within the above listed topics. Query or send complete ms. Length: Open, but most features run approximately 2,500 words or 3-4 magazine pages. **Pays $100-450 for well-researched technical articles.**

Photos Photographers have a much better chance of having their photos published if the photos accompany a written article. Prefers JPEGs scanned at 300 dpi and sent via e-mail or CD-ROM, or prints, slides, and transparencies. Buys one-time rights. Ms payment includes payment for photos. Captions, technical information required.

Tips "Study the magazine! Virtually all writers we publish are readers of the magazine. We are now more receptive than ever to articles about photographers, history, aesthetics, and informative backgrounders about specific areas of the photo industry or specific techniques. Successful writers for our magazine are doing what they write about."

$ PICTURE MAGAZINE

41 Union Square W., Suite 504, New York NY 10003. (212)352-2700. Fax: (212)352-2155. E-mail: picmag@aol.com. Web site: www.picturemagazine.com. **100% freelance written.** Bimonthly magazine covering professional photography topics. Estab. 1995. Circ. 16,000. Pays on publication. Publishes ms an average of 2 months after acceptance. Byline given. Buys one-time rights. Editorial lead time 3 months. Submit seasonal material 3 months in advance. Accepts queries by e-mail. Accepts previously published material. Accepts simultaneous submissions. Sample copy for free. Writer's guidelines free.

Nonfiction General interest, how-to, interview/profile, new product, photo feature, technical. **Buys 5 mss/year.** Send complete ms. Length: 1,500-2,500 words. **Pays $150.** Pays expenses of writers on assignment.

Photos State availability with submission. Buys one-time rights. Offers no additional payment for photos accepted with ms. Captions required.

⊘ POPULAR PHOTOGRAPHY & IMAGING

Hachette Filipacchi Media U.S., Inc., 1633 Broadway, New York NY 10019. (212)767-6000. Fax: (212)767-5602. E-mail: popeditor@aol.com. Web site: www.popphoto.com. Managing Editor: Miriam Leuchter. **Contact:** Jason Schneider, editor-in-chief. Monthly magazine edited for amateur to professional photographers. Provides incisive instructional articles, authoritative tests of photographic equipment; covers still and digital imaging; travel, color, nature, and large-format columns, plus up-to-date industry information. Circ. 453,944. Editorial lead time 2 months.

- Query before submitting.

$ $ VIDEOMAKER

Videomaker, Inc., P.O. Box 4591, Chico CA 95927-4591. (530)891-8410. Fax: (530)891-8443. E-mail: editor@videomaker.com. Web site: www.videomaker.com. Editor-in-Chief: John Burkhart. Managing Editor: Jennifer O'Rourke. **Contact:** Charles Fulton, associate editor. Monthly magazine covering audio and video production, camcorders, editing, computer video, DVDs. Estab. 1985. Circ. 62,311. Pays on publication. Publishes ms an average of 4 months after acceptance. Byline given. Buys electronic, all rights. Editorial lead time 5 months.

Submit seasonal material 5 months in advance. Accepts queries by mail, e-mail. Responds in 3 weeks to queries. Sample copy and writer's guidelines online.

- The magazine's voice is friendly, encouraging; never condescending to the audience.

Nonfiction How-to, technical. Special issues: Annual Buyer's Guide in October (13th issue of the year). **Buys 34 mss/year.** Query. Length: 800-1,500 words. **Pays $100-300.** Sometimes pays expenses of writers on assignment.

Photos Melissa Hageman, art director. Negotiates payment individually. Model releases required.

Fiction Storyboards for readers to reproduce. **Buys 3 mss/year.** Query. Length: 400-600 words. **Pays $150-200.**

POLITICS & WORLD AFFAIRS

THE AMERICAN SPECTATOR

1611 N. Kent St., Suite 901, Arlington VA 22209. (703)807-2011. Fax: (703)807-2013. E-mail: editor@spectator.org. Web site: www.spectator.org. Managing Editor: Amy Mitchell. Monthly magazine. ''For many years, one ideological viewpoint dominated American print and broadcast journalism. Today, that viewpoint still controls the entertainment and news divisions of the television networks, the mass-circulation news magazines, and the daily newspapers. *American Spectator* has attempted to balance the Left's domination of the media by debunking its perceived wisdom and advancing alternative ideas through spirited writing, insightful essays, humor and, most recently, through well-researched investigative articles that have themselves become news.'' Estab. 1967. Circ. 50,000. Pays on other. Accepts queries by mail.

Nonfiction ''Topics include politics, the press, foreign relations, the economy, culture. Stories most suited for publication are timely articles on previously unreported topics with national appeal. Articles should be thoroughly researched with a heavy emphasis on interviewing and reporting, and the facts of the article should be verifiable. We prefer articles in which the facts speak for themselves and shy away from editorial and first person commentary. No unsolicited poetry, fiction, satire, or crossword puzzles. Query with résumé, clips and SASE.

Columns/Departments The Continuing Crisis and Current Wisdom (humor); On the Prowl (''Washington insider news''). Query with résumé, clips and SASE.

$$ CHURCH & STATE

Americans United for Separation of Church and State, 518 C St. NE, Washington DC 20002. (202)466-3234. Fax: (202)466-3353. E-mail: americansunited@au.org. Web site: www.au.org. **Contact:** Joseph Conn, editor. **10% freelance written.** Monthly magazine emphasizing religious liberty and church/state relations matters. Strongly advocates separation of church and state. Readership is well-educated. Estab. 1947. Circ. 40,000. **Pays on acceptance.** Publishes ms an average of 2 months after acceptance. Buys all rights. Accepts queries by mail. Accepts simultaneous submissions. Responds in 2 months to queries. Sample copy and writer's guidelines for 9×12 SAE with 3 first-class stamps.

Nonfiction Exposé, general interest, historical/nostalgic, interview/profile. **Buys 11 mss/year.** Query. Length: 800-1,600 words. **Pays $150-300 for assigned articles.** Sometimes pays expenses of writers on assignment.

Reprints Send tearsheet, photocopy or typed ms with rights for sale noted and information about when and where the material previously appeared.

Photos Send photos with submission. Buys one-time rights. Pays negotiable fee for b&w prints. Captions required.

Tips ''We're looking for feature articles on underreported local church-state controversies. We also consider 'viewpoint' essays that offer a unique or personal take on church-state issues. We are not a religious magazine. You need to see our magazine before you try to write for it.''

$ COMMONWEAL

A Review of Public Affairs, Religion, Literature and the Arts, Commonweal Foundation, 475 Riverside Dr., Room 405, New York NY 10115. (212)662-4200. Fax: (212)662-4183. E-mail: editors@commonwealmagazine.org. Web site: www.commonwealmagazine.org. Editor: Paul Baumann. **Contact:** Patrick Jordan, managing editor. Biweekly journal of opinion edited by Catholic lay people, dealing with topical issues of the day on public affairs, religion, literature, and the arts. Estab. 1924. Circ. 20,000. Pays on publication. Byline given. Buys all rights. Submit seasonal material 2 months in advance. Responds in 2 months to queries. Sample copy for free. Writer's guidelines online.

Nonfiction Essays, general interest, interview/profile, personal experience, religious. **Buys 30 mss/year.** Query with published clips. Length: 2,000-2,500 words. **Pays $75-100.**

Columns/Departments Upfronts (brief, newsy reportorials, giving facts, information and some interpretation behind the headlines of the day), 750-1,000 words; Last Word (usually of a personal nature, on some aspect of the human condition: spiritual, individual, political, or social), 800 words.

Poetry Rosemary Deen, editor. Free verse, traditional. **Buys 20 poems/year. Pays 75¢/line.**
Tips "Articles should be written for a general but well-educated audience. While religious articles are always topical, we are less interested in devotional and churchy pieces than in articles which examine the links between 'worldly' concerns and religious beliefs."

$ $ THE FREEMAN: IDEAS ON LIBERTY

30 S. Broadway, Irvington-on-Hudson NY 10533. (914)591-7230. Fax: (914)591-8910. E-mail: freeman@fee.org. Web site: www.fee.org. Publisher: Foundation for Economic Education. **85% freelance written.** Monthly Publication for "the layman and fairly advanced students of liberty." Estab. 1946. Pays on publication. Publishes ms an average of 5 months after acceptance. Byline given. all rights, including reprint rights. Sample copy for 7½×10½ SASE with 4 first-class stamps.

- Eager to work with new/unpublished writers.

Nonfiction "We want nonfiction clearly analyzing and explaining various aspects of the free market, private property, limited-government philosophy. Though a necessary part of the literature of freedom is the exposure of collectivistic cliches and fallacies, our aim is to emphasize and explain the positive case for individual responsibility and choice in a free-market economy. We avoid name-calling and personality clashes. Ours is an intelligent analysis of the principles underlying a free-market economy. No political strategies or tactics." **Buys 100 mss/year.** Query with SASE. Length: 3,500 words. **Pays 10¢/word.** Sometimes pays expenses of writers on assignment.
Tips "It's most rewarding to find freelancers with new insights, fresh points of view. Facts, figures and quotations cited should be fully documented, to their original source, if possible."

$ $ THE NATION

33 Irving Place, New York NY 10003. (212)209-5400. Fax: (212)982-9000. Web site: www.thenation.com. **75% freelance written.** Works with a small number of new/unpublished writers each year. Weekly magazine "firmly committed to reporting on the issues of labor, national politics, business, consumer affairs, environmental politics, civil liberties, foreign affairs and the role and future of the Democratic Party." Estab. 1865. Pays on other. Buys first rights. Accepts queries by mail, e-mail, fax. Sample copy for free. Writer's guidelines online.

- See the Contests & Awards section for the Discovery-*The Nation* poetry contest.

Nonfiction "We welcome all articles dealing with the social scene, from an independent perspective." Queries encouraged. **Buys 100 mss/year. Pays $350-500.** Sometimes pays expenses of writers on assignment.
Columns/Departments Editorial, 500-700 words. **Pays $150.**
Poetry *The Nation* publishes poetry of outstanding aesthetic quality. Send poems with SASE. See the Contests & Awards section for the Discovery—*The Nation* poetry contest. **Payment negotiable.**
Tips "We are a journal of left/liberal political opinion covering national and international affairs. We are looking both for reporting and for fresh analysis. On the domestic front, we are particularly interested in civil liberties; civil rights; labor, economics, environmental and feminist issues and the role and future of the Democratic Party. Because we have readers all over the country, it's important that stories with a local focus have real national significance. In our foreign affairs coverage we prefer pieces on international political, economic and social developments. As the magazine which published Ralph Nader's first piece (and there is a long list of *Nation* "firsts"), we are seeking new writers."

NATIONAL REVIEW

215 Lexington Ave., New York NY 10016. (212)679-7330. E-mail: submissions@nationalreview.com. Web site: www.nationalreview.com. **Contact:** Rich Lowry, editor.

THE NATIONAL VOTER

League of Women Voters, 1730 M St. NW, Suite 1000, Washington DC 20036. (202)429-1965. Fax: (202)429-0854. E-mail: nationalvoter@lwv.org. Web site: www.lwv.org. Magazine published 3 times/year. "*The National Voter* provides background, perspective and commentary on public policy issues confronting citizens and their leaders at all levels of government. And it empowers people to make a difference in their communities by offering guidance, maturation and models for action." Estab. 1951. Circ. 100,000. Pays on publication. Byline given. Makes work-for-hire assignments. Editorial lead time 2 months. Accepts queries by mail, e-mail. Sample copy for free.
Nonfiction Exposé, general interest, interview/profile. No essays, personal experience, religious,opinion. **Buys 2-3 mss/year.** Query with published clips. Length: 200-4,000 words. **Payment always negotiated.** Pays expenses of writers on assignment.
Photos State availability with submission. Reviews contact sheets. Buys one-time rights. Offers no additional payment for photos accepted with ms. Captions, identification of subjects required.

THE NEW REPUBLIC

1331 H St. NW, Suite 700, Washington DC 20005. (202)508-4444. Fax: (202)628-9383. E-mail: letters@tnr.com. Web site: www.tnr.com. Editor-in-Chief: Martin Peretz. Editor: Franklin Foer. Weekly magazine. "*The New Republic* covers issues before they hit the mainstream, from energy to the environment, from foreign to fiscal policy. By publishing the best writing from a variety of view points, *The New Republic* continues to be America's best and most influential journal of opinion." Responds in 6-8 weeks to queries; 6-8 weeks to mss.

Tips "Poetry submissions should be sent by regular mail. No phone calls please."

⊘ THE ONION

Onion, Inc., 536 Broadway, 10th Floor, New York NY 10012. (212)627-1972. Fax: (212)627-1711. E-mail: infomat@theonion.com. Web site: www.theonion.com. Editor-in-Chief: Carol Kolb. Weekly magazine. "*The Onion* offers satirical editorial which uses invented names in all its stories, except when public figures are being satirized." Circ. 153,000.

- Does not buy freelance material or use freelance writers.

$ PROGRESSIVE POPULIST

Journal from America's Heartland, P.O. Box 819, Manchaca TX 78652. (512)828-7245. E-mail: populist@usa.net. Web site: www.populist.com. **Contact:** Jim Cullen, editor. **90% freelance written.** Biweekly tabloid covering politics and economics. "We cover issues of interest to workers, small businesses, and family farmers and ranchers." Estab. 1995. Circ. 15,000. Pays quarterly. Publishes ms an average of 1 month after acceptance. Byline given. Buys first North American serial, second serial (reprint) rights. Editorial lead time 3 weeks. Submit seasonal material 1 month in advance. Accepts queries by mail, e-mail, fax, phone. Accepts previously published material. Accepts simultaneous submissions. Sample copy and writer's guidelines free.

Nonfiction "We cover politics and economics. We are interested not so much in the dry reporting of campaigns and elections, or the stock markets and GNP, but in how big business is exerting more control over both the government and ordinary people's lives, and what people can do about it." Essays, exposé, general interest, historical/nostalgic, humor, interview/profile, opinion. "We are not much interested in 'sound-off' articles about state or national politics, although we accept letters to the editor. We prefer to see more 'journalistic' pieces, in which the writer does enough footwork to advance a story beyond the easy realm of opinion." **Buys 400 mss/year.** Query. Length: 600-1,000 words. **Pays $15-50.** Pays writers with contributor copies or other premiums if preferred by writer.

Reprints Send photocopy with rights for sale noted and information about when and where the material previously appeared.

Photos State availability with submission. Buys one-time rights. Negotiates payment individually. Identification of subjects required.

Tips "We do prefer submissions by e-mail. I find it's easier to work with e-mail and for the writer it probably increases the chances of getting a response."

$ $ THE PROGRESSIVE

409 E. Main St., Madison WI 53703. (608)257-4626. Fax: (608)257-3373. E-mail: editorial@progressive.org. Web site: www.progressive.org. **Contact:** Matthew Rothschild, editor. **75% freelance written.** Monthly Estab. 1909. Pays on publication. Publishes ms an average of 6 weeks after acceptance. Byline given. Accepts queries by mail. Responds in 1 month to queries. Sample copy for 9×12 SAE with 4 first-class stamps or sample articles online. Writer's guidelines online.

Nonfiction Investigative reporting (exposé of corporate malfeasance and governmental wrongdoing); electoral coverage (a current electoral development that has national implications); social movement pieces (important or interesting event or trend in the labor movement, or the GLBT movement, or in the area of racial justice, disability rights, the environment, women's liberation); foreign policy pieces (a development of huge moral importance where the US role may not be paramount); interviews (a long Q&A with a writer, activist, political figure, or musician who is widely known or doing especially worthwhile work); activism (highlights the work of activists and activist groups; increasingly, we are looking for good photographs of a dynamic or creative action, and we accompany the photos with a caption); book reviews (cover two or three current titles on a major issue of concern). Primarily interested in articles that interpret, from a progressive point of view, domestic and world affairs. Occasional lighter features. "*The Progressive* is a *political* publication. General interest is inappropriate. We do not want editorials, satire, historical pieces, philosophical peices or columns." Query. Length: 500-4,000 words. **Pays $500-1,300.**

Poetry Publishes 1 original poem a month. "We prefer poems that connect up—in one fashion or another, however obliquely—with political concerns. **Pays $150.**

Tips "Sought-after topics include electoral coverage, social movement, foreign policy, activism and book reviews."

$$$$ REASON

Free Minds and Free Markets, Reason Foundation, 3415 S. Sepulveda Blvd., Suite 400, Los Angeles CA 90034. (310)391-2245. Fax: (310)390-8986. E-mail: jsanchez@reason.com. Web site: www.reason.com. Editor-in-Chief: Nick Gillespie. **Contact:** Brian Doherty (by mail) or Julian Sanchez (by e-mail). **30% freelance written.** Monthly magazine covering politics, current events, culture, ideas. "*Reason* covers politics, culture and ideas from a dynamic libertarian perspective. It features reported works, opinion pieces, and book reviews." Estab. 1968. Circ. 55,000. **Pays on acceptance.** Byline given. Offers kill fee. Buys first North American serial, first, all rights. Editorial lead time 2 months. Submit seasonal material 3 months in advance. Accepts queries by mail, e-mail. Responds in 6 weeks to queries; 2 months to mss. Sample copy for $4. Writer's guidelines online.

Nonfiction Book excerpts, essays, exposé, general interest, humor, interview/profile, opinion. No products, personal experience, how-to, travel. **Buys 50-60 mss/year.** Query with published clips. Length: 850-5,000 words. **Pays $300-2,000.** Sometimes pays expenses of writers on assignment.

The online magazine carries original content not found in the print edition and includes writer's guidelines. Contact: Nick Gillespie.

Tips "We prefer queries of no more than one or two pages with specifically developed ideas about a given topic rather than more general areas of interest. Enclosing a few published clips also helps."

U.S. NEWS & WORLD REPORT

U.S. News & World Report, Inc., 1050 Thomas Jefferson St. NW, Washington DC 20007. (202)955-2000. Web site: www.usnews.com. Weekly magazine devoted largely to reporting and analyzing national and international affairs, politics, business, health, science, technology and social trends. Circ. 2,018,621. Editorial lead time 10 days.

- Query before submitting.

$$ WASHINGTON MONTHLY

The Washington Monthly Co., 1319 F St. NW, Suite 710, Washington DC 20004. (202)393-5155. Fax: (202)393-2444. E-mail: editors@washingtonmonthly.com. Web site: www.washingtonmonthly.com. Editor-in-Chief: Paul Glastris. **50% freelance written.** Monthly magazine covering politics, policy, media. "We are a neo-liberal publication with a long history and specific views—please read our magazine before submitting." Estab. 1969. Circ. 28,000. Pays on publication. Publishes ms an average of 2 months after acceptance. Byline given. Buys all rights. Editorial lead time 2 months. Submit seasonal material 4 months in advance. Accepts queries by mail, e-mail, fax, phone. Responds in 3 weeks to queries; 2 months to mss. Sample copy for 11×17 SAE with 5 first-class stamps or by e-mail. Writer's guidelines online.

Nonfiction Book excerpts, essays, exposé, general interest, historical/nostalgic, interview/profile, opinion, personal experience, technical, first-person political. "No humor, how-to, or generalized articles." **Buys 20 mss/year.** Query with or without published clips or send complete ms. Length: 1,500-5,000 words. **Pays 10¢/word.**

Photos State availability with submission. Reviews contact sheets, prints. Buys one-time rights. Negotiates payment individually.

Columns/Departments 10 Miles Square (about DC); On Political Books, Booknotes (both reviews of current political books), 1,500-3,000 words. **Buys 10 mss/year.** Query with published clips or send complete ms. **Pays 10¢/word.**

Tips "Call our editors to talk about ideas. Always pitch articles showing background research. We're particularly looking for first-hand accounts of working in government. We also like original work showing that the government is or is not doing something important. We have writer's guidelines, but do your research first."

N THE WEEKLY STANDARD

News America, Inc., 1150 17th St., NW, Suite 505, Washington DC 20036. E-mail: editor@weeklystandard.com. Web site: www.weeklystandard.com. Publisher: Terry Eastland. **Contact:** William Kristol, editor; Fred Barnes, executive editor. Weekly magazine.

- Query before submitting.

PSYCHOLOGY & SELF-IMPROVEMENT

$$$$ PSYCHOLOGY TODAY

Sussex Publishers, Inc., 115 E. 23rd St., 9th Floor, New York NY 10010. (212)260-7210. Fax: (212)260-7445. E-mail: jay@psychologytoday.com. Web site: www.psychologytoday.com. Associate Editor: Carlin Flora. **Contact:** Jay Dixit, senior editor. Bimonthly magazine. "*Psychology Today* explores every aspect of human behavior, from the cultural trends that shape the way we think and feel to the intricacies of modern neuroscience. We're sort of a hybrid of a science magazine, a health magazine and a self-help magazine. While we're read by many psychologists, therapists and social workers, most of our readers are simply intelligent and curious people interested in the psyche and the self.'' Estab. 1967. Circ. 331,400. 30 days after publication. Publishes ms an average of 3 months after acceptance. Byline given. Buys first North American serial rights. Editorial lead time 5 months. Accepts queries by mail, e-mail. Responds in 1 month to queries. Sample copy for $3.50. Writer's guidelines online.

Nonfiction ''Nearly any subject related to psychology is fair game. We value originality, insight and good reporting; we're not interested in stories or topics that have already been covered *ad nauseum* by other magazines unless you can provide a fresh new twist and much more depth. We're not interested in simple-minded 'pop psychology.' '' No fiction, poetry or first-person essays on ''How I Conquered Mental Disorder X.'' **Buys 20-25 mss/year.** Query with published clips. Length: 1,500-4,000 words. **Pays $1,000-2,500.**

Columns/Departments News Editor. News & Trends, 150-300 words. Query with published clips. **Pays $150-300.**

$ ROSICRUCIAN DIGEST

Rosicrucian Order, AMORC, 1342 Naglee Ave., San Jose CA 95191-0001. (408)947-3600. Web site: www.rosicrucian.org. **Contact:** Robin M. Thompson, editor-in-chief. Quarterly magazine (international) emphasizing mysticism, science, philosophy, and the arts for educated men and women of all ages seeking alternative answers to life's questions. **Pays on acceptance.** Publishes ms an average of 6 months after acceptance. Byline given. Buys first, second serial (reprint) rights. Accepts queries by mail, phone. Responds in 3 months to queries. Writer's guidelines for #10 SASE.

Nonfiction How to deal with life—and all it brings us—in a positive and constructive way. Informational articles—new ideas and developments in science, the arts, philosophy, and thought. Historical sketches, biographies, human interest, psychology, philosophical, and inspirational articles. ''We are always looking for good articles on the contributions of ancient civilizations to today's civilizations, the environment, ecology, inspirational (nonreligious) subjects. Know your subject well and be able to capture the reader's interest in the first paragraph. Be willing to work with the editor to make changes in the manuscript.'' No religious, astrological, or political material, or articles promoting a particular group or system of thought. Most articles are written by members or donated, but we're always open to freelance submissions. No book-length mss. Query. Length: 1,500-2,000 words. **Pays 6¢/word.**

Reprints Prefers typed ms with rights for sale noted and information about when and where the article previously appeared, but tearsheet or photcopy acceptable. Pays 50% of amount paid for an original article.

Tips ''We're looking for more pieces on these subjects: our connection with the past—the important contributions of ancient civilizations to today's world and culture and the relevance of this wisdom to now; how to channel teenage energy/angst into positive, creative, constructive results (preferably written by teachers or others who work with young people—written for frustrated parents); and the vital necessity of raising our environmental consciousness if we are going to survive as a species on this planet.''

SCIENCE OF MIND MAGAZINE

2600 W. Magnolia Blvd., Burbank CA 91505. (818)526-7757. E-mail: edit@scienceofmind.com. Web site: www.scienceofmind.com. Editor: Amanda Pisani. **30% freelance written.** Monthly magazine featuring articles on spirituality, self-help, and inspiration. ''Our publication centers on oneness of all life and spiritual empowerment through the application of *Science of Mind* principles.'' **Pays on acceptance.** Publishes ms an average of 5 months after acceptance. Byline given. Buys first North American serial rights. Submit seasonal material 6 months in advance. Writer's guidelines online.

Nonfiction Book excerpts, essays, inspirational, interview/profile, personal experience (of Science of Mind), spiritual. **Buys 35-45 mss/year.** Length: 750-2,000 words. **Payment varies. Pays in copies for some features written by readers.**

Tips ''We are interested in how to use spiritual principles in worldly situations or other experiences of a spiritual nature having to do with *Science of Mind* principles.''

SHARED VISION

Raven Eagle Partners Co., 873 Beatty St., Suite 203, Vancouver BC V6B 2H6 Canada. (604)733-5062. Fax: (604)731-1050. E-mail: editor@shared-vision.com. Web site: www.shared-vision.com. **Contact:** Ian Hanington, editor. **75% freelance written.** Monthly magazine covering health and wellness, environment, personal growth, spirituality, social justice, and issues related to food. Estab. 1988. Circ. 40,000 monthly. Byline given. Editorial lead time 3 months. Submit seasonal material 3 months in advance. Accepts queries by mail, e-mail, fax. Accepts previously published material. Sample copy for $3 Canadian, postage paid. Writer's guidelines by e-mail.

Nonfiction Book excerpts, general interest, inspirational, personal experience, travel, health, environment. Query with published clips.

Columns/Departments Footnotes (first-person inspirational). Query with published clips.
Tips "Reading the magazine is the optimum method. E-mail the editor for writer's guidelines."

N $ SPOTLIGHT ON RECOVERY MAGAZINE

R. Graham Publishing Company, 1454 Rockaway Parkway, #140, Brooklyn NY 11236. (646)641-6646. E-mail: rgraham_100@msn.com. Web site: www.spotlightonrecovery.com. Editor: Lisa Roma. **Contact:** Robin Graham, publisher/managing editor. **85% freelance written.** Quarterly magazine covering self-help, recovery, and empowerment. "This is the premiere outreach and resource magazine in New York. Its goal is to be the catalyst for which the human spirit could heal. Everybody knows somebody who has mental illness, substance abuse issues, parenting problems, educational issues, or someone who is homeless, unemployed, physically ill, or the victim of a crime. Many people suffer in silence. *Spotlight on Recovery* will provide a voice to those who suffer in silence and begin the dialogue of recovery." Estab. 2001. Circ. 1,500-2,500. Pays on publication. Publishes ms an average of 2 months after acceptance. Byline sometimes given. Buys second serial (reprint), electronic rights. Editorial lead time 1 month. Submit seasonal material 1 month in advance. Accepts queries by mail, e-mail. Accepts simultaneous submissions. Responds in 2 weeks to queries; 1 month to mss. Sample copy and writer's guidelines free.
Nonfiction Book excerpts, interview/profile, opinion, personal experience. **Buys 30-50 mss/year.** Query with published clips. Length: 150-1,500 words. **Pays 5¢/word or $75-80/article.**
Photos State availability with submission. Reviews GIF/JPEG files. Buys one-time rights. Pays $5-10/photo. Identification of subjects required.
Columns/Departments Buys 4 mss/year. Query with published clips. **Pays 5¢/word or $75-80/column.**
Fiction Ethnic, mainstream, slice-of-life vignettes.
Fillers Facts, newsbreaks, short humor. **Buys 2/year. Pays 5¢/word.**
Tips "Send a query and give a reason why you would choose the subject posted to write about."

REGIONAL

GENERAL

$ CHRONOGRAM

Luminary Publishing, P.O. Box 459, New Paltz NY 12561. Fax: (914)256-0349. E-mail: info@chronogram.com. Web site: www.chronogram.com. **Contact:** Brian K. Mahoney, editor. **50% freelance written.** Monthly magazine covering regional arts and culture. "*Chronogram* features accomplished, literary writing on issues of cultural, spiritual, and idea-oriented interest." Estab. 1994. Circ. 20,000. Pays on publication. Publishes ms an average of 3 months after acceptance. Byline given. Buys one-time rights. Editorial lead time 2 months. Submit seasonal material 3 months in advance. Accepts queries by mail, e-mail. Accepts simultaneous submissions. Responds in 2 weeks to queries; 6-8 weeks to mss. Sample copy and writer's guidelines online.
Nonfiction Book excerpts, essays, exposé, general interest, historical/nostalgic, humor, interview/profile, opinion, personal experience, photo feature, religious, travel. "No health practitioners writing about their own healing modality." **Buys 24 mss/year.** Query with published clips. Length: 1,000-3,500 words. **Pays $75-150.**
Photos State availability with submission. Reviews contact sheets. Buys one-time rights. Negotiates payment individually. Captions required.
Poetry Phillip Levine, poetry editor. Avant-garde, free verse, haiku, traditional.
Tips "The editor's ears are always open for new voices and all story ideas are invited for pitching. *Chronogram* welcomes all voices and viewpoints as long as they are expressed well. We discriminate solely based on the quality of the writing, nothing else. Clear, thoughtful writing on any subject will be considered for publication in *Chronogram*. We publish a good deal of introspective first-person narratives and find that in the absence of objectivity, subjectivity at least is a quantifiable middle ground between ranting opinion and useless facts."

$$$$ COWBOYS & INDIANS MAGAZINE

The Premier Magazine of the West, USFR Media Group, 6688 N. Central Expressway, Suite 650, Dallas TX 75206. E-mail: queries@cowboysindians.com. Web site: www.cowboysindians.com. **Contact:** Queries. **60% freelance written.** Magazine published 8 times/year covering people and places of the American West. "The Premier Magazine of the West, *Cowboys & Indians* captures the romance, drama, and grandeur of the American frontier—both past and present—like no other publication. Undeniably exclusive, the magazine covers a broad range of lifestyle topics: art, home interiors, travel, fashion, Western film, and Southwestern cuisine." Estab. 1993. Circ. 101,000. Pays on publication. Publishes ms an average of 2 months after acceptance. Byline given. Offers 20% kill fee. Buys first North American serial, electronic rights. Editorial lead time 4 months. Submit seasonal material 6 months in advance. Accepts queries by mail, e-mail, fax. Sample copy for $5. Writer's guidelines by e-mail.

Nonfiction Book excerpts, exposé, general interest, historical/nostalgic, interview/profile, photo feature, travel, art. No essays, humor, poetry, or opinion. **Buys 40-50 mss/year.** Query. Length: 500-3,000 words. **Pays $250-5,000 for assigned articles; $250-1,000 for unsolicited articles.**

Photos State availability with submission. Reviews contact sheets, $2\frac{1}{4} \times 2\frac{1}{4}$ transparencies. Buys one-time rights. Negotiates payment individually. Captions, identification of subjects required.

Columns/Departments Art; Travel; Music; Home Interiors; all 200-1,000 words. **Buys 50 mss/year.** Query. **Pays $200-1,500.**

Tips "Our readers are educated, intelligent, and well-read Western enthusiasts, many of whom collect Western Americana, read other Western publications, attend shows and have discerning tastes. Therefore, articles should assume a certain level of prior knowledge of Western subjects on the part of the reader. Articles should be readable and interesting to the novice and general interest reader as well. Please keep your style lively, above all things, and fast-moving, with snappy beginnings and endings. Wit and humor are always welcome."

N $ $ $ ESTATES WEST MAGAZINE

Media That Deelivers, Inc., 8132 N. 87th Place, Scottsdale AZ 85258. (480)460-5203. Fax: (480)443-1517. E-mail: editorial@estateswest.com; afier@estateswest.com. Web site: www.estateswest.com. **Contact:** Amanda Fier, editor. **30% freelance written.** Bimonthly magazine affluent living, real estate, architecture, design, and travel throughout the West. Estab. 2000. Circ. 60,000. **Pays on acceptance.** Publishes ms an average of 10 months after acceptance. Byline given. Editorial lead time 3-4 months. Submit seasonal material 4 month in advance. Accepts queries by mail, e-mail. Responds in 1 month to queries. Sample copy and writer's guidelines for #10 SASE.

"Break in by submitting clips and several potential story ideas that suit our readers."

Nonfiction Interview/profile (designers, builders, realtors, architects), new product, travel, decor, real estate. **Buys 10-15 mss/year.** Query with published clips. Length: 900-2,000 words. **Pays 50-60¢/word for assigned articles.**

Photos Send photos with submission per discussion with editor. Photos must be high resolution. Buys one-time rights. Negotiates payment individually.

$ $ GUESTLIFE

Monterey Bay/New Mexico/El Paso/Houston/Vancouver, Desert Publications, Inc., 303 N. Indian Canyon Dr., Palm Springs CA 92262. (760)325-2333. Fax: (760)325-7008. E-mail: steven@palmspringslife.com. Web site: www.guestlife.com. **Contact:** Steven R. Biller, editorial director. **95% freelance written.** Annual prestige hotel room magazine covering history, highlights, and activities of the area named (i.e., *Monterey Bay GuestLife*). "*GuestLife* focuses on its respective area and is placed in hotel rooms in that area for the affluent vacationer." Estab. 1979. Pays on publication. Publishes ms an average of 9 months after acceptance. Byline given. Offers negotiable kill fee. Buys electronic, all rights. Editorial lead time 6 months. Submit seasonal material 8 months in advance. Accepts queries by e-mail. Responds in 1 month to queries; 1 month to mss. Sample copy for $10. Writer's guidelines not available.

Nonfiction General interest (regional), historical/nostalgic, photo feature, travel. **Buys 3 mss/year.** Query with published clips. Length: 300-1,500 words. **Pays $100-500.**

Photos State availability with submission. Reviews contact sheets. Buys all rights. Negotiates payment individually. Identification of subjects required.

Fillers Facts. **Buys 3/year.** Length: 50-100 words. **Pays $50-100.**

N $ $ LAKE

Resort Lifestyle on Lake Michigan, Small Newspaper Group, 701 State St., La Porte IN 46350. E-mail: info@lakemagazine.com. Web site: www.lakemagazine.com. Editor: Lucinda Hahn. Senior Editor: Edward McClelland. **Contact:** Ted McClelland, senior editor; Lisa Panzica, production editor. **80% freelance written.** Magazine published 10 times/year covering Lake Michigan, in particular the resort communities of Southeast Michigan and Northwest Indiana. Estab. 2000. Circ. 35,000. **Pays on acceptance.** Publishes ms an average of 2 months after acceptance. Byline given. Offers 15% kill fee. Buys first North American serial rights. Editorial lead time 2 months. Submit seasonal material 4-5 months in advance. Accepts queries by e-mail. Accepts previously published material. Accepts simultaneous submissions. Sample copy online.

Nonfiction Book excerpts, essays, general interest, historical/nostalgic, humor, interview/profile, new product, personal experience, photo feature, travel. Special issues: Travel (May and September issues); Kids (June issue). Does not want fiction, poetry. **Buys 100 mss/year.** Query with published clips or send complete ms. Length: 250-2,000 words. **Pays 30-50¢/word.** Sometimes pays expenses of writers on assignment.

Columns/Departments Lake's Grapes (wine), 550 words; Field to Table (regional food); My Lake (well-known

Harbor Country residents), 1,000 words; Postcard (profile of Harbor County community), 1,000 words. **Buys 40-50 mss/year.** Query with published clips or send complete ms. **Pays 30-50¢/word.**

Tips "Pitch shorter stories for our front-of-book section. Send well thought out, in-depth queries explaining what angle you'd use and why it's a good or important story for *Lake* to run."

N $ MIDWEST LIVING

Meredith Corp., 1716 Locust St., Des Moines IA 50309-3038. (515)284-3000. Fax: (515)284-3836. E-mail: mwl@mdp.com. Web site: www.midwestliving.com. Bimonthly magazine covering Midwestern families. Regional service magazine that celebrates the interest, values, and lifestyles of Midwestern families. Estab. 1987. Circ. 915,000. **Pays on acceptance.** Buys all rights. Editorial lead time 6 months. Accepts queries by mail, e-mail. Sample copy for $3.95. Writer's guidelines by e-mail.

Nonfiction General interest (good eating, festivals and fairs), historical/nostalgic (interesting slices of Midwestern history, customs, traditions and the people who preserve them), interview/profile (towns, neighborhoods, families,people whose stories exemplify the Midwest spirit an values), travel (Midwestern destinations with emphasis on the fun and affordable). Query.

Photos State availability with submission.

Tips "As general rule of thumb, we're looking for stories that are useful to the reader with information of ideas they can act on in their own lives. Most important, we want stories that have direct relevance to our Midwest audience."

$ $ NOW AND THEN

The Appalachian Magazine, Center for Appalachian Studies and Services, P.O. Box 70556-ETSU, Johnson City TN 37614. (423)439-7865. Fax: (423)439-7870. E-mail: nowandthen@etsu.edu. Web site: cass.etsu.edu/n&t/. **80% freelance written.** Triannual magazine covering Appalachian region from Southern New York to Northern Mississippi. "*Now & Then* accepts a variety of writing genres: fiction, poetry, nonfiction, essays, interviews, memoirs, and book reviews. All submissions must relate to Appalachia and to the issue's specific theme. Our readership is educated and interested in the region." Estab. 1984. Circ. 1,000. Pays on publication. Publishes ms an average of 4 months after acceptance. Byline given. Buys all, holds copyright rights. Editorial lead time 6 months. Accepts queries by mail, e-mail, fax. Accepts simultaneous submissions. Responds in 5 months to queries; 5 months to mss. Sample copy for $5. Writer's guidelines online.

Nonfiction Book excerpts, essays, general interest, historical/nostalgic, humor, interview/profile, opinion, personal experience, photo feature, book reviews from and about Appalachia. "We don't consider articles which have nothing to do with Appalachia; articles which blindly accept and employ regional stereotypes (dumb hillbillies, poor and downtrodden hillfolk, and miners)." Query with published clips. Length: 1,000-2,500 words. **Pays $30-250 for assigned articles; $30-100 for unsolicited articles.** Sometimes pays expenses of writers on assignment.

Reprints Send ms with rights for sale noted and information about when and where the material previously appeared. Pays 100% of amount paid for original article (typically $15-60).

Photos State availability with submission. Buys one-time rights. Offers no additional payment for photos accepted with ms. Captions, identification of subjects required.

Fiction "Fiction has to relate to Appalachia and to the issue's theme in some way." Adventure, ethnic, experimental, fantasy, historical, humorous, mainstream, slice-of-life vignettes, excerpted novel, prose poem. "Absolutely has to relate to Appalachian theme. Can be about adjustment to new environment, themes of leaving and returning, for instance. Nothing unrelated to region." **Buys 3-4 mss/year.** Send complete ms. Length: 750-2,500 words. **Pays $30-100.**

Poetry Free verse, haiku, light verse, traditional. "No stereotypical work about the region. I want to be surprised and embraced by the language, the ideas, even the form." **Buys 25-30 poems/year.** Submit maximum 5 poems. **Pays $10.**

Tips "Get a copy of the magazine and read it. Then make sure your submission has a connection to Appalachia (check out http://cass.etsu.edu/cass/apregion.htm) and fits in with an upcoming theme."

N $ $ PINNACLE LIVING/MOUNTAIN HOMES

P.O. Box 21535, Roanoke VA 24018. **Contact:** Norma Lugar, editor. Bimonthly magazine celebrating the best of upscale living in the Southern mountains—the homes, the events, the art, the style, the food, and the cities and towns that people today are increasingly seeking out for retirement or as an escape from big city living. "Our territory extends from the Shenandoah Valley of Virginia down into northern Georgia and includes all territory in the mountain regions of Virginia, North Carolina, South Carolina, West Virginia, Tennessee, Maryland and Georgia." Pays on publication. Buys first North American serial rights. Accepts queries by mail. Sample copy for $3 and magazine-sized envelope.

Nonfiction General interest, interview/profile, travel. Query. **Pays $250-400.**

Photos "We assign photography according to story needs." Buys one-time rights.

Columns/Departments Destinations (everything there is to tell about a great Southern mountain town, city or locale); Food and Wine (covering Southern vinters, chefs and restaurants); Mountain Style (new trends and sources for unique products); Homes and Gardens (spotlight on homes and gardens;often of those who have chosen to relocate to the mountains), 750-2,000 words. Query. **Pays $250-400.**

Tips "Anything that is well-researched, well-written and tied to the Southern mountains, the second-home and retirement demographic trends, and the area's upscale lifestyle would get strong consideration."

SOUTHERN LIVING

Southern Progress Corp., 2100 Lakeshore Dr., Birmingham AL 35209. (205)445-6000. Fax: (205)445-6700. E-mail: sara_askew_jones@timeinc.com. Web site: www.southernliving.com. Editor: John Floyd. Managing Editor: Clay Norden. **Contact:** Sara Askew Jones. Monthly magazine covering the southern lifestyle. Publication addressing the tastes and interest of contemporary southerners. Estab. 1966. Circ. 2,526,799. Buys all rights. Editorial lead time 3 months. Accepts queries by mail. Sample copy for $4.99 at newsstands. Writer's guidelines by e-mail.

N $ $ $ $ SUNSET MAGAZINE

Sunset Publishing Corp., 80 Willow Rd., Menlo Park CA 94025-3691. (650)321-3600. Fax: (650)327-7537. E-mail: travelquery@sunset.com. Web site: www.sunset.com. Monthly magazine covering the lifestyle of the Western states. "*Sunset* is a Western lifestyle publication for educated, active consumers. Editorial provides localized information on gardening and travel, food and entertainment, home building and remodeling." Freelance articles should be timely and only about the 13 Western states. Garden section accepts queries by mail. Travel section prefers queries by e-mail. **Pays on acceptance.** Byline given. Writer's guidelines online.

Nonfiction "Travel items account for the vast majority of *Sunset's* freelance assignments, although we also contract out some short garden items. However *Sunset* is largely staff-written." Travel (in the West). **Buys 50-75 mss/year.** Query. Length: 550-750 words. **Pays $1/word.**

Columns/Departments Building & Crafts, Food, Garden, Travel. Travel Guide length: 300-350 words. Direct queries to specific editorial department.

Tips "Here are some subjects regularly treated in *Sunset*'s stories and Travel Guide items: Outdoor recreation (i.e., bike tours, bird-watching spots, walking or driving tours of historic districts); indoor adventures (i.e., new museums and displays, hands-on science programs at aquariums or planetariums, specialty shopping); special events (i.e., festivals that celebrate a region's unique social, cultural, or agricultural heritage). Also looking for great weekend getaways, backroad drives, urban adventures and culinary discoveries such as ethnic dining enclaves. Planning and assigning begins a year before publication date."

YANKEE

Yankee Publishing, Inc., P.O. Box 520, Dublin NH 03444-0520. (603)563-8111. Fax: (603)563-8298. Web site: www.yankeemagazine.com. Editor: Michael Carlton. **Contact:** (Ms.) Sam Darley, editorial assistant. **60% freelance written.** Monthly magazine covering the New England states of Connecticut, Massachusetts, Maine, New Hampshire, Rhode Island, and Vermont. "Our feature articles, as well as the departments of Home, Food, and Travel, reflect what is happening currently in these New England states. Our mission is to express and perhaps, indirectly, preserve the New England culture—and to do so in an entertaining way. Our audience is national and has 1 thing in common—it loves New England." Estab. 1935. Circ. 500,000. **Pays on acceptance.** Byline given. Offers kill fee. Buys all rights. Editorial lead time 6 months. Submit seasonal material 1 year in advance. Accepts queries by mail. Accepts simultaneous submissions. Responds in 2 months to queries. Writer's guidelines online.

Nonfiction Essays, general interest, interview/profile. Does not want "good old days" pieces or dialect, humor, or anything outside New England. **Buys 30 mss/year.** Query with published clips and SASE. Length: Not to exceed 2,500 words. **Pays per assignment.** Pays expenses of writers on assignment when appropriate.

Photos All photos and art are assigned to experienced professionals. If interested, send a portfolio with 35 mm, $2^1/4''$, or $4\times5''$ color transparencies. Do not send any unsolicited original photos or artwork. Heather Marcus, photo editor.

Tips "Submit lots of ideas. Don't censor yourself—let us decide whether an idea is good or bad. We might surprise you. Remember we've been publishing for 65 years, so chances are we've already done every 'classic' New England subject. Try to surprise us—it isn't easy. Study the ones we publish—the format should be apparent. It is to your advantage to read several issues of the magazine before sending us a query or a manuscript. *Yankee* does not publish fiction, poetry, humor, history, memoir, or cartoons as a routine format, nor do we solicit submissions."

ALABAMA

$ $ ALABAMA HERITAGE

University of Alabama, Box 870342, Tuscaloosa AL 35487-0342. (205)348-7467. Fax: (205)348-7473. Web site: www.alabamaheritage.com. **Contact:** Donna L. Cox, editor. **90% freelance written.** "*Alabama Heritage* is a nonprofit historical quarterly published by the University of Alabama and the Alabama Department of Archives and History for the intelligent lay reader. We are interested in lively, well-written, and thoroughly researched articles on Alabama/Southern history and culture. Readability and accuracy are essential." Estab. 1986. Pays on publication. Byline given. Buys all rights. Accepts queries by mail, e-mail. Sample copy for $6, plus $2.50 for shipping. Writer's guidelines for #10 SASE or online.

Nonfiction Buys 12-16 feature mss/year and 10-14 short pieces. Historical. "We do not publish fiction, poetry, articles on current events or living artists, and personal/family reminiscences." Query. Length: 750-4,000 words. **Pays $50-350.** Sends 10 copies to each author.

Photos Reviews contact sheets. Buys one-time rights. Identification of subjects required.

Tips "Authors need to remember that we regard history as a fascinating subject, not as a dry recounting of dates and facts. Articles that are lively and engaging, in addition to being well researched, will find interested readers among our editors. No term papers, please. All areas are open to freelance writers. Best approach is a written query."

$ $ ALABAMA LIVING

Alabama Rural Electric Assn., P.O. Box 244014, Montgomery AL 36124. (334)215-2732. Fax: (334)215-2733. E-mail: info@areapower.com. Web site: www.alabamaliving.com. Editor: Darryl Gates. **Contact:** Editor. **80% freelance written.** Monthly magazine covering topics of interest to rural and suburban Alabamians. "Our magazine is an editorially balanced, informational and educational service to members of rural electric cooperatives. Our mix regularly includes Alabama history, Alabama features, gardening, outdoor, and consumer pieces." Estab. 1948. Circ. 380,000. **Pays on acceptance.** Byline given. Not copyrighted. Editorial lead time 4 months. Submit seasonal material 4 months in advance. Accepts queries by mail, e-mail. Accepts simultaneous submissions. Responds in 1 month to queries. Sample copy for free.

O→ Break in with a bit of history or nostalgia about Alabama or the Southeast and pieces about "little-known" events in Alabama history or "little-known" sites.

Nonfiction Historical/nostalgic (rural-oriented), inspirational, personal experience (Alabama). Special issues: Gardening (March); Travel (April); Home Improvement (May); Holiday Recipes (December). **Buys 20 mss/year.** Send complete ms. Length: 500-750 words. **Pays $250 minimum for assigned articles; $100 minimum for unsolicited articles.**

Reprints Send ms with rights for sale noted. Pays $75.

N MOBILE BAY MONTHLY

PMT Publishing, P.O. Box 66200, Mobile AL 36660. (251)473-6269. Fax: (251)479-8822. E-mail: snpotts@pmtpublishing.com. Web site: www.mobilebaymonthly.com. Publisher: TJ Potts. Editorial Director: Judsen Culbreth. Associate Editor: Laura VanLandingham. **Contact:** Stephen Potts, assistant editor. **25% freelance written.** "*Mobile Bay Monthly* is a monthly lifestyle magazine for the South Alabama/Gulf Coast region focusing on the people, ideas, issues, arts, homes, food, culture, and businesses that make Mobile Bay an interesting place." Estab. 1990. Circ. 10,000. Pays on publication. Publishes ms an average of 4 months after acceptance. Byline given. Buys first rights. Editorial lead time 4 months. Submit seasonal material 6 months in advance. Accepts queries by mail, e-mail, fax. Sample copy for $2. Writer's guidelines not available.

Nonfiction General interest, historical/nostalgic, how-to (home renovations, etc.), interview/profile, personal experience, photo feature, travel (must be along the Gulf Coast). Query with published clips. Length: 1,200-3,000 words.

Photos State availability with submission. Buys one-time rights. Negotiates payment individually. Identification of subjects required.

Tips "We use mostly local writers. Strong familiarity with the Mobile area is a must. No phone calls; please send query letters with writing samples."

ALASKA

$ $ $ ALASKA

Exploring Life on the Last Frontier, 301 Arctic Slope Ave., Suite 300, Anchorage AK 99518. (907)272-6070. E-mail: andy.hall@alaskamagazine.com. Web site: www.alaskamagazine.com. **Contact:** Andy Hall, editor. **70% freelance written.** Eager to work with new/unpublished writers. Magazine published 10 times/year covering topics "uniquely Alaskan." Estab. 1935. Circ. 180,000. Pays on publication. Publishes ms an average of 6 months after acceptance. Byline given. Buys first, one-time rights. Submit seasonal material 1 year in advance. Accepts queries by mail. Responds in 2 months to queries; 2 months to mss. Sample copy for $3 and 9×12 SAE with 7 first-class stamps. Writer's guidelines online.

Break in by "doing your homework. Make sure a similar story has not appeared in the magazine within the last 5 years. It must be about Alaska."

Nonfiction Historical/nostalgic, humor, interview/profile, personal experience, photo feature, travel, adventure, outdoor recreation (including hunting, fishing), Alaska destination stories. No fiction or poetry. **Buys 40 mss/year.** Query. Length: 100-2,500 words. **Pays $100-1,250.**

Photos Send photos with submission. Reviews 35mm or larger transparencies, slides labeled with your name. Captions, identification of subjects required.

Tips "We're looking for top-notch writing—original, well researched, lively. Subjects must be distinctly Alaskan. A story on a mall in Alaska, for example, won't work for us; every state has malls. If you've got a story about a Juneau mall run by someone who is also a bush pilot and part-time trapper, maybe we'd be interested. The point is *Alaska* stories need to be vivid, focused and unique. Alaska is like nowhere else—we need our stories to be the same way."

ARIZONA

N $ $ ARIZONA FOOTHILLS MAGAZINE

Media That Deelivers, Inc., 8132 N. 87th Place, Scottsdale AZ 85258. (480)460-5203. Fax: (480)443-1517. E-mail: editorial@azfoothillsmag.com. Web site: www.azfoothillsmag.com. **Contact:** Elizabeth Smith, executive editor. **10% freelance written.** Monthly magazine covering Arizona lifesyle. Estab. 1996. Circ. 60,000. Pays on publication. Publishes ms an average of 6 months after acceptance. Byline given. Editorial lead time 6 months. Submit seasonal material at least 4 months in advance. Accepts queries by mail, e-mail. Responds in 1 month to queries. Sample copy for #10 SASE.

Break in by submitting a story with a local angle and having several reader-service sidebars in mind.

Nonfiction General interest, photo feature, travel, fashion, decor, arts, interview. **Buys 10 mss/year.** Query with published clips. Length: 900-2,000 words. **Pays 35-40¢/word for assigned articles.**

Photos Photos may be requested. Reviews contact sheets, transparencies. Occasionally buys one-time rights. Negotiates payment individually. Captions, identification of subjects, model releases required.

Columns/Departments Travel, dining, fashion, home decor, design, architecture, wine, shopping, golf, performance & visual arts.

Tips "We prefer stories that appeal to our affluent audience written with an upbeat, contemporary approach and reader service in mind."

$ $ $ $ ARIZONA HIGHWAYS

2039 W. Lewis Ave., Phoenix AZ 85009-9988. (602)712-2024. Fax: (602)254-4505. E-mail: queryeditor@azhighways.com. Web site: www.arizonahighways.com. **Contact:** Beth Deveny, senior editor. **100% freelance written.** Magazine that is state-owned, designed to help attract tourists into and through Arizona. Estab. 1925. Circ. 425,000. **Pays on acceptance.** Buys first North American serial rights. Accepts queries by mail, e-mail, fax. Responds in 1 month to queries; 1 month to mss. Sample copy not available. Writer's guidelines online.

Break in with "a concise query written with flair, backed by impressive clips that reflect the kind of writing that appears in *Arizona Highways*. The easiest way to break into the magazine for writers new to us is to propose short items for the Off-Ramp section or submit 750-word pieces for the Along the Way column."

Nonfiction Feature subjects include narratives and exposition dealing with history, anthropology, nature, wildlife, armchair travel, out of the way places, small towns, Old West history, Indian arts and crafts, travel, etc. Travel articles are experience-based. All must be oriented toward Arizona. "We deal with professionals only, so include a list of current credits." **Buys 50 mss/year.** Query with a lead paragraph and brief outline of story. Length: 600-1,800 words. **Pays up to $1/word.** Pays expenses of writers on assignment.

Photos "We use transparencies of medium format, 4×5, and 35mm when appropriate to the subject matter, or they display exceptional quality or content. If submitting 35mm, we prefer 100 ISO or slower. Each transparency must be accompanied by information attached to each photograph: where, when, what. No photography will be reviewed by the editors unless the photographer's name appears on each and every transparency. For digital requirements, contact the photography department." Peter Ensenberger, director of photography. Buys one-time rights. Pays $125-600.

Columns/Departments Focus on Nature (short feature in first or third person dealing with the unique aspects of a single species of wildlife), 800 words; Along the Way (short essay dealing with life in Arizona, or a personal experience keyed to Arizona), 750 words; Back Road Adventure (personal back-road trips, preferably off the beaten path and outside major metro areas), 1,000 words; Hike of the Month (personal experiences on trails anywhere in Arizona), 500 words. **Pays $50-1,000, depending on department.**

The online magazine carries original content not found in the print edition. Contact: Beth Deveny, senior editor.

Tips "Writing must be of professional quality, warm, sincere, in-depth, well peopled, and accurate. Avoid themes that describe first trips to Arizona, the Grand Canyon, the desert, Colorado River running, etc. Emphasis is to be on Arizona adventure and romance as well as flora and fauna, when appropriate, and themes that can be photographed. Double check your manuscript for accuracy. Our typical reader is a 50-something person with the time, the inclination, and the means to travel."

$ $ DESERT LIVING

2525 E. Camelback Rd., Suite 120, Phoenix AZ 85016. (602)667-9798. Fax: (602)508-9454. E-mail: david@desertlivingmag.com. Web site: www.desertlivingmag.com. **Contact:** David Tyda, editor. **75% freelance written.** Lifestyle and culture magazine published 8 times/year "with an emphasis on modern design, culinary trends, cultural trends, fashion, great thinkers of our time and entertainment." Estab. 1997. Circ. 50,000. Pays 1 month after publication. Byline given. Offers 50% kill fee. Buys first, electronic rights. Editorial lead time 3 months. Submit seasonal material 3 months in advance. Accepts queries by mail, e-mail, fax. Responds in 3 weeks to queries; 2 months to mss. Sample copy for e-mail request. Writer's guidelines free.

Nonfiction General interest, interview/profile, new product, photo feature, travel, architecture. Query with published clips. Length: 300-1,500 words. **Pays $25-600.**

Photos State availability with submission. Reviews contact sheets, negatives, transparencies, prints. Buys one-time or electronic rights. Negotiates payment individually. Identification of subjects, model releases required.

Columns/Departments See Web site.

N $ $ TRENDS MAGAZINE

Trends Publishing, 6045 N. Scottsdale Rd., Suite 205, Scottsdale AZ 85250. (480)990-9007. Fax: (480)990-0048. E-mail: bdougherty@trendspublishing.com. Web site: www.trendspublishing.com. Editor: Wendy Miller. **Contact:** Bill Dougherty, publisher. **20% freelance written.** Monthly magazine covering society, affluent lifestyle, luxury goods and services. "*Trends Magazine* has a focus on the affluent community, especially in Arizona." Estab. 1982. Circ. 45,000. Byline given. Offers 100% kill fee. Buys one-time rights. Editorial lead time 2-3 months. Submit seasonal material 2-3 months in advance. Accepts queries by mail, e-mail, fax, phone. Accepts previously published material. Accepts simultaneous submissions. Responds in 1 month to queries; 1 month to mss. Sample copy for free. Writer's guidelines by e-mail.

Nonfiction General interest, humor, interview/profile, travel. Does not want technical, religious, or political. Query with published clips. Length: 700-1,200 words. **Pays $350-600.** Sometimes pays expenses of writers on assignment.

Tips "Just think about subjects that would appeal to affluent readers."

N $ $ TUCSON LIFESTYLE

Conley Publishing Group, Ltd., Suite 12, 7000 E. Tanque Verde Rd., Tucson AZ 85715-5318. (520)721-2929. Fax: (520)721-8665. E-mail: scott@tucsonlifestyle.com. **Contact:** Scott Barker, executive editor. **90% freelance written.** Prefers to work with published/established writers. Monthly magazine covering Southern Arizona-related events and topics. Estab. 1982. Circ. 32,000. **Pays on acceptance.** Publishes ms an average of 6 months after acceptance. Byline given. Buys one-time, second serial (reprint) rights. Submit seasonal material 1 year in advance. Accepts queries by mail, e-mail. Responds in 2 months to queries; 3 months to mss. Sample copy for $2.95, plus $3 postage. Writer's guidelines free.

Features are not open to freelancers.

Nonfiction All stories need a Southern Arizona angle. "Avoid obvious tourist attractions and information that most residents of the Southwest are likely to know. No anecdotes masquerading as articles. Not interested in fish-out-of-water, Easterner-visiting-the-Old-West pieces." **Buys 20 mss/year. Pays $50-500.**

Photos Query about electronic formats. Reviews contact sheets, $2\frac{1}{4} \times 2\frac{1}{4}$ transparencies, 5×7 prints. Buys one-time and reprint rights. Pays $25-100/photo. Identification of subjects required.

Tips "Read the magazine before submitting anything."

CALIFORNIA

$ $ BRENTWOOD MAGAZINE

PTL Productions, 2118 Wilshire Blvd., #1060, Santa Monica CA 90403. (310)390-0251. Fax: (310)390-0261. E-mail: dawnya@brentwoodmagazine.com. Web site: www.brentwoodmagazine.com. **Contact:** Dawnya Pring, editor. **100% freelance written.** Bimonthly magazine covering entertainment, business, lifestyles, reviews.

"Wanting in-depth interviews with top entertainers, politicians, and similar individuals. Also travel, sports, adventure." Estab. 1995. Circ. 50,000. Pays on publication. Byline given. Editorial lead time 3 months. Submit seasonal material 3 months in advance. Accepts queries by mail, e-mail, phone. Accepts simultaneous submissions. Sample copy for $5. Writer's guidelines available.

O→ Break in with "strong editorial pitches on unique personalities, trends, or travel destinations."

Nonfiction Book excerpts, exposé, general interest, historical/nostalgic, humor, interview/profile, new product, opinion, personal experience, photo feature, travel. **Buys 80 mss/year.** Query with published clips. Length: 1,000-2,500 words. **Pays 20¢/word.**

Photos State availability with submission. Reviews contact sheets, negatives, prints. Offers no additional payment for photos accepted with ms. Captions, identification of subjects required.

Columns/Departments Reviews (film/books/theater/museum), 100-500 words; Sports (Southern California angle), 200-600 words. **Buys 20 mss/year.** Query with or without published clips or send complete ms. **Pays 15¢/word.**

Tips "Los Angeles-based writers preferred for most articles."

N $ $ CARLSBAD MAGAZINE

Wheelhouse Media, 2911 State St., Suite I, Carlsbad CA 92008. (760)729-9010. Fax: (760)729-9011. E-mail: meredith@carlsbadmagazine.com. Web site: www.clickoncarlsbad.com. Editor: Tim Wrisley. **Contact:** Meredith Hoyer, managing editor. **80% freelance written.** Bimonthly magazine covering people, places, events, arts in Carlsbad, California. "We are a regional magazine highlighting all things pertaining specifically to Carlsbad. We focus on history, events, people and places that make Carlsbad interesting and unique. Our audience is both Carlsbad residents and visitors or anyone interested in learning more about Carlsbad. We favor a conversational tone that still adheres to standard rules of writing." Estab. 2004. Circ. 35,000. Pays on publication. Publishes ms an average of 6 months after acceptance. Byline given. Buys first North American serial rights. Editorial lead time 4 months. Submit seasonal material 6-12 months in advance. Accepts queries by mail, e-mail. Accepts simultaneous submissions. Responds in 2 months to queries; 2 months to mss. Sample copy for $2.31. Writer's guidelines by e-mail.

Nonfiction Historical/nostalgic, interview/profile, photo feature, home, garden, arts, events. Does not want self-promoting articles for individuals or businesses, real estate how-to's, advertorials. **Buys 3 mss/year.** Query with published clips. Length: 300-2,700 words. **Pays 20-30¢/word for assigned articles; 20¢/word for unsolicited articles.** Sometimes pays expenses of writers on assignment.

Photos State availability with submission. Reviews GIF/JPEG files. Buys one-time rights. Offers $15-400/photo.

Columns/Departments Carlsbad Arts (people, places or things related to cultural arts in Carlsbad); Happenings (events that take place in Carlsbad); Carlsbad Character (unique Carlsbad residents who have contributed to Carlsbad's character); Commerce (Carlsbad business profiles); Surf Scene (subjects pertaining to the beach/surf in Carlsbad), all 500-700 words. Garden (Carlsbad garden feature); Home (Carlsbad home feature), both 700-1,200 words. **Buys 60 mss/year.** Query with published clips. **Pays $50 flat fee or 20¢/word.**

Tips "The main thing to remember is that any pitches need to be subjects directly related to Carlsbad. If the subjects focus on surrounding towns, they aren't going to make the cut. We are looking for well-written feature magazine-style articles. E-mail is the preferred method for queries; you will get a response."

$ $ $ $ DIABLO MAGAZINE

The Magazine of the East Bay, Diablo Publications, 2520 Camino Diablo, Walnut Creek CA 94597. Fax: (925)943-1045. E-mail: dmail@diablopubs.com. Web site: www.diablomag.com. **50% freelance written.** Monthly magazine covering regional travel, food, homestyle, and profiles in Contra Costa and southern Alameda counties and selected areas of Oakland and Berkeley. Estab. 1979. Circ. 45,000. **Pays on acceptance.** Publishes ms an average of 3 months after acceptance. Byline given. Offers 25% kill fee. Buys first rights. Editorial lead time 3 months. Submit seasonal material 5 months in advance. Accepts queries by mail, e-mail, fax. Sample copy and writer's guidelines online.

Nonfiction General interest, interview/profile, new product, photo feature, technical, travel. No restaurant profiles, out of country travel, nonlocal topics. **Buys 60 mss/year.** Query with published clips. Length: 600-3,000 words. **Pays $300-2,000.** Sometimes pays expenses of writers on assignment.

Photos State availability with submission. Buys one-time rights. Negotiates payment individually.

Columns/Departments Education; Parenting; Homestyle; Food; Books; Health; Profiles; Regional Politics. Query with published clips.

Tips "We prefer San Francisco Bay area writers who are familiar with the area."

N $ $ THE EAST BAY MONTHLY

The Berkeley Monthly, Inc., 1301 59th St., Emeryville CA 94608. (510)658-9811. Fax: (510)658-9902. E-mail: editorial@themonthly.com. **Contact:** Andrea Lampros and Julia Park, co-editors. **95% freelance written.**

Monthly tabloid. "We feature distinctive, intelligent articles of interest to *East Bay* readers." Estab. 1970. Circ. 80,000. Pays on publication. Byline given. Buys first, second serial (reprint) rights. Editorial lead time 2+ months. Submit seasonal material 3 months in advance. Accepts queries by mail, e-mail. Accepts simultaneous submissions. Responds in 1 month to queries; 1 month to mss. Sample copy for $1. Writer's guidelines for #10 SASE or by e-mail.

Nonfiction All articles must have a local angle. Topics include essays (first person), exposés, general interest, humor, interview/profile, personal experience, arts, culture, lifestyles. No fiction or poetry. Query with published clips. Length: 1,500-3,000 words. **Pays $200-700.**

Reprints Send tearsheet and information about when and where the material previously appeared.

Photos State availability with submission. Negotiates payment individually. Identification of subjects required.

Columns/Departments Shopping Around (local retail news), 2,000 words; First Person, 2,000 words. Query with published clips.

N $ NOB HILL GAZETTE

An Attitude: Not an Address, Nob Hill Gazette, Inc., 5 Third St., San Francisco CA 94103. (415)227-0190. Fax: (415)974-5103. E-mail: nobhillnews@nobhillgazette.com. Web site: www.nobhillgazette.com. Editor: Merla Zellerbach. **Contact:** Marlowe Rafelle, associate editor (marlowe@nobhillgazette.com). **95% freelance written.** Monthly magazine covering upscale lifestyles in the Bay Area. "*Nob Hill Gazette* is for an upscale readership." Estab. 1978. Circ. 82,000. Pays on 15th of month following publication. Publishes ms an average of 2-3 months after acceptance. Byline given. Offers $50 kill fee. Buys all rights. Editorial lead time 1-2 months. Submit seasonal material 1-2 months in advance. Accepts queries by e-mail. Accepts previously published material. Responds in 2 weeks to queries; 2 months to mss. Sample copy online. Writer's guidelines free.

Nonfiction General interest, historical/nostalgic, interview/profile, opinion, photo feature, trends, lifestyles, fashion, health, fitness, entertaining, decor, real estate, charity and philanthropy, culture and the arts. Does not want first person articles, anything commercial (from a business or with a product to sell), profiles of people not active in the community, anything technical, anything on people or events not in the Bay Area. **Buys 75 mss/year.** Query with published clips. Length: 1,200-2,000 words. **Pays $100.** Sometimes pays expenses of writers on assignment.

Photos Contact Shara Hall, photo coordinator. State availability with submission. Reviews GIF/JPEG files. Buys one-time rights. Offers no additional payment for photos accepted with ms. Captions, identification of subjects required.

Columns/Departments Contact Lois Lehrman, publisher. "All our columnists are freelancers, but they write for us regularly, so we don't take other submissions."

Tips "Before submission, a writer should look at our publication and read the articles to get some idea of our style and range of subjects."

N $ $ $ $ OCEAN MAGAZINE

Shoreline Publications, 3334 E. Coast Hwy. #125, Corona del Mar CA 92625. E-mail: editor@oceanmagonline.com. Web site: www.oceanmagazine.com. **Contact:** Molly Chizzick, editor. **90% freelance written.** Quarterly magazine covering beauty, fashion, health, decor. "A perfect blend of the hippest trends and freshest ideas, *Ocean* stands apart as the first women's beauty, lifestyle and fashion-forward resource for Southern California. Capturing the essence of one of the most stylish, affluent and globally sought after destinations, *Ocean* appeals to all style-seeking women in search of the inside scoop on West Coast style, shopping, beauty and travel." Estab. 2005. Circ. 45,000. Pays on publication. Publishes ms an average of 1 month after acceptance. Offers 25% kill fee. Buys all rights. Editorial lead time 3 months. Submit seasonal material 3 months in advance. Accepts queries by e-mail. Writer's guidelines by e-mail.

Nonfiction General interest, interview/profile, new product. Query with published clips. Length: 800-1,000 words. **Pays 45¢-$1/word.** Sometimes pays expenses of writers on assignment.

Photos Send photos with submission. Reviews GIF/JPEG files. Buys one-time rights. Negotiates payment individually. Model releases required.

$ $ ORANGE COAST MAGAZINE

The Magazine of Orange County, Orange Coast Kommunications, Inc., 3701 Birch St., Suite 100, Newport Beach CA 92660. (949)862-1133. Fax: (949)862-0133. Web site: www.orangecoastmagazine.com. **Contact:** Paul Sterman, editor. **90% freelance written.** Monthly magazine "designed to inform and enlighten the educated, upscale residents of Orange County, California; highly graphic and well researched." Estab. 1974. Circ. 52,000. Pays on publication. Publishes ms an average of 4 months after acceptance. Byline given. Offers 20% kill fee. Buys first North American serial rights. Editorial lead time 5 months. Submit seasonal material 6 months in advance. Accepts queries by mail. Accepts simultaneous submissions. Responds in 3 months to queries; 3 months to mss. Sample copy for #10 SASE and 6 first-class stamps. Writer's guidelines for #10 SASE.

O→ Break in with Short Cuts (topical briefs of about 250 words), **pays 30¢/word.**

Nonfiction Absolutely no phone queries. General interest (with Orange County focus), inspirational, interview/profile (prominent Orange County citizens), personal experience, celebrity profiles, guides to activities and services. Special issues: Health, Beauty, and Fitness (January); Dining (March and August); International Travel (April); Home Design (June); Arts (September); Local Travel (October). "Except for our celebrity cover stories, we do not accept stories that do not have specific Orange County angles. We want profiles on local people, stories on issues going on in our community, informational stories using Orange County-based sources. We cannot emphasize the local angle enough." **Buys up to 65 mss/year.** Query with published clips. Length: 1,000-2,000 words. **Pays 30¢/word for assigned articles.**

Photos State availability with submission. Buys one-time rights. Negotiates payment individually. Captions, identification of subjects required.

Columns/Departments Short Cuts (stories for the front of the book that focus on Orange County issues, people, and places), 150-250 words. **Buys up to 25 mss/year.** Query with published clips. **Pays 30¢/word.**

Tips "We're looking for more local personality profiles, analysis of current local issues, local takes on national issues. Most features are assigned to writers we've worked with before. Don't try to sell us 'generic' journalism. *Orange Coast* prefers articles with specific and unusual angles focused on Orange County. A lot of freelance writers ignore our Orange County focus. We get far too many generalized manuscripts."

$ $ PALM SPRINGS LIFE

The California Prestige Magazine, Desert Publications, Inc., 303 N. Indian Canyon, Palm Springs CA 92262. (760)325-2333. Fax: (760)325-7008. E-mail: steven@palmspringslife.com. **Contact:** Steven R. Biller, editor. **80% freelance written.** Monthly magazine covering "affluent Palm Springs-area desert resort communities. *Palm Springs Life* celebrates the good life." Estab. 1958. Circ. 20,000. Pays on publication. Publishes ms an average of 3 months after acceptance. Byline given. Offers negotiable kill fee. Buys one-time rights (negotiable). Submit seasonal material 6 months in advance. Responds in 4-6 weeks to queries. Sample copy for $3.95. Writer's guidelines online.

• Increased focus on desert style, home, fashion, art, culture, personalities, celebrities.

Nonfiction Book excerpts, essays, interview/profile, feature stories, celebrity, fashion, spa, epicurean. Query with published clips. Length: 500-2,500 words. **Pays $100-500.**

Photos State availability with submission. Reviews contact sheets. Buys one-time rights. Pays $75-350/photo. Captions, identification of subjects, model releases required.

Columns/Departments The Good Life (art, fashion, fine dining, philanthropy, entertainment, luxury living, luxury auto, architecture), 250-750 words. **Buys 12 mss/year.** Query with or without published clips. **Pays $200-350.**

$ $ $ SACRAMENTO MAGAZINE

Sacramento Magazines Corp., 706 56th St., Suite 210, Sacramento CA 95819. (916)452-6200. Fax: (916)452-6061. E-mail: krista@sacmag.com. Web site: www.sacmag.com. Managing Editor: Darlena Belushin McKay. **Contact:** Krista Minard, editor. **80% freelance written.** Works with a small number of new/unpublished writers each year. Monthly magazine with a strictly local angle on local issues, human interest and consumer items for readers in the middle to high income brackets. Prefers to work with writers local to Sacramento area. Estab. 1975. Circ. 50,000. Pays on publication. Publishes ms an average of 3 months after acceptance. Generally buys shared North American serial rights and electronic rights. Accepts queries by mail. Responds in 3 months to queries; 3 months to mss. Sample copy for $4.50. Writer's guidelines for #10 SASE.

O→ Break in with submissions to UpFront.

Nonfiction Local issues vital to Sacramento quality of life. "No e-mail, fax or phone queries will be answered." **Buys 5 unsolicited feature mss/year.** Query. Length: 1,500-3,000 words, depending on author, subject matter and treatment. **Pays $400 and up.** Sometimes pays expenses of writers on assignment.

Photos Send photos with submission. Buys one-time rights. Payment varies depending on photographer, subject matter and treatment. Captions, identification of subjects, location and date required.

Columns/Departments Business, home and garden, first person essays, regional travel, gourmet, profile, sports, city arts, health, home and garden, profiles of local people (1,000-1,800 words); UpFront (250-300 words). **Pays $600-800.**

$ $ SACRAMENTO NEWS & REVIEW

Chico Community Publishing, 1015 20th St., Sacramento CA 95814. (916)498-1234. Fax: (916)498-7920. E-mail: nancyw@newsreview.com; cosmog@newsreview.com. Web site: www.newsreview.com. **Contact:** Nancy Brands Ward, editor; Becca Costello, arts and lifestyle editor. **25% freelance written.** Magazine "We are an alternative news and entertainment weekly. We maintain a high literary standard for submissions; unique or alternative slant. Publication aimed at a young, intellectual audience; submissions should have an edge and strong voice. We have a decided preference for stories with a strong local slant." Estab. 1989. Circ. 87,000. Pays on publication. Publishes ms an average of 2 months after acceptance. Byline given. Offers 10% kill fee. Buys first, electronic rights. Editorial lead time 2 months. Submit seasonal material 2 months in advance. Accepts queries by mail, e-mail, fax, phone. Accepts simultaneous submissions. Responds in 1 month to queries; 2 months to mss. Sample copy for 50¢.

- Prefers to work with Sacramento-area writers.

Nonfiction Essays, exposé, general interest, humor, interview/profile, personal experience. Does not want to see travel, product stories, business profile. **Buys 20-30 mss/year.** Query with published clips. Length: 750-5,000 words. **Pays $40-500.** Sometimes pays expenses of writers on assignment.

Photos State availability with submission. Reviews 8×10 prints. Buys one-time rights. Negotiates payment individually. Identification of subjects required.

Columns/Departments In the Mix (CD/TV/book reviews), 150-750 words. **Buys 10-15 mss/year.** Query with published clips. **Pays $10-200.**

$ $ SAN DIEGO MAGAZINE

San Diego Magazine Publishing Co., 1450 Front St., San Diego CA 92101. (619)230-9292. Fax: (619)230-0490. E-mail: tblair@sandiegomag.com. Web site: www.sandiegomag.com. **Contact:** Tom Blair, editor-in-chief. **30% freelance written.** Monthly magazine. "We produce informative and entertaining features and investigative reports about politics; community and neighborhood issues; lifestyle; sports; design; dining; arts; and other facets of life in San Diego." Estab. 1948. Circ. 55,000. Pays on publication. Publishes ms an average of 2 months after acceptance. Byline given. Offers 25% kill fee. Buys first North American serial, second serial (reprint) rights. Editorial lead time 2 months. Submit seasonal material 4 months in advance. Accepts simultaneous submissions.

Nonfiction Exposé, general interest, historical/nostalgic, how-to, interview/profile, travel, lifestyle. **Buys 12-24 mss/year.** Query with published clips or send complete ms. Length: 1,000-3,000 words. **Pays $250-750.** Sometimes pays expenses of writers on assignment.

Photos State availability with submission. Buys one-time rights. Offers no additional payment for photos accepted with ms.

$ $ $ $ SAN FRANCISCO

Focus on the Bay Area, 243 Vallejo St., San Francisco CA 94111. (415)398-2800. Fax: (415)398-6777. Web site: sanfranmag.com. **Contact:** Bruce Kelley, editor-in-chief. **50% freelance written.** Prefers to work with published/established writers. Monthly city/regional magazine. Estab. 1968. Circ. 180,000. Pays on publication. Publishes ms an average of 2 months after acceptance. Byline given. Offers 25% kill fee. Submit seasonal material 5 months in advance. Responds in 2 months to queries; 2 months to mss. Sample copy for $3.95.

Nonfiction All stories should relate in some way to the San Francisco Bay Area (travel excepted). Exposé, interview/profile, travel, arts; politics; public issues; sports; consumer affairs. Query with published clips. Length: 200-4,000 words. **Pays $100-2,000 and some expenses.**

$ $ $ SAN JOSE

The Magazine for Silicon Valley, Renaissance Publications, Inc., 25 Metro Dr., Suite 550, San Jose CA 95110. (408)975-9300. Fax: (408)975-9900. E-mail: gilbert@sanjosemagazine.com. Web site: www.sanjosemagazine.com. Managing Editor: Jodi Engle. **Contact:** Gilbert Sangari, publisher/editor. **10% freelance written.** Monthly magazine. "As the lifestyle magazine for those living at center of the technological revolution, we cover the people and places that make Silicon Valley the place to be for the new millennium. All stories must have a local angle, though they should be of national relevance." Estab. 1997. Circ. 60,000. Pays on publication. Publishes ms an average of 3 months after acceptance. Byline given. Offers 10% kill fee. Buys first North American serial rights. pays a flat $25 electronic rights fee. Editorial lead time 18 weeks. Submit seasonal material 6 months in advance. Accepts queries by mail, e-mail, fax. Accepts simultaneous submissions. Responds in 1 month to queries. Sample copy for $5. Writer's guidelines for #10 SASE.

- "Get your feet wet by writing smaller pieces (200-500 words). Writers can get into my good graces by agreeing to write some of our unsigned pieces. What impresses the editor the most is meeting the assigned length and meeting deadlines."

Nonfiction General interest, interview/profile, photo feature, travel. "No technical, trade or articles without a tie-in to Silicon Valley." **Buys 12 mss/year.** Query with published clips. Length: 1,000-2,000 words. **Pays 35¢/word.**

Photos State availability with submission. Offers no additional payment for photos accepted with ms. Captions, identification of subjects, model releases required.

Columns/Departments Fast Forward (a roundup of trends and personalities and news that has Silicon Valley buzzing; topics include health, history, politics, nonprofits, education, Q&As, business, technology, dining, wine and fashion). **Buys 5 mss/year.** Query. **Pays 35¢/word.**

Tips "Study our magazine for style and content. Nothing is as exciting as reading a tightly written query and discovering a new writer."

N $ SAN LUIS OBISPO COUNTY JOURNAL

793 Higuera St., Suite 10, San Luis Obispo CA 93401. (805)546-0609 or (805)544-8711. Fax: (805)546-8827. E-mail: slojournal@fix.net. **Contact:** Steve Owens, publisher. "*The Journal* is strictly local to the Central Coast of California, and the writers are local as well."

Nonfiction General interest. Query.

N $ $ SEASON IN THE SUN

Truth, beauty and charity on the California desert, Season in the Sun, Inc., P.O. Box 536, Palm Desert CA 92261-0536. (760)770-5033. Fax: (760)770-3705. E-mail: trafficseason@dc.rr.com. Web site: www.seasoninthesun.com. **Contact:** Sarah Hagerty, editor. **80% freelance written.** Magazine published 7 times/year covering philanthrophy and luxurious desert living. Estab. 2002. Circ. 12,000. Pays on publication. Publishes ms an average of 3 months after acceptance. Byline given. Offers 25% kill fee. Buys first North American serial, electronic rights. Editorial lead time 4 months. Submit seasonal material 6 months in advance. Accepts queries by mail. Accepts previously published material. Responds in 2 months to queries. Sample copy for $8.

Nonfiction Book excerpts, historical/nostalgic, humor, interview/profile, photo feature, travel, desert charities. Does not want articles without supportive detail, examples, quotes, or research. Query with published clips. Length: 500-2,500 words. **Pays $50-1,500 for assigned articles.** Sometimes pays expenses of writers on assignment.

Photos State availability with submission. Buys one-time rights. Negotiates payment individually. Identification of subjects, model releases required.

Fiction Serializes 1 chapter of fiction/issue. Condensed novels, humorous, serialized novels. **Pays $400.**

Tips "Know desert history, personalities, and charities."

N 7x7

Hartle Media, 59 Grant Ave., 4th Floor, San Francisco CA 94108. E-mail: chris@7x7mag.com. Web site: www.7x7sf.com. Editorial & Creative Director: Heather Luplow Hartle. **Contact:** Christine Ryan, executive editor. **15% freelance written.** Monthly magazine covering the city of San Francisco. Estab. 2001. Circ. 45,000. Pays 60 days following publication. Byline given. Offers 25% kill fee. Buys first North American serial, electronic, nonexclusive reprint rights rights. Editorial lead time 3 months. Submit seasonal material 3-6 months in advance. Accepts queries by mail. Sample copy for $4. Writer's guidelines free.

Nonfiction "Although the majority of the magazine is written inhouse, *7x7* accepts freelance queries for both its features section and various departments in the magazine." **Buys 6-10 mss/year.** Query with published clips. **Pays negotiable amount.** Sometimes pays expenses of writers on assignment.

Photos Contact Stefanie Michejda, photo editor.

Tips "Please read the magazine. Stories must appeal to an educated, San Francisco-based audience and, ideally, provide a first-person perspective. Most articles are 500-1,000 words in length."

COLORADO

$ $ $ ASPEN MAGAZINE

Ridge Publications, 720 E. Durant Ave., Suite E8, Aspen CO 81611. (970)920-4040. Fax: (970)920-4044. E-mail: judge@aspenmagazine.com. Web site: www.aspenmagazine.com. Editor: Janet C. O'Grady. **Contact:** Liz Judge, managing editor. **30% freelance written.** Bimonthly magazine covering Aspen and the Roaring Fork Valley. "All things Aspen, written in a sophisticated, insider-oriented tone." Estab. 1974. Circ. 20,000. Pays within 3 months of publication. Byline sometimes given. Offers 10% kill fee. Buys first North American serial, electronic rights. Editorial lead time 2 months. Accepts queries by mail, e-mail, fax. Accepts simultaneous submissions. Responds in 2 months to queries; 6 months to mss. Sample copy for 9×12 SAE and 10 first-class stamps. Writer's guidelines for #10 SASE.

- Responds only to submissions including a SASE.

Nonfiction Essays, new product, photo feature, historical, environmental and local issues, architecture and design, sports and outdoors, arts. "We do not publish general interest articles without a strong Aspen hook. We do not publish 'theme' (skiing in Aspen) or anniversary (40th year of Aspen Music Festival) articles, fiction, poetry, or prewritten manuscripts." **Buys 30-60 mss/year.** Query with published clips. Length: 50-4,000 words. **Pays $50-1,000.** Sometimes pays expenses of writers on assignment.

Photos State availability with submission. Reviews contact sheets, negatives, transparencies, prints. Identification of subjects, model releases required.

[N] MUNDO MUJER MAGAZINE

7845 Elder Circle, Denver CO 80221. E-mail: mundomujer@msn.com. Editor: Ruth Rosales. **Contact:** Felipe Gomez, editor. **50% freelance written.** Bimonthly magazine covering fashion, beauty, entertaining and culture. Estab. 2005. Circ. 20,000. Submit seasonal material 1 month in advance. Accepts queries by mail, e-mail. Accepts simultaneous submissions. Sample copy by e-mail.
Nonfiction Book excerpts, general interest, opinion. Does not want obscene or religious writing.
Fiction Historical.

$ $ STEAMBOAT MAGAZINE

100 Park Ave., Suite 209, Steamboat Springs CO 80487. (970)871-9413. Fax: (970)871-1922. E-mail: info@steamboatmagazine.com. Web site: www.steamboatmagazine.com. **Contact:** Stacey Kramer, editor. **80% freelance written.** Semiannual magazine "showcasing the history, people, lifestyles, and interests of Northwest Colorado. Our readers are generally well-educated, well-traveled, upscale, active people visiting our region to ski in winter and recreate in summer. They come from all 50 states and many foreign countries. Writing should be fresh, entertaining, and informative." Estab. 1978. Circ. 30,000. Pays 50% on acceptance, 50% on publication. Publishes ms an average of 6 months after acceptance. Byline given. Buys exclusive rights. Submit seasonal material 1 year in advance. Accepts queries by mail, e-mail, fax, phone. Responds in 3 months to queries. Sample copy for $4.95 and SAE with 10 first-class stamps. Writer's guidelines free.
Nonfiction Book excerpts, essays, general interest, historical/nostalgic, humor, interview/profile, photo feature, travel. **Buys 10-15 mss/year.** Query with published clips. Length: 150-1,500 words. **Pays $50-300 for assigned articles.** Sometimes pays expenses of writers on assignment.
Photos "Prefers to review viewing platforms, JPEGs, and dupes. Will request original transparencies when needed." State availability with submission. Buys one-time rights. Pays $50-250/photo. Captions, identification of subjects required.
Tips "Stories must be about Steamboat Springs and the Yampa Valley to be considered. We're looking for new angles on ski/snowboard stories in the winter and activity-related stories, all year round. Please query first with ideas to make sure subjects are fresh and appropriate. We try to make subjects and treatments 'timeless' in nature because our magazine is a 'keeper' with a multi-year shelf life."

[N] $ $ VAIL-BEAVER CREEK MAGAZINE

Rocky Mountain Media, LLC, P.O. Box 1397, Avon CO 81620. (970)476-6600. Fax: (970)845-0069. E-mail: bergerd@vail.net. Web site: www.vailbeavercreekmag.com. **Contact:** Don Berger, editor. **80% freelance written.** Semiannual magazine showcasing the lifestyles and history of the Vail Valley. "We are particularly interested in personality profiles, home and design features, the arts, winter and summer recreation/adventure stories, and environmental articles." Estab. 1975. Circ. 30,000. **Pays on acceptance.** Publishes ms an average of 6 months after acceptance. Byline given. Offers 100% kill fee. Buys one-time rights. Editorial lead time 1 year. Submit seasonal material 1 year in advance. Accepts queries by mail, e-mail. Accepts simultaneous submissions. Responds in 1 month to queries; 2 months to mss. Sample copy for $5.95 and SAE with 10 first-class stamps. Writer's guidelines free.
Nonfiction Essays, general interest, historical/nostalgic, humor, interview/profile, personal experience, photo feature. **Buys 20-25 mss/year.** Query with published clips. Length: 500-3,000 words. **Pays 20-30¢/word.** Sometimes pays expenses of writers on assignment.
Reprints Send ms with rights for sale noted and information about when and where the material previously appeared.
Photos State availability with submission. Reviews transparencies. Buys one-time rights. Offers $50-250/photo. Captions, identification of subjects, model releases required.
Tips "Be familiar with the Vail Valley and its personality. Approach a story that will be relevant for several years to come. We produce a magazine that is a 'keeper.' "

CONNECTICUT

$ $ $ CONNECTICUT MAGAZINE

Journal Register Co., 35 Nutmeg Dr., Trumbull CT 06611. (203)380-6600. Fax: (203)380-6610. E-mail: dsalm@connecticutmag.com. Web site: www.connecticutmag.com. Editor: Charles Monagan. **Contact:** Dale Salm, managing editor. **75% freelance written.** Prefers to work with published/established writers who know the state and live/have lived here. Monthly magazine "for an affluent, sophisticated, suburban audience. We want only articles that pertain to living in Connecticut." Estab. 1971. Circ. 93,000. Pays on publication. Publishes ms an average of 4 months after acceptance. Byline given. Offers 20% kill fee. Buys first North American serial rights. Submit seasonal material 4 months in advance. Accepts queries by mail, e-mail, fax. Responds in 6 weeks to queries. Sample copy not available. Writer's guidelines for #10 SASE.

Freelancers can best break in with "First" (short, trendy pieces with a strong Connecticut angle); find a story that is offbeat and write it in a lively, interesting manner.

Nonfiction Interested in seeing hard-hitting investigative pieces and strong business pieces (not advertorial). Book excerpts, exposé, general interest, interview/profile, topics of service to Connecticut readers. Special issues: Dining/entertainment, northeast/travel, home/garden and Connecticut bride twice/year. Also, business (January) and healthcare once/year. No personal essays. **Buys 50 mss/year.** Query with published clips. Length: 3,000 words maximum. **Pays $600-1,200.** Sometimes pays expenses of writers on assignment.

Photos Send photos with submission. Reviews contact sheets, transparencies. Buys one-time rights. Pays $50 minimum/photo. Identification of subjects, model releases required.

Columns/Departments Business, Health, Politics, Connecticut Calendar, Arts, Dining Out, Gardening, Environment, Education, People, Sports, Media, From the Field (quirky, interesting regional stories with broad appeal). Length: 1,500-2,500 words. **Buys 50 mss/year.** Query with published clips. **Pays $400-700.**

Fillers Short pieces about Connecticut trends, curiosities, interesting short subjects, etc. Length: 150-400 words. **Pays $75-150.**

The online magazine carries original content not found in the print edition. Contact: Charles Monagan, online editor.

Tips "Make certain your idea has not been covered to death by the local press and can withstand a time lag of a few months. Again, we don't want something that has already received a lot of press."

N $$$$ NORTHEAST MAGAZINE

The Hartford Courant, 285 Broad St., Hartford CT 06115-2510. (860)241-3700. Fax: (860)241-3853. E-mail: northeast@courant.com. Web site: www.ctnow.com. Editor: Jennifer Frank. **Contact:** Stephanie Summers or David Funkhouser. **30% freelance written.** Weekly magazine for a Connecticut audience. Estab. 1982. Circ. 281,000. **Pays on acceptance.** Publishes ms an average of 5 months after acceptance. Byline given. Accepts queries by mail. Responds in 3 months to queries. Writer's guidelines available.

Nonfiction "We are primarily interested in hard-hitting nonfiction articles spun off the news and compelling personal stories. We have a strong emphasis on Connecticut subject matter." General interest (has to have a strong Connecticut tie-in), historical/nostalgic, in-depth investigations of stories behind the news (has to have strong Connecticut tie-in), personal essays (humorous or anecdotal). No poetry. **Buys 40-50 mss/year.** Query. Length: 750-4,000 words. **Pays $200-1,500.**

Photos Most are assigned. "Do not send originals." State availability with submission.

Fiction Rare; "we run an occasional fiction issue and more frequently excerpts of soon-to-be published books by Connecticut authors or with Connecticut tie-ins." Length: 750-1,500 words.

Tips "Less space available for all types of writing means our standards for acceptance will be much higher. It is to your advantage to read several issues of the magazine before submitting a manuscript or query. Virtually all our pieces are solicited and assigned by us, with a small percentage of what we publish coming in 'over the transom.' "

DELAWARE

$$ DELAWARE TODAY

3301 Lancaster Pike, Suite 5C, Wilmington DE 19805. (302)656-1809. Fax: (302)656-5843. E-mail: editors@delawaretoday.com. Web site: www.delawaretoday.com. **50% freelance written.** Monthly magazine geared toward Delaware people, places and issues. "All stories must have Delaware slant. No pitches such as Delawareans will be interested in a national topic." Estab. 1962. Circ. 25,000. Pays on publication. Publishes ms an average of 4 months after acceptance. Byline given. Offers 50% kill fee. all rights for 1 year. Editorial lead time 3 months. Submit seasonal material 6 months in advance. Responds in 2 months to queries. Sample copy for $2.95.

Nonfiction Historical/nostalgic, interview/profile, photo feature, lifestyles, issues. Special issues: Newcomer's Guide to Delaware. **Buys 40 mss/year.** Query with published clips. Length: 100-3,000 words. **Pays $50-750 for assigned articles.** Sometimes pays expenses of writers on assignment.

Photos State availability with submission. Buys one-time rights. Negotiates payment individually. Identification of subjects required.

Columns/Departments Business, Health, History, People, all 1,500 words. **Buys 24 mss/year.** Query with published clips. **Pays $150-250.**

Fillers Anecdotes, newsbreaks, short humor. **Buys 10/year.** Length: 100-200 words. **Pays $50-75.**

Tips "No story ideas that we would know about, i.e., a profile of the governor. Best bets are profiles of quirky/unique Delawareans that we'd never know about or think of."

DISTRICT OF COLUMBIA

$ $ WASHINGTON CITY PAPER

2390 Champlain St. NW, Washington DC 20009. (202)332-2100. Fax: (202)332-8500. E-mail: kmarsh@washingtoncitypaper.com. Web site: www.washingtoncitypaper.com. **Contact:** Kate Marsh. **50% freelance written.** "Relentlessly local alternative weekly in nation's capital covering city and regional politics, media and arts. No national stories." Estab. 1981. Circ. 93,000. Pays on publication. Publishes ms an average of 6 weeks after acceptance. Byline given. Offers 10% kill fee for assigned stories. Buys first rights. Editorial lead time 7-10 days. Responds in 1 month to queries. Writer's guidelines online.

Nonfiction "Our biggest need for freelancers is in the District Line section of the newspaper: short, well-reported and local stories. These range from carefully-drawn profiles to sharp, hooky approaches to reporting on local institutions. We don't want op-ed articles, fiction, poetry, service journalism or play by play accounts of news conferences or events. We also purchase, but more infrequently, longer 'cover-length' stories that fit the criteria stated above. Full guide to freelance submissions can be found on Web site." **Buys 100 mss/year.** Query by e-mail with published clips or send complete ms. Length: District Line: 800-1,500 words; Covers: 2,500-10,000 words. **Pays 10-40¢/word.** Sometimes pays expenses of writers on assignment.

Photos Make appointment to show portfolio to Pete Morelewicz, art director. Pays minimum of $75.

Columns/Departments Music Writing (eclectic). **Buys 100 mss/year.** Query with published clips or send complete ms. **Pays 10-40¢/word.**

Tips "Think local. Great ideas are a plus. We are willing to work with anyone who has a strong idea, regardless of vita."

$ $ $ THE WASHINGTONIAN

1828 L St. NW, Suite 200, Washington DC 20036. (202)296-3600. E-mail: editorial@washingtonian.com. Web site: www.washingtonian.com. **20-25% freelance written.** Monthly magazine. "Writers should keep in mind that we are a general interest city-and-regional magazine. Nearly all our articles have a hard Washington connection. And, please, no political satire." Estab. 1965. Circ. 160,000. Pays on publication. Publishes ms an average of 3 months after acceptance. Byline given. Buys first North American serial, limited, nonexclusive electronic rights. Editorial lead time 10 weeks. Accepts queries by mail, fax. Writer's guidelines online.

Nonfiction Book excerpts, exposé, general interest, historical/nostalgic (with specific Washington, D.C. focus), interview/profile, personal experience, photo feature, travel. **Buys 15-30 mss/year.** Query with published clips. **Pays 50¢/word.** Sometimes pays expenses of writers on assignment.

Columns/Departments First Person (personal experience that somehow illuminates life in Washington area), 650-700 words. **Buys 9-12 mss/year.** Query. **Pays $325.**

Tips "The types of articles we publish include service pieces; profiles of people; investigative articles; rating pieces; institutional profiles; first-person articles; stories that cut across the grain of conventional thinking; articles that tell the reader how Washington got to be the way it is; light or satirical pieces (send the complete manuscript, not the idea, because in this case execution is everything). Subjects of articles include the federal government, local government, dining out, sports, business, education, medicine, fashion, environment, how to make money, how to spend money, real estate, performing arts, visual arts, travel, health, nightlife, home and garden, self-improvement, places to go, things to do, and more. Again, we are interested in almost anything as long as it relates to the Washington area. We don't like puff pieces or what we call 'isn't-it-interesting' pieces. In general, we try to help our readers understand Washington better, to help our readers live better, and to make Washington a better place to live. Also, remember—a magazine article is different from a newspaper story. Newspaper stories start with the most important facts, are written in short paragraphs with a lot of transitions, and usually can be cut from the bottom up. A magazine article usually is divided into sections that are like 400-word chapters of a very short book. The introductory section is very important—it captures the reader's interest and sets the tone for the article. Scenes or anecdotes often are used to draw the reader into the subject matter. The next section then might foreshadow what the article is about without trying to summarize it—you want to make the reader curious. Each succeeding section develops the subject. Any evaluations or conclusions come in the closing section."

FLORIDA

N $ $ ATTITUDES MAGAZINE

Southern Broadcasting Corporation, P.O. Box 987, Sarasota FL 34230-0987. (941)538-3142. Fax: (941)758-7923. E-mail: atteditor@tampabay.rr.com. Editor: Diana Bogan. **80% freelance written.** Monthly tabloid. "*Attitudes Magazine* is published to celebrate the lifestyle attitudes of the cultural coast of Florida (Sarasota and its surrounding Gulfcoast communities). We strive to offer content that is meaningful to those who live in Sarasota year-round, as well as the many tourists who continue to discover our community.'' Estab. 1992. **Pays on acceptance.** Publishes ms an average of 1 month after acceptance. Byline given. Makes work-for-hire assignments. Editorial lead time 1 month. Submit seasonal material 1 month in advance. Accepts queries by mail, e-mail. Responds in 1 month to queries. Sample copy for free.

Nonfiction General interest, historical/nostalgic, how-to, inspirational, interview/profile, personal experience, travel. Query. Length: 500-1,200 words. **Pays $200.**

Photos State availability with submission. Offers no additional payment for photos accepted with ms.

Tips ''I am open to queries, but they must fit the themes from our editorial calendar. Request a copy of our editorial calendar, because the main features to fit these topics are always assigned freelance writers.''

$ $ $ $ BOCA RATON MAGAZINE

JES Publishing, 6413 Congress Ave., Suite 100, Boca Raton FL 33487. (561)997-8683. Fax: (561)997-8909. Web site: www.bocamag.com. **Contact:** Marie Speed, editor-in-chief. **70% freelance written.** Bimonthly lifestyle magazine ''devoted to the residents of South Florida, featuring fashion, interior design, food, people, places, and issues that shape the affluent South Florida market.'' Estab. 1981. Circ. 20,000. **Pays on acceptance.** Publishes ms an average of 3 months after acceptance. Byline given. Buys second serial (reprint) rights. Submit seasonal material 7 months in advance. Accepts simultaneous submissions. Responds in 1 month to queries. Sample copy for $4.95 and 10×13 SAE with 10 first-class stamps. Writer's guidelines for #10 SASE.

Nonfiction General interest, historical/nostalgic, humor, interview/profile, photo feature, travel. Special issues: Interior Design (September-October); Real Estate (March-April); Best of Boca (July-August). Query with published clips or send complete ms. Length: 800-2,500 words. **Pays $350-1,500.**

Reprints Send tearsheet. Payment varies.

Photos Send photos with submission.

Columns/Departments Body & Soul (health, fitness and beauty column, general interest); Hitting Home (family and social interactions); History or Arts (relevant to South Florida), all 1,000 words. Query with published clips or send complete ms. **Pays $350-400.**

Tips ''We prefer shorter manuscripts, highly localized articles, excellent art/photography.''

$ $ COASTAL ELEGANCE & WEALTH

Naples Daily News/E.W. Scripps, 1075 Central Ave., Naples FL 34102. (239)403-6133. Fax: (239)263-4708. E-mail: dwlindley@naplesnews.com. Web site: www.ceandw.com. **Contact:** Daniel Lindley, editor. **25% freelance written.** Monthly magazine covering upscale audience in southwest Florida. ''*Coastal Elegance & Wealth* is a regional lifestyle magazine that circulates mainly to high-income households in southwest Florida. Our main themes include travel, food & wine, art, the season, homes & gardens, sports & outdoors, wealth and health.'' Estab. 2005. Circ. 32,000. **Pays on acceptance.** Publishes ms an average of 1-3 months after acceptance. Byline given. Offers $50 kill fee. Buys all rights. Editorial lead time 3-6 months. Submit seasonal material 6 months in advance. Accepts queries by mail, e-mail. Accepts previously published material. Accepts simultaneous submissions. Responds in 1 month to queries; 2 months to mss. Sample copy for $3.95. Writer's guidelines free.

Nonfiction ''It helps to have a regional focus, or one related to southwest Florida.'' Book excerpts, general interest, historical/nostalgic, interview/profile, new product, personal experience, photo feature, travel. Special issues: Homes & Gardens (January); Outdoors/Sports/Recreation (February); Wealth, Fortune and Finance (March); Health (April); Travel (July); Food & Wine (October); The Arts (November); The Season (December). **Buys 20-30 mss/year.** Query. Length: 1,000-5,000 words. **Pays $250-350.**

Photos State availability with submission. Reviews GIF/JPEG files. Buys all rights. Negotiates payment individually. Captions, identification of subjects required.

Columns/Departments Traveler (high-end travel), 1,000-2,000 words; Parting Shot (funny/unusual photo with long caption), 50-100 words. **Buys 6 mss/year.** Query. **Pays $250.**

Tips ''Read the magazine. Keep material relevant to southwest Florida. Think upscale. We place a premium on good writing and good photography.''

$ $ CORAL GABLES LIVING

Accentuating a Miami Lifestyle, Metropical Media Corp., 2655 Le Jeune Rd., Suite 500, Coral Gables FL 33134. (786)552-6464. E-mail: editor@gablesliving.com. Web site: www.gablesliving.com. Editor: Jacqueline Sousa. **80% freelance written.** Bimonthly magazine capturing Miami's unique lifestyle. ''Stories highlight interesting trends and events taking place in the region, profile the city's most colorful people, feature local foods and flavors, and explore travel destinations of interest to our readers.'' Accepts queries by e-mail. Editorial calendar online.

Nonfiction ''First person stories are preferred, particularly stories that take the reader along on an experience an include the writer's observations about the subject.'' General interest, how-to, interview/profile, new product, travel. Query. Length: 1,200-1,500 words. **Pays $150-500.**

Photos Reviews GIF/JPEG files (8×10 at 300 dpi). Buys one-time rights. Offers no additional payment for photos accepted with ms.

Columns/Departments Your Body (health, beauty, fitness or mental health), **$300**; First Person (first-person piece in which writer tells of a unique, life-learning experience), **$150**; Getaways and At Your Leisure (travel and leisure stories on destinations in Florida, the Caribbean and Latin America), **$300** for story and photography; Personalities (well-researched profile of person of local interest), **$500**. Query.

Tips ''Stories must have a unique angle or peg and not consist simply of general information about the destination or subject. Before purchasing a story, *CGL* editors will research other stories written on the subject or destination. If the proposed story offers nothing new and different from what already has been written elsewhere (including local and national publications and Web sites), then the story is not likely to accepted.''

$ $ EMERALD COAST MAGAZINE

Rowland Publishing, Inc., 1932 Miccosukee Rd., Tallahassee FL 32308. (850)878-0554. Fax: (850)656-1871. Web site: www.rowlandinc.com. **50% freelance written.** Bimonthly magazine. Lifestyle publication celebrating life on Florida's Emerald Coast. ''All content has an Emerald Coast (Northwest Florida) connection. This includes Panama City, Seaside, Sandestin, Destin, Fort Walton Beach, and Pensacola.'' Estab. 2000. Circ. 18,000. **Pays on acceptance.** Publishes ms an average of 3 months after acceptance. Byline given. Buys first North American serial rights. Editorial lead time 4 months. Submit seasonal material 6 months in advance. Accepts queries by mail, e-mail. Accepts previously published material. Accepts simultaneous submissions. Responds in 3 months to queries; 3 months to mss. Sample copy for $4. Writer's guidelines by e-mail.

Nonfiction All must have an Emerald Coast slant. Book excerpts, essays, historical/nostalgic, inspirational, interview/profile, new product, personal experience, photo feature. No fiction, poetry, or travel. No general interest—''we are Northwest Florida specific.'' **Buys 10-15 mss/year.** Query with published clips. Length: 1,800-2,000 words. **Pays $100-250.** Pays in contributor copies as special arrangements through publisher.

Photos Send photos with submission. Reviews prints, GIF/JPEG files. Buys one-time rights. Negotiates payment individually. Captions, identification of subjects, model releases required.

Tips ''We're looking for fresh ideas and new slants that are related to Florida's Emerald Coast. Because we work so far in advance, it is difficult to be timely, so be sure to give us ideas that aren't too time specific.''

N $ $ $ $ FLORIDA INSIDE OUT

Sobe News Group, 404 Washington Ave., Suite 650, Miami Beach FL 33139. (305)532-2544. E-mail: info@floridainsideout.com. Web site: www.floridainsideout.com. Editor: Linda Lee. **Contact:** Tali Jaffe, managing editor. **60% freelance written.** Bimonthly magazine covering architecture and interior design. ''*Florida Inside Out* is a smart publication for those interested in design, architecture and interiors. It is product-heavy, but also includes many newsy features on the fields we cover. No press releases or pre-packaged features will be published. We accept original material only.'' Estab. 2004. Circ. 55,000. Pays on publication. Publishes ms an average of 1-2 months after acceptance. Byline given. Offers 20% kill fee. Buys one-time rights. Editorial lead time 2-3 months. Submit seasonal material 3 months in advance. Accepts queries by mail, e-mail, phone. Accepts simultaneous submissions.

Nonfiction Book excerpts, essays, general interest, historical/nostalgic, interview/profile, new product, travel. Does not want pre-packaged material. Query with published clips. Length: 150-1,400 words. **Pays $1/word.** Pays expenses of writers on assignment.

Photos Contact Reynaldo Martin, associate art director. Send photos with submission. Reviews GIF/JPEG files. Buys one-time rights. Negotiates payment individually. Identification of subjects required.

Columns/Departments Green Matters (landscape, agriculture), 1,000-1,200 words; Fin, Feather, Hoof & Paw (pets and pet-related), 850-1,000 words; History Books (Florida-related history), 850-1,000 words. **Buys 18-20 mss/year.** Query. **Pays $1/word.**

Tips ''Do not approach with anything that has already been published. We assign all of our features, departments, etc. But we do always look for new contributors with fresh ideas.''

$ $ FLORIDA MONTHLY MAGAZINE

Florida Media, Inc., 801 Douglas Ave., Suite 100, Altamonte Springs FL 32714. (407)816-9596. Fax: (407)816-9373. E-mail: exec-editor@floridamagazine.com. Web site: www.floridamagazine.com. Publisher: E. Douglas Cifers. Monthly lifestyle magazine covering Florida travel, food and dining, heritage, homes and gardens, and all aspects of Florida lifestyle. Full calendar of events each month. Estab. 1981. Circ. 225,235. Pays on publication. Publishes ms an average of 5 months after acceptance. Byline given. Buys first rights. Editorial lead time 3 months. Submit seasonal material 6 months in advance. Accepts queries by mail, e-mail, fax. Responds in 2 months to queries. Sample copy for $5. Writer's guidelines for #10 SASE.

- Interested in material on areas outside of the larger cities.

O╖ Break in with stories specific to Florida showcasing the people, places, events, and things that are examples of Florida's rich history and culture.

Nonfiction Historical/nostalgic, interview/profile, travel, general Florida interest, out-of-the-way Florida places, dining, attractions, festivals, shopping, resorts, bed & breakfast reviews, retirement, real estate, business, finance, health, recreation, sports. **Buys 50-60 mss/year.** Query with published clips. Length: 500-2,500 words. **Pays $100-400 for assigned articles; $50-250 for unsolicited articles.**

Photos Send photos with submission. Reviews 3×5 color prints and slides. Offers $6/photo. Captions required.

Columns/Departments Golf; Homes & Gardenings; Heritage (all Florida-related); 750 words. **Buys 24 mss/year.** Query with published clips. **Pays $75-250.**

$ FT. MYERS MAGAZINE

And Pat, LLC, 15880 Summerlin Rd., Suite 189, Fort Myers FL 33908. E-mail: ftmyers@optonline.net. Web site: www.ftmyersmagazine.com. Director/Designer: Andrew Elias. **Contact:** Pat Simms-Elias, editorial director. **90% freelance written.** Bimonthly magazine covering regional arts and living. Audience: Educated, active, successful and creative residents of Fort Myers and Lee County, Florida, and guests at resorts and hotels in Lee County. Content: Arts, entertainment, media, travel, sports, health, home. Estab. 2001. Circ. 20,000. Pays on publication. Publishes ms an average of 3 months after acceptance. Byline given. Offers 50% kill fee. Buys one-time, second serial (reprint) rights. Editorial lead time 3 months. Submit seasonal material 3 months in advance. Accepts queries by e-mail. Accepts simultaneous submissions. Responds in 3 months to queries; 3 months to mss. Writer's guidelines for #10 SASE or by e-mail.

Nonfiction Essays, general interest, historical/nostalgic, how-to, humor, interview/profile, personal experience, reviews, previews, news, informational. **Buys 60-75 mss/year.** Query with or without published clips or send complete ms. Length: 300-1,500 words. **Pays $40-150.** Will pay in copies or in ad barter at writer's request. Sometimes pays expenses of writers on assignment.

Reprints Accepts previously published submissions.

Photos State availability of or send photos with submission. Reviews 4×5 to 8×10 prints. Buys one-time rights. Negotiates payment individually; generally offers $100/photo or art. Captions, identification of subjects required.

Columns/Departments Media: books, music, video, film, theater, Internet, software (news, previews, reviews, interviews, profiles), 300-1,500 words. Lifestyles: art & design, science & technology, house & garden, health & fitness, sports & recreation, travel & leisure, food & drink (news, interviews, previews, reviews, profiles, advice), 300-1,500 words. **Buys 60 mss/year.** Query with or without published clips or send complete ms. **Pays $40-150.**

$$$ GULFSHORE LIFE

9051 N. Tamiami Trail, Suite 202, Naples FL 34108. (239)594-9980. Fax: (239)594-9986. E-mail: hobartr@gulfshorelifemag.com. Web site: www.gulfshorelifemag.com. **Contact:** Hobart Rowland, senior editor. **75% freelance written.** Magazine published 10 times/year for "southwest Florida, the workings of its natural systems, its history, personalities, culture and lifestyle." Estab. 1970. Circ. 35,000. Pays on publication. Publishes ms an average of 4 months after acceptance. Byline given. Submit seasonal material 8 months in advance. Accepts queries by mail, e-mail, fax. Accepts simultaneous submissions. Sample copy for 9×12 SAE and 10 first-class stamps.

Nonfiction All articles must be related to southwest Florida. Historical/nostalgic, interview/profile, issue/trend. **Buys 100 mss/year.** Query with published clips. Length: 500-3,000 words. **Pays $100-1,000.**

Photos Send photos with submission. Reviews 35mm transparencies, 5×7 prints. Buys one-time rights. Pays $50-100. Identification of subjects, model releases required.

Tips "We buy superbly written stories that illuminate southwest Florida personalities, places and issues. Surprise us!"

$$ JACKSONVILLE

White Publishing Co., 534 Lancaster St., Jacksonville FL 32204. (904)358-8330. Fax: (904)358-8668. Web site: www.jacksonvillemag.com. **Contact:** Joseph White, editor/publisher. **50% freelance written.** Monthly magazine covering life and business in northeast Florida "for upwardly mobile residents of Jacksonville and the Beaches, Orange Park, St. Augustine and Amelia Island, Florida." Estab. 1985. Circ. 25,000. Pays on publication. Byline given. Offers 25-33% kill fee to writers on assignment. Buys first North American serial, second serial (reprint) rights. Editorial lead time 3 months. Submit seasonal material 4 months in advance. Responds in 6 weeks to queries; 1 month to mss. Sample copy for $5 (includes postage).

Nonfiction All articles *must* have relevance to Jacksonville and Florida's First Coast (Duval, Clay, St. John's, Nassau, Baker counties). Book excerpts, exposé, general interest, historical/nostalgic, how-to (service articles), humor, interview/profile, personal experience, photo feature, travel, commentary; local business successes; trends; personalities; community issues; how institutions work. **Buys 50 mss/year.** Query with published clips. Length: 1,200-3,000 words. **Pays $50-500 for feature length pieces.** Sometimes pays expenses of writers on assignment.

Reprints Send photocopy. Payment varies.

Photos State availability with submission. Reviews contact sheets, transparencies. Buys one-time rights. Negotiates payment individually. Captions, model releases required.

Columns/Departments Business (trends, success stories, personalities), 1,000-1,200 words; Health (trends, emphasis on people, hopeful outlooks), 1,000-1,200 words; Money (practical personal financial advice using local people, anecdotes and examples), 1,000-1,200 words; Real Estate/Home (service, trends, home photo features), 1,000-1,200 words; Travel (weekends; daytrips; excursions locally and regionally), 1,000-1,200 words; occasional departments and columns covering local history, sports, family issues, etc. **Buys 40 mss/year. Pays $150-250.**

Tips "We are a writer's magazine and demand writing that tells a story with flair."

N MIAMI MONTHLY MAGAZINE

2980 McFarlane Rd., Suite 204, Miami FL 33133. (305)446-1989. Fax: (305)446-1049. E-mail: editor@massmediamiami.com. Web site: www.miamimonthlymagazine.com. **Contact:** Judith C. Faerron, managing editor. Monthly magazine focusing on news and information of value to those who live in—or have an interest in—Miami, and its environs. "We welcome queries (no full length stories, please), but emphatically request that suggestions be limited to the parameters stated above and be of legitimate interest. We do not welcome thinly veiled sales pitches or marketing ploys." Accepts queries by e-mail.

Nonfiction "Our areas of interest include: profiles of interesting Miamians from all walks of life; longer Miami-related feature stories of compelling interest or newsworthiness; real estate trend pieces; travel (anywhere in the world, however, we do *not* pay for travel pieces). **Pays negotiable amount decided on case-by-case basis.**

Tips "We look for solid, lively writing."

N MY WEDDING SOUTH FLORIDA

HCP/Aboard Publishing, One Herald Plaza, Miami FL 33132. Fax: (305)376-5276. Web site: www.experiencedestinations.com. **Contact:** Vanessa Molina, director of editorial and design. **80% freelance written.** Semiannual magazine covering weddings and planning for South Florida brides. "Writers for this publication write about honeymoon destinations, preparations for weddings, etc., who know about this subject." Estab. 2005. Circ. 15,000. **Pays on acceptance.** Byline given. Buys all rights. Editorial lead time 2 months. Submit seasonal material 2 months in advance. Accepts queries by fax. Accepts simultaneous submissions. Responds in 1 week to queries. Sample copy and writer's guidelines online.

Nonfiction General interest, how-to, travel.

Photos Contact J. Kevin Foltz, photo editor. State availability with submission. Reviews transparencies, GIF/JPEG files. Buys all rights. Negotiates payment individually. Model releases required.

N $ $ PENSACOLA MAGAZINE

Ballinger Publishing, 41 N. Jefferson St., Suite 402, Pensacola FL 32502. E-mail: shannon@ballingerpublishing.com. Web site: www.ballingerpublishing.com. **Contact:** Shannon Lord, executive editor. **75% freelance written.** Monthly magazine. "*Pensacola Magazine*'s articles are written in a casual, conversational tone. We cover a broad range of topics that citizens of Pensacola relate to. Most of our freelance work is assigned, so it is best to send a résumé, cover letter and 3 clips to the above e-mail address." Estab. 1987. Circ. 10,000. Pays at end of shelf life. Byline given. Offers 20% kill fee. Buys first rights, makes work-for-hire assignments. Editorial lead time 1 month. Submit seasonal material 6 months in advance. Accepts queries by e-mail. Accepts previously published material. Accepts simultaneous submissions. Responds in 2 weeks to queries. Sample copy for $1, SASE and 1 First-Class stamp. Writer's guidelines online.

Nonfiction Special issues: Wedding (February); Home & Garden (May). Query with published clips. Length: 700-2,100 words. **Pays 10-15¢/word.** Sometimes pays expenses of writers on assignment.

Photos State availability of or send photos with submission. Reviews GIF/JPEG files. Buys one-time rights. Offers $7/photo. Captions, identification of subjects, model releases required.

Tips "We accept submissions for *Pensacola Magazine*, *Northwest Florida's Business Climate*, and *Coming of Age*. Please query by topic via e-mail to shannon@ballingerpublishing.com. If you do not have a specific query topic, please send a résumé and three clips via e-mail, and you will be given story assignments if your writing style is appropriate. You do not have to be locally or regionally located to write for us."

$ $ TALLAHASSEE MAGAZINE

Rowland Publishing, Inc., 1932 Miccosukee Rd., Tallahassee FL 32308. E-mail: editorial@rowlandpublishing.com. Web site: www.rowlandpublishing.com. **Contact:** Rosanne Dunkelberger, editor. **20% freelance written.**

Bimonthly magazine covering life in Florida's Capital Region. "All content has a Tallahassee, Florida connection." Estab. 1978. Circ. 18,000. **Pays on acceptance.** Publishes ms an average of 2 months after acceptance. Byline given. Buys first North American serial rights. Editorial lead time 4 months. Submit seasonal material 6 months in advance. Accepts queries by mail, e-mail. Accepts simultaneous submissions. Responds in 3 months to queries; 3 months to mss. Sample copy for $4. Writer's guidelines by e-mail.

Nonfiction All must have a Tallahassee slant. Book excerpts, essays, historical/nostalgic, inspirational, interview/profile, new product, personal experience, photo feature, travel, sports, business, Calendar items. No fiction, poetry, or travel. No general interest—"we are Tallahassee, Florida specific." **Buys 15 mss/year.** Query with published clips. Length: 1,000-2,000 words. **Pays $100-250.**

Photos Send photos with submission. Reviews prints, GIF/JPEG files. Buys one-time rights. Negotiates payment individually. Captions, identification of subjects, model releases required.

Tips "We're looking for fresh ideas and new slants that are related to Florida's Capital Region. Because we work so far in advance, it is difficult to be timely, so be sure to give us ideas that aren't too time specific."

N $ $ TIMES OF THE ISLANDS

Southwest Florida's Island Coast Magazine, Times of the Islands Inc., P.O. Box 1227, Sanibel FL 33957. (239)472-0205. Fax: (239)395-2125. E-mail: editor@toti.com. Web site: www.toti.com. Editor: Beth Luberecki. Managing Editor: Lauren Davies. **Contact:** Maria Dispenza, editorial assistant. **98% freelance written.** Bimonthly magazine. "*Times of the Islands* is a magazine that captures the true essence of island living. It is a high-quality, intriguing publication that captures the beauty, style and spirit of island life; a magazine with vision and substance that appeals not only to residents of Sanibel, Captiva and the barrier islands of Southwest Florida, but to vacationers and mainlanders as well—anyone who shares a passion for the island mystique and lifestyle." Estab. 1997. Circ. 25,000. Pays on publication. Publishes ms an average of 4 months after acceptance. Byline given. Buys one-time, electronic rights. Editorial lead time 4 months. Submit seasonal material 4 months in advance. Accepts queries by e-mail. Accepts simultaneous submissions. Responds in 1 week to queries; 1 month to mss. Sample copy for free. Writer's guidelines online.

Nonfiction General interest, humor, interview/profile, photo feature, travel, cuisine. Query with published clips. Length: 1,000-2,000 words. **Pays $250-400.**

Photos Send photos with submission. Reviews contact sheets. Buys one-time rights. Offers $25-50/published photo. Captions, identification of subjects required.

Columns/Departments Habitats (homes and living spaces); Arts; Profile (profile of notable person); Coastal Commerce (profile of local business person); Explorer (fun weekend exploration trip); Getaways (traveling trip); Outdoors (outdoor activity); To Your Health (informative health and medical), all 1,000 words. Plus, Making Waves (notable SW Floridians), 300 words. Query with published clips. **Pays $150-250.**

Tips "We are looking for exciting, fresh material on subjects that cover anything pertaining to Southwest Florida living."

GEORGIA

N $ $ $ ATLANTA LIFE MAGAZINE

2500 Hospital Blvd., Roswell GA 30076. (770)664-6466. Fax: (770)664-6465. E-mail: cklinger@atlantalifemag.com. Web site: www.atlantalifemag.com. Editor-in-Chief: Tom Boc. **Contact:** Cindy Klinger, assistant editor. **50% freelance written.** Monthly magazine. "We are an upscale lifestyle magazine that covers the northern part of Atlanta. We cover a variety of topics, including sports, fashion, travel, health, finances, home design, etc." Estab. 2006. **Pays on acceptance.** Byline given. Editorial lead time 2 months. Submit seasonal material 4 months in advance. Accepts queries by e-mail. Sample copy for free. Writer's guidelines free.

Nonfiction Essays, exposé, general interest, historical/nostalgic, how-to, humor, inspirational, interview/profile, new product, personal experience, travel. **Buys 35 mss/year.** Query with published clips. Length: 750-2,000 words. **Pays 25-75¢/word.** Sometimes pays expenses of writers on assignment.

Photos Contact Natalie Zieky, creative director. State availability of or send photos with submission. Reviews GIF/JPEG files. Buys one-time rights. Negotiates payment individually. Captions, identification of subjects, model releases required.

Columns/Departments Travel; Health/Medical; Sports; Fashion, all 750-1,100 words. Also, Mountain Life and CD/Book Reviews, 750-1,200 words. Query with published clips.

Fillers Anecdotes, facts, gags to be illustrated by cartoonist, short humor. **Buys 12/year.** Length: 150-350 words.

Tips "Submit previously published samples. Have high resolution photo support for your article if possible."

$ $ $ $ ATLANTA MAGAZINE

260 Peachtree St., Suite 300, Atlanta GA 30303. (404)527-5500. Fax: (404)527-5575. Web site: www.atlantamagazine.com. "The magazine's mission is to engage our community through provacative writing, authoritative

reporting, superlative design that illuminates the people, trends, and events that define our city." Circ. 69,000. **Pays on acceptance.** Byline given. Buys first North American serial rights. Accepts queries by mail. Responds in 3 months to queries. Sample copy online.

- Almost all content staff written except fiction.

Nonfiction "*Atlanta* magazine articulates the special nature of Atlanta and appeals to an audience that wants to understand and celebrate the uniqueness of the city." General interest, interview/profile, travel. **Buys 15-20 mss/year.** Query with published clips. Length: 250-5,000 words. **Pays $200-2,000.**

Fiction Need short stories for annual reading issue (Summer). "We prefer all fiction to be by Georgia writers and/or have a Georgia/Southern theme. Length: 1,500-5,000 words.

Tips "It's *Atlanta* magazine. If your idea isn't about Atlanta, we're not interested."

$ $ATLANTA TRIBUNE: THE MAGAZINE

Black Atlanta's Business & Politics, L&L Communications, 875 Old Roswell Rd, Suite C-100, Roswell GA 30076. (770)587-0501. Fax: (770)642-6501. E-mail: frobinson@atlantatribune.com. Web site: www.atlantatribune.com. **Contact:** Fred Robinson, editor. **30% freelance written.** Monthly magazine covering African-American business, careers, technology, wealth-building, politics, and education. "The *Atlanta Tribune* is written for Atlanta's black executives, professionals and entrepreneurs with a primary focus of business, careers, technology, wealth-building, politics, and education. Our publication serves as an advisor that offers helpful information and direction to the black entrepreneur." Estab. 1987. Circ. 30,000. Pays on publication. Byline given. Offers 10% kill fee. Buys electronic, all rights. Editorial lead time 3 months. Submit seasonal material 4 months in advance. Accepts queries by e-mail. Responds in 6 weeks to queries. Sample copy online or mail a request. Writer's guidelines online.

- Break in with "the ability to write feature stories that give insight into Black Atlanta's business community, technology, businesses, and career and wealth-building opportunities. Also, stories with real social, political or economic impact."

Nonfiction "Our special sections include Black History; Real Estate; Scholarship Roundup." Book excerpts, how-to (business, careers, technology), interview/profile, new product, opinion, technical. **Buys 100 mss/year.** Query with published clips. Length: 1,400-2,500 words. **Pays $250-600.** Sometimes pays expenses of writers on assignment.

Photos State availability with submission. Reviews $2^1/_4 \times 2^1/_4$ transparencies. Buys one-time rights. Negotiates payment individually. Identification of subjects, model releases required.

Columns/Departments Business; Careers; Technology; Wealth-Building; Politics and Education; all 400-600 words. **Buys 100 mss/year.** Query with published clips. **Pays $100-200.**

Tips "Send a well-written, convincing query by e-mail that demonstrates that you have thoroughly read previous issues and reviewed our online writer's guidelines."

N $FLAGPOLE MAGAZINE

P.O. Box 1027, Athens GA 30603. (706)549-9523. Fax: (706)548-8981. E-mail: editor@flagpole.com. Web site: www.flagpole.com. **Contact:** Pete McCommons, editor. **75% freelance written.** Local "alternative" weekly with a special emphasis on popular (and unpopular) music. "Will consider stories on national, international musicians, authors, politicians, etc., even if they don't have a local or regional news peg. However, those stories should be original and irreverent enough to justify inclusion. Of course, local/Southern news/feature stories are best. We like reporting and storytelling more than opinion pieces." Estab. 1987. Circ. 16,000. Pays on publication. Publishes ms an average of 1 month after acceptance. Byline given. Makes work-for-hire assignments. Editorial lead time 2 months. Submit seasonal material 2 months in advance. Responds in 2 weeks to queries; 1 month to mss. Sample copy online.

Nonfiction Book excerpts, essays, exposé, interview/profile, new product, personal experience. **Buys 50 mss/year.** Query by e-mail. Length: 600-2,000 words.

Reprints Send tearsheet, photocopy or typed ms with rights for sale noted and information about when and where the material previously appeared.

Photos State availability with submission. Reviews prints. Buys one-time rights. Negotiates payment individually. Captions required.

Tips "Read our publication online before querying, but don't feel limited by what you see. We can't afford to pay much, so we're open to young/inexperienced writer-journalists looking for clips. Fresh, funny/insightful voices make us happiest, as does reportage over opinion. If you've ever succumbed to the temptation to call a pop record 'ethereal' we probably won't bother with your music journalism. No faxed submissions, please."

$ $GEORGIA BACKROADS

Legacy Communications, Inc., P.O. Box 585, Armuchee GA 30105. E-mail: info@georgiabackroads.com. Web site: www.georgiahistory.ws. **Contact:** Daniel M. Roper, editor/publisher. **70% freelance written.** Quarterly magazine "for readers interested in travel, history, and lifestyles in Georgia." Estab. 1984. Circ. 18,861. Pays on publication. Publishes ms an average of 5 months after acceptance. Byline given. Offers 25% kill fee. Buys Usually buys all rights. Rights negotiable rights. Editorial lead time 3 months. Submit seasonal material 6 months in advance. Accepts queries by mail, e-mail, fax. Sample copy for 9×12 SAE and 8 first-class stamps, or online. Writer's guidelines for #10 SASE.

Nonfiction Historical/nostalgic, how-to (survival techniques; mountain living; do-it-yourself home construction and repairs, etc.), interview/profile (celebrity), personal experience (anything unique or unusual pertaining to Georgia history), photo feature (any subject of a historic nature which can be photographed in a seasonal context, i.e., old mill with brilliant yellow jonquils in foreground), travel (subjects highlighting travel opportunities in north Georgia). Query with published clips. **Pays $75-350.**

Photos Send photos with submission. Reviews contact sheets, transparencies. Rights negotiable. Negotiates payment individually. Captions, identification of subjects, model releases required.

Fiction Novel excerpts.

Tips "Good photography is crucial to acceptance of all articles. Send written queries then *wait* for a response. *No telephone calls, please.* The most useful material involves a first-person experience of an individual who has explored a historic site or scenic locale and *interviewed* a person or persons who were involved with or have first-hand knowledge of a historic site/event. Interviews and quotations are crucial. Articles should be told in writer's own words."

$ $ GEORGIA MAGAZINE

Georgia Electric Membership Corp., P.O. Box 1707, Tucker GA 30085. (770)270-6950. E-mail: ann.orowski@georgiaemc.com. Web site: www.georgiamagazine.org. **Contact:** Ann Orowski, editor. **50% freelance written.** "We are a monthly magazine for and about Georgians, with a friendly, conversational tone and human interest topics." Estab. 1945. Circ. 460,000. Pays on publication. Publishes ms an average of 4 months after acceptance. Byline given. Buys first North American serial, electronic rights. Editorial lead time 2 months. Submit seasonal material 6 months in advance. Accepts simultaneous submissions. Responds in 1 month to subjects of interest to queries. Sample copy for $2. Writer's guidelines for #10 SASE.

Nonfiction General interest (Georgia-focused), historical/nostalgic, how-to (in the home and garden), humor, inspirational, interview/profile, photo feature, travel. **Buys 24 mss/year.** Query with published clips. Length: 800-1,000 words; 500 words for smaller features and departments. **Pays $150-500.**

Photos State availability with submission. Reviews contact sheets, transparencies, prints. Buys one-time rights. Negotiates payment individually. Identification of subjects, model releases required.

$ $ KNOW ATLANTA MAGAZINE

New South Publishing, 1303 Hightower Trail, Suite 101, Atlanta GA 30350. (770)650-1102. Fax: (770)650-2848. E-mail: editor1@knowatlanta.com. Web site: www.knowatlanta.com. **Contact:** Riley McDermid, editor. **80% freelance written.** Quarterly magazine covering the Atlanta area. "Our articles offer information on Atlanta that would be useful to newcomers—homes, schools, hospitals, fun things to do, anything that makes their move more comfortable." Estab. 1986. Circ. 192,000. Pays on publication. Byline given. Offers 100% kill fee. Buys first North American serial rights. Editorial lead time 2 months. Submit seasonal material 2 months in advance. Accepts queries by mail, e-mail, fax. Accepts previously published material. Sample copy for free.

O→ "Know the metro Atlanta area, especially hot trends in real estate. Writers who know about international relocation trends and commercial real estate topics are hot."

Nonfiction General interest, how-to (relocate), interview/profile, personal experience, photo feature. No fiction. **Buys 20 mss/year.** Query with clips. Length: 1,000-2,000 words. **Pays $100-500 for assigned articles; $100-300 for unsolicited articles.** Sometimes pays expenses of writers on assignment.

Reprints Accepts previously published submissions.

Photos Send photos with submission, if available. Reviews contact sheets. Buys one-time rights. Negotiates payment individually. Captions, identification of subjects required.

N THE PIEDMONT REVIEW

A review of Atlanta's finest people, places, things, P.O. Box 12047, Atlanta GA 30355. Fax: (404)257-3008. E-mail: mneiman@piedmontreview.com. Web site: piedmontreview.com. **Contact:** Miles K. Neiman, publisher/founder. Monthly magazine covering local business, dining, cultural and charity events, fashion, home and garden features, art reviews, travel and various personal success stories. "*The Piedmont Review* is one of Atlanta's most popular lifestyle magazines." Accepts queries by e-mail.

Nonfiction General interest, interview/profile, new product, opinion, personal experience. Query with published clips.

$ $ POINTS NORTH MAGAZINE

Serving Atlanta's Stylish Northside, All Points Interactive Media Corp., 568 Peachtree Pkwy., Cumming GA 30041-6820. (770)844-0969. Fax: (770)844-0968. E-mail: julie@ptsnorth.com. Web site: www.ptsnorth.com. **Contact:** Julie Clark, editor. **85% freelance written.** Monthly magazine covering lifestyle (regional). "*Points North* is a first-class lifestyle magazine for affluent residents of suburban communities in north metro Atlanta." Estab. 2000. Circ. 81,000. Pays on publication. Publishes ms an average of 1 month after acceptance. Byline given. Offers negotiable (for assigned articles only) kill fee. Buys electronic, first serial (in the southeast with a 6 month moratorium) rights. Editorial lead time 3 months. Submit seasonal material 6 months in advance. Accepts queries by mail, e-mail, fax. Accepts previously published material. Responds in 6-8 weeks to queries; 6-8 months to mss. Sample copy for $3.

Nonfiction Managing Editor. General interest (only topics pertaining to Atlanta area), historical/nostalgic, interview/profile, travel. **Buys 50-60 mss/year.** Query with published clips. Length: 1,200-2,500 words. **Pays $250-500.**

Photos "We do not accept photos until article acceptance. Do not send photos with query." State availability with submission. Reviews slide transparencies, 4×6 prints, GIF/JPEG files. Offers no additional payment for photos accepted with ms. Captions, identification of subjects, model releases required.

Tips "The best way for a freelancer, who is interested in being published, is to get a sense of the types of articles we're looking for by reading the magazine."

N $ $ SAVANNAH MAGAZINE

Morris Publishing Group, P.O. Box 1088, Savannah GA 31402-1088. Fax: (912)525-0611. E-mail: linda.wittish@savannahnow.com. Web site: www.savannahmagazine.com. **Contact:** Linda Wittish, editor. **90% freelance written.** Bimonthly magazine covering coastal lifestyle of Savannah and South Carolina area. "*Savannah Magazine* publishes articles about people, places and events of interest to the residents of the greater Savannah areas, as well as coastal Georgia and the South Carolina lowcountry. We strive to provide our readers with information that is both useful and entertaining—written in a lively, readable style." Estab. 1990. Circ. 12,000. Pays on publication. Publishes ms an average of 2 months after acceptance. Byline given. Offers 20% kill fee. Buys first North American serial, second serial (reprint) rights. Editorial lead time 2 months. Submit seasonal material 4 months in advance. Accepts queries by mail, e-mail, fax. Accepts simultaneous submissions. Responds in 3 weeks to queries; 1 month to mss. Sample copy for free. Writer's guidelines by e-mail.

Nonfiction General interest, historical/nostalgic, humor, interview/profile, travel. Does not want fiction or poetry. Query with published clips. Length: 1,000-1,800 words. **Pays $250-450.**

Photos Contact Michelle Karner, art director. State availability with submission. Reviews GIF/JPEG files. Buys one-time rights. Negotiates payment individually. Offers no additional payment for photos accepted with ms.

N ⊘ SOUTHCOMM PUBLISHING COMPANY, INC.

2600 Abbey Ct., Alpharetta GA 30004. (678)624-1075. Fax: (678)624-1079. E-mail: cwwalker@southcomm.com. Web site: www.southcomm.com. Managing Editor: Jodi Drinkard. **Contact:** Carolyn Williams-Walker, editor. "Our magazines primarily are used as marketing and economic development pieces, but they are also used as tourism guides and a source of information for newcomers. As such, our editorial supplies entertaining and informative reading for those visiting the communities for the first time, as well as those who have lived in the area for any period of time. We are looking for writers who are interested in writing dynamic copy about Georgia, Tennessee, South Carolina, North Carolina, Alabama, Virginia, Florida, Pennsylvania, and Texas." Estab. 1985. Pays 2 weeks after acceptance. Publishes ms an average of 1-2 months after acceptance. Byline given. Buys all rights. Accepts queries by mail, e-mail, fax. Accepts previously published material. Accepts simultaneous submissions. Sample copy and writer's guidelines free.

Nonfiction "Our articles are informative pieces about the communities we're covering. We have 2 types of publications. Our "Classic" pieces are term paper-style publications, providing a comprehensive overview of all the community has to offer. Our "StandOut" magazines provide snapshots of community life through articles with a lifestyle publication slant (require interviews and quotes). Classic: Lifestyle; Recreation/Culture; Education; Healthcare; History (community changes over the years); Economic Development; Community/Newcomer Information (important phone numbers and Web sites). StandOut: Report Card (education stories); Vital Signs (movers an shakers in healthcare); Business Portfolio (what makes the economy work); Claim to Fame (who's who in the community). "We are not looking for article submissions. We will assign stories to writers in which we're interested. Queries should include samples of published works and biographical information." **Buys 50+ mss/year.** Quer or send complete ms. Length: 100-1,000 words. **Pays $25-200.**

Tips "It is not necessary for writers to live in the areas about which they are writing, but it does sometimes help to be familiar with them. We are not looking for writers to submit articles. We solely are interested in contacting writers for articles that we generate with our clients."

HAWAII

$ $ HONOLULU MAGAZINE

PacificBasin Communications, 1000 Bishop St., Suite 405, Honolulu HI 96813. (808)537-9500. Fax: (808)537-6455. E-mail: kam@pacificbasin.net. Web site: www.honolulumagazine.com. **Contact:** A. Kam Napier, editor. Prefers to work with published/established writers. Monthly magazine covering general interest topics relating to Hawaii residents. Estab. 1888. Circ. 30,000. Pays on publication. Byline given. Makes work-for-hire assignments. Accepts queries by mail, e-mail. Writer's guidelines online.

Nonfiction Historical/nostalgic, interview/profile, sports, politics, lifestyle trends, all Hawaii-related. "We write for Hawaii residents, so travel articles about Hawaii are not appropriate." Query with published clips or send complete ms. Length: determined when assignments discussed. **Pays $100-700.** Sometimes pays expenses of writers on assignment.

Photos Jayson Harper, creative director. State availability with submission. Pays $50-200/shot. Captions, identification of subjects, model releases required.

Columns/Departments Length determined when assignments discussed. Query with published clips or send complete ms. **Pays $100-300.**

IDAHO

$ $ SUN VALLEY MAGAZINE

Valley Publishing, LLC, 12 E. Bullion, Suite B, Hailey ID 83333. (208)788-0770. Fax: (208)788-3881. E-mail: edit@sunvalleymag.com. Web site: www.sunvalleymag.com. **95% freelance written.** Quarterly magazine covering the lifestyle of the Sun Valley area. *Sun Valley Magazine* "presents the lifestyle of the Sun Valley area and the Wood River Valley, including recreation, culture, profiles, history and the arts." Estab. 1973. Circ. 17,000. Pays on publication. Publishes ms an average of 5 months after acceptance. Byline given. Buys first North American serial, electronic rights. Editorial lead time 1 year. Submit seasonal material 14 months in advance. Accepts queries by mail. Accepts previously published material. Accepts simultaneous submissions. Responds in 5 weeks to queries; 2 months to mss. Sample copy for $4.95 and $3 postage. Writer's guidelines for #10 SASE.

Nonfiction "All articles are focused specifically on Sun Valley, the Wood River Valley and immediate surrounding areas." Historical/nostalgic, interview/profile, photo feature, travel. Special issues: Sun Valley home design and architecture, Spring; Sun Valley weddings/wedding planner, summer. Query with published clips. **Pays $40-500.** Sometimes pays expenses of writers on assignment.

Reprints Only occasionally purchases reprints.

Photos State availability with submission. Reviews transparencies. Buys one-time rights and some electronic rights. Offers $60-275/photo. Identification of subjects, model releases required.

Columns/Departments Conservation issues, winter/summer sports, health & wellness, mountain-related activities and subjects, home (interior design), garden. All columns must have a local slant. Query with published clips. **Pays $40-300.**

Tips "Most of our writers are locally based. Also, we rarely take submissions that are not specifically assigned, with the exception of fiction. However, we always appreciate queries."

ILLINOIS

$ $ $ $ CHICAGO MAGAZINE

435 N. Michigan Ave., Suite 1100, Chicago IL 60611. (312)222-8999. E-mail: stritsch@chicagomag.com. Web site: www.chicagomag.com. Senior Editor: Cassie Walker (cwalker@chicagomag.com). Special Publications Editor: Jan Parr (jparr@chicagomag.com). **Contact:** Shane Tritsch, managing editor. **50% freelance written.** Prefers to work with published/established writers. Monthly magazine for an audience which is "95% from Chicago area; 90% college educated; upper income, overriding interests in the arts, politics, dining, good life in the city and suburbs. Most are in 25-50 age bracket, well-read and articulate." Estab. 1968. Circ. 182,000. **Pays on acceptance.** Publishes ms an average of 3 months after acceptance. Buys first rights. Submit seasonal material 4 months in advance. Accepts queries by mail, e-mail. Responds in 1 month to queries. For sample copy, send $3 to Circulation Dept. Writer's guidelines for #10 SASE.

> "Try starting with the 'Arena' section, which features short, trend-driven articles, roundups, and charts. Everything must be centered around Chicago."

Nonfiction "On themes relating to the quality of life in Chicago: Past, present, and future." Writers should have "a general awareness that the readers will be concerned, influential, longtime Chicagoans. We generally publish material too comprehensive for daily newspapers." Exposé, humor, personal experience, think pieces, profiles, spot news, historical articles. Does not want anything about events outside the city or profiles on people who no longer live in the city. **Buys 100 mss/year.** Query; indicate specifics, knowledge of city and market, and demonstrable access to sources. Length: 200-6,000 words. **Pays $100-3,000 and up.** Pays expenses of writers on assignment.

Photos Usually assigned separately, not acquired from writers. Reviews 35mm transparencies, color and b&w glossy prints.

Tips "Submit detailed queries, be business-like, and avoid cliché ideas."

$ $ $ $ CHICAGO READER

Chicago's Free Weekly, Chicago Reader, Inc., 11 E. Illinois St., Chicago IL 60611. (312)828-0350. Fax: (312)828-9926. E-mail: mail@chicagoreader.com. Web site: www.chicagoreader.com. Editor: Alison True. **Contact:** Kiki Yablon, managing editor. **50% freelance written.** Weekly Alternative tabloid for Chicago. Estab. 1971. Circ. 120,000. Pays on publication. Publishes ms an average of 2 weeks after acceptance. Byline given. Buys one-time rights. Editorial lead time up to 6 months. Accepts queries by mail, e-mail, fax. Accepts simultaneous submissions. Responds if interested to queries. Sample copy for free. Writer's guidelines free or online.

Nonfiction Magazine-style features; also book excerpts, essays, humor, interview/profile, opinion, personal experience, photo feature. **Buys 500 mss/year.** Send complete ms. Length: 500-50,000 words. **Pays $100-3,000.** Sometimes pays expenses of writers on assignment.

Reprints Occasionally accepts previously published submissions.

Columns/Departments Local color, 500-2,500 words; arts and entertainment reviews, up to 1,200 words.

Tips "Our greatest need is for full-length magazine-style feature stories on Chicago topics. We're *not* looking for: hard news (What the Mayor Said About the Schools Yesterday); commentary and opinion (What I Think About What the Mayor Said About the Schools Yesterday); poetry. We are not particularly interested in stories of national (as opposed to local) scope, or in celebrity for celebrity's sake (_ la *Rolling Stone, Interview*, etc.). More than half the articles published in the *Reader* each week come from freelancers, and once or twice a month we publish one that's come in 'over the transom'—from a writer we've never heard of and may never hear from again. We think that keeping the *Reader* open to the greatest possible number of contributors makes a fresher, less predictable, more interesting paper. We not only publish unsolicited freelance writing, we depend on it. Our last issue in December is dedicated to original fiction."

$ $ $ ⊘ CS

Chicago Social, Modern Luxury, Inc., 200 W. Hubbard, Chicago IL 60610. (312)274-2500. Web site: www.modernluxury.com. **70% freelance written.** Monthly Luxury lifestyle magazine. "We cover the good things in life—fashion, fine dining, the arts, etc.—from a sophisticated, cosmopolitan, well-to-do perspective." Circ. 75,000. Pays 2 months after receipt of invoice. Byline given. Offers kill fee. first rights and all rights in this market. Editorial lead time 6 months. Submit seasonal material 3-6 months in advance. Responds in 1 month to queries. Sample copy for $7.15 for current issue; $8.20 for back issue. Writer's guidelines not available.

Nonfiction General interest, how-to (gardening, culinary, home design), interview/profile, photo feature (occasional), travel. No fiction. *No unsolicited mss.* Query with published clips only. Length: 500-4,500 words. **Pays $50-900.** Pays expenses of writers on assignment.

Photos State availability with submission. Reviews transparencies, prints. Buys one-time rights. We pay for film and processing only.

Columns/Departments Few Minutes With (Q&A), 800 words; City Art, Home Design, 2,000 words. Query with published clips only. **Pays $150-400.**

Tips "Send résumé, clips and story ideas. Mention interest and expertise in cover letter. We need writers who are knowledgeable about home design, architecture, art, culinary arts, entertainment, fashion and retail."

$ ILLINOIS ENTERTAINER

Chicago's Music Monthly, Roberts Publishing Co., 124 W. Polk, #103, Chicago IL 60605. (312)922-9333. Fax: (312)922-9369. E-mail: ieeditors@aol.com. Web site: www.illinoisentertainer.com. **Contact:** Steve Forstneger, editor. **80% freelance written.** Monthly free magazine covering "popular and alternative music, as well as other entertainment: film, media." Estab. 1974. Circ. 55,000. Pays on publication. Publishes ms an average of 2 months after acceptance. Byline given. Offers 50% kill fee. Buys first North American serial rights. Editorial lead time 2 months. Submit seasonal material 2 months in advance. Accepts queries by mail. Accepts simultaneous submissions. Responds in 2 months to queries. Sample copy for $5.

Nonfiction Exposé, how-to, humor, interview/profile, new product, reviews. No personal, confessional, inspirational articles. **Buys 75 mss/year.** Query with published clips. Length: 600-2,600 words. **Pays $15-160.** Sometimes pays expenses of writers on assignment.

Reprints Send ms with rights for sale noted and information about when and where the material previously appeared. Pays 100% of amount paid for an original article.

Photos Send photos with submission. Reviews contact sheets, transparencies, 5×7 prints. Buys one-time rights. Offers $20-200/photo. Captions, identification of subjects, model releases required.

Columns/Departments Spins (LP reviews), 100-400 words. **Buys 200-300 mss/year.** Query with published clips. **Pays $8-25.**

The online version contains material not found in the print edition. Contact: Steve Forstneger.

Tips "Send clips, résumé, etc. and be patient. Also, sending queries that show you've seen our magazine and have a feel for it greatly increases your publication chances. Don't send unsolicited material. No e-mail solicitations or queries of any kind."

N $ MIDWESTERN FAMILY MAGAZINE

P.O. Box 9302, Peoria IL 61612. (309)679-9539. E-mail: jburnitz@midwesternfamily.com. Web site: www.midwesternfamily.com. Editor: Jim Burnitz. **90% freelance written.** Bimonthly magazine covering family living in Central Illinois. "*Midwestern Family* is a comprehensive guide to fun, health and happiness for Central Illinois families." Estab. 2003. Circ. 23,000. Pays on publication. Publishes ms an average of 2 months after acceptance. Byline given. Buys all rights. Editorial lead time 4-6 weeks. Submit seasonal material 4-6 weeks in advance. Accepts queries by e-mail. Responds in 2 weeks to queries; 4 months to mss. Sample copy for $1.50. Writer's guidelines by e-mail.

Nonfiction Query. Length: 1,000-1,500 words. **Pays $100.** Sometimes pays expenses of writers on assignment.

Photos State availability with submission. Reviews GIF/JPEG files. Buys all rights. Negotiates payment individually. Identification of subjects, model releases required.

Columns/Departments Home; Fun; Life; Food; Health; Discovery, all 1,000-1,250 words. **Buys 40 mss/year.** Query. **Pays $100.**

$ $ NEWCITY

Chicago's News and Arts Weekly, New City Communications, Inc., 770 N. Halsted, Chicago IL 60622. (312)243-8786. Fax: (312)243-8802. E-mail: brian@newcity.com. Web site: www.newcitychicago.com. **Contact:** Brian Hieggelke, editor. **50% freelance written.** Weekly magazine. Estab. 1986. Circ. 50,000. Pays 2-4 months after publication. Publishes ms an average of 1 month after acceptance. Byline given. Offers 20% kill fee in certain cases . . . first rights and non-exclusive electronic rights. Editorial lead time 2 months. Submit seasonal material 2 months in advance. Accepts queries by e-mail. Responds in 1 month to mss. Sample copy for $3. Writer's guidelines online.

Nonfiction Essays, exposé, general interest, interview/profile, personal experience, travel (related to traveling from Chicago and other issues particularly affecting travelers from this area), service. **Buys 100 mss/year.** Query by e-mail only. Length: 100-4,000 words. **Pays $15-450.** Rarely pays expenses of writers on assignment.

Photos State availability with submission. Reviews contact sheets. Buys one-time rights. Captions, identification of subjects, model releases required.

Columns/Departments Lit (literary supplement), 300-2,000 words; Music, Film, Arts (arts criticism), 150-800 words; Chow (food writing), 300-2,000 words. **Buys 50 mss/year.** Query by e-mail. **Pays $15-300.**

Tips "E-mail a solid, sharply written query that has something to do with what our magazine publishes."

N $ $ OUTDOOR ILLINOIS

Illinois Department of Natural Resources, One Natural Resources Way, Springfield IL 62702. (217)782-7454. E-mail: dnr.editor@illinois.gov. Web site: www.dnr.state.il.us/oi. Editor: Kathleen M. Andrews. **25% freelance written.** Monthly magazine covering Illinois cultural and natural resources. "*Outdoor Illinois* promotes outdoor activities, Illinois State parks, Illinois natural and cultural resources." Estab. 1973. Circ. 30,000. **Pays on acceptance.** Byline given. Buys one-time rights. Editorial lead time 4 months. Submit seasonal material 1 year in advance. Accepts queries by mail, e-mail. Responds in 2 weeks to queries. Sample copy for free. Writer's guidelines by e-mail.

Nonfiction Historical/nostalgic, how-to, humor, interview/profile, photo feature, travel. Does not want first person unless truly has something to say. Query with published clips. Length: 350-1,500 words. **Pays $100-250.**

Photos Contact Adele Hodde, photography manager. Reviews contact sheets, GIF/JPEG files. Buys one-time rights. Negotiates payment individually. Captions, identification of subjects, model releases required.

Tips "Write with an Illinois slant to encourage participation in outdoor activities/events."

N $ $ WEST SUBURBAN LIVING

C2 Publishing, Inc., 775 Church Rd., Elmhurst IL 60126. (630)834-4994. Fax: (630)834-4996. Web site: www.westsuburbanliving.net. Managing Editor: Brittany Ashcroft. **Contact:** Chuck Cozette, editor. **80% freelance written.** Bimonthly magazine focusing on the western suburbs of Chicago. Estab. 1996. Circ. 25,000. Pays on publication. Publishes ms an average of 2-4 months after acceptance. Byline given. Buys first, electronic rights.

Accepts queries by mail, fax. Accepts previously published material. Accepts simultaneous submissions. Sample copy online.

Nonfiction General interest, how-to, travel. Does not want anything that does not have an angle or tie-in to the area we cover—Chicago's western suburbs. **Buys 15 mss/year. Pays $100-500.** Sometimes pays expenses of writers on assignment.

Photos State availability with submission. Offers $50-700/photo; negotiates payment individually. Model releases required.

INDIANA

$ $ EVANSVILLE LIVING

Tucker Publishing Group, 100 NW Second St., Suite 220, Evansville IN 47708. (812)426-2115. Fax: (812)426-2134. E-mail: ktucker@evansvilleliving.com. Web site: www.evansvilleliving.com. **Contact:** Kristen Tucker, editor/publisher. **80-100% freelance written.** Bimonthly magazine covering Evansville, Indiana, and the greater area. "*Evansville Living* is the only full-color, glossy, 100+ page city magazine for the Evansville, Indiana, area. Regular departments include: Home Style, Garden Style, Day Tripping, Sporting Life, and Local Flavor (menus)." Estab. 2000. Circ. 50,000. **Pays on acceptance.** Publishes ms an average of 3 months after acceptance. Byline given. Buys all rights. Editorial lead time 6 months. Submit seasonal material 6 months in advance. Accepts queries by mail, e-mail, fax. Accepts previously published material. Sample copy for $5 or online. Writer's guidelines for free or by e-mail.

Nonfiction Essays, general interest, historical/nostalgic, photo feature, travel. **Buys 60-80 mss/year.** Query with published clips. Length: 200-2,000 words. **Pays $100-300.** Sometimes pays expenses of writers on assignment.

Reprints Accepts previously published submissions.

Photos State availability with submission. Reviews contact sheets, negatives, transparencies, prints. Buys all rights. Negotiates payment individually. Captions, identification of subjects required.

Columns/Departments Home Style (home); Garden Style (garden); Sporting Life (sports); Local Flavor (menus), all 1,500 words. Query with published clips. **Pays $100-300.**

$ $ $ INDIANAPOLIS MONTHLY

Emmis Publishing Corp., 1 Emmis Plaza, 40 Monument Circle, Suite 100, Indianapolis IN 46204. (317)237-9288. Web site: www.indianapolismonthly.com. **30% freelance written.** Prefers to work with published/established writers. "*Indianapolis Monthly* attracts and enlightens its upscale, well-educated readership with bright, lively editorial on subjects ranging from personalities to social issues, fashion to food. Its diverse content and attention to service make it the ultimate source by which the Indianapolis area lives." Estab. 1977. Circ. 45,000. **Pays on acceptance.** Publishes ms an average of 2 months after acceptance. Byline given. Offers negotiable kill fee. Buys first North American serial, one-time rights. Editorial lead time 3 months. Submit seasonal material 3 months in advance. Accepts queries by mail, e-mail. Accepts simultaneous submissions. Responds in 3 weeks to queries. Sample copy for $6.10.

- This magazine is using more first-person essays, but they must have a strong Indianapolis or Indiana tie. It will consider nonfiction book excerpts of material relevant to its readers.

Nonfiction Must have a strong Indianapolis or Indiana angle. Book excerpts (by Indiana authors or with strong Indiana ties), essays, exposé, general interest, interview/profile, photo feature. No poetry, fiction, or domestic humor; no "How Indy Has Changed Since I Left Town," "An Outsider's View of the 500," or generic material with no or little tie to Indianapolis/Indiana. **Buys 35 mss/year.** Query by mail with published clips. Length: 200-3,000 words. **Pays $50-1,000.**

Reprints Send ms with rights for sale noted and information about when and where the material previously appeared. *Accepts reprints only from noncompeting markets.*

Photos State availability with submission. Buys one-time rights. Negotiates payment individually. Captions, identification of subjects, model releases required.

Tips "Our standards are simultaneously broad and narrow: Broad in that we're a general interest magazine spanning a wide spectrum of topics, narrow in that we buy only stories with a heavy emphasis on Indianapolis (and, to a lesser extent, Indiana). Simply inserting an Indy-oriented paragraph into a generic national article won't get it: All stories must pertain primarily to things Hoosier. Once you've cleared that hurdle, however, it's a wide-open field. We've done features on national celebrities—Indianapolis native David Letterman and *Mir* astronaut David Wolf of Indianapolis, to name 2—and we've published 2-paragraph items on such quirky topics as an Indiana gardening supply house that sells insects by mail. Query with clips showing lively writing and solid reporting. No phone queries, please."

IOWA

N DES MOINES WOMAN

P.O. Box 957, Des Moines IA 50304. (515)284-8000. E-mail: ropeters@dmreg.com. Managing Editor: Jane Schorer Meisner. **Contact:** Roberta J. Peterson, editor-in-chief. Magazine published 10 times/year covering local women making a difference, beauty/fashion, and local events, issues, and opportunities. "*Des Moines Woman* targets central Iowa women aged 40-59." Circ. 80,000. Byline given. Accepts queries by e-mail.

Nonfiction "I want published women writers who live in central Iowa. Des Moines area or surrounding suburbs/ cities is ideal. We assign the articles, but we need writers who can get beneath the surface and tell a woman's story or mine a topic in-depth. We need writers who can make readers feel elated, angry, cry, care, or who can just help them have fun." General interest, interview/profile. Does not want first person or essays. Query with published clips. **Pays variable amount.**

Tips "There is a lot of opportunity to write for this publication (and a few others) for writers in the area. We do only by assignment. No unsolicited manuscripts. We want to hear from people who want writing assignments. We welcome ideas, but only very local ones."

N $ $ THE IOWAN

Pioneer Communications, Inc., 218 6th Ave., Suite 610, Des Moines IA 50309. Fax: (515)282-0125. E-mail: iowan@thepioneergroup.com. Web site: www.iowan.com. Managing Editor: Jill Brimeyer. **Contact:** Abbie Hansen, editor. **75% freelance written.** Bimonthly magazine covering the state of Iowa. "Our mission statement is: To celebrate the people and communities, the history and traditions, and the culture and events of Iowa that make our readers proud of our state." Estab. 1952. Circ. 25,000. **Pays on acceptance.** Publishes ms an average of 3 months after acceptance. Byline given. Offers $100 kill fee. Buys first rights. Editorial lead time 8-12 months. Submit seasonal material 6 months in advance. Accepts queries by mail, e-mail. Responds to queries received twice/year to queries. Sample copy for $4.50 + s&h.

Nonfiction Book excerpts, essays, general interest, historical/nostalgic, interview/profile, photo feature, travel. **Buys 30 mss/year.** Query with published clips. Length: 1,000-2,000 words. **Pays $250-450.** Sometimes pays expenses of writers on assignment.

Photos Send photos with submission. Reviews contact sheets, GIF/JPEG files (8×10 at 300 dpi min). Buys one-time rights. Negotiates payment individually, according to space rates. Captions, identification of subjects, model releases required.

Columns/Departments Last Word (essay), 800 words. **Buys 6 mss/year.** Query with published clips. **Pays $100.**

Tips "Must have submissions in writing, either via e-mail or snail mail. Submitting published clips is preferred."

KANSAS

$ $ KANSAS!

Kansas Department of Commerce, 1000 SW Jackson St., Suite 100, Topeka KS 66612-1354. (785)296-3479. Fax: (785)296-6988. E-mail: ksmagazine@kansascommerce.com. Web site: www.kansmag.com. **90% freelance written.** Quarterly magazine emphasizing Kansas travel attractions and events. Estab. 1945. Circ. 38,000. **Pays on acceptance.** Publishes ms an average of 1 year after acceptance. Byline given. Buys one-time rights. Submit seasonal material 8 months in advance. Accepts queries by mail. Responds in 2 months to queries. Writer's guidelines online.

Nonfiction "Material must be Kansas-oriented and have good potential for color photographs. The focus is on travel with articles about places and events that can be enjoyed by the general public and experimental travel. In other words, events must be open to the public, places also. Query letter should clearly outline story. We are especially interested in Kansas freelancers who can supply their own quality photos." General interest, photo feature, travel. Query by mail. Length: 750-1,250 words. **Pays $200-350.** Pays mileage only for writers on assignment within the State of Kansas.

Photos "We are a full-color photo/manuscript publication." Send photos (original transparencies only or CD with images available in high resolution) with query. Pays $50-75 (generally included in ms rate) for 35mm or larger format transparencies. Captions required.

Tips "History and nostalgia or essay stories do not fit into our format because they can't be illustrated well with color photos. Submit a query letter describing 1 appropriate idea with outline for possible article and suggestions for photos. Do not send unsolicited manuscripts."

N $ $ RELOCATING IN KANSAS CITY

Network Communicatons, Inc., 5301 W. 75th St., Prairie Village KS 66208. (913)648-5757. Fax: (913)648-5783. Editor: Andrea Darr. Annual relocation guide. Estab. 1986. Pays on publication. Buys continual rights. Editorial lead time 4 months. Submit seasonal material 4 months in advance. Accepts queries by mail, fax. Accepts previously published material. Accepts simultaneous submissions. Responds in 1 month to queries; 1 month to mss. Sample copy for $5.

Nonfiction Local issues. **Buys 8 mss/year.** Query with published clips. Length: 600-1,000 words. **Pays $60-350.**

Reprints Accepts previously published submissions.

Photos Reviews transparencies. Buys continual rights. Offers no additional payment for photos accepted with ms. Identification of subjects required.

Tips "Understand the Kansas City market and the issues relocators face."

KENTUCKY

N $ BACK HOME IN KENTUCKY

Back Home in Kentucky, Inc., P.O. Box 710, Clay City KY 40312-0710. (606)663-1011. Fax: (606)663-1808. E-mail: info@backhomeinky.com. **Contact:** Jerlene Rose, editor/publisher. **50% freelance written.** Bimonthly magazine "covering Kentucky heritage, people, places, events. We reach Kentuckians and 'displaced' Kentuckians living outside the state." Estab. 1977. Circ. 8,000. Pays on publication. Publishes ms an average of 6 months after acceptance. Byline given. Buys first North American serial rights. Submit seasonal material 6 months in advance. Responds in 2 months to queries. Sample copy for $3 and 9×12 SAE with $1.23 postage affixed. Writer's guidelines for #10 SASE.

- Interested in profiles of Kentucky people and places, especially historic interest.

Nonfiction Historical/nostalgic (Kentucky-related eras or profiles), photo feature (Kentucky places and events), travel (unusual/little-known Kentucky places), profiles (Kentucky cooks, gardeners, and craftspersons), memories (Kentucky related). No inspirational or religion. **Buys 20-25 mss/year.** Query with or without published clips or send complete ms. Length: 500-2,000 words. **Pays $50-150 for assigned articles; $50-100 for unsolicited articles.** "In addition to normal payment, writers receive 2 copies of issue containing their article."

Photos Looking for color transparencies, slides, or digital (high resolution) for covers (inquire for specific topics). Vertical format. Pays $50-150. Photo credits given. For inside photos, send photos with submission. Reviews transparencies, 4×6 prints. Rights purchased depends on situation. Occasionally offers additional payment for photos accepted with ms. Identification of subjects, model releases required.

Columns/Departments Travel, crafts, profile, and cookbooks (all Kentucky related), 500-750 words. **Buys 10-12 mss/year.** Query with published clips. **Pays $15-40.**

Tips "We work mostly with unpublished or emerging writers who have a feel for Kentucky's people, places, and events. Areas most open are little known places in Kentucky, unusual history, and profiles of interesting Kentuckians, and Kentuckians with unusual hobbies or crafts."

$ $ KENTUCKY MONTHLY

Vested Interest Publications, 213 St. Clair St., Frankfort KY 40601. (502)227-0053. Fax: (502)227-5009. E-mail: jackie@kentuckymonthly.com or steve@kentuckymonthly.com. Web site: www.kentuckymonthly.com. Publisher: Stephen M. Vest. **Contact:** Jackie Hollenkamp Bentley, editor. **75% freelance written.** Monthly magazine. "We publish stories about Kentucky and by Kentuckians, including those who live elsewhere." Estab. 1998. Circ. 40,000. Pays within 3 months of publication. Publishes ms an average of 3 months after acceptance. Byline given. Buys first North American serial rights. Editorial lead time 3 months. Submit seasonal material 4 months in advance. Accepts queries by mail, e-mail, fax. Accepts simultaneous submissions. Responds in 1 month to queries; 1 month to mss. Sample copy and writer's guidelines online.

Nonfiction Book excerpts, general interest, historical/nostalgic, how-to, humor, interview/profile, photo feature, religious, travel, all with a Kentucky angle. **Buys 60 mss/year.** Query with or without published clips. Length: 300-2,000 words. **Pays $25-350 for assigned articles; $20-100 for unsolicited articles.**

Photos State availability with submission. Reviews negatives. Buys all rights. Captions required.

Fiction Adventure, historical, mainstream, novel excerpts. **Buys 10 mss/year.** Query with published clips. Length: 1,000-5,000 words. **Pays $50-100.**

Tips "We're looking for more home and garden, first-person experience, mystery. Please read the magazine to get the flavor of what we're publishing each month. We accept articles via e-mail, fax, and mail."

LOUISIANA

$ $ SUNDAY ADVOCATE MAGAZINE

P.O. Box 588, Baton Rouge LA 70821-0588. (225)383-1111 ext. 0199. Fax: (225)388-0351. E-mail: glangley@theadvocate.com. Web site: www.theadvocate.com. **Contact:** Tim Belehrad, news/features editor. **5% freelance**

written. "Freelance features are put on our Web site." Estab. 1925. Pays on publication. Publishes ms an average of 3 months after acceptance. Byline given. Buys one-time rights.

O→ Break in with travel articles.

Nonfiction Well-illustrated, short articles; must have local, area, or Louisiana angle, in that order of preference. **Buys 24 mss/year. Pays $100-200.**

Reprints Send tearsheet or typed ms with rights for sale noted and information about when and where the material previously appeared. Pays $100-200.

Photos Photos purchased with ms. Pays $30/published color photo.

Tips "Style and subject matter vary. Local interest is most important. No more than 4 to 5 typed, double-spaced pages."

MAINE

N $ DISCOVER MAINE MAGAZINE

10 Exhcange St., Suite 208, Portland ME 04101. (207)874-7720. Fax: (207)874-7721. E-mail: dmm@discovermainemag.com. Editor: Bruce Little. **Contact:** Jim Burch, publisher. **100% freelance written.** Monthly magazine covering Maine history and nostalgia. Sports and hunting/fishing topics are also included. Estab. 1992. Circ. 12,000. Pays on publication. Publishes ms an average of 2-3 months after acceptance. Byline given. Buys one-time rights. Editorial lead time 3 months. Submit seasonal material 3 months in advance. Accepts queries by mail, fax, phone. Accepts previously published material. Accepts simultaneous submissions. Responds in 2 weeks to queries; 1 month to mss.

Nonfiction Historical/nostalgic. Does not want to receive poetry. **Buys 200 mss/year.** Send complete ms. Length: 500-2,000 words. **Pays $20-30.**

Photos Send photos with submission. Buys one-time rights. Negotiates payment individually.

Tips Call first and talk with the publisher.

MARYLAND

$ $ BALTIMORE MAGAZINE

Inner Harbor E. 1000 Lancaster St., Suite 400, Baltimore MD 21202. (410)752-4200. Fax: (410)625-0280. Web site: www.baltimoremagazine.net. **Contact:** Appropriate Editor. **50-60% freelance written.** Monthly. "Pieces must address an educated, active, affluent reader and must have a very strong Baltimore angle." Estab. 1907. Circ. 70,000. Pays within 1 month of publication. Byline given. first rights in all media Submit seasonal material 4 months in advance. Accepts queries by mail, e-mail. Sample copy for $4.45. Writer's guidelines online.

O→ Break in through "Baltimore Inc. and B-Side—these are our shortest, newsiest sections and we depend heavily on tips and reporting from strangers. Please note that we are exclusively local. Submissions without a Baltimore angle may be ignored." Look online for appropriate editor to query via e-mail.

Nonfiction Book excerpts (Baltimore subject or author), essays, exposé, general interest, historical/nostalgic, humor, interview/profile (with a Baltimorean), new product, personal experience, photo feature, travel (local and regional to Maryland *only*). "Nothing that lacks a strong Baltimore focus or angle." Query by mail with published clips or send complete ms. Length: 1,600-2,500 words. **Pays 30-40¢/word.** Sometimes pays expenses of writers on assignment.

Columns/Departments Hot Shot, Health, Education, Sports, Parenting, Politics. Length: 1,000-2,500 words. Query with published clips.

Tips "Writers who live in the Baltimore area can send résumé and published clips to be considered for first assignment. Must show an understanding of writing that is suitable to an educated magazine reader and show ability to write with authority, describe scenes, help reader experience the subject. Too many writers send us newspaper-style articles. We are seeking: 1) *Human interest features*—strong, even dramatic profiles of Baltimoreans of interest to our readers. 2) *First-person accounts* of experience in Baltimore, or experiences of a Baltimore resident. 3) *Consumer*—according to our editorial needs, and with Baltimore sources. Writers should read/familiarize themselves with style of *Baltimore Magazine* before submitting."

CHESAPEAKE LIFE MAGAZINE

Alter Communications, 1040 Park Ave., Suite 200, Baltimore MD 21201. (443)451-6023. Fax: (443)451-6027. E-mail: editor@chesapeakelifemag.com. Web site: www.chesapeakelifemag.com. **Contact:** Kessler Burnett, editor. **80% freelance written.** Bimonthly magazine covering restaurant reviews, personalities, home design, travel, regional calendar of events, feature articles, gardening. "*Chesapeake Life* is a regional magazine covering the Chesapeake areas of Maryland, Virginia, and Southern Delaware." Estab. 1995. Circ. 85,000. Pays on publication. Byline given. Buys first North American serial rights. Editorial lead time 2 months. Accepts queries by mail, e-mail, fax, phone.

Nonfiction Book excerpts, general interest, historical/nostalgic, interview/profile, photo feature, travel. Query with published clips. Length: Open.

Photos Send photos with submission. Buys one-time rights. Negotiates payment individually.

MASSACHUSETTS

N BOSTON GLOBE MAGAZINE

P.O. Box 55819, Boston MA 02205-5819. (617)929-2000. Web site: www.boston.com/magazine. **Contact:** Doug Most, magazine editor. **75% freelance written.** Weekly magazine. Circ. 706,153. Pays on publication. Publishes ms an average of 2 months after acceptance. Buys non exclusive electronic rights Editorial lead time 2 months. Submit seasonal material 3 months in advance. Sample copy for 9×12 SAE and 2 first-class stamps.

Nonfiction Book excerpts (first serial rights only), Q&A, narratives, trend pieces, profiles. Especially interested in medicine, science, higher education, sports, and the arts. No travelogs or poetry. **Buys up to 100 mss/year.** Query; SASE must be included with ms or queries for return. Length: 1,000-4,000 words.

Photos Purchased with accompanying ms or on assignment. Reviews contact sheets. Pays standard rates according to size used. Captions required.

⊘ BOSTON MAGAZINE

300 Massachusetts Ave., Boston MA 02115. (617)262-9700. Fax: (617)267-1774. E-mail: editor@bostonmagazine.com. Web site: www.bostonmagazine.com. **Contact:** James Burnett, editor. **10% freelance written.** Monthly magazine covering the city of Boston. Estab. 1962. Circ. 125,000. Pays on publication. Publishes ms an average of 3 months after acceptance. Byline given. Offers 20% kill fee. Buys first North American serial rights. Editorial lead time 2 months. Submit seasonal material 4 months in advance. Accepts queries by mail, fax.

Nonfiction Book excerpts, exposé, general interest, interview/profile, politics; crime; trends; fashion. **Buys 20 mss/year.** Query. *No unsolicited mss.* Length: 1,200-12,000 words. Pays expenses of writers on assignment.

Photos State availability with submission. Buys one-time rights. Negotiates payment individually.

Columns/Departments Dining, City Journal, City Style, Politics, Ivory Tower, Media, Boston Inc., Culture, Power, Society. Query.

Tips "Read *Boston*, and pay attention to the types of stories we use. Suggest which column/department your story might best fit, and keep your focus on the city and its environs. We like a strong narrative style, with a slightly 'edgy' feel—we rarely do 'remember when' stories. Think *city* magazine."

$ $ CAPE COD LIFE

including Martha's Vineyard and Nantucket, Cape Cod Life, Inc., 270 Communication Way, Building #6, Hyannis MA 02601. (508)775-9800. Fax: (508)775-9801. Web site: www.capecodlife.com. **Contact:** Janice Rohlf, editor-in-chief. **80% freelance written.** Magazine published 7 times/year focusing on "area lifestyle, history and culture, people and places, business and industry, and issues and answers for year-round and summer residents of Cape Cod, Nantucket, and Martha's Vineyard as well as nonresidents who spend their leisure time here." Circ. 45,000. Pays 90 days after acceptance. Byline given. Offers 20% kill fee. Buys first North American serial rights, makes work-for-hire assignments. Submit seasonal material 6 months in advance. Accepts queries by mail. Responds in 3 months to queries; 3 months to mss. Sample copy for $5. Writer's guidelines for #10 SASE.

Nonfiction Book excerpts, general interest, historical/nostalgic, interview/profile, photo feature, travel, outdoors, gardening, nautical, nature, arts, antiques. **Buys 20 mss/year.** Query with or without published clips. Length: 800-1,500 words. **Pays $200-400.**

Photos Photo guidelines for #10 SASE. Buys first rights with right to reprint. Pays $25-225. Captions, identification of subjects required.

Tips "Freelancers submitting *quality* spec articles with a Cape Cod and Islands angle have a good chance at publication. We like to see a wide selection of writer's clips before giving assignments. We also publish *Cape Cod & Islands Home* covering architecture, landscape design, and interior design with a Cape and Islands focus."

N $ $ CAPE COD MAGAZINE

Rabideau Publishing, 396 Main St., Suite 8, Hyannis MA 02601. (508)771-6549. Fax: (508)771-3769. E-mail: editor@capecodmagazine.com. Web site: www.capecodmagazine.com. **Contact:** Scott Lajoie, editor. **80% freelance written.** Magazine published 9 times/year covering Cape Cod lifestyle. Estab. 1996. Circ. 16,000. Pays 30 days after publication. Publishes ms an average of 3 months after acceptance. Byline given. Offers 25% kill fee. Buys first North American serial, electronic rights. Editorial lead time 6 months. Submit seasonal material

1 year in advance. Accepts queries by mail, e-mail. Responds in 3 weeks to queries; 2 months to mss. Sample copy for $5. Writer's guidelines by e-mail.

Nonfiction Book excerpts, essays, general interest, historical/nostalgic, humor, interview/profile, personal experience. Does not want cliched pieces, interviews, and puff features. **Buys 3 mss/year.** Query with or without published clips or send complete ms. Length: 800-2,500 words. **Pays $300-500 for assigned articles; $100-300 for unsolicited articles.** Sometimes pays expenses of writers on assignment.

Photos State availability of or send photos with submission. Reviews GIF/JPEG files. Buys one-time rights. Negotiates payment individually.

Columns/Departments Last Word (personal observations in typical back page format), 700 words. **Buys 4 mss/year.** Query with or without published clips or send complete ms. **Pays $150-300.**

Tips "Read good magazines. We strive to offer readers the quality they find in good national magazines, so the more informed they are of what good writing is, the better the chance they'll get published in our magazine. Think of art opportunities. Ideas that do not have good art potential are harder to sell than those that do."

N $ $ CHATHAM MAGAZINE

Rabideau Publishing, 396 Main St., Suite 8, Hyannis MA 02601. (508)771-6549. Fax: (508)771-3769. E-mail: editor@capecodmagazine.com. Web site: www.chathammag.com. **Contact:** Scott Lajoie, editor. **80% freelance written.** Annual magazine covering Chatham lifestyle. Estab. 2006. Pays 30 days after publication. Publishes ms an average of 3 months after acceptance. Byline given. Offers 25% kill fee. Buys first North American serial, electronic rights. Editorial lead time 6 months. Submit seasonal material 1 year in advance. Accepts queries by mail, e-mail. Responds in 3 weeks to queries; 2 months to mss. Sample copy for $5. Writer's guidelines by e-mail.

Nonfiction Book excerpts, essays, general interest, historical/nostalgic, humor, interview/profile, personal experience. Query with or without published clips or send complete ms. Length: 800-2,500 words. **Pays $300-500 for assigned articles; $100-300 for unsolicited articles.** Sometimes pays expenses of writers on assignment.

Photos State availability of or send photos with submission. Reviews GIF/JPEG files. Buys one-time rights. Negotiates payment individually.

Columns/Departments Hooked (fishing issues), 700 words. **Buys 4 mss/year.** Query with or without published clips or send complete ms. **Pays $150-300.**

Tips "Read good magazines. We strive to offer readers the quality they find in good national magazines, so the more informed they are of what good writing is, the better the chance they'll get published in our magazine. Think of art opportunities. Ideas that do not have good art potential are harder to sell than those that do."

N $ $ PROVINCETOWN ARTS

Provincetown Arts, Inc., 650 Commercial St., P.O. Box 35, Provincetown MA 02657. (508)487-3167. E-mail: cbusa@comcast.net. Web site: www.provincetownarts.org. **Contact:** Christopher Busa, editor. **90% freelance written.** Annual magazine covering contemporary art and writing. "*Provincetown Arts* focuses broadly on the artists and writers who inhabit or visit the Lower Cape, and seeks to stimulate creative activity and enhance public awareness of the cultural life of the nation's oldest continuous art colony. Drawing upon a 75-year tradition rich in visual art, literature, and theater, *Provincetown Arts* offers a unique blend of interviews, fiction, visual features, reviews, reporting, and poetry." Estab. 1985. Circ. 8,000. Pays on publication. Publishes ms an average of 4 months after acceptance. Offers 50% kill fee. Buys first, one-time, second serial (reprint) rights. Editorial lead time 6 months. Submit seasonal material 6 months in advance. Accepts simultaneous submissions. Responds in 3 weeks to queries; 2 months to mss. Sample copy for $10. Writer's guidelines for #10 SASE.

Nonfiction Book excerpts, essays, humor, interview/profile. **Buys 40 mss/year.** Send complete ms. Length: 1,500-4,000 words. **Pays $150 minimum for assigned articles; $125 minimum for unsolicited articles.**

Photos Send photos with submission. Reviews 8×10 prints. Buys one-time rights. Offers $20-$100/photo. Identification of subjects required.

Fiction Mainstream, novel excerpts. **Buys 7 mss/year.** Send complete ms. Length: 500-5,000 words. **Pays $75-300.**

Poetry Buys 25 poems/year. Submit maximum 3 poems. **Pays $25-150.**

$ $ WORCESTER MAGAZINE

172 Shrewsbury St., Worcester MA 01604-4636. (508)755-8004. Fax: (508)755-4734. E-mail: mwarshaw@worcestermag.com. Web site: www.worcestermag.com. **Contact:** Michael Warshaw, editor. **10% freelance written.** Weekly tabloid emphasizing the central Massachusetts region, especially the city of Worcester. Estab. 1976. Circ. 40,000. Pays on publication. Publishes ms an average of 3 weeks after acceptance. Byline given. Buys all rights. Submit seasonal material 2 months in advance. Accepts queries by mail, e-mail, fax.

- Does not respond to unsolicited material.

O→ Break in with "back of the book arts and entertainment articles."

Nonfiction "We are interested in any piece with a local angle." Essays, exposé (area government, corporate), general interest, historical/nostalgic, humor, opinion (local), personal experience, photo feature, religious, interview (local). **Buys less than 75 mss/year.** Length: 500-1,500 words. **Pays 10¢/word.**

MICHIGAN

$ $ $ ANN ARBOR OBSERVER

Ann Arbor Observer Co., 201 E. Catherine, Ann Arbor MI 48104. Fax: (734)769-3375. E-mail: hilton@aaobserver.com. Web site: www.arborweb.com. **Contact:** John Hilton, editor. **50% freelance written.** Monthly magazine. "We depend heavily on freelancers and we're always glad to talk to new ones. We look for the intelligence and judgment to fully explore complex people and situations, and the ability to convey what makes them interesting." Estab. 1976. Circ. 63,500. Pays on publication. Publishes ms an average of 2 months after acceptance. Byline given. Accepts queries by mail, e-mail, fax, phone. Responds in 3 weeks to queries; several months to mss. Sample copy for 12½×15 SAE with $3 postage. Writer's guidelines for #10 SASE.

Nonfiction Historical, investigative features, profiles, brief vignettes. Must pertain to Ann Arbor. **Buys 75 mss/year.** Length: 100-5,000 words. **Pays up to $1,000.** Sometimes pays expenses of writers on assignment.

Columns/Departments Up Front (short, interesting tidbits), 150 words. **Pays $75.** Inside Ann Arbor (concise stories), 300-500 words. **Pays $150.** Around Town (unusual, compelling ancedotes), 750-1,500 words. **Pays $150-200.**

Tips "If you have an idea for a story, write a 100-200-word description telling us why the story is interesting. We are open most to intelligent, insightful features of up to 5,000 words about interesting aspects of life in Ann Arbor."

N $ $ $ COMMUNITY OBSERVER

A Quarterly Magazine for Western Washtenaw County, Ann Arbor Observer Co., 201 Catherine St., Ann Arbor MI 48104. (734)769-3175. Fax: (734)769-3375. E-mail: michael@aaobserver.com. Web site: www.washtenawguide.com. **Contact:** Michael Betzold, editor. **50% freelance written.** Quarterly magazine covering the communities of Chelsea, Dexter, Manchester and Saline Michigan. "*The Community Observer* serves 4 historic communities facing rapid change. We provide an intelligent, informed perspective on the most important news and events in the communities we cover." Estab. 1999. Circ. 22,000. Pays on publication. Publishes ms an average of 2 months after acceptance. Byline given. Buys all rights. Editorial lead time 2 months. Submit seasonal material 3 months in advance. Accepts queries by mail, e-mail, phone. Accepts previously published material. Responds in 2 weeks to queries; 1 month to mss. Sample copy for $3. Writer's guidelines for #10 SASE.

Nonfiction Essays, exposé, general interest, historical/nostalgic, interview/profile, personal experience. **Buys 30 mss/year.** Query with or without published clips or send complete ms. Length: 500-4,000 words. **Pays $100-1,000.**

Photos Michael Betzold. State availability with submission. Reviews contact sheets, negatives, transparencies, prints, GIF/JPEG files. Buys one-time rights. Negotiates payment individually. Identification of subjects required.

Columns/Departments Front Porch (short news items), 500 words; Back Yard (personal reflections on life in the CMO area), 1,250 words. **Buys 30 mss/year.** Query with or without published clips or send complete ms. **Pays $100-300.**

Tips "If you have an idea for a story, send a 100- to 200-word e-mail telling us why the story is interesting. We are most open to intelligent, insightful stories about interesting aspects of life in Chelsea, Dexter, Manchester and Saline."

$ $ GRAND RAPIDS MAGAZINE

Gemini Publications, 549 Ottawa Ave. NW, Suite 201, Grand Rapids MI 49503-1444. (616)459-4545. Fax: (616)459-4800. E-mail: cvalade@geminipub.com. Web site: www.grmag.com. **Contact:** Carole Valade, editor. "*Grand Rapids* is a general interest life and style magazine designed for those who live in the Grand Rapids metropolitan area or desire to maintain contact with the community." Estab. 1964. Pays on publication. Byline given. Editorial lead time 2 months. Submit seasonal material 2 months in advance. Sample copy for $2 and an SASE with $1.50 postage. Writer's guidelines for #10 SASE.

Nonfiction "*Grand Rapids Magazine* is approximately 60 percent service articles—dining guide, calendar, travel, personal finance, humor and reader service sections—and 40 percent topical and issue-oriented editorial that centers on people, politics, problems and trends in the region. In 2003, the editors added a section called 'Design,' which provides a focus on every aspect of the local design community—from Maya Lin's urban park installation and the new 125-acre sculpture park to architecture and the world's Big Three office furniture manufacturers headquartered here." Query. **Pays $25-500.**

HOUR DETROIT

Hour Media, LLC, 117 W. Third St., Royal Oak MI 48067. (248)691-1800. Web site: www.hourdetroit.com. **50% freelance written.** Monthly magazine. "General interest/lifestyle magazine aimed at a middle- to upper-income readership aged 17-70." Estab. 1996. Circ. 45,000. **Pays on acceptance.** Publishes ms an average of 2 months after acceptance. Byline given. Offers 30% kill fee. Buys first North American serial rights. Editorial lead time 2 months. Submit seasonal material 1 year in advance. Accepts queries by mail. Sample copy for $6.
Nonfiction Exposé, general interest, historical/nostalgic, interview/profile, new product, photo feature, technical. **Buys 150 mss/year.** Query with published clips. Length: 300-2,500 words.
Photos State availability with submission.

$ $ TRAVERSE

Northern Michigan's Magazine, Prism Publications, 148 E. Front St., Traverse City MI 49684. (231)941-8174. Fax: (231)941-8391. Web site: www.traversemagazine.com. **20% freelance written.** Monthly magazine covering northern Michigan life. "*Traverse* is a celebration of the life and environment of northern Michigan." Estab. 1981. Circ. 30,000. **Pays on acceptance.** Byline given. Offers 10% kill fee. Buys first North American serial rights. Editorial lead time 1 year. Submit seasonal material 1 year in advance. Accepts queries by mail, fax, phone. Accepts simultaneous submissions. Responds in 2 months to queries. Sample copy for $3. Writer's guidelines for #10 SASE.
Nonfiction Book excerpts, essays, general interest, historical/nostalgic, humor, interview/profile, personal experience, photo feature, travel. No fiction or poetry. **Buys 24 mss/year.** Query with published clips or send complete ms. Length: 1,000-3,200 words. **Pays $150-500.** Sometimes pays expenses of writers on assignment.
Photos State availability with submission. Buys one-time rights. Negotiates payment individually.
Columns/Departments Up in Michigan Reflection (essays about northern Michigan); Reflection on Home (essays about northern homes), both 700 words. **Buys 18 mss/year.** Query with published clips or send complete ms. **Pays $100-200.**
Tips "When shaping an article for us, consider first that it must be strongly rooted in our region. The lack of this foundation element is one of the biggest reasons for our rejecting material. If you send us a piece about peaches, even if it does an admirable job of relaying the history of peaches, their medicinal qualities, their nutritional magnificence, and so on, we are likely to reject if it doesn't include local farms as a reference point. We want sidebars and extended captions designed to bring in a reader not enticed by the main subject. We cover the northern portion of the Lower Peninsula and to a lesser degree the Upper Peninsula. General categories of interest include nature and the environment, regional culture, personalities, the arts (visual, performing, literary), crafts, food & dining, homes, history, and outdoor activities (e.g., fishing, golf, skiing, boating, biking, hiking, birding, gardening). We are keenly interested in environmental and land-use issues but seldom use material dealing with such issues as health care, education, social services, criminal justice, and local politics. We use service pieces and a small number of how-to pieces, mostly focused on small projects for the home or yard. Also, we value research. We need articles built with information. Many of the pieces we reject use writing style to fill in for information voids. Style and voice are strongest when used as vehicles for sound research."

MINNESOTA

$ $ LAKE COUNTRY JOURNAL MAGAZINE

Evergreen Press of Brainerd, 201 W. Laurel St., P.O. Box 465, Brainerd MN 56401. (218)828-6424, ext. 14. Fax: (218)825-7816. E-mail: jodi@lakecountryjournal.com. Web site: www.lakecountryjournal.com. **Contact:** Jodi Schwen, editor or Tenlee Lund, assistant editor. **90% freelance written.** Bimonthly magazine covering central Minnesota's lake country. "We target a specific geographical niche in central Minnesota. The writer must be familiar with our area. We promote positive family values, foster a sense of community, increase appreciation for our natural and cultural environments, and provide ideas for enhancing the quality of our lives." Estab. 1996. Circ. 14,500. Pays on publication. Publishes ms an average of 6 months after acceptance. Byline given. Offers 25% kill fee. Buys first North American serial, second serial (reprint), electronic rights. Submit seasonal material 1 year in advance. Accepts queries by mail, e-mail. Responds in 2 months to queries; 3 months to mss. Sample copy for $6. Writer's guidelines online.

O— Break in by "submitting department length first—they are not scheduled as far in advance as features. Always in need of original fillers."

Nonfiction Essays, general interest, how-to, humor, interview/profile, personal experience, photo feature. "No articles that come from writers who are not familiar with our target geographical location." **Buys 30 mss/year.** Query with or without published clips. Length: 1,000-1,500 words. **Pays $100-200.** Sometimes pays expenses of writers on assignment.
Reprints Accepts previously published submissions.

Photos State availability with submission. Reviews transparencies. Buys one-time rights. Negotiates payment individually. Identification of subjects, model releases required.

Columns/Departments Profile-People from Lake Country, 800 words; Essay, 800 words; Health (topics pertinent to central Minnesota living), 500 words. **Buys 40 mss/year.** Query with published clips. **Pays $50-75.**

Fiction Adventure, humorous, mainstream, slice-of-life vignettes, literary, also family fiction appropriate to Lake Country and seasonal fiction. **Buys 6 mss/year.** Length:1,500 words. **Pays $100-200.**

Poetry Free verse. "Never use rhyming verse, avant-garde, experimental, etc." **Buys 6 poems/year.** Submit maximum 4 poems. Length: 8-32 lines. **Pays $25.**

Fillers Anecdotes, short humor. **Buys 20/year.** Length: 100-300 words. **Pays $25.**

Tips "Most of the people who will read your articles live in the north central Minnesota lakes area. All have some significant attachment to the area. We have readers of various ages, backgrounds, and lifestyles. After reading your article, we hope to have a deeper understanding of some aspect of our community, our environment, ourselves, or humanity in general."

$ $ LAKE SUPERIOR MAGAZINE

Lake Superior Port Cities, Inc., P.O. Box 16417, Duluth MN 55816-0417. (218)722-5002. Fax: (218)722-4096. E-mail: edit@lakesuperior.com. Web site: www.lakesuperior.com. **Contact:** Konnie LeMay, editor. **40% freelance written.** Works with a small number of new/unpublished writers each year. Please include phone number and address with e-mail queries. Bimonthly magazine covering contemporary and historic people, places and current events around Lake Superior. Estab. 1979. Circ. 20,000. Pays on publication. Publishes ms an average of 10 months after acceptance. Byline given. Buys first North American serial, second serial (reprint) rights. Submit seasonal material 1 year in advance. Accepts queries by mail, e-mail. Responds in 3 months to queries. Sample copy for $3.95 and 5 first-class stamps. Writer's guidelines for #10 SASE.

Nonfiction Book excerpts, general interest, historical/nostalgic, humor, interview/profile (local), personal experience, photo feature (local), travel (local), city profiles, regional business, some investigative. **Buys 15 mss/year.** Query with published clips. Length: 300-2,200 words. **Pays $60-600.** Sometimes pays expenses of writers on assignment.

Photos "Quality photography is our hallmark." Send photos with submission. Reviews contact sheets, 2×2 and larger transparencies, 4×5 prints. Offers $50/image; $150 for covers. Captions, identification of subjects, model releases required.

Columns/Departments Current events and things to do (for Events Calendar section), less than 300 words; Around The Circle (media reviews; short pieces on Lake Superior; Great Lakes environmental issues; themes, letters and short pieces on events and highlights of the Lake Superior Region); I Remember (nostalgic lake-specific pieces), up to 1,100 words; Life Lines (single personality profile with photography), up to 900 words. Other headings include Destinations, Wild Superior, Lake Superior Living, Heritage, Shipwreck, Chronicle, Lake Superior's Own. **Buys 20 mss/year.** Query with published clips. **Pays $60-90.**

Fiction Ethnic, historic, humorous, mainstream, novel excerpts, slice-of-life vignettes, ghost stories. Must be targeted regionally. "Wants stories that are Lake Superior related." **Buys 2-3 mss/year.** Query with published clips. Length: 300-2,500 words. **Pays $50-125.**

The online magazine carries original content not found in the print edition. Contact: Konnie LeMay, online editor.

Tips "Well-researched queries are attended to. We actively seek queries from writers in Lake Superior communities. We prefer manuscripts to queries. Provide enough information on why the subject is important to the region and our readers, or why and how something is unique. We want details. The writer must have a thorough knowledge of the subject and how it relates to our region. We prefer a fresh, unused approach to the subject which provides the reader with an emotional involvement. Almost all of our articles feature quality photography, color or black and white. It is a prerequisite of all nonfiction. All submissions should include a *short* biography of author/photographer; mug shot sometimes used. Blanket submissions need not apply."

$ $ $ MPLS. ST. PAUL MAGAZINE

MSP Communications, 220 S. 6th St., Suite 500, Minneapolis MN 55402. (612)339-7571. Fax: (612)339-5806. E-mail: edit@mspmag.com. Web site: www.mspmag.com. Editor: Brian Anderson. Managing Editor: Jean Marie Hamilton. Monthly magazine. "*Mpls. St. Paul Magazine* is a city magazine serving upscale readers in the Minneapolis-St. Paul metro area." Circ. 80,000. Pays on publication. Buys all rights. Editorial lead time 3 months. Accepts queries by mail, e-mail, fax. Sample copy for $9.25. Writer's guidelines online.

Nonfiction Book excerpts, essays, general interest, historical/nostalgic, interview/profile, personal experience, photo feature, travel. **Buys 150 mss/year.** Query with published clips. Length: 500-4,000 words. **Pays 50¢/word for assigned articles.**

MISSISSIPPI

$ $ MISSISSIPPI MAGAZINE

Downhome Publications, 5 Lakeland Circle, Jackson MS 39216. (601)982-8418. Fax: (601)982-8447. Web site: www.mississippimagazine.com. **Contact:** Kelli Bozeman, editor. **90% freelance written.** Bimonthly magazine covering Mississippi—the state and its lifestyles. "We are interested in positive stories reflecting Mississippi's rich traditions and heritage and focusing on the contributions the state and its natives have made to the arts, literature, and culture. In each issue we showcase homes and gardens, in-state travel, food, design, art, and more." Estab. 1982. Circ. 40,000. Pays on publication. Publishes ms an average of 6 months after acceptance. Byline given. Offers 25% kill fee. Buys first North American serial rights. Editorial lead time 6 months. Submit seasonal material 1 year in advance. Accepts queries by mail, fax. Responds in 2 months to queries. Writer's guidelines for #10 SASE or online.

Nonfiction General interest, historical/nostalgic, how-to (home decor), interview/profile, personal experience, travel (in-state). "No opinion, political, sports, exposé." **Buys 15 mss/year.** Query. Length: 900-1,500 words. **Pays $150-350.**

Photos Send photos with query. Reviews transparencies, prints, digital images on CD. Buys one-time rights. Negotiates payment individually. Captions, identification of subjects, model releases required.

Columns/Departments Gardening (short informative article on a specific plant or gardening technique), 750-1,000 words; Culture Center (story about an event or person relating to Mississippi's art, music, theatre, or literature), 750-1,000 words; Made in Mississippi (short article about a nationally or internationally known Mississippian or Mississippi company in any field), 600-700 words; On Being Southern (personal essay about life in Mississippi; only ms submissions accepted), 750 words. **Buys 6 mss/year.** Query. **Pays $150-225.**

MISSOURI

N $ $ 417 MAGAZINE

The Magazine of Springfield & Southwest Missouri, Whitaker Publishing, 2111 S. Eastgate Ave., Springfield MO 65809. (417)883-7417. Fax: (417)889-7417. E-mail: editor@417mag.com. Web site: www.417mag.com. **Contact:** Gregory Holman, editor. **50% freelance written.** Monthly magazine. "*417 Magazine* is a regional title serving southwest Missouri. Our editorial mix includes service journalism and lifestyle content on home, fashion and the arts; as well as narrative and issues pieces. The audience is affluent, educated, mostly female." Estab. 1998. Circ. 15,000. **Pays on acceptance.** Publishes ms an average of 2-3 months after acceptance. Byline given. Buys first, second serial (reprint), simultaneous, electronic rights. Editorial lead time 6 months. Accepts queries by mail, e-mail, fax. Responds in 1-2 months to queries. Sample copy by e-mail. Writer's guidelines online.

Nonfiction Essays, exposé, general interest, how-to, humor, inspirational, interview/profile, new product, personal experience, photo feature, travel, local book reviews. "We are a local magazine, so anything not reflecting our local focus is something we have to pass on." **Buys 175 mss/year.** Query with published clips. Length: 300-3,500 words. **Pays $30-500.** Sometimes pays expenses of writers on assignment.

Tips "Read the magazine before contacting us. Send specific ideas with your queries. Submit story ideas of local interest. Send published clips. Be a curious reporter, and ask probing questions."

$ $ KANSAS CITY HOMES & GARDENS

Network Communications, Inc., 5301 W. 75th St., Prairie Village KS 66208. (913)648-5757. Fax: (913)648-5783. E-mail: adarr@kc-hg.com. Web site: kchandg.com. Publisher: Keith Sauro. Managing Editor: Andrea Darr. Bimonthly magazine with 2 annual issues: Kitchen & Bath and Holiday. "Since 1986, Kansas City residents (mainly women) have embraced a local publication that speaks to them. Their home, lifestyle and family are featured with emphasis on high-quality, upscale decorating, building and living." Estab. 1986. Circ. 18,000. Pays on publication. Byline given. Buys one-time rights. Editorial lead time 4 months. Submit seasonal material 4 months in advance. Accepts queries by mail, e-mail, fax. Accepts previously published material. Accepts simultaneous submissions. Responds in 1 month to queries; 1 month to mss. Sample copy for $7.50 or online.

Nonfiction Home and garden. **Buys 8 mss/year.** Query with published clips. Length: 600-1,000 words. **Pays $100-350.** Sometimes pays expenses of writers on assignment.

Reprints Accepts previously published submissions.

Photos State availability of or send photos with submission. Reviews transparencies. Buys continual rights. Offers no additional payment for photos accepted with ms. Identification of subjects required.

Tips "Focus on the high-end homeowner."

$ $ MISSOURI LIFE

Missouri Life, Inc., P.O. Box 421, Fayette MO 65248-0421. (660)248-3489. Fax: (660)248-2310. E-mail: info@missourilife.com. Web site: www.missourilife.com. Editor-in-Chief: Danita Allen Wood. **Contact:** Amy Stapleton, advertising coordinator/calendar editor. **85% freelance written.** Bimonthly magazine covering the state of Missouri. "*Missouri Life*'s readers are mostly college-educated people with a wide range of travel and lifestyle interests. Our magazine discovers the people, places, and events—both past and present—that make Missouri a great place to live and/or visit." Estab. 1973. Circ. 20,000. Pays on publication. Byline given. Buys all, nonexclusive rights. Editorial lead time 3 months. Submit seasonal material 6 months in advance. Accepts queries by mail, e-mail, fax. Responds in 2 months to queries. Writer's guidelines online.

Nonfiction General interest, historical/nostalgic, travel, all Missouri related. Length: 300-2,000 words. **Pays $50-600; 20¢/word.**

Photos State availability in query; buys all rights nonexclusive. Offers $50-150/photo. Captions, identification of subjects, model releases required.

Columns/Departments All Around Missouri (people and places, past and present, written in an almanac style), 300 words; Missouri Artist (features a Missouri artist), 500 words; Made in Missouri (products and businesses native to Missouri), 500 words; Missouri Memory (a personal memory of Missouri gone by), 500 words.

N $ $ RELOCATING TO THE LAKE OF THE OZARKS

Cliffside Corporate Center, 2140 Bagnell Dam Blvd., Suite 303E, Lake Ozark MO 65049. (573)365-2323. Fax: (573)365-2351. E-mail: mindy.whittle@gmail.com. Web site: www.relocatingtothelakeoftheozarks.com/. Publisher: Dave Leathers (spublishingco@msn.com). **Contact:** Mindy Whittle, editor. Annual relocation guides, free for people moving to the area. Pays on publication. Publishes ms an average of 6 months after acceptance. Byline given. Accepts queries by e-mail. Sample copy for $8.95. Writer's guidelines online.

Nonfiction Historical/nostalgic, travel, local issues. Length: 600-1,000 words.

Photos Purchases images portraying recreational activities, tourism, nature, business development, cultural events, historical sites, and the people of the lake area. Send color positive film in 35mm or larger format, or send high-resoultion digital images. State availability of or send photos with submission. Buys one-time rights. Pays $20-300, depending on size. Identification of subjects required.

Tips "Read the magazine and understand our audience."

$ RIVER HILLS TRAVELER

Todd Publishing, Route 4, Box 4396, Piedmont MO 63957. (573)223-7143. Fax: (573)223-2117. E-mail: btodd@riverhillstraveler.com. Web site: www.riverhillstraveler.com. **Contact:** Bob Todd, online editor. **50% freelance written.** Monthly tabloid covering "outdoor sports and nature in the southeast quarter of Missouri, the east and central Ozarks. Topics like those in *Field & Stream* and *National Geographic*." Estab. 1973. Circ. 7,500. Pays on publication. Publishes ms an average of 2 months after acceptance. Byline given. Buys one-time rights. Editorial lead time 2 months. Submit seasonal material 1 year in advance. Accepts queries by e-mail. Accepts simultaneous submissions. Responds in 2 months to queries. Sample copy for SAE or online. Writer's guidelines online.

Nonfiction Historical/nostalgic, how-to, humor, opinion, personal experience, photo feature, technical, travel. "No stories about other geographic areas." **Buys 80 mss/year.** Query with writing samples. Length: 1,500 word maximum. **Pays $15-50.** Sometimes pays expenses of writers on assignment.

Reprints Send ms with rights for sale noted and information about when and where the material previously appeared.

Photos Send photos with submission. Reviews JPEG/TIFF files. Buys one-time rights. Negotiates payment individually. Pays $25 for covers.

The online magazine carries original content not found in the print edition and includes writer's guidelines. Contact: Bob Todd, online editor.

Tips "We are a 'poor man's' *Field & Stream* and *National Geographic*—about the eastern Missouri Ozarks. We prefer stories that relate an adventure that causes a reader to relive an adventure of his own or consider embarking on a similar adventure. Think of an adventure in camping or cooking, not just fishing and hunting. How-to is great, but not simple instructions. We encourage good first-person reporting. We like to get stories as part of an e-mail, not an attached document."

N $ RURAL MISSOURI MAGAZINE

Association of Missouri Electric Cooperatives, P.O. Box 1645, Jefferson City MO 65102. E-mail: hberry@ruralmissouri.coop. Web site: www.ruralmissouri.coop. Editor: Jim McCarty. Managing Editor: Bob McEowen. **Contact:** Heather Berry, associate editor. **5% freelance written.** Monthly magazine covering rural interests in Missouri; people, places and sights in Missouri. "Our audience is comprised of rural electric cooperative members in Missouri. We describe our magazine as 'being devoted to the rural way of life.' " Estab. 1948. Circ. 515,000. **Pays on acceptance.** Publishes ms an average of 6 months after acceptance. Byline given. Buys one-time rights. Editorial lead time 6 months. Submit seasonal material 6 months in advance. Accepts queries by mail, e-mail. Responds in 6-8 weeks to queries; 6-8 weeks to mss. Sample copy and writer's guidelines online.

Nonfiction General interest, historical/nostalgic. Does not want personal experiences or nostalgia pieces. Query with published clips or send complete ms. Length: 1,000-1,100 words. **Pays variable amount for each piece.**
Tips "We look for tight, well-written history pieces. Remember: History doesn't mean boring. Bring it to life for us—attribute quotes. Make us feel what you're describing to us."

N $ $ SPRINGFIELD! MAGAZINE

Springfield Communications, Inc., P.O. Box 4749, Springfield MO 65808-4749. (417)882-4917. **Contact:** Robert Glazier, editor. **85% freelance written.** Eager to work with a small number of new/unpublished writers each year. "This is an extremely local and provincial monthly magazine. No *general* interest articles." Estab. 1979. Circ. 10,000. Pays on publication. Publishes ms an average of 3-24 months after acceptance. Byline given. First serial rights. Submit seasonal material 1 year in advance. Responds in 3 months to queries; 6 months to mss. Sample copy for $5.30 and 9½×12½ SAE.
Nonfiction Local interest *only*; no material that could appeal to other magazines elsewhere. Book excerpts (Springfield authors only), exposé (local topics only), historical/nostalgic (top priority, but must be local history), how-to, humor, interview/profile (needs more on females than males), personal experience, photo feature, travel (1 page/month). **Buys 150 mss/year.** Query with published clips by mail only or send complete ms with SASE. Length: 500-3,000 words. **Pays $35-250 for assigned articles.**
Photos Send photos with query or ms. "Needs more photo features of a nostalgic bent." Reviews contact sheets, 4×6 color, 5×7 b&w glossy prints. Buys one-time rights. Pays $5-$35 for b&w, $10-50 for color. Captions, identification of subjects, model releases required.
Columns/Departments Buys 150 mss/year. Query by mail or send complete ms.
Tips "We prefer writers read 8 or 10 copies of our magazine prior to submitting any material for our consideration. The magazine's greatest need is for features which comment on these times in Springfield. We are overstocked with nostalgic pieces right now. We also need profiles about young women and men of distinction."

MONTANA

$ $ MONTANA MAGAZINE

Lee Enterprises, P.O. Box 5630, Helena MT 59604-5630. Fax: (406)443-5480. E-mail: editor@montanamagazine.com. Web site: www.montanamagazine.com. **Contact:** Beverly R. Magley, editor. **90% freelance written.** Bimonthly magazine. "Strictly Montana-oriented magazine that features community profiles, contemporary issues, wildlife and natural history, travel pieces." Estab. 1970. Circ. 40,000. Publishes ms an average of 1 year after acceptance. Byline given. Buys one-time rights. Submit seasonal material 1 year in advance. Accepts simultaneous submissions. Responds in 6 months to queries. Sample copy for $5 or online. Writer's guidelines online.

- Accepts queries by e-mail. No phone calls.

Nonfiction Query by September for summer material; March for winter material. Essays, general interest, interview/profile, photo feature, travel. Special issues: Special features on summer and winter destination points. No 'me and Joe' hiking and hunting tales; no blood-and-guts hunting stories; no poetry; no fiction; no sentimental essays. **Buys 30 mss/year.** Query with samples and SASE. Length: 300-3,000 words. **Pays 20¢/word.** Sometimes pays expenses of writers on assignment.
Reprints Send photocopy of article with rights for sale noted and information about when and where the material previously appeared. Pays 50% of amount paid for an original article.
Photos Send photos with submission. Reviews contact sheets, 35mm or larger format transparencies, 5×7 prints. Buys one-time rights. Offers additional payment for photos accepted with ms. Captions, identification of subjects, model releases required.
Columns/Departments Memories (reminisces of early-day Montana life), 800-1,000 words; Outdoor Recreation, 1,500-2,000 words; Community Festivals, 500 words, plus b&w or color photo; Montana-Specific Humor, 800-1,000 words. Query with samples and SASE.
Tips "We avoid commonly known topics so Montanans won't ho-hum through more of what they already know. If it's time to revisit a topic, we look for a unique slant."

NEVADA

N $ NEVADA HOME MAGAZINE

House and Garden Living, Nevada Home LLC, 780 Smithridge Dr., #200, Reno NV 89502. (775)825-4344. Fax: (775)825-4644. E-mail: cturner@nvhome.biz. Web site: www.nevadahomemag.com. Managing Editor: John Seelmeyer. **Contact:** Judith Harlan, editor. **80% freelance written.** Monthly magazine covering do-it-yourself home design, food/cooking, home improvement, gardening and landscaping specific to the Washoe County,

Nevada region. "Stories are all specific to the Reno and Sparks areas. All use local sources as experts. In gardening, the stories must present an understanding of the microclimates here in this area. In home improvement, they must reflect needs and timing based on the local climate and aesthetics." Estab. 2005. Circ. 40,000. **Pays on acceptance.** Publishes ms an average of 2 months after acceptance. Byline given. Buys first rights plus usage in all media thereafter, though ownership reverts to writer. Editorial lead time 3 months. Submit seasonal material 4 months in advance. Accepts queries by mail, e-mail. Responds in 3 weeks to queries. Sample copy online. Writer's guidelines by e-mail.

Nonfiction House and garden in Washoe County NV. **Buys 100 mss/year.** Query. Length: 200-1,200 words. **Pays $50-150 for assigned articles; $50-100 for unsolicited articles.**

Photos State availability with submission. Reviews GIF/JPEG files. Buys first rights plus usage in all media thereafter, though ownership reverts to photographer. Negotiates payment individually. Captions, identification of subjects, model releases required.

Tips "If you have expertise in either home improvement (construction-related work) or gardening, let me know. Depth of related experience counts. Also, all stories are local to the Washoe County, Nevada area. Include your knowledge of, and time spent in, this area."

$ $ NEVADA MAGAZINE

401 N. Carson St., Carson City NV 89701-4291. (775)687-5416. Fax: (775)687-6159. E-mail: editor@nevadamagazine.com. Web site: www.nevadamagazine.com. Editor: Joyce Hollister. **Contact:** Matt Brown, associate editor. **50% freelance written.** Works with a small number of new/unpublished writers each year. Bimonthly magazine published by the state of Nevada to promote tourism. Estab. 1936. Circ. 80,000. Pays on publication. Publishes ms an average of 8 months after acceptance. Byline given. Buys first North American serial rights. Submit seasonal material 6 months in advance. Accepts queries by mail, e-mail. Responds in 1 month to queries.

Nonfiction "We use stories and photos on speculation." Nevada topics only. Photo feature, travel, lifestyle, dining, recreational. **Buys 40 unsolicited mss/year.** Send detailed query. Length: 300-800 words. **Pays $50-500.**

Photos Query art director Matt Smith (matt@nevadamagazine.com). Reviews digital images. Buys one-time rights. Pays $20-100.

Tips "Keep in mind the magazine's purpose is to promote Nevada tourism and lifestyle. We look for a light, enthusiastic tone of voice without being too cute."

N $ $ RELOCATING TO LAS VEGAS

Network Communications, Inc., 5301 W. 75th St., Prairie Village KS 66208. (913)648-5757. Fax: (913)648-5783. Editor: Andrea Darr. Triannual relocation guides, free for people moving to the area. Pays on publication. Publishes ms an average of 6 months after acceptance. Buys continual rights. Editorial lead time 4 months. Submit seasonal material 4 months in advance. Accepts queries by mail, e-mail. Responds in 1 month to queries; 1 month to mss. Sample copy for $5.

Nonfiction Historical/nostalgic, travel, local issues. **Buys 8 mss/year.** Query with published clips. Length: 650-1,000 words. **Pays $60-350.** Sometimes pays expenses of writers on assignment.

Reprints Accepts previously published submissions.

Photos State availability with submission. Reviews transparencies. Buys continual rights. Offers no additional payment for photos accepted with ms. Identification of subjects required.

Tips "Understand the Las Vegas market and the issues relocators face."

NEW HAMPSHIRE

$ $ NEW HAMPSHIRE MAGAZINE

McLean Communications, Inc., 150 Dow St., Manchester NH 03101. (603)624-1442. E-mail: editor@nhmagazine.com. Web site: www.nhmagazine.com. **Contact:** Rick Broussard, editor. **50% freelance written.** Monthly magazine devoted to New Hampshire. "We want stories written for, by, and about the people of New Hampshire with emphasis on qualities that set us apart from other states. We feature lifestyle, adventure, and home-related stories with a unique local angle." Estab. 1986. Circ. 32,000. Pays on publication. Byline given. Offers 25% kill fee. Buys all rights. Editorial lead time 3 months. Submit seasonal material 3 months in advance. Accepts queries by mail, e-mail, fax. Accepts simultaneous submissions. Responds in 2 months to queries; 3 months to mss. Writer's guidelines online. Editorial calendar online.

Nonfiction Essays, general interest, historical/nostalgic, photo feature, business. **Buys 30 mss/year.** Query with published clips. Length: 800-2,000 words. **Pays $50-500.** Sometimes pays expenses of writers on assignment.

Photos State availability with submission. Rights purchased vary. Possible additional payment for photos accepted with ms. Captions, identification of subjects, model releases required.

Fillers Upfront items, sidebars. Length: 200-400 words.

The online magazine carries original content not found in the print edition. Contact: Rick Broussard, online editor.

Tips McLean Communications publishes 1 monthly magazine entitled *New Hampshire Magazine* and a "specialty" publication called *Destination New Hampshire*. "In general, our articles deal with the people of New Hampshire—their lifestyles and interests. We also present localized stories about national and international issues, ideas, and trends. We will only use stories that show our readers how these issues have an impact on their daily lives. We cover a wide range of topics, including healthcare, politics, law, real-life dramas, regional history, medical issues, business, careers, environmental issues, the arts, the outdoors, education, food, recreation, etc. Many of our readers are what we call 'The New Traditionalists'—aging Baby Boomers who have embraced solid American values and contemporary New Hampshire lifestyles."

NEW JERSEY

$ $ $ $ NEW JERSEY MONTHLY

The Magazine of the Garden State, New Jersey Monthly, LLC, 55 Park Place, P.O. Box 920, Morristown NJ 07963-0920. (973)539-8230. Fax: (973)538-2953. E-mail: editor@njmonthly.com. Web site: www.njmonthly.com. **Contact:** Christopher Hann, senior editor. **75-80% freelance written.** Monthly magazine covering "just about anything to do with New Jersey, from news, politics, and sports to decorating trends and lifestyle issues. Our readership is well-educated, affluent, and on average our readers have lived in New Jersey 20 years or more." Estab. 1976. Circ. 95,000. Pays on completion of fact-checking. Publishes ms an average of 3 months after acceptance. Byline given. Offers 20% kill fee. Buys first North American serial rights. Editorial lead time 3 months. Submit seasonal material 6 months in advance. Accepts queries by mail, e-mail, fax, phone. Accepts simultaneous submissions. Responds in 2 months to queries.

- This magazine continues to look for strong investigative reporters with novelistic style and solid knowledge of New Jersey issues.

Nonfiction Book excerpts, essays, exposé, general interest, historical/nostalgic, humor, interview/profile, personal experience, photo feature, travel (within New Jersey), arts, sports, politics. "No experience pieces from people who used to live in New Jersey or general pieces that have no New Jersey angle." **Buys 90-100 mss/year.** Query with published magazine clips and SASE. Length: 800-3,000 words. **Pays $750-2,500.** Pays reasonable expenses of writers on assignment with prior approval.

Photos Donna Panagakos, art director. State availability with submission. Reviews transparencies, prints. Buys one-time rights. Payment negotiated. Identification of subjects, model releases required.

Columns/Departments Exit Ramp (back page essay usually originating from personal experience but written in a way that tells a broader story of statewide interest), 1,200 words. **Buys 12 mss/year.** Query with published clips. **Pays $400.**

Fillers Anecdotes (for front-of-book). **Buys 12-15/year.** Length: 200-250 words. **Pays $100.**

Tips "The best approach: Do your homework! Read the past year's issues to get an understanding of our well-written, well-researched articles that tell a tale from a well-established point of view."

$ $ NEW JERSEY SAVVY LIVING

CTB, LLC, 30B Vreeland Rd., Florham Park NJ 07932. (973)966-0997. Fax: (973)966-0210. E-mail: njsavvyliving@ctbintl.com. Web site: www.njsavvyliving.com. **90% freelance written.** Bimonthly magazine covering New Jersey residents with affluent lifestyles. "*Savvy Living* is a regional magazine for an upscale audience, ages 35-65. We focus on lifestyle topics such as home design, fashion, the arts, travel, personal finance, and health and well being." Estab. 1997. Circ. 50,000. Pays on publication. Publishes ms an average of 3 months after acceptance. Byline given. Offers $50 kill fee. variable rights. Editorial lead time 3 months. Accepts queries by mail. Accepts simultaneous submissions. Response time varies to queries. Sample copy for 9×12 SAE.

Nonfiction Interview/profile (people of national and regional importance), photo feature, travel, home/decorating, finance, health, fashion, beauty. No investigative, fiction, personal experience, and non-New Jersey topics (excluding travel). **Buys 50 mss/year.** Query with published clips. Length: 900-2,000 words. **Pays $250-500.**

Photos State availability with submission. Buys one-time rights. Offers no additional payment for photos accepted with ms. Captions, identification of subjects, model releases required.

Columns/Departments Savvy Shoppers (inside scoop on buying); Dining Out (restaurant review); Home Gourmet (gourmet cooking and entertaining). **Buys 25 mss/year.** Query with published clips. **Pays $300.**

Tips "Offer ideas of interest to a savvy, upscale New Jersey readership. We love articles that utilize local sources and are well focused and keep our readers informed about trends affecting their lives. We work with experienced and stylish writers. Please provide clips."

$ $ THE SANDPAPER

Newsmagazine of the Jersey Shore, The SandPaper, Inc., 1816 Long Beach Blvd., Surf City NJ 08008-5461. (609)494-5900. Fax: (609)494-1437. E-mail: letters@thesandpaper.net. Weekly tabloid covering subjects of interest to Long Island Beach area residents and visitors. "Each issue includes a mix of news, human interest features, opinion columns, and entertainment/calendar listings." Estab. 1976. Circ. 60,000. Pays on publication. Publishes ms an average of 1 month after acceptance. Byline given. Offers 100% kill fee. Buys first, all rights. Submit seasonal material 3 months in advance. Accepts queries by mail, e-mail, fax, phone. Accepts simultaneous submissions. Responds in 1 month to queries.

O→ "The opinion page and columns are most open to freelancers." Send SASE for return of ms.

Columns/Departments Speakeasy (opinion and slice-of-life, often humorous); Commentary (forum for social science perspectives); both 1,000-1,500 words, preferably with local or Jersey Shore angle. **Buys 50 mss/year.** Send complete ms. **Pays $30.**

NEW MEXICO

$ $ NEW MEXICO MAGAZINE

Lew Wallace Bldg., 495 Old Santa Fe Trail, Santa Fe NM 87501. (505)827-7447. E-mail: submissions@nmmagazine.com. Web site: www.nmmagazine.com. Editor-in-Chief: Emily Drabanski. Managing Editor: Walter K. Lopez. Associate Editor/Photo Editor: Steve Larese. Editorial Assistant: Carol Kay. **Contact:** Any editor. Monthly magazine emphasizing New Mexico for a college-educated readership with above-average income and interest in the Southwest. Estab. 1923. Circ. 120,000. **Pays on acceptance.** Publishes ms an average of 8 months after acceptance. Buys first North American serial rights. Submit seasonal material 1 year in advance. Accepts queries by mail. Accepts previously published material. Responds in 2 months to queries. Sample copy for $3.95. Writer's guidelines for SASE.

Nonfiction New Mexico subjects of interest to travelers. Historical, cultural, informational articles. "We are looking for more short, light and bright stories for the 'Poquito Mas' section. Also, we are buying 12 mss per year for our MakinTracks series." Send those submissions to Steve Larese. **Buys 7-10 mss/issue**. General interest, historical/nostalgic, interview/profile, travel. "No columns, cartoons, poetry or non-New Mexico subjects." Query by mail with 3 published writing samples. No phone or fax queries. Length: 250-2,500 words. **Pays 30¢/word.**

Reprints Rarely publishes reprints but sometimes publishes excerpts from novels and nonfiction books.

Photos Purchased as portfolio or on assignment. "Photographers interested in photo assignments should send tearsheets to photo editor Steve Larese; slides or transparencies with complete caption information are accepted. Photographers name and telephone number should be affixed to the image mount." Buys one-time rights. Captions, model releases required.

Tips "Your best bet is to write a fun, lively short feature (200-250 words) for our Poquito Mas section that is a superb short manuscript on a little-known person, aspect of history or place to see in New Mexico. Faulty research will ruin a writer's chances for the future. Good style, good grammar. No generalized odes to the state or the Southwest. No sentimentalized, paternalistic views of Indians or Hispanics. No glib, gimmicky 'travel brochure' writing. No first-person vacation stories. We're always looking for well-researched pieces on unusual aspects of New Mexico and lively writing."

N $ NEW MEXICO WOMAN

New Mexico Woman, Inc., P.O. Box 12955, Albuquerque NM 87195. (505)247-9195. Fax: (505)842-5129. E-mail: heygals@nmwoman.com. Web site: www.nmwoman.com. **Contact:** M.T. Hyatt, editor. **90% freelance written.** Monthly magazine covering women in business and professional women. Estab. 1983. Circ. 15,000. Pays on publication. Publishes ms an average of 3 months after acceptance. Buys one-time rights. Editorial lead time 2 months. Submit seasonal material 2-3 months in advance. Accepts queries by mail, e-mail, fax. Accepts previously published material. Accepts simultaneous submissions. Writer's guidelines online.

Nonfiction "We are interested primarily in education, opportunities, career options, self improvement, women's health issues, and occasionally articles about home, hobby, travel, lifestyle, or nonprofit programs that serve women in the community." General interest, historical/nostalgic, how-to, humor, inspirational, new product, personal experience. **Buys 5-10 mss/year.** Query. Length: 800-1,600 words. **Pays 5¢/word.**

Photos State availability with submission. Reviews GIF/JPEG files. Buys one-time rights. Offers no additional payment for photos accepted with ms. Captions required.

Columns/Departments From My Perspective (personal experience); The Inner You (self-improvement); Young Women to Watch (talented young women), all 600 words; and The Seasons of Fitness (fitness advice), 400 words. **Buys 12 mss/year.** Query with published clips. **Pays 5¢/word.**

Fillers Anecdotes, facts, short humor. Length: 100-150 words. **Pays 5¢/word.**

NEW YORK

$ $ ADIRONDACK LIFE

P.O. Box 410, Jay NY 12941-0410. (518)946-2191. Fax: (518)946-7461. E-mail: aledit@adirondacklife.com. Web site: www.adirondacklife.com. **Contact:** Mary Thill and Galen Crane, co-editors. **70% freelance written.** Prefers to work with published/established writers. Magazine published 8 issues/year, including special Annual Outdoor Guide, emphasizes the Adirondack region and the North Country of New York State in articles covering outdoor activities, history, and natural history directly related to the Adirondacks. Estab. 1970. Circ. 50,000. Pays 2-3 months after acceptance. Publishes ms an average of 6 months after acceptance. Byline given. Buys first North American serial, web rights. Submit seasonal material 1 year in advance. Accepts queries by mail, e-mail. Sample copy for $3 and 9×12 SAE. Writer's guidelines online.

O-ᵣ "For new writers, the best way to break in to the magazine is through departments."

Nonfiction "*Adirondack Life* attempts to capture the unique flavor and ethos of the Adirondack mountains and North Country region through feature articles directly pertaining to the qualities of the area." Special issues: Outdoors (May); Single-topic Collector's issue (September). **Buys 20-25 unsolicited mss/year.** Query with published clips. Length: 2,000-4,000 words. **Pays 25¢/word.** Sometimes pays expenses of writers on assignment.

Photos All photos must have been taken in the Adirondacks. Each issue contains a photo feature. Purchased with or without ms on assignment. All photos must be individually identified as to the subject or locale and must bear the photographer's name. Send photos with submission. Reviews color transparencies, b&w prints. Pays $150 for full page, b&w, or color; $400 for cover (color only,vertical in format). Credit line given.

Columns/Departments Special Places (unique spots in the Adirondack Park); Watercraft; Barkeater (personal to political essays); Wilderness (environmental issues); Working (careers in the Adirondacks); Home; Yesteryears; Kitchen; Profile; Historic Preservation; Sporting Scene. Length: 1,200-2,400 words. Query with published clips. **Pays 25¢/word.**

Fiction Considers first-serial novel excerpts in its subject matter and region.

Tips "Do not send a personal essay about your meaningful moment in the mountains. We need factual pieces about regional history, sports, culture, and business. We are looking for clear, concise, well-organized manuscripts that are strictly Adirondack in subject. Check back issues to be sure we haven't already covered your topic. Please do not send unsolicited manuscripts via e-mail. Check out our guidelines online."

$ BEYOND THE BADGE

(formerly *Police Officer's Quarterly*), 47-01 Greenpoint Ave., #114, Sunnyside NY 11104-1709. Fax: (718)732-2998. E-mail: editor@beyondthebadgemag.com. Web site: www.badgemag.com. **Contact:** Liz Martinez, editor. Quarterly magazine. *Beyond the Badge* is distributed to police officers, peace officers, federal agents, corrections officers, auxiliary police officers, probation and parole officers, civilian employees of law enforcement agencies, etc., in the Long Island, New York area (Nassau and Suffolk Counties), plus NYPD precincts in Eastern Queens, adjacent to Nassau County. Estab. 2001. Buys one-time rights. Accepts queries by e-mail. Accepts previously published material. Accepts simultaneous submissions. Sample copy for $5, plus a 9×12 SASE. Writer's guidelines by e-mail.

Nonfiction "We are seeking stories on travel; law enforcement product/news; books with a LE hook; movies and other entertainment that our readers would enjoy knowing about; worthy LE-related Internet sites; the latest developments in forensics and technology; health articles with a LE spin; investigation techniques; innovative international, national, regional, or local (inside and outside of the New York area) approaches to LE or crime prevention issues; other topics of interest to our reader population. General interest. Special issues: Summer Camps (Summer 2005); Education (Fall 2005); Washington D.C. Travel/Police Week (Winer 2006); Family Vacation Guide (Spring 2006). Please submit supplemental and seasonal topics 5 months in advance. "We see too many pieces that are dry and not enjoyable to read. Even if the topic is serious or scientific, present the material as though you were telling a friend about it." Query. Length: 1,000-1,500 words. **Pays $100.**

Photos Photos are very helpful and much appreciated; however, there is no additional pay for photos. Inclusion of photos does increase chances of publication.

Columns/Departments Book'Em (book reviews/excerpts/author interviews); Internet Guide; Screening Room (movie reviews); Your Finances; Management in Focus; Health Department; Forensics Lab; Technology. Query. **Pays $75.**

Tips "Writers should keep in mind that this is a lifestyle magazine whose readers happen to be cops, not a cop magazine with some lifestyle topics in it."

$ $ BUFFALO SPREE MAGAZINE

David Laurence Publications, Inc., 6215 Sheridan Dr., Buffalo NY 14221. (716)634-0820. Fax: (716)810-0075. E-mail: elicata@buffalospree.com. Web site: www.buffalospree.com. **Contact:** Elizabeth Licata, editor. **90%**

freelance written. City regional magazine published 8 times/year. Estab. 1967. Circ. 25,000. Pays on publication. Publishes ms an average of 1 month after acceptance. Byline given. Buys first North American serial rights. Accepts queries by mail, e-mail, fax. Responds in 6 months to queries. Sample copy for $3.95 and 9×12 SAE with 9 first-class stamps.

Nonfiction "Most articles are assigned not unsolicited." Interview/profile, travel, issue-oriented features, arts, living, food, regional. Query with résumé and published clips. Length: 1,000-2,000 words. **Pays $125-250.**

Tips "Send a well-written, compelling query or an interesting topic, and *great* clips. We no longer regularly publish fiction or poetry. Prefers material that is Western New York related."

$$$$ CITY LIMITS

New York's Urban Affairs News Magazine, City Limits Community Information Service, 120 Wall St., 20th Floor, New York NY 10005. (212)479-3344. Fax: (212)344-6457. E-mail: citylimits@citylimits.org. Web site: www.citylimits.org. **Contact:** Alyssa Katz, editor. **50% freelance written.** Monthly magazine covering urban politics and policy. "*City Limits* is a 29-year-old nonprofit magazine focusing on issues facing New York City and its neighborhoods, particularly low-income communities. The magazine is strongly committed to investigative journalism, in-depth policy analysis and hard-hitting profiles." Estab. 1976. Circ. 4,000. Pays on publication. Publishes ms an average of 3 months after acceptance. Byline given. Offers 50% kill fee. Buys first North American serial, second serial (reprint) rights. Editorial lead time 2 months. Accepts queries by mail, e-mail, fax. Accepts simultaneous submissions. Sample copy for $2.95. Writer's guidelines free.

Nonfiction Book excerpts, exposé, humor, interview/profile, opinion, photo feature. No essays, polemics. **Buys 25 mss/year.** Query with published clips. Length: 400-3,500 words. **Pays $150-2,000 for assigned articles; $100-800 for unsolicited articles.** Pays expenses of writers on assignment.

Photos State availability with submission. Reviews contact sheets, negatives, transparencies. Offers $50-100/photo.

Columns/Departments Making Change (nonprofit business); Big Idea (policy news); Book Review, all 800 words; Urban Legend (profile); First Hand (Q&A), both 350 words. **Buys 15 mss/year.** Query with published clips.

Tips "*City Limits'* specialty is covering low-income communities. We want to report untold stories about news affecting neighborhoods at the grassroots. We're looking for stories about housing, health care, criminal justice, child welfare, education, economic development, welfare reform, politics and government."

$$$ HUDSON VALLEY

Today Media, Inc., 22 IBM Rd., Suite 108, Poughkeepsie NY 12601. (845)463-0542. Fax: (845)463-1544. E-mail: rsparling@hvmag.com. Web site: www.hudsonvalleymagazine.com. **Contact:** Reed Sparling, editor-in-chief. Monthly magazine for residents of the Hudson Valley. Byline given. Offers 25% kill fee. Buys first North American serial rights. Accepts queries by mail, e-mail. Accepts simultaneous submissions. Responds in 3 months to queries. Sample copy for free. Writer's guidelines for #10 SASE.

Nonfiction Buys 50-80 mss/year. Query with published clips. Length: 200-5,000 words. **Pays $400-800/feature, $50-250/department article, $25-75/short piece.**

IN NEW YORK

261 Madison Ave., 9th Floor, New York NY 10016. (212)716-8562. E-mail: trisha.mcmahon@in-newyorkmag.com. Web site: www.in-newyorkmag.com. Editor: Trisha S. McMahon. Monthly magazine created exclusively for sophisticated travelers to the New York Metropolitan area and distributed at most hotels, tourist centers, VIP lounges of Amtrak Acela, airlines and popular sights. Circ. 125,000. Sample copy for free in upscale hotels at concierge desk.

$$$$ NEW YORK MAGAZINE

New York Media Holdings, LLC, 444 Madison Ave., 4th Floor, New York NY 10022. Web site: www.newyorkmetro.com. **Contact:** Ben Mathis-Lilley. **25% freelance written.** Weekly magazine focusing on current events in the New York metropolitan area. Circ. 433,813. **Pays on acceptance.** Offers 25% kill fee. Buys electronic, first world serial rights rights. Submit seasonal material 2 months in advance. Responds in 1 month to queries. Sample copy for $3.50 or on Web site. Writer's guidelines not available.

Nonfiction New York-related journalism that covers lifestyle, politics and business. Query by mail. No unsolicited mss. **Pays $1/word.** Pays expenses of writers on assignment.

N NEW YORK SPACES

Wainscot Media, 110 Summit Ave., Montvale NJ 07645. (201)571-7003. Fax: (201)782-5319. E-mail: nyspaces@wainscotmedia.com. Web site: www.nyspacesmagazine.com. **Contact:** Rita Guarna, editor-in-chief. Bimonthly magazine celebrating the best of New York area design. "*New York Spaces* is dedicated to helping affluent, acquisitive users enhance their private worlds—making it a remarkable showcase for the design community and advertisers alike."

Nonfiction General interest, how-to. Query.

Photos "Submit scouting shots (color prints, copies or low-resjpg files on CD) for consideration. These images are used solely for the purpose of reviewing and selecting which projects we will publish. We'll be in touch to let you know if your project has been selected." State availability of or send photos with submission. Reviews 2¼, 4×5, etc. or 35mm slides transparencies, high-resolution digital photos on CD. Captions, identification of subjects required.

$ $ SYRACUSE NEW TIMES

A. Zimmer, Ltd., 1415 W. Genesee St., Syracuse NY 13204. Fax: (315)422-1721. E-mail: editorial@syracusenewtimes.com. Web site: www.syracusenewtimes.com. **Contact:** Molly English, editor. **50% freelance written.** Weekly tabloid covering news, sports, arts, and entertainment. "*Syracuse New Times* is an alternative weekly that can be topical, provocative, irreverent, and intensely local." Estab. 1969. Circ. 46,000. Pays on publication. Publishes ms an average of 1 month after acceptance. Byline given. Buys one-time rights. Editorial lead time 3 months. Submit seasonal material 3 months in advance. Accepts simultaneous submissions. Responds in 2 weeks to queries; 1 month to mss. Sample copy for 9×12 SAE and 2 first-class stamps. Writer's guidelines for #10 SASE.

Nonfiction Essays, general interest. **Buys 200 mss/year.** Query by mail with published clips. Length: 250-2,500 words. **Pays $25-200.**

Photos State availability of or send photos with submission. Reviews 8×10 prints, color slides. Buys one-time rights. Offers $10-25/photo or negotiates payment individually. Identification of subjects required.

Tips "Move to Syracuse and query with strong idea."

TIME OUT NEW YORK

Time Out New York Partners, LP, 475 10th Ave., 12th Floor, New York NY 10018. (646)432-3000. Fax: (646)432-3160. E-mail: letters@timeoutny.com. Web site: www.timeoutny.com. **Contact:** Erin Clements, editorial assistant. **20% freelance written.** Weekly magazine covering entertainment in New York City. "Those who want to contribute to *Time Out New York* must be intimate with New York City and its environs." Estab. 1995. Circ. 120,000. Pays on publication. Publishes ms an average of 1 month after acceptance. Byline sometimes given. Offers 25% kill fee. Makes work-for-hire assignments. Accepts queries by mail, fax, phone. Responds in 2 months to queries.

> O‑ Pitch ideas to the editor of the section to which you would like to contribute (i.e., film, music, dance, etc.). Be sure to include clips or writing samples with your query letter. No unsolicited mss.

Nonfiction Essays, general interest, how-to, humor, interview/profile, new product, travel (primarily within NYC area), reviews of various entertainment topics. No essays, articles about trends, unpegged articles. Query with published clips. Length: 250-1,500 words.

Columns/Departments Around Town (Ethan LaCroix); Art (Andrea Scott); Books & Poetry (Maureen Shelly); Cabaret (Adam Feldman); Check Out (Marissa Patlingrao Cooley); Clubs (Bruce Tantum); Comedy (Jane Borden); Dance (Gia Kourlas); Eat Out (Maile Carpenter); Film (Darren S'Addario); Gay & Lesbian (Beth Greenfield); Kids (Barbara Aria); Music (Mike Wolf); Radio/TV/Video (Andrew Johnston); Sports (Reed Tucker); Theater (David Cote).

Tips "We're always looking for quirky, less-known news about what's going on in New York City."

N $ $ $ WESTCHESTER MAGAZINE

Spotlight Publications, LLC, 100 Clearbrook Rd., Elmsford NY 10523. (914)345-0601. Web site: www.westchestermagazine.com. Managing Editor: John Turiano. **Contact:** Esther Davidowitz, editor-in-chief. **35% freelance written.** Monthly magazine covering culture and lifestyle of Westchester County, New York. "*Westchester Magazine* is an upscale, high-end regional lifestyle publication covering issues specific to Westchester County, New York. All stories must have a local slant." Estab. 2001. Circ. 65,475. Pays on publication. Publishes ms an average of 5 months after acceptance. Byline given. Offers 25% kill fee. Buys all rights. Editorial lead time 3 months. Submit seasonal material 3 months in advance. Accepts queries by mail. Sample copy online.

Nonfiction Exposé, general interest, interview/profile, local service. Does not want personal essays, reviews, stories not specific to Westchester. **Buys 36 mss/year.** Query with published clips. Length: 150-5,000 words. **Pays $50-900.** Sometimes pays expenses of writers on assignment.

Photos Contact Aiko Masazumi, creative director. State availability with submission. Reviews GIF/JPEG files. Negotiates rights individually. Negotiates payment individually. Captions, identification of subjects required.

Columns/Departments Contact Catherine Censor, senior editor. Our Neighbor (profile of a local celebrity), 500 words; Westchester Chronicles (short items of local interest), 300 words; County Golf (articles about the local golf scene), 500 words. **Buys 36 mss/year.** Query with published clips. **Pays $30-200.**

Tips "Be sure to query ideas applicable *only* to Westchester County that we have not written about before."

NORTH CAROLINA

N $ $ AAA CAROLINAS GO MAGAZINE

6600 AAA Dr., Charlotte NC 28212. Fax: (704)569-7815. Web site: www.aaacarolinas.com. Managing Editor: Sarah B. Davis. **Contact:** Tom Crosby, editor. **20% freelance written.** Member publication for the Carolina affiliate of American Automobile Association covering travel, auto-related issues. "We prefer stories that focus on travel and auto safety in North and South Carolina and surrounding states." Estab. 1922. Circ. 800,000. Pays on publication. Byline given. Buys all rights. Editorial lead time 2 months. Accepts queries by mail. Sample copy and writer's guidelines for #10 SASE.

Nonfiction Travel, auto safety. Length: 750 words. **Pays $150.**

Photos Send photos with submission. Reviews slides. Buys all rights. Offers no additional payment for photos accepted with ms. Identification of subjects required.

The online magazine carries original content not found in the print edition. Contact: Sarah B. Davis.

Tips "Submit regional stories relating to Carolinas travel."

$ $ CARY MAGAZINE

Cherokee Publishing Co., Westview at Weston, 301 Cascade Pointe Lane, #101, Cary NC 27513. (919)674-6020. Fax: (919)674-6027. E-mail: editor@carymagazine.com. Web site: www.carymagazine.com. **Contact:** Danielle Caspar. **40% freelance written.** Bimonthly magazine. Lifestyle publication for the affluent communities of Cary, Apex, Morrisville, Holly Springs, Fuquay-Varina and RTP. "Our editorial objective is to entertain, enlighten and inform our readers with unique and engaging editorial and vivid photography." Estab. 2004. Circ. 23,000. Byline given. Buys first North American serial rights. Editorial lead time 3 months. Submit seasonal material 3 months in advance. Accepts queries by mail, e-mail. Responds in 2-4 weeks to queries; 1 month to mss. Sample copy for $4.95. Writer's guidelines free.

Nonfiction Historical/nostalgic (specific to Western Wake County, North Carolina), inspirational, interview/profile (human interest), personal experience. "Don't submit articles with no local connection." **Buys 2 mss/year.** Query with published clips. Sometimes pays expenses of writers on assignment.

Photos Freelancers should state the availability of photos with their submission or send the photos with their submission. Reviews GIF/JPEG files. Buys one-time rights. Negotiates payment individually. Identification of subjects required.

Tips Prefer experienced feature writers with exceptional interviewing skills who can take a fresh perspective on a topic; writes with a unique flare, but clearly with a good hook to engage the reader and evoke emotion; adheres to AP Style and follows basic journalism conventions; and takes deadlines seriously. E-mail inquiries preferred.

$ $ CHARLOTTE MAGAZINE

Abarta Media, 127 W. Worthington Ave., Suite 208, Charlotte NC 28203. (704)335-7181. Fax: (704)335-3739. E-mail: richard.thurmond@charlottemagazine.com. Web site: www.charlottemagazine.com. **Contact:** Richard H. Thurmond, editorial director. **75% freelance written.** Monthly magazine covering Charlotte life. "This magazine tells its readers things they didn't know about Charlotte, in an interesting, entertaining, and sometimes provocative style." Circ. 30,000. Pays within 30 days of acceptance. Publishes ms an average of 3 months after acceptance. Byline given. Offers 25% kill fee. Buys first North American serial rights. Editorial lead time 3 months. Submit seasonal material 6 months in advance. Accepts queries by mail, e-mail. Accepts simultaneous submissions. Responds in 6 months to mss. Sample copy for $8\frac{1}{2} \times 11$ SAE and $2.09.

Nonfiction Book excerpts, exposé, general interest, historical/nostalgic, interview/profile, photo feature, travel. **Buys 90-100 mss/year.** Query with published clips. Length: 200-3,000 words. **Pays 20-40¢/word.** Sometimes pays expenses of writers on assignment.

Photos State availability with submission. Buys one-time rights. Negotiates payment individually. Identification of subjects required.

Columns/Departments Buys 35-50 mss/year. Pays 20-40¢/word.

Tips "A story for *Charlotte* magazine could only appear in *Charlotte* magazine. That is, the story and its treatment are particularly germane to this area."

N $ $ FIFTEEN 501

Connecting Life in Durham, Orange and Chatham Counties, Weiss and Hughes Publishing, 5870 Faringdon Place, Raleigh NC 27609. (919)870-1722. Fax: (919)719-5260. E-mail: eshugg@wakeliving.com. Web site: www.fifteen501.com. **Contact:** Elizabeth Shugg, editor-in-chief. **50% freelance written.** Quarterly magazine covering lifestyle issues relevant to residents in the US 15/501 corridor of Durham, Orange and Chatham counties. "We cover issues important to residents of Durham, Orange and Chatham counties. We're committed to improving our readers' overall quality of life and keeping them informed of the lifestyle amenities there." Estab. 2006.

Circ. 25,000. within 30 days of publication. Publishes ms an average of 2 months after acceptance. Byline given. Offers 25% kill fee. Buys all rights. Editorial lead time 2-3 months. Submit seasonal material 6 months in advance. Accepts queries by mail, e-mail. Accepts simultaneous submissions. Responds in 2-4 weeks to queries. Sample copy online. Writer's guidelines by e-mail.

Nonfiction General interest, historical/nostalgic, how-to (home interiors, landscaping, gardening, technology), inspirational, interview/profile, personal experience, photo feature, technical, travel. Does not want opinion pieces, political or religious topics. Query. Length: 600-1,200 words. **Pays 35¢/word.** Sometimes pays expenses of writers on assignment.

Photos State availability with submission. Reviews transparencies, GIF/JPEG files. Rights are negotiable. Offers no additional payment for photos accepted with ms. Captions, identification of subjects required.

Columns/Departments Around Town (local lifestyle topics), 1,000 words; Hometown Stories, 600 words; Travel (around North Carolina), 1,000 words; Home Interiors/Landscaping (varies), 1,000 words; Restaurants (local, fine dining), 600-1,000 words. **Buys 20-25 mss/year.** Query. **Pays 35¢/word.**

Tips "All queries must be focused on the issues that make Durham, Chapel Hill, Carrboro, Hillsborough and Pittsboro unique and wonderful places to live."

$ $ OUR STATE

Down Home in North Carolina, Mann Media, P.O. Box 4552, Greensboro NC 27404. (336)286-0600. Fax: (336)286-0100. E-mail: editorial@ourstate.com. Web site: www.ourstate.com. **95% freelance written.** Monthly magazine covering North Carolina. "*Our State* is dedicated to providing editorial about the history, destinations, out-of-the-way places, and culture of North Carolina." Estab. 1933. Circ. 130,000. Pays on publication. Publishes ms an average of 6-24 months after acceptance. Byline given. Buys first North American serial rights. Editorial lead time 4-6 months. Submit seasonal material 4 months in advance. Accepts queries by mail, e-mail, fax. Responds in 6 weeks to queries; 2 months to mss. Sample copy for $6. Writer's guidelines for #10 SASE.

Nonfiction Historical/nostalgic, travel, North Carolina culture, folklore. **Buys 250 mss/year.** Send complete ms. Length: 1,400-1,600 words. **Pays $300-500.**

Photos State availability with submission. Reviews 35mm or 4×6 transparencies, digital. Buys one-time rights. Negotiates payment individually.

Columns/Departments Tar Heel Memories (remembering something specific about North Carolina), 1,000 words; Tar Heel Profile (profile of interesting North Carolinian), 1,500 words; Tar Heel Literature (review of books by North Carolina writers and about North Carolina), 300 words.

Tips "We are developing a style for travel stories that is distinctly *Our State*. That style starts with outstanding photographs, which not only depict an area, but interpret it and thus become an integral part of the presentation. Our stories need not dwell on listings of what can be seen. Concentrate instead on the experience of being there, whether the destination is a hiking trail, a bed and breakfast, a forest, or an urban area. What thoughts and feelings did the experience evoke? We want to know why you went there, what you experienced, and what impressions you came away with. With at least 1 travel story an issue, we run a short sidebar called, 'If You're Going.' It explains how to get to the destination; rates or admission costs if there are any; a schedule of when the attraction is open or list of relevant dates; and an address and phone number for readers to write or call for more information. This sidebar eliminates the need for general-service information in the story."

N $ $ WAKE LIVING

Wake County's Premier Lifestyle Publication, Weiss and Hughes Publishing, 5870 Faringdon Place, Suite 100, Raleigh NC 27609. (919)870-1722. Fax: (919)719-5260. E-mail: eshugg@wakeliving.com. Web site: www.wakeliving.com. **Contact:** Elizabeth Shugg, editor-in-chief. **50% freelance written.** Quarterly magazine covering lifestyle issues in Wake County, North Carolina. "We cover issues important to residents of Wake County. We are committed to improving our readers' overall quality of life and keeping them informed of the lifestyle amenities here." Estab. 2003. Circ. 35,000. within 30 days of publication. Publishes ms an average of 2 months after acceptance. Byline given. Offers 25% kill fee. Buys all rights. Editorial lead time 2-3 months. Submit seasonal material 6 months in advance. Accepts queries by mail, e-mail. Accepts simultaneous submissions. Responds in 2-4 weeks to queries. Sample copy and writer's guidelines online.

Nonfiction General interest, historical/nostalgic, how-to (home interiors, technology, landscaping, gardening), inspirational, interview/profile, personal experience, photo feature, technical, travel. Does not want opinion pieces, political topics, religious articles. Query. Length: 600-1,200 words. **Pays 35¢/word.** Sometimes pays expenses of writers on assignment.

Photos State availability with submission. Reviews transparencies, GIF/JPEG files. Offers no additional payment for photos accepted with ms. Captions, identification of subjects required.

Columns/Departments Around Town (local lifestyle topics); Hometown Stories, 600 words; Travel (around North Carolina); Home Interiors/Landscaping, all 1,000 words. Restaurants (local restaurants, fine dining), 600-1,000 words. **Buys 20-25 mss/year.** Query. **Pays 35¢/word.**

Tips "Articles must be specifically focused on Wake County/Raleigh metro issues. We like unusual angles about what makes living here unique from other areas."

NORTH DAKOTA

N $ $ NORTH DAKOTA LIVING MAGAZINE

North Dakota Association of Rural Electric Cooperatives, 3201 Nygren Dr. NW, P.O. Box 727, Mandan ND 58554-0727. (701)663-6501. Fax: (701)663-3745. E-mail: kbrick@ndarec.com. Web site: www.ndarec.com. **Contact:** Kent Brick, editor. **20% freelance written.** Monthly magazine covering information of interest to memberships of electric cooperatives and telephone cooperatives. "We publish a general interest magazine for North Dakotans. We treat subjects pertaining to living and working in the northern Great Plains. We provide progress reporting on electric cooperatives and telephone cooperatives." Estab. 1954. Circ. 70,000. **Pays on acceptance.** Publishes ms an average of 6 months after acceptance. Byline given. Buys one-time rights, makes work-for-hire assignments. Editorial lead time 6 months. Submit seasonal material 6 months in advance. Accepts queries by mail, e-mail. Accepts previously published material. Accepts simultaneous submissions. Sample copy and writer's guidelines not available.

Nonfiction General interest, historical/nostalgic, how-to, humor, interview/profile, new product, travel. **Buys 20 mss/year.** Query with published clips. Length: 1,500-2,000 words. **Pays $100-500 minimum for assigned articles; $300-600 for unsolicited articles.** Sometimes pays expenses of writers on assignment.

Photos State availability with submission. Reviews contact sheets. Buys one-time rights. Negotiates payment individually. Identification of subjects required.

Columns/Departments Energy Use and Financial Planning, both 750 words. **Buys 6 mss/year.** Query with published clips. **Pays $100-300.**

Fiction Historical, humorous, slice-of-life vignettes, western. **Buys 1 mss/year.** Query with published clips. Length: 1,000-2,500 words. **Pays $100-400.**

Tips "Deal with what's real: real data, real people, real experiences, real history, etc."

OHIO

$ BEND OF THE RIVER MAGAZINE

P.O. Box 859, Maumee OH 43537. (419)893-0022. **Contact:** R. Lee Raizk, publisher. **98% freelance written.** This magazine reports that it is eager to work with all writers. "We buy material that we like whether it is by an experienced writer or not." Monthly magazine for readers interested in northwestern Ohio history and nostalgia. Estab. 1972. Circ. 7,500. Pays on publication. Publishes ms an average of 6 months after acceptance. Byline given. Buys one-time rights. Submit seasonal material 2 months in advance. Responds in 1 month to queries. Sample copy for $1.25. Writer's guidelines not available.

Nonfiction "We are looking for Toledo area articles and ones about famous people and events of Ohio, Michigan and Indiana." Historical/nostalgic. **Buys 75 unsolicited mss/year.** Query with or without published clips or send complete ms. Length: 1,500 words. **Pays $50 and up.**

Tips "Our stockpile is low. Send us something!"

$ $ $ CLEVELAND MAGAZINE

City Magazines, Inc., 1422 Euclid Ave., Suite 730, Cleveland OH 44115. (216)771-2833. Fax: (216)781-6318. E-mail: editorial@clevelandmagazine.com. Web site: www.clevelandmagazine.com. **Contact:** Steve Gleydura, editorial director. **60% freelance written.** Mostly by assignment. Monthly magazine with a strong Cleveland/Northeast Ohio angle. Estab. 1972. Circ. 50,000. Pays on publication. Publishes ms an average of 3 months after acceptance. Byline given. Buys first, second serial (reprint), electronic rights. Editorial lead time 6 months. Submit seasonal material 8 months in advance. Accepts queries by mail, e-mail, fax. Accepts simultaneous submissions. Responds in 2 months to queries. Sample copy not available.

Nonfiction General interest, historical/nostalgic, humor, interview/profile, travel, home and garden. Query with published clips. Length: 800-4,000 words. **Pays $250-1,200.**

Columns/Departments My Town (Cleveland first-person stories), 1,100-1,500 words. Query with published clips. **Pays $300.**

$ $ $ COLUMBUS MONTHLY

P.O. Box 29913, Columbus OH 43229-7513. (614)888-4567. Fax: (614)848-3838. Editor: Ray Paprocki. **40% freelance written.** Prefers to work with published/established writers. Monthly magazine emphasizing subjects specifically related to Columbus and Central Ohio. Circ. 38,000. Pays on publication. Publishes ms an average of 2 months after acceptance. Byline given. Buys all rights. Responds in 1 month to queries. Sample copy for $6.50. Writer's guidelines not available.

Nonfiction "We like query letters that are well written, indicate the author has some familiarity with *Columbus Monthly,* give us enough detail to make a decision and include at least a basic résumé of the writer and clips." **Buys 2-3 unsolicited mss/year.** Query. Length: 250-4,500 words. **Pays $85-900.** Sometimes pays expenses of writers on assignment.

Tips "It makes sense to start small—something for our City Journal section, perhaps. Stories for that section run between 250-500 words."

$ $ $ NORTHERN OHIO LIVE

Rightup Media LLC, 2026 Murray Hill Rd., Suite 103, Cleveland OH 44106. (216)721-7850. Fax: (216)721-7851. E-mail: editor@rightupmedia.com. **Contact:** Sarah R. Sphar, editor. **70% freelance written.** Monthly magazine covering Northern Ohio politics, arts, entertainment, education, and dining. "Reader demographic is 59% female, median age 48 years. Our readers are well-educated, many with advanced degrees. They're interested in Northern Ohio's cultural scene and support it." Estab. 1980. Circ. 35,000. Pays end of publication month. Publishes ms an average of 1 month after acceptance. Byline given. Offers negotiable kill fee. Buys first North American serial rights. Editorial lead time 3 months. Submit seasonal material 4 months in advance. Responds in 3 weeks to queries; 2 months to mss. Sample copy for $3. Writer's guidelines not available.

Nonfiction All submission/pitches should have a Northern Ohio slant. Essays, exposé, general interest, humor, interview/profile, photo feature, travel. Special issues: Gourmet Guide (restaurants) (May). Query with published clips. Length: 1,000-2,500 words.

Tips "Don't send submissions not having anything to do with Northern Ohio. Must have some tie to the Northeast Quadrant of Ohio. We are not interested in stories appearing in every other outlet in town. What is the new angle?"

$ $ $ OHIO MAGAZINE

Great Lakes Publishing Co., 1422 Euclid Ave., Suite 730, Cleveland OH 44115. (216)771-2833. E-mail: editorial@ohiomagazine.com. Web site: www.ohiomagazine.com. **Contact:** Richard Osborne, editorial director. **50% freelance written.** Monthly magazine emphasizing Ohio-based travel, news and feature material that highlights what's special and unique about the state. Estab. 1978. Circ. 80,000. Pays on publication. Publishes ms an average of 6 months after acceptance. Byline given. Buys first North American serial, one-time, second serial (reprint), all rights. First serial rights Submit seasonal material 6 months in advance. Accepts queries by mail, e-mail, fax. Responds in 3 months to queries; 3 months to mss. Sample copy for $3.95 and 9×12 SAE or online. Writer's guidelines online.

- Break in by "knowing the magazine—read it thoroughly for several issues. Send good clips—that show your ability to write on topics we cover. We're looking for thoughtful stories on topics that are more contextual and less shallow. I want queries that show the writer has some passion for the subject."

Nonfiction Length: 1,000-3,000 words. **Pays $300-1,200.** Sometimes pays expenses of writers on assignment.

Reprints Send tearsheet or photocopy and information about when and where the material previously appeared. Pays 50% of amount paid for an original article.

Photos Rob McGarr, art director. Rate negotiable.

Columns/Departments Buys minimum 5 unsolicited mss/year. Pays $100-600.

Tips "Freelancers should send all queries in writing (either by mail or e-mail), not by telephone. Successful queries demonstrate an intimate knowledge of the publication. We are looking to increase our circle of writers who can write about the state in an informative and upbeat style. Strong reporting skills are highly valued."

OKLAHOMA

N $ $ INTERMISSION

Langdon Publishing, 110 E. 2nd St., Tulsa OK 74103-3212. (918)596-2368. Fax: (918)596-7144. E-mail: nhermann@ci.tulsa.ok.us. Web site: www.tulsapac.com. Managing Editor: Nancy Bizjack. **Contact:** Nancy Hermann, editor-in-chief. **30% freelance written.** Monthly magazine covering entertainment. "We feature profiles of entertainers appearing at our center, Q&As, stories on the events and entertainers slated for the Tulsa PAC." Pays on publication. Publishes ms an average of 1 month after acceptance. Byline given. Offers 50% kill fee. Buys one-time rights. Editorial lead time 2 months. Submit seasonal material 2 months in advance. Accepts queries by mail, e-mail. Accepts simultaneous submissions. Responds in 2 weeks to queries. Sample copy online. Writer's guidelines by e-mail.

Nonfiction General interest, interview/profile. Does not want personal experience. **Buys 35 mss/year.** Query with published clips. Length: 600-1,400 words. **Pays $100-200.**

Columns/Departments Q&A (personalities and artists tied into the events at the Tulsa PAC), 1,100 words. **Buys 12 mss/year.** Query with published clips. **Pays $100-150.**

Tips "Look ahead at our upcoming events, find an interesting slant on an event. Interview someone who would be of general interest."

$ $ OKLAHOMA TODAY

P.O. Box 1468, Oklahoma City OK 73101. (405)521-2496. Fax: (405)522-4588. E-mail: mccune@oklahomatoday.com. Web site: www.oklahomatoday.com. **Contact:** Louisa McCune, editor-in-chief. **80% freelance written.** Works with approximately 25 new/unpublished writers each year. Bimonthly magazine covering people, places, and things Oklahoman. "We are interested in showing off the best Oklahoma has to offer; we're pretty serious about our travel slant but regularly run history, nature, and personality profiles." Estab. 1956. Circ. 45,000. Pays on publication. Publishes ms an average of 6 months after acceptance. Byline given. Buys first worldwide serial rights. Submit seasonal material 1 year in advance. Accepts queries by mail, e-mail. Responds in 4 months to queries. Sample copy for $3.95 and 9×12 SASE or online. Writer's guidelines online.

- O→ "Start small. Look for possibilities for 'The Range.' Even letters to the editor are good ways to 'get some ink.'"

Nonfiction Book excerpts (on Oklahoma topics), historical/nostalgic (Oklahoma only), interview/profile (Oklahomans only), photo feature (in Oklahoma), travel (in Oklahoma). No phone queries. **Buys 20-40 mss/year.** Query with published clips. Length: 250-3,000 words. **Pays $25-750.**

Photos "We are especially interested in developing contacts with photographers who live in Oklahoma or have shot here. Send samples." Photo guidelines for SASE. Reviews 4×5, 2¼×2¼, and 35mm color transparencies, high-quality transparencies, slides, and b&w prints. Buys one-time rights to use photos for promotional purposes. Pays $50-750 for color. Captions, identification of subjects required.

Fiction Novel excerpts, occasionally short fiction.

Tips "The best way to become a regular contributor to *Oklahoma Today* is to query us with 1 or more story ideas, each developed to give us an idea of your proposed slant. We're looking for lively, concise, well-researched and reported stories, stories that don't need to be heavily edited and are not newspaper style. We have a 3-person full-time editorial staff, and freelancers who can write and have done their homework get called again and again."

OREGON

$ $ OREGON COAST

4969 Highway 101 N. #2, Florence OR 97439. (541)997-8401. Web site: www.northwestmagazines.com. **65% freelance written.** Bimonthly magazine covering the Oregon Coast. Estab. 1982. Circ. 50,000. Pays after publication. Publishes ms an average of up to 1 year after acceptance. Byline given. Offers 33% (on assigned stories only, not on stories accepted on spec) kill fee. Buys first North American serial rights. Submit seasonal material 6 months in advance. Accepts queries by mail. Responds in 3 months to queries. Sample copy for $4.50. Writer's guidelines for #10 SASE.

- This company also publishes *Northwest Travel.*
- O→ Break in with "great photos with a story that has a great lead and no problems during fact-checking. Like stories that have a slightly different take on 'same-old' subjects and have good anecdotes and quotes. Stories should have satisfying endings."

Nonfiction "A true regional with general interest, historical/nostalgic, humor, interview/profile, personal experience, photo feature, travel, and nature as pertains to Oregon Coast." **Buys 55 mss/year.** Query with published clips. Length: 500-1,500 words. **Pays $75-250, plus 2-5 contributor copies.**

Reprints Send tearsheet or photocopy and information about when and where the material previously appeared. Pays an average of 60% of the amount paid for an original article.

Photos Photo submissions with no ms or stand alone or cover photos. Send photos with submission. Reviews 35mm or larger transparencies. Buys one-time rights. Captions, identification of subjects, model releases (for cover), photo credits required.

Fillers Newsbreaks (no-fee basis).

Tips "Slant article for readers who do not live at the Oregon Coast. At least 1 historical article is used in each issue. Manuscript/photo packages are preferred over manuscripts with no photos. List photo credits and captions for each historic print or color slide. Check all facts, proper names, and numbers carefully in photo/manuscript packages. Must pertain to Oregon Coast somehow."

PENNSYLVANIA

$ $ BERKS COUNTY LIVING

West Lawn Graphic Communications, P.O. Box 642, Shillington PA 19607. (610)775-0640. Fax: (610)775-7412. E-mail: editor@berkscountyliving.com. Web site: www.berkscountyliving.com. **Contact:** Kristin Kramer, editor. **90% freelance written.** Bimonthly magazine covering topics of interest to people living in Berks County, Pennsylvania. Estab. 2000. Circ. 36,000. Pays on publication. Publishes ms an average of 4 months after acceptance. Byline given. Offers 25% kill fee. Buys first North American serial rights. Editorial lead time 3 months. Submit seasonal material 4 months in advance. Accepts queries by mail, e-mail. Accepts previously published material. Accepts simultaneous submissions. Responds in 1 week to queries; 1 month to mss. Sample copy for 9×12 SAE and 2 first-class stamps. Writer's guidelines online.

Nonfiction Articles must be associated with Berks County, Pennsylvania. Exposé, general interest, historical/nostalgic, how-to, humor, inspirational, interview/profile, new product, photo feature, travel, food, health. **Buys 25 mss/year.** Query. Length: 750-2,000 words. **Pays $150-400.** Sometimes pays expenses of writers on assignment.

Reprints Accepts previously published submissions.

Photos State availability with submission. Reviews 35mm or greater transparencies, any size prints. Buys one-time rights. Negotiates payment individually. Captions, identification of subjects, model releases required.

N $ $ LEHIGH VALLEY LIVING

The Morning Call, 101 N. 6th St., Allentown PA 18105. (610)820-6773. Fax: (610)820-6663. E-mail: lori.mcferran@mcall.com. Web site: www.mcall.com. Managing Editor: Jerry Brahm. **Contact:** Lori McFerran, editor. **100% freelance written.** Monthly magazine covering regional Lehigh Valley lifestyle. "*Lehigh Valley Living* aims to provide information and ideas that will entice and motivate readers to enjoy a high-quality life in our community. Written and edited for those interested in a stylish, aesthetic lifestyle." Estab. 2005. Circ. 33,000. **Pays on acceptance.** Publishes ms an average of 3 months after acceptance. Byline given. Offers 100% kill fee. Buys all rights. Editorial lead time 4 months. Accepts queries by mail, e-mail. Accepts simultaneous submissions. Sample copy online.

Nonfiction General interest, historical/nostalgic, interview/profile, travel, health, entertainment, finance, automotive. Special issues: "We do a bridal focus in May and October." Does not want anything that does not have a distinct Lehigh Valley focus. **Buys 36-40 mss/year.** Query with published clips. Length: 500-650 words. **Pays $300.**

Photos State availability with submission. Reviews contact sheets, GIF/JPEG files. Buys all rights. Offers $50/photo. Identification of subjects, model releases required.

Tips "Be familiar with the Allentown, Bethlehem, Easton areas. Stories about new happenings, events, businesses, or news in the region will get the editor's attention."

N $ $ MAIN LINE TODAY

Today Media, Inc., 4699 West Chester Pike, Newtown Square PA 19073. (610)848-6037. Fax: (610)325-5215. E-mail: hrowland@mainlinetoday.com. Web site: www.mainlinetoday.com. Senior Editor: Tara Bertan. **Contact:** Hobart Rowland, editor. **60% freelance written.** Monthly magazine serving Philadelphia's main line and western suburbs. Estab. 1996. Circ. 20,000. Pays on publication. Publishes ms an average of 3 months after acceptance. Byline given. Offers 25% kill fee. Buys first North American serial rights. Editorial lead time 5 months. Submit seasonal material 5 months in advance. Accepts queries by e-mail, fax. Accepts simultaneous submissions. Responds in 2 weeks to queries; 1 month to mss. Sample copy for free. Writer's guidelines free.

Nonfiction Book excerpts, historical/nostalgic, how-to, humor, interview/profile, opinion, photo feature, travel. Special issues: Health & Wellness Guide (September and March). Query with published clips. Length: 400-3,000 words. **Pays $125-650.** Sometimes pays expenses of writers on assignment.

Photos Contact Ingrid Lynch, art director. State availability with submission. Reviews GIF/JPEG files. Buys one-time rights. Negotiates payment individually. Identification of subjects, model releases required.

Columns/Departments Profile (local personality); Neighborhood (local people/issues); End of the Line (essay/humor); Living Well (health/wellness), all 1,600 words. **Buys 50 mss/year.** Query with published clips. **Pays $125-350.**

$ $ PENNSYLVANIA

Pennsylvania Magazine Co., P.O. Box 755, Camp Hill PA 17001-0755. (717)697-4660. E-mail: pamag@aol.com. Web site: www.pa-mag.com. Publisher: Albert E. Holliday. **Contact:** Matt Holliday, editor. **90% freelance written.** Bimonthly magazine covering people, places, events, and history in Pennsylvania. Estab. 1981. Circ. 33,000. Pays on acceptance except for articles (by authors unknown to us) sent on speculation. Publishes ms an average of 9 months after acceptance. Byline given. 25% kill fee for assigned articles. Buys first North

American serial, one-time rights. Submit seasonal material 9 months in advance. Accepts queries by mail, e-mail. Responds in 4-6 weeks to queries. Sample copy for $2.95. Writer's guidelines for #10 SASE or by e-mail.

O⊸ Break in with "a text/photo package—learn to take photos or hook up with a photographer who will shoot for our rates."

Nonfiction Features include general interest, historical, photo feature, vacations and travel, people/family success stories—all dealing with or related to Pennsylvania. Send photocopies of possible illustrations with query or ms. Include SASE. Nothing on Amish topics, hunting, or skiing. **Buys 75-120 mss/year.** Query. Length: 750-2,500 words. **Pays 10-15¢/word.**

Reprints Send photocopy with rights for sale noted and information about when and where the material previously appeared. Pays 5¢/word.

Photos No original slides or transparencies. Photography Essay (highlights annual photo essay contest entries and showcase individual photographers). Reviews 35mm 2¼×2¼ color transparencies, 5×7 to 8×10 color prints, digital photos (send printouts and CD). Buys one-time rights. Pays $15-25 for inside photos; $100 for covers. Captions, thumbnail sheet for digital submissions required.

Columns/Departments Round Up (short items about people, unusual events, museums, historical topics/events, family and individually owned consumer-related businesses), 250-1,300 words; Town and Country (items about people or events illustrated with commissioned art), 500 words. Include SASE. Query. **Pays 12-15¢/word.**

Tips "Our publication depends upon freelance work—send queries."

$ $ PENNSYLVANIA HERITAGE

Pennsylvania Historical and Museum Commission and the Pennsylvania Heritage Society, Commonwealth Keystone Bldg., Plaza Level, 400 North St., Harrisburg PA 17120-0053. (717)787-7522. Fax: (717)787-8312. E-mail: miomalley@state.pa.us. Web site: www.paheritage.org. **Contact:** Michael J. O'Malley III, editor. **90% freelance written.** Prefers to work with published/established writers. Quarterly magazine. "*Pennsylvania Heritage* introduces readers to Pennsylvania's rich culture and historic legacy; educates and sensitizes them to the value of preserving that heritage; and entertains and involves them in such a way as to ensure that Pennsylvania's past has a future. The magazine is intended for intelligent lay readers." Estab. 1974. Circ. 10,000. Pays on publication. Publishes ms an average of 1 year after acceptance. Byline given. Buys all rights. Accepts queries by mail, e-mail. Responds in 10 weeks to queries; 8 months to mss. Sample copy for $5 and 9×12 SAE or online. Writer's guidelines for #10 SASE or online.

- *Pennsylvania Heritage* is now considering freelance submissions that are shorter in length (2,000-3,000 words); pictorial/photographic essays; biographies of famous (and not-so-famous) Pennsylvanians; and interviews with individuals who have helped shape, make, and preserve the Keystone State's history and heritage.

Nonfiction "Our format requires feature-length articles. Manuscripts with illustrations are especially sought for publication. We are now looking for shorter (2,000 words) manuscripts that are heavily illustrated with publication-quality photographs or artwork. We are eager to work with experienced travel writers for destination pieces on historical sites and museums that make up 'The Pennsylvania Trail of History.' " Art, science, biographies, industry, business, politics, transportation, military, historic preservation, archaeology, photography, etc. No articles which do not relate to Pennsylvania history or culture. **Buys 20-24 mss/year.** Prefers to see mss with suggested illustrations. Length: 2,000-3,500 words. **Pays $100-500.**

Photos State availability of or send photos with submission. Buys one-time rights. $25-200 for transparencies; $5-75 for b&w photos. Captions, identification of subjects required.

Tips "We are looking for well-written, interesting material that pertains to any aspect of Pennsylvania history or culture. Potential contributors should realize that, although our articles are popularly styled, they are not light, puffy, or breezy; in fact they demand strident documentation and substantiation (sans footnotes). The most frequent mistake made by writers in completing articles for us is making them either too scholarly or too sentimental or nostalgic. We want material which educates, but also entertains. Authors should make history readable and enjoyable. Our goal is to make the Keystone State's history come to life in a meaningful, memorable way."

N $ $ PHILADELPHIA LIFE

American City Business Journals, 400 Market St., Suite 1200, Philadelphia PA 19106. Fax: (215)238-9489. E-mail: ssherwood@bizjournals.com. Web site: www.philadelphia.bizjournals.com/philadelphia. **Contact:** Sonja Sherwood, editor. **90% freelance written.** Quarterly magazine covering all of the counties touching Philadelphia county, including 3 in South Jersey. "*Philadelphia Life* is an offshoot of the *Philadelphia Business Journal* newspaper. Our readers are accustomed to enjoying the finer things in life. *Philadelphia Life* taps into the readership of the region's trusted business news provider in an entirely new way, providing a guide for living well beyond the office." Estab. 2006. Circ. 12,000. Pays on publication. Publishes ms an average of 3 months after acceptance. Byline given. Offers $25 kill fee. Buys all rights. Editorial lead time 3-4 months. Submit seasonal material 3-4 months in advance. Accepts queries by e-mail. Responds in 2 weeks to queries. Sample copy by e-mail. Writer's guidelines free.

Nonfiction General interest, historical/nostalgic, how-to, interview/profile, photo feature, travel. Does not want first-person stories or stories about homes in which the owners are not identified. Query with published clips. Length: 900-1,300 words. **Pays $200-300.**

Tips "Bring fresh ideas and local examples to illustrate your pitch."

PHILADELPHIA MAGAZINE

1818 Market St., 36th Floor, Philadelphia PA 19103. (215)564-7700. Web site: www.phillymag.com. **Contact:** Editor: Larry Platt. Monthly magazine. "*Philadelphia* is edited for the area's community leaders and their families. It provides in-depth reports on crucial and controversial issues confronting the region—business trends, political analysis, metropolitan planning, sociological trends—plus critical reviews of the cultural, sports and entertainment scene." Estab. 1908. Circ. 133,083. **Pays on acceptance.** Accepts queries by mail.

- Break in by sending queries along with clips. "Remember that we are a general interest magazine that focuses exclusively on topics of interest in the Delaware Valley."

Nonfiction "Articles range from law enforcement to fashion, voting trends to travel, transportation to theater, also includes the background studies of the area newsmakers." Query with clips and SASE.

Tips "*Philadelphia Magazine* readers are an affluent, interested and influential group who can afford the best the region has to offer. They're the greater Philadelphia area residents who care about the city and its politics, lifestyles, business and culture."

$ $ PHILADELPHIA STYLE

Philadelphia's Premier Magazine for Lifestyle & Fashion, Philadelphia Style Magazine, LLC, 141 League St., Philadelphia PA 19147. (215)468-6670. Fax: (215)468-6530. E-mail: pete@phillystylemag.com. Web site: www.phillystylemag.com. Executive Editor: Susan M. Stapleton. **Contact:** Peter Mazzaccaro, articles editor. **90% freelance written.** Bimonthly magazine covering upscale living in the Philadelphia region. Topics include: fashion (men's and women's), home and design, real estate, dining, beauty, travel, arts and entertainment, and more. "Our magazine is a positive look at the best ways to live in the Philadelphia region. Submitted articles should speak to an upscale, educated audience of professionals that live in the Delaware Valley." Estab. 1999. Circ. 45,000. Pays on publication. Publishes ms an average of 3 months after acceptance. Byline given. Offers 25% kill fee. Buys first rights. Editorial lead time 2-4 months. Submit seasonal material 6 months in advance. Accepts queries by mail, e-mail, fax.

- Break in "with ideas for our real estate section (reviews/stories of area neighborhoods, home and design, architecture, and other new ideas you may have)."

Nonfiction General interest, interview/profile, travel, region-specific articles. "We are not looking for articles that do not have a regional spin." **Buys 100+ mss/year.** Query with published clips or send complete ms. Length: 300-2,500 words. **Pays $50-500.**

Columns/Departments Life in the City (fresh, quirky, regional reporting on books, real estate, art, retail, dining, events, and little-known stories/facts about the region), 100-500 words; Vanguard (people on the forefront of Philadelphia's arts, media, fashion, business, and social scene), 500-700 words; In the Neighborhood (reader-friendly reporting on up-and-coming areas of the region including dining, shopping, attractions, and recreation), 2,000-2,500 words. Query with published clips or send complete ms. **Pays $50-500.**

Tips "Mail queries with clips or manuscripts. Articles should speak to a stylish, educated audience."

$ $ $ $ PITTSBURGH MAGAZINE

WQED Pittsburgh, 4802 Fifth Ave., Pittsburgh PA 15213. (412)622-1360. Web site: www.pittsburghmag.com. **Contact:** Stephen Segal, managing editor. **70% freelance written.** Monthly magazine. "*Pittsburgh* presents issues, analyzes problems, and strives to encourage a better understanding of the community. Our region is Western Pennsylvania, Eastern Ohio, Northern West Virginia, and Western Maryland." Estab. 1970. Circ. 75,000. Pays on publication. Publishes ms an average of 2 months after acceptance. Byline given. Offers kill fee. Buys first North American serial, second serial (reprint) rights. Submit seasonal material 6 months in advance. Accepts queries by mail. Responds in 2 months to queries. Sample copy for $2 (old back issues). Writer's guidelines online or via SASE.

- The editor reports a need for more hard news and stories targeting readers in their 30s and 40s, especially those with young families. Prefers to work with published/established writers. The monthly magazine is purchased on newsstands and by subscription, and is given to those who contribute $40 or more/year to public TV in western Pennsylvania.

Nonfiction "Without exception—whether the topic is business, travel, the arts, or lifestyle—each story is clearly oriented to Pittsburghers of today and to the greater Pittsburgh region of today." Must have greater Pittsburgh angle. No fax, phone, or e-mail queries. No complete mss. Exposé, lifestyle, sports, informational, service, business, medical, profile. "We have minimal interest in historical articles and we do not publish fiction, poetry, advocacy, or personal reminiscence pieces." Query in writing with outline and clips. Length: 1,200-4,000 words. **Pays $300-1,500+.**

Photos Query. Pays prenegotiated expenses of writer on assignment. Model releases required.

Columns/Departments The Front (short, front-of-the-book items). Length: 300 words maximum. **Pays $50-150.**

Tips "Best bet to break in is through hard news with a region-wide impact or service pieces or profiles with a regional interest. The point is that we want more stories that reflect our region, not just a tiny part. And we *never* consider any story without a strong regional focus. We do not respond to fax and e-mail queries."

$ SUSQUEHANNA LIFE

Central Pennsylvania's Lifestyle Magazine, ELS & Associates, 637 Market St., Lewisburg PA 17837. Fax: (570)524-7796. E-mail: info@susquehannalife.com. Web site: www.susquehannalife.com. **Contact:** Erica Shames, publisher. **80% freelance written.** Quarterly magazine covering Central Pennsylvania lifestyle. Estab. 1993. Circ. 45,000. Pays on publication. Publishes ms an average of 6-9 months after acceptance. Byline given. Offers 50% kill fee. Not copyrighted. Buys first North American serial, electronic rights. Editorial lead time 3-6 months. Submit seasonal material 4-6 months in advance. Accepts queries by e-mail. Responds in 4-6 weeks to queries; 1-3 months to mss. Sample copy for $4.95, plus 5 first-class stamps. Writer's guidelines for #10 SASE.

Nonfiction Book excerpts, general interest, historical/nostalgic, how-to, inspirational, interview/profile, photo feature, travel. Does not want poetry or fiction. **Buys 30-40 mss/year.** Query or send complete ms. Length: 800-1,200 words. **Pays $75-125.** Sometimes pays expenses of writers on assignment.

Photos Send photos with submission. Reviews contact sheets, prints, GIF/JPEG files. Buys one-time rights. Offers $20-25/photo. Captions, identification of subjects, model releases required.

Tips "When you query, do not address letter to 'Dear Sir'—address the letter to the name of the publisher/editor. Demonstrate your ability to write. You need to be familiar with the type of articles we use and the particular flavor of the region."

$ $ WESTSYLVANIA

Westsylvania Heritage Corp., 105 Zee Plaza, Hollidaysburg PA 16648-0565. (814)696-9380. Fax: (814)696-9569. E-mail: jschumacher@westsylvania.org. Web site: www.westsylvania.com. **Contact:** Jerilynn "Jerry" Schumacher, editor. **50% freelance written.** Quarterly magazine in Western Pennsylvania, plus parts of Ohio, Maryland, West Virginia, Virginia, and Kentucky. "*Westsylvania* magazine celebrates the cultural and natural heritages of south-central and southwestern Pennsylvania. Articles must reflect the writer's keen knowledge of the region. Writers should strive to show what residents are doing to preserve and protect their natural and cultural heritages. This is not a typical history or travel magazine. Stories should show how building on the region's history can make it a great place to live and visit." Estab. 1997. Circ. 10,000-14,000. Pays on publication. Publishes ms an average of 4 months after acceptance. Byline given. Buys first North American serial, web rights. Editorial lead time 6-24 months. Accepts queries by mail, e-mail, fax. Sample copy sent with request for writer's or photographer's guidelines.

- Break in with "a well-written query that spotlights stories on what people are doing to preserve their own heritage, such as cleaning up a trout stream, protecting endangered species, finding new uses for historic buildings, or helping others understand the past through art or music. First-person accounts accepted only for assigned columns."

Nonfiction Book excerpts, historical/nostalgic, interview/profile, religious, travel (heritage), business, wildlife, outdoors, photography. *No unsolicited mss.* **Buys 30 mss/year.** Query with published clips. Length: 750-2,200 words. **Pays $75-300 for assigned articles.**

Photos State photo ideas or availability with submission. Use of high-quality digital images a must. Gives assignments to experienced photographers who supply introductory letters, résumés, and samples of past work. Buys one-time rights for magazine and Web site. Negotiates payments individually. Captions, identification of subjects, model releases required.

Columns/Departments On the Back Porch (introduces readers to a special time or place in Westsylvania), 750 words; Vintage Ventures (stories about businesses 100 or more years old), 750 words. **Buys 8 mss/year.** Query with published clips. **Pays with free subscription or check up to $125, depending.**

Tips Poorly written queries will receive no response. "Look for stories that are uniquely Westsylvania. We will not accept generic articles that do not have a Westsylvania slant."

RHODE ISLAND

$ $ $ RHODE ISLAND MONTHLY

The Providence Journal Co., 280 Kinsley Ave., Providence RI 02903. (401)277-8200. Web site: www.rimonthly.com. **50% freelance written.** Monthly magazine. "*Rhode Island Monthly* is a general interest consumer magazine with a strict Rhode Island focus." Estab. 1988. Circ. 41,000. **Pays on acceptance.** Publishes ms an average of 3 months after acceptance. Byline given. Offers 25% kill fee. Buys all rights for 90 days from date of publication. Editorial lead time 3 months. Submit seasonal material 6 months in advance. Accepts queries by mail, e-mail, fax. Responds in 6 weeks to queries. Writer's guidelines free.

Nonfiction Exposé, general interest, interview/profile, photo feature. **Buys 40 mss/year.** Query with published clips. Length: 1,800-3,000 words. **Pays $600-1,200.** Sometimes pays expenses of writers on assignment.

SOUTH CAROLINA

CHARLESTON MAGAZINE

P.O. Box 1794, Mt. Pleasant SC 29465-1794. (843)971-9811. E-mail: dshankland@charlestonmag.com. Web site: charlestonmag.com. **Contact:** Darcy Shankland, editor. **80% freelance written.** Bimonthly magazine covering current issues, events, arts and culture, leisure pursuits, travel, and personalities, as they pertain to the city of Charleston and surrounding areas. "A Lowcountry institution for more than 30 years, *Charleston Magazine* captures the essence of Charleston and her surrounding areas—her people, arts and architecture, culture and events, and natural beauty." Estab. 1972. Circ. 25,000. Pays 1 month after publication. Byline given. Buys one-time rights. Submit seasonal material 4 months in advance. Accepts queries by mail, e-mail, fax. Sample copies may be ordered at cover price from office. Writer's guidelines for #10 SASE.

Nonfiction "Must pertain to the Charleston area and its present culture." General interest, humor, interview/profile, opinion, photo feature, travel, food, architecture, sports, current events/issues, art. "Not interested in 'Southern nostalgia' articles or gratuitous history pieces." **Buys 40 mss/year.** Query with published clips and SASE. Length: 150-1,500 words. **Payment negotiated.** Sometimes pays expenses of writers on assignment.

Reprints Send photocopy and information about when and where the material previously appeared. Payment negotiable.

Photos Send photos with submission. Reviews contact sheets, transparencies, slides. Buys one-time rights. Identification of subjects required.

Columns/Departments Channel Markers (general local interest), 50-400 words; Local Seen (profile of local interest), 500 words; In Good Taste (restaurants and culinary trends in the city), 1,000-1,200 words, plus recipes; Chef at Home (profile of local chefs), 1,200 words, plus recipes; On the Road (travel opportunities near Charleston), 1,000-1,200 words; Southern View (personal experience about Charleston life), 750 words; Doing Business (profiles of exceptional local businesses and entrepreneurs), 1,000-1,200 words; Native Talent (local profiles), 1,000-1,200 words; Top of the Shelf (reviews of books with Southern content or by a Southern author), 750 words.

Tips "Charleston, although a city with a 300-year history, is a vibrant, modern community with a tremendous dedication to the arts and no shortage of newsworthy subjects. We're looking for the freshest stories about Charleston—and those don't always come from insiders, but also outsiders who are keenly observant."

$ $ HILTON HEAD MONTHLY

Frey Media, Inc., 2 Park Lane, Hilton Head Island SC 29928. Fax: (843)842-5743. E-mail: bkaufman@freymedia.com; blt1@freymedia.com. Web site: www.hiltonheadmonthly.com. **Contact:** Blanche L. Tomaszewski, editor; Barry Kaufman, assistant editor. **75% freelance written.** Monthly magazine covering the business, people, and lifestyle of Hilton Head, South Carolina. "Our mission is to provide fresh, upbeat reading about the residents, lifestyle and community affairs of Hilton Head Island, an upscale, intensely pro-active resort community on the East Coast. We are not even remotely 'trendy,' but we like to see how national trends/issues play out on a local level. Especially interested in: home design and maintenance, entrepreneurship, health issues, nature, area history, golf/tennis/boating, volunteerism." Circ. 28,000. Pays on publication. Publishes ms an average of 6 months after acceptance. Byline given. Offers 50% kill fee. Buys first North American serial rights, makes work-for-hire assignments. Editorial lead time 3 months. Submit seasonal material 4 months in advance. Accepts queries by mail, e-mail, fax. Accepts previously published material. Accepts simultaneous submissions. Responds in 1 week to queries; 4 months to mss. Sample copy for $3.

Nonfiction General interest, historical/nostalgic (history only), how-to (home related), humor, interview/profile (Hilton Head residents only), opinion (general humor or Hilton Head Island community affairs), personal experience, travel. No "exposé interviews with people who are not Hilton Head residents; profiles of people, events, or businesses in Beaufort, South Carolina; Savannah, Georgia; Charleston; or other surrounding cities, unless it's within a travel piece." **Buys 225-250 mss/year.** Query with published clips.

Photos State availability with submission. Reviews contact sheets, prints, slides; any size. Buys one-time rights. Negotiates payment individually.

Columns/Departments News; Business; Lifestyles (hobbies, health, sports, etc.); Home; Around Town (local events, charities and personalities); People (profiles, weddings, etc.). Query with synopsis. **Pays 15¢/word.**

Tips "Give us concise, bullet-style descriptions of what the article covers (in the query letter); choose upbeat, pro-active topics; delight us with your fresh (not trendy) description and word choice."

$ SANDLAPPER

The Magazine of South Carolina, The Sandlapper Society, Inc., P.O. Box 1108, Lexington SC 29071-1108. (803)359-9941. Fax: (803)359-0629. E-mail: aida@sandlapper.org. Web site: www.sandlapper.org. Editor Emeritus: Robert P. Wilkins. **Contact:** Aida Rogers, editor. **60% freelance written.** Quarterly magazine focusing on the positive aspects of South Carolina. "*Sandlapper* is intended to be read at those times when people want to relax with an attractive, high-quality magazine that entertains and informs them about their state." Estab. 1989. Circ. 18,000 with a readership of 60,000. Pays during the dateline period. Publishes ms an average of 1 year after acceptance. Byline given. Buys first North American serial rights and the right to reprint. Submit seasonal material 6 months in advance. Accepts queries by mail, e-mail, fax. Sample copy online. Writer's guidelines for #10 SASE.

Nonfiction Feature articles and photo essays about South Carolina's interesting people, places, cuisine, history and culture, things to do. Essays, general interest, humor, interview/profile, photo feature. Query with clips and SASE. Length: 500-2,500 words. **Pays $100/published page.** Sometimes pays expenses of writers on assignment.

Photos "*Sandlapper* buys b&w prints, color transparencies, and art. Photographers should submit working cutlines for each photograph. We accept prints, slides and digital images." Pays $25-75, $100 for cover or centerspread photo.

The online version contains material not found in the print edition. Contact: Dan Harmon.

Tips "We're not interested in articles about topical issues, politics, crime, or commercial ventures. Avoid first-person nostalgia and remembrances of places that no longer exist. We look for top-quality literature. Humor is encouraged. Good taste is a standard. Unique angles are critical for acceptance. Dare to be bold, but not too bold."

SOUTH DAKOTA

$ DAKOTA OUTDOORS

South Dakota, P.O. Box 669 333 W. Dakota Ave., Pierre SD 57501-0669. (605)224-7301. Fax: (605)224-9210. E-mail: dakotaoutdoors@capjournal.com. **Contact:** Kevin Hipple, editor. **85% freelance written.** Monthly magazine on Dakota outdoor life, focusing on hunting and fishing. Estab. 1974. Circ. 7,000. Pays on publication. Publishes ms an average of 1-2 months after acceptance. Byline given. Submit seasonal material 3 months in advance. Accepts queries by mail, e-mail. Accepts simultaneous submissions. Responds in 3 months to queries. Sample copy for 9×12 SAE and 3 first-class stamps. Writer's guidelines by e-mail.

Nonfiction "Topics should center on fishing and hunting experiences and advice. Other topics such as boating, camping, hiking, environmental concerns and general nature will be considered as well." General interest, how-to, humor, interview/profile, personal experience, technical (all on outdoor topics-prefer in the Dakotas). **Buys 120 mss/year.** Send complete ms. Length: 500-2,000 words. **Pays $5-50. Sometimes pays in contributor's copies or other premiums (inquire).**

Reprints Send ms with rights for sale noted and information about when and where the material previously appeared. 50% of amount paid for an original article.

Photos Send photos with submission. Reviews 3×5 or 5×7 prints. Buys one-time rights. Offers no additonal payment for photos accepted with ms or negotiates payment individually. Identification of subjects required.

Columns/Departments Kids Korner (outdoors column addressing kids 12-16 years of age). Length: 50-500 words. **Pays $5-15.**

Fiction Adventure, humorous. Does not want stories about vacations or subjects that don't include hunting and fishing. **Buys 15 mss/year.** Send complete ms. Length: 750-1,500 words.

Fillers Anecdotes, facts, gags to be illustrated by cartoonist, newsbreaks, short humor, line drawings of fish and game. **Buys 10/year.**

Tips "Submit samples of manuscript or previous works for consideration; photos or illustrations with manuscript are helpful."

TENNESSEE

N $ $ AT HOME TENNESSEE

Pinpoint Publishing Group, 671 N. Ericson Rd., Suite 200, Cordova TN 38018. (901)684-4155. Fax: (901)684-4156. Web site: www.athometn.com. Editorial Director/Publisher: Margaret Monger. **Contact:** Laura Blanton, managing editor. **10% freelance written.** Monthly magazine. Estab. 2002. Circ. 30,000. Pays on publication. Byline given. Offers 100% kill fee. Not copyrighted. Makes work-for-hire assignments. Editorial lead time 2-3 months. Submit seasonal material 2-3 months in advance. Accepts queries by mail. Accepts simultaneous submissions. Responds in 1-2 months to queries. Sample copy for $4.95. Writer's guidelines free.

Nonfiction General interest, how-to, interview/profile, travel, gardenings, arts, design, architecture. Does not want opinion. Query with published clips. Length: 400-900 words. **Pays $50-350.**

Photos Contact Matt Lunn, art director. Send photos with submission. Reviews GIF/JPEG files.

$ $ MEMPHIS

Contemporary Media, P.O. Box 1738, Memphis TN 38101. (901)521-9000. Fax: (901)521-0129. E-mail: memmag@memphismagazine.com. Web site: www.memphismagazine.com. **30% freelance written.** Works with a small number of new/unpublished writers. Monthly magazine covering Memphis and the local region. "Our mission is to provide Memphis with a colorful and informative look at the people, places, lifestyles and businesses that make the Bluff City unique." Estab. 1976. Circ. 24,000. Pays on publication. Buys first North American serial rights. Submit seasonal material 3 months in advance. Accepts queries by mail, e-mail, fax.

Nonfiction "Virtually all of our material has strong Memphis area connections." Essays, general interest, historical/nostalgic, interview/profile, photo feature, travel, Interiors/exteriors, local issues and events. Special issues: Restaurant Guide and City Guide. **Buys 20 mss/year.** Query with published clips. Length: 500-3,000 words. **Pays 10-30¢/word.** Sometimes pays expenses of writers on assignment.

Photos State availability with submission. Reviews contact sheets, transparencies. Buys one-time rights.

Fiction One story published annually as part of contest. Open only to those within 150 miles of Memphis. See Web site for details.

N $ $ MEMPHIS DOWNTOWNER MAGAZINE

Downtown Productions, Inc., 408 S. Front St., Suite 109, Memphis TN 38103. Fax: (901)525-7128. E-mail: editor@memphisdowntowner.com. Web site: www.memphisdowntowner.com. Publisher: Jodie Vance. **Contact:** Terre Gorham, editor. **50% freelance written.** Monthly magazine covering features on positive aspects with a Memphis tie-in, especially to downtown. "We feature people, companies, nonprofits and other issues that the general Memphis public would find interesting, entertaining, and informative. All editorial focuses on the positives Memphis has. No negative commentary or personal judgements. Controversial subjects should be treated fairly and balanced without bias." Estab. 1991. Circ. 30,000. Pays on 15th of month in which assignment is published. Publishes ms an average of 2-6 months after acceptance. Byline given. Offers 25% kill fee. Buys all rights for 90 days, with relicensing rights thereafter. Editorial lead time 3-6 months. Submit seasonal material 3-6 months in advance. Accepts queries by mail, e-mail, fax. Accepts previously published material. Responds in 2 weeks to queries. Sample copy for free. Writer's guidelines by e-mail.

Nonfiction General interest, historical/nostalgic, how-to, humor, interview/profile, personal experience, photo feature. **Buys 40-50 mss/year.** Query with published clips. Length: 600-2,000 words. **Pays Pay scales vary depending on scope of assignment, but typically runs 15¢/word.** Sometimes pays expenses of writers on assignment.

Photos State availability with submission. Reviews GIF/JPEG files (300 dpi). Negotiates payment individually. Identification of subjects required.

Columns/Departments So It Goes (G-rated humor), 600-800 words. **Buys 6 mss/year.** Query with published clips. **Pays $85-100.**

Fillers Unusual, interesting, or how-to or "what to look for" appealing to a large, general audience. Facts.

Tips "Always pitch an actual story idea. E-mails that simply let us know you're a freelance writer mysteriously disappear from our inboxes. Actually read the magazine before you pitch. Get to know the regular columns and departments. In your pitch, explain where in the magazine you think your story idea would best fit."

TEXAS

$ HILL COUNTRY SUN

Sun Country Publications, Inc., P.O. Box 1482, Wimberley TX 78676. (512)847-5162. Fax: (512)847-5162. E-mail: melissa@hillcountrysun.com. Web site: www.hillcountrysun.com. **Contact:** Melissa Gilmere, editor. **75% freelance written.** Monthly tabloid covering traveling in the Central Texas Hill Country. "We publish stories of interesting people, places and events in the Central Texas Hill Country.'' Estab. 1990. Circ. 40,000. **Pays on acceptance.** Publishes ms an average of 2 months after acceptance. Byline given. Buys one-time rights. Editorial lead time 1 month. Submit seasonal material 2 months in advance. Accepts queries by mail, e-mail. Responds in 1 week to queries; 1 month to mss. Sample copy for free. Writer's guidelines online.

Nonfiction Interview/profile, travel. No first person articles. **Buys 50 mss/year.** Query. Length: 600-800 words. **Pays $50-60.**

Photos State availability of or send photos with submission. Reviews 5×7 prints. Buys one-time rights. No additional payment for photos accepted with ms. Identification of subjects required.

Tips ''Writers must be familiar with both the magazine's style and the Texas Hill Country.''

$ $ $ HOUSTON PRESS

New Times, Inc., 1621 Milam, Suite 100, Houston TX 77002. (713)280-2400. Fax: (713)280-2444. E-mail: melissa.sonzala@houstonpress.com. Web site: www.houstonpress.com. Editor: Margaret Downing. Managing Editor: George Flynn. Associate Editor: Cathy Matusow. **Contact:** Melissa Sonzala, editorial assistant. **40% freelance written.** Weekly tabloid covering ''news and arts stories of interest to a Houston audience. If the same story could run in Seattle, then it's not for us.'' Estab. 1989. Pays on publication. Publishes ms an average of 2 weeks after acceptance. Byline given. Buys first North American serial, Web site rights. Editorial lead time 2 months. Submit seasonal material 3 months in advance. Sample copy for $3.

Nonfiction Exposé, general interest, interview/profile, arts reviews; music. Query with published clips. Length: 300-4,500 words. **Pays $10-1,000.** Sometimes pays expenses of writers on assignment.

Photos State availability with submission. Buys all rights. Negotiates payment individually. Identification of subjects required.

$ $ $ PAPERCITY

Dallas Edition, Urban Publishers, 3303 Lee Parkway, #340, Dallas TX 75219. (214)521-3439. Fax: (214)521-3178. E-mail: brooke@papercitymag.com. **Contact:** Brooke Hortenstine, Dallas co-editor; Holly Moore, editor-in-chief. **5% freelance written.** Monthly magazine. ''*Papercity* covers fashion, food, entertainment, home design and decoratives for urban Dallas, Houston, San Francisco, and Atlanta. Our writing is lively, brash, sexy—it's where to read about the hottest restaurants, great chefs, where to shop, what's cool to buy, where to go and the chicest places to stay—from sexy, small hotels in New York, Los Angeles, London and Morocco, to where to buy the newest trends in Europe. We cover local parties with big photo spreads, and a hip nightlife column.'' Estab. 1994 (Houston); 1998 (Dallas); 2002 (San Francisco); 2004 (Atlanta). Circ. 85,000 (Dallas). Pays on publication. Publishes ms an average of 1 month after acceptance. Byline given. Offers 10% kill fee. Buys first North American serial rights. Editorial lead time 2 months. Submit seasonal material 4 months in advance. Accepts queries by mail, e-mail, fax. Accepts simultaneous submissions. Responds in 3 weeks to queries; 1 month to mss. Sample copy for 9×12 SAE with $1.50 in first-class stamps. Writer's guidelines for #10 SASE or by e-mail.

Nonfiction General interest, interview/profile, new product, travel, home decor, food. Special issues: Bridal (February); Travel (April); Restaurants (October). No straight profiles on anyone, especially celebrities. **Buys 10-12 mss/year.** Query with published clips. Length: 150-3,000 words. **Pays 35-50¢/word.**

Photos State availability with submission. Reviews contact sheets, transparencies, prints. Buys one-time rights. Negotiates payment individually.

Tips ''Read similar publications such as *W*, *Tattler*, *Wallpaper*, *Martha Stewart Living* for new trends, style of writing, hip new restaurants. We try to be very 'of the moment' so give us something in Dallas, Houston, Atlanta, San Francisco, New York, Los Angeles, London, etc., that we haven't heard yet. Chances are if other hip magazines are writing about it so will we.''

$ $ $ TEXAS HIGHWAYS

The Travel Magazine of Texas, Box 141009, Austin TX 78714-1009. (512)486-5858. Fax: (512)486-5879. E-mail: letters05@texashighways.com. Web site: www.texashighways.com. **70% freelance written.** Monthly magazine ''encourages travel within the state and tells the Texas story to readers around the world.'' Estab. 1974. Circ. 250,000. **Pays on acceptance.** Publishes ms an average of 1 year after acceptance. Buys first North American serial, electronic rights. Accepts queries by mail. Responds in 2 months to queries. Writer's guidelines online.

Nonfiction ''Subjects should focus on things to do or places to see in Texas. Include historical, cultural, and geographical aspects if appropriate. Text should be meticulously researched. Include anecdotes, historical references, quotations and, where relevant, geologic, botanical, and zoological information.'' Query with description, published clips, additional background materials (charts, maps, etc.) and SASE. Length: 1,200-1,500 words. **Pays 40-50¢/word.**

Tips "We like strong leads that draw in the reader immediately and clear, concise writing. Be specific and avoid superlatives. Avoid overused words. Don't forget the basics—who, what, where, when, why, and how."

N $$$$ TEXAS MONTHLY

Emmis Publishing LP, P.O. Box 1569, Austin TX 78767. (512)320-6900. Fax: (512)476-9007. E-mail: info@texasmonthly.com. Web site: www.texasmonthly.com. Managing Editor: Patricia McConnico. **Contact:** Evan Smith, editor. **10% freelance written.** Monthly magazine covering Texas. Estab. 1973. Circ. 300,000. **Pays on acceptance.** Publishes ms an average of 1-3 months after acceptance. Byline given. Buys first North American serial, first, one-time, electronic rights. Editorial lead time 2 months. Submit seasonal material 3 months in advance. Accepts queries by mail, e-mail, fax. Responds in 2 months to queries; 2 months to mss. Sample copy for $7. Writer's guidelines online.

Nonfiction Contact John Broders, assistant editor. Book excerpts, essays, exposé, general interest, interview/profile, personal experience, photo feature, travel. Does not want articles without a Texas connection. **Buys 15 mss/year.** Query. Length: 2,000-5,000 words. **Pays $1/word.** Pays expenses of writers on assignment.

Photos Contact Leslie Baldwin, photography editor (lbaldwin@texasmonthly.com).

Tips "Stories must appeal to an educated Texas audience. We like solidly researched reporting that uncovers issues of public concern, reveals offbeat and previously unreported topics, or uses a novel approach to familiar topics. Any issue of the magazine would be a helpful guide. We do not use fiction, poetry, or cartoons."

$$ TEXAS PARKS & WILDLIFE

3000 South I.H. 35, Suite 120, Austin TX 78704. (512)912-7000. Fax: (512)707-1913. E-mail: robert.macias@tpwd.state.tx.us. Web site: www.tpwmagazine.com. **Contact:** Robert Macias, editorial director. **80% freelance written.** Monthly magazine featuring articles about Texas hunting, fishing, birding, outdoor recreation, game and nongame wildlife, state parks, environmental issues. All articles must be about Texas. Estab. 1942. Circ. 150,000. **Pays on acceptance.** Publishes ms an average of 4 months after acceptance. Byline given. Kill fee determined by contract, usually $200-250. Buys first rights. Accepts queries by mail. Responds in 1 month to queries; 3 months to mss. Sample copy and writer's guidelines online.

- *Texas Parks & Wildlife* needs more short items for front-of-the-book scout section and wildlife articles written from a natural history perspective (not for hunters).

Nonfiction General interest (Texas only), how-to (outdoor activities), photo feature, travel (state parks and small towns). **Buys 60 mss/year.** Query with published clips; follow up by e-mail 1 month after submitting query. Length: 500-2,500 words. **Pays 50¢/word. for assigned articles.**

Photos Send photos to photo editor. Reviews transparencies. Buys one-time rights. Offers $65-500/photo. Captions, identification of subjects required.

Tips "Queries with a strong seasonal peg are preferred. Our planning progress begins 7 months before the date of publication. That means you have to think ahead. What will Texas outdoor enthusiasts want to read about 7 months from today?"

VERMONT

$$ VERMONT LIFE MAGAZINE

6 Baldwin St., Montpelier VT 05602-2109. (802)828-3241. Fax: (802)828-3366. E-mail: tom.slayton@state.vt.us. Web site: www.vermontlife.com. **Contact:** Thomas K. Slayton, editor-in-chief. **90% freelance written.** Prefers to work with published/established writers. Quarterly magazine. "*Vermont Life* is interested in any article, query, story idea, photograph or photo essay that has to do with Vermont. As the state magazine, we are most favorably impressed with pieces that present positive aspects of life within the state's borders." Estab. 1946. Circ. 75,000. Publishes ms an average of 9 months after acceptance. Byline given. Offers kill fee. Buys first North American serial rights. Submit seasonal material 1 year in advance. Accepts queries by mail, e-mail, fax. Responds in 1 month to queries. Writer's guidelines online.

O→ Break in with "short humorous Vermont anecdotes for our 'Postboy' column."

Nonfiction Wants articles on today's Vermont, those which portray a typical or, if possible, unique aspect of the state or its people. Style should be literate, clear, and concise. Subtle humor favored. No "Vermont clichés," and please do not send first-person accounts of your vacation trip to Vermont. **Buys 60 mss/year.** Query by letter essential. Length: 1,500 words average. **Pays 25¢/word.**

Photos Buys photos with mss; buys seasonal photographs alone. Prefers b&w contact sheets to look at first on assigned material. Color submissions must be 4×5 or 35mm transparencies. Gives assignments but only with experienced photographers. Query in writing. Buys one-time rights. Pays $75-200 inside color; $500 for cover. Captions, identification of subjects, model releases required.

The online version contains material not found in the print edition. Contact: Andrew Jackson.

Tips "Writers who read our magazine are given more consideration because they understand that we want authentic articles about Vermont. If a writer has a genuine working knowledge of Vermont, his or her work usually shows it. Vermont is changing and there is much concern here about what this state will be like in years ahead. It is a beautiful, environmentally sound place now and the vast majority of residents want to keep it so. Articles reflecting such concerns in an intelligent, authoritative, non-hysterical way will be given very careful consideration. The growth of tourism makes us interested in intelligent articles about specific places in Vermont, their history and attractions to the traveling public.''

VIRGINIA

$ $ ALBEMARLE

Living in Jefferson's Virginia, Carden Jennings Publishing, 375 Greenbrier Dr., Suite 100, Charlottesville VA 22901. (434)817-2000. Fax: (434)817-2020. Web site: www.cjp.com. **80% freelance written.** Bimonthly magazine. ''Lifestyle magazine for central Virginia.'' Estab. 1987. Circ. 10,000. Pays on publication. Publishes ms an average of 4 months after acceptance. Byline given. Offers 30% kill fee. Buys first North American serial rights. Editorial lead time 6 months. Submit seasonal material 6 months in advance. Accepts queries by mail, fax. Accepts simultaneous submissions. Responds in 1 month to queries; 2 months to mss. Sample copy for 10×12 SAE and 5 first-class stamps. Writer's guidelines for #10 SASE.

- Break in with ''a strong idea backed by good clips to prove abilities. Ideas should be targeted to central Virginia and lifestyle, which can be very broad—a renaissance man or woman approach to living.''

Nonfiction Essays, historical/nostalgic, interview/profile, photo feature, travel. ''No fiction, poetry or anything without a direct tie to central Virginia.'' **Buys 30-35 mss/year.** Query with published clips. Length: 900-3,500 words. **Pays $75-225 for assigned articles; $75-175 for unsolicited articles.** Sometimes pays expenses of writers on assignment.

Photos State availability with submission. Reviews transparencies. Buys one-time rights. Negotiates payment individually. Captions, identification of subjects, model releases required.

Columns/Departments Etcetera (personal essay), 900-1,200 words; Flavors of Virginia (food), 900-1,100 words; Leisure (travel, sports), 3,000 words. **Buys 20 mss/year.** Query with published clips. **Pays $75-150.**

Tips ''Be familiar with the central Virginia area and lifestyle. We prefer a regional slant, which should include a focus on someone or something located in the region, or a focus on someone or something from the region making an impact in other parts of the world. Quality writing is a must. Story ideas that lend themselves to multiple sources will give you a leg up on the competition.''

$ $ HAMPTON ROADS SHIELD

A Magazine for Law Enforcement Officers and Enthusiasts in Hampton Roads, One Offer Publishing, P.O. Box 99052, Norfolk VA 23509-9052. E-mail: queries@hamptonroadsshield.com. **Contact:** Cindy Smith. **85% freelance written.** Monthly magazine covering all subjects of interest to law enforcement officers in the Hampton Roads, Virginia area. ''We cover items of interest that are both job related and non-job related.'' This magazine is specifically for law enforcement, correctional and security officers working in the Hampton Roads, Virginia area. Estab. 2004. Circ. 5,000. **Pays on acceptance.** Publishes ms an average of 3-4 months after acceptance. Byline given. Offers 10% kill fee. Buys one-time rights. Editorial lead time 4-6 months. Submit seasonal material 6 months in advance. Accepts queries by mail, e-mail. Responds in 6-8 weeks to queries; 1-2 months to mss. Writer's guidelines by e-mail.

- ''This is not a trade magazine, but rather a magazine that strives to bring stories of humor, interest and information to our audience.''

Nonfiction Essays, general interest, historical/nostalgic, humor, inspirational, interview/profile, new product, opinion, personal experience, photo feature. Doesn't want anything anti-law enforcement or anything overly dramatic or flowery. **Buys 30/year mss/year.** Query. Length: 300-1,000 words. **Pays 10-15¢/word.**

Photos State availability with submission. Reviews prints, GIF/JPEG files. Buys one-time rights. Negotiates payment individually. Captions, identification of subjects required.

Columns/Departments Excuses, Excuses! (stories of humorous excuses offered by criminals), any word length; Shield Gear (highlights law enforcement-related products), 300-500 words; Brother to Brother (written by law enforcement officials), 300-700 words.

Poetry Poems must be related to law enforcement. Avant-garde, free verse, light verse, traditional. **Buys 2-3/year poems/year.** Submit maximum 5 poems. Length: 10-30 lines.

Fillers Anecdotes, facts, short humor. **Buys 50-60/year.** Length: Maximum of 250 words.

Tips Remember the audience and speak to them. ''We also welcome ideas for regular departments. New writers are welcome, but please be sure your idea will be of interest to law enforcement officers in Hampton Roads, Virginia. You do not need to be from this area to write effectively for this audience.''

$ $ THE ROANOKER

Leisure Publishing Co., 3424 Brambleton Ave., P.O. Box 21535, Roanoke VA 24018-9900. (540)989-6138. Fax: (540)989-7603. E-mail: krheinheimer@leisurepublishing.com. Web site: www.theroanoker.com. **Contact:** Kurt Rheinheimer, editor. **75% freelance written.** Works with a small number of new/unpublished writers each year. Magazine published 6 times/year. "*The Roanoker* is a general interest city magazine for the people of Roanoke, Virginia and the surrounding area. Our readers are primarily upper-income, well-educated professionals between the ages of 35 and 60. Coverage ranges from hard news and consumer information to restaurant reviews and local history." Estab. 1974. Circ. 12,000. Pays on publication. Publishes ms an average of 4 months after acceptance. Byline given. Buys all rights, makes work-for-hire assignments. Submit seasonal material 4 months in advance. Accepts queries by mail, e-mail, fax. Responds in 2 months to queries. Sample copy for $2 and 9×12 SAE with 5 first-class stamps or online. Editorial calendar online.

Nonfiction "We're looking for more photo feature stories based in western Virginia. We place special emphasis on investigative and exposé articles." Exposé, historical/nostalgic, how-to (live better in western Virginia), interview/profile (of well-known area personalities), photo feature, travel (Virginia and surrounding states), periodic special sections on fashion, real estate, media, banking, investing. **Buys 30 mss/year.** Query with published clips or send complete ms. Length: 1,400 words maximum. **Pays $35-200.**

Photos Send photos with submission. Reviews color transparencies, digital submissions. Rights purchased vary. Pays $25-50/published photograph. Captions, model releases required.

Columns/Departments Skinny (shorts on people, Roanoke-related books, local issues, events, arts and culture).

Tips "We're looking for more pieces on contemporary history (1930s-70s). It helps if freelancer lives in the area. The most frequent mistake made by writers in completing an article for us is not having enough Roanoke-area focus: use of area experts, sources, slants, etc."

$ $ VIRGINIA LIVING

Cape Fear Publishing, 109 E. Cary St., Richmond VA 23219. (804)343-7539. Fax: (804)649-0306. E-mail: editor@capefear.com. Web site: www.virginialiving.com. **Contact:** Garland Pollard, editor; Tina Ennulat, associate editor. **95% freelance written.** Bimonthly magazine covering life and lifestyle in Virginia. "We are a large-format (10×13) glossy magazine covering life in Virginia, from food, architecture, and gardening, to issues, profiles, and travel. Estab. 2002. Circ. 60,000. Pays on publication. Publishes ms an average of 1 year after acceptance. Byline given. Buys first North American serial rights. Editorial lead time 6-12 months. Submit seasonal material 1 year in advance. Accepts queries by mail. Accepts simultaneous submissions. Responds in 1 month to queries; 1 month to mss. Sample copy for $5.

Nonfiction Book excerpts, essays, exposé, general interest, historical/nostalgic, interview/profile, new product, personal experience, photo feature, travel, architecture, design. No fiction, poetry, previously published articles, or stories with a firm grasp of the obvious. **Buys 180 mss/year.** Query with published clips or send complete ms. Length: 300-3,000 words. **Pays $100-1,000.**

Photos Tyler Darden, art director. Reviews contact sheets, 6×7 transparencies, 8×10 prints, GIF/JPEG files. Buys one-time rights. Negotiates payment individually. Captions, identification of subjects, model releases required.

Columns/Departments Beauty; Travel; Books; Events; Sports (all with a unique Virginia slant), all 1,000-1,500 words. **Buys 50 mss/year.** Send complete ms. **Pays $120-200.**

Tips "A freelancer would get the best reception if they send clips via mail before they query. I can then sit down with them and read them. In addition, queries should be about fresh subjects in Virginia. Avoid stories about Williamsburg, Chincoteague ponies, Monticello, the Civil War, and other press release-type topics. We prefer to introduce new subjects, faces, and ideas, and get beyond the many clichés of Virginia. Freelancers would also do well to think about what time of the year they are pitching stories for, as well as art possibilities. We are a large-format magazine close to the size of the old-look magazine, so photography is a key component to our stories."

WASHINGTON

$ $ SEATTLE MAGAZINE

Tiger Oak Publications Inc., 1505 Western Ave., Suite 500, Seattle WA 98101. (206)284-1750. Fax: (206)284-2550. E-mail: rachel@seattlemag.com. Web site: www.seattlemagazine.com. **Contact:** Rachel Hart, editor. Monthly magazine "serving the Seattle metropolitan area. Articles should be written with our readers in mind. They are interested in social issues, the arts, politics, homes and gardens, travel and maintaining the region's high quality of life." Estab. 1992. Circ. 45,000. Pays on or about 30 days after publication. Publishes ms an average of 3 months after acceptance. Byline given. Offers 25% kill fee. Buys first rights. Editorial lead time 6 months. Submit seasonal material 6 months in advance. Accepts queries by mail, e-mail, fax. Responds in 2 months to queries. Sample copy for #10 SASE. Writer's guidelines online.

O-π Break in by "suggesting short, newsier stories with a strong Seattle focus."
Nonfiction Book excerpts (local), essays, exposé, general interest, humor, interview/profile, photo feature, travel, local/regional interest. No longer accepting queries by mail. Query with published clips. Length: 100-2,000 words. **Pays $50 minimum.**
Photos State availability with submission. Buys one-time rights. Negotiates payment individually.
Columns/Departments Scoop, Urban Safari, Voice, Trips, People, Environment, Hot Button, Fitness, Fashion, Eat and Drink. Query with published clips. **Pays $225-400.**
Tips "The best queries include some idea of a lead and sources of information, plus compelling reasons why the article belongs specifically in *Seattle Magazine*. In addition, queries should demonstrate the writer's familiarity with the magazine. New writers are often assigned front- or back-of-the-book contents, rather than features. However, the editors do not discourage writers from querying for longer articles and are especially interested in receiving trend pieces, in-depth stories with a news hook and cultural criticism with a local angle."

$ $ $ SEATTLE WEEKLY

Village Voice, 1008 Western Ave., Suite 300, Seattle WA 98104. (206)623-0500. Fax: (206)467-4377. Web site: seattleweekly.com. **Contact:** Appropriate Editor. **20% freelance written.** Weekly tabloid covering arts, politics, food, business and books with local and regional emphasis. Estab. 1976. Circ. 105,000. Pays on publication. Publishes ms an average of 1 month after acceptance. Byline given. Offers variable kill fee. Buys first North American serial rights. Submit seasonal material 2 months in advance. Responds in 1 month to queries. Sample copy for $3. Writer's guidelines online.

O-π Read online guide for freelancers for specific editors and e-mail addresses.
Nonfiction Book excerpts, exposé, general interest, historical/nostalgic (Northwest), humor, interview/profile, opinion. **Buys 6-8 mss/year.** Query with cover letter, résumé, published clips and SASE. Length: 300-4,000 words. **Pays $50-800.** Sometimes pays expenses of writers on assignment.
Reprints Send tearsheet. Payment varies.
Tips "The *Seattle Weekly* publishes stories on Northwest politics and art, usually written by regional and local writers, for a mostly upscale, urban audience; writing is high-quality magazine style."

WISCONSIN

N LABOR PAPER EXTRA!!

Serving Southern Wisconsin, Union-Cooperative Publishing, 3030 39th Ave., Suite 110, Kenosha WI 53144. (262)657-6116. Fax: (262)657-6153. **Contact:** Mark T. Onosko, publisher. **30% freelance written.** Monthly tabloid covering union/labor news. Estab. 2002. Circ. 12,000. Pays on publication. Publishes ms an average of 2 months after acceptance. Byline given. Buys all rights. Editorial lead time 1 month. Submit seasonal material 1 month in advance. Accepts queries by mail, fax. Accepts simultaneous submissions. Sample copy and writer's guidelines free.
Nonfiction Exposé, general interest, historical/nostalgic, humor, inspirational. **Buys 4 mss/year.** Query with published clips. Length: 300-1,000 words. Sometimes pays expenses of writers on assignment.
Photos State availability with submission. Negotiates payment individually. Captions required.

N $ $ MADISON MAGAZINE

The magazine of lifestyle and business, Morgan Murphy Media, 7025 Raymond Rd., Madison WI 53719. (608)270-3600. Fax: (608)270-3636. E-mail: bnardi@madisonmagazine.com. Web site: www.madisonmagazine.com. **Contact:** Brennan Nardi, editor. **75% freelance written.** Monthly magazine. Estab. 1978. Circ. 18,600. Pays on publication. Publishes ms an average of 2 months after acceptance. Byline given. Offers 33% kill fee. Editorial lead time 3 months. Submit seasonal material 3-4 months in advance. Accepts queries by mail, e-mail. Accepts simultaneous submissions. Responds in 3 weeks to queries; 3 weeks to mss. Sample copy for free. Writer's guidelines online.
Nonfiction Book excerpts, essays, exposé, general interest, historical/nostalgic, how-to, humor, inspirational, interview/profile, new product, opinion, personal experience, photo feature, religious, technical, travel.
Photos State availability with submission. Reviews contact sheets. Buys one-time rights. Negotiates payment individually.
Columns/Departments Your Town (local events) and OverTones (local arts/entertainment), both 300 words; Habitat (local house/garden) and Business (local business), both 800 words. **Buys 120 mss/year.** Query with published clips. **Pays variable amount.**
Fillers Anecdotes, facts, gags to be illustrated by cartoonist, newsbreaks, short humor. Length: 100 words. **Pays 20-30¢/word.**
Tips "Our magazine is local so only articles pertaining to Madison are considered. Specific queries are heavily appreciated. We like fresh, new content taken in a local perspective. Show us what you're like to write for us."

$$$$ MILWAUKEE MAGAZINE

417 E. Chicago St., Milwaukee WI 53202. (414)273-1101. Fax: (414)273-0016. E-mail: milmag@qg.com. Web site: www.milwaukeemagazine.com. **Contact:** Bruce Murphy, editor. **40% freelance written.** Monthly magazine. "We publish stories about Milwaukee, of service to Milwaukee-area residents and exploring the area's changing lifestyle, business, arts, politics, and dining." Circ. 40,000. Pays on publication. Publishes ms an average of 2 months after acceptance. Byline given. Offers 20% kill fee. Buys first rights. Submit seasonal material 6 months in advance. Accepts queries by mail, e-mail. Responds in 6 weeks to queries. Sample copy for $4.

Nonfiction Essays, exposé, general interest, historical/nostalgic, interview/profile, photo feature, travel, food and dining, and other services. "No articles without a strong Milwaukee or Wisconsin angle." Length: 2,500-6,000 words for full-length features; 800 words for 2-page "breaker" features (short on copy, long on visuals). **Buys 30-50 mss/year.** Query with published clips. **Pays $400-1,800 for full-length, $150-400 for breaker.** Sometimes pays expenses of writers on assignment.

Columns/Departments Insider (inside information on Milwaukee, exposé, slice-of-life, unconventional angles on current scene), up to 500 words; Mini Reviews for Insider, 125 words. Query with published clips.

Tips "Pitch something for the Insider, or suggest a compelling profile we haven't already done. Submit clips that prove you can do the job. The department most open is Insider. Think short, lively, offbeat, fresh, people-oriented. We are actively seeking freelance writers who can deliver lively, readable copy that helps our readers make the most out of the Milwaukee area. Because we're only human, we'd like writers who can deliver copy on deadline that fits the specifications of our assignment. If you fit this description, we'd love to work with you."

$$ WISCONSIN TRAILS

P.O. Box 317, Black Earth WI 53515-0317. (608)767-8000. Fax: (608)767-5444. E-mail: lkearney@wistrails.com. Web site: wisconsintrails.com. **Contact:** Laura Kearney, managing editor. **40% freelance written.** Bimonthly magazine for readers interested in Wisconsin and its contemporary issues, personalities, recreation, history, natural beauty, and arts. Estab. 1960. Circ. 55,000. Pays 1 month from publication. Publishes ms an average of 6 months after acceptance. Byline given. Buys first North American serial, one-time rights. Submit seasonal material 1 year in advance. Accepts queries by mail, e-mail, fax. Responds in 4 months to queries. Sample copy for $4.95. Writer's guidelines for #10 SASE or online.

> O→ "We're looking for active articles about people, places, events, and outdoor adventures in Wisconsin. We want to publish 1 in-depth article of statewide interest or concern/issue, and several short (600-1,500 words) articles about short trips, recreational opportunities, personalities, restaurants, inns, history, and cultural activities. We're looking for more articles about out-of-the-way Wisconsin places that are exceptional in some way and engaging pieces on Wisconsin's little-known and unique aspects."

Nonfiction "Our articles focus on some aspect of Wisconsin life: an interesting town or event, a person or industry, history or the arts, and especially outdoor recreation. No fiction. No articles that are too local for our regional audience, or articles about obvious places to visit in Wisconsin. We need more articles about the new and little-known." **Buys 3 unsolicited mss/year.** Query or send outline. Length: 1,000-3,000 words. **Pays 25¢/word for assigned articles.** Sometimes pays expenses of writers on assignment.

Photos Photographs purchased with or without mss, or on assignment. Color photos usually illustrate an activity, event, region, or striking scenery. Prefer photos with people in scenery. Reviews 35mm or larger transparencies. Pays $45-175 for inside color; $250 for covers. Captions, labels with photographer's name required.

Tips "When querying, submit well-thought-out ideas about stories specific to people, places, events, arts, outdoor adventures, etc., in Wisconsin. Include published clips with queries. Do some research—many queries we receive are pitching ideas for stories we recently have published. Know the tone, content, and audience of the magazine. Refer to our writer's guidelines, or request them, if necessary."

WYOMING

$ WYOMING RURAL ELECTRIC NEWS (WREN)

P.O. Box 549, Gillette WY 82717. (307)682-7527. Fax: (307)682-7528. E-mail: wren@coffey.com. **Contact:** Kris Wendtland, editor. **20% freelance written.** Monthly magazine for audience of small town residents, vacation-home owners, farmers, and ranchers. Estab. 1954. Circ. 39,000. **Pays on acceptance.** Publishes ms an average of 2 months after acceptance. Byline given. Buys one-time rights. Submit seasonal material 2 months in advance. Accepts queries by mail, e-mail, fax, phone. Responds in 3 months to queries. Sample copy for $2.50 and 9×12 SASE. Writer's guidelines for #10 SASE.

> O→ "You have just learned something. It is so amazing you just have to find out more. You call around. You search on the Web. You go to the library. Everything you learn about it makes you want to know

more. In a matter of days, all your friends are aware that you are into something. You don't stop talking about it. You're totally confident that they find it interesting too. Now, write it down and send it to us. We are excited just wondering what you find so amazing! Come on, tell us! Tell us!"

Nonfiction "We print science, ag, how-to, and human interest but not fiction. Topics of interest in general include: hunting, cooking, gardening, commodities, sugar beets, wheat, oil, coal, hard rock mining, beef cattle, electric technologies such as lawn mowers, car heaters, air cleaners and assorted gadgets, surge protectors, pesticators, etc." Wants science articles with question/answer quiz at end—test your knowledge. Buys electrical appliance articles. Articles welcome that put present and/or future in positive light. No nostalgia, sarcasm, or tongue-in-cheek. **Buys 4-10 mss/year.** Send complete ms. Length: 500-800 words. **Pays up to $140, plus 4 copies.**

Reprints Send tearsheet or photocopy and information about when and where the material previously appeared.

Photos Color only.

Tips "Always looking for fresh, new writers. Submit entire manuscript. Don't submit a regionally set story from some other part of the country. Photos and illustrations (if appropriate) are always welcomed. We want factual articles that are blunt, to the point, accurate."

CANADIAN & INTERNATIONAL

$ $ ABACO LIFE

Caribe Communications, P.O. Box 37487, Raleigh NC 27627. (919)859-6782. Fax: (919)859-6769. E-mail: jimkerr@mindspring.com. Web site: www.abacolife.com. Managing Editor: Cathy Kerr. **Contact:** Jim Kerr, editor/publisher. **50% freelance written.** Quarterly magazine covering Abaco, an island group in the Northeast Bahamas. "*Abaco Life* editorial focuses entirely on activities, history, wildlife, resorts, people and other subjects pertaining to the Abacos. Readers include locals, vacationers, second-home owners, and other visitors whose interests range from real estate and resorts to scuba, sailing, fishing, and beaches. The tone is upbeat, adventurous, humorous. No fluff writing for an audience already familiar with the area." Estab. 1979. Circ. 10,000. Pays on publication. Publishes ms an average of 2 months after acceptance. Byline given. Offers 40% kill fee. Buys one-time rights. Editorial lead time 2 months. Submit seasonal material 4 months in advance. Accepts queries by mail, e-mail. Accepts simultaneous submissions. Responds in 2 weeks to queries; 2 months to mss. Sample copy for $2. Writer's guidelines free.

Nonfiction General interest, historical/nostalgic, how-to, interview/profile, personal experience, photo feature, travel. "No general first-time impressions. Articles must be specific, show knowledge and research of the subject and area—'Abaco's Sponge Industry'; 'Diving Abaco's Wrecks'; 'The Hurricane of '36.' " **Buys 8-10 mss/year.** Query or send complete ms. Length: 700-2,000 words. **Pays $400-1,000.**

Photos State availability of or send photos with submission. Reviews transparencies, prints. Buys one-time rights. Offers $25-100/photo. Negotiates payment individually. Captions, identification of subjects, model releases required.

The online magazine carries original content not found in the print edition. Contact: Jim Kerr, online editor.

Tips "Travel writers must look deeper than a usual destination piece, and the only real way to do that is spend time in Abaco. Beyond good writing, which is a must, we like submissions on Microsoft Word, but that's optional. Color slides are also preferred over prints, and good ones go a long way in selling the story. We prefer digital photos saved to a disc at 300 dpi minimum JPEG format. Read the magazine to learn its style."

$ $ THE ATLANTIC CO-OPERATOR

Promoting Community Ownership, Atlantic Co-operative Publishers, 123 Halifax St., Moncton, New Brunswick E1C 8N5 Canada. Fax: (506)858-6615. E-mail: editor@theatlanticco-operator.coop. Web site: www.theatlanticco-operator.coop. **Contact:** Mark Higgins, editor. **95% freelance written.** Bimonthly tabloid covering co-operatives. "We publish articles of interest to the general public, with a special focus on community ownership and community economic development in Atlantic Canada." Estab. 1933. Pays on publication. Publishes ms an average of 2 months after acceptance. Byline given. Editorial lead time 2 months. Submit seasonal material 2 months in advance. Accepts queries by mail, e-mail, fax. Accepts simultaneous submissions. Responds in 3 weeks to queries. Sample copy not available.

Nonfiction Exposé, general interest, historical/nostalgic, interview/profile. No political stories, economical stories, sports. **Buys 90 mss/year.** Query with published clips. Length: 500-2,000 words. **Pays 22¢/word.** Pays expenses of writers on assignment.

Reprints Accepts previously published submissions.

Photos State availability with submission. Reviews prints, GIF/JPEG files. Buys one-time rights. Offers $25/photo. Identification of subjects required.

Columns/Departments Health and Lifestyle (anything from recipes to travel), 800 words; International Page (co-operatives in developing countries, good ideas from around the world). **Buys 10 mss/year.** Query with published clips.

AUSTRALIANA

The Australiana Society, Inc., P.O. Box 2335, Bondi Junction NSW 1355 Australia. (61)(2)9389-4404. E-mail: info@australiana.org. Web site: www.australiana.org. Co-editor: Kevin Fahy AM. **Contact:** John Wade, co-editor. Quarterly magazine covering various aspects of Australiana.

Nonfiction General interest, historical/nostalgic, how-to, interview/profile, photo feature, reviews. Query.

$ $ $ THE BEAVER

Canada's History Magazine, Canada's National History Society, 478-167 Lombard Ave., Winnipeg MB R3B 0T6 Canada. (204)988-9300. Fax: (204)988-9309. E-mail: articlequeries@historysociety.ca. Web site: www.thebeaver.ca. **50% freelance written.** Bimonthly magazine covering Canadian history. Estab. 1920. Circ. 46,000. **Pays on acceptance.** Byline given. Offers $200 kill fee. Buys first North American serial, electronic rights. Editorial lead time 4 months. Submit seasonal material 8 months in advance. Accepts queries by mail. Accepts simultaneous submissions. Responds in 6 weeks to queries; 2 months to mss. Sample copy for 9×12 SAE and 2 first-class stamps. Writer's guidelines online.

Break in with a "new interpretation based on solid new research; entertaining magazine style."

Nonfiction Photo feature (historical), historical (Canadian focus). Does not want anything unrelated to Canadian history. **Buys 30 mss/year.** Query with published clips. Length: 600-3,500 words. **Pays $400-1,000 for assigned articles; $300-600 for unsolicited articles.** Sometimes pays expenses of writers on assignment.

Photos State availability with submission. Buys one-time rights. Offers no additional payment for photos accepted with ms. Identification of subjects, model releases required.

Columns/Departments Book and other media reviews and Canadian history subjects, 600 words ("These are assigned to freelancers with particular areas of expertise, i.e., women's history, labour history, French regime, etc."). **Buys 15 mss/year. Pays $125.**

Tips "*The Beaver* is directed toward a general audience of educated readers, as well as to historians and scholars. We are in the market for lively, well-written, well-researched, and informative articles about Canadian history that focus on all parts of the country and all areas of human activity. Subject matter covers the whole range of Canadian history, with particular emphasis on social history, politics, exploration, discovery and settlement, aboriginal peoples, business and trade, war, culture and sport. Articles are obtained through direct commission and by submission. Queries should be accompanied by a stamped, self-addressed envelope. *The Beaver* publishes articles of various lengths, including long features (from 1,500-3,500 words) that provide an in-depth look at an event, person or era; short, more narrowly focused features (from 600-1,500 words). Longer articles may be considered if their importance warrants publication. Articles should be written in an expository or interpretive style and present the principal themes of Canadian history in an original, interesting and informative way."

$ $ $ CANADIAN GEOGRAPHIC

39 McArthur Ave., Ottawa ON K1L 8L7 Canada. (613)745-4629. Fax: (613)744-0947. E-mail: editorial@canadiangeographic.ca. Web site: www.canadiangeographic.ca. **Contact:** Rick Boychuk, editor. **90% freelance written.** Works with a small number of new/unpublished writers each year. Bimonthly magazine. "*Canadian Geographic*'s colorful portraits of our ever-changing population show readers just how important the relationship between the people and the land really is." Estab. 1930. Circ. 240,000. **Pays on acceptance.** Publishes ms an average of 3 months after acceptance. Buys first Canadian rights. Accepts queries by mail, e-mail, fax. Responds in 1 month to queries. Sample copy for $5.95 (Canadian) and 9×12 SAE or online.

• *Canadian Geographic* reports a need for more articles on earth sciences. Canadian writers only.

Nonfiction Buys authoritative geographical articles, in the broad geographical sense, written for the average person, not for a scientific audience. Predominantly Canadian subjects by Canadian authors. **Buys 30-45 mss/year.** Query. Length: 1,500-3,000 words. **Pays 80¢/word minimum.** Sometimes pays expenses of writers on assignment.

Photos Pays $75-400 for color photos, depending on published size.

$ $ COTTAGE MAGAZINE

The Best in Recreational Living, OP Publishing, Ltd., 900-1080 Howe St., Vancouver BC V62 2T1 Canada. (604)606-4644. Fax: (604)687-1925. E-mail: editor@cottagemagazine.com. Web site: www.cottagemagazine.com. **Contact:** David Webb, editor. **80% freelance written.** Bimonthly magazine covering do-it-yourself projects, profiles of people and their innovative solutions to building and maintaining their country homes, issues that affect rural individuals and communities, and the R&R aspect of country living. "Our readers want solid, practical information about living in the country—including alternative energy and sustainable living. The also like to have fun in a wide range of recreational pursuits, from canoeing, fishing, and sailing to water skiing, snowmobiling, and entertaining.'' Estab. 1992. Circ. 20,000. Pays within 1 month of publication. Publishes ms an average of 6 months after acceptance. Byline given. Offers 50% kill fee. Buys first North American serial rights. Accepts queries by e-mail. Accepts simultaneous submissions. Responds in 1 month to queries. Writer's guidelines online.

Nonfiction Buys 18-24 mss/year. Query. Length: Up to 1,500 words. **Pays $200-450 (including visuals).**

Photos Send photos with submission. Reviews with negatives prints, slides, digital. Pays $25-250. Cover submissions also accepted.

Columns/Departments Utilities (solar and/or wind power), 800 words; Weekend Project (a how-to most homeowners can do themselves), 800 words; Government (new regulations, processes, problems), 800 words; Diversions (advisories, ideas, and how-tos about the fun things that people do), 800 words; InRoads (product reviews), 50-600 words; This Land (personal essays or news-based story with a broader context), 800 words; Last Word or Cabin Life (personal essays and experiences), 800 words; Elements (short articles focusing on a single feature of cottage), 600 words; Alternatives (applied alternative energy), 600 words. Query. **Pays 20¢/published word.**

Fillers Anecdotes, facts, newsbreaks, seasonal tips. **Buys 12/year.** Length: 50-200 words. **Pays 20¢/word.**

Tips ''We serve all of Western Canada, so while it's OK to have a main focus on one region, reference should be made to similarities/differences in other provinces. Even technical articles should have some anecdotal content. Some of our best articles come from readers themselves or from writers who can relay that 'personal' feeling. Cottaging is about whimsy and fun as well as maintenance and chores. Images, images, images: We require sharp, quality photos, and the more, the better.''

N $ DEVON LIFE

Archant Life Ltd, Archant House, Babbage Road, Totnes Devon TQ9 5JA United Kingdom. (44)(180)386-0910. Fax: (44)(180)386-0922. E-mail: devonlife@archant.co.uk. Web site: www.devonlife.co.uk. **Contact:** Jan Barwick (jan.barwick@archant.co.uk). Accepts queries by mail, e-mail. Sample copy online. Writer's guidelines by e-mail.

''It is wise to submit a synopsis that indicates why the article would appeal to *Devon Life*. Include clips and your publishing history. You can attach the complete manuscript, but there is no guarantee it will be used.''

Nonfiction Length: 600-800 words/single-page articles; 1,000-2,000 words/2-page articles. **Pays £60-75/up to 1,200 words; £40-50/up to 800 words.**

Photos Send photos with submission. Reviews transparencies, prints, 300 dpi digital images. Captions required.

N $$$$ HAMILTON MAGAZINE

Town Media, 1074 Cooke Blvd., Burlington ON L7T 4A8 Canada. Phone/Fax: (905)634-8003. E-mail: info@townmedia.ca. Web site: www.hamiltonmagazine.com.; www.townmedia.ca. Associate Editor: Garine Tcholakian. **Contact:** David Young, editor. **50% freelance written.** Quarterly magazine devoted to the Greater Hamilton and Golden Horseshoe area. ''Our mandate: to entertain and inform by spotlighting the best of what our city and region has to offer. We invite readers to take part in a vibrant community by supplying them with authoritative and dynamic coverage of local culture, food, fashion and design. We dig into an eclectic range of issues and satisfy curiosity about them all. Each story strives to expand your view of the area, every issue an essential resource for exploring, understanding and unlocking the region. Packed with insight, intrigue and suspense, *Hamilton Magazine* delivers the city to your doorstep.'' Estab. 1978. Pays on publication. Byline given. Offers 50% kill fee. Buys first North American serial, second serial (reprint) rights, makes work-for-hire assignments. Editorial lead time 2-3 months. Submit seasonal material 2-3 months in advance. Accepts queries by e-mail. Responds in 1 week to queries; 1 month to mss. Sample copy for #10 SASE. Writer's guidelines by e-mail.

Nonfiction Book excerpts, essays, exposé, historical/nostalgic, how-to, humor, inspirational, interview/profile, personal experience, photo feature, religious, travel. Does not want generic articles that could appear in any mass-market publication. Query with published clips or send complete ms. Length: 800-2,000 words. **Pays $200-1,600 for assigned articles; $100-800 for unsolicited articles.** Sometimes pays expenses of writers on assignment.

Photos Contact John Bullock, art director. State availability of or send photos with submission. Reviews 8×10 prints, JPEG files (8×10 at 300 dpi). Buys one-time rights. Negotiates payment individually. Identification of subjects required.

Columns/Departments A&E Art, 1,200-2,000 words; A&E Music, 1,200-2,000 words; A&E Books, 1,200-1,400 words. **Buys 12 mss/year.** Send complete ms. **Pays $200-400.**

Tips ''Unique local voices are key and a thorough knowledge of the area's history, politics and culture is invaluable.''

MONDAY MAGAZINE

Black Press Ltd., 818 Broughton St., Victoria BC V8W 1E4 Canada. E-mail: editorial@mondaymag.com. Web site: www.mondaymag.com. Editor: Alisa Gordaneer. Arts Editor: John Threlfall. **Contact:** Editor. **40% freelance written.** Weekly tabloid covering local news. "*Monday Magazine* is Victoria's only alternative newsweekly. For 30 years, we have published fresh, informative and alternative perspectives on local events. We prefer lively, concise writing with a sense of humor and insight." Estab. 1975. Circ. 40,000. Pays 1-2 months after publication. Publishes ms an average of 1 month after acceptance. Byline given. Buys first North American serial, second serial (reprint), electronic rights, makes work-for-hire assignments. Editorial lead time 1-2 months. Submit seasonal material 2 months in advance. Accepts queries by e-mail. Responds in 2-4 weeks to queries; up to 3 months to mss. Sample copy not available. Writer's guidelines free.

Nonfiction Exposé, general interest, humor, interview/profile, opinion, personal experience, technical, travel. Special issues: Body, Mind, Spirit (October); Student Survival Guide (August). Does not want fiction, poetry, or conspiracy theories. Query with published clips or send complete ms. Length: 300-2,000 words. **Pays $25-400.**

Photos Send photos with submission. Reviews GIF/JPEG files (300 dpi at 4×6). Buys one-time rights. Offers no additional payment for photos accepted with ms. Captions, identification of subjects required.

Tips "Local writers tend to have an advantage, as they are familiar with the issues and concerns of interest to a Victoria audience. However, we are interested in perspectives from elsewhere as well, especially on universal topics."

$ $ OUTDOOR CANADA MAGAZINE

25 Sheppard Ave. W., Suite 100, Toronto ON M2N 6S7 Canada. (416)733-7600. Fax: (416)227-8296. E-mail: editorial@outdoorcanada.ca. Web site: www.outdoorcanada.ca. **Contact:** Patrick Walsh, editor-in-chief. **90% freelance written.** Works with a small number of new/unpublished writers each year. Magazine published 8 times/year emphasizing hunting, fishing, and related pursuits in Canada *only*. Estab. 1972. Circ. 80,000. Pays on publication. Publishes ms an average of 8 months after acceptance. Byline given. Buys first rights. Submit seasonal material 1 year in advance. Accepts queries by mail, e-mail. Responds in 1 month to queries. Writer's guidelines online.

Nonfiction How-to, fishing, hunting, outdoor issues, outdoor destinations in Canada. **Buys 35-40 mss/year.** Query. Length: 2,500 words. **Pays $500 and up for assigned articles.**

Reprints Send information about when and where the article previously appeared. Payment varies.

Photos Emphasize people in the Canadian outdoors. Pays $100-250 for 35mm transparencies and $400/cover. Captions, model releases required.

Fillers Short news pieces. **Buys 30-40/year.** Length: 100-500 words. **Pays $50 and up.**

The online magazine carries original content not found in the print edition. Contact: Aaron Kylie, online editor.

$ $ $ $ TORONTO LIFE

111 Queen St. E., Suite 320, Toronto ON M5C 1S2 Canada. (416)364-3333. Fax: (416)861-1169. E-mail: editorial @torontolife.com. Web site: www.torontolife.com. **Contact:** John Macfarlane, editor. **95% freelance written.** Prefers to work with published/established writers. Monthly magazine emphasizing local issues and social trends, short humor/satire, and service features for upper income, well-educated and, for the most part, young Torontonians. Circ. 92,039. **Pays on acceptance.** Publishes ms an average of 4 months after acceptance. Byline given. Pays 50% kill fee for commissioned articles only. Buys first North American serial rights. Responds in 3 weeks to queries. Sample copy for $4.95 with SAE and IRCs.

Nonfiction Uses most types of articles. **Buys 17 mss/issue**. Query with published clips and SASE. Length: 1,000-6,000 words. **Pays $500-5,000.**

Columns/Departments Query with published clips and SASE. **Pays $2,000.**

Tips "Submissions should have strong Toronto orientation."

UP HERE

Explore Canada's Far North, Up Here Publishing, Ltd., P.O. Box 1350, Yellowknife NT X1A 2N9 Canada. (867)766-6710. Fax: (867)873-9876. E-mail: jake@uphere.ca. Web site: www.uphere.ca. **Contact:** Jake Kennedy, editor. **50% freelance written.** Magazine published 8 times/year covering general interest about Canada's Far North. "We publish features, columns, and shorts about people, wildlife, native cultures, travel, and adventure in Yukon, Northwest Territories, and Nunavut. Be informative, but entertaining." Estab. 1984. Circ. 30,000. Pays on publication. Byline given. Offers 50% kill fee. Buys first North American serial rights. Editorial lead time 6 months. Accepts queries by mail, e-mail, fax. Sample copy for $3.95 (Canadian) and 9×12 SASE.

Break in with "precise queries with well-developed focuses for the proposed story."

Nonfiction Essays, general interest, how-to, humor, interview/profile, personal experience, photo feature, tech-

Consumer Magazines

nical, travel, lifestyle/culture, historical. **Buys 25-30 mss/year.** Query. Length: 1,500-3,000 words. **Fees are negotiable.**

Photos "*Please* do not send unsolicited original photos, slides." Send photos with submission. Reviews transparencies, prints. Buys one-time rights. Captions, identification of subjects required.

Columns/Departments **Buys 25-30 mss/year.** Query with published clips.

$ $ $ VANCOUVER MAGAZINE

Transcontinental Publications, Inc., Suite 500, 2608 Granville St., Vancouver BC V6H 3V3 Canada. E-mail: mail@vancouvermagazine.com. Web site: www.vancouvermagazine.com. **Contact:** Matthew Mallon, editor. **70% freelance written.** Monthly magazine covering the city of Vancouver. Estab. 1967. Circ. 65,000. **Pays on acceptance.** Byline given. Offers negotiable kill fee. Buys first North American serial rights. Editorial lead time 2 months. Submit seasonal material 6 months in advance. Accepts queries by mail, e-mail, fax, phone. Accepts simultaneous submissions. Responds in 2 weeks to queries; 1 month to mss. Sample copy for $5. Writer's guidelines for #10 SASE or by e-mail.

Nonfiction "We prefer to work with writers from a conceptual stage and have a 6-week lead time. Most stories are under 1,500 words. Please be aware that we don't publish poetry and rarely publish fiction." Book excerpts, essays, historical/nostalgic, humor, interview/profile, new product, personal experience, photo feature, travel. **Buys 200 mss/year.** Query. Length: 200-3,000 words. **Pays 50¢/word.** Sometimes pays expenses of writers on assignment.

Photos State availability with submission. Reviews contact sheets, negatives, transparencies, prints, GIF/JPEG files. Buys negotiable rights. Negotiates payment individually. Captions, identification of subjects, model releases required.

Columns/Departments Sport; Media; Business; City Issues, all 1,500 words. Query. **Pays 50¢/word.**

Tips "Read back issues of the magazine, or visit our Web site. Almost all of our stories have a strong Vancouver angle. Submit queries by e-mail. Do not send complete stories."

RELATIONSHIPS

$ $ MARRIAGE PARTNERSHIP

Christianity Today International, 465 Gundersen Dr., Carol Stream IL 60188. Fax: (630)260-0114. E-mail: mp@marriagepartnership.com. Web site: www.marriagepartnership.com. **Contact:** Ginger E. Kolbaba, managing editor. **50% freelance written.** Quarterly magazine covering Christian marriages. "Our readers are married Christians. Writers must understand our readers." Estab. 1988. Circ. 55,000. **Pays on acceptance.** Publishes ms an average of 9 months after acceptance. Byline given. Offers 50% kill fee. Buys first North American serial rights. Editorial lead time 6 months. Submit seasonal material 1 year in advance. Accepts queries by mail, e-mail, fax. Responds in 10 weeks to queries; 2 months to mss. Sample copy for $5 or online. Writer's guidelines online.

- Does not accept unsolicited mss.

Nonfiction Book excerpts, essays, how-to, humor, inspirational, interview/profile, opinion, personal experience, religious. **Buys 20 mss/year.** Query with or without published clips. Length: 1,000-2,000 words. **Pays 15-30¢/word for assigned articles; 15¢/word for unsolicited articles.**

Columns/Departments Starting Out (opinion by/for newlyweds), 1,000 words; Soul to Soul (inspirational), 1,500 words; Work It Out (problem-solving), 1,000 words; Back from the Brink (marriage in recovery), 1,800 words. **Buys 10 mss/year.** Query with or without published clips. **Pays 15-30¢/word.**

Tips "Think of topics with a fresh slant. Be ever mindful of our readers. Writers who can communicate with freshness, clarity, and insight will receive serious consideration. We are looking for writers who are willing to candidly speak about their own marriages. We strongly urge writers who are interested in contributing to *Marriage Partnership* to read several issues to become thoroughly acquainted with our tone and slant."

RELIGIOUS

ALIVE NOW

1908 Grand Ave., P.O. Box 340004, Nashville TN 37203-0004. E-mail: alivenow@upperroom.org. Web site: www.alivenow.org. **Contact:** JoAnn Evans Miller. Bimonthly thematic magazine for a general Christian audience interested in reflection and meditation. Circ. 70,000. Writer's guidelines online.

Nonfiction Length: 250-500 words. **Pays $35 and up.**

Fiction Length: 250-500 words. **Pays $35 and up.**

Poetry Avant-garde, free verse. Length: 10-45 lines.

$ $ AMERICA

106 W. 56th St., New York NY 10019. (212)581-4640. Fax: (212)399-3596. E-mail: articles@americamagazine.org. Web site: www.americamagazine.org. **Contact:** The Rev. Drew Christiansen, editor. Published weekly for adult, educated, largely Roman Catholic audience. Estab. 1909. **Pays on acceptance.** Byline given. Buys all rights. Responds in 3 weeks to queries. Writer's guidelines online.

Nonfiction "We publish a wide variety of material on religion, politics, economics, ecology, and so forth. We are not a parochial publication, but almost all pieces make some moral or religious point." Articles on theology, spirituality, current political, social issues. "We are not interested in purely informational pieces or personal narratives which are self-contained and have no larger moral interest." Length: 1,500-2,000 words. **Pays $50-300.**

Poetry Only 10-12 poems published a year, thousands turned down. Contact: Rev. James S. Torrens, poetry editor. **Buys 10-12 poems/year.** Length: 15-30 lines.

$ THE ANNALS OF SAINT ANNE DE BEAUPRÉ

Redemptorist Fathers, P.O. Box 1000, St. Anne De Beaupré QC G0A 3C0 Canada. (418)827-4538. Fax: (418)827-4530. Editor: Father Bernard Mercier, C.Ss.R. **20% freelance written.** Releases 10 issues/year. religious magazine. "Our mission statement includes dedication to Christian family values and devotion to St. Anne." Estab. 1885. Circ. 32,000. **Pays on acceptance.** Buys first North American rights. "Please state rights for sale." Editorial lead time 6 months. Submit seasonal material 6 months in advance. Responds in 4-6 weeks to queries. Sample copy and writer's guidelines for 8½×11 SAE and IRCs.

- No e-mail or fax queries.

Nonfiction Inspirational, religious. **Buys 40 mss/year.** Send complete ms. Length: 500-1,250 words. **Pays 3-4¢/word, plus 3 copies.**

Fiction Religious. No senseless mockery or anti-Christian materials. **Buys 25 mss/year.** Send complete ms. Length: 500-1,250 words. **Pays 3-4¢/word, plus 3 copies.**

Tips "Write something uplifting and/or inspirational. Report-writing is simply not remarkable. We maintain an article bank of unsolicited manuscripts awaiting publication. It may take 5 or more years to see any new article in print."

AUSTRALIAN CATHOLICS

Australian Catholics, Ltd., P.O. Box 553, Richmond VIC 3121 Australia. (61)(3)9427-7311. Fax: (61)(3)9428-4450. E-mail: auscaths@jespub.jesuit.org.au. Web site: www.australiancatholics.com.au. **Contact:** Michael McVeigh, editor. Magazine published 5 times/year covering the faith and life of Australians. "*Australian Catholics* is aimed at all members of the Catholic community, especially young people and the families of students in Catholic schools." Writer's guidelines online.

Nonfiction Religious. Send complete ms. Length: 1,000 words. **Pays negotiable amount.**

Tips "We are looking for 'good news' stories."

$ $ BGC WORLD

Magazine of the Baptist General Conference, Baptist General Conference, 2002 S. Arlington Heights Rd., Arlington Heights IL 60005. Fax: (847)228-5376. E-mail: bputman@baptistgeneral.org. Web site: www.bgcworld.org. **Contact:** Bob Putman, editor. **35% freelance written.** Nonprofit, religious, evangelical Christian magazine published 10 times/year covering the Baptist General Conference. "*BGC-WORLD* is the official magazine of the Baptist General Conference (BGC). Articles related to the BGC, our churches, or by/about BGC people receive preference." Circ. 46,000. Pays on publication. Byline given. Offers 50% kill fee. Buys first rights. Editorial lead time 6 months. Submit seasonal material 6 months in advance. Accepts queries by e-mail. Responds in 1 month to queries; 3 months to mss. Sample copy for #10 SASE. Writer's guidelines, theme list free.

Nonfiction General interest, photo feature, religious, profile, infographics, sidebars related to theme. No sappy religious pieces, articles not intended for our audience. Ask for a sample instead of sending anything first. **Buys 20-30 mss/year.** Query with published clips. Length: 300-1,500 words. **Pays $60-280.** Sometimes pays expenses of writers on assignment.

Photos State availability with submission. Reviews prints, some high-resolution digital. Buys one-time rights. Offers $15-60/photo. Captions, identification of subjects, model releases required.

Columns/Departments Around BGC (blurbs of news happening in the BGC), 50-150 words. Send complete ms. **Pays $15-20.**

Tips "Please study the magazine and the denomination. We will send sample copies to interested freelancers and give further information about our publication needs upon request. Freelancers who are interested in working on assignment are welcome to express their interest."

$$ CATHOLIC DIGEST

P.O. Box 6015, 1 Montauk Ave., Suite 200, New London CT 06320. (800)321-0411. Fax: (860)457-3013. E-mail: cdsubmissions@bayard-inc.com. Web site: www.catholicdigest.com. Editor: Daniel Connors. **Contact:** Articles Editor. **12% freelance written.** Monthly magazine. "Publishes features and advice on topics ranging from health, psychology, humor, adventure, and family, to ethics, spirituality, and Catholics, from modern-day heroes to saints through the ages. Helpful and relevant reading culled from secular and religious periodicals." Estab. 1936. Circ. 275,000. Pays on publication. Byline given. Buys first, one-time, second serial (reprint) rights. Editorial lead time 3 months. Submit seasonal material 5 months in advance. Accepts queries by mail, e-mail. Responds in 2 months to mss. Sample copy free.

Nonfiction "Most articles we use are reprinted." Book excerpts, essays, general interest, historical/nostalgic, how-to, humor, inspirational, interview/profile, personal experience, religious, travel. Send complete ms. Length: 750-2,000 words. **Pays $200-400.**

Reprints Send tearsheet or typed ms with rights for sale noted and information about when and where the material previously appeared. Pays $100.

Photos State availability with submission. Reviews contact sheets, transparencies, prints. Negotiates payment individually. Captions, identification of subjects, model releases required.

Fillers Filler Editor. Open Door (statements of true incidents through which people are brought into the Catholic faith, or recover the Catholic faith they had lost), 200-320 words. Also publishes jokes, short anecdotes, and factoids. Finder fees given, depending on length of submission. **Buys 200/year.** Length: 1 line minimum, 500 words maximum. **Pays $2/per published line (full page width) upon publication.**

Tips "Spiritual, self-help, and all wellness is a good bet for us. We would also like to see material with an innovative approach to daily living, articles that show new ways of looking at old ideas, problems. You've got to dig beneath the surface."

$$ CATHOLIC FORESTER

Catholic Order of Foresters, 355 Shuman Blvd., P.O. Box 3012, Naperville IL 60566-7012. Fax: (630)983-3384. E-mail: magazine@catholicforester.com. Web site: www.catholicforester.com. **Contact:** Mary Ann File, editor. **20% freelance written.** Quarterly magazine for members of the Catholic Order of Foresters, a fraternal insurance benefit society. *Catholic Forester* articles cover varied topics to create a balanced issue for the purpose of informing, educating, and entertaining our readers. Circ. 100,000. **Pays on acceptance.** Buys first North American serial rights. Editorial lead time 6 months. Submit seasonal material 6 months in advance. Responds in 3 months to mss. Sample copy for 9×12 SAE and 4 first-class stamps. Writer's guidelines online.

Nonfiction Inspirational, religious, travel, health, parenting, financial, money management, humor. **Buys 12-16 mss/year.** Send complete ms by mail, fax, or e-mail. Rejected material will not be returned without accompanying SASE. Length: 500-1,500 words. **Pays 30¢/word.**

Photos State availability with submission. Buys one-time rights. Negotiates payment individually.

Fiction Humorous, religious. **Buys 12-16 mss/year.** Length: 500-1,500 words. **Pays 30¢/word.**

Poetry Light verse, traditional. **Buys 3 poems/year.** Length: 15 lines maximum. **Pays 30¢/word.**

Tips "Our audience includes a broad age spectrum, ranging from youth to seniors. Nonfiction topics that appeal to our members include health and wellness, money management and budgeting, parenting and family life, interesting travels, insurance, nostalgia, and humor. A good children's story with a positive lesson or message would rate high on our list."

$$$ CHARISMA & CHRISTIAN LIFE

The Magazine About Spirit-Led Living, Strang Communications Co., 600 Rinehart Rd., Lake Mary FL 32746. (407)333-0600. Fax: (407)333-7133. E-mail: charisma@strang.com. Web site: www.charismamag.com. Editor: J. Lee Grady. Managing Editor: Jimmy Stewart. **Contact:** Adrienne Gaines, associate editor. **80% freelance written.** Monthly magazine covering items of interest to the Pentecostal or independent charismatic reader. "More than half of our readers are Christians who belong to Pentecostal or independent charismatic churches, and numerous others participate in the charismatic renewal in mainline denominations." Estab. 1975. Circ. 250,000. Pays on publication. Publishes ms an average of 3 months after acceptance. Byline given. Offers $50 kill fee. Buys all rights. Editorial lead time 4 months. Submit seasonal material 5 months in advance. Accepts queries by mail, e-mail. Sample copy for free. Writer's guidelines by e-mail.

Nonfiction Andy Butcher, senior writer. Book excerpts, exposé, general interest, interview/profile, religious. No fiction, poetry, columns/departments, or sermons. **Buys 40 mss/year.** Query. Length: 2,000-3,000 words. **Pays $1,000 (maximum) for assigned articles.** Pays expenses of writers on assignment.

Photos Rachel Campbell. State availability with submission. Reviews contact sheets, $2\frac{1}{4} \times 2\frac{1}{4}$ transparencies, 3×5 or larger prints, GIF/JPEG files. Buys one-time rights. Negotiates payment individually. Model releases required.

Tips "Be especially on the lookout for news stories, trend articles, or interesting personality profiles that relate specifically to the Christian reader."

$ $ THE CHRISTIAN CENTURY

104 S. Michigan Ave., Suite 700, Chicago IL 60603-5901. (312)263-7510. Fax: (312)263-7540. E-mail: main@christiancentury.org. Web site: www.christiancentury.org. **Contact:** David Heim, executive editor. **90% freelance written.** Works with new/unpublished writers. Biweekly magazine for ecumenically-minded, progressive Protestant church people, both clergy and lay. "Authors must have a critical and analytical perspective on the church and be familiar with contemporary theological discussion." Estab. 1884. Circ. 30,000. Pays on publication. Byline given. Buys all rights. Editorial lead time 1 month. Submit seasonal material 4 months in advance. Accepts queries by mail, e-mail. Responds in 1 week to queries; 3 months to mss. Sample copy for $3. Writer's guidelines online.

Nonfiction "We use articles dealing with social problems, ethical dilemmas, political issues, international affairs, and the arts, as well as with theological and ecclesiastical matters. We focus on issues of church and society, and church and culture." Essays, humor, interview/profile, opinion, religious. No inspirational. **Buys 150 mss/year.** Send complete ms; query appreciated, but not essential. Length: 1,000-3,000 words. **Pays variable amount for assigned articles; $75-150 for unsolicited articles.**

Photos State availability with submission. Reviews any size prints. Buys one-time rights. Offers $25-100/photo.

Fiction Humorous, religious, slice-of-life vignettes. No moralistic, unrealistic fiction. Send complete ms. Length: 1,000-3,000 words. **Pays $75-200.**

Poetry Jill Pelàez Baumgaertner, poetry editor. Avant-garde, free verse, haiku, traditional. No sentimental or didactic poetry. **Buys 50 poems/year.** Length: 20 lines. **Pays $50.**

Tips "We seek manuscripts that articulate the public meaning of faith, bringing the resources of Christian tradition to bear on such topics as poverty, human rights, economic justice, international relations, national priorities, and popular culture. We are equally interested in articles that probe classical theological themes. We welcome articles that find fresh meaning in old traditions and which adapt or apply religious traditions to new circumstances. Authors should assume that readers are familiar with main themes in Christian history and theology; are not threatened by the historical-critical study of the Bible; and are already engaged in relating faith to social and political issues. Many of our readers are ministers or teachers of religion at the college level."

$ $ CHRISTIAN HOME & SCHOOL

Christian Schools International, 3350 E. Paris Ave. SE, Grand Rapids MI 49512. (616)957-1070, ext. 239. Fax: (616)957-5022. E-mail: rogers@csionline.org. Executive Editor: Gordon L. Bordewyk. **Contact:** Roger Schmurr, senior editor. **30% freelance written.** Works with a small number of new/unpublished writers each year. Magazine published 4 times/year during the school year covering family life and Christian education. "*Christian Home & School* is designed for parents in the United States and Canada who send their children to Christian schools and are concerned about the challenges facing Christian families today. These readers expect a mature, Biblical perspective in the articles, not just a Bible verse tacked onto the end." Estab. 1922. Circ. 67,000. Pays on publication. Publishes ms an average of 4 months after acceptance. Byline given. Buys first North American serial rights. Submit seasonal material 4 months in advance. Accepts queries by mail, e-mail. Responds in 1 month to queries. Sample copy and writer's guidelines for 9×12 SAE with 4 first-class stamps. Writer's guidelines only for #10 SASE or online.

- The editor reports an interest in seeing articles on how to experience and express forgiveness in your home, make summer interesting and fun for your kids, help your child make good choices, and raise kids who are opposites, and promote good educational practices in Christian schools.

O┑ Break in by picking a contemporary parenting situation/problem and writing to Christian parents.

Nonfiction "We publish features on issues that affect the home and school." Book excerpts, interview/profile, opinion, personal experience, articles on parenting and school life. **Buys 30 mss/year.** Send complete ms. Length: 1,000-2,000 words. **Pays $175-250.**

Tips "Features are the area most open to freelancers. We are publishing articles that deal with contemporary issues that affect parents. Use an informal easy-to-read style rather than a philosophical, academic tone. Try to incorporate vivid imagery and concrete, practical examples from real life. We look for manuscripts with a mature Christian perspective."

N ⊘ CHRISTIAN NEWS NORTHWEST

P.O. Box 974, Newberg OR 97132. Web site: www.cnnw.com.

- *Chiristan News Northwest* does not need freelance writers.

$ $ CHRISTIAN RESEARCH JOURNAL

30162 Tomas, Suite 101, Rancho Santa Margarita CA 92688-2124. (949)858-6100. Fax: (949)858-6111. E-mail: submissions@equip.org. Web site: www.equip.org. Managing Editor: Melanie Cogdill. **Contact:** Elliot Miller, editor-in-chief. **75% freelance written.** Quarterly magazine. "The *Journal* is an apologetics magazine probing today's religious movements, promoting doctrinal discernment and critical thinking, and providing reasons for Christian faith and ethics." Pays on publication. Publishes ms an average of 3 months after acceptance. Byline given. Offers 50% kill fee. Buys first rights. Submit seasonal material 4 months in advance. Accepts queries by mail, e-mail. Accepts simultaneous submissions. Responds in 4 months to queries; 4 months to mss. Sample copy for $6. Writer's guidelines by e-mail at guidelines@equip.org.

Nonfiction Opinion (religious viewpoint), religious, ethics, book reviews, features on cults, witnessing tips. No fiction or general Christian living topics. Query with or without published clips or send complete ms.

Columns/Departments Features, 4,500 words; Effective Evangelism, 1,700 words; Viewpoint, 875 words; News Watch, 2,500 words. Query with or without published clips or send complete ms.

Tips "We are most open to features on cults, apologetics, Christian discernment, ethics, book reviews, opinion pieces, and witnessing tips. Be familiar with the *Journal* in order to know what we are looking for."

$ $ CHRISTIANITY TODAY

465 Gundersen Dr., Carol Stream IL 60188-2498. (630)260-6200. Fax: (630)260-8428. E-mail: cteditor@christianitytoday.com. Web site: www.christianitytoday.com. **80% freelance written, but mostly assigned**. Works with a small number of new/unpublished writers each year. Monthly magazine. *Christianity Today* believes that the vitality of the American church depends on its adhering to and applying the biblical teaching as it meets today's challenges. It attempts to biblically assess people, events, and ideas that shape evangelical life, thought, and mission. It employs analytical reporting, commentary, doctrinal essays, interviews, cultural reviews, and the occasional realistic narrative." Estab. 1956. Circ. 154,000. Publishes ms an average of 6 months after acceptance. Buys first rights. Submit seasonal material at least 8 months in advance. Accepts queries by mail, e-mail, fax. Responds in 3 months to queries. Sample copy and writer's guidelines for 9×12 SAE with 3 first-class stamps.

Nonfiction Buys 20 unsolicited mss/year. Query. Length: 1,200-5,200 words. **Pays 25-35¢/word.** Sometimes pays expenses of writers on assignment.

Reprints Rarely accepts previously published submissions. Pays 25% of amount paid for an original article.

Columns/Departments The CT Review (books, the arts, and popular culture). Length: 700-1,500 words. **Buys 6 mss/year.** Query only.

The online magazine carries original content not found in the print edition.

Tips "We are developing more of our own manuscripts and requiring a much more professional quality from others. By query only; e-mail preferred."

$ $ CONSCIENCE

The Newsjournal of Catholic Opinion, Catholics for a Free Choice, 1436 U St. NW, Suite 301, Washington DC 20009-3997. (202)986-6093. E-mail: conscience@catholicsforchoice.org. Web site: www.catholicsforchoice.org. **Contact:** David J. Nolan, editor. **60% freelance written.** Sometimes works with new/unpublished writers. Quarterly newsjournal covering reproductive health and rights including, but not limited to, abortion rights in the church, and church-state issues in US and worldwide. "A feminist, pro-choice perspective is a must, and knowledge of Christianity and specifically Catholicism is helpful." Estab. 1980. Circ. 12,000. Pays on publication. Publishes ms an average of 2 months after acceptance. Byline given. Buys first North American serial rights, makes work-for-hire assignments. Accepts queries by mail, e-mail. Responds in 4 months to queries. Sample copy for 9×12 SAE and 4 first-class stamps. Writer's guidelines for #10 SASE.

Nonfiction Especially needs material that recognizes the complexity of reproductive issues and decisions, and offers original, honest insight. "Writers should be aware that we are a nonprofit organization." Book excerpts, interview/profile, opinion, personal experience (a small amount), issue analysis. **Buys 4-8 mss/year.** Query with published clips or send complete ms. Length: 1,500-3,500 words. **Pays $200 negotiable.**

Reprints Send ms with rights for sale noted and information about when and where the material previously appeared. Pays 20-30% of amount paid for an original article.

Photos Prefers b&w prints. State availability with submission. Identification of subjects required.

Columns/Departments Book Reviews, 600-1,200 words. **Buys 4-8 mss/year. Pays $75.**

Tips "Say something new on the issue of abortion, or sexuality, or the role of religion or the Catholic church, or women's status in the church. Thoughtful, well-researched, and well-argued articles needed. The most frequent mistakes made by writers in submitting an article to us are lack of originality and wordiness."

$ $ DECISION

Billy Graham Evangelistic Association, 1 Billy Graham Parkway, Charlotte NC 28201. (704)401-2432. Fax: (704)401-3009. E-mail: submissions@bgea.org. Web site: www.decisionmag.org. **Contact:** Bob Paulson, managing editor. **5% freelance written.** Works each year with small number of new/unpublished writers. Magazine published 11 times/year with a mission "to extend the ministry of Billy Graham Evangelistic Association; to communicate the Good News of Jesus Christ in such a way that readers will be drawn to make a commitment to Christ; and to encourage, strengthen and equip Christians in evangelism and discipleship." Estab. 1960. Circ. 800,000. Pays on publication. Publishes ms an average of up to 18 months after acceptance. Byline given. Offers 50% kill fee. Buys first rights. Assigns work-for-hire mss, articles, projects. Editorial lead time 6 months. Submit seasonal material 6 months in advance. Sample copy for 9×12 SAE and 4 first-class stamps. Writer's guidelines online.

- Include telephone number with submission.

O‑ "The best way to break in to our publication is to submit an article that has some connection to the Billy Graham Evangelistic Association or Samaritan's Purse, but also has strong takeaway for the personal lives of the readers."

Nonfiction Personal experience, testimony. **Buys approximately 8 mss/year.** Send complete ms. Length: 400-1,500 words. **Pays $200-400.** Pays expenses of writers on assignment.
Photos State availability with submission. Reviews prints. Buys one-time rights. Captions, identification of subjects, model releases required.
Columns/Departments Finding Jesus (people who have become Christians through Billy Graham Ministries), 500-600 words. **Buys 11 mss/year.** Send complete ms. **Pays $200.**
Poetry Amanda Knoke, assistant editor. Free verse, light verse, traditional. **Buys 6 poems/year.** Submit maximum 7 poems. Length: 4-16 lines. **Pays $1/word.**
Tips "Articles should have some connection to the ministry of Billy Graham or Franklin Graham. For example, you may have volunteered in one of these ministries or been touched by them. The article does not need to be entirely about that connection, but it should at least mention the connection. Testimonies and personal experience articles should show how God intervened in your life and how you have been transformed by God. SASE required with submissions."

DEVO'ZINE

Just for Teens, 1908 Grand Ave., P.O. Box 340004, Nashville TN 37203-0004. (615)340-7247. Fax: (615)340-1783. E-mail: smiller@upperroom.org. Web site: www.devozine.org. Editor: Sandy Miller. Bimonthly magazine for youth ages 12-18. Offers meditations, scripture, prayers, poems, stories, songs, and feature articles to "aid youth in their prayer life, introduce them to spiritual disciplines, help them shape their concept of God, and encourage them in the life of discipleship." Writer's guidelines online.
Nonfiction General interest, inspirational, personal experience, religious, devotional.
Poetry Length: 20 lines.

$ $ DISCIPLESHIP JOURNAL

NavPress, a division of The Navigators, P.O. Box 35004, Colorado Springs CO 80935-0004. (719)548-9222. Fax: (719)598-7128. E-mail: dj.writers@navpress.com. Web site: www.discipleshipjournal.com. **Contact:** Sue Kline, editor. **90% freelance written.** Works with a small number of new/unpublished writers each year. Bimonthly magazine. "The mission of *Discipleship Journal* is to help believers develop a deeper relationship with Jesus Christ, and to provide practical help in understanding the scriptures and applying them to daily life and ministry. We prefer those who have not written for us before to begin with nontheme articles about almost any aspect of Christian living. We'd like more articles that explain a Bible passage and show how to apply it to everyday life, as well as articles about developing a relationship with Jesus; reaching the world; growing in some aspect of Christian character; or specific issues related to leadership and helping other believers grow." Estab. 1981. Circ. 100,000. **Pays on acceptance.** Publishes ms an average of 8-12 months after acceptance. Byline given. Buys first North American serial, second serial (reprint), electronic rights. Submit seasonal material 9 months in advance. Accepts queries by mail, e-mail, fax. Responds in 6-8 weeks to queries. Sample copy for $2.56 and 9×12 SAE or online. Writer's guidelines online.

O‑ Break in through departments (DJ Plus guidelines available online) and with nontheme feature articles.

Nonfiction Book excerpts (rarely), how-to (grow in Christian faith and disciplines; help others grow as Christians; serve people in need; understand and apply the Bible), inspirational, interpretation/application of the Bible. No personal testimony; humor; poetry; anything not directly related to Christian life and faith; politically partisan articles; purely theological material; Bible studies; personal profiles. **Buys 80 mss/year.** Query with published clips and SASE only. Length: 500-2,500 words. **Pays 25¢/word for first rights.** Sometimes pays expenses of writers on assignment.
Reprints Send tearsheet and information about when and where the material previously appeared. Pays 5¢/word for reprints.
Tips "Our articles are meaty, not fluffy. Study writer's guidelines and back issues and try to use similar approaches. Don't preach. Polish before submitting. We are looking for more practical articles on ministering to others and more articles on growing in Christian character. Be vulnerable. Show the reader that you have wrestled with the subject matter in your own life. Use personal illustrations. We can no longer accept unsolicited manuscripts. Query first."

$ $ DISCIPLESWORLD

A Journal of News, Opinion, and Mission for the Christian Church, DisciplesWorld, Inc., 6235 N. Guilford Ave., Suite 213, Indianapolis IN 46220. (317)375-8846. Fax: (317)375-8849. E-mail: editor@disciplesworld.com. Web site: www.disciplesworld.com. **75% freelance written.** Monthly magazine covering faith issues, especially those with a "Disciples slant. We are the journal of the Christian Church (Disciples of Christ) in North America. Our denomination numbers roughly 800,000. Disciples are a mainline Protestant group. Our readers are mostly laity, active in their churches, and interested in issues of faithful living, political and church news, ethics, and contemporary social issues." Estab. 2002. Circ. 14,000. Pays on publication. Publishes ms an average of 6 months after acceptance. Byline given. Buys first North American serial rights. Editorial lead time 3 months. Submit seasonal material 3 months in advance. Accepts queries by mail, e-mail. Accepts simultaneous submissions. Responds in 2 weeks to queries; 2 months to mss. Sample copy for #10 SASE. Writer's guidelines online.

Nonfiction Essays, general interest, inspirational, interview/profile, opinion, personal experience, religious. Does not want preachy or didactic articles. "Our style is conversational rather than academic." **Buys 40 mss/year.** Query with or without published clips or send complete ms. Length: 400-1,500 words. **Pays $100-300 for assigned articles; $25-300 for unsolicited articles.** Sometimes pays expenses of writers on assignment.

Photos Send photos with submission. Buys one-time rights. Negotiates payment individually. Identification of subjects, model releases required.

Columns/Departments Browsing the Bible (short reflections on the applicability of books of the Bible), 500 words; Speak Out (opinion pieces about issues facing the church), 700 words. **Buys 12-15 mss/year.** Send complete ms. **Pays $100.**

Fiction Ethnic, mainstream, novel excerpts, religious, serialized novels, slice-of-life vignettes. "We're a religious publication, so use common sense! Stories do not have to be overtly 'religious,' but they should be uplifting and positive." **Buys 8-10 mss/year.** Send complete ms. Length: 700-1,500 words. **16¢/word.**

Poetry Free verse, light verse, traditional. **Buys 6-10 poems/year.** Submit maximum 3 poems. Length: 30 maximum lines.

Fillers Anecdotes, short humor. **Buys 20/year.** Length: 25-400 words. **Pays $0-100.**

Tips "Send a well-written (and well-proofed!) query explaining what you would like to write about and why you are the person to do it. Write about what you're passionate about. We are especially interested in social justice issues, and we like our writers to take a reasoned and well-argued stand."

N $ DOVETAIL

A Journal By and For Jewish/Christian Families, Dovetail Institute for Interfaith Family Resources, 775 Simon Greenwell Lane, Boston KY 40107. (502)549-5499. Fax: (502)549-3543. E-mail: di-ifr@bardstown.com. Web site: www.dovetailinstitute.org. **Contact:** Mary Rosenbaum, editor. **75% freelance written.** Quarterly newsletter for interfaith families. "All articles must pertain to life in an interfaith (primarily Jewish/Christian) family. We are broadening our scope to include other sorts of interfaith mixes. We accept all kinds of opinions related to this topic." Estab. 1992. Circ. 1,500. Pays on publication. Publishes ms an average of 9 months after acceptance. Byline given. Buys first, one-time, second serial (reprint) rights. Editorial lead time 6 months. Submit seasonal material 6 months in advance. Accepts queries by mail, e-mail, fax, phone. Accepts previously published material. Accepts simultaneous submissions. Responds in 3 months to queries. Sample copy and writer's guidelines online.

O━ Break in with "a fresh approach to standard interfaith marriage situations."

Nonfiction Book reviews, 500 words. **Pays $15, plus 2 copies**. Book excerpts, interview/profile, opinion, personal experience. No fiction. **Buys 5-8 mss/year.** Send complete ms. Length: 800-1,000 words. **Pays $25, plus 2 copies.**

Photos Send photos with submission. Reviews 5×7 prints. Buys one-time rights. Offers no additional payment for photos accepted with ms. Identification of subjects, model releases required.

Tips "Write on concrete, specific topics related to Jewish/Christian or other dual-faith intermarriage: no proselytizing, sermonizing, or general religious commentary. Successful freelancers are part of an interfaith family themselves, or have done solid research/interviews with members of interfaith families. We look for honest, reflective personal experience. We're looking for more on alternative or nontraditional families, e.g., interfaith gay/lesbian, single parent raising child in departed partner's faith."

$ $ EFCA TODAY

Evangelical Free Church of America, 418 Fourth St., NE, Charlottesville VA 22902. E-mail: dianemc@journeygroup.com. Web site: www.efca.org/today. **Contact:** Diane J. McDougall, editor. **30% freelance written.** Quarterly magazine. "*EFCA Today* informs readers of the vision and activities of the Evangelical Free Church of America. Its readers are EFCA leaders—pastors, elders, deacons, Sunday-school teachers, ministry volunteers." Estab. 1931. Circ. 44,000. **Pays on acceptance.** Publishes ms an average of 3 months after acceptance. Byline given. Offers 50% kill fee. Buys first North American serial, electronic, efca-related church use (if free) rights, makes work-for-hire assignments. Editorial lead time 5 months. Submit seasonal material 6 months in advance. Accepts queries by mail, e-mail. Accepts previously published material. Accepts simultaneous submissions. Sample copy for $1 with SAE and 5 first-class stamps. Writer's guidelines free.

Nonfiction Interview/profile, religious. No general-interest "inspirational" articles. Send complete ms. Length: 200-1,100 words. **Pays $75-325 for assigned articles; $46-250 for unsolicited articles.** Sometimes pays expenses of writers on assignment.

Columns/Departments On the Radar (significant trends/news of EFCA), 200-700 words; Breakthrough (innovative outreaches and practices of the EFCA); Impressions (thoughts from EFCA leaders); Among All People (celebration of EFCA diversity); Across the Movement (stories of God at work in the EFCA); all 500-1,000 words. Send complete ms. **Pays $46-250.**

$ $ ENRICHMENT

The General Council of the Assemblies of God, 1445 N. Boonville Ave., Springfield MO 65802. (417)862-2781. Fax: (417)862-0416. E-mail: enrichmentjournal@ag.org. Web site: www.enrichmentjournal.ag.org. Executive Editor: Gary Allen. **Contact:** Rick Knoth, managing editor. **15% freelance written.** Quarterly journal covering church leadership and ministry. "*Enrichment* offers enriching and encouraging information to equip and empower spirit-filled leaders." Circ. 33,000. Pays on publication. Publishes ms an average of 1 year after acceptance. Byline given. Buys first rights. Editorial lead time 18 months. Submit seasonal material 18 months in advance. Accepts queries by mail, e-mail, fax, phone. Sample copy for $7. Writer's guidelines free.

Nonfiction Religious. Query with or without published clips or send complete ms. Length: 1,000-3,000 words. **Pays up to 10¢/word.**

$ THE EVANGELICAL BAPTIST

Fellowship of Evangelical Baptist Churches in Canada, 18 Louvigny, Lorraine QC J6Z 1T7 Canada. (450)621-3248. Fax: (450)621-0253. E-mail: eb@fellowship.ca. Web site: www.fellowship.ca. **Contact:** Ginette Cotnoir, managing editor. **10% freelance written.** Magazine published 4 times/year covering religious, spiritual, Christian living, denominational, and missionary news. "We exist to enhance the life and ministry of the church leaders and members in Fellowship Congregations." Estab. 1953. Circ. 3,000. Pays on publication. Publishes ms an average of 6 months after acceptance. Byline given. Buys one-time, second serial (reprint) rights. Editorial lead time 4 months. Accepts queries by e-mail. Accepts previously published material. Accepts simultaneous submissions. Sample copy and writer's guidelines online.

Nonfiction Religious. No poetry, fiction, puzzles. **Buys 4-6 mss/year.** Send complete ms. Length: 500-900 words. **Pays $50.**

$ EVANGELICAL MISSIONS QUARTERLY

A Professional Journal Serving the Missions Community, Billy Graham Center/Wheaton College, P.O. Box 794, Wheaton IL 60189. (630)752-7158. Fax: (630)752-7155. E-mail: emqjournal@aol.com. Web site: www.billygrahamcenter.org/emis. Editor: A. Scott Moreau. **Contact:** Managing Editor. **67% freelance written.** Quarterly magazine covering evangelical missions. "This is a professional journal for evangelical missionaries, agency executives, and church members who support global missions ministries." Estab. 1964. Circ. 7,000. Pays on publication. Publishes ms an average of 18 months after acceptance. Byline given. Offers negotiable kill fee. Buys electronic, all rights. Editorial lead time 1 year. Accepts queries by mail, e-mail, fax, phone. Responds in 2 weeks to queries. Sample copy free. Writer's guidelines online.

Nonfiction Essays, interview/profile, opinion, personal experience, religious. No sermons, poetry, straight news. **Buys 24 mss/year.** Query. Length: 800-3,000 words. **Pays $50-100.**

Photos Send photos with submission. Buys first rights. Offers no additional payment for photos accepted with ms. Identification of subjects required.

Columns/Departments In the Workshop (practical how to's), 800-2,000 words; Perspectives (opinion), 800 words. **Buys 8 mss/year.** Query. **Pays $50-100.**

N $ $ EVANGELIZING TODAY'S CHILD

Child Evangelism Fellowship, Inc., Box 348, Warrenton MO 63383-0348. (636)456-4321. Fax: (636)456-4321. E-mail: etceditor@cefonline.com. Web site: www.cefonline.com/etcmag. **Contact:** Elsie Lippy, editor. **50% freelance written.** Bimonthly magazine. "Our purpose is to equip Christians to win the world's children to Christ and disciple them. Our readership is Sunday school teachers, Christian education leaders, and children's workers in every phase of Christian ministry to children 4-12 years old." Estab. 1942. Circ. 12,000. Pays within 2 months of acceptance. Publishes ms an average of 6 months after acceptance. Byline given. Offers kill fee if assigned. Buys first North American serial, electronic rights. Submit seasonal material 6 months in advance. Accepts queries by mail, e-mail. Responds in 1 month to queries. Sample copy for $2. Writer's guidelines online.

Nonfiction Unsolicited articles welcomed from writers with Christian education training or current experience in working with children. **Buys 50 mss/year.** Query. Length: 900 words. **Pays 12-15¢/word.**

Reprints Send photocopy and information about when and where the material previously appeared. Pays 35% of amount paid for an original article.

N $ $ FAITH & FRIENDS

Inspiration for Living, The Salvation Army, 2 Overlea Blvd., Toronto ON M4H 1P4 Canada. (416)422-6226. Fax: (416)422-6120. E-mail: faithandfriends@can.salvationarmy.org. Web site: www.faithandfriends.ca. Editor: Ray Moulton. **Contact:** Geoff Moulton, senior editor. **25% freelance written.** Monthly magazine covering Christian living and religion. "Our mission statement: to show Jesus Christ at work in the lives of real people, and to provide spiritual resources for those who are new to the Christian faith." Estab. 1996. Circ. 43,000. **Pays on acceptance.** Publishes ms an average of 3 months after acceptance. Byline given. Offers $50 kill fee. Buys first, electronic rights. Editorial lead time 2 months. Submit seasonal material 6 months in advance. Accepts queries by mail, e-mail. Accepts previously published material. Responds in 1 week to queries; 1 month to mss. Sample copy online. Writer's guidelines by e-mail.

Nonfiction Book excerpts, humor, inspirational, interview/profile, personal experience, photo feature, religious, travel. Does not want sermons, devotionals, or "Christian-ese." **Buys 12-18 mss/year.** Query. Length: 500-1,250 words. **Pays $50-200.**

Photos Send photos with submission. Reviews prints, GIF/JPEG files. Buys one-time rights. Negotiates payment individually. Captions required.

Columns/Departments God in My Life (how life changed by accepting Jesus); Someone Cares (how life changed through someone's intervention), 750 words. **Buys 12-18 mss/year.** Query. **Pays $50.**

$ $ FAITH TODAY

To Connect, Equip and Inform Evangelical Christians in Canada, Evangelical Fellowship of Canada, MIP Box 3745, Markham ON L3R 0Y4 Canada. (905)479-5885. Fax: (905)479-4742. E-mail: fteditor@efc-canada.com. Web site: www.faithtoday.ca. Bimonthly magazine. "*FT* is the magazine of an association of more than 40 evangelical denominations, but serves evangelicals in all denominations. It focuses on church issues, social issues and personal faith as they are tied to the Canadian context. Writing should explicitly acknowledge that Canadian evangelical context." Estab. 1983. Circ. 18,000. Pays on publication. Publishes ms an average of 4 months after acceptance. Byline given. Offers 30-50% kill fee. Buys first rights. Editorial lead time 4 months. Accepts queries by mail, e-mail, fax. Responds in 6 weeks to queries. Sample copy for SASE in Canadian postage. Writer's guidelines online.

- Break in by "researching the Canadian field and including in your query a list of the Canadian contacts (Christian or not) that you intend to interview."

Nonfiction Book excerpts (Canadian authors only), essays (Canadian authors only), interview/profile (Canadian subjects only), opinion, religious, news feature. **Buys 75 mss/year.** Query. Length: 400-2,000 words. **Pays $100-500 Canadian.** Sometimes pays expenses of writers on assignment.

Reprints Send photocopy. Rarely used. Pays 50% of amount paid for an original article.

Photos State availability with submission. Reviews contact sheets. Buys one-time rights. Identification of subjects (except for concept/stock photos) required.

Tips "Query should include brief outline and names of the sources you plan to interview in your research. Use Canadian postage on SASE."

$ FORWARD IN CHRIST

The Word from the WELS, WELS, 2929 N. Mayfair Rd., Milwaukee WI 53222-4398. (414)256-3210. Fax: (414)256-3862. E-mail: fic@sab.wels.net. Web site: www.wels.net. **Contact:** John A. Braun, executive editor. **5% freelance written.** Monthly magazine covering WELS news, topics, issues. The material usually must be written by or about WELS members. Estab. 1913. Circ. 56,000. Pays on publication. Publishes ms an average of 6 months after acceptance. Byline given. Buys one-time rights. Editorial lead time 3 months. Submit seasonal material 4 months in advance. Accepts queries by mail, e-mail, fax. Responds in 2 months to queries. Sample copy and writer's guidelines free.

Nonfiction Personal experience, religious. Query. Length: 550-1,200 words. **Pays $75/page, $125/2 pages.** Sometimes pays expenses of writers on assignment.

Photos State availability with submission. Reviews contact sheets. Buys one-time rights, plus 1 month on Web and in archive. Negotiates payment individually. Captions, identification of subjects, model releases required.

Tips "Topics should be of interest to the majority of the members of the synod—the people in the pews. Articles should have a Christian viewpoint, but we don't want sermons. We suggest you carefully read at least 5 or 6 issues with close attention to the length, content, and style of the features."

FOURSQUARE WORLD ADVANCE

International Church of the Foursquare Gospel, 1910 W. Sunset Blvd., Suite 400, Los Angeles CA 90026. E-mail: bshepson@foursquare.org. Web site: www.advancemagazine.org. **Contact:** Bill Shepson, editorial director. **90% freelance written.** Quarterly magazine covering devotional/religious material, news, book and product reviews. "The official publication of the International Church of the Foursquare Gospel is distributed without charge to members and friends of the Foursquare Church." Estab. 1917. Circ. 98,000. Pays on publication. Buys all rights. Accepts queries by mail, e-mail. Accepts previously published material. Responds in 2 weeks to queries. Sample copy for free. Writer's guidelines online.

- Does not accept unsolicited mss.

$ $ GROUP MAGAZINE

Group Publishing, Inc., P.O. Box 481, Loveland CO 80539. Fax: (970)292-4373. E-mail: greditor@youthministry.com. Web site: www.groupmag.com. **Contact:** Kathy Dietrich. **60% freelance written.** Bimonthly magazine covering youth ministry. "Writers must be actively involved in youth ministry. Articles we accept are practical, not theoretical, and focused for local church youth workers." Estab. 1974. Circ. 57,000. **Pays on acceptance.** Publishes ms an average of 6 months after acceptance. Byline given. Offers $20 kill fee. Buys all rights. Submit seasonal material 7 months in advance. Responds in 2 months to queries. Sample copy for $2 and 9×12 SAE. Writer's guidelines online.

Nonfiction How-to (youth ministry issues). No personal testimony, theological or lecture-style articles. **Buys 50-60 mss/year.** Query. Length: 250-2,200 words. **Pays $40-350.** Sometimes pays expenses of writers on assignment.

Tips "Submit a youth ministry idea to one of our mini-article sections—we look for tried-and-true ideas youth ministers have used with kids."

$ $ GUIDEPOSTS MAGAZINE

16 E. 34th St., New York NY 10016-4397. (212)251-8100. Web site: www.guideposts.com. **Contact:** James McDermott, articles editor. **40% freelance written.** Works with a small number of new/unpublished writers each year. Monthly magazine. "*Guideposts* is an inspirational monthly magazine for people of all faiths, in which men and women from all walks of life tell in true, first-person narrative how they overcame obstacles, rose above failures, handled sorrow, gained new spiritual insight, and became more effective people through faith in God." Estab. 1945. Pays on publication. Publishes ms an average of several months after acceptance. Offers 20% kill fee on assigned stories, but not to first-time freelancers. Buys all rights. Writer's guidelines online.

- "Many of our stories are ghosted articles, so the writer would not get a byline unless it was his/her own story. Because of the high volume of mail the magazine receives, we regret we *cannot* return manuscripts, and will contact writers only if their material can be used."

Nonfiction Articles and features should be true stories written in simple, anecdotal style with an emphasis on human interest. Short mss of approximately 250-750 words (pays $100-250) considered for such features as "Angels Among Us," "His Mysterious Ways," and general 1-page stories. Address short items to Celeste McCauley. For full-length mss, 750-1,500 words, pays $250-500. All mss should be typed, double-spaced, and accompanied by e-mail address, if possible. Annually awards scholarships to high school juniors and seniors in writing contest. **Buys 40-60 unsolicited mss/year.** Length: 250-1,500 words. **Pays $100-500.** Pays expenses of writers on assignment.

Tips "Study the magazine before you try to write for it. Each story must make a single spiritual point that readers can apply to their own daily lives. And it may be easier to just sit down and write them than to have to go through the process of preparing a query. They should be warm, well written, intelligent, and upbeat. We require personal narratives that are true and have some spiritual aspect, but the religious element can be subtle and should *not* be sermonic. A writer succeeds with us if he or she can write a true article using short-story techniques with scenes, drama, tension, and a resolution of the problem presented."

$ HORIZONS

The Magazine for Presbyterian Women, 100 Witherspoon St., Louisville KY 40202-1396. (502)569-5897. Fax: (502)569-8085. Web site: www.pcusa.org/horizons/. Bimonthly magazine owned and operated by Presbyterian women offering "information and inspiration for Presbyterian women by addressing current issues facing the church and the world." Estab. 1988. Circ. 25,000. Pays on publication. Publishes ms an average of 4 months after acceptance. Buys all rights. Sample copy for $4 and 9×12 SAE. Writer's guidelines for #10 SASE.

Fiction Send complete ms. Length: 800-1,200 words. **Pays $50/600 words and 2 contributor's copies.**

$ JEWISH FRONTIER

Ameinu, 114 W. 26th St., #1006, New York NY 10001. (212)366-1194. Fax: (212)675-7685. Web site: www.ameinu.net. **Contact:** Mark Seal, executive editor. **100% freelance written.** Bimonthly intellectual journal covering progressive Jewish issues. "Reportage, essays, reviews, and occasional fiction and poetry, with a progressive Jewish perspective, and a particular interest in Israeli and Jewish-American affairs." Estab. 1934. Circ. 2,600. **Pays on acceptance.** Publishes ms an average of 4 months after acceptance. Byline given. Buys first, second serial (reprint), electronic rights. Editorial lead time 4 months. Submit seasonal material 2 months in advance. Accepts queries by mail, e-mail. Accepts previously published material. Accepts simultaneous submissions. Responds in 1 month to queries; 2 months to mss. Sample copy for 9×12 SASE and 3 first-class stamps, and online at Web site. Writer's guidelines online.

Nonfiction Must have progressive Jewish focus or will not be considered. Book excerpts, essays, exposé, historical/nostalgic, interview/profile, opinion, personal experience. **Buys 20 mss/year.** Query. Length: 1,000-2,500 words. **Pays 5¢/word.**

Photos State availability with submission. Buys all rights. Offers no additional payment for photos accepted with ms. Captions, identification of subjects required.

Columns/Departments Essays (progressive Jewish opinion), 1,000-2,500 words; Articles (progressive Jewish reportage), 1,000-2,500 words; Reviews, 500-1,000 words. **Buys 12 mss/year.** Query. **Pays 5¢/word.**

Poetry Avant-garde, free verse, haiku, traditional. **Buys 12 poems/year.** Submit maximum 3 poems. Length: 7-25 lines. **Pays 5¢/word.**

Tips "Send queries with strong ideas first. *Jewish Frontier* particularly appreciates original thinking on its topics related to progressive Jewish matters."

$ $ LIGHT AND LIFE MAGAZINE

Free Methodist Church of North America, P.O. Box 535002, Indianapolis IN 46253-5002. (317)244-3660. Fax: (317)248-9055. E-mail: llmauthors@fmcna.org. Web site: www.freemethodistchurch.org/magazine. **Contact:** Doug Newton, editor; Cynthia Schnereger, managing editor. Works with a small number of new/unpublished writers each year. Bimonthly magazine for maturing Christians emphasizing a holiness lifestyle, contemporary issues, and a Christ-centered worldview. Includes pull-out discipleship and evangelism tools and encouragement cards, leadership tips and profiles, denominational news. Estab. 1868. Circ. 50,000. **Pays on acceptance.** Byline given. Buys first North American serial rights. Sample copy for $4. Writer's guidelines online.

Nonfiction Query. Length: 1,000-1,500 words (LifeNotes 1,000 words). **Pays 15¢/word.**

$ $ LIGUORIAN

One Liguori Dr., Liguori MO 63057-9999. (636)464-2500. Fax: (636)464-8449. E-mail: liguorianeditor@liguori.org. Web site: www.liguorian.org. Managing Editor: Cheryl Plass. **Contact:** Fr. William J. Parker, CSSR, editor-in-chief. **25% freelance written.** Prefers to work with published/established writers. Magazine published 10 times/year for Catholics. "Our purpose is to lead our readers to a fuller Christian life by helping them better understand the teachings of the gospel and the church and by illustrating how these teachings apply to life and the problems confronting them as members of families, the church, and society." Estab. 1913. Circ. 180,000. **Pays on acceptance.** Offers 50% kill fee. Buys first rights. Submit seasonal material 8 months in advance. Accepts queries by mail, e-mail, fax, phone. Responds in 3 months to mss. Sample copy for 9×12 SAE with 3 first-class stamps or online. Writer's guidelines for #10 SASE and on Web site.

Nonfiction Pastoral, practical, and personal approach to the problems and challenges of people today. "No travelogue approach or unresearched ventures into controversial areas. Also, no material found in secular publications—fad subjects that already get enough press, pop psychology, negative or put-down articles." **Buys 40-50 unsolicited mss/year.** Length: 400-2,000 words. **Pays 10-15¢/word.** Sometimes pays expenses of writers on assignment.

Photos Photographs on assignment only unless submitted with and specific to article.

Fiction Religious, senior citizen/retirement. Send complete ms. Length: 1,500-2,000 words preferred. **Pays 10-15¢/word and 5 contributor's copies.**

$ $ THE LOOKOUT

For Today's Growing Christian, Standard Publishing, 8121 Hamilton Ave., Cincinnati OH 45231-9981. (513)931-4050. Fax: (513)931-0950. E-mail: lookout@standardpub.com. Web site: www.lookoutmag.com. Administrative Assistant: Sheryl Overstreet. **Contact:** Shawn McMullen, editor. **50% freelance written.** Weekly magazine for Christian adults, with emphasis on spiritual growth, family life, and topical issues. "Our purpose is to provide Christian adults with practical, Biblical teaching and current information that will help them mature as believers." Estab. 1894. Circ. 100,000. **Pays on acceptance.** Publishes ms an average of 1 year after acceptance. Byline given. Offers 33% kill fee. Buys first, one-time rights. Editorial lead time 9 months. Submit seasonal material 1 year in advance. Accepts simultaneous submissions. Responds in 4-6 weeks to queries; 10 weeks to mss. Sample copy for $1. Writer's guidelines by e-mail.

- Audience is mainly conservative Christians. Manuscripts only accepted by mail.

Nonfiction "Writers need to send for current theme list. We also use inspirational short pieces." Inspirational, interview/profile, opinion, personal experience, religious. No fiction or poetry. **Buys 100 mss/year.** Query with or without published clips or send complete ms. Length: Check guidelines. **Pays 5-12¢/word.** Sometimes pays expenses of writers on assignment.

Photos State availability with submission. Buys one-time rights. Offers no additional payment for photos accepted with ms. Identification of subjects required.

Tips "*The Lookout* publishes from a theologically conservative, nondenominational, and noncharismatic perspective. It is a member of the Evangelical Press Association. We have readers in every adult age group, but we aim primarily for those aged 30-55. Most readers are married and have elementary to young adult children, but a large number come from other home situations as well. Our emphasis is on the needs of ordinary Christians who want to grow in their faith, rather than on trained theologians or church leaders. As a Christian general-interest magazine, we cover a wide variety of topics—from individual discipleship to family concerns to social involvement. We value well-informed articles that offer lively and clear writing as well as strong application. We often address tough issues and seek to explore fresh ideas or recent developments affecting today's Christians."

$ THE LUTHERAN DIGEST

The Lutheran Digest, Inc., P.O. Box 4250, Hopkins MN 55343. (952)933-2820. Fax: (952)933-5708. E-mail: tldi@lutherandigest.com. Web site: www.lutherandigest.com. **Contact:** David L. Tank, editor. **95% freelance written.** Quarterly magazine covering Christianity from a Lutheran perspective. "Articles frequently reflect a Lutheran Christian perspective, but are not intended to be sermonettes. Popular stories show how God has intervened in a person's life to help solve a problem." Estab. 1953. Circ. 100,000. **Pays on acceptance.** Publishes ms an average of 6 months after acceptance. Byline given. Buys first, second serial (reprint) rights. Editorial lead time 9 months. Submit seasonal material 9 months in advance. Accepts queries by mail. Accepts previously published material. Accepts simultaneous submissions. Responds in 1 month to queries; 4 months to mss. Sample copy for $3.50. Writer's guidelines online.

- Break in with "reprints from other publications that will fill less than three pages of *TLD*. Articles of 1 or 2 pages are even better. As a digest, we primarily look for previously published articles to reprint, however, we do publish about twenty to thirty percent original material. Articles from new writers are always welcomed and seriously considered."

Nonfiction General interest, historical/nostalgic, how-to (personal or spiritual growth), humor, inspirational, personal experience, religious, nature, God's unique creatures. Does not want to see "personal tributes to deceased relatives or friends. They are seldom used unless the subject of the article is well known. We also avoid articles about the moment a person finds Christ as his or her personal savior." **Buys 50-60 mss/year.** Send complete ms. Length: 1,500 words. **Pays $35-50.**

Reprints Accepts previously published submissions. "We prefer this as we are a digest and 70-80% of our articles are reprints."

Photos "We seldom print photos from outside sources." State availability with submission. Buys one-time rights.

Tips "An article that tugs on the 'heart strings' just a little and closes leaving the reader with a sense of hope is a writer's best bet to breaking into *The Lutheran Digest*."

$ THE LUTHERAN JOURNAL

Apostolic Publishing Co., Inc., P.O. Box 28158, Oakdale MN 55128. (651)702-0086. Fax: (651)702-0074. Publisher: Vance Lichty. **Contact:** Editorial Assistant. Semiannual Magazine published 2 times/year for Lutheran Church members, middle age and older. "A family magazine providing wholesome and inspirational reading material for the enjoyment and enrichment of Lutherans." Estab. 1938. Circ. 200,000. Pays on publication. Byline given. Buys first, all rights. Accepts simultaneous submissions. Responds in 4 months to queries. Sample copy for 9×12 SAE with 60¢ postage.

Nonfiction Historical/nostalgic, how-to, humor, inspirational, interview/profile, personal experience, religious, interesting or unusual church projects, think articles. **Buys 25-30 mss/year.** Send complete ms. Length: 1,500 words maximum; occasionally 2,000 words. **Pays 1-4¢/word.**

Reprints Send tearsheet, photocopy or typed ms with rights for sale noted and information about when and where the material previously appeared. Pays up to 50% of amount paid for an original article.

Photos Send photocopies of b&w and color photos with accompanying ms. Please do not send original photos.

Fiction Religious, romance, senior citizen/retirement. Must be appropriate for distribution in the churches. Send complete ms. Length: 1,000-1,500 words. **Pays $20-50 and one contributor's copy.**

Poetry Buys 2-3 poems/issue, as space allows. Pays $10-30.

Tips "We strongly prefer a warm, personal style of writing that speaks directly to the reader. In general, writers should seek to convey information rather than express personal opinion, though the writer's own personality should be reflected in the article's style. Send submissions with SASE so we may respond."

$ LUTHERAN PARTNERS

Augsburg Fortress, Publishers, ELCA (VE), 8765 W. Higgins Rd., Chicago IL 60631-4101. (773)380-2884. Fax: (773)380-2829. E-mail: lutheran.partners@elca.org. Web site: www.elca.org/lutheranpartners. **Contact:** William A. Decker, editor. **40% freelance written.** Bimonthly magazine covering issues of religious leadership. ''Lutheran Partners provides a forum for the discussion of issues surrounding gospel-centered ministry which are vital to scripture, theology, leadership, and mission in congregations and other settings of the church.'' Estab. 1979. Circ. 20,000. Pays on publication. Publishes ms an average of 6 months after acceptance. Byline given. Buys first, one-time, second serial (reprint), electronic rights. Editorial lead time 6 months. Submit seasonal material 6 months in advance. Accepts queries by mail, e-mail, fax, phone. Accepts previously published material. Accepts simultaneous submissions. Responds in 3 months to queries; 6 months to mss. Sample copy for $2. Writer's guidelines online.

- The editor reports an interest in seeing articles on various facets of ministry from the perspectives of ELCA Lutheran ethnic authors (Hispanic, African-American, Asian, Native American, Arab-American), as well as material on youth leadership and ministry, parish education, outreach, and preaching.

Nonfiction Historical/nostalgic, how-to (leadership in faith communities), humor (religious cartoon), inspirational, opinion (religious leadership issues), religious, book and DVD reviews (query review editors). ''No exposés, articles primarily promoting products/services, or anti-religion.'' **Buys 10-15 mss/year.** Query with published clips or send complete ms. Length: 500-1,500 words. **Pays $25-170.** Pays in copies for book reviews.

Photos State availability with submission. Buys one-time rights. Generally offers no additional payment for photos accepted with ms. Captions, identification of subjects required.

Columns/Departments Review Editor. Partners Review (book reviews), 700 words. Query. **Pays in copies.**

Fiction Rarely accepts religious fiction. Query.

Poetry Free verse, haiku, light verse, traditional, hymns. **Buys 3-6 poems/year.** Submit maximum 4 poems. **Pays $50-75.**

Fillers Practical ministry (education, music, youth, social service, administration, worship, etc.) in congregation. **Buys 1-3/year.** Length: 500 words. **Pays $25.**

Tips ''Know congregational life, especially from the perspective of leadership, including both ordained pastor and lay staff. Think current and future leadership needs. It would be good to be familiar with ELCA rostered pastors, lay ministers, and congregations.''

$ $ THE LUTHERAN

Magazine of the Evangelical Lutheran Church in America, 8765 W. Higgins Rd., Chicago IL 60631-4183. (773)380-2540. Fax: (773)380-2751. E-mail: lutheranutheran.org. Web site: www.thelutheran.org. Managing Editor: Sonia Solomonson. **Contact:** David L. Miller, editor. **15% freelance written.** Monthly magazine for ''lay people in church. News and activities of the Evangelical Lutheran Church in America, news of the world of religion, ethical reflections on issues in society, personal Christian experience.'' Estab. 1988. Circ. 600,000. **Pays on acceptance.** Publishes ms an average of 6 months after acceptance. Byline given. Offers 50% kill fee. Buys first rights. Submit seasonal material 4 months in advance. Accepts queries by mail, e-mail. Responds in 6 weeks to queries. Sample copy free. Writer's guidelines online.

O- Break in by checking out the theme list on the Web site and querying with ideas related to these themes.

Nonfiction Inspirational, interview/profile, personal experience, photo feature, religious. ''No articles unrelated to the world of religion.'' **Buys 40 mss/year.** Query with published clips. Length: 400-1,400 words. **Pays $75-600.** Pays expenses of writers on assignment.

Photos Send photos with submission. Reviews contact sheets, transparencies, prints. Buys one-time rights. Offers $50-175/photo. Captions, identification of subjects required.

Columns/Departments Lite Side (humor—church, religious), In Focus, Living the Faith, Values & Society, In Our Churches, Our Church at Work, 25-100 words. Send complete ms. **Pays $10.**

Tips ''Writers have the best chance selling us feature articles.''

$ MENNONITE BRETHREN HERALD

1310 Taylor Ave., Winnipeg MB R3M 3Z6 Canada. (888)669-6575. Fax: (204)654-1865. E-mail: mbherald@mbconf.ca. Web site: www.mbherald.com. **Contact:** Laura Kalman, editor. **25% freelance written.** Monthly family publication ''read mainly by people of the Mennonite Brethren faith, reaching a wide cross section of professional and occupational groups. Readership includes people from both urban and rural communities. It is intended to inform members of events in the church and the world, serve personal and corporate spiritual needs, serve as a vehicle of communication within the church, serve conference agencies and reflect the history and theology of the Mennonite Brethren Church.'' Estab. 1962. Circ. 17,000. Pays on publication. Publishes ms an average of 6 months after acceptance. Byline given. Not copyrighted. Buys one-time rights. Accepts queries by e-mail, fax. Responds in 6 months to queries. Sample copy for $1 and 9×12 SAE with 2 IRCs. Writer's guidelines online.

• "Articles and manuscripts not accepted for publication will be returned if a SASE (Canadian stamps or IRCs) is provided by the writers."

Nonfiction Articles with a Christian family orientation; youth directed, Christian faith and life, and current issues. Wants articles critiquing the values of a secular society, attempting to relate Christian living to the practical situations of daily living; showing how people have related their faith to their vocations. Send complete ms. Length: 250-1,500 words. **Pays $30-40.** Pays expenses of writers on assignment.

Reprints Send tearsheet, photocopy or typed ms with rights for sale noted and information about when and where the material previously appeared. Pays 70% of amount paid for an original article.

Photos Photos purchased with ms.

Columns/Departments Viewpoint (Christian opinion on current topics), 850 words. Crosscurrent (Christian opinion on music, books, art, TV, movies), 350 words.

Poetry Length: 25 lines maximum.

Tips "We like simple style, contemporary language and fresh ideas. Writers should take care to avoid religious cliches."

$ $ MESSAGE MAGAZINE

Review and Herald Publishing Association, 55 West Oak Ridge Dr., Hagerstown MD 21740. (301)393-4099. Fax: (301)393-4103. E-mail: message@rhpa.org. Web site: www.messagemagazine.org. **Contact:** Dr. Ron C. Smith, editor. **10-20% freelance written.** Bimonthly magazine. "*Message* is the oldest religious journal addressing ethnic issues in the country. Our audience is predominantly Black and Seventh-day Adventist; however, *Message* is an outreach magazine geared to the unchurched." Estab. 1898. Circ. 110,000. **Pays on acceptance.** Publishes ms an average of 12 months after acceptance. Byline given. first North American serial rights Editorial lead time 6 months. Submit seasonal material 6 months in advance. Responds in 9 months to queries. Sample copy by e-mail. Writer's guidelines by e-mail.

Nonfiction General interest (to a Christian audience), how-to (overcome depression; overcome defeat; get closer to God; learn from failure, etc.), inspirational, interview/profile (profiles of famous African Americans), personal experience (testimonies), religious. **Buys variable number of mss/year.** Send complete ms. Length: 800-1,200 words. **Payment varies.**

Photos State availability with submission. Buys one-time rights. Identification of subjects required.

Columns/Departments Voices in the Wind (community involvement/service/events/health info); Message, Jr. (stories for children with a moral, explain a biblical or moral principle); Recipes (no meat or dairy products—12-15 recipes and an intro); Healthspan (health issues); all 500 words. Send complete ms. for Message, Jr. and Healthspan. Query editor with published clips for Voices in the Wind and Recipes. **Pays $50-300.**

Tips "Please look at the magazine before submitting manuscripts. *Message* publishes a variety of writing styles as long as the writing style is easy to read and flows—please avoid highly technical writing styles."

$ THE MESSENGER OF THE SACRED HEART

Apostleship of Prayer, 661 Greenwood Ave., Toronto ON M4J 4B3 Canada. (416)466-1195. **Contact:** Rev. F.J. Power, S.J., editor. **20% freelance written.** Monthly magazine for "Canadian and U.S. Catholics interested in developing a life of prayer and spirituality; stresses the great value of our ordinary actions and lives." Estab. 1891. Circ. 11,000. **Pays on acceptance.** Byline given. Buys first North American serial, first rights. Submit seasonal material 5 months in advance. Responds in 1 month to queries. Sample copy for $1 and 7½×10½ SAE. Writer's guidelines for #10 SASE.

Fiction Rev. F.J. Power, S.J. and Alfred DeManche, editors. Religious, stories about people, adventure, heroism, humor, drama. No poetry. **Buys 12 mss/year.** Send complete ms. Length: 750-1,500 words. **Pays 8¢/word, and 3 contributor's copies.**

Tips "Develop a story that sustains interest to the end. Do not preach, but use plot and characters to convey the message or theme. Aim to move the heart as well as the mind. Before sending, cut out unnecessary or unrelated words or sentences. If you can, add a light touch or a sense of humor to the story. Your ending should have impact, leaving a moral or faith message for the reader."

$ THE MONTANA CATHOLIC

Diocese of Helena, P.O. Box 1729, Helena MT 59624. (406)442-5820. Fax: (406)442-5191. E-mail: rstmartin@diocesehelena.org. **Contact:** Renee St. Martin Wizeman, editor. **5% freelance written.** Monthly tabloid. "We publish news and features from a Catholic perspective, particularly as they pertain to the church in western Montana." Estab. 1932. Circ. 9,200. **Pays on acceptance.** Publishes ms an average of 6 months after acceptance. Byline given. Offers 25% kill fee. Buys first, one-time, simultaneous rights. Editorial lead time 1 month. Accepts queries by mail, e-mail. Accepts simultaneous submissions. Responds in 1 month to queries. Writer's guidelines for #10 SASE.

Nonfiction Special issues: Vocations (January); Lent; Easter; Advent; Christmas. **Buys 5 mss/year.** Send complete ms with SASE for reply and/or return of ms. Length: 400-1,200 words. **Pays 10¢/word for assigned articles; 5¢/word for unsolicited articles.**

Photos Reviews contact sheets, prints. Buys one-time rights. Offers $5-20/photo. Identification of subjects required.

Tips "Best bets are seasonal pieces, topics related to our special supplements, and features with a tie-in to western Montana—always with a Catholic angle. No poetry, please."

N $ MONTGOMERY'S JOURNEY

Sharing Hope, Buidling Community, Keep Sharing, 555 Farmington Rd., Montgomery AL 36109. E-mail: deanne @montgomerysjourney.com. **Contact:** DeAnne Watson, editor. **50% freelance written.** Monthly magazine covering Christian living. Includes Protestant Christian writing, topical articles on Christian living, and Christian living articles with helpful information for walking with Christ daily. Estab. 1999. Circ. 8,000. Pays on publication. Publishes ms an average of 6-12 months after acceptance. Byline given. Offers 25% kill fee. Buys one-time, second serial (reprint) rights. Editorial lead time 1 year. Submit seasonal material 1 year in advance. Accepts queries by e-mail. Accepts previously published material. Accepts simultaneous submissions. Sample copy for $1.75 and self-addressed magazine-size envelope. Writer's guidelines by e-mail.

Nonfiction Inspirational, religious. No fiction, poetry, or autobiography. Submit query or complete ms. Length: 1,300-2,200 words. **Pays $25-50 for assigned articles; $25 for unsolicited articles.**

$ $ MY DAILY VISITOR

Our Sunday Visitor, Inc., 200 Noll Plaza, Huntington IN 46750. (260)356-8400. Fax: (260)356-8472. E-mail: mdvisitor@osv.com. Web site: www.osv.com. **99% freelance written.** Bimonthly magazine of Scripture meditations based on the day's Catholic Mass readings. Circ. 33,000. **Pays on acceptance.** Publishes ms an average of 6 months after acceptance. Byline given. Not copyrighted. Buys one-time rights. Accepts queries by mail, e-mail. Responds in 2 months to queries. Sample copy and writer's guidelines for #10 SAE with 3 first-class stamps.

- Sample meditations and guidelines online. Each writer does 1 full month of meditations on assignment basis only.

Nonfiction Inspirational, personal experience, religious. **Buys 12 mss/year.** Query with published clips. Length: 130-140 words times the number of days in month. **Pays $500 for 1 month (28-31) of meditations and 5 free copies.**

Tips "Previous experience in writing Scripture-based Catholic meditations or essays is helpful."

$ $ ON MISSION

North American Mission Board, SBC, 4200 North Point Pkwy., Alpharetta GA 30022-4176. E-mail: cpipes@namb .net. Web site: www.onmission.com. **50% freelance written.** Quarterly lifestyle magazine that popularizes evangelism, church planting and missions. "*On Mission*'s primary purpose is to help readers and churches become more intentional about personal evangelism, church planting, and missions. *On Mission* equips Christians for leading people to Christ and encourages churches to reach new people through new congregations." Estab. 1997. Circ. 100,000. **Pays on acceptance.** Publishes ms an average of 6 months after acceptance. Byline given. Buys first, electronic, first north american rights. Editorial lead time 9 months. Submit seasonal material 9 months in advance. Accepts queries by mail, e-mail. Responds in 6 months to queries; 6 months to mss. Sample copy free or online. Writer's guidelines online.

O→ Break in with a 600-word how-to article.

Nonfiction How-to, humor, personal experience (stories of sharing your faith in Christ with a non-Christian). **Buys 30 mss/year.** Query with published clips. Length: 350-1,200 words. **Pays 25¢/word, more for cover stories.** Pays expenses of writers on assignment.

Photos Most are shot on assignment. Buys one-time rights. Captions, identification of subjects required.

Columns/Departments Buys 2 mss/year. Query. **Pays 25¢/word.**

Tips "Readers might be intimidated if those featured appear to be 'super Christians' who seem to live on a higher spiritual plane. Try to introduce subjects as three-dimensional, real people. Include anecdotes or examples of their fears and failures, including ways they overcame obstacles. In other words, take the reader inside the heart of the on mission Christian and reveal the inevitable humanness that makes that person not only believable, but also approachable. We want the reader to feel encouraged to become on mission by identifying with people like them who are featured in the magazine."

$ $ ONE

Catholic Near East Welfare Association, 1011 First Ave., New York NY 10022-4195. (212)826-1480. Fax: (212)826-8979. E-mail: cnewa@cnewa.org. Web site: www.cnewa.org. **75% freelance written.** Bimonthly magazine for a Catholic audience with interest in the Near East, particularly its current religious, cultural and political aspects. Estab. 1974. Circ. 100,000. Pays on publication. Publishes ms an average of 6 months after acceptance. Byline given. Buys all rights. Accepts queries by mail, fax. Responds in 1 month to queries. Sample copy and writer's guidelines for 7½×10½ SAE with 2 first-class stamps.

Nonfiction "Cultural, devotional, political, historical material on the Near East, with an emphasis on the Eastern Christian churches. Style should be simple, factual, concise. Articles must stem from personal acquaintance with subject matter, or thorough up-to-date research." Length: 1,200-1,800 words. **Pays 20¢/edited word.**

Photos "Photographs to accompany manuscript are welcome; they should illustrate the people, places, ceremonies, etc. which are described in the article. We prefer color transparencies but occasionally use b&w." Pay varies depending on use—scale from $50-300.

Tips "We are interested in current events in the Near East as they affect the cultural, political and religious lives of the people."

$ $ OUR SUNDAY VISITOR

Our Sunday Visitor, Inc., 200 Noll Plaza, Huntington IN 46750. (260)356-8400. Fax: (260)356-8472. E-mail: jduriga@osv.com. Web site: www.osv.com. **Contact:** Joyce Duriga. **10% freelance written.** (Mostly assigned). Weekly tabloid covering world events and culture from a Catholic perspective. Estab. 1912. Circ. 70,000. **Pays on acceptance.** Publishes ms an average of 2-3 months after acceptance. Byline given. Buys first rights. Accepts queries by mail, e-mail.

$ $ OUTREACH MAGAZINE

Outreach, Inc., 2560 Progress St., Vista CA 92081-8422. (760)940-0600. Fax: (760)597-2314. E-mail: lwarren@outreach.com. Web site: www.outreachmagazine.com. Editor: Lynne Marian. **Contact:** Lindy Warren, managing editor. **80% freelance written.** Bimonthly magazine covering outreach. "*Outreach* is designed to inspire, challenge, and equip churches and church leaders to reach out to their communities with the love of Jesus Christ." Circ. 30,000, plus newsstand. Pays on publication. Publishes ms an average of 2 months after acceptance. Byline given. Offers 10% kill fee. Buys first North American serial, electronic rights. Editorial lead time 6 months. Submit seasonal material 6 months in advance. Accepts queries by mail, e-mail, fax. Accepts previously published material. Accepts simultaneous submissions. Responds in 2 months to queries; 8 months to mss. Sample copy and writer's guidelines free.

Nonfiction Book excerpts, how-to, humor, inspirational, interview/profile, personal experience, photo feature, religious. Special issues: Vacation Bible School (January); America's Fastest-Growing Churches (July/August). Does not want fiction, poetry, non-outreach-related articles. **Buys 30 mss/year.** Query with published clips. Length: 1,200-2,000 words. **Pays $375-600 for assigned articles; $375-500 for unsolicited articles.** Sometimes pays expenses of writers on assignment.

Photos Christi Osselaer, lead designer. Send photos with submission. Reviews GIF/JPEG files. Buys all rights. Negotiates payment individually. Identification of subjects required.

Columns/Departments Outreach Pulse (short stories about outreach-oriented churches and ministries), 75-250 words; Questions & Perspectives (a first-person expert perspective on a question related to outreach), 300-400 words; Soulfires (an as-told-to interview with a person about the stories and people that have fueled their passion for outreach), 900 words; From the Front Line (a profile of a church that is using a transferable idea or concept for outreach), 800 words, plus sidebar; Soujourners (short interviews with everyday people about the stories and people that have informed their worldview and faith perspective), 800 words. **Buys 6 mss/year.** Query with published clips. **Pays $100-375.**

Fillers Facts, gags to be illustrated by cartoonist. **Buys 6/year.** Length: 25-100 words. **Pays negotiated fee.**

Tips "Study our writer's guidelines. Send published clips that showcase tight, bright writing as well as your ability to interview, research, and organize numerous sources into an article, and your ability to write a 100-word piece as well as a 1,600-word piece."

N $ $ $ $ PAKN TREGER

National Yiddish Book Center, 1021 West St., Amherst MA 01002. E-mail: aatherley@bikher.org. Web site: www.yiddishbookcenter.org. **Contact:** Nancy Sherman, editor. **50% freelance written.** Magazine published 3 times/year covering modern and contemporary Yiddish and Jewish culture. Estab. 1980. Circ. 30,000. Pays on publication. Publishes ms an average of 4 months after acceptance. Byline given. Buys one-time rights, makes work-for-hire assignments. Editorial lead time 4 months. Submit seasonal material 4 months in advance. Accepts queries by mail, e-mail, fax. Accepts simultaneous submissions. Responds in 2 weeks to queries; 2 months to mss. Sample copy online. Writer's guidelines by e-mail.

Nonfiction Book excerpts, essays, humor, interview/profile, travel, graphic novels. Does not want personal memoirs or poetry. **Buys 4 mss/year.** Query. Length: 1,200-5,000 words. **Pays $1,000-2,500 for assigned articles; $350-1,000 for unsolicited articles.** Sometimes pays expenses of writers on assignment.

Photos Contact Betsey Wolfson, designer. State availability with submission. Reviews GIF/JPEG files. Buys one-time rights. Negotiates payment individually. Identification of subjects required.
Columns/Departments Let's Learn Yiddish (Yiddish lesson), 1 page Yid/English; Translations (Yiddish-English), 1,200-2,500 words. **Buys 2 mss/year.** Query. **Pays $350-1,000.**
Fiction Historical, humorous, mystery, novel excerpts, serialized novels, slice-of-life vignettes. **Buys 2 mss/year.** Query. Length: 1,200-5,000 words. **Pays $800-1,500.**
Fillers Anecdotes, facts, short humor. **Buys 6/year.** Length: 250-600 words. **Pays $200-400.**
Tips "Read the magazine and visit our Web site."

$ $ ⊘ THE PLAIN TRUTH

Christianity Without the Religion, Plain Truth Ministries, 300 W. Green St., Pasadena CA 91129. Fax: (626)304-8172. E-mail: managing.editor@ptm.org. Web site: www.ptm.org. **90% freelance written.** Bimonthly magazine. "We seek to reignite the flame of shattered lives by illustrating the joy of a new life in Christ." Estab. 1935. Circ. 70,000. Pays on publication. Publishes ms an average of 8 months after acceptance. Byline given. Offers $50 kill fee. Buys all-language rights for *The Plain Truth* and its affiliated publications. Editorial lead time 6 months. Submit seasonal material 6 months in advance. Accepts queries by mail, e-mail. Accepts simultaneous submissions. Sample copy for 9×12 SAE and 5 first-class stamps. Writer's guidelines online.
Nonfiction Inspirational, interview/profile, personal experience, religious. **Buys 48-50 mss/year.** Query with published clips and SASE. *No unsolicited mss.* Length: 750-2,500 words. **Pays 25¢/word.**
Reprints Send tearsheet or photocopy of article or typed ms with rights for sale noted and information about when and where the article previously appeared with SASE for response. Pays 15¢/word.
Photos State availability with submission. Reviews transparencies, prints. Buys one-time rights. Negotiates payment individually. Captions required.
Tips "Material should offer Biblical solutions to real-life problems. Both first-person and third-person illustrations are encouraged. Articles should take a unique twist on a subject. Material must be insightful and practical for the Christain reader. All articles must be well researched and Biblically accurate without becoming overly scholastic. Use convincing arguments to support your Christian platform. Use vivid word pictures, simple and compelling language, and avoid stuffy academic jargon. Captivating anecdotes are vital."

$ PRAIRIE MESSENGER

Catholic Journal, Benedictine Monks of St. Peter's Abbey, P.O. Box 190, Muenster SK S0K 2Y0 Canada. (306)682-1772. Fax: (306)682-5285. E-mail: pm.canadian@stpeters.sk.ca. Web site: www.stpeters.sk.ca/prairie_messenger. Managing Editor: Peter Novecosky, OSB. **Contact:** Maureen Weber, associate editor. **10% freelance written.** Weekly Catholic journal with strong emphasis on social justice, Third World, and ecumenism. Estab. 1904. Circ. 7,300. Pays on publication. Publishes ms an average of 4 months after acceptance. Byline given. Not copyrighted. Buys first North American serial, first, one-time, second serial (reprint), simultaneous rights. Submit seasonal material 3 months in advance. Accepts queries by mail, e-mail, fax, phone. Responds in 2 months to queries. Sample copy for 9×12 SAE with $1 Canadian postage or IRCs. Writer's guidelines online.
Nonfiction Interview/profile, opinion, religious. "No articles on abortion." **Buys 15 mss/year.** Send complete ms. Length: 250-600 words. **Pays $40-60.** Sometimes pays expenses of writers on assignment.
Photos Send photos with submission. Reviews 3×5 prints. Buys all rights. Offers $20/photo. Captions required.

$ ⊘ PRESBYTERIAN RECORD

50 Wynford Dr., Toronto ON M3C 1J7 Canada. (416)444-1111. Fax: (416)441-2825. E-mail: dharris@presbyterian.ca. Web site: www.presbyterian.ca/record. **Contact:** Andrew Faiz, managing editor. **5% freelance written.** Monthly magazine for a church-oriented, family audience. Circ. 41,000. Pays on publication. Publishes ms an average of 4 months after acceptance. Buys first North American serial, one-time, simultaneous rights. Submit seasonal material 4 months in advance. Accepts queries by e-mail. Sample copy for 9×12 SAE with $1 Canadian postage or IRCs.

- Responds in 2 months on accepted ms.

Nonfiction Check a copy of the magazine for style. Inspirational, interview/profile, personal experience, religious. Special issues: Evangelism; Spirituality; Education. No material solely or mainly US in context. No sermons, accounts of ordinations, inductions, baptisms, receptions, church anniversaries, or term papers. Query. Length: 700-1,500 words. **Pays $75-150 (Canadian).** Sometimes pays expenses of writers on assignment.
Reprints Send tearsheet, photocopy or typed ms with rights for sale noted and information about when and where the material previously appeared.
Photos When possible, photos should accompany ms; e.g., current events, historical events, and biographies. Pays $50 (Canadian) for glossy photos.
Columns/Departments Items of contemporary and often controversial nature, 700 words; Mission Knocks (new ideas for congregational mission and service), 700 words.

Tips "There is a trend away from maudlin, first-person pieces redolent with tragedy and dripping with simplistic, pietistic conclusions. Writers often leave out those parts which would likely attract readers, such as anecdotes and direct quotes. Using active rather than passive verbs also helps most manuscripts."

$ $ PRESBYTERIANS TODAY

Presbyterian Church (U.S.A.), 100 Witherspoon St., Louisville KY 40202-1396. (502)569-5637. Fax: (502)569-8632. E-mail: today@pcusa.org. Web site: www.pcusa.org/today. **Contact:** Eva Stimson, editor. **25% freelance written.** Prefers to work with published/established writers. Denominational magazine published 10 times/year covering religion, denominational activities, and public issues for members of the Presbyterian Church (U.S.A.). "The magazine's purpose is to increase understanding and appreciation of what the church and its members are doing to live out their Christian faith." Estab. 1867. Circ. 58,000. **Pays on acceptance.** Publishes ms an average of 6 months after acceptance. Byline given. Offers 50% kill fee. Buys first North American serial rights. Editorial lead time 3 months. Submit seasonal material 3 months in advance. Accepts queries by mail, e-mail, fax, phone. Responds in 2 weeks to queries; 1 month to mss. Sample copy free. Writer's guidelines online.

O→ Break in with a "short feature for our 'Spotlight' department (300 words)."

Nonfiction "Most articles have some direct relevance to a Presbyterian audience; however, *Presbyterians Today* also seeks well-informed articles written for a general audience that help readers deal with the stresses of daily living from a Christian perspective." How-to (everyday Christian living), inspirational, Presbyterian programs, issues, people. **Buys 20 mss/year.** Send complete ms. Length: 1,000-1,800 words. **Pays $300 maximum for assigned articles; $75-300 for unsolicited articles.**

Photos State availability with submission. Reviews contact sheets, transparencies, color prints, digital images. Buys one-time rights. Negotiates payment individually. Identification of subjects required.

$ $ PRISM MAGAZINE

America's Alternative Evangelical Voice, Evangelicals for Social Action, 6 E. Lancaster Ave., Wynnewood PA 19096. (610)645-9391. Fax: (610)649-8090. E-mail: kristyn@esa-online.org. Web site: www.esa-online.org. **Contact:** Kristyn Komarnicki, editor. **50% freelance written.** Bimonthly magazine covering Christianity and social justice. For holistic, Biblical, socially-concerned, progressive Christians. Estab. 1993. Circ. 5,000. Pays on publication. Publishes ms an average of 4-6 months after acceptance. Byline given. Buys first North American serial rights. Editorial lead time 4 months. Submit seasonal material 4 months in advance. Accepts queries by mail, e-mail. Responds in 1 month to queries; 3 months to mss. Sample copy for $3. Writer's guidelines free.

• "We're a nonprofit, some writers are pro bono." Occasionally accepts previously published material.

Nonfiction Book excerpts (to coincide with book release date), essays, interview/profile (ministry). **Buys 10-12 mss/year.** Send complete ms. Length: 500-3,000 words. **Pays $75-300 for assigned articles; $25-200 for unsolicited articles.**

Photos Send photos with submission. Reviews prints, JPEG files. Buys one-time rights. Pays $25/photo published; $150 if photo used on cover.

Tips "We look closely at stories of holistic ministry. It's best to request a sample copy to get to know *PRISM*'s focus/style before submitting—we receive so many submissions that are not appropriate."

$ PURPOSE

616 Walnut Ave., Scottdale PA 15683-1999. (724)887-8500. Fax: (724)887-3111. E-mail: horsch@mph.org. Web site: www.mph.org. **Contact:** James E. Horsch, editor. **95% freelance written.** Monthly magazine in weekly parts "for adults, young and old, general audience with varied interests. Magazine focuses on Christian discipleship—how to be a faithful Christian in the midst of everday life situations. Uses personal story form to present models and examples to encourage Christians in living a life of faithful discipleship." Estab. 1968. Circ. 8,500. **Pays on acceptance.** Publishes ms an average of 18 months after acceptance. Buys one-time rights. Submit seasonal material 1 year in advance. Accepts queries by e-mail. Accepts previously published material. Accepts simultaneous submissions. Responds in 3 months to queries. Sample copy and writer's guidelines for 6×9 SAE and $2.

Nonfiction Inspirational stories from a Christian perspective. "I want upbeat stories that deal with issues faced by believers in family, business, politics, religion, gender, and any other areas—and show how the Christian faith resolves them. *Purpose* conveys truth through quality fiction or true life stories. Our magazine accents Christian discipleship. Christianity affects all of life, and we expect our material to demonstrate this. I would like story-type articles about individuals, groups, and organizations who are intelligently and effectively working at such problems as hunger, poverty, international understanding, peace, justice, etc., because of their faith. Essays, fiction, and how-to-do-it pieces must include a lot of anecdotal, life exposure examples." **Buys 160 mss/year.** E-mail submissions preferred.

Reprints Send tearsheet, photocopy or typed ms with rights for sale noted and information about when and where the material previously appeared.
Photos Photos purchased with ms must be sharp enough for reproduction; requires prints in all cases. Captions required.
Fiction "Produce the story with specificity so that it appears to take place somewhere and with real people." Historical, humorous, religious. No militaristic/narrow patriotism or racism. Send complete ms. Length: 600 words. **Pays up to 6¢ for stories, and 2 contributor's copies.**
Poetry Free verse, light verse, traditional, blank verse. **Buys 130 poems/year.** Length: 12 lines. **Pays $7.50-20/poem depending on length and quality. Buys one-time rights only.**
Fillers Anecdotal items up to 400 words. **Pays 5¢/word maximum.**

$ $ REFORM JUDAISM

Union for Reform Judaism, 633 Third Ave. 7th Floor, New York NY 10017-6778. (212)650-4240. Fax: (212)650-4249. E-mail: rjmagazine@urj.org. Web site: www.reformjudaismmag.org. **Contact:** Joy Weinberg, managing editor. **30% freelance written.** Quarterly magazine of Jewish issues for contemporary Jews. "*Reform Judaism* is the official voice of the Union for Reform Judaism, linking the institutions and affiliates of Reform Judaism with every Reform Jew. *RJ* covers developments within the Movement while interpreting events and Jewish tradition from a Reform perspective." Estab. 1972. Circ. 310,000. Pays on publication. Publishes ms an average of 3 months after acceptance. Byline given. Offers kill fee for commissioned articles. Buys first North American serial rights. Submit seasonal material 6 months in advance. Accepts previously published material. Accepts simultaneous submissions. Responds in 2 months to queries; 2 months to mss. Sample copy for $3.50. Writer's guidelines online.
Nonfiction Book excerpts, exposé, general interest, historical/nostalgic, inspirational, interview/profile, opinion, personal experience, photo feature, travel. **Buys 30 mss/year.** Submit complete ms with SASE. Length: Cover stories: 2,500-3,500 words; major feature: 1,800-2,500 words; secondary feature: 1,200-1,500 words; department (e.g., Travel): 1,200 words; letters: 200 words maximum; opinion: 525 words maximum. **Pays 30¢/published word.** Sometimes pays expenses of writers on assignment.
Reprints Send tearsheet, photocopy or typed ms with rights for sale noted and information about when and where the material previously appeared. Usually does not publish reprints.
Photos Send photos with submission. Reviews 8×10/color or slides, b&w prints, and printouts of electronic images. Buys one-time rights. Payment varies. Identification of subjects required.
Fiction Humorous, religious, ophisticated, cutting-edge, superb writing. **Buys 4 mss/year.** Send complete ms. Length: 600-2,500 words. **Pays 30¢/published word.**
The online magazine carries original content not found in the print edition and includes writer's guidelines.
Tips "We prefer a stamped postcard including the following information/checklist: __Yes, we are interested in publishing; __No, unfortunately the submission doesn't meet our needs; __Maybe, we'd like to hold on to the article for now. Submissions sent this way will receive a faster response."

$ $ RELEVANT

Relevant Media Group, 100 S. Lake Destiny Dr., Suite 200, Orlando FL 32810. (407)660-1411. Fax: (407)660-8555. E-mail: editorial@relevantmagazine.com. Web site: www.relevantmagazine.com. Editor: Cara Davis. **Contact:** Adam Smith, managing editor. **80% freelance written.** Biweekly magazine covering God, life, and progressive culture. *Relevant* is a lifestyle magazine for Christians in their 20s. Estab. 2002. Circ. 70,000. Pays 45 days after publication. Publishes ms an average of 6 months after acceptance. Byline given. Offers 50% kill fee. Buys first North American serial rights. Editorial lead time 4 months. Submit seasonal material 5 months in advance. Accepts queries by e-mail. Accepts simultaneous submissions. Responds in 6 weeks to queries; 3 months to mss. Sample copy and writer's guidelines online.
Nonfiction General interest, how-to, inspirational, interview/profile, new product, personal experience, religious. Don't submit anything that doesn't target ages 18-34. Query with published clips. Length: 1,000-1,500 words. **Pays 10-15¢/word for assigned articles; 10¢/word for unsolicited articles.** Sometimes pays expenses of writers on assignment.
Tips "The easiest way to get noticed by our editors is to first submit (donate) stories for online publication."

$ $ THE REPORTER

Women's American ORT, Inc., 250 Park Ave. S., Suite 600, New York NY 10003. (212)505-7700. Fax: (212)674-3057. E-mail: dasher@waort.org. Web site: www.waort.org. **Contact:** Dana Asher, editor. **85% freelance written.** Semiannual nonprofit journal published by Jewish women's organization covering Jewish women celebrities, issues of contemporary Jewish culture, Israel, anti-Semitism, women's rights, Jewish travel and the international Jewish community. Estab. 1966. Circ. 50,000. **Pays on acceptance.** Publishes ms an average of 1 year after acceptance. Byline given. Buys first North American serial rights. Submit seasonal material 6 months in advance. Accepts queries by mail, e-mail. Responds in 3 months to queries. Sample copy for 9×12 SAE and 3 first-class stamps. Writer's guidelines for #10 SASE.

O-ᴛ Break in with "a different look at a familiar topic, i.e., 'Jews without God' (Winter 2000). Won't consider handwritten or badly-typed queries. Unpublished writers are welcome. Others, include credits."

Nonfiction Cover feature profiles a dynamic Jewish woman making a difference in Judaism, women's issues, education, entertainment, profiles, business, journalism, arts. Essays, exposé, humor, inspirational, opinion, personal experience, photo feature, religious, travel. Query. Length: 1,800 words maximum. **Pays $200 and up.**

Photos Send photos with submission. Identification of subjects required.

Columns/Departments Education Horizon; Destination (Jewish sites/travel); Inside Out (Advocacy); Women's Business; Art Scene (interviews, books, films); Lasting Impression (uplifting/inspirational).

Fiction Publishes novel excerpts and short stories as part of Lasting Impressions column. Length: 800 words. **Pays $150-300.**

Tips "Send query only by e-mail or postal mail. Show us a fresh look, not a rehash. Particularly interested in stories of interest to younger readers."

$ REVIEW FOR RELIGIOUS

3601 Lindell Blvd., Room 428, St. Louis MO 63108-3393. (314)977-7363. Fax: (314)977-7362. E-mail: review@slu.edu. Web site: www.reviewforreligious.org. **Contact:** David L. Fleming, S.J., editor. **100% freelance written.** Quarterly magazine for Roman Catholic priests, brothers, and sisters. Estab. 1942. Pays on publication. Publishes ms an average of 9 months after acceptance. Byline given. Buys first North American serial rights. Rarely buys second serial (reprint) rights. Accepts queries by mail, fax. Responds in 2 months to queries. Writer's guidelines online.

Nonfiction Spiritual, liturgical, canonical matters only. Not for general audience. Length: 1,500-5,000 words. **Pays $6/page.**

Tips "The writer must know about religious life in the Catholic Church and be familiar with prayer, vows, community life, and ministry."

$ $ $ SCIENCE & SPIRIT

Heldref Publications, 162 Old Colony Ave., 3rd Floor, Quincy MA 02170. Fax: (617)847-5924. E-mail: freelance@science-spirit.org. Web site: www.science-spirit.org. Editor: Marc Kaufman. **Contact:** Heather Wax, features editor. **75% freelance written.** Bimonthly magazine covering science and spirituality. "*Science & Spirit* explores the integration of the scientific and spiritual aspects of our culture in a way that is accessible and relevant to everyday living. Examining life's complexities through the lenses of both science and spirituality offers insight neither provides alone. We look for solidly reported pieces relayed in a narrative voice." Circ. 7,500. **Pays on acceptance.** Publishes ms an average of 4 months after acceptance. Byline given. Makes work-for-hire assignments. Editorial lead time 4-6 months. Submit seasonal material 6 months in advance. Accepts queries by e-mail. Responds in 1 month to queries. Sample copy and writer's guidelines online.

Nonfiction Essays, interview/profile, religious, science, reported pieces. "No New Age pieces. In general, we look for solidly reported articles." **Buys 40 mss/year.** Query with published clips. Length: 1,200-2,500 words. **Pays 20-75¢/word for assigned articles; 20-50¢/word for unsolicited articles.** Sometimes pays expenses of writers on assignment.

Tips "The best way to improve odds of publication is to really familiarize yourself with the magazine. The most successful submissions are focused pieces that contain unique information about the relationship between science and spirituality. We already know that science, faith, and ethics intersect—we're looking for angles we've never heard before, explored in new and innovative ways."

$ THE SECRET PLACE

National Ministries, ABC/USA, P.O. Box 851, Valley Forge PA 19482-0851. (610)768-2240. E-mail: thesecretplace@abc-usa.org. **Contact:** Kathleen Hayes, senior editor. **100% freelance written.** Quarterly devotional covering Christian daily devotions. Estab. 1938. Circ. 100,000. **Pays on acceptance.** Byline given. Buys first rights. Editorial lead time 1 year. Submit seasonal material 9 months in advance. For free sample and guidelines, send 6×9 SASE.

Nonfiction Inspirational. **Buys about 400 mss/year.** Send complete ms. Length: 100-200 words. **Pays $15.**

Poetry Avant-garde, free verse, light verse, traditional. **Buys 12-15/year poems/year.** Submit maximum 6 poems. Length: 4-30 lines. **Pays $15.**

Tips Accepts submissions via e-mail.

[N] $ $ $ $ [icon] SHAMBHALA SUN

1660 Hollis St., Suite 701, Halifax NS B3J 1V7 Canada. Fax: (902)423-2701. E-mail: magazine@shambhalasun.com. Web site: www.shambhalasun.com. Editor: Melvin McLeod. Managing Editor: Andrea McQuillin. **Contact:** Editorial Assistant. **80% freelance written.** Bimonthly magazine covering contemporary life from a Buddhist perspective; Buddhism. "We're interested in how a contemplative spiritual practice informs one's view of modern life and experience of it." Estab. 1992. Circ. 75,000. Pays on publication. Publishes ms an average of 2-4 months after acceptance. Byline given. Buys one-time, electronic rights. Editorial lead time 3 months. Submit seasonal material 6 months in advance. Accepts queries by e-mail, fax. Accepts simultaneous submissions. Responds in 2 weeks to queries; 1-2 months to mss. Sample copy for free. Writer's guidelines free.

Nonfiction Book excerpts, essays, how-to, humor, inspirational, interview/profile, opinion, personal experience, photo feature, religious, travel. Does not want unsolicited poetry. **Buys 20 mss/year.** Query with or without published clips or send complete ms. Length: 800-3,900 words. **Pays $250-2,000 for assigned articles; $100 for unsolicited articles.** Sometimes pays expenses of writers on assignment.

Photos State availability with submission. Reviews contact sheets, negatives, transparencies, prints, GIF/JPEG files. Buys one-time rights. Negotiates payment individually. Captions, identification of subjects required.

Columns/Departments About a Poem (short essay on a favorite poem), 300 words. **Buys 6 mss/year.** Query. **Pays $0-250.**

$ $ SHARING THE VICTORY

Fellowship of Christian Athletes, 8701 Leeds Rd., Kansas City MO 64129. (816)921-0909. Fax: (816)921-8755. E-mail: stv@fca.org. Web site: www.fca.org. Editor: Jill Ewert. **50% freelance written.** Prefers to work with published/established writers, but works with a growing number of new/unpublished writers each year. Published 9 times/year. "We seek to serve as a ministry tool of the Fellowship of Christian Athletes by informing, inspiring and involving coaches, athletes and all whom they influence, that they may make an impact for Jesus Christ." Estab. 1959. Circ. 80,000. Pays on publication. Publishes ms an average of 4 months after acceptance. Byline given. Buys first rights. Submit seasonal material 6 months in advance. Responds in 3 months to queries; 3 months to mss. Sample copy for $1 and 9×12 SAE with 3 first-class stamps. Writer's guidelines online.

Nonfiction "Must have FCA connection." Inspirational, interview/profile (with name athletes and coaches solid in their faith), personal experience, photo feature. **Buys 5-20 mss/year.** Query. Length: 500-1,000 words.

Photos State availability with submission. Reviews contact sheets. Buys one-time rights. Pay based on size of photo.

Tips "Profiles and interviews of particular interest to coed athlete, primarily high school and college age. Our graphics and editorial content appeal to youth. The area most open to freelancers is profiles on or interviews with well-known athletes or coaches (male, female, minorities) who have been or are involved in some capacity with FCA."

[N] $ SPIRITUAL LIFE

2131 Lincoln Rd. NE, Washington DC 20002-1199. (202)832-5505. Fax: (202)832-8967. E-mail: edodonnell@aol.com. Web site: www.spiritual-life.org. **Contact:** Br. Edward O'Donnell, O.C.D., editor. **80% freelance written.** Prefers to work with published/established writers. Quarterly magazine for "largely Christian, well-educated, serious readers." Circ. 12,000. **Pays on acceptance.** Publishes ms an average of 1 year after acceptance. Buys first North American serial rights. Responds in 2 months to queries. Sample copy and writer's guidelines for 7x10 or larger SAE with 5 first-class stamps.

Nonfiction Serious articles of contemporary spirituality and its pastoral application to everday life. High quality articles about our encounter with God in the present day world. Language of articles should be college level. Technical terminology, if used, should be clearly explained. Material should be presented in a postive manner. Buys inspirational and think pieces. "Brief autobiographical information (present occupation, past occupations, books and articles published, etc.) should accompany article." Sentimental articles or those dealing with specific devotional practices not accepted.No fiction or poetry. **Buys 20 mss/year.** Length: 3,000-5,000 words. **Pays $50 minimum, and 2 contributor's copies.**

$ $ ST. ANTHONY MESSENGER

28 W. Liberty St., Cincinnati OH 45202-6498. (513)241-5615. Fax: (513)241-0399. E-mail: stanthony@americancatholic.org. Web site: www.americancatholic.org. **Contact:** Father Pat McCloskey, O.F.M., editor. **55% freelance written.** Monthly general interest magazine for a national readership of Catholic families, most of which have children or grandchildren in grade school, high school, or college. "*St. Anthony Messenger* is a Catholic family magazine which aims to help its readers lead more fully human and Christian lives. We publish articles which report on a changing church and world, opinion pieces written from the perspective of Christian faith and values, personality profiles, and fiction which entertains and informs." Estab. 1893. Circ. 305,000. **Pays on acceptance.** Publishes ms an average of 1 year after acceptance. Byline given. Buys first North American

serial, electronic rights. first worldwide serial rights. Submit seasonal material 6 months in advance. Accepts queries by mail, e-mail, fax. Responds in 3 weeks to queries; 2 months to mss. Sample copy for 9×12 SAE with 4 first-class stamps. Writer's guidelines online.

Nonfiction How-to (on psychological and spiritual growth, problems of parenting/better parenting, marriage problems/marriage enrichment), humor, inspirational, interview/profile, opinion (limited use; writer must have special qualifications for topic), personal experience (if pertinent to our purpose), photo feature, informational, social issues. **Buys 35-50 mss/year.** Query with published clips. Length: 1,500-2,500 words. **Pays 20¢/word.** Sometimes pays expenses of writers on assignment.

Fiction Mainstream, religious, senior citizen/retirement. "We do not want mawkishly sentimental or preachy fiction. Stories are most often rejected for poor plotting and characterization; bad dialogue—listen to how people talk; inadequate motivation. Many stories say nothing, are 'happenings' rather than stories." No fetal journals, no rewritten Bible stories. **Buys 12 mss/year.** Send complete ms. Length: 2,000-3,000 words. **Pays 16¢/word maximum and 2 contributor's copies; $1 charge for extras.**

Poetry "Our poetry needs are very limited." Submit maximum 4-5 poems. Length: Up to 20-25 lines; the shorter, the better. **Pays $2/line; $20 minimum.**

Tips "The freelancer should consider why his or her proposed article would be appropriate for us, rather than for *Redbook* or *Saturday Review.* We treat human problems of all kinds, but from a religious perspective. Articles should reflect Catholic theology, spirituality, and employ a Catholic terminology and vocabulary. We need more articles on prayer, scripture, Catholic worship. Get authoritative information (not merely library research); we want interviews with experts. Write in popular style; use lots of examples, stories, and personal quotes. Word length is an important consideration."

$ $ TODAY'S CHRISTIAN

Stories of Faith, Hope and God's Love, Christianity Today, 465 Gundersen Dr., Carol Stream IL 60188. (630)260-6200. Fax: (630)480-2004. E-mail: tceditor@todays-christian.com. Web site: www.christianitytoday.com/todayschristian. Editor: Edward Gilbreath. **Contact:** Cynthia Thomas, editorial coordinator. **25% freelance written.** Bimonthly magazine for adult evangelical Christian audience. Estab. 1963. Circ. 125,000. Pays on acceptance; on publication for humor pieces. Byline given. Editorial lead time 5 months. Submit seasonal material 8 months in advance. Accepts queries by mail. Accepts simultaneous submissions. Responds in 1 month to queries. Sample copy for 5×8 SAE and 4 first-class stamps. Writer's guidelines online.

Nonfiction Book excerpts, general interest, historical/nostalgic, humor, inspirational, interview/profile, personal experience, photo feature, religious. **Buys 100-125 mss/year.** Query with or without published clips or send complete ms. Length: 250-1,500 words. **Pays $125-600 depending on length.** Pays expenses of writers on assignment.

Reprints Send tearsheet, photocopy or typed ms with rights for sale noted and information about when and where the material previously appeared. Pays 35-50% of amount paid for an original article.

Photos Send photos with submission. Reviews transparencies, prints. Buys one-time rights. Negotiates payment individually. Identification of subjects required.

Columns/Departments Humor Us (adult church humor, kids say and do funny things, and humorous wedding tales), 50-200 words. **Pays $35.**

Fillers Anecdotes, short fillers. **Buys 10-20/year.** Length: 100-250 words. **Pays $35.**

Tips "Most of our articles are reprints or staff written. Freelance competition is keen, so tailor submissions to meet our needs by observing the following: *Today's Christian* audience is truly a general interest one, including men and women, urban professionals and rural homemakers, adults of every age and marital status, and Christians of every church affiliation. We seek to publish a magazine that people from the variety of ethnic groups in North America will find interesting and relevant."

$ $ TODAY'S PENTECOSTAL EVANGEL

The General Council of the Assemblies of God, 1445 N. Boonville, Springfield MO 65802-1894. (417)862-2781. Fax: (417)862-0416. E-mail: tpe@ag.org. Web site: www.tpe.ag.org. Editor: Hal Donaldson. Managing Editor: Ken Horn. **Contact:** Scott Harrup, associate editor. **5-10% freelance written.** Weekly magazine emphasizing news of the Assemblies of God for members of the Assemblies and other Pentecostal and charismatic Christians. "Articles should be inspirational without being preachy. Any devotional writing should take a literal approach to the Bible. A variety of general topics and personal experience accepted with inspirational tie-in." Estab. 1913. Circ. 200,000. **Pays on acceptance.** Publishes ms an average of 6 months after acceptance. Byline given. Offers 100% kill fee. Buys first North American serial, one-time rights. Editorial lead time 3 months. Submit seasonal material 6 months in advance. Accepts queries by e-mail. Accepts previously published material. Responds in 2 weeks to queries; 2 months to mss. Sample copy for free. Writer's guidelines online.

Nonfiction Book excerpts, general interest, inspirational, personal experience, religious. Does not want poetry, fiction, self-promotional. **Buys 10-15 mss/year.** Send complete ms. Length: 700-1,200 words. **Pays $25-200.** Pays expenses of writers on assignment.

Tips "We publish first-person articles concerning spiritual experiences; that is, answers to prayer for help in a particular situation, of unusual conversions or healings through faith in Christ. All articles submitted to us should be related to religious life. We are Protestant, evangelical, Pentecostal, and any doctrines or practices portrayed should be in harmony with the official position of our denomination (Assemblies of God)."

$ TOGETHER

Shalom Publishers, 1251 Virginia Ave., Harrisonburg VA 22802. E-mail: tgether@aol.com. Web site: www.churchoutreach.com. Managing Editor: Dorothy Hartman. **Contact:** Melodie M. Davis, editor. **90% freelance written.** Quarterly tabloid covering religion and inspiration for a nonchurched audience. "*Together* is is directed as an outreach publication to those who are not currently involved in a church; therefore, we need general inspirational articles that tell stories of personal change, especially around faith issues. Also, stories that will assist our readers in dealing with the many stresses and trials of everday life—family, financial, career, community. Estab. 1980. Circ. 50,000. Pays on publication. Publishes ms an average of 6-12 months after acceptance. Byline given. Buys first, electronic rights. Editorial lead time 6-9 months. Submit seasonal material 6 months in advance. Accepts queries by mail, e-mail. Accepts previously published material. Accepts simultaneous submissions. Responds in 2 months to queries; 4 months to mss. Sample copy and writer's guidelines online.

O→ "We aim for articles that are well written, understandable, challenging (not the same old thing you've read elsewhere); that stimulate readers to dig a little deeper, but not too deep with academic or technical lanugage; that are interesting and fitting for our theological perspective (Christian), but are not preachy or overly patriotic. No mentions of smoking, drinking, cursing, etc."

Nonfiction Essays, general interest, how-to, humor, inspirational, interview/profile, personal experience (testimony), religious. No pet stories. "We have limited room for stories about illness, dying, or grief, but we do use them occasionally. We publish in March, June, September, and December, so holidays that occur in other months are not usually the subject of articles." **Buys 16 mss/year.** Query with or without published clips or send complete ms. Length: 500-1,200 words. **Pays $35-60.**

Photos Dorothy Hartman. State availability with submission. Reviews 4×6 prints, GIF/JPEG files. Buys one-time rights. Offers $15-25/photo. Captions, identification of subjects, model releases required.

Tips "We prefer 'good news' stories that are uplifting and noncontroversial in nature. We can use stories of change and growth in religious journey from a Christian slant, including 'salvation' stories. We generally want articles that tell stories of people solving problems and dealing with personal issues rather than essays or 'preaching.' If you submit electronically, it is very helpful if you put the specific title of the submission in the subject line and include your e-mail address in the body of the e-mail or on your manuscript. Also, always include your address and phone number."

TRICYCLE

The Buddhist Review, 92 Vandam St., New York NY 10013. (212)645-1143. Fax: (212)645-1493. E-mail: editorial@tricycle.com. Web site: www.tricycle.com. Editor-in-Chief: James Shaheen. **Contact:** Andrew Merz, associate editor. **80% freelance written.** Quarterly magazine covering the impact of Buddhism on Western culture. "*Tricycle* readers tend to be well educated and open minded." Estab. 1991. Circ. 60,000. Pays on publication. Byline given. Offers 25% kill fee. Buys one-time rights. Editorial lead time 3 months. Accepts queries by mail, e-mail, fax. Accepts simultaneous submissions. Responds in 3 months to queries; 3 months to mss. Sample copy for $7.95 or online at Web site. Writer's guidelines online.

Nonfiction Book excerpts, essays, general interest, historical/nostalgic, humor, inspirational, interview/profile, personal experience, photo feature, religious, travel. **Buys 4-6 mss/year.** Length: 1,000-5,000 words.

Photos State availability with submission. Reviews contact sheets. Buys one-time rights. Negotiates payment individually. Captions, identification of subjects required.

Columns/Departments Buys 6-8 mss/year. Query.

Tips "*Tricycle* is a Buddhist magazine, and we can only consider Buddhist-related submissions."

$ $ U.S. CATHOLIC

Claretian Publications, 205 W. Monroe St., Chicago IL 60606. (312)236-7782. Fax: (312)236-8207. E-mail: editors@uscatholic.org. Web site: www.uscatholic.org. Editor: Fr. John Molyneux, CMF. Managing Editor: Heidi Schlumpf. Executive Editor: Meinrad Scherer-Emunds. **Contact:** Fran Hurst, editorial assistant. **100% freelance written.** Monthly magazine covering Roman Catholic spirituality. "*U.S. Catholic* is dedicated to the belief that it makes a difference whether you're Catholic. We invite and help our readers explore the wisdom of their faith tradition and apply their faith to the challenges of the 21st century." Estab. 1935. Circ. 40,000. **Pays on acceptance.** Publishes ms an average of 2-3 months after acceptance. Byline given. Buys all rights. Editorial lead time 8 months. Submit seasonal material 6 months in advance. Accepts queries by mail, e-mail, fax, phone. Responds in 1 month to queries; 2 months to mss. Sample copy for large SASE. Guidelines by e-mail or on Web site.

- Please include SASE with written ms.

Nonfiction Essays, inspirational, opinion, personal experience, religious. **Buys 100 mss/year.** Send complete ms. Length: 2,500-3,500 words. **Pays $250-600.** Sometimes pays expenses of writers on assignment.

Photos State availability with submission.

Columns/Departments **Pays $250-600.**

Fiction Maureen Abood, literary editor. Ethnic, mainstream, religious, slice-of-life vignettes. **Buys 4-6 mss/year.** Send complete ms. Length: 2,500-3,000 words. **Pays $300.**

Poetry Maureen Abood, literary editor. Free verse. "No light verse." **Buys 12 poems/year.** Submit maximum 5 poems. Length: 50 lines. **Pays $75.**

THE UNITED CHURCH OBSERVER

478 Huron St., Toronto ON M5R 2R3 Canada. (416)960-8500. Fax: (416)960-8477. E-mail: dnwilson@ucobserver.org. Web site: www.ucobserver.org. **Contact:** David Wilson, editor. **20% freelance written.** Prefers to work with published/established writers. Monthly newsmagazine for people associated with The United Church of Canada. Deals primarily with events, trends, and policies having religious significance. Most coverage is Canadian, but reports on international or world concerns will be considered. Pays on publication. Publishes ms an average of 4 months after acceptance. Byline usually given. first serial rights and occasionally all rights. Accepts queries by mail, e-mail, fax.

Nonfiction Occasional opinion features only. Extended coverage of major issues is usually assigned to known writers. Submissions should be written as news, no more than 1,200 words length, accurate, and well-researched. No poetry. Queries preferred. **Rates depend on subject, author, and work involved.** Pays expenses of writers on assignment as negotiated.

Reprints Send tearsheet or photocopy and information about when and where the material previously appeared. Payment negotiated.

Photos Buys color photographs with mss. Send via e-mail. Payment varies.

Tips "The writer has a better chance of breaking in at our publication with short articles; this also allows us to try more freelancers. Include samples of previous *news* writing with query. Indicate ability and willingness to do research, and to evaluate that research. The most frequent mistakes made by writers in completing an article for us are organizational problems, lack of polished style, short on research, and a lack of inclusive language."

$ THE UPPER ROOM

Daily Devotional Guide, P.O. Box 340004, Nashville TN 37203-0004. (615)340-7252. Fax: (615)340-7267. E-mail: theupperroommagazine@upperroom.org. Web site: www.upperroom.org. Editor and Publisher: Stephen D. Bryant. **Contact:** Marilyn Beaty, editorial assistant. **95% freelance written.** Eager to work with new/unpublished writers. Bimonthly magazine "offering a daily inspirational message which includes a Bible reading, text, prayer, 'Thought for the Day,' and suggestion for further prayer. Each day's meditation is written by a different person and is usually a personal witness about discovering meaning and power for Christian living through scripture study which illuminates daily life." Circ. 2.2 million (U.S.); 385,000 outside U.S. Pays on publication. Publishes ms an average of 1 year after acceptance. Byline given. Buys first North American serial, translation rights. Submit seasonal material 14 months in advance. Sample copy and writer's guidelines with a 4×6 SAE and 2 first-class stamps. Guidelines only for #10 SASE or online.

- "Manuscripts are not returned. If writers include a stamped, self-addressed postcard, we will notify them that their writing has reached us. This does not imply acceptance or interest in purchase. Does not respond unless material is accepted for publication."

Nonfiction Inspirational, personal experience, Bible-study insights. Special issues: Lent and Easter; Advent. No poetry, lengthy "spiritual journey" stories. **Buys 365 unsolicited mss/year.** Send complete ms by mail or e-mail. Length:300 words. **Pays $25/meditation.**

Tips "The best way to break in to our magazine is to send a well-written manuscript that looks at the Christian faith in a fresh way. Standard stories and sermon illustrations are immediately rejected. We very much want to find new writers and welcome good material. We are particularly interested in meditations based on Old Testament characters and stories. Good repeat meditations can lead to work on longer assignments for our other publications, which pay more. A writer who can deal concretely with everyday situations, relate them to the Bible and spiritual truths, and write clear, direct prose should be able to write for *The Upper Room*. We want material that provides for interaction on the part of the reader—meditation suggestions, journaling suggestions, space to reflect and link personal experience with the meditation for the day. Meditations that are personal, authentic, exploratory, and full of sensory detail make good devotional writing."

N $ $ THE WAR CRY

The Salvation Army, 615 Slaters Lane, Alexandria VA 22314. (703)684-5500. Fax: (703)684-5539. E-mail: war_cry@usn.salvationarmy.org. Web site: www.salpubs.com. Managing Editor: Jeff McDonald. **Contact:** Major Ed Forster, editor-in-chief. **5% freelance written.** Biweekly magazine covering army news and Christian devotional writing. Estab. 1881. Circ. 250,000. **Pays on acceptance.** Publishes ms an average of 2 months-1 year after acceptance. Byline given. Buys first, one-time rights. Editorial lead time 6 weeks. Submit seasonal material 1 year in advance. Responds in 2 months to mss. Sample copy, theme list, and writer's guidelines free for #10 SASE or online.

"A best bet would be a well-written profile of an exemplary Christian or a recounting of a person's experiences that deepened the subject's faith and showed God in action. Most popular profiles are of Salvation Army programs and personnel."

Nonfiction Inspirational, interview/profile, personal experience, religious. No missionary stories, confessions. **Buys 25 mss/year.** Send complete ms. **Pays 15-25¢/word for unsolicited articles.**

Photos Buys one-time rights. Offers up to $200/full page or cover; $50/inside. Identification of subjects required.

Fillers Anecdotes (inspirational). **Buys 10-20/year.** Length: 200-500 words. **Pays 15¢/word.**

$ WESLEYAN LIFE

The Wesleyan Publishing House, P.O. Box 50434, Indianapolis IN 46250-0434. (317)774-7909. Fax: (317)774-7913. E-mail: communications@wesleyan.org. Editor: Dr. Norman G. Wilson. **Contact:** Jerry Brecheisen, managing editor. Quarterly magazine of The Wesleyan Church. Estab. 1842. Circ. 50,000. Pays on publication. Byline given. Buys first rights or simultaneous rights (prefers first rights). Submit seasonal material 6 months in advance. Accepts simultaneous submissions.

Nonfiction Inspirational, religious. No poetry accepted. Send complete ms. Length: 250-400 words. **Pays $25-150.**

N ⊘ WHAT IS ENLIGHTENMENT?

P.O. Box 2360, Lenox MA 01240. Web site: www.wie.org..

- *WIE* does not accept freelance submissions.

$ $ THE WITTENBURG DOOR

(formerly *The Door*), P.O. Box 1444, Waco TX 76703-1444. (214)827-2625. Fax: (254)752-4915. E-mail: dooreditor@earthlink.net. Web site: www.thedoormagazine.com. **Contact:** Robert Darden, senior editor. **90% freelance written.** Works with a large number of new/unpublished writers each year. Bimonthly magazine. "*The Wittenburg Door* is the world's only oldest and largest religious humor and satire magazine." Estab. 1969. Circ. 7,500. Pays on publication. Publishes ms an average of 1 year after acceptance. Buys first rights. Accepts queries by mail. Responds in 3 months to mss. Sample copy for $5.95. Writer's guidelines online.

Read several issues of the magazine first! Get the writer's guidelines.

Nonfiction Looking for humorous/satirical articles on church renewal, Christianity and organized religion. Exposé, humor, interview/profile, religious. No book reviews or poetry. **Buys 45-50 mss/year.** Send complete ms. Length: 1,500 words maximum; 750-1,000 preferred. **Pays $50-250.** Sometimes pays expenses of writers on assignment.

Reprints Send ms with rights for sale noted and information about when and where the material previously appeared.

The online magazine carries original content not found in the print edition. Contact: Robert Darden.

Tips "We look for someone who is clever, on our wave length, and has some savvy about the evangelical church. We are very picky and highly selective. The writer has a better chance of breaking in with our publication with short articles since we are a bimonthly publication with numerous regular features and the magazine is only 52 pages. The most frequent mistake made by writers is that they do not understand satire. They see we are a humor magazine and consequently come off funny/cute (like *Reader's Digest*) rather than funny/satirical (like *National Lampoon*)."

N $ WOMAN ALIVE

Christian Publishing and Outreach, Garcia Estate, Canterbury Road, Worthing West Sussex BN13 1BW United Kingdom. (44)(190)360-4352. Fax: (44)(190)383-0066. E-mail: womanalive@cpo.org.uk. Web site: www.womanalive.co.uk. Editor: Jackie Stead. Administrator: Wendy Steele. Christian magazine geared specifically toward women. It covers all denominations and seeks to inspire, encourage, and resource women in their faith, helping them to grow in their relationship with God and providing practical help and biblical perspective on the issues impacting their lives. Pays on publication. Accepts queries by mail, e-mail. Sample copy for £1.50, plus postage. Writer's guidelines by e-mail.

O→ Articles should be personal in tone and draw on real-life anecdotes, as well as quotes from Christian professionals or related sources. Articles should be practical, accessible, and offer a Christian perspective, but writers should avoid using language that assumes a reader's familiarity with Christian or church-oriented terminology. All Bible quotes should be taken from the New International Version.

Nonfiction Contemporary issues (social/domestic issues affecting the church and women), reports from around the country giving a brief overview of the town and what churches/individuals are doing there, lifestyle, money matters, ethical shopping, work/life balance, homestyle, fashion, creative cookery. How-to (build life skills and discipleship), interview/profile (with Christian women in prominent positions or who are making a difference in their communities/jobs), personal experience (women facing difficult challenges or taking on new challenges), travel (affordable holiday destinations written from a Christian perspective). Submit clips, bio, article summary, ms, SASE. Length: 750-900/1-page article; 1,200-1,300/-page article; 1,500-1,600/3-page article. **Pays £65/1-page article; £90/2-page article; £120/3-page article.**

Photos Send photos with submission. Reviews 300 dpi digital images.

RETIREMENT

N $ $ $ $ AARP THE MAGAZINE

AARP, 601 E St. NW, Washington DC 20049. (202)434-6880. E-mail: member@aarp.org. Web site: www.aarp.org. **Contact:** Editorial Submissions. **50% freelance written.** Prefers to work with published/established writers. Bimonthly magazine. "*AARP The Magazine* is devoted to the varied needs and active life interests of AARP members, age 50 and over, covering such topics as financial planning, travel, health, careers, retirement, relationships, and social and cultural change. Its editorial content serves the mission of AARP seeking through education, advocacy and service to enhance the quality of life for all by promoting independence, dignity, and purpose." Circ. 21,500,000. **Pays on acceptance.** Publishes ms an average of 6 months after acceptance. Byline given. Offers 25% kill fee. Buys exclusive first worldwide publication rights. Submit seasonal material 6 months in advance. Accepts queries by mail, e-mail. Responds in 3 months to queries. Sample copy for free. Writer's guidelines online.

Nonfiction Articles can cover finance, health, food, travel, consumerism, general interest topics, and profiles/first-person accounts. Query with published clips. *No unsolicited mss.* Length: Up to 2,000 words. **Pays $1/word.** Sometimes pays expenses of writers on assignment.

Photos Photos purchased with or without accompanying mss. Pays $250 and up for color; $150 and up for b&w.

Tips "The most frequent mistake made by writers in completing an article for us is poor follow-through with basic research. The outline is often more interesting than the finished piece. We do not accept unsolicited manuscripts."

N $ $ FIFTY PLUS

Richmond Publishing, 5511 Staples Mill Rd., Suite 103, Richmond VA 23228. E-mail: mail@richmondpublishing.com. Web site: www.richmondpublishing.com. Editor: Angela Lehman-Rios. **85% freelance written.** Monthly tabloid covering mature living. "Our publication intends to reflect and enhance 50-plus lifestyles and to encourage reader dialogue and input." Estab. 1996. Circ. 30,000. Pays on publication. Publishes ms an average of 2 months after acceptance. Byline given. Buys first North American serial rights. Editorial lead time 3 months. Submit seasonal material 3-4 months in advance. Accepts queries by mail, e-mail. Accepts previously published material. Accepts simultaneous submissions. Responds in 1 month to queries; 2 months to mss. Sample copy and writer's guidelines online

Nonfiction General interest, historical/nostalgic, interview/profile, personal experience, travel, informational (senior issues). Does not want humorous, religious. **Buys 10 mss/year.** Query with published clips. Length: 425-1,750 words. **Pays $52-360.**

Photos Contact Denine D'Angelo, art director. Send photos with submission. Reviews GIF/JPEG files. Buys one-time rights. Negotiates payment individually. Captions, model releases required

Tips "I'm looking for writers who can identify and present topics of relevance to people over 65 and people over 45, using real examples and reputable sources."

$ MATURE YEARS

The United Methodist Publishing House, 201 Eighth Ave. S., Nashville TN 37202-0801. (615)749-6292. Fax: (615)749-6512. E-mail: matureyears@umpublishing.org. **Contact:** Marvin W. Cropsey, editor. **50% freelance written.** Prefers to work with published/established writers. Quarterly magazine "designed to help persons in and nearing the retirement years understand and appropriate the resources of the Christian faith in dealing with specific problems and opportunities related to aging." Estab. 1954. Circ. 55,000. **Pays on acceptance.**

Publishes ms an average of 1 year after acceptance. Buys first North American serial rights. Submit seasonal material 14 months in advance. Responds in 2 weeks to queries; 2 months to mss. Sample copy for $6 and 9×12 SAE. Writer's guidelines for #10 SASE or by e-mail.

Nonfiction Especially important are opportunities for older adults to read about service, adventure, fulfillment, and fun. How-to (hobbies), inspirational, religious, travel (special guidelines), older adult health, finance issues. **Buys 75-80 mss/year.** Send complete ms; e-mail submissions preferred. Length: 900-2,000 words. **Pays $45-125.** Sometimes pays expenses of writers on assignment.

Reprints Send tearsheet, photocopy or typed ms with rights for sale noted and information about when and where the material previously appeared. Pays at same rate as for previously unpublished material.

Photos Send photos with submission. Typically buys one-time rights. Negotiates pay individually. Captions, model releases required.

Columns/Departments Health Hints (retirement, health), 900-1,500 words; Going Places (travel, pilgrimage), 1,000-1,500 words; Fragments of Life (personal inspiration), 250-600 words; Modern Revelations (religious/inspirational), 900-1,500 words; Money Matters (personal finance), 1,200-1,800 words; Merry-Go-Round (cartoons, jokes, 4-6 line humorous verse); Puzzle Time (religious puzzles, crosswords). **Buys 4 mss/year.** Send complete ms. **Pays $25-45.**

Fiction Marvin Cropsey, editor. Humorous, religious, slice-of-life vignettes, retirement years nostalgia, intergenerational relationships. "We don't want anything poking fun at old age, saccharine stories or anything not for older adults. Must show older adults (age 55 plus) in a positive manner." **Buys 4 mss/year.** Send complete ms. Length: 1,000-2,000 words. **Pays $60-125.**

Poetry Free verse, haiku, light verse, traditional. **Buys 24 poems/year poems/year.** Submit maximum 6 poems. Length: 3-16 lines. **Pays $5-20.**

N $PLUS

Life's Second Half on the Central Coast, 793 Higuera St., Suite 10, San Luis Obispo CA 93401. (805)544-8711. Fax: (805)546-8827. E-mail: slojournal@fix.net. Web site: slojournal.com. **Contact:** Steve Owens, publisher. **60% freelance written.** Monthly magazine covering seniors to inform and entertain the "over-50" but young-at-heart audience. Estab. 1981. Circ. 60,000. Pays on publication. Publishes ms an average of 2 months after acceptance. Byline given. Buys one-time rights. Editorial lead time 2 months. Submit seasonal material 2 months in advance. Accepts queries by mail. Accepts simultaneous submissions. Responds in 2 weeks to queries; 1 month to mss. Sample copy for 9×12 SAE with $2 postage.

Nonfiction "We favor up-beat articles concerning nostalgia, personality profiles, subtle, not heavy-handed humor, travel, book reviews, entertainment and health." Historical/nostalgic, humor, interview/profile, personal experience, travel, book reviews, entertainment, health. Special issues: Christmas (December); Travel (October, April). No finance, automotive, heavy humor, poetry, or fiction. **Buys 60-70 mss/year.** Query with or without published clips or send complete ms. Length: 600-1,400 words. **Pays $50-75.**

Photos Send photos with submission.

Tips "Request and read a sample copy before submitting."

ROMANCE & CONFESSION

N MY WEEKLY

D.C. Thomson & Co Ltd, 80 Kingsway East, Dundee DD4 8SL United Kingdom. (44)(138)246-2276. E-mail: gsmart@dcthomson.co.uk. Editor: Harrison Watson. **Contact:** Gillian Smart. Weekly magazine aimed at "young" women of all ages. "We like our stories to deal with real, down-to-earth themes that related to the lives of our readers." **Pays on acceptance.** Submit seasonal material 3 months in advance. Writer's guidelines by e-mail.

Fiction Historical, humorous, mystery, romance, serialized novels, thriller, drama, seasonal. Does not want stories containing gratuitous sex or violence. Send complete ms. Length: 1,500-4,000 words.

$TRUE ROMANCE

Dorchester Media, 333 Seventh Ave., New York NY 10001. (212)780-3500. E-mail: nmiller@dorchestermedia.c om. Web site: www.trueromancemag.com. Associate Editor: Gia Portfolio. **Contact:** Nell Miller, senior editor. **100% freelance written.** Monthly magazine for women, teens through retired, offering compelling confession stories based on true happenings, with reader identification and strong emotional tone. No third-person material. Estab. 1923. Circ. 225,000. Pays 1 month after publication. Buys all rights. Submit seasonal material 6 months in advance. Accepts queries by mail, e-mail, fax. Responds in 8 months to queries.

Nonfiction Confessions, true love stories, mini-adventures; problems and solutions; dating and marital difficulties. Realistic, yet unique stories dealing with current problems, everyday events; strong emotional appeal;

controversial topics of interest to women. **Buys 180 mss/year.** Submit ms. Length: 6,000-9,000 words. **Pays 3¢/word; slightly higher rates for short-shorts.**

Columns/Departments Happily Ever After; Family Recipe; Loving Pets; Let It Out!, **all pay $50;** Cupid's Corner, **pays $100**; Passages, **pays 3¢/word.**

Poetry Light romantic poetry. Length: 24 lines maximum. **Pays $10-50.**

Tips "A timely, well-written story that is told by a sympathetic narrator who sees the central problem through to a satisfying resolution is *all* important to break into *True Romance*. We are always looking for interesting, emotional, identifiable stories."

RURAL

$ $ THE COUNTRY CONNECTION

Ontario's Magazine of Choice, Pinecone Publishing, P.O. Box 100, Boulter ON K0L 1G0 Canada. (613)332-3651. E-mail: editor@pinecone.on.ca. Web site: www.pinecone.on.ca. **Contact:** Gus Zylstra, editor. **100% freelance written.** Magazine published 4 times/year covering nature, environment, history, heritage, nostalgia, travel and the arts. "*The Country Connection* is a magazine for true nature lovers and the rural adventurer. Building on our commitment to heritage, cultural, artistic, and environmental themes, we continually add new topics to illuminate the country experience of people living within nature. Our goal is to chronicle rural life in its many aspects, giving 'voice' to the countryside." Estab. 1989. Circ. 4,000. Pays on publication. Publishes ms an average of 4 months after acceptance. Byline given. Buys first rights. Editorial lead time 4 months. Accepts queries by mail, e-mail, phone. Sample copy for $5.64. Writer's guidelines online.

Nonfiction General interest, historical/nostalgic, humor, opinion, personal experience, travel, lifestyle, leisure, art and culture, vegan recipes. No hunting, fishing, animal husbandry, or pet articles. **Buys 60 mss/year.** Send complete ms. Length: 500-2,000 words. **Pays 10¢/word.**

Photos Send photos with submission. Reviews transparencies, prints, digital photos on CD. Buys one-time rights. Offers $10-50/photo. Captions required.

Fiction Adventure, fantasy, historical, humorous, slice-of-life vignettes, country living. **Buys 10 mss/year.** Send complete ms. Length: 500-1,500 words. **Pays 10¢/word.**

Tips "Canadian content only with a preference for Ontario subject matter. Send manuscript with appropriate support material such as photos, illustrations, maps, etc."

$ $ FARM & RANCH LIVING

Reiman Media Group, 5925 Country Lane, Greendale WI 53129. (414)423-0100. Fax: (414)423-8463. E-mail: editors@farmandranchliving.com. Web site: www.farmandranchliving.com. **Contact:** Nick Pabst, editor. **30% freelance written.** Eager to work with new/unpublished writers. Bimonthly magazine aimed at families that farm or ranch full time. "*F&RL* is *not* a 'how-to' magazine—it focuses on people rather than products and profits." Estab. 1978. Circ. 400,000. Pays on publication. Publishes ms an average of 6 months after acceptance. Byline given. Buys first, one-time rights. Submit seasonal material 6 months in advance. Accepts queries by mail, e-mail, fax. Responds in 6 weeks to queries. Sample copy for $2. Writer's guidelines for #10 SASE.

Break in with "photo-illustrated stories about present-day farmers and ranchers."

Nonfiction Humor (rural only), inspirational, interview/profile, personal experience (farm/ranch related), photo feature, nostalgia, prettiest place in the country (photo/text tour of ranch or farm). No issue-oriented stories (pollution, animal rights, etc.). **Buys 30 mss/year.** Query with or without published clips or send complete ms. Length: 600-1,200 words. **Pays up to $300 for text/photo package. Payment for Prettiest Place negotiable.**

Reprints Send photocopy with rights for sale noted. Payment negotiable.

Photos Scenic. State availability with submission. Buys one-time rights. Pays $75-200 for 35mm color slides.

Tips "Our readers enjoy stories and features that are upbeat and positive. A freelancer must see *F&RL* to fully appreciate how different it is from other farm publications—ordering a sample is strongly advised (not available on newsstands). Photo features (about interesting farm or ranch families) and personality profiles are most open to freelancers."

$ $ HOBBY FARMS

Rural Living for Pleasure and Profit, Bowtie, Inc., P.O. Box 8237, Lexington KY 40533. Fax: (859)260-9814. E-mail: hobbyfarms@bowtieinc.com. Web site: www.hobbyfarms.com. Associate Editor: Sarah Coleman. **Contact:** Karen Keb Acevedo, editor. **75% freelance written.** Bimonthly magazine covering small farms and rural lifestyle. "*Hobby Farms* is the magazine for rural enthusiasts. Whether you have a small garden or 100 acres, there is something in *Hobby Farms* to educate, enlighten or inspire you." Estab. 2001. Circ. 90,000. Pays on publication. Publishes ms an average of 6 months after acceptance. Byline given. Buys first North American serial rights, makes work-for-hire assignments. Editorial lead time 3 months. Submit seasonal material 6 months in advance. Accepts queries by mail, e-mail. Responds in 2 months to queries; 2 months to mss. Sample copy for 10×12 SAE and 3 first-class stamps. Writer's guidelines free.

- Writing tone should be conversational, but authoritative.

Nonfiction Historical/nostalgic, how-to (farm or livestock management, equipment, etc.), interview/profile, personal experience, technical, breed or crop profiles. **Buys 10 mss/year.** Query with or without published clips or send complete ms. Length: 1,500-2,500 words. Sometimes pays expenses of writers on assignment.

Photos State availability of or send photos with submission. Reviews transparencies, GIF/JPEG files. Buys one-time rights. Negotiates payment individually. Identification of subjects, model releases required.

Tips "Please state your specific experience with any aspect of farming (livestock, gardening, equipment, marketing, etc)."

$ MOTHER EARTH NEWS

Ogden Publications, 1503 SW 42nd St., Topeka KS 66609-1265. (785)274-4300. E-mail: letters@motherearthnews.com. Web site: www.motherearthnews.com. Managing Editor: Nancy Smith. **Contact:** Cheryl Long, editor. Mostly written by staff and team of established freelancers. Bimonthly magazine emphasizing country living, country skills, natural health and sustainable technologies for both long-time and would-be ruralists. "*Mother Earth News* is dedicated to presenting information that helps readers be more self-sufficient, financially independent, and environmentally aware." Circ. 350,000. Pays on publication. Byline given. Submit seasonal material 5 months in advance. Responds in 6 months to mss. Sample copy for $5. Writer's guidelines for #10 SASE.

Nonfiction How-to, alternative energy systems; organic gardening; home building; home retrofit and maintenance; energy-efficient structures; seasonal cooking; home business. No fiction, please. **Buys 35-50 mss/year.** Query. "Sending us a short, to-the-point paragraph is often enough. If it's a subject we don't need at all, we can answer it immediately. If it tickles our imagination, we'll ask to take a look at the whole piece." Length: 300-3,000 words. **Pays $25-100.**

Columns/Departments Country Lore (down-home solutions to everyday problems); Herbs & Remedies (home healing, natural medicine); Energy & Environment (ways to conserve energy while saving money; also alternative energy).

Tips "Probably the best way to break in is to study our magazine, digest our writer's guidelines, and send us a concise article illustrated with color transparencies that we can't resist. When folks query and we give a go-ahead on speculation, we often offer some suggestions. Failure to follow those suggestions can lose the sale for the author. We want articles that tell what real people are doing to take charge of their own lives. Articles should be well-documented and tightly written treatments of topics we haven't already covered."

$ RANGE MAGAZINE

The Cowboy Spirit on America's Outback, Purple Coyote Corp., 106 E. Adams St., Suite 201, Carson City NV 89706. (775)884-2200. Fax: (775)884-2213. Web site: www.rangemagazine.com. **Contact:** C.J. Hadley, editor. **70% freelance written.** Quarterly magazine. "*RANGE* magazine covers ranching and farming as available resources." Estab. 1991. Pays on publication. Publishes ms an average of 6 months after acceptance. Buys first North American serial rights, makes work-for-hire assignments. Accepts queries by mail. Responds in 6-8 weeks to queries; 3-6 months to mss. Sample copy for $2. Writer's guidelines online.

Nonfiction Book excerpts, humor, interview/profile, personal experience, photo feature. No rodeos or anything by a writer not familiar with *RANGE*. Query. Length: 1,000-1,500 words. **Pays $100.** Sometimes pays expenses of writers on assignment.

Photos C.J. Hadley, editor/publisher. State availability with submission. Reviews 35mm transparencies, 4×6 prints. Buys one-time rights. Negotiates payment individually. Captions, identification of subjects, model releases required.

$ RURAL HERITAGE

281 Dean Ridge Lane, Gainesboro TN 38562-5039. (931)268-0655. E-mail: editor@ruralheritage.com. Web site: www.ruralheritage.com. Publisher: Allan Damerow. **Contact:** Gail Damerow, editor. **98% freelance written.** Willing to work with a small number of new/unpublished writers. Bimonthly magazine devoted to the training and care of draft animals. Estab. 1976. Circ. 9,500. Pays on publication. Publishes ms an average of 6 months after acceptance. Byline given. Buys first English language rights. Submit seasonal material 6 months in advance. Accepts queries by mail, e-mail. Responds in 3 months to queries. Sample copy for $8. Writer's guidelines online.

Nonfiction How-to (farming with draft animals), interview/profile (people using draft animals), photo feature. No articles on *mechanized* farming. **Buys 200 mss/year.** Query or send complete ms. Length: 1,200-1,500 words. **Pays 5¢/word.**

Photos Six covers/year, animals in harness $200. Photo guidelines for #10 SASE or on Web site. Buys one-time rights. Pays $10. Captions, identification of subjects required.

Poetry Traditional. **Pays $5-25.**

Tips "Thoroughly understand our subject: working draft animals in harness. We'd like more pieces on plans and instructions for constructing various horse-drawn implements and vehicles. Always welcome are: 1.) Detailed descriptions and photos of horse-drawn implements, 2.) Prices and other details of draft animal and implement auctions and sales."

$ $ RURALITE

P.O. Box 558, Forest Grove OR 97116-0558. (503)357-2105. Fax: (503)357-8615. E-mail: ruralite@ruralite.org. Web site: www.ruralite.org. **Contact:** Curtis Condon, editor-in-chief. **80% freelance written.** Works with new, unpublished writers. Monthly magazine aimed at members of consumer-owned electric utilities throughout 10 western states, including Alaska. Publishes 48 regional editions. Estab. 1954. Circ. 325,000. **Pays on acceptance.** Byline given. Buys first, sometimes reprint rights. Accepts queries by mail. Responds in 1 month to queries. Sample copy for 10×13 SAE with 4 first-class stamps; guidelines also online. Writer's guidelines online.

Nonfiction Looking for well-written nonfiction, dealing primarily with human interest topics. Must have strong Northwest perspective and be sensitive to Northwest issues and attitudes. Wide range of topics possible, from energy-related subjects to little-known travel destinations to interesting people living in areas served by consumer-owned electric utilities. Family-related issues, Northwest history (no encyclopedia rewrites), people and events, unusual tidbits that tell the Northwest experience are best chances for a sale. **Buys 50-60 mss/year.** Query. Length: 100-2,000 words. **Pays $50-500.**

Reprints Send ms with rights for sale noted and information about when and where the material previously appeared.

Photos "Illustrated stories are the key to a sale. Stories without art rarely make it. Color prints/negatives, color slides, all formats accepted. No black & white."

Tips "Study recent issues. Follow directions when given an assignment. Be able to deliver a complete package (story and photos). We're looking for regular contributors to whom we can assign topics from our story list after they've proven their ability to deliver quality mss."

SCIENCE

$ $ $ $ AMERICAN ARCHAEOLOGY

The Archaeological Conservancy, 5301 Central Ave. NE, #902, Albuquerque NM 87108-1517. (505)266-9668. Fax: (505)266-0311. E-mail: tacmag@nm.net. Web site: www.americanarchaeology.org. Assistant Editor: Tamara Stewart. **Contact:** Michael Bawaya, editor. **60% freelance written.** Quarterly magazine. "We're a popular archaeology magazine. Our readers are very interested in this science. Our features cover important digs, prominent archaeologists, and most any aspect of the science. We only cover North America." Estab. 1997. Circ. 35,000. **Pays on acceptance.** Publishes ms an average of 3 months after acceptance. Byline given. Offers 20% kill fee. Buys one-time, electronic rights. Editorial lead time 3 months. Accepts queries by mail, e-mail, fax. Responds in 3 weeks to queries; 1 month to mss.

Nonfiction Archaeology. No fiction, poetry, humor. **Buys 15 mss/year.** Query with published clips. Length: 1,500-3,000 words. **Pays $700-1,500.** Pays expenses of writers on assignment.

Photos State availability with submission. Reviews transparencies, prints. Buys one-time rights. Offers $400-600/photo shoot. Negotiates payment individually. Identification of subjects required.

Tips "Read the magazine. Features must have a considerable amount of archaeological detail."

$ $ $ $ ARCHAEOLOGY

Archaeological Institute of America, 36-36 33rd St., Long Island NY 11106. (718)472-3050. Fax: (718)472-3051. E-mail: peter@archaeology.org. Web site: www.archaeology.org. **Contact:** Peter A. Young, editor-in-chief. **50% freelance written.** Magazine. "*Archaeology* combines worldwide archaeological findings with photography, specially rendered maps, drawings, and charts. Articles cover current excavations and recent discoveries, and include personality profiles, technology updates, adventure, travel and studies of ancient cultures. The only magazine of its kind to bring worldwide archaeology to the attention of the general public." Estab. 1948. Circ. 220,000. **Pays on acceptance.** Byline given. Offers 25% kill fee. Buys world rights. Submit seasonal material 6 months in advance. Accepts queries by mail, e-mail, fax. Accepts simultaneous submissions. Sample copy and writer's guidelines free.

Nonfiction Essays, general interest. **Buys 6 mss/year.** Query preferred. Length: 1,000-3,000 words. **Pays $1,500 maximum.** Sometimes pays expenses of writers on assignment.

Photos Send photos with submission. Reviews 4×5 color transparencies, 35mm color slides. Identification of subjects, credits required.

The online magazine carries original content not found in the print edition. Contact: Mark Rose, online editor.

Tips "We reach nonspecialist readers interested in art, science, history, and culture. Our reports, regional commentaries, and feature-length articles introduce readers to recent developments in archaeology worldwide."

$ $ ASTRONOMY

Kalmbach Publishing, 21027 Crossroads Circle, P.O. Box 1612, Waukesha WI 53187-1612. (262)796-8776. Fax: (262)798-6468. Web site: www.astronomy.com. Editor: David J. Eicher. Managing Editor: Dick McNally. **50% of articles submitted and written by science writers; includes commissioned and unsolicited.** Monthly magazine covering the science and hobby of astronomy. "Half of our magazine is for hobbyists (who are active observers of the sky); the other half is directed toward armchair astronomers who are intrigued by the science." Estab. 1973. Circ. 137,000. **Pays on acceptance.** Byline given. Buys first North American serial, one-time, all rights. Responds in 1 month to queries; 3 months to mss. Writer's guidelines for #10 SASE or online.

- "We are governed by what is happening in astronomical research and space exploration. It can be up to a year before we publish a manuscript." Query for electronic submissions.

Nonfiction Book excerpts, new product (announcements), photo feature, technical, space, astronomy. **Buys 75 mss/year.** Query. Length: 500-3,000 words. **Pays $100-1,000.**

Photos Send photos with submission. Pays $25/photo. Captions, identification of subjects, model releases required.

Tips "Submitting to *Astronomy* could be tough. (Take a look at how technical astronomy is.) But if someone is a physics teacher or an amateur astronomer, he or she might want to study the magazine for a year to see the sorts of subjects and approaches we use, and then submit a proposal."

N $ $ $ CHEMICAL HERITAGE

Newsmagazine of the Chemical Heritage Foundation, Chemical Heritage Foundation (CHF), 315 Chestnut St., Philadelphia PA 19106-2702. (215)925-2222. E-mail: editor@chemheritage.org. Web site: www.chemheritage.org. Editor: Audra J. Wolfe. **Contact:** Jocelyn Hammond, production editor. **40% freelance written.** Quarterly magazine covers history of chemistry and molecular sciences. "*Chemical Heritage* reports on the history of the chemical and molecular sciences and industries, on CHF activities, and on other activities of interest to our readers." Estab. 1982. Circ. 25,000. **Pays on acceptance.** Publishes ms an average of 6-12 months after acceptance. Byline given. Buys all rights. Editorial lead time 3 months. Accepts queries by mail, e-mail, phone. Responds in 1 month to queries; 1 month to mss. Sample copy for free. Editorial calendar free.

Nonfiction "We are always particularly interested in celebrating historical anniversaries or discoveries." Book excerpts, essays, historical/nostalgic, interview/profile. No exposés or excessively technical material. "Many of our readers are highly educated professionals, but they may not be familiar with, for example, specific chemical processes." **Buys 10 mss/year.** Query. Length: 1,000-3,500 words. **Pays 50¢/word.**

Photos State availability with submission. Buys one-time rights. Offers no additional payment for photos accepted with ms. Captions required.

Columns/Departments Content Editor: Christopher Munden (christopherm@chemheritage.org). Book reviews and CHF collecting, both 600 words; Conferences, 500 words; History in the Making, 500-1,000 words. **Buys 10 mss/year.** Query.

Tips "CHF operates exhibits at many scientific trade shows and scholarly conferences. Our representatives are always happy to speak to potential authors genuinely interested in the past, present and future of chemistry. We are a good venue for scholars who want to reach a broader audience or for science writers who want to bolster their scholarly credentials."

N Ø DISCOVER

90 Fifth Ave., New York NY 10011. E-mail: editorial@discover.com. Web site: www.discover.com. Executive Editor: Corey S. Powell.

- *Discover* does not accept freelance submissions.

POPULAR SCIENCE

The What's New Magazine, Time4Media, 2 Park Ave., 9th Floor, New York NY 10016. Web site: www.popsci.com. Deputy Editor: Glenn Coleman. **Contact:** Editorial Department. **50% freelance written.** Monthly magazine for the well-educated adult, interested in science, technology, new products. "*Popular Science* is devoted to exploring (and explaining) to a nontechnical, but knowledgeable, readership the technical world around us. We cover all of the sciences, engineering, and technology, and above all, products. We are largely a 'thing'-oriented publication: things that fly or travel down a turnpike, or go on or under the sea, or cut wood, or reproduce music, or build buildings, or make pictures. We are especially focused on the new, the ingenious, and the useful. Contributors should be as alert to the possibility of selling us pictures and short features as they are to major articles. Freelancers should study the magazine to see what we want and avoid irrelevant submissions.'' Estab. 1872. Circ. 1,450,000. **Pays on acceptance.** Byline given. Offers 25% kill fee. Buys first North American serial, second serial (reprint) rights. Editorial lead time 3 months. Accepts queries by mail, e-mail, fax. Responds in 1 month to queries. Writer's guidelines online.

Nonfiction ''We publish stories ranging from hands-on product reviews to investigative feature stories, on everything from black holes to black-budget airplanes.'' Query.

Tips ''Probably the easiest way to break in here is by covering a news story in science and technology that we haven't heard about yet. We need people to be acting as scouts for us out there, and we are willing to give the most leeway on these performances. We are interested in good, sharply focused ideas in all areas we cover. We prefer a vivid, journalistic style of writing, with the writer taking the reader along with him, showing the reader what he saw, through words.''

$ $ $ $ SCIENTIFIC AMERICAN

415 Madison Ave., New York NY 10017. (212)754-0550. E-mail: editors@sciam.com. Web site: www.sciam.com. Monthly magazine covering developments and topics of interest in the world of science. Query before submitting. ''*Scientific American* brings its readers directly to the wellspring of exploration and technological innovation. The magazine specializes in first-hand accounts by the people who actually do the work. Their personal experience provides an authoritative perspective on future growth. Over 100 of our authors have won Nobel Prizes. Complementing those articles are regular departments written by *Scientific American*'s staff of professional journalists, all specialists in their fields. *Scientific American* is the authoritative source of advance information. Authors are the first to report on important breakthroughs, because they're the people who make them. It all goes back to *Scientific American*'s corporate mission: to link those who use knowledge with those who create it.'' Estab. 1845. Circ. 710,000.

Nonfiction Freelance opportunities mostly in the news scan section; limited opportunity in feature well. **Pays $1/word average.** Pays expenses of writers on assignment.

$ $ SKY & TELESCOPE

The Essential Magazine of Astronomy, New Track Media, 49 Bay State Rd., Cambridge MA 02138. (617)864-7360. Fax: (617)576-0336. E-mail: editors@skyandtelescope.com. Web site: skyandtelescope.com. **Contact:** Richard Tresch Fienberg, editor. **15% freelance written.** Monthly magazine covering astronomy. ''*Sky & Telescope* is the magazine of record for astronomy. We cover amateur activities, research news, equipment, book, and software reviews. Our audience is the amateur astronomer who wants to learn more about the night sky.'' Estab. 1941. Circ. 110,000. Pays on publication. Publishes ms an average of 6 months after acceptance. Byline given. Buys first rights. Editorial lead time 4 months. Submit seasonal material 1 year in advance. Accepts queries by mail, e-mail, fax. Responds in 3 weeks to queries; 1 month to mss. Sample copy for $6.99. Writer's guidelines online.

Nonfiction Essays, historical/nostalgic, how-to, opinion, personal experience, photo feature, technical. No poetry, crosswords, New Age, or alternative cosmologies. **Buys 10 mss/year.** Query. Length: 1,500-2,500 words. **Pays at least 25¢/word.** Sometimes pays expenses of writers on assignment.

Photos Send photos with submission. Reviews contact sheets. Buys one-time rights. Negotiates payment individually. Identification of subjects required.

Columns/Departments Focal Point (opinion), 700 words; Books & Beyond (reviews), 800 words; The Astronomy Scene (profiles), 1,500 words. **Buys 20 mss/year.** Query. **Pays 25¢/word.**

Tips ''We're written exclusively by astronomy professionals, hobbyists, and insiders. Good artwork is key. Keep the text lively and provide captions.''

$ $ $ $ ☒ STARDATE

University of Texas, 1 University Station, A2100, Austin TX 78712. (512)471-5285. Fax: (512)471-5060. Web site: stardate.org. **80% freelance written.** Bimonthly magazine covering astronomy. ''*StarDate* is written for people with an interest in astronomy and what they see in the night sky, but no special astronomy training or background.'' Estab. 1975. Circ. 10,000. **Pays on acceptance.** Publishes ms an average of 4 months after acceptance. Byline given. Offers 25% kill fee. Buys first North American serial, electronic rights. Editorial lead time 6 months. Submit seasonal material 6 months in advance. Accepts queries by mail, e-mail, fax. Responds in 6 weeks to queries. Sample copy and writer's guidelines free.

- No unsolicited mss.

O→ ''*StarDate* magazine covers a wide range of topics related to the science of astronomy, space exploration, skylore, and skywatching. Many of our readers rely on the magazine for most of their astronomy information, so articles may cover recent discoveries or serve as a primer on basic astronomy or astrophysics. We also introduce our readers to historical people and events in astronomy and space exploration, as well as look forward to what will make history next year or 50 years from now. *StarDate* topics should appeal to a wide audience, not just professional or amateur astronomers. Topics are not limited to hard-core science. When considering topics, look for undercovered subjects, or give a familiar topic a unique spin. Research findings don't have to make the front page of every newspaper in the country to be interesting. Also, if you'd like to write an historical piece, look for offbeat items and events; we've already covered Copernicus, Kepler, Tycho, Newton and the like pretty well.''

Nonfiction General interest, historical/nostalgic, interview/profile, photo feature, technical, travel, research in astronomy. ''No first-person; first stargazing experiences; paranormal.'' **Buys 8 mss/year.** Query with published clips. Length: 1,500-3,000 words. **Pays $500-1,500.** Sometimes pays expenses of writers on assignment.

Photos Send photos with submission. Reviews transparencies, prints. Buys one-time rights. Negotiates payment individually. Identification of subjects required.

Columns/Departments Astro News (short astronomy news item), 250 words. **Buys 6 mss/year.** Query with published clips. **Pays $100-200.**

Tips ''Keep up to date with current astronomy news and space missions. No technical jargon.''

N $ SUPER SCIENCE

Scholastic, Inc., 557 Broadway, New York NY 10012-3999. (212)343-6470. Fax: (212)343-4459. E-mail: www.superscience@scholastic.com. Web site: www.scholastic.com. Magazine published 8 times/year. Designed as a hands on science magazine to turn kids on to science through experiments and science news that touches their lives. Circ. 200,000.

Nonfiction Send résumé and several published clips.

$ $ WEATHERWISE

The Magazine About the Weather, Heldref Publications, 1319 18th St. NW, Washington DC 20036. (202)296-6267. Fax: (202)296-5149. E-mail: ww@heldref.org. Web site: www.weatherwise.org. Associate Editor: Amy Souza. **Contact:** Lynn Elsey, managing editor. **75% freelance written.** Bimonthly magazine covering weather and meteorology. ''*Weatherwise* is America's only magazine about the weather. Our readers range from professional weathercasters and scientists to basement-bound hobbyists, but all share a common interest in craving information about weather as it relates to the atmospheric sciences, technology, history, culture, society, art, etc.'' Estab. 1948. Circ. 22,000. Pays on publication. Publishes ms an average of 6 months after acceptance. Byline given. Buys all rights. Editorial lead time 6-9 months. Submit seasonal material 9 months in advance. Accepts queries by mail, e-mail, fax, phone. Responds in 2 months to queries. Sample copy for $4 and 9×12 SAE with 10 first-class stamps. Writer's guidelines online.

> ''First, familiarize yourself with the magazine by taking a close look at the most recent issues. (You can also visit our Web site, which features the full text of many recent articles.) This will give you an idea of the style of writing we prefer in *Weatherwise*. Then, read through our writer's guidelines (available from our office or on our Web site) which detail the process for submitting a query letter. As for the subject matter, keep your eyes and ears open for the latest research and/or current trends in meteorology and climatology that may be appropriate for the general readership of *Weatherwise*. And always keep in mind weather's awesome power and beauty—its 'fun, fury, and fascination' that so many of our readers enjoy.''

Nonfiction Book excerpts, essays, general interest, historical/nostalgic, how-to, interview/profile, new product, opinion, personal experience, photo feature, technical, travel. Special issues: Photo Contest (September/October deadline June 1). ''No blow-by-blow accounts of the biggest storm to ever hit your backyard.'' **Buys 15-18 mss/year.** Query with published clips. Length: 1,000-2,000 words. **Pays $200-500 for assigned articles; $0-300 for unsolicited articles.**

Photos Reviews contact sheets, negatives, prints, electronic files. Buys one-time rights. Negotiates payment individually. Captions, identification of subjects required.

Columns/Departments Front & Center (news, trends, opinion), 300-400 words; Weather Talk (folklore and humor), 650-1,000 words. **Buys 12-15 mss/year.** Query with published clips. **Pays $0-200.**

Tips ''Don't query us wanting to write about broad types like the Greenhouse Effect, the Ozone Hole, El Niño, etc. Although these are valid topics, you can bet you won't be able to cover it all in 2,000 words. With these topics and all others, find the story within the story. And whether you're writing about a historical storm or new technology, be sure to focus on the human element—the struggles, triumphs, and other anecdotes of individuals.''

SCIENCE FICTION, FANTASY & HORROR

N $ ALL POSSIBLE WORLDS

A magazine of science fiction and fantasy stories, Zeta Centauri, Inc., 3156 Portman Rd., Columbus OH 43232. E-mail: allpossibleworlds@zetacentauri.com. Web site: www.allpossibleworlds.net. **Contact:** Jason Champion, editor. **98% freelance written.** Quarterly magazine covering science fiction and fantasy short stories. Estab. 2006. Circ. 100. **Pays on acceptance.** Publishes ms an average of 6 months after acceptance. Byline given. Buys first North American serial, electronic rights. Editorial lead time 3 months. Submit seasonal material 3-6 months in advance. Accepts queries by e-mail. Responds in 1-2 weeks to queries; 1-2 months to mss. Sample copy for $5.95. Writer's guidelines online.

Photos Send photos with submission. Reviews GIF/JPEG files. Buys one-time rights. Offers $10-12/photo.

Fiction Fantasy, science fiction. Does not want religious, poetry, stream of consciousness, "waking up from a dream" stories. **Buys 40 mss/year.** Send complete ms. Length: 500-6,000 words. **Pays $6-72.**

Fillers Gags to be illustrated by cartoonist. **Buys 1-2/year.** Length: 0-100 words. **Pays $10-45.**

Tips "Read guidelines thoroughly."

$ $ ANALOG SCIENCE FICTION & FACT

Dell Magazine Fiction Group, 475 Park Ave. S., 11th Floor, New York NY 10016. (212)686-7188. Fax: (212)686-7414. E-mail: analog@dellmagazines.com. Web site: www.analogsf.com. **Contact:** Dr. Stanley Schmidt, editor. **100% freelance written.** Eager to work with new/unpublished writers. Monthly magazine for general future-minded audience. Estab. 1930. Circ. 50,000. **Pays on acceptance.** Publishes ms an average of 10 months after acceptance. Byline given. Not copyrighted. Buys first North American serial, nonexclusive foreign serial rights. Sample copy for $5. Writer's guidelines online.

Break in by telling an "unforgettable story in which an original, thought-provoking, plausible idea plays an indispensible role."

Nonfiction Looking for illustrated technical articles dealing with subjects of not only current but future interest, i.e., topics at the present frontiers of research whose likely future developments have implications of wide interest. **Buys 11 mss/year.** Send complete ms. Length: 5,000 words. **Pays 6¢/word.**

Fiction "Basically, we publish science fiction stories. That is, stories in which some aspect of future science or technology is so integral to the plot that, if that aspect were removed, the story would collapse. The science can be physical, sociological, or psychological. The technology can be anything from electronic engineering to biogenetic engineering. But the stories must be strong and realistic, with believable people doing believable things—no matter how fantastic the background might be." Science fiction. "No fantasy or stories in which the scientific background is implausible or plays no essential role." **Buys 60-100 unsolicited mss/year.** Send complete ms. Length: 2,000-80,000 words. **Pays 4¢/word for novels; 5-6¢/word for novelettes; 6-8¢/word for shorts under 7,500 words; $450-600 for intermediate lengths.**

Tips "In query give clear indication of central ideas and themes and general nature of story line—and what is distinctive or unusual about it. We have no hard-and-fast editorial guidelines, because science fiction is such a broad field that I don't want to inhibit a new writer's thinking by imposing 'Thou Shalt Not's.' Besides, a really good story can make an editor swallow his preconceived taboos. I want the best work I can get, regardless of who wrote it—and I need new writers. So I work closely with new writers who show definite promise, but of course it's impossible to do this with every new writer. No occult or fantasy."

$ APEX DIGEST

Apex Science Fiction and Horror Digest, Apex Publications, LLC, P.O. Box 2223, Lexington KY 40588. (859)312-3974. E-mail: jason@apexdigest.com. Web site: www.apexdigest.com. **Contact:** Jason Sizemore, editor-in-chief. **75% freelance written.** Quarterly magazine covering dark science fiction and science-horror. "An elite repository for new and seasoned authors with an other-worldly interest in the unquestioned and slightly bizarre parts of the universe." Estab. 2004. Circ. 2,500. Pays on publication. Publishes ms an average of 2 months after acceptance. Byline given. Offers 100% kill fee. Buys first North American serial rights. Editorial lead time 2 months. Submit seasonal material 2 months in advance. Accepts queries by e-mail. Responds in 1 month to queries; 1 month to mss. Sample copy for $6. Writer's guidelines online.

Fiction Horror, science fiction. **Buys 44 mss/year.** Send complete ms. Length: 100-10,000 words. **Pays $10-100.**

$ ASIMOV'S SCIENCE FICTION

Dell Magazine Fiction Group, 475 Park Ave. S., 11th Floor, New York NY 10016. (212)686-7188. Fax: (212)686-7414. E-mail: asimovs@dellmagazines.com. Web site: www.asimovs.com. **Contact:** Sheila Williams, editor. **98% freelance written.** Works with a small number of new/unpublished writers each year. Magazine published 10 times/year, including 2 double issues. Magazine consists of science fiction and fantasy stories for adults and young adults. Publishes "the best short science fiction available." Estab. 1977. Circ. 50,000. **Pays on acceptance.** Publishes ms an average of 6-12 months after acceptance. Buys first North American serial, nonexclusive foreign serial rights; reprint rights occasionally. Accepts queries by mail. Responds in 2 months to queries; 3 months to mss. Sample copy for $5. Writer's guidelines for #10 SASE or online.

Fiction Science fiction primarily. Some fantasy and humor but no "sword and sorcery." No explicit sex or violence that isn't integral to the story. "It is best to read a great deal of material in the genre to avoid the use of some very old ideas." **Buys 10mss/issue.** Send complete ms and SASE with *all* submissions. Fantasy, science fiction. No horror or psychic/supernatural. Would like to see more hard science fiction. Length: 750-15,000 words. **Pays 5-8¢/word.**

Poetry Length: 40 lines maximum. **Pays $1/line.**

Tips "In general, we're looking for 'character-oriented' stories, those in which the characters, rather than the science, provide the main focus for the reader's interest. Serious, thoughtful, yet accessible fiction will constitute the majority of our purchases, but there's always room for the humorous as well. Borderline fantasy is fine, but no Sword & Sorcery, please. A good overview would be to consider that all fiction is written to examine or illuminate some aspect of human existence, but that in science fiction the backdrop you work against is the size of the universe. Please do not send us submissions on disk or via e-mail. We've bought some of our best stories from people who have never sold a story before."

$ BOOK OF DARK WISDOM

A Magazine of Dark Fiction, Elder Signs Press, Inc., P.O. Box 389, Lake Orion MI 48361-0389. E-mail: submissions@darkwisdom.com. Web site: www.darkwisdom.com. **Contact:** William Jones, editor (editor@darkwisdom.com). **95% freelance written.** Triannual digest-sized magazine covering dark fiction and strange facts (science/folklore). "The important ingredients for publication in *Book of Dark Wisdom* are origniality and well-written stories of dark fiction. Stories can be set in any time period or most any genre. Explicit violence, sex, or gore are not elements of dark fiction; rather, exploring the human condition through strong character and interesting settings/atmospheres are what make good tales for the magazine. We do publish some 'Lovecraft'-type stories, but they must be original—not pastiches—and they must be innovative. Do not reproduce Lovecraft's writing, build upon it." Estab. 2002. Circ. 6,000+. Pays on publication. Publishes ms an average of up to 1 year after acceptance. Byline given. Offers 10% kill fee. Buys first North American serial rights. Editorial lead time 5 months. Submit seasonal material 4 months in advance. Accepts queries by mail, e-mail. Accepts previously published material. Responds in up to 1 month to queries; 5 months to mss. Sample copy and writer's guidelines online or via e-mail.

Nonfiction Essays, historical/nostalgic. No true ghost stories, true crimes, or tales about serial killers. **Buys 3+ mss/year.** Send complete ms. Length: 1,200-2,000 words. **Pays 3-5¢/word for assigned articles; 1-5¢/word for unsolicited articles.** Sometimes pays expenses of writers on assignment.

Photos Send photos with submission. Reviews GIF/JPEG files. Buys one-time rights. Negotiates payment individually. Captions, identification of subjects, model releases required.

Columns/Departments Strange Happenings (true facts, science, new discoveries, unusal news), 1,500 words; Dark Library (book/film/music/art reviews), 500 words. **Buys 25+ mss/year.** Query. **Pays 1-5¢/word.**

Fiction Adventure, horror, science fiction, suspense, dark fiction. No tales with elves, trolls and pixies set in fantastic worlds. No serial killer or splatterpunk stories. Vampire and zombie stories must be very original. **Buys 35+ mss/year.** Send complete ms. Length: 100-5,000 words. **Pays 1-5¢/word.**

Poetry Avant-garde, free verse, haiku, light verse, traditional. **Buys 24 poems/year.** Submit maximum 4 poems. Length: 1-30 lines.

$ LEADING EDGE

Science Fiction and Fantasy, 4064 JFSB, Provo UT 84602. E-mail: editor@leadingedgemagazine.com. Web site: www.leadingedgemagazine.com/. **Contact:** Matthew Gibbons, editor. **100% freelance written.** Semiannual magazine covering science fiction and fantasy. "*Leading Edge* is a magazine dedicated to new and upcoming talent in the field of science fiction and fantasy." Estab. 1980. Circ. 400. Pays on publication. Publishes ms an average of 2-4 months after acceptance. Byline given. Buys first North American serial rights. Accepts queries by mail. Responds in 2-4 months to queries. Sample copy for $4.95. Writer's guidelines online.

- *No unsolicited submissions.*

Nonfiction Accepts scholarly articles on science fiction, science, fantasy, mythology, speculative anthropology, psychology, sociology, biology, chemistry, geology, or astronomy. Literary reviews are also encouraged. Book reviews (not book reports) should cover significant works published within the last year. Send complete ms. Length: 5,000 words maximum for scholarly articles; 500-1,000 words for book reviews. **Pays in contributor copies for nonfiction.**

Fiction Fantasy, science fiction. **Buys 14-16 mss/year.** Send complete ms. Length: Length: 17,000 words maximum. **Pays 1¢/word; $10 minimum.**

Poetry Publishes 2-4 poems per issue. Poetry should reflect both literary value and popular appeal and should deal with science fiction- or fantasy-related themes. Avant-garde, haiku, light verse, traditional. Submit maximum 10 poems. Length: Pays $10 for first 4 pages; $1.50/each subsequent page.

$ THE MAGAZINE OF FANTASY & SCIENCE FICTION

Spilogale, Inc., P.O. Box 3447, Hoboken NJ 07030. E-mail: fandsf@aol.com. Web site: www.fsfmag.com. **Contact:** Gordon Van Gelder, editor. **100% freelance written.** Monthly magazine covering fantasy fiction and science fiction. "*The Magazine of Fantasy and Science Fiction* publishes various types of science fiction and fantasy short stories and novellas, making up about 80% of each issue. The balance of each issue is devoted to articles about science fiction, a science column, book and film reviews, cartoons, and competitions." Estab. 1949. Circ. 40,000. **Pays on acceptance.** Publishes ms an average of 9-12 months after acceptance. Byline given. Buys first North American serial, foreign serial rights. Submit seasonal material 8 months in advance. Accepts previously published material. Responds in 2 months to queries. Sample copy for $5. Writer's guidelines for SASE, by e-mail or on Web site.

Fiction Prefers character-oriented stories. "We receive a lot of fantasy fiction, but never enough science fiction." Adventure, fantasy, horror, science fiction. No electronic submissions. **Buys 70-100 mss/year.** Send complete ms. Length: Up to 25,000 words. **Pays 5-9¢/word; additional copies $2.10.**

Tips "We need more hard science fiction and humor."

N $ NECROLOGY MAGAZINE

Isis International, P.O. Box 510232, Saint Louis MO 63151. E-mail: editor@necrologymag.com. Web site: www.necrologymag.com. Editor: John Ferguson. **100% freelance written.** Quarterly magazine dedicated to horror. "We also publish sci-fi and fantasy that contain elements of horror and macabre." Estab. 2006. Circ. 575. **Pays on acceptance.** Publishes ms an average of 9 months after acceptance. Byline sometimes given. Offers 100% kill fee. Buys first North American serial rights. Editorial lead time 6 months. Submit seasonal material 9 months in advance. Accepts queries by e-mail. Responds in 6 weeks to queries; 2 months to mss. Sample copy for $5. Writer's guidelines online.

Nonfiction Humor, interview/profile. Send complete ms. Length: 1,000-5,000 words. **Pays $50-150 for assigned articles; $10-25 for unsolicited articles.** Sometimes pays expenses of writers on assignment.

Photos Send photos with submission. Reviews GIF/JPEG files. Buys one-time rights. Offers no additional payment for photos accepted with ms; offers $5-25/photo. Identification of subjects, model releases required

Columns/Departments Buys 8 mss/year. Send complete ms. **Pays $10-25.**

Fiction Fantasy, horror, science fiction. Does not want to see gore and violence type fiction. "We'd prefer Lovecraftian style fiction." **Buys 16-20 mss/year.** Send complete ms. Length: 5,000-15,000 words. **Pays $10-25.**

Poetry Avant-garde, free verse, haiku, light verse, traditional. **Buys 12-15 poems/year.** Submit maximum 5 poems. Length: 5-100 lines.

Fillers Facts, newsbreaks. **Buys 8-16/year.** Length: 10-500 words. **Pays $1-25.**

Tips "We prefer Lovecraftian style horror and macabre. Do not repeat his works, but expand them into new dark and demented tales."

$ ON SPEC

P.O. Box 4727, Station South, Edmonton AB T6E 5G6 Canada. (780)413-0215. Fax: (780)413-1538. E-mail: onspec@onspec.ca. Web site: www.onspec.ca/. **Contact:** Diane L. Walton, fiction editor. Barry Hammond, poetry editor. **95% freelance written.** Quarterly magazine covering Canadian science fiction, fantasy and horror. "We publish speculative fiction and poetry by new and established writers, with a strong preference for Canadian authored works." Estab. 1989. Circ. 2,000. **Pays on acceptance.** Publishes ms an average of 6-18 months after acceptance. Byline given. Buys first North American serial rights. Editorial lead time 6 months. Accepts queries by mail. Accepts simultaneous submissions. Responds in 2 weeks to queries 3 months after deadline to mss to mss. Sample copy for $7. Writer's guidelines for #10 SASE or on Web site.

- Submission deadlines are February 28, May 31, August 31, and November 30.

Nonfiction Commissioned only.

Fiction Fantasy, horror, science fiction, magic realism, ghost stories, fairy stories. No media tie-in or shaggy-alien stories. No condensed or excerpted novels, religious/inspirational stories, fairy tales. **Buys 50 mss/year.** Send complete ms. Length: 1,000-6,000 words. **Pays $50-180 for fiction. Short stories (under 1,000 words): $50 plus 1 contributor's copy.**

Poetry Avant-garde, free verse. No rhyming or religious material. **Buys 6 poems/year.** Submit maximum 10 poems. Length: 4-100 lines. **Pays $20.**

Tips "We want to see stories with plausible characters, a well-constructed, consistent, and vividly described setting, a strong plot and believable emotions; characters must show us (not tell us) their emotional responses to each other and to the situation and/or challenge they face. Also: don't send us stories written for television. We don't like media tie-ins, so don't watch TV for inspiration! Read, instead! Absolutely no e-mailed or faxed submissions. Strong preference given to submissions by Canadians."

$ PENNY BLOOD

New York NY 10012. E-mail: editor@pennyblood.com. Web site: www.pennyblood.com. Editor: Nick Louras. **70% freelance written.** Quarterly magazine covering horror in entertainment. "*Penny Blood Magazine* is a survey of horror and cult entertainment. We are looking for horror movie retrospectives and interviews with genre personalities." Estab. 2004. Circ. 8,000. **Pays on acceptance.** Byline given. Offers 100% kill fee. Buys all rights. Accepts queries by e-mail. Responds in 2 weeks to queries; 1 month to mss. Sample copy not available. Writer's guidelines online.

Nonfiction Essays, interview/profile. **Buys 20-30 mss/year.** Send complete ms. **Pays 3¢/word.** Pays in contributor copies for filler material.

Tips "We accept submissions by e-mail only. We are seeking interviews particularly and our highest pay rates go for these."

$ RED SCREAM

Red Scream LLC, 166 Kelvin Dr., Buffalo NY 14223. E-mail: williams.redscream@gmail.com. Web site: www.redscream.com. **Contact:** David R. Williams, publisher/editor. **100% freelance written.** Quarterly magazine covering horror and alt-culture. "*Red Scream* publishes extreme horror and dark erotica fiction, indepth film analysis of transgressive cinema and articles on fringe culture online and offline." Estab. 2005. Pays on publication. Publishes ms an average of 2-6 months after acceptance. Byline given. Offers $25 kill fee. Buys first rights, makes work-for-hire assignments. Editorial lead time 2-6 months. Accepts queries by e-mail. Responds in 1-2 weeks to queries; 1-2 months to mss. Sample copy for $5.95. Writer's guidelines online.

Nonfiction Book excerpts, interview/profile, new product, film analysis. Does not want puff pieces, interviews of old school writers, actors, directors. "Read our magazine before submitting." **Buys 30-50 mss/year.** Query. Length: 500-5,000 words. **Pays 1-5¢/word.**

Fiction Erotica, experimental, horror. Does not want any horror that is not extreme. Any erotica that is not dark and disturbing. **Buys 30-50 mss/year.** Query. Length: 500-5,000 words. **Pays 1-5¢/word.**

N $ SCIWEB BEM

Science Fiction & Fantasy Audiozine, Riamac Group, P.O. Box 691298, Charlotte NC 28227. (704)545-8844. E-mail: editor@scywebbem.com. Web site: www.scywebbem.com. **Contact:** Cameron Harne, editor. **100% freelance written.** Quarterly audiozine (CDROM and MP3 download) covering science fiction and fantasy. "*SCYWEB BEM* strongly encourages contributors not to alter their writing style to accommodate an audio format, but simply to write the best story possible. They should also go to the 'Submissions' tab on the Web site and click on the link 'a side note about narratives and human psychology.' " Estab. 2005. Circ. 2,000. **Pays on acceptance.** Publishes ms an average of 3-6 months after acceptance. Byline given. Buys first North American serial, electronic, first offer on world anthology rights. Editorial lead time 3-6 months. Submit seasonal material 6-9 months in advance. Accepts queries by mail, e-mail. Responds in 1 month to queries; 2 months to mss. Sample copy for $7.95. Writer's guidelines online.

Fiction Fantasy, science fiction. Does not want graphic sexual content or horror. **Buys 25 mss/year.** Send complete ms. Length: 8,500 words. **Pays $10-50.**

Tips "There are a few things that do not translate easily from the written word to the spoken word. Beyond this, writers should do what they've always done: concentrate on telling a good story."

$ $ STARLOG MAGAZINE

The Science Fiction Universe, Starlog Group, 1372 Broadway, 2nd Floor, New York NY 10018-6113. Fax: (212)889-7933. E-mail: allan.dart@starloggroup.com. Web site: www.starlog.com. **Contact:** David McDonnell, editor. **90% freelance written.** Monthly magazine covering "the science fiction/fantasy genre: its films, TV, books, art, and personalities. We often provide writers with a list of additional questions for them to ask interviewees. Manuscripts must be submitted by e-mail. We are somewhat hesitant to work with unpublished writers. We concentrate on interviews with actors, directors, writers, producers, special effects technicians, and others. Be aware that 'science fiction' and 'Trekkie' are seen as derogatory terms by our readers and by us." Estab. 1976. Pays on publication. Publishes ms an average of 3 months after acceptance. Byline given. Offers kill fee only to mss. Buys all rights. Accepts queries by mail, e-mail, fax. Responds in 1 month to queries. Sample copy for $7. Writer's guidelines for #10 SASE.

- Break in by "doing something fresh, imaginative or innovative—or all 3, or by getting an interview we can't get or didn't think of. The writers who sell to us try hard and manage to meet 1 or more challenges. It helps to read the magazine."

Nonfiction "We also sometimes cover science fiction/fantasy animation. We prefer article format as opposed to Q&A interviews." Book excerpts (having directly to do with science fiction films, TV, or literature), interview/profile (actors, directors, screenwriters—who've done science fiction films—and science fiction novelists), movie/TV set visits. No personal opinion think pieces/essays. No first person. Avoids articles on horror films/

creators (which are covered by sister magazine *Fangoria*). Query first with published clips. Length: 500-3,000 words. **Pays $35 (500 words or less); $50-75 (sidebars); $150-300 (1,000-4,000 words).** Pays $50 for each reprint in each foreign edition or such.

Photos "No separate payment for photos provided by film studios or TV networks." State availability with submission. Buys all rights. Photo credit given. Pays $10-25 for color digital images depending on quality. Captions, identification of subjects, credit line required.

Columns/Departments Booklog (book reviews by assignment only). **Buys 150 reviews/year.** Book review, 125 words maximum. No kill fee. Query with published clips. **Pays $15 each.**

This online magazine carries original content not found in the print edition. Contact: David McDonnell, online editor.

Tips "Absolutely no fiction. We do not publish it, and we throw away fiction manuscripts from writers who can't be bothered to include SASE. Nonfiction only please! We are always looking for fresh angles on the various *Star Trek* shows and *Star Wars*. Read the magazine more than once, and don't just rely on this listing. Know something about science fiction films, TV, and literature. Most full-length major assignments go to freelancers with whom we're already dealing. But if we like your clips and ideas, it's possible we'll give you a chance. No phone calls for any reason please—we mean that!"

$ TABARD INN

Tales of Questionable Taste, Edgewood Ent., 468 E. Vallette St., Elmhurst IL 60126. E-mail: tabardinnedgewoodent@yahoo.com. **Contact:** John Bruni, editor. **100% freelance written.** Magazine published as funds allow. "I publish stories so edgy, extreme and weird that other magazines would usually not print them." Estab. 2005. Circ. 560. Pays on publication. Publishes ms an average of 6 months after acceptance. Byline given. Buys first North American serial rights. Editorial lead time 1 month. Accepts queries by mail, e-mail. Accepts simultaneous submissions. Responds in 2 weeks to queries; 1 month to mss. Sample copy for $6. Writer's guidelines for #10 SASE or via e-mail.

Fiction Adventure, erotica, ethnic, experimental, historical, horror, humorous, mainstream, mystery, religious, science fiction, slice-of-life vignettes, suspense, western, anything out of the ordinary. Does not want children's or fantasy. **Buys 12 mss/year.** Send complete ms. Length: 1-5,000 words. **Pays $1.**

Tips "All content, no matter how extreme, gruesome or bizarre, is welcome, but there must be characterization and plot. These are stories, not gladiator pits. No blatant preaching. Follow your heart. Write what you want to, not what you think has a good shot at getting published."

N $ TALEBONES

5203 Quincy Ave. SE, Auburn WA 98092. E-mail: info@talebones.com. Web site: www.talebones.com. Associate Editor: Kevin Kerr. **Contact:** Patrick and Honna Swenson, editors. **100% freelance written.** Magazine covering science fiction and dark fantasy. "*Talebones* publishes an eclectic mix of speculative fiction. We want literate stories that entertain readers." Estab. 1995. Circ. 1,000. Pays before publication. Publishes ms an average of 6 months after acceptance. Byline given. Offers 100% kill fee. Buys first North American serial, electronic rights. Accepts queries by mail, e-mail. Responds in 1 week to queries; 2 months to mss. Sample copy for $7. Writer's guidelines online.

Fiction Fantasy, horror, science fiction. Does not want vampire stories, writer stories, or stories about or narrated by young adults or children. **Buys 16 mss/year.** Send complete ms. Length: 6,000 words maximum. **Pays 1-2¢/word.**

Poetry Avant-garde, free verse, light verse, traditional. **Buys 3-8 poems/year.** Submit maximum 8 poems. **Pays $10 maximum.**

Tips "We publish a wide variety of speculative fiction. Reading a sample copy of *Talebones* will help the writer understand our eclectic tastes. Be professional and humble. We do publish a lot of new writers."

$ TALES OF THE TALISMAN

Hadrosaur Productions, P.O. Box 2194, Mesilla Park NM 88047-2194. E-mail: hadrosaur@zianet.com. Web site: www.zianet.com/hadrosaur. **Contact:** David Lee Summers, editor. **95% freelance written.** Quarterly magazine covering science fiction and fantasy. "*Tales of the Talisman* is a literary science fiction and fantasy magazine published 3 times a year. We publish short stories, poetry, and articles with themes related to science fiction and fantasy. Above all, we are looking for thought-provoking ideas and good writing. Speculative fiction set in the past, present, and future is welcome. Likewise, contemporary or historical fiction is welcome as long as it has a mythic or science fictional element. Our target audience includes adult fans of the science fiction and fantasy genres along with anyone else who enjoys thought-provoking and entertaining writing." Estab. 1995. Circ. 200. **Pays on acceptance.** Publishes ms an average of 9 months after acceptance. Byline given. Offers 100% kill fee. Buys one-time rights. Editorial lead time 9-12 months. Submit seasonal material 1 year in advance.

Accepts queries by mail, e-mail. Accepts previously published material. Responds in 1 week to queries; 1 month to mss. Sample copy for $8. Writer's guidelines online.

Nonfiction Interview/profile, technical, articles on the craft of writing. "We do not want to see unsolicited articles—please query first if you have an idea that you think would be suitable for *Tales of the Talisman*'s audience. We do not want to see negative or derogatory articles." **Buys 1-3 mss/year.** Query. Length: 1,000-3,000 words. **Pays $4-6 for assigned articles.**

Fiction David L. Summers, editor. Fantasy, horror, science fiction. "We do not want to see stories with graphic violence. Do not send 'mainstream' fiction with no science fictional or fantastic elements. Do not send stories with copyrighted characters, unless you're the copyright holder." **Buys 25-30 mss/year.** Send complete ms. Length: 1,000-6,000 words. **Pays $6-10.**

Poetry Avant-garde, free verse, haiku, light verse, traditional. "Do not send 'mainstream' poetry with no science fictional or fantastic elements. Do not send poems featuring copyrighted characters, unless you're the copyright holder." **Buys 24-30 poems/year.** Submit maximum 5 poems. Length: 3-50 lines.

Tips "Let your imagination soar to its greatest heights and write down the results. Above all, we are looking for thought-provoking ideas and good writing. Our emphasis is on character-oriented science fiction and fantasy. If we don't believe in the people living the story, we generally won't believe in the story itself. Queries are accepted year-round. Please submit complete manuscripts only during our annual reading periods: May 1-June 15 and November 1-December 15."

SEX

N $BLACK MALE FOR MEN

Go West Media Group, LLC, 3230 E. Flamingo Rd. #8-171, Las Vegas NV 89121. (877)446-8682. Fax: (702)974-0585. E-mail: wes@gowestmediagroup.com. Web site: www.blackmaleformen.com. **Contact:** Wes Miller, Raul Mangubat. **80% freelance written.** Works with a small number of new/unpublished writers each year. Monthly covering the gay black male lifestyle, gay humor, entertainment, and erotica. Estab. 1998. Circ. 60,000. Pays on publication. Byline given, pseudonym OK. Buys Buys unlimted rights to print (magazine and anthology) and electronic (Web site) publication rights. Accepts queries by mail, e-mail, fax. Accepts simultaneous submissions. Responds in 2 months to queries. Sample copy for $7.99. Writer's guidelines online.

- Break in with "a clear, solid story that can be sent on disk, uploaded on the Web site, or sent via e-mail."

Nonfiction Black entertainment and music/movie interests. **Buys 12-18 mss/year.** Send complete ms. Length: 3,000-3,500 words. **Pays $50-125.**

Photos Send photos with submission. Reviews contact sheets, transparencies, prints. Buys one-time print rights and electronic (Web site) posting rights. Offers $25/photo. Captions, identification of subjects, model releases, also buys up to 36 illustrations/year to complement erotic fiction (pays $125) required.

Fiction Gay black male erotica. **Buys up to 36 mss/year.** Send complete ms. Length: 3,000-3,500 words. **Pays $75-125.**

Fillers Short humor. **Buys 12-18/year.** Length: 1,500-2,500 words. **Pays $25-35.**

Tips "Our publications feature male nude photos, plus 2-3 fiction pieces, several articles, cartoons, humorous comments on items from the media, photo features, and entertainment/music information. We present the positive aspects of gay lifestyle, with an emphasis on humor and fitness. Humorous pieces may be erotic in nature. We are open to all submissions that fit our gay male format; the emphasis, however, is on humor and the upbeat. We receive many fiction manuscripts, but not nearly enough unique, innovative, or even experimental material."

N $$EXOTIC MAGAZINE

X Publishing, 818 SW 3rd Ave. #1324, Portland OR 97204. Fax: (503)241-7239. E-mail: vivacide@hotmail.com. Web site: www.xmag.com. Monthly magazine covering adult entertainment, sexuality. "*Exotic* is pro-sex, informative, amusing, mature, intelligent. Our readers rent and/or buy adult videos, visit strip clubs and are interested in topics related to the adult entertainment industry and sexuality/culture. Don't talk down to them or fire too far over their heads. Many readers are computer literate and well-traveled. We're also interested in insightful fetish material. We are not a 'hard core' publication." Estab. 1993. Circ. 120,000. Pays 30 days after publication. Byline given. Buys first North American serial rights; and online rights; may negotiate second serial (reprint) rights. Accepts queries by fax. Accepts simultaneous submissions. Responds in 2 weeks to queries; 2 months to mss. Sample copy for 9×12 SAE and 5 first-class stamps. Writer's guidelines for #10 SASE.

Nonfiction Interested in seeing articles about Viagra, auto racing, gambling, insider porn industry and real sex worker stories. Exposé, general interest, historical/nostalgic, how-to, humor, interview/profile, travel, News. No "men writing as women, articles about being a horny guy, opinion pieces pretending to be fact pieces."

Buys 36 mss/year. Send complete ms. Length: 1,000-1,800 words. **Pays 10¢/word up to $150.**
Reprints Send ms with rights for sale noted and information about when and where the material previously appeared. Pays 100% of amount paid for an original article.
Photos Rarely buys photos. Most provided by staff. Reviews prints. Negotiates payment individually. Model releases required.
Fiction "We are currently overwhelmed with fiction submissions. Please only send fiction if it's really amazing." Erotica, slice-of-life vignettes. Send complete ms. Length: 1,000-1,800 words. **Pays 10¢/word up to $150.**
Tips "Read adult publications, spend time in the clubs doing more than just tipping and drinking. Look for new insights in adult topics. For the industry to continue to improve, those who cover it must also be educated consumers and affiliates. Please type, spell-check and be realistic about how much time the editor can take 'fixing' your manuscript."

$ $ $ $ HUSTLER

HG Inc., 8484 Wilshire Blvd., Suite 900, Beverly Hills CA 90211. Fax: (323)651-2741. E-mail: features fp.com. Web site: www.hustler.com. Editor: Bruce David. **Contact:** Carolyn Sinclair, features editor. **60% freelance written.** Magazine published 13 times/year. "*Hustler* is the no-nonsense men's magazine, one that is willing to speak frankly about society's sacred cows and exposé its hypocrites. The *Hustler* reader expects honest, unflinching looks at hard topics—sexual, social, political, personality profile, true crime." Estab. 1974. Circ. 750,000. Pays as boards ship to printer. Publishes ms an average of 3 months after acceptance. Byline given. Offers 20% kill fee. Buys all rights. Editorial lead time 4 months. Submit seasonal material 6 months in advance. Accepts queries by mail, e-mail, fax. Responds in 2 weeks to queries; 1 month to mss. Writer's guidelines for #10 SASE.

- *Hustler* is most interested in well-researched nonfiction reportage focused on sexual practices and subcultures.

Nonfiction Book excerpts, exposé, general interest, how-to, interview/profile, personal experience, trends. **Buys 30 mss/year.** Query. Length: 3,500-4,000 words. **Pays $1,500.** Sometimes pays expenses of writers on assignment.
Columns/Departments Sex play (some aspect of sex that can be encapsulated in a limited space), 2,500 words. **Buys 13 mss/year.** Send complete ms. **Pays $750.**
Fillers Jokes and "Graffilthy," bathroom wall humor. **Pays $50-100.**
Tips "Don't try and mimic the *Hustler* style. If a writer needs to be molded into our voice, we'll do a better job of it than he or she will. Avoid first- and second-person voice. The ideal manuscript is quote-rich, visual and is narratively driven by events and viewpoints that push one another forward."

N $ IN TOUCH FOR MEN

Go West Media Group, LLC, 3230 E. Flamingo Rd. #8-171, Las Vegas NV 89121. (877)446-8682. Fax: (702)974-0585. E-mail: wes@gowestmediagroup.com. Web site: www.intouchformen.com. **Contact:** Wes Miller, Raul Mangubat. **80% freelance written.** Works with a small number of new/unpublished writers each year. Monthly magazine covering the gay male lifestyle, gay humor, and erotica. Estab. 1973. Circ. 70,000. Pays on publication. Byline given, pseudonym OK. Buys Buys unlimited rights to print (magazine and anthology) and electronic (Web site) publication rights. Accepts queries by mail, e-mail, fax. Accepts simultaneous submissions. Responds in 2 months to queries. Sample copy for $7.99. Writer's guidelines online.

- Break in with "a clear, solid story that can be sent on disk, uploaded on the Web site, or sent via e-mail."

Nonfiction Rarely buys nonfiction. Send complete ms. Length: 3,000-3,500 words. **Pays $50-125.**
Photos Send photos with submission. Reviews contact sheets, transparencies, prints. Buys one-time and electronic (Web site) posting rights. Offers $25/photo. Captions, identification of subjects, model releases, also buys up to 36 illustrations/year to complement erotic fiction (pays $125) required.
Fiction Gay male erotica. **Buys up to 36 mss/year.** Send complete ms. Length: 3,000-3,500 words. **Pays $75-125.**
Fillers Short humor. **Buys 12-18/year.** Length: 1,500-2,500 words. **Pays $25-35.**
Tips "Our publications feature male nude photos, plus 2-3 fiction pieces, several articles, cartoons, humorous comments on items from the media, and photo features. We present the positive aspects of gay lifestyle, with an emphasis on humor. Humorous pieces may be erotic in nature. We are open to all submissions that fit our gay male format; the emphasis, however, is on humor and the upbeat. We receive many fiction manuscripts but not nearly enough unique, innovative, or even experimental material."

N $ INDULGE FOR MEN

Go West Media Group, LLC, 3230 E. Flamingo Rd. #8-171, Las Vegas NV 89121. (877)446-8682. Fax: (702)974-0585. E-mail: wes@gowestmediagroup.com. Web site: www.indulgeformen.com. **Contact:** Wes Miller, Raul

Mangubat. **80% freelance written.** Works with a small number of new/unpublished writers each year. Monthly magazine covering the gay male lifestyle, gay humor, fitness, and erotica. Estab. 1985. Circ. 60,000. Pays on publication. Byline given, pseudonym OK. Buys Buys unlimited rights to print (magazine and anthology) and electronic (Web site) publication rights. Accepts queries by mail, e-mail, fax. Accepts simultaneous submissions. Responds in 2 months to queries. Sample copy for $7.99. Writer's guidelines online.

O‑ Break in with "a clear, solid story that can be sent on disk, uploaded on the Web site, or sent via e-mail."

Nonfiction Fitness and health interests. **Buys 12-18 mss/year.** Send complete ms. Length: 3,000-3,500 words. **Pays $50-125.**

Photos Send photos with submission. Reviews contact sheets, transparencies, prints. Buys one-time print rights and electronic (Web site) posting rights. Offers $25/photo. Captions, identification of subjects, model releases, also buys up to 36 illustrations/year to complement erotic fiction (pays $125) required.

Fiction Gay male erotica. **Buys up to 36 mss/year.** Send complete ms. Length: 3,000-3,500 words. **Pays $75-125.**

Fillers Short humor. **Buys 12-18/year.** Length: 1,500-2.500 words. **Pays $25-35.**

Tips "Our publications feature male nude photos, plus 2-3 fiction pieces, several articles, cartoons, humorous comments on items from the meda, photo features, fitness training, and wellness information. We present the positive aspects of gay lifestyle, with an emphasis on humor and fitness. Humorous pieces may be erotic in nature. We are open to all submissions that fit our gay male format; the emphasis, however, is on humor and the upbeat. We receive many fiction manuscripts, but not nearly enough unique, innovative, or even experimental material."

$ $ $ $ PENTHOUSE

General Media Communications, 2 Penn Plaza, 11th Floor, New York NY 10121. (212)702-6000. Fax: (212)702-6279. E-mail: peter.bloch@pmgi.com. Web site: www.penthouse.com. Monthly magazine. "*Penthouse* is for the sophisticated male. Its editorial scope ranges from outspoken contemporary comment to photography essays of beautiful women. *Penthouse* features interviews with personalities, sociological studies, humor, travel, food and wine, and fashion and grooming for men." Estab. 1969. Circ. 640,000. Pays 2 months after acceptance. Byline given. Offers 25% kill fee. Buys all rights. Editorial lead time 3 months. Accepts simultaneous submissions. Writer's guidelines for #10 SASE.

Nonfiction Exposé, general interest (to men), interview/profile. **Buys 50 mss/year.** Query with published clips or send complete ms. Length: 4,000-6,000 words. **Pays $3,000.**

Columns/Departments Buys 25 mss/year. Query with published clips or send complete ms. **Pays $500.**

Tips "Because of our long lead time, writers should think at least 6 months ahead. We take chances. Go against the grain; we like writers who look under rocks and see what hides there."

⊘ PLAYBOY MAGAZINE

730 Fifth Ave., New York NY 10019. Web site: www.playboy.com. Monthly magazine.

- As of November 2006, *Playboy* no longer accepts unsolicited mss of any kind, including fiction, nonfiction or poetry.

N $ $ $ PLAYGIRL

801 Second Ave., 9th Floor, New York NY 10017. (212)661-7878. Fax: (212)697-6343. E-mail: editorial@playgirlmag.com. Editor-in-Chief: Michele Zipp. **25% freelance written.** Prefers to work with published/established writers. Monthly magazine. "*PLAYGIRL* addresses the needs, interests and desires of women 18 years of age and older. We provide something no other American women's magazine can: An uninhibited approach to exploring sexuality and fantasy that empowers, enlightens, and entertains. We publish features articles of all sorts: interviews with top celebrities; essays and humor pieces on sexually-related topics; first-person accounts of sensual adventures; articles on the latest trends in sex, love, romance, and dating; and how-to stories that give readers sexy news they can use. We also publish erotic fiction and reader fantasies from first-person. The common thread—besides, of course, good, lively writing and scrupulous research—is a fresh, open-minded, inquisitive attitude." Circ. 500,000. Pays within 6 weeks of acceptance. Publishes ms an average of 5 months after acceptance. Byline given. Buys first rights. Submit seasonal material 6 months in advance. Accepts queries by mail. Sample copy not available. Writer's guidelines for #10 SASE.

O‑ Break in with pieces for Erotic Encounters. "This section is devoted to female fantasies and pleasures of the flesh. Be creative, wild, and uninhibited in your writings. Write what turns you on, not what you think turns other people on. All submissions considered must be sexually explorative fantasies that empower, enlighten, and entertain. Any fantasies that involve pain, degradation, or extreme negativity will not be published." Send complete ms and mark 'Erotic Encounters' on the envelope.

Nonfiction Average issue: 3 articles; 1 celebrity interview. Essays, exposé (related to women's issues), general interest, interview/profile (Q&A format with major celebrities—pitch first), new product, articles on sexuality, medical breakthroughs, relationships, insightful, lively articles on current issues, investigative pieces particularly geared to *PLAYGIRL*'s focus on sex/dating/relationships. **Buys 6 mss/year.** Query with published clips. Length: 800-1,200 for Erotic Encounters; 1,600-2,500 for articles. **Pays $300-1,000 (varies); $25 for some fantasies, more for celeb interviews.**

Tips "Best bet for first-time writers: Erotic Encounters. No phone calls, please."

SPORTS

ARCHERY & BOWHUNTING

$ $ BOW & ARROW HUNTING

Action Pursuit Group, 265 S. Anita Dr., Suite 120, Orange CA 92868-3310. (714)939-9991. Fax: (714)939-9909. E-mail: editorial@bowandarrowhunting.com. Web site: www.bowandarrowhunting.com. **Contact:** Joe Bell, editor. **70% freelance written.** Magazine published 9 times/year covering bowhunting. "Dedicated to serve the serious bowhunting enthusiast. Writers must be willing to share their secrets so our readers can become better bowhunters." Estab. 1962. Circ. 90,000. Pays on publication. Publishes ms an average of 2 months after acceptance. Byline given. Buys all rights. Submit seasonal material 6 months in advance. Accepts queries by mail, e-mail. Accepts simultaneous submissions. Responds in 1 month to queries; 6 weeks to mss. Sample copy and writer's guidelines free.

Nonfiction How-to, humor, interview/profile, opinion, personal experience, technical. **Buys 60 mss/year.** Send complete ms. Length: 1,700-3,000 words. **Pays $200-450.**

Photos Send photos with submission. Reviews contact sheets, 35mm and 2¼×2¼ transparencies, 5×7 prints. Buys one-time or all rights. Offers no additional payment for photos accepted with ms. Captions required.

Fillers Facts, newsbreaks. **Buys 12/year.** Length: 500 words. **Pays $20-100.**

Tips "Inform readers how they can become better at the sport, but don't forget to keep it fun! Sidebars are recommended with every submission."

$ $ BOWHUNTER

The Number One Bowhunting Magazine, InterMedia Outdoors, 6405 Flank Dr., Harrisburg PA 17112. (717)657-9555. Fax: (717)657-9552. E-mail: bowhunter_magazine@primediamags.com. Web site: www.bowhunter.com. **Contact:** Jeff Waring, publisher. **50% freelance written.** Bimonthly magazine covering hunting big and small game with bow and arrow. "We are a special-interest publication, produced by bowhunters for bowhunters, covering all aspects of the sport. Material included in each issue is designed to entertain and inform readers, making them better bowhunters." Estab. 1971. Circ. 155,000. **Pays on acceptance.** Publishes ms an average of 3 months to 2 years after acceptance. Byline given. Buys exclusive first, worldwide publication rights. Submit seasonal material 8 months in advance. Accepts queries by mail, e-mail, fax. Responds in 1 month to queries; 2 months to mss. Sample copy for $2 and 8 ½×11 SAE with appropriate postage. Writer's guidelines for #10 SASE or on Web site.

Nonfiction "We publish a Big Game Special each July but need all material by mid-April. Another annual publication, Whitetail Special, is staff written or by assignment only. Our latest special issue is the Gear Special, which highlights the latest in equipment. We don't want articles that graphically deal with an animal's death. And, please, no articles written from the animal's viewpoint." General interest, how-to, interview/profile, opinion, personal experience, photo feature. **Buys 60 plus mss/year.** Query. Length: 250-2,000 words. **Pays $500 maximum for assigned articles; $100-400 for unsolicited articles.** Sometimes pays expenses of writers on assignment.

Photos Send photos with submission. Reviews 35mm and 2¼×2¼ transparencies, 5×7 and 8×10 prints, hi-res digital images. Buys one-time rights. Offers $75-250/photo. Captions required.

Fiction Dwight Schuh, editor. Bowhunting, outdoor adventure. Send complete ms. Length: 500-2,000 words. **Pays $100-350.**

Tips "A writer must know bowhunting and be willing to share that knowledge. Writers should anticipate *all* questions a reader might ask, then answer them in the article itself or in an appropriate sidebar. Articles should be written with the reader foremost in mind; we won't be impressed by writers seeking to prove how good they are—either as writers or bowhunters. We care about the reader and don't need writers with 'I' trouble. Features are a good bet because most of our material comes from freelancers. The best advice is: Be yourself. Tell your story the same as if sharing the experience around a campfire. Don't try to write like you think a writer writes."

$ $ BOWHUNTING WORLD

Grand View Media Group, 14505 21 st Ave North, Suite 202, Plymouth MN 55447. (763)473-5800. E-mail: mikes@grandviewmedia.com. Web site: www.bowhuntingworld.com. **Contact:** Mike Strandlund, editor. **50% freelance written.** Bimonthly magazine with 3 additional issues for bowhunting and archery enthusiasts who participate in the sport year-round. Estab. 1952. Circ. 95,000. **Pays on acceptance.** Publishes ms an average of 5 months after acceptance. Byline given. Buys first, second serial (reprint) rights. Responds in 1 week (e-mail queries) to queries; 6 weeks to mss. Sample copy for $3 and 9×12 SAE with 10 first-class stamps. Writer's guidelines for #10 SASE.

- Accepts queries by mail, but prefers e-mail.

Nonfiction How-to articles with creative slants on knowledgeable selection and use of bowhunting equipment and bowhunting methods. Articles must emphasize knowledgeable use of archery or hunting equipment, and/or specific bowhunting techniques. Contributors must be authorities in the areas of archery and bowhunting. Straight hunting adventure narratives and other types of articles now appear only in special issues. Equipment-oriented aricles must demonstrate wise and insightful selection and use of archery equipment and other gear related to the archery sports. Some product-review, field-test, equipment how-to, and technical pieces will be purchased. We are not interested in articles whose equipment focuses on random mentioning of brands. Technique-oriented aricles most sought are those that briefly cover fundamentals and delve into leading-edge bowhunting or recreational archery methods. **Buys 60 mss/year.** Query with or without published clips or send complete ms. Length: 1,500-2,500 words. **Pays $350-600.**

Photos "We are seeking cover photos that depict specific behavioral traits of the more common big game animals (scraping whitetails, bugling elk, etc.) and well-equipped bowhunters in action. Must include return postage."

Tips "Writers are strongly advised to adhere to guidelines and become familiar with our format, as our needs are very specific. Writers are urged to query by e-mail. We prefer detailed outlines of 6 or so article ideas/query. Assignments are made for the next 18 months."

PETERSEN'S BOWHUNTING

Inter Media Partners, 7819 Highland Scenic Rd., Baxter MN 56425. (218)824-2549. Fax: (218)829-2371. Web site: www.bowhuntingmag.com. Editor: Jay Michael Strangis. **70% freelance written.** Magazine published 9 times/year covering bowhunting. "Very equipment oriented. Our readers are 'superenthusiasts,' therefore our writers must have an advanced knowledge of hunting archery." Circ. 175,000. **Pays on acceptance.** Byline given. Buys all rights. Editorial lead time 6 months. Submit seasonal material 6 months in advance. Accepts queries by mail. Responds in 1 month to queries. Writer's guidelines free.

Nonfiction Emphasis is on how-to instead of personal. How-to, humor, interview/profile, new product, opinion, personal experience, photo feature. **Buys 50 mss/year.** Query. Length: 2,100 words.

Photos Send photos with submission. Reviews contact sheets, 35mm transparencies, 5×7 prints, digital. Buys one-time rights. Captions, model releases required.

Columns/Departments Query.

Fillers Facts, newsbreaks. **Buys 12/year.** Length: 150-400 words. **Pays Other.**

BASEBALL

N BASEBALL AMERICA

Baseball America, Inc., P.O. Box 2089, Durham NC 27702. (919)682-9635. Fax: (919)682-2880. E-mail: willingo@baseballamerica.com. Web site: www.baseballamerica.com. Editor: Will Lingo. Managing Editor: J.J. Cooper. **10% freelance written.** Biweekly tabloid covering baseball. "*Baseball America* is read by industry insiders and passionate, knowledgeable fans. Writing should go beyond routine baseball stories to include more depth or a unique angle." Estab. 1981. Circ. 80,000. Pays on publication. Publishes ms an average of 2 months after acceptance. Byline given. Buys one-time rights. Editorial lead time 1 month. Submit seasonal material 2 months in advance. Accepts previously published material. Accepts simultaneous submissions. Sample copy for $3.25.

- "We use little freelance material, in part because we have a large roster of excellent correspondents and because much of what we receive is too basic or superficial for our readership. Sometimes writers stray too far the other way and get too arcane. But we're always interested in great stories that baseball fans haven't heard yet."

Nonfiction Historical/nostalgic, interview/profile, theme or issue-oriented baseball features. No major league player features that don't cover new ground or superficial treatments of baseball subjects. Send complete ms. Length: 100-2,000 words.

Photos State availability with submission. Buys one-time rights. Negotiates payment individually. Identification of subjects required.

$ FANTASY BASEBALL

Krause Publications, Inc., 700 E. State St., Iola WI 54990-0001. (715)445-2214. Fax: (715)445-4087. E-mail: info@fwpubs.com. Web site: www.collect.com. Editor: Greg Ambrosius. Quarterly magazine. Published for fantasy baseball league players. Circ. 130,000. Editorial lead time 6 weeks.

$ JUNIOR BASEBALL

America's Youth Baseball Magazine, 2D Publishing, P.O. Box 9099, Canoga Park CA 91309. (818)710-1234. Fax: (818)710-1877. E-mail: dave@juniorbaseball.com. Web site: www.juniorbaseball.com. **Contact:** Dave Destler, editor/publisher. **25% freelance written.** Bimonthly magazine covering youth baseball. "Focused on youth baseball players ages 7-17 (including high school) and their parents/coaches. Edited to various reading levels, depending upon age/skill level of feature." Estab. 1996. Circ. 50,000. Pays on publication. Publishes ms an average of 4 months after acceptance. Byline given. Buys all rights. Editorial lead time 3 months. Submit seasonal material 4 months in advance. Accepts simultaneous submissions. Responds in 2 weeks to queries; 1 month to mss. Sample copy for $5 and online.

Nonfiction How-to (skills, tips, features, how to play better baseball, etc.), interview/profile (with major league players; only on assignment), personal experience (from coaches' or parents' perspective). "No trite first-person articles about your kid." No fiction or poetry. **Buys 8-12 mss/year.** Query. Length: 500-1,000 words. **Pays $50-100.**

Photos Photos can be e-mailed in 300 dpi JPEGs. State availability with submission. Reviews 35mm transparencies, 3×5 prints. Offers $10-100/photo; negotiates payment individually. Captions, identification of subjects required.

Columns/Departments When I Was a Kid (a current Major League Baseball player profile); Parents Feature (topics of interest to parents of youth ball players); all 1,000-1,500 words. In the Spotlight (news, events, new products), 50-100 words; Hot Prospect (written for the 14 and older competitive player. High school baseball is included, and the focus is on improving the finer points of the game to make the high school team, earn a college scholarship, or attract scouts, written to an adult level), 500-1,000 words. **Buys 8-12 mss/year. Pays $50-100.**

Tips "Must be well-versed in baseball! Having a child who is very involved in the sport, or have extensive hands-on experience in coaching baseball, at the youth, high school or higher level. We can always use accurate, authoritative skills information and good photos to accompany is a big advantage! This magazine is read by experts. No fiction, poems, games, puzzles, etc."

N $ $ $ $ 108

Celebrating Baseball, Sandlot Media, 517 N. Mountain Ave., #237, Upland CA 91786. (909)912-0134. Fax: (909)912-0197. E-mail: info@108mag.com. Web site: www.108mag.com. Editor: Randy Merritt. **Contact:** Phil Osterholt, managing editor. **75% freelance written.** Quarterly magazine covering baseball. "*108* celebrates baseball's contribution to and role in American history, culture, and community through in-depth feature articles, short fiction, photography and original artwork." Estab. 2006. Circ. 40,000. Pays on publication. Publishes ms an average of 1-2 months after acceptance. Byline given. Buys first North American serial, one-time, electronic rights, makes work-for-hire assignments. Editorial lead time 3-6 months. Submit seasonal material 3-6 months in advance. Accepts queries by mail, e-mail. Sample copy for $7.95. Writer's guidelines by e-mail.

Nonfiction Submit nonfiction to features@108mag.com. Essays, historical/nostalgic, humor, inspirational, interview/profile, personal experience, photo feature. **Buys 20-30 mss/year.** Query with or without published clips or send complete ms. Length: 1,000-7,000 words. **Pays 50¢-$2/word for assigned articles; 50¢-$1/word for unsolicited articles.** Sometimes pays expenses of writers on assignment.

Photos State availability of or send photos with submission. Reviews GIF/JPEG files. Buys one-time rights. Negotiates payment individually. Captions, identification of subjects, model releases required.

Columns/Departments Growing Up (children of MLB players, what it's like); Beyond the Boxscore (greater significance of a single game/moment); Whatever Happened To (profile on player who fell out of the limelight); Teammates (tales of extraordinary baseball friendships), all 1,500-2,000 words. **Buys 16 mss/year.** Query with or without published clips or send complete ms. **Pays 50¢-$1/word.**

Fiction "As long as baseball is an integral part of the story, we'll take a look." Submit to fiction@108mag.com. Historical, horror, humorous, mainstream, mystery, slice-of-life vignettes, suspense, baseball. **Buys 10-15 mss/year.** Send complete ms. Length: 2,000-7,000 words. **Pays 50¢-$2/word.**

Poetry Publishes baseball-related poetry. **Buys 4-6 poems/year.** Submit maximum 3 poems. **Pays 50¢-$1/word.**

Tips "We tell the great stories that help make baseball the great game it is. We're looking for great stories—not statistical-laden entries from a baseball encyclopedia. We prefer complete manuscripts to queries."

BASKETBALL

[N] WOMEN'S BASKETBALL

420 Boylston St., 5th Floor, Boston MA 02116. E-mail: mmiazga@madavor.com. Web site: www.wbmagazine.com. **Contact:** Mike Miazga, editor-in-chief. Bimonthly magazine covering all aspects of women's basketball from youth to college to WNBA/Olympics. "We are the only printed national publication devoted exclusively to girls and women's basketball." Accepts queries by e-mail.

Nonfiction "Looking for experienced freelance writers who have covered the girls/women's game for a daily newspaper or bona fide national magazine. Also looking for credentialed fitness and instructional writers. No phone calls or faxes." General interest, how-to, interview/profile. Query with published clips. **Payment based on work being published.**

BICYCLING

$ $ $ ADVENTURE CYCLIST

Adventure Cycling Assn., Box 8308, Missoula MT 59807. (406)721-1776, ext. 222. Fax: (406)721-8754. E-mail: editor@adventurecycling.org. Web site: www.adventurecycling.org. **Contact:** Mike Deme, editor. **75% freelance written.** Magazine published 9 times/year for Adventure Cycling Association members. Estab. 1975. Circ. 30,000. Pays on publication. Byline given. Buys first rights. Submit seasonal material 9 months in advance. Sample copy and guidelines for 9×12 SAE with 4 first-class stamps.

Nonfiction How-to, humor, interview/profile, photo feature, technical, travel, U.S. or foreign tour accounts; special focus (on tour experience). **Buys 20-25 mss/year.** Query with or without published clips or send complete ms. Length: 800-2,500 words. **Pays $450-1,500.**

Photos Bicycle, scenery, portraits. State availability with submission. Reviews color transparencies. Identification of subjects, model releases required.

BICYCLING

Rodale Press, Inc., 135 N. Sixth St., Emmaus PA 18098. (610)967-8722. Fax: (610)967-8960. E-mail: bicycling@rodale.com. Web site: www.bicycling.com. **Contact:** William Strickland, executive editor. **50% freelance written.** Magazine published 11 times/year. "*Bicycling* features articles about fitness, training, nutrition, touring, racing, equipment, clothing, maintenance, new technology, industry developments, and other topics of interest to committed bicycle riders. Editorially, we advocate for the sport, industry, and the cycling consumer." Estab. 1961. Circ. 280,000. **Pays on acceptance.** Byline given. Buys all rights. Submit seasonal material 6 months in advance. Accepts previously published material. Responds in 2 months to queries. Sample copy for $3.50. Writer's guidelines for #10 SASE.

- "There are 2 great break-in opportunities for writers: 1.) 'Noblest Invention' (750-word column) offers writers a chance to tell us why the bicycle is the greatest bit of machinery ever created. 2.) 'Ask the Wrench' maintenance feature showcases a local bike mechanic's know-how. If you know a great mechanic, this is a chance to get in the magazine."

Nonfiction "We are a cycling lifestyle magazine. We seek readable, clear, well-informed pieces that show how cycling is part of our readers' lives. We sometimes run articles that are inspirational, and inspiration might flavor even our most technical pieces. No fiction or poetry." How-to (on all phases of bicycle touring, repair, maintenance, commuting, new products, clothing, riding technique, nutrition for cyclists, conditioning), photo feature (on cycling events), technical (opinions about technology), travel (bicycling must be central here), fitness. **Buys 10 unsolicited mss/year.** Query. **Payment varies.** Sometimes pays expenses of writers on assignment.

Reprints Send tearsheet or photocopy and information about when and where the material previously appeared.

Photos State availability of or send photos with submission. Pays $15-250/photo. Captions, model releases required.

Tips "Don't send us travel pieces about where you went on summer vacation. Travel/adventure stories have to be about something larger than just visiting someplace on your bike and meeting quirky locals."

BIKE CULTURE MAGAZINE

East Coast, (formerly *The Ride*), P.O. Box 441, Lexington MA 02420. (781)641-9515. Fax: (781)652-9575. E-mail: bikeculture@bikeculture.com. Web site: www.bikeculture.com. Editor: Richard Fries. **Contact:** Deb Fries. **25% freelance written.** Magazine published 8 times/year covering cycling on the East Coast. *Bike Culture Magazine* probes and merges the different genres of cyclists that make up East Coast bike culture. "Our readers look to the magazine as their main resource for provocative articles on racing, advocacy, industry, history, travel, and tourism." Estab. 1993. Circ. 10,000. Pays on publication. Publishes ms an average of 2 months after acceptance. Byline given. Buys first rights. Editorial lead time 2-3 months. Submit seasonal material 4 months in advance. Accepts queries by mail, e-mail. Accepts simultaneous submissions. Responds in 1 month to queries; 2 months to mss. Sample copy for $5.

Nonfiction "We seek articles with distinct and intriguing East Coast angles. We look for articles that report on people, places, industries, and things that help shape bike culture in our region." Exposé, interview/profile, travel. "No fiction or poetry, and please don't send a proposal for a bike ride you took in our region unless it is uniquely tied in with the topics we cover." Query with published clips. Length: 500-1,500 words. **Payment varies.**

Columns/Departments Lanterne Rouge (personal experience), 700-1,100 words; Racing (race reporting), 500-700 words; Urban Fringe (urban riding/racing and couriers), 500-700 words; Outta' Here (travel by bike). Query with published clips. **Payment varies.**

Tips "That a bike-related event occurs in our region is a basic foundation for our articles, but we want to show our readers how/why it matters (i.e. politically, historically, recreationally, or culturally)."

$ $ BIKE MAGAZINE

Primedia Enthusiast, P.O. Box 1028, Dana Point CA 92629. (949)496-5922. Fax: (949)496-7849. E-mail: bikemag@primedia.com. Web site: www.bikemag.com. **Contact:** Ron Ige, editor. **35% freelance written.** Magazine publishes 8 times/year covering mountain biking. Estab. 1993. Circ. 170,000. Pays on publication. Publishes ms an average of 2 months after acceptance. Byline given. Offers 25% kill fee. Buys first North American serial rights. Editorial lead time 4 months. Submit seasonal material 6 months in advance. Responds in 2 months to queries. Sample copy for $8. Writer's guidelines for #10 SASE.

> O→ *Bike* receives many travel-related queries and is seeking more investigative journalism on matters that affect mountain bikers. Writers have a much better chance of publication if they tackle larger issues that affect mountain bikers, such as trail access or sport controversies (i.e., drugs in cycling). If you do submit a travel article, know that a great location is not a story in itself—there must also be a theme. Examine back issues before submitting a travel story; if *Bike* has covered your location before, they won't again (for at least 4-5 years).

Nonfiction Writers should submit queries in March (April 1 deadline) for consideration for the following year's editions. All queries received by April 1 will be considered and editors will contact writers about stories they are interested in. Queries should include word count. Humor, interview/profile, personal experience, photo feature, travel. **Buys 20 mss/year.** Length: 1,000-2,500 words. **Pays 50¢/word.** Sometimes pays expenses of writers on assignment.

Photos David Reddick, photo editor. Send photos with submission. Reviews color transparencies, b&w prints. Buys one-time rights. Negotiates payment individually. Captions, identification of subjects required.

Columns/Departments Splatter (news), 300 words; Urb (details a great ride within 1 hour of a major metropolitan area), 600-700 words. Query year-round for Splatter and Urb. **Buys 20 mss/year. Pays 50¢/word.**

Tips "Remember that we focus on hard core mountain biking, not beginners. We're looking for ideas that deliver the excitement and passion of the sport in ways that aren't common or predictable. Ideas should be vivid, unbiased, irreverent, probing, fun, humorous, funky, quirky, smart, good. Great feature ideas are always welcome, especially features on cultural matters or issues in the sport. However, you're much more likely to get published in *Bike* if you send us great ideas for short articles. In particular we need stories for our Splatter, a front-of-the-book section devoted to news, funny anecdotes, quotes, and odds and ends. These stories range from 50 to 300 words. We also need personality profiles of 600 words or so for our People Who Ride section. Racers are OK but we're more interested in grassroots people with interesting personalities—it doesn't matter if they're Mother Theresas or scumbags, so long as they make mountain biking a little more interesting. Short descriptions of great rides are very welcome for our Urb column; the length should be from 600-700 words."

$ $ CYCLE CALIFORNIA! MAGAZINE

1702-L Meridian Ave., #289, San Jose CA 95125. (408)924-0270. Fax: (408)292-3005. E-mail: tcorral@cyclecalifornia.com. Web site: www.cyclecalifornia.com. **Contact:** Tracy L. Corral, editor/publisher. **75% freelance written.** Magazine published 11 times/year "covering Northern California bicycling events, races, people. Issues (topics) covered include bicycle commuting, bicycle politics, touring, racing, nostalgia, history, anything at all to do with riding a bike." Estab. 1995. Circ. 26,000. Pays on publication. Publishes ms an average of 3 months after acceptance. Byline given. Buys first North American serial rights. Editorial lead time 6 weeks. Submit seasonal material 6 weeks in advance. Accepts queries by mail, e-mail. Accepts simultaneous submissions. Responds in 1 month to queries. Sample copy for 10×13 SAE with 3 first-class stamps. Writer's guidelines for #10 SASE.

Nonfiction Historical/nostalgic, how-to, interview/profile, opinion, personal experience, technical, travel. Special issues: Bicycle Tour & Travel (January/February). No articles about any sport that doesn't relate to bicycling, no product reviews. **Buys 36 mss/year.** Query with or without published clips. Length: 500-1,500 words. **Pays 3-10¢/word.**

Photos Send photos with submission. Reviews 3×5 prints. Buys one-time rights. Negotiates payment individually. Identification of subjects required.

Columns/Departments Buys 2-3 mss/year. Query with published clips. **Pays 3-10¢/word.**

Tips "E-mail editor with good ideas. While we don't exclude writers from other parts of the country, articles really should reflect a Northern California slant, or be of general interest to bicyclists. We prefer stories written by people who like and use their bikes."

CYCLE WORLD

Hachette Filipacchi Media U.S., Inc., 1499 Monrovia Ave., Newport Beach CA 92663. (949)720-5300. Web site: www.cycleworld.com. Monthly magazine geared towards motorcycle owners and buyers, accesory buyers, potential buyers and enthusiasts of the overall sport of motorcycling. Circ. 319,489.

- Query before submitting.

MOUNTAIN BIKE

Rodale, Inc., 135 N. 6th Street, Emmaus PA 18049-2441. (610)967-8722. Fax: (610)967-8960. Web site: www.mountainbike.com. Editor-in-Chief: Stephen Madden. Magazine published 11 times/year covering every aspect of the bicycle sport including new products and technology, riding techniques, destinations, health and fitness as well as racing and enviromental issues. Circ. 150,328.

- Query before submitting.

N $ $ VELONEWS

The Journal of Competitive Cycling, Inside Communications, Inc., 1830 N. 55th St., Boulder CO 80301. (303)440-0601. Fax: (303)444-6788. Web site: www.velonews.com. **Contact:** Editor. **40% freelance written.** Monthly tabloid covering bicycle racing. Estab. 1972. Circ. 48,000. Pays on publication. Publishes ms an average of 1 month after acceptance. Byline given. Buys one-time worldwide rights. Accepts previously published material. Responds in 3 weeks to queries.

Nonfiction Freelance opportunities include race coverage, reviews (book and videos), health-and-fitness departments. **Buys 80 mss/year.** Query. Length: 300-1,200 words. **Pays $100-400.**

Reprints Send ms with rights for sale noted and information about when and where the material previously appeared.

Photos State availability with submission. Buys one-time rights. Captions, identification of subjects required.

BOATING

N AUSTRALIAN YACHTING

Yaffa Publishing, 17-21 Bellevue St., Surry Hills NSW 2010 Australia. (61)(2)9281-2333. Fax: (61)(2)9281-2750. E-mail: yaffa@yaffa.com.au. Web site: www.yaffa.com.au. Monthly magazine aimed at the owners and crews of yachts over 20 feet. "*Australian Yachting* covers monohulls, multihulls, inshore and offshore racing, coastal cruising and passage making."

Nonfiction General interest, how-to, interview/profile, new product. Query.

BASS & WALLEYE BOATS

The Magazine of Performance Fishing Boats, Poole Publications, Inc., 20700 Belshaw Ave., Carson CA 90746. (310)537-6322. Fax: (310)537-8735. E-mail: info@bassandwalleyeboats.com. Web site: www.bassandwalleyeboats.com. Editor: Steve Quinlan. **Contact:** Sylvia Alarid, managing editor. **50% freelance written.** "*Bass & Walleye Boats* is published 9 times/year for the bass and walleye fisherman/boater. Directed to give priority to the boats, the tech, the how-to, the after-market add-ons and the devices that help anglers enjoy their boating experience." Estab. 1994. Circ. 65,000. **Pays on acceptance.** Byline given. Offers 25% kill fee. Buys first North American serial rights. Editorial lead time 2 months. Submit seasonal material 3 months in advance. Accepts queries by mail. Sample copy for $3.95 and 9×12 SAE with 7 first-class stamps. Writer's guidelines free.

Nonfiction General interest, how-to, interview/profile, photo feature, technical. No fiction. **Buys about 120 mss/year.** Query. Length: 1,000-3,000 words.

Photos State availability with submission. Reviews transparencies, 35mm slides. Buys one-time rights. Negotiates payment individually. Captions, identification of subjects required.

Tips "Write from and for the bass and walleye boaters' perspective."

$ $ BOATWORKS

98 N. Washington St., 2nd Floor, Boston MA 02114. (617)720-8600. Fax: (617)723-0912. E-mail: bwmail@boatworksmagazine.com. Web site: www.boatworksmagazine.com. Editor: Peter Nielsen. **Contact:** Mark Corke, sen-

ior editor. **50% freelance written.** Quarterly DIY magazine for practically-minded boat owners. Explains how boat systems work in easy-to-understand, profusely illustrated features. Each issue has several step-by-step photographic guides to carrying out maintenance and improvement projects. Explains boat design and construction, and all technical aspects of sailing and boating. Readers are encouraged to submit stories based on their own projects and experiences.

Nonfiction Buys 30 mss/year. Length: 250-3,000 words. **Pays $100-750.**

Photos Prefers high resolution digital photos (300 dpi). Transparencies are also accepted, as are high-quality color prints. Prints should have negatives attached. Pays $25 and up, depending on the size used.

$ $ $ CANOE & KAYAK MAGAZINE

Action Sports Group, 950 Calle Amanecer, Suite C, San Clemente CA 92673. Web site: www.canoekayak.com. Editor: Frederick Reimers. **75% freelance written.** Bimonthly magazine. "*Canoe & Kayak Magazine* is North America's No. 1 paddlesports resource. Our readers include flatwater and whitewater canoeists and kayakers of all skill levels. We provide comprehensive information on destinations, technique and equipment. Beyond that, we cover canoe and kayak camping, safety, the environment, and the history of boats and sport." Estab. 1972. Circ. 70,000. Pays on publication. Publishes ms an average of 6 months after acceptance. Byline given. first international rights, which includes electronic and anthology rights Editorial lead time 6 months. Submit seasonal material 8 months in advance. Accepts queries by mail, e-mail. Responds in 2 months to queries. Sample copy and writer's guidelines for 9×12 SAE with 7 first-class stamps.

- Break in with good out-of-the-way destination or Put-In (news) pieces with excellent photos. "Take a good look at the types of articles we publish before sending us any sort of query."

Nonfiction Historical/nostalgic, how-to (canoe, kayak camp, load boats, paddle whitewater, etc.), personal experience, photo feature, technical, travel. Special issues: Whitewater Paddling; Beginner's Guide; Kayak Touring; Canoe Journal. "No cartoons, poems, stories in which bad judgement is portrayed or 'Me and Molly' articles." **Buys 25 mss/year.** Query with or without published clips or send complete ms. Length: 400-2,500 words. **Pays $100-800 for assigned articles; $100-500 for unsolicited articles.**

Photos "Some activities we cover are canoeing, kayaking, canoe fishing, camping, canoe sailing or poling, backpacking (when compatible with the main activity) and occasionally inflatable boats. We are not interested in groups of people in rafts, photos showing disregard for the environment or personal safety, gasoline-powered engines unless appropriate to the discussion, or unskilled persons taking extraordinary risks." State availability with submission. Reviews 35mm transparencies, 4×6 prints. Buys one-time rights. Offers $75-500/photo. Captions, identification of subjects, model releases required.

Columns/Departments Put In (environment, conservation, events), 500 words; Destinations (canoe and kayak destinations in US, Canada), 1,500 words; Essays, 750 words. **Buys 40 mss/year.** Send complete ms. **Pays $100-350.**

Fillers Anecdotes, facts, newsbreaks. **Buys 20/year.** Length: 200-500 words. **Pays $25-50.**

Tips "Start with Put-In articles (short featurettes) or short, unique equipment reviews. Or give us the best, most exciting article we've ever seen—with great photos. Read the magazine before submitting."

$ $ $ CHESAPEAKE BAY MAGAZINE

Boating at Its Best, Chesapeake Bay Communications, 1819 Bay Ridge Ave., Annapolis MD 21403. (410)263-2662. Fax: (410)267-6924. E-mail: editor@cbmmag.net. **Contact:** Ann Levelle, managing editor. **60% freelance written.** Monthly magazine covering boating and the Chesapeake Bay. "Our readers are boaters. Our writers should know boats and boating. Read the magazine before submitting." Estab. 1972. Circ. 46,000. Pays within 2 months after acceptance. Publishes ms an average of 1 year after acceptance. Byline given. Buys first North American serial rights. Editorial lead time 1 year. Submit seasonal material 1 year in advance. Accepts queries by mail, e-mail, fax, phone. Accepts simultaneous submissions. Responds in 2 months to queries; 3 months to mss. Sample copy for $5.19 prepaid.

- "Read our Channel 9 column and give us some new ideas. These are short news items, profiles, and updates (200-800 words)."

Nonfiction Destinations, boating adventures, how-to, marina reviews, history, nature, environment, lifestyles, personal and institutional profiles, boat-type profiles, boatbuilding, boat restoration, boating anecdotes, boating news. **Buys 30 mss/year.** Query with published clips. Length: 300-3,000 words. **Pays $100-1,000.** Pays expenses of writers on assignment.

Photos Buys one-time rights. Offers $75-250/photo, $400/day rate for assignment photography. Captions, identification of subjects required.

Tips "Send us unedited writing samples (not clips) that show the writer can write, not just string words together. We look for well-organized, lucid, lively, intelligent writing."

$ $ $ $ CRUISING WORLD

The Sailing Co., 5 John Clarke Rd., Newport RI 02840-0992. (401)845-5100. Fax: (401)845-5180. Web site: www.cruisingworld.com. Editor: Herb McCormick. Managing Editor: Elaine Lembo. **Contact:** Tim Murphy, executive editor. **60% freelance written.** Monthly magazine covering sailing, cruising/adventuring, do-it-yourself boat improvements. "*Cruising World* is a publication by and for sailboat owners who spend time in home waters as well as voyaging the world. Its readership is extremely loyal, savvy, and driven by independent thinking." Estab. 1974. Circ. 155,000. **Pays on acceptance for articles;** on publication for photography. Publishes ms an average of 18 months after acceptance. Byline given. Buys 6-month, all-world, first time rights (amendable). Editorial lead time 3 months. Submit seasonal material 1 year in advance. Accepts queries by mail. Responds in 1 month to queries; 4 months to mss. Sample copy for free. Writer's guidelines online.

Nonfiction Book excerpts, essays, exposé, general interest, historical/nostalgic, how-to, humor, interview/profile, new product, opinion, personal experience, photo feature, technical, travel. No travel articles that have nothing to do with cruising aboard sailboats from 20-50 feet in length. **Buys dozens of mss/year.** Send complete ms. **Pays $50-1,500 for assigned articles; $50-1,000 for unsolicited articles.** Sometimes pays expenses of writers on assignment.

Photos Send photos with submission. Reviews negatives, transparencies, color slides preferred. Buys one-time rights. Negotiates payment individually. Also buys stand-alone photos. Captions required.

Columns/Departments Shoreline (sailing news, people, and short features; contact Nim Marsh), 500 words maximum; Hands-on Sailor (refit, voyaging, seamanship, how-to; contact Darrell Nicholson), 1,000-1,500 words. **Buys dozens of mss/year.** Query with or without published clips or send complete ms. **Pays $100-700.**

Tips "*Cruising World's* readers know exactly what they want to read, so our best advice to freelancers is to carefully read the magazine and envision which exact section or department would be the appropriate place for proposed submissions."

$ $ GO BOATING MAGAZINE

America's Family Boating Magazine, Duncan McIntosh Co., 17782 Cowan, Suite C, Irvine CA 92614. (949)660-6150. E-mail: editorial@goboatingamerica.com. Web site: www.goboatingamerica.com. **Contact:** Mike Telleria, managing editor. **60% freelance written.** Magazine published 8 times/year covering recreational trailer boats. Typical reader "owns a power boat between 14 and 32 feet long and has 3-9 years experience. Boat reports are mostly written by staff while features and most departments are provided by freelancers. We are looking for freelancers who can write well and who have at least a working knowledge of recreational power boating and the industry behind it." Estab. 1997. Circ. 100,000. Pays on publication. Publishes ms an average of 4 months after acceptance. Accepts simultaneous submissions. Responds in 3 months to queries. Sample copy for free. Writer's guidelines for #10 SASE.

Nonfiction General interest, how-to, humor, new product, personal experience, travel. **Buys 20-25 mss/year.** Query. Length: 1,400-1,600 words. **Pays $150-450.** Sometimes pays expenses of writers on assignment.

Photos State availability with submission. Reviews transparencies, prints, digital images. Buys one-time rights. Offers $50-250/photo. Identification of subjects, model releases required.

Fillers Anecdotes, facts, newsbreaks. Length: 250-500 words. **Pays $50-100.**

Tips "We are looking for solid writers who are familiar with power boating and who can educate, entertain, and enlighten our readers with well-written and researched feature stories."

GOOD OLD BOAT

The Sailing Magazine for the Rest of Us, Partnership for Excellence, Inc., 7340 Niagara Lane N., Maple Grove MN 55311. (763)420-8923. Fax: (763)420-8921. E-mail: karen@goodoldboat.com. Web site: www.goodoldboat.com. **Contact:** Karen Larson, editor. **90% freelance written.** Bimonthly magazine covering sailing. "*Good Old Boat* magazine focuses on maintaining, upgrading, and loving cruising sailboats that are 10 years old and older. Readers see themselves as part of a community of sailors who share similar maintenance and replacement concerns which are not generally addressed in the other sailing publications. Our readers do much of the writing about projects they have done on their boats and the joy they receive from sailing them." Estab. 1998. Circ. 30,000. Pays 2 months in advance of publication. Publishes ms an average of 12-18 months after acceptance. Buys first North American serial rights. Editorial lead time 4 months. Submit seasonal material 12-15 months in advance. Accepts queries by mail, e-mail, fax. Accepts simultaneous submissions. Responds in 1-2 weeks to queries; 2-6 months to mss. Sample copy for free. Writer's guidelines online.

Nonfiction General interest, historical/nostalgic, how-to, interview/profile, personal experience, photo feature, technical. "Articles which are written by nonsailors serve no purpose for us." **Buys 150 mss/year.** Query or send complete ms. **Payment varies, refer to published rates on Web site.**

Photos State availability of or send photos with submission. "We do not pay additional fees for photos except when they run as covers, center spread photo features, or are specifically requested to support an article."

Tips "Our shorter pieces are the best way to break into our magazine. We publish many Simple Solutions and

Quick & Easy pieces. These are how-to tips that have worked for sailors on their boats. In addition, our readers send lists of projects which they've done on their boats and which they could write for publication. We respond to these queries with a thumbs up or down by project. Articles are submitted on speculation, but they have a better chance of being accepted once we have approved of the suggested topic.''

$ $ HEARTLAND BOATING

The Waterways Journal, Inc., 319 N. Fourth St., Suite 650, St. Louis MO 63102. (314)241-4310. Fax: (314)241-4207. E-mail: lbraff@heartlandboating.com. Web site: www.heartlandboating.com. **Contact:** Lee Braff, editor. **90% freelance written.** Magazine published 9 times/year covering recreational boating on the inland waterways of mid-America, from the Great Lakes south to the Gulf of Mexico and over to the east. ''Our writers must have experience with, and a great interest in, boating, particularly in the area described above. *Heartland Boating*'s content is both informative and humorous—describing boating life as the heartland boater knows it. We are boaters and enjoy the outdoor, water-oriented way of life. The content reflects the challenge, joy, and excitement of our way of life afloat. We are devoted to both power and sailboating enthusiasts throughout middle America; houseboats are included. The focus is on the freshwater inland rivers and lakes of the heartland, primarily the waters of the Arkansas, Tennessee, Cumberland, Ohio, Missouri, Illinois, and Mississippi rivers, the Tennessee-Tombigbee Waterway, The Gulf Intracoastal Waterway, and the lakes along these waterways.'' Estab. 1989. Circ. 12,000. Pays on publication. Byline given. Buys first North American serial, first, electronic rights. Editorial lead time 3 months. Submit seasonal material 1 year in advance. Accepts queries by mail, e-mail, phone. Accepts previously published material. Responds in 2 months to queries. Sample copy for $5. Writer's guidelines by e-mail.

Nonfiction How-to (articles about navigation maintenance, upkeep, or making time spent aboard easier and more comfortable), humor, personal experience, technical, travel (along waterways and on-land stops). Special issues: Annual houseboat issue in March looks at what is coming out on the houseboat market for the coming year. **Buys 100 mss/year.** Query with published clips or send complete ms. Length: 850-1,500 words. **Pays $40-285.**

Reprints Send tearsheet, photocopy or typed ms and information about when and where the material previously appeared.

Photos Send photos with submission. Reviews prints, digital images. Buys one-time rights. Offers no additional payment for photos accepted with ms.

Columns/Departments Books Aboard (assigned book reviews), 400 words. **Buys 8-10 mss/year. Pays $40.** Handy Hints (boat improvement or safety projects), 850 words. **Buys 9 mss/year. Pays $180.** Heartland Haunts (waterside restaurants, bars or B&Bs), 1,000 words. **Buys 9 mss/year. Pays $155.** Query with published clips or send complete ms.

Tips ''We plan the next year's schedule starting in mid-May. So submitting material between May and July will be most helpful for planning.''

$ $ ⊘ HOUSEBOAT MAGAZINE

The Family Magazine for the American Houseboater, Harris Publishing, Inc., 360 B St., Idaho Falls ID 83402. Fax: (208)522-5241. E-mail: hbeditor@houseboatmagazine.com. Web site: www.houseboatmagazine.com. **Contact:** Steve Smede, editor. **60% freelance written.** Monthly magazine for houseboaters, who enjoy reading everything that reflects the unique houseboating lifestyle. If it is not a houseboat-specific article, please do not query. Estab. 1990. Circ. 25,000. **Pays on acceptance.** Publishes ms an average of 3 months after acceptance. Byline given. Offers 25% kill fee. Buys first North American serial, electronic rights. Editorial lead time 6 months. Submit seasonal material 6 months in advance. Accepts simultaneous submissions. Responds in 1 month to queries. Sample copy for $5. Writer's guidelines online.

- No unsolicited mss. Accepts queries by mail and fax, but e-mail strongly preferred.

Nonfiction How-to, interview/profile, new product, personal experience, travel. **Buys 36 mss/year.** Query. Length: 1,500-2,200 words. **Pays $200-500.**

Photos Often required as part of submission package. Color prints discouraged. Digital prints are unacceptable. Seldom purchases photos without ms, but occasionally buys cover photos. Reviews transparencies, high-resolution electronic images. Buys one-time rights. Offers no additional payment for photos accepted with ms. Captions, model releases required.

Columns/Departments Pays $150-300.

Tips ''As a general rule, how-to articles are always in demand. So are stories on unique houseboats or houseboaters. You are less likely to break in with a travel piece that does not revolve around specific people or groups. Personality profile pieces with excellent supporting photography are your best bet.''

$ $ LAKELAND BOATING

The Magazine for Great Lakes Boaters, O'Meara-Brown Publications, Inc., 727 S. Dearborn, Suite 812, Chicago IL 60605. (312)276-0610. Fax: (312)276-0619. E-mail: lb@lakelandboating.com. Web site: www.lakelandboatin

g.com. **50% freelance written.** Magazine covering Great Lakes boating. Estab. 1946. Circ. 60,000. Pays on publication. Byline given. Buys first North American serial rights. Accepts queries by e-mail. Responds in 4 months to queries. Sample copy for $5.50 and 9×12 SAE with 6 first-class stamps. Writer's guidelines free.
Nonfiction Book excerpts, historical/nostalgic, how-to, interview/profile, personal experience, photo feature, technical, travel, must relate to boating in Great Lakes. No inspirational, religious, exposé or poetry. **Buys 20-30 mss/year.** Length: 300-1,500 words. **Pays $100-600.**
Photos State availability with submission. Reviews prefers 35mm transparencies, high-res digital shots. Buys one-time rights. Captions required.
Columns/Departments Bosun's Locker (technical or how-to pieces on boating), 100-1,000 words. **Buys 40 mss/year.** Query. **Pays $25-200.**

$LIVING ABOARD

P.O. Box 91299, Austin TX 78709-1299. (512)892-4446. Fax: (512)892-4448. E-mail: editor@livingaboard.com. Web site: www.livingaboard.com. Publisher: Fred Walters. **Contact:** Linda Ridihalgh, editor. **95% freelance written.** Bimonthly magazine covering living on boats/cruising. Estab. 1973. Circ. 10,000. Pays on publication. Publishes ms an average of 3-6 months after acceptance. Byline given. Buys first North American serial, first, one-time, second serial (reprint) rights. Accepts queries by mail, e-mail, fax. Responds in 1-2 weeks to queries; 1-2 months to mss. Sample copy online. Writer's guidelines free.
Nonfiction How-to (buy, furnish, maintain, provision a boat), interview/profile, personal experience, technical (as relates to boats), travel (on the water), Cooking Aboard with Recipes. Send complete ms. **Pays 5¢/word.**
Photos Pays $5/photo; $50/cover photo.
Columns/Departments Cooking Aboard (how to prepare healthy and nutritious meals in the confines of a galley; how to entertain aboard a boat), 1,000-1,500 words; Environmental Notebook (articles pertaining to clean water, fish, waterfowl, water environment), 750-1,000 words. **Buys 6 mss/year.** Send complete ms. **Pays 5¢/word.**
Tips "Articles should have a positive tone and promote the liveaboard lifestyle."

MOTOR BOATING

Time 4 Media, 18 Marshall St., Suite 114, Norwalk CT 06854-2237. (203)299-5950. Fax: (203)299-5951. Web site: www.motorboating.com. Monthly magazine geared toward the owners of power boats 20' to 60'. Devoted to helping its readers make educated decisions about how to buy, equip, maintain, and enjoy their boats. Circ. 155,000. Editorial lead time 6 weeks. Accepts queries by mail. Responds in 6-8 weeks to queries.
Nonfiction "We look for articles on adventure travel by boat; investigative stories on issues important to recreational power boaters; and informative service pieces on boat/engine care and maintenance." Short tips on boat maintenance and repair. Query with published clips. Length: 1,500-2,000 words.

$NORTHERN BREEZES, SAILING MAGAZINE

Northern Breezes, Inc., 3949 Winnetka Ave. N, Minneapolis MN 55427. E-mail: alan@sailingbreezes.com. Web site: www.sailingbreezes.com. **Contact:** Alan Kretzschmar. **70% freelance written.** Magazine published 8 times/year for the Great Lakes and Midwest sailing community. Focusing on regional cruising, racing, and day sailing. Estab. 1989. Circ. 22,300. Pays on publication. Byline given. Buys first North American serial rights. Editorial lead time 1 months. Submit seasonal material 3 months in advance. Accepts queries by mail, e-mail, fax, phone. Accepts previously published material. Responds in 1 month to queries; 2 months to mss. Sample copy for free. Writer's guidelines online.
Nonfiction Book excerpts, how-to (sailing topics), humor, inspirational, interview/profile, new product, personal experience, photo feature, technical, travel. No boating reviews. **Buys 24 mss/year.** Query with published clips. Length: 300-3,500 words.
Reprints Accepts previously published submissions.
Photos Send photos with submission. Reviews negatives, 35mm slides, 3×5 or 4×6 prints. Buys one-time rights. Offers no additional payment for photos accepted with ms. Captions required.
Columns/Departments This Old Boat (sailboat), 500-1,000 words; Surveyor's Notebook, 500-800 words. **Buys 8 mss/year.** Query with published clips. **Pays $50-150.**
Tips "Query with a regional connection already in mind."

$$$$OFFSHORE

Northeast Boating at Its Best, Offshore Communications, Inc., 500 Victory Rd., Marina Bay, North Quincy MA 02171. (617)221-1400. Fax: (617)847-1871. E-mail: editors@offshoremag.net. Web site: www.offshoremag.net. **Contact:** Editorial Department. **80% freelance written.** Monthly magazine covering power and sailboating on the coast from Maine to New Jersey. Estab. 1976. Circ. 35,000. **Pays on acceptance.** Publishes ms an average of 5 months after acceptance. Byline given. Offers 50% kill fee. Buys first North American serial rights. Submit seasonal material 6 months in advance. Accepts queries by mail. Accepts simultaneous submissions. Writer's guidelines for #10 SASE.

Nonfiction Articles on boats, boating, New York, New Jersey, and New England coastal places and people, Northeast coastal history. **Buys 90 mss/year.** Query with or without published clips or send complete ms. Length: 1,200-2,500 words. **Pays $500-1,500 for features, depending on length.**

Photos Reviews 35mm slides and digital images. Buys one-time rights. Pays $150-800. Identification of subjects required.

Tips "Writers must demonstrate a familiarity with boats and with the Northeast coast. Specifically we are looking for articles on boating destinations, boating events (such as races, rendezvous, and boat parades), on-the-water boating adventures, boating culture, maritime museums, maritime history, boating issues (such as safety and the environment), seamanship, fishing, how-to stories, and essays. Note: Since *Offshore* is a regional magazine, all stories must focus on the area from New Jersey to Maine. We are always open to new people, the best of whom may gradually work their way into regular writing assignments. Important to ask for (and follow) our writer's guidelines if you're not familiar with our magazine."

$ $ PACIFIC YACHTING

Western Canada's Premier Boating Magazine, OP Publishing, Ltd., 1080 Howe St., Suite 900, Vancouver BC V6Z 2T1 Canada. (604)606-4644. Fax: (604)687-1925. E-mail: editor@pacificyachting.com. Web site: www.pacificyachting.com. **90% freelance written.** Monthly magazine covering all aspects of recreational boating on British Columbia's coast. "The bulk of our writers and photographers not only come from the local boating community, many of them were long-time *PY* readers before coming aboard as a contributor. The *PY* reader buys the magazine to read about new destinations or changes to old haunts on the British Columbia coast and to learn the latest about boats and gear." Circ. 19,000. Pays on publication. Publishes ms an average of 6 months after acceptance. Byline given. Buys first North American serial, simultaneous rights. Editorial lead time 4 months. Submit seasonal material 6 months in advance. Accepts queries by mail, e-mail, fax. Sample copy for $5.95, plus postage charged to credit card. Writer's guidelines free.

Nonfiction Historical/nostalgic (British Columbia coast only), how-to, humor, interview/profile, personal experience, technical (boating related), travel, cruising, and destination on the British Columbia coast. "No articles from writers who are obviously not boaters!" Query. Length: 1,500-2,000 words. **Pays $150-500.** Pays expenses of writers on assignment.

Photos Send photos with submission. Reviews transparencies, 4×6 prints, and slides. Buys one-time rights. Offers no additional payment for photos accepted with ms. Offers $25-300 for photos accepted alone. Identification of subjects required.

Columns/Departments Currents (current events, trade and people news, boat gatherings, and festivities), 50-250 words. Reflections; Cruising, both 800-1,000 words. Query. **Pay varies.**

Tips "Our reader wants you to balance important navigation details with first-person observations, blending the practical with the romantic. Write tight, write short, write with the reader in mind, write to inform, write to entertain. Be specific, accurate, and historic."

$ $ PONTOON & DECK BOAT

Harris Publishing, Inc., 360 B. St., Idaho Falls ID 83402. (208)524-7000. Fax: (208)522-5241. E-mail: blk@pdbmagazine.com. Web site: www.pdbmagazine.com. **Contact:** Brady L. Kay, editor. **15% freelance written.** Magazine published 11 times/year. "We are a boating niche publication geared toward the pontoon and deck boating lifestyle and consumer market. Our audience is comprised of people who utilize these boats for varied family activities and fishing. Our magazine is promotional of the PDB industry and its major players. We seek to give the reader a twofold reason to read our publication: to celebrate the lifestyle, and to do it aboard a first-class craft." Estab. 1995. Circ. 84,000. Pays on publication. Byline given. Buys one-time rights. Editorial lead time 2 months. Submit seasonal material 3 months in advance. Accepts simultaneous submissions. Responds in 6 weeks to queries; 3 months to mss. Sample copy and writer's guidelines free.

Nonfiction How-to, personal experience, technical, remodeling, rebuilding. "We are saturated with travel pieces, no general boating, humor, fiction, or poetry." **Buys 15 mss/year.** Query with or without published clips or send complete ms. Length: 600-2,000 words. **Pays $50-300.** Sometimes pays expenses of writers on assignment.

Photos State availability with submission. Reviews transparencies. Rights negotiable. Captions, model releases required.

Columns/Departments No Wake Zone (short, fun quips); Better Boater (how-to). **Buys 6-12 mss/year.** Query with published clips. **Pays $50-150.**

Tips "Be specific to pontoon and deck boats. Any general boating material goes to the slush pile. The more you can tie together the lifestyle, attitudes, and the PDB industry, the more interest we'll take in what you send us."

$ $ $ POWER & MOTORYACHT

Primedia, Inc., 260 Madison Ave., 8th Floor, New York NY 10016. (917)256-2276. Fax: (917)256-2282. E-mail: diane.byrne@primedia.com. Web site: www.powerandmotoryacht.com. Editor: Richard Thiel. Managing Editor: Eileen Murphy. **Contact:** Diane M. Byrne, executive editor. **25% freelance written.** Monthly magazine covering powerboats 24 feet and larger with special emphasis on the 35-foot-plus market. "Readers have an average of 33 years experience boating, and we give them accurate advice on how to choose, operate, and maintain their boats as well as what electronics and gear will help them pursue their favorite pastime. In addition, since powerboating is truly a lifestyle and not just a hobby for them, *Power & Motoryacht* reports on a host of other topics that affect their enjoyment of the water: chartering, sportfishing, and the environment, among others. Articles must therefore be clear, concise, and authoritative; knowledge of the marine industry is mandatory. Include personal experience and information for marine industry experts where appropriate." Estab. 1985. Circ. 157,000. **Pays on acceptance.** Publishes ms an average of 4-6 months after acceptance. Byline given. Offers 33% kill fee. Buys all rights. Editorial lead time 4-6 months. Submit seasonal material 4-6 months in advance. Accepts queries by mail, e-mail. Responds in 1 month to queries. Sample copy for 10×12 SASE. Writer's guidelines for #10 SASE.

Nonfiction How-to, interview/profile, personal experience, photo feature, travel. No unsolicited mss or articles about sailboats and/or sailing yachts (including motorsailers or cruise ships). **Buys 20-25 mss/year.** Query with published clips. Length: 800-1,500 words. **Pays $500-1,000 for assigned articles.** Sometimes pays expenses of writers on assignment.

Photos Aimee Colon, art director. State availability with submission. Reviews 8×10 transparencies, GIF/JPEG files (minimum 300 dpi). Buys one-time print and Web rights. Offers no additional payment for photos accepted with ms. Captions, identification of subjects required.

Tips "Take a clever or even unique approach to a subject, particularly if the topic is dry/technical. Pitch us on yacht cruises you've taken, particularly if they're in off-the-beaten-path locations."

$ $ POWER BOATING CANADA

1020 Brevik Place, Suites 4 & 5, Mississauga ON L4W 4N7 Canada. (905)624-8218. Fax: (905)624-6764. E-mail: editor@powerboating.com. Web site: www.powerboating.com. **70% freelance written.** Bimonthly magazine covering recreational power boating. "*Power Boating Canada* offers boating destinations, how-to features, boat tests (usually staff written), lifestyle pieces—with a Canadian slant—and appeal to recreational power boaters across the country." Estab. 1984. Circ. 42,000. Pays on publication. Publishes ms an average of 3 months after acceptance. Byline given. Buys first North American serial rights. Editorial lead time 2 months. Submit seasonal material 3 months in advance. Accepts previously published material. Responds in 1 month to queries; 2 months to mss. Sample copy for free.

Nonfiction "Any articles related to the sport of power boating, especially boat tests." Historical/nostalgic, how-to, interview/profile, personal experience, travel (boating destinations). No general boating articles or personal anectdotes. **Buys 40-50 mss/year.** Query. Length: 1,200-2,500 words. **Pays $150-300 (Canadian).** Sometimes pays expenses of writers on assignment.

Reprints Send photocopy with rights for sale noted and information about when and where the material previously appeared.

Photos Send photos with submission. Reviews contact sheets, negatives, transparencies, prints. Buys one-time rights. Pay varies; no additional payment for photos accepted with ms. Captions, identification of subjects required.

$ $ $ POWERBOAT

Nordskog Publishing Inc., 1691 Spinnaker Dr., #206, Ventura CA 93001. (805)639-2222. Fax: (805)639-2220. Web site: www.powerboatmag.com. **25% freelance written.** Magazine published 11 times/year covering performance boating. Estab. 1973. Circ. 50,000. Pays on publication. Publishes ms an average of 3 months after acceptance. Byline given. Offers negotiable kill fee. Buys first North American serial, electronic rights. Editorial lead time 3 months. Submit seasonal material 4 months in advance. Accepts queries by mail, e-mail, fax. Sample copy online.

- No unsolicited mss.

Nonfiction Features highly focused storied on performance boats and boating. How-to, interview/profile, new product, photo feature. No general interest boating stories. **Buys numerous mss/year.** Query. Length: 300-2,000 words. **Pays $125-1,200.** Sometimes pays expenses of writers on assignment.

Photos State availability with submission. Reviews negatives. Buys one-time rights. Captions required.

$ $ $ SAIL

98 N. Washington St., 2nd Floor, Boston MA 02114. (617)720-8600. Fax: (617)723-0912. E-mail: sailmail@primediasi.com. Web site: www.sailmagazine.com or www.sailbuyersguide.com. Editor: Peter Nielsen. **Contact:**

Amy Ullrich, managing editor. **30% freelance written.** Monthly magazine "written and edited for everyone who sails—aboard a coastal or bluewater cruiser, trailerable, one-design or offshore racer, or daysailer. How-to and technical articles concentrate on techniques of sailing and aspects of design and construction, boat systems, and gear; the feature section emphasizes the fun and rewards of sailing in a practical and instructive way." Estab. 1970. Circ. 180,000. **Pays on acceptance.** Publishes ms an average of 1 year after acceptance. Byline given. Buys first North American and other rights. Accepts queries by mail, e-mail, fax. Responds in 3 months to queries. Writer's guidelines for SASE or online (download).

Nonfiction How-to, personal experience, technical, distance cruising, destinations. Special issues: "Cruising, chartering, commissioning, fitting-out, special race (e.g., America's Cup), Top 10 Boats." **Buys 50 mss/year.** Query. Length: 1,500-3,000 words. **Pays $200-800.** Sometimes pays expenses of writers on assignment.

Photos Prefers transparencies. High-resolution digital photos (300 dpi) are also accepted, as are high-quality color prints (preferably with negatives attached). Payment varies, up to $1,000 if photo used on cover. Captions, identification of subjects, credits required.

Columns/Departments Sailing Memories (short essay); Sailing News (cruising, racing, legal, political, environmental); Under Sail (human interest). Query. **Pays $50-400.**

The online magazine carries original content not found in the print edition and includes writer's guidelines. Contact: Kimball Livingston, online editor.

Tips "Request an articles' specification sheet. We look for unique ways of viewing sailing. Skim old issues of *Sail* for ideas about the types of articles we publish. Always remember that *Sail* is a sailing magazine. Stay away from gloomy articles detailing all the things that went wrong on your boat. Think constructively and write about how to avoid certain problems. You should focus on a theme or choose some aspect of sailing and discuss a personal attitude or new philosophical approach to the subject. Notice that we have certain issues devoted to special themes—for example, chartering, electronics, commissioning, and the like. Stay away from pieces that chronicle your journey in the day-by-day style of a logbook. These are generally dull and uninteresting. Select specific actions or events (preferably sailing events, not shorebound activities), and build your articles around them. Emphasize the sailing."

$ $ $ SAILING MAGAZINE

125 E. Main St., Port Washington WI 53074-0249. (262)284-3494. Fax: (262)284-7764. E-mail: editorial@sailingmagazine.net. Web site: www.sailingonline.com. Publisher: William F. Schanen. Managing Editor: Greta Schanen. Monthly magazine for the experienced sailor. Estab. 1966. Circ. 45,000. Pays after publication. Buys one-time rights. Accepts queries by mail, e-mail. Responds in 2 months to queries. Editorial calendar online.

"Let us get to know your writing with short, newsy, sailing-oriented pieces with good slides for our Splashes section. Query for upcoming theme issues; read the magazine; writing must show the writer loves sailing as much as our readers. We are always looking for fresh stories on new destinations with vibrant writing and top-notch photography. Always looking for short (100-1,500 word) articles or newsy items."

Nonfiction "Experiences of sailing, cruising, and racing or cruising to interesting locations, whether a small lake near you or islands in the Southern Ocean, with first-hand knowledge and tips for our readers. Top-notch photos with maps, charts, cruising information complete the package. No regatta sports unless there is a story involved." Book excerpts, how-to (tech pieces on boats and gear), interview/profile, personal experience, travel (by sail). **Buys 15-20 mss/year.** Length: 750-2,500 words. **Pays $100-800.**

Photos Reviews color transparencies. Pays $50-400. Captions required.

Tips Prefers text in Word on disk for Mac or to e-mail address.

$ $ SAILING WORLD

World Publications, 55 Hammarlund Way, Middletown RI 02842. (401)845-5100. Fax: (401)848-5180. E-mail: editorial@sailingworld.com. Web site: www.sailingworld.com. **40% freelance written.** Magazine published 10 times/year covering performance sailing. Estab. 1962. Circ. 60,000. Pays on publication. Publishes ms an average of 4 months after acceptance. Byline given. Buys first North American serial rights. world serial rights Responds in 1 month to queries. Sample copy for $5.

Break in with short articles and fillers such as regatta news reports from your own area.

Nonfiction How-to (for racing and performance-oriented sailors), interview/profile, photo feature, Regatta sports and charter. No travelogs. **Buys 5-10 unsolicited mss/year.** Query. Length: 400-1,500 words. **Pays $400 for up to 2,000 words.** Does not pay expenses of writers on assignment unless pre-approved.

Tips "Send query with outline and include your experience. Prospective contributors should study recent issues of the magazine to determine appropriate subject matter. The emphasis here is on performance sailing: keep in mind that the *Sailing World* readership is relatively educated about the sport. Unless you are dealing with a totally new aspect of sailing, you can and should discuss ideas on an advanced technical level. 'Gee-whiz' impressions from beginning sailors are generally not accepted."

$ $ SEA KAYAKER

Sea Kayaker, Inc., P.O. Box 17029, Seattle WA 98127. (206)789-1326. Fax: (206)781-1141. E-mail: editorial@seakayakermag.com. Web site: www.seakayakermag.com. Editor: Christopher Cunningham. **Contact:** Connie Chaplan, editorial assistant. **95% freelance written.** "*Sea Kayaker* is a bimonthly publication with a worldwide readership that covers all aspects of kayak touring. It is well known as an important source of continuing education by the most experienced paddlers." Estab. 1984. Circ. 30,000. Pays on publication. Publishes ms an average of 6 months after acceptance. Byline given. Offers 10% kill fee. Buys first North American serial rights. Editorial lead time 4 months. Submit seasonal material 4 months in advance. Accepts queries by mail, e-mail, fax, phone. Responds in 2 months to queries. Sample copy for $7.30 (US), samples to other countries extra. Writer's guidelines online.

Nonfiction Essays, historical/nostalgic, how-to (on making equipment), humor, new product, personal experience, technical, travel. Unsolicited gear reviews are not accepted. **Buys 50 mss/year.** Query with or without published clips or send complete ms. Length: 1,500-5,000 words. **Pays 18-20¢/word for assigned articles; 15-17¢/word for unsolicited articles.**

Photos Send photos with submission. Reviews transparencies, prints. Buys one-time rights. Offers $15-400. Captions, identification of subjects required.

Columns/Departments Technique; Equipment; Do-It-Yourself; Food; Safety; Health; Environment; Book Reviews; all 1,000-2,500 words. **Buys 40-45 mss/year.** Query. **Pays 15-20¢/word.**

Tips "We consider unsolicited manuscripts that include a SASE, but we give greater priority to brief descriptions (several paragraphs) of proposed articles accompanied by at least 2 samples—published or unpublished—of your writing. Enclose a statement as to why you're qualified to write the piece and indicate whether photographs or illustrations are available to accompany the piece."

SEA MAGAZINE

America's Western Boating Magazine, Duncan McIntosh Co., 17782 Cowan, Suite A, Irvine CA 92614. (949)660-6150. Fax: (949)660-6172. Web site: www.goboatingamerica.com. **Contact:** Holly Simpson, managing editor. Monthly magazine covering West Coast power boating. Estab. 1908. Circ. 50,000. Pays on publication. Publishes ms an average of 6 months after acceptance. Byline given. Buys first North American serial rights. Editorial lead time 3 months. Submit seasonal material 6 months in advance. Accepts simultaneous submissions. Responds in 3 months to queries.

Nonfiction "News you can use" is kind of our motto. All articles should aim to help power boat owners make the most of their boating experience. How-to, new product, personal experience, technical, travel. **Buys 36 mss/year.** Query with or without published clips or send complete ms. Length: 1,000-1,500 words. **Payment varies.** Pays expenses of writers on assignment.

Photos State availability with submission. Reviews transparencies, hi-res digital. Buys one-time rights. Offers $50-250/photo. Captions, identification of subjects, model releases required.

$ $ SOUTHERN BOATING MAGAZINE

The South's Largest Boating Magazine, Southern Boating & Yachting, Inc., 330 N. Andrews Ave., Ft. Lauderdale FL 33301. (954)522-5515. Fax: (954)522-2260. E-mail: sboating@southernboating.com. Web site: southernboating.com. Editor: Skip Allen. **Contact:** Bill Lindsey, executive editor. **50% freelance written.** Monthly magazine. Upscale monthly yachting magazine focusing on the Southeast U.S., Bahamas, Caribbean, and Gulf of Mexico. Estab. 1972. Circ. 40,000. Pays within 30 days of publication. Publishes ms an average of 3 months after acceptance. Byline given. Buys one-time rights. Editorial lead time 3 months. Submit seasonal material 3 months in advance. Accepts queries by e-mail. Sample copy for $8.

O‑ Break in with destination, how-to, and technical articles.

Nonfiction How-to (boat maintenance), travel (boating related, destination pieces). **Buys 10 mss/year.** Query. Length: 1,000 words. **Pays $500 with art.**

Photos State availability of or send photos with submission. Reviews transparencies, prints. Buys one-time rights. Offers $50/photo maximum. Captions, identification of subjects, model releases required.

Columns/Departments Weekend Workshop (how-to/maintenance), 1,000 words; What's New in Electronics (electronics), 1,000 words; Engine Room (new developments), 1,000 words. **Buys 24 mss/year.** Query. **Pays $500.**

$ $ $ TRAILER BOATS MAGAZINE

Ehlert Publishing Group, Inc., 20700 Belshaw Ave., Carson CA 90746-3510. (310)537-6322. Fax: (310)537-8735. Web site: www.trailerboats.com. Editor: Ron Eldridge. **50% freelance written.** Monthly magazine covering legally trailerable power boats and related powerboating activities. Estab. 1971. Circ. 100,000. **Pays on acceptance.** Publishes ms an average of 3 months after acceptance. Byline given. Buys all rights. Editorial lead time

3 months. Submit seasonal material 5 months in advance. Responds in 1 month to queries. Sample copy for 9×12 SAE with 7 first-class stamps.

Nonfiction General interest (trailer boating activities), historical/nostalgic (places, events, boats), how-to (repair boats, installation, etc.), interview/profile, personal experience, photo feature, technical, travel (boating travel on water or highways), product evaluations. No "How I Spent My Summer Vacation" stories, or stories not directly connected to trailerable boats and related activities. **Buys 3-4 unsolicited mss/year.** Query. Length: 1,000-2,500 words. **Pays $150-1,000.** Sometimes pays expenses of writers on assignment.

Photos Send photos with submission. Reviews transparencies, 2¼×2¼ and 35mm slides, and high-resolution digital images (300 dpi). Buys all rights. Captions, identification of subjects, model releases required.

Columns/Departments Over the Transom (funny or strange boating photos); Dock Talk (short pieces on boating news, safety, products, profiles of people using boats to do their jobs), all 1,000-1,500 words. **Buys 12-13 mss/year.** Query. **Pays $250-500.**

Tips "Query should contain short general outline of the intended material; what kind of photos; how the photos illustrate the piece. Write with authority, covering the subject with quotes from experts. Frequent mistakes are not knowing the subject matter or the audience. The writer may have a better chance of breaking in at our publication with short articles and fillers if they are typically hard-to-find articles. We do most major features in-house, but try how-to stories dealing with repairs, installation and towing tips, boat trailer repair. Good color photos will win our hearts every time."

$ WATERFRONT NEWS

Ziegler Publishing Co., Inc., 1515 SW 1st Ave., Ft. Lauderdale FL 33315. (954)524-9450. Fax: (954)524-9464. E-mail: editor@waterfront-news.com. Web site: www.waterfront-news.com. **Contact:** Jennifer Heit, editor. **20% freelance written.** Monthly tabloid covering marine and boating topics for the Greater Ft. Lauderdale waterfront community. Estab. 1984. Circ. 39,000. Pays on publication. Publishes ms an average of 2 months after acceptance. Byline given. Buys first, second serial (reprint), simultaneous rights in certain circumstances rights. Submit seasonal material 3 months in advance. Responds in 1 month to queries. Sample copy for 9×12 SAE and 4 first-class stamps.

O‑ Travel pieces written for recreational boaters are most needed. Include photos, prints or digital.

Nonfiction Interview/profile (of people important in boating, i.e., racers, boat builders, designers, etc. from south Florida), Regional articles on south Florida's waterfront issues; marine communities. Length: 500-1,000 words. **Pays $100-125 for assigned articles.**

Photos Send photos with submission. Reviews JPEG/TIFF files.

Tips "No fiction. Keep it under 1,000 words. Photos or illustrations help. Send for a sample copy of *Waterfront News* so you can acquaint yourself with our publication and our unique audience. Although we're not necessarily looking for technical articles, it helps if the writer has sailing or powerboating experience. Writers should be familiar with the region and be specific when dealing with local topics."

$ $ WATERWAY GUIDE

326 First St., Suite 400, Annapolis MD 21403. (443)482-9377. Fax: (443)482-9422. E-mail: greich@waterwayguide.com. Web site: www.waterwayguide.com. **Contact:** Gary Reich, editor. **90% freelance written.** Triannual magazine covering intracoastal waterway travel for recreational boats. "Writer must be knowledgeable about navigation and the areas covered by the guide." Estab. 1947. Circ. 30,000. Pays on publication. Publishes ms an average of 3 months after acceptance. Byline given. Buys first North American serial, electronic rights, makes work-for-hire assignments. Editorial lead time 4 months. Submit seasonal material 3 months in advance. Accepts queries by mail, phone. Responds in 6 weeks to queries; 2 months to mss. Sample copy for $39.95 with $3 postage.

Nonfiction Essays, historical/nostalgic, how-to, photo feature, technical, travel. **Buys 6 mss/year.** Query with or without published clips or send complete ms. Length: 250-5,000 words. **Pays $50-500.** Pays in contributor copies or other premiums for helpful tips and useful information.

Photos Send photos with submission. Reviews transparencies, 3×5 prints. Buys all rights. Offers $25-50/photo. Captions, identification of subjects required.

Tips "Must have on-the-water experience and be able to provide new and accurate information on geographic areas covered by *Waterway Guide*."

N ⊕ WATERWAYS WORLD

Waterways World Ltd, 151 Station St., Burton-on-Trent Staffordshire DE14 1BG United Kingdom. (44)(128)374-2952. E-mail: richard.fairhurst@wwonline.co.uk; chris.daniels@wwonline.co.uk. Editor: Richard Fairhurst. Assistant Editor: Chris Daniels. Monthly magazine publishing news, photographs, and illustrated articles on all aspects of inland waterways in Britain, and on limited aspects of waterways abroad. Estab. 1972. Pays on publication. Editorial lead time 2 months. Accepts queries by mail, e-mail. Writer's guidelines by e-mail.

Nonfiction "We are interested in all canals and navigable rivers, whether operational or derelict." Topics include: waterways, boats/boating, waterway history, and current waterway affairs. Does not want poetry or fiction. Submit query letter or complete ms, SAE.

Photos Reviews transparencies, gloss prints, 300 dpi digital images, maps/diagrams. Captions required.

$ WAVELENGTH MAGAZINE

Pacific Edge Publishing, 1773 El Verano Dr., Gabriola Island BC V0R 1X6 Canada. (250)247-9093. Fax: (250)247-9083. E-mail: diana@wavelengthmagazine.com. Web site: www.wavelengthmagazine.com. **Contact:** Diana Mumford, editor. **75% freelance written.** Bimonthly magazine covering sea kayaking. "We promote safe paddling, guide paddlers to useful products and services and explore coastal environmental issues." Estab. 1991. Circ. 65,000 print and electronic readers. Pays on publication. Publishes ms an average of 4 months after acceptance. Byline given. Offers 10% kill fee. Buys first North American serial, electronic rights. Editorial lead time 4 months. Submit seasonal material 4 months in advance. Accepts queries by mail, e-mail. Sample copy and writer's guidelines online.

"Sea kayaking content, even if from a beginner's perspective, is essential. We like a light approach to personal experiences and humor is appreciated. Good detail (with maps and pics) for destinations material. Write to our feature focus."

Nonfiction How-to (paddle, travel), humor, new product, personal experience, technical, travel, trips; advice. **Buys 25 mss/year.** Query. Length: 1,000-1,500 words. **Pays $50-75.**

Photos State availability with submission. Reviews low res JPEGs. Buys first and electronic rights. Offers $25-50/photo. Captions, identification of subjects required.

Tips "You must know paddling—although novice paddlers are welcome. A strong environmental or wilderness appreciation component is advisable. We are willing to help refine work with flexible people. E-mail queries preferred. Check out our Editorial Calendar for our upcoming features."

$ $ WOODENBOAT MAGAZINE

The Magazine for Wooden Boat Owners, Builders, and Designers, WoodenBoat Publications, Inc., P.O. Box 78, Brooklin ME 04616. (207)359-4651. Fax: (207)359-8920. Web site: www.woodenboat.com. Editor-in-Chief: Jonathan A. Wilson. Senior Editor: Mike O'Brien. Associate Editor: Tom Jackson. **Contact:** Matthew P. Murphy, editor. **50% freelance written.** Bimonthly magazine for wooden boat owners, builders, and designers. "We are devoted exclusively to the design, building, care, preservation, and use of wooden boats, both commercial and pleasure, old and new, sail and power. We work to convey quality, integrity, and involvement in the creation and care of these craft, to entertain, inform, inspire, and to provide our varied readers with access to individuals who are deeply experienced in the world of wooden boats." Estab. 1974. Circ. 90,000. Pays on publication. Publishes ms an average of 1 year after acceptance. Byline given. Offers variable kill fee. Buys first North American serial rights. Accepts previously published material. Accepts simultaneous submissions. Responds in 2 months to queries; 2 months to mss. Sample copy for $5.99. Writer's guidelines online.

Nonfiction Technical (repair, restoration, maintenance, use, design, and building wooden boats). No poetry, fiction. **Buys 50 mss/year.** Query with published clips. Length: 1,500-5,000 words. **Pays $300/1,000 words.** Sometimes pays expenses of writers on assignment.

Reprints Send tearsheet or typed ms with rights for sale noted and information about when and where the material previously appeared.

Photos Send photos with submission. Reviews negatives. Buys one-time rights. Pays $15-75 b&w, $25-350 color. Identification of subjects required.

Columns/Departments Currents pays for information on wooden boat-related events, projects, boatshop activities, etc. Uses same columnists for each issue. Length: 250-1,000 words. Send complete information. **Pays $5-50.**

Tips "We appreciate a detailed, articulate query letter, accompanied by photos, that will give us a clear idea of what the author is proposing. We appreciate samples of previously published work. It is important for a prospective author to become familiar with our magazine. Most work is submitted on speculation. The most common failure is not exploring the subject material in enough depth."

N $ $ $ YACHTING

18 Marshall St., Suite 114, South Norwalk CT 06854. (203)299-5900. Fax: (203)299-5901. E-mail: kwooten@yachtingnet.com. Web site: www.yachtingmagazine.com. Publisher: Peter Beckenbach. Editor-in-Chief: Kenny Wooton. **30% freelance written.** Monthly magazine. "Monthly magazine written and edited for experienced, knowledgeable yachtsmen." Estab. 1907. Circ. 132,000. **Pays on acceptance.** Byline given. Buys first North American serial, electronic rights. Editorial lead time 2 months. Submit seasonal material 6 months in advance. Accepts queries by mail, e-mail, fax. Responds in 1 month to queries; 3 months to mss. Sample copy for free. Writer's guidelines online. Editorial calendar online.

Nonfiction Personal experience, technical. **Buys 50 mss/year.** Query with published clips. Length: 750-800 words. **Pays $150-1,500.** Pays expenses of writers on assignment.

Photos Send photos with submission. Reviews transparencies. Negotiates payment individually. Captions, identification of subjects, model releases required.

Tips "We require considerable expertise in our writing because our audience is experienced and knowledgeable. Vivid descriptions of quaint anchorages and quainter natives are fine, but our readers want to know how the yachtsmen got there, too. They also want to know how their boats work. *Yachting* is edited for experienced, affluent boatowners—power and sail—who don't have the time or the inclination to read sub-standard stories. They love carefully crafted stories about places they've never been or a different spin on places they have, meticulously reported pieces on issues that affect their yachting lives, personal accounts of yachting experiences from which they can learn, engaging profiles of people who share their passion for boats, insightful essays that evoke the history and traditions of the sport and compelling photographs of others enjoying the game as much as they do. They love to know what to buy and how things work. They love to be surprised. They don't mind getting their hands dirty or saving a buck here and there, but they're not interested in learning how to make a masthead light out of a mayonnaise jar. If you love what they love and can communicate like a pro (that means meeting deadlines, writing tight, being obsessively accurate and never misspelling a proper name), we'd love to hear from you."

YACHTING MONTHLY

IPC Media Ltd, Room 2215, King's Reach Tower, Stamford Street, London England SE1 9LS United Kingdom. (44)(207)261-6580. Fax: (44)(207)261-7555. E-mail: dick_durham@ipcmedia.com. Editor: Paul Gelder (paul_gelder@ipcmedia.com). **Contact:** Dick Durham, features editor. Monthly magazine covering practical and technical articles on all aspects of seamanship, navigation, and the handling of small craft and their design, construction, and equipment. Also accepts cruising narratives about sailing almost anywhere in the world and carefully researched pilotage articles on anchorages and cruising areas. Accepts queries by mail, e-mail. Writer's guidelines for £10, plus shipping. Editorial calendar available via e-mail.

Nonfiction Humor, technical, cruising narratives, lessons learned from mistakes/mishaps. Submit 150-word synopsis or complete ms. Length: 450-1,800 words. **Fees are quoted on acceptance.**

Photos Send photos with submission. Reviews transparencies, prints, 300 dpi digital images, original artwork/ sketches. Captions, identification of subjects required.

YACHTING WORLD

King's Reach Tower, Stamford St., London England SE1 9LS United Kingdom. (44)(207)261-6800. Fax: (44)(207)261-6818. E-mail: yachting_world@ipcmedia.com. Web site: www.yachtingworld.com. Magazine Assistant: Joanne Cackett. **Contact:** Elaine Bunting, features editor. Accepts queries by mail, e-mail. Writer's guidelines by e-mail.

"Over 50% of our circulation is outside the UK. We cater to all disciplines of sailing, racing, cruising, charter, and superyachting. The emphasis is on quality of writing, photography, and the topics covered."

Nonfiction Query with or without published clips or send complete ms. Length: 2,500-3,000 words.

Photos Reviews prints, slides, sketches of maps/diagrams.

BOWLING

BOWLING THIS MONTH

P.O. Box 966, San Marcos TX 78667. (512)353-8906. Fax: (512)353-8690. Web site: www.bowlingthismonth.com.

- *Bowling This Month* does not use freelance articles.

GENERAL INTEREST

$ $ METROSPORTS

New York, MetroSports Publishing, Inc., 259 W. 30th St., 3rd Floor, New York NY 10001. (212)563-7329. Fax: (212)563-7573. E-mail: jshweder@metrosports.com. Web site: www.metrosportsny.com. **Contact:** Jeremy Shweder, editor. **50% freelance written.** Monthly magazine covering amateur sports and fitness. "We focus on participatory sports (not team sports) for an active, young audience that likes to exercise." Estab. 1987. Circ. 100,000. Pays on publication. Byline given. Offers 50% kill fee. Buys first, electronic rights. Editorial lead time 3 months. Submit seasonal material 6 months in advance. Accepts queries by mail, e-mail, fax. Accepts previously published material. Accepts simultaneous submissions. Responds in 3-4 weeks to queries; 1-2 months to mss. Sample copy online. Writer's guidelines by e-mail.

Nonfiction Essays, general interest, historical/nostalgic, how-to (train for a triathlon, train for an adventure race, etc.), humor, inspirational, interview/profile, new product, opinion, personal experience, technical, travel. Special issues: Holiday Gift Guide (December). "We don't publish anything related to team sports (basketball, baseball, football, etc.), golf, tennis." **Buys 24 mss/year.** Query with published clips. Length: 800-3,000 words. **Pays $100-300.** Sometimes pays expenses of writers on assignment.

Photos State availability with submission. Reviews slides transparencies, 3×5 prints, GIF/JPEG files (300 dpi). Buys one-time rights. Negotiates payment individually. Captions, identification of subjects required.

Columns/Departments Running (training, nutrition, profiles); Cycling (training, nutrition, profiles), both 800 words. **Buys 15 mss/year.** Query with published clips. **Pays $100-250.**

Tips "Read the magazine, know what we cover. E-mail queries or mail with published clips. No phone calls, please."

$ OUTDOORS NW

PMB 3311, 10002 Aurora Ave. N. #36, Seattle WA 98133. (206)418-0747. Fax: (206)418-0746. E-mail: info@outdoorsnw.com. Web site: www.outdoorsnw.com. **Contact:** Carolyn Price, editor. **80% freelance written.** Monthly magazine covering outdoor recreation in the Pacific Northwest. "Writers must have a solid knowledge of the sport they are writing about. They must be doers." Estab. 1988. Circ. 40,000. Pays on publication. Publishes ms an average of 3 months after acceptance. Byline given. Buys first rights. Editorial lead time 2 months. Submit seasonal material 4 months in advance. Accepts queries by mail, e-mail, fax. Accepts previously published material. Accepts simultaneous submissions. Sample copy and writer's guidelines for $3.

- Publication changed it's name from Sports Etc.

Nonfiction Interview/profile, new product, travel. Query with published clips. Length: 750-1,500 words. **Pays $25-125.** Sometimes pays expenses of writers on assignment.

Photos Send photos with submission. Reviews electronic images only. Buys all rights. Captions, identification of subjects, model releases required.

Columns/Departments Faces, Places, Puruits (750 words). **Buys 10-12 mss/year.** Query with published clips. **Pays $40-75.**

Tips "*Outdoors NW* is written for the serious Pacific Northwest outdoor recreationalist. The magazine's look, style and editorial content actively engage the reader, delivering insightful perspectives on the sports it has come to be known for—alpine skiing, bicycling, adventure racing, triathlon and multi-sport, hiking, kayaking, marathons, mountain climbing, Nordic skiing, running, and snowboarding. *Outdoors NW* magazine wants vivid writing, telling images, and original perspectives to produce its smart, entertaining monthly."

$ $ ROCKY MOUNTAIN SPORTS MAGAZINE

Rocky Mountain Sports, Inc., 2525 15th St., #1A, Denver CO 80211. (303)477-9770. Fax: (303)477-9747. E-mail: rheaton@rockymountainsports.com. Web site: www.rockymountainsports.com. Publisher: Doug Kaplan. **Contact:** Rebecca Heaton, editor. **50% freelance written.** Monthly magazine covering nonteam-related sports in Colorado. "*Rocky* is a magazine for sports-related lifestyles and activities. Our mission is to reflect and inspire the active lifestyle of Rocky Mountain residents." Estab. 1986. Circ. 95,000. Pays 60-90 days after publication. Publishes ms an average of 1 month after acceptance. Byline given. Offers 50% kill fee. Buys first North American serial rights. Editorial lead time 3 months. Submit seasonal material 6 months in advance. Accepts queries by e-mail. Accepts previously published material. Accepts simultaneous submissions. Responds in 1 month to queries; 2 months to mss. Writer's guidelines by e-mail.

- The editor says she wants to see mountain outdoor sports writing *only*. No ball sports, hunting, or fishing.
- Break in with "Rocky Mountain angle—off-the-beaten-path."

Nonfiction General interest, how-to, humor, inspirational, interview/profile, new product, personal experience, travel. Special issues: Skiing & Snowboarding (November); Nordic/Snowshoeing (December); Marathon (January); Running (March); Adventure Travel (April); Triathlon (May); Paddling and Climbing (June); Road Cycling & Camping (July); Organic (August); Women's Sports & Marathon (September); Health Club (October). Query with published clips. Length: 500-1,500 words. **Pays $50-300.**

Reprints Send photocopy and information about when and where the material previously appeared. Pays 20-25% of amount paid for original article.

Photos State availability with submission. Reviews GIF/JPEG files. Buys one-time rights. Negotiates payment individually. Identification of subjects, model releases required.

Columns/Departments Starting Lines (short newsy items); Running; Cycling; Climbing; Triathlon; Fitness, Nutrition; Sports Medicine; Off the Beaten Path (sports we don't usually cover). **Buys 20 mss/year.** Query. **Pays $25-300.**

Tips "Have a Colorado angle to the story, a catchy cover letter, good clips, and demonstrate that you've read and understand our magazine and its readers."

$ SILENT SPORTS

Waupaca Publishing Co., P.O. Box 152, Waupaca WI 54981-9990. (715)258-5546. Fax: (715)258-8162. E-mail: info@silentsports.net. Web site: www.silentsports.net. **75% freelance written.** Monthly magazine covering running, cycling, cross-country skiing, canoeing, kayaking, snowshoeing, in-line skating, camping, backpacking, and hiking aimed at people in Wisconsin, Minnesota, northern Illinois, and portions of Michigan and Iowa. "Not a coffee table magazine. Our readers are participants from rank amateur weekend athletes to highly competitive racers." Estab. 1984. Circ. 10,000. Pays on publication. Publishes ms an average of 3 months after acceptance. Byline given. Offers 20% kill fee. Buys one-time rights. Submit seasonal material 4 months in advance. Accepts queries by mail, e-mail, fax. Accepts previously published material. Responds in 3 months to queries. Sample copy and writer's guidelines for 10×13 SAE with 7 first-class stamps.

- The editor needs local angles on in-line skating, recreation bicycling, and snowshoeing.

Nonfiction All stories/articles must focus on the Upper Midwest. General interest, how-to, interview/profile, opinion, technical, travel. **Buys 25 mss/year.** Query. Length: 2,500 words maximum. **Pays $15-100.** Sometimes pays expenses of writers on assignment.

Reprints Send ms with rights for sale noted and information about when and where the material previously appeared. Pays 50% of amount paid for an original article.

Photos State availability with submission. Reviews transparencies. Buys one-time rights. Pays $5-15 for b&w story photos; $50-100 for color covers.

Tips "Where-to-go and personality profiles are areas most open to freelancers. Writers should keep in mind that this is a regional, Midwest-based publication. We want only stories/articles with a focus on our region."

$ $ TWIN CITIES SPORTS

Twin Cities Sports Publishing, Inc., 3009 Holmes Ave. S., Minneapolis MN 55408. (612)825-1034. Fax: (612)825-6452. E-mail: kyle@metrosports.com. Web site: www.twincitiessports.com. Editor: Jeff Banowetz. **Contact:** Kyle Ryan, managing editor. **75% freelance written.** Monthly magazine covering amateur sports and fitness. "We focus on participatory sports (not team sports) for an active, young audience that likes to exercise." Estab. 1987. Circ. 40,000. Pays on publication. Publishes ms an average of 2 months after acceptance. Byline given. Offers 50% kill fee. Buys first, electronic rights. Editorial lead time 3 months. Submit seasonal material 6 months in advance. Accepts queries by mail, e-mail, fax. Accepts previously published material. Accepts simultaneous submissions. Responds in 3-4 weeks to queries; 1-2 months to mss. Sample copy online. Writer's guidelines by e-mail.

Nonfiction Essays, general interest, historical/nostalgic, how-to (train for a triathlon, set a new 5K P.R., train for an adventure race), humor, inspirational, interview/profile, new product, opinion, personal experience, technical, travel. Special issues: Holiday Gift Guide (December). "We don't publish anything related to team sports (basketball, baseball, football, etc.), golf, tennis. **Buys 24 mss/year.** Query with published clips. Length: 800-3,000 words. **Pays $100-300.** Sometimes pays expenses of writers on assignment.

Photos State availability with submission. Reviews slides transparencies, 3×5 prints, GIF/JPEG files (300 dpi). Buys one-time rights. Negotiates payment individually. Captions, identification of subjects required.

Columns/Departments Running (training, nutrition, profiles), 800 words; Cycling (training, nutrition, profiles), 800 words; Cool Down (first-person essay), 800-1,000 words. **Buys 15 mss/year.** Query with published clips. **Pays $100-250.**

Tips "Read the magazine, know what we cover. E-mail queries or mail with published clips. No phone calls, please."

GOLF

N $ $ AFRICAN AMERICAN GOLFER'S DIGEST

Nation's leading publication for avid black golfers, 139 Fulton St., Suite 209, New York NY 10038. (212)571-6559. E-mail: debertcook@aol.com. Web site: www.africanamericangolfersdigest.com. **Contact:** Debert Cook, CMP, publisher/editor. **100% freelance written.** Quarterly magazine covering golf lifestyle, health, travel destinations and reviews, golf equipment, golfer profiles. "Editorial should focus on interests of our market demographic of African Americans with historical, artistic, musical, educational (higher learning), automotive, sports, fashion, entertainment, and other categories of high interest to them." Estab. 2003. Circ. 20,000. Publishes ms an average of 3 months after acceptance. Byline given. Buys all rights. Editorial lead time 3-6 months. Submit seasonal material 3-6 months in advance. Accepts queries by e-mail. Accepts simultaneous submissions. Responds in 3 weeks to queries; 3 months to mss. Sample copy for $4.50. Writer's guidelines by e-mail.

Nonfiction How-to, interview/profile, new product, personal experience, photo feature, technical, travel, golf-related. **Buys 3 mss/year.** Query. Length: 250-1,500 words. **Pays 25-50¢/word.**
Photos State availability with submission. Reviews GIF/JPEG files (300 dpi or higher at 4×6). Buys all rights. Negotiates payment individually. Captions, identification of subjects, model releases required.
Columns/Departments Profiles (celebrities, national leaders, entertainers, corporate leaders, etc., who golf); Travel (destination/golf course reviews); Golf Fashion (jewelry, clothing, accessories). **Buys 3 mss/year.** Query. **Pays 25-50¢/word.**
Fillers Anecdotes, facts, gags to be illustrated by cartoonist, newsbreaks, short humor. **Buys 3/year.** Length: 20-125 words. **Pays 25-50¢/word.**
Tips "Emphasize golf and African American appeal."

$ $ ARIZONA, THE STATE OF GOLF

Arizona Golf Association, 7226 N. 16th St., Suite 200, Phoenix AZ 85020. (602)944-3035. Fax: (602)944-3228. Web site: www.azgolf.org. **50% freelance written.** Quarterly magazine covering golf in Arizona, the official publication of the Arizona Golf Association. Estab. 1999. Circ. 45,000. **Pays on acceptance.** Byline given. Buys all rights. Editorial lead time 6 months. Submit seasonal material 3 months in advance. Accepts queries by mail. Accepts previously published material. Accepts simultaneous submissions. Sample copy and writer's guidelines free.
Nonfiction Book excerpts, essays, historical/nostalgic, how-to (golf), humor, inspirational, interview/profile, new product, opinion, personal experience, photo feature, travel (destinations). **Buys 5-10 mss/year.** Query with or without published clips. Length: 500-2,000 words. **Pays $50-500.** Sometimes pays expenses of writers on assignment.
Reprints Accepts previously published submissions.
Photos State availability with submission. Reviews contact sheets. Rights purchased varies. Negotiates payment individually. Captions, identification of subjects required.
Columns/Departments Short Strokes (golf news and notes), Improving Your Game (golf tips), Out of Bounds (guest editorial, 800 words). Query.

[N] EXECUTIVE GOLFER

Pazdur Publishing, 2171 Campus Dr., Suite 330, Irvine CA 92612. (949)752-6474. Fax: (949)752-0398. Web site: www.executivegolfermagazine.com. Editor: Mark Pazdur. **20% freelance written.** Bimonthly magazine covering golf. Estab. 1972. Circ. 100,000. **Pays on acceptance.** Byline sometimes given. Buys all rights. Accepts queries by fax, phone. Sample copy and writer's guidelines for SASE.
Nonfiction General interest, humor, travel. Query.

$ $ $ GOLF CANADA

Official Magazine of the Royal Canadian Golf Association, RCGA/Relevant Communications, Golf House Suite 1, 1333 Dorval Dr., Oakville ON L6M 4X7 Canada. (905)849-9700. Fax: (905)845-7040. E-mail: golfcanada@rcga.org. Web site: www.rcga.org. **Contact:** John Tenpenny, editor. **80% freelance written.** Magazine published 5 times/year covering Canadian golf. "*Golf Canada* is the official magazine of the Royal Canadian Golf Association, published to entertain and enlighten members about RCGA-related activities and to generally support and promote amateur golf in Canada." Estab. 1994. Circ. 159,000. **Pays on acceptance.** Byline given. Offers 100% kill fee. Buys first translation, electronic rights. Editorial lead time 3 months. Submit seasonal material 6 months in advance. Accepts queries by mail, e-mail, fax, phone. Accepts previously published material. Sample copy for free.
Nonfiction Historical/nostalgic, interview/profile, new product, opinion, photo feature, travel. No professional golf-related articles. **Buys 42 mss/year.** Query with published clips. Length: 750-3,000 words. **Pays 60¢/word, including electronic rights.** Sometimes pays expenses of writers on assignment.
Photos State availability with submission. Reviews contact sheets, negatives, transparencies, prints. Buys all rights. Negotiates payment individually. Captions required.
Columns/Departments Guest Column (focus on issues surrounding the Canadian golf community), 700 words. Query. **Pays 60¢/word, including electronic rights.**
Tips "Keep story ideas focused on Canadian competitive golf."

[N] $ $ $ $ GOLF CONNOISSEUR

Patience Publishing, 4311 Oak Lawn Ave., Dallas TX 75219. E-mail: jfrank@golfconnoisseur.com. Web site: www.golfconnoisseur.com. **Contact:** James A. Frank, editor-in-chief. **90% freelance written.** Bimonthly magazine covering upscale lifestyle. "We are not a golf magazine but an upscale lifestyle book aimed at the members of the finest private golf clubs. Our golf coverage is about the great places to play (resorts, clubs, courses, real-estate communities, etc.) and the people in the game, as well as equipment and other areas, but not instruction.

The rest of the editorial is about the wide world of what interests this well-to-do, educated, experienced, well-traveled readership, which is just about everything from products to travel to ideas: business, sports, products, transportation, enjoyment, lifestyle . . . and more.'' Estab. 2004. Circ. 205,000. within 30 days of acceptance. Publishes ms an average of 2-3 months after acceptance. Byline given. Offers 20% kill fee. Buys exclusive serial for print and electronic for 120 days rights. Editorial lead time 3-6 months. Submit seasonal material 4-6 months in advance. Accepts queries by e-mail. Accepts simultaneous submissions. Responds in 1-2 weeks to queries. Writer's guidelines by e-mail.

Nonfiction Essays, general interest, interview/profile, new product, travel. Does not want personal golf experiences. **Buys 100 mss/year.** Query. Length: 300-2,500 words. **Pays $350-3,000.** Sometimes pays expenses of writers on assignment.

Photos State availability with submission. Buys one-time rights. Negotiates payment individually.

Tips ''Writers should put themselves in the shoes of someone they know who is upscale, well-traveled, educated, etc. These people have likely done all the 'first-timer' stuff; they probably drive the expensive car and know how to order a good bottle of wine. But everyone wants to know more, do more, see more, and be the first in their crowd do so. We want them to know about the newest, best, most interesting. Not always the most expensive, although income certainly helps make some choices. These people want to have 'experiences,' not just take trips and buy things. I'm more than willing to discuss ideas, to help shape an idea and help a new writer who shows promise, but it starts with having some understanding of the audience and a feel for writing for these people.''

⊘ GOLF DIGEST

The Golf Digest Companies, 20 Westport Rd., Box 20, Wilton CT 06897. (203)761-5100. Fax: (203)761-5129. E-mail: editor@golfdigest.com. Web site: www.golfdigest.com. Editor: Jerry Tarde. Managing Editor: Roger Schiffman. **Contact:** Craig Bestrom; features editor. Monthly magazine covering the sport of golf. Written for all golf enthusiasts, whether recreational, amateur, or professional player. Estab. 1950. Circ. 1,550,000. Editorial lead time 6 months. Accepts queries by mail. Sample copy for $3.95.

- *Golf Digest* does not accept any unsolicited materials.

Nonfiction Query.

GOLF FOR WOMEN

The Golf Digest Companies, P.O. Box 850, Wilton CT 06897. (203)761-5100. E-mail: editors@golfforwomen.com. Web site: www.golfdigest.com/gfw. Managing Editor: Iris Sutcliffe. **50% freelance written.** Bimonthly magazine covering golf instruction, travel, lifestyle. ''Our magazine is the leading authority on the game for women. We celebrate the traditions and lifestyle of golf, explore issues surrounding the game with incisive features, and we present traditional women's and fashion magazine fare—fashion, beauty, relationship stories—all with a strong golf angle. Travel is also a big component of our coverage. We package everything in a modern, sophisticated way that suits our affluent, educated readers.'' Circ. 500,000. **Pays on acceptance.** Byline given. Offers variable kill fee (25% standard). Buys all rights, including online. Accepts queries by mail, e-mail, fax.

Nonfiction Book excerpts, essays, general interest, historical/nostalgic, how-to (golf related), humor, inspirational, interview/profile, new product, personal experience, photo feature, travel. **Buys 50 mss/year.** Query. Length: 250-2,500 words. **Payment negotiated.** Sometimes pays expenses of writers on assignment.

Photos State availability with submission. Buys one-time rights and online usage rights. Negotiates payment individually. Model releases required.

Columns/Departments Fitness; Beauty; Get There (travel); Fashion; First Person; Health. **Pays per piece or per word; fees negotiated.**

N GOLF ILLUSTRATED

NatCom, Inc., 7580 E. 151st St., Bixby OK 74008. (918)366-6191. Fax: (918)366-6512. Web site: www.golfillustrated.com. Bimonthly magazine targeted to avid players who are big on equipment, clothing, and accessories. Circ. 143,719. Editorial lead time 3 months.

N GOLF MAGAZINE

Time4 Media, Inc., 2 Park Ave., New York NY 10016. (212)779-5000. Fax: (212)779-5522. E-mail: golfletters@golfonline.com. Web site: www.golfonline.com. Editor: David Clark. Monthly magazine written for all levels of golf enthusiasts, including beginners, experts and pros. Circ. 1,403,685. Editorial lead time 6 weeks.

$ $ GOLF NEWS MAGAZINE

Premier Golf Magazine Since 1984, Golf News Magazine, P.O. Box 1040, Rancho Mirage CA 92270. (760)321-8800. Fax: (760)328-3013. E-mail: golfnews@aol.com. Web site: www.golfnewsmag.com. **Contact:** Dan Poppers, editor/publisher. **70% freelance written.** Monthly magazine covering golf. ''Our publication specializes

Consumer Magazines

in the creative treatment of the sport of golf, offering a variety of themes and slants as related to golf. If it's good writing and relates to golf, we're interested." Estab. 1984. Circ. 15,000. **Pays on acceptance.** Publishes ms an average of 4 months after acceptance. Byline given. Buys first rights, makes work-for-hire assignments. Editorial lead time 2 months. Submit seasonal material 2 months in advance. Accepts queries by mail, e-mail, fax. Accepts previously published material. Accepts simultaneous submissions. Responds in 1 month to queries; 3 months to mss. Sample copy for $2 and 9×12 SAE with 4 first-class stamps.
Nonfiction "We will consider any topic related to golf that is written well with high standards." Book excerpts, essays, exposé, general interest, historical/nostalgic, how-to, humor, inspirational, interview/profile, opinion, personal experience, photo feature, technical, real estate. **Buys 20 mss/year.** Query with published clips. **Pays $75-350.**
Photos State availability with submission. Buys one-time rights. Negotiates payment individually. Identification of subjects required.
Columns/Departments Buys 10 mss/year. Query with published clips.
Tips "Solid, creative, good, professional writing. Stay away from cliches and the hackneyed. Only good writers need apply. We are a national award-winning magazine looking for the most creative writers we can find."

$ $ $ GOLF TIPS

The Game's Most In-Depth Instruction & Equipment Magazine, Werner Publishing Corp., 12121 Wilshire Blvd., Suite 1200, Los Angeles CA 90025. E-mail: editors@golftipsmag.com. Web site: www.golftipsmag.com. **95% freelance written.** Magazine published 9 times/year covering golf instruction and equipment. "We provide mostly concise, very clear golf instruction pieces for the serious golfer." Estab. 1986. Pays on publication. Publishes ms an average of 2 months after acceptance. Byline given. Offers 33% kill fee. Buys first, second serial (reprint) rights. Editorial lead time 3 months. Submit seasonal material 4 months in advance. Accepts previously published material. Responds in 1 month to queries. Sample copy free. Writer's guidelines online.
Nonfiction Book excerpts, how-to, interview/profile, new product, photo feature, technical, travel, all golf related. "Generally golf essays rarely make it." **Buys 125 mss/year.** Send complete ms. Length: 250-2,000 words. **Pays $300-1,000 for assigned articles; $300-800 for unsolicited articles.** Occassionally negotiates other forms of payment. Sometimes pays expenses of writers on assignment.
Photos State availability with submission. Reviews 2×2 transparencies. Buys all rights. Negotiates payment individually. Captions, identification of subjects required.
Columns/Departments Stroke Saver (very clear, concise instruction), 350 words; Lesson Library (book excerpts—usually in a series), 1,000 words; Travel Tips (formatted golf travel), 2,500 words. **Buys 40 mss/year.** Query with or without published clips or send complete ms. **Pays $300-850.**
Tips "Contact a respected PGA Professional and find out if they're interested in being published. A good writer can turn an interview into a decent instruction piece."

N $ $ $ GOLFING MAGAZINE

Golfer Magazine, Inc., 205 Broad St., Wethersfield CT 06109. (860)563-1633. Fax: (646)607-3001. E-mail: tlanders@golfingmagazine.net. Web site: www.golfingmagazineonline.com. Editor: Mike Stinton. **Contact:** Tom Landers, publisher. **30% freelance written.** Bimonthly magazine covering golf, including travel, products, player profiles and company profiles. Estab. 1999. Circ. 175,000. Pays on publication. Byline given. Offers negotiable kill fee. Buys one-time, simultaneous rights. Editorial lead time 2 months. Submit seasonal material 2 months in advance. Accepts queries by mail, e-mail. Accepts previously published material. Sample copy for free.
Nonfiction All articles must include golf-related tips. Book excerpts, new product, photo feature, travel. **Buys 4-5 mss/year.** Query. Length: 700-2,500 words. **Pays $250-1,000 for assigned articles; $100-500 for unsolicited articles.**
Photos State availability with submission. Reviews GIF/JPEG files. Negotiates payment and rights individually. Captions required.
Fillers Facts, gags to be illustrated by cartoonist. **Buys 2-3/year. Pays payment individually determined.**

N $ $ $ MINNESOTA GOLFER

6550 York Ave. S., Suite 211, Edina MN 55435. (952)927-4643. Fax: (952)927-9642. E-mail: editor@mngolf.org. Web site: www.mngolfer.com. **Contact:** W.P. Ryan, editor. **75% freelance written.** Bimonthly magazine covering golf in Minnesota, the official publication of the Minnesota Golf Association. Estab. 1975. Circ. 66,000. Pays on acceptance or publication. Byline given. Buys first rights. Editorial lead time 3 months. Accepts queries by mail, e-mail, fax.
Nonfiction Historical/nostalgic, interview/profile, new product, travel, book reviews, instruction, golf course previews. Query with published clips. Length: 400-2,000 words. **Pays $50-750.** Sometimes pays expenses of writers on assignment.
Photos State availability with submission. Reviews contact sheets, transparencies, digital images. Image rights

by assignment. Negotiates payment individually. Captions, identification of subjects required.
Columns/Departments Punch shots (golf news and notes); Q School (news and information targeted to beginners, junior golfers and women); Great Drives (featuring noteworthy golf holes in Minnesota); Instruction.

TRAVEL + LEISURE GOLF

(formerly *T&L Golf*), American Express Publishing Corp., 1120 Avenue of the Americas, 11th Floor, New York NY 10036. E-mail: tlgletters@tlgolf.com. Web site: www.tlgolf.com. Editor: Yossi Langer. **95% freelance written.** Bimonthly magazine for those who see golf not only as a game but as a lifestyle. Circ. 600,000. **Pays on acceptance.** Buys first time world rights rights.
Nonfiction Query through Web site.
Tips "It is rare we will assign a feature article to a writer with whom we have not worked. The best sections to start with are departments in the front of the magazine."

$ $ VIRGINIA GOLFER

TPG Sports, Inc., 600 Founders Bridge Blvd., Midlothian VA 23113. (804)378-2300. Fax: (804)378-2369. Web site: www.vsga.org. **Contact:** Andrew Blair, editor. **65% freelance written.** Bimonthly magazine covering golf in Virginia, the official publication of the Virginia State Golf Association. Estab. 1983. Circ. 45,000. Pays on publication. Byline given. Buys all rights. Editorial lead time 6 months. Submit seasonal material 3 months in advance. Accepts queries by mail, e-mail. Accepts previously published material. Accepts simultaneous submissions. Sample copy and writer's guidelines free.
Nonfiction Book excerpts, essays, historical/nostalgic, how-to (golf), humor, inspirational, interview/profile, personal experience, photo feature, technical (golf equipment), where to play, golf business. **Buys 30-40 mss/year.** Query with or without published clips or send complete ms. Length: 500-2,500 words. **Pays $50-200.** Sometimes pays expenses of writers on assignment.
Reprints Accepts previously published submissions.
Photos State availability with submission. Reviews contact sheets. Rights purchased varies. Negotiates payment individually. Captions, identification of subjects required.
Columns/Departments Chip ins & Three Putts (news notes), Rules Corner (golf rules explanations and discussion), Pro Tips, Golf Travel (where to play), Great Holes, Q&A, Golf Business (what's happening?), Fashion. Query.

GUNS

$ $ GUN DIGEST

Krause Publications, 700 E. State St., Iola WI 54990. (888)457-2873. Fax: (715)445-4087. **Contact:** Ken Ramage, editor-in-chief. **50% freelance written.** Prefers to work with published/established writers, but works with a small number of new/unpublished writers each year. Annual journal covering guns and shooting. Estab. 1944. **Pays on acceptance.** Publishes ms an average of 20 months after acceptance. Byline given. Buys all rights. Accepts queries by mail. Responds as time allows to queries.
Nonfiction Buys 25 mss/year. Query. Length: 500-5,000 words. **Pays $100-600 for text/art package.**
Photos Prefers color images. Slides, transparencies OK. Digital OK as 300 dpi TIFF. State availability with submission. Payment for photos included in payment for ms. Captions required.
Tips Award of $1,000 to author of best article (juried) in each edition.

$ $ MUZZLE BLASTS

National Muzzle Loading Rifle Association, P.O. Box 67, Friendship IN 47021. (812)667-5131. Fax: (812)667-5137. E-mail: mblastdop@seidata.com. Web site: www.nmlra.org. Editor: Eric A. Bye. **Contact:** Terri Trowbridge, director of publications. **65% freelance written.** Monthly magazine. "Articles must relate to muzzleloading or the muzzleloading era of American history." Estab. 1939. Circ. 20,000. Pays on publication. Publishes ms an average of 6 months after acceptance. Byline given. Offers $50 kill fee. Buys first North American serial, one-time, second serial (reprint) rights. Editorial lead time 4 months. Submit seasonal material 6 months in advance. Responds in 1 month to mss. Sample copy and writer's guidelines free.
Nonfiction Book excerpts, general interest, historical/nostalgic, how-to, humor, interview/profile, new product, personal experience, photo feature, technical, travel. "No subjects that do not pertain to muzzleloading." **Buys 80 mss/year.** Query. Length: 2,500 words. **Pays $150 minimum for assigned articles; $50 minimum for unsolicited articles.**
Photos Send photos with submission. Reviews 5×7 prints. Buys one-time rights. Negotiates payment individually. Captions, model releases required.
Columns/Departments Buys 96 mss/year. Query. **Pays $50-200.**

Fiction Must pertain to muzzleloading. Adventure, historical, humorous. **Buys 6 mss/year.** Query. Length: 2,500 words. **Pays $50-300.**

Fillers Facts. **Pays $50.**

$ $ SHOTGUN NEWS

Primedia, 2 News Plaza, 2nd Floor, Peoria IL 61614. (800)521-2885. Fax: (309)679-5476. E-mail: sgnews@primedia.com. Web site: www.shotgunnews.com. **95% freelance written.** Tabloid published every 10 days covering firearms, accessories, ammunition and militaria. "The nation's oldest and largest gun sales publication. Provides up-to-date market information for gun trade and consumers." Estab. 1946. Circ. 100,000. **Pays on acceptance.** Publishes ms an average of 3 months after acceptance. Byline given. Buys first North American serial rights. Editorial lead time 1 month. Submit seasonal material 3 months in advance. Responds in 1 month to queries. Sample copy for free.

Nonfiction Historical/nostalgic, how-to, technical. No political pieces, fiction or poetry. **Buys 50 mss/year.** Query. Length: 1,000-3,000 words. **Pays $200-500 for assigned articles.** Sometimes pays expenses of writers on assignment.

Photos Send photos with submission. Reviews prints. Buys one-time rights. Offers no additional payment for photos accepted with ms. Captions required.

HIKING & BACKPACKING

$ $ $ $ BACKPACKER

Rodale, 33 E. Minor St., Emmaus PA 18098. (610)967-8296. Fax: (610)967-8181. E-mail: pflax@backpacker.com. Web site: www.backpacker.com. **Contact:** Peter Flax, deputy editor. **50% freelance written.** Magazine published 9 times/year covering wilderness travel for backpackers. Estab. 1973. Circ. 295,000. **Pays on acceptance.** Byline given. Buys one-time, all rights. Accepts queries by mail, e-mail, fax. Responds in 6 weeks to queries. Writer's guidelines online.

Nonfiction "What we want are features that let us and the readers 'feel' the place, and experience your wonderment, excitement, disappointment, or other emotions encountered 'out there.' If we feel like we've been there after reading your story, you've succeeded." Essays, exposé, historical/nostalgic, how-to, humor, inspirational, interview/profile, new product, personal experience, technical, travel. No step-by-step accounts of what you did on your summer vacation—stories that chronicle every rest stop and gulp of water. Query with published clips. Length: 750-4,000 words. **Pays 60¢-$1/word.**

Photos State availability with submission. Buys one-time rights. Payment varies.

Columns/Departments Signpost, "News From All Over" (adventure, environment, wildelife, trails, techniques, organizations, special interests—well-written, entertaining, short, newsy item), 50-500 words; Getaways (great hiking destinations, primarily North America), includes weekend, 250-500 words, weeklong, 250-1000, multi-destination guides, 500-1500 words, and dayhikes, 50-200 words, plus travel news and other items; Fitness (in-the-field health column), 750-1,200 words; Food (food-related aspects of wilderness: nutrition, cooking techniques, recipes, products and gear), 500-750 words; Know How (ranging from beginner to expert focus, written by people with solid expertise, details ways to improve performance, how-to-do-it instructions, information on equipment manufacturers, and places readers can go), 300-1,000 words; Senses (capturing a moment in backcountry through sight, sound, smell, and other senses, paired with an outstanding photo), 150-200 words. **Buys 50-75 mss/year.**

Contact: Sarah James, online editor.

Tips "Our best advice is to read the publication—most freelancers don't know the magazine at all. The best way to break in is with an article for the Weekend Wilderness, Know How, or Signpost Department."

OUTSIDE

Mariah Media, Inc., Outside Plaza, 400 Market St., Santa Fe NM 87501. Web site: www.outsidemag.com. Editor: Hal Espen. Managing Editor: Aaron Gulley. **Contact:** Editorial Department. **90% freelance written.** Monthly magazine. "*Outside* is a monthly national magazine for active, educated, upscale adults who love the outdoors and are concerned about its preservation." Estab. 1977. Circ. 550,000. Pays after acceptance. Publishes ms an average of 3 months after acceptance. Byline given. Offers 25% kill fee. Buys first North American serial rights. Submit seasonal material 5 months in advance. Writer's guidelines online. Editorial calendar online.

Nonfiction Book excerpts, essays, general interest, how-to, interview/profile (major figures associated with sports, travel, environment, outdoor), photo feature (outdoor photography), technical (reviews of equipment, how-to), travel (adventure, sports-oriented travel). Do not want to see articles about sports that we don't cover (basketball, tennis, golf, etc.). **Buys 40 mss/year.** Query with published clips. Length: 1,500-5,000 words. Pays expenses of writers on assignment.

Photos "Do not send photos; if we decide to use a story, we may ask to see the writer's photos." Reviews transparencies. Buys one-time rights. Captions, identification of subjects required.
Columns/Departments Dispatches (news, events, short profiles relevant to outdoors), 100-8,000 words; Destinations (places to explore, news, and tips for adventure travelers), 300-1,000 words; Review (evaluations of products), 200-1,500 words. **Buys 180 mss/year.** Query with published clips.
Tips "Prospective writers should study the magazine before querying. Look at the magazine for our style, subject matter, and standards." The departments are the best areas for freelancers to break in.

HOCKEY

$ $ MINNESOTA HOCKEY JOURNAL

Official Publication of Minnesota Hockey, Inc., % TPG Sports, Inc., 6160 Summit Dr., Suite 375, Minneapolis MN 55430. (763)595-0808. Fax: (763)595-0016. E-mail: greg@tpgsports.com. Web site: www.tpgsports.com. Editor: Greg Anzlec. **50% freelance written.** Journal published 4 times/year. Estab. 2000. Circ. 40,000. Pays on publication. Byline given. Buys all rights. Editorial lead time 6 months. Submit seasonal material 4 months in advance. Accepts previously published material. Accepts simultaneous submissions. Sample copy and writer's guidelines free.
Nonfiction Essays, general interest, historical/nostalgic, how-to (play hockey), humor, inspirational, interview/profile, new product, opinion, personal experience, photo feature, travel, hockey camps, pro hockey, juniors, college, Olympics, youth, etc. **Buys 3-5 mss/year.** Query. Length: 500-1,500 words. **Pays $100-300.**
Reprints Accepts previously published submissions.
Photos State availability with submission. Reviews contact sheets. Rights purchased vary. Negotiates payment individually. Captions, identification of subjects required.

N $ $ $ USA HOCKEY MAGAZINE

Official Publication of USA Hockey, TPG Sports, Inc., 6160 Summit Dr., Suite 375, Minneapolis MN 55430. (763)595-0808, ext. 114. Fax: (763)595-0016. E-mail: info@tpgsports.com. Web site: www.usahockey.com. Managing Editor: Harry Thompson. **Contact:** Greg Anzelc, publications manager. **60% freelance written.** Magazine published 10 times/year covering amateur hockey in the US. "The world's largest hockey magazine, *USA Hockey Magazine* is the official magazine of USA Hockey, Inc., the national governing body of hockey." Estab. 1980. Circ. 444,000. Pays on acceptance or publication. Byline given. Buys all rights. Editorial lead time 6 months. Submit seasonal material 4 months in advance. Accepts previously published material. Accepts simultaneous submissions. Sample copy and writer's guidelines free.
Nonfiction Essays, general interest, historical/nostalgic, how-to (play hockey), humor, inspirational, interview/profile, new product, opinion, personal experience, photo feature, travel, hockey camps, pro hockey, juniors, college, NCAA hockey championships, Olympics, youth, etc. **Buys 20-30 mss/year.** Query. Length: 500-5,000 words. **Pays $50-750.** Pays expenses of writers on assignment.
Reprints Accepts previously published submissions.
Photos State availability with submission. Reviews contact sheets. Rights purchased varies. Negotiates payment individually. Captions, identification of subjects required.
Columns/Departments Short Cuts (news and notes); Coaches' Corner (teaching tips); USA Hockey; Inline Notebook (news and notes). **Pays $150-250.**
Fiction Adventure, humorous, slice-of-life vignettes. **Buys 10-20 mss/year. Pays $150-1,000.**
Fillers Anecdotes, facts, gags to be illustrated by cartoonist, newsbreaks, short humor. **Buys 20-30/year.** Length: 10-100 words. **Pays $25-250.**
Tips Writers must have a general knowledge and enthusiasm for hockey, including ice, inline, street, and other. The primary audience is youth players in the US.

HORSE RACING

N THE AMERICAN QUARTER HORSE RACING JOURNAL

American Quarter Horse Association, P.O. Box 32470, Amarillo TX 79120. (806)376-4811. Web site: www.aqha.com/magazines. **10% freelance written.** Monthly magazine promoting American Quarter Horse racing. Articles include training, breeding, nutrition, sports medicine, health, history, etc. Estab. 1988. Circ. 9,000. **Pays on acceptance.** Publishes ms an average of 3 months after acceptance. Buys first North American serial rights. Submit seasonal material 3 months in advance. Accepts queries by mail. Accepts previously published material. Responds in 1 month to queries. Sample copy and writer's guidelines free.
Nonfiction Historical/nostalgic (must be on Quarter Horses or people associated with them), how-to (training), opinion, nutrition, health, breeding. Query. Length: 700-1,500 words.

Reprints Send photocopy and information about when and where the material previously appeared.
Photos Send photos with submission. Additional payment for photos accepted with ms might be offered. Captions, identification of subjects required.
Tips "Query first—you must be familiar with Quarter Horse racing and be knowledgeable of the sport. The *Journal* directs its articles to those who own, train and breed racing Quarter Horses, as well as fans and handicappers. Most open to features covering breeding, raising, training, nutrition and health care utilizing knowledgeable sources with credentials."

$ $ AMERICAN TURF MONTHLY

All Star Sports, Inc., 747 Middle Neck Rd., Suite 103, Great Neck NY 11024. (516)773-4075. Fax: (516)773-2944. E-mail: editor@americanturf.com. Web site: www.americanturf.com. **Contact:** James Corbett, editor-in-chief. **90% freelance written.** Monthly magazine covering Thoroughbred racing, handicapping, and wagering. "Squarely focused on Thoroughbred handicapping and wagering. *ATM* is a magazine for horseplayers, not owners, breeders, or 12-year-old girls enthralled with ponies." Estab. 1946. Circ. 28,000. Pays on publication. Publishes ms an average of 4 months after acceptance. Byline given. Makes work-for-hire assignments. Editorial lead time 2 months. Submit seasonal material 2 months in advance. Accepts queries by mail, e-mail. Responds in 1 month to queries. Sample copy and writer's guidelines free.
Nonfiction Handicapping and wagering features. Special issues: Triple Crown/Kentucky Derby (May); Saratoga/Del Mar (August); Breeder's Cup (November). No historical essays, bilious 'guest editorials,' saccharine poetry, fiction. **Buys 50 mss/year.** Query. Length: 800-2,000 words. **Pays $75-300 for assigned articles; $100-500 for unsolicited articles.**
Photos Send photos with submission. Reviews 3×5 transparencies, prints, 300 dpi TIF images on CD-ROM. Buys one-time rights. Offers $25 interior; $150 for cover. Identification of subjects required.
Fillers Newsbreaks, short humor. **Buys 5/year.** Length: 400 words.**Pays $25.**
The online magazine carries original content not found in the print version.
Tips "Send a good query letter specifically targeted at explaining how this contribution will help our readers to cash a bet at the track!"

$ $ HOOF BEATS

United States Trotting Association, 750 Michigan Ave., Columbus OH 43215. Fax: (614)222-6791. E-mail: hoofbeats@ustrotting.com. Web site: www.ustrotting.com. **Contact:** Nicole Kraft, executive editor (nkraft@ustrotting.com). **50% freelance written.** Monthly magazine covering harness racing for the participants of the sport of harness racing. "We cover all aspects of the sport—racing, breeding, selling, etc." Estab. 1933. Circ. 13,500. Pays on publication. Publishes ms an average of 3 months after acceptance. Byline given. Buys negotiable rights. Submit seasonal material 4 months in advance. Responds in 1 months to mss. Free sample copy postpaid.
Nonfiction General interest, historical/nostalgic, humor, inspirational, interview/profile, new product, personal experience, photo feature, horse care. **Buys 15-20 mss/year.** Length: open. **Pays $100-400.**
Photos State availability with submission. Reviews prints, electronic images. Buys one-time rights. Negotiates payment individually. Identification of subjects required.

HUNTING & FISHING

$ $ ALABAMA GAME & FISH

Game & Fish, 2250 Newmarket Parkway, Suite 110, Marietta GA 30067. (770)953-9222. Fax: (770)933-9510. E-mail: jimmy.jacobs@primedia.com. Web site: www.alabamagameandfish.com. **Contact:** Jimmy Jacobs, editor. See *Game & Fish*.

$ $ AMERICAN ANGLER

the Magazine of Fly Fishing & Fly Tying, Abenaki Publishers, Inc., P.O. Box 4100, Bennington VT 05201. E-mail: americanangler@flyfishingmagazines.com. Web site: www.flyfishingmagazines.com. **Contact:** Philip Monahan, editor. **95% freelance written.** Bimonthly magazine covering fly fishing. "*American Angler* is dedicated to giving fly fishers practical information they can use—wherever they fish, whatever they fish for." Estab. 1976. Circ. 60,000. Pays on publication. Publishes ms an average of 6 months after acceptance. Byline given. Buys first North American serial, one-time rights. Editorial lead time 3 months. Submit seasonal material 5 months in advance. Accepts queries by mail, fax. Accepts previously published material. Accepts simultaneous submissions. Responds in 6 weeks to queries; 2 months to mss. Sample copy for $6. Writer's guidelines for #10 SASE.
Nonfiction How-to (most important), personal experience, photo feature (seldom), technical. No promotional flack fo pay back free trips or freebies, no superficial, broad-brush coverage of subjects. **Buys 45-60 mss/year.**

Query with published clips. Length: 800-2,200 words. **Pays $200-400.** Send information about when and where the material previously appeared. Pay negotiable.

Photos "Photographs are important. A fly-tying submission should always include samples of flies to send to our staff photographer, even if photos of the flies are included." Send photos with submission. Reviews contact sheets, transparencies. Buys one-time rights. Offers no additional payment for photos accepted with ms. Captions, identification of subjects required.

Columns/Departments One-page shorts (problem solvers), 350-750 words. Query with published clips. **Pays $100-300.**

Tips "If you are new to this editor, please submit complete queries."

$ $ $ AMERICAN HUNTER

11250 Waples Mill Rd., Fairfax VA 22030-9400. (703)267-1335. Fax: (703)267-3971. E-mail: publications@nrahq.org. Web site: www.nra.org. Editor-in-Chief: J. Scott Olmsted. **Contact:** Frank Miniter, executive editor. Monthly magazine for hunters who are members of the National Rifle Association. "*American Hunter* contains articles dealing with various sport hunting and related activities both at home and abroad. With the encouragement of the sport as a prime game management tool, emphasis is on technique, sportsmanship and safety. In each issue hunting equipment and firearms are evaluated, legislative happenings affecting the sport are reported, lore and legend are retold and the business of the Association is recorded in the Official Journal section." Circ. 1,000,000. **Pays on acceptance.** Byline given. Buys first North American serial, second serial (reprint) rights. Accepts queries by mail, e-mail. Responds in 6 months to queries. Writer's guidelines for #10 SASE.

Nonfiction Factual material on all phases of hunting: Expository how-to, where-to, and general interest pieces; humor: personal narratives; and semi-technical articles on firearms, wildlife management or hunting. Features fall into five categories: Deer, upland birds, waterfowl, big game and varmints/small game. Special issues: Pheasants, whitetail tactics, black bear feed areas, mule deer, duck hunters' transport by land and sea, tech topics to be decided; rut strategies, muzzleloader moose and elk, fall turkeys, staying warm, goose talk, long-range muzzleloading. Not interested in material on fishing, camping, or firearms knowledge. Query. Length: 1,800-2,000 words. **Pays up to $800.**

Reprints Send ms with rights for sale noted and information about when and where the material previously appeared.

Photos No additional payment made for photos used with ms; others offered from $75-600.

Columns/Departments Hunting Guns, Hunting Loads and Public Hunting Grounds. Study back issues for appropriate subject matter and style. Length: 1,200-1,500 words. **Pays $300-450.**

Tips "Although unsolicited manuscripts are welcomed, detailed query letters outlining the proposed topic and approach are appreciated and will save both writers and editors a considerable amount of time. If we like your story idea, you will be contacted by mail or phone and given direction on how we'd like the topic covered. NRA Publications accept all manuscripts and photographs for consideration on a specualtion basis only. Story angles should be narrow, but coverage must have depth. How-to articles are popular with readers and might range from methods for hunting to techniques on making gear used on successful hunts. Where-to articles should contain contacts and information needed to arrange a similar hunt. All submissions are judged on three criteria: Story angle (it should be fresh, interesting, and informative); quality of writing (clear and lively—capable of holding the readers' attention throughout); and quality and quantity of accompanying photos (sharpness, reproduceability, and connection to text are most important.)"

N $ $ $ ARIZONA WILDLIFE VIEWS

Arizona Game and Fish Department, IEPB, 2221 W. Greenway Rd., Phoenix AZ 85053. E-mail: awv@azgfd.gov. Web site: www.azgfd.gov. Editor: Heidi Hougham. **Contact:** Julie Hammonds, associate editor. **50% freelance written.** Bimonthly magazine covering Arizona wildlife, wildlife management and outdoor recreation (specifically hunting, fishing, wildlife watching, boating and off-highway vehicle recreation). "*Arizona Wildlife Views* is a general interest magazine about Arizona wildlife, wildlife management and outdoor recreation. We publish material that conforms to the mission and policies of the Arizona Game and Fish Department. In addition to Arizona wildlife and wildlife management, topics include habitat issues, outdoor recreation involving wildlife, boating, fishing, hunting, bird-watching, animal observation, off-highway vehicle use, etc., and historical articles about wildlife and wildlife management." Estab. 1953. Circ. 22,000. Pays on publication. Publishes ms an average of 10 months after acceptance. Byline given. Buys one-time rights. Editorial lead time 1 year. Submit seasonal material 2 months in advance. Accepts queries by mail, e-mail. Accepts simultaneous submissions. Responds in 1 month to queries; 2 months to mss. Sample copy for free. Writer's guidelines free.

Nonfiction General interest, historical/nostalgic, how-to, interview/profile, photo feature, technical, travel, scientific for a popular audience. Does not want "me and Joe" articles, anthropomorphism of wildlife or opinionated pieces not based on confirmable facts. **Buys 20 mss/year.** Query. Length: 1,000-2,500 words. **Pays $450-800.**

Photos Send photos with submission. Reviews transparencies, GIF/JPEG files. Buys one-time rights. Offers $150-400/photo. Captions required.
Columns/Departments Outdoor Tips (how to hunt, fish, boat, or use an OHV); Watchable Wildlife (where and how to watch Arizona wildlife and what you will see there), both 1,600 words. **Buys 12 mss/year.** Query. **Pays $450-800.**
Tips "We look for writers with a scientific background who are familiar with Arizona. The preferred writing style entertains and informs a popular auidence."

$ $ ARKANSAS SPORTSMAN

Game & Fish, 2250 Newmarket Parkway, Suite 110, Marietta GA 30067. (770)953-9222. Fax: (770)933-9510. E-mail: ronell.smith@primedia.com. Web site: www.arkansassportsmanmag.com. **Contact:** Ronell Smith, editor. See *Game & Fish*.

$ $ BASSMASTER MAGAZINE

B.A.S.S. Publications, 5845 Carmichael Pkwy., Montgomery AL 36117. (334)272-9530. Fax: (334)396-8230. E-mail: editorial@bassmaster.com. Web site: www.bassmaster.com. **Contact:** James Hall, editor. **80% freelance written.** Magazine published 11 times/year about largemouth, smallmouth, and spotted bass, offering "how-to" articles for dedicated beginning and advanced bass fishermen, including destinations and new product reviews. Estab. 1968. Circ. 600,000. **Pays on acceptance.** Publishes ms an average of less than 1 year after acceptance. Byline given. Buys electronic rights. Editorial lead time 2 months. Submit seasonal material 6 months in advance. Accepts queries by mail, e-mail. Responds in 2 months to queries. Sample copy for $2. Writer's guidelines for #10 SASE.

- Needs destination stories (how to fish a certain area) for the Northwest and Northeast.

Nonfiction Historical/nostalgic, how-to (patterns, lures, etc.), interview/profile (of knowledgeable people in the sport), new product (reels, rods, and bass boats), travel (where to go fish for bass), conservation related to bass fishing. "No first-person, personal experience-type articles." **Buys 100 mss/year.** Query. Length: 500-1,500 words. **Pays $100-600.**
Photos Send photos with submission. Reviews transparencies. Buys all rights. Offers no additional payment for photos accepted with ms, but pays $700 for color cover transparencies. Captions, model releases required.
Columns/Departments Short Cast/News/Views/Notes/Briefs (upfront regular feature covering news-related events such as new state bass records, unusual bass fishing happenings, conservation, new products, and editorial viewpoints). Length: 250-400 words. **Pays $100-300.**
Fillers Anecdotes, newsbreaks. **Buys 4-5/year.** Length: 250-500 words. **Pays $50-100.**
Tips "Editorial direction continues in the short, more direct how-to article. Compact, easy-to-read information is our objective. Shorter articles with good graphics, such as how-to diagrams, step-by-step instruction, etc., will enhance a writer's articles submitted to *Bassmaster Magazine*. The most frequent mistakes made by writers in completing an article for us are poor grammar, poor writing, poor organization, and superficial research. Send in detailed queries outlining specific objectives of article, obtain writer's guidelines. Be as concise as possible."

BC OUTDOORS SPORT FISHING AND OUTDOOR ADVENTURE

OP Publishing, 1080 Howe St., Suite 900, Vancouver BC V6Z 2T1 Canada. (604)678-2586. E-mail: editor@bcosportfishing.com. Web site: www.bcosportfishing.com. **Contact:** D. Ryan Pohl, editor. **80% freelance written.** Magazine published 6 times/year covering fresh and saltwater fishing, camping, and backroads. Pays on publication. Publishes ms an average of 3 months after acceptance. Byline given. Offers kill fee. Buys first North American serial rights. Writer's guidelines for 8×10 SAE with 7 Canadian first-class stamps.
Nonfiction "We would like to receive how-to, where-to features dealing with fishing in British Columbia." How-to (new or innovative articles on fishing subjects), personal experience (outdoor adventure), outdoor topics specific to British Columbia. Query features in early spring. Length: 1,700-2,000 words.
Photos State availability with submission. Buys one-time rights. Captions, identification of subjects required.
Tips "Wants in-depth information, professional writing only. Emphasis on environmental issues. Those pieces with a conservation component have a better chance of being published. Subject must be specific to British Columbia. We receive many manuscripts written by people who obviously do not know the magazine or market. The writer has a better chance of breaking in with short, lesser-paying articles and fillers, because we have a stable of regular writers who produce most main features."

$ $ THE BIG GAME FISHING JOURNAL

Informational Publications, Inc., 1800 Bay Ave., Point Pleasant NJ 08742. Fax: (732)223-2449. Web site: www.biggamefishingjournal.com. **90% freelance written.** Bimonthly magazine covering big game fishing. "We require highly instructional articles prepared by qualified writers/fishermen." Estab. 1994. Circ. 45,000. Pays on publication. Byline given. Offers 50% kill fee. Buys first North American serial rights. Editorial lead time 3 months. Submit seasonal material 3 months in advance. Accepts queries by mail, e-mail. Accepts simultaneous submissions. Responds in 2 weeks to queries; 1 month to mss. Writer's guidelines free.

Nonfiction How-to, interview/profile, technical. **Buys 50-70 mss/year.** Send complete ms. Length: 2,000-3,000 words. **Pays $200-400.** Sometimes pays expenses of writers on assignment.

Photos Send photos with submission. Reviews transparencies. Buys one-time rights. Offers no additional payment for photos accepted with ms. Captions required.

Tips "Our format is considerably different than most publications. We prefer to receive articles from qualified anglers on their expertise—if the author is an accomplished writer, all the better. We require highly-instructional articles that teach both novice and expert readers."

N $ CALIFORNIA BUCKS

Outdoor News Service, P.O. Box 9007, San Bernardino CA 92427-0007. (909)887-3444. Fax: (909)887-8180. E-mail: cabucks@earthlink.net. Web site: www.outdoornewsservice.com. Editor: Jim Matthews. **Contact:** Rick Bean, managing editor. **25% freelance written.** Quarterly newsletter covering strictly the hunting of deer in California—when, where and how. Estab. 2005. Circ. 500. Pays on publication. Publishes ms an average of 1-2 months after acceptance. Byline given. Editorial lead time 3-12 months. Submit seasonal material 3-12 months in advance. Accepts queries by mail, e-mail, fax. Accepts previously published material. Accepts simultaneous submissions. Sample copy by e-mail. Writer's guidelines by e-mail.

Nonfiction Exposé, historical/nostalgic, how-to, new product, personal experience, technical. Does not want anything that does not deal with deer hunting in California. **Buys 12-18 mss/year.** Query. Length: 200-1,200 words. **Pays $75/printed page.**

Photos State availability with submission. Reviews TIFF/JPEG files. Buys one-time rights. Offers no additional payment for photos accepted with ms; pays $25-50/photo separately. Captions, identification of subjects required.

Tips "We are always looking for individual research pieces on hunters who are successful on taking deer on public lands, especially if the piece details—with maps—where the hunt took place and gives detailed information for our readers."

$ $ CALIFORNIA GAME & FISH

Game & Fish, 2250 Newmarket Parkway, Suite 110, Marietta GA 30067. (770)953-9222. Fax: (770)933-9510. E-mail: john.geiger@primedia.com. Web site: www.californiagameandfish.com. **Contact:** John Geiger, editor. See *Game & Fish*.

N $ CALIFORNIA HOG HUNTER

A Newsletter Dedicated to Hunting Wild Pigs, Outdoor News Service, P.O. Box 9007, San Bernardino CA 92427-0007. (909)887-3444. Fax: (909)887-8180. E-mail: cahoghunter@earthlink.net. Web site: www.outdoornewsservice.com. Editor: Jim Matthews. **Contact:** Rick Bean, managing editor. **25% freelance written.** Quarterly newsletter covering strictly the hunting of wild hogs in California—when, where and how. Estab. 1998. Circ. 1,000. Pays on publication. Publishes ms an average of 1-2 months after acceptance. Byline given. Offers kill fee. Editorial lead time 3-12 months. Submit seasonal material 3-12 months in advance. Accepts queries by mail, e-mail, fax. Accepts previously published material. Accepts simultaneous submissions. Responds in 1 month to queries. Sample copy by e-mail. Writer's guidelines by e-mail.

Nonfiction Exposé, historical/nostalgic, how-to, new product, personal experience, technical. Does not want anything not dealing with hog hunting in California. **Buys 12-18 mss/year.** Query. Length: 200-1,200 words. **Pays $75/printed page.**

Photos State availability with submission. Reviews GIF/JPEG files. Buys one-time rights. Offers no additional payment for photos accepted with ms; offers $25-50/photo for those sold separately. Captions, identification of subjects required.

Tips "We are always looking for individual research pieces on hunters who are successful on taking wild hogs on public lands, especially if the piece details—with maps—where the hunt took place and gives detailed information for our readers."

N $ $ THE DRAKE MAGAZINE

For Those Who Fly-Fish, 34145 PCH #319, Dana Point CA 92629. E-mail: info@drakemag.com. Web site: www.drakemag.com. **Contact:** Tom Bie, managing editor. **70% freelance written.** Annual magazine for people who love fishing. Pays 1 month after publication. Publishes ms an average of 1 year after acceptance. Byline given. Buys first North American serial rights. Editorial lead time 1 year. Submit seasonal material 1 year in advance. Accepts queries by mail. Responds in 6 months to mss. Writer's guidelines online.

O→ To break in "Tippets is the best bet: Short, 200-600 word essays on any aspect of the fishing world. Rodholders is another good area (profiles of people who fish)."

Nonfiction Book excerpts, essays, general interest, historical/nostalgic, humor, interview/profile, opinion, personal experience, photo feature, travel (fishing related). **Buys 8 mss/year.** Query. Length: 250-3,000 words. **Pays 10-20¢/word "depending on the amount of work we have to put into the piece."**

Photos State availability with submission. Reviews contact sheets, negatives, transparencies. Buys one-time rights. Offers $25-250/photo.

$ $ $ FIELD & STREAM

2 Park Ave., Time 4 Media, New York NY 10016-5695. (212)779-5000. Fax: (212)779-5114. E-mail: fsletters@time4.com. Web site: fieldandstream.com. **Contact:** Sid Evans, editor. **50% freelance written.** Monthly magazine. "Broad-based service magazine for the hunter and fisherman. Editorial content consists of articles of penetrating depth about national hunting, fishing, and related activities. Also humor, personal essays, profiles on outdoor people, conservation, sportsmen's insider secrets, tactics and techniques, and adventures." Estab. 1895. Circ. 1,500,000. Pays on acceptance for most articles. Byline given. Buys first rights. Accepts queries by mail. Responds in 1 month to queries. Sample copy not available. Writer's guidelines online.

Nonfiction Length: 1,500 words for features. Payment varies depending on the quality of work, importance of the article. **Pays $800-1,000 and more on a sliding scale for major features.** Query by mail.

Photos Send photos with submission. Reviews slides (prefers color). Buys first rights. When purchased separately, pays $450 minimum for color.

▣ Online version of magazine carries original content not contained in the print edition. Contact: Elizabeth Burnham.

Tips "Writers are encouraged to submit queries on article ideas. These should be no more than a paragraph or 2, and should include a summary of the idea, including the angle you will hang the story on, and a sense of what makes this piece different from all others on the same or a similar subject. Many queries are turned down because we have no idea what the writer is getting at. Be sure that your letter is absolutely clear. We've found that if you can't sum up the point of the article in a sentence or 2, the article doesn't have a point. Pieces that depend on writing style, such as humor, mood, and nostalgia or essays often can't be queried and may be submitted in manuscript form. The same is true of short tips. All submissions to *Field & Stream* are on an on-spec basis. Before submitting anything, however, we encourage you to *study*, not simply read, the magazine. Many pieces are rejected because they do not fit the tone or style of the magazine, or fail to match the subject of the article with the overall subject matter of *Field & Stream*. Above all, study the magazine before submitting anything."

$ FISHING & HUNTING NEWS

Outdoor Empire Publishing, 424 N. 130th St., Seattle WA 98133. (206)624-3845. Fax: (206)695-8512. E-mail: staff@fishingandhuntingnews.com. Web site: www.fhnews.com/. **Contact:** John Marsh, managing editor. **95% freelance written.** Bimonthly magazine covering fishing and hunting. "We focus on upcoming fishing and hunting opportunities in your area—where to go and what to do once you get there." Estab. 1954. Circ. 96,000. Pays on publication. Publishes ms an average of 1 month after acceptance. Byline given. Buys first North American serial, second serial (reprint), electronic rights. Editorial lead time 1 month. Submit seasonal material 2 months in advance. Accepts queries by mail, e-mail. Sample copy and writer's guidelines free.

Nonfiction How-to (local fishing and hunting), where-to. **Buys 5,000 mss/year.** Query with published clips. Length: 350-2,000 words. **Pays $25-125 and up.** Seldom pays expenses of writers on assignment.

Photos State availability with submission. Buys all rights. Captions required.

Tips "*F&H News* is published in 7 local editions across the western U.S., Great Lakes, and mid-Atlantic states. We look for reports of current fishing and hunting opportunity, plus technique- or strategy-related articles that can be used by anglers and hunters in these areas."

$ $ FLORIDA GAME & FISH

Game & Fish, 2250 Newmarket Parkway, Suite 110, Marietta GA 30067. (770)953-9222. Fax: (770)933-9510. E-mail: jimmy.jacobs@primedia.com. Web site: www.floridagameandfish.com. **Contact:** Jimmy Jacobs, editor. See *Game & Fish*.

$ $ FLORIDA SPORTSMAN

Wickstrom Communications Division of Primedia Special Interest Publications, 2700 S. Kanner Hwy., Stuart FL 34994. (772)219-7400. Fax: (772)219-6900. E-mail: editor@floridasportsman.com. Web site: www.floridasportsman.com. **Contact:** Jeff Weakley, editor. **30% freelance written.** Monthly magazine covering fishing, boating, and related sports—Florida and Caribbean only. "*Florida Sportsman* is edited for the boatowner and offshore, coastal, and fresh water fisherman. It provides a how, when, and where approach in its articles, which also includes occasional camping, diving, and hunting stories—plus ecology; in-depth articles and editorials attempting to protect Florida's wilderness, wetlands, and natural beauty." Circ. 115,000. **Pays on acceptance.** Publishes ms an average of 6 months after acceptance. Byline given. Buys nonexclusive additional rights. Submit seasonal material 6 months in advance. Accepts queries by mail. Responds in 2 months to queries; 1 month to mss. Sample copy for free. Writer's guidelines for #10 SASE.

Nonfiction "We use reader service pieces almost entirely—how-to, where-to, etc. One or 2 environmental pieces/issue as well. Writers must be Florida based, or have lengthy experience in Florida outdoors. All articles must have strong Florida emphasis. We do not want to see general how-to-fish-or-boat pieces which might well appear in a national or wide-regional magazine." Essays (environment or nature), how-to (fishing, hunting, boating), humor (outdoors angle), personal experience (in fishing, etc.), technical (boats, tackle, etc., as particularly suitable for Florida specialities). **Buys 40-60 mss/year.** Query. Length: 1,500-2,500 words. **Pays $475.**

Photos Send photos with submission. Reviews 35mm transparencies, 4×5 and larger prints. Buys all rights. Offers no additional payment for photos accepted with ms. Pays up to $750 for cover photos.

Tips "Feature articles are most open to freelancers; however there is little chance of acceptance unless contributor is an accomplished and avid outdoorsman *and* a competent writer-photographer with considerable experience in Florida."

$ FLY FISHERMAN MAGAZINE

Primedia Enthusiast Group, 6405 Flank Dr., Harrisburg PA 17112. (717)540-6704. Fax: (717)657-9552. Web site: www.flyfisherman.com. Editor: John Randolph. Published 6 times/year covering fly fishing. Written for anglers who fish primarily with a fly rod and for other anglers who would like to learn more about fly fishing. Circ. 120,358. Sample copy not available.

$ $ FLY FISHING IN SALT WATERS

World Publications, Inc., 460 N. Orlando Ave., Suite 200, Winter Park FL 32789-7061. (407)571-4901. Fax: (407)571-4902. E-mail: editor@flyfishinsalt.com. Web site: www.flyfishinsalt.com. **Contact:** Capt. Ted Lund, editor. **90% freelance written.** Bimonthly magazine covering fly fishing in salt waters anywhere in the world. Estab. 1994. Circ. 44,000. Pays on publication. Publishes ms an average of 1 year after acceptance. Byline given. Buys first North American serial, electronic rights. Editorial lead time 3 months. Submit seasonal material 2 months in advance. Accepts queries by mail, e-mail. Responds in 1 month to queries; 2 months to mss. Sample copy for $3, plus $1 S&H. Writer's guidelines for #10 SASE.

- Break in with "well written original material that is oriented toward teaching a new idea, concept, location, technique, etc."

Nonfiction Book excerpts, essays, historical/nostalgic, how-to, interview/profile, new product, personal experience, photo feature, technical, travel, resource issues (conservation). **Buys 40-50 mss/year.** Query with or without published clips. Length: 1,500-2,500 words. **Pays $400-500.**

Photos Send photos with submission. Reviews 35mm color transparencies. Buys one-time rights. Offers no additional payment for photos accepted with ms; pays $80-300/photo if purchased separately. Captions, identification of subjects required.

Columns/Departments Legends/Reminiscences (history-profiles-nostalgia), 2,000-2,500 words; Resource (conservation issues), 1,000-1,500 words; Fly Tier's Bench (how to tie saltwater flies), 1,000-1,500 words, photos or illustrations critical; Boating (technical how-to), 2,000-2,500 words; Saltwater 101 (for beginners, tackle tips and techniques), 1,000-2,000 words. **Buys 25-30 mss/year.** Query. **Pays $400-500.**

Fiction Adventure, humorous, mainstream, all dealing with fly fishing. **Buys 2-3 mss/year.** Send complete ms. Length: 2,000-3,000 words. **Pays $500.**

Fillers Most fillers are staff written.

The online magazine carries content not found in the print edition. Contact: David Ritchie, online editor.

Tips "Follow up on your inquiry with a phone call."

$ $ FLYFISHING & TYING JOURNAL

A Compendium for the Complete Fly Fisher, Frank Amato Publications, P.O. Box 82112, Portland OR 97282. (503)653-8108. Fax: (503)653-2766. E-mail: dave@amatobooks.com. Web site: www.amatobooks.com. **Contact:** Dave Hughes, editor. Quarterly magazine covering flyfishing and fly tying for both new and veteran anglers. Every issue is seasonally focused: Spring, Summer, Fall, and Winter. Estab. 1980. Circ. 60,000. Pays on publication. Byline given. Buys first rights. Editorial lead time up to 1 year. Submit seasonal material up to 1 year in advance. Accepts queries by mail, e-mail. Responds in 2 months to queries; 2 months to mss. Writer's guidelines for #10 SASE, Attn: Kim Koch.

Nonfiction How-to. **Buys 55-60 mss/year.** Query. Length: 1,000-2,000 words. **Pays $200-600.**

Photos State availability with submission. Reviews transparencies. Buys one-time rights. Offers no additional payment for photos accepted with ms. Captions, identification of subjects, model releases required.

$ $ FUR-FISH-GAME

2878 E. Main, Columbus OH 43209-9947. E-mail: ffgcox@ameritech.net. **Contact:** Mitch Cox, editor. **65% freelance written.** Monthly magazine for outdoorsmen of all ages who are interested in hunting, fishing, trapping, dogs, camping, conservation, and related topics. Estab. 1900. Circ. 111,000. **Pays on acceptance.** Publishes ms an average of 7 months after acceptance. Byline given. Buys first, all rights. Responds in 2 months to queries. Sample copy for $1 and 9×12 SAE. Writer's guidelines for #10 SASE.

Nonfiction "We are looking for informative, down-to-earth stories about hunting, fishing, trapping, dogs, camping, boating, conservation, and related subjects. Nostalgic articles are also used. Many of our stories are 'how-to' and should appeal to small-town and rural readers who are true outdoorsmen. Some recents articles have told how to train a gun dog, catch big-water catfish, outfit a bowhunter, and trap late-season muskrat. We also use personal experience stories and an occasional profile, such as an article about an old-time trapper. 'Where-to' stories are used occasionally if they have broad appeal." Query. Length: 500-3,000 words. **Pays $50-250 or more for features depending upon quality, photo support, and importance to magazine.**

Photos Send photos with submission. Reviews transparencies, color 5×7 or 8×10 prints, digital photos on CD only with thumbnail sheet of small images and a numbered caption sheet. Pays $25 for separate freelance photos. Captions, credits required.

Tips "We are always looking for quality how-to articles about fish, game animals, or birds that are popular with everyday outdoorsmen but often overlooked in other publications, such as catfish, bluegill, crappie, squirrel, rabbit, crows, etc. We also use articles on standard seasonal subjects such as deer and pheasant, but like to see a fresh approach or new technique. Instructional trapping articles are useful all year. Articles on gun dogs, ginseng, and do-it-yourself projects are also popular with our readers. An assortment of photos and/or sketches greatly enhances any manuscript, and sidebars, where applicable, can also help. No phone queries, please."

$ $ GAME & FISH

2250 Newmarket Pkwy., Suite 110, Marietta GA 30067. (770)953-9222. Fax: (770)933-9510. E-mail: ken.dunwoody@primedia.com. Web site: www.gameandfishmag.com. **Contact:** Ken Dunwoody, editorial director. **90% freelance written.** Publishes 30 different monthly outdoor magazines, each one covering the fishing and hunting opportunities in a particular state or region (see individual titles to contact editors). Estab. 1975. Circ. 570,000. Pays 3 months prior to cover date of issue. Publishes ms an average of 7 months after acceptance. Byline given. Offers negotiable kill fee. Buys first North American serial rights. Submit seasonal material 8 months in advance. Accepts queries by mail, e-mail, fax. Responds in 3 months to queries. Sample copy for $3.50 and 9×12 SASE. Writer's guidelines for #10 SASE.

Nonfiction Prefers queries over unsolicited mss. Length: 1,500-2,400 words. **Pays $150-300; additional payment made for electronic rights.**

Photos Reviews transparencies, prints, digital images. Buys one-time rights. Cover photos $250, inside color $75, and b&w $25. Captions, identification of subjects required.

Online magazine occasionally carries original content not found in the print edition.

Tips "Our readers are experienced anglers and hunters, and we try to provide them with useful, specific articles about where, when, and how to enjoy the best hunting and fishing in their state or region. We also cover topics concerning game and fish management. Most articles should be tightly focused and aimed at outdoorsmen in 1 particular state. After familiarizing themselves with our magazine(s), writers should query the appropriate state editor (see individual listings) or send to Ken Dunwoody."

$ $ GEORGIA SPORTSMAN

Game & Fish, 2250 Newmarket Parkway, Suite 110, Marietta GA 30067. (770)953-9222. Fax: (770)933-9510. E-mail: jimmy.jacobs@primedia.com. Web site: www.georgiasportsmanmag.com. **Contact:** Jimmy Jacobs, editor. See *Game & Fish*.

$ $ GREAT PLAINS GAME & FISH

Game & Fish, 2250 Newmarket Parkway, Suite 110, Marietta GA 30067. (770)953-9222. Fax: (770)933-9510. E-mail: nick.gilmore@primedia.com. Web site: www.greatplainsgameandfish.com. **Contact:** Nick Gilmore, editor. See *Game & Fish*.

N Ø GUN WORLD

Y-Visionary Publishing, L.P., 265 Anita Dr., Suite 120, Orange CA 92868-3310. (714)939-9991. Fax: (714)939-9909. E-mail: editorial@gunworld.com. Web site: www.gunworld.com. Editor: Jan Libourel. Monthly magazine edited for hunters and target shooters, with frequent articles on new innovations in police and military armament. Circ. 126,402. Editorial lead time 2 months.

- Query before submitting.

GUNS & AMMO

Primedia Enthusiast Group, 6420 Wilshire Blvd., Los Angeles CA 90048. (323)782-2000. Fax: (323)782-2867. E-mail: gunsandammo@primedia.com. Web site: www.gunsandammomag.com. Editor: J. Scott Rupp. Monthly magazine. Created for recreational shooters, hunters, target shooters, plinkers and collectors. Circ. 450,000. Editorial lead time 4 months. Sample copy not available.

$ $ ILLINOIS GAME & FISH

Game & Fish, 2250 Newmarket Parkway, Suite 110, Marietta GA 30067. (770)953-9222. Fax: (770)933-9510. E-mail: dennis.schmidt@primedia.com. Web site: www.illinoisgameandfish.com. **Contact:** Dennis Schmidt, editor. See *Game & Fish*.

$ $ INDIANA GAME & FISH

Game & Fish, 2250 Newmarket Parkway, Suite 110, Marietta GA 30067. (770)953-9222. Fax: (770)933-9510. E-mail: ken.freel@primedia.com. Web site: www.indianagameandfish.com. **Contact:** Ken Freel, editor. See *Game & Fish*.

⊘ IN-FISHERMAN

Primedia Enthusiast Group, 7819 Highland Scenic Rd., Baxter MN 56425. (218)829-1648. Web site: www.in-fisherman.com. Magazine published 8 times/year for freshwaters anglers from beginners to professionals. Circ. 301,258. Editorial lead time 2 months.

- Query before submitting.

$ $ IOWA GAME & FISH

Game & Fish, 2250 Newmarket Parkway, Suite 110, Marietta GA 30067. (770)953-9222. Fax: (770)933-9510. E-mail: ronell.smith@primedia.com. Web site: www.iowagameandfish.com. **Contact:** Ronell Smith, editor. See *Game & Fish*.

$ $ KENTUCKY GAME & FISH

Game & Fish, 2250 Newmarket Parkway, Suite 110, Marietta GA 30067. (770)953-9222. Fax: (770)933-9510. E-mail: ken.freel@primedia.com. Web site: www.kentuckygameandfish.com. **Contact:** Ken Freel, editor. See *Game & Fish*.

$ $ LOUISIANA GAME & FISH

Game & Fish, 2250 Newmarket Parkway, Suite 110, Marietta GA 30067. (770)953-9222. Fax: (770)933-9510. E-mail: ronell.smith@primedia.com. Web site: www.lagameandfish.com. **Contact:** Ronell Smith, editor. See *Game & Fish*.

$ $ MARLIN

The International Sportfishing Magazine, World Publications, Inc., P.O. Box 8500, Winter Park FL 32790. (407)628-4802. Fax: (407)628-7061. E-mail: editor@marlinmag.com. Web site: www.marlinmag.com. **Contact:** Dave Ferrell, editor. **90% freelance written.** Magazine published 8 times/year covering the sport of big game fishing (billfish, tuna, dorado, and wahoo). Our readers are sophisticated, affluent, and serious about their sport—they expect a high-class, well-written magazine that provides information and practical advice.'' Estab. 1982. Circ. 50,000. **Pays on acceptance.** Publishes ms an average of 3 months after acceptance. Byline given. Buys first North American serial rights. Submit seasonal material 3 months in advance. Accepts previously published material. Sample copy free with SASE. Writer's guidelines online.

Nonfiction General interest, how-to (bait-rigging, tackle maintenance, etc.), new product, personal experience, photo feature, technical, travel. ''No freshwater fishing stories. No 'Me & Joe went fishing' stories.'' **Buys 30-50 mss/year.** Query with published clips. Length: 800-3,000 words. **Pays $250-500.**

Reprints Send photocopy and information about when and where the material previously appeared. Pays 50-75% of amount paid for original article.

Photos State availability with submission. Reviews original slides. Buys one-time rights. Offers $50-300 for inside use, $1,000 for a cover.

Columns/Departments Tournament Reports (reports on winners of major big game fishing tournaments), 200-400 words; Blue Water Currents (news features), 100-400 words. **Buys 25 mss/year.** Query. **Pays $75-250.**

Tips ''Tournament reports are a good way to break in to *Marlin*. Make them short but accurate, and provide photos of fishing action or winners' award shots (*not* dead fish hanging up at the docks). We always need how-tos and news items. Our destination pieces (travel stories) emphasize where and when to fish, but also include information on where to stay. For features: Crisp, high-action stories with emphasis on exotic nature, adventure, personality, etc.—nothing flowery or academic. Technical/how-to: concise and informational—specific details. News: Again, concise with good details—watch for legislation affecting big game fishing, outstanding catches, new clubs and organizations, new trends, and conservation issues."

$ MICHIGAN OUT-OF-DOORS

P.O. Box 30235, Lansing MI 48909. (517)371-1041. Fax: (517)371-1505. E-mail: magazine@mucc.org. Web site: www.mucc.org. **Contact:** Tony Hansen, editor. **75% freelance written.** Monthly magazine emphasizing Michigan outdoor recreation, especially hunting and fishing, conservation, nature, and environmental affairs. Estab. 1947. Circ. 90,000. **Pays on acceptance.** Publishes ms an average of 6 months after acceptance. Byline given. Buys first North American serial rights. Submit seasonal material 6 months in advance. Accepts queries by mail, phone. Responds in 1 month to queries. Sample copy for $3.50. Writer's guidelines for free or on Web site.

O‑ Break in by "writing interestingly about an *unusual* aspect of Michigan natural resources and/or outdoor recreation.

Nonfiction "Stories must have a Michigan slant unless they treat a subject of universal interest to our readers." Exposé, historical/nostalgic, how-to, interview/profile, opinion, personal experience, photo feature. Special issues: Archery Deer and Small Game Hunting (October); Firearm Deer Hunting (November); Cross-country Skiing and Early-ice Lake Fishing (December or January); Camping/Hiking (May); Family Fishing (June). No humor or poetry. **Buys 96 mss/year.** Send complete ms. Length: 1,000-2,000 words. **Pays $90 minimum for feature stories.**

Photos Buys one-time rights. Offers no additional payment for photos accepted with ms; others $20-175. Captions required.

Tips "Top priority is placed on true accounts of personal adventures in the out-of-doors—well-written tales of very unusual incidents encountered while hunting, fishing, camping, hiking, etc."

$ $ MICHIGAN SPORTSMAN

Game & Fish, 2250 Newmarket Parkway, Suite 110, Marietta GA 30067. (770)953-9222. Fax: (770)933-9510. E-mail: dennis.schmidt@primedia.com. Web site: www.michigansportsmanmag.com. **Contact:** Dennis Schmidt, editor. See *Game & Fish*.

$ $ MID-ATLANTIC GAME & FISH

Game & Fish, 2250 Newmarket Parkway, Suite 110, Marietta GA 30067. (770)953-9222. Fax: (770)933-9510. E-mail: ken.freel@primedia.com. Web site: www.midatlanticgameandfish.com. **Contact:** Ken Freel, editor. See *Game & Fish*.

$ MIDWEST OUTDOORS

MidWest Outdoors, Ltd., 111 Shore Dr., Burr Ridge IL 60527-5885. (630)887-7722. Fax: (630)887-1958. Web site: www.midwestoutdoors.com. **Contact:** Gene Laulunen, editor. **100% freelance written.** Monthly tabloid emphasizing fishing, hunting, camping, and boating. Estab. 1967. Circ. 45,000. Pays on publication. Publishes ms an average of 3 months after acceptance. Byline given. Buys simultaneous rights. Submit seasonal material 2 months in advance. Accepts previously published material. Accepts simultaneous submissions. Responds in 3 weeks to queries. Sample copy for $1 or online. Writer's guidelines for #10 SASE or online.

- Submissions must be e-mailed to info@midwestoutdoors.com (Microsoft Word format preferred).

Nonfiction How-to (fishing, hunting, camping in the Midwest), where-to-go (fishing, hunting, camping within 500 miles of Chicago). "We do not want to see any articles on 'my first fishing, hunting, or camping experiences,' 'cleaning my tackle box,' 'tackle tune-up,' 'making fishing fun for kids,' or 'catch and release.' " **Buys 1,800 unsolicited mss/year.** Send complete ms. Length: 1,000-1,500 words. **Pays $15-30.**

Reprints Send tearsheet.

Photos Reviews slides and b&w prints. Buys all rights. Offers no additional payment for photos accompanying ms. Captions required.

Columns/Departments Fishing; Hunting. Send complete ms. **Pays $30.**

Tips "Break in with a great unknown fishing hole or new technique within 500 miles of Chicago. Where, how, when, and why. Know the type of publication you are sending material to."

$ $ MINNESOTA SPORTSMAN

Game & Fish, 2250 Newmarket Parkway, Suite 110, Marietta GA 30067. (770)953-9222. Fax: (770)933-9510. E-mail: dennis.schmidt@primedia.com. Web site: www.minnesotasportsmanmag.com. **Contact:** Dennis Schmidt, editor. See *Game & Fish*.

$ $ MISSISSIPPI GAME & FISH

Game & Fish, 2250 Newmarket Parkway, Suite 110, Marietta GA 30067. (770)953-9222. Fax: (770)933-9510. E-mail: jimmy.jacobs@primedia.com. Web site: www.mississippigameandfish.com. **Contact:** Jimmy Jacobs, editor. See *Game & Fish*.

$ $ MISSOURI GAME & FISH

Game & Fish, 2250 Newmarket Parkway, Suite 110, Marietta GA 30067. (770)953-9222. Fax: (770)933-9510. E-mail: ronell.smith@primedia.com. Web site: www.missourigameandfish.com. **Contact:** Ronell Smith, editor. See *Game & Fish*.

N $ $ MUSKY HUNTER MAGAZINE

P.O. Box 340, St. Germain WI 54558. (715)477-2178. Fax: (715)477-8858. Editor: Jim Saric. **Contact:** Steve Heiting. **90% freelance written.** Bimonthly magazine on musky fishing. "Serves the vertical market of musky fishing enthusiasts. We're interested in how-to, where-to articles." Estab. 1988. Circ. 34,000. Pays on publication. Publishes ms an average of 4 months after acceptance. Byline given. Buys first, one-time rights. Submit seasonal material 4 months in advance. Responds in 2 months to queries. Sample copy for 9×12 SAE with $1.93 postage. Writer's guidelines for #10 SASE.

Nonfiction Historical/nostalgic (related only to musky fishing), how-to (modify lures, boats, and tackle for musky fishing), personal experience (must be musky fishing experience), technical (fishing equipment), travel (to lakes and areas for musky fishing). **Buys 50 mss/year.** Send complete ms. Length: 1,000-2,500 words. **Pays $100-300 for assigned articles; $50-300 for unsolicited articles.** Payment of contributor copies or other premiums negotiable.

Photos Send photos with submission. Reviews 35mm transparencies, 3×5 prints. Buys one-time rights. Offers no additional payment for photos accepted with ms. Identification of subjects required.

$ $ NEW ENGLAND GAME & FISH

Game & Fish, 2250 Newmarket Parkway, Suite 110, Marietta GA 30067. (770)953-9222. Fax: (770)933-9510. E-mail: steve.carpenteri@primedia.com. Web site: www.newenglandgameandfish.com. **Contact:** Steve Carpenteri, editor. See *Game & Fish*.

N $ $ NEW JERSEY LAKE SURVEY FISHING MAPS GUIDE

Freshwater Angler's Edge, P.O. Box 2355, Willingboro NJ 08046. (609)932-5627. Fax: (609)871-3921. **Contact:** Marty Klapa, editor/publisher. **40% freelance written.** Biannual magazine covering freshwater lake fishing. "*New Jersey Lake Survey Fishing Maps Guide* is edited for freshwater fishing for trout, bass, perch, catfish, and other species. It contains 140 pages and approximately 100 full-page maps of the surveyed lakes that illustrate contours, depths, bottom characteristics, shorelines, and vegetation present at each location. The guide includes a 10-page chart which describes over 250 fishing lakes in New Jersey. It also includes more than 125 fishing tips and 'Bass'n Notes.' " Estab. 1989. Circ. 3,500. **Pays on acceptance.** Publishes ms an average of 6 months after acceptance. Byline given. Buys first rights, makes work-for-hire assignments. Editorial lead time 6 months. Accepts queries by mail, fax. Sample copy for $14.50 postage paid.

Nonfiction How-to fishing, freshwater fishing. Length: 500-2,000 words. **Pays $75-250.**

Photos State availability with submission. Reviews transparencies, 4×5 slides, or 4×6 prints. Buys one-time rights. Captions, identification of subjects, model releases required.

Tips "We want queries with published clips of articles describing fishing experiences on New Jersey lakes and ponds."

$ $ NEW YORK GAME & FISH

Game & Fish, 2250 Newmarket Parkway, Suite 110, Marietta GA 30067. (770)953-9222. Fax: (770)933-9510. E-mail: steve.carpenteri@primedia.com. Web site: www.newyorkgameandfish.com. **Contact:** Steve Carpenteri, editor. See *Game & Fish*.

$ $ NORTH AMERICAN WHITETAIL

The Magazine Devoted to the Serious Trophy Deer Hunter, Game & Fish, 2250 Newmarket Pkwy., Suite 110, Marietta GA 30067. (770)953-9222. Fax: (770)933-9510. Web site: northamericanwhitetail.com. **Contact:** Duncan Dobie, editor. **70% freelance written.** Magazine published 8 times/year about hunting trophy-class white-tailed deer in North America, primarily the US. "We provide the serious hunter with highly sophisticated information about trophy-class whitetails and how, when, and where to hunt them. We are not a general hunting magazine or a magazine for the very occasional deer hunter." Estab. 1982. Circ. 130,000. Pays 65 days prior to cover date of issue. Publishes ms an average of 6 months after acceptance. Byline given. Offers negotiable kill fee. Buys first North American serial rights. Submit seasonal material 10 months in advance. Accepts queries by mail, fax, phone. Responds in 3 months to mss. Sample copy for $3.50 and 9×12 SAE with 7 first-class stamps. Writer's guidelines for #10 SASE.

Nonfiction How-to, interview/profile. **Buys 50 mss/year.** Query. Length: 1,000-3,000 words. **Pays $150-400.**

Photos Send photos with submission. Reviews 35mm transparencies, color prints, high quality digital images. Buys one-time rights. Offers no additional payment for photos accepted with ms. Captions, identification of subjects required.

Columns/Departments Trails and Tails (nostalgic, humorous, or other entertaining styles of deer-hunting material, fictional or nonfictional), 1,200 words. **Buys 8 mss/year.** Send complete ms. **Pays $150.**

Tips "Our articles are written by persons who are deer hunters first, writers second. Our hard-core hunting audience can see through material produced by nonhunters or those with only marginal deer-hunting expertise. We have a continual need for expert profiles/interviews. Study the magazine to see what type of hunting expert it takes to qualify for our use, and look at how those articles have been directed by the writers. Good photography of the interviewee and his hunting results must accompany such pieces."

$ $ NORTH CAROLINA GAME & FISH

Game & Fish, 2250 Newmarket Parkway, Suite 110, Marietta GA 30067. (770)953-9222. Fax: (770)933-9510. E-mail: david.johnson@primedia.com. Web site: www.ncgameandfish.com. **Contact:** David Johnson, editor. See *Game & Fish.*

$ $ OHIO GAME & FISH

Game & Fish, 2250 Newmarket Parkway, Suite 110, Marietta GA 30067. (770)953-9222. Fax: (770)933-9510. E-mail: steve.carpenteri@primedia.com. Web site: www.ohiogameandfish.com. **Contact:** Steve Carpenteri, editor. See *Game & Fish.*

$ $ OKLAHOMA GAME & FISH

Game & Fish, 2250 Newmarket Parkway, Suite 110, Marietta GA 30067. (770)953-9222. Fax: (770)933-9510. E-mail: nick.gilmore@primedia.com. Web site: www.oklahomagameandfish.com. **Contact:** Nick Gilmore, editor. See *Game & Fish.*

$ $ ONTARIO OUT OF DOORS

Roger's Media, 1 Mt. Pleasant Rd., Isabella Tower, Toronto ON M4Y 2Y5 Canada. (416)764-1652. Fax: (416)764-1751. Web site: www.ontariooutofdoors.com. Editor: Burt Myers. **Contact:** John Kerr, managing editor. **90% freelance written.** Magazine published 10 times/year covering the outdoors (hunting, fishing, camping). Estab. 1968. Circ. 93,865. **Pays on acceptance.** Publishes ms an average of 6 months after acceptance. Byline given. Buys first, electronic rights. Editorial lead time 6 months. Submit seasonal material 6 months in advance. Accepts queries by mail, e-mail, fax. Responds in 3 months to queries. Sample copy and writer's guidelines free.

Nonfiction Book excerpts, essays, exposé, how-to (fishing and hunting), humor, inspirational, interview/profile, new product, opinion, personal experience, photo feature, technical, travel (where-to), wildlife management; environmental concerns. "No 'Me and Joe' features or articles written from a women's point of view on how to catch a bass." **Buys 100 mss/year.** Length: 500-2,500 words. **Pays $750 maximum for assigned articles; $700 maximum for unsolicited articles.** Sometimes pays expenses of writers on assignment.

Photos Send photos with submission. Reviews transparencies. Buys one time and electronic rights. Pays $450-750 for covers. Captions required.

Columns/Departments Trips & Tips (travel pieces), 50-150 words; Short News, 50-500 words. **Buys 30-40 mss/year.** Query. **Pays $50-250.**

Fiction Humorous, novel excerpts. **Buys 6 mss/year.** Send complete ms. Length: 1,000 words. **Pays $500 maximum.**

Fillers Facts, newsbreaks. **Buys 40/year.** Length: 25-100 words. **Pays $15-50.**

Tips "With the exception of short news stories, it is suggested that writers query prior to submission."

$ THE OUTDOORS MAGAZINE

For the Better Hunter, Angler & Trapper, Elk Publishing, Inc., 531 Main St., Colchester VT 05446. (800)499-0447. Fax: (802)879-2015. E-mail: james@elkpublishing.com. Web site: www.outdoorsmagazine.net. **Contact:** James Ehlers, publisher. **80% freelance written.** Monthly magazine covering wildlife conservation. "New England hunting, fishing, and trapping magazine covering news, tips, destinations, and good old-fashioned stories." Estab. 1996. Circ. 14,000. Pays on publication. Publishes ms an average of 1 year after acceptance. Byline given. Offers 10% kill fee. Buys first North American serial rights. Editorial lead time 1 year. Submit seasonal material 6 months in advance. Accepts queries by mail. Accepts previously published material. Responds in 1 month to queries; 3 month to mss. Sample copy online or by e-mail. Writer's guidelines free.

Nonfiction Book excerpts, essays, exposé, general interest, historical/nostalgic, how-to, interview/profile, new product, opinion, personal experience, technical. **Buys 200 mss/year.** Query with published clips. Length: 750-2,500 words. **Pays $20-150 for assigned articles.**
Photos State availability with submission. Reviews contact sheets. Buys one-time rights. Pays $15-75/photo. Identification of subjects required.
Columns/Departments **Buys 100 mss/year.** Query with published clips. **Pays $20-60.**
Fillers Anecdotes, facts.
Tips "*Know* the publication, not just read it, so you understand the audience. Patience and thoroughness will go a long way."

$ $ ⊘ PENNSYLVANIA ANGLER & BOATER

Pennsylvania Fish & Boat Commission, P.O. Box 67000, Harrisburg PA 17106-7000. (717)705-7844. E-mail: amichaels@state.pa.us. Web site: www.fish.state.pa.us. **Contact:** Art Michaels, editor. **40% freelance written.** Bimonthly magazine covering fishing, boating, and related conservation topics in Pennsylvania. Circ. 30,000. Pays 2 months after acceptance. Publishes ms an average of 8 months after acceptance. Byline given. Submit seasonal material 8 months in advance. Responds in 1 month to queries; 2 months to mss. Sample copy for 9×12 SAE with 9 first-class stamps. Writer's guidelines for #10 SASE.

- No unsolicited mss.

Nonfiction How-to (and where-to), technical. No saltwater or hunting material. **Buys 75 mss/year.** Query. Length: 500-2,500 words. **Pays $25-300.**
Photos Send photos with submission. Reviews 35mm and larger transparencies, digital submissions (preferred). Rights purchased vary. Offers no additional payment for photos accompanying mss. Captions, identification of subjects, model releases required.

$ $ PENNSYLVANIA GAME & FISH

Game & Fish, 2250 Newmarket Parkway, Suite 110, Marietta GA 30067. (770)953-9222. Fax: (770)933-9510. E-mail: steve.carpenteri@primedia.com. Web site: www.pagameandfish.com. **Contact:** Steve Carpenteri, editor. See *Game & Fish*.

PETERSEN'S HUNTING

Primedia Enthusiast Group, 6420 Wilshire Blvd., Los Angeles CA 90048. (323)782-2563. Fax: (323)782-2477. Web site: www.huntingmag.com. **Contact:** Scott Rupp, editor. **10% freelance written.** Magazine published 10 times/year covering sport hunting. "We are a 'how-to' magazine devoted to all facets of sport hunting, with the intent to make our readers more knowledgeable, more successful and safer hunters." Circ. 350,000. Pays on scheduling. Publishes ms an average of 9 months after acceptance. Byline given. Buys all rights. Writer's guidelines on request.
Nonfiction General interest, how-to (on hunting techniques), travel. **Buys 15 mss/year.** Query. Length: 2,400 words.
Photos Send photos with submission. Reviews 35mm transparencies. Buys one-time rights. Captions, identification of subjects, model releases required.

PETERSEN'S RIFLE SHOOTER

Primedia Enthusiast Group, 6420 Wilshire Blvd., 14th Floor, Los Angeles CA 90048. (323)782-2000. Fax: (323)782-2867. E-mail: rifles@primedia.com. Web site: www.rifleshootermag.com. Editor: Jerry Lee. Bimonthly magazine. Published and edited for the dedicated and serious rifle enthusiast. Circ. 150,000. Editorial lead time 4 months. Sample copy not available.

$ $ RACK MAGAZINE

Adventures in Trophy Hunting, Buckmasters, Ltd., P.O. Box 244022, Montgomery AL 36124-4022. (800)240-3337. Fax: (334)215-3535. E-mail: mhandley@buckmasters.com. Web site: www.rackmag.com. **Contact:** Mike Handley, editor. **10-15% freelance written.** Hunting magazine published monthly (July-December). "*Rack Magazine* caters to deer hunters and chasers of other big game animals who prefer short stories detailing the harvests of exceptional specimens. There are no how-to, destination, or human interest stories; only pieces describing particular hunts." Estab. 1999. Circ. 100,000. Pays on publication. Publishes ms an average of 1 year after acceptance. Byline given. Buys first North American serial, second serial (reprint) rights. Editorial lead time 9 months. Accepts queries by e-mail, phone. Accepts previously published material. Accepts simultaneous submissions. Responds in 1 month to queries. Sample copy for free. Writer's guidelines by e-mail.
Nonfiction Interview/profile, personal experience. *Rack Magazine* does not use how-to, destination, humor, general interest, or hunter profiles. **Buys 35-40 mss/year.** Query. Length: 500-1,000 words. **Pays $175 ($325 to professional outdoors writers).**

Reprints Accepts previously published submissions.
Photos Send photos with submission. Reviews transparencies. Captions, identification of subjects required.
Tips "We're only interested in stories about record book animals (those scoring high enough to qualify for BTR, B&C, P&Y, SCI, or Longhunter). Whitetails must be scored by a certified BTR/Buckmasters measurer and their antlers must register at least 160-inches on the BTR system. Deer scoring 190 or better on the B&C or P&Y scales would be candidates, but the hunter would have to have his or her buck scored by a BTR measurer."

$ $ ROCKY MOUNTAIN GAME & FISH

Game & Fish, 2250 Newmarket Parkway, Suite 110, Marietta GA 30067. (770)935-9222. Fax: (770)933-9510. E-mail: john.geiger@primedia.com. Web site: www.rmgameandfish.com. **Contact:** John Geiger, editor. See *Game & Fish*.

$ $ SALT WATER SPORTSMAN MAGAZINE

2 Park Ave., New York NY 10016. (212)779-5003. Fax: (212)779-5025. E-mail: editor@saltwatersportsman.com. Web site: www.saltwatersportsman.com. **Contact:** David Dibenedetto, editor. **85% freelance written.** Monthly magazine. "*Salt Water Sportsman* is edited for serious marine sport fishermen whose lifestyle includes the pursuit of game fish in US waters and around the world. It provides information on fishing trends, techniques, and destinations, both local and international. Each issue reviews offshore and inshore fishing boats, high-tech electronics, innovative tackle, engines, and other new products. Coverage also focuses on sound fisheries management and conservation." Circ. 170,000. **Pays on acceptance.** Publishes ms an average of 5 months after acceptance. Byline given. Offers kill fee. Buys first North American serial rights. Submit seasonal material 8 months in advance. Accepts queries by mail, e-mail, fax. Responds in 1 month to queries. Sample copy for #10 SASE. Writer's guidelines online.
Nonfiction "Readers want solid how-to, where-to information written in an enjoyable, easy-to-read style. Personal anecdotes help the reader identify with the writer." How-to, personal experience, technical, travel (to fishing areas). **Buys 100 mss/year.** Query. Length: 1,200-2,000 words. **Pays $300-750.**
Reprints Send tearsheet. Pays up to 50% of amount paid for original article.
Photos Reviews color slides. Pays $1,500 minimum for 35mm, 2¼×2¼ or 8×10 transparencies for cover. Captions required.
Columns/Departments Sportsman's Tips (short, how-to tips and techniques on salt water fishing, emphasis is on building, repairing, or reconditioning specific items or gear). Send complete ms.
Tips "There are a lot of knowledgeable fishermen/budding writers out there who could be valuable to us with a little coaching. Many don't think they can write a story for us, but they'd be surprised. We work with writers. Shorter articles that get to the point which are accompanied by good, sharp photos are hard for us to turn down. Having to delete unnecessary wordage—conversation, clichés, etc.—that writers feel is mandatory is annoying. Often they don't devote enough attention to specific fishing information."

$ $ SHOTGUN SPORTS MAGAZINE

P.O. Box 6810, Auburn CA 95604. (530)889-2220. Fax: (530)889-9106. E-mail: shotgun@shotgunsportsmagazine.com. **Contact:** Linda Martin, production coordinator. **50% freelance written.** Welcomes new writers. Monthly magazine covering all the shotgun sports and shotgun hunting—sporting clays, trap, skeet, hunting, gunsmithing, shotshell patterning, shotsell reloading, mental training for the shotgun sports, shotgun tests, anything "shotgun." Pays on publication. Publishes ms an average of 1-6 months after acceptance. Buys all rights. Sample copy and writer's guidelines available by contacting Linda Martin, production coordinator.
● Responds within 3 weeks. Subscription: $32.95 (U.S.); $39.95 (Canada); $60 (foreign).
Nonfiction Current needs: "Anything with a 'shotgun' subject. Tests, think pieces, roundups, historical, interviews, etc. No articles promoting a specific club or sponsored hunting trip, etc." Submit complete ms with photos by mail with SASE. Can submit by e-mail. Length: 1,000-5,000 words. **Pays $50-200.**
Photos "5×7 or 8×10 b&w or 4-color with appropriate captions. On disk or e-mailed at least 5-inches and 300 dpi (contact Graphics Artist for details)." Reviews transparencies (35 mm or larger), b&w, or 4-color. Send photos with submission.
Tips "Do not fax manuscript. Send good photos. Take a fresh approach. Create a professional, yet friendly article. Send diagrams, maps, and photos of unique details, if needed. For interviews, more interested in 'words of wisdom' than a list of accomplishments. Reloading articles must include source information and backup data. Check your facts and data! If you can't think of a fresh approach, don't bother. If it's not about shotguns or shotgunners, don't send it. Never say, 'You don't need to check my data; I never make mistakes.' "

$ $ SOUTH CAROLINA GAME & FISH

Game & Fish, 2250 Newmarket Parkway, Suite 110, Marietta GA 30067. (770)953-9222. Fax: (770)933-9510. E-mail: david.johnson@primedia.com. Web site: www.scgameandfish.com. **Contact:** David Johnson, editor. See *Game & Fish*.

N $ $ $ $ SPORT FISHING

The Magazine of Saltwater Fishing, World Publications, 460 N. Orlando Ave., Suite 200, Winter Park FL 32789. (417)628-4802. Fax: (417)628-7061. E-mail: doug.olander@worldpub.net. Web site: www.sportfishingmag.com. Managing Editor: Mike Mazur. **Contact:** Doug Olander, editor-in-chief. **50% freelance written.** Magazine published 10 times/year covering saltwater angling—saltwater fish and fisheries. "*Sport Fishing*'s readers are middle-aged, affluent, mostly male, who are generally proficient in and very educated to their sport. We are about fishing from boats—not from surf or jetties." Estab. 1985. Circ. 250,000. **Pays on acceptance.** Publishes ms an average of 6-12 months after acceptance. Byline given. Offers 25% kill fee. Buys first North American serial, electronic rights. Editorial lead time 2-12 months. Submit seasonal material 1 year in advance. Accepts queries by e-mail. Responds in 1 week to queries; 1 month to mss. Sample copy for #10 SASE. Writer's guidelines online.

Nonfiction General interest, how-to. Query. Length: 2,000-2,500 words. **Pays $500-2,000.**

Photos State availability with submission. Reviews GIF/JPEG files. Buys one-time rights. Offers $75-400/photo.

Tips "Meet or beat deadlines. Include quality photos when you can. Quote the experts. Balance information with readability. Include sidebars."

N $ $ $ SPORTS AFIELD

The Premier Hunting Adventure Magazine, Field Sports Publishing, 15621 Chemical Lane, Huntington Beach CA 92649. E-mail: letters@sportsafield.com. Web site: www.sportsafield.com. **Contact:** Diana Rupp, editor-in-chief. **60% freelance written.** Magazine published 9 times/year covering big game hunting. "We cater to the upscale hunting market, especially hunters who travel to exotic destinations like Alaska and Africa. We are not a deer hunting magazine, and we do not cover fishing." Estab. 1887. Circ. 50,000. Pays 1 month prior to publication. Publishes ms an average of 6 months after acceptance. Byline given. Buys first North American serial, first, electronic rights. Editorial lead time 4 months. Submit seasonal material 5 months in advance. Accepts queries by mail, e-mail. Responds in 2 months to queries; 2 months to mss. Sample copy for $6.99. Writer's guidelines online.

Nonfiction Personal experience, travel. **Buys 25 mss/year.** Query. Length: 1,500-2,500 words. **Pays $500-800.**

Photos State availability with submission. Reviews 35mm slides transparencies, GIF/JPEG files. Buys one-time rights. Offers no additional payment for photos accepted with ms. Captions, model releases required.

Fillers Newsbreaks. **Buys 30/year.** Length: 200-500 words. **Pays $75-150.**

$ $ TENNESSEE SPORTSMAN

Game & Fish, 2250 Newmarket Parkway, Suite 110, Marietta GA 30067. (770)953-9222. Fax: (770)933-9510. E-mail: david.johnson@primedia.com. Web site: www.tennesseesportsmanmag.com. **Contact:** David Johnson, editor. See *Game & Fish*.

$ $ TEXAS SPORTSMAN

Game & Fish, 2250 Newmarket Parkway, Suite 110, Marietta GA 30067. (770)953-9222. Fax: (770)933-9510. E-mail: nick.gilmore@primedia.com. Web site: www.texassportsmanmag.com. **Contact:** Nick Gilmore, editor. See *Game & Fish*.

N $ $ TIDE MAGAZINE

Coastal Conservation Association, 6919 Portwest Dr., Suite 100, Houston TX 77024. (713)626-4222. Fax: (713)626-5852. E-mail: tide@joincca.org. **Contact:** Ted Venker, editor. Bimonthly magazine on saltwater fishing and conservation of marine resources. Estab. 1977. Circ. 80,000. Pays on publication. Byline given. Buys one-time rights. Submit seasonal material 6 months in advance. Responds in 1 month to queries.

Nonfiction Essays, exposé, general interest, historical/nostalgic, humor, opinion, personal experience, travel, Related to saltwater fishing and Gulf/Atlantic coastal habitats. **Buys 40 mss/year.** Query with published clips. Length: 1,200-1,500 words. **Pays $300-400 for ms/photo package.**

Photos Reviews negatives, 35mm transparencies, color prints, high-res digital. Buys one-time rights. Pays $50-200. Captions required.

$ $ TURKEY & TURKEY HUNTING

Krause Publications, a Division of F+W Publications, Inc., 700 E. State St., Iola WI 54990-0001. Web site: www.turkeyandturkeyhunting.com. **Contact:** James Schlender, editor. **50% freelance written.** Bimonthly magazine filled with practical and comprehensive information for wild turkey hunters. Estab. 1982. Circ. 40,000. **Pays on acceptance.** Publishes ms an average of 8 months after acceptance. Byline given. Offers 50% kill fee. Buys one-time rights. Editorial lead time 1 year. Submit seasonal material 1 year in advance. Accepts queries by mail. Responds in 1 month to queries; 6 months to mss. Sample copy for $4. Ms and photo guidelines online.

Nonfiction Does not want "Me and Joe went hunting and here's what happened" articles. **Buys 20 mss/year.** Send complete ms. Length: 1,500-2,500 words. **Pays $275-400.**
Photos Send photos with submission. Reviews 2 X 2 transparencies, any size prints, digital images with contact sheets. Buys one-time rights. Offers $75-200/photo. Negotiates payment individually. Identification of subjects required.
Tips "Turkey hunting is a continually growing and changing sport. Search for topics that reflect this trend. Our audience is sophisticated and experienced. We have several contributing editors who write most of our how-to articles, so we buy few articles of this type from freelancers. Well-written mood/essay articles are always welcome for review. If you have not written for *Turkey & Turkey Hunting*, it is best to send a finished manuscript. We do not assign articles based on query letters."

$ $ VIRGINIA GAME & FISH

Game & Fish, 2250 Newmarket Parkway, Suite 110, Marietta GA 30067. (770)953-9222. Fax: (770)933-9510. E-mail: david.johnson@primedia.com. Web site: www.virginiagameandfish.com. **Contact:** David Johnson, editor. See *Game & Fish*.

$ $ WASHINGTON-OREGON GAME & FISH

Game & Fish, 2250 Newmarket Parkway, Suite 110, Marietta GA 30067. (770)953-9222. Fax: (770)933-9510. E-mail: john.geiger@primedia.com. Web site: www.wogameandfish.com. **Contact:** John Geiger, editor. See *Game & Fish*.

$ $ WEST VIRGINIA GAME & FISH

Game & Fish, 2250 Newmarket Parkway, Suite 110, Marietta GA 30067. (770)953-9222. Fax: (770)933-9510. E-mail: ken.freel@primedia.com. Web site: www.wvgameandfish.com. **Contact:** Ken Freel, editor. See *Game & Fish*.

$ $ WESTERN OUTDOORS

185 Avenida La Pata, San Clemente CA 92673. (949)366-0030. Fax: (949)366-0804. E-mail: lew@wonews.com. **Contact:** Lew Carpenter, editor. **60% freelance written.** Magazine emphasizing fishing, boating for California, Oregon, Washington, Baja California, and Alaska. "We are the West's leading authority on fishing techniques, tackle and destinations, and all reports present the latest and most reliable information." Estab. 1961. Circ. 100,000. **Pays on acceptance.** Publishes ms an average of 6 months after acceptance. Buys first North American serial rights. Submit seasonal material 6 months in advance. Accepts queries by mail, e-mail, fax. Responds in 6 weeks to queries. Sample copy for free. Writer's guidelines for #10 SASE.
Nonfiction Where-to (catch more fish, improve equipment, etc.), how-to informational, photo feature. "We do not accept poetry or fiction." **Buys 36-40 assigned mss/year.** Query. Length: 1,500-2,000 words. **Pays $450-600.**
Photos Reviews 35mm slides. Offers no additional payment for photos accepted with ms; pays $350-500 for covers. Captions required.
Tips "Provide a complete package of photos, map, trip facts and manuscript written according to our news feature format. Excellence of color photo selections make a sale more likely. Include sketches of fishing patterns and techniques to guide our illustrators. Graphics are important. The most frequent mistake made by writers in completing an article for us is that they don't follow our style. Our guidelines are quite clear. One query at a time via mail, e-mail, fax. No phone calls. You can become a regular *Western Outdoors* byliner by submitting professional quality packages of fine writing accompanied by excellent photography. Pros anticipate what is needed, and immediately provide whatever else we request. Furthermore, they meet deadlines!"

$ $ WISCONSIN SPORTSMAN

Game & Fish, 2250 Newmarket Parkway, Suite 110, Marietta GA 30067. (770)953-9222. Fax: (770)933-9510. E-mail: dennis.schmidt@primedia.com. Web site: www.wisconsinsportsmanmag.com. **Contact:** Dennis Schmidt, editor. See *Game & Fish*.

MARTIAL ARTS

$ $ BLACK BELT

Black Belt Communications, LLC, 24900 Anza Dr., Unit E, Valencia CA 91355. Fax: (661)257-3028. E-mail: byoung@aimmedia.com. Web site: www.blackbeltmag.com. **Contact:** Robert Young, executive editor. **80% freelance written.** Works with a small number of new/unpublished writers each year. Monthly magazine emphasizing martial arts for both experienced practitioner and layman. Estab. 1961. Circ. 100,000. Pays on publication. Publishes ms an average of 1 year after acceptance. Buys all rights. Accepts queries by mail, e-mail, fax. Accepts simultaneous submissions. Responds in 3 weeks to queries. Writer's guidelines online.

Nonfiction Exposé, how-to, interview/profile, new product, personal experience, technical, travel, Informational; Health/fitness; Training. "We never use personality profiles." **Buys 40-50 mss/year.** Query with outline. Length: 1,200 words minimum. **Pays $100-300.**

Photos Very seldom buys photographs without accompanying ms. Total purchase price for ms includes payment for photos. Captions, model releases required.

N $ $ JOURNAL OF ASIAN MARTIAL ARTS

Via Media Publishing Co., 941 Calle Mejia #822, Santa Fe NM 87501. Web site: www.goviamedia.com. **Contact:** Michael A. DeMarco, publisher. **90% freelance written.** Quarterly magazine covering "all historical and cultural aspects related to Asian martial arts, offering a mature, well-rounded view of this uniquely fascinating subject. Although the journal treats the subject with academic accuracy (references at end), writing need not lose the reader!" Estab. 1991. Pays on publication. Publishes ms an average of 1 year after acceptance. Byline given. Buys first, second serial (reprint) rights. Submit seasonal material 6 months in advance. Responds in 1 month to queries; 2 months to mss. Sample copy for $10. Writer's guidelines for #10 SASE.

Nonfiction "All articles should be backed with solid, reliable reference material." Essays, exposé, historical/nostalgic, how-to (martial art techniques and materials, e.g., weapons), interview/profile, personal experience, photo feature (place or person), religious, technical, travel. "No articles overburdened with technical/foreign/scholarly vocabulary, or material slanted as indirect advertising or for personal aggrandizement." **Buys 30 mss/year.** Query with short background and martial arts experience. Length: 2,000-10,000 words. **Pays $150-500.**

Photos State availability with submission. Reviews contact sheets, negatives, transparencies, prints. Buys one-time and reprint rights. Offers no additional payment for photos accepted with ms. Identification of subjects, model releases required.

Columns/Departments Location (city, area, specific site, Asian or non-Asian, showing value for martial arts, researchers, history); Media Review (film, book, video, museum for aspects of academic and artistic interest).-**Length:** 1,000-2,500 words. **Buys 16 mss/year.** Query. **Pays $50-200.**

Fiction Adventure, historical, humorous, slice-of-life vignettes, translation. No material that does not focus on martial arts culture. **Buys 1 mss/year.** Query. Length: 1,000-10,000 words. **Pays $50-500, or copies.**

Poetry Avant-garde, free verse, haiku, light verse, traditional, translation. "No poetry that does not focus on martial arts culture." **Buys 2 poems/year.** Submit maximum 10 poems. **Pays $10-100, or copies.**

Fillers Anecdotes, facts, gags to be illustrated by cartoonist, newsbreaks, short humor. **Buys 2/year.** Length: 25-500 words. **Pays $1-50, or copies.**

Tips "Always query before sending a manuscript. We are open to varied types of articles; most however require a strong academic grasp of Asian culture. For those not having this background, we suggest trying a museum review, or interview, where authorities can be questioned, quoted, and provide supportive illustrations. We especially desire articles/reports from Asia, with photo illustrations, particularly of a martial art style, so readers can visually understand the unique attributes of that style, its applications, evolution, etc. 'Location' and media reports are special areas that writers may consider, especially if they live in a location of martial art significance."

$ KUNG FU TAI CHI

Wisdom for Body and Mind, Pacific Rim Publishing, 40748 Encyclopedia Circle, Fremont CA 94538. (510)656-5100. Fax: (510)656-8844. E-mail: gene@kungfumagazine.com. Web site: www.kungfumagazine.com. **Contact:** Gene Ching. **70% freelance written.** Bimonthly magazine covering Chinese martial arts and culture. "*Kung Fu Tai Chi* covers the full range of Kung Fu culture, including healing, philosophy, meditation, yoga, Fengshui, Buddhism, Taoism, history, and the latest events in art and culture, plus insightful features on the martial arts." Circ. 50,000. Pays on publication. Byline given. Buys first North American serial, electronic rights. Editorial lead time 4 months. Submit seasonal material 4 months in advance. Accepts queries by mail, e-mail, fax, phone. Responds in 2 months to queries; 3 months to mss. Sample copy for $3.99 or online. Writer's guidelines online.

Nonfiction General interest, historical/nostalgic, how-to, interview/profile, personal experience, photo feature, religious, technical, travel, cultural perspectives. No poetry or fiction. **Buys 70 mss/year.** Query. Length: 500-2,500 words. **Pays $35-125.**

Photos Send photos with submission. Reviews 5×7 prints, GIF/JPEG files. Buys one-time rights. Offers no additional payment for photos accepted with ms. Captions, identification of subjects required.

Tips "Check out our Web site and get an idea of past articles."

$ $ T'AI CHI

Leading International Magazine of T'ai Chi Ch'uan, Wayfarer Publications, P.O. Box 39938, Los Angeles CA 90039. (323)665-7773. Fax: (323)665-1627. E-mail: taichi@tai-chi.com. Web site: www.tai-chi.com/magazine.h

tm. **Contact:** Marvin Smalheiser, editor. **90% freelance written.** Bimonthly magazine covering T'ai Chi Ch'uan as a martial art and for health and fitness. "Covers T'ai Chi Ch'uan and other internal martial arts, plus qigong and Chinese health, nutrition, and philosophical disciplines. Readers are practitioners or laymen interested in developing skills and insight for self-defense, health, and self-improvement." Estab. 1977. Circ. 50,000. Pays on publication. Publishes ms an average of 2 months after acceptance. Byline given. Buys first North American serial rights. Editorial lead time 3 months. Submit seasonal material 6 months in advance. Accepts queries by mail, e-mail, fax. Responds in 3 weeks to queries; 3 months to mss. Sample copy for $3.95. Writer's guidelines online.

O━ Break in by "understanding the problems our readers have to deal with learning and practicing T'ai Chi, and developing an article that deals with 1 or more of those problems.

Nonfiction Book excerpts, essays, how-to (on T'ai Chi Ch'uan, qigong, and related Chinese disciplines), interview/profile, personal experience. "Do not want articles promoting an individual, system, or school." **Buys 100-120 mss/year.** Query with or without published clips or send complete ms. Length: 1,200-4,500 words. **Pays $75-500.**

Photos Send photos with submission. Reviews color transparencies, color or b&w 4×6 or 5×7 prints, digital files suitable for print production. Buys one-time and reprint rights. Offers no additional payment for photos accepted with ms, but overall payment takes into consideration the number and quality of photos. Captions, identification of subjects, model releases required.

Tips "Think and write for practitioners and laymen who want information and insight, and who are trying to work through problems to improve skills and their health. No promotional material."

MISCELLANEOUS

$ ACTION PURSUIT GAMES

2655 S. Anita Dr., Suite 120, Orange CA 92868. E-mail: editor@actionpursuitgames.com. Web site: www.actionpursuitgames.com. **Contact:** Daniel Reeves, editor. **60% freelance written.** Monthly magazine covering paintball. Estab. 1987. Circ. 85,000. Pays on publication. Publishes ms an average of 2 months after acceptance. Byline given. Buys electronic rights. print rights Editorial lead time 3 months. Submit seasonal material 6 months in advance. Accepts queries by e-mail. Sample copy for 9×12 SAE and 5 first-class stamps. Writer's guidelines online.

Nonfiction Essays, exposé, general interest, historical/nostalgic, how-to, humor, interview/profile, new product, opinion, personal experience, technical, travel, all paintball-related. No sexually oriented material. **Buys 100+ mss/year.** Length: 500-1,000 words. **Pays $100.** Sometimes pays expenses of writers on assignment.

Photos Send photos with submission. Reviews transparencies, prints. Buys all rights, web and print. Negotiates payment individually. Captions, identification of subjects, model releases required.

Columns/Departments Guest Commentary, 400 words; TNT (tournament news), 500-800 words; Young Guns, 300 words; Scenario Game Reporting, 300-500 words. **Buys 24 mss/year. Pays $100.**

Fiction Adventure, historical, must be paintball related. **Buys 1-2 mss/year.** Send complete ms. Length: 500 words. **Pays $100.**

Poetry Avant-garde, free verse, haiku, light verse, traditional, must be paintball related. **Buys 1-2 poems/year.** Submit maximum 1 poems. Length: 20 lines.

Fillers Anecdotes, gags to be illustrated by cartoonist. **Buys 2-4/year.** Length: 20-50 words. **Pays $25.**

Tips "Good graphic support is critical. Read writer's guidelines at Web site; read Web site, www.actionpursuitgames.com, and magazine."

$ $ AMERICAN CHEERLEADER

Lifestyle Media, Inc., 110 William St., 23rd Floor, New York NY 10038. (646)459-4800. Fax: (646)459-4900. E-mail: mwalker@americancheerleader.com. Web site: www.americancheerleader.com. Senior Editor: Jennifer Smith. **Contact:** Marisa Walker, editor-in-chief. **30% freelance written.** Bimonthly magazine covering high school, college, and competitive cheerleading. "We try to keep a young, informative voice for all articles—'for cheerleaders, by cheerleaders.' " Estab. 1995. Circ. 200,000. Pays on publication. Publishes ms an average of 4 months after acceptance. Byline given. Offers 25% kill fee. Buys all rights. Editorial lead time 3 months. Submit seasonal material 4 months in advance. Accepts queries by mail, e-mail. Responds in 4 weeks to queries; 2 months to mss. Sample copy for $2.95. Writer's guidelines free.

Nonfiction How-to (cheering techniques, routines, pep songs, etc.), interview/profile (celebrities and media personalities who cheered). Special issues: Tryouts (April); Camp Basics (June); College (October); Competition (December). No professional cheerleading stories, i.e., no Dallas Cowboy cheerleaders. **Buys 12-16 mss/year.** Query with published clips. Length: 400-1,500 words. **Pays $100-250 for assigned articles; $100 maximum for unsolicited articles.** Sometimes pays expenses of writers on assignment.

Photos State availability with submission. Reviews transparencies, 5×7 prints. Rights purchased varies. Offers $50/photo. Model releases required.

Columns/Departments Gameday Beauty (skin care, celeb how-tos), 600 words; Health & Fitness (teen athletes), 1,000 words; Profiles (winning squads), 1,000 words. **Buys 12 mss/year.** Query with published clips. **Pays $100-250.**

The online magazine carries original content not found in the print edition.

Tips "We invite proposals from freelance writers who are involved in or have been involved in cheerleading—i.e., coaches, sponsors, or cheerleaders. Our writing style is upbeat and 'sporty' to catch and hold the attention of our teenaged readers. Articles should be broken down into lots of sidebars, bulleted lists, Q&As, etc."

$ $ $ ATV MAGAZINE/ATV SPORT

Ehlert Publishing, 6420 Sycamore Lane, Maple Grove MN 55369. Fax: (763)383-4499. E-mail: terickson@ehlertpublishing.com. Web site: www.atvnews.com. **Contact:** Tim Erickson, editor. **20% freelance written.** Bimonthly magazine covering all-terrain vehicles. "Devoted to covering all the things ATV owners enjoy, from hunting to racing, farming to trail riding." Pays on magazine shipment to printer. Byline given. Buys all rights. Editorial lead time 6 months. Accepts queries by mail, e-mail, fax. Responds in 3 weeks to queries. Sample copy and writer's guidelines for #10 SASE.

Nonfiction How-to, interview/profile, new product, personal experience, photo feature, technical, travel. **Buys 15-20 mss/year.** Query with published clips. Length: 200-2,000 words. **Pays $100-1,000.** Sometimes pays expenses of writers on assignment.

Photos State availability with submission. Rights purchased vary. Negotiates payment individually. Captions, identification of subjects required.

Tips "Writers must have experience with ATVs, and should own one or have regular access to at least one ATV."

N $ $ BVM

Beach Volleyball Magazine, STN Media Co., 700 Torrance Blvd., Suite C, Redondo Beach CA 90277. (310)792-2226. Fax: (310)792-2231. E-mail: ryan@bvmag.com. Web site: www.bvmag.com. General Manager: Branden Smeltzer. **Contact:** Ryan Gray, editor. **60% freelance written.** Semiannual magazine covering all things, all ages of beach volleyball from an enthusiast slant. "Writers must possess a Gen X/Y voice with an understanding of beach culture. Beach volleyball players and/or fans preferred. Writers should at least be familiar with the sport of volleyball and its application in the sand. This includes rules and regulations and leading personalities of the sport." Estab. 2006. Circ. 30,000. Pays on publication. Byline given. Buys one-time rights. Editorial lead time 2 months. Submit seasonal material 2 months in advance. Accepts queries by e-mail. Accepts simultaneous submissions. Sample copy for free. Writer's guidelines free.

Nonfiction General interest, historical/nostalgic, how-to, humor, inspirational, interview/profile, new product, opinion, personal experience, photo feature, travel. Does not want game reporting. "*BVM* is a lifestyle magazine looking for lifestyle feature content." Query with published clips. Length: 600-1,200 words. **Pays $150-300.**

Photos Contact Vince Rios, art director. Send photos with submission. Reviews contact sheets, GIF/JPEG files. Buys all rights. Negotiates payment individually. Captions, identification of subjects, model releases required.

Columns/Departments Health & Fitness (training and nutrition tips for all ages); Beach News (current events), both 500 words. **Buys 12 mss/year.** Query with published clips. **Pays $150-300.**

Fillers Anecdotes, facts, newsbreaks. Length: 50-150 words. **Pays $0-50.**

Tips "This is an enthusiast magazine. Writers should be able to exhibit familiarity with and interest in beach volleyball and the surrounding culture. Previous sports writing and/or lifestyle feature experience preferred. Story ideas should have a firm grasp on topics of interest to beach volleyball community. Playing experience a definite plus, as is a demonstrated knowledge of sport history and knowledge, or the ability to quickly come up to speed and take direction."

$ CANADIAN RODEO NEWS

Canadian Rodeo News, Ltd., #223, 2116 27th Ave. NE, Calgary AB T2E 7A6 Canada. (403)250-7292. Fax: (403)250-6926. E-mail: editor@rodeocanada.com. Web site: www.rodeocanada.com. **Contact:** Darell Hartlen, editor. **80% freelance written.** Monthly tabloid covering "Canada's professional rodeo (CPRA) personalities and livestock. Read by rodeo participants and fans." Estab. 1964. Circ. 4,000. Pays on publication. Publishes ms an average of 1 month after acceptance. Byline given. Buys first, second serial (reprint) rights. Editorial lead time 1 month. Submit seasonal material 1 month in advance. Accepts queries by mail, e-mail, fax. Accepts simultaneous submissions. Responds in 1 month to queries; 2 months to mss.

Nonfiction General interest, historical/nostalgic, interview/profile. **Buys 70-80 mss/year.** Query. Length: 400-1,200 words. **Pays $30-60.**

Reprints Send photocopy of article or typed ms with rights for sale noted and information about when and where the material previously appeared. Pays 100% of amount paid for an original article.

Photos Send photos with submission. Reviews digital only. Buys one-time rights. Offers $15-25/cover photo.

Tips "Best to call first with the story idea to inquire if it is suitable for publication. Readers are very knowledgeable of the sport, so writers need to be as well."

N $FANTASY SPORTS

Krause Publications, Inc., 700 E. State St., Iola WI 54990-0001. (715)445-2214. Fax: (715)445-4087. E-mail: fb@fwpubs.com. Web site: fanatasysportsmag.com. **Contact:** Greg Ambrosius, Tom Kessenich. **10% freelance written.** Quarterly magazine covering fantasy baseball and football. "Fantasy advice—how-to win." Estab. 1989. Circ. 100,000. Pays on publication. Publishes ms an average of 3 months after acceptance. Byline given. Offers negotiable kill fee. Makes work-for-hire assignments. Editorial lead time 4 months. Submit seasonal material 4 months in advance. Accepts queries by e-mail. Sample copy for free. Writer's guidelines not available.

Tips "Send an e-mail suggestion to ambrosiusg@krause.com."

$ $FENCERS QUARTERLY MAGAZINE

848 S. Kimbrough, Springfield MO 65806. (417)866-4370. E-mail: editor@fencersquarterly.com. Editor-in-Chief: Nick Evangelista. **Contact:** Justin Evangelista, managing editor. **60% freelance written.** Quarterly magazine covering fencing, fencers, history of sword/fencing/dueling, modern techniques and systems, controversies, personalities of fencing, personal experience. "This is a publication for all fencers and those interested in fencing; we favor the grassroots level rather than the highly-promoted elite. Readers will have a grasp of terminology of the sword and refined fencing skills—writers must be familiar with fencing and current changes and controversies. We are happy to air any point of view on any fencing subject, but the material must be well-researched and logically presented." Estab. 1996. Circ. 5,000. Pays prior to or at publication. Publishes ms an average of 6 months after acceptance. Byline given. Offers 25% kill fee. Buys first North American serial, second serial (reprint), electronic rights, makes work-for-hire assignments. Editorial lead time 3 months. Submit seasonal material 6 months in advance. Accepts queries by mail, e-mail. Accepts simultaneous submissions. Sample copy by request. Writer's guidelines by request.

- Responds in 1 week or less for e-mail; 1 month for snail mail if SASE; no reply if no SASE and material not usable.

Nonfiction "All article types acceptable—however, we have seldom used fiction or poetry (though will consider if has special relationship to fencing)." How-to should reflect some aspect of fencing or gear. Personal experience welcome. No articles "that lack logical progression of thought, articles that rant, 'my weapon is better than your weapon' emotionalism, puff pieces, or public relations stuff." **Buys 100 mss/year.** Query with or without published clips or send complete ms. Length: 100-4,000 words. **Pays $100-200 (rarely) for assigned articles; $10-60 for unsolicited articles.**

Photos Send photos by mail or as e-mail attachment. Prefers prints, all sizes. Buys all rights. Negotiates payment individually. Captions, identification of subjects, model releases required.

Columns/Departments Cutting-edge news (sword or fencing related), 100 words; Reviews (books/films), 300 words; Fencing Generations (profile), 200-300 words; Tournament Results (veteran events only, please), 200 words. **Buys 40 mss/year.** Send complete ms. **Pays $10-20.**

Fiction Will consider all as long as strong fencing/sword slant is major element. No erotica. Query with or without published clips or send complete ms. Length: 1,500 words maximum. **Pays $25-100.**

Poetry Will consider all which have distinct fencing/sword element as central. No erotica. Submit maximum 10 poems. Length: Up to 100 lines. **Pays $10.**

Fillers Anecdotes, facts, gags to be illustrated by cartoonist, newsbreaks. **Buys 30/year.** Length: 100 words maximum. **Pays $5.**

Tips "We love new writers! Professionally presented work impresses us. We prefer complete submissions, and e-mail or disk (in rich text format) are our favorites. Ask for our writer's guidelines. Always aim your writing to knowledgeable fencers who are fascinated by this subject, take their fencing seriously, and want to know more about its history, current events, and controversies. Action photos should show proper form—no flailing or tangled-up images, please. We want to know what the 'real' fencer is up to these days, not just what the Olympic contenders are doing. If we don't use your piece, we'll tell you why not."

N $LACROSSE MAGAZINE

US Lacrosse, 113 W. University Pkwy., Baltimore MD 21210. (410)235-6882. Fax: (410)366-6735. E-mail: pkrome@uslacrosse.org. Web site: www.uslacrosse.org. **Contact:** Paul Krome, editor. **75% freelance written.** Magazine published 8 times/year , monthly during lacrosse season, bimonthly off-season, by U.S. Lacrosse for its members "*Lacrosse Magazine* is the only national feature publication devoted to the sport of lacrosse. It is a benefit of membership in U.S. Lacrosse, a nonprofit organization devoted to promoting the growth of lacrosse and preserving its history." Estab. 1978. Circ. 180,000. Pays on publication. Publishes ms an average of 2 months after acceptance. Byline given. Buys one-time rights. Editorial lead time 2 months. Submit seasonal material 2 months in advance. Sample copy for free. Writer's guidelines free.

Nonfiction Book excerpts, general interest, historical/nostalgic, how-to (drills, conditioning, x's and o'x, etc.), interview/profile, new product, opinion, personal experience, photo feature, technical. **Buys 30-40 mss/year.** Length: 500-1,750 words. **Payment negotiable.** Sometimes pays expenses of writers on assignment.

Photos State availability with submission. Reviews contact sheets, 4×6 prints. Buys one-time rights. Negotiates payment individually. Captions, identification of subjects required.

Columns/Departments First Person (personal experience), 1,000 words; Fitness (conditioning/strength/exercise), 500-1,000 words; How-to, 500-1,000 words. **Buys 10-15 mss/year. Payment negotiable.**

Tips "As the national development center of lacrosse, we are particularly interested in stories about the growth of the sport in non-traditional areas of the U.S. and abroad, written for an audience already knowledgeable about the game."

$ $ POINTE MAGAZINE

Ballet At Its Best, Lifestyle Media, Inc., 110 William St., 23rd Floor, New York NY 10038. (646)459-4800. Fax: (646)459-4900. E-mail: pointe@lifestylemedia.com. Web site: www.pointemagazine.com. Editor-in-Chief: Virginia Johnson. Managing Editor: Jocelyn Anderson. Bimonthly magazine covering ballet. "*Pointe Magazine* is the only magazine dedicated to ballet. It offers practicalities on ballet careers as well as news and features." Estab. 2000. Circ. 38,000. Pays on publication. Byline given. Buys all rights. Accepts simultaneous submissions. Responds in 1 month to queries; 1 month to mss. Sample copy for 9×12 SAE and 6 first-class stamps.

Nonfiction Historical/nostalgic, how-to, interview/profile, biography, careers, health, news. **Buys 60 mss/year.** Query with published clips. Length: 400-1,500 words. **Pays $125-400.**

Photos Colin Fowler, photo editor. State availability with submission. Reviews 2¼×2¼ or 35mm transparencies, 8×11 prints. Buys one-time rights. Negotiates payment individually. Captions required.

$ $ POLO PLAYERS' EDITION

Rizzo Management Corp., 3500 Fairlane Farms Rd., Suite 9, Wellington FL 33414. (561)793-9524. Fax: (561)793-9576. E-mail: info@poloplayersedition.com. Web site: www.poloplayersedition.com. **Contact:** Gwen Rizzo, editor. Monthly magazine on polo—the sport and lifestyle. "Our readers are affluent, well educated, well read, and highly sophisticated." Circ. 6,150. **Pays on acceptance.** Publishes ms an average of 2 months after acceptance. Kill fee varies. Buys first North American serial rights, makes work-for-hire assignments. Submit seasonal material 3 months in advance. Accepts queries by mail, e-mail, fax. Accepts simultaneous submissions. Responds in 3 months to queries. Writer's guidelines for #10 SAE with 2 stamps.

Nonfiction Historical/nostalgic, interview/profile, personal experience, photo feature, technical, travel. Special issues: Annual Art Issue/Gift Buying Guide; Winter Preview/Florida Supplement. **Buys 20 mss/year.** Query with published clips or send complete ms. Length: 800-3,000 words. **Pays $150-400 for assigned articles; $100-300 for unsolicited articles.** Sometimes pays expenses of writers on assignment.

Reprints Send tearsheet or typed ms with rights for sale noted and information about when and where the material previously appeared. Pays 50% of amount paid for an original article.

Photos State availability of or send photos with submission. Reviews contact sheets, transparencies, prints. Buys one-time rights. Offers $20-150/photo. Captions required.

Columns/Departments Yesteryears (historical pieces), 500 words; Profiles (clubs and players), 800-1,000 words. **Buys 15 mss/year.** Query with published clips. **Pays $100-300.**

Tips "Query us on a personality or club profile or historic piece or, if you know the game, state availability to cover a tournament. Keep in mind that ours is a sophisticated, well-educated audience."

$ PRORODEO SPORTS NEWS

Professional Rodeo Cowboys Association, 101 ProRodeo Dr., Colorado Springs CO 80919. (719)593-8840. Fax: (719)548-4889. Web site: www.prorodeo.com. **Contact:** Kendra Santos. **10% freelance written.** Biweekly magazine covering professional rodeo. "Our readers are extremely knowledgeable about the sport of rodeo, and anyone who writes for us should have that same in-depth knowledge." Estab. 1952. Circ. 30,000. Pays on publication. Publishes ms an average of 1 month after acceptance. Byline given. Buys first, one-time rights, makes work-for-hire assignments. Editorial lead time 2 months. Submit seasonal material 2 months in advance. Responds in 2 weeks to queries. Sample copy for #10 SASE. Writer's guidelines free.

Nonfiction Historical/nostalgic, how-to, humor, interview/profile, photo feature, technical. **Pays $50-100.**

Photos State availability with submission. Reviews digital images and hard copy portfolios. Buys one-time rights. Offers $15-85/photo. Identification of subjects required.

$ RUGBY MAGAZINE

Rugby Press, Ltd., 459 Columbus Ave., #1200, New York NY 10024. (212)787-1160. Fax: (212)787-1161. E-mail: rugbymag@aol.com. Web site: www.rugbymag.com. **75% freelance written.** Monthly magazine. "*Rugby Magazine* is the journal of record for the sport of rugby in the U.S. Our demographics are among the best in the country." Estab. 1975. Circ. 10,000. Pays on publication. Publishes ms an average of 2 months after acceptance. Byline given. Buys all rights. Editorial lead time 1 month. Submit seasonal material 2 months in advance. Accepts queries by mail, e-mail, fax, phone. Accepts simultaneous submissions. Responds in 2 weeks to queries; 1 month to mss. Sample copy for $4. Writer's guidelines free.

Nonfiction Book excerpts, essays, general interest, historical/nostalgic, how-to, humor, interview/profile, new product, opinion, personal experience, photo feature, technical, travel. **Buys 15 mss/year.** Send complete ms. Length: 600-2,000 words. **Pays $50 minimum.** Pays expenses of writers on assignment.

Reprints Send tearsheet or typed ms with rights for sale noted and information about when and where the material previously appeared. Payment varies.

Photos Send photos with submission. Reviews negatives, transparencies, prints. Buys all rights. Offers no additional payment for photos accepted with ms.

Columns/Departments Nutrition (athletic nutrition), 900 words; Referees' Corner, 1,200 words. **Buys 2-3 mss/year.** Query with published clips. **Pays $50 maximum.**

Fiction Condensed novels, humorous, novel excerpts, slice-of-life vignettes. **Buys 1-3 mss/year.** Query with published clips. Length: 1,000-2,500 words. **Pays $100.**

Tips "Give us a call. Send along your stories or photos; we're happy to take a look. Tournament stories are a good way to get yourself published in *Rugby Magazine.*"

⊘ SKATEBOARDER

Primedia Enthusiast Group, P.O. Box 1028, Dana Point CA 92629. (949)661-5150. E-mail: peech@skateboardermag.com. Web site: www.skateboardermag.com. Editor: Brian Peech. Monthly magazine for begining and experienced skateboarders. Circ. 105,000.

- Query before submitting.

$ SKYDIVING

1725 N. Lexington Ave., DeLand FL 32724. (386)736-4793. Fax: (386)736-9786. E-mail: editor@skydivingmagazine.com. Web site: skydivingmagazine.com. **Contact:** Sue Clifton, editor. **25% freelance written.** Monthly tabloid featuring skydiving for sport parachutists, worldwide dealers and equipment manufacturers. "*Skydiving* is a news magazine. Its purpose is to deliver timely, useful and interesting information about the equipment, techniques, events, people and places of parachuting. Our scope is national. *Skydiving*'s audience spans the entire spectrum of jumpers, from first-jump students to veterans with thousands of skydives. Some readers are riggers with a keen interest in the technical aspects of parachutes, while others are weekend 'fun' jumpers who want information to help them make travel plans and equipment purchases." Circ. 14,200. Pays on publication. Publishes ms an average of 3 months after acceptance. Byline given. Buys one-time rights. Accepts previously published material. Accepts simultaneous submissions. Responds in 1 month to queries. Sample copy for $2. Writer's guidelines online.

Nonfiction Average issue includes 3 feature articles and 3 columns of technical information. "Send us news and information on how-to, where-to, equipment, techniques, events and outstanding personalities who skydive. We want articles written by people who have a solid knowledge of parachuting." No personal experience or human interest articles. Query. Length: 500-1,000 words. **Pays $25-100.** Sometimes pays expenses of writers on assignment.

Photos State availability with submission. Reviews 5×7 and larger b&w glossy prints. Offers no additional payment for photos accepted with ms. Captions required.

Fillers Newsbreaks. Length: 100-200 words. **Pays $25 minimum.**

Tips "The most frequent mistake made by writers in completing articles for us is that the writer isn't knowledgeable about the sport of parachuting. Articles about events are especially time-sensitive so yours must be submitted quickly. We welcome contributions about equipment. Even short, 'quick look' articles about new products are appropriate for *Skydiving*. If you know of a drop zone or other place that jumpers would like to visit, write an article describing its features and tell them why you liked it and what they can expect to find if they visit it. Avoid first-person articles."

N TENNIS MAGAZINE

Miller Publishing Group, 79 Madison Ave., 8th Floor, New York NY 10016. (212)636-2700. Web site: www.tennis.com. Editor-in-Chief: James Martin. Magazine published 10 times/year covering the sport of tennis.

Nonfiction Query with published clips.

$ $ TENNIS WEEK

Tennis News, Inc., 15 Elm Place, Rye NY 10580. (914)967-4890. Fax: (914)967-8178. **Contact:** Andre Christopher, managing editor. **10% freelance written.** Monthly magazine covering tennis. "For readers who are either tennis fanatics or involved in the business of tennis." Estab. 1974. Circ. 107,253. Pays on publication. Byline given. Buys all rights. Editorial lead time 1 month. Submit seasonal material 1 month in advance. Responds in 1 month to queries. Sample copy for $4.

Nonfiction Buys 15 mss/year. Query with or without published clips. Length: 1,000-2,000 words. **Pays $300.**

⊘ TRANSWORLD SKATEBOARDING

Time 4 Media, 353 Airport Rd., Oceanside CA 92054. (760)722-7777. Web site: www.skateboarding.com. Managing Editor: Carleton Curtis. Monthly magazine for skateboarding enthusiasts. Circ. 243,000. Editorial lead time 3 months.

- Query before submitting.

N VOLLEYBALL MAGAZINE

420 Boylston St., 5th Floor, Boston MA 02116. E-mail: mmiazga@madavor.com. Web site: www.volleyballmag.com. **Contact:** Mike Miazga, editor-in-chief. "Only printed monthly publication devoted exclusively to all aspects of the sport of volleyball. We cover anything volleyball-related from the expanding juniors scene, to the college, professional and Olympic-International levels, both indoor and outdoor." Accepts queries by e-mail.

Nonfiction "Looking for experienced freelance writers who have a strong knowledge of volleyball. Also looking for credentialed fitness and instructional writers. No phone calls or faxes." General interest, how-to, interview/profile. Query with published clips. **Payment based on work being published.**

$ $ WINDY CITY SPORTS

Windy City Publishing, 1450 W. Randolph St., Chicago IL 60607. (312)421-1551. Fax: (312)421-1454. E-mail: jeff@windycitysports.com. Web site: www.windycitysports.com. **Contact:** Jeff Banowetz, editorial director. **50% freelance written.** Monthly tabloid. "Writers should have knowledge of the sport they've been hired to cover. In most cases, these are endurance sports, such as running, cycling, triathlon, or adventure racing. Please read the magazine and visit the Web site to famliarize yourself with our subject matter and our style. Poorly-tailored queries reflect badly on your journalistic skills. If you query us on a golf story, you will not only suffer the shame of rejection, but your name shall be added to our 'clueless freelancer' list, and we will joke about you at the water cooler." Circ. 110,000. Pays on publication. Publishes ms an average of 1 month after acceptance. Byline given. Buys one-time rights. Editorial lead time 2 months. Accepts queries by e-mail. Sample copy and writer's guidelines online.

Nonfiction Essays, general interest, how-to, humor, interview/profile, opinion, personal experience, photo feature, technical. **Buys up to 35 mss/year.** Query with published clips. Length: 700-1,500 words. **Pays $150-300 for assigned articles; $0-300 for unsolicited articles.** Sometimes pays expenses of writers on assignment.

Photos Send photos with submission. Reviews prints. Buys one-time rights. Negotiates payment individually. Captions, identification of subjects required.

Columns/Departments Cool Down (humorous, personal experience), 800-1,000 words; Nutrition (advice and information on diet), 500-800 words; Health/Wellness (advice and information on general health), 500-800 words. Query with published clips. **Pays $50-150.**

Tips "You should try to make it fun. We like to see anecdotes, great quotes and vivid descriptions. Quote Chicago area people as often as possible. If that's not possible, try to stick to the Midwest or people with Chicago connections."

MOTOR SPORTS

$ DIRT RIDER

Primedia Enthusiast Group, 6420 Wilshire Blvd., 17th Floor, Los Angeles CA 90048. (323)782-2390. Fax: (323)782-2372. E-mail: drmail@primedia.com. Web site: www.dirtrider.com. Editor: Jimmy Lewis. Managing Editor: Terry Masaoka. Monthly magazine devoted to the sport of off-road motorcycle riding that showcases the many ways enthusiast can enjoy dirt bikes. Circ. 201,342. Sample copy not available.

N 4-WHEEL & OFF ROAD

Primedia Enthusiast Group, 6420 Wilshire Blvd., Los Angeles CA 90048. (323)782-2000. Fax: (323)782-2704. E-mail: 4wheeloffroad@primedia.com. Web site: www.4wheeloffroad.com. Editor: Rick Pewe. Monthly magazine covering off road driving. Intended for the connoisseur of four wheel drive vehicles and their specific applications. Estab. 1977. Circ. 379,284. Sample copy not available.

Nonfiction How-to, new product (product evaluations), travel (trail destinations), legal issues.

$ THE HOOK MAGAZINE

The Magazine for Antique & Classic Tractor Pullers, Greer Town, Inc., 209 S. Marshall, Box 16, Marshfield MO 65706. (417)468-7000. Fax: (417)859-6075. E-mail: editor@hookmagazine.com. Web site: www.hookmagazine.com. **Contact:** Dana Greer Marlin, owner/president. **80% freelance written.** Bimonthly magazine covering tractor pulling. Estab. 1992. Circ. 6,000. Pays on publication. Byline given. Buys one-time, electronic rights. Editorial lead time 6 months. Submit seasonal material 6 months in advance. Accepts queries by mail, e-mail, fax. Accepts previously published material. Accepts simultaneous submissions. Responds in 3 weeks to queries; 2 months to mss. Sample copy for 8½×11 SAE with 4 first-class stamps or online. Writer's guidelines for #10 SASE.

O→ "Our magazine is easy to break into. Puller profiles are your best bet. Features on individuals and their tractors, how they got into the sport, what they want from competing."

Nonfiction How-to, interview/profile, new product, personal experience, photo feature, technical, event coverage. **Buys 25 mss/year.** Send complete ms. Length: 500-1,500 words. **Pays $70 for technical articles; $35 for others.**

Photos Send photos with submission. Reviews 3×5 prints. Buys one-time and online rights. Negotiates payment individually. Captions, identification of subjects, model releases required.

Fillers Anecdotes, short humor. **Buys 6/year.** Length: 100 words.

Tips "Write 'real'; our readers don't respond well to scholarly tomes. Use your everyday voice in all submissions and your chances will go up radically."

$ $ SAND SPORTS MAGAZINE

Wright Publishing Co., Inc., P.O. Box 2260, Costa Mesa CA 92628. (714)979-2560, ext. 107. Fax: (714)979-3998. Web site: www.sandsports.net. **Contact:** Michael Sommer, editor. **20% freelance written.** Bimonthly magazine covering vehicles for off-road and sand dunes. Estab. 1995. Circ. 35,000. Pays on publication. Byline given. Buys first, one-time rights. Editorial lead time 3 months. Submit seasonal material 6 months in advance. Accepts queries by mail. Sample copy and writer's guidelines free.

Nonfiction How-to (technical-mechanical), photo feature, technical. **Buys 20 mss/year.** Query. Length: 1,500 words minimum. **Pays $175/page.** Sometimes pays expenses of writers on assignment.

Photos Send photos with submission. Reviews color slides or high res digital images. Buys one-time rights. Negotiates payment individually. Captions, identification of subjects, model releases required.

$ $ SPEEDWAY ILLUSTRATED

Performance Media, LLC, 107 Elm St., Salisbury MA 01952. (978)465-9099. Fax: (978)465-9033. E-mail: editorial@speedwayillustrated.com. Web site: www.speedwayillustrated.com. Executive Editor: Dick Berggren. **40% freelance written.** Monthly magazine covering stock car racing. Estab. 2000. Circ. 146,000. Pays on publication. Byline given. Buys first rights. Editorial lead time 6 weeks. Accepts queries by mail, e-mail, fax. Responds in 2 weeks to queries. Sample copy for free.

Nonfiction Interview/profile, opinion, personal experience, photo feature, technical. **Buys 30 mss/year.** Query. **Pays variable rate.**

Photos Send photos with submission. Reviews transparencies, digital. Buys all rights. Offers $40-250/photo. Captions, identification of subjects, model releases required.

Tips "We seek short, high-interest value pieces that are accompanied by strong photography, in short—knock our socks off."

OLYMPICS

USA GYMNASTICS

201 S. Capitol Ave., Suite 300, Pan American Plaza, Indianapolis IN 46225. (317)237-5050. Fax: (317)237-5069. E-mail: lpeszek@usa-gymnastics.org. Web site: www.usa-gymnastics.org. **Contact:** Luan Peszek, editor. **5% freelance written.** Bimonthly magazine covering gymnastics—national and international competitions. Designed to educate readers on fitness, health, safety, technique, current topics, trends, and personalities related to the gymnastics/fitness field. Readers are gymnasts ages 7-18, parents, and coaches. Estab. 1981. Circ. 100,000. Pays on publication. Publishes ms an average of 4 months after acceptance. Byline given. Buys all rights. Submit seasonal material 4 months in advance. Accepts queries by e-mail, fax. Accepts simultaneous submissions. Responds in 2 months to queries. Sample copy for $5.

Nonfiction General interest, how-to (related to fitness, health, gymnastics), inspirational, interview/profile, photo feature. **Buys 1-2 mss/year.** Query. Length: 1,500 words maximum. **Payment negotiable.**

Reprints Send photocopy.

Photos Send photos with submission. Buys all rights. Offers no additional payment for photos accepted with ms. Identification of subjects required.

Tips "Any articles of interest to gymnasts (men, women, rhythmic gymnastics, trampoline, and tumbling and acrobatic gymnastics), coaches, judges, and parents. This includes nutrition, toning, health, safety, trends, techniques, timing, etc."

RUNNING

$ INSIDE TEXAS RUNNING

14201 Memorial Dr., Suite 204, Houston TX 77079. (281)759-0555. Fax: (281)759-7766. E-mail: lance@runningmags.com. Web site: www.insidetexasrunning.com. **Contact:** Lance Phegley, editor. **70% freelance written.** Monthly (except June and August) tabloid covering running and running-related events. "Our audience is made up of Texas runners who may also be interested in cross training." Estab. 1977. Circ. 10,000. Pays on publication. Publishes ms an average of 2 months after acceptance. Byline given. Buys one-time, exclusive Texas rights. Submit seasonal material 2 months in advance. Responds in 1 month to mss. Sample copy for $4.95. Writer's guidelines for #10 SASE.

"The best way to break in to our publication is to submit brief (2 or 3 paragraphs) fillers for our Texas Roundup section."

Nonfiction Various topics of interest to runners: Profiles of newsworthy Texas runners of all abilities; unusual events; training interviews. Special issues: Shoe Review (March); Fall Race Review (September); Marathon Focus (October); Resource Guide (December). **Buys 20 mss/year.** Send complete ms. Length: 500-1,500 words. **Pays $100 maximum for assigned articles; $50 maximum for unsolicited articles.**

Reprints Send tearsheet, photocopy or typed ms with rights for sale noted and information about when and where the material previously appeared.

Photos Send photos with submission. Buys one-time rights. Offers $25 maximum/photo. Captions required.

The online magazine carries original content not found in the print edition.

Tips "Writers should be familiar with the sport and the publication."

$$ NEW YORK RUNNER

New York Road Runners, 9 E. 89th St., New York NY 10128. (212)423-2260. Fax: (212)423-0879. E-mail: newyorkrun@nyrr.org. Web site: www.nyrr.org. **Contact:** Gordon Bakoulis, editor. Quarterly magazine covering running, walking, nutrition, and fitness. Estab. 1958. Circ. 45,000. **Pays on acceptance.** Byline given. Buys first North American serial rights. Submit seasonal material 4 months in advance. Accepts queries by mail, e-mail, fax. Responds in 2 months to queries. Sample copy for $3. Writer's guidelines for #10 SASE.

- Material should be of interest to members of the New York Road Runners.

Nonfiction Running and marathon articles. Interview/profile (of runners). **Buys 15 mss/year.** Query. Length: 750-1,000 words. **Pays $50-350.**

Columns/Departments Running Briefs (anything noteworthy in the running world), 250-500 words. Query.

Tips "Be knowledgeable about the sport of running."

$$$$ RUNNER'S WORLD

Rodale, 135 N. 6th St., Emmaus PA 18098. (610)967-5171. Fax: (610)967-8883. E-mail: rwedit@rodale.com. Web site: www.runnersworld.com. Managing Editor: Sean Downey. **Contact:** David Willey, editor-in-chief. **5% freelance written.** Monthly magazine on running, mainly long-distance running. "The magazine for and about distance running, training, health and fitness, nutrition, motivation, injury prevention, race coverage, personalities of the sport." Estab. 1966. Circ. 500,000. Pays on publication. Publishes ms an average of 6 months after acceptance. Byline given. Buys all rights. Submit seasonal material 6 months in advance. Accepts queries by mail. Responds in 2 months to queries. Writer's guidelines online.

Break in through columns 'Human Race' and 'Finish Line.' Also 'Warmups,' which mixes international running news with human interest stories. If you can send us a unique human interest story from your region, we will give it serious consideration.

Nonfiction How-to (train, prevent injuries), interview/profile, personal experience. No "my first marathon" stories. No poetry. **Buys 5-7 mss/year.** Query. **Pays $1,500-2,000.** Pays expenses of writers on assignment.

Photos State availability with submission. Buys one-time rights. Identification of subjects required.

Columns/Departments Finish Line (back-of-the-magazine essay, personal experience—humor). **Buys 24 mss/year.** Send complete ms. **Pays $300.**

Tips "We are always looking for 'Adventure Runs' from readers—runs in wild, remote, beautiful, and interesting places. These are rarely race stories but more like backtracking/running adventures. Great color slides are crucial, 2,000 words maximum."

$$ RUNNING TIMES

The Runner's Best Resource, Fitness Publishing, Inc., 15 River Rd., Suite 230, Wilton CT 06897. (203)761-1113. Fax: (203)761-9933. E-mail: editor@runningtimes.com. Web site: www.runningtimes.com. Managing Editor:

Marc Chalufour. **Contact:** Jonathan Beverly, editor-in-chief. **40% freelance written.** Magazine published 10 times/year covering distance running and racing. "*Running Times* is the national magazine for the experienced running participant and fan. Our audience is knowledgeable about the sport and active in running and racing. All editorial relates specifically to running: improving performance, enhancing enjoyment, or exploring events, places, and people in the sport." Estab. 1977. Circ. 75,000. Pays on publication. Publishes ms an average of 3 months after acceptance. Byline given. Buys first North American serial, second serial (reprint), electronic rights. Editorial lead time 4-6 months. Submit seasonal material 6 months in advance. Accepts queries by mail, e-mail. Responds in 1 month to queries; 2 months to mss. Sample copy for $5. Writer's guidelines online.

Nonfiction Book excerpts, essays, historical/nostalgic, how-to (training), humor, inspirational, interview/profile, new product, opinion, personal experience (with theme, purpose, evidence of additional research and/or special expertise), photo feature, travel, news, reports. No basic, beginner how-to, generic fitness/nutrition, or generic first-person accounts. **Buys 25 mss/year.** Query. Length: 1,500-3,000 words. **Pays $200-600 for assigned articles; $100-300 for unsolicited articles.** Sometimes pays expenses of writers on assignment.

Photos State availability with submission. Buys one-time rights. Negotiates payment individually. Identification of subjects required.

Columns/Departments Training (short topics related to enhancing performance), 1,000 words; Sports-Med (application of medical knowledge to running), 1,000 words; Nutrition (application of nutritional principles to running performance), 1,000 words. **Buys 10 mss/year.** Query. **Pays $50-200.**

Fiction Any genre, with running-related theme or characters. Buys 1 ms/year. Send complete ms. Length: 1,500-3,000 words. **Pays $100-500.**

Tips "Thoroughly get to know runners and the running culture, both at the participant level and the professional, elite level."

$ $ TRAIL RUNNER

The Magazine of Running Adventure, Big Stone Publishing, 1101 Village Rd. UL-4D, Carbondale CO 81623. (970)704-1442. Fax: (970)963-4965. E-mail: mbenge@bigstonepub.com. Web site: www.trailrunnermag.com. **Contact:** Michael Benge, editor. **65% freelance written.** Bimonthly magazine covering all aspects of off-road running. "The only nationally circulated 4-color glossy magazine dedicated to covering trail running." Estab. 1999. Circ. 20,000. Pays on publication. Publishes ms an average of 2 months after acceptance. Byline given. Offers $50 kill fee. Buys first North American serial, electronic rights. Editorial lead time 3 months. Submit seasonal material 5 months in advance. Accepts queries by mail, e-mail. Accepts simultaneous submissions. Responds in 3 weeks to queries; 2 months to mss. Sample copy for $3. Writer's guidelines online.

Nonfiction Essays, exposé, general interest, historical/nostalgic, how-to, humor, inspirational, interview/profile, new product, opinion, personal experience, photo feature, technical, travel, racing. No gear reviews, race results. **Buys 30-40 mss/year.** Query with published clips. Length: 800-2,000 words. **Pays 30¢/word.** Sometimes pays expenses of writers on assignment.

Photos Send photos with submission. Reviews 35mm transparencies, prints. Buys one-time rights. Offers $50-250/photo. Identification of subjects, model releases required.

Columns/Departments Garett Graubins, senior editor. Training (race training, altitude training, etc.), 800 words; Adventure (off-beat aspects of trail running), 600-800 words; Wanderings (personal essay on any topic related to trail running), 600 words; Urban Escapes (urban trails accessible in and around major US sites), 800 words; Personalities (profile of a trail running personality), 1,000 words. **Buys 5-10 mss/year.** Query with published clips. **Pays 30-40¢/word.**

Fiction Adventure, fantasy, slice-of-life vignettes. **Buys 1-2 mss/year.** Query with published clips. Length: 1,000-1,500 words. **Pays 25-35¢/word.**

Fillers Anecdotes, facts, gags to be illustrated by cartoonist, newsbreaks, short humor. **Buys 50-60/year.** Length: 75-400 words. **Pays 25-35¢/word.**

Tips "Best way to break in is with interesting and unique trail running news, notes, and nonsense from around the world. Also, check the Web site for more info."

$ $ TRIATHLETE MAGAZINE

The World's Largest Triathlon Magazine, Triathlon Group of North America, 328 Encinitas Blvd., Suite 100, Encinitas CA 92024. (760)634-4100. Fax: (760)634-4110. E-mail: cam@triathletemag.com. Web site: www.triathletemag.com. **Contact:** Cameron Elford, managing editor. **50% freelance written.** Monthly magazine. "In general, articles should appeal to seasoned triathletes, as well as eager newcomers to the sport. Our audience includes everyone from competitive athletes to people considering their first event." Estab. 1983. Circ. 53,864. Pays on publication. Byline given. Buys second serial (reprint), all rights. Editorial lead time 3 months. Submit seasonal material 6 months in advance. Accepts queries by mail, e-mail. Accepts simultaneous submissions. Sample copy for $5.

Nonfiction How-to, interview/profile, new product, photo feature, technical. "No first-person pieces about your experience in triathlon or my-first-triathlon stories.'' **Buys 36 mss/year.** Query with published clips. Length: 1,000-3,000 words. **Pays $200-600.** Sometimes pays expenses of writers on assignment.

Photos State availability with submission. Reviews transparencies. Buys first North American rights. Offers $50-300/photo.

Tips ''Writers should know the sport and be familiar with the nuances and history. Training-specific articles that focus on new, but scientifically based, methods are good, as are seasonal training pieces.''

N $ WASHINGTON RUNNING REPORT

Capital Running Company, 13710 Ashby Rd., Rockville MD 20853-2903. (301)871-0005. Fax: (301)871-0006. E-mail: kathy@runwashington.com. Web site: www.runwashington.com. **Contact:** Kathy Freedman, publisher/editor. **90% freelance written.** Bimonthly tabloid covering running and racing in Washington, DC, metropolitan area, including Baltimore and Richmond metro areas. ''*Washington Running Report* is written by runners for runners. Features include runner rankings, training tips and advice, feature articles on races, race results, race calendar, humor, product reviews, and other articles of interest to runners.'' Estab. 1984. Circ. 35,000. Pays on publication. Publishes ms an average of 2-4 months after acceptance. Byline given. Buys first, one-time, second serial (reprint), simultaneous, electronic rights, makes work-for-hire assignments. Editorial lead time 1 month. Submit seasonal material 3 months in advance. Accepts queries by mail, e-mail, fax, phone. Accepts previously published material. Accepts simultaneous submissions. Responds in 2-3 weeks to queries; 1-2 months to mss. Sample copy for free.

Nonfiction Book excerpts, essays, exposé, general interest, historical/nostalgic, how-to, humor, inspirational, interview/profile, new product, opinion, personal experience, photo feature, technical, travel. **Buys 10-12 mss/year.** Query. Length: 500-2,800 words. **Pays $75 for assigned articles; $50 for unsolicited articles.**

Photos Send photos with submission. Reviews contact sheets, 4×6 prints, GIF/JPEG files. Buys all rights. Offers $20-50/photo. Captions, identification of subjects required.

Columns/Departments Traveling Runner (races in exotic locales), 1,400 words; Training Tips (how to run faster, racing strategy), 750 words; Sports Medicine (new developments in the field), 750 words. **Buys 3-4 mss/year.** Query with or without published clips or send complete ms. **Pays $50.**

Fiction Adventure, condensed novels, experimental, fantasy, historical, humorous, mainstream, mystery, slice-of-life vignettes. **Buys 1-2 mss/year.** Send complete ms. Length: 750-1,500 words. **Pays $50.**

Fillers Anecdotes, facts, gags to be illustrated by cartoonist, newsbreaks, short humor. **Buys 6/year.** Length: 50-250 words. **Pays $50.**

Tips ''Submit timely articles about running and racing in the DC area; original humor pieces; coverage of a large race in our area.''

SKIING & SNOW SPORTS

$ AMERICAN SNOWMOBILER

The Enthusiast Magazine, Kalmbach Publishing Co., P.O. Box 1612, Waukesha WI 53187. Web site: www.amsnow.com. **30% freelance written.** Magazine published 6 times seasonally covering snowmobiling. Estab. 1985. Circ. 70,000. **Pays on acceptance.** Publishes ms an average of 4 months after acceptance. Byline given. Buys all rights. Editorial lead time 4 months. Submit seasonal material 6 months in advance. Accepts queries by mail, e-mail, fax. Responds in 1 month to queries; 2 months to mss. Writer's guidelines for #10 SASE.

- Break in with ''a packet complete with résumé, published clips and photos (or color copies of available photos) and a complete query with a few paragraphs to get me interested and to give an idea of the angle the writer will be taking.''

Nonfiction Seeking race coverage for online version. General interest, historical/nostalgic, how-to, interview/profile, new product, personal experience, photo feature, travel. **Buys 10 mss/year.** Query with published clips. Length: 500-1,500 words. **Pay varies for assigned articles; $100 minimum for unsolicited articles.**

Photos State availability with submission. Buys all rights. Offers no additional payment for photos accepted with ms. Captions, identification of subjects, model releases required.

$ $ $ SKI MAGAZINE

Times Mirror Magazines, 929 Pearl St., Suite 200, Boulder CO 80302. E-mail: editor@skimag.com. Web site: www.skimag.com. **Contact:** Kendall Hamilton, editor-in-chief. **60% freelance written.** Magazine published 8 times/year. ''*Ski* is a ski-lifestyle publication written and edited for recreational skiers. Its content is intended to help them ski better (technique), buy better (equipment and skiwear), and introduce them to new experiences, people, and adventures.'' Estab. 1936. Circ. 430,000. **Pays on acceptance.** Publishes ms an average of 3 months after acceptance. Byline given. Offers 15% kill fee. Buys first North American serial rights. Submit seasonal material 8 months in advance. Accepts queries by mail, e-mail. Sample copy for 9×12 SAE and 5 first-class stamps.

Consumer Magazines

• Does not accept unsolicited mss, and assumes no responsibility for their return.

Nonfiction Essays, historical/nostalgic, how-to, humor, interview/profile, personal experience. **Buys 5-10 mss/year.** Send complete ms. Length: 1,000-3,500 words. **Pays $500-1,000 for assigned articles; $300-700 for unsolicited articles.** Pays expenses of writers on assignment.

Photos Send photos with submission. Buys one-time rights. Offers $75-300/photo. Captions, identification of subjects, model releases required.

Fillers Facts, short humor. **Buys 10/year.** Length: 60-75 words. **Pays $50-75.**

Tips "Writers must have an extensive familiarity with the sport and know what concerns, interests, and amuses skiers. Start with short pieces ('hometown hills,' 'dining out,' 'sleeping in'). Columns are most open to freelancers."

$ $ $ $ SKIING

Time 4 Media, Inc., 929 Pearl St., Suite 200, Boulder CO 80302. (303)448-7600. Fax: (303)448-7676. E-mail: evelynspence@time4.com. Web site: www.skiingmag.com. Editor-in-Chief: Marc Peruzzi. **Contact:** Evelyn Spence, articles editor. Magazine published 7 times/year for skiers who deeply love winter, who live for travel, adventure, instruction, gear, and news. "*Skiing* is the user's guide to winter adventure. It is equal parts jaw-dropping inspiration and practical information, action and utility, attitude and advice. It relates the lifestyles of dedicated skiers and captures their spirit of daring and exploration. Dramatic photography transports readers to spine-tingling mountains with breathtaking immediacy. Reading *Skiing* is almost as much fun as being there." Estab. 1948. Circ. 400,000. Byline given. Offers 40% kill fee.

Nonfiction Buys 10-15 feature (1,500-2,000 words) and 12-24 short (100-500 words) mss/year. Query. **Pays $1,000-2,500/feature; $100-500/short piece.**

Columns/Departments Buys 2-3 mss/year. Query. **Pays $150-1,000.**

The online magazine carries original content not found in the print edition. Contact: Doug Sabonosh, online managing editor.

Tips "Consider less obvious subjects: smaller ski areas, specific local ski cultures, unknown aspects of popular resorts. Be expressive, not merely descriptive. We want readers to feel the adventure in your writing—to tingle with the excitement of skiing steep powder, of meeting intriguing people, of reaching new goals or achieving dramatic new insights. We want readers to have fun, to see the humor in and the lighter side of skiing and their fellow skiers."

$ $ SNOW GOER

Ehlert Publishing Group, 6420 Sycamore Lane, Maple Grove MN 55369. Fax: (763)383-4499. E-mail: terickson@ehlertpublishing.com. Web site: www.snowmobilenews.com. **Contact:** Tim Erickson, editor. **5% freelance written.** Magazine published 7 times/year covering snowmobiling. "*Snow Goer* is a hard-hitting, tell-it-like-it-is magazine designed for the ultra-active snowmobile enthusiast. It is fun, exciting, innovative, and on the cutting edge of technology and trends." Estab. 1967. Circ. 64,000. Pays on publication. Publishes ms an average of 5 months after acceptance. Byline given. Buys first, one-time rights. Editorial lead time 5 months. Submit seasonal material 6 months in advance. Accepts queries by mail, e-mail, fax. Accepts simultaneous submissions. Responds in 3 months to queries. Sample copy for 8×10 SAE and 4 first-class stamps.

Nonfiction General interest, how-to, interview/profile, new product, personal experience, photo feature, technical, travel. **Buys 6 mss/year.** Query. Length: 500-4,000 words. **Pays $50-500.** Sometimes pays expenses of writers on assignment.

Photos State availability with submission. Reviews contact sheets, prints. Buys one-time rights or all rights. Negotiates payment individually. Captions, identification of subjects required.

N $ $ SNOW WEEK

The Snowmobile Racing Authority, Ehlert Publishing Group, 6420 Sycamore Lane N., Maple Grove MN 55369. (763)383-4400. Fax: (763)383-4499. E-mail: lkeillor@ehlertpublishing.com. Web site: www.snowweek.com. Associate Editors: Andy Swanson. **Contact:** Lynn Keillor, editor. **15% freelance written.** Magazine published 4 times/year covering snowmobile racing. "We cover snowmobile racing from coast to coast for hard core fans. We get in the pits, inside the race trailers and pepper our race coverage with behind the scenes details." Estab. 1973. Circ. 26,000. Pays on publication. Publishes ms an average of 2 months after acceptance. Byline given. Buys first, one-time, simultaneous rights. Editorial lead time 2 weeks. Accepts queries by mail, e-mail, fax, phone. Sample copy for 8×11 SAE and 4 first-class stamps.

Nonfiction Technical, feature, race coverage. **Buys 20 mss/year.** Query. Length: 500-4,000 words. **Pays 50-450.** Sometimes pays expenses of writers on assignment.

Photos State availability with submission. Reviews contact sheets, prints. Buys one-time rights. Offers no additional payment for photos accepted with ms. Captions, identification of subjects required.

Tips "Writers should also be fans of the sport, know how to write and photograph races."

⊘ SNOWBOARDER

Primedia Enthusiast Group, P.O. Box 1028, Dana Point CA 92629-5028. (949)496-5922. Fax: (949)496-7849. E-mail: pat.bridges@primedia.com. Web site: www.snowboardermag.com. Editor: Pat Bridges. Magazine published 8 times/year edited primarily for male youths who are snowboard enthusiasts. Circ. 137,800. Editorial lead time 3 months.

- Query before submitting.

$ $ SNOWEST MAGAZINE

Harris Publishing, 360 B St., Idaho Falls ID 83402. (208)524-7000. Fax: (208)522-5241. E-mail: lindstrm@snowest.com. Web site: snowest.com. Publisher: Steve Janes. **Contact:** Lane Lindstrom, editor. **10-25% freelance written.** Monthly magazine. "*SnoWest* covers the sport of snowmobiling, products, and personalities in the western states. This includes mountain riding, deep powder, and trail riding, as well as destination pieces, tech tips, and new model reviews." Estab. 1972. Circ. 150,000. Pays on publication. Publishes ms an average of 2 months after acceptance. Byline given. Buys first North American serial rights. Editorial lead time 6 months. Submit seasonal material 3 months in advance. Sample copy and writer's guidelines free.

Nonfiction How-to (fix a snowmobile, make it high performance), new product, technical, travel. **Buys 3-5 mss/year.** Query with published clips. Length: 500-1,500 words. **Pays $150-300.**

Photos Send photos with submission. Buys one-time rights. Negotiates payment individually. Captions, identification of subjects required.

⊘ TRANSWORLD SNOWBOARDING

Transworld Media, 353 Airport Rd., Oceanside CA 92054. (760)722-7777. Fax: (760)722-0653. Web site: www.transworldsnowboarding.com. Editor: Kurt Hoy. Magazine published 8 times/year edited for the snowboarding enthusiast. Circ. 250,000. Editorial lead time 3 months.

- Query before submitting.

WATER SPORTS

N ⊘ BOATING

Hachette Filipacchi Media U.S., Inc., 1633 Broadway, 41st Floor, New York NY 10019. (212)767-6041. Fax: (212)767-4831. Web site: www.boatingmag.com. Monthly magazine dedicated to manufactures, distributors and consumers involved in the boating industry. Circ. 201,171. Editorial lead time 3 months.

- Query before submitting.

$ DIVER

241 E. 1st St., North Vancouver BC V7L 1B4 Canada. (604)948-9337. Fax: (604)948-9985. E-mail: divermag@axion.net. Web site: www.divermag.com. Magazine published 8 times/year emphasizing scuba diving, ocean science, and technology for a well-educated, outdoor-oriented readership. Circ. 7,000. Accepts queries by mail, e-mail.

Nonfiction "Well-written and illustrated Canadian and North American regional dive destination articles. Most travel articles are committed up to a year in advance, and there is limited scope for new material." Reading period for unsolicited articles July through August. Length: 500-1,000 words. **Pays $2.50/column inch.**

Photos Reviews 5×7 prints, JPEG/TIFF files (300 dpi), slides, maps, drawings. Captions, identification of subjects required.

$ $ PADDLER MAGAZINE

World's No. 1 Canoeing, Kayaking and Rafting Magazine, Paddlesport Publishing, 12040 98th Ave. NE, Suite 205, Kirkland WA 98034. E-mail: mike@paddlermagazine.com. Web site: www.paddlermagazine.com. **Contact:** Mike Kord, editor. **70% freelance written.** Bimonthly magazine covering paddle sports. "*Paddler* magazine is written by and for those knowledgeable about river running, flatwater canoeing and sea kayaking. Our core audience is the intermediate to advanced paddler, yet we strive to cover the entire range from beginners to experts. Our editorial coverage is divided between whitewater rafting, whitewater kayaking, canoeing and sea kayaking. We strive for balance between the Eastern and Western U.S. paddling scenes and regularly cover international expeditions. We also try to integrate the Canadian paddling community into each publication." Estab. 1991. Circ. 40,000. Pays on publication. Publishes ms an average of 6 months after acceptance. Byline given. Buys first North American serial, one-time electronic rights rights. Editorial lead time 3 months. Submit seasonal material 6 months in advance. Accepts queries by mail, e-mail. Responds in 6 months to queries. Sample copy for $3 with 8 ½×11 SASE. Writer's guidelines online.

O→ Break in through "The Hotline section at the front of the magazine."

Nonfiction Book excerpts, essays, general interest, historical/nostalgic, how-to, humor, inspirational, interview/

profile, new product, opinion, personal experience, photo feature, technical, travel (must be paddlesport related). **Buys 75 mss/year.** Query. Length: 100-3,000 words. **Pays 10-25¢/word (more for established writers) for assigned articles; 10-20¢/word for unsolicited articles.** Sometimes pays expenses of writers on assignment.
Photos Submissions should include photos or other art. State availability with submission. Reviews contact sheets, negatives, transparencies. Buys one-time rights. Offers $25-200/photo.
Columns/Departments Hotline (timely news and exciting developments relating to the paddling community. Stories should be lively and newsworthy), 150-750 words; Paddle People (unique people involved in the sport and industry leaders), 600-800 words; Destinations (informs paddlers of unique places to paddle—we often follow regional themes and cover all paddling disciplines); submissions should include map and photo, 800 words. Marketplace (gear reviews, gadgets and new products, and is about equipment paddlers use, from boats and paddles to collapsible chairs, bivy sacks and other accessories), 250-800 words. Paddle Tales (short, humorous anecdotes), 75-300 words. Skills (a "How-to" forum for experts to share tricks of the trade, from playboating techniques to cooking in the backcountry), 250-1,000 words. Query. **Pays 20-25¢/word.**
Tips "We prefer queries, but will look at manuscripts on speculation. No phone queries please. Be familiar with the magazine and offer us unique, exciting ideas. Most positive responses to queries are on spec, but we will occasionally make assignments."

SAILING

Sailing Publications CC, P.O. Box 1849, Westville 3630 South Africa. (27)(31)709-6087. Fax: (27)(31)709-6143. E-mail: editor@sailing.co.za. Web site: www.sailingmag.co.za. **Contact:** Richard Crockett, editor. Monthly magazine. Estab. 1984. Circ. 5,000. Pays on publication. Byline given.

$ SURFER MAGAZINE

Primedia Enthusiast Group, P.O. Box 1028, Dana Point CA 92629-5028. (949)661-5150. E-mail: chris.mauro@primedia.com. Web site: www.surfermag.com. Editor: Chris Mauro. Monthly magazine edited for the avid surfers and those who follow the beach, wave riding scene. Circ. 118,570. Editorial lead time 10 weeks.

- Query before submitting.

SURFING

Primedia Enthusiast Group, 950 Calle Amanecer, Suite C, San Clemente CA 93673. (949)492-7873. E-mail: matt.walker@primedia.com. Web site: www.surfingthemag.com. Editor: Evan Slater. **Contact:** Matt Walker, senior editor. Monthly magazine covering surfing. Edited for the active surfing enthusiast who enjoys the beach lifestyle. Estab. 1964. Circ. 108,035. Sample copy for $3.99.

- Query before submitting.

$ $ SWIMMING WORLD MAGAZINE

Sports Publications International, P.O. Box 20337, Sedona AZ 86341. (928)284-4005. Fax: (928)284-2477. E-mail: editorial@swimmingworldmagazine.com. Web site: www.swimmingworldmagazine.com. Publisher: Brent Rutemiller. Senior Editor: Bob Ingram. **30% freelance written.** Bimonthly magazine about competitive swimming. Readers are fitness-oriented adults from varied social and professional backgrounds who share swimming as part of their lifestyle. Submit 250-word synopsis of your article. Estab. 1960. Circ. 50,000. Pays on publication. Byline given. Buys all rights. Editorial lead time 2 months. Submit seasonal material 3 months in advance. Accepts queries by mail, e-mail, fax. Accepts simultaneous submissions. Responds in 1 month to queries. Writer's guidelines online.

- Included in this publication are *Swimming Technique*, *Swim Magazine*, and *Junior Swimmer*.

Nonfiction "Articles need to be informative as well as interesting. In addition to fitness and health articles, we are interested in exploring fascinating topics dealing with swimming for the adult reader." Book excerpts, essays, exposé, general interest, historical/nostalgic, how-to (training plans and techniques), humor, inspirational, interview/profile (people associated with fitness and competitive swimming), new product (articles describing new products for fitness and competitive training), personal experience, photo feature, technical, travel, general health. **Buys 30 mss/year.** Query with or without published clips. Length: 250-2,500 words. **Pays $75-400.**
Photos Send photos with submission. Reviews high-resolution digital images. Negotiates payment individually. Captions, identification of subjects, model releases required.

TRANSWORLD SURF

Transworld Media (a division of Time 4 Media), 353 Airport Rd., Oceanside CA 92054. (760)722-7777. Fax: (760)722-0653. Web site: www.transworldsurf.com. Editor-in-Chief: Joel Patterson. Monthly magazine designed to promote the growth of the sport of surfing. Circ. 85,000.

WAKE BOARDING MAGAZINE

World Publications, Inc., P.O. Box 2456, Winter Park FL 32790. (407)571-4672. E-mail: editor@wakeboardingmag.com. Web site: www.wakeboardingmag.com. Managing Editor: Luke Woodling. Photo Editor: Bill Doster. **Contact:** Matt Hickman, editor (matt.hickman@worldpub.net). **10% freelance written.** Magazine published 9 times/year covering wakeboarding. "*Wake Boarding Magazine* is the leading publication for wakeboarding in the world. Articles must focus on good riding, first and foremost, then good fun and good times. Covers competition, travel, instruction, personalities, and humor." Estab. 1994. Circ. 60,000. Pays on publication. Publishes ms an average of 3 months after acceptance. Byline given. Buys all rights. Editorial lead time 4 months. Submit seasonal material 4 months in advance. Accepts queries by mail, e-mail. Accepts simultaneous submissions. Responds in 1 week to queries; 1 month to mss. Sample copy and writer's guidelines free.

Nonfiction General interest, how-to (wakeboarding instruction), humor, interview/profile, new product, photo feature, travel. "No Weekend Wallys having fun on the lake. Serious riders only. Nothing to do with waterskiing or barefooting." Send complete ms. Length: 1,000-2,500 words.

Photos Send photos with submission. Reviews transparencies, slides. Buys all rights. Negotiates payment individually. Captions, identification of subjects required.

Tips "Contact us first before presuming article is worthy. What may be cool to you might not fit our readership. Remember, *WBM*'s readership is made up of a lot of teenagers, so buck authority every chance you get."

$ THE WATER SKIER

USA Water Ski, 1251 Holy Cow Rd., Polk City FL 33868-8200. (863)324-4341. Fax: (863)325-8259. E-mail: satkinson@usawaterski.org. Web site: www.usawaterski.org. Scott Atkinson, editor. **10-20% freelance written.** Magazine published 9 times/year. "*The Water Skier* is the membership magazine of USA Water Ski, the national governing body for organized water skiing in the United States. The magazine has a controlled circulation and is available only to USA Water Ski's membership, which is made up of 20,000 active competitive water skiers and 10,000 members who are supporting the sport. These supporting members may participate in the sport but they don't compete. The editorial content of the magazine features distinctive and informative writing about the sport of water skiing only." Estab. 1951. Circ. 30,000. Byline given. Offers 30% kill fee. Editorial lead time 4 months. Submit seasonal material 6 months in advance. Responds in 2 weeks to queries. Sample copy for $3.50. Writer's guidelines for #10 SASE.

Most open to material for feature articles (query editor with your idea).

Nonfiction Historical/nostalgic (has to pertain to water skiing), interview/profile (call for assignment), new product (boating and water ski equipment), travel (water ski vacation destinations). **Buys 10-15 mss/year.** Query. Length: 1,500-3,000 words. **Pays $100-150.**

Reprints Send photocopy. Payment negotiable.

Photos State availability with submission. Reviews contact sheets. Buys all rights. Negotiates payment individually. Captions, identification of subjects required.

Columns/Departments Query. **Pays $50-100.**

The online magazine carries original content not found in the print edition. Contact: Scott Atkinson, online editor.

Tips "Contact the editor through a query letter (please, no phone calls) with an idea. Avoid instruction, these articles are written by professionals. Concentrate on articles about the people of the sport. We are always looking for interesting stories about people in the sport. Also, short news features which will make a reader say to himself, 'Hey, I didn't know that.' Keep in mind that the publication is highly specialized about the sport of water skiing."

WATERSKI MAGAZINE

World Publications, 460 N. Orlando Ave., Suite 200, Winter Park FL 32703. (407)628-4802. E-mail: editor@waterskimag.com. Web site: www.waterskimag.com. Managing Editor: Luke Woodling. Associate Editor: Adrianne Brice. Photo Editor: Bill Doster. **Contact:** Todd Ristorcelli, editor (todd.ristorcelli@worldpub.net). **25% freelance written.** Magazine published 9 times/year for water skiing and related watersports. "*WaterSki* instructs, advises, enlightens, informs and creates an open forum for skiers around the world. It provides definitive information on instruction, products, people and travel destinations." Estab. 1978. Circ. 105,000. **Pays on acceptance.** Publishes ms an average of 4 months after acceptance. Buys first North American serial, second serial (reprint) rights. Editorial lead time 2 months. Submit seasonal material 2 months in advance. Responds in 1 month to queries; 2 months to mss. Sample copy for $8\frac{1}{2} \times 11$ SAE and 4 first-class stamps. Writer's guidelines for #10 SASE.

Nonfiction General interest, historical/nostalgic, how-to (water ski instruction boating-related), interview/profile, new product, photo feature, technical, travel. Nothing unrelated to water skiing. **Buys 10 mss/year.** Query with published clips. Length: 800-2,000 words. **Pays negotiable amount.** Sometimes pays expenses of writers on assignment.

Photos Send photos with submission. Reviews transparencies, slides. Buys one-time rights on color, all rights on b&w. Negotiates payment individually. Identification of subjects required.
Columns/Departments Shortline (interesting news of the sport), 300 words. Query with published clips.
Fillers Anecdotes, facts, gags to be illustrated by cartoonist, newsbreaks, short humor. Length: 200-500 words.
Tips "Writers should have some interest in the sport and understand its people, products, and lifestyle. The features sections offer the most opportunity for freelancers. One requirement: It must have a positive, strong water skiing slant, whether it be personality, human interest, or travel."

TEEN & YOUNG ADULT

BOP

Laufer Media, Inc., 6430 Sunset Blvd., Suite 700, Hollywood CA 90028. (323)462-4267. Fax: (323)462-4341. Web site: www.bopmag.com. Editor: Leesa Coble. Monthly magazine. Top teen entertainment magazine covers today's hottest stars. Features, news, gossip, quizzes. Does not want poetry, fiction or real-person stories. Circ. 200,000. Sample copy not available.

$ $ BREAKAWAY MAGAZINE

Focus on the Family, 8605 Explorer Dr., Colorado Springs CO 80920. (719)531-3400. Web site: www.breakawaymag.com. **Contact:** Michael Ross, editor. **25% freelance written.** Monthly magazine covering extreme sports, Christian music artists, and new technology relevant to teen boys. "This fast-paced, 4-color publication is designed to creatively teach, entertain, inspire, and challenge the emerging teenager. It also seeks to strengthen a boy's self-esteem, provide role models, guide a healthy awakening to girls, make the Bible relevant, and deepen their love for family, friends, church, and Jesus Christ." Estab. 1990. Circ. 96,000. **Pays on acceptance.** Publishes ms an average of 5-12 months after acceptance. Byline given. Offers $25 kill fee. Buys first North American serial, first, one-time, electronic rights. Editorial lead time 5 months. Submit seasonal material 8 months in advance. Accepts queries by mail. Responds in 2-3 months to queries; 2-3 months to mss. Sample copy for $1.50 and 9×12 SASE with 3 first-class stamps. Writer's guidelines for #10 SASE.
Nonfiction Inspirational, interview/profile, personal experience. **Buys up to 6 mss/year.** Send complete ms. Length: 700-2,000 words. **Pays 12-15¢/word.**
Columns/Departments Epic Truth (spiritual/Biblical application devotional for teen guys), 800 words; Weird, Wild, WOW! (technology, culture, science), 200-400 words. **Buys 2-3 mss/year.** Send complete ms. **Pays 12-15¢/word.**
Fiction Adventure, humorous, religious, suspense. "Avoid Christian jargon, clichés, preaching, and other dialogue that isn't realistic or that interrupts the flow of the story." **Buys 3-4 mss/year.** Send complete ms. Length: 600-2,000 words. **Pays 15-20¢/word.**
Tips "Some of our readers get spiritual nurture at home and at church; many don't. To reach both groups, the articles must be written in ways that are compelling, bright, out of the ordinary. Nearly every adult in a boy's life is an authority figure. We would like you, through the magazine, to be seen as a friend! We also want *Breakaway* to be a magazine any pre-Christian teen could pick up and understand without first learning 'Christianese.' Stories should spiritually challenge, yet be spiritually inviting."

$ $ CICADA MAGAZINE

Cricket Magazine Group, 140 S. Dearborn St., Suite 1450, Chicago IL 60603. (312)701-1720. Fax: (312)701-1728. Web site: www.cricketmag.com. Editor-in-Chief: Marianne Carus. Executive Editor: Deborah Vetter. Editorial Assistant: Pete Coco. Art Director: John Sandford. **Contact:** Submissions Editor. **80% freelance written.** Bimonthly literary magazine for ages 14 and up. Publishes original short stories, poems, and first-person essays written for teens and young adults. Estab. 1998. Circ. 17,000. Pays on publication. Byline given. Accepts previously published material. Accepts simultaneous submissions. Responds in 3 months to mss. Writer's guidelines online.
Nonfiction Looking for first-person experiences that are relevant and interesting to teenagers. Essays, personal experience, book reviews. Submit complete ms, SASE. Length: 5,000 words maximum; 300-500 words/book reviews. **Pays up to 25¢/word.**
Reprints Send ms. Payment varies.
Photos Send photocopies/tearsheets of artwork.
Fiction The main protagonist should be at least 14 and preferably older. Stories should have a genuine teen sensibility and be aimed at readers in high school or college. Adventure, fantasy, historical, humorous, mainstream, novel excerpts, romance, science fiction, contemporary, realistic, novellas (1/issue). Length: 5,000 words maximum (up to 15,000 words/novellas). **Pays up to 25¢/word.**
Poetry Free verse, light verse, traditional, serious, humorous, rhyming. Length: 25 lines maximum. **Pays up to $3/line.**

$ COLLEGEBOUND TEEN MAGAZINE

The College Bound Network, 1200 South Ave., Suite 202, Staten Island NY 10314. (718)761-4800. Fax: (718)761-3300. E-mail: editorial@collegebound.net. Web site: www.collegeboundteen.com. Editor-in-Chief: Gina LaGuardia. **Contact:** Dawn Papandrea, managing editor. **70% freelance written.** Monthly magazine. "*CollegeBound Teen Magazine* is designed to provide high school students with an inside look at all aspects of college life academics and socials. College students from around the country (and those young at heart!) are welcome to serve as correspondents to provide our teen readership with real-life accounts and cutting-edge, expert advice on the college admissions process and beyond." Estab. 1987. Circ. 100,000 (regional issues). Pays 6 weeks upon publication. Publishes ms an average of 3-4 months after acceptance. Byline given. Buys first North American serial, first, electronic rights. Editorial lead time 4 months. Submit seasonal material 4 months in advance. Accepts queries by mail, e-mail. Responds in 6 weeks to queries; 2 months to mss. Sample copy for 9×12 SAE and $3.85 postage. Writer's guidelines online.

Nonfiction How-to (apply for college, prepare for the interview, etc.), unique teen stories related to college admission and college life. No fillers, poetry, or fiction. **Buys 100 mss/year.** Query with published clips. Length: 650-1,500 words. **Pays $50-100, plus 2 issues of magazine.**

Photos Gina LaGuardia, editor-in-chief. State availability with submission. Buys one-time rights. Offers no additional payment for photos accepted with ms. Captions, identification of subjects required.

Columns/Departments Buys 15 mss/year. Query with published clips. **Pays $40-70.**

Tips "We're looking for well-researched, well-reported articles packed with real-life student anecdotes and expert insight on everything from dealing with dorm life, choosing the right college, and joining a fraternity or sorority, to college dating, cool campus happenings, scholarship scoring strategies, and other college issues."

$ $ GUIDEPOSTS SWEET 16

1050 Broadway, Suite 6, Chesterton IN 46304. (219)929-4429. Fax: (219)926-3839. E-mail: writers@sweet16mag.com. Web site: www.sweet16mag.com. Editor-in-Chief: Mary Lou Carney. **Contact:** Betsy Kohn, managing editor. **90% freelance written.** Bimonthly magazine serving as an inspiration for teens. "*Sweet 16* is a general interest magazine for teenage girls (ages 11-17). We are an inspirational publication that offers true, first-person stories about real teens. Our watchwords are 'wholesome,' 'current,' 'fun,' and 'inspiring.' We also publish shorter pieces on fashion, beauty, celebrity, boys, embarrassing moments, and advice columns." Estab. 1998. Circ. 145,000. **Pays on acceptance.** Byline sometimes given. Offers 25% kill fee. Buys all rights. Editorial lead time 6 months. Submit seasonal material 6 months in advance. Accepts queries by mail, e-mail. Accepts simultaneous submissions. Responds in 6 weeks to queries; 6 weeks to mss. Sample copy for $4.50. Writer's guidelines online.

Nonfiction Nothing written from an adult point of view. How-to, humor, inspirational, interview/profile, personal experience. **Buys 80 mss/year.** Query. Length: 200-1,500 words. **Pays $300-500 for assigned articles; $100-300 for unsolicited articles.** Pays expenses of writers on assignment.

Photos State availability with submission. Buys one-time rights. Negotiates payment individually. Identification of subjects required.

Columns/Departments Quiz (teen-related topics/teen language), 500-600 words; Positive Thinker (first-person stories of teen who've overcome something remarkable and kept a positive outlook), 300 words; Mysterious Moments (first-person "strange-but-true" stories), 250 words; Too Good to be True (profile of a cute wholesome teen guy who has more than looks/has done something very cool/has overcome something extraordinary), 400 words. **Buys 40 mss/year.** Query with published clips. **Pays $175-400.**

Tips "We are eagerly looking for a number of things: teen profiles, quizzes, DIYs. Most of all, though, we are about TRUE STORIES in the *Guideposts* tradition. Teens in dangerous, inspiring, miraculous situations. These first-person (ghostwritten) true narratives are the backbone of *Sweet 16*—and what sets us apart from other publications."

$ GUMBO MAGAZINE

The National Magazine Written by Teens for Teens, Strive Media Institute, 1818 N. Dr. Martin Luther King Dr., Milwaukee WI 53212. (414)374-3511. Fax: (414)374-3512. E-mail: info@mygumbo.com. Web site: www.mygumbo.com. Editor-in-Chief: Robyn Lockett. **Contact:** Carrie Trousil, managing editor. **25% freelance written.** Bimonthly magazine covering teen issues (arts, entertainment, social issues, etc.). "All articles must be written by teens (13-19 year-olds) and for teens. Tone is modern, hip, and urban. No adults may write for magazine." Estab. 1998. Circ. 25,000. Pays on publication. Publishes ms an average of 6 months after acceptance. Byline given. Buys one-time rights. Editorial lead time 6 months. Submit seasonal material 6 months in advance. Accepts queries by mail, e-mail, fax. Accepts previously published material. Accepts simultaneous submissions. Responds in 2 weeks to queries; 2 months to mss. Sample copy for free. Writer's guidelines free.

Nonfiction General interest, humor, inspirational, interview/profile, opinion, personal experience, photo feature, technical, book & CD reviews. Does not want unsolicited articles or fiction other than poetry. All news stories require approval from Managing Editor prior to submission. **Buys 50-70 mss/year.** Query. Length: 500-1,000 words. **Pays $25.** Sometimes pays expenses of writers on assignment.

Photos State availability of or send photos with submission. Reviews prints, GIF/JPEG files. Buys one-time rights. Offers no additional payment for photos accepted with ms. Captions, identification of subjects required.

Poetry Any poetry is acceptable provided author is 13-19 years of age. Avant-garde, free verse, haiku, light verse, traditional. Submit maximum 3 poems. Length: 5-50 lines.

Tips "Writers need to apply online or mail in an application from an issue of the magazine."

$ $ ⊘ IGNITE YOUR FAITH

(formerly *Campus Life*), Christianity Today, Intl., 465 Gundersen Dr., Carol Stream IL 60188. (630)260-6200. Fax: (630)480-2004. E-mail: iyf@igniteyourfaith.com. Web site: www.igniteyourfaith.com. **Contact:** Chris Lutes, editor. **35% freelance written.** Bimonthly magazine published 9 times/year for the Christian life as it relates to today's teen. "*Ignite Your Faith* is a magazine for high-school teenagers. Our editorial slant is not overtly religious. The indirect style is intended to create a safety zone with our readers and to reflect our philosophy that God is interested in all of life. Therefore, we publish 'message stories' side by side with general interest, humor, etc. We are also looking for stories that help high school students consider a Christian college education." Estab. 1942. Circ. 100,000. **Pays on acceptance.** Publishes ms an average of 5 months after acceptance. Byline given. Offers 50% kill fee. Buys first, one-time rights. Editorial lead time 4 months. Responds in 6 weeks to queries. Sample copy for $3 and $9\frac{1}{2} \times 11$ SAE with 3 first-class stamps. Writer's guidelines online.

- No unsolicited mss.

Nonfiction Humor, personal experience, photo feature. **Buys 15-20 mss/year.** Query with published clips. Length: 750-1,500 words. **Pays 15-20¢/word minimum.**

Reprints Send tearsheet, photocopy or typed ms with rights for sale noted and information about when and where the material previously appeared. Pays $50.

Fiction Buys 1-5 mss/year. Query. Length: 1,000-1,500 words. **Pays 20-25¢/word, and 2 contributor's copies.**

Tips "The best way to break in to *Ignite Your Faith* is through writing first-person or as-told-to first-person stories. We want stories that capture a teen's everyday 'life lesson' experience. A first-person story must be highly descriptive and incorporate fictional technique. While avoiding simplistic religious answers, the story should demonstrate that Christian values or beliefs brought about a change in the young person's life. But query first with theme information telling the way this story would work for our audience."

$ INSIGHT

Because Life Is Full of Decisions, The Review and Herald Publishing Association, 55 W. Oak Ridge Dr., Hagerstown MD 21740. E-mail: insight@rhpa.org. Web site: www.insightmagazine.org. **Contact:** Dwain Neilson Esmond, editor. **80% freelance written.** Weekly magazine covering spiritual life of teenagers. "*Insight* publishes true dramatic stories, interviews, and community and mission service features that relate directly to the lives of Christian teenagers, particularly those with a Seventh-day Adventist background." Estab. 1970. Circ. 20,000. Pays on publication. Publishes ms an average of 4 months after acceptance. Byline given. Buys first, second serial (reprint) rights. Editorial lead time 6 months. Submit seasonal material 6 months in advance. Accepts queries by mail, e-mail, fax. Responds in 1 month to mss. Sample copy for $2 and #10 SASE. Writer's guidelines online.

- " 'Big Deal' appears in *Insight* often, covering a topic of importance to teens. Each feature contains: An opening story involving real teens (can be written in first-person), "Scripture Picture" (a sidebar that discusses what the Bible says about the topic) and another sidebar (optional) that adds more perspective and help.

Nonfiction How-to (teen relationships and experiences), humor, interview/profile, personal experience, photo feature, religious. **Buys 120 mss/year.** Send complete ms. Length: 500-2,000 words. **Pays $25-150 for assigned articles; $25-125 for unsolicited articles.**

Reprints Send ms with rights for sale noted and information about when and where the material previously appeared. Pays $50.

Photos State availability with submission. Reviews contact sheets, negatives, transparencies, prints. Buys one-time rights. Negotiates payment individually. Model releases required.

Columns/Departments Send complete ms. **Pays $25-125.**

Tips "Skim 2 months of *Insight*. Write about your teen experiences. Use informed, contemporary style and vocabulary. Follow Jesus' life and example."

$ $ LISTEN MAGAZINE

Celebrating Positive Choices, The Health Connection, 55 W. Oak Ridge Dr., Hagerstown MD 21740. (301)393-4010. E-mail: editor@listenmagazine.org. Web site: www.listenmagazine.org. **Contact:** Celeste Perrino-Walker, editor. **80% freelance written.** Monthly magazine specializing in tobacco, drug, and alcohol prevention, presenting positive alternatives to various tobacco, drug, and alcohol dependencies. "*Listen* is used in many high school classes and by professionals: medical personnel, counselors, law enforcement officers, educators, youth workers, etc. *Listen* publishes true-to-life stories about giving teens choices about real-life situations and moral issues in a secular way." Circ. 20,000. Publishes ms an average of 6 months after acceptance. Byline given. Pays on acceptance for first rights for use in *Listen*, reprints, and associated material. Accepts queries by mail, e-mail. Accepts previously published material. Accepts simultaneous submissions. Responds in 2 months to queries. Sample copy for $2 and 9×12 SASE. Writer's guidelines online.

O━ Break in with true stories or an article on a new trend in drug use.

Nonfiction Seeks articles on positive, practical ways in which teens can cope with everyday conflicts and develop self-esteem. Subjects may or may not have a direct connection to drug use. Especially interested in youth-slanted articles or personality interviews encouraging nonalcoholic and nondrug ways of life and showing positive alternatives. Also interested in good activity articles of interest to teens; sports or hobbies to interest a teen. Teenage point of view is essential. **Pays $150 for Personalities (1,000 words); $125 for hobby/sport/activity (1,000 words); $100 for factuals (800 words); $80 for true stories (800 words); $50 for quizzes/shorts (500 words); and 3 contributor's copies (additional copies $2). Buys 30-50 unsolicited mss/year.** Query.

Reprints Send photocopy of article or typed ms with rights for sale noted and information about when and where the material previously appeared. Pays their regular rates.

Photos Color photos preferred, but b&w acceptable. Purchased with accompanying ms. Captions required.

Tips "In query, briefly summarize article idea and logic of why you feel it's good. Make sure you've read the magazine to understand our approach. Yearly theme lists available on our Web site."

$ $ LIVE

A Weekly Journal of Practical Christian Living, Gospel Publishing House, 1445 N. Boonville Ave., Springfield MO 65802-1894. (417)862-2781. Fax: (417)862-6059. E-mail: rl-live@gph.org. Web site: www.radiantlife.org. **Contact:** Richard Bennett, LIVE editor. **100% freelance written.** Weekly magazine for weekly distribution covering practical Christian living. "*LIVE* is a take-home paper distributed weekly in young adult and adult Sunday school classes. We seek to encourage Christians in living for God through fiction and true stories which apply Biblical principles to everyday problems." Estab. 1928. Circ. 50,000. **Pays on acceptance.** Publishes ms an average of 18 months after acceptance. Byline given. Buys first, second serial (reprint) rights. Editorial lead time 12 months. Submit seasonal material 18 months in advance. Accepts queries by mail, e-mail. Accepts simultaneous submissions. Responds in 2 weeks to queries; 6 weeks to mss. Sample copy for #10 SASE. Writer's guidelines for #10 SASE.

O━ Break in with "true stories that demonstrate how the principles in the Bible work in everyday circumstances as well as crises."

Nonfiction Inspirational, religious. No preachy articles or stories that refer to religious myths (e.g., Santa Claus, Easter Bunny, etc.). **Buys 50-100 mss/year.** Send complete ms. Length: 400-1,200 words. **Pays 7-10¢/word.**

Reprints Send tearsheet, photocopy or typed ms with rights for sale noted and information about when and where the material previously appeared. Pays 7¢/word.

Photos Send photos with submission. Reviews 35mm transparencies and 3×4 prints or larger. Buys one-time rights. Offers $35-60/photo. Identification of subjects required.

Fiction Paul W. Smith, editor. Religious, inspirational, prose poem. No preachy fiction, fiction about Bible characters, or stories that refer to religious myths (e.g., Santa Claus, Easter Bunny, etc.). No science or Bible fiction. No controversial stories about such subjects as feminism, war or capital punishment. **Buys 20-50 mss/year.** Send complete ms. Length: 800-1,200 words. **Pays 7-10¢/word.**

Poetry Free verse, haiku, light verse, traditional. **Buys 15-24 poems/year.** Submit maximum 3 poems. Length: 12-25 lines. **Pays $35-60.**

Fillers Anecdotes, short humor. **Buys 12-36/year.** Length: 300-600 words. **Pays 7-10¢/word.**

Tips "Don't moralize or be preachy. Provide human interest articles with Biblical life application. Stories should consist of action, not just thought-life; interaction, not just insight. Heroes and heroines should rise above failures, take risks for God, prove that scriptural principles meet their needs. Conflict and suspense should increase to a climax! Avoid pious conclusions. Characters should be interesting, believable, and realistic. Avoid stereotypes. Characters should be active, not just pawns to move the plot along. They should confront conflict and change in believable ways. Describe the character's looks and reveal his personality through his actions to such an extent that the reader feels he has met that person. Readers should care about the character enough to finish the story. Feature racial, ethnic, and regional characters in rural and urban settings."

$ $ THE NEW ERA

50 E. North Temple, Salt Lake City UT 84150. (801)240-2951. Fax: (801)240-2270. E-mail: newera@ldschurch.org. Web site: www.lds.org. **Contact:** Richard M. Romney, managing editor. **20% freelance written.** Monthly

magazine for young people (ages 12-18) of the Church of Jesus Christ of Latter-day Saints (Mormon), their church leaders and teachers. Estab. 1971. Circ. 230,000. **Pays on acceptance.** Publishes ms an average of 1 year after acceptance. Byline given. Buys all rights. Submit seasonal material 1 year in advance. Accepts queries by mail, e-mail, fax. Responds in 2 months to queries. Sample copy for $1.50. Writer's guidelines online.

Nonfiction Material that shows how the Church of Jesus Christ of Latter-day Saints is relevant in the lives of young people today. Must capture the excitement of being a young Latter-day Saint. Special interest in the experiences of young Mormons in other countries. No general library research or formula pieces without the *New Era* slant and feel. How-to, humor, inspirational, interview/profile, personal experience, informational. Query. Length: 150-1,200 words. **Pays 3-12¢/word.** Pays expenses of writers on assignment.

Photos Uses b&w photos and transparencies with manuscripts. Individual photos used for *Photo of the Month*. Payment depends on use, $10-125 per photo.

Columns/Departments What's Up? (news of young Mormons around the world); How I Know; Scripture Lifeline. **Pays 3-12¢/word.**

Poetry Must relate to editorial viewpoint. Free verse, light verse, traditional, blank verse, all other forms. **Pays 25¢/line minimum.**

Tips "The writer must be able to write from a Mormon point of view. We're especially looking for stories about successful family relationships and personal growth. Well-written, personal experiences are always in demand."

SCHOLASTIC ACTION

Scholastic, Inc., 557 Broadway, New York NY 10012-3902. (212)343-6100. Fax: (212)343-6945. E-mail: actionmag@scholastic.com. Web site: www.scholastic.com. Published 14 times/year written for teenagers with profiles of TV and movie celebrities and famous athletes. It also includes true teen nonfiction articles and vocabulary activities. Circ. 200,000. Editorial lead time 2 months.

SCHOLASTIC ART

Scholastic, Inc., 557 Broadway, New York NY 10012-3902. (212)343-6100. Fax: (212)343-6945. E-mail: art@scholastic.com. Web site: www.scholastic.com. Published 6 times/year. Edited for use by young students and their teachers. Includes student artist profiles, lessons on classic and contemporary artists, and a critics corner. Circ. 261,975.

SCHOLASTIC CHOICES

Scholatic, Inc., 557 Broadway, New York NY 10012-3902. (212)343-6100. Fax: (212)343-6945. E-mail: choicesmag@scholastic.com. Web site: www.scholastic.com. Magazine published 6 times/year for 6th-12th graders focusing on personal development, family, child care, nutrition, consumer life and practical living skills (quizzes, puzzles, Q&As). Also includes lively articles featuring celebrities and teen role models. Circ. 200,000. Editorial lead time 2 months.

$ $ $ $ SEVENTEEN

1440 Broadway, 13th Floor, New York NY 10018. (917)934-6500. Fax: (917)934-6574. Web site: www.seventeen.com. Features Assistant: Melanie Abrahams. Features Editor: Sarah Nanus. **20% freelance written.** Monthly magazine. "*Seventeen* is a young woman's first fashion and beauty magazine. Tailored for young women in their teens and early twenties, *Seventeen* covers fashion, beauty, health, fitness, food, college, entertainment, fiction, plus crucial personal and global issues." Estab. 1944. Circ. 2,400,000. **Pays on acceptance.** Publishes ms an average of 6 months after acceptance. Byline given. Offers 25% kill fee. Buys one-time rights. Accepts queries by mail. Responds in 3 months to queries. Sample copy not available. Writer's guidelines available online.

- "We no longer accept fiction submissions."

O- Break in with the Who Knew section, which contains shorter items, or *Quiz*.

Nonfiction Articles and features of general interest to young women who are concerned with intimate relationships and how to realize their potential in the world; strong emphasis on topicality and service. Send brief outline and query, including typical lead paragraph, summing up basic idea of article, with clips of previously published works. Articles are commissioned after outlines are submitted and approved. Length: 1,200-2,500 words. **Pays $1/word, occasionally more for assigned articles.** Pays expenses of writers on assignment.

Photos Photos usually by assignment only. Elizabeth Kildahl, photo editor.

The online magazine carries original content not found in the print edition. Contact: Fiona Gibb, editorial director.

Tips "Writers have to ask themselves whether or not they feel they can find the right tone for a *Seventeen* article—a tone which is empathetic, yet never patronizing; lively, yet not superficial. Not all writers feel comfortable with, understand, or like teenagers. If you don't like them, *Seventeen* is the wrong market for you. An excellent way to break in to the magazine is by contributing ideas for quizzes or the 'My Story' (personal essay) column."

$ $ TEEN MAGAZINE

Hearst Magazines, 3000 Ocean Park Blvd., Suite 3048, Santa Monica CA 90405. (310)664-2950. Fax: (310)664-2959. Web site: www.teenmag.com. **Contact:** Jane Fort, editor-in-chief (fashion, beauty, TeenPROM); Kelly Bryant, entertainment editor (entertainment, movies, TV, music, books, covers); Heather Hewitt, managing editor (manufacturing, advertising, new products, tech). Quarterly magazine. for a pure Jr. high school female audience. *TEEN* teens are upbeat and want to be informed. Estab. 1957. **Pays on acceptance.** Buys all rights.

- No unsolicited materials accepted.

Nonfiction Arts/crafts, games/puzzles, careers, cooking, health, multicultural, problem-solving, social issues. Does not want to see adult-oriented, adult point of view.'' **Pays $50-500.**

Fiction Does not want to see ''that which does not apply to our market—i.e., science fiction, history, religious, adult-oriented.'' **Pays $100-400.**

TIGER BEAT

Laufer Media, Inc., 6430 Sunset Blvd., Suite 700, Hollywood CA 90028. (323)462-4267. Fax: (323)462-4341. Web site: www.tigerbeatmag.com. Editor: Leesa Coble. Monthly magazine. Leading teen entertainment magazine written for girls. Features news, gossip and features on today's hottest stars. Does not want poetry, fiction, or real-person stories. Circ. 200,000. Editorial lead time 2 months. Sample copy not available.

TWIST

Bauer Publishing, 270 Sylvan Ave., Englewood Cliffs NJ 07632. E-mail: twistmail@twistmagazine.com. Web site: www.twistmagazine.com. **5% freelance written.** Monthly entertainment magazine targeting 14- to 19-year-old girls. Estab. 1997. Circ. 700,000. **Pays on acceptance.** Publishes ms an average of 3 months after acceptance. Offers 20% kill fee. Buys first North American serial rights. Editorial lead time 3 months. Submit seasonal material 4 months in advance. Accepts queries by mail. Accepts simultaneous submissions. Responds in 1 month to queries. Writer's guidelines online.

Nonfiction ''No articles written from an adult point of view about teens—i.e., a mother's or teacher's personal account.'' Personal experience (real teens' experiences, preferably in first person). **Payment varies according to assignment.** Pays expenses of writers on assignment.

Photos State availability with submission. Negotiates payment individually. Identification of subjects, model releases required.

Tips ''Tone must be conversational, neither condescending to teens nor trying to be too slangy. If possible, send clips that show an ability to write for the teen market. We are in search of real-life stories, and writers who can find teens with compelling real-life experiences (who are willing to use their full names and photographs in the magazine). Please refer to a current issue to see examples of tone and content. No e-mail queries or submissions, please.''

$ WINNER

Saying No To Drugs and Yes To Life, The Health Connection, 55 W. Oak Ridge Dr., Hagerstown MD 21740. (301)393-4082. Fax: (301)393-4055. E-mail: jschleifer@rhpa.org. Web site: www.winnermagazine.org. **Contact:** Jan Schleifer, editor. **30% freelance written.** Monthly magazine covering positive lifestyle choices for students in grades 4-6. ''*Winner* is a teaching tool to help students learn the dangers in abusive substances, such as tobacco, alcohol, and other drugs, as well as at-risk behaviors. It also focuses on everyday problems such as dealing with divorce, sibling rivalry, coping with grief, and healthy diet, to mention just a few.'' Estab. 1956. Circ. 12,000. **Pays on acceptance.** Publishes ms an average of 6-9 months after acceptance. Byline sometimes given. Offers 50% kill fee. Buys first North American serial, first rights. Editorial lead time 5 months. Submit seasonal material 6-8 months in advance. Accepts queries by mail, e-mail, fax, phone. Accepts simultaneous submissions. Responds in 4-6 weeks to queries; 2-3 months to mss. Sample copy for $2 and 9×12 SAE with 2 first-class stamps. Writer's guidelines for SASE, by e-mail, fax or on Web site.

Nonfiction General interest, humor, drug/alcohol/tobacco activities, personalities, family relationships, friends. No occult, mysteries. ''I prefer true-to-life stories.'' Query or send complete ms. Length: 600-650 words. **Pays $50-80.** Sometimes pays expenses of writers on assignment.

Photos State availability of or send photos with submission. Reviews GIF/JPEG files. Buys one-time rights. Negotiates payment individually. Model releases required.

Columns/Departments Personality (kids making a difference in their community), 600-650 words; Fun & Games (dangers of tobacco, alcohol, and other drugs), 400 words. **Buys 9 mss/year.** Query. **Pays $50-80.**

Fiction True-to-life stories dealing with problems preteens face. No suspense or mystery. **Buys 18 mss/year.** Send complete ms. Length: 600-650 words. **Pays $50-80.**

$ WITH

The Magazine for Radical Christian Youth, Faith and Life Press, 722 Main St., P.O. Box 347, Newton KS 67114-0347. (620)367-8432. Fax: (620)367-8218. E-mail: carold@mennoniteusa.org. Web site: www.withonline.org.

Contact: Carol Duerksen, editor. **60% freelance written.** Magazine published 6 times/year for teenagers. "We are a Christian youth magazine that strives to help youth be radically commited to a personal relationship with Jesus Christ, to peace and justice, and to sharing God's good news through word and action." Estab. 1968. Circ. 3,000. **Pays on acceptance.** Publishes ms an average of 1 year after acceptance. Byline given. Buys one-time rights. Submit seasonal material 6 months in advance. Accepts queries by mail, fax. Accepts previously published material. Accepts simultaneous submissions. Responds in 1 month to queries; 2 months to mss. Sample copy for 9×12 SAE with 4 first-class stamps. Writer's guidelines and theme list for #10 SASE. Additional detailed guidelines for first-person stories, how-to articles, and/or fiction available for #10 SASE.

O- Break in with "well-written true stories from teen's standpoint."

Nonfiction How-to, humor, personal experience, religious, youth. **Buys 15 mss/year.** Send complete ms. Length: 400-1,800 words. **Pays 5¢/word for simultaneous rights, higher rates for articles written on assignment; 3¢/word for reprint rights and for unsolicited articles.** Sometimes pays expenses of writers on assignment.

Reprints Send ms with rights for sale noted and information about when and where the material previously appeared. Pays 60% of amount paid for an original article.

Photos Send photos with submission. Reviews 8×10 color prints. Buys one-time rights. Offers $10-50/photo. Identification of subjects required.

Fiction Ethnic, humorous, mainstream, religious, youth, parables. **Buys 15 mss/year.** Send complete ms. Length: 500-1,500 words. **Pays 5¢/word for simultaneous rights, higher rates for articles written on assignment; 3¢/word for reprint rights and for unsolicited articles.**

Poetry Avant-garde, free verse, haiku, light verse, traditional. **Buys 10-12 poems/year. Pays $10-25.**

Tips "Most of all, we are looking for true stories, along with some humor, fiction, light verse, and cartoons. Please don't send manuscripts that aren't related to our themes."

$ $ YOUNG SALVATIONIST

The Salvation Army, P.O. Box 269, Alexandria VA 22313-0269. (703)684-5500. Fax: (703)684-5539. E-mail: ys@usn.salvationarmy.org. **Contact:** Capt. Curtiss A. Hartley. **80% freelance written.** Monthly magazine for high school and early college youth. "Only material with Christian perspective with practical real-life application will be considered." Circ. 48,000. **Pays on acceptance.** Publishes ms an average of 6 months after acceptance. Byline given. Buys first North American serial, first, one-time, second serial (reprint) rights. Submit seasonal material 6 months in advance. Responds in 2 months to mss. Sample copy for 9×12 SAE with 3 first-class stamps or on Web site. Writer's guidelines and theme list for #10 SASE or on Web site.

- Works with a small number of new/unpublished writers each year. Accepts complete mss by mail and e-mail.

O- "Our greatest need is for nonfiction pieces based in real life rather than theory or theology. Practical living articles are especially needed. We receive many fiction submissions but few good nonfiction."

Nonfiction "Articles should deal with issues of relevance to teens (high school students) today; avoid 'preachiness' or moralizing." How-to, humor, inspirational, interview/profile, personal experience, photo feature, religious. **Buys 60 mss/year.** Send complete ms. Length: 1,000-1,500 words. **Pays 15¢/word for first rights.**

Reprints Send tearsheet, photocopy or typed ms with rights for sale noted and information about when and where the material previously appeared. Pays 10¢/word for reprints.

Fiction Only a small amount is used. Adventure, fantasy, humorous, religious, romance, science fiction, (all from a Christian perspective). **Buys few mss/year.** Length: 500-1,200 words. **Pays 15¢/word.**

Tips "Study magazine, familiarize yourself with the unique 'Salvationist' perspective of *Young Salvationist*; learn a little about the Salvation Army; media, sports, sex, and dating are strongest appeal."

TRAVEL, CAMPING & TRAILER

N $ AAA GOING PLACES

Magazine for Today's Traveler, AAA Auto Club South, 1515 N. Westshore Blvd., Tampa FL 33607. (813)289-5923. Fax: (813)288-7935. Editor-In-Chief: Sandy Klim. **50% freelance written.** Bimonthly magazine on auto tips, cruise travel, tours. Estab. 1982. Circ. 2,500,000. Pays on publication. Publishes ms an average of 6 months after acceptance. Byline given. Buys one-time rights. Submit seasonal material 9 months in advance. Accepts simultaneous submissions. Responds in 2 months to mss. Sample copy not available. Writer's guidelines for SAE.

Nonfiction Travel stories feature domestic and international destinations with practical information and where to stay, dine, and shop, as well as personal anecdotes and historical background. Historical/nostalgic, how-to, humor, interview/profile, personal experience, photo feature, travel. **Buys 15 mss/year.** Send complete ms. Length: 500-1,200 words. **Pays $50/printed page.**

Photos State availability with submission. Reviews 2×2 transparencies, 300 dpi digital images. Offers no additional payment for photos accepted with ms. Captions required.
Columns/Departments What's Happening (local attractions in Florida, Georgia, or Tennessee).
Tips "We prefer lively, upbeat stories that appeal to a well-traveled, sophisticated audience, bearing in mind that AAA is a conservative company."

$ $ AAA MIDWEST TRAVELER

AAA Auto Club of Missouri, 12901 N. 40 Dr., St. Louis MO 63141. (314)523-7350 ext. 6301. Fax: (314)523-6982. E-mail: dreinhardt@aaamissouri.com. Editor: Michael J. Right. **Contact:** Deborah Reinhardt, managing editor. **80% freelance written.** Bimonthly magazine covering travel and automotive safety. "We provide members with useful information on travel, auto safety and related topics." Estab. 1901. Circ. 465,000. **Pays on acceptance.** Byline given. Offers $50 kill fee. Not copyrighted. Buys first North American serial, second serial (reprint), electronic rights. Editorial lead time 1 year. Submit seasonal material 6 months in advance. Accepts queries by mail, e-mail, fax. Accepts simultaneous submissions. Responds in 1 month to queries; 1 month to mss. Sample copy for 10×13 SAE and 4 first-class stamps. Writer's guidelines for #10 SASE.
Nonfiction Travel. No humor, fiction, poetry or cartoons. **Buys 20-30 mss/year.** Query; query with published clips the first time. Length: 800-1,200 words. **Pays $250-350.**
Photos State availability with submission. Reviews transparencies, prints. Buys one-time and electronic rights. Offers no additional payment for photos accepted with ms. Captions required.
Tips "Send queries between December and February, as we plan our calendar for the following year. Request a copy. Serious writers ask for media kit to help them target their piece. Send a SASE or download online. Travel destinations and tips are most open to freelancers; all departments and auto-related news handled by staff. We see too many 'Here's a recount of our family vacation' manuscripts. Go easy on first-person accounts."

$ $ ARUBA NIGHTS

Nights Publications, Inc., 1751 Richardson St., Suite 5.530, Montreal QC H3K 1G6 Canada. (514)931-1987. Fax: (514)931-6273. E-mail: editor@nightspublications.com. Web site: www.nightspublications.com. Editor: Jennifer McMorran. **90% freelance written.** Annual magazine covering the Aruban vacation lifestyle experience with an upscale, upbeat touch. Estab. 1988. Circ. 245,000. **Pays on acceptance.** Publishes ms an average of 9 months after acceptance. Byline given for feature articles. Buys North American and Caribbean serial rights. Editorial lead time 1 month. Accepts queries by mail, e-mail, fax. Responds in 2 weeks to queries; 1 month to mss. Writer's guidelines by e-mail.

Aruba Nights is looking for more articles on nightlife experiences.

Nonfiction General interest, historical/nostalgic, how-to (relative to Aruba vacationers), humor, inspirational, interview/profile, opinion, personal experience, photo feature, travel, ecotourism, Aruban culture, art, activities, entertainment, topics relative to vacationers in Aruba. "No negative pieces." **Buys 5-10 mss/year.** Send complete ms, include SAE with Canadian postage or IRC. Length: 250-750 words. **Pays $100-250.**
Photos State availability with submission. Reviews transparencies. Buys one-time rights. Pays $50/photo. Captions, identification of subjects, model releases required.
Tips "Be descriptive and entertaining and make sure stories are factually correct. Stories should immerse the reader in a sensory adventure. Focus on specific, individual aspects of the Aruban lifestyle and vacation experience (e.g., art, music, culture, a colorful local character, a personal experience, etc.), rather than generalized overviews. Provide an angle that will be entertaining to vacationers who are already there. E-mail submissions preferred."

$ $ ASU TRAVEL GUIDE

ASU Travel Guide, Inc., 448 Ignacio Blvd. #333, Novato CA 94949. (415)898-9500. Fax: (415)898-9501. E-mail: editor@asutravelguide.com. Web site: www.asutravelguide.com. **Contact:** The Editor. **80% freelance written.** Quarterly guidebook covering international travel features and travel discounts for well-traveled airline employees. Estab. 1970. Circ. 36,000. **Pays on acceptance.** Publishes ms an average of 4 months after acceptance. Byline given. Buys first North American serial, first, second serial (reprint) rights. Submit seasonal material 6 months in advance. Accepts previously published material. Accepts simultaneous submissions. Responds in 1 year to queries; 1 year to mss. Sample copy for 6×9 SAE and 5 first-class stamps. Writer's guidelines for #10 SASE.
Nonfiction International travel articles "similar to those run in consumer magazines. Not interested in amateur efforts from inexperienced travelers or personal experience articles that don't give useful information to other travelers." Destination pieces only; no "Tips on Luggage" articles. Unsolicited mss or queries without SASE will not be acknowledged. No telephone queries. Travel (international). **Buys 12 mss/year.** Length: 1,800 words. **Pays $200.**

Reprints Send tearsheet and information about when and where the material previously appeared. Pays 100% of amount paid for an original article.

Photos "Interested in clear, high-contrast photos." Reviews 5×7 and 8×10 b&w or color prints, JPEGs (300 dpi). Payment for photos is included in article price; photos from tourist offices are acceptable.

Tips "Query with samples of travel writing and a list of places you've recently visited. We appreciate clean and simple style. Keep verbs in the active tense and involve the reader in what you write. Avoid 'cute' writing, coined words, and stale clichés. The most frequent mistakes made by writers in completing an article for us are: 1) Lazy writing—using words to describe a place that could describe any destination such as 'there is so much to do in (fill in destination) that whole guidebooks have been written about it'; 2) Including fare and tour package information—our readers make arrangements through their own airline."

$ BONAIRE NIGHTS

Nights Publications, Inc., 1751 Richardson St., Suite 5.530, Montreal QC H3K 1G6 Canada. (514)931-1987. Fax: (514)931-6273. E-mail: editor@nightspublications.com. Editor: Jennifer McMorran. **90% freelance written.** Annual magazine covering Bonaire vacation experience. Estab. 1993. Circ. 80,000. Byline given for features. Buys North American and Caribbean serial rights. Editorial lead time 1 month. Accepts queries by mail, e-mail, fax. Responds in 2 weeks to queries; 1 month to mss. Writer's guidelines by e-mail.

Nonfiction General interest, historical/nostalgic, how-to, humor, interview/profile, opinion, personal experience, photo feature, travel, lifestyle, local culture, art, architecture, activities, scuba diving, snorkeling, ecotourism. **Buys 6-9 mss/year.** E-mail submissions preferred. Mailed mss must include an e-mail address for correspondence. Length: 250-750 words. **Pays $100.**

Photos State availability with submission. Pays $50/published photo. Captions, identification of subjects, model releases required.

Tips "Focus on the Bonaire lifestyle, what sets it apart from other islands. We want personal experience on specific attractions and culture, not generalized overviews. Be positive and provide an angle that will appeal to vacationers who are already there. Our style is upbeat, friendly, fluid, and descriptive."

$ CAMPERWAYS, MIDWEST RV TRAVELER, FLORIDA RV TRAVELER, NORTHEAST OUTDOORS, SOUTHERN RV

Woodall Publications Corp., 2575 Vista Del Mar Dr., Ventura CA 93001. (800)323-9076. Fax: (805)667-4122. E-mail: editor@woodallpub.com. Web site: www.woodalls.com. **Contact:** Preston Gratiot, managing editor. **75% freelance written.** Monthly tabloids covering RV lifestyle. "We're looking for articles of interest to RVers. Lifestyle articles, destinations, technical tips, interesting events and the like make up the bulk of our publications. We also look for region-specific travel and special interest articles." Circ. 30,000. **Pays on acceptance.** Byline given. Offers 50% kill fee. Buys first North American serial rights. Accepts queries by mail, e-mail. Sample copy for free. Writer's guidelines for #10 SASE.

- Accepts queries in June, July, and August for upcoming year.

Nonfiction How-to, personal experience, technical, travel. No "Camping From Hell" articles. **Buys approximately 500 mss/year.** Length: 500-2,000 words. **Payment varies.**

Photos Prefers slides and large (5×7, 300 dpi) digital images. State availability with submission. Reviews negatives, 4×5 transparencies, 4×5 prints. Buys first North American serial rights. Captions, identification of subjects required.

Tips "Be an expert in RVing. Make your work readable to a wide variety of readers, from novices to full-timers."

$ CAMPING TODAY

Official Publication of the Family Campers & RVers, 126 Hermitage Rd., Butler PA 16001-8509. (724)283-7401. **Contact:** DeWayne Johnston, June Johnston, editors. **30% freelance written.** Monthly official membership publication of the FCRV. *Camping Today* is "the largest nonprofit family camping and RV organization in the United States and Canada. Members are heavily oriented toward RV travel, both weekend and extended vacations. Concentration is on member activities in chapters. Group is also interested in conservation and wildlife. The majority of members are retired." Estab. 1983. Circ. 10,000. Pays on publication. Publishes ms an average of 6 months after acceptance. Byline given. Buys one-time rights. Submit seasonal material 3 months in advance. Accepts simultaneous submissions. Responds in 2 months to queries; 2 months to mss. Sample copy and guidelines for 4 first-class stamps. Writer's guidelines for #10 SASE.

Nonfiction Humor (camping or travel related), interview/profile (interesting campers), new product, technical (RVs related), travel (interesting places to visit by RV, camping). **Buys 10-15 mss/year.** Query by mail only or send complete ms with photos. Length: 750-2,000 words. **Pays $50-150.**

Reprints Send ms with rights for sale noted and information about when and where the material previously appeared. Pays 35-50% of amount paid for original article.

Photos "Need b&w or sharp color prints inside (we can make prints from slides) and vertical transparencies for cover." Send photos with submission. Captions required.

Tips "Freelance material on RV travel, RV maintenance/safety, and items of general camping interest throughout the United States and Canada will receive special attention. Good photos increase your chances."

$ $ $ COAST TO COAST MAGAZINE

Affinity Group, Inc., 2575 Vista Del Mar Dr., Ventura CA 93001. (805)667-4100. Fax: (805)667-4217. E-mail: vlaw@affinitygroup.com. Web site: www.coastresorts.com. **Contact:** Valerie Law, editorial director. **80% freelance written.** Magazine published 8 times/year for members of Coast to Coast Resorts. "*Coast to Coast* focuses on travel, recreation, and good times, with most stories targeted to recreational vehicle owners." Estab. 1983. Circ. 125,000. **Pays on acceptance.** Publishes ms an average of 4 months after acceptance. Byline given. Offers 33% kill fee. Buys first North American serial rights. Editorial lead time 5 months. Submit seasonal material 5 months in advance. Accepts queries by mail, e-mail, fax. Accepts previously published material. Accepts simultaneous submissions. Responds in 6-8 weeks to queries; 1-2 months to mss. Sample copy for $4 and 9×12 SASE. Writer's guidelines for #10 SASE.

Nonfiction Book excerpts, essays, general interest, how-to, interview/profile, new product, personal experience, photo feature, technical, travel. No poetry, cartoons. **Buys 70 mss/year.** Query with published clips or send complete ms. Length: 800-2,500 words. **Pays $75-1,200.**

Reprints Send photocopy and information about when and where the material previously appeared. Pays approximately 50% of amount paid for original article.

Columns/Departments Pays $150-400.

Tips "Send clips or other writing samples with queries, or story ideas will not be considered."

$ $ CURACAO NIGHTS

Nights Publications, Inc., 1751 Richardson St., Suite 5.530, Montreal QC H3K 1G6 Canada. (514)931-1987. Fax: (514)931-6273. E-mail: editor@nightspublications.com. Editor: Jennifer McMorran. **90% freelance written.** Annual magazine covering the Curacao vacation experience. "We are seeking upbeat, entertaining lifestyle articles; colorful profiles of locals; lively features on culture, activities, nightlife, ecotourism, special events, gambling, how-to features, humor. Our audience is North American vacationers." Estab. 1989. Circ. 155,000. Byline given. Buys North American and Caribbean serial rights. Editorial lead time 1 month. Accepts queries by mail, e-mail, fax. Responds in 2 weeks to queries; 1 month to mss. Writer's guidelines by e-mail.

Nonfiction General interest, historical/nostalgic, how-to (help a vacationer get the most from their vacation), humor, interview/profile, opinion, personal experience, photo feature, travel, ecotourism, lifestyle, local culture, art, activities, nightlife, topics relative to vacationers in Curacao. "No negative pieces, generic copy, or stale rewrites." **Buys 5-10 mss/year.** Query with published clips, include SASE and either Canadian postage or IRC, though e-mail submissions are preferred. Length: 250-750 words. **Pays $100-300.**

Photos State availability with submission. Reviews transparencies. Buys one-time rights. Pays $50/photo. Captions, identification of subjects, model releases required.

Tips "Demonstrate your voice in your query letter. Focus on individual aspects of the island lifestyle and vacation experience (e.g., art, music, culture, a colorful local character, a personal experience, etc.), rather than a generalized overview. Provide an angle that will be entertaining to vacationers who are already on the island. Our style is upbeat, friendly, and fluid."

$ $ DURANGO MAGAZINE

For People Who Love Durango, Schultz & Associates, Inc., P.O. Box 3408, Durango CO 81302. (970)385-4030. Fax: (970)385-4436. E-mail: drgomag@animas.net. Web site: www.durangomagazine.com. **Contact:** Julianne W. Schultz, editor/publisher. **75% freelance written.** Semiannual magazine covering travel and tourism, city and regional. "Readers want to know what to see and do in the Durango area. Locals need more in-depth information than visitors, but subjects of interest to both are covered. People profiles, area attractions, history, arts & culture, outdoor pursuits, entertainment are subjects covered." Estab. 1986. Circ. 325,000. Pays on publication. Publishes ms an average of 3 months after acceptance. Byline given. Offers 50% kill fee. Buys first North American serial rights. Editorial lead time 4 months. Submit seasonal material 5 months in advance. Accepts queries by mail, e-mail. Accepts previously published material. Accepts simultaneous submissions. Responds in 6 weeks to queries. Sample copy for $3.95, plus mailing. Writer's guidelines free.

Nonfiction Book excerpts, historical/nostalgic, humor, interview/profile, personal experience, photo feature, travel. Does not want to see anything not assigned. Query with or without published clips. **Pays 30-50¢/word.** Sometimes pays expenses of writers on assignment.

Photos State availability of or send photos with submission. Buys one-time rights. Negotiates payment individually. Identification of subjects required.

$$$$ ENDLESS VACATION MAGAZINE

Endless Vacation, 9998 N. Michigan Rd., Carmel IN 46032-9640. Fax: (317)805-9507. Web site: www.evmediakit.com.; www.rci.com. **Contact:** Julie Woodard, senior editor. Prefers to work with published/established writers. Bimonthly magazine. "*Endless Vacation* is the vacation-idea magazine edited for people who love to travel. Each issue offers articles for America's dedicated and frequent leisure travelers—time-share owners. Articles and features explore the world through a variety of vacation opportunities and options for travelers who average 4 weeks of leisure travel each year. The goal of the magazine is to provide vibrant, interesting and informative editorial that engages and inspires the reader to travel, focusing more on active, 'do-able' dream vacations rather than aspirational arm-chair travel." Estab. 1974. Circ. 1,541,107. **Pays on acceptance.** Publishes ms an average of 6 months after acceptance. Byline given. Buys first North American serial rights. Accepts queries by mail, e-mail, fax. Accepts simultaneous submissions. Responds in 2 months to queries. Sample copy for $5 and 9×12 SAE with 5 first-class stamps. Writer's guidelines for #10 SASE.

Nonfiction Most articles are from established writers already published in *Endless Vacation. Accepts very few unsolicited pieces.* **Buys 30 feature mss/year.** Query with published clips (no phone calls). Length: 500-1,500 words. **Pays $500-1,500 for feature articles.** Sometimes pays expenses of writers on assignment.

Photos Reviews transparencies, 35mm slides. Buys one-time rights. Pays $300-1,300/photo. Identification of subjects required.

Columns/Departments Weekender (on domestic weekend vacation travel); Healthy Traveler; Cruise Currents; Family Vacationing; Value Travel Destinations, up to 1,200 words. Also Taste (on food-related travel topics) and news items for Ready, Set, Go column on products and the useful and unique in travel, 100-200 words. **Pays $100-900.**

Tips "Study the magazine and the writer's guidelines before you query us. Also check out www.evmediakit.com, which includes a reader profile and the magazine's current editorial calendar. The best way to break in to writing for *Endless Vacation* is through departments (Weekender, for example) and smaller pieces (Ready, Set, Go and Taste). Queries should be well developed."

⊘ EXECUTIVE TRAVEL

American Express Publishing, 1120 Avenue of the Americas, New York NY 10036. E-mail: editor@executivetravelmag.com. Web site: www.skyguide.net. Editor: Janet Libert. Quarterly magazine for affluent, educated professionals who are constantly on the go. Circ. 130,000.

- Query before submitting.

$$ FAMILY MOTOR COACHING

Official Publication of the Family Motor Coach Association, 8291 Clough Pike, Cincinnati OH 45244. (513)474-3622. Fax: (513)388-5286. E-mail: magazine@fmca.com. Web site: www.fmca.com. Publishing Director: Pamela Wisby Kay. **Contact:** Robbin Gould, editor. **80% freelance written.** "We prefer that writers be experienced RVers." Monthly magazine emphasizing travel by motorhome, motorhome mechanics, maintenance, and other technical information. "*Family Motor Coaching* magazine is edited for the members and prospective members of the Family Motor Coach Association who own or are about to purchase self-contained, motorized recreational vehicles known as motorhomes. Featured are articles on travel and recreation, association news and activities, plus articles on new products and motorhome maintenance and repair. Approximately 1/3 of editorial content is devoted to travel and entertainment, 1/3 to association news, and 1/3 to new products, industry news, and motorhome maintenance." Estab. 1963. Circ. 140,000. **Pays on acceptance.** Publishes ms an average of 8 months after acceptance. Byline given. Buys first North American serial rights. Submit seasonal material 4 months in advance. Accepts queries by mail, e-mail, fax. Responds in 3 months to queries. Sample copy for $3.99; $5 if paying by credit card. Writer's guidelines for #10 SASE.

Nonfiction How-to (do-it-yourself motorhome projects and modifications), humor, interview/profile, new product, technical, motorhome travel (various areas of North America accessible by motorhome), bus conversions, nostalgia. **Buys 90-100 mss/year.** Query with published clips. Length: 1,000-2,000 words. **Pays $100-500, depending on article category.**

Photos State availability with submission. Prefers North American serial rights but will consider one-time rights on photos only. Offers no additional payment for b&w contact sheets, 35mm 2¼×2¼ color transparencies, or high-resolution electronic images (300 dpi and at least 4×5 in size). Captions, model releases, photo credits required.

Tips "The greatest number of contributions we receive are travel; therefore, that area is the most competitive. However, it also represents the easiest way to break in to our publication. Articles should be written for those traveling by self-contained motorhome. The destinations must be accessible to motorhome travelers and any peculiar road conditions should be mentioned."

$ GO MAGAZINE

AAA Carolinas, 6600 AAA Dr., Charlotte NC 28212. (704)569-7733. Fax: (704)569-7815. E-mail: trcrosby@mailaaa.com. Web site: www.aaacarolinas.com. **Contact:** Sarah Davis, assistant editor. Bimonthly magazine covering travel, automotive, safety (traffic), and insurance. "Consumer-oriented membership publication providing information on things such as car buying, vacations, travel safety problems, etc." Estab. 1928. Circ. 910,000. Pays on publication. Makes work-for-hire assignments. Editorial lead time 3-4 months. Accepts queries by mail, fax. Responds in 6 weeks to queries; 3 months to mss. Sample copy for 1 SAE and 4 first-class stamps. Writer's guidelines for #10 SASE.

Nonfiction How-to (fix auto, travel safety, etc.), travel, automotive insurance, traffic safety. **Buys 16-18 mss/year.** Query with published clips. Length: 600-900 words. **Pays $150/published story.**

Photos Send photos with submission. Buys one-time rights. Offers no additional payment for photos accepted with ms.

$ $ HIGHWAYS

The Official Publication of the Good Sam Club, Affinity Group, Inc., 2575 Vista Del Mar Dr., Ventura CA 93001. (805)667-4100. Fax: (805)667-4454. E-mail: goodsam@goodsamclub.com. Web site: www.goodsamclub.com/highways. **Contact:** Dee Reed, managing editor. **30% freelance written.** Monthly magazine covering recreational vehicle lifestyle. "All of our readers own some type of RV—a motorhome, trailer, pop-up, tent—so our stories need to include places that you can go with large vehicles, and campgrounds in and around the area where they can spend the night." Estab. 1966. Circ. 975,000. **Pays on acceptance.** Publishes ms an average of 6 months after acceptance. Byline given. Offers 50% kill fee. Buys first North American serial, electronic rights. Accepts queries by e-mail. Responds in 2 weeks to queries. Sample copy and writer's guidelines free or online.

Nonfiction How-to (repair/replace something on an RV), humor, technical, travel (all RV related). **Buys 15-20 mss/year.** Query. Length: 800-1,100 words.

Photos Do not send or e-mail unless approved by staff.

Columns/Departments On the Road (issue related); RV Insight (for people new to the RV lifestyle); Action Line (consumer help); Tech Topics (tech Q&A); Camp Cuisine (cooking in an RV); Product Previews (new products). No plans on adding new columns/departments.

Tips "Know something about RVing. People who drive motorhomes or pull trailers have unique needs that have to be incorporated into our stories. We're looking for well-written, first-person stories that convey the fun of this lifestyle and way to travel."

N $ THE INTERNATIONAL RAILWAY TRAVELER

Hardy Publishing Co., Inc., P.O. Box 3747, San Diego CA 92163. (619)260-1332. Fax: (619)296-4220. E-mail: irteditor@aol.com. Web site: www.irtsociety.com. **Contact:** Gena Holle, editor. **100% freelance written.** Monthly newsletter covering rail travel. Estab. 1983. Circ. 3,500. Pays within 1 month of the publication date. Byline given. Offers 25% kill fee. Buys first North American serial, all electronic rights. Editorial lead time 4 months. Submit seasonal material 6 months in advance. Responds in 1 month to queries; 2 months to mss. Sample copy for $6. Writer's guidelines for #10 SASE or via e-mail.

Nonfiction General interest, how-to, interview/profile, new product, opinion, personal experience, travel, book reviews. **Buys 48-60 mss/year.** Query with published clips or send complete ms. Length: 800-1,200 words. **Pays 3¢/word.**

Photos Include SASE for return of photos. Send photos with submission. Reviews contact sheets, negatives, transparencies, 8×10 (preferred) and 5×7 prints, digital photos preferred (minimum 300 dpi). Buys first North American serial rights, all electronic rights. Offers $10 b&w; $20 cover photo. Costs of converting slides and negatives to prints are deducted from payment. Captions, identification of subjects required.

Tips "We want factual articles concerning world rail travel which would not appear in the mass-market travel magazines. *IRT* readers and editors love stories and photos on off-beat train trips as well as more conventional train trips covered in unconventional ways. With *IRT,* the focus is on the train travel experience, not a blow-by-blow description of the view from the train window. Be sure to include details (prices, passes, schedule info, etc.) for readers who might want to take the trip. E-mail queries, submissions encouraged. Digital photo submissions (at least 300 dpi) are encouraged. Please stay within word-count guidelines."

$ $ $ $ ISLANDS

World Publications, 460 N. Orlando Ave., Suite 200, Winter Park FL 32789. (407)628-4802. E-mail: storyideas@islands.com. Web site: www.islands.com. Executive Editor: Christine Richard. Features Editor: Megan Padilla. **80% freelance written.** Magazine published 8 times/year "We cover accessible and once-in-a-lifetime islands from many different perspectives: travel, culture, lifestyle. We ask our authors to give us the essence of the island and do it with literary flair." Estab. 1981. Circ. 220,000. Pays on publication. Publishes ms an average of 8 months after acceptance. Byline given. Offers 25% kill fee. Buys all rights. Accepts queries by mail, e-mail, fax. Responds in 2 months to queries; 6 weeks to mss. Sample copy for $6. Writer's guidelines for #10 SASE or online.

O→ "A freelancer can best break in to our publication with front- or back-of-the-book stories. It's rare that we will use a writer new to us for a feature story or column. We would consider it in certain instances, but would want to see the manuscript on spec."

Nonfiction Book excerpts, essays, general interest, interview/profile, photo feature, travel, service shorts, island-related material. **Buys 25 feature mss/year.** Query with published clips or send complete ms. Length: 2,000-4,000 words. **Pays $750-2,500.** Sometimes pays expenses of writers on assignment.

Photos "Fine color photography is a special attraction of *Islands*, and we look for superb composition, technical quality, and editorial applicability." Will not accept or be responsible for unsolicited images or artwork.

Columns/Departments Discovers section (island related news), 100-600 words; Island Life (travel experiences-that illuminate culture), 700-1,000 words; Adventures (things to do), 800 words. **Buys 50 mss/year.** Query with published clips. **Pays $25-1,000.**

$ $ MOTORHOME

TL Enterprises, 2575 Vista Del Mar Dr., Ventura CA 93001. (805)667-4100. Fax: (805)667-4484. Web site: www.motorhomemagazine.com. Editor/Publisher: Bob Livingston. **Contact:** Eileen Hubbard, senior managing editor. **60% freelance written.** Monthly magazine. "*MotorHome* is a magazine for owners and prospective buyers of motorized recreational vehicles who are active outdoorsmen and wide-ranging travelers. We cover all aspects of the RV lifestyle; editorial material is both technical and nontechnical in nature. Regular features include tests and descriptions of various models of motorhomes, travel adventures, and hobbies pursued in such vehicles, objective analysis of equipment and supplies for such vehicles, and do-it-yourself articles. Guides within the magazine provide listings of manufacturers, rentals, and other sources of equipment and accessories of interest to enthusiasts. Articles must have an RV slant and excellent transparencies accompanying text." Estab. 1968. Circ. 150,000. **Pays on acceptance.** Publishes ms an average of within 1 year after acceptance. Byline given. Offers 30% kill fee. Buys first North American serial, electronic rights. Editorial lead time 4 months. Submit seasonal material 6 months in advance. Accepts queries by mail, fax. Responds in 1 month to queries; 2 months to mss. Sample copy for free. Writer's guidelines for #10 SASE.

O→ Break in with *Crossroads* items.

Nonfiction General interest, historical/nostalgic, how-to, humor, interview/profile, new product, personal experience, photo feature, technical, travel, celebrity profiles, recreation, lifestyle, legislation, all RV related. No diaries of RV trips or negative RV experiences. **Buys 120 mss/year.** Query with or without published clips. Length: 250-2,500 words. **Pays $300-600.**

Photos Digital photography accepted depending upon topic/anticipated use. Send photos with submission. Reviews 35mm slides. Buys one-time rights. Offers no additional payment for art accepted with ms. Pays $500 (minimum) for covers. Captions, identification of subjects, model releases required.

Columns/Departments Crossroads (offbeat briefs of people, places, and events of interest to travelers), 100-200 words; Keepers (tips, resources). Query with or without published clips or send complete ms. **Pays $100.**

Tips "If a freelancer has an idea for a good article, it's best to send a query and include possible photo locations to illustrate the article. We prefer to assign articles and work with the author in developing a piece suitable to our audience. We are in a specialized field with very enthusiastic readers who appreciate articles by authors who actually enjoy motorhomes. The following areas are most open: Crossroads—brief descriptions of places to see or special events, with 1 photo/slide, 100-200 words; travel—places to go with a motorhome, where to stay, what to see and do, etc; and how-to—personal projects on author's motorhomes to make travel easier, unique projects, accessories. Also articles on motorhome-owning celebrities, humorous experiences. Be sure to submit appropriate photography (35mm slides) with at least 1 good motorhome shot to illustrate travel articles. No phone queries, please."

N $ $ NORTH AMERICAN INNS MAGAZINE

Harworth Publishing Inc., Box 998, Guelph ON N1H 6N1 Canada. (519)767-6059. Fax: (519)821-0479. E-mail: editor@harworthpublishing.com. Web site: www.northamericaninns.com. **Contact:** Mary Hughes, editor-in-chief/publisher. "*North American Inns* is a national publication for travel, dining and pastimes. It focuses on inns, beds & breakfasts, resorts and travel in North America. The magazine is targeted to travelers looking for exquisite getaways." Accepts queries by e-mail. Writer's guidelines by e-mail.

Nonfiction General interest, interview/profile, new product, opinion, personal experience, travel. Query. Length: 300-600 words. **Pays $175-250 (Canadian).**

Fillers Short quips or nominations at 75 words are **$25 each**. All stories submitted have to accompany photos. Please e-mail photos to designer@harworthpublishing.com.

$ $ NORTHWEST TRAVEL

Northwest Regional Magazines, 4969 Hwy. 101 N., Suite 2, Florence OR 97439. (541)997-8401 or (800)348-8401. Fax: (541)902-0400. Web site: www.northwestmagazines.com. **Contact:** Candise Montemayor, editor. **60% freelance written.** Bimonthly magazine. "We like energetic writing about popular activities and destinations in the Pacific Northwest. *Northwest Travel* aims to give readers practical ideas on where to go in the region. Magazine covers Oregon, Washington, Idaho, British Columbia, and western Montana; occasionally Alaska." Estab. 1991. Circ. 50,000. Pays after publication. Publishes ms an average of 8 months after acceptance. Buys first North American serial rights. Submit seasonal material 6 months in advance. Accepts queries by mail, e-mail. Responds in 3 months to queries; 3 months to mss. Sample copy for $4.50. Writer's guidelines online.

- Have good slides to go with a story that is lively with compelling leads, quotes, anecdotes, and no grammar problems.

Nonfiction Book excerpts, general interest, historical/nostalgic, interview/profile (rarely), photo feature, travel (only in Northwest region). "No cliché-ridden pieces on places that everyone covers." **Buys 40 mss/year.** Query with or without published clips. Submit hard copy of ms, plus copy on CD or via e-mail. Length: 1,000-1,500 words. **Pays $100-500 for feature articles, and 2-5 contributor copies.**

Reprints Send photocopy and information about when and where the material previously appeared. Pays 50% of amount paid for original article.

Photos "Provide credit and model release information on cover photos." Digital photos on CD (300 dpi 8½×11 ½). State availability with submission. Reviews transparencies, prefers dupes. Buys one-time rights. Pays $425 for cover; $100 for stand-alone photos; $100 for Back Page. Captions, identification of subjects required.

Columns/Departments Worth a Stop (brief items describing places "worth a stop"), 300-700 words. **Pays $50-100.** Back Page (photo and text package on a specific activity, season, or festival with some technical photo info), 80 words and 1 slide. **Pays $100. Buys 25-30 mss/year.**

Tips "Write fresh, lively copy (avoid clichés), and cover exciting travel topics in the region that haven't been covered in other magazines. A story with stunning photos will get serious consideration. The department most open to freelancers is the Worth a Stop department. Take us to fascinating places we may not otherwise discover."

$ PATHFINDERS

Travel Information for People of Color, 6325 Germantown Ave., Philadelphia PA 19144. (215)438-2140. Fax: (215)438-2144. E-mail: editors@pathfinderstravel.com. Web site: www.pathfinderstravel.com. **Contact:** Joseph P. Blake, managing editor. **75% freelance written.** Quarterly magazine covering travel for people of color, primarily African-Americans. "We look for lively, original, well-written stories that provide a good sense of place, with useful information and fresh ideas about travel and the travel industry. Our main audience is African-Americans, though we do look for articles relating to other persons of color: Native Americans, Hispanics and Asians." Estab. 1997. Circ. 100,000. **Pays on acceptance.** Byline given. Buys first North American serial, electronic rights. Accepts queries by mail, e-mail. Responds in 1 month to queries; 2 months to mss. Sample copy at bookstores (Barnes & Noble, Borders, Waldenbooks). Writer's guidelines online.

- Break in through *Looking Back*, 600-word essay on travel from personal experience that provides a historical perspective and U.S. travel with cultural perspective. Also Chef's Table column, featuring information on African American chefs.

Nonfiction Interested in seeing more Native American stories, places that our readers can visit and rodeos (be sure to tie-in African-American cowboys). Essays, historical/nostalgic, how-to, personal experience, photo feature, travel (all vacation travel oriented). "No more pitches on Jamaica. We get these all the time." **Buys 16-20 mss/year.** Send complete ms. Length: 1,200-1,400 words for cover stories; 1,000-1,200 words for features. **Pays $150.**

Photos State availability with submission.

Columns/Departments Chef's Table, Post Cards from Home; Looking Back; City of the Month, 500-600 words. Send complete ms. **Pays $150.**

Tips "We prefer seeing finished articles rather than queries. All articles are submitted on spec. Articles should be saved in either WordPerfect of Microsoft Word, double-spaced and saved as a text-only file. Include a hard copy. E-mail articles are accepted only by request of the editor. No historical articles."

$ $ PILOT GETAWAYS MAGAZINE

Airventure Publishing LLC, P.O. Box 550, Glendale CA 91209-0550. (818)241-1890. Fax: (818)241-1895. E-mail: editor@pilotgetaways.com. Web site: www.pilotgetaways.com. **Contact:** John Kounis, editor. **90% freelance written.** Bimonthly magazine covering aviation travel for private pilots. "*Pilot Getaways* is a travel magazine for private pilots. Our articles cover destinations that are easily accessible by private aircraft, including details such as airport transportation, convenient hotels, and attractions. Other regular features include Fly-in dining, Flying Tips, and Bush Flying." Estab. 1998. Circ. 20,000. Pays on publication. Byline given. Buys first North American serial, electronic rights. Editorial lead time 4 months. Submit seasonal material 9 months in advance.

Accepts queries by mail, e-mail, fax, phone. Accepts simultaneous submissions. Responds in 2 weeks to queries; 2 months to mss. Sample copy and writer's guidelines free.

Nonfiction Travel (specifically travel guide articles). "We rarely publish articles about events that have already occurred, such as travel logs about trips the authors have taken or air show reports." **Buys 30 mss/year.** Query. Length: 1,000-3,500 words. **Pays $100-500.**

Reprints Accepts previously published submissions.

Photos State availability with submission. Reviews contact sheets, negatives, 35mm transparencies, prints, GIF/JPEG/TIFF files. Buys one-time rights. Negotiates payment individually. Captions, identification of subjects required.

Columns/Departments Weekend Getaways (short fly-in getaways), 2,000 words; Fly-in Dining (reviews of airport restaurants), 1,200 words; Flying Tips (tips and pointers on flying technique), 1,000 words; Bush Flying (getaways to unpaved destinations), 1,500 words. **Buys 20 mss/year.** Query. **Pays $100-500.**

Tips "*Pilot Getaways* follows a specific format, which is factual and informative. We rarely publish travel logs that chronicle a particular journey. Rather, we prefer travel guides with phone numbers, addresses, prices, etc., so that our readers can plan their own trips. The exact format is described in our writer's guidelines."

$ $ $ PORTHOLE CRUISE MAGAZINE

The PPI Group, 4517 NW 31st Ave., Ft. Lauderdale FL 33309-3403. (954)377-7777. Fax: (954)377-7000. E-mail: jornstein@ppigroup.com. Web site: www.porthole.com. **Contact:** Jodi Ornstein, managing editor; Jeffrey Laign, editorial director. **70% freelance written.** Bimonthly magazine covering the cruise industry. "*Porthole Cruise Magazine* entices its readers to take a cruise vacation by delivering information that is timely, accurate, colorful, and entertaining." Estab. 1992. Circ. 2,000,000. Pays on publication. Publishes ms an average of 6 months after acceptance. Byline given. Offers 20% kill fee. Buys first North American serial, electronic rights. Editorial lead time 8 months. Submit seasonal material 5 months in advance. Accepts queries by e-mail. Accepts simultaneous submissions.

Nonfiction General interest (cruise related), historical/nostalgic, how-to (pick a cruise, not get seasick, travel tips), humor, interview/profile (crew on board or industry executives), new product, personal experience, photo feature, travel (off-the-beaten-path, adventure, ports, destinations, cruises), onboard fashion, spa articles, duty-free shopping, port shopping, ship reviews. No articles on destinations that can't be reached by ship. **Buys 30 mss/year.** Length: 1,000-1,200 words. **Pays $500-600 for assigned feature articles.**

Photos Linda Douthat, creative director. State availability with submission. Reviews digital images and original transparencies. Buys one-time rights. Rates available upon request to ldouthat@ppigroup.com. Captions, identification of subjects, model releases required.

RV LIFESTYLE MAGAZINE

1020 Brevik Place, Unit 5, Mississauga ON L4W 4N7 Canada. (905)624-8218. Fax: (905)624-6764. E-mail: editor@rvlifemag.com. Web site: www.rvlifemag.com. **50% freelance written.** Magazine published 7 times/year (monthly December-May and October). "*RV Lifestyle Magazine* is geared to readers who enjoy travel/camping. Upbeat pieces only. Readers vary from owners of towable trailers or motorhomes to young families and entry-level campers (no tenting)." Estab. 1971. Circ. 45,000. Pays on publication. Byline given. Buys first North American serial rights. Editorial lead time 2 months. Responds in 1 month to queries; 2 months to mss. Sample copy for free.

Nonfiction How-to, personal experience, technical, travel. No inexperienced, unresearched, or too general pieces. **Buys 30-40 mss/year.** Query. Length: 1,200-2,000 words. **Payment varies.**

Photos Send photos with submission. Reviews low-ISO 35mm slides or JPEG/TIFF files saved at 300 dpi minimum at 5×7. Buys one-time rights. Offers no additional payment for photos accepted with ms.

Tips "Pieces should be slanted toward RV living. All articles must have an RV slant. Canadian content regulations require 95% Canadian writers."

$ $ THE SOUTHERN TRAVELER

AAA Auto Club of Missouri, 12901 N. Forty Dr., St. Louis MO 63141. (314)523-7350. Fax: (314)523-6982. Web site: www.aaatravelermags.com. Editor: Michael J. Right. **Contact:** Deborah Reinhardt, managing editor. **80% freelance written.** Bimonthly magazine. Estab. 1997. Circ. 170,000. **Pays on acceptance.** Byline given. Not copyrighted. Buys first North American serial, second serial (reprint) rights. Accepts simultaneous submissions. Responds in 1 month to queries; 1 month to mss. Sample copy for 12½×9½ SAE and 3 first-class stamps. Writer's guidelines online. Editorial calendar online.

Query, with best chance for good reception January-March for inclusion in following year's editorial calendar.

Nonfiction "We feature articles on regional and world travel, area history, auto safety, highway and transportation news." **Buys 30 mss/year.** Query. Length: 2,000 words maximum. **Pays $300 maximum.**

Reprints Send ms with rights for sale noted and information about when and where the material previously appeared. Pays $125-200.

Photos State availability with submission. Reviews transparencies. One-time photo reprint rights. Offers no additional payment for photos accepted with ms. Captions required.

Tips "Editorial schedule is set 6-9 months in advance (available online). Some stories available throughout the year, but most are assigned early. Travel destinations and tips are most open to freelancers; auto-related topics handled by staff. Make story bright and quick to read. We see too many 'Here's what I did on my vacation' manuscripts. Go easy on first-person accounts."

$ $ $ $ SPA

Healthy Living, Travel & Renewal, World Publications, 135 E. Ortego St., Santa Barbara CA 93101. (805)690-9850. Fax: (805)690-9855. Web site: www.spamagazine.com. Bimonthly magazine covering health spas: treatments, travel, cuisine, fitness, beauty. "Approachable and accessible, authoritative and full of advice, *Spa* is the place to turn for information and tips on nutrition, spa cuisine/recipes, beauty, health, skin care, spa travel, fitness, well-being and renewal." Byline given. Offers 25% kill fee. Buys first North American serial, all rights. Editorial lead time 3 months. Accepts queries by mail. Sample copy for $6.

Columns/Departments In Touch (spa news, treatments, destinations); Body (nutrition, health & fitness, spa therapies); Rituals (spa at home, beauty, home, books & music, mind/body).

N $ $ SPA LIFE

Harworth Publishing, Inc., Box 998, Guelph ON N1H 6N1 Canada. (519)767-6059. Fax: (519)821-0479. E-mail: editor@harworthpublishing.com. **Contact:** Mary Hughes, editor-in-chief/publisher. "*Spa Life* is about more than just spas. With favorite recipes from featured spa destinations, mouth-watering treats are at your fingertips. *Spa Life* is also dedicated to personal and health issues." Estab. 2000. Accepts queries by e-mail. Writer's guidelines by e-mail.

Nonfiction General interest, interview/profile, new product, personal experience, travel. Length: 300-600 words. **Pays $175-250 (Canadian).**

Fillers Short quips or nominations are 75 words. **Pays $25/each.** Should include photos submitted to designer@harworthpublishing.com.

Tips "Describe the treatments/food and surroundings. Include all information to make it easy for readers to get more info and make reservations. Make it personal and fun; the reader has to feel they know you and can relate."

$ $ ST. MAARTEN NIGHTS

Nights Publications, Inc., 1751 Richardson St., Suite 5.530, Montreal QC H3K 1G6 Canada. (514)931-1987. Fax: (514)931-6273. E-mail: editor@nightspublications.com. Web site: www.nightspublications.com. Editor: Jennifer McMorran. **90% freelance written.** Annual magazine covering the St. Maarten/St. Martin vacation experience seeking "upbeat, entertaining, lifestyle articles. Our audience is the North American vacationer." Estab. 1981. Circ. 225,000. **Pays on acceptance.** Publishes ms an average of 9 months after acceptance. Byline given. Buys North American and Caribbean serial rights. Editorial lead time 1 month. Accepts queries by mail, e-mail, fax. Responds in 2 weeks to queries; 1 month to mss. Writer's guidelines by e-mail.

- E-mail queries preferred. All submissions must include an e-mail address for correspondence.
- "Let the reader experience the story; utilize the senses; be descriptive."

Nonfiction Lifestyle with a lively, upscale touch. Include SASE with Canadian postage or IRC. General interest, historical/nostalgic, how-to (gamble), humor, interview/profile, opinion, personal experience, photo feature, travel, colorful profiles of islanders, sailing, ecological, ecotourism, local culture, art, activities, entertainment, nightlife, special events, topics relative to vacationers in St. Maarten/St. Martin. **Buys 8-10 mss/year.** Query with published clips. Length: 250-750 words. **Pays $100-300.**

Photos State availability with submission. Reviews transparencies. Buys one-time rights. Pays $50/photo. Captions, identification of subjects, model releases required.

Tips "Our style is upbeat, friendly, fluid, and descriptive. Our magazines cater to tourists who are already at the destination, so ensure your story is of interest to this particular audience. We welcome stories that offer fresh angles to familiar tourist-related topics."

$ $ TIMES OF THE ISLANDS

The International Magazine of the Turks & Caicos Islands, Times Publications, Ltd., P.O. Box 234, Southwind Plaza, Providenciales Turks & Caicos Islands British West Indies. (649)946-4788. Fax: (649)946-4788. E-mail: timespub@tciway.tc. Web site: www.timespub.tc. **Contact:** Kathy Borsuk, editor. **60% freelance written.** Quarterly magazine covering the Turks & Caicos Islands. "*Times of the Islands* is used by the public and private sector to inform visitors and potential investors/developers about the Islands. It goes beyond a superficial overview of tourist attractions with in-depth articles about natural history, island heritage, local personalities, new development, offshore finance, sporting activities, visitors' experiences, and Caribbean fiction." Estab. 1988. Circ. 10,000. Pays on publication. Publishes ms an average of 6 months after acceptance. Byline given. Buys second serial (reprint) rights. Publication rights for 6 months with respect to other publications distributed in Caribbean. Editorial lead time 4 months. Submit seasonal material at least 4 months in advance. Accepts queries by mail, fax. Accepts simultaneous submissions. Responds in 6 weeks to queries; 2 months to mss. Sample copy for $6. Writer's guidelines online.

Nonfiction Book excerpts, essays, general interest (Caribbean art, culture, cooking, crafts), historical/nostalgic, humor, interview/profile (locals), personal experience (trips to the Islands), photo feature, technical (island businesses), travel, book reviews, nature, ecology, business (offshore finance), watersports. **Buys 20 mss/year.** Query. Length: 500-3,000 words. **Pays $200-600.**

Reprints Send photocopy and information about when and where the material previously appeared. Payment varies.

Photos Send photos with submission. Reviews slides, prints, digital photos. Pays $15-100/photo. Identification of subjects required.

Columns/Departments On Holiday (unique experiences of visitors to Turks & Caicos), 500-1,500 words. **Buys 4 mss/year.** Query. **Pays $200.**

Fiction Adventure, ethnic, historical, humorous, mystery, novel excerpts. **Buys 2-3 mss/year.** Query. Length: 1,000-3,000 words. **Pays $250-400.**

Tips "Make sure that the query/article specifically relates to the Turks and Caicos Islands. The theme can be general (ecotourism, for instance), but the manuscript should contain specific and current references to the Islands. We're a high-quality magazine, with a small budget and staff, and are very open-minded to ideas (and manuscripts). Writers who have visited the Islands at least once would probably have a better perspective from which to write."

$ $ TRAILER LIFE

America's No. 1 RV Magazine, Affinity Group, Inc., 2575 Vista Del Mar Dr., Ventura CA 93001. Fax: (805)667-4484. E-mail: info@trailerlife.com. Web site: www.trailerlife.com. **40% freelance written.** Monthly magazine. "*Trailer Life* magazine is written specifically for active people whose overall lifestyle is based on travel and recreation in their RV. Every issue includes product tests, travel articles, and other features—ranging from lifestyle to vehicle maintenance." Estab. 1941. Circ. 270,000. **Pays on acceptance.** Publishes ms an average of 6 months after acceptance. Byline given. Offers 30% kill fee for assigned articles that are not acceptable. Buys first North American serial, electronic rights. Editorial lead time 4 months. Submit seasonal material 6 months in advance. Accepts queries by mail. Responds in 2 months to queries; 2 months to mss. Sample copy for free. Writer's guidelines for #10 SASE.

O→ Break in with a "small piece for the Campground Spotlight or Etc. section; a short article on an interesting RV trip."

Nonfiction Historical/nostalgic, how-to (technical), humor, new product, opinion, personal experience, travel. No vehicle tests, product evaluations or road tests; tech material is strictly assigned. No diaries or trip logs, no non-RV trips; nothing without an RV-hook. **Buys 75 mss/year.** Query with or without published clips. Length: 250-2,500 words. **Pays $125-700.** Sometimes pays expenses of writers on assignment.

Photos Send photos with submission. Reviews transparencies, b&w contact sheets. Buys one-time and occasionally electronic rights. Offers no additional payment for photos accepted with ms, does pay for supplemental photos. Identification of subjects, model releases required.

Columns/Departments Campground Spotlight (report with 1 photo of campground recommended for RVers), 250 words; Around the Bend (news, trends of interest to RVers), 100 words; Etcetera (useful tips and information affecting RVers), 240 words. **Buys 70 mss/year.** Query or send complete ms. **Pays $75-250.**

Tips "Prerequisite: Must have RV focus. Photos must be magazine quality. These are the two biggest reasons why manuscripts are rejected. Our readers are travel enthusiasts who own all types of RVs (travel trailers, truck campers, van conversions, motorhomes, tent trailers, fifth-wheels) in which they explore North America and beyond, embrace the great outdoors in national, state and private parks. They're very active and very adventurous."

$ TRANSITIONS ABROAD

P.O. Box 745, Bennington VT 05201. Phone/Fax: (802)442-4827. E-mail: editor@transitionsabroad.com. Web site: www.transitionsabroad.com. **Contact:** Sherry Schwarz, editor. **80-90% freelance written.** Bimonthly magazine resource for low-budget international travel, often with an educational or volunteer/work component. Focus is on enriching, informed, affordable, and responsible travel. Estab. 1977. Circ. 12,000. Pays on publication. Byline given. Buys first, second serial (reprint) rights. Accepts queries by e-mail. Responds in 1 month to queries; 1 month to mss. Sample copy for $6.45. Writer's guidelines online.

O→ Break in by sending "a concisely written fact-filled article—or even a letter to Info Exchange—of no more than 1,000 words with up-to-date practical information, based on your own experience, on how readers can combine travel and learning or travel and work."

Nonfiction Lead articles (up to 1,500 words) provide first-hand practical information on independent travel to featured country or region (see topics schedule). Also, how to find educational and specialty travel opportunities, practical information (evaluation of courses, special interest and study tours, economy travel), travel (new learning and cultural travel ideas). Foreign travel only. Few destination ("tourist") pieces or first-person narratives. *Transitions Abroad* is a resource magazine for independent, educated, and adventurous travelers, not for armchair travelers or those addicted to packaged tours or cruises. Emphasis on information—which must be usable by readers—and on interaction with people in host country. **Buys 120 unsolicited mss/year.** Prefer e-mail queries that indicate familiarity with the magazine. Query with credentials and SASE. Include author's bio and e-mail with submissions. Length: 500-1,500 words. **Pays $2/column inch.**

Photos Send photos when submission is accepted. Buys one-time rights. Pays $10-25 for color prints or color slides (prints preferred), $150 for covers. Captions, identification of subjects required.

Columns/Departments Worldwide Travel Bargains (destinations, activities, and accommodations for budget travelers—featured in every issue); Tour and Program Notes (new courses or travel programs); Travel Resources (new information and ideas for independent travel); Working Traveler (how to find jobs and what to expect); Activity Vacations (travel opportunities that involve action and learning, usually by direct involvement in host culture); Responsible Travel (information on community-organized tours). Length: 1,000 words maximum. **Buys 60 mss/year.** Send complete ms. **Pays $2/column inch.**

Fillers Info Exchange (information, preferably first hand—having to do with travel, particularly offbeat educational travel and work or study abroad). **Buys 30/year.** Length: 750 words maximum. **Pays complimentary 1-year subscription.**

The online magazine carries original content not found in the print edition and includes writer's guidelines.

Tips "We like nuts and bolts stuff, practical information, especially on how to work, live, and cut costs abroad. Our readers want usable information on planning a travel itinerary. Be specific: names, addresses, current costs. We are very interested in educational and long-stay travel and study abroad for adults and senior citizens. *Overseas Travel Planner* published each year in July provides best information sources on work, study, and independent travel abroad. Each bimonthly issue contains a worldwide directory of educational and specialty travel programs."

$$$$ TRAVEL + LEISURE

American Express Publishing Corp., 1120 Ave. of the Americas, New York NY 10036. (212)382-5600. Web site: www.travelandleisure.com. Editor-in-Chief: Nancy Novogrod. Managing Editor: Michael S. Cain. **Contact:** Editor. **80% freelance written.** "*Travel + Leisure* is a monthly magazine edited for affluent travelers. It explores the latest resorts, hotels, fashions, foods, and drinks, as well as political, cultural, and economic issues affecting travelers." Circ. 925,000. **Pays on acceptance.** Byline given. Offers 25% kill fee. Buys first world rights, as well as rights to republish in international editions and online. Accepts queries by mail, e-mail. Responds in 6 weeks to queries; 6 weeks to mss. Sample copy for $5.50 from (800)888-8728. Writer's guidelines online.

O→ There is no single editorial contact for *Travel + Leisure*. It is best to find the name of the editor of each section, as appropriate for your submission.

Nonfiction Travel. **Buys 40-50 feature (3,000-5,000 words) and 200 short (125-500 words) mss/year.** Query (e-mail preferred). **Pays $4,000-6,000/feature; $100-500/short piece.** Pays expenses of writers on assignment.

Photos Discourages submission of unsolicited transparencies. Buys one-time rights. Payment varies. Captions required.

Columns/Departments Length: 2,500-3,500 words. **Buys 125-150 mss/year. Pays $2,000-3,500.**

Tips "Queries should not be generic, but should specify what is new or previously uncovered in a destination or travel-related subject area."

N $ TRAVEL NATURALLY

Internaturally, Inc., P.O. Box 317-W, Newfoundland NJ 07435-0317. (973)697-3552. Fax: (973)697-8313. E-mail: naturally@internaturally.com. Web site: www.internaturally.com. **Contact:** Bernard Loibl, editor. **90% freelance written.** Quarterly magazine covering wholesome family nude recreation and travel locations. "*Travel Naturally* looks at why millions of people believe that removing clothes in public is a good idea, and at places specifically created for that purpose—with good humor, but also in earnest. *Travel Naturally* takes you to places where your personal freedom is the only agenda, and to places where textile-free living is a serious commitment." Estab. 1981. Circ. 35,000. Pays on publication. Byline given. Buys first, one-time rights. Editorial lead time 4 months. Submit seasonal material 4 months in advance. Accepts queries by mail, e-mail, fax. Accepts simultaneous submissions. Sample copy for $9. Writer's guidelines online.

Nonfiction Frequent contributors and regular columnists, who develop a following through *Travel Naturally*, are paid from the Frequent Contributors Budget. Payments increase on the basis of frequency of participation. General interest, interview/profile, personal experience, photo feature, travel. **Buys 12 mss/year.** Send complete ms. Length: 2 pages. **Pays $80/published page, including photos.**
Reprints Accepts previously published submissions. Pays 50% of original rate.
Photos Send photos with submission. Reviews contact sheets, negatives, transparencies, prints, high resolution digital images. Buys one-time rights.
Fillers Anecdotes, facts, gags to be illustrated by cartoonist, newsbreaks, short humor, poems, artwork. **Pays payment is pro-rated based on length.**
Tips "*Travel Naturally* invokes the philosophies of naturism and nudism, but also activities and beliefs in the mainstream that express themselves, barely: spiritual awareness, New Age customs, pagan and religious rites, alternative and fringe lifestyle beliefs, artistic expressions, and many individual nude interests. Our higher purpose is simply to help restore our sense of self. Although the term 'nude recreation' may, for some, conjure up visions of sexual frivolities inappropriate for youngsters—because that can also be technically true—these topics are outside the scope of *Travel Naturally* magazine. Here the emphasis is on the many varieties of human beings, of all ages and backgrounds, recreating in their most natural state, at extraordinary places, their reasons for doing so, and the benefits they derive. We incorporate a travel department to advise and book vacations in locations reviewed in travel articles."

$ TRAVEL SMART

Communications House, Inc., P.O. Box 397, Dobbs Ferry NY 10522. E-mail: travelsmartnow@aol.com. Web site: travelsmartnewsletter.com. **Contact:** Nancy Dunnan, editor. Monthly newsletter covering information on "good-value travel." Estab. 1976. Circ. 20,000. Pays on publication. Buys all rights. Accepts queries by mail, e-mail. Responds in 6 weeks to queries; 6 weeks to mss. Sample copy for 9×12 SAE and 3 first-class stamps. Writer's guidelines for 9×12 SAE with 3 first-class Stamps.
Nonfiction "Interested primarily in bargains or little-known deals on transportation, lodging, food, unusual destinations that are really good values. No destination stories on major Caribbean islands, London, New York, no travelogs, 'my vacation,' poetry, fillers. No photos or illustrations other than maps. Just hard facts. We are not part of 'Rosy fingers of dawn.' school." Write for guidelines, then query. Query. Length: 100-1,500 words. **Pays $150 maximum.**
Tips "When you travel, check out small hotels offering good prices, good restaurants, and send us brief rundown (with prices, phone numbers, addresses). Information must be current. Include your phone number with submission, because we sometimes make immediate assignments."

$ $ VOYAGEUR

The Magazine of Carlson Hospitality Worldwide, Pace Communications, 1301 Carolina St., Greensboro NC 27401. (336)378-6065. Fax: (336)378-8272. Editor: Mark Caskie. **Contact:** Sarah Lindsay, senior editor. **90% freelance written.** Quarterly in-room magazine for Radisson hotels and affiliates. "*Voyageur* is an international magazine published quarterly for Carlson Hospitality Worldwide and distributed in the rooms of Radisson Hotels & Resorts, Park Plaza and Park Inn hotels, and Country Inns & Suites By Carlson throughout North and South America, Europe, Australia, Africa, Asia, and the Middle East. All travel-related stories must be in destinations where Carlson has a presence." Estab. 1992. Circ. 160,000. Pays on publication. Publishes ms an average of 2 months after acceptance. Offers 25% kill fee. Buys first North American serial rights. Editorial lead time 4 months. Submit seasonal material 6 months in advance. Accepts queries by mail. Responds in 2 months to queries; 2 months to mss. Sample copy for $5. Writer's guidelines for #10 SASE.

- Break in with a "well-thought-out, well-written, well-researched query on a city or area the writer lives in or knows well—one where Carlson has a presence (Radisson, Country Inns, or Park)."

Nonfiction The cover story is "a multi-destination feature with an overall theme, such as romantic weekend getaways. We like these articles to capture the distinctive atmosphere of a destination, while at the same time providing readers with a possible itinerary for a visit. All destinations are locations where Carlson has a major presence. We have a strong preference for writers who live in the city/region covered by the story. Typically, we use 4 different writers for 4 separate destinations in a single issue." Length: 425 words, plus sidebar of contact information for travelers. Adventures are first-person articles (with an "in-the-moment" feel) that "focus on active travel opportunities that reflect the unique aspects of a destination. They usually describe adventures that can be accomplished in a weekend or less (i.e., traditional outdoor sports, visits to historic sites, a 1-day cooking class at a local cooking school). Activities must be near destinations with Carlson properties." Length: 475 words. Travel. Query with published clips. **Pays $500-525/piece.** Sometimes pays expenses of writers on assignment.
Photos State availability with submission. Reviews contact sheets, transparencies, prints. Buys one-time rights. Negotiates payment individually. Identification of subjects, model releases required.

Columns/Departments A place-specific shopping story with cultural context and upscale attitude, 300 words and 50-word mini-sidebar; Agenda (insights into conducting business and traveling for business internationally), 350 words; Port of Call (an evocative first-person look back at an appealing destination visited by Radisson Seven Seas Cruises), 350 words. **Buys 28-32 mss/year.** Query with published clips. **Pays $375.**
Tips "We look for authoritative, energetic, and vivid writing to inform and entertain business and leisure travelers, and we are actively seeking writers with an authentic European, Asian, Latin American, African, or Australian perspective. Travel stories should be authoritative yet personal."

N $ WESTERN RV NEWS & RECREATION

Fax: (503)214-8291. Web site: www.westernrvnews.com. **Contact:** Tom and Darlene O'Connor, Publishers and Editors. Monthly magazine for owners of recreational vehicles and those interested in the RV lifestyle. Estab. 1966. Byline given. Buys first, second serial (reprint) rights. Accepts queries by e-mail. Accepts simultaneous submissions. Writer's guidelines online.

- All correspondence should come through links on the Web site. Do not send snail mail, call or e-mail directly. Visit the Web pages for submission guidelines and contact forms.

Nonfiction How-to (RV oriented, purchasing considerations, maintenance), humor (RV experiences), new product (with ancillary interest to RV lifestyle), personal experience (varying or unique RV lifestyles), technical (RV systems or hardware), travel. "No articles without an RV slant." **Buys 100 mss/year.** Submit complete ms on paper, disk, or by e-mail. Length: 250-1,400 words. **Pays 8¢/word for first rights.**
Reprints Photocopy of article or typed ms with rights for sale noted and information about when and where the material previously appeared. Pays 5¢/word.
Photos Color slides and prints are accepted with article at a rate of $5/photo used. Digital photos are also accepted through e-mail or on disk (CD, Zip, etc.), but must be at a minimum resolution of 300 dpi at published size (generally, 5×7 inches is adequate). Captions, identification of subjects, model releases required.
Fillers Encourage anecdotes, RV-related tips, and short humor. Length: 50-250 words. **Pays $5-25.**
Tips "our editorial mix strives to provide full-color travel features and destinations, useful repair and technical articles, how-to advice, and product reviews. Regular columns written by on-the-road RVers share the backroads and first-hand experiences of the part-time and full-time RV lifestyle. Our readers say that generations of their families have subscribed to Western RV News & Recreation for many years, and they continue to enjoy Western RV News & Recreation from cover to cover."

$ $ WOODALL'S REGIONALS

2575 Vista Del Mar Dr., Ventura CA 93001. Web site: www.woodalls.com. Monthly magazine for RV and camping enthusiasts. Woodall's Regionals include *Camper Ways, Midwest RV Traveler, Northeast Outdoors, Florida RV Traveler, Southern RV, Texas RV*, and *Southwest RV Traveler.* Byline given. Buys first rights. Accepts queries by mail, e-mail. Responds in 1-2 months to queries. Sample copy for free. Writer's guidelines free.
Nonfiction "We need interesting and tightly focused feature stories on RV travel and lifestyle, campground spotlights and technical articles that speak to both novices and experienced RVers." **Buys 500 mss/year.** Query with published clips. Length: 500-1,700 words. **Pays $180-250/feature; $75-100/department article and short piece.**

WOMEN'S

N ALL YOU MAGAZINE

Time Inc., 1271 Avenue of the Americas, New York NY 10020. E-mail: feedback@allyou.com. Web site: www.allyou.com..

- Query before submitting.

N ⊘ ALLURE

Conde Nast Publications, 4 Times Square, 10th Floor, New York NY 10036. (212)286-7441. Fax: (212)286-2690. E-mail: alluremag@aol.com. Web site: www.allure.com. Editor: Linda Wells. Senior Editor: Brooke Le Poer Trench. Deputy Editor: Jill Mackenzie. Articles Editor: Sarah Van Boven. Monthly magazine covering fashion, beauty, fitness, etc. Geared toward the professional modern woman. Circ. 957,276. Sample copy not available.

$ $ $ BRIDAL GUIDE

R.F.P., LLC, 3 E. 54th St., 15th Floor, New York NY 10022. (212)838-7733. Fax: (212)308-7165. Web site: www.bridalguide.com. **Contact:** Susan Schneider, executive editor; Jennifer Dennis, travel editor. **20% freelance written.** Bimonthly magazine covering relationships, sexuality, fitness, wedding planning, psychology, finance, travel. Only works with experienced/published writers. **Pays on acceptance.** Accepts queries by mail.

Responds in 3 months to queries; 3 months to mss. Sample copy for $5 and SAE with 4 first-class stamps. Writer's guidelines available.

Nonfiction "Please do not send queries concerning beauty, fashion, or home design stories since we produce them in-house. We do not accept personal wedding essays, fiction, or poetry. Address travel queries to travel editor." All correspondence accompanied by an SASE will be answered. **Buys 100 mss/year.** Query with published clips from national consumer magazines. Length: 1,000-2,000 words. **Pays 50¢/word.**

Photos Photography and illustration submissions should be sent to the art department.

Tips "We are looking for service-oriented, well-researched pieces that are journalistically written. Writers we work with use at least 3 top expert sources, such as physicians, book authors, and business people in the appropriate field. Our tone is conversational, yet authoritative. Features are also generally filled with real-life anecdotes. We also do features that are completely real-person based—such as roundtables of bridesmaids discussing their experiences, or grooms-to-be talking about their feelings about getting married. In queries, we are looking for a well-thought-out idea, the specific angle of focus the writer intends to take, and the sources he or she intends to use. Queries should be brief and snappy—and titles should be supplied to give the editor an even better idea of the direction the writer is going in."

$$$$ CHATELAINE

One Mount Pleasant Rd., 8th Floor, Toronto ON M4Y 2Y5 Canada. (416)764-2879. Fax: (416)764-2981. Web site: www.chatelaine.com. Executive Editor: Craig Offman. Monthly magazine. "*Chatelaine* is edited for Canadian women ages 25-49, their changing attitudes and lifestyles. Key editorial ingredients include health, finance, social issues and trends, as well as fashion, beauty, food and home decor. Regular departments include Health pages, Entertainment, Humour, How-to." **Pays on acceptance.** Byline given. Offers 25-50% kill fee. Buys first, electronic rights. Accepts queries by mail. Sample copy not available.

Nonfiction Seeks "agenda-setting reports on Canadian national issues and trends as well as pieces on health, careers, personal finance and other facts of Canadian life." **Buys 50 mss/year.** Query with published clips and SASE. Length: 1,000-2,500 words. **Pays $1,000-2,500.** Pays expenses of writers on assignment.

Columns/Departments Length: 500-1,000 words. Query with published clips and SASE. **Pays $500-750.**

$$ COMPLETE WOMAN

For All The Women You Are, Associated Publications, Inc., 875 N. Michigan Ave., Suite 3434, Chicago IL 60611. (312)266-8680. Editor-in-Chief: Bonnie L. Krueger. **Contact:** Lora Wintz, executive editor. **90% freelance written.** Bimonthly magazine. "Manuscripts should be written for today's busy women, in a concise, clear format with useful information. Our readers want to know about the important things: sex, love, relationships, career, and self-discovery. Examples of true-life anecdotes incorporated into articles work well for our readers, who are always interested in how other women are dealing with life's ups and downs." Estab. 1980. Circ. 300,000. Pays 45 days after acceptance. Publishes ms an average of 6 months after acceptance. Byline given. Buys first North American serial, second serial (reprint), simultaneous rights. Editorial lead time 6 months. Submit seasonal material 5 months in advance. Accepts queries by mail. Accepts simultaneous submissions. Responds in 2 months to queries; 2 months to mss. Sample copy not available. Writer's guidelines for #10 SASE.

"Break in with writing samples that relate to the magazine. Also, the editor reports a need for more relationship stories."

Nonfiction "We want self-help articles written for today's woman. Articles that address dating, romance, sexuality, and relationships are an integral part of our editorial mix, as well as inspirational and motivational pieces." Book excerpts, exposé (of interest to women), general interest, how-to (beauty/diet-related), humor, inspirational, interview/profile (celebrities), new product, personal experience, photo feature, sex, love, relationship advice. **Buys 60-100 mss/year.** Query with published clips or send complete ms. Length: 800-2,000 words. **Pays $160-500.** Sometimes pays expenses of writers on assignment.

Reprints Send tearsheet, photocopy or typed ms with rights for sale noted and information about when and where the material previously appeared.

Photos Photo features with little or no copy should be sent to Kourtney McKay. Send photos with submission. Reviews 2.25 or 35mm transparencies, 5×7 prints. Buys one-time rights. Pays $35-100/photo. Captions, identification of subjects, model releases required.

Tips "Freelance writers should review publication, review writer's guidelines, then submit their articles for review. We're looking for new ways to explore the usual topics, written in a format that will be easy for our readers (ages 24-40+) to understand. We also like sidebar information that readers can review quickly before or after reading the article. Our focus is relationship-driven, with an editorial blend of beauty, health, and career."

N $ $ $ $ CONCEIVE MAGAZINE

Celebrating the Creation of Families, Intellectual Capital Productions Inc., 622 E. Washington St., Suite 440, Orlando FL 32801. (407)447-2456. Fax: (407)770-1760. Web site: www.conceiveonline.com. **Contact:** Beth Weinhouse, editor-in-chief. **50% freelance written.** Quarterly magazine covering fertility, conception, adoption. Estab. 2004. Circ. 200,000+. **Pays on acceptance.** Publishes ms an average of 4 months after acceptance. Byline given. Offers 25% kill fee. Buys all rights. Editorial lead time 6 months. Submit seasonal material 8 months in advance. Accepts queries by mail, e-mail, fax. Writer's guidelines online.

- E-mail queries should be sent through online contact form.

Nonfiction Book excerpts, essays, interview/profile, new product, personal experience. "I am inundated with queries from writers who want to recount their own 'journey to parenthood.' I have plenty of personal stories; I need well-reported, well-written health and lifestyle pieces." Query with published clips. Length: 500-2,000 words. **Pays $250-2,000.** Pays expenses of writers on assignment.

Columns/Departments Adam + Eve (marriage/relationship), 750-1,000 words; Boxers + Briefs (men/fertility), 750 words; Family is Born (success stories), 750-1,500 words; Conceived (early pregnancy), 750-1,500 words. Query with published clips. **Pays $250-1,000.**

Tips "We are the first and only consumer magazine in the pre-pregnancy (fertility and conception) category. We are not a pregnancy or parenting journal, or an infertility magazine."

COUNTRY WOMAN

Reiman Publications, 5925 Country Lane, Greendale WI 53129. (414)423-0100. E-mail: editors@countrywomanmagazine.com. Web site: www.countrywomanmagazine.com. **75-85% freelance written.** Bimonthly magazine. "*Country Woman* is for contemporary rural women of all ages and backgrounds and from all over the U.S. and Canada. It includes a sampling of the diversity that makes up rural women's lives—love of home, family, farm, ranch, community, hobbies, enduring values, humor, attaining new skills and appreciating present, past and future all within the context of the lifestyle that surrounds country living." Estab. 1970. **Pays on acceptance.** Byline given. Buys first North American serial, one-time, second serial (reprint) rights. Submit seasonal material 5 months in advance. Accepts queries by mail. Accepts previously published material. Accepts simultaneous submissions. Responds in 2 months to queries; 3 months to mss. Sample copy for $2 and SASE. Writer's guidelines for #10 SASE.

- Break in with "fiction, nostalgia and inspirational pieces. Study the magazine carefully before submitting."

Nonfiction Articles must be written in a positive, light and entertaining manner. General interest, historical/nostalgic, how-to (crafts, community projects, decorative, antiquing, etc.), humor, inspirational, interview/profile, personal experience, photo feature (packages profiling interesting country women-all pertaining to rural women's interests). Query. Length: 1,000 words maximum.

Reprints Send ms with rights for sale noted and information about when and where the material previously appeared. Payment varies.

Photos Uses only excellent quality color photos. No b&w. "We pay for photo/feature packages." State availability of or send photos with submission. Reviews 35mm or 2.25 transparencies, excellent-quality color prints. Buys one-time rights. Captions, identification of subjects, model releases required.

Columns/Departments Why Farm Wives Age Fast (humor), I Remember When (nostalgia) and Country Decorating. Length: 500-1,000 words. **Buys 10-12 mss/year.** Query or send ms.

Fiction Kathleen Anderson, managing editor. Main character *must* be a country woman. All fiction must have a country setting. Fiction must have a positive, upbeat message. Includes fiction in every issue. Would buy more fiction if stories suitable for our audience were sent our way. "No contemporary, urban pieces that deal with divorce, drugs, etc." Send complete ms. Length: 750-1,000 words.

Poetry Light verse, traditional. "Poetry must have rhythm and rhyme! It must be country-related, positive and upbeat. Always looking for seasonal poetry." **Buys 6-12 poems/year.** Submit maximum 6 poems. Length: 4-24 lines.

Tips "We have broadened our focus to include 'country' women, not just women on farms and ranches but also women who live in a small town or country home and/or simply have an interest in country-oriented topics. This allows freelancers a wider scope in material. Write as clearly and with as much zest and enthusiasm as possible. We love good quotes, supporting materials (names, places, etc.) and strong leads and closings. Readers relate strongly to where they live and the lifestyle they've chosen. They want to be informed and entertained, and that's just exactly why they subscribe. Readers are busy—not too busy to read—but when they do sit down, they want good writing, reliable information and something that feels like a reward. How-to, humor, personal experience and nostalgia are areas most open to freelancers. Profiles, to a certain degree, are also open. Be accurate and fresh in approach."

$$$$ ELLE

Hachette Filipacchi Media U.S., Inc., 1633 Broadway, 44th Floor, New York NY 10019. (212)767-5800. Fax: (212)489-4211. Web site: www.elle.com. **Contact:** Editorial Department. Monthly magazine. Edited for the modern, sophisticated, affluent, well-traveled woman in her twenties to early thirties. Circ. 1,100,000. Editorial lead time 3 months.

- Query first.

ESSENCE

135 W. 50th St., New York NY 10020. Web site: www.essence.com. Executive Editor: Vanessa Bush. Entertainment Editor: Cori Murray. **Contact:** Editorial Department. Monthly magazine. "*Essence* is the magazine for today's Black women. Edited for career-minded, sophisticated and independent achievers, *Essence*'s editorial is dedicated to helping its readers attain their maximum potential in various lifestyles and roles. The editorial content includes career and educational opportunities; fashion and beauty; investing and money management; health and fitness; parenting; information on home decorating and food; travel; cultural reviews; fiction; and profiles of achievers and celebrities." Estab. 1970. Circ. 1,000,000. **Pays on acceptance.** Byline given. Offers 25% kill fee. Makes assignments on a one-time serial rights basis. Editorial lead time 6 months. Submit seasonal material 6 months in advance. Accepts queries by mail, fax. Accepts previously published material. Responds in 2 months to queries; 2 months to mss. Sample copy for $3.25. Writer's guidelines online.

- To contact this magazine, first see their online instructions at www.essence.com/essence/writers_guidelines.

Nonfiction Book excerpts, novel excerpts. **Buys 200 mss/year.** Query. Length: Will be given upon assignment. **Pays by the word.**

Reprints Send tearsheet and information about when and where the material previously appeared. Pays 50% of the amount paid for the original article.

Photos "We particularly would like to see photographs for our travel section that feature Black travelers." State availability with submission. Pays from $200 up depending on the size of the image. Model releases required.

Tips "Please note that *Essence* no longer accepts unsolicited mss for fiction or nonfiction, except for the Brothers, Where There's a Will, Making Love Work, Our World, Back Talk and Interiors columns. So please only send query letters for nonfiction story ideas."

FIRST FOR WOMEN

Bauer Publishing Co., 270 Sylvan Ave., Englewood Cliffs NJ 07632-2523. (201)569-6699. Fax: (201)569-6264. E-mail: firstfw@aol.com. Web site: www.firstforwomen.com. Editor: Carol Brooks. Magazine. Designed for the busy woman. Articles concering health, beauty, real life stories, home and food. Circ. 1,500,000. Editorial lead time 3 months. Sample copy not available.

$$$$ FLARE MAGAZINE

One Mt. Pleasant Rd., 8th Floor, Toronto ON M4Y 2Y5 Canada. (416)764-2863. Fax: (416)764-2866. E-mail: editors@flare.com. Web site: www.flare.com. Monthly magazine for women ages 17-34. Byline given. Offers 50% kill fee. Buys first North American serial, electronic rights. Accepts queries by e-mail. Response time varies to queries. Sample copy for #10 SASE. Writer's guidelines online.

Nonfiction Looking for "women's fashion, beauty, health, sociological trends and celebrities." **Buys 24 mss/year.** Query. Length: 200-1,200 words. **Pays $1/word.** Pays expenses of writers on assignment.

Tips "Study our masthead to determine if your topic is handled by regular contributing staff or a staff member."

$$$$ GLAMOUR

Conde Nast Publications, Inc., 4 Times Square, 16th floor, New York NY 10036. (212)286-2860. Fax: (212)286-7731. Web site: www.glamour.com. Editor-in-Chief: Blaine Zuckerman. Senior Beauty Editor: Laurel Naversen. Articles Editor: Abigail Pesta. Monthly magazine covering subjects ranging from fashion, beauty and health, personal relationships, career, travel, food and entertainment. *Glamour* is edited for the contemporary woman, and informs her of the trends and recommends how she can adapt them to her needs, and motivates her to take action. Estab. 1939.

Nonfiction Personal experience (relationships), travel.

$$$$ GOOD HOUSEKEEPING

Hearst Corp., 250 W. 55th St., New York NY 10019. (212)649-2200. Fax: (212)649-2340. Web site: www.goodhousekeeping.com. Editor-in-Chief: Rosemary Ellis. **Contact:** Judith Coyne, executive editor. Monthly magazine. "*Good Housekeeping* is edited for the 'New Traditionalist.' Articles which focus on food, fitness, beauty, and child care draw upon the resources of the Good Housekeeping Institute. Editorial includes human interest stories, articles that focus on social issues, money management, health news, travel.'' Circ. 5,000,000. **Pays on acceptance.** Byline given. Offers 25% kill fee. Buys first North American serial rights. Submit seasonal material 6 months in advance. Responds in 2-3 months to queries; 2-3 months to mss. For sample copy, call (212)649-2359. Writer's guidelines for #10 SASE.

Nonfiction Consumer, social issues, dramatic narrative, nutrition, work, relationships, psychology, trends. **Buys 4-6 mss/issue mss/year.** Query. Length: 1,500-2,500 words. Pays expenses of writers on assignment.

Photos Photos purchased on assignment mostly. Melissa Paterno, art director. Toni Paciello, photo editor. State availability with submission. Pays $100-350 for b&w; $200-400 for color photos. Model releases required.

Columns/Departments Profiles (inspirational, activist or heroic women), 400-600 words. Query with published clips. **Pays $1/word for items 300-600 words.**

Fiction Laura Mathews, fiction editor. No longer accepts unagented fiction submissions. Because of heavy volume of fiction submissions, *Good Housekeeping* is not accepting unsolicited submissions at this time. Agented submissions only. Length: 1,500 words (short-shorts); novel according to merit of material; average 5,000 word short stories. **Pays $1,000 minimum.**

Tips ''Always send a SASE and clips. We prefer to see a query first. Do not send material on subjects already covered in-house by the Good Housekeeping Institute—these include food, beauty, needlework and crafts.''

$ $ GRACE ORMONDE WEDDING STYLE

Elegant Publishing, Inc., P.O. Box 89, Barrington RI 02806. (401)245-9726. Fax: (401)245-5371. E-mail: yanni@weddingstylemagazine.com. Web site: www.weddingstylemagazine.com. Editor: Grace Ormonde. **Contact:** Yannis Tzoumas, editorial director/publisher. Annual magazine covering wedding and special event planning with editorial covering home and home decorating, women's health issues, cooking, beauty, and travel. Estab. 1997. Circ. 400,000. Pays on publication. Publishes ms an average of 4 months after acceptance. Accepts queries by mail, e-mail, fax. Sample copy not available. Writer's guidelines not available.

Nonfiction General interest, how-to, interview/profile, personal experience, travel. **Buys 35 mss/year.** Query. Length: 300-3,500 words. **Pays $100-300.**

Photos State availability with submission. Reviews transparencies. Negotiates payment individually.

Columns/Departments Wedding related (flowers, beauty, etc.), 450 words; Women's Health, 3,000 words; Home Decorating/Cooking, 400 words; Travel, 350 words. Query. **Pays $100-300.**

$ $ HER SPORTS

Active Sports Lifestyles, Wet Dog Media, 245 Central Ave., Suite C, St. Petersburg FL 33701. E-mail: editorial@hersports.com. Web site: www.hersports.com. **Contact:** Christina Gandolfo, editor-in-chief. **60% freelance written.** Bimonthly magazine covering women's outdoor, individual sports. ''*Her Sports* is for active women ages 25-49 who regard sports and being active an important part of their lifestyle. Our readers are beyond 'quick-fix diets' and '5-minute' exercise routines, and are looking for a way to balance being active and healthy with a busy lifestyle. We focus on health, nutrition, and sports, and sports training, travel, and profiles on everyday athletes and professional athletes with unique and motivational stories.'' Estab. 2004. Circ. 50,000. Pays on publication. Publishes ms an average of 3 months after acceptance. Byline given. Offers 50% kill fee. Buys all rights. Editorial lead time 3 months. Submit seasonal material 6-8 months in advance. Accepts queries by e-mail. Responds in 2 weeks to queries; 1 month to mss. Sample copy for $4.99 and SASE with 5 first-class stamps. Writer's guidelines online.

Nonfiction Personal experience. ''Please do not send articles pertaining to team sports; we cover only outdoor individual sports.'' **Buys 6 mss/year.** Query with published clips. Length: 800-1,200 words. **Pays $200-300 for assigned articles.**

Photos Kristin Mayer, creative director. State availability with submission. Reviews GIF/JPEG files. Buys one-time rights. Negotiates payment individually. Captions, identification of subjects required.

Columns/Departments Body & Mind (nutrition, mental training, fitness training, body/mind exercise), 1,200 words; Adventure Journal (personal experience with a sport or outdoor adventure), 800-1,200 words; Discoveries (travel articles of interest to active women), 1,500-2,000 words; Weekend Warrior (how-to tips for mastering the sports we cover), 1,000-1,200 words; Her Story (short profile on ''everyday athletes'' who are an inspiration to others), 650 words. **Buys at least 24 mss/year.** Query. **Pays $250-350.**

Tips ''Persistence pays off but burying the editor with multiple submissions will quickly lose you points. If you're asked to check back in 2 months, do so, but if the editor tells you she's on deadline, simply inquire about a better time to get back in touch.''

INSTYLE

Time, Inc., 1271 Avenue of the Americas, 18th Floor, New York NY 10020. (212)522-1212. Fax: (212)522-0867. E-mail: letters@instylemag.com. Web site: www.instyle.com. Editor: Norman Pearlstine. Managing Editor:

Charla Lawhon. Monthly magazine. Written to be the most trusted style adviser and lifestyle resource for women. Circ. 1,670,000. Editorial lead time 4 months. Sample copy not available.

JANE

Fairchild Publications, Inc., 7 W. 34th St., 3rd Floor, New York NY 10001. (212)630-3900. Fax: (212)630-3925. E-mail: jane@fairchildpub.com. Web site: www.janemag.com. Editor-in-Chief: Brandon Holley. Managing Editor: Brekke Fletcher. Beauty/Health Director: Erin Flaherty. Deputy Editor: Stephanie Trong. Assistant Beauty Editor: Jill Schuck. Monthly magazine for confident, media-savvy 18-34 year old women. Written in an honest, first person tone by women (and some men) who are living the lifestyle they are covering. Circ. 678,000. Sample copy not available.

- Only accepting submissions for fiction and column called "It happened to me." Most writing is done in-house.

$ $ $ $ ⊘ LADIES' HOME JOURNAL

Meredith Corp., 125 Park Ave., 20th Floor, New York NY 10017-5516. (212)557-6600. Fax: (212)455-1313. E-mail: lhj@mdp.com. Web site: www.lhj.com. Editor-in-Chief: Diane Salvatore. **Contact:** Margot Gilman, articles editor. **50% freelance written.** Monthly magazine focusing on issues of concern to women 30-45. They cover a broader range of news and political issues than many women's magazines. "*Ladies' Home Journal* is for active, empowered women who are evolving in new directions. It addresses informational needs with highly focused features and articles on a variety of topics: self, style, family, home, world, health, and food." Estab. 1882. Circ. 4.1 million. **Pays on acceptance.** Publishes ms an average of 4-12 months after acceptance. Offers 25% kill fee. Buys first North American serial rights. Rights bought vary with submission. Editorial lead time 4 months. Accepts queries by mail, e-mail. Accepts simultaneous submissions. Responds in 3 months to queries. Sample copy not available. Writer's guidelines online.

Nonfiction Submissions on the following subjects should be directed to the editor listed for each: investigative reports, news-related features, psychology/relationships/sex, celebrities/entertainment. Send 1-2 page query, SASE, résumé, clips via mail or e-mail (preferred). Length: 2,000-3,000 words. **Pays $2,000-4,000.** Pays expenses of writers on assignment.

Photos *LHJ* arranges for its own photography almost all the time. State availability with submission. Rights bought vary with submission. Offers variable payment for photos accepted with ms. Captions, identification of subjects, model releases required.

Fiction Only short stories and novels submitted by an agent or publisher will be considered. No poetry of any kind. **Buys 12 mss/year.** Send complete ms. Length: 2,000-2,500.

$ $ ✪ THE LINK & VISITOR

Baptist Women of Ontario and Quebec, 1-315 Lonsdale Rd., Toronto ON M4V 1X3 Canada. (416)544-8550. E-mail: linkvis@baptistwomen.com. Web site: www.baptistwomen.com. **Contact:** Editor. **50% freelance written.** Magazine published 6 times/ year "designed to help Baptist women grow their world, faith, relationships, creativity, and mission vision-evangelical, egalitarian, Canadian." Estab. 1878. Circ. 3,500. Pays on publication. Publishes ms an average of 6 months after acceptance. Byline given. Buys one-time, second serial (reprint), simultaneous rights, makes work-for-hire assignments. Editorial lead time 2 months. Submit seasonal material 4 months in advance. Accepts simultaneous submissions. Sample copy for 9×12 SAE with 2 first-class Canadian stamps. Writer's guidelines online.

Nonfiction "Articles must be Biblically literate. No easy answers, American mindset or U.S. focus, retelling of Bible stories, sermons." Inspirational, interview/profile, religious. **Buys 30-35 mss/year.** Send complete ms. Length: 750-2,000 words. **Pays 5-12¢/word (Canadian).** Sometimes pays expenses of writers on assignment.

Photos State availability with submission. Buys one-time rights. Offers no additional payment for photos accepted with ms. Captions required.

Tips "We cannot use unsolicited manuscripts from non-Canadian writers. When submitting by e-mail, please send stories as messages, not as attachments."

$ LONG ISLAND WOMAN

Maraj, Inc., P.O. Box 176, Malverne NY 11565. E-mail: editor@liwomanonline.com. Web site: www.liwomanonline.com. **Contact:** A. Nadboy, managing editor. **40% freelance written.** Monthly magazine covering issues of importance to women—health, family, finance, arts, entertainment, fitness, travel, home. Estab. 2001. Circ. 40,000. Pays within 1 month of publication. Publishes ms an average of 3 months after acceptance. Byline given. Offers 33% kill fee. Buys one-time rights for print and online use. Editorial lead time 3 months. Submit seasonal material 3 months in advance. Accepts queries by mail, e-mail. Accepts previously published material. Accepts simultaneous submissions. Responds in 8 weeks to queries; 3 months to mss. Sample copy for $5. Writer's guidelines online. Editorial calendar online.

• Responds if interested in using reprints that were submitted.

Nonfiction Book excerpts, general interest, how-to, humor, interview/profile, new product, travel, reviews. **Buys 25-30 mss/year.** Query with published clips or send complete ms. Length: 500-1,800 words. **Pays $35-150.**

Reprints Accepts previously published submissions.

Photos State availability of or send photos with submission. Reviews 5×7 prints. Captions, identification of subjects, model releases required.

Columns/Departments Humor; Health Issues; Family Issues; Financial and Business Issues; Book Reviews and Books; Arts and Entertainment; Travel and Leisure; Home and Garden; Fitness.

$ $ $ $ MARIE CLAIRE

The Hearst Publishing Corp., 1790 Broadway, 3rd Floor, New York NY 10019. (212)649-5000. Fax: (212)649-5050. E-mail: marieclaire@hearst.com. Web site: www.marieclaire.com. Editor-in-Chief: Joanna Coles. Deputy Editor: Marty Munson. Senior Editor: Colleen Oakley. Associate Editor: Kelly Marages. Monthly magazine written for today's younger working woman with a smart service-oriented view. Estab. 1937. Circ. 952,223. Editorial lead time 6 months. Sample copy not available.

MORE MAGAZINE

Meredith Corp., 375 Lexington Ave., 9th Floor, New York NY 10017. Fax: (212)455-1433. Web site: www.more.com. Editor-in-Chief: Peggy Northrop. **90% freelance written.** Magazine published 10 times/year covering smart, sophisticated women from 40-60. Estab. 1998. Circ. 1,000,000. **Pays on acceptance.** Publishes ms an average of 3 months after acceptance. Byline given. Offers 25% kill fee. Buys first North American serial, first, all rights. Editorial lead time 4 months. Submit seasonal material 6 months in advance. Accepts queries by mail, e-mail, fax. Responds in 3 months to queries; 3 months to mss. Sample copy not available. Writer's guidelines for #10 SASE.

Nonfiction Essays, exposé, general interest, interview/profile, personal experience, travel, crime; food. **Buys 50 mss/year.** Query with published clips. Length: 300-2,500 words. **Pays variable rate depending on writer and/or story length.** Pays expenses of writers on assignment.

Photos State availability with submission. Negotiates payment individually. Captions, identification of subjects, model releases required.

Columns/Departments Buys 20 mss/year. Query with published clips.

$ $ $ $ MS. MAGAZINE

433 S. Beverly Dr., Beverly Hills CA 90212. (310)556-2515. Fax: (310)556-2514. E-mail: info@msmagazine.com. Web site: www.msmagazine.com. **Contact:** Manuscripts Editor. **30% freelance written.** Quarterly magazine on women's issues and news. Estab. 1972. Circ. 150,000. Byline given. Offers 30% kill fee. Buys all rights. Responds in 2 months to queries; 2 months to mss. Sample copy for $9. Writer's guidelines online.

• No unsolicited fiction or poetry.

Nonfiction International and national (U.S.) news, the arts, books, popular culture, feminist theory and scholarship, ecofeminism, women's health, spirituality, political and economic affairs, photo essays. **Buys 4-5 feature (3,500 words) and 4-5 short (500 words) mss/year.** Query with published clips. Length: 300-3,500 words. **Pays $1/word, 50¢/word for news stories.** Pays expenses of writers on assignment.

Reprints Send tearsheet or typed ms with rights for sale noted and information about when and where the material previously appeared. Pays 50% of amount paid for original article.

Photos State availability with submission. Buys one-time rights. Identification of subjects, model releases required.

Columns/Departments Buys 4-5 mss/year. Pays $1/word.

Tips Needs "international and national women's news, investigative reporting, personal narratives, humor, world-class fiction and poetry, and prize-winning journalists and feminist thinkers."

$ $ $ ⊘ REDBOOK MAGAZINE

Hearst Corp., 224 W. 57th St., 6th Floor, New York NY 10019. Web site: www.redbookmag.com. Monthly magazine. "*Redbook* addresses young married women between the ages of 28 and 44. Most of our readers are married with children 10 and under; over 60 percent work outside the home. The articles entertain, educate and inspire our readers to confront challenging issues. Each article must be timely and relevant to *Redbook* readers' lives." Estab. 1903. Circ. 2,300,000. **Pays on acceptance.** Publishes ms an average of 6 months after acceptance. Rights purchased vary with author and material. Responds in 3 months to queries; 3 months to mss. Sample copy not available. Writer's guidelines online.

O→ "Please review at least the past six issues of *Redbook* to better understand subject matter and treatment."

Nonfiction Subjects of interest: Social issues, parenting, sex, marriage, news profiles, true crime, dramatic narratives, health. Query with published clips and SASE. Length: 2,500-3,000 words/articles; 1,000-1,500 words/short articles.

Tips "Most *Redbook* articles require solid research, well-developed anecdotes from on-the-record sources, and fresh, insightful quotes from established experts in a field that pass our 'reality check' test. Articles must apply to women in our demographics."

$$$$ SELF

Condé Nast, 4 Times Square, New York NY 10036. (212)286-2860. Fax: (212)286-8110. E-mail: comments@self.com. Web site: www.self.com. Editor-in-Chief: Lucy Danziger. **Contact:** Dana Points, executive editor. Monthly magazine for women ages 20-45. "Self-confidence, self-assurance, and a healthy, happy lifestyle are pivotal to *Self* readers. This healthy lifestyle magazine delivers by addressing real-life issues from the inside out, with unparalleled energy and authority. From beauty, fitness, health and nutrition to personal style, finance, and happiness, the path to total well-being begins with *Self*." Circ. 1,300,000. **Pays on acceptance.** Byline given on features and most short items. Buys one-time rights. Accepts simultaneous submissions. Responds in 1 month to queries. Sample copy not available. Writer's guidelines for #10 SASE.

- *SELF* magazine does not accept unsolicited mss.
- Break in with "an original, news-driven story idea conveyed with lively and compelling writing and storytelling."

Nonfiction Considers proposals for major pieces on health, nutrition, psychology, fitness, family relationships and sociological issues. **Buys 40 mss/year.** Query with published clips. Length: 1,500-5,000 words. **Pays $1-2/word.**

Columns/Departments Buys 50 mss/year. Query with published clips. **Pays $1-2/word.**

The online version contains material not found in the print edition. Contact: Catherine Winters.

N $$ SKIRT! MAGAZINE

Morris Communications, 7 Radcliffe St., Suite 302, Charleston SC 29403. (843)958-0028. Fax: (843)958-0029. E-mail: editor@skirtmag.com. Web site: www.skirtmag.com. Publisher/Founder/Editor: Nikki Hardin. **Contact:** Kelly Love Johnson, senior editor. **50% freelance written.** Monthly magazine covering women's interest. "*Skirt!* is all about women—their work, play, families, creativity, style, health, wealth, bodies, and souls. The magazine's attitude is spirited, independent, outspoken, serious, playful, irreverent, sometimes controversial, and always passionate." Estab. 1994. Circ. 285,000. Pays on publication. Publishes ms an average of 2 months after acceptance. Byline given. Buys one-time rights. Editorial lead time 2-3 months. Submit seasonal material 2-3 months in advance. Accepts queries by e-mail. Accepts simultaneous submissions. Responds in 6-8 weeks to queries; 1-2 months to mss. Sample copy for $5. Writer's guidelines online.

Nonfiction Essays, humor, personal experience. Do not send feature articles. "We only accept submissions of completed personal essays." **Buys 100+ mss/year.** Send complete ms. Length: 900-1,200 words. **Pays $150-250.** Sometimes pays expenses of writers on assignment.

Photos "We feature a different color photo, painting, or illustration on the cover each month. Each issue also features a b&w photo by a female photographer. Submit artwork via e-mail or mail (include SASE)." Reviews Slides, high-resolution digital files. Does not pay for photos or artwork, but the artist's bio is published.

Tips "Surprise and charm us. We look for fearless essays that take chances with content and subject. *Skirt!* is not your average women's magazine. We push the envelope and select content that makes our readers think."

$$ TODAY'S BRIDE

Family Communications, 65 The East Mall, Toronto ON M8Z SW3 Canada. (416)537-2604. Fax: (416)538-1794. E-mail: info@canadianbride.com. Web site: www.todaysbride.ca.; www.canadianbride.com. Editor: Bettie Bradley. **Contact:** Susan Pennell-Sebekos, assistant editor; Diane Jermyn, assistant editor. **20% freelance written.** Semiannual magazine. "Magazine provides information to engaged couples on all aspects of wedding planning, including tips, fashion advice, etc. There are also beauty, home, groom, and honeymoon travel sections." Estab. 1979. Circ. 102,000. **Pays on acceptance.** Byline given. Buys all rights. Editorial lead time 6 months. Accepts queries by mail, e-mail, fax. Accepts simultaneous submissions. Responds in 2 weeks-1 month to queries. Sample copy not available. Writer's guidelines not available.

Nonfiction Humor, opinion, personal experience. No travel pieces. Query with or without published clips or send complete ms. Length: 800-1,400 words. **Pays $250-300.**

Photos Send photos with submission. Reviews transparencies, prints. Rights purchased negotiated on individual basis. Negotiates payment individually. Identification of subjects required.

Tips "Send us tight writing about topics relevant to all brides and grooms. Stories for grooms, especially those written by/about grooms, are also encouraged."

$ $ ☒ TODAY'S CHRISTIAN WOMAN

465 Gundersen Dr., Carol Stream IL 60188-2498. (630)260-6200. Fax: (630)260-0114. E-mail: tcwedit@christianitytoday.com. Web site: www.todayschristianwoman.com. Editor: Jane Johnson Struck. Managing Editor: Camerin Courtney. **Contact:** Lisa Cockrel, associate editor. **50% freelance written.** Bimonthly magazine for Christian women of all ages, single and married, homemakers, and career women. "*Today's Christian Woman* seeks to help women deal with the contemporary issues and hot topics that impact their lives, as well as provide depth, balance, and a Biblical perspective to the relationships they grapple with daily in the following arenas: family, friendship, faith, marriage, single life, self, work, and health." Estab. 1978. Circ. 230,000. **Pays on acceptance.** Publishes ms an average of 6-12 months after acceptance. Byline given. Buys first rights. Submit seasonal material 9 months in advance. Accepts queries by mail, e-mail, fax. Responds in 2 months to queries; 2 months to mss. Sample copy for $5. Writer's guidelines for #10 SASE or online.

Nonfiction How-to, narrative, inspirational. *Practical* spiritual living articles, 1,200-1,500 words. Humor (light, first-person pieces that include some spiritual distinctive), 1,000 words. Issues (third-person, anecdotal articles that report on scope of trends or hot topics, and provide perspective and practical take away on issues, plus sidebars), 1,500 words. How-to, inspirational. Query. No unsolicited mss. "The query should include article summary, purpose, and reader value, author's qualifications, suggested length, date to send, and SASE for reply." **Pays 20-25¢/word.**

Tips "Articles should be practical and contain a distinct evangelical Christian perspective. While *TCW* adheres strictly to this underlying perspective in all its editorial content, articles should refrain from using language that assumes a reader's familiarity with Christian or church-oriented terminology. Bible quotes and references should be used selectively. All Bible quotes should be taken from the New International Version if possible. All articles should be highly anecdotal, personal in tone, and universal in appeal."

N TRACE MAGAZINE

TRACE Inc., 476 Broome St., 2nd Floor, New York NY 10013. (212)625-1192. Fax: (212)625-1195. E-mail: editorial@trace212.com. Web site: www.trace212.com. Editor-in-Chief: Claude Grunitzky. **Contact:** Angela Cravens, executive editor. **25% freelance written.** Lifestyle magazine published 10 times/year covering fashion, music, and art. "*TRACE Magazine* is a leading international transcultural style magazine that mixes music, fashion, lifestyle and art through cutting-edge editorial." Estab. 1996. Circ. 100,000. Pays 30 days after publication. Publishes ms an average of 2 months after acceptance. Byline given. Buys first, second serial (reprint), electronic rights. Editorial lead time 2 months. Submit seasonal material 2 months in advance. Accepts queries by e-mail, phone. Accepts simultaneous submissions. Responds in 2 weeks to queries.

Nonfiction Book excerpts, essays, exposé, general interest, interview/profile, new product, personal experience, photo feature, technical, travel. Query with published clips. **Pays variable amount.** Sometimes pays expenses of writers on assignment.

Photos Contact Katie Constans, creative director. State availability of or send photos with submission. Reviews contact sheets, negatives, transparencies, prints, GIF/JPEG files. Buys exclusive worldwide first time, second serial, and electronic rights. Negotiates payment individually. Identification of subjects, model releases required.

Tips "Read the magazine and be familiar with style and tone. Also, queries that represent a knowledge of international subcultures and trends affecting young people are most often picked up by *TRACE*."

N $ $ $ $ VOGUE

Condé Nast, 4 Times Square, 12th Floor, New York NY 10036-6518. (212)286-2860. Web site: www.vogue.com. **Contact:** Laurie Jones, managing editor. Monthly magazine. "*Vogue* mirrors the changing roles and concerns of women, covering not only evolutions in fashion, beauty and style, but the important issues and ideas of the arts, health care, politics and world affairs." Estab. 1892. Circ. 1,174,677. **Pays on acceptance.** Byline sometimes given. Offers 25% kill fee. Responds in 3 months to queries. Sample copy not available. Writer's guidelines for #10 SASE.

Nonfiction "Needs fresh voices on unexpected topics." **Buys 5 unsolicited mss/year.** Query with published clips. Length: 2,500 words maximum. **Pays $1-2/word.**

Tips "Sophisticated, surprising and compelling writing a must." Please note: *Vogue* accepts *very* few unsolicited manuscripts. Most stories are generated in-house and are written by staff.

W

Fairchild Publications, Inc., 750 3rd Ave., New York NY 10017. (212)630-4900. Fax: (212)630-4919. Web site: www.wmagazine.com. Vice President/Publisher: Nina Lawrence. Monthly magazine covering pop culture, fashion, beauty, the arts, celebrities, homes, hotels, and more. Written for today's contemporary woman whose fashion sensibility and sense of style define her own look, in her own way. Circ. 463,000. Editorial lead time 6 weeks. Sample copy not available.

⊘ WEDDING CHANNEL MAGAZINE

(formerly *Weddingbells, (U.S.)*), 34 King St. E., Suite 1200, Toronto ON M5C 2X8 Canada. (416)363-1574. Fax: (416)363-6004. E-mail: editorialdept@weddingchannel.com. Web site: www.weddingchannel.com. Editor: Crys Stewart. **Contact:** Helen Cotellier, managing editor. **10% freelance written.** Quarterly magazine covering bridal, wedding, setting up home. Estab. 2000. Circ. 350,000. Pays on completion of assignment. Publishes ms an average of 6 months after acceptance. Byline sometimes given. Offers 25% kill fee. Buys first North American serial, second serial (reprint), electronic rights. Accepts queries by mail, fax. Responds in 2 months to queries.

- Does not accept unsolicited materials.

Nonfiction Book excerpts, bridal service pieces. **Buys 22 mss/year.** Query with published clips. **Pays variable rates for assigned articles.**

$ $ $ $ WISH

St. Joseph Media, 111 Queen St. E., Suite 320, Toronto ON M5C 1S2 Canada. E-mail: jane@wish.ca. Web site: www.wish.ca. **Contact:** Jane Francisco, editor-in-chief. **Pays on acceptance.** Writer's guidelines online.

Nonfiction Fashion, beauty, home decor, food, family, relationships, health & wellness, fitness. Query. **Pays $1/word.**

N $ $ WOMAN INTERNATIONAL

Emblem Media LLC, 9768 Belladonna Dr., San Raman CA 94582. (925)336-9252. Fax: (603)794-5923. E-mail: editorinchief@womanintl.com. Web site: www.womanintl.com. Managing Editor: Lynn Bolinger. **Contact:** Siara Nazir, editor-in-chief. **100% freelance written.** Quarterly magazine covering Asian women, ethnic women, women's fashion, beauty, health, relationships, celebrity. "Slant towards community activity, spirituality, and emphasis on womanhood rather than ethnicity." Estab. 2005. Circ. 15,000. Pays on publication. Publishes ms an average of 4-5 months after acceptance. Byline given. Offers $25 kill fee. Buys first, electronic rights. Editorial lead time 3 months. Submit seasonal material 3-4 months in advance. Accepts queries by mail, e-mail, fax. Accepts previously published material. Accepts simultaneous submissions. Responds in 2 weeks to queries. Sample copy for $3, SAE and 7 First-Class stamps. Writer's guidelines online.

Nonfiction Book excerpts, essays, exposé, general interest, how-to, humor, inspirational, interview/profile, new product, personal experience, photo feature, travel, women's causes. Does not material not in line with our demographics. **Buys 1-2 mss/year.** Query with published clips. Length: 500-700 words. **Pays 10¢/word.**

Photos State availability with submission. Reviews GIF/JPEG files. Buys one-time rights. Offers no additional payment for photos accepted with ms. Captions, identification of subjects, model releases required.

Columns/Departments He Said, She Said (all Asians quotes, funny, humor), 10-15 words each quote/6-8 quotes total; Events International (international women's events), 300 words; Just Did It (Asian women who have success), 500 words; Cover Profile (profile of a celebrity of Asian descent), 500-700 words. **Buys 1-2 mss/year.** Query with published clips. **Pays 10¢/word.**

Fiction Buys 3 mss/year. Query with published clips. Length: 500-700 words. **Pays 10¢/word.**

Fillers Facts, gags to be illustrated by cartoonist, short humor. **Buys 20-25/year.** Length: 15-20 words. **Pays 10¢/word.**

Tips "Just e-mail us, follow up with a phone call, and check back after 2 weeks."

$ $ WOMAN'S LIFE

A Publication of Woman's Life Insurance Society, 1338 Military St., P.O. Box 5020, Port Huron MI 48061-5020. (800)521-9292. Fax: (810)985-6970. E-mail: wkrabach@womanslifeins.com. Web site: www.womanslifeins.com. Editor: Janice U. Whipple. **Contact:** Wendy L. Krabach, director of sales and marketing. **30% freelance written.** Quarterly magazine published for a primarily female membership to help them care for themselves and their families. Estab. 1892. Circ. 32,000. Pays on publication. Publishes ms an average of 1 year after acceptance. Byline given. Not copyrighted. Buys one-time, second serial (reprint), simultaneous rights. Submit seasonal material 6 months in advance. Accepts queries by mail, e-mail, fax. Accepts simultaneous submissions. Responds in 1 year to queries; 1 year to mss. Sample copy for 9×12 SAE and 4 first-class stamps. Writer's guidelines for #10 SASE.

- Works only with published/established writers.

Nonfiction Looking primarily for general interest stories for women aged 25-55 regarding physical, mental, and emotional health and fitness; and financial/fiscal health and fitness. "We would like to see more creative financial pieces that are directed at women." **Buys 4-10 mss/year.** Send complete ms. Length: 1,000-2,000 words. **Pays $150-500.**

Reprints Send tearsheet, photocopy or typed ms with rights for sale noted and information about when and where the material previously appeared. Pays 15% of amount paid for an original article.

Photos Only interested in photos included with ms. Identification of subjects, model releases required.

$WOMEN ALIVE

Encouraging Excellence in Holy Living, Women Alive, Inc., P.O. Box 480052, Kansas City MO 64145. Phone/Fax: (913)402-1369. E-mail: ahinthorn@kc.rr.com. Web site: www.womenalivemagazine.org. Managing Editor: Jeanette Littleton. **Contact:** Aletha Hinthorn, editor. **50% freelance written.** Bimonthly magazine covering Christian living. "*Women Alive* encourages and equips women to live holy lives through teaching them to live out Scripture." Estab. 1984. Circ. 4,000. Pays on publication. Publishes ms an average of 6 months after acceptance. Byline given. Buys first North American serial, first, one-time, second serial (reprint), simultaneous rights. Editorial lead time 4 months. Submit seasonal material 4 months in advance. Accepts queries by mail, e-mail. Accepts simultaneous submissions. Responds in 6 weeks to mss. Sample copy for 9×12 SAE and 3 first-class stamps. Writer's guidelines for 9×12 SAE with 3 first-class stamps.

Nonfiction Inspirational, opinion, personal experience, religious. **Buys 30 mss/year.** Send complete ms. Length: 500-1,500 words.

Photos State availability with submission. Offers no additional payment for photos accepted with ms.

$WOMEN IN BUSINESS

American Business Women's Association (The ABWA Co., Inc.), 9100 Ward Pkwy., P.O. Box 8728, Kansas City MO 64114-0728. (816)361-6621. Fax: (816)361-4991. E-mail: abwa@abwa.org. Web site: www.abwa.org. **Contact:** Kathleen Isaacson, editor. **30% freelance written.** Bimonthly magazine covering issues affecting working women. "How-to features for career women on business trends, small-business ownership, self-improvement, and retirement issues. Profiles business women." Estab. 1949. Circ. 45,000. **Pays on acceptance.** Publishes ms an average of 3 months after acceptance. Byline given. Buys first North American serial rights. Editorial lead time 3 months. Accepts queries by mail, e-mail, fax. Accepts simultaneous submissions. Responds in 3 weeks to queries; 2 months to mss. Sample copy for 9×12 SAE and 4 first-class stamps. Writer's guidelines for #10 SASE.

🔑 Break in by "having knowledge of the business world and how women fit into it."

Nonfiction How-to, interview/profile, computer/Internet. No fiction or poetry. **Buys 3% of submitted mss/year.** Query. Length: 500-1,000 words. **Pays $100/500 words.**

Photos State availability with submission. Reviews prints. Buys all rights. Offers no additional payment for photos accepted with ms. Identification of subjects required.

Columns/Departments Life After Business (concerns of retired business women); It's Your Business (entrepreneurial advice for business owners); Health Spot (health issues that affect women in the work place). Length: 500-750 words. Query. **Pays $100/500 words.**

N 🌐 YORKSHIRE WOMEN'S LIFE

P.O. Box 113, Leeds LS8 2WX United Kingdom. E-mail: ywlmagenquiries@btinternet.com. Web site: www.yorkshirewomenslife.co.uk. **Contact:** India Jones, assistant editor. Magazine published 3 times/year covering news, women's issues, fashion, travel, art, and lifestyle. Writer's guidelines by e-mail.

Nonfiction General interest (women's issues), personal experience (author descibes some aspect of her life in first person), reviews of theatres/art exhibitions/books. Does not want cooking/recipes, short stories, or poetry. Submit 200-word proposal, published clips, bio, SAE.

Photos Accepts color copies via post from female visual artists. Include a short CV.

MARKETS

Trade Journals

Many writers who pick up *Writer's Market* for the first time do so with the hope of selling an article to one of the popular, high-profile consumer magazines found on newsstands and in bookstores. Many of those writers are surprised to find an entire world of magazine publishing exists outside the realm of commercial magazines—trade journals. Writers who *have* discovered trade journals have found a market that offers the chance to publish regularly in subject areas they find interesting, editors who are typically more accessible than their commercial counterparts, and pay rates that rival those of the big-name magazines. **(Note: All of the magazines listed in the Trade Journals section are paying markets. However, some of the magazines are not identified by payment rates ($-$$$$) because the magazines preferred not to disclose specific payment information.)**

Trade journal is the general term for any publication focusing on a particular occupation or industry. Other terms used to describe the different types of trade publications are business, technical, and professional journals. They are read by truck drivers, bricklayers, farmers, fishermen, heart surgeons, and just about everyone else working in a trade or profession. Trade periodicals are sharply angled to the specifics of the professions on which they report. They offer business-related news, features, and service articles that will foster their readers' professional development.

Trade journal editors tell us their audience is made up of a knowledgeable and highly interested readers. Writers for trade journals have to either possess knowledge about the field in question or be able to report it accurately from interviews with those who do. Writers who have or can develop a good grasp of a specialized body of knowledge will find trade magazine editors who are eager to hear from them.

An ideal way to begin your foray into trade journals is to write for those that report on your present profession. Whether you've been teaching dance, farming, or working as a paralegal, begin by familiarizing yourself with the magazines that serve your occupation. After you've read enough issues to have a feel for the kinds of pieces the magazines run, approach the editors with your own article ideas. If you don't have experience in a profession but can demonstrate an ability to understand (and write about) the intricacies and issues of a particular trade that interests you, editors will still be willing to hear from you.

Information on trade publications listed in the previous edition of *Writer's Market*, but not included in this edition, can be found in the General Index.

ADVERTISING, MARKETING & PR

N $ $ $ ADVANTAGES MAGAZINE

The Advertising Specialty Institute, 4800 Street Rd., Trevose PA 19053. (215)953-3337. E-mail: khuston@asicentral.com. Web site: www.advantagesinfo.com. Managing Editor: Joe Haley. **Contact:** Kathy Huston, editor. **40% freelance written.** Monthly magazine covering promotional products (branded T-shirts, mugs, pens, etc.). "*Advantages* is a 15-issue publication targeted to promotional products salespeople. Its main objective is to be a comprehensive source of sales strategies, information and inspiration through articles, columns, case histories and product showcases. The magazine is presented in a fun and easy-to-read format to keep busy salespeople interested and entertained. The easy-to-use reader response system makes it fast and simple to request product information from suppliers featured in showcases. We want our subscribers to look forward to its arrival and to believe that *Advantages* is the one magazine they can't do without." Estab. 1997. Circ. 40,000. **Pays on acceptance.** Publishes ms an average of 1-2 months after acceptance. Byline given. Buys all rights. Editorial lead time 1 month. Submit seasonal material 1 month in advance. Accepts queries by e-mail, phone. Accepts simultaneous submissions. Sample copy for free. Writer's guidelines free.

Nonfiction Full-length features on market opportunities and selling-related topics. **Buys 40 mss/year.** Query. Length: 2,500-3,500 words. **Pays $500-1,000+.**

Tips "Just send me an e-mail, especially if you have any previous experience writing on the promotional products industry and/or sales topics in general."

$ $ BIG IDEA

Detroit's Connection to the Communication Arts, Big Idea, 2145 Crooks Rd., Suite 208, Troy MI 48084. (248)458-5500. Fax: (248)458-7099. E-mail: info@bigideaweb.com. Web site: www.bigideaweb.com. **Contact:** Kate Grace, managing editor. **75% freelance written.** Monthly magazine covering creative and communication arts in the Midwest. "We are a trade magazine specifically for creative professionals in the advertising, marketing and communication arts industry in the Midwest. We are the resource for anyone in the agency: film and video, printing, post production, interactive, art and design, illustration, or photography." Estab. 1994. Circ. 10,000. **Pays on acceptance.** Publishes ms an average of 2 months after acceptance. Byline given. Editorial lead time 2 months. Accepts queries by mail, e-mail, fax. Responds in 6 weeks to queries.

Nonfiction Buys 10-12 mss/year. Query with published clips. Length: 1,500-2,500 words. **Pays $100-350 for assigned articles.** Sometimes pays expenses of writers on assignment.

Photos State availability with submission. Reviews GIF/JPEG files. Offers no additional payment for photos accepted with ms. Captions, identification of subjects, model releases required.

$ $ $ BRAND PACKAGING

Stagnito Communications, 155 Pfingsten Rd., Suite 205, Deerfield IL 60015. (847)405-4000. Fax: (847)405-4100. E-mail: jacevedo@stagnito.com. Web site: www.brandpackaging.com. Senior Editor: Pauline Tingas. **Contact:** Jennifer Acevedo, editor-in-chief. **15% freelance written.** Magazine published 10 times/year covering how packaging can be a marketing tool. "We publish strategies and tactics to make products stand out on the shelf. Our market is brand managers who are marketers but need to know something about packaging." Estab. 1997. Circ. 33,000. **Pays on acceptance.** Publishes ms an average of 2 months after acceptance. Byline given. Makes work-for-hire assignments. Editorial lead time 3 months. Submit seasonal material 3 months in advance. Accepts queries by mail, fax. Sample copy for free.

Nonfiction How-to, interview/profile, new product. **Buys 10 mss/year.** Send complete ms. Length: 600-2,400 words. **Pays 40-50¢/word.**

Photos State availability with submission. Reviews contact sheets, 35mm transparencies, 4×5 prints. Buys one-time rights. Negotiates payment individually. Identification of subjects required.

Columns/Departments Emerging Technology (new packaging technology), 600 words. **Buys 10 mss/year.** Query. **Pays $150-300.**

Tips "Be knowledgeable on marketing techniques and be able to grasp packaging techniques. Be sure you focus on packaging as a marketing tool. Use concrete examples. We are not seeking case histories at this time."

N $ $ $ COLORADO MEETINGS & EVENTS MAGAZINE

Tiger Oak Publications, 900 S. 3rd St., Minneapolis MN 55401. Fax: (612)338-0532. Web site: www.meetingsandeventsmags.com. **Contact:** Barbara Knox, editor. **80% freelance written.** Quarterly magazine covering meetings and events industry. "*Colorado Meetings & Events* magazine is the premier trade publication for meeting planners and hospitality service providers in the state. This magazine aims to report on and promote businesses involved in the meetings and events industry. The magazine covers current and emerging trends, people and venues in the meetings and events industry in the state." Estab. 1993. Circ. 20,000. **Pays on acceptance.** Publishes ms an average of 4 months after acceptance. Byline given. Offers 20% kill fee. Buys first North

American serial rights. Editorial lead time 4-6 months. Submit seasonal material 6 months in advance. Accepts queries by mail. Accepts simultaneous submissions. Responds in 1-2 weeks to queries.

Nonfiction General interest, historical/nostalgic, interview/profile, new product, opinion, personal experience, photo feature, technical, travel. **Buys 30 mss/year.** Query with published clips. Length: 600-1,500 words. **Pays $400-800.**

Photos State availability with submission. Buys one-time rights. Negotiates payment individually. Identification of subjects, model releases required.

Columns/Departments Meet + Eat (restaurant reviews); Facility Focus (venue reviews); Regional Spotlight (city review), 1,000 words. **Buys 30 mss/year.** Query with published clips. **Pays $400-600.**

Tips "Familiarization with the meetings and events industry is critical, as well as knowing how to write for a trade magazine. Writers experienced in writing for the trade magazine business industry are preferred."

$ DECA DIMENSIONS

1908 Association Dr., Reston VA 20191. (703)860-5000. Fax: (703)860-4013. E-mail: decainc@aol.com. Web site: www.deca.org. **30% freelance written.** Quarterly magazine covering marketing, professional development, business, career training during school year (no issues published May-August). "*DECA Dimensions* is the membership magazine for DECA—The Association of Marketing Students—primarily ages 15-19 in all 50 states, the U.S. territories, Germany, and Canada. The magazine is delivered through the classroom. Students are interested in developing professional, leadership, and career skills." Estab. 1947. Circ. 160,000. Pays on publication. Byline given. Buys first, second serial (reprint) rights. Editorial lead time 3 months. Submit seasonal material 4 months in advance. Accepts queries by mail, e-mail, fax, phone. Accepts simultaneous submissions. Sample copy for free.

Nonfiction "Interested in seeing trends/forecast information of interest to audience (How do you forecast? Why? What are the trends for the next 5 years in fashion or retail?)." Essays, general interest, how-to (get jobs, start business, plan for college, etc.), interview/profile (business leads), personal experience (working), leadership development. **Buys 10 mss/year.** Send complete ms. Length: 800-1,000 words. **Pays $125 for assigned articles; $100 for unsolicited articles.**

Reprints Send ms and information about when and where the material previously appeared. Pays 85% of amount paid for an original article.

Columns/Departments Professional Development; Leadership, 350-500 words. **Buys 6 mss/year.** Send complete ms. **Pays $75-100.**

$ $ $ ILLINOIS MEETINGS & EVENTS MAGAZINE

Tiger Oak Publications, 900 S. 3rd St., Minneapolis MN 55401. Fax: (612)338-0532. Web site: www.meetingsandeventsmags.com. **Contact:** Barbara Knox, editor. **80% freelance written.** Quarterly magazine covering meetings and events industry. "*Illinois Meetings & Events* magazine is the premier trade publication for meetings planners and hospitality service providers in the state. This magazine aims to report on and promote businesses involved in the meetings and events industry. The magazine covers current and emerging trends, people and venues in the meetings and events industry in the state." Estab. 1993. Circ. 20,000. **Pays on acceptance.** Publishes ms an average of 4 months after acceptance. Byline given. Offers 20% kill fee. Buys first North American serial rights. Editorial lead time 4-6 months. Submit seasonal material 6 months in advance. Accepts queries by mail. Accepts simultaneous submissions. Responds in 1-2 weeks to queries.

Nonfiction General interest, historical/nostalgic, interview/profile, new product, opinion, personal experience, photo feature, technical, travel. **Buys 30 mss/year.** Query with published clips. Length: 600-1,500 words. **Pays $400-800.**

Photos State availability with submission. Buys one-time rights. Negotiates payment individually. Identification of subjects, model releases required.

Columns/Departments Meet + Eat (restaurant reviews); Facility Focus (venue reviews); Regional Spotlight (city review), 1,000 words. **Buys 30 mss/year.** Query with published clips. **Pays $400-600.**

Tips "Familiarization with the meetings and events industry is critical, as well as knowing how to write for a trade magazine. Writers experienced in writing for the trade magazine business industry are preferred."

$ $ $ MICHIGAN MEETINGS & EVENTS MAGAZINE

Tiger Oak Publications, 900 S. 3rd St., Minneapolis MN 55401. Fax: (612)338-0532. Web site: www.meetingsandeventsmags.com. **Contact:** Laurie Berger. **80% freelance written.** Quarterly magazine covering meetings and events industry. "*Michigan Meetings & Events* magazine is the premier trade publication for meetings planners and hospitality service providers in the state. This magazine aims to report on and promote businesses involved in the meetings and events industry. The magazine covers current and emerging trends, people and venues in the meetings and events industry in the state." Estab. 1993. Circ. 20,000. **Pays on acceptance.** Publishes ms an average of 4 months after acceptance. Byline given. Offers 20% kill fee. Buys first North American serial rights. Editorial lead time 4-6 months. Submit seasonal material 6 months in advance. Accepts queries by mail. Accepts simultaneous submissions. Responds in 1-2 weeks to queries.

Nonfiction General interest, historical/nostalgic, interview/profile, new product, opinion, personal experience, photo feature, technical, travel. **Buys 30 mss/year.** Query with published clips. Length: 600-1,500 words. **Pays $400-800.**

Photos State availability with submission. Buys one-time rights. Negotiates payment individually. Identification of subjects, model releases required.

Columns/Departments Meet + Eat (restaurant reviews); Family Focus (venue reviews); Regional Spotlight (city review), 1,000 words. Query with published clips. **Pays $400-600.**

Tips "Familiarization with the meetings and events industry is critical, as well as knowing how to write for a trade magazine. Writers experienced in writing for the trade magazine business industry are preferred."

$ $ $ MINNESOTA MEETINGS & EVENTS MAGAZINE

Tiger Oak Publications, 900 S. 3rd St., Minneapolis MN 55401. Fax: (612)338-0532. Web site: www.meetingsand eventsmags.com. **Contact:** Barbara Knox, editor. **80% freelance written.** Quarterly magazine covering meetings and events industry. "*Minnesota Meetings & Events* magazine is the premier trade publication for meetings planners and hospitality service providers in the state. This magazine aims to report on and promote businesses involved in the meetings and events industry. The magazine covers current and emerging trends, people and venues in the meetings and events industry in the state." Estab. 1993. Circ. 20,000. **Pays on acceptance.** Publishes ms an average of 4 months after acceptance. Byline given. Offers 20% kill fee. Buys first North American serial rights. Editorial lead time 4-6 months. Submit seasonal material 4 months in advance. Accepts queries by mail. Accepts simultaneous submissions. Responds in 1-2 weeks to queries.

Nonfiction General interest, historical/nostalgic, interview/profile, new product, opinion, personal experience, photo feature, technical, travel. **Buys 30 mss/year.** Query with published clips. Length: 600-1,500 words. **Pays $400-800.**

Photos State availability with submission. Buys one-time rights. Negotiates payment individually. Identification of subjects, model releases required.

Columns/Departments Meet + Eat (restaurant reviews); Facility Focus (venue reviews); Regional Spotlight (city review), 1,000 words. **Buys 30 mss/year.** Query with published clips. **Pays $400-600.**

Tips "Familiarization with the meetings and events industry is critical, as well as knowing how to write for a trade magazine. Writers experienced in writing for the trade magazine business industry are preferred."

N $ $ O'DWYER'S PR REPORT

271 Madison Ave., #600, New York NY 10016. E-mail: jack@odwyerpr.com. Web site: www.odwyerpr.com. **Contact:** Jack O'Dwyer. Monthly magazine providing PR articles. "Many of the contributors are PR people publicizing themselves while analyzing something." Byline given. Accepts queries by mail.

Nonfiction "We use op-ed pieces and news articles about PR trends." Opinion. Query. **Pays $250.**

N P-O-P TIMES

Hoyt Publishing Co., 7400 Skokie Blvd., Skokie IL 60077. (847)675-7400. Fax: (847)675-7494. E-mail: dan_ochw at@instoremarketer.org. Web site: www.instoremarketer.org.; www.hoytpub.com/poptimes. Editor: Bill Schober. **Contact:** Dan Ochwat, managing editor. **90% freelance written.** Monthly tabloid covering anything that pertains to in-store marketing and the point-of-purchase industry. "We cover in-store marketing from the perspective of the marketer. The stories are geared toward marketing professionals at consumer product goods companies that develop marketing programs launched at retail. This includes large product branded fixtures and floor displays, packaging, digital media, signage, temporary product displays, sweepstakes and event marketing, and anything that markets a brand in stores. Our readers are marketers and retailers, and a small selection of P-O-P producers (the guys that build the displays). We essentially cover individual campaigns; and we cover large category reports and retailer reports, company profiles and any breaking news in the industry." Estab. 1988. Circ. 20,000. **Pays on acceptance.** Byline given. Offers 100% kill fee. Buys all rights. Editorial lead time 2 months. Submit seasonal material 3 months in advance. Accepts queries by mail, e-mail. Accepts simultaneous submissions. Responds in 1 month to queries. Sample copy for free. Writer's guidelines free.

$ $ $ PROMO MAGAZINE

Insights and Ideas for Building Brands, Primedia, 11 Riverbend Dr., Stamford CT 06907. (203)358-4226. Fax: (203)358-9900. E-mail: kjoyce@prismb2b.com. Web site: www.promomagazine.com. **Contact:** Kathleen Joyce, editorial director. **5% freelance written.** Monthly magazine covering promotion marketing. "*Promo* serves marketers, and stories must be informative, well written, and familiar with the subject matter." Estab. 1987. Circ. 25,000. Pays on publication. Publishes ms an average of 2 months after acceptance. Byline given. Offers

25% kill fee. Buys first North American serial rights. Editorial lead time 3 months. Submit seasonal material 3 months in advance. Responds in 1 month to queries. Sample copy for $5.

Nonfiction Exposé, general interest, how-to (marketing programs), interview/profile, new product (promotion). "No general marketing stories not heavily involved in promotions." Generally does not accept unsolicited mss, query first. **Buys 6-10 mss/year.** Query with published clips. Length: Variable. **Pays $1,000 maximum for assigned articles; $500 maximum for unsolicited articles.** Sometimes pays expenses of writers on assignment.

Photos State availability with submission. Reviews contact sheets, negatives. Negotiates payment individually. Captions, identification of subjects, model releases required.

Tips "Understand that our stories aim to teach marketing professionals about successful promotion strategies. Case studies or new promos have the best chance."

$ $ SIGN BUILDER ILLUSTRATED

The How-To Magazine, Simmons-Boardman Publishing Corp., 345 Hudson St., 12th Floor, New York NY 10014. (212)620-7223. E-mail: cytuarte@sbpub.com. Web site: www.signshop.com. Associate Editor: Chris Ytuarte. **Contact:** Jeff Wooten, editor. **40% freelance written.** Monthly magazine covering sign and graphic industry. "*Sign Builder Illustrated* targets sign professionals where they work: on the shop floor. Our topics cover the broadest spectrum of the sign industry, from design to fabrication, installation, maintenance and repair. Our readers own a similarly wide range of shops, including commercial, vinyl, sign erection and maintenance, electrical and neon, architectural, and awnings." Estab. 1987. Circ. 14,500. **Pays on acceptance.** Publishes ms an average of 3 months after acceptance. Byline given. Offers 10% kill fee. Buys all rights. Editorial lead time 3 months. Submit seasonal material 4 months in advance. Accepts queries by mail, e-mail, fax, phone. Accepts simultaneous submissions. Responds in 1 month to queries. Sample copy and writer's guidelines free.

Nonfiction Historical/nostalgic, how-to, humor, interview/profile, photo feature, technical. **Buys 50-60 mss/year.** Query. Length: 1,000-1,500 words. **Pays $250-550 for assigned articles.**

Photos Send photos with submission. Reviews 3×5 prints. Buys all rights. Negotiates payment individually. Captions, identification of subjects required.

Tips "Be very knowledgeable about a portion of the sign industry you are covering. We want our readers to come away from each article with at least one good idea, one new technique, or one more 'trick of the trade.' At the same time, we don't want a purely textbook listing of 'do this, do that.' Our readers enjoy *Sign Builder Illustrated* because the publication speaks to them in a clear and lively fashion, from one sign professional to another. We want to engage the reader who has been in the business for some time. While there might be a place for basic instruction in new techniques, our average paid subscriber has been in business over 20 years, employs over seven people, and averages $800,000 in annual sales. These people aren't neophytes content with retread articles they can find anywhere. It's important for our writers to use anecdotes and examples drawn from the daily sign business."

$ $ SIGNS OF THE TIMES

The Industry Journal Since 1906, ST Publications, Dept. WM, 407 Gilbert Ave., Cincinnati OH 45202-2285. (513)421-2050. Fax: (513)421-5144. Web site: www.signweb.com. Editor/Publisher: Wade Swormstedt. **15-30% freelance written.** Monthly magazine covering the sign and outdoor advertising industries. Estab. 1906. Circ. 17,000. Pays on publication. Publishes ms an average of 3 months after acceptance. Byline given. Buys variable rights. Accepts queries by mail, e-mail, fax, phone. Responds in 3 months to queries. Sample copy and writer's guidelines for 9×12 SAE with 10 first-class stamps.

Nonfiction Historical/nostalgic (regarding the sign industry), how-to (carved signs, goldleaf, etc.), interview/profile (focusing on either a signshop or a specific project), photo feature (query first), technical (sign engineering, etc.). Nothing "nonspecific on signs, an example being a photo essay on 'signs I've seen.' We are a trade journal with specific audience interests." **Buys 15-20 mss/year.** Query with published clips. **Pays $150-500.**

Reprints Send tearsheet or typed ms with rights for sale noted and information about when and where the material previously appeared. Payment is negotiated.

Photos "Sign industry-related photos only. We sometimes accept photos with funny twists or misspellings." Send photos with submission.

Fillers Open to queries; request rates.

The online version contains material not found in the print edition.

Tips "Be thoroughly familiar with the sign industry, especially in the CAS-related area. Have an insider's knowledge plus an insider's contacts."

N $ $ $ SOCAL MEETINGS & EVENTS MAGAZINE

Tiger Oak Publications, 251 First Ave. N., Suite 401, Minneapolis MN 55401. Fax: (612)338-0532. Web site: www.meetingsandeventsmags.com. **Contact:** Suzy Feine, editorial director. **80% freelance written.** Quarterly magazine covering meetings and events industry. "*SoCal Meetings & Events* magazine is the premier trade publication for meetings planners and hospitality service providers in Southern California. This magazine aims to report on and promote businesses involved in the meetings and events industry. The magazine covers current and emerging trends, people and venues in the meetings and events industry in Southern California.'' Estab. 1993. Circ. 20,000. **Pays on acceptance.** Publishes ms an average of 4 months after acceptance. Byline given. Offers 20% kill fee. Buys first North American serial rights. Editorial lead time 4-6 months. Submit seasonal material 6 months in advance. Accepts queries by mail. Accepts simultaneous submissions. Responds in 1-2 weeks to queries.

Nonfiction General interest, historical/nostalgic, interview/profile, new product, opinion, personal experience, photo feature, technical, travel. **Buys 30 mss/year.** Query with published clips. Length: 600-1,500 words. **Pays $400-800.** Buys one-time rights. Negotiates payment individually. Identification of subjects, model releases required.

Columns/Departments Meet + Eat (restaurant reviews); Facility Focus (venue reviews); Regional Spotlight (city review), 1,000 words. **Buys 30 mss/year.** Query with published clips. **Pays $400-600.**

Tips ''Familiarization with the meetings and events industry is critical, as well as knowing how to write for a trade magazine. Writers experienced in writing for the trade magazine business industry are preferred.''

$ $ $ TEXAS MEETINGS & EVENTS MAGAZINE

Tiger Oak Publications, 900 S. 3rd St., Minneapolis MN 55401. Fax: (612)338-0532. Web site: www.meetingsandeventsmags.com. **Contact:** Barbara Knox, editor. **80% freelance written.** Quarterly magazine covering meetings and events industry. ''*Texas Meetings & Events* magazine is the premier trade publication for meetings planners and hospitality service providers in the state. This magazine aims to report on and promote businesses involved in the meetings and events industry. The magazine covers current and emerging trends, people and venues in the meetings and events industry in the state.'' Estab. 1993. Circ. 20,000. **Pays on acceptance.** Publishes ms an average of 4 months after acceptance. Byline given. Offers 20% kill fee. Buys first North American serial rights. Editorial lead time 4-6 months. Submit seasonal material 6 months in advance. Accepts queries by mail. Accepts simultaneous submissions. Responds in 1-2 weeks to queries.

Nonfiction General interest, historical/nostalgic, interview/profile, new product, opinion, personal experience, photo feature, technical, travel. **Buys 30 mss/year.** Query with published clips. Length: 600-1,500 words. **Pays $400-800.**

Photos State availability with submission. Buys one-time rights. Negotiates payment individually. Identification of subjects, model releases required.

Columns/Departments Meet + Eat (restaurant reviews); Facility Focus (venue reviews); Regional Spotlight (city review), 1,000 words. **Buys 30 mss/year.** Query with published clips. **Pays $400-600.**

Tips ''Familiarization with the meetings and events industry is critical, as well as knowing how to write for a trade magazine. Writers experienced in writing for the trade magazine business industry are preferred.''

ART, DESIGN & COLLECTIBLES

$ $ AIRBRUSH ACTION MAGAZINE

Action, Inc., 3209 Atlantic Ave., P.O. Box 438, Allenwood NJ 08720. (732)223-7878. Fax: (732)223-2855. E-mail: editor@airbrushaction.com. Web site: www.airbrushaction.com. **80% freelance written.** Bimonthly magazine covering the spectrum of airbrush applications: automotive and custom paint applications, illustration, T-shirt airbrushing, fine art, automotive and sign painting, hobby/craft applications, wall murals, fingernails, temporary tattoos, artist profiles, reviews, and more. Estab. 1985. Circ. 35,000. Pays 1 month after publication. Publishes ms an average of 6 months after acceptance. Byline given. Buys all rights. Editorial lead time 6 months. Submit seasonal material 6 months in advance. Accepts queries by mail, e-mail, fax, phone. Accepts simultaneous submissions.

Nonfiction Current primary focus is on automotive, motorcycle, and helmet kustom kulture arts. How-to, humor, inspirational, interview/profile, new product, personal experience, technical. Nothing unrelated to airbrush. Query with published clips. **Pays 15¢/word.** Sometimes pays expenses of writers on assignment.

Photos Digital images preferred. Send photos with submission. Buys all rights. Negotiates payment individually. Captions, identification of subjects, model releases required.

Columns/Departments Query with published clips.

The online version contains material not found in the print edition.

Tips ''Send bio and writing samples. Send well-written technical information pertaining to airbrush art. We publish a lot of artist profiles—they all sound the same. Looking for new pizzazz!''

$ $ ANTIQUEWEEK

DMG World Media (USA), P.O. Box 90, Knightstown IN 46148-0090. (800)876-5133, ext. 189. Fax: (800)695-8153. E-mail: connie@antiqueweek.com. Web site: www.antiqueweek.com. Managing Editor: Connie Swaim.

80% freelance written. Weekly tabloid covering antiques and collectibles with 3 editions: Eastern, Central and National, plus monthly *AntiqueWest*. "*AntiqueWeek* has a wide range of readership from dealers and auctioneers to collectors, both advanced and novice. Our readers demand accurate information presented in an entertaining style." Estab. 1968. Circ. 50,000. Pays on publication. Byline given. Offers 10% kill fee or $25. Buys first, second serial (reprint) rights. Submit seasonal material 1 month in advance. Accepts queries by mail, e-mail. Sample copy for free. Writer's guidelines by e-mail.

Nonfiction Historical/nostalgic, how-to, interview/profile, opinion, personal experience, antique show and auction reports, feature articles on particular types of antiques and collectibles. **Buys 400-500 mss/year.** Query. Length: 1,000-2,000 words. **Pays $50-250.**

Reprints Send electronic copy with rights for sale noted and information about when and where the material previously appeared.

Photos All material must be submitted electronically via e-mail or on CD. Send photos with submission. Identification of subjects required.

Tips "Writers should know their topics thoroughly. Feature articles must be well researched and clearly written. An interview and profile article with a knowledgeable collector might be the break for a first-time contributor. We seek a balanced mix of information on traditional antiques and 20th century collectibles."

ARCHITECTURAL RECORD

McGraw-Hill, 2 Penn Plaza, 9th Floor, New York NY 10121. (212)904-2594. Fax: (212)904-4256. Web site: www.architecturalrecord.com. Editor: Robert Ivy, FAIA. Managing Editor: Elisabeth Broome. **50% freelance written.** Monthly magazine covering architecture and design. "Our readers are architects, designers, and related professionals." Estab. 1891. Circ. 110,000. Pays on publication. Publishes ms an average of 2 months after acceptance. Byline given. Offers 25% kill fee. Buys all rights. Editorial lead time 2 months. Submit seasonal material 2 months in advance. Accepts queries by mail. Responds in 2 weeks to queries; 2 months to mss. Sample copy and writer's guidelines online.

$ $ ART CALENDAR MAGAZINE

The Business Magazine for Visual Artists, P.O. Box 2675, Salisbury MD 21802. Fax: (410)749-9626. E-mail: info@artcalendar.com. Web site: www.artcalendar.com. **Contact:** Carolyn Proeber, publisher. **100% freelance written.** Monthly magazine. Estab. 1986. Circ. 23,000. Pays on publication. Accepts previously published material. Sample copy for $5. Writer's guidelines online.

- "We welcome nuts-and-bolts, practical articles of interest to serious visual artists, emerging or professional. Examples: marketing how-to's, first-person stories on how an artist has built his career or an aspect of it, interviews with artists (business/career-building emphasis), and pieces on business practices and other topics of use to artists. The tone of our magazine is practical, can-do, and uplifting. Writers may use as many or as few words as necessary to tell the whole story."

Nonfiction Essays (the psychology of creativity), how-to, interview/profile (successful artists with a focus on what made them successful—not necessarily rich and famous artists, but the guy next door who paints all day and makes a decent living doing it), personal experience (artists making a difference—art teachers working with disabled students, bringing a community together, etc.), technical (new equipment, new media, computer software, Internet sites that are way cool that no one has heard of yet), cartoons, art law, including pending legislation that affects artists (copyright law, Internet regulations, etc.). "We like nuts-and-bolts information about making a living as an artist. We do not run reviews or art historical pieces, nor do we like writing characterized by 'critic-speak,' philosophical hyperbole, psychological arrogance, politics, or New Age religion. Also, we do not condone a get-rich-quick attitude." Send complete ms. **Pays $200.** We can make other arrangements in lieu of pay, i.e. a subscription or copies of the magazine in which your article appears.

Reprints Send photocopy or typed ms and information about when and where the material previously appeared. Pays $50.

Photos Reviews b&w glossy or color prints. Pays $25.

Columns/Departments "If an artist or freelancer sends us good articles regularly, and based on results we feel that he is able to produce a column at least 3 times per year, we will invite him to be a contributing writer. If a gifted artist-writer can commit to producing an article on a monthly basis, we will offer him a regular column and the title contributing editor." Send complete ms.

$ $ ART MATERIALS RETAILER

Fahy-Williams Publishing, P.O. Box 1080, Geneva NY 14456. (315)789-0458. Fax: (315)789-4263. E-mail: tmanzer@fwpi.com. Web site: www.artmaterialsretailer.com. **Contact:** Tina Manzer, editorial director. **10% freelance written.** Quarterly magazine. Estab. 1998. Pays on publication. Byline given. Buys one-time rights. Editorial lead time 2 months. Submit seasonal material 3 months in advance. Accepts simultaneous submissions. Responds in 3 weeks to queries; 3 months to mss. Sample copy and writer's guidelines free.

Nonfiction Book excerpts, how-to, interview/profile, personal experience. **Buys 2 mss/year.** Send complete ms. Length: 1,500-3,000 words. **Pays $50-250.** Sometimes pays expenses of writers on assignment.
Photos State availability with submission. Reviews transparencies. Buys one-time rights. Offers no additional payment for photos accepted with ms. Identification of subjects required.
Fillers Anecdotes, facts, newsbreaks. **Buys 5/year.** Length: 500-1,500 words. **Pays $50-125.**
Tips "We like to review manuscripts rather than queries. Artwork (photos, drawings, etc.) is a real plus. We enjoy (our readers enjoy) practical, nuts-and-bolts, news-you-can-use articles."

$ ARTS MANAGEMENT

110 Riverside Dr., Suite 4E, New York NY 10024. (212)579-2039. **Contact:** A.H. Reiss, editor. **1% freelance written.** Magazine published 5 times/year for cultural institutions. Estab. 1962. Circ. 6,000. Pays on publication. Byline given. Buys all rights. Accepts queries by mail. Responds in 2 months to queries. Writer's guidelines for #10 SASE.

- *Arts Management* is almost completely staff-written and uses very little outside material.

Nonfiction Short articles, 400-900 words, tightly written, expository, explaining how arts administrators solved problems in publicity, fund raising, and general administration; actual case histories emphasizing the how-to. Also short articles on the economics and sociology of the arts and important trends in the nonprofit cultural field. Must be fact filled, well organized, and without rhetoric. No photographs or pictures. **Pays 2-4¢/word.**

$ $ CNA

Craft & Needlework Age, Turning Creative Ideas Into Profits™, Krause Publications, a Division of F+W Publications, Inc., 700 E. State St., Iola WI 54990. (715)445-2214. Fax: (715)445-4087. E-mail: anconak@fwpubs.com. Web site: www.cnamag.com. Associate Editor: Robyn Austin. **Contact:** Karen Ancona, editor-in-chief. **60% freelance written.** Monthly magazine covering the industry, including crafts, scrapbooking, needlecrafts, art materials, paper crafts, educational business articles, and resource articles for small businesses. Also publishes niche supplements in February, March, May, June, September, and November, and a directory in December. "*CNA* is a trade magazine that services companies conducting commerce in the creative leisure industry. Readers are manufacturers, retailers, e-retailers, investors, designers, and wholesalers. Focus is on product, technique, and solid business information including marketing, competing, accounting, and everyday challenges that businesses face." Estab. 1954. Circ. 22,000. Pays on publication. Publishes ms an average of 3 months after acceptance. Byline given. Buys all rights. Editorial lead time 3 months. Submit seasonal material 8 months in advance. Accepts queries by mail, e-mail. Sample copy for 11×13 SASE with 5 first-class stamps.
Nonfiction Business, trends relating to creative leisure industry. Special issues: Scrapbooking; Beading; Knit & Crochet; Fashion. Does not want articles with a consumer voice. **Buys 12 mss/year.** Query. Length: 800-1,200 words. **Pays $150-350 for assigned articles.** Sometimes pays expenses of writers on assignment.
Photos Robyn Austin, associate editor. Send photos with submission. Reviews transparencies, prints, GIF/JPEG files. Offers no additional payment for photos accepted with ms. Captions, identification of subjects required.

⊘ COIN PRICES MAGAZINE

Krause Publications, a Division of F+W Publications, Inc., 700 E. State St., Iola WI 54990-0001. Web site: www.coinpricesmagazine.net. "*Coin Prices Magazine* offers complete retail value listings for all U.S. coins since 1972 in various collectible grades. Each issue also contains a special pricing supplement for either U.S. paper money, Canadian coins, Mexican coins, U.S. Territorial gold coins, or Colonial coins."

- Magazine does not contain editorial content other than pricing. Does not accept freelance material.

⊘ COINS MAGAZINE

Krause Publications, a Division of F+W Publications, Inc., 700 E. State St., Iola WI 54990-0001. Web site: www.coinsmagazine.net. "*Coins Magazine* features articles on the history and lore of coins and coin collecting, as well as basic information on collecting, investing, and buying and selling coins. Coverage is largely for U.S. coins since 1792."

- Does not accept freelance material.

N $ $ FAITH + FORM

The Interfaith Journal of Religion, Art and Architecture, % SWA, 50 Washington St., Norwalk CT 06854. (203)857-0200. Fax: (203)852-0741. E-mail: mcrosbie@faithandform.com. Web site: www.faithandform.com. **Contact:** Michael J. Crosbie, editor. **50% freelance written.** Quarterly magazine covering relgious buildings and art. "Writers must be knowledgeable about environments for worship, or able to explain them." Estab. 1967. Circ. 2,000. Pays on publication. Publishes ms an average of 6 months after acceptance. Byline given. Offers 25% kill fee. Buys one-time rights. Editorial lead time 6 months. Submit seasonal material 6 months in advance. Accepts queries by mail, e-mail, fax, phone. Accepts previously published material. Accepts simultaneous submissions. Responds in 2 weeks to queries; 1 month to mss. Sample copy online.

Nonfiction Book excerpts, essays, how-to, inspirational, interview/profile, opinion, personal experience, photo feature, religious, technical. **Buys 6 mss/year.** Query. Length: 500-2,500 words. **Pays $50-200.**

Photos State availability with submission. Reviews GIF/JPEG files. Buys one-time rights. Offers no additional payment for photos accepted with ms. Captions required.

Columns/Departments News, 250-750 words; Book Reviews, 250-500 words. **Buys 3 mss/year.** Query. **Pays $0-100.**

$ $ $ HOW

Design Ideas at Work, F+W Publications, Inc., 4700 E. Galbraith Rd., Cincinnati OH 45236. (513)531-2222. Fax: (513)531-2902. E-mail: editorial@howdesign.com. Web site: www.howdesign.com. **Contact:** Bryn Mooth, editor. **75% freelance written.** Bimonthly magazine covering graphic design profession. "*HOW: Design Ideas at Work* strives to serve the business, technological and creative needs of graphic-design professionals. The magazine provides a practical mix of essential business information, up-to-date technological tips, the creative whys and hows behind noteworthy projects, and profiles of professionals who are impacting design. The ultimate goal of *HOW* is to help designers, whether they work for a design firm or for an inhouse design department, run successful, creative, profitable studios." Estab. 1985. Circ. 40,000. **Pays on acceptance.** Byline given. Buys first North American serial rights. Responds in 6 weeks to queries. Sample copy for cover price plus $1.50 (cover price varies per issue). Writer's guidelines and editorial calendar online.

Nonfiction Features cover noteworthy design projects, interviews with leading creative professionals, profiles of established and up-and-coming firms, business and creativity topics for graphic designers. Special issues: Self-Promotion Annual (September/October); Business Annual (November/December); International Annual of Design (March/April); Creativity/Paper/Stock Photography (May/June); Digital Design Annual (July/August). No how-to articles for beginning artists or fine-art-oriented articles. **Buys 40 mss/year.** Query with published clips and samples of subject's work, artwork or design. Length: 1,500-2,000 words. **Pays $700-900.** Sometimes pays expenses of writers on assignment.

Photos State availability with submission. Reviews Information updated and verified. Buys one-time rights. Captions required.

Columns/Departments Design Disciplines (focuses on lucrative fields for designers/illustrators); Workspace (takes an inside look at the design of creatives' studios), 1,200-1,500 words. **Buys 35 mss/year.** Query with published clips. **Pays $250-400.**

Tips "We look for writers who can recognize graphic designers on the cutting-edge of their industry, both creatively and business-wise. Writers must have an eye for detail, and be able to relay *HOW*'s editorial style in an interesting, concise manner—without omitting any details. Showing you've done your homework on a subject—and that you can go beyond asking 'those same old questions'—will give you a big advantage."

$ $ INTERIOR LANDSCAPE BUSINESS MAGAZINE

(formerly *Interior Business Magazine*), GIE Media, Inc., 4012 Bridge Ave., Cleveland OH 44113. (800)456-0707. Fax: (216)961-0364. E-mail: ccode@gie.net. Web site: www.interiorbusinessonline.com. **Contact:** Cyndi Code, editorial director. **5-10% freelance written.** Magazine covering interior landscaping. "*Interior Business* addresses the concerns of the professional interior landscape contractor. It's devoted to the business management needs of interior landscape professionals." Estab. 2000. Circ. 6,000. Pays on publication. Publishes ms an average of 3 months after acceptance. Editorial lead time 3 months. Submit seasonal material 5 months in advance. Responds in 1 week to queries.

Nonfiction Interior landscaping. "No articles oriented to the consumer or homeowner." **Buys 2 mss/year.** Length: 1,000-2,500 words. **Pays $250-500.**

Tips "Know the audience. It's the professional business person, not the consumer."

$ $ $ PRINT

America's Graphic Design Magazine, F+W Publications, 38 E. 29th St., 3rd Floor, New York NY 10016. (212)447-1400. Fax: (212)447-5231. E-mail: info@printmag.com. Web site: www.printmag.com. **75% freelance written.** Bimonthly magazine covering graphic design and visual culture. "*PRINT*'s articles, written by design specialists and cultural critics, focus on the social, political, and historical context of graphic design, and on the places where consumer culture and popular culture meet. We aim to produce a general interest magazine for professionals with engagingly written text and lavish illustrations. By covering a broad spectrum of topics, both international and local, we try to demonstrate the significance of design in the world at large." Estab. 1940. Circ. 45,000. **Pays on acceptance.** Publishes ms an average of 3 months after acceptance. Byline given. Offers 25% kill fee. Buys first North American serial rights. Editorial lead time 3 months. Submit seasonal material 3 months in advance. Accepts queries by e-mail. Responds in 2 weeks to queries; 1 month to mss. Sample copy not available.

Nonfiction Essays, interview/profile, opinion. **Buys 35-40 mss/year.** Query with published clips. Length: 1,000-2,500 words. **Pays $1,250.** Sometimes pays expenses of writers on assignment.

Columns/Departments Query with published clips. **Pays $800.**

Tips "Be well versed in issues related to the field of graphic design; don't submit ideas that are too general or geared to nonprofessionals."

$ TEXAS ARCHITECT

Texas Society of Architects, 816 Congress Ave., Suite 970, Austin TX 78701. (512)478-7386. Fax: (512)478-0528. Web site: www.texasarchitect.org. **Contact:** Stephen Sharpe, editor. **30% freelance written.** Mostly written by unpaid members of the professional society. Bimonthly journal covering architecture and architects of Texas. "*Texas Architect* is a highly visually-oriented look at Texas architecture, design, and urban planning. Articles cover varied subtopics within architecture. Readers are mostly architects and related building professionals." Estab. 1951. Circ. 12,000. Pays on publication. Publishes ms an average of 3 months after acceptance. Byline given. Buys one-time, all rights, makes work-for-hire assignments. Submit seasonal material 4 months in advance. Accepts queries by mail, e-mail. Responds in 6 weeks to queries. Writer's guidelines online.

Nonfiction Interview/profile, photo feature, technical, book reviews. Query with published clips. Length: 100-2,000 words. **Pays $50-100 for assigned articles.**

Photos Send photos with submission. Reviews contact sheets, 35mm or 4×5 transparencies, 4×5 prints. Buys one-time rights. Offers no additional payment for photos accepted with ms. Identification of subjects required.

Columns/Departments News (timely reports on architectural issues, projects, and people), 100-500 words. **Buys 10 mss/year.** Query with published clips. **Pays $50-100.**

AUTO & TRUCK

$ $ AUTOINC.

Automotive Service Association, P.O. Box 929, Bedford TX 76095. (800)272-7467. Fax: (817)685-0225. E-mail: editor@asashop.org. Web site: www.autoinc.org. Assistant Editor: Levy Joffrion. **Contact:** Leona Dalavai Scott, editor. **10% freelance written.** Monthly magazine covering independent automotive repair. "The mission of *AutoInc.*, ASA's official publication, is to be the informational authority for ASA and industry members nationwide. Its purpose is to enhance the professionalism of these members through management, technical and legislative articles, researched and written with the highest regard for accuracy, quality, and integrity." Estab. 1952. Circ. 14,000. Pays on publication. Publishes ms an average of 3 months after acceptance. Byline given. Buys all rights. Editorial lead time 2 months. Accepts queries by mail, e-mail, fax. Accepts simultaneous submissions. Responds in 6 weeks to queries; 2 months to mss. Sample copy for $5 or online. Writer's guidelines online.

Nonfiction How-to (automotive repair), technical. No coverage of staff moves or financial reports. **Buys 6 mss/year.** Query with published clips. Length: 1,200 words. **Pays $300.** Sometimes pays phone expenses of writers on assignment.

Photos State availability of or send photos with submission. Reviews 2×3 transparencies, 3×5 prints, high resolution digital images. Buys one-time and electronic rights. Negotiates payment individually. Captions, identification of subjects, model releases required.

Tips "Learn about the automotive repair industry, specifically the independent shop segment. Understand the high-tech requirements needed to succeed today. We target professional repair shop owners rather than consumers."

$ $ BUSINESS FLEET

Bobit Publishing, 3520 Challenger St., Torrance CA 90501-1711. (310)533-2400. E-mail: chris.brown@bobit.com. Web site: www.businessfleet.com. **Contact:** Chris Brown, senior editor. **10% freelance written.** Bimonthly magazine covering businesses which operate 10-50 company vehicles. "While it's a trade publication aimed at a business audience, *Business Fleet* has a lively, conversational style. The best way to get a feel for our 'slant' is to read the magazine." Estab. 2000. Circ. 100,000. Pays on publication. Publishes ms an average of 3 months after acceptance. Byline given. Offers 25% kill fee. Buys first, second serial (reprint), electronic rights. Editorial lead time 2 months. Submit seasonal material 2 months in advance. Accepts queries by mail, e-mail, fax. Responds in 3 weeks to queries; 2 months to mss. Sample copy and writer's guidelines free.

Nonfiction How-to, interview/profile, new product, personal experience, photo feature, technical. **Buys 16 mss/year.** Query with published clips. Length: 500-2,000 words. **Pays $100-400.** Pays with contributor copies or other premiums by prior arrangement. Sometimes pays expenses of writers on assignment.

Photos State availability with submission. Reviews 3×5 prints. Buys one-time, reprint, and electronic rights. Negotiates payment individually. Captions required.

Tips "Our mission is to educate our target audience on more economical and efficient ways of operating company vehicles, and to inform the audience of the latest vehicles, products, and services available to small commercial companies. Be knowledgeable about automotive and fleet-oriented subjects."

$ $ CASP

Canadian Aftermarket Service Professional, Publications Rousseau et Associes, Inc., 2938 Terrasse Abenaquis, Longueuil QC J4M 2B3 Canada. (450)448-2220. Fax: (450)448-1041. E-mail: admin@p-rousseau.com. Web site: www.publicationsrousseau.com. Editor: Remy L. Rousseau. **Contact:** Valerie St. Cyr, production manager. **30% freelance written.** Magazine published 8 times/year covering the Canadian automotive aftermarket. "*CASP* presents many aspects of the automotive aftermarket: new products, technology, industry image, HR, management." Estab. 2003. Circ. 18,000. Pays on publication. Publishes ms an average of 2 months after acceptance. Byline given. Not copyrighted. Buys first, second serial (reprint), electronic rights. Editorial lead time 2 months. Submit seasonal material 2 months in advance. Accepts queries by e-mail. Accepts previously published material. Accepts simultaneous submissions. Responds in 2 weeks to queries; 2 months to mss. Sample copy for free. Writer's guidelines by e-mail.

Nonfiction General interest, how-to, inspirational, interview/profile, new product, technical. Does not want opinion pieces. **Buys 6 mss/year.** Query with published clips. Length: 550-610 words. **Pays up to $200 (Canadian).**

Photos Send photos with submission. Reviews GIF/JPEG files. Buys all rights. Offers no additional payment for photos accepted with ms. Captions required.

Fillers Facts. **Buys 2/year.** Length: 550-610 words. **Pays $0-200.**

$ $ FENDERBENDER

Your Leading Source for Complete Collision Coverage, Dewitt Publishing, 1043 Grand Ave. #372, St. Paul MN 55105. (651)224-6207. Fax: (651)224-6212. E-mail: editor@fenderbender.com. Web site: www.fenderbender.com. **Contact:** Eric Skogman, editor. **70% freelance written.** Monthly magazine covering automotive collision repair. Estab. 1999. Circ. 30,000. Pays on publication. Publishes ms an average of 2 months after acceptance. Byline given. Offers 20% kill fee. Buys first North American serial, second serial (reprint), electronic rights. Editorial lead time 3 months. Submit seasonal material 6 months in advance. Accepts queries by e-mail. Accepts simultaneous submissions. Responds in 1-2 months to queries; 2-3 months to mss. Sample copy for 10×13 SAE and 6 first-class stamps. Writer's guidelines online.

Nonfiction Exposé, how-to, inspirational, interview/profile, technical. Does not want personal narratives or any other first-person stories. No poems or creative writing manuscripts. Query with published clips. Length: 1,800-2,500 words. **Pays 25-35¢/word.** Sometimes pays expenses of writers on assignment.

Photos Send photos with submission. Reviews 35mm transparencies, 5×7 prints, GIF/JPEG files. Buys one-time rights. Offers no additional payment for photos accepted with ms. Captions, identification of subjects, model releases required.

Columns/Departments Q&A, 600 words; Shakes, Rattles & Rollovers; FenderBender Report. Query with published clips. **Pays 25-35¢/word.**

Tips "Potential writers need to be knowledgeable about the auto collision repair industry. They should also know standard business practices and be able to explain to shop owners how they can run their businesses better."

$ $ FLEET EXECUTIVE

The Magazine of Vehicle Management, The National Association of Fleet Administrators, Inc., 100 Wood Ave. S., Suite 310, Iselin NJ 08830-2716. (732)494-8100. Fax: (732)494-6789. E-mail: publications@nafa.org. Web site: www.nafa.org. **Contact:** Carolann McLoughlin, managing editor. **30% freelance written.** Magazine published 8 times/year covering automotive fleet management. "*NAFA Fleet Executive* focuses on car, van, and light-duty truck management in US and Canadian corporations, government agencies, and utilities. Editorial emphasis is on general automotive issues; improving jobs skills, productivity, and professionalism; legislation and regulation; alternative fuels; safety; interviews with prominent industry personalities; technology; association news; public service fleet management; and light-duty truck fleet management." Estab. 1957. Circ. 4,000. Pays on publication. Publishes ms an average of 4 months after acceptance. Buys all rights. Editorial lead time 2 months. Accepts queries by mail, e-mail, fax. Accepts simultaneous submissions. Responds in 1 month to queries. Sample copy online. Writer's guidelines free.

Nonfiction "NAFA hosts its Fleet Management Institute, an educational conference and trade show, which is held in a different city in the US and Canada each year. *Fleet Executive* would consider articles on regional attractions, particularly those that might be of interest to the automotive industry, for use in a conference preview issue of the magazine. The preview issue is published one month prior to the conference. Information about the conference, its host city, and conference dates in a given year may be found on NAFA's Web site, www.nafa.org, or by calling the association at (732)494-8100." Interview/profile, technical. **Buys 24 mss/year.** Query with published clips. Length: 500-3,000 words. **Pays $500 maximum.**

Photos State availability with submission. Reviews electronic images.

Tips "The sample articles online at www.nafa.org/fleetexecutive should help writers get a feel of the journalistic style we require."

$ $ LIGHT TRUCK & SUV ACCESSORY BUSINESS & PRODUCT NEWS

Cygnus Business Media, 1233 Janesville Ave., Fort Atkinson WI 53538. (920)563-6388. Fax: (920)563-1702. E-mail: pat.walker@cygnusb2b.com. Web site: www.sportstruck.com. **Contact:** Pat Walker, editor. **25% freelance written.** "*Light Truck & SUV Accessory Business & Product News* is a bimonthly trade magazine designed to provide light truck accessory dealers and installers with advice on improving their retail business practices, plus timely information about industry trends and events. Each issue's editorial package includes a dealer profile, plus features aimed at meeting the distinct needs of store owners, managers and counter sales people. The magazine also provides aftermarket, OEM and trade association news, three separate new product sections, plus an analysis of light truck sales." Estab. 1996. Circ. 15,000. Pays 30 days after publication. Publishes ms an average of 3 months after acceptance. Byline given. Buys first North American serial rights. Editorial lead time 3 months. Submit seasonal material 4 months in advance. Accepts simultaneous submissions. Responds in 1 month to queries. Sample copy, writer's guidelines free.

O— Break in with "a feature on a top truck or SUV retailer in your area."

Nonfiction General interest, interview/profile, new product, technical, Considers cartoons. No travel, installation how-to's. **Buys 20-30 mss/year.** Query. Length: 1,000-2,000 words. **Pays $300-500.**

Photos Send photos with submission. Reviews transparencies, prints. Buys one-time rights. Negotiates payment individually. Model releases required.

Tips "Send query with or without completed manuscripts. Background/experience and published clips are required."

$ $ $ OVERDRIVE

The Voice of the American Trucker, Randall Publishing Co./Overdrive, Inc., 3200 Rice Mine Rd., Tuscaloosa AL 35406. (205)349-2990. Fax: (205)750-8070. E-mail: mheine@randallpub.com. Web site: www.etrucker.com. Editor: Linda Longton. **Contact:** Max Heine, editorial director. **5% freelance written.** Monthly magazine for independent truckers. Estab. 1961. Circ. 100,000. Pays on publication. Publishes ms an average of 2 months after acceptance. Byline given. Offers 10% kill fee. Buys all North American rights, including electronic rights. Responds in 2 months to queries. Sample copy for 9×12 SASE.

Nonfiction All must be related to independent trucker interest. Essays, exposé, how-to (truck maintenance and operation), interview/profile (successful independent truckers), personal experience, photo feature, technical. Query with or without published clips or send complete ms. Length: 500-2,500 words. **Pays $300-1,500 for assigned articles.**

Photos Buys all rights. Photo fees negotiable.

Tips "Talk to independent truckers. Develop a good knowledge of their concerns as small-business owners, truck drivers, and individuals. We prefer articles that quote experts, people in the industry, and truckers, to first-person expositions on a subject. Get straight facts. Look for good material on truck safety, on effects of government regulations, and on rates and business relationships between independent truckers, brokers, carriers, and shippers."

$ PML

The Market Letter for Porsche Automobiles, PML Consulting, P.O. Box 567, Socorro NM 87801. Fax: (505)838-1222. Web site: www.pmletter.com. **100% freelance written.** Monthly magazine covering technical tips, personality profiles and race coverage of Porsche automobiles. Estab. 1981. Circ. 1,500. Pays on publication. Publishes ms an average of 2 months after acceptance. Byline given. Buys one-time rights. Editorial lead time 2 months. Submit seasonal material 2 months in advance. Accepts queries by mail, e-mail, fax, phone. Accepts previously published material. Accepts simultaneous submissions. Responds in 2 weeks to queries; 1 month to mss. Sample copy for $5. Writer's guidelines for #10 SASE.

Nonfiction General interest, historical/nostalgic, how-to, humor, interview/profile, new product, personal experience, photo feature, technical, travel, race results. **Buys 30-40 mss/year.** Query with published clips. Length: 500-2,000 words. **Pays $30-50 and up, depending on length and topic.** Sometimes pays expenses of writers on assignment.

Photos Send photos with submission. Reviews 8×10 b&w prints. Buys one-time rights. Negotiates payment individually. Captions, identification of subjects, model releases required.

Fillers Anecdotes, facts, gags to be illustrated by cartoonist, newsbreaks, short humor. **Pays negotiable amount.**

Tips "Check any auto-related magazine for types, styles of articles. We are looking for people doing anything unusual or interesting in the Porsche world. Submit well-prepared, thoroughly-edited articles with photos."

$ ROAD KING MAGAZINE

For the Professional Driver, Parthenon Publishing, 28 White Bridge Rd., Suite 209, Nashville TN 37205. (615)627-2250. Fax: (615)690-3401. Web site: www.roadking.com. **80% freelance written.** Bimonthly magazine. "*Road King* is published bimonthly for long-haul truckers. It celebrates the lifestyle and work and profiles interesting and/or successful drivers. It also reports on subjects of interest to our audience, including outdoors, vehicles, music, and trade issues." Estab. 1963. Circ. 229,900. Pays 3 weeks after acceptance. Publishes ms an average of 4 months after acceptance. Byline given. Offers negotiable kill fee. Buys first North American serial, electronic rights. Editorial lead time 4 months. Submit seasonal material 6 months in advance. Accepts queries by mail, e-mail. Responds in 2 months to queries. Sample copy for 9×12 SAE and 5 first-class stamps. Writer's guidelines online.

Nonfiction How-to (trucking-related), interview/profile, new product, photo feature, technical, travel. Special issues: Road Gear (the latest tools, techniques and industry developments to help truckers run a smarter, more efficient trucking business); At Home on the Road ("creature comfort" products, services, and information for the road life, including what's new, useful, interesting, or fun for cyber-trucking drivers). "No fiction, poetry." **Buys 20 mss/year.** Query with published clips. Length: 850-2,000 words. **Payment negotiable.** Sometimes pays expenses of writers on assignment.

Photos State availability with submission. Reviews contact sheets. Buys negotiable rights. Negotiates payment individually. Identification of subjects, model releases required.

Columns/Departments Lead Driver (profile of outstanding trucker), 250-500 words; Roadrunner (new products, services suited to the business of trucking or to truckers' lifestyles), 100-250 words. **Buys 6-10 mss/year.** Query. **Payment negotiable.**

Fillers Anecdotes, facts, gags to be illustrated by cartoonist, short humor. Length: 100-250 words. **Pays $50.**

The online magazine of *Road King* carries original content not found in the print edition.

N $ $ TIRE NEWS

Publications Rousseau et Associes Inc., 2938 Terrasse Abenaquis, Longueuil QC J4M 2B3 Canada. (450)448-2220. Fax: (450)448-1041. E-mail: admin@p-rousseau.com. Web site: www.publicationsrousseau.com. Editor: Remy L. Rousseau. **Contact:** Valerie St. Cyr, production manager. Bimonthly magazine covering Canadian tire industry. "*Tire News* focuses on education/training, industry image, management, new tires, new techniques, marketing, HR, etc." Estab. 2004. Circ. 16,000. Pays on publication. Publishes ms an average of 2 months after acceptance. Byline given. Not copyrighted. Buys first, second serial (reprint), electronic rights. Editorial lead time 2 months. Submit seasonal material 2 months in advance. Accepts queries by e-mail. Accepts previously published material. Accepts simultaneous submissions. Responds in 2 weeks to queries; 2 months to mss. Sample copy for free. Writer's guidelines by e-mail.

Nonfiction General interest, how-to, inspirational, interview/profile, new product, technical. Does not want opinion pieces. **Buys 5 mss/year.** Query with published clips. Length: 550-610 words. **Pays up to $200 (Canadian).**

Photos Send photos with submission. Reviews GIF/JPEG files. Buys all rights. Offers no additional payment for photos accepted with ms. Captions required.

Fillers Facts. **Buys 2/year.** Length: 550-610 words. **Pays $0-200.**

$ $ TODAY'S TRUCKING

New Communications Group, 451 Attwell Dr., Toronto ON M9W 5C4 Canada. (416)614-2200. Fax: (416)614-8861. Web site: www.todaystrucking.com. Editor: Peter Carter. **Contact:** Rolf Lockwood. **15% freelance written.** Monthly magazine covering the trucking industry in Canada. "We reach nearly 30,000 fleet owners, managers, owner-operators, shop supervisors, equipment dealers, and parts distributors across Canada. Our magazine has a strong service slant, combining useful how-to journalism with analysis of news, business issues, and heavy-duty equipment trends. Before you sit down to write, please take time to become familiar with *Today's Trucking*. Read a few recent issues." Estab. 1987. Circ. 30,000. **Pays on acceptance.** Byline given. Buys first North American serial, second serial (reprint) rights. Editorial lead time 2 months. Submit seasonal material 3 months in advance. Accepts queries by mail, e-mail, fax. Sample copy and writer's guidelines free.

Nonfiction How-to, interview/profile, technical. **Buys 20 mss/year.** Query with published clips. Length: 500-2,000 words. **Pays 40¢/word.** Sometimes pays expenses of writers on assignment.

Photos State availability with submission.

Columns/Departments Pays 40¢/word.

TRUCK NEWS

Business Information Group, 12 Concorde Place, Suite 800, Toronto ON M3C 4J2 Canada. Web site: www.trucknews.com. **Contact:** James Menzies. **15% freelance written.** Monthly magazine covering trucking industry. Estab. 1981. **Pays on acceptance.** Publishes ms an average of 1 month after acceptance. Byline given. Buys first, one-time, electronic rights. Editorial lead time 1 month. Submit seasonal material 2 months in advance. Accepts queries by mail. Accepts simultaneous submissions.

Nonfiction General interest, new product, technical. **Buys 20 mss/year.** Query.

WARD'S AUTOWORLD

Primedia Business Magazines and Media, 3000 Town Center, Suite 2750, Southfield MI 48075-1245. (248)357-0800. Fax: (248)357-0810. Web site: www.wardsauto.com. Monthly magazine. for personnel involved in the original equipment manufacturing industry. Circ. 101,349. Editorial lead time 1 month.

- Query before submitting.

WARD'S DEALER BUSINESS

Primedia Business Magazines and Media, 3000 Town Center, Suite 2750, Southfield MI 48075-1245. (248)357-0800. Fax: (248)357-0810. Web site: www.wardsauto.com. Monthly magazine edited for personnel involved in aftermarket sales. Circ. 30,000. Editorial lead time 1 month.

- Query before submitting.

$ $ WESTERN CANADA HIGHWAY NEWS

Craig Kelman & Associates, 2020 Portage Ave., 3rd Floor, Winnipeg MB R3J 0K4 Canada. (204)985-9785. Fax: (204)985-9795. E-mail: terry@kelman.ca. **Contact:** Terry Ross, managing editor. **30% freelance written.** Quarterly magazine covering trucking. "The official magazine of the Alberta, Saskatchewan, and Manitoba trucking associations." Estab. 1995. Circ. 4,500. Pays on publication. Publishes ms an average of 2 months after acceptance. Byline given. Buys one-time rights. Editorial lead time 3 months. Submit seasonal material 3 months in advance. Accepts simultaneous submissions. Responds in 1 month to queries; 1 month to mss. Sample copy for 10×13 SAE with 1 IRC. Writer's guidelines for #10 SASE.

Nonfiction Essays, general interest, how-to (run a trucking business), interview/profile, new product, opinion, personal experience, photo feature, technical, profiles in excellence (bios of trucking or associate firms enjoying success). **Buys 8-10 mss/year.** Query. Length: 500-3,000 words. **Pays 18-25¢/word.** Sometimes pays expenses of writers on assignment.

Photos State availability with submission. Reviews 4×6 prints. Buys one-time rights. Identification of subjects required.

Columns/Departments Safety (new safety innovation/products), 500 words; Trade Talk (new products), 300 words. Query. **Pays 18-25¢/word.**

Tips "Our publication is fairly time sensitive regarding issues affecting the trucking industry in Western Canada. Current 'hot' topics are international trucking, security, driver fatigue, health and safety, emissions control, and national/international highway systems."

AVIATION & SPACE

$ $ AIR LINE PILOT

The Magazine of Professional Flight Deck Crews, Air Line Pilots Association, 1625 Massachusetts Ave. NW, Washington DC 20036. E-mail: magazine@alpa.org. Web site: www.alpa.org. **2% freelance written.** Prefers to work with published/established writers; works with a small number of new/unpublished writers each year. Magazine published 10 times/year for airline pilots covering commercial aviation industry information—economics, avionics, equipment, systems, safety—that affects a pilot's life in a professional sense. Also includes information about management/labor relations trends, contract negotiations, etc. Estab. 1931. Circ. 90,000. **Pays on acceptance.** Publishes ms an average of 6 months after acceptance. Offers 50% kill fee. Buys all rights except book rights. Submit seasonal material 6 months in advance. Responds in 2 months to queries. Sample copy for $2. Writer's guidelines online.

Nonfiction Humor, inspirational, photo feature, technical. **Buys 5 mss/year.** Query with or without published clips or send complete ms and SASE. Length: 700-3,000 words. **Pays $100-600 for assigned articles; $50-600 for unsolicited articles.**

Reprints Send photocopy of article or typed ms with rights for sale noted and information about when and where the material previously appeared. Payment varies.

Photos "Our greatest need is for strikingly original cover photographs featuring ALPA flight deck crew members and their airlines in their operating environment. See list of airlines with ALPA Pilots online." Send photos with submission. Reviews contact sheets, 35mm transparencies, 8×10 prints, digital must be 300 dpi at 8×11. Will review low res thumbnail images. Buys all rights for cover photos, one-time rights for inside color. Offers $10-35/b&w photo, $30-50 for color used inside and $450 for color used as cover. For cover photography, shoot vertical rather than horizontal. Identification of subjects required.

Tips "For our feature section, we seek aviation industry information that affects the life of a professional pilot's career. We also seek material that affects a pilot's life from a job security and work environment standpoint. Any airline pilot featured in an article must be an Air Line Pilot Association member in good standing. Our readers are very experienced and require a high level of technical accuracy in both written material and photographs."

$ $ AIRCRAFT MAINTENANCE TECHNOLOGY

Cygnus Business Media, 1233 Janesville Ave., Fort Atkinson WI 53538. (920)563-6388. Fax: (920)569-4603. E-mail: joe.escobar@cygnusb2b.com. Web site: www.amtonline.com. Editor: Joe Escobar. **10% freelance written.** Magazine published 10 times/year covering aircraft maintenance. "*Aircraft Maintenance Technology* provides aircraft maintenance professionals worldwide with a curriculum of technical, professional, and managerial development information that enables them to more efficiently and effectively perform their jobs. Estab. 1989. Circ. 41,500 worldwide. Pays on publication. Publishes ms an average of 2 months after acceptance. Byline given. Buys all rights, makes work-for-hire assignments. Editorial lead time 3 months. Submit seasonal material 6 months in advance. Accepts queries by mail, e-mail, fax. Accepts simultaneous submissions. Responds in 2 weeks to queries; 1 month to mss. Sample copy for free. Writer's guidelines for #10 SASE or by e-mail.

Nonfiction How-to, technical, safety; human factors. Special issues: Aviation career issue (August). No travel/pilot-oriented pieces. **Buys 10-12 mss/year.** Query with published clips. Length: 600-1,500 words, technical articles 2,000 words. **Pays $200.**

Photos State availability with submission. Buys one-time rights. Offers no additional payment for photos accepted with ms. Captions, identification of subjects, model releases required.

Columns/Departments Professionalism, 1,000-1,500 words; Safety Matters, 600-1,000 words; Human Factors, 600-1,000 words. **Buys 10-12 mss/year.** Query with published clips. **Pays $200.**

Tips "This is a technical magazine approved by the FAA and Transport Canada for recurrency training for technicians. Freelancers should have a strong background in aviation, particularly maintenance, to be considered for technical articles. Columns/Departments: Freelancers still should have a strong knowledge of aviation to slant professionalism, safety, and human factors pieces to that audience."

$ $ AIRPORT OPERATIONS

Flight Safety Foundation, Suite 300, 601 Madison St., Alexandria VA 22314-1756. (703)739-6700. Fax: (703)739-6708. Web site: www.flightsafety.org. **25% freelance written.** Bimonthly newsletter covering safety aspects of airport operations. "*Airport Operations* directs attention to ground operations that involve aircraft and other equipment, airport personnel and services, air traffic control (ATC), and passengers." Estab. 1974. Circ. 2,000. Pays on publication. Publishes ms an average of 3 months after acceptance. Byline given. Buys all rights. Editorial lead time 3 months. Accepts queries by mail, e-mail, fax. Accepts previously published material. Responds in 3 weeks to queries. Sample copy and writer's guidelines online.

Nonfiction Technical. No argumentation, crusading, inspiration, anecdotes, or humor. **Buys 6 mss/year.** Query. Length: 2,500-8,750 words. **Pays $200/printed page, plus 6 copies of publication.**

Photos Send photos with submission. Reviews contact sheets, negatives, 35mm or larger transparencies, 5×7 minimum prints, GIF/JPEG files. Buys all rights. Offers $25/photo. Captions, identification of subjects, model releases required.

Tips "Study the guidelines carefully. Be concerned above all with accuracy, fairness, and objectivity, but if you have information that you believe meets those standards, do not hesitate to query even if you aren't sure of format or style. If you have the content we need, our editorial staff will work with you to put the material into shape."

$ $ AVIATION INTERNATIONAL NEWS

The Convention News Co., 214 Franklin Ave., Midland Park NJ 07432. (201)444-5075. Fax: (201)444-4647. E-mail: rpadfield@ainonline.com. Web site: www.ainonline.com. Editor *AIN* Monthly Edition: Nigel Moll. **Contact:** R. Randall Padfield, editor-in-chief. **30-40% freelance written.** Monthly magazine (with onsite issues published at 3 conventions and 2 international air shows each year) covering business and commercial aviation with news features, special reports, aircraft evaluations, and surveys on business aviation worldwide, written for business pilots and industry professionals. "While the heartbeat of *AIN* is driven by the news it carries, the human touch is not neglected. We pride ourselves on our people stories about the industry's 'movers and shakers' and others in aviation who make a difference." Estab. 1972. Circ. 40,000. **Pays on acceptance and upon receipt of writer's invoice**. Publishes ms an average of 2 months after acceptance. Byline given. Offers variable kill fee. Buys first North American serial and second serial (reprint) rights and makes work-for-hire assignments. Editorial lead time 2 months. Submit seasonal material 3 months in advance. Accepts queries by mail, e-mail, fax. Responds in 6 weeks to queries; 2 months to mss. Sample copy for $10. Writer's guidelines for 9×12 SAE with 3 first-class stamps.

- Do not send mss by e-mail unless requested.
- O→ Break in with "local news stories relating to business, commercial and regional airline aviation—think turbine-powered aircraft (no stories about national airlines, military aircraft, recreational aviation or history."

Nonfiction "We hire freelancers to work on our staff at 3 aviation conventions and 2 international airshows each year. Must have strong reporting and writing skills and knowledge of aviation." How-to (aviation), interview/profile, new product, opinion, personal experience, photo feature, technical. No puff pieces. "Our readers expect serious, real news. We don't pull any punches. *AIN* is not a 'good news' publication: It tells the story, both good and bad." **Buys 150-200 mss/year.** Query with published clips. Length: 200-3,000 words. **Pays 30¢/word to first timers, higher rates to proven *AIN* freelancers.** Pays expenses of writers on assignment.

Photos Send photos with submission. Reviews contact sheets, transparencies, prints, TIFF files (300 dpi). Buys one-time rights. Negotiates payment individually. Captions required.

Tips "Our core freelancers are professional pilots with good writing skills, or good journalists and reporters with an interest in aviation (some with pilot licenses) or technical experts in the aviation industry. The ideal *AIN* writer has an intense interest in and strong knowledge of aviation, a talent for writing news stories, and journalistic cussedness. Hit me with a strong news story relating to business aviation that takes me by surprise—something from your local area or area of expertise. Make it readable, fact-filled, and in the inverted-pyramid style. Double-check facts and names. Interview the right people. Send me good, clear photos and illustrations. Send me well-written, logically ordered copy. Do this for me consistently and we may take you along on our staff to one of the conventions in the U.S. or an airshow in Paris, Singapore, London, or Dubai."

$ $ AVIATION MAINTENANCE

Access Intelligence, 4 Choke Cherry Rd., 2nd Floor, Rockville MD 20850. (301)354-1831. Fax: (301)340-8741. E-mail: mthurber@accessintel.com. Web site: www.aviationmx.com. Managing Editor: Joy Finnegan. **Contact:** Matt Thurber, editor. **40% freelance written.** Monthly magazine covering aircraft maintenance from small to large aircraft. *Aviation Maintenance* delivers news and information about the aircraft maintenance business for mechanics and management at maintenance shops, airlines, and corporate flight departments. Estab. 1982. Circ. 25,000. **Pays on acceptance.** Publishes ms an average of 2 months after acceptance. Byline given. Kill fee varies. Buys all rights. Editorial lead time 3 months. Submit seasonal material 3 months in advance. Accepts queries by mail, e-mail, fax, phone. Responds in 1 week to queries; 1 month to mss. Sample copy online. Writer's guidelines free.

Nonfiction Exposé, interview/profile, technical. No fiction, technical how-to, or poetry. **Buys 20 mss/year.** Query with or without published clips. Length: 200-500 words. **Pays 50¢/word.** Pays expenses of writers on assignment.

Photos State availability with submission. Buys all rights. Negotiates payment individually. Captions, identification of subjects required.

Columns/Departments Buys 12 mss/year. Query with or without published clips. **Pays $500.**

Tips "Writer must be intimately familiar with, or involved in, aviation, either as a pilot or preferably a mechanic or a professional aviation writer. Best place to break in is in the Intelligence News section or the Industry Insights column (see Web site)."

$ AVIATION MECHANICS BULLETIN

Flight Safety Foundation, Suite 300, 601 Madison St., Alexandria VA 22314-1756. (703)739-6700. Fax: (703)739-6708. Web site: www.flightsafety.org. **25% freelance written.** Bimonthly newsletter covering safety aspects of aviation maintenance (airline and corporate). Estab. 1953. Circ. 2,000. Pays on publication. Publishes ms an average of 3 months after acceptance. Byline given. Buys all rights. Editorial lead time 3 months. Accepts queries by mail, e-mail, fax. Accepts previously published material. Responds in 3 weeks to queries. Sample copy and writer's guidelines online.

Nonfiction Technical. No argumentation, crusading, inspiration, anecdotes, or humor. **Buys 6 mss/year.** Query. Length: 2,000-5,500 words. **Pays $100/printed pocket-sized page, plus 6 copies of publication.**

Photos Send photos with submission. Reviews contact sheets, negatives, 35mm or larger transparencies, 5×7 minimum prints, GIF/JPEG files. Buys all rights. Offers $25/photo. Captions, identification of subjects, model releases required.

Tips "Study guidelines carefully. Be concerned above all with accuracy, but if you have information that you believe meets those standards, do not hesitate to query even if you aren't sure of format or style. If you have the content we need, our editorial staff will work with you to put the material into shape."

$ $ CABIN CREW SAFETY

Flight Safety Foundation, Suite 300, 601 Madison St., Alexandria VA 22314-1756. (703)739-6700. Fax: (703)739-6708. Web site: www.flightsafety.org. **25% freelance written.** Bimonthly newsletter covering safety aspects of aircraft cabins (airline and corporate aviation) for cabin crews and passengers. Estab. 1956. Circ. 2,000. Pays on publication. Publishes ms an average of 3 months after acceptance. Byline given. Buys all rights. Editorial lead time 3 months. Accepts queries by mail, e-mail, fax. Accepts previously published material. Responds in 3 weeks to queries. Sample copy and writer's guidelines online.

Nonfiction Technical. No argumentation, crusading, inspiration, anecdotes, or humor. **Buys 6 mss/year.** Query. Length: 2,500-8,750 words. **Pays $200/printed page, plus 6 copies of publication.**

Photos Send photos with submission. Reviews contact sheets, negatives, 35mm or larger transparencies, 5×7 minimum prints, GIF/JPEG files. Buys all rights. Offers $25/photo. Captions, identification of subjects, model releases required.

Tips "Study guidelines carefully. Be concerned above all with accuracy, fairness, and objectivity, but if you have information that you believe meets those standards, do not hesitate to query even if you aren't sure of format or style. If you have the content we need, our editorial staff will work with you to put the material into shape."

$ $ FLIGHT SAFETY DIGEST

Flight Safety Foundation, Suite 300, 601 Madison St., Alexandria VA 22314-1756. (703)739-6700. Fax: (703)739-6708. Web site: www.flightsafety.org. **25% freelance written.** Monthly magazine covering significant issues in airline and corporate aviation safety. "*Flight Safety Digest* offers the page space to explore subjects in greater detail than in other Foundation periodicals." Estab. 1982. Circ. 2,000. Pays on publication. Publishes ms an average of 3 months after acceptance. Byline given. Buys all rights. Editorial lead time 3 months. Accepts queries by mail, e-mail, fax. Accepts previously published material. Responds in 3 weeks to queries. Sample copy and writer's guidelines online.

Nonfiction Technical. No argumentation, crusading, inspiration, anecdotes, or humor. **Buys 6 mss/year.** Query. Length: 4,000-15,000 words. **Pays $200/printed page, plus 6 copies of publication.**

Photos Send photos with submission. Reviews contact sheets, negatives, 35mm or larger transparencies, 5×7 minimum prints, GIF/JPEG files. Buys all rights. Offers $25/photo. Captions, identification of subjects, model releases required.

Tips "Study guidelines carefully. Be concerned above all with accuracy, fairness, and objectivity, but if you have information that you believe meets those standards, do not hesitate to query even if you aren't sure of format or style. If you have the content we need, our editorial staff will work with you to put the material into shape."

$ $ GROUND SUPPORT MAGAZINE

Cygnus Business Media, 1233 Janesville Ave., Fort Atkinson WI 53538. (920)563-1622. Fax: (920)563-1699. E-mail: karen.reinhardt@cygnuspub.com. Web site: www.groundsupportmagazine.com. **Contact:** Karen Reinhardt, editor. **20% freelance written.** Magazine published 10 times/year. "Our readers are those aviation professionals who are involved in ground support—the equipment manufacturers, the suppliers, the ramp operators, ground handlers, airport and airline managers. We cover issues of interest to this community—deicing, ramp safety, equipment technology, pollution, etc." Estab. 1993. Circ. 15,000. Pays on publication. Publishes ms an average of 2 months after acceptance. Buys all rights. Editorial lead time 2 months. Accepts queries by mail, e-mail, fax. Responds in 3 weeks to queries; 3 months to mss. Sample copy for 9×11 SAE and 5 first-class stamps.

Nonfiction How-to (use or maintain certain equipment), interview/profile, new product, opinion, photo feature, technical aspects of ground support and issues, industry events, meetings, new rules and regulations. **Buys 12-20 mss/year.** Send complete ms. Length: 500-2,000 words. **Pays $100-300.**

Photos Send photos with submission. Reviews 35mm prints, electronic preferred, slides. Buys all rights. Offers additional payment for photos accepted with ms. Identification of subjects required.

Tips "Write about subjects that relate to ground services. Write in clear and simple terms—personal experience is always welcome. If you have an aviation background or ground support experience, let us know."

$ $ HELICOPTER SAFETY

Flight Safety Foundation, Suite 300, 601 Madison St., Alexandria VA 22314-1756. (703)739-6700. Fax: (703)739-6708. Web site: www.flightsafety.org. **50% freelance written.** Bimonthly newsletter covering safety aspects of helicopter operations. "*Helicopter Safety* highlights the broad spectrum of real-world helicopter operations. Topics have ranged from design principles and primary training to helicopter utilization in offshore applications and in emergency medical service (EMS)." Estab. 1956. Circ. 2,000. Pays on publication. Publishes ms an average of 3 months after acceptance. Byline given. Buys all rights. Editorial lead time 3 months. Accepts queries by mail, e-mail, fax. Accepts previously published material. Responds in 3 weeks to queries. Sample copy and writer's guidelines online.

Nonfiction Technical. No argumentation, crusading, inspiration, anecdotes, or humor. **Buys 6 mss/year.** Query. Length: 2,500-8,750 words. **Pays $200/printed page, plus 6 copies of publication.**

Photos Send photos with submission. Reviews contact sheets, negatives, 35mm or larger transparencies, 5×7 minimum prints. Buys all rights. Offers $25/photo. Captions, identification of subjects, model releases required.

Tips "Study guidelines carefully. Be concerned above all with accuracy, fairness, and objectivity, but if you have information that you believe meets those standards, do not hesitate to query even if you aren't sure of format or style. If you have the content we need, our editorial staff will work with you to put the material into shape."

$ $ HUMAN FACTORS & AVIATION MEDICINE

Flight Safety Foundation, Suite 300, 601 Madison St., Alexandria VA 22314-1756. (703)739-6700. Fax: (703)739-6708. Web site: www.flightsafety.org. **50% freelance written.** Bimonthly newsletter covering medical aspects of aviation, primarily for airline and corporate aviation pilots. "*Human Factors & Aviation Medicine* allows specialists, researchers, and physicians to present information critical to the training, performance, and health of aviation professionals." Estab. 1953. Circ. 2,000. Pays on publication. Publishes ms an average of 3 months after acceptance. Byline given. Buys all rights. Editorial lead time 3 months. Accepts queries by mail, e-mail, fax. Accepts previously published material. Responds in 3 weeks to queries. Sample copy and writer's guidelines online.

Nonfiction Technical. No argumentation, crusading, inspiration, anecdotes, or humor. **Buys 6 mss/year.** Query. Length: 2,500-8,750 words. **Pays $200/printed page, plus 6 copies of publication.**

Photos Send photos with submission. Reviews contact sheets, negatives, 35mm or larger transparencies, 5×7 minimum prints, GIF/JPEG files. Buys all rights. Offers $25/photo. Captions, identification of subjects, model releases required.

Tips "Study guidelines carefully. Be concerned above all with accuracy, fairness, and objectivity, but if you have information that you believe meets those standards, do not hesitate to query even if you aren't sure of format or style. If you have the content we need, our editorial staff will work with you to put the material into shape."

$ $ $ PROFESSIONAL PILOT

Queensmith Communications, 30 S. Quaker Lane, Suite 300, Alexandria VA 22314. (703)370-0606. Fax: (703)370-7082. E-mail: editorial@propilotmag.com. Web site: www.propilotmag.com. **Contact:** Phil Rose, managing editor. **75% freelance written.** Monthly magazine covering regional airline, corporate and various other types of professional aviation. "The typical reader has a sophisticated grasp of piloting/aviation knowledge and is interested in articles that help him/her do the job better or more efficiently." Estab. 1967. Circ. 44,000. Pays on publication. Publishes ms an average of 2-3 months after acceptance. Byline given. Kill fee negotiable. Buys all rights. Accepts queries by mail, e-mail, fax, phone.

O━ "Affiliation with an active flight department, weather activity of Air Traffic Control (ATC) is helpful. Our readers want tool tech stuff from qualified writers with credentials."

Nonfiction "Typical subjects include new aircraft design, new product reviews (especially avionics), pilot techniques, profiles of regional airlines, fixed base operations, profiles of corporate flight departments and technological advances." All issues have a theme such as regional airline operations, maintenance, avionics, helicopters, etc. **Buys 40 mss/year.** Query. Length: 750-2,500 words. **Pays $200-1,000, depending on length. A fee for the article will be established at the time of assignment.** Sometimes pays expenses of writers on assignment.

Photos Prefers transparencies or slides. Send photos with submission. Buys all rights. Additional payment for photos negotiable. Captions, identification of subjects required.

Tips Query first. "Freelancer should be a professional pilot or have background in aviation. Authors should indicate relevant aviation experience and pilot credentials (certificates, ratings and hours). We place a greater emphasis on corporate operations and pilot concerns."

BEAUTY & SALON

$ $ BEAUTY STORE BUSINESS

Creative Age Communications, 7628 Densmore Ave., Van Nuys CA 91406-2042. (818)782-7328, ext. 353. Fax: (818)782-7450. E-mail: mbirenbaum@creativeage.com. **Contact:** Marc Birenbaum, executive editor. **50% freelance written.** Monthly magazine covering beauty store business management, news and beauty products. "The primary readers of the publication are owners, managers, and buyers at open-to-the-public beauty stores, including general-market and multicultural market-oriented ones with or without salon services. Our secondary readers are those at beauty stores only open to salon industry professionals. We also go to beauty distributors." Estab. 1994. Circ. 15,000. **Pays on acceptance.** Publishes ms an average of 3 months after acceptance. Byline given. Offers negotiable kill fee. Buys all rights. Editorial lead time 3 months. Submit seasonal material 4 months in advance. Accepts queries by mail, e-mail, fax. Responds in 1 week to queries Responds in 2 weeks, if interested, to mss. Sample copy for free.

Nonfiction "If your business-management article will help a specialty retailer or small business owner, it should be of assistance to our readers. If you're a writer who is/was a hairstylist, nail tech or esthetician, has an interest in professional beauty products or is fluent in Korean, we'd like to talk to you. We're also interested in hearing from illustrators/cartoonists and puzzle writers." How-to (business management, merchandising, e-commerce, retailing), interview/profile (industry leaders/beauty store owners). **Buys 20-30 mss/year.** Query. Length: 1,800-2,200 words. **Pays $250-525 for assigned articles.** Sometimes pays expenses of writers on assignment.

Photos Do not send computer art electronically. State availability with submission. Reviews transparencies, computer art (artists work on Macs, request 300 dpi, on CD or Zip disk, saved as JPEG, TIFF, or EPS). Buys all rights. Negotiates payment individually. Captions, identification of subjects required.

N $ $ COSMETICS

Canada's Business Magazine for the Cosmetics, Fragrance, Toiletry, and Personal Care Industry, Rogers, 1 Mt. Pleasant Rd., 7th Floor, Toronto ON M4Y 2Y5 Canada. (416)764-1680. Fax: (416)764-1704. E-mail: dave.lackie@cosmetics.rogers.com. Web site: www.cosmeticsmag.com. **Contact:** Dave Lackie, editor. **10% freelance written.** Bimonthly magazine. "Our main reader segment is the retail trade—department stores, drugstores, salons, estheticians—owners and cosmeticians/beauty advisors; plus manufacturers, distributors, agents, and suppliers to the industry." Estab. 1972. Circ. 13,000. **Pays on acceptance.** Publishes ms an average of 3 months after acceptance. Byline given. Offers 50% kill fee. Buys all rights. Editorial lead time 4 months. Submit seasonal material 4 months in advance. Accepts queries by mail. Responds in 1 month to queries. Sample copy for $6 (Canadian) and 8% GST.

Nonfiction General interest, interview/profile, photo feature. **Buys 1 mss/year.** Query. Length: 250-1,200 words. **Pays 25¢/word.** Sometimes pays expenses of writers on assignment.

Photos Send photos with submission. Reviews 2½ up to 8×10 transparencies, 4×6 up to 8×10 prints, 35mm slides, e-mail pictures in 300 dpi JPEG format. Buys all rights. Offers no additional payment for photos accepted with ms. Captions, identification of subjects, model releases required.

The online magazine carries original content not found in the print edition. Contact: Jim Hicks, publisher/online editor.

Tips "Must have broad knowledge of the Canadian cosmetics, fragrance, and toiletries industry and retail business. 99.9% of freelance articles are assigned by the editor to writers involved with the Canadian cosmetics business."

$ $ DAYSPA

The Premiere Spa Business Source, Creative Age Publications, 7628 Densmore Ave., Van Nuys CA 91406. (818)782-7328. Fax: (818)782-7450. E-mail: dayspa@creativeage.com. Web site: www.dayspamagazine.com. Managing Editor: Linda Jacobson-Kossoff. **Contact:** Amy E. Haymaker, executive editor. **50% freelance written.** Monthly magazine covering the business of day spas, skin care salons, wellness centers. "*Dayspa* includes only well-targeted business articles directed at the owners and managers of high-end, multi-service salons, day spas, resort spas, and destination spas." Estab. 1996. Circ. 31,000. **Pays on acceptance.** Publishes ms an average of 4 months after acceptance. Byline given. Buys first, one-time rights. Editorial lead time 4 months. Submit seasonal material 4 months in advance. Accepts queries by mail, e-mail, fax, phone. Responds in 2 months to queries. Sample copy for $5.

Nonfiction Buys 40 mss/year. Query. Length: 1,200-3,000 words. **Pays $150-500.**

Photos Send photos with submission. Buys one-time rights. Negotiates payment individually. Identification of subjects, model releases required.

Columns/Departments Legal Pad (legal issues affecting salons/spas); Money Matters (financial issues); Management Workshop (spa management issues), all 1,200-1,500 words. **Buys 20 mss/year.** Query. **Pays $150-300.**

MASSAGE & BODYWORK

Associated Bodywork & Massage Professionals, 1271 Sugarbush Dr., Evergreen CO 80439-9766. (303)674-8478 or (800)458-2267. Fax: (303)674-0859. E-mail: editor@abmp.com. Web site: www.massageandbodywork.com. **Contact:** Leslie A. Young, PhD, editor-in-chief. **85% freelance written.** Bimonthly magazine covering therapeutic massage/bodywork. "A trade publication for the massage therapist, and bodyworker. An all-inclusive publication encompassing everything from traditional Swedish massage to energy work to other complementary therapies (i.e., homeopathy, herbs, aromatherapy, etc.)." **Pays on acceptance.** Publishes ms an average of 6 months after acceptance. Buys first North American serial, one-time, electronic rights. Editorial lead time 6 months. Submit seasonal material 6 months in advance. Accepts queries by e-mail. Responds in 1 month to queries; 5 months to mss. Writer's guidelines online.

Nonfiction Essays, exposé, how-to (technique/modality), interview/profile, opinion, personal experience, technical. No fiction. **Buys 60-75 mss/year.** Query with published clips. Length: 1,000-3,000 words.

Reprints Accepts previously published submissions.

Photos Not interested in photo submissions separate from feature queries. State availability with submission. Reviews digital images (300 dpi). Buys one-time rights. Negotiates payment individually. Captions, identification of subjects, model releases required.

Columns/Departments Buys 20 mss/year.

Tips "Know your topic. Offer suggestions for art to accompany your submission. *Massage & Bodywork* looks for interesting, tightly focused stories concerning a particular modality or technique of massage, bodywork, and somatic therapies. The editorial staff welcomes the opportunity to review manuscripts which may be relevant to the field of massage and bodywork. In addition to more general pieces pertaining to complementary and alternative medicine. This would include the widely varying modalities of massage and bodywork (from Swedish massage to Polarity therapy), specific technical or ancillary therapies, including such topics as biomagnetics, aromatherapy, and facial rejuvenation. Reference lists relating to technical articles should include the author, title, publisher, and publication date of works cited according to Chicago Manual of Style. Word count: 1,500-4,000 words; longer articles negotiable."

$ $ MASSAGE MAGAZINE

Exploring Today's Touch Therapies, 5150 Palm Valley Rd., Suite 103, Ponte Vedra Beach FL 32082. (904)285-6020. E-mail: kmenahan@massagemag.com. Web site: www.massagemag.com. **Contact:** Karen Menehan, editor. **60% freelance written.** Bimonthly magazine covering massage and other touch therapies. Estab. 1985. Circ. 50,000. Pays on publication. Publishes ms an average of 4 months-1 year after acceptance. Byline given. Buys first North American serial rights. Accepts queries by e-mail. Responds in 2 months to queries; 3 months to mss. Sample copy for $6.95. Writer's guidelines online.

Nonfiction Book excerpts, essays, general interest, how-to, interview/profile, personal experience, photo feature, technical, experiential. Length: 600-2,000 words. **Pays $75-300 for assigned articles.**

Reprints Send tearsheet of article and electronic ms with rights for sale noted and information about when and where the material previously appeared. Pays 50-75% of amount paid for an original article.

Photos Send photos with submission via e-mail. Buys one-time rights. Offers $25-100/photo. Identification of subjects, identification of photographer required.

Columns/Departments Profiles; News and Current Events; Practice Building (business); Technique; Body/Mind. Length: 800-1,200 words. **$75-300 for assigned articles.**

Fillers Facts, newsbreaks. Length: 100-800 words. **Pays $125 maximum.**

Tips "Our readers seek practical information on how to help their clients, improve their techniques, and/or make their businesses more successful, as well as feature articles that place massage therapy in a positive or inspiring light. Since most of our readers are professional therapists, we do not publish articles on topics like 'How Massage Can Help You Relax.' Please study a few back issues so you know what types of topics and tone we're looking for."

$ $ NAILPRO

The Magazine for Nail Professionals, Creative Age Publications, 7628 Densmore Ave., Van Nuys CA 91406. (818)782-7328. Fax: (818)782-7450. E-mail: jmills@creativeage.com. Web site: www.nailpro.com. **Contact:** Jodi Mills, executive editor. **75% freelance written.** Monthly magazine written for manicurists and nail technicians working in full-service salons or nails-only salons. It covers technical and business aspects of working in and operating a nail-care service, as well as the nail-care industry in general. Estab. 1989. Circ. 65,000. **Pays on acceptance.** Publishes ms an average of 6 months after acceptance. Byline given. Buys first North American serial rights. Editorial lead time 3 months. Submit seasonal material 3 months in advance. Accepts queries by mail, e-mail, fax. Accepts simultaneous submissions. Responds in 6 weeks to queries. Sample copy for $2 and $8\frac{1}{2} \times 11$ SASE.

Nonfiction Book excerpts, how-to, humor, inspirational, interview/profile, personal experience, photo feature, technical. No general interest articles or business articles not geared to the nail-care industry. **Buys 50 mss/year.** Query. Length: 1,000-3,000 words. **Pays $150-450.**

Reprints Send ms with rights for sale noted and information about when and where the material previously appeared. Pays 25-50% of amount paid for an original article.

Photos Send photos with submission. Reviews transparencies, prints. Buys one-time rights. Negotiates payment individually. Identification of subjects, model releases required.

Columns/Departments Building Business (articles on marketing nail services/products), 1,200-2,000 words; Shop Talk (aspects of operating a nail salon), 1,200-2,000 words. **Buys 50 mss/year.** Query. **Pays $200-300.**

The online magazine carries original content not found in the print edition. Contact: Jodi Mills.

$ $ NAILS

Bobit Business Media, 3520 Challenger St., Torrance CA 90503. (310)533-2400. Fax: (310)533-2507. E-mail: hannah.lee@bobit.com. Web site: www.nailsmag.com. **Contact:** Hannah Lee, editor. **10% freelance written.** Monthly magazine. "*NAILS* seeks to educate its readers on new techniques and products, nail anatomy and health, customer relations, working safely with chemicals, salon sanitation, and the business aspects of running a salon." Estab. 1983. Circ. 55,000. **Pays on acceptance.** Byline given. Buys all rights. Submit seasonal material 4 months in advance. Accepts queries by mail, e-mail, fax. Responds in 3 months to queries. Sample copy and writer's guidelines for #10 SASE.

Nonfiction Historical/nostalgic, how-to, inspirational, interview/profile, personal experience, photo feature, technical. "No articles on one particular product, company profiles or articles slanted toward a particular company or manufacturer." **Buys 20 mss/year.** Query with published clips. Length: 1,200-3,000 words. **Pays $200-500.** Sometimes pays expenses of writers on assignment.

Photos State availability with submission. Reviews contact sheets, transparencies, prints (any standard size acceptable). Buys all rights. Offers $50-200/photo. Captions, identification of subjects, model releases required.

The online version contains material not found in the print edition. Contact: Hannah Lee.

Tips "Send clips and query; *do not send unsolicited manscripts.* We would like to see ideas for articles on a unique salon or a business article that focuses on a specific aspect or problem encountered when working in a salon. The Modern Nail Salon section, which profiles nail salons and full-service salons, is most open to freelancers. Focus on an innovative business idea or unique point of view. Articles from experts on specific business issues—insurance, handling difficult employees, cultivating clients—are encouraged."

N $ $ PULSE MAGAZINE

The Magazine for the Spa Professional, HOST Communications Inc., 2365 Harrodsburg Rd., Suite A325, Lexington KY 40511. Fax: (859)226-4445. E-mail: pulse@ispastaff.com. Web site: www.experienceispa.com/ispa/pulse. Editor: Julie Wilson. **Contact:** Rachel Zawila, editorial assistant. **30% freelance written.** Magazine published 8 times/year covering spa industry. "*Pulse* is the magazine for the spa professional. As the official publication of the International SPA Association, its purpose is to advance the business of the spa professionals by informing them of the latest trends and practices and promoting the wellness aspects of spa. *Pulse* connects people, nurtures their personal and professional growth, and enhances their ability to network and succeed in the spa industry." Estab. 1991. Circ. 5,300. Pays on publication. Publishes ms an average of 1 month after acceptance. Byline given. Buys all rights. Editorial lead time 3 months. Submit seasonal material 4 months in advance. Accepts queries by e-mail. Sample copy for #10 SASE. Writer's guidelines by e-mail.

Nonfiction General interest, how-to, interview/profile, new product. Does not want articles focused on spas that are not members of ISPA, consumer-focused articles (market is the spa industry professional), or features on hot tubs (not *that* spa industry). **Buys 8-10 mss/year.** Query with published clips. Length: 800-2,000 words. **Pays $250-450.** Sometimes pays expenses of writers on assignment.

Photos Contact Rachel Zawila, editorial assistant. Send photos with submission. Reviews GIF/JPEG files. Buys one-time rights. Negotiates payment individually. Captions required.

Tips "Understand the nuances of association publishing (different than consumer and B2B). Send published clips, not Word documents. Experience in writing for health and wellness market is helpful. Only feature ISPA member companies in the magazine; visit our Web site to learn more about our industry and to see if your pitch includes member companies before making contact."

$ $ SKIN INC. MAGAZINE

The Complete Business Guide for Spa Professionals, Allured Publishing Corp., 362 S. Schmale Rd., Carol Stream IL 60188. (630)653-2155. Fax: (630)653-2192. E-mail: taschetta-millane@allured.com. Web site: www.skininc.com. Publisher: Annette Delagrange. **Contact:** Melinda Taschetta-Millane, editor. **30% freelance written.** Magazine published 12 times/year. "Manuscripts considered for publication that contain original and new information in the general fields of skin care and makeup, dermatological and esthetician-assisted surgical techniques. The subject may cover the science of skin, the business of skin care and makeup, and plastic surgeons on healthy (i.e., nondiseased) skin." Estab. 1988. Circ. 20,000. Pays on publication. Publishes ms an average of 6 months after acceptance. Byline given. Buys all rights. Editorial lead time 6 months. Submit seasonal material 1 year in advance. Accepts queries by mail, e-mail, fax, phone. Responds in 3 weeks to queries; 1 month to mss. Sample copy and writer's guidelines free.

Nonfiction General interest, how-to, interview/profile, personal experience, technical. **Buys 6 mss/year.** Query with published clips. Length: 2,000 words. **Pays $100-300 for assigned articles; $50-200 for unsolicited articles.**
Photos State availability with submission. Reviews 3×5 prints. Buys one-time rights. Offers no additional payment for photos accepted with ms. Captions, identification of subjects, model releases required.
Columns/Departments Finance (tips and solutions for managing money), 2,000-2,500 words; Personnel (managing personnel), 2,000-2,500 words; Marketing (marketing tips for salon owners), 2,000-2,500 words; Retail (retailing products and services in the salon environment), 2,000-2,500 words. Query with published clips. **Pays $50-200.**
Fillers Facts, newsbreaks. **Buys 6/year.** Length: 250-500 words. **Pays $50-100.**
Tips "Have an understanding of the skin care industry."

BEVERAGES & BOTTLING

$ $ BAR & BEVERAGE BUSINESS MAGAZINE

Mercury Publications, Ltd., 1740 Wellington Ave., Winnipeg MB R3H 0E8 Canada. (204)954-2085. Fax: (204)954-2057. E-mail: editorial@mercury.mb.ca. Web site: www.barandbeverage.com. Editor: Kelly Gray. **Contact:** Carly Peters, editorial production manager. **33% freelance written.** Bimonthly magazine providing information on the latest trends, happenings, buying-selling of beverages and product merchandising. Estab. 1998. Circ. 16,077. Pays 30-45 days from receipt of invoice. Byline given. Offers 33% kill fee. Buys all rights. Submit seasonal material 3 months in advance. Accepts simultaneous submissions. Sample copy and writer's guidelines free or by e-mail.

- Does not accept queries for specific stories. Assigns stories to Canadian writers.

Nonfiction How-to (making a good drink, training staff, etc.), interview/profile. Industry reports, profiles on companies. Query with published clips. Length: 500-9,000 words. **Pays 25-35¢/word.** Sometimes pays expenses of writers on assignment.
Photos State availability with submission. Reviews negatives, transparencies, 3×5 prints, JPEG, EPS or TIFF files. Buys all rights. Negotiates payment individually. Captions required.
Columns/Departments Out There (bar & bev news in various parts of the country), 100-500 words. Query. **Pays $0-100.**

N $ $ THE BEVERAGE JOURNAL

Michigan Edition, MI Licensed Beverage Association, P.O. Box 4067, East Lansing MI 48826. (517)374-9611. Fax: (517)374-1165. E-mail: editor@mlba.org. Web site: www.mlba.org. **40-50% freelance written.** Monthly magazine covering hospitality industry. "A monthly trade magazine devoted to the beer, wine, and spirits industry in Michigan. It is dedicated to serving those who make their living serving the public and the state through the orderly and responsible sale of beverages." Estab. 1983. Circ. 4,200. Pays on publication. Buys one-time, second serial (reprint) rights, makes work-for-hire assignments. Editorial lead time 3 months. Submit seasonal material 3 months in advance. Accepts queries by mail, e-mail. Responds in 2 weeks to queries; 1 month to mss. Sample copy for $5 or online.
Nonfiction Essays, general interest, historical/nostalgic, how-to (make a drink, human resources, tips, etc.), humor, interview/profile, new product, opinion, personal experience, photo feature, technical. **Buys 24 mss/year.** Send complete ms. Length:1,000 words. **Pays $20-200.**
Reprints Accepts previously published submissions.
Columns/Departments Interviews (legislators, others), 750-1,000 words; personal experience (waitstaff, customer, bartenders), 500 words. **Buys 12 mss/year.** Send complete ms. **Pays $25-100.**
Tips "We are particularly interested in nonfiction concerning responsible consumption/serving of alcohol. We are looking for product reviews, company profiles, personal experiences, and news articles that would benefit our audience. Our audience is a busy group of business owners and hospitality professionals striving to obtain pertinent information that is not too wordy."

$ $ PATTERSON'S CALIFORNIA BEVERAGE JOURNAL

Interactive Color, Inc., 4910 San Fernando Rd., Glendale CA 91204. (818)291-1125. Fax: (818)547-4607. E-mail: mmay@interactivecolor.com. Web site: www.beveragelink.com. **Contact:** Meridith May, associate publisher/senior editor. **25% freelance written.** Monthly magazine covering the alcohol, beverage, and wine industries. "*Patterson's* reports on the latest news in product information, merchandising, company appointments, developments in the wine industry, and consumer trends. Our readers can be informed, up-to-date and confident in their purchasing decisions." Estab. 1962. Circ. 25,000. Byline given. Offers negotiable kill fee. Editorial lead time 1 month. Submit seasonal material 1 month in advance. Accepts queries by mail, e-mail, fax. Sample copy and writer's guidelines free.

Nonfiction Interview/profile, new product, market reports. "No consumer-oriented articles or negative slants on industry as a whole." **Buys 200 mss/year.** Query with published clips. Length: 500-750 words. **Pays $60-200.**

Photos State availability with submission. Reviews transparencies. Buys all rights. Offers no additional payment for photos accepted with ms. Captions, identification of subjects required.

Columns/Departments Query with published clips.

$ $ $ VINEYARD & WINERY MANAGEMENT

P.O. Box 2358, Windsor CA 95492-2358. (707)836-6820. Fax: (707)836-6825. Web site: www.vwm-online.com. **70% freelance written.** Bimonthly magazine of professional importance to grape growers, winemakers, and winery sales and business people. Estab. 1975. Circ. 6,500. Pays on publication. Byline given. Buys first North American serial, simultaneous rights. Accepts queries by e-mail. Responds in 3 weeks to queries; 1 month to mss. Sample copy for free. Writer's guidelines for #10 SASE.

Nonfiction Subjects are technical in nature and explore the various methods people in these career paths use to succeed and the equipment and techniques they use successfully. Business articles and management topics are also featured. The audience is national with western dominance. How-to, interview/profile, new product, technical. **Buys 30 mss/year.** Query. Length: 1,800-5,000 words. **Pays $30-1,000.** Sometimes pays expenses of writers on assignment.

Photos State availability with submission. Reviews contact sheets, negatives, transparencies, digital photos. Black & white often purchased for $20 each to accompany story material; 35mm and/or 4×5 transparencies for $50 and up; 6/year of vineyard and/or winery scene related to story. Captions, identification of subjects required.

Tips "We're looking for long-term relationships with authors who know the business and write well. Electronic submissions required; query for formats."

$ $ WINES & VINES MAGAZINE

The Authoritative Voice of the Grape and Wine Industry Since 1919, Wine Communications Group, 1800 Lincoln Ave., San Rafael CA 94901. (415)453-9700. Fax: (415)453-2517. E-mail: edit@winesandvines.com. Web site: www.winesandvines.com. **50% freelance written.** Monthly magazine covering the international winegrape and winemaking industry. "Since 1919 *Wines & Vines Magazine* has been the authoritative voice of the wine and grape industry—from prohibition to phylloxera, we have covered it all. Our paid circulation reaches all 50 states and many foreign countries. Because we are intended for the trade—including growers, winemakers, winery owners, wholesalers, restauranteurs, and serious amateurs—we accept more technical, informative articles. We do not accept wine reviews, wine country tours, or anything of a wine consumer nature." Estab. 1919. Circ. 5,000. Pays 30 days after acceptance. Publishes ms an average of 3 months after acceptance. Byline given. Buys first, electronic rights. Editorial lead time 2 months. Submit seasonal material 4 months in advance. Accepts queries by e-mail. Responds in 2-3 weeks to queries. Sample copy for $5. Writer's guidelines free.

Nonfiction Interview/profile, new product, technical. No wine reviews, wine country travelogues, 'lifestyle' pieces, or anything aimed at wine consumers. "Our readers are professionals in the field." **Buys 60 mss/year.** Query with published clips. Length: 1,000-2,000 words. **Pays flat fee of $500 for assigned articles.**

Photos Prefers JPEG files (JPEG, 300 dpi minimum). Can use high-quality prints. State availability of or send photos with submission. Does not pay for photos submitted by author, but will give photo credit. Captions, identification of subjects required.

BOOK & BOOKSTORE

$ $ FOREWORD MAGAZINE

ForeWord Magazine, Inc., 129½ E. Front St., Traverse City MI 49684. (231)933-3699. Fax: (231)933-3899. Web site: www.forewordmagazine.com. **Contact:** Alex Moore, managing editor. **95% freelance written.** Bimonthly magazine covering independent and university presses for booksellers and librarians with articles, news, book reviews. Estab. 1998. Circ. 8,000. Pays 2 months after publication. Publishes ms an average of 2-3 months after acceptance. Byline given. Buys all rights. Editorial lead time 3-4 months. Submit seasonal material 5 months in advance. Accepts queries by mail, e-mail. Responds in 1 month to queries; 1 month to mss. Sample copy for $10 and 8½×11 SASE with $1.50 postage.

Nonfiction Reviews, 85% nonfiction and 15% fiction/poetry. Query with published clips. Length: 400-1,500 words. **Pays $25-200 for assigned articles.**

Tips "Be knowledgeable about the needs of booksellers and librarians—remember we are an industry trade journal, not a how-to or consumer publication. We review books prior to publication, so book reviews are always assigned—but send us a note telling subjects you wish to review, as well as a résumé."

THE HORN BOOK MAGAZINE

The Horn Book, Inc., 56 Roland St., Suite 200, Boston MA 02129. (617)628-0225. Fax: (617)628-0882. Web site: www.hbook.com. **Contact:** Roger Sutton, editor-in-chief. **75% freelance written.** Prefers to work with published/established writers. Bimonthly magazine covering children's literature for librarians, booksellers, professors, teachers and students of children's literature. Estab. 1924. Circ. 16,000. Pays on publication. Publishes ms an average of 4 months after acceptance. Byline given. Submit seasonal material 6 months in advance. Accepts queries by mail, e-mail, fax. Accepts simultaneous submissions. Responds in 3 months to queries. Sample copy and writer's guidelines online.

Nonfiction Interested in seeing strong, authoritative pieces about children's books and contemporary culture. Writers should be familiar with the magazine and its contents. Interview/profile (children's book authors and illustrators), topics of interest to the children's bookworld. **Buys 20 mss/year.** Query or send complete ms. Length: 1,000-2,800 words. **Pays honorarium upon publication.**

Tips "Writers have a better chance of breaking into our publication with a query letter on a specific article they want to write."

BRICK, GLASS & CERAMICS

$ $ GLASS MAGAZINE

For the Architectural Glass Industry, National Glass Association, 8200 Greensboro Dr., Suite 302, McLean VA 22102. (866)342-5642. Fax: (703)442-0630. E-mail: editorialinfo@glass.org. Web site: www.glass.org. **Contact:** Nancy Davis, editor-in-chief. **10% freelance written.** Prefers to work with published/established writers. Monthly magazine covering the architectural glass industry. Circ. 28,289. **Pays on acceptance.** Publishes ms an average of 6 months after acceptance. Byline given. Kill fee varies. Buys first rights. Accepts queries by mail, e-mail, fax. Responds in 2 months to mss. Sample copy for $5 and 9×12 SAE with 10 first-class stamps.

Nonfiction Interview/profile (of various glass businesses; profiles of industry people or glass business owners), new product, technical (about glazing processes). **Buys 5 mss/year.** Query with published clips. Length: 1,000 words minimum. **Pays $150-300 for assigned articles.**

Photos State availability with submission.

Tips *Glass Magazine* is doing more inhouse writing; freelance cut by half. "Do not send in general glass use stories. Research the industry first, then query."

$ $ US GLASS, METAL & GLAZING

Key Communications, Inc., P.O. Box 569, Garrisonville VA 22463. (540)720-5584. Fax: (540)720-5687. E-mail: info@glass.com. Web site: www.usglassmag.com. **25% freelance written.** Monthly magazine for companies involved in the flat glass trades. Estab. 1966. Circ. 27,000. Pays on publication. Publishes ms an average of 3 months after acceptance. Byline given. Buys all rights. Editorial lead time 3 months. Submit seasonal material 2 months in advance. Accepts queries by mail, e-mail, fax. Accepts simultaneous submissions. Responds in 1 month to queries; 2 months to mss. Sample copy and writer's guidelines online.

Nonfiction Buys 12 mss/year. Query with published clips. **Pays $300-600 for assigned articles.** Sometimes pays expenses of writers on assignment.

Photos State availability with submission. Reviews contact sheets. Buys first North American rights. Offers no additional payment for photos accepted with ms. Captions, identification of subjects required.

BUILDING INTERIORS

N $ $ FABRICS + FURNISHINGS INTERNATIONAL

SIPCO Publications + Events, 1133 Pleasantville Rd., P.O. 161, Briarcliff NY 10510. (914)923-0616. Fax: (914)923-0018. E-mail: rgoldberg@sipco.net. Web site: www.sipco.net. **Contact:** Rebecca Goldberg, editor. **10% freelance written.** Bimonthly magazine covering commercial, hospitality interior design, manufacturing. "*F+FI* covers news from vendors who supply hospitality interiors industry." Estab. 1990. Circ. 11,000+. Pays on publication. Byline given. Offers $100 kill fee. Editorial lead time 3 months. Submit seasonal material 3 months in advance. Accepts queries by e-mail. Accepts simultaneous submissions. Sample copy online.

Nonfiction Interview/profile, technical. Does not opinion, consumer pieces. "Our readers must learn something from our stories." Query with published clips. Length: 500-1,000 words. **Pays $250-350.**

Photos Send photos with submission. Reviews GIF/JPEG files. Offers no additional payment for photos accepted with ms. Captions, identification of subjects required.

Tips "Give us a lead on a new project that we haven't heard about. Have pictures of space and ability to interview designer on how they made it work."

N FLOOR COVERING NEWS

The publication more retailers prefer, Ro-El Productions, 550 W. Old Country Rd., Suite 204, Hicksville NY 11801. (516)932-7860. Fax: (516)932-7639. E-mail: fcnews@optonline.net. Web site: www.floorcoveringnews.net. Editor: Al Wahnon. **Contact:** Matthew Spieler, executive editor. **15% freelance written.** Biweekly tabloid covering the floor covering industry for retailers, salespeople, installers, distributors and designers, as well as manufacturers. "We are a journalistic-style publication that writes for the flooring industry. While we use industry jargon and have our own nuances, we use the AP and New York Times stylebooks as general guidelines." Estab. 1986. Circ. 16,000. **Pays on acceptance.** Publishes ms an average of 1 month after acceptance. Byline given. Buys exclusivity rights for within the flooring industry trades, which includes the Internet. Editorial lead time 2 months. Accepts previously published material. Accepts simultaneous submissions. Responds in 2-3 weeks to queries. Sample copy for $4.

Nonfiction Book excerpts, exposé, historical/nostalgic, interview/profile, new product, photo feature, technical. Does not want puff pieces and commercials. **Buys 30-40 mss/year.** Query. **Pays negotiable amount.** Pays expenses of writers on assignment.

Photos Send photos with submission. Reviews contact sheets, prints, JPEG/TIFF files (300 dpi, 4×4 minimum). Offers no additional payment for photos accepted with ms; negotiates payment individually. Captions, identification of subjects, model releases required.

N HOME TEXTILES TODAY

The Business and Fashion Newspaper of the Home Textiles Industry, Reed Business Information, 360 Park Ave. S., New York NY 10010. (646)746-7290. Fax: (646)746-7300. E-mail: jnegley@reedbusiness.com. Web site: www.hometextilestoday.com. Editor: Jennifer Marks. **Contact:** James Mammarella, managing editor. **5% freelance written.** Tabloid published 33 times/year covering home textiles retailers, manufacturers and importers/exporters. "Our readers are interested in business trends and statistics about business trends related to their niche in the home furnishings market." Estab. 1979. Circ. 7,700. Pays on publication. Publishes ms an average of 2 weeks after acceptance. Byline given. Offers 30% kill fee. Buys all rights. Editorial lead time 1-2 weeks. Submit seasonal material 3 weeks in advance. Accepts queries by mail, e-mail, fax, phone. Accepts simultaneous submissions. Responds in 2 weeks to queries; 2 weeks to mss. Sample copy for free. Writer's guidelines free.

Tips "Information has to be focused on home textiles business—sheets, towels, bedding, curtains, rugs, table linens, kitchen textiles, curtains. Most of our readers are doing volume business at discount chains, mass market retailers, big boxes and department stores."

N $ $ KITCHEN & BATH DESIGN NEWS

Cygnus Business Media, 3 Huntington Quadrangle, Suite 301N, Melville NY 11747. Fax: (631)845-7218. E-mail: janice.costa@cygnuspub.com. Web site: www.kitchenbathdesign.com. Senior Editors: Anita Shaw, John Filippelli. **Contact:** Janice Costa, editor. **15% freelance written.** Monthly tabloid for kitchen and bath dealers and design professionals, offering design, business and marketing advice to help our readers be more successful. It is not a consumer publication about design, a book for do-it-yourselfers, or a magazine created to showcase pretty pictures of kitchens and baths. "Rather, we cover the professional kitchen and bath design industry in depth, looking at the specific challenges facing these professionals, and how they address these challenges." Estab. 1983. Circ. 51,000. Pays on publication. Publishes ms an average of 2-3 months after acceptance. Byline given. Buys all rights. Editorial lead time 2 months. Accepts queries by mail, e-mail, fax. Responds in 2-4 weeks to queries. Sample copy online. Writer's guidelines by e-mail.

Nonfiction How-to, interview/profile. Does not want consumer stories; generic business stories; "I remodeled my kitchen and it's so beautiful" stories. "This is a magazine for trade professionals, so stories need to be both slanted for these professionals, as well as sophisticated enough so that people who have been working in the field 30 years can still learn something from them." **Buys 16 mss/year.** Query with published clips. Length: 1,100-3,000 words. **Pays $200-650.** Sometimes pays expenses of writers on assignment.

Photos Send photos with submission. Offers no additional payment for photos accepted with ms. Identification of subjects required.

Tips "This is a trade magazine for kitchen and bath dealers and designers, so trade experience and knowledge of the industry are essential. We look for writers who already know the unique challenges facing this industry, as well as the major players, acronyms, etc. This is not a market for beginners, and the vast majority of our freelancers are either design professionals, or experienced in the industry."

$ $ PWC

Painting & Wallcovering Contractor, Finan Publishing Co., Inc., 15 W. Moody Ave., St. Louis MO 63119. (314)961-6644. Fax: (314)961-4809. E-mail: pdowns@finan.com. Web site: www.paintstore.com. **Contact:** Peter Downs, editor. **90% freelance written.** Bimonthly magazine. "*PWC* provides news you can use: information helpful to the painting and wallcovering contractor in the here and now." Estab. 1928. Circ. 30,000. Pays 1 month after publication. Publishes ms an average of 1 month after acceptance. Byline given. Offers variable kill fee. Buys first North American serial rights. Editorial lead time 2 months. Submit seasonal material 2 months in advance. Accepts simultaneous submissions. Responds in 2 weeks to queries. Sample copy for free.

Nonfiction Essays, exposé, how-to (painting and wallcovering), interview/profile, new product, opinion, personal experience. **Buys 40 mss/year.** Query with published clips. Length: 1,500-2,500 words. **Pays $300 minimum.** Pays expenses of writers on assignment.

Reprints Send photocopy and information about when and where the material previously appeared. Negotiates payment.

Photos State availability of or send photos with submission. Reviews contact sheets, negatives, transparencies, digital prints. Buys all rights. Offers no additional payment for photos accepted with ms. Identification of subjects required.

Columns/Departments Anything of interest to the small businessman, 1,250 words. **Buys 2 mss/year.** Query with published clips. **Pays $50-100.**

Tips "We almost always buy on an assignment basis. The way to break in is to send good clips, and I'll try and give you work."

$ $ QUALIFIED REMODELER

The Business Management Tool for Professional Remodelers, Cygnus Business Media, P.O. Box 803, Fort Atkinson WI 53538. E-mail: chaya.chang@cygnuspub.com. Web site: www.qualifiedremodeler.com. Editor-in-Chief: Patrick O'Toole. **Contact:** Chaya Chang, managing editor. **5% freelance written.** Monthly magazine covering residential remodeling. Estab. 1975. Circ. 83,500. **Pays on acceptance.** Publishes ms an average of 1 month after acceptance. Byline given. Buys all rights. Editorial lead time 3 months. Submit seasonal material 2 months in advance. Accepts queries by mail, e-mail, fax, phone. Sample copy online.

Nonfiction How-to (business management), new product, photo feature, best practices articles, innovative design. **Buys 12 mss/year.** Query with published clips. Length: 1,200-2,500 words. **Pays $300-600 for assigned articles; $200-400 for unsolicited articles.** Sometimes pays expenses of writers on assignment.

Photos Send photos with submission. Reviews negatives, transparencies. Buys one-time rights. Negotiates payment individually.

Columns/Departments Query with published clips. **Pays $400.**

The online version contains material not found in the print edition.

Tips "We focus on business management issues faced by remodeling contractors. For example, sales, marketing, liability, taxes, and just about any matter addressing small business operation."

$ $ $ $ REMODELING

HanleyWood, LLC, One Thomas Circle NW, Suite 600, Washington DC 20005. (202)452-0800. Fax: (202)785-1974. E-mail: ibush@hanleywood.com. Web site: www.remodelingmagazine.com. Editor-in-Chief: Sal Alfano. **Contact:** Ingrid Bush, managing editor. **10% freelance written.** Monthly magazine covering residential and light commercial remodeling. "We cover the best new ideas in remodeling design, business, construction and products." Estab. 1985. Circ. 80,000. Pays on publication. Publishes ms an average of 3 months after acceptance. Byline given. Offers 5¢/word kill fee. Buys first North American serial rights. Accepts queries by mail, e-mail, fax. Sample copy for free.

Nonfiction Interview/profile, new product, technical, small business trends. **Buys 6 mss/year.** Query with published clips. Length: 250-1,000 words. **Pays $1/word.** Sometimes pays expenses of writers on assignment.

Photos State availability with submission. Reviews 4×5 transparencies, slides, 8×10 prints. Buys one-time rights. Offers $25-125/photo. Captions, identification of subjects, model releases required.

The online magazine carries original content not included in the print edition.

Tips "We specialize in service journalism for remodeling contractors. Knowledge of the industry is essential."

$ $ WALLS & CEILINGS

2401 W. Big Beaver Rd., Suite 700, Troy MI 48084. (248)244-6404. Fax: (248)362-5103. E-mail: wyattj@bnpmedia.com. Web site: www.wconline.com. **Contact:** John Wyatt, managing editor. **20% freelance written.** Monthly magazine for contractors involved in lathing and plastering, drywall, acoustics, fireproofing, curtain walls, and movable partitions, together with manufacturers, dealers, and architects. Estab. 1938. Circ. 30,000. Pays on publication. Publishes ms an average of 6 months after acceptance. Byline given. Buys all rights. Submit seasonal material 4 months in advance. Accepts queries by mail, e-mail, phone. Accepts simultaneous submissions.

Responds in 6 months to queries. Sample copy for 9 × 12 SAE with $2 postage. Writer's guidelines for #10 SASE.

O→ Break in with technical expertise in drywall, plaster, stucco.

Nonfiction How-to (drywall and plaster construction and business management), technical. **Buys 20 mss/year.** Query or send complete ms. Length: 1,000-1,500 words. **Pays $50-500.** Sometimes pays expenses of writers on assignment.

Reprints Send tearsheet or photocopy with rights for sale noted and information about when and where the material previously appeared. Pays 50% of the amount paid for an original article.

Photos Send photos with submission. Reviews contact sheets, negatives, transparencies, prints. Buys one-time rights. Captions, identification of subjects required.

The online magazine carries original content not included in the print edition.

BUSINESS MANAGEMENT

N $ $ ASSOCIATION & MEETING DIRECTOR

Canada's Number One Association Management & Meeting Magazine, August Communications, 225-530 Century St., Winnipeg MB R3H 0Y4 Canada. (888)573-1136. Fax: (866)957-0217. E-mail: r.mcilroy@august.ca. Web site: www.associationdirector.ca. **Contact:** Randal McIlroy, editor. **70% freelance written.** Bimonthly magazine covering association management and corporate meeting planners. "*Association & Meeting Director* is direct mailed to Canadian association executives and corporate meeting professionals. It has the aim of exploring both the Canadian corporate and association marketplace." Estab. 2000. Circ. 15,000. Pays 1 month after publication. Publishes ms an average of 2 months after acceptance. Byline given. Buys all rights. Editorial lead time 3 months. Submit seasonal material 3 months in advance. Accepts queries by mail, e-mail, fax. Responds in 1 week to queries. Sample copy and writer's guidelines free.

Nonfiction How-to, inspirational, interview/profile, new product, technical, travel. **Buys 18 mss/year.** Query with published clips. Length: 700-2,000 words. **Pays 20-40¢/word for assigned articles.**

Photos State availability with submission. Reviews GIF/JPEG files. Buys all rights. Negotiates payment individually. Identification of subjects required.

Columns/Departments Buys 12 mss/year. Query with published clips. **Pays 20-40¢/word.**

N BEDROOM MAGAZINE

The Marketing Arm Group, Inc., P.O. Box 79258, Charlotte NC 79258. (704)841-8323. Fax: (704)841-0616. E-mail: daler@rtppub.com. Web site: www.bedroom-mag.com. **Contact:** Dale T. Read, publisher/editor-in-chief. Quarterly magazine mailed to more than 18,000 home furnishings retailers, buyers, owners and managers. "We only cover one thing: mattresses, beds, top-of-bed, sleep products. We are a narrow, long-standing trade journal." Circ. 20,000.

$ $ $ $ BEDTIMES

The Business Journal for the Sleep Products Industry, International Sleep Products Association, 501 Wythe St., Alexandria VA 22314-1917. (703)683-8371. E-mail: jpalm@sleepproducts.org. Web site: www.sleepproducts.org. **Contact:** Julie Palm, editor-in-chief. **20-40% freelance written.** Monthly magazine covering the mattress manufacturing industry. "Our news and features are straightforward—we are not a lobbying vehicle for our association. No special slant." Estab. 1917. Circ. 3,700. **Pays on acceptance.** Publishes ms an average of 3 months after acceptance. Byline given. Buys first North American serial rights. Editorial lead time 2 months. Accepts queries by e-mail. Accepts simultaneous submissions. Responds in 1 month to queries. Sample copy for $4. Writer's guidelines by e-mail.

O→ Break in with short news stories. "We also use freelancers for monthly features including Newsmakers, company and individual profiles, and other features."

Nonfiction "No pieces that do not relate to business in general or mattress industry in particular." **Buys 15-25 mss/year.** Query with published clips. Length: 500-2,500 words. **Pays 50¢-$1/word for short features; $2,000 for cover story.**

Photos State availability with submission. Buys one-time rights. Negotiates payment individually. Identification of subjects required.

Tips "Cover topics have included annual industry forecast; physical expansion of industry facilities; e-commerce; flammability and home furnishings; the risks and rewards of marketing overseas; the evolving family business; the shifting workplace environment; and what do consumers really want?"

$ $ $ $ BLACK MBA MAGAZINE

Official Publication of NBMBAA, P&L Publishing Ltd., 9730 S. Western Ave., Suite 605, Evergreen Park IL 60805. (708)422-1506. Fax: (708)422-1507. E-mail: robert@blackmbamagazine.net. Web site: www.blackmba

magazine.net. Managing Editor: Robert Miller. **80% freelance written.** Quarterly magazine covering business career strategy, economic development, and financial management. Estab. 1997. Circ. 45,000. Pays after publication. Publishes ms an average of 1 month after acceptance. Byline given. Offers 10-20% or $500 kill fee. Buys all rights. Editorial lead time 2-3 months. Submit seasonal material 3-4 months in advance. Accepts queries by mail, e-mail, fax. Sample copy not available.

Photos State availability of or send photos with submission. Reviews ZIP disk. Buys one-time rights. Offers no additional payment for photos accepted with ms. Identification of subjects required.

Columns/Departments Management Strategies (leadership development), 1,200-1,700 words; Features (business management, entreprenuerial finance); Finance; Technology. Send complete ms. **Pays $500-1,000.**

N $ $ $ BUSINESS TRAVEL EXECUTIVE

Managed Travel & Procurement Solutions, 11 Ryerson Ave., Suite 200, Pompton Plains NJ 07405. E-mail: jferring@askbte.com. Web site: www.askbte.com. Managing Editor: Judith Ferring. **90% freelance written.** Monthly magazine covering corporate procurement of travel services. "We are not a travel magazine. We publish articles designed to help corporate purchasers of travel negotiate contracts, enforce policy, select automated services, track business travelers and account for their safety and expenditures, understand changes in the various industries associated with travel. Do not submit manuscripts without an assignment. Look at the Web site for an idea of what we publish." Pays on publication. Publishes ms an average of 2 months after acceptance. Byline given. Buys first North American serial rights. Editorial lead time 0-3 months. Accepts queries by e-mail.

Nonfiction How-to, technical. **Buys 48 mss/year.** Query. Length: 800-2,000 words. **Pays $200-800.**

Columns/Departments Meeting Place (meeting planning and management); Hotel Pulse (hotel negotiations, contracting and compliance); Security Watch (travel safety), all 1,000 words. **Buys 24 mss/year.** Query. **Pays $200-400.**

$ $ CBA MARKETPLACE

CBA Service Corp., P.O. Box 62000, Colorado Springs CO 80962. Fax: (719)272-3510. E-mail: info@cbaonline.org. Web site: www.cbaonline.org. **20% freelance written.** Monthly magazine covering the Christian retail industry. "Writers must have knowledge of and direct experience in the Christian retail industry. Subject matter must specifically pertain to the Christian retail audience." Estab. 1968. **Pays on acceptance.** Publishes ms an average of 3 months after acceptance. Byline given. Buys all rights. Editorial lead time 3 months. Submit seasonal material 6 months in advance. Accepts queries by mail, e-mail. Responds in 2 months to queries. Sample copy for $9.50 or online.

Nonfiction Christian retail. **Buys 24 mss/year.** Query. Length: 750-1,500 words. **Pays 20-30¢/word.**

Fillers Cartoons. **Buys 12/year. Pays $150.**

Tips "Only experts on Christian retail industry, completely familiar with retail audience and their needs and considerations, should submit a query. Do not submit articles unless requested."

⊘ CIO INSIGHT

Ziff-Davis Media, Inc., 28 E. 28th St., New York NY 10016. (212)503-3500. Fax: (212)503-5636. Web site: www.cioinsight.com. Editor-in-Chief: Ellen Pearlman. Managing Editor: Pat Perkowski. **Contact:** Editorial Assistant. Monthly magazine covering team management, wireless strategies, investment planning and profits, and Web-hosting security issues. "Written for senior-level executives with key interests in strategic information technology, including CIOs, chief technology officers and IS/IT/MIS vice presidents and managers." Accepts queries by e-mail. Accepts previously published material. Writer's guidelines online.

- No unsolicited mss.

Nonfiction "We welcome well-thought out story proposals from experienced journalists and experts in technology and business subjects. If you have a compelling and/or original story idea, you may send us your pitch via e-mail. We are particularly interested in case studies, trend and analysis articles, and ideas for whiteboards. Story pitches should be clear about the focus of the proposed article, why the topic is timely, and the key questions to be answered in the article."

$ $ CONTRACT MANAGEMENT

National Contract Management Association, 8260 Greensboro Dr., Suite 200, McLean VA 22102. (571)382-0082. Fax: (703)448-0939. E-mail: miedema@ncmahq.org. Web site: www.ncmahq.org. **Contact:** Amy Miedema, editor-in-chief. **10% freelance written.** Monthly magazine covering contract and business management. "Most of the articles published in *Contract Management (CM)* are written by members, although one does not have to be an NCMA member to be published in the magazine. Articles should concern some aspect of the contract management profession, whether at the level of a beginner or that of the advanced practitioner." Estab. 1960. Circ. 23,000. Pays on publication. Publishes ms an average of 3 months after acceptance. Byline given. Buys one-time rights. Editorial lead time 10 weeks. Submit seasonal material 3 months in advance. Accepts queries by mail, e-mail, fax, phone. Accepts previously published material. Accepts simultaneous submissions. Responds in 2 weeks to queries; 1 month to mss. Sample copy and writer's guidelines free.

Nonfiction Essays, general interest, how-to, humor, inspirational, new product, opinion, technical. No company or CEO profiles—please read a copy of publication before submitting. **Buys 6-10 mss/year.** Query with published clips. Length: 2,500-3,000 words. **Pays $300, association members paid in 3 copies.**

Reprints Accepts previously published submissions.

Photos State availability with submission. Buys one-time rights. Offers no additional payment for photos accepted with ms. Captions, identification of subjects required.

Columns/Departments Professional Development (self-improvement in business), 1,000-1,500 words; Back to Basics (basic how-tos and discussions), 1,500-2,000 words. **Buys 2 mss/year.** Query with published clips. **Pays $300.**

Tips "Query and read at least 1 issue. Visit Web site to better understand our audience."

$ $ CONTRACTING PROFITS

Trade Press Publishing, 2100 W. Florist Ave., Milwaukee WI 53209. (414)228-7701. Fax: (414)228-1134. Web site: www.cleanlink.com/cp. **Contact:** Stacie Rosenzweig, editor. **40% freelance written.** Magazine published 10 times/year covering "building service contracting, business management advice." "We are the pocket MBA for this industry—focusing not only on cleaning-specific topics, but also discussing how to run businesses better and increase profits through a variety of management articles." Estab. 1995. Circ. 32,000. Pays within 30 days of acceptance. Byline given. Buys all rights. Editorial lead time 2 months. Submit seasonal material 3 months in advance. Accepts queries by mail, e-mail. Sample copy online. Writer's guidelines free.

Nonfiction Exposé, how-to, interview/profile, technical. "No product-related reviews or testimonials." **Buys 30 mss/year.** Query with published clips. Length: 1,000-1,500 words. **Pays $100-500.** Sometimes pays expenses of writers on assignment.

Columns/Departments Query with published clips.

Tips "Read back issues on our Web site and be able to understand some of those topics prior to calling."

$ $ EXECUTIVE UPDATE

Greater Washington Society of Association Executives, Reagan Building & International Trade Center, 1300 Pennsylvania Ave. NW, Washington DC 20004. (202)326-9545. Fax: (202)326-0999. Web site: www.executiveupdate.com. **Contact:** Scott Briscoe, editor. **60% freelance written.** Monthly magazine "exploring a broad range of association management issues and for introducing and discussing management and leadership philosophies. It is written for individuals at all levels of association management, with emphasis on senior staff and CEOs." Estab. 1979. Circ. 14,000. **Pays on acceptance.** Publishes ms an average of 6 months after acceptance. Byline given. Offers 20% kill fee. Buys first rights. Editorial lead time 3 months. Submit seasonal material 6 months in advance. Accepts queries by mail, e-mail, fax, phone. Accepts simultaneous submissions. Responds in 1 month to queries; 2 months to mss. Sample copy for free. Writer's guidelines online.

Nonfiction How-to, humor, interview/profile, opinion, personal experience, travel, management and workplace issues. **Buys 24-36 mss/year.** Query with published clips. Length: 2,000-2,500 words. **Pays $500-700.** Pays expenses of writers on assignment.

Columns/Departments Intelligence (new ways to tackle day-to-day issues), 500-700 words; Off the Cuff (guest column for association executives). Query. **Pays $100-200.**

$ $ $ EXPO

Atwood Publishing, LLC, 11600 College Blvd., Overland Park KS 66210. (913)344-1303. Fax: (913)344-1486. E-mail: dtormohlen@ascendmedia.com. Web site: www.expoweb.com. **Contact:** Danica Tormohlen, editor-in-chief. **80% freelance written.** Magazine covering expositions. "*EXPO* is the information and education resource for the exposition industry. It is the only magazine dedicated exclusively to the people with direct responsibility for planning, promoting and operating trade and consumer shows. Our readers are show managers and their staff, association executives, independent show producers and industry suppliers. Every issue of *EXPO* contains in-depth, how-to features and departments that focus on the practical aspects of exposition management, including administration, promotion and operations." Pays on publication. Byline given. Offers 50% kill fee. Buys first North American serial rights. Editorial lead time 3 months. Accepts queries by mail, e-mail, fax. Responds in 3 weeks to queries. Sample copy for free. Writer's guidelines online.

Nonfiction How-to, interview/profile. Query with published clips. Length: 600-2,400 words. **Pays 50¢/word.** Pays expenses of writers on assignment.

Photos State availability with submission.

Columns/Departments Profile (personality profile), 650 words; Exhibitor Matters (exhibitor issues) and EXPO-Tech (technology), both 600-1,300 words. **Buys 10 mss/year.** Query with published clips.

Tips "*EXPO* now offers shorter features and departments, while continuing to offer in-depth reporting. Editorial is more concise, using synopsis, bullets and tidbits whenever possible. Every article needs sidebars, call-outs, graphs, charts, etc., to create entry points for readers. Headlines and leads are more provocative. And writers should elevate the level of shop talk, demonstrating that *EXPO* is the leader in the industry. We plan our editorial calendar about one year in advance, but we are always open to new ideas. Please query before submitting a story to *EXPO*—tell us about your idea and what our readers would learn. Include your qualifications to write about the subject and the sources you plan to contact."

$ $ $ FAMILY BUSINESS

The Guide for Family Companies, Family Business Publishing Co., 1845 Walnut St., Philadelphia PA 19103. Fax: (215)405-6078. E-mail: bspector@familybusinessmagazine.com. Web site: www.familybusinessmagazine.com. **Contact:** Barbara Spector, editor-in-chief. **50% freelance written.** Quarterly magazine covering family-owned companies. "Written expressly for family company owners and advisors. Focuses on business and human dynamic issues unique to family enterprises. Offers practical guidance and tried-and-true solutions for business stakeholders." Estab. 1989. Circ. 6,000. **Pays on acceptance.** Publishes ms an average of 9-12 months after acceptance. Byline given. Offers 30% kill fee. Buys first, electronic rights. Editorial lead time 4 months. Submit seasonal material 6 months in advance. Accepts queries by e-mail. Writer's guidelines online.

Nonfiction Book excerpts, how-to (family business related only), interview/profile, personal experience. No "articles that aren't specifically related to multi-generational family companies (no general business advice). No success stories—there must be an underlying family or business lesson." **No payment for articles written by family business advisors and other service providers. Buys 24 mss/year.** Query with published clips. Length: 1,500-2,000 words. **Pays $50-1,000 for articles written by freelance reporters.**

Photos State availability with submission. Buys one-time rights. Offers $50-500 maximum/shoot. Captions, identification of subjects, model releases required.

$ $ INTENTS

The Magazine for the Tent-Rental and Special-Event Industries, Industrial Fabrics Association International, 1801 County Rd. B W., Roseville MN 55113-4061. (651)225-6970. Fax: (651)225-6966. E-mail: intents@ifai.com. Web site: www.ifai.com. **Contact:** Katie Harholdt, editor. **50% freelance written.** Bimonthly magazine covering tent-rental and special-event industries. Estab. 1994. Circ. 12,000. **Pays on acceptance.** Publishes ms an average of 2 months after acceptance. Byline given. Buys all rights. Editorial lead time 3 months. Accepts queries by mail, e-mail, fax. Sample copy and writer's guidelines free.

- Break in with familiarity of tent rental, special events, tent manufacturing, and fabric structure industries, or lively, intelligent writing on technical subjects.

Nonfiction How-to, interview/profile, new product, photo feature, technical. **Buys 12-18 mss/year.** Query. Length: 800-2,000 words. **Pays $300-500.** Sometimes pays expenses of writers on assignment.

Photos State availability with submission. Reviews contact sheets, negatives, prints, digital images. Negotiates payment individually. Captions, identification of subjects, model releases required.

Tips "We look for lively, intelligent writing that makes technical subjects come alive."

$ $ MAINEBIZ

Maine's Business News Source, Mainebiz Publications, Inc., 30 Milk St., 3rd Floor, Portland ME 04101. (207)761-8379. Fax: (207)761-0732. E-mail: sdonahue@mainebiz.biz. Web site: www.mainebiz.biz. **Contact:** Sean Donahue, editor. **25% freelance written.** Biweekly tabloid covering business in Maine. "*Mainebiz* is read by business decision makers across the state. They look to the publication for business news and analysis." Estab. 1994. Circ. 13,000. Pays on publication. Publishes ms an average of 1 month after acceptance. Byline given. Offers 10% kill fee. Buys all rights. Editorial lead time 1 month. Submit seasonal material 2 months in advance. Accepts queries by mail, e-mail. Responds in 3 weeks to queries. Sample copy and writer's guidelines online.

Nonfiction "All pieces are reported and must comply with accepted journalistic standards. We only publish stories about business in Maine." Essays, exposé, interview/profile, business trends. Special issues: See Web site for editorial calendar. **Buys 50+ mss/year.** Query with published clips. Length: 500-2,500 words. **Pays $50-250.** Pays expenses of writers on assignment.

Photos State availability with submission. Reviews GIF/JPEG files. Buys one-time rights. Negotiates payment individually. Identification of subjects required.

Tips "Stories should be well thought out with specific relevance to Maine. Arts and culture-related queries are welcome, as long as there is a business angle. We appreciate unusual angles on business stories and regularly work with new freelancers. Please, no queries unless you have read the paper."

N $ $ NATIVE AMERICAN CASINO

Dellas Publications LLC, 1446 Front St., Suite 200, San Diego CA 92101. (619)223-0782. Fax: (619)223-0761. E-mail: mdellas@nacasino.com. Web site: www.nacasino.com. **Contact:** Melanie Dellas, publisher/editor-in-chief. **30% freelance written.** Monthly magazine covering the Indian casino industry. "*Native American Casino* (NAC) is a monthly, business-to-business magazine dedicated to the growth and prosperity of the Native American businessperson. Our articles aid casino managers in running their various departments, articles also focus on new or expanding Indian casinos, interviews, and topics that people can use to improve any business they wish to pursue. Our readers are the casino managers and tribal leaders/members." Estab. 2000. Circ. 30,000. Pays on publication. Publishes ms an average of 2 months after acceptance. Byline given. Buys all rights. Editorial lead time 2 months. Submit seasonal material 2 months in advance. Accepts queries by e-mail. Accepts simultaneous submissions. Sample copy for free. Writer's guidelines by e-mail.

Nonfiction Historical/nostalgic, how-to, inspirational, interview/profile, technical, travel. Does not want advertorials, articles degrading or giving any kind of negative impression on Native Americans or the gaming industry, or articles with sexual content or profanity. **Buys 24-36 mss/year.** Query with published clips. Length: 900-2,000 words. **Pays $200-300.**

Photos Contact Kristina Ushakov, creative director. State availability with submission. Reviews 5×7 prints, GIF/JPEG files (300 dpi). Buys one-time rights. Offers no additional payment for photos accepted with ms. Captions, identification of subjects, model releases required.

Tips "I encourage all freelancers interested to visit our Web site to get familiar with *NAC*. I would also like them to visit www.indiangaming.com to read about the National Indian Gaming Association and become familiar with our industry."

$ $ PROGRESSIVE RENTALS

The Voice of the Rental-Purchase Industry, Association of Progressive Rental Organizations, 1504 Robin Hood Trail, Austin TX 78703. (800)204-2776. Fax: (512)794-0097. Web site: www.aprovision.org. **50% freelance written.** Bimonthly magazine covering the rent-to-own industry. "*Progressive Rentals* is the only publication representing the rent-to-own industry and members of APRO. The magazine covers timely news and features affecting the industry, association activities, and member profiles. Awarded best 4-color magazine by the American Society of Association Executives in 1999." Estab. 1980. Circ. 5,500. **Pays on acceptance.** Publishes ms an average of 2 months after acceptance. Byline given. Offers 25% kill fee. Buys first North American serial rights. Editorial lead time 2 months. Submit seasonal material 4 months in advance. Accepts queries by mail, e-mail, fax, phone. Accepts simultaneous submissions. Responds in 1 month to queries; 2 months to mss. Sample copy for free.

Nonfiction Exposé, general interest, how-to, inspirational, interview/profile, technical, industry features. **Buys 12 mss/year.** Query with published clips. Length: 1,200-2,500 words. **Pays $150-700.** Sometimes pays expenses of writers on assignment.

RENTAL MANAGEMENT

American Rental Association, 1900 19th St., Moline IL 61265. (309)764-2475. Fax: (309)764-1533. Web site: www.rentalmanagementmag.com. **Contact:** Wayne Walley, editor. **50% freelance written.** Monthly magazine for the equipment rental industry worldwide (*not* property, real estate, appliances, furniture, or cars), emphasizing management topics in particular but also marketing, merchandising, technology, etc. Estab. 1970. Circ. 18,500. **Pays on acceptance.** Publishes ms an average of 3 months after acceptance. Byline given. Buys first North American serial rights. Editorial lead time 2 months. Submit seasonal material 3 months in advance. Accepts queries by mail, e-mail, fax.

Nonfiction Business management and marketing. **Buys 25-30 mss/year.** Query with published clips. Does not respond to unsolicited work unless being considered for publication. Length: 600-1,500 words. **Payment negotiable.** Sometimes pays expenses of writers on assignment.

Reprints Send tearsheet or typed ms with rights for sale noted and information about when and where the material previously appeared.

Photos Reviews contact sheets, negatives (35mm or 2¼), transparencies, prints (any size), digital (300 dpi EPS/TIFF/JPEG on e-mail or CD). State availability with submission. Buys one-time rights. Negotiates payment individually. Identification of subjects required.

Tips "Show me you can write maturely, cogently, and fluently on management matters of direct and compelling interest to the small-business owner or manager in a larger operation; no sloppiness, no unexamined thoughts, no stiffness or affectation—genuine, direct, and worthwhile English. Knowledge of the equipment rental industry is a distinct plus."

$ $ RETAIL INFO SYSTEMS NEWS

Where Retail Management Shops for Technology, Edgell Communications, 4 Middlebury Blvd., Randolph NJ 07869. (973)252-0100. Fax: (973)252-9020. Web site: www.risnews.com. Managing Editor: Debbie Hauss. **Contact:** Joe Skorupa, editor. **65% freelance written.** Monthly magazine. "Readers are functional managers/executives in all types of retail and consumer goods firms. They are making major improvements in company operations and in alliances with customers/suppliers.'' Estab. 1988. Circ. 20,000. Pays on publication. Publishes ms an average of 2 months after acceptance. Byline sometimes given. Buys first North American serial, second serial (reprint), electronic, all rights. Editorial lead time 3 months. Submit seasonal material 3 months in advance. Accepts queries by mail. Sample copy online.

Nonfiction Essays, exposé, how-to, humor, interview/profile, technical. **Buys 80 mss/year.** Query with published clips. Length: 700-1,900 words. **Pays $600-1,200 for assigned articles.** Sometimes pays in contributor copies as negotiated. Sometimes pays expenses of writers on assignment.

Photos State availability of or send photos with submission. Buys one-time rights plus reprint, if applicable. Negotiates payment individually. Identification of subjects required.

Columns/Departments News/trends (analysis of current events), 150-300 words. **Buys 4 mss/year.** Query with published clips. **Pays $100-300.**

Tips ''Case histories about companies achieving substantial results using advanced management practices and/or advanced technology are best.''

N $ $ SECURITY DEALER

Cygnus Publishing, 445 Broad Hollow Rd., Melville NY 11747. (631)845-2700. Fax: (631)845-2736. E-mail: susan.brady@secdealer.com. Managing Editor: Erin Harrington. **Contact:** Susan A. Brady, editor-in-chief. **25% freelance written.** Monthly magazine for electronic alarm dealers, burglary and fire installers, with technical, business, sales and marketing information. Circ. 25,000. Pays 3 weeks after publication. Publishes ms an average of 4 months after acceptance. Byline sometimes given. Buys first North American serial rights. Accepts simultaneous submissions.

Nonfiction How-to, interview/profile, technical. No consumer pieces. Query by mail only. Length: 1,000-3,000 words. **Pays $300 for assigned articles; $100-200 for unsolicited articles.** Sometimes pays expenses of writers on assignment.

Photos State availability with submission. Reviews contact sheets, transparencies. Offers $25 additional payment for photos accepted with ms. Captions, identification of subjects required.

Columns/Departments Closed Circuit TV, Access Control (both on application, installation, new products), 500-1,000 words. **Buys 25 mss/year.** Query by mail only. **Pays $100-150.**

Tips ''The areas of our publication most open to freelancers are technical innovations, trends in the alarm industry, and crime patterns as related to the business as well as business finance and management pieces.''

$ $ ⊘ SMART BUSINESS

Pittsburgh Edition, SBN, Inc., 11632 Frankstown Rd., #313, Pittsburgh PA 15235. (412)371-0451. Fax: (412)371-0452. E-mail: rmarano@sbnonline.com. Web site: www.sbnonline.com. **Contact:** Ray Marano, editor. Monthly magazine. ''We provide information and insight designed to help companies grow. Our focus is on CEOs of local companies with 100 or more employees and their successful business strategies, with the ultimate goal of educating their peers. Our target audience is business owners and other top executives.'' Estab. 1994. Circ. 12,000. Editorial lead time 2 months.

Nonfiction How-to, interview/profile, opinion. ''No basic profiles about 'interesting' companies or stories about companies with no ties to Pittsburgh.''

Photos Reviews high resolution digital images.

Tips ''We have articles localized to the Pittsburgh and surrounding areas. The short description of what we do is tell readers how CEOs do their jobs. Our feature stories focus exclusively on CEOs. Our readers are their peers, and want information and guidance that can help them to better manage their organizations.''

$ $ SMART BUSINESS

Smart Business Network, Inc., 835 Sharon Dr., Cleveland OH 44145. (440)250-7000. Fax: (440)250-7001. E-mail: dsklein@sbnonline.com. Web site: www.sbnonline.com. **Contact:** Dustin S. Klein, executive editor. **5% freelance written.** Monthly business magazine with an audience made up of business owners and top decision makers. ''*Smart Business* is one of the fastest growing national chains of regional management journals for corporate executives. Every issue delves into the minds of the most innovative executives in each of our regions to report on how market leaders got to the top and what strategies they use to stay there.'' Estab. 1989. Pays on publication. Publishes ms an average of 2 months after acceptance. Byline given. Offers 50% kill fee. Buys first North American serial, second serial (reprint), electronic rights. Editorial lead time 3 months. Submit seasonal material 3 months in advance. Accepts queries by mail, e-mail. Responds in 2 weeks to queries; 1 month to mss. Sample copy online. Writer's guidelines by e-mail.

- Publishes local editions in Philadephia, Cincinnati, Detroit, Los Angeles, Broward/Palm Beach, Cleveland, Akron/Canton, Columbus, Pittsburgh, Atlanta, Chicago, and Indianapolis.

Nonfiction How-to, interview/profile. No breaking news or news features. **Buys 10-12 mss/year.** Query with published clips. Length: 1,150-2,000 words. **Pays $200-500.** Sometimes pays expenses of writers on assignment.

Reprints Accepts previously published submissions.

Photos State availability with submission. Reviews negatives, prints. Buys one-time, reprint, or Web rights. Offers no additional payment for photos accepted with ms. Identification of subjects required.

The online magazine carries original content not found in the print edition. Contact: Dustin S. Klein, executive editor.

Tips "The best way to submit to *Smart Business* is to read us—either online or in print. Remember, our audience is made up of top level business executives and owners."

$ $ STAMATS MEETINGS MEDIA

550 Montgomery St., Suite 750, San Francisco CA 94111. Fax: (415)788-1358. E-mail: tyler.davidson@meetingsmedia.com. Web site: www.meetingsmedia.com. Destinations Editor: Lori Tenny. **Contact:** Tyler Davidson, editorial director (columnists, cover stories). **75% freelance written.** Monthly tabloid covering meeting, event, and conference planning. Estab. 1986. Circ. *Meetings East* and *Meetings South* 22,000; *Meetings West* 26,000. Pays 1 month after publication. Publishes ms an average of 1 month after acceptance. Byline given. Buys first North American serial, electronic rights. Editorial lead time 3 months. Submit seasonal material 3 months in advance. Accepts queries by mail, e-mail, fax. Responds in 3 weeks to queries. Sample copy for 9×13 SAE and 5 first-class stamps. Editorial calendar online.

Queries and pitches are accepted on columns and cover stories only. All other assignments (Features and Site Inspections) are based exclusively on editorial calendar. Interested writers should send a résumé and 2-3 relevant clips, which must show familiarity with meetings/conventions topics, by e-mail.

Nonfiction How-to, travel (as it pertains to meetings and conventions). "No first-person fluff. We are a business magazine." **Buys 150 mss/year.** Query with published clips. Length: 1,200-2,000 words. **Pays $500 flat rate/package.**

Photos State availability with submission. Buys one-time rights. Offers no additional payment for photos accepted with ms. Identification of subjects required.

Tips "We're always looking for freelance writers who are local to our destination stories. For Site Inspections, get in touch in late September or early October, when we usually have the following year's editorial calendar available."

N $ SUPERVISION MAGAZINE

National Research Bureau, 320 Valley St., Burlington IA 52601. (319)752-5415. E-mail: national@willinet.net. Web site: www.national-research-bureau.com. **Contact:** Todd Darnall, editor. **80% freelance written.** Monthly magazine covering management and supervision. "*SuperVision Magazine* explains complex issues in a clear and understandable format. Articles written by both experts and scholars provide practical and concise answers to issues facing today's supervisors and managers." Estab. 1939. Circ. 500. **Pays on acceptance.** Publishes ms an average of 1 month after acceptance. Byline given. Buys all rights. Editorial lead time 1 month. Submit seasonal material 2 months in advance. Accepts queries by e-mail. Sample copy for free. Writer's guidelines free.

Nonfiction Personal experience. Send complete ms. Length: 1,500-1,800 words. **Pays 4¢/word.**

$ $ SUSTAINABLE INDUSTRIES JOURNAL NW

Sustainable Industries Media, LLC, 3941 SE Hawthorne Blvd., Portland OR 97214. (503)226-7798. Fax: (503)226-7917. E-mail: brian@celilo.net. Web site: www.sijournal.com. Associate Editors: Michael Burnham and Celeste LeCompte. **Contact:** Brian J. Back, editor. **20% freelance written.** Monthly magazine covering environmental innovation in business (Northwest focus). "We seek high quality, balanced reporting aimed at business readers. More compelling writing than is typical in standard trade journals." Estab. 2003. Circ. 2,500. Pays on publication. Publishes ms an average of 1-3 months after acceptance. Byline sometimes given. Not copyrighted. Buys all rights. Editorial lead time 1-2 months. Accepts queries by mail, e-mail, fax. Accepts simultaneous submissions.

Nonfiction General interest, how-to, interview/profile, new product, opinion, news briefs. Special issues: Themes rotate on the following topics: Agriculture & Natural Resources; Green Building; Energy; Government; Manufacturing & Technology; Retail & Service; Transportation & Tourism—though all topics are covered in each issue. No prosaic essays or extra-long pieces. Query with published clips. Length: 500-1,500 words. **Pays $0-500.**

Photos State availability with submission. Reviews prints, GIF/JPEG files. Buys all rights. Offers no additional payment for photos accepted with ms.

Columns/Departments Business trade columns on specific industries, 500-1,000 words. Query.

$ $ $ WORLD TRADE

452 25th St., Hermosa Beach CA 90254. (310)980-5537. E-mail: laras@worldtrademag.com. Web site: www.worldtrademag.com. Editorial Director: Neil Shister. **Contact:** Lara Sowinski, managing editor. **50% freelance**

written. Monthly magazine covering international business. Estab. 1988. Circ. 75,000. Pays on publication. Publishes ms an average of 1 month after acceptance. Byline given. Buys all rights. Editorial lead time 3 months. Accepts queries by mail, fax.

Nonfiction "See our editorial calendar online." Interview/profile, technical, market reports, finance, logistics. **Buys 40-50 mss/year.** Query with published clips. Length: 450-1,500 words. **Pays 50¢/word.**

Photos State availability with submission. Reviews transparencies, prints. Buys all rights. Negotiates payment individually. Identification of subjects required.

Columns/Departments International Business Services, 800 words; Shipping, Supply Chain Management, Logistics, 800 words; Software & Technology, 800 words; Economic Development (US, International), 800 words. **Buys 40-50 mss/year. Pays 50¢/word.**

Tips "We seek writers with expertise in their subject areas, as well as solid researching and writing skills. We want analysts more than reporters. We don't accept unsolicited manuscripts, and we don't want phone calls. Please read *World Trade* before sending a query."

CHURCH ADMINISTRATION & MINISTRY

THE AFRICAN AMERICAN PULPIT

P.O. Box 381587, Germantown TN 38183. Web site: www.theafricanamericanpulpit.com. **100% freelance written.** Quarterly magazine covering African American preaching. "*The African American Pulpit* is a quarterly journal that serves as a repository for the very best of African American preaching and provides practical and creative resources for persons in ministry." Estab. 1997. Circ. 3,000. Pays on publication. Publishes ms an average of 6 months after acceptance. Byline always given. Editorial lead time 9 months. Submit seasonal material 1 year in advance. Accepts queries by mail, e-mail, fax, phone. Accepts simultaneous submissions. Writer's guidelines online.

Nonfiction Sermons and articles relating to African American preaching and the African American Church. Book excerpts, essays, how-to (craft a sermon), inspirational, interview/profile, opinion, religious. **Buys 60 mss/year.** Send complete ms. Length: 1,500-3,000 words.

$ CHRISTIAN COMMUNICATOR

9118 W. Elmwood Dr., #1G, Niles IL 60714-5820. (847)296-3964. Fax: (847)296-0754. E-mail: ljohnson@wordprocommunications.com. **Contact:** Lin Johnson, managing editor. **90% freelance written.** Monthly magazine covering Christian writing and speaking. Circ. 4,000. Pays on publication. Publishes ms an average of 6-12 months after acceptance. Byline given. Buys first, second serial (reprint) rights. Editorial lead time 3 months. Submit seasonal material 9 months in advance. Accepts queries by e-mail. Responds in 4-6 weeks to queries; 6-8 weeks to mss. Sample copy for SAE and 5 first-class stamps. Writer's guidelines for SASE or by e-mail.

Nonfiction How-to, interview/profile, opinion, book reviews. **Buys 90 mss/year.** Query or send complete ms only by e-mail. Length: 500-1,000 words. **Pays $10.**

Columns/Departments Speaking, 650-1,000 words. **Buys 11 mss/year.** Query. **Pays $10.**

Poetry Free verse, light verse, traditional. **Buys 11 poems/year.** Submit maximum 3 poems. Contact: Gretchen Sousa, poetry editor (gretloriat@earthlink.net) Length: 4-20 lines. **Pays $5.**

Fillers Anecdotes, short humor. **Buys 10-30/year.** Length: 75-300 words. **Pays cassette tape.**

Tips "We primarily use 'how to' articles and personality features on experienced writers and editors. However, we're willing to look at any other pieces geared to the writing life."

$ $ GROUP MAGAZINE

Group Publishing, Inc., P.O. Box 481, Loveland CO 80539. E-mail: kdieterich@grouppublishing.com. Web site: www.groupmag.com. **Contact:** Kathy Dieterich, assistant editor. **50% freelance written.** Bimonthly magazine for Christian youth workers. "*Group* is the interdenominational magazine for leaders of Christian youth groups. *Group*'s purpose is to supply ideas, practical help, inspiration, and training for youth leaders." Estab. 1974. Circ. 55,000. **Pays on acceptance.** Byline sometimes given. Buys all rights. Editorial lead time 4 months. Submit seasonal material 5 months in advance. Accepts queries by mail, e-mail, fax. Responds in 6 weeks to queries; 2 months to mss. Sample copy for $2, plus 10×12 SAE and 3 first-class stamps. Writer's guidelines online.

Nonfiction Inspirational, personal experience, religious. No fiction. **Buys 100 mss/year.** Query. Length: 175-2,000 words. **Pays $150-250.** Sometimes pays expenses of writers on assignment.

Columns/Departments Try This One (short ideas for group use), 300 words; Hands-On-Help (tips for youth leaders), 175 words; Strange But True (profiles remarkable youth ministry experience), 500 words. **Pays $40.**

$ $ THE JOURNAL OF ADVENTIST EDUCATION

General Conference of SDA, 12501 Old Columbia Pike, Silver Spring MD 20904-6600. (301)680-5069. Fax: (301)622-9627. E-mail: rumbleb@gc.adventist.org. Web site: education.gc.adventist.org/jae. **Contact:** Beverly

J. Robinson-Rumble, editor. Bimonthly (except skips issue in summer) professional journal covering teachers and administrators in Seventh Day Adventist school systems. Estab. 1939. Circ. 7,500. Pays on publication. Publishes ms an average of 1 year after acceptance. Byline given. Buys first rights. Editorial lead time 1 year. Accepts queries by mail, e-mail, fax, phone. Responds in 6 weeks to queries; 4 months to mss. Sample copy for 10×12 SAE and 5 first-class stamps. Writer's guidelines online.

Nonfiction Theme issues have assigned authors. Book excerpts, essays, how-to (education-related), personal experience, photo feature, religious, education. "No brief first-person stories about Sunday Schools." Query. Length: 1,000-1,500 words. **Pays $25-300.**

Reprints Send tearsheet or photocopy and information about when and where the material previously appeared.

Photos Submit glossy prints, high resolution (300 dpi) scans or digital photos in TIFF/JPEG format. No PowerPoint presentations or photos imbedded in Word documents. Include photo of author with submission. State availability of or send photos with submission. Buys one-time rights. Negotiates payment individually. Captions required.

Tips "Articles may deal with educational theory or practice, although the *Journal* seeks to emphasize the practical. Articles dealing with the creative and effective use of methods to enhance teaching skills or learning in the classroom are especially welcome. Whether theoretical or practical, such essays should demonstrate the skillful integration of Seventh-day Adventist faith/values and learning."

$ $ LEADERSHIP

Real Ministry in a Complex World, Christianity Today International, 465 Gundersen Dr., Carol Stream IL 60188. (630)260-6200. Fax: (630)260-0114. E-mail: ljeditor@leadershipjournal.net. Web site: www.leadershipjournal.net. Editor: Marshall Shelley. Managing Editor: Eric Reed. **Contact:** Elizabeth Diffin, editorial coordinator. **75% freelance written.** Works with a small number of new/unpublished writers each year. Quarterly magazine. Writers must have a "knowledge of and sympathy for the unique expectations placed on pastors and local church leaders. Each article must support points by illustrating from real life experiences in local churches." Estab. 1980. Circ. 57,000. **Pays on acceptance.** Publishes ms an average of 6 months after acceptance. Byline given. Offers 33% kill fee. Buys first, electronic rights. Editorial lead time 6 months. Submit seasonal material 6 months in advance. Accepts queries by mail, e-mail, fax. Responds in 3 weeks to queries; 2 months to mss. Sample copy for $5 or online. Writer's guidelines online.

Nonfiction How-to, humor, interview/profile, personal experience, sermon illustrations. "No articles from writers who have never read our journal." **Buys 60 mss/year.** Query. Length: 300-3,000 words. **Pays $35-400.** Sometimes pays expenses of writers on assignment.

Columns/Departments Eric Reed, managing editor. Toolkit (book/software reviews), 500 words. **Buys 8 mss/year.** Query.

Tips "Every article in *Leadership* must provide practical help for problems that church leaders face. *Leadership* articles are not essays expounding a topic or editorials arguing a position or homilies explaining Biblical principles. They are how-to articles, based on first-person accounts of real-life experiences in ministry. They allow our readers to see 'over the shoulder' of a colleague in ministry who then reflects on those experiences and identifies the lessons learned. As you know, a magazine's slant is a specific personality that readers expect (and it's what they've sent us their subscription money to provide). Our style is that of friendly conversation rather than directive discourse—what I learned about local church ministry rather than what you need to do."

$ $ OUTREACH MAGAZINE

Outreach Inc., 2230 Oak Ridge Way, Vista CA 92081-8341. (760)940-0600. Fax: (760)597-2314. E-mail: lwarren@outreach.com. Web site: www.outreachmagazine.com. **Contact:** Lindy Lowry, editor & director of publishing. **80% freelance written.** Bimonthly magazine designed to inspire, challenge and equip churches and church leaders to reach out to their communities with the love of Jesus Christ. Circ. 30,000. Pays on publication. Publishes ms an average of 2 months after acceptance. Byline given. Offers 10% kill fee. Buys first North American serial, electronic rights. Editorial lead time 6 months. Submit seasonal material 6 months in advance. Accepts queries by mail, e-mail, fax. Accepts previously published material. Accepts simultaneous submissions. Responds in 2 months to queries; 8 months to mss. Sample copy and writer's guidelines free.

Nonfiction Book excerpts, how-to, humor, inspirational, interview/profile, personal experience, photo feature, religious. Special issues: Vacation Bible School (January); America's Fastest Growing Churches (July/August 2005). Does not want fiction, poetry, or non-outreach-related articles. **Buys 30 mss/year.** Query with published clips. Length: 1,200-2,000 words. **Pays $375-600 for assigned articles; $375-400 for unsolicited articles.** Pays some expenses of writers on assignment.

Photos Christi Riddell, lead designer. Send photos with submission. Reviews GIF/JPEG files. Buys all rights. Negotiates payment individually. Identification of subjects required.

Columns/Departments Outreach Pulse (short stories about outreach-oriented churches and ministries), 75-250 words; Questions & Perspectives (first-person expert perspective on a question related to outreach), 300-400 words; Soulfires (interview piece with a person about the stories and people that have fueled their passion for outreach), 900 words; From the Front Line (profile of a church that is using a transferable idea for outreach), 800 words plus sidebars; Sounourners (short interviews with everyday people about the stories and people that have informed their worldview and faith perspective), 800 words; Frames (short personality profiles); POV (2-page interview with a significant voice in the church). **Buys at least 6 mss/year.** Query with published clips. **Pays $100-375.**

Fillers Facts, gags to be illustrated by cartoonist. **Buys 2/year.** Length: 25-100 words. **Pays payment is negotiated.**

Tips "Study our writer's guidelines. Send published clips that showcase tight, bright writing, as well as your ability to interview, research, organize numerous sources into an article, and write a 100-word piece as well as a 1,600-word piece."

$ $ THE PRIEST

Our Sunday Visitor, Inc., 200 Noll Plaza, Huntington IN 46750-4304. (260)356-8400. Fax: (260)359-9117. E-mail: tpriest@osv.com. Web site: www.osv.com. **40% freelance written.** Monthly magazine. "We run articles that will aid priests in their day-to-day ministry. Includes items on spirituality, counseling, administration, theology, personalities, the saints, etc." **Pays on acceptance.** Byline given. Buys first North American serial rights. Editorial lead time 3 months. Submit seasonal material 4 months in advance. Accepts queries by mail, e-mail, fax, phone. Responds in 5 weeks to queries; 3 months to mss. Sample copy and writer's guidelines free.

Nonfiction Essays, historical/nostalgic, humor, inspirational, interview/profile, opinion, personal experience, photo feature, religious. **Buys 96 mss/year.** Send complete ms. Length: 1,500 words. **Pays $200 minimum for assigned articles; $50 minimum for unsolicited articles.**

Photos Send photos with submission. Reviews transparencies, prints. Buys one-time rights. Negotiates payment individually. Captions, identification of subjects required.

Tips "Please do not stray from the magisterium of the Catholic Church."

$ $ REV! MAGAZINE

P.O. Box 481, Loveland CO 80539-0481. (970)669-3836. Fax: (970)292-4392. E-mail: lsparks@group.com. Web site: www.revmagazine.com. Editor: Lee Sparks. **25% freelance written.** Bimonthly magazine for pastors. "We offer practical solutions to revolutionize and revitalize ministry." Estab. 1997. Circ. 45,000. **Pays on acceptance.** Publishes ms an average of 6 months after acceptance. Byline given. Makes work-for-hire assignments. Editorial lead time 6 months. Submit seasonal material 8 months in advance. Accepts queries by mail, e-mail. Responds in 2 months to queries. Writer's guidelines online.

O-π Break in with short, practical department pieces.

Nonfiction Ministry, leadership, and personal articles with practical application. "No devotions, articles for church members, theological pieces." **Buys 18-24 mss/year.** Query or send complete ms. Length: 1,800-2,000 words. **Pays $300-400.**

Columns/Departments Work (preaching, worship, discipleship, outreach, church business & administration, leadership); Life (personal growth, pastor's family); Culture (trends, facts), all 250-3,000 words. **Buys 25 mss/year.** Send complete ms. **Pays $100-500.**

Fillers Cartoons. **Buys 3/year. Pays $50.**

Tips "We are looking for creative and practical ideas that pastors and other leaders of churches of all sizes can use."

$ RTJ

The Magazine for Catechist Formation, Twenty-Third Publications, P.O. Box 180, Mystic CT 06355. (800)321-0411. Fax: (860)437-6246. E-mail: aberger@twenty-thirdpublications.com. Web site: www.religionteachersjournal.com. **Contact:** Alison Berger, editor. Monthly magazine for Catholic catechists and religion teachers. "The mission of *RTJ* is to encourage and assist Catholic DREs and catechists in their vocation to proclaim the gospel message and lead others to the joy of following Jesus Christ. *RTJ* provides professional support, theological content, age appropriate methodology and teaching tools." Estab. 1966. Circ. 30,000. **Pays on acceptance.** Publishes ms an average of 3-20 months after acceptance. Byline given. Buys first, one-time rights. Editorial lead time 4 months. Submit seasonal material 6 months in advance. Accepts queries by mail, e-mail. Accepts simultaneous submissions. Responds in 1-2 weeks to queries; 1-2 months to mss. Sample copy for 9×12 SAE and 3 first-class stamps. Writer's guidelines free.

Nonfiction How-to, inspirational, personal experience, religious, articles on celebrating church seasons, sacraments, on morality, on prayer, on saints. Special issues: Sacraments; Prayer; Advent/Christmas; Lent/Easter. "All should be written by people who have experience in religious education, or a good background in Catholic faith." Does not want fiction, poems, plays, articles written for Catholic school teachers (i.e., math, English, etc.), or articles that are academic rather than catechetical in nature. **Buys 35-40 mss/year.** Query with or without published clips or send complete ms. Length: 600-1,300 words. **Pays $100-125 for assigned articles; $75-125 for unsolicited articles.**

Columns/Departments Catechist to Catechist (brief articles on crafts, games, etc., for religion lessons); Faith and Fun (full page religious word games, puzzles, mazes, etc., for children). **Buys 30 mss/year.** Send complete ms. **Pays $20-125.**

Tips "We look for clear, concise articles written from experience. Articles should help readers move from theory/doctrine to concrete application. Unsolicited manuscripts not returned without SASE. No fancy formatting; no handwritten manuscripts. Author should be able to furnish article on disk or via e-mail if possible."

$ TEACHERS INTERACTION

Concordia Publishing House, 3558 S. Jefferson Ave., St. Louis MO 63118-3968. (314)268-1083. Fax: (314)268-1329. E-mail: tom.nummela@cph.org. **Contact:** Tom Nummela, editor. **5% freelance written.** Quarterly magazine of practical, inspirational, theological articles for volunteer Sunday school teachers. Material must be true to the doctrines of the Lutheran Church—Missouri Synod. Estab. 1960. Circ. 12,000. Pays on publication. Publishes ms an average of 1 year after acceptance. Byline given. Buys all rights. Submit seasonal material 1 year in advance. Accepts queries by mail, e-mail, fax. Responds in 3 weeks to mss. Sample copy for $5.50. Writer's guidelines for #10 SASE.

Nonfiction How-to (practical help/ideas used successfully in own classroom), inspirational, personal experience (of Sunday School teachers). No freelance theological articles. **Buys 6 mss/year.** Send complete ms. Length: 1,200 words. **Pays up to $120.**

Fillers "*Teachers Interaction* buys short 'Toolbox' items—activities and ideas planned and used successfully in a church school classroom." **Buys 48/year.** Length: 200 words maximum. **Pays $20-40.**

Tips "Practical or 'it happened to me' articles would have the best chance. Also short items—ideas used in classrooms; seasonal and in conjunction with our Sunday school material. Our format emphasizes volunteer Sunday school teachers."

$ $ TODAY'S CATHOLIC TEACHER

Peter Li Education Group, 2621 Dryden Rd., Suite 300, Dayton OH 45439. (937)293-1415. Fax: (937)293-1310. E-mail: mnoschang@peterli.com. Web site: www.catholicteacher.com. **Contact:** Mary C. Noschang, editor. **60% freelance written.** Magazine published 6 times/year during school year covering Catholic education for grades K-12. "We look for topics of interest and practical help to teachers in Catholic elementary schools in all curriculum areas including religion technology, discipline, motivation." Estab. 1972. Circ. 50,000. Pays on publication. Publishes ms an average of 2 months after acceptance. Byline given. Buys first and all rights and makes work-for-hire assignments. Editorial lead time 3 months. Submit seasonal material 6 months in advance. Accepts queries by mail, e-mail, fax. Accepts simultaneous submissions. Responds in 1 month to queries; 3 months to mss. Sample copy for $3 or on Web site. Writer's guidelines online.

Nonfiction Interested in articles detailing ways to incorporate Catholic values into academic subjects other than religion class. Essays, how-to, humor, interview/profile, personal experience. "No articles pertaining to public education." **Buys 15 mss/year.** Query or send complete ms. Length: 1,500-3,000 words. **Pays $150-300.** Sometimes pays expenses of writers on assignment.

Photos State availability with submission. Reviews transparencies, prints. Buys one-time rights. Offers $20-50/photo. Captions, identification of subjects, model releases required.

Tips "Although our readership is primarily classroom teachers, *Today's Catholic Teacher* is also read by principals, supervisors, superintendents, boards of education, pastors, and parents. *Today's Catholic Teacher* aims to be for Catholic educators a source of information not available elsewhere. The focus of articles should span the interests of teachers from early childhood through junior high. Articles may be directed to just one age group, yet have wider implications. Preference is given to material directed to teachers in grades 4-8. The desired magazine style is direct, concise, informative, and accurate. Writing should be enjoyable to read, informal rather than scholarly, lively, and free of educational jargon."

$ TODAY'S CHRISTIAN PREACHER

Right Ideas, Inc., P.O. Box 100, Morgantown PA 19543. (610)856-6830. Fax: (610)856-6831. E-mail: publications@rightideas.us. Editor: Jerry Thacker. **Contact:** Elaine Williams, assistant editor. **10% freelance written.** Quarterly magazine offering articles for pastors. "*Today's Christian Preacher* is designed to meet the personal needs of the man of God." Estab. 1992. Circ. 25,000. Pays on publication. Publishes ms an average of 1 year after acceptance. Buys simultaneous rights. Editorial lead time 1 year. Submit seasonal material 1 year in advance. Accepts queries by mail, e-mail, fax. Accepts simultaneous submissions. Responds in 1 month to queries; 3 months to mss. Sample copy for 9×12 SAE and 4 first-class stamps. Writer's guidelines for #10 SASE.

O→ Break in with "concise, practical information for the pastor in his personal life, not sermons or church issues."

Nonfiction Inspirational, religious, articles to help the man of God in his personal life. **Buys 2 mss/year.** Send complete ms. Length: 800-1,000 words. **Pays $150 for assigned articles.**
Photos Offers no additional payment for photos accepted with ms.

$ $ $ WORSHIP LEADER MAGAZINE

26311 Junipero Serra, #130, San Juan Capistrano CA 92675. (949)240-9339. Fax: (949)240-0038. E-mail: editor@wlmag.com. Web site: www.worshipleader.com. **80% freelance written.** Bimonthly magazine covering all aspects of Christian worship. "*Worship Leader Magazine* exists to challenge, serve, equip, and train those involved in leading the 21st century church in worship. The intended readership is the worship team (all those who plan and lead) of the local church." Estab. 1992. Circ. 50,000. Pays on publication. Byline given. Offers 50% kill fee. Buys first North American serial, all rights. Editorial lead time 3 months. Submit seasonal material 6 months in advance. Responds in 6 weeks to queries; 3 months to mss. Sample copy for $5. Writer's guidelines online.
Nonfiction General interest, how-to (related to purpose/audience), inspirational, interview/profile, opinion. **Buys 15-30 mss/year.** Query with published clips. Length: 1,200-2,000 words. **Pays $200-800 for assigned articles; $200-500 for unsolicited articles.** Sometimes pays expenses of writers on assignment.
Photos State availability with submission. Buys one-time rights. Negotiate payment individually. Identification of subjects required.
Tips "Our goal has been and is to provide the tools and information pastors, worship leaders, and ministers of music, youth, and the arts need to facilitate and enhance worship in their churches. In achieving this goal, we strive to maintain high journalistic standards, Biblical soundness, and theological neutrality. Our intent is to present the philosophical, scholarly insight on worship, as well as the day-to-day, 'putting it all together' side of worship, while celebrating our unity and diversity."

$ $ YOUR CHURCH

Helping You With the Business of Ministry, Christianity Today, Inc., 465 Gundersen Dr., Carol Stream IL 60188. (630)260-6200. Fax: (630)260-0114. E-mail: yceditor@yourchurch.net. Web site: www.yourchurch.net. Managing Editor: Mike Schreiter. **90% freelance written.** Bimonthly magazine covering church administration and products. "Articles pertain to the business aspects of ministry pastors are called upon to perform: administration, purchasing, management, technology, building, etc." Estab. 1955. Circ. 85,000 (controlled). **Pays on acceptance.** Publishes ms an average of 3-4 months after acceptance. Byline given. Buys first, electronic rights. Editorial lead time 6 weeks. Submit seasonal material 5 months in advance. Accepts queries by mail, e-mail, fax. Accepts previously published material. Responds in 1 month to queries; 3 months to mss. Sample copy for 9×12 SAE and 4 first-class stamps. Writer's guidelines free.
Nonfiction How-to, new product, technical. **Buys 50-60 mss/year.** Send complete ms. Length: 1,000-4,000 words. **Pays 15-20¢/word.** Sometimes pays expenses of writers on assignment.
Tips "The editorial is generally geared toward brief and helpful articles dealing with some form of church business. Concise, bulleted points from experts in the field are typical for our articles."

$ $ YOUTHWORKER JOURNAL

Salem Publishing, 104 Woodmont Blvd., Suite 300, Nashville TN 37205-9759. E-mail: articles@youthworker.com. Web site: www.youthworker.com. **Contact:** Steve Rabey, editor. **100% freelance written.** Bimonthly magazine covering professional youth ministry in the church and parachurch. "We exist to help meet the personal and professional needs of career, Christian youth workers in the church and parachurch. Proposals accepted on the posted theme, according to the writer's guidelines on our Web site. It's not enough to write well—you must know youth ministry." Estab. 1984. Circ. 20,000. Pays on publication. Publishes ms an average of 3 months after acceptance. Byline given. "Articles must be first published with us, and we buy unrestricted use for print and electronic media." Editorial lead time 6 months. Submit seasonal material 6 months in advance. Accepts queries by e-mail. Responds in 6 months to queries. Sample copy for $5. Writer's guidelines online.
Nonfiction Essays, new product (youth ministry books only), personal experience, photo feature, religious. Query. Length: 250-3,000 words. **Pays $50-200.** Pays in contributor copies at the request of the author. Sometimes pays expenses of writers on assignment.
Photos Send photos with submission. Reviews GIF/JPEG files. Negotiates payment individually.

CLOTHING

$ $ EMB-EMBROIDERY/MONOGRAM BUSINESS

1145 Sanctuary Parkway, Suite 355, Alpharetta GA 30004. (770)291-5534. Fax: (770)777-8733. E-mail: rlebovitz@embmag.com. Web site: www.embmag.com. **Contact:** Richard Lebovitz, editor-in-chief. **30% freelance writ-**

ten. Monthly magazine covering computerized embroidery and digitizing design. "Readable, practical business and/or technical articles that show our readers how to succeed in their profession." Estab. 1994. Circ. 20,000. Pays on publication. Publishes ms an average of 3 months after acceptance. Byline given. Buys all rights. Editorial lead time 3 months. Submit seasonal material 6 months in advance. Accepts queries by mail, e-mail. Accepts simultaneous submissions. Sample copy for $10. Writer's guidelines not available.

Nonfiction How-to (embroidery, sales, marketing, design, general business info), interview/profile, new product, photo feature, technical (computerized embroidery). **Buys 40 mss/year.** Query. Length: 800-2,000 words. **Pays $200 and up for assigned articles.**

Photos Send photos with submission. Reviews transparencies, prints. Negotiates payment individually.

Tips "Show us you have specified knowledge, experience, or contacts in the embroidery industry or a related field."

N $ $ $ FOOTWEAR PLUS

Symphony Publishing, 8 W. 38th St., New York NY 10018. (646)278-1550. Fax: (646)278-1553. E-mail: nyeditorial@symphonypublishing.com. Web site: www.footwearplusmagazine.com. **Contact:** Greg Dutter, editorial director. **20% freelance written.** Monthly magazine covering footwear fashion and business. "A business-to-business publication targeted at footwear retailers. Covering all categories of footwear and age ranges with a focus on new trends, brands and consumer buying habits, as well as retailer advice on operating the store more effectively." Estab. 1990. Circ. 18,000. Pays on publication. Publishes ms an average of 1-2 months after acceptance. Byline given. Buys second serial (reprint), electronic rights. Editorial lead time 1-2 months. Accepts queries by e-mail. Sample copy for $5.

Nonfiction Interview/profile, new product, technical. Does not want pieces unrelated to footwear/fashion industry. **Buys 10-20 mss/year.** Query. Length: 500-2,500 words. **Pays $1,000 maximum.** Sometimes pays expenses of writers on assignment.

$ $ MADE TO MEASURE

Halper Publishing Co., 830 Moseley Rd., Highland Park IL 60035. Fax: (847)780-2902. E-mail: mtm@halper.com. Web site: www.madetomeasuremag.com. **Contact:** Rick Levine, editor/publisher. **50% freelance written.** Semiannual magazine covering uniforms and career apparel. "A semi-annual magazine/buyers' reference containing leading sources of supply, equipment, and services of every description related to the Uniform, Career Apparel, and allied trades, throughout the entire US." Estab. 1930. Circ. 25,000. **Pays on acceptance.** Publishes ms an average of 2 months after acceptance. Byline given. Buys first North American serial rights. Editorial lead time 4 months. Submit seasonal material 4 months in advance. Accepts queries by mail, e-mail. Accepts simultaneous submissions. Responds in 3 weeks to queries. Sample copy online.

Nonfiction "Please only consider sending queries related to companies that wear or make uniforms, career apparel, or identify apparel." Interview/profile, new product, personal experience, photo feature, technical. **Buys 6-8 mss/year.** Query with published clips. Length: 1,000-3,000 words. **Pays $300-500.** Sometimes pays expenses of writers on assignment.

Photos State availability with submission. Reviews contact sheets, any prints. Buys one-time rights. Negotiates payment individually.

Tips "We look for features about large and small companies who wear uniforms (restaurants, hotels, industrial, medical, public safety, etc.)."

$ $ TEXTILE WORLD

Billian Publishing Co., 2100 Powers Ferry Rd., Suite 300, Atlanta GA 30339. (770)955-5656. Fax: (770)952-0669. E-mail: editor@textileindustries.com. Web site: www.textileindustries.com. **Contact:** James Borneman, editor-in-chief. **5% freelance written.** Bimonthly magazine covering "the business of textile, apparel, and fiber industries with considerable technical focus on products and processes. No puff pieces pushing a particular product." Estab. 1868. Pays on publication. Byline given. Buys first North American serial rights.

Nonfiction Technical, business. **Buys 10 mss/year.** Query. Length: 500 words minimum. **Pays $200/published page.**

Photos Send photos with submission. Reviews prints. Buys one-time rights. Offers no additional payment for photos accepted with ms. Captions required.

CONSTRUCTION & CONTRACTING

$ $ ADVANCED MATERIALS & COMPOSITES NEWS PLUS COMPOSITES ENEWS

International Business & Technology Intelligence on High Performance M&P, Composites Worldwide, Inc., 991-C Lomas Santa Fe Dr., MC469, Solana Beach CA 92075-2125. (858)755-1372. E-mail: info@compositesnews.c om. Web site: www.compositesnews.com. Managing Editor: Susan Loud. **Contact:** Steve Loud, editor. **1% freelance written.** Bimonthly newsletter covering advanced materials and fiber-reinforced polymer composites, plus a weekly electronic version called *Composite eNews*, reaching over 15,000 subscribers and many more pass-along readers. *Advanced Materials & Composites News* "covers markets, applications, materials, processes, and organizations for all sectors of the global hi-tech materials world. Audience is management, academics, researchers, government, suppliers, and fabricators. Focus on news about growth opportunities." Estab. 1978. Circ. 15,000+. Pays on publication. Publishes ms an average of 1 month after acceptance. Byline sometimes given. Buys all rights. Editorial lead time 2 weeks. Submit seasonal material 1 month in advance. Accepts queries by e-mail. Responds in 1 week to queries; 1 month to mss. Sample copy for #10 SASE.

- "We target, contact, and use freelancers with the most industry knowledge, usually people we know personally from the FRP composites industry."

Nonfiction New product, technical, industry information. **Buys 4-6 mss/year.** Query. Length: 300 words. **Pays $200/final printed page.**

Photos State availability with submission. Reviews 4×5 transparencies, prints, 35mm slides, JPEGs (much preferred). Buys all rights. Offers no additional payment for photos accepted with ms. Captions, identification of subjects, model releases required.

$ $ AUTOMATED BUILDER

CMN Associates, Inc., 1445 Donlon St., Suite 16, Ventura CA 93003. (805)642-9735. Fax: (805)642-8820. E-mail: info@automatedbuilder.com. Web site: www.automatedbuilder.com. Editor-in-Chief: Don Carlson. **Contact:** Olaf Wolff. **10% freelance written.** Monthly magazine specializing in management for industrialized (manufactured) housing and volume home builders. "Our material is technical in content and concerned with new technologies or improved methods for in-plant building and components related to building. Online content is uploaded from the monthly print material." Estab. 1964. Circ. 25,000. **Pays on acceptance.** Publishes ms an average of 3 months after acceptance. Byline given. Buys first North American serial rights. Editorial lead time 2 months. Submit seasonal material 2 months in advance. Accepts queries by mail, e-mail, fax. Responds in 2 weeks to queries. Sample copy for free.

Nonfiction Case history articles on successful home building companies which may be 1) production (big volume) home builders; 2) mobile home manufacturers; 3) modular home manufacturers; 4) prefabricated (panelized) home manufacturers; 5) house component manufacturers; or 6) special unit (in-plant commercial building) manufacturers. Also uses interviews, photo features, and technical articles. "No architect or plan 'dreams.' Housing projects must be built or under construction." **Buys 6-8 mss/year.** Query. Phone queries OK. Length: 250-500 words. **Pays $300.**

Photos Wants 4×5, 5×7, or 8×10 glossies or disks. State availability with submission. Offers no additional payment for photos accepted with ms. Captions, identification of subjects required.

Tips "Stories often are too long, too loose; we prefer 500-750 words. We prefer a phone query on feature articles. If accepted on query, article usually will not be rejected later."

$ $ BUILDERNEWS MAGAZINE

Pacific NW Sales & Marketing, Inc., 500 W. 8th St., Suite 270, Vancouver WA 98660. (360)906-0793. Fax: (360)906-0794. Web site: www.buildernewsmag.com. "Articles must address pressing topics for builders in our region with a special emphasis on the business aspects of construction." Estab. 1996. Circ. 35,000. Pays on acceptance of revised ms. Publishes ms an average of 1 month after acceptance. Byline given. Buys first North American serial, electronic rights. Editorial lead time 2 months. Submit seasonal material 3 months in advance. Accepts queries by mail, e-mail, fax. Responds in 1 week to queries; 1 month to mss. Sample copy for free or online. Writer's guidelines free.

Nonfiction How-to, interview/profile, new product, technical. No personal bios unless they teach a valuable lesson to those in the building industry. **Buys 400 mss/year.** Query. Length: 500-2,500 words. **Pays $200-500.** Sometimes pays expenses of writers on assignment.

Photos State availability with submission. Buys first North American serial and electronic rights. Offers no additional payment for photos accepted with ms. Captions, identification of subjects, model releases required.

Columns/Departments Query.

Tips "Writers should have an understanding of the residential building industry and its terminology and be prepared to provide a résumé, writing samples, and story synopsis."

$ $ CONCRETE CONSTRUCTION

Hanley-Wood, LLC., 426 S. Westgate St., Addison IL 60101. (630)543-0870. Fax: (630)543-3112. E-mail: preband @hanleywood.com. Web site: www.worldofconcrete.com. Editor: William Palmer. **Contact:** Pat Reband, managing editor. **20% freelance written.** Monthly magazine for concrete contractors, engineers, architects, specifiers, and others who design and build residential, commercial, industrial, and public works, cast-in-place concrete structures. It also covers job stories and new equipment in the industry. Estab. 1956. Circ. 80,000. **Pays on acceptance.** Publishes ms an average of 4 months after acceptance. Byline given. Editorial lead time 4 months. Submit seasonal material 4 months in advance. Accepts queries by mail, e-mail, fax. Responds in 2 weeks to queries; 1 month to mss. Sample copy and writer's guidelines free.

Nonfiction How-to, new product, personal experience, photo feature, technical, job stories. **Buys 7-10 mss/year.** Query with published clips. Length: 2,000 words maximum. **Pays $250 or more for assigned articles; $200 minimum for unsolicited articles.** Pays expenses of writers on assignment.

Photos Send photos with submission. Reviews contact sheets, negatives, transparencies, prints. Buys one-time rights. Offers no additional payment for photos accepted with ms. Captions required.

Tips "Have a good understanding of the concrete construction industry. How-to stories accepted only from industry experts. Job stories must cover procedures, materials, and equipment used as well as the project's scope."

$ $ $ THE CONCRETE PRODUCER

Hanley-Wood, LLC, 426 S. Westgate St., Addison IL 60101. (630)543-0870. Fax: (630)543-3112. Web site: www.theconcreteproducer.com. **Contact:** Rick Yelton, editor. **25% freelance written.** Monthly magazine covering concrete production. "Our audience consists of producers who have succeeded in making concrete the preferred building material through management, operating, quality control, use of the latest technology, or use of superior materials." Estab. 1982. Circ. 18,000. **Pays on acceptance.** Publishes ms an average of 2 months after acceptance. Byline given. Editorial lead time 4 months. Accepts queries by mail, e-mail, fax, phone. Responds in 1 week to queries; 2 months to mss. Sample copy for $4. Writer's guidelines free.

Nonfiction How-to (promote concrete), new product, technical. **Buys 10 mss/year.** Send complete ms. Length: 500-2,000 words. **Pays $200-1,000.** Sometimes pays expenses of writers on assignment.

Photos Scan photos at 300 dpi. State availability with submission. Reviews transparencies, prints. Offers no additional payment for photos accepted with ms. Captions, identification of subjects required.

$ $ FRAME BUILDING NEWS

The Official Publication of the National Frame Builders Association, Krause Publications, a Division of F+W Publications, Inc., 700 E. State St., Iola WI 54990-0001. (715)445-4612, ext. 428. Fax: (715)445-4087. E-mail: scott.tappa@fwpubs.com. Web site: www.framebuildingnews.com. Associate Editor: Jim Austin. **Contact:** Scott Tappa, editor. **10% freelance written.** Magazine published 5 times/year covering building. "*Frame Building News* is the official publication of the National Frame Builders Association, which represents contractors who specialize in post-frame building construction." Estab. 1990. Circ. 20,000. Pays on publication. Publishes ms an average of 3 months after acceptance. Byline given. Buys all rights. Editorial lead time 3 months. Submit seasonal material 3 months in advance. Accepts queries by mail. Accepts simultaneous submissions. Sample copy for free.

Nonfiction Book excerpts, historical/nostalgic, how-to, interview/profile, new product, opinion, photo feature, technical. No advertorials. **Buys 15 mss/year.** Query with published clips. Length: 750 words minimum. **Pays $100-500 for assigned articles.**

Photos Send photos with submission. Reviews GIF/JPEG files. Buys all rights. Negotiates payment individually. Captions, identification of subjects required.

Columns/Departments Money Talk (taxes for business); Tech Talk (computers for builders); Tool Talk (tools); Management Insights (business management), all 1,000 words. **Buys 15 mss/year.** Send complete ms. **Pays $0-500.**

Tips "Read our magazine online for a sense of our typical subject matter and audience. Contact by regular mail is best. No advertorials, please."

$ HARD HAT NEWS

Lee Publications, Inc., 6113 State Highway 5, Palatine Bridge NY 13428. (518)673-3237. Fax: (518)673-2381. E-mail: hrieser@leepub.com. Web site: www.hardhat.com. **Contact:** Holly Rieser. **80% freelance written.** Biweekly tabloid covering heavy construction, equipment, road, and bridge work. "Our readers are contractors and heavy construction workers involved in excavation, highways, bridges, utility construction, and underground construction." Estab. 1980. Circ. 58,000. Byline given. Editorial lead time 2 weeks. Submit seasonal material 2 weeks in advance. Accepts queries by mail, e-mail, fax, phone. Sample copy and writer's guidelines free.

> O‑ "We especially need writers with some knowledge of heavy construction, although anyone with good composition and interviewing skills is welcome. Focus on major construction in progress in your area."

Nonfiction Job stories (a brief overall description of the project, the names and addresses of the companies and contractors involved, and a description of the equipment used, including manufacturers' names and model numbers; quotes from the people in charge, as well as photos, are important, as are the names of the dealers providing the equipment). Interview/profile, new product, opinion, photo feature, technical. Send complete ms. Length: 800-2,000 words. **Pays $2.50/inch.** Sometimes pays expenses of writers on assignment.

Photos Send photos with submission. Reviews prints, digital preferred. Offers $15/photo. Captions, identification of subjects required.

Columns/Departments Association News; Parts and Repairs; Attachments; Trucks and Trailers; People on the Move.

Tips "Every issue has a focus—see our editorial calender. Special consideration is given to a story that coincides with the focus. A color photo is necessary for the front page. Vertical shots work best. We need more writers in metro NY area. Also, we are expanding our distribution into the Mid-Atlantic states and need writers in Virginia, Tennessee, North Carolina, Michigan, New Jersey and South Carolina."

$ $ MC MAGAZINE

The Voice of the Manufactured Concrete Products Industry, National Precast Concrete Association, 10333 N. Meridian St., Suite 272, Indianapolis IN 46290. (317)571-9500. Fax: (317)571-0041. E-mail: rhyink@precast.org. Web site: www.precast.org. **Contact:** Ron Hyink, managing editor. **75% freelance written.** Bimonthly magazine covering manufactured concrete products. "*MC Magazine* is a publication for owners and managers of factory-produced concrete products used in construction. We publish business articles, technical articles, company profiles, safety articles, and project profiles, with the intent of educating our readers in order to increase the quality and use of precast concrete." Estab. 1995. Circ. 8,500. **Pays on acceptance.** Publishes ms an average of 6 months after acceptance. Byline given. Buys first North American serial, second serial (reprint), all rights. Editorial lead time 3 months. Accepts queries by mail, e-mail, fax. Accepts simultaneous submissions. Responds in 1 month to queries; 2 months to mss. Sample copy and writer's guidelines online.

Nonfiction How-to (business), interview/profile, technical (concrete manufacturing). "No humor, essays, fiction, or fillers." **Buys 8-14 mss/year.** Query or send complete ms. Length: 1,500-2,500 words. **Pays $250-750.** Sometimes pays expenses of writers on assignment.

Photos State availability with submission. Buys all rights. Offers no additional payment for photos accepted with ms. Captions required.

Tips "Understand the audience and the purpose of the magazine. Understanding audience interests and needs is important and expressing a willingness to tailor a subject to get the right slant is critical. Our primary freelance needs are about general business or technology topics. Of course, if you are an engineer or a writer specializing in industry, construction, or manufacturing technology, other possibilities may exist. Writing style should be concise, yet lively and entertaining. Avoid clichés. We require a third-person perspective, and encourage a positive tone and active voice. For stylistic matters, follow the *AP Style Book*."

$ $ METAL ROOFING MAGAZINE

Krause Publications, a Division of F + W Publications, Inc., 700 E. Iola St., Iola WI 54990-0001. (715)445-4612, ext. 281. Fax: (715)445-4087. E-mail: jim.austin@fwpubs.com. Web site: www.metalroofingmag.com. **Contact:** Jim Austin, associate editor. **10% freelance written.** Bimonthly magazine covering roofing. "*Metal Roofing Magazine* offers contractors, designers, suppliers, and others in the construction industry a wealth of information on metal roofing—a growing segment of the roofing trade." Estab. 2000. Circ. 25,000. Pays on publication. Publishes ms an average of 3 months after acceptance. Byline given. Buys all rights. Editorial lead time 3 months. Submit seasonal material 3 months in advance. Accepts queries by mail. Accepts simultaneous submissions. Sample copy for free.

Nonfiction Book excerpts, historical/nostalgic, how-to, interview/profile, new product, opinion, photo feature, technical. No advertorials. **Buys 15 mss/year.** Query with published clips. Length: 750 words minimum. **Pays $100-500 for assigned articles.**

Photos Send photos with submission. Reviews GIF/JPEG files. Buys all rights. Negotiates payment individually. Captions, identification of subjects required.

Columns/Departments Money Talk (taxes for business); Tech Talk (computers for builders); Tool Talk (tools); Management Insights (business management), all 1,000 words. **Buys 15 mss/year.** Send complete ms. **Pays $0-500.**

Tips "Read our magazine online for a sense of our typical subject matter and audience. Contact by regular mail is best. No advertorials, please."

MICHIGAN CONTRACTOR & BUILDER

1917 Savannah Lane, Ypsilanti MI 48198-3674. (734)482-0272. Fax: (734)482-0291. E-mail: akalousdian@reedbusiness.com. **Contact:** Aram Kalousdian. **25% freelance written.** Weekly magazine covering the commercial construction industry in Michigan (no home building). "*Michigan Contractor & Builder's* audience is contractors, equipment suppliers, engineers, and architects. The magazine reports on construction projects in Michigan. It does not cover homebuilding. Stories should focus on news or innovative techniques or materials in construction." Estab. 1907. Pays 1 month after publication. Byline given. Buys all rights. Accepts queries by mail, e-mail, fax, phone. Sample copy for free.

Nonfiction Michigan construction projects. Query with published clips. Length: 1,000 words with 5-7 photos. **Payment is negotiable.**

Photos Send photos with submission. Reviews high resolution digital photos. Buys all rights. Offers no additional payment for photos accepted with ms. Captions required.

N $ $ PENNSYLVANIA BUILDER

Pennsylvania Builders Association, 600 N. 12th St., Lemoyne PA 17043. (717)730-4380. Fax: (717)730-4396. E-mail: pba@pahomes.org. Web site: www.pahomes.org. **10% freelance written.** "Quarterly trade publication for builders, remodelers, subcontractors, and other affiliates of the home building industry in Pennsylvania." Estab. 1988. Circ. 12,200. Pays on publication. Publishes ms an average of 1 year after acceptance. Byline given. Buys one-time rights. Editorial lead time 3 months. Submit seasonal material 9 months in advance. Accepts queries by mail, e-mail. Accepts simultaneous submissions. Responds in 2 weeks to queries; 3 months to mss. Sample copy for free. Writer's guidelines by e-mail. Editorial calendar online.

Nonfiction General interest, how-to, new product, technical. No personnel or company profiles. **Buys 1-2 mss/year.** Send complete ms. Length: 800-1,200 words. **Pays $250.** Sometimes pays expenses of writers on assignment.

Reprints Accepts previously published submissions.

Photos Send photos with submission. Reviews negatives, transparencies, prints. Buys one-time rights. Negotiates payment individually. Captions, identification of subjects required.

$ $ PERMANENT BUILDINGS & FOUNDATIONS (PBF)

R.W. Nielsen Co., 575 E. Center St., Provo UT 84606. (801)794-1393. Fax: (801)804-6691. E-mail: rnielsen@permanentbuildings.com. Web site: www.permanentbuildings.com. **Contact:** Roger W. Nielsen, editor. **80% freelance written.** Magazine published 8 times/year. "*PBF* readers are general contractors who build residential and light commercial concrete buildings. Editorial focus is on new technologies to build solid, energy efficient structures, insulated concrete walls, waterproofing, underpinning, roofing and the business of contracting and construction." No highway, bridge or large industrial construction. Estab. 1989. Circ. 30,000. Pays on publication. Byline given. Buys first North American serial rights. Editorial lead time 1 month. Submit seasonal material 2 months in advance. Accepts queries by mail, e-mail, phone. Responds immediately to queries; 1 month to mss. Sample copy for 9×12 SASE or online. Writer's guidelines free or online.

Nonfiction How-to (construction methods, management techniques), humor, interview/profile, new product, technical, tool reviews, environment/green building. **Buys 90-100 mss/year.** Query. Length: 500-1,500 words. **Pays 30-60¢/word.**

Photos State availability with submission. Reviews digital images (300 dpi). Buys North American rights. Offers no additional payment for photos accepted with ms. Captions, identification of subjects required.

Columns/Departments Marketing Tips, 250-500 words; Q&A (solutions to contractor problems), 200-500 words. Query.

N PROFESSIONAL BUILDER

Reed Business Information, 2000 Clearwater Dr., Oak Brook IL 60523. (630)288-8198. Fax: (630)288-8145. E-mail: erin.hallstrom@reedbusiness.com. Web site: probuilder.com. Editorial Director: Paul Deffenbaugh. Managing Editor: Erin Hallstrom-Erickson. Senior Editors: Laura Butalla, Bill Lurz, Mark Jarasek, Felicia Oliver. Magazine published 17 times/year covering the business of building. Designed as a resource to help builders run succesful and profitable businesses. Circ. 127,277. Editorial lead time 6 months. Accepts queries by mail, e-mail.

$ $ REEVES JOURNAL

Business News Publishing Co., 23241 South Pointe Dr., Suite 280, Laguna Hills CA 92654. (949)830-0881. Fax: (949)859-7845. E-mail: jack@reevesjournal.com. Web site: www.reevesjournal.com. **Contact:** Jack Sweet, editor. **25% freelance written.** Monthly magazine covering the plumbing and radiant heating industries in the 14 western states. Estab. 1920. Circ. 13,800. Pays on publication. Byline given. Buys first North American serial, electronic rights. Editorial lead time 3 months. Accepts queries by mail, e-mail, fax. Responds in 1 month to queries; 2 months to mss. Sample copy for free. Writer's guidelines for #10 SASE.

"Knowledge of building construction, water science, radiant heating, hydronics, codes and engineering is extremely helpful. Even better—former plumbing or radiant experience and a great command of the English language. We do not consider unsolicited 'generic' business articles."

Nonfiction "We are only interested in articles applicable to the plumbing and radiant heating subcontracting trades affecting contractors in the western US." How-to, interview/profile, new product, technical. Query with published clips. Length: 1,500-2,000 words. **Pays $100-350.**

Photos State availability with submission. Buys all rights. Negotiates payment individually. Captions, identification of subjects required.

The online magazine carries original content not found in the print edition. Contact: Jack Sweet.

Tips "Know the market. We're not just another builder publication and we do not publish or even consider publishing canned, generic articles, so don't even bother querying us with them. Our target audience is the plumbing and radiant heating contractor—new construction, residential, commercial, and service and repair. We cover the western US (plus Texas)."

$ $ RURAL BUILDER

The Business Management Magazine for Rural Contractors, Krause Publications, a Division of F+W Publications, Inc., 700 E. State St., Iola WI 54990-0001. (715)445-4612, ext. 428. Fax: (715)445-4087. E-mail: scott.tappa@fwpubs.com. Web site: www.ruralbuilder.com. Associate Editor: Jim Austin. **Contact:** Scott Tappa, editor. **10% freelance written.** Magazine published 7 times/year covering building. "*Rural Builder* serves diversified town and country builders, offering them help managing their businesses through editorial and advertising material about metal, wood, post-frame, and masonry construction." Estab. 1967. Circ. 30,000. Pays on publication. Publishes ms an average of 3 months after acceptance. Byline given. Buys all rights. Editorial lead time 3 months. Submit seasonal material 3 months in advance. Accepts queries by mail. Accepts simultaneous submissions. Sample copy for free.

Nonfiction Book excerpts, historical/nostalgic, how-to, interview/profile, new product, opinion, photo feature, technical. No advertorials. **Buys 15 mss/year.** Query with published clips. Length: 750 words minimum. **Pays $100-500.**

Photos Send photos with submission. Reviews GIF/JPEG files. Buys all rights. Negotiates payment individually. Captions, identification of subjects required.

Columns/Departments Money Talk (taxes for business); Tech Talk (computers for builders); Tool Talk (tools); Management Insights (business management); all 1,000 words. **Buys 15 mss/year.** Send complete ms. **Pays $0-500.**

Tips "Read our magazine online for a sense of our typical subject matter and audience. Contact by regular mail is best. No advertorials, please."

$ $ UNDERGROUND CONSTRUCTION

Oildom Publishing Co. of Texas, Inc., P.O. Box 941669, Houston TX 77094-8669. (281)558-6930. Fax: (281)558-7029. E-mail: rcarpenter@oildom.com. Web site: www.oildompublishing.com. **Contact:** Robert Carpenter, editor. **35% freelance written.** Monthly magazine covering underground oil and gas pipeline, water and sewer pipeline, cable construction for contractors and owning companies. Circ. 34,500. Publishes ms an average of 6 months after acceptance. Buys first North American serial rights. Accepts queries by mail, e-mail, fax, phone. Responds in 1 month to mss.

Nonfiction How-to, job stories. Query with published clips. Length: 1,000-2,000 words. **Pays $3-500.** Sometimes pays expenses of writers on assignment.

Photos Send photos with submission. Reviews color prints and slides. Buys one-time rights. Captions required.

Tips "We supply guidelines outlining information we need. The most frequent mistake made by writers in completing articles is unfamiliarity with the field."

DRUGS, HEALTHCARE & MEDICAL PRODUCTS

$ $ $ VALIDATION TIMES

Bio Research Compliance Report, Adverse Event Reporting News, Washington Information Source Co., 208 S. King St., Suite 303, Leesburg VA 20175. (703)779-8777. Fax: (703)779-2508. E-mail: publisher@fdainfo.com. Web site: www.fdainfo.com. **Contact:** Ken Reid, editor. Monthly Newsletters covering regulation of pharmaceutical and medical devices. "We write to executives who have to keep up on changing FDA policies and regulations, and on what their competitors are doing at the agency." Estab. 1992. Pays on publication. Publishes ms an average of 1 month after acceptance. Byline given. Makes work-for-hire assignments. Editorial lead time 1 month. Submit seasonal material 1 month in advance. Accepts queries by mail. Responds in 1 month to queries. Sample copy and writer's guidelines free.

Nonfiction How-to, technical, regulatory. No lay interest pieces. **Buys 50-100 mss/year.** Query. Length: 600-1,500 words. **Pays $100/half day; $200 full day "to cover meetings and same rate for writing."** Sometimes pays expenses of writers on assignment.

Tips "If you're covering a conference for non-competing publications, call me with a drug or device regulatory angle."

EDUCATION & COUNSELING

$ ARTS & ACTIVITIES

Publishers' Development Corp., Dept. WM, 12345 World Trade Dr., San Diego CA 92128. (858)605-0242. Fax: (858)605-0247. E-mail: ed@artsandactivities.com. Web site: www.artsandactivities.com. **Contact:** Maryellen Bridge, editor-in-chief. **95% freelance written.** Eager to work with new/unpublished writers. Monthly (except July and August) magazine covering art education at levels from preschool through college for educators and therapists engaged in arts and crafts education and training. Estab. 1932. Circ. 20,000. Pays on publication. Publishes ms an average of 1 year after acceptance. Byline given. Buys first North American serial rights. Submit seasonal material 6 months in advance. Accepts queries by mail. Responds in 3 months to queries. Sample copy for 9×12 SAE and 8 first-class stamps. Writer's guidelines online.

- Editors here are seeking more materials for upper elementary and secondary levels on printmaking, ceramics, 3-dimensional design, weaving, fiber arts (stitchery, tie-dye, batik, etc.), crafts, painting, and multicultural art.

Nonfiction Historical/nostalgic (arts, activities, history), how-to (classroom art experiences, artists' techniques), interview/profile (of artists), opinion (on arts activities curriculum, ideas of how to do things better, philosophy of art education), personal experience (this ties in with the how-to, we like it to be personal, no recipe style), articles of exceptional art programs. **Buys 80-100 mss/year.** Length: 200-2,000 words. **Pays $35-150.**

Tips "Frequently in unsolicited manuscripts, writers obviously have not studied the magazine to see what style of articles we publish. Send for a sample copy to familiarize yourself with our style and needs. The best way to find out if his/her writing style suits our needs is for the author to submit a manuscript on speculation. We prefer an anecdotal style of writing, so that readers will feel as though they are there in the art room as the lesson/project is taking place. Also, good quality photographs of student artwork are important. We are a visual art magazine!"

AUSTRALIAN JOURNAL OF EARLY CHILDHOOD

Early Childhood Australia, Inc., P.O. Box 7105, Watson ACT 2602 Australia. (61)(2)6242-1800. Fax: (61)(2)6242-1818. E-mail: publishing@earlychildhood.org.au. Web site: www.earlychildhoodaustralia.org.au. Inhouse Editor: David Kingwell. Quarterly magazine designed to impart new information and encourage the critical exchange of ideas among practitioners in early childhood field. Writer's guidelines online.

Nonfiction Essays. Send complete ms. Length: 3,000-6,500 words.

AUSTRALIAN SCREEN EDUCATION

P.O. Box 2040, St. Kilda West VIC 3182 Australia. (61)(3)9525-5302. Fax: (61)(3)9537-2325. E-mail: assistanteditor@atom.org.au. Web site: www.metromagazine.com.au. **Contact:** Peter Tapp or Zoe Tovey. Quarterly magazine written by and for teachers and students in secondary and primary schools, covering all curriculum areas. Writer's guidelines online.

Nonfiction General interest, interview/profile, reviews, classroom activities. E-mail proposals or complete article. Length: 1,000-3,000 words.

Photos Reviews TIFF/JPEG files.

CATECHIST

Peter Li, Inc., 2621 Dryden Rd., Suite 300, Dayton OH 45439. E-mail: kdotterweich@peterli.com. Web site: www.catechist.com. **Contact:** Kass Dotterweich, editor. **75% freelance written.** Magazine published 7 times/year covering Catholic education, grades K-6. "Our articles target teachers of children in religious education parish programs." Estab. 1961. Circ. 52,000. Pays on publication. Publishes ms an average of 8 months after acceptance. Byline given. Buys first North American serial rights. Editorial lead time 1 year. Submit seasonal material 1 year in advance. Accepts queries by mail, e-mail, fax. Responds in 2 weeks to queries; 2 months to mss. Sample copy for $3.50. Writer's guidelines online.

Nonfiction How-to, personal experience, religious. Special issues: Advent/Christmas (November-December); Sacrament (January). Does not want product profiles. **Buys 15 mss/year.** Query. Length: 500-1,000 words. **Pays negotiable amount.**

Tips "Call the editor with specific questions."

$ $ EARLYCHILDHOOD NEWS

Excelligence Learning Corp., 2 Lower Ragsdale, Suite 200, Monterey CA 93940. (831)333-5771. Fax: (831)333-5595. E-mail: batkinson@excelligencemail.com. Web site: www.earlychildhoodnews.com. **Contact:** Barbara Atkinson, managing editor. **80% freelance written.** Monthly magazine covering early childhood education. Targets teachers and parents of young children (infants to age 8). Estab. 1988. Circ. 55,000. Pays on publication. Publishes ms an average of 2-3 months after acceptance. Byline given. Buys all rights. Editorial lead time 2-4 months. Submit seasonal material 4 months in advance. Accepts queries by mail, e-mail, fax. Responds in 4-6 weeks to queries; 2-4 months to mss. Writer's guidelines online.

Nonfiction Essays, general interest, inspirational, interview/profile, research-based. Special issues: Why Humor is the Best Teacher, Classroom Design (January/February); Promoting Development Through Play (March/April); Sizzling Summer Programs, Summer Reading (May/June); Meeting the Needs of Infants & Toddlers, Safety, Preschool Behavior (August/September); How to Measure Learning, Directors' Choice Awards (October); Crystal Clear Communication with Parents, Music, Teaching Kids with Special Needs (November/December). No personal stories or fiction. **Buys 40-50 mss/year.** Query. Length: 500-1,200 words. **Pays $100-300 for assigned articles; $100-300 for unsolicited articles.**

Poetry "Poems should have a teacher-directed audience." Light verse, traditional. No "poetry not related to children, teachers, or early childhood." **Buys 6 poems/year.** Length: 10-60 lines. **Pays $50-250.**

Tips "Knowing about the publication and the types of articles we publish is greatly appreciated. Query letters are preferred over complete manuscripts."

N $ THE FORENSIC TEACHER

Wide Open Minds Educational Services, P.O. Box 5263, Wilmington DE 19808. E-mail: admin@theforensicteacher.com. Web site: www.theforensicteacher.com. **Contact:** Mark R. Feil, Ed.D., editor. **70% freelance written.** Quarterly magazine covering forensic education. "Our readers are middle, high and post-secondary teachers who are looking for better, easier and more engaging ways to teach forensics. Our writers understand this and are writing from a forensic or educational background, or both." Estab. 2006. Circ. 7,000. Pays 30 days after publication. Publishes ms an average of 6 months after acceptance. Byline given. Buys first North American serial, second serial (reprint), electronic rights. Editorial lead time 6 months. Submit seasonal material 6 months in advance. Accepts queries by mail, e-mail. Accepts simultaneous submissions. Responds in 2 weeks to queries; 2 months to mss. Sample copy for $5. Writer's guidelines online.

Nonfiction How-to, personal experience, photo feature, technical, lesson plans. Does not want poetry, fiction or anything unrelated to medicine, law, forensics or teaching. **Buys 18 mss/year.** Query with or without published clips or send complete ms. Length: 400-2,000 words. **Pays 5¢/word.**

Photos State availability with submission. Reviews GIF/JPEG files/pdf. Buys one-time rights. Negotiates payment individually. Captions required.

Fillers Facts, newsbreaks. **Buys 15/year.** Length: 50-200 words. **Pays 5¢/word.**

Tips "Your article will benefit forensics teachers and their students. It should inform, entertain and enlighten the teacher and the students. Would you read it if you were a busy forensics teacher?"

$ $ HISPANIC OUTLOOK IN HIGHER EDUCATION

210 Route 4 E., Suite 310, Paramus NJ 07652. (201)587-8800, ext 100. Fax: (201)587-9105. E-mail: sloutlook@aol.com. Web site: www.hispanicoutlook.com. Editor: Adalyn Hixson. **Contact:** Sue Lopez-Isa, managing editor. **50% freelance written.** Biweekly magazine. "We're looking for higher education story articles, with a focus on Hispanics and the advancements made by and for Hispanics in higher education." Circ. 28,000. Pays on publication. Publishes ms an average of 2 months after acceptance. Byline given. Editorial lead time 2 months. Submit seasonal material 3 months in advance. Accepts queries by mail, e-mail, fax. Accepts simultaneous submissions. Sample copy for free.

O→ Break with "issues articles such as new laws in higher education."

Nonfiction Historical/nostalgic, interview/profile (of academic or scholar), opinion (on higher education), personal experience, all regarding higher education only. **Buys 20-25 mss/year.** Query with published clips. Length: 1,800-2,200 words. **Pays $500 minimum for assigned articles.** Pays expenses of writers on assignment.

Photos Send photos with submission. Reviews color or b&w prints, digital images must be 300 dpi (call for e-mail photo address). Offers no additional payment for photos accepted with ms.

Tips "Articles explore the Hispanic experience in higher education. Special theme issues address sports, law, health, corporations, heritage, women, and a wide range of similar issues; however, articles need not fall under those umbrellas."

N INSTRUCTOR MAGAZINE

For Teachers of Grades K-8, Scholastic, Inc., P.O. Box 713, New York NY 10013. E-mail: instructor@scholastic.com. Web site: www.scholastic.com/instructor. Magazine 8 times/year geared toward teachers, curriculum coordinators, principals, and supervisors of kindergarten through 8th grade classes. Circ. 200,391. Editorial lead time 4 months. Submit seasonal material 6 months in advance. Accepts queries by mail, e-mail. Sample copy available by calling (866)436-2455. Writer's guidelines online.

Nonfiction Classroom management and practice, education trends and issues, professional development, lesson plans. Query with or without published clips or send complete ms. Length: 800-1,200 words.

Columns/Departments Activities and Tips (for teachers), 250 words; Lesson Units (lesson-planning units on a specific curriculum area or theme), 400-800 words. Send complete ms.

Tips "As you write, think: How can I make this article most useful for teachers? Write in your natural voice. We shy away from wordy, academic prose. Let us know what grade/subject you teach and name and location of your school."

$ $ PTO TODAY

The Magazine for Parent Group Leaders, PTO Today, Inc., 100 Stonewall Blvd., Suite 3, Wrentham MA 02093. (800)644-3561. Fax: (508)384-6108. E-mail: editor@ptotoday.com. Web site: www.ptotoday.com. **Contact:** Craig Bystrynski, editor-in-chief. **65% freelance written.** Magazine published 6 times during the school year covering the work of school parent-teacher groups. "We celebrate the work of school parent volunteers and provide resources to help them do that work more effectively." Estab. 1999. Circ. 80,000. Pays on publication. Publishes ms an average of 2-4 months after acceptance. Byline given. Offers 30% kill fee. Buys first North American serial, electronic, all rights. Editorial lead time 4 months. Submit seasonal material 4 months in advance. Accepts queries by e-mail. Sample copy online. Writer's guidelines by e-mail.

Nonfiction Exposé, general interest, how-to (anything related to PTO/PTA), interview/profile, new product, personal experience. **Buys 40 mss/year.** Query. Length: 600-2,000 words. **Pays 20-40¢/word for assigned articles; $50-500 for unsolicited articles.** Sometimes pays expenses of writers on assignment.

Photos State availability with submission. Buys one-time rights. Negotiates payment individually. Identification of subjects required.

Tips "It's difficult for us to find talented writers with strong experience with parent groups. This experience is a big plus. Also, it helps to review our writer's guidelines before querying."

$ SCHOOLARTS MAGAZINE

50 Portland St., Worcester MA 01608-9959. Fax: (610)683-8229. Web site: www.davis-art.com. **Contact:** Editor. **85% freelance written.** Monthly magazine (September-May), serving arts and craft education profession, K-12, higher education, and museum education programs written by and for art teachers. Estab. 1901. Pays on publication. Publishes ms an average of 3 months after acceptance. Buys all rights. Accepts queries by mail, phone. Responds in 3 months to queries. Writer's guidelines online.

Break in with "professional quality photography to illustrate art lessons."

Nonfiction Articles on art and craft activities in schools. Should include description and photos of activity in progress, as well as examples of finished artwork. Query or send complete ms and SASE. Length: 600-1,400 words. **Pays $30-150.**

The online version contains material not found in the print edition.

Tips "We prefer articles on actual art projects or techniques done by students in actual classroom situations. Philosophical and theoretical aspects of art and art education are usually handled by our contributing editors. Our articles are reviewed and accepted on merit and each is tailored to meet our needs. Keep in mind that art teachers want practical tips above all—more hands-on information than academic theory. Write your article with the accompanying photographs in hand." The most frequent mistakes made by writers are "bad visual material (photographs, drawings) submitted with articles, a lack of complete descriptions of art processes, and no rationale behind programs or activities. Familiarity with the field of art education is essential. Review recent issues of *SchoolArts*."

$ $ $ TEACHER MAGAZINE

Editorial Projects in Education, 6935 Arlington Rd., Suite 100, Bethesda MD 20814. (310)280-3100. Fax: (301)280-3150. Web site: www.teachermagazine.org. **Contact:** Scott Cech, executive editor. **40% freelance written.** Magazine published 6 times/year covering the teaching profession. "One of the major thrusts of the current school reform movement is to make teaching a true profession. *Teacher Magazine* plays a central role in that effort. It is a national communications network that provides teacher-leaders with the information they need to be better practitioners." Estab. 1989. Circ. 120,000. Pays on publication. Publishes ms an average of 1 month after acceptance. Byline given. Offers 25% kill fee. Buys first North American serial, electronic rights. Editorial lead time 3 months. Submit seasonal material 4 months in advance. Accepts queries by mail, fax. Responds in 2 months to queries. Sample copy online. Writer's guidelines free.

Nonfiction Book excerpts, essays, interview/profile, personal experience, photo feature, investigative. **Buys 56 mss/year.** Query with published clips. Length: 600-5,000 words. **Pays 50¢/word.** Sometimes pays expenses of writers on assignment.

Photos State availability with submission. Reviews contact sheets, transparencies, prints. Buys one-time rights. Negotiates payment individually. Identification of subjects, model releases required.

Columns/Departments Current events, forum. Query with published clips. **Pays 50¢/word.**

Tips "Sending us a well-researched query letter accompanied by clips that demonstrate you can tell a good story is the best way to break into *Teacher Magazine*. Describe the characters in your proposed article. What scenes do you hope to include in the piece?"

$ $ $ $ TEACHING TOLERANCE

The Southern Poverty Law Center, 400 Washington Ave., Montgomery AL 36104. (334)956-8200. Fax: (334)956-8488. Web site: www.teachingtolerance.org. **30% freelance written.** Semiannual magazine. "*Teaching Tolerance* is dedicated to helping K-12 teachers promote tolerance and understanding between widely diverse groups of students. Includes articles, teaching ideas, and reviews of other resources available to educators." Estab. 1991. Circ. 600,000. **Pays on acceptance.** Byline given. Buys all rights. Editorial lead time 6 months. Submit seasonal material 6 months in advance. Accepts queries by mail, fax. Sample copy and writer's guidelines free or online.

Nonfiction Essays, how-to (classroom techniques), personal experience (classroom), photo feature. "No jargon, rhetoric or academic analysis. No theoretical discussions on the pros/cons of multicultural education." **Buys 2-4 mss/year.** Submit outlines or complete mss. Length: 1,000-3,000 words. **Pays $500-3,000 for assigned articles.** Pays expenses of writers on assignment.

Photos State availability with submission. Reviews contact sheets, transparencies. Buys one-time rights. Captions, identification of subjects required.

Columns/Departments Essays (personal reflection, how-to, school program), 400-800 words; Idea Exchange (special projects, successful anti-bias activities), 250-500 words; Student Writings (short essays dealing with diversity, tolerance, justice), 300-500 words. **Buys 8-12 mss/year.** Query with published clips. **Pays $50-1,000.**

The online magazine carries original content not found in the print edition and includes writer's guidelines. Contact: Brian Willoughby, managing editor.

Tips "We want lively, simple, concise writing. The writing style should be descriptive and reflective, showing the strength of programs dealing successfully with diversity by employing clear descriptions of real scenes and interactions, and by using quotes from teachers and students. We ask that prospective writers study previous issues of the magazine before making submission. Most open to articles that have a strong classroom focus. We are interested in approaches to teaching tolerance and promoting understanding that really work—approaches we might not have heard of. We want to inform our readers; we also want to inspire and encourage them. We know what's happening nationally; we want to know what's happening in your neighborhood classroom."

ELECTRONICS & COMMUNICATION

$ $ THE ACUTA JOURNAL OF TELECOMMUNICATIONS IN HIGHER EDUCATION

ACUTA, 152 W. Zandale Dr., Suite 200, Lexington KY 40503-2486. (859)278-3338. Fax: (859)278-3268. E-mail: pscott@acuta.org. Web site: www.acuta.org. **Contact:** Patricia Scott, communications manager. **20% freelance written.** Quarterly professional association journal covering telecommunications in higher education. "Our audience includes, primarily, middle to upper management in the telecommunications department on college/university campuses. They are highly skilled, technology-oriented professionals who provide data, voice, and video communications services for residential and academic purposes." Estab. 1997. Circ. 2,200. Pays on publication. Publishes ms an average of 6 months after acceptance. Byline given. Buys first rights. Editorial lead time 6 months. Accepts queries by mail, e-mail, fax, phone. Responds in 1 month to queries; 2 months to mss. Sample copy for 9×12 SAE and 6 first-class stamps. Writer's guidelines free.

Break in with a campus study or case profile. "Contact me with your idea for a story. Convince me you can handle the level of technical depth required."

Nonfiction "Each issue has a focus. Available with writer's guidelines. We are only interested in articles described in article types." How-to (telecom), technical (telecom), case study, college/university application of technology. **Buys 6-8 mss/year.** Query. Length: 1,200-4,000 words. **Pays 8-10¢/word.** Sometimes pays expenses of writers on assignment.

Photos State availability with submission. Reviews prints. Offers no additional payment for photos accepted with ms. Captions, model releases required.

Tips "Our audience expects every article to be relevant to telecommunications on the college/university campus, whether it is related to technology, facilities, or management. Writers must read back issues to understand this focus and the level of technicality we expect."

AMERICA'S NETWORK

Advanstar Communications, 201 E. Sandpointe Ave., Suite 500, Santa Ana CA 92707. Web site: www.americasnetwork.com. Magazine published 18 times/year. Edited for telecommunications executives and professionals who are responsible for the design, construction, sales, purchase, operations and maintenance of telephone/telecom systems. Circ. 43,533. Editorial lead time 3 months.

COMPUTERWORLD

The Voice of IT Management, IDG, Inc., One Speen St., Framingham MA 01701. (508)879-0700. Web site: www.computerworld.com. **Contact:** Editor. Weekly magazine. "We provide readers with a lively variety of everything from the latest IT news, in-depth analysis and feature stories, to special reports, case studies, industry updates, product information, advice and opinion." Estab. 1967. Circ. 180,000.

- Contact specific editor.

Nonfiction How-to, opinion. Query.

N $ $ DIGITAL OUTPUT

The Only Magazine Dedicated to Capture, Creation, Output and Finishing, The Doyle Group, 5150 Palm Valley Rd., Suite 103, Ponte Vedra Beach FL 32082. (904)285-6020. Fax: (904)285-9944. E-mail: cmason@digitaloutput.net. Web site: www.digitaloutput.net. **Contact:** Cathy Mason, editor-in-chief. **70% freelance written.** Monthly magazine covering electronic prepress, desktop publishing, and digital imaging, with articles ranging from digital capture and design to electronic prepress and digital printing. "*Digital Output* is a national business publication for electronic publishers and digital imagers, providing monthly articles which examine the latest technologies and digital methods and discuss how to profit from them. Our readers include service bureaus, prepress and reprographic houses, designers, commercial printers, wide-format printers, ad agencies, corporate communications, sign shops, and others." Estab. 1994. Circ. 30,000. Pays on publication. Publishes ms an average of 2 months after acceptance. Byline given. Offers 10-20% kill fee. Buys one-time rights including electronic rights for archival posting. Editorial lead time 3 months. Submit seasonal material 3 months in advance. Accepts queries by mail, e-mail. Responds in 3 weeks to queries; 1 month to mss. Sample copy for $4.50 or online.

Nonfiction How-to, interview/profile, technical, case studies. **Buys 36 mss/year.** Query with published clips or hyperlinks to posted clips. Length: 1,500-4,000 words. **Pays $250-600.**

Photos Send photos with submission.

Tips "Our readers are graphic arts professionals. The freelance writers we use are deeply immersed in the technology of commercial printing, desktop publishing, digital imaging, color management, PDF workflow, inkjet printing, and similar topics."

N $ $ ELECTRONIC SERVICING & TECHNOLOGY

The Professional Magazine for Electronics and Computer Servicing, P.O. Box 12487, Overland Park KS 66282-2487. (913)492-4857. Fax: (913)492-4857. E-mail: cpersedit@aol.com. **Contact:** Conrad Persson, editor. **80% freelance written.** Monthly magazine for service technicians, field service personnel, and avid servicing enthusiasts, who service audio, video, and computer equipment. Estab. 1950. Circ. 15,000. Pays on publication. Publishes ms an average of 4 months after acceptance. Byline given. Buys one-time rights. Editorial lead time 2 months. Accepts queries by mail, e-mail, fax, phone. Accepts simultaneous submissions. Responds in 1 month to queries; 2 months to mss. Sample copy for free. Writer's guidelines free.

- Break in by knowing how to service consumer electronics products and being able to explain it in writing in good English.

Nonfiction Book excerpts, how-to (service consumer electronics), new product, technical. **Buys 40 mss/year.** Query or send complete ms. **Pays $50/page.**

Reprints Send ms with rights for sale noted and information about when and where the material previously appeared.

Photos Send photos with submission. Buys one-time rights. Offers no additional payment for photos accepted with ms.

Columns/Departments Business Corner (business tips); Computer Corner (computer servicing tips); Video Corner (understanding/servicing TV and video), all 1,000-2,000 words. **Buys 30 mss/year.** Query, or send complete ms. **Pays $100-300.**

Tips "Writers should have a strong background in electronics, especially consumer electronics servicing. Understand the information needs of consumer electronics service technicians, and be able to write articles that address specific areas of those needs."

N HOME THEATER

Primedia Enthusiast Group, 6420 Wilshire Blvd., Los Angeles CA 90048-5502. (323)782-2000. Fax: (323)782-2080. E-mail: htletters@primedia.com. Web site: www.hometheatermag.com. Executive Editor: Adrienne Maxwell. **Contact:** Maureen Jenson, editor. Monthly magazine covering audio, video, high-end components, and

movies and music. Covers the home theater lifestyle. Estab. 1995. Circ. 109,422. Accepts queries by e-mail. Sample copy for $4.95.
Nonfiction Send résumé.
Columns/Departments Query with published clips.

N $ $ $ SOUND & VIDEO CONTRACTOR

Primedia Business, 6400 Hollis St., Suite 12, Emeryville CA 94608. (510)985-3203. Fax: (510)653-5142. E-mail: mjohnson@primediabusiness.com. **Contact:** Mark Johnson, editor. **60% freelance written.** Monthly magazine covering "professional audio, video, security, acoustical design, sales, and marketing." Estab. 1983. Circ. 24,000. **Pays on acceptance.** Publishes ms an average of 3 months after acceptance. Byline given. Buys one-time, all rights. Editorial lead time 3 months. Accepts queries by mail, e-mail, fax, phone. Accepts simultaneous submissions. Responds ASAP to queries and to mss. Sample copy and writer's guidelines free.
Nonfiction Historical/nostalgic, how-to, photo feature, technical, professional audio/video applications, installations, product reviews. No opinion pieces, advertorial, interview/profile, exposé/gossip. **Buys 60 mss/year.** Query. Length: 1,000-2,500 words. **Pays $200-1,200 for assigned articles; $200-650 for unsolicited articles.**
Reprints Accepts previously published submissions.
Photos Send photos with submission. Reviews transparencies, prints. Offers no additional payment for photos accepted with ms. Identification of subjects required.
Columns/Departments Security Technology Review (technical install information); Sales & Marketing (techniques for installation industry); Video Happenings (Pro video/projection/storage technical info), all 1,500 words. **Buys 30 mss/year.** Query. **Pays $200-350.**
Tips "We want materials and subject matter that would be of interest to audio/video/security/low-voltage product installers/contractors/designers professionals. If the piece allows our readers to save time, money and/or increases their revenues, then we have reached our goals. Highly technical is desirable."

$ $ SQL SERVER MAGAZINE

Penton Media, 221 E. 29th St., Loveland CO 80538. (970)663-4700. Fax: (970)667-2321. E-mail: articles@sqlmag.com. Web site: www.sqlmag.com. **35% freelance written.** Monthly magazine covering Microsoft SQL Server. "*SQL Server Magazine* is the only magazine completely devoted to helping developers and DBAs master new and emerging SQL Server technologies and issues. It provides practical advice and lots of code examples for SQL Server developers and administrators, and includes how-to articles, tips, tricks, and programming techniques offered by SQL Server experts." Estab. 1999. Circ. 20,000. Pays on publication. Publishes ms an average of 6 months after acceptance. Byline given. Offers $100 kill fee. Buys all rights. Editorial lead time 4+ months. Accepts queries by mail, e-mail. Responds in 6 weeks to queries; 2-3 months to mss. Sample copy and writer's guidelines online.
Nonfiction How-to, technical, SQL Server administration and programming. Nothing promoting third-party products or companies. **Buys 25-35 mss/year.** Query with or without published clips or send complete ms. Length: 1,800-3,000 words. **Pays $200 for feature articles; $500 for Focus articles.** Pays in contributor copies if the writer requests the substitution.
Columns/Departments R2R Editor. Reader to Reader (helpful SQL Server hints and tips from readers), 200-400 words. **Buys 6-12 mss/year.** Send complete ms. **Pays $50.**
Tips "Read back issues and make sure that your proposed article doesn't overlap previous coverage. When proposing articles, state specifically how your article would contain new information compared to previously published information, and what benefit your information would be to *SQL Server Magazine*'s readership."

ENERGY & UTILITIES

$ $ ALTERNATIVE ENERGY RETAILER

Zackin Publications, Inc., P.O. Box 2180, Waterbury CT 06722. (800)325-6745. Fax: (203)755-3480. E-mail: griffin@aer-online.com. Web site: www.aer-online.com/aer/. **Contact:** Michael Griffin, editor. **5% freelance written.** Prefers to work with published/established writers. Monthly magazine on selling home hearth products—chiefly solid fuel and gas-burning appliances. "We seek detailed how-to tips for retailers to improve business. Most freelance material purchased is about retailers and how they succeed." Estab. 1980. Circ. 10,000. Pays on publication. Publishes ms an average of 2 months after acceptance. Buys first North American serial rights. Submit seasonal material 4 months in advance. Accepts queries by mail, e-mail, fax, phone. Responds in 2 weeks to queries. Sample copy for 9×12 SAE and 4 first-class stamps. Writer's guidelines online.

O→ Submit articles that focus on hearth market trends and successful sales techniques.

Nonfiction How-to (improve retail profits and business know-how), interview/profile (of successful retailers in this field). No "general business articles not adapted to this industry." **Buys 10 mss/year.** Query. Length: 1,000 words. **Pays $200.**

Photos State availability with submission. Reviews color transparencies. Buys one-time rights. Pays $25-125 maximum for 5×7 b&w prints. Identification of subjects required.

Tips "A freelancer can best break into our publication with features about readers (retailers). Stick to details about what has made this person a success."

$ $ ELECTRICAL APPARATUS

The Magazine of Electromechanical & Electronic Application & Maintenance, Barks Publications, Inc., 400 N. Michigan Ave., Chicago IL 60611-4198. (312)321-9440. Fax: (312)321-1288. **Contact:** Elsie Dickson, editorial director. Monthly magazine for persons working in electrical and electronic maintenance, in industrial plants and service and sales centers, who install and service electrical motors, transformers, generators, controls, and related equipment. Estab. 1967. Circ. 16,000. Pays on publication. Publishes ms an average of 1 month after acceptance. Byline given. Buys all rights unless other arrangements made. Accepts queries by mail, fax. Responds in 1 week to queries; 2 weeks to mss.

Nonfiction Technical. Length: 1,500-2,500 words. **Pays $250-500 for assigned articles.**

Tips "All feature articles are assigned to staff and contributing editors and correspondents. Professionals interested in appointments as contributing editors and correspondents should submit résumé and article outlines, including illustration suggestions. Writers should be competent with a camera, which should be described in résumé. Technical expertise is absolutely necessary, preferably an E.E. degree, or practical experience. We are also book publishers and some of the material in *EA* is now in book form, bringing the authors royalties. Also publishes an annual directory, subtitled *ElectroMechanical Bench Reference.*"

$ $ ELECTRICAL BUSINESS

CLB Media, Inc., 240 Edward St., Aurora ON L4G 3S9 Canada. (905)727-0077. Fax: (905)727-0017. E-mail: acapkun@clbmedia.ca. Web site: www.ebmag.com. **Contact:** Anthony Capkun, editor. **35% freelance written.** Tabloid published 10 times/year covering the Canadian electrical industry. "*Electrical Business* targets electrical contractors and electricians. It provides practical information readers can use right away in their work and for running their business and assets." Estab. 1964. Circ. 18,097. **Pays on acceptance.** Publishes ms an average of 1-2 months after acceptance. Byline given. Offers 50% kill fee. Buys simultaneous rights. Editorial lead time 3 months. Submit seasonal material 6 months in advance. Accepts queries by e-mail, phone. Accepts simultaneous submissions. Responds in 1 month to queries; 1 month to mss. Sample copy online. Writer's guidelines free.

Nonfiction How-to, technical. Special issues: Summer Blockbuster issue (June/July); Special Homebuilders' issue (November/December). **Buys 15 mss/year.** Query. Length: 800-1,200 words. **Pays 40¢/word.** Sometimes pays expenses of writers on assignment.

Photos State availability with submission. Reviews GIF/JPEG files. Buys simultaneous rights. Negotiates payment individually. Captions, identification of subjects, model releases required.

Columns/Departments Atlantic Focus (stories from Atlantic Canada); Western Focus (stories from Western Canada, including Manitoba); Trucks for the Trade (articles pertaining to the vehicles used by electrical contractors); Tools for the Trade (articles pertaining to tools used by contractors); all 800 words. **Buys 6 mss/year.** Query. **Pays 40¢/word.**

Tips "Call me, and we'll talk about what I need, and how you can provide it. Stories must have Canadian content."

$ $ FAR NORTH OIL & GAS

Up Here Publishing, Ltd., #800 4920 52nd St., Yellowknife NT X1A 3T1 Canada. (867)920-4343. Fax: (867)873-2844. E-mail: jake@uphere.ca. Web site: www.fnog.ca. Managing Editor: Darren Campbell. **Contact:** Jake Kennedy, editor. **60% freelance written.** Quarterly magazine covering the oil and gas industry in the far North (Alaska, Yukon, NWT, Nunavut). "*Far North Gas & Oil* is the leading authority on the oil and gas industry in the far North of Canada and the U.S." Estab. 1998. Circ. 10,000. Pays on publication. Publishes ms an average of 3 months after acceptance. Byline given. Offers 50% kill fee. Buys first, electronic rights. Editorial lead time 1 year. Submit seasonal material 6 months in advance. Accepts queries by mail, e-mail, fax. Responds in 2 weeks to queries; 1 month to mss. Sample copy for free.

Nonfiction Essays, general interest, historical/nostalgic, interview/profile, new product, opinion, photo feature, technical. **Buys 10 mss/year.** Query. Length: 1,800-2,500 words. **Pays 30-50¢/word.** Sometimes pays expenses of writers on assignment.

Photos State availability with submission. Reviews contact sheets, negatives, transparencies, prints, GIF/JPEG files. Buys one-time rights. Negotiates payment individually. Captions, identification of subjects required.

Columns/Departments Border Patrol (updates/opinions on Alaska's oil and gas), 1,100 words; Opinion (opinions on oil and gas industry), 1,100 words; Final Say (parting thoughts, back page), 800 words. **Buys 12 mss/year.** Query. **Pays $200-400.**

Tips "Query with story ideas, and be familiar with the magazine. You don't need expertise in the oil/gas industry, but you do need to be a good writer."

$ $ PUBLIC POWER

Dept. WM, 2301 M St. NW, Washington DC 20037-1484. (202)467-2948. Fax: (202)467-2910. E-mail: jlabella@appanet.org. Web site: www.appanet.org. **Contact:** Jeanne LaBella, editor. **60% freelance written.** Prefers to work with published/established writers. Bimonthly trade journal. Estab. 1942. **Pays on acceptance.** Publishes ms an average of 3 months after acceptance. Byline given. Accepts queries by mail, e-mail, fax. Responds in 6 months to queries. Sample copy and writer's guidelines free.

Nonfiction Features on municipal and other local publicly owned electric utilities. **Pays $600 and up.**

Photos Reviews electronic photos (minimum 300 dpi at reproduction size), transparencies, slides, and prints.

Tips "We look for writers who are familiar with energy policy issues."

$ $ $ TEXAS CO-OP POWER

Texas Electric Cooperatives, Inc., 2550 S. IH-35, Austin TX 78704. (512)454-0311. Web site: www.texascooppower.com. Editor: Kaye Northcott. Managing Editor: Carol Moczygemba. **50% freelance written.** Monthly magazine covering rural and suburban Texas life, people, and places. "*Texas Co-op Power* provides 1 million households and businesses educational and technical information about electric cooperatives in a high-quality and entertaining format to promote the general welfare of cooperatives, their member-owners, and the areas in which they serve." Estab. 1948. Circ. 1 million. **Pays on acceptance.** Publishes ms an average of 6 months after acceptance. Byline given. Buys first, electronic rights. Editorial lead time 4-5 months. Submit seasonal material 6 months in advance. Accepts queries by mail, e-mail, fax. Accepts simultaneous submissions. Responds in 1 month to queries; 3 months to mss. Sample copy online. Writer's guidelines for #10 SASE.

Nonfiction General interest, historical/nostalgic, interview/profile, photo feature, travel. **Buys 30 mss/year.** Query with published clips. Length: 800-1,200 words. **Pays $400-1,000.** Sometimes pays expenses of writers on assignment.

Photos State availability with submission. Reviews transparencies, prints. Buys one-time rights. Negotiates payment individually. Identification of subjects, model releases required.

Tips "We're looking for Texas-related, rural-based articles, often first-person, always lively and interesting."

ENGINEERING & TECHNOLOGY

$ $ $ ☐ CABLING NETWORKING SYSTEMS

12 Concorde Place, Suite 800, North York ON M3C 4J2 Canada. (416)510-6752. Fax: (416)510-5134. E-mail: pbarker@cnsmagazine.com. Web site: www.cablingsystems.com. **Contact:** Paul Barker. **50% freelance written.** Magazine published 8 times/year covering structured cabling/telecommunications industry. "*Cabling Systems* is written for engineers, designers, contractors, and end users who design, specify, purchase, install, test and maintain structured cabling and telecommunications products and systems." Estab. 1998. Circ. 11,000. Pays on publication. Publishes ms an average of 1 month after acceptance. Byline given. Buys all rights. Editorial lead time 3 months. Submit seasonal material 1 month in advance. Accepts queries by mail, e-mail, phone. Accepts simultaneous submissions. Sample copy online. Writer's guidelines free.

Nonfiction Technical (case studies, features). "No reprints or previously written articles. All articles are assigned by editor based on query or need of publication." **Buys 12 mss/year.** Query with published clips. Length: 1,500-2,500 words. **Pays 40-50¢/word.** Sometimes pays expenses of writers on assignment.

Photos State availability with submission. Reviews contact sheets, prints. Negotiates payment individually. Captions, identification of subjects required.

Columns/Departments Focus on Engineering/Design; Focus on Installation; Focus on Maintenance/Testing, all 1,500 words. **Buys 7 mss/year.** Query with published clips. **Pays 40-50¢/word.**

Tips "Visit our Web site to see back issues, and visit links on our Web site for background."

$ $ $ ☐ CANADIAN CONSULTING ENGINEER

Business Information Group, 12 Condorde Place, Suite 800, Toronto ON M3C 4J2 Canada. (416)510-5119. Fax: (416)510-5134. E-mail: bparsons@ccemag.com. Web site: www.canadianconsultingengineer.com. **Contact:** Bronwen Parsons, editor. **20% freelance written.** Bimonthly magazine covering consulting engineering in private practice. Estab. 1958. Circ. 8,900. Pays on publication. Publishes ms an average of 4 months after acceptance. Byline given depending on length of story. Offers 50% kill fee. Buys first North American serial rights. Editorial lead time 6 months. Responds in 3 months to mss. Sample copy for free.

• Canadian content only. Impartial editorial required.

Nonfiction Historical/nostalgic, new product, technical, engineering/construction projects, environmental/construction issues. **Buys 8-10 mss/year.** Length: 300-1,500 words. **Pays $200-1,000 (Canadian).** Sometimes pays expenses of writers on assignment.

Photos State availability with submission. Buys one-time rights. Negotiates payment individually.

Columns/Departments Export (selling consulting engineering services abroad); Management (managing consulting engineering businesses); On-Line (trends in CAD systems); Employment, all 800 words. **Buys 4 mss/year.** Query with published clips. **Pays $250-400.**

$ $ COMPOSITES MANUFACTURING MAGAZINE

The Official Publication of the American Composites Manufacturers Association, (formerly *Composites Fabrication Magazine*), American Composites Manufacturers Association, 1010 N. Glebe Rd., Suite 450, Arlington VA 22201. (703)525-0511. Fax: (703)525-0743. E-mail: arusnak@acmanet.org. Web site: www.cfmagazine.org. **Contact:** Andrew Rusnak, editor. Monthly magazine covering any industry that uses reinforced composites: marine, aerospace, infrastructure, automotive, transportation, corrosion, architecture, tub and shower, sports, and recreation. "Primarily, we publish educational pieces, the how-to of the shop environment. We also publish marketing, business trends, and economic forecasts relevant to the composites industry." Estab. 1979. Circ. 12,000. **Pays on acceptance.** Publishes ms an average of 2-3 months after acceptance. Byline given. Buys all rights. Editorial lead time 2 months. Accepts queries by e-mail. Accepts previously published material. Accepts simultaneous submissions. Responds in 1 week to queries; 1 month to mss. Sample copy for free. Writer's guidelines by e-mail.

Nonfiction How-to (composites manufacturing), new product, technical, marketing, related business trends and forecasts. Special issues: "Each January we publish a World Market Report where we cover all niche markets and all geographic areas relevant to the composites industry. Freelance material will be considered strongly for this issue. No need to query company or personal profiles unless there is an extremely unique or novel angle." **Buys 5-10 mss/year.** Query. Length: 1,500-4,000 words. **Pays 20-40¢/word (negotiable).** Sometimes pays expenses of writers on assignment.

Columns/Departments Query. **Pays $300-350.**

Tips "The best way to break into the magazine is to empathize with the entrepreneurial and technical background of readership, and come up with an exclusive, original, creative story idea. We pride ourselves on not looking or acting like any other trade publication (composites industry or otherwise). Our editor is very open to suggestions, but they must be unique. Don't waste his time with canned articles dressed up to look exclusive. This is the best way to get on the 'immediate rejection list.' "

N $ $ INTERFACE TECH NEWS

Northern New England's Technology Newspaper, Millyard Communications, Inc., 670 N. Commercial St., Suite 110, Manchester NH 03101. (603)626-6354. Fax: (603)626-6359. E-mail: msaturley@millyardcommunications.com. Web site: www.interfacetechnews.com. **Contact:** Michelle Saturley, managing editor. **85% freelance written.** Monthly newspaper covering people, companies and cutting edge technology in Northern New England. "Stories must have a local, northern New England angle. Who are the people shaping tomorrow's tech industry? Why should you care?" Estab. 1997. Circ. 11,000. Pays on publication. Publishes ms an average of 2-3 months after acceptance. Byline given. Offers 25% kill fee. Buys first North American serial rights. Editorial lead time 3 months. Submit seasonal material 3 months in advance. Accepts queries by mail, e-mail. Accepts previously published material. Responds in 2 weeks to queries. Sample copy for free. Writer's guidelines free.

Nonfiction How-to, interview/profile, new product, opinion, technical, case studies. Does not want stories about companies, people or products not based in northern New England. **Buys 60 mss/year.** Query with published clips. Length: 600-1,500 words. **Pays $150-300.** Sometimes pays expenses of writers on assignment.

Photos Contact Greg Duval, creative director. Send photos with submission. Reviews GIF/JPEG files. Buys one-time rights. Offers $25-50/photo. Identification of subjects required.

Columns/Departments Industry Watch (exploring tech advancements in specific industries), 600-800 words; From the Bench (case law, legislation, lobbyist activity), 600-800 words; Tech Download (explanation of bleeding-edge tech), 800 words; Interface Case Study (in-depth look at a problem solved by technology), 800-900 words. **Buys 50 mss/year.** Query with published clips. **Pays $200-250.**

Tips "We usually start off new writers with a shorter piece, around 600 words. If they work out, we start assigning longer stories. Experience in journalism and a working knowledge of tech required."

LASER FOCUS WORLD MAGAZINE

PennWell, 98 Spit Brook Rd., Nashua NH 03062-2801. (603)891-0123. Fax: (603)891-0574. Web site: www.laserfocusworld.com. Associate Publisher: Stephen G. Anderson. **Contact:** Carol Settino, managing editor. **1% freelance written.** Monthly magazine for physicists, scientists, and engineers involved in the research and development, design, manufacturing, and applications of lasers, laser systems, and all other segments of optoelectronic technologies. Estab. 1968. Circ. 66,000. Publishes ms an average of 6 months after acceptance. Byline given unless anonymity requested. Buys all rights. Accepts queries by mail, e-mail, fax, phone. Responds in 1 month to queries. Sample copy for free. Writer's guidelines online.

- Check online guidelines for specific contacts.

Nonfiction Lasers, laser systems, fiberoptics, optics, detectors, sensors, imaging, and other optoelectronic materials, components, instrumentation, and systems. "Each article should serve our reader's need by either stimulating ideas, increasing technical competence, or improving design capabilities in the following areas: natural light and radiation sources, artificial light and radiation sources, light modulators, optical materials and components, image detectors, energy detectors, information displays, image processing, information storage and processing, subsystem and system testing, support equipment, and other related areas. No flighty prose, material not written for our readership, or irrelevant material. Query first with a clear statement and outline of why the article would be important to our readers."

Photos Drawings: Rough drawings accepted and finished by staff technical illustrator. Send photos with submission. Reviews 4×5 color transparencies, 8×10 b&w glossies.

Tips "The writer has a better chance of breaking in at our publication with short articles because shorter articles are easier to schedule, but they must address more carefully our requirements for technical coverage. Most of our submitted materials come from technical experts in the areas we cover. The most frequent mistake made by writers in completing articles for us is that the articles are too commercial, i.e., emphasize a given product or technology from one company. Also, articles are not the right technical depth, too thin, or too scientific."

$ $ LD+A

Lighting Design & Application, Illuminating Engineering Society of North America, 120 Wall St., 17th Floor, New York NY 10005. (212)248-5000. Fax: (212)248-5017. E-mail: ptarricone@iesna.org. Web site: www.iesna.org. **Contact:** Paul Tarricone, editor. **10% freelance written.** Monthly magazine. "*LD+A* is geared to professionals in lighting design and the lighting field in architecture, retail, entertainment, etc." Estab. 1971. Circ. 10,000. **Pays on acceptance.** Publishes ms an average of 4 months after acceptance. Byline given. Buys all rights. Editorial lead time 2 months. Submit seasonal material 4 months in advance. Accepts queries by mail, e-mail, fax, phone. Accepts simultaneous submissions. Responds in 2 weeks to queries. Sample copy for free.

Nonfiction "Every year we have entertainment, outdoor, retail and arts, and exhibits issues." Historical/nostalgic, how-to, opinion, personal experience, photo feature, technical. "No articles blatantly promoting a product, company, or individual." **Buys 6-10 mss/year.** Query. Length: 1,500-2,200 words.

Photos Send photos with submission. Reviews JPEG/TIFF files. Offers no additional payment for photos accepted with ms. Captions required.

Columns/Departments Essay by Invitation (industry trends), 1,200 words. Query. **Does not pay for columns.**

Tips "Most of our features detail the ins and outs of a specific lighting project. From museums to stadiums and highways, *LD+A* gives its readers an in-depth look at how the designer(s) reached their goals."

$ $ $ MINNESOTA TECHNOLOGY

Inside Technology and Manufacturing Business, Minnesota Technology, Inc., 111 Third Ave. S., Minneapolis MN 55401. (612)373-2900. Fax: (612)373-2901. E-mail: editor@mntech.org. Web site: mntechnologymag.com. **Contact:** Chris Mikko, editor. **90% freelance written.** Magazine published 5 times/year. "*Minnesota Technology* is read 5 times a year by owners and top management of Minnesota's technology and manufacturing companies. The magazine covers technology trends and issues, global trade, management techniques, and finance. We profile new and growing companies, new products, and the innovators and entrepreneurs of Minnesota's technology sector." Estab. 1991. Circ. 16,000. Pays on publication. Publishes ms an average of 3 months after acceptance. Byline given. Offers 10% kill fee. Buys first North American serial rights for print and Web version of magazine. Editorial lead time 1 month. Submit seasonal material 1 year in advance. Accepts queries by mail, e-mail. Writer's guidelines online.

Nonfiction General interest, how-to, interview/profile. **Buys 60 mss/year.** Query with published clips. **Pays $150-1,000.**

Columns/Departments Feature Well (Q&A format, provocative ideas from Minnesota business and industry leaders), 2,000 words; Up Front (mini profiles, anecdotal news items), 250-500 words. Query with published clips.

$ $ MINORITY ENGINEER

An Equal Opportunity Career Publication for Professional and Graduating Minority Engineers, Equal Opportunity Publications, Inc., 445 Broad Hollow Rd., Suite 425, Melville NY 11747. (631)421-9421. Fax: (516)421-0359. E-mail: jschneider@eop.com. Web site: www.eop.com. **Contact:** James Schneider, editor. **60% freelance written.** Prefers to work with published/established writers. Triannual magazine covering career guidance for minority engineering students and minority professional engineers. Estab. 1969. Circ. 15,000. Pays on publication. Publishes ms an average of 6 months after acceptance. Byline given. Buys first rights. Accepts queries by mail, e-mail, fax, phone. Accepts simultaneous submissions. Sample copy and writer's guidelines for 9×12 SAE with 5 first-class stamps.

Nonfiction "We're interested in articles dealing with career guidance and job opportunities for minority engineers." Book excerpts, general interest (on specific minority engineering concerns), how-to (land a job, keep a job, etc.), interview/profile (minority engineer role models), opinion (problems of ethnic minorities), personal experience (student and career experiences), technical (on career fields offering opportunities for minority engineers), articles on job search techniques, role models. No general information. Query. Length: 1,000-2,000 words. **Pays 10¢/word.** Sometimes pays expenses of writers on assignment.

Reprints Send ms with rights for sale noted and information about when and where the material previously appeared. Pays 100% of amount paid for an original article.

Photos State availability with submission.

Tips "Articles should focus on career guidance, role model and industry prospects for minority engineers. Prefer articles related to careers, not politically or socially sensitive."

N PROFESSIONAL SURVEYOR MAGAZINE

Reed Business Geo, Inc., 100 Tuscanny Drive, Frederick MD 21702-5958. (301)682-6101. Fax: (301)682-6105. E-mail: psm@gitcamerica.com. Web site: www.profsurv.com. Tom Gibson, editor. **Contact:** Tom Gibson, editor. **50% freelance written.** Monthly magazine Surveying. This publication covers all facets of surveying and related activities such as satellite positioning (GPS), laser scanning, remote sensing, photogrammetry and mapping. The audience is mainly surveyors. Estab. 1982. Circ. 40,000. Pays on publication. Publishes ms an average of 2 months after acceptance. Byline given. Buys first North American serial, second serial (reprint) rights. Editorial lead time 3 months. Accepts queries by e-mail. Responds in 2 weeks to queries; 1 month to mss. Sample copy online. Writer's guidelines not available.Book excerpts, general interest, historical/nostalgic, how-to, humor, interview/profile, new product, opinion, personal experience, technical, case histories. Special issues: Aerial Mapping Supplement. Length: 1000-2000 words. **Pays $300-500 for assigned articles.** Sometimes pays expenses of writers on assignment. Reviews GIF/JPEG files. offers no additional money for photos. Captions required.

Columns/Departments Shelly Cox, managing editor. Book Review, Aerial Perspective, 3D Scanning, Business Angle (all 1,250 words). **Buys 50 mss/year.** Query. **Pays $$200-$400.**

Tips "For features, we're always looking for surveying-related case histories or discussions of new technology. We also seek contributors for our columns."

$ $ WOMAN ENGINEER

An Equal Opportunity Career Publication for Graduating Women and Experienced Professionals, Equal Opportunity Publications, Inc., 445 Broad Hollow Rd., Suite 425, Melville NY 11747. (631)421-9421. Fax: (631)421-0359. E-mail: lrusso@eop.com. Web site: www.eop.com. **Contact:** Lana Russo, editor. **60% freelance written.** Works with a small number of new/unpublished writers each year. Triannual magazine covering career guidance for women engineering students and professional women engineers. Estab. 1968. Circ. 16,000. Pays on publication. Publishes ms an average of 1 year after acceptance. Byline given. Buys first North American serial rights. Accepts queries by e-mail. Responds in 3 months to queries. Sample copy and writer's guidelines free.

Nonfiction "Interested in articles dealing with career guidance and job opportunities for women engineers. Looking for manuscripts showing how to land an engineering position and advance professionally. We want features on job-search techniques, engineering disciplines offering career opportunities to women; companies with career advancement opportunities for women; problems facing women engineers and how to cope with such problems; and role-model profiles of successful women engineers, especially in major U.S. corporations." Query. Length: 1,000-2,500 words. **Pays 10¢/word.**

Photos Reviews color slides but will accept b&w. Buys all rights. Captions, identification of subjects required.

Tips "We are looking for 800-1,000 word first-person 'As I See It, personal perspectives.' "

ENTERTAINMENT & THE ARTS

$ $ $ AMERICAN CINEMATOGRAPHER

The International Journal of Film & Digital Production Techniques, American Society of Cinematographers, 1782 N. Orange Dr., Hollywood CA 90028. (323)969-4333. Fax: (323)876-4973. E-mail: stephen@ascmag.com. Web site: www.theasc.com. Senior Editor: Rachael Bosley. **Contact:** Stephen Pizzello, executive editor. **90% freelance written.** Monthly magazine covering cinematography (motion picture, TV, music video, commercial). "*American Cinematographer* is a trade publication devoted to the art and craft of cinematography. Our readers are predominantly film-industry professionals.'' Estab. 1919. Circ. 45,000. Pays on publication. Publishes ms an average of 2-3 months after acceptance. Byline given. Offers 50% kill fee. Buys all rights. Editorial lead time 2 months. Submit seasonal material 3 months in advance. Accepts queries by mail, e-mail, phone. Responds in 2 weeks to queries; 2 months to mss. Sample copy and writer's guidelines free.

Nonfiction Stephen Pizzello, editor. Interview/profile, new product, technical. No reviews, opinion pieces. **Buys 20-25 mss/year.** Query with published clips. Length: 1,500-4,000 words. **Pays $600-1,200.** Pays in contributor copies if the writer is promoting his/her own product or company. Sometimes pays expenses of writers on assignment.

Tips ''Familiarity with the technical side of film production and the ability to present that information in an articulate fashion to our audience are crucial.''

$ $ BOXOFFICE MAGAZINE

Media Enterprises LP, 155 S. El Molino Ave., Suite 100, Pasadena CA 91101. (626)396-0250. Fax: (626)396-0248. E-mail: editorial@boxoffice.com. Web site: www.boxoffice.com. Editor-in-Chief/VP-Editorial: Kim Williamson. Senior Editor: Francesca Dinglasan. Film & Technology Editor: Annlee Ellingson. **Contact:** Christine James, managing editor. **15% freelance written.** Magazine about the motion picture industry for executives and managers working in the film business, including movie theater owners and operators, Hollywood studio personnel and leaders in allied industries. Estab. 1920. Circ. 6,000. Pays on publication. Publishes ms an average of 3 months after acceptance. Byline given. Buys first print and all electronic rights. Submit seasonal material 5 months in advance. Accepts queries by mail, e-mail, fax. Sample copy for $5 in US; $10 outside US.

O━ ''*Boxoffice Magazine* is particularly interested in freelance writers who can write business articles on the movie theater industry or technical writers who are familiar with projection/sound equipment and new technologies such as digital cinema.''

Nonfiction ''We are a business news magazine about the motion picture industry in general and the theater industry in particular, and as such publish stories on business trends, developments, problems, and opportunities facing the industry. Almost any story will be considered, including corporate profiles, but we don't want gossip, film or celebrity coverage.'' Book excerpts, essays, interview/profile, new product, personal experience, photo feature, technical, investigative ''all regarding movie theatre business.'' Query with published clips. Length: 800-2,500 words. **Pays 10¢/word.**

Photos State availability with submission. Reviews prints, slides and JPEG files. Pays $10 per published image. Captions required.

The online version of this magazine carries original content. Contact: Kim Williamson.

Tips Purchase a sample copy and read it. Then, write a clear, comprehensive outline of the proposed story, and enclose a résumé and published clips to the managing editor.

$ $ CAMPUS ACTIVITIES

Cameo Publishing Group, P.O. Box 509, Prosperity SC 29127. (800)728-2950. Fax: (803)712-6703. E-mail: cameopublishing@earthlink.net. Web site: www.campusactivitiesmagazine.com; www.cameopublishing.com; www.americanentertainmentmagazine.com. **75% freelance written.** Magazine published 8 times/year covering entertainment on college campuses. *Campus Activities* goes to entertainment buyers on every campus in the U.S. Features stories on artists (national and regional), speakers, and the programs at individual schools. Estab. 1991. Circ. 9,872. Pays on publication. Publishes ms an average of 2 months after acceptance. Byline given. Offers 15% kill fee if accepted and not run. Buys first, second serial (reprint), electronic rights. Editorial lead time 2 months. Submit seasonal material 2 months in advance. Accepts queries by mail, e-mail, fax. Accepts simultaneous submissions. Responds in 1 month to queries; 2 months to mss. Sample copy for $3.50. Writer's guidelines free.

Nonfiction Interview/profile, photo feature. Accepts no unsolicited articles. **Buys 40 mss/year.** Query. Length: 1,400-3,000 words. **Pays 13¢/word.** Sometimes pays expenses of writers on assignment.

Photos State availability with submission. Reviews contact sheets, negatives, 3×5 transparencies, 8×10 prints, electronic media at 300 dpi or higher. Buys one-time rights. Negotiates payment individually. Identification of subjects required.

Tips ''Writers who have ideas, proposals, and special project requests should contact the publisher prior to any commitment to work on such a story. The publisher welcomes innovative and creative ideas for stories and works with writers on such proposals which have significant impact on our readers.''

$ $ CREATE MAGAZINE

Fueling the Professional Creative Community, Brahn Communications, Inc., 5762 S. Semoran Blvd., Orlando FL 32822. Fax: (407)207-0405. E-mail: contribute@createmagazine.com. Web site: www.createmagazine.com. **Contact:** Rebecca Bredholt, associate editor (localized stories); Katherine Johnson, associate editor (national sotries). **90% freelance written.** Quarterly magazine covering advertising, design, photography, printing, film

& video, audio & music, animation, new media. *Create Magazine* is the largest trade publication serving the creative community. "We are looking for experts in our respective industries who have writing experience. We are constantly looking for local writers in the 20 cities where we are published to get the latest scoop on the local creative community." Estab. 2000. Circ. 100,000. Pays on publication. Publishes ms an average of 4 months after acceptance. Byline given. Buys first North American serial, electronic rights. Editorial lead time 4-12 months. Submit seasonal material 5 months in advance. Accepts queries by e-mail, fax. Accepts simultaneous submissions. Sample copy for $7.95. Writer's guidelines online.

"Feature stories are assigned, not received, but queries are accepted for departments. Writers familiar with the fields covered by our trade publication and the people who serve them are encouraged to inquire."

Nonfiction How-to (use design/photo software), inspirational, new product, photo feature, technical. Does not want downtrodden musings and frustrations of particular industries. How poorly certain products perform and stream of consciousness writings are not accepted. Query with published clips. Length: 500-2,500 words. **Pays minimum $300 for assigned articles.** "Pays in contributor copies or other premiums if the writer is an 'expert' in his/her field and we publish company info and details."

Photos State availability with submission. Reviews GIF/JPEG files. Offers no additional payment for photos accepted with ms. Captions required.

Tips "Have plenty of contacts in these industries: advertising, new media, photography, film & video, design, printing, audio & music. Be located in one of our 20 markets (Central Florida, South Florida, Southern California, Atlanta, Chicago, New York—see Web site for all 20)."

$ $ DANCE TEACHER

The Practical Magazine of Dance, McFadden Performing Arts Media, 110 William St., 23rd Floor, New York NY 10038. Fax: (646)459-4000. E-mail: jtu@dancemedia.com. Web site: www.dance-teacher.com. **60% freelance written.** Monthly magazine. "Our readers are professional dance educators, business persons, and related professionals in all forms of dance." Estab. 1979. Circ. 25,000. Pays on publication. Publishes ms an average of 3 months after acceptance. Byline given. Negotiates rights and permission to reprint on request. Submit seasonal material 6 months in advance. Accepts queries by mail, e-mail, fax, phone. Responds in 3 months to mss. Sample copy for 9×12 SAE and 6 first-class stamps. Writer's guidelines online.

Nonfiction How-to (teach, health, business, legal). Special issues: Summer Programs (January); Music & More (May); Costumes and Production Preview (November); College/Training Schools (December). No PR or puff pieces. All articles must be well researched. **Buys 50 mss/year.** Query. Length: 700-2,000 words. **Pays $100-300.**

Photos Send photos with submission. Reviews contact sheets, negatives, transparencies, prints. Limited photo budget.

Tips "Read several issues—particularly seasonal. Stay within writer's guidelines."

$ $ DRAMATICS MAGAZINE

Educational Theatre Association, 2343 Auburn Ave., Cincinnati OH 45219-2815. (513)421-3900. Fax: (513)421-7077. E-mail: dcorathers@edta.org. Web site: www.edta.org. **Contact:** Donald Corathers, editor-in-chief. **70% freelance written.** Monthly magazine for theater arts students, teachers, and others interested in theater arts education. "*Dramatics* is designed to provide serious, committed young theater students and their teachers with the skills and knowledge they need to make better theater; to be a resource that will help high school juniors and seniors make an informed decision about whether to pursue a career in theater, and about how to do so; and to prepare high school students to be knowledgeable, appreciative audience members for the rest of their lives." Estab. 1929. Circ. 40,000. **Pays on acceptance.** Publishes ms an average of 3 months after acceptance. Byline given. Buys first North American serial rights. Submit seasonal material 3 months in advance. Accepts queries by mail, e-mail, fax. Accepts previously published material. Accepts simultaneous submissions. Responds in 3 months to queries; more than 3 months to mss. Sample copy for 9×12 SAE with 5 first-class stamps. Writer's guidelines online.

"The best way to break in is to know our audience—drama students, teachers, and others interested in theater—and to write for them."

Nonfiction How-to (technical theater, directing, acting, etc.), humor, inspirational, interview/profile, photo feature, technical. **Buys 30 mss/year.** Send complete ms. Length: 750-3,000 words. **Pays $50-400.** Sometimes pays expenses of writers on assignment.

Reprints Send tearsheet, photocopy or typed ms with rights for sale noted and information about when and where the material previously appeared. Pays up to 75% of amount paid for original.

Photos Query. Purchased with accompanying ms. Reviews high-res JPEG files on CD. Total price for ms usually includes payment for photos.

Fiction Drama (one-act and full-length plays). Prefers unpublished scripts that have been produced at least once. "No plays for children, Christmas plays, or plays written with no attention paid to the conventions of theater." **Buys 5-9 mss/year.** Send complete ms. **Pays $100-400.**

Tips "Writers who have some practical experience in theater, especially in technical areas, have a leg-up here, but we'll work with anybody who has a good idea. Some freelancers have become regular contributors, others ignore style suggestions included in our writer's guidelines."

$ $ $ EMMY MAGAZINE

Academy of Television Arts & Sciences, 5220 Lankershim Blvd., North Hollywood CA 91601-3109. Web site: www.emmys.tv. **Contact:** Editor. **90% freelance written.** Prefers to work with published/established writers. Bimonthly magazine on television for TV professionals. Circ. 14,000. Pays on publication or within 6 months. Publishes ms an average of 4 months after acceptance. Byline given. Offers 25% kill fee. Buys first North American serial rights. Accepts queries by mail. Responds in 1 month to queries. Sample copy for 9×12 SAE and 6 first-class stamps. Writer's guidelines online.

Nonfiction Articles on contemporary issues, trends, and VIPs (especially those behind the scenes) in broadcast and cable TV; programming and new technology. "Looking for profiles of fascinating people who work 'below the line' in television. Also, always looking for new writers who understand technology and new media and can write about it in an engaging manner. We require TV industry expertise and clear, lively writing." Query with published clips. Length: 1,500-2,000 words. **Pays $1,000-1,200.**

Columns/Departments Most written by regular contributors, but newcomers can break in with filler items in In the Mix or short profiles in Labors of Love. Length: 250-500 words, depending on department. Query with published clips. **Pays $250-500.**

Tips "Please review recent issues before querying us. Query with published, television-related clips. No fanzine, academic, or nostalgic approaches, please. Demonstrate experience in covering the business of television and your ability to write in a lively and compelling manner about programming trends and new technology. Identify fascinating people behind the scenes, not just in the executive suites but in all ranks of the industry."

N $ $ MAKE-UP ARTIST MAGAZINE

Motion Picture, Television, Theatre, Print, 4018 NE 112th Ave., Suite D-8, Vancouver WA 98682. (360)882-3488. E-mail: news@makeupmag.com. Web site: www.makeupmag.com. Editor: Michael Key. **Contact:** Elizabeth Grattan, managing editor. **90% freelance written.** Bimonthly magazine covering all types of professional make-up artistry. "Our audience is a mixture of high-level make-up artists, make-up students, and movie buffs. Writers should be comfortable with technical writing, and should have substantial knowledge of at least one area of makeup, such as effects or fashion. This is an entertainment-industry magazine so writing should have an element of fun and storytelling. Good interview skills required." Estab. 1996. Circ. 12,000. Pays within 30 days of publication. Byline given. Buys all rights. Editorial lead time 6 weeks. Submit seasonal material 2 months in advance. Accepts queries by mail, e-mail, phone. Accepts simultaneous submissions. Sample copy for $7. Writer's guidelines by e-mail.

Nonfiction Book excerpts, essays, historical/nostalgic, how-to, humor, inspirational, interview/profile, new product, opinion, personal experience, photo feature, technical, travel. Does not want fluff pieces about consumer beauty products. **Buys 20+ mss/year.** Query with published clips. Length: 500-3,000 words. **Pays 20-50¢/word.** Sometimes pays expenses of writers on assignment.

Photos Contact Elizabeth Grattan, make-up artist. Send photos with submission. Reviews prints, GIF/JPEG files. Buys all rights. Negotiates payment individually. Captions, identification of subjects required.

Columns/Departments Cameo (short yet thorough look at a makeup artist not covered in a feature story), 800 words (15 photos); Lab Tech (how-to advice for effects artists, usually written by a current makeup artist working in a lab), 800 words (3 photos); Backstage (analysis, interview, tips and behind the scenes info on a theatrical production's makeup), 800 words (3 photos). **Buys 30 mss/year.** Query with published clips. **Pays $100.**

Tips "Read books about professional makeup artistry (see list in FAQ section of our Web site). Read online interviews with makeup artists. Read makeup-oriented mainstream magazines, such as *Allure*. Read *Cinefex* and other film-industry publications. Meet and talk to makeup artists and makeup students."

$ $ RELEASE PRINT

The Magazine of Film Arts Foundation, Film Arts Foundation, 145 9th St., Suite 101, San Francisco CA 94103. (415)552-8760. Fax: (415)552-0882. E-mail: releaseprint@filmarts.org. Web site: www.filmarts.org. Editor: Shari Kizirian. **Contact:** Editor. **80% freelance written.** Bimonthly magazine covering US independent filmmaking. "We have a knowledgeable readership of film and videomakers. They are interested in the financing, production, exhibition, and distribution of independent films and videos. They are interested in practical, technical issues and, to a lesser extent, aesthetic ones." Estab. 1977. Circ. 5,000. Pays on publication. Publishes ms an average of 3 months after acceptance. Byline given. Buys all rights for commissioned works. For works submitted on spec, buys first rights and requests acknowledgement of Release Print in any subsequent publication. Editorial lead time 4 months. Accepts queries by e-mail. Responds in 6 weeks to queries; 2 months to mss. Sample copy for $5 (payable to Film Arts Foundation) and 9×12 SASE with $1.52 postage.

O→ Break in with a proposal for an article or interview of an American experimental, documentary or very low budget feature film/video maker with ties to the San Francisco Bay area (or an upcoming screening in this area). Submit at least 4 months prior to publication date.

Nonfiction Interview/profile, technical, book recommendations, case studies. No film criticism or reviews. **Buys 70-72 mss/year.** Query. Length: 500-2,000 words. Sometimes pays expenses of writers on assignment.

Photos Send photos with submission. Reviews prints. Buys one-time rights. Offers no additional payment for photos accepted with ms. Identification of subjects required.

Columns/Departments Query. **Pays 10¢/word.**

FARM

AGRICULTURAL EQUIPMENT

$ $ IMPLEMENT & TRACTOR

Agri USA, 2302 W. First St., Cedar Falls IA 50613. (319)277-3599. Fax: (319)277-3783. E-mail: mshepherd@cfu.net. Web site: www.implementandtractor.com. **Contact:** Mary Shepherd, editor. **10% freelance written.** Bimonthly magazine covering the agricultural equipment industry. "*Implement & Tractor* offers equipment reviews and business news for agricultural equipment dealers, ag equipment manufacturers, distributors, and aftermarket suppliers." Estab. 1895. Circ. 5,000. Pays on publication. Publishes ms an average of 3-4 months after acceptance. Byline given. Buys all rights. Editorial lead time 2 months. Accepts queries by mail, e-mail, fax. Responds in 2 months to queries. Sample copy for $6.

O→ The biggest freelance opportunity is for dealership profiles.

Nonfiction No fiction, cartoons, how-to, general farm machinery articles or farmer profiles articles. Length: 600-1,200 words. **Pays $100-200 (including photos).**

Tips "Know the retail agricultural equipment industry, have an engineer's outlook for analyzing machinery and a writer's skills to communicate that information. Technical background is helpful, as is mechanical aptitude."

CROPS & SOIL MANAGEMENT

$ $ AMERICAN AND WESTERN FRUIT GROWER

Meister Media Worldwide, 37733 Euclid Ave., Willoughby OH 44094. (440)942-2000. E-mail: bdsparks@meistermedia.com. Web site: www.fruitgrower.com. **Contact:** Brian Sparks, managing editor. **3% freelance written.** Annual magazine covering commercial fruit growing. "How-to" articles are best. Estab. 1880. Circ. 44,000. Pays on publication. Publishes ms an average of 4 months after acceptance. Byline given. Buys first rights. Editorial lead time 2 months. Submit seasonal material 4 months in advance. Accepts queries by mail, e-mail, fax, phone. Responds in 2 weeks to queries; 2 months to mss. Sample copy and writer's guidelines free.

Nonfiction How-to (better grow fruit crops). **Buys 6-10 mss/year.** Query with published clips or send complete ms. Length: 800-1,200 words. **Pays $200-250.** Sometimes pays expenses of writers on assignment.

Photos Send photos with submission. Reviews prints, slides. Buys one-time rights. Negotiates payment individually.

N ⊕ THE AUSTRALIAN & NEW ZEALAND GRAPEGROWER AND WINEMAKER

Ryan Publications, Ltd., P.O. Box 54, Goodwood SA 5034 Australia. (61)(8)8375-9888. Fax: (61)(8)8351-5899. E-mail: editor@grapeandwine.com.au. Web site: www.grapeandwine.com.au. Editor: Penny Boothman. Monthly magazine providing vignerons and winemakers with an abundance of practical information to assist them to make premium quality wines for domestic and discerning export markets. Estab. 1963.

Nonfiction General interest, how-to, interview/profile, new product, personal experience, technical. Query.

$ $ COTTON GROWER MAGAZINE

Meister Media Worldwide, 65 Germantown Court, #202, Cordova TN 38018. (901)756-8822. E-mail: frgiles@meistermedia.com. **Contact:** Frank Giles, editor. **5% freelance written.** Monthly magazine covering cotton production, cotton markets and related subjects. Readers are mostly cotton producers who seek information on production practices, equipment and products related to cotton. Estab. 1901. Circ. 43,000. **Pays on acceptance.** Publishes ms an average of 2 months after acceptance. Byline given. Buys first rights. Editorial lead time 2 months. Submit seasonal material 2 months in advance. Accepts queries by mail, e-mail, fax, phone. Accepts simultaneous submissions. Sample copy for free. Writer's guidelines not available.

Nonfiction Interview/profile, new product, photo feature, technical. No fiction or humorous pieces. **Buys 5-10 mss/year.** Query with published clips. Length: 500-800 words. **Pays $200-400.** Sometimes pays expenses of writers on assignment.
Photos State availability with submission. Reviews transparencies. Buys all rights. Offers no additional payment for photos accepted with ms. Captions, identification of subjects required.

$ THE FRUIT GROWERS NEWS

Great American Publishing, P.O. Box 128, Sparta MI 49345. (616)887-9008. Fax: (616)887-2666. E-mail: editor@fruitgrowersnews.com. Web site: www.fruitgrowersnews.com. Publisher: Matt McCallum. **Contact:** Kimberly Warren, editor. **25% freelance written.** Monthly tabloid covering agriculture. "Our objective is to provide commercial fruit growers of all sizes with information to help them succeed." Estab. 1970. Circ. 28,000. Pays on publication. Publishes ms an average of 2 months after acceptance. Makes work-for-hire assignments. Editorial lead time 1 month. Submit seasonal material 1 month in advance. Accepts queries by mail, e-mail, fax. Accepts simultaneous submissions. Responds in 2 weeks to queries; 1 month to mss. Sample copy for free.
Nonfiction General interest, interview/profile, new product. No advertorials, other "puff pieces." **Buys 72 mss/year.** Query with published clips. Length: 800-1,200 words. **Pays $100-125.** Sometimes pays expenses of writers on assignment.
Photos Send photos with submission. Reviews prints. Buys one-time rights. Offers $15/photo. Captions required.

$ GRAIN JOURNAL

Country Publications, Inc., 3065 Pershing Ct., Decatur IL 62526. Fax: (217)877-6647. E-mail: ed@grainnet.com. Web site: www.grainnet.com. **Contact:** Ed Zdrojewski, editor. **5% freelance written.** Bimonthly magazine covering grain handling and merchandising. "*Grain Journal* serves the North American grain industry, from the smallest country grain elevators and feed mills to major export terminals." Estab. 1972. Circ. 12,000. Pays on publication. Publishes ms an average of 2 months after acceptance. Byline sometimes given. Buys first rights. Editorial lead time 2 months. Submit seasonal material 2 months in advance. Accepts simultaneous submissions. Sample copy for free.
Nonfiction How-to, interview/profile, new product, technical. Query. Length: 750 words maximum. **Pays $100.**
Photos Send photos with submission. Reviews contact sheets, negatives, transparencies, 3×5 prints. Buys one-time rights. Offers $50-100/photo. Captions, identification of subjects required.
Tips "Call with your idea. We'll let you know if it is suitable for our publication."

NEW ZEALAND COMMERCIAL GROWER

P.O. Box 10-232, Wellington New Zealand. (64)(4)472-3795. Fax: (64)(4)471-2861. E-mail: comgrow@xtra.co.nz. Web site: www.thegrower.co.nz. **Contact:** David Paterson, editor. Trade journal published 11 times/year covering information for commercial growers of fresh vegetables, including potatoes, tomatoes, asparagus, and buttercup squash. Circ. 4,500.

- Query before submitting.

$ SPUDMAN

Great American Publishing, P.O. Box 128, Sparta MI 49345. Fax: (616)887-2666. Web site: www.spudman.com. **Contact:** Kimberly Warren, editorial director. **15% freelance written.** Monthly magazine covering potato industry—growing, packing, processing, chipping. Estab. 1964. Circ. 10,000. Pays on publication. Publishes ms an average of 2 months after acceptance. Byline given. Offers $75 kill fee. Not copyrighted. Buys first North American serial, electronic rights. Editorial lead time 2 months. Submit seasonal material 4 months in advance. Accepts queries by mail, fax. Accepts previously published material. Responds in 2-3 weeks to queries. Sample copy for 8½×11 SAE and 3 first-class stamps. Writer's guidelines for #10 SASE.

$ THE VEGETABLE GROWERS NEWS

Great American Publishing, P.O. Box 128, Sparta MI 49345. (616)887-9008. Fax: (616)887-2666. E-mail: editor@vegetablegrowersnews.com. Web site: www.vegetablegrowersnews.com. Publisher: Matt McCallum. **Contact:** Kimberly Warren, editor. **25% freelance written.** Monthly tabloid covering agriculture. "Our objective is to provide commercial vegetable growers of all sizes with information to help them succeed." Estab. 1970. Circ. 28,000. Pays on publication. Publishes ms an average of 2 months after acceptance. Makes work-for-hire assignments. Editorial lead time 1 month. Submit seasonal material 1 month in advance. Accepts queries by mail, e-mail, fax. Accepts simultaneous submissions. Responds in 2 weeks to queries; 1 month to mss. Sample copy for free.
Nonfiction General interest, interview/profile, new product. No advertorials, other "puff pieces." **Buys 72 mss/**

year. Query with published clips. Length: 800-1,200 words. **Pays $100-125.** Sometimes pays expenses of writers on assignment.

Photos Send photos with submission. Reviews prints. Buys one-time rights. Offers $15/photo. Captions required.

DAIRY FARMING

$ DAIRY GOAT JOURNAL

Central Countryside Publications, Ltd., 145 Industrial Dr., Medford WI 54451. (715)785-7979. Fax: (715)785-7414. Web site: www.dairygoatjournal.com. **Contact:** Jennifer Stultz, editor. **45% freelance written.** Monthly journal. "We are looking for clear and accurate articles about dairy goat owners, their herds, cheesemaking, and other ways of marketing products. Some readers own two goats; others own 1,500 and are large commercial operations." Estab. 1917. Circ. 8,000, including copies to more than 70 foreign countries. Pays on publication. Byline given.

Nonfiction Information on personalities and on public issues affecting dairy goats and their owners. How-to articles with plenty of practical information. Health and husbandry articles should be written with appropriate experience or academic credentials. **Buys 100 mss/year.** Query with published clips. Length: 750-2,500 words. **Pays $50-150.** Pays expenses of writers on assignment.

Photos Color or b&w. Vertical cover. Goats and/or people. Pays $100 maximum for covers; $20-70 for inside use or for b&w. Identification of subjects required.

$ $ HOARD'S DAIRYMAN

W.D. Hoard and Sons, Co., P.O. Box 801, Fort Atkinson WI 53538. (920)563-5551. Fax: (920)563-7298. E-mail: hoards@hoards.com. Web site: www.hoards.com. Tabloid published 20 times/year covering dairy industry. "We publish semi-technical information published for dairy-farm families and their advisors." Estab. 1885. Circ. 100,000. **Pays on acceptance.** Publishes ms an average of 4 months after acceptance. Byline given. Buys first rights. Editorial lead time 2 months. Submit seasonal material 3 months in advance. Accepts queries by mail, e-mail, fax. Responds in 2 weeks to queries; 1 month to mss. Sample copy for 12×15 SAE and $3. Writer's guidelines for #10 SASE.

Nonfiction How-to, technical. **Buys 60 mss/year.** Query. Length: 800-1,500 words. **Pays $150-350.**

Photos Send photos with submission. Reviews 2×2 transparencies. Offers no additional payment for photos accepted with ms.

$ ✪ WESTERN DAIRY FARMER

Bowes Publishers, Ltd., 4504—61 Ave., Leduc AB T9E 3Z1 Canada. (780)980-7488. Fax: (780)986-6397. E-mail: editor-wdf-caf@webcoleduc.com. Web site: www.westerndairyfarmer.com. **Contact:** Diana Macleod, editor. **70% freelance written.** Bimonthly magazine covering the dairy industry. "*Western Dairy Farmer* is a trade publication dealing with issues surrounding the dairy industry. The magazine features innovative articles on animal health, industry changes, new methods of dairying, and personal experiences. Sometimes highlights successful farmers." Estab. 1991. Circ. 6,300. Pays on publication. Publishes ms an average of 4 months after acceptance. Byline given. Buys all rights. Editorial lead time 2 months. Submit seasonal material 2 months in advance. Accepts queries by mail, e-mail, fax. Responds in 2 weeks to queries; 2 months to mss. Sample copy for 9×12 SAE.

Nonfiction "All topics/submissions must be related to the dairy industry." General interest, how-to, interview/profile, new product, personal experience (only exceptional stories), technical. "Not interested in anything vague, trite, or not dairy related." **Buys 50 mss/year.** Query or send complete ms. Length: 900-1,200 words. **Pays $75-150.**

Photos State availability with submission. Reviews GIF/JPEG files. Buys all rights. Offers no additional payment for photos accepted with ms. Captions, identification of subjects, model releases required.

Tips "Know the industry inside and out. Provide contact names and phone numbers (both for writers and subjects) with submissions. Remember, this is a specialized trade publication, and our readers are well-aquainted with the issues and appreciate new up-to-date information."

$ $ WESTERN DAIRYBUSINESS

Dairy Business Communications, Heritage Complex, Suite 218, 4500 S. Laspina, Tulare CA 93274. (559)687-3160. Fax: (559)687-3166. E-mail: rgoble@dairybusiness.com. Web site: www.dairybusiness.com. **Contact:** Ron Goble, editor. **10% freelance written.** Prefers to work with published/established writers. Monthly magazine dealing with large-herd commercial dairy industry. Rarely publishes information about non-Western producers or dairy groups and events. Estab. 1922. Circ. 17,000. Pays on publication. Publishes ms an average of 3 months after acceptance. Byline given. Buys first North American serial rights. Submit seasonal material 3 months in advance. Accepts queries by mail, e-mail. Responds in 1 month to queries. Sample copy for 9×12 SAE and 4 first-class stamps.

Nonfiction Special emphasis on: environmental stewardship, herd management systems, business management, facilities/equipment, forage/cropping. Interview/profile, new product, opinion, industry analysis. "No religion, nostalgia, politics, or 'mom and pop' dairies." Query, or send complete ms. Length: 300-1,500 words. **Pays $25-400 for assigned articles.**

Reprints Seldom accepts previously published submissions. Send information about when and where the article previously appeared. Pays 50% of amount paid for an original article.

Photos Photos are a critical part of story packages. Send photos with submission. Reviews contact sheets, 35mm or 2¼×2¼ transparencies. Buys one-time rights. Pays $25 for b&w; $50-100 for color. Captions, identification of subjects required.

Tips "Know the market and the industry, be well-versed in large-herd dairy management and business."

LIVESTOCK

$ $ ANGUS BEEF BULLETIN

Angus Productions, Inc., 3201 Frederick Ave., St. Joseph MO 64506. (816)383-5270. Fax: (816)233-6575. E-mail: shermel@angusjournal.com. Web site: www.angusbeefbulletin.com. **Contact:** Shauna Rose Hermel, editor. **45% freelance written.** Tabloid published 4 times/year covering commercial cattle industry. "The *Bulletin* is mailed free to commercial cattlemen who have purchased an Angus bull and had the registration transferred to them and to others who sign a request card." Estab. 1985. Circ. 67,000. Pays on publication. Publishes ms an average of 3 months after acceptance. Byline given. Buys first, electronic rights. Editorial lead time 3 months. Submit seasonal material 3 months in advance. Accepts queries by mail, e-mail. Accepts simultaneous submissions. Responds in 3 weeks to queries; 3 months to mss. Sample copy for $5. Writer's guidelines for #10 SASE.

Nonfiction How-to (cattle production), interview/profile, technical (cattle production). **Buys 10 mss/year.** Query with published clips. Length: 800-2,500 words. **Pays $50-600.** Pays expenses of writers on assignment.

Photos Send photos with submission. Reviews 5×7 transparencies, 5×7 glossy prints. Buys all rights. Offers $25/photo. Identification of subjects required.

Tips "Read the publication and have a firm grasp of the commercial cattle industry and how the Angus breed fits in that industry."

$ $ $ ANGUS JOURNAL

Angus Productions Inc., 3201 Frederick Ave., St. Joseph MO 64506-2997. (816)383-5270. Fax: (816)233-6575. E-mail: shermel@angusjournal.com. Web site: www.angusjournal.com. **Contact:** Shauna Rose Hermel, editor. **40% freelance written.** Monthly magazine covering Angus cattle. "The *Angus Journal* is the official magazine of the American Angus Association. Its primary function as such is to report to the membership association activities and information pertinent to raising Angus cattle." Estab. 1919. Circ. 17,000. Pays on publication. Publishes ms an average of 3 months after acceptance. Byline given. Buys first, electronic rights. Editorial lead time 2 months. Submit seasonal material 3 months in advance. Accepts queries by mail, e-mail, fax. Accepts simultaneous submissions. Responds in 3 weeks to queries; 2 months to mss. Sample copy for $5. Writer's guidelines for #10 SASE.

Nonfiction How-to (cattle production), interview/profile, technical (related to cattle). **Buys 20-30 mss/year.** Query with published clips. Length: 800-3,500 words. **Pays $50-1,000.** Pays expenses of writers on assignment.

Photos Send photos with submission. Reviews 5×7 glossy prints. Buys all rights. Offers $25-400/photo. Identification of subjects required.

Tips "Read the magazine and have a firm grasp of the cattle industry."

$ $ THE CATTLEMAN

Texas and Southwestern Cattle Raisers Association, 1301 W. 7th St., Ft. Worth TX 76102-2660. E-mail: lionel@texascattleraisers.org. Web site: www.thecattlemanmagazine.com. **Contact:** Lionel Chambers, editor. **25% freelance written.** Monthly magazine covering the Texas/Oklahoma beef cattle industry. "We specialize in in-depth, management-type articles related to range and pasture, beef cattle production, animal health, nutrition, and marketing. We want 'how-to' articles." Estab. 1914. Circ. 15,400. **Pays on acceptance.** Publishes ms an average of 2 months after acceptance. Byline given. Buys exclusive and one-time rights, plus rights to post on Web site in month of publication. Editorial lead time 2 months. Submit seasonal material 6 months in advance. Accepts queries by mail, e-mail. Sample copy for free. Writer's guidelines online.

O- Break in with "clips from other cattle magazines and demonstrated knowledge of our audiences."

Nonfiction How-to, interview/profile, new product, personal experience, technical, ag research. Special issues: Editorial calendar themes include: Horses (January); Range and Pasture (February); Livestock Marketing (July); Hereford and Wildlife (August); Feedlots (September); Bull Buyers (October); Ranch Safety (December). Does not want to see anything not specifically related to beef production in the Southwest. **Buys 20 mss/year.** Query with published clips. Length: 1,500-2,000 words. **Pays $200-350 for assigned articles; $100-350 for unsolicited articles.** Sometimes pays expenses of writers on assignment.

Photos Reviews transparencies, prints, digital files. Buys one-time rights. Offers no additional payment for photos accepted with ms. Identification of subjects required.

Tips "In our most recent readership survey, subscribers said they were most interested in the following topics in this order: range/pasture, property rights, animal health, water, new innovations, and marketing. *The Cattleman* prefers to work on an assignment basis. However, prospective contributors are urged to write the managing editor of the magazine to inquire of interest on a proposed subject. Occasionally, the editor will return a manuscript to a potential contributor for cutting, polishing, checking, rewriting, or condensing. Be able to demonstrate background/knowledge in this field. Include tearsheets from similar magazines."

$ $ FEED LOT MAGAZINE

Feed Lot Magazine, Inc., P.O. Box 850, Dighton KS 67839. (620)397-2838. Fax: (620)397-2839. E-mail: feedlot@st-tel.net. Web site: www.feedlotmagazine.com. **Contact:** Robert A. Strong, editor (rstrong@st-tel.net). **40% freelance written.** Bimonthly magazine. "The editorial information content fits a dual role: large feedlots and their related cow/calf operations, and large 500pl cow/calf, 100pl stocker operations. The information covers all phases of production from breeding, genetics, animal health, nutrition, equipment design, research through finishing fat cattle. *Feed Lot* publishes a mix of new information and timely articles which directly affect the cattle industry." Estab. 1993. Circ. 12,000. Pays on publication. Publishes ms an average of 2 months after acceptance. Byline given. Offers 50% kill fee. Buys all rights. Editorial lead time 2 months. Submit seasonal material 6 months in advance. Accepts queries by mail, e-mail, fax. Responds in 1 month to queries. Sample copy and writer's guidelines for $1.50.

Nonfiction Interview/profile, new product (cattle-related), photo feature. Send complete ms. Length: 100-400 words. **Pays 20¢/word.**

Reprints Send tearsheet or typed ms with rights for sale noted and information about when and where the material previously appeared. Pays 50% of amount paid for an original article.

Photos State availability of or send photos with submission. Reviews contact sheets. Buys all rights. Negotiates payment individually. Captions, model releases required.

Tips "Know what you are writing about—have a good knowledge of the subject."

$ SHEEP! MAGAZINE

Countryside Publications, Ltd., 145 Industrial Dr., Medford WI 54451. (715)785-7979. Fax: (715)785-7414. Web site: www.sheepmagazine.com. **Contact:** Nathan Griffin, editor. **35% freelance written.** Prefers to work with published/established writers. Bimonthly magazine. "We're looking for clear, concise, useful information for sheep raisers who have a few sheep to a 1,000 ewe flock." Estab. 1980. Circ. 8,000. Pays on publication. Byline given. Offers $30 kill fee. Buys all rights or makes work-for-hire assignments. Submit seasonal material 3 months in advance.

Nonfiction Health and husbandry articles should be written by someone with extensive experience or appropriate credentials (i.e., a veterinarian or animal scientist). Accepts informative articles (on personalities and/or political, legal, or environmental issues affecting the sheep industry); features (on small businesses that promote wool products and stories about local and regional sheep producers' groups and their activities); and first-person narratives. Book excerpts, how-to (on innovative lamb and wool marketing and promotion techniques, efficient record-keeping systems, or specific aspects of health and husbandry), interview/profile (on experienced sheep producers who detail the economics and management of their operation), new product (of value to sheep producers; should be written by someone who has used them), technical (on genetics health and nutrition). **Buys 80 mss/year.** Query with published clips or send complete ms. Length: 750-2,500 words. **Pays $45-150.**

Photos Color—vertical compositions of sheep and/or people—for cover. Use only b&w inside magazine. Black & white, 35mm photos or other visuals improve chances of a sale. Buys all rights. Identification of subjects required.

Tips "Send us your best ideas and photos! We love good writing!"

MANAGEMENT

$ $ NEW HOLLAND NEWS

P.O. Box 1895, New Holland PA 17557-0903. Web site: www.newholland.com/na. **Contact:** Editor. **60% freelance written.** Works with a small number of new/unpublished writers each year. Magazine published 8 times/year covering agriculture and non-farm country living; designed to entertain and inform farm families and provide ideas for small acreage outdoor projects. Estab. 1960. **Pays on acceptance.** Publishes ms an average of 10 months after acceptance. Byline given. Offers negotiable kill fee. Buys first North American serial rights. Submit seasonal material 6 months in advance. Accepts queries by mail. Responds in 2 months to queries. Sample copy and writer's guidelines for 9×12 SAE with 2 first-class stamps.

O→ Break in with an "agricultural 'economic' success story with all the management details."

Nonfiction "We need strong photo support for articles of 1,200-1,700 words on farm management, farm human interest and rural lifestyles." Inspirational, photo feature. **Buys 40 mss/year.** Query. **Pays $700-900.** Pays expenses of writers on assignment.

Photos Send photos with submission. Reviews color photos in any format. Buys one-time rights. Pays $50-300, $500 for cover shot. Captions, identification of subjects, model releases required.

Tips "The writer must have an emotional understanding of agriculture and the farm family and must demonstrate in the article an understanding of the unique economics that affect farming in North America. We want to know about the exceptional farm managers, those leading the way in agriculture. Use anecdotes freely."

N $ SMALLHOLDER MAGAZINE

Newsquest Media Group, Hook House, Hook Road, Wimblington, March Cambs PE15 0QL United Kingdom. Phone/Fax: (44)(135)474-1538. E-mail: liz.wright1@btconnect.com. Web site: www.smallholder.co.uk. **Contact:** Liz Wright. Accepts queries by e-mail. Sample copy online. Writer's guidelines by e-mail.

Nonfiction Length: 700-1,400 words. **Pays 4£/word.**

Photos Send photos with submission. Reviews 300 dpi digital images. Pays £5-50.

MISCELLANEOUS

N $ $ ACRES U.S.A.

The Voice of Eco-Agriculture, P.O. Box 91299, Austin TX 78709-1299. (512)892-4400. Fax: (512)892-4448. E-mail: editor@acresusa.com. Web site: www.acresusa.com. Managing Editor: Fred C. Walters. **Contact:** Samuel Bruce, editor. Monthly trade journal written by people who have a sincere interest in the principles of organic and sustainable agriculture. Estab. 1970. Circ. 18,000. Pays on publication. Byline given. Buys first North American serial rights. Editorial lead time 4 months. Submit seasonal material 6 months in advance. Accepts queries by mail, e-mail, fax. Accepts simultaneous submissions. Sample copy and writer's guidelines free.

Nonfiction Exposé, how-to, personal experience. Special issues: Seeds (January), Soil Fertility & Testing (March), Cattle & Grazing (May), Poultry (July), Composting/Compost Tea (September), Tillage & Equipment (November). Does not want poetry, fillers, product profiles, or anything with a promotional tone. **Buys about 50 mss/year.** Query with or without published clips or send complete ms. Length: 1,000-2,500 words. **Pays 10¢/word.**

Photos State availability of or send photos with submission. Reviews GIF/JPEG files. Buys one-time rights. Negotiates payment individually. Captions, identification of subjects required.

$ $ BEE CULTURE

P.O. Box 706, Medina OH 44256-0706. Fax: (330)725-5624. E-mail: kim@beeculture.com. Web site: www.beeculture.com. **Contact:** (Mr.) Kim Flottum, editor. **50% freelance written.** Monthly magazine for beekeepers and those interested in the natural science of honey bees, with environmentally-oriented articles relating to honey bees or pollination. Estab. 1873. Pays on publication. Publishes ms an average of 4 months after acceptance. Buys first North American serial rights. Accepts queries by mail, e-mail, fax, phone. Responds in 1 month to mss. Sample copy for 9×12 SAE and 5 first-class stamps. Writer's guidelines online.

O→ Break in with marketing strategies, interviews of successful beekeepers or beekeeping science, making management of bees easier or less expensive.

Nonfiction Interested in articles giving new ideas on managing bees. Also looking for articles on honey bee/environment connections or relationships. Also uses success stories about commercial beekeepers. Interview/profile, personal experience, photo feature. No "how I began beekeeping" articles. No highly advanced, technical, and scientific abstracts, or impractical advice. Length: 2,000 words average. **Pays $100-250.**

Reprints Send photocopy and information about when and where the material previously appeared. Pays about the same as for an original article, on negotiation.

Photos "B&W or color prints, 5×7 standard, but 3×5 are OK. 35mm slides, mid-format transparencies are excellent. Electronic images accepted and encouraged." Pays $7-10 each, $50 for cover photos.

Tips "Do an interview story on commercial beekeepers who are cooperative enough to furnish accurate, factual information on their operations. Frequent mistakes made by writers in completing articles are that they are too general in nature and lack management knowledge."

N $ $ $ PRODUCE BUSINESS

Phoenix Media Network Inc., P.O. Box 810425, Boca Raton FL 33481-0425. (561)994-1110. E-mail: kwhitacre@phoenixmedianet.com. Editor: James Prevor. Managing Editor: Jan Fialkow. **Contact:** Ken Whitacre. **90% free-**

lance written. Monthly magazine covering produce and floral marketing. "We address the buying end of the produce/floral industry, concentrating on supermarkets, chain restaurants, etc." Estab. 1985. Circ. 16,000. Pays 30 days after publication. Byline given. Offers $50 kill fee. Buys all rights. Editorial lead time 2 months. Accepts queries by e-mail. Sample copy for free. Writer's guidelines free.

Nonfiction "All articles are assigned to conform to our editorial calendar." Does not want unsolicited articles. **Buys 150 mss/year.** Query with published clips. Length: 1,200-10,000 words. **Pays $240-1,200.** Pays expenses of writers on assignment.

REGIONAL

$ CENTRAL ALBERTA FARMER

Bowes Publishers, Ltd., 4504—61 Ave., Leduc AB T9E 3Z1 Canada. (780)986-2271. Fax: (780)986-6397. E-mail: editor-wdf-caf@webcoleduc.com. Web site: www.albertafarmer.com. **Contact:** Diana MacLeod, editor. **10% freelance written.** Monthly tabloid covering farming issues specific to or affecting farmers in central Alberta, Canada. "*Central Alberta Farmer* is an industry magazine-type product that deals with issues in farming. It also highlights value-added efforts in agriculture and features stories on rural lifestyles." Estab. 1993. Circ. 36,000. Pays on publication. Publishes ms an average of 3 months after acceptance. Byline given. Buys all rights. Editorial lead time 3 months. Submit seasonal material 4 months in advance. Accepts queries by mail, e-mail, fax. Accepts simultaneous submissions. Responds in 2 weeks to queries; 2 months to mss. Sample copy for 9×12 SAE.

Nonfiction "All articles must be related to an aspect of farming in the area *Central Alberta Farmer* covers. Freelance articles must be exceptional. Not many are accepted." General interest, how-to, interview/profile, new product, personal experience, technical. "Not interested in anything trite or trivial." **Buys 5 mss/year.** Query or send complete ms. Length: 1,000-1,500 words. **Pays $20-30.**

Photos State availability with submission. Reviews GIF/JPEG files. Buys all rights. Offers no additional payment for photos accepted with ms. Captions, identification of subjects, model releases required.

Tips "Know the industry well. Provide names and phone numbers with submissions (both yours and the people in the article). This is a difficult publication to break into because most copy is generated in-house. So, your submission must be far above average."

$ $ FLORIDA GROWER

The Voice of Florida Agriculture for More Than 90 Years, Meister Media Worldwide, 1555 Howell Branch Rd., Suite C-204, Winter Park FL 32789. (407)539-6552. Fax: (407)539-6544. E-mail: rcpadrick@meistermedia.com. Web site: www.floridagrower.net. **Contact:** Roy Padrick, managing editor. **10% freelance written.** Monthly magazine "edited for the Florida farmer with commercial production interest primarily in citrus, vegetables, and other ag endeavors. Our goal is to provide articles which update and inform on such areas as production, ag financing, farm labor relations, technology, safety, education, and regulation." Estab. 1907. Circ. 12,200. Pays on publication. Byline given. Buys all rights. Editorial lead time 2 months. Submit seasonal material 3 months in advance. Accepts queries by mail, e-mail, fax, phone. Responds in 1 month to queries. Sample copy for 9×12 SAE and 5 first-class stamps. Writer's guidelines free.

Nonfiction Interview/profile, photo feature, technical. Query with published clips. Length: 700-1,000 words. **Pays $150-250.**

Photos Send photos with submission.

$ THE LAND

Minnesota's Favorite Ag Publication, Free Press Co., P.O. Box 3169, Mankato MN 56002-3169. (507)345-4523. E-mail: kschulz@thelandonline.com. Web site: www.thelandonline.com. **Contact:** Kevin Schulz, editor. **40% freelance written.** Weekly tabloid covering farming in Minnesota. "Although we're not tightly focused on any one type of farming, our articles must be of interest to farmers. In other words, will your article topic have an impact on people who live and work in rural areas?" Prefers to work with Minnesota writers. Estab. 1976. Circ. 33,000. **Pays on acceptance.** Publishes ms an average of 2 months after acceptance. Byline given. Buys first North American serial rights. Editorial lead time 2 months. Submit seasonal material 2 months in advance. Accepts queries by mail, e-mail. Responds in 3 weeks to queries; 2 months to mss. Sample copy for free. Writer's guidelines for #10 SASE.

Nonfiction General interest (ag), how-to (crop, livestock production, marketing). **Buys 80 mss/year.** Query. Length: 500-750 words. **Pays $40-70 for assigned articles.**

Photos Send photos with submission. Reviews contact sheets. Buys one-time rights. Negotiates payment individually.

Columns/Departments Query. **Pays $10-50.**

Tips "Be enthused about rural Minnesota life and agriculture and be willing to work with our editors. We try to stress relevance. When sending me a query, convince me the story belongs in a Minnesota farm publication."

$ $ MAINE ORGANIC FARMER & GARDENER

Maine Organic Farmers & Gardeners Association, 662 Slab City Rd., Lincolnville ME 04849. (207)763-3043. E-mail: jenglish@midcoast.com. Web site: www.mofga.org. **Contact:** Jean English, editor. **40% freelance written.** Prefers to work with published/established local writers. Quarterly newspaper. "The *MOF&G* promotes and encourages sustainable agriculture and environmentally sound living. Our primary focus is organic farming, gardening, and forestry, but we also deal with local, national, and international agriculture, food, and environmental issues." Estab. 1976. Circ. 10,000. Pays on publication. Publishes ms an average of 8 months after acceptance. Byline and bio offered. Buys first North American serial, first, one-time, second serial (reprint) rights. Submit seasonal material 1 year in advance. Accepts queries by mail, e-mail. Accepts simultaneous submissions. Responds in 2 months to queries. Sample copy for $2 and SAE with 7 first-class stamps from MOFGA, P.O. Box 170, Unity ME 04988. Writer's guidelines free.

Nonfiction Book reviews; how-to based on personal experience, research reports, interviews; profiles of farmers, gardeners, plants; information on renewable energy, recycling, nutrition, health, nontoxic pest control, organic farm management and marketing. "We use profiles of New England organic farmers and gardeners and news reports (500-1,000 words) dealing with U.S./international sustainable ag research and development, rural development, recycling projects, environmental and agricultural problems and solutions, organic farms with broad impact, cooperatives and community projects." **Buys 30 mss/year.** Query with published clips or send complete ms. Length: 250-3,000 words. **Pays $25-300.**

Reprints Send ms with rights for sale noted and information about when and where the material previously appeared. Pays 50% of amount paid for an original article.

Photos State availability of b&w photos with query; or send 3×5 b&w photos with ms. Buys one-time rights. Captions, identification of subjects, model releases required.

Tips "We are a nonprofit organization. Our publication's primary mission is to inform and educate, but we also want readers to enjoy the articles."

FINANCE

$ $ $ ADVISOR'S EDGE

Canada's Magazine for the Financial Professional, Rogers Media, Inc., 156 Front St. W., 4th Floor, Toronto ON M5J 2L6 Canada. E-mail: deanne.gage@advisor.rogers.com. Web site: www.advisorsedge.ca. Assistant Editor: Heidi Staseson. **Contact:** Deanne Gage, managing editor. Monthly magazine covering the financial industry (financial advisors and investment advisors). "*Advisor's Edge* focuses on sales and marketing opportunities for the financial advisor (how they can build their business and improve relationships with clients." Estab. 1998. Circ. 36,000. Pays on publication. Publishes ms an average of 3 months after acceptance. Byline given. Offers 25% kill fee. Buys one-time, electronic rights. Editorial lead time 3 months. Accepts queries by e-mail. Sample copy online.

Nonfiction "We are looking for articles that help advisors do their jobs better." How-to, interview/profile. No articles that aren't relevant to how a financial advisor does his/her job. **Buys 12 mss/year.** Query with published clips. Length: 1,500-2,000 words. **Pays $900 (Canadian).** Pays in contributor copies only if an industry contributor (i.e., an advisor).

$ $ $ $ BLOOMBERG WEALTH MANAGER

Bloomberg L.P., 731 Lexington Ave., New York NY 10022. E-mail: rkoreto@highlinemedia.com. Web site: wealth.bloomberg.com. Editor-in-Chief: Richard J. Korreto. **90% freelance written.** published 10 times/year magazine for financial advisors. "Stories should provide insight and information for the financial adviser. Put yourself on the adviser's side of the table and cover the issues thoroughly from his/her perspective. The piece should delve beneath the surface. We need specific examples, professional caveats, advice from professionals." Estab. 1999. Circ. 50,000. **Pays on acceptance.** Publishes ms an average of 3 months after acceptance. Byline given. Offers 30% kill fee. Buys first North American serial rights. Editorial lead time 2 months. Submit seasonal material 2 months in advance. Accepts queries by mail, e-mail, fax, phone. Responds in 1 month to queries.

Nonfiction Book excerpts, interview/profile, technical. Do not submit anything that does not deal with financial planning issues or the financial markets. **Buys 30-40 mss/year.** Query with published clips. Length: 1,500-3,000 words. **Pays $1.50-2/word for assigned articles.** Sometimes pays expenses of writers on assignment.

Columns/Departments Expertly Speaking, Tax Strategies, Retirement, Executive Compensation (all financial planning), all 1,900 words. **Buys 10-15 mss/year.** Query with published clips. **Pays $1.50-2/word.**

Tips "*Wealth Manager* is a trade magazine. All pieces should be written from the perspective of a financial adviser who has wealthy clients."

$ $ $ COLLECTIONS & CREDIT RISK

The Authority for Commercial and Consumer Professionals, Thomson Media, 300 S. Wacker Dr., Suite 1800, Chicago IL 60606. Web site: www.creditcollectionsworld.com. **Contact:** John Frank, editor. **33% freelance written.** Monthly journal covering debt collections and credit risk management. "*Collections & Credit Risk* reports and analyzes events and trends affecting consumer and commercial credit practices and debt collections. The entire credit cycle is covered from setting credit policy and making loan decisions to debt recovery, collections, bankruptcy, and debt sales." Estab. 1996. Circ. 30,000. **Pays on acceptance.** Publishes ms an average of 3 months after acceptance. Byline given. Kill fee determined case by case. Buys all rights. Editorial lead time 3 months. Accepts queries by mail. Sample copy free or online.

- Break in with "a query with clips of business trend stories using 8-10 sources and demonstrating strong analysis."

Nonfiction Interview/profile, technical, business news and analysis. "No unsolicited submissions accepted—freelancers work on assignment only." **Buys 30-40 mss/year.** Query with published clips. Length: 1,000-2,500 words. **Pays $800-1,000.** Sometimes pays expenses of writers on assignment.

Tips "This is a business news and analysis magazine focused on events and trends affecting the credit-risk management and collections professions. Our editorial approach is modeled after *Business Week, Forbes, Fortune, Wall Street Journal.* No fluff accepted."

$ $ COMMUNITY BANKER

900 19th St. NW, Suite 400, Washington DC 20006. Fax: (202)296-8716. Web site: www.americascommunitybankers.com/magazine. **25% freelance written.** Monthly magazine. "*America's Community Banker* is written for senior managers and executives of community financial institutions. The magazine covers all aspects of financial institution management, with an emphasis on strategic business issues and trends. Recent features have included bank technology, trends in home mortgage finance and alternative bank funding." Circ. 14,000. **Pays on acceptance.** Publishes ms an average of 2 months after acceptance. Byline given. Buys first North American serial rights. Editorial lead time 3 months. Submit seasonal material 6 months in advance. Responds in 1 month to queries. Sample copy and writer's guidelines free.

Nonfiction "Articles must be well-researched and backed up by a variety of sources, preferably senior managers of financial institutions or experts associated with the banking industry." How-to (articles on various aspects of a financial institution's operations). **Buys 6 mss/year.** Query with published clips. Length: 1,000-2,700 words. **Pays 50¢/word.**

Photos Send photos with submission. Reviews contact sheets, negatives, prints. Buys one-time rights. Identification of subjects required.

Columns/Departments Nationwide News (news items on banking and finance), 100-500 words; Technology Report (news on techology for community bankers); and Surveys and Trends (information on the banking business and business in general). **Buys 25 mss/year.** Query with published clips.

Tips "The best way to develop a relationship with *America's Community Banker* is through our 2 departments, Nationwide News and Technology Report. If writers can prove themselves reliable there first, major feature assignments may follow."

N $ $ $ CREDIT TODAY

Tomorrow's Tools for Today's Credit Professionals, P.O. Box 720, Roanoke VA 24004. (540)343-7500. E-mail: editor@credittoday.net. Web site: www.credittoday.net. **Contact:** Rob Lawson, editor. **50% freelance written.** Monthly newsletter covering business or "trade" credit. "Make pieces actionable, personable, and a quick read." Estab. 1997. **Pays on acceptance.** Publishes ms an average of 2 months after acceptance. Buys all rights. Editorial lead time 1-2 months. Accepts queries by e-mail. Sample copy for free. Writer's guidelines free.

Nonfiction How-to, interview/profile, technical. Does not want puff pieces promoting a particular product or vendor. **Buys 20 mss/year.** Query with published clips or send complete ms. Length: 700-1,800 words. **Pays $200-1,400.**

$ $ CREDIT UNION MANAGEMENT

Credit Union Executives Society, 5510 Research Park Dr., Madison WI 53711. Web site: www.cumanagement.org. **Contact:** Theresa Witham, editors. **44% freelance written.** Monthly magazine covering credit union, banking trends, management, HR, marketing issues. "Our philosophy mirrors the credit union industry of cooperative financial services." Estab. 1978. Circ. 7,413. **Pays on acceptance.** Publishes ms an average of 2 months after acceptance. Editorial lead time 3 months. Submit seasonal material 4 months in advance. Accepts queries by mail. Accepts simultaneous submissions. Responds in 2 weeks to queries; 1 month to mss. Sample copy and writer's guidelines free.

Nonfiction Book excerpts, how-to (be a good mentor/leader, recruit, etc.), interview/profile, technical. **Buys 74 mss/year.** Query with published clips. Length: 700-2,400 words. **$250-350 for assigned features.** Pays phone expenses only of writers on assignment.

Columns/Departments Management Network (book/Web reviews, briefs), 300 words; e-marketing, 700 words; Point of Law, 700 words; Best Practices (new technology/operations trends), 700 words. Query with published clips.

Tips "The best way is to e-mail an editor; include résumé, cover letter and clips. Knowledge of financial services is very helpful."

$ $ EQUITIES MAGAZINE, LLC

2118 Wilshire Blvd. #722, Santa Monica CA 90403. (914)723-6702. Fax: (914)723-0176. E-mail: equitymag@aol.com. Web site: www.equitiesmagazine.com. Editor: Robert Flaherty. **50% freelance written.** "We are a seven-issues-a-year financial magazine covering the fastest-growing public companies in the world. We study the management of companies and act as critics reviewing their performances. We aspire to be 'The Shareholder's Friend.' We want to be a bridge between quality public companies and sophisticated investors." Estab. 1951. Circ. 18,000. Pays on publication. Publishes ms an average of 2 months after acceptance. Byline given. Buys all rights. Accepts queries by mail. Sample copy for 9×12 SAE and 5 first-class stamps.

Nonfiction "We must know the writer first as we are careful about whom we publish. A letter of introduction with résumé and clips is the best way to introduce yourself. Financial writing requires specialized knowledge and a feel for people as well, which can be a tough combination to find." Carries guest columns by famous money managers who are not writing for cash payments, but to showcase their ideas and approach. Exposé, new product, technical. **Buys 30 mss/year.** Query with published clips. Length: 300-1,500 words. **Pays $250-750 for assigned articles, more for very difficult or investigative pieces.** Pays expenses of writers on assignment.

Photos Send color photos with submission. Reviews contact sheets, negatives, transparencies, prints. Offers no additional payment for photos accepted with ms. Identification of subjects required.

Columns/Departments Pays $25-75 for assigned items only.

Tips "Give us an idea for a story on a specific publically-owned company, whose stock is traded on NASDAQ, the NYSE, or American Stock Exchange. Anyone who enjoys analyzing a business and telling the story of the people who started it, or run it today, is a potential *Equities* contributor. But to protect our readers and ourselves, we are careful about who writes for us. We do not want writers who are trading the stocks of the companies they profile. Business writing is an exciting area and our stories reflect that. If a writer relies on numbers and percentages to tell his story, rather than the individuals involved, the result will be numbingly dull."

$ $ $ THE FEDERAL CREDIT UNION

National Association of Federal Credit Unions, 3138 N. 10th St., Arlington VA 22201. (703)522-4770. Fax: (703)524-1082. E-mail: tfcu@nafcu.org. Web site: www.nafcu.org. Executive Editor: Jay Morris. **Contact:** Robin Johnston, publisher/managing editor. **30% freelance written.** "Looking for writers with financial, banking, or credit union experience, but will work with inexperienced (unpublished) writers based on writing skill. Published bimonthly, *The Federal Credit Union* is the official publication of the National Association of Federal Credit Unions. The magazine is dedicated to providing credit union management, staff, and volunteers with in-depth information (HR, technology, security, board management, etc.) they can use to fulfill their duties and better serve their members. The editorial focus includes coverage of management issues, operations, and technology as well as volunteer-related issues." Estab. 1967. Circ. 8,000. Pays on publication. Publishes ms an average of 3 months after acceptance. Byline given. Buys first North American serial rights, rights to publish and archive online. Submit seasonal material 5 months in advance. Accepts queries by mail, e-mail, fax. Accepts simultaneous submissions. Responds in 2 months to queries. Sample copy for 10×13 SAE and 5 first-class stamps. Writer's guidelines for #10 SASE.

- Break in with "pithy, informative, thought-provoking items for our 'Management Insight' section (for free or a small fee of $50-200)."

Nonfiction Humor, inspirational, interview/profile. Query with published clips and SASE. Length: 1,200-2,000 words. **Pays $400-1,000.**

Photos Send photos with submission. Reviews 35mm transparencies, 5×7 prints, high-resolution photos. Buys all rights. Offers no additional payment for photos accepted with ms. Pays $50-500. Identification of subjects, model releases required.

- The online magazine carries original content not found in the print edition, as well as some print copy. Contact: Robin Johnston.

Tips "We would like more articles on how credit unions are using technology to serve their members and more articles on leading-edge technologies they can use in their operations. If you can write on current trends in technology, human resources, or strategic planning, you stand a better chance of being published than if you wrote on other topics."

ILLINOIS BANKER

Illinois Bankers Association, 133 S. Fourth St., Suite 300, Springfield IL 62701. (217)789-9340. Fax: (217)789-5410. **Contact:** Debbie Jemison, editor. "Our audience is approximately 3,000 bankers and vendors related to the banking industry. The purpose of the publication is to educate and inform readers on major public policy issues affecting banking today, as well as provide new ideas that can be applied to day-to-day operations and management. Writers may not sell or promote a product or service." Estab. 1891. Circ. 2,800. Publishes ms an average of 3 months after acceptance. Byline given. Buys first North American serial rights. Editorial lead time 2 months. Accepts simultaneous submissions. Responds in 3 months to queries. Sample copy and writer's guidelines free.

Nonfiction "It is *IBA* policy that writers do not sell or promote a particular product, service, or organization within the content of an article written for publication." Essays, historical/nostalgic, interview/profile, new product, opinion, personal experience. Query. Length: 1,000-1,500 words.

Photos State availability with submission. Reviews contact sheets, negatives, transparencies, prints. Captions, identification of subjects required.

Tips "Articles published in *Illinois Banker* address current issues of key importance to the banking industry in Illinois. Our intention is to keep readers informed of the latest industry news, developments, and trends, as well as provide necessary technical information. We publish articles on any topic that affects the banking industry, provided the content is in agreement with Association policy and position. Because we are a trade association, most articles need to be reviewed by an advisory committee before publication; therefore, the earlier they are submitted the better. Some recent topics include: agriculture, bank architecture, commercial and consumer credit, marketing, operations/cost control, security, and technology. In addition, articles are also considered on the topics of economic development and business/banking trends in Illinois and the Midwest region."

$ $ $ $ ON WALL STREET

Source Media, One State St. Plaza, 26th Floor, New York NY 10004. (212)803-8783. E-mail: frances.mcmorris@sourcemedia.com. Web site: www.onwallstreet.com. **Contact:** Frances A. McMorris, executive editor. **50% freelance written.** Monthly magazine for retail stockbrokers. "We help 95,000+ stockbrockers build their business." Estab. 1991. Circ. 95,000. Pays on publication. Publishes ms an average of 1-2 months after acceptance. Byline given. Buys all rights. Editorial lead time 3 months. Submit seasonal material 4 months in advance. Accepts queries by e-mail. Responds in 1-2 months to queries; 2 month to mss. Sample copy for $10.

Nonfiction How-to, interview/profile. "No investment-related articles about hot stocks, nor funds or hot alternative investments." **Buys 30 mss/year.** Query. Length: 1,000-3,000 words. **Pays $1/word.**

Photos State availability with submission. Reviews contact sheets. Buys all rights. Negotiates payment individually. Identification of subjects required.

Tips "Articles should be written for a professional, not consumer, audience."

$ $ SERVICING MANAGEMENT

The Magazine for Loan Servicing Professionals, Zackin Publications, P.O. Box 2180, Waterbury CT 06722. (800)325-6745. Fax: (203)755-3480. E-mail: bates@sm-online.com. Web site: www.sm-online.com. **Contact:** Michael Bates, editor. **15% freelance written.** Monthly magazine covering residential mortgage servicing. Estab. 1989. Circ. 20,000. **Pays on acceptance.** Publishes ms an average of 2 months after acceptance. Byline given. Buys all rights. Accepts queries by mail, e-mail, fax. Responds in 2 weeks to queries. Sample copy for free. Writer's guidelines online.

O→ Break in by "submitting a query for Servicing Reports, a monthly department featuring news and information about mortgage servicing and the industry. It should be informative, topical and include comments by industry professionals."

Nonfiction How-to, interview/profile, new product, technical. **Buys 10 mss/year.** Query. Length: 1,500-2,500 words. Will pay industry experts with contributor copies or other premiums rather than a cash payment.

Photos State availability with submission. Reviews contact sheets. Buys all rights. Offers no additional payment for photos accepted with ms. Identification of subjects required.

Columns/Departments **Buys 5 mss/year.** Query. **Pays $200.**

N TRANSACTION WORLD MAGAZINE

Transaction World, Inc., P.O. Box 2255, Wylie TX 75098. E-mail: editorinchief@transactionworld.net. Web site: www.transactionworld.net. **Contact:** Cynthia Bailey, president/editor. **40% freelance written.** Monthly magazine covering bankcard processing, electronic transactions. Estab. 2000. Circ. 15,500. Pays on publication. Publishes ms an average of 2 months after acceptance. Byline given. Editorial lead time 2-3 months. Submit seasonal material 4 months in advance. Accepts queries by e-mail. Accepts simultaneous submissions. Responds in 2 weeks to queries. Sample copy online. Writer's guidelines by e-mail.

Nonfiction Query. Length: 1,500-3,000 words. **Pays negotiable amount.**

Photos State availability with submission. Reviews GIF/JPEG files. Buys all rights. Offers no additional payment for photos accepted with ms.

Tips "Review Web site to understand industry and nature of accepted contributions."

FISHING

$ $ PACIFIC FISHING

Northwest Publishing Center, 1710 S. Norman St., Seattle WA 98144. (206)709-1840. Fax: (206)324-8939. E-mail: jholland@pfmag.com. Web site: www.pfmag.com. **Contact:** Jon Holland, editor. **75% freelance written.** Works with some new/unpublished writers. Monthly magazine for commercial fishermen and others in the commercial fishing industry throughout Alaska, the west coast, and the Pacific. "*Pacific Fishing* views the fisherman as a small businessman and covers all aspects of the industry, including harvesting, processing, and marketing." Estab. 1979. Circ. 8,000. Pays on publication. Publishes ms an average of 2 months after acceptance. Byline given. Buys first North American serial and unlimited re-use rights. Accepts queries by mail, e-mail, fax, phone. Variable response time to queries. Sample copy and writer's guidelines for 9×12 SAE with 10 first-class stamps.

O→ Study the magazine before querying.

Nonfiction "Articles must be concerned specifically with commercial fishing. We view fishermen as small business operators and professionals who are innovative and success-oriented. To appeal to this reader, *Pacific Fishing* offers 4 basic features: technical, how-to articles that give fishermen hands-on tips that will make their operation more efficient and profitable; practical, well-researched business articles discussing the dollars and cents of fishing, processing, and marketing; profiles of a fisherman, processor, or company with emphasis on practical business and technical areas; and in-depth analysis of political, social, fisheries management, and resource issues that have a direct bearing on commercial fishermen." **Buys 20 mss/year.** Query noting whether photos are available, and enclose samples of previous work and SASE. Length: Varies, one-paragraph news items to 3,000-word features. **Pays 20¢/word for most assignments.** Sometimes pays expenses of writers on assignment.

Photos "We need good, high-quality photography, especially color, of commercial fishing. We prefer 35mm color slides or JPEG files of at least 300 dpi." Our rates are $200 for cover; $50-100 for inside color; $25-75 for b&w; $10 for table of contents.

Tips "Read the magazine before sending a query. Make your pitch fit the magazine. If you haven't read it, don't waste your time and ours."

FLORISTS, NURSERIES & LANDSCAPERS

$ $ DIGGER

Oregon Association of Nurseries, 29751 SW Town Center Loop W., Wilsonville OR 97070. (503)682-5089. Fax: (503)682-5727. E-mail: csivesind@oan.org. Web site: www.oan.org. **Contact:** Cam Sivesind, manager of publications and communications. **50% freelance written.** Monthly magazine covering nursery and greenhouse industry. "Our readers are mainly nursery and greenhouse operators and owners who propagate nursery stock/crops, so we write with them in mind." Circ. 8,000. Pays on receipt of copy. Publishes ms an average of 2 months after acceptance. Byline given. Offers 100% kill fee. Buys first North American serial rights. Editorial lead time 6 weeks. Submit seasonal material 2 months in advance. Accepts queries by mail, e-mail, fax, phone. Sample copy and writer's guidelines free.

Nonfiction General interest, how-to (propagation techniques, other crop-growing tips), interview/profile, personal experience, technical. Special issues: Farwest Edition (August)—this is a triple-size issue that runs in tandem with our annual trade show (14,500 circulation for this issue). "No articles not related or pertinent to nursery and greenhouse industry." **Buys 20-30 mss/year.** Query. Length: 800-2,000 words. **Pays $125-400 for assigned articles; $100-300 for unsolicited articles.** Sometimes pays expenses of writers on assignment.

Photos State availability with submission. Reviews high-res digital images sent by e-mail or on CD preferred. Buys one-time rights, which includes Web posting. Offers $25-150/photo. Captions, identification of subjects required.

Tips "Our best freelancers are familiar with or have experience in the horticultural industry. Some 'green' knowledge is a definite advantage."

$ GROWERTALKS

Ball Publishing, 335 N. River St., P.O. Box 9, Batavia IL 60510. (630)208-9080. Fax: (630)208-9350. E-mail: beytes@growertalks.com. Web site: www.growertalks.com. **Contact:** Chris Beytes, editor. **50% freelance written.** Monthly magazine. "*GrowerTalks* serves the commercial greenhouse grower. Editorial emphasis is on floricultural crops: bedding plants, potted floral crops, foliage and fresh cut flowers. Our readers are growers, managers, and owners. We're looking for writers who've had experience in the greenhouse industry." Estab. 1937. Circ. 9,500. Pays on publication. Publishes ms an average of 3 months after acceptance. Byline given. Buys first North American serial rights. Editorial lead time 4 months. Submit seasonal material 3 months in advance. Accepts queries by mail, e-mail, fax. Responds in 1 month to queries. Sample copy and writer's guidelines free.

Nonfiction How-to (time- or money-saving projects for professional flower/plant growers), interview/profile (ornamental horticulture growers), personal experience (of a grower), technical (about growing process in greenhouse setting). "No articles that promote only one product." **Buys 36 mss/year.** Query. Length: 1,200-1,600 words. **Pays $125 minimum for assigned articles; $75 minimum for unsolicited articles.**

Photos State availability with submission. Reviews 2½×2½ slides and 3×5 prints. Buys one-time rights. Negotiates payment individually. Captions, identification of subjects, model releases required.

Tips "Discuss magazine with ornamental horticulture growers to find out what topics that have or haven't appeared in the magazine interest them."

$ $ THE GROWING EDGE

New Moon Publishing, Inc., P.O. Box 1027, Corvallis OR 97339. (541)757-8477. Fax: (541)757-0028. Web site: www.growingedge.com. **Contact:** Tom Weller, editor. **85% freelance written.** Bimonthly magazine covering indoor and outdoor high-tech gardening techniques and tips. Estab. 1980. Circ. 20,000. Pays on publication. Publishes ms an average of 3 months after acceptance. Byline given. Buys first serial and reprint rights. Submit seasonal material 6 months in advance. Accepts queries by mail, e-mail. Responds in 3 months to queries. Sample copy for $3. Writer's guidelines online.

O➛ Break in with "a detailed, knowledgeable e-mail story pitch."

Nonfiction How-to, interview/profile, personal experience (must be technical), book reviews, general horticulture and agriculture. Query. Length: 500-3,500 words. **Pays 20¢/word (10– for first rights, 5– for nonexclusive reprint and nonexclusive electronic rights).**

Reprints Send tearsheet, photocopy or typed ms with rights for sale noted and information about when and where the material previously appeared. Payment negotiable.

Photos Buys first and reprint rights. Pays $25-175. Pays on publication. Credit line given.

Tips Looking for more hydroponics articles and information that will give the reader/gardener/farmer the "growing edge" in high-tech gardening and farming on topics such as high intensity grow lights, water conservation, drip irrigation, advanced organic fertilizers, new seed varieties, and greenhouse cultivation.

$ $ ORNAMENTAL OUTLOOK

Your Connection To The South's Horticulture Industry, Meister Media Worldwide, 1555 Howell Branch Rd., Suite C204, Winter Park FL 32789. (407)539-6552. Fax: (407)539-6544. E-mail: tlcallies@meistermedia.com. Web site: www.ornamentaloutlook.com. **Contact:** Tacy Callies, editor. **20% freelance written.** Monthly magazine. "*Ornamental Outlook* is written for commercial growers of ornamental plants and landscapers in the Southeast US. Our goal is to provide interesting and informative articles on such topics as production, legislation, safety, technology, pest control, water management, and new varieties, as they apply to Southeast growers and landscapers." Estab. 1991. Circ. 11,000. Pays on publication. Publishes ms an average of 4 months after acceptance. Byline given. Buys all rights. Editorial lead time 2 months. Submit seasonal material 3 months in advance. Accepts queries by mail, e-mail, fax, phone. Responds in 3 months to queries. Sample copy for 9×12 SAE and 5 first-class stamps. Writer's guidelines free.

Nonfiction Interview/profile, photo feature, technical. "No first-person articles. No word-for-word meeting transcripts or all-quote articles." Query with published clips. Length: 600-1,000 words. **Pays $150-300/article including photos.**

Photos Send photos with submission. Reviews contact sheets, transparencies, prints. Buys one-time rights. Captions, identification of subjects required.

Tips "I am most impressed by written queries that address specific subjects of interest to our audience, which is the Southeast landscaper and grower of commercial horticulture. Our biggest demand is for features, about 700 words, that follow subjects listed on our editorial calendar (which is sent with guidelines). Please do not send articles of national or consumer interest."

$ $ TREE CARE INDUSTRY MAGAZINE

Tree Care Industry Association, 3 Perimeter Rd. Unit 1, Manchester NH 03103-3341. (800)733-2622 or (603)314-5380. Fax: (603)314-5386. E-mail: staruk@treecareindustry.org. Web site: www.treecareindustry.org. Managing Editor: Don Staruk. **50% freelance written.** Monthly magazine covering tree care and landscape maintenance. Estab. 1990. Circ. 27,500. Pays within 1 month of publication. Publishes ms an average of 3 months after acceptance. Byline given. Buys all rights. Editorial lead time 10 weeks. Submit seasonal material 3 months in advance. Accepts queries by e-mail. Responds in 2 weeks to queries; 2 months to mss. Sample copy for 9×12 SAE and 6 first-class stamps or view PDFs online. Writer's guidelines free.

Nonfiction Book excerpts, historical/nostalgic, interview/profile, new product, technical. **Buys 60 mss/year.** Query with published clips. Length: 900-3,500 words. **Pays negotiable rate.**

Photos Send photos with submission by e-mail or FTP site. Reviews prints. Buys one-time and Web rights. Negotiate payment individually. Captions, identification of subjects required.

Columns/Departments Buys 40 mss/year. Send complete ms. **Pays $100 and up.**

Tips "Preference is given to writers with background and knowledge of the tree care industry; our focus is relatively narrow."

GOVERNMENT & PUBLIC SERVICE

CANADIAN FIREFIGHTER AND EMS QUARTERLY

51 MacDonald Ave., Oromocto NB E2V 1A1 Canada. (506)446-4836. E-mail: canfirefight@annexweb.com. Web site: www.firefightingincanada.com. Editor: James Haley. Quarterly magazine covering fire fighting in Canada.

Nonfiction General interest, how-to, interview/profile, technical. Query.

N $ $ COUNTY

Texas Association of Counties, P.O. Box 2131, Austin TX 78768. (512)478-8753. Fax: (512)477-1324. E-mail: jiml@county.org. Web site: www.county.org. **Contact:** Jim Lewis, editor. **15% freelance written.** Bimonthly magazine covering county and state government in Texas. "We provide elected and appointed county officials with insights and information that help them do their jobs and enhances communications among the independent office-holders in the courthouse." Estab. 1988. Circ. 5,500. **Pays on acceptance.** Publishes ms an average of 2 months after acceptance. Byline given. Makes work-for-hire assignments. Editorial lead time 2 months. Submit seasonal material 4 months in advance. Accepts queries by mail, e-mail, phone. Responds in 2 weeks to queries; 1 month to mss. Sample copy and writer's guidelines for 8×10 SAE with 3 first-class stamps.

Nonfiction Historical/nostalgic, photo feature, government innovations. **Buys 5 mss/year.** Query with published clips. Length: 1,000-3,000 words. **Pays $500-700.** Sometimes pays expenses of writers on assignment.

Photos State availability with submission. Buys all rights. Negotiates payment individually. Captions, identification of subjects, model releases required.

Columns/Departments Safety; Human Resources; Risk Management (all directed toward education of Texas county officials), maximum length 1,000 words. **Buys 2 mss/year.** Query with published clips. **Pays $500.**

Tips "Identify innovative practices or developing trends that affect Texas county officials, and have the basic journalism skills to write a multi-sourced, informative feature."

$ $ FIRE CHIEF

Primedia Business, 330 N. Wabash, Suite 2300, Chicago IL 60611. (312)840-8410. Fax: (312)595-0295. E-mail: jwilmoth@primediabusiness.com. Web site: www.firechief.com. **Contact:** Janet Wilmoth, editor. **60% freelance written.** Monthly magazine. "*Fire Chief* is the management magazine of the fire service, addressing the administrative, personnel, training, prevention/education, professional development, and operational issues faced by chiefs and other fire officers, whether in paid, volunteer, or combination departments. We're potentially interested in any article that can help them do their jobs better, whether that's as incident commanders, financial managers, supervisors, leaders, trainers, planners, or ambassadors to municipal officials or the public." Estab. 1956. Circ. 53,000. Pays on publication. Publishes ms an average of 6 months after acceptance. Byline given. Kill fee negotiable. Buys first, one-time, second serial (reprint), all rights. Editorial lead time 2 months. Submit seasonal material 4 months in advance. Accepts queries by mail, e-mail, fax. Responds in 1 month to queries; 2 months to mss. Sample copy and writer's guidelines free or online.

Nonfiction "If your department has made some changes in its structure, budget, mission, or organizational culture (or really did reinvent itself in a serious way), an account of that process, including the mistakes made and lessons learned, could be a winner. Similarly, if you've observed certain things that fire departments typically could do a lot better and you think you have the solution, let us know." How-to, technical. **Buys 50-60 mss/year.** Query with published clips. Length: 1,500-8,000 words. **Pays $50-400.** Sometimes pays expenses of writers on assignment.

Photos State availability with submission. Reviews transparencies, prints. Buys one-time or reprint rights. Captions, identification of subjects required.

Columns/Departments Training Perspectives; EMS Viewpoints; Sound Off; Volunteer Voice; all 1,000-1,800 words.

Tips "Writers who are unfamiliar with the fire service are very unlikely to place anything with us. Many pieces that we reject are either too unfocused or too abstract. We want articles that help keep fire chiefs well informed and effective at their jobs."

N FIRE ENGINEERING

21-00 Route 208 S., Fair Lawn NJ 07410. (800)962-6484, ext. 5047. E-mail: dianef@pennwell.com. Web site: www.fireengineering.com. **Contact:** Diane Feldman. Monthly magazine covering issues of importance to firefighters. Accepts queries by mail, e-mail. Responds in 2-3 months to mss. Writer's guidelines online.

Nonfiction Themes: Training/Instructor Development, Engine Company Operations, Technical Rescue, Fire Protection, EMS, Truck Company Operations, Apparatus, Fire Technology, Firefighter Safety and Health, Officer Development, and Leadership and Management. How-to, new product, incident reports, training. Send complete ms.

Photos Reviews transparencies, prints, JPEG/TIFF/EPS files (300 dpi).

Columns/Departments Volunteers Corner; Training Notebook; Rescue Company; The Engine Company; The Truck Company; Fire Prevention Bureau; Apparatus; The Shops; Fire Service EMS; Fire Service Court; Speaking of Safety; Fire Commentary; Technology Today; and Innovations: Homegrown. Send complete ms.

FIRE FIGHTING IN CANADA

Canada's National Fire Magazine, 51 MacDonald Ave., Oromocto NB E2V 1A1 Canada. (506)446-4836. E-mail: firefightcan@annexweb.com. Web site: www.firefightingincanada.com. Editor: James Haley. Magazine published 8 times/year covering fire fighting in Canada.

Nonfiction General interest, interview/profile, technical. Query.

$ $ FIREHOUSE MAGAZINE

Cygnus Business Media, 3 Huntington Quadrangle, Suite 301N, Melville NY 11747. (631)845-2700. Fax: (631)845-7218. E-mail: editors@firehouse.com. Web site: www.firehouse.com. Editor-in-Chief: Harvey Eisner. **Contact:** Elizabeth Neroulas, managing editor. **85% freelance written.** Works with a small number of new/unpublished writers each year. Monthly magazine. "*Firehouse* covers major fires nationwide, controversial issues and trends in the fire service, the latest firefighting equipment and methods of firefighting, historical fires, firefighting history and memorabilia. Fire-related books, fire safety education, hazardous-materials incidents, and the emergency medical services are also covered." Estab. 1976. Circ. 127,000. Pays on publication. Byline given. Accepts queries by mail, e-mail, fax. Sample copy for 9×12 SAE and 8 first-class stamps. Writer's guidelines online.

Nonfiction Book excerpts (of recent books on fire, EMS, and hazardous materials), historical/nostalgic (great fires in history, fire collectibles, the fire service of yesteryear), how-to (fight certain kinds of fires, buy and maintain equipment, run a fire department), technical (on almost any phase of firefighting, techniques, equipment, training, administration), trends in the fire service. No profiles of people or departments that are not unusual or innovative, reports of nonmajor fires, articles not slanted toward firefighters' interests. No poetry. **Buys 100 mss/year.** Query with or without published clips. Length: 500-3,000 words. **Pays $50-400 for assigned articles.**

Photos Send photos with submission. Pays $25-200 for transparencies and color prints. Cannot accept negatives. Captions, identification of subjects required.

Columns/Departments Training (effective methods); Book Reviews; Fire Safety (how departments teach fire safety to the public); Communicating (PR, dispatching); Arson (efforts to combat it). Length: 750-1,000 words. **Buys 50 mss/year.** Query or send complete ms. **Pays $100-300.**

Tips "Have excellent fire service credentials and be able to offer our readers new information. Read the magazine to get a full understanding of the subject matter, the writing style, and the readers before sending a query or manuscript. Send photos with manuscript or indicate sources for photos. Be sure to focus articles on firefighters."

$ $ FIRE-RESCUE MAGAZINE

Jems Communications, 525 B St., Suite 1900, San Diego CA 92101. Fax: (619)699-6396. E-mail: jems.editor@elsevier.com. Web site: www.jems.com. **75% freelance written.** Monthly magazine covering technical aspects of being a firefighter/rescuer. Estab. 1988. Circ. 50,000. Pays on publication. Buys first North American serial, one-time rights. Submit seasonal material 6 months in advance. Accepts queries by mail. Responds in 3 weeks to queries; 2 months to mss. Sample copy and writer's guidelines for 9×12 SAE with 5 first-class stamps or online. Writer's guidelines online.

Nonfiction How-to, new product, photo feature, technical, incident review/report. Special issues: fire suppression, incident command, vehicle extrication, rescue training, mass-casualty incidents, water rescue/major issues facing the fire service. **Buys 15-20 mss/year.** Query with published clips or send complete ms. Length: 1,000-3,000 words. **Pays $125-250.** Sometimes pays expenses of writers on assignment.

Photos Send photos with submission. Reviews contact sheets, negatives, 2×2 and 35mm transparencies, 5×7 prints. Buys one-time rights. Offers $20-200.

Tips "Read our magazine, spend some time with a fire department. We focus on all aspects of fire and rescue. Emphasis on techniques and new technology, with color photos as support."

$ $ HSTODAY

Insight and Analysis for Homeland Security Decisionmakers, KMD Media LLC, P.O. Box 9789, McLean VA. (703)757-0520. Fax: (866)503-5758. E-mail: editor@hstoday.us. Web site: www.hstoday.us. Senior Correspondent: Anthony Kimery. **Contact:** David Silverberg, editor. **100% freelance written.** Monthly magazine covering homeland security and everything related to public safety, security, and emergency management. "This is a magazine designed for government officials with decision and policy-making authority and homeland security responsibilities at the federal, state, and local levels. While written for professionals, we want to be accessible to all readers. Accordingly, we seek good, accurate, comprehensive reporting and analysis that delivers new and useful information to our readers in a lively and engaging style. We encourage articles from everyone in the homeland security community, especially people with firsthand knowledge of HS topics or relevant personal experience." Estab. 2004. Circ. 30,000. Pays on publication. Publishes ms an average of 6 weeks after acceptance. Byline given. Buys first North American serial rights. Editorial lead time 6 weeks. Accepts queries by e-mail. Sample copy for #10 SASE. Writer's guidelines free.

Nonfiction "We are looking for analysis and insight related to homeland security topics and best practices in the field. The editor should be contacted by e-mail (editor@hstoday.us) before making any proposal." Opinion (essays from people in the homeland security community; must deal with government policy), reporting/analysis. Special issues: *HSToday* has 1 ongoing special feature: regional reports. In the regional reports, we report on homeland security measures taken in each of these cities and their surrounding regions along with tips on the procurement practices in each municipality. "No vague, alarmist articles chiefly of interest to general consumer audiences. While being aware of the threat, we concentrate on solutions rather than vulnerability. Our audience of government officials, law enforcement, and first responders is very well aware of homeland security vulnerabilities." Query. Length: Length: 1,500 words. **Pays $500.**

Photos State availability with submission. Reviews JPEG files. Offers no additional payment for photos accepted with ms. Captions required.

Columns/Departments After Action (analysis and lessons learned from past terrorism-related incidents or events), 1,500 words. **Buys 10-12 mss/year.** Query. **Pays $500.**

Tips "Best approach is to query editor by e-mail. Some background in reporting on government, law enforcement, defense, homeland security, and/or government procurement is helpful but not essential. We don't publish corporate bylines, technology White Papers, or one product/one company articles. Our best articles are on government practices, innovative solutions to homeland security challenges, and what homeland security professionals are doing in their jurisdictions. While based in the Washington DC area, we're always looking for articles from towns and cities around the country, and we want to build a network of local and international correspondents. We have a particular need for good reporting on funding, appropriations, and federal grantmaking in homeland security."

$ $ THE JOURNAL OF SAFE MANAGEMENT OF DISRUPTIVE AND ASSAULTIVE BEHAVIOR

Crisis Prevention Institute, Inc., 3315-K N. 124th St., Brookfield WI 53005. Fax: (262)783-5906. E-mail: editor@crisisprevention.com. Web site: www.crisisprevention.com. **Contact:** Jerilyn Dufresne, director of communications. **75% freelance written.** Semiannual journal covering safe management of disruptive and assaultive behavior. "Our audience consists of human service and business professionals concerned about workplace violence issues, and who want to stay on the cutting edge of crisis trends and solutions in workplaces." Estab. 1980. Circ. 20,000. Pays on publication. Publishes ms an average of 6 months after acceptance. Byline given. Offers 50% kill fee. Buys full publication rights for original work and one-time rights for reprints. Editorial lead time 6 months. Submit seasonal material 3 months in advance. Responds in 1 month to queries. Sample copy and writer's guidelines free.

Nonfiction "Each issue is specifically devoted to one topic. Inquire about topics by e-mail or read journal for editorial calendar." Interview/profile, new product, opinion, personal experience, research. **Buys 5-10 mss/year.** Query. Length: 1,500-3,000 words. **Pays $100-300 for assigned articles; $100 for unsolicited articles.**

Tips "It's wise to know about CPI before attempting to write for us. We specialize in nonviolent and respectful interventions."

$ $ LAW AND ORDER

Hendon Co., 130 N. Waukegan Rd., Deerfield IL 60015. (847)444-3300. Fax: (847)444-3333. E-mail: esanow@hendonpub.com. Web site: www.lawandordermag.com. **Contact:** Ed Sanow, editorial director. **90% freelance written.** Prefers to work with published/established writers. Monthly magazine covering the administration and operation of law enforcement agencies, directed to police chiefs, sheriffs, and supervisors. Estab. 1953. Circ. 42,000. Pays on publication. Publishes ms an average of 6 months after acceptance. Byline given. Buys all rights. Submit seasonal material 3 months in advance. Accepts queries by mail, e-mail, fax, phone. Responds in 1 month to queries. Sample copy for 9×12 SAE. Writer's guidelines online.

Nonfiction General police interest. How-to (do specific police assignments), new product (how applied in police operation), technical (specific police operation). Special issues: Weapons (January); Buyers Guide (February); S.W.A.T. (March); Community Relations (April); Science & Technology (May); Training (June); Mobile Patrol (July); Communications (August); Uniforms (September); IACP (October); Investigative (November); Computing & the Internet (December). No articles dealing with courts (legal field) or convicted prisoners. No nostalgic, financial, travel, or recreational material. **Buys 150 mss/year.** Query; no simultaneous queries. Length: 2,000-3,000 words. **Pays 10-25¢/word.**

Photos Send photos with submission. Reviews transparencies, prints. Buys all rights. Pays $25-40/photo. Identification of subjects required.

Tips "*L&O* is a respected magazine that provides up-to-date information that police chiefs can use. Writers must know their subject as it applies to this field. Case histories are well received. We are upgrading editorial quality—stories must show some understanding of the law enforcement field. A frequent mistake is not getting photographs to accompany article."

$ $ LAW ENFORCEMENT TECHNOLOGY

Cygnus Business Media, P.O. Box 803, 1233 Janesville Ave., Fort Atkinson WI 53538-0803. (920)563-1726. Fax: (920)563-1702. E-mail: ronnie.garrett@cygnuspub.com. Editor: Ronnie Garrett. **50% freelance written.** Monthly magazine covering police management and technology. Estab. 1974. Circ. 35,000. Pays on publication. Publishes ms an average of 6 months after acceptance. Byline given. Offers 25% kill fee. Buys first North American serial rights. Editorial lead time 6 months. Submit seasonal material 6 months in advance. Responds in 1 month to queries; 2 months to mss. Writer's guidelines for #10 SASE.

Nonfiction Book excerpts, how-to, interview/profile, photo feature, police management and training. **Buys 15 mss/year.** Query. Length: 800-1,800 words. **Pays $75-400 for assigned articles.**

Reprints Send ms with rights for sale noted and information about when and where the material previously appeared. Payment negotiable.

Photos Send photos with submission. Reviews contact sheets, negatives, 5×7 or 8×10 prints. Buys one-time rights. Offers no additional payment for photos accepted with ms. Captions required.

Tips "Writer should have background in police work or currently work for a police agency. Most of our articles are technical or supervisory in nature. Please query first after looking at a sample copy."

$ $ NATIONAL FIRE & RESCUE

SpecComm International, Inc., 5808 Faringdon Place, Suite 200, Raleigh NC 27609. (919)872-5040. Fax: (919)876-6531. E-mail: mike@nfrmag.com. Web site: www.nfrmag.com. **Contact:** Mike Macdonald, managing editor. **80% freelance written.** "*National Fire & Rescue* is a bimonthly magazine devoted to informing the nation's fire and rescue services, with special emphasis on fire departments serving communities of less than 100,000. It is the *Popular Science* for fire and rescue with easy-to-understand information on science, technology, and training." Estab. 1980. Circ. 30,000. Pays on publication. Publishes ms an average of 5 months after acceptance. Byline given. Offers 50% kill fee. Buys first North American serial rights. Editorial lead time 2 months. Submit seasonal material 3 months in advance. Accepts simultaneous submissions. Responds in 1 month to queries. Call for writer's guidelines.

Nonfiction Book excerpts, how-to, humor, inspirational, interview/profile, new product, personal experience, photo feature. No pieces marketing specific products or services. **Buys 40 mss/year.** Query with published clips. Length: 1,800-3,000 words. **Pays $100-350 for assigned articles; $100-200 for unsolicited articles.** Pays expenses of writers on assignment.

Photos State availability with submission. Buys one-time rights. Offers $50-200/photo. Identification of subjects required.

Columns/Departments Leadership (management); Training; Special Operations; all 1,800 words. **Buys 16 mss/year.** Send complete ms. **Pays $100-200.**

Tips "Discuss your story ideas with the editor."

$ $ 9-1-1 MAGAZINE

Official Publications, Inc., 18201 Weston Place, Tustin CA 92780-2251. (714)544-7776. Fax: (714)838-9233. E-mail: publisher@9-1-1magazine.com. Web site: www.9-1-1magazine.com. **Contact:** Randall Larson, editor

(editor@9-1-1magazine.com). **85% freelance written.** Trade magazine published 9 times/year for knowledgeable emergency communications professionals and those associated with this respectful profession. "Serving law enforcement, fire, and emergency medical services, with an emphasis on communications, *9-1-1 Magazine* provides valuable information to readers in all aspects of the public safety communications and response community. Each issue contains a blending of product-related, technical, operational, and people-oriented stories, covering the skills, training, and equipment which these professionals have in common." Estab. 1989. Circ. 15,000. Pays on publication. Publishes ms an average of 4-6 months after acceptance. Byline given. Offers 20% kill fee. Buys one-time, second serial (reprint) rights. Accepts queries by mail, e-mail, fax. Responds in 1 month to queries; 1 month to mss. Sample copy for 9×12 SAE and 5 first-class stamps. Writer's guidelines online.

Nonfiction New product, photo feature, technical, incident report. **Buys 15-25 mss/year.** Query by e-mail. "We prefer queries, but will look at manuscripts on speculation. Most positive responses to queries are considered on spec, but occasionally we will make assignments." Length: 1,000-2,500 words. **Pays 10¢/word.**

Photos Send photos with submission. Reviews color transparencies, prints, high-resolution digital (300 dpi). Buys one-time rights. Offers $50-100/interior, $300/cover. Captions, identification of subjects required.

The online version of this magazine contains material not found in the print version.

Tips "We are looking for writers knowledgable in this field. As a trade magazine, stories should be geared for professionals in the emergency services and dispatch field, not the lay public. We do not use poetry or fiction. Our primary considerations in selecting material are: quality, appropriateness of material, brevity, knowledge of our readership, accuracy, accompanying photography, originality, wit and humor, a clear direction and vision, and proper use of language."

$ $ P I MAGAZINE

Journal of Professional Investigators, P I Magazine, Inc., 4400 Route 9 S., Suite 1000, P.O. Box 7198, Freehold NJ 07728-7198. (732)308-3800. Fax: (732)308-3314. E-mail: editor@pimagazine.com. Web site: www.pimagazine.com. Publisher/Editor-in-Chief: Jimmie Mesis. **Contact:** Don Johnson, editor. **90% freelance written.** Magazine published 6 times/year. "Audience includes US, Canada, and professional investigators in 20-plus countries, law enforcement, attorneys, process servers, paralegals, and other legal professionals." Estab. 1988. Pays on publication. Accepts queries by mail, e-mail. Sample copy for free. Writer's guidelines online.

- No payment for unsolicited materials.

Nonfiction "Manuscripts must include educational material for professional investigators. Profiles are accepted if they offer information on how other professionals can use the knowledge or expertise utilized by the person profiled. Accounts of real cases are used only as part of an educational piece. Investigators with special expertise should query for educational articles to exceed 1,000 words." **Buys up to 75 mss/year.** Query. Length: 750-2,500 words. **Pays $50-500 upon acceptance.**

Photos State availability with submission. May offer additional payment for photos accepted with ms. Identification of subjects, model releases required.

Tips "*P I Magazine* has a new publisher and editor-in-chief, a new editor, and a new focus! Please review the current issue online to understand the magazine before submitting a query. Avoid clichés and television inspired concepts of PIs. Great way to get the editor's attention: There are numerous special sections that need shorts of 500 words or less. $10-75."

$ $ $ PLANNING

American Planning Association, 122 S. Michigan Ave., Suite 1600, Chicago IL 60603. (312)431-9100. Fax: (312)431-9985. E-mail: slewis@planning.org. Web site: www.planning.org. **Contact:** Sylvia Lewis, editor. **30% freelance written.** Monthly magazine emphasizing urban planning for adult, college-educated readers who are regional and urban planners in city, state, or federal agencies or in private business, or university faculty or students. Estab. 1972. Circ. 42,000. Pays on publication. Publishes ms an average of 2 months after acceptance. Byline given. Buys all rights. Accepts queries by mail, e-mail, fax. Responds in 5 weeks to queries. Sample copy for 9×12 SAE with 6 first-class stamps. Writer's guidelines online.

Nonfiction "It's best to query with a fairly detailed, 1-page letter or e-mail. We'll consider any article that's well written and relevant to our audience. Articles have a better chance if they are timely and related to planning, and if they appeal to a national audience. All articles should be written in magazine-feature style." Exposé (on government or business, but topics related to planning, housing, land use, zoning), general interest (trend stories on cities, land use, government), how-to (successful government or citizen efforts in planning, innovations, concepts that have been applied), technical (detailed articles on the nitty-gritty of planning, transportation, computer mapping, but no footnotes or mathematical models). Special issues: Transportation Issue; Technology Issue. Also needs news stories up to 500 words. **Buys 44 features and 33 news story mss/year.** Length: 500-3,000 words. **Pays $150-1,500.**

Photos "We prefer authors supply their own photos, but we sometimes take our own or arrange for them in other ways.'' State availability with submission. Buys one-time rights. Pays $100 minimum for photos used on inside pages and $300 for cover photos. Captions required.

$ $ POLICE AND SECURITY NEWS

DAYS Communications, Inc., 1208 Juniper St., Quakertown PA 18951-1520. (215)538-1240. Fax: (215)538-1208. E-mail: jdevery@policeandsecuritynews.com. **Contact:** James Devery, editor. **40% freelance written.** Bimonthly tabloid on public law enforcement and Homeland Security. ''Our publication is designed to provide educational and entertaining information directed toward management level. Technical information written for the expert in a manner the nonexpert can understand.'' Estab. 1984. Circ. 22,000. Pays on publication. Publishes ms an average of 2 months after acceptance. Byline given. Buys first North American serial rights. Accepts queries by mail, e-mail, fax, phone. Accepts simultaneous submissions. Sample copy and writer's guidelines for 9×12 SAE with $2.44 postage.

Nonfiction Al Menear, articles editor. Exposé, historical/nostalgic, how-to, humor, interview/profile, opinion, personal experience, photo feature, technical. **Buys 12 mss/year.** Query. Length: 200-4,000 words. **Pays 10¢/word. Sometimes pays in trade-out of services.**

Reprints Send tearsheet, photocopy or typed ms with rights for sale noted and information about when and where the material previously appeared.

Photos State availability with submission. Reviews 3×5 prints. Buys one-time rights. Offers $10-50/photo.

Fillers Facts, newsbreaks, short humor. **Buys 6/year.** Length: 200-2,000 words. **Pays 10¢/word.**

N THE UTAH PEACE OFFICER

Utah Peace Officers Association, P.O. Box 277, West Jordan UT 84084. Fax: (801)313-0761. Web site: www.upoa.org. Editor: Les Langford. Quarterly magazine for law enforcement officers and their families in the State of Utah.

Nonfiction General interest, humor, inspirational, interview/profile. Query.

N $ $ WILDLAND FIREFIGHTER MAGAZINE

Jems Communications, 525 B St., Suite 1900, San Diego CA 92101. E-mail: m.garrido@elsevier.com. Web site: www.wildlandfirefighter.com. **Contact:** Michelle Garrido, editor. Monthly magazine focusing on stories from the fireline, practical information, news, techniques and product reviews to assist wildland firefighters and fire managers. Estab. 1994. Pays on publication. Responds in 3 months to mss. Writer's guidelines online.

Nonfiction General interest, how-to, interview/profile, new product, technical. Query. Length: 200-2,200 words. **Pays $25-250.**

GROCERIES & FOOD PRODUCTS

$ $ $ CAMPUS DINING TODAY

The National Association of College & University Food Services, 1405 S. Harrison Rd., Suite 305, East Lansing MI 48824-5242. (517)332-2494. Fax: (517)332-8144. E-mail: jsmith@nacufs.org. Web site: www.nacufs.org. **Contact:** Jodi L. Smith, NACUFS marketing manager. **65% freelance written.** Semiannual magazine. ''*Campus Dining Today* provides current industry information on college dining trends and techniques.'' Estab. 1998. Circ. 3,900. Pays on publication. Publishes ms an average of 2-3 months after acceptance. Byline given. Buys all rights. Editorial lead time 3 months. Submit seasonal material 6 weeks in advance. Accepts queries by mail, e-mail, phone. Sample copy for $15. Writer's guidelines free.

Nonfiction Essays, general interest, how-to, interview/profile, photo feature, technical. **Buys 6-8 mss/year.** Query. Length: 600-3,000 words. **Pays $300-1,000.**

Photos Send photos with submission. Reviews GIF/JPEG files. Buys one time and electronic rights. Offers no additional payment for photos accepted with ms. Captions required.

$ $ $ DISTRIBUTION CHANNELS

AWMA's Magazine for Candy, Tobacco, Grocery, Foodservice and General Merchandise Marketers, American Wholesale Marketers Association, 2750 Prosperity Ave., Suite 530, Fairfax VA 22031. Fax: (703)573-5738. E-mail: tracic@awmanet.org. Web site: www.awmanet.org. **Contact:** Traci Carneal, editor-in-chief. **70% freelance written.** Magazine published 10 times/year. ''We cover trends in candy, tobacco, groceries, beverages, snacks, and other product categories found in convenience stores, grocery stores, and drugstores, plus distribution topics. Contributors should have prior experience writing about the food, retail, and/or distribution industries. Editorial includes a mix of columns, departments, and features (2-6 pages). We also cover AWMA programs.'' Estab. 1948. Circ. 11,000. **Pays on acceptance.** Publishes ms an average of 2 months after acceptance. Byline given. Editorial lead time 4 months. Accepts queries by mail, e-mail, fax. Writer's guidelines online.

Nonfiction How-to, technical, industry trends; also profiles of distribution firms. No comics, jokes, poems, or other fillers. **Buys 40 mss/year.** Query with published clips. Length: 1,200-3,600 words. **Pays 50¢/word.** Sometimes pays industry members who author articles. Pays expenses of writers on assignment.
Photos Authors must provide artwork (with captions) with articles.
Tips "We're looking for reliable, accurate freelancers with whom we can establish a long-term working relationship. We need writers who understand this industry. We accept very few articles on speculation. Most are assigned. To consider a new writer for an assignment, we must first receive his or her résumé, at least 2 writing samples, and references."

N $ $ $ $ FOOD PRODUCT DESIGN MAGAZINE
Weeks Publishing, 3400 Dundee Rd., Suite 100, Northbrook IL 60062. (847)559-0385. Fax: (847)559-0389. E-mail: weeksfpd@aol.com. **Contact:** Lynn Kuntz, editor. **50% freelance written.** Monthly magazine covering food processing industry. "The magazine written for food technologists by food technologists. No foodservice/restaurant, consumer, or recipe development." Estab. 1991. Circ. 30,000. **Pays on acceptance.** Publishes ms an average of 2 months after acceptance. Byline given. Buys one-time, all rights, makes work-for-hire assignments. Editorial lead time 4 months. Sample copy for 9×12 SAE and 5 first-class stamps.
Nonfiction Technical. **Buys 30 mss/year.** Length: 1,500-7,000 words. **Pays $100-1,500.** Sometimes pays expenses of writers on assignment.
Reprints Accepts previously published submissions depending on where it was published.
Photos State availability with submission. Reviews transparencies, prints. Buys rights depending on photo. Offers no additional payment for photos accepted with ms. Captions required.
Columns/Departments Pays $100-500.
Tips "If you haven't worked in the food industry in research & development, or QA/QC, don't bother to call us. If you can't communicate technical information in a way that is clear, easy-to-understand and well organized, don't bother to call us. While perfect grammar is not expected, good grammar and organization is."

$ $ FOODSERVICE DIRECTOR
VNU Business Media, 90 Broad St., Suite 402, New York NY 10004. (646)708-7318. Fax: (646)708-7399. E-mail: jpond@fsdmag.com. Web site: www.fsdmag.com. Editor-In-Chief: James Pond. Senior Editor: Karen Weisberg. News Editor: Jennifer Alexis. **20% freelance written.** Monthly tabloid covering noncommercial foodservice operations for operators of kitchens and dining halls in schools, colleges, hospitals/health care, office and plant cafeterias, military, airline/transportation, correctional institutions. Estab. 1988. Circ. 45,000. Pays on publication. Byline sometimes given. Buys all rights for print and online usage. Submit seasonal material 3 months in advance. Accepts simultaneous submissions. Sample copy for free.
Nonfiction How-to, interview/profile. **Buys 60-70 mss/year.** Query with published clips. Length: 700-900 words. **Pays $250-500.**
Photos Send photos with submission. Reviews transparencies. Buys all rights. Offers no additional payment for photos accepted with ms. Identification of subjects required.
Columns/Departments Equipment (case studies of kitchen/serving equipment in use), 700-900 words; Food (specific category studies per publication calendar), 750-900 words. Query.

N $ FRESH CUT MAGAZINE
The Magazine for Value-added Produce, Great American Publishing, P.O. Box 128, 75 Applewood Dr., Suite A, Sparta MI 49345. (616)887-9008. Editorial Director: Kimberly Warren. Publisher: Matt McCallum. Assistant Editor: Scott Christie. **20% freelance written.** Monthly magazine covering the value-added and pre-cut fruit and vegetable industry. The editor is interested in articles that focus on what different fresh-cut processors are doing. Estab. 1993. Circ. 16,000. Pays on publication. Publishes ms an average of 2 months after acceptance. Byline given. Buys all rights. Editorial lead time 2 months. Accepts queries by mail, e-mail, fax, phone. Responds in 1 month to queries; 2 months to mss. Sample copy for 9×12 SAE. Writer's guidelines for #10 SASE.

O→ "We want to hear of new products, packaging, food safety programs, how they deal with transportation issues—anything of interest to the industry. We're also interested in the use of pre-cut fruit and vegetable products in retail and foodservice—growth trends and perception by chefs, store managers and others."

Nonfiction Historical/nostalgic, new product, opinion, technical. **Buys 2-4 mss/year.** Query with published clips.
Reprints Send tearsheet with rights for sale noted and information about when and where the material previously appeared. Pays 50% of amount paid for an original article.
Photos Send photos with submission. Reviews transparencies. Buys one-time rights. Offers no additional payment for photos accepted with ms. Identification of subjects required.
Columns/Departments Packaging; Food Safety; Processing/Engineering. **Buys 20 mss/year.** Query. **Pays $125-200.**

N $ $ $ NATURAL FOOD NETWORK MAGAZINE

Supporting the Business of Natural & Organic Food Supply, Rich's Business Media, 604 Price Ave., Suite 100, Redwood City CA 94063. (650)363-1023. Fax: (650)362-1026. E-mail: news@naturalfoodnet.com. Web site: www.naturalfoodnet.com. Managing Editor: Samantha Molineaux. **Contact:** Dan Bolton, editor. **70% freelance written.** Bimonthly magazine covering natural and certified organic food industry (domestic and international). Estab. 2003. Circ. 15,000. Pays on publication. Publishes ms an average of 2 months after acceptance. Byline given. Offers 10% up to $50 maximum kill fee. Buys first North American serial rights. Editorial lead time 2 months. Submit seasonal material 2 months in advance. Accepts queries by e-mail. Accepts simultaneous submissions. Responds in 1 week to queries; 1 month to mss. Sample copy for free. Writer's guidelines free.

Nonfiction "Our publication circulates entirely to retail and supply professionals." Does not want work with a consumer angle. **Buys 50 mss/year.** Query. Length: 250-1,500 words. **Pays $250-750.** Sometimes pays expenses of writers on assignment.

Photos State availability with submission. Reviews JPEG files. Buys all rights. Offers no additional payment for photos accepted with ms. Captions, identification of subjects required.

Columns/Departments Q&A with industry leaders (natural and organic specialists in academia, trade associations and business); Worldview (interviews with internationally recognized leaders in organic food supply), both 750 words. **Buys 6 mss/year.** Query. **Pays $500.**

Tips "Our magazine encourages writers to work closely with editors using online story pitch and assignment software. This collaborative software permits writers to see what is being pitched (anonymously) and to track their own assignments, download materials like story guidelines and monitor deadlines."

$ $ PRODUCE MERCHANDISING

Vance Publishing Corp., 10901 W. 84th Terrace, Lenexa KS 66214. (913)438-8700. Fax: (913)438-0691. E-mail: eashby@producemerchandising.com. Web site: www.producemerchandising.com. **Contact:** Elizabeth Ashby, editor. **10% freelance written.** Monthly magazine. "The magazine's editorial purpose is to provide information about promotions, merchandising, and operations in the form of ideas and examples. *Produce Merchandising* is the only monthly journal on the market that is dedicated solely to produce merchandising information for retailers." Circ. 12,000. **Pays on acceptance.** Publishes ms an average of 3 months after acceptance. Byline given. Buys all rights. Editorial lead time 3 months. Accepts queries by mail. Responds in 2 weeks to queries. Sample copy for free.

Nonfiction How-to, interview/profile, new product, photo feature, technical (contact the editor for a specific assignment). **Buys 48 mss/year.** Query with published clips. Length: 1,000-1,500 words. **Pays $200-600.** Pays expenses of writers on assignment.

Photos State availability of or send photos with submission. Reviews color slides and 3×5 or larger prints. Buys all rights. Offers no additional payment for photos accepted with ms. Captions, identification of subjects, model releases required.

Columns/Departments Contact editor for a specific assignment. **Buys 30 mss/year.** Query with published clips. **Pays $200-450.**

Tips "Send in clips and contact the editor with specific story ideas. Story topics are typically outlined up to a year in advance."

$ $ THE PRODUCE NEWS

800 Kinderkamack Rd., Suite 100, Oradell NJ 07649. (201)986-7990. Fax: (201)986-7996. E-mail: groh@theproducenews.com. Web site: www.theproducenews.com. Publisher: Gordon M. Hochberg. **Contact:** John Groh, editor. **10% freelance written.** Works with a small number of new/unpublished writers each year. Weekly magazine for commercial growers and shippers, receivers and distributors of fresh fruits and vegetables, including chain store produce buyers and merchandisers. Estab. 1897. Pays on publication. Publishes ms an average of 2 weeks after acceptance. Accepts queries by mail, e-mail, fax. Responds in 1 month to queries. Sample copy and writer's guidelines for 10×13 SAE and 4 first-class stamps.

Nonfiction News stories (about the produce industry). Buys profiles, spot news, coverage of successful business operations and articles on merchandising techniques. Query. **Pays $1/column inch minimum.** Sometimes pays expenses of writers on assignment.

Photos Black and white glossies or color prints. Pays $8-10/photo.

Tips "Stories should be trade oriented, not consumer oriented. As our circulation grows in the next year, we are interested in stories and news articles from all fresh-fruit-growing areas of the country."

$ $ WESTERN GROCER MAGAZINE

Mercury Publications Ltd., 1740 Wellington Ave., Winnipeg MB R3H 0E8 Canada. (204)954-2085. Fax: (204)954-2057. Web site: www.mercury.mb.ca/. **75% freelance written.** Bimonthly magazine covering the grocery industry. Reports profiles on independent food stores, supermarkets, manufacturers and food processors, brokers, distributors, and wholesalers. Estab. 1916. Circ. 15,500. Pays 30-45 days from receipt of invoice. Byline given. Offers 33% kill fee. Buys all rights. Submit seasonal material 3 months in advance. Sample copy and writer's guidelines free.

- Assigns stories to Canadian writers based on editorial needs of publication.

Nonfiction How-to, interview/profile. Industry reports and profiles on companies. Query with published clips. Length: 500-9,000 words. **Pays 25-35¢/word.** Sometimes pays expenses of writers on assignment.

Photos State availability with submission. Reviews negatives, transparencies, 3×5 prints, JPEG, EPS, or TIF files. Buys all rights. Negotiates payment individually. Captions required.

Tips "E-mail, fax, or mail a query outlining your experience, interest, and pay expectations. Include clippings."

HOME FURNISHINGS & HOUSEHOLD GOODS

N $ $ HOME FURNISHINGS RETAILER

National Home Furnishings Association (NHFA), 3910 Tinsley Dr., High Point NC 27265. (336)801-6156. Fax: (336)801-6102. E-mail: tkemerly@nhfa.org. **Contact:** Trisha Kemerly, editor. **75% freelance written.** Monthly magazine published by NHFA covering the home furnishings industry. "We hope home furnishings retailers view our magazine as a profitability tool. We want each issue to help them make or save money." Estab. 1927. Circ. 15,000. **Pays on acceptance.** Publishes ms an average of 6 weeks after acceptance. Byline given. Buys first North American serial rights. Editorial lead time 3 months. Accepts queries by mail, e-mail. Responds in 1 month to queries. Sample copy available with proper postage. Writer's guidelines for #10 SASE.

O→ Break in by "e-mailing queries that pertain to our market—furniture retailers. We publish articles that give our readers tangible ways to improve their business."

Nonfiction Query with published clips. Length: 3,000-5,000 words (features). **Pays $350-500 for assigned articles.**

Photos State availability with submission. Reviews transparencies. Buys one-time rights. Negotiates payment individually. Identification of subjects required.

Columns/Departments Query with published clips.

Tips "Our readership includes owners of small 'Ma and Pa' furniture stores, executives of medium-sized chains (2-10 stores), and executives of big chains. Articles should be relevant to retailers and provide them with tangible information, ideas, and products to better their business."

HOME LIGHTING & ACCESSORIES

Doctorow Communications, Inc., 1011 Clifton Ave., Clifton NJ 07013. (973)779-1600. Fax: (973)779-3242. Web site: www.homelighting.com. **25% freelance written.** Prefers to work with published/established writers. Monthly magazine for lighting showrooms/department stores. Estab. 1923. Circ. 10,000. Pays on publication. Publishes ms an average of 6 months after acceptance. Buys first rights. Submit seasonal material 6 months in advance. Accepts queries by mail. Responds in 2 months to queries. Sample copy for 9×12 SAE and 4 first-class stamps.

Nonfiction Interview/profile (with lighting retailers), personal experience (as a businessperson involved with lighting), technical (concerning lighting or lighting design), profile (of a successful lighting retailer/lamp buyer). Special issues: Outdoor (March); Tribute To Tiffanies (August). **Buys less than 10 mss/year.** Query.

Reprints Send tearsheet and information about when and where the material previously appeared.

Photos State availability with submission. Offers no additional payment for 5×7 or 8×10 b&w glossy prints. Captions required.

Tips "Have a unique perspective on retailing lamps and lighting fixtures. We often use freelancers located in a part of the country where we'd like to profile a specific business or person. Anyone who has published an article dealing with any aspect of home furnishings will have high priority."

HOSPITALS, NURSING & NURSING HOMES

ALZHEIMER'S CARE GUIDE

Freiberg Press Inc., P.O. Box 612, Cedar Falls IA 50613. (319)553-0642. Fax: (319)553-0644. E-mail: bfreiberg@cfu.net. Web site: www.care4elders.com. **Contact:** Bill Freiberg, editor. **25% freelance written.** Bimonthly magazine covering Alzheimer's care. Aimed at caregivers of Alzheimer's patients. Interested in either inspirational first-person type stories or features/articles involving authoritative advice or caregiving tips. Estab. 1992. Circ. 10,000. **Pays on acceptance.** Byline sometimes given. Buys all rights. Accepts queries by e-mail.

- Query first. Only pays for assigned articles.

Nonfiction Book excerpts, interview/profile, personal experience, technical. **Buys 50 mss/year.** Query. Length: 500-2,000 words.

N $ $ CURRENT NURSING IN GERIATRIC CARE

Freiberg Press Inc., P.O. Box 612, Cedar Falls IA 50613. (319)553-0642. E-mail: bfreiberg@cfu.net. Web site: www.care4elders.com. **Contact:** Bill Freiberg, editor. **25% freelance written.** Bimonthly trade journal covering medical information and new developments in research for geriatric nurses and other practitioners. Estab. 2006. **Pays on acceptance.** Byline sometimes given. Buys all rights. Accepts queries by e-mail. Sample copy for free.

Nonfiction Query. Length: 500-1,500 words. **Pays 15¢/word for assigned articles.**

Photos State availability with submission.

$ $ $ HOSPITALS & HEALTH NETWORKS

Health Forum, 1 N. Franklin, 29th Floor, Chicago IL 60606. (312)422-2100. E-mail: bsantamour@healthforum.com. Web site: www.hhnmag.com. **Contact:** Bill Santamour, managing editor. **25% freelance written.** Monthly magazine covering hospitals. "We are a business publication for hospital and health system executives. We use only writers who are thoroughly familiar with the hospital field. Submit résumé and up to 5 samples of health care-related articles. We assign all articles and do not consider manuscripts." Estab. 1926. Circ. 85,000. **Pays on acceptance.** Publishes ms an average of 3 months after acceptance. Byline given. Offers variable kill fee. Buys all rights. Editorial lead time 2-3 months. Accepts queries by e-mail. Responds in 2-4 months to queries.

Nonfiction Interview/profile, technical. Query with published clips. Length: 350-2,000 words. **Pays $300-1,500 for assigned articles.**

Tips "If you demonstrate via published clips that you are thoroughly familiar with the business issues facing health-care executives, and that you are a polished reporter and writer, we will consider assigning you an article for our InBox section to start out. These are generally 350 words on a specific development of interest to hospitals and health system executives. Persistence does not pay with us. Once you've sent your résumé and clips, we will review them. If we have no assignment at that time, we will keep promising freelance candidates on file for future assignments."

$ $ LONG TERM CARE

The Ontario Long Term Care Association, 345 Renfrew Dr., Suite 102-202, Markham ON L3R 9S9 Canada. (905)470-8995. Fax: (905)470-9595. E-mail: hlrpublishing@bellnet.ca. Web site: www.oltca.com. Co-Editor: Tracey Ann Coveart. **Contact:** Heather Lang, editor. Quarterly magazine covering "professional issues and practical articles of interest to staff working in a long-term care setting (nursing home, retirement home): Information must be applicable to a Canadian setting; focus should be on staff and for resident well being." Estab. 1990. Circ. 6,000. Pays on publication. Publishes ms an average of 4 months after acceptance. Byline given. Buys one-time rights. Editorial lead time 3 months. Submit seasonal material 5 months in advance. Responds in 3 months to queries. Sample copy for free. Writer's guidelines online.

Nonfiction General interest, how-to (practical, of use to long term care practitioners), inspirational, interview/profile. No product-oriented articles. Query with published clips. Length: 800-1,500 words. **Pays up to $500 (Canadian).**

Photos Send photos with submission. Reviews contact sheets, 5×5 prints. Buys one-time rights. Offers no additional payment for photos accepted with ms. Captions, model releases required.

Columns/Departments Query with published clips. **Pays up to $500 (Canadian).**

Tips "Articles must be positive, upbeat, and contain helpful information that staff and managers working in the long term care field can use. Focus should be on staff and resident well being. Articles that highlight new ways of doing things are particularly useful. Please call the editor to discuss ideas. Must be applicable to Canadian settings."

NURSEWEEK

NurseWeek Publishing, 6860 Santa Teresa Blvd., San Jose CA 95119. (800)859-2091. Fax: (408)249-3756. Web site: www.nurseweek.com. *NurseWeek* is an independent biweekly news magazine supported by advertising revenue, sales of continuing education, and trade shows. Its editorial mission is to provide nurses with the latest news, resources, and opportunities to help them succeed in their lives and careers. Five regional editions: California, Mountain West, South Central, Midwest, and Great Lakes. Assigns articles. **Pays on acceptance.**

NurseWeek.com is updated daily with news content and posts new job listings on a daily basis.

$ $ $ NURSING SPECTRUM

Florida Edition, Nursing Spectrum, 1001 W. Cypress Creek Rd., Suite 330, Ft. Lauderdale FL 33309. (954)776-1455. Fax: (954)776-1456. Web site: www.nursingspectrum.com. **Contact:** Phyllis Class, RN, editorial director. **80% freelance written.** Biweekly magazine covering registered nursing. "We support and recognize registered nurses. All articles must have at least one RN in byline. We prefer articles that feature nurses in our region, but articles of interest to all nurses are welcome, too. We look for substantive, yet readable articles. Our bottom line—timely, relevant, and compelling articles that support nurses and help them excel in their clinical and professional careers.'' Estab. 1991. Circ. 60,000. Pays on publication. Byline given. Buys all rights. Editorial lead time 3 months. Submit seasonal material 4 months in advance. Accepts queries by mail, fax, phone. Responds in 1 month to queries; 4 months to mss. Sample copy for free. Writer's guidelines online.

O→ ''Having an original idea is paramount and the first step in writing an article. We are looking for success stories, nurses to be proud of, and progress that is helping patients. If you and your colleagues have dealt with and learned from a thorny issue, tell us how. What is new in your field? Consider your audience: all RNs, well educated, and of various specialties. Will they relate, be inspired, learn something? The best articles are both interesting and informative.''

Nonfiction General interest, how-to (career management), humor, interview/profile, personal experience, photo feature. Special issues: Critical Care; Nursing Management. **Buys 125 plus mss/year.** Length: 700-1,200 words. **Pays $50-800 for assigned articles.** Sometimes pays expenses of writers on assignment.

Photos Buys one-time rights. Negotiates payment individually. Captions, identification of subjects, model releases required.

Columns/Departments Humor Infusion (cartoon, amusing anecdotes). **Buys 75 mss/year.** Query with published clips. **Pays $50-120.**

Tips ''Write in 'magazine' style—as if talking to another RN. Use to-the-point, active language. Narrow your focus. Topics such as 'The Future of Nursing' or 'Dealing With Change' are too broad and nonspecific. Use informative but catchy titles and subheads (we can help with this). If quoting others, be sure quotes are meaningful and add substance to the piece. To add vitality, you may use statistics and up-to-date references. Try to paint a complete picture, using pros and cons. Be both positive and realistic.''

$ $ $ NURSING SPECTRUM

Greater Philadelphia/Tri-State edition, Nursing Spectrum, 1 Presidential Blvd., Suite 412, Bala Cynwyd PA 19004. (610)617-7355. Fax: (610)617-3106. Web site: www.nursingspectrum.com. **Contact:** Donna Novak, editorial director. **80% freelance written.** Biweekly magazine covering registered nursing. ''We support and recognize registered nurses. We prefer articles that feature nurses in our region, but articles of interest to all nurses are welcome, too. We look for substantive, yet readable articles. Our bottom line—timely, relevant, and compelling articles that support nurses and help them excel in their clinical and professional careers.'' Estab. 1992. Circ. 67,000. Byline given. Writer's guidelines online.

- See *Nursing Spectrum, Florida Edition* for article needs.

$ $ $ NURSING SPECTRUM

Washington, DC/Baltimore edition, Nursing Spectrum, 803 W. Broad St., Suite 500, Falls Church VA 22046. (703)237-6515. Fax: (703)237-6299. Web site: www.nursingspectrum.com. **Contact:** Pam Meredith, RN, editor. **80% freelance written.** Biweekly journal covering registered nursing. ''We support and recognize registered nurses. We prefer articles that feature nurses in our region, but articles of interest to all nurses are welcome, too. We look for substantive, yet readable articles. Our bottom line—timely, relevant, and compelling articles that support nurses and help them excel in their clinical and professional careers.'' Estab. 1990. Circ. 1 million. Writer's guidelines online.

- See *Nursing Spectrum, Florida Edition* for article needs.

HOTELS, MOTELS, CLUBS, RESORTS & RESTAURANTS

$ $ BARTENDER MAGAZINE

Foley Publishing, P.O. Box 158, Liberty Corner NJ 07938. (908)766-6006. Fax: (908)766-6607. Web site: www.bartender.com. **100% freelance written.** Prefers to work with published/established writers; eager to work with new/unpublished writers. Quarterly magazine emphasizing liquor and bartending for bartenders, tavern owners, and owners of restaurants with full-service liquor licenses. Circ. 148,225. Pays on publication. Publishes ms an average of 3 months after acceptance. Byline given. Buys first North American serial, first, one-time, second serial (reprint), simultaneous, all rights. Submit seasonal material 3 months in advance. Accepts simultaneous submissions. Responds in 2 months to mss. Sample copy for 9×12 SAE and 4 first-class stamps.

Nonfiction General interest, historical/nostalgic, how-to, humor, interview/profile (with famous bartenders or ex-bartenders), new product, opinion, personal experience, photo feature, travel, nostalgia, unique bars, new techniques, new drinking trends, bar sports, bar magic tricks. Special issues: Annual Calendar and Daily Cocktail Recipe Guide. Send complete ms and SASE. Length: 100-1,000 words.

Reprints Send tearsheet and information about when and where the material previously appeared. Pays 25% of amount paid for an original article.

Photos Send photos with submission. Pays $7.50-50 for 8×10 b&w glossy prints; $10-75 for 8×10 color glossy prints. Captions, model releases required.
Columns/Departments Bar of the Month; Bartender of the Month; Creative Cocktails; Bar Sports; Quiz; Bar Art; Wine Cellar; Tips from the Top (from prominent figures in the liquor industry); One For the Road (travel); Collectors (bar or liquor-related items); Photo Essays. **Length:** 200-1,000 words. Query by mail only with SASE. **Pays $50-200.**
Fillers Anecdotes, newsbreaks, short humor, clippings, jokes, gags. Length: 25-100 words. **Pays $5-25.**
Tips "To break in, absolutely make sure that your work will be of interest to all bartenders across the country. Your style of writing should reflect the audience you are addressing. The most frequent mistake made by writers in completing an article for us is using the wrong subject."

CHEF

The Food Magazine for Professionals, Talcott Communications Corp., 20 W. Kinzie, 12th Floor, Chicago IL 60610. (312)849-2220. Fax: (312)849-2174. Web site: www.chefmagazine.com. **Contact:** Editor. **40% freelance written.** Monthly magazine covering chefs in all food-service segments. "*Chef* is the one magazine that communicates food production to a commercial, professional audience in a meaningful way." Circ. 42,000. Byline given. Buys first North American serial, second serial (reprint) rights. Editorial lead time 2 months. Submit seasonal material 4 months in advance. Accepts queries by mail, e-mail, fax. Writer's guidelines free.
Nonfiction Book excerpts, essays, exposé, general interest, historical/nostalgic, how-to (create a dish or perform a technique), inspirational, interview/profile, new product, opinion, personal experience, photo feature, technical. **Buys 30-50 mss/year.** Query. Length: 750-1,500 words.
Reprints Accepts previously published submissions.
Photos State availability with submission. Reviews transparencies. Buys one-time rights. Captions, identification of subjects required.
Columns/Departments Flavor (traditional and innovative applications of a particular flavor) 1,000-1,200 words; Dish (professional chef profiles), 1,000-1,200 words; Savor (themed recipes), 1,000-1,500 words. **Buys 12-18 mss/year.** Query.
Tips "Know food and apply it to the business of chefs. Always query first, after you've read our magazine. Tell us how your idea can be used by our readers to enhance their businesses in some way."

CLUB MANAGEMENT

The Resource for Successful Club Operations, Finan Publishing Co., 107 W. Pacific Ave., St. Louis MO 63119. (314)961-6644. Fax: (314)961-4809. Web site: www.club-mgmt.com. Bimonthly magazine covering club management, private club market, hospitality industry. Estab. 1925. Circ. 16,702. Pays on publication. Publishes ms an average of 2 months after acceptance. Buys first North American serial, electronic rights. Accepts queries by mail, e-mail, fax.
Nonfiction General interest, historical/nostalgic, how-to, interview/profile, personal experience, photo feature, technical, travel. **Buys 100 mss/year.** Query with published clips. Length: 2,000-2,500 words.
Photos State availability with submission.
Columns/Departments Sports (private club sports: golf, tennis, yachting, fitness, etc.).
Tips "We don't accept blind submissions. Please submit a résumé and clips of your work. Send copies, not originals."

$ $ EL RESTAURANTE MEXICANO

P.O. Box 2249, Oak Park IL 60303-2249. (708)488-0100. Fax: (708)488-0101. E-mail: kfurore@restmex.com. **Contact:** Kathleen Furore, editor. Bimonthly magazine covering Mexican restaurants. "*El Restaurante Mexicano* offers features and business-related articles that are geared specifically to owners and operators of Mexican, Tex-Mex, Southwestern, and Latin cuisine restaurants." Estab. 1997. Circ. 27,000. Pays on publication. Publishes ms an average of 3 months after acceptance. Byline given. Buys first North American serial rights. Responds in 2 months to queries. Sample copy for free.
Nonfiction Looking for stories about unique Mexican restaurants and about business issues that affect Mexican restaurant owners. "No specific knowledge of food or restaurants is needed; the key qualification is to be a good reporter who knows how to slant a story toward the Mexican restaurant operator." **Buys 4-6 mss/year.** Query with published clips. Length: 800-1,500 words. **Pays $250-300.** Pays expenses of writers on assignment.
Tips "Query with a story idea, and tell how it pertains to Mexican restaurants."

N $ $ FLORIDA HOTEL & MOTEL JOURNAL

The Official Publication of the Florida Hotel & Motel Association, Accommodations, Inc., P.O. Box 1529, Tallahassee FL 32302-1529. (850)224-2888. Fax: (850)668-2884. E-mail: journal@flhma.net. Web site: www.flahotel.com. **Contact:** Lytha Page Belrose, editor. **10% freelance written.** Prefers to work with published/established writers. Bimonthly magazine acting as a reference tool for managers and owners of Florida's hotels, motels, and resorts. Estab. 1978. Circ. 8,500. Pays on publication. Publishes ms an average of 1-2 months after acceptance. Byline given. Buys first rights. Editorial lead time 1-9 months. Submit seasonal material 4-5 months in advance. Accepts queries by mail. Accepts previously published material. Responds in 2-4 months to queries. Sample copy for free. Writer's guidelines online.

O➛ Preference is given to articles that include references to member properties and general managers affiliated with the Florida Hotel and Motel Association. Since the association acquires new members weekly, queries may be made prior to the scheduling of interviews. This does not preclude the use of materials or ideas based on non-member properties, but member property sources are preferable.

Nonfiction How-to (pertaining to hotel management), interview/profile, new product, personal experience, technical. No travel tips or articles aimed at the traveling public, and no promotion of individual property, destination, product, or service. Query with published clips. Length: 500-1,500 words. **Pays 10¢/published word.** Pays in contributor copies if the article is reprinted with persmission, or the author is a paid representative of a company which is publicized in some manner through the article. Sometimes pays expenses of writers on assignment.

Photos State availability with submission. Buys all rights. Offers no additional payment for photos accepted with ms. Captions, identification of subjects, model releases required.

Columns/Departments Management Monograph, 500-1,000 words (expert information for hotel and motel management); Florida Scene, 500 words (Florida-specific, time-sensitive information for hotel managers or owners); National Scene, 500-1,000 words (USA-specific, time-sensitive information for hotel managers or owners); Fillers and Features, 500-700 words (information specific to editorial focus for the issue). Query. **Pays in contributor copies.**

Fillers Anecdotes, facts, short humor. Length: 50-1,000 words. **Pays in contributor copies.**

Tips "We use press releases provided to this office that fit the profile of our magazine's departments, targeting items of interest to the general managers of Florida's lodging operations. Feature articles are written based on an editorial calendar. We also publish an annual buyer's guide that provides a directory of all FH&MA member companies and allied member companies."

$ $ $ $ ⊘ HOSPITALITY TECHNOLOGY

Edgell Communications, 4 Middlebury Blvd., Randolph NJ 07869. (973)252-0100. Fax: (973)252-9020. E-mail: rpaul@edgellmail.com. Web site: www.htmagazine.com. **Contact:** Reid Paul, editor-in-chief. **70% freelance written.** Magazine published 9 times/year. "We cover the technology used in foodservice and lodging. Our readers are the operators, who have significant IT responsibilities." Estab. 1996. Circ. 16,000. **Pays on acceptance.** Publishes ms an average of 1 month after acceptance. Byline given. Buys all rights, makes work-for-hire assignments. Editorial lead time 2 months. Accepts queries by mail, e-mail, fax, phone. Responds in 2 weeks to queries.

Nonfiction How-to, interview/profile, new product, technical. Special issues: "We publish 2 studies each year, the Restaurant Industry Technology Study and the Lodging Industry Technology Study." No unsolicited mss. **Buys 40 mss/year.** Query with published clips. Length: 800-1,200 words. **Pays $1/word.** Sometimes pays expenses of writers on assignment.

$ $ HOTELIER

Kostuch Publications, Ltd., 23 Lesmill Rd., Suite 101, Don Mills ON M3B 3P6 Canada. (416)447-0888. Fax: (416)447-5333. E-mail: rcaira@foodservice.ca. Web site: www.foodserviceworld.com. Managing Editor: Iris Benaroia. **Contact:** Rosanna Caira, editor. **40% freelance written.** Magazine published 8 times/year covering the Canadian hotel industry. Estab. 1989. Circ. 9,000. Pays on publication. Byline given. Buys first North American serial rights. Editorial lead time 3 months. Submit seasonal material 2 months in advance. Accepts queries by mail, fax. Sample copy and writer's guidelines free.

Nonfiction How-to, new product. No case studies. **Buys 30-50 mss/year.** Query with or without published clips. Length: 700-1,500 words. **Pays 35¢/word (Canadian) for assigned articles.** Sometimes pays expenses of writers on assignment.

Photos Send photos with submission. Offers $30-75/photo.

$ $ INSITE

Christian Camp & Conference Association, P.O. Box 62189, Colorado Springs CO 80962-2189. (719)260-9400. Fax: (719)260-6398. E-mail: editor@ccca-us.org. Web site: www.ccca-us.org. **Contact:** Justin Boles, managing editor; Alison Hayhoe, editor. **75% freelance written.** Prefers to work with published/established writers. Bimonthly magazine emphasizing the broad scope of organized camping with emphasis on Christian camps and conference centers. "All who work in youth camps and adult conferences read our magazine for inspiration and to get practical help in ways to serve in their operations." Estab. 1963. Circ. 9,000. Pays on publication.

Publishes ms an average of 4 months after acceptance. Byline given. Buys negotiable rights. Submit seasonal material 6 months in advance. Accepts queries by mail, e-mail. Responds in 1 month to queries. Sample copy for $4.95 plus 9×12 SASE. Writer's guidelines online.

Nonfiction General interest (trends in organized camping in general, Christian camping in particular), how-to (anything involved with organized camping, including motivating staff, programming, record keeping, and camper follow-up), inspirational, interview/profile (with movers and shakers in Christian camping; submit a list of basic questions first). **Buys 15-20 mss/year.** Query required. Length: 500-1,500 words. **Pays 16¢/word.**

Reprints Send photocopy and information about when and where the material previously appeared. Pays 50% of amount paid for an original article.

Photos Price negotiable for 35mm color transparencies and high-quality digital photos.

Tips "The most frequent mistake made by writers is that they send articles unrelated to our readers. Review our publication guidelines first. Interviews are the best bet for freelancers."

N $ $ MOUNTAIN RESORT MAGAZINE

Skinner Media, Vail CO 81657. Phone/Fax: (252)261-3437. E-mail: editor@mountainresortmag.com. Web site: www.mountainresortmag.com. **Contact:** Gard Skinner, editor. **50% freelance written.** Bimonthly magazine covering the ski and snowboard resort industry. "We are exclusively an area operations, marketing, and management resource for local, regional, and national mountain destinations. We combine humor with information and images with explanations, and understand the spark it takes to work in black snow pants 175 days a year. We will gladly trade publishing credits for real experience on the front lines. And, we readily understand that although travel writers and old-school journalists are invariably handsome, brilliant, and uber-masters of the sport, they have little cred with those who actually do the job. We do not preach, but utilize the voices in the industry to help share authentic experience." Estab. 2004. Circ. 4,200. **Pays on acceptance.** Byline given. Offers 20% kill fee. Buys first North American serial rights. Editorial lead time 2 months. Submit seasonal material 3 months in advance. Accepts queries by e-mail. Accepts simultaneous submissions. Responds in 1 week to queries; 1 month to mss. Writer's guidelines by e-mail.

Nonfiction Historical/nostalgic, how-to, humor, interview/profile, new product, technical. Please do not confuse the retail or travel end of skiing and riding with the operations community (management, marketing, lift operators). **Buys 15 mss/year.** Query. Length: 1,200-2,000 words. **Pays $500.**

Photos "Please contact the editor if you have taken operations photography. (This does not include pictures of your buddy doing some trick in the park.)"

Columns/Departments Bullwheel (informative spew about interesting and funny operations developments), 200 words. **Buys 1 mss/year.** Query. **Pays $100 maximum.**

Tips "Our angle is experience from the front lines. We've of course had dozens of travel writers pawning their wares, but are more interested in actual resort employees' voices than consumer writing credits. Shoot ideas by e-mail, and please include any relevant on-hill experience. Be young; be funny. Tell us a story you heard in a locker room rather than drone on about what's happening in a board room."

$ $ $ PIZZA TODAY

The Monthly Professional Guide to Pizza Profits, Macfadden Protech, LLC, 908 S. 8th St., Suite 200, Louisville KY 40203. (502)736-9500. Fax: (502)736-9502. E-mail: jwhite@pizzatoday.com. Web site: www.pizzatoday.com. **Contact:** Jeremy White, editor-in-chief. **40% freelance written.** Works with published/established writers; occasionally works with new writers. Monthly magazine for the pizza industry, covering trends, features of successful pizza operators, business and management advice, etc. Estab. 1983. Circ. 47,000. **Pays on acceptance.** Publishes ms an average of 2 months after acceptance. Byline given. Offers 10-30% kill fee. Buys all rights. Submit seasonal material 3 months in advance. Accepts queries by mail, e-mail, fax. Responds in 2 months to queries; 3 weeks to mss. Sample copy for 10×13 SAE and 6 first-class stamps. Writer's guidelines for #10 SASE.

Nonfiction Interview/profile, entrepreneurial slants, pizza production and delivery, employee training, hiring, marketing, and business management. No fillers, humor, or poetry. **Buys 85 mss/year.** Length: 1,000 words. **Pays 50¢/word, occasionally more.** Sometimes pays expenses of writers on assignment.

Photos Reviews contact sheets, negatives, transparencies, color slides, 5×7 prints. Captions required.

Tips "We currently need articles that cover ways pizzeria operators can implement effective marketing plans. Our readers are not looking for generic advice, however. They need truly unique, applicable marketing advice that can be immediately instituted at acceptable costs."

$ $ WESTERN HOTELIER MAGAZINE

Mercury Publications, Ltd., 1740 Wellington Ave., Winnipeg MB R3H 0E8 Canada. (204)954-2085. Fax: (204)954-2057. Web site: www.mercury.mb.ca/. **33% freelance written.** Quarterly magazine covering the hotel industry. "*Western Hotelier* is dedicated to the accommodation industry in Western Canada and U.S.

western border states. *WH* offers the West's best mix of news and feature reports geared to hotel management. Feature reports are written on a sector basis and are created to help generate enhanced profitability and better understanding.'' Circ. 4,342. Pays 30-45 days from receipt of invoice. Byline given. Offers 33% kill fee. Buys all rights. Submit seasonal material 3 months in advance. Accepts queries by mail, fax. Accepts simultaneous submissions. Responds in 2 weeks to queries. Sample copy and writer's guidelines free.

Nonfiction How-to (train staff), interview/profile. Industry reports and profiles on companies. Query with published clips. Length: 500-9,000 words. **Pays 25-35¢/word.** Sometimes pays expenses of writers on assignment.

Photos State availability with submission. Reviews negatives, transparencies, 3×5 prints, JPEG, EPS or TIF files. Buys all rights. Negotiates payment individually. Captions required.

Tips ''E-mail, fax, or mail a query outlining your experience, interests and pay expectations. Include clippings.''

$ $ WESTERN RESTAURANT NEWS

Mercury Publications, Ltd., 1740 Wellington Ave., Winnipeg MB R3H 0E8 Canada. (204)954-2085. Fax: (204)954-2057. Web site: www.mercury.mb.ca/. **20% freelance written.** Bimonthly magazine covering the restaurant trade. Reports profiles and industry reports on associations, regional business developments, etc. ''*Western Restaurant News Magazine* is the authoritative voice of the foodservice industry in Western Canada. Offering a total package to readers, *WRN* delivers concise news articles, new product news, and coverage of the leading trade events in the West, across the country, and around the world.'' Estab. 1994. Circ. 14,532. Pays 30-45 days from receipt of invoice. Byline given. Offers 33% kill fee. Buys all rights. Submit seasonal material 3 months in advance. Accepts queries by mail, fax. Accepts simultaneous submissions. Sample copy and writer's guidelines free.

Nonfiction How-to, interview/profile. Industry reports and profiles on companies. Query with published clips. Length: 500-9,000 words. **Pays 25-35¢/word.** Sometimes pays expenses of writers on assignment.

Photos State availability with submission. Reviews negatives, transparencies, 3×5 prints, JPEG, EPS, or TIFF files. Buys all rights. Negotiates payment individually. Captions required.

Tips ''E-mail, fax, or mail a query outlining your experience, interests and pay expectations. Include clippings.''

INDUSTRIAL OPERATIONS

$ $ CAST POLYMER CONNECTION

International Cast Polymer Alliance of the American Composites Manufacturers Association, 1010 N. Glebe Rd., Suite 450, Arlington VA 22201-5761. (703)525-0511. Fax: (703)525-0743. E-mail: jgorman@acmanet.org. Web site: www.icpa-hq.org. Assistant Editor: Jen McCabe Gorman. **Contact:** Andrew Rusnak, editor. Bimonthly magazine covering cultured marble and solid surface industries. ''Articles should focus on small business owners and manufacturers.'' Circ. 2,000. Pays on publication. Publishes ms an average of 3 months after acceptance. Byline given. Buys all rights. Accepts queries by mail, e-mail.

Nonfiction ''We are interested in how-to articles on technical processes, industry-related manufacturing techniques, and small-business operations.'' Historical/nostalgic, how-to, interview/profile, photo feature, technical. **Buys 3-5 mss/year.** Query. Length: 2,000-5,000 words. **Pays $200-350.** Occasionally arrange ad space to swap for editorial. Sometimes pays expenses of writers on assignment.

$ $ COMMERCE & INDUSTRY

Mercury Publications, Ltd., 1740 Wellington Ave., Winnipeg MB R3H 0E8 Canada. (204)954-2085. Fax: (204)954-2057. Web site: www.mercury.mb.ca/. **75% freelance written.** Bimonthly magazine covering the business and industrial sectors. Industry reports and company profiles provide readers with an in-depth insight into key areas of interest in their profession. Estab. 1947. Circ. 18,876. Pays 30-45 days from receipt of invoice. Byline given. Offers 33% kill fee. Buys all rights. Submit seasonal material 3 months in advance. Accepts queries by mail, e-mail, fax. Accepts simultaneous submissions. Responds in 2 weeks to queries. Sample copy and writer's guidelines free or by e-mail.

Nonfiction How-to, interview/profile. Industry reports and profiles on companies. Query with published clips. Length: 500-9,000 words. **Pays 25-35¢/word.** Sometimes pays expenses of writers on assignment.

Photos State availability with submission. Reviews negatives, transparencies, 3×5 prints, JPEG, EPS or TIF files. Buys all rights. Negotiates payment individually. Captions required.

Tips ''E-mail, fax, or mail a query outlining your experience, interests and pay expectations. Include clippings.''

$ $ MODERN MATERIALS HANDLING

Reed Business Information, 275 Washington St., Newton MA 02458. (617)558-4374. Fax: (617)558-4327. E-mail: noel.bodenburg@reedbusiness.com. Web site: www.mmh.com. **40% freelance written.** Magazine published 11 times/year covering warehousing, distribution centers, inventory. "*Warehousing Management* is an 11 times-a-year glossy national magazine read by managers of warehouses and distribution centers. We focus on lively, well-written articles telling our readers how they can achieve maximum facility productivity and efficiency. Heavy management components. We cover technology, too." Estab. 1945. Circ. 42,000. Pays on acceptance (allow 4-6 weeks for invoice processing). Publishes ms an average of 1 month after acceptance. Byline given. Editorial lead time 3 months. Accepts queries by mail, e-mail, fax. Sample copy for free. Writer's guidelines free.

Nonfiction Articles must be on-point, how-to pieces for managers. How-to, new product, technical. Special issues: State-of-the-Industry Report, Peak Performer, Salary and Wage survey, Warehouse of the Year. Doesn't want to see anything that doesn't deal with our topic—warehousing. No general-interest profiles or interviews. **Buys 25 mss/year.** Query with published clips. **Pays $300-650.**

Photos State availability with submission. Reviews negatives, transparencies, prints. Buys all rights. Offers no additional payment for photos accepted with ms. Captions, identification of subjects required.

Tips "Learn a little about warehousing, distributors and write well. We typically don't accept specific article queries, but welcome introductory letters from journalists to whom we can assign articles. But authors are welcome to request an editorial calendar and develop article queries from it."

$ $ $ PEM PLANT ENGINEERING & MAINTENANCE

CLB Media, Inc., 240 Edward St., Aurora ON L4G 3S9 Canada. (905)727-0077. Fax: (905)727-0017. E-mail: rrobertson@clbmedia.ca. Web site: www.pem-mag.com. **Contact:** Rob Robertson, editor. **30% freelance written.** Bimonthly magazine looking for "informative articles on issues that affect plant floor operations and maintenance." Circ. 18,500. Pays on publication. Publishes ms an average of 3 months after acceptance. Byline given. Buys one-time rights. Editorial lead time 4 months. Submit seasonal material 4 months in advance. Accepts simultaneous submissions. Responds in 3 weeks to queries; 1 month to mss. Sample copy for free. Writer's guidelines online.

Nonfiction How-to (keep production downtime to a minimum, better operate an industrial operation), new product, technical. **Buys 6 mss/year.** Query with published clips. Length: 750-4,000 words. **Pays $500-1,400 (Canadian).** Sometimes pays expenses of writers on assignment.

Photos State availability with submission. Reviews transparencies, prints. Buys one-time rights. Negotiates payment individually. Captions required.

Tips "Information can be found at our Web site. Call us for sample issues, ideas, etc."

N $ $ WEIGHING & MEASUREMENT

WAM Publishing Co., P.O. Box 2247, Hendersonville TN 37077. (615)824-6920. Fax: (615)824-7092. E-mail: wampub@wammag.com. Web site: www.wammag.com. **Contact:** David M. Mathieu, editor. Bimonthly magazine for users of industrial scales. Estab. 1914. Circ. 13,900. **Pays on acceptance.** Byline given. Offers 20% kill fee. Buys all rights. Accepts queries by mail, e-mail, fax, phone. Responds in 2 weeks to queries. Sample copy for $2.

Nonfiction Interview/profile (with presidents of companies), personal experience (guest editorials on government involvement in business, etc.), technical, Profile (about users of weighing and measurement equipment); Product reviews. **Buys 15 mss/year.** Query on technical articles; submit complete ms for general interest material. Length: 1,000-2,500 words. **Pays $175-300.**

INFORMATION SYSTEMS

$ $ $ CARD TECHNOLOGY

The Magazine of Smart Cards, Networks, and ID Solutions, 550 W. Van Buren, Suite 1110, Chicago IL 60607. (312)983-6152. Fax: (312)913-1369. E-mail: don.davis@sourcemedia.com. Web site: www.cardtechnology.com. Publisher: Andy Rowe. **Contact:** Don Davis, editor/associate publisher. **20% freelance written.** Monthly magazine covering smart cards, biometrics, and related technologies. "*Card Technology* covers all uses of smart cards worldwide, as well as other advanced plastic card technologies. Aimed at senior management, not technical staff. Our readership is global, as is our focus." Estab. 1996. Circ. 22,000. **Pays on acceptance.** Byline given. Offers negotiable kill fee. Buys all rights. Editorial lead time 1 month. Submit seasonal material 2 months in advance. Accepts queries by e-mail. Responds in 1 week to queries; 1 month to mss. Sample copy for free.

Nonfiction Interview/profile, opinion. **Buys 15 mss/year.** Query with published clips. Length: 2,000-4,000 words. **Pays $500-1,500.** Sometimes pays expenses of writers on assignment.

Photos State availability with submission. Reviews contact sheets, negatives, transparencies, prints. Rights negotiable. Negotiates payment individually. Identification of subjects required.

Tips "We are especially interested in finding freelancers outside of North America who have experience writing about technology issues for business publications."

$ $ COMPUTER GRAPHICS WORLD

PennWell, 98 Spit Brook Rd., Nashua NH 03062-2801. (603)891-0123. Fax: (603)891-0539. E-mail: kdove@pennwell.com. Web site: www.cgw.com. **Contact:** Kelly Dove, editor-in-chief. **25% freelance written.** Monthly magazine. "*Computer Graphics World* specializes in covering computer-aided 3D modeling, animation, and visualization, and their uses in entertainment applications." Estab. 1978. Circ. 50,000. **Pays on acceptance.** Publishes ms an average of 3 months after acceptance. Byline given. Offers 20% kill fee. Buys all rights. Editorial lead time 4 months. Submit seasonal material 3 months in advance. Sample copy for free.

Nonfiction New product, opinion, technical, user application stories, professional-user, techonology innovations. "We do not want to run articles that are geared to computer programmers. Our focus as a magazine is on users involved in specific applications." **Buys 10-20 mss/year.** Query with published clips. Length: 1,200-2,000 words. **Pays $500 minimum.**

Columns/Departments Technology stories (describes innovation and its implication for computer graphics users), 750-1,000 words; Reviews (offers hands-on review of important new products), 750 words. Query with published clips. **Pays $300-500.**

Tips "Freelance writers will be most successful if they have some familiarity with computers and know how to write from a user's perspective. They do not need to be computer experts, but they do have to understand how to explain the impact of the technology and the applications in which a user is involved. Our feature section, and our application story section are open to freelancers. The trick to winning acceptance for your story is to have a well-developed idea that highlights a fascinating new trend or development in computer graphics technology or profiles a unique use of the technology by a single user or a specific class of users."

$ $ $ DESKTOP ENGINEERING

Design Solutions from Concept Through Manufacture, Helmers Publishing, P.O. Box 1039, Dublin NH 03444. (603)563-1631. Fax: (603)563-8192. E-mail: de-editors@deskeng.com. Web site: www.deskeng.com. **Contact:** Jonathan Gourlay, features editor. **90% freelance written.** Monthly magazine covering microcomputer hardware/software for hands-on design and mechanical engineers and engineering management. 4 special supplements/year. Estab. 1995. Circ. 63,000. Pays on publication. Publishes ms an average of 2 months after acceptance. Byline given. Buys all rights. Editorial lead time 3 months. Accepts queries by mail, e-mail, fax, phone. Responds in 1 week to queries; 1 month to mss. Sample copy for free with 8×10 SASE. Writer's guidelines by e-mail to jgourlay@helmers.com.

Nonfiction How-to (design), new product, technical, reviews. "No fluff." **Buys 50-70 mss/year.** Query. Length: 750-1,500 words. **Pays 60¢/word for assigned articles; negotiable for unsolicited articles.** Sometimes pays expenses of writers on assignment.

Photos Send photos with submission. Negotiates payment individually. Captions required.

Columns/Departments Product Briefs (new products), 50-100 words; Reviews (software, hardware), 500-1,500 words.

The online magazine carries original content not found in the print edition. Contact: Jonathan Gourlay.

Tips "Call the editors or e-mail them for submission tips."

$ $ $ GAME DEVELOPER

CMP Media LLC, 600 Harrison St., 6th Floor, San Francisco CA 94107. (415)947-6000. Fax: (415)947-6090. E-mail: jduffy@cmp.com. Web site: www.gdmag.com. **Contact:** Jill Duffy, managing editor. **90% freelance written.** Monthly magazine covering computer game development. Estab. 1994. Circ. 35,000. Pays on publication. Publishes ms an average of 3-6 months after acceptance. Byline given. Buys first North American serial, first, electronic, all rights. Editorial lead time 3 months. Submit seasonal material 4 months in advance. Accepts queries by e-mail. Sample copy for free. Writer's guidelines online.

Nonfiction How-to, personal experience, technical. **Buys 50 mss/year.** Query. Length: 3,000-5,000 words. **Pays $150/page.**

Photos State availability with submission.

Tips "We're looking for writers who are professional game developers with published game titles. We do not target the hobbyist or amateur market."

$ $ $ $ GOVERNMENT COMPUTER NEWS

Post Newsweek Tech Media, 10 G St., NE, Suite 500, Washington DC 20002. (202)772-2540. Fax: (202)772-2516. E-mail: wkash@postnewsweektech.com. Web site: www.gcn.com. **Contact:** Wyatt Kash, editorial director. Biweekly for government information technology managers. **Pays on acceptance.** Byline given. Offers variable kill fee. Buys all rights. Responds in 1 month to queries. Sample copy for free. Writer's guidelines for #10 SASE.

Nonfiction Buys 30 mss/year. Query. Length: 600-750 words. **Pays $800-2,000.** Pays expenses of writers on assignment.

Columns/Departments Buys 75 mss/year. Query. **Pays $250-400.**

Fillers Buys 10/year. Length: 300-500 words. **Pays $250-450.**

Tips Needs "technical case histories of applications of computers to governmental missions and trends in information technology."

$ $ $ $ INFORMATION WEEK

600 Community Dr., Manhasset NY 11030. (516)562-5036. Fax: (516)562-5036. E-mail: jpfoley@cmp.com. Web site: www.informationweek.com. Editor: John Foley. **20% freelance written.** Weekly magazine for information systems managers. Estab. 1985. Circ. 440,000. **Pays on acceptance.** Publishes ms an average of 1 month after acceptance. Byline given. Offers 25% kill fee. Buys first rights. Non-exclusive serial rights Accepts simultaneous submissions. Responds in 1 month to mss. Sample copy for free. Writer's guidelines for #10 SASE.

Nonfiction Book excerpts, how-to, interview/profile, new product, technical, News analysis, company profiles. **Buys 30 mss/year.** Query with published clips. Length: 1,500-4,000 words. **Pays $1.10/word minimum.** Pays expenses of writers on assignment.

Reprints Considers previously published submissions.

Tips Needs "feature articles on technology trends—all with a business angle. We look at implementations by users, new products, management issues, intranets, the Internet, web, networks, PCs, objects, workstations, sewers, etc. Our competitors are tabloids—we're better written, more selective, and more analytical."

$ $ $ INTELLIGENT ENTERPRISE

Enterprise Solutions for Business Intelligence, CMP Media Inc., 2800 Campus Dr., San Mateo CA 94403. (650)513-4490. Fax: (650)513-4613. E-mail: dstodder@cmp.com. Web site: www.intelligententerprise.com. **Contact:** David Stodder, editor-in-chief. **98% freelance written.** 18 times/year magazine covering e-business and business intelligence. "Intelligent Enterprise is a new magazine covering the strategies, trends and products for managing enterprise information solutions in a cohesive, coherent infrastructure—what we call the information supply chain. Most of our readers work within or are consultants serving the needs of corporate information systems organizations. Our readers are educated, technically astute, and experienced; they use their knowledge to guide them through a dynamic, market-driven industry. They are expoloring business intelligence, data warehousing, knowledge management, multitier client/server, the Internet/intranet, and object technology." Estab. 1998. Circ. 100,000. Pays on publication. Publishes ms an average of 3 months after acceptance. Byline given. Buys all rights. Submit seasonal material 4 months in advance. Accepts queries by mail, e-mail, phone. Sample copy and writer's guidelines online.

Nonfiction Technical. **Buys 60 mss/year.** Query. Length: 350-3,000 words. **Pays $0-1,000.** Sometimes pays expenses of writers on assignment.

The online version of *Intelligent Enterprise* contains material not found in the print edition.

Tips "To write for *Intelligent Enterprise,* you must have a minimum of three years field experience. You must also have a working knowledge of theories and techniques beyond your own personal experience (unless you've done absolutely everything there is to do). Be familiar with the magazine in terms of style, content, and editorial focus. *Intelligent Enterprise* readers make the best *Intelligent Enterprise* writers and have enthusiasm for the job."

$ $ $ ISERIES NEWS

Penton Technology Media, 221 E. 29th St., Loveland CO 80538. (970)203-2824. Fax: (970)663-3285. E-mail: editors@iseriesnetwork.com; vhamende@penton.com. Web site: www.iseriesnetwork.com. **Contact:** Vicki Hamende. **40% freelance written.** Magazine published 14 times/year. "Programming, networking, IS management, technology for users of IBM AS/400 platform." Estab. 1982. Circ. 30,000 (international). Pays on publication. Publishes ms an average of 3 months after acceptance. Byline given. Offers 50% kill fee. Buys first, second serial (reprint), all rights. Editorial lead time 4 months. Submit seasonal material 4 months in advance. Accepts queries by mail, e-mail, fax, phone. Responds in 3 weeks to queries; 5 weeks to mss. Writer's guidelines online.

Nonfiction Book excerpts, opinion, technical. **Buys 70 mss/year.** Query. Length: 1,500-2,500 words. **Pays 17-50¢/word for assigned articles.** Pays in contributor copies upon request of the author. Sometimes pays expenses of writers on assignment.

Reprints Send photocopy. Payment negotiable.

Photos State availability with submission. Offers no additional payment for photos accepted with ms.

Columns/Departments Dialog Box (computer industry opinion), 1,500 words; Load'n'go (complete utility). **Buys 24 mss/year.** Query. **Pays $250-1,000.**

Tips "Be familiar with IBM AS/400 computer platform."

$ JOURNAL OF INFORMATION ETHICS

McFarland & Co., Inc., Publishers, P.O. Box 611, Jefferson NC 28640. (336)246-4460. E-mail: hauptman@stcloudstate.edu. **Contact:** Robert Hauptman, editor: P.O. Box 32, West Wardsboro VT 05360. **90% freelance written.** Semiannual scholarly journal. "Addresses ethical issues in all of the information sciences with a deliberately interdisciplinary approach. Topics range from electronic mail monitoring to library acquisition of controversial material. The *Journal*'s aim is to present thoughtful considerations of ethical dilemmas that arise in a rapidly evolving system of information exchange and dissemination." Estab. 1992. Pays on publication. Publishes ms an average of 2 years after acceptance. Byline given. Buys all rights. Submit seasonal material 8 months in advance. Accepts queries by mail, e-mail, fax, phone. Sample copy for $30. Writer's guidelines free.

Nonfiction Essays, opinion, book reviews. **Buys 10 mss/year.** Send complete ms. Length: 500-3,500 words. **Pays $25-50 depending on length.**

Tips "Familiarize yourself with the many areas subsumed under the rubric of information ethics, e.g., privacy, scholarly communication, errors, peer review, confidentiality, e-mail, etc. Present a well-rounded discussion of any fresh, current, or evolving ethical topic within the information sciences or involving real-world information collection/exchange."

$ $ $ $ TECHNOLOGY REVIEW

MIT, 1 Main St., 7th Floor, Cambridge MA 02142. (617)475-8000. Fax: (617)475-8042. Web site: www.technologyreview.com. Editor-in-Chief: Jason Pontin. Magazine published 10 times/year covering information technology, biotech, material science, and nanotechnology. "*Technology Review* promotes the understanding of emerging technologies and their impact." Estab. 1899. Circ. 310,000. **Pays on acceptance.** Byline given. Accepts queries by mail, e-mail.

- Contact specific editor via e-mail using firstname.lastname@technologyreview.com

Nonfiction "We place a high premium on in-depth, original reporting that produces stories rich in description, containing lively quotes from key researchers and industry analysts. Summaries of other companies or labratories doing similar work typically supplement articles. Looking for feature articles." Length: 2,000-4,000 words. **Pays $1-3/word.**

Fillers Short tidbits that relate laboratory prototypes on their way to market in 1-5 years. Length: 150-250 words. **Pays $1-3/word.**

INSURANCE

$ $ $ $ ADVISOR TODAY

NAIFA, 2901 Telestar Court, Falls Church VA 22042. (703)770-8204. E-mail: amseka@naifa.org. Web site: www.advisortoday.com. **Contact:** Ayo Mseka, editor-in-chief. **25% freelance written.** Monthly magazine covering life insurance and financial planning. "Writers must demonstrate an understanding at what insurance agents and financial advisors do to earn business and serve their clients." Estab. 1906. Circ. 110,000. Pays on acceptance or publication (by mutual agreement with editor). Publishes ms an average of 3 months after acceptance. Makes work-for-hire assignments. Editorial lead time 3 months. Submit seasonal material 6 months in advance. Accepts queries by mail, e-mail, fax, phone. Sample copy for free. Writer's guidelines online.

O→ Break in with queries for "pieces about sales techniques and product disclosure issues."

Nonfiction Insurance. **Buys 8 mss/year.** Query. Length: 1,500-6,000 words. **Pays $800-2,000.**

$ $ GEICO DIRECT

K.L. Publications, 2001 Killebrew Dr., Suite 105, Bloomington MN 55425-1879. (952)854-0155. Fax: (952)854-9440. E-mail: klpub@aol.com. **Contact:** Jan Brenny, editor. **60% freelance written.** Semiannual magazine published for the Government Employees Insurance Company (GEICO) policyholders. Estab. 1988. Circ. 5,000,000. **Pays on acceptance.** Byline given. Accepts queries by mail. Responds in 3 months to queries. Writer's guidelines for #10 SASE.

O→ Break in by "submitting an idea (or editorial approach) for auto/home safety or themed regional travel—one theme with several destinations around the country—that is unique, along with proof of research and writing ability."

Nonfiction Americana, home and auto safety, car care, financial, lifestyle. How-to (auto/home related only), technical (auto), travel. Query with published clips. Length: 1,000-2,200 words. **Pays $300-650.**

Photos Reviews 35mm transparencies, Web sites. Payment varies.

Columns/Departments Moneywise; Your Car. Length: 500-600 words. Query with published clips. **Pays $175-350.**

Tips "We prefer work from published/established writers, especially those with specialized knowledge of the insurance industry, safety issues, and automotive topics."

JEWELRY

$ $ CANADIAN DIAMONDS AND JEWELLERY

(formerly *Canadian Diamonds*), Up Here Publishing, Ltd., #800 4920 52nd St., Yellowknife NT X1A 3T1 Canada. (867)920-4343. Fax: (867)873-2844. E-mail: jake@uphere.ca. Web site: www.canadiandiamondsmagazine.ca. Managing Editor: Tara Fraser. **Contact:** Jake Kennedy, editor. **60% freelance written.** Quarterly magazine "covering the Canadian diamond industry, from mine to exploration, from the boardroom to the jeweller's display case." Estab. 2000. Circ. 5,000. Pays on publication. Publishes ms an average of 3 months after acceptance. Byline given. Offers 50% kill fee. Buys first rights. Editorial lead time 1 year. Submit seasonal material 6 months in advance. Accepts queries by mail, e-mail, phone. Responds in 1 week to queries; 1 month to mss. Sample copy for free.

Nonfiction Book excerpts, essays, exposé, general interest, historical/nostalgic, how-to, interview/profile, new product, opinion, photo feature, technical, travel. **Buys 10 mss/year.** Query. Length: 1,800-2,500 words. **Pays 30-50¢/word.** Sometimes pays expenses of writers on assignment.

Photos State availability with submission. Reviews contact sheets, negatives, transparencies, prints, GIF/JPEG files. Buys one-time rights. Negotiates payment individually. Captions, identification of subjects required.

Columns/Departments Points (back page, general opinion), 750 words; Retail (retail diamond issues), 1,100 words. **Buys 6 mss/year.** Query. **Pays $200-400.**

$ $ COLORED STONE

Lapidary Journal/Primedia, Inc., 300 Chesterfield Parkway, Suite 100, Malvern PA 19355. (610)232-5700. Fax: (610)232-5756. E-mail: morgan.beard@primedia.com. Web site: www.colored-stone.com. **Contact:** Morgan Beard, editor-in-chief. **50% freelance written.** Bimonthly magazine covering the colored gemstone industry. "*Colored Stone* covers all aspects of the colored gemstone (i.e., no diamonds) trade. Our readers are manufacturing jewelers and jewelry designers, gemstone dealers, miners, retail jewelers, and gemologists." Estab. 1987. Circ. 11,000. **Pays on acceptance.** Publishes ms an average of 2 months after acceptance. Byline given. Buys one-time, all rights. Editorial lead time 2 months. Submit seasonal material 4 months in advance. Accepts queries by mail, e-mail, fax. Accepts simultaneous submissions. Responds in 1 month to queries; 2 months to mss. Sample copy for free. Writer's guidelines online.

Nonfiction Exposé, interview/profile, new product, technical. "No articles intended for the general public." **Buys 35-45 mss/year.** Query with published clips. Length: 400-2,200 words. **Pays $200-600.**

Photos State availability with submission. Reviews any size transparencies, 4×6 prints and up. Buys one-time rights. Offers $15-50/photo. Captions, identification of subjects, model releases required.

Tips "A background in the industry is helpful but not necessary. Please, no recycled marketing/new technology/etc. pieces."

$ THE DIAMOND REGISTRY BULLETIN

580 Fifth Ave., #806, New York NY 10036. (212)575-0444. Fax: (212)575-0722. Web site: www.diamondregistry.com. **50% freelance written.** Monthly newsletter. Estab. 1969. Pays on publication. Buys all rights. Submit seasonal material 1 month in advance. Accepts queries by mail, e-mail. Accepts simultaneous submissions. Responds in about 3 weeks to mss. Sample copy for $5.

Nonfiction How-to (ways to increase sales in diamonds, improve security, etc.), interview/profile (of interest to diamond dealers or jewelers), prevention advice (on crimes against jewelers). Send complete ms. Length: 50-500 words. **Pays $75-150.**

Tips "We seek ideas to increase sales of diamonds."

$ $ THE ENGRAVERS JOURNAL

P.O. Box 318, Brighton MI 48116. (810)229-5725. Fax: (810)229-8320. E-mail: editor@engraversjournal.com. Web site: www.engraversjournal.com. Publisher: Michael J. Davis. **Contact:** Claudia Sinta, managing editor. **70% freelance written.** Monthly magazine covering the recognition and identification industry (engraving, marking devices, awards, jewelry, and signage). "We provide practical information for the education and advancement of our readers, mainly retail business owners." Estab. 1975. **Pays on acceptance.** Publishes ms an average of 1 year after acceptance. Byline given. Buys one-time rights, makes work-for-hire assignments. Accepts queries by mail, e-mail, fax. Responds in 2 weeks to mss. Sample copy for free. Writer's guidelines free.

- To break in, submit well-written, fairly in-depth general business articles. Topics and article style should focus on the small retail business owner, and should be helpful and informative.

Nonfiction General interest (industry related), how-to (small business subjects, increase sales, develop new markets, use new sales techniques, etc.), technical. No general overviews of the industry. Length: 1,000-5,000 words. **Pays $200 and up.**

Reprints Send tearsheet, photocopy or typed ms with rights for sale noted and information about when and where the material previously appeared. Pays 50-100% of amout paid for original article.
Photos Send photos with submission. Pays variable rate. Captions, identification of subjects, model releases required.
Tips "Articles should always be down to earth, practical, and thoroughly cover the subject with authority. We do not want the 'textbook' writing approach, vagueness, or theory—our readers look to us for sound practical information. We use an educational slant, publishing both trade-oriented articles and general business topics of interest to a small retail-oriented readership."

$ $ LUSTRE

The Luxury Jeweler's Design & Lifestyle Magazine, Cygnus Publishing Co., 19 W. 44th St., Suite 1401, New York NY 10036. (212)921-1091. Fax: (212)921-5539. Web site: www.lustremag.com. Editor-in-Chief: Lorraine DePasque. Bimonthly magazine covering fine jewelry and related accessories. "*Lustre*'s focus is on the latest lifestyle and fashion trends of the most affluent consumers in the United States. Editorial includes model fashion and still life photography with emphasis on forecasting trends 6-8 months prior to retail deliveries." Estab. 1997. Circ. 5,000. Pays on publication. Publishes ms an average of 4 months after acceptance. Byline given. Offers 50% kill fee. Buys all rights. Editorial lead time 4 months. Submit seasonal material 4 months in advance. Accepts queries by mail. Responds in 4 weeks to queries. Sample copy for free.
Nonfiction How-to, new product. **Buys 18 mss/year.** Query with published clips. Length: 1,000-2,500 words. **Pays $500.** Sometimes pays expenses of writers on assignment.
Photos State availability with submission. Buys one-time rights, plus usage for 1 year after publication date (but not exclusive usage). Offers no additional payment for photos accepted with ms. Captions, identification of subjects required.
Columns/Departments Trend Talk (color, society, runway, item), 500-1,000 words; Marketing/Merchandising (to the affluent market), 1,000-2,000 words.

MODERN JEWELER

Cygnus Business Media, 3 Huntington Quadrangle, Suite 301N, Melville NY 11747. (631)845-2700. Fax: (631)845-7109. Web site: www.modernjeweler.com. Publisher: Tim Murphy. **20% freelance written.** Monthly magazine covering fine jewelry and watches. Estab. 1901. Circ. 33,000. **Pays on acceptance.** Publishes ms an average of 2 months after acceptance. Byline given. Buys all rights. Editorial lead time 2 months. Submit seasonal material 2 months in advance. Accepts queries by mail, fax. Responds in 3 weeks to queries; 3 months to mss. Sample copy for SAE.
Nonfiction Technical.
Photos State availability with submission. Reviews transparencies, prints.
Tips "Requires knowledge of retail business, experience in dealing with retail and manufacturing executives and analytical writing style. We don't frequently use writers who have no ties to or experience with the jewelry manufacturing industry."

JOURNALISM & WRITING

$ $ $ $ AMERICAN JOURNALISM REVIEW

1117 Journalism Bldg., University of Maryland, College Park MD 20742. (301)405-8803. Fax: (301)405-8323. E-mail: editor@ajr.umd.edu. Web site: www.ajr.org. Editor: Rem Rieder. **Contact:** Rachel Smolkin, managing editor. **80% freelance written.** Bimonthly magazine covering print, broadcast, and online journalism. "Mostly journalists subscribe. We cover ethical issues, trends in the industry, coverage that falls short." Circ. 25,000. Pays within 1 month after publication. Publishes ms an average of 2 months after acceptance. Byline given. Offers 25% kill fee. Buys first North American serial, electronic rights. Editorial lead time 1 month. Accepts queries by mail, e-mail, fax. Responds in 1 month to queries. Sample copy for $4.95 pre-paid or online. Writer's guidelines online.
Nonfiction Exposé, personal experience, ethical issues. **Buys many mss/year.** Query with published clips or send complete ms. Length: 2,000-4,000 words. **Pays $1,500-2,000.** Pays expenses of writers on assignment.
Fillers Anecdotes, facts, short humor, short pieces. Length: 150-1,000 words. **Pays $100-250.**
Tips "Write a short story for the front-of-the-book section. We prefer queries to completed articles. Include in a page what you'd like to write about, who you'll interview, why it's important, and why you should write it."

$ BOOK DEALERS WORLD

North American Bookdealers Exchange, P.O. Box 606, Cottage Grove OR 97424. (541)942-7455. Web site: www.bookmarketingprofits.com. **Contact:** Al Galasso, editorial director. **50% freelance written.** Quarterly magazine covering writing, self-publishing, and marketing books by mail. Circ. 20,000. Pays on publication. Publishes ms an average of 3 months after acceptance. Byline given. Buys first North American serial, second serial (reprint) rights. Accepts simultaneous submissions. Responds in 1 month to queries. Sample copy for $3.

Nonfiction Book excerpts (writing, mail order, direct mail, publishing), how-to (home business by mail, advertising), interview/profile (of successful self-publishers), positive articles on self-publishing, new writing angles, marketing. **Buys 10 mss/year.** Send complete ms. Length: 1,000-1,500 words. **Pays $25-50.**

Reprints Send ms with rights for sale noted and information about when and where the material previously appeared. Pays 80% of amount paid for an original article.

Columns/Departments Publisher Profile (on successful self-publishers and their marketing strategy). Length: 250-1,000 words. **Buys 20 mss/year.** Send complete ms. **Pays $5-20.**

Fillers Fillers concerning writing, publishing, or books. **Buys 6/year.** Length: 100-250 words. **Pays $3-10.**

Tips "Query first. Get a sample copy of the magazine."

N $ $ CANADIAN SCREENWRITER

Writers Guild of Canada, 366 Adelaide St. W., Suite 401, Toronto ON M5V 1R9 Canada. (416)979-7907. Fax: (416)979-9273. E-mail: b.farwell@wgc.ca. Web site: www.wgc.ca/magazine. **Contact:** Barb Farwell, editor. **80% freelance written.** Magazine published 3 times/year covering screenwriting for television, film, radio and digital media. "*Canadian Screenwriter* profiles Canadian screenwriters, provides industry news and offers practical writing tips for screenwriters." Estab. 1998. Circ. 4,000. **Pays on acceptance.** Publishes ms an average of 1 month after acceptance. Byline given. Offers 50% kill fee. Buys first, electronic rights. Editorial lead time 2 months. Submit seasonal material 2 months in advance. Accepts queries by e-mail. Accepts previously published material. Responds in 1 week to queries; 1 month to mss. Sample copy for free. Writer's guidelines by e-mail.

Nonfiction How-to, humor, interview/profile. Does not want writing on foreign screenwriters. The focus is on Canadian-resident screenwriters. **Buys 12 mss/year.** Query with published clips. Length: 750-2,200 words. **Pays 50¢/word.** Sometimes pays expenses of writers on assignment.

Photos State availability with submission. Reviews GIF/JPEG files. Buys one-time rights. Negotiates payment individually. Identification of subjects required.

Tips "Read other Canadian film and television publications."

$ CANADIAN WRITER'S JOURNAL

P.O. Box 1178, New Liskeard ON P0J 1P0 Canada. (705)647-5424. Fax: (705)647-8366. E-mail: cwj@cwj.ca. Web site: www.cwj.ca. **Contact:** Deborah Ranchuk, editor. **75% freelance written.** Bimonthly magazine for writers. Accepts well-written articles by all writers. Estab. 1984. Circ. 350. Pays on publication. Publishes ms an average of 9 months after acceptance. Byline given. Buys one-time rights. Accepts queries by mail, e-mail, fax, phone. Responds in 2 months to queries. Sample copy for $8, including postage. Writer's guidelines online.

Nonfiction Looking for articles on how to break into niche markets. How-to (articles for writers). **Buys 200 mss/year.** Query optional. **Pays $7.50/published magazine page (approx. 450 words).**

Reprints Send ms with rights for sale noted and information about when and where the material previously appeared.

Fiction Requirements being met by annual contest. Send SASE for rules, or see guidelines on Web site. "Does not want gratuitous violence, sex subject matter."

Poetry Short poems or extracts used as part of articles on the writing of poetry.

Tips "We prefer short, tightly written, informative how-to articles. U.S. writers note that U.S. postage cannot be used to mail from Canada. Obtain Canadian stamps, use IRCs, or send small amounts in cash."

N $ $ $ E CONTENT MAGAZINE

Digital Content Strategies & Resources, Online, Inc., 88 Danbury Rd., Suite 1D, Wilton CT 06897. (203)761-1466. Fax: (203)761-1444. E-mail: michelle.manafy@infotoday.com. Web site: www.econtentmag.com. **Contact:** Michelle Manafy, editor. **90% freelance written.** Monthly magazine covering digital content trends, strategies, etc. "*E Content* is a business publication. Readers need to stay on top of industry trends and developments." Estab. 1979. Circ. 12,000. Pays within 1 month of publication. Byline given. Offers 20-50% kill fee. Buys all rights. Editorial lead time 4 months. Accepts queries by e-mail. Responds in 3 weeks to queries; 1 month to mss. Sample copy and writer's guidelines online.

Nonfiction Exposé, how-to, interview/profile, new product, opinion, technical, news features, strategic and solution-oriented features. No academic or straight Q&A. **Buys 48 mss/year.** Query with published clips. Length: 500-700 words. **Pays 40-50¢/word.** Sometimes pays expenses of writers on assignment.

Photos State availability with submission. Buys one-time rights. Negotiates payment individually. Captions required.

Columns/Departments Profiles (short profile of unique company, person or product), 1,200 words; New Features (breaking news of content-related topics), 500 words maximum. **Buys 40 mss/year.** Query with published clips. **Pays 30-40¢/word.**

Tips "Take a look at the Web site. Most of the time, an e-mail query with specific article ideas works well. A general outline of talking points is good, too. State prior experience."

$ $ FREELANCE WRITER'S REPORT

CNW Publishing, Inc., 45 Main St., P.O. Box A, North Stratford NH 03590-0167. (603)922-8338. E-mail: fwrwm @writers-editors.com. Web site: www.writers-editors.com. **Contact:** Dana K. Cassell, editor. **25% freelance written.** Monthly newsletter. "*FWR* covers the marketing and business/office management aspects of running a freelance writing business. Articles must be of value to the established freelancer; nothing basic." Estab. 1982. Pays on publication. Publishes ms an average of 6 months after acceptance. Byline given. Buys one-time rights. Editorial lead time 2 months. Submit seasonal material 2 months in advance. Accepts simultaneous submissions. Responds in 1 week to queries; 2 weeks to mss. Sample copy for 6×9 SAE with 2 first-class stamps (for back copy); $4 for current copy. Writer's guidelines online.

O→ Most needed are filler tips of up to 400 words.

Nonfiction Book excerpts, how-to (market, increase income or profits). No articles about the basics of freelancing. **Buys 50 mss/year.** Send complete ms by e-mail. Length: Up to 900 words. **Pays 10¢/word.**

Reprints Accepts previously published submissions.

Tips "Write in a terse, newsletter style."

N KIRKUS REVIEWS

VNU Business Media, 770 Broadway, 6th Floor, New York NY 10003. (646)654-5000. Fax: (646)654-4706. E-mail: info@kirkusreviews.com. Web site: www.kirkusreviews.com. Editor-in-Chief: Jerome Kramer. Managing Editor: Chuck Shelton. Children's Editor: Karen Breen. **Contact:** Eric Liebetrau, associate editor. **100% freelance written.** Biweekly trade journal that reviews 5,000 pre-publication books each year—mainstream fiction, nonfiction, children's books, and young adult books—for libraries, booksellers, publishers, producers, and agents. Estab. 1933. Circ. 2,100. **Pays on acceptance.** Editorial lead time 3-4 months.

Tips "Please visit our Web site for details."

$ $ $ MASTHEAD

The Magazine About Magazines, North Island Publishing, 1606 Sedlescomb Dr., Unit 8, Mississauga ON L4X 1M6 Canada. (905)625-7070. Fax: (905)625-4856. E-mail: wshields@masthead.ca. Web site: www.mastheadonline.com. **40% freelance written.** Journal published 6 times/year covering the Canadian magazine industry. "With its lively mix of in-depth features, news stories, service pieces, surveys, tallies, and spirited commentary, this independent journal provides detailed coverage and analysis of the events, issues, personalities, and technologies shaping Canada's magazine industry." Estab. 1987. Circ. 2,400. Pays on publication. Publishes ms an average of 2 months after acceptance. Byline given. Offers 50% kill fee. Buys first North American serial rights. Editorial lead time 1 month. Accepts queries by mail. Accepts simultaneous submissions. Responds in 2 weeks to queries. Sample copy for free. Writer's guidelines by e-mail.

Nonfiction "We generally pay $600-850 for a cover story running 2,000-2,500 words, depending on the amount of research, etc., required. For the most part, *Masthead* generates feature ideas in-house and then assigns the stories to regular contributors. When space permits, we sometimes run shorter features or service pieces (1,000-1,500 words) for a flat rate of $350." Book excerpts, essays, exposé, historical/nostalgic, how-to, humor, interview/profile, new product, opinion, personal experience, technical. No articles that have nothing to do with Canadian magazines. Length: 100-3,000 words. **Pays $30-850 (Canadian).** Pays expenses of writers on assignment.

Photos State availability with submission. Negotiates payment individually. Identification of subjects required.

Fiction Novel excerpts. No excerpts that have nothing to do with Canadian magazines. Query with published clips.

Tips "Have a solid understanding of the Canadian magazine industry. A good way to introduce yourself is to propose small articles on new magazines."

$ $ MSLEXIA

For Women Who Write, Mslexia Publications Ltd., P.O. Box 656, Newcastle upon Tyne NE99 1PZ United Kingdom. (44)(191)261-6656. E-mail: postbag@mslexia.demon.co.uk. Web site: www.mslexia.co.uk. **Contact:** Daneet Steffens, editor. **60% freelance written.** Quarterly magazine offering advice and publishing opportunities for women writers, plus poetry and prose submissions on a different theme each issue. "*Mslexia* tells you all you need to know about exploring your creativity and getting into print. No other magazine provides *Mslexia*'s unique mix of advice and inspiration; news, reviews, interviews; competitions, events, grants; all served up with a challenging selection of new poetry and prose. *Mslexia* is read by authors and absolute beginners. A quarterly master class in the business and psychology of writing, it's the essential magazine for women who write." Estab. 1998. Circ. 12,000. Pays on publication. Publishes ms an average of 1 month after acceptance. Byline given. Offers 50% kill fee. Buys one-time rights. Editorial lead time 3 months. Submit seasonal material 3 months in advance. Accepts queries by mail, e-mail, phone. Accepts simultaneous submissions. Responds in 3 months to mss. Sample copy online. Writer's guidelines online or by e-mail.

- This publication does not accept e-mail submissions except from overseas writers.

Nonfiction How-to, interview/profile, opinion, personal experience. No general items about women or academic features. "We are only interested in features (for tertiary-educated readership) about women's writing and literature." **Buys 40 mss/year.** Query with published clips. Length: 500-2,000 words. **Pays $70-400 for assigned articles; $70-300 for unsolicited articles. Pays $40/poem and $20/1,000 words for submissions published in the New Writing section of the magazine.** Sometimes pays expenses of writers on assignment.
Columns/Departments "We are open to suggestions, but would only commission 1 new column/year, probably from a UK-based writer." **Buys 12 mss/year.** Query with published clips.
Fiction Helen Christie, editorial assistant. "See guidelines on our Web site. Submissions not on one of our current themes will be returned (if submitted with a SASE) or destroyed." **Buys 30 mss/year.** Send complete ms. Length: 50-3,000 words.
Poetry Helen Christie, editorial assistant. Avant-garde, free verse, haiku, traditional. **Buys 40 poems/year.** Submit maximum 4 poems.
Tips "Read the magazine; subscribe if you can afford it. *Mslexia* has a particular style and relationship with its readers which is hard to assess at a quick glance. The majority of our readers live in the UK, so feature pitches should be aware of this. We never commission work without seeing a written sample first. We rarely accept unsolicited manuscripts, but prefer a short letter suggesting a feature, plus a brief bio and writing sample."

$ NEW WRITER'S MAGAZINE

Sarasota Bay Publishing, P.O. Box 5976, Sarasota FL 34277-5976. (941)953-7903. E-mail: newriters@aol.com. **Contact:** George S. Haborak, editor. **95% freelance written.** Bimonthly magazine. "*New Writer's Magazine* believes that *all* writers are *new* writers in that each of us can learn from one another. So, we reach pro and nonpro alike." Estab. 1986. Circ. 5,000. Pays on publication. Byline given. Buys first rights. Accepts queries by mail. Responds in 1 month to queries; 1 month to mss. Sample copy for $3. Writer's guidelines for #10 SASE.
Nonfiction General interest, how-to (for new writers), humor, interview/profile, opinion, personal experience (with pro writer). **Buys 50 mss/year.** Send complete ms. Length: 700-1,000 words. **Pays $10-50.**
Photos Send photos with submission. Reviews 5×7 prints. Offers no additional payment for photos accepted with ms. Captions required.
Fiction Experimental, historical, humorous, mainstream, slice-of-life vignettes. "Again, we do *not* want anything that does not have a tie-in with the writing life or writers in general." **Buys 2-6 mss/year.** Send complete ms. Length: 700-800 words. **Pays $20-40.**
Poetry Free verse, light verse, traditional. Does not want anything *not* for writers. **Buys 10-20 poems/year.** Submit maximum 3 poems. Length: 8-20 lines. **Pays $5 minimum.**
Fillers For cartoons, writing lifestyle slant. Buys 20-30/year. Pays $10 maximum. Anecdotes, facts, newsbreaks, short humor. **Buys 5-15/year.** Length: 20-100 words. **Pays $5 maximum.**
Tips "Any article with photos has a good chance, especially an up close and personal interview with an established professional writer offering advice, etc. Short profile pieces on new authors also receive attention."

$ $ NOVEL & SHORT STORY WRITER'S MARKET

F+W Publications, Inc., 4700 E. Galbraith Rd., Cincinnati OH 45236. E-mail: rachel.mcdonald@fwpubs.com. **Contact:** Rachel McDonald, editor. **80% freelance written.** Annual resource book covering the fiction market. "In addition to thousands of listings for places to get fiction published, we feature articles on the craft and business of fiction writing, as well as interviews with successful fiction writers, editors, and agents. Our articles are unique in that they always offer an actionable take-away. In other words, readers must learn something immediately useful about the creation or marketing of fiction." Estab. 1981. **Pays on acceptance.** Byline given. Offers 25% kill fee. Buys exclusive first serial rights and nonexclusive electronic rights for reproduction on Web site. Accepts queries by mail, e-mail. Responds in 1 week to queries. Sample copy not available.

- Accepts proposals during the summer.
- "We're especially in need of writers who can cover the genre markets—romance, horror, science fiction, mystery."

Nonfiction How-to (write, sell and promote fiction; find an agent; etc.), interview/profile, personal experience. **Buys 15 mss/year.** Length: 750-2,500 words. **Pays $200-600.**
Photos Send photos with submission. Reviews prints, GIF/JPEG files (hi-res). Offers no additional payment for photos accepted with ms. Identification of subjects required.
Tips "The best way to break into this book is to review the last few years' editions and look for aspects of the

fiction industry that we haven't covered recently. Send me a specific, detailed pitch stating the topic, angle, and 'takeaway' of the piece, what sources you intend to use, and what qualifies you to write this article. Freelancers who have published fiction and/or have contacts in the industry have an advantage.''

$ OHIO WRITER

Poets' & Writers' League of Greater Cleveland, 12200 Fairhill Rd., Townhouse #3A, Cleveland OH 44120. (216)421-0403. Fax: (216)421-8874. E-mail: pwlgc@yahoo.com. Web site: www.pwlgc.com. **75% freelance written.** Bimonthly magazine covering writing and Ohio writers. Estab. 1987. Pays on publication. Publishes ms an average of 4 months after acceptance. Byline given. Buys one-time, second serial (reprint) rights. Editorial lead time 4 months. Submit seasonal material 4 months in advance. Accepts queries by mail, e-mail, fax, phone. Responds in 6 weeks to mss. Sample copy for $2.50. Writer's guidelines for #10 SASE.

Nonfiction ''All articles must be related to the writing life of Ohio writers, or the Ohio publishing scene.'' Essays, how-to, humor, inspirational, interview/profile, opinion, personal experience. **Buys 24 mss/year.** Send complete ms and SASE. Length: 750-2,500 words. **Pays $25 minimum, up to $50 for lead article, other payment under arrangement with writer.**

Reprints Send ms with rights for sale noted and information about when and where the material previously appeared. Pays $10 for reprints.

Columns/Departments Buys 6 mss/year. Send complete ms. **Pays $25-50; $5/book review.**

Tips ''We look for articles about writers and writing, with a special emphasis on activities in our state. However, we publish articles by writers throughout the country that offer something helpful about the writing life. Profiles and interviews of writers who live in Ohio are always needed. *Ohio Writer* is read by both beginning and experienced writers and hopes to create a sense of community among writers of different genres, abilities, and backgrounds. We want to hear a personal voice, one that engages the reader. We're looking for intelligent, literate prose that isn't stuffy.''

$ $ POETS & WRITERS MAGAZINE

72 Spring St., New York NY 10012. E-mail: editor@pw.org. Web site: www.pw.org. **Contact:** The Editors. **95% freelance written.** Bimonthly professional trade journal for poets and fiction writers and creative nonfiction writers. Estab. 1987. Circ. 60,000. Pays on acceptance of finished draft. Publishes ms an average of 4 months after acceptance. Byline given. Offers 25% kill fee. Buys first North American serial, nonexclusive reprint rights shared 50/50 thereafter rights. Submit seasonal material 4 months in advance. Accepts queries by mail, e-mail. Responds in 2 months to mss. Sample copy for $4.95 to Sample Copy Dept. Writer's guidelines online.

- No poetry or fiction submissions.

Nonfiction How-to (craft of poetry, fiction or creative nonfiction writing), interview/profile (with poets or writers of fiction and creative nonfiction). ''We do not accept submissions by fax.'' **Buys 35 mss/year.** Query with published clips or send complete ms. Length: 500-2,500 (depending on topic) words.

Photos State availability with submission. Reviews b&w prints. Offers no additional payment for photos accepted with ms.

Columns/Departments Literary and Publishing News, 500-1,000 words; Profiles of Emerging and Established Poets, Fiction Writers and Creative Nonfiction Writers, 2,000-3,000 words; Regional Reports (literary activity in US), 1,000-2,000 words. Query with published clips or send complete ms. **Pays $150-500.**

N $ $ $ QUILL MAGAZINE

Society of Professional Journalists, 3909 N. Meridian St., Indianapolis IN 46208. Fax: (317)920-4789. E-mail: jskeel@spj.org. Web site: www.spj.org/quill.asp. Editor: Joe Skeel. **75% freelance written.** Monthly magazine covering journalism and the media industry. ''*Quill* is a how-to magazine written by journalists. We focus on the industry's biggest issues while providing tips on how to become better journalists.'' Estab. 1912. Circ. 10,000. **Pays on acceptance.** Publishes ms an average of 2 months after acceptance. Byline given. Offers 25% kill fee. Buys first, electronic rights. Editorial lead time 2-3 months. Submit seasonal material 2-3 months in advance. Accepts queries by e-mail. Accepts previously published material. Accepts simultaneous submissions. Sample copy online.

Nonfiction General interest, how-to, technical. Does not want personality profiles and straight research pieces. **Buys 12 mss/year.** Query. Length: 800-2,500 words. **Pays $150-800.**

$ $ THE WRITER

Kalmbach Publishing Co., 21027 Crossroads Circle, P.O. Box 1612, Waukesha WI 53187-1612. E-mail: queries@writermag.com. Web site: www.writermag.com. **Contact:** Elfrieda Abbe, editor. **90% freelance written.** Prefers to buy work of published/established writers. Estab. 1887. **Pays on acceptance.** Buys first North American serial rights. Accepts queries by mail, e-mail. Sample copy for $5.50. Writer's guidelines online.

• No phone queries.

Nonfiction Practical articles for writers on how to write for publication, and how and where to market manuscripts in various fields. Considers all submissions generally in 1-2 months. Assignments go to writers who have published in the magazine. Length: 700-3,400 words. **Pays $50-500.**

Reprints Send tearsheet or photocopy and information about when and where the material previously appeared.

Tips "We are looking for articles with plenty of practical, specific advice, tips, and techniques that aspiring and beginning writers can apply to their own work. New types of publications and our continually updated market listings in all fields will determine changes of focus and fact."

$ $ $ WRITER'S DIGEST

F+W Publications, Inc., 4700 E. Galbraith Rd., Cincinnati OH 45236. (513)531-2690. E-mail: wdsubmissions@fwpubs.com. Web site: www.writersdigest.com. **Contact:** Submissions Editor. **70% freelance written.** Bimonthly magazine for those who want to write better, get published and participate in the vibrant culture of writers. "Our readers look to us for specific ideas and tips that will help them succeed, whether success means getting into print, finding personal fulfillment through writing or building and maintaining a thriving writing career and network." Estab. 1920. Circ. 140,000. **Pays on acceptance.** Publishes ms an average of 9-12 months after acceptance. Byline given. Offers 25% kill fee. Buys first world serial rights for one-time editorial use, possible electronic posting, and magazine promotional use. Pays 25% reprint fee and 10% for electronic use in fee-charging mediums. Accepts queries by mail, e-mail. Responds in 2 months to queries; 2 months to mss. Writer's guidelines online.

• The magazine does not accept or read e-queries with attachments.

Nonfiction "Although we welcome the work of new writers, we believe the established writer can better instruct our readers. Please include your publishing credentials related to your topic with your submission." Essays, how-to, humor, inspirational, interview/profile, opinion. Does not accept phone or fax queries. "We don't buy newspaper clippings or reprints of articles previously published in other writing magazines. Book and software reviews are handled in-house, as are *WD* interviews." **Buys 75 mss/year.** Query with published clips or send complete ms. Length: 800-1,500 words. **Pays 30-50¢/word.**

Tips "InkWell is the best place for new writers to break in. Other sections you can pitch include: Author Profiles; Essays; Writer's Workbook; Writing Technique Articles; and Market Reports. Check our writer's guidelines for more details."

$ WRITERS' JOURNAL

The Complete Writer's Magazine, Val-Tech Media, P.O. Box 394, Perham MN 56573-0394. (218)346-7921. Fax: (218)346-7924. E-mail: writersjournal@writersjournal.com. Web site: www.writersjournal.com. Managing Editor: John Ogroske. **Contact:** Leon Ogroske, editor (editor@writersjournal.com). **60% freelance written.** Bimonthly magazine covering writing. "*Writers' Journal* is read by thousands of aspiring writers whose love of writing has taken them to the next step: writing for money. We are an instructional manual giving writers the tools and information necessary to get their work published. We also print works by authors who have won our writing contests." Estab. 1980. Circ. 22,000. Pays on publication. Publishes ms an average of 4 months after acceptance. Byline given. Buys first, second serial (reprint) rights. Accepts queries by mail, e-mail, fax. Responds in 6 weeks to queries; 6 months to mss. Sample copy for $5. Writer's guidelines online.

Nonfiction How-to (write, publish, market). **Buys 25 mss/year.** Send complete ms. Length: 800-2,500 words. **Pays $30 for assigned articles. Pays with a 1-year subscription, money depending on article and budget, and in contributor copies or other premiums if author agrees.**

Photos Send photos with submission. Reviews transparencies, 8×10 prints, GIF/JPEG files. Buys one-time rights. Offers no addition payment for photos accepted with ms; offers $50/cover photo. Model releases required.

Fiction "We only publish winners of our fiction contests—16 contests/year." Length: 2,000 words.

Poetry Contact Esther Leiper, poetry editor. Light verse, anything about writing. Does not want anything boring. **Buys 30 poems/year.** Submit maximum 2 poems. Length: 15 lines. **Pays $5.**

Fillers Facts, gags to be illustrated by cartoonist, short humor. **Buys 20/year.** Length: 10-200 words. **Pays up to $10.**

Tips "Appearance must be professional with no grammatical or spelling errors, submitted on white paper, double spaced with easy-to-read font. We want articles that will help writers improve technique in writing, style, editing, publishing, and story construction. We are interested in how writers use new and fresh angles to break into the writing markets."

$ WRITING THAT WORKS

The Business Communications Report, Communications Concepts, Inc., 7481 Huntsman Blvd., #720, Springfield VA 22153-1648. (703)643-2200. Fax: (703)643-2329. Web site: www.apexawards.com. **Contact:** John De Lellis, editor/publisher. Monthly newsletter on business writing and communications. "Our readers are company writers, editors, communicators, and executives. They need specific, practical advice on how to write well as part of their job." Estab. 1983. Pays within 45 days of acceptance. Publishes ms an average of 3 months after acceptance. Byline sometimes given. Buys all rights. Editorial lead time 3 months. Accepts queries by mail, e-mail. Responds in 1 month to queries. Sample copy and writer's guidelines online.

Nonfiction Practical, short, how-to articles and quick tips on business writing techniques geared to company writers, editors, publication staff and communicators. "We're always looking for shorts—how-to tips on business writing." How-to. **Buys 120 mss/year.** Accepts electronic final mss. Length: 100-500 words. **Pays $35-150.**

Columns/Departments Writing Techniques (how-to business writing advice); Style Matters (grammar, usage, and editing); Online Publishing (writing, editing, and publishing for the Web); Managing Publications; PR & Marketing (writing).

Fillers Short tips on writing or editing. Mini-reviews of communications Web sites for business writers, editors, and communicators. Length: 100-150 words. **Pays $35.**

Tips "We do not use material on how to get published or how to conduct a freelancing business. Format your copy to follow *Writing That Works* style. Include postal and e-mail addresses, phone numbers, Web site URLs, and prices for products/services mentioned in articles."

$ $ $ $ WRITTEN BY

The Magazine of the Writers Guild of America, West, 7000 W. Third St., Los Angeles CA 90048. (323)782-4522. Fax: (323)782-4800. Web site: www.wga.org. **40% freelance written.** Magazine published 9 times/year. "*Written By* is the premier magazine written by and for America's screen and TV writers. We focus on the craft of screenwriting and cover all aspects of the entertainment industry from the perspective of the writer. We are read by all screenwriters and most entertainment executives." Estab. 1987. Circ. 12,000. **Pays on acceptance.** Publishes ms an average of 2 months after acceptance. Byline given. Offers 10% kill fee. Buys first North American serial, electronic rights. Editorial lead time 4 months. Submit seasonal material 4 months in advance. Accepts queries by mail, e-mail, fax, phone. Writer's guidelines for #10 SASE.

O→ Break in with "an exclusive profile or Q&A with a major TV or screenwriter."

Nonfiction Book excerpts, essays, historical/nostalgic, humor, interview/profile, opinion, personal experience, photo feature, technical (software). No beginner pieces on "how to break into Hollywood," or "how to write scripts." **Buys 20 mss/year.** Query with published clips. Length: 500-3,500 words. **Pays $500-3,500 for assigned articles.** Sometimes pays expenses of writers on assignment.

Photos State availability with submission. Reviews transparencies. Buys one-time rights. Offers no additional payment for photos accepted with ms. Captions, identification of subjects, model releases required.

Columns/Departments Pays $1,000 maximum.

Tips "We are looking for more theoretical essays on screenwriting past and/or present. Also, the writer must always keep in mind that our audience is made up primarily of working writers who are inside the business; therefore all articles need to have an 'insider' feel and not be written for those who are still trying to break in to Hollywood. We prefer a hard copy of submission or e-mail."

LAW

$ $ $ $ ABA JOURNAL

The Lawyer's Magazine, American Bar Association, 321 N. Clark St., Chicago IL 60610. (312)988-6018. Fax: (312)988-6014. E-mail: releases@abanet.org. Web site: www.abajournal.com. Editor: Danial J. Kim. **Contact:** Debra Cassens Weiss, managing editor. **10% freelance written.** Monthly magazine covering law. "The *ABA Journal* is an independent, thoughtful, and inquiring observer of the law and the legal profession. The magazine is edited for members of the American Bar Association." Circ. 380,000. **Pays on acceptance.** Byline given. Makes work-for-hire assignments. Accepts queries by mail, e-mail. Sample copy for free. Writer's guidelines online.

Nonfiction Legal features. "We don't want anything that does not have a legal theme. No poetry or fiction." **Buys 5 mss/year.** Query with published clips. Length: 500-3,500 words. **Pays $300-2,000 for assigned articles.**

Columns/Departments Buys 25 mss/year. Query with published clips. **Pays $300, regardless of story length.**

$ $ $ BENCH & BAR OF MINNESOTA

Minnesota State Bar Association, 600 Nicollet Mall #380, Minneapolis MN 55402. (612)333-1183. Fax: (612)333-4927. Web site: www.mnbar.org. **5% freelance written.** Magazine published 11 times/year. "Audience is mostly Minnesota lawyers. *Bench & Bar* seeks reportage, analysis, and commentary on trends and issues in the law and the legal profession, especially in Minnesota. Preference to items of practical/human interest to professionals in law." Estab. 1931. Circ. 16,000. **Pays on acceptance.** Publishes ms an average of 3 months after acceptance. Byline given. Buys first North American serial rights, makes work-for-hire assignments. Responds in 1 month to queries. Writer's guidelines for free online or by mail.

Nonfiction How-to (handle particular types of legal/ethical problems in office management, representation, etc.), humor, interview/profile, technical (legal). "We do not want one-sided opinion pieces or advertorial." **Buys 2-3 mss/year.** Query with or without published clips or send complete ms. Length: 1,500-3,000 words. **Pays $300-800.** Sometimes pays expenses of writers on assignment.

Photos State availability with submission. Reviews 5×7 prints. Buys one-time rights. Pays $25-100 upon publication. Identification of subjects, model releases required.

$ $ $ $ CALIFORNIA LAWYER

Daily Journal Corp., 44 Montgomery St., Suite 250, San Francisco CA 94104. (415)296-2400. Fax: (415)296-2440. E-mail: tema_goodwin@dailyjournal.com. Web site: www.dailyjournal.com. **Contact:** Tema Goodwin, managing editor. **30% freelance written.** Monthly magazine of law-related articles and general-interest subjects of appeal to lawyers and judges. "Our primary mission is to cover the news of the world as it affects the law and lawyers, helping our readers better comprehend the issues of the day and to cover changes and trends in the legal profession. Our readers are all California lawyers, plus judges, legislators, and corporate executives. Although we focus on California and the West, we have subscribers in every state. *California Lawyer* is a general interest magazine for people interested in law. Our writers are journalists." Estab. 1981. Circ. 140,000. **Pays on acceptance.** Publishes ms an average of 3 months after acceptance. Byline given. Offers 25% kill fee. Buys first North American serial, electronic rights. Editorial lead time 3 months. Accepts queries by mail, e-mail, fax. Sample copy and writer's guidelines for #10 SASE.

O→ Break in by "showing us clips—we usually start people on short news stories."

Nonfiction Essays, general interest, interview/profile, news and feature articles on law-related topics. "We are interested in concise, well-written and well-researched articles on issues of current concern, as well as well-told feature narratives with a legal focus. We would like to see a description or outline of your proposed idea, including a list of possible sources." **Buys 12 mss/year.** Query with or without published clips or send complete ms. Length: 500-5,000 words. **Pays $50-2,000.** Pays expenses of writers on assignment.

Photos Jake Flaherty, art director. State availability with submission. Reviews prints. Identification of subjects, model releases required.

Columns/Departments California Esq. (current legal trends), 300 words. **Buys 6 mss/year.** Query with or without published clips. **Pays $50-250.**

$ $ $ $ INSIDECOUNSEL

(formerly *Corporate Legal Times*), 222 S. Riverside Plaza, Suite 620, Chicago IL 60606. (312)654-3500. E-mail: rvasper@insidecounsel.com. Web site: www.insidecounsel.com. **Contact:** Robert Vosper, editor. **50% freelance written.** Monthly tabloid. "*InsideCounsel* is a monthly national magazine that gives general counsel and inhouse attorneys information on legal and business issues to help them better manage corporate law departments. It routinely addresses changes and trends in law departments, litigation management, legal technology, corporate governance and inhouse careers. Law areas covered monthly include: intellectual property, international, technology, project finance, e-commerce and litigation. All articles need to be geared toward the inhouse attorney's perspective." Estab. 1991. Circ. 45,000. Pays on publication. Publishes ms an average of 3 months after acceptance. Byline given. Buys all rights. Editorial lead time 3 months. Submit seasonal material 3 months in advance. Accepts queries by mail, e-mail. Responds in 3 weeks to queries. Sample copy for $17. Writer's guidelines online.

Nonfiction Interview/profile, news about legal aspects of business issues and events. **Buys 12-25 mss/year.** Query with published clips. Length: 500-3,000 words. **Pays $500-2,000.**

Photos Freelancers should state availability of photos with submission. Reviews color transparencies, b&w prints. Buys all rights. Offers $25-150/photo. Identification of subjects required.

Tips "Our publication targets general counsel and inhouse lawyers. All articles need to speak to them—not to the general attorney population. Query with clips and a list of potential in-house sources."

$ $ $ JOURNAL OF COURT REPORTING

National Court Reporters Association, 8224 Old Courthouse Rd., Vienna VA 22182. (703)556-6272. Fax: (703)556-6291. E-mail: jschmidt@ncrahq.org. **Contact:** Jacqueline Schmidt, editor. **20% freelance written.** Monthly (bimonthly July/August and November/December) magazine. "The *Journal of Court Reporting* has two complementary purposes: to communicate the activities, goals and mission of its publisher, the National Court Reporters Association; and, simultaneously, to seek out and publish diverse information and views on matters significantly related to the information/court reporting and captioning profession." Estab. 1905. Circ. 34,000. **Pays on acceptance.** Publishes ms an average of 3 months after acceptance. Byline given. Buys one-time rights, makes work-for-hire assignments. Editorial lead time 3 months. Accepts simultaneous submissions. Sample copy for $6. Writer's guidelines free.

Nonfiction Essays, historical/nostalgic, how-to, interview/profile, new product, technical. **Buys 10 mss/year.** Query. Length: 1,200 words. **Pays $55-1,000.** Sometimes pays expenses of writers on assignment.

Photos State availability with submission. Buys one-time rights. Offers no additional payment for photos accepted with ms. Captions, identification of subjects, model releases required.

$ LEGAL ASSISTANT TODAY

James Publishing, Inc., P.O. Box 25202, Santa Ana CA 92799. (714)755-5468. Fax: (714)751-5508. E-mail: rhughes@jamespublishing.com. Web site: www.legalassistanttoday.com. **Contact:** Rod Hughes. Bimonthly magazine ''geared toward all legal assistants/paralegals throughout the United States and Canada, regardless of specialty (litigation, corporate, bankruptcy, environmental law, etc.). How-to articles to help paralegals perform their jobs more effectively are most in demand, as are career and salary information, and timely news and trends pieces.'' Estab. 1983. Circ. 8,000. Pays on publication. Byline given. Buys first North American Serial rights, electronic rights, non-exclusive rights to use the article, author's name, image, and biographical data in advertising and promotion. Editorial lead time 10 weeks. Submit seasonal material 3 months in advance. Accepts queries by mail, e-mail, fax. Accepts simultaneous submissions. Responds in 2 months to mss. Sample copy and writer's guidelines free. Writer's guidelines online.

Nonfiction Interview/profile (unique and interesting paralegals in unique and particular work-related situations), news (brief, hard news topics regarding paralegals), features (present information to help paralegals advance their careers). **Pays $25-100.**

Photos Send photos with submission.

Tips ''Fax a detailed outline of a 2,500 to 3,000-word feature about something useful to working legal assistants. Writers must understand our audience. There is some opportunity for investigative journalism as well as the usual features, profiles, and news. How-to articles are especially desired. If you are a great writer who can interview effectively, and really dig into the topic to grab readers' attention, we need you.''

$ $ THE NATIONAL JURIST

Cypress Magazines, P.O. Box 939039, San Diego CA 92193. (858)300-3220. Fax: (858)503-7588. E-mail: rebecca@cypressmagazines.com. **Contact:** Rebecca Luczycki, editor-in-chief. **25% freelance written.** Bimonthly magazine covering law students and issues of interest to law students. Estab. 1991. Circ. 100,000. Pays on publication. Buys all rights. Accepts queries by mail, e-mail, fax, phone.

Nonfiction General interest, how-to, humor, interview/profile. **Buys 4 mss/year.** Query. Length: 750-3,000 words. **Pays $100-500 for assigned articles.**

Photos State availability with submission. Reviews contact sheets. Negotiates payment individually.

Columns/Departments Pays $100-500.

$ $ THE PENNSYLVANIA LAWYER

Pennsylvania Bar Association, P.O. Box 186, 100 South St., Harrisburg PA 17108-0186. E-mail: editor@pabar.org. Executive Editor: Marcy Carey Mallory. Editor: Geoff Yuda. **Contact:** Donald C. Sarvey, editorial director. **25% freelance written.** Prefers to work with published/established writers. Bimonthly magazine published as a service to the legal profession and the members of the Pennsylvania Bar Association. Estab. 1979. Circ. 30,000. **Pays on acceptance.** Publishes ms an average of 6 months after acceptance. Byline given. Buys first, one-time rights. Submit seasonal material 6 months in advance. Accepts queries by mail, e-mail. Responds in 2 months to queries; 2 months to mss. Sample copy for $2. Writer's guidelines for #10 SASE or by e-mail.

Nonfiction All features must relate in some way to Pennsylvania lawyers or the practice of law in Pennsylvania. How-to, interview/profile, law-practice management, technology. **Buys 8-10 mss/year.** Query. Length: 1,200-2,000 words. **Pays $50 for book reviews; $75-400 for assigned articles; $150 for unsolicited articles.** Sometimes pays expenses of writers on assignment.

Photos State availability with submission. Reviews contact sheets. Buys one-time rights. Negotiates payment individually. Identification of subjects required.

LUMBER

$ $ PALLET ENTERPRISE

Industrial Reporting Inc., 10244 Timber Ridge Dr., Ashland VA 23005. (804)550-0323. Fax: (804)550-2181. E-mail: editor@ireporting.com. Web site: www.palletenterprise.com. Assistant Publisher: Chaille Brindley. **Contact:** Tim Cox, editor. **40% freelance written.** Monthly magazine covering lumber and pallet operations. Articles should offer technical, solution-oriented information. Anti-forest articles are not accepted. Articles should focus on machinery and unique ways to improve profitability/make money. Estab. 1981. Circ. 14,500. Pays on publication. Buys first, one-time, electronic rights. Makes work-for-hire assignments. May buy all rights. Rights purchased depends on the writer and the article. Editorial lead time 2 months. Submit seasonal material 2 months in advance. Accepts queries by mail, e-mail, fax, phone. Accepts previously published material. Accepts simultaneous submissions. Sample copy online. Writer's guidelines free.

Nonfiction "We only want articles of interest to pallet manufacturers, pallet recyclers, and lumber companies/sawmills." Interview/profile, new product, opinion, technical, industry news, environmental, forests operation/plant features. No lifestyle, humor, general news, etc. **Buys 20 mss/year.** Query with published clips. Length: 1,000-3,000 words. **Pays $200-400 for assigned articles; $100-400 for unsolicited articles.** Call editor to discuss circumstances under which writers are paid in contributor copies. Sometimes pays expenses of writers on assignment.

Photos State availability with submission. Reviews 3×5 prints. Buys one time rights and Web rights. Negotiates payment individually. Captions, identification of subjects required.

Columns/Departments Green Watch (environmental news/opinion affecting US forests), 1,500 words. **Buys 12 mss/year.** Query with published clips. **Pays $200-400.**

Tips "Provide unique environmental or industry-oriented articles. Many of our freelance articles are company features of sawmills, pallet manufacturers, pallet recyclers, and wood waste processors."

$ $ SOUTHERN LUMBERMAN

Hatton-Brown Publishers, P.O. Box 2268, Montgomery AL 36102. (334)834-1170. Fax: (334)834-4525. E-mail: rich@hattonbrown.com. Web site: www.southernlumberman.com. **Contact:** Rich Donnell, editor. **20% freelance written.** Works with a small number of new/unpublished writers each year. Monthly journal for the sawmill industry. Estab. 1881. Circ. 15,000. Pays on publication. Publishes ms an average of 3 months after acceptance. Byline given. Buys first North American serial rights. Submit seasonal material 6 months in advance. Responds in 1 month to queries; 2 months to mss. Sample copy for $3 and 9×12 SAE with 5 first-class stamps. Writer's guidelines for #10 SASE.

Nonfiction How-to (sawmill better), technical, equipment analysis, sawmill features. **Buys 10-15 mss/year.** Query with or without published clips or send complete ms. Length: 500-2,000 words. **Pays $150-350 for assigned articles; $100-250 for unsolicited articles.** Sometimes pays expenses of writers on assignment.

Reprints Send tearsheet or photocopy of article and information about when and where the article previously appeared. Pays 25-50% of amount paid for an original article.

Photos Always looking for news feature types of photos featuring forest products, industry materials, or people. Send photos with submission. Reviews transparencies, 4×5 color prints. Pays $10-25/photo. Captions, identification of subjects required.

Tips "Like most, we appreciate a clearly-worded query listing the merits of a suggested story—what it will tell our readers they need/want to know. We want quotes, we want opinions to make others discuss the article. Best hint? Find an interesting sawmill operation owner and start asking questions—what's he doing bigger, better, different. I bet a story idea develops. We need color photos, too. We're interested in new facilities, better marketing, and improved production."

$ $ TIMBERLINE

Timber Industry Newsline/Trading Post, Industrial Reporting, Inc., 10244 Timber Ridge Dr., Ashland VA 23005. (804)550-0323. Fax: (804)550-2181. E-mail: editor@ireporting.com. Web site: www.timberlinemag.com. Assistant Publisher: Chaille Brindley. **Contact:** Tim Cox, editor. **50% freelance written.** Monthly tabloid covering the forest products industry. Articles should offer technical, solution-oriented information. Anti-forest products, industry articles are not accepted. Articles should focus on machinery and unique ways to improve profitability and make money. Estab. 1994. Circ. 30,000. Pays on publication. Byline given. Buys first, one-time, electronic rights. Makes work-for-hire assignments. May purchase all rights. Rights purchased depends on the writer and the article. Editorial lead time 2 months. Submit seasonal material 2 months in advance. Accepts queries by mail, e-mail, fax, phone. Accepts previously published material. Accepts simultaneous submissions. Sample copy online. Writer's guidelines free.

Nonfiction "We only want articles of interest to loggers, sawmills, wood treatment facilities, etc. Readers tend to be pro-industry/conservative, and opinion pieces must be written to appeal to them." Historical/nostalgic, interview/profile, new product, opinion, technical, industry news, environmental operation/plant features. No lifestyles, humor, general news, etc. **Buys 25 mss/year.** Query with published clips. Length: 1,000-3,000 words. **Pays $200-400 for assigned articles; $100-400 for unsolicited articles.** Call editor to discuss circumstances under which writers are paid in contributor copies. Sometimes pays expenses of writers on assignment.

Photos State availability with submission. Reviews 3×5 prints. Buys one time rights and Web rights. Negotiates payment individually. Captions, identification of subjects required.

Columns/Departments From the Hill (legislative news impacting the forest products industry), 1,800 words;

Green Watch (environmental news/opinion affecting US forests), 1,500 words. **Buys 12 mss/year.** Query with published clips. **Pays $200-400.**

Tips "Provide unique environmental or industry-oriented articles. Many of our freelance articles are company features of logging operations or sawmills."

N $ $ TIMBERWEST

Timber/West Publications, LLC, P.O. Box 610, Edmonds WA 98020-0160. Fax: (425)771-3623. E-mail: timberwest@forestnet.com. Web site: www.forestnet.com. **Contact:** Diane Mettler, managing editor. **75% freelance written.** Monthly magazine covering logging and lumber segment of the forestry industry in the Northwest. "We publish primarily profiles on loggers and their operations—with an emphasis on the machinery—in Washington, Oregon, Idaho, Montana, Northern California, and Alaska. Some timber issues are highly controversial and although we will report on the issues, this is a pro-logging publication. We don't publish articles with a negative slant on the timber industry." Estab. 1975. Circ. 10,000. **Pays on acceptance.** Byline given. Not copyrighted. Buys first North American serial, second serial (reprint) rights. Editorial lead time 3 months. Accepts queries by mail, fax. Responds in 3 weeks to queries. Sample copy for $2. Writer's guidelines for #10 SASE.

Nonfiction Historical/nostalgic, interview/profile, new product. No articles that put the timber industry in a bad light—such as environmental articles against logging. **Buys 50 mss/year.** Query with published clips. Length: 1,100-1,500 words. **Pays $350.** Pays expenses of writers on assignment.

Photos Send photos with submission. Reviews contact sheets, transparencies, prints, GIF/JPEG files. Buys all rights. Offers no additional payment for photos accepted with ms. Captions, identification of subjects required.

Fillers Facts, newsbreaks. **Buys 10/year.** Length: 400-800 words. **Pays $100-250.**

Tips "We are always interested in profiles of loggers and their operations in Alaska, Oregon, Washington, Montana, and Northern California. We also want articles pertaining to current industry topics, such as fire abatement, sustainable forests, or new technology. Read an issue to get a clear idea of the type of material *TimberWest* publishes. The audience is primarily loggers and topics that focus on an 'evolving' timber industry versus a 'dying' industry will find a place in the magazine. When querying, a clear overview of the article will enhance acceptance."

MACHINERY & METAL

N $ $ $ AMERICAN MACHINIST

Penton Media, 1300 E. 9th St., Cleveland OH 44144. (216)931-9240. Fax: (216)931-9524. E-mail: ameditor@penton.com. Web site: www.americanmachinist.com. **Contact:** Bruce Vernyi, editor-in-chief. **10% freelance written.** Monthly magazine covering all forms of metalworking. "*American Machinist* is the oldest magazine dedicated to metalworking in the United States. Our readers are the owners and managers of metalworking shops. We publish articles that provide the managers and owners of job shops, contract shops, and captive shops the information they need to make their operations more efficient, more productive, and more profitable. Our articles are technical in nature and must be focused on technology that will help these shops to become more competitive on a global basis. Our readers are skilled machinists. This is not the place for lightweight items about manufacturing, and we are not interested in articles on management theories." Estab. 1877. Circ. 80,000. Publishes ms an average of 1-2 months after acceptance. Byline sometimes given. Offers 20% kill fee. Buys all rights, makes work-for-hire assignments. Editorial lead time 3-6 months. Submit seasonal material 4-6 months in advance. Accepts queries by mail, e-mail, phone. Responds in 1-2 weeks to queries; 1 month to mss. Sample copy online.

Nonfiction General interest, how-to, new product, opinion, personal experience, photo feature, technical. Query with published clips. Length: 600-2,400 words. **Pays $300-1,200.** Sometimes pays expenses of writers on assignment.

Photos State availability with submission. Reviews GIF/JPEG files. Buys all rights. Negotiates payment individually. Captions, identification of subjects, model releases required.

Fillers Anecdotes, facts, gags to be illustrated by cartoonist, newsbreaks, short humor. **Buys 12-18/year.** Length: 50-200 words. **Pays $25-100.**

Tips "With our exacting audience, a writer would do well to have some background working with machine tools."

$ $ $ CUTTING TOOL ENGINEERING

CTE Publications, Inc., 400 Skokie Blvd., Suite 395, Northbrook IL 60062-7903. (847)714-0175. Fax: (847)559-4444. E-mail: alanr@jwr.com. Web site: www.ctemag.com. Publisher: Don Nelson. **Contact:** Alan Richter, editor. **40% freelance written.** Monthly magazine covering industrial metal cutting tools and metal cutting operations. "*Cutting Tool Engineering* serves owners, managers and engineers who work in manufacturing, specifically manufacturing that involves cutting or grinding metal or other materials. Writing should be geared toward improving manufacturing processes.'' Circ. 40,000. Pays on publication. Publishes ms an average of 2 months after acceptance. Byline given. Offers 50% kill fee. Buys all rights. Editorial lead time 2 months. Accepts queries by mail, fax. Responds in 2 months to mss. Sample copy and writer's guidelines free.

Nonfiction How-to, opinion, personal experience, technical. ''No fiction or articles that don't relate to manufacturing.'' **Buys 10 mss/year.** Length: 1,500-3,000 words. **Pays $450-1,000.** Pays expenses of writers on assignment.

Photos State availability with submission. Reviews transparencies, prints. Buys all rights. Negotiates payment individually. Captions required.

Tips ''For queries, write 2 clear paragraphs about how the proposed article will play out. Include sources that would be in the article.''

$ $ $ THE FABRICATOR

833 Featherstone Rd., Rockford IL 61107. (815)399-8700. Fax: (815)381-1370. E-mail: kateb@thefabricator.com. Web site: www.thefabricator.com. **Contact:** Kate Bachman, associate editor. **15% freelance written.** Monthly magazine covering metal forming and fabricating. Our purpose is to disseminate information about modern metal forming and fabricating techniques, machinery, tooling, and management concepts for the metal fabricator. Estab. 1971. Circ. 58,000. Pays on publication. Byline given. Buys all rights. Editorial lead time 6 months. Accepts queries by mail, e-mail. Responds in 2 weeks to queries; 1 month to mss. Sample copy for free. Writer's guidelines online.

Nonfiction How-to, technical, company profile. Query with published clips. Length: 1,200-2,000 words. **Pays 40-80¢/word.**

Photos Request guidelines for digital images. State availability with submission. Reviews transparencies, prints. Rights purchased depends on photographer requirements. Negotiates payment individually. Captions, identification of subjects required.

N $ $ $ GASES & WELDING DISTRIBUTOR

Penton Media, 1300 E. 9th St., Cleveland OH 44144. (216)931-9240. Fax: (216)931-9524. E-mail: weldingeditor@penton.com. Web site: www.weldingdesign.com. **Contact:** Bruce Vernyi, editor-in-chief. **10% freelance written.** Bimonthly magazine covering the distribution business for welding supplies and industrial gases. ''*Gases & Welding Distributor* provides information to the owners and managers of distributorships that sell welding equipment and industrial gases. We include information on federal regulations, business technology for distributorships, technological developments in welding, and feature stories on how our distributors are doing business with the goal of helping our readers to be more productive, efficient and competitive. These shops are very local in nature, and need to be addressed as small businessmen in a field that is consolidating and becoming more challenging. We do not write about business management theory as much as we write about putting into practice good management techniques that have proved to work at similar businesses.'' Estab. 1966. Circ. 20,000. Pays on publication. Publishes ms an average of 1-2 months after acceptance. Byline sometimes given. Offers 20% kill fee. Buys all rights, makes work-for-hire assignments. Editorial lead time 3-6 months. Submit seasonal material 4-6 months in advance. Accepts queries by mail, e-mail, phone. Responds in 1-2 weeks to queries; 1 month to mss. Sample copy online.

Nonfiction General interest, how-to, new product, opinion, personal experience, photo feature, technical. Query with published clips. Length: 600-2,400 words. **Pays $300-1,200.** Sometimes pays expenses of writers on assignment.

Photos State availability with submission. Reviews GIF/JPEG files. Buys all rights. Negotiates payment individually. Captions, identification of subjects, model releases required.

Fillers Anecdotes, facts, gags to be illustrated by cartoonist, newsbreaks, short humor. **Buys 12-18/year.** Length: 50-200 words. **Pays $25-100.**

Tips ''Writers should be familiar with welding and/or the industrial distribution business. With that, calling or e-mailing me directly is the next best approach. We are interested in information that will help to make machine shops more competitive, and a writer should have a very specific idea before approaching me.''

$ $ ORNAMENTAL AND MISCELLANEOUS METAL FABRICATOR

National Ornamental And Miscellaneous Metals Association, 1535 Pennsylvania Ave., McDonough GA 30253. (423)413-6436. Fax: (770)288-2006. E-mail: rachel@nomma.org. **Contact:** Rachel Bailey, editor. **20% freelance written.** Bimonthly magazine ''to inform, educate, and inspire members of the ornamental and miscellaneous metalworking industry.'' Estab. 1959. Circ. 9,000. Pays on publication. Byline given. Buys one-time rights. Editorial lead time 2 months. Accepts queries by mail, e-mail, fax. Responds by e-mail in 1 month (include e-mail address in query) to queries. Writer's guidelines by e-mail.

Nonfiction Book excerpts, essays, exposé, general interest, historical/nostalgic, how-to, humor, inspirational, interview/profile, new product, opinion, personal experience, photo feature, technical. **Buys 8-12 mss/year.** Query. Length: 1,200-2,000 words. **Pays $375-400.** Pays expenses of writers on assignment.

Reprints Send tearsheet, photocopy or typed ms with rights for sale noted and information about when and where the material previously appeared. Pays 100% of amount paid for an original article.

Photos Artwork and sidebars preferred. State availability with submission. Reviews contact sheets, negatives, transparencies, prints. May offer additional payment for artwork accepted with ms. Model releases required.

Columns/Departments 700-900 words. **Pays $50-100.**

Tips "Please request and review recent issues. Contacting the editor for guidance on article topics is welcome."

$ $ $ PRACTICAL WELDING TODAY

FMA Communications, Inc., 833 Featherstone Rd., Rockford IL 61107-6302. (815)399-8700. Fax: (815)381-1370. E-mail: stephaniev@thefabricator.com. Web site: www.thefabricator.com. **Contact:** Stephanie Vaughan, associate editor. **15% freelance written.** Bimonthly magazine covering welding. "We generally publish how-to and educational articles that teach people about a process or how to do something better." Estab. 1997. Circ. 40,000. Pays on publication. Byline given. Buys all rights. Editorial lead time 6 months. Accepts queries by mail, e-mail. Responds in 2 weeks to queries; 2 months to mss. Sample copy for free. Writer's guidelines online.

Nonfiction How-to, technical, company profiles. Special issues: Forecast issue on trends in welding (January/February). No promotional, one-sided, persuasive articles or unsolicited case studies. **Buys 5 mss/year.** Query with published clips. Length: 800-1,200 words. **Pays 40-80¢/word.** Sometimes pays expenses of writers on assignment.

Photos State availability with submission. Reviews contact sheets. Rights purchased depends on photographer requirements. Negotiates payment individually. Captions, identification of subjects required.

Tips "Follow our author guidelines and editorial policies to write a how-to piece from which our readers can benefit."

$ $ SPRINGS

The International Magazine of Spring Manufacturers, Spring Manufacturers Institute, 2001 Midwest Rd., Suite 106, Oak Brook IL 60523-1335. (630)495-8588. Fax: (630)495-8595. Web site: www.smihq.org. **Contact:** Rita Schauer, editor. **10% freelance written.** Quarterly magazine covering precision mechanical spring manufacture. Articles should be aimed at spring manufacturers. Estab. 1962. Circ. 10,800. Pays on publication. Publishes ms an average of 3-6 months after acceptance. Byline given. Buys first rights. Editorial lead time 4 months. Accepts simultaneous submissions. Sample copy free. Writer's guidelines online.

Nonfiction General interest, how-to, interview/profile, opinion, personal experience, technical. **Buys 4-6 mss/year.** Length: 2,000-10,000 words. **Pays $100-600 for assigned articles.**

Photos State availability with submission. Reviews prints, digital photos. Buys one-time rights. Offers no additional payment for photos accepted with ms. Captions required.

Tips "Call the editor. Contact springmakers and spring industry suppliers and ask about what interests them. Include interviews/quotes from people in the spring industry in the article. The editor can supply contacts."

$ $ $ STAMPING JOURNAL

Fabricators & Manufacturers Association (FMA), 833 Featherstone Rd., Rockford IL 61107. (815)399-8700. Fax: (815)381-1370. E-mail: katm@thefabricator.com. Web site: www.thefabricator.com. **Contact:** Kathleen McLaughlin, associate editor. **15% freelance written.** Bimonthly magazine covering metal stamping. "We look for how-to and educational articles—nonpromotional." Estab. 1989. Circ. 35,000. Pays on publication. Byline given. Buys all rights. Editorial lead time 6 months. Accepts queries by mail, e-mail, fax, phone. Responds in 2 weeks to queries; 2 months to mss. Sample copy and writer's guidelines free.

Nonfiction How-to, technical, company profile. Special issues: Forecast issue (January). No unsolicited case studies. **Buys 5 mss/year.** Query with published clips. Length: 1,000 words. **Pays 40-80¢/word.** Sometimes pays expenses of writers on assignment.

Photos State availability with submission. Reviews contact sheets. Rights purchased depends on photographer requirements. Negotiates payment individually. Captions, identification of subjects required.

Tips "Articles should be impartial and should not describe the benefits of certain products available from certain companies. They should not be biased toward the author's or against a competitor's products or technologies. The publisher may refuse any article that does not conform to this guideline."

$ $ $ TPJ—THE TUBE & PIPE JOURNAL

Fabricators & Manufacturers Association (FMA), 833 Featherstone Rd., Rockford IL 61107. (815)399-8700. Fax: (815)381-1370. Web site: www.thefabricator.com. **15% freelance written.** Magazine published 8 times/year covering metal tube and pipe. Educational perspective—emphasis is on "how-to" articles to accomplish a particular task or improve on a process. New trends and technologies are also important topics. Estab. 1990.

Circ. 30,000. Pays on publication. Byline given. Buys all rights. Editorial lead time 6 months. Accepts queries by mail, e-mail. Responds in 2 weeks to queries; 2 months to mss. Sample copy for free. Writer's guidelines online.

Nonfiction Any new or improved tube production or fabrication process—includes manufacturing, bending, and forming tube (metal tube only). How-to, technical. Special issues: Forecast issue (January). No unsolicited case studies. **Buys 5 mss/year.** Query with published clips. Length: 800-1,200 words. **Pays 40-80¢/word.** Sometimes pays expenses of writers on assignment.

Photos State availability with submission. Reviews contact sheets. Rights purchased depends on photographer requirements. Negotiates payment individually. Captions, identification of subjects required.

Tips "Submit a detailed proposal, including an article outline, to the editor."

N $ $ $ WELDING DESIGN & FABRICATION

Penton Media, 1300 E. 9th St., Cleveland OH 44144. (216)931-9240. Fax: (216)931-9524. E-mail: weldingeditor@penton.com. Web site: www.weldingdesign.com. **Contact:** Bruce Vernyi, editor-in-chief. **10% freelance written.** Bimonthly magazine covering all facets of welding and running a welding business. "*Welding Design & Fabrication* provides information to the owners and managers of welding shops, including business, technology and trends. We include information on engineering and technological developments that could change the business as it is currently known, and feature stories on how welders are doing business with the goal of helping our readers to be more productive, effecient, and competitive. Welding shops are very local in nature and need to be addressed as small businessmen in a field that is consolidating and becoming more challenging and more global. We do not write about business management theory as much as we write about putting into practice good management techniques that have proved to work at similar businesses." Estab. 1930. Circ. 40,000. Pays on publication. Publishes ms an average of 1-2 months after acceptance. Byline given. Offers 20% kill fee. Buys all rights, makes work-for-hire assignments. Editorial lead time 3-6 months. Submit seasonal material 4-6 months in advance. Accepts queries by mail, e-mail, phone. Responds in 1-2 weeks to queries; 1 month to mss. Sample copy online.

Nonfiction General interest, how-to, new product, opinion, personal experience, photo feature, technical. Query with or without published clips. Length: 600-2,400 words. **Pays $300-1,200.** Sometimes pays expenses of writers on assignment.

Photos State availability with submission. Reviews GIF/JPEG files (300 dpi). Buys all rights. Negotiates payment individually. Captions, identification of subjects, model releases required.

Fillers Anecdotes, facts, gags to be illustrated by cartoonist, newsbreaks, short humor. **Buys 12-18/year.** Length: 50-200 words. **Pays $25-100.**

Tips "Writers should be familiar with welding and/or metalworking and metal joining techniques. With that, calling or e-mailing me directly is the next best approach. We are interested in information that will help to make welding shops more competitive, and a writer should have a very specific idea before approaching me."

$ $ WIRE ROPE NEWS & SLING TECHNOLOGY

Wire Rope News LLC, P.O. Box 871, Clark NJ 07066. (908)486-3221. Fax: (732)396-4215. Web site: www.wireropenews.com. **100% freelance written.** Bimonthly magazine "published for manufacturers and distributors of wire rope, chain, cordage, related hardware, and sling fabricators. Content includes technical articles, news and reports describing the manufacturing and use of wire rope and related products in marine, construction, mining, aircraft and offshore drilling operations." Estab. 1979. Circ. 4,300. **Pays on acceptance.** Publishes ms an average of 6 months after acceptance. Byline sometimes given. Buys all rights. Editorial lead time 2 months. Submit seasonal material 2 months in advance. Accepts queries by mail, fax. Accepts simultaneous submissions.

Nonfiction General interest, historical/nostalgic, interview/profile, photo feature, technical. **Buys 30 mss/year.** Send complete ms. Length: 2,500-5,000 words. **Pays $300-500.**

Photos Send photos with submission. Reviews contact sheets, 5×7 prints, digital. Buys all rights. Offers no additional payment for photos accepted with ms. Identification of subjects required.

Tips "We are accepting more submissions and queries by e-mail."

MAINTENANCE & SAFETY

$ $ AMERICAN WINDOW CLEANER MAGAZINE

Voice of the Professional Window Cleaner, P.O. Box 98, Bedford NY 10506. (914)234-2630. Fax: (914)234-2632. Web site: www.awcmag.com. **20% freelance written.** Bimonthly magazine window cleaning. "Articles to help window cleaners become more profitable, safe, professional, and feel good about what they do." Estab. 1986. Circ. 8,000. **Pays on acceptance.** Publishes ms an average of 4-8 months after acceptance. Byline given. Offers 33% kill fee. Buys first rights. Editorial lead time 2 months. Submit seasonal material 3 months in advance.

Responds in 2 weeks to queries; 1 month to mss. Sample copy for free. Writer's guidelines online.

Nonfiction How-to, humor, inspirational, interview/profile, personal experience, photo feature, technical. ''We do not want PR-driven pieces. We want to educate—not push a particular product.'' **Buys 20 mss/year.** Query. Length: 500-5,000 words. **Pays $50-250.**

Photos State availability with submission. Reviews contact sheets, transparencies, 4×6 prints. Buys one-time rights. Offers $10 per photo. Captions required.

Columns/Departments Window Cleaning Tips (tricks of the trade); 1,000-2,000 words; Humor-anecdotes-feel good-abouts (window cleaning industry); Computer High-Tech (tips on new technology), all 1,000 words. **Buys 12 mss/year.** Query. **Pays $50-100.**

Tips ''*American Window Cleaner Magazine* covers an unusual niche that gets people's curiosity. Articles that are technical in nature and emphasize practical tips or safety, and how to work more efficiently, have the best chances of being published. Articles include: window cleaning unusual buildings, landmarks; working for well-known people/celebrities; window cleaning in resorts/casinos/unusual cities; humor or satire about our industry or the public's perception of it. At some point, we make phone contact and chat to see if our interests are compatible.''

$ CLEANING BUSINESS

3693 E. Marginal Way S., Seattle WA 98134. Fax: (206)622-6876. Web site: www.cleaningbusiness.com. **80% freelance written.** Quarterly magazine. ''We cater to those who are self-employed in any facet of the cleaning and maintenance industry and seek to be top professionals in their field. *Cleaning Business* is published for self-employed cleaning professionals, specifically carpet, upholstery and drapery cleaners; janitorial and maid services; window washers; odor, water and fire damage restoration contractors. Our readership is small but select. We seek concise, factual articles, realistic but definitely upbeat.'' Circ. 6,000. Pays 1 month after publication. Publishes ms an average of 3 months after acceptance. Byline given. Buys all rights, makes work-for-hire assignments. Submit seasonal material 6 months in advance. 3 months or less to mss. Sample copy for $3 and 8×10 SAE with 3 first-class stamps. Writer's guidelines for #10 SASE.

Nonfiction Exposé (safety/health business practices), how-to (on cleaning, maintenance, small business management), humor (clean jokes, cartoons), interview/profile, new product (must be unusual to rate full article—mostly obtained from manufacturers), opinion, personal experience, technical. Special issues: ''What's New?'' (February). No ''wordy articles written off the top of the head, obviously without research, and needing more editing time than was spent on writing.'' **Buys 40 mss/year.** Query with or without published clips. Length: 500-3,000 words.

Photos ''Magazine size is 8½×11—photos need to be proportionate. Also seeks full-color photos of relevant subjects for cover.'' State availability with submission. Buys one-time rights. Pays $5-25 for. Captions, identification of subjects, model releases required.

Columns/Departments Buys 36 mss/year. Query with or without published clips. **Pays $15-85.**

Fillers Anecdotes, gags to be illustrated by cartoonist, newsbreaks, short humor, jokes, gags, poetry. **Buys 40/year.** Length: 3-200 words. **Pays $1-20.**

Tips ''We are constantly seeking quality freelancers from all parts of the country. A freelancer can best break in to our publication with fairly technical articles on how to do specific cleaning/maintenance jobs; interviews with top professionals covering this and how they manage their business; and personal experience. Our readers demand concise, accurate information. Don't ramble. Write only about what you know and/or have researched. Editors don't have time to rewrite your rough draft. Organize and polish before submitting.''

$ $ EXECUTIVE HOUSEKEEPING TODAY

The International Executive Housekeepers Association, 1001 Eastwind Dr., Suite 301, Westerville OH 43081. (614)895-7166. Fax: (614)895-1248. E-mail: avance@ieha.org. Web site: www.ieha.org. **Contact:** Andi Vance, editor. **50% freelance written.** Monthly magazine for ''nearly 5,000 decision makers responsible for housekeeping management (cleaning, grounds maintenance, laundry, linen, pest control, waste management, regulatory compliance, training) for a variety of institutions: hospitality, healthcare, education, retail, government.'' Estab. 1930. Circ. 5,500. **Pays on acceptance.** Publishes ms an average of 6 months after acceptance. Byline given. Buys first North American serial rights. Editorial lead time 2 months. Submit seasonal material 3 months in advance. Accepts queries by mail, e-mail, fax, phone.

Nonfiction General interest, interview/profile, new product (related to magazine's scope), personal experience (in housekeeping profession), technical. **Buys 30 mss/year.** Query with published clips. Length: 500-1,500 words. **Pays $150-250.**

Photos State availability with submission. Buys one-time rights. Offers no additional payment for photos accepted with ms. Identification of subjects required.

Columns/Departments Federal Report (OSHA/EPA requirements), 1,000 words; Industry News; Management

Perspectives (industry specific), 500-1,500 words. Query with published clips. **Pays $150-250.**
Tips "Have a background in the industry or personal experience with any aspect of it."

N $ $ PEST CONTROL MAGAZINE

7500 Old Oak Blvd., Cleveland OH 44130. (440)243-8100. Fax: (440)891-2675. E-mail: pestcon@advanstar.com. Web site: www.pestcontrolmag.com. **Contact:** Frank H. Andorka, Jr., editorial director. Monthly magazine for professional pest management professionals and sanitarians. Estab. 1933. Circ. 20,000. Pays on publication. Licenses rights. Submit seasonal material 3 months in advance. Accepts queries by mail, e-mail, phone. Responds in 1 month to mss. Sample copy not available. Writer's guidelines online.

- Break in with "information directly relating to the field¢citing sources that are either industry experts (university or otherwise) or direct quotes from pest/management professionals."

Nonfiction Prefers contributors with pest control industry background. All articles must have trade or business orientation. How-to, humor, inspirational, interview/profile, new product, personal experience (stories about pest management operations and their problems), case histories, new technological breakthroughs. No general information type of articles desired. **Buys 3 mss/year.** Query. Length: 1,000-1,400 words. **Pays $150-400 minimum.**
Photos Digital photos accepted; please query on specs. State availability with submission. No additional payment for photos used with ms.
Columns/Departments Regular columns use material oriented to this profession, 550 words.

MANAGEMENT & SUPERVISION

$ $ $ HUMAN RESOURCE EXECUTIVE

LRP Publications Magazine Group, P.O. Box 980, Harsham PA 19044. (215)784-0910. Fax: (215)784-0275. E-mail: dshadovitz@lrp.com. Web site: www.hrexecutive.com. **Contact:** David Shadovitz, editor. **30% freelance written.** "Monthly magazine serving the information needs of chief human resource professionals/executives in companies, government agencies, and nonprofit institutions with 500 or more employees." Estab. 1987. Circ. 75,000. **Pays on acceptance.** Publishes ms an average of 2 months after acceptance. Byline given. Pays 50% kill fee on assigned stories. Buys all rights. Accepts queries by mail, e-mail, fax. Responds in 1 month to mss. Writer's guidelines online.
Nonfiction Book excerpts, interview/profile. **Buys 16 mss/year.** Query with published clips. Length: 1,800 words. **Pays $200-1,000.** Sometimes pays expenses of writers on assignment.
Photos State availability with submission. Reviews contact sheets. Buys first and repeat rights. Offers no additional payment for photos accepted with ms. Identification of subjects required.

$ $ INCENTIVE

VNU Business Publications, 770 Broadway, New York NY 10003. (646)654-7636. Fax: (646)654-7650. E-mail: wflanagan@vnubuspubs.com. Web site: www.incentivemag.com. **Contact:** William Flanagan, editor-in-chief. Monthly magazine covering sales promotion and employee motivation: managing and marketing through motivation. Estab. 1905. Circ. 41,000. **Pays on acceptance.** Publishes ms an average of 3 months after acceptance. Byline given. Buys all rights. Accepts queries by mail, e-mail, fax. Responds in 1 month to queries; 2 months to mss. Sample copy for 9×12 SAE.
Nonfiction General interest (motivation, demographics), how-to (types of sales promotion, buying product categories, using destinations), interview/profile (sales promotion executives), travel (incentive-oriented), corporate case studies. **Buys 48 mss/year.** Query with published clips. Length: 1,000-2,000 words. **Pays $250-700 for assigned articles; does not pay for unsolicited articles.** Pays expenses of writers on assignment.
Reprints Send tearsheet and information about when and where the material previously appeared. Pays 50% of the amount paid for an original article.
Photos Send photos with submission. Reviews contact sheets, transparencies. Offers some additional payment for photos accepted with ms. Identification of subjects required.
Tips "Read the publication, then query."

N PEOPLE MANAGEMENT

Chartered Institute of Personnel and Development, 17-18 Britton St., London England EC1M 5TP United Kingdom. (44)(207)324-2729. E-mail: editorial@peoplemanagement.co.uk. Web site: www.peoplemanagement.co.uk. Editor: Steve Crabb. Managing Editor: Rima Evans. Editorial Assistant: Harriet Wraith. **Contact:** Commissioning Editor. Biweekly magazine publishing articles on all aspects of managing and developing people at work. Circ. 120,000. Editorial lead time 2 months. Only responds to proposals if interested to queries. Writer's guidelines online.

Nonfiction General interest (features with a theoretical/strategic/policy theme or investigations of current developments/case studies), how-to (step-by-step hints/tips for best practices to use in everyday work). Submit 2-page proposal, bio. Length: 1,000-2,500 words.
Columns/Departments Learning Centre (training/development matters aimed to provoke discussion), 350 words; Viewpoint (addresses a key topical issue), 600 words; Research (academics summarize their latest findings or review other research in a particular area), 500 words); Troubleshooter (overview of a HR dilemma and/or a solution to that dilemma), 350 words/dilemma and 400 words/solution.

$ $ TODAY'S PLAYGROUND

The National Magazine for Today's Playground Design & Standards, Harris Publishing, 360 B St., Idaho Falls ID 83402. (208)542-2271. Fax: (208)522-5241. E-mail: shannon@todaysplayground.com. Web site: www.todaysplayground.com. Editor: Shannon Stockwell. **25% freelance written.** Magazine published 7 times/year covering playgrounds, play-related issues, equipment and industry trends. "*Today's Playground* targets a park and recreation management, elementary school teachers and administrators, child care facilities and parent-group leader readership. Articles should focus on play and the playground market as a whole, including aquatic play and surfacing." Estab. 2000. Circ. 35,000. Pays on publication. Publishes ms an average of 6 months after acceptance. Byline given. Buys first North American serial, electronic rights. Editorial lead time 2 months. Submit seasonal material 1 year in advance. Accepts queries by mail, e-mail. Accepts simultaneous submissions. Responds in 1 month to queries; 2 months to mss. Sample copy for $5. Writer's guidelines for #10 SASE.
Nonfiction How-to, interview/profile, new product, opinion, personal experience, photo feature, technical, travel. "*Today's Playground* does not publish any articles that do not directly relate to play and the playground industry." **Buys 4-6 mss/year.** Query with or without published clips. Length: 800-1,500 words. **Pays $50-300 for assigned articles.** Sometimes pays expenses of writers on assignment.
Photos State availability of or send photos with submission. Reviews 35mm transparencies, GIF/JPEG files (350 dpi or better). Buys one-time rights. Offers no additional payment for photos accepted with ms. Captions, identification of subjects, model releases required.
Columns/Departments Playground Profile (an article that profiles a unique play area and focuses on community involvement, unique design, or human interest), 800-1,200 words. **Buys 2 mss/year.** Query. **Pays $100-300.**
Tips "We are looking for articles that managers can use as a resource when considering playground construction, management, safety, etc. Writers should find unique angles to playground-related features. We are a trade journal that offers up-to-date industry news and features that promote play and the playground industry."

MARINE & MARITIME INDUSTRIES

$ $ MARINE BUSINESS JOURNAL

The Voice of the Marine Industries Nationwide, 330 N. Andrews Ave., Ft. Lauderdale FL 33301. (954)522-5515. Fax: (954)522-2260. E-mail: sboating@southernboating.com. Web site: www.marinebusinessjournal.com. **Contact:** Bill Lindsey, executive editor. **25% freelance written.** Bimonthly magazine that covers the recreational boating industry. "*The Marine Business Journal* is aimed at boating dealers, distributors and manufacturers, naval architects, yacht brokers, marina owners and builders, marine electronics dealers, distributors and manufacturers, and anyone involved in the U.S. marine industry. Articles cover news, new product technology, and public affairs affecting the industry." Estab. 1986. Circ. 26,000. Pays on publication. Publishes ms an average of 1 month after acceptance. Byline given. Buys first North American serial, one-time, second serial (reprint) rights. Accepts queries by mail, e-mail. Responds in 2 weeks to queries. Sample copy for $2.50, 9×12 SAE with 7 first-class stamps.
Nonfiction Buys 20 mss/year. Query with published clips. Length: 500-1,000 words. **Pays $200-500.**
Photos State availability with submission. Reviews 35mm or larger transparencies, 5×7 prints. Buys one-time rights. Offers $50/photo. Captions, identification of subjects, model releases required.
Tips "Query with clips. It's a highly specialized field, written for professionals by professionals, almost all on assignment or by staff."

$ $ PROFESSIONAL MARINER

Journal of the Maritime Industry, Navigator Publishing, P.O. Box 569, Portland ME 04112. (207)822-4350. Fax: (207)772-2879. E-mail: editors@professionalmariner.com. Web site: www.professionalmariner.com. **Contact:** John Gormley, editor. **75% freelance written.** Bimonthly magazine covering professional seamanship and maritime industry news. Estab. 1993. Circ. 29,000. Pays on publication. Byline given. Buys all rights. Editorial lead time 3 months. Accepts queries by mail, e-mail, fax, phone. Accepts simultaneous submissions.
Nonfiction For professional mariners on vessels and ashore. Seeks submissions on industry news, regulations, towing, piloting, technology, engineering, business, maritime casualties, and feature stories about the maritime

industry. Does accept "sea stories" and personal professional experiences as correspondence pieces. **Buys 15 mss/year.** Query. Length: varies; short clips to long profiles/features. **Pays 20¢/word.** Sometimes pays expenses of writers on assignment.

Photos Send photos with submission. Reviews prints, slides. Buys one-time rights. Negotiates payment individually. Captions, identification of subjects required.

Tips "Remember that our audience comprises maritime industry professionals. Stories must be written at a level that will benefit this group."

SEA BREEZES

Mannin Media Group Ltd, Media House, Cronkbourne, Douglas Isle of Man IM4 4SB. E-mail: seabreezes@manninmedia.co.im. Web site: www.seabreezes.co.im. Editor: Captain A.C. Douglas. **Contact:** Steve Robinson, senior administrator. *Sea Breezes* publishes factual tales of ships, seamen, and the sea that are of interest to professional seamen or those with a deep knowledge of ships and shipping. Estab. 1919. Pays at the end of each publication month. Accepts queries by mail, e-mail. Writer's guidelines by e-mail.

"The best guide to our requirements is a close study of the magazine. The most readily acceptable work will show it's clearly the result of first-hand experience or extensive and accurate research."

Nonfiction Does not accept fiction, poetry, cartoons, crosswords, quizzes, puzzles, or anything that smacks of "the romance of the sea." Length: 1,000-6,000 words. **Pays 14£/page.**

Photos State availability of or send photos with submission. 5£/photo; 10£/cover photo; 30£/centrespread photo. Captions required.

MEDICAL

$ $ ADVANCE FOR HEALTHY AGING

Merion Publications, 2900 Horizon Dr., King of Prussia PA 19406. (800)355-5627. Fax: (610)278-1425. E-mail: mlandsmann@merion.com. Web site: www.advanceweb.com/healthyaging. Editor: Maria Wolf. **Contact:** Marci Landsmann, managing editor. **5% freelance written.** Bimonthly magazine covering health care—the science of aging well. "*Healthy Aging* is a magazine for physicians who are interested in providing wellness and skin services to their baby boomer patients. Writers should be able to write to a physician's level. This means researching studies and doing thorough interviewing to understand medical topics, ranging from nutraceuticals, and preventative health topics. Articles must be well-researched and objective—speaking to the mission of the magazine." Estab. 2005. Circ. 30,000. Pays on publication. Publishes ms an average of 3 months after acceptance. Byline given. Buys first North American serial rights. Editorial lead time 5 months. Submit seasonal material 3 months in advance. Accepts queries by mail. Responds in 3 months to queries. Writer's guidelines online.

Nonfiction Interview/profile, technical. Nothing touting miracle cures for aging or favoring a product or specific approach. Articles must be research-driven and provide realistic portrayals. **Buys 6 mss/year.** Query with published clips. Length: 1,800-2,500 words. **Pays $150-300.**

Tips "Authors should be able to take medical information and make it easy to read for a physician-level audience, and prove their information will be objective with research, interviews, etc. We are looking for consumer-oriented articles that are taken a part for physician's practical use."

$ ADVANCE FOR RESPIRATORY CARE PRACTITIONERS

Merion Publications, Inc., 2900 Horizon Dr., King of Prussia PA 19406-0956. (610)278-1400. Fax: (516)275-1425. E-mail: venge@merion.com. Web site: www.advanceweb.com?rcp. **Contact:** Vern Enge, editor. **50% freelance written.** Biweekly magazine covering respiratory diseases and therapies. "*ADVANCE for Respiratory Care Practitioners* is available only to respiratory therapists and related health care personnel. We are a forum for educating our readers about new therapies and equipment and some of the changes and innovations taking place in the field of respiratory care." Estab. 1988. Circ. 45,500. Pays on publication. Publishes ms an average of 6 months after acceptance. Byline given. Offers 75% kill fee. Buys all rights. Editorial lead time 1 month. Submit seasonal material 3 months in advance. Accepts queries by mail, e-mail, fax, phone. Accepts simultaneous submissions. Responds in 2 weeks to queries; up to 6 months to mss. Sample copy and writer's guidelines online.

Nonfiction Technical. "Because we are an exclusive respiratory care publication, we do not want to see articles beyond that reach. We also do not want to get general information articles about specific respiratory care related diseases. For example, our audience is all too familiar with cystic fibrosis, asthma, COPD, bronchitis, Alpha 1 Antitrypsin Defiency, pulmonary hypertension and the like." **Buys 2-3 mss/year.** Query. **Pays $150.** Sometimes pays expenses of writers on assignment.

Photos State availability with submission. Reviews GIF/JPEG files. Buys all rights. Negotiates payment individually. Captions, identification of subjects, model releases required.

Tips "The only way to truly break into the market for this publication on a freelance basis is to have a background in health care (preferably in respiratory care). All of our columnists are caregivers; most of our freelancers are caregivers. Any materials that come in of a general nature like 'contact me for freelance writing assignments or photography' are discarded."

N $ ADVANCE NEWSMAGAZINES

Merion Publications Inc., 2900 Horizon Dr., King of Prussia PA 19406. (610)278-1400. Fax: (610)278-1425. Web site: www.advanceweb.com. **Contact:** Lynn Nace and Linda Jones, editorial department coordinators/directors. More than 30 magazines covering allied health fields, nursing, age management, long-term care and more. Pays on publication. Byline given. Buys first North American serial rights. Editorial lead time 3 months. Accepts queries by e-mail, phone.

Nonfiction Interview/profile, new product, personal experience, technical. Query with published clips. Length: 2,000 words.

N $ $ $ AHIP COVERAGE

America's Health Insurance Plans, 601 Pennsylvania Ave., Suite 500, Washington DC 20004. (202)778-8493. Fax: (202)331-7487. E-mail: lakey@ahip.org. Web site: www.ahip.org. **Contact:** Larry Akey, editor. **75% freelance written.** Bimonthly magazine. "*AHIP Coverage* is geared toward administrators in America's health insurance companies. Articles should inform and generate interest and discussion about topics on anything from patient care to regulatory issues." Estab. 1990. Circ. 12,000. Pays within 30 days of acceptance of article in final form. Publishes ms an average of 2 months after acceptance. Byline given. Offers 30% kill fee. Buys all rights. Editorial lead time 2 months. Submit seasonal material 4 months in advance. Accepts queries by mail, e-mail, fax. Accepts simultaneous submissions. Sample copy for free.

Nonfiction Book excerpts, how-to (how industry professionals can better operate their health plans), opinion. "We do not accept stories that promote products." Query with published clips or send complete ms. Length: 1,800-2,500 words. **Pays 65¢/word minimum for assigned articles.** Pays phone expenses of writers on assignment. Buys all rights.

Tips "Look for health plan success stories in your community; we like to include case studies on a variety of topics—including patient care, provider relations, regulatory issues—so that our readers can learn from their colleagues. Our readers are members of our trade association and look for advice and news. Topics relating to the quality of health plans are the ones more frequently assigned to writers, whether a feature or department. We also welcome story ideas. Just send us a letter with the details."

N $ $ $ AMA ALLIANCE TODAY

American Medical Association Alliance, Inc., 515 N. State St., 9th Floor, Chicago IL 60610. (312)464-4470. Fax: (312)464-5020. E-mail: amaa@ama-assn.org. Web site: www.ama-assn.org/go/alliance. **Contact:** Megan Pellegrini, editor. **25% freelance written.** Magazine published 3 times/year for physicians' spouses. Works with both established and new writers. Estab. 1965. Circ. 35,000. **Pays on acceptance.** Publishes ms an average of 6 months after acceptance. Buys first rights. Accepts queries by mail, e-mail, fax. Accepts simultaneous submissions. Sample copy for 9×12 SAE and 2 first-class stamps.

- Break in with a "solid understanding of issues affecting physicians and their families with a special emphasis on the perspective of the physician's spouse or child."

Nonfiction All articles must be related to the experiences of physicians' spouses. Current health issues; financial topics, physicians' family circumstances, business management and volunteer leadership how-to's. Query with clear outline of article—what points will be made, what conclusions drawn, what sources will be used. Length: 1,000 words. **Pays $300-800.**

Photos Uses all color visuals. State availability with submission.

Tips "Emphasize trends in healthcare as they affect the spouses and children of physicians."

$ AT THE CENTER

Scepter Institute, P.O. Box 100, Morgantown PA 19543. (610)856-6830. Fax: (610)856-6831. E-mail: publications@rightideas.us. Web site: www.atcmag.com. Editor: Jerry Thacker. **Contact:** Elaine Williams, assistant editor. **20% freelance written.** Magazine published 3 times/year that provides encouragement and education to the staff, volunteers, and board members working in crisis pregnancy centers. Estab. 2000. Circ. 30,000. Pays on publication. Publishes ms an average of 1 year after acceptance. Byline given. Buys first North American serial, first, one-time, electronic rights. Editorial lead time 6 months. Submit seasonal material 1 year in advance. Accepts queries by mail, e-mail, fax. Accepts simultaneous submissions. Responds in 1 month to queries; 3-4 months to mss. Sample copy for 9×12 SAE and 4 stamps, or online. Writer's guidelines for #10 SASE or by e-mail.

Nonfiction Relevant topics include abstinence programs and counseling, adoption, counseling pregnant moms in a crisis, post-abortion stress. **Buys about 12 mss/year.** Query. Length: 800-1,200 words. **Pays $150 for assigned articles; $50-150 for unsolicited articles.**

Tips "Generally, we don't have enough space to print personal stories. If your story is relevant to the things you want to share with staff and volunteers of the centers, your best chance to get it published is to keep it brief (a couple paragraphs). Any scripture references should be quoted from KJV or NKJV."

$ $ $ BIOTECHNOLOGY HEALTHCARE

A Guide for Decision Makers on the Biotechnology Revolution, BioCommunications LLC, 780 Township Line Rd., Yardley PA 19067. (267)685-2782. Fax: (267)685-2966. E-mail: editors@biotechnologyhealthcare.com. Web site: www.biotechnologyhealthcare.com. **Contact:** Michael D. Dalzell, editor. **80% freelance written.** Bimonthly magazine. "We are a business magazine (not an academic journal) that covers the economic, regulatory, and health policy aspects of biotech therapies and diagnostics. Our audience includes third-party payers, employer purchasers of healthcare, public healthcare agencies, and healthcare professionals who prescribe biotech therapies. Articles should be written in business magazine-style prose and should be focused on the concerns of these audiences." Estab. 2004. Circ. 35,000. **Pays on acceptance.** Publishes ms an average of 3 months after acceptance. Byline given. Offers $300 kill fee. Buys all rights. Editorial lead time 4 months. Accepts queries by mail, e-mail, fax. Responds in 2 weeks to queries; 1 month to mss. Sample copy online. Writer's guidelines by e-mail.

Nonfiction Book excerpts, essays, how-to (manage the cost of biologics, case studies), interview/profile, opinion, technical (about biotech therapies, diagnostics, or devices), regulatory developments, cost analyses studies, coverage of hot-button issues in the field. **Buys 30 mss/year.** Query with published clips. Length: 1,650-3,300 words. **Pays 75-85¢/word; $300-1,870 for unsolicited articles.** Pays expenses of writers on assignment.

Photos Philip Denlinger, design director. State availability with submission. Reviews contact sheets, 4×6 or larger, color only prints, PowerPoint slides, TIF files that are 200 dpi or higher. Buys one-time rights. Negotiates pay individually. Captions, identification of subjects required.

Columns/Departments "Our columns are 'spoken for,' but I am always interested in pitches for new columns from qualified writers." **Buys 24 mss/year.** Query with published clips. **Pays $300 minimum for a full piece; 75¢/word maximum for ms 600-1,200 words.**

Fillers Gags to be illustrated by cartoonist. **Buys 3 cartoons/year. Pays $300 for cartoons upon publication.**

Tips "Biotechnology represents a new age of medicine, and our readers—who struggle with how to provide healthcare benefits to employees and health insurance enrollees in an affordable way—have a strong interest in learning about how these cutting-edge, but very expensive, treatments will affect how they do their jobs. Keep in mind the interests of the managed care medical or pharmacy director, the employer HR/benefits department, the state Medicaid director, or the clinician who provides biotech therapies to patients. Our audience is highly educated, but not versed in the deep science of biotechnology, so write up to their level but be conversational and stay away from jargon. Please avoid sending consumer-health pitches, as we are not a consumer publication."

N EMERGENCY MEDICINE NEWS

Emergency Medicine's Only Independent News Magazine, Lippincott Williams & Wilkins, Wolters Kluwer Health, 333 7th Ave., 19th Floor, New York NY 10001. E-mail: emn@lww.com. Web site: www.em-news.com. **Contact:** Lisa Hoffman, editor. **100% freelance written.** Monthly tabloid covering emergency medicine only, not emergency nursing, EMTs, PAs. "*Emergency Medicine News* provides breaking coverage of advances, trends and issues within the field, as well as clinical commentary with a CME activity by Editorial Board Chairman James R. Roberts, MD, a leader in the field." Estab. 1978. Circ. 25,000. **Pays on acceptance.** Byline given. Offers 25% kill fee. Buys first North American serial, electronic rights. Editorial lead time 2 months. Submit seasonal material 4 months in advance. Accepts queries by e-mail. Responds in 2 weeks to queries; 1 month to mss. Sample copy online.

Nonfiction Query.

$ $ JEMS

The Journal of Emergency Medical Services, Jems Communications, 525 B St., Suite 1900, San Diego CA 92101. Fax: (619)699-6396. E-mail: jems.editor@elsevier.com. Web site: www.jems.com. **95% freelance written.** Monthly magazine directed to personnel who serve the pre-hospital emergency medicine industry: paramedics, EMTs, emergency physicians and nurses, administrators, EMS consultants, etc. Estab. 1980. Circ. 45,000. Pays on publication. Publishes ms an average of 6 months after acceptance. Byline given. Buys all North American serial rights. Submit seasonal material 6 months in advance. Accepts queries by mail, e-mail, fax. Responds in 2-3 months to queries. Sample copy and writer's guidelines free. Writer's guidelines online.

Nonfiction Essays, exposé, general interest, how-to, humor, interview/profile, new product, opinion, personal experience, photo feature, technical, continuing education. **Buys 50 mss/year.** Query. **Pays $200-400.**

Photos State availability with submission. Reviews 4×6 prints. Buys one-time rights. Offers $25 minimum per photo. Identification of subjects, model releases required.

Columns/Departments Length: 850 words maximum. Query with or without published clips. **Pays $50-250.**

Tips "Please submit a 1-page query letter before you send a manuscript. Your query should answer these questions: 1) What specifically are you going to tell *JEMS* readers? 2) Why do *JEMS* readers need to know this? 3) How will you make your case (i.e., literature review, original research, interviews, personal experience, observation)? Your query should explain your qualifications, as well as include previous writing samples."

$ $ $ MANAGED CARE

780 Township Line Rd., Yardley PA 19067-4200. (267)685-2784. Fax: (267)685-2966. E-mail: editors@managedcaremag.com. Web site: www.managedcaremag.com. **Contact:** John Marcille, editor. **75% freelance written.** Monthly magazine. "We emphasize practical, usable information that helps HMO medical directors and pharmacy directors cope with the options, challenges, and hazards in the rapidly changing health care industry." Estab. 1992. Circ. 44,000. **Pays on acceptance.** Publishes ms an average of 6 weeks after acceptance. Byline given. Offers 20% kill fee. Buys all rights. Editorial lead time 3 months. Submit seasonal material 4 months in advance. Accepts queries by mail, e-mail, fax. Responds in 3 weeks to queries; 2 months to mss. Sample copy for free. Writer's guidelines on request.

Nonfiction "I strongly recommend submissions via e-mail. You'll get a faster response." Book excerpts, general interest (trends in health-care delivery and financing, quality of care, and employee concerns), how-to (deal with requisites of managed care, such as contracts with health plans, affiliation arrangements, accredidation, computer needs, etc.), original research and review articles that examine the relationship between health care delivery and financing. Also considered occasionally are personal experience, opinion, interview/profile, and humor pieces, but these must have a strong managed care angle and draw upon the insights of (if they are not written by) a knowledgeable managed care professional. **Buys 40 mss/year.** Query with published clips. Length: 1,000-3,000 words. **Pays 75¢/word.** Pays expenses of writers on assignment.

Photos State availability with submission. Reviews contact sheets, negatives, transparencies, prints. Buys first-time rights. Negotiates payment individually.

Tips "Know our audience (health plan executives) and their needs. Study our Web site to see what we cover."

N MEDESTHETICS

Business Education for Medical Practitioners, Creative Age Publications, 7628 Densmore Ave., Van Nuys CA 91406. E-mail: llewis@creativeage.com. Web site: www.medestheticsmagazine.com. **Contact:** Linda W. Lewis, executive editor. **50% freelance written.** Bimonthly magazine covering noninvasive medical aesthetic services such as laser hair removal, skin rejuvenation, injectable fillers, and neuromodulators. "*Medesthetics* is a business to business magazine written for and distributed to dermatologists, plastic surgeons and other physicians offering noninvasive medical aesthetic services. We cover the latest equipment and products as well as legal and management issues specific to medspas, laser centers and other medical aesthetic practices." Estab. 2005. Circ. 17,000. **Pays on acceptance.** Publishes ms an average of 3 months after acceptance. Byline given. Buys first, electronic rights. Editorial lead time 3 months. Submit seasonal material 3 months in advance. Accepts queries by e-mail. Responds in 1 month to queries.

Nonfiction New product, technical. Does not want articles directed at consumers. **Buys 25 mss/year.** Query.

Photos State availability with submission. Reviews transparencies, prints. Buys one-time rights. Negotiates payment individually. Identification of subjects, model releases required.

Tips "We work strictly on assignment. Query with article ideas; do not send manuscripts. We respond to queries with article assignments that specify article requirements."

$ $ $ $ MEDICAL ECONOMICS

5 Paragon Dr., Montvale NJ 07645-1742. (973)847-5343. Fax: (973)847-5390. E-mail: jsabatie@advanstar.com. Web site: www.memag.com. **Contact:** Jeanne Sabatie, acquisitions editor. Semimonthly magazine (24 times/year). "*Medical Economics* is a national business magazine read by M.D.s and D.O.s in office-based practice. Our purpose is to be informative and useful to practicing physicians in the professional and financial management of their practices. We look for contributions from writers who know—or will make the effort to learn—the nonclinical concerns of today's physician. These writers must be able to address those concerns in feature articles that are clearly written and that convey authoritative information and advice. Our articles focus very narrowly on a subject and explore it in depth." Circ. 170,000. **Pays on acceptance.** Offers 25% kill fee. Buys all rights. Accepts queries by mail, e-mail, fax. Sample copy and writer's guidelines online.

Nonfiction Articles about private physicians in innovative, pioneering, and/or controversial situations affecting medical care delivery, patient relations, or malpractice prevention/litigation; personal finance topics. "We do not want overviews or pieces that only skim the surface of a general topic. We address physician readers in a conversational, yet no-nonsense tone, quoting recognized experts on office management, personal finance, patient relations, and medical-legal issues." Query with published clips. Length: 1,000-1,800 words. **Pays $1,200-2,000 for assigned articles.** Pays expenses of writers on assignment.
Photos Will negotiate an additional fee for photos accepted for publication.
Tips "We look for articles about physicians who run high-quality, innovative practices suited to the age of managed care. We also look for how-to service articles—on practice-management and personal-finance topics—which must contain anecdotal examples to support the advice. Read the magazine carefully, noting its style and content. Then send detailed proposals or outlines on subjects that would interest our mainly primary-care physician readers."

MEDICAL IMAGING

6100 Center Dr., Suite 1000, Los Angeles CA 90045. (310)642-4400. Fax: (310)641-0831. E-mail: alucas@ascendmedia.com. Web site: www.medicalimagingmag.com. **Contact:** Andi Lucas, editor. **80% freelance written.** Monthly magazine covering diagnostic imaging equipment and technology. Estab. 1986. Circ. 26,000. Pays on publication. Publishes ms an average of 2 months after acceptance. Byline given. Buys all rights. Editorial lead time 2 months. Sample copy on request.
Nonfiction Interview/profile, technical. "No general interest/human interest stories about healthcare. Articles *must* deal with our industry, diagnostic imaging." **Buys 6 mss/year.** Query with published clips. Length: 1,500-2,500 words.
Photos State availability with submission. Reviews negatives. Buys all rights. Offers no additional payment for photos accepted with ms. Identification of subjects, model releases required.
Tips "Send an e-mail or a letter with an interesting story idea that is applicable to our industry, diagnostic imaging. Then follow up with a phone call. Areas most open to freelancers are features and technology profiles. You don't have to be an engineer or radiologist, but you have to know how to talk and listen to them."

$ $ $ $ MODERN PHYSICIAN

Essential Business News for the Executive Physician, Crain Communications, 360 N. Michigan Ave., 5th Floor, Chicago IL 60601. (312)649-5439. Fax: (312)280-3183. E-mail: dburda@crain.com. Web site: www.modernphysician.com. **Contact:** David Burda, editor. **10% freelance written.** Monthly magazine covering business and management news for doctors. "*Modern Physician* offers timely topical news features with lots of business information—revenues, earnings, financial data." Estab. 1997. Circ. 32, 552. **Pays on acceptance.** Publishes ms an average of 2 months after acceptance. Byline given. Buys all rights. Editorial lead time 2 months. Accepts queries by mail, e-mail. Responds in 6 weeks to queries. Sample copy for free. Writer's guidelines sent after query.

O→ Break in with a regional story involving business or physicians.

Nonfiction Length: 750-1,000 words. **Pays 75¢-$1/word.**
Tips "Read the publication, know our audience, and come up with a good story idea that we haven't thought of yet."

N 🌐 THE NEW ZEALAND MEDICAL JOURNAL

Dept. of Surgery, Christchurch Hospital, P.O. Box 4345, Christchurch New Zealand. (64)(3)364-1277. Fax: (64)(3)364-1683. E-mail: brennan.edwardes@cdhb.govt.nz. Web site: www.nzma.org.nz/journal. Editor: Frank Frizelle. **Contact:** Brennan Edwardes. Accepts queries by e-mail. Writer's guidelines online.
Nonfiction Editorials (1,200 words), Obituaries (600 words and a photo), Case Reports (600 words and a photo), Viewpoints (3,000 words), Medical Image (50-200 words and 1-4 images). Send complete ms.

N $ $ PLASTIC SURGERY NEWS

American Society of Plastic Surgeons, 444 E. Algonquin Rd., Arlington Heights IL 60005. Fax: (847)981-5458. E-mail: mss@plasticsurgery.org. Web site: www.plasticsurgery.org. **Contact:** Mike Stokes, managing editor. **15% freelance written.** Monthly tabloid covering plastic surgery. "*Plastic Surgery News* readership is comprised primarily of plastic surgeons and those involved with the specialty (nurses, techs, industry). The magazine is distributed via subscription and to all members of the American Society of Plastic Surgeons. The magazine covers a variety of specialty-specific news and features, including trends, legislation and clinical information." Estab. 1960. Circ. 7,000. **Pays on acceptance.** Publishes ms an average of 1-2 months after acceptance. Byline given. Offers 25% kill fee. Buys first North American serial, simultaneous, electronic rights. Editorial lead time 1-3 months. Accepts queries by e-mail. Accepts simultaneous submissions. Responds in 2 weeks to queries; 3 months to mss. Sample copy for 10 First-Class stamps. Writer's guidelines by e-mail.

Nonfiction Exposé, how-to, new product, technical. Does not want celebrity or entertainment based pieces. **Buys 20 mss/year.** Query with published clips. Length: 1,000-3,500 words. **Pays 20-40¢/word.** Sometimes pays expenses of writers on assignment.

Columns/Departments Digital Plastic Surgeon (technology), 1,500-1,700 words.

$ $ PODIATRY MANAGEMENT

Kane Communications, Inc., P.O. Box 750129, Forest Hills NY 11375. (718)897-9700. Fax: (718)896-5747. E-mail: bblock@podiatrym.com. Web site: www.podiatrym.com. Publisher: Scott C. Borowsky. **Contact:** Barry Block, editor. Magazine published 9 times/year for practicing podiatrists. "Aims to help the doctor of podiatric medicine to build a bigger, more successful practice, to conserve and invest his money, to keep him posted on the economic, legal, and sociological changes that affect him." Estab. 1982. Circ. 14,500. Pays on publication. Byline given. Buys first North American serial, second serial (reprint) rights. Submit seasonal material 4 months in advance. Accepts queries by e-mail. Accepts simultaneous submissions. Responds in 2 weeks to queries. Sample copy for $5 and 9×12 SAE. Writer's guidelines for #10 SASE.

Nonfiction Book excerpts, general interest (taxes, investments, estate, estate planning, recreation, hobbies), how-to (establish and collect fees, practice management, organize office routines, supervise office assistants, handle patient relations), interview/profile (about interesting or well-known podiatrists), personal experience. "These subjects are the mainstay of the magazine, but offbeat articles and humor are always welcome." **Buys 35 mss/year.** Length: 1,500-3,000 words. **Pays $350-600.**

Reprints Send photocopy. Pays 33% of amount paid for an original article.

Photos State availability with submission. Buys one-time rights. Pays $15 for b&w contact sheet.

Tips "We have been persuading writers to use e-mail for the past few years because of the speed, ease of editing, and general efficiency of the process. The tragic events of 9/11/01 along with the anthrax issue now make the policy mandatory—and the trees will also appreciate it!"

N $ $ PRIMARY CARE OPTOMETRY NEWS

The Leading Clinical Newspaper for Optometrists, SLACK Incorporated, 6900 Grove Rd., Thorofare NJ 08086. (856)848-1000. Fax: (856)848-6091. E-mail: pconsupersiteeditor@slackinc.com. Web site: www.pconsupersite.com. Editor: Michael D. DePaolis, OD. **Contact:** Nancy Hemphill, ELS, editor-in-chief. **5% freelance written.** Monthly tabloid covering optometry. "*Primary Care Optometry News* strives to be the optometric professional's definitive information source by delivering timely, accurate, authoritative and balanced reports on clinical issues, socioeconomic and legislative affairs, ophthalmic industry and research developments, as well as updates on diagnostic and thereapeutic regimens and techniques to enhance the quality of patient care." Estab. 1996. Circ. 39,000. Pays on publication. Publishes ms an average of 2 months after acceptance. Byline given. Offers 50% kill fee. Buys all rights. Editorial lead time 2 months. Accepts queries by mail, e-mail, fax, phone. Responds in 2 weeks to queries. Sample copy online. Writer's guidelines by e-mail.

Nonfiction How-to, interview/profile, new product, opinion, technical. **Buys 20 mss/year.** Query. Length: 800-1,600 words. **Pays $350-700.** Sometimes pays expenses of writers on assignment.

Photos State availability with submission. Reviews GIF/JPEG files. Buys all rights. Offers no additional payment for photos accepted with ms. Captions, model releases required.

Columns/Departments What's Your Diagnosis (case presentation), 800 words. **Buys 40 mss/year.** Query. **Pays $100-500.**

Tips "Either e-mail or call the editor-in-chief with questions or story ideas."

$ $ STITCHES

The Journal of Medical Humour, Stitches Publishing, Inc., 240 Edward St., Aurora ON L4G 3S9 Canada. (905)713-4336. Fax: (905)727-0017. E-mail: simon@stitchesmagazine.com. **Contact:** Simon Hally, editor. **90% freelance written.** Bimonthly magazine covering humor for physicians. "*Stitches* is read primarily by physicians in Canada. Stories with a medical slant are particularly welcome, but we also run a lot of nonmedical material. It must be funny and, of course, brevity is the soul of wit." Estab. 1990. Circ. 44,000. Pays on publication. Publishes ms an average of 3-4 months after acceptance. Byline given. Buys first North American serial, electronic rights. Editorial lead time 1 month. Submit seasonal material 4 months in advance. Responds in 6 weeks to queries; 2 months to mss. Sample copy and writer's guidelines free.

Nonfiction Humor, personal experience. **Buys 20 mss/year.** Send complete ms. Length: 200-1,500 words. **Pays 25¢/word to US contributors.**

Fiction Humorous. **Buys 20 mss/year.** Send complete ms. Length: 200-1,500 words. **Pays 25¢/word (US) to US contributors.**

Poetry Humorous. **Buys 5 poems/year.** Submit maximum 5 poems. Length: 2-30 lines. **Pays 35¢/word (US) to US contributors.**

Tips "Due to the nature of humorous writing, we have to see a completed manuscript, rather than a query, to determine if it is suitable for us. Along with a short cover letter, that's all we require."

$ $ ⊘ STRATEGIC HEALTH CARE MARKETING

Health Care Communications, 11 Heritage Lane, P.O. Box 594, Rye NY 10580. (914)967-6741. Fax: (914)967-3054. E-mail: healthcomm@aol.com. Web site: www.strategichealthcare.com. **Contact:** Michele von Dambrowski, editor. **90% freelance written.** Monthly newsletter covering health care marketing and management in a wide range of settings, including hospitals, medical group practices, home health services, and managed care organizations. Emphasis is on strategies and techniques employed within the health care field and relevant applications from other service industries. Works with published/established writers only. Estab. 1984. Pays on publication. Publishes ms an average of 2 months after acceptance. Byline given. Offers 25% kill fee. Buys first North American serial rights. Accepts queries by mail, e-mail. Responds in 1 month to queries. Sample copy for 9×12 SAE and 3 first-class stamps. Guidelines sent with sample copy only.

- *Strategic Health Care Marketing* is specifically seeking writers with expertise/contacts in managed care, patient satisfaction, and e-health.

Nonfiction "Preferred format for feature articles is the case history approach to solving marketing problems. Crisp, almost telegraphic style." How-to, interview/profile, new product, technical. **Buys 50 mss/year.** *No unsolicited mss.* Length: 700-3,000 words. **Pays $100-500.** Sometimes pays expenses of writers on assignment with prior authorization.

Photos Photos, unless necessary for subject explanation, are rarely used. State availability with submission. Reviews contact sheets. Buys one-time rights. Offers $10-30/photo. Captions, model releases required.

The online magazine carries original content not found in the print edition. Contact: Mark Gothberg.

Tips "Writers with prior experience on the business beat for newspapers or newsletters will do well. We require a sophisticated, in-depth knowledge of health care and business. This is not a consumer publication—the writer with knowledge of both health care and marketing will excel. Absolutely no unsolicited manuscripts; any received will be returned or discarded unread."

$ $ $ $ UNIQUE OPPORTUNITIES

The Physician's Resource, U O, Inc., 214 S. 8th St., Suite 502, Louisville KY 40202. Fax: (502)587-0848. E-mail: bett@uoworks.com. Web site: www.uoworks.com. Editor: Mollie Vento Hudson. **Contact:** Bett Coffman, associate editor. **55% freelance written.** Bimonthly magazine covering physician relocation and career development. "Published for physicians interested in a new career opportunity. It offers physicians useful information and first-hand experiences to guide them in making informed decisions concerning their first or next career opportunity. It provides features and regular columns about specific aspects of the search process, practice management and career development." Estab. 1991. Circ. 80,000 physicians. Pays 1 month after acceptance. Publishes ms an average of 2 months after acceptance. Byline given. Offers 10% kill fee. Buys first North American serial, electronic rights. Editorial lead time 3 months. Submit seasonal material 6 months in advance. Responds in 2 months to queries. Sample copy for 9×12 SAE and 6 first-class stamps. Writer's guidelines online.

Nonfiction Features: Practice options and information of interest to physicians in career transition. **Buys 14 mss/year.** Query with published clips. Length: 1,500-3,500 words. **Pays $750-2,000.** Sometimes pays expenses of writers on assignment.

Photos State availability with submission. Buys electronic rights. Negotiates payment individually. Identification of subjects, model releases required.

Columns/Departments Remarks (opinion from physicians and industry experts on physician career issues), 900-1,500 words. **No payment**.

The online magazine carries original content not found in the print edition.

Tips "Submit queries via letter or e-mail with ideas for articles that directly pertain to physician career issues, such as specific or unusual practice opportunities, relocation, or practice establishment subjects, etc. Feature articles are most open to freelancers. Physician sources are most important with tips and advice from both the physicians and business experts. Physicians like to know what other physicians think and do, and appreciate suggestions from other business people."

MUSIC

CLAVIER MAGAZINE

The Instrumentalist Publishing Co., 200 Northfield Rd., Northfield IL 60093. (847)446-5000. Fax: (847)446-6263. **Contact:** Judy Nelson, editor. **1% freelance written.** Magazine published 10 times/year featuring practical information on teaching subjects that are of value to studio piano teachers and interviews with major artists.

Estab. 1937. Circ. 14,000. Pays on publication. Publishes ms an average of 18 months after acceptance. Byline given. Buys all rights. Submit seasonal material 6 months in advance. Accepts queries by mail, fax, phone. Responds in 6 weeks to queries. Sample copy and writer's guidelines free.

Nonfiction "Articles should be of interest and direct practical value to concert pianists, harpsichordists, and organists who are teachers of piano, organ, harpsichord, and electronic keyboards. Topics may include pedagogy, technique, performance, ensemble playing, and accompanying." Historical/nostalgic, how-to, interview/profile, photo feature. Length: 10-12 double-spaced pages. **Pays small honorarium.**

Reprints Occasionally we will reprint a chapter in a book.

Photos Digital artwork should be sent in TIFF, EPS, JPEG files for Photoshop at 300 dpi. Send photos with submission. Reviews negatives, 2¼×2¼ transparencies, 3×5 prints. Buys all rights. Offers no additional payment for photos accepted with ms. Identification of subjects required.

$ ⊘ INTERNATIONAL BLUEGRASS

International Bluegrass Music Association, 2 Music Circle S., Suite 100, Nashville TN 37203. (615)256-3222. Fax: (615)256-0450. E-mail: info@ibma.org. Web site: www.ibma.org.; www.discoverbluegrass.com. **Contact:** Nancy Cardwell. **10% freelance written.** Bimonthly newsletter. "We are the business publication for the bluegrass music industry. IBMA believes that our music has growth potential. We are interested in hard news and features concerning how to reach that potential and how to conduct business more effectively." Estab. 1985. Circ. 4,500. Pays on publication. Publishes ms an average of 2 months after acceptance. Byline given. Not copyrighted. Buys one-time rights. Submit seasonal material 4 months in advance. Accepts queries by mail, e-mail, phone. Accepts simultaneous submissions. Responds in 1 month to queries. Sample copy for 6×9 SAE and 2 first-class stamps.

Nonfiction Unsolicited mss are not accepted, but unsolicited news about the industry is accepted. Book excerpts, essays, how-to (conduct business effectively within bluegrass music), new product, opinion. No interview/profiles/feature stories of performers (rare exceptions) or fans. **Buys 6 mss/year.** Query with or without published clips. Length: 1,000-1,200 words. **Pays up to $150/article for assigned articles.**

Reprints Send photocopy of article and information about when and where the article previously appeared. Does not pay for reprints.

Photos Send photos with submission. Buys one-time rights. Offers no additional payment for photos accepted with ms. Captions, identification of subjects, photographer's name required.

Tips "We're interested in a slant strongly toward the business end of bluegrass music. We're especially looking for material dealing with audience development and how to book bluegrass bands outside of the existing market."

$ $ $ MIX MAGAZINE

Primedia Business Magazines, 6400 Hollis St., Suite 12, Emeryville CA 94608. Fax: (510)653-5142. E-mail: gpetersen@primediabusiness.com. Web site: www.mixonline.com. Editorial Director: George Petersen. **50% freelance written.** Monthly magazine covering pro audio. "*Mix* is a trade publication geared toward professionals in the music/sound production recording and post-production industries. We include stories about music production, sound for picture, live sound, etc. We prefer in-depth technical pieces that are applications-oriented." Estab. 1977. Circ. 50,000. Pays on publication. Publishes ms an average of 3 months after acceptance. Byline given. Offers 50% kill fee. Buys all rights. Editorial lead time 10 weeks. Submit seasonal material 3 months in advance. Responds in 2 weeks to queries; 1 month to mss. Sample copy for $6. Writer's guidelines free.

Nonfiction How-to, interview/profile, new product, technical, project/studio spotlights. Special issues: Sound for picture supplement (April, September), Design issue. **Buys 60 mss/year.** Query. Length: 500-2,000 words. **Pays $300-800 for assigned articles; $300-400 for unsolicited articles.**

Photos State availability with submission. Reviews 4×5 transparencies, prints. Buys one-time rights. Negotiates payment individually. Captions, identification of subjects required.

N $ $ THE MUSIC & SOUND RETAILER

Testa Communications, 25 Willowdale Ave., Port Washington NY 11050. E-mail: bberk@testa.com. Web site: www.msretailer.com. Managing Editor: Michelle Loeb. **Contact:** Brian Berk, editor. **25% freelance written.** Monthly magazine covering music instrument retailers. "*The Music & Sound Retailer* covers the music instrument and specializes in guitars, percussion, pro audio, and DJ products. Our readers are all independent and chain retailers throughout the United States." Estab. 1978. Circ. 11,911. Pays on publication. Publishes ms an average of 2 months after acceptance. Byline given. Offers $100 kill fee. Buys first North American serial rights. Editorial lead time 1 month. Submit seasonal material 1 month in advance. Accepts queries by e-mail. Sample copy for #10 SASE. Writer's guidelines free.

Nonfiction General interest, interview/profile, new product. Does not want product reviews, opinion pieces, stories on music itself that do not pertain to instruments (new songs, singers, etc.). Query with published clips. Length: 1,000-2,000 words. **Pays $300-450.** Sometimes pays expenses of writers on assignment.

Photos State availability with submission. Reviews GIF/JPEG files. Buys one-time rights. Identification of subjects required.

$ $ $ OPERA NEWS

Metropolitan Opera Guild, Inc., 70 Lincoln Center Plaza, New York NY 10023-6593. (212)769-7080. Fax: (212)769-8500. Web site: www.operanews.com. Editor: F. Paul Driscoll. **Contact:** Kitty March, editor. **75% freelance written.** Monthly magazine for people interested in opera; the opera professional as well as the opera audience. Estab. 1936. Circ. 105,000. Pays on publication. Publishes ms an average of 4 months after acceptance. Byline given. Buys first serial rights only. Editorial lead time 4 months. Sample copy for $5. Writer's guidelines not available.

- Break in by ''showing incisive knowledge of opera and the opera scene. We look for knowledgeable and informed writers who are capable of discussing opera in detailed musical terms—but in an engaging way.''

Nonfiction Most articles are commissioned in advance. Monthly issues feature articles on various aspects of opera worldwide. Emphasis is on high quality writing and an intellectual interest to the opera-oriented public. Historical/nostalgic, interview/profile, informational, think pieces, opera, CD, and DVD reviews. Query. Length: 1,500-2,800 words. **Pays $450-1,200.** Sometimes pays expenses of writers on assignment.

Photos State availability with submission. Buys one-time rights.

Columns/Departments Buys 24 mss/year.

$ $ VENUES TODAY

The News Behind the Headlines, 18350 Mount Langley, #200, Fountain Valley CA 92708. Fax: (714)378-0040. E-mail: linda@venuestoday.com. Web site: www.venuestoday.com. Editor: Linda Deckard. **Contact:** Dave Brooks, staff writer. **70% freelance written.** Weekly magazine covering the live entertainment industry and the buildings that host shows and sports. ''We need writers who can cover an exciting industry from the business side, not the consumer side. The readers are venue managers, concert promoters, those in the concert and sports business, not the audience for concerts and sports. So we need business journalists who can cover the latest news and trends in the market.'' Estab. 2002. Pays on publication. Publishes ms an average of 1 month after acceptance. Byline given. Buys all rights. Editorial lead time 1-2 months. Submit seasonal material 1-2 months in advance. Accepts queries by mail, e-mail, fax. Accepts simultaneous submissions. Responds in 1 week to queries. Sample copy online. Writer's guidelines free.

Nonfiction Interview/profile, photo feature, technical, travel. Does not want customer slant, marketing pieces. Query with published clips. Length: 500-1,500 words. **Pays $100-250.** Pays expenses of writers on assignment.

Photos State availability with submission. Reviews GIF/JPEG files. Buys one-time rights. Negotiates payment individually. Captions, identification of subjects required.

Columns/Departments Venue News (new buildings, trend features, etc.); Bookings (show tours, business side); Marketing (of shows, sports, convention centers); Concessions (food, drink, merchandise). Length: 500-1,200 words. **Buys 250 mss/year.** Query with published clips. **Pays $100-250.**

Fillers Gags to be illustrated by cartoonist. **Buys 6/year. Pays $100-300.**

OFFICE ENVIRONMENT & EQUIPMENT

$ $ OFFICE DEALER

Updating the Office Products Industry, OfficeVision, Inc., 252 N. Main St., Suite 200, Mt. Airy NC 27030. (336)783-0000. Fax: (336)783-0045. E-mail: scullen@os-od.com. Web site: www.os-od.com. **Contact:** Scott Cullen, managing editor. **80% freelance written.** Bimonthly magazine covering the office product industry. ''*Office Dealer* serves independent resellers of office supplies, furniture, and equipment.'' Estab. 1987. Circ. 15,300. Pays on publication. Byline given. Buys all rights. Editorial lead time 3 months. Submit seasonal material 5 months in advance. Accepts queries by mail, e-mail, fax. Accepts simultaneous submissions. Responds in 1 month to queries. Sample copy and writer's guidelines free.

Nonfiction Interview/profile, new product, technical. **Buys 10 mss/year.** Length: 700-1,500 words. **Pays $300-500.**

Tips ''See editorial calendar posted online. Feature articles are written by our staff or by freelance writers. We may accept corporate 'byline' articles. Queries should be a single page or less and include an SASE for response. Samples of a writer's past work and clips concerning the proposed story are helpful.''

$ $ OFFICE SOLUTIONS

The Magazine for Office Professionals, OfficeVision Inc., 252 N. Main St., Suite 200, Mt. Airy NC 27030. (336)783-0000. Fax: (336)783-0045. E-mail: scullen@os-od.com. Web site: www.os-od.com. **Contact:** Scott Cullen, managing editor. **80% freelance written.** Bimonthly magazine covering the office personnel and environment. "*Office Solutions* subscribers are responsible for the management of their personnel and office environments." Estab. 1984. Circ. 81,250. Pays on publication. Byline given. Buys all rights. Editorial lead time 3 months. Submit seasonal material 4 months in advance. Accepts queries by mail, e-mail, fax. Accepts simultaneous submissions. Responds in 1 month to queries. Sample copy and writer's guidelines free.

Nonfiction "Our audience is responsible for general management of an office environment and personnel, so articles should be broad in scope and not too technical in nature." Interview/profile, new product, technical, human resources. **Buys 18 mss/year.** Query. Length: 1,500-2,200 words. **Pays $200-450.**

Tips "See editorial calendar posted online. Feature articles are written by our staff or by freelance writers. Queries should be a single page or less and include an SASE for response. Samples of a writer's past work and clips concerning the proposed story are helpful."

PAPER

N $ $ THE PAPER STOCK REPORT

News and Trends of the Paper Recycling Markets, McEntee Media Corp., 9815 Hazelwood Ave., Cleveland OH 44149. (440)238-6603. Fax: (440)238-6712. E-mail: psr@recycle.cc. Web site: www.recycle.cc. **Contact:** Ken McEntee, editor. Biweekly newsletter covering market trends, news in the paper recycling industry. "Audience is interested in new innovative markets, applications for recovered scrap paper, as well as new laws and regulations impacting recycling." Estab. 1990. Circ. 2,000. Pays on publication. Publishes ms an average of 1 month after acceptance. Byline given. Buys first, all rights. Editorial lead time 2 months. Submit seasonal material 2 months in advance. Accepts queries by mail, e-mail, fax, phone. Accepts simultaneous submissions. Responds in 1 month to queries. Sample copy for #10 SAE with 55¢ postage.

Nonfiction Book excerpts, essays, exposé, general interest, historical/nostalgic, interview/profile, new product, opinion, photo feature, technical, all related to paper recycling. **Buys 0-13 mss/year.** Send complete ms. Length: 250-1,000 words. **Pays $50-250 for assigned articles; $25-250 for unsolicited articles.** Pays expenses of writers on assignment.

Photos State availability with submission. Reviews contact sheets. Negotiates payment individually. Identification of subjects required.

The online magazine carries original content not found in the print edition. Contact: Ken McEntee, online editor.

Tips "Article must be valuable to readers in terms of presenting new market opportunities or cost-saving measures."

N $ $ RECYCLED PAPER NEWS

Independent Coverage of Environmental Issues in the Paper Industry, McEntee Media Corp., 9815 Hazelwood Ave., Cleveland OH 44149. (440)238-6603. Fax: (440)238-6712. E-mail: rpn@recycle.cc. Web site: www.recycle.cc. **Contact:** Ken McEntee, president. **10% freelance written.** Monthly newsletter. "We are interested in any news impacting the paper recycling industry, as well as other environmental issues in the paper industry, i.e., water/air pollution, chlorine-free paper, forest conservation, etc., with special emphasis on new laws and regulations." Estab. 1990. Pays on publication. Publishes ms an average of 2 months after acceptance. Buys first, all rights. Editorial lead time 1 month. Submit seasonal material 1 month in advance. Accepts queries by mail, e-mail, fax, phone. Accepts simultaneous submissions. Responds in 2 months to queries. Sample copy for 9×12 SAE and 55– postage. Writer's guidelines for #10 SASE.

Nonfiction Book excerpts, essays, how-to, interview/profile, new product, opinion, personal experience, photo feature, technical, new business, legislation, regulation, business expansion. **Buys 0-5 mss/year.** Query with published clips. **Pays $10-500.** Pays writers with contributor copies or other premiums by prior agreement.

Reprints Accepts previously published submissions.

Columns/Departments Query with published clips. **Pays $10-500.**

Tips "We appreciate leads on local news regarding recycling or composting, i.e., new facilities or businesses, new laws and regulations, unique programs, situations that impact supply and demand for recyclables, etc. International developments are also of interest."

PETS

N $ $ PET AGE

H.H. Backer Associates, Inc., 200 S. Michigan Ave., Suite 840, Chicago IL 60604-2383-2404. (312)663-4040. Fax: (312)663-5676. E-mail: petage@hhbacker.com. Editor-In-Chief/Associate Publisher: Karen Long MacLeod. **Contact:** Cathy Foster, senior editor. **90% freelance written.** Monthly magazine for pet/pet supplies retailers, covering the complete pet industry. Prefers to work with published/established writers. Will consider new writers. Estab. 1971. Circ. 23,022. **Pays on acceptance.** Publishes ms an average of 3 months after acceptance. Byline given. Buys first North American serial, one-time rights. Sample copy and writer's guidelines available.

Nonfiction How-to articles on marketing/merchandising companion animals and supplies; how-to articles on retail store management; industry trends and issues; animal health care and husbandry. No profiles of industry members and/or retail establishments or consumer-oriented pet articles. **Buys 80 mss/year.** Query with published clips. Length: 1,500-2,200 words. **Pays 15¢/word for assigned articles.** Pays documented telephone expenses.

Photos Reviews transparencies, slides, and 5×7 glossy prints. Buys one-time rights. Captions, identification of subjects required.

Tips "This is a business publication for busy people, and must be very informative in easy-to-read, concise style. Articles about animal care or business practices should have the pet-retail angle or cover issues specific to this industry."

$ $ PET PRODUCT NEWS INTERNATIONAL

BowTie News, P.O. Box 6050, Mission Viejo CA 92690. (949)855-8822. Fax: (949)855-3045. **Contact:** Carol Boker, editor. **70% freelance written.** Monthly magazine. "*Pet Product News* covers business/legal and economic issues of importance to pet product retailers, suppliers, and distributors, as well as product information and animal care issues. We're looking for straightforward articles on the proper care of dogs, cats, birds, fish, and exotics (reptiles, hamsters, etc.) as information the retailers can pass on to new pet owners." Estab. 1947. Circ. 26,000. Pays on publication. Byline given. Offers $50 kill fee. Buys first North American serial rights. Editorial lead time 3 months. Submit seasonal material 4 months in advance. Accepts queries by mail, fax. Responds in 2 weeks to queries. Sample copy for $5.50. Writer's guidelines for #10 SASE.

Nonfiction General interest, interview/profile, new product, photo feature, technical. "No cute animal stories or those directed at the pet owner." **Buys 150 mss/year.** Query. Length: 500-1,500 words. **Pays $175-350.**

Columns/Departments The Pet Dealer News™ (timely news stories about business issues affecting pet retailers), 800-1,000 words; Industry News (news articles representing coverage of pet product suppliers, manufacturers, distributors, and associations), 800-1,000 words; Pet Health News™ (pet health and articles relevant to pet retailers); Dog & Cat (products and care of), 1,000-1,500 words; Fish & Bird (products and care of), 1,000-1,500 words; Small Mammals (products and care of), 1,000-1,500 words; Pond/Water Garden (products and care of), 1,000-1,500 words. **Buys 120 mss/year.** Query. **Pays $150-300.**

Tips "Be more than just an animal lover. You have to know about health, nutrition, and care. Product and business articles are told in both an informative and entertaining style. Talk to pet store owners and see what they need to know to be better business people in general, who have to deal with everything from balancing the books and free trade agreements to animal rights activists. All sections are open, but you have to be knowledgeable on the topic, be it taxes, management, profit building, products, nutrition, animal care, or marketing."

PLUMBING, HEATING, AIR CONDITIONING & REFRIGERATION

N $ $ HEATING PLUMBING AIR CONDITIONING

One Mount Pleasant Rd., Toronto ON M4Y 2Y5 Canada. (416)764-1549. **Contact:** Kerry Turner, editor. **20% freelance written.** Monthly magazine. For a prompt reply, "enclose a sheet on which is typed a statement either approving or rejecting the suggested article which can either be checked off, or a quick answer written in and signed and returned." Estab. 1923. Circ. 16,500. Pays on publication. Publishes ms an average of 3 months after acceptance. Accepts queries by mail, e-mail, phone. Responds in 2 months to queries.

Break in with technical, "how-to," Canadian-specific applications/stories.

Nonfiction News, business management articles that inform, educate, motivate, and help readers to be more efficient and profitable. Readers design, manufacture, install, sell, service maintain, or supply all mechanical components and systems in residential, commercial, institutional, and industrial installations across Canada. How-to, technical. Length: 1,000-1,500 words. **Pays 25¢/word.** Sometimes pays expenses of writers on assignment.

Reprints Send tearsheet or photocopy with rights for sale noted and information about when and where the material previously appeared.

Photos Prefers 4×5 or 5×7 glossies, high resolution JPEGS. Photos purchased with ms.

Tips "Topics must relate directly to the day-to-day activities of *HPAC* readers in Canada. Must be detailed, with specific examples, quotes from specific people or authorities—show depth. We specifically want material from other parts of Canada besides southern Ontario. U.S. material must relate to Canadian readers' concerns. We primarily want articles that show *HPAC* readers how they can increase their sales and business step-by-step based on specific examples of what others have done."

N $ $ HVACR NEWS

Trade News International, 4444 Riverside Dr., #202, Burbank CA 91505-4048. Fax: (818)848-1306. E-mail: news@hvacrnews.com. Web site: www.hvacrnews.com. **Contact:** Gary McCarty. Monthly tabloid covering heating, ventilation, air conditioning, and refrigeration. "We are a national trade publication writing about news and trends for those in the trade." Estab. 1981. Circ. 50,000. Pays on publication. Byline sometimes given. Buys first North American serial rights. Editorial lead time 2 months. Submit seasonal material 2 months in advance. Accepts queries by mail, e-mail. Responds in 1 month to queries. Sample copy online. Writer's guidelines by e-mail.

Nonfiction General interest, how-to, interview/profile, photo feature, technical. **Buys 25 mss/year.** Query with published clips. Length: 250-1,000 words. **Pays 25¢/word.** Sometimes pays expenses of writers on assignment.

Photos Send photos with submission. Buys one-time rights. Offers $10 minimum. Negotiates payment individually. Identification of subjects required.

Columns/Departments Buys 24 mss/year. Pays 20¢/word.

Tips "Writers must be knowledgeable about the HVACR industry."

$ $ SNIPS MAGAZINE

BNP Media, 2401 W. Big Beaver Rd., Suite 700, Troy MI 48084. (248)244-6416. Fax: (248)362-0317. E-mail: mcconnellm@bnpmedia.com. Web site: www.snipsmag.com. **Contact:** Michael McConnell, editor. **2% freelance written.** Monthly magazine for sheet metal, heating, ventilation, air conditioning, and metal roofing contractors. Estab. 1932. Publishes ms an average of 3 months after acceptance. Buys all rights. Accepts queries by mail, e-mail, fax, phone. Call for writer's guidelines.

O→ Break in with a "profile of a local contractor in our industries."

Nonfiction Material should deal with information about contractors who do sheet metal, heating, air conditioning, ventilation, and metal roofing work; also about successful advertising and/or marketing campaigns conducted by these contractors and the results. Length: Under 1,000 words unless on special assignment. **Pays $200-300.**

Photos Negotiable.

PRINTING

$ $ IN-PLANT GRAPHICS

North American Publishing Co., 1500 Spring Garden St., Suite 1200, Philadelphia PA 19130. (215)238-5321. Fax: (215)238-5457. E-mail: bobneubauer@napco.com. Web site: www.ipgonline.com. **Contact:** Bob Neubauer, editor. **50% freelance written.** "*In-Plant Graphics* features articles designed to help in-house printing departments increase productivity, save money, and stay competitive. *IPG* features advances in graphic arts technology and shows in-plants how to put this technology to use. Our audience consists of print shop managers working for (nonprint related) corporations (i.e., hospitals, insurance companies, publishers, nonprofits), universities, and government departments. They often oversee graphic design, prepress, printing, bindery, and mailing departments." Estab. 1951. Circ. 24,100. Pays on publication. Publishes ms an average of 3 months after acceptance. Byline given. Buys all rights. Editorial lead time 2 months. Submit seasonal material 3 months in advance. Accepts queries by mail, e-mail, fax. Writer's guidelines online.

Nonfiction "Stories include profiles of successful in-house printing operations (not commercial or quick printers); updates on graphic arts technology (new features, uses); reviews of major graphic arts and printing conferences (seminar and new equipment reviews)." New product (graphic arts), technical (graphic arts/printing/prepress). No articles on desktop publishing software or design software. No Internet publishing articles. **Buys 5 mss/year.** Query with published clips. Length: 800-1,500 words. **Pays $350-500.** Pays writers with contributor copies or other premiums for consultants who agree to write just for exposure.

Photos State availability with submission. Reviews transparencies, prints. Buys one-time rights. Negotiates payment individually. Captions, identification of subjects required.

The online magazine carries original content not found in the print edition. Contact: Bob Neubauer.

Tips "To get published in *IPG*, writers must contact the editor with an idea in the form of a query letter that includes published writing samples. Writers who have covered the graphic arts in the past may be assigned stories for an agreed-upon fee. We don't want stories that tout only one vendor's products and serve as glorified commercials. All profiles must be well balanced, covering a variety of issues. If you can tell us about an in-house printing operation is doing innovative things, we will be interested."

$ $ SCREEN PRINTING

407 Gilbert Ave., Cincinnati OH 45202-2285. (513)421-2050. Fax: (513)421-5144. E-mail: tom.frecska@stmediagroup.com. Web site: www.screenweb.com. **Contact:** Tom Frecska, editor. **30% freelance written.** Monthly magazine for the screen printing industry, including screen printers (commercial, industrial, and captive shops), suppliers and manufacturers, ad agencies, and allied professions. Works with a small number of new/unpublished writers each year. Estab. 1953. Circ. 17,500. Pays on publication. Publishes ms an average of 3 months after acceptance. Byline given. Buys all rights. Accepts queries by mail, e-mail, fax. Sample copy available. Writer's guidelines for #10 SASE.

Nonfiction "Because the screen printing industry is a specialized but diverse trade, we do not publish general interest articles with no pertinence to our readers. Subject matter is open, but should fall into 1 of 4 categories—technology, management, profile, or news. Features in all categories must identify the relevance of the subject matter to our readership. Technology articles must be informative, thorough, and objective—no promotional or 'advertorial' pieces accepted. Management articles may cover broader business or industry specific issues, but they must address the screen printer's unique needs. Profiles may cover serigraphers, outstanding shops, unique jobs and projects, or industry personalities; they should be in-depth features, not PR puff pieces, that clearly show the human interest or business relevance of the subject. News pieces should be timely (reprints from nonindustry publications will be considered) and must cover an event or topic of industry concern." Unsolicited mss not returned. **Buys 10-15 mss/year.** Query. **Pays $400 minimum for major features.**

Photos Cover photos negotiable; b&w or color. Published material becomes the property of the magazine.

Tips "Be an expert in the screen-printing industry with supreme or special knowledge of a particular screen-printing process, or have special knowledge of a field or issue of particular interest to screen-printers. If the author has a working knowledge of screen printing, assignments are more readily available. General management articles are rarely used."

PROFESSIONAL PHOTOGRAPHY

N $ $ IMAGING BUSINESS

(formerly *Photographic Processing*), Cygnus Business Media, 3 Huntington Quad., Suite 301N, Melville NY 11747. (631)845-2700. Fax: (631)845-7109. E-mail: bill.schiffner@cygnusb2b.com. Web site: www.labsonline.com. Publisher: Arthur Hotz. **Contact:** Bill Schiffner, editor-in-chief. **30% freelance written.** Monthly magazine covering photographic (commercial/minilab) and electronic processing markets. Estab. 1965. Circ. 19,000. Pays on publication. Publishes ms an average of 4 months after acceptance. Byline given. Offers $75 kill fee. Editorial lead time 3 months. Submit seasonal material 3 months in advance. Accepts simultaneous submissions. Sample copy and writer's guidelines free.

Nonfiction How-to, interview/profile, new product, photo processing/digital imaging features. **Buys 20-30 mss/year.** Query with published clips. Length: 1,500-2,200 words. **Pays $275-350 for assigned articles; $250-275 for unsolicited articles.**

Photos Looking for digitally manipulated covers. Send photos with submission. Reviews 4×5 transparencies, 4×6 prints. Buys one-time rights. Offers no additional payment for photos accepted with ms. Captions required.

Columns/Departments Surviving in 2000 (business articles offering tips to labs on how to make their businesses run better), 1,500-1,800 words; Business Side (getting more productivity out of your lab). **Buys 10 mss/year.** Query with published clips. **Pays $150-250.**

$ $ NEWS PHOTOGRAPHER

National Press Photographers Association, Inc., 6677 Whitemarsh Valley Walk, Austin TX 78746. E-mail: magazine@nppa.org. Web site: www.nppa.org. **Contact:** Donald R. Winslow, editor. Published 12 times/year. "*News Photographer* magazine is dedicated to the advancement of still and television news photography. The magazine presents articles, interviews, profiles, history, new products, electronic imaging, and news related to the practice of photojournalism." Estab. 1946. Circ. 11,000. **Pays on acceptance.** Publishes ms an average of 4 months after acceptance. Byline given. Offers 100% kill fee. Buys one-time and archival electronic rights. Editorial lead time 2 months. Submit seasonal material 2 months in advance. Accepts queries by mail, e-mail, fax, phone.

Accepts previously published material. Accepts simultaneous submissions. Responds in 1 month to queries. Sample copy for 9×12 SAE and 3 first-class stamps. Writer's guidelines free.

Nonfiction Historical/nostalgic, how-to, interview/profile, new product, opinion, personal experience, photo feature, technical. **Buys 10 mss/year.** Query. Length: 1,500 words. **Pays $300.** Pays expenses of writers on assignment.

Photos State availability with submission. Reviews high resolution, digital images only. Buys one-time rights. Negotiates payment individually. Captions, identification of subjects required.

Columns/Departments Query.

$ $ THE PHOTO REVIEW

140 E. Richardson Ave., Suite 301, Langhorne PA 19047. (215)891-0214. Fax: (215)891-9358. E-mail: info@photoreview.org. Web site: www.photoreview.org. **Contact:** Stephen Perloff, editor-in-chief. **50% freelance written.** Quarterly magazine covering art photography and criticism. "*The Photo Review* publishes critical reviews of photography exhibitions and books, critical essays, and interviews. We do not publish how-to or technical articles." Estab. 1976. Circ. 2,000. Pays on publication. Publishes ms an average of 9-12 months after acceptance. Byline given. Buys first rights. Editorial lead time 3 months. Submit seasonal material 6 months in advance. Accepts queries by mail. Accepts simultaneous submissions. Responds in 2 months to queries; 3 months to mss. Sample copy for $7. Writer's guidelines for #10 SASE.

Nonfiction Interview/profile, photography essay, critical review. No how-to articles. **Buys 20 mss/year.** Send complete ms. Length: 2-20 typed pages. **Pays $10-250.**

Reprints Send tearsheet, photocopy or typed ms with rights for sale noted and information about when and where the material previously appeared. Payment varies.

Photos Send photos with submission. Reviews contact sheets, transparencies, prints. Buys all rights. Offers no additional payment for photos accepted with ms. Captions required.

REAL ESTATE

$ $ AREA DEVELOPMENT MAGAZINE

Sites and Facility Planning, Halcyon Business Publications, Inc., 400 Post Ave., Westbury NY 11590. (516)338-0900, ext. 211. Fax: (516)338-0100. E-mail: gerri@areadevelopment.com. Web site: www.areadevelopment.com. **Contact:** Geraldine Gambale, editor. **80% freelance written.** Prefers to work with published/established writers. Bimonthly magazine covering corporate facility planning and site selection for industrial chief executives worldwide. Estab. 1965. Circ. 45,000. Pays on publication. Publishes ms an average of 2 months after acceptance. Byline given. Buys all rights. Accepts queries by mail, e-mail, fax. Responds in 3 months to queries. Sample copy for free. Writer's guidelines for #10 SASE.

Nonfiction Related areas of site selection and facility planning such as taxes, labor, government, energy, architecture, and finance. Historical/nostalgic (if it deals with corporate facility planning), how-to (experiences in site selection and all other aspects of corporate facility planning), interview/profile (corporate executives and industrial developers). **Buys 75 mss/year.** Query. Length: 1,500-2,000 words. **Pays 40¢/word.** Sometimes pays expenses of writers on assignment.

Photos State availability with submission. Reviews JPEGS of at least 300 dpi. Negotiates payment individually. Captions, identification of subjects required.

The online version of this publication contains material not found in the print edition.

$ $ CANADIAN PROPERTY MANAGEMENT

Mediaedge Communications Inc., 5255 Yonge St., Suite 1000, Toronto ON M2N 6P4 Canada. (416)512-8186. Fax: (416)512-8344. E-mail: barbc@mediaedge.ca. Web site: www.mediaedge.ca. **Contact:** Barb Carss, editor. **10% freelance written.** Magazine published 8 times/year covering Canadian commercial, industrial, institutional (medical and educational), residential properties. "*Canadian Property Management* magazine is a trade journal supplying building owners and property managers with Canadian industry news, case law reviews, technical updates for building operations and events listings. Building and professional profile articles are regular features." Estab. 1985. Circ. 14,500. Pays on publication. Publishes ms an average of 3 months after acceptance. Byline given. Buys all rights. Editorial lead time 2 months. Submit seasonal material 2 months in advance. Accepts queries by mail, e-mail, fax, phone. Accepts simultaneous submissions. Responds in 3 weeks to queries; 2 months to mss. Sample copy for $5, subject to availability. Writer's guidelines free.

Nonfiction Interview/profile, technical. "No promotional articles (i.e., marketing a product or service geared to this industry)!" Query with published clips. Length: 700-1,200 words. **Pays 35¢/word.**

Photos State availability with submission. Reviews transparencies, 3×5 prints, digital (at least 300 dpi). Offers no additional payment for photos accepted with ms. Captions, identification of subjects, model releases required.

Tips "We do not accept promotional articles serving companies or their products. Freelance articles that are strong, information-based pieces that serve the interests and needs of property managers and building owners stand a better chance of being published. Proposals and inquiries with article ideas are appreciated the most. A good understanding of the real estate industry (management structure) is also helpful for the writer."

$ $ THE COOPERATOR

The Co-op and Condo Monthly, Yale Robbins, Inc., 102 Madison Ave., 5th Floor, New York NY 10016. (212)683-5700. Fax: (212)545-0764. E-mail: editorial@cooperator.com. Web site: www.cooperator.com. **70% freelance written.** Monthly tabloid covering real estate in the New York City metro area. "*The Cooperator* covers condominium and cooperative issues in New York and beyond. It is read by condo unit owners and co-op shareholders, real estate professionals, board members and managing agents, and other service professionals." Estab. 1980. Circ. 40,000. Pays on publication. Publishes ms an average of 3 months after acceptance. Byline given. Buys all rights, makes work-for-hire assignments. Submit seasonal material 3 months in advance. Accepts queries by mail, e-mail, fax. Responds in 1 month to queries. Sample copy and writer's guidelines free.

Nonfiction All articles related to co-op and condo ownership. Interview/profile, new product, personal experience. No submissions without queries. Query with published clips. Length: 1,500-2,000 words. **Pays $300.** Sometimes pays expenses of writers on assignment.

Photos State availability with submission. Reviews contact sheets, negatives, transparencies, prints, digital. Rights purchased vary. Negotiates payment individually. Captions, identification of subjects required.

Columns/Departments Profiles of co-op/condo-related businesses with something unique; Building Finance (investment and financing issues); Buying and Selling (market issues, etc.); Interior Design (architectural and interior/exterior design, lobby renovation, etc.); Building Maintenance (issues related to maintaining interior/exterior, facades, lobbies, elevators, etc.); Legal Issues Related to Co-Ops/Condos; Real Estate Trends, all 1,500 words. **Buys 50 mss/year.** Query with published clips. **Pays $300.**

Tips "You must have experience in business, legal, or financial. Must have published clips to send in with résumé and query."

$ $ FLORIDA REALTOR MAGAZINE

Florida Association of Realtors, 7025 Augusta National Dr., Orlando FL 32822-5017. (407)438-1400. Fax: (407)438-1411. E-mail: flrealtor@far.org. Web site: floridarealtormagazine.com. Associate Editor: Leslie Stone. **Contact:** Doug Damerst, editor-in-chief. **50% freelance written.** Journal published 11 times/year covering the Florida real estate profession. "As the official publication of the Florida Association of Realtors, we provide helpful articles for our 150,000 members. We try to stay up on the trends and issues that affect business in Florida's real estate market." Estab. 1925. Circ. 150,000. Pays on publication. Publishes ms an average of 2 months after acceptance. Byline given. Editorial lead time 3 months. Accepts queries by mail, e-mail, fax. Sample copy online.

Nonfiction Book excerpts, how-to, inspirational, interview/profile, new product—all with a real estate angle. Florida-specific is good. No fiction or poetry. **Buys varying number of mss/year.** Query with published clips. Length: 800-1,500 words. **Pays $500-700.** Sometimes pays expenses of writers on assignment.

Photos State availability with submission. Buys one-time print rights and internet use rights. Negotiates payment individually. Captions, identification of subjects, model releases required.

Columns/Departments Mostly written in-house: Know the Law, 900 words; You Inc., 900 words; Technology & You, 1,000 words; Realtor Advantage, 1,000 words. **Buys varying number of mss/year. Payment varies.**

Tips "Build a solid reputation for specializing in real estate writing in state/national publications. Query with specific article ideas."

JOURNAL OF PROPERTY MANAGEMENT

Institute of Real Estate Management, 430 N. Michigan Ave., 7th Floor, Chicago IL 60611. Web site: www.irem.org. **30% freelance written.** Bimonthly magazine covering real estate management. "The *Journal* has a feature/information slant designed to educate readers in the application of new techniques and to keep them abreast of current industry trends." Circ. 20,000. **Pays on acceptance.** Publishes ms an average of 3 months after acceptance. Byline given. Buys all rights. Accepts queries by mail, e-mail, fax. Responds in 6 weeks to queries; 1 month to mss. Sample copy for free. Writer's guidelines online.

Nonfiction Demographic shifts in business employment and buying patterns, marketing. How-to, interview/profile, technical (building systems/computers). "No non-real estate subjects, personality, or company humor." **Buys 8-12 mss/year.** Query with published clips. Length: 750-1,500 words. Sometimes pays expenses of writers on assignment.

Reprints Send tearsheet, photocopy or typed ms. Pays 35% of amount paid for an original article.

Photos State availability with submission. Reviews contact sheets. Buys one-time rights. May offer additional payment for photos accepted with ms. Identification of subjects, model releases required.

Columns/Departments **Buys 6-8 mss/year.** Query.

$ $ OFFICE BUILDINGS MAGAZINE

Yale Robbins, Inc., 102 Madison Ave., New York NY 10016. (212)683-5700. Fax: (212)545-0764. Web site: www.officebuildingsmagazine.com. **15% freelance written.** "Annual magazine covering market statistics, trends, and thinking of area professionals on the current and future state of the real estate market." Estab. 1987. Circ. 10,500. Pays 1 month after publication. Byline sometimes given. Offers kill fee. Buys all rights. Editorial lead time 2 months. Accepts queries by mail, e-mail, fax. Sample copy and writer's guidelines free.

Nonfiction Survey of specific markets. **Buys 15-20 mss/year.** Query with published clips. Length: 1,500-2,000 words. **Pays $600-700.** Sometimes pays expenses of writers on assignment.

$ $ PROPERTIES MAGAZINE

Properties Magazine, Inc., P.O. Box 112127, Cleveland OH 44111. (216)251-0035. Fax: (216)251-0064. E-mail: kkrych@propertiesmag.com. Editor: Kenneth C. Krych. **25% freelance written.** Monthly magazine covering real estate, residential, commerical construction. "*Properties Magazine* is published for executives in the real estate, building, banking, design, architectural, property management, tax, and law community—busy people who need the facts presented in an interesting and informative format." Estab. 1946. Circ. over 10,000. Pays on publication. Publishes ms an average of 2 months after acceptance. Byline given. Buys first rights. Editorial lead time 2 months. Submit seasonal material 2 months in advance. Accepts queries by mail, fax. Responds in 3 weeks to queries. Sample copy for $3.95.

Nonfiction General interest, how-to, humor, new product. Special issues: Environmental issues (September); Security/Fire Protection (October); Tax Issues (November); Computers In Real Estate (December). **Buys 30 mss/year.** Send complete ms. Length: 500-2,000 words. **Pays 50¢/column line.** Sometimes pays expenses of writers on assignment.

Photos Send photos with submission. Reviews prints. Buys one-time rights. Offers no additional payment for photos accepted with ms. Negotiates payment individually. Captions required.

Columns/Departments Buys 25 mss/year. Query or send complete ms. **Pays 50¢/column line.**

$ $ REM

The Real Estate Magazine, House Publications, 808 Coxwell Ave., Toronto ON M4C 3E4 Canada. (416)425-3504. Fax: (416)406-0882. E-mail: jim@remonline.com. Web site: www.remonline.com. **Contact:** Jim Adair, editor. **35% freelance written.** Monthly trade journal covering real estate. "*REM* provides Canadian real estate agents and brokers with news and opinions they can't get anywhere else. It is an independent publication and not affiliated with any real estate board, association, or company." Estab. 1989. Circ. 50,000. **Pays on acceptance.** Publishes ms an average of 2 months after acceptance. Offers 25% kill fee. Buys first Canadian serial rights. Editorial lead time 3 months. Submit seasonal material 3 months in advance. Accepts queries by mail, e-mail, fax. Accepts previously published material. Accepts simultaneous submissions. Sample copy for free.

Nonfiction Book excerpts, exposé, inspirational, interview/profile, new product, personal experience. No articles geared to consumers about market conditions or how to choose a realtor. Must have Canadian content. **Buys 60 mss/year.** Query. Length: 500-1,500 words. **Pays $200-400.**

Photos Send photos with submission. Reviews transparencies, prints, GIF/JPEG files. Buys one-time rights. Offers $25/photo. Captions, identification of subjects required.

Tips "Stories must be of interest or practical use for Canadian realtors. Check out our Web site to see the types of stories we require."

RESOURCES & WASTE REDUCTION

N $ $ COMPOSTING NEWS

The Latest News in Composting and Scrap Wood Management, McEntee Media Corp., 9815 Hazelwood Ave., Cleveland OH 44149. (440)238-6603. Fax: (440)238-6712. E-mail: cn@recycle.cc. **Contact:** Ken McEntee, editor. **5% freelance written.** Monthly newsletter. "We are interested in any news impacting the composting industry including new laws, regulations, new facilities/programs, end-uses, research, etc." Estab. 1992. Circ. 1,000. Pays on publication. Publishes ms an average of 1 month after acceptance. Buys first, all rights. Editorial lead time 1 month. Submit seasonal material 1 month in advance. Accepts queries by mail, e-mail, fax, phone. Accepts previously published material. Accepts simultaneous submissions. Responds in 2 months to queries. Sample copy for 9×12 SAE and 55– postage. Writer's guidelines for #10 SASE.

Nonfiction Book excerpts, essays, general interest, how-to, interview/profile, new product, opinion, personal experience, photo feature, technical, new business, legislation, regulation, business expansion. **Buys 0-5 mss/year.** Query with published clips. Length: 100-5,000 words. **Pays $10-500.** Pays writers with contributor copies or other premiums by prior agreement.

Columns/Departments Query with published clips. **Pays $10-500.**

The online magazine carries original content not found in the print edition. Contact: Ken McEntee.
Tips "We appreciate leads on local news regarding composting, i.e., new facilities or business, new laws and regulations, unique programs, situations that impact supply and demand for composting. International developments are also of interest."

$ $ $ EROSION CONTROL

The Journal for Erosion and Sediment Control Professionals, Forester Communications, Inc., 2946 De La Vina St., Santa Barbara CA 93105. (805)682-1300. Fax: (805)682-0200. E-mail: eceditor@forester.net. Web site: www.erosioncontrol.com. **Contact:** Janice Kaspersen, editor. **60% freelance written.** Magazine published 7 times/year covering all aspects of erosion prevention and sediment control. "*Erosion Control* is a practical, hands-on, 'how-to' professional journal. Our readers are civil engineers, landscape architects, builders, developers, public works officials, road and highway construction officials and engineers, soils specialists, farmers, landscape contractors, and others involved with any activity that disturbs significant areas of surface vegetation." Estab. 1994. Circ. 20,000. Pays 1 month after acceptance. Publishes ms an average of 3 months after acceptance. Byline given. Buys all rights. Editorial lead time 4 months. Submit seasonal material 4 months in advance. Accepts queries by mail, e-mail, fax, phone. Responds in 3 weeks to queries. Sample copy and writer's guidelines free.
Nonfiction Photo feature, technical. **Buys 15 mss/year.** Query with published clips. Length: 3,000-4,000 words. **Pays $700-850.** Sometimes pays expenses of writers on assignment.
Photos Send photos with submission. Reviews transparencies, prints. Buys all rights. Offers no additional payment for photos accepted with ms. Captions, identification of subjects, model releases required.
Tips "Writers should have a good grasp of technology involved and good writing and communication skills. Most of our freelance articles include extensive interviews with engineers, contractors, developers, or project owners, and we often provide contact names for articles we assign."

$ $ MSW MANAGEMENT

The Journal for Municipal Solid Waste Professionals, Forester Communications, Inc., P.O. Box 3100, Santa Barbara CA 93130. (805)682-1300. Fax: (805)682-0200. E-mail: editor@forester.net. Web site: www.mswmanagement.net. **Contact:** John Trotti, editor. **70% freelance written.** Bimonthly magazine. "*MSW Management* is written for public sector solid waste professionals—the people working for the local counties, cities, towns, boroughs, and provinces. They run the landfills, recycling programs, composting, incineration. They are responsible for all aspects of garbage collection and disposal; buying and maintaining the associated equipment; and designing, engineering, and building the waste processing facilities, transfer stations, and landfills." Estab. 1991. Circ. 25,000. Pays on publication. Byline given. Buys all rights. Editorial lead time 4 months. Submit seasonal material 4 months in advance. Accepts queries by mail, e-mail, fax, phone. Accepts simultaneous submissions. Responds in 6 weeks to queries; 2 months to mss. Sample copy and writer's guidelines free. Writer's guidelines online.
Nonfiction Photo feature, technical. "No rudimentary, basic articles written for the average person on the street. Our readers are experienced professionals with years of practical, in-the-field experience. Any material submitted that we judge as too fundamental will be rejected." **Buys 15 mss/year.** Query. Length: 3,000-4,000 words. **Pays $350-750.** Sometimes pays expenses of writers on assignment.
Photos Send photos with submission. Reviews transparencies, prints. Buys all rights. Offers no additional payment for photos accepted with ms. Captions, identification of subjects, model releases required.
Tips "We're a small company, easy to reach. We're open to any and all ideas as to possible editorial topics. We endeavor to provide the reader with usable material, and present it in full color with graphic embellishment whenever possible. Dry, highly technical material is edited to make it more palatable and concise. Most of our feature articles come from freelancers. Interviews and quotes should be from public sector solid waste managers and engineers—not PR people, not manufacturers. Strive to write material that is 'over the heads' of our readers. If anything, attempt to make them 'reach.' Anything submitted that is too basic, elementary, fundamental, rudimentary, etc., cannot be accepted for publication."

$ $ $ STORMWATER

The Journal for Surface Water Quality Professionals, Forester Communications, Inc., 2946 De La Vina St., Santa Barbara CA 93105. (805)682-1300. Fax: (805)682-0200. E-mail: sweditor@forester.net. Web site: www.stormh2o.com. **Contact:** Janice Kaspersen, editor. **10% freelance written.** Magazine published 8 times/year. "*Stormwater* is a practical business journal for professionals involved with surface water quality issues, protection, projects, and programs. Our readers are municipal employees, regulators, engineers, and consultants concerned with stormwater management." Estab. 2000. Circ. 20,000. Pays 1 month after acceptance. Publishes ms an average of 3 months after acceptance. Byline given. Editorial lead time 4 months. Submit seasonal material 4 months in advance. Accepts queries by mail, e-mail. Responds in 3 weeks to queries. Writer's guidelines free.

Nonfiction Technical. **Buys 8-10 mss/year.** Query with published clips. Length: 3,000-4,000 words. **Pays $700-850.** Sometimes pays expenses of writers on assignment.

Photos Send photos with submission. Buys all rights. Offers no additional payment for photos accepted with ms. Captions, identification of subjects, model releases required.

Tips "Writers should have a good grasp of the technology and regulations involved in stormwater management and good interviewing skills. Our freelance articles include extensive interviews with engineers, stormwater managers, and project owners, and we often provide contact names for articles we assign. See past editorial content online."

$ $ WATER WELL JOURNAL

National Ground Water Association, 601 Dempsey Rd., Westerville OH 43081. Fax: (614)898-7786. Web site: www.ngwa.org. **Contact:** Thad Plumley, director of publications. **15% freelance written.** Monthly magazine covering the ground water industry; well drilling. "Each month the *Water Well Journal* covers the topics of drilling, rigs and heavy equipment, pumping systems, water quality, business management, water supply, on-site waste water treatment, and diversification opportunities, including geoexchange installations, environmental remediation, irrigation, dewatering, and foundation installation. It also offers updates on regulatory issues that impact the ground water industry." Estab. 1948. Circ. 26,500. Pays on publication. Publishes ms an average of 3 months after acceptance. Byline given. Buys all rights. Editorial lead time 2 months. Submit seasonal material 3 months in advance. Accepts queries by mail. Responds in 2 weeks to queries; 1 month to mss. Writer's guidelines free.

Nonfiction Essays (sometimes), historical/nostalgic (sometimes), how-to (recent examples include how to chlorinate a well; how to buy a used rig; how to do bill collections), interview/profile, new product, personal experience, photo feature, technical, business management. No company profiles or extended product releases. **Buys up to 20 mss/year.** Query with published clips. Length: 1,000-4,000 words. **Pays $100-400.**

Photos State availability with submission. Offers $50-250/photo. Captions, identification of subjects required.

Tips "Some previous experience or knowledge in groundwater/drilling/construction industry helpful. Published clips are a must."

SELLING & MERCHANDISING

N $ THE AMERICAN SALESMAN

National Research Bureau, 320 Valley St., Burlington IA 52601. (319)752-5415. E-mail: national@willinet.net. Web site: www.national-research-bureau.com. **Contact:** Todd Darnall, editor. **80% freelance written.** Monthly magazine covering sales and marketing. "*The American Salesman Magazine* is designed for sales professionals. Its primary objective is to provide informative articles which develop the attitudes, skills, personal and professional qualities of sales representatives, allowing them to use more of their potential to increase productivity and achieve goals." Publishes ms an average of 1 month after acceptance. Byline given. Buys all rights. Editorial lead time 1 month. Submit seasonal material 2 months in advance. Accepts queries by e-mail. Sample copy for free. Writer's guidelines by e-mail.

Nonfiction Personal experience. **Buys 24 mss/year.** Send complete ms. Length: 500-1,000 words. **Pays 4¢/word.**

AUSTRALIAN GIFTGUIDE

The Intermedia Group, Ltd., P.O. Box 55, Glebe NSW 2037 Australia. (61)(2)9660-2113. Fax: (61)(2)9660-4419. E-mail: rhoswyn@intermedia.com.au. Web site: www.intermedia.com.au. **Contact:** Rhoswyn Joyce, editor. Quarterly magazine covering the very latest products, trends, industry news and trade fairs around the world. "*Australian Giftguide* magazine has been serving the gift and homewares industry for 30 years and is widely regarded as 'the bible of the trade.' It is recognized as an essential business tool by tens of thousands of gift and homewares retailers throughout Australia and New Zealand."

Nonfiction General interest. Query.

$ $ BALLOONS AND PARTIES MAGAZINE

Partilife Publications, 65 Sussex St., Hackensack NJ 07601. (201)441-4224. Fax: (201)342-8118. E-mail: mark@balloonsandparties.com. Web site: www.balloonsandparties.com. **Contact:** Mark Zettler, publisher. **10% freelance written.** International trade journal published 4 times/year for professional party decorators and gift delivery businesses. Estab. 1986. Circ. 7,000. Pays on publication. Publishes ms an average of 3 months after acceptance. Byline given. Buys all rights. Submit seasonal material 6 months in advance. Accepts queries by mail, e-mail, fax, phone. Responds in 6 weeks to queries. Sample copy for 9×12 SAE.

Nonfiction Essays, how-to, interview/profile, new product, personal experience, photo feature, technical, craft.

Buys 12 mss/year. Query with or without published clips or send complete ms. Length: 500-1,500 words. **Pays $100-300 for assigned articles; $50-200 for unsolicited articles.** Sometimes pays expenses of writers on assignment.

Reprints Send ms with rights for sale noted and information about when and where the material previously appeared Length: up to 2,500 words. Pays 10¢/word.

Photos Send photos with submission. Reviews 2×2 transparencies, 3×5 prints. Buys all rights. Captions, identification of subjects, model releases required.

Columns/Departments Problem Solver (small business issues); Recipes That Cook (centerpiece ideas with detailed how-to), 400-1,000 words. Send complete ms with photos.

Tips "Show unusual, lavish, and outstanding examples of balloon sculpture, design and decorating, and other craft projects. Offer specific how-to information. Be positive and motivational in style."

$ $ $ $ CONSUMER GOODS TECHNOLOGY

Edgell Communications, 4 Middlebury Blvd., Randolph NJ 07869. (973)252-0100. Fax: (973)252-9020. E-mail: tclark@edgellmail.com. Web site: www.consumergoods.com. **Contact:** Tim Clark, managing editor. **40% freelance written.** Monthly tabloid benchmarking business technology performance. Estab. 1987. Circ. 25,000. Pays on publication. Publishes ms an average of 2 months after acceptance. Byline given. Buys first North American serial, second serial (reprint), electronic, all rights. Editorial lead time 3 months. Accepts queries by e-mail. Sample copy online. Writer's guidelines by e-mail.

Nonfiction "We create several supplements annually, often using freelance." Essays, exposé, interview/profile. **Buys 60 mss/year.** Query with published clips. Length: 700-1,900 words. **Pays $600-1,200.** Sometimes pays expenses of writers on assignment.

Photos Buys all rights. Negotiates payment individually. Identification of subjects, model releases required.

Columns/Departments Columns 400-750 words—featured columnists. **Buys 4 mss/year.** Query with published clips. **Pays 75¢-$1/word.**

Tips "All stories in *Consumer Goods Technology* are told through the voice of the consumer goods executive. We only quote VP-level or C-level CG executives. No vendor quotes. We're always on the lookout for freelance talent. We look in particular for writers with an in-depth understanding of the business issues faced by consumer goods firms and the technologies that are used by the industry to address those issues successfully. 'Bits and bytes' tech writing is not sought; our focus is on benchmarketing the business technology performance of CG firms, CG executives, CG vendors, and CG vendor products. Our target reader is tech-savvy, CG C-level decision maker. We write to, and about, our target reader."

$ $ CONVENIENCE STORE DECISIONS

Penton Media, Inc., Two Greenwood Square, #410, Bensalem PA 19020. (215)245-4555. Fax: (215)245-4060. E-mail: jgordon@penton.com. Web site: www.c-storedecisions.com. Editorial Director: Jay Gordon. **15-20% freelance written.** Monthly magazine covering convenience retail/petroleum marketing. "*CSD* is received by top-level executives in the convenience retail and petroleum marketing industry. Writers should have knowledge of the industry and the subjects it encompasses." Estab. 1990. Circ. 42,000. Pays on publication. Byline given. Buys all rights, makes work-for-hire assignments. Editorial lead time 2-4 months. Submit seasonal material 3 months in advance. Accepts queries by mail, e-mail, fax. Accepts simultaneous submissions. Responds in 3 weeks to queries. Sample copy and writer's guidelines free.

- Break in with a "demonstrated knowledge of finance and business, with special emphasis on retail. Keen powers of observation and attention to detail are also prized."

Nonfiction Interview/profile (retailers), photo feature, technical. No self-serving, vendor-based stories. **Buys 12-15 mss/year.** Query with published clips. Length: 400-2,000 words. **Pays $200-600 for assigned articles.** Sometimes pays expenses of writers on assignment.

Photos State availability with submission. Buys all rights. Negotiates payment individually. Identification of subjects required.

Tips Offer experience. "We get queries from freelancers daily. We are looking for writers with industry experience. We need real-life, retailer-based work. Bring us a story."

$ $ COUNTRY SAMPLER'S COUNTRY BUSINESS

The Magazine for Retailers of Country Gifts and Accessories, Emmis Publishing LP, 707 Kautz Rd., St. Charles IL 60174. (630)377-8000. Fax: (630)377-8194. E-mail: cbiz@sampler.emmis.com. Web site: www.country-business.com. **Contact:** Susan Wagner, editor. **50% freelance written.** Magazine published 7 times/year covering independent retail, gift and home decor. *Country Business* is a trade publication for independent retailers of gifts and home accents. Estab. 1993. Circ. 32,000. Pays 1 month after acceptance of final ms. Publishes ms an average of 4-6 months after acceptance. Byline given. Offers $50 kill fee. Buys all rights. Editorial lead time 4-6 months. Submit seasonal material 8-10 months in advance. Accepts queries by mail, e-mail, fax. Accepts previously published material. Accepts simultaneous submissions. Usually responds in 4-6 weeks (only if accepted) to queries. Sample articles are available on Web site. Writer's guidelines by e-mail.

- Articles cover new products and trends in the gift industry, as well as topics related to running retail and small businesses.

Nonfiction How-to (pertaining to retail), interview/profile, new product, finance, legal, marketing, small business. No fiction, poetry, fillers, photos, artwork, or profiles of businesses, unless queried and first assigned. **Buys 20 mss/year.** Query with published clips or send complete ms. Length: 1,000-2,500 words. **Pays $275-500 for assigned articles; $200-350 for unsolicited articles.** Sometimes pays expenses of writers on assignment.

Columns/Departments Display & Design (store design and product display), 1,500 words; Retailer Profile (profile of retailer—assigned only), 1,800 words; Vendor Profile (profile of manufacturer—assigned only), 1,200 words; Technology (Internet, computer-related articles as applies to small retailers), 1,500 words; Marketing (marketing ideas and advice as applies to small retailers), 1,500 words; Finance (financial tips and advice as applies to small retailers), 1,500 words; Legal (legal tips and advice as applies to small retailers), 1,500 words; Employees (tips and advice on hiring, firing, and working with employees as applies to small retailers), 1,500 words. **Buys 15 mss/year.** Query with published clips or send complete ms. **Pays $250-350.**

N $ $ $ $ DIRECT SELLING NEWS

Video Plus, 200 Swisher Rd., Lake Dallas TX 75067. E-mail: nlaichas@directsellingnews.com. Web site: www.directsellingnews.com. **Contact:** Nancy Laichas, managing editor. **20% freelance written.** Monthly magazine covering direct selling/network marketing industry. "Though we are a business publication, we prefer feature-style writing rather than a newsy approach." Circ. 6,000. Pays 30 days after publication. Publishes ms an average of 1-2 months after acceptance. Byline given. Makes work-for-hire assignments. Editorial lead time 3 months. Submit seasonal material 3 months in advance. Accepts queries by e-mail. Responds in 3 weeks to queries. Sample copy online.

Nonfiction General interest, how-to. Query. Length: 1,500-3,000 words. **Pays 50¢-$1/word.**

$ $ GIFTWARE NEWS

Talcott Corp., 20 W. Kinzie, 12th Floor, Chicago IL 60610. (312)849-2220. Fax: (312)849-2174. **Contact:** John Saxtan, editor-in-chief. **20% freelance written.** Monthly magazine covering gifts, collectibles, and tabletops for giftware retailers. Estab. 1976. Circ. 35,000. Pays on publication. Publishes ms an average of 2 months after acceptance. Byline given. Buys all rights. Submit seasonal material 6 months in advance. Responds in 2 months to mss. Sample copy for $8.

Nonfiction How-to (sell, display), new product. **Buys 20 mss/year.** Query with published clips or send complete ms. Length: 1,500-2,000 words. **Pays $400-500 for assigned articles; $200-300 for unsolicited articles.**

Photos Send photos with submission. Reviews 4×5 transparencies, 5×7 prints, electronic images. Offers no additional payment for photos accepted with ms. Identification of subjects required.

Columns/Departments Buys 10 mss/year. Send complete ms. **Pays $100-250.**

Tips "We are not looking so much for general journalists but rather experts in particular fields who can also write."

N GREETINGS & GIFTS

Yaffa Publishing, 17-21 Bellevue St., Surry Hills NSW 2010 Australia. (61)(2)9281-2333. Fax: (61)(2)9281-2750. E-mail: alisonleader@yaffa.com.au. Web site: www.yaffa.com.au. Bimonthly magazine for owners and managers of gift and specialist greeting card shops.

Nonfiction General interest, how-to, interview/profile, new product, technical. Query.

$ $ NEW AGE RETAILER

2183 Alpine Way, Bellingham WA 98225. (800)463-9243. Fax: (360)676-0932. E-mail: ray@newageretailer.com. Web site: www.newageretailer.com. **Contact:** Ray Hemachandra, editor-in-chief. **60% freelance written.** Bimonthly magazine for retailers of spiritual and New Age books, music, and giftware. "The goal of the articles in *New Age Retailer* is usefulness—we strive to give store owners and managers practical, in-depth information they can begin using immediately. We have 3 categories of articles: retail business methods that give solid information about the various aspects of running an independent store; inventory articles that discuss a particular New Age subject or trend; and education articles that help storeowners and managers gain knowledge and stay current in New Age subjects." Estab. 1987. Circ. 10,000. Pays on publication. Publishes ms an average of 4 months after acceptance. Byline given. Offers 10% kill fee. Buys first North American serial, second serial (reprint), simultaneous, electronic rights. Editorial lead time 4 months. Submit seasonal material 4 months in advance. Accepts queries by mail, e-mail, fax, phone. Accepts simultaneous submissions. Responds in 1 month to queries; 2 months to mss. Sample copy for $5. Writer's guidelines online.

Nonfiction Book excerpts, how-to, interview/profile, new product, opinion, personal experience, technical, business principles, spiritual. No self-promotion for writer's company or product. Writer must understand independent retailing or New Age subjects. **Buys approximately 25 mss/year.** Query with published clips. Length: 2,500-3,500 words. **Pays $150-350 for assigned articles; $100-300 for unsolicited articles.**

Photos State availability of or send photos with submission. Reviews 2X3 minimum size prints, digital images at 300 dpi. Buys one-time rights. Negotiates payment individually. Captions required.

Tips "Describe your expertise in independent retailing or the New Age market and independent retailing. Have an idea for an article ready to pitch. Promise only what you can deliver."

$ $ NICHE

The Magazine For Craft Gallery Retailers, The Rosen Group, 3000 Chestnut Ave., Suite 304, Baltimore MD 21211. (410)889-3093. Fax: (410)243-7089. E-mail: kstewart@rosengrp.com. **Contact:** Kristina Stewart, editor-in-chief. **80% freelance written.** Quarterly trade magazine for the progressive craft gallery retailer. Each issue includes retail gallery profiles, store design trends, management techniques, financial information, and merchandising strategies for small business owners, as well as articles about craft artists and craft mediums. Estab. 1988. Circ. 25,000. Pays on publication. Publishes ms an average of 9 months after acceptance. Byline given. Buys first North American serial rights. Editorial lead time 9 months. Submit seasonal material 1 year in advance. Accepts queries by mail, e-mail, fax. Responds in 6-8 weeks to queries; 3 months to mss. Sample copy for $3.

Nonfiction *Niche* is looking for in-depth articles on store security, innovative merchandising/display, design trends, or marketing and promotion. Stories of interest to independent retailers, such as gallery owners, may be submitted. Interview/profile, photo feature, articles targeted to independent retailers and small business owners. **Buys 20-28 mss/year.** Query with published clips. **Pays $300-700.** Sometimes pays expenses of writers on assignment.

Photos Send photos with submission. Reviews transparencies, slides, e-images. Negotiates payment individually. Captions required.

Columns/Departments Retail Details (short items at the front of the book, general retail information); Artist Profiles (biographies of American Craft Artists); Retail Resources (including book/video/seminar reviews and educational opportunities pertaining to retailers). Query with published clips. **Pays $25-100.**

$ O&A MARKETING NEWS

KAL Publications, Inc., 559 S. Harbor Blvd., Suite A, Anaheim CA 92805. (714)563-9300. Fax: (714)563-9310. E-mail: kathy@kalpub.com. Web site: www.kalpub.com. **Contact:** Kathy Laderman, editor-in-chief. **3% freelance written.** Bimonthly tabloid. "*O&A Marketing News* is editorially directed to people engaged in the distribution, merchandising, installation, and servicing of gasoline, oil, TBA, quick lube, carwash, convenience store, alternative fuel, and automotive aftermarket products in the 13 Western states." Estab. 1966. Circ. 7,500. Pays on publication. Publishes ms an average of 2 months after acceptance. Byline sometimes given. Buys first, electronic rights. Editorial lead time 1 month. Submit seasonal material 1 month in advance. Accepts queries by mail, e-mail, fax. Accepts simultaneous submissions. Responds in 2 months to queries; 2 months to mss. Sample copy for 9×13 SAE and 10 first-class stamps. Writer's guidelines not available.

Nonfiction Interview/profile, photo feature, industry news. Nothing that doesn't pertain to the petroleum marketing industry in the 13 Western states. **Buys 35 mss/year.** Send complete ms. Length: 100-500 words. **Pays $1.25/column inch.**

Photos State availability of or send photos with submission. Reviews contact sheets, 4×6 prints. Buys electronic rights. Offers $5/photo. Captions, identification of subjects required.

Columns/Departments Oregon News (petroleum marketing news in state of Oregon). **Buys 7 mss/year.** Send complete ms. **Pays $1.25/column inch.**

Fillers Gags to be illustrated by cartoonist, short humor. **Buys 7/year.** Length: 1-200 words. **Pays per column inch.**

Tips "Seeking Western industry news pertaining to the petroleum marketing industry. It can be something simple—like a new gas station or quick lube opening. News from 'outlying' states such as Montana, Idaho, Wyoming, New Mexico, and Hawaii is always needed—but any timely, topical news-oriented stories will also be considered."

N $ $ $ $ OPERATIONS & FULFILLMENT

Primedia, Inc., 11 Riverbend Dr. S., P.O. Box 4949, Stamford CT 06907-2524. (203)358-4106. E-mail: barnn@primediabusiness.com. Web site: www.opsandfulfillment.com. **Contact:** Barbara Arnn, managing editor. **25% freelance written.** Monthly magazine covering catalog/direct mail operations. "*Operations & Fulfillment (O&F)* is a monthly publication that offers practical solutions for catalog online, and direct response operations management. The magazine covers such critical areas as material handling, bar coding, facility planning, transportation, call centers, warehouse management, information systems, online fulfillment and human resources." Estab. 1993. Circ. 17,600. Pays on publication. Publishes ms an average of 2 months after acceptance. Buys first North

American serial rights. Editorial lead time 2 months. Accepts queries by mail, e-mail, phone. Responds in 1 week to queries. Sample copy and writer's guidelines free.

Nonfiction Book excerpts, how-to, interview/profile, new product, technical. **Buys 4-6 mss/year.** Query with published clips. Length: 2,500-3,000 words. **Pays $1,000-1,800.**

Photos "In addition to the main article, you must include at least one sidebar of about 400 words that contains a detailed example or case study of how a direct-to-customer catalog company implements or benefits from the process you're writing about; a check list or set of practical guidelines (i.e., "Twelve Ways to Ship Smarter") that describe how to implement what you suggest in the article; supporting materials such as flow charts, graphs, diagrams, illustrations and photographs (these must be clearly labeled and footnoted); and an author biography of no more than 75 words." Send photos with submission. Captions, identification of subjects required.

Tips "Writers need some knowledge of the direct-to-customer industry. They should be able to deal clearly with highly technical material and provide attention to detail and painstaking research."

PARTY & PAPER RETAILER

P.O. Box 128, Sparta MI 49345. (616)887-9008. Fax: (616)887-2666. Web site: www.partypaper.com. Editor at Large: Sarah Schwartz. **80% freelance written.** Monthly magazine covering "every aspect of how to do business better for owners of party and stationery shops. Tips and how-tos on display, marketing, success stories, merchandising, operating costs, e-commerce, retail technology, etc." Estab. 1986. Circ. 20,000. Pays on publication. Offers 15% kill fee. Buys first North American serial rights. Editorial lead time 6 months. Submit seasonal material 6 months in advance. Accepts queries by mail, e-mail, fax. Responds in 2 months to queries. Sample copy for $6.

- Especially interested in news items on party retail industry for our Press Pages. Also, new column on Internet retailing ("Cyberlink") which covers all Web-related topics.

Nonfiction Book excerpts, how-to (retailing related), new product. No articles written in first person. **Buys 100 mss/year.** Query with published clips. Length: 800-1,500 words. Pays phone expenses only of writers on assignment.

Reprints Send tearsheet or photocopy of article and information about when and where the article previously appeared.

Photos State availability with submission. Reviews transparencies. Buys one-time rights. Negotiates payment individually. Captions, identification of subjects required.

Columns/Departments Shop Talk (successful party/stationery store profile), 1,500 words; Storekeeping (selling, employees, market, running store), 800 words; Cash Flow (anything finance related), 800 words. **Buys 30 mss/year.** Query with published clips. **Payment varies.**

$ $ TRAVEL GOODS SHOWCASE

The source for luggage, business cases, and accessories, Travel Goods Association, 5 Vaughn Dr., Suite 105, Princeton NJ 08540. (609)720-1200. Fax: (609)720-0620. E-mail: john@travel-goods.org. Web site: www.travel-goods.org. Editor and Publisher: Michele M. Pittenger. **Contact:** John Misiano, senior editor. **5-10% freelance written.** Magazine published 5 times/year. covering travel goods, accessories, trends, and new products. "*Travel Goods Showcase* contains articles for retailers, dealers, manufacturers, and suppliers about luggage, business cases, personal leather goods, handbags, and accessories. Special articles report on trends in fashion, promotions, selling and marketing techniques, industry statistics, and other educational and promotional improvements and advancements." Estab. 1975. Circ. 11,000. **Pays on acceptance.** Publishes ms an average of 2 months after acceptance. Byline given. Offers $50 kill fee. Editorial lead time 3 months. Submit seasonal material 2 months in advance. Accepts queries by mail, e-mail. Responds in 2 weeks to queries; 1 month to mss. Sample copy and writer's guidelines free.

Nonfiction Interview/profile, new product, technical, travel, retailer profiles with photos. "No manufacturer profiles." **Buys 3 mss/year.** Query with published clips. Length: 1,200-1,600 words. **Pays $200-400.**

$ $ $ VERTICAL SYSTEMS RESELLER

The news source for channel management, Edgell Communications, Inc., 4 Middlebury Blvd., Suite 1, Randolph NJ 07869. (973)252-0100. Fax: (973)252-9020. E-mail: alorden@edgellmail.com. Web site: www.verticalsystemsreseller.com. Publisher: Michael Kachmar. **Contact:** Abby Lorden, managing editor. **60% freelance written.** Monthly journal covering channel strategies that build business. Estab. 1992. Circ. 30,000. **Pays on acceptance.** Publishes ms an average of 2 months after acceptance. Byline given. Editorial lead time 3 months. Accepts queries by mail, e-mail, fax. Accepts simultaneous submissions. Responds in 2 weeks to queries; 2 months to mss. Sample copy online.

Nonfiction Interview/profile, opinion, technical, technology/channel issues. **Buys 36 mss/year.** Query with

published clips. Length: 1,000-1,700 words. **Pays $200-800 for assigned articles.** Sometimes pays expenses of writers on assignment.
Photos Send photos with submission. Offers no additional payment for photos accepted with ms. Identification of subjects, model releases required.

N $$$ VM+SD

S.T. Media Group International, 407 Gilbert Ave., Cincinnati OH 45202. (513)421-2050. Fax: (513)421-5144. E-mail: steve.kaufman@stmediagroup.com. Web site: www.vmsd.com. Editor: Steve Kaufman. **Contact:** Matthew Hall, managing editor. **10% freelance written.** Monthly magazine covering retailing—store design, store planning, visual merchandising, brand marketing. "Our articles need to get behind the story, tell not only what retailers did when building a new store, renovating an existing store, mounting a new in-store merchandise campaign, but also why they did what they did: specific goals, objectives, strategic initiatives, problems to solve, target markets to reach, etc. Estab. 1872. Circ. 20,000. **Pays on acceptance.** Publishes ms an average of 1-2 months after acceptance. Byline given. Offers $100 kill fee. Buys all rights. Editorial lead time 2-3 months. Submit seasonal material 3-4 months in advance. Accepts queries by e-mail. Sample copy for free. Writer's guidelines free.
Nonfiction Buys 2-3 mss/year. Query. Length: 500-1,000 words. **Pays $400-1,000.**
Photos Contact Matthew Hall, managing editor. Send photos with submission. Reviews GIF/JPEG files. Buys one-time rights. Negotiates payment individually.
Columns/Departments Contact Anne Dinardo, senior associate editor. Please ask for an editorial calendar. **Buys 5-6 mss/year.** Query. **Pays $500-750.**
Tips "We need to see a demonstrated understanding of our industry, its issues and major players; strong reporting and interviewing skills are also important. Merely facile writing is not enough for us."

SPORT TRADE

$$ AQUATICS INTERNATIONAL

Hanley-Wood, LLC, 4160 Wilshire Blvd., Los Angeles CA 90010. Fax: (323)801-4986. E-mail: gthill@hanleywood.com. Web site: www.aquaticsintl.com. **Contact:** Gary Thill, editor. Magazine published 10 times/year covering public swimming pools and waterparks. Estab. 1989. Circ. 30,000. Pays on publication. Publishes ms an average of 3 months after acceptance. Byline given. international rights in perpetuity and makes work-for-hire assignments. Editorial lead time 3 months. Responds in 1 month to queries. Sample copy for $10.50.
Nonfiction How-to, interview/profile, technical. **Buys 6 mss/year.** Query with published clips. Length: 1,500-2,500 words. **Pays $525 for assigned articles.**
Columns/Departments Pays $250.
Tips "Send query letter with samples."

$$ ARROWTRADE MAGAZINE

A Magazine for Retailers, Distributors & Manufacturers of Bowhunting Equipment, Arrow Trade Publishing Corp., 3479 409th Ave. NW, Braham MN 55006. (320)396-3473. Fax: (320)396-3206. E-mail: arrowtrade@northlc.com. **Contact:** Tim Dehn, editor and publisher. **40% freelance written.** Bimonthly magazine covering the archery industry. "Our readers are interested in articles that help them operate their business better. They are primarily owners or managers of sporting goods stores and archery pro shops." Estab. 1996. Circ. 11,000. **Pays on acceptance.** Publishes ms an average of 2 months after acceptance. Byline given. Buys first North American serial rights. Editorial lead time 2 months. Accepts queries by mail, e-mail, fax. Responds in 2 weeks to queries; 2 weeks to mss. Sample copy for 9×12 SAE and 10 first-class stamps. Writer's guidelines not available.

> *ArrowTrade Magazine* needs queries from veterans interested in writing for our industry audience. Our readers are primarily retailers of bowhunting equipment. "Find an unusual business combination, like someone selling archery plus cowboy boots, motorcycles, taxidermy—and submit it (1,100-1,400 words) for 'Archery Plus.'"

Nonfiction Interview/profile, new product. "Generic business articles won't work for our highly specialized audience." **Buys 24 mss/year.** Query with published clips. Length: 1,800-3,800 words. **Pays $350-550.**
Photos Send photos with submission. Reviews contact sheets, negatives, 35mm transparencies, 4×6 prints, digital photos on CD or DVD. Offers no additional payment for photos accepted with ms. Captions required.
Columns/Departments Dealer Workbench (repair and tuning bows), 1,600 words; Bow Report (tests and evaluations of current models), 2,400 words; Archery Plus (short profiles of retailers who combine archery with other product lines); Product Focus (digging into the design and function of an innovative single product); Behind the Brand (profiling a firm that's important to the bowhunting industry). **Buys 12 mss/year.** Query with published clips. **Pays $250-375.**

Tips "Our readers are hungry for articles that help them decide what to stock and how to do a better job selling or servicing it. Articles needed typically fall into one of these categories: business profiles on outstanding retailers, manufacturers or distributors; equipment articles that cover categories of gear, citing trends in the market and detailing why products have been designed a certain way and what type of use they're best suited for; basic business articles that help dealers do a better job of promoting their business, managing their inventory, training their staff, etc. Good interviewing skills are a must, as especially in the equipment articles we like to see a minimum of 6 sources."

$ $ BOATING INDUSTRY INTERNATIONAL

The Management Magazine for the Recreational Marine Industry, Ehlert Publishing Group, 6420 Sycamore Lane, Suite 100, Maple Grove MN 55369. (763)383-4448. Fax: (763)383-4499. Web site: www.boating-industry.com. **10-20% freelance written.** Bimonthly magazine covering recreational marine industry management. "We write for those in the industry—not the consumer. Our subject is the business of boating. All of our articles must be analytical and predictive, telling our readers where the industry is going, rather than where it's been." Estab. 1929. Circ. 23,000. **Pays on acceptance.** Publishes ms an average of 2 months after acceptance. Byline given. Offers 50% kill fee. Buys first, electronic rights. Editorial lead time 2 months. Submit seasonal material 2 months in advance. Accepts queries by mail, e-mail, fax. Responds in 1 month to queries. Sample copy online. Writer's guidelines free.

O⊸ "We actively solicit items for our electronic news service. See the News Flash section of our Web site. This is an excellent way to break in, especially for writers based outside the US."

Nonfiction Technical, business. **Buys 30 mss/year.** Query with published clips. Length: 250-2,500 words. **Pays $25-250.** Sometimes pays expenses of writers on assignment.

Photos State availability with submission. Reviews 2×2 transparencies, 4×6 prints. Buys one-time rights. Negotiates payment individually. Captions, identification of subjects required.

N $ $ BOWLING CENTER MANAGEMENT

Trade Magazine for Bowling Center Operators, Luby Publishing, 122 S. Michigan Ave., Suite 1506, Chicago IL 60603. (312)341-1110. Fax: (312)341-1469. E-mail: mikem@lubypublishing.com. Web site: www.bcmmag.com. **Contact:** Michael Mazek, editor. **50% freelance written.** Monthly magazine covering bowling centers, family entertainment. "Our readers are looking for novel ways to draw more customers. Accordingly, we look for articles that effectively present such ideas." Estab. 1995. Circ. 12,000. **Pays on acceptance.** Publishes ms an average of 3 months after acceptance. Byline given. Buys first North American serial rights. Editorial lead time 3 months. Submit seasonal material 6 months in advance. Accepts queries by e-mail. Accepts previously published material. Accepts simultaneous submissions. Responds in 2-3 weeks to queries. Sample copy for $10.

Nonfiction How-to, interview/profile. **Buys 10-20 mss/year.** Query. Length: 750-1,500 words. **Pays $150-350.**

Tips "Send a solid, clever query by e-mail with knowledge and interest in an industry trend."

N $ $ CROSSFIRE

Paintball Digest, 570 Mantus Rd., P.O. Box 690, Sewell NJ 08080. (888)834-6026. E-mail: editor@paintball2xtremes.com. Web site: www.crossfiremag.com. **Contact:** John Amodea, executive editor. **100% freelance written.** Monthly magazine covering paintball sport. "*Crossfire* will cover all aspects of the paintball industry from tactics to safety." Pays on publication. Byline given. Makes work-for-hire assignments. Editorial lead time 1 year. Submit seasonal material 2 months in advance. Accepts queries by mail, e-mail, fax. Accepts simultaneous submissions. Responds in 2 weeks to queries. Sample copy for free.

Nonfiction How-to, humor, interview/profile, new product, personal experience, photo feature, technical, travel, Tournament coverage, industry news. **Buys 1-3 mss/year.** Send complete ms. Length: 700-1,900 words. **Pays 7-22¢/word.**

Photos Send photos with submission. Reviews negatives. Buys all rights. Negotiates payment individually. Captions, identification of subjects, model releases required.

Fillers Facts, gags to be illustrated by cartoonist, newsbreaks. **Buys 24/year.** Length: 25-100 words. **Pays 7-22¢/word.**

Tips "Paintball or extreme sport participation is a plus."

$ $ FITNESS MANAGEMENT

Issues and Solutions in Fitness Services, Athletic Business Publications, P.O. Box 409, Danville PA 17821. (800)722-8764. Fax: (570)271-1202. E-mail: edit@fitnessmanagement.com. Web site: www.fitnessmanagement.com. **Contact:** Ronale Tucker Rhodes, editor. **50% freelance written.** Monthly magazine. "Readers are owners, managers, and program directors of physical fitness facilities. *FM* helps them run their enterprises safely, efficiently, and profitably. Ethical and professional positions in health, nutrition, sports medicine, management, etc., are consistent with those of established national bodies." Estab. 1985. Circ. 26,000. Pays on publication.

Publishes ms an average of 5 months after acceptance. Byline given. Offers 50% kill fee. Buys all rights (all articles published in *FM* are also published and archived on its Web site). Submit seasonal material 6 months in advance. Accepts queries by mail, e-mail, fax. Responds in 3 months to queries. Sample copy for $5. Writer's guidelines for #10 SASE.

Nonfiction How-to (manage fitness center and program), new product (no pay), photo feature (facilities/programs), technical, news of fitness research and major happenings in fitness industry. No exercise instructions or general ideas without examples of fitness businesses that have used them successfully. **Buys 50 mss/year.** Query. Length: 750-2,000 words. **Pays $60-300 for assigned articles.** Pays expenses of writers on assignment.

Photos Send photos with submission. Reviews contact sheets, 2×2 and 4×5 transparencies, prefers glossy prints (5×7 to 8×10). Captions, model releases required.

Tips "We seek writers who are experts in a business or science field related to the fitness-service industry or who are experienced in the industry. Be current with the state of the art/science in business and fitness and communicate it in human terms (avoid intimidating academic language; tell the story of how this was learned and/or cite examples or quotes of people who have applied the knowledge successfully)."

$ $ GOLF COURSE MANAGEMENT

Golf Course Superintendents Association of America, 1421 Research Park Dr., Lawrence KS 66049. (800)472-7878. Fax: (785)832-3665. E-mail: shollister@gcsaa.org. Web site: www.gcsaa.org. **Contact:** Scott Hollister, editor. **50% freelance written.** Monthly magazine covering the golf course superintendent. "*GCM* helps the golf course superintendent become more efficient in all aspects of their job." Estab. 1924. Circ. 40,000. **Pays on acceptance.** Publishes ms an average of 6 months after acceptance. Byline given. Buys first North American serial rights, Web rights, and makes work-for-hire assignments. Editorial lead time 6 months. Submit seasonal material 6 months in advance. Accepts simultaneous submissions. Responds in 3 weeks to queries; 1 month to mss. Sample copy and writer's guidelines free.

Nonfiction How-to, interview/profile. No articles about playing golf. **Buys 40 mss/year.** Query. Length: 1,500-2,500 words. **Pays $300-450 for assigned articles.** Sometimes pays expenses of writers on assignment.

Photos Send photos with submission. Buys all rights. Offers no additional payment for photos accepted with ms. Identification of subjects required.

Tips "Writers should have prior knowledge of the golf course superintendent profession."

IDEA FITNESS JOURNAL

IDEA Health & Fitness Association, Inc., 10455 Pacific Center Court, San Diego CA 92121. (858)535-8979. Fax: (858)535-8234. E-mail: websters@ideafit.com. Web site: www.ideafit.com. **Contact:** Sandy Todd Webster, editor-in-chief. **70% freelance written.** Magazine published 10 times/year "for fitness professionals—personal trainers, group fitness instructors, and studio and health club owners—covering topics such as exercise science, nutrition, injury prevention, entrepreneurship in fitness, fitness-oriented research, and program design." Estab. 1984. Circ. 20,000. **Pays on acceptance.** Publishes ms an average of 4 months after acceptance. Byline given. Buys all rights. Accepts queries by mail, e-mail, fax. Accepts simultaneous submissions. Responds in 2 months to queries. Sample copy for $5. Writer's guidelines online.

Nonfiction How-to, technical. No general information on fitness; our readers are pros who need detailed information. **Buys 15 mss/year.** Query. Length: 1,000-3,000 words. **Payment varies.**

Photos State availability with submission. Buys all rights. Offers no additional payment for photos with ms. Model releases required.

Columns/Departments Research (detailed, specific info—must be written by expert), 750-1,500 words; Industry News (short reports on research, programs, and conferences), 150-300 words; Fitness Handout (exercise and nutrition info for participants), 750 words. **Buys 80 mss/year.** Query. **Payment varies.**

Tips "We don't accept fitness information for the consumer audience on topics such as why exercise is good for you. Writers who have specific knowledge of, or experience working in, the fitness industry have an edge."

N $ $ INTERNATIONAL BOWLING INDUSTRY

B2B Media, Inc., 13245 Riverside Dr., Suite 501, Sherman Oaks CA 91423. Fax: (818)789-2812. E-mail: info@bowlingindustry.com. Web site: www.bowlingindustry.com. Editor: Scott Frager. **Contact:** Fred Groh, managing editor. **40% freelance written.** Monthly magazine covering ownership and management of bowling centers (alleys) and pro shops. "IBI publishes articles in all phases of bowling center and bowling pro shop ownership and management, among them finance, promotion, customer service, relevant technology, architecture and capital improvement. The magazine also covers the operational areas of bowling centers and pro shops such as human resources, food and beverage, corporate and birthday parties, ancillary attractions (go-karts, gaming and the like), and retailing. Articles must have strong how-to emphasis. They must be written specifically in terms of the bowling industry, although content may be applicable more widely." Estab. 1993. Circ. 10,200. **Pays on acceptance.** Publishes ms an average of 3 months after acceptance. Byline given. Offers $50 kill fee.

Buys all rights. Submit seasonal material 3 months in advance. Accepts queries by mail, e-mail, fax. Accepts simultaneous submissions. Responds in 2 weeks to queries; 1 month to mss. Sample copy for #10 SASE. Writer's guidelines free.

Nonfiction How-to, interview/profile, new product, technical. **Buys 40 mss/year.** Send complete ms. Length: 1,100-1,400 words. **Pays $250.** Sometimes pays expenses of writers on assignment.

Photos State availability with submission. Reviews JPEG photos. Buys all rights. Offers no additional payment for photos accepted with ms. Identification of subjects required.

Tips "Please supply writing samples, applicable list of credits and bio."

$ $ NSGA RETAIL FOCUS

National Sporting Goods Association, 1601 Feehanville Dr., Suite 300, Mt. Prospect IL 60056-6035. (847)296-6742. Fax: (847)391-9827. E-mail: info@nsga.org. Web site: www.nsga.org. **Contact:** Larry N. Weindruch, editor/publisher. **20% freelance written.** Works with a small number of new/unpublished writers each year. Bimonthly magazine. "*NSGA Retail Focus* serves as a bimonthly trade journal for sporting goods retailers who are members of the association." Estab. 1948. Circ. 2,000. Pays on publication. Publishes ms an average of 1 month after acceptance. Byline given. Offers kill fee. Buys first, second serial (reprint), electronic rights. Submit seasonal material 6 months in advance. Accepts queries by e-mail. Sample copy for 9×12 SAE and 5 first-class stamps.

Nonfiction Interview/profile, photo feature. "No articles written without sporting goods retail businesspeople in mind as the audience. In other words, no generic articles sent to several industries." **Buys 12 mss/year.** Query with published clips. **Pays $150-300.** Sometimes pays expenses of writers on assignment.

Photos State availability with submission. Reviews high-resolution, digital images. Buys one-time rights. Payment negotiable.

Columns/Departments Personnel Management (succinct tips on hiring, motivating, firing, etc.); Sales Management (in-depth tips to improve sales force performance); Retail Management (detailed explanation of merchandising/inventory control); Store Design; Visual Merchandising, all 1,500 words. **Buys 12 mss/year.** Query. **Pays $150-300.**

$ $ PADDLE DEALER

The Trade Magazine for Paddlesports, Paddlesport Publishing, Inc., P.O. Box 775450, Steamboat Springs CO 80477. (970)879-1450. Fax: (970)870-1404. E-mail: jeff@paddlermagazine.com. Web site: www.paddlermagazine.com. Editor: Eugene Buchanan. **Contact:** Jeff Moag, managing editor. **70% freelance written.** Quarterly magazine covering the canoeing, kayaking and rafting industry. Estab. 1993. Circ. 7,500. 1 month after publication. Publishes ms an average of 6 months after acceptance. Byline given. Buys first North American serial and one-time electronic rights. Editorial lead time 2 months. Submit seasonal material 6 months in advance. Accepts queries by mail, e-mail. Accepts simultaneous submissions. Responds in 3 months to queries. Sample copy for 8½×11 SAE and $1.78. Writer's guidelines for #10 SASE.

Nonfiction New product, technical, business advice. **Buys 8 mss/year.** Query or send complete ms. Length: 2,300 words. **Pays 15-20¢/word.** Sometimes pays expenses of writers on assignment.

Photos State availability with submission. Reviews transparencies, hi-res digital images (300 dpi at 5×7). Buys one-time rights.

Columns/Departments Profiles, how-to, great ideas, computer corner. **Buys 12 mss/year.** Query or send complete ms. **Pays 10-20¢/word.**

$ $ POOL & SPA NEWS

Hanley-Wood, LLC, 6222 Wilshire Blvd., Los Angeles CA 90048. (323)801-4972. Fax: (323)801-4986. E-mail: etaylor@hanleywood.com. Web site: poolspanews.com. **Contact:** Erika Taylor, editor. **15% freelance written.** Semimonthly magazine covering the swimming pool and spa industry for builders, retail stores, and service firms. Estab. 1960. Circ. 16,300. Pays on publication. Publishes ms an average of 2 months after acceptance. Buys all rights. Accepts queries by mail, e-mail. Responds in 1 month to queries. Sample copy for $5 and 9×12 SAE and 11 first-class stamps.

Nonfiction Interview/profile, technical. Send résumé with published clips. Length: 500-2,000 words. **Pays $150-550.** Pays expenses of writers on assignment.

Reprints Send ms with rights for sale noted and information about when and where the material previously appeared. Payment varies.

Photos Payment varies.

Columns/Departments Payment varies.

The online magazine carries original content not found in the print edition. Contact: Margi Millunzi, online editor.

$ $ REFEREE

Referee Enterprises, Inc., P.O. Box 161, Franksville WI 53126. Fax: (262)632-5460. E-mail: submissions@referee.com. Web site: www.referee.com. **75% freelance written.** Monthly magazine covering sports officiating. "*Referee* is a magazine for and read by sports officials of all kinds with a focus on baseball, basketball, football, softball, and soccer officiating." Estab. 1976. Circ. 40,000. **Pays on acceptance.** Publishes ms an average of 6 months after acceptance. Byline given. Kill fee negotiable. Buys all rights. Editorial lead time 6 months. Accepts queries by mail, e-mail, fax. Responds in 2 weeks to queries; 1 month to mss. Sample copy for #10 SASE. Writer's guidelines online.

Nonfiction Book excerpts, essays, historical/nostalgic, how-to (sports officiating related), humor, interview/profile, opinion, photo feature, technical (as it relates to sports officiating). "We don't want to see articles with themes not relating to sport officiating. General sports articles, although of interest to us, will not be published." **Buys 40 mss/year.** Query with published clips. Length: 500-2,500 words. **Pays $100-400.** Sometimes pays expenses of writers on assignment.

Photos State availability with submission. Reviews contact sheets, negatives, transparencies, prints. Purchase of rights negotiable. Offers $35-40 per photo. Identification of subjects required.

Tips "Query first and be persistent. We may not like your idea but that doesn't mean we won't like your next one. Professionalism pays off."

N $ $ THE RINKSIDER

Independent Voice of the Industry, Target Publishing Co., Inc., 2470 E. Main St., Columbus OH 43209. (614)235-1022. Fax: (614)235-3584. E-mail: rinksider@rinksider.com. Web site: www.rinksider.com. **Contact:** Suzy Weinland, editor. **90% freelance written.** Bimonthly magazine of interest to owners/operators of roller skating facilities¢promotions, games, snack bars, roller hockey competitive programs, music, decor, features on new or successful skating centers, competitive amusements, etc. Estab. 1953. Circ. 1,600. Pays on publication. Publishes ms an average of 2 months after acceptance. Byline given. Offers 100% (unless poorly done) kill fee. Buys first, exclusive of competitive journals rights. Editorial lead time 1 month. Accepts queries by e-mail. Accepts previously published material. Accepts simultaneous submissions. Responds in 2 weeks to queries; 1 month to mss. Sample copy for $5. Writer's guidelines free.

Nonfiction Essays, historical/nostalgic, how-to, humor, inspirational, interview/profile, new product, personal experience, photo feature, travel. Does not want opinion pieces. Query with published clips. Length: 250-1,000 words. **Pays $75-200.**

Photos Send photos with submission. Reviews prints. Buys all rights. Offers no additional payment for photos accepted with ms.

Columns/Departments Finance; Roller Skating News; Marketing; Technology. **Buys 20 mss/year.** Query with published clips. **Pays $75-200.**

$ $ SKI AREA MANAGEMENT

Beardsley Publications, P.O. Box 644, Woodbury CT 06798. (203)263-0888. Fax: (203)266-0452. Web site: www.saminfo.com. **Contact:** Rick Kahl, editor. **85% freelance written.** Bimonthly magazine covering everything involving the management and development of ski resorts. "We are the publication of record for the North American ski industry. We report on new ideas, developments, marketing, and regulations with regard to ski and snowboard resorts. Everyone from the CEO to the lift operator of winter resorts reads our magazine to stay informed about the people and procedures that make ski areas successful." Estab. 1962. Circ. 4,500. Pays on publication. Byline given. Offers kill fee. Buys all rights. Editorial lead time 2 months. Submit seasonal material 3 months in advance. Accepts queries by mail, e-mail. Responds in 2 weeks to queries. Sample copy for 9×12 SAE with $3 postage or online. Writer's guidelines for #10 SASE.

Nonfiction Historical/nostalgic, how-to, interview/profile, new product, opinion, personal experience, technical. "We don't want anything that does not specifically pertain to resort operations, management, or financing." **Buys 25-40 mss/year.** Query. Length: 500-2,500 words. **Pays $50-400.**

Reprints Accepts previously published submissions.

Photos Send photos with submission. Reviews transparencies, prints. Buys one-time rights or all rights. Offers no additional payment for photos accepted with ms. Identification of subjects required.

Tips "Know what you are writing about. We are read by people dedicated to skiing and snowboarding and to making the resort experience the best possible for their customers. It is a trade publication read by professionals."

$ $ THOROUGHBRED TIMES

Thoroughbred Times Co., Inc., 2008 Mercer Rd., P.O. Box 8237, Lexington KY 40533. (859)260-9800. **Contact:** Tom Law, managing editor. **10% freelance written.** Weekly tabloid "written for professionals who breed and/or race thoroughbreds at tracks in the US. Articles must help owners and breeders understand racing to help them realize a profit.'' Estab. 1985. Circ. 20,000. Pays on publication. Publishes ms an average of 1 month after acceptance. Byline given. Offers 50% kill fee. Buys first publication rights. Submit seasonal material 2 months in advance. Responds in 2 weeks to mss. Sample copy not available.

Nonfiction Historical/nostalgic, interview/profile, technical. **Buys 52 mss/year.** Query. Length: 500-2,500 words. **Pays 10-20¢/word.** Sometimes pays expenses of writers on assignment.

Photos State availability with submission. Reviews prints. Buys one-time rights. Offers $50/photo. Identification of subjects required.

Columns/Departments Vet Topics; Business of Horses; Pedigree Profiles; Bloodstock Topics; Tax Matters; Viewpoints; Guest Commentary.

Tips ''We are looking for farm stories and profiles of owners, breeders, jockeys, and trainers.''

STONE, QUARRY & MINING

$ $ CANADIAN MINING JOURNAL

Business Information Group, 12 Concorde Place, Suite 800, Toronto ON M3C 4J2 Canada. (416)510-6742. Fax: (416)510-5138. E-mail: jwerniuk@canadianminingjournal.com. **Contact:** Jane Werniuk, editor. **5% freelance written.** Magazine covering mining and mineral exploration by Canadian companies. ''*Canadian Mining Journal* provides articles and information of practical use to those who work in the technical, administrative, and supervisory aspects of exploration, mining, and processing in the Canadian mineral exploration and mining industry.'' Estab. 1882. Circ. 10,000. Pays on publication. Publishes ms an average of 3 months after acceptance. Byline given. Buys one-time, electronic rights. Makes work-for-hire assignments. Submit seasonal material 3 months in advance. Accepts queries by mail, e-mail, fax, phone. Responds in 1 week to queries; 1 month to mss.

Nonfiction Opinion, technical, operation descriptions. **Buys 6 mss/year.** Query with published clips. Length: 500-1,400 words. **Pays $100-600.** Pays expenses of writers on assignment.

Photos State availability with submission. Reviews 4×6 prints or high-resolution files. Buys one-time rights. Negotiates payment individually. Captions, identification of subjects, credits required.

Columns/Departments Guest editorial (opinion on controversial subject related to mining industry), 600 words. **Buys 3 mss/year.** Query with published clips. **Pays $150.**

Tips ''I need articles about mine sites it would be expensive/difficult for me to reach. I also need to know the writer is competent to understand and describe the technology in an interesting way.''

$ COAL PEOPLE MAGAZINE

Al Skinner, Inc., Dept. WM, 629 Virginia St. W, P.O. Box 6247, Charleston WV 25362. (304)342-4129. Fax: (304)343-3124. Editor/Publisher: Al Skinner. **Contact:** Christina Karawan, president. **50% freelance written.** Monthly magazine. ''Most stories are about people or historical—either narrative or biographical on all levels of coal people, past and present—from coal execs down to grass roots miners. Most stories are upbeat—showing warmth of family or success from underground up!'' Estab. 1976. Circ. 11,000. Pays on publication. Publishes ms an average of 3 months after acceptance. Byline given. Buys first, second serial (reprint) rights, makes work-for-hire assignments. Submit seasonal material 2 months in advance. Responds in 3 months to mss. Sample copy for 9×12 SAE and 10 first-class stamps.

Nonfiction Book excerpts (and film if related to coal), historical/nostalgic (coal towns, people, lifestyles), humor (including anecdotes and cartoons), interview/profile (for coal personalities), personal experience (as relates to coal mining), photo feature (on old coal towns, people, past and present). Special issues: Calendar issue for more than 300 annual coal shows, association meetings, etc. (January); Surface Mining/Reclamation Award (July); Christmas in Coal Country (December). No poetry, fiction, or environmental attacks on the coal industry. **Buys 32 mss/year.** Query with published clips. Length: 5,000 words. **Pays $90 for assigned articles.**

Reprints Send tearsheet and information about when and where the material previously appeared. Pays 50% of amount paid for an original article.

Photos Send photos with submission. Reviews contact sheets, transparencies, 5×7 prints. Buys one-time reprint rights. Captions, identification of subjects required.

Columns/Departments Editorials—anything to do with current coal issues (nonpaid); Mine'ing Our Business (bull pen column—gossip—humorous anecdotes); Coal Show Coverage (freelance photojournalist coverage of any coal function across the US). **Buys 10 mss/year.** Query. **Pays $50.**

Fillers Anecdotes. Length: 300 words. **Pays $35.**

Tips ''We are looking for good feature articles on coal professionals, companies—past and present, color slides (for possible cover use), and b&w photos to complement stories. Writers wanted to take photos and do journalistic coverage on coal events across the country. Slant stories more toward people and less on historical. More faces and names than old town, company store photos. Include more quotes from people who lived these moments!'' The following geographical areas are covered: North America and overseas.

$ $ PIT & QUARRY

Advanstar Communications, 600 Superior Ave. E., Suite 1100, Cleveland OH 44114. (216)706-3725. Fax: (216)706-3710. E-mail: mkuhar@questex.com. Web site: www.pitandquarry.com. Managing Editor: Darren Constantino. **Contact:** Mark S. Kuhar, editor. **10-20% freelance written.** Monthly magazine covering nonmetallic minerals, mining, and crushed stone. Audience has ''knowledge of construction-related markets, mining, minerals processing, etc.'' Estab. 1916. Circ. 25,000. **Pays on acceptance.** Publishes ms an average of 6 months after acceptance. Byline given. Buys first North American serial rights. Editorial lead time 6 months. Accepts queries by mail, e-mail, fax, phone. Accepts simultaneous submissions. Responds in 1 month to queries; 4 months to mss. Sample copy for 9×12 SAE and 4 first-class stamps.

Nonfiction How-to, interview/profile, new product, technical. No humor or inspirational articles. **Buys 12-15 mss/year.** Query. Length: 1,000-1,500 words. **Pays $250-700 for assigned articles; $250-500 for unsolicited articles.** Pays writers with contributor copies or other premiums for simple news items, etc. Sometimes pays expenses of writers on assignment.

Photos State availability with submission. Buys one-time rights. Offers no additional payment for photos accepted with ms. Identification of subjects, model releases required.

Columns/Departments Brand New; Techwatch; E-business; Software Corner; Equipment Showcase. Length: 250-750 words. **Buys 5-6 mss/year.** Query. **Pays $250-300.**

The online magazine sometimes carries original content not found in the print edition.

Tips ''Be familiar with quarry operations (crushed stone or sand and gravel), as opposed to coal or metallic minerals mining. Know construction markets. We always need equipment-focused features on specific quarry operations.''

TOY, NOVELTY & HOBBY

N $ $ MODEL RETAILER

21027 Crossroads Circle, P.O. Box 1612, Waukesha WI 53187. (262)796-8776. Fax: (262)796-1383. E-mail: hmiller@modelretailer.com. Web site: www.modelretailer.com. Publisher: Kevin Keefe. Associate Editors: Jim Faber, Andy Lilienthal. **Contact:** Hal Miller, editor. **5% freelance written.** Monthly magazine. ''*Model Retailer* covers the business of hobbies, from financial and shop management issues to industry trends and the latest product releases. Our goal is to provide hobby shop entrepreneurs with the tools and information they need to be successful retailers.'' Estab. 1987. Circ. 6,000. **Pays on acceptance.** Publishes ms an average of 3 months after acceptance. Byline given. Buys one-time, electronic rights. Editorial lead time 3 months. Submit seasonal material 6 months in advance. Accepts queries by mail, e-mail, fax. Sample copy and writer's guidelines free. Writer's guidelines online.

Nonfiction How-to (business), new product. ''No articles that do not have a strong hobby or small retail component.'' **Buys 2-3 mss/year.** Query with published clips. Length: 750-1,500 words. **Pays $250-500 for assigned articles; $100-250 for unsolicited articles.** Sometimes pays expenses of writers on assignment.

Photos State availability with submission. Reviews 4×6 prints. Buys one-time rights. Negotiates payment individually. Captions, identification of subjects required.

Columns/Departments Shop Management; Sales Marketing; Technology Advice; Industry Trends, all 500-750 words. **Buys 2-3 mss/year.** Query with published clips. **Pays $100-200.**

PEN WORLD

World Publications, Inc., 3946 Glade Valley Dr., Kingwood TX 77339-2059. (281)359-4363. Fax: (281)359-5748. E-mail: editor@penworld.com. Web site: www.penworld.com. Editor: Marie Picon. Magazine published 6 times/year. Published for writing instrument enthusiasts. Circ. 30,000.

TRANSPORTATION

$ $ METRO MAGAZINE

Bobit Publishing Co., 3520 Challenger St., Torrance CA 90503. (310)533-2400. Fax: (310)533-2502. E-mail: joseph.campbell@bobit.com. Web site: www.metro-magazine.com. Editor: Steve Hirano. **Contact:** Joseph Campbell, managing editor. **10% freelance written.** Magazine published 10 times/year covering transit bus, passenger rail, and motorcoach operations. ''*Metro Magazine* delivers business, government policy, and technology developments that are *industry specific* to public transportation.'' Estab. 1904. Circ. 20,500. **Pays on accep-**

tance. Publishes ms an average of 2 months after acceptance. Byline given. Offers 10% kill fee. Buys all rights. Editorial lead time 3 months. Submit seasonal material 3 months in advance. Accepts queries by e-mail. Responds in 2 weeks to queries; 1 month to mss. Sample copy for $8. Writer's guidelines by e-mail.

Nonfiction How-to, interview/profile (of industry figures), new product (related to transit—bus and rail—private bus), technical. **Buys 6-10 mss/year.** Query. Length: 400-1,500 words. **Pays $80-400.**

Photos State availability with submission. Buys all rights. Negotiates payment individually. Captions, identification of subjects, model releases required.

Columns/Departments Query. **Pays 20¢/word.**

$ $ SCHOOL BUS FLEET

Bobit Business Media, 3520 Challenger St., Torrance CA 90503. (310)533-2400. Fax: (310)533-2512. E-mail: sbf@bobit.com. Web site: www.schoolbusfleet.com. **Contact:** Steve Hirano, editor. **10% freelance written.** Magazine covering school transportation of K-12 population. "Most of our readers are school bus operators, public and private." Estab. 1956. Circ. 24,000. **Pays on acceptance.** Publishes ms an average of 3 months after acceptance. Byline given. Offers 25% kill fee or $50. Buys first North American serial rights. Editorial lead time 3 months. Submit seasonal material 3 months in advance. Accepts queries by mail, e-mail, fax. Responds in 1 month to queries. Sample copy for free. Writer's guidelines free.

Nonfiction Interview/profile, new product, technical. **Buys 6 mss/year.** Query with published clips. Length: 600-1,800 words. **Pays 20-25¢/word.** Sometimes pays expenses of writers on assignment.

Photos State availability with submission. Reviews transparencies, 4×6 prints, digital photos. Buys one-time rights. Negotiates payment individually. Captions, identification of subjects required.

Columns/Departments Shop Talk (maintenance information for school bus mechanics), 650 words. **Buys 2 mss/year.** Query with published clips. **Pays $100-150.**

Tips "Freelancers should submit ideas about innovations in school bus safety and operations."

TRAVEL

$ $ $ CRUISE INDUSTRY NEWS

Cruise Industry News, 441 Lexington Ave., Suite 809, New York NY 10017. (212)986-1025. Fax: (212)986-1033. E-mail: oivind@cruiseindustrynews.com. Web site: www.cruiseindustrynews.com. **Contact:** Oivind Mathisen, editor. **20% freelance written.** Quarterly magazine covering cruise shipping. "We write about the business of cruise shipping for the industry. That is, cruise lines, shipyards, financial analysts, etc." Estab. 1991. Circ. 10,000. Pays on acceptance or on publication. Publishes ms an average of 4 months after acceptance. Byline given. Offers 25% kill fee. Buys first rights. Editorial lead time 3 months. Accepts queries by mail. Reponse time varies to queries. Sample copy for $15. Writer's guidelines for #10 SASE.

Nonfiction Interview/profile, new product, photo feature, business. No travel stories. **Buys more than 20 mss/year.** Query with published clips. Length: 500-1,500 words. **Pays $500-1,000 for assigned articles.** Sometimes pays expenses of writers on assignment.

Photos State availability with submission. Buys one-time rights. Pays $25-50/photo.

$ $ LEISURE GROUP TRAVEL

Premier Tourism Marketing, 4901 Forest Ave., Downers Grove IL 60515. (630)964-1431. Fax: (630)852-0414. E-mail: johnk@premiertourismmarketing.com. Web site: www.premiertourismmarketing.com. **Contact:** John Kloster, editor-in-chief. **35% freelance written.** Bimonthly magazine covering group travel. We cover destinations and editorial relevant to the group travel market. Estab. 1994. Circ. 15,012. Pays on publication. Byline given. Buys first rights, including online publication rights. Editorial lead time 6 months. Submit seasonal material 6 months in advance. Accepts queries by mail, e-mail. Sample copy online.

Nonfiction Travel. **Buys 75 mss/year.** Query with published clips. Length: 1,200-3,000 words. **Pays $0-1,000.**

Tips "Experience in writing for 50+ travel marketplace a bonus."

N $ $ $ RV BUSINESS

TL Enterprises, Inc., 2575 Vista del Mar Dr., Ventura CA 93001. (805)667-4100. Fax: (805)667-4484. E-mail: bhampson@affinitygroup.com. Web site: www.rvbusiness.com. **Contact:** Bruce Hampson, editor. **50% freelance written.** Monthly magazine. "*RV Business* caters to a specific audience of people who manufacture, sell, market, insure, finance, service and supply, components for recreational vehicles." Estab. 1972. Circ. 21,000. **Pays on acceptance.** Publishes ms an average of 2 months after acceptance. Byline given. Offers kill fee. Buys first North American serial rights. Editorial lead time 3 months. Accepts queries by mail, e-mail. Sample copy for free.

Nonfiction New product, photo feature, industry news and features. "No general articles without specific

application to our market." **Buys 300 mss/year.** Query with published clips. Length: 125-2,200 words. **Pays $50-1,500.** Sometimes pays expenses of writers on assignment.
Columns/Departments Top of the News (RV industry news), 75-400 words; Business Profiles, 400-500 words; Features (indepth industry features), 800-2,000 words. **Buys 300 mss/year.** Query. **Pays $50-1,500.**
Tips "Query. Send 1 or several ideas and a few lines letting us know how you plan to treat it/them. We are always looking for good authors knowledgeable in the RV industry or related industries. We need more articles that are brief, factual, hard hitting, and business oriented. Review other publications in the field, including enthusiast magazines."

N $ $ SCHOOL TRANSPORTATION NEWS

STN Media Co., 700 Torrance Blvd., Suite C, Redondo Beach CA 90277. (310)792-2226. Fax: (310)792-2231. E-mail: info@stnonline.com. Web site: www.stnonline.com. Publisher: Bill Paul. **Contact:** Ryan Gray, senior editor. **20% freelance written.** Monthly magazine covering school bus and pupil transportation industries in North America. "Contributors to *School Transportation News* must have a basic understanding of K-12 education and automotive fleets and specifically of school buses. Articles cover such topics as manufacturing, operations, maintenance and routing software, GPS, security and legislative affairs. A familiarity with these principles is preferred. Additional industry information is availabe on our Web site. New writers must perform some research of the industry or exhibit core competencies in the subject matter." Estab. 1991. Circ. 22,824. Pays on publication. Byline given. Buys one-time rights. Editorial lead time 1-2 months. Submit seasonal material 2 months in advance. Accepts queries by e-mail. Accepts simultaneous submissions. Sample copy for free. Writer's guidelines free.
Nonfiction Book excerpts, general interest, historical/nostalgic, humor, inspirational, interview/profile, new product, personal experience, photo feature, technical. Does not want strictly localized editorial. "We want articles that put into perspective the issues of the day." Query with published clips. Length: 600-1,200 words. **Pays $150-300.** Sometimes pays expenses of writers on assignment.
Photos Contact Vince Rios, art director. Reviews GIF/JPEG files. Buys all rights. Offers $150-200/photo. Captions, model releases required.
Columns/Departments Back of the Bus (nontraditional side of school bus industry); Book/Video Reviews (new programs/publications/training for pupil transporters), both 600 words. **Buys 40 mss/year.** Query with published clips. **Pays $150.**
Tips "Potential freelancers should exhibit a basic proficiency in understanding school bus issues and demonstrate the ability to report on education, legislative and business affairs, as well as a talent with feature writing. It would be helpful if the writer has previous contacts within the industry. Article pitches should be e-mailed only."

$ $ SPECIALTY TRAVEL INDEX

Alpine Hansen, P.O. Box 458, San Anselmo CA 94979. (415)455-1643. Fax: (415)455-1648. E-mail: info@specialtytravel.com. Web site: www.specialtytravel.com. **90% freelance written.** Semiannual magazine covering adventure and special interest travel. Estab. 1980. Circ. 35,000. Pays on receipt and acceptance of all materials. Byline given. Buys one-time rights. Editorial lead time 3 month. Submit seasonal material 3 months in advance. Accepts queries by mail, e-mail. Writer's guidelines on request.
Nonfiction How-to, personal experience, photo feature, travel. **Buys 15 mss/year.** Query. Length: 1,250 words. **Pays $300 minimum.**
Reprints Send tearsheet. Pays 100% of amount paid for an original article.
Photos State availability with submission. Reviews EPS/TIFF files. Negotiates payment individually. Captions, identification of subjects required.
Tips "Write about group travel and be both creative and factual. The articles should relate to both the travel agent booking the tour and the client who is traveling."

N TRAVEL AGENT MAGAZINE

Questex Media, 1 Park Ave., 2nd Floor, New York NY 10016. (917)326-6196. E-mail: omcdonald@advanstar.com. Web site: www.travelagentcentral.com/travelagentcentral. Editor: Owen McDonald. Weekly magazine serving travel agents.
Nonfiction General interest, interview/profile, travel. Query.

N $ $ TRAVEL TIPS

Premier Tourism Marketing, 4901 Forest Ave., Downers Grove IL 60515. (630)964-1431. Fax: (630)852-0414. E-mail: johnk@premiertourismmarketing.com. Web site: www.premiertourismmarketing.com. **Contact:** John Kloster, editor-in-chief. **75% freelance written.** Bimonthly magazine covering group travel. "We cover destinations and editorial relevant to the group travel market." Estab. 1994. Circ. 12,500. Pays on publication. Byline

given. Buys first, electronic rights. Editorial lead time 6 months. Submit seasonal material 6 months in advance. Accepts queries by mail, e-mail. Sample copy online.
Nonfiction Travel. **Buys 36-50 mss/year.** Query with published clips. Length: 1,200-3,000 words. **Pays $0-500.**
Tips "Experience in writing for 50+ travel marketplace a bonus."

VETERINARY

$ $ VETERINARY ECONOMICS

Business Solutions for Practicing Veterinarians, Advanstar Veterinary Healthcare Communications, 8033 Flint, Lenexa KS 66214. (913)492-4300. Fax: (913)492-4157. E-mail: ve@advanstar.com. Web site: www.vetecon.com. **20% freelance written.** Monthly magazine covering veterinary practice management. "We address the business concerns and management needs of practicing veterinarians." Estab. 1960. Circ. 54,000. Pays on publication. Publishes ms an average of 6 months after acceptance. Byline given. Buys all rights. Editorial lead time 3 months. Submit seasonal material 3 months in advance. Accepts queries by mail, e-mail, fax. Accepts simultaneous submissions. Responds in 3 months to queries. Sample copy for free. Writer's guidelines online.
Nonfiction How-to, interview/profile, personal experience. **Buys 24 mss/year.** Query with or without published clips or send complete ms. Length: 1,000-2,000 words. **Pays $50-400.**
Photos Send photos with submission. Reviews transparencies, prints. Buys one-time rights. Offers no additional payment for photos accepted with ms. Captions, identification of subjects required.
Columns/Departments Practice Tips (easy, unique business tips), 200-300 words. Send complete ms. **Pays $40.**
Tips "Among the topics we cover: veterinary hospital design, client relations, contractual and legal matters, investments, day-to-day management, marketing, personal finances, practice finances, personnel, collections, and taxes. We also cover news and issues within the veterinary profession; for example, articles might cover the effectiveness of Yellow Pages advertising, the growing number of women veterinarians, restrictive-covenant cases, and so on. Freelance writers are encouraged to submit proposals or outlines for articles on these topics. Most articles involve interviews with a nationwide sampling of veterinarians; we will provide the names and phone numbers if necessary. We accept only a small number of unsolicited manuscripts each year; however, we do assign many articles to freelance writers. All material submitted by first-time contributors is read on speculation, and the review process usually takes 12-16 weeks. Our style is concise yet conversational, and all manuscripts go through a fairly rigorous editing process. We encourage writers to provide specific examples to illustrate points made throughout their articles."

MARKETS

Newspapers

Over the past several years, newspapers have struggled, but it would be foolish to think they're dead or dying. There are still thousands of dailies and weeklies covering city and regional beats across the country. And while most newspapers have been forced to consolidate efforts and cut staff to remain competitive, they also still need to provide newsworthy content to fill pages, which opens the door of opportunity for freelancers.

Staff writers will continue to handle the obvious stories of national, regional and local importance, but a freelancer can make sales by searching out those stories of real interest that are not as obvious, as well as the stories that take special connections or a certain sensitivity to write. Your uniqueness as a freelancer is something you should communicate in your query letter. (For more information on query letters, read "Query Letter Clinic," on page 20.)

Listings

We selected the 50 highest circulation newspapers from the WritersMarket.com database, which lists more than 400 newspapers. As a result of these being the highest circulation newspapers, the information they freely share with freelancers is scarce. While it is always advised that you query before submitting to a newspaper, that rule holds especially true for the higher circulation papers.

In addition, most newspapers have several departments with a specific editor handling all the material within each. It is important that you take the extra step to find out who the current contact is for the department you wish to submit your query. While it can seem like a lot of legwork, that is exactly the kind of professionalism that will be required if you expect to successfully freelance for newspapers.

For more information

To find out more on the relationship between freelancers and newspapers, including the best ways to break in and work with editors, read "Freelance Newspaper Writing 101" on page 13.

AKRON BEACON JOURNAL
Knight Ridder, P.O. Box 640, Akron OH 44309. (330)996-3000. Fax: (330)376-9235. Web site: www.ohio.com/mld/beaconjournal. Estab. 1839. Circ. 141,000. Daily.

- Mostly staff written.

ALBANY TIMES UNION
Capital Newspapers, P.O. Box 15000, Albany NY 12212-5000. (518)454-5420. Fax: (518)454-5628. Web site: www.timesunion.com. Circ. 101,290. Daily.

- Query before submitting. Mostly staff written.

ARIZONA DAILY STAR
Pulitzer Newspapers, P.O. Box 26807, Tucson AZ 85726-6807. (520)573-4220. Fax: (520)573-4141. E-mail: letters@azstarnet.com. Web site: www.azstarnet.com. Circ. 100,000. Daily.

- Query before submitting. Mostly staff written.

ATLANTA JOURNAL-CONSTITUTION
Cox Newspapers, Inc., P.O. Box 4689, Atlanta GA 30302. (404)526-5151. Fax: (404)526-5610. Web site: www.ajc.com. Circ. 405,000. Daily.

- Mostly staff written.

THE BLADE
The Toledo Blade Company, 541 N. Superior St., Toledo OH 43660. (419)724-6000. Fax: (419)724-6439. Web site: www.toledoblade.com. Estab. 1835. Circ. 138,000. Daily.

- Mostly staff written. Query first.

CHATTANOOGA TIMES FREE PRESS
Chattanooga Publishing Company, Inc., 400 E. 11th St., Chattanooga TN 37403. (423)756-6900. Fax: (423)757-6383. Web site: www.timesfreepress.com. Circ. 77,065. Daily.

- Mostly staff written.

CHICAGO SUN-TIMES
Sun-Times Media Group, Inc., 350 N. Orleans, Chicago IL 60654. (312)321-3000. Fax: (312)321-3084. Web site: www.suntimes.com. Circ. 450,000. Daily.

- Mostly staff written, but accepts freelance queries by mail.

CHICAGO TRIBUNE
Tribune Co., 435 N. Michigan Ave., Chicago IL 60611. (312)222-3232. Fax: (312)222-2550. Web site: www.chicagotribune.com. Estab. 1847. Circ. 689,000. Daily.

- Mostly staff written.

THE CINCINNATI ENQUIRER
Gannett Newspapers, 312 Elm St., Cincinnati OH 45202. (513)768-8000. Fax: (513)768-8340. Web site: www.enquirer.com. Circ. 191,000. Daily.

- Mostly staff written.

THE CLARION-LEDGER
Gannett Newspapers, P.O. Box 40, Jackson MS 39205-0040. (601)961-7230. Fax: (601)961-7211. Web site: www.clarionledger.com. Circ. 94,600. Daily.

- Query before submitting. Mostly staff written.

THE COLORADO SPRINGS GAZETTE
Freedom Communications, Inc., 30 S. Prospect St., Colorado Springs CO 80903. Fax: (719)632-5511. Web site: www.gazette.com. Circ. 95,220. Daily.

- Query before submitting. Mostly staff written.

THE COLUMBUS DISPATCH
The Dispatch Printing Co., 34 S. 3rd St., Columbus OH 43215. (614)461-5000. Fax: (614)461-7580. Web site: www.dispatch.com. Circ. 261,000. Daily.

- Mostly staff written.

THE COMMERCIAL APPEAL

E.W. Scripps Co., 495 Union Ave., Memphis TN 38103. (901)529-2345. Fax: (901)529-2522. Web site: www.commercialappeal.com. Estab. 1841. Circ. 161,000. Daily.

- Mostly staff written.

THE COURIER-JOURNAL

Gannett Newspapers, P.O. Box 740031, Louisville KY 40201. (502)582-4011. Fax: (502)582-4200. Web site: www.courier-journal.com. Estab. 1868. Circ. 223,000. Daily.

- Mostly staff written.

DAILY PRESS

Tribune Company, P.O. Box 746, 7505 Warwick Blvd., Newport News VA 23607. (757)247-4730. Fax: (757)245-8618. Web site: www.dailypress.com. Circ. 91,780. Daily.

- Query before submitting. Mostly staff written.

DAYTON DAILY NEWS

Cox Newspapers, Inc., P.O. Box 1287, Dayton OH 45401. (937)222-5700. Fax: (937)225-2088. Web site: www.daytondailynews.com. Estab. 1898. Circ. 134,000. Daily.

- Mostly staff written.

FLINT JOURNAL

Newhouse Newspapers, 200 E. 1st St., Flint MI 48502-1925. (810)766-6100. Fax: (810)767-7518. Web site: www.mlive.com/flintjournal/. Circ. 84,897. Daily.

- Mostly staff written.

FLORIDA TODAY

Gannett Newspapers, P.O. Box 419000, Melbourne FL 39241-9000. (321)242-3620. Fax: (321)242-6620. Web site: www.floridatoday.com. Estab. 1966. Circ. 90,870. Daily.

- Query before submitting. Mostly staff written.

THE GREENVILLE NEWS

Gannett Newspapers, P.O. Box 1688, Greeville SC 29602-1688. (864)298-4100. Fax: (864)298-4395. Web site: www.greenvilleonline.com. Estab. 1874. Circ. 87,622. Daily.

- Mostly staff written. Direct story ideas to the appropriate section editor (e-mail addresses provided on website).

THE HARTFORD COURANT

Tribune Co., 285 Broad St., Hartford CT 06115. (860)241-6200. Fax: (860)241-3865. Web site: www.ctnow.com. Circ. 190,000. Daily.

- Mostly staff written. Submit story ideas to the appropriate section editor (e-mail addresses provided on website).

LAS VEGAS REVIEW-JOURNAL

Stephens Media Group, P.O. Box 70, Las Vegas NV 89125. (702)383-0211. Fax: (702)383-4676. Web site: www.lvrj.com. Estab. 1905. Circ. 170,000. Daily.

- Mostly staff written.

LEXINGTON HERALD-LEADER

Knight Ridder, 100 Midland Ave., Lexington KY 40508. (859)231-3100. Fax: (859)231-1659. Web site: www.kentucky.com. Circ. 113,000. Daily.

- Mostly staff written.

LONG BEACH PRESS-TELEGRAM

MediaNews Group, 300 Oceangate, Long Beach CA 90844. (562)435-1161. Fax: (562)437-7892. Web site: www.presstelegram.com. Circ. 100,000. Daily.

- Query before submitting. Mostly staff written.

METRO NEW YORK

Metro International, 44 Wall St., New York NY 10005-2401. (212)952-1500. Fax: (212)952-1242. E-mail: letters@metro.us. Web site: www.metro.us. Circ. 300,000. Daily.

- Query before submitting. Mostly staff written.

MILWAUKEE JOURNAL SENTINEL

Journal Communications, P.O. Box 661, Milwaukee WI 53201. (414)224-2413. Fax: (414)224-2047. Web site: www.jsonline.com. Estab. 1837. Circ. 257,000. Daily.

- Mostly staff written.

NEW HAVEN REGISTER

Journal Register Company, 40 Sargent Dr., New Haven CT 06511. (203)789-5650. Fax: (203)865-7894. Web site: www.nhregister.com. Circ. 91,480. Daily.

- Query before submitting. Mostly staff written.

NEW YORK POST

News America Publishing, Inc., 1211 Avenue of the Americas, New York NY 10036. (212)930-8000. Fax: (212)930-8540. Web site: www.nypost.com. Circ. 620,000. Daily.

- Mostly staff written.

THE NEWS & OBSERVER

McClatchy Newspapers, P.O. Box 191, Raleigh NC 27602. (919)829-4500. Fax: (919)829-4529. Web site: www.newsobserver.com. Estab. 1865. Circ. 169,000. Daily.

- Mostly staff written.

THE NEWS JOURNAL

Gannett Newspapers, P.O. Box 15505, Wilmington DE 19850. (302)324-2500. Fax: (302)324-2595. Web site: www.delawareonline.com. Circ. 119,000. Daily.

- Mostly staff written.

THE NEWS TRIBUNE

McClatchy Newspapers, P.O. Box 11000, Tacoma WA 98411. (253)597-8742. Fax: (253)597-8274. Web site: www.tribnet.com. Estab. 1880. Circ. 130,000. Daily.

- Mostly staff written.

NEWS-PRESS (FORTH MYERS)

Gannett Newspapers, 2442 Dr. MLK Jr. Blvd., Fort Myers FL 33901. (239)335-0200. Fax: (239)334-0708. Web site: www.news-press.com. Circ. 79,766. Daily.

- Mostly staff written.

THE OKLAHOMAN

Oklahoma Publishing Co., P.O. Box 25125, Oklahoma City OK 73125. (405)478-7171. Fax: (405)475-3970. Web site: www.newsok.com. Circ. 222,000. Daily.

- Mostly staff written; submit story ideas through the website.

OMAHA WORLD-HERALD

MediaNews Group, World-Herald Square, Omaha NE 68102. (402)444-1000. Fax: (402)345-0183. Web site: www.omaha.com. Estab. 1885. Circ. 200,000. Daily.

- Mostly staff written.

ORLANDO SENTINEL

Tribune Co., 633 N. Orange Ave., Orlando FL 32801. (407)420-5000. Fax: (407)420-5350. Web site: www.orlandosentinel.com. Circ. 266,000. Daily.

- Mostly staff written.

PORTLAND PRESS HERALD

Blethen Maine Newspapers, P.O. Box 1460, Portland ME 04104-5009. (207)791-6650. Fax: (207)791-6920. Web site: www.mainetoday.com. Circ. 77,487. Daily.

- Mostly staff written.

⊘ THE POST AND COURIER
Evening Post Publishing Co., 134 Columbus St., Charleston SC 29403. (843)577-7111. Fax: (843)937-5579. Web site: www.charleston.net. Estab. 1803. Circ. 118,000. Daily.

- Mostly staff written.

⊘ THE PRESS OF ATLANTIC CITY
Abarta, Inc., 11 Devins Lane, Pleasantville NJ 08232. (609)272-7000. Fax: (609)272-7224. Web site: www.pressofatlanticcity.com. Estab. 1895. Circ. 76,645. Daily.

- Mostly staff written.

⊘ QUICK
A.H. Belo Corporation, 508 Young St., Dallas TX 75202-4893. (214)977-7888. Fax: (214)977-8319. Web site: www.quickdfw.com. Circ. 150,000. Daily.

- Query before submitting. Mostly staff written.

⊘ THE ROANOKE TIMES
Landmark Communications, Inc., P.O. Box 2491, Roanoke VA 24010-2491. (540)981-3341. Fax: (540)981-3346. Web site: www.roanoketimes.com. Circ. 100,440. Daily.

- Query before submitting. Mostly staff written.

⊘ SACRAMENTO BEE
McClatchy Newspapers, P.O. Box 15779, Sacramento CA 95816. (916)321-1000. Fax: (916)321-1109. Web site: www.sacbee.com. Estab. 1857. Circ. 300,000. Daily.

- Mostly staff written.

⊘ THE SALT LAKE TRIBUNE
MediaNews Group, 90 S. 400 West, Suite 700, Salt Lake City UT 84101. (801)257-8742. Fax: (801)257-8525. Web site: www.sltrib.com. Circ. 135,730. Daily.

- Query before submitting. Mostly staff written.

⊘ SANTA ROSA PRESS DEMOCRAT
The New York Times Company, P.O. Box 569, Santa Rosa CA 95402-0910. (707)546-2020. Fax: (707)521-5330. Web site: www.pressdemocrat.com. Circ. 88,722. Daily.

- Mostly staff written.

⊘ THE TIMES (MUNSTER)
Lee Enterprises, Inc., 601 W. 45th Ave., Munster IN 46321-2819. (219)933-3200. Fax: (219)933-3307. Web site: www.nwitimes.com. Circ. 86,474. Daily.

- Mostly staff written.

⊘ TIMES HERALD RECORD (MIDDLETOWN)
Ottaway Newspapers, P.O. Box 2046, 40 Mulberry St., Middletown NY 10940. (845)341-1100. Fax: (845)343-2170. Web site: www.recordonline.com. Estab. 1851. Circ. 82,130. Daily.

- Mostly staff written.

⊘ THE TRIBUNE (FORT PIERCE)
E.W. Scripps Co., 600 Edwards Rd., Fort Pierce FL 34982. (772)461-2050. Fax: (772)464-4447. Web site: www.tcpalm.com. Circ. 107,122. Daily.

- Mostly staff written. Submit story ideas through website.

⊘ TUCSON CITIZEN
Gannett Newspapers, P.O. Box 26767, Tucson AZ 85726-6767. (520)573-4561. Fax: (520)573-4569. Web site: www.tucsoncitizen.com. Circ. 100,000. Daily.

- Query before submitting. Mostly staff written.

⊘ THE VIRGINIAN-PILOT

Landmark Communications, Inc., P.O. Box 449, Norfolk VA 23501. (757)446-2000. Fax: (757)446-2414. Web site: www.pilotonline.com. Circ. 201,000. Daily.

- Mostly staff written.

⊘ THE WASHINGTON TIMES

The Washington Times, Inc., 3600 New York Ave. NE, Washington DC 20002-1947. (202)636-3000. Fax: (202)636-8906. Web site: www.washtimes.com. Circ. 102,255. Daily.

- Query before submitting. Mostly staff written.

⊘ THE WICHITA EAGLE

Knight Ridder, 825 E. Douglas, Wichita KS 67201-0820. (316)268-6000. Fax: (316)268-6627. Web site: www.wichitaeagle.com. Circ. 87,366. Daily.

- Mostly staff written.

⊘ WISCONSIN STATE JOURNAL

Capital Newspapers, P.O. Box 8056, Madison WI 53708-8056. (608)252-6100. Fax: (608)252-6119. Web site: www.wisconsinstatejournal.com. Circ. 89,000. Daily.

- Query before submitting. Mostly staff written.

MARKETS

Screenwriting

Writers do not often get into screenwriting for the fame. Most of the glory shines on the directors, actors and actresses. But every great movie and TV show relies upon a great script that was crafted by a screenwriter. And though there may not be much in the way of fame, successful screenwriters do tend to bring in a healthy income. In fact, ''How Much Should I Charge?'' on page 64 states that screenwriters make anywhere from $56,500 to $106,070 for an original screenplay.

Writing for TV

To break into TV you must have spec scripts—work written for free that serves as a calling card and gets you in the door. A spec script showcases your writing abilities and gets your name in front of influential people. Whether a network has invited you in to pitch some ideas, or a movie producer has contacted you to write a first draft for a feature film, the quality of writing in your spec script got their attention and that may get you the job.

It's a good idea to have several spec scripts, perhaps one each for three of the top five shows in the format you prefer to work, whether it's sitcom (half-hour comedies), episodic (one-hour series), or movie of the week (two-hour dramatic movies). For TV and cable movies, you should have completed original scripts (not sequels to existing movies) and you might also have a few for episodic TV shows.

In choosing the shows you write spec scripts for, you must remember one thing: Don't write a script for a show you want to work on. If you want to write for *CSI*, for example, you'll send a *Cold Case* script and vice versa. It may seem contradictory, but it's standard practice. It reduces the chances of lawsuits, and writers and producers can feel very proprietary about their shows and their stories. They may not be objective enough to fairly evaluate your writing. In submitting another similar type of show you'll avoid these problems while demonstrating comparable skills.

Writing for the movies

An original movie script contains characters you have created, with story lines you design, allowing you more freedom than you have in TV. However, your writing must still convey believable dialogue and realistic characters, with a plausible plot and high-quality writing carried through roughly 120 pages.

Many novice screenwriters tend to write too many visual cues and camera directions into their scripts. Your goal should be to write something readable, like a ''compressed novella.'' Write succinct resonant scenes and leave the camera technique to the director and producer.

ALLIANCE FILMWORKS

9595 Wilshire Blvd., Suite 900, Beverly Hills CA 90212. Web site: www.alliancefilmworks.com. Estab. 2001. Produces 3 movies/year. *Alliance is not accepting unsolicited TV or film submissions, screenplays, pitches, log lines or treatments at this time.* **Pays option; makes outright purchase.**

Produces all genres. Budgets are $1.5 million plus.

ALLIED ARTISTS, INC.

9360 W. Flamingo Rd., Unit 110-189, Las Vegas NV 89147. (702)991-9011. E-mail: query@alliedartistsonline.com. Web site: www.alliedartistsonline.com. Estab. 1990. Produces material for broadcast and cable television, home video, and film. **Buys 3-5 script(s)/year. Works with 10-20 writer(s)/year.** Buys first or all rights. Accepts previously produced material. Submit synopsis, outline. Responds in 2 months to queries; 3 months to scripts. **Pays in accordance with WGA standards.**

Needs Films, videotapes, social issue TV specials (30-60 minutes), special-interest home video topics, positive values feature screenplays.

Tips "We are looking for positive, uplifting dramatic stories involving 'real people' situations. Future trend is for more reality-based programming, as well as interactive television programs for viewer participation. Send brief e-mail query only. Do not send scripts or additional material until requested. No phone pitches accepted."

AMERICAN WORLD PICTURES, INC.

16027 Ventura Blvd., Suite 320, Encino CA 91436. (818)380-9100. Fax: (818)380-0050. E-mail: clayton@americanworldpictures.com. Web site: www.americanworldpictures.com. **Contact:** Clayton Boen, acquisitions. **Buys 4 script(s)/year. Works with 5 writer(s)/year.** Buys all rights. Accepts previously produced material. Query. Responds in 2 months to queries; 3 months to scripts. **Pays only $15,000 for scripts. Do not contact if price is more than that.**

Needs feature-length films. Send DVD/VHS to the Acquisitions Department.

Tips "Use strong characters and strong dialogue."

BIG EVENT PICTURES

3940 Laurel Canyon Blvd., #1137, Studio City CA 91604. E-mail: bigevent1@bigeventpictures.com. **Contact:** Michael Cargile, president. Produces G, PG, and R-rated feature films for theaters, cable TV, and home video. Query by e-mail. Producers will respond if interested.

Needs All film genres.

Tips "Interesting query letters intrigue us—and tell us something about the writer. Query letter should include a short log line or pitch encapsulating what this story is about and should be no more than 1 page in length. We look for unique stories with strong characters and would like to see more action and science fiction submissions. We make movies that we would want to see. Producers are known for encouraging new/unproduced screenwriters and giving real consideration to their scripts."

SAM BLATE ASSOCIATES, LLC

10331 Watkins Mill Dr., Montgomery Village MD 20886-3950. (301)840-2248. Fax: (301)990-0707. E-mail: info@writephotopro.com. Web site: www.writephotopro.com. **Contact:** Sam Blate, CEO. Produces educational and multimedia for marine, fishing, boating, business, education, institutions and state and federal governments. **Works with 2 local writers/year on a per-project basis—it varies as to business conditions and demand.** Buys first rights when possible. Query with writing samples and SASE for return. Responds in 1 month to queries. **Payment depends on contact with client. Pays some expenses.**

Needs Scripts on technical, business, and outdoor subjects.

Tips "Writers must have a strong track record of technical and aesthetic excellence."

BRIGHTON COAST ENTERTAINMENT

Warner Center, 21550 Oxnard St., 3rd Floor, Woodland Hills CA 91367. (818)592-6379. Fax: (818)888-5219. E-mail: info@trihughes.com. Web site: www.trihughes.com. **Contact:** Faye, creative executive, Producer: Patrick Hughes. Estab. 2002. Produces 10 movies/year. Does not return submissions. Send query and synopsis, or submit complete ms. Mostly accepts agented submissions. Responds in 3 weeks to queries.

"We are looking to produce and develop feature-length screenplays, produced stage plays, well-developed pitches, and detailed treatments. Focus is on broad comedies, black comedies, socially smart comedies, family films (family adventure), ground-breaking abstract projects, and new writers/directors with an extremely unique and unparalleled point of view. Don't focus on budget, cast, or locations. The story is key to getting things done here."

Tips "We do not want to see talking-heads projects with no point in sight, projects that scream 'You've seen me before' or projects that try too hard to be different. Be yourself. Don't try to be different to get noticed. Never talk about budget and a star that's attached that pre-sold in Egypt for $100 million. We don't care. We care about a unique voice—a filmmaker willing to take risks. Scripts that push the limits without trying for shock value. We care about filmmakers here."

CPC ENTERTAINMENT

353 W. 57th St., #2227, New York NY 10019. (212)554-6447. E-mail: development@cpcentertainment.com. Web site: www.cpcentertainment.com. **Contact:** Peggy Chane, producer/director; Sylvie de la Riviere, vice president creative affairs. Feature and TV. **Buys 2 script(s)/year. Works with 3 writer(s)/year.** Buys all rights. Submit résumé, 1 sentence premise, and 3 sentence synopsis. Prefers e-mail queries. Responds in 2 weeks to queries; 3 months to scripts. **Makes outright purchase. Pays in accordance with WGA standards.**

LEE DANIELS ENTERTAINMENT

39 W. 131st St., Suite 2, New York NY. (646)548-0930. Fax: (646)548-9883. E-mail: info@leedanielsentertainment.com. Web site: www.leedanielsentertainment.com. **Contact:** Nova Smith, VP of development. "We work in all aspects of entertainment, including film, television, and theater." All nonagency scripts must be accompanied by a signed copy of our submission release form, which can be downloaded from our Web site. All scripts should be registered or copyrighted for your protection. All scripts should be in standard screenplay format. Include a synopsis, logline, and character breakdown (including lead and supporting roles). Do not send any extraneous materials.

Tips Lee Daniels produced *Monster's Ball, The Woodsman* and produced/directed *Shadowboxer*. He is the first African-American sole producer of an Academy Award winning film.

EDCON PUBLISHING GROUP

30 Montauk Blvd., Oakdale NY 11769-1399. (631)567-7227. Fax: (631)567-8745. E-mail: editor@edconpublishing.com. Web site: www.edconpublishing.com. **Contact:** Janice Cobas, editor. Estab. 1971. Produces supplementary materials for elementary-high school students, either on grade level or in remedial situations. **100% freelance written.** "All scripts/titles are by assignment only. Do not send manscripts." Employs video, CD, book, and personal computer media. Buys all rights. Writing samples kept on file unless return requested. Include return envelope and postage if return desired. Responds in 1 month to outline, 6 weeks on final scripts. **Pays $300 and up.**

Tips "Writers must be highly creative and disciplined. We are interested in high interest/low readability materials. Send writing samples, published or unpublished."

ENERGY ENTERTAINMENT

999 N. Doheny Dr., #711, Los Angeles CA 90069. (310)274-3440. Web site: www.energyentertainment.net. **Contact:** Brooklyn Weaver, owner/manager-producer. Estab. 2001. Submit query via Web site.

ENTERTAINMENT PRODUCTIONS, INC.

2118 Wilshire Blvd., #744, Santa Monica CA 90403. (310)456-3143. Fax: (310)456-8950. **Contact:** Mary Lee, story editor; Edward Coe, producer. Estab. 1971. Produces theatrical and television productions for worldwide distribution. Query with synopsis and a Writer Submission Release in any form. Responds to queries only if SASE is included. **Purchases rights by negotiations.**

Tips "Submit your 1 strongest writing."

FAST CARRIER PICTURES, INC.

820 Majorca Place, Los Angeles CA 90049. (213)300-1896. E-mail: steven@fastcarrier.com. Web site: www.fastcarrier.com. **Contact:** Steve Rubin, president. Estab. 2000. Mass market motion picture/TV audience. **Buys 1-2 script(s)/year. Works with 1-2 writer(s)/year.** No options or cash up front. No previously produced material. Query with synopsis. Responds to queries immediately; 1-2 months to scripts.

O─ "Our bread basket is cable, broadcast, and smaller theatrical films in the following genres: women in jeopardy, low-budget family movies tied to a holiday, low-budget westerns, horror, and romantic comedy." No teen sex comedies, large science fiction movies, historical epics, serial killer movies, or gross violence and humor at the expense of women, children, or minorities.

GINTY FILMS

16255 Ventura Blvd., Suite 625, Encino CA 91436. (310)277-1408. E-mail: rwginty@aol.com. Web site: www.robertginty.com. **Contact:** Cheri Williams, assistant. Estab. 1989. Commercial audience. **Buys 12-15 script(s)/year. Works with 10-20 writer(s)/year.** Buys first rights, all rights. Accepts previously produced material.

Query with synopsis, production history. Responds in 1 month to queries; 1 month to scripts. **Pays in accordance with WGA standards.**
Needs Films.

GREY LINE ENTERTAINMENT

115 W. California Blvd., #310, Pasadena CA 91105-3005. (626)943-0950. E-mail: submissions@greyline.net. Web site: www.greyline.net. **Contact:** Sara Miller, submissions coordinator. "Grey Line Entertainment is a full-service motion picture production and literary management company. We offer direct management of all services associated with the exploitation of stories. When our clients' motion picture screenplays are ready for the marketplace, we place them directly with studios or with major co-producers who can assist in packaging cast and/or director before approaching financiers (Warner Bros., New Line, Fox, Disney, etc.), or broadcasters (HBO, Showtime, etc.)." Query via e-mail only. No attachments. Review online submission gudielines before sending. Responds in 2 weeks to queries.

O→ Queries for screenplays and treatments should consist of a compelling and business-like letter giving us a brief overview of your story and a 1-sentence pitch. Be sure to include your return address and a phone number. No multiple submissions. Treatments and screenplays submitted without a completed and signed Grey Line submission form will be discarded. Include SASE for reply. "We recommend you register your screenplays/treatments with the copyright office or WGA before submitting."

Tips "Your work must be finished and properly edited before seeking our representation (meaning proofread, spell-checked, and rewritten until it's perfect)."

BETH GROSSBARD PRODUCTIONS

9696 Culver Blvd., Suite 208, Culver City CA 90232. (310)841-2555. Fax: (310)841-5934 or (818)705-7366. **Contact:** Jessica Roach, development executive; Beth Grossbard, executive producer. Estab. 1994. Buys first rights and true-life story rights. Query with synopsis, treatment/outline. Responds in 1 month to queries.
Tips "Company develops material for television and the feature film markets. Interested in women's stories/issues, compelling true stories, social issues, contemporary legal issues, literary material, including young adult, children's titles, and small press books. We are also interested in plays, short stories, and original ideas."

INTERNATIONAL HOME ENTERTAINMENT

1440 Veteran Ave., Suite 650, Los Angeles CA 90024. (323)663-6940. **Contact:** Jed Leland, Jr., assistant to the president. Estab. 1976. Buys first rights. Query. Responds in 2 months to queries. **Pays in accordance with WGA standards.**

O→ Looking for material that is international in scope.

Tips "Our response time is faster on average now (3-6 weeks), but no replies without a SASE. No unsolicited mss. We do not respond to unsolicited phone calls or e-mail."

ARNOLD LEIBOVIT ENTERTAINMENT

P.O. Box 33544, Santa Fe NM 87594-3544. E-mail: director@scifistation.com. Web site: www.scifistation.com. **Contact:** Barbara Schimpf, vice president, production; Arnold Leibovit, director/producer. Estab. 1988. Produces material for motion pictures and television. **Works with 1 writer(s)/year.** Query with log line and synopsis via e-mail. Do not send full script unless requested. A submission release must be included with all scripts. Responds in 2 months to queries. **Pays in accordance with WGA standards.**
Needs Films (35mm), videotapes. Does not want novels, plays, poems, treatments, or submissions on disk.

LEO FILMS

6249 Langdon Ave., Van Nuys CA 91411. (818)782-6541. Fax: (818)782-3320. E-mail: lustgar@pacbell.net. Web site: www.leofilms.com. **Contact:** Steve Lustgarten, president. Estab. 1989. Has released over 75 feature films. **Buys 5 script(s)/year. Works with 8 writer(s)/year.** Buys all rights. Query by e-mail with synopsis. Responds in 1 week to queries; 2 months to scripts. **Payment varies—options and sales.**
Tips "Will also consider novels, short stories, and treatments that have true movie potential."

MAINLINE RELEASING

A Film & TV Production and Distribution Co., 301 Arizona Ave., 4th Floor, Santa Monica CA 90401. (301)255-1200. Fax: (310)255-1201. E-mail: joe@mainlinereleasing.com. Web site: www.mainlinereleasing.com. **Contact:** Joseph Dickstein, vice president of acquisitions. Estab. 1997. Produces family films, drama, thrillers, and erotic features.

THE MARSHAK/ZACHARY CO.

8840 Wilshire Blvd., 1st Floor, Beverly Hills CA 90211. Fax: (310)358-3192. E-mail: marshakzachary@aol.com; alan@themzco.com. **Contact:** Alan W. Mills, associate. Estab. 1981. Audience is film goers of all ages and

television viewers. **Buys 3-5 script(s)/year. Works with 10 writer(s)/year.** Rights purchased vary. Query with synopsis. Responds in 2 weeks to queries; 3 months to scripts. **Payment varies.**
Tips "Submit logline (1-line description), a short synopsis of storyline, and a short biographical profile (focus on professional background). SASE required for all mailed inquiries. If submissions are sent via e-mail, subject must include specific information or else run the risk of being deleted as junk mail. All genres accepted, but ideas must be commercially viable, high concept, original, and marketable."

MONAREX HOLLYWOOD CORP.
11605 W. Pico Blvd., Suite 200, Los Angeles CA 90064. (310)478-6666. Fax: (310)478-6866. E-mail: monarexcorp @aol.com. **Contact:** Chris D. Nebe, president. Estab. 1978. All audiences. **Buys 3-4 script(s)/year. Works with 5-10 writer(s)/year.** Buys all rights. Query with synopsis. Responds in 1 month to queries. **Pays in accordance with WGA standards.**

NHO ENTERTAINMENT
11962 Darlington Ave., Los Angeles CA 90049. E-mail: mark.costa@nhoentertainment.com; ford.oelman@nhoentertainment.com. Web site: www.nhoentertainment.com. **Contact:** Mark Costa, partner. Estab. 1999. All audiences. **Buys 5 script(s)/year. Works with 10 writer(s)/year.** Buys all rights. Accepts previously produced material. Catalog for #10 SASE. Query with synopsis, résumé, writing samples, production history. Via e-mail. Responds in 1 month to queries. **Pays in accordance with WGA standards.**
Needs Films, videotapes, multimedia kits, tapes and cassettes.

NITE OWL PRODUCTIONS
126 Hall Rd., Aliquippa PA 15001. (724)775-1993. Fax: (801)881-3017. E-mail: niteowlprods@aol.com; mark@niteowlproductionsltd.com. Web site: www.niteowlproductionsltd.com. **Contact:** Bridget Petrella. Estab. 2001. Send a 1-page, single-spaced query letter via e-mail or mail.

O- "We will be producing at least 5-10 feature films in the next 2-5 years. We are searching for polished, well-structured, well-written, and professional-looking screenplays that are ready for production. If your screenplay does not meet these standards, do not send us a query. All screenplays must be in English and be in standard industry format. Provide a working title for your screenplay.

Tips "All submissions must include a dated and signed Submission Release Form or they will be discarded immediately. All full-length feature film screenplays must be 80-130 pages in length. One-hour TV spec scripts must be 55-65 pages in length. Do not send us computer disks. One hardcopy of your screenplay will suffice. Do not cheat on your margins—we will notice. Proofread your screenplay thoroughly before submitting to avoid typos and punctuation and grammar mistakes. Copyright your script with the US Copyright Office and register it with the WGA. All screenplays must be firmly bound and include a cover page with the title of the work and your name, address, and contact information. Your materials will not be returned."

POP/ART FILM FACTORY
23679 Calabasas Rd., Suite 686, Calabasas CA 91302. E-mail: dzpff@earthlink.net. Web site: popartfilmfactory.com. **Contact:** Daniel Zirilli, CEO/director. Estab. 1990. Produces material for all audiences/feature films. Query with synopsis. Will look at. **Pays on per project basis.**

O- "We also have domestic and international distribution, and are always looking for finished films. We're producing 3 feature films/year and 15-20 music-oriented projects. Also exercise and other special-interest videos."

Needs Films (35mm), multimedia kits, documentaries.
Tips "Send a query/pitch letter and let me know if you are willing to write on spec (for the first job only; you will be paid if the project is produced). Be original. Do not play it safe. If you don't receive a response from anyone you have ever sent your ideas to, or you continually get rejected, don't give up if you believe in yourself. Good luck and keep writing!"

PRODUCTION LOGISTICS, INC.
E-mail: productionlogistics@msn.com. **Contact:** L.G. Friedman, producer. Buys first rights. No previously produced material. Query with synopsis by e-mail only. **Payment is negotiated on a per picture/per development basis.**
Needs Films (35mm).
Tips "Keep inquiries short, succinct, and impactful."

THE PUPPETOON STUDIOS
P.O. Box 33544, Santa Fe NM 87594-3544. E-mail: director@scifistation.com. Web site: www.scifistation.com. **Contact:** Arnold Leibovit, director/producer. Estab. 1987. Wants plays geared toward a broad audience. **Works**

with 1 writer(s)/year. Query with logline and synopsis via e-mail. Do not send script unless requested. Submission release required with all scripts. Responds in 2 month to queries. **Pays in accordance with WGA standards.**
Needs Films (35mm). No novels, plays, poems, treatments, or submissions on disk.

RANDWELL PRODUCTIONS, INC.

185 Pier Ave., Suite 103, Santa Monica CA 90405. E-mail: randwellprods@yahoo.com. Web site: www.randwell.com. **Contact:** Christina Wanke, development. Estab. 1997. TV and features audience. **Buys 3-4 script(s)/year. Works with 2-3 writer(s)/year.** Buys all rights. Query with synopsis. Responds in 2 weeks to queries; 3 months to scripts. **Pays in accordance with WGA standards.**
Needs Films (35mm). No sci-fi, no westerns.
Tips "Please keep synopsis to no more than one page. We hardly if ever request a copy of unsolicited material so don't be surprised if we pass."

SHORELINE ENTERTAINMENT, INC.

1875 Century Park E., Suite 600, Los Angeles CA 90067. (310)551-2060. Fax: (310)201-0729. E-mail: info@shorelineentertainment.com. Web site: www.shorelineentertainment.com. Estab. 1993. Mass audience. **Buys 8 script(s)/year. Works with 8 writer(s)/year.** Buys all rights. Query. Responds in 1 week to queries.
Needs Films (35, 70mm).
Tips "Looking for character driven films that are commercial as well as independent. Completed screenplays only. Especially looking for big-budget action, thrillers. We accept submissions by mail, e-mail or fax. No unsolicited screenplays, please."

SILENT SOUND FILMS, LTD.

United Kingdom. E-mail: thj@silentsoundfilms.co.uk. Web site: www.silentsoundfilms.co.uk. **Contact:** Timothy Foster, MD. Estab. 1997. Stage and fiction movies only. No TV or publishing. No previously produced material. Query with synopsis. Responds in 2 weeks to queries; 1-2 months to scripts. **Writers paid in accordance with WGA standards or the UK 'pact' agreement, if British production.**

"We are interested in excellent writing (specifically musicals, art house, stage plays) with well-developed plot themes and original characters. So if you have a story that is nonparochial, we would be interested to see an e-mailed package that comprises: a 1-page synopsis, no more than 8 pages of scenario, and brief biography. Do not send images, complete screenplays, or large attachments. If it's something that grabs our attention, you will certainly hear from us."

Needs Films (35mm). Does not want "U.S.-based movies, nor storylines with principally American characters set anywhere else. Nothing personal, it's just that we are involved in what is unreliably called art house films and the best American art house films are made by Americans. So why compete?"
Tips "We seek material that may well include a good 'pitchable idea' but also one that goes a lot deeper. I suppose the filmic equivalent of literature as opposed to bestseller."

SPENCER PRODUCTIONS, INC.

P.O. Box 2247, Westport CT 06880. E-mail: spencerprods@yahoo.com. **Contact:** Bruce Spencer, general manager; Alan Abel, creative director. Produces material for high school students, college students and adults. Occasionally uses freelance writers with considerable talent. Query. Responds in 1 month to queries. **Payment negotiable.**
Needs Tapes and cassettes.
Tips "For a comprehensive view of our humor requirements, we suggest viewing our feature film production, *Is There Sex After Death* (Rated R), starring Buck Henry. It is available at video stores. Or read *Don't Get Mad . . . Get Even* and *How to Thrive on Rejection* by Alan Abel (published by W.W. Norton), both available from Barnes & Noble or Amazon." Also Books-on-Tape. "Send brief synopsis (one page) and outline (2-4 pages)."

TALCO PRODUCTIONS

279 E. 44th St., New York NY 10017-4354. (212)697-4015. Fax: (212)697-4827. **Contact:** Alan Lawrence, president; Marty Holberton, vice president. Estab. 1968. Produces variety of material for TV, radio, business, trade associations, nonprofit organizations, public relations (chiefly political and current events), etc. Audiences range from young children to senior citizens. **20-40% freelance written. Buys scripts from published/produced writers only.** Buys all rights. No previously produced material. Submit résumé, production history. Responds in 3 weeks to queries. **Makes outright purchase. Pays in accordance with WGA standards. Sometimes pays the expenses of writers on assignment.**
Needs Films, videotapes, CDs, DVDs.
Tips "We maintain a file of writers and call on those with experience in the same general category as the project in production. *We do not accept unsolicited manuscripts.* We prefer to receive a writer's résumé listing credits.

If his/her background merits, we will be in touch when a project seems right. We are doing more public relations-oriented work (print and DVD) and are concentrating on TV productions. Production budgets are tighter."

TOO NUTS PRODUCTIONS, L.P.

4200 Park Blvd., Suite 241, Oakland CA 94602. (310)967-4532. E-mail: toonutsproductions@yahoo.com. **Contact:** R. Scott and D. Simpson, co-executive producers. Estab. 1994. Produces illustrated kids books and books with CDs/cassettes, and half-hour video and educational TV with a twist. Storylines for the current TV and multimedia, audio books, and TV slate include: "Toad Pizza," "The Salivating Salamander," "The Contest-Ants," "The De-Stinkified Skunk," and "Sneeks Peaks." Audience is children, typically ages 5-11. Always looking for talented, new kidlit illustrators as well. **Buys 4-10 script(s)/year. Works with 4-6 writer(s)/year.** Buys both first and all rights. Query with creative but brief cover letter/e-mail, synopsis, résumé, 1-3 writing samples, production history. Illustrators query with creative but brief cover letter, 1 sample of work by e-mail or snail mail, hyperlink to your online portfolio. Responds in less than 3 months to queries; 6 months to scripts. **Pays royalty, makes outright purchase.**

Needs Videotapes, multimedia kits, tapes and cassettes, synopses, audio CDs, CD-ROMs.

Tips "Suggestion: Use the words 'Too Nuts' at least twice in your query. (Do the math.) If you don't know how to giggle all the way to the bank, you may want to try someone else. If you've already exorcised your inner child, lizard, monkey, etc., don't contact us either!"

TREASURE ENTERTAINMENT

468 N. Camden Dr., Suite 200, Beverly Hills CA 90210. (310)860-7490. Fax: (310)943-1488. E-mail: info@treasureentertainment.net. Web site: www.treasureentertainment.net. **Contact:** Mark Heidelberger, Treasure Entertainment co-chairman/chief executive officer. Estab. 2000. Management consideration given to writers with produced credits only. Intended audience is theatrical, festival, television, home video/DVD, Internet. **Buys 1-2 script(s)/year. Works with 8-10 writer(s)/year.** Accepts previously produced material. Does not return submissions unless SASE is included. No Catalog. Query. Responds in up to 6 months to queries; up to 6 months to scripts. **Pays 1-10% royalty, makes outright purchase $1-100,000.**

Needs Films (35 mm and 16mm), videotapes, multimedia kits.

Tips "We reserve the right to reject or return any unsolicited material. We also reserve the right not to purchase any material if we don't feel that any submissions are of sufficient merit. Our needs tend to change with the market and will vary from year to year. We are agreeing to look at writer's queries only. Queries should be sent by mail or e-mail only."

VALEO FILMS

P.O. Box 5876, Longview TX 75608. (903)797-6489. E-mail: screenplays@valeofilms.com. Web site: www.valeofilms.com. Query by e-mail or mail.

- Currently considering projects that contain 1 or more of the following: character or story driven, identifies moral values, romance/love story, educational/documentary, presents the human condition, strong visual imagery, coming of age/learning, or intellectual drama/mystery.

Tips "We require that you provide your name, phone number, address, title of your work, and WGA registration or copyright number. We will send and Unsolicited Project Release letter for you to sign and return with a sing copy of your screenplay/treatment. We don't want projects that contain the following characteristics: 1 character saves the world, SFX based, highly action based, extreme/grotesque violence, high sexual content, or strong explicit language. Although we do have a vast array of production resources available to us, we are a relatively small production copmany who prefers to limit the number of projects we have in production. Consequently, we tend to be very selective when it comes to choosing new material."

VANGUARD PRODUCTIONS

12111 Beatrice St., Culver City CA 90230. **Contact:** Terence M. O'Keefe, president. Estab. 1985. **Buys 1 script(s)/year.** Buys all rights. Accepts previously produced material. Query with synopsis, résumé. Responds in 3 months to queries; 6 months to scripts. **Pays in accordance with WGA standards. Negotiated option.**

Needs Films (35mm), videotapes.

YOUR HALF PICTURES, LLC

1752 Garfield Place, Hollywood CA 90028. Web site: www.yourhalf.com. **Contact:** Rusty Gray, development executive/producer. Estab. 1998. Intended audience is for those who see motion pictures. **Works with 5 writer(s)/year.** Buys all rights. Accepts previously produced material. Does not return submissions sent with SASE. No Catalog. Query with synopsis. Responds in 2 weeks to queries; 2 months to scripts. **Payment varies according to project.**

Needs Films (35 mm), videotapes.

MARKETS

Playwriting

Where TV and movies have a diminished role for writers in the collaboration that produces the final product, whether a show or a film, theater places a very high value on the playwright. This may have something to do with the role of the scripts in the different settings.

Screenplays are often in a constant state of ''in progress,'' where directors make changes; producers make changes; and even actors and actresses make changes throughout the filming of the TV show or movie. Plays, on the other hand, must be as solid as a rock, because the script must be performed live night after night.

As a result, playwrights tend to have more involvement in the productions of their scripts, a power screenwriters can only envy. Counterbalancing the greater freedom of expression are the physical limitations inherent in live performance: a single stage, smaller cast, limited sets and lighting, and, most importantly, a strict, smaller budget. These conditions not only affect what but also how you write.

Listings

The following listings include contact information, submission details, current needs, and other helpful tips to help you find a home for your finished and polished play. As with any market, it is advised that after you pinpoint a listing that you then follow up with them to find out their most current submission policy and to ask who you should address your submission. This might seem like a lot of work, but writing plays is a competitive business. Your professionalism will go a long way in separating you from other ''wanna-be'' playwrights.

For more information

To find out more about writing and submitting plays, contact the Dramatists Guild (www.dramaguild.com) and the Writers Guild of America (www.wga.org). Both organizations are great for networking and for learning the basics needed to build a successful career crafting plays.

ABINGDON THEATRE CO.

312 W. 36th St., 6th Floor, New York NY 10036. (212)868-2055. Fax: (212)868-2056. E-mail: mail@abingdontheatre.org. Web site: www.abingdontheatre.org. Artistic Director: Pamela Paul. Estab. 1993. **Produces 3 Mainstage and 3 Stage II plays/year.** Professional productions for a general audience. Submit full-length script in hard copy. No one-act. Responds in 4 months. Buys variable rights. **Payment is negotiated.** Include SASE for return of manuscript.

Needs All scripts should be suitable for small stages. No musicals where the story line is not very well-developed and the driving force of the piece.

ACT II PLAYHOUSE

P.O. Box 555, Ambler PA 19002. (215)654-0200. Fax: (215)654-9050. Web site: www.act2.org. **Contact:** Stephen Blumenthal, literary manager. Estab. 1998. **Produces 5 plays/year.** Query and synopsis. Responds in 1 month. **Payment negotiable.**

Needs Contemporary comedy, drama, musicals. Full length. 6 character limitation; 1 set or unit set. Does not want period pieces. Limited number of scenes per act.

ACTORS THEATRE OF LOUISVILLE

316 W. Main St., Louisville KY 40202-4218. (502)584-1265. Fax: (502)561-3300. E-mail: ahansel@actorstheatre.org. Web site: www.actorstheatre.org. **Contact:** Adrien-Alice Hansel, literary manager. Estab. 1964. **Produces approximately 30 new plays of varying lengths/year.** Professional productions are performed for subscription audience from diverse backgrounds. Agented submissions only for full-length plays. Open submissions to National Ten-Minute Play Contest (plays 10 pages or less) are due November 1. Responds in 9 months to submissions, mostly in the fall. Buys variable rights. **Offers variable royalty.**

Needs "We are interested in full-length, one-act and 10-minute plays and in plays of ideas, language, humor, experiment and passion."

ALLEYWAY THEATRE

1 Curtain Up Alley, Buffalo NY 14202. (716)852-2600. Fax: (716)852-2266. E-mail: newplays@alleyway.com. Web site: www.alleyway.com. **Contact:** Literary Manager. Estab. 1980. **Produces 4-5 full-length, 6-12 one-act plays/year.** Submit complete script; include CD for musicals. Responds in 6 months. Seeks first production rights. **Pays 7% royalty.**

- Alleyway Theatre also sponsors the Maxim Mazumdar New Play Competition. See the Contest & Awards section for more information.

Needs Wants works written uniquely for the theatre. Theatricality, breaking the fourth wall, and unusual settings are of particular interest. "We are less interested in plays which are likely to become TV or film scripts."

ALLIANCE THEATRE

1280 Peachtree St. NE, Atlanta GA 30309. (404)733-4650. Web site: www.alliancetheatre.org. **Contact:** Freddie Ashley, literary manager. Estab. 1969. **Produces 11 plays/year.** Professional production for local audience. Query with synopsis and sample or submit through agent. Enclose SASE. Responds in 9 months.

Needs Full-length scripts and scripts for young audiences no longer than 60 minutes.

Tips "As the premier theater of the southeast, the Alliance Theatre sets the highest artistic standards, creating the powerful experience of shared theater for diverse people. Please submit via snail mail."

⊘ AMERICAN CONSERVATORY THEATER

30 Grant Ave., 6th Floor, San Francisco CA 94108-5800. (415)834-3200. Web site: www.act-sf.org. Artistic Director: Carey Perloff. **Contact:** Johanna Pfaelzer, associate artistic director. Estab. 1965. **Produces 8 plays/year.** Plays are performed in Geary Theater, a 1,000-seat classic proscenium. No unsolicited scripts.

APPLE TREE THEATRE

1850 Green Bay Rd., Suite 100, Highland Park IL 60035. (847)432-8223. Fax: (847)432-5214. E-mail: info@appletreetheatre.com. Web site: www.appletreetheatre.com. Artistic Director: Eileen Boevers. **Contact:** Literary Assistant. Estab. 1983. **Produces 5 plays/year.** "Professional productions intended for an adult audience mix of subscriber base and single-ticket holders. Our subscriber base is extremely theater-savvy and intellectual." Submit query and synopsis, along with tapes for musicals. Rights obtained vary. **Pays variable royalty.** Return SASE submissions only if requested.

Needs "We produce a mixture of musicals, dramas, classical, contemporary, and comedies." Length: 90 minutes-2½ hours. Small space, unit set required. No fly space, 3¼ thrust stage. Maximum actors 15.

Tips "No farces or large-scale musicals. Theater needs small shows with 1-unit sets due to financial concerns.

Also note the desire for nonlinear pieces that break new ground. *Please do not submit unsolicited manuscripts—send letter and description*; if we want more, we will request it."

ARENA STAGE

1101 6th St. SW, Washington DC 20024. (202)554-9066. Fax: (202)488-4056. Web site: www.arenastage.org. Artistic Director: Molly Smith. **Contact:** Michelle Hall, literary manager. Estab. 1950. **Produces 8 plays/year.** The Kreeger Theater seats 514 (modified thrust stage). The Fichandler Stage seats 827 (arena stage). Only accepts scripts from writers with agent or theatrical representation.

Needs Plays about the diverse voices in America (racial, cultural, political). Plays that provoke thought about the individual and collective American consciousness (past, present, and future). Seeks only full-length plays and musicals in all genres.

ARIZONA THEATRE CO.

P.O. Box 1631, Tucson AZ 85702. (520)884-8210. Fax: (520)628-9129. E-mail: info@arizonatheatre.org. Web site: arizonatheatre.org. **Contact:** Literary Department. Estab. 1966. **Produces 6-8 plays/year.** Arizona Theatre Company is the State Theatre of Arizona and plans the season with the population of the state in mind. Only Arizona writers may submit unsolicited scripts, along with production history (if any), brief bio, and SASE. Out-of-state writers can send a synopsis, 10-page sample dialogue, production history (if any), brief bio, and SASE. Responds in 4-6 months. **Payment negotiated.**

Needs Full length plays of a variety of genres and topics and full length musicals. No one-acts.

Tips "Please include in the cover letter a bit about your current situation and goals. It helps in responding to plays."

ARTISTS REPERTORY THEATRE

1516 S.W. Alder St., Portland OR 97205. Web site: www.artistsrep.org. Estab. 1982. **Produces.** Plays performed in professional theater with a subscriber-based audience. Send synopsis, résumé, and sample (maximum 10 pages). No unsolicited mss accepted. Responds in 6 months. **Pays royalty.**

Needs Full-length, hard-hitting, emotional, intimate, actor-oriented shows with small casts (rarely exceeds 10-13, usually 2-7). Language and subject matter are not a problem. No one-acts or children's scripts.

ASIAN AMERICAN THEATER CO.

690 5th St., Suite 211, San Francisco CA 94107. (415)543-5738. Fax: (415)543-5638. E-mail: info@asianamericantheater.org. Web site: www.asianamericantheater.org. **Contact:** Sean Lim, artistic director. Estab. 1973. **Produces 4 plays/year.** Produces professional productions for San Francisco Bay Area audiences. Submit complete script. **Payment varies.**

Needs The new voice of Asian American theater. No limitations in cast, props or staging.

Tips Looking for plays from the new Asian American theater aesthetic—bold, substantive, punchy. Scripts from Asian Pacific Islander American women and under-represented Asian Pacific Islander ethnic groups are especially welcome.

ASOLO THEATRE CO.

5555 N. Tamiami Trail, Sarasota FL 34234. (941)351-8000. Web site: www.asolo.org. Estab. 1960. **Produces 7-8 plays/year.** A LORT theater with 2 intimate performing spaces. **Negotiates rights and payment.**

- Not currently accepting new scripts.

Needs Play must be full length. "We operate with a resident company in rotating repertory."

ATTIC THEATRE & FILM CENTRE

5429 W. Washington Blvd., Los Angeles CA 90016-1112. (323)525-0600. E-mail: attictheatre1@attictheatre.org. Web site: www.attictheatre.org. Artistic Director: James Carey. **Contact:** Literary Manager. Estab. 1987. **Produces 4 plays/year.** "We are based in Los Angeles and play to industry and regular joes. We use professional actors; however, our house is very small, and the salaries we pay, including the royalties are very small because of that." Send query and synopsis or check out Web site. Responds in 4 months. Buys first producer rights. **Payment is negotiated on a case by case basis.**

Needs "We will consider any type of play except musicals and large cast historical pieces with multiple hard sets." Must be original 1-act plays no longer than 45 minutes in length. Deadline for 2006 One-Act Marathon is December 31, 2005. Submissions after this date may be entered into 2007 festival. "Plays featuring elderly casts cannot be done because of our acting ages."

Tips "Please send an SASE and read our guidelines on the Web site. Follow all the directions."

BAILIWICK REPERTORY

Bailiwick Arts Center, 1229 W. Belmont Ave., Chicago IL 60657-3205. (773)883-1090. Fax: (773)883-2017. E-mail: bailiwicktheater@aol.com. Web site: www.bailiwick.org. **Contact:** David Zak, artistic director. Estab. 1982. **Produces 5 mainstage plays (classic and newly commissioned) each year; 12 one-acts in annual Directors Festival.** Pride Performance Series (gay and lesbian), includes one-acts, poetry, workshops, and staged adaptations of prose. Submit year-round. One-act play fest runs July-August. Responds in 9 months for full-length only. **Pays 6% royalty.**

Needs "We need daring scripts that break the mold. Large casts or musicals are OK. Creative staging solutions are a must."

Tips "Know the rules, then break them creatively and boldly! Please send SASE for manuscript submission guidelines *before you submit* or get manuscript guidelines at our Web site."

BAKER'S PLAYS PUBLISHING CO.

P.O. Box 699222, Quincy MA 02269-9222. (617)745-0805. E-mail: publications@bakersplays.com. Web site: www.bakersplays.com. **Contact:** Associate Editor. Estab. 1845. **Publishes 20-30 straight plays and musicals. Works with 2-3 unpublished/unproduced writers annually. 80% freelance written. 75% of scripts unagented submissions**. Plays performed by amateur groups, high schools, children's theater, churches and community theater groups. Submit complete script with news clippings, résumé. Submit complete cassette of music with musical submissions. Responds in 4 months. **Pay varies; negotiated royalty split of production fees; 10% book royalty.**

Needs "We are finding strong support in our new division—plays from young authors featuring contemporary pieces for high school production."

Tips "We are particularly interested in adaptation of lesser-known folk tales from around the world. Also of interest are plays which feature a multicultural cast and theme. Collections of one-act plays for children and young adults tend to do very well. Also, high school students: Write for guidelines for our High School Playwriting Contest."

MARY BALDWIN COLLEGE THEATRE

Mary Baldwin College, Staunton VA 24401. Fax: (540)887-7139. Web site: www.mbc.edu/theatre/. **Contact:** Virginia R. Francisco, professor of theater. Estab. 1842. **Produces 5 plays/year.** 15% of scripts are unagented submissions. Works with up to 1 unpublished/unproduced writer annually. An undergraduate women's college theater with an audience of students, faculty, staff and local community (adult, conservative). Query with synopsis. Responds in 1 year. Buys performance rights only. **Pays $10-50 per performance.**

Needs Full-length and short comedies, tragedies, and music plays geared particularly toward young women actresses, dealing with women's issues both contemporary and historical. Experimental/studio theater not suitable for heavy sets. Cast should emphasize women. No heavy sex; minimal explicit language.

Tips "A perfect play for us has several roles for young women, few male roles, minimal production demands, a concentration on issues relevant to contemporary society, and elegant writing and structure."

BLOOMSBURG THEATRE ENSEMBLE

226 Center St., Bloomsburg PA 17815. (570)784-5530. Fax: (570)784-4912. E-mail: jsatherton@bte.org. Web site: www.bte.org. Ensemble Director: Daniel Roth. **Contact:** J. Scott Atherton, director of development. Estab. 1979. **Produces 6 plays/year.** Professional productions for a non-urban audience. Query and synopsis. Responds in 9 months. Buys negotiable rights **Pays 6-9% royalty. Pays $50-70 per performance.** "Because of our non-urban location, we strive to exposé our audience to a broad range of theatre—both classical and contemporary. We are drawn to language and ideas and to plays that resonate in our community. We are most in need of articulate comedies and cast sizes under 6."

Tips "Because of our non-urban setting we are less interested in plays that focus on dilemmas of city life in particular. Most of the comedies we read are cynical. Many plays we read would make better film scripts; static/relationship-heavy scripts that do not use the 'theatricality' of the theatre to an advantage."

BOARSHEAD THEATER

425 S. Grand Ave., Lansing MI 48933. (517)484-7800. Fax: (517)484-2564. E-mail: boarshead@boarshead.org. Web site: www.boarshead.org. **Contact:** Kristine Thatcher, artistic director. Estab. 1966. **Produces 8 plays/year (6 mainstage, 2 Young People's Theater productions inhouse), 4 or 5 staged readings.** Mainstage Actors' Equity Association company; also Youth Theater—touring to schools by our intern company. Submit synopsis, character breakdown, 20 pages of sample dialogue, bio, production history (if any) via mail or e-mail. **Pays royalty for mainstage productions, transport/per diem for staged readings.**

Needs Thrust stage. Cast usually 8 or less; occasionally up to 20; no one-acts and no musicals considered. Prefers staging which depends on theatricality rather than multiple sets. "Send materials for full-length plays (only) to

Kristine Thatcher, artistic director. For Young People's Theater, send one-act plays (only); 4-5 characters."
Tips "Plays should not have multiple realistic sets—too many scripts read like film scripts. Focus on intelligence, theatricality, crisp, engaging humorous dialogue. Write a good play and prove it with 10 pages of great, precise dialogue."

BROADWAY PLAY PUBLISHING

56 E. 81st St., New York NY 10028-0202. (212)772-8334. Fax: (212)772-8358. E-mail: sara@broadwayplaypubl.com; broadwaypl@aol.com. Web site: www.broadwayplaypubl.com. **Contact:** Christopher Gould. This publisher does not read play mss. It will only publish a play if: the playwright is an American-born resident; the play is not in print elsewhere; the play is full-length (at least 1 hour); the play has contemporary subject matter; the play is for at least 2 actors; the play has been professionally produced for at least 12 pefromances; there is acceptable color artwork for the cover; ther are a few sentences from print media complimenting the play.

CELEBRATION THEATRE

7985 Santa Monica Blvd., #109-1, Los Angeles CA 90046. E-mail: celebrationthtr@earthlink.net. Web site: www.celebrationtheatre.com. Managing Artistic Director: Michael Matthews. **Contact:** Literary Management Team. Estab. 1983. **Produces 4 plays/year.** Performed in a small theatre in Los angeles. For all audiences, but with gay and lesbian characters at the center of the plays. Query and synopsis. Responds in 5 months. **Pays 6-7% royalty.**
Needs Produce works with gay and lesbian characters at the center of the narrative. There aren't any limitations, but simple productions work best. Don't send coming-out plays/stories.

CHILDSPLAY, INC.

P.O. Box 517, Tempe AZ 85280. (480)350-8101. Fax: (480)350-8584. E-mail: info@childsplayaz.org. Web site: childsplayaz.org. **Contact:** David Saar, artistic director. Estab. 1978. **Produces 5-6 plays/year.** "Professional touring and in-house productions for youth and family audiences." Submit synopsis, character descriptions and 7- to 10-page dialogue sample. Responds in 6 months. **Pays royalty of $20-35/performance (touring) or pays $3,000-8,000 commission. Holds a small percentage of royalties on commissioned work for 3-5 years.**
Needs Seeking theatrical plays on a wide range of contemporary topics. "Our biggest market is K-6. We need intelligent theatrical pieces for this age group that meet touring requirements and have the flexibility for in-house staging. The company has a reputation, built up over 30 years, of maintaining a strong aesthetic. We need scripts that respect the audience's intelligence and support their rights to dream and to have their concerns explored. Innovative, theatrical and small is a constant need." Touring shows limited to 5 actors; in-house shows limited to 6-10 actors.
Tips No traditionally-handled fairy tales. "Theater for young people is growing up and is able to speak to youth and adults. The material must respect the artistry of the theater and the intelligence of our audience. Our most important goal is to benefit children. If you wish your materials returned send SASE."

CIRCUIT PLAYHOUSE/PLAYHOUSE ON THE SQUARE

51 S. Cooper, Memphis TN 38104. (901)725-0776. **Contact:** Jackie Nichols, artistic director. **Produces 16 plays/year. 100% of scripts unagented submissions. Works with 1 unpublished/unproduced writer/year.** Professional plays performed for the Memphis/Mid-South area. Member of the Theatre Communications Group. Contest held each fall. Submit complete script. Responds in 6 months. Buys percentage of royalty rights for 2 years. **Pays $500.**
Needs All types; limited to single or unit sets. Casts of 20 or fewer.
Tips "Each play is read by 3 readers through the extended length of time a script is kept. Preference is given to scripts for the southeastern region of the US."

I.E. CLARK PUBLICATIONS

P.O. Box 246, Schulenburg TX 78956-0246. E-mail: email@ieclark.com. Web site: www.ieclark.com. Estab. 1956. Publishes 10-15 plays/year for educational theater, children's theater, religious theater, regional professional theater and community theater. Publishes unagented submissions. Catalog online. Writer's guidelines for #10 SASE. Submit complete script, 1 at a time with SASE. Responds in 6 months. Buys all available rights; "We serve as an agency as well as a publisher." **Pays standard book and performance royalty, amount and percentages dependent upon type and marketability of play.**

- "One of our specialties is "Young Adult Awareness Drama"—plays for ages 13 to 25 dealing with sex, drugs, popularity, juvenile, crime, and other problems of young adults. We also need plays for children's theatre, especially dramatizations of children's classic literature."

Needs "We are interested in plays of all types—short or long. Audiotapes of music or videotapes of a performance are requested with submissions of musicals. We require that a play has been produced (directed by someone other than the author); photos, videos and reviews of the production are helpful. No limitations in cast, props, staging, etc. Plays with only one or two characters are difficult to sell. We insist on literary quality. We like plays that give new interpretations and understanding of human nature. Correct spelling, punctuation and grammar (befitting the characters, of course) impress our editors."

Tips Publishes plays only. "Entertainment value and a sense of moral responsibility seem to be returning as essential qualities of a good play script. The era of glorifying the negative elements of society seems to be fading rapidly. Literary quality, entertainment value and good craftsmanship rank in that order as the characteristics of a good script in our opinion. 'Literary quality' means that the play must—in beautiful, distinctive, and untrite language—say something; preferably something new and important concerning man's relations with his fellow man or God; and these 'lessons in living' must be presented in an intelligent, believable and creative manner. Plays for children's theater are tending more toward realism and childhood problems, but fantasy and dramatization of fairy tales are also needed."

CLEVELAND PLAY HOUSE

8500 Euclid Ave., Cleveland OH 44106. E-mail: sgordon@clevelandplayhouse.com. Web site: www.clevelandplayhouse.com. Artistic Director: Michael Bloom. **Contact:** Seth Gordon, associate artistic director. Estab. 1915. **Produces 10 plays/year.** "We have five theatres, 100-550 seats." Submit 10-page sample with synopsis. Responds in 6 months. **Payment is negotiable.**

Needs All styles and topics of new plays.

COLONY THEATRE CO.

555 N. Third St., Burbank CA 91502. (818)558-7000. Fax: (818)558-7110. E-mail: colonytheatre@colonytheatre.org. Web site: www.colonytheatre.org. **Contact:** Michael David Wadler, literary manager. **Produces 6 plays/year.** Professional 276-seat theater with thrust stage. Casts from resident company of professional actors. Agented submissions only. Negotiated rights. **Pays royalty for each performance.**

Needs Full length (90-120 minutes) with a cast of 4-12. No musicals or experimental works.

Tips "We seek works of theatrical imagination and emotional resonance on universal themes."

CONFRONTATION, A Literary Journal

C.W. Post of Long Island University, Brookville NY 11548-1300. (516)299-2720. Fax: (516)299-2735. E-mail: martin.tucker@liu.edu. **Contact:** Martin Tucker, editor. Estab. 1968. **Publishes 2 plays/year.** Submit complete script. Responds in 2 months. Obtains first serial and reprint rights. **Pays up to $50.**

Needs "We have an annual one-act play contest, open to all forms and styles. Award is $200 and publication."

CONTEMPORARY DRAMA SERVICE

Meriwether Publishing Ltd., P.O. Box 7710, Colorado Springs CO 80933. Fax: (719)594-9916. E-mail: merpcds@aol.com. Web site: www.contemporarydrama.com. Associate Editor: Arthur Zapel. **Contact:** Theodore Zapel, associate editor. Estab. 1969. **Publishes 50-60 plays/year.** "We are specialists in theater arts books and plays for middle grades, high schools, and colleges. We publish textbooks for drama courses of all types. We also publish for mainline liturgical churches—drama activities for church holidays, youth activities, and fundraising entertainments. These may be plays, musicals, or drama-related books." Query with synopsis or submit complete script. Responds in 6 weeks. Obtains either amateur or all rights. **Pays 10% royalty or negotiates purchase.**

- Contemporary Drama Service is now looking for play or musical adaptations of classic stories by famous authors and playwrights. Also looking for parodies of famous movies or historical and/or fictional characters (i.e., Robin Hood, Rip Van Winkle, Buffalo Bill, Huckleberry Finn).

Needs "Most of the plays we publish are one-acts 15-45 minutes in length. We also publish full-length two-act musicals or three-act plays 90 minutes in length. We prefer comedies. Musical shows should have large casts for 20-25 performers. Comedy sketches, monologues, and plays are welcome. We prefer simple staging appropriate to middle school, high school, college, or church performance. We like playwrights who see the world with a sense of humor. Offbeat themes and treatments are accepted if the playwright can sustain a light touch. In documentary or religious plays we look for good research and authenticity. We are publishing many scenebooks for actors (which can be anthologies of great works excerpts), scenebooks on special themes, and speech and theatrical arts textbooks. We also publish many books of monologs for young performers. We are especially interested in authority-books on a variety of theater-related subjects."

Tips "Contemporary Drama Service is looking for creative books on comedy, monologs, staging amateur theatricals, and Christian youth activities. Our writers are usually highly experienced in theatre as teachers or performers. We welcome books that reflect their experience and special knowledge. Any good comedy writer of monologs and short scenes will find a home with us."

A CONTEMPORARY THEATRE

700 Union St., Seattle WA 98101. (206)292-7660. Fax: (206)292-7670. Web site: www.acttheatre.org. Estab. 1965. **Produces 5-6 mainstage plays/year.** "ACT performs a subscription-based season on 3 stages: 2 main stages (a thrust and an arena) and a smaller, flexible 99-seat space. Although our focus is towards our local Seattle audience, some of our notable productions have gone on to other venues in other cities." *Agented submissions only* or through theatre professional's recommendation. Query and synopsis only for Northwest playwrights. Responds in 6 months. **Pays 5-10% royalty.**

Needs "ACT produces full-length contemporary scripts ranging from solo pieces to large ensemble works, with an emphasis on plays that embrace the contradictions and mysteries of our contemporary world and that resonate with audiences of all backgrounds through strong storytelling and compelling characters."

Tips "ACT is looking for plays that offer strong narrative, exciting ideas, and well-drawn, dimensional characters that will engage an audience emotionally and intellectually. These may sound like obvious prerequisites for a play, but often it seems that playwrights are less concerned with the story they have to tell than with the way they're telling it, emphasizing flashy, self-conscious style over real substance and solid structure."

CREEDE REPERTORY THEATRE

P.O. Box 269, Creede CO 81130-0269. (719)658-2541. E-mail: crt@creederep.com. Web site: www.creederep.org. **Contact:** Maurice LaMee, artistic director. Estab. 1966. **Produces 6 plays/year.** Plays performed for a smaller audience. Query and synopsis. Responds in 1 year. **Royalties negotiated with each author—paid on a per performance basis.**

Needs One-act children's scripts. Special consideration given to plays focusing on the cultures and history of the American West and Southwest.

Tips "We seek new adaptations of classical or older works as well as original scripts."

DALLAS CHILDREN'S THEATER

Rosewood Center for Family Arts, 5938 Skillman, Dallas TX 75231. E-mail: artie@dct.org. Web site: www.dct.org. **Contact:** Artie Olaisen, associate artistic director. Estab. 1984. **Produces 11 plays/year.** Professional theater for family and student audiences. Query with synopsis, number of actors required, any material regarding previous productions of the work, and a demo tape or lead sheets (for musicals). Responds in 8 months. Rights negotiable. **Pays negotiable royalty.** No materials will be returned without a SASE included.

Needs Substantive material appropriate for youth and family audiences. Most consideration given to full-length, non-musical works, especially classic and contemporary adaptations of literature. Also interested in social, topical issue-oriented material. Very interested in scripts which enlighten diverse cultural experiences, particularly Hispanic and African-American experiences. Prefers scripts with no more than 15 cast members; 6-12 is ideal.

Tips "No adult experience material. We are a family theater. Not interested in material intended for performance by children or in a classroom. Productions are performed by professional adults. Children are cast in child-appropriate roles. We receive far too much light musical material that plays down to children and totally lacks any substance. Be patient. We receive an enormous amount of submissions. Most of the material we have historically produced has had previous production. We are not against perusing non-produced material, but it has rarely gone into our season unless we have been involved in its development."

DARLINGHURST THEATRE COMPANY

19 Greenknowe Ave., Potts Pointe NSW 2011, Australia. (61)(2)9331-3107. E-mail: theatre@darlinghursttheatre.com. Web site: www.darlinghursttheatre.com. Submission period ends September 15. Seeks to exposé the audience to a diverse range of work, included narratives, non-narratives, Australian content, and international work. Classics are not excluded, though work new to Sydney is encouraged. Financial issues are a part of the selection process, so discuss your proposal with Glenn Terry before submitting. If asked, send complete ms or outline. See Web site for more submission details.

DETROIT REPERTORY THEATRE

13103 Woodrow Wilson, Detroit MI 48238-3686. (313)868-1347. Fax: (313)868-1705. **Contact:** Barbara Busby, literary manager. Estab. 1957. **Produces 4 plays/year.** Professional theater, 194 seats operating on A.E.A. SPT contract Detroit metropolitan area. Submit complete ms in bound folder, cast list, and description with SASE. Responds in 6 months. **Pays royalty.**

Needs Wants issue-oriented works. Cast limited to no more than 7 characters. No musicals or one-act plays.

DIVERSIONARY THEATRE

4545 Park Blvd., Suite 101, San Diego CA 92116. (619)220-6830. E-mail: dkirsch@diversionary.org. Web site: www.diversionary.org. **Contact:** Dan Kirsch, executive director. Estab. 1986. **Produces 5-6 plays/year.** Non-professional full-length productions of gay, lesbian, bisexual and transgender content. Ideal cast size is 2-6. Submit application and 10-15 pages of script. Responds in 6 months.

DIXON PLACE

258 Bowery, 2nd Floor, New York NY 10012. (212)219-0736. Fax: (212)219-0761. Web site: www.dixonplace.org. **Contact:** Leslie Strongwater, artistic associate. Estab. 1986. **Produces 12 plays/year.** Submit full script. Does not accept submissions from writers outside the NYC area. **Pays flat fee.**

- Not currently operating at full capacity due to a pending move.

Needs Musicals, one-acts, full-length plays, not already read or workshopped in New York. Particularly interested in non-traditional, either in character, content, structure and/or themes. "We almost never produce kitchen sink, soap opera-style plays about AIDS, coming out, unhappy love affairs, getting sober or lesbian parenting. We regularly present new works, plays with innovative structure, multi-ethnic content, non-naturalistic dialogue, irreverent musicals and the elegantly bizarre. We are an established performance venue with a very diverse audience. We have a reputation for bringing our audience the unexpected. Submissions accepted year-round."

[A] DORSET THEATRE FESTIVAL

Box 510, Dorset VT 05251-0510. (802)867-2223. Web site: www.dorsettheatrefestival.org. Estab. 1976. **Produces 5 plays/year (1 a new work).** "Our plays will be performed in our Equity theater and are intended for a sophisticated community." Agented submissions only. **Rights and compensation negotiated.**

Needs Looking for full-length contemporary American comedy or drama. Limited to a cast of 6.

Tips "Language and subject matter must be appropriate to general audience."

THE DRAMA PLACE

P.O. Box 88196, Colorado Springs CO 80908-8191. (719)331-8834. E-mail: thedramaplace@yahoo.com. Web site: www.thedramaplace.com. Estab. 2006. **Publishes 15 plays/year.** Publish plays for family audiences. e-mail. Responds in 1 month. Buys all rights. Buys All rights. **Pays writers in royalties (10% on script sales, 50% on productions).**

Needs "We publish plays for elementary school through high school. All genres are acceptable, but we prefer plays that are adaptations of well-known stories. We're especially interested in working with published authors on the dramatization of their novels. We're also interested in Christmas plays and other Bible-based scripts for church youth groups. We prefer large-cast plays (24-30 roles) that are easy to produce, with simple staging, costuming and props." Does not want mature themes. "We're looking for plays that are fresh, fast and funny. No long, boring monologues. No stale, corny jokes. Physical humor is a plus."

Tips "We will consider simultaneous submissions. We do not require that plays be produced before they're submitted to us. Mail or e-mail your submissions."

DRAMATIC PUBLISHING

311 Washington St., Woodstock IL 60098. (815)338-7170. Fax: (815)338-8981. Web site: www.dramaticpublishing.com. **Publishes 40-50 titles/year.** Publishes paperback acting editions of original plays, musicals, adaptations, and translations. **Receives 250-500 queries and 600 mss/year.** Catalog and script guidelines free. **Pays 10% royalty on scripts; performance royalty varies.**

Needs Interested in playscripts appropriate for children, middle and high schools, colleges, community, stock and professional theaters. Send full ms.

Tips "We publish all kinds of plays for the professional, stock, amateur, high school, elementary and children's theater markets: full lengths, one acts, children's plays, musicals, adaptations."

DRAMATICS MAGAZINE

2343 Auburn Ave., Cincinnati OH 45219. (513)421-3900. Fax: (513)421-7077. E-mail: dcorathers@edta.org. Web site: www.edta.org. **Contact:** Don Corathers, editor. Estab. 1929. **Publishes 7 plays/year.** For high school theater students and teachers. Submit complete script. Responds in 3 months. Buys first North American serial rights only.

Needs "We are seeking one-acts to full-lengths that can be produced in an educational theater setting."

Tips "No melodrama, musicals, farce, children's theater, or cheap knock-offs of TV sitcoms or movies. Fewer writers are taking the time to learn the conventions of theater—what makes a piece work on stage, as opposed to film and television—and their scripts show it. We're always looking for good interviews with working theatre professionals."

EAST WEST PLAYERS

120 N. Judge John Aiso St., Los Angeles CA 90012. (213)625-7000. Fax: (213)625-7111. E-mail: info@eastwestplayers.org. Web site: www.eastwestplayers.org. Artistic Director: Tim Dang. **Contact:** Jeff Liu, literary manager.

Estab. 1965. **Produces 5 plays/year.** Professional 240-seat theater performing under LOA-BAT contract, presenting plays which explore the Asian-Pacific or Asian-American experience. Submit ms with title page, résumé, cover letter, and SASE. Responds in 3-9 months. **Pays royalty against percentage of box office.**

Needs "Whether dramas, comedies, performance art or musicals, all plays must either address the Asian-American experience or have a special resonance when cast with Asian-American actors."

Tips "We are especially looking for comedies."

ELDRIDGE PUBLISHING CO.

P.O. Box 14367, Tallahassee FL 32317. (800)447-8243. Fax: (800)453-5179. E-mail: editorial@histage.com. Web site: www.histage.com. Managing Editor: Nancy Vorhis. **Contact:** Editor: Susan Shore. Estab. 1906. **Publishes 65 new plays/year for junior high, senior high, church, and community audience.** Query with synopsis (acceptable) or submit complete ms (preferred). Please send CD with any musicals. Responds in 1-2 months. Buys all dramatic rights. Buys All rights. **Pays 50% royalties for amateur productions, 80% for professional productions and 10% copy sales in general market. Makes outright purchase of $100-600 in religious market.**

Needs "We are most interested in full-length plays and musicals for our school and community theater market. Nothing lower than junior high level, please. We always love comedies but also look for serious, high caliber plays reflective of today's sophisticated students. We also need one-acts and plays for children's theater. In addition, in our religious market we're always searching for holiday plays." No plays which belong in a classroom setting as part of a lesson plan. Unless it is for Christmas, no other religious musicals considered.

Tips "Please have your work performed, if at all possible, before submitting. The quality will improve substantially."

THE ENSEMBLE STUDIO THEATRE

549 W. 52nd St., New York NY 10019. (212)247-4982. Fax: (212)664-0041. E-mail: est@ensemblestudiotheatre.org. Web site: www.ensemblestudiotheatre.org. Artistic Director: Curt Dempster. **Contact:** Literary Manager. Estab. 1972. **Produces 250 projects/year for off-off Broadway developmental theater in a 100-seat house, 60-seat workshop space.** Do not fax mss or résumés. Submit complete ms. Responds in 10 months.

Needs Full-length plays with strong dramatic actions and situations and solid one-acts, humorous and dramatic, which can stand on their own. Special programs include Going to the River Series, which workshops new plays by African-American women, and the Sloan Project, which commissions new works on the topics of science and technology. Seeks "original plays with strong dramatic action, believable characters and dynamic ideas. We are interested in writers who respect the power of language." No verse-dramas or elaborate costume dramas. Accepts new/unproduced work only.

ENSEMBLE THEATRE OF CINCINNATI

1127 Vine St., Cincinnati OH 45248. (513)421-3555. Fax: (513)562-4104. Web site: cincyetc.com. **Contact:** D. Lynn Meyers, producing artistic director. Estab. 1987. **Produces 12 plays/year, including a staged reading series.** Professional year-round theater. Query with synopsis, submit complete ms or submit through agent. Responds in 6 months. **Pays 5-10% royalty.**

Needs Dedicated to good writing of any style for a small, contemporary cast. Small technical needs, big ideas.

THE ESSENTIAL THEATRE

995 Greenwood Ave. #6, Atlanta GA 30306. (404)212-0815. E-mail: pmhardy@aol.com. Web site: www.essentialtheatre.com. **Contact:** Peter Hardy, artistic director. Estab. 1987. **Produces 3 plays/year.** "Professional theatre on a small budget, for adventurous theatregoers interested in new plays." Submit complete script. Responds in 6 months. Include SASE for return of submission.

Needs Accepts full-length, unproduced plays by Georgia residents only, to be considered for Essential Theatre Playwriting Award.

FOUNTAIN THEATRE

5060 Fountain Ave., Los Angeles CA 90029. (323)663-2235. Fax: (323)663-1629. E-mail: ftheatre@aol.com. Web site: fountaintheatre.com. Artistic Directors: Deborah Lawlor, Stephen Sachs. **Contact:** Simon Levy, dramaturg. Estab. 1990. Produces both a theater and dance season. Produced at Fountain Theatre (99-seat equity plan). *Professional recommendation only.* Query with synopsis to Simon Levy, producing director/dramaturg. Responds in 6 months. Rights acquired vary. **Pays royalty.**

Needs Original plays, adaptations of American literature, material that incorporates dance or language into text with unique use and vision.

THE FREELANCE PRESS

P.O. Box 548, Dover MA 02030-2207. (508)785-8250. Fax: (508)785-8291. **Contact:** Narcissa Campion, managing director. Estab. 1984. Submit complete ms with SASE. Responds in 4 months. **Pays 70% of performance royalties to authors. Pays 10% script and score royalty.**

Needs ''We publish original musical theater to be performed by young people, dealing with issues of importance to them. Also adapt 'classics' into musicals for 8- to 16-year-old age groups to perform.'' Large cast, flexible.

SAMUEL FRENCH, INC.

45 W. 25th St., New York NY 10010. (212)206-8990. Fax: (212)206-1429. E-mail: info@samuelfrench.net. Web site: www.samuelfrench.com. **Contact:** Lawrence Harbison, senior editor. Estab. 1830. **Publishes 50-60 titles/year.** Publishes paperback acting editions of plays. Receives 1,500 submissions/year, mostly from unagented playwrights. 10% of publications are from first-time authors; 20% from unagented writers. **Pays 10% royalty on retail price, plus amateur and stock royalties on productions.**

Needs Comedies, mysteries, children's plays, high school plays.

Tips ''Broadway and Off-Broadway hit plays, light comedies and mysteries have the best chance of selling to our firm. Our market is comprised of theater producers—both professional and amateur—actors and students. Read as many plays as possible of recent vintage to keep apprised of today's market; write plays with good female roles; and be 100% professional in approaching publishers and producers. We recommend (not require) that submissions be in the format used by professional playwrights in the US, as illustrated in *Guidelines*, available for $4 (postpaid).''

WILL GEER THEATRICUM BOTANICUM

P.O. Box 1222, Topanga CA 90290. (310)455-2322. Fax: (310)455-3724. E-mail: egtilee@theatricum.com. Web site: www.theatricum.com. **Contact:** Ellen Geer, artistic director. Estab. 1973. **Produces 3 classical and 1 new play if selected/year.** Professional productions for summer theater. ''Botanicum Seedlings'' new plays selected for readings and one play each year developed. Contact: Jennie Webb. Send synopsis, sample dialogue and tape if musical. Responds in 6 months. **Pays 6% royalty or $150 per show.**

Needs Socially relevant plays, musicals; all full-length. Cast size of 4-10 people. ''We are a large outdoor theatre—small intimate works could be difficult.''

Tips ''September submissions have best turn around for main season; year-round for 'Botanicum Seedlings.' ''

⊘ GEORGE STREET PLAYHOUSE

9 Livingston Ave., New Brunswick NJ 08901. (732)246-7717. Web site: www.georgestplayhouse.org. Artistic Director: David Saint. **Contact:** Literary Associate. **Produces 6 plays/year.** Professional regional theater (LORT C). Proscenium/thurst stage with 367 seats. Query with synopsis, character breakdown, SASE, and up to 10 sample pages. *No unsolicited scripts. Agent or professional recommendation only.* Responds in 8-10 months to scripts.

Needs Full-length dramas and comedies with a fresh perspective on society. Prefers cast size of 5-7 characters; one unit set.

Tips ''It is our firm belief that theater reaches the mind via the heart and the funny bone. Our work tells a compelling, personal, human story that entertains, challenges and stretches the imagination.''

GEVA THEATRE CENTER

75 Woodbury Blvd., Rochester NY 14607. (585)232-1366. **Contact:** Marge Betley, literary manager. **Produces 7-11 plays/year.** Professional and regional theater, modified thrust, 552 seats; second stage has 180 seats. Subscription and single-ticket sales. Query with sample pages, synopsis, and résumé. Responds in 3 months.

Needs Full-length plays, translations, and adaptations.

THE GOODMAN THEATRE

170 N. Dearborn St., Chicago IL 60601-3205. (312)443-3811. Fax: (312)443-3821. E-mail: staff@goodman-theatre.org. Web site: www.goodman-theatre.org. **Contact:** Tanya Palmer, literary manager. Estab. 1925. **Produces 9 plays/year.** ''The Goodman is a professional, not-for-profit theater producing a series in both the Albert Theatre and the Owen Theatre, which includes an annual New Play Series. The Goodman does not accept unsolicited scripts, nor will it respond to synopsis of plays submitted by playwrights, unless accompanied by a stamped, self-addressed postcard. The Goodman may request plays to be submitted for production consideration after receiving a letter of inquiry or telephone call from recognized literary agents or producing organizations.'' Responds in 6 months. Buys variable rights. **Pays variable royalty.**

Needs Full-length plays, translations, musicals; special interest in social or political themes.

GRETNA THEATRE
P.O. Box 578, Mt. Gretna PA 17064. Fax: (717)964-2189. E-mail: larryfrenock@gretnatheatre.com. Web site: www.mtgretna.com/theatre. **Contact:** Larry Frenock, producing director. Estab. 1923. ''Plays are performed at a professional equity theater during summer.'' Agented submissions only. **Pays negotiable royalty (6-12%).**

Needs ''We produce full-length plays for a summer audience—subject, language and content are important.'' Prefer ''package'' or vehicles which have ''star'' role.

Tips ''No one-acts or romantic comedies.''

GRIFFIN THEATRE COMPANY
13 Craigend St., Kings Cross NSW 2011, Australia. (61)(2)9332-1052. Fax: (61)(2)9331-1524. Web site: www.griffintheatre.com.au. Gives consideration and feedback if the author has had a play professionally produced, has an agent, has been shortlisted for the Griffin Award, or has had a play workshopped at Griffin. ''If you don't meet these requirements, you may still send a 1-page outline and a 10-page sample. If interested, we will request the full manuscript.''

THE HARBOR THEATRE
160 W. 71st St., PHA, New York NY 10023. (212)787-1945. E-mail: swarmflash@harbortheatre.org. Web site: www.harbortheatre.org. **Contact:** Stuart Warmflash, artistic director. Estab. 1993. **Produces 1-2 plays/year.** Off-off Broadway showcase. Query and synopsis. Responds in 10 weeks.

Needs Full-length and one-act festival. *''We only produce plays developed in our workshop.''*

HARTFORD STAGE CO.
50 Church St., Hartford CT 06103. (860)525-5601. E-mail: info@hartfordstage.org. Web site: www.hartfordstage.org. Estab. 1963. **Produces 6 plays/year.** Regional theater productions with a wide range in audience.

Needs Classics, new plays, musicals. *Agented submissions only.* No queries or synopses.

HORIZON THEATRE CO.
P.O. Box 5376, Atlanta GA 31107. (404)523-1477. Web site: www.horizontheatre.com. **Contact:** J. Caleb Boyd, artistic director. Estab. 1983. **5+ plays/year, and workshops 6-10 plays as part of New South Playworks Festival.** Professional productions. Accepts unsolicited résumés, samples, treatments, and summaries with SASE. Responds in 1 year. Buys rights to produce in Atlanta area.

Needs ''We produce contemporary plays that seek to bridge cultures and communities, utilizing a realistic base but with heightened visual or language elements. Particularly interested in comedy, satire, plays that are entertaining and topical, but thought provoking. Also particular interest in plays by women, African-Americans, or that concern the contemporary South.'' No more than 8 in cast.

ILLINOIS THEATRE CENTRE
371 Artists' Walk, P.O. Box 397, Park Forest IL 60466. (708)481-3510. Fax: (708)481-3693. E-mail: ilthctr@sbcglobal.net. Web site: www.ilthctr.org. Artistic Director: Etel Billig. Estab. 1976. **Produces 8 plays/year.** Professional Resident Theatre Company in our own space for a subscription-based audience. Query with synopsis or agented submission. Responds in 2 months. Buys casting and directing and designer selection rights. **Pays 7-10% royalty.**

Needs All types of 2-act plays, musicals, dramas. Prefers cast size of 6-10.

Tips Always looking for mysteries and comedies. ''Make sure your play arrives between November and January when play selections are made.''

INDIANA REPERTORY THEATRE
140 W. Washington St., Indianapolis IN 46204-3465. (317)635-5277. E-mail: rroberts@irtlive.com. Web site: www.irtlive.com. Artistic Director: Janet Allen. Dramaturg: Richard Roberts. Modified proscenium stage with 600 seats; thrust stage with 300 seats. Send synopsis with résumé via e-mail to the dramaturg. No unsolicited scripts. Submit year-round (season chosen by January). Responds in 6 month.

Needs Full-length plays, translations, adaptations, solo pieces. Also interested in adaptations of classic literature and plays that explore cultural/ethnic issues with a midwestern voice. Special program: Discovery Series (plays for family audiences with a focus on youth). Cast size should be 6-8.

Tips ''The IRT employs a playwright-in-residence from whom the majority of our new work is commissioned. We occasionally place other subject-specific commissions.''

INTERACT THEATRE CO.
The Adrienne, 2030 Sansom St., Philadelphia PA 19103. (215)568-8077. Fax: (215)568-8095. E-mail: pbonilla@interacttheatre.org. Web site: www.interacttheatre.org. **Contact:** Peter Bonilla, literary associate. Estab. 1988.

Produces 4 plays/year. Produces professional productions for adult audience. Query with synopsis and bio. No unsolicited scripts. Responds in 6 months. **Pays 2-8% royalty or $25-100/performance.**

Needs Contemporary dramas and comedies that explore issues of political, social, cultural or historical significance. "Virtually all of our productions have political content in the foregound of the drama." Prefer plays that raise interesting questions without giving easy, predictable answers. "We are interested in new plays." Limit cast to 8. No romantic comedies, family dramas, agit-prop.

A INTIMAN THEATRE

201 Mercer St., Seattle WA 98109. (206)269-1901. Fax: (206)269-1928. E-mail: kate@intiman.org. Web site: www.intiman.org. Artistic Director: Bartlett Sher. **Contact:** Kate Goodman. Estab. 1972. **Produces 6 plays/year.** LORT C Regional Theater in Seattle. Best submission time is October through March. *Agented submissions only* or by professional recommendation. Responds in 4 months.

Needs Well-crafted dramas and comedies by playwrights who fully utilize the power of language and character relationships to explore enduring themes. Prefers nonnaturalistic plays and plays of dynamic theatricality.

JEWEL BOX THEATRE

3700 N. Walker, Oklahoma City OK 73118-7099. (405)521-1786. Fax: (405)525-6562. **Contact:** Charles Tweed, production director. Estab. 1956. **Produces 6 plays/year.** Amateur productions. 3,000 season subscribers and general public. **Pays $500 contest prize.**

Needs Annual Playwriting Competition: Send SASE in September-October. Deadline: mid-January.

JEWISH ENSEMBLE THEATRE

6600 W. Maple Rd., West Bloomfield MI 48322. (248)788-2900. E-mail: orbach@jettheatre.org. Web site: www.jettheatre.org. **Contact:** Evelyn Orbach, artistic director. Estab. 1989. **Produces 4-6 plays/year.** Professional productions at the Aaron DeRoy Theatre (season), The Detroit Institue of Arts Theatre, and Scottish Rite Cathedral Theatre (schools), as well as tours to schools. Submit complete script. Responds in 1 year. "Obtains rights for our season productions and staged readings for festival." **Pays 6-8% royalty for full production or honorarium for staged reading—$100/full-length play.**

Needs "We do few children's plays except original commissions; we rarely do musicals." Cast limited to a maximum of 8 actors.

Tips "We are a theater of social conscience with the following mission: to produce work on the highest possible professional level; to deal with issues of community & humanity from a Jewish perspective; to provide a platform for new voices and a bridge for understanding to the larger community."

KITCHEN DOG THEATER

3120 McKinney Ave., Dallas TX 75204. (214)953-2258. Fax: (214)953-1873. **Contact:** Chris Carlos, co-artistic director. Estab. 1990. **Produces 5 plays/year.** Kitchen Dog has two performance spaces: a 100-seat black box and a 150-seat thrust. Submit complete manuscript with SASE. Each year the deadline for submissions is March 1 (received by). Writers are notified by May 15. Buys rights to full production. **Pays $1,000 for winner of New Works Festival.**

Needs "We are interested in experimental plays, literary adaptations, historical plays, political theater, gay and lesbian work, culturally diverse work, and small musicals. Ideally, cast size would be 1-5, or more if doubling roles is a possibility." No romantic/light comedies or material that is more suited for television than the theater.

Tips "We are interested in plays that are theatrical and that challenge the imagination—plays that are for the theater, rather than TV or film."

KUMU KAHUA

46 Merchant St., Honolulu HI 96813. (808)536-4222. Fax: (808)536-4226. E-mail: kumukahuatheatre@hawaiiantel.net. Web site: kumukahua.org. **Contact:** Harry Wong, artistic director. Estab. 1971. **Produces 5 productions, 3-4 public readings/year.** "Plays performed at new Kumu Kahua Theatre, flexible 120-seat theater, for community audiences." Submit complete script. Responds in 4 months. **Pays royalty of $50/performance; usually 20 performances of each production.**

Needs "Plays must have some interest for local Hawai'i audiences."

LILLENAS PUBLISHING CO.

P.O. Box 419527, Kansas City MO 64141-6527. (816)931-1900. Fax: (816)412-8390. E-mail: drama@lillenas.com. Web site: www.lillenasdrama.com. **Contact:** Kim Messer, product manager. Estab. 1926. "We publish on 2 levels: 1) Program Builders—seasonal and topical collections of recitations, sketches, dialogues, and short plays; 2) Drama Resources which assume more than 1 format: a) full-length scripts; b) one-acts, shorter plays, and sketches all by 1 author; c) collection of short plays and sketches by various authors. All program and play resources are produced with local church and Christian school in mind. Therefore there are taboos." Queries are encouraged, but synopses and complete scripts are read. Responds in 3 months. "First rights are purchased for Program Builders scripts. For Drama Resources, we purchase all print rights." **Drama Resources are paid on a 12% royalty, whether full-length scripts, one-acts, or sketches. No advance.**

- This publisher is interested in collections of and individual sketches. There is also a need for short pieces that are seasonal and on current events.

Needs 98% of Program Builders materials are freelance written. Scripts selected for these publications are outright purchases; verse is minimum of 25¢/line, prose (play scripts) are minimum of $5/double-spaced page. "Lillenas Drama Resources is a line of play scripts that are, for the most part, written by professionals with experience in productions as well as writing. While we do read unsolicited scripts, more than half of what we publish is written by experienced authors whom we have already published."

Tips "All plays need to be presented in standard play script format. We welcome a summary statement of each play. Purpose statements are always desirable. Approximate playing time, cast and prop lists, etc., are important to include. Contemporary settings generally have it over Biblical settings. Christmas and Easter scripts must have a bit of a twist. Secular approaches to these seasons (Santas, Easter bunnies, and so on), are not considered. We sell our product in 10,000 Christian bookstores and by catalog. We are in the forefront as a publisher of religious drama resources. Request a copy of our newsletter and/or catalog."

LIVE BAIT THEATER

3914 N. Clark St., Chicago IL 60613. (773)871-1212. Web site: www.livebaittheater.org. Artistic Director: Sharon Evans. **Contact:** Literary Department. Estab. 1987. **Produces 2-3 plays/year.** "Professional, non-Equity productions here at our space in Chicago, for sophisticated local audiences." Send brief synopsis, query letter, and 10-page dialogue sample. Responds in 6 months. Include SASE for return of submitted materials.

Needs "We produce only new works by local Chicago playwrights only. We produce both original plays and original adaptations of literature to the stage. We seek properties that put a heavy emphasis on the visual element, use rich and compelling language, and explore unconventional subject matter." Prefers plays with smaller casts (6-8 max.), suitable for an intimate 50-70 seat space with no wing or fly space.

A ⊘ LONG WHARF THEATRE

222 Sargent Dr., New Haven CT 06511. (203)787-4284. Fax: (203)776-2287. Web site: www.longwharf.org. **Contact:** Literary Department. Estab. 1965. **Produces 6-8 plays/year.** Professional regional theater. *Agented submissions only.*

Needs Full-length plays, translations, adaptations. Special interest: Dramatic plays and comedies about human relationships, social concerns, ethical and moral dilemmas.

Tips "We no longer accept queries."

LOS ANGELES DESIGNERS' THEATRE

P.O. Box 1883, Studio City CA 91614-0883. E-mail: ladesigners@juno.com. **Contact:** Richard Niederberg, artistic director. Estab. 1970. **Produces 8-20 plays/year.** Professional shows/industry audience. Submit proposal only (i.e., 1 page in #10 SASE). Reports in 3 months (minimum) to submission Purchases rights by negotiation, first refusal for performance/synchronization rights only. **Payment varies.**

- "We want highly commercial work without liens, 'understandings,' or promises to anyone."

Needs All types. No limitations—"We seek design challenges." No boring material. Shorter plays with musical underscores are desirable; nudity, street language, and political themes are OK."

MAGIC THEATRE

Fort Mason Center, Bldg. D, 3rd Floor, San Francisco CA 94123. (415)441-8001. Fax: (415)771-5505. E-mail: info@magictheatre.org. Web site: www.magictheatre.org. Artistic Director: Chris Smith. **Contact:** Mark Routhier, literary manager. Estab. 1967. **Produces 6 mainstage plays/year, plus monthly reading series and several festivals each year which contain both staged readings and workshop productions.** Regional theater. Bay area residents can send complete ms or query with cover letter, résumé, 1-page synopsis, SASE, dialogue sample (10-20 pages). Those outside the Bay area can query or submit through an agent. Responds in 6-8 months. **Pays royalty or per performance fee.**

Needs Plays that are innovative in theme and/or craft, cutting-edge sociopolitical concerns, intelligent comedy. Full-length only, strong commitment to multicultural work.

Tips "Not interested in classics, conventional approaches and cannot produce large-cast (over 10) plays. Send query to Mark Routhier, literary manager."

MALTHOUSE THEATRE

113 Sturt St., Southbank VIC 3006, Australia. (61)(3)9685-5100. Fax: (61)(3)9685-5111. E-mail: admin@malthousetheatre.com.au. Web site: www.malthousetheatre.com.au. **Contact:** Michael Kantor, artistic director. "We

are dedicated to contemporary Australian theatre.'' Writers should have had at least 1 professional production of their work. Proposals are called for on March 1, July 1, and October 1. Mail 1-page synopsis, brief author bio, and 10-page sample. Responds in 3 months if interested.

MANHATTAN THEATRE CLUB

311 W. 43rd St., 8th Floor, New York NY 10036. (212)399-3000. Fax: (212)399-4329. E-mail: questions@mtc-nyc.org. Web site: www.manhattantheatreclub.com. Director of Artistic Development: Paige Evans. **Contact:** Emily Shooltz, literary manager. **Produces 7-8 plays/year.** One Broadway and 2 Off-Broadway theatres, using professional actors. *Solicited and agented submissions only.* No queries. Responds within 6 months.
Needs ''We present a wide range of new work, from this country and abroad, to a subscription audience. We want plays about contemporary concerns and people. All genres are welcome. MTC also maintains an extensive play development program.''

MCCARTER THEATRE

91 University Place, Princeton NJ 08540. E-mail: literary@mccarter.org. Web site: www.mccarter.org. Artistic Director: Emily Mann. **Contact:** Literary Manager. **Produces 5 plays/year; 1 second stage play/year.** Produces professional productions for a 1,077-seat and 360-seat theaters. Agented submissions only. Responds in 4-6 months. **Pays negotiable royalty.**
Needs Full length plays, musicals, translations.

MELBOURNE THEATRE COMPANY

129 Ferrars St., Southbank VIC 3006, Australia. (61)(3)9684-4500. Fax: (61)(3)9696-2627. E-mail: info@mtc.com.au. Web site: www.mtc.com.au. **Contact:** Simon Phillips, artistic director. ''We are interested in timeless classics, modern classics, and the best new plays from Australia and overseas. Victorian work is given emphasis.'' Submissions are accepted February-October. Unsolicited scripts are only accepted if they satisfy 2 of these requirements: the author has had 1 script professionally produced or workshopped, the script is submitted by an agent, or the script is recommended by a professional theatre company or script development agency. Responds in 3 months.

MERIWETHER PUBLISHING, LTD.

885 Elkton Dr., Colorado Springs CO 80907-3557. Fax: (719)594-9916. E-mail: merpcds@aol.com. Web site: www.meriwether.com. President: Mark Zapel. Associate Editor: Arthur L. Zapel. **Contact:** Ted Zapel, associate editor. Estab. 1969. ''We publish how-to theatre materials in book and video formats. We are interested in materials for middle school, high school, and college-level students only.'' Query with synopsis/outline, résumé of credits, sample of style, and SASE. Catalog available for $2 postage. Responds in 1 month to queries; 2 months to full-length mss. **Offers 10% royalty or makes outright purchase.**
Needs Musicals for a large cast of performers, one-act or two-act comedy plays with large casts, and book mss on theatrical arts subjects—especially books of short scenes for amateur and professional actors. ''We are now looking for scenebooks with special themes: scenes for young women, comedy scenes for 2 actors, etc. These need not be original, provided the compiler can get letters of permission from the original copyright owner. We are interested in all textbook candidates for theater arts subjects. Christian children's activity book manuscripts also accepted. We will consider elementary-level religious materials and plays, but no elementary-level children's secular plays.''
Tips ''We publish a wide variety of speech contest materials for high-school students. We are publishing more full-length play scripts and musicals parodies based on classic literature or popular TV shows. Our educational books are sold to teachers and students at college and high-school levels. Our religious books are sold to youth activity directors, pastors, and choir directors. Another group of buyers is the professional theater, radio, and TV category. We will be especially interested in full-length (two- or three-act) plays with name recognition (either the playwright or the adaptation source).''

METROSTAGE

1201 N. Royal St., Alexandria VA 22314. (703)548-9044. Fax: (703)548-9089. Web site: www.metrostage.org. **Contact:** Carolyn Griffin, producing artistic director. Estab. 1984. **Produces 5-6 plays/year.** Professional productions for 130-seat theatre, general audience. Agented submissions only. Responds in 3 months. **Pays royalty.**
Needs Contemporary themes, small cast (up to 6 actors), unit set.
Tips ''Plays should have *already* had readings and workshops before being sent for our review. Do not send plays that have never had a staged reading.''

MOVING ARTS

P.O. Box 481145, Los Angeles CA 90048. (323)666-3259. E-mail: treynichols@movingarts.org. Web site: www.movingarts.org. Artistic Director: Paul Nicolai Stein. **Contact:** Trey Nichols, literary director. Estab. 1992. **Pro-**

duces 10 plays/year. Professional productions produced under Actors Equity Association 99-Seat Plan. "Our audiences are progressive, culturally adventurous, diverse adults." Query with synopsis, 10-20 page dialogue sample, bio, cover letter. Responds in 9 months. Obtains 5% of future income for 5-year period. **Pays 6% of box office gross.** Include SASE for return of submissions.

Needs Full-length and one-act plays. (One-act plays accepted *only* for Premiere One-Act Competition. $10 entry fee, $200 1st prize. Submission period is November 1-January 31. Send SASE or e-mail for full guidelines.) Original drama or comedy that is bold, challenging, and edgy; plays that speak to the human condition in a fresh and startling way. "We are not limited to any particular style or genre; we are confined only by the inherent truth of the material." Cast limit of 8. Theatre is a 60-seat black box. Limited backstage space, no fly space, limited wing space. "No plays that are like sitcoms or showcases, or too 'well-made.' We don't do plays for children (although we welcome young audiences) and tend to stay away from period pieces, heavy dramas, and performance art."

Tips "If you're a Southern California playwright, come see our play readings and shows. Party with us! Get to know us, our spirit, and our work. If not, control the controllable. Keep your cover letter brief, polite, and to the point. If you've been referred by a writer or director or seen prior productions, mention it. If you've seen prior productions, we appreciate it. When we read your work, we respond to the writing, but professionalism (or lack thereof) affects our evaluation in terms of potential artistic relationship. Three-hole punched script, 2-3 fasteners, SASE, clean copy, it all matters. Be patient with our process. Don't pester with follow-up queries. We love playwrights, so trust that your work will recieve as much time and attention as our limited but committed resources allow."

NEBRASKA THEATRE CARAVAN

6915 Cass St., Omaha NE 68132. Fax: (402)553-6288. E-mail: info@omahaplayhouse.com. Web site: www.omahaplayhouse.com. Artistic Director: Carl Beck. **Contact:** Brynna Cool, director of development. Estab. 1976. **Produces 4-5 plays/year.** "Nebraska Theatre Caravan is a touring company which produces professional productions in schools, arts centers, and small and large theaters for elementary, middle, high school and family audiences." Query and synopsis. Responds in 3 weeks. Negotiates production rights "unless the work is commissioned by us." **Pays $20-50 per performance.**

Needs "All genres are acceptable bearing in mind the student audiences. We are truly an ensemble and like to see that in our choice of shows; curriculum ties are very important for elementary and hich school shows; 75 minutes for middle/high school shows. No sexually explicit material."

Tips "We tour eight months of the year to a variety of locations. Flexibility is important as we work in both beautiful performing arts facilities and school multipurpose rooms."

THE NEW GROUP

410 W. 42nd St., New York NY 10036. (212)244-3380. Fax: (212)244-3438. E-mail: info@thenewgroup.org. Web site: www.thenewgroup.org. Artistic Director: Scott Elliott. **Contact:** Ian Morgan, associate artistic director. Estab. 1991. **Produces 4 plays/year.** Off-Broadway theater. Submit 10-page sample, cover letter, résumé, synopsis, and SASE. Responds in 9 months to submissions. **Pays royalty. Makes outright purchase.**

- No submissions that have already been produced in NYC.

Needs "We produce challenging, character-based scripts with a contemporary sensibility." Does not want to receive musicals, historical scripts or science fiction.

NEW JERSEY REPERTORY CO.

179 Broadway, Long Branch NJ 07740. (732)229-3166. Web site: www.njrep.org. Artistic Director: SuzAnne Barabas. **Contact:** Literary Manager. Estab. 1997. **Produces 6 plays/year and 25 script-in-hand readings.** Professional productions year round. Previously unproduced plays and musicals only. Submit script with SASE. Responds in 1 year. Rights negotiable.

Needs Full-length plays with a cast size no more than 5. Unit or simple set.

NEW PLAYS, INC.

P.O. Box 5074, Charlottesville VA 22905. (434)823-7555. E-mail: pat@newplaysforchildren.com. Web site: www.newplaysforchildren.com. **Contact:** Patricia Whitton Forrest, publisher. Estab. 1964. **Publishes 3-6 plays/year.** Publishes for children's or youth theaters. Submit complete script. Attempts to respond in 2 months, sometimes longer. Buys all semi-professional and amateur rights in US and Canada. **Pays 50% royalty on productions, 10% on sale of books.**

Needs "I have eclectic taste—plays must have quality and originality in whatever genres, topics, styles or lengths the playwright chooses."

Tips "No adaptations of stuff that has already been adapted a million times, i.e., *Tom Sawyer*, *A Christmas Carol*, or plays that sound like they've been written by the guidance counselor. There will be more interest in youth theater productions with moderate to large casts (15 people). Plays must have been produced and directed by someone other than the author or author's spouse. People keep sending us material suitable for adults—this is not our market. Read our online catalog."

NEW REPERTORY THEATRE

200 Dexter Ave., Waterton MA 02472. (617)923-8487. Fax: (617)923-7625. E-mail: info@newrep.org. Web site: www.newrep.org. **Contact:** Rick Lombardo, producing artistic director. Estab. 1984. **Produces 5 plays/year.** Professional theater, general audience. Query with synopsis and dialogue sample. Buys production and subsidiary rights. **Pays 5-10% royalty.**

Needs Idea laden, all styles, full-length only. New musicals.

Tips No sitcom-like comedies. Incorporating and exploring styles other than naturalism.

NEW STAGE THEATRE

1100 Carlisle, Jackson MS 39202. (601)948-3533. Fax: (601)948-3538. E-mail: newstage@netdoor.com. Web site: www.newstagetheatre.com. **Contact:** Artistic Director. Estab. 1965. **Produces 8 plays/year.** "Professional productions, 8 mainstage, 1 in our 'second space.' We play to an audience comprised of Jackson, the state of Mississippi and the Southeast." Query and synopsis. Exclusive premiere contract upon acceptance of play for mainstage production. **Pays 5-8% royalty. Pays $25-60 per performance.**

Needs Southern themes, contemporary issues, small casts (5-8), single set plays.

NEW THEATRE

4120 Laguna St., Coral Gables FL 33146. (305)443-5373. Fax: (305)443-1642. E-mail: playsubmissions@newtheatre.org. Web site: www.new-theatre.org. **Contact:** Literary Manager. Estab. 1986. **Produces 7 plays/year.** Professional productions. Submit query and synopsis. Responds in 3-6 months. Rights subject to negotiation. **Payment negotiable.**

Needs Interested in full-length, non-realistic, moving, intelligent, language-driven plays with a healthy dose of humor. No musicals or large casts.

Tips "No kitchen sink realism. Send a simple query with synopsis. Be mindful of social issues."

NEW THEATRE

542 King St., Newtown NSW 2042, Australia. (61)(2)9519-3403. Fax: (61)(2)9519-8960. E-mail: newtheatre@bigpond.com. Web site: www.newtheatre.org.au. **Contact:** Administrator. Estab. 1932. "We welcome the submission of new scripts." Submissions are assessed by playreaders and the artistic director. Submit complete ms and SASE.

NEW YORK THEATRE WORKSHOP

83 E. 4th St., New York NY 10003. Fax: (212)460-8996. Web site: nytw.org. Artistic Director: James C. Nicoloa. **Contact:** Literary Department. Estab. 1979. **Produces 6-7 full productions and approximately 50 readings/year.** Plays are performed off-Broadway. Audience is New York theater-going audience and theater professionals. Query with cover letter, synopsis, 10-page dialogue sample, 2 letters of recommendation. Include tape/CD/video where appropriate. Responds in 6-10 months.

Needs Full-length plays, translations/adaptations, music theater pieces; proposals for performance projects. Socially relevant issues, innovative form, and language.

Tips "No overtly commercial and conventional musicals or plays."

NORTH SHORE MUSIC THEATRE AT DUNHAM WOODS

P.O. Box 62, Beverly MA 01915. (978)232-7200. Fax: (978)921-7874. E-mail: jlarock@nsmt.org. Web site: www.nsmt.org. **Contact:** John La Rock, producer. Estab. 1955. **Produces 8 plays/year.** Plays are performed at Arena theater for 27,500 subscribers. Submit letter of interest, synopsis, production details, music tape/CD, SASE. Responds in 4 months. Rights negotiable. **Payment negotiable.**

Needs Musicals only (adult and children's), with cast size under 20.

Tips No straight plays, opera.

NORTHLIGHT THEATRE

9501 Skokie Blvd., Skokie IL 60077. (847)679-9501. Fax: (847)679-1879. Web site: www.northlight.org. **Contact:** Rosanna Forrest, artistic associate. Estab. 1975. **Produces 5 plays/year.** "We are a professional, equity theater, LORT C. We have a subscription base of over 8,000 and have a significant number of single ticket buyers." Query with 10-page dialogue sample, synopsis, résumé/bio, and SASE/SASPC for response. Responds in 3-4 months. Buys production rights, plus royalty on future mountings. **Pays royalty.**

Needs "Full-length plays, translations, adaptations, musicals. Interested in plays of 'ideas'; plays that are

passionate and/or hilarious; accessible plays that challenge, incite, and reflect the beliefs of our society/community. Generally looking for cast size of 6 or fewer, but there are exceptions made for the right play."
Tips "As a mainstream regional theater, we are unlikely to consider anything overtly experimental or absurdist. We seek good stories, vivid language, rich characters, and strong understandings of theatricality."

THE O'NEILL PLAYWRIGHTS CONFERENCE

305 Great Neck Rd., Waterford CT 06385. (860)443-5378. Fax: (860)443-9653. E-mail: info@theoneill.org; playwrights@theoneill.org. Web site: www.theoneill.org. Artistic Director: Wendy C. Goldberg. **Contact:** Jill Mauritz, production manager. Estab. 1964. **Produces 7-8 plays/year.** The O'Neill Center theater is located in Waterford, Connecticut, and operates under an Equity LORT contract. There are 4 theaters: Barn—250 seats, Edith Oliver Theater—150 seats, Dina Merrill—188 seats. "Please send #10 SASE for guidelines in the fall, or check online." Decision by late April. We accept submissions September 1-October 1 of each year. Conference takes place during June/July each summer. Playwrights selected are in residence for one month and receive a four-day workshop and two script-in-hand readings with professional actors and directors. **Pays stipend plus room, board and transportation.**

EUGENE O'NEILL THEATER CENTER, O'NEILL MUSIC THEATER CONFERENCE

305 Great Neck Rd., Waterford CT 06385. (860)443-5378. Fax: (860)443-9653. Web site: www.oneilltheatercenter.org. Executive Director: Amy Sullivan. Developmental process for new music theater works. Creative artists are in residence with artistic staff and equity company of actors/singers. Public and private readings, script in hand, piano only. For guidelines and application deadlines, send SASE to address above. **Pays stipend, room and board.**

ODYSSEY THEATRE ENSEMBLE

2055 S. Sepulveda Blvd., Los Angeles CA 90025. (310)477-2055. Fax: (310)444-0455. **Contact:** Sally Essex-Lopresti, director of literary programs. Estab. 1969. **Produces 9 plays/year.** Plays performed in a 3-theater facility. "All 3 theaters are Equity 99-seat theater plan. We have a subsciption audience of 4,000 for a nine-play main season, and they are offered a discount on our rentals and co-productions. Remaining seats are sold to the general public." No unsolicited material. Query with résumé, synopsis, 10 pages of sample dialogue, and cassette if musical. Responds in 2 weeks. Buys negotiable rights. **Pays 5-7% royalty.** Does not return scripts without SASE.
Needs "Full-length plays only with either an innovative form and/or provocative subject matter. We desire highly theatrical pieces that explore possibilities of the live theater experience. We are not reading one-act plays or light situation comedies."

OMAHA THEATER CO./ROSE THEATER

2001 Farnam St., Omaha NE 68102. (402)345-9718. E-mail: jlarsonotc@msn.com. Web site: www.rosetheater.org. **Contact:** James Larson, artistic director. **Produces 6-10 plays/year.** "Our target audience is children, preschool-high school and their parents." Query and synopsis. Responds in 9 months. **Pays royalty.**
Needs "Plays must be geared to children and parents (PG rating). Titles recognized by the general public have a stronger chance of being produced." Cast limit: 25 (8-10 adults). No adult scripts.
Tips "Unproduced plays may be accepted only after a letter of inquiry (familiar titles only!)."

ONE ACT PLAY DEPOT

Box 335, Spiritwood Saskatchewan S0J 2M0, Canada. E-mail: submissions@oneactplays.net. Web site: oneactplays.net. Accepts unsolicited submissions only in February of each year. Submit complete script by mail or via e-mail as a plaintxt file or pasted into the body of the message.
Needs Interested only in one-act plays. Does not want musicals or farces. Do not mail originals. "Our main focus will be black comedy, along with well-written dramatic and comedic pieces."

OREGON SHAKESPEARE FESTIVAL

15 S. Pioneer St., Ashland OR 97520. Fax: (541)482-0446. Web site: www.osfashland.org. Artistic Director: Bill Rauch. **Contact:** Director of Literary Development and Dramaturgy. Estab. 1935. **Produces 11 plays/year.** OSF directly solicits playwright or agent, and does not accept unsolicited submissions.

PERTH THEATRE COMPANY

P.O. Box Y3514, East St. George Terrace, Perth WA 6832, Australia. (61)(8)9323-3433. Fax: (61)(8)9323-3455. E-mail: admin@perththeatre.com.au. Web site: www.perththeatre.com.au. **Contact:** Alan Becher, artistic director. Estab. 1983. Seeks to develop new West Australian theatre and provide opportunities to talented local artists. Develops most of its scripts through the Writer's Lab program. Do not send an unsolicited ms unless it is submitted by or accompanied by a letter of recommendation from a writer's agency, script development organization, or professional theatre company. Make sure to include a SASE.

PIONEER DRAMA SERVICE, INC.

P.O. Box 4267, Englewood CO 80155-4267. (303)779-4035. Fax: (303)779-4315. E-mail: submissions@pioneerdrama.com. Web site: www.pioneerdrama.com. Publisher: Steven Fendrich. **Contact:** Lori Conary, submissions editor. Estab. 1963. **Publishes 30 plays/year.** Plays are performed by schools, colleges, community theaters, recreation programs, churches, and professional children's theaters for audiences of all ages. Query or submit complete ms. Responds in about 2 weeks to queries; 4-6 months to submissions. Retains all rights. Buys All rights. **Pays royalty.**

- All submissions automatically entered in Shubert Fendrich Memorial Playwriting Contest.

Needs Musicals, comedies, mysteries, dramas, melodramas, and children's theater. Two-acts up to 90 minutes; children's theater (1 hour); one-acts. Prefers large ensemble casts with many female roles, simple sets, and costumes. Plays need to be appropriate for amateur groups and family audiences. Interested in adaptations of classics of public domain works appropriate for children and teens. Also plays that deal with social issues for teens and preteens.

Tips "Check out our Web site to see what we carry and if your material would be appropriate for our market. Make sure to include proof of productions and a SASE if you want your material returned."

PLAYSCRIPTS, INC.

325 W. 38th St., Suite 305, New York NY 10018. E-mail: submissions@playscripts.com. Web site: www.playscripts.com. Estab. 1998. Audience is professional, community, college, high school and children's theaters worldwide. See Web site for complete submission guidelines. Response time varies. Buys exclusive publication and performance licensing rights. **Pays negotiated book and production royalties.**

Needs "We are open to a wide diversity of writing styles and content. Musicals are not accepted."

Tips "Playscripts, Inc. is a play publishing company dedicated to new work by established and emerging playwrights. We provide all of the same licensing and book production services as a traditional play publisher, along with unique promotional features that maximize the exposure of each dramatic work. Be sure to view our guidelines before submitting."

PLAYWRIGHTS HORIZONS

416 W. 42nd St., New York NY 10036. (212)564-1235. Fax: (212)594-0296. Web site: www.playwrightshorizons.org. Artistic Director: Tim Sanford. **Contact:** Steven Levenson, literary assistant (plays); send musicals Attn: Christie Evangelisto, Director of Musical Theater. Estab. 1971. **Produces 6 plays/year.** Plays performed off-Broadway for a literate, urban, subscription audience. Submit complete ms with author bio; include CD for musicals. Responds in 6-8 months. Negotiates for future rights. **Pays royalty. Makes outright purchase.**

Needs "We are looking for new, full-length plays and musicals by American authors."

Tips "No adaptations, children's theater, one-person shows, biographical or historical plays. We dislike synopses, because we accept unsolicited manuscripts. We look for plays with a strong sense of language and a clear dramatic action that truly use the resources of the theater."

[A] PLAYWRIGHTS THEATRE OF NEW JERSEY

P.O. Box 1295, Madison NJ 07940-1295. (973)514-1787. Fax: (973)514-2060. E-mail: phays@ptnj.org. Web site: www.ptnj.org. Artistic Director: John Pietrowski. **Contact:** Peter Hays, director of new play development. Estab. 1986. **Produces 3 plays/year.** "We operate under a Small Professional Theatre Contract (SPT), a development theatre contract with Actors Equity Association. Readings are held under a staged reading code." Responds in 1 year. "For productions we ask the playwright to sign an agreement that gives us exclusive rights to the play for the production period and for 30 days following. After the 30 days we give the rights back with no strings attached, except for commercial productions. We ask that our developmental work be acknowledged in any other professional productions." **Makes outright purchase of $750.**

- 10-page submission program has been discontinued. Accepts agented submission only.

Needs Any style or length; full length, one acts, musicals.

Tips "We are looking for American plays in the early stages of development—plays of substance, passion, and light (comedies and dramas) that raise challenging questions about ourselves and our communities. We prefer plays *that can work only on the stage* in the most theatrical way possible—plays that are not necessarily 'straight-on' realistic, but rather ones that use imagery, metaphor, poetry and musicality in new and interesting ways. Plays can go through a 3-step development process: A roundtable, a concert reading, and then a workshop production."

THE PLAYWRIGHTS' CENTER'S PLAYLABS

2301 Franklin Ave. E., Minneapolis MN 55406. (612)332-7481. Fax: (612)332-6037. E-mail: info@pwcenter.org. Web site: www.pwcenter.org. Producing Artistic Director: Polly K. Carl. Estab. 1971. "Playlabs is a 2-week developmental workshop for new plays. The program is held in Minneapolis and is open by script competition. Up to 5 new plays are given reading performances. Announcements of playwrights by May 1. Playwrights receive honoraria, travel expenses, room and board.

Needs "We are interested in playwrights with ambitions for a sustained career in theater, and scripts that could benefit from development involving professional dramaturgs, directors, and actors." US citizens or permanent residents only. Participants must attend entire festival. Send SASE after August 15 for application or see Web site. Submission deadline: October 26. Call for information on competitions. No previously produced materials.

Tips "We are a service organization that provides programs for developmental work on scripts for members."

PLAYWRIGHTS' PLATFORM

P.O. Box 267, State House Post Office, Boston MA 02133-0267. (781)894-0081. Web site: www.playwrightsplatfo rm.org. **Contact:** Jerry Bisantz, producing director. Estab. 1972. **Produces approximately 50 readings/year.** Plays are read in staged readings at Hovey Players on Spring St. (Walthan MA). Accepts scripts on a face-to-face basis. Submit script and SASE (or e-mail or hand deliver). Responds in 2 months.

Needs Any types of plays. "We will not accept scripts we think are sexist or racist." Massachusetts residents only. There are no restrictions on length or number of characters, but it's more difficult to schedule full-length pieces.

[A] PLOWSHARES THEATRE CO.

2870 E. Grand Blvd., Suite 600, Detroit MI 48202-3146. (313)872-0279. Fax: (313)872-0067. Web site: www.plow shares.org. **Contact:** Gary Anderson, producing artistic director. Estab. 1989. **Produces 5 plays/year.** Professional productions of plays by African-American writers for African-American audience and those who appreciate African-American culture. *Agented submissions only.* Responds in 8 months.

Tips "Submissions are more likely to be accepted if written by an African-American with the willingness to be developed. It must also be very good, and the writer should be ready to make a commitment."

PORTLAND STAGE CO.

P.O. Box 1458, Portland ME 04104. (207)774-1043. Fax: (207)774-0576. E-mail: info@portlandstage.com. Web site: www.portlandstage.com. Artistic Director: Anita Stewart. **Contact:** Daniel Burson, literary manager. Estab. 1974. **Produces 7 plays/year.** Professional productions at Portland Stage Company. Send first 10 pages with synopsis. Responds in 3 months. Buys 3- or 4-week run in Maine. **Pays royalty.**

Needs Developmental Staged Readings: Little Festival of the Unexpected.

Tips "Work developed in Little Festival generally will be more strongly considered for future production."

PRINCE MUSIC THEATER

100 S. Broad St., Suite 650, Philadelphia PA 19110. (215)972-1000. Fax: (215)972-1020. Web site: www.princem usictheater.org. **Contact:** Majorie Samoff, producing artistic director. Estab. 1984. **Produces 4 musicals/year.** Professional musical productions. Send synopsis and sample audio tape with no more than 4 songs. Responds in 6 months. **Pays royalty.**

Needs Song-driven music theater, varied musical styles. Nine in orchestra, 10-14 cast, 36x60 stage.

Tips Innovative topics and use of media, music, technology a plus. Sees trends of arts in technology (interactive theater, virtual reality, sound design); works are shorter in length (1-1æ hours with no intermissions or 2 hours with intermission).

PRINCETON REP COMPANY

One Palmer Square, Suite 541, Princeton NJ 08542. E-mail: prcreprap@aol.com. Web site: www.princetonrep.o rg. **Contact:** New Play Submissions. Estab. 1984. Plays are performed in site-specific venues, outdoor amphitheatres, and indoor theatres with approximately 199 seats. "Princeton Rep Company works under Actors' Eequity contracts, and its directors are members of the SSDC." Query with synopsis, SASE, résumé, and 10 pages of sample dialogue. Responds in up to 2 years. Rights are negotiated on a play-by-play basis. **Payment negotiated on a play-by-play basis.**

Needs Stories that investigate the lives of middle and working class people. "If the play demands a cast of thousands, please don't wste your time and postage." Love stories of the rich, famous, and fatuous, and no drama or comedy set in a prep school or ivy league college.

THE PUBLIC THEATER

425 Lafayette St., New York NY 10003. (212)539-8500. Web site: www.publictheater.org. Artistic Director: Oskar Eustis. **Contact:** Literary Department. Estab. 1964. **Produces 6 plays/year.** Professional productions.

Query with synopsis,10-page sample, letter of inquiry, cassette with 3-5 songs for musicals/operas. Responds in 1 month.

Needs Full-length plays, translations, adapatations, musicals, operas, and solo pieces. All genres, no one-acts.

PULSE ENSEMBLE THEATRE

266 W. 36th St., 22nd Floor, New York NY 10018. (212)695-1596. Fax: (212)594-4208. E-mail: theatre@pulseensembletheatre.org. Web site: www.pulseensembletheatre.org. **Contact:** Brian Richardson. Estab. 1989. **Produces 3 plays/year.** No unsolicited submissions. Only accepts new material through the Playwright's Lab. Buys variable rights. **Usually pays 2% of gross.**

Needs Meaningful theater. No production limitations. Does not want to see fluff or vanity theater.

THE PURPLE ROSE THEATRE CO.

P.O. Box 220, Chelsea MI 48118. (734)433-7782. Fax: (734)475-0802. Web site: www.purplerosetheatre.org. **Contact:** Guy Sanville, artistic director. Estab. 1990. **Produces 4 plays/year.** PRTC is a regional theater with an S.P.T. equity contract which produces plays intended for Midwest/Middle American audience. Query with synopsis, character breakdown, and 10-page dialogue sample. Responds in 9 months. **Pays 5-10% royalty.**

Needs Modern, topical full length, 75-120 minutes. Prefers scripts that use comedy to deal with serious subjects. 12 cast maximum. No fly space, unit set preferable but not required. Intimate 168 seat ¾ thrust house.

QUEENSLAND THEATRE COMPANY

P.O. Box 3310, South Brisbane QLD 4101, Australia. (61)(7)3010-7600. Fax: (61)(7)3010-7699. E-mail: mail@qldtheatreco.com.au. Web site: www.qldtheatreco.com.au. **Contact:** Michael Gow, artistic director. Seeks timeless classis, modern classics, and new plays from Australia and overseas. Only considers unsolicited scripts if the playwright has had at least 1 play professionally produced, or if the script has been workshopped, submitted by an agent, or recommended by a professional theatre company or script development agency. Responds in 3 months.

Needs Works specifically aimed at child/youth audiences are less likely to be considered.

RED LADDER THEATRE CO.

3 St. Peter's Buildings, York St., Leeds LS9 1AJ, United Kingdom. (44)(113)245-5311. E-mail: wendy@redladder.co.uk. Web site: www.redladder.co.uk. **Contact:** Rod Dixon, artistic director. Estab. 1969. **Produces 2 plays/year.** "Our work tours nationally to young people, aged 13-25, in youth clubs, community venues and small scale theatres." Query and synopsis. Responds in 6 months. **Offers ITC/Equity writers contract.**

Needs One hour in length for cast size no bigger than 5. Work that connects with a youth audience that both challenges them and offers them new insights. "We consider a range of styles and are seeking originality." Small scale touring. Does not want to commission single issue drama. The uses of new technologies in production (DVD, video projection). Young audiences are sophisticated.

Tips "Please do not submit full length plays. Get in touch with us first. Tell us about yourself and why you would like to write for Red Ladder. We like to hear about ideas you may have in the first instance."

RESOURCE PUBLICATIONS

160 E. Virginia St., Suite 290, San Jose CA 95112-5876. (408)286-8505. Fax: (408)287-8748. E-mail: editor@rpinet.com. Web site: www.resourcepublications.com. Editorial Director: William Burns. Estab. 1973. Audience includes laity and ordained seeking resources (books/periodicals/software) in Christian ministry, worship, faith formation, education, and counseling (primarily Roman Catholic, but not all). Submit query and synopsis via e-mail. Responds in 3 months.

Needs Needs materials for those in pastoral ministry, faith formation, youth ministry, and parish administration. No fiction, children's books, or music.

SALTWORKS THEATRE CO.

569 N. Neville St., Pittsburgh PA 15213. (412)621-6150. Fax: (412)621-6010. E-mail: nalrutz@saltworks.org. Web site: www.saltworks.org. **Contact:** Norma Alrutz, executive director. Estab. 1981. **Produces 8-10 plays/year.** Query and synopsis. Responds in 2 months. Obtains regional performance rights for educational grants. **Pays $25 per performance.**

Needs Wants plays for children, youth, and families that address social issues like violence prevention, sexual responsibility, peer pressures, tobacco use, bullying, racial issues/diversity, drug and alcohol abuse (grades 1-12). Limited to 5 member cast, 2 men/2 women/1 either.

Tips "Check Web site for current play contest rules and deadlines."

SEATTLE REPERTORY THEATRE

P.O. Box 900923, Seattle WA 98109. Web site: www.seattlerep.org. Artistic Director: David Esbjornson. **Contact:** Braden Abraham, literary manager. Estab. 1963. **Produces 8 plays/year.** Send query, résumé, synopsis and 10 sample pages. Responds in 6 months. Buys percentage of future royalties. **Pays royalty.**

Needs "The Seattle Repertory Theatre produces eclectic programming. We welcome a wide variety of writing."

SHAW FESTIVAL THEATRE

P.O. Box 774, Niagara-on-the-Lake ON L0S 1J0, Canada. (905)468-2153. Fax: (905)468-7140. Web site: www.shawfest.com. **Contact:** Jackie Maxwell, artistic director. Estab. 1962. **Produces 12 plays/year.** "Professional theater company operating 3 theaters (Festival: 869 seats; Court House: 327 seats; Royal George: 328 seats). Shaw Festival presents the work of George Bernard Shaw and his contemporaries written during his lifetime (1856-1950) and in 2000 expanded the mandate to include contemporary works written about the period of his lifetime." Query with SASE or SAE and IRC's, depending on country of origin. "We prefer to hold rights for Canada and northeastern US, also potential to tour." **Pays 5-10% royalty.**

Needs "We operate an acting ensemble of up to 75 actors; and we have sophisticated production facilities. During the summer season (April-November) the Academy of the Shaw Festival organizes workshops of new plays commissioned for the company."

SOUTH COAST REPERTORY

P.O. Box 2197, Costa Mesa CA 92628-2197. (714)708-5500. Fax: (714)545-0391. Web site: www.scr.org. Artistic Director: Martin Benson. **Contact:** Megan Monaghan, literary manager. Estab. 1964. **Produces 14 plays/year.** Professional nonprofit theater; a member of LORT and TCG. "We operate in our own facility which houses the 507-seat Segerstrom stage and 336-seat Julianne Argyros stage. We have a combined subscription audience of 18,000." Query with synopsis and 10 sample pages of dialogue, or submit full script through an agent. Responds in 4 months. Acquires negotiable rights. **Pays royalty.**

Needs "We produce full-length contemporary plays, as well as theatre for young audiences scripts with a running time of approximately 65 minutes. We prefer plays that address contemporary concerns and are dramaturgically innovative. A play whose cast is larger than 15-20 will need to be extremely compelling, and its cast size must be justifiable."

Tips "We don't look for a writer to write for us—he or she should write for him or herself. We look for honesty and a fresh voice. We're not likely to be interested in writers who are mindful of any trends. Originality and craftsmanship are the most important qualities we look for."

SOUTHERN APPALACHIAN REPERTORY THEATRE (SART)

Mars Hill College, P.O. Box 1720, Mars Hill NC 28754. (828)689-1384. E-mail: sart@mhc.edu. Managing Director: Rob Miller. Estab. 1975. **Produces 5-6 plays/year.** Since 1975 the Southern Appalachian Repertory Theatre has produced over 50 world premieres in the 166-seat Owen Theatre on the Mars Hill College campus. SART is a professional summer theater company whose audiences range from students to senior citizens. SART also conducts an annual playwrights conference in which 4-5 playwrights are invited for a weekend of public readings of their new scripts. The conference is held in March or May each year. Submissions must be postmarked by September 30. If a script read at the conference is selected for production, it will be given a fully-staged production in the following summer season. Playwrights receive honorarium and housing. Enclose SASE for return of script.

Needs Comedies, dramas and musicals. No screenplays, translations, or adaptations. Please send complete scripts of full-length plays and musicals, synopsis, and a recording of at least 4 songs (for musicals). Include name and contact information only on a cover sheet. New plays are defined as those that are unpublished and have not received a fully-staged professional production. "Workshops and other readings do not constitute a fully-staged production."

STAGE LEFT THEATRE

3408 N. Sheffield, Chicago IL 60657. (773)883-8830. E-mail: scripts@stagelefttheatre.com. Web site: www.stagelefttheatre.com. **Contact:** LaRonika Thomas, literary manager. Estab. 1982. **Produces 3-4 plays/year.** Professional productions (usually in Chicago), for all audiences (usually adult). Submit script through an agent or query with cover letter, 10-page excerpt, 1-page synopsis, SASE, supporting material, and résumé. Responds in 3 months. **Pays 6% royalty.**

Needs "Any length, any genre, any style that fits the Stage Left mission—to produce plays that raise debate on political and social issues. We do have an emphasis on new work."

STAMFORD THEATRE WORKS

307 Atlantic St., Stamford CT 06901. (203)359-4414. Fax: (203)356-1846. E-mail: stwct@aol.com. Web site: www.stamfordtheatreworks.org. **Contact:** Steve Karp, producing director. Estab. 1988. **Produces 4-6 plays/**

year. Professional productions for an adult audience. *Agented submissions* or queries with a professional recommendation. Responds in 3 months. **Pays 5-8% royalty.** Include SASE for return of submission.
Needs Plays of social relevance; contemporary work. Limited to unit sets; maximum cast of about 8.

STEPPENWOLF THEATRE CO.

758 W. North Ave., 4th Floor, Chicago IL 60610. (312)335-1888. Fax: (312)335-0808. Web site: www.steppenwolf.org. Artistic Director: Martha Lavey. **Contact:** Edward Sobel, director of new play development. Estab. 1976. **Produces 9 plays/year.** 500-, 250- and 100-seat performance venues. Many plays produced at Steppenwolf have gone to Broadway. "We currently have 20,000 savvy subscribers." Agented submissions only with full scripts. Others please check our Web site for submission guidelines. Unrepresented writers may send a 10-page sample along with cover letter, bio, and synopsis. Responds in 6-8 months. Buys commercial, film, television, and production rights. **Pays 5% royalty.**
Needs "Actor-driven works are crucial to us, plays that explore the human condition in our time. We max at around 10 characters."
Tips No musicals, one-person shows, or romantic/light comedies. Plays get produced at STC based on ensemble member interest.

STONEHAM THEATRE

395 Main St., Stoneham MA 02180. E-mail: weylin@stonehamtheatre.org. Web site: www.stonehamtheatre.org. **Contact:** Weylin Symes, artistic director. Estab. 1999. **Produces 7 plays/year.** "Plays will be produced on-stage in our 350-seat SPT-7 theater—either as part of the Mainstage Season or our Emerging stages series of new works." Submit complete script via mail or e-mail. Responds in 3 months. Rights acquired varies according to script. **Pays royalty.**
Needs "Anything of quality will be considered. We look for exciting new work with a fresh voice, but that can still appeal to a relatively mainstream audience." Does not want anything with a cast size over 18 for a musical or 9 for a play.

STUDIO ARENA THEATRE

710 Main St., Buffalo NY 14202. (716)856-8025. E-mail: jblaha@studioarena.com. Web site: www.studioarena.org. **Contact:** Jana Blaha, executive assistant. Estab. 1965. **Produces 6-8 plays/year.** Professional productions. Agented submissions only.
Needs Full-length plays. No fly space.
Tips "Do not fax or send submissions via the Internet. Submissions should appeal to a diverse audience. We do not generally produce musicals. Please send a character breakdown and 1-page synopsis for a faster reply."

TADA!

15 W. 28th St., 3rd Floor, New York NY 10001. (212)252-1619. Fax: (212)252-8763. E-mail: ewilson@tadatheater.com. Web site: www.tadatheater.com. **Contact:** Literary Manager. Estab. 1984. **Produces 3 musical plays/year.** "TADA! produces original musicals performed by children and teens, ages 8-18. Productions are for family audiences." Submit a brief summary of the musical, 10 pages from the scripts, and a CD or cassette with songs from the score. Responds in 2-3 months. **Pays 5% royalty. Commission fee.**

- TADA! also sponsors an annual one-act playwriting contest for their Spring Staged Reading Series. Works must be original, unproduced and unpublished one-acts. Plays must be geared toward teen audiences. Call or e-mail for guidelines.

Needs Generally pieces run 1 hour long. Must be enjoyed by children and adults and performed by a cast of children ages 8-18.
Tips "No redone fairy tales or pieces where children are expected to play adults. Plays with animals and nonhuman characters are highly discouraged. Be careful not to condescend when writing for children's theater."

THE TEN-MINUTE MUSICALS PROJECT

P.O. Box 461194, West Hollywood CA 90046. E-mail: info@tenminutemusicals.org. Web site: www.tenminutemusicals.org. **Contact:** Michael Koppy, producer. Estab. 1987. **Produces 1-10 plays/year.** "Plays performed in Equity regional theaters in the US and Canada." Deadline August 31; notification by November 30. Submit complete script, lead sheets and, cassette/CD. Buys first performance rights. **Pays $250 royalty advance upon selection, against equal share of performance royalties when produced.**
Needs Looking for complete short stage musicals lasting 7-14 minutes. Limit cast to 10 (5 women, 5 men).

THEATER AT LIME KILN

P.O. Box 1244, Lexington VA 24450. Web site: www.theateratlimekiln.com. Estab. 1984. **Produces 3 (1 new) plays/year.** Outdoor summer theater (May through October) and indoor space (October through May, 144

seats). Query and synopsis. Responds in 3 months. Buys performance rights. **Pays $25-75 per performance.**
Needs Plays that explore the history and heritage of the Appalachian region. Minimum set required.
Tips "Searching for plays that can be performed in outdoor space. Prefer plays that explore the cultural and/or history of the Appalichian region."

THEATER BY THE BLIND

306 W. 18th St., New York NY 10011. (212)243-4337. Fax: (212)243-4337. E-mail: gar@nyc.rr.com. Web site: www.tbtb.org. **Contact:** Ike Schambelan, artistic director. Estab. 1979. **Produces 2 plays/year.** "Off Broadway, Theater Row, general audiences, seniors, students, disabled. If play transfers, we'd like a piece." Submit complete script. Responds in 3 months. **Pays $1,000-1,500/production.**
Needs Genres about blindness.

THEATRE BUILDING CHICAGO

1225 W. Belmont Ave., Chicago IL 60657. (773)929-7367 ext. 22. Fax: (773)327-1404. E-mail: tim@theatrebuildingchicago.org. Web site: www.theatrebuildingchicago.org. **Contact:** John Sparks, artistic director. **Produces mostly readings of new works, 4 skeletal productions, and Stages Festival.** "Mostly developed in our workshop. Some scripts produced are unagented submissions. Plays performed in 3 small off-Loop theaters are seating 148 for a general theater audience, urban/suburban mix." Submit synopsis, sample scene, CD or cassette tape and piano/vocal score of three songs, and author bios. Responds in 3 months.
Needs Musicals *only*. "We're interested in all forms of musical theater including more innovative styles. Our production capabilities are limited by the lack of space, but we're very creative and authors should submit anyway. The smaller the cast, the better. We are especially interested in scripts using a younger (35 and under) ensemble of actors. We mostly look for authors who are interested in developing their scripts through workshops, readings and production." No one-man shows or 'single author' pieces.
Tips "We would like to see the musical theater articulating something about the world around us, as well as diverting an audience's attention from that world." Offers Script Consultancy—A new program designed to assist authors and composers in developing new musicals through private feedback sessions with professional dramaturgs and musical directors. For further info contact (773)929-7367, ext. 222.

THEATRE IV

114 W. Broad St., Richmond VA 23220. (804)783-1688. Fax: (804)775-2325. E-mail: info@theatreivrichmond.org. Web site: www.theatreiv.org. **Contact:** Janine Serresseque. Estab. 1975. **Produces approximately 20 plays/year.** National tour of plays for young audiences—maximum cast of 5, maximum length of an hour. Mainstage plays for young audiences in 600 or 350 seat venues. Query and synopsis. Responds in 1 month. Buys standard production rights. **Payment varies.**
Needs Touring and mainstage plays for young audiences. Touring—maximum cast of 5, length of 60 minutes.

THEATRE THREE

P.O. Box 512, 412 Main St., Port Jefferson NY 11777-0512. (631)928-9202. Fax: (631)928-9120. Web site: www.theatrethree.com. **Contact:** Jeffrey Sanzel, artistic director. Estab. 1969. "We produce an Annual Festival of One-Act Plays on our Second Stage." Deadline for submission is September 30. Send SASE for festival guidelines or visit Web site. Responds in 6 months. "We ask for exclusive rights up to and through the festival." **Pays $75 for the run of the festival.**
Needs One-act plays. Maximum length: 40 minutes. "Any style, topic, etc. We require simple, suggested sets and a maximum cast of 6. No adaptations, musicals or children's works."
Tips "Too many plays are monologue-dominant. Please—reveal your characters through action and dialogue."

THEATRE WEST

3333 Cahuenga Blvd. W., Hollywood CA 90068-1365. (323)851-4839. Fax: (323)851-5286. E-mail: theatrewest@theatrewest.org. Web site: www.theatrewest.org. **Contact:** Chris DiGiovanni and Doug Haverty, moderators of the Writers Workshop. Estab. 1962. "99-seat waiver productions in our theater. Audiences are primarily young urban professionals." Residence in Southern California is vital as it's a weekly workshop. Submit script, résumé and letter requesting membership. Responds in 4 months. Contracts a percentage of writer's share to other media if produced on MainStage by Theatre West. **Pays royalty based on gross box office.**
Needs Full-length plays only, no one-acts. Uses minimalistic scenery, no fly space.
Tips "Theatre West is a dues-paying membership company. Only members can submit plays for production. So you must first seek membership to the Writers Workshop. We accept all styles of theater writing, but theater only—no screenplays, novels, short stories or poetry will be considered for membership."

THEATREWORKS

1100 Hamilton Court, Menlo Park CA 94025-1425. (650)463-7126. Fax: (650)463-1963. E-mail: kent@theatreworks.org. Web site: www.theatreworks.org. **Contact:** Kent Nicholson, new works director. Estab. 1970. **Produces 8 plays/year.** Specializes in development of new musicals. Plays are professional productions intended for an adult audience. Submit synopsis, 10 pages of sample dialogue, and SASE. Responds in 6-8 months. Buys performance rights. **Payment varies per contract.**

Needs TheatreWorks has a high standard for excellence. "We prefer well-written, well-constructed plays that celebrate the human spirit through innovative productions and programs inspired by our exceptionally diverse community. There is no limit on the number of characters, and we favor plays with multi-ethnic casting possibilities. We are a LORT C company. Plays are negotiated per playwright." Does not want one-acts, plays with togas. "We are particularly interested in plays with musical elements."

Tips "Guidelines are online—check out our Web site for Submission Checklist Request and the New Works Program under New Works."

UNICORN THEATRE

3828 Main St., Kansas City MO 64111. (816)531-7529 ext. 22. Fax: (816)531-0421. Web site: www.unicorntheatre.org. Producing Artistic Director: Cynthia Levin. **Contact:** Herman Wilson, literary assistant. **Produces 6-8 plays/year.** "We are a professional Equity Theatre. Typically, we produce plays dealing with contemporary issues." Send complete script (to Herman Wilson) with brief synopsis, cover letter, bio, character breakdown. Send #10 SASE for results. Does not return scripts. Responds in 4-8 months.

Needs Prefers contemporary (post-1950) scripts. Does not accept musicals, one-acts, or historical plays. A royalty/prize of $1,000 will be awarded the playwright of any play selected through this process, The New Play Development Award. This script receives production as part of the Unicorn's regular season.

URBAN STAGES

17 E. 47th St., New York NY 10017. (212)421-1380. Fax: (212)421-1387. E-mail: urbanstage@aol.com. Web site: www.urbanstages.org. **Contact:** Frances Hill. Estab. 1986. **Produces 2-4 plays/year.** Professional productions off Broadway—throughout the year. General audience. Submit complete script. Responds in 4 months. If produced, option for 1 year. **Pays royalty.**

- Enter Emerging Playwright Award competition at $10/play. Prize is $8,500, plus NYC production.

Needs Full-length; generally 1 set or styled playing dual. Good imaginative, creative writing. Cast limited to 3-6.

Tips "We tend to reject 'living-room' plays. We look for imaginative settings. Be creative and interesting. No one acts. No e-mail submissions, scripts are not returned."

UTAH SHAKESPEAREAN FESTIVAL

New American Playwright's Program, 351 W. Center St., Cedar City UT 84720-2498. (435)586-7884. Fax: (435)865-8003. Founder/Executive Producer Emeritus: Fred C. Adams. **Contact:** Charles Metten, director. Estab. 1993. **Produces 9 plays/year.** Travelling audiences ranging in ages from 6-80. Programming includes classic plays, musicals, new works. Submit complete script; no synopsis. No musicals. Responds in 3-4 months. **Pays travel, housing, and tickets for USF productions only.**

Needs The USF is only interested in material that explores characters and ideas that focus on the West and our western experience, spirit, and heritage. Preference is given to writers whose primary residence is in the western United States. New plays are for staged readings only. These are not fully mountable productions. Cast size is a consideration due to the limited time of rehearsal and the actors available during the USF production period. Does not want plays that do not match criteria or plays longer than 90 pages.

Tips "We want previously unproduced plays with western themes by western playwrights."

WALNUT STREET THEATRE

Ninth and Walnut Streets, Philadelphia PA 19107. (215)574-3550. Fax: (215)574-3598. Producing Artistic Director: Bernard Havard. **Contact:** Literary Office. Estab. 1809. **Produces 10 plays/year.** "Our plays are performed in our own space. WST has 3 theaters—a proscenium (mainstage), 1,052 seats; and 2 studios, 79-99 seats. We have a subscription audience—the largest in the nation." Query with synopsis, 10-20 pages of dialogue, character breakdown, and bio. Include SASE for return of materials. Responds in 5 months. Rights negotiated per project. **Pays negotiable royalty or makes outright purchase.**

Needs Full-length dramas and comedies, musicals, translations, adaptations, and revues. The studio plays must have a cast of no more than 4 and use simple sets.

Tips "Bear in mind that on the mainstage we look for plays with mass appeal, Broadway-style. The studio spaces are our off-Broadway. No children's plays. Our mainstage audience goes for work that is entertaining and light. Our studio season is where we look for plays that have bite and are more provocative."

WILLOWS THEATRE CO.

1425 Gasoline Alley, Concord CA 94520. (925)798-1824. Fax: (925)676-5726. Web site: www.willowstheatre.org. Artistic Director: Richard Elliott. **Produces 6 plays/year.** "Professional productions for a suburban audience." Accepts new manuscripts in March and April only; accepts queries year-round. Responds in 6-12 months to scripts. **Pays standard royalty.**

Needs "Commercially viable, small-medium size musicals or comedies that are popular, rarely produced, or new. Certain stylized plays or musicals with a contemporary edge to them (e.g., *Les Liasons Dangereuses, La Bete, Candide*)." No more than 15 actors. Unit or simple sets with no fly space, no more than 7 pieces. "We are not interested in 1-character pieces."

Tips "Our audiences want light entertainment, comedies, and musicals. Also, have an interest in plays and musicals with a historical angle." Submission guidelines are on Web site.

[A] THE WILMA THEATER

265 S. Broad St., Philadelphia PA 19107. (215)893-9456. Fax: (215)893-0895. E-mail: wcb@wilmatheater.org. Web site: www.wilmatheater.org. **Contact:** Walter Bilderback, dramaturg and literary manager. Estab. 1980. **Produces 4 plays/year.** LORT-C 300-seat theater, 7,500 subscribers. *Agented submissions only* for full mss. Accepts queries with cover letter, résumé, synopsis, and sample if recommended by a literary manager, dramaturg, or other theater professional. Responds in 6 months.

Needs Full-length plays, translations, adaptations, and musicals from an international repertoire with emphasis on innovative, bold staging; world premieres; ensemble works; works with poetic dimension; plays with music; multimedia works; social issues. Prefers maximum cast size of 12. Stage 44′×46′.

Tips "Before submitting any material to The Wilma Theater, please research our production history. Considering the types of plays we have produced in the past, honestly assess whether or not your play would suit us. In general, I believe researching the various theaters to which you send your play is important in the long and short run. Different theaters have different missions and therefore seek out material corresponding with those goals. In other words, think through what is the true potential of your play and this theater, and if it is a compatible relationship."

WOMEN'S PROJECT AND PRODUCTIONS

55 West End Ave., New York NY 10023. (212)765-1706. Fax: (212)765-2024. Web site: www.womensproject.org. **Contact:** Megan E. Carter, artistic associate. Estab. 1978. **Produces 3 plays/year.** Professional Off-Broadway productions. Query with synopsis and 10 sample pages of dialogue. Responds in 8-12 months.

Needs "We are looking for full-length plays written by women."

[A] WOOLLY MAMMOTH THEATRE CO.

641 D St. NW, Washington DC 20004. (202)289-2443. Fax: (202)289-2446. E-mail: info@woollymammoth.net. Web site: www.woollymammoth.net. Artistic Director: Howard Shalwitz. **Contact:** Elissa Goetschius, literary associate. Estab. 1980. **Produces 5 plays/year.** Produces professional productions for the general public. Solicited submissions only. Responds in 6 months to scripts; very interesting scripts often take much longer. Buys first- and second-class production rights. **Pays variable royalty.**

Needs "We look for plays with a distinctive authorial voice. Our work is word and actor driven. One-acts and issue-driven plays are not used." Cast limit of 5.

MARKETS

Greeting Cards

Greeting cards are an intricate part of American culture. There are, of course, cards tied to holidays, birthdays, graduations, and weddings. There are ''thinking of you'' cards, condolences cards, thank you cards, get well cards, and humor cards. And many of these cards are specialized to mom, dad, mother-in-law, father-in-law, son, daughter, cousin, and even ex-girlfriend's roommate from college (okay, that may be stretching it—but only slightly). Point is, they are here; they've all got a special message to deliver; and someone has to write them.

Freelance realities

Writers who make a decent income writing greeting cards are almost always staff writers or those who are on contract. Freelance writers do not typically earn enough to use greeting card sales as any more than a supplemental source of income.

In the most recent ''How Much Should I Charge?'' survey (on page 64), freelancers made $50 on the low end to $300 on the high end per card. And that is from a more experienced set of freelancers. It is known that some freelancers settle for payment as low as $5 to $10 per card idea, which makes it harder for newer writers to negotiate higher payments.

Listings

Each listing includes contact information, submission specs, needs, and payment details. While we work to give you the most up-to-date listing information, it is still recommended that you either contact the companies or check out their Web sites to confirm specific submission policies and needs. This little bit of extra work is what often sets apart professional writers from the rest of the pack. In a competitive market such as greeting cards, professionalism goes a long way toward ensuring success.

For more information

To learn even more about the greeting card industry, check out the Greeting Card Association (GCA) Web site at www.greetingcard.org. It provides industry statistics, tips, and information on specific greeting card companies.

AMERICAN GREETINGS

One American Rd., Cleveland OH 44144-2398. (216)252-7300. Fax: (216)252-6778. Web site: www.americangreetings.com. No unsolicited material. Experienced, talented writers should submit a cover letter and résumé describing their education and content experience for contract-to-permanent staff writing positions.

Needs Humorous.

Tips "In this competitive arena, we're only looking for gifted humor writers and cartoonists who are interested in adapting their skillsets to the uniqueness of greeting card composition."

BLUE MOUNTAIN ARTS, INC.

P.O. Box 1007, Boulder CO 80306. (303)449-0536. Fax: (303)447-0939. E-mail: editorial@sps.com. Web site: www.sps.com. **Acquisitions:** Editorial Department. Estab. 1971. **Bought over 200 freelance ideas last year.** Submit seasonal/holiday material 4 months in advance. Responds in 2-4 months. Buys worldwide, exclusive rights, or anthology rights. Pays on publication. Request writer's guidelines through Web site.

"We like to receive original, sensitive poetry and prose on love, friendship, family, philosophies, and any other topic that one person might want to communicate or share with another person. Writings on special occasions (birthday, anniversary, congratulations, etc.) as well as the challenges, difficulties, and aspirations of life are also considered. Important note: Because of the large volume of poetry we receive written to mothers, sons, and daughters, we are only accepting highly original and creative poetry that expresses new thoughts and sentiments on these themes." "Submissions should reflect a message, feeling, or sentiment that one person would want to share with another. Full book manuscripts or proposals are also accepted for possible publication by our book division, Blue Mountain Press." **Pays $300 for the first work chosen for publication on a card (payment scale escalates after that); $50 for anthology rights; payment schedule for books will be discussed at time of acceptance.**

Other Product Lines Calendars, gift books, prints, mugs.

Tips "We strongly suggest that you familiarize yourself with our products before submitting material, although we caution you not to study them too hard. We do not need more poems that sound like something we've already published. We're looking for poetry that expresses real emotions and feelings, so we suggest that you have someone specific in mind (a friend, relative, etc.) as you write. We do not wish to receive rhymed poetry, religious verse, or one-liners. We prefer that submissions be typewritten, one poem per page, with name and address on every page. Only a small portion of the freelance material we receive is selected each year, either for publication on a notecard or in a gift anthology, and the review process can also be lengthy, but please be assured that every manuscript is given serious consideration."

BRILLIANT ENTERPRISES

117 W. Valerio St., Santa Barbara CA 93101-2927. **Acquisitions:** Ashleigh Brilliant, president. Estab. 1967. Responds in 2 weeks. Buys all rights. Catalog and sample set for $2.

Needs Postcards. "Messages should be of a highly original nature, emphasizing subtlety, simplicity, insight, wit, profundity, beauty and felicity of expression. Accompanying art should be in the nature of oblique commentary or decoration rather than direct illustration. Messages should be of universal appeal, capable of being appreciated by all types of people and of being easily translated into other languages. Because our line of cards is highly unconventional, it is essential that freelancers study it before submitting. No topical references or subjects limited to American culture or puns." Submit words and art in black on $3\frac{1}{2} \times 3\frac{1}{2}$ horizontal, thin white paper in batches of no more than 15. Limit of 17 words/card. **Pays $60 for "complete, ready-to-print word and picture design."**

COMSTOCK CARDS

600 S. Rock Blvd., Suite 15, Reno NV 89502. (775)856-9400. Fax: (775)856-9406. E-mail: production@comstockcards.com. Web site: www.comstockcards.com. **Acquisitions:** Editorial Department. Estab. 1986. **35% freelance written. Receives 2,000 submissions/year; bought 150 freelance ideas last year.** months in advance. Responds in 5 weeks. Buys all rights. **Pays on acceptance.** Writer's guidelines for #10 SASE or online.

Seeks middle-of-the-road humor to wildly risqué on these subjects: birthday, get well, bachelor/bachelorette, divorce, thank you, anniversary, get married, retirement, congratulations, and love/friendship.

Needs Humorous, informal, invitations. Puns, put-downs, put-ons, outrageous humor aimed at a sophisticated, adult audience. Also risqué cartoon cards. No conventional, soft line, or sensitivity (hearts and flowers, etc). Submit via e-mail or mail (include SASE). **Pays $50-75/card idea.**

Other Product Lines Notepads, cartoon cards, invitations, gift bags and coupon books.

Tips "Ideas must be simple and concisely delivered. A combination of strong image and strong gag line make a successful greeting card. Consumers relate to themes of work, sex, and friendship combined with current social, political and economic issues."

DESIGNER GREETINGS

P.O. Box 140729, Staten Island NY 10314. (718)981-7700. Fax: (718) 981-0151. E-mail: info@designergreetings.com. Web site: www.designergreetings.com. **Acquisitions:** Fern Gimbelman, art director. Estab. 1978. **50% freelance written. Receives 200-300 submissions/year.** Submit seasonal/holiday material 6 months in advance. Responds in 2 months. Buys greeting card rights. **Pays on acceptance.** Writer's guidelines online at Web site.

O⊸ Themes include holidays, pets, animals, children, florals, and scenic views.

Needs Conventional, humorous, informal, inspirational, juvenile, sensitivity, soft line, studio. Query with SASE. Accepts rhymed or unrhymed verse.

DUCK AND COVER PRODUCTIONS

P.O. Box 21640, Oakland CA 94620. E-mail: duckcover@aol.com. **Acquisitions:** Jim Buser, editor. Estab. 1990. **50% freelance written. Receives 1,000 submissions/year; bought 120 freelance ideas last year.** Responds in 3 weeks. Buys all rights. Pays on publication. Writer's guidelines/market list for #10 SASE

Other Product Lines ''We do not make greeting cards.'' Buttons, magnets and bumper stickers only. **Pays $40/idea.**

Tips ''Duck and Cover holds the trump card for intelligent, contemporary humor. We are a smorgasbord of existential angst, psychotic babble, dry wit, and outrageous zingers. Our products appeal to anyone with an offbeat, irreverent sense of humor. We sell to novelty stores, head shops, record stores, bookstores, sex shops, comic stores, etc. There are no taboos for our writers; we encourage them to be as weird and/or rude as they like, as long as they are funny. Let your inner child thumb his nose at society. Cerebral material that makes use of contemporary pop vocabulary is a plus. We do not want to see old clichés or slogans already in the market. Drink a six pack, read the newspaper from beginning to end, and then try to make humorous reflections about what you've just read.''

EPHEMERA, INC.

P.O. Box 490, Phoenix OR 97535. E-mail: mail@ephemera-inc.com. Web site: www.ephemera-inc.com. **Acquisitions:** Ed Polish. Estab. 1980. **95% freelance written. Receives 2,000 submissions/year.** Buys nearly 200 slogans for novelty buttons, stickers,and magnets each year. Responds in 1-5 months. Buys all rights. **Pays on acceptance.** Writer's guidelines for SASE or online. Complete full-color catalog online or for $4. ''We produce irreverent, provocative, and outrageously funny buttons, magnets, and stickers. You'll find them in cutting-edge shops that sell cards, gifts, books, music, coffee, pipes, porn, etc. We're looking for snappy slogans about politics, women and bitchiness, work, parenting, coffee, booze, pot, drugs, religion, food, aging, teens, gays and lesbians, sexual come-ons and put-downs, etc. Pretty please, don't limit yourself to these topics. Surprise us!'' **Pays $50/slogan.**

Tips ''We're looking for fresh, interesting, original material. Our buttons and magnets are small, so we crave concise and high-impact gems of wit. We urge you to be as off-the-wall and obscene as you like. We want humor that makes us laugh out loud.''

GALLANT GREETINGS CORP.

4300 United Parkway, Schiller Park IL 60176. Web site: www.gallantgreetings.com. Gallant is a publisher of traditional, religious, and humorous greeting cards for all occasions and seasons. All card ideas are purchased from freelance writers. Payment is $45/card idea purchased.

⊘ HALLMARK CARDS

P.O. Box 419034, Kansas City MO 64141. Web site: www.hallmark.com. ''At this time, Hallmark does not accept unsolicited freelance submissions, and our employment opportunities would involve relocating to the Kansas City area.''

KATE HARPER DESIGNS

E-mail: kidquotes@gmail.com. Web site: kidcards.blogspot.com/. **Acquisitions:** Via e-mail (quotesub@aol.com). Estab. 1993. **100% freelance written. Pays on acceptance.** Writer's guidelines online or via e-mail.

O⊸ Kate Harper Designs is seeking out submissions for its ''Kid's Quotes'' greeting card line. All work must be original and written/spoken by a child 12 years or younger. If quote is selected, the child will receive $25, name credit on the card, free greeting cards, and—with parental permissions—press releases will be sent to local newspapers.

KALAN LP

97 S. Union Ave., Lansdowne PA 19050. E-mail: editorial@kalanlp.com. Web site: www.kalanlp.com. **Acquisitions:** Editorial Department. Estab. 1973. **80% freelance written. Receives 500-800 submissions/year; bought**

80-100 freelance ideas last year. Submit seasonal/holiday material 8-10 Responds in 6-8. Material copyrighted. Buys all rights. **Pays on acceptance.** Writer's guidelines/market list for free.

O→ Categories include: birthday, retirement, congratulations, office occasions, weddings, friendship, Christmas, and Valentine's Day.

Needs Humorous. Send typed submissions with SASE. Accepts rhymed or unrhymed verse. **Pays $100/card concept; $60/one-liners.**

Other Product Lines Bumper stickers; post cards; posters; key rings; shot glasses; lighters; buttons; mugs; magnets.

Tips "Target to contemporary women of all ages. We want humor anywhere from subtle, to risqué, to downright rude. No flowery prose"

KOEHLER COMPANIES, INC.

8758 Woodcliff Rd., Bloomington MN 55438. (952)942-5666. Fax: (952)942-5208. E-mail: bob@koehlercompanies.com. Web site: www.koehlercompanies.com. **Acquisitions:** Bob Koehler. Estab. 1988. "We manufacture a decorative plaque line that utilizes verse and art. We are not a greeting card company. We combine art and message to create a product that a consumer will like enough to want to look at for a year or longer." **65% freelance written. Receives 100 submissions/year; bought 25 freelance ideas last year.** Responds in 1 month. **Pays on acceptance.**

O→ "Topics that works best includes: golf, fishing, pets, and other passions; verse that speaks to women, sisters, mom, family; words to inspire without getting preachy; humorous verse for men. See Web site for examples of our work."

Needs Humorous, inspirational. **"We pay $125/selected verse and limit the use to our products so that writers may resell their work for other uses."**

Other Product Lines Decorative wall plaques.

Tips "We sell wholesale to the retail market and the mail order catalog industry as well. Lengthy verse is sometimes challenging. Usually under 6 lines is best. We prefer to have work submitted by e-mail or mail."

NOVO CARD PUBLISHERS, INC.

3630 W. Pratt Ave., Lincolnwood IL 60712. (847)763-0077. Fax: (847)763-0020. E-mail: art@novocard.net. Web site: www.novocard.net. Estab. 1926. **80% freelance written. Receives 500 submissions/year; bought 200 freelance ideas last year.** Submit seasonal/holiday material 8 months in advance. Responds in 2 months. Buys worldwide greeting card rights. **Pays on acceptance.** Writer's guidelines/market list for #10 SASE. Market list available to writer on mailing list basis.

Needs Announcements, conventional, humorous, informal, inspirational, invitations, juvenile, soft line, religious, inspirational, etc.

OATMEAL STUDIOS

P.O. Box 138W3, Rochester VT 05767. (802)767-3171. Web site: www.oatmealstudios.com. **Acquisitions:** Helene Lehrer, creative director. Estab. 1979. **85% freelance written. Bought 200-300 freelance ideas last year.** Responds in 6 weeks. **Pays on acceptance.** Current market list for #10 SASE

- "Humor—conversational in tone and format—sells best for us."

Needs Humorous, birthday, friendship, anniversary, get well cards, etc. Will review concepts. Humorous material (clever and very funny) year-round. Prefers unrhymed verse ideas. **Current pay schedule available with guidelines.**

Other Product Lines Notepads, stick-on notes.

Tips "The greeting card market has become more competitive with a greater need for creative and original ideas. We are looking for writers who can communicate situations, thoughts, and relationships in a funny way and apply them to a birthday, get well, etc., greeting. We are willing to work with them in targeting our style. We will be looking for material that says something funny about life in a new way."

P.S. GREETINGS

5730 N. Tripp Ave., Chicago IL 60646. Fax: (773)267-6055. Web site: www.psgreetings.com. **Acquisitions:** Design Director. **Bought 200-300 freelance ideas last year.** Submit seasonal/holiday material 6 months in advance. Responds in 1 month. **Pays on acceptance.** Writer's guidelines/market list for #10 SASE or online.

Needs Conventional, humorous, inspirational, invitations, juvenile, sensitivity, soft line, studio, Christmas. Send typed submissions with SASE. Accepts rhymed or unrhymed verse. Submit 10 ideas/batch. **Pays one-time flat fee.**

Other Product Lines Stationary, notepads.

THE PAPER MAGIC GROUP, INC.

401 Adams Ave., Scranton PA 18501. (800)278-4085. Web site: www.papermagic.com. **Acquisitions:** Creative Director. Estab. 1907. **50% freelance written. Receives 500 submissions/year.** Submit seasonal/holiday material 6 months in advance. **Pays on acceptance.** No market list. Christmas boxed cards only. Submit Christmas sentiments only. No relative titles, juvenile. Submit 6-12 ideas/batch.

PAPYRUS DESIGN

500 Chadbourne Rd., Box 6030, Fairfield CA 94533. Fax: (707) 428-0641. Web site: www.papyrusonline.com. **Acquisitions:** Portfolio Review (design), Editorial Department (text). Estab. 1950. **10% freelance written. Receives 500 submissions/year; bought 35 freelance ideas last year.** Responds in 2 months. **Pays on acceptance.** Writer's guidelines/market list for #10 SASE. Inspirational, sentimental, contemporary, romance, friendship, seasonal, and everyday categories. Send humor ideas to: Laffs by Marcel at address above. Prefers unrhymed verse, but on juvenile cards rhyme is OK. Submit 10-15 ideas/batch.

Tips "Clever, sophisticated, fresh text concepts needed for traditional and humorous greeting cards. Seeking text that goes beyond the standard generic verse. We have specialized needs in the areas of verses for men, positive messages about aging, and workplace-related greetings. Poetry and off-color humor are not appropriate to our line. Sentimental text works best if it's short and elegant. The target market is upscale, professional, and well-educated."

PORTAL PUBLICATIONS

201 Almeda Del Prado, Novato CA 94949. Fax: (415)382-3377. E-mail: reception@portalpub.com. Web site: www.portalpub.com. **Acquisitions:** Editorial Department. Estab. 1954. **25% freelance written. Receives 400 submissions/year; bought 100 freelance ideas last year.** Responds in 2 months. **Pays on acceptance.**

Needs Humorous, informal, inspirational, whimsical, alternative. "Send 10-15 samples of your work with SASE. If in the future, we have need for writers for our greeting cards or other products we will contact you. No phone calls." **Pays flat fees. Buys exclusive rights.**

Other Product Lines Calendars, posters, matted/framed prints.

Tips "Upscale, cute, alternative, humorous cards for bookstores, card stores, chain stores, and college bookstores."

RECYCLED PAPER GREETINGS

3636 N. Broadway, Chicago IL 60613. (800)777-9494. Web site: www.recycledpapergreetings.com. **Acquisitions:** The Art Department. Estab. 1971. **100% freelance written. Bought 3,000 freelance ideas last year.** Responds in 2 months. "Please send ideas for specific occasions, such as birthday, friendship, thank you, miss you, and thinking of you." Submit up to 10 ideas/batch.

Tips "Find our guidelines online. We do not accept submissions that include a message without any accompanying artwork. Be sure to label each card idea with your name, address, and phone number, and include a SASE. We accept simultaneous submissions."

RENAISSANCE GREETING CARDS

P.O. Box 845, Springvale ME 04083. (207)324-4153. Fax: (207)324-9564. E-mail: cmarino@marianheath.com. Web site: www.rencards.com. **Acquisitions:** Licensing Department. Estab. 1977. **90% freelance written. Receives 75-100 submissions/year; bought 200-250 freelance ideas last year.** Submit seasonal/holiday material 4 months in advance. Responds in 2 weeks. Buys greeting card rights. Pays on publication. Writer's guidelines/market list for #10 SASE. Accepts wide range of writing styles—casual or coversational, meaningful, inspirational, humorous. Prefers unrhymed verse ideas. Submit 25 ideas/batch.

Tips "Verses that are sincere and complimentary in a conversational tone tend to do best. For humor, we avoid 'put down' type of jokes and try to stay positive. Target audience is women over 18 and Baby Boomers."

ROCKSHOTS, INC.

20 Vandam St., New York NY 10013. (212)243-9661. Fax: (212)604-9060. Web site: www.rockshots.com. **Acquisitions:** Bob Vesce, editor. Estab. 1979. **Bought 75 greeting card verse (or gag) freelance ideas last year.** Responds in 1 month. Buys greeting card rights. Writer's guidelines/market list for #10 SASE.

Needs Humorous. Looking for a combination of sexy and humorous come-on type greeting ("sentimental is not our style"); and insult cards ("looking for cute insults"). "Card gag can adopt a sentimental style, then take an ironic twist and end on an off-beat note." No sentimental or conventional material. Prefers gag lines on 8×11 paper with name, address, and phone and social security numbers in right corner, or individually on 3×5 cards. Submit 10 ideas/batch. **Pays $50/gag line.**

Tips "Rockshots is an outrageous, witty, adult, and sometimes shocking card company. Our range of style starts at cute and whimsical and runs the gamut all the way to totally outrageous and unbelievable. Rockshots' cards definitely stand out from all the 'mainstream' products on the market today. Some of the images we are famous for include 'sexy' photos of 500- to 600-pound female models, smart-talking grannies, copulating animals, and, of course, incredibly sexy shots of nude and seminude men and women. Some of our best-selling cards are photos with captions that start out leading the reader in one direction, and then zings them with a punch line totally out of left field, but also hysterically apropos. As you can guess, we do not shy away from much. Be creative, be imaginative, be funny, but most of all, be different. Do not hold back because of society's imposed standards, but let it all pour out. It's always good to mix sex and humor, as sex always sells. Remember that 70% to 80% of our audience is women, so get in touch with your 'feminine' side, your bitchy feminine side. Your gag line will be illustrated by a Rockshots photograph or drawing, so try and think visually. It's always a good idea to preview our cards at your local store, if this is possible, to give you a feeling of our style."

SNAFU DESIGNS, INC.

2500 University Ave. W., Suite C10, St. Paul MN 55114. E-mail: info@snafucards.com. Web site: www.snafudesigns.com. **Acquisitions:** Scott F. Austin, editor. Estab. 1985. Responds in 6 weeks. Buys all rights. **Pays on acceptance.** Writer's guidelines/market list for #10 SASE.

Needs Cartoon, informal. Specifically seeking birthday, friendship, thank you, anniversary, congratulations, get well, new baby, Christmas, wedding, pregnancy, retirement, Valentines Day and Mother's Day ideas. Submit no more than 10 ideas/batch. **Pays $100/idea.**

Tips "Our cards use clever ideas that are simple and concisely delivered and are aimed at a smart, adult audience. We like 'off the wall' irreverent humor that often has a little bite to it. Well done 'bathroom humor' is great! Please do not submit anything cute."

SUZY'S ZOO

P.O. Box 85490, San Diego CA 92186. Web site: www.suzyszoo.com. Estab. 1968. Submit seasonal/holiday material 18 months in advance. Responds in 4 months. Material copyrighted. Buys all rights. **Pays on acceptance.** Writer's guidelines/market list for #10 SASE.

Needs Announcements, conventional, humorous, informal, inspirational, invitations. Prefers unrhymed verse ideas. Submit 15 ideas/batch.

Tips "Cards that make people smile, touches their heart no matter what the occasion. Suzy's Zoo greeting cards are purchased primarily by women to give to their family and friends. We are looking for fresh, happy, witty verse that reflects the culture of today's family."

Contests & Awards

The contests and awards listed in this section are arranged by subject. Nonfiction writers can turn immediately to nonfiction awards listed alphabetically by the name of the contest or award. The same is true for fiction writers, poets, playwrights and screenwriters, journalists, children's writers, and translators. You'll also find general book awards, fellowships offered by arts councils and foundations, and multiple category contests.

New contests and awards are announced in various writer's publications nearly every day. However, many lose their funding or fold—and sponsoring magazines go out of business just as often. We have contacted the organizations whose contests and awards are listed here with the understanding that they are valid through 2007-2008. **Contact names, entry fees,** and **deadlines** have been highlighted and set in bold type for your convenience.

To make sure you have all the information you need about a particular contest, always send a SASE to the contact person in the listing before entering a contest. The listings in this section are brief, and many contests have lengthy, specific rules and requirements that we could not include in our limited space. Often a specific entry form must accompany your submission.

When you receive a set of guidelines, you will see that some contests are not applicable to all writers. The writer's age, previous publication, geographic location, and length of the work are common matters of eligibility. Read the requirements carefully to ensure you don't enter a contest for which you are not qualified. You should also be aware that every year, more and more contests, especially those sponsored by "little" literary magazines, are charging entry fees.

Winning a contest or award can launch a successful writing career. Take a professional approach by doing a little extra research. Find out who the previous winner of the award was by investing in a sample copy of the magazine in which the prize-winning article, poem, or short story appeared. Attend the staged reading of an award-winning play. Your extra effort will be to your advantage in competing with writers who simply submit blindly.

Information on contests and awards listed in the previous edition of *Writer's Market*, but not included in this edition, can be found in the General Index.

GENERAL

THE ANISFIELD-WOLF BOOK AWARDS

The Cleveland Foundation, 700 W. St. Clair Ave., #414, Cleveland OH 44113. Web site: www.anisfield-wolf.org. **Contact:** Laura Scharf. "The Anisfield-Wolf Book Award annually honors books which contribute to our understanding of racism or our appreciation of the diversity of human culture published during the year of the award." Any work addressing issues of racial bias or human diversity may qualify. **Deadline: January 31.** Prize: $10,000.

ANNUAL DREAM GRANT

The Hobson Foundation, 18 Circle Dr., Gettysburg PA 17325. E-mail: writers@hobsonfoundation.com. Web site: www.hobsonfoundation.com. **Contact:** Cyndy Phillips, director. Annually. **Deadline: June 1. Charges $15 processing fee.** Prize: up to $800 for the grant winner, as well as the winners' grant idea displayed on our Web site along with the author's contact information. Judged by a panel of professional writers and writing professors. Open to any writer.

ARTSLINK PROJECTS AWARD

CEC Artslink, 435 Hudson St., 8th Floor, New York NY 10014. (212)643-1985, ext. 21. Fax: (212)643-1996. E-mail: tmiller@cecartslink.org. Web site: www.cecartslink.org. **Contact:** Tamalyn Miller, program manager. Offered annually to enable artists of all media to work in Central Europe, Russia, and Eurasia with colleagues there on collaborative projects. Check Web site for deadline and other information. Prize: Up to $10,000.

THE MARIAN ENGEL AWARD

The Writers' Trust of Canada, 90 Richmond St. E., Suite 200, Toronto ON M5C 1P1, Canada. (416)504-8222. Fax: (416)504-9090. E-mail: info@writerstrust.com. Web site: www.writerstrust.com. **Contact:** James Davies. The Engel Award is presented annually at the Writers' Trust Awards Event, held in Toronto each Spring, to a female Canadian writer for a body of work in hope of continued contribution to the richness of Canadian literature. Prize: $15,000. Open to Canadian residents only.

THE TIMOTHY FINDLEY AWARD

The Writers' Trust of Canada, 90 Richmond St. E., Suite 200, Toronto ON M5C 1P1, Canada. (416)504-8222. Fax: (416)504-9090. E-mail: info@writerstrust.com. Web site: www.writerstrust.com. **Contact:** James Davies. The Findley Award is presented annually at The Writers' Trust Awards Event, held in Toronto each Spring, to a male Canadian writer for a body of work in hope of continued contribution to the richness of Canadian literature. Prize: $15,000. Open to Canadian residents only.

ROSALIE FELMING MEMORIAL HUMOR PRIZE

National League of American Pen Women, The Webhallow House, 1544 Sweetwood Dr., Colma CA 94015-20029. E-mail: pennobhill@aol.com. Web site: www.soulmakingcontest.us. **Contact:** Eileen Malone. Make the judge laugh in 2,500 words or less. Must be original and unpublished. Any form (poem, story, essay, etc) is acceptable. Only 1 piece allowed/entry. Indicate category on first page. Identify only with 3×5 card. **Deadline: November 30.** Guidelines for SASE. **Charges $5/ entry (make checks payable to NLAPW, Nob Hill Branch).** Prize: 1st Place: $100; 2nd Place: $50; 3rd Place: $45. Open to any writer.

THE FOUNTAINHEAD ESSAY CONTEST

The Ayn Rand Institute, Dept. W, P.O. Box 57044, Irvine CA 92619-7044. E-mail: essay@aynrand.org. Web site: www.aynrand.org/contests/. Estab. 1985. Offered annually to encourage analytical thinking and excellence in writing, and to exposé students to the philosophic ideas of Ayn Rand. "For information contact your English teacher or guidance counselor, or visit our Web site." Length: 800-1,600 words. **Deadline: April 25.** Prize: 1st Place: $10,000; 2nd Place (5): $2,000; 3rd Place (10): $1,000; Finalist (45): $100; Semifinalist (175): $50. Open to 11th and 12th graders.

INSCRIBE FALL CONTEST

InScribe Christian Writers' Fellowship, 333 Hunter's Run, Edmonton AB T6R 2N9, Canada. E-mail: info@inscribe.org. Web site: www.inscribe.org. **Contact:** Contest Director. Annual contest for unpublished writing; purpose is to encourage quality writing. Categories usually include devotional (500 words), free verse (40-60 lines), rhymed verse (40 lines), short story (1,500-2,000 words), and nonfiction (up to 2,000 words). See Web site for details. Guidelines for SASE (use Canadian stamps or IRCs). **Deadline: the first Saturday in August. Charges $10 (Canadian or US dollars); add $5 if you want a critique.** Prize: 1st Place: $100; 2nd Place: $50; 3rd Place:

$30. InScribe reserves the right to publish winning entries in its newsletter, *FellowScript*. Judged by different judges for each category. Judging is blind. Open to any writer.

JACK KAVANAGH MEMORIAL YOUTH BASEBALL RESEARCH AWARD

Society for American Baseball Research (SABR), Clinton High School, 75 Chenango Ave., Clinton NY 13323. E-mail: rthunt@ccs.edu. Web site: www.sabr.org. **Contact:** Richard Hunt. Estab. 1999. Offered annually for unpublished work. Purpose is to stimulate interest in baseball research by youth under age of 21. **Deadline: June 1.** Prize: Award is $200 cash prize, publication in *SABR Journal* and/or Web site, 3-year SABR membership, plaque honoring award. Up to 3 finalists also receive 1-year SABR membership. Judged by the Youth/Education Awards Committee. Acquires nonexclusive rights to SABR to publish the entrants' submissions in printed and/or electronic form. Writers must be under 21 as of June 1 of the year the award is given. Writers must submit a copy of birth certificate or drivers license with their submission as proof of age.

DOROTHEA LANGE—PAUL TAYLOR PRIZE

Center for Documentary Studies, 1317 W. Pettigrew St., Duke University, Durham NC 27705. (919)660-3663. Fax: (919)681-7600. Web site: cds.aas.duke.edu/l-t/. Offered annually to "promote the collaboration between a writer and a photographer in the formative or fieldwork stages of a documentary project. Collaborative submissions on any subject are welcome." Guidelines for SASE or on Web site. **Deadline: January 31. Submissions accepted during January only. Charges $35.** Prize: $20,000.

THE W.O. MITCHELL LITERARY PRIZE

The Writers' Trust of Canada, 90 Richmond St. E., Suite 200, Toronto ON M5C 1P1, Canada. (416)504-8222. Fax: (416)504-9090. E-mail: info@writerstrust.com. Web site: www.writerstrust.com. **Contact:** James Davies. Offered annually to a writer who has produced an outstanding body of work and has acted during his/her career as a "caring mentor" for other writers. They must also have published a work of fiction or had a new stage play produced during the 3-year period for each competition. Every third year the W.O. Mitchell Literary Prize will be awarded to a writer who works in French. Prize: $15,000. Open to Canadian residents only.

MLA PRIZE IN UNITED STATES LATINA & LATINO AND CHICANA & CHICANO LITERARY AND CULTURAL STUDIES

Modern Language Association of America, 26 Broadway, 3rd Floor, New York NY 10004-1789. (646)576-5141. Fax: (646)458-0030. E-mail: awards@mla.org. Web site: www.mla.org. **Contact:** Coordinator of Book Prizes. Award for an outstanding scholarly study in any language of United States Latina & Latino and Chicana & Chicano literature or culture. Open to current MLA members only. Authors or publishers may submit titles. **Deadline: May 1.** Guidelines for SASE. Prize: $1,000, and a certificate to be presented at the Modern Language Association's annual convention in December.

OHIOANA WALTER RUMSEY MARVIN GRANT

Ohioana Library Association, 274 E. First Ave., Suite 300, Columbus OH 43201. (614)466-3831. Fax: (614)728-6974. E-mail: ohioana@sloma.state.oh.us. Web site: www.ohioana.org. **Contact:** Linda Hengst. Offered annually to encourage young writers; open to writers under age 30 who have not published a book. Entrants must have been born in Ohio or have lived in Ohio for at least 5 years. Enter 1-6 pieces of prose totaling 10-60 pages (double space, 12 pt. font). **Deadline: January 31.** Prize: $1,000.

PEN CENTER USA LITERARY AWARDS

PEN Center USA, 400 Corporate Pointe, Culver City CA 90230. (310)862-1555. E-mail: awards@penusa.org. Web site: www.penusa.org. **Contact:** Literary Awards Coordinator. Offered for work published or produced in the previous calendar year. Open to writers living west of the Mississippi River. Award categories: drama, screenplay, teleplay, journalism. Guidelines for SASE or download from Web site. **Deadline: 4 copies must be received by January 31. Charges $35.** Prize: $1,000.

PULITZER PRIZES

The Pulitzer Prize Board, Columbia University, 709 Journalism Building, 2950 Broadway, New York NY 10027. (212)854-3841. E-mail: pulitzer@www.pulitzer.org. Web site: www.pulitzer.org. **Contact:** Sig Gissler, administrator. Estab. 1917. Journalism in US newspapers (published daily or weekly), and in letters, drama, and music by Americans. **Deadline: January 15 (music); February 1 (journalism); June 15 and October 15 (letters); December 31 (drama). Charges $50.** Prize: $10,000.

PUSHCART PRIZE

Pushcart Press, P.O. Box 380, Wainscott NY 11975. (631)324-9300. Web site: www.pushcartprize.com. **Contact:** Bill Henderson. Estab. 1976. All short stories, poetry, and essays must be nominated by an editor from a publishing house or little magazine. **Deadline: October 15.** Guidelines for SASE.

THE GROLLO RUZZENE FOUNDATION PRIZE FOR WRITING ABOUT ITALIANS IN AUSTRALIA

Victorian Premier's Literary Awards, State Library of Victoria, 328 Swanston St., Melbourne VIC 3000, Australia. (61)(3)8664-7277. E-mail: pla@slv.vic.gov.au. Web site: www.slv.vic.gov.au/pla. **Contact:** Project Officer. Biennial prize (held in odd-numbered years) for a ms published May 1-April 30 that encourages people from all backgrounds to write about the experiences of Italians in Australia. Migration studies, histories, travel narratives, published plays and screenplays, biographies, and collections of poems/novels for adults/children are accepted. **Deadline: May 5.** Guidelines for SASE. Prize: $15,000. Open to Australian citizens or permanent residents.

WILLIAM SANDERS SCARBOROUGH PRIZE

Modern Language Association of America, 26 Broadway, 3rd Floor, New York NY 10004-1789. (646)576-5141. Fax: (646)458-0030. E-mail: awards@mla.org. Web site: www.mla.org. **Contact:** Coordinator of book prizes. Offered annually for work published in the previous year. Given in honor of a distinguished man of letters and the first African-American member of the Modern Language Association, this prize will be awarded to an outstanding scholarly study of black American literature or culture. Open to MLA members and nonmembers. Authors or publishers may enter titles. Guidelines for SASE or by e-mail. **Deadline: May 1.** Prize: $1,000 and a certificate to be presented at the Modern Language Association's annual convention in December.

TRILLIUM BOOK AWARD/PRIX TRILLIUM

Ontario Media Development Corp., 175 Bloor St. E., SouthTower, Suite 501, Toronto ON M4W 3R8, Canada. (416)314-6698. Fax: (416)314-6876. E-mail: jhawkins@omdc.on.ca. Web site: www.omdc.on.ca. **Contact:** Janet Hawkins. Estab. 1987. Offered annually for books of any genre. Publishers submit titles on behalf of authors. Authors must have been Ontario residents 3 of the last 5 years. Guidelines online or for SASE. **Deadline: December 9 for titles published between January and October; January 9 for books published in November and December.** Prize: The winning author in each category (English and French) receives $20,000; the winning publisher in each category receives $2,500. Judged by a jury of writers, poets, and other members of the literary community.

WHITING WRITERS' AWARDS

Mrs. Giles Whiting Foundation, 1133 Avenue of the Americas, 22nd Floor, New York NY 10036-6710. Web site: whitingfoundation.org. Estab. 1985. "The Foundation gives annually $35,000 each to up to 10 writers of poetry, fiction, nonfiction, and plays. The awards place special emphasis on exceptionally promising emerging talent." Direct applications and informal nominations are not accepted by the Foundation. Literary professionals are contacted by the foundation to make nominations. Judged by 6-7 writers of distinction and accomplishment.

NONFICTION

AMWA MEDICAL BOOK AWARDS COMPETITION

American Medical Writers Association, 40 W. Gude Dr., Suite 101, Rockville MD 20850-1192. (301)294-5303. Fax: (301)294-9006. E-mail: slynn@amwa.org. Web site: www.amwa.org. **Contact:** Book Awards Committee. Offered annually to honor the best medical book published in the previous year in each of 3 categories: Books for Physicians, Books for Allied Health Professionals, and Trade Books. **Deadline: March 1. Charges $50 fee.**

ANTHEM ESSAY CONTEST

The Ayn Rand Institute, P.O. Box 57044, Irvine CA 92619-7044. (949)222-6550. Fax: (949)222-6558. E-mail: essay@aynrand.org. Web site: www.aynrand.org/contests. Estab. 1992. Offered annually to encourage analytical thinking and excellence in writing (600-1,200 word essay), and to exposé students to the philosophic ideas of Ayn Rand. "For information contact your English teacher or guidance counselor or visit our Web site." **Deadline: March 20.** Prize: 1st Place: $2,000; 2nd Place (5): $500; 3rd Place (10): $200; Finalist (45): $50; Semifinalist (175): $30. Open to 9th and 10th graders.

ATLAS SHRUGGED ESSAY CONTEST

Dept. W, The Ayn Rand Institute, P.O. Box 57044, Irvine CA 92619-7044. (949)222-6550. Fax: (949)222-6558. E-mail: essay@aynrand.org. Web site: www.aynrand.org/contests. Offered annually to encourage analytical thinking and excellence in writing, and to exposé students to the philosophic ideas of Ayn Rand. Essays are judged both on style and content. Essay length: 1,000-1,200 words. Guidelines on Web site. Open to students enrolled full-time in an undergraduate or graduate program. **Deadline: September 15.** Prize: 1st Place: $5,000; 2nd Place (3 awards): $1,000; 3rd Place (5 awards): $400; Finalists (20 awards): $100; Semifinalists (20 awards): $50.

BANCROFT PRIZE

Columbia University, % Office of the University Librarian, 517 Butter Library, Mail Code 1101, 535 W. 114th St., New York NY 10027. Web site: www.columbia.edu/cu/lweb/eguides/amerihist/bancroft.html. **Contact:** Bancroft Prize Committee. Offered annually for work published in previous year. Winning submissions will be chosen in either or both of the following categories: American history (including biography) and diplomacy. **Deadline: November 1.** Guidelines for SASE. Prize: $10,000 for the winning entry in each category. Open to all writers except previous recipients of the Bancroft Prize.

BIOGRAPHERS' CLUB PRIZE

Biographers' Club, The Secretary, 36 Great Smith St., London SW1P 3BU, United Kingdom. (44)(20)7222 7574. Fax: (44)(20)7222 7576. E-mail: lownie@globalnet.co.uk. Web site: www.biographersclub.co.uk. **Contact:** Andrew Lownie. The annual prize is sponsored by the *Daily Mail*, and all previous winners have gone on to secure publishing contracts—some for 6-figure sums. Entries should consist of a 15-20 page synopsis and 10 pages of a sample chapter for a biography. **Deadline: August 1.** Prize: £1,000. Judged by 3 distinguished biographers. Judges have included Michael Holroyd, Victoria Glendinning, Selina Hastings, Frances Spalding, Lyndall Gordon, Anne de Courcy, Nigel Hamilton, Anthony Sampson, and Mary Lovell. Open to any biographer who has not previously been commissioned or written a book.

JOHN BULLEN PRIZE

Canadian Historical Association, 395 Wellington St., Ottawa ON K1A 0N4, Canada. (613)233-7885. Fax: (613)567-3110. E-mail: cha-shc@lac-bac.gc.ca. Web site: www.cha-shc.ca. Offered annually for an outstanding historical dissertation for a doctoral degree at a Canadian university. Open only to Canadian citizens or landed immigrants. **Deadline: November 30.** Guidelines for SASE. Prize: $500.

CANADIAN AUTHORS ASSOCIATION LELA COMMON AWARD FOR CANADIAN HISTORY

Box 419, 320 S. Shores Rd., Campbellford ON K0L 1L0, Canada. (705)653-0323. Fax: (705)653-0593. E-mail: admin@canauthors.org. Web site: www.canauthors.org. **Contact:** Alec McEachern. Offered annually for a work of historical nonfiction on a Canadian topic by a Canadian author. Entry form required. Obtain entry form from contact name or download from Web site. **Deadline: December 15.** Guidelines for SASE. **Charges $35 (Canadian) entry fee.** Prize: $2,500 and a silver medal.

THE DOROTHY CHURCHILL CAPPON CREATIVE NONFICTION AWARD

New Letters, 5101 Rockhill Rd., Kansas City MO 64110. (816)235-1168. Fax: (816)235-2611. E-mail: newletters@umkc.edu. Web site: www.newsletters.org. **Contact:** Amy Lucas. Contest is offered annually for unpublished work to discover and reward emerging writers and to give experienced writers a place to try new genres. Acquires first North American serial rights. Open to any writer. Guidelines for SASE or online. **Deadline: Third week of May. Charges $15 fee (includes a 1-year subscription).** Prize: 1st Place: $1,500 and publication in a volume of *New Letters*; runner-up will receive a copy of a recent book of poetry or fiction courtesy of BkMk Press. All entries will receive consideration for publication in future editions of *New Letters*.

MORTON N. COHEN AWARD

Modern Language Association of America, 26 Broadway, 3rd Floor, New York NY 10004-1789. (646)576-5141. Fax: (646)458-0030. E-mail: awards@mla.org. Web site: www.mla.org. **Contact:** Coordinator of Book Prizes. Estab. 1989. Awarded in odd-numbered years for a distinguished edition of letters. At least 1 volume of the edition must have been published during the previous 2 years. Editors need not be members of the MLA. **Deadline: May 1.** Guidelines for SASE. Prize: $1,000 and a certificate.

CARR P. COLLINS AWARD

The Texas Institute of Letters, 6335 W. Northwest Hwy., #618, Dallas TX 75225. (214)363-7253. E-mail: franvick@aol.com. Web site: www.wtamu.edu/til/awards.htm. **Contact:** Fran Vick. Offered annually for work published January 1-December 31 of the previous year to recognize the best nonfiction book by a writer who was born in Texas, who has lived in the state for at least 2 consecutive years at one point, or a writer whose work has some notable connection with Texas. See Web site for guidelines. **Deadline: January 3.** Prize: $5,000.

COMPETITION FOR WRITERS OF BC HISTORY

British Columbia Historical Federation, 2477 140th St., Surrey BC V4P 2C5 Canada. (604)274-6449. E-mail: robert_mukai@telus.net. Web site: www.bchistory.ca. **Contact:** Bob Mukai. Offered annually to nonfiction books containing a facet of BC history and published during contest year. Books become the property of BC Historical Federation. **Deadline: December 31.** Prize: Cash, a certificate of merit, and an invitation to the BCHF annual conference. Open to any writer.

CREATIVE NONFICTION PRIZE

National League of American Pen Women, Nob Hill, San Francisco Branch, The Webhallow House, 1544 Sweetwood Dr., Colma CA 94015. E-mail: pennobhill@aol.com. Web site: www.soulmakingcontest.us. **Contact:** Eileen Malone. All prose works must be typed, page numbered, stapled, and double-spaced. Each essay/entry up to 3,000 words. Identify only with 3×5 card. **Deadline: November 30.** Guidelines for SASE. **Charges $5/entry (make checks payable to NLAPW, Nob Hill Branch).** Prize: 1st Place: $100; 2nd Place: $50; 3rd Place: $25. Open annually to any writer.

THE ALFRED DEAKIN PRIZE FOR AN ESSAY ADVANCING PUBLIC DEBATE

Victorian Premier's Literary Awards, State Library of Victoria, 328 Swanston St., Melbourne VIC 3000 Australia. (61)(3)8664-7277. E-mail: pla@slv.vic.gov.au. Web site: www.slv.vic.gov.au/pla. **Contact:** Project Officer. Prize for an individual essay that contributes to the national debate through the quality of its writing. Must have been published between May 1 and April 30 in the form of a book or a print, electronic, or newspaper article. **Deadline: May 8.** Guidelines for SASE. Prize: $15,000. Open to Australian citizens or permanent residents.

ANNIE DILLARD AWARD IN CREATIVE NONFICTION

Bellingham Review, Mail Stop 9053, Western Washington University, Bellingham WA 98225. (360)650-4863. E-mail: bhreview@cc.wwu.edu. Web site: www.wwu.edu/~bhreview. **Contact:** Brenda Miller. Offered annually for unpublished essays on any subject and in any style. Guidelines for SASE or online. **Deadline: December 1-March 15. Charges $15/1st entry, $10/additional entry.** Prize: 1st Place: $1,000, plus publication and copies. All finalists considered for publication. All entrants receive subscription.

THE DONNER PRIZE

The Award for Best Book on Canadian Public Policy, The Donner Canadian Foundation, 394A King St. E., Toronto ON M5A 1K9, Canada. (416)368-8253 or (416)368-3763. Fax: (416)363-1448. E-mail: meisnerpublicity@sympatico.ca. Web site: www.donnerbookprize.com. **Contact:** Sherry Naylor, Susan Meisner. Offered annually for nonfiction published January 1-December 31 that highlights the importance of public policy and to reward excellent work in this field. Entries must be published in either English or French. Open to Canadian citizens. **Deadline: November 30.** Guidelines for SASE. Prize: $30,000; 5 shortlist authors get $5,000 each.

THE FREDERICK DOUGLASS BOOK PRIZE

Gilder Lehrman Center for the Study of Slavery, Resistance and Abolition, Yale Center for International & Area Studies, 34 Hillhouse Ave., New Haven CT 06511-8936. (203)432-3339. Fax: (203)432-6943. E-mail: gilder.lehrman.center@yale.edu. Web site: www.yale.edu/glc. **Contact:** Dana Schaffer. Estab. 1999. Offered annually for books published the previous year. Annual prize awarded for the most outstanding book published on the subject of slavery, resistance, and/or abolition. Works related to the American Civil War are eligble only if their primary focus is slavery, resistance, or abolition. **Deadline: April 3.** Guidelines for SASE. Prize: $25,000.

THE DRAINIE-TAYLOR BIOGRAPHY PRIZE

The Writers' Trust of Canada, 90 Richmond St. E., Suite 200, Toronto ON M5C 1P1, Canada. (416)504-8222. Fax: (416)504-9090. E-mail: info@writerstrust.com. Web site: www.writerstrust.com. **Contact:** James Davies. Awarded annually to a Canadian author for a significant work of biography, autobiography, or personal memoir. Award presented at the Writers' Trust Awards event held in Toronto each Spring. Prize: $10,000.

EDUCATOR'S AWARD

The Delta Kappa Gamma Society International, P.O. Box 1589, Austin TX 78767-1589. (512)478-5748. Fax: (512)478-3961, ext. 113. E-mail: jillf@deltakappagamma.org. Web site: www.deltakappagamma.org. **Contact:** Jill Foltz, program/membership services administrator. Offered annually for quality research and nonfiction published January-December of previous year. This award recognizes educational research and writings of female authors whose work may influence the direction of thought and action necessary to meet the needs of today's complex society. The book must be written by 1 or 2 women who are citizens of any country in which The Delta Kappa Gamma Society International is organized: Canada, Costa Rica, El Salvador, Finland, Germany,

Great Britain, Guatemala, Iceland, Mexico, The Netherlands, Norway, Puerto Rico, Sweden, US. Guidelines (required) for SASE. **Deadline: February 1.** Prize: $2,500.

EVERETT E. EDWARDS MEMORIAL AWARD

Agricultural History, P.O. Box 5075, Minard Hall 203, NDSU, Fargo ND 58105-5075. (701)231-5831. Fax: (701)231-5832. E-mail: ndsu.agricultural.history@ndsu.nodak.edu. Web site: agriculturalhistory.ndsu.nodak.edu. **Contact:** Claire Strom. Offered annually for best graduate paper written during the calendar year on any aspect of agricultural and rural studies (broadly interpreted). Open to submission by any graduate student. **Deadline: December 31.** Prize: $200 and publication of the paper in the scholarly journal, *Agricultural History*.

EVANS BIOGRAPHY & HANDCART AWARDS

Mountain West Center for Regional Studies, Utah State University, 0735 Old Main Hill, Logan UT 84322-0735. (435)797-3630. Fax: (435)797-3899. E-mail: mwc@cc.usu.edu. Web site: www.usu.edu/mountainwest/evans.html. Estab. 1983. Offered to encourage the writing of biography about people who have played a role in Mormon Country (not the religion, the country—Intermountain West with parts of Southwestern Canada and Northwestern Mexico). Publishers or authors may nominate books. Criteria for consideration: Work must be a biography or autobiography on "Mormon Country"; must be submitted for consideration for publication year's award; new editions or reprints are not eligible; mss are not accepted. Submit 5 copies. **Deadline: January 1.** Guidelines for SASE. Prize: $10,000 and $1,000.

EVENT CREATIVE NONFICTION CONTEST

Event, The Douglas College Review, P.O. Box 2503, New Westminster BC V3L 5B2, Canada. (604)527-5293. Fax: (604)527-5095. E-mail: event@douglas.bc.ca. Web site: event.douglas.bc.ca. Offered annually for unpublished creative nonfiction. Maximum length: 5,000 words. **Deadline: April 15. Charges $29.95 entry fee, which includes 1-year subscription; American and overseas residents pay in U.S. funds.** Prize: 3 winners will each receive $500, plus payment for publication. Acquires Acquires first North American serial rights for the 3 winning entries. Open to any writer, except Douglas College employees.

DINA FEITELSON RESEARCH AWARD

International Reading Association, Division of Research & Policy, 800 Barksdale Rd., Newark DE 19714-8139. (302)731-1600, ext. 423. Fax: (302)731-1057. E-mail: research@reading.org. Web site: www.reading.org. **Contact:** Marcella Moore. Award for an exemplary work published in English in a refereed journal that reports on an empirical study investigating aspects of literacy acquisition, such as phonemic awareness, the alphabetic principle, bilingualism, or cross-cultural studies of beginning reading. Mss may be submitted for consideration by researchers, authors, and others. **Deadline: September 1.** Prize: Monetary award and recognition at the International Reading Association's annual convention. Open to any writer.

WALLACE K. FERGUSON PRIZE

Canadian Historical Association, 395 Wellington St., Ottawa ON K1A 0N4, Canada. (613)233-7885. Fax: (613)567-3110. E-mail: cha-shc@lac-bac.gc.ca. Web site: www.cha-shc.ca. Offered to a Canadian who has published the outstanding scholarly book in a field of history other than Canadian history. **Deadline: December 2.** Guidelines for SASE. Prize: $1,000. Open to Canadian citizens and landed immigrants only.

GILBERT C. FITE DISSERTATION AWARD

Agricultural History, P.O. Box 5075, Minard Hall 203, NDSU, Fargo ND 58105-5075. (701)231-5831. Fax: (701)231-5832. E-mail: ndsu.agricultural.history@ndsu.nodak.edu. Web site: agriculturalhistory.ndsu.nodak.edu. **Contact:** Claire Strom. Award is presented to the author of the best dissertation on agricultural history, broadly construed, completed during the calendar year. **Deadline: December 31.** Guidelines for SASE. Prize: $300 honorararium.

N DIXON RYAN FOX MANUSCRIPT PRIZE

New York State Historical Association, P.O. Box 800, Lake Rd., Cooperstown NY 13326. (607)547-1491. Fax: (607)547-1405. E-mail: goodwind@nysha.org. Web site: www.nysha.org. **Contact:** Daniel Goodwin, editor. Offered annually for the best unpublished book-length ms dealing with some aspect of the history of New York State. Send 2 unbound copies and a cover letter. Guidelines online or for SASE. **Deadline: January 20.** Prize: $3,000. Open to any writer.

N FREELANCE SUCCESS STORIES

Writer's Market, 4700 E. Galbraith Rd., Cincinnati OH 45236. Fax: (513)531-2686. E-mail: writersmarket@fwpubs.com. Web site: www.writersmarket.com. **Contact:** Robert Lee Brewer, editor *Writer's Market*. Estab. 2006.

This contest is open to writers who have achieved some form of freelance writing success. Writers can write about their first sale, first byline, an interesting or unlikely sale, or any other type of success. The main rules are to keep the focus on freelance writing success and keep it personal (this is your story). Length should be 800-1,500 words. Submissions only accepted via e-mail—any questions should be sent via e-mail as well. **Deadline: December 1.** Prize: 1st Place: $250 contract to have story published in *Writer's Market*; 2nd Place: $150 contract to have story published in *Writer's Market*; 3rd Place: $100 contract to have story published in *Writer's Market*. Judged by Robert Lee Brewer, editor *Writer's Market*. Open to any writer.

LIONEL GELBER PRIZE

Munk Center for International Studies, University of Toronto, 1 Devonshire Place, Toronto ON M5S 3K7, Canada. (416)946-8901. Fax: (416)946-8915. E-mail: gelberprize.munk@utoronto.ca. Web site: www.utoronto.ca/mcis/gelber. **Contact:** Prize Manager. Estab. 1989. Offered annually for the year's most outstanding work of nonfiction in the field of international relations. Books must be published in English or English translation between January 1 and December 31 of the current year, and submitted by the publisher. Publishers should submit 6 copies of each title (up to 3 titles can be submitted). **Deadline: October 31.** Prize: $15,000 (Canadian funds).

GENEii AWARDS

Southern California Genealogical Society, 417 Irving Dr., Burbank CA 91504-2408. (818)843-7247. E-mail: scgs@scgsgenealogy.com. Web site: www.scgsgenealogy.com. **Contact:** Beth Uyehara, contest coordinator. Offered annually to promote family history writing, including memoirs, character sketches, and local history. There are 2 categories: works under 1,000 words and works of 1,000-2,000 words. The best entries will illuminate the era and/or the historical or social context of the subject. **Deadline: Entries are only accepted November 1-December 31 of each year.** Guidelines for SASE. **Charges $10/US submissions; no fee for entries outside the US.** Prize: $25-200. Winning entries may be published in the society's quarterly journal, in an anthology, or online.

GOVERNOR GENERAL'S LITERARY AWARD FOR LITERARY NONFICTION

Canada Council for the Arts, 350 Albert St., P.O. Box 1047, Ottawa ON K1P 5V8, Canada. (613)566-4414, ext. 5573. Fax: (613)566-4410. Web site: www.canadacouncil.ca/prizes/ggla. Offered for work published September 1-September 30. Publishers submit titles for consideration. **Deadline: March 15, June 1 or August 7, depending on the book's publication date.** Prize: Each laureate receives $15,000; nonwinning finalists receive $1,000.

JAMES T. GRADY—JAMES H. STACK AWARD FOR INTERPRETING CHEMISTRY FOR THE PUBLIC

American Chemical Society, 1155 16th St. NW, Washington DC 20036-4800. E-mail: awards@acs.org. Web site: www.acs.org/awards/grady-stack.html. Offered annually for previously published work to recognize, encourage, and stimulate outstanding reporting directly to the public, which materially increases the public's knowledge and understanding of chemistry, chemical engineering, and related fields. Guidelines online at Web site. Rules of eligibility: A nominee must have made noteworthy presentations through a medium of public communication to increase the American public's understanding of chemistry and chemical progress. This information shall have been disseminated through the press, radio, television, films, the lecture platform, books, or pamphlets for the lay public. **Deadline: February 1.** Prize: $3,000, medallion with a presentation box, and certificate, plus travel expenses to the meeting at which the award will be presented.

JOHN GUYON NONFICTION PRIZE

Crab Orchard Review, English Department, Southern Illinois University Carbondale, Carbondale IL 62901-4503. E-mail: jtribble@siu.edu. Web site: www.siu.edu/~crborchd. **Contact:** Jon C. Tribble, managing editor. Offered annually for unpublished work. This competition seeks to reward excellence in the writing of creative nonfiction. This is not a prize for academic essays. *Crab Orchard Review* acquires first North American serial rights to submitted works. **Deadline: February 1-April 1.** Guidelines for SASE. **Charges $15/essay (limit of 3 essays of up to 6,500 words each).** Prize: $1,500 and publication. Open to US citizens only.

ALBERT J. HARRIS AWARD

International Reading Association, Division of Research and Policy, 800 Barksdale Rd., Newark DE 19714-8139. (302)731-1600, ext. 423. Fax: (302)731-1057. E-mail: research@reading.org. Web site: www.reading.org. **Contact:** Marcella Moore. Offered annually to recognize outstanding published works focused on the identification, prevention, assessment, or instruction of learners experiencing difficulty learning to read. Articles may be nominated by researchers, authors, and others. Copies of the applications and guidelines can be downloaded in PDF format from the Web site. **Deadline: September 1.** Prize: Monetary award and recognition at the International Reading Association's annual convention.

HENDRICKS MANUSCRIPT AWARD

The New Netherland Institute, % New Netherland Project, New York State Library, CEC, 8th Floor, Albany NY 12230. (518)474-6067. Fax: (518)473-0472. E-mail: cgehring@mail.nysed.gov. Web site: www.nnp.org. **Contact:** Charles Gehring. Offered annually for the best published or unpublished ms focusing on any aspect of the Dutch colonial experience in North America. **Deadline: March 1.** Guidelines for SASE. Prize: $2,000. Judged by a 4-member panel of scholars.

THE KIRIYAMA PRIZE

Kiriyama Pacific Rim Voices, 650 Delancey St., Suite 101, San Francisco CA 94107. (415)777-1628. Fax: (415)777-1646. E-mail: admin@kiriyamaprize.org. Web site: www.kiriyamaprize.org. **Contact:** Jeannine Stronach, prize manager. Offered for work published from January 1 through December 31 of the current prize year to promote books that will contribute to greater mutual understanding and increased cooperation throughout the Pacific Rim and South Asia. Guidelines and entry form on request, or may be downloaded from the Web site. Books must be submitted for entry by the publisher. Proper entry forms must be submitted. **Deadline: late Fall each year.** Prize: $30,000 to be divided equally between the author of 1 fiction and 1 nonfiction book.

KATHERINE SINGER KOVACS PRIZE

Modern Language Association of America, 26 Broadway, 3rd Floor, New York NY 10004-1789. (646)576-5141. Fax: (646)458-0030. E-mail: awards@mla.org. Web site: www.mla.org. **Contact:** Coordinator of Book Prizes. Estab. 1990. Offered annually for a book published during the previous year in English in the field of Latin American and Spanish literatures and cultures. Books should be broadly interpretive works that enhance understanding of the interrelations among literature, the other arts, and society. Author need not be a member of the MLA. **Deadline: May 1.** Guidelines for SASE. Prize: $1,000 and a certificate.

LITERARY NONFICTION CONTEST

(formerly Rogers Communication Literary Nonfiction Contest), PRISM International, Creative Writing Program, UBC, Buch E462—1866 Main Mall, Vancouver BC V6T 1Z1, Canada. (604)822-2514. Fax: (604)822-3616. E-mail: prism@interchange.ubc.ca. Web site: prism.arts.ubc.ca. **Contact:** Zoya Harris, executive editor. Offered annually for published and unpublished writers to promote and reward excellence in literary nonfiction writing. *PRISM* buys first North American serial rights upon publication. "We also buy limited Web rights for pieces selected for the Web site." Open to anyone except students and faculty of the Creative Writing Program at UBC or people who have taken a creative writing course at UBC in the 2 years prior to contest deadline. All entrants receive a 1-year subscription to *PRISM*. Guidelines for SASE (Canadian postage only), via e-mail, or online. **Deadline: September 30. Charges $27/piece; $7/additional entry (outside Canada use US funds).** Prize: $500 for the winning entry, plus $20/page for the publication of the winner in *PRISM*'s winter issue.

JAMES RUSSELL LOWELL PRIZE

Modern Language Association of America, 26 Broadway, 3rd Floor, New York NY 10004-1789. (646)576-5141. Fax: (646)458-0030. E-mail: awards@mla.org. Web site: www.mla.org. **Contact:** Coordinator of Book Prizes. Offered annually for literary or linguistic study, or critical edition or biography published in previous year. *Open to MLA members only.* **Deadline: March 1.** Guidelines for SASE. Prize: $1,000 and a certificate.

SIR JOHN A. MACDONALD PRIZE

Canadian Historical Association, 395 Wellington St., Ottawa ON K1A 0N4, Canada. (613)233-7885. Fax: (613)567-3110. E-mail: cha-shc@lac-bac-gc.ca. Web site: www.cha-shc.ca. Offered annually to award a previously published nonfiction work of Canadian history judged to have made the most significant contribution to an understanding of the Canadian past. Open to Canadian citizens only. **Deadline: December 2.** Guidelines for SASE. Prize: $1,000.

HOWARD R. MARRARO PRIZE

Modern Language Association of America, 26 Broadway, 3rd Floor, New York NY 10004-1789. (646)576-5141. Fax: (646)458-0030. E-mail: awards@mla.org. Web site: www.mla.org. **Contact:** Coordinator of Book Prizes. Offered in even-numbered years for a scholarly book or essay on any phase of Italian literature or comparative literature involving Italian, published in previous year. Authors must be members of the MLA. **Deadline: May 1.** Guidelines for SASE. Prize: $1,000 and a certificate.

KENNETH W. MILDENBERGER PRIZE

Modern Language Association of America, 26 Broadway, 3rd Floor, New York NY 10004-1789. (646)576-5141. Fax: (646)458-0030. E-mail: awards@mla.org. Web site: www.mla.org. **Contact:** Coordinator of Book Prizes. Offered annually for a publication from the previous year in the field of language culture, literacy, or literature with a strong application to the teaching of languages other than English. Author need not be a member. **Deadline: May 1.** Guidelines for SASE. Prize: $1,000, a certificate, and a year's membership in the MLA.

MLA PRIZE FOR A DISTINGUISHED BIBLIOGRAPHY

Modern Language Association of America, 26 Broadway, 3rd Floor, New York NY 10004-1789. (646)576-5141. Fax: (646)458-0030. E-mail: awards@mla.org. Web site: www.mla.org. **Contact:** Coordinator of Book Prizes. Offered in even-numbered years for enumerative and descriptive bibliographies published in monographic, book, or electronic format in the 2 years prior to the competition. Open to any writer or publisher. **Deadline: May 1.** Guidelines for SASE. Prize: $1,000 and a certificate.

MLA PRIZE FOR A DISTINGUISHED SCHOLARLY EDITION

Modern Language Association of America, 26 Broadway, 3rd Floor, New York NY 10004-1789. (646)576-5141. Fax: (646)458-0030. E-mail: awards@mla.org. Web site: www.mla.org. **Contact:** Coordinator of Book Prizes. Offered in odd-numbered years. To qualify for the award, an edition should be based on an examination of all available relevant textual sources; the source texts and the edited text's deviations from them should be fully described; the edition should employ editorial principles appropriate to the materials edited, and those principles should be clearly articulated in the volume; the text should be accompanied by appropriate textual and other historical contextual information; the edition should exhibit the highest standards of accuracy in the presentation of its text and apparatus; and the text and apparatus should be presented as accessibly and elegantly as possible. Editor need not be a member of the MLA. **Deadline: May 1.** Guidelines for SASE. Prize: $1,000 and a certificate.

MLA PRIZE FOR A FIRST BOOK

Modern Language Association of America, 26 Broadway, 3rd Floor, New York NY 10004-1789. (646)576-5141. Fax: (646)458-0030. E-mail: awards@mla.org. Web site: www.mla.org. **Contact:** Coordinator of Book Prizes. Offered annually for the first book-length scholarly publication by a current member of the association. To qualify, a book must be a literary or linguistic study, a critical edition of an important work, or a critical biography. Studies dealing with literary theory, media, cultural history, and interdisciplinary topics are eligible; books that are primarily translations will not be considered. **Deadline: April 1.** Guidelines for SASE. Prize: $1,000 and a certificate.

MLA PRIZE FOR INDEPENDENT SCHOLARS

Modern Language Association of America, 26 Broadway, 3rd Floor, New York NY 10004-1789. (646)576-5141. Fax: (646)458-0030. E-mail: awards@mla.org. Web site: www.mla.org. **Contact:** Coordinator of Book Prizes. Offered annually for a book in the field of English, or another modern language, or literature published in the previous year. Authors who are enrolled in a program leading to an academic degree or who hold tenured or tenure-track positions in higher education are not eligible. Authors need not be members of MLA. Guidelines and application form for SASE. **Deadline: May 1.** Prize: $1,000, a certificate, and a year's membership in the MLA.

LINDA JOY MYERS MEMOIR PRIZE

National League of American Pen Women, Nob Hill, San Francisco Branch, Webhallow House, 1544 Sweetwood Dr., Colma CA 94015-20029. E-mail: pennobhill@aol.com. Web site: www.soulmakingcontest.us. **Contact:** Eileen Malone. One memoir/entry, up to 3,000 words, double spaced. Previously published material is acceptable. Indicate category on first page. Identify only with 3×5 card. **Deadline: November 30.** Guidelines for SASE. **Charges $5/entry (make checks payable to NLAPW, Nob Hill Branch).** Prize: 1st Place: $100; 2nd Place $50; 3rd Place $45. Open annually to any writer.

GEORGE JEAN NATHAN AWARD FOR DRAMATIC CRITICISM

Cornell University, Department of English, Goldwin Smith Hall, Ithaca NY 14853. (607)255-6801. Fax: (607)255-6661. Web site: www.arts.cornell.edu/english/nathan/index.html. **Contact:** Chair, Department of English. Offered annually to the American who has written the best piece of drama criticism during the theatrical year (July 1-June 30), whether it is an article, essay, treatise, or book. Only published work may be submitted; author must be an American citizen. Guidelines for SASE. Prize: $10,000 and a trophy.

NATIONAL WRITERS ASSOCIATION NONFICTION CONTEST

The National Writers Association, 10940 S. Parker Rd., #508, Parker CO 80134. (303)841-0246. Fax: (303)841-2607. E-mail: authorsandy@hotmail.com. Web site: www.nationalwriters.com. **Contact:** Sandy Whelchel, director. Annual contest to encourage writers in this creative form and to recognize those who excel in nonfiction writing. **Deadline: December 31.** Guidelines for SASE. **Charges $18 fee.** Prize: 1st Place: $200; 2nd Place: $100; 3rd Place: $50.

OUTSTANDING DISSERTATION OF THE YEAR AWARD

International Reading Association, 800 Barksdale Rd., P.O. Box 8139, Newark DE 19714-8139. (302)731-1600, ext. 423. Fax: (302)731-1057. E-mail: research@reading.org. Web site: www.reading.org. **Contact:** Marcella Moore. Offered annually to recognize dissertations in the field of reading and literacy. *Applicants must be members of the International Reading Association*. Copies of the applications and guidelines can be downloaded in PDF format from the Web site. **Deadline: October 1.** Prize: $1,000.

FRANK LAWRENCE AND HARRIET CHAPPELL OWSLEY AWARD

Southern Historical Association, Dept. of History, University of Georgia, Athens GA 30602-1602. (706)542-8848. Fax: (706)542-2455. Web site: www.uga.edu/sha. **Contact:** Secretary-Treasurer. Estab. 1934. Editor: John B. Boles. Offered in odd-numbered years for recognition of a distinguished book in Southern history published in even-numbered years. Publishers usually submit the books. **Deadline: March 1.**

THE NETTIE PALMER PRIZE FOR NONFICTION

Victorian Premier's Literary Awards, State Library of Victoria, 328 Swanston St., Melbourne VIC 3000 Australia. (61)(3)8664-7277. E-mail: pla@slv.vic.gov.au. Web site: www.slv.vic.gov.au/pla. **Contact:** Project Officer. Prize for a work of nonfiction published May 1-April 30. **Deadline: May 4.** Guidelines for SASE. **Charges $35.** Prize: $30,000. Open to Australian citizens or permanent residents.

PRESERVATION FOUNDATION CONTESTS

The Preservation Foundation, Inc., 2213 Pennington Bend, Nashville TN 37214. E-mail: preserve@storyhouse.org. Web site: www.storyhouse.org. **Contact:** Richard Loller. Contest offered annually for unpublished nonfiction. General nonfiction category (1,500-5,000 words)—any appropriate nonfiction topic. Travel nonfiction category (1,500-5,000 words)—must be true story of trip by author or someone known personally by author." E-mail entries only (no mss). **First entry in each category is free; $5 fee for each additional entry (limit 3 entires/category). Deadline: September 30.** Prize: 1st Place: $100 in each category; certificates for finalists. Open to any previously unpublished writer.

THE PRIZE FOR SCIENCE WRITING

Victorian Premier's Literary Awards, State Library of Victoria, 328 Swanston St., Melbourne VIC 3000 Australia. (61)(3)8664-7277. E-mail: pla@slv.vic.gov.au. Web site: www.slv.vic.gov.au/pla. **Contact:** Project Officer. Biennial prize (held in odd-numbered years) for popular science books for nonspecialist readers published May 1-April 30. The prize aims to encourage discussion and understanding of scientific ideas in their broadest sense in the wider community and nurture a culture of innovation in Victoria. **Deadline: May 5.** Guidelines for SASE. Prize: $15,000. Open to Australian citizens or permanent residents.

EVELYN RICHARDSON NONFICTION AWARD

Writers' Federation of Nova Scotia, 1113 Marginal Rd., Halifax NS B3H 4P7, Canada. (902)423-8116. Fax: (902)422-0881. E-mail: talk@writers.ns.ca. Web site: www.writers.ns.ca. **Contact:** Jane Buss, executive director. This annual award is named for Nova Scotia writer Evelyn Richardson, whose book *We Keep a Light* won the Governor General's Literary Award for nonfiction in 1945. There is **no entry fee** or form. Full-length books of nonfiction written by Nova Scotians, and published as a whole for the first time in the previous calendar year, are eligible. Publishers: Send 4 copies and a letter attesting to the author's status as a Nova Scotian, and the author's current mailing address and telephone number. **Deadline: First Friday in December.** Prize: $2,000.

THE CORNELIUS RYAN AWARD

The Overseas Press Club of America, 40 W. 45th St., New York NY 10036. (212)626-9220. Fax: (212)626-9210. Web site: www.opcofamerica.org. **Contact:** Sonya Fry, executive director. Offered annually for excellence in a nonfiction book on international affairs. Generally publishers nominate the work, but writers may also submit in their own name. The work must be published and on the subject of foreign affairs. **Deadline: End of January. Charges $150 fee.** Prize: $1,000 and a certificate.

THEODORE SALOUTOS AWARD

Agricultural History, P.O. Box 5075, Minard Hall, NDSU, Fargo ND 58105-5075. (701)231-5831. Fax: (701)231-5832. E-mail: ndsu.agricultural.history@ndsu.nodak.edu. Web site: agriculturalhistory.ndsu.nodak.edu. **Contact:** Claire Strom. Offered annually for best book on US agricultural history (broadly interpreted). Open nominations. **Deadline: December 31.** Prize: $500.

SASKATCHEWAN NONFICTION AWARD

Saskatchewan Book Awards, Inc., Box 1921, Regina SK S4P 3E1, Canada. (306)569-1585. Fax: (306)569-4187. E-mail: director@bookawards.sk.ca. Web site: www.bookawards.sk.ca. **Contact:** Glenda James, executive director. Offered annually for work published September 15-September 14. This award is presented to a Saskatchewan author for the best book of nonfiction, judged on the quality of writing. **Deadline: First deadline: July 31; Final deadline: September 14.** Guidelines for SASE. **Charges $20 (Canadian).** Prize: $2,000.

SASKATCHEWAN SCHOLARLY WRITING AWARD

Saskatchewan Book Awards, Inc., Box 1921, Regina SK S4P 3E1, Canada. (306)569-1585. Fax: (306)569-4187. E-mail: director@bookawards.sk.ca. Web site: www.bookawards.sk.ca. **Contact:** Glenda James, executive director. Offered annually for work published September 15-September 14 annually. This award is presented to a Saskatchewan author for the best contribution to scholarship. The work must recognize or draw on specific theoretical work within a community of scholars, and participate in the creation and transmission of knowledge. **Deadline: First deadline: July 31; Final deadline: September 14.** Guidelines for SASE. **Charges $20 (Canadian).** Prize: $2,000.

ALDO AND JEANNE SCAGLIONE PRIZE FOR COMPARATIVE LITERARY STUDIES

Modern Language Association of America, 26 Broadway, 3rd Floor, New York NY 10004-1789. (646)576-5141. Fax: (646)458-0030. E-mail: awards@mla.org. Web site: www.mla.org. **Contact:** Coordinator of Book Prizes. Offered annually for outstanding scholarly work published in the preceding year in the field of comparative literary studies involving at least 2 literatures. *Author must be a member of the MLA.* Works of scholarship, literary history, literary criticism, and literary theory are eligible; books that are primarily translations are not eligible. **Deadline: May 1.** Guidelines for SASE. Prize: $2,000 and a certificate.

ALDO AND JEANNE SCAGLIONE PRIZE FOR FRENCH AND FRANCOPHONE STUDIES

Modern Language Association of America, 26 Broadway, 3rd Floor, New York NY 10004-1789. (646)576-5141. Fax: (646)458-0030. E-mail: awards@mla.org. Web site: www.mla.org. **Contact:** Coordinator of Book Prizes. Offered annually for work published in the preceding year that is an outstanding scholarly work in the field of French or francophone linguistic or literary studies. *Author must be a member of the MLA.* Works of scholarship, literary history, literary criticism, and literary theory are eligible; books that are primarily translations are not eligible. **Deadline: May 1.** Guidelines for SASE. Prize: $2,000 and a certificate.

ALDO AND JEANNE SCAGLIONE PRIZE FOR ITALIAN STUDIES

Modern Language Association of America, 26 Broadway, 3rd Floor, New York NY 10004-1789. (646)576-5141. Fax: (646)458-0030. E-mail: awards@mla.org. Web site: www.mla.org. **Contact:** Coordinator of Book Prizes. Offered in odd-numbered years for a scholarly book on any phase of Italian literature or culture, or comparative literature involving Italian, including works on literary or cultural theory, science, history, art, music, society, politics, cinema, and linguistics, preferably but not necessarily relating other disciplines to literature. Books must have been published in year prior to competition. *Authors must be members of the MLA.* **Deadline: May 1.** Guidelines for SASE. Prize: $2,000 and a certificate.

ALDO AND JEANNE SCAGLIONE PRIZE FOR STUDIES IN GERMANIC LANGUAGES & LITERATURE

Modern Language Association of America, 26 Broadway, 3rd Floor, New York NY 10004-1789. (646)576-5141. Fax: (646)458-0030. E-mail: awards@mla.org. Web site: www.mla.org. **Contact:** Coordinator of Book Prizes. Offered in even-numbered years for outstanding scholarly work appearing in print in the previous 2 years and written by a member of the MLA on the linguistics or literatures of the Germanic languages. Works of literary history, literary criticism, and literary theory are eligible; books that are primarily translations are not eligible. **Deadline: May 1.** Guidelines for SASE. Prize: $2,000 and a certificate.

ALDO AND JEANNE SCAGLIONE PRIZE FOR STUDIES IN SLAVIC LANGUAGES AND LITERATURES

Modern Language Association of America, 26 Broadway, 3rd Floor, New York NY 10004-1789. (646)576-5141. Fax: (646)458-0030. E-mail: awards@mla.org. Web site: www.mla.org. **Contact:** Coordinator of Book Prizes. Offered in odd-numbered years for books published in the previous 2 years. Membership in the MLA is not required. Works of literary history, literary criticism, philology, and literary theory are eligible; books that are primarily translations are not eligible. **Deadline: May 1.** Guidelines for SASE. Prize: $2,000 and a certificate.

MINA P. SHAUGHNESSY PRIZE

Modern Language Association of America, 26 Broadway, 3rd Floor, New York NY 10004-1789. (646)576-5141. Fax: (646)458-0030. E-mail: awards@mla.org. Web site: www.mla.org. **Contact:** Coordinator of Book Prizes. Offered annually for a scholarly book in the fields of language, culture, literacy or literature with strong application to the teaching of English published during preceding year. Authors need not be members of the MLA. **Deadline: May 1.** Guidelines for SASE. Prize: $1,000, a certificate, and a 1-year membership in the MLA.

TURNING WHEEL YOUNG WRITER'S AWARD

Turning Wheel: The Journal of Socially Engaged Buddhism, P.O. Box 3470, Berkeley CA 94703. (510)655-6169, ext. 302. Fax: (510)655-1369. E-mail: turningwheel@bpf.org. Web site: www.bpf.org. **Contact:** Susan Moon, editor. Contest for "essays (1,500-4,000 words) from a socially engaged Buddhist perspective by emerging writers (30 and under) on an aspect of the issue's theme." Contest is ongoing—award is given twice per year. Open to writers 30 and under who have not previously published in *Turning Wheel*. **Deadline: March 7.** Guidelines for SASE. Prize: $500, and publication in *Turning Wheel*. Judged by *Turning Wheel* Editor Susan Moon, and the *Turning Wheel* Editorial Committee. Acquires first publication rights.

WRITERS' JOURNAL ANNUAL TRAVEL WRITING CONTEST

Val-Tech Media, P.O. Box 394, Perham MN 56573. (218)346-7921. Fax: (218)346-7924. E-mail: writersjournal@writersjournal.com. Web site: www.writersjournal.com. **Contact:** Leon Ogroske. Offered annually for unpublished work (maximum 2,000 words). No e-mail submissions accepted. Guidelines for SASE or online. **Deadline: November 30. Charges $7 fee.** Prize: 1st Place: $250; 2nd Place: $100; 3rd Place: $50, plus honorable mentions. Prize-winning stories and selected honorable mentions will be published in *Writer's Journal* magazine. Open to any writer.

THE WRITERS' TRUST OF CANADA'S SHAUGHNESSY COHEN PRIZE FOR POLITICAL WRITING

The Writers' Trust of Canada, 90 Richmond St. E., Suite 200, Toronto ON M5C 1P1, Canada. (416)504-8222. Fax: (416)504-9090. E-mail: info@writerstrust.com. Web site: www.writerstrust.com. **Contact:** James Davies. Awarded annually for "a nonfiction book of outstanding literary merit that enlarges our understanding of contemporary Canadian political and social issues." Presented at the Politics & the Pen event each spring in Ottawa. **Deadline: November 1.** Prize: $15,000; $2,000 to other finalists.

LAMAR YORK PRIZE FOR NONFICTION CONTEST

The Chattahoochee Review, Georgia Perimeter College, 2101 Womack Rd., Dunwoody GA 30338-4497. (770)274-5145. Web site: www.chattahoochee-review.org. Offered annually for unpublished creative nonfiction and nonscholarly essays up to 5,000 words. *The Chattahoochee Review* buys first rights only for winning essay/ms for the purpose of publication in the summer issue. **Deadline: October 1-January 31.** Guidelines for SASE. **Charges $10 fee/entry.** Prize: $1,000, plus publication for 1 or more winners. Judged by the editorial staff of *The Chattahoochee Review*. Open to any writer.

FICTION

AIM MAGAZINE SHORT STORY CONTEST

P.O. Box 390, Milton WA 98354. (253)815-9030. E-mail: apiladoone@aol.com. Web site: www.aimmagazine.org. **Contact:** Ruth Apilado, editor. Estab. 1974. $100 prize offered to contest winner for best unpublished short story (4,000 words maximum) "promoting brotherhood among people and cultures." **Deadline: August 15.** Open to any writer.

SHERWOOD ANDERSON SHORT FICTION AWARD

Mid-American Review, Dept. of English, Box WM, Bowling Green State University, Bowling Green OH 43403. (419)372-2725. E-mail: mikeczy@bgnet.bgsu.edu. Web site: www.bgsu.edu/midamericanreview. **Contact:** Michael Czyzniejewski, fiction editor. Offered annually for unpublished mss (6,000 word limit). Contest is open to all writers not associated with a judge or *Mid-American Review*. Guidelines available online or for SASE. **Deadline: October 1. Charges $10.** Prize: $1,000, plus publication in the spring issue of *Mid-American Review*. Judged by editors and a well-known writer, i.e., Steve Almond or Aimee Bender.

ANNUAL GIVAL PRESS NOVEL AWARD

Gival Press, LLC, P.O. Box 3812, Arlington VA 22203. (703)351-0079. E-mail: givalpress@yahoo.com. Web site: www.givalpress.com. **Contact:** Robert L. Giron. Offered annually for a previously unpublished original novel (not a translation). It must be in English with at least 30,000-100,000 words of literary quality. Guidelines online, via e-mail, or by mail with SASE. **Deadline: May 30. Charges $50 (USD) reading fee.** Prize: $3,000, plus publication of book with a standard contract. Open to any writer.

ANNUAL GIVAL PRESS SHORT STORY AWARD

Gival Press, LLC, P.O. Box 3812, Arlington VA 22203. (703)351-0079. E-mail: givalpress@yahoo.com. Web site: www.givalpress.com. **Contact:** Robert L. Giron. Offered annually for a previously unpublished original short story (not a translation). It must be in English with at least 5,000-15,000 words of literary quality. Guidelines by mail with SASE, by e-mail, or online. **Deadline: August 8. Charges $20 (USD) reading fee.** Prize: $1,000, plus publication on Web site. Open to any writer.

THE BALTIMORE REVIEW FICTION CONTEST

The Baltimore Review, P.O. Box 36418, Towson MD 21286. Web site: www.baltimorereview.org. **Contact:** Susan Muaddi Darraj. **Deadline: December 1. Charges $20; $25 for fee and 1-year subscription.** Prize: 1st Place: $500 and publication; 2nd Place: $250; 3rd Place: $100. Open to any writer.

BARD FICTION PRIZE

Bard College, P.O. Box 5000, Annandale-on-Hudson NY 12504-5000. (845)758-7087. E-mail: bfp@bard.edu. Web site: www.bard.edu/bfp. Estab. 2001. **Deadline: July 15.** Guidelines for SASE. Prize: $30,000 and appointment as writer-in-residence at Bard College for 1 semester. Open to younger American writers.

BEST PRIVATE EYE NOVEL CONTEST

Private Eye Writers of America and St. Martin's Press, 175 Fifth Ave., New York NY 10010. (212)674-5151. Fax: (212)254-4553. **Contact:** Toni Plummer. Offered annually for unpublished, book-length mss in the "private-eye" genre. Open to authors who have not published a mystery novel. **Deadline: July 1.** Guidelines for SASE. Prize: Advance against future royalties of $10,000, and publication by St. Martin's Minotaur.

BOSTON REVIEW SHORT STORY CONTEST

Boston Review, 35 Medford St., Suite 302, Somerville MA 02143. Web site: bostonreview.net. Stories should not exceed 4,000 words and must be previously unpublished. **Deadline: October 1. Charges $20 fee (check or money order payable to** *Boston Review*). Prize: $1,000 and publication in a later issue of *Boston Review*.

BOULEVARD SHORT FICTION CONTEST FOR EMERGING WRITERS

Boulevard Magazine, 6614 Clayton Rd., PMB #325, Richmond Heights MO 63117. (314)862-2643. Web site: www.richardburgin.net/boulevard. **Contact:** Richard Burgin, senior editor. Offered annually for unpublished short fiction to a writer who has not yet published a book of fiction, poetry, or creative nonfiction with a nationally distributed press. "We hold first North American rights on anything not previously published." Open to any writer with no previous publication by a nationally known press. Guidelines for SASE or on Web site. **Deadline: December 15. Charges $15 fee/story; includes 1-year subscription to** *Boulevard*. Prize: $1,500, and publication in 1 of the next year's issues.

CANADIAN AUTHORS ASSOCIATION MOSAID TECHNOLOGIES INC. AWARD FOR FICTION

Box 419, 320 South Shores Rd., Campbellford ON K0L 1L0, Canada. (705)653-0323 or (866)216-6222. Fax: (705)653-0593. E-mail: admin@canauthors.org. Web site: www.canauthors.org. **Contact:** Alec McEachern. Offered annually for a full-length novel by a Canadian citizen or landed immigrant. Entry form required. Obtain entry form from contact name or download from Web site. **Deadline: December 15.** Guidelines for SASE. **Charges $35 fee (Canadian).** Prize: $2,500 and a silver medal.

CAPE FEAR CRIME FESTIVAL SHORT STORY CONTEST

P.O. Box 12295, Wilmington NC 28405. Web site: www.capefearcrimefestival.org. "The CFCF Short Story Contest was created in concert with the annual Cape Fear Crime Festival, a mystery writer and reader's conference held in North Carolina. The purpose of the annual story contest is to provide a forum in which to discover, publish, and promote new writers, and to introduce readers to promising authors through the publication of the contest's annual chapbook. Contest organizers are also interested in bridging the imagined gap between genre and nongenre fiction." Entries must be unpublished, no longer than 4,000 words, and have a strong mystery or crime theme. Guidelines online or for SASE. **Deadline: June 1. Charges $8/entry (unlimited entries).** Prize: 1st Place: $100; 2nd Place: $75; 3rd Place: $50. All winning stories will be published in the story contest chapbook, which is distributed to hundreds of festival attendees. Winning authors will also receive free registration to the Cape Fear Crime Festival, and a free Saturday night dinner featuring a celebrated mystery author. Each winning story is subject to editorial review and will be copyedited for grammatical errors, spelling mistakes, and libelous language. All editorial changes will be shared with the winning authors before the chapbook goes to press. Judged by a panel of local bookstore employees, editors, and librarians to determine the semifinalists. Semifinalist stories are then passed on to a celebrity judge who determines which stories win 1st, 2nd, and 3rd place. Open to any writer.

THE ALEXANDER PATTERSON CAPPON FICTION AWARD

New Letters, 5101 Rockhill Rd., Kansas City MO 64110. (816)235-1168. Fax: (816)235-2611. E-mail: newletters@umkc.edu. Web site: www.newletters.org. **Contact:** Amy Lucas. Offered annually for unpublished work to discover and reward new and upcoming writers. Buys first North American serial rights. Open to any writer. **Deadline: Third week in May.** Guidelines for SASE. **Charges $15 (includes a 1-year subscription).** Prize: 1st Place: $1,500 and publication in a volume of *New Letters*; runner-up will receive a complimentary copy of a recent book of poetry or fiction courtesy of BkMk Press. All entries will be given consideration for publication in future issues of *New Letters*.

G.S. SHARAT CHANDRA PRIZE FOR SHORT FICTION

BkMk Press, University of Missouri-Kansas City, 5100 Rockhill Rd., Kansas City MO 64110. (816)235-2558. Fax: (816)235-2611. E-mail: bkmk@umkc.edu. Web site: www.umkc.edu/bkmk. Offered annually for the best book-length ms collection (unpublished) of short fiction in English by a living author. Translations are not eligible. Initial judging is done by a network of published writers. Final judging is done by a writer of national reputation. Guidelines for SASE, by e-mail, or on Web site. **Deadline: January 15 (postmarked). Charges $25 fee.** Prize: $1,000, plus book publication by BkMk Press.

CAROLYN A. CLARK FLASH FICTION PRIZE

National League of American Pen Women, Nob Hill, San Francisco Branch, The Webhallow House, 1544 Sweetwood Dr., Colma CA 94015-2029. E-mail: pennobhill@aol.com. Web site: www.soulmakingcontest.us. **Contact:** Eileen Malone. Three flash fiction (short-short) stories per entry, under 500 words. Previously published material is accepted. Indicate category on each poem. Identify only with 3 × 5 card. **Deadline: November 30.** Guidelines for SASE. **Charges $5/entry (make checks payable to NLAPW, Nob Hill Branch).** Prize: 1st Place: $100; 2nd Place: $50; 3rd Place: $25. Open annually to any writer.

CROSSTIME SCIENCE FICTION CONTEST

Crossquarter Publishing Group, P.O. Box 23749, Santa Fe NM 87502. (505)438-9846. Fax: (505)438-4789. E-mail: info@crossquarter.com. Web site: www.crossquarter.com. **Contact:** Therese Francis. Annual contest for short science fiction (up to 7,500 words) showcasing the best in the human spirit. No horror or dystopia. Guidelines and entry form available online. **Deadline: January 6. Charges $15; $10/each additional entry.** Prize: 1st Place: $250; 2nd Place: $125; 3rd Place: $75; 4th Place: $50. Winners are also combined into an anthology. Open to any writer.

DAME THROCKMORTON FICTION CONTEST

Coffeehousefiction.com, P.O. Box 399, Forest Hill MD 21050. E-mail: info@coffeehousefiction.com. Web site: www.coffeehousefiction.com. **Contact:** Sherri Cook Woosley, contest director. Estab. 2004. Annual contest to encourage unpublished fiction writers who have chosen a vocation with such a high frustration rate. ''Each of our judges either loves literature or is a writer, and understands firsthand the emotional highs and lows of the road to publication.'' Guidelines for SASE, via e-mail, or online. Writers keep all rights to their work. Annually, Must Be Unpublished. **Deadline: Jan. 31, 2007.** Guidelines for SASE. **Charges $15.** Prize: 1st Place: $500; 2nd Place: $125; 3rd Place: 75; 4th Place: $50. All winners are published on Coffeehousefiction.com with bios and pictures. Judged by Andrew Stauffer, an associate professor of English literature at Boston University; Sherri Cook Woosley Elyse, M.A. in English literature from University of Maryland; Beaulieu-Lucey, M.A. in English literature from University of Maryland; Nancy Adler, graduate work from Johns Hopkins University. Acquires None. Open to any writer.

WILLIAM F. DEECK MALICE DOMESTIC GRANTS FOR UNPUBLISHED WRITERS

Malice Domestic, P.O. Box 8007, Gaithersburg MD 20898. E-mail: grants@malicedomestic.org. Web site: www.malicedomestic.org. **Contact:** Grants chair. Offered annually for unpublished work in the mystery field. Malice awards 2 grants to unpublished writers in the malice domestic genre at its annual convention in May. The competition is designed to help the next generation of malice authors get their first work published and to foster quality malice literature. Malice domestic literature is loosely described as mystery stories of the Agatha Christie type, i.e., traditional mysteries, which usually feature an amateur detective, characters who know each other, and no excessive gore, gratuitous violence, or explicit sex. Writers who have been published previously in the mystery field, including publication of a mystery novel, short story, or nonfiction work, are ineligible to apply. Members of the Malice Domestic Board of Directors and their families are ineligible to apply. Malice encourages applications from minority candidates. Guidelines online. **Deadline: December 15.** Prize: $1,000.

JACK DYER FICTION PRIZE

Crab Orchard Review, Dept. of English, Southern Illinois University Carbondale, Carbondale IL 62901-4503. E-mail: jtribble@siu.edu. Web site: www.siu.edu/~crborchd. **Contact:** Jon C. Tribble, managing editor. Offered annually for unpublished short fiction. *Crab Orchard Review* acquires first North American serial rights to all submitted work. Open to any writer. **Deadline: February 1-April 1.** Guidelines for SASE. **Charges $15/entry**

Contests & Awards

(can enter up to 3 stories, each story submitted requires a separate fee and can be up to 6,000 words), which includes a 1-year subscription to *Crab Orchard Review*. Prize: $1,500 and publication. Open to US citizens only.

H.E. FRANCIS SHORT STORY AWARD

University of Alabama in Huntsville, Department of English, Huntsville AL 35899. Web site: www.uah.edu/colleges/liberal/english/whatnewcontest.html. Offered annually for unpublished work, not to exceed 5,000 words. Acquires first-time publication rights. **Deadline: December 31.** Guidelines for SASE. **Charges $15 reading fee (make check payable to the Ruth Hindman Foundation).** Prize: $1,000. Judged by a panel of nationally recognized, award-winning authors, directors of creative writing programs, and editors of literary journals.

DANUTA GLEED LITERARY AWARD FOR FIRST BOOK OF SHORT FICTION

The Writers' Union of Canada, 90 Richmond St. E., Suite 200, Toronto ON M5C 1P1, Canada. (416)703-8982. Fax: (416)504-9090. E-mail: projects@writersunion.ca. Web site: www.writersunion.ca. **Contact:** Deborah Windsor. Offered annually to Canadian writers for the best first collection of published short stories in the English language. Must have been published in the previous calendar year. Submit 4 copies. **Deadline: January 31.** Guidelines for SASE. Prize: 1st Place: $10,000; $500 to each of 2 runners-up.

GLIMMER TRAIN'S FALL SHORT-STORY AWARD FOR NEW WRITERS

Glimmer Train Press, Inc., 1211 NW Glisan St., Suite 207, Portland OR 97209. (503)221-0836. Fax: (503)221-0837. E-mail: eds@glimmertrain.org. Web site: www.glimmertrain.org. **Contact:** Linda Swanson-Davies. Offered for any writer whose fiction hasn't appeared in a nationally-distributed publication with a circulation over 5,000. Maximum 12,000 words. **Open August 1-September 30.** Follow submission procedure on Web site. Notification on January 2. **Charges $15 fee/story.** Prize: Winner receives $1,200, publication in *Glimmer Train Stories,* and 20 copies of that issue; runners-up receive $500/$300, respectively.

GLIMMER TRAIN'S SPRING SHORT-STORY AWARD FOR NEW WRITERS

Glimmer Train Press, Inc., 1211 NW Glisan St., Suite 207, Portland OR 97209. (503)221-0836. Fax: (503)221-0837. E-mail: eds@glimmertrain.org. Web site: www.glimmertrain.org. **Contact:** Linda Swanson-Davies. Offered for any writer whose fiction hasn't appeared in a nationally-distributed publication with a circulation over 5,000. Maximum 12,000 words. **Open February 1-March 31.** Follow submission procedure on Web site. Notification on July 1. **Charges $15 fee/story.** Prize: Winner receives $1,200, publication in *Glimmer Train Stories* and 20 copies of that issue; runners-up receive $500/$300, respectively.

GLIMMER TRAIN'S SUMMER FICTION OPEN

Glimmer Train Press, Inc., 1211 NW Glisan St., Suite 207, Portland OR 97209. (503)221-0836. Fax: (503)221-0837. E-mail: eds@glimmertrain.org. Web site: www.glimmertrain.org. **Contact:** Linda Swanson-Davies. Offered annually for unpublished stories as a platform for all themes, all lengths (up to 25,000 words), all writers. Follow submission procedure on Web site. **Deadline: June 30. Charges $20 fee/story.** Prize: 1st Place: $2,000, publication in *Glimmer Train Stories*, and 20 copies of that issue; 2nd Place: $1,000; 3rd Place: $600.

GLIMMER TRAIN'S SUMMER VERY SHORT FICTION CONTEST

Glimmer Train Press, Inc., 1211 NW Glisan St., 207, Portland OR 97209. (503)221-0836. Fax: (503)221-0837. E-mail: eds@glimmertrain.org. Web site: www.glimmertrain.org. **Contact:** Linda Swanson-Davies. Offered to encourage the art of the very short story. Word count: 3,000 maximum. Open May 1-July 31. Follow submission process online. Results will be e-mailed to all entrants on November 1. **Charges $15 fee/story.** Prize: Winner receives $1,200, publication in Glimmer Train Stories (circ. 13,000), and 20 copies of that issue; runners-up receive $500/300, respectively, and consideration for publication.

GLIMMER TRAIN'S WINTER FICTION OPEN

Glimmer Train, Inc., 1211 NW Glisan St., Suite 207, Portland OR 97209. (503)221-0836. Fax: (503)221-0837. E-mail: eds@glimmertrain.org. Web site: www.glimmertrain.org. **Contact:** Linda Swanson-Davies. Offered annually for unpublished work as a platform for all themes, all lengths (up to 25,000 words), and all writers. Follow submission procedure on Web site. **Deadline: January 15. Charges $20/story.** Prize: 1st Place: $2,000, publication in *Glimmer Train Stories*, and 20 copies of that issue; 2nd Place: $1,000; 3rd Place: $600. Open to any writer.

GLIMMER TRAIN'S WINTER VERY SHORT FICTION AWARD

Glimmer Train Press, Inc., 1211 NW Glisan St., #207, Portland OR 97209. (503)221-0836. Fax: (503)221-0837. E-mail: eds@glimmertrain.org. Web site: www.glimmertrain.org. **Contact:** Linda Swanson-Davies. Offered twice yearly to encourage the art of the very short story. Word count: 2,000 maximum. Open November 1-January 31. Follow online submission process on Web site. Results will be e-mailed to all entrants on May 1. **Charges $10 fee/story.** Prize: Winner receives $1,200, publication in *Glimmer Train Stories* (circulation 13,000), and 20 copies of that issue; runners-up receive $500/$300, respectively, and consideration for publication.

GOVERNOR GENERAL'S LITERARY AWARD FOR FICTION

Canada Council for the Arts, 350 Albert St., P.O. Box 1047, Ottawa ON K1P 5V8, Canada. (613)566-4414, ext. 4582. Fax: (613)566-4410. Web site: www.canadacouncil.ca/prizes/ggla. Offered annually for the best English-language and the best French-language work of fiction by a Canadian. Publishers submit titles for consideration. **Deadline: June 1 or August 7, depending on the book's publication date.** Prize: Each laureate receives $15,000; nonwinning finalists receive $1,000.

LYNDALL HADOW/DONALD STUART SHORT STORY COMPETITION

Fellowship of Australian Writers (WA), P.O. Box 312, Cottesloe WA 6911. (61)(8)9384-4771. Fax: (61)(8)9384-4854. E-mail: admin@fawwa.org.au. Web site: www.fawwa.org.au. Annual contest for unpublished short stories (maximum 3,000 words). "We reserve the right to publish entries in an FAWWA publication or on its Web site." Guidelines online or for SASE. **Deadline: June 1. Charges $7/story.** Prize: 1st Place: $400; 2nd Place; $100; Highly Commended: $50. Open to any writer.

ERNEST HEMINGWAY FOUNDATION PEN AWARD FOR FIRST FICTION

PEN New England, Emerson College, 120 Boylston St., Boston MA 02116. (617)824-8820. E-mail: pen_ne@emerson.edu. Web site: www.pen-ne.org. **Contact:** Karen Wulf. Estab. 1976. Offered for first-published novel or short story collection by an unpublished American author. Guidelines and entry form for SASE. **Deadline: December 9. Charges $35.** Prize: $8,000; 2 finalists and 2 runners-up will be awarded a residency at UCross Foundation in Wyoming.

LORIAN HEMINGWAY SHORT STORY COMPETITION

Hemingway Days Festival, P.O. Box 993, Key West FL 33041-0993. (305)294-0320. E-mail: calico2419@aol.com. Web site: www.shortstorycompetition.com. Estab. 1981. Offered annually for unpublished short stories up to 3,000 words. Guidelines available via mail, e-mail, or online. **Deadline: May 15. Charges $10/story postmarked by May 1, $15/story postmarked by May 15; no stories accepted after May 15.** Prize: 1st Place: $1,000; 2nd-3rd Place: $500; honorable mentions will also be awarded.

TOM HOWARD/JOHN H. REID SHORT STORY CONTEST

% Winning Writers, 351 Pleasant St., PMB 222, Northampton MA 01060-3961. (866)946-9748. E-mail: adam@winningwriters.com. Web site: www.winningwriters.com. **Contact:** Adam Cohen. Estab. 1993. Both unpublished and published work accepted (maximum 5,000 words). Guidlines for SASE or online. **Deadline: March 31. Charges $12 USD/story/essay/prose work.** Prize: 1st Place: $1,200; 2nd Place: $800; 3rd Place: $400; plus 4 high distinction awards of $200 each. The top 10 entries will be publishing on the Winning Writers Web site. Judged by John H. Reid; assisted by Dee C. Konrad. Open to any writer.

L. RON HUBBARD'S WRITERS OF THE FUTURE CONTEST

P.O. Box 1630, Los Angeles CA 90078. (323)466-3310. E-mail: contests@authorservicesinc.com. Web site: www.writersofthefuture.com. **Contact:** Contest Administrator. Offered for unpublished work to find, reward, and publicize new speculative fiction writers so they may more easily attain professonal writing careers. Open to new and amateur writers who have not professionally published a novel or short novel, more than 1 novelette, or more than 3 short stories. Eligible entries are short stories or novelettes (under 17,000 words) of science fiction or fantasy. Guidelines for SASE, online, or via e-mail. No entry fee. Entrants retain all rights to their stories. **Deadline: December 31, March 31, June 30, September 30.** Prize: Awards quarterly 1st Place: $1,000; 2nd Place: $750; and 3rd Place: $500. Annual Grand Prize: $5,000. Judged by professional writers only.

INDIANA REVIEW FICTION CONTEST

Indiana Review, Ballantine Hall 465, Indiana University, Bloomington IN 47405-7103. (812)855-3439. Fax: (812)855-4253. E-mail: inreview@indiana.edu. Web site: www.indiana.edu/~inreview. Maximum story length is 15,000 words (no minimum). Offered annually for unpublished work. Guidelines on Web site and with SASE request. **Deadline: October 15. Charges $15 fee (includes a 1-year subscription).** Prize: $1,000. Judged by guest judges; 2005 prize judged by Rick Moody. Open to any writer.

INNERMOONLIT AWARD FOR BEST FIRST CHAPTER OF A NOVEL

E-mail: timescythe@cetlink.net. Web site: www.brianagincourtmassey.com. **Contact:** Brian Agincourt Massey. Annual contest for an unpublished first chapter of a novel (2,000 words maximum). All genres are accepted.

Guidelines available online. No entry fee. **Deadline: March 1.** Prize: 1st Place: $100; 2nd Place: $50. Judged by Brian and Maria Massey. Open to all writers 18 years and older.

INNERMOONLIT AWARD FOR BEST SHORT-SHORT STORY

E-mail: timescythe@cetlink.net. Web site: www.brianagincourtmassey.com. **Contact:** Brian Agincourt Massey. Annual contest for unpublished short-short stories that do not exceed 500 words. Guidelines available online. No entry fee. **Deadline: September 1.** Prize: 1st Place: $100; 2nd Place: $50. Judged by Brian and Maria Massey. Open to all writers 18 years and older.

INTERNATIONAL 3-DAY NOVEL CONTEST

200-341 Water St., Vancouver BC V6B 1B8 Canada. E-mail: info@3daynovel.com. Web site: www.3daynovel.com. **Contact:** Melissa Edwards. Estab. 1977. Offered annually for the best novel written in 3 days (Labor Day weekend). To register, send SASE (IRC if from outside Canada) for details, or entry form available online. **Deadline: Friday before Labor Day weekend. Charges $50 fee (lower group rates available).** Prize: 1st place receives publication; 2nd place receives $500; 3rd place receives library of books. Open to all writers. Writing may take place in any location.

JAMES JONES FIRST NOVEL FELLOWSHIP

Wilkes University, Department of English, 245 S. River St., Wilkes-Barre PA 18766. (570)408-4534. Fax: (570)408-7829. E-mail: cwriting@wilkes.edu. Web site: www.wilkes.edu. Offered annually for unpublished novels, novellas, and closely-linked short stories (all works in progress). "The award is intended to honor the spirit of unblinking honesty, determination, and insight into modern culture exemplified by the late James Jones." The competition is open to all American writers who have not previously published novels. **Deadline: March 1. Charges $20 fee.** Prize: $10,000; runner-up gets $250 honorarium.

JUST DESSERTS SHORT-SHORT FICTION CONTEST

Passages North, Dept. of English, Northern Michigan University, 1401 Presque Isle Ave., Marquette MI 49855. (906)227-1203. Fax: (906)227-1096. E-mail: passages@nmu.edu. Web site: myweb.nmu.edu/~passages. **Contact:** Jennifer Howard. Offered every even year to publish new voices in literary fiction (maximum 1,000 words). Guidelines available for SASE or online. **Deadline: Submit September 15-January 15. Charges $10 reading fee/story.** Prize: $1,000, and publication for the winner; 2 honorable mentions also published; all entrants receive a copy of *Passages North*.

SERENA MCDONALD KENNEDY AWARD

Snake Nation Press, 110 W. Force St., Valdosta GA 31601. (229)244-0752. E-mail: jeana@snakenationpress.org. Web site: www.snakenationpress.org. **Contact:** Jean Arambula. Contest for a collection of unpublished short stories by a new or underpublished writer. Entries accepted all year. **Deadline: April 30.** Guidelines for SASE. **Charges $25 reading fee.** Prize: $1,000 and publication. Judged by an independent judge. Open to any writer.

E.M. KOEPPEL SHORT FICTION AWARD

Writecorner Press, Koeppel Contest, P.O. Box 140310, Gainesville FL 32614-0310. Web site: writecorner.com. **Contact:** Mary Sue Koeppel, Robert B. Gentry. Estab. 2004. Any number of unpublished stories may be entered by any writer. Send 2 title pages. Put only the title on one title page. List the title and the author's name, address, phone, e-mail, and short bio on the second title page. Guidelines for SASE or online. **Deadline: October 1-April 30. Charges $15/story; $10/additional story.** Prize: 1st Place: $1,100; Editor's Choices: $100 each; P.L. Titus Scholarship: $500. Open to any writer.

LA BELLE LETTRE SHORT STORY CONTEST

P.O. Box 2009, Longview WA 98632. E-mail: admin@labellelettre.com. Web site: www.labellelettre.com. **Contact:** Jennifer Hill, executive director. Contest offered seasonally with Spring deadline of May 1, Summer deadline of August 1, Fall deadline of November 1, Winter deadline of February 1. Guidelines on Web site or for SASE. **Charges $6.** Prize: 1st Place: $150 + critique; 2nd Place: $75 + critique; 3rd Place: $50 + critique. Judged by Jennifer Hill, executive director, and Mary Stone, assistant director. Additional judges as determined by contest. Open to any writer.

LAWRENCE HOUSE CENTRE FOR THE ARTS SHORT STORY CONTEST

Lawrence House Centre for the Arts, 127 Christina St. S., Sarnia ON N7T 2M8, Canada. (519)337-0507. Fax: (519)337-0482. E-mail: lhcarts@hotmail.com. Web site: www.lawrencehouse.ca. **Contact:** Literary Representative on Board of Directors. Annual contest to promote unpublished fiction entries up to 2,500 words. Open to Canadian citizens and landed immigrants. Guidelines online or for SASE. **Deadline: September 30. Charges**

$20 (Canadian) entry fee. Prize: 1st Place: $250; 2nd Place: $150; 3rd Place: $100. Judged by college professors of English and/or teachers of creative writing.

N THE LEDGE ANNUAL FICTION AWARDS COMPETITION

The Ledge Magazine, 40 Maple Avenue, Bellport NY 11713. E-mail: info@theledgemagazine.com. Web site: www.theledgemagazine.com. **Contact:** Timothy Monaghan. Stories must be unpublished and 7,500 words or less. There are no restrictions on form or content. Guidelines online or for SASE. **Deadline: March 1. Charges $10/first story; $6/additional story.** Prize: 1st Place: $1,000 and publication; 2nd Place: $250 and publication; 3rd Place: $100 and publication. Open to any writer.

LITERAL LATTÉ FICTION AWARD

Literal Latté, 200 E. 10th St., Suite 240, New York NY 10003. (212)260-5532. E-mail: litlatte@aol.com. Web site: www.literal-latte.com. **Contact:** Edward Estlin, contributing editor. Award to provide talented writers with 3 essential tools for continued success: money, publication, and recognition. Offered annually for unpublished fiction (maximum 6,000 words). Guidelines for SASE, by e-mail, or online. Open to any writer. **Deadline: January 15.** Prize: 1st Place: $1,000 and publication in *Literal Latté*; 2nd Place: $300; 3rd Place: $200; plus up to 7 honorable mentions.

LONG STORY CONTEST, INTERNATIONAL

White Eagle Coffee Store Press, P.O. Box 383, Fox River Grove IL 60021. (847)639-9200. E-mail: wecspress@aol.com. Web site: members.aol.com/wecspress. **Contact:** Frank E. Smith, publisher. Offered annually since 1993 for unpublished work to recognize and promote long short stories of 8,000-14,000 words (about 30-50 pages). Sample of previous winner: $5.95, including postage. Open to any writer; no restrictions on materials. **Deadline: December 15.** Guidelines for SASE. **Charges $15 fee; $10 for second story in same envelope.** Prize: $500, publication, and 25 copies of chapbook.

THE MALAHAT REVIEW NOVELLA PRIZE

The Malahat Review, University of Victoria, P.O. Box 1700 STN CSC, Victoria BC V8W 2Y2, Canada. (250)721-8524. E-mail: malahat@uvic.ca. Web site: malahatreview.ca. **Contact:** Editor. "In alternate years, we hold the Long Poem and Novella contests." Offered to promote unpublished novellas. Obtains first world rights. After publication rights revert to the author. Open to any writer. **Deadline: February 1 (even years).** Guidelines for SASE. **Charges $35 fee (includes a 1-year subscription to** *Malahat*). Prize: $500, plus payment for publication ($35/page) and an additional year's subscription.

MARY MCCARTHY PRIZE IN SHORT FICTION

Sarabande Books, P.O. Box 4456, Louisville KY 40204. (502)458-4028. Fax: (502)458-4065. E-mail: info@sarabandebooks.org. Web site: www.sarabandebooks.org. **Contact:** Kirby Gann, managing editor. Offered annually to publish an outstanding collection of stories, novellas, or short novel (less than 250 pages). All finalists considered for publication. **Deadline: January 1-February 15.** Guidelines for SASE. **Charges $25 fee.** Prize: $2,000 and publication (standard royalty contract).

MARJORIE GRABER MCINNIS SHORT STORY AWARD

ACT Writers Centre, Gorman House Arts Centre, Ainslie Ave., Braddon ACT 2612, Australia. Phone/Fax: (61)(2)6262-9191. E-mail: admin@actwriters.org.au. Web site: www.actwriters.org.au. Open theme for a short story with 1,500-3,000 words. Guidelines available on Web site. **Deadline: September 23. Charges $7.50/nonmembers; $5/members.** Prize: $600 and publication. Five runners-up receive book prizes. All winners may be published in the ACT writers centre newsletter and on the ACT writers centre Web site. Open to unpublished emerging writers residing within the ACT or region.

N MICHIGAN LITERARY FICTION AWARDS

University of Michigan Press, 839 Greene St., Ann Arbor MI 48104-3209. E-mail: ump.fiction@umich.edu. Web site: www.press.umich.edu/fiction. **Contact:** Chris Hebert, fiction editor. Submit an unpublished novel of at least 100 pages (no genre fiction). Entrants must have previously published at least 1 literary novel or story collection in English. **Deadline: February 1-July 1.** Prize: $1,000 advance and publication. Closed to university students, faculty, graduates, and staff. Entrants may only submit once per year. Simultaneous submissions are allowed.

MILKWEED NATIONAL FICTION PRIZE

Milkweed Editions, 1011 Washington Ave. S., Suite 300, Minneapolis MN 55415. (612)332-3192. Fax: (612)215-2550. Web site: www.milkweed.org. **Contact:** The Editors. Estab. 1986. Annual award for unpublished works.

Milkweed is looking for a novel, novella, or a collection of short stories written in English. Mss should be of high literary quality and must be double-spaced and between 150-400 pages in length. Enclose a SASE for response, or a mailer-sized SASE with postage or a $5 check for return of ms. All mss submitted to Milkweed will automatically be considered for the prize. Submission directly to the contest is no longer necessary. Writers are recommended to have previously published a book of fiction or 3 short stories (or novellas) in magazines/journals with national distribution. Catalog available on request for $1.50. Guidelines for SASE or online. **Deadline: Open.** Prize: Publication by Milkweed Editions and a cash advance of $5,000 against royalties agreed upon in the contractual arrangement negotiated at the time of acceptance.

C. WRIGHT MILLS AWARD

The Society for the Study of Social Problems, Dept. of Sociology and Anthropology, University of La Verne, 1950 3rd Street, La Verne CA 91750. (865)689-1531. Fax: (865)689-1534. E-mail: delgadoh@utk.edu. Web site: www.sssp1.org. **Contact:** Michele Smith Koontz, administrative officer. Offered annually for a book published the previous year that most effectively critically addresses an issue of contemporary public importance; brings to the topic a fresh, imaginative perspective; advances social scientific understanding of the topic; displays a theoretically informed view and empirical orientation; evinces quality in style of writing; and explicitly or implicitly contains implications for courses of action. **Deadline: January 16.** Prize: $500 stipend.

KATHLEEN MITCHELL AWARD

Cauz Group Pty., Ltd., P.O. Box 777, Randwick NSW 2031 Australia. (61)(2)9326-5507. Fax: (61)(2)9326-5514. E-mail: psalter@cauzgroup.com.au. **Contact:** Petrea Salter. Estab. 1996. Offered in even years for novels published in the previous 2 years. Author must have been under age 30 when the novel was published. Entrants must be Australian or British born or naturalized Australian citizens, and have resided in Australia for the last year. The award is for a novel of the highest literary merit. **Deadline: February 8, 2008.** Guidelines for SASE. Prize: $7,500 (Australian).

NATIONAL WRITERS ASSOCIATION NOVEL WRITING CONTEST

The National Writers Association, 10940 S. Parker Rd. #508, Parker CO 80134. (303)841-0246. Fax: (303)841-2607. **Contact:** Sandy Whelchel, director. Annual contest to help develop creative skills, to recognize and reward outstanding ability, and to increase the opportunity for the marketing and subsequent publication of novel mss. **Deadline: April 1. Charges $35 fee.** Prize: 1st Place: $500; 2nd Place: $300; 3rd Place: $200.

NATIONAL WRITERS ASSOCIATION SHORT STORY CONTEST

The National Writers Association, 10940 S. Parker Rd. #508, Parker CO 80134. (303)841-0246. Fax: (303)841-2607. **Contact:** Sandy Whelchel, director. Annual contest to encourage writers in this creative form, and to recognize those who excel in fiction writing. **Deadline: July 1.** Guidelines for SASE. **Charges $15 fee.** Prize: 1st Place: $200; 2nd Place: $100; 3rd Place: $50.

THE NELLIGAN PRIZE FOR SHORT FICTION

Colorado Review/Center for Literary Publishing, Dept. of English, Colorado State University, Ft. Collins CO 80523. (970)491-5449. E-mail: creview@colostate.edu. Web site: coloradoreview.colostate.edu. **Contact:** Stephanie G'Schwind, editor. Offered annually to an unpublished short story. Guidelines for SASE or online. **Deadline: March 15. Charges $10.** Prize: $1,000 and publication of story in *Colorado Review*.

FRANK O'CONNOR AWARD FOR SHORT FICTION

descant, Texas Christian University's literary journal, TCU Box 297270, Fort Worth TX 76129. (817)257-6537. Fax: (817)257-6239. E-mail: descant@tcu.edu. Web site: www.descant.tcu.edu. **Contact:** Dave Kuhne, editor. Offered annually for unpublished short stories. Publication retains copyright but will transfer it to the author upon request. **Deadline: September-March.** Guidelines for SASE. Prize: $500.

THE OHIO STATE UNIVERSITY PRIZE IN SHORT FICTION

The Ohio State University Press and the MFA Program in Creative Writing at The Ohio State University, 180 Pressey Hall, 1070 Carmack Rd., Columbus OH 43210-1002. (614)292-1462. Fax: (614)292-2065. E-mail: ohiostatepress@osu.edu. Web site: ohiostatepress.org. Offered annually to published and unpublished writers. Submissions may include short stories, novellas, or a combination of both. Manuscripts must be 150-300 typed pages; novellas must not exceed 125 pages. No employee or student of The Ohio State University is eligible. **Deadline: Entry must be postmarked during the month of January. Charges $20 fee.** Prize: $1,500 and publication under a standard book contract.

ONCEWRITTEN.COM FICTION CONTEST

Oncewritten.com, 1850 N. Whitley Ave., #404, Hollywood CA 90028. E-mail: fictioncontest@oncewritten.com. Web site: www.oncewritten.com. The purpose of this biannual contest is to find high quality short fiction to feature on the Web site and in *Off the Press*, our monthly newsletter, which is distributed specifically to people interested in reading about new authors.'' **Deadline: April 30 and October 31.** Guidelines for SASE. **Charges $5/story.** Prize: 1st Place: $100. Judged by editor and 1 industry professional. Open to any writer.

ORANGE PRIZE FOR FICTION

Orange PCS, % Booktrust, Book House, 45 E. Hill, Wandsworth, London SW18 2QZ United Kingdom. Fax: (44)(208)516-2978. E-mail: tarryn@booktrust.org.uk. Web site: www.orangeprize.co.uk. **Contact:** Tarryn McKay. This annual award is for a full-length novel written by a woman which fulfills the criteria of excellence in writing, relevance to people's everyday and imaginative lives, accessibility, and originality. The award is open to any full-length novel written in English between April 1 and the following March 31 by a woman of any nationality and published in the UK by a UK publisher. Translations are not eligible, neither are novellas or collections of short stories. Books from all genres are encouraged, but all books must be unified and substantial works written by a single author. All entries must be published in the UK between the publication dates, but may have been previously published outside the UK. **Deadline: End of November.** Prize: £30,000 and a statuette known as ''The Bessie.'' Judged by a panel of women.

OTTAWA PUBLIC LIBRARY ANNUAL ADULT SHORT STORY CONTEST

Ottawa Public Library, Community Partnerships and Programming, Ben Franklin Place, 2nd Floor, 101 Centrepointe Dr., Ottawa ON K2G 5K7, Canada. (613)580-2424, ext. 41307. E-mail: eva-marie.pigeon-seguin@library.ottawa.on.ca. Web site: www.library.ottawa.on.ca. **Contact:** Eva Pigeon-Seguin. Offered annually for unpublished short stories (written in French or English) to encourage writing in the community. Open to residents of Ottawa, Ontario, age 18 or older. Call for guidelines, or go online. **Deadline: March 14. Charges $10/story.** Prize: 1st Place: $500; 2nd Place: $250; 3rd Place: $100.

THE VANCE PALMER PRIZE FOR FICTION

Victorian Premier's Literary Awards, State Library of Victoria, 328 Swanston St., Melbourne VIC 3000 Australia. (61)(3)8664-7277. E-mail: pla@slv.vic.gov.au. Web site: www.slv.vic.gov.au/pla. **Contact:** Project Officer. Prize for a novel or collection of short stories published May 1-April 30. **Deadline: May 5.** Guidelines for SASE. **Charges $35.** Prize: $30,000. Open to Australian citizens or permanent residents.

PATERSON FICTION PRIZE

PCCC, Poetry Center, One College Blvd., Paterson NJ 07505-1179. (973)684-6555. Fax: (973)523-6085. E-mail: mgillan@pccc.edu. Web site: www.pccc.edu/poetry. **Contact:** Maria Mazziotti Gillan, director. Offered annually for a novel or collection of short fiction published the previous calendar year. Guidelines for SASE or online. **Deadline: April 1.** Prize: $1,000.

PEN/FAULKNER AWARDS FOR FICTION

PEN/Faulkner Foundation, 201 E. Capitol St., Washington DC 20003. (202)675-0345. Fax: (202)608-1719. E-mail: jneely@folger.edu. Web site: www.penfaulkner.org. **Contact:** Jessica Neely, executive director. Offered annually for best book-length work of fiction by an American citizen published in a calendar year. **Deadline: October 31.** Prize: $15,000 (one winner); $5,000 (4 nominees).

PHOEBE WINTER FICTION CONTEST

Phoebe, MSN 2D6, George Mason University, 4400 University Dr., Fairfax VA 22030. (703)993-2915. E-mail: phoebe@gmu.edu. Web site: www.gmu.edu/pubs/phoebe. Offered annually for an unpublished story (25 pages maximum). Guidelines online or for SASE. **Deadline: December 1. Charges $15.** Prize: $1,000 and publication in the Fall issue. All entrants receive a free issue. Judged by a recognized fiction writer hired by *Phoebe* (changes each year). Acquires first serial rights if work is accepted for publication. Open to any writer.

POCKETS FICTION-WRITING CONTEST

1908 Grand Ave., P.O. Box 340004, Nashville TN 37203-0004. (615)340-7333. E-mail: pockets@upperroom.org. Web site: www.pockets.org. **Contact:** Lynn W. Gilliam. Offered annually for unpublished work (1,000-1,600 words) to discover new writers. **Deadline: March 1-August 15.** Guidelines for SASE. Prize: $1,000, and publication in *Pockets*.

THE KATHERINE ANNE PORTER PRIZE FOR FICTION

Nimrod International Journal, The University of Tulsa, 600 S. College Ave., Tulsa OK 74104. (918)631-3080. Fax: (918)631-3033. E-mail: nimrod@utulsa.edu. Web site: www.utulsa.edu/nimrod. **Contact:** Francine Ringold. This annual award was established to discover new, unpublished writers of vigor and talent. **Deadline: April 30.** Guidelines for SASE. **Charges $20 (includes a 1-year subscription to** *Nimrod*). Prize: 1st Place: $2,000 and publication; 2nd Place: $1,000 and publication. *Nimrod* retains the right to publish any submission. Judged by the *Nimrod* editors (finalists), and a recognized author selects the winners. Open to US residents only.

PRISM INTERNATIONAL ANNUAL SHORT FICTION CONTEST

Prism International, Creative Writing Program, UBC, Buch E462, 1866 Main Mall, Vancouver BC V6T 1Z1, Canada. (604)822-2514. Fax: (604)822-3616. E-mail: prism@interchange.ubc.ca. Web site: prism.arts.ubc.ca. **Contact:** Fiction Contest Manager. Offered annually for unpublished work to award the best in contemporary fiction. Works of translation are eligible. Guidelines for SASE, by e-mail, or on Web site. Acquires first North American serial rights upon publication, and limited Web rights for pieces selected for Web site. Open to any writer except students and faculty in the Creative Writing Department at UBC, or people who have taken a creative writing course at UBC within 2 years of the contest deadline. **Deadline: January 31. Charges $27/story; $7 each additional story (outside Canada pay US currency); includes subscription.** Prize: 1st Place: $2,000; Runners-up (3): $200 each; winner and runners-up published.

THE PRIZE FOR AN UNPUBLISHED MANUSCRIPT BY AN EMERGING VICTORIAN WRITER

Victorian Premier's Literary Awards, State Library of Victoria, 328 Swanston St., Melbourne VIC 3000 Australia. (61)(3)8664-7277. E-mail: pla@slv.vic.gov.au. Web site: www.slv.vic.gov.au/pla. **Contact:** Project Officer. Prize for an unpublished ms which may be a novel or a collection of short stories. **Deadline: May 5.** Guidelines for SASE. Prize: $15,000 and 20 hours of professional assistance from the Victorial Writers' Centre. Open to unpublished authors who have been citizens or residents of Australia for at least 1 year before the award.

THOMAS H. RADDALL ATLANTIC FICTION PRIZE

Writers' Federation of Nova Scotia, 1113 Marginal Rd., Halifax NS B3H 4P7, Canada. (902)423-8116. Fax: (902)422-0881. E-mail: talk@writers.ns.ca. Web site: www.writers.ns.ca. **Contact:** Jane Buss, executive director. Estab. 1990. Purpose is to recognize the best Atlantic Canadian adult fiction. There is no entry fee or form. Full-length books of fiction written by Atlantic Canadians, and published as a whole for the first time in the previous calendar year, are eligible. Entrants must be native or resident Atlantic Canadians who have either been born in Newfoundland, Prince Edward Island, Nova Scotia, or New Brunswick, and spent a substantial portion of their lives living there, or who have lived in 1 or a combination of these provinces for at least 24 consecutive months prior to entry deadline date. Publishers: Send 4 copies and a letter attesting to the author's status as an Atlantic Canadian, and the author's current mailing address and telephone number. **Deadline: First Friday in December.** Prize: $10,000.

THE ROGERS WRITERS' TRUST FICTION PRIZE

The Writers' Trust of Canada, 90 Richmond St. E., Suite 200, Toronto ON M5C 1P1, Canada. (416)504-8222. Fax: (416)504-9090. E-mail: info@writerstrust.com. Web site: www.writerstrust.com. **Contact:** James Davies. Awarded annually for a distinguished work of fiction—either a novel or short story collection—published within the previous year. Presented at the Writers' Trust Awards event held in Toronto each Spring. Prize: $15,000. Open to Canadian residents only.

RROFIHE TROPHY

Open City, 341 Lafayette St., #974, New York NY 10012. Web site: www.opencity.org/rrofihe. **Contact:** Rick Rofihe, contest judge. Third annual contest for an unpublished short story (up to 5,000 words). Stories should be typed, double-spaced, on 8½×11 paper with the author's name and contact information on the first page, and name and story title on the upper right corner of remaining pages. Limit 1 submission/author. Author must not have been previously published in *Open City*. Enclose SASE to receive names of winner and honorable mentions. All mss are nonreturnable and will be recycled. **Deadline: September 15 (postmarked).** Guidelines for SASE. **Charges $10 (make check payable to RRofihe).** Prize: $500, a trophy, and publication in *Open City*. Acquires first North American serial rights (from winner only).

SASKATCHEWAN FICTION AWARD

Saskatchewan Book Awards, Inc., Box 1921, Regina SK S4P 3E1, Canada. (306)569-1585. Fax: (306)569-4187. E-mail: director@bookawards.sk.ca. Web site: www.bookawards.sk.ca. **Contact:** Glenda James, executive director. Offered annually for work published September 15-September 14 annually. This award is presented to a Saskatchewan author for the best book of fiction (novel or short fiction), judged on the quality of writing. **Deadline: First deadline: July 31; Final deadline: September 14.** Guidelines for SASE. **Charges $20 (Canadian).** Prize: $2,000.

SCIENCE FICTION/FANTASY SHORT STORY CONTEST

Science Fiction Writers of Earth, P.O. Box 121293, Fort Worth TX 76121. Web site: www.flash.net/~sfwoe. Contest for unpublished science fiction/fantasy stories (2,000-7,500 words). The winning story is eligible to appear on the SFOE Web site. **Deadline: October 30.** Guidelines for SASE. **Charges $5; $2/additional entry.** Prize: 1st Prize: $200; 2nd Prize: $100; 3rd Prize: $50. Judged by author Edward Bryant. Open to any writer.

JOANNA CATHERINE SCOTT NOVEL EXCERPT PRIZE

National League of American Pen Women, Nob Hill, San Francisco Bay Area Branch, The Webhallow House, 1544 Sweetwood Dr., Colma CA 94015. E-mail: pennobhill@aol.com. Web site: www.soulmakingcontest.us. **Contact:** Eileen Malone. Send first chapter or the first 20 pages, whichever comes first. Include a 1-page synopsis indicating category at top page. Identify with 3×5 card only. **Deadline: November 30.** Guidelines for SASE. **Charges $5/entry (make checks payable to NLAPW, Nob Hill Branch).** Prize: 1st Place: $100; 2nd Place: $50; 3rd Place: $25. Open annually to any writer.

MICHAEL SHAARA AWARD FOR EXCELLENCE IN CIVIL WAR FICTION

Civil War Institute at Gettysburg College, 300 N. Washington St., Campus Box 435, Gettysburg PA 17325. (717)337-6590. Fax: (717)337-6596. E-mail: civilwar@gettysburg.edu. Web site: www.gettysburg.edu. **Contact:** Gabor S. Boritt, director. Estab. 1997. Offered annually for fiction published for the first time in January 1-December 31 of the year of the award "to encourage examination of the Civil War from unique perspectives or by taking an unusual approach." All Civil War novels are eligible. To nominate a novel, send 5 copies of the novel to the address above with a cover letter. Nominations should be made by publishers, but authors and critics can nominate as well. **Deadline: December 31.** Guidelines for SASE. Prize: $2,500.

MARY WOLLSTONECRAFT SHELLEY PRIZE FOR IMAGINATIVE FICTION

Rosebud, N3310 Asje Rd., Cambridge WI 53523. (608)423-4750. Fax: (608)423-9976. E-mail: jrodclark@smallbytes.net. Web site: www.rsbd.net. **Contact:** J. Roderick Clark, editor. Biennial (odd years) contest for unpublished stories. Entries are welcome any time. Acquires first rights. Open to any writer. **Deadline: October 15. Charges $10/story.** Prize: $1,000, plus publication in *Rosebud*.

ELIZABETH SIMPSON SMITH AWARD

8032 S. Dorchester Trace, Fort Mill SC 29715. E-mail: anniemaier453@msn.com. Web site: www.charlottewritersclub.org. **Contact:** Annie Maier. Offered annually for unpublished short stories (maxiumum 4,000 words) by North Carolina and South Carolina residents. Send SASE or check online for guidelines. **Deadline: May 31. Charges $15 fee.** Prize: $500 and publication in anthology.

SPOKANE PRIZE FOR SHORT FICTION

Eastern Washington University Press, 705 W. First Ave., Spokane WA 99201. (800)508-9095. Fax: (509)623-4283. E-mail: ewupress@mail.ewu.edu. Web site: ewupress.ewu.edu. **Contact:** Christopher Howell. Annual award to publish the finest work the literary world has to offer. **Deadline: May 15.** Guidelines for SASE. **Charges $25.** Prize: $1,500 and publication. Open to any writer.

THE PETER TAYLOR PRIZE FOR THE NOVEL

Knoxville Writers' Guild and University of Tennessee Press, P.O. Box 2565, Knoxville TN 37901. Web site: www.knoxvillewritersguild.org. Offered annually for unpublished work to discover and publish novels of high literary quality. Guidelines for SASE or online. Open to US residents writing in English. Members of the Knoxville Writers' Guild do the initial screening. A widely published novelist chooses the winner from a pool of finalists. **Deadline: February 1-April 30. Charges $25 fee.** Prize: $1,000 and publication by University of Tennessee Press (a standard royalty contract).

THOROUGHBRED TIMES FICTION CONTEST

P.O. Box 8237, Lexington KY 40533. (859)260-9800. Fax: (859)260-9812. E-mail: copy@thoroughbredtimes.com. Web site: www.thoroughbredtimes.com. **Contact:** Amy Owens. Offered every 2 years for unpublished work to recognize outstanding fiction written about the Thoroughbred racing industry. Maximum length: 5,000 words. *Thoroughbred Times* receives first North American serial rights and reserves the right to publish any and all entries in the magazine. **Deadline: December 31.** Prize: 1st Place: $800 and publication in *Thoroughbred Times*; 2nd Place: $400 and publication; 3rd Place: $250 and publication.

THE DAME LISBET THROCKMORTON SHORT FICTION CONTEST

Coffeehousefiction.com, P.O. Box 399, Forest Hill MD 21050. E-mail: contest@coffeehousefiction.com. Web site: www.coffeehousefiction.com. **Contact:** Sherri Cook Woosley. First annual contest for unpublished fiction.

It's meant to encourage writers who have chosen a vocation with such a high frustration rate. Each judge either loves literature or is a writer and understands firsthand the emotional highs and lows of the road to publication. **Deadline: April 30.** Guidelines for SASE. **Charges $15.** Prize: 1st Prize: $500; 2nd Prize: $125; 3rd Prize: $75; 4th Prize: $50. Depending on the quality of submissions, there is also a possibility of publishing an anthology. Judged by writers or teachers with graduate degrees, including Sherri Cook Woosley, Elyse Beaulieu-Lucey, and Nancy Adler. Open to any writer.

TICKLED BY THUNDER FICTION CONTEST

Tickled by Thunder fiction magazine, 14076 86A Ave., Surrey BC V3W 0V9, Canada. E-mail: info@tickledbythunder.com. Web site: www.tickledbythunder.com. **Contact:** Larry Lindner. Annual contest to encourage unpublished fiction writers. **Deadline: February 15.** Guidelines for SASE. **Charges $10/story (free for subscribers).** Prize: $150, subscription, publication, and 2 copies of the magazine. Judged by the publisher and other various writers he knows who have not entered the contest. Open to any writer.

N 24-HOUR SHORT STORY CONTEST

WritersWeekly.com, P.O. Box 2399, Bangor ME 04402. E-mail: writersweekly@writersweekly.com. Web site: www.writersweekly.com/misc/contest.php. **Contact:** Angela Hoy. Quarterly contest in which registered entrants receive a topic at start time (usually noon CST) and have 24 hours to write a story on that topic. All submissions should be returned via e-mail. Each contest is limited to 500 people. Guidelines via e-mail or online. **Deadline: Quarterly—see Web site for dates. Charges $5.** Prize: 1st Place: $300; 2nd Place: $250; 3rd Place: $200. There are also 20 honorable mentions and 60 "door" prizes. The top 3 winners' entries are posted on WritersWeekly.com (non-exclusive electronic rights only). Writers retain all rights to their work. Judged by Angela Hoy (publisher of WritersWeekly.com and Booklocker.com) and Jon Huntress (author/journalist). Open to any writer.

WAASMODE FICTION CONTEST

Passages North, Dept. of English, Northern Michigan University, 1401 Presque Isle Ave., Marquette MI 49855. (906)227-1203. Fax: (906)227-1096. E-mail: passages@nmu.edu. Web site: myweb.nmu.edu/~passages. **Contact:** Kate Myers Hanson. Offered every 2 years to publish new voices in literary fiction. Guidelines for SASE or online. **Deadline: Submit September 15-January 15. Charges $10 reading fee/story.** Prize: $1,000 and publication for winner; 2 honorable mentions are also published; all entrants receive a copy of *Passages North*.

WCDR SHORT FICTION CONTEST

The Writers' Circle of Durham Region, Bayly Postal Outlet, P.O. Box 14558, 75 Bayly St. W., Ajax ON L1S 7K7, Canada. E-mail: shortstory@wcdr.org. Web site: www.wcdr.org. **Contact:** Sherry Hinman, Barbara Hunt. Annual contest for unpublished short fiction. **Deadline: June 1. Charges $10 (Canadian).** Prize: 1st Place: 25% of entry fees; 2nd Place: 15% of entry fees; 3rd Place: 10% of entry fees. Open to all writers 18 years or older.

WD POPULAR FICTION AWARDS

Writer's Digest, 4700 E. Galbraith Rd., Cincinnati OH 45236. (513)531-2690, ext. 1328. E-mail: popularfictionawards@fwpubs.com. Web site: www.writersdigest.com. **Contact:** Terri Boes. Contest for 4,000-word mss in the categories of romance, mystery/crime fiction, sci-fi/fantasy, thriller/suspense, and horror. Entries must be original, in English, unpublished, and not accepted by any other publisher at the time of submission. *Writer's Digest* retains one-time rights to the winning entries. **Deadline: November 1. Charges $12.50.** Prize: Grand Prize: $2,500, $100 of Writer's Digest Books, and a ms critique and marketing advice from a *Writer's Digest* editor; 1st Place: $500, $100 of Writer's Digest Books, and a ms critique and marketing advice from a *Writer's Digest* editor; Honoroable Mentions: promotion in *Writer's Digest*.

WHIM'S PLACE CHANGING OF THE SEASONS FLASH FICTION WRITING CONTEST

WhimsPlace.com, P.O. Box 14931, Lenexa KS 66285. E-mail: contest@whimsplace.com. Web site: www.whimsplace.com/contest/contest.asp. **Contact:** Betsy Gallup. Offered quarterly for flash fiction. "We love flash fiction! That's why we're having a contest. We also feel that contests are a great way to boost an ego, enhance a résumé, and to just have some plain old fashion fun with your writing. We expect good writing, however. It must be tightly written, organized, and proofread at least 100 times." Submissions are accepted only through Whim's Place online submission form. Entries over 500 words will automatically be disqualified. **Deadline: March 30; June 30; September 30; December 30. Charges $5.** Prize: 1st Place: $250; 2nd Place: $150; 3rd Place: $100; Honorable Mentions (8): $50. Judged by Whim's Place staff members, and an appointed guest judge each season. The special judge will be a published author or an editor. Open to any writer.

GARY WILSON SHORT FICTION AWARD

descant, Texas Christian University's literary journal, TCU, Box 297270, Fort Worth TX 76129. (817)257-6537. Fax: (817)257-6239. E-mail: descant@tcu.edu. Web site: www.descant.tcu.edu. **Contact:** David Kuhne, editor. Offered annually for an outstanding story in an issue. Guidelines for SASE. Prize: $250. Open to any writer.

TOBIAS WOLFF AWARD IN FICTION

Bellingham Review, Mail Stop 9053, Western Washington University, Bellingham WA 98225. (360)650-4863. E-mail: bhreview@cc.wwu.edu. Web site: www.wwu.edu/~bhreview/. **Contact:** Brenda Miller. Offered annually for unpublished work. Guidelines for SASE or online. **Deadline: December 1-March 15. Charges $15 entry fee for 1st entry; $10 for each additional entry.** Prize: $1,000, plus publication and subscription. All finalists considered for publication. All entrants receive subscription.

WRITER'S DIGEST SHORT SHORT STORY COMPETITION

Writer's Digest, 4700 E. Galbraith Rd., Cincinnati OH 45236. (513)531-2690, ext. 1328. E-mail: short-short-competition@fwpubs.com. Web site: www.writersdigest.com. **Contact:** Terri Boes. "We're looking for fiction that's bold, brilliant, and brief. Send us your best in 1,500 words or fewer." All entries must be original, unpublished, and not submitted elsewhere until the winners are announced. *Writer's Digest* reserves one-time publication rights to the 1st-25th winning entries. **Deadline: December 1. Charges $12.** Prize: 1st Place: $3,000; 2nd Place: $1,500; 3rd Place: $500; 4th-10th Place: $100; 11th-25th Place: $50 gift certificate for Writer's Digest Books.

WRITERS' JOURNAL ANNUAL FICTION CONTEST

Val-Tech Media, P.O. Box 394, Perham MN 56573. (218)346-7921. Fax: (218)346-7924. E-mail: writersjournal@writersjournal.com. Web site: www.writersjournal.com. **Contact:** Leon Ogroske (editor@writersjournal.com). Offered annually for previously unpublished fiction. Open to any writer. Guidelines for SASE or online. **Deadline: January 30. Charges $15 reading fee.** Prize: 1st Place: $500; 2nd Place: $200; 3rd Place: $100; plus honorable mentions. Prize-winning stories and selected honorable mentions are published in *Writers' Journal*.

WRITERS' JOURNAL ANNUAL HORROR/GHOST CONTEST

Val-Tech Media, P.O. Box 394, Perham MN 56573. (218)346-7921. Fax: (218)346-7924. E-mail: writersjournal@writersjournal.com. Web site: www.writersjournal.com. **Contact:** Leon Ogroske. Offered annually for previously unpublished works. Open to any writer. Guidelines for SASE or online. **Deadline: March 30. Charges $7 fee.** Prize: 1st Place: $250; 2nd Place: $100; 3rd Place: $50; plus honorable mentions. Prize-winning stories and selected honorable mentions are published in *Writers' Journal*.

WRITERS' JOURNAL ANNUAL ROMANCE CONTEST

Val-Tech Media, P.O. Box 394, Perham MN 56573. (218)346-7921. Fax: (218)346-7924. E-mail: writersjournal@writersjournal.com. Web site: www.writersjournal.com. **Contact:** Leon Ogroske. Offered annually for previously unpublished works. Open to any writer. Guidelines for SASE or online. **Deadline: July 30. Charges $7 fee.** Prize: 1st Place: $250; 2nd Place: $100; 3rd Place: $50; plus honorable mentions. Prize-winning stories and selected honorable mentions are published in *Writers' Journal*.

WRITERS' JOURNAL ANNUAL SHORT STORY CONTEST

Val-Tech Media, P.O. Box 394, Perham MN 56573. (218)346-7921. Fax: (218)346-7924. E-mail: writersjournal@writersjournal.com. Web site: www.writersjournal.com. **Contact:** Leon Ogroske. Offered annually for previously unpublished short stories. Open to any writer. Guidelines for SASE or online. **Deadline: May 30. Charges $10 reading fee.** Prize: 1st Place: $350; 2nd Place: $125; 3rd Place: $75; plus honorable mentions. Prize-winning stories and selected honorable mentions are published in *Writers' Journal*.

ZOETROPE SHORT FICTION CONTEST

Zoetrope: All-Story, 916 Kearny St., San Francisco CA 94133. Web site: www.all-story.com. **Contact:** Francis Ford Coppola, publisher. Annual contest for unpublished short stories. Guidelines by SASE or on Web site. Open to any writer. Please clearly mark envelope "short fiction contest." **Deadline: October 1. Charges $15 fee.** Prize: 1st Place: $1,000, 2nd Place: $500, 3rd Place: $250, plus 10 honorable mentions.

POETRY

ACORN-PLANTOS AWARD FOR PEOPLES POETRY

Acorn-Plantos Award Committee, 36 Sunset Ave., Hamilton ON L8R 1V6, Canada. E-mail: jeffseff@allstream.net. **Contact:** Jeff Seffinga. Annual contest for work that appeared in print between January 1, 2006 and December

31, 2006. This award is given to the Canadian poet who best (through the publication of a book of poems) exemplifies populist or "peoples" poetry in the tradition of Milton Acorn, Ted Plantos, et al. Work may be entered by the poet or the publisher; the award goes to the poet. Entrants must submit 5 copies of each title. **Deadline: June 30. Charges $25 (CDN)/title.** Prize: $500 (CDN) and a medal. Judged by a panel of poets in the tradition who are not entered in the current year. Poet must be a citizen of Canada or a landed immigrant. Publisher need not be Canadian.

AKRON POETRY PRIZE

University of Akron Press, 374B Bierce Library, Akron OH 44325-1703. (330)972-5342. Fax: (330)972-6896. E-mail: eglaser@uakron.edu. Web site: www.uakron.edu/uapress/poetry.html. **Contact:** Elton Glaser, poetry editor. Annual book contest for unpublished poetry. "The Akron Poetry Prize brings to the public writers with original and compelling voices. Books must exhibit 3 essential qualities: mastery of language, maturity of feeling, and complexity of thought." Guidelines available online or for SASE. The final selection will be made by a nationally prominent poet. The University of Akron Press has the right to publish the winning ms, inherent with winning the poetry prize. Open to all poets writing in English. **Deadline: May 15-June 30. Charges $25 fee.** Prize: Winning poet receives $1,000 and publication of book.

ANNUAL GIVAL PRESS OSCAR WILDE AWARD

Gival Press, LLC, P.O. Box 3812, Arlington VA 22203. (703)351-0079. E-mail: givalpress@yahoo.com. Web site: www.givalpress.com. **Contact:** Robert L. Giron. Award given to the best previously unpublished original poem—written in English of any length, in any style, typed, double-spaced on 1 side only—which best relates gay/lesbian/bisexual/transgendered life, by a poet who is 18 or older. Entrants are asked to submit their poems without any kind of identification (with the exception of titles) and with a separate cover page with the following information: name, address (street, city, and state with zip code), telephone number, e-mail address (if available) and a list of poems by title. Checks drawn on American banks should be made out to Gival Press, LLC. **Deadline: June 27 (postmarked). Charges $5 (USD) reading fee/poem.** Prize: $100 (USD), and the poem, along with information about the poet, will be published on the Gival Press Web site. Open to any writer.

ANNUAL GIVAL PRESS POETRY AWARD

Gival Press, LLC, P.O. Box 3812, Arlington VA 22203. (703)351-0079. E-mail: givalpress@yahoo.com. Web site: www.givalpress.com. **Contact:** Robert L. Giron. Offered annually for a previously unpublished poetry collection of at least 45 pages, which may include previously published poems. The competition seeks to award well-written, original poetry in English on any topic, in any style. Guidelines for SASE, by e-mail, or online. Entrants are asked to submit their poems without any kind of identification (with the exception of the titles) and with a separate cover page with the following information: name, address (street, city, state, and zip code), telephone number, e-mail address (if available), short bio, and a list of the poems by title. Checks drawn on American banks should be made out to Gival Press, LLC. **Deadline: December 15 (postmarked). Charges $20 reading fee (USD).** Prize: $1,000, publication, standard contract, and 20 author's copies. Open to any writer.

THE ANNUAL PRAIRIE SCHOONER STROUSSE AWARD

Prairie Schooner, 201 Andrews Hall, P.O. Box 880334, Lincoln NE 68588-0334. (402)472-0911. Fax: (402)472-9771. E-mail: kgrey2@unl.edu. Web site: www.unl.edu/schooner/psmain.htm. **Contact:** Hilda Raz. Offered annually for the best poem or group of poems published in *Prairie Schooner* in the previous year. Prize: $500.

ATLANTIC POETRY PRIZE

Writers' Federation of Nova Scotia, 1113 Marginal Rd., Halifax NS B3H 4P7, Canada. (902)423-8116. Fax: (902)422-0881. E-mail: talk@writers.ns.ca. Web site: www.writers.ns.ca. **Contact:** Jane Buss, executive director. Full-length books of adult poetry written by Atlantic Canadians, and published as a whole for the first time in the previous calendar year, are eligible. Entrants must be native or resident Atlantic Canadians who have either been born in Newfoundland, Prince Edward Island, Nova Scotia, or New Brunswick, and spent a susbstantial portion of their lives living there, or who have lived in one or a combination of these provinces for at least 24 consecutive months prior to entry deadline date. Publishers: Send 4 copies and a letter attesting to the author's status as an Atlantic Canadian and the author's current mailing address and telephone number. **Deadline: First Friday in December.** Prize: $2,000.

THE BALTIMORE REVIEW POETRY CONTEST

The Baltimore Review, P.O. Box 36418, Towson MD 21286. Web site: www.baltimorereview.org. **Contact:** Susan Muaddi Darraj. **Deadline: July 1. Charges $15; $20 for fee and 1-year subscription.** Prize: 1st Place: $300 and publication; 2nd Place: $150; 3rd Place: $50. Open to any writer.

THE BASKERVILLE PUBLISHERS POETRY AWARD & THE BETSY COLQUITT POETRY AWARD

descant, Texas Christian University's literary journal, TCU, Box 297270, Fort Worth TX 76129. (817)257-6537. Fax: (817)257-6239. E-mail: descant@tcu.edu. Web site: www.descant.tcu.edu. **Contact:** Dave Kuhne, editor. Annual award for an outstanding poem published in an issue of *descant*. **Deadline: September-April.** Guidelines for SASE. Prize: $250 for Baskerville Award; $500 for Betsy Colquitt Award. Publication retains copyright, but will transfer it to the author upon request. Open to any writer.

N THE BINGHAMTON UNIVERSITY MILT KESSLER POETRY BOOK AWARD

Binghamton Center for Writers, Dept. of English, General Literature & Rhetoric, Library North, Room 1149, Vestal Parkway E., P.O. Box 6000, Binghamton NY 13902-6000. (607)777-2713. E-mail: cwpro@binghamton.edu. Web site: www.binghamton.edu/english/cwpro/BookAwards/KesslerGuidelines.htm. **Contact:** Maria Mazziotti Gillan, creative writing program director. Estab. 2001. Offered annually for previously published work. Books must be 48 pages or more with a press run of 500 copies or more. Each book submitted must be accompanied by an application form. Publisher may submit more than 1 book for prize consideration. Send 3 copies of each book. Guidelines available online or for SASE. **Deadline: March 1.** Prize: $1,000. Judged by professional poet not on Binghamton University faculty. Open to any writer over the age of 40.

N BLUE LYNX PRIZE FOR POETRY

Eastern Washington University Press, 705 W. First Ave., Spokane WA 99201. (800)508-9095. Fax: (509)623-4283. E-mail: ewupress@mail.ewu.edu. Web site: ewupress.ewu.edu. **Contact:** Christopher Howell. Annual award to publish the finest work the literary world has to offer. Send book-length mss of at least 48 pages. Guidelines available online or for SASE. Entries are judged anonymously. **Deadline: May 15. Charges $25.** Prize: $1,500 and publication. Open to any writer.

BLUE MOUNTAIN ARTS/SPS STUDIOS POETRY CARD CONTEST

P.O. Box 1007, Boulder CO 80306. (303)449-0536. Fax: (303)447-0939. E-mail: poetrycontest@sps.com. Web site: www.sps.com. "We're looking for original poetry that is rhyming or nonrhyming, although we find nonrhyming poetry reads better. Poems may also be considered for possible publication on greeting cards or in book anthologies." Contest is offered biannually. Guidelines available online. **Deadline: December 31 and June 30.** Prize: 1st Place: $300; 2nd Place: $150; 3rd Place: $50. Judged by Blue Mountain Arts editorial staff. Open to any writer.

THE FREDERICK BOCK PRIZE

Poetry, 444 North Michigan Ave., Suite 1850, Chicago IL 60610. (312)787-7070. E-mail: poetry@poetrymagazine.org. Web site: www.poetrymagazine.org. Estab. 1981. Offered annually for poems published in *Poetry* during the preceding year (October through September). *Poetry* buys all rights to the poems published in the magazine. Copyrights are returned to the authors on request. Any writer may submit poems to *Poetry*. Guidelines for SASE. Prize: $500.

THE BORDIGHERA ITALIAN-AMERICAN POETRY PRIZE

Sonia Raiziss-Giop Foundation, Bordighera Press @ John D. Calandra Italian American Institute, Graduate Center, The City University of New York, 25 West 43rd St., 17th Floor, New York NY 10036. E-mail: daniela@garden.net. Web site: www.italianamericanwriters.com. **Contact:** Alfredo de Palchi. Offered annually to find the best unpublished manuscripts of poetry in English, by an American of Italian descent, to be translated into quality Italian and published bilingually. No Italian-American themes required, just excellent poetry. Guidelines for SASE or online. Judges change every 2 years. Former judges include Daniela Gioseffi, Felix Stefanile, Dorothy Barresi, W.S. DePiero, Donna Masini. **Deadline: May 31.** Prize: $2,000 and bilingual book publication to be divided between poet and consigned translator.

BOSTON REVIEW POETRY CONTEST

Boston Review, 35 Medford St., Suite 302, Somerville MA 02143. Web site: bostonreview.net. Submit up to 5 unpublished poems, no more than 10 pages total. **Deadline: June 1. Charges $15 fee (check or money order payable to** *Boston Review*). Prize: $1,000 and publication in the October/November issue of *Boston Review*.

BP NICHOL CHAPBOOK AWARD

Phoenix Community Works Foundation, 316 Dupont St., Toronto ON M5R 1V9, Canada. (416)964-7919. Fax: (416)964-6941. E-mail: info@pcwf.ca. Web site: www.pcwf.ca. **Contact:** Philip McKenna, award director. Offered annually to a chapbook (10-48 pages) of poetry in English, published in Canada in the previous year. Must submit 3 nonreturnable copies. **Deadline: March 30.** Prize: $1,000 (Canadian). Open to any writer. Author or publisher may make submissions. Send 3 copies (nonreturnable), plus a short author cv.

BARBARA BRADLEY PRIZE

New England Poetry Club, 16 Cornell St., Arlington MA 02476. E-mail: contests@nepoetryclub.org. Web site: www.nepoetryclub.org/contests.htm. **Contact:** NEPC Contest Coordinator. Offered annually for a poem under 20 lines, written by a woman. **Deadline: June 30.** Guidelines for SASE. **Charges $10 for 3 poems.** Prize: $200.

N BRIGHT HILL PRESS ANNUAL POETRY BOOK COMPETITION

Bright Hill Press, P.O. Box 193, Treadwell NY 13846. Phone/Fax: (607)829-5055. E-mail: wordthur@stny.rr.com. Web site: www.brighthillpress.org. **Contact:** Bertha Rogers. Send 48-65 pages, bio, TOC, acknowledgments page, and 2 title pages (1 with name, address, etc; 1 with title only). Poems can be published in journals or anthologies. Guidelines online, for SASE, or via e-mail. **Deadline: November 30. Charges $22 fee.** Prize: $1,000, publication, and 25 copies of the winning book.

N BRIGHT HILL PRESS ANNUAL POETRY CHAPBOOK COMPETITION

Bright Hill Press, P.O. Box 193, Treadwell NY 13846. Phone/Fax: (607)829-5055. E-mail: wordthur@stny.rr.com. Web site: www.brighthillpress.org. **Contact:** Bertha Rogers. Send 16-24 pages, bio, TOC, acknowledgments page, and 2 title pages (1 with name, address, etc; 1 with title only). Guidelines online, for SASE, or via e-mail. **Deadline: July 31. Charges $10 fee.** Prize: $300, publication, and 25 copies of the winning chapbook.

BRITTINGHAM PRIZE IN POETRY/FELIX POLLAK PRIZE IN POETRY

University of Wisconsin Press, Dept. of English, 600 N. Park St., University of Wisconsin, Madison WI 53706. E-mail: rwallace@wisc.edu. Web site: www.wisc.edu/wisconsinpress/poetryguide.html. **Contact:** Ronald Wallace, contest director. Estab. 1985. Offered for unpublished book-length mss of original poetry. Submissions must be received by the press during the month of September, accompanied by a SASE for contest results. Does not return mss. One entry fee covers both prizes. Guidelines for SASE or online. **Charges $25 fee (payable to University of Wisconsin Press).** Prize: $2,500 ($1,000 cash prize and $1,500 honorarium for campus reading) and publication of the 2 winning mss.

THE DOROTHY BRUNSMAN POETRY PRIZE

Bear Star Press, 185 Hollow Oak Dr., Cohasset CA 95973. (530)891-0360. E-mail: bspencer@bearstarpress.com. Web site: www.bearstarpress.com. Offered annually to support the publication of 1 volume of poetry. Guidelines on Web site. Open to poets living in the Western States (those in Mountain or Pacific time zones, plus Alaska and Hawaii). **Deadline: November 30. Charges $20 fee.** Prize: $1,000 and publication.

GERALD CABLE BOOK AWARD

Silverfish Review Press, P.O. Box 3541, Eugene OR 97403. (541)344-5060. E-mail: sfrpress@earthlink.net. Web site: www.silverfishreviewpress.com. **Contact:** Rodger Moody, series editor. Purpose is to publish a poetry book by a deserving author who has yet to publish a full-length book collection. Open to any writer. Guidelines for SASE or by e-mail. **Deadline: October 15. Charges $20 reading fee.** Prize: $1,000, 10% of the press run, and publication by the press for a book-length ms of original poetry.

CATFISH POETRY PUBLICATION PRIZE

Catfish Publishing, 32 Joness St., Historic Norcross GA 30071. (678)261-8880. E-mail: editor@catfishpoetry.com. Web site: www.catfishpoetry.com. **Contact:** Heather Richie. Annual contest for unpublished poetry and/or poetry published since 2000. Ms must be 48-80 pages of poetry, including a table of contents, acknowledgments, and a bio. Buys first North American serial rights. **Deadline: December 31.** Guidelines for SASE. **Charges $20/ms (donated to The Rural-Urban Literacy Education Resource Syndicate www.therulers.org).** Prize: $500, publication, and residency at Salmon Publishing (located in County Clare, Ireland). Judged by Jessie Lendennie of Salmon Publishing and other guest judges. Open to any writer.

JOHN CIARDI POETRY AWARD FOR LIFETIME ACHIEVEMENT

Italian Americana, URI/CCE, 80 Washington St., Providence RI 02903-1803. Fax: (401)277-5100. E-mail: bonomoal@etal.uri.edu. Web site: www.uri.edu/prov/italian/italian.html. **Contact:** Carol Bonomo Albright, editor. Offered annually for lifetime achievement to a mature Italian American poet who has published in all aspects of poetry: creative, critical, etc. Applicants should have at least 2 books published and engage in activities promoting poetry. Open to Italian-Americans only. Prize: $1,000.

JOHN CIARDI PRIZE FOR POETRY

BkMk Press, University of Missouri-Kansas City, 5100 Rockhill Rd., Kansas City MO 64110. (816)235-2558. Fax: (816)235-2611. E-mail: bkmk@umkc.edu. Web site: www.umkc.edu/bkmk. Offered annually for the best book-length collection (unpublished) of poetry in English by a living author. Translations are not eligible. Initial judging is done by a network of published writers. Final judging is done by a writer of national reputation. Guidelines for SASE, by e-mail, or on Web site. **Deadline: January 15 (postmarked). Charges $25 fee.** Prize: $1,000, plus book publication by BkMk Press.

CLEVELAND STATE UNIVERSITY POETRY CENTER PRIZES

Cleveland State University Poetry Center, 2121 Euclid Ave., Cleveland OH 44115-2214. (216)687-3986. Fax: (216)687-6943. E-mail: poetrycenter@csuohio.edu. Web site: www.csuohio.edu/poetrycenter. **Contact:** Rita Grabowski, poetry center manager. Estab. 1987. Offered annually to identify, reward, and publish the best unpublished book-length poetry ms (minimum 40 pages) in 2 categories: First Book and Open Competition (for poets who have published a collection at least 48 pages long, with a press run of 500). Submission implies willingness to sign standard contract for publication if manuscript wins. Does not return mss. Guidelines for SASE or online. **Deadline: Submissions accepted November 1-February 1. Charges $20 fee.** Prize: $1,000 in each category and publication.

THE COLORADO PRIZE FOR POETRY

Colorado Review/Center for Literary Publishing, Dept. of English, Colorado State University, Ft. Collins CO 80523. (970)491-5449. E-mail: creview@colostate.edu. Web site: coloradoreview.colostate.edu. **Contact:** Stephanie G'Schwind, editor. Offered annually to an unpublished collection of poetry. Guidelines for SASE or online. **Deadline: January 12. Charges $25 fee (includes subscription).** Prize: $1,500 and publication of book.

CRAB ORCHARD OPEN COMPETITION SERIES IN POETRY

1000 Faner Dr., Southern Illinois University, Carbondale IL 62901. Web site: www.siu.edu/ ~ crborchd. **Contact:** Jon C. Tribble, series editor. Offered annually for collections of unpublished poetry. Visit Web site for current deadlines. Guidelines for SASE. **Charges $25 fee.** Prize: 1st Place: $3,500 and publication; 2nd Place: $2,000 and publication. Open to US citizens and permanent residents.

THE CJ DENNIS PRIZE FOR POETRY

Victorian Premier's Literary Awards, State Library of Victoria, 328 Swanston St., Melbourne VIC 3000 Australia. (61)(3)8664-7277. E-mail: pla@slv.vic.gov.au. Web site: www.slv.vic.gov.au/pla. **Contact:** Project Officer. Prize for a significant selection of new work by a poet published in a book between May 1 and April 30. **Deadline: May 4.** Guidelines for SASE. Prize: $15,000. Open to Australian citizens or permanent residents.

ALICE FAY DI CASTAGNOLA AWARD

Poetry Society of America, 15 Gramercy Park S., New York NY 10003. (212)254-9628. Fax: (212)673-2352. Web site: www.poetrysociety.org. **Contact:** Programs Associate. Offered annually for a manuscript-in-progress of poetry or verse-drama. Guidelines for SASE or online. Award open only to PSA members. It is strongly encouraged that applicants read the complete contest guidelines on the PSA Web site before submitting. **Deadline: October 1-December 21.** Prize: $1,000. Open to members only.

MILTON DORFMAN POETRY PRIZE

Rome Art & Community Center, 308 W. Bloomfield St., Rome NY 13440. (315)336-1040. Fax: (315)336-1090. E-mail: racc2@cnymail.com. Web site: www.romeart.org. Estab. 1990. Award offers poets an outlet for their craft. All submissions must be previously unpublished. **Deadline: April 30.** Guidelines for SASE. **Charges $15 fee/poem.** Prize: 1st Place: $500; 2nd Place: $250; 3rd Place: $150. Judged by a professional, published poet. Awards ceremony and poetry reading in June.

T.S. ELIOT PRIZE FOR POETRY

Truman State University Press, 100 E. Normal St., Kirksville MO 63501-4221. (660)785-7336. Fax: (660)785-4480. E-mail: tsup@truman.edu. Web site: tsup.truman.edu. **Contact:** Nancy Rediger. Annual competition for unpublished poetry collection. Guidelines for SASE, online, or by e-mail. **Deadline: October 31 (postmarked). Charges $25 fee.** Prize: $2,000 and publication.

ROBERT G. ENGLISH/POETRY IN PRINT

P.O. Box 30981, Albuquerque NM 87190-0981. (505)888-3937. Fax: (505)888-3937. Web site: www.poets.com/RobertEnglish.html. **Contact:** Robert G. English. Offered annually to help a poetry writer accomplish their own personal endeavors. Hopefully the prize amount of the Poetry in Print award will grow to a higher significance. The contest is open to any writer of any age. Hopefully to prepare writers other than just journalists with a stronger desire to always tell the truth. No limit to number of entries; 60-line limit/poem. Please enclose SASE. **Deadline: August 1. Charges $10/poem.** Prize: $1,000.

JANICE FARRELL POETRY PRIZE

National League of American Pen Women, Nob Hill, San Francisco Branch, The Webhallow House, 1544 Sweetwood Dr., Colma CA 94015-2029. E-mail: pennobhill@aol.com. Web site: www.soulmakingcontest.us. **Contact:** Eileen Malone. Poetry may be double- or single-spaced. One-page poems only, and only 1 poem/page. All poems must be titled. 3 poems/entry. Indicate category on each poem. Identify with 3×5 card only. **Deadline: November 30.** Guidelines for SASE. **Charges $5/entry (make checks payable to NLAPW, Nob Hill Branch).** Prize: 1st Place: $100; 2nd Place: $50; 3rd Place: $25. Judged by a local San Francisco successfully published poet. Open annually to any writer.

FIELD POETRY PRIZE

Oberlin College Press/FIELD, 50 N. Professor St., Oberlin OH 44074-1091. (440)775-8408. Fax: (440)775-8124. E-mail: oc.press@oberlin.edu. Web site: www.oberlin.edu/ocpress. **Contact:** Linda Slocum, managing editor. Offered annually for unpublished work. Contest seeks to encourage the finest in contemporary poetry writing. Open to any writer. **Deadline: Submit in May only.** Guidelines for SASE. **Charges $22 fee, which includes a 1-year subscription.** Prize: $1,000 and the book is published in Oberlin College Press's FIELD Poetry Series.

FIVE POINTS JAMES DICKEY PRIZE FOR POETRY

Five Points, Georgia State University, P.O. Box 3999, Atlanta GA 30302-3999. (404)651-0071. Fax: (404)651-3167. Web site: www.webdelsol.com/Five_Points. Offered annually for unpublished poetry. Send 3 unpublished poems, no longer than 50 lines each, name and addresses on each poem, SASE for receipt and notification of winner. Winner announced in Spring issue. **Deadline: November 30.** Guidelines for SASE. **Charges $20 fee (includes 1-year subscription).** Prize: $1,000, plus publication.

THE 49th PARALLEL POETRY AWARD

Bellingham Review, Mail Stop 9053, Western Washington University, Bellingham WA 98225. (360)650-4863. E-mail: bhreview@cc.wwu.edu. Web site: www.wwu.edu/~bhreview/. **Contact:** Brenda Miller. Estab. 1977. Offered annually for unpublished poetry. Guidelines available online or for SASE. **Deadline: December 1-March 15. Charges $15/first entry (up to 3 poems), $10/additional entry.** Prize: $1,000 and publication. All finalists considered for publication; all entrants receive a subscription.

FOUR WAY BOOKS POETRY PRIZES

Four Way Books, P.O. Box 535, Village Station, New York NY 10014. E-mail: 2007prize@fourwaybooks.com. Web site: www.fourwaybooks.com. Four Way Books runs different prizes annually. For guidelines send a SASE or download from Web site. **Deadline: March 31. Charges $25.** Prize: $1,000 and book publication.

ALLEN GINSBERG POETRY AWARDS

The Poetry Center at Passaic County Community College, One College Blvd., Paterson NJ 07505-1179. (973)684-6555. Fax: (973)684-5843. E-mail: mgillan@pccc.edu. Web site: www.pccc.edu/poetry. **Contact:** Maria Mazziotti Gillan, executive director. Offered annually for unpublished poetry to honor Allen Ginsberg's contribution to American literature. The college retains first publication rights. Open to any writer. **Deadline: April 1.** Guidelines for SASE. **Charges $15, which includes the cost of a subscription to *The Paterson Literary Review*.** Prize: $1,000.

GOVERNOR GENERAL'S LITERARY AWARD FOR POETRY

Canada Council for the Arts, 350 Albert St., P.O. Box 1047, Ottawa ON K1P 5V8, Canada. (613)566-4414, ext. 5573. Fax: (613)566-4410. Web site: www.canadacouncil.ca/prizes/ggla. **Contact:** Diane Miljours. Offered for the best English-language and the best French-language work of poetry by a Canadian. **Deadline: June 1.** Prize: Each laureate receives $15,000; nonwinning finalists receive $1,000.

GREEN ROSE PRIZE IN POETRY

New Issues Poetry & Prose, Dept. of English, Western Michigan University, 1903 W. Michigan Ave., Kalamazoo MI 49008-5331. (269)387-8185. Fax: (269)387-2562. E-mail: herbert.scott@wmich.edu. Web site: www.wmich.edu/newissues. **Contact:** Herbert Scott, editor. Offered annually for unpublished poetry. The university will publish a book of poems by a poet writing in English who has published 1 or more full-length books of poetry. Guidelines for SASE or online. *New Issues Poetry & Prose* obtains rights for first publication. Book is copyrighted in the author's name. **Deadline: May 1-September 30. Charges $20 fee.** Prize: $2,000 and publication of book. Author also receives 10% of the printed edition.

THE GRIFFIN POETRY PRIZE

The Griffin Trust for Excellence in Poetry, 6610 Edwards Blvd., Mississauga ON L5T 2V6, Canada. (905)565-5993. E-mail: info@griffinpoetryprize.com. Web site: www.griffinpoetryprize.com. **Contact:** Ruth Smith. Offered annually for work published between January 1 and December 31. **Deadline: December 31.** Prize: Two $50,000 (Canadian) prizes. One prize will go to a living Canadian poet or translator, the other to a living poet or translator from any country, which may include Canada. Judged by a panel of qualified English-speaking judges of stature. Judges are chosen by the Trustees of The Griffin Trust For Excellence in Poetry.

N GREG GRUMMER POETRY AWARD

Phoebe, MSN 2D6, George Mason University, 4400 University Dr., Fairfax VA 22030. (703)993-2915. E-mail: phoebe@gmu.edu. Web site: www.gmu.edu/pubs/phoebe. **Contact:** Kati Fargo. Offered annually for unpublished work. Submit up to 4 poems. Guidelines online or for SASE. **Deadline: December 1. Charges $15 fee.** Prize: $1,000 and publication in the Fall issue. Judged by a recognized poet hired by *Phoebe* each year. Acquires first serial rights, if work is to be published. Open to any writer.

KATHRYN HANDLEY PROSE-POEM PRIZE

National League of American Pen Women, Nob Hill, San Francisco Branch, The Webhallow House, 1544 Sweetwood Dr., Colma CA 94015-2029. E-mail: pennobhill@aol.com. Web site: www.soulmakingcontest.us. **Contact:** Eileen Malone. Poetry may be double- or single-spaced. One-page poems only, and only 1 poem/page. Three poems/entry. Indicate category on each poem. Identify only with 3×5 card. **Deadline: November 30.** Guidelines for SASE. **Charges $5/entry (make checks payable to NLAPW, Nob Hill Branch).** Prize: 1st Place: $100; 2nd Place: $50; 3rd Place: $25. Open annually to any writer.

THE BEATRICE HAWLEY AWARD

Alice James Poetry Cooperative, 238 Main St., Farmington ME 04938. Phone/Fax: (207)778-7071. E-mail: ajb@umf.maine.edu. Web site: www.alicejamesbooks.org. **Contact:** Lacy Simons, managing editor. Offered annually for unpublished poetry. Open to US residents only. Guidelines online or for SASE. **Deadline: December 1. Charges $25.** Prize: $2,000, and publication.

CECIL HEMLEY MEMORIAL AWARD

Poetry Society of America, 15 Gramercy Park, New York NY 10003. (212)254-9628. Fax: (212)673-2352. E-mail: tom@poetrysociety.org. Web site: www.poetrysociety.org. **Contact:** Thomas Hummel, awards coordinator. Offered for unpublished lyric poems on a philosophical theme. Line limit: 100. Guidelines subject to change. *Open to PSA members only*. Guidelines for SASE or online. **Deadline: October 1-December 23.** Guidelines for SASE. Prize: $500.

THE BESS HOKIN PRIZE

Poetry, 444 North Michigan Ave. Suite 1850, Chicago IL 60611. (312)787-7070. E-mail: poetry@poetrymagazine.org. Web site: www.poetrymagazine.org. Estab. 1947. Offered annually for poems published in *Poetry* during the preceding year (October-September). *Poetry* buys all rights to the poems published in the magazine. Copyrights are returned to the authors on request. Any writer may submit poems to *Poetry*. Guidelines for SASE. Prize: $500.

IRA LEE BENNETT HOPKINS PROMISING POET AWARD

International Reading Association, P.O. Box 8139, Newark DE 19714-8139. (302)731-1600. Fax: (302)731-1057. E-mail: exec@reading.org. Web site: www.reading.org. Offered every 3 years to a promising new poet of children's poetry (for children and young adults up to grade 12) who has published no more than 2 books of children's poetry. Download application from Web site after May 2009. **Deadline: December 1, 2009 for published poem books during 2007-2009.** Guidelines for SASE. Prize: $500.

FIRMAN HOUGHTON PRIZE

New England Poetry Club, 16 Cornell St., Arlington MA 02476. E-mail: contests@nepoetryclug.org. Web site: www.nepoetryclub.org/contests.htm. **Contact:** NEPC Contest Coordinator. Offered annually for a lyric poem in English. **Deadline: June 30.** Guidelines for SASE. **Charges $10 for 3 poems.** Prize: $250.

IOWA POETRY PRIZES

University of Iowa Press, 100 Kuhl House, Iowa City IA 52242. (319)335-2000. Fax: (319)335-2055. Web site: www.uiowapress.org. Offered annually to encourage poets and their work. Submit mss by April 30; put name on title page only. Open to writers of English (US citizens or not). Manuscripts will not be returned. Previous winners are not eligible. **Deadline: April. Charges $20 fee.**

RANDALL JARRELL/HARPERPRINTS POETRY CHAPBOOK COMPETITION

North Carolina Writers' Network, Appalachian State University, Department of English, Box 32052, Boone NC 28608. E-mail: bathantjr@appstate.edu. Web site: www.ncwriters.org. **Contact:** Joseph Bathani. Offered annually for unpublished work "to honor Randall Jarrell and his life at UNC-Greensboro by recognizing the best poetry submitted." Competition is open to North Carolina residents who have not published a full-length collection of poems. **Deadline: January 31. Charges $10 (NCWN members); $15 (nonmembers) entry fee.** Prize: $200, chapbook publication, and a reading and reception.

ROBINSON JEFFERS TOR HOUSE PRIZE FOR POETRY

Robinson Jeffers Tor House Foundation, P.O. Box 223240, Carmel CA 93922. (831)624-1813. Fax: (831)624-3696. E-mail: thf@torhouse.org. Web site: www.torhouse.org. **Contact:** Poetry Prize Coordinator. The contest honors well-crafted, unpublished poetry in all styles, ranging from experimental work to traditional forms, including short narrative poems. **Deadline: November 1-March 15.** Guidelines for SASE. **Charges $10 for first 3 poems; $15 for up to 6 poems; $2.50 for each additional poem.** Prize: $1,000; $200 for Honorable Mention. Judged by a distinguished panel of published poets and editors (preliminary judging). Final judging by a nationally known poet. Open to any writer.

THE JUNIPER PRIZE

University of Massachusetts Press, East Experiment Station, 671 N. Pleasant St., Amherst MA 01003. (413)545-2217. Fax: (413)545-1226. E-mail: info@umpress.umass.edu. Web site: www.umass.edu/umpress/juniper.html. **Contact:** Carla J. Potts, promotion manager. Estab. 1964. Awarded annually for an original ms of poems. Chapbook must be 50-70 pages. Self-published work doesn't meet requirements. In alternating years, the program is open to poets either with or without previously published books. **Deadline: August 1-September 30. Charges $20 fee.** Prize: $1,500.

BARBARA MANDIGO KELLY PEACE POETRY AWARDS

Nuclear Age Peace Foundation, PMB 121, 1187 Coast Village Rd., Suite 1, Santa Barbara CA 93108-2794. (805)965-3443. Fax: (805)568-0466. E-mail: communications@napf.org. Web site: www.wagingpeace.org. **Contact:** Carah Ong. The Barbara Mandigo Kelly Peace Poetry Contest was created to encourage poets to explore and illuminate positive visions of peace and the human spirit. The annual contest honors the late Barbara Kelly, a Santa Barbara poet and longtime supporter of peace issues. Awards are given in 3 categories: adult (over 18 years), youth between 12 and 18 years, and youth under 12. All submitted poems should be unpublished. **Deadline: July 1 (postmarked).** Guidelines for SASE. **Charges $15/up to 3 poems; no fee for youth entries.** Prize: Adult: $1,000; Youth (13-18): $200; Youth (12 and under): $200. Honorable Mentions may also be awarded. Judged by a committee of poets selected by the Nuclear Age Peace Foundation. The foundation reserves the right to publish and distribute the award-winning poems, including honorable mentions. Open to any writer.

HELEN AND LAURA KROUT MEMORIAL OHIOANA POETRY AWARD

Ohioana Library Association, 274 E. First Ave., Suite 300, Columbus OH 45201. (614)466-3831. Fax: (614)728-6974. E-mail: ohioana@sloma.state.oh.us. Web site: www.ohioana.org. **Contact:** Linda R. Hengst. Estab. 1984. Offered annually "to an individual whose body of published work has made, and continues to make, a significant contribution to poetry, and through whose work interest in poetry has been developed." Recipient must have been born in Ohio or lived in Ohio at least 5 years. **Deadline: December 31.** Guidelines for SASE. Prize: $1,000.

GERALD LAMPERT MEMORIAL AWARD

The League of Canadian Poets, 920 Yonge St., Suite 608, Toronto ON M4W 3C7, Canada. (416)504-1657. Fax: (416)504-0096. E-mail: marketing@poets.ca. Web site: www.poets.ca. Offered annually for a first book of poetry by a Canadian poet published in the preceding year. Guidelines for SASE or online. **Deadline: November 1. Charges $15 fee.** Prize: $1,000. Open to Canadian citizens and landed immigrants only.

THE LEDGE ANNUAL POETRY CHAPBOOK CONTEST

The Ledge Magazine, 40 Maple Ave., Bellport NY 11713. E-mail: info@theledgemagazine.com. Web site: www.theledgemagazine.com. **Contact:** Timothy Monaghan. Offered annually to publish an outstanding collection of poems. No restrictions on form or content. Send 16-32 pages, titles page, bio, acknowledgments, SASE. Guidelines online or for SASE. Open to any writer. **Deadline: October 31. Charges $15 fee.** Prize: $1,000 and publication in and 50 copies of the chapbook.

THE LEDGE POETRY AWARDS COMPETITION

The Ledge Magazine, 40 Maple Ave., Bellport NY 11713. E-mail: info@theledgemagazine.com. Web site: www.theledgemagazine.com. **Contact:** Timothy Monaghan. Offered annually for unpublished poems of exceptional quality and significance. No restrictions on form or content. All poems are considered for publication in the magazine. Guidelines online or for SASE. Open to any writer. **Deadline: April 30. Charges $10/first 3 poems;**

$3/additional poem. Prize: 1st Place: $1,000 and publication in *The Ledge Magazine*; 2nd Place: $250 and publication; 3rd Place: $100 and publication.

LENA-MILES WEVER TODD POETRY SERIES

Pleiades Press & Winthrop University, Dept. of English, Central Missouri State University, Warrensburg MO 64093. (660)543-8106. Fax: (660)543-8544. E-mail: kdp8106@cmsu2.cmsu.edu. Web site: www.cmsu.edu/englphil/pleiades. **Contact:** Kevin Prufer. Offered annually for an unpublished book of poetry by an American or Canadian poet. Guidelines for SASE or by e-mail. The winning book is copyrighted by the author and Pleiades Press. **Deadline: Generally September 30; e-mail for firm deadline. Charges $15, which includes a copy of the winning book.** Prize: $1,000 and publication of winning book in paperback edition. Distribution through Louisiana State University Press. Open to any writer living in the US or Canada.

THE LEVINSON PRIZE

Poetry, 444 North Michigan Ave., Suite 1850, Chicago IL 60611. (312)787-7070. E-mail: poetry@poetrymagazine.org. Web site: www.poetrymagazine.org. Estab. 1914. Offered annually for poems published in *Poetry* during the preceding year (October-September). *Poetry* buys all rights to the poems published in the magazine. Copyrights are returned to the authors on request. Any writer may submit poems to *Poetry*. Guidelines for SASE. Prize: $500.

LEVIS READING PRIZE

Virginia Commonwealth University, Dept. of English, P.O. Box 842005, Richmond VA 23284-2005. (804)828-1329. Fax: (804)828-8684. E-mail: eng_grad@vcu.edu. Web site: www.has.vcu.edu/eng/resources/levis_prize.htm. **Contact:** Jeff Lodge. Offered annually for books of poetry published in the previous year to encourage poets early in their careers. The entry must be the writer's first or second published book of poetry. Previously published books in other genres, or previously published chapbooks, do not count as books for this purpose. **Deadline: January 15.** Guidelines for SASE. Prize: $1,000 honorarium and an expense-paid trip to Richmond to present a public reading.

THE RUTH LILLY POETRY PRIZE

The Modern Poetry Association, 444 North Michigan Ave., Suite 1850, Chicago IL 60610. E-mail: poetry@poetrymagazine.org. Web site: www.poetrymagazine.org. Estab. 1986. Offered annually to a poet whose accomplishments in the field of poetry warrant extraordinary recognition. No applicants or nominations are accepted. **Deadline: Varies.** Prize: $100,000.

LITERAL LATTÉ POETRY AWARD

Literal Latté, 200 E. 10th St., Suite 240, New York NY 10003. (212)260-5532. E-mail: LitLatte@aol.com. Web site: www.literal-latte.com. **Contact:** Edwin Estlin, contributing editor. Offered annually for unpublished poetry (maximum 2,000 words). All styles welcome. **Deadline: July 19.** Guidelines for SASE. **Charges $10/up to 4 poems; $15/set of 8 poems.** Prize: 1st Place: $1,000; 2nd Place: $300; 3rd Place: $200; winners published in *Literal Latté*. Open to any writer.

FRANCES LOCKE MEMORIAL POETRY AWARD

The Bitter Oleander Press, 4983 Tall Oaks Dr., Fayetteville NY 13066-9776. (315)637-3047. Fax: (315)637-5056. E-mail: info@bitteroleander.com. Web site: www.bitteroleander.com. **Contact:** Paul B. Roth. Offered annually for unpublished, imaginative poetry. Open to any writer. **Deadline: June 15.** Guidelines for SASE. **Charges $10 for 5 poems; $2/additional poem.** Prize: $1,000 and 5 copies of the issue.

LOUISIANA LITERATURE PRIZE FOR POETRY

Louisiana Literature, SLU—Box 792, Southeastern Louisiana University, Hammond LA 70402. (504)549-5022. Fax: (504)549-5021. E-mail: lalit@selu.edu. Web site: www.selu.edu/orgs/lalit/. **Contact:** Jack Bedell, contest director. Estab. 1984. Offered annually for unpublished poetry. All entries considered for publication. **Deadline: April 1.** Guidelines for SASE. **Charges $12 fee.** Prize: $400.

LOUISE LOUIS/EMILY F. BOURNE STUDENT POETRY AWARD

Poetry Society of America, 15 Gramercy Park S., New York NY 10003. (212)254-9628. Fax: (212)673-2352. Web site: www.poetrysociety.org. **Contact:** Programs Associate. Offered annually for unpublished work to promote excellence in student poetry. Open to American high school or preparatory school students (grades 9-12). Guidelines for SASE and online. Judged by prominent American poets. It is strongly encouraged that applicants read the complete contest guidelines before submitting. **Deadline: October 1-December 21. Charges $5 for a student submitting a single entry; $20 for a high school submitting unlimited number of its students' poems.** Prize: $250.

PAT LOWTHER MEMORIAL AWARD

920 Yonge St., Suite 608, Toronto ON M4W 3C7, Canada. (416)504-1657. Fax: (416)504-0096. E-mail: marketing @poets.ca. Web site: www.poets.ca. Estab. 1966. Offered annually for a book of poetry by a Canadian woman published in the preceding year. Guidelines for SASE or online. **Deadline: November 1. Charges $15 fee.** Prize: $1,000. Open to Canadian citizens and landed immigrants only.

LUMINA NATIONAL POETRY CONTEST

Sarah Lawrence College, 1 Mead Way, Bronxville NY 10708. E-mail: lumina@slc.edu. Web site: pages.slc.edu/~lumina. This contest provides a place for the publication of the best original poetry written in English. Previously published poems and translations are not eligible. Please submit up to 3 poems of up to 40 lines each. "We reserve the right to publish winning poems on our Web site." **Deadline: January 1.** Guidelines for SASE. **Charges $10.** Prize: 1st Place: $500; 2nd Place: $100: 3rd Place: $50, plus publication and 2 copies of the journal. Judged by Mark Doty. Open to any writer except current Sarah Lawrence College graduate students.

LYRIC POETRY AWARD

Poetry Society of America, 15 Gramercy Park, New York NY 10003. (212)254-9628. Fax: (212)673-2352. E-mail: tom@poetrysociety.org. Web site: www.poetrysociety.org. **Contact:** Thomas Hummel, awards coordinator. Offered annually for unpublished work to promote excellence in lyric poetry. Line limit 50. Guidelines subject to change. *Open to PSA members only*. Guidelines for SASE or online. **Deadline: October 1-December 23.** Guidelines for SASE. Prize: $500.

THE MACGUFFIN NATIONAL POET HUNT

The MacGuffin, 18600 Haggerty Rd., Livonia MI 48152. E-mail: macguffin@schoolcraft.edu. Web site: www.schoolcraft.edu/macguffin. **Contact:** Managing Editor. Each submission is judged blindly in its own right and on its own merits. "We assure writers who enter the contest that their work will be read by a renowned published poet." Offered annually for unpublished work. Guidelines available by fax, e-mail, or for SASE. **Deadline: April 3-June 5 (postmarked). Charges $15 for a 5-poem entry.** Prize: 1st Place: $500; 2 Honorable Mentions will be published. Judged by Thomas Lux in 2007. Past judges include Molly Peacock, Gary Gildner, Richard Tillinghast, Bob Hicok, Laurence Lieberman, and Conrad Hilberry. Acquires first rights (if published). Once published, all rights revert to the author. Open to any writer.

NAOMI LONG MADGETT POETRY AWARD

Lotus Press, Inc., P.O. Box 21607, Detroit MI 48221. E-mail: lotuspress@aol.com. Web site: www.lotuspress.org. **Contact:** Constance Withers. Offered annually to recognize an unpublished poetry ms. Guidelines for SASE, by e-mail, or online. **Deadline: January 2-March 31.** Prize: $500 and publication by Lotus Press.

MAHONEY RESEARCH LIBRARY POETRY CONTEST

Mahoney Research Library, 206 E. Colbert Dr., Minden LA 71055-6363. (318)377-0053. E-mail: poet@mahoneyresearchlibrary.org. Web site: www.mahoneyresearchlibrary.org. **Contact:** Michael Mahoney, president. Annual contest to encourage and reward the difficult work of poets who reside in the US in a meaningful way. **Deadline: March 31.** Guidelines for SASE. **Charges $10/poem, $20/3 poems.** Prize: $1,000 and a certificate. Judged by executive committee of the Mahoney Research Library. Open to US residents only.

THE MALAHAT REVIEW LONG POEM PRIZE

The Malahat Review, Box 1700 STN CSC, Victoria BC V8W 2Y2, Canada. E-mail: malahat@uvic.ca (queries only). Web site: malahatreview.ca. **Contact:** Editor. Offered in alternate years with the Novella Contest. Open to unpublished long poems. Preliminary reading by editorial board; final judging by the editor and 2 recognized poets. Obtains first world rights. After publication rights revert to the author. Open to any writer. **Deadline: February 1 (odd years).** Guidelines for SASE. **Charges $35 fee (includes a 1-year subscription to the** ***Malahat***, published quarterly). Prize: 2 prizes of $400, plus payment for publication ($35/page), and additional 1-year subscription.

MORTON MARR POETRY PRIZE

Southwest Review, P.O. Box 750374, Dallas TX 75275-0374. (214)768-1037. Fax: (214)768-1408. E-mail: swr@mail.smu.edu. Web site: www.southwestreview.org. **Contact:** Willard Spiegelman. Annual award given to a poem by a writer who has not yet published a first book. Contestants may submit no more than 6 poems in a traditional form (i.e., sonnet, sestina, villanelle, rhymed stanzas, blank verse, etc.). A cover letter with name, address, and other relevant information may accompany the poems which must be printed without any identifying information. Guidelines for SASE or online. **Deadline: September 30. Charges $5/poem.** Prize: 1st Place: $1,000; 2nd Place: $500; publication in *The Southwest Review*. Open to any writer who has not yet published a first book.

LUCILLE MEDWICK MEMORIAL AWARD

Poetry Society of America, 15 Gramercy Park, New York NY 10003. (212)254-9628. Fax: (212)673-2352. E-mail: tom@poetrysociety.org. Web site: www.poetrysociety.org. **Contact:** Thomas Hummel, awards coordinator. Original poem in any form on a humanitarian theme. Line limit: 100. Guidelines subject to change. *Open to PSA members only*. Guidelines for SASE or online. **Deadline: October 1-December 23.** Guidelines for SASE. Prize: $500.

MORSE POETRY PRIZE

Northeastern University English Department, 406 Holmes Hall, Boston MA 02115. (617)437-2512. E-mail: g.rotella@neu.edu. Web site: www.casdn.neu.edu/~english. **Contact:** Guy Rotella. Offered annually for previously published poetry book-length mss of first or second books. **Deadline: September 15. Charges $10 fee.** Prize: $1,000 and publication by NU/UPNE.

KATHRYN A. MORTON PRIZE IN POETRY

Sarabande Books, P.O. Box 4456, Louisville KY 40204. (502)458-4028. Fax: (502)458-4065. E-mail: info@sarabandebooks.org. Web site: www.sarabandebooks.org. **Contact:** Kristina McGrath, associate editor. Offered annually to publish an outstanding collection of poetry. All finalists considered for publication. **Deadline: January 1-February 15.** Guidelines for SASE. **Charges $25 fee.** Prize: $2,000 and publication with standard royalty contract.

SHEILA MOTTON AWARD

New England Poetry Club, 16 Cornell St., Apt. 2, Arlington MA 02476-7710. E-mail: contests@nepoetryclub.org. Web site: www.nepoetryclub.org/contests.htm. For a poetry book published in the last 2 years. Send 2 copies of the book and **$10 entry fee**. Prize: $500.

ERIKA MUMFORD PRIZE

New England Poetry Club, 16 Cornell St., Arlington MA 02476-7710. E-mail: contests@nepoetryclub.org. Web site: www.nepoetryclub.org/contests.htm. Offered annually for a poem in any form about foreign culture or travel. **Deadline: June 30.** Guidelines for SASE. **Charges $10/up to 3 entries in NEPC contests.** Prize: $250.

NATIONAL WRITERS ASSOCIATION POETRY CONTEST

The National Writers Association, 10940 S. Parker Rd. #508, Parker CO 80134. (303)841-0246. Fax: (303)841-2607. **Contact:** Sandy Whelchel, director. Annual contest to encourage the writing of poetry, an important form of individual expression but with a limited commercial market. Guidelines for SASE. **Charges $10 fee.** Prize: 1st Place: $100; 2nd Place: $50; 3rd Place: $25.

HOWARD NEMEROV SONNET AWARD

The Formalist, 320 Hunter Dr., Evansville IN 47711. Web site: www2.evansville.edu/theformalist. Offered annually for an unpublished sonnet to encourage poetic craftsmanship and to honor the memory of the late Howard Nemerov, third US Poet Laureate. Acquires first North American serial rights for those sonnets chosen for publication. Upon publication all rights revert to the author. Open to the international community of writers. Guidelines available online. **Deadline: November 15. Charges $3/sonnet.** Prize: $1,000 and publication in *Measure: An Annual Review of Formal Poetry*.

THE PABLO NERUDA PRIZE FOR POETRY

Nimrod International Journal, 600 S. College Ave., Tulsa OK 74104. (918)631-3080. Fax: (918)631-3033. E-mail: nimrod@utulsa.edu. Web site: www.utulsa.edu/nimrod. **Contact:** Francine Ringold. Annual award to discover new writers of vigor and talent. **Deadline: April 30.** Guidelines for SASE. **Charges $20 (includes a 1-year subscription).** Prize: 1st Place: $2,000 and publication; 2nd Place: $1,000 and publication. *Nimrod* retains the right to publish any submission. Judged by the *Nimrod* editors (finalists). A recognized author selects the winners. Open to US residents only.

NEW ISSUES FIRST BOOK OF POETRY PRIZE

New Issues Poetry & Prose, Dept. of English, Western Michigan University, 1903 W. Michigan Ave., Kalamazoo MI 49008-5331. (269)387-8185. Fax: (269)387-2562. E-mail: herbert.scott@wmich.edu. Web site: www.wmich.edu/newissues. **Contact:** Herbert Scott, editor. Offered annually for publication of a first book of poems by a poet writing in English who has not previously published a full-length collection of poems in an edition of 500 or more copies. *New Issues Poetry & Prose* obtains rights for first publication. Book is copyrighted in author's name. Guidelines for SASE or online. **Deadline: November 30. Charges $15.** Prize: $2,000 and publication of book. Author also receives 10% of the printed edition.

THE JOHN FREDERICK NIMS MEMORIAL PRIZE

Poetry, 444 North Michigan Ave., Suite 1850, Chicago IL 60611. (312)787-7070. E-mail: poetry@poetrymagazine.org. Web site: www.poetrymagazine.org. Offered annually for poems published in *Poetry* during the preceding year (October-September). Judged by the editors of *Poetry*. *Poetry* buys all rights to the poems published in the magazine. Copyrights are returned to the authors on request. Any writer may submit poems to *Poetry*. Guidelines for SASE. Prize: $500.

ONCEWRITTEN.COM POETRY CONTEST

Oncewritten.com, 1850 N. Whitley Ave., #404, Hollywood CA 90028. E-mail: poetrycontest@oncewritten.com. Web site: www.oncewritten.com. The purpose of this biannual contest is "to find high quality, previously unpublished poetry to feature on the Web site and in *Off the Press*, our monthly newsletter, which is distributed specifically for people interested in reading about new authors." **Deadline: February 28 and August 31.** Guidelines for SASE. **Charges $15.** Prize: 1st Prize: $500; Runner-Up: $100. Judged by the editor and industry professionals. Open to any writer.

THE OPEN WINDOW

Hidden Brook Press, 109 Bayshore Rd., RR#4, Brighton ON K0K 1H0, Canada. (613)475-2368. E-mail: writers@hiddenbrookpress.com. Web site: www.hiddenbrookpress.com. An annual poetry anthology contest. A wide open window theme including family, nature, death, rhyming, city, country, war and peace, social—long, short haiku, or any other genre. Send sets of 3 poems with short bio (35-40 words) and a SASE. Electronic and hard copy submissions required. Previously published and simultaneous submissions are welcome. **Deadline: November 30. Charges $15/3 poems.** Prize: 1st Place: $100; 2nd Place: $75; 3rd Place: $50; 4th Place: $40; 5th Place: $30; 6th Place: $25; 7th Place: $20; 8th Place: $15; 9th-10th Place: $10; plus up to 12 honorable mentions. All winners, honorable mentions, and runners up receive 1 copy of the book for each published poem. Authors retain copyright. Open to any writer.

GUY OWEN AWARD

Southern Poetry Review, Dept. of Languages, Literature, and Philosophy, Armstrong Atlantic State University, 11935 Abercorn St., Savannah GA 31419-1997. (912)921-5633. Fax: (912)927-5399. E-mail: smithjam@mail.armstrong.edu. Web site: www.spr.armstrong.edu. **Contact:** James Smith. Send 3-5 unpublished poems (maximum 10 pages). Please indicate simultaneous submissions. **Deadline: March 1-June 15 (postmarked).** Guidelines for SASE. **Charges $15 entry fee (includes 1-year subscription).** Prize: $1,000 and publication of winning poem in *Southern Poetry Review*. Judged by a distinguished poet. Open to any writer.

THE PATERSON POETRY PRIZE

The Poetry Center at Passaic County Community College, One College Blvd., Paterson NJ 07505-1179. Fax: (973)523-6085. E-mail: mgillan@pccc.edu. Web site: www.pccc.edu/poetry. **Contact:** Maria Mazziotti Gillan, director. Offered annually for a book of poetry published in the previous year. Guidelines available online. **Deadline: February 1.** Prize: $1,000.

PEARL POETRY PRIZE

Pearl Editions, 3030 E. Second St., Long Beach CA 90803. (562)434-4523. Fax: (562)434-4523. E-mail: pearlmag@aol.com. Web site: www.pearlmag.com. **Contact:** Marilyn Johnson, editor/publisher. Offered annually to provide poets with further opportunity to publish their poetry in book-form and find a larger audience for their work. Mss must be original works written in English. Guidelines for SASE or online. **Deadline: July 15. Charges $20.** Prize: $1,000 and publication by Pearl Editions. Open to all writers.

PEN/JOYCE OSTERWEIL AWARD FOR POETRY

PEN American Center, 588 Broadway, Suite 303, New York NY 10012. (212)334-1660, ext. 108. E-mail: awards@pen.org. Web site: www.pen.org. **Contact:** Andrew Proctor, coordinator. *Candidates may only be nominated by members of PEN.* This award recognizes the high literary character of the published work to date of a new and emerging American poet of any age, and the promise of further literary achievement. Nominated writer may not have published more than 1 book of poetry. Offered in odd-numbered years. **Deadline: January 7.** Prize: $5,000. Judged by a panel of 3 judges selected by the PEN Awards Committee.

PERUGIA PRESS PRIZE

Perugia Press, P.O. Box 60364, Florence MA 01062. E-mail: info@perugiapress.com. Web site: www.perugiapress.com. **Contact:** Susan Kan. The contest is for first or second poetry books by women. Some poems in the submission may be previously published, but the ms as a whole must be unpublished. Send SASE or visit our Web site for guidelines. **Deadline: November 15. Charges $20.** Prize: $1,000 and publication. Judged by previous winners of the Perugia Press Prize, plus other poets, teachers, scholars, booksellers, and poetry lovers. The contest is open to women poets who are US residents and who have not published more than 1 book.

PHILBRICK POETRY AWARD

Providence Athenaeum, 251 Benefit St., Providence RI 02903. (401)421-6970. Fax: (401)421-2860. E-mail: smarkley@providenceathenaeum.org. Web site: www.providenceathenaeum.org. **Contact:** Sandy Markley. Offered annually for New England poets who have not yet published a book. Previous publication of individual poems in journals or anthologies is allowed. Judged by nationally-known poets. Guidelines for SASE or online. **Deadline: June 15-October 15. Charges $8 fee (includes copy of previously published chapbook).** Prize: $500, publication of winning ms as a chapbook, and a public reading at Providence Athenaeum with the final judge/award presenter.

POET'S CORNER AWARD

BS Poetry Society, Box 596 Stn. A, Fredericton NB E3B 5A6, Canada. (506)454-5127. Estab. 1998. Offered annually to recognize the best book-length ms by a poet. Guidelines on Web site at www.brokenjaw.com/poetscorner.htm. **Deadline: September 1. Charges $20 fee (which includes copy of winning book upon publication).** Prize: $500, plus trade publication of poetry ms.

POETIC LICENCE CONTEST FOR CANADIAN YOUTH

League of Canadian Poets, 920 Yonge St., Suite 608, Toronto ON M4W 3C7, Canada. (416)504-1657. Fax: (416)504-0096. E-mail: marketing@poets.ca. Web site: www.poets.ca; www.youngpoets.ca. Offered annually for unpublished work to seek and encourage new poetic talent in 2 categories: grades 7-9 and 10-12. Entry is by e-mail only. Open to Canadian citizens and landed immigrants only. Guidelines for SASE or on Web site. See Web site for more information about the contest. **Deadline: December 1.** Prize: 1st Place: $150; 2nd Place: $100; 3rd Place: $50.

POETRY SOCIETY OF VIRGINIA CONTESTS

Poetry Society of Virginia, P.O. Box 35685, Richmond VA 23235. E-mail: contest@poetrysocietyofvirginia.org. Web site: www.poetrysocietyofvirginia.org. **Contact:** Norma Richardson, adult categories; Shann Palmer, student categories. Annual contest for unpublished poetry in 28 categories. Most categories are open to any writer, several are open only to members or students. Guidelines for SASE or online. **Deadline: January 19. Charges $3/poem for nonmembers; free for members and students.** Prize: $10-300, depending on the category.

POETS OUT LOUD PRIZE

Poets Out Loud, Fordham University at Lincoln Center, 113 W. 60th St., Room 924-I, New York NY 10023. (212)636-6792. Fax: (212)636-7153. E-mail: pol@fordham.edu. Web site: www.poetsoutloud.com. Annual competition for an unpublished, full-length poetry ms (50-80 pages). **Deadline: November 30.** Guidelines for SASE. **Charges $25 entry fee.** Prize: $1,000 and book publication. Judged by Alberto Ríos in 2005-2006. Open to any writer.

MARGARET REID POETRY CONTEST FOR TRADITIONAL VERSE

℅ Winning Writers, 351 Pleasant St., PMB 222, Northampton MA 01060-3961. (866)946-9748. E-mail: adam@winningwriters.com. Web site: www.winningwriters.com. **Contact:** Adam Cohen. Estab. 2004. Seeks poems in traditional verse forms, such as sonnets and haiku. Both unpublished and published work accepted. Guidelines for SASE or on Web site. **Deadline: June 30. Charges $6/25 lines of poetry.** Prize: 1st Place: $1,000; 2nd Place: $400; 3rd Place: $200; plus 7 high distinction awards of $100 each; 10 highly commended awards of $70 each; 30 commended awards of $50 each. The top 10 entries will be published on the Winning Writers Web site. Judged by John H. Reid and Dee C. Konrad. Open to any writer.

BENJAMIN SALTMAN POETRY AWARD

Red Hen Press, P.O. Box 3537, Granada Hills CA 91394. (818)831-0649. Fax: (818)831-6659. E-mail: editors@redhen.org. Web site: www.redhen.org. **Contact:** Kate Gale. Offered annually for unpublished work to publish a winning book of poetry. Open to any writer. **Deadline: October 31.** Guidelines for SASE. **Charges $25 fee.** Prize: $3,000 and publication.

SUE SANIEL ELKIND POETRY CONTEST

Kalliope, 11901 Beach Blvd., Jacksonville FL 32246. (904)646-2081. Web site: www.fccj.org/kalliope. Offered annually for unpublished work. Poetry may be in any style and on any subject. Maximum poem length is 50 lines. Only unpublished poems are eligible. No limit on number of poems entered by any 1 poet. The winning poem is published, as are the finalists' poems. Copyright then returns to the authors. Guidelines for SASE or online. **Deadline: November 1. Charges $5/poem; $1⅔ poems.** Prize: $1,000 and publication in *Kalliope*.

SASKATCHEWAN POETRY AWARD

Saskatchewan Book Awards, Inc., Box 1921, Regina SK S4P 3E1, Canada. (306)569-1585. Fax: (306)569-4187. E-mail: director@bookawards.sk.ca. Web site: www.bookawards.sk.ca. **Contact:** Glenda James, executive director. Offered annually for work published September 15-September 14. This award is presented to a Saskatchewan author for the best book of poetry, judged on the quality of writing. **Deadline: First deadline: July 31; Final deadline: September 14.** Guidelines for SASE. **Charges $20 (Canadian).** Prize: $2,000.

SEEDS

Hidden Brook Press, 109 Bayshore Rd., RR#4, Brighton ON K0K 1H0, Canada. (613)475-2368. E-mail: writers@hiddenbrookpress.com. Web site: www.hiddenbrookpress.com. "The *SEEDS* International Poetry Chapbook Anthology Contest is interested in all types and styles of poetry. See the *SEEDS* Web site for examples of the type of poetry we have published in the past." Previously published and multiple submissions are welcome. **Deadline: October 1. Charges $15/3 poems.** Prize: 1st Place: $100; 2nd Place: $75; 3rd Place: $50; 4th Place: $40; 5th Place: $30; 6th Place: $25; 7th Place: $20; 8th Place: $15; 9th-10th Place: $10; plus 15-25 Honorable Mentions. Winning poems published in the *SEEDS International Poetry Chapbook Anthology*. All winning and honorable mention submissions receive 1 copy of the book for each published poem. Authors retain copyright. Open to any writer.

SLAPERING HOL PRESS CHAPBOOK COMPETITION

The Hudson Valley Writers' Center, 300 Riverside Dr., Sleepy Hollow NY 10591. (914)332-5953. Fax: (914)332-4825. E-mail: info@writerscenter.org. Web site: www.writerscenter.org. **Contact:** Margo Stever, editor. The annual competition is open to poets who have not published a book or chapbook, though individual poems may have already appeared. Limit: 16-20 pages. The press was created in 1990 to provide publishing opportunities for emerging poets. **Deadline: May 15.** Guidelines for SASE. **Charges $15 fee.** Prize: $1,000, publication of chapbook, 10 copies of chapbook, and a reading at The Hudson Valley Writers' Center.

SLIPSTREAM ANNUAL POETRY CHAPBOOK COMPETITION

Slipstream, Box 2071, Niagara Falls NY 14301. E-mail: editors@slipstreampress.org. Web site: www.slipstreampress.org. **Contact:** Dan Sicoli, co-editor. Offered annually to help promote a poet whose work is often overlooked or ignored. Open to any writer. **Deadline: December 1.** Guidelines for SASE. **Charges $15.** Prize: $1,000 and 50 copies of published chapbook.

THE SOW'S EAR CHAPBOOK PRIZE

The Sow's Ear Poetry Review, 355 Mount Lebanon Rd., Donalds SC 29638-9115. (864)379-8061. E-mail: errol@kitenet.net. **Contact:** Errol Hess, managing editor. Estab. 1988. Offered for poetry mss of 22-26 pages. Guidelines for SASE, by e-mail, or on Web site. **Deadline: Submit March-April. Charges $20 fee; includes subscription.** Prize: $1,000, 25 copies, and distribution to subscribers.

THE SOW'S EAR POETRY PRIZE

The Sow's Ear Poetry Review, 355 Mount Lebanon Rd., Donalds SC 29638-9115. (864)379-8061. E-mail: errol@kitenet.net. **Contact:** Errol Hess, managing editor. Estab. 1988. Offered for previously unpublished poetry. Guidelines for SASE or by e-mail. All submissions considered for publication. **Deadline: November 1 postmark. Submit September-October. Charges $20, covering up to 5 poems.** Prize: $1,000, publication of winner and top finalists. Contestants receive a year's subscription.

SPOON RIVER POETRY REVIEW EDITORS' PRIZE

Spoon River Poetry Review, Campus Box 4241, English Department, Illinois State University, Normal IL 61790-4241. (309)438-7906. Web site: www.litline.org/spoon. Offered annually for unpublished poetry to identify and reward excellence. Guidelines available online. Open to all writers. **Deadline: April 15. Charges $16 (entitles entrant to a 1-year subscription valued at $15).** Prize: 1st Place: $1,000 and publication; Runners-Up (2): $100 each and publication.

THE EDWARD STANLEY AWARD

Prairie Schooner, 201 Andrews Hall, P.O. Box 880334, Lincoln NE 68588-0334. (402)472-0911. Fax: (402)472-9771. E-mail: kgrey2@unl.edu. Web site: www.unl.edu/schooner/psmain.htm. **Contact:** Hilda Raz. Offered annually for poetry published in *Prairie Schooner* in the previous year. Prize: $1,000.

THE ELIZABETH MATCHETT STOVER MEMORIAL AWARD

Southwest Review, P.O. Box 750374, Dallas TX 75275-0374. (214)768-1037. Fax: (214)768-1408. E-mail: swr@mail.smu.edu. Web site: www.southwestreview.org. **Contact:** Jennifer Cranfill, Willard Spiegelman. Offered annually for unpublished poems or group of poems. Please note that mss are submitted for publication, not for the prizes themselves. Guidelines for SASE and online. Prize: $250. Judged by Jennifer Cranfill, managing editor, and Willard Spiegelman, editor-in-chief. Open to any writer.

THE DAN SULLIVAN MEMORIAL POETRY CONTEST

The Writers' Circle of Durham Region, P.O. Box 14558, 75 Bayly St. W., Ajax ON L1S 7K7, Canada. (905)686-0211. E-mail: dansullivan@wcdr.org. Web site: www.wcdr.org. Estab. 1995. Annual contest for unpublished poetry. **Deadline: February 15. Charges $15/submission for adults; free entry for children & youth. Payment must be payable in Canadian funds by money order to The Writers' Circle of Dunham Region or via PayPal on the Web site.** Prize: **Children:** 1st Prize: $45; 2nd Prize: $35; 3rd Prize: $25; **Youth:** 1st Prize: $45; 2nd Prize: $35; 3rd Prize: $25; **Adult:** 1st Prize: $300; 2nd Prize: $200; 3rd Prize: $100. Open to any writer.

HOLLIS SUMMERS POETRY PRIZE

Ohio University Press, 19 Circle Dr., The Ridges, Athens OH 45701. (740)593-1155. Fax: (740)593-4536. Web site: www.ohio.edu/oupress. **Contact:** David Sanders. Offered annually for unpublished poetry mss. Mss will be eligible even if individual poems or sections have been published previously. Open to any writer. Guidelines for SASE or online. **Deadline: October 31. Charges $20.** Prize: $1,000 and publication of the ms in book form.

MAY SWENSON POETRY AWARD

Utah State University Press, 7800 Old Main Hill, Logan UT 84322-7800. (435)797-1362. Fax: (435)797-0313. E-mail: michael.spooner@usu.edu. Web site: www.usu.edu/usupress. **Contact:** Michael Spooner. Offered annually in honor of May Swenson, one of America's major 20th century poets. Contest for unpublished mss in English, 50-100 pages; not only a "first book" competition. Entries are screened by 6 professional writers and teachers. The finalists are judged by a nationally known poet. Former judges include Alice Quinn, Alicia Ostriker, Mark Doty, John Hollander, and Mary Oliver. Guidelines on Web site. Open to any writer. **Deadline: September 30. Charges $25 fee.** Prize: $1,000, publication of ms, and royalties.

TICKLED BY THUNDER POETRY CONTEST

Tickled by Thunder fiction magazine, 14076 86A Ave., Surrey BC V3W 0V9, Canada. E-mail: info@tickledbythunder.com. Web site: www.tickledbythunder.com. **Contact:** Larry Lindner. Annual contest to encourage unpublished poets. **Deadline: February 15, May 15, August 15 and October 15.** Guidelines for SASE. Prize: $75 (Canada), subscription, publication, and 2 copies of the magazine. Judged by the publisher and others he knows who have not entered the contest. Open to any writer.

TRANSCONTINENTAL POETRY AWARD

Pavement Saw Press, P.O. Box 6291, Columbus OH 43206. (614)445-0534. E-mail: info@pavementsaw.org. Web site: pavementsaw.org. **Contact:** David Baratier, editor. Offered annually for a first book of poetry. Judged by the editor and a guest judge. Guidelines available online. **Deadline: August 15. Charges $18 fee.** Prize: $1,500, 30 copies for judge's choice, and standard royalty contract for editor's choice. All writers receive 1 free book for entering. Open to any writer.

N TRILLIUM BOOK AWARD FOR POETRY

Ontario Media Development Corp., 175 Bloor St. E., South Tower, Suite 501, Toronto ON M4W 3R8, Canada. (416)314-6698. Fax: (416)314-6876. E-mail: jhawkins@omdc.on.ca. Web site: www.omdc.on.ca. **Contact:** Janet Hawkins. Estab. 2003. Offered annually for a published book of poetry. Publishers submit titles on behalf of authors. Authors must have been Ontario residents 3 of the last 5 years. Guidelines online or for SASE. **Deadline: December 9 for books published between January and October; January 9 for books published in November and December.** Prize: The winning author in each category (English and French) receives $10,000; the winning publisher in each category receives $2,000. Judged by a jury of writers, poets, and other members of the literary community.

UTMOST CHRISTIAN POETRY CONTEST

Utmost Christian Writers Foundation, 121 Morin Maze, Edmonton AB T6K 1V1, Canada. Web site: www.utmostchristianwriters.com. The purpose of this annual contest is "to promote excellence in poetry by poets of Christian faith. All entries are eligible for most of the cash awards, but special categories (each with a $100 prize) have been created for: Best Poem by a US Citizen; Best Poem by a Canadian Citizen; Best Formal Poem (specific form); Best Poem by a Young Poet (under 21)." All entries must be unpublished. **Deadline: February 28.**

Guidelines for SASE. **Charges $15/poem (maximum 7 poems).** Prize: 1st Place: $1,000; 2nd Place: $500; 3rd Place: $150. Rights are acquired to post winning entries on the organization's Web site. Judged by a committee of the Directors of Utmost Christian Writers Foundation (who work under the direction of Barbara Mitchell, chief judge). Open to any writer.

DANIEL VAROUJAN AWARD

New England Poetry Club, 16 Cornell St., Arlington MA 02476-7710. E-mail: contests@nepoetryclub.org. Web site: www.nepoetryclub.org/contests.htm. Offered annually for an unpublished poem worthy of Daniel Varoujan, a poet killed by the Turks at the onset of the first genocide of the 20th century which decimated three-fourths of the Armenian population. Send poems in duplicate, with name and address of poet on one copy only. **Deadline: June 30.** Guidelines for SASE. **Charges $10/up to 3 entries in NEPC contests.** Prize: $1,000. Open to any writer.

N DEANE WAGNER POETRY CONTEST

St. Louis Writers Guild, P.O. Box 724, St. Louis MO 63026. (314)821-3823. E-mail: contest@stlwritersguild.org. Web site: www.stlwritersguild.org. **Contact:** Robin Theiss, president. Annual contest for exceptional unpublished poems. All entrants release one-time rights so the St. Louis Writers Guild can publish the winning entries on its Web site. **Deadline: June 17. Charges $10/first poem; $5/additional poem (unlimited entries).** Prize: 1st Place: $100 or 40% of money received from submissions (whichever is more); 2nd Place: $75 or 30% of money from submissions; 3rd Place: $50 or 15% or money from submissions. Judged by Albert J. Montesi, professor emeritus from St. Louis University with a specialty in American poetry. Open to any writer.

CHAD WALSH POETRY PRIZE

Beloit Poetry Journal, P.O. Box 151, Farmington ME 04938. (207)778-0020. Web site: www.bpj.org. **Contact:** Lee Sharkey and John Rosenwald, editors. Offered annually to honor the memory of poet Chad Walsh, a founder of the *Beloit Poetry Journal*. The editors select an outstanding poem or group of poems from the poems published in the journal that year. Prize: $3,000.

WAR POETRY CONTEST

Winning Writers, 351 Pleasant St., PMB 222, Northampton MA 01060-3961. (866)946-9748. Fax: (413)280-0539. E-mail: adam@winningwriters.com. Web site: www.winningwriters.com. **Contact:** Adam Cohen. Estab. 2002. This annual contest seeks outstanding, unpublished poetry on the theme of war. Up to 3 poems can be submitted, with a maximum total of 500 lines. English language—no translations, please. Submit online or by mail. Guidelines for SASE or see Web site. **Deadline: November 15-May 31. Charges $15.** Prize: 1st Place: $2,000 and publication on WinningWriters.com; 2nd Place: $1,200 and publication; 3rd Place: $600 and publication; Honorable Mentions (12): $100. Judged by award-winning poet Jendi Reiter. Acquires nonexclusive right to publish submissions on WinningWriters.com, in e-mail newsletter, and in press releases. Open to any writer.

THE WASHINGTON PRIZE

The Word Works, Inc., 3201 Taylor St., Mt. Rainier MD 20712. E-mail: editor@wordworksdc.com. Web site: www.wordworksdc.com. **Contact:** Steven Rogers, Washington Prize Director. Estab. 1981. Offered annually "for the best full-length poetry manuscript (48-64 pp.) submitted to The Word Works each year. The Washington Prize contest is the only forum in which we consider unsolicited manuscripts." Acquires first publication rights. Open to any American writer. **Deadline: January 15-March 1.** Guidelines for SASE. **Charges $20 fee.** Prize: $1,500 and book publication; all entrants receive a copy of the winning book.

WERGLE FLOMP HUMOR POETRY CONTEST

Winning Writers, 351 Pleasant St., PMB 222, Northampton MA 01060-3961. (866)946-9748. Fax: (413)280-0539. E-mail: adam@winningwriters.com. Web site: www.winningwriters.com. **Contact:** Adam Cohen. Estab. 2002. This annual contest seeks the best parody poem that has been sent to a vanity poetry contest as a joke. Vanity contests are characterized by low standards. Their main purpose is to entice poets to buy expensive products like anthologies, chapbooks, CDs, plaques, and silver bowls. Vanity contests will often praise remarkably bad poems in their effort to sell as much stuff to as many people as possible. The Wergle Flomp Prize will be awarded for the best bad poem. One poem of any length should be submitted, along with the name of the vanity contest that was spoofed. The poem should be in English. Inspired gibberish is also accepted. See Web site for guidelines, examples, and to submit your poem." **Deadline: August 15-April 1.** Prize: 1st Place: $1,190; 2nd Place: $169; 3rd Place: $60. Honorable Mentions get $38 each. All prize winners receive publication at WinningWriters.com. Non-US winners will be paid in US currency (or PayPal) if a check is inconvenient. Judged by Jendi Reiter. Acquires nonexclusive right to publish submissions on WinningWriters.com, in e-mail newsletter, and in press releases. Open to any writer.

WHITE PINE PRESS POETRY PRIZE

White Pine Press, P.O. Box 236, Buffalo NY 14201. E-mail: wpine@whitepine.org. Web site: www.whitepine.org. **Contact:** Elaine LaMattina, managing editor. Offered annually for previously published or unpublished poets. Manuscript: Up to 80 pages of original work; translations are not eligible. Poems may have appeared in magazines or limited-edition chapbooks. Open to any US citizen. **Deadline: November 30 (postmarked). Charges $20 fee.** Prize: $1,000 and publication. Judged by a poet of national reputation. All entries are screened by the editorial staff of White Pine Press.

STAN AND TOM WICK POETRY PRIZE

Wick Poetry Center, 301 Satterfield Hall, Kent State University, P.O. Box 5190, Kent OH 44242-0001. (330)672-2067. Fax: (330)672-3333. E-mail: wickpoet@kent.edu. Web site: dept.kent.edu/wick. **Contact:** Maggie Anderson, director. Open to anyone writing in English who has not previously published a full-length book of poems (a volume of 50 pages or more published in an edition of 500 or more copies). Send SASE or visit the Web site for guidelines. **Deadline: May 1. Charges $20 reading fee.** Prize: $2,000 and publication by the Kent State University Press.

WILLIAM CARLOS WILLIAMS AWARD

Poetry Society of America, 15 Gramercy Park S., New York NY 10003. (212)254-9628. Fax: (212)673-2352. Web site: www.poetrysociety.org. **Contact:** Programs Associate. Offered annually for a book of poetry published by a small press, nonprofit, or university press. Winning books are distributed to PSA Lyric Circle members while supplies last. Books must be submitted directly by publishers. Entry forms are required. It is strongly encouraged that applicants read the complete contest guidelines on the PSA Web site before submitting. **Deadline: October 1-December 21. Charges $20 fee.** Prize: $500-1,000.

ROBERT H. WINNER MEMORIAL AWARD

Poetry Society of America, 15 Gramercy Park, New York NY 10003. (212)254-9628. Fax: (212)673-2352. E-mail: tom@poetrysociety.org. Web site: www.poetrysociety.org. **Contact:** Thomas Hummel, awards coordinator. This award acknowledges original work being done in mid-career by a poet who has not had substantial recognition. Send manuscript of 10 poems (up to 20 pages). Guidelines for SASE or online. **Deadline: October 1-December 23. Charges $15/nonmembers; free to PSA members.** Prize: $2,500. Open to poets over 40 who are unpublished or have 1 book.

THE J. HOWARD AND BARBARA M.J. WOOD PRIZE

Poetry, 444 North Michigan Ave., Suite 1850, Chicago IL 60611. (312)787-7070. E-mail: poetry@poetrymagazine.org. Web site: www.poetrymagazine.org. Estab. 1994. Offered annually for poems published in *Poetry* during the preceding year (October-September). *Poetry* buys all rights to the poems published in the magazine. Copyrights are returned to the authors on request. Any writer may submit poems to *Poetry*. Guidelines for SASE. Prize: $5,000.

THE WRITER MAGAZINE/EMILY DICKINSON AWARD

Poetry Society of America, 15 Gramercy Park, New York NY 10003. (212)254-9628. Fax: (212)673-2352. E-mail: tom@poetrysociety.org. Web site: www.poetrysociety.org. **Contact:** Thomas Hummel, awards coordinator. Offered annually for a poem inspired by Emily Dickinson, though not necessarily in her style. Line limit: 30. Guidelines for SASE or online. Guidelines subject to change. *Open to PSA members only.* **Deadline: October 1-December 23.** Prize: $250.

WRITERS' JOURNAL POETRY CONTEST

Val-Tech Media, P.O. Box 394, Perham MN 56573. (218)346-7921. Fax: (218)346-7924. E-mail: writersjournal@writersjournal.com. Web site: www.writersjournal.com. **Contact:** Esther M. Leiper. Offered for previously unpublished poetry. Guidelines for SASE or online. **Deadline: April 30, August 30, December 30. Charges $3/poem.** Prize: 1st Place: $50; 2nd Place: $25; 3rd Place: $15. First, second, third, and selected honorable mention winners will be published in *Writers' Journal* magazine.

PLAYWRITING & SCRIPTWRITING

ALBERTA PLAYWRITING COMPETITION

Alberta Playwrights' Network, 2633 Hochwald Ave. SW, Calgary AB T3E 7K2, Canada. (403)269-8564. Fax: (403)265-6773. Web site: www.albertaplaywrights.com. Offered annually for unproduced plays with full-length and Discovery categories. Discovery is open only to previously unproduced playwrights. Open only to residents of Alberta. **Deadline: March 31. Charges $40 fee (Canadian).** Prize: Full length: $3,500 (Canadian); Discovery: $1,500 (Canadian); plus a written critique, workshop of winning play, and reading of winning plays at a Showcase Conference.

APPALACHIAN FESTIVAL OF PLAYS & PLAYWRIGHTS

Barter Theatre, Box 867, Abingdon VA 24212-0867. (276)619-3314. Fax: (276)619-3335. E-mail: apfestival@bartertheatre.com. Web site: www.bartertheatre.com. **Contact:** Nick Piper. "With the annual Appalachian Festival of New Plays & Playwrights, Barter Theatre wishes to celebrate new, previously unpublished/unproduced plays by playwrights from the Appalachian region. If the playwrights are not from Appalachia, the plays themselves must be about the region." **Deadline: April 23.** Guidelines for SASE. Prize: $250, a staged reading performed at Barter's Stage II theater, and some transportation compensation and housing during the time of the festival. There may be an additional award for the best staged readings. Judged by the Barter Theatre's artistic director and associate director.

BAY AREA PLAYWRIGHTS FESTIVAL

Produced by Playwrights Foundation, 131 10th St., 3rd Floor, San Francisco CA 94103. E-mail: literary@playwrightsfoundation.org. Web site: www.playwrightsfoundation.org. **Contact:** Jonathan Spector; jonathan@just-theater.org. Offered annually for unpublished plays by established and emerging theater writers to support and encourage development of a new work. Unproduced full-length play only. **Deadline: January 15 (postmarked). Charges $20.** Prize: Small stipend and in-depth development process with dramaturg and director, and a professionally staged reading in San Francisco. Open to any writer.

N BIENNIAL PROMISING PLAYWRIGHT CONTEST

Colonial Players, Inc., 108 East St., Annapolis MD 21401. (410)268-7373. E-mail: cpartisticdir@yahoo.com. Web site: www.cplayers.com. Offered every 2 years for unproduced full-length plays and one-acts with 10 actor or fewer. Musicals are not eligible. Open to any aspiring playwright residing in West Virginia, Washington DC, or any of the states descendant from the original 13 colonies (Connecticut, Delaware, Georgia, Maryland, Massachusetts, New Hampshire, New Jersey, New York, North Carolina, Pennsylvania, Rhode Island, South Carolina, and Virginia). Next contest runs September 1-December 1, 2008. Guidelines available online beginning summer 2008. Prize: $1,000, a weekend workshop, and a public reading.

CAA CAROL BOLT AWARD FOR DRAMA

Canadian Authors Association with the support of the Playwrights Guild of Canada and Playwrights Canada Press, 320 S. Shores Rd., P.O. Box 419, Campbellford ON K0L 1L0, Canada. (705)653-0323 or (866)216-6222. Fax: (705)653-0593. E-mail: admin@canauthors.org. Web site: www.canauthors.org. **Contact:** Alec McEachern. Annual contest for the best English-language play for adults by an author who is Canadian or a landed immigrant. Obtain form from contact name or download from Web site. **Deadline: December 15; plays published or performed in December are due January 15. Charges $35 (Canadian funds).** Prize: $1,000 and a silver medal. Judged by a trustee for the award (appointed by the CAA). The trustee appoints up to 3 judges. The identities of the trustee and judges are confidential. Short lists are not made public. Decisions of the trustee and judges are final, and they may choose not to award a prize.

COE COLLEGE PLAYWRITING FESTIVAL

Coe College, 1220 First Ave. NE, Cedar Rapids IA 52402-5092. (319)399-8624. Fax: (319)399-8557. E-mail: swolvert@coe.edu. Web site: www.theatre.coe.edu. **Contact:** Susan Wolverton. Estab. 1993. Offered biennially for unpublished work to provide a venue for new works for the stage. "There is usually a theme for the festival. We are interested in full-length productions, not one-acts or musicals. There are no specific criteria although a current résumé and synopsis is requested." Open to any writer. **Deadline: November 1. Notification: January 15.** Guidelines for SASE. Prize: $350, plus 1-week residency as guest artist with airfare, room and board provided.

DAYTON PLAYHOUSE FUTUREFEST

The Dayton Playhouse, 1301 E. Siebenthaler Ave., Dayton OH 45414-5357. (937)424-8477. Web site: www.daytonplayhouse.org. **Contact:** Adam J. Leigh, executive director. Three plays selected for full productions, 3 for readings at July FutureFest weekend. The 6 authors will be given travel and lodging to attend the festival. Professionally adjudicated. Guidelines for SASE or online. **Deadline: October 31.** Prize: $1,000; $100 goes to the other 5 playwrights.

DRURY UNIVERSITY ONE-ACT PLAY CONTEST

Drury University, 900 N. Benton Ave., Springfield MO 65802-3344. E-mail: msokol@drury.edu. **Contact:** Mick Sokol. Offered in even-numbered years for unpublished and professionally unproduced plays. One play/playwright. Guidelines for SASE or by e-mail. **Deadline: December 1.**

DUBUQUE FINE ARTS PLAYERS ANNUAL ONE-ACT PLAY CONTEST

Dubuque Fine Arts Players, 1686 Lawndale, Dubuque IA 52001. E-mail: gary.arms@clarke.edu. **Contact:** Gary Arms. "We select 3 one-act plays each year. We award cash prizes of up to $600 for a winning entry. We produce the winning plays in August." Offered annually for unpublished work. Guidelines and application form for SASE. **Deadline: January 31. Charges $10.** Prize: 1st Place: $600; 2nd Place: $300; 3rd Place: $200. Judged by 3 groups who read all the plays; each play is read at least twice. Plays that score high enough enter the second round. The top 10 plays are read by a panel consisting of 3 directors and 2 other final judges. Open to any writer.

[N] EMERGING PLAYWRIGHT'S AWARD

Urban Stages, 17 E. 47th St., New York NY 10017-1920. (212)421-1380. Fax: (212)421-1387. E-mail: sonia@urbanstages.org. Web site: www.urbanstages.org. **Contact:** Sonia Kozlova, managing director. Estab. 1986. Submissions must be unproduced in New York City. Prefers full-length plays; subject matter and charager variations are open (no translations or adapatations). Cast size is limited to 9 actors. Send script, bio, production history, character breakdown, synopsis, and SASE. Submissions are accepted year-round and plays are selected in the spring. **Deadline: Ongoing.** Prize: $500 (in lieu of royalties), and a staged production of winning play in New York City. Open to US residents only.

ESSENTIAL THEATRE PLAYWRITING AWARD

The Essential Theatre, P.O. Box 8172, Atlanta GA 30306. (404)212-0815. E-mail: pmhardy@aol.com. Web site: www.essentialtheatre.com. **Contact:** Peter Hardy. Offered annually for unproduced, full-length plays by Georgia resident writers. No limitations as to style or subject matter. **Deadline: April 23.** Prize: $500 and full production.

THE LOUIS ESSON PRIZE FOR DRAMA

Victorian Premier's Literary Awards, State Library of Victoria, 328 Swanston St., Melbourne VIC 3000 Australia. (61)(3)8664-7277. E-mail: pla@slv.vic.gov.au. Web site: www.slv.vic.gov.au/pla. **Contact:** Project Officer. Prize for theatre or radio scripts produced between May 1 and April 30. The State Library of Victoria reserves the right to place a copy of all nominated works in its collection. Further copyright remains with the author. **Deadline: May 4.** Guidelines for SASE. Prize: $15,000. Open to Australian citizens or permanent residents.

FEATURE LENGTH SCREENPLAY COMPETITION

Austin Film Festival, 1604 Nueces St., Austin TX 78701. (512)478-4795. Fax: (512)478-6205. E-mail: info@austinfilmfestival.com. Web site: www.austinfilmfestival.com. Offered annually for unpublished screenplays. The Austin Film Festival is looking for quality screenplays which will be read by industry professionals. Two competitions: Adult/Family Category and Comedy Category. Guidelines for SASE or call (800)310-3378. The writer must hold the rights when submitted; it must be original work. The screenplay must be 90-130 pages and it must be in industry standard screenplay format. **Deadline: May 15 (early); June 1 (late). Charges $40/early entry; $50/late entry.** Prize: $5,000 in each category.

SHUBERT FENDRICH MEMORIAL PLAYWRITING CONTEST

Pioneer Drama Service, Inc., P.O. Box 4267, Englewood CO 80155. (303)779-4035. Fax: (303)779-4315. E-mail: submissions@pioneerdrama.com. Web site: www.pioneerdrama.com. **Contact:** Lori Conary, assistant editor. Offered annually for unpublished, but previously produced, submissions to encourage the development of quality theatrical material for educational and community theater. Rights acquired only if published. Authors already published by Pioneer Drama are not eligible. **Deadline: December 31 (postmarked).** Guidelines for SASE. Prize: $1,000 royalty advance and publication.

[N] FESTIVAL OF NEW AMERICAN PLAYS

Firehouse Theatre Project, 1609 W. Broad St., Richmond VA 23220. (804)355-2001. E-mail: info@firehousetheatre.org. Web site: www.firehousetheatre.org. **Contact:** Carol Piersol, artistic director. Annual contest designed to support new and emerging American playwrights. Scripts must be full-length and previously unpublished/unproduced. (Readings are acceptable if no admission was charged.) Submissions should be mailed in hard copy form and accompanied by a letter of recommendation from a theater company or individual familiar with your work. **Deadline: July 31.** Annual deadline is adjusted depending on the volume of plays received. Prize: 1st Place: $1,000 and a staged reading; 2nd Place: $500 and a staged reading. All plays are initially read by a panel of individuals with experience in playwriting and literature. Previous judges have included Lloyd Rose (former *Washington Post* theatre critic), Bill Patton (frequent Firehouse director), Richard Toscan (dean of the Virginia Commonwealth University School for the Arts), and Israel Horovitz (playwright). All finalists are asked to sign a contract with the Firehouse Theatre Project that guarantees performance rights for the staged reading in January and printed credit for Firehouse Theatre Project if the play is produced/published in the future. All American playwrights are welcome to submit their work.

FIREHOUSE THEATRE PROJECT NEW PLAY COMPETITION

The Firehouse Theatre Project, 1609 W. Broad St., Richmond VA 23220. (804)355-2001. Web site: www.firehousetheatre.org. **Contact:** Literary Manager FTP. Calls for previously unpublished full-length works with non-musical and non-children's themes. Submissions must be in standard play format. Scripts should be accompanied by a letter of recommendation from a company or individual familiar with your work. Submissions must be unpublished. Visit Web site for complete submission guidelines. "We're receptive to unusual, but well-wrought works." **Deadline: July 31.** Prize: 1st Prize: $1,000; 2nd Prize: $500. Judged by a committee selected by the executive board of the Firehouse Theatre Project. Acquires the right to produce the winning scripts for the FTP Festival of New American Plays. Following the Festival production dates, all rights are relinquished to the author. Open to US residents only.

JOHN GASSNER MEMORIAL PLAYWRITING COMPETITION

New England Theatre Conference, 215 Knob Hill Dr., Hamden CT 06158. Fax: (203)288-5938. E-mail: mail@netconline.org. Web site: www.netconline.org. Offered annually to unpublished full-length plays and scripts. Open to New England residents and NETC members. Playwrights living outside New England may participate by joining NETC. **Deadline: April 15.** Guidelines for SASE. **Charges $10 fee.** Prize: 1st Place: $1,000; 2nd Place: $500.

Contests & Awards

GOVERNOR GENERAL'S LITERARY AWARD FOR DRAMA

Canada Council for the Arts, 350 Albert St., P.O. Box 1047, Ottawa ON K1P 5V8, Canada. (613)566-4414, ext. 5573. Fax: (613)566-4410. Web site: www.canadacouncil.ca/prizes/ggla. Offered for the best English-language and the best French-language work of drama by a Canadian. **Deadline: March 15 or August 7, depending on the book's publication date.** Prize: Each laureate receives $15,000; nonwinning finalists receive $1,000.

AURAND HARRIS MEMORIAL PLAYWRITING AWARD

The New England Theatre Conference, Inc., 215 Knob Hill Dr., Hamden CT 06518. Fax: (203)288-5938. E-mail: mail@netconline.org. Web site: www.netconline.org. Offered annually for an unpublished full-length play for young audiences. Guidelines for SASE. "No phone calls, please." Open to New England residents and/or members of the New England Theatre Conference. **Deadline: May 1.** Guidelines for SASE. **Charges $20 fee.** Prize: 1st Place: $1,000; 2nd Place: $500. Open to any writer.

HENRICO THEATRE COMPANY ONE-ACT PLAYWRITING COMPETITION

Henrico Recreation & Parks, P.O. Box 27032, Richmond VA 23273. (804)501-5138. Fax: (804)501-5284. E-mail: per22@co.henrico.va.us. Web site: www.co.henrico.va.us/rec. **Contact:** Amy A. Perdue. Offered annually for previously unpublished or unproduced plays or musicals to produce new dramatic works in one-act form. Scripts with small casts and simpler sets given preference. Controversial themes and excessive language should be avoided. **Deadline: July 1.** Guidelines for SASE. Prize: $300; Runner-Up: $200. Winning entries may be produced; videotape sent to author.

HOLLYWOOD SCREENPLAY AWARDS

433 N. Camden Dr., Suite 600, Beverly Hills CA 90210. (310)288-3040. Fax: (310)288-0060. E-mail: hollyinfo@hollywoodnetwork.com. Web site: www.hollywoodawards.com. Annual contest that bridges the gap between writers and the established entertainment industry and provides winning screenwriters what they need most: access to key decision-makers. Only non-produced, non-optioned screenplays can be submitted. **Deadline: March 31.** Guidelines for SASE. **Charges $55 fee.** Prize: 1st Prize $1,000; 2nd Prize $500; 3rd Prize $250. Scripts are also introduced to major studios and winners receive 2 VIP passes to the Hollywood Film Festival. Judged by reputable industry professionals (producers, development executives, story analysts). Open to any writer.

N THE KAUFMAN & HART PRIZE FOR NEW AMERICAN COMEDY

Arkansas Repertory Theatre, P.O. Box 110, Little Rock AR 72201. (501)378-0445. Web site: www.therep.org. **Contact:** Brad Mooy, literary manager. Offered every 2 years for unpublished, unproduced, full-length comedies (no musicals or children's plays). Scripts may be submitted with the recommendation of an agent or theater professional only. Must be at least 65 pages, with minimal set requirements and a cast limit of 12. One entry/playwright. Open to US citizens only. **Deadline: February 1.** Prize: $10,000, a staged reading, and transportation.

MAXIM MAZUMDAR NEW PLAY COMPETITION

Alleyway Theatre, 1 Curtain Up Alley, Buffalo NY 14202. (716)852-2600. Fax: (716)852-2266. E-mail: newplays@alleyway.com. Web site: www.alleyway.com. **Contact:** Literary Manager. Estab. 1989. Annual competition. Full Length: Not less than 90 minutes, no more than 10 performers. One-Act: Less than 20 minutes, no more than 6 performers. Musicals must be accompanied by audio CD/tape. Finalists announced October 1; winners announced November 1. Playwrights may submit work directly. There is no entry form. Writers may submit once in each category, but pay only 1 fee. Please specify if submission is to be included in competition. Alleyway Theatre must receive first production credit in subsequent printings and productions. **Deadline: July 1. Charges $25.** Prize: Full length: $400, production, and royalties; One-act: $100, production, and royalties. Open to any writer.

MCLAREN MEMORIAL COMEDY PLAY WRITING COMPETITION

Midland Community Theatre, 2000 W. Wadley, Midland TX 79705. (432)682-2544. Fax: (432)682-6136. Web site: www.mctmidland.org. Estab. 1990. Offered annually in 2 divisions: one-act and full-length. All entries must be comedies for adults, teens, or children; musical comedies accepted. Work must have never been professionally produced or published. See Web site for competition guidelines and required entry form. **Deadline: December 1-January 31. Charges $15/script.** Prize: $400 for winning full-length play; $200 for winning one-act play; staged readings for finalists in each category.

N MOVING ARTS PREMIERE ONE-ACT COMPETITION

Moving Arts, P.O. Box 481145, Los Angeles CA 90048. (213)622-8906. Fax: (213)622-8946. E-mail: info@movingarts.org. Web site: www.movingarts.org. **Contact:** Trey Nichols. Offered annually for unproduced one-act plays in the Los Angeles area (single set; maximum cast of 8 people). All playwrights are eligible except Moving Arts resident artists. Send 5-70 pages, cover letter, and SASE. Guidelines online, for SASE, or by e-mail. **Deadline: November 1-February 1 (postmarked). Charges $10 fee/script.** Prize: 1st Place: $200, plus a full production with a 4-8 week run; finalists get program mention and possible production.

NATIONAL CANADIAN ONE-ACT PLAYWRITING COMPETITION

Ottawa Little Theatre, 400 King Edward Ave., Ottawa ON K1N 7M7, Canada. (613)233-8948. Fax: (613)233-8027. E-mail: olt@on-aibn.com. Web site: www.ottawalittletheatre.com. **Contact:** Elizabeth Holden, office administrator. Estab. 1913. Purpose is to encourage literary and dramatic talent in Canada. Guidelines for #10 SASE with Canadian postage or #10 SAE with 1 IRC. **Deadline: August 31.** Prize: 1st Place: $1,000; 2nd Place: $700; 3rd Place: $500.

NATIONAL CHILDREN'S THEATRE FESTIVAL

Actors' Playhouse at the Miracle Theatre, 280 Miracle Mile, Coral Gables FL 33134. (305)444-9293, ext. 615. Fax: (305)444-4181. E-mail: maulding@actorsplayhouse.org. Web site: www.actorsplayhouse.org. **Contact:** Earl Maulding. Offered annually for unpublished musicals for young audiences. Target age is 3-12. Script length should be 45-60 minutes. Maximum of 8 actors to play any number of roles. Prefer settings which lend themselves to simplified scenery. Bilingual (English/Spanish) scripts are welcomed. Call or visit Web site for guidelines. Open to any writer. **Deadline: May 1. Charges $10 fee.** Prize: $500 and full production.

NATIONAL TEN-MINUTE PLAY CONTEST

Actors Theatre of Louisville, 316 W. Main St., Louisville KY 40202-4218. (502)584-1265. Web site: www.actorstheatre.org. Offered annually for previously (professionally) unproduced 10-minute plays (10 pages or less). "Entries must *not* have had an Equity or Equity-waiver production." One submission/playwright. Scripts are not returned. Please write or call for submission guidelines. Open to US residents. **Deadline: November 1 (postmarked).** Prize: $1,000.

NEW WORKS FOR THE STAGE

COE College Theatre Arts Department, 1220 First Ave. NE, Cedar Rapids IA 52402. (319)399-8624. Fax: (319)399-8557. E-mail: swolvert@coe.edu. Web site: www.public.coe.edu/departments/theatre. **Contact:** Susan Wolverton. Offered in odd-numbered years to encourage new work, to provide an interdisciplinary forum for the discussion of issues found in new work, and to offer playwright contact with theater professionals who can provide response to new work. Full-length, original, unpublished and unproduced scripts only. No musicals, adaptations, translations, or collaborations. Submit 1-page synopsis, résumé, and SASE if the script is to be returned. **Deadline: November 1.** Prize: $325, plus travel, room and board for residency at the college.

DON AND GEE NICHOLL FELLOWSHIPS IN SCREENWRITING

Academy of Motion Picture Arts & Sciences, 1313 N. Vine St., Hollywood CA 90028-8107. (310)247-3010. E-mail: nicholl@oscars.org. Web site: www.oscars.org/nicholl. Estab. 1985. Offered annually for unproduced screenplays to identify talented new screenwriters. **Deadline: May 1. Charges $30 fee.** Prize: Up to five $30,000 fellowships awarded each year. Open to writers who have not earned more than $5,000 writing for films or TV.

ONE ACT MARATHON

Attic Theatre Ensemble, 5429 W. Washington Blvd., Los Angeles CA 90016-1112. (323)525-0600. E-mail: info@attictheatre.org. Web site: www.attictheatre.org. **Contact:** Literary Manager. Offered annually for unpublished and unproduced work. Scripts should be intended for mature audiences. Length should not exceed 45 minutes. Guidelines for SASE or online. **Deadline: December 31. Charges $15.** Prize: 1st Place: $300; 2nd Place: $100.

N THE PAGE INTERNATIONAL SCREENWRITING AWARDS

The PAGE Awards Committee, 7510 Sunset Blvd., #610, Hollywood CA 90046-3408. E-mail: info@internationalscreenwritingawards.com. Web site: www.internationalscreenwritingawards.com. **Contact:** Jennifer Berg, administrative director. Annual competition to discover the most talented new screenwriters from across the country and around the world. Each year, awards are presented to 28 screenwriters in 9 different categories: action/adventure, comedy, drama, family film, science fiction/fantasy, thriller/horror, short film script, 1-hour TV pilot, half-hour TV pilot. Guidelines and entry forms are online. **Deadline: January 31 (early); March 15 (regular); April 30 (late). Charges $39 (early); $49 (regular); $59 (late).** Prize: "Each year we present more than $25,000 in cash and prizes, including a $10,000 grand prize, plus gold, silver, and bronze prizes in all 9 categories. Most importantly, the award-winning writers receive extensive publicity and industry exposure." Judging is done entirely by Hollywood professionals, including script readers, consultants, agents, managers, producers, and development executives. Entrants retain all rights to their work. The contest is open to all writers 18 years of age and older who have not previously earned more than $25,000 writing for film and/or television. Go online for a complete list of rules and regulations.

MILDRED & ALBERT PANOWSKI PLAYWRITING AWARD

Forest Roberts Theatre, Northern Michigan University, Marquette MI 49855-5364. (906)227-2559. Fax: (906)227-2567. Web site: www.nmu.edu/theatre. **Contact:** Award Coordinator. Estab. 1977. Offered annually for unpublished, unproduced, full-length plays. Guidelines and application for SASE. **Deadline: July 15-October 31.** Prize: $2,000, a summer workshop, a fully-mounted production, and transportation to Marquette to serve as Artist-in-Residence the week of the show.

ROBERT J. PICKERING AWARD FOR PLAYWRIGHTING EXCELLENCE

Coldwater Community Theater, % 89 Division, Coldwater MI 49036. (517)279-7963. Fax: (517)279-8095. **Contact:** J. Richard Colbeck, committee chairperson. Estab. 1982. Contest to encourage playwrights to submit their work and to present a previously unproduced play in full production. Must be previously unproduced monetarily. Submit script with SASE. "We reserve the right to produce winning script." **Deadline: December 31.** Guidelines for SASE. Prize: 1st Place: $300; 2nd Place: $100; 3rd Place: $50.

PLAYING BY THE LAKE SCRIPTWRITING CONTEST

Lake County Repertory Theater, 4388, Clearlake CA 95422. E-mail: ljaltman2@mchsi.com. Web site: lcrt_festival.home.mchsi.com/homepage.htm. **Contact:** Linda J. Altman, contest coordinator. Award offered every even-numbered year for unproduced scripts to help new playwrights and bring original theater to local audiences. Guidelines and entry form for SASE or online. **Deadline: January 1-April 15. Charges $10.** Prize: $300, full production by LCRT, video of performance, and consideration by a major play publisher. Judged by a panel of professional writers, actors, directors, and teachers. Open to any writer.

PLAYS FOR THE 21ST CENTURY

Playwrights Theater, 6732 Orangewood Dr., Dallas TX 75248-5024. E-mail: contest@playwrightstheater.org. Web site: www.playwrightstheater.org. Annual contest for unpublished or professionally unproduced plays (at time of submission). **Deadline: March 22. Charges $20.** Prize: $1,500 first prize; $500 each for second and third prizes. First prize receives a rehearsed reading. The judges decide on readings for second and third prizes. "Winners and their bios and contact info are posted on our Web site with a 15-page sample of the play (with playwright's permission)." All rights remain with the author. Judged by an outside panel of 3 theater professionals. The judges are different each year. Open to any writer.

PLAYWRIGHTS/SCREENWRITERS FELLOWSHIPS

NC Arts Council, Dept. of Cultural Resources, Raleigh NC 27699-4632. (919)807-6512. Fax: (919)807-6525. E-mail: debbie.mcgill@ncmail.net. Web site: www.ncarts.org. **Contact:** Deborah McGill, literature director. Offered every even year to support the development and creation of new work. See Web site for guidelines and other elegibility requirements. **Deadline: November 1.** Prize: $8,000 grant. Judged by a panel of film and theater professionals (playwrights, screenwriters, directors, producers, etc.). Artists must be current North Carolina residents who have lived in the state for at least 1 year as of the application deadline. Grant recipients must maintain their North Carolina status during the grant year and may not pursue academic or professional degrees during that period.

PRINCESS GRACE AWARDS PLAYWRIGHT FELLOWSHIP

Princess Grace Foundation—USA, 150 E. 58th St., 25th Floor, New York NY 10155. (212)317-1470. Fax: (212)317-1473. E-mail: pgfusa@pgfusa.com. Web site: www.pgfusa.com. **Contact:** Christine Giancatarino, grants coordinator. Offered annually for unpublished, unproduced submissions to support playwright-through-residency program with New Dramatists, Inc., located in New York City. Entrants must be US citizens or have permanent US status. Guidelines for SASE or on Web site. **Deadline: March 31.** Prize: $7,500, plus residency with New Dramatists, Inc., in New York City, and representation/publication by Samuel French, Inc.

THE SCREENWRITER'S PROJECT

Indiefest: Film Festival & Market, P.O. Box 148849, Chicago IL 60614-8849. (773)665-7600. Fax: (773)665-7660. E-mail: info@indiefestchicago.com. Web site: www.indiefestchicago.com. Offered annually to give both experienced and first-time writers the opportunity to begin a career as a screenwriter. **Deadline: January 1; March 1; April 1.** Guidelines for SASE. **Charges $40-100.** Prize: Various cash awards and prizes.

N SCRIPT PIMP SCREENWRITING COMPETITION

Script P.I.M.P., 5723 Melrose Ave., Suite 100, Los Angeles CA 90038. (310)401-1155. Fax: (310)564-2021. E-mail: competition@scriptpimp.com. Web site: scriptpimp.com. **Contact:** Chadwick Clough. Annual international competition open to all original English-written feature film screenplays that have yet to be produced, optioned, or sold. ''We're looking for the best stories told by the best screenwriters demonstrating the best craft.'' The awards ceremony gathers hundreds of film industry professionals who meet with the finalists to provide advice and potential leads. Guidelines available for SASE or online. **Deadline: May 1. Charges $40.** Prize: Four grand-prize winners will each receive $2,500. In addition to mentor meetings, each of the 20 finalists will be guaranteed circulation of their script to over 20 companies, free 5-year memberships to Script P.I.M.P.'s Writers Database, and featured posting of their script in the Script Pimp Finalist listing on InkTip‹. Judged by a panel of working literary agents, literary managers, and development directors from the film industry. Each screenplay is guaranteed 2 reads from the panel of judges. Script P.I.M.P. does not acquire any rights to materials submitted through the contest. Open to writers 18 years and older who are the exclusive owner of all rights, titles, and interest in the script. Entrants must not have received sole or shared writing, directing, or producing credit on any film, series, or episode that has been produced for presentation in theatres or on TV. Individuals who have sold or optioned any screenplay for $15,000 or more are ineligible.

SCRIPTAPALOOZA SCREENWRITING COMPETITION

Supported by Writers Guild of America West and sponsored by Write Brothers, Inc., 7775 Sunset Blvd., PMB #200, Hollywood CA 90046. (323)654-5809. E-mail: info@scriptapalooza.com. Web site: www.scriptapalooza.com. Annual competition for unpublished scripts from any genre. Open to any writer, 18 or older. Submit 1 copy of a 90- 130-page screenplay. Body pages must be numbered, and scripts must be in industry-standard format. All entered scripts will be read and judged by over 60 production companies. **Deadline: Early Deadline: January 5; Deadline: March 3; Late Deadline: April 14.** Guidelines for SASE. **Charges $40 (early); $45 (regular deadline); $50 (late).** Prize: 1st Place: $10,000 and software package from Write Brothers, Inc; 2nd Place, 3rd Place, and 10 Runners-Up: Software package from Write Brothers, Inc. The top 13 scripts will be considered by over 60 production companies.

SCRIPTAPALOOZA TELEVISION WRITING COMPETITION

7775 Sunset Blvd., PMB #200, Hollywood CA 90046. (323)654-5809. E-mail: info@scriptapalooza.com. Web site: www.scriptapaloozatv.com. Biannual competition accepting entries in 4 categories: reality shows, sitcoms, original pilots, and 1-hour dramas. There are more than 25 producers, agents, and managers reading the winning scripts. Two past winners won Emmys because of Scriptapalooza and 1 past entrant now writes for Comedy Central. **Deadline: October 15 and April 15.** Guidelines for SASE. **Charges $40.** Prize: 1st Place: $500; 2nd Place: $200; 3rd Place: $100 (in each category). Open to any writer.

REVA SHINER FULL-LENGTH PLAY CONTEST

Bloomington Playwrights Project, 107 W. 9th St., Bloomington IN 47404. E-mail: bppwrite@newplays.org. Web site: www.newplays.org. **Contact:** Literary Manager. Annual award for unpublished/unproduced plays. The Bloomington Playwrights Project is a script-developing organization. Winning playwrights are expected to become part of the development process, working with the director in person or via long-distance. **Deadline:**

Contests & Awards

October 31. Guidelines for SASE. **Charges $10 reading fee.** Prize: $500, a reading, and possible production. Judged by the literary committee of the BPP. Open to any writer.

SIENA COLLEGE INTERNATIONAL PLAYWRIGHTS COMPETITION

Siena College Theatre Program, 515 Loudon Rd., Loudonville NY 12211-1462. (518)783-2381. Fax: (518)783-2381. E-mail: maciag@siena.edu. Web site: www.siena.edu/theatre. **Contact:** Gary Maciag, director. Offered every 2 years for unpublished plays to allow students to explore production collaboration with the playwright. In addition, it provides the playwright an important development opportunity. Plays should be previously unproduced, unpublished, full-length, nonmusicals, and free of copyright and royalty restrictions. Plays should require unit set, or minimal changes, and be suitable for a college-age cast of 3-10. There is a required 4-6 week residency. Guidelines for SASE. Guidelines are available after November 1 in odd-numbered years. Winning playwright must agree that the Siena production will be the world premiere of the play. **Deadline: February 1-June 30 in even-numbered years.** Prize: $2,000 honorarium, up to $2,000 to cover expenses for required residency, and full production of winning script.

DOROTHY SILVER PLAYWRITING COMPETITION

The Jewish Community Center of Cleveland, 26001 S. Woodland, Beachwood OH 44122. (216)831-0700. Fax: (216)831-7796. E-mail: dbobrow@clevejcc.org. Web site: www.clevejcc.org. **Contact:** Deborah Bobrow, competition coordinator. Estab. 1948. All entries must be original works, not previously produced, suitable for a full-length presentation, and directly concerned with the Jewish experience. **Deadline: December 31.** Prize: Cash award and a staged reading.

N SLAMDANCE SCREENPLAY COMPETITION

WGA-West/*Script Magazine*/Final Draft/Writers Bootcamp, 5634 Melrose Ave., Los Angeles CA 90038. (323)466-1786. E-mail: screenplay@slamdance.com. Web site: www.slamdance.com/screencomp. **Contact:** John Stoddard. Annual competition to discover and support emerging screenwriting talent. Entrants must be first-time writers and cannot submit material that has been previously optioned, purchased, or produced by non-indepenedent means. Entrants cannot have won awards from other competitions, nor can they have any previously produced/distributed projects. Applications are available online. **Deadline: June 1. Charges $40.** Prize: $7,000, Writers Bookcamp certificates, Final Draft software, *Script Magazine* subscription, Slamdance Film Festival passes, staged reading in Los Angeles, and elgibility for membership in the WGA's Independent Writers Caucus. No rights are required—register your work before entering the competition. Judged by Slamdance alumni screenwriters, filmmakers, professional writers, journalists, playwrights, and readers with a background in development/production.

N SOUTHEASTERN CREATIVE MEDIA COMPETITION

GAMMA, P.O. Box 50238, Summerville SC 29485. (843)276-1875. E-mail: gammamotionpictures@yahoo.com. Web site: www.geocities.com/gammamotionpictures. **Contact:** Kirk and Kelly Lowe. Annual competition to promote and encourage media development in the Charleston, S.C. area, the southeastern US, and the world. Categories include: motion picture (short), motion picture (feature), screenplay, and music (includes music video). **Deadline: September 15. Charges $8-10.** Prize: $100 for the best entry in each category. Non-cash awards (certificates) will also be given for the best in each genre/style under each category. Judged by the general partners of GAMMA and other drama/media-related volunteers. Open to any writer.

SOUTHEASTERN THEATRE CONFERENCE NEW PLAY PROJECT

Department of Theatre & Dance, Southeast Missouri State University, 1 University Plaza: MS 2800, Cape Girardeau MO 63701. E-mail: kstilson@semo.edu. Web site: www.setc.org. **Contact:** Kenn Stilson. Annual award for full-length plays. No musicals or children's plays. Submissions must be unproduced/unpublished. Submit application, synopsis, and 1 copy of script on CD or as an e-mail attachment (preferred). Send SASE or visit Web site for application. **Deadline: June 1.** Prize: $1,000 and a staged reading.

SOUTHERN PLAYWRIGHTS COMPETITION

Jacksonville State University, 700 Pelham Rd. N., Jacksonville AL 36265-1602. (256)782-5414. Fax: (256)782-5441. E-mail: jmaloney@jsu.edu; swhitton@jsu.edu. Web site: www.jsu.edu/depart/english/southpla.htm. **Contact:** Joy Maloney, Steven J. Whitton. Estab. 1988. Offered annually to identify and encourage the best of Southern playwriting. Playwrights must be a native or resident of Alabama, Arkansas, Florida, Georgia, Kentucky, Louisiana, Missouri, North Carolina, South Carolina, Tennessee, Texas, Virginia, or West Virginia. **Deadline: February 15.** Guidelines for SASE. Prize: $1,000 and production of the play.

TELEPLAY COMPETITION
Austin Film Festival, 1604 Nueces St., Austin TX 78701. (512)478-4795. Fax: (512)478-6205. E-mail: info@austinfilmfestival.con. Web site: www.austinfilmfestival.com. Offered annually for unpublished work to discover talented television writers and introduce their work to production companies. Categories: drama and sitcom (must be based on current television program). Contest open to writers who do not earn a living writing for television or film. **Deadline: June 1.** Guidelines for SASE. **Charges $30.** Prize: $1,000 in each category.

10-MINUTE PLAY FESTIVAL
Fire Rose Productions & International Arts Group, 11246 Magnolia Blvd., NoHo Theatre & Arts District CA 91601. E-mail: info@fireroseproductions.com. Web site: www.fireroseproductions.com. **Contact:** Kaz Matamura, director. Contest is offered twice a year for unpublished and unproduced plays that are 8-12 minutes long. Fire Rose Productions & International Arts Group are nonprofit organizations that are committed to discovering new playwrights and giving them opportunities to work with directors and producers. **Deadline: June 30 and December 31.** Guidelines for SASE. **Charges $5; $2/additional submission.** Prize: 1st Place: $250; 2nd Place: $100; profesionally mounted production for winners and semi-finalists. Guest judges are entertainment professionals including writers, producers, directors, and agents. Fire Rose Productions does the first evaluation. Acquires right to produce and mount the plays if chosen as festival finalists or semi-finalists. No royalties are gathered for those performances. Open to any writer.

THE PEN IS A MIGHTY SWORD
The Virtual Theatre Project, P.O. Box 29340, Los Angeles CA 90029. (323)663-0112. Fax: (323)660-5097. E-mail: info@virtualtheatreproject.com. Web site: www.virtualtheatreproject.org. **Contact:** Whit Andrews. Annual contest open to unproduced plays written specifically for the stage. Plays should be bold, compelling, and passionate. Guidelines for SASE or online. **Deadline: June 30. Charges $35.** Prize: 1st Place: $2,000 and full, 6-week premiere production; 2nd Place: $1,000 and a staged reading; 3rd Place: $500 and a reading. In addition, up to 7 honorable mentions receive $100 each. Judged by a panel of professional writers, directors, and producers. Open to any writer.

THEATRE BC'S ANNUAL CANADIAN NATIONAL PLAYWRITING COMPETITION
Theatre BC, P.O. Box 2031, Nanaimo BC V9R 6X6, Canada. (250)714-0203. Fax: (250)714-0213. E-mail: pwc@theatrebc.org. Web site: www.theatrebc.org. **Contact:** Robb Mowbray, executive director. Offered annually to unpublished plays to promote the development and production of previously unproduced new plays (no musicals) at all levels of theater. Categories: Full Length (75 minutes or longer); One-Act (less than 75 minutes); and an open Special Merit (juror's discretion). Guidelines for SASE or online. Winners are also invited to New Play Festival: Up to 16 hours with a professional dramaturg, registrant actors, and a public reading in Kamloops (every Spring). Production and publishing rights remain with the playwright. Open to Canadian residents. All submissions are made under pseudonyms. E-mail inquiries welcome. **Deadline: Fourth Monday in July. Charges $40/entry; optional $25 for written critique.** Prize: Full Length: $1,000; One-Act: $750; Special Merit: $500.

THEATRE CONSPIRACY ANNUAL NEW PLAY CONTEST
Theatre Conspiracy, 10091 McGregor Blvd., Ft. Myers FL 33919. (239)936-3239. Fax: (239)936-0510. E-mail: info@theatreconspiracy.org. **Contact:** Bill Taylor, artistic director. Offered annually for full-length plays that are unproduced or have received up to 3 productions with 8 or less characters and simple to moderate production demands. No musicals. One entry per year. Send SASE for contest results. **Deadline: March 30. Charges $5 fee.** Prize: $700 and full production. Open to any writer.

THEATRE PUBLICUS PRIZE FOR DRAMATIC LITERATURE
Media Darlings Literature, Art & Sound, 5201 Great America Parkway, Suite 320, Santa Clara CA 95054. E-mail: dropbox@mediadarlings.org. Web site: www.mediadarlings.org/publicus. Annual competition to recognize the work of emerging playwrights and to provide promotional and financial support to innovative new talent who may be overlooked by mainstream literary or theater circles. Submissions are accepted regardless of content, genre, or theme. No musicals, please. **Deadline: August 31.** Guidelines for SASE. **Charges $10/one-act plays; $20/full-length plays.** Prize: $200 for jury prize (best overall); $150 each for best one-act and full-length plays. Judged by the staff of Media Darlings Literature, Art & Sound—an arts collective based in the San Francisco Bay area. The staff includes published fiction writers, editors, and former industry professionals. Open to all American and Canadian playwrights over the age of 18 who have completed a one-act or full-length play since 2003.

THEATREPEI NEW VOICES PLAYWRITING COMPETITION

P.O. Box 1573, Charlottetown PE C1A 7N3, Canada. (902)894-3558. Fax: (902)368-7180. E-mail: theatre@isn.net. Web site: theatrepei.org. **Contact:** Dawn Binkley, general manager. Offered annually. Open to individuals who have been residents of Prince Edward Island for 6 months preceding the deadline for entries. Guidelines online or for SASE. **Deadline: February 14. Charges $5 fee.** Prize: Full-length Plays—1st Place: $500; 2nd Place: $300. One-Act Plays—1st Place: $200; 2nd Place: $100. High School Entries—Winning English-language play: $100; Winning French-languagle play: $100.

TRUSTUS PLAYWRIGHTS' FESTIVAL

Trustus Theatre, Box 11721, Columbia SC 29211-1721. (803)254-9732. Fax: (803)771-9153. E-mail: trustus@trustus.org. Web site: www.trustus.org. **Contact:** Jon Tuttle, literary manager. Offered annually for professionally unproduced full-length plays; cast limit of 8. Prefers challenging, innovative dramas and comedies. No musicals, plays for young audiences, or "hillbilly" southern shows. Send SASE or consult Trustus Web site for guidelines and application. **Deadline: December 1, 2008-February 28, 2009.** Prize: $500 and a 1-year development period with full production and travel/accommodations to attend the public opening.

UNICORN THEATRE NEW PLAY DEVELOPMENT

Unicorn Theatre, 3828 Main St., Kansas City MO 64111. (816)531-7529, ext. 22. Fax: (816)531-0421. Web site: www.unicorntheatre.org. **Contact:** Herman Wilson, literary assistant. Offered annually to encourage and assist the development of an unpublished and unproduced play. "We look for nonmusical, issue-oriented, thought-provoking plays set in contemporary times (post 1950s) with a cast limit of 10." Submit cover letter, brief bio/résumé, short synopsis, complete character breakdown, complete ms, SASE. Does not return scripts. **Deadline: Ongoing.** Guidelines for SASE. Prize: $1,000 royalty and production. Acquires 2% subsidiary rights of future productions for a 5-year period.

VERMONT PLAYWRIGHT'S AWARD

The Valley Players, P.O. Box 441, Waitsfield VT 05673. (802)496-3751. E-mail: valleyplayer@madriver.com. Web site: www.valleyplayers.com. **Contact:** Jennifer Howard, chair. Offered annually for unpublished, nonmusical, full-length plays suitable for production by a community theater group to encourage development of playwrights in Vermont, New Hampshire, and Maine. **Deadline: February 1.** Prize: $1,000.

THE HERMAN VOADEN NATIONAL PLAYWRITING COMPETITION

Drama Department, Queen's University, Kingston ON K7L 3N6, Canada. (613)533-2104. E-mail: hannaca@post.queensu.ca. Web site: www.queensu.ca/drama. **Contact:** Carol Anne Hanna. Offered every 2 years for unpublished plays to discover and develop new Canadian plays. See Web site for deadlines and guidelines. Open to Canadian citizens or landed immigrants. **Charges $30 entry fee.** Prize: $3,000, $2,000, and 8 honorable mentions. 1st- and 2nd-prize winners are offered a 1-week workshop and public reading by professional director and cast. The 2 authors will be playwrights-in-residence for the rehearsal and reading period.

WRITE A PLAY! NYC

Young Playwrights, Inc., P.O. Box 5134, New York NY 10185. (212)594-5440. Fax: (212)684-4902. Web site: youngplaywrights.org. **Contact:** Literary Department. Offered annually for plays by NYC elementary, middle, and high school students only. **Deadline: March 20.** Prize: Varies.

YEAR END SERIES (YES) NEW PLAY FESTIVAL

Dept. of Theatre, Nunn Dr., Northern Kentucky University, Highland Heights KY 41099-1007. (859)572-6362. Fax: (859)572-6057. E-mail: forman@nku.edu. **Contact:** Sandra Forman, project director. Receives submissions from May 1-October 1 in even-numbered years for the festivals which occur in April of odd-numbered years. Open to all writers. **Deadline: October 1.** Guidelines for SASE. Prize: $500 and an expense-paid visit to Northern Kentucky University to see the play produced.

ANNA ZORNIO MEMORIAL CHILDREN'S THEATRE PLAYWRITING COMPETITION

University of New Hampshire, Dept. of Theatre and Dance, PCAC, 30 College Rd., Durham NH 03824-3538. (603)862-3044. E-mail: mike.wood@unh.edu. Web site: www.unh.edu/theatre-dance/zornio.html. **Contact:** Michael Wood. Offered every 4 years for unpublished well-written plays or musicals appropriate for young audiences with a maximum length of 60 minutes. May submit more than 1 play, but not more than 3. All plays will be performed by adult actors and must be appropriate for a children's audience within the K-12 grades. Guidelines and entry forms available as downloads on the Web site. **Deadline: March 3, 2008.** Prize: $1,000. The play is also produced and underwritten as part of the 2009-2010 season by the UNH Department of Theatre and Dance. Winner will be notified in November 2008. Open to all playwrights in US and Canada. All ages are invited to participate.

JOURNALISM

AAAS SCIENCE JOURNALISM AWARDS

American Association for the Advancement of Science, Office of News and Information, 1200 New York Ave. NW, Washington DC 20005. Web site: www.aaas.org. **Contact:** Awards Coordinator. Estab. 1945. Offered annually for previously published work to reward excellence in reporting on the sciences, engineering, and mathematics. Sponsored by Johnson & Johnson. **Deadline: August 1.** Prize: $3,000 and a trip to AAAS Annual Meeting. Judged by committees of reporters, editors, and scientists.

THE AMERICAN LEGION FOURTH ESTATE AWARD

The American Legion, 700 N. Pennsylvania, Indianapolis IN 46204. (317)630-1253. E-mail: pr@legion.org. Web site: www.legion.org. Offered annually for journalistic works published the previous calendar year. "Subject matter must deal with a topic or issue of national interest or concern. Entry must include cover letter explaining entry, and any documention or evidence of the entry's impact on the community, state, or nation. No printed entry form." Guidelines for SASE or on Web site. **Deadline: January 31.** Prize: $2,000 stipend to defray expenses of recipient accepting the award at The American Legion National Convention in August.

AMY WRITING AWARDS

The Amy Foundation, P.O. Box 16091, Lansing MI 48901. (517)323-6233. Fax: (517)323-7293. E-mail: amyfoundtn@aol.com. Web site: www.amyfound.org. Estab. 1985. Offered annually for nonfiction articles containing scripture published in the previous calendar year in the secular media. **Deadline: January 31.** Prize: 1st Prize: $10,000; 2nd Prize: $5,000; 3rd Prize: $4,000; 4th Prize: $3,000; 5th Prize: $2,000; and 10 prizes of $1,000.

JOHN AUBUCHON FREEDOM OF THE PRESS AWARD

General Manager's Office, National Press Club, National Press Bldg., 529 14th St. NW, Washington DC 20045. (202)662-7532. Fax: (202)662-7512. E-mail: jbooze@npcpress.org. Web site: npc.press.org. **Contact:** Joann Booze. Offered annually to recognize members of the news media who have, through the publishing or broadcasting of news, promoted or helped to protect the freedom of the press during the previous calendar year. Categories: A US journalist or team for work published or broadcast in the US; a foreign journalist or team for work published or broadcast in their home country. Guidelines available online. Open to professional journalists. **Deadline: April 1.** Prize: $1,000 in each category.

THE WHITMAN BASSOW AWARD

Overseas Press Club of America, 40 W. 45th St., New York NY 10036. (212)626-9220. Fax: (212)626-9210. Web site: www.opcofamerica.org. **Contact:** Sonya Fry, executive director. Offered annually for best reporting in any medium on international environmental issues. Work must be published by US-based publications or broadcast. **Deadline: End of January. Charges $150 fee.** Prize: $1,000 and a certificate.

MIKE BERGER AWARD

Columbia University Graduate School of Journalism, 2950 Broadway, MC 3800, New York NY 10027-7004. (212)854-6468. Fax: (212)854-3800. E-mail: lsr21@columbia.edu. Web site: www.jrn.columbia.edu. **Contact:** Lisa S. Redd, program coordinator. Offered annually honoring in-depth and enterprising reporting on individuals in the tradition of the late Meyer "Mike" Berger. All newspaper reporters who cover the eastern seaboard from Maine to Washington DC are eligible—whether they report for dailies, weeklies, or monthlies. "We welcome and encourage members of the English-language ethnic press to submit nominations." **Deadline: March 1.** Prize: Cash.

THE WORTH BINGHAM PRIZE

The Worth Bingham Memorial Fund, 1211 Connecticut Ave. N.W. #310, Washington DC 20036. (202)737-3700. Fax: (202)737-0530. E-mail: info@worthbinghamprize.com. Web site: www.worthbinghamprize.org. **Contact:** Jackie Blumenthal. Offered annually to articles published during the year of the award. The prize honors newspaper or magazine investigative reporting of stories of national significance where the public interest is being ill-served. Entries may include a single story, a related series of stories, or up to 3 unrelated stories. "Please contact us for guidelines and entry form, or check our Web site." **Deadline: January 3.** Prize: $10,000.

NICHOLAS BLAKE FOREIGN FREE-LANCE REPORTING GRANT

Nicholas Blake Grant Program, 7715 Crittenden St., Box 239, Philadelphia PA 19118-4421. E-mail: nblake.grant@verizon.net. Estab. 2001. Contest offered annually for material published January 1, 2006 through December 31, 2007. The purpose of the grant program is to support current freelance print journalists who specialize in foreign reporting on national (or significant regional) political or armed conflicts within foreign countries. The grant program was created in honor of Nicholas C. Blake, an American freelance journalist who was murdered by security forces in 1985 while pursuing a story on the Guatemalan civil war. The grant program seeks to recognize that freelance foreign reporting is an important but under-emphasized branch of print journalism and to reward high-quality, innovative foreign reporting by these journalists. The program is intended to recognize the difficult conditions under which many freelance foreign print reporters work, and to foster their important role in foreign reporting by providing them financial support. An additional goal is to assist in the career development of these individuals, whether it is freelance reporting or as foreign correspondents with news organizations. Complete grant submission guidelines can be obtained via e-mail. **Deadline: September 1-December 31, 2007.** Prize: $5,000 grant to 1 journalist annually. Open to freelance print journalists who have filed reports from foreign countries.

HEYWOOD BROUN AWARD

The Newspaper Guild-CWA, 501 Third St. NW, Washington DC 20001-2797. (202)434-7173. Fax: (202)434-1472. E-mail: azipser@cwa-union.org. Web site: www.newsguild.org. **Contact:** Andy Zipser. Offered annually for works published the previous year. ''This annual competition is intended to encourage and recognize individual journalistic achievement by members of the working media, particularly if it helps right a wrong or correct an injustice. First consideration will be given to entries on behalf of individuals or teams of no more than 2.'' Guidelines for SASE or online. **Deadline: Last Friday in January.** Prize: $5,000 and plaque.

HARRY CHAPIN MEDIA AWARDS

World Hunger Year, 505 Eighth Ave., Suite 2100, New York NY 10018-6582. (212)629-8850, ext. 22. Fax: (212)465-9274. E-mail: media@worldhungeryear.org. Web site: www.worldhungeryear.org. **Contact:** Lisa Ann Batitto. Estab. 1982. Open to works published the previous calendar year. Critical issues of domestic and world hunger, poverty and development (newspaper, periodical, TV, radio, photojournalism, books). **Deadline: Early February. Charges $25 for 1 entry, $40 for 2 entries, $50 for 3-5 entries.** Prize: Several prizes from $1,000-2,500.

CONSUMER JOURNALISM AWARD

National Press Club, General Manager's Office, National Press Bldg., 529 14th St. NW, Washington DC 20045. (202)662-8744. Fax: (202)662-7512. E-mail: jbooze@npcpress.org. Web site: npc.press.org. **Contact:** Joann Booze. Offered annually to recognize excellence in reporting on consumer topics in the following categories: newspapers, periodicals, television, and radio. Entries must have been published/broadcast in the previous calendar year. Include a letter detailing how the piece or series resulted in action by consumers, the government, the community, or an individual. Guidelines available online. **Deadline: April 1.** Prize: $500 for each category.

ANN COTTRELL FREE ANIMAL REPORTING AWARD

National Press Club, General Manager's Office, National Press Bldg., 529 14th St. NW, Washington DC 20045. (202)662-8744. Fax: (202)662-7512. E-mail: jbooze@npcpress.org. Web site: npc.press.org. **Contact:** Joann Booze. Prize recognizing serious work by journalists that informs and educates the public about threats facing animals. Categories: print/online and broadcast. Entries must consist of a single article or broadcast or a series of related articles or broadcasts, which will be judged as a unit. Guidelines available online. Guidelines for SASE. Prize: $1,000 for each category. Open to any writer.

THE JANE CUNNINGHAM CROLY/GFWC PRINT JOURNALISM AWARD

The General Federation of Women's Clubs, 1734 N St. NW, Washington DC 20036-2990. (202)347-3168. Fax: (202)835-0246. Web site: www.gfwc.org. **Contact:** Contest Coordinator. An annual award ''to honor the print journalist whose writing demonstrates a concern for the rights and the advancement of women in our society and/or an awareness of women's sensitivity, strength, and courage, and/or an attempt to counteract existing sexism.'' Open to women and men who write for newspapers or magazines—either on staff or in a freelance capacity. Three articles must be submitted by each person. Articles must have been published during the previous calendar year. **Deadline: March 20.** Guidelines for SASE. **Charges $50.** Prize: $1,000 presented at GFWC's Annual International Convention. GFWC pays airfare and expenses. Judged by 2 prominent journalists, and 1 leader of a major woman's organization.

ROBIN GOLDSTEIN AWARD FOR WASHINGTON REGIONAL REPORTING

General Manager's Office, National Press Club, National Press Bldg., 529 14th St. NW, Washington DC 20045. (202)662-8744. E-mail: jbooze@npcpress.org. Web site: npc.press.org. **Contact:** Joann Booze. Offered annually for a Washington newspaper correspondent who best exemplifies the standards set by the late Robin Goldstein. Working alone in each bureau, Goldstein proved that one dedicated reporter can do it all for the hometown readers—news, features, enterprise, analysis and columns. This contest honors reporters who demonstrate excellence and versatility in covering Washington from a local angle. Categories: print and online. Submit up to 6 pieces. Guidelines available online. **Deadline: April 1.** Prize: $1,000. Open to professional reporters.

EDWIN M. HOOD AWARD FOR DIPLOMATIC CORRESPONDENCE

General Manager's Office, National Press Club, National Press Bldg., 529 14th St. NW, Washington DC 20045. (202)662-8744. E-mail: jbooze@npcpress.org. Web site: npc.press.org. **Contact:** Joann Booze. Offered annually to recognize excellence in reporting on diplomatic and foreign policy issues. Categories: print, online, and broadcast. Guidelines available online. **Deadline: April 1.** Prize: $500 in each category.

SANDY HUME MEMORIAL AWARD FOR EXCELLENCE IN POLITICAL JOURNALISM

National Press Club, General Manager's Office, National Press Bldg., 529 14th St. NW, Washington DC 20045. (202)662-8744. Fax: (202)662-7512. E-mail: jbooze@npcpress.org. Web site: npc.press.org. **Contact:** Joann Booze. Offered annually for work published in the previous calendar year. This award honors excellence and objectivity in political coverage. This prize can be awarded for a single story of great distinction or for continuing coverage of 1 political topic. Categories: print and online. Guidelines available online. Open to professional journalists aged 34 or younger. **Deadline: April 1.** Prize: $1,000.

ICIJ AWARD FOR OUTSTANDING INTERNATIONAL INVESTIGATIVE REPORTING

International Consortium of Investigative Journalists, A Project of the Center for Public Integrity, 910 17th St. NW, 7th Floor, Washington DC 20006. (202)466-1300. Fax: (202)466-1101. E-mail: info@icij.org. Web site: www.icij.org. Offered annually for works produced in print, broadcast, and online media. Work requires the use of sources in 2 or more countries. Guidelines and application form are on the Web site. **Deadline: February 15.** Prize: 1st Place: $20,000; up to 5 finalist awards of $1,000 each.

INVESTIGATIVE JOURNALISM GRANT

Fund For Investigative Journalism, P.O. Box 60184, Washington DC 20039-0184. (202)362-0260. Fax: (301)576-0804. E-mail: johnchyde@yahoo.com. Web site: www.fij.org. **Contact:** John Hyde. Estab. 1969. Offered 3 times/year for original investigative newspaper and magazine stories, radio and TV documentaries, books and media criticism. Guidelines online or by e-mail. The fund also offers an annual $25,000 FIJ Book Prize in November for the best book chosen by the board during the year. **Deadline: February 1, June 1, and October 1.** Prize: Grants of $500-10,000.

ANSON JONES, M.D. AWARD

Texas Medical Association, 401 W. 15th St., Austin TX 78701-1680. (512)370-1381. Fax: (512)370-1629. E-mail: brent.annear@texmed.org. Web site: www.texmed.org. **Contact:** Brent Annear, media relations manager. Offered annually to the media of Texas for excellence in communicating health information to the public. Open only to Texas general interest media for work published or aired in Texas during the previous calendar year. Guidelines posted online. **Deadline: January 15.** Prize: $1,000 for winners in each of the categories.

ROBERT L. KOZIK AWARD FOR ENVIRONMENTAL REPORTING

General Manager's Office, National Press Club, National Press Bldg., 529 14th St. NW, Washington DC 20045. (202)662-8744. E-mail: jbooze@npcpress.org. Web site: npc.press.org. **Contact:** Joann Booze. Offered annually to recognize excellence in environmental reporting at the local, national, or international level that impacted or prompted action to remedy an environmental situation. Categories: print, online, and broadcast. Guidelines available online. **Deadline: April 1.** Prize: $500 and Kozik medal in each category.

LIVINGSTON AWARDS FOR YOUNG JOURNALISTS

Mollie Parnis Livingston Foundation, Wallace House, 620 Oxford, Ann Arbor MI 48104. (734)998-7575. Fax: (734)998-7979. E-mail: livingstonawards@umich.edu. Web site: www.livawards.org. **Contact:** Charles Eisendrath. Offered annually for journalism published January 1-December 31 the previous year to recognize and further develop the abilities of young journalists. Includes print, online, and broadcast. Guidelines available online. **Deadline: February 1.** Prize: $10,000 each for local reporting, national reporting, and international reporting. Judges include Charles Gibson, Ellen Goodman, and Tom Brokaw. Open to journalists who are 34 years or younger as of December 31 of previous year and whose work appears in US-controlled print or broadcast media.

FRANK LUTHER MOTT-KAPPA TAU ALPHA RESEARCH AWARD IN JOURNALISM

University of Missouri School of Journalism, 76 Gannett Hall, Columbia MO 65211-1200. (573)882-7685. E-mail: umcjourkta@missouri.edu. Web site: www.kappataualpha.org. **Contact:** Dr. Keith Sanders, executive director, Kappa Tau Alpha. Offered annually for best researched book in mass communication. Submit 6 copies; no forms required. **Deadline: December 9.** Prize: $1,000.

NATIONAL MAGAZINE AWARDS

National Magazine Awards Foundation, 425 Adelaide St. W., Suite 700, Toronto ON M5V 3C1, Canada. (416)422-1358. E-mail: staff@magazine-awards.com. Web site: www.magazine-awards.com. Offered annually for work by Canadian citizens or landed immigrants published in a Canadian magazine during the previous calendar year. Awards presented for writers, art directors, illustrators and photographers in written and visual categories. **Deadline: January 10. Charges $75/entry.** Prize: Monetary rewards. Open to Canadian residents only.

O. HENRY AWARD

The Texas Institute of Letters, 5307 Preston Haven Dr., Dallas TX 75229. Web site: www.smu.edu/english/creativewriting/The_Texas_Institute_of_Letters.htm. **Contact:** Ben Fountain, chair. Offered annually for work published January 1-December 31 of previous year to recognize the best-written work of journalism appearing in a magazine or weekly newspaper. Judged by a panel chosen by the TIL Council. Writer must have been born in Texas, have lived in Texas for at least 2 consecutive years at some time, or the subject matter of the work should be associated with Texas. See Web site for guidelines. **Deadline: January 9.** Prize: $1,000.

ONLINE JOURNALISM AWARD

National Press Club, General Manager's Office, National Press Bldg., 529 14th St. NW, Washington DC 20045. (202)662-8744. Fax: (202)662-7512. E-mail: jbooze@npcpress.org. Web site: npc.press.org. **Contact:** Joann Booze. Offered annually to recognize the most significant contributions to journalism by the online media in 2 categories: Best Journalism Site (this award honors the best journalistic use of the online medium); and Distinguished Online Contribution (this award goes to the best individual contribution to public service using online technology). Guidelines available online. **Deadline: April 1.** Prize: $1,000 in each category.

ALICIA PATTERSON JOURNALISM FELLOWSHIP

Alicia Patterson Foundation, 1025 F St. NW Suite 700, Washington DC 20004. (202)393-5995. Fax: (301)951-8512. E-mail: director@aliciapatterson.org. Web site: www.aliciapatterson.org. **Contact:** Margaret Engel. Offered annually for previously published submissions to give 8-10 full-time print journalists or photojournalists 6 months or one year of in-depth research and reporting. Applicants must have 5 years of professional print journalism experience and be US citizens. Fellows write 4 magazine-length pieces for the *Alicia Patterson Reporter*, a quarterly magazine, during their fellowship year. Fellows must take 6-12 months' leave from their jobs, but may do other freelance articles during the year. Write, call, fax, or check Web site for applications. **Deadline: October 1.** Prize: $35,000 stipend for calendar year; $17,500 for 6 months.

THE MADELINE DANE ROSS AWARD

Overseas Press Club of America, 40 W. 45th St., New York NY 10036. (212)626-9220. Fax: (212)626-9210. E-mail: sonya@opcofamerica.org. Web site: www.opcofamerica.org. **Contact:** Sonya Fry, executive director. Offered annually for best international reporting in any medium showing a concern for the human condition. Work must be published by US-based publications or broadcast. Printable application available online. **Deadline: Late January; date changes each year. Charges $125 fee.** Prize: $1,000 and certificate.

JOSEPH D. RYLE AWARD FOR EXCELLENCE IN WRITING ON THE PROBLEMS OF GERIATRICS

National Press Club, General Manager's Office, National Press Bldg., 529 14th St. NW, Washington DC 20045. (202)662-8744. Fax: (202)662-7512. E-mail: jbooze@npcpress.org. Web site: npc.press.org. **Contact:** Joann Booze. Offered annually for work published in the previous year. This award emphasizes excellence and objectivity in coverage of the problems faced by the elderly. Guidelines available online. Open to professional print journalists. **Deadline: April 1.** Prize: $2,000.

SANOFI PASTEUR MEDAL FOR EXCELLENCE IN HEALTH RESEARCH JOURNALISM

Canadians for Health Research, P.O. Box 126, Westmount QC H3Z 2T1, Canada. (514)398-7478. Fax: (514)398-8361. E-mail: info@chrcrm.org. Web site: www.chrcrm.org. Offered annually for work published the previous calendar year in Canadian newspapers or magazines. Applicants must have demonstrated an interest and effort in reporting health research issues within Canada. Guidelines available from CHR or on Web site. **Deadline: February.** Prize: $2,500 and a medal.

SCIENCE IN SOCIETY AWARDS

National Association of Science Writers, Inc., P.O. Box 890, Hedgesville WV 25427. (304)754-5077. E-mail: diane@nasw.org. Web site: www.nasw.org. **Contact:** Diane McGurgan. Estab. 1972. Offered annually for investigative or interpretive reporting about the sciences and their impact for good and bad. Six categories: newspaper, magazine, television, radio, book, and Internet. Material may be a single article or broadcast, or a series. Works must have been first published or broadcast in North America between June 1 and May 31 of the previous year. **Deadline: February 1.** Prize: $1,000, and a certificate of recognition in each category. Open to any writer.

SCIENCE IN SOCIETY JOURNALISM AWARDS

Canadian Science Writers' Association, P.O. Box 75, Station A, Toronto ON M5W 1A2, Canada. (800)796-8595. E-mail: awards@sciencewriters.ca. Web site: www.sciencewriters.ca. Offered annually for work published/aired during the previous year to recognize outstanding contributions to journalism in print and electronic media (3 newspaper, 3 TV, 3 radio). Each material becomes property of CSWA. Does not return mss. Open to Canadian citizens or residents of Canada. **Deadline: February 1. Charges $10 entry fee.** Prize: $1,000 and a plaque.

WASHINGTON CORRESPONDENCE AWARD

National Press Club, General Manager's Office, National Press Bldg., 529 14th St. NW, Washington DC 20045. (202)662-8744. Fax: (202)662-7512. E-mail: jbooze@npcpress.org. Web site: npc.press.org. **Contact:** Joann Booze. Offered annually to honor the work of reporters who cover Washington for the benefit of the hometown audience. This award is for a single report or series on one topic, not for national reporting, nor for a body of work. Entrants must demonstrate a clear knowledge of how Washington works and what it means to the folks back home. Categories: print and online. Guidelines available online. **Deadline: April 1.** Prize: $1,000.

WRITING FOR CHILDREN & YOUNG ADULTS

ASTED/GRAND PRIX DE LITTERATURE JEUNESSE DU QUEBEC-ALVINE-BELISLE

Association pour l'avancement des sciences et des techniques de la documentation, 3414 Avenue du Parc, Bureau 202, Montreal QC H2X 2H5, Canada. (514)281-5012. Fax: (514)281-8219. E-mail: info@asted.org. Web site: www.asted.org. **Contact:** Brigitte Moreau and Olivia Marleau, co-presidents. Prize granted for the best work in youth literature edited in French in the Quebec Province. Authors and editors can participate in the contest. Offered annually for books published during the preceding year. **Deadline: June 1.** Prize: $1,000.

BOSTON GLOBE-HORN BOOK AWARDS

The Boston Globe, Horn Book, Inc., 56 Roland St., Suite 200, Boston MA 02129. (617)628-0225. Fax: (617)628-0882. E-mail: aamato@hbook.com. Web site: www.hbook.com/awards. **Contact:** Alison Amato. Estab. 1967. Offered annually for excellence in literature for children and young adults (published June 1-May 31). Categories: picture book, fiction and poetry, nonfiction. Judges may also name several honor books in each category. Books must be published in the US, but may be written or illustrated by citizens of any country. Guidelines for SASE or online. **Deadline: May 5.** Prize: Winners receive $500 and an engraved silver bowl; honor book recipients receive an engraved silver plate. Judged by a panel of 3 judges selected each year.

SANDRA CARON YOUNG ADULT POETRY PRIZE

National League of American Pen Women, Nob Hill, San Francisco Branch, The Webhallow House, 1544 Sweetwood Dr., Colma CA 94015-2029. E-mail: pennobhill@aol.com. Web site: www.soulmakingcontest.us. **Contact:** Eileen Malone. Three poems/entry; 1 poem/page; 1-page poems only from someone in grades 9-12. Indicate age and category on each poem. Identify with 3×5 card only. **Deadline: November 30.** Guidelines for SASE. **Charges $5/entry (make checks payable to NLAPW, Nob Hill Branch).** Prize: 1st Place: $100; 2nd Place: $50; 3rd Place: $25. Open annually to any young adult writer.

DELACORTE PRESS CONTEST FOR A FIRST YOUNG ADULT NOVEL

Random House, Inc., 1745 Broadway, 9th Floor, New York NY 10019. Web site: www.randomhouse.com/kids/games/delacorte.html. Offered annually "to encourage the writing of contemporary young adult fiction." Open to US and Canadian writers who have not previously published a young adult novel. Guidelines on Web site. **Deadline: October 1-December 31 (postmarked).** Prize: $1,500 cash, publication, and $7,500 advance against royalties. Judged by the editors of Delacorte Press Books for Young Readers.

DELACORTE YEARLING CONTEST FOR A FIRST MIDDLE-GRADE NOVEL

Delacorte Press Books for Young Readers, Random House, Inc., 1745 Broadway, New York NY 10019. (212)782-9000. Fax: (212)782-9452. Web site: www.randomhouse.com/kids. Estab. 1992. Offered annually for an unpublished fiction ms (96-160 pages) suitable for readers 9-12 years of age, set in North America, either contemporary or historical. Guidelines available online. **Deadline: April 1-June 30.** Prize: $1,500, publication, and $7,500 advance against royalties. World rights acquired.

GOVERNOR GENERAL'S LITERARY AWARD FOR CHILDREN'S LITERATURE

Canada Council for the Arts, 350 Albert St., P.O. Box 1047, Ottawa ON K1P 5V8, Canada. (613)566-4414, ext. 4582. Fax: (613)566-4410. Web site: www.canadacouncil.ca/prizes/ggla. Offered for the best English-language and the best French-language works of children's literature by a Canadian in 2 categories: text and illustration. Publishers submit titles for consideration. **Deadline: April 15 or August 7, depending on the book's publication date.** Prize: Each laureate receives $15,000; nonwinning finalists receive $1,000.

THE VICKY METCALF AWARD FOR CHILDREN'S LITERATURE

The Writers' Trust of Canada, 90 Richmond St. E., Suite 200, Toronto ON M5C 1P1, Canada. (416)504-8222. Fax: (416)504-9090. E-mail: info@writerstrust.com. Web site: www.writerstrust.com. **Contact:** James Davies. The Metcalf Award is presented to a Canadian writer for a body of work in children's literature at The Writers' Trust Awards event in Toronto each Spring. Prize: $15,000. Open to Canadian residents only.

MILKWEED PRIZE FOR CHILDREN'S LITERATURE

Milkweed Editions, 1011 Washington Ave. S., Suite 300, Minneapolis MN 55415. (612)332-3192. Fax: (612)215-2550. Web site: www.milkweed.org. **Contact:** The Editors. Estab. 1993. Annual prize for unpublished works. The Milkweed Prize for Children's Literature will be awarded to the best ms for children ages 8-13 that Milkweed accepts for publication during each calendar year by a writer not previously published by Milkweed Editions. Mss should be of high literary quality and must be double-spaced, 90-200 pages in length. All mss submitted to Milkweed will automatically be considered for the prize. Submission directly to the contest is not necessary. Must review guidelines, available online or for SASE. Catalog for $1.50 postage. Prize: $10,000 advance on royalties agreed upon at the time of acceptance.

PATERSON PRIZE FOR BOOKS FOR YOUNG PEOPLE

The Poetry Center at Passaic County Community College, One College Blvd., Paterson NJ 07505-1179. (973)684-6555. Fax: (973)523-6085. E-mail: mgillan@pccc.edu. Web site: www.pccc.edu/poetry. **Contact:** Maria Mazziotti Gillan, executive director. Offered annually for books published the previous calendar year. Three categories: pre-kindergarten-grade 3; grades 4-6; grades 7-12. Open to any writer. **Deadline: March 15.** Guidelines for SASE. Prize: $500 in each category.

PEN/PHYLLIS NAYLOR WORKING WRITER FELLOWSHIP

PEN American Center, 588 Broadway, Suite 303, New York NY 10012. (212)334-1660, ext. 108. Fax: (212)334-2181. E-mail: awards@pen.org. **Contact:** Nick Burd. Offered annually to a writer of children's or young-adult fiction in financial need, who has published 2-5 books in the past 10 years, which may have been well reviewed and warmly received by literary critics, but which have not generated sufficient income to support the author. Writers must be nominated by an editor or fellow writer. **Deadline: January 15.** Prize: $5,000.

PRIX ALVINE-BELISLE

Association pour L'avancement des sciences et des techniques de la documentation, ASTED, Inc., 3414 av. Parc #202, Montreal QC H2X 2H5, Canada. (514)281-5012. Fax: (514)281-8219. E-mail: info@asted.org. Web site: www.asted.org. **Contact:** Louis Cabral, executive director. Offered annually for work published the year before the award to promote authors of French youth literature in Canada. **Deadline: April 1.** Prize: $1,000.

SASKATCHEWAN CHILDREN'S LITERATURE AWARD

Saskatchewan Book Awards, Inc., Box 1921, Regina SK S4P 3E1, Canada. (306)569-1585. Fax: (306)569-4187. E-mail: director@bookawards.sk.ca. Web site: www.bookawards.sk.ca. **Contact:** Glenda James, executive director. Offered annually for work published September 15-September 14. This award is presented to a Saskatchewan author for the best book of children's or young adult's literature, judged on the quality of writing. **Deadline: First Deadline: July 31; Final Deadline: September 14.** Guidelines for SASE. **Charges $20 (Canadian).** Prize: $2,000.

TEDDY AWARD FOR BEST CHILDREN'S BOOK

Writers' League of Texas, 1501 W. Fifth St., Suite E-2, Austin TX 78703. (512)499-8914. Fax: (512)499-0441. E-mail: wlt@writersleague.org. Web site: www.writersleague.org. **Contact:** Kristy Bordine, membership director. Offered annually for work published January 1-December 31. Honors 2 outstanding books for children published by members of the Writers' League of Texas. Writer's League of Texas dues may accompany entry fee. **Deadline: May 31.** Guidelines for SASE. **Charges $25 fee.** Prize: Two prizes of $1,000, teddy bears, and trophies.

RITA WILLIAMS YOUNG ADULT PROSE PRIZE

National League of American Pen Women, Nob Hill, San Francisco Branch, The Webhallow House, 1544 Sweetwood Dr., Colma CA 94015-2029. E-mail: pennobhill@aol.com. Web site: www.soulmakingcontest.us. **Contact:** Eileen Malone. Up to 3,000 words in story, essay, journal entry, creative nonfiction, or memoir by someone in grades 9-12. Indicate age and category on each first page. Identify with 3×5 card only. **Deadline: November 30.** Guidelines for SASE. **Charges $5/entry (make checks payable to NLAPW, Nob Hill Branch).** Prize: 1st Place: $100; 2nd Place: $50; 3rd Place: $25. Open annually to any young adult writer.

ALICE WOOD MEMORIAL OHIOANA AWARD FOR CHILDREN'S LITERATURE

Ohioana Library Association, 274 E. First Ave., Suite 300, Columbus OH 43201. (614)466-3831. Fax: (614)728-6974. E-mail: ohioana@sloma.state.oh.us. Web site: www.ohioana.org. **Contact:** Linda R. Hengst. Offered to an author whose body of work has made, and continues to make, a significant contribution to literature for children or young adults, and through their work as a writer, teacher, administrator, and community member, interest in children's literature has been encouraged and children have become involved with reading. Nomination forms for SASE. Recipient must have been born in Ohio or lived in Ohio at least 5 years. **Deadline: December 31.** Prize: $1,000.

WORK-IN-PROGRESS GRANT

Society of Children's Book Writers and Illustrators (SCBWI), 8271 Beverly Blvd., Los Angeles CA 90048. (323)782-1010. E-mail: scbwi@scbwi.org. Web site: www.scbwi.org. Two grants—1 designated specifically for a contemporary novel for young people—to assist SCBWI members in the completion of a specific project. Open to SCBWI members only. **Deadline: March 1.** Guidelines for SASE.

WRITING FOR CHILDREN COMPETITION

The Writers' Union of Canada, 90 Richmond St. E., Suite 200, Toronto ON M5C 1P1. (416)703-8982, ext. 223. Fax: (416)504-9090. E-mail: projects@writersunion.ca. Web site: www.writersunion.ca. **Contact:** Projects Coordinator. Offered annually to discover developing Canadian writers of unpublished children's/young adult fiction or nonfiction. Open to Canadian citizens or landed immigrants who have not been published in book format and who do not currently have a contract with a publisher. **Deadline: April 24. Charges $15 entry fee.** Prize: $1,500; the winner and 11 finalists' pieces will be submitted to 3 Canadian publishers of children's books.

THE YOUNG ADULT FICTION PRIZE

Victorian Premier's Literary Awards, State Library of Victoria, 328 Swanston St., Melbourne VIC 3000 Australia. (61)(3)8664-7277. E-mail: pla@slv.vic.gov.au. Web site: www.slv.vic.gov.au/pla. **Contact:** Project Officer. Prize for a work of fiction or collection of short stories published May 1-April 30 and written for ages 13-18. **Deadline: May 5.** Guidelines for SASE. **Charges $35.** Prize: $15,000. Open to Australian citizens or permanent residents.

TRANSLATION

ALTA NATIONAL TRANSLATION AWARD

American Literary Translators Association, UTD, Box 830688-JO51, Richardson TX 75083-0688. (972)883-2093. Fax: (972)883-6303. E-mail: jeffrey.green@utdallas.edu. Web site: www.literarytranslators.org. **Contact:** Jeffrey Green. Each year, ALTA invites publishers to nominate book-length translations published in the preceding calendar year. Publication must be by a US or Canadian publisher and the submission must be a book-length work in English of fiction, poetry, drama, or creative nonfiction (literary criticism and philosophy are not eligible). For nominated books selected as finalists, publishers will be asked to provide an original-language version of the text. For each nominated book, send a letter of nomination, $25 entry fee, and 4 copies of the book. **Deadline: March 31.** Guidelines for SASE. Prize: $2,500; winner announced and featured at annual ALTA conference in the fall; press release distributed to major publications. Judged by panel of translators. Open to any translator/writer.

DIANA DER-HOVANESSIAN TRANSLATION PRIZE

New England Poetry Club, 16 Cornell St., Arlington MA 02476. E-mail: contests@nepoetryclub.org. Web site: www.nepoetryclub.org/contests.htm. Annual contest for a poem translated into English. **Deadline: June 30.** Guidelines for SASE. **Charges $10/up to 3 poems.** Prize: $200. Open to any writer.

FELLOWSHIPS FOR TRANSLATORS

National Endowment for the Arts, Room 815, 1100 Pennsylvania Ave. NW, Washington DC 20506-0001. (202)682-5034. Web site: www.arts.gov. **Contact:** Heritage and Preservation Division. "Grants are available to published translators of literature for projects that involve specific translation of prose (fiction, creative nonfiction and drama) or poetry (including verse drama) from other languages into English. We encourage translations of writers and of work which are insufficiently represented in English translation." Guidelines on Web site or by phone request. **Deadline: December 1-January 10.** Prize: Grants are for $10,000 or $20,000, depending on the artistic excellence and merit of the project.

GERMAN PRIZE FOR LITERARY TRANSLATION

American Translators Association, 225 Reinekers Ln., Suite 590, Alexandria VA 22314. (703)683-6100, ext. 3006. Fax: (703)683-6122. E-mail: ata@atanet.org. Web site: www.atanet.org. **Contact:** Walter W. Bacak. Offered in odd-numbered years for a previously published book translated from German to English. In even-numbered years, the Lewis Galentiere Prize is awarded for translations other than German to English. **Deadline: May 15.** Prize: $1,000, a certificate of recognition, and up to $500 toward expenses for attending the ATA Annual Conference.

JOHN GLASSCO TRANSLATION PRIZE

Literary Translators' Association of Canada, SB 335 Concordia University, 1455 boul. de Maisonneuve Ouest, Montréal QC H3G 1M8, Canada. (514)848-8702. E-mail: info@attlc-ltac.org. Web site: www.attlc-ltac.org/glasscoe.htm. **Contact:** Glassco Price Committee. Estab. 1981. Offered annually for a translator's first book-length literary translation into French or English, published in Canada during the previous calendar year. The translator must be a Canadian citizen or permanent resident. Eligible genres include fiction, creative nonfiction, poetry, and children's books. **Deadline: July 31.** Prize: $1,000.

GOVERNOR GENERAL'S LITERARY AWARD FOR TRANSLATION

Canada Council for the Arts, 350 Albert St., P.O. Box 1047, Ottawa ON K1P 5V8, Canada. (613)566-4414, ext. 4082. Fax: (613)566-4410. Web site: www.canadacouncil.ca/prizes/ggla. Offered for the best English-language and the best French-language work of translation by a Canadian. **Deadline: March 15 or August 7, depending on the book's publication date.** Prize: Each laureate receives $15,000; nonwinning finalists receive $1,000.

JAPAN-U.S. FRIENDSHIP COMMISSION PRIZE FOR THE TRANSLATION OF JAPANESE LITERATURE

Donald Keene Center of Japanese Culture at Columbia University, 507 Kent Hall, MC 3920, Columbia University, New York NY 10027. (212)854-5036. Fax: (212)854-4019. E-mail: donald-keene-center@columbia.edu. Web site: www.donaldkeenecenter.org. Annual award of $5,000 in Japan-U.S. Friendship Commission Prizes for the translation of Japanese literature. A prize is given for the best translation of a modern work or a classical work, or the prize is divided between equally distinguished translations. To qualify, works must be book-length translations of Japanese literary works: novels, collections of short stories, literary essays, memoirs, drama, or poetry. Submissions are judged on the literary merit of the translation and the accuracy with which it reflects the spirit of the Japanese original. Eligible works include unpublished mss, works in press, or books published during the 2 years prior to the prize year. Applications are accepted from translators or their publishers. Previous winners are ineligible. **Deadline: February 1.**

THE HAROLD MORTON LANDON TRANSLATION AWARD

The Academy of American Poets, 584 Broadway, Suite 604, New York NY 10012-3210. (212)274-0343. Fax: (212)274-9427. E-mail: rmurphy@poets.org. Web site: www.poets.org. **Contact:** Ryan Murphy, awards coordinator. Offered annually to recognize a published translation of poetry from any language into English. Open to living US citizens. Anthologies by a number of translators are ineligible. **Deadline: December 31.** Guidelines for SASE. Prize: $1,000.

FENIA AND YAAKOV LEVIANT MEMORIAL PRIZE IN YIDDISH STUDIES

Modern Language Association of America, 26 Broadway, 3rd Floor, New York NY 10004-1789. (646)576-5141. Fax: (646)458-0030. E-mail: awards@mla.org. Web site: www.mla.org. **Contact:** Coordinator of book prizes. This prize is to honor, in alternating years, an outstanding English translation of a Yiddish literary work or an outstanding scholarly work in any language in the field of Yiddish. Offered every two years. In 2008 it will be awarded to a scholarly work published between 2004 and 2007. Open to MLA members and nonmembers. Authors or publishers may submit titles. Guidelines for SASE or by e-mail. **Deadline: May 1.** Prize: $1,000, and a certificate, to be presented at the Modern Language Association's annual convention in December.

PEN AWARD FOR POETRY IN TRANSLATION

PEN American Center, 588 Broadway, Suite 303, New York NY 10012. (212)334-1660, ext. 108. E-mail: awards@pen.org. Web site: www.pen.org. **Contact:** Literary awards manager. This award recognizes book-length transla-

Contests & Awards

tions of poetry from any language into English, published during the current calendar year. All books must have been published in the US Translators may be of any nationality. US residency/citizenship not required. **Deadline: December 15.** Prize: $3,000. Judged by a single translator of poetry appointed by the PEN Translation Committee.

PEN/BOOK-OF-THE-MONTH CLUB TRANSLATION PRIZE

PEN American Center, 588 Broadway, Suite 303, New York NY 10012. (212)334-1660, ext. 108. Fax: (212)334-2181. E-mail: awards@pen.org. **Contact:** Literary Awards Manager. Offered for a literary book-length translation into English published in the calendar year. No technical, scientific, or reference books. Publishers, agents, or translators may submit 3 copies of each eligible title. All eligible titles must have been published in the US. **Deadline: December 14.** Prize: $3,000.

N THE RAIZISS/DE PALCHI TRANSLATION BOOK PRIZE

The Academy of American Poets, 584 Broadway, Suite 604, New York NY 10012. (212)274-0343, ext. 17. Fax: (212)274-9427. E-mail: rmurphy@poets.org. Web site: www.poets.org. **Contact:** Ryan Murphy. Offered in alternate years to recognize outstanding unpublished translations of modern Italian poetry into English. Applicants must verify permission to translate the poems or that the poems are in the public domain. Open to any US citizen. Guidelines online or for SASE. **Deadline: January 15.** Prize: $5,000.

LOIS ROTH AWARD FOR A TRANSLATION OF A LITERARY WORK

Modern Language Association, 26 Broadway, 3rd Floor, New York NY 10004-1789. (646)576-5141. Fax: (646)458-0030. E-mail: awards@mla.org. Web site: www.mla.org. **Contact:** Coordinator of Book Prizes. Offered every 2 years (odd years) for an outstanding translation into English of a book-length literary work published the previous year. Translators need not be members of the MLA. **Deadline: April 1.** Guidelines for SASE. Prize: $1,000 and a certificate.

ALDO AND JEANNE SCAGLIONE PRIZE FOR A TRANSLATION OF A LITERARY WORK

Modern Language Association, 26 Broadway, 3rd Floor, New York NY 10004-1789. (646)576-5141. Fax: (646)458-0030. E-mail: awards@mla.org. Web site: www.mla.org. **Contact:** Coordinator of Book Prizes. Offered in even-numbered years for the translation of a book-length literary work appearing in print during the previous year. Translators need not be members of the MLA. **Deadline: April 1.** Guidelines for SASE. Prize: $2,000 and a certificate.

ALDO AND JEANNE SCAGLIONE PRIZE FOR A TRANSLATION OF A SCHOLARLY STUDY OF LITERATURE

Modern Language Association of America, 26 Broadway, 3rd Floor, New York NY 10004-1789. (646)576-5141. Fax: (646)458-0030. E-mail: awards@mla.org. Web site: www.mla.org. **Contact:** Coordinator of Book Prizes. Offered in odd-numbered years for an outstanding translation into English of a book-length work of literary history, literary criticism, philology, or literary theory published during the previous biennium. Translators need not be members of the MLA. **Deadline: May 1.** Guidelines for SASE. Prize: $2,000 and a certificate.

MULTIPLE WRITING AREAS

ABILENE WRITERS GUILD ANNUAL CONTEST

Abilene Writers Guild, P.O. Box 2562, Abilene TX 79604. E-mail: AWG@abilenewritersguild.org. Web site: www.abilenewritersguild.org. Offered annually for unpublished work in the following categories: Rhymed Poetry (up to 50 lines); Unrhymed Poetry (up to 50 lines); Children's Stories for ages 3-10 (1,000 words maximum); Articles of General Interest (1,200 words maximum); Compositions of Inspiration (1,200 words maximum); Memoir/Composition of Nostalgia (1,200 words maximum); Fiction for Adults (1,200 words maximum); Adventure, Science Fiction, Mystery, Fantasy, Horror Novels (first 10 pages and synopsis); Mainstream, Romance, Western, Other Novel (first 10 pages and synopsis). All rights remain with the writer. **Deadline: July 1-August 1.** Guidelines for SASE. **Charges $5 for each short piece; $10 for novel entries.** Prize: 1st Place: $100; 2nd Place: $65; 3rd Place: $35 (in each category). Judged by professional writers and editors; different ones each year and for each category. Open to any writer.

THE ALLEGHENY REVIEW LITERATURE & ART AWARDS

The Allegheny Review, Allegheny College, Box 32, Allegheny College, Meadville PA 16335. E-mail: review@allegheny.edu. Web site: review.allegheny.edu. **Contact:** Senior Editor. Offered annually for unpublished works of poetry, fiction, creative nonfiction, and art. **Deadline: January 1. Charges $5/entry.** Prize: $250 and guaranteed publication. Open to currently enrolled undergraduate students.

ALLIGATOR JUNIPER AWARD

Alligator Juniper/Prescott College, 220 Grove Ave., Prescott AZ 86301. (928)350-2012. E-mail: aj@prescott.edu. Web site: www.prescott.edu/highlights/alligator_juniper. **Contact:** Rachel Yoder, managing editor. Offered annually for unpublished fiction, nonfiction and poetry. Guidelines online. **Deadline: October 1. Charges $10 (includes the winning issue).** Prize: $500 and publication. Judged by the staff and occasional guest judges. Acquires first North American rights. Open to any writer.

AMERICAN LITERARY REVIEW CONTEST

American Literary Review, P.O. Box 311307, University of North Texas, Denton TX 76203-1307. (940)565-2755. E-mail: americanliteraryreview@yahoo.com. Web site: www.engl.unt.edu/alr. **Contact:** Managing Editor. Offered annually for unpublished work. This contest alternates annually between poetry and fiction. Open to any writer. Guidelines for SASE or online. **Deadline: Varies each year. Charges $10 entry fee.** Prize: $1,000 and publication.

AMERICAN MARKETS NEWSLETTER COMPETITION

American Markets Newsletter, 1974 46th Ave., San Francisco CA 94116. E-mail: sheila.oconnor@juno.com. **Contact:** Sheila O'Connor. "Accepts fiction and nonfiction up to 2,000 words. Entries are eligible for cash prizes and all entries are eligible for worldwide syndication whether they win or not. Here's how it works: Send us your double-spaced manuscripts with your story/article title, byline, word count, and address on the first page above your article/story's first paragraph (no need for separate cover page). There is no limit to the number of entries you may send." **Deadline: December 31 and July 31.** Guidelines for SASE. **Charges $12 for 1 entry; $15 for 2 entries; $20 for 3 entries; $25 for 4 entries; $30 for 5 entries.** Prize: 1st Place: $300; 2nd Place: $100; 3rd Place: $50. Judged by a panel of independent judges. Open to any writer.

ANNUAL FICTION/NONFICTION WRITING CONTEST

The Hobson Foundation, 18 Circle Dr., Gettysburg PA 17325. E-mail: writers@hobsonfoundation.com. Web site: www.hobsonfoundation.com. **Contact:** Cyndy Phillips, director. **Deadline: July 1. Charges $20/first entry; $10/additional entry.** Prize: Over $1,000 of cash prizes for 1st-3rd place entries, in addition to a full critique of their work and their stories displayed with judges comments on our Web site. Judged by a panel of professional writers and writing professors. Acquires rights to display prize winning stories on our Web site. Writers retain all other rights. Open to any writer.

ARIZONA AUTHORS' ASSOCIATION ANNUAL NATIONAL LITERARY CONTEST AND BOOK AWARDS

Arizona Authors' Association, P.O. Box 87857, Phoenix AZ 85080-7857. (623)847-9343. E-mail: info@azauthors.com; gmanville@aol.com. Web site: www.azauthors.com. **Contact:** Greta Manville. Offered annually for previously unpublished poetry, short stories, essays, novels, and articles. New awards for published books in fiction, anthology, nonfiction, and children's. Winners announced at an award banquet in Phoenix in November, and short pieces and excerpts published in *Arizona Literary Magazine*. **Deadline: July 1. Charges $10 fee for poetry; $15 for short stories and essays; $30 for unpublished novels and published books.** Prize: $100 and publication, and/or feature in the *Arizona Literary Magazine*.

ARTS & LETTERS PRIZES

Arts & Letters Journal of Contemporary Culture, Campus Box 89, GC&SU, Milledgeville GA 31061. (478)445-1289. E-mail: al@gcsu.edu. Web site: al.gcsu.edu. **Contact:** The Editors. Offered annually for unpublished work. **Deadline: March 15 (postmarked). Charges $15/entry (payable to GC&SU), which includes a 1-year subscription to the journal.** Prize: $1,000 for winners in fiction, poetry, creative nonfiction and drama (one-act play). Fiction and poetry winners will attend a weekend program in the fall, and the creative nonfiction and drama winner will attend a Spring program that includes readings and a production of the prize-winning play. Judged by editors (initial screening); see Web site for final judges and further details about submitting work. Open to any writer.

ATLANTIC WRITING COMPETITION FOR UNPUBLISHED MANUSCRIPTS

Writers' Federation of Nova Scotia, 1113 Marginal Rd., Halifax NS B3H 4P7. (902)423-8116. Fax: (902)422-0881. E-mail: talk@writers.ns.ca. Web site: www.writers.ns.ca. **Contact:** Susan Mersereau, executive assistant. Estab. 1975. Annual contest for beginners to try their hand in a number of categories: novel, short story, poetry, writing for younger children, writing for juvenile/young adult, magazine article/essay. Only 1 entry/category is allowed. Established writers are also eligible, but must work in an area that's new to them. "Because our aim is to help Atlantic Canadian writers grow, judges return written comments when the competition is concluded." **Deadline: First Friday in December. Charges $25 fee for novel ($20 for WFNS members); $15 fee for all other categories ($10 for WFNS members).** Prize: **Novel**—1st Place: $200; 2nd Place: $150; 3rd Place: $100. **Writing for Younger Children and Juvenile/Young Adult**—1st Place: $150; 2nd Place: $75; 3rd Place: $50. **Poetry, Essay/Magazine Article, and Short Story**—1st Place: $100; 2nd Place: $75; 3rd Place: $50. Judged by a team of 2-3 professional writers, editors, booksellers, librarians, or teachers. Anyone residing in the Atlantic Provinces for at least 6 months prior to the contest deadline is eligible to enter.

AWP AWARD SERIES

Association of Writers & Writing Programs, Carty House, Mail Stop 1E3, George Mason University, Fairfax VA 22030. (703)993-4301. Fax: (703)993-4302. E-mail: awp@awpwriter.org. Web site: awpwriter.org. **Contact:** Supriya Bhatnagar. Offered annually to foster new literary talent. Categories: poetry (Donald Hall Poetry Prize), short fiction (Grace Paley Prize in Short Fiction), novel, and creative nonfiction. Guidelines for SASE or online. Open to any writer. **Deadline: January 1-February 28 (postmarked). Charges $20/nonmembers; $10/members.** Prize: Cash honorarium—4,000 for Donald Hall Prize for Poetry and Grace Paley Prize in Short Fiction, and $2,000 each for novel and creative nonfiction—and publication by a participating press.

AWP INTRO JOURNALS PROJECT

The Association of Writers & Writing Programs, Dept. of English, Bluffton University, 1 University Dr., Bluffton OH 45817-2104. E-mail: awp@awpwriter.org. Web site: www.awpwriter.org. **Contact:** Jeff Gundy. "This is a prize for students in AWP member-university creative writing programs only. Authors are nominated by the head of the Creative Writing Department. Each school may nominate no more than 1 work of nonfiction, 1 work of short fiction, and 3 poems." **Deadline: December 1.** Guidelines for SASE. Prize: $100, plus publication in participating journal. Judged by AWP. Open to students in AWP member-university creative writing programs only.

BOROONDARA LITERARY AWARDS

City of Boroondara, Private Bag 1, Camberwell VIC 3124, Australia. E-mail: bla@boroondara.vic.gov.au. Web site: www.boroondara.vic.gov.au. **Contact:** Awards Coordinator. Contest for unpublished work in 2 categories: Young Writers, 7th-9th grade and 10th-12th grade (prose and poetry on any theme) and Open Short Story (2,000-3,000 words). Entries are only eligible if submitted on floppy disk or CD-ROM. **Deadline: August 31.** Guidelines for SASE. **Charges $7.30/short story; free entry for Young Writers.** Prize: **Young Writers**—1st Place: $300; 2nd Place: $150; 3rd Place: $100. **Open Short Story**—1st Place: $1,500; 2nd Place: $500; 3rd Place $250.

THE BOSTON AUTHORS CLUB BOOK AWARDS

The Boston Authors Club, 79 Moore Road, Wayland MA 01778. E-mail: pattywolcott@comcast.net. Web site: www.bostonauthorsclub.org. **Contact:** Patty Wolcott. Julia Ward Howe Prize offered annually for books published the previous year. Two awards are given, 1 for trade books of fiction, nonfiction, or poetry, and the second for children's books. Authors must live or have lived within 100 miles of Boston. No picture books or subsidized publishers. **Deadline: January 15.** Prize: $1,000 in each category. Books may also be cited as "Finalist" or "Recommended" with no cash award.

THE BRIAR CLIFF POETRY, FICTION AND CREATIVE NONFICTION COMPETITION

The Briar Cliff Review, Briar Cliff University, 3303 Rebecca St., Sioux City IA 51104-0100. Web site: www.briarcliff.edu/bcreview. **Contact:** Tricia Currans-Sheehan, editor. Offered annually for unpublished poetry, fiction and essay. **Deadline: August 1-November 1. No mss returned.** Guidelines for SASE. **Charges $15.** Prize: $1,000 and publication in Spring issue. Judged by editors. "We guarantee a considerate reading." Open to any writer.

BURNABY WRITERS' SOCIETY CONTEST

E-mail: info@bws.bc.ca. Web site: www.bws.bc.ca. **Contact:** Eileen Kernaghan. Offered annually for unpublished work. Open to all residents of British Columbia. Categories vary from year to year. Send SASE for current rules. Purpose is to encourage talented writers in all genres. **Deadline: May 31. Charges $5 fee.** Prize: 1st Place: $200; 2nd Place: $100; 3rd Place: $50; and public reading.

BYLINE MAGAZINE AWARDS

P.O. Box 111, Albion NY 14411. Web site: www.bylinemag.com. Contest includes several monthly contests, open to anyone, in various categories that include fiction, nonfiction, poetry, and children's literature; an annual poetry chapbook award which is open to any poet; and an annual *ByLine* Short Fiction and Poetry Award open only to our subscribers. For chapbook award and subscriber awards, publication constitutes part of the prize, and winners grant first North American rights to *ByLine*. **Deadline: Varies. Charges $3-5 for monthly contests; $15 for chapbook contest.** Prize: **Monthly contests:** Cash and listing in magazine; **Chapbook Award:** Publication of chapbook, 50 copies, and $200; ***ByLine* Short Fiction and Poetry Award:** $250 in each category, plus publication in the magazine.

CANADIAN AUTHORS ASSOCIATION AWARDS PROGRAM

P.O. Box 419, Campbellford ON K0L 1L0, Canada. (705)653-0323 or (866)216-6222. Fax: (705)653-0593. E-mail: admin@canauthors.org. Web site: www.canauthors.org. **Contact:** Alec McEachern. Offered annually for fiction, poetry, history, and drama. Entrants must be Canadians by birth, naturalized Canadians, or landed immigrants. Entry form required for all awards. Obtain entry form from contact name or download from Web site. **Deadline: December 15.** Guidelines for SASE. **Charges $35 (Canadian) fee/title entered.** Prize: Cash and a silver medal.

CANADIAN HISTORICAL ASSOCIATION AWARDS

Canadian Historical Association, 395 Wellington, Ottawa ON K1A 0N3, Canada. (613)233-7885. Fax: (613)567-3110. E-mail: cha-shc@lac-bac.gc.ca. Web site: www.cha-shc.ca. **Contact:** Joanne Mineault. Offered annually. Categories: Regional history, Canadian history, history (not Canadian), women's history (published articles, English or French), doctoral dissertations. Open to Canadian writers. **Deadline: Varies.** Guidelines for SASE. Prize: Varies.

CBC LITERARY AWARDS/PRIX LITTÈRAIRES RADIO-CANADA

CBC Radio/Radio Canada, Canada Council for the Arts, *enRoute* magazine, P.O. Box 6000, Montreal QC H3C 3A8, Canada. (877)888-6788. E-mail: literary_awards@cbc.ca. Web site: www.cbc.ca/literaryawards. **Contact:** Carolyn Warren, executive producer. The CBC Literary Awards Competition is the only literary competition that celebrates original, unpublished works in Canada's 2 official languages. There are 3 categories: short story, poetry, and travel writing. Submissions to the short story and travel category must be 2,000-2,500 words; poetry submissions must be 1,500-2,500 words. Poetry submissions can take the form of a long narrative poem, a sequence of connected poems, or a group of unconnected poems. **Deadline: November.** Guidelines for SASE. **Charges $20 CDN.** Prize: There is a first prize of $6,000 and second prize of $4,000 for each category, in both English and French, courtesy of the Canada Council for the Arts. In addition, winning entries are published in Air Canada's *enRoute* magazine and broadcast on CBC radio. First publication rights are granted by winners to *enRoute* magazine and broadcast rights are given to CBC radio. Submissions are judged blind by a jury of qualified writers and editors from around the country. Each category has 3 jurors. Canadian citizens, living in Canada or abroad, and permanent residents of Canada are eligible to enter.

CHAUTAUQUA LITERARY JOURNAL ANNUAL CONTESTS

Chautauqua Literary Journal, P.O. Box 2039, York Beach ME 03910 (for contest entries only). E-mail: cljeditor@aol.com. Web site: writers.ciweb.org. **Contact:** Richard Foerster, editor. Offered annually for unpublished work to award literary excellence in the categories of poetry and prose (short stories and/or creative nonfiction). Guidelines for SASE, online, or via e-mail. **Deadline: September 30 (postmarked). Charges $15/entry.** Prize: $1,500 in each of the 2 categories of poetry and prose, plus publication in *Chautauqua Literary Journal*. Judged by the editor and editorial advisory staff of the *Chautauqua Literary Journal*. Acquires first rights and one-time nonexclusive reprint rights. Open to any writer.

CHICANO/LATINO LITERARY CONTEST

Dept. of Spanish and Portuguese, University of California-Irvine, 322 Humanities Hall, Irvine CA 92697. (949)824-5443. Fax: (949)824-2803. E-mail: cllp@uci.edu. Web site: www.hnet.uci.edu/spanishandportuguese/contest.html. **Contact:** Evelyn Flores. Estab. 1974. Offered annually to promote the dissemination of unpublished Chicano/Latino literature in Spanish or English, and to encourage its development. The call for entries will be genre specific, rotating through 4 categories: drama (2006), novel (2007), short story (2008), and poetry (2009). The contest is open to all US citizens and permanent residents. **Deadline: June 1.** Prize: 1st Place: $1,000, publication, and transportation to the award ceremony; 2nd Place: $500; 3rd Place: $250.

THE CITY OF VANCOUVER BOOK AWARD

Office of Cultural Affairs, 453 W. 12th Ave., Vancouver BC V5Y 1V4, Canada. (604)871-6434. Fax: (604)871-6005. E-mail: marnie.rice@vancouver.ca. Web site: www.vancouver.ca/culture. Offered annually for books published in the previous year which exhibit excellence in the categories of content, illustration, design, and format. The book must contribute significantly to the appreciation and understanding of the city of Vancouver and heighten awareness of 1 or more of the following: Vancouver's history, the city's unique character, or achievements of the city's residents. The book may be fiction, nonfiction, poetry, or drama written for adults or children, and may deal with any aspects of the city—history, geography, current affairs, or the arts. Guidelines online. Prize: $2,000.

CNW/FFWA ANNUAL FLORIDA STATE WRITING COMPETITION

Florida Freelance Writers Association, P.O. Box A, North Stratford NH 03590-0167. E-mail: contest@writers-editors.com. Web site: www.writers-editors.com. **Contact:** Dana K. Cassell, executive director. Annual award to recognize publishable talent. Categories: Nonfiction (previously published article/essay/column/nonfiction book chapter; unpublished or self-published article/essay/column/nonfiction book chapter); Fiction (unpublished or self-published short story or novel chapter); Children's Literature (unpublished or self-published short story/nonfiction article/book chapter/poem); Poetry (unpublished or self-published free verse/traditional). **Deadline: March 15.** Guidelines for SASE. **Charges $5 (active or new CNW/FFWA members) or $10 (nonmembers) for each fiction/nonfiction entry under 3,000 words; $10 (members) or $20 (nonmembers) for each entry of 3,000 words or longer; $3 (members) or $5 (nonmembers) for each poem.** Prize: 1st Place: $100; 2nd Place: $75; 3rd Place: $50. All winners and Honorable Mentions will receive certificates as warranted. Judged by editors, librarians, and writers. Open to any writer.

COLORADO BOOK AWARDS

Colorado Center for the Book, 1490 Lafayette St., Suite 101, Denver CO 80218. (303)894-7951, ext. 19. Fax: (303)864-9361. E-mail: ccftb@ceh.org. Web site: www.coloradocenterforthebook.org. **Contact:** Margaret Coval, executive director. Offered annually for work published by December of previous year or current calendar year. The purpose is to champion all Colorado authors and in particular to honor the award winners and a reputation for Colorado as a state whose people promote and support reading, writing, and literacy through books. The categories are children, young adult, fiction, nonfiction, and poetry, and other categories as determined each year. Open to authors who reside or have resided in Colorado. **Deadline: January 15.** Guidelines for SASE. **Charges $45 fee.** Prize: $250 in each category, and an annual gala event where winners are honored.

COMMONWEALTH CLUB OF CALIFORNIA BOOK AWARDS

595 Market St., San Francisco CA 94105. (415)597-4846. Fax: (415)597-6729. E-mail: bookawards@commonwealthclub.org. Web site: www.commonwealthclub.org/bookawards. **Contact:** Scott Davis, book award producer. Estab. 1931. Offered annually for published submissions appearing in print January 1-December 31 of the previous year. Purpose of award is the encouragement and production of literature in California. Categories include: fiction, nonfiction, poetry, first work of fiction, juvenile up to 10 years old, juvenile 11-16, works in translation, notable contribution to publishing and Californiana. Can be nominated by publisher as well. Open to California residents (or residents at time of publication). Guidelines available online. **Deadline: December 15.** Prize: Medals and cash prizes to be awarded at publicized event.

CONTEST IN POETRY, FICTION, AND NONFICTION

Columbia: A Journal of Literature and Art, 415 Dodge Hall, 2960 Broadway, New York NY 10027. Web site: arts.columbia.edu/journal/contests.htm. Annual contest to acknowledge and print a single remarkable piece of unpublished poetry, fiction, and nonfiction in *Columbia: A Journal of Literature and Art*. **Deadline: January 15.** Guidelines for SASE. **Charges $12.** Prize: $500 in each category. Judged by established writers. Open to any writer.

N CORDON D'OR GOLD RIBBON ANNUAL INTERNATIONAL CULINARY ACADEMY AWARDS

Cordon d'Or Gold Ribbon Inc., P.O. Box 40660, St. Petersburg FL 33743-0660. (727)347-2437. E-mail: awards@cordonorcuisine.com. Web site: www.cordonorcuisine.com; www.goldribboncookery.com. **Contact:** Noreen Kinney. Contest promotes recognition of food authors, writers, culinary magazines, food stylists and food photographers and other professionals in the culinary field. Full details on all categories can be found on the Web site. Annually. **Deadline: July 31.** Prize: Cordon d'Or Gold Ribbon Crystal Globe Trophies (with stands) will be presented to winners in each category. An outstanding winner chosen by the judges from among all entries will also win a cash award of $1,000. Judged by professionals in the fields covered in the awards program. Open to any writer. The only criteria is that all entries must be in the English language.

VIOLET CROWN BOOK AWARDS

Writers' League of Texas, 1501 W. Fifth St., Suite E-2, Austin TX 78703. (512)499-8914. Fax: (512)499-0441. E-mail: wlt@writersleague.org. Web site: www.writersleague.org. **Contact:** Kristy Bordine, membership director. Offered annually for work published June 1-May 31. Honors 3 outstanding books published in fiction, nonfiction, and literary categories by Writers' League of Texas members. Membership dues may accompany entry fee. **Deadline: May 31.** Guidelines for SASE. **Charges $25 fee.** Prize: Three $1,000 prizes and trophies.

CWW ANNUAL AWARDS COMPETITION

Council for Wisconsin Writers, 1909 E. Menlo Blvd., Milwaukee WI 53211. Web site: www.wisconsinwriters.org/index.htm. Offered annually for work published by Wisconsin writers the previous calendar year. Thirteen awards: major/life achievement; short fiction; scholarly book; short nonfiction; nonfiction book; juvenile fiction book; children's picture book; poetry book; fiction book; outdoor writing; juvenile nonfiction book; drama (produced); outstanding service to Wisconsin writers. Open to Wiscconsin residents. Guidelines on Web site. **Deadline: January 31. Charges $25 fee for nonmembers; $10 for members.** Prize: $500 and a certificate.

DANA AWARDS IN PORTFOLIO, THE NOVEL, SHORT FICTION AND POETRY

200 Fosseway Dr., Greensboro NC 27445. (336)644-8028. E-mail: danaawards@pipeline.com. **Contact:** Mary Elizabeth Parker, chair. Four awards offered annually for unpublished work written in English. Purpose is monetary award for work that has not been previously published or received monetary award, but will accept work published simply for friends and family. Works previously published online are not eligible. No work accepted by or for persons under 16 for any of the 4 awards. Awards: **Portfolio**—For any combination of 3 mss in novel, short fiction or poetry. For this 3-mss award (as for the single mss award), each novel mss must be the first 50 pages only; each short fiction mss must be 1 short story only; and each poetry mss must be 5 poems only. **Novel**—For the first 50 pages of a novel completed or in progress. **Fiction**—Short fiction (no memoirs) up to 10,000 words. **Poetry**—For best group of 5 poems based on excellence of all 5 (no light verse, no single poem over 100 lines). See Web site for full guidelines on varied reading fees. **Deadline: October 31 (postmarked). Charges See fee schedule in online guidelines.** Prize: $3,000 for portfolio award; $1,000 each for other categories.

N EDITORS' PRIZE IN FICTION, ESSAY AND POETRY

The Missouri Review, 357 McReynolds Hall, Columbia MO 65211. (573)882-4474. Fax: (573)884-4671. E-mail: contest_question@missourireview.com. Web site: www.missourireview.com. **Contact:** Richard Sowienski. Offered annually for unpublished work in 3 categories: fiction, essay, and poetry. Guidelines online or for SASE. **Deadline: October 1. Charges $20 (includes a 1-year subscription).** Prize: $2,000 and publication for each category winner; 3 finalists in each category receive a minimum of $100.

N EMERGING LESBIAN WRITERS FUND AWARD

ASTRAEA Lesbian Foundation for Justice, 116 E. 16th St., 7th Floor, New York NY 10003. (212)529-8021. Fax: (212)982-3321. E-mail: grants@astraeafoundation.org. Web site: www.astraeafoundation.org. Estab. 1990. Offered annually to encourage and support the work of new lesbian writers of fiction and poetry. Guidelines for SASE or online. Entrants must be a lesbian writer of either fiction or poetry who has had at least 1 piece of writing (in any genre) published in a newspaper, magazine, journal, anthology, or professional Web site. **Deadline: June 30. Charges $5 fee.** Prize: $10,000 grants for awardees; $1,500 for 2 runners-up.

THE VIRGINIA FAULKNER AWARD FOR EXCELLENCE IN WRITING

Prairie Schooner, 201 Andrews Hall, P.O. Box 880334, Lincoln NE 68588-0334. (402)472-0911. Fax: (402)472-9771. E-mail: kgrey2@unl.edu. Web site: www.unl.edu/schooner/psmain.htm. **Contact:** Hilda Raz. Offered annually for work published in *Prairie Schooner* in the previous year. Prize: $1,000.

FINELINE COMPETITION FOR PROSE POEMS, SHORT SHORTS, AND ANYTHING IN BETWEEN

Mid-American Review, Dept. of English, Box W, Bowling Green State University, Bowling Green OH 43403. (419)372-2725. Web site: www.bgsu.edu/midamericanreview. **Contact:** Michael Czyzniejewski, editor-in-chief. Offered annually for previously unpublished submissions. Contest open to all writers not associated with current judge or *Mid-American Review*. **Deadline: June 1.** Guidelines for SASE. **Charges $5/prose poem or short; $10 for set of 3. All $10-and-over participants receive prize issue.** Prize: $1,000, plus publication in spring issue of *Mid-American Review*; 10 finalists receive notation plus possible publication. Judged by 2005 Judge: Alice Fulton. Open to any writer.

THE FLORIDA REVIEW EDITOR'S PRIZE

Dept. of English, P.O. Box 161346, University of Central Florida, Orlando FL 32816. (407)823-2038. E-mail: flreview@mail.ucf.edu. Web site: www.flreview.com. Annual awards for the best unpublished fiction, poetry, and creative nonfiction. **Deadline: Spring Yearly. Check Web site for specifics.** Guidelines for SASE. **Charges $15.** Prize: $1,000 (in each genre) and publication in *The Florida Review*. Judged by the editors in each genre. Judging is blind, so names should not appear on mss. Acquires first rights. Open to any writer.

FOREWORD MAGAZINE BOOK OF THE YEAR AWARDS

ForeWord Magazine, 129½ E. Front St., Traverse City MI 49684. (231)933-3699. Fax: (231)933-3899. Web site: www.forewordmagazine.com. Awards offered annually. Eligibility: Books must have a 2006 copyright.

Contests & Awards

Deadline: January 15. Prize: $1,500 cash prizes will be awarded to a Best Fiction and Best Nonfiction choice as determined by the editors of *ForeWord Magazine*. Judged by a jury of librarians, booksellers, and reviewers who are selected to judge the categories for entry and select winners and finalists in 52 categories based on editorial excellence and professional production as well as the originality of the narrative and the value the book adds to its genre. Open to any writer.

FREEFALL SHORT FICTION AND POETRY CONTEST

The Alexandra Writers' Centre Society, 922 9th Ave. SE, Calgary AB T2G 0S4, Canada. (403)264-4730. E-mail: awcs@telusplanet.net. Web site: www.alexandrawriters.org. Offered annually for unpublished work in the categories of poetry (5 poems/entry) and fiction (3,000 words or less). The purpose of the award in both categories is to recognize writers and offer publication credits in a literary magazine format. Contest theme and application online. **Deadline: October 1. Charges $20 entry fee.** Prize: 1st Place: $200 (Canadian); 2nd Place: $100 (Canadian). Both prizes include publication in the spring edition of *FreeFall Magazine*. Winners will also be invited to read at the launch of that issue if such a launch takes place. Honorable mentions in each category will be published and may be asked to read. Travel expenses not included. Judged by current *FreeFall* editors (who are also published authors in Canada). Acquires first Canadian serial rights (ownership reverts to author after one-time publication). Open to any writer.

FUGUE'S PROSE AND POETRY CONTEST

Fugue, 200 Brink Hall, English Department, University of Idaho, Moscow ID 83844-1102. Web site: www.uidaho.edu/fugue/contest. **Contact:** Senior Editor. Annual award for fiction, every 2 years for nonfiction and poetry, to recognize the most compelling work being produced. **Deadline: May 1.** Guidelines for SASE. **Charges $20/submission.** Prize: $1,000 and publication for 1st-place winner; publication for 2nd- and 3rd-place winners. Acquires first North American serial rights and electronic rights. Open to any writer.

GSU REVIEW WRITING CONTEST

GSU Review, Attn: Annual Contest, Georgia State University Plaza, Campus Box 1894, MSC 8R0322, Unit 8, Atlanta GA 30303-3083. (404)651-4804. Web site: www.review.gsu.edu. **Contact:** Christopher Bundy, editor. Offered annually to publish the most promising work of up-and-coming writers of poetry (3-5 poems, none over 50 lines) and fiction (8,000 word limit). Rights revert to writer upon publication. Guidelines for SASE or online. **Deadline: March 4.** Guidelines for SASE. **Charges $15 fee.** Prize: 1st Place: $1,000 in each category; 2nd Place: $250; plus a copy of winning issue to each paid submission.

N HACKNEY LITERARY AWARDS

Birmingham-Southern College, Box 549003, Birmingham AL 35254. (205)226-4921. E-mail: sbarr@bsc.edu. Web site: www.writingtoday.org. **Contact:** Sandy Barr. Estab. 1969. Offered annually for unpublished novels, short stories (maximum 5,000 words) and poetry (50 line limit). Guidelines on Web site (click on Hackney Awards) or send SASE. **Deadline: September 30 (novels), December 31 (short stories and poetry). Charges $25/novels; $10/short stories and poetry.** Prize: $5,000 in annual prizes for poetry and short fiction ($2,500 national and $2,500 state level; 1st Place: $600; 2nd Place: $400; 3rd Place: $250), plus $5,000 for an unpublished novel. Competition winners will be announced at the annual Writing Today Conference held the second weekend in March. Open to any writer.

THE JULIA WARD HOWE/BOSTON AUTHORS AWARD

The Boston Authors Club, 79 Moore Rd., Wayland MA 01778. (781)259-7966. E-mail: bostonauthors@aol.com. Web site: www.bostonauthorsclub.org. **Contact:** Patty Wolcott. This annual award honors Julia Ward Howe and her literary friends who founded the Boston Authors Club in 1900. It also honors the membership over 107 years, consisting of novelists, biographers, historians, governors, senators, philosophers, poets, playwrights, and other luminaries. There are 2 categories: adult books and books for young readers (beginning with chapter books through young adult books). Illustrated books and works of fiction, nonfiction, memoir, poetry, and biography are eligible. Authors must live or have lived (college counts) within a 100-mile radius of Boston. Subsidized books and picture books are not eligible. **Deadline: January 1.** Prize: $1,000 in each category.

INSIGHT WRITING CONTEST

Insight Magazine, 55 W. Oak Ridge Dr., Hagerstown MD 21740. Fax: (301)393-4055. E-mail: insight@rhpa.org. Web site: www.insightmagazine.org. **Contact:** Dwain Esmond, editor. Annual contest for unpublished writers in the categories of student short story, general short story, and student poetry. **Deadline: June 1.** Guidelines for SASE. Prize: **Student Short Story** and **General Short Story:** 1st Prize: $250; 2nd Prize: $200; 3rd Prize: $150. **Student Poetry:** 1st Prize: $100; 2nd Prize: $75; 3rd Prize: $50. Judged by editors. General category is open to all writers; student categories must be age 22 and younger.

ROBERT F. KENNEDY BOOK AWARDS

1367 Connecticut Ave., NW, Suite 200, Washington DC 20036. (202)463-7575. Fax: (202)463-6606. E-mail: pellish@rfkmemorial.org. Web site: www.rfkmemorial.org. **Contact:** Book Award Director. Offered annually for fiction and nonfiction works published the previous year which most faithfully and forcefully reflect Robert Kennedy's purposes—his concern for the poor and the powerless, his struggle for honest and even-handed justice, his conviction that a decent society must assure all young people a fair chance, and his faith that a free democracy can act to remedy disparities of power and opportunity. **Deadline: January 20. Charges $50 fee.** Prize: $2,500 and a bust of Robert F. Kennedy.

LABYRINTH SOCIETY WRITING CONTEST

The Labyrinth Society, P.O. Box 736, Trumansburg NY 14886-0736. Web site: www.labyrinthsociety.org. Estab. 2004. The Labyrinth Society is looking for short stories, essays, and poems that reflect the many experiences available through the labyrinth. "We want to see your best writing. Stories will be judged on creativity, content, general appeal, and the extent to which the labyrinth is highlighted." Entry forms are available online or by sending a request and SASE to The Labyrinth Society. **Deadline: June 15 (postmarked). Charges $10 (send checks only).** Prize: Grand Prize: free registration for The Labyrinth Society's Annual Gathering/Conference ($500+ value), or $150 if unable to attend; 1st Prize: $75; 2nd Prize: $50; 3rd Prize: $25 in each of the 3 categories. Open to any writer.

N LAMBDA LITERARY AWARDS

The Lambda Literary Foundation, 16 W. 32nd St., Suite 10E, New York NY 10001-3808. (212)239-6575. Fax: (212)239-6576. E-mail: asklambda@earthlink.net. Web site: www.lambdaliterary.org. **Contact:** Charles Flowers. Annual contest for published books in 25 categories: Anthology; Arts & Culture; Bisexual; Chilren's/Young Adult; Debut Fiction (1 gay, 1 lesbian); Erotica (1 gay, 1 lesbian); Fiction (1 gay, 1 lesbian); Humor; LGBT Nonfiction; LGBT Studies; Memoir/Biography (1 gay, 1 lesbian); Mystery (1 gay, 1 lesbian); Poetry (1 gay, 1 lesbian); Romance (1 gay, 1 lesbian); Science Fiction/Fantasy/Horror; Spirituality; Transgender. **Deadline: December 1. Charges $20.** Prize: The debut gay and lesbian fiction awards are for $1,000 each.

LET'S WRITE LITERARY CONTEST

The Gulf Coast Writers Association, P.O. Box 6445, Gulfport MS 39506. E-mail: gcwriters@aol.com. Web site: www.gcwriters.org. **Contact:** Victoria Olsen. **Deadline: April 15.** Guidelines for SASE. **Charges $10 for each fiction or nonfiction entry and $5/additional entry (adults); $1 for entry in each category (children).** Prize: **Adult** 1st Prize: $75; 2nd Prize: $50; 3rd Prize: $25. **Young Writer** 1st Prize: $25; 2nd Prize: $15; 3rd Prize: $10. Judged by 5 professional writers. Open to any writer.

THE HUGH J. LUKE AWARD

Prairie Schooner, 201 Andrews Hall, P.O. Box 880334, Lincoln NE 68588-0334. (402)472-0911. Fax: (402)472-9771. E-mail: kgrey2@unl.edu. Web site: www.unl.edu/schooner/psmain.htm. **Contact:** Hilda Raz. Offered annually for work published in *Prairie Schooner* in the previous year. Prize: $250.

THE LUSH TRIUMPHANT

subTerrain Magazine, P.O. Box 3008, MPO, Vancouver BC V6B 3X5, Canada. E-mail: subter@portal.ca. Web site: www.subterrain.ca. Annual contest for fiction, poetry, and creative nonfiction. All entries must be previously unpublished and not currently under consideration in any other contest or competition. Entries will not be returned. Results of the competition will be announced in the Summer issue of *subTerrain*. All entrants receive a complimentary 1-year subscription to *subTerrain*. **Deadline: May 15. Charges $20/entry (entrants may submit as many entries in as many categories as they like).** Prize: The winning entries in each category will receive $500 and will be published in the Fall issue of *subTerrain*. The 1st runner-up in each category will be published in a future issue of *subTerrain*. Open to any writer.

BRENDA MACDONALD RICHES FIRST BOOK AWARD

Saskatchewan Book Awards, Inc., 205B-2314 11th Ave., Regina SK S4P 0K1, Canada. (306)569-1585. Fax: (306)569-4187. E-mail: director@bookawards.sk.ca. Web site: www.bookawards.sk.ca. **Contact:** Glenda James, executive director. Offered annually for work published September 15 of year past to September 14 of current year. This award is presented to a Saskatchewan author for the best first book, judged on the quality of writing. Books from the following categories will be considered: children's; drama; fiction (short fiction by a single author, novellas, novels); nonfiction (all categories of nonfiction writing except cookbooks, directories, how-to books, or bibliographies of minimal critical content); poetry. **Deadline: First deadline: July 31; Final deadline: September 14.** Guidelines for SASE. **Charges $20 (Canadian).** Prize: $2,000.

MANITOBA WRITING AND PUBLISHING AWARDS

% Manitoba Writers' Guild, 206-100 Arthur St., Winnipeg MB R3B 1H3, Canada. (204)942-6134 or (888)637-5802. Fax: (204)942-5754. E-mail: info@mbwriter.mb.ca. Web site: www.mbwriter.mb.ca. **Contact:** Robyn Maharaj, Jamis Paulson. Offered annually: The McNally Robinson Book of Year Award (adult); The McNally Robinson Book for Young People Awards (8 and under and 9 and older); The John Hirsch Award for Most Promising Manitoba Writer; The Mary Scorer Award for Best Book by a Manitoba Publisher; The Carol Shields Winnipeg Book Award; The Eileen McTavish Sykes Award for Best First Book; The Margaret Laurence Award for Fiction; The Alexander Kennedy Isbister Award for Non-Fiction; The Manuela Dias Book Design of the Year Award; The Best Illustrated Book of the Year Award; and the biennial Le Prix Littéraire Rue-Deschambault. Guidelines and submission forms available online (accepted until mid-January). Open to Manitoba writers only. Prize: Several prizes up to $5,000 (Canadian).

THE MCGINNIS-RITCHIE MEMORIAL AWARD

Southwest Review, P.O. Box 750374, Dallas TX 75275-0374. (214)768-1037. Fax: (214)768-1408. E-mail: swr@mail.smu.edu. Web site: www.southwestreview.org. **Contact:** Jennifer Cranfill, Willard Spiegelman. The McGinnis-Ritchie Memorial Award is given annually to the best works of fiction and nonfiction that appeared in the magazine in the previous year. Manuscripts are submitted for publication, not for the prizes themselves. Guidelines for SASE or online. Prize: Two cash prizes of $500 each. Judged by Jennifer Cranfill, managing editor, and Willard Spiegelman, editor-in-chief. Open to any writer.

MIDLAND AUTHORS AWARD

Society of Midland Authors, P.O. Box 10419, Chicago IL 60610-0419. E-mail: writercc@aol.com. Web site: www.midlandauthors.com. **Contact:** Carol Jean Carlson. Offered annually for published fiction, nonfiction, poetry, biography, children's fiction, and children's nonfiction pbulished in the previous calendar year. Authors must reside in, have been born in, or have strong connections to the states of Illinois, Indiana, Iowa, Kansas, Michigan, Minnesota, Missouri, Nebraska, North Dakota, South Dakota, Wisconsin, or Ohio. Guidelines online. **Deadline: February 15.** Prize: Monetary award given to winner in each category.

MISSISSIPPI REVIEW PRIZE

Mississippi Review, U.S.M. 118 College Dr., #5144, Hattiesburg MS 39406-0011. (601)266-4321. Fax: (601)266-5757. E-mail: rief@mississippireview.com. Web site: www.mississippireview.com. **Contact:** Rie Fortenberry, contest director. Offered annually for unpublished fiction and poetry. Guidelines available online or for SASE. **Deadline: October 1. Charges $15 fee.** Prize: $1,000 each for fiction and poetry winners; plus winners are published in the magazine. Open to all US writers except current or former students and employees of USM.

NEW ENGLAND WRITERS FREE VERSE AND FICTION CONTESTS

New England Writers, P.O. Box 5, Windsor VT 05089-0005. (802)674-2315. E-mail: newvtpoet@aol.com. Web site: www.newenglandwriters.org. **Contact:** Dr. Frank and Susan Anthony. Poetry line limit: 30 lines. Fiction word limit: 1,000 words. Guidelines for SASE or online. **Deadline: Postmarked June 15. Charges $5 for 3 poems or 1 fiction (multiple entries welcome).** Prize: The winning poems and fiction are published in *The Anthology of New England Writers*. The free verse contest has Robert Penn Warren Awards of $300, $200, and $100, with 10 Honorable Mentions of $20. The short fiction contest has 1 Marjory Bartlett Sanger Award of $300, with 5 Honorable Mentions of $30. Judged by published, working university professors of the genre. Open to any writer, not just New England.

NEW MILLENNIUM WRITING AWARDS

New Millennium Writings, Room M2, P.O. Box 2463, Knoxville TN 37901. Web site: www.newmillenniumwritings.com/awards.html. **Contact:** Contest Coordinator. Offered twice annually for unpublished fiction, poetry, essays or nonfiction prose to encourage new writers and bring them to the attention of the publishing industry. **Deadline: June 17. Charges $17/submission.** Prize: $1,000 each for best poem, fiction, and nonfiction; winners published in *NMW* and on Web site.

THE NOMA AWARD FOR PUBLISHING IN AFRICA

Kodansha Ltd., Japan, P.O. Box 128, Witney, Oxon OX8 5XU, United Kingdom. (44)(1993)775-235. Fax: (44)(1993)709-265. E-mail: maryljay@aol.com. Web site: www.nomaaward.org. **Contact:** Mary Jay, secretary to the Noma Award Managing Committee. Estab. 1979. "The Noma Award is open to African writers and scholars whose work is published in Africa. The spirit within which the annual award is given is to encourage and reward genuinely autonomous African publishers, and African writers. The award is given for an outstanding new book in any of these 3 categories: scholarly or academic; books for children; and literature and creative writing (including fiction, drama, poetry, and essays on African literature)." Entries must be submitted by publishers in Africa, who are limited to 3 entries (in any combination of the eligible categories). The award is open to any author who is indigenous to Africa (a national, irrespective of place of domicile). Guidelines at Web site or from Secretariat. **Deadline: March 31.** Prize: $10,000 (US). Judged by an impartial committee chaired by Mr. Walter Bgoya, comprising African scholars, book experts, and representatives of the international book community. This Managing Committee is the jury. The jury is assisted by independent opinion and assessment from a large and distinguished pool of subject specialists from throughout the world, including many in Africa.

OHIOANA BOOK AWARDS

Ohioana Library Association, 274 E. 1st Ave., Suite 300, Columbus OH 43201-3673. (614)466-3831. Fax: (614)728-6974. E-mail: ohioana@sloma.state.oh.us. Web site: www.ohioana.org. **Contact:** Linda Hengst, director. Offered annually to bring national attention to Ohio authors and their books (published in the last 2 years). Categories: Fiction, nonfiction, juvenile, poetry, and books about Ohio or an Ohioan. Books about Ohio or an Ohioan need not be written by an Ohioan. For other book categories, writers must have been born in Ohio or lived in Ohio for at least 5 years. **Deadline: December 31.** Guidelines for SASE.

OURECHO CONTESTS FOR BEST POSTS

OurEcho.com, P.O. Box 725008, Atlanta GA 31139. E-mail: admin@ourecho.com. Web site: www.ourecho.com. **Contact:** Scott Lupo. For the monthly contests, one post from the previous month is selected to receive a prize of $100. OurEcho.com also administers a number of contests dedicated to specific types of content. These provide a $50 prize for the post that best represents the content category (biography, local history, photograph, diary/journal entry, letter, travel, things to do, period piece, fiction, family history, foreign, only here, local legend, poem). See Web site for specific deadlines. All intellectual and property rights (including copyright) remain with the artist. By submitting, the artist agrees to let OurEcho print the story in its newsletter. Open to any writer.

PEACE WRITING INTERNATIONAL WRITING AWARDS

Peace and Justice Studies Association and Omni: Center for Peace, Justice & Ecology, 2582 Jimmie, Fayetteville AR 72703-3420. (479)442-4600. E-mail: jbennet@uark.edu. Web site: www.omnicenter.org. **Contact:** Dick Bennett. Offered annually for unpublished books. PeaceWriting encourages writing about war and international nonviolent peacemaking and peacemakers. PeaceWriting seeks book manuscripts about the causes, consequences, and solutions to violence and war, and about the ideas and practices of nonviolent peacemaking and the lives of nonviolent peacemakers. Three categories: Nonfiction Prose (history, political science, memoirs); Imaginative Literature (novels, plays, collections of short stories, collections of poetry, collections of short plays); and Works for Young People. Open to any writer. **Deadline: December 1.** Prize: $500 in each category.

PEN CENTER USA ANNUAL LITERARY AWARDS

PEN Center USA, 400 Corporate Pointe, Culver City CA 90230. E-mail: awards@penusa.org. Web site: www.penusa.org. **Contact:** Literary Awards Coordinator. Estab. 1982. Offered annually for fiction, nonfiction, poetry, children's literature, or translation published January 1-December 31 of the current year. Open to authors west of the Mississippi River. Guidelines for SASE or online. **Deadline: December 16 (book categories); January 31 (nonbook categories). Charges $35 fee.** Prize: $1,000.

PEN WRITING AWARDS FOR PRISONERS

PEN American Center, 588 Broadway, Suite 303, New York NY 10012. Web site: www.pen.org. Offered annually to the authors of the best poetry, plays, short fiction, and nonfiction received from prison writers in the U.S. **Deadline: Submit January 1-September 1.** Guidelines for SASE. Prize: 1st Place: $200; 2nd Place: $100; 3rd Place: $50 (in each category).

PNWA LITERARY CONTEST

Pacific Northwest Writers Association, PMB 2717-1420 NW Gilman Blvd, Ste, Issaquah WA 98027. (425)673-2665. Fax: (425)771-9588. E-mail: pnwa@pnwa.org. Web site: www.pnwa.org. **Contact:** Brenda Stav. Annual contest for unpublished mss that awards prize money in 11 categories. Categories include: Romance Genre; Screenwriting; Poetry; Adult Genre Novel; Jean Auel Adult Mainstream Novel; Adult Short Story; Juvenile/Young Adult Novel; Juvenile Short Story or Picture Book; Nonfiction Book/Memoir; Adult Article/Essay/Short Memoir; Young Writer. Each entry receives 2 critiques. **Deadline: February.** Guidelines for SASE. **Charges $35/entry (members); $45/entry (nonmembers).** Prize: 1st Place: $600; 2nd Place: $300; 3rd Place: $150. Each prize is awarded in all 10 categories. Judged by industry experts. Open to any writer.

POSTCARD STORY COMPETITION

The Writers' Union of Canada, 90 Richmond St. E., Suite 200, Toronto ON M5C 1P1, Canada. (416)703-8982. Fax: (416)504-9090. Web site: www.writersunion.ca. **Contact:** Competitions Coordinator. Offered annually for original and unpublished fiction, nonfiction, prose, verse, dialogue, etc., with a maximum length of 250 words. Open to Canadian citizens or landed immigrants only. **Deadline: February 14.** Guidelines for SASE. **Charges $5 entry fee.** Prize: $500.

THE PRESIDIO LA BAHIA AWARD

Sons of the Republic of Texas, 1717 Eighth St., Bay City TX 77414-5033. (979)245-6644. Fax: (979)244-3819. E-mail: srttexas@srttexas.org. Web site: www.srttexas.org. **Contact:** Scott Dunbar, chairman. Offered annually to promote suitable preservation of relics, appropriate dissemination of data, and research into Texas heritage, with particular attention to the Spanish Colonial period. **Deadline: September 30.** Guidelines for SASE. Prize: $2,000 total; 1st Place: Minimum of $1,200, 2nd and 3rd prizes at the discretion of the judges. Judged by members of the Sons of the Republic of Texas on the Presidio La Bahia Award Committee. Open to any writer.

N PUDDING HOUSE CHAPBOOK COMPETITION

Pudding House Publications, 81 Shadymere Ln., Columbus OH 43213. (614) 986-1881. E-mail: jen@puddinghouse.com. Web site: www.puddinghouse.com. **Contact:** Jennifer Bosveld. Ms must be 10-36 pages (prefers around 24-28 pages). Some poems may be previously published but not the collection as a whole. Guidelines on Web site. Past winners include David Hernandez, Rebecca Baggett, Willie Abraham Howard Jr., Michael Day, Bill Noble, William Keener, Mark Taksa, and Ron Moran. **Deadline: September 30. Charges $12 fee.** Prize: $2,000 (split between the author and a shelter program for the homeless), publication, and 20 copies of the chapbook.

N QWF LITERARY AWARDS

Quebec Writers' Federation, 1200 Atwater Ave., Montreal QC H3Z 1X4, Canada. (514)933-0878. E-mail: info@qwf.org. Web site: www.qwf.org/awards. Offered annually for a book published October 1-September 30 to honor excellence in English-language writing in Quebec. Categories: fiction, nonfiction, poetry, first book, and translation. Author must have resided in Quebec for 3 of the past 5 years. Guidelines online or for SASE. **Deadline: May 31 for books published before May 16; August 15 for books/bound proofs published after May 16. Charges $20/entry.** Prize: $2,000 in each category.

REGINA BOOK AWARD

Saskatchewan Book Awards, Inc., 205B-2314 11th Ave., Regina SK S4P 0K1, Canada. (306)569-1585. Fax: (306)569-4187. E-mail: director@bookawards.sk.ca. Web site: www.bookawards.sk.ca. **Contact:** Glenda James, executive director. Offered annually for work published September 15 of year past to September 14 of current year. In recognition of the vitality of the literary community in Regina, this award is presented to a Regina author for the best book, judged on the quality of writing. Books from the following categories will be considered: children's; drama; fiction (short fiction by a single author, novellas, novels); nonfiction (all categories of nonfiction writing except cookbooks, directories, how-to books, or bibliographies of minimal critical content); poetry. **Deadline: First deadline: July 31; Final deadline: September 14.** Guidelines for SASE. **Charges $20 (Canadian).** Prize: $2,000.

SUMMERFIELD G. ROBERTS AWARD

Sons of the Republic of Texas, 1717 Eighth St., Bay City TX 77414-5033. (979)245-6644. Fax: (979)244-3819. E-mail: srttexas@srttexas.org. Web site: www.srttexas.org. **Contact:** J. Richard Reese, chairman. Offered annually for submissions published during the previous calendar year to encourage literary effort and research about historical events and personalities during the days of the Republic of Texas, 1836-1846, and to stimulate interest in the period. **Deadline: January 15.** Guidelines for SASE. Prize: $2,500. Judged by the last 3 winners of the contest. Open to any writer.

SASKATCHEWAN BOOK OF THE YEAR AWARD

Saskatchewan Book Awards, Inc., Box 1921, Regina SK S4P 3E1, Canada. (306)569-1585. Fax: (306)569-4187. E-mail: director@bookawards.sk.ca. Web site: www.bookawards.sk.ca. **Contact:** Glenda James, executive director. Offered annually for work published September 15-September 14 annually. This award is presented to a Saskatchewan author for the best book, judged on the quality of writing. Books from the following categories will be considered: children's; drama; fiction (short fiction by a single author, novellas, novels); nonfiction (all categories of nonfiction writing except cookbooks, directories, how-to books, or bibliographies of minimal critical content); poetry. Visit Web site for more details. **Deadline: First deadline: July 31; Final deadline: September 14.** Guidelines for SASE. **Charges $20 (Canadian).** Prize: $3,000.

Contests & Awards

SASKATOON BOOK AWARD

Saskatchewan Book Awards, Inc., Box 1921, Regina SK S4P 3E1, Canada. (306)569-1585. Fax: (306)569-4187. E-mail: director@bookawards.sk.ca. Web site: www.bookawards.sk.ca. **Contact:** Glenda James, executive director. Offered annually for work published September 15-September 14. In recognition of the vitality of the literary community in Saskatoon, this award is presented to a Saskatoon author for the best book, judged on the quality of writing. Books from the following categories will be considered: children's; drama; fiction (short fiction by a single author, novellas, novels); nonfiction (all categories of nonfiction writing except cookbooks, directories, how-to books, or bibliographies of minimal critical content); poetry. **Deadline: First deadline: July 31; Final deadline: September 14.** Guidelines for SASE. **Charges $20 (Canadian).** Prize: $2,000.

MARGARET & JOHN SAVAGE FIRST BOOK AWARD

Halifax Public Libraries, 60 Alderney Dr., Dartmouth NS B2Y 4P8, Canada. (902)490-5991. Fax: (902)490-5889. E-mail: evansj@halifaxpubliclibraries.ca. Web site: www.halifax.ca/bookawards. **Contact:** Jennifer Evans. Recognizes the best first book of fiction or nonfiction written by a first-time published author residing in Atlantic Canada. Books may be of any genre, but must contain a minimum of 40% text, be at least 49 pages long, and be available for sale. No anthologies. Publishers: Send 4 copies of each title and submission form for each entry. **Deadline: First Monday in December. Charges $10 (made payable to the Halifax Regional Municipality).** Prize: $500.

THE MONA SCHREIBER PRIZE FOR HUMOROUS FICTION & NONFICTION

15442 Vista Haven Place, Sherman Oaks CA 91403. (310)471-3280. E-mail: brashcyber@pcmagic.net. Web site: www.brashcyber.com. **Contact:** Brad Schreiber. **Deadline: December 1. Charges $5 fee/entry (payable to Mona Schreiber Prize).** Prize: 1st Place: $500; 2nd Place: $250; 3rd Place: $100. All winners receive a copy of *What Are You Laughing At?: How to Write Funny Screenplays, Stories and More*, by Brad Schreiber. Judged by Brad Schreiber, author, journalist, consultant, and instructor at MediaBistro.com. Complete rules and previous winning entries on Web site. Open to any writer.

SHORT GRAIN WRITING CONTEST

Grain Magazine, Box 67, Saskatoon SK S7K 3K1, Canada. (306)244-2828. Fax: (306)244-0255. E-mail: grainmag@sasktel.net. Web site: www.grainmagazine.ca. **Contact:** Sue Stewart. Offered annually for unpublished dramatic monologues, postcard stories (narrative fiction) and prose (lyric) poetry, and nonfiction creative prose. Maximum length for short entries: 500 words. Entry guidelines online. All entrants receive a 1-year subscription to *Grain Magazine*. *Grain* purchases first Canadian serial rights only. Open to any writer. No fax or e-mail submissions. **Deadline: January 31. Charges $28 fee for 2 entries; $8 for 3 additional entries; US and international entries $28, plus $6 postage in US funds.** Prize: $6,000; 3 prizes of $500 in each category.

SHORT PROSE COMPETITION FOR DEVELOPING WRITERS

The Writers' Union of Canada, 90 Richmond St. E., Suite 200, Toronto ON M5C 1P1, Canada. (416)703-8982. Fax: (416)504-9090. Web site: www.writersunion.ca. **Contact:** Competitions Coordinator. Offered annually "to discover developing Canadian writers of unpublished prose: fiction and nonfiction." Length: 2,500 words maximum. Open to Canadian citizens or landed immigrants who have not been published in book format, and who do not currently have a contract with a publisher. **Deadline: November 3.** Guidelines for SASE. **Charges $25 entry fee.** Prize: $2,500 and possible publication in a literary journal.

KAY SNOW WRITING AWARDS

Willamette Writers, 9045 SW Barbur Blvd., Suite 5A, Portland OR 97219. (503)452-1592. Fax: (503)452-0372. E-mail: wilwrite@willamettewriters.com. Web site: www.willamettewriters.com. Contest offered annually to "offer encouragement and recognition to writers with unpublished submissions." Acquires right to publish excerpts from winning pieces 1 time in their newsletter. **Deadline: May 15.** Guidelines for SASE. **Charges $15 fee; no fee for student writers.** Prize: 1st Place: $300; 2nd Place: $150; 3rd Place: $50; excerpts published in Willamette Writers newsletter, and winners acknowledged at banquet during writing conference. Student writers win $50 in categories for grades 1-5, 6-8, and 9-12. $500 Liam Callen Memorial Award goes to best overall entry.

SOCIETY OF MIDLAND AUTHORS AWARDS

Society of Midland Authors, P.O. Box 10419, Chicago IL 60610-0419. Web site: midlandauthors.com. **Contact:** Thomas Frisbie, president. Annual contest for previously published writing in several categories. **Deadline: February 1.** Guidelines for SASE. Prize: at least $300 and a plaque awarded at the SMA annual banquet. Judged by panel of 3 judges for each category that includes a mix of experienced authors, reviewers, book sellers, university faculty and librarians. Open to any writer.

SOUTHWEST WRITERS ANNUAL CONTEST

SWW, 3721 Morris St. NE, Suite A, Albuquerque NM 87111-3611. (505)265-9485. Fax: (505)265-9483. E-mail: swwriters@juno.com. Web site: www.southwestwriters.org. **Contact:** Jeanne Shannon, contest chair. **Deadline: May 1. Charges $18/poetry entry (members); $28/poetry entry (nonmembers); $29 for all other entries (members); $44 for all other entries (nonmembers).** Prize: 1st Place: $150; 2nd Place: $100; 3rd Place: $50 in each category, as well as a certificate of achievement. First-place winners also compete for the $1,000 Storyteller Award. Finalists in all categories are notified by mail and are listed on the SWW Web site. Winners will be honored at a contest awards banquet. Writer maintains all rights to the work. Judged by editors and literary agents who review all entries and critique the top 3 entries in each category. All entries receive a written critique by a qualified consultant (usually—but not always—a published author). Judges are chosen by the contest chairs. Also monthly writing contest on various themes (see Web site for details). Open to any writer.

TENNESSEE WRITERS ALLIANCE LITERARY COMPETITION

Tennessee Writers Alliance, P.O. Box 120396, Nashville TN 37212. Web site: www.tn-writers.org. Offered annually for unpublished short fiction and poetry. Membership open to all, regardless of residence, for $25/year; $15/year for students. "For more information and guidelines visit our Web site or send a SASE." **Deadline: February 28. Charges $10/members; $15/nonmembers.** Prize: 1st Place: $500; 2nd Place: $250; 3rd Place: $100.

TORONTO BOOK AWARDS

City of Toronto % Toronto Protocol, 100 Queen St. W., 2nd Floor, West Tower, City Hall, Toronto ON M5H 2N2, Canada. (416)392-8191. Fax: (416)392-1247. E-mail: bkurmey@toronto.ca. Web site: www.toronto.ca/book_awards. **Contact:** Bev Kurmey, protocol officer. Offered annually for previously published fiction, nonfiction, or juvenile books that are evocative of Toronto. Previously published entries must have appeared in print between January 1 and December 31 the year prior to the contest year. **Deadline: February 28.** Guidelines for SASE. Prize: Awards total $15,000; $1,000 goes to shortlist finalists (usually 4-6) and the remainder goes to the winner. Judged by independent judging committee of 5 people chosen through an application and selection process.

WESTERN MAGAZINE AWARDS

Western Magazine Awards Foundation, 1506 East 11th Avenue, Garden Unit, Vancouver BC V5N 4Y7, Canada. (604)669-3717. Fax: (604)669-3701. E-mail: wma@direct.ca. Web site: www.westernmagazineawards.com. Offered annually for magazine work published January 1-December 31 of previous calendar year. Entry categories include business, culture, science, technology and medicine, entertainment, fiction, political issues, and much more. The work must have been published in a magazine whose main editorial office is in Western Canada, the Northwest Territories, and Yukon. Guidelines for SASE or online. **Deadline: February 25. Charges $27 for work in magazines with circulation under 20,000; $35 for work in magazines with circulation over 20,000.** Prize: $500 in each category. Applicant must be a Canadian citizen or full-time resident.

WILLA LITERARY AWARD

Women Writing the West, 8547 East Arapaho Road, Box 5-541, Greenwood Village CO 80112-1436. Phone/Fax: (541)565-3475. E-mail: jane@jkbook.com. Web site: www.womenwritingthewest.org. **Contact:** Jane Kirkpatrick, contest director. "The Willa Literary Award honors the best in literature featuring women's stories set in the West published each year. Women Writing the West (WWW), a nonprofit association of writers and other professionals writing and promoting the Women's West, underwrites and presents the nationally recognized award annually (for work published between January 1 and December 31). The award is named in honor of Pulitzer Prize winner Willa Cather, one of the country's foremost novelists. The award is given in 7 categories: historical fiction, contemporary fiction, original softcover, nonfiction, memoir/essay nonfiction, poetry, and children's/young adult fiction/nonfiction." **Deadline: February 1.** Guidelines for SASE. **Charges $50 entry fee.** Prize: Each winner receives $100 and a trophy. Each finalist receives a plaque. Award announcement is in early August, and awards are presented to the winners and finalists at the annual WWW Fall Conference. Judged by professional librarians not affiliated with WWW. Open to any writer.

L.L. WINSHIP/PEN NEW ENGLAND AWARD

PEN New England, Emerson College, 120 Boylston St., Boston MA 02116. Web site: www.pen-ne.org. Offered annually for work published in the previous calendar year. This annual prize is offered for the best book by a New England author or with a New England topic or setting. Open to fiction, nonfiction, and poetry. **Deadline: December 22.** Guidelines for SASE. **Charges $35.**

JOHN WOOD COMMUNITY COLLEGE CREATIVE WRITING CONTEST

1301 S. 48th St., Quincy IL 62305. (217)641-4940. Fax: (217)641-4900. Web site: www.jwcc.edu. **Contact:** Janet McGovern, education specialist. Categories include nonfiction and fiction. No identification should appear on manuscripts, but send a separate 3×5 card for each entry with name, address, phone number, e-mail address, word count, title of work, and category in which each work should be entered. Only for previously unpublished work: poetry (2 page/poem maximum), fiction (2,000 words maximum), nonfiction (2,000 words maximum). Accepts traditional rhyming poetry, nonrhyming poetry, and other poetry forms such as hauku, limericks, etc. Entries are accepted March 1-April 3. Guidelines for SASE or online. **Charges $5/poem; $7/fiction or nonfiction. Critiquing service is available for $5/poem; $15/story (3 page maximum).** Prize: Cash prizes dictated by the number of entries received.

N THE WORD GUILD CANADIAN WRITING AWARDS

The Word Guild, Box 34, Port Pery ON L9L 1B6. (905)985-1212. E-mail: info@thewordguild.com. Web site: www.thewordguild.com. Awards offered to encourage first-time Canadian authors to write fiction and nonfiction books expressing Christian faith in a clear, original, and inspiring way. The Castle Quay Books Canada and Essence Publishing Award is open to Canadian citizens only and someone who has never had a book published. The God Uses Ink Awards is for a theme-based article, short story, book, or script submitted by an unpublished author. The Word Guild Canadian Christian Writing Awards for work published in the previous year include: Nonfiction Books (life stories, personal growth, relationships, culture, leadership and philosophy, and special—books of poetry, anthology, etc.); Novels (literary/mainstream); Children & Young Adult Books (novels and nonfiction); Self-Published Books; Articles (news, feature, column/editorial/opinion, personal experience, devotional/inspirational, humor); Letter to the Editor; Short Story (fiction); Children & Young Adult (articles and short stories); Poetry (rhymed or free verse; maximum of 40 lines). **Deadline: January for published work; February for unpublished work. Charges $50 (Canadian)/$30 (US) for published books; $20 (Canadian)/$15 (US) for short items.** Prize: Book Awards: $200; Short Items: $100; Castle Quay Books Award: Ms will be published; God Uses ink Award: Registration at the God Uses Ink conference, plus runners-up awards. Judged by writers, editors, etc.

WORLD OF EXPRESSION SCHOLARSHIP PROGRAM

Bertelsmann, 1745 Broadway, New York NY 10019. E-mail: worldofexpression@randomhouse.com. Web site: www.worldofexpression.org. Offered annually for unpublished work to NYC public high school seniors. Three categories: poetry, fiction/drama, and personal essay. **Deadline: February 1.** Guidelines for SASE. Prize: Awards range from $500-10,000. Applicants must be seniors (under age 21) at a New York high school. No college essays or class assignments will be accepted.

WORLD'S BEST SHORT SHORT STORY FICTION CONTEST & SOUTHEAST REVIEW POETRY CONTEST

English Department, Florida State University, Tallahassee FL 32306. Web site: www.english.fsu.edu/southeastreview. Estab. 1979. Annual award for unpublished short short stories (no more than 500 words). **Deadline: March 7. Charges $10 fee for up to 3 stories or poems.** Prize: $500 and publication in *The Southeast Review*. Nine finalists in each genre will also be published.

WRITER'S DIGEST WRITING COMPETITION

Writer's Digest, 4700 E. Galbraith Rd., Cincinnati OH 45236. (513)531-2690, ext. 1328. E-mail: writing-competition@fwpubs.com. Web site: www.writersdigest.com. **Contact:** Terri Boes. Writing contest with 10 categories: Inspirational Writing (spiritual/religious, maximum 2,500 words); Memoir/Personal Essay (maximum 2,000 words); Magazine Feature Article (maximum 2,000 words); Short Story (genre, maximum 4,000 words); Short Story (mainstream/literary, maximum 4,000 words); Rhyming Poetry (maximum 32 lines); Nonrhyming Poetry (maximum 32 lines); Stage Play (first 15 pages and 1-page synopsis); TV/Movie Script (first 15 pages and 1-page synopsis). Entries must be original, in English, unpublished/unproduced (except for Magazine Feature Articles), and not accepted by another publisher/producer at the time of submission. *Writer's Digest* retains one-time publication rights to the winning entries in each category. **Deadline: June 1. Charges $10/first poetry entry; $5/additional poem. All other entries are $15/first ms; $10/additional ms.** Prize: Grand Prize: $2,500 and a trip to New York City to meet with editors and agents; 1st Place: $1,000, ms critique and marketing advice from a *Writer's Digest* editor, commentary from an agent, and $100 of Writer's Digest Books; 2nd Place: $500 and $100 of Writer's Digest Books; 3rd Place: $250 and $100 of Writer's Digest Books; 4th Place: $100 and a subscription to *Writer's Digest*; 5th Place: $50 and a subscription to *Writer's Digest*.

ARTS COUNCILS & FOUNDATIONS

ALABAMA STATE COUNCIL ON THE ARTS FELLOWSHIP-LITERATURE

Alabama State Council on the Arts, 201 Monroe St., Montgomery AL 36130-1800. (334)242-4076, ext. 224. Fax: (334)240-3269. E-mail: randy.shoults@arts.alabama.gov. Web site: www.arts.state.al.us. **Contact:** Randy Shoults. Literature fellowship offered every year (for previously published or unpublished work) to set aside time to create and improve skills. Two-year Alabama residency required. Guidelines available. **Deadline: March 1.** Prize: $10,000 or $5,000.

ALASKA STATE COUNCIL ON THE ARTS CAREER OPPORTUNITY GRANT AWARD

Alaska State Council on the Arts, 411 W. 4th Ave., Suite 1E, Anchorage AK 99501-2343. (907)269-6610. Fax: (907)269-6601. E-mail: aksca_info@eed.state.ak.us. Web site: www.eed.state.ak.us/aksca. **Contact:** Charlotte Fox, executive director. Grants help artists take advantage of impending, concrete opportunities that will significantly advance their work or careers. **Deadline: Applications accepted quarterly.** Prize: Up to $1,000. Open to residents of Alaska only.

N AMERICAN PRINTING HISTORY ASSOCIATION FELLOWSHIP IN PRINTING HISTORY

American Printing History Association, P.O. Box 4519, Grand Central Station, New York NY 10163. E-mail: sgcrook@printinghistory.com. Web site: www.printinghistory.org. **Contact:** Stephen Crook, executive secretary. Estab. 1976. Annual award for research in any area of the history of printing in all its forms, including all the arts and technologies relevant to printing, the book arts, and letter forms. Applications are especially welcome from those working in the area of American printing history, but the subject of research has no geographical or chronological limitations, and may be national or regional in scope, biographical, analytical, technical, or bibliographic in nature. Printing history-related study with a recognized printer or book artist may also be supported. The fellowship can be used to pay for travel, living, and other expenses. Applicants are asked to submit an application form, a curriculum vitae, and a 1-page proposal. Two confidential letters of recommendation specific to this fellowship should be sent separately by the recommenders. **Deadline: December 1.** Guidelines for SASE. Prize: Up to $2,000. Judged by a committee. Open to any writer.

ARROWHEAD REGIONAL ARTS COUNCIL INDIVIDUAL ARTIST CAREER DEVELOPMENT GRANT

Arrowhead Regional Arts Council, 1301 Rice Lake Rd., Suite 111, Duluth MN 55811. (218)722-0952 or (800)569-8134. Fax: (218)722-4459. E-mail: aracouncil@aol.com. Web site: www.aracouncil.org. **Contact:** Robert DeArmond, executive director. **Deadline: November 24 and April 29.** Guidelines for SASE. Prize: Up to $1,000. Judged by ARAC Board. Applicants must live in the 7-county region of Northeastern Minnesota.

ARTIST TRUST/WASHINGTON STATE ARTS COMMISSION FELLOWSHIP AWARDS

Artist Trust, 1835 12th Ave., Seattle WA 98122-2437. (206)467-8734. E-mail: info@artisttrust.org. Web site: www.artisttrust.org. **Contact:** Heatherjoy Helbach-Olds, director of programs. Estab. 1987. "The fellowship is a merit-based award of $6,000 to practicing professional Washington State artists of exceptional talent and demonstrated ability." Literature fellowships are offered every other year, and approximately six $6,000 literature fellowships are awarded. The award is made on the basis of work of the past 5 years. Applicants must be individual artists; Washington State residents; not matriculated students; and generative artists. Offered every 2 years in odd years. Guidelines and application online or for SASE. **Deadline: June.** Prize: $6,000. Judged by a selection panel of artists and/or arts professionals in the field chosen by the Artist Trust staff.

GEORGE BENNETT FELLOWSHIP

Phillips Exeter Academy, 20 Main St., Box #2339, Exeter NH 03833-2460. Web site: www.exeter.edu. Estab. 1968. Annual award for a fellow to provide time and freedom from material considerations to a person seriously contemplating or pursuing a career as a writer. Applicants should have a manuscript in progress which they intend to complete during the fellowship period. The recipient's duties are to be in residency for the academic year and to be available informally to students interested in writing. Guidelines for SASE or online. The committee favors writers who have not yet published a book with a major publisher. Residence at the academy during the fellowship period required. **Deadline: December 1.** Prize: $10,000 stipend and room and board.

CREATIVE & PERFORMING ARTISTS & WRITERS FELLOWSHIP

American Antiquarian Society, 185 Salisbury St., Worcester MA 01609. (508)471-2131. Fax: (508)753-3311. Web site: www.americanantiquarian.org. **Contact:** James David Moran. Annual contest for published writers and performers to conduct research in pre-20th century history. **Deadline: October 5.** Prize: $1,200 monthly stipend, plus travel expenses of up to $400. Judged by AAS staff and outside reviewers. Open to any writer.

DELAWARE DIVISION OF THE ARTS

820 N. French St., Wilmington DE 19801. (302)577-8278. Fax: (302)577-6561. E-mail: kristin.pleasanton@state.de.us. Web site: www.artsdel.org. **Contact:** Kristin Pleasanton, coordinator. Award offered annually to help further the careers of Delaware's emerging and established professional artists. **Deadline: August 1.** Guidelines for SASE. Prize: $10,000 for masters; $5,000 for established professionals; $2,000 for emerging professionals. Judged by out-of-state professionals in each division. Open to Delaware residents only.

DOBIE/PAISANO FELLOWSHIPS

J. Frank Dobie House, 702 E. Dean Keeton St., Austin TX 78705. Fax: (512)471-9997. E-mail: aslate@mail.utexas.edu. Web site: www.utexas.edu/ogs/Paisano. **Contact:** Audrey Slate. The annual Dobie-Paisano Fellowships provide an opportunity for creative writers to live for an extended period of time at a place of literary association. At the time of the application, the applicant must: be a native Texan; have lived in Texas at some time for at least 3 years; or have published writing that has a Texas subject. Criteria for making the awards include quality of work, character of proposed project, and suitability of the applicant for life at Paisano. Applicants must submit examples of their work in triplicate. Guidelines for SASE or online. **Deadline: January 26. Charges $10 fee.** Prize: 2 fellowships of $2,000/month for 6 months, and 6 months in residence at the late J. Frank Dobie's ranch near Austin, Texas—the first beginning September 1 and the second March 1. The fellowships are known as the Ralph A. Johnston Memorial Fellowship and the Jesse H. Jones Writing Fellowship. Winners are announced in early May. Three copies of the application must be submitted with the rest of the entry and mailed in 1 package. Entries must be submitted on the form.

DOCTORAL DISSERTATION FELLOWSHIPS IN JEWISH STUDIES

National Foundation for Jewish Culture, 330 7th Ave., 21st Floor, New York NY 10001. (212)629-0500, ext. 215. Fax: (212)629-0508. E-mail: grants@jewishculture.org. Web site: www.jewishculture.org/grants. **Contact:** Kristen L. Runk. **Deadline: February 1.** Guidelines for SASE. Prize: $8,000-10,000 grant. Open annually to students who have completed their course work and need funding for research in order to write their dissertation thesis or a PhD in a Jewish field of study.

N FELLOWSHIPS FOR CREATIVE WRITERS

National Endowment for the Arts, 1100 Pennsylvania Ave. NW, Washington DC 20506. (202)682-5400. Web site: www.arts.gov. Fellowships enable recipients to set aside time for writing, research, travel, and general career advancement. The program operates on a 2-year cycle, with prose (fiction and creative nonfiction) 1 year and poetry the next. Guidelines available online. **Deadline: March 1.** Prize: $25,000 grants.

FELLOWSHIPS TO ASSIST RESEARCH AND ARTISTIC CREATION

John Simon Guggenheim Memorial Foundation, 90 Park Ave., New York NY 10016. (212)687-4470. Fax: (212)697-3248. E-mail: fellowships@gf.org. Web site: www.gf.org. Offered annually to assist scholars and artists to engage in research in any field of knowledge and creation in any of the arts, under the freest possible conditions and irrespective of race, color, or creed. Application form is required. **Deadline: October 1.**

GAP (GRANTS FOR ARTIST PROJECTS) PROGRAM

Artist Trust, 1835 12th Ave., Seattle WA 98122. (206)467-8734. Fax: (206)467-9633. E-mail: info@artisttrust.org. Web site: www.artisttrust.org. **Contact:** Director of Grant Programs. Estab. 1987. "The GAP is awarded annually to approximately 50 artists, including writers. The award is meant to help finance a specific project, which can be in very early stages or near completion. Full-time students are not eligible. Open to Washington state residents only. **Deadline: The last Friday of February.** Guidelines for SASE. Prize: Up to $1,400 for artist-generated projects.

GRANTS FOR WRITERS

NC Arts Council, Department of Cultural Resources, Raleigh NC 27699-4632. (919)807-6512. E-mail: debbie.mcgill@ncmail.net. Web site: www.ncarts.org. **Contact:** Debbie McGill, literature director. Offered every 2 years "to serve writers of fiction, poetry, literary nonfiction, and literary translation in North Carolina, and to recognize the contribution they make to this state's creative environment." Guidelines available on Web site. Writer must have been a resident of NC for at least a year as of the application deadline and may not be enrolled in any degree-granting program at the time of application. Prize: $8,000 grants every 2 years.

THE HODDER FELLOWSHIP

The Council of the Humanities, Joseph Henry House, Princeton University, Princeton NJ 08544. Web site: www.princeton.edu/~humcounc/. The Hodder Fellowship is awarded to exceptional humanists at the early stages of their careers, typically after they have published one book and are working on a second. Preference is given to individuals outside academia. Hodder Fellows spend an academic year in residence in Princeton, pursuing independent projects. Candidates are invited to submit a résumé, a sample of previous work (10-page maximum, not returnable), a project proposal of 2-3 pages, and SASE for acknowledgement. Letters of recommendation are not required. **Deadline: November 1 (postmarked).** Prize: $58,000 stipend.

ILLINOIS ART COUNCIL ARTISTS FELLOWSHIP PROGRAM IN POETRY & PROSE

Illinois Art Council, 100 W. Randolph, Suite 10-500, Chicago IL 60601. (312)814-6750. Fax: (312)814-1471. E-mail: iac.info@illinois.gov. Web site: www.state.il.us/agency/iac. **Contact:** Director of Literature. Offered biannually for Illinois writers of exceptional talent to enable them to pursue their artistic goals. Applicant must have been a resident of Illinois for at least 1 year prior to the deadline. Guidlines for SASE. Prize: Nonmatching award of $7,000; finalist award of $700.

INDIVIDUAL PROJECT GRANTS

Rhode Island State Council on the Arts, One Capitol Hill, 3rd Floor, Providence RI 02908. (401)222-3880. Fax: (401)222-3018. E-mail: cristina@arts.ri.gov. Web site: www.arts.ri.gov. **Contact:** Cristina DiChiera, director of individual artist & public art programs. "Request for Proposal grants enable an artist to create new work and/or complete works-in-progress by providing direct financial assistance. By encouraging significant development in the work of an individual artist, these grants recognize the central contribution artists make to the creative environment of Rhode Island." Guidelines online. Open to Rhode Island residents age 18 or older; students not eligible. **Deadline: October 1 and April 1.** Prize: Nonmatching grants typically under $5,000.

CHRISTOPHER ISHERWOOD FELLOWSHIPS

Christopher Isherwood Foundation, PMB 139, 1223 Wilshire Blvd., Santa Monica CA 90403-5040. E-mail: james@isherwoodfoundation.org. Web site: www.isherwoodfoundation.org. **Contact:** James P. White, executive director. Several awards are given annually to selected writers who have published a novel. **Deadline: September 1-October 1 (send to the address posted on the Web site).** Prize: Fellowship consists of $3,000. Judged by advisory board.

KANSAS ARTS COMMISSION INDIVIDUAL ARTIST FELLOWSHIPS/MINI-FELLOWSHIPS

Kansas Arts Commission, 700 SW Jackson St., Suite 1004, Topeka KS 66603-3761. (785)296-3335. Fax: (785)296-4989. E-mail: kac@arts.state.ks.us. Web site: arts.state.ks.us. **Contact:** Tom Klocke. Offered annually for Kansas artists, both published and unpublished. Fellowships are offered in 10 artistic disciplines, rotating 5 disciplines every other year, and are awarded based on artistic merit. The fellowship disciplines are: music composition; choreography; film/video; interdisciplinary/performance art; playwriting; fiction; poetry; 2-dimensional visual art; 3-dimensional visual art; and crafts. Mini-fellowships (up to 12) are awarded annually to emerging artists in the same 10 disciplines. Guidelines available online. **Deadline: Varies.** Prize: Fellowship: $5,000; Mini-fellowship: $500. Open to Kansas residents only.

LITERARY GIFT OF FREEDOM

A Room of Her Own Foundation, P.O. Box 778, Placitas NM 87043. E-mail: info@aroomofherownfoundation.org. Web site: www.aroomofherownfoundation.org. **Contact:** Darlene Chandler Bassett. Award offered every other year to provide very practical help—both materially and in professional guidance and moral support—to women who need assistance in making their creative contribution to the world. Guidelines available online. **Deadline: February 1 (for fiction writers). Charges $35.** Prize: Up to $50,000 over 2 years, also a mentor for advice and dialogue, and access to the Advisory Council for professional and business consultation. Judged by a nationally known independent panel. Open to any female resident citizen of the US.

MASSACHUSETTS CULTURAL COUNCIL ARTISTS GRANTS PROGRAM

Massachusetts Cultural Council, 10 St. James Ave., 3rd Floor, Boston MA 02116-3803. (617)727-3668. Fax: (617)727-0044. E-mail: mcc@art.state.ma.us. Web site: www.massculturalcouncil.org. Awards in poetry, fiction, creative nonfiction, and playwriting/new theater works (among other discipline categories) are $5,000 each in recognition of exceptional original work. Criteria: Artistic excellence and creative ability, based on work submitted for review. Judged by independent peer panels composed of artists and art professionals. Must be 18 years or older and a legal residents of Massachusetts for the last 2 years and at time of award. This excludes students in directly-related degree programs and grant recipients within the last 3 years.

MINNESOTA STATE ARTS BOARD ARTIST INITIATIVE GRANT

Minnesota State Arts Board, Park Square Court, 400 Sibley St., Suite 200, St. Paul MN 55101-1928. (651)215-1600 or (800)866-2787. Fax: (651)215-1602. E-mail: nicole.simoneaux@arts.state.mn.us. Web site: www.arts.state.mn.us. **Contact:** Nicole Simoneaux. The grant is meant to support and assist artists at various stages in their careers. It encourages artistic development, nurtures artistic creativity, and recognizes the contributions individual artists make to the creative environment of the state of Minnesota. Literary categories include prose, poetry, playwriting, and screenwriting. Open to Minnesota residents. Prize: Bi-annual grants of $2,000-6,000.

THE MOONDANCER FELLOWSHIP FOR NATURE AND OUTDOOR WRITING

The Writers' Colony at Dairy Hollow, 515 Spring St., Eureka Springs AR 72632. (479)253-7444. Fax: (479)253-9859. E-mail: director@writerscolony.org. Web site: www.writerscolony.org. **Contact:** Jane Tucker, colony coordinator. **Deadline: November 15.** Guidelines for SASE. **Charges $35 application fee.** Prize: 1-month residency, all-expense paid fellowship at the Writers' Colony at Dairy Hollow. Transportation to and from the colony is not included. Judged by professional writers in the nature/outdoor writing genre. Open annually to any writer.

JENNY McKEAN/MOORE VISITING WRITER

English Department, George Washington University, Washington DC 20052. (202)994-6180. Fax: (202)994-7915. E-mail: dmca@gwu.edu. Web site: www.gwu.edu/~english. **Contact:** David McAleavey. Offered annually to provide 1-year visiting writers to teach 1 George Washington course and 1 free community workshop each semester. Guidelines for SASE or online. This contest seeks someone specializing in a different genre each year. **Deadline: November 15.** Prize: Annual stipend of approximately $50,000, plus reduced-rent townhouse (not guaranteed).

LARRY NEAL WRITERS' COMPETITION

DC Commission on the Arts and Humanities, 410 Eighth St., NW 5th Floor, Washington DC 20004. (202)724-5613. Fax: (202)727-4135. Web site: www.dcarts.dc.gov. **Contact:** Lisa Richards, arts program coordinator. Offered annually for unpublished poetry, fiction, essay, and dramatic writing. Call or visit Web site for current deadlines. Open to Washington DC residents only. Prize: Cash awards.

NEBRASKA ARTS COUNCIL INDIVIDUAL ARTISTS FELLOWSHIPS

Nebraska Arts Council, 1004 Farnam St., Plaza Level, Omaha NE 68102. (402)595-2122. Fax: (402)595-2334. E-mail: jhutton@nebraskaartscouncil.org. Web site: www.nebraskaartscouncil.org. **Contact:** J.D. Hutton. Estab. 1991. Offered every 3 years (literature alternates with other disciplines) to recognize exemplary achievements by originating artists in their fields of endeavor and support the contributions made by Nebraska artists to the quality of life in this state. Generally, distinguished achievement awards are $5,000 and merit awards are $1,000-2,000. Funds available are announced in September prior to the deadline. Must be a resident of Nebraska for at least 2 years prior to submission date; 18 years of age; and not enrolled in an undergraduate, graduate, or certificate-granting program in English, creative writing, literature, or related field. **Deadline: November 15.**

NEW JERSEY STATE COUNCIL ON THE ARTS FELLOWSHIP PROGRAM

P.O. Box 306, Trenton NJ 08625. (609)292-6130. Fax: (609)989-1440. Web site: www.njartscouncil.org. Offered every other year. Writers may apply in either poetry, playwriting, or prose. Fellowship awards are intended to provide support for the artist during the year to enable him/her to continue producing new work. Send for guidelines and application, or visit Web site. Must be New Jersey residents; may *not* be undergraduate or graduate matriculating students. **Deadline: July 15.** Prize: $7,000-12,000.

NEW YORK FOUNDATION FOR THE ARTS ARTISTS' FELLOWSHIPS

New York Foundation for the Arts, 155 Avenue of the Americas, 14th Floor, New York NY 10013-1507. (212)366-6900. E-mail: nyfaafp@nyfa.org. Web site: www.nyfa.org. Estab. 1985. Fellowships are awarded in 16 disciplines on a biannual rotation made to individual originating artists living and working in the State of New York. Awards are based upon the recommendations of peer panels and are not project support. The Fellowships may be used by each recipient as she/he sees fit. **Deadline: October 3.** Prize: Grants of $7,000. All applicants must be 18 years of age, and a New York resident for 2 years prior to the time of application.

NORTH CAROLINA ARTS COUNCIL REGIONAL ARTIST PROJECT GRANTS

North Carolina Arts Council, Dept. of Cultural Resources, Raleigh NC 27699-4634. (919)807-6512. Fax: (919)807-6532. E-mail: debbie.mcgill@ncmail.net. Web site: www.ncarts.org. **Contact:** Debbie McGill, literature director. **Deadline: Generally late summer/early fall.** Prize: $500-2,000 awarded to writers to pursue projects that further their artistic development. Open to any writer living in North Carolina. See Web site for contact information for the local arts councils that distribute these grants.

NORTH CAROLINA WRITERS' FELLOWSHIPS

North Carolina Arts Council, Dept. of Cultural Resources, Raleigh NC 27699-4632. (919)807-6512. Fax: (919)807-6532. E-mail: debbie.mcgill@ncmail.net. Web site: www.ncarts.org. **Contact:** Deborah McGill, literature director. Offered every even year to support writers of fiction, poetry, literary nonfiction, literary translation, and spoken word. See Web site for guidelines and other eligibility requirements. **Deadline: November 1, 2008.** Prize: $8,000 grant. Judged by a panel of literary professionals (writers, editors). Writers must be current residents of North Carolina for at least 1 year, must remain in residence in North Carolina during the grant year, and may not pursue academic or professional degrees while receiving grant.

OREGON LITERARY FELLOWSHIPS

Literary Arts, Inc., 224 NW 13th Ave., Suite 306, Portland OR 97209. (503)227-2583. E-mail: la@literary-arts.org. Web site: www.literary-arts.org. **Contact:** Susan Denning, program coordinator. The annual Oregon Literary Fellowships support Oregon writers with a monetary award. Guidelines for SASE or online. **Deadline: last Friday in June.** Prize: $500-3,000. Judged by out-of-state judges who are selected for their expertise in a genre. Open to Oregon residents only.

THE PULLIAM JOURNALISM FELLOWSHIPS

The Indianapolis Star, a Gannett Co. publication, P.O. Box 145, Indianapolis IN 46206-0145. (317)444-6001. E-mail: rpulliam@indystar.com. Web site: www.indystar.com/pjf. **Contact:** Russell B. Pulliam. Offered annually as an intensive 10-week summer "training school" for college students with firm commitments to, and solid training in, newspaper journalism. "Call or e-mail us in September, and we'll send an application packet." **Deadline: November 15.** Prize: $6,500 for 10-week session, June-August.

RHODE ISLAND ARTIST FELLOWSHIPS AND INDIVIDUAL PROJECT GRANTS

Rhode Island State Council on the Arts, One Capitol Hill, 3rd Floor, Providence RI 02908. (401)222-3880. Fax: (401)222-3018. E-mail: cristina@arts.ri.gov. Web site: www.arts.ri.gov. **Contact:** Cristina DiChiera, director of individual artist & public art programs. Annual fellowship competition is based upon panel review of mss for poetry, fiction, and playwriting/screenwriting. Project grants provide funds for community-based arts projects. **Deadline: April 1 and October 1.** Prize: Fellowship awards: $5,000 and $1,000. Grants range from $500-10,000 with an average of around $3,000. Rhode Island artists may apply without a nonprofit sponsor. Applicants for all RSCA grant and award programs must be at least 18 years and not currently enrolled in an arts-related degree program.

THE SOCIETY FOR THE SCIENTIFIC STUDY OF SEXUALITY STUDENT RESEARCH GRANT

The Society for the Scientific Study of Sexuality, P.O. Box 416, Allentown PA 18105-0416. (610)530-2483. Fax: (610)530-2485. E-mail: thesociety@sexscience.org. Web site: www.sexscience.org. **Contact:** Peter Anderson. Offered twice a year for unpublished works. The student research grant helps support graduate student research on a variety of sexually related topics. Guidelines and entry forms for SASE. Open to SSSS students pursuing graduate study. **Deadline: February 1 and September 1.** Prize: $1,000.

WALLACE STEGNER FELLOWSHIPS

Creative Writing Program, Stanford University, Dept. of English, Stanford CA 94305-2087. (650)723-0011 or (650)725-1208. Fax: (650)723-3679. E-mail: mpopek@stanford.edu. Web site: www.stanford.edu/dept/english/cw/. **Contact:** Mary Popek, program administrator. A 2-year, non-degree granting program at Stanford offered annually for emerging writers to attend the Stegner workshop to practice and perfect their craft under the guidance of the creative writing faculty. Guidelines available online. **Deadline: December 1 (postmarked). Charges $60 fee.** Prize: Living stipend (currently $22,000/year) and required workshop tuition of $6,500/year.

TENNESSEE ARTS COMMISSION LITERARY FELLOWSHIP

Tennessee Arts Commission, 401 Charlotte Ave., Nashville TN 37243-0780. Fax: (615)741-8559. E-mail: lee.baird@state.tn.us. Web site: www.arts.state.tn.us. **Contact:** Lee Baird, director of literary programs. Awarded annually in recognition of professional Tennessee artists, i.e., individuals who have received financial compensation for their work as professional writers. Applicants must have a publication history other than vanity press. Two fellowships awarded annually to outstanding literary artists who live and work in Tennessee. Categories are in fiction and poetry. **Deadline: January 30.** Guidelines for SASE. Prize: $5,000. Judged by an out-of-state adjudicator.

VERMONT ARTS COUNCIL

136 State St., Drawer 33, Montpelier VT 05633-6001. (802)828-3291. Fax: (802)828-3363. E-mail: mbailey@vermontartscouncil.org. Web site: www.vermontartscouncil.org. **Contact:** Michele Bailey. Offered twice a year for previously published or unpublished works. Opportunity Grants are for specific projects of writers (poetry, playwriters, fiction, nonfiction) as well as not-for-profit presses. Also available are Artist Development funds

to provide technical assistance for Vermont writers. Write or call for entry information. Open to Vermont residents only. Prize: $250-5,000.

WISCONSIN ARTS BOARD ARTIST FELLOWSHIP AWARDS

Wisconsin Arts Board, 101 E. Wilson St., 1st Floor, Madison WI 53702. (608)266-0190. Fax: (608)267-0380. E-mail: artsboard@arts.state.wi.us. Web site: www.arts.state.wi.us. **Contact:** Mark Fraire, grant programs and services specialist. Offered in even years to reward outstanding, professionally active Wisconsin artists by supporting their continued development, enabling them to create new work, complete work in progress, or pursue activities which contribute to their artistic growth. If the deadline falls on a weekend, the deadline is extended to the following Monday. Application is found on the Wisconsin Arts Board Web site. The Arts Board requires permission to use the work sample, or a portion thereof, for publicity or educational purposes. Contest open to professionally active artists who have resided in Wisconsin 1 year prior to application. Artists who are full or part-time students pursuing a degree in the fine arts at the time of application are not eligible. **Deadline: September 15.** Prize: $8,000 fellowship awarded to 7 Wisconsin writers.

WRITERS' RESIDENCIES—HEADLANDS CENTER FOR THE ARTS

NC Arts Council, Dept. of Cultural Resources, Raleigh NC 27699-4634. (919)715-1519. Fax: (919)807-6512. E-mail: debbie.mcgill@ncmail.net. Web site: www.ncarts.org. **Contact:** Deborah McGill, literature director. **Deadline: first Friday in June.** Prize: Room, board, round-trip travel, and a $500 monthly stipend for 2-month residency. Judged by a panel assembled by Headlands. In addition, a member of the Headlands staff comes to North Carolina to interview a short list of finalists in order to narrow that list down to 1 grant recipient. Applicants must be residents of North Carolina and have lived in the state at least 1 year prior to the application deadline. NCAC grant recipients must maintain their North Carolina residency status during the grant year and may not pursue academic or professional degrees during that period. See Web site for other eligibility requirements. E-mail or call for guidelines.

RESOURCES

Professional Organizations

AGENTS' ORGANIZATIONS

Association of Authors' Agents (AAA), 20 John St., London WC1N 2DR, United Kingdom. (44)(20)7405-6774. E-mail: aaa@apwatt. Web site: www.agentsassoc.co.uk.

Association of Authors' Representatives (AAR), 676A 9th Ave., #312, New York NY 10036. (212)840-5777. E-mail: aarinc@mindspring.com. Web site: www.aar-online.org.

Association of Talent Agents (ATA), 9255 Sunset Blvd., Suite 930, Los Angeles CA 90069. (310)274-0628. Fax: (310)274-5063. E-mail: shellie@agentassociation.com. Web site: www.agentassociation.com.

WRITERS' ORGANIZATIONS

Academy of American Poets, 584 Broadway, Suite 604, New York NY 10012-5243. (212)274-0343. Fax: (212)274-9427. E-mail: academy@poets.org. Web site: www.poets.org.

American Crime Writers League (ACWL), 17367 Hilltop Ridge Dr., Eureka MO 63205. Web site: www.acwl.org.

American Medical Writers Association (AMWA), 40 W. Gude Dr., Suite 101, Rockville MD 20850-1192. (301)294-5303. Fax: (301)294-9006. E-mail: amwa@amwa.org. Web site: www.amwa.org.

American Screenwriters Association (ASA), 269 S. Beverly Dr., Suite 2600, Beverly Hills CA 90212-3807. (866)265-9091. E-mail: asa@goasa.com. Website: www.asascreenwriters.com.

American Translators Association (ATA), 225 Reinekers Lane, Suite 590, Alexandria VA 22314. (703)683-6100. Fax: (703)683-6122. E-mail: ata@atanet.org. Web site: www.atanet.org.

Education Writers Association (EWA), 2122 P St. NW, Suite 201, Washington DC 20037. (202)452-9830. Fax: (202)452-9837. E-mail: ewa@ewa.org. Web site: www.ewa.org.

Garden Writers Association (GWA), 10210 Leatherleaf Ct., Manassas VA 20111. (703)257-1032. Fax: (703)257-0213. Web site: www.gardenwriters.org.

Horror Writers Association (HWA), 244 5th Ave., Suite 2767, New York NY 10001. E-mail: hwa@horror.org. Web site: www.horror.org.

The International Women's Writing Guild (IWWG),P.O. Box 810, Gracie Station, New York

NY 10028-0082. (212)737-7536. Fax: (212)737-9469. E-mail: dirhahn@iwwg.org. Web site: www.iwwg.com.

Mystery Writers of America (MWA), 17 E. 47th St., 6th Floor, New York NY 10017. (212)888-8171. Fax: (212)888-8107. E-mail: mwa@mysterywriters.org. Web site: www.mysterywriters.org.

National Association of Science Writers (NASW), P.O. Box 890, Hedgesville WV 25427. (304)754-5077. Fax: (304)754-5076. E-mail: diane@nasw.org. Web site: www.nasw.org.

National Association of Women Writers (NAWW), 24165 IH-10 W., Suite 217-637, San Antonio TX 78257. Web site: www.naww.org.

Organization of Black Screenwriters (OBS). Web site: www.obswriter.com.

Outdoor Writers Association of America (OWAA), 121 Hickory St., Suite 1, Missoula MT 59801. (406)728-7434. Fax: (406)728-7445. E-mail: krhoades@owaa.org. Web site: www.owaa.org.

Poetry Society of America (PSA), 15 Gramercy Park, New York NY 10003. (212)254-9628. Web site: www.poetrysociety.org.

Poets & Writers, 72 Spring St., Suite 301, New York NY 10012. (212)226-3586. Fax: (212)226-3963. Web site: www.pw.org.

Romance Writers of America (RWA), 16000 Stuebner Airline Rd., Suite 140, Spring TX 77379. (832)717-5200. E-mail: info@rwanational.org. Web site: www.rwanational.org.

Science Fiction and Fantasy Writers of America (SFWA), P.O. Box 877, Chestertown MD 21620. E-mail: execdir@sfwa.org. Web site: www.sfwa.org.

Society of American Business Editors & Writers (SABEW), University of Missouri, School of Journalism, 385 McReynolds, Columbia MO 65211. (573)882-7862. Fax: (573)884-1372. E-mail: sabew@missouri.edu. Web site: www.sabew.org.

Society of American Travel Writers (SATW), 1500 Sunday Dr., Suite 102, Raleigh NC 27607. (919)861-5586. Fax: (919)787-4916. E-mail: satw@satw.org. Web site: www.satw.org.

Society of Children's Book Writers & Illustrators (SCBWI), 8271 Beverly Blvd., Los Angeles CA 90048. (323)782-1010. Fax: (323)782-1892. E-mail: scbwi@scbwi.org. Web site: www.scbwi.org.

Washington Independent Writers (WIW), 1001 Connecticut Ave. NW, Suite 701, Washington DC 20036. (202)775-5150. Fax: (202)775-5810. E-mail: info@washwriter.org. Web site: www.washwriter.org.

Western Writers of America (WWA). E-mail: wwa@unm.edu. Web site: www.westernwriters.org.

INDUSTRY ORGANIZATIONS

American Booksellers Association (ABA), 200 White Plains Rd., Tarrytown NY 10591. (914)591-2665. Fax: (914)591-2720. E-mail: info@bookweb.org. Web site: www.bookweb.org.

American Society of Journalists & Authors (ASJA), 1501 Broadway, Suite 302, New York NY 10036. (212)997-0947. Fax: (212)937-2315. E-mail: execdir@asja.org. Web site: www.asja.org.

Association for Women in Communications (AWC), 3337 Duke St., Alexandria VA 22314. (703)370-7436. Fax: (703)370-7437. E-mail: info@womcom.org. Web site: www.womcom.org.

Association of American Publishers (AAP), 71 5th Ave., 2nd Floor, New York NY 10003. (212)255-0200. Fax: (212)255-7007. Or, 50 F St. NW, Suite 400, Washington DC 20001. (202)347-3375. Fax: (202)347-3690. Web site: www.publishers.org.

The Association of Writers & Writing Programs (AWP), The Carty House, Mail stop 1E3, George Mason University, Fairfax VA 22030. (703)993-4301. Fax: (703)993-4302. E-mail: services@awpwriter.org. Web site: www.awpwriter.org.

The Authors Guild, Inc., 31 E. 32nd St., 7th Floor, New York NY 10016. (212)563-5904. Fax: (212)564-5363. E-mail: staff@authorsguild.org. Web site: www.authorsguild.org.

Canadian Authors Association (CAA), Box 419, Campbellford ON K0L 1L0 Canada. (705)653-0323. Fax: (705)653-0593. E-mail: admin@canauthors.org. Web site: www.canauthors.org.

Christian Booksellers Association (CBA), P.O. Box 62000, Colorado Springs CO 80962-2000. (800)252-1950. Fax: (719)272-3510. E-mail: info@cbaonline.org. Web site: www.cbaonline.org.

The Dramatists Guild of America, 1501 Broadway, Suite 701, New York NY 10036. (212)398-9366. Fax: (212)944-0420. Web site: www.dramaguild.com.

National League of American Pen Women (NLAPW), 1300 17th St. NW, Washington DC 20036-1973. (202)785-1997. Fax: (202)452-8868. Website: www.americanpenwomen.org.

National Writers Association (NWA), 10940 S. Parker Rd., #508, Parker CO 80134. (303)841-0246. Fax: (303)841-2607. E-mail: anitaedits@aol.com. Web site: www.nationalwriters.com.

National Writers Union (NWU), 113 University Place, 6th Floor, New York NY 10003. (212)254-0279. Fax: (212)254-0673. E-mail: nwu@nwu.org. Web site: www.nwu.org.

PEN American Center, 588 Broadway, Suite 303, New York NY 10012-3225. (212)334-1660. Fax: (212)334-2181. E-mail: pen@pen.org. Web site: www.pen.org.

The Playwrights Guild of Canada (PGC), 54 Wolseley St., 2nd Floor, Toronto ON M5T 1A5 Canada. (416)703-0201. Fax: (416)703-0059. E-mail: info@playwrightsguild.ca. Web site: www.playwrightsguild.com.

Volunteer Lawyers for the Arts (VLA), One E. 53rd St., 6th Floor, New York NY 10022. (212)319-2787. Fax: (212)752-6575. Web site: www.vlany.org.

Women in Film (WIF), 8857 W. Olympic Blvd., Suite 201, Beverly Hills CA 90211. (310)657-5144. E-mail: info@wif.org. Web site: www.wif.org.

Women in the Arts Foundation (WIA), 32-35 30th St., D24, Long Island City NY 11106. (212)941-0130. E-mail: reginas@anny.org. Web site: www.anny.org/2/orgs/womeninarts/.

Women's National Book Association (WNBA), 2166 Broadway, #9-E, New York NY 10024. (212)208-4629. Web site: www.wnba-books.org.

Writers Guild of Alberta (WGA), 11759 Groat Rd., Edmonton AB T5M 3K6 Canada. (780)422-8174. Fax: (780)422-2663. E-mail: mail@writersguild.ab.ca. Web site: writersguild.ab.ca.

Writers Guild of America-East (WGA), 555 W. 57th St., Suite 1230, New York NY 10019. (212)767-7800. Fax: (212)582-1909. Web site: www.wgaeast.org.

Writers Guild of America-West (WGA), 7000 W. Third St., Los Angeles CA 90048. (323)951-4000. Fax: (323)782-4800. Web site: www.wga.org.

Writers Union of Canada (TWUC), 90 Richmond St. E., Suite 200, Toronto ON M5C 1P1 Canada. (416)703-8982. Fax: (416)504-9090. E-mail: info@writersunion.ca. Web site: www.writersunion.ca.

Book Publishers Subject Index

This index will help you find publishers that consider books on specific subjects. Remember that a publisher may be listed here only under a general subject category such as Art and Architecture, while the company publishes *only* art history or how-to books. Be sure to consult each company's individual listing, its book catalog, and several of its books before you send your query or proposal.

FICTION

Adventure

Comic Books

Confession

Erotica

Ethnic

Experimental

Fantasy

Feminist

Gay/Lesbian

Gothic

Hi-Lo

Historical

Horror

Humor

Juvenile

Literary

Mainstream/Contemporary

Military/War

Subject Index

Multicultural

Multimedia

Mystery

Occult

Picture Books

Plays

Poetry (Including Chapbooks)

Subject Index

Poetry In Translation

Regional

Religious

Romance

Science Fiction

Short Story Collections

Spiritual (New Age, etc.)

Sports

Suspense

Western

Subject Index

Young Adult

NONFICTION

Agriculture/Horticulture

Subject Index

Americana

Animals

Anthropology/Archeology

Subject Index

Art/Architecture

Biography

Business/Economics

Child Guidance/Parenting

Children's/Juvenile

Coffee Table Book

Computers/Electronic

Contemporary Culture

Cookbook

Cooking/Foods/Nutrition

Creative Nonfiction

Education

Subject Index

Ethnic

Fashion/Beauty

Film/Cinema/Stage

Gardening

Gay/Lesbian

General Nonfiction

Gift Book

Subject Index

Government/Politics

Health/Medicine

History

Hobbies

How-To

Subject Index

Humor

Illustrated Book

Language/Literature

Memoirs

Military/War

Money/Finance

Multicultural

Subject Index

Multimedia

Music/Dance

Nature/Environment

Subject Index

New Age

Philosophy

Photography

Psychology

Recreation

Reference

Subject Index

Regional

Subject Index

Religion

Subject Index

Science

Subject Index

Self-Help

Sex

Sociology

Software

Spirituality

Sports

Writer's Digest

DISCOVER A WORLD OF WRITING SUCCESS!

Are you ready to be praised, published, and paid for your writing? It's time to invest in your future with *Writer's Digest!* Beginners and experienced writers alike have been relying on *Writer's Digest*, the world's leading magazine for writers, for more than 80 years — and it keeps getting better!

Each issue is brimming with:

- technique articles geared toward specific genres, including fiction, nonfiction, business writing and more
- business information specifically for writers, such as organizational advice, tax tips, and setting fees
- tips and tricks for rekindling your creative fire
- the latest and greatest markets for print, online and e-publishing
- and much more!

NO RISK!

Send No Money Now!

☐ **Yes!** Please rush me my FREE issue of *Writer's Digest* — the world's leading magazine for writers. If I like what I read, I'll get a full year's subscription (6 issues, including the free issue) for only $19.96. That's 44% off the newsstand rate! If I'm not completely satisfied, I'll write "cancel" on your invoice, return it and owe nothing. The FREE issue is mine to keep, no matter what!

Name (please print)

Address

City State ZIP

E-mail (to contact me regarding my subscription)

☐ YES! Also e-mail me *Writer's Digest*'s FREE e-newsletter and other information of interest. *(We will not sell your e-mail address to outside companies.)*

Subscribers in Canada will be charged an additional US$10 (includes GST/HST) and invoiced. Outside the U.S. and Canada, add US$10 and remit payment in U.S. funds with this order. Annual newsstand rate: $35.94. Please allow 4-6 weeks for first-issue delivery.

Writer's Digest www.writersdigest.com

J7FWMK

Get a FREE TRIAL ISSUE of Writer's Digest

Packed with creative inspiration, advice, and tips to guide you on the road to success, *Writer's Digest* offers everything you need to take your writing to the next level! You'll discover how to:

- create dynamic characters and page-turning plots
- submit query letters that publishers won't be able to refuse
- find the right agent or editor
- make it out of the slush-pile and into the hands of publishers
- write award-winning contest entries
- and more!

See for yourself — order your FREE trial issue today!

RUSH!
Free Issue!

NO POSTAGE NECESSARY IF MAILED IN THE UNITED STATES

BUSINESS REPLY MAIL
FIRST-CLASS MAIL PERMIT NO. 340 FLAGLER BEACH FL
POSTAGE WILL BE PAID BY ADDRESSEE

Writer's Digest
PO BOX 421365
PALM COAST FL 32142-7104

Technical

Textbook

Translation

Travel

True Crime

Women's Issues/Studies

World Affairs

General Index

A

C

D

E

G

H

J

N

O

P

S

General Index

X

Y

Z